Webster's

Kiribati
–
English

Thesaurus Dictionary

PROCEEDS BENEFIT

Webster's Online Dictionary
(www.websters-online-dictionary.org)

EDITED BY

Philip M. Parker, Ph.D.
INSEAD (Fontainebleau & Singapore)

Published by ICON Group International, Inc.
7404 Trade St
San Diego, CA 92122 USA
Phone: (858) 635-9410
Fax: (858) 635-9414
iconsubs@san.rr.com

www.icongrouponline.com

This edition published by ICON Classics in 2008
Printed in the United States of America.

Webster's Kiribati – English Thesaurus Dictionary

ISBN 0-497-83553-3

PREFACE

This is an English thesaurus designed for Kiribati speakers who wish to better understand the ambiguities and richness of the English language. The first chapter is a full English thesaurus organized by 6889 Kiribati subject words. For each Kiribati subject word, one or more corresponding English subject words (translations) are provided. Synonyms are then given for the English translations for all relevant parts of speech (even in cases where the Kiribati subject word has a unique part of speech). This process results in over 15202 English synonyms.

The second chapter gives an index of these English synonyms back to the Kiribati subject words (a potentially useful chapter to English speakers interested in basic Kiribati vocabulary). The third chapter has short vocabulary lists organized by parts-of-speech. English teachers or students can use these bilingual lists to create flash cards, basic lesson plans, and English as a Second Language (ESL) study lists.

While creating an English thesaurus for Kiribati speakers seems simple enough, it can be tricky. What's the problem? Translations do not always follow strict transitivity. Normally, if $a=b$ and $b=c$, then $c=a$. This is not necessarily true in linguistics when b is an English word that has more than one part of speech. For example, "test" is a verb, noun and adjective. What is the correct English synonym for "a" (in Kiribati) when "b" (in English) has synonyms ("c") having many parts of speech? Furthermore, what if "a" (in Kiribati) is ambiguous and has several translations into English ("b")? This thesaurus embraces this ambiguity by giving as much information to the reader as possible. This was accomplished in two phases. In the first phase, maximum-likelihood English translations of the Kiribati subject words are given. For all the languages covered in Webster's Online Dictionary translations are determined using rather massive content analyses of translations from various sources including translations of United Nations documents, translations of the Holy Bible (and similar sources), training manuals, popular works, and academic sources. An English translation having the highest probability of being used is reported first, then the second most probable is reported second, and so on.

Reference: Webster's Online Dictionary (www.websters-online-dictionary.org)

In the second phase, English synonyms for all parts of speech, including those not related to the original Kiribati subject, are given for each English translation generated by the first phase. If an English entry is most used as a certain part of speech (estimated based on an English language corpus), then English synonyms for that part of speech are listed first. This indicates to the speaker of Kiribati how the English subject word is most used. Other parts of speech are listed based on their frequency of usage in English. Within each part of speech, synonyms most likely to be used in English are listed first. Readers who seek further information on any of the words in this book, including translations to other world languages, can freely refer to Webster's Online Dictionary (www.websters-online-dictionary.org).

The goal of Webster's Online Dictionary is to give all people of the world free access to a complete mapping of all known words to and from all written languages. In fulfillment of this goal, Webster's Online Dictionary (www.websters-online-dictionary.org) also offers as much information as possible for each word, including definitions, translations, images, trade name usage, quotations, and encyclopedic knowledge. The proceeds generated by the sale of this Kiribati–English thesaurus dictionary as well as other books extracted from the project will be used to augment the contents of the Webster's Online Dictionary.

This book may be the first Kiribati-English thesaurus ever published. All the errors and omissions are mine. I will certainly revise and improve this book at some later date, so if you wish to see better editions published in the future, please send any suggestions, corrections, or translations to webstersedits2@hotmail.com. Thank you for purchasing this book and supporting Webster's Online Dictionary.

Philip M. Parker, Ph.D., editor
Chair Professor of Management Science
INSEAD (Singapore & Fontainebleau, France)

CONTENTS

Reference: Webster's Online Dictionary (www.websters-online-dictionary.org)

VOCABULARY STUDY LISTS 607

Kiribati to English Thesaurus

A

a 1. just; *synonyms* (*adv*) exactly, hardly, newly, (*adj*) fair, right, correct, equitable, accurate, honest, impartial, barely, fit, good, reasonable, righteous; *antonyms* (*adj*) unfair, biased, wrong, 2. gape; *synonyms* (*n*) gaze, (*v*) gawk, open, yawn, glare, goggle, split, dehisce, look, (*adj*) stare, 3. are, 4. yawn; *synonyms* (*n*) yawning, nod, (*v*) gape, ope, yaw.

aa yawn; *synonyms* (*n*) yawning, nod, (*v*) gape, open, ope, yaw.

aai four; *synonyms* (*n*) quaternity, foursome, quadruplet, quaternary, quaternion, tetrad, quarter, square, ace, air, appearence, cast, casting, contrivance, direction.

aba 1. country; *synonyms* (*n*) state, nation, home, land, area, commonwealth, kingdom, place, realm, region, soil, territory, (*adj*) rural, rustic, public; *antonyms* (*n*) city, (*adj*) urban, 2. earth; *synonyms* (*n*) dirt, world, dust, ground, clay, lair, creation, ball, country, den, globe, hole, nature, orb, sphere, 3. land; *synonyms* (*n*) field, domain, estate, empire, demesne, property, (*v*) disembark, debark, alight, get, drop, arrive, bring, down, perch; *antonym* (*adj*) aquatic.

ababa inherit; *synonyms* (*v*) succeed, heir, get, own, receive, follow, obtain, ascend, attain, promote, prosper, pursue.

ababaki 1. great; *synonyms* (*adj*) eminent, famous, gigantic, big, distinguished, extensive, extreme, grand, large, chief, ample, capital, celebrated, considerable, dignified; *antonyms* (*adj*) small, awful, insignificant, tiny, mild, 2. inherited; *synonyms* (*adj*) hereditary, inborn, familial, genetic, ancestral, congenital, incarnate, inherent, transmissible, 3. big; *synonyms* (*adj*) major, heavy, important, significant, thick, sturdy, generous, adult, bad, burly, great, hefty, high, liberal, magnanimous; *antonyms* (*adj*) little, puny, 4. spacious; *synonyms* (*adj*) roomy, broad, wide, capacious, commodious, vast, comprehensive, expansive, extended, open, airy, full, comfortable, sizable, voluminous; *antonyms* (*adj*) cramped, narrow.

abakae huge; *synonyms* (*adj*) big, enormous, gigantic, immense, large, vast, colossal, extensive, great, elephantine, ample, considerable, excessive, gargantuan, giant; *antonyms* (*adj*) tiny, insignificant, miniature, small.

abakaei 1. massive; *synonyms* (*adj*) bulky, large, gigantic, huge, big, enormous, great, heavy, immense, monumental, gross, colossal, considerable, gargantuan, impressive; *antonyms* (*adj*) tiny, small, insignificant, miniature, 2. immense; *synonyms* (*adj*) vast, immeasurable, boundless, giant, infinite, endless, extensive, extreme, incalculable, massive, prodigious, untold, whopping, broad, super, 3. stupendous; *synonyms* (*adj*) terrific, tremendous, fantastic, mighty, mammoth, miraculous, astonishing, extraordinary, marvelous, towering, wonderful, fabulous, spectacular, amplitudinous, (*v*) monstrous, 4. titanic; *synonym* (*adj*) stupendous, 5. terrific; *synonyms* (*adj*) shocking, dreadful, formidable, appalling, brilliant, frightful, magnificent, marvellous, splendid, superb, grand, rattling, awful, howling, (*v*) terrible, 6. tremendous; *synonyms* (*adj*) fearful, awesome, devastating, excellent, horrible, horrid, intense, phenomenal, wondrous, (*v*) thrilling, 7. vast; *synonyms* (*adj*) spacious, wide, unlimited, unbounded, limitless, ample, roomy, voluminous, open, illimitable, cavernous, substantial, deep, expansive, interminable; *antonyms* (*adj*) limited, narrow, cramped.

abanaba 1. instantaneously; *synonyms* (*adv*) directly, immediately, instantly, forthwith, outright, 2. forthwith; *synonyms* (*adv*) now, straight, incontinently, presently, right, soon, straightaway, (*adj*) quickly, 3. directly; *synonyms* (*adv*) bluntly, direct, frankly, personally, sheer, flat, promptly, slap, rapidly, precisely, absolutely, exactly, flatly, honestly, (*adj*) forthright; *antonyms* (*adv*) indirectly, obliquely, later, 4. immediately; *synonyms* (*adv*) readily, instantaneously, momentarily, summarily, speedily, straightway, swiftly, completely, correctly, hastily, (*adj*) instanter; *antonym* (*adv*) slowly, 5. instantly; *synonym* (*adv*) suddenly; *antonym* (*adv*) eventually, 6. presently; *synonyms* (*adv*) shortly, currently, just.

abina prepare; *synonyms* (*v*) arrange, fix, form, plan, dress, coach, devise, lay, make, set, adjust, concoct, cook, equip, fit.

abinaki prepared; *synonyms* (*adj*) disposed, fit, willing, fitted, fain, finished, ready, ripe, competent, inclined, primed, completed, efficient, mature, apt; *antonyms* (*adj*) unprepared, spontaneous.

abo aboriginal; *synonyms* (*adj*) native, original, early, autochthonous, first, indigenous, primaeval, primal, primary, primeval, primordial, (*n*) aborigine; *antonym* (*adj*) nonnative.

aboabo 1. aboriginal; *synonyms* (*adj*) native, original, early, autochthonous, first, indigenous, primaeval, primal, primary, primeval, primordial, (n) aborigine; *antonym* (adj) nonnative, **2.** gusty; *synonyms* (adj) breezy, blustery, stormy, windy, blowy, squally, tempestuous, blustering, blusterous, dirty; *antonym* (adj) still, **3.** polite; *synonyms* (adj) courteous, cultured, civil, courtly, genteel, gentle, proper, refined, attentive, kind, friendly, chivalrous, civilized, complaisant, considerate; *antonyms* (adj) impolite, rude, bad-mannered, discourteous, boorish.

aboabonaomata humane; *synonyms* (adj) benevolent, compassionate, beneficent, clement, charitable, kind, merciful, good, benignant, tender, (n) gentle, gracious, kindly, sympathetic, caring; *antonyms* (adj) cruel, inhumane.

aboka 1. initiate; *synonyms* (v) begin, found, commence, inaugurate, launch, activate, induct, institute, introduce, originate, start, enter, undertake, broach, (n) entrant, **2.** begin; *synonyms* (v) arise, become, initiate, rise, create, dawn, embark, open, build, happen, induce, attack, attempt, bring, cause; *antonyms* (v) finish, end, stop, **3.** commence; *synonyms* (v) approach, develop, get, **4.** starting; *synonyms* (n) commencement, first, outset, departure, kickoff, origin, source, advantage, (adj) opening, initial, incipient, original, introductory, (prep) beginning, from, **5.** start; *synonyms* (v) drive, spring, flinch, set, startle, actuate, break, depart, establish, (n) jump, onset, shock, leap, threshold, genesis; *antonyms* (v) conclude, halt, (n) conclusion.

Abotoro apostle; *synonyms* (n) disciple, follower, propagandist, believer, missionary, advocate, munshi, proselyte, saint, evangelist, pioneer, companion, converter, proponent, proselytizer.

abu 1. end; *synonyms* (n) close, aim, closure, destination, conclusion, death, cause, demise, object, (v) cease, complete, finish, discontinue, conclude, (prep) consequence; *antonyms* (n) beginning, maintenance, opening, middle, (v) start, begin, continue, **2.** extremity; *synonyms* (n) end, extreme, member, boundary, bound, appendage, ending, limit, emergency, need, crisis, exigency, border, edge, height, **3.** top; *synonyms* (adj) maximum, superlative, (n) crown, peak, acme, apex, crest, cover, pinnacle, summit, (v) best, cap, exceed, head, outdo; *antonyms* (adj) worst, (n) bottom, base, nadir.

abuabu 1. massage; *synonyms* (n) manipulation, friction, (v) rub, knead, manipulate, press, caress, touch, abrade, abrase, apply, arrange, cajole, corrade, daub, **2.** seize; *synonyms* (v) capture, catch, grab, arrest, apprehend, clutch, get, grapple, receive, annex, assume, clasp, confiscate, conquer, grasp; *antonym* (v) release, **3.** scoop; *synonyms* (n) ladle, spade, exclusive, pocket, scoopful, shovel,

article, report, (v) draw, dig, excavate, hollow, best, outdo, outflank.

abuabuaki seized; *synonyms* (adj) confiscate, confiscated, appropriated, condemned, apprehended, detained, held, censured, convicted, forfeit, forfeited, obsessed.

abue lukewarm; *synonyms* (adj) tepid, cold, indifferent, warm, listless, cool, halfhearted, mild, unenthusiastic, apathetic, frigid, genial, hot; *antonym* (adj) enthusiastic.

abunaña shoulder; *synonyms* (n) elbow, back, (v) bear, carry, push, hold, jostle, support, sustain, assume, accept, shove, take, thrust, undertake.

abuta scoop; *synonyms* (n) ladle, spade, exclusive, pocket, scoopful, shovel, article, report, (v) draw, dig, excavate, hollow, best, outdo, outflank.

abwabwaki long; *synonyms* (adj) extended, lengthy, dragging, far, (v) aspire, desire, hanker, languish, yearn, ache, hunger, wish, crave, (n) extensive, large; *antonyms* (adj) short, brief.

abwi forty; *synonyms* (n) forties, (adj) twoscore.

aea 1. sliver; *synonyms* (n) splinter, shred, fragment, bit, shaving, scrap, shiver, part, crumb, slip, (v) chip, flake, slice, shave, cut, **2.** split; *synonyms* (v) crack, fracture, slit, burst, divide, separate, divorce, breach, cleave, (n) break, rip, rupture, tear, cleavage, cleft; *antonyms* (v) join, unite, merge.

aeae 1. infiltrate; *synonyms* (v) soak, enter, penetrate, permeate, inculcate, indoctrinate, instill, **2.** striped; *synonyms* (adj) streaked, stripy, paled, virgated, zoned, hooped, zonate.

aeaea tow; *synonyms* (n) towage, (v) pull, drag, draw, haul, lug, tug, heave, trail, rake, taw; *antonym* (v) push.

aeaki split; *synonyms* (v) crack, cut, fracture, slit, burst, divide, separate, divorce, breach, cleave, (n) break, rip, rupture, tear, cleavage; *antonyms* (v) join, unite, merge.

aebai handle; *synonyms* (v) administer, conduct, feel, wield, control, deal, direct, finger, manage, manipulate, touch, treat, (n) grip, clutch, grasp.

aeka 1. classify; *synonyms* (v) arrange, class, assort, categorize, order, separate, distinguish, group, rank, organize, regulate, dispose, characterize, codify, (n) sort; *antonym* (v) declassify, **2.** describe; *synonyms* (v) define, delineate, depict, outline, report, represent, state, draw, relate, qualify, designate, explain, name, narrate, recite, **3.** assorted; *synonyms* (adj) different, mixed, miscellaneous, sundry, various, diverse, heterogeneous, motley, varied, manifold, multiple; *antonyms* (adj) homogeneous, uniform, **4.** ride; *synonyms* (n) outing, run, lift, jaunt, voyage, (v) drive, bait, float, mount, rag, tease, harass, annoy, drift, (adj) bestride, **5.** vary; *synonyms* (v) alter, change, differ, modify, alternate, deviate, diverge, diversify, modulate, depart, disagree, fluctuate, shift, variegate, contrast, **6.** queer; *synonyms* (*adj*) fantastic, eccentric, odd, curious, funny, fishy, gay, peculiar, quaint, strange, outlandish, comical, fanciful, droll, (*v*) baffle, **7.** rank; *synonyms* (*n*) range, place, file, gradation, line, degree, quality, rate, post, (*adj*) putrid, (*v*) classify, grade, position, array, estimate; *antonym* (*adj*) fresh, **8.** such; *synonyms* (*adv*) what, (*adj*) like, sic, sich, slik, swich, resembling, **9.** sort; *synonyms* (*n*) kind, type, assortment, breed, description, form, variety, pattern, fashion, nature, appearance, brand, (*v*) divide, (*adj*) manner, character, **10.** withdraw; *synonyms* (*v*) extract, remove, retire, retract, retreat, abandon, cancel, disengage, leave, recall, recede, secede, go, repeal, rescind; *antonyms* (*v*) advance, extend, give, offer, present, propose, deposit.

aekaki 1. classified; *synonyms* (*adj*) confidential, secret, clandestine, private, hush-hush, inside, chronological, exclusive, personal, privileged, regular, concealed, confidence, undisclosed, **2.** described; *synonyms* (*adj*) alleged, detailed, **3.** varied; *synonyms* (*adj*) assorted, diverse, miscellaneous, mixed, various, different, diversified, sundry, heterogeneous, manifold, motley, many, dissimilar, versatile, odd; *antonyms* (*adj*) boring, dull, homogeneous, uniform, **4.** sorted; *synonyms* (*adj*) grouped, fixed, straight, **5.** withdrawn; *synonyms* (*adj*) reserved, secluded, retiring, solitary, indrawn, cloistered, reclusive, uncommunicative, lonely, taciturn, unsociable, introverted, reticent, shy, aloof; *antonym* (*adj*) outgoing, **6.** ranked; *synonyms* (*adj*) graded, bedded, graveled, stratified.

aera done; *synonyms* (*adj*) finished, complete, completed, over, gone, through, (*adv*) ended; *antonym* (*adj*) unfinished.

aerake land; *synonyms* (*n*) ground, country, soil, field, kingdom, domain, estate, nation, realm, state, (*v*) disembark, debark, alight, get, drop; *antonym* (*adj*) aquatic.

aeraki done; *synonyms* (*adj*) finished, complete, completed, over, gone, through, (*adv*) ended; *antonym* (*adj*) unfinished.

aerona stoke; *synonyms* (*v*) hit, paddle, tap, touch, stab, stick, thrust.

aetorake vertical; *synonyms* (*adj*) upright, perpendicular, straight, erect, sheer, standing, plumb, unbowed; *antonyms* (*adj*) horizontal, prone.

ahine girl; *synonyms* (*n*) damsel, lady, daughter, fille, lass, maid, wench, virgin, quean, female, girlfriend, woman.

ahoua four; *synonyms* (*n*) quaternity, foursome, quadruplet, quaternary, quaternion, tetrad, quarter, square, ace, air, appearence, cast, casting, contrivance, direction.

ai 1. heap; *synonyms* (*n*) pile, stack, accumulation, collection, amass, group, lot, mass, mound, bulk, bunch, congeries, (*v*) aggregate, bank, collect, **2.** fire; *synonyms* (*n*) discharge, ardor, conflagration, explode, fervor, flame, (*v*) excite, eject, blaze, dismiss, ignite, kindle, expel, animate, arouse; *antonym* (*v*) hire, **3.** me; *synonym* (*n*) myself, **4.** accumulate; *synonyms* (*v*) gather, store, accrue, assemble, compile, cumulate, heap, hoard, drift, add, concentrate, conglomerate, cull, gain, garner; *antonyms* (*v*) disperse, distribute, dwindle.

aia yes; *synonyms* (*int*) surely, (*n*) consent, acceptance, nod, (*adv*) ay, yea, certainly, positively, precisely, (*v*) acquiesce, agree, allow, grovel, (*adj*) obedient, submissive.

aiaki 1. heaped; *synonyms* (*adj*) piled, coacervate, collective, cumulative, dense, thick, cumulous, **2.** accumulated; *synonyms* (*adj*) accrued, amassed, assembled, collected, accumulate, aggregate, congregate, massed, store, upheaped, equanimous, poised.

aibiko excited; *synonyms* (*adj*) agitated, ablaze, emotional, enthusiastic, frantic, ardent, aroused, delirious, fervent, heated, impassioned, passionate, warm, elated, (*v*) animated; *antonyms* (*adj*) calm, cool, unexcited.

aiewe 1. misplace; *synonyms* (*v*) lose, displace, mislay, derange, dislocate, disorganize, confuse, disarrange, disestablish, dishevel, dislodge, disorder, displant, disturb, drop; *antonym* (*v*) find, **2.** lose; *synonyms* (*v*) forfeit, sacrifice, fail, clear, hurt, regress, retrogress, destroy, misplace, recede, suffer, waste, escape; *antonyms* (*v*) gain, acquire, earn, get, obtain, recover, secure, win, beat, defeat, keep, succeed.

aieweaki 1. misplaced; *synonyms* (*adj*) lost, mislaid, absent, disordered, misguided, missing, wrong, gone, omitted, vanished, (*v*) misjoined, mismatched; *antonyms* (*adj*) present, found, **2.** lost; *synonyms* (*v*) abandoned, (*adj*) doomed, forlorn, extinct, hopeless, bewildered, disoriented, forgotten, helpless, broken, confused, irrecoverable, astray, dead, missed; *antonym* (*adj*) existing.

aika 1. who; *synonyms* (*pron*) one, (*adj*) which, what, **2.** with; *synonyms* (*prep*) by, for, alongside, among, plus, (*adv*) on, beside, (*adj*) including, (*n*) withe.

aikoa never; *synonyms* (*adv*) ne'er, nevermore, nor, tomorrow; *antonym* (*adv*) always.

aimaka glow; *synonyms* (*n*) beam, color, glare, sparkle, blaze, flash, (*v*) blush, flush, gleam, glimmer, shine, burn, flare, fire, flame; *antonym* (*n*) dullness.

aine female; *synonyms* (*adj*) distaff, feminine, pistillate, (*n*) lady, woman, girl, (*obj*) she; *antonyms* (*adj*) masculine, (*n*) male, man.

ainenuma matron; *synonyms* (*n*) lady, wife, woman, matriarch, female, companion, administrator, biddy, mother, superintendent, (*v*) matronage, matronhood.

ainga 1. illuminated; *synonyms* (*adj*) bright, lighted, lit, luminous, enlightened, clear, ablaze, brilliant, burning, irradiate, intelligent, intelligible, **2**. enlighten; *synonyms* (*v*) elucidate, advise, clarify, edify, educate, inform, apprise, illuminate, instruct, notify, acquaint, solve, tell, train, (*adj*) lighten; *antonym* (*v*) confuse, puzzle, **3**. clear; *synonyms* (*adj*) clean, certain, open, apparent, distinct, empty, light, (*v*) acquit, absolute, free, net, absolve, definite, discharge, exculpate; *antonyms* (*adj*) cloudy, opaque, unclear, dark, fuzzy, hazy, incomprehensible, obscure, uncertain, vague, ambiguous, blurry, confused, confusing, (*v*) convict.

aingaki enlightened; *synonyms* (*adj*) educated, liberal, disillusioned, progressive, aware, cultured, informed, learned, lettered, refined, (*v*) wise, savant, shrewd; *antonyms* (*adj*) mystified, puzzled, unenlightened.

aini creak; *synonyms* (*n*) creaking, (*v*) squeak, pipe, screech, jangle, skreigh, twang, confess, screak, skreak, sound, crepitate, shrill, speak, (*adj*) ancient.

ainikai squeak; *synonyms* (*n*) cry, screech, chirp, (*v*) shriek, scream, peep, creak, screak, yell, scrape, howl, cheep, wail, yelp, shrill.

aintoa 1. titan; *synonyms* (*n*) giant, colossus, behemoth, heavyweight, monster, hulk, whale, (*adj*) gigantic, titanic, **2**. warrior; *synonyms* (*n*) fighter, soldier, combatant, champion, militant, hero, boxer, captain, chieftain, contestant, defender, enemy, leader, mercenary, protagonist, **3**. strong; *synonyms* (*adj*) intense, powerful, able, deep, firm, stable, steady, cogent, durable, forcible, good, hard, influential, lusty, potent; *antonyms* (*adj*) weak, bland, delicate, faint, feeble, frail, mild, pale, slight, unconvincing, cowardly, diluted, dull, exhausted, flimsy.

aioro 1. collide; *synonyms* (*v*) bump, clash, conflict, impact, crash, strike, beat, hit, hurtle, jar, knock, smash, quarrel, (*n*) bang, **2**. clash; *synonyms* (*n*) battle, brush, clang, discord, encounter, struggle, wrangle, argument, (*v*) fight, brawl, clank, collide, dispute, scuffle, squabble; *antonyms* (*n*) agreement, (*v*) agree.

aiota 1. daybreak; *synonyms* (*n*) dawn, sunrise, morning, prime, aurora, cockcrow, dawning, daylight, dayspring, light, sunup; *antonyms* (*n*) dusk, sunset, **2**. dawn; *synonyms* (*n*) beginning, commencement, onset, origin, start, birth, genesis, inception, opening, (*v*) break, begin, appear, originate, rise, (*adj*) daybreak; *antonyms* (*n*) twilight, (*v*) end, finish.

airi 1. accompany; *synonyms* (*v*) attend, follow, associate, companion, company, guide, lead, walk, consort, bring, concur, conduct, convoy, join, (*n*) escort, **2**. inseparable; *synonyms* (*adj*) indivisible, inherent, built-in, close, essential, inborn, inbred, indiscerptible, indispensable, innate, inseverable, tenacious, thick, (*v*) severable, united; *antonym* (*adj*) divisible.

airiaki accompanied; *synonym* (*adj*) attended.

airo 1. dusk; *synonyms* (*n*) dark, nightfall, twilight, darkness, gloaming, gloom, night, shade, sunset, shadow, evenfall, evening, eventide, sundown, (*adj*) dusky; *antonyms* (*n*) dawn, sunrise, daybreak, light, **2**. bump; *synonyms* (*n*) bang, crash, blow, bulge, clash, hit, knock, blast, collision, concussion, jar, push, (*v*) bash, jolt, break, **3**. eve; *synonyms* (*n*) apex, cover, top, lid, point, summit, verge, vertex, **4**. twilight; *synonyms* (*n*) dusk, crepuscule, curfew, decline, fall, (*adj*) aurora.

airua 1. mistake; *synonyms* (*n*) blunder, fault, defect, error, failure, misapprehension, misconception, demerit, inaccuracy, (*v*) err, misapprehend, slip, confuse, misjudge, misunderstand, **2**. blunder; *synonyms* (*n*) mistake, gaffe, bloomer, blooper, botch, lapse, misstep, oversight, trip, blemish, boner, (*v*) stumble, fail, fumble, boob, **3**. error; *synonyms* (*n*) deviation, wrong, delusion, crime, guilt, misunderstanding, falsehood, confusion, erroneousness, fallacy, misprint, omission, sin, transgression, breakdown; *antonym* (*n*) correctness.

airuaki mistaken; *synonyms* (*adj*) incorrect, erroneous, false, wrong, misguided, inaccurate, fallacious, untrue, misleading; *antonym* (*adj*) correct.

aitao 1. covered; *synonyms* (*adj*) hidden, veiled, concealed, covert, coated, masked, obscured, secret, shrouded, thick, wrapped, (*prep*) cloaked; *antonyms* (*adj*) bare, naked, **2**. overflowing; *synonyms* (*v*) inundation, deluge, (*adj*) abundant, full, copious, exuberant, flooding, bountiful, generous, brimming, profuse, superfluous, afloat, ample, (*n*) flood; *antonym* (*adj*) empty, **3**. submerged; *synonyms* (*adj*) immersed, subaqueous, submersed, sunken, underwater, subaquatic, submarine, covered, bathed, deep, engrossed, recessed, semiaquatic, suffused, (*pron*) drowned.

aitau 1. expedient; *synonyms* (*adj*) fit, adequate, advisable, becoming, desirable, apt, appropriate, convenient, suitable, handy, (*n*) contrivance, makeshift, artifice, device, resource, **2**. timely; *synonyms* (*adj*) opportune, punctual, early, prompt, propitious, pat, providential, auspicious, favorable, fortunate, timeful, (*v*) seasonable, (*adv*) apropos, seasonably; *antonyms* (*adj*) untimely, inopportune.

aitibo contact; *synonyms* (*n*) touch, connection, collision, communication, link, impact, tangency, acquaintance, (*v*) call, meet, adjoin, communicate, reach, butt, join.

aitiotiriti isosceles; *synonym* (*adj*) equicrural.

aiûri like; *synonyms* (v) corresponding, enjoy, identical, care, desire, fancy, (adj) equal, equivalent, alike, analogous, comparable, same, parallel, (n) love, relish; *antonyms* (prep) unlike, (v) dislike, (adj) different.

aiwau 1. delirious; *synonyms* (adj) crazy, frantic, frenzied, wild, wandering, demented, excited, frenetic, insane, mad; *antonym* (adj) sane, **2.** rave; *synonyms* (n) rage, rant, (v) fume, jabber, wander, gush, bluster, storm, tear, acclaim, babble, (adj) foam, boil, flame, seethe.

akawa fish; *synonyms* (n) bird, insect, mollusk, shellfish, worm, amphibian, beginner, blacktail, (v) angle, seek, hunt, pursue, grope, rummage, beg.

ake 1. comb; *synonyms* (n) cockscomb, combing, crest, (v) brush, ransack, search, dress, groom, rake, scour, (adj) weed, **2.** hackle; *synonyms* (v) comb, chop, haggle, hatchel, heckle, lacerate, scamble, slice, chip, clean, (adj) awn, bur, burr, catchweed, cleavers, **3.** card; *synonyms* (n) bill, board, ticket, label, carte, menu, notice, placard, postal, scorecard, wit, (v) tease, **4.** strip; *synonyms* (n) band, slip, (v) deprive, despoil, divest, peel, plunder, rifle, denude, pillage, pluck, pare, sack, bare, bereave; *antonym* (v) decorate.

akea 1. no; *synonyms* (n) refusal, rejection, denial, number, nix, rebuff, nobelium, ordinal, (adv) nay, (adj) zero, naught, none, non, nul, **2.** absent; *synonyms* (adj) off, wanting, inattentive, absentminded, abstracted, faraway, lost, missing, nonexistent, out, preoccupied, (adv) away; *antonym* (adj) present, **3.** none; *synonyms* (adj) nil, no, **4.** empty; *synonyms* (adj) discharge, hollow, destitute, bare, blank, barren, abandoned, deserted, vain, (v) drain, clear, deplete, desolate, pour, spill; *antonyms* (adj) full, crowded, meaningful, packed, brimming, inhabited, occupied, swarming, cultivated, filled, laden, (v) fill, **5.** emptiness; *synonyms* (n) blankness, vacancy, vanity, void, vacuity, futility, inanition, inanity, space, worthlessness, conceit, oblivion, vacuousness; *antonyms* (n) overcrowding, richness, fullness, value, **6.** nothing; *synonyms* (n) cipher, nobody, nihil, nonentity, aught, cypher, null, trifle, nada, zilch, zip, (adj) worthless; *antonym* (pron) something, **7.** zero; *synonyms* (n) nothing, nought, nullity, root, **8.** space; *synonyms* (n) length, gap, opening, period, place, scope, margin, distance, emptiness, extent, interval, latitude, location, range, room, **9.** zilch.

akêa 1. not; *synonyms* (adv) no, nay, nor, nowise, never, (adj) shaven, shorn, **2.** no; *synonyms* (n) refusal, rejection, denial, number, nix, rebuff, nobelium, ordinal, (adj) zero, naught, none, non, nul.

akeaki 1. carded, **2.** combed, **3.** stripped; *synonyms* (adj) bare, naked, nude, exposed, fleeced, undressed, desolate, stark, unclothed.

aki 1. a; *synonyms* (n) amp, ampere, angstrom, axerophthol, forenoon, morn, morning, (v) grammar, initiation, (adj) cream, elite, flower, masterpiece, pick, prime, **2.** not; *synonyms* (adv) no, nay, nor, nowise, never, (adj) shaven, shorn, **3.** about; *synonyms* (prep) encircling, for, encompassing, circa, concerning, (adv) around, approximately, almost, nearly, most, roughly, in, nearby, (adj) some, near; *antonyms* (prep) exactly, precisely, **4.** slightly; *synonyms* (adv) rather, little, somewhat, lightly, slight, fairly, moderately, slenderly, faintly, small, hardly, barely, slimly, scarcely; *antonyms* (adv) very, excessively, infinitely, significantly, terribly, tremendously, considerably, much, particularly, solidly, **5.** superficially; *synonyms* (adv) outwardly, apparently, hastily, allegedly, cheaply, dismissively, externally, frivolously, glibly, ostensibly, ostentatiously, seemingly, showily, supposedly, tackily; *antonyms* (adv) deeply, thoroughly, seriously, **6.** un; *synonyms* (n) death, (v) discharge.

akî not; *synonyms* (adv) no, nay, nor, nowise, never, (adj) shaven, shorn.

akiako rude; *synonyms* (adj) gross, rough, impudent, blunt, coarse, bold, brutal, crude, discourteous, impolite, mean, abusive, barbarous, churlish, (n) abrupt; *antonyms* (adj) polite, respectful, chivalrous, courteous, refined, civil, decent, proper, well-mannered.

akibakatae frugal; *synonyms* (adj) economical, chary, thrifty, abstemious, sparing, austere, careful, moderate, parsimonious, provident, prudent, slender, economic, scarce, (v) spare; *antonyms* (adj) spendthrift, extravagant.

akideria deep; *synonyms* (adj) thick, profound, absorbed, abstruse, broad, dark, rich, sound, strong, wide, esoteric, bright, large, abysmal, (v) intense; *antonyms* (adj) shallow, superficial, high, high-pitched, light, soft, weak.

akikaubwai 1. destitute; *synonyms* (adj) indigent, bankrupt, broke, forlorn, impoverished, needy, poor, helpless, impecunious, necessitous, penniless, void, wanting, bare, (v) devoid; *antonym* (adj) rich, **2.** poor; *synonyms* (adj) bad, low, miserable, paltry, deplorable, destitute, evil, inadequate, insufficient, pathetic, piteous, pitiful, meagre, (v) meager, (n) mean; *antonyms* (adj) wealthy, excellent, first-rate, privileged, well-off, admirable, good.

ako careful; *synonyms* (adj) accurate, attentive, thrifty, alert, deliberate, economical, frugal, mindful, prudent, thoughtful, assiduous, aware, cagey, cautious, (v) anxious; *antonyms* (adj) careless, reckless, slapdash, neglectful.

akoa 1. minister; *synonyms* (n) pastor, envoy, priest, deputy, divine, ambassador, churchman, clergyman, cleric, curate, ecclesiastic, agent, messenger, (v) supply, administer, **2**. welcome; *synonyms* (adj) acceptable, pleasant, agreeable, pleasing, enjoyable, (v) accept, greet, invite, receive, hail, entertain, (n) salute, hospitality, reception, embrace; *antonyms* (adj) unwelcome, unwanted, (v) reject.

akoi 1. kind; *synonyms* (n) form, helpful, sort, benign, brand, breed, class, gentle, type, variety, (adj) friendly, generous, good, humane, affectionate; *antonyms* (adj) unkind, callous, cruel, hardhearted, mean, merciless, nasty, spiteful, uncaring, upsetting, disagreeable, unfeeling, **2**. liberal; *synonyms* (adj) bountiful, free, handsome, abundant, benevolent, big, large, kind, ample, bounteous, broad, charitable, giving, tolerant, lavish; *antonyms* (adj) strict, oppressive, totalitarian, intolerant, (n) conservative.

aman month; *synonyms* (n) moon, day, hour, minute, quarter, quinquennium, year, moneth, moonshine, second, time, week.

amarake 1. eat; *synonyms* (v) devour, consume, bite, dine, munch, corrode, deplete, drink, feed, finish, gnaw, gobble, gorge, graze, (adj) digest, **2**. dine; *synonyms* (v) eat, lunch, breakfast, entertain, taste, touch.

añ wind; *synonyms* (n) air, gust, (v) coil, twist, curl, meander, turn, bend, curve, twine, blow, crook, entwine, roll, weave.

ana 1. receive; *synonyms* (v) accept, admit, get, assume, adopt, bear, have, obtain, welcome, make, acknowledge, embrace, gather, greet, take, **2**. get; *synonyms* (v) acquire, gain, attain, become, catch, earn, buy, come, fall, fetch, achieve, beget, bring, capture, cause; *antonyms* (v) lose, give, leave, **3**. bereave; *synonyms* (v) deprive, divest, rob, strip, despoil, oust, disinherit, widow, depose, destroy, dismantle, outstrip, pass, skin, uncover, **4**. bring; *synonyms* (v) convey, carry, conduct, put, reduce, afford, bestow, deliver, land, move, provide, attract, accompany, arrest, contribute, **5**. below; *synonyms* (adv) beneath, under, down, infra, downstairs, (prep) underneath, (adj) low, after; *antonyms* (prep) above, over, **6**. bottom; *synonyms* (n) base, basis, backside, bed, behind, foot, footing, back, arse, ass, bum, butt, buttocks, craft, floor; *antonyms* (n) top, pinnacle, (adj) highest, **7**. sap; *synonyms* (n) chump, fool, liquid, mug, muggins, (v) debilitate, deplete, drain, exhaust, enfeeble, enervate, dig, consume, (adj) juice, mine, **8**. subtract; *synonyms* (v) deduct, calculate, add, discount, diminish, subduct, withhold, deduce, withdraw, cipher, compute, figure, infer, score, **9**.

take; *synonyms* (v) hold, clutch, return, borrow, pick, appropriate, claim, demand, grab, interpret, require, select, steal, (n) seize, (phr) receive; *antonyms* (v) refuse, abstain, **10**. withdraw; *synonyms* (v) extract, remove, retire, retract, retreat, abandon, cancel, disengage, draw, recall, recede, secede, depart, go, repeal; *antonyms* (v) advance, extend, offer, present, propose, deposit, **11**. taken; *synonyms* (adj) occupied, full, interpreted, besotted, crazed, enamored, engaged, interested, lovesick, obsessed, overcome, preferred, rapt, reserved, unavailable, **12**. recite; *synonyms* (v) enumerate, relate, tell, describe, narrate, recount, detail, rehearse, repeat, say, lecture, report, state, read, (n) declaim.

aña shoulder; *synonyms* (n) elbow, back, (v) bear, carry, push, hold, jostle, support, sustain, assume, accept, shove, take, thrust, undertake.

anai 1. pick; *synonyms* (v) clean, gather, harvest, opt, break, (n) alternative, elite, best, choice, option, selection, (adj) cream, select, mattock, flower, **2**. subtract; *synonyms* (v) deduct, reduce, calculate, add, discount, diminish, subduct, withhold, deduce, withdraw, cipher, compute, figure, infer, score.

anaia 1. retrieve; *synonyms* (v) recover, regain, reclaim, recoup, rescue, obtain, get, redeem, recuperate, renew, resume, fetch, find, recall, recollect; *antonym* (v) lose, **2**. open; *synonyms* (adj) frank, obvious, artless, exposed, free, honest, bare, forthright, guileless, ingenuous, naked, (v) expand, give, (n) candid, clear; *antonyms* (v) devious, secretive, concealed, furtive, hidden, limited, repressive, reserved, restricted, secret, blocked, cautious, (v) shut, end, (tr v) close.

anákara slave; *synonyms* (n) serf, servant, bondman, inferior, thrall, bondsman, captive, vassal, dependent, (v) labor, drudge, fag, toil, work, moil.

anaki 1. bereaved; *synonyms* (adj) bereft, grieving, mourning, orbate, sad, sorrowing, childless, fatherless, lovelorn, unbeloved, (v) minus, denuded, **2**. received; *synonyms* (v) receiving, ascertained, current, recognized, (adj) accepted, acknowledged, conventional, acceptable, canonical, orthodox, customary, established, inward, known, legitimate, **3**. taken; *synonyms* (v) take, (adj) occupied, full, interpreted, besotted, crazed, enamored, engaged, interested, lovesick, obsessed, overcome, preferred, rapt, reserved, **4**. subtracted, **5**. withdrawn; *synonyms* (adj) secluded, retiring, solitary, indrawn, cloistered, reclusive, uncommunicative, lonely, taciturn, unsociable, introverted, reticent, shy, aloof, detached; *antonym* (adj) outgoing.

ananau 1. long; *synonyms* (adj) extended, lengthy, dragging, far, (v) aspire, desire, hanker, languish, yearn, ache, hunger, wish, crave, (n) extensive, large; *antonyms* (adj) short, brief, **2**. towering; *synonyms* (adj) high, lofty, eminent, tall, great, soaring, elevated, mighty, exalted, monumental, distinguished, imposing, magnificent, prodigious, stately, **3**. tall; *synonyms* (adj) big, lanky, towering, unbelievable, strapping, long, exaggerated, gangling, grandiloquent, magniloquent; *antonyms* (adj) low, small.

anânau 1. long; *synonyms* (adj) extended, lengthy, dragging, far, (v) aspire, desire, hanker, languish, yearn, ache, hunger, wish, crave, (n) extensive, large; *antonyms* (adj) short, brief, **2**. tall; *synonyms* (adj) lofty, elevated, high, exalted, big, lanky, towering, eminent, unbelievable, strapping, long, exaggerated, gangling, grandiloquent, magniloquent; *antonyms* (adj) low, small.

anangaki receive; *synonyms* (v) accept, admit, get, assume, adopt, bear, have, obtain, welcome, make, acknowledge, embrace, gather, greet, take.

anangakiaki received; *synonyms* (v) receiving, ascertained, current, recognized, (adj) accepted, acknowledged, conventional, acceptable, canonical, orthodox, customary, established, inward, known, legitimate.

anaukaei stretched; *synonyms* (adj) taut, extended, stiff, tense, tight, strained, expanded, outstretched, elongated, outspread, prolonged, protracted, assiduous, close, delayed; *antonym* (adj) brief.

ane surely; *synonyms* (adv) definitely, absolutely, positively, sure, undoubtedly, confidently, clearly, firmly, indeed, securely, truly, unquestionably, (int) certainly, (adj) really, doubtless; *antonym* (adv) doubtfully.

aneang mast; *synonyms* (n) post, column, tower, aerial, prop, pillar, stick, support, timber, arm, mass, acorns, nuts, receiver, transmitter.

anena foreign; *synonyms* (adj) alien, extraneous, extrinsic, exotic, exterior, external, strange, oversea, adventitious, outlandish, peregrine, remote, unfamiliar, unknown, different; *antonyms* (adj) native, familiar, domestic, internal.

anene sing; *synonyms* (v) chant, hymn, chirp, hum, drone, pipe, twitter, vocalize, carol, snitch, betray, harmonize, poetize, squeal, (n) squeak.

ang 1. direction; *synonyms* (n) administration, conduct, bearing, command, course, guidance, address, charge, control, instruction, rule, aspect, aim, counsel, (v) management, **2**. tepid; *synonyms* (adj) lukewarm, warm, mild, cool, indifferent, genial, hot, **3**. warm; *synonyms* (adj) affectionate, tender, ardent, cordial, fervent, lively, fond, loving, earnest, caring, enthusiastic, glowing, hearty, tepid, (v) heat; *antonyms* (adj) aloof, cold, unfriendly, reserved, hostile, (v) chill.

anga 1. contribute; *synonyms* (v) conduce, bestow, bring, administer, aid, impart, provide, supply, tend, afford, endow, advance, assist, donate, give,

2. donate; *synonyms* (v) contribute, confer, grant, offer, present, extend, gift, award, bequeath, **3**. dish; *synonyms* (n) bowl, beauty, disk, plate, platter, saucer, container, dishful, bag, (v) hollow, serve, **4**. grant; *synonyms* (n) concession, donation, permit, allowance, (v) allow, admit, concede, acknowledge, accord, direct, handle, minister, oversee, run, supervise, treat, apportion, (n) command, control, **7**. impart; *synonyms* (v) announce, disclose, divulge, hand, reveal, tell, instill, express, display, add, break, declare, discover, lend, render, **8**. deliver; *synonyms* (v) consign, bear, carry, rescue, save, abandon, liberate, pronounce, return, send, utter, drop, acquit, remit, birth, **9**. assign; *synonyms* (v) delegate, appoint, ascribe, accredit, allocate, appropriate, attribute, depute, place, put, designate, detail, entrust, impute, (n) adjudge, **10**. extend; *synonyms* (v) expand, enlarge, amplify, broaden, dilate, widen, augment, continue, elongate, go, spread, develop, increase, crane, (adj) stretch; *antonyms* (v) shorten, limit, narrow, shrink, **11**. given; *synonyms* (adj) apt, disposed, prone, liable, granted, inclined, set, (n) assumption, particular, presumption, fact, **12**. offer; *synonyms* (v) introduce, perform, propose, tender, lay, furnish, sacrifice, submit, (n) bid, proposal, proposition, approach, crack, fling, overture; *antonym* (v) refuse.

angaanga offer; *synonyms* (v) give, bestow, put, advance, extend, impart, introduce, perform, propose, tender, lay, (n) bid, proposal, go, proposition; *antonyms* (v) withdraw, refuse.

angaangaki given; *synonyms* (adj) apt, disposed, prone, liable, granted, inclined, set, (n) assumption, particular, presumption, fact.

angabaibuaka insult; *synonyms* (n) dishonor, abuse, affront, contumely, disgrace, indignity, outrage, contempt, wound, derision, harm, injury, (v) flout, taunt, cut; *antonyms* (v) compliment, praise.

angabe ungrateful; *synonyms* (adj) thankless, unmindful, unappreciative, unthankful, unnatural, ingrate, distasteful, displeasing, unkind, childless, cruel, harsh, ingrateful, offensive, unacceptable; *antonyms* (adj) grateful, thankful.

angabuaka 1. inconvenience; *synonyms* (n) bother, disadvantage, difficulty, nuisance, awkwardness, unsuitableness, encumbrance, ineptness, (v) trouble, discommode, incommode, disoblige, annoy, disquiet, disturb; *antonym* (n) convenience, **2**.

trouble; *synonyms* (*n*) distress, pain, anxiety, fuss, torment, care, concern, (*v*) inconvenience, disorder, worry, afflict, agitate, burden, distract, (*adj*) affliction; *antonyms* (*v*) calm, please.

angaki 1. donated; *synonyms* (*adj*) complimentary, unpaid, **2**. dished; *synonyms* (*v*) befooled, stultified, (*adj*) concave, hollow, dipped; *antonym* (*adj*) convex, **3**. delivered, **4**. given; *synonyms* (*adj*) apt, disposed, prone, liable, granted, inclined, set, (*n*) assumption, particular, presumption, fact, **5**. granted; *synonyms* (*adj*) given, assumed, fixed, approved, arranged, blessed, decided, legal, privileged, settled, contracted, established, (*adv*) yes, **6**. assigned; *synonyms* (*adj*) destined, definite, **7**. extended; *synonyms* (*adj*) broad, expanded, ample, extensive, long, wide, elongated, enlarged, lengthened, lengthy, prolonged, protracted, open, comprehensive, continued; *antonyms* (*adj*) brief, short, condensed, unextended.

angama 1. confused; *synonyms* (*adj*) abashed, bewildered, baffled, befuddled, bemused, chaotic, confounded, disjointed, disordered, dizzy, incoherent, indistinct, ambiguous, (*n*) cloudy, (*adv, adj*) topsy-turvy; *antonyms* (*adj*) clear, enlightened, alert, clearheaded, clear-headed, orderly, **2**. fearful; *synonyms* (*adj*) afraid, cowardly, dreadful, anxious, apprehensive, awful, craven, terrible, timid, dire, eerie, formidable, frightful, appalling, awesome; *antonyms* (*adj*) brave, calm, rational, bold, confident, unimpressed, **3**. embarrassed; *synonyms* (*adj*) ashamed, awkward, uncomfortable, disconcerted, bashful, shamefaced, sheepish, shy, chagrined, discomfited, humiliated, mortified; *antonyms* (*adj*) proud, relaxed, **4**. timid; *synonyms* (*adj*) fearful, diffident, cautious, coy, nervous, frightened, modest, retiring, faint, fainthearted, pusillanimous, reserved, scared, spineless, coward; *antonym* (*adj*) fearless.

angamaran 1. slippery; *synonyms* (*adj*) cunning, crafty, glib, elusive, glossy, oily, shifty, slick, slippy, tricky, untrustworthy, wily, dishonest, (*v*) precarious, questionable, **2**. sloping; *synonyms* (*adj*) oblique, slanting, aslant, aslope, inclined, slanted, diagonal, leaning, sloped, slope, tilted, declivous, (*v*) slant, (*adv*) sideways; *antonym* (*adj*) level.

angamatoa strong; *synonyms* (*adj*) intense, powerful, able, deep, firm, stable, steady, cogent, durable, forcible, good, hard, influential, lusty, potent; *antonyms* (*adj*) weak, bland, delicate, faint, feeble, frail, mild, pale, slight, unconvincing, cowardly, diluted, dull, exhausted, flimsy.

angana 1. hand; *synonyms* (*n*) deal, aid, applause, employee, paw, worker, (*v*) deliver, give, pass, commit, bestow, afford, communicate, reach, grant, **2**. present; *synonyms* (*adj*) confer, current, (*n*) gift, donation, offering, presentation, (*v*) display,

introduce, prefer, donate, offer, perform, gratuity, award, exhibit; *antonyms* (*adj*) missing, (*n*) past, future, history, (*v*) withdraw, (*adv*) absent.

anganai fetch; *synonyms* (*v*) carry, bring, convey, draw, elicit, attract, catch, get, retrieve, transport, conduct, extract, earn, bear, (*adj*) feint.

anganako 1. lent; *synonyms* (*n*) lenten, meager, plain, somber, spare, unostentatious, (*adj*) gentle, lento, mild, slow, **2**. lend; *synonyms* (*v*) loan, advance, give, grant, add, bestow, bring, contribute, impart, confer, provide; *antonym* (*v*) borrow.

anganakoaki lent; *synonyms* (*n*) lenten, meager, plain, somber, spare, unostentatious, (*adj*) gentle, lento, mild, slow.

angang 1. ardent; *synonyms* (*adj*) burning, enthusiastic, fervent, passionate, eager, impassioned, keen, vehement, warm, acute, affectionate, avid, devoted, earnest, fervid; *antonyms* (*adj*) indifferent, apathetic, **2**. lively; *synonyms* (*adj*) brisk, active, agile, cheerful, energetic, busy, fresh, gay, jolly, jovial, alert, animated, bright, live, merry; *antonyms* (*adj*) dull, inactive, lethargic, listless, lifeless, unexciting.

angangana 1. hand; *synonyms* (*n*) deal, aid, applause, employee, paw, worker, (*v*) deliver, give, pass, commit, bestow, afford, communicate, reach, grant, **2**. present; *synonyms* (*adj*) confer, current, (*n*) gift, donation, offering, presentation, (*v*) display, introduce, prefer, donate, offer, perform, gratuity, award, exhibit; *antonyms* (*adj*) missing, (*n*) past, future, history, (*v*) withdraw, (*adv*) absent.

angi 1. greater; *synonyms* (*adj*) more, higher, major, superior, most, great, additional, best, considerable, high, sizeable, upper, advanced, copious, (*adv*) better; *antonyms* (*adj*) lesser, inferior, smaller, **2**. much; *synonyms* (*adv*) greatly, frequently, almost, awfully, considerably, far, often, pretty, highly, nearly, (*n*) lot, heap, multitude, (*adj*) practically, muckle; *antonym* (*adv*) slightly, **3**. many; *synonyms* (*adj*) manifold, abundant, countless, frequent, various, innumerable, much, multiple, numerous, plentiful, several, different, numberless, (*n*) number; *antonym* (*n*) few, **4**. numerous; *synonyms* (*adj*) many, multitudinous, populous, myriad, rife, common, incalculable, thick.

angibue 1. lukewarm; *synonyms* (*adj*) tepid, cold, indifferent, warm, listless, cool, halfhearted, mild, unenthusiastic, apathetic, frigid, genial, hot; *antonym* (*adj*) enthusiastic, **2**. warm; *synonyms* (*adj*) affectionate, tender, ardent, cordial, fervent, lively, fond, loving, earnest, caring, glowing, hearty, heartfelt, burning, (*v*) heat; *antonyms* (*adj*) aloof, unfriendly, reserved, hostile, (*v*) chill, **3**. tepid; *synonym* (*adj*) lukewarm.

angita stimulate; *synonyms* (*v*) excite, incite, arouse, encourage, enliven, inspire, prompt, provoke, animate, awaken, drive, energize, exhilarate, goad, (*adj*) quicken; *antonym* (*v*) defuse.

angitaba impeding; *synonyms* (*adj*) hindering, obstructive, clogging, counter, disadvantageous, disconducive, impeditive, meddlesome, (*n*) resistance.

angitannene changeable; *synonyms* (*adj*) variable, capricious, erratic, inconsistent, irregular, fickle, giddy, mercurial, mobile, mutable, slippery, temperamental, uncertain, unsettled, unstable; *antonyms* (*adj*) constant, fixed, stable, unchangeable, consistent, dependable, predictable, regular.

angitannenne gusty; *synonyms* (*adj*) breezy, blustery, stormy, windy, blowy, squally, tempestuous, blustering, blusterous, dirty; *antonym* (*adj*) still.

angitoi 1. daze; *synonyms* (*n*) fog, shock, stupor, trance, confusion, (*v*) astonish, astound, bedazzle, amaze, befuddle, bewilder, dazzle, stun, surprise, flabbergast, **2.** shock; *synonyms* (*n*) blow, daze, impact, collision, outrage, concussion, fright, (*v*) jar, offend, revolt, startle, appall, clash, disgust, dismay; *antonym* (*v*) comfort, **3.** stun; *synonyms* (*v*) baffle, stagger, deaden, numb, bemuse, dumbfound, floor, perplex, petrify, electrify, galvanize, paralyze, overwhelm, (*n*) stupefy, (*adj*) deafen.

angitoiaki 1. dazed; *synonyms* (*adj*) confused, bewildered, stunned, dizzy, dumbfounded, muzzy, stupefied, amazed, astounded, bleary, groggy, stupid; *antonym* (*adj*) alert, **2.** stunned; *synonyms* (*adj*) astonished, dazed, flabbergasted, staggered, astonied, shocked, surprised, kayoed, out, unconscious, **3.** shocked; *synonyms* (*adj*) dismayed, aghast, distressed, afraid, appalled, speechless, upset; *antonym* (*adj*) delighted, indifferent.

angkoro 1. angle; *synonyms* (*n*) hook, incline, view, aspect, cant, corner, outlook, perspective, pitch, position, viewpoint, (*v*) slant, lean, tilt, fish, **2.** angular; *synonyms* (*adj*) angulate, bony, gaunt, skinny, spare, scrawny, aquiline, bent, gangling, rangy, serrated, uncinated, rude, stilted, angulous; *antonym* (*adj*) rounded.

angkoroaki angled; *synonyms* (*adj*) angulated, bent, forked, oblique, aslant, diagonal, inclined, leaning, sideways, sloping; *antonym* (*adj*) level.

angoa scratch; *synonyms* (*n*) score, mark, nick, scrabble, dent, abrasion, cut, groove, (*v*) graze, notch, rub, scrape, chafe, rake, grate.

angoaki scratched; *synonyms* (*adj*) scraped, hurt, abraded, dented, injured, raw, sgraffito, spoiled, broken, skinned, smashed.

anibana 1. agree; *synonyms* (*v*) accord, admit, acknowledge, acquiesce, adjust, accede, bargain, concord, correspond, fit, harmonize, suit, compromise, align, (*n*) coincide; *antonyms* (*v*)

disagree, oppose, differ, argue, object, refuse, refute, **2.** obey; *synonyms* (*v*) follow, comply, mind, heed, listen, keep, fulfill, hear, conform, serve, mark, observe, respect, submit; *antonyms* (*v*) disobey, break, defy, **3.** yield; *synonyms* (*n*) produce, return, give, output, proceeds, (*v*) surrender, allow, concede, cede, grant, relinquish, bow, afford, bear, consent; *antonyms* (*v*) resist, persevere, **4.** submit; *synonyms* (*v*) obey, present, resign, bend, convey, defer, deliver, exhibit, offer, proffer, propose, relegate, render, succumb, yield; *antonym* (*v*) withdraw.

anibange subordinate; *synonyms* (*adj*) subject, inferior, dependent, lower, secondary, subaltern, petty, junior, lesser, lowly, minor, less, ancillary, (*n*) assistant, underling; *antonyms* (*adj*) senior, (*n*) chief, superior, major.

anikai grating; *synonyms* (*adj*) rough, harsh, hoarse, strident, discordant, gravelly, gruff, rasping, raspy, raucous, (*n*) grate, grid, austere, (*v*) lattice, cutting; *antonyms* (*adj*) soft, pleasing.

anima scoop; *synonyms* (*n*) ladle, spade, exclusive, pocket, scoopful, shovel, article, report, (*v*) draw, dig, excavate, hollow, best, outdo, outflank.

animana scoop; *synonyms* (*n*) ladle, spade, exclusive, pocket, scoopful, shovel, article, report, (*v*) draw, dig, excavate, hollow, best, outdo, outflank.

annan scoop; *synonyms* (*n*) ladle, spade, exclusive, pocket, scoopful, shovel, article, report, (*v*) draw, dig, excavate, hollow, best, outdo, outflank.

annanau long; *synonyms* (*adj*) extended, lengthy, dragging, far, (*v*) aspire, desire, hanker, languish, yearn, ache, hunger, wish, crave, (*n*) extensive, large; *antonyms* (*adj*) short, brief.

anneanea mind; *synonyms* (*n*) intellect, brain, head, inclination, intelligence, psyche, regard, (*v*) care, look, attend, beware, keep, listen, notice, (*adj*) heed; *antonym* (*v*) forget.

anneaneaki minded; *synonyms* (*adj*) willing, prone, ready, partial, predisposed, prepared, (*prep*) inclined, disposed, jolly.

anni bark; *synonyms* (*n*) snarl, yelp, rind, bay, crust, peel, shout, boat, (*v*) yap, skin, cry, growl, roar, bellow, cough; *antonyms* (*v*) mutter, whisper.

ano inside; *synonyms* (*adv*) indoors, inwardly, within, (*n*) interior, middle, center, stomach, bosom, contents, (*adj*) inner, internal, indoor, inland, inward, private; *antonyms* (*prep*) outside, (*n*) exterior, (*adj*) free.

anoa beckon; *synonyms* (*v*) wave, attract, signal, summon, call, gesture, invite, motion, sign.

anoano 1. call; *synonyms* (*v*) cry, bellow, name, shout, bid, summon, howl, address, baptize, cite, (*n*) appeal, yell, appoint, command, demand; *antonym* (*v*) dismiss, **2.** beckon; *synonyms* (*v*) wave, attract, signal, call, gesture, invite, motion, sign, **3.** page;

synonyms (*n*) attendant, footboy, usher, note, pageboy, varlet, context, donzel, (*v*) paginate.

anoanoaki 1. called; *synonyms* (*v*) nempt, ycleped, (*adj*) named, chosen, qualified, **2. paged**.

anra undermine; *synonyms* (*v*) subvert, weaken, mine, cave, damage, sabotage, break, impair, burrow, counteract, countermine, (*n*) overthrow, (*adj*) sap, dig, delve; *antonyms* (*v*) strengthen, bolster.

antai 1. desist; *synonyms* (*v*) cease, abstain, discontinue, refrain, avoid, leave, end, forbear, halt, pause, quit, stop; *antonym* (*v*) persist, **2**. forbear; *synonyms* (*v*) desist, help, relinquish, (*n*) forebear, **3**. who; *synonyms* (*pron*) one, (*adj*) which, what.

antena strange; *synonyms* (*adj*) extraneous, foreign, peculiar, abnormal, curious, extraordinary, irregular, mysterious, new, odd, outlandish, unusual, rare, alien, anomalous; *antonyms* (*adj*) normal, ordinary, familiar, typical.

anti wild; *synonyms* (*adj*) desert, waste, fierce, boisterous, violent, reckless, desolate, ferocious, furious, raging, rude, stormy, untamed, giddy, barbarous; *antonyms* (*adj*) calm, orderly, domestic, manageable, sane, cultivated, restrained, tame.

antibuaka 1. clumsy; *synonyms* (*adj*) bumbling, bungling, cumbersome, unwieldy, gawky, inapt, inept, maladroit, rude, ungainly, unskilled, wooden, incompetent, lumbering, (*n*) awkward; *antonyms* (*adj*) graceful, nimble, clever, dexterous, skillful, adroit, deft, **2**. handy; *synonyms* (*adj*) available, convenient, apt, expert, good, accessible, easy, commodious, functional, near, nearby, practical, useful, able, (*n*) ready; *antonyms* (*adj*) useless, clumsy, fixed, **3**. awkward; *synonyms* (*adj*) inconvenient, crude, embarrassing, sticky, uncomfortable, untoward, left-handed, annoying, difficult, graceless, heavy, inelegant, rough, rustic, thorny; *antonyms* (*adj*) manageable, straightforward, helpful, rotund, simple, **4**. skillful; *synonyms* (*adj*) accomplished, adept, capable, proficient, knowing, artful, efficient, handy, practiced, skilled, nice, slick, (*v*) crafty, judicious, (*n*) cunning, **5**. sharp; *synonyms* (*adj*) acute, bitter, intelligent, acid, acrid, harsh, incisive, intense, penetrating, piercing, pointed, pungent, quick, (*n*) keen, (*v*) biting; *antonyms* (*adj*) blunt, dull, mild, gentle, rounded, sweet, bland, blurred, naive, round, smooth.

antingoa 1. hold; *synonyms* (*v*) keep, detain, endure, adhere, bear, comprise, contain, entertain, have, arrest, carry, (*n*) grasp, grip, clasp, clutch; *antonym* (*v*) release, **2**. whine; *synonyms* (*n*) groan, cry, complaint, wail, drone, (*v*) moan, complain, whimper, grumble, howl, sigh, squeal, buzz, gripe, grizzle, **3**. whimper; *synonyms* (*n*) whine, (*v*) sob, weep, pule, snivel, blubber, mewl, bleat, bibber, greet, growl, grunt, pipe, **4**. retard; *synonyms* (*v*)

delay, check, hinder, impede, lag, obstruct, slow, decelerate, procrastinate, curb, prevent, encumber, (*n*) defer, moron, (*adj*) deaden; *antonym* (*v*) accelerate, **5**. retain; *synonyms* (*v*) preserve, reserve, continue, hold, maintain, employ, engage, hire, own, possess, defend, occupy, remember, restrain, save.

antingoaki 1. held; *synonyms* (*adj*) absorbed, confined, alleged, assumed, believed, bound, caged, captive, detained, fast, immersed, obsessed, occupied, protected, (*adv*) on, **2**. retarded; *synonyms* (*adj*) backward, slow, tardy, imbecile, defective, deferred, dull, half-baked, leisurely, obtuse, simple, birdbrained, dim, dim-witted, dopey, **3**. retained; *synonyms* (*adj*) maintained, reserved, aeonian, durable, eonian, eternal, everlasting, haunting, lasting, permanent, persistent, relentless, repaired, serviced, unrelenting.

anua 1. assume; *synonyms* (*v*) affect, accept, adopt, appropriate, arrogate, feign, take, presume, sham, simulate, suppose, understand, usurp, feel, acquire, **2**. unintelligent; *synonyms* (*adj*) stupid, dull, silly, senseless, foolish, mindless, idiotic, inane, obtuse, petty, shallow, stolid, thick, ungifted; *antonyms* (*adj*) intelligent, bright, clever, **3**. same; *synonyms* (*adj*) alike, identical, corresponding, equal, like, equivalent, similar, uniform, even, consistent, matching, comparable, duplicate, monotonous, self; *antonym* (*adj*) different.

anuaki assumed; *synonyms* (*adj*) false, sham, affected, counterfeit, fake, feigned, fictitious, pretended, reputed, artificial, alleged, assumptive, hypothetical, phony, spurious.

ao 1. lament; *synonyms* (*n*) cry, dirge, complaint, elegy, (*v*) bemoan, complain, deplore, grieve, bewail, keen, moan, mourn, regret, wail, howl; *antonyms* (*n*) celebration, (*v*) revel, **2**. cry; *synonyms* (*n*) shout, bark, scream, yell, clamor, roar, bay, crying, (*v*) call, bellow, shriek, weep, exclaim, outcry, screech; *antonyms* (*v*) laugh, whisper, **3**. moan; *synonyms* (*n*) groan, gripe, whine, lament, grievance, grouse, protest, sob, murmur, (*v*) grumble, bleat, whimper, mutter, hum, growl, **4**. and; *synonyms* (*conj*) with, (*adv*) also, additionally, (*prep*) plus, including, (*adj*) more, **5**. sigh; *synonyms* (*n*) suspire, breath, suspiration, sike, (*v*) breathe, languish, pine, **6**. regret; *synonyms* (*v*) sorrow, repent, rue, (*n*) grief, compunction, contrition, penitence, remorse, repentance, disappointment, woe, mourning, qualm, contriteness, dissatisfaction, **7**. then; *synonyms* (*adv*) so, accordingly, afterward, again, consequently, later, (*conj*) therefore, **8**. over; *synonyms* (*adv*) beyond, across, by, o'er, on, too, crosswise, (*prep*) above, during, (*n*) overs, (*adj*) finished, done, extra, odd, past.

aoao regret; *synonyms* (*v*) bewail, grieve, bemoan, deplore, lament, mourn, sorrow, repent, (*n*) grief, compunction, contrition, penitence, remorse, repentance, disappointment.

aoaoraki sickly; *synonyms* (*adj*) feeble, infirm, sick, ailing, diseased, indisposed, morbid, pale, poorly, sallow, peaked, pasty, (*n*) invalid, (*v*) faint, frail; *antonyms* (*adj*) healthy, bitter.

aoaoria lounge; *synonyms* (*n*) couch, saunter, sofa, bar, (*v*) loiter, loll, loaf, recline, rest, dawdle, linger, relax, sprawl, bask, lie.

aobaki reject; *synonyms* (*v*) refuse, decline, deny, disapprove, discard, dismiss, eliminate, exclude, rebuff, abandon, disallow, disown, ignore, renounce, (*n*) cull; *antonyms* (*v*) accept, approve, choose, select, acknowledge, grant.

aoi 1. dewy; *synonyms* (*adj*) wet, dank, bedewed, humid, moist, damp, fresh, new, roric, irriguous, juicy, misty, roral, rorid, roscid, **2.** mold; *synonyms* (*n*) cast, matrix, frame, mould, stamp, die, (*v*) model, form, fashion, shape, carve, fit, figure, cut, forge, **3.** damp; *synonyms* (*adj*) muggy, clammy, cool, dampish, (*v*) break, check, chill, deaden, benumb, dampen, depress, discourage, (*n*) dampness, moisture, clamminess; *antonyms* (*adj*) dry, (*n*) dryness, **4.** humid; *synonyms* (*adj*) sultry, oppressive, soggy, steamy, sticky, watery, wettish, hot, **5.** moldy; *synonyms* (*adj*) musty, fusty, rancid, mouldy, bad, rank, rotten, (*v*) mildewed, rusty, decayed, **6.** wet; *synonyms* (*adj*) drenched, soaked, sodden, rainy, saturated, (*v*) moisten, water, wash, douse, irrigate, drench, bedew, splash, humidify, (*n*) humidity; *antonyms* (*adj*) dehydrated, parched.

aoiaki molded; *synonyms* (*adj*) formed, shaped, affected, characterized, figulated, inseparable, plastic, tough, wrought.

aoka dampen; *synonyms* (*v*) deaden, muffle, depress, dishearten, dull, moisten, mute, soften, wet, blunt, chill, cool, check, dash, (*n*) damp; *antonym* (*v*) stimulate.

aokabu illuminated; *synonyms* (*adj*) bright, lighted, lit, luminous, enlightened, clear, ablaze, brilliant, burning, irradiate, intelligent, intelligible.

aokangare 1. comical; *synonyms* (*adj*) amusing, comic, funny, laughable, absurd, humorous, ridiculous, zany, droll, jocose, entertaining, facetious, fantastic, farcical, jocular; *antonyms* (*adj*) serious, tragic, **2.** humorous; *synonyms* (*adj*) comical, witty, hilarious, playful, jovial, merry, pleasant, waggish, diverting, **3.** amusing; *synonyms* (*adj*) fun, agreeable, enjoyable, pleasing, risible, readable, amusive, charming, delightful, interesting, mirthful, pleasurable; *antonyms* (*adj*) dull, boring, **4.** laughable; *synonyms* (*adj*) ludicrous, foolish, derisory, preposterous, odd, burlesque, nonsensical, silly, gay, **5.** funny;

synonyms (*adj*) eccentric, fishy, peculiar, strange, curious, queer, suspicious, unusual, whimsical, abnormal, jolly, quaint, (*adv*) funnily, oddly, (*n*) jest; *antonym* (*adj*) grave.

aokua 1. arched; *synonyms* (*adj*) bowed, curved, arcuate, bent, vaulted, convex, arciform, arced, **2.** convex; *synonyms* (*adj*) bulging, gibbous, biconvex, hunched, bulgy, bellied, bellying, bulbous, deformed, outbowed, bulged, curving, (*n*) crescent, (*v*) projecting, curve; *antonym* (*adj*) concave, **3.** arch; *synonyms* (*n*) arc, acute, bend, curvature, dome, archway, (*v*) bow, vault, (*adj*) shrewd, sly, wily, round, crafty, consummate, astute; *antonym* (*v*) straightness.

aokuaki arched; *synonyms* (*adj*) bowed, curved, arcuate, bent, vaulted, convex, arciform, arced.

aomara 1. dangerous; *synonyms* (*adj*) critical, grave, serious, severe, adventurous, unhealthy, chancy, dicey, hazardous, hurtful, perilous, precarious, threatening, unsafe, poisonous; *antonyms* (*adj*) safe, secure, stable, **2.** hazardous; *synonyms* (*adj*) dangerous, risky, insecure, uncertain, awkward, explosive, treacherous, venturesome, venturous, (*n*) daring, **3.** smooth; *synonyms* (*adj*) easy, calm, level, oily, facile, flat, flowing, fluent, fluid, glossy, graceful, greasy, (*v*) quiet, facilitate, even; *antonyms* (*adj*) rough, uneven, abrasive, coarse, crumpled, flaking, harsh, jerky, lined, peeling, prickly, ridged, wrinkled, corrugated, (*v*) wrinkle, **4.** slippery; *synonyms* (*adj*) cunning, crafty, glib, elusive, shifty, slick, slippy, tricky, untrustworthy, wily, dishonest, icy, artful, shady, (*v*) questionable.

aomata 1. mortal; *synonyms* (*adj*) deadly, fatal, human, lethal, deathly, earthly, implacable, fateful, (*n*) individual, man, creature, person, being, body, soul; *antonyms* (*adj*) eternal, (*n*) immortal, **2.** human; *synonyms* (*adj*) humane, corporeal, worldly, carnal, (*n*) mortal, homo, gay, party, life, someone, homosexual, (*adv*) fleshly, **3.** being; *synonyms* (*n*) existence, animal, entity, essence, presence, matter, nature, organism, reality, self, spirit, substance, thing, (*adj*) present; *antonyms* (*n*) death, nonexistence, **4.** people; *synonyms* (*n*) nation, community, family, folk, multitude, populace, clan, mob, flock, citizenry, crowd, (*v*) inhabit, occupy, reside, dwell, **5.** party; *synonyms* (*n*) gang, band, company, assembly, association, crew, gathering, group, affair, bevy, celebration, do, faction, meeting, club, **6.** population; *synonyms* (*n*) inhabitants, people, public, society, citizens, stock, universe, **7.** populous; *synonyms* (*adj*) multitudinous, crowded, multiple, teeming, numerous, thick, large, manifold, multinominal, multiplied, (*v*) dense, peopled; *antonym* (*adj*) deserted.

aomatata 1. clear; *synonyms* (*adj*) clean, certain, open, apparent, distinct, empty, (*v*) bright, acquit, absolute, free, net, absolve, clarify, definite, discharge; *antonyms* (adj) cloudy, opaque, unclear, dark, fuzzy, hazy, incomprehensible, obscure, uncertain, vague, ambiguous, blurry, confused, confusing, (v) convict, **2.** bare; *synonyms* (adj) naked, austere, bald, stark, bleak, desolate, devoid, exposed, mere, nude, plain, vacant, vacuous, (v) show, disclose; *antonyms* (adj) covered, cultivated, ornate, concealed, (v) cover, **3.** plain; *synonyms* (adj) ordinary, comprehensible, intelligible, clear, downright, easy, evident, homely, humble, level, manifest, obvious, simple, perspicuous, (n) flat; *antonyms* (adj) elaborate, fancy, mottled, multicolored, attractive, fussy, two-colored.

aomate unfruitful; *synonyms* (adj) barren, infertile, sterile, acarpous, arid, fruitless, unproductive, effete, addled, infecund, inoperative, lean, unfertile.

aomwaimwai humid; *synonyms* (adj) moist, wet, damp, dank, sultry, clammy, muggy, oppressive, soggy, steamy, sticky, watery, wettish, hot; *antonyms* (adj) dry, fresh.

aona 1. excuse; *synonyms* (n) apology, alibi, evasion, palliate, pretext, color, (v) pardon, absolve, acquit, condone, exculpate, forgive, justify, apologise, apologize; *antonym* (v) punish, **2.** miss; *synonyms* (v) lack, lose, fail, jump, omit, overlook, long, drop, escape, (n) maid, girl, want, fille, missy, (adj) fault; *antonym* (v) perceive, **3.** overcome; *synonyms* (v) conquer, beat, crush, subdue, vanquish, defeat, master, overpower, hurdle, overwhelm, prevail, subjugate, surmount, demolish, (adj) beaten; *antonyms* (adj) victorious, unimpressed, **4.** omit; *synonyms* (v) neglect, disregard, delete, forget, except, exclude, ignore, leave, pretermit, expunge, erase, eliminate, default, (adj) skip, (n) forsake; *antonym* (v) include, **5.** surpass; *synonyms* (v) pass, exceed, outdo, better, excel, outstrip, overcome, overrun, best, outgo, outshine, outweigh, overstep, top, break.

aonaki 1. missed; *synonyms* (adj) lost, baffled, befuddled, bemused, bewildered, confounded, confused, disoriented, forgotten, helpless, irretrievable, mazed, preoccupied, **2.** excused; *synonyms* (adj) exempt, immune, privileged, excepted, **3.** overcome; *synonyms* (v) conquer, beat, crush, subdue, vanquish, defeat, master, overpower, hurdle, overwhelm, prevail, subjugate, surmount, demolish, (adj) beaten; *antonyms* (v) fail, (adj) victorious, unimpressed.

aoneiney 1. marshy; *synonyms* (adj) boggy, muddy, marsh, miry, quaggy, sloughy, swampy, paludal, moist, dirty, cloudy, coastal, dingy, moory, morassy, **2.** swampy; *synonyms* (adj) marshy, mucky.

aonikai 1. monopolize; *synonyms* (v) engross, control, forestall, absorb, consume, monopolise,

occupy, **2.** rascally; *synonyms* (adj) dirty, contemptible, abject, mean, mischievous, roguish, scabby, scoundrelly, scurvy, shabby, blackguardly, devilish, groveling, little, paltry, **3.** prevail; *synonyms* (v) predominate, dominate, triumph, obtain, outweigh, overcome, persist, carry, govern, conquer, rule, succeed, win, (n) reign, (adj) preponderate, **4.** triumph; *synonyms* (n) glory, conquest, exultation, victory, success, achievement, accomplishment, celebration, defeat, (v) exult, prevail, crow, joy, rejoice, gloat; *antonyms* (n) failure, sorrow, (v) fail, lose, **5.** villainous; *synonyms* (adj) nefarious, base, heinous, atrocious, depraved, evil, vile, wicked, black, vicious, corrupt, bad, criminal, (v) infamous, shameful.

aonikaia 1. master; *synonyms* (n) captain, instructor, head, boss, leader, gentleman, (v) conquer, control, command, defeat, dominate, (adj) chief, original, ace, expert, **2.** usurp; *synonyms* (v) assume, appropriate, arrogate, seize, commandeer, capture, borrow, confiscate, take, **3.** seize; *synonyms* (v) catch, grab, arrest, apprehend, clutch, get, grapple, receive, annex, clasp, grasp, grip, nail, carry, impound; *antonym* (v) release, **4.** supplant; *synonyms* (v) substitute, replace, succeed, supersede, displace, change, follow, **5.** overcome; *synonyms* (v) beat, crush, subdue, vanquish, master, overpower, hurdle, overwhelm, prevail, subjugate, surmount, demolish, affect, cross, (adj) beaten; *antonyms* (v) fail, (adj) victorious, unimpressed, **6.** oppress; *synonyms* (v) persecute, afflict, harass, press, burden, pinch, depress, encumber, repress, load, harry, harrow, distress, (adj) aggrieve, wrong.

aonikaiaki 1. mastered; *synonyms* (adj) down, beaten, blue, cut, declining, depressed, dispirited, downcast, downhearted, low, tame, shut, **2.** oppressed; *synonyms* (adj) downtrodden, laden, persecuted, broken, burdened, aggrieved, beleaguered, browbeaten, despairing, drawn, forlorn, gloomy, haggard, heavy, ladened, **3.** seized; *synonyms* (adj) confiscate, confiscated, appropriated, condemned, apprehended, detained, held, censured, convicted, forfeit, forfeited, obsessed, **4.** overcome; *synonyms* (v) conquer, beat, crush, subdue, vanquish, defeat, master, overpower, hurdle, overwhelm, prevail, subjugate, surmount, demolish, affect; *antonyms* (v) fail, (adj) victorious, unimpressed, **5.** usurped.

aonkaia subdue; *synonyms* (v) conquer, crush, defeat, overpower, quash, quell, reduce, repress, chasten, curb, overcome, restrain, soften, subjugate, (adv) control; *antonym* (v) surrender.

aonkaiaki subdued; *synonyms* (adj) muffled, quiet, soft, dull, muted, restrained, tame, faint, resigned, repressed, low, meek, broken, delicate, sober; *antonyms* (adj) loud, enthusiastic, lively.

aontabuki 1. hilly; *synonyms* (*adj*) craggy, mountainous, rugged, steep, cragged, knobby, prominent, tumulous, high, precipitous, tumulose, **2**. rough; *synonyms* (*adj*) coarse, hard, harsh, raw, crude, cruel, grating, gross, hoarse, jagged, approximate, gruff, inclement, (*n*) boisterous, draft; *antonyms* (*adj*) gentle, smooth, polished, precise, refined, silky, soft, sophisticated, even, exact, glossy, pleasant, **3**. uneven; *synonyms* (*adj*) rough, unequal, irregular, erratic, patchy, spotty, disproportionate, ragged, crooked, unbalanced, variable, asymmetrical, changeable, disparate, (*v*) broken; *antonyms* (*adj*) straight, equal, symmetrical.

aoraba 1. fortunate; *synonyms* (*adj*) favorable, auspicious, lucky, advantageous, blessed, favored, fortuitous, happy, prosperous, successful, well, felicitous, golden, good, propitious; *antonyms* (*adj*) unfortunate, unlucky, **2**. lucky; *synonyms* (*adj*) favourable, flourishing, chance, providential, encouraging, promising, (*v*) fortunate; *antonyms* (*adj*) hapless, ill-fated.

aoraia save; *synonyms* (*v*) deliver, economize, rescue, conserve, free, hoard, keep, maintain, preserve, liberate, protect, redeem, retain, defend, (*prep*) except; *antonyms* (*v*) spend, squander, waste.

aoraiaki saved; *synonyms* (*adj*) protected, blessed, secure.

aoraki 1. ail; *synonyms* (*v*) afflict, pain, suffer, trouble, worry, distress, disturb, hurt, upset, **2**. diseased; *synonyms* (*adj*) morbid, ailing, bad, ill, sick, sickly, unsound, infected, pathological, unhealthy; *antonym* (*adj*) healthy, **3**. ill; *synonyms* (*adj*) diseased, adverse, harmful, nauseous, (*adv*) badly, poorly, amiss, (*n*) evil, harm, complaint, ailment, mischief, damage, calamity, detriment; *antonym* (*adv*) well, **4**. sick; *synonyms* (*adj*) queasy, indisposed, weary, invalid, poor, crazy, disgusted, nauseated, perverted, distressed, (*v*) unwell, puke, vomit, heave, disgorge, **5**. patient; *synonyms* (*adj*) forbearing, passive, calm, enduring, resigned, tolerant, uncomplaining, stoical, lenient, meek, persistent, considerate, indefatigable; *antonym* (*adj*) impatient.

aorakiaki sickly; *synonyms* (*adj*) feeble, infirm, sick, ailing, diseased, indisposed, morbid, pale, poorly, sallow, peaked, pasty, (*n*) invalid, (*v*) faint, frail; *antonyms* (*adj*) healthy, bitter.

aorakina sick; *synonyms* (*adj*) ill, queasy, ailing, indisposed, poorly, weary, invalid, diseased, morbid, sickly, nauseous, poor, crazy, disgusted, (*v*) unwell; *antonyms* (*adj*) well, healthy.

aoranti orange; *synonyms* (*adj*) amber, ocher, orangey, orangish, tawny, ginger, red, (*n*) orangeness, lemon, etc, lime, apricot, bittersweet, coral, peach.

aoraoi 1. even; *synonyms* (*adv*) yet, (*adj*) direct, equal, constant, equable, equivalent, flat, horizontal, identical, plane, regular, steady, (*v*) level, balance, smooth; *antonyms* (*adj*) uneven, inconsistent, irregular, jagged, unequal, **2**. level; *synonyms* (*n*) grade, degree, category, class, (*adj*) even, (*v*) flatten, floor, aim, demolish, destroy, dismantle, raze, bulldoze, equalize, fell; *antonyms* (*adj*) inclined, slanting, angled, (*v*) build, raise, **3**. flat; *synonyms* (*adj*) dull, bland, plain, insipid, tasteless, dreary, boring, absolute, dead, downright, fixed, lifeless, monotonous, (*n*) apartment, (*v*) uninteresting; *antonyms* (*adj*) exciting, high-pitched, bumpy, **4**. plain; *synonyms* (*adj*) ordinary, comprehensible, intelligible, apparent, clear, easy, evident, homely, humble, manifest, obvious, simple, perspicuous, overt, outspoken; *antonyms* (*adj*) elaborate, fancy, unclear, mottled, multicolored, ornate, attractive, concealed, confused, fussy, two-colored.

aorek doctor; *synonyms* (*n*) physician, doc, medico, (*v*) cure, adulterate, attend, fix, heal, mend, remedy, repair, cook, debase, falsify, leech; *antonym* (*v*) break.

aori imperative; *synonyms* (*adj*) essential, necessary, absolute, commanding, exigent, imperious, peremptory, prerequisite, pressing, urgent, vital, domineering, dictatorial, important, (*v*) authoritative; *antonyms* (*adj*) trivial, unimportant.

aotakaka 1. impulsive; *synonyms* (*adj*) impetuous, capricious, hasty, driving, rash, changeable, hotheaded, instinctive, headlong, passionate, quick-tempered, automatic, brainish, emotional, extemporaneous; *antonyms* (*adj*) cautious, considered, predictable, **2**. scared; *synonyms* (*adj*) afraid, frightened, fearful, anxious, horrified, intimidated, nervous, terrified, timid, panicky, (*adv*) cowardly; *antonyms* (*adj*) calm, confident, fearless.

aotaningo 1. impenetrable; *synonyms* (*adj*) dense, impassable, incomprehensible, thick, hard, heavy, impervious, mysterious, obscure, opaque, unfathomable, unintelligible, compact, enigmatic, impermeable; *antonyms* (*adj*) clear, penetrable, readable, **2**. inscrutable; *synonyms* (*adj*) impenetrable, inexplicable, weird, cryptic, cryptical, deep, hidden, arcane, indecipherable, mystic, unsearchable, blank, expressionless, impassive, incognizable, **3**. distant; *synonyms* (*adj*) cold, aloof, remote, chill, cool, detached, far, reserved, long, faraway, icy, indifferent, removed, (*adv*) apart, (*n*) chilly; *antonyms* (*adj*) close, adjacent, friendly, near, nearby, neighboring, warm, pending, alert, intimate, involved, **4**. discreet; *synonyms* (*adj*) circumspect, prudent, careful, cautious, chary, discerning, tactful, wise, diplomatic, considerate, judicious, modest, politic, sensible, thoughtful; *antonyms* (*adj*) conspicuous, elaborate, tactless, careless, indiscreet, **5**. deep;

synonyms (*adj*) profound, absorbed, abstruse, broad, dark, rich, sound, strong, wide, esoteric, bright, large, abysmal, bass, (*v*) intense; *antonyms* (*adj*) shallow, superficial, high, high-pitched, light, soft, weak, **6.** sullen; *synonyms* (*adj*) morose, gloomy, gruff, cross, glum, grim, moody, sour, dismal, dour, lowering, peevish, surly, black, (*n*) sulky; *antonym* (*adj*) cheerful.

aotiki 1. stiff; *synonyms* (*adj*) rigid, hard, difficult, formal, inflexible, firm, numb, rigorous, severe, solid, sturdy, (*adv*) tight, (*n*) stark, cadaver, corpse; *antonyms* (*adj*) relaxed, flexible, floppy, soft, supple, free, pliable, **2.** rigid; *synonyms* (*adj*) harsh, fixed, stiff, austere, set, strict, exacting, stern, tense, tough, determined, resolute, immovable, precise, adamant; *antonym* (*adj*) elastic.

aoua fool; *synonyms* (*n*) blockhead, dunce, clown, ass, buffoon, dolt, (*v*) dupe, deceive, bamboozle, befool, cheat, con, defraud, delude, gull.

aouki indiscreet; *synonyms* (*adj*) foolish, careless, imprudent, incautious, ill-advised, rash, unadvised, unwise, impolitic, hasty, inadvisable, inconsiderate, tactless, thoughtless, heedless; *antonym* (*adj*) discreet.

aoun enemy; *synonyms* (*n*) adversary, antagonist, foe, opponent, opposition, competitor, assailant, foeman, hostile, challenger, contender, (*adj*) rival; *antonyms* (*n*) ally, friend, supporter.

aouti 1. rough; *synonyms* (*adj*) coarse, hard, harsh, raw, crude, cruel, grating, gross, hoarse, jagged, approximate, gruff, inclement, (*n*) boisterous, draft; *antonyms* (*adj*) gentle, smooth, polished, refined, silky, soft, sophisticated, even, exact, glossy, pleasant, **2.** swollen; *synonyms* (*adj*) bloated, inflated, bombastic, puffed, puffy, turgid, egotistic, high, bulging, tumescent, tumid, conceited, (*v*) distended, blown, (*prep*) pompous.

apâpaki great; *synonyms* (*adj*) eminent, famous, gigantic, big, distinguished, extensive, extreme, grand, large, chief, ample, capital, celebrated, considerable, dignified; *antonyms* (*adj*) small, awful, insignificant, tiny, mild.

apéi basket; *synonyms* (*n*) basketful, bassinet, cradle, gondola, case, coffin, handbasket, hoop, leap, ped, pottle, stomach, whisket, bound, corbeille.

ara 1. friend; *synonyms* (*n*) fellow, acquaintance, ally, colleague, crony, advocate, assistant, booster, buddy, mate, connection, wellwisher, (*adj*) associate, companion, comrade; *antonyms* (*n*) enemy, foe, stranger, rival, **2.** name; *synonyms* (*n*) call, title, epithet, address, appellation, (*v*) appoint, baptize, describe, cite, designate, entitle, enumerate, identify, list, mention, **3.** very; *synonyms* (*adv*) extremely, greatly, highly, really, completely, entirely, most, quite, truly, actually, too, awfully, (*adj*) much, identical, (*n*) self; *antonyms* (*adv*) abysmally, slightly, somewhat.

arana 1. name; *synonyms* (*n*) call, title, epithet, address, appellation, (*v*) appoint, baptize, describe, cite, designate, entitle, enumerate, identify, list, mention, **2.** call; *synonyms* (*v*) cry, bellow, name, shout, bid, summon, howl, dub, invite, scream, (*n*) appeal, yell, command, demand, request; *antonym* (*v*) dismiss.

aranaki 1. named; *synonyms* (*v*) benempt, nempt, ycleped, promised, styled, vowed, (*adj*) called, nominative, chosen, nominal, nominated, preferred, titular, tokenish, **2.** called; *synonyms* (*adj*) named, qualified.

aranna title; *synonyms* (*n*) call, designation, caption, claim, designate, appellation, denomination, epithet, interest, (*v*) name, style, term, entitle, (*adj*) right, ownership.

arannaki titled; *synonyms* (*adj*) noble, aristocratic, coroneted, highborn, patrician, big, fair, generous, posh, upright, worthy, (*n*) princely.

arara monotone; *synonyms* (*n*) monotony, drone, droning, bourdon, dawdler, laggard, lagger, trailer, (*adj*) humdrum, monotonic, monotonous, blah, dim, pedestrian.

ararâ thread; *synonyms* (*n*) string, line, yarn, rope, twine, wire, cord, fiber, (*v*) file, range, penetrate, lace, pass, run, meander.

ararake 1. ascend; *synonyms* (*v*) rise, arise, mount, climb, scale, uprise, increase, appear, escalate, jump, lift, soar; *antonyms* (*v*) descend, drop, **2.** climb; *synonyms* (*v*) ascend, clamber, scramble, bestride, fly, (*n*) ascent, acclivity, advance, ascending, ascension, climbing, hike, mounting, raise, upgrade.

ararakea scale; *synonyms* (*n*) flake, gamut, degree, graduation, measure, yardstick, rate, chip, (*v*) ascend, climb, gauge, mount, weigh, rise, (*adj*) balance; *antonym* (*v*) descend.

ararakeaki scaled; *synonyms* (*adj*) scaly, lepidote, leprose, scabrous, scaley, scurfy.

are tie; *synonyms* (*n*) band, connection, draw, lace, association, relationship, sleeper, (*v*) link, bond, attach, bind, join, knot, connect, fasten; *antonyms* (*v*) disconnect, untie, undo.

areaki tied; *synonyms* (*adj*) fastened, connected, even, fixed, laced, united, attached, binding, buttoned, joined, legato, liable, mixed, powerless, responsible; *antonym* (*adj*) separate.

areare 1. inadequate; *synonyms* (*adj*) insufficient, faulty, defective, deficient, flimsy, poor, feeble, imperfect, inappropriate, incapable, incompetent, ineffective, short, improper, impotent; *antonyms* (*adj*) adequate, ample, enough, passable, competent, reasonable, strong, **2.** lavish; *synonyms* (*adj*) extravagant, exuberant, generous, copious, prodigal, abundant, bountiful, excessive, improvident, lush, munificent, plush, rich, (*v*) dissipate, profuse; *antonym* (*adj*) meager, **3.**

adequate; *synonyms* (*adj*) sufficient, acceptable, right, condign, effectual, satisfactory, agreeable, decent, equal, fair, fit, full, good, qualified, able; *antonyms* (*adj*) inadequate, unsatisfactory, **4**. enough; *synonyms* (*adv*) rather, plenty, amply, adequately, satisfaction, fairly, fully, only, sufficiently, considering, (*n*) adequacy, fill, sufficiency, (*int*) basta, **5**. plenty; *synonyms* (*n*) abundance, affluence, copiousness, many, much, plenteousness, exuberance, opulence, plenitude, galore, flood, multitude, heap, lot, (*adj*) plentiful; *antonym* (*n*) few.

arei 1. inattentive; *synonyms* (*adj*) heedless, forgetful, neglectful, negligent, careless, reckless, remiss, unaware, inadvertent, inconsiderate, indifferent, mindless, regardless, slack, thoughtless; *antonyms* (*adj*) attentive, alert, observant, **2**. careless; *synonyms* (*adj*) cursory, haphazard, inattentive, insouciant, hasty, imprudent, incautious, lax, listless, messy, nonchalant, oblivious, perfunctory, rash, sloppy; *antonyms* (*adj*) careful, cautious, prudent, diligent, meticulous, thorough, thoughtful, guarded, methodical, strict, wary, **3**. sloppy; *synonyms* (*adj*) slipshod, muddy, slapdash, dirty, disheveled, untidy, filthy, casual, slovenly, squalid, thick, unkempt, inefficient, (*v*) dripping, sodden; *antonym* (*adj*) conscientious, **4**. there; *synonyms* (*adv*) here, thither, present, thereat, apparent, convenient, visible, (*adj*) adept, competent, expert, professional, reliable, skillful, trustworthy, unfailing.

arena tie; *synonyms* (*n*) band, connection, draw, lace, association, relationship, sleeper, (*v*) link, bond, attach, bind, join, knot, connect, fasten; *antonyms* (*v*) disconnect, untie, undo.

arenaki tied; *synonyms* (*adj*) fastened, connected, even, fixed, laced, united, attached, binding, buttoned, joined, legato, liable, mixed, powerless, responsible; *antonym* (*adj*) separate.

arenang babble; *synonyms* (*n*) drivel, burble, gibberish, (*v*) murmur, chat, gab, gossip, ripple, talk, blab, blather, bubble, chatter, guggle, gurgle; *antonyms* (*v*) quietness, silence, stillness.

aretau 1. dumb; *synonyms* (*adj*) mute, dense, dim, dull, silent, speechless, inarticulate, obtuse, slow, stupid, idiotic, quiet, taciturn, thick, voiceless, **2**. simple; *synonyms* (*adj*) plain, homely, pure, elementary, humble, innocent, mere, natural, rustic, honest, bare, chaste, childish, (*v*) clear, downright; *antonyms* (*adj*) complex, complicated, compound, elaborate, difficult, multiple, obscure, ornate, confused, confusing, cunning, multifaceted, problematical, sophisticated.

ari 1. bitter; *synonyms* (*adj*) acrimonious, biting, acrid, sharp, acerbic, acid, caustic, keen, malicious, resentful, sour, virulent, acerb, cutting, (*n*) acerbity; *antonyms* (*adj*) mild, sweet, charitable, hot, kind,

sugary, **2**. eyebrow; *synonyms* (*n*) brow, hair, supercilium, hilltop, **3**. yonder; *synonyms* (*adv*) beyond, abroad, farther, further, (*adj*) yon, distant, **4**. there; *synonyms* (*adv*) here, thither, present, thereat, apparent, convenient, visible, (*adj*) adept, competent, expert, professional, reliable, skillful, trustworthy, unfailing.

aria calm; *synonyms* (*adj*) quiet, peaceful, tranquil, (*v*) assuage, appease, cool, still, allay, pacify, easy, moderate, mollify, steady, (*n*) lull, equanimity; *antonyms* (*adj*) agitated, angry, nervous, stormy, wild, annoyed, anxious, enraged, frantic, frightened, intense, irritable, (*v*) agitate, upset, (*n*) agitation.

ariki placid; *synonyms* (*adj*) calm, mild, peaceful, composed, easygoing, equable, cool, gentle, peaceable, quiet, serene, tranquil, impassive, collected, meek.

arira tighten; *synonyms* (*v*) contract, strain, brace, compress, constrict, fasten, narrow, reduce, squeeze, stiffen, stretch, screw, secure, constrain, frap; *antonyms* (*v*) loosen, relax.

ariraki 1. taut; *synonyms* (*adj*) close, firm, tight, drawn, rigid, stiff, tense, strained, stringent, inflexible, taught, (*v*) fast; *antonyms* (*adj*) loose, limp, **2**. tightened.

aro kind; *synonyms* (*n*) form, helpful, sort, benign, brand, breed, class, gentle, type, variety, (*adj*) friendly, generous, good, humane, affectionate; *antonyms* (*adj*) unkind, callous, cruel, hardhearted, mean, merciless, nasty, spiteful, uncaring, upsetting, disagreeable, unfeeling.

arobaba 1. corny; *synonyms* (*adj*) banal, hackneyed, stale, trite, commonplace, threadbare, platitudinous, stereotyped, timeworn, bromidic, clichéd, unoriginal; *antonym* (*adj*) original, **2**. inane; *synonyms* (*adj*) blank, empty, foolish, fatuous, hollow, idiotic, vacuous, asinine, mindless, pointless, senseless, silly, stupid, daft, meaningless; *antonym* (*adj*) sensible, **3**. dumb; *synonyms* (*adj*) mute, dense, dim, dull, silent, speechless, inarticulate, obtuse, slow, quiet, taciturn, thick, voiceless, aphonous, **4**. silly; *synonyms* (*adj*) absurd, ridiculous, childish, fool, frivolous, irrational, preposterous, unreasonable, crazy, dizzy, ludicrous, nonsensical, sappy, simple, (*n*) imbecile; *antonyms* (*adj*) mature, wise, **5**. simple; *synonyms* (*adj*) plain, homely, pure, elementary, humble, innocent, mere, natural, rustic, honest, bare, chaste, childlike, (*v*) clear, downright; *antonyms* (*adj*) complex, complicated, compound, elaborate, difficult, multiple, obscure, ornate, confused, confusing, cunning, multifaceted, problematical, sophisticated.

arobaia serve; *synonyms* (*v*) help, act, aid, assist, attend, benefit, do, function, operate, tend, answer, facilitate, go, (*n*) avail, officiate.

Reference: Webster's Online Dictionary (www.websters-online-dictionary.org)

aroboi 1. sniff; *synonyms* (*v*) scent, inhale, nose, smell, snuff, breathe, whiff, sniffle, smoke; *antonym* (*v*) exhale, **2**. smell; *synonyms* (*n*) odor, fragrance, savor, aroma, bouquet, odour, savour, stench, flavor, smack, feel, flavour, (*v*) reek, perfume, stink.

aroka smell; *synonyms* (*n*) odor, fragrance, savor, aroma, bouquet, odour, savour, stench, flavor, smack, (*v*) reek, nose, perfume, scent, stink.

arokana appropriate; *synonyms* (*adj*) pertinent, proper, true, agreeable, apposite, apt, congruous, correct, particular, peculiar, right, (*v*) annex, allocate, adopt, seize; *antonyms* (*adj*) inappropriate, unsuitable, unrelated, untimely, wrong, (*v*) surrender.

arokanaki appropriated; *synonyms* (*adj*) destined, condemned, confiscate, confiscated, reserved, seized, censured, convicted, forfeit, forfeited.

aroki smell; *synonyms* (*n*) odor, fragrance, savor, aroma, bouquet, odour, savour, stench, flavor, smack, (*v*) reek, nose, perfume, scent, stink.

aron 1. finish; *synonyms* (*v*) end, complete, achieve, execute, accomplish, cease, determine, discontinue, consume, do, (*n*) close, consummate, conclusion, death, conclude; *antonyms* (*v*) start, begin, continue, (*n*) beginning, **2**. complete; *synonyms* (*adj*) perfect, absolute, whole, full, stark, accomplished, all, finished, (*v*) finish, act, attain, clear, effect, fulfill, implement; *antonyms* (*adj*) incomplete, partial, unfinished, abridged, shortened, sketchy, lacking, narrow, qualified, (*v*) neglect, **3**. about; *synonyms* (*prep*) encircling, for, encompassing, circa, concerning, (*adv*) around, approximately, almost, nearly, most, roughly, in, nearby, (*adj*) some, near; *antonyms* (*prep*) exactly, precisely.

arona 1. lead; *synonyms* (*v*) head, guide, conduct, contribute, direct, chair, conduce, control, go, govern, bring, convey, give, (*n*) clue, advantage; *antonym* (*v*) follow, **2**. direct; *synonyms* (*adj*) straight, blunt, immediate, transparent, (*v*) aim, channel, address, charge, dictate, administer, lead, level, order, point, (*n*) command; *antonyms* (*adj*) indirect, roundabout, circuitous, oblique, second-hand, sideways, unplanned, (*v*) request, **3**. guide; *synonyms* (*n*) escort, directory, attendant, usher, chief, director, pilot, rule, steer, adviser, introduction, (*v*) drive, advise, cicerone, show, **4**. conduct; *synonyms* (*n*) behavior, administration, manage, demeanor, performance, behaviour, (*v*) act, carriage, acquit, bearing, carry, comport, accompany, bear, behave, **5**. rule; *synonyms* (*n*) decree, dominion, law, ordinance, principle, regulate, reign, authority, government, line, precept, regulation, (*v*) influence, dominate, measure, **6**. predominate; *synonyms* (*v*) outweigh, domineer, excel, (*adj*) predominant,

prevail, preponderate, paramount, master, overriding.

aronaki 1. guided; *synonym* (*adj*) conducted, **2**. directed; *synonyms* (*adj*) absorbed, concentrating, destined, focussed, formal, intent, prescript, subject, engaged, fixed, prescribed, rapt, (*adv*) under, **3**. completed; *synonyms* (*adj*) complete, done, accomplished, finished, ended, perfect, ready, through, whole, (*adv*) over, **4**. finished; *synonyms* (*adj*) completed, consummate, absolute, polished, ripe, ruined, spent, round, capable, decided, final, elegant, concluded, exhausted, fitted; *antonyms* (*adj*) unfinished, incomplete, remaining, rough, **5**. led, **6**. ruled; *synonyms* (*adj*) lined, lawful, feint, hatched.

arora 1. extend; *synonyms* (*v*) expand, enlarge, amplify, broaden, dilate, widen, augment, continue, elongate, go, spread, carry, develop, increase, (*adj*) stretch; *antonyms* (*v*) withdraw, shorten, limit, narrow, shrink, **2**. spread; *synonyms* (*v*) scatter, reach, disperse, extend, broadcast, circulate, diffuse, disseminate, propagate, deploy, distribute, (*n*) span, dissemination, expanse, expansion; *antonym* (*adj*) concentrated, **3**. stretch; *synonyms* (*n*) extent, run, extension, range, effort, spell, area, space, (*v*) strain, lengthen, prolong, draw, distend, pull, sprawl.

aroraki 1. extended; *synonyms* (*adj*) broad, expanded, ample, extensive, long, wide, elongated, enlarged, lengthened, lengthy, prolonged, protracted, open, comprehensive, continued; *antonyms* (*adj*) brief, short, condensed, unextended, **2**. spread; *synonyms* (*v*) scatter, reach, disperse, expand, extend, broadcast, circulate, diffuse, disseminate, increase, propagate, stretch, broaden, deploy, (*n*) span; *antonym* (*adj*) concentrated, **3**. stretched; *synonyms* (*adj*) taut, extended, stiff, tense, tight, strained, outstretched, outspread, assiduous, close, delayed, firm, inflated, intense, intensive.

arotau fair; *synonyms* (*adj*) equitable, clear, beautiful, average, dispassionate, fine, impartial, reasonable, sweet, candid, (*adv*) clean, (*n*) bazaar, blonde, carnival, (*v*) bright; *antonyms* (*adj*) unfair, biased, dark, exceptional, unjust, partial, foul, imbalanced, mismatched, prejudiced, unwarranted.

article master; *synonyms* (*n*) captain, instructor, head, boss, leader, gentleman, (*v*) conquer, control, command, defeat, dominate, (*adj*) chief, original, ace, expert.

at liver; *synonyms* (*n*) denizen, resident.

ata 1. interlace; *synonyms* (*v*) intertwine, entwine, tangle, braid, enlace, lace, twine, entangle, plait, interlock, intersect, interweave, twist, weave, distort, **2**. know; *synonyms* (*v*) discern, comprehend, can, distinguish, have, recognize, understand, feel, acknowledge, agnise, agnize, apprehend, fathom, appreciate, (n) ken, **3.** understand; *synonyms* (v) interpret, catch, hear, learn, realize, see, assume, believe, construe, deduce, gather, grasp, perceive, read, (adj) take; *antonyms* (v) misinterpret, misconstrue, misunderstand, **4.** weave; *synonyms* (v) knit, wind, waver, fabricate, tissue, lurch, interlace, reel, join, meander, sway, thread, totter, (n) texture, wander.

atabai knowledgeable; *synonyms* (adj) intelligent, wise, clever, erudite, educated, informed, knowing, sagacious, smart, conversant, experienced, learned, versed, enlightened, aware; *antonyms* (adj) ignorant, inexperienced.

ataei 1. child; *synonyms* (n) baby, boy, babe, bairn, brat, girl, infant, juvenile, kid, minor, toddler, tot, youngster, innocent, imp; *antonym* (n) adult, **2.** childish; *synonyms* (adj) boyish, childlike, babyish, immature, naive, frivolous, infantile, puerile, silly, simple, young, absurd, adolescent, stupid, peevish; *antonyms* (adj) mature, grown-up, old, sensible, **3.** kid; *synonyms* (n) child, teenager, kidskin, lad, nipper, offspring, (v) joke, jest, banter, chaff, mock, fool, jolly, dupe, rag, **4.** youth; *synonyms* (n) adolescence, juvenility, puberty, stripling, younker, puppy, infancy, childhood, guy, prime, youthfulness, fellow; *antonyms* (n) adulthood, ripeness, **5.** young; *synonyms* (adj) green, fresh, new, raw, callow, childish, early, tender, unripe, youthful, recent, inexperienced, little, (n) progeny, issue; *antonym* (n) aged, **6.** offspring; *synonyms* (n) brood, children, family, descendant, descendants, lineage, posterity, race, seed, successor, consequence, (v) breed, fruit, generation, increase, **7.** youthful; *synonyms* (adj) vernal, beardless.

ataeinaine 1. damsel; *synonyms* (n) damosel, damozel, demoiselle, damoiselle, girl, maid, wench, nymph, **2.** maid; *synonyms* (n) amah, domestic, housemaid, maiden, virgin, maidservant, servant, woman, **3.** maiden; *synonyms* (adj) first, initiatory, unmarried, celibate, inaugural, initiative, (n) damsel, **4.** lassie; *synonym* (n) lass, **5.** lass; *synonyms* (n) lassie, drab, harlot, youngster, schoolgirl, strumpet, teenager, trollop.

ataeinimwane laddie; *synonyms* (n) cub, lad, chap, blighter, cuss, fella, feller, fellow, gent, greenhorn, sonny, rookie.

ataeinimwani lad; *synonyms* (n) boy, fellow, blighter, chap, cub, cuss, fella, laddie, youngster, schoolboy, kid, companion, stripling, youth, gent.

atai 1. who; *synonyms* (pron) one, (adj) which, what, **2.** right; *synonyms* (adj) correct, appropriate, due, just, proper, decent, good, even, perfect, accurate, exact, fair, faithful, fit, (n) privilege; *antonyms* (adj)

inappropriate, unjustified, immoral, incorrect, (n) left, (v) wrong.

ataia 1. misunderstand; *synonyms* (v) misapprehend, misconceive, misconstrue, misinterpret, mistake, misjudge, misread, miscalculate, miscomprehend; *antonym* (v) understand, **2.** know; *synonyms* (v) discern, comprehend, can, distinguish, have, recognize, feel, acknowledge, agnise, agnize, apprehend, fathom, appreciate, cognize, (n) ken, **3.** identify; *synonyms* (v) detect, discover, name, ascertain, find, know, mark, pinpoint, place, see, spot, tell, describe, differentiate, perceive, **4.** misunderstood; *synonyms* (adj) confused, vague, **5.** sure; *synonyms* (adj) certain, reliable, secure, safe, firm, indisputable, dependable, assured, confident, definite, infallible, positive, bound, (adv) certainly, (v) steady; *antonyms* (adj) doubtful, uncertain, unsure, hesitant, **6.** recognize; *synonyms* (v) identify, admit, allow, confess, realize, notice, descry, accredit, own, agree, hail, discriminate, espy, experience, recognise.

ataiaki 1. misunderstood; *synonyms* (adj) confused, vague, **2.** known; *synonyms* (adj) well-known, familiar, conscious, certain, accepted, acknowledged, plain, published, understood, evident, recognized, apparent, aware, common, apprised; *antonyms* (adj) nameless, unknown, secret, unidentified, **3.** identified; *synonyms* (adj) coherent, synonymous, branded, celebrated, famous, notorious, renowned, **4.** recognized; *synonyms* (v) ascertained, (adj) established, noted, recognised, received, distinguished, illustrious, known, official; *antonyms* (adj) unofficial, concealed.

ataibai 1. clever; *synonyms* (adj) adroit, capable, acute, able, apt, intelligent, smart, astute, cunning, expert, ingenious, quick, sharp, skillful, (v) brilliant; *antonyms* (adj) stupid, clumsy, unintelligent, dim, dull, inept, **2.** competent; *synonyms* (adj) adequate, clever, effective, efficient, fit, sufficient, commensurate, accomplished, adept, appropriate, enough, experienced, good, professional, proficient; *antonyms* (adj) incompetent, useless.

atainimari magnanimous; *synonyms* (adj) generous, liberal, great, noble, bountiful, exalted, big, handsome, lofty, charitable, considerate, large, elevated, chivalrous, high.

atake abridged; *synonyms* (adj) abbreviated, condensed, shortened, concise, abbreviate, capsule, compendious, cut, incomplete, pocket, tail, censored, compact, comprehensive, (v) abrege; *antonym* (adj) complete.

ataki 1. aware; *synonyms* (adj) awake, attentive, conscious, heedful, mindful, vigilant, sentient, alert, enlightened, knowing, knowledgeable, observant, sensible, wary, watchful; *antonyms* (adj) unaware, unconscious, **2**. known; *synonyms* (adj) well-known, familiar, certain, accepted, acknowledged, plain, published, understood, evident, recognized, apparent, aware, common, apprised, approved; *antonyms* (adj) nameless, unknown, secret, unidentified, **3**. misunderstand; *synonyms* (v) misapprehend, misconceive, misconstrue, misinterpret, mistake, misjudge, misread, miscalculate, miscomprehend; *antonym* (v) understand, **4**. misunderstood; *synonyms* (adj) confused, vague, **5**. interlaced; *synonyms* (adj) fretted, complicated, interfretted, latticed, latticelike, **6**. understood; *synonyms* (v) admitted, (adj) implicit, tacit, implied, silent, assumed; *antonyms* (adj) explicit, spoken.

atakiaki misunderstood; *synonyms* (adj) confused, vague.

atakin 1. practice; *synonyms* (n) exercise, fashion, convention, discipline, experience, habit, form, observance, application, employment, (v) custom, drill, use, act, apply; *antonym* (n) performance, **2**. recognize; *synonyms* (v) acknowledge, know, discern, distinguish, identify, admit, discover, allow, appreciate, confess, realize, notice, descry, accredit, agnize.

atakinaki practiced; *synonyms* (adj) experienced, adept, expert, skillful, accomplished, proficient, versed, practised, skilful, skilled, trained, able, good, qualified; *antonym* (adj) amateur.

atama pebbles; *synonyms* (n) shingle, grit, gravel, sand.

atamana cover; *synonyms* (v) coat, conceal, top, bury, cloak, (n) blind, blanket, screen, binding, camouflage, cap, covering, lid, mask, shield; *antonyms* (v) reveal, expose, uncover.

atamanaki covered; *synonyms* (adj) hidden, veiled, concealed, covert, coated, masked, obscured, secret, shrouded, thick, wrapped, (prep) cloaked; *antonyms* (adj) bare, naked.

atamaumau 1. large; *synonyms* (adj) big, ample, extensive, generous, broad, bulky, considerable, handsome, high, heavy, abundant, capacious, great, gross, hefty; *antonyms* (adj) small, cramped, insignificant, **2**. deep; *synonyms* (adj) thick, profound, absorbed, abstruse, dark, rich, sound, strong, wide, esoteric, bright, large, abysmal, bass, (v) intense; *antonyms* (adj) shallow, superficial, high-pitched, light, soft, weak, **3**. deepen; *synonyms* (v) enhance, intensify, amplify, develop, darken, heighten, increase, magnify, rise, strengthen, change, compound, **4**. thicken; *synonyms* (v) congeal, condense, clot, set, coagulate, stiffen, gel, gather, harden, incrassate, jell, reduce, (n) curdle; *antonym* (v) thin, **5**. thick; *synonyms* (adj) dense, compact, stupid, crowded, dull, opaque, slow, stocky, close, deep, dim, familiar, fat,

intimate, (n) midst; *antonyms* (adj) intelligent, sparse, clever, diluted, fine, slight, transparent.

atamaumauaki 1. deepened; *synonyms* (adj) collected, gathered, **2**. thickened; *synonyms* (adj) calloused, thick, concentrated, incrassated, inspissated, spissated, stiff.

atataiaomata 1. benevolent; *synonyms* (adj) charitable, good, compassionate, generous, gracious, kind, kindly, philanthropic, loving, considerate, gentle, humane, (n) beneficent, nice, sympathetic; *antonyms* (adj) malevolent, malicious, unfeeling, **2**. kind; *synonyms* (n) form, helpful, sort, benign, brand, breed, class, type, variety, benevolent, description, (adj) friendly, affectionate, genial, hospitable; *antonyms* (adj) unkind, callous, cruel, hardhearted, mean, merciless, nasty, spiteful, uncaring, upsetting, disagreeable, **3**. forgiving; *synonyms* (adj) lenient, tolerant, remissive, magnanimous, merciful, mild, absolvitory, easy, exonerative, patient; *antonym* (adj) intolerant, **4**. good; *synonyms* (adj) able, benefit, delicious, right, efficient, capable, excellent, fine, superior, well, advantageous, agreeable, desirable, (n) advantage, gain; *antonyms* (adj) disobedient, poor, wicked, unpleasant, (n) evil, bad, **5**. merciful; *synonyms* (adj) clement, forgiving, tender, sparing, benignant, indulgent, pitiful, propitious, forbearing; *antonym* (adj) pitiless.

atataibai 1. experienced; *synonyms* (adj) accomplished, capable, educated, competent, expert, knowledgeable, old, practiced, proficient, skillful, sophisticated, trained, able, conversant, informed; *antonyms* (adj) inexperienced, naive, immature, **2**. expert; *synonyms* (adj) adept, adroit, dexterous, clever, experienced, ace, apt, deft, veteran, knowing, (n) professional, critic, authority, connoisseur, dab; *antonyms* (adj) unskilled, inept, inferior, untrained, (n) amateur, beginner, **3**. clever; *synonyms* (adj) acute, intelligent, smart, astute, cunning, ingenious, quick, sharp, artful, learned, brainy, bright, cagey, (v) brilliant, brisk; *antonyms* (adj) stupid, clumsy, unintelligent, dim, dull, **4**. knowledgeable; *synonyms* (adj) wise, erudite, sagacious, versed, enlightened, aware, cognizant, discerning, intellectual, scholarly, skilled, cultured, intimate, perceptive; *antonym* (adj) ignorant.

atatainimari 1. lavish; *synonyms* (adj) extravagant, exuberant, generous, ample, copious, prodigal, abundant, bountiful, excessive, improvident, lush, munificent, plush, (v) dissipate, profuse; *antonym* (adj) meager, **2**. liberal; *synonyms* (adj) free, handsome, benevolent, big, large, kind, bounteous, broad, charitable, giving, tolerant, lavish, easy, bighearted, enlightened; *antonyms* (adj) strict, oppressive, totalitarian, intolerant, (n) conservative.

ati 1. child; *synonyms* (*n*) baby, boy, babe, bairn, brat, girl, infant, juvenile, kid, minor, toddler, tot, youngster, innocent, imp; *antonym* (*n*) adult, **2**. much; *synonyms* (*adv*) greatly, frequently, almost, awfully, considerably, far, most, often, pretty, highly, (*n*) lot, heap, (*adj*) great, considerable, practically; *antonym* (*adv*) slightly, **3**. large; *synonyms* (*adj*) big, ample, extensive, generous, broad, bulky, handsome, high, heavy, abundant, capacious, gross, hefty, huge, important; *antonyms* (*adj*) small, cramped, insignificant, **4**. fireplace; *synonyms* (*n*) chimney, fire, hearth, fireside, ingle, barbecue, blaze, favourite, flame, paramour, sweetheart, **5**. thatch; *synonyms* (*n*) thatching, ceiling, roof, teach, tile, hair, mop.

atia 1. already; *synonyms* (*adv*) beforehand, previously, before, formerly, once, earlier, finally, (*adj*) erewhile, present, **2**. recently; *synonyms* (*adv*) newly, freshly, lately, latterly, new, fresh, late, anew, (*n*) yesterday, (*adj*) afresh.

atiati 1. granular; *synonyms* (*adj*) grainy, gritty, chondritic, coarse, granulated, granulous, granulose, sandy, dusty, farinaceous, powdery, **2**. gritty; *synonyms* (*adj*) courageous, fearless, game, granular, spirited, brave, gravelly, mettlesome, resolute, rough, spunky, gamey, gamy, (*v*) firm; *antonym* (*adj*) smooth, **3**. sandy; *synonyms* (*adj*) light, arenaceous, sabulous, loose, mealy, branny, creamy, flaxen, flocculent, floury, friable, furfuraceous, luteous, nimble, pulverulent.

atinkinaki recognized; *synonyms* (*v*) ascertained, (*adj*) acknowledged, accepted, established, noted, recognised, received, distinguished, illustrious, known, famous, notorious, official; *antonyms* (*adj*) unknown, unofficial, concealed.

ato 1. thatch; *synonyms* (*n*) thatching, ceiling, roof, teach, tile, hair, mop, **2**. weave; *synonyms* (*v*) twine, twist, braid, knit, entwine, interweave, wind, waver, plait, fabricate, tissue, lurch, interlace, reel, (*n*) texture.

atoa 1. gorge; *synonyms* (*n*) abyss, chasm, cleft, esophagus, ravine, canyon, (*v*) devour, glut, cram, fill, gobble, engorge, satiate, stuff, bolt; *antonyms* (*n*) hill, (*v*) nibble, fast, **2**. fill; *synonyms* (*v*) block, clog, charge, line, accomplish, execute, complete, brim, close, flood, fulfill, occupy, (*n*) crowd, filling, packing; *antonyms* (*v*) empty, free, **3**. stuff; *synonyms* (*n*) material, cloth, force, gear, matter, goods, stock, (*v*) jam, pack, pad, ram, squeeze, gorge, load, shove; *antonym* (*v*) unstuff, **4**. pour; *synonyms* (*v*) gush, shed, decant, flow, pelt, scatter, stream, discharge, emit, jet, run, spill, teem, (*n*) overflow, rain; *antonym* (*v*) drizzle.

atoaki 1. filled; *synonyms* (*adj*) replete, packed, crowded, fraught, teeming, (*adv*) full, **2**. gorged; *synonyms* (*adj*) satiated, sated, stuffed, bursting, congested, satisfied, surfeited, glutted, **3**. poured; *synonym* (*adj*) concrete, **4**. stuffed; *synonyms* (*v*) farctate, (*adj*) crammed, loaded, chock-full, abounding, big, brimming, concentrated, distended, overcrowded, overflowing, overfull, overloaded, plentiful, swollen; *antonyms* (*adj*) empty, hungry.

atonga 1. say; *synonyms* (*v*) remark, articulate, express, pronounce, assert, enunciate, observe, maintain, order, read, speak, state, tell, (*n*) declare, voice, **2**. remark; *synonyms* (*n*) observation, regard, mind, commentary, heed, observance, reflection, (*v*) comment, notice, note, mention, perceive, mark, discern, (*adj*) look, **3**. pronounce; *synonyms* (*v*) affirm, say, deliver, utter, announce, decree, judge, proclaim, rule, vocalize, pass, adjudicate, (*n*) allege, give, adjudge, **4**. utter; *synonyms* (*adj*) absolute, complete, extreme, pure, sheer, total, thorough, unmitigated, rank, (*v*) breathe, emit, talk, reveal, disclose, exclaim; *antonyms* (*adj*) partial, qualified.

atongaki 1. noteworthy; *synonyms* (*adj*) important, notable, eminent, remarkable, significant, considerable, distinguished, famous, extraordinary, outstanding, particular, signal, memorable, noted, noticeable; *antonym* (*adj*) insignificant, **2**. eminent; *synonyms* (*adj*) celebrated, high, elevated, brilliant, big, conspicuous, illustrious, noble, renowned, dignified, exalted, grand, great, prominent, sublime; *antonym* (*adj*) unknown, **3**. famous; *synonyms* (*adj*) splendid, famed, capital, known, notorious, stunning, glorious, magnificent, popular, proverbial, wonderful; *antonyms* (*adj*) infamous, ordinary, **4**. distinguished; *synonyms* (*adj*) reputable, superior, distinct, ace, excellent, lofty, majestic, preeminent, recognized, shining, swell, unusual, **5**. renowned; *synonyms* (*adj*) well-known, acknowledged, familiar, legendary, **6**. pronounced; *synonyms* (*adj*) marked, clear, emphatic, definite, obvious, salient, bold, decided, demonstrative, striking.

atsina mother; *synonyms* (*n*) mamma, parent, (*v*) father, beget, engender, generate, care, sire, fuss, get.

atu bundle; *synonyms* (*n*) cluster, pile, sheaf, batch, group, heap, load, package, packet, parcel, stack, wad, (*v*) bunch, pack, clump.

atua divine; *synonyms* (*adj*) beautiful, sacred, wonderful, almighty, blessed, holy, exquisite, splendid, hallowed, celestial, (*v*) anticipate, augur, conjecture, guess, (*n*) clergyman.

atubibitaki dumb; *synonyms* (*adj*) mute, dense, dim, dull, silent, speechless, inarticulate, obtuse, slow, stupid, idiotic, quiet, taciturn, thick, voiceless.

atubitaki 1. changeable; *synonyms* (*adj*) variable, capricious, erratic, inconsistent, irregular, fickle, giddy, mercurial, mobile, mutable, slippery, temperamental, uncertain, unsettled, unstable; *antonyms* (*adj*) constant, fixed, stable, unchangeable, consistent, dependable, predictable, regular, **2.** fickle; *synonyms* (*adj*) volatile, changeful, inconstant, shifting, skittish, unfaithful, irresolute, light, unpredictable, faithless, unreliable, flighty, moody, quicksilver, (*v*) changeable; *antonyms* (*adj*) resolute, untiring, **3.** dizzy; *synonyms* (*adj*) dazed, faint, frivolous, silly, vertiginous, featherbrained, muzzy, unsteady, airheaded, woozy, (*v*) daze; *antonyms* (*adj*) alert, clear-headed, **4.** capricious; *synonyms* (*adj*) arbitrary, fanciful, freakish, whimsical, fantastic, impulsive, aimless, eccentric, fitful, wayward, alterable, undependable, untrustworthy, **5.** unstable; *synonyms* (*adj*) precarious, insecure, shaky, unsound, fluid, fluctuating, rickety, unbalanced, wobbly, neurotic, perilous, unsafe, uneasy, infirm, (*v*) perishable; *antonym* (*adj*) steady.

atumara bald; *synonyms* (*adj*) bare, hairless, simple, austere, meager, threadbare, raw, barefaced, dry, forthright, mere, naked, nude, plain, stark; *antonym* (*adj*) hairy.

atumeamea blonde; *synonyms* (*adj*) blond, fair, golden, (*n*) towheaded, buff, girl, albino, auricomous, bleached, champagne, leucous, light, pale, platinum, sallow; *antonym* (*n*) brunet.

atuna 1. head; *synonyms* (*n*) chief, captain, front, point, boss, foam, froth, crown, chieftain, executive, chair, brain, (*v*) capital, direct, lead; *antonyms* (*n*) end, subordinate, (*v*) follow, **2.** direct; *synonyms* (*adj*) straight, blunt, immediate, (*v*) aim, channel, conduct, address, charge, control, dictate, head, administer, guide, level, (*n*) command; *antonyms* (*adj*) indirect, roundabout, circuitous, oblique, second-hand, sideways, unplanned, (*v*) request, **3.** headed, **4.** conduct; *synonyms* (*n*) behavior, administration, manage, demeanor, performance, (*v*) act, bring, carriage, acquit, bearing, carry, comport, show, accompany, bear, **5.** preside; *synonyms* (*v*) rule, moderate, hold, sit, celebrate, oversee, solemnize.

atunaki directed; *synonyms* (*adj*) absorbed, concentrating, destined, focussed, formal, intent, prescript, subject, engaged, fixed, prescribed, rapt, (*adv*) under.

atunipai wrist; *synonyms* (*n*) carpus, (*v*) finger, hand, paw.

atutababa 1. disheveled; *synonyms* (*adj*) untidy, unkempt, sloppy, tousled, uncombed, dishevelled, messy, scruffy, slovenly, tangled, grubby; *antonyms* (*adj*) tidy, free, neat, **2.** ruffled; *synonyms* (*adj*) disheveled, frilled, frilly, rippled, disordered, upset, crinkled, crinkly, disconcerted, excited, nervous, rough, shaggy, turbulent, wavelike.

atutarere 1. abandoned; *synonyms* (*adj*) forlorn, immoral, deserted, empty, profligate, shameless, stranded, wicked, lonely, corrupt, debauched, depraved, derelict, desolate, discarded; *antonyms* (*adj*) restrained, inhabited, orderly, overcrowded, **2.** solitary; *synonyms* (*adj*) lonesome, alone, lone, only, single, sole, unaccompanied, isolated, secluded, separate, one, forsaken, private, (*n*) hermit, recluse.

atutekonaua 1. hypocritical; *synonyms* (*adj*) deceitful, false, insincere, dishonest, disingenuous, pharisaical, sanctimonious, hollow, (*adv*) counterfeit; *antonyms* (*adj*) genuine, sincere, **2.** untrustworthy; *synonyms* (*adj*) unreliable, unfaithful, treacherous, faithless, slippery, undependable, untrue, dubious, untrusty, disloyal, fallible, irresponsible, questionable, shady, (*v*) fickle; *antonyms* (*adj*) trustworthy, reliable, dependable, faithful, honest, **3.** sly; *synonyms* (*adj*) crafty, cunning, wily, furtive, artful, clever, secret, shrewd, designing, arch, astute, clandestine, devious, foxy, guileful; *antonyms* (*adj*) open, naive.

atuu head; *synonyms* (*n*) chief, captain, front, point, boss, foam, froth, crown, chieftain, executive, chair, brain, (*v*) capital, direct, lead; *antonyms* (*n*) end, subordinate, (*v*) follow.

au 1. caulked, **2.** extract; *synonyms* (*n*) excerpt, essence, juice, quotation, quote, citation, (*v*) draw, abstract, derive, educe, elicit, distill, express, get, extort, **3.** h; *synonyms* (*n*) asshole, bastard, buck, bull, bullshit, buncombe, bunk, bunkum, cavalry, cocksucker, crap, damn, darn, debris, detritus, **4.** waterproof; *synonyms* (*adj*) rainproof, impervious, waterproofed, proof, bombproof, resistant, resilient, solid, (*n*) mackintosh, raincoat, slicker, cagoule, oilskin, (*v*) weatherproof, seal; *antonym* (*adj*) permeable, **5.** sealed; *synonyms* (*adj*) closed, certain, plastered, tight, airtight, assured, besotted, blotto, crocked, destined, fuddled, guaranteed, loaded, pissed, pixilated, **6.** seal; *synonyms* (*n*) mark, stamp, cachet, hallmark, imprint, impression, signet, (*v*) plug, bar, close, shut, stop, clinch, lock, (*adj*) conclude; *antonyms* (*v*) open, unseal, **7.** watertight; *synonyms* (*adj*) unassailable, waterproof, firm, impregnable, ironclad, leakproof, unshakable; *antonym* (*adj*) indefensible, **8.** slow; *synonyms* (*adj*) dull, late, easy, sluggish, heavy, dense, dim, gradual, inactive, indolent, lazy, stupid, (*v*) slack, (*adv*) behind, behindhand; *antonyms* (*adj*) fast, intelligent, rapid, bright, alert, brisk, hasty, prompt, quick, speedy, hurried, observant, rushed, (*v*) accelerate.

aua 1. dwindle; *synonyms* (*v*) abate, decline, decrease, diminish, contract, fade, fall, lessen, recede, reduce, wane, decay, drop, ebb, fail; *antonym* (*v*) increase, **2.** four; *synonyms* (*n*) quaternity, foursome, quadruplet, quaternary, quaternion, tetrad, quarter, square, ace, air, appeerence, cast, casting, contrivance, direction, **3.** dawdle; *synonyms* (*v*) dally, linger, delay, lag, amble, procrastinate, hesitate, idler, loiter, lounge, saunter, drag; *antonyms* (*v*) hurry, rush, **4.** lag; *synonyms* (*n*) backwardness, interim, interval, retardation, (*v*) dawdle, gaol, immure, imprison, incarcerate, jail, jug, crawl, slacken, (*adj*) slouch, last, **5.** straggle; *synonyms* (*n*) wander, hover, nomadize, (*v*) sprawl, stray, ramble, depart, deviate, digress, range, roam, rove, sidetrack.

auaki sealed; *synonyms* (*adj*) closed, certain, plastered, tight, airtight, assured, besotted, blotto, crocked, destined, fuddled, guaranteed, impervious, loaded, pissed.

auáta many; *synonyms* (*adj*) manifold, abundant, countless, frequent, various, innumerable, much, multiple, numerous, plentiful, several, different, numberless, (*n*) number; *antonym* (*n*) few.

auba 1. frightened; *synonyms* (*adj*) afraid, fearful, scared, terrified, timid, anxious, apprehensive, horrified, intimidated, restless, worried, (*adv*) cowardly; *antonyms* (*adj*) calm, confident, unimpressed, brave, fearless, **2.** dumbfounded; *synonyms* (*adj*) astonished, astounded, amazed, staggered, bewildered, dazed, speechless, stunned, stupefied, flabbergasted, **3.** scared; *synonyms* (*adj*) frightened, nervous, panicky, **4.** startled; *synonyms* (*adj*) dumbfounded, aghast, distressed, shocked, alarmed, troubled, upset, **5.** perplexed; *synonyms* (*v*) complicated, intricate, (*adj*) confused, involved, lost, baffled, confounded, doubtful, puzzled, distracted, uneasy, bemused, questioning, quizzical, entangled; *antonym* (*adj*) enlightened, **6.** shy; *synonyms* (*adj*) diffident, abashed, reserved, ashamed, coy, modest, reticent, self-conscious, backward, careful, (*v*) fling, cast, chuck, pitch, (*n*) throw; *antonyms* (*adj*) brash, bold, demonstrative, forward, outgoing.

aubanga 1. rob; *synonyms* (*v*) filch, pinch, deprive, pilfer, pillage, plunder, rifle, fleece, lift, purloin, steal, pick, divest, defraud, despoil, **2.** steal; *synonyms* (*v*) abstract, creep, misappropriate, rob, snatch, sneak, plagiarize, slip, thieve, hook, poach, prowl, appropriate, (*n*) bargain, theft, **3.** swindle; *synonyms* (*n*) cheat, imposture, beguile, deception, fraud, hoax, trick, deceit, (*v*) con, do, deceive, bamboozle, bilk, bunco, diddle.

aubangaki 1. robed; *synonyms* (*adj*) appareled, attired, clothed, dressed, garbed, garmented, habilimented, fixed, polished, vested, **2.** stolen; *synonyms* (*adj*) purloined, furtive, misbegotten, secret, sly, stealthy.

aubeabea 1. belated; *synonyms* (*adj*) late, tardy, behindhand, overdue, slow, behind, benighted, delayed, **2.** delayed; *synonyms* (*adj*) belated, protracted, deferred; *antonyms* (*adj*) brief, early.

auderia devil; *synonyms* (*n*) demon, fiend, ghost, daemon, deuce, monster, imp, rogue, (*v*) rag, torment, harass, bedevil, crucify, annoy, bother.

aukou back; *synonyms* (*adv*) before, backward, (*n*) rear, (*adj*) assist, (*v*) support, advocate, endorse, recede, second, stake, vouch, guarantee, aid, champion, encourage; *antonyms* (*n*) face, (*v*) front, oppose, advance.

aumua bake; *synonyms* (*v*) burn, broil, cook, fire, fry, roast, grill, heat, parch, scorch, singe, toast.

auoumaraki sick; *synonyms* (*adj*) ill, queasy, ailing, indisposed, poorly, weary, invalid, diseased, morbid, sickly, nauseous, poor, crazy, disgusted, (*v*) unwell; *antonyms* (*adj*) well, healthy.

aupoui forty; *synonyms* (*n*) forties, (*adj*) twoscore.

aurama 1. await; *synonyms* (*v*) expect, anticipate, abide, bide, tarry, wait, attend, look, hope, approach, loom, **2.** wait; *synonyms* (*v*) stop, ambush, await, lurk, stay, linger, remain, hesitate, watch, loiter, (*n*) delay, pause, hold, rest, holdup.

auta gouge; *synonyms* (*n*) nick, rut, (*v*) excavate, swindle, deceive, dig, fleece, groove, scoop, dent, extort, cut, cheat, furrow, squeeze.

auti 1. house; *synonyms* (*n*) family, home, dwelling, firm, abode, domicile, building, edifice, habitation, housing, establishment, structure, ancestry, (*v*) accommodate, lodge, **2.** dwell; *synonyms* (*v*) abide, inhabit, reside, bide, live, stay, be, belong, brood, continue, delay, occupy, remain, settle, consist, **3.** reside; *synonyms* (*v*) exist, populate, lie, people, repose, rest, domiciliate, shack, last, perch, (*adj*) dwell, roost.

awa seethe; *synonyms* (*v*) boil, churn, foam, fume, stew, cook, bubble, simmer, rage, froth, effervesce, ferment, fizz, buzz, digest.

aweawe 1. slender; *synonyms* (*adj*) lean, narrow, little, thin, fine, lithe, slight, delicate, faint, feeble, flimsy, gaunt, light, lissom, (*v*) meager; *antonyms* (*adj*) plump, stocky, fat, wide, **2.** pointed; *synonyms* (*adj*) penetrating, keen, poignant, acute, piquant, cutting, marked, pithy, biting, acuminate, barbed, prickly, pungent, sharp, short; *antonym* (*adj*) rounded, **3.** straight; *synonyms* (*adv*) level, right, directly, (*adj*) erect, honest, even, flat, upright, fair, correct, just, perpendicular, proper, accurate, (*v*) direct; *antonyms* (*adv*) indirectly, (*adj*) curly, curved, diluted, winding, zigzag, askew, bent, curvy, knotted, twisted, twisting, wavy, circuitous, guarded.

Á

áñara axe; *synonyms* (*n*) knife, blade, (*v*) ax, chop, abort, destroy.

Â

â four; *synonyms* (*n*) quaternity, foursome, quadruplet, quaternary, quaternion, tetrad, quarter, square, ace, air, appearence, cast, casting, contrivance, direction.

âio there; *synonyms* (*adv*) here, thither, present, thereat, apparent, convenient, visible, (*adj*) adept, competent, expert, professional, reliable, skillful, trustworthy, unfailing.

âua four; *synonyms* (*n*) quaternity, foursome, quadruplet, quaternary, quaternion, tetrad, quarter, square, ace, air, appearence, cast, casting, contrivance, direction.

B

b d; *synonyms* (*n*) calciferol, cholecarciferol, ergocalciferol, viosterol, euchre, (*v*) e, f.

ba 1. hard; *synonyms* (*adj*) austere, bad, difficult, grave, severe, strong, arduous, callous, cruel, grueling, knotty, tough, (*adv*) firm, (*v*) acute, (*n*) rough; *antonyms* (*adj*) easy, soft, kind, merciful, simple, soggy, tender, yielding, (*adv*) gently, lightly, 2. but; *synonyms* (*conj*) while, (*adv*) alone, only, though, barely, however, merely, simply, yet, exclusively, if, just, (*prep*) besides, except, excluding, 3. firm; *synonyms* (*n*) company, (*adj*) constant, hard, stable, close, compact, determined, fixed, resolute, solid, steadfast, steady, dense, (*v*) faithful; *antonyms* (*adj*) irresolute, weak, hesitant, limp, liquid, 4. as; *synonyms* (*conj*) qua, because, since, considering, whilst, (*prep*) during, like, (*adv*) equally, from, (*n*) arsenic, 5. repulsive; *synonyms* (*adj*) odious, offensive, abominable, detestable, ugly, disagreeable, nauseous, abhorrent, disgusting, hideous, loathsome, obnoxious, execrable, distasteful, (*v*) hateful; *antonyms* (*adj*) attractive, pleasant, 6. repugnant; *synonyms* (*adj*) repulsive, contradictory, adverse, inimical, obscene, opposite, antagonistic, gruesome, incompatible, nasty, (*v*) hostile, (*n*) irreconcilable, discordant, contrary, inconsistent, 7. solid; *synonyms* (*adj*) consistent, real, good, massive, secure, substantial, fast, hearty, heavy, material, potent, reliable, rigid, sturdy, thick; *antonyms* (*adj*) unreliable, loose, gaseous, permeable, runny, transparent, watery, 8. tasteless; *synonyms* (*adj*) insipid, bland, flavorless, flat, dull, flashy, flavourless, gaudy, vulgar, garish, stale, uninteresting, diluted, indelicate, showy; *antonyms* (*adj*) tasteful, tasty, delicious.

bâ 1. oil; *synonyms* (*n*) petroleum, fat, ointment, salve, cream, fuel, cerate, lotion, (*v*) lubricate, anoint, anele, glycerine, 2. rock; *synonyms* (*n*) boulder, calculus, pillar, (*v*) jar, sway, cradle, jolt, shake, toss, waver, quake, pitch, reel, (*adj*) pebble, stone.

bä thunder; *synonyms* (*n*) boom, bang, roll, bellow, clap, (*v*) roar, howl, rumble, fulminate, blast, storm, growl, (*adj*) peal, explode, detonate.

baang pale; *synonyms* (*adj*) ghastly, faint, wan, dull, light, pallid, weak, watery, cadaverous, (*v*) dim, blanch, (*n*) boundary, confine, border, bound; *antonyms* (*adj*) dark, rosy, strong, brown.

baba 1. idiot; *synonyms* (*n*) fool, dolt, dunce, dimwit, moron, ass, cretin, imbecile, oaf, changeling, dumbbell, half-wit, innocent, jerk, natural, 2. cracked; *synonyms* (*adj*) broken, nutty, batty, chapped, crazy, balmy, wacky, bats, crackers, crackled, crazed, deranged, dotty, insane, kookie, 3. drown; *synonyms* (*v*) deluge, drench, overwhelm, sink, submerge, choke, engulf, flood, inundate, suffocate, swamp, asphyxiate, extinguish, (*adj*) duck, immerse, 4. disturbed; *synonyms* (*adj*) agitated, concerned, anxious, confused, disquieted, restless, upset, worried, disordered, bothered, disconcerted, distracted, distressed, nervous, tumultuous; *antonyms* (*adj*) rational, calm, relaxed, 5. club; *synonyms* (*n*) association, bat, circle, society, stick, baton, company, cudgel, fraternity, gang, group, guild, (*v*) beat, bludgeon, hit, 6. crazy; *synonyms* (*adj*) mad, madcap, wild, absurd, brainsick, cracked, demented, eccentric, foolish, ludicrous, preposterous, silly, bonkers, outrageous, barmy; *antonyms* (*adj*) sane, sensible, 7. hood; *synonyms* (*n*) cap, bonnet, cowl, cover, hat, coif, headdress, hoodlum, thug, malefactor, gangster, helmet, hooligan, punk, cowling, 8. fool; *synonyms* (*n*) blockhead, clown, buffoon, idiot, joke, (*v*) dupe, deceive, bamboozle, befool, cheat, con, defraud, delude, gull, beguile, 9. foolish; *synonyms* (*adj*) childish, daft, dopey, dull, dumb, fatuous, stupid, unwise, anserine, dopy, idiotic, imprudent, irrational, nonsensical, ridiculous; *antonyms* (*adj*) wise, prudent, shrewd, visionary, 10. insane; *synonyms* (*adj*) delirious, lunatic, frantic, furious, possessed, psychotic, rabid, harebrained, 11. silly; *synonyms* (*adj*) frivolous, unreasonable, dizzy, sappy, senseless, simple, insignificant, puerile, babyish, featherbrained, giddy, goofy, inane, inept, injudicious; *antonym* (adj) mature, **12.** stupid; *synonyms* (adj) crass, dim, pointless, slow, booby, dense, doltish, heavy, insipid, obtuse, stolid, torpid, uninteresting, (n) dullard, (adv) thoughtless; *antonyms* (adj) bright, clever, intelligent.

babae indebted; *synonyms* (adj) grateful, appreciative, thankful, obliged, broke, deferred, gratified, insolvent, accountable, chargeable, duty-bound, honor-bound, hooked, (prep) beholden, debted.

babaenikai 1. linger; *synonyms* (v) dally, delay, hover, loiter, hesitate, stay, procrastinate, dawdle, remain, saunter, tarry, abide, endure, continue, (adv) lag; *antonyms* (v) leave, hurry, **2.** loiter; *synonyms* (v) linger, loaf, prowl, idle, loll, drag, footle, lallygag, lurk, (adj) lounge, poke, (adv) crawl, creep, drawl.

babaina 1. appropriate; *synonyms* (adj) pertinent, proper, true, agreeable, apposite, apt, congruous, correct, particular, peculiar, right, (v) annex, allocate, adopt, seize; *antonyms* (adj) inappropriate, unsuitable, unrelated, untimely, wrong, (v) surrender, **2.** own; *synonyms* (v) acknowledge, admit, have, concede, allow, grant, hold, possess, confess, get, accept, avow, enjoy, occupy, (adj) individual, **3.** use; *synonyms* (n) custom, practice, benefit, habit, application, function, (v) exercise, employ, employment, expend, profit, advantage, exploit, operate, (adj) usage; *antonym* (v) conserve, **4.** possess; *synonyms* (v) wield, bear, keep, maintain, obsess, retain, consume, feature, (n) hazard, (adj) own.

babainaki 1. appropriated; *synonyms* (adj) destined, condemned, confiscate, confiscated, reserved, seized, censured, convicted, forfeit, forfeited, **2.** owned; *synonyms* (v) behoove, ought, owed, (adj) own, proprietary, **3.** used; *synonyms* (adj) secondhand, exploited, accustomed, decrepit, depleted, exhausted, faded, habituated, hand-me-down, spent, threadbare, tried, victimised, victimized, wont; *antonyms* (adj) pristine, new, spanking, unused.

babaireia control; *synonyms* (n) rule, authority, care, hold, influence, sway, ascendancy, ascendency, (v) command, check, curb, bridle, conduct, handle, conquer; *antonyms* (n) freedom, weakness, (v) intensify, share.

babaireiaki controlled; *synonyms* (adj) limited, restrained, restricted, temperate, subdued, inhibited, banned, calm, chaste, composed, confidential, conscious, conservative, contained, deliberate; *antonym* (adj) spontaneous.

babaiwae lag; *synonyms* (n) backwardness, interim, interval, (v) dawdle, delay, linger, dally, drag, gaol, immure, imprison, incarcerate, jail, jug, loiter.

babakaine neglect; *synonyms* (n) disregard, slight, carelessness, delinquency, negligence, omission,

mistake, (v) fail, forget, ignore, overlook, default, drop, omit, disdain; *antonyms* (n) development, surveillance, (v) attention, care, complete, do, protect.

babakaineaki neglected; *synonyms* (adj) abandoned, dilapidated, disregarded, ignored, derelict, deserted, ancient, antiquated, antique, disused, forsaken, obsolete, shabby, unnoticed.

babakanikawai 1. fraudulent; *synonyms* (adj) deceitful, false, dishonest, fallacious, crooked, corrupt, deceptive, dishonorable, counterfeit, crafty, devious, mendacious, mock, (v) bogus, sham; *antonym* (adj) honest, **2.** iniquitous; *synonyms* (adj) wicked, immoral, sinful, evil, impious, bad, heinous, injurious, wrong, criminal, villainous, inequitable, (adv) infamous, nefarious, atrocious, **3.** cheat; *synonyms* (v) trick, beguile, betray, defraud, fake, beat, deceive, fleece, fob, (n) swindle, con, fraud, bilk, impostor, charlatan, **4.** defraud; *synonyms* (v) cheat, bamboozle, mislead, rob, victimize, circumvent, bluff, chouse, cozen, diddle, do, dupe, fiddle, gull, gyp, **5.** grasping; *synonyms* (adj) avaricious, covetous, acquisitive, greedy, avid, grabby, rapacious, voracious, mercenary, miserly, ravenous, sordid, stingy, envious, (n) seizing; *antonym* (adj) generous, **6.** mean; *synonyms* (v) intend, design, imply, denote, involve, (adj) middle, base, common, hateful, ignoble, medium, abject, (n) average, contemptible, low; *antonym* (adj) kind, **7.** villainous; *synonyms* (adj) depraved, vile, black, vicious, mischievous, felonious, (v) shameful, **8.** treacherous; *synonyms* (adj) perfidious, unfaithful, dangerous, disloyal, faithless, fraudulent, insidious, unreliable, unsafe, perilous, traitorous, tricky, untrue, rotten, risky; *antonyms* (adj) faithful, loyal, **9.** unjust; *synonyms* (adj) unfair, partial, foul, unrighteous, wrongful, improper, unjustified, unmerited, iniquitous, undue, unreasonable, hard, illegal, oppressive, rough; *antonyms* (adj) fair, just, equitable, reasonable, rightful.

babakanikora voracious; *synonyms* (adj) greedy, gluttonous, hungry, rapacious, ravenous, avid, edacious, esurient, grasping, insatiable, ravening, famished, predatory, avaricious, devouring.

babakanikoroa 1. ravenous; *synonyms* (adj) greedy, hungry, avid, famished, gluttonous, voracious, edacious, insatiable, rapacious, covetous, predatory, avaricious, esurient, grasping, ravening; *antonym* (adj) full, **2.** rapacious; *synonyms* (adj) acquisitive, ravenous, ferocious, raptorial, vulturous, predacious, predaceous, marauding, stingy, vulturine, aggressive, (v) extortionate, lupine, mercenary, sordid.

babaki drowned; *synonyms* (v) drenched, drent, (adj) prostrate, (pron) submerged.

bâbaki 1. great; *synonyms* *(adj)* eminent, famous, gigantic, big, distinguished, extensive, extreme, grand, large, chief, ample, capital, celebrated, considerable, dignified; *antonyms* *(adj)* small, awful, insignificant, tiny, mild, **2.** large; *synonyms* *(adj)* generous, broad, bulky, handsome, high, heavy, abundant, capacious, great, gross, hefty, huge, important, roomy, stout; *antonym* *(adj)* cramped.

babako 1. bent; *synonyms* *(adj)* arched, curved, bended, crooked, deformed, intent, *(n)* aptitude, inclination, propensity, fancy, ability, bias, flair, gift, leaning; *antonym* *(adj)* straight, **2.** cuddle; *synonyms* *(n)* caress, *(v)* hug, nestle, snuggle, squeeze, clasp, embrace, nuzzle, stroke, clinch, enfold, fondle, huddle, pet, hold, **3.** adapt; *synonyms* *(v)* adjust, accommodate, acclimate, fashion, alter, arrange, assimilate, change, edit, familiarize, gear, modify, shape, suit, *(adj)* fit, **4.** nurse; *synonyms* *(n)* nurture, doctor, amah, *(v)* nourish, attend, cherish, entertain, foster, harbor, lactate, cradle, cultivate, keep, raise, breastfeed.

babakoa cuddle; *synonyms* *(n)* caress, *(v)* hug, nestle, snuggle, squeeze, clasp, embrace, nuzzle, stroke, clinch, enfold, fondle, huddle, pet, hold.

babakoaki 1. adapted; *synonyms* *(v)* convenient, *(adj)* altered, fit, agreeable, appropriate, conformable, fitted, prepared; *antonyms* *(adj)* mass-produced, unaccustomed, **2.** nursed; *synonym* *(adj)* suckled.

babana 1. lust; *synonyms* *(n)* appetite, craving, lecherousness, libido, cupidity, lechery, wantonness, *(v)* desire, hunger, itch, covet, crave, thirst, long, *(adj)* concupiscence, **2.** love; *synonyms* *(n)* affection, dear, fondness, liking, benevolence, charity, attachment, beloved, darling, devotion, honey, sweetheart, *(v)* cherish, enjoy, like; *antonyms* *(n)* abhorrence, hatred, aversion, *(v)* hate, dislike, abhor, **3.** dote; *synonyms* *(v)* drivel, doat, fond, slaver, *(n)* dotard, imbecile, *(adj)* ramble, wander, rave, trifle.

babanaine infatuate; *synonyms* *(v)* enamor, befool, fascinate, besot, captivate, craze, affatuate, assot, beguile, deceive, fool, *(adj)* madden, dementate, doltish, dull.

babanaineaki infatuated; *synonyms* *(adj)* enamored, fanatical, crazy, dotty, gaga, mad, obsessed, smitten, foolish, loving, *(v)* besotted, confined, illiberal.

babanaki loved; *synonyms* *(adj)* dear, beloved, cherished, pet, precious, appreciated, esteemed, prized, respected, treasured, valued, important, *(n)* darling.

babane nimble; *synonyms* *(adj)* active, adroit, agile, lively, brisk, spry, alert, clever, energetic, expeditious, lithe, quick, deft, lissome, *(v)* light; *antonym* *(adj)* clumsy.

babanga 1. inapt; *synonyms* *(adj)* inadequate, inappropriate, unbecoming, inapposite, awkward, clumsy, improper, inept, unsuitable, undue, unseemly, inapplicable, irrelevant, incongruous, unapt, **2.** inexpert; *synonyms* *(adj)* incompetent, inapt, amateur, amateurish, inexperienced, unprofessional, incapable, green, unskilled, crude, inefficient, unfit, unqualified, untrained; *antonym* *(adj)* trained, **3.** ignorant; *synonyms* *(adj)* unconscious, illiterate, rude, uneducated, unwitting, blind, dull, innocent, naive, unaware, uninformed, unlearned, barbarous, shallow, dark; *antonyms* *(adj)* knowledgeable, conscious, **4.** incompetent; *synonyms* *(adj)* impotent, unable, feeble, insufficient, powerless, useless, feckless, hopeless, ineffective, ineligible, weak, bungling, deficient, fumbling, *(n)* bungler; *antonyms* *(adj)* competent, capable, skillful, **5.** unqualified; *synonyms* *(adj)* sheer, absolute, total, unconditional, complete, unmitigated, utter, perfect, pure, categorical, flat, outright, positive, thorough, unlimited; *antonyms* *(adj)* qualified, prepared, **6.** unskillful; *synonyms* *(adj)* maladroit, botchy, butcherly.

babangaki 1. crossing; *synonyms* *(n)* cross, ford, transit, crossbreeding, hybridization, intersection, passage, voyage, crossroad, crosswalk, crossway, cruise, flight, interbreeding, junction, **2.** crosswise; *synonyms* *(adv)* across, crossways, athwart, diagonally, traverse, *(adj)* diagonal; *antonym* *(adj)* lengthwise, **3.** swollen; *synonyms* *(adj)* bloated, inflated, bombastic, puffed, puffy, turgid, egotistic, high, bulging, tumescent, tumid, conceited, *(v)* distended, blown, *(prep)* pompous.

babaraki upset; *synonyms* *(v)* overturn, agitate, disquiet, overthrow, bother, confuse, disturb, perturb, reverse, *(adj)* unsettled, hurt, *(n)* disorder, trouble, distress, disturbance; *antonyms* *(v)* calm, please, encourage, soothe, *(adj)* pleased, confident.

babarantiko 1. chatterbox; *synonyms* *(n)* chatterer, babbler, gossip, talker, cackler, busybody, communicator, conversationalist, spouter, cotinga, mouth, raconteur, **2.** chatter; *synonyms* *(n)* prattle, gab, chattering, chaffer, *(v)* babble, chat, jabber, cackle, blab, blabber, natter, patter, tattle, *(adj)* prate, palaver, **3.** gossip; *synonyms* *(n)* rumor, chitchat, chatterbox, conversation, comment, talk, blabbermouth, hearsay, scandal, talebearer, tattletale, telltale, *(v)* chatter, confabulate, converse; *antonym* *(n)* fact, **4.** talkative; *synonyms* *(adj)* loquacious, chatty, garrulous, gabby, verbose, gossipy, glib, communicative, talky, wordy, bigmouthed, blabbermouthed, blabby, effusive, expansive; *antonyms* *(adj)* taciturn, reserved, mute, quiet, shy, silent, **5.** tattle; *synonyms* *(n)* gabble, *(v)* blather, snitch, blither, betray, jaw, squeal, clack, divulge, gibber, piffle, twaddle, blether, peach, sing.

babaro 1. empty; *synonyms* (*adj*) discharge, hollow, destitute, bare, blank, barren, abandoned, deserted, vain, (*v*) drain, clear, deplete, desolate, pour, spill; *antonyms* (*adj*) full, crowded, meaningful, packed, brimming, inhabited, occupied, swarming, cultivated, filled, laden, (*v*) fill, **2.** pour; *synonyms* (*v*) gush, shed, decant, flow, pelt, scatter, stream, emit, jet, run, teem, effuse, deluge, (*n*) overflow, rain; *antonym* (*v*) drizzle, **3.** overflow; *synonyms* (*n*) flood, inundation, excess, flooding, outpouring, runoff, torrent, affluence, flowage, abundance, (*v*) inundate, drown, overrun, submerge, brim.

babaroaki 1. emptied; *synonyms* (*adj*) void, voided, depleted, annulled, open, vacuous, evacuated, invalidated, **2.** poured; *synonym* (*adj*) concrete.

babetitoa christen; *synonyms* (*v*) call, baptize, dub, entitle, name, baptise, designate, style, term.

babobo yellow; *synonyms* (*adj*) jaundiced, amber, chicken, chickenhearted, fearful, xanthous, craven, spineless, yellowish, flavous, golden, (*n*) coward, (*adv*) cowardly.

babu calm; *synonyms* (*adj*) quiet, peaceful, tranquil, (*v*) assuage, appease, cool, still, allay, pacify, easy, moderate, mollify, steady, (*n*) lull, equanimity; *antonyms* (*adj*) agitated, angry, nervous, stormy, wild, annoyed, anxious, enraged, frantic, frightened, intense, irritable, (*v*) agitate, upset, (*n*) agitation.

bae 1. indebted; *synonyms* (*adj*) grateful, appreciative, thankful, obliged, broke, deferred, gratified, insolvent, accountable, chargeable, duty-bound, honor-bound, hooked, (*prep*) beholden, debted, **2.** engaged; *synonyms* (*adj*) busy, occupied, betrothed, affianced, employed, engrossed, reserved, absorbed, working, pledged, bespoken, booked, immersed, intent, rapt; *antonyms* (*adj*) available, free.

baebaeta 1. abuse; *synonyms* (*n*) affront, misuse, harm, outrage, reproach, invective, (*v*) insult, mistreat, injure, assault, censure, damage, exploit, hurt, (*adj*) maltreat; *antonyms* (*v*) praise, respect, **2.** discredit; *synonyms* (*v*) degrade, disbelieve, decry, impeach, distrust, compromise, belittle, (*n*) disgrace, disrepute, dishonor, doubt, shame, defame, slur, contempt; *antonyms* (*v*) honor, believe, credit, dignify, **3.** cry; *synonyms* (*n*) shout, bark, scream, yell, clamor, roar, bay, crying, (*v*) call, bellow, shriek, weep, exclaim, howl, moan; *antonyms* (*v*) laugh, whisper, **4.** wail; *synonyms* (*n*) lament, complaint, lamentation, plaint, (*v*) cry, ululate, bawl, bewail, mewl, sob, whimper, whine, squall, grieve, mourn.

baebaetaki 1. discredited; *synonyms* (*adj*) disgraced, damaged, besmirched, dishonored, shamed, flyblown, guilty, hangdog, shamefaced, spotted,

stained, sullied, tainted, tarnished, **2.** abused; *synonyms* (*adj*) maltreated, mistreated, downtrodden, dull, perverted, battered, harmed, injured, molested, neglected.

baebaeti wail; *synonyms* (*n*) lament, moan, scream, complaint, lamentation, plaint, (*v*) howl, cry, ululate, bellow, bawl, bewail, mewl, roar, sob.

baebaetia wail; *synonyms* (*n*) lament, moan, scream, complaint, lamentation, plaint, (*v*) howl, cry, ululate, bellow, bawl, bewail, mewl, roar, sob.

baekeke 1. domineering; *synonyms* (*adj*) arrogant, dictatorial, overbearing, arbitrary, autocratic, authoritative, bossy, commanding, dominant, imperious, lordly, masterful, despotic, haughty, magisterial; *antonyms* (*adj*) submissive, subservient, **2.** controlling; *synonyms* (*adj*) ruling, capital, chief, influential, predominant, **3.** dominating; *synonyms* (*adj*) ascendant, ascendent, inextinguishable, unquenchable, authoritarian, autocratical, leading, ascensive, distinguished, impregnable, indomitable, invincible, irresistible, overlooking, peremptory, **4.** obtrusive; *synonyms* (*adj*) noticeable, blatant, conspicuous, officious, prominent, pushy, saucy, forward, precocious, presumptuous, rude, salient, busy, glaring, brassy; *antonyms* (*adj*) inconspicuous, unobtrusive.

baenikai 1. delay; *synonyms* (*n*) pause, arrest, deferment, wait, stay, deferral, extension, (*v*) defer, check, postpone, reserve, adjourn, break, detain, hesitate; *antonyms* (*n*) punctuality, decisiveness, (*v*) rush, advance, **2.** hamper; *synonyms* (*n*) basket, bond, disadvantage, (*v*) clog, cramp, block, fetter, hinder, curb, interfere, confine, delay, embarrass, encumber, handicap, **3.** delayed; *synonyms* (*adj*) belated, late, tardy, protracted, deferred, slow, (*adv*) behind; *antonyms* (*adj*) brief, early, **4.** hinder; *synonyms* (*adj*) posterior, hind, (*v*) bar, impede, hamper, obstruct, resist, counteract, frustrate, preclude, prevent, prohibit, restrain, stop, balk; *antonyms* (*v*) help, assist, facilitate, **5.** late; *synonyms* (*adj*) former, dead, deceased, behindhand, delayed, modern, dull, defunct, bygone, posthumous, erstwhile, (*adv*) dilatory, fresh, backward, belatedly; *antonyms* (*adj*) ahead, (*adv*) punctually, promptly, punctual.

baenikaiaki delayed; *synonyms* (*adj*) belated, late, tardy, protracted, deferred, slow, (*adv*) behind; *antonyms* (*adj*) brief, early.

bai very; *synonyms* (*adv*) extremely, greatly, highly, really, completely, entirely, most, quite, truly, actually, too, awfully, (*adj*) much, identical, (*n*) self; *antonyms* (*adv*) abysmally, slightly, somewhat.

baia gristly; *synonyms* (*adj*) cartilaginous, stringy, rubbery, tough, chewy, fibrous, hard, leathery, sinewy, stiff, rubberlike; *antonym* (*adj*) tender.

baiati 1. giving; *synonyms* (n) gift, endowment, donation, presentation, (adj) generous, liberal, bighearted, charitable, big, bounteous, bountiful, freehanded, humanitarian, openhanded, **2.** generous; *synonyms* (adj) ample, full, abundant, benevolent, copious, fair, flush, kind, spacious, rich, benign, broad, considerable, handsome, (n) free; *antonyms* (adj) stingy, meager, mean, measly, miserly, small, tightfisted, avaricious, greedy, ungenerous, **3.** benevolent; *synonyms* (adj) good, compassionate, gracious, kindly, philanthropic, loving, considerate, gentle, humane, tender, altruistic, affable, (n) beneficent, nice, sympathetic; *antonyms* (adj) malevolent, malicious, unfeeling.

baibai 1. own; *synonyms* (v) acknowledge, admit, have, concede, allow, grant, hold, possess, confess, get, accept, avow, enjoy, (adj) individual, proper, **2.** possess; *synonyms* (v) occupy, wield, bear, keep, maintain, obsess, retain, consume, feature, (n) hazard, (adj) own, **3.** use; *synonyms* (n) custom, practice, benefit, habit, application, function, (v) exercise, employ, employment, expend, profit, advantage, exploit, operate, (adj) usage; *antonym* (v) conserve.

baibaiaki 1. owned; *synonyms* (v) behoove, ought, owed, (adj) own, proprietary, **2.** used; *synonyms* (adj) secondhand, exploited, accustomed, decrepit, depleted, exhausted, faded, habituated, hand-me-down, spent, threadbare, tried, victimised, victimized, wont; *antonyms* (adj) pristine, new, spanking, unused.

baibainanti 1. deformed; *synonyms* (adj) crooked, bent, distorted, malformed, misshapen, ugly, crippled, contorted, deform, grotesque, shapeless, twisted, warped, (v) crump, **2.** freak; *synonyms* (n) crotchet, caprice, eccentric, crank, oddity, fanatic, fad, fit, monster, nut, whim, abnormality, whimsy, (v) fancy, capriccio.

baibait 1. sound; *synonyms* (n) echo, peal, (v) ring, chime, fast, (adj) reasonable, complete, healthy, fit, good, just, rational, right, sane, sensible; *antonyms* (n) silence, (adj) illogical, unsound, confused, **2.** strong; *synonyms* (adj) intense, powerful, able, deep, firm, stable, steady, cogent, durable, forcible, hard, influential, lusty, potent, rigid; *antonyms* (adj) weak, bland, delicate, faint, feeble, frail, mild, pale, slight, unconvincing, cowardly, diluted, dull, exhausted, flimsy.

baibake miss; *synonyms* (v) lack, lose, fail, jump, omit, overlook, long, drop, escape, (n) maid, girl, want, fille, missy, (adj) fault; *antonym* (v) perceive.

baibakeaki missed; *synonyms* (adj) lost, baffled, befuddled, bemused, bewildered, confounded, confused, disoriented, forgotten, helpless, irretrievable, mazed, preoccupied.

baibao miss; *synonyms* (v) lack, lose, fail, jump, omit, overlook, long, drop, escape, (n) maid, girl, want, fille, missy, (adj) fault; *antonym* (v) perceive.

baibaoaki missed; *synonyms* (adj) lost, baffled, befuddled, bemused, bewildered, confounded, confused, disoriented, forgotten, helpless, irretrievable, mazed, preoccupied.

baibati 1. impetuous; *synonyms* (adj) boisterous, furious, hasty, impulsive, fiery, headlong, heady, hot, brash, fierce, foolhardy, hotheaded, impatient, rash, vehement; *antonyms* (adj) cautious, considered, **2.** strong; *synonyms* (adj) intense, powerful, able, deep, firm, stable, steady, cogent, durable, forcible, good, hard, influential, lusty, potent; *antonyms* (adj) weak, bland, delicate, faint, feeble, frail, mild, pale, slight, unconvincing, cowardly, diluted, dull, exhausted, flimsy.

baibuaka 1. awkward; *synonyms* (adj) clumsy, inconvenient, crude, embarrassing, inept, sticky, uncomfortable, ungainly, untoward, left-handed, annoying, bungling, cumbersome, difficult, graceless; *antonyms* (adj) graceful, easy, adroit, manageable, straightforward, convenient, dexterous, helpful, rotund, simple, **2.** clumsy; *synonyms* (adj) bumbling, unwieldy, gawky, inapt, maladroit, rude, unskilled, wooden, incompetent, lumbering, boorish, gross, heavy, (n) awkward, gauche; *antonyms* (adj) nimble, clever, skillful, deft.

baiene basket; *synonyms* (n) basketful, bassinet, cradle, gondola, case, coffin, handbasket, hoop, leap, ped, pottle, stomach, whisket, bound, corbeille.

baikiaro inelegant; *synonyms* (adj) awkward, clumsy, graceless, coarse, crude, gawky, maladroit, rude, ungraceful, crass, vulgar, gross, rustic, rough, tasteless; *antonyms* (adj) graceful, elegant.

baikimoa 1. thief; *synonyms* (n) robber, burglar, bandit, pirate, plunderer, crook, filcher, stealer, despoiler, freebooter, pillager, rifler, **2.** shyster; *synonyms* (n) pettifogger, attorney, caviler, caviller, cheat, counselor, impostor, lawyer, quibbler, rascal, **3.** robber; *synonyms* (n) thief, highwayman, outlaw, depredator, spoiler.

baikonaki comparative; *synonyms* (adj) relative, qualified, proportionate, approximate, illustrative, near, allusive, analogous, approaching, conditional, connected, contingent, contrastive, correlative, (n) compeer.

baikoraki 1. shrewd; *synonyms* (adj) astute, calculating, crafty, knowing, sagacious, sharp, clever, cunning, keen, piercing, bright, ingenious, cautious, acute, (v) prudent; *antonyms* (adj) stupid, foolish, gullible, **2.** quaint; *synonyms* (adj) fantastic, odd, funny, picturesque, comical, fanciful, curious, droll, peculiar, queer, quizzical, strange, whimsical, eccentric, outlandish; *antonyms* (adj) modern, normal, **3.** odd; *synonyms* (adj) grotesque, exceptional, abnormal, extraordinary, singular, chance, novel, anomalous, bizarre, individual, irregular, unusual, laughable, erratic, particular; *antonyms* (*adj*) ordinary, even, typical.

baimatoa 1. subdue; *synonyms* (*v*) conquer, crush, defeat, overpower, quash, quell, reduce, repress, chasten, curb, overcome, restrain, soften, subjugate, (*adv*) control; *antonym* (*v*) surrender, **2.** overcome; *synonyms* (*v*) beat, subdue, vanquish, master, hurdle, overwhelm, prevail, surmount, demolish, affect, cross, exceed, outdo, (*adj*) beaten, conquered; *antonyms* (*v*) fail, (*adj*) victorious, unimpressed.

baimatoaki 1. subdued; *synonyms* (*adj*) muffled, quiet, soft, dull, muted, restrained, tame, faint, resigned, repressed, low, meek, broken, delicate, sober; *antonyms* (*adj*) loud, enthusiastic, lively, **2.** overcome; *synonyms* (*v*) conquer, beat, crush, subdue, vanquish, defeat, master, overpower, hurdle, overwhelm, prevail, subjugate, surmount, demolish, (*adj*) beaten; *antonyms* (*v*) fail, (*adj*) victorious, unimpressed.

baina 1. appropriate; *synonyms* (*adj*) pertinent, proper, true, agreeable, apposite, apt, congruous, correct, particular, peculiar, right, (*v*) annex, allocate, adopt, seize; *antonyms* (*adj*) inappropriate, unsuitable, unrelated, untimely, wrong, (*v*) surrender, **2.** own; *synonyms* (*v*) acknowledge, admit, have, concede, allow, grant, hold, possess, confess, get, accept, avow, enjoy, occupy, (*adj*) individual.

bainaka 1. honored; *synonyms* (*v*) completed, consummated, crowned, excessive, (*adj*) esteemed, reputable, honoured, respected, privileged, distinguished, glorious, exalted, advantaged, estimable, famous, **2.** sacred; *synonyms* (*adj*) hallowed, holy, consecrated, dedicated, divine, religious, pious, blessed, inviolable, spiritual, consecrate, celestial, devoted, (*v*) solemn, majestic; *antonyms* (*adj*) secular, profane.

bainaki 1. appropriated; *synonyms* (*adj*) destined, condemned, confiscate, confiscated, reserved, seized, censured, convicted, forfeit, forfeited, **2.** owned; *synonyms* (*v*) behoove, ought, owed, (*adj*) own, proprietary.

bainanti 1. extraordinary; *synonyms* (*adj*) distinguished, curious, exceptional, odd, abnormal, amazing, astonishing, bizarre, extra, phenomenal, rare, special, strange, unusual, famous; *antonyms* (*adj*) ordinary, normal, everyday, **2.** abnormal; *synonyms* (*adj*) aberrant, anomalous, atypical, irregular, monstrous, perverted, uncommon, unnatural, perverse, improper, preternatural, grotesque, defective, divergent, eccentric; *antonyms* (*adj*) typical, usual, **3.** exceptional; *synonyms* (*adj*) excellent, extraordinary, particular, prodigious, singular, exceeding, outstanding, single, superior, unique, especial, infrequent, great,

incomparable, individual; *antonyms* (*adj*) common, mediocre, average, abysmal, inferior, poor, **4.** singular; *synonyms* (*adj*) peculiar, quaint, queer, separate, one, outlandish, remarkable, solitary, comical, noteworthy, scarce, distinctive, funny, rum, rummy; *antonym* (*n*) plural.

bainataei unusual; *synonyms* (*adj*) strange, peculiar, odd, quaint, uncommon, curious, eccentric, exceptional, exotic, extraordinary, irregular, rare, remarkable, special, unprecedented; *antonyms* (*adj*) usual, normal, common, customary, ordinary, typical, familiar, conventional, routine.

bain-ganai if; *synonyms* (*conj*) provided, although, providing, whether, though, and, so, an, gin, (*n*) but, conditionally, condition, stipulation, proviso, (*adv*) peradventure.

bainikirina 1. maltreat; *synonyms* (*v*) abuse, mistreat, harm, mishandle, misuse, damage, hurt, injure, molest, oppress, outrage, persecute, wrong, assail, **2.** mock; *synonyms* (*adj*) counterfeit, (*v*) deride, ridicule, burlesque, gibe, ape, flout, mimic, scoff, scorn, sham, taunt, bemock, (*n*) jeer, derision; *antonyms* (*adj*) genuine, real, **3.** mistreat; *synonyms* (*v*) maltreat, torture, manhandle, torment, assault, blackguard, clapperclaw, corrupt, exploit, knock, manipulate, pervert, vilify, backbite, bash, **4.** torment; *synonyms* (*n*) harass, agony, anguish, annoy, pain, suffering, curse, (*v*) tease, distress, afflict, badger, irritate, pester, rack, worry, **5.** oppress; *synonyms* (*v*) press, burden, pinch, depress, encumber, crush, repress, load, harry, harrow, control, bully, jam, overload, (*adj*) aggrieve, **6.** persecute; *synonyms* (*v*) chase, follow, plague, bait, beset, bother, crucify, grind, pursue, heckle, beleaguer, vex.

bainikirinaki 1. mistreated; *synonyms* (*adj*) abused, maltreated, battered, aggrieved, downtrodden, harmed, injured, neglected, wronged, ignored, offended, persecuted, victimized, **2.** maltreated; *synonym* (*adj*) mistreated, **3.** tormented; *synonyms* (*adj*) anguished, tortured, worried, hagridden, beleaguered, beset, besieged, cruciate, cruciform, distraught, distressed, miserable, obsessed, plagued, suffering; *antonym* (*adj*) content, **4.** oppressed; *synonyms* (*adj*) laden, broken, burdened, browbeaten, despairing, downcast, drawn, forlorn, gloomy, haggard, heavy, ladened, loaded, subjugated, demoralized.

bainingare 1. laughable; *synonyms* (*adj*) funny, absurd, amusing, humorous, comical, droll, farcical, ludicrous, ridiculous, comic, foolish, jocular, derisory, preposterous, risible, **2.** ridiculous; *synonyms* (*adj*) laughable, inane, nonsensical, irrational, outrageous, silly, inconsistent, grotesque, crazy, daft, extravagant, incongruous, senseless, unreasonable, unwise; *antonyms* (*adj*) sensible, inspiring, reasonable.

bainingareakina 1. mock; *synonyms* (*adj*)
counterfeit, (*v*) deride, ridicule, burlesque, gibe,
ape, flout, mimic, scoff, scorn, sham, taunt, bemock,
(*n*) jeer, derision; *antonyms* (*adj*) genuine, real, **2.**
ridicule; *synonyms* (*n*) irony, mockery, insult,
contempt, disdain, sarcasm, sneer, disparagement,
(*v*) banter, mock, tease, rib, chaff, joke, (*adj*)
lampoon; *antonyms* (*v*) praise, respect, **3.** scoff;
synonyms (*v*) quip, jest, gird, barrack, (*n*) jibe, hoot,
jeering, scoffing, hiss, (*adj*) blaspheme, desecrate,
profane, revile.

bainraraea insult; *synonyms* (*n*) dishonor, abuse,
affront, contumely, disgrace, indignity, outrage,
contempt, wound, derision, harm, injury, (*v*) flout,
taunt, cut; *antonyms* (*v*) compliment, praise.

bainraraeaki insulted; *synonyms* (*adj*) affronted,
huffy, disrespected, hurt, slighted, snubbed, upset.

baira 1. clumsy; *synonyms* (*adj*) bumbling, bungling,
cumbersome, unwieldy, gawky, inapt, inept,
maladroit, rude, ungainly, unskilled, wooden,
incompetent, lumbering, (*n*) awkward; *antonyms*
(*adj*) graceful, nimble, clever, dexterous, skillful,
adroit, deft, **2.** awkward; *synonyms* (*adj*) clumsy,
inconvenient, crude, embarrassing, sticky,
uncomfortable, untoward, left-handed, annoying,
difficult, graceless, heavy, inelegant, rough, rustic;
antonyms (*adj*) easy, manageable, straightforward,
convenient, helpful, rotund, simple.

bairaoi 1. generous; *synonyms* (*adj*) ample, full,
abundant, benevolent, copious, bountiful,
charitable, fair, flush, kind, liberal, spacious, rich,
benign, (*n*) free; *antonyms* (*adj*) stingy, meager,
mean, measly, miserly, small, tightfisted,
avaricious, greedy, ungenerous, **2.** apt; *synonyms*
(*adj*) appropriate, adroit, apropos, apposite,
intelligent, good, able, adequate, convenient,
dexterous, efficient, fit, ready, smart, clever;
antonym (*adj*) inappropriate, **3.** impartial;
synonyms (*adj*) just, disinterested, dispassionate,
equitable, unbiased, unprejudiced, even-handed,
candid, even, balanced, detached, evenhanded,
honest, impersonal, indifferent; *antonyms* (*adj*)
biased, partial, **4.** clever; *synonyms* (*adj*) capable,
acute, apt, astute, cunning, expert, ingenious,
quick, sharp, skillful, artful, learned, adept, brainy,
(*v*) brilliant; *antonyms* (*adj*) stupid, clumsy,
unintelligent, dim, dull, inept, **5.** handy;
synonyms (*adj*) available, deft, accessible, easy,
commodious, functional, near, nearby, practical,
useful, close, portable, effective, expedient, (*n*)
applicable; *antonyms* (*adj*) useless, fixed, **6.**
skillful; *synonyms* (*adj*) accomplished, proficient,
knowing, handy, practiced, skilled, nice, slick,
competent, experienced, skilful, (*v*) crafty,
judicious, nimble, (*n*) neat; *antonym* (*adj*)
incompetent, **7.** proficient; *synonyms* (*adj*)
professional, crack, qualified, gifted,

knowledgeable, talented, versed, facile, finished, (*n*)
master.

bairawata 1. robber; *synonyms* (*n*) thief,
highwayman, bandit, outlaw, burglar, crook,
pillager, pirate, plunderer, depredator, despoiler,
spoiler, rifler, **2.** thief; *synonyms* (*n*) robber, filcher,
stealer, freebooter.

baire 1. arrange; *synonyms* (*v*) adjust, appoint, dress,
order, set, settle, pack, adapt, agree, classify,
compose, decorate, do, engineer, fix; *antonyms* (*v*)
disturb, disarrange, **2.** gauge; *synonyms* (*n*)
criterion, caliber, gage, calibre, (*v*) estimate,
measure, calculate, assess, compute, fathom, make,
reckon, forecast, scale, appraise, **3.** rule; *synonyms*
(*n*) govern, decree, dominion, law, ordinance,
principle, regulate, reign, authority, dictate, (*v*)
command, control, influence, direct, dominate, **4.**
regulate; *synonyms* (*v*) arrange, manage,
determine, modulate, regularize, align, check,
correct, decide, guide, organize, rectify, shape,
accommodate, (*n*) form, **5.** organize; *synonyms* (*v*)
establish, coordinate, constitute, devise, institute,
conduct, found, orchestrate, organise, plan,
prepare, systematize, unionize, categorize, erect;
antonym (*v*) disorganize.

bairea measure; *synonyms* (*n*) amount, criterion,
extent, beat, benchmark, degree, estimate,
measurement, meter, quantity, act, allotment,
action, (*v*) grade, appraise.

baireaki 1. measured; *synonyms* (*adj*) careful,
deliberate, moderate, calculated, reasonable,
temperate, regular, leisurely, metrical, sober, cool,
slow, **2.** arranged; *synonyms* (*adj*) set, settled,
fixed, orderly, organized, prepared, ready, neat,
ordered, straight, tidy, **3.** regulated; *synonyms*
(*adj*) arranged, consistent, lawful, logical,
regulatory, systematic, (*adv*) synchronized, **4.**
ruled; *synonyms* (*adj*) lined, subject, feint, hatched,
5. organized; *synonyms* (*adj*) organised, organic,
methodical, shipshape, efficient; *antonyms* (*adj*)
untidy, disorganized, muddled.

bairean measure; *synonyms* (*n*) amount, criterion,
extent, beat, benchmark, degree, estimate,
measurement, meter, quantity, act, allotment,
action, (*v*) grade, appraise.

baireanaki measured; *synonyms* (*adj*) careful,
deliberate, moderate, calculated, reasonable,
temperate, regular, leisurely, metrical, sober, cool,
slow.

bairekereke catch; *synonyms* (*v*) arrest, capture,
hook, apprehend, get, acquire, ensnare, intercept,
(*n*) haul, hitch, trick, bolt, clasp, grab, pawl;
antonym (*v*) release.

bairemwe slow; *synonyms* (*adj*) dull, late, easy,
sluggish, heavy, dense, dim, gradual, inactive,
indolent, lazy, stupid, (*v*) slack, (*adv*) behind,
behindhand; *antonyms* (*adj*) fast, intelligent, rapid,

bright, alert, brisk, hasty, prompt, quick, speedy, hurried, observant, rushed, (v) accelerate.

baitabare 1. meddlesome; *synonyms* (*adj*) intrusive, busy, inquisitive, interfering, officious, obtrusive, nosy, curious, pragmatical, prying, busybodied, impertinent, meddling, **2**. thief; *synonyms* (*n*) robber, burglar, bandit, pirate, plunderer, crook, filcher, stealer, despoiler, freebooter, pillager, rifler.

baitangako 1. licentious; *synonyms* (*adj*) dissolute, immoral, lewd, filthy, abandoned, debauched, lascivious, depraved, lecherous, fast, loose, unchaste, wanton, wild, carnal, **2**. untidy; *synonyms* (*adj*) slovenly, disheveled, disordered, disorderly, messy, sloppy, unkempt, confused, disorganized, frowzy, scruffy, sluttish, slipshod, dowdy, tousled; *antonyms* (*adj*) tidy, neat, elegant.

baitata 1. fast; *synonyms* (*adj*) dissolute, firm, agile, debauched, fixed, hurried, instant, quick, rapid, staunch, brisk, (*adv*) soon, hard, close, (*n*) diet; *antonyms* (*adj*) sluggish, loose, (*adv*) slow, slowly, leisurely, (*v*) gorge, (*n*) binge, **2**. expeditious; *synonyms* (*adj*) prompt, swift, fast, hasty, speedy, fleet, immediate, nimble, ready, punctual, **3**. brisk; *synonyms* (*adj*) active, bracing, alive, bright, lively, acute, alert, energetic, smart, sprightly, adroit, animated, crisp, fresh, invigorating; *antonym* (*adj*) soporific, **4**. agile; *synonyms* (*adj*) spry, deft, lithe, supple, quick-witted, dexterous, flexible, light, limber, lissom, vivacious, graceful; *antonym* (*adj*) clumsy, **5**. smart; *synonyms* (*adj*) crafty, dapper, shrewd, sly, astute, chic, clever, intelligent, jaunty, natty, neat, (*v*) ache, hurt, (*n*) pain, sharp; *antonyms* (*adj*) scruffy, stupid, dim, shabby, unkempt.

baiteke 1. dexterous; *synonyms* (*adj*) adroit, adept, crafty, deft, skillful, able, clever, expert, agile, cunning, apt, artful, good, handy, neat; *antonym* (*adj*) clumsy, **2**. coordinated; *synonyms* (*adj*) cooperative, harmonious, interconnected, matching, unified, corresponding, duplicate, harmonized, incorporate, incorporated, interrelated, matched, merged, synchronized, twinned.

baito 1. steal; *synonyms* (*v*) abstract, lift, purloin, creep, filch, misappropriate, pilfer, pinch, plunder, rob, snatch, sneak, plagiarize, slip, (*n*) bargain, **2**. stole; *synonyms* (*n*) scarf, wrap, stolon, robe, alb, cassock, chasuble, cope, dalmatic, gown, mozetta, pallium, scapulary, surplice, tunicle.

baitoaki stolen; *synonyms* (*adj*) purloined, furtive, misbegotten, secret, sly, stealthy.

baiturua 1. mark; *synonyms* (*n*) brand, evidence, score, character, heed, impression, imprint, sign, feature, (*v*) blemish, characterize, distinguish, grade, label, (*adj*) notice, **2**. imprint; *synonyms* (*n*) stamp, print, effect, feeling, depression, embossment, (*v*) impress, mark, engrave, inscribe, dent, cast, make, form, **3**. stamp; *synonyms* (*n*)

seal, cachet, emblem, die, earmark, hallmark, mold, mould, pestle, (*v*) trample, punch, shape, note, emboss, mint.

baituruaki 1. marked; *synonyms* (*adj*) distinct, conspicuous, noticeable, pronounced, remarkable, distinguished, apparent, definite, notable, obvious, signal, striking, strong, clear, appreciable; *antonyms* (*adj*) plain, unblemished, **2**. stamped; *synonyms* (*v*) imprinted, engraved, fixed, carved, impressed, (*adj*) beaten, embossed.

baka 1. miss; *synonyms* (*v*) lack, lose, fail, jump, omit, overlook, long, drop, escape, (*n*) maid, girl, want, fille, missy, (*adj*) fault; *antonym* (*v*) perceive, **2**. feign; *synonyms* (*v*) affect, assume, dissemble, fake, pretend, simulate, dissimulate, deceive, act, counterfeit, sham, fabricate, cheat, forge, play, **3**. conspire; *synonyms* (*v*) collude, complot, concur, cabal, connive, plan, plot, contribute, collaborate, confederate, intrigue, machinate, scheme, conduce, conjure, **4**. collapse; *synonyms* (*n*) crash, breakdown, fall, subsidence, bust, debacle, (*v*) break, slump, buckle, crack, crumble, crumple, faint, flop, burst, **5**. abate; *synonyms* (*v*) subside, allay, bate, decline, diminish, fade, flag, lessen, relax, relieve, remit, slack, slake, wane, (*adj*) slacken; *antonym* (*v*) increase, **6**. lost; *synonyms* (*v*) gone, missing, abandoned, (*adj*) doomed, forlorn, extinct, hopeless, bewildered, disoriented, forgotten, helpless, broken, confused, irrecoverable, absent; *antonyms* (*adj*) present, found, existing, **7**. lose; *synonyms* (*v*) forfeit, mislay, sacrifice, clear, hurt, regress, retrogress, destroy, misplace, recede, suffer, waste; *antonyms* (*v*) gain, find, acquire, earn, get, obtain, recover, secure, win, beat, defeat, keep, succeed, **8**. missed; *synonyms* (*adj*) lost, baffled, befuddled, bemused, confounded, irretrievable, mazed, preoccupied, **9**. overripe; *synonyms* (*adj*) decadent, effete, decayed, degenerate, fracid, overmellow, **10**. scandalize; *synonyms* (*v*) outrage, defame, disgust, scandalise, shock, slander, offend, malign, calumniate, libel, reproach, appal, appall, **11**. pretend; *synonyms* (*v*) feign, imagine, imitate, profess, mask, masquerade, disguise, kid, move, trick, claim, (*adj*) pretended, false, (*n*) allege, contend; *antonyms* (*v*) real, (*adj*) genuine, natural, **12**. succumb; *synonyms* (*v*) submit, defer, yield, bow, accede, decease, die, go, perish, surrender, capitulate, give, cede, pass, accept; *antonyms* (*v*) endure, resist.

bakabua hoarse; *synonyms* (*adj*) harsh, gruff, husky, grating, raucous, strident, guttural, rough, throaty, croaking, (*v*) coarse, hollow, sepulchral; *antonym* (*adj*) soft.

bakaea pretend; *synonyms* (*v*) assume, feign, dissimulate, counterfeit, act, affect, dissemble, imagine, imitate, profess, mask, (*adj*) sham, fake, play, (n) allege; **antonyms** (v) real, (adj) genuine, natural.

bakaki feigned; *synonyms* (adj) artificial, false, sham, affected, assumed, counterfeit, dummy, fictitious, spurious, unnatural, fake, fabulous, (v) mock, pretended, supposititious.

bakamoamoa 1. braggart; *synonyms* (n) boaster, blowhard, braggadocio, bragger, vaunter, swaggerer, talker, babbler, rodomont, (v) magniloquent, pretentious, flaming, gasconading, (adj) braggy, crowing, **2.** boaster; *synonyms* (n) braggart, bouncer, huff, pretension, rage, **3.** hypocrite; *synonyms* (n) dissembler, impostor, pretender, trickster, fraud, cheat, fake.

bakannaioro rebound; *synonyms* (n) bound, kick, backlash, repercussion, return, echo, reaction, (v) bounce, recoil, glance, ricochet, rally, boomerang, jump, backfire.

bakantang 1. desire; *synonyms* (n) ambition, hope, aspiration, will, wish, craving, dream, impulse, (v) fancy, aspire, seek, want, aim, choose, crave; *antonyms* (n) aversion, reality, (v) dislike, hate, **2.** covetous; *synonyms* (adj) avaricious, avid, acquisitive, envious, grasping, greedy, sordid, hungry, jealous, miserly, ravenous, voracious, selfish, (n) desirous, (v) mercenary; *antonym* (adj) generous, **3.** envious; *synonyms* (adj) covetous, invidious, jaundiced, malicious, resentful, green, grudging, begrudging, **4.** jealous; *synonyms* (adj) distrustful, suspicious.

bakantangaki desired; *synonyms* (adj) coveted, craved, desirable, chosen, favorite, wanted, needed, welcome, beloved, adored, appropriate, pet, preferred, (v) complying, consenting; *antonym* (adj) undesirable.

bakara 1. startle; *synonyms* (v) alarm, frighten, jump, scare, astonish, shock, astound, amaze, shake, dismay, electrify, rouse, stagger, (n) start, (adv) surprise, **2.** shock; *synonyms* (n) blow, daze, impact, collision, outrage, concussion, fright, (v) jar, offend, revolt, startle, appall, clash, disgust, horrify; *antonym* (v) comfort, **3.** scare; *synonyms* (n) dread, fear, menace, anxiety, (v) intimidate, daunt, awe, affright, discourage, terrify, terrorize, (adj) panic, consternation, horror, terror, **4.** surprise; *synonyms* (n) amazement, astonishment, surprisal, wonder, admiration, miracle, (v) jolt, stun, catch, bewilder, confound, overwhelm, overtake, capture, discover.

bakarae 1. messy; *synonyms* (adj) untidy, dirty, confused, careless, disheveled, disordered, disorganized, grimy, grubby, scruffy, slovenly, unkempt, chaotic, muddled, (v) mussy; *antonyms* (adj) tidy, neat, clean, **2.** forsaken; *synonyms* (adj) deserted, desolate, abandoned, lonely, forlorn, derelict, desert, jilted, empty, solitary, friendless, isolated, **3.** disordered; *synonyms* (adj) broken,

deranged, incoherent, messy, sick, upset, disconnected, disjointed, disorderly, ill, jumbled, mixed, scattered, complex, discontinuous; *antonyms* (adj) orderly, ordered, **4.** untidy; *synonyms* (adj) sloppy, frowzy, sluttish, slipshod, dowdy, tousled, ragged, slatternly; *antonym* (adj) elegant, **5.** scattered; *synonyms* (adj) dispersed, dissipated, sparse, sporadic, thin, diffuse, distributed, rare, separate, spread, stray, strewn, garbled, illogical; *antonym* (adj) concentrated, **6.** unkept; *synonyms* (adj) busted, crushed, humbled, humiliated, impoverished, low, rugged.

bakaraki 1. scared; *synonyms* (adj) afraid, frightened, fearful, anxious, horrified, intimidated, nervous, terrified, timid, panicky, (adv) cowardly; *antonyms* (adj) calm, confident, fearless, **2.** surprised; *synonyms* (adj) astonished, amazed, astounded, dumbfounded, shocked, stunned, bewildered, startled, aghast, confused, curious, puzzled, questioning, quizzical, baffled; *antonym* (adj) indifferent, **3.** startled; *synonyms* (adj) scared, distressed, alarmed, flabbergasted, staggered, troubled, upset, worried, **4.** shocked; *synonyms* (adj) dismayed, surprised, appalled, speechless; *antonym* (adj) delighted.

bakarerea transfix; *synonyms* (v) impale, pierce, spike, fascinate, thrust, spellbind, stab, stick, empale, grip.

bakarereaki transfixed; *synonyms* (v) absorbed, rapt, riveted, (adj) fascinated, spellbound, hypnotised, hypnotized, mesmerised, mesmerized, motionless.

bakaruru 1. hungry; *synonyms* (adj) avid, eager, esurient, famished, greedy, ravenous, starving, desirous, meager, starveling, barren, keen, peckish, (v) craving, (adv) empty; *antonyms* (adj) full, sated, satiated, **2.** fatigued; *synonyms* (adj) exhausted, tired, weary, beat, worn, jaded, spent, fagged; *antonyms* (adj) fresh, refreshed, **3.** shaky; *synonyms* (adj) rickety, precarious, insecure, ramshackle, unsafe, unstable, broken, quaking, shaking, trembling, unsound, unsteady, weak, wobbly, (v) crazy; *antonyms* (adj) stable, steady, strong, **4.** shake; *synonyms* (v) agitate, jar, brandish, disturb, excite, flutter, totter, wag, drop, bump, (n) tremble, jolt, quiver, wave, (adj) quake, **5.** quiver; *synonyms* (n) palpitate, shake, quaver, thrill, tremor, vibration, chill, palpitation, tingle, (v) shiver, shudder, flicker, pulsate, vibrate, waver, **6.** starve; *synonyms* (v) famish, fast, crave, hunger, lust, pinch, thirst, benumb, bite, clem, (adj) begrudge, gripe, grudge, lack, screw.

bakaruruaki 1. starved; *synonyms* (adj) hungry, famished, starving, ravenous, meager, emaciated, esurient, malnourished, thin, **2.** shaken; *synonyms* (v) broken, lame, passe, shaky, threadbare, wilted, shattered, stale, (adj) jolted, dazed, disconcerted, fallen, scared, stunned, surprised.

bakatae 1. extravagant; *synonyms* (adj) excessive, wasteful, exaggerated, luxurious, prodigal, costly, expensive, immoderate, lavish, profligate, profuse, egregious, exorbitant, fantastic, improvident; *antonyms* (adj) economical, restrained, frugal, parsimonious, plain, stingy, understated, **2**. lavish; *synonyms* (adj) extravagant, exuberant, generous, ample, copious, abundant, bountiful, lush, munificent, plush, rich, free, (v) dissipate, waste, consume; *antonym* (adj) meager, **3**. prodigal; *synonyms* (adj) spendthrift, liberal, dissipated, flush, plentiful, luxuriant, opulent, squandering, unsparing, unstinted, overgenerous, (n) spender, squanderer, (v) waster.

bakataea 1. squander; *synonyms* (v) waste, fritter, dissipate, exhaust, lavish, spend, blow, expend, desolate, lose, scatter, trifle, deplete, devour, (adj) consume; *antonyms* (v) save, conserve, **2**. waste; *synonyms* (n) desert, refuse, damage, trash, dissipation, garbage, loss, (adj) spoil, barren, (v) ruin, squander, ravage, destruction, devastate, languish.

bakataeaki 1. squandered; *synonyms* (v) alienated, bewildered, (adj) lost, wasted, dissipated, atrophied, blasted, bony, cadaverous, desolate, desolated, devastated, diminished, dissolute, emaciated, **2**. wasted; *synonyms* (v) rotten, effete, languishing, (adj) squandered, thin, gaunt, decayed, haggard, pointless, skeletal, depleted, destroyed, faded, futile, ineffectual; *antonyms* (adj) worthwhile, bloated.

bakati squirt; *synonyms* (n) jet, spurt, spirt, fountain, child, nobody, (v) spray, gush, spout, eject, emit, splash, flow, burst, discharge.

bakatoki stubborn; *synonyms* (adj) obstinate, contrary, hard, intractable, perverse, determined, obdurate, persistent, refractory, rigid, tenacious, inveterate, contumacious, difficult, firm; *antonyms* (adj) compliant, flexible, irresolute, amenable.

bakaunun 1. bragging; *synonyms* (n) boasting, brag, swagger, bluff, bluster, (adj) arrogant, big, boastful, **2**. swaggering; *synonyms* (adj) blustering, hectoring, disdainful, haughty, lordly, prideful, roistering, sniffy, supercilious, swashbuckling, (n) bravado, ostentation.

bake 1. bent; *synonyms* (adj) arched, curved, bended, crooked, deformed, intent, (n) aptitude, inclination, propensity, fancy, ability, bias, flair, gift, leaning; *antonym* (adj) straight, **2**. crooked; *synonyms* (adj) bent, awry, corrupt, irregular, askew, dishonest, indirect, lopsided, unfair, unscrupulous, angular, asymmetrical, bowed, dishonorable, (v) wry; *antonyms* (adj) honest, even, principled, **3**. awkward; *synonyms* (adj) clumsy, inconvenient, crude, embarrassing, inept, sticky, uncomfortable, ungainly, untoward, left-handed, annoying, bungling, cumbersome, difficult, graceless; *antonyms* (adj) graceful, easy, adroit, manageable, straightforward, convenient, dexterous, helpful, rotund, simple.

bakete light; *synonyms* (adj) fair, clear, facile, easy, faint, flimsy, (n) flame, brightness, daylight, (v) fire, kindle, inflame, glow, ignite, dismount; *antonyms* (adj) fattening, nauseating, (n) dark, darkness, gloom, shade, night, (v) extinguish, darken, (alt sp) heavy.

baki 1. hungry; *synonyms* (adj) avid, eager, esurient, famished, greedy, ravenous, starving, desirous, meager, starveling, barren, keen, peckish, (v) craving, (adv) empty; *antonyms* (adj) full, sated, satiated, **2**. grouped; *synonyms* (adj) sorted, collective, **3**. accumulated; *synonyms* (adj) accrued, amassed, assembled, collected, accumulate, aggregate, congregate, massed, store, upheaped, equanimous, poised, **4**. hunger; *synonyms* (n) desire, thirst, appetite, wish, itch, eagerness, famine, longing, starvation, yen, (v) crave, want, ache, long, lust; *antonym* (n) moderation, **5**. crowd; *synonyms* (n) huddle, swarm, collection, crew, press, circle, cluster, army, assembly, concourse, congregation, (v) bunch, flock, squeeze, compress; *antonym* (v) disperse, **6**. stuffed; *synonyms* (v) farctate, (adj) crammed, packed, congested, replete, loaded, chock-full, crowded, fraught, abounding, big, brimming, concentrated, distended, overcrowded; *antonym* (adj) hungry, **7**. piled; *synonyms* (adj) heaped, cumulous, dense, pointed.

bakibora 1. battered; *synonyms* (adj) beaten, worn, damaged, hurt, maltreated, ragged, tattered, abused, aching, bruised, decrepit, dilapidated, injured, (v) seedy, shattered, **2**. deformed; *synonyms* (adj) crooked, bent, distorted, malformed, misshapen, ugly, crippled, contorted, deform, grotesque, shapeless, twisted, warped, (v) crump, **3**. dented; *synonyms* (v) indented, (adj) crumpled, bended, bowed, concave, creased, spoiled, broken, inclined, rumpled, scratched, smashed, stooped, **4**. smashed; *synonyms* (adj) drunk, inebriated, intoxicated, plastered, sloshed, blotto, tipsy, besotted, pissed, tight; *antonym* (adj) sober.

bakikangenge 1. emaciate; *synonyms* (v) thin, waste, consume, macerate, blow, desolate, devastate, emacerate, languish, liquidate, ravage, rot, squander, ware, **2**. skinny; *synonyms* (adj) lean, meager, emaciated, scrawny, gaunt, scraggy, underweight, weedy, lank, angular, slender, slight, spare, (v) cortical, cutaneous; *antonyms* (adj) fat, plump, brawny, well-built, **3**. thin; *synonyms* (adj) flimsy, light, tenuous, fine, rare, slim, sparse, narrow, bony, (v) dilute, sheer, subtle, scanty, adulterate, cut; *antonyms* (*adj*) thick, concentrated, chubby, wide, broad, heavy, (*v*) thicken.

bakikangengeaki 1. emaciated; *synonyms* (*adj*) cadaverous, bony, gaunt, lean, thin, haggard, meager, skinny, wasted, slender, slim, atrophied, lanky, pinched, poor; *antonyms* (*adj*) plump, fat, **2.** thinned; *synonyms* (*adj*) cut, dilute, adulterate, attenuate, attenuated, diminished, down, emasculated, faded, gashed, gelded, hurt, lessened, mown, shortened.

bakin greatness; *synonyms* (*n*) grandeur, excellence, dimension, dignity, bulk, bigness, enormity, enormousness, grandness, magnitude, size, fame, eminence, glory, quantity.

bakiriro starve; *synonyms* (*v*) famish, fast, crave, hunger, lust, pinch, thirst, benumb, bite, clem, (*adj*) begrudge, gripe, grudge, lack, screw.

bakiriroaki starved; *synonyms* (*adj*) hungry, famished, starving, ravenous, meager, emaciated, esurient, malnourished, thin.

bakiruru starve; *synonyms* (*v*) famish, fast, crave, hunger, lust, pinch, thirst, benumb, bite, clem, (*adj*) begrudge, gripe, grudge, lack, screw.

bakiruruaki starved; *synonyms* (*adj*) hungry, famished, starving, ravenous, meager, emaciated, esurient, malnourished, thin.

bakitaia 1. frail; *synonyms* (*adj*) brittle, fragile, delicate, flimsy, breakable, light, rickety, slender, slim, dainty, decrepit, fine, (*v*) weak, feeble, faint; *antonyms* (*adj*) strong, substantial, robust, **2.** meager; *synonyms* (*adj*) lean, emaciated, gaunt, inadequate, insufficient, spare, frugal, deficient, dry, exiguous, insignificant, jejune, (*v*) bare, barren, (*adv*) stingy; *antonyms* (*adj*) abundant, generous, lavish, **3.** skinny; *synonyms* (*adj*) meager, scrawny, thin, scraggy, underweight, weedy, lank, angular, slight, starving, (*v*) cortical, cutaneous, cuticular, dermal; *antonyms* (*adj*) fat, plump, brawny, well-built, **4.** rickety; *synonyms* (*adj*) shaky, unstable, wobbly, dilapidated, insecure, ramshackle, rachitic, precarious, unsteady, wonky, awkward, clumsy, gross; *antonyms* (*adj*) stable, steady.

bakitoutou 1. admirable; *synonyms* (*adj*) beautiful, excellent, fine, outstanding, commendable, creditable, good, grand, great, lovely, praiseworthy, worthy, valuable, exquisite, handsome; *antonyms* (*adj*) disgraceful, appalling, poor, unworthy, **2.** magnificent; *synonyms* (*adj*) imposing, brilliant, splendid, gorgeous, illustrious, grandiose, elegant, glorious, superb, divine, fabulous, luxurious, majestic, rich, royal, **3.** beautiful; *synonyms* (*adj*) attractive, good-looking, bright, beauteous, picturesque, pleasant, pretty, striking, sweet, adorned, ornate, dainty, stylish, bonny, charming; *antonyms* (*adj*) ugly, unattractive.

bako bent; *synonyms* (*adj*) arched, curved, bended, crooked, deformed, intent, (*n*) aptitude, inclination,

propensity, fancy, ability, bias, flair, gift, leaning; *antonym* (*adj*) straight.

bakoa faint; *synonyms* (*adj*) collapse, dim, dizzy, feeble, indistinct, weak, dull, gentle, soft, vague, delicate, distant, (*v*) languish, swoon, droop; *antonyms* (*adj*) distinct, strong, clear, obvious, considerable, loud, pungent.

bákoa shark; *synonyms* (*n*) cheat, fraud, swindler, charlatan, crook, harpy, trickster, thug, predator, wizard, expert, master, professional, scavenger, (*v*) lend.

bakoko 1. mean; *synonyms* (*v*) intend, design, imply, denote, involve, (*adj*) middle, base, common, hateful, ignoble, medium, miserly, (*n*) average, contemptible, low; *antonyms* (*adj*) generous, kind, **2.** miserly; *synonyms* (*adj*) stingy, mean, close, parsimonious, closefisted, grasping, avaricious, measly, mingy, penurious, tight, greedy, cheap, covetous, (*adv*) ungenerous, **3.** miser; *synonyms* (*n*) churl, curmudgeon, hunks, muckworm, niggard, skinflint, accumulator, collector, magpie, muckerer, pickpenny, pinchfist, saver, scrapepenny, snudge.

bakora 1. hero; *synonyms* (*n*) champion, character, leader, protector, worthy, protagonist, warrior, bomber, celebrity, combatant, conqueror, defender, fighter, **2.** champion; *synonyms* (*n*) advocate, backer, partisan, ace, hero, champ, exponent, paladin, patron, supporter, (*v*) defend, support, back, maintain, uphold; *antonym* (*v*) oppose, **3.** giant; *synonyms* (*adj*) colossal, gargantuan, gigantic, jumbo, elephantine, enormous, huge, immense, large, mammoth, vast, (*n*) monster, behemoth, colossus, ogre; *antonyms* (*adj*) small, tiny, miniature, **4.** outstanding; *synonyms* (*adj*) eminent, due, conspicuous, great, owing, famous, distinguished, excellent, exceptional, notable, noteworthy, prominent, unpaid, major, brilliant; *antonyms* (*adj*) ordinary, paid, inferior.

baku 1. behead; *synonyms* (*v*) decapitate, decollate, cut, bowstring, electrocute, head, execute, murder, unhead, direct, lead, oppose, **2.** decapitate; *synonyms* (*v*) behead, guillotine, top, **3.** truncate; *synonyms* (*v*) curtail, abridge, shorten, clip, abbreviate, reduce, mutilate, crop, deface, deform, disfigure, maim; *antonym* (*v*) lengthen.

bakuaki 1. beheaded; *synonyms* (*adj*) decapitated, headless, foolish, obstinate, rash, **2.** decapitated; *synonyms* (*adj*) beheaded, decollated, **3.** truncated; *synonyms* (*adj*) abbreviated, shortened, cut, docked, garbled, lopped, mutilated, truncate.

bakuaku 1. relieve; *synonyms* (*v*) assuage, comfort, ease, allay, mitigate, calm, aid, assist, console, excuse, free, help, (*n*) alleviate, redress, (*adj*) absolve; *antonyms* (*v*) worsen, burden, **2.** succor; *synonyms* (*n*) relief, assistance, ministration, consolation, favor, alleviation, countenance, encouragement, opitulation, (*v*) support, relieve, succour, promote, benefit, encourage.

bakurakura squat; *synonyms* (*adj*) dumpy, short, chunky, squatty, stumpy, thick, low, squab, (*v*) crouch, perch, sit, bend, settle, couch, cower.

bam pump; *synonyms* (*n*) heart, pumps, ticker, (*v*) interrogate, draw, examine, milk, question.

bamaiu verdant; *synonyms* (*adj*) green, lush, leafy, flourishing, fresh, raw, verdurous; *antonym* (*adj*) arid.

bamaki pumped; *synonym* (*adj*) wired.

bâmuti beads; *synonyms* (*n*) rosary, censer, cross, crucifix, host, patera, pax, pyx, reliquary, rood, thurible, jewelry, lot, relics.

bana sling; *synonyms* (*n*) cast, bow, (*v*) catapult, pitch, fling, hurl, suspend, dangle, chuck, heave, throw, toss, shoot, drive, (*adj*) hang.

banaonao turbulent; *synonyms* (*adj*) tempestuous, tumultuous, rough, furious, boisterous, disorderly, noisy, riotous, violent, wild, rude, troubled, unruly, agitated, (*n*) stormy; *antonym* (*adj*) calm.

bane 1. finished; *synonyms* (*v*) done, (*adj*) complete, completed, ended, perfect, consummate, absolute, accomplished, polished, ripe, ruined, spent, round, capable, (*adv*) over; *antonyms* (*adj*) unfinished, incomplete, remaining, rough, **2.** done; *synonyms* (*adj*) finished, gone, through, **3.** entirely; *synonyms* (*adv*) absolutely, all, altogether, totally, wholly, clean, fully, solely, bodily, alone, exclusively, only, quite, right, (*adj*) completely; *antonyms* (*adv*) partly, partially, **4.** exhausted; *synonyms* (*v*) weak, (*adj*) drained, fatigued, tired, dry, beat, depleted, empty, enervated, faint, jaded, weary, expended, dead, poor; *antonyms* (*adj*) energetic, fresh, refreshed, strong, **5.** fully; *synonyms* (*adv*) entirely, downright, enough, amply, full, thoroughly, utterly, well, abundantly, adequately, considerably, favorably, very, carefully, outright; *antonym* (*adv*) superficially, **6.** wholly; *synonyms* (*adv*) whole, exactly, unreservedly, extremely, really, (*adj*) perfectly, simply.

banebane indebted; *synonyms* (*adj*) grateful, appreciative, thankful, obliged, broke, deferred, gratified, insolvent, accountable, chargeable, duty-bound, honor-bound, hooked, (*prep*) beholden, debted.

banei turbulent; *synonyms* (*adj*) tempestuous, tumultuous, rough, furious, boisterous, disorderly, noisy, riotous, violent, wild, rude, troubled, unruly, agitated, (*n*) stormy; *antonym* (*adj*) calm.

bang 1. indistinct; *synonyms* (*adj*) confused, dim, faint, inarticulate, indefinite, dull, fuzzy, hazy, indeterminate, dark, neutral, ambiguous, blurred, doubtful, (*n*) cloudy; *antonyms* (*adj*) distinct, clear, **2.** wan; *synonyms* (*v*) pale, (*adj*) pallid, cadaverous,

ghastly, sickly, haggard, ashen, colorless, pasty, sallow, bloodless, lurid, weak, ashy, thin; *antonym* (*adj*) strong.

bangaaomata 1. cruel; *synonyms* (*adj*) barbarous, brutal, hard, harsh, heartless, unkind, bitter, bloody, atrocious, biting, fierce, inhuman, merciless, ruthless, savage; *antonyms* (*adj*) gentle, kind, merciful, humane, liberal, sympathetic, **2.** inhumane; *synonyms* (*adj*) cruel, ferocious, truculent, remorseless, pitiless, unmerciful, misanthropic, **3.** selfish; *synonyms* (*adj*) mean, greedy, mercenary, egocentric, egoistic, egotistic, egotistical, self-centered, stingy, covetous, inconsiderate, sordid, thoughtless, exclusive, (*v*) contracted; *antonyms* (*adj*) unselfish, selfless, altruistic, generous, **4.** ungrateful; *synonyms* (*adj*) thankless, unmindful, unappreciative, unthankful, unnatural, ingrate, distasteful, displeasing, childless, ingrateful, offensive, unacceptable, unappreciated, careless, demanding; *antonyms* (*adj*) grateful, thankful.

bangabanga 1. hollow; *synonyms* (*adj*) blank, concave, empty, false, insincere, (*n*) cavity, hole, cave, depression, groove, excavation, (*v*) excavate, dent, scoop, dig; *antonyms* (*adj*) convex, (*n*) solid, hump, **2.** breached, **3.** opened; *synonyms* (*v*) blown, distended, exhausted, inflated, (*adj*) open, candid, exposed, assailable, blatant, blazing, clear, conspicuous, lawless, loose, through, **4.** pierced; *synonyms* (*adj*) perforated, punctured, perforate, cleft, entered, **5.** perforated; *synonyms* (*adj*) pierced, penetrated.

bangabwai 1. dunce; *synonyms* (*n*) blockhead, dolt, ass, bonehead, booby, dullard, dunderhead, ignoramus, loggerhead, numskull, dumbbell, dummy, fool, hammerhead, idiot, **2.** ignorant; *synonyms* (*adj*) unconscious, illiterate, rude, uneducated, unwitting, blind, dull, innocent, naive, unaware, uninformed, unlearned, barbarous, crude, shallow; *antonyms* (*adj*) knowledgeable, conscious.

bangaki 1. across; *synonyms* (*prep*) athwart, cross, overthwart, (*adv*) over, crossways, crosswise, (*adj*) crossed; *antonyms* (*adv*) along, (*adj*) uncrossed, **2.** crosswise; *synonyms* (*adv*) across, diagonally, traverse, (*adj*) diagonal; *antonym* (*adj*) lengthwise, **3.** crossed; *synonyms* (*v*) matted, unhinged, frustrated, (*adj*) crossbred, decussated, hybrid, interbred, intercrossed, mixed, intersected.

banganibai provident; *synonyms* (*adj*) circumspect, frugal, prudent, sparing, careful, cautious, economical, farsighted, sagacious, wise, discreet, thrifty, wary, (*v*) precautionary; *antonym* (*adj*) improvident.

banganikoko stingy; *synonyms* (*adj*) parsimonious, avaricious, mean, miserly, low, penurious, skimpy, greedy, niggard, frugal, cheap, closefisted, measly,

(v) narrow, close; *antonyms* (adj) generous, spendthrift.

banganikou mean; *synonyms* (v) intend, design, imply, denote, involve, (adj) middle, base, common, hateful, ignoble, medium, miserly, (n) average, contemptible, low; *antonyms* (adj) generous, kind.

banganrino particular; *synonyms* (adj) special, fastidious, careful, definite, delicate, exact, finicky, fussy, individual, detailed, certain, choosy, circumstantial, (n) detail, item; *antonyms* (adj) careless, easy, vague, ordinary, (n) general.

bangantauti mean; *synonyms* (v) intend, design, imply, denote, involve, (adj) middle, base, common, hateful, ignoble, medium, miserly, (n) average, contemptible, low; *antonyms* (adj) generous, kind.

banganuaru 1. meddlesome; *synonyms* (adj) intrusive, busy, inquisitive, interfering, officious, obtrusive, nosy, curious, pragmatical, prying, busybodied, impertinent, meddling, **2.** meddling; *synonyms* (adj) meddlesome, dabbling, **3.** pragmatic; *synonyms* (adj) practical, hardheaded, realistic, useful, functional, sensible, empirical, helpful.

banganun quarrelsome; *synonyms* (adj) argumentative, pugnacious, belligerent, contentious, combative, aggressive, cantankerous, disputatious, currish, ugly, contrary, termagant, arguing, factious, (v) fretful; *antonym* (adj) peaceable.

baniaki fried; *synonyms* (adj) daft, deranged, done, inebriated, intoxicated.

baniia fry; *synonyms* (n) chicken, child, chrysalis, cub, nestling, (v) cook, burn, singe, grill, roast, toast, electrocute, heat.

baniiaki fried; *synonyms* (adj) daft, deranged, done, inebriated, intoxicated.

banikai 1. leaf; *synonyms* (n) blade, page, foliage, folio, leafage, slip, (v) sheet, leave, flick, flip, **2.** leaves; *synonyms* (n) plants, vegetation.

ba-ni-mata temple; *synonyms* (n) church, tabernacle, shrine, brow, synagogue, forehead, chapel, kirk, meetinghouse, basilica, chantry, conventicle, memorial, oratory, side.

banin 1. stark; *synonyms* (adj) austere, bare, bleak, desolate, mere, plain, severe, simple, bald, positive, absolute, barren, harsh, sheer, naked, **2.** solid; *synonyms* (adj) firm, dense, compact, consistent, hard, real, strong, good, fixed, massive, secure, substantial, fast, hearty, (v) close; *antonyms* (adj) soft, unreliable, loose, gaseous, permeable, runny, transparent, watery, (n) liquid, **3.** sound; *synonyms* (n) echo, peal, (v) ring, chime, blow, (adj) reasonable, complete, healthy, fit, just, rational, right, sane, sensible, robust; *antonyms* (n) silence, (adj) illogical, unsound, confused.

banuea 1. noble; *synonyms* (adj) dignified, imposing, magnificent, glorious, distinguished, elevated, exalted, generous, high, impressive, majestic, patrician, (n) grand, excellent, (v) great; *antonyms* (adj) lower-class, selfish, shameful, humble, dishonorable, lowly, **2.** royal; *synonyms* (adj) regal, imperial, kingly, noble, princely, purple, sovereign, stately, grandiose, monarchical, splendid, **3.** princely; *synonyms* (adj) munificent, lordly, luxurious, opulent, royal, magnanimous, liberal, sumptuous, deluxe, gilded, (v) proud, honorable.

bao 1. moderate; *synonyms* (adj) temperate, abstemious, middling, mild, easy, (v) calm, mitigate, allay, curb, diminish, lessen, ease, cool, abate, (adv) check; *antonyms* (adj) extreme, immoderate, radical, (v) increase, intensify, **2.** abate; *synonyms* (v) subside, bate, decline, fade, flag, relax, relieve, remit, slack, slake, wane, weaken, qualify, abolish, (adj) slacken, **3.** shelves; *synonym* (n) gondola, **4.** shelf; *synonyms* (n) ledge, rack, bank, flat, projection, board, frame, shallows, stand, support, bench, bracket, breakers, (adj) shallow.

baoaki moderated; *synonyms* (adj) subdued, certified, dependant, dependent, equal, graduated, limited, measured, qualified, restricted, uniform.

baobao 1. pile; *synonyms* (n) heap, stack, mass, congeries, mound, bunch, accumulation, bundle, collection, hoard, jam, (v) pack, accumulate, amass, crowd, **2.** shelves; *synonym* (n) gondola, **3.** shelf; *synonyms* (n) ledge, rack, bank, flat, projection, board, frame, shallows, stand, support, bench, bracket, breakers, (adj) shallow.

baokoko 1. bent; *synonyms* (adj) arched, curved, bended, crooked, deformed, intent, (n) aptitude, inclination, propensity, fancy, ability, bias, flair, gift, leaning; *antonym* (adj) straight, **2.** stooped; *synonyms* (adj) bent, hunched, stooping, asymmetrical, bowed, convex, corrupt, crumpled, dented, droopy, hooked, inclined, rounded.

baotabare meddling; *synonyms* (adj) interfering, busy, curious, inquisitive, intrusive, meddlesome, officious, prying, nosy, busybodied, dabbling, impertinent.

baoti swamp; *synonyms* (n) marsh, mire, bog, morass, quagmire, (v) flood, inundate, overwhelm, submerge, sink, deluge, drench, drown, overflow, engulf; *antonym* (n) desert.

baotiaki swamped; *synonyms* (v) grounded, (adj) flooded, inundated, overcome, busy, engulfed, overpowered, overwhelmed, (adv) aground.

baoua 1. crowded; *synonyms* (adj) close, compact, congested, busy, dense, full, packed, populous, jammed, cramped, teeming, thick, tight, (n) thronged; *antonyms* (adj) empty, sparse, **2.** crooked; *synonyms* (adj) bent, awry, corrupt, irregular, askew, curved, deformed, dishonest, indirect, lopsided, unfair, unscrupulous, angular, asymmetrical, (v) wry; *antonyms* (adj) straight, honest, even, principled, **3**. curved; *synonyms* (adj) crooked, curve, round, bend, curving, curvy, hooked, rounded, tortuous, twisted, (v) bowed; *antonym* (adj) concave, **4**. bend; *synonyms* (n) bow, arch, arc, elbow, twist, angle, curvature, (v) turn, crouch, stoop, crook, curl, flex, deflect, fold; *antonyms* (v) straighten, square, **5**. bent; *synonyms* (adj) arched, bended, intent, set, (n) aptitude, inclination, propensity, fancy, ability, bias, flair, gift, leaning, mind, proclivity.

baouaki bent; *synonyms* (adj) arched, curved, bended, crooked, deformed, intent, (n) aptitude, inclination, propensity, fancy, ability, bias, flair, gift, leaning; *antonym* (adj) straight.

bara 1. dirty; *synonyms* (adj) foul, dirt, contemptible, bawdy, contaminated, dingy, impure, despicable, (v) muddy, corrupt, soil, contaminate, begrime, bemire, (n) defile; *antonyms* (adj) hygienic, pure, spotless, immaculate, (v) clean, **2**. dirt; *synonyms* (n) dust, filth, grime, crap, ground, mire, scandal, contamination, smudge, dirtiness, foulness, impurity, land, muck, pollution.

barairai fizzle; *synonyms* (v) fizz, fail, effervesce, buzz, ferment, sparkle, fatigue, die, fold, (n) sizzle, frustration, disappointment.

baraki 1. busy; *synonyms* (adj) active, brisk, assiduous, engaged, occupied, agile, crowded, industrious, meddlesome, officious, live, diligent, earnest, (v) occupy, employ; *antonyms* (adj) idle, free, inactive, **2**. working; *synonyms* (adj) operative, practical, busy, acting, effective, operating, operational, (n) running, functioning, play, agency, movement, performance, go; *antonyms* (adj) passive, unemployed.

barakia endeavor; *synonyms* (n) attempt, try, effort, essay, trial, enterprise, shot, work, endeavour, (v) struggle, strive, aim, labor, strain, offer; *antonym* (v) neglect.

baranna wear; *synonyms* (v) dress, endure, bear, fatigue, tire, waste, fray, frazzle, (n) clothing, apparel, attire, clothes, garb, erosion, garment; *antonym* (v) refresh.

barannaki worn; *synonyms* (v) decayed, (adj) haggard, shabby, tired, ragged, tattered, threadbare, drawn, jaded, exhausted, fatigued, careworn, decrepit, faded, frayed; *antonyms* (adj) fresh, new.

barantauti mean; *synonyms* (v) intend, design, imply, denote, involve, (adj) middle, base, common, hateful, ignoble, medium, miserly, (n) average, contemptible, low; *antonyms* (adj) generous, kind.

barara 1. low; *synonyms* (adj) contemptible, abject, humble, ignoble, base, blue, common, deep, dejected, depressed, down, downcast,

downhearted, (adv) gentle, (n) depression; *antonyms* (adj) cheerful, happy, high-pitched, loud, important, piercing, (n) high, **2**. sweating; *synonyms* (adj) perspiring, sweaty, (n) perspiration, exudation, sweat, diaphoresis, hidrosis, extravasation, fermentation, sudation, **3**. perspiring; *synonyms* (adj) sweating, perspirable, sudatory, sweltering, warm, clammy, damp, moist, sticky.

bararai disgusted; *synonyms* (adj) sick, ill, sickened, weary, aghast, appalled, brainsick, corrupted, crazy, demented, horrified, shocked, squeamish, abhorred, dismayed; *antonym* (adj) delighted.

bare 1. equal; *synonyms* (adj) agree, comparable, adequate, balanced, commensurate, equivalent, (v) match, compare, correspond, even, parallel, rival, equalize, (n) compeer, peer; *antonyms* (adj) unequal, different, repressive, disproportionate, inconsistent, uneven, unlike, (v) differ, **2**. hasten; *synonyms* (v) speed, expedite, further, forward, dispatch, advance, hurry, dash, hie, rush, bustle, dart, (adj) accelerate, quicken, (n) haste; *antonym* (v) delay, **3**. hurry; *synonyms* (n) flurry, celerity, hastiness, hurriedness, press, (v) hasten, scurry, fly, run, zip, drive, race, scamper, scuttle, flit; *antonyms* (n) slowness, (v) dawdle, **4**. same; *synonyms* (adj) alike, identical, corresponding, equal, like, similar, uniform, consistent, matching, duplicate, monotonous, self, very, indistinguishable, interchangeable.

bareaki hurried; *synonyms* (adj) hasty, fast, headlong, quick, rapid, speedy, sudden, swift, abrupt, cursory, careless, precipitate, prompt, rash, slapdash; *antonyms* (adj) slow, unhurried, leisurely.

bareka 1. accelerate; *synonyms* (v) quicken, advance, hurry, speed, dispatch, rush, expedite, forward, further, hasten, heighten, increase, intensify, precipitate, (adj) vivify; *antonyms* (v) decelerate, stop, **2**. hasten; *synonyms* (v) dash, hie, bustle, dart, facilitate, race, run, fly, gallop, sprint, drive, (adj) accelerate, course, go, (n) haste; *antonym* (v) delay, **3**. expedite; *synonym* (v) assist, **4**. muddy; *synonyms* (adj) boggy, cloudy, filthy, turbid, foul, dark, dingy, dull, grimy, marshy, miry, murky, sloppy, (v) dirty, blur; *antonyms* (adj) clear, clean, dry, **5**. hurry; *synonyms* (n) flurry, celerity, hastiness, hurriedness, press, flutter, rapidity, expedition, trot, (v) scurry, zip, scamper, scuttle, flit, hotfoot; *antonyms* (n) slowness, (v) dawdle, **6**. impure; *synonyms* (adj) defiled, bastard, sordid, squalid, unclean, immoral, profane, contaminated, indecent, lewd, libidinous, licentious, muddy, obscene, coarse; *antonym* (adj) pure, **7**. dirty; *synonyms* (adj) dirt, contemptible, bawdy, impure, despicable, nasty, shabby, (v) corrupt, soil, contaminate, begrime, bemire, pollute, spoil, (n) defile; *antonyms* (adj) hygienic, spotless, immaculate, **8**. stained; *synonyms* (adj) besmirched, spotted, sullied, tainted, tarnished, black, damaged, discolored, flyblown, painted, (v) polluted; *antonym* (adj) unspoiled, **9.** quick; *synonyms* (adj) bright, prompt, active, agile, clever, hasty, intelligent, nimble, speedy, alert, alive, cursory, dexterous, expeditious, (adv) fast; *antonyms* (adj) slow, leisurely, **10.** spotted; *synonyms* (v) mildewed, moldy, rusty, (adj) mottled, dappled, speckled, blotchy, dotted, piebald, multicolored, spotty, stained, freckled, patched; *antonym* (adj) plain.

barekaki 1. expedited, **2.** hurried; *synonyms* (adj) hasty, fast, headlong, quick, rapid, speedy, sudden, swift, abrupt, cursory, careless, precipitate, prompt, rash, slapdash; *antonyms* (adj) slow, unhurried, leisurely, **3.** accelerated; *synonyms* (adj) intensive, express.

barekareka 1. grubby; *synonyms* (adj) dirty, grimy, nasty, filthy, unclean, impure, begrimed, dingy, foul, messy, muddy, seedy, sordid, squalid, unkempt; *antonym* (adj) clean, **2.** dirty; *synonyms* (adj) dirt, contemptible, bawdy, contaminated, despicable, shabby, (v) corrupt, soil, contaminate, begrime, bemire, pollute, spoil, blemish, (n) defile; *antonyms* (adj) hygienic, pure, spotless, immaculate.

barekatia rejoice; *synonyms* (v) cheer, delight, gladden, glory, joy, jubilate, revel, triumph, gratify, gloat, exhilarate, please, celebrate, recreate, (n) exult; *antonyms* (v) lament, mourn.

barekia hustle; *synonyms* (n) hurry, haste, ado, cheat, commotion, con, fuss, (v) jostle, bustle, elbow, hasten, flurry, push, shove, work.

bari 1. curved; *synonyms* (adj) bent, crooked, curve, round, bend, curving, curvy, deformed, hooked, rounded, tortuous, twisted, (v) bowed; *antonyms* (adj) straight, concave, **2.** unequal; *synonyms* (adj) dissimilar, different, unlike, inadequate, lopsided, rough, uneven, unfair, disparate, disproportionate, unbalanced, unsymmetrical, inconsistent, insufficient, various; *antonyms* (adj) equal, even.

barik dirty; *synonyms* (adj) foul, dirt, contemptible, bawdy, contaminated, dingy, impure, despicable, (v) muddy, corrupt, soil, contaminate, begrime, bemire, (n) defile; *antonyms* (adj) hygienic, pure, spotless, immaculate, (v) clean.

barino finicky; *synonyms* (adj) fastidious, finical, fussy, choosy, dainty, exacting, particular, picky, squeamish, demanding, meticulous, nice, persnickety, scrupulous, selective; *antonym* (adj) easy.

baro spill; *synonyms* (v) fall, shed, drop, empty, flow, pour, slop, stream, upset, cast, overrun, flood, disgorge, (n) overflow, discharge.

baroa 1. spit; *synonyms* (n) broach, saliva, cape, expectoration, spittle, (v) drizzle, impale, expectorate, skewer, spew, sprinkle, drool, spike,

hiss, spatter, **2.** salivate; *synonyms* (v) dribble, drivel, **3.** overwhelm; *synonyms* (v) defeat, flood, inundate, overcome, overpower, overthrow, crush, deluge, drown, engulf, astound, beat, overrun, overtake, overturn, **4.** spat; *synonyms* (v) bicker, clap, row, (n) quarrel, squabble, altercation, tiff, dispute, gaiter, argument, wrangle, bickering, fuss, disagreement, fight.

baroaki 1. spat; *synonyms* (v) bicker, clap, row, (n) quarrel, squabble, altercation, tiff, dispute, gaiter, argument, wrangle, bickering, fuss, disagreement, fight, **2.** overwhelmed; *synonyms* (v) overborne, (adj) overcome, beaten, overpowered, vanquished, conquered, dumbfounded, engulfed, flooded, inundated, overthrown; *antonyms* (adj) victorious, unimpressed.

baroakina 1. crowd; *synonyms* (n) huddle, swarm, collection, crew, press, circle, cluster, army, assembly, concourse, congregation, (v) bunch, flock, squeeze, compress; *antonym* (v) disperse, **2.** invade; *synonyms* (v) encroach, assail, assault, infringe, intrude, occupy, overrun, impinge, raid, infest, seize, penetrate, permeate, (n) attack, charge, **3.** spill; *synonyms* (v) fall, shed, drop, empty, flow, pour, slop, stream, upset, cast, flood, disgorge, drain, (n) overflow, discharge, **4.** pour; *synonyms* (v) gush, decant, pelt, scatter, emit, jet, run, spill, teem, effuse, deluge, funnel, tip, spout, (n) rain; *antonym* (v) drizzle, **5.** overrun; *synonyms* (v) invade, inundate, overwhelm, conquer, rout, exceed, ravage, distribute, makeup, mortise, offset, (n) excess, overproduction, (adj) infested.

baroakinaki 1. crowded; *synonyms* (adj) close, compact, congested, busy, dense, full, packed, populous, jammed, cramped, teeming, thick, tight, (n) thronged; *antonyms* (adj) empty, sparse, **2.** overrun; *synonyms* (v) overflow, deluge, flood, infest, invade, occupy, inundate, overwhelm, conquer, rout, exceed, ravage, spill, distribute, (n) excess, **3.** poured; *synonym* (adj) concrete.

baronga 1. assemble; *synonyms* (v) amass, accumulate, aggregate, convene, gather, meet, call, collect, compile, concentrate, converge, group, make, rally, edit; *antonyms* (v) dismantle, disperse, disband, disassemble, **2.** unite; *synonyms* (v) combine, associate, blend, coalesce, connect, join, link, amalgamate, attach, fuse, merge, tie, unify, couple, agree; *antonyms* (v) separate, divide.

barongaki 1. assembled; *synonyms* (adj) accumulated, amassed, collected, collective, united, accrued, aggregate, built, congregate, massed, equanimous, fabricated, fancied, fictional, fictitious, **2.** united; *synonyms* (adj) joined, joint, combined, cooperative, connected, allied, mutual, concerted, mixed, common, conjunctive, undivided, conjunct, unanimous, (v) consolidated; *antonyms* (adj) individual, separate, divided.

baronria 1. chew; *synonyms* (*v*) champ, munch, chomp, crunch, gnaw, manducate, masticate, mouth, eat, jaw, (*n*) bite, chaw, chewing, cud, mastication, **2.** suck; *synonyms* (*v*) draw, drink, imbibe, nurse, absorb, lactate, suckle, drain, puff, aspirate, pull, breastfeed, (*n*) sucking, suction.

baroro verdant; *synonyms* (*adj*) green, lush, leafy, flourishing, fresh, raw, verdurous; *antonym* (*adj*) arid.

baru crave; *synonyms* (*v*) beg, ask, beseech, covet, implore, want, desire, entreat, long, wish, fancy, claim, adjure, demand, hunger.

baruaki craved; *synonyms* (*adj*) desired, coveted.

barukuruku wrinkled; *synonyms* (*adj*) furrowed, creased, crumpled, lined, puckered, wizened, wrinkly, gnarled, unironed, (*n*) rough, rugged; *antonym* (*adj*) smooth.

bataka 1. dry; *synonyms* (*adj*) thirsty, arid, barren, boring, dehydrated, dull, bald, hoarse, jejune, plain, (*v*) dehydrate, desiccate, drain, uninteresting, sardonic; *antonyms* (*adj*) wet, damp, moist, saturated, soaked, boggy, drenched, rainy, sodden, interesting, fresh, humid, juicy, succulent, (*v*) drench, **2.** parched; *synonyms* (*adj*) dry, adust, torrid, desiccated, scorched, baked.

batana 1. inhabit; *synonyms* (*v*) dwell, reside, abide, occupy, live, lodge, people, settle, be, bide, exist, roost, domicile, (*n*) habit, (*adj*) perch, **2.** dwell; *synonyms* (*v*) inhabit, stay, belong, brood, continue, delay, remain, consist, domiciliate, endure, keep, last, lie, ponder, populate.

batanaki inhabited; *synonyms* (*v*) populous, accustomed, arrayed, clothed, dressed, habited, (*adj*) peopled, occupied, housing, colonized, suburban, uninhabited, uptown; *antonyms* (*adj*) empty, unoccupied.

batata scorched; *synonyms* (*adj*) parched, baked, adust, burnt, dry, seared; *antonym* (*adj*) wet.

bataua measure; *synonyms* (*n*) amount, criterion, extent, beat, benchmark, degree, estimate, measurement, meter, quantity, act, allotment, action, (*v*) grade, appraise.

batauaki measured; *synonyms* (*adj*) careful, deliberate, moderate, calculated, reasonable, temperate, regular, leisurely, metrical, sober, cool, slow.

batete 1. decline; *synonyms* (*n*) decay, declension, decrease, dip, declination, (*v*) wane, drop, reject, fall, abate, ebb, fail, refuse, sink, deny; *antonyms* (*n*) improvement, recovery, development, growth, rebirth, (*v*) increase, rise, accept, flourish, improve, **2.** drunk; *synonyms* (*adj*) intoxicated, tipsy, tight, wet, inebriated, delirious, high, (*n*) inebriate, drunkard, rummy, sot; *antonym* (*adj*) sober, **3.** slope; *synonyms* (*n*) incline, declivity, decline,

descent, grade, gradient, hill, inclination, (*v*) pitch, slant, cant, lean, bank, tilt, (*adj*) obliquity.

bateteaki sloped; *synonyms* (*adj*) slanted, slanting, oblique, sloping, aslant, aslope, diagonal, biased, coloured.

bati 1. adroit; *synonyms* (*adj*) dexterous, ingenious, skillful, able, adept, artful, clever, expert, intelligent, slick, politic, cunning, deft, handy, neat; *antonyms* (*adj*) clumsy, awkward, dim, maladroit, **2.** expert; *synonyms* (*adj*) adroit, experienced, accomplished, ace, apt, practiced, veteran, knowing, capable, (*n*) professional, proficient, critic, authority, connoisseur, dab; *antonyms* (*adj*) unskilled, inept, inferior, untrained, (*n*) amateur, beginner, **3.** effective; *synonyms* (*adj*) beneficial, practical, effectual, efficacious, operative, strong, actual, fruitful, positive, active, forceful, important, influential, (*n*) competent, efficient; *antonyms* (*adj*) ineffective, useless, weak, inoperative, **4.** many; *synonyms* (*adj*) manifold, abundant, countless, frequent, various, innumerable, much, multiple, numerous, plentiful, several, different, numberless, (*n*) number; *antonym* (*n*) few, **5.** much; *synonyms* (*adv*) greatly, frequently, almost, awfully, considerably, far, most, often, pretty, highly, (*n*) lot, heap, (*adj*) great, considerable, practically; *antonym* (*adv*) slightly, **6.** skilled; *synonyms* (*adj*) old, learned, sophisticated, versed, gifted, perfect, masterly, crack, masterful, consummate, conversant, educated, fit, knowledgeable, qualified; *antonyms* (*adj*) incompetent, inexperienced, **7.** numerous; *synonyms* (*adj*) many, multitudinous, copious, populous, myriad, rife, common, incalculable, thick, **8.** professional; *synonyms* (*adj*) specialist, occupational, technical, skilled, (*n*) master, pro, maestro, whiz; *antonyms* (*adj*) unpaid, unprofessional, **9.** skillful; *synonyms* (*adj*) good, ready, nice, quick, skilful, fine, practised, gracious, sagacious, subtle, talented, trained, (*v*) crafty, judicious, nimble.

batia 1. gather; *synonyms* (*v*) deduce, convene, accumulate, amass, assemble, collect, compile, congregate, flock, garner, meet, tuck, earn, rally, (*n*) fold; *antonyms* (*v*) disperse, scatter, **2.** creased; *synonyms* (*adj*) crumpled, furrowed, lined, rumpled, wrinkled, wrinkly, corrugated, bent, craggy, crinkly, dented, disheveled, dishevelled, frowzled, puckered; *antonym* (*adj*) smooth, **3.** crumbled; *synonyms* (*adj*) broken, fragmented, rotten, disconnected, disunited, split, **4.** arrange; *synonyms* (*v*) adjust, appoint, dress, order, set, settle, pack, adapt, agree, classify, compose, decorate, do, engineer, fix; *antonyms* (*v*) disturb, disarrange, **5.** bundle; *synonyms* (*n*) cluster, pile, sheaf, batch, group, heap, load, package, packet, parcel, stack, wad, collection, (*v*) bunch, clump, **6.** crease; *synonyms* (*n*) wrinkle, line, plait, pleat, pucker, bend, crimp, groove, (v) crinkle, crumple, cockle, furrow, rumple, crush, ruck, **7. pack;** *synonyms* (n) bundle, mob, bevy, company, herd, backpack, box, gang, horde, knapsack, (v) crowd, compress, cram, fill, jam; *antonym* (v) unpack, **8. wrap;** *synonyms* (v) cloak, cover, envelop, enfold, roll, shroud, swathe, wind, enclose, bind, drape, enwrap, hide, involve, (n) coat; *antonyms* (v) unwrap, uncover.

batiaki 1. gathered; *synonyms* (adj) collected, deepened, accumulated, amassed, assembled, collective, congregate, equanimous, massed, poised, **2.** creased; *synonyms* (adj) crumpled, furrowed, lined, rumpled, wrinkled, wrinkly, corrugated, bent, craggy, crinkly, dented, disheveled, dishevelled, frowzled, puckered; *antonym* (adj) smooth, **3.** arranged; *synonyms* (adj) set, settled, fixed, orderly, organized, prepared, ready, regular, neat, ordered, straight, tidy, **4.** wrapped; *synonyms* (adj) clothed, draped, enwrapped, absorbed, cloaked, intent, rapt, engrossed, mantled, (prep) covered, **5.** packed; *synonyms* (adj) crowded, compact, full, filled, jammed, overcrowded, congested, dense, thick, brimming, close, cramped, teeming; *antonyms* (adj) empty, deserted.

batiatia wrinkled; *synonyms* (adj) furrowed, creased, crumpled, lined, puckered, wizened, wrinkly, gnarled, unironed, (n) rough, rugged; *antonym* (adj) smooth.

batiboa 1. beat; *synonyms* (v) batter, flap, pulsate, throb, tick, trounce, whip, bat, baste, break, (n) pulse, thump, knock, round, cadence; *antonym* (v) lose, **2.** thrash; *synonyms* (v) flog, lash, beat, defeat, pound, clobber, drub, lam, lick, whack, bang, belabor, crush, flail, hammer, **3.** trounce; *synonyms* (v) thrash, castigate, rout, chastise, overpower, slash, reprimand, thresh, scourge, pummel, pip, lambaste, overcome, scold, smash, **4.** smite; *synonyms* (v) afflict, strike, buffet, affect, cut, impress, punish, touch, animate, excite, impassion, inspire, interest, move, **5.** whop; *synonyms* (n) hit, (v) wallop, whap, bash, bop, wham, bonk, sock, **6.** strike; *synonyms* (n) assault, clap, rap, tap, attack, (v) slap, box, bump, clout, coin, collide, mint, hew, clash, cuff, **7.** thump; *synonyms* (n) punch, crack, crash, blow, stroke, thwack, swipe, (v) thud, clump, smack, palpitate, poke, boom, bounce, spank.

batiboaki beaten; *synonyms* (v) beat, (adj) battered, overpowered, conquered, routed, overcome; *antonym* (adj) victorious.

batikora 1. strong; *synonyms* (adj) intense, powerful, able, deep, firm, stable, steady, cogent, durable, forcible, good, hard, influential, lusty, potent; *antonyms* (adj) weak, bland, delicate, faint, feeble, frail, mild, pale, slight, unconvincing, cowardly,

diluted, dull, exhausted, flimsy, **2.** vigorous; *synonyms* (adj) robust, strong, energetic, hardy, lively, strenuous, active, athletic, hearty, mighty, healthy, smart, brawny, (n) brave, (v) brisk; *antonyms* (adj) lethargic, unenergetic.

batirae 1. wander; *synonyms* (v) ramble, digress, stray, deviate, err, roam, travel, depart, divagate, gad, meander, (n) saunter, stroll, tramp, drift, **2.** stray; *synonyms* (adj) erratic, scattered, random, errant, (v) range, wander, rove, straggle, diverge, gallivant, go, swerve, adrift, (n) vagabond, waif.

bato 1. flat; *synonyms* (adj) dull, bland, even, plain, insipid, level, plane, tasteless, dreary, boring, absolute, dead, downright, (n) apartment, (v) uninteresting; *antonyms* (adj) exciting, high-pitched, bumpy, **2.** collapsed; *synonyms* (adj) bent, bowed, broken, buckled, depleted, distorted, fallen, flat, malformed, misshapen, warped, shrunken, **3.** coward; *synonyms* (n) craven, cur, sneak, weakling, cocktail, coistril, niding, alarmist, baby, deserter, invertebrate, jellyfish, lily-liver, (adj) gutless, (v) frighten.

batoara alternate; *synonyms* (adj) reciprocal, secondary, (v) reciprocate, change, fluctuate, interchange, vary, swerve, alter, (n) substitute, alternative, surrogate, standby, replacement, deputy; *antonym* (n) original.

batua slide; *synonyms* (n) glide, chute, decline, transparency, gliding, (v) drop, slip, fall, slither, run, slump, coast, skid, descend, (adj) shift.

bau 1. assembled; *synonyms* (adj) accumulated, amassed, collected, collective, united, accrued, aggregate, built, congregate, massed, equanimous, fabricated, fancied, fictional, fictitious, **2.** grouped; *synonym* (adj) sorted.

baua 1. catch; *synonyms* (v) arrest, capture, hook, apprehend, get, acquire, ensnare, intercept, (n) haul, hitch, trick, bolt, clasp, grab, pawl; *antonym* (v) release, **2.** encircle; *synonyms* (v) beset, surround, besiege, circle, embrace, bound, circumvent, enclose, encompass, environ, hem, begird, circumscribe, beleaguer, (adv) compass, **3.** circle; *synonyms* (n) round, association, band, ring, field, range, beat, circuit, company, gang, scope, set, (v) turn, whirl, encircle, **4.** lasso; *synonyms* (n) lariat, noose, cestus, garter, girdle, girth, halter, (v) rope, catch, **5.** surround; *synonyms* (v) gird, border, inclose, skirt, envelop, entwine, blockade, edge, enfold, fence, invest, smother, (n) environment, environs, wreathe.

bauaki 1. encircled; *synonyms* (adj) surrounded, enclosed, bounded, annular, annulate, annulated, bordered, circinate, circular, delimited, ingirt, ringed, wreathed, **2.** surrounded; *synonyms* (v) beset, begone, furnished, (adj) encircled, circumstanced, conditioned, entrenched, fixed, inside, rooted, implanted.

bauarira 1. promise; *synonyms* (*n*) engagement, assurance, bargain, engage, hope, plight, word, (*v*) pledge, covenant, guarantee, contract, vow, augur, assure, undertake, **2.** vow; *synonyms* (*n*) promise, oath, undertaking, parole, behest, commitment, profession, (*v*) swear, betroth, behight, command, commit, consecrate, devote, order.

bauariraki promised; *synonyms* (*v*) benempt, named, (*adj*) engaged, pledged, affianced, betrothed, busy, devoted, earnest, employed, intended, involved, occupied, prospective, votary.

baubau soft; *synonyms* (*adj*) gentle, easy, light, limp, balmy, delicate, quiet, slack, loose, clement, faint, flabby, flaccid, (*v*) feeble, low; *antonyms* (*adj*) hard, firm, harsh, loud, hoarse, rough, solid, stiff, alcoholic, shrill, strong.

baun golden; *synonyms* (*adj*) aureate, fortunate, gilded, auspicious, gilt, gold, lucky, advantageous, fair, favorable, favored.

bauna 1. lasso; *synonyms* (*n*) lariat, noose, cestus, garter, girdle, girth, halter, (*v*) rope, catch, **2.** snare; *synonyms* (*n*) trap, lure, decoy, net, pitfall, trick, (*v*) mesh, gin, ambush, ensnare, entrap, hook, capture, enmesh, entangle.

baurana 1. explode; *synonyms* (*v*) erupt, detonate, crack, discharge, break, fulminate, blast, disprove, fire, shoot, expand, discredit, shatter, (*n*) burst, flare; *antonym* (*v*) implode, **2.** detonate; *synonyms* (*v*) explode, (*adj*) thunder, bounce; *antonym* (*v*) defuse.

bauranaki exploded; *synonyms* (*adj*) antebellum, antediluvian, elapsed, expired, extinct, lapsed, forgotten, irrecoverable, refuted.

baurawata monopolize; *synonyms* (*v*) engross, control, forestall, absorb, consume, monopolise, occupy.

bauta 1. bind; *synonyms* (*v*) attach, tie, bandage, bundle, combine, fasten, fetter, fix, lace, truss, affix, bond, cement, gird, (*n*) band; *antonyms* (*v*) untie, release, unbind, **2.** bandage; *synonyms* (*n*) swathe, (*v*) bind, wrap, dress, **3.** tie; *synonyms* (*n*) connection, draw, association, relationship, sleeper, strap, string, cord, deadlock, fastening, (*v*) link, join, knot, connect, leash; *antonyms* (*v*) disconnect, undo.

bautaki 1. bound; *synonyms* (*v*) leap, border, bounce, limit, circumscribe, confine, pounce, rebound, (*n*) spring, jump, boundary, edge, barrier, compass, hop; *antonym* (*adj*) free, **2.** bandaged; *synonyms* (*adj*) bound, apprenticed, articled, destined, indentured, obligate, **3.** tied; *synonyms* (*adj*) fastened, connected, even, fixed, laced, united, attached, binding, buttoned, joined, legato, liable, mixed, powerless, responsible; *antonym* (*adj*) separate.

bauwar spittle; *synonyms* (*n*) saliva, slaver, spit, sputum, expectoration, slabber, spattle, spatula, spawl, spet, spitting, spital, tongue.

baware 1. dribble; *synonyms* (*n*) trickle, dribbling, (*v*) drip, drool, drop, drivel, slobber, distill, flow, ooze, spout, trill, leak, seep, slabber, **2.** drool; *synonyms* (*n*) bosh, humbug, tosh, twaddle, baloney, bilgewater, boloney, (*v*) dribble, salivate, slaver, spit, **3.** salivate, **4.** spat; *synonyms* (*v*) bicker, clap, row, (*n*) quarrel, squabble, altercation, tiff, dispute, gaiter, argument, wrangle, bickering, fuss, disagreement, fight, **5.** spit; *synonyms* (*n*) broach, saliva, cape, expectoration, spittle, (*v*) drizzle, impale, expectorate, skewer, spew, sprinkle, spike, hiss, spatter, disgorge.

bawareaki spat; *synonyms* (*v*) bicker, clap, row, (*n*) quarrel, squabble, altercation, tiff, dispute, gaiter, argument, wrangle, bickering, fuss, disagreement, fight.

be 1. naughty; *synonyms* (*adj*) bad, blue, impish, mischievous, improper, disobedient, insubordinate, wicked, evil, lewd, dark, defiant, racy, rebellious, risque; *antonyms* (*adj*) well-behaved, good, **2.** evil; *synonyms* (*adj*) corrupt, criminal, ill, depraved, destructive, harmful, malign, sinister, (*n*) damage, adversity, detriment, disaster, depravity, malice, mischief; *antonyms* (*adj*) kindhearted, (*n*) goodness, righteousness, **3.** bad; *synonyms* (*adj*) adverse, immoral, naughty, poisonous, sad, malicious, infamous, appalling, awful, damaging, devilish, disagreeable, dreadful, hurtful, (*v*) decayed; *antonyms* (*adj*) fresh, pleasant, well, **4.** conceited; *synonyms* (*adj*) arrogant, cocky, egotistic, vain, boastful, proud, smug, affected, assuming, egotistical, haughty, pompous, complacent, narcissistic, priggish; *antonyms* (*adj*) humble, modest, **5.** mischievous; *synonyms* (*adj*) injurious, detrimental, deleterious, maleficent, playful, arch, baneful, sly, malignant, noisome, noxious, pernicious, puckish, implike, mean, **6.** flirtatious; *synonyms* (*adj*) coquettish, coy, brassy, fast, kittenish, seductive, sexy, amorous, come-hither, come-on, dallying, enticing, libidinous, nymphomaniac, philandering, **7.** vile; *synonyms* (*adj*) foul, contemptible, despicable, low, ignoble, disgusting, filthy, nasty, offensive, revolting, sorry, sordid, vicious, (*n*) dirty, (*v*) base; *antonym* (*adj*) attractive, **8.** unpleasant; *synonyms* (*adj*) harsh, obnoxious, ugly, sour, awkward, forbidding, repulsive, hard, rude, abhorrent, bitter, horrible, objectionable, odious, (*n*) difficult; *antonyms* (*adj*) agreeable, delightful, comfortable, enjoyable, nice, wonderful, charming, **9.** rude; *synonyms* (*adj*) gross, rough, impudent, blunt, coarse, bold, brutal, crude, discourteous, impolite, abusive, barbarous, churlish, crass, (*n*) abrupt; *antonyms* (*adj*) polite, respectful, chivalrous, courteous, refined, civil, decent, proper, well-mannered, **10**. ugly; *synonyms* (*adj*) frightful, gruesome, hideous, homely, surly, atrocious, deformed, grotesque, monstrous, ominous, plain, shocking, vile, sullen, threatening; *antonyms* (*adj*) beautiful, good-looking, flowing, ornamental.

beako 1. jumbled; *synonyms* (*adj*) confused, disorderly, disordered, disorganized, untidy, cluttered, mixed, muddled, chaotic, incoherent, topsy-turvy; *antonyms* (*adj*) neat, tidy, **2**. entangled; *synonyms* (*adj*) involved, complicated, intricate, embroiled, complex, foul, matted, tangled; *antonym* (*adj*) free, **3**. matted; *synonyms* (*adj*) mat, entangled, flat, knotted, matt, matte, knotty, bland, categoric, categorical, compressed, fixed, flavorless, flavourless, (*v*) crossed, **4**. tangled; *synonyms* (*adj*) convoluted, difficult, disheveled, tousled, kinky, labyrinthine, perplexed, raveled, tortuous.

bebádoa cockroach; *synonym* (*n*) roach.

bebe 1. unsteady; *synonyms* (*adj*) unstable, changeable, dizzy, insecure, rickety, shaky, unbalanced, unsettled, unsound, precarious, uneven, irregular, erratic, fluctuating, (*n*) uncertain; *antonym* (*adj*) steady, **2**. stagger; *synonyms* (*v*) falter, astonish, lurch, startle, flabbergast, flounder, hobble, reel, shake, shock, pitch, amaze, dumbfound, stun, (*adj*) bewilder, **3**. sway; *synonyms* (*n*) influence, reign, rock, authority, empire, power, (*v*) command, rule, oscillate, control, stagger, bias, careen, persuade, roll, **4**. waver; *synonyms* (*v*) vacillate, flicker, fluctuate, hesitate, quiver, hover, totter, wave, pause, tremble, vibrate, scruple, wobble, (*n*) flutter, faltering, **5**. reel; *synonyms* (*n*) bobbin, coil, spool, (*v*) spin, waver, teeter, dance, gyrate, quake, stumble, whirl, wind, sway, swing, twirl.

bebebebe 1. reel; *synonyms* (*n*) bobbin, coil, roll, spool, (*v*) lurch, rock, spin, stagger, totter, waver, teeter, falter, fluctuate, dance, gyrate, **2**. totter; *synonyms* (*v*) reel, shake, stumble, toddle, waddle, shamble, dodder, sway, tremble, limp, quiver, hobble, quake, walk, wobble, **3**. stagger; *synonyms* (*v*) astonish, startle, flabbergast, flounder, shock, pitch, amaze, dumbfound, stun, surprise, astound, baffle, careen, (*adj*) bewilder, petrify.

bebei 1. lurch; *synonyms* (*v*) careen, stumble, pitch, reel, stagger, tilt, cant, rock, shake, sway, swing, teeter, totter, wobble, flounder, **2**. stagger; *synonyms* (*v*) falter, astonish, lurch, startle, flabbergast, hobble, shock, amaze, dumbfound, stun, surprise, astound, limp, (*adj*) bewilder, petrify.

bebentekura perpendicular; *synonyms* (*adj*) erect, upright, vertical, plumb, steep, straight, normal, orthogonal, precipitous, right, sheer; *antonym* (*adj*) horizontal.

beberino 1. fussy; *synonyms* (*adj*) fastidious, finicky, busy, particular, choosy, crabbed, crabby, difficult, fidgety, finical, picky, meticulous, critical, exacting, (*v*) crotchety; *antonyms* (*adj*) easy, plain, **2**. particular; *synonyms* (*adj*) special, careful, definite, delicate, exact, fussy, individual, detailed, certain, circumstantial, distinct, especial, exceptional, (*n*) detail, item; *antonyms* (*adj*) careless, vague, ordinary, (*n*) general.

bebete 1. easy; *synonyms* (*adj*) comfortable, convenient, gentle, familiar, graceful, lenient, light, clear, contented, cozy, casual, comfy, cushy, (*adv*) soft, easily; *antonyms* (*adj*) difficult, arduous, demanding, hard, laborious, burdensome, particular, strenuous, tough, awkward, formal, testing, uneasy, **2**. mild; *synonyms* (*adj*) kindly, gracious, benign, easy, docile, humble, balmy, calm, clement, delicate, kind, meek, sweet, affable, fine; *antonyms* (*adj*) intense, extreme, pungent, severe, sharp, spicy, barbed, fierce, great, hot, incisive, passionate, powerful, scathing, wintry, **3**. light; *synonyms* (*adj*) fair, facile, faint, flimsy, (*n*) flame, brightness, daylight, illumination, (*v*) fire, kindle, inflame, glow, ignite, dismount, illuminate; *antonyms* (*adj*) fattening, nauseating, (*n*) dark, darkness, gloom, shade, night, (*v*) extinguish, darken, (*alt sp*) heavy, **4**. simple; *synonyms* (*adj*) plain, homely, pure, elementary, innocent, mere, natural, rustic, honest, bare, chaste, childish, childlike, foolish, (*v*) downright; *antonyms* (*adj*) complex, complicated, compound, elaborate, multiple, obscure, ornate, confused, confusing, cunning, multifaceted, problematical, sophisticated.

beebete 1. easy; *synonyms* (*adj*) comfortable, convenient, gentle, familiar, graceful, lenient, light, clear, contented, cozy, casual, comfy, cushy, (*adv*) soft, easily; *antonyms* (*adj*) difficult, arduous, demanding, hard, laborious, burdensome, particular, strenuous, tough, awkward, formal, testing, uneasy, **2**. simple; *synonyms* (*adj*) plain, homely, pure, elementary, humble, innocent, mere, natural, rustic, honest, bare, chaste, childish, childlike, (*v*) downright; *antonyms* (*adj*) complex, complicated, compound, elaborate, multiple, obscure, ornate, confused, confusing, cunning, multifaceted, problematical, sophisticated.

beeboro purple; *synonyms* (*adj*) mauve, violet, imperial, lilac, regal, royal, embellished, majestic, (*n*) empurpled, magenta, purpleness, damask, ermine, mantle, (*v*) empurple.

bei skim; *synonyms* (*v*) glide, slip, browse, skip, sweep, brush, fly, graze, race, read, scan, shave, glance, (*n*) cream, slide.

beibeti 1. afloat; *synonyms* (*adj*) buoyant, floating, current, aimless, directionless, flooded, inundated, overflowing, planless, rudderless, undirected, rife, *(adv)* adrift, *(v)* afoot, *(n)* prevalent, **2.** float; *synonyms* *(n)* buoy, raft, bob, fleet, *(v)* drift, swim, blow, hover, ride, waft, fly, glide, hang, range, sail; *antonym* *(v)* sink.

beireina 1. instruct; *synonyms* *(v)* charge, advise, direct, educate, enlighten, teach, command, drill, indoctrinate, inform, apprise, bid, coach, discipline, edify; *antonym* *(v)* request, **2.** educate; *synonyms* *(v)* civilize, cultivate, instruct, train, breed, develop, groom, nurture, rear, school, condition, refine, guide, nourish, tutor, **3.** form; *synonyms* *(n)* figure, design, arrange, ceremony, shape, class, conformation, *(v)* cast, make, fashion, build, constitute, establish, carve, construct, **4.** inform; *synonyms* *(v)* communicate, acquaint, impart, announce, tell, familiarize, explain, advertise, state, warn, describe, declare, animate, notify, report, **5.** teach; *synonyms* *(v)* learn, lecture, form, catechize, demonstrate, discover, ground, improve, inculcate, prepare, *(adj)* show.

beireinaki 1. educated; *synonyms* *(v)* instructed, *(adj)* cultured, erudite, enlightened, learned, lettered, trained, informed, refined, taught; *antonyms* *(adj)* uneducated, ignorant, **2.** formed; *synonyms* *(adj)* wrought, settled, shaped, affected, characterized, conceived, defined, fashioned, built, constructed, established, firm, adapted, adjusted, arranged, **3.** informed; *synonyms* *(adj)* aware, cognizant, educated, conscious, knowledgeable, familiar, apprised, wise, conversant, experienced, *(adv)* abreast, **4.** instructed; *synonyms* *(v)* leaned, *(adj)* tutored, furnished, instruct, intelligent, qualified, schooled, provided, **5.** taught; *synonyms* *(v)* close, fast, overwrought, taut, tense, tight, *(adj)* gentle, scholarly, well-bred, skilled.

beka 1. excrete; *synonyms* *(v)* discharge, eliminate, emit, defecate, exude, crap, excern, evacuate, secrete, egest, pass, **2.** defecate; *synonyms* *(v)* clarify, dung, shit, clear, excrete, refine, stool, attain, betray, bricks, build, cause, constitute, construct, cook, **3.** shit; *synonyms* *(n)* bullshit, cocksucker, dump, junk, poop, bull, bunk, bunkum, damn, guff, *(v)* grass, *(adj)* excrement, faeces, feces, ordure.

bekan 1. infidel; *synonyms* *(adj)* skeptic, *(n)* atheist, heathen, pagan, gentile, unbeliever, deist, freethinker, **2.** nude; *synonyms* *(adj)* bare, bald, raw, stark, uncovered, undressed, defenseless, *(v)* naked, **3.** naked; *synonyms* *(adj)* exposed, nude, open, barren, bleak, unclothed, defenceless, undraped, alone, denuded, destitute, mere, simple, unaided, unvarnished; *antonyms* *(adj)* covered, concealed, **4.** pagan; *synonyms* *(adj)* heathenish, ethnic, irreligious, *(n)* idolater, infidel.

bekobeko cough; *synonyms* *(n)* coughing, sneeze, *(v)* choke, convulse, vomit.

bekoko numerous; *synonyms* *(adj)* manifold, many, abundant, frequent, multiple, multitudinous, copious, innumerable, plentiful, populous, great, myriad, rife, several, various; *antonym* *(adj)* few.

bekorara 1. growl; *synonyms* *(n)* snarl, roar, bark, thunder, cry, *(v)* grumble, gnarl, howl, mutter, yap, moan, complain, croak, grunt, murmur, **2.** roar; *synonyms* *(n)* boom, shout, noise, peal, clamor, *(v)* bellow, bawl, clatter, blare, call, holler, rave, scream, yell, *(adj)* bluster; *antonym* *(v)* whisper.

bekua thump; *synonyms* *(n)* beat, cuff, punch, strike, crack, crash, tap, *(v)* bang, bump, knock, thud, hit, pound, clump, pulsate.

ben 1. coconut; *synonyms* *(n)* coco, cocoanut, head, **2.** painting; *synonyms* *(n)* picture, portrait, likeness, depiction, icon, design, image, coat, drawing, art.

benga 1. open; *synonyms* *(adj)* frank, obvious, artless, exposed, free, honest, bare, forthright, guileless, ingenuous, naked, *(v)* expand, give, *(n)* candid, clear; *antonyms* *(adj)* devious, secretive, concealed, furtive, hidden, limited, repressive, reserved, restricted, secret, blocked, cautious, *(v)* shut, end, *(tr v)* close, **2.** separate; *synonyms* *(adj)* detached, *(v)* detach, divorce, part, insulate, scatter, cut, dissociate, disconnect, discrete, discriminate, disjoin, disperse, distinguish, divide; *antonyms* *(adj)* connected, joined, simultaneous, *(v)* unite, merge, mix, combine, fuse, join, link, associate, **3.** opened; *synonyms* *(v)* blown, distended, exhausted, inflated, stale, swollen, tired, *(adj)* open, assailable, blatant, blazing, conspicuous, lawless, loose, through, **4.** separated; *synonyms* *(adj)* disconnected, separate, apart, divided, isolated, disjointed, disjunct, removed, dislocated, independent, lone, single, *(prep)* disjoined, distinct.

bengaki 1. separated; *synonyms* *(adj)* disconnected, separate, apart, detached, divided, isolated, disjointed, free, disjunct, removed, dislocated, independent, lone, *(prep)* disjoined, distinct, **2.** opened; *synonyms* *(v)* blown, distended, exhausted, inflated, *(adj)* open, candid, exposed, assailable, blatant, blazing, clear, conspicuous, lawless, loose, through.

benoinoi 1. mischievous; *synonyms* *(adj)* bad, evil, injurious, detrimental, hurtful, naughty, deleterious, harmful, impish, maleficent, playful, arch, baneful, sly, disobedient; *antonym* *(adj)* good, **2.** wicked; *synonyms* *(adj)* atrocious, sinful, vicious, depraved, immoral, mischievous, unholy, vile, corrupt, criminal, diabolical, foul, hellish, iniquitous, nasty; *antonyms* *(adj)* innocent, kind, moral, pious, pure.

benono 1. curved; *synonyms* *(adj)* bent, crooked, curve, round, bend, curving, curvy, deformed, hooked, rounded, tortuous, twisted, *(v)* bowed; *antonyms* *(adj)* straight, concave, **2.** pliable; *synonyms* *(adj)* flexible, elastic, plastic, ductile, pliant, flexile, malleable, soft, fictile, supple, susceptible, yielding, docile, (v) lithe, limber; *antonyms* (adj) rigid, stiff.

beo matted; *synonyms* (adj) mat, entangled, tangled, flat, knotted, matt, matte, knotty, bland, categoric, categorical, compressed, fixed, flavorless, (v) crossed; *antonym* (adj) tidy.

berebitero priest; *synonyms* (n) clergyman, minister, ecclesiastic, churchman, cleric, parson, pastor, presbyter, chaplain, monk, (adj) divine.

berino particular; *synonyms* (adj) special, fastidious, careful, definite, delicate, exact, finicky, fussy, individual, detailed, certain, choosy, circumstantial, (n) detail, item; *antonyms* (adj) careless, easy, vague, ordinary, (n) general.

berita 1. commit; *synonyms* (v) commend, assign, charge, consign, apply, confide, dedicate, entrust, submit, deliver, devote, give, intrust, leave, send, 2. promising; *synonyms* (adj) likely, auspicious, bright, favorable, encouraging, hopeful, propitious, budding, optimistic, probable, fortunate, rosy, potential; *antonyms* (adj) unpromising, hopeless, inauspicious, 3. promise; *synonyms* (n) engagement, assurance, bargain, engage, hope, plight, word, (v) pledge, covenant, guarantee, contract, vow, augur, assure, undertake, 4. plight; *synonyms* (n) condition, predicament, fix, quandary, dilemma, case, gage, scrape, state, troth, category, corner, (v) promise, affiance, betroth.

beritaki promised; *synonyms* (v) benempt, named, (adj) engaged, pledged, affianced, betrothed, busy, devoted, earnest, employed, intended, involved, occupied, prospective, votary.

beroro 1. multiple; *synonyms* (adj) manifold, many, complex, diverse, populous, compound, multiplex, multiplied, multitudinous, various, (n) coefficient; *antonym* (adj) simple, 2. frequent; *synonyms* (adj) continual, everyday, familiar, ordinary, incessant, habitual, accustomed, commonplace, chronic, (v) common, customary, usual, haunt, patronize, attend; *antonyms* (adj) rare, infrequent, occasional, 3. close; *synonyms* (adj) near, adjacent, nearby, accurate, tight, approximate, narrow, (v) compact, stop, conclude, (adv) by, about, (v) end, finish, conclusion; *antonyms* (adj) distant, airy, fresh, loose, far, (v) open, start, 4. numerous; *synonyms* (adj) abundant, frequent, multiple, copious, innumerable, plentiful, great, myriad, rife, several, numberless, countless, incalculable, thick, different; *antonym* (adj) few.

berurare 1. feet; *synonyms* (n) fete, meter, rescue, arm, fact, performance, (v) legs, pegs, pins, trotters, 2. plural; *synonym* (adj) several; *antonym* (n) singular.

beta 1. bet; *synonyms* (v) gamble, play, lay, risk, venture, (n) wager, stake, stakes, 2. bid; *synonyms*

(n) offer, tender, attempt, proffer, suggestion, (v) ask, call, command, invite, adjure, beseech, charge, direct, instruct, order.

betanga 1. many; *synonyms* (adj) manifold, abundant, countless, frequent, various, innumerable, much, multiple, numerous, plentiful, several, different, numberless, (n) number; *antonym* (n) few, 2. much; *synonyms* (adv) greatly, frequently, almost, awfully, considerably, far, most, often, pretty, highly, (n) lot, heap, (adj) great, considerable, practically; *antonym* (adv) slightly.

betanna 1. exaggerate; *synonyms* (v) boast, aggravate, amplify, dramatize, overdo, overdraw, enhance, enlarge, magnify, overstate, embellish, heighten, hyperbolize, increase, inflate; *antonyms* (v) understate, minimize, 2. exaggerated; *synonyms* (adj) enlarged, extravagant, theatrical, immoderate, hypertrophied, affected, excessive, hyperbolic, inflated, magnified, overdone, overstated, pretentious, melodramatic; *antonyms* (adj) understated, restrained.

betannaki exaggerated; *synonyms* (adj) enlarged, extravagant, theatrical, immoderate, hypertrophied, affected, excessive, hyperbolic, inflated, magnified, overdone, overstated, pretentious, melodramatic; *antonyms* (adj) understated, restrained.

bete light; *synonyms* (adj) fair, clear, facile, easy, faint, flimsy, (n) flame, brightness, daylight, (v) fire, kindle, inflame, glow, ignite, dismount; *antonyms* (adj) fattening, nauseating, (n) dark, darkness, gloom, shade, night, (v) extinguish, darken, (alt sp) heavy.

betinako adrift; *synonyms* (adj) astray, disoriented, asunder, insular, isolated, planless, rudderless, undirected, derelict, lost, careless, (adv) directionless, afloat, amiss, wrong.

betingaingai 1. foul; *synonyms* (adj) base, disgusting, filthy, nasty, evil, dingy, putrid, unclean, abominable, (n) soil, (v) dirty, corrupt, coarse, defile, befoul; *antonyms* (adj) pleasant, fair, (v) clean, pure, 2. nasty; *synonyms* (adj) loathsome, foul, awful, mean, disagreeable, distasteful, hurtful, obnoxious, raw, repulsive, unpleasant, vile, impure, dangerous, (adv) beastly; *antonyms* (adj) agreeable, kind, nice, charitable, lovely, 3. soiled; *synonyms* (adj) grubby, grimy, muddy, black, mucky, polluted, squalid, stained, contaminated, lousy.

betirake 1. ascending; *synonyms* (adj) uphill, ascendent, assurgent, climbing, rising, (n) ascension, ascent, rise, 2. floating; *synonyms* (adj) drifting, buoyant, aimless, current, loose, (adv) afloat, 3. float; *synonyms* (n) buoy, raft, bob, fleet, (v) drift, swim, blow, hover, ride, waft, fly, glide, hang, range, sail; *antonym* (v) sink, 4. ascend; *synonyms* (v) arise, mount, climb, scale, uprise, increase, appear, escalate, jump, lift, soar;

antonyms (*v*) descend, drop, **5**. rising; *synonyms* (*adj*) emergent, emerging, (*n*) ascending, mutiny, rebellion, revolt, insurrection, outbreak, advance, upheaval, uprising, revolution, heave, (*adv*) increasing, growing; *antonyms* (*adj*) plummeting, decreasing, plunging.

betiti 1. dirty; *synonyms* (*adj*) foul, dirt, contemptible, bawdy, contaminated, dingy, impure, despicable, (*v*) muddy, corrupt, soil, contaminate, begrime, bemire, (*n*) defile; *antonyms* (*adj*) hygienic, pure, spotless, immaculate, (*v*) clean, **2**. filthy; *synonyms* (*adj*) dirty, nasty, unclean, disgusting, squalid, awful, grimy, grubby, indecent, ribald, smutty, sordid, vile, vulgar, distasteful; *antonym* (*adj*) decent.

betoto rude; *synonyms* (*adj*) gross, rough, impudent, blunt, coarse, bold, brutal, crude, discourteous, impolite, mean, abusive, barbarous, churlish, (*n*) abrupt; *antonyms* (*adj*) polite, respectful, chivalrous, courteous, refined, civil, decent, proper, well-mannered.

betunga 1. criticize; *synonyms* (*v*) attack, belittle, berate, blame, censure, chide, comment, denounce, rebuke, reprimand, scold, condemn, criticise, deplore, disparage; *antonyms* (*v*) praise, approve, commend, admire, **2**. scrutinize; *synonyms* (*v*) inspect, examine, review, analyze, audit, consider, explore, investigate, scan, search, check, observe, probe, study, (*n*) canvass.

betuntun 1. constrained; *synonyms* (*adj*) uneasy, bound, forced, stiff, strained, awkward, compelled, limited, affected, confined, cramped, restricted, rigid, stilted; *antonyms* (*adj*) free, unrestricted, **2**. numerous; *synonyms* (*adj*) manifold, many, abundant, frequent, multiple, multitudinous, copious, innumerable, plentiful, populous, great, myriad, rife, several, various; *antonym* (*adj*) few.

beu 1. awkward; *synonyms* (*adj*) clumsy, inconvenient, crude, embarrassing, inept, sticky, uncomfortable, ungainly, untoward, left-handed, annoying, bungling, cumbersome, difficult, graceless; *antonyms* (*adj*) graceful, easy, adroit, manageable, straightforward, convenient, dexterous, helpful, rotund, simple, **2**. malformed; *synonyms* (*adj*) deformed, misshapen, distorted, warped, grotesque, odd, freakish, faulty, aberrant, anomalous, atypical, bent, contorted, deviant, irregular.

beuakora 1. bent; *synonyms* (*adj*) arched, curved, bended, crooked, deformed, intent, (*n*) aptitude, inclination, propensity, fancy, ability, bias, flair, gift, leaning; *antonym* (*adj*) straight, **2**. stooped; *synonyms* (*adj*) bent, hunched, stooping, asymmetrical, bowed, convex, corrupt, crumpled, dented, droopy, hooked, inclined, rounded.

bewa tangled; *synonyms* (*adj*) involved, complex, knotted, intricate, complicated, entangled, convoluted, knotty, difficult, disheveled, tousled, kinky, labyrinthine, muddled, perplexed; *antonym* (*adj*) free.

bewawa 1. nasty; *synonyms* (*adj*) dirty, loathsome, disgusting, filthy, foul, awful, mean, abominable, coarse, disagreeable, distasteful, evil, hurtful, obnoxious, raw; *antonyms* (*adj*) agreeable, kind, pleasant, nice, charitable, lovely, **2**. foul; *synonyms* (*adj*) base, nasty, dingy, putrid, unclean, fetid, grimy, offensive, revolting, (*n*) soil, (*v*) corrupt, defile, befoul, contaminate, pollute; *antonyms* (*adj*) fair, (*v*) clean, pure, **3**. squalid; *synonyms* (*adj*) seedy, sordid, abject, grubby, seamy, sleazy, mangy, shabby, impure, miserable, black, scruffy, low, poor, wretched, **4**. sticky; *synonyms* (*adj*) adhesive, awkward, clammy, muggy, embarrassing, glutinous, gummy, humid, difficult, slimy, gluey, gooey, hard, mucilaginous, pasty; *antonyms* (*adj*) dry, fresh, easy.

bigúgu pregnant; *synonyms* (*adj*) pithy, significant, fraught, enceinte, expectant, gravid, heavy, big, meaning, teeming, important, (*v*) telling, emphatic.

bikoukou pregnant; *synonyms* (*adj*) pithy, significant, fraught, enceinte, expectant, gravid, heavy, big, meaning, teeming, important, (*v*) telling, emphatic.

bimaung 1. reek; *synonyms* (*n*) smoke, stench, fetor, malodor, malodour, vapor, fumes, (*v*) fume, stink, emit, exhale, fumigate, smack, smell, (*adj*) gas, **2**. stink; *synonyms* (*n*) foetor, (*v*) reek, odor.

bina appear; *synonyms* (*v*) occur, rise, seem, sound, emerge, show, break, arise, arrive, begin, feel, happen, look, surface, (*n*) come; *antonyms* (*v*) disappear, vanish.

binainga 1. sensitive; *synonyms* (*adj*) delicate, excitable, sensible, sore, tender, painful, impressionable, emotional, gentle, irritable, perceptive, receptive, susceptible, nice, nervous; *antonyms* (*adj*) insensitive, numb, hardhearted, tactless, thick-skinned, **2**. timid; *synonyms* (*adj*) fearful, afraid, cowardly, diffident, shy, bashful, cautious, coy, apprehensive, frightened, modest, retiring, craven, anxious, faint; *antonyms* (*adj*) confident, bold, fearless, (*n*) brave.

binenea 1. coax; *synonyms* (*v*) wheedle, allure, cajole, entice, charm, blarney, inveigle, persuade, seduce, flatter, induce, (*n*) tempt, captivate, conciliate, fascinate, **2**. urge; *synonyms* (*n*) goad, spur, drive, impulse, (*v*) push, advocate, press, force, impel, incite, inspire, instigate, prompt, promote, (*adj*) quicken; *antonym* (*v*) discourage.

binenga prefer; *synonyms* (*v*) choose, pick, advance, elect, elevate, favor, like, opt, favour, promote, select, want, dignify, fancy, desire.

bing 1. ground; *synonyms* (*n*) base, cause, land, floor, reason, dirt, field, soil, account, country, basis, (*v*) bottom, found, establish, fix; *antonym* (*n*) ceiling, **2**.

grind; *synonyms* (v) labor, toil, comminute, crunch, drudge, grate, abrade, chew, crush, file, mash, scrape, sharpen, (n) mill, drudgery, **3**. resonant; *synonyms* (adj) ringing, sonorous, vibrant, deep, full, melodious, resounding, reverberating, reverberative, rich, bass, booming, cavernous, echoing, loud; *antonym* (adj) weak, **4**. tinkle; *synonyms* (n) chink, ring, chime, sound, clang, (v) jingle, clink, tink, ting, clank, buzz.

bingaki ground; *synonyms* (n) base, cause, land, floor, reason, dirt, field, soil, account, country, basis, (v) bottom, found, establish, fix; *antonym* (n) ceiling.

bingibing resonant; *synonyms* (adj) ringing, sonorous, vibrant, deep, full, melodious, resounding, reverberating, reverberative, rich, bass, booming, cavernous, echoing, loud; *antonym* (adj) weak.

bingingi 1. minute; *synonyms* (n) instant, flash, jiffy, note, memorandum, moment, second, (adj) little, delicate, microscopic, atomic, careful, circumstantial, diminutive, elaborate; *antonyms* (adj) enormous, huge, big, gigantic, **2**. tiny; *synonyms* (adj) minute, infinitesimal, midget, petite, petty, puny, slight, teeny, exiguous, baby, insignificant, miniature, bantam, (phr) minuscule, small; *antonyms* (adj) vast, large.

bingore 1. sickly; *synonyms* (adj) feeble, infirm, sick, ailing, diseased, indisposed, morbid, pale, poorly, sallow, peaked, pasty, (n) invalid, (v) faint, frail; *antonyms* (adj) healthy, bitter, **2**. puny; *synonyms* (adj) little, petty, weak, small, tiny, minute, measly, paltry, runty, trifling, trivial, exiguous, meager; *antonyms* (adj) brawny, muscular, **3**. stunted; *synonyms* (adj) scrubby, scrawny, diminutive, puny, short, spare, (v) strangulated.

binibing hollow; *synonyms* (adj) blank, concave, empty, false, insincere, (n) cavity, hole, cave, depression, groove, excavation, (v) excavate, dent, scoop, dig; *antonyms* (adj) convex, (n) solid, hump.

bino serenade; *synonyms* (n) canon, cheer, divertimento, fugue, quodlibet, serenate, (v) court, sing.

binoka 1. twine; *synonyms* (n) coil, string, cord, rope, thread, (v) wind, entwine, lace, enlace, interlace, intertwine, meander, twist, weave, braid; *antonym* (v) untwist, **2**. spin; *synonyms* (n) turn, twirl, whirl, revolution, roll, ride, eddy, (v) revolve, run, drive, reel, fabricate, gyrate, invent, narrate, **3**. span; *synonyms* (n) length, space, distance, bridge, couple, range, period, extent, reach, pair, width, scope, (v) cross, stretch, arch, **4**. twist; *synonyms* (n) twine, spin, kink, loop, strain, (v) bend, distort, curl, contort, deform, curve, pervert, wrench, pull, sprain; *antonym* (v) straighten, **5**. ravel; *synonyms* (n) involve, (v) entangle, tangle, disentangle,

unravel, unwind, knot, embrangle, snarl, dishevel, fray, imbrangle, (adj) embarrass, enmesh, encumber.

binokaia twine; *synonyms* (n) coil, string, cord, rope, thread, (v) wind, entwine, lace, enlace, interlace, intertwine, meander, twist, weave, braid; *antonym* (v) untwist.

binokaiaki twined; *synonyms* (adj) twisted, bent, contorted, distorted, misrepresented, perverted.

binokaki 1. twined; *synonyms* (adj) twisted, bent, contorted, distorted, misrepresented, perverted, **2**. twisted; *synonyms* (adj) crooked, deformed, coiled, misshapen, curved, twined, winding, wry, gnarled, tortuous, awry, kinky, wrong, warped, askew; *antonyms* (adj) straight, tidy.

bïr lizard; *synonyms* (n) loafer, purse.

bira 1. braid; *synonyms* (n) plait, pigtail, tress, band, braiding, (v) plat, twine, entwine, intertwine, mat, (adj) knit, string, embroider, lace, tie; *antonym* (v) unbraid, **2**. whistle; *synonyms* (n) whistling, pennywhistle, (v) pipe, sing, twitter, hiss, cry, warble, cheep, tweet, chirp, wheeze.

biraki braided; *synonyms* (adj) plaited, artful, breaded, tressed, folded, intricate, (v) broidered.

biri run; *synonyms* (v) flow, rule, dash, gush, race, career, conduct, direct, function, go, (n) pass, campaign, course, drive, (adj) stream.

biria 1. wreathe; *synonyms* (v) twine, twist, entwine, wind, weave, encircle, coil, infold, curve, inweave, nose, scent, worm, wreath, **2**. seize; *synonyms* (v) capture, catch, grab, arrest, apprehend, clutch, get, grapple, receive, annex, assume, clasp, confiscate, conquer, grasp; *antonym* (v) release, **3**. occupy; *synonyms* (v) hold, have, engage, engross, fill, absorb, employ, inhabit, invade, possess, busy, keep, take, (n) entertain, interest; *antonym* (v) leave.

biriaki 1. occupied; *synonyms* (adj) busy, engaged, employed, diligent, absorbed, active, engrossed, working, affianced, betrothed, concerned, industrious, involved; *antonyms* (adj) empty, vacant, available, uninhabited, free, idle, **2**. wreathed; *synonyms* (adj) encircled, ringed, annular, annulate, annulated, bent, circinate, circular, coiled, curled, curved, deceitful, erroneous, indirect, oblique, **3**. seized; *synonyms* (adj) confiscate, confiscated, appropriated, condemned, apprehended, detained, held, censured, convicted, forfeit, forfeited, obsessed.

biriakinnako elope; *synonyms* (v) abscond, escape, flee, desert, bolt, decamp, absquatulate, dispel, leave, abandon, disappear, photocopy, skip, waste.

birianena ramble; *synonyms* (n) journey, stroll, excursion, hike, promenade, walk, amble, (v) meander, roam, saunter, wander, range, rove, tramp, digress.

biriao overstep; *synonyms* (*v*) exceed, encroach, surpass, transcend, trespass, overrun, overtake, pass, transgress, intrude, outdo.

birikewe bluff; *synonyms* (*n*) bravado, cheat, hill, cliff, deception, (*v*) beguile, blague, (*adj*) brusque, blunt, direct, rough, candid, peak, abrupt, bold.

birimaka 1. dash; *synonyms* (*n*) rush, sprint, animation, beat, bit, bolt, line, (*v*) dart, touch, strike, break, charge, crash, hurry, jog; *antonym* (*n*) lethargy, **2.** fast; *synonyms* (*adj*) dissolute, firm, agile, debauched, fixed, hurried, instant, quick, rapid, staunch, brisk, (*adv*) soon, hard, close, (*n*) diet; *antonyms* (*adj*) sluggish, loose, (*adv*) slow, slowly, leisurely, (*v*) gorge, (*n*) binge, **3.** quick; *synonyms* (*adj*) bright, prompt, active, clever, hasty, intelligent, nimble, speedy, alert, alive, cursory, dexterous, expeditious, immediate, (*adv*) fast; *antonym* (*adj*) dull, **4.** swift; *synonyms* (*adj*) fleet, lively, sudden, abrupt, express, ready, sprightly, impetuous, unexpected, keen, brief, impulsive, meteoric, (*n*) cylinder, (*adv*) swiftly; *antonym* (*adj*) considered, **5.** sprint; *synonyms* (*n*) dash, race, (*v*) run, gallop, scurry, hasten, speed, fly, trot.

birimakaki dashed; *synonyms* (*v*) abashed, ashamed, sunk, (*adj*) dejected, discouraged, dotted, flecked, specked, speckled, stippled.

birimara slow; *synonyms* (*adj*) dull, late, easy, sluggish, heavy, dense, dim, gradual, inactive, indolent, lazy, stupid, (*v*) slack, (*adv*) behind, behindhand; *antonyms* (*adj*) fast, intelligent, rapid, bright, alert, brisk, hasty, prompt, quick, speedy, hurried, observant, rushed, (*v*) accelerate.

birinako 1. evacuate; *synonyms* (*v*) deplete, void, discharge, quit, clear, drain, abandon, displace, eject, eliminate, leave, pass, vacate, annul, (*adj*) empty, **2.** escape; *synonyms* (*v*) elude, break, dodge, avoid, evade, run, bolt, circumvent, duck, bilk, abscond, (*n*) leak, avoidance, evasion, outlet; *antonyms* (*v*) capture, return, **3.** evade; *synonyms* (*v*) escape, equivocate, parry, hedge, sidestep, skirt, fudge, neglect, omit, prevaricate, quibble, shun, block, eschew, deflect; *antonym* (*v*) confront.

birinakoaki 1. evacuated; *synonyms* (*adj*) empty, annulled, emptied, voided, invalidated, **2.** escaped; *synonyms* (*v*) escaping, (*adj*) free, loose, easy, runaway, wild, fugitive, idle, informal, lax, liberal, light, open, promiscuous, slack.

biririmoa 1. foreseen; *synonyms* (*adj*) accidental, adventitious, casual, coming, concourse, contingent, foretold, predictable, predicted, fortuitous, incidental, intelligence, observer, occasional, prearranged, **2.** foresee; *synonyms* (*v*) envision, expect, forecast, anticipate, envisage, foreknow, previse, prophesy, predict, provide, see, counter, **3.** anticipate; *synonyms* (*v*) antedate, forestall, foretell, think, calculate, estimate, apprehend, divine, guess, presume, prevent,

intercept, trust, await, forebode, **4.** assert; *synonyms* (*v*) affirm, allege, claim, declare, say, argue, aver, avow, insist, maintain, protest, show, swear, announce, assure; *antonym* (*v*) deny, **5.** precede; *synonyms* (*v*) lead, head, antecede, forego, forerun, introduce, pass, preface, direct, go; *antonym* (*v*) follow, succeed.

biririmoaki 1. anticipated; *synonyms* (*adj*) likely, expected, predictable, appointed, awaited, coming, forthcoming, future, natural, planned, probable, projected, proposed, scheduled, **2.** asserted, **3.** foreseen; *synonyms* (*v*) provided, (*adj*) accidental, adventitious, casual, concourse, contingent, foretold, predicted, fortuitous, incidental, intelligence, observer, occasional, prearranged, premeditated.

biririmwi miss; *synonyms* (*v*) lack, lose, fail, jump, omit, overlook, long, drop, escape, (*n*) maid, girl, want, fille, missy, (*adj*) fault; *antonym* (*v*) perceive.

biririmwiaki missed; *synonyms* (*adj*) lost, baffled, befuddled, bemused, bewildered, confounded, confused, disoriented, forgotten, helpless, irretrievable, mazed, preoccupied.

biritaetae 1. foretold; *synonyms* (*v*) annunciate, preannounced, (*adj*) predicted, foreseen, **2.** foretell; *synonyms* (*v*) anticipate, augur, divine, forecast, announce, bode, predict, presage, calculate, forebode, foreshadow, foreshow, portend, prognosticate, prophesy.

biritaetaeaki foretold; *synonyms* (*v*) annunciate, preannounced, (*adj*) predicted, foreseen.

biritana 1. abandon; *synonyms* (*v*) quit, relinquish, renounce, resign, vacate, desert, evacuate, leave, waive, depart, abdicate, chuck, ditch, drop, forfeit; *antonyms* (*v*) keep, support, maintain, (*n*) restraint, **2.** leave; *synonyms* (*v*) forsake, go, abandon, escape, flee, lead, lay, allow, bequeath, (*n*) furlough, holiday, permission, permit, break, (*adj*) empty; *antonyms* (*v*) arrive, enter, stay, remain, approach, change, come.

biritanaki abandoned; *synonyms* (*adj*) forlorn, immoral, deserted, empty, profligate, shameless, stranded, wicked, lonely, corrupt, debauched, depraved, derelict, desolate, discarded; *antonyms* (*adj*) restrained, inhabited, orderly, overcrowded.

biroa 1. tighten; *synonyms* (*v*) contract, strain, brace, compress, constrict, fasten, narrow, reduce, squeeze, stiffen, stretch, screw, secure, constrain, frap; *antonyms* (*v*) loosen, relax, **2.** twist; *synonyms* (*n*) twine, wind, spin, twirl, entwine, (*v*) turn, bend, distort, curl, coil, contort, deform, curve, pervert, wrench; *antonyms* (*v*) straighten, untwist, **3.** screw; *synonyms* (*n*) fuck, propeller, fucking, gaoler, jailer, (*v*) cheat, pin, bonk, jockey, (*adj*) bolt, nail, stint, gripe, pinch, clamp.

biroaki 1. twisted; *synonyms (adj)* crooked, deformed, perverted, bent, distorted, coiled, misshapen, contorted, curved, twined, winding, wry, gnarled, tortuous, awry; *antonyms (adj)* straight, tidy, **2.** tightened; *synonyms (adj)* tight, firm.

bita 1. modify; *synonyms (v)* alter, qualify, adapt, change, limit, adjust, amend, assuage, convert, moderate, restrict, vary, commute, fit, revise, **2.** change; *synonyms (n)* shift, alteration, barter, modification, variation, move, adjustment, *(v)* exchange, alternate, cash, switch, transpose, turn, twist, affect; *antonyms (v)* stay, leave, idle, maintain, **3.** invert; *synonyms (v)* reverse, capsize, overturn, upset, annul, subvert, **4.** turn; *synonyms (v)* revolve, deviate, get, revolution, spin, *(n)* bend, curve, roll, coil, go, bout, round, bent, circle, tour.

bitabao 1. distorted; *synonyms (adj)* crooked, contorted, deformed, misshapen, perverted, twisted, wry, bent, misrepresented, malformed, *(adv)* awry; *antonyms (adj)* straight, unchanged, **2.** altered; *synonyms (v)* battered, seedy, shattered, *(adj)* adapted, transformed, changed, diversified, distorted, varied, affected, corrupt, different, misused, neutered, new; *antonym (adj)* unaltered, **3.** misconstrue; *synonyms (v)* misapprehend, misunderstand, misconceive, misinterpret, misjudge, misread, mistake; *antonym (v)* understand, **4.** deformed; *synonyms (adj)* ugly, crippled, deform, grotesque, shapeless, warped, *(v)* crump.

bitaki 1. inverted; *synonyms (adj)* inverse, upside-down, anatropous, backward, overturned, topsy-turvy, converted, debased, gay, hyperbatic, invert, upturned, transposed; *antonym (adj)* upright, **2.** changed; *synonyms (adj)* altered, transformed, varied, affected, changeling, different, disguised, distorted, malformed, misshapen, new, reformed, rehabilitated, tainted, diversified; *antonym (adj)* unchanged, **3.** modified; *synonyms (adj)* limited, qualified, circumscribed, conditional, mediocre, variant, bespoke, customized, personalized, special, tailored; *antonym (adj)* mass-produced, **4.** turned; *synonyms (adj)* off, sour, curved, rancid, twisted, askew, awry, bent, bowed, cancelled, crooked, dark, deflected, dour, dull.

bitanikai 1. dodge; *synonyms (v)* circumvent, avoid, evade, maneuver, duck, elude, escape, fudge, hedge, parry, *(n)* contrivance, stratagem, cheat, device, quibble, **2.** trick; *synonyms (n)* deceit, deception, joke, prank, dupe, knack, *(v)* swindle, deceive, fraud, sham, con, mislead, beguile, bamboozle, defraud, **3.** pretend; *synonyms (v)* assume, feign, dissimulate, counterfeit, act, affect, dissemble, imagine, imitate, profess, mask, masquerade, *(adj)* fake, play, *(n)* allege; *antonyms (v)* real, *(adj)* genuine, natural.

bitara 1. contradictory; *synonyms (adj)* conflicting, incompatible, inconsistent, contrary, discordant, antagonistic, opposite, ironic, discrepant, incoherent, incongruous, opposed, opposing, repugnant, *(n)* disagreeing; *antonyms (adj)* consistent, similar, compatible, **2.** contradict; *synonyms (v)* deny, oppose, belie, conflict, confute, contravene, controvert, disprove, dissent, impugn, invalidate, refute, disaffirm, disclaim, counteract; *antonyms (v)* confirm, agree, match, **3.** contrary; *synonyms (adj)* contradictory, adverse, reverse, unfavorable, alien, cross, different, disobedient, obstinate, perverse, averse, hostile, *(n)* antithesis, converse, *(adv)* counter, **4.** invert; *synonyms (v)* change, transpose, capsize, overturn, turn, upset, annul, subvert, **5.** opposite; *synonyms (adj)* diametric, diametrical, unlike, across, contra, *(n)* opponent, adversary, contradiction, antonym, inverse, negation, counterpart, antagonist, opposition, *(pron)* other, **6.** oppose; *synonyms (v)* object, contest, contend, contradict, resist, fight, disagree, combat, confront, defend, dispute, gainsay, hinder, repel, thwart; *antonyms (v)* support, advocate, back, advise.

bitaraki 1. inverted; *synonyms (adj)* inverse, upside-down, anatropous, backward, overturned, topsy-turvy, converted, debased, gay, hyperbatic, invert, upturned, transposed; *antonym (adj)* upright, **2.** opposed; *synonyms (adj)* conflicting, contradictory, hostile, contrary, antagonistic, opposing, adverse, averse, contrasted, repugnant, incompatible, irreconcilable, counter, against, opposite.

biti 1. iron; *synonyms (n)* chain, irons, chains, *(v)* firm, flatten, press, smooth, *(adj)* hard, adamant, inflexible, steel, tenacious, **2.** knife; *synonyms (n)* dagger, tongue, whittle, clapper, couteau, cuttle, cuttlefish, *(v)* stab, wound, jab, slit, betray, dig, *(adj)* blade, cutlery, **3.** knives.

bitia reverse; *synonyms (adj)* opposite, converse, inverse, *(v)* annul, repeal, rescind, countermand, overturn, revoke, rear, nullify, cancel, invert, overrule, *(n)* contrary; *antonym (n)* front.

bitiaki reversed; *synonyms (adj)* inverted, converse, inverse, reverse, overturned, upside-down, contrary, opposite; *antonym (adj)* upright.

biwa feverish; *synonyms (adj)* hectic, febrile, feverous, hot, fiery, frenzied, fanatical, flushed, sick, *(n)* hysterical; *antonym (adj)* cool.

bo 1. knock; *synonyms (v)* hit, blow, bump, cuff, punch, strike, boot, clip, *(n)* rap, bang, tap, bash, crash, whack, clap; *antonym (v)* praise, **2.** combat; *synonyms (n)* fight, encounter, action, brawl, conflict, contest, fighting, fray, war, hostility, affray, contention, engagement, *(v)* battle, clash, **3.** accord; *synonyms (n)* agreement, assent, consensus, harmony, consonance, *(v)* agree, concord, consent, give, bestow, grant, harmonize, suit, adjust, comply; *antonyms* (*n*) disagreement, discord, strife, **4.** battle; *synonyms* (*n*) combat, struggle, scuffle, warfare, feud, row, tussle, bout, campaign, (*v*) quarrel, scrap, wrestle, contend, dispute, grapple, **5.** answer; *synonyms* (*n*) reply, respond, retort, return, solution, defense, echo, reaction, (*v*) counter, resolve, serve, acknowledge, correspond, do, (*adj*) pay; *antonyms* (*v*) question, ask, **6.** compensate; *synonyms* (*v*) balance, recompense, reimburse, counterbalance, recoup, remunerate, repay, reward, cover, correct, expiate, indemnify, offset, redeem, redress, **7.** equalize; *synonyms* (*v*) compensate, equate, even, compare, equalise, level, match, counteract, (*adj*) equal, **8.** hit; *synonyms* (*v*) attain, belt, collide, club, contact, lick, (*n*) knock, smash, touch, chance, beat, collision, play, clout, crack; *antonyms* (*n*) failure, flop, **9.** hurt; *synonyms* (*v*) pain, wound, afflict, injure, ail, cost, (*adj*) evil, (*n*) harm, damage, detriment, ache, disadvantage, abuse, distress, lesion; *antonyms* (*v*) encourage, (*adj*) uninjured, unhurt, **10.** fight; *synonyms* (*v*) argue, bicker, compete, box, crusade, drive, defend, brush, disagree, (*n*) squabble, competition, confrontation, altercation, argument, hassle; *antonyms* (*v*) retreat, withdrawal, **11.** blow; *synonyms* (*n*) blast, shock, wallop, gust, jolt, thump, (*v*) puff, bloom, blossom, pant, slap, squander, stroke, waft, (*adj*) gasp; *antonyms* (*v*) calm, save, **12.** contact; *synonyms* (*n*) connection, communication, link, impact, tangency, acquaintance, interaction, juxtaposition, (*v*) call, meet, adjoin, communicate, reach, butt, join, **13.** touch; *synonyms* (*n*) feel, tinge, feeling, hint, tincture, (*v*) affect, border, regard, concern, handle, interest, move, taste, tint, allude, **14.** thump; *synonyms* (*n*) pulse, thwack, (*v*) thud, pound, clump, pulsate, throb, flap, buffet, thrash, smack, palpitate, batter, poke, boom, **15.** stroke; *synonyms* (*n*) caress, mark, apoplexy, attack, line, streak, cut, dint, seizure, accomplishment, (*v*) fondle, pat, smite, pet, measure, **16.** reward; *synonyms* (*n*) guerdon, payment, wage, bribe, fee, premium, award, bonus, payoff, price, (*v*) compensation, meed, prize, requite, honor; *antonym* (*v*) punish.

bô exchange; *synonyms* (*n*) commutation, swap, switch, commerce, conversion, substitute, (*v*) change, barter, interchange, commute, counterchange, alternate, alter, cash, convert.

boa 1. admonish; *synonyms* (*v*) warn, chide, rebuke, remonstrate, remind, advise, caution, censure, lecture, reprimand, reproach, reprove, scold, accuse, blame; *antonym* (*v*) praise, **2.** answer; *synonyms* (*n*) reply, respond, retort, return, solution, defense, echo, (*v*) counter, resolve, serve, acknowledge, agree, correspond, do, (*adj*) pay;

antonyms (*v*) question, ask, **3.** blame; *synonyms* (*v*) arraign, charge, fault, attribute, criticize, knock, (*n*) attack, rap, onus, accusation, allegation, condemnation, inculpation, responsibility, indictment; *antonyms* (*v*) pardon, absolve, **4.** smite; *synonyms* (*v*) afflict, strike, buffet, affect, cut, impress, punish, touch, animate, excite, impassion, inspire, interest, move, **5.** rate; *synonyms* (*n*) price, worth, pace, value, percentage, (*v*) assess, estimate, evaluate, appreciate, appraise, compute, count, calculate, merit, put, **6.** scold; *synonyms* (*v*) berate, abuse, rail, admonish, castigate, grouch, grumble, jaw, lash, vituperate, rate, (*n*) nag, nagger, (*adj*) shrew, curse, **7.** reprimand; *synonyms* (*n*) admonition, chastisement, reproof, castigation, reprehension, admonishment, scolding, (*v*) chastise, discipline, correct, condemn, criminate, reprehend, check, chasten; *antonym* (*v*) commend, **8.** rebuke; *synonyms* (*n*) rebuff, chiding, lesson, criticism, punishment, reproval, warning, slight, sneap, (*v*) lambaste, upbraid, resist, rag, snub, lambast; *antonym* (*v*) compliment, **9.** strike; *synonyms* (*n*) assault, clap, smash, tap, (*v*) bang, beat, hit, slap, box, bump, clout, coin, collide, mint, whack, **10.** smack; *synonyms* (*n*) blow, flavor, wallop, crack, cuff, relish, (*v*) savor, kiss, buss, bash, punch, savour, taste, thwack, (*adj*) dash, **11.** reprove; *synonym* (*v*) disapprove.

boaia lecture; *synonyms* (*n*) address, discourse, harangue, reprimand, speech, talk, oration, censure, declaim, homily, (*v*) rebuke, sermon, chide, preach, instruct.

boaki 1. embattled; *synonyms* (*adj*) crenelate, crenelated, crenellate, crenellated, battlemented, beleaguered, castellated, castled, depressed, indented, militant, targeted, besieged, (*v*) battled, **2.** hit; *synonyms* (*v*) strike, attain, belt, blow, bump, collide, encounter, (*n*) knock, bang, smash, touch, chance, bash, beat, collision; *antonyms* (*n*) failure, flop, **3.** admonished; *synonyms* (*adj*) chastened, rebuked, reprimanded, reproved, **4.** hurt; *synonyms* (*v*) pain, wound, afflict, injure, ail, cost, (*adj*) evil, (*n*) harm, damage, detriment, ache, disadvantage, abuse, distress, lesion; *antonyms* (*v*) encourage, (*adj*) uninjured, unhurt, **5.** blown; *synonyms* (*v*) distended, (*adj*) breathless, puffy, panting, swollen, winded, dissipated, flushed, gasping, high, late, mighty, misspent, pursy, spent, **6.** blamed; *synonyms* (*adj*) damned, goddam, goddamn, goddamned, infernal, damnable, aeonian, ageless, answerable, beatified, blame, blasted, blessed, damn, darned, **7.** compensated; *synonyms* (*v*) paid, contented, hired, satisfied, (*adj*) remunerated, salaried, compensable, stipendiary, remunerative; *antonym* (*adj*) unpaid, **8.** reproved; *synonym* (*adj*) admonished, **9.** rebuked, **10.** rated;

synonym (*adj*) nominal, **11.** touched; *synonyms* (*v*) compassionate, pitiful, sympathetic, bad, decayed, lentiginous, mildewed, moldy, (*adj*) affected, cracked, crazy, daft, insane, tinged, interested; *antonym* (*adj*) untouched, **12.** reprimanded.

boba cheat; *synonyms* (*v*) trick, beguile, betray, defraud, fake, beat, deceive, fleece, (*n*) swindle, con, fraud, bilk, impostor, sham, charlatan.

bobai 1. bargain; *synonyms* (*n*) contract, agreement, covenant, deal, treaty, arrangement, buy, chaffer, compact, promise, purchase, steal, (*v*) exchange, agree, (*adj*) cheap; *antonym* (*n*) rip-off, **2.** buy; *synonyms* (*v*) acquire, bribe, take, shop, accept, believe, get, admit, attain, corrupt, hold, obtain, procure, (*n*) bargain, acquisition; *antonym* (*v*) sell, **3.** trade; *synonyms* (*n*) business, barter, commerce, swap, switch, clientele, craft, employment, interchange, occupation, profession, calling, custom, (*v*) change, merchandise; *antonym* (*adj*) charitable.

bobaiaki traded; *synonyms* (*adj*) practiced, professional.

bobaraki 1. bow; *synonyms* (*n*) arc, curve, obeisance, turn, curvature, (*v*) bend, arch, stoop, duck, buckle, crouch, incline, kowtow, crook, defer, **2.** stoop; *synonyms* (*v*) bow, deign, condescend, descend, squat, couch, cringe, flex, grovel, lean, huddle, hunch, droop, demean, (*n*) porch.

bobarakiaki bowed; *synonyms* (*adj*) bent, arched, curved, crooked, inclined, arced, arching, arciform, arcuate, bandy; *antonyms* (*adj*) straight, concave.

bobaranako 1. miss; *synonyms* (*v*) lack, lose, fail, jump, omit, overlook, long, drop, escape, (*n*) maid, girl, want, fille, missy, (*adj*) fault; *antonym* (*v*) perceive, **2.** pass; *synonyms* (*v*) flow, deliver, give, happen, lead, move, offer, overtake, live, advance, die, elapse, exceed, (*adj*) go, run.

bobaranakoaki missed; *synonyms* (*adj*) lost, baffled, befuddled, bemused, bewildered, confounded, confused, disoriented, forgotten, helpless, irretrievable, mazed, preoccupied.

bobitia nail; *synonyms* (*n*) arrest, pin, (*v*) catch, apprehend, collar, hook, strike, capture, cop, fasten, hit, nab, secure, spike, (*adj*) tack.

bobo 1. hammer; *synonyms* (*n*) pound, gavel, (*v*) strike, bang, beat, knock, tap, club, forge, hit, thrash, drive, drum, rap, batter, **2.** hit; *synonyms* (*v*) attain, belt, blow, bump, collide, encounter, clash, contact, (*n*) smash, touch, chance, bash, collision, play, clout; *antonyms* (*n*) failure, flop, **3.** strike; *synonyms* (*n*) assault, clap, (*v*) impress, slap, move, affect, box, buffet, coin, mint, whack, lash, hew, whip, afflict.

boboaki 1. hit; *synonyms* (*v*) strike, attain, belt, blow, bump, collide, encounter, (*n*) knock, bang, smash, touch, chance, bash, beat, collision; *antonyms* (*n*)

failure, flop, **2.** hammered; *synonyms* (*adj*) beaten, drunk.

bobonga complete; *synonyms* (*adj*) perfect, absolute, consummate, whole, full, stark, accomplished, all, (*v*) accomplish, achieve, close, finish, execute, act, attain; *antonyms* (*adj*) incomplete, partial, unfinished, abridged, shortened, sketchy, lacking, narrow, qualified, (*v*) neglect.

bobono 1. blockhead; *synonyms* (*n*) ass, dunderhead, beetlehead, dolt, dunce, fool, idiot, loggerhead, bonehead, dummy, fuckhead, knucklehead, moron, muttonhead, (*v*) block, **2.** obstinate; *synonyms* (*adj*) headstrong, obdurate, determined, inflexible, intractable, inveterate, disobedient, contrary, dogged, firm, stubborn, uncompromising, wayward, willful, contumacious; *antonyms* (*adj*) compliant, amenable, flexible, **3.** stupid; *synonyms* (*adj*) foolish, silly, dull, fatuous, idiotic, ridiculous, senseless, crass, insane, childish, dim, pointless, (*n*) simple, absurd, dullard; *antonyms* (*adj*) sensible, bright, clever, intelligent, shrewd, wise, **4.** stubborn; *synonyms* (*adj*) obstinate, hard, perverse, persistent, refractory, rigid, tenacious, difficult, recalcitrant, resolute, stiff, tough, opinionated, restive, strong; *antonym* (*adj*) irresolute.

bobota muster; *synonyms* (*v*) assemble, congregate, gather, collect, convene, marshal, rally, accumulate, amass, aggregate, call, garner, (*n*) levy, draft, gathering.

bobouro 1. astonished; *synonyms* (*adj*) amazed, astonish, dumbfounded, flabbergasted, stunned, aghast, astounded, bewildered, thunderstruck, astonied, **2.** surprised; *synonyms* (*adj*) astonished, shocked, startled, confused, curious, puzzled, questioning, quizzical, baffled, bemused, confounded, dazed, incredulous, inquiring, overcome; *antonym* (*adj*) indifferent.

bobuaka 1. fight; *synonyms* (*v*) combat, contest, quarrel, feud, argue, bicker, campaign, clash, contend, (*n*) battle, dispute, engagement, conflict, contention, (*adj*) brawl; *antonyms* (*v*) agree, retreat, withdrawal, **2.** costly; *synonyms* (*adj*) expensive, dear, precious, valuable, extravagant, high, luxurious, pricey, rich, sumptuous, invaluable, beloved, plush, priceless, pricy; *antonyms* (*adj*) cheap, worthless, **3.** jar; *synonyms* (*n*) jangle, blow, crock, container, jog, shake, amphora, bottle, crash, (*v*) jolt, creak, bump, collide, jounce, grate, **4.** expensive; *synonyms* (*adj*) costly, lavish, overpriced, exclusive, fine, exorbitant, splendid; *antonyms* (*adj*) inexpensive, reasonable, **5.** odd; *synonyms* (*adj*) grotesque, exceptional, funny, abnormal, curious, droll, eccentric, extraordinary, singular, strange, chance, novel, anomalous, bizarre, fantastic; *antonyms* (*adj*) normal, ordinary, even, typical, **6.** unequal; *synonyms* (*adj*) dissimilar, different, unlike, inadequate, lopsided, rough, uneven, unfair, disparate, disproportionate, unbalanced, unsymmetrical, inconsistent, insufficient, various; *antonym* (*adj*) equal.

boê gone; *synonyms* (*v*) extinct, (*adj*) dead, past, absent, deceased, exhausted, away, bygone, departed, desperate, bypast, foregone, hopeless, late, lost; *antonym* (*adj*) present.

boi 1. smell; *synonyms* (*n*) odor, fragrance, savor, aroma, bouquet, odour, savour, stench, flavor, smack, (*v*) reek, nose, perfume, scent, stink, **2.** property; *synonyms* (*n*) characteristic, capital, peculiarity, feature, belongings, character, asset, estate, goods, nature, place, wealth, (*adj*) attribute, quality, (*v*) possession.

boibarabara musty; *synonyms* (*adj*) moldy, fusty, rancid, stale, mouldy, bad, rank, obsolete, rotten, stuffy, threadbare, trite, damp, frowsty, (*v*) decayed; *antonym* (*adj*) fresh.

boibuako 1. associate; *synonyms* (*v*) affiliate, connect, company, link, relate, consort, (*n*) ally, assistant, companion, fellow, partner, accomplice, adjunct, acquaintance, colleague; *antonyms* (*v*) avoid, dissociate, distance, (*adj*) chief, (*n*) stranger, **2.** sociable; *synonyms* (*adj*) affable, amicable, friendly, outgoing, amiable, companionable, congenial, cordial, genial, social, gracious, agreeable, clubbable, conversable, convivial; *antonym* (*adj*) unsociable.

boibuakoaki associated; *synonyms* (*adj*) connected, related, affiliated, allied, united, attendant, attached, confederate, joined, linked, alike; *antonym* (*adj*) unrelated.

boituta unlucky; *synonyms* (*adj*) unfortunate, hapless, luckless, unhappy, untoward, inauspicious, sinister, adverse, disastrous, ominous, unsuccessful, doomed, unfavorable, poor, fatal; *antonyms* (*adj*) lucky, fortunate.

bokewe lye; *synonyms* (*n*) fable, fiction, law, lea, ley, lie, falsehood, siding, untruth.

boki book; *synonyms* (*n*) bible, journal, pamphlet, tome, volume, writing, text, manuscript, (*v*) order, reserve, apply, inscribe, list, record, arrest.

bôki 1. greatness; *synonyms* (*n*) grandeur, excellence, dimension, dignity, bulk, bigness, enormity, enormousness, grandness, magnitude, size, fame, eminence, glory, quantity, **2.** size; *synonyms* (*n*) measure, capacity, dimensions, extent, largeness, glue, amount, breadth, degree, mass, measurement, sizing, proportion, (*v*) gauge, scale; *antonyms* (*n*) length, slenderness.

bomaki grazed; *synonyms* (*adj*) hurt, raw.

bomanea 1. entrap; *synonyms* (*v*) enmesh, entangle, catch, ensnare, trap, deceive, decoy, entice, tangle, delude, frame, hook, inveigle, snare, allure, **2.** encircle; *synonyms* (*v*) beset, surround, besiege,

circle, embrace, bound, circumvent, enclose, encompass, environ, hem, begird, circumscribe, beleaguer, (*adv*) compass, **3.** surround; *synonyms* (*v*) encircle, gird, border, inclose, ring, round, skirt, envelop, entwine, blockade, edge, enfold, fence, (*n*) environment, environs.

bomaneaki 1. encircled; *synonyms* (*adj*) surrounded, enclosed, bounded, annular, annulate, annulated, bordered, circinate, circular, delimited, ingirt, ringed, wreathed, **2.** surrounded; *synonyms* (*v*) beset, begone, furnished, (*adj*) encircled, circumstanced, conditioned, entrenched, fixed, inside, rooted, implanted.

bomatoa 1. expensive; *synonyms* (*adj*) costly, sumptuous, dear, extravagant, luxurious, valuable, lavish, overpriced, exclusive, fine, high, precious, rich, exorbitant, invaluable; *antonyms* (*adj*) cheap, inexpensive, reasonable, worthless, **2.** overcharge; *synonyms* (*n*) extortion, (*v*) surcharge, overburden, overload, fleece, burden, swindle, bleed, gazump, hook, ornament, **3.** overprice; *synonym* (*v*) cheat.

bomatoaki overpriced; *synonyms* (*adj*) expensive, steep, dear, costly, exorbitant, extravagant, high, (*adv*) excessive, inflated, ridiculous.

bon 1. do; *synonyms* (*v*) act, cheat, commit, accomplish, complete, conduct, perform, achieve, make, practice, defraud, answer, arrange, (*n*) function, occasion; *antonyms* (*v*) neglect, unmake, **2.** indeed; *synonyms* (*adv*) actually, certainly, exactly, much, really, surely, greatly, absolutely, clearly, definitely, positively, precisely, so, truly, (*int*) forsooth; *antonym* (*adv*) possibly, **3.** have; *synonyms* (*v*) contain, gain, bear, carry, get, hold, possess, accept, acquire, eat, suffer, take, allow, bring, attain, **4.** fertilize; *synonyms* (*v*) impregnate, enrich, fecundate, feed, fertilise, fructify, cultivate, inseminate, **5.** done; *synonyms* (*adj*) finished, completed, over, gone, through, (*adv*) ended; *antonym* (*adj*) unfinished, **6.** am; *synonyms* (*n*) morning, americium, amateur, mama, mamma, mammy, mater, milliampere, mom, momma, mommy, mum, mummy, red, **7.** definitely; *synonyms* (*adv*) decidedly, specifically, undoubtedly, unquestionably, completely, determinately, distinctly, emphatically, explicitly, finally, firmly, indeed, indubitably, particularly, plainly; *antonyms* (*adv*) perhaps, doubtfully, maybe, vaguely, **8.** certainly; *synonyms* (*adv*) assuredly, necessarily, sure, inevitably, undeniably, verily, (*int*) yes; *antonym* (*adv*) questionably, **9.** are, **10.** actually; *synonyms* (*adv*) quite, presently, correctly, literally, authentically, right, physically, bodily, easily, effectually, indisputably, truthfully, accurately, actively, directly, **11.** quite; *synonyms* (*adv*) altogether, all, entirely, fully, sheer, enough, even, fairly, rather, stark, totally, well, wholly,

awfully, (adj) just; *antonym* (adv) extremely, **12.**
really; *synonyms* (adv) honestly, genuinely, real,
very, simply, practically, essentially, highly,
legitimately, substantially, faithfully, rattling, (adj)
sincerely, earnestly, **13.** sheer; *synonyms* (adj)
absolute, pure, mere, bold, diaphanous, filmy,
gauzy, gossamer, simple, steep, transparent,
regular, perpendicular, (n) perfect, entire;
antonyms (adj) gentle, thick, **14.** truly; *synonyms*
(adv) loyally, rightfully; *antonym* (adv) falsely, **15.**
real; *synonyms* (adj) genuine, material, physical,
true, concrete, literal, natural, positive, native,
good, certain, honest, sincere, (n) authentic, (v)
actual; *antonyms* (adj) unreal, imaginary, apparent,
artificial, fake, bogus, deceptive, false, fantasy,
imitation, insubstantial, mock, nominal, (v) pretend,
16. perfectly; *synonyms* (adv) thoroughly, utterly,
dead, flawlessly, clean; *antonyms* (adv) badly,
imperfectly, **17.** surely; *synonyms* (adv)
confidently, securely, (adj) doubtless, **18.** stark;
synonyms (adj) austere, bare, bleak, desolate, plain,
severe, bald, barren, harsh, naked, nude, hollow,
empty, hard, inhospitable.

boñ night; *synonyms* (n) dark, evening, dusk,
darkness, nighttime, twilight, (adj) nocturnal;
antonyms (n) day, light.

bonaki 1. done; *synonyms* (adj) finished, complete,
completed, over, gone, through, (adv) ended;
antonym (adj) unfinished, **2.** fertilized; *synonyms*
(adj) fertilised, impregnated, inseminated.

bonanga worth; *synonyms* (n) merit, value, cost,
price, virtue, importance, excellence, dignity,
quality, benefit, goodness, import, good, substance,
fortune; *antonym* (n) worthlessness.

bong 1. dark; *synonyms* (adj) black, dismal, cheerless,
dim, obscure, blind, blue, deep, gloomy, murky,
mysterious, (n) cloudy, darkness, evening, night;
antonyms (adj) bright, sunny, fair, clear, pale, pallid,
sunlit, (n) light, day, **2.** day; *synonyms* (n) daylight,
generation, age, daytime, epoch, time, crisis;
antonym (n) nighttime.

bongana 1. important; *synonyms* (adj) essential,
grave, fundamental, significant, chief, crucial, key,
remarkable, serious, earnest, authoritative, big,
central, consequential, considerable; *antonyms* (adj)
unimportant, insignificant, trivial, minor,
irrelevant, low, worthless, **2.** substantial;
synonyms (adj) actual, solid, firm, real, strong,
important, palpable, momentous, sturdy, sound,
concrete, ample, corporeal, durable, hearty;
antonyms (adj) insubstantial, small, ethereal, fine, **3.**
valuable; *synonyms* (adj) costly, estimable,
precious, beneficial, expensive, helpful, useful,
worthy, admirable, dear, invaluable, priceless,
profitable, rich, (n) treasure; *antonym* (adj) useless,
4. useful; *synonyms* (adj) handy, practical,

advantageous, convenient, effective, valuable,
functional, clever, constructive, efficient, gainful,
serviceable, usable, good, suitable; *antonym* (adj)
ineffective.

bonganga 1. momentous; *synonyms* (adj) important,
grave, significant, big, material, weighty,
consequential, memorable, considerable, critical,
crucial, major, serious, solemn, influential;
antonyms (adj) insignificant, trivial, **2.** pertinent;
synonyms (adj) apt, apropos, apposite, appropriate,
relevant, applicable, fitting, germane, pat, related,
suitable, felicitous; *antonyms* (adj) irrelevant,
inappropriate, unrelated.

bongata 1. durable; *synonyms* (adj) constant, lasting,
stable, permanent, enduring, firm, serviceable,
strong, sturdy, tough, abiding, continuing, eternal,
fixed, (v) fast; *antonyms* (adj) fragile, weak, flimsy,
lightweight, **2.** lasting; *synonyms* (adj) durable,
everlasting, continuous, perpetual, immortal,
aeonian, ageless, continual, eonian, persistent,
standing, chronic, continued, long, immovable;
antonyms (adj) short-lived, temporary, fleeting.

boni quite; *synonyms* (adv) altogether, absolutely, all,
completely, entirely, fully, sheer, exactly, enough,
even, fairly, rather, right, stark, (adj) just; *antonym*
(adv) extremely.

boniba notch; *synonyms* (n) cut, gap, mark, nick,
score, scratch, degree, grade, groove, (v) dent, hack,
indent, nock, hollow, jag.

bonibaki notched; *synonyms* (adj) jagged, serrated,
jaggy, serrate, toothed, erose, rough, uneven.

bonnano 1. agree; *synonyms* (v) accord, admit,
acknowledge, acquiesce, adjust, accede, bargain,
concord, correspond, fit, harmonize, suit,
compromise, align, (n) coincide; *antonyms* (v)
disagree, oppose, differ, argue, object, refuse,
refute, **2.** contract; *synonyms* (n) compact, charter,
agree, (v) covenant, concentrate, condense, narrow,
catch, compress, constrict, shrink, wrinkle,
abbreviate, (adj) abridge, shorten; *antonyms* (v)
expand, widen, stretch.

bonnanoaki contracted; *synonyms* (v) shrunk, (adj)
narrow, insular, contract, constricted, tight, bound.

bono 1. constipated; *synonyms* (adj) costive,
bellybound, close, cold, formal, impermeable,
reserved, unyielding, (v) bound, certain, destined,
resolved, **2.** closed; *synonyms* (v) tight, accurate,
adjoining, attentive, (adj) blind, blocked, finished,
shut, congested, fastened, exclusive, insular,
stopped, airtight, benighted; *antonym* (adj) open, **3.**
dull; *synonyms* (adj) dim, blunt, dense, dreary,
sluggish, bland, boring, cloudy, dark, dismal,
inactive, inert, obtuse, (v) deaden, dampen;
antonyms (adj) bright, lively, sharp, exciting,
interesting, lustrous, stimulating, amusing,
exhilarating, glittery, glossy, glowing, high-
pitched, intense, luminous, **4.** stupid; *synonyms*

(adj) foolish, silly, dull, fatuous, idiotic, ridiculous, senseless, crass, insane, childish, pointless, (n) simple, absurd, dullard, idiot; *antonyms* (adj) sensible, clever, intelligent, shrewd, wise, **5.** shut; *synonyms* (v) bar, seal, fasten, exclude, lock, (adj) closed, cut, (n) end, finish, confine, **6.** stopped; *synonyms* (adj) halted, unmoving, chinked, clogged, immobile, motionless, static, stationary, bunged, crashed, still, **7.** obstructed; *synonyms* (adj) hindered, foiled, frustrated, impedite, stymied, thwarted; *antonym* (adj) successful.

bonoike 1. choke; *synonyms* (v) asphyxiate, block, throttle, stifle, clog, foul, gag, obstruct, smother, strangle, suffocate, check, die, close, congest; *antonym* (v) unclog, **2.** suffocate; *synonyms* (v) choke, drown, extinguish, quench, garrote, hang, kill.

bonoikeaki 1. choked; *synonyms* (adj) clogged, suffocated, congested, anxious, high-strung, insecure, neurotic, strained, suffocate, tense, clotted, **2.** suffocated; *synonyms* (v) asphyxied, (adj) choked.

bononano 1. anger; *synonyms* (n) displeasure, fury, rage, indignation, resentment, annoyance, (v) enrage, incense, aggravate, displease, exasperate, irritate, offend, wrath, fume; *antonyms* (n) pleasure, composure, (v) please, placate, pacify, calm, **2.** mad; *synonyms* (adj) frantic, frenzied, demented, foolish, insane, delirious, angry, crazy, distracted, frenetic, lunatic, wild, irate, (n) furious, anger; *antonyms* (adj) sane, sensible, **3.** irritate; *synonyms* (v) chafe, fret, gall, harass, annoy, bother, goad, grate, infuriate, provoke, vex, disturb, inflame, irk, itch; *antonym* (v) soothe, **4.** irritated; *synonyms* (adj) annoyed, exasperated, aggravated, enraged, incensed, displeased, inflamed, nettled, provoked, sore, disgruntled, infuriated, mad, riled; *antonyms* (adj) unprovoked, pleased, **5.** displeased; *synonyms* (v) pained, afflicted, (adj) discontented, dissatisfied, irritated, peeved, unhappy, **6.** angry; *synonyms* (adj) fierce, raging, vehement, maddened, fuming, outraged, piqued, splenetic, angered, boiling, choleric, hot, huffy, indignant, irascible; *antonym* (adj) gentle, **7.** cross; *synonyms* (n) crisscross, affliction, check, (v) intersect, baffle, cover, thwart, bilk, (adj) crabbed, crabby, cantankerous, grouchy, grumpy, traverse, cranky; *antonyms* (v) uncross, (adj) good-tempered, **8.** displease; *synonyms* (v) disgust, affront, rile, pique, trouble, discompose; *antonym* (v) satisfy.

bononanoaki 1. displeased; *synonyms* (v) pained, afflicted, (adj) discontented, disgruntled, angry, dissatisfied, annoyed, irritated, peeved, unhappy; *antonym* (adj) pleased, **2.** crossed; *synonyms* (v) matted, unhinged, frustrated, (adj) across, crossbred, decussated, hybrid, interbred, intercrossed, mixed, intersected, **3.** irritated;

synonyms (adj) exasperated, aggravated, enraged, furious, incensed, irate, displeased, inflamed, nettled, provoked, sore, infuriated, mad, riled; *antonyms* (adj) calm, unprovoked, **4.** angered; *synonyms* (adj) huffy, maddened, spleened, ferocious, fierce, savage, tempestuous, wild.

bonota 1. close; *synonyms* (adj) near, adjacent, nearby, accurate, tight, approximate, narrow, (v) compact, stop, conclude, (adv) by, about, (n) end, finish, conclusion; *antonyms* (adj) distant, airy, fresh, loose, far, (v) open, start, **2.** block; *synonyms* (n) bar, barricade, pad, clog, cluster, barrier, (v) arrest, hinder, encumber, halt, lock, obstruct, parry, plug, (adj) lump; *antonyms* (v) free, unblock, **3.** mend; *synonyms* (v) repair, improve, correct, cure, amend, better, doctor, heal, restore, convalesce, ameliorate, bushel, (n) fix, patch, botch; *antonym* (v) break, **4.** shut; *synonyms* (v) close, seal, fasten, exclude, (adj) closed, cut, (n) confine, **5.** patch; *synonyms* (n) darn, fleck, mend, plot, bed, blot, freckle, bit, blotch, dapple, field, maculation, clout, (v) piece, cobble, **6.** obstruct; *synonyms* (v) block, check, choke, delay, hamper, impede, screen, intercept, debar, blockade, counteract, dam, embarrass, frustrate, interrupt; *antonyms* (v) encourage, facilitate, **7.** stop; *synonyms* (v) stand, catch, disrupt, dwell, pause, desist, discontinue, (n) hold, stay, cease, curb, recess, cessation, closure, (adj) quit; *antonyms* (v) continue, begin, permit, prolong.

bonotaki 1. blocked; *synonyms* (adj) jammed, clogged, locked, barren, blind, congested, foiled, fruitless, frustrated, infertile, lodged, plugged, sterile, stiff, stuck; *antonyms* (adj) successful, free, **2.** closed; *synonyms* (v) close, tight, accurate, adjoining, attentive, (adj) blocked, finished, shut, fastened, exclusive, insular, stopped, airtight, benighted, black; *antonym* (adj) open, **3.** shut; *synonyms* (v) bar, seal, fasten, exclude, lock, (adj) closed, cut, (n) end, finish, confine, **4.** obstructed; *synonyms* (adj) hindered, impedite, stymied, thwarted, **5.** stopped; *synonyms* (adj) halted, unmoving, chinked, immobile, motionless, static, stationary, bunged, crashed, still, **6.** patched; *synonyms* (adj) besmirched, damaged, flyblown, mean, ragged, spotted, sullied, tainted, tarnished.

bonotakiaki shut; *synonyms* (v) close, bar, seal, fasten, exclude, lock, (adj) closed, cut, tight, (n) end, finish, confine; *antonym* (v) open.

bonotaninga 1. indocile; *synonyms* (adj) disobedient, uncontrollable, fractious, intractable, ungovernable, unruly, untoward, boisterous, indocible, untrained, unwilling, robustious, rumbustious, uncorrectable, unteachable, **2.** disobedient; *synonyms* (adj) contrary, insubordinate, defiant, disorderly, naughty, rebellious, wayward, headstrong, willful, contumacious, froward, perverse, refractory, unmanageable, bad; *antonyms* (*adj*) obedient, compliant, good, well-behaved, orderly, **3**. deaf; *synonyms* (*adj*) earless, blind, indifferent, unhearing, aspirated, atonic, deve, inattentive, oblivious, regardless, surd, thoughtless, unaware, unconcerned, (*v*) deafen; *antonym* (*adj*) hearing.

bonu tattoo; *synonym* (*v*) drumroll.

bonua sketch; *synonyms* (*n*) plan, drawing, outline, scheme, cartoon, project, (*v*) design, paint, draft, draw, picture, chart, delineate, depict, describe.

boo correspondingly; *synonyms* (*adv*) accordingly, similarly, according, agreeably, agreeingly, alike, also, appropriately, consequently, equally, like, suitably, conformably, fittingly, (*adj*) likewise.

boongata 1. rancid; *synonyms* (*adj*) bad, putrid, high, musty, rank, sour, fetid, rotten, stale, tainted, offensive, reasty, foul, (*v*) decayed, moldy; *antonym* (*adj*) fresh, **2**. stale; *synonyms* (*adj*) old, commonplace, hackneyed, banal, corny, flat, insipid, stagnant, trite, dull, obsolete, cold, rancid, shabby, (*v*) dry; *antonyms* (*adj*) original, innovative, **3**. sour; *synonyms* (*adj*) morose, sharp, acid, bitter, severe, gruff, dour, glum, grim, pungent, sullen, (*v*) acidify, ferment, (*n*) harsh, acidity; *antonyms* (*adj*) sweet, kindly.

booraoi 1. fair; *synonyms* (*adj*) equitable, clear, beautiful, average, dispassionate, fine, impartial, reasonable, sweet, candid, (*adv*) clean, (*n*) bazaar, blonde, carnival, (*v*) bright; *antonyms* (*adj*) unfair, biased, dark, exceptional, unjust, partial, foul, imbalanced, mismatched, prejudiced, unwarranted, **2**. just; *synonyms* (*adv*) exactly, hardly, newly, simply, (*adj*) fair, right, correct, accurate, honest, barely, fit, good, righteous, upright, appropriate; *antonym* (*adj*) wrong.

boota 1. gather; *synonyms* (*v*) deduce, convene, accumulate, amass, assemble, collect, compile, congregate, flock, garner, meet, tuck, earn, rally, (*n*) fold; *antonyms* (*v*) disperse, scatter, **2**. collect; *synonyms* (*v*) gather, pick, accrue, acquire, aggregate, cluster, collate, cull, harvest, hoard, raise, accept, catch, derive, gain; *antonym* (*v*) distribute.

bootaki 1. gathered; *synonyms* (*adj*) collected, deepened, accumulated, amassed, assembled, collective, congregate, equanimous, massed, poised, **2**. collected; *synonyms* (*v*) composed, (*adj*) calm, cool, sober, tranquil, unflappable, dispassionate, gathered, imperturbable, peaceful, placid, quiet, sedate, serene, staid; *antonym* (*adj*) agitated.

boou 1. improved; *synonyms* (*adj*) better, enhanced, new, reformed, advanced, amplified, augmented, bigger, changed, converted, enlarged, finer, greater, healthier, higher; *antonyms* (*adj*) inferior, worse, lesser, **2**. new; *synonyms* (*adj*) green, modern,

novel, original, additional, inexperienced, innovative, raw, recent, strange, unaccustomed, unprecedented, young, (*adv*) fresh, lately; *antonyms* (*adj*) old, familiar, outgoing, second-hand, traditional, used, less, old-fashioned, stale, (*adv*) past.

bora 1. expensive; *synonyms* (*adj*) costly, sumptuous, dear, extravagant, luxurious, valuable, lavish, overpriced, exclusive, fine, high, precious, rich, exorbitant, invaluable; *antonyms* (*adj*) cheap, inexpensive, reasonable, worthless, **2**. exorbitant; *synonyms* (*adj*) excessive, unreasonable, immoderate, enormous, inordinate, outrageous, steep, unconscionable, extortionate, extreme, preposterous, undue, usurious, expensive; *antonym* (*adj*) affordable, **3**. overprice; *synonyms* (*v*) cheat, fleece, swindle, **4**. overcharge; *synonyms* (*n*) extortion, (*v*) surcharge, overburden, overload, burden, bleed, gazump, hook, ornament, **5**. shelf; *synonyms* (*n*) ledge, rack, bank, flat, projection, board, frame, shallows, stand, support, bench, bracket, breakers, (*adj*) shallow.

borababaua 1. plain; *synonyms* (*adj*) ordinary, comprehensible, intelligible, apparent, clear, downright, easy, evident, homely, humble, level, manifest, obvious, simple, (*n*) flat; *antonyms* (*adj*) elaborate, fancy, unclear, mottled, multicolored, ornate, attractive, concealed, confused, fussy, two-colored, **2**. stretched; *synonyms* (*adj*) taut, extended, stiff, tense, tight, strained, expanded, outstretched, elongated, outspread, prolonged, protracted, assiduous, close, delayed; *antonym* (*adj*) brief.

borabi crease; *synonyms* (*n*) wrinkle, line, plait, pleat, pucker, bend, crimp, groove, (*v*) fold, crinkle, crumple, cockle, furrow, rumple, crush; *antonym* (*v*) smooth.

borabiaki creased; *synonyms* (*adj*) crumpled, furrowed, lined, rumpled, wrinkled, wrinkly, corrugated, bent, craggy, crinkly, dented, disheveled, dishevelled, frowzled, puckered; *antonym* (*adj*) smooth.

boraitia plane; *synonyms* (*n*) airplane, face, aeroplane, aircraft, degree, stage, surface, (*v*) flatten, shave, (*adj*) level, even, flat, horizontal, smooth, flush.

boraitiaki planned; *synonyms* (*adj*) deliberate, intended, intentional, calculated, designed, aforethought, plotted, premeditated, scheduled, fixed, future, prepared, studied; *antonyms* (*adj*) spontaneous, unplanned.

borake ascend; *synonyms* (*v*) rise, arise, mount, climb, scale, uprise, increase, appear, escalate, jump, lift, soar; *antonyms* (*v*) descend, drop.

boraki overpriced; *synonyms* (*adj*) expensive, steep, dear, costly, exorbitant, extravagant, high, (*adv*) excessive, inflated, ridiculous.

boraoi 1. balanced; *synonyms* *(adj)* equal, even, firm, regular, stable, steady, harmonious, impartial, steadfast, symmetrical, uniform, fast, fixed, secure, unprejudiced; *antonyms* *(adj)* biased, unbalanced, unfair, **2.** adjust; *synonyms* *(v)* temper, accommodate, adapt, align, acclimatize, balance, fit, fix, reconcile, regulate, set, alter, arrange, *(adj)* dress, *(n)* square, **3.** fit; *synonyms* *(v)* agree, meet, suit, correspond, accord, befit, *(adj)* decorous, apt, applicable, appropriate, becoming, *(n)* adjust, convulsion, attack, burst; *antonyms* *(adj)* unfit, inappropriate, unwell, **4.** agree; *synonyms* *(v)* admit, acknowledge, acquiesce, accede, bargain, concord, harmonize, compromise, assent, check, concur, consent, consort, contract, *(n)* coincide; *antonyms* *(v)* disagree, oppose, differ, argue, object, refuse, refute, **5.** evening; *synonyms* *(n)* dusk, dark, eve, eventide, nightfall, sunset, twilight, night, sundown; *antonyms* *(n)* dawn, daybreak, **6.** equalize; *synonyms* *(v)* compensate, equate, compare, counterbalance, equalise, level, match, counteract, **7.** equal; *synonyms* *(adj)* comparable, adequate, balanced, commensurate, equivalent, alike, coordinate, corresponding, fair, identical, *(v)* parallel, rival, equalize, *(n)* compeer, peer; *antonyms* *(adj)* unequal, different, repressive, disproportionate, inconsistent, uneven, unlike, **8.** balance; *synonyms* *(n)* poise, symmetry, excess, remainder, account, complement, counterpoise, credit, equality, parity, proportion, *(v)* offset, contrast, settle, audit; *antonyms* *(n)* imbalance, *(v)* unbalance, **9.** flatten; *synonyms* *(v)* fell, demolish, press, drop, roll, squash, depress, destroy, ruin, smash, smooth, unfold, bulldoze, deflate, trample; *antonyms* *(v)* build, crumple, **10.** conform; *synonyms* *(v)* assimilate, observe, comply, follow, frame, obey, answer, acclimate, fulfill, integrate; *antonym* *(v)* deviate, **11.** equivalent; *synonyms* *(adj)* analogous, like, matching, same, equipollent, akin, reciprocal, related, similar, tantamount, *(n)* counterpart, eq, substitute, *(v)* consideration; *antonym* *(n)* dissimilar, **12.** flat; *synonyms* *(adj)* dull, bland, plain, insipid, plane, tasteless, dreary, boring, absolute, dead, downright, lifeless, monotonous, *(n)* apartment, *(v)* uninteresting; *antonyms* *(adj)* exciting, high-pitched, bumpy, **13.** matched; *synonyms* *(adj)* fitting, complementary, fitted, conformable, duplicate, coordinated, dual, engaged, exact, harmonized, jump, right, suitable, synchronized, twin, **14.** even; *synonyms* *(adv)* yet, all, e'en, nevertheless, notwithstanding, *(adj)* direct, constant, equable, flat, horizontal, clear, equitable, flush, homogeneous, *(v)* regularize; *antonyms* *(adj)* irregular, jagged, **15.** match; *synonyms* *(n)* competition, couple, bout, contest, game, tally, associate, catch, *(v)* mate, harmonise, fellow, pair, jibe, marry, conform; *antonyms* *(v)* clash,

contradict, **16.** unify; *synonyms* *(v)* combine, amalgamate, consolidate, merge, blend, join, unite, wed, coalesce, mix, fuse, connect, unitize, commix, mingle, **17.** suitable; *synonyms* *(adj)* good, proper, convenient, eligible, apposite, correct, desirable, pertinent, due, respectable, befitting, compatible, competent, decent, *(n)* seasonable; *antonyms* *(adj)* unsuitable, wrong, improper, **18.** quantify; *synonyms* *(v)* measure, gauge, evaluate, assess, determine, quantitate, calculate, appraise, compute, mensurate, rate, valuate, value, **19.** regular; *synonyms* *(adj)* normal, orderly, common, customary, general, methodical, ordinary, formal, accurate, habitual, commonplace, accustomed, consistent, *(n)* familiar, *(v)* conventional; *antonyms* *(adj)* erratic, unusual, variable, asymmetrical, extraordinary, straight, **20.** same; *synonyms* *(adj)* self, very, indistinguishable, interchangeable.

boraoiaki 1. balanced; *synonyms* *(adj)* equal, even, firm, regular, stable, steady, harmonious, impartial, steadfast, symmetrical, uniform, fast, fixed, secure, unprejudiced; *antonyms* *(adj)* biased, unbalanced, unfair, **2.** matched; *synonyms* *(adj)* fitting, complementary, fitted, conformable, duplicate, level, alike, coordinated, corresponding, dual, engaged, exact, harmonized, jump, right, **3.** flattened; *synonyms* *(adj)* compressed, depressed, planate, trodden, unconscious, compacted, firmed, trampled; *antonym* *(adj)* loose, **4.** equalized; *synonyms* *(adj)* equalised, coordinate, poised, **5.** adjusted; *synonyms* *(adj)* adapted, altered, set, applied, familiarised, familiarized, prepared, ready, resigned, associate, balanced, calm, equable, equally, equitable, **6.** unified; *synonyms* *(adj)* incorporated, integrated, united, amalgamated, incorporate, interconnected, merged, allied, collective, combined, concurrent, corporate, entire, inseparable, intermingled.

borata flat; *synonyms* *(adj)* dull, bland, even, plain, insipid, level, plane, tasteless, dreary, boring, absolute, dead, downright, *(n)* apartment, *(v)* uninteresting; *antonyms* *(adj)* exciting, high-pitched, bumpy.

borau navigate; *synonyms* *(v)* cruise, guide, sail, fly, pilot, voyage, cross, maneuver.

borauakina 1. journey; *synonyms* *(n)* jaunt, excursion, expedition, passage, trip, way, course, flight, outing, pilgrimage, *(v)* go, travel, cruise, fare, navigate, **2.** embark; *synonyms* *(v)* ship, leave, enter, sail, start, undertake, venture, open, emplane, adventure, approach, imbark, inship, enrol, enroll; *antonym* *(v)* disembark, **3.** navigate; *synonyms* *(v)* guide, fly, pilot, voyage, cross, maneuver.

boreitiman 1. constable; *synonyms* *(n)* policeman, alderman, burgomaster, portreeve, alguazil, tipstaff, beagle, committeeman, councilman, councilwoman, detective, seneschal, sheriff, shrieve, warden, **2**. policeman; *synonyms* (*n*) cop, officer, watchman, peon, crest, messenger, officeholder, pawn, poon, servant, (*adj*) patrolman.

borengarenga spotted; *synonyms* (*adj*) mottled, dappled, speckled, blotchy, dotted, flyblown, piebald, multicolored, dirty, spotty, stained, tainted, besmirched, damaged, freckled; *antonym* (*adj*) plain.

boretia print; *synonyms* (*n*) imprint, mark, impression, engraving, copy, lettering, picture, facsimile, letterpress, reproduction, (*v*) impress, photograph, issue, engrave, stamp.

boretiaki printed; *synonyms* (*adj*) print, imprinted, stamped, embossed, marked.

boria tainted; *synonyms* (*v*) rotten, reasty, blighted, cankered, (*adj*) corrupt, rancid, rank, bad, contaminated, faulty, musty, vitiated, putrid, dirty, besmirched; *antonyms* (*adj*) pure, unadulterated, unchanged, untarnished.

botaki 1. group; *synonyms* (*n*) bunch, brigade, collection, crowd, flock, gang, association, clump, company, gathering, (*v*) assemblage, class, cluster, rank, sort, **2**. assemble; *synonyms* (*v*) amass, accumulate, aggregate, convene, gather, meet, call, collect, compile, concentrate, converge, group, make, rally, edit; *antonyms* (*v*) dismantle, disperse, disband, disassemble, **3**. assembled; *synonyms* (*adj*) accumulated, amassed, collected, collective, united, accrued, built, congregate, massed, equanimous, fabricated, fancied, fictional, fictitious, invented, **4**. grouped; *synonym* (*adj*) sorted, **5**. gather; *synonyms* (*v*) deduce, assemble, garner, tuck, earn, reap, derive, extract, acquire, conclude, crease, cull, gain, glean, (*n*) fold; *antonym* (*v*) scatter, **6**. affiliate; *synonyms* (*n*) member, chapter, (*v*) associate, ally, unite, adopt, assort, band, consort, join, **7**. unite; *synonyms* (*v*) combine, blend, coalesce, connect, link, amalgamate, attach, fuse, merge, tie, unify, couple, agree, conjoin, league; *antonyms* (*v*) separate, divide, **8**. reunite; *synonyms* (*v*) reconcile, reunify, integrate, conciliate, appease, pacify, placate, propitiate, reannex, settle, square, resolve, **9**. party; *synonyms* (*n*) assembly, crew, affair, bevy, celebration, do, faction, meeting, club, knot, body, circle, entertainment, festivity, function.

botakiaki 1. assembled; *synonyms* (*adj*) accumulated, amassed, collected, collective, united, accrued, aggregate, built, congregate, massed, equanimous, fabricated, fancied, fictional, fictitious, **2**. affiliated; *synonyms* (*adj*) connected, attached, allied, related, (*v*) associated, **3**. grouped; *synonym* (*adj*) sorted, **4**. gathered; *synonyms* (*adj*) deepened, assembled, poised, **5**. united; *synonyms* (*adj*) joined, joint, combined, cooperative, mutual, concerted, mixed, common,

conjunctive, undivided, conjunct, unanimous, conjoint, linked, (*v*) consolidated; *antonyms* (*adj*) individual, separate, divided.

botam 1. caress; *synonyms* (*n*) rub, touch, endearment, (*v*) fondle, stroke, pat, pet, tickle, coddle, cuddle, kiss, **2**. stroke; *synonyms* (*n*) beat, caress, hit, mark, apoplexy, attack, bang, impact, knock, line, streak, (*v*) buffet, lick, move, (*adj*) blow.

botau 1. mixed; *synonyms* (*adj*) miscellaneous, assorted, composite, heterogeneous, integrated, medley, impure, amalgamated, diverse, intermingled, motley, varied, indiscriminate, (*v*) blended, mingled; *antonyms* (*adj*) homogeneous, insular, pure, **2**. equal; *synonyms* (*adj*) agree, comparable, adequate, balanced, commensurate, equivalent, (*v*) match, compare, correspond, even, parallel, rival, equalize, (*n*) compeer, peer; *antonyms* (*adj*) unequal, different, repressive, disproportionate, inconsistent, uneven, unlike, (*v*) differ, **3**. match; *synonyms* (*n*) equal, competition, couple, duplicate, bout, (*v*) mate, meet, accord, harmonise, harmonize, balance, fellow, fit, pair, coincide; *antonyms* (*v*) clash, contradict, **4**. suit; *synonyms* (*n*) lawsuit, plea, action, case, petition, cause, courtship, (*v*) accommodate, adapt, answer, become, please, adjust, satisfy, befit, **5**. sufficient; *synonyms* (*adj*) enough, satisfactory, competent, proper, good, acceptable, ample, full, plenty, due, abundant, comfortable, decent, fair, suitable; *antonyms* (*adj*) inadequate, insufficient, **6**. suitable; *synonyms* (*adj*) appropriate, apt, right, convenient, eligible, apposite, correct, desirable, fitting, pertinent, decorous, respectable, fitted, (*n*) seasonable, (*v*) becoming; *antonyms* (*adj*) inappropriate, unsuitable, wrong, improper.

botauaki 1. matched; *synonyms* (*adj*) fitting, complementary, equal, fitted, conformable, duplicate, level, alike, coordinated, corresponding, dual, engaged, exact, harmonized, jump, **2**. suited; *synonyms* (*v*) fit, convenient, (*adj*) suitable, proper, appropriate, adapted, apt, good, capable, eligible, useful, desirable, seemly.

boti 1. merge; *synonyms* (*v*) amalgamate, blend, combine, melt, coalesce, fuse, commingle, integrate, meld, unite, absorb, aggregate, consolidate, incorporate, (*adj*) immerse; *antonyms* (*v*) separate, split, **2**. muster; *synonyms* (*v*) assemble, congregate, gather, collect, convene, marshal, rally, accumulate, amass, call, garner, summon, (*n*) levy, draft, gathering.

botia boss; *synonyms* (*n*) chief, governor, head, overseer, superior, ruler, administrator, captain, director, executive, foreman, leader, (*v*) administer, govern, direct.

botitibaua obtuse; *synonyms* (*adj*) dim, dull, blunt, dense, stupid, heavy, slow, insensitive, doltish, dumb, thick, simple, flat, gross, pointless; *antonym* (adj) bright.

boto 1. essential; *synonyms* (adj) necessary, crucial, important, inherent, requisite, constituent, basic, elementary, fundamental, natural, central, constitutional, (n) necessity, base, (v) imperative; *antonyms* (adj) minor, secondary, (n) inessential, optional, option, unimportant, peripheral, luxury, **2**. basic; *synonyms* (adj) first, cardinal, initial, primary, primordial, basal, bottom, introductory, key, plain, primitive, simple, vital, (n) essential, staple; *antonyms* (adj) complex, extra, **3**. principled; *synonyms* (adj) conscientious, ethical, moral, scrupulous, upstanding; *antonyms* (adj) unprincipled, dishonest, immoral.

botonaine pretty; *synonyms* (adv) very, fairly, (adj) beautiful, fair, graceful, lovely, attractive, charming, handsome, good-looking, picturesque, dainty, cute, elegant, (n) nice; *antonym* (adj) ugly.

botonimwaane handsome; *synonyms* (adj) elegant, beautiful, fair, charming, fine, generous, attractive, bountiful, comely, bonny, big, bounteous, exquisite, gorgeous, graceful; *antonyms* (adj) ugly, unattractive.

botu 1. fatigued; *synonyms* (adj) exhausted, tired, weary, beat, worn, jaded, spent, fagged; *antonyms* (adj) fresh, refreshed, **2**. fatigue; *synonyms* (n) exhaustion, tiredness, weariness, lethargy, boredom, (v) exhaust, tire, bore, enervate, fag, harass, jade, wear, drain, (adj) flag; *antonyms* (n) energy, (v) refresh, **3**. bore; *synonyms* (v) dig, bother, annoy, drill, perforate, pierce, plague, tap, (n) caliber, diameter, nuisance, well, annoyance, calibre, (adj) pother; *antonyms* (v) interest, excite, fascinate, **4**. bored; *synonyms* (adj) uninterested, listless, sick, blasé, discontented, droopy, inattentive, indifferent, lazy, lethargic, sophisticated, unconcerned, cynical, lackluster, melancholic, **5**. boring; *synonyms* (adj) dull, tedious, tiresome, annoying, arid, bland, dreary, monotonous, prosaic, tame, uninteresting, wearisome, vapid, drab, (n) drilling; *antonyms* (adj) exciting, fascinating, interesting, gripping, original, thrilling, varied, **6**. tired; *synonyms* (adj) fatigued, hackneyed, banal, commonplace, stale, threadbare, trite, haggard, stock, drowsy, whacked, corny, limp, weak, enervated; *antonyms* (adj) invigorated, alert, energetic, strong, **7**. tire; *synonyms* (v) fatigue, pall, prostrate, disturb, molest, tease, pester, drudge, irritate, outwear, perplex, sap, (n) tyre, labor, **8**. weary; *synonyms* (adj) aweary, languid, irksome, gloomy, (v) irk, depress, cloy, toil, vex, **9**. wear; *synonyms* (v) dress, endure, bear, waste, fray, frazzle, assume, break, (n) clothing, apparel, attire, clothes, garb, erosion, garment.

botuaki 1. fatigued; *synonyms* (adj) exhausted, tired, weary, beat, worn, jaded, spent, fagged; *antonyms* (adj) fresh, refreshed, **2**. bored; *synonyms* (adj) uninterested, listless, sick, blasé, discontented, droopy, inattentive, indifferent, lazy, lethargic, sophisticated, unconcerned, cynical, lackluster, melancholic, **3**. worn; *synonyms* (v) decayed, rotten, (adj) haggard, shabby, ragged, tattered, threadbare, drawn, fatigued, careworn, decrepit, faded, frayed, raddled, seedy; *antonym* (adj) new.

botuakina 1. endure; *synonyms* (v) bear, stand, suffer, accept, undergo, allow, bide, brook, defy, dwell, last, (n) abide, be, (adj) continue, support; *antonyms* (v) succumb, perish, **2**. consistent; *synonyms* (adj) coherent, uniform, agreeable, compatible, congruous, constant, logical, conformable, consonant, regular, unchanging, concurrent, unvarying, accordant, equable; *antonyms* (adj) inconsistent, erratic, contradictory, illogical, unpredictable, unreliable, **3**. persevere; *synonyms* (v) persist, endure, keep, pursue, remain, apply; *antonyms* (v) stop, surrender, yield, **4**. support; *synonyms* (n) help, aid, comfort, maintenance, patronage, (v) assist, prop, back, brace, encourage, maintain, boost, carry, confirm, corroborate; *antonyms* (n) hindrance, (v) oppose, neglect, undermine, abandon, reject, weaken, **5**. tenacious; *synonyms* (adj) stubborn, adhesive, dogged, obstinate, firm, persistent, resolute, tough, sticky, determined, glutinous, persevering, pertinacious, (v) retentive, strong, **6**. preserve; *synonyms* (v) defend, guard, hold, save, cure, pickle, protect, uphold, perpetuate, observe, (n) conserve, jam, jelly, conserves, marmalade; *antonym* (v) destroy, **7**. persistent; *synonyms* (adj) durable, continual, insistent, lasting, permanent, continuous, chronic, consistent, incessant, perpetual, relentless, unrelenting, habitual, indefatigable, (n) frequent; *antonyms* (adj) contained, occasional.

botuakinaki 1. supported; *synonyms* (v) borne, carried, conveyed, supporting, (adj) bolstered, based, (adv) on, **2**. preserved; *synonyms* (adj) condite, pickled, safe, whole, potted, sealed.

botumara slack; *synonyms* (adj) loose, lax, idle, indolent, negligent, baggy, flaccid, limp, flabby, neglectful, dilatory, inattentive, (v) remiss, dull, slow; *antonyms* (adj) tight, strict, taut, thorough.

bou 1. current; *synonyms* (adj) common, contemporary, fashionable, instant, actual, fresh, modern, new, popular, (n) flow, stream, run, afloat, movement, (prep) course; *antonyms* (adj) obsolete, past, old, old-fashioned, previous, **2**. advanced; *synonyms* (adj) sophisticated, progressive, senior, higher, precocious, late, cultured, developed, elevated, forward, liberal, ripe, superior, innovative; *antonyms* (adj) conservative, inferior, **3**.

novel; *synonyms* (*n*) fiction, romance, book, narrative, (*adj*) curious, different, unprecedented, original, newfangled, recent, strange, unfamiliar, unique, extraordinary, abnormal, **4**. new; *synonyms* (*adj*) green, novel, additional, inexperienced, raw, unaccustomed, young, current, unknown, virgin, extra, immature, (*adv*) lately, freshly, recently; *antonyms* (*adj*) familiar, outgoing, second-hand, traditional, used, less, stale, **5**. modern; *synonyms* (*adj*) advanced, latest, present, stylish, chic, latter, up-to-date, existing, modernistic, modish, groundbreaking, later, mod, topical, (*n*) neoteric; *antonyms* (*adj*) ancient, antiquated, prehistoric, neurotic, old-time, primordial, **6**. latest; *synonyms* (*adj*) final, last, hot, ultimate, newest, (*n*) vogue, **7**. recent; *synonym* (*adj*) immediate, **8**. trendy; *synonyms* (*adj*) smart, in, voguish; *antonyms* (*adj*) unfashionable, out-of-date, unpopular.

boua 1. open; *synonyms* (*adj*) frank, obvious, artless, exposed, free, honest, bare, forthright, guileless, ingenuous, naked, (*v*) expand, give, (*n*) candid, clear; *antonyms* (*adj*) devious, secretive, concealed, furtive, hidden, limited, repressive, reserved, restricted, secret, blocked, cautious, (*v*) shut, end, (*tr v*) close, **2**. sunder; *synonyms* (*v*) divide, part, separate, dissever, tear, share, cleave, detach, (*n*) sever, divorce, fragment, **3**. spike; *synonyms* (*n*) pin, point, barb, ear, needle, prickle, plug, peak, quill, (*v*) impale, pierce, nail, spear, transfix, lace, **4**. split; *synonyms* (*v*) crack, cut, fracture, slit, burst, breach, division, fork, rift, (*n*) break, rip, rupture, cleavage, cleft, parting; *antonyms* (*v*) join, unite, merge.

bouaia chop; *synonyms* (*v*) ax, chip, cleave, cut, hack, hash, hew, mince, slash, slice, smite, crop, crunch, divide, grind.

bouaiaki chopped; *synonyms* (*adj*) shredded, sliced.

bouaki 1. split; *synonyms* (*v*) crack, cut, fracture, slit, burst, divide, separate, divorce, breach, cleave, (*n*) break, rip, rupture, tear, cleavage; *antonyms* (*v*) join, unite, merge, **2**. spiked; *synonyms* (*adj*) pointed, laced, thorny, sharp, acute, altered, firm, jagged, tied, **3**. opened; *synonyms* (*v*) blown, distended, exhausted, inflated, (*adj*) open, candid, exposed, assailable, blatant, blazing, clear, conspicuous, lawless, loose, through.

boubu tired; *synonyms* (*adj*) exhausted, fatigued, hackneyed, weary, banal, commonplace, stale, threadbare, trite, beat, haggard, jaded, stock, worn, drowsy; *antonyms* (*adj*) fresh, invigorated, alert, refreshed, energetic, original, strong.

bowi deliberate; *synonyms* (*adj*) careful, calculated, circumspect, slow, thoughtful, conscious, (*v*) consider, cogitate, consult, debate, think, confer, contemplate, ponder, reflect; *antonyms* (*adj*)

accidental, chance, unintentional, hasty, ingenuous, involuntary, spontaneous.

brok frozen; *synonyms* (*adj*) cold, frosty, arctic, frigid, glacial, wintry, freezing, icy, stiff, congealed, chilled, chilly, gelid, iced, set; *antonyms* (*adj*) hot, moving.

btaona ravel; *synonyms* (*n*) involve, (*v*) entangle, tangle, disentangle, unravel, unwind, knot, embrangle, snarl, dishevel, fray, imbrangle, (*adj*) embarrass, enmesh, encumber.

bu 1. budding; *synonyms* (*adj*) young, blossoming, emergent, green, juvenile, youthful, **2**. mate; *synonyms* (*n*) match, companion, partner, associate, compeer, consort, fellow, friend, spouse, husband, colleague, (*v*) equal, copulate, couple, (*adj*) comrade, **3**. emerge; *synonyms* (*v*) appear, arise, emanate, spring, transpire, develop, issue, occur, rise, surface, begin, escape, loom, materialize, originate, **4**. partner; *synonyms* (*n*) copartner, accomplice, ally, collaborator, mate, pal, confederate, wife, accessory, assistant, cooperator, pardner, helper, man, (*v*) escort, **5**. spouse; *synonyms* (*n*) woman, (*v*) neogamist.

bû spouse; *synonyms* (*n*) consort, husband, partner, wife, man, mate, match, companion, woman, (*v*) neogamist.

bü but; *synonyms* (*conj*) while, (*adv*) alone, only, though, barely, however, merely, simply, yet, exclusively, if, just, (*prep*) besides, except, excluding.

bua 1. mouth; *synonyms* (*n*) jaw, lip, aperture, lips, edge, entrance, brim, (*v*) grimace, articulate, pronounce, speak, utter, vocalize, blab, deliver, **2**. casualty; *synonyms* (*n*) accident, loss, prey, damage, disaster, fatality, chance, circumstance, contingency, death, misfortune, victim, adventure, hazard, **3**. missing; *synonyms* (*v*) lost, (*adj*) lacking, absent, gone, wanting, deficient, away, misplaced, nonexistent; *antonym* (*adj*) present, **4**. solid; *synonyms* (*adj*) firm, dense, compact, consistent, hard, real, strong, good, fixed, massive, secure, substantial, fast, hearty, (*v*) close; *antonyms* (*adj*) soft, unreliable, loose, gaseous, permeable, runny, transparent, watery, (*n*) liquid, **5**. thick; *synonyms* (*adj*) stupid, crowded, dull, heavy, opaque, slow, stocky, deep, dim, familiar, fat, gross, intimate, muddy, (*n*) midst; *antonyms* (*adj*) thin, intelligent, bright, sparse, clever, diluted, fine, slight.

buaakaka bad; *synonyms* (*adj*) evil, adverse, harmful, immoral, naughty, poisonous, sad, sinister, wicked, malicious, infamous, appalling, awful, damaging, (*v*) decayed; *antonyms* (*adj*) fresh, pleasant, well, well-behaved, (*n*) good.

buabeka 1. glutton; *synonyms* (*n*) epicure, wolverine, gormandizer, gourmand, trencherman, guttler, carcajou, beast, epicurean, gulch, gulist, hedonist, lurcher, connoisseur, crammer, **2**.

insatiable; *synonyms* (*adj*) greedy, gluttonous, insatiate, ravenous, voracious, avaricious, avid, unsatiable, **3.** gluttonous; *synonyms* (*adj*) insatiable, edacious, hoggish, **4.** greedy; *synonyms* (*adj*) eager, covetous, desirous, acquisitive, glutton, grasping, piggish, esurient, grabby, hungry, selfish, envious, keen, predatory, (*v*) mercenary; *antonym* (*adj*) generous, **5.** voracious; *synonyms* (*adj*) rapacious, ravening, famished, devouring, starved, **6.** overeat; *synonyms* (*v*) cram, fill, gorge, jam, overindulge, stuff, binge, block, englut, engorge, flood, glut, gormandise, gormandize, gourmandize; *antonym* (*v*) nibble.

buabua 1. lumpy; *synonyms* (*adj*) chunky, coarse, dull, dumpy, gawky, gritty, indolent, rude, squat, squatty, stumpy, (*v*) lumpish, (*n*) failure, **2.** thick; *synonyms* (*adj*) dense, compact, stupid, crowded, heavy, opaque, slow, stocky, close, deep, dim, familiar, fat, gross, intimate; *antonyms* (*adj*) thin, intelligent, bright, sparse, clever, diluted, fine, slight, transparent.

buai beard; *synonyms* (*n*) awn, hair, whiskers, disguise, sloven, (*v*) dare, defy, camouflage, mask, (*adj*) brave.

buaiai smoky; *synonyms* (*adj*) reeky, murky, hazy, fumid, vaporous, muddy, opaque, burnt, choleric, famish, filthy, foul, (*v*) smutty, sooty, dusty.

buaka 1. false; *synonyms* (*adj*) bastard, counterfeit, untrue, deceitful, dishonest, erroneous, artificial, assumed, deceptive, disloyal, faithless, fake, fictitious, sham, ersatz; *antonyms* (*adj*) true, real, correct, factual, faithful, genuine, natural, truthful, honest, valid, **2.** fight; *synonyms* (*v*) combat, contest, quarrel, feud, argue, bicker, campaign, clash, contend, (*n*) battle, dispute, engagement, conflict, contention, (*adj*) brawl; *antonyms* (*v*) agree, retreat, withdrawal, **3.** improper; *synonyms* (*adj*) false, inappropriate, illicit, illegitimate, bad, coarse, indecent, indecorous, unsuitable, wrong, amiss, faulty, undue, gross, impolite; *antonyms* (*adj*) proper, suitable, fitting, polite, **4.** combat; *synonyms* (*n*) fight, encounter, action, fighting, fray, war, hostility, affray, struggle, (*v*) oppose, resist, wrestle, tilt, attack, engage, **5.** bad; *synonyms* (*adj*) evil, adverse, harmful, immoral, naughty, poisonous, sad, sinister, wicked, malicious, infamous, appalling, awful, damaging, (*v*) decayed; *antonyms* (*adj*) fresh, pleasant, well, well-behaved, (*n*) good, **6.** battle; *synonyms* (*n*) scuffle, warfare, row, strife, tussle, bout, competition, crusade, hostilities, skirmish, confrontation, (*v*) scrap, grapple, compete, disagree, **7.** wrong; *synonyms* (*adj*) harm, ill, improper, incorrect, abuse, criminal, inaccurate, iniquitous, unjust, (*n*) damage, injure, injury, injustice, crime, hurt; *antonyms* (*adj*) law-abiding, (*adv*) correctly, (*v*) right, (*n*) justice, **8.**

offensive; *synonyms* (*adj*) foul, disgusting, distasteful, abusive, aggressive, loathsome, nauseous, abominable, disagreeable, impertinent, insulting, (*n*) assault, (*v*) odious, nasty, hateful; *antonyms* (*adj*) complimentary, inoffensive, defensive, tasteful, **9.** unbecoming; *synonyms* (*adj*) unseemly, indelicate, untoward, unworthy, shameful, unbefitting, incongruous, inept, unbeseeming, uncomely, unfit, degrading, low, misbecoming, rude; *antonyms* (*adj*) becoming, dignified, **10.** unjust; *synonyms* (*adj*) unfair, partial, injurious, inequitable, unrighteous, wrongful, unjustified, unmerited, unreasonable, hard, illegal, oppressive, rough, sinful, undeserved; *antonyms* (*adj*) fair, just, equitable, reasonable, rightful, **11.** struggle; *synonyms* (*n*) strain, effort, exertion, scramble, pull, flounder, (*v*) attempt, endeavor, labor, strive, aim, essay, push, tug, clamber; *antonyms* (*v*) flourish, glide.

buakaka 1. evil; *synonyms* (*adj*) bad, corrupt, criminal, ill, wicked, depraved, destructive, harmful, malign, (*n*) damage, adversity, detriment, disaster, depravity, malice; *antonyms* (*adj*) kindhearted, (*n*) good, goodness, righteousness, **2.** disagreeable; *synonyms* (*adj*) difficult, distasteful, nasty, offensive, uncomfortable, cantankerous, cross, ungrateful, abhorrent, bitter, horrible, objectionable, obnoxious, painful, sour; *antonyms* (*adj*) agreeable, friendly, pleasant, good-natured, amiable, **3.** malicious; *synonyms* (*adj*) malevolent, evil, spiteful, venomous, vicious, cruel, envious, mean, mischievous, pernicious, poisonous, unkind, wanton, despiteful, ill-natured; *antonyms* (*adj*) benevolent, kind, harmless, **4.** corrupt; *synonyms* (*adj*) rotten, canker, dishonest, impure, (*n*) poison, (*v*) adulterate, contaminate, taint, bribe, debase, defile, infect, buy, pervert, pollute; *antonyms* (*adj*) honest, moral, principled, pure, **5.** bad; *synonyms* (*adj*) adverse, immoral, naughty, sad, sinister, malicious, infamous, appalling, awful, damaging, devilish, disagreeable, dreadful, hurtful, (*v*) decayed; *antonyms* (*adj*) fresh, well, well-behaved, **6.** hurtful; *synonyms* (*adj*) deleterious, detrimental, baneful, cutting, injurious, baleful, noisome, noxious, prejudicial, snide, grievous, dangerous, distressing, inimical, ruinous; *antonym* (*adj*) pleasing, **7.** impure; *synonyms* (*adj*) defiled, dirty, bastard, filthy, foul, sordid, squalid, unclean, profane, contaminated, indecent, lewd, libidinous, licentious, muddy; *antonyms* (*adj*) noxious; *synonyms* (*adj*) deadly, lethal, malignant, nocuous, pestilent, toxic, unhealthy, insanitary, disadvantageous, fatal, insalubrious, pestilential, unwholesome, corrupting; *antonym* (*adj*) innocuous, **9.** rancid; *synonyms* (*adj*) putrid, high, musty, rank, fetid, stale, tainted, reasty, fulsome, smelly, malodorous, off, strong, (*v*) moldy, **10.** vile; *synonyms* (*adj*) contemptible, despicable, low, ignoble, disgusting, revolting, sorry, atrocious, beastly, loathsome, nauseating, repulsive, shameful, sickening, (v) base; *antonym* (adj) attractive, **11.** vicious; *synonyms* (adj) brutal, barbarous, savage, profligate, fierce, ferocious, reprobate, heinous, dissolute, fell, furious, harsh, violent, sinful, perverse; *antonym* (adj) gentle, **12.** pernicious; *synonyms* (adj) mortal, calamitous, virulent, cursed, insidious, **13.** wicked; *synonyms* (adj) unholy, vile, diabolical, hellish, iniquitous, ungodly, impious, black, dark, diabolic, fiendish, infernal, nefarious, severe, terrible; *antonyms* (adj) innocent, pious.

buakaki embattled; *synonyms* (adj) crenelate, crenelated, crenellate, crenellated, battlemented, beleaguered, castellated, castled, depressed, indented, militant, targeted, besieged, (v) battled.

buakana 1. attack; *synonyms* (n) incursion, thrust, aggression, fit, onset, onslaught, seizure, (v) assault, assail, attempt, aggress, charge, invade, raid, accuse; *antonyms* (n) defense, (v) defend, protect, retreat, **2.** combat; *synonyms* (n) fight, encounter, action, brawl, conflict, contest, fighting, fray, war, hostility, affray, contention, engagement, (v) battle, clash, **3.** fight; *synonyms* (v) combat, quarrel, feud, argue, bicker, campaign, contend, compete, box, crusade, (n) dispute, squabble, struggle, competition, confrontation; *antonyms* (v) agree, withdrawal.

buakoako dense; *synonyms* (adj) compact, thick, close, crowded, deep, crass, dim, dull, heavy, impenetrable, solid, stupid, concentrated, dumb, firm; *antonyms* (adj) bright, insightful, loose, clever, intelligent, readable, simple, sparse.

buaraku musty; *synonyms* (adj) moldy, fusty, rancid, stale, mouldy, bad, rank, obsolete, rotten, stuffy, threadbare, trite, damp, frowsty, (v) decayed; *antonym* (adj) fresh.

buariki greedy; *synonyms* (adj) eager, avid, gluttonous, covetous, desirous, acquisitive, glutton, grasping, piggish, esurient, grabby, hungry, insatiable, ravenous, (v) avaricious; *antonym* (adj) generous.

buata 1. bound; *synonyms* (v) leap, border, bounce, limit, circumscribe, confine, pounce, rebound, (n) spring, jump, boundary, edge, barrier, compass, hop; *antonym* (adj) free, **2.** plan; *synonyms* (n) aim, map, figure, chart, intent, outline, pattern, scheme, invent, form, (v) design, devise, intend, plot, arrange.

buataki 1. bounded; *synonyms* (adj) finite, restricted, delimited, limited, encircled, enclosed, local, qualified, surrounded, belted, compassed, contiguous, defined, definite, determinate, **2.** planned; *synonyms* (adj) deliberate, intended, intentional, calculated, designed, aforethought, plotted, premeditated, scheduled, fixed, future,

prepared, studied; *antonyms* (adj) spontaneous, unplanned.

bubai 1. plunder; *synonyms* (v) loot, pillage, despoil, harry, spoil, devastate, destroy, maraud, ransack, strip, divest, forage, (n) booty, depredation, despoliation, **2.** rob; *synonyms* (v) filch, pinch, deprive, pilfer, plunder, rifle, fleece, lift, purloin, steal, pick, defraud, hook, pluck, sack, **3.** undress; *synonyms* (v) disrobe, unclothe, discase, doff, unrobe, uncase, (n) dishabille, disarray; *antonym* (v) dress, **4.** strip; *synonyms* (n) band, slip, ribbon, shred, zone, (v) peel, denude, pare, bare, bereave, dismantle, skin, undress, decorticate, disarm; *antonym* (v) decorate.

bubaiaki 1. plundered; *synonyms* (adj) looted, pillaged, despoiled, fleeced, ransacked, ravaged, sacked, **2.** robed; *synonyms* (adj) appareled, attired, clothed, dressed, garbed, garmented, habilimented, fixed, polished, vested, **3.** undressed; *synonyms* (adj) nude, naked, unclad, unclothed, bare, raw, unappareled, unattired; *antonym* (adj) covered, **4.** stripped; *synonyms* (adj) exposed, undressed, desolate, stark.

bubu 1. foggy; *synonyms* (adj) cloudy, hazy, misty, brumous, bleary, blurred, fuzzy, murky, opaque, thick, blear, dark, clouded, muddy, muzzy; *antonym* (adj) clear, **2.** misty; *synonyms* (adj) foggy, dim, indistinct, nebulous, dull, wet, gloomy, damp, obscure, steamy, turbid, unclear, vague, blurry, cloud, **3.** blunt; *synonyms* (adj) bluff, candid, direct, forthright, frank, outspoken, plain, round, abrupt, brusque, downright, obtuse, plainspoken, (v) deaden, numb; *antonyms* (adj) sharp, devious, pointed, (v) hone, sharpen, **4.** dusty; *synonyms* (adj) powdery, dirty, sandy, sooty, dry, mealy, branny, pulverulent, unclean, **5.** smoky; *synonyms* (adj) reeky, fumid, vaporous, burnt, choleric, famish, filthy, foul, fumacious, fumous, gray, hot, reechy, (v) smutty, dusty, **6.** pulverized; *synonyms* (adj) powdered, fine, pulverised, crushed, broken, minute, minced, pounded, **7.** powdery; *synonyms* (adj) pulverized, psammous, sabulous, crumbly, brittle, gritty, powdry, arenaceous, arenose, crumbling, flaky, grainy, gravelly, impalpable.

bubua 1. grind; *synonyms* (v) labor, toil, comminute, crunch, drudge, grate, abrade, chew, crush, file, mash, scrape, sharpen, (n) mill, drudgery, **2.** rub; *synonyms* (v) fray, gall, chafe, caress, fret, furbish, graze, irritate, massage, scratch, shine, wipe, (n) check, brush, hitch, **3.** pulverize; *synonyms* (v) grind, pound, powder, demolish, smash, bruise, disintegrate, pulverise, shatter, bray, granulate, powderize.

bubuaka 1. bad; *synonyms* (adj) evil, adverse, harmful, immoral, naughty, poisonous, sad, sinister, wicked, malicious, infamous, appalling, awful, damaging, (*v*) decayed; *antonyms* (*adj*) fresh, pleasant, well, well-behaved, (*n*) good, **2. useless;** *synonyms* (*adj*) futile, pointless, unnecessary, needless, abortive, fruitless, hopeless, worthless, idle, barren, superfluous, bootless, incompetent, ineffective, ineffectual; *antonyms* (*adj*) useful, helpful, competent, effective, convenient, necessary, valuable.

bubuaki 1. ground; *synonyms* (*n*) base, cause, land, floor, reason, dirt, field, soil, account, country, basis, (*v*) bottom, found, establish, fix; *antonym* (*n*) ceiling, **2.** pulverized; *synonyms* (*adj*) powdery, powdered, fine, pulverised, crushed, broken, minute, minced, pounded.

bubuônibai elbow; *synonyms* (*n*) bend, cubitus, angle, joint, (*v*) poke, jostle, nudge, push, shove, jolt, crowd, hustle.

bubuôniwai knee; *synonyms* (*n*) elbow, genu, scythe, sickle, zigzag, angle, hinge, junction, know, stifle.

bubura 1. big; *synonyms* (*adj*) ample, major, heavy, important, significant, thick, sturdy, generous, adult, bad, burly, considerable, great, hefty, (*adv*) large; *antonyms* (*adj*) little, puny, (*adv*) small, (*syn*) tiny, **2.** great; *synonyms* (*adj*) eminent, famous, gigantic, big, distinguished, extensive, extreme, grand, chief, capital, celebrated, dignified, fantastic, fine, glorious; *antonyms* (*adj*) awful, insignificant, mild, **3.** monstrous; *synonyms* (*adj*) enormous, atrocious, grotesque, heinous, huge, monster, immense, dreadful, flagitious, grievous, preposterous, ugly, inordinate, exorbitant, abnormal, **4.** fat; *synonyms* (*adj*) stout, corpulent, dense, bulky, fatty, fertile, fleshy, gainful, greasy, gross, obese, (*n*) avoirdupois, blubber, cream, (*v*) fatten; *antonyms* (*adj*) thin, slim, skinny, slender, **5.** gigantic; *synonyms* (*adj*) colossal, mammoth, giant, stupendous, gargantuan, massive, monstrous, vast, monumental, terrific, gigantean, infinite, prodigious, tremendous, whopping, **6.** broad; *synonyms* (*adj*) wide, comprehensive, general, sweeping, free, blanket, capacious, deep, full, inclusive, liberal, spacious, tolerant, widespread, (*n*) female; *antonyms* (*adj*) narrow, specific, **7.** chubby; *synonyms* (*adj*) buxom, fat, plump, round, chunky, pudgy, tubby, overweight, **8.** grand; *synonyms* (*adj*) excellent, gorgeous, elevated, exalted, majestic, superb, beautiful, high, brilliant, heroic, impressive, lordly, magnificent, proud, (*n*) noble; *antonyms* (*adj*) unimpressive, humble, modest, **9.** bulky; *synonyms* (*adj*) unwieldy, cumbersome, substantial, awkward, clumsy, ponderous, stocky, voluminous, weighty, brawny, (*adv*) portly; *antonyms* (*adj*) compact, manageable, **10.** huge; *synonyms* (*adj*) elephantine, excessive, jumbo, untold, cavernous, cosmic, mighty, mountainous, roomy; *antonym* (*adj*) miniature, **11.** stout; *synonyms* (*adj*) bold, hardy, husky, robust,

strong, fearless, hearty, gallant, brave, chubby, healthy, lusty, resolute, solid, stalwart; *antonym* (*adj*) flimsy, **12.** thick; *synonyms* (*adj*) stupid, crowded, dull, opaque, slow, close, dim, familiar, intimate, muddy, obtuse, broad, impenetrable, concentrated, (*n*) midst; *antonyms* (*adj*) intelligent, bright, sparse, clever, diluted, slight, transparent.

bûbura large; *synonyms* (*adj*) big, ample, extensive, generous, broad, bulky, considerable, handsome, high, heavy, abundant, capacious, great, gross, hefty; *antonyms* (*adj*) small, cramped, insignificant.

buburakaei 1. immense; *synonyms* (*adj*) huge, vast, colossal, enormous, gigantic, great, immeasurable, big, boundless, giant, infinite, large, endless, extensive, extreme; *antonyms* (*adj*) small, tiny, **2.** titanic; *synonyms* (*adj*) massive, mammoth, stupendous, immense, **3.** terrific; *synonyms* (*adj*) marvelous, tremendous, fantastic, wonderful, shocking, dreadful, formidable, appalling, brilliant, fabulous, frightful, magnificent, marvellous, splendid, (*v*) terrible; *antonym* (*adj*) awful.

buburamaiu 1. forceful; *synonyms* (*adj*) assertive, cogent, dynamic, effective, emphatic, pithy, strenuous, active, compelling, convincing, energetic, insistent, passionate, persuasive, powerful; *antonyms* (*adj*) weak, unconvincing, lightweight, mild, **2.** insistent; *synonyms* (*adj*) exigent, stubborn, pressing, clamant, crying, importunate, instant, persistent, imperative, adamant, dogged, forceful, obstinate, unremitting, unyielding; *antonym* (*adj*) halfhearted, **3.** headstrong; *synonyms* (*adj*) intractable, disobedient, froward, rash, unruly, wayward, willful, headlong, contumacious, heady, inflexible, mulish, perverse, pigheaded, (*v*) ungovernable; *antonym* (*adj*) biddable, **4.** insist; *synonyms* (*v*) affirm, assert, contend, claim, asseverate, declare, maintain, urge, importune, press, argue, force, dwell, hold, persist, **5.** obstinate; *synonyms* (*adj*) headstrong, obdurate, determined, inveterate, contrary, firm, uncompromising, cussed, defiant, refractory, resolute, stiff, sullen, tenacious, unbending; *antonyms* (*adj*) compliant, amenable, flexible, **6.** stubborn; *synonyms* (*adj*) hard, rigid, difficult, recalcitrant, tough, opinionated, restive, strong, fractious, pertinacious, steadfast, immovable, sturdy, inexorable, set; *antonym* (*adj*) irresolute, **7.** vivacious; *synonyms* (*adj*) animated, lively, spirited, cheerful, sprightly, vibrant, brisk, buoyant, effervescent, gay, merry, spry, vigorous, exuberant, agile; *antonyms* (*adj*) dull, lethargic, listless.

buburatautau round; *synonyms* (*adv*) about, around, (*adj*) circular, plump, entire, chubby, complete, (*n*) circle, bout, ring, beat, circuit, (*v*) compass, turn, gird; *antonyms* (*adj*) slim, sharp.

buburerei 1. sparkling; *synonyms* *(adj)* lively, effervescent, bright, brilliant, radiant, bubbly, glittering, glittery, scintillant, scintillating, shining, bubbling, *(n)* sparkle, scintillation, glitter; *antonyms* *(adj)* still, dull, **2.** shrinking; *synonyms* *(v)* lessening, *(adj)* timid, fearful, shy, bashful, cowardly, nervous, delicacy, demur, qualm, *(n)* shrinkage, contraction, decrease, recoil, reduction; *antonym* *(n)* growth.

bubutei 1. foggy; *synonyms* *(adj)* cloudy, hazy, misty, brumous, bleary, blurred, fuzzy, murky, opaque, thick, blear, dark, clouded, muddy, muzzy; *antonym* *(adj)* clear, **2.** misty; *synonyms* *(adj)* foggy, dim, indistinct, nebulous, dull, wet, gloomy, damp, obscure, steamy, turbid, unclear, vague, blurry, cloud, **3.** hazy; *synonyms* *(adj)* faint, ambiguous, uncertain, filmy, overcast, weak, confused, imprecise, indefinite, loose, shadowy, wooly, fuliginous, groggy, rough; *antonyms* *(adj)* bright, distinct, precise.

bubuteiaki fogged; *synonyms* *(adj)* blurred, bleary, blurry, brumous, dazed, foggy, fuzzy, groggy, hazy, logy, muzzy, stuporous.

bubuti 1. apply; *synonyms* *(v)* dedicate, devote, employ, ask, consume, exercise, resort, use, utilize, lay, appeal, address, administer, consecrate, *(n)* give, **2.** beseech; *synonyms* *(v)* entreat, beg, adjure, crave, implore, pray, request, conjure, importune, plead, solicit, sue, supplicate, bid, demand, **3.** importune; *synonyms* *(v)* beseech, badger, besiege, pester, press, tease, worry, bother, harass, beset, molest, persecute, harry, nag, plague, **4.** borrow; *synonyms* *(v)* adopt, appropriate, assume, take, accept, acquire, plagiarize, cadge, obtain, sponge, usurp, charter, copy, imitate, *(n)* pledge; *antonym* *(v)* lend, **5.** beg; *synonyms* *(v)* desire, require, get, borrow, invite, invoke, petition, seek, woo, lobby, quest, *(n)* bey, **6.** demand; *synonyms* *(n)* claim, requirement, requisition, sale, call, want, application, *(v)* command, need, charge, expect, involve, necessitate, challenge, clamor; *antonym* *(v)* supply, **7.** petition; *synonyms* *(n)* entreaty, invocation, asking, prayer, plea, supplication, orison, grace, suit, wish, adroitness, communion, *(v)* apply, discourse, **8.** plead; *synonyms* *(v)* defend, argue, justify, urge, *(n)* allege, **9.** solicit; *synonyms* *(v)* court, entice, attract, accost, procure, inquire, move, allure, tempt, proposition, question, romance, *(n)* canvass, **10.** request; *synonyms* *(n)* invitation, inquiry, offer, bidding, behest, *(v)* order, query, summon, exact, propose, will, bespeak, tell.

bûbuti deep; *synonyms* *(adj)* thick, profound, absorbed, abstruse, broad, dark, rich, sound, strong, wide, esoteric, bright, large, abysmal, *(v)* intense; *antonyms* *(adj)* shallow, superficial, high, high-pitched, light, soft, weak.

bubutiaki 1. borrowed; *synonyms* *(adj)* foreign, rubato, secondary, rented, robbed, **2.** applied; *synonyms* *(adj)* practical, useful, concrete, activated, adjusted, correlated, devoted, exercised, practiced, related, tested, utilized; *antonym* *(adj)* theoretical, **3.** solicited.

bue 1. burn; *synonyms* *(v)* bite, glow, blaze, incinerate, scorch, sting, bake, beam, boil, cremate, flare, ignite, sunburn, *(n)* fire, *(adj)* flush; *antonym* *(v)* dawdle, **2.** aflame; *synonyms* *(adj)* ablaze, burning, excited, afire, passionate, alight, fiery, flaming, **3.** glow; *synonyms* *(n)* color, glare, sparkle, flash, brilliance, effulgence, fervor, *(v)* blush, gleam, glimmer, shine, burn, flame, kindle, warmth; *antonym* *(n)* dullness, **4.** burning; *synonyms* *(adj)* ardent, blazing, boiling, hot, aflame, fervent, impassioned, live, pressing, scorching, *(n)* combustion, firing, glowing, zealous, enthusiastic; *antonyms* *(adj)* cold, cool, trivial, **5.** burnt; *synonyms* *(v)* brent, *(adj)* burned, adust, baked, heated, sunburnt, adusted, arid, combust, dry, overcooked, overdone, consumed, dehydrated, desiccated; *antonym* *(adj)* underdone, **6.** hot; *synonyms* *(adj)* warm, feverish, fresh, blistering, eager, fast, peppery, pungent, spicy, angry, new, acrid, close, furious, gingery; *antonyms* *(adj)* mild, freezing, airy, bland, chilly, **7.** warm; *synonyms* *(adj)* affectionate, tender, cordial, lively, fond, loving, earnest, caring, genial, hearty, tepid, heartfelt, friendly, lukewarm, *(v)* heat; *antonyms* *(adj)* aloof, unfriendly, reserved, hostile, *(v)* chill.

bueaki burnt; *synonyms* *(v)* brent, *(adj)* burned, adust, baked, heated, sunburnt, adusted, arid, combust, dry, overcooked, overdone, consumed, dehydrated, desiccated; *antonym* *(adj)* underdone.

buia shelf; *synonyms* *(n)* ledge, rack, bank, flat, projection, board, frame, shallows, stand, support, bench, bracket, breakers, *(adj)* shallow.

buibuina 1. screen; *synonyms* *(n)* shade, blind, riddle, disguise, partition, veil, guard, *(v)* cover, shield, conceal, hide, mask, protect, shelter, cloak, **2.** shelter; *synonyms* *(n)* refuge, asylum, harbor, protection, sanctuary, security, hut, covert, haven, lee, lodge, *(v)* screen, defend, keep, *(adj)* defense; *antonym* *(v)* expose.

buibuinaki 1. screened; *synonyms* *(adj)* hidden, covered, concealed, hazy, invisible, isolated, secluded, select, shady, **2.** sheltered; *synonyms* *(adj)* secure, comfortable, safe, screened, cozy, *(v)* protected, private; *antonym* *(adj)* desolate.

buiérar fragrant; *synonyms* *(adj)* aromatic, balmy, odorous, spicy, sweet, odorant, odoriferous, redolent, savory, scented; *antonym* *(adj)* stinking.

buînai 1. loam; *synonyms* *(n)* clay, dirt, soil, land, glebe, ground, **2.** earth; *synonyms* *(n)* world, dust, lair, creation, ball, country, den, globe, hole, nature, orb, sphere, terra, ashes, cosmos.

buir 1. fault; *synonyms* (*n*) defect, blemish, error, failing, blame, blot, crime, delinquency, flaw, blunder, break, demerit, weakness, (*v*) deficiency, culpability; *antonyms* (*n*) merit, strength, **2.** error; *synonyms* (*n*) deviation, fault, mistake, wrong, delusion, lapse, oversight, guilt, misunderstanding, falsehood, confusion, erroneousness, fallacy, inaccuracy, misprint; *antonym* (*n*) correctness, **3.** sin; *synonyms* (*n*) evil, iniquity, misdeed, offense, wickedness, immorality, peccancy, transgression, vice, infraction, (*v*) offend, err, trespass, misbehave, fall; *antonyms* (*n*) virtue, piety.

buira fetid; *synonyms* (*adj*) foul, malodorous, noisome, putrid, smelly, rank, stinking, disgusting, rotten, foetid, rancid, decayed, dirty, unclean; *antonyms* (*adj*) fragrant, fresh.

buirābuir froth; *synonyms* (*n*) foam, effervescence, bubbles, spindrift, spray, (*v*) bubble, fizz, spume, boil, suds, effervesce, sparkle, ferment, seethe, (*adj*) scum.

bukarakara musty; *synonyms* (*adj*) moldy, fusty, rancid, stale, mouldy, bad, rank, obsolete, rotten, stuffy, threadbare, trite, damp, frowsty, (*v*) decayed; *antonym* (*adj*) fresh.

buki 1. fall; *synonyms* (*v*) decline, dip, decrease, descend, dive, rain, diminish, dwindle, sink, alight, (*n*) drop, descent, downfall, plunge, pitch; *antonyms* (*v*) rise, increase, ascend, climb, triumph, win, (*n*) ascent, **2.** thud; *synonyms* (*n*) thump, bang, crash, clunk, clump, boom, noise, (*v*) bump, beat, hit, rap, crump, crunch, knock, pound.

bukibuki 1. beat; *synonyms* (*v*) batter, flap, pulsate, throb, tick, trounce, whip, bat, baste, break, (*n*) pulse, thump, knock, round, cadence; *antonym* (*v*) lose, **2.** throb; *synonyms* (*n*) pulsation, thrill, pain, pounding, (*v*) beat, quiver, ache, pound, flutter, palpitate, shudder, smart, tingle, pant, shiver, **3.** pulsate; *synonyms* (*v*) shake, vibrate, **4.** paddle; *synonyms* (*n*) blade, oar, vane, (*v*) dabble, dodder, row, pull, spank, toddle, totter, coggle, larrup, **5.** palpitate; *synonyms* (*v*) flicker, tremble, (*n*) heave, **6.** thud; *synonyms* (*n*) bang, crash, clunk, clump, boom, noise, (*v*) bump, hit, rap, crump, crunch, scrunch, sound.

bukibukiaki 1. beaten; *synonyms* (*v*) beat, (*adj*) battered, overpowered, conquered, routed, overcome; *antonym* (*adj*) victorious, **2.** pulsated.

bukimake 1. emaciated; *synonyms* (*adj*) cadaverous, bony, gaunt, lean, thin, haggard, meager, skinny, wasted, slender, slim, atrophied, lanky, pinched, poor; *antonyms* (*adj*) plump, fat, **2.** thin; *synonyms* (*adj*) flimsy, light, slight, tenuous, emaciated, fine, rare, sparse, narrow, (*v*) dilute, sheer, subtle, scanty,

adulterate, cut; *antonyms* (*adj*) thick, concentrated, chubby, wide, broad, heavy, (*v*) thicken.

bukina 1. denounce; *synonyms* (*v*) condemn, censure, accuse, brand, criticize, decry, damn, reproach, arraign, betray, excoriate, fulminate, impeach, scold, charge; *antonym* (*v*) praise, **2.** blame; *synonyms* (*v*) reprimand, chide, fault, rebuke, attribute, knock, (*n*) attack, rap, onus, accusation, allegation, condemnation, inculpation, responsibility, indictment; *antonyms* (*v*) pardon, absolve, **3.** accuse; *synonyms* (*v*) incriminate, criminate, defame, denounce, indict, admonish, impute, inculpate, sue, (*n*) tax, **4.** incriminate; *synonyms* (*v*) involve, implicate, imply, **5.** indict; *synonyms* (*v*) blame, prosecute, (*n*) apprehend, cite, **6.** suspect; *synonyms* (*v*) doubt, distrust, mistrust, suppose, conjecture, guess, surmise, believe, disbelieve, divine, (*adj*) fishy, questionable, shady, suspicious, dubious; *antonyms* (*v*) trust, (*adj*) trustworthy, **7.** trim; *synonyms* (*adj*) tidy, neat, spruce, orderly, shipshape, (*v*) cut, dress, clip, garnish, shave, adorn, embellish, lop, prune, reduce; *antonym* (*adj*) fat.

bukinaki 1. accused; *synonyms* (*n*) panel, perpetrator, **2.** blamed; *synonyms* (*adj*) damned, goddam, goddamn, goddamned, infernal, damnable, aeonian, ageless, answerable, beatified, blame, blasted, blessed, damn, darned, **3.** trimmed; *synonyms* (*adj*) cut, cunning, demure, down, emasculated, gashed, gelded, level, mown, neat, shortened, slashed, sly, smooth, snoD.

bukinanganga 1. forebode; *synonyms* (*v*) augur, bode, prognosticate, anticipate, betoken, foretell, portend, predict, divine, guess, foreshadow, presage, abode, announce, call, **2.** prognosticate; *synonyms* (*v*) forecast, forebode, foreshow, prophesy, foresee, herald, foretoken, omen, calculate, prefigure.

bukinibaia 1. elbow; *synonyms* (*n*) bend, cubitus, angle, joint, (*v*) poke, jostle, nudge, push, shove, jolt, crowd, hustle, **2.** jostle; *synonyms* (*v*) jog, joggle, bump, encounter, shoulder, thrust, drive, squeeze, hurtle, (*n*) elbow, jostling, justle, (*adj*) clash, jar, **3.** nudge; *synonyms* (*v*) dig, prod, punch, (*n*) jab, touch, jerk, bother, glance, leer, shake, stab.

bukinimata 1. jeer; *synonyms* (*v*) deride, hiss, mock, taunt, barrack, insult, sneer, (*n*) gibe, flout, ridicule, scoff, mockery, banter, boo, derision; *antonym* (*v*) cheer, **2.** covet; *synonyms* (*v*) begrudge, desire, envy, long, aspire, crave, grudge, hanker, want, fancy, wish, **3.** sneer; *synonyms* (*n*) leer, smirk, grin, hoot, gleek, slight, dig, jibe, giggle, (*v*) jeer, scorn, gird, grimace, fling, jest.

bukinimataki coveted; *synonyms* (*adj*) desired, craved, exceptional, impressive, marketable.

bukiniwae heel; *synonyms* (*n*) blackguard, counter, dog, cad, scoundrel, shoe, sole, villain, bounder, (*v*) list, lean.

buki-ni-wai heel; *synonyms* (*n*) blackguard, counter, dog, cad, scoundrel, shoe, sole, villain, bounder, (*v*) list, lean.

bukinna 1. condemn; *synonyms* (*v*) blame, censure, reproach, castigate, criticize, decry, deplore, doom, excoriate, knock, sentence, upbraid, boo, chide, adjudge; *antonyms* (*v*) praise, approve, commend, free, pardon, 2. imprecate; *synonyms* (*v*) curse, damn, execrate, beshrew, blaspheme, cuss, swear, anathematize, accurse, anathemize, bedamn, impetrate.

bukinnaki condemned; *synonyms* (*adj*) damned, censured, guilty, convicted, doomed, appropriated, destined.

bukiruru tumble; *synonyms* (*n*) fall, drop, (*v*) jumble, stumble, collapse, crumble, plunge, slip, spill, topple, confuse, downfall, toss, crash, crumple.

bukiruruaki tumbled; *synonyms* (*adj*) disordered, upset.

bukirurunga 1. tumble; *synonyms* (*n*) fall, drop, (*v*) jumble, stumble, collapse, crumble, plunge, slip, spill, topple, confuse, downfall, toss, crash, crumple, 2. thud; *synonyms* (*n*) thump, bang, clunk, clump, boom, noise, (*v*) bump, beat, hit, rap, crump, crunch, knock, pound, pulsate.

bukirurungaki tumbled; *synonyms* (*adj*) disordered, upset.

bukitau 1. tumble; *synonyms* (*n*) fall, drop, (*v*) jumble, stumble, collapse, crumble, plunge, slip, spill, topple, confuse, downfall, toss, crash, crumple, 2. thud; *synonyms* (*n*) thump, bang, clunk, clump, boom, noise, (*v*) bump, beat, hit, rap, crump, crunch, knock, pound, pulsate.

bukitaua crash; *synonyms* (*n*) clash, collision, smash, clank, clatter, fall, impact, (*v*) bang, collapse, break, clang, crack, dash, plunge, ram.

bukitauaki tumbled; *synonyms* (*adj*) disordered, upset.

bukitiotio roam; *synonyms* (*v*) ramble, stray, wander, gallivant, meander, range, gad, drift, journey, rove, stroll, tramp, walk, prowl, (*adj*) err.

bukuna denounce; *synonyms* (*v*) condemn, censure, accuse, brand, criticize, decry, damn, reproach, arraign, betray, excoriate, fulminate, impeach, scold, charge; *antonym* (*v*) praise.

bukunaki suspected; *synonyms* (*adj*) suspect, supposed, distrusted, assumed.

bumbing 1. fit; *synonyms* (*v*) agree, accommodate, meet, suit, adapt, correspond, square, accord, dress, (*adj*) decorous, apt, applicable, appropriate, (*n*) adjust, convulsion; *antonyms* (*adj*) unfit, inappropriate, unwell, 2. muscular; *synonyms* (*adj*) athletic, brawny, strong, burly, hefty, powerful,

robust, husky, stalwart, stout, sturdy, manly, cogent, hardy, rugged; *antonyms* (*adj*) puny, slight, 3. strong; *synonyms* (*adj*) intense, able, deep, firm, stable, steady, durable, forcible, good, hard, influential, lusty, potent, rigid, secure; *antonyms* (*adj*) weak, bland, delicate, faint, feeble, frail, mild, pale, unconvincing, cowardly, diluted, dull, exhausted, flimsy, imperceptible.

bumoa 1. lead; *synonyms* (*v*) head, guide, conduct, contribute, direct, chair, conduce, control, go, govern, bring, convey, give, (*n*) clue, advantage; *antonym* (*v*) follow, 2. mount; *synonyms* (*v*) ascend, rise, climb, board, arise, advance, jump, bestride, grow, increase, ride, scale, (*n*) hill, frame, mountain; *antonyms* (*v*) descend, drop, (*n*) valley, 3. initiate; *synonyms* (*v*) begin, found, commence, inaugurate, launch, activate, induct, institute, introduce, originate, start, enter, undertake, broach, (*n*) entrant, 4. launch; *synonyms* (*n*) boat, inauguration, initiation, launching, (*v*) initiate, dart, fire, toss, establish, hurl, cast, fling, open, shoot, throw; *antonym* (*v*) end.

bumoaki 1. mounted; *synonyms* (*adj*) equestrian, firm, 2. led.

bün just; *synonyms* (*adv*) exactly, hardly, newly, (*adj*) fair, right, correct, equitable, accurate, honest, impartial, barely, fit, good, reasonable, righteous; *antonyms* (*adj*) unfair, biased, wrong.

buna 1. deaf; *synonyms* (*adj*) earless, blind, indifferent, unhearing, aspirated, atonic, deve, inattentive, oblivious, regardless, surd, thoughtless, unaware, unconcerned, (*v*) deafen; *antonym* (*adj*) hearing, 2. marry; *synonyms* (*v*) join, link, conjoin, splice, tie, unite, wive, couple, combine, merge, connect, unify, match, (*n*) espouse, wed; *antonym* (*v*) divorce, 3. wed; *synonyms* (*v*) marry, married.

buña chin; *synonyms* (*n*) talk, jaw, jawbone, rap, mentum, button, cheek, chops, mouth, point, (*v*) speak, confer, utter.

bunaki married; *synonyms* (*adj*) marital, wedded, conjugal, matrimonial, connubial, nuptial; *antonyms* (*adj*) single, unmarried.

bunau tainted; *synonyms* (*v*) rotten, reasty, blighted, cankered, (*adj*) corrupt, rancid, rank, bad, contaminated, faulty, musty, vitiated, putrid, dirty, besmirched; *antonyms* (*adj*) pure, unadulterated, unchanged, untarnished.

bung 1. descend; *synonyms* (*v*) alight, condescend, settle, deign, derive, dismount, down, drop, subside, tumble, come, decline, dip, fall, sink; *antonyms* (*v*) rise, ascend, climb, 2. down; *synonyms* (*adv*) below, (*adj*) cut, dejected, depressed, downward, despondent, dispirited, downcast, downhearted, (*n*) feather, fur, fuzz, (*v*) consume, devour, drink; *antonyms* (*adv*) up, (*adj*) cheerful, happy, upward, 3. spawn; *synonyms* (*v*) engender, generate, cause, make, spat, father, create, produce, beget, (*n*) egg, offspring, breed, progeny, seed, brood.

bungata rank; *synonyms* (*n*) range, place, file, gradation, line, degree, quality, (*v*) arrange, order, class, classify, grade, position, array, group; *antonym* (*adj*) fresh.

bungia birth; *synonyms* (*n*) beginning, ancestry, descent, extraction, genesis, parturition, blood, labor, lineage, nascency, nativity, onset, (*v*) delivery, bear, deliver; *antonym* (*n*) death.

bungiaki born; *synonyms* (*v*) deliver, (*adj*) native, natural, elder, uneducated, untrained, untutored, built-in, cognate, deep-seated, essential, instinctive, intrinsic.

bungintaai sunset; *synonyms* (*n*) dusk, evening, nightfall, sundown, twilight; *antonym* (*n*) dawn.

buni good; *synonyms* (*adj*) able, benefit, delicious, right, efficient, capable, excellent, fine, nice, superior, well, advantageous, (*n*) benign, advantage, gain; *antonyms* (*adj*) disobedient, poor, wicked, unpleasant, (*n*) evil, bad.

bunin round; *synonyms* (*adv*) about, around, (*adj*) circular, plump, entire, chubby, complete, (*n*) circle, bout, ring, beat, circuit, (*v*) compass, turn, gird; *antonyms* (*adj*) slim, sharp.

buno 1. fuck; *synonyms* (*v*) screw, bang, bonk, hump, jazz, fornicate, (*n*) fucking, nookie, shag, ass, 2. intercourse; *synonyms* (*n*) communion, contact, acquaintance, coition, coitus, communication, conversation, dealings, converse, commerce, congress, copulation, fellowship, dealing, (*adj*) familiarity.

bunong 1. leak; *synonyms* (*n*) leakage, crevice, breach, disclosure, chink, escape, fissure, hole, (*v*) dribble, reveal, release, disclose, drip, drop, ooze, 2. squirt; *synonyms* (*n*) jet, spurt, spirt, fountain, child, nobody, (*v*) spray, gush, spout, eject, emit, splash, flow, burst, discharge, 3. spray; *synonyms* (*n*) mist, froth, aerosol, atomizer, foam, branch, squirt, bouquet, bubble, bunch, (*v*) shower, dust, scatter, spatter, sprinkle.

bunra relinquish; *synonyms* (*v*) abandon, abdicate, cede, leave, quit, renounce, discard, disclaim, concede, desert, forgo, forsake, give, surrender, waive; *antonym* (*v*) retain.

bunraki relinquished; *synonyms* (*adj*) abandoned, deserted, derelict, surrendered.

buoguínyikai woods; *synonyms* (*n*) wood, forest, woodland, timber.

buoka 1. collaborate; *synonyms* (*v*) cooperate, unite, assist, concur, combine, agree, assemble, bargain, confer, consult, discuss, interact, league, parley, settle, 2. assist; *synonyms* (*v*) aid, support, abet, serve, contribute, boost, attend, avail, back, comfort, encourage, expedite, facilitate, (*n*) help,

assistance; *antonym* (*v*) hinder, 3. cooperate; *synonyms* (*v*) collaborate, join, participate, 4. aid; *synonyms* (*n*) encouragement, relief, backing, care, cure, favor, hand, lift, patronage, recourse, (*v*) benefit, ease, minister, countenance, relieve; *antonym* (*n*) hindrance, 5. help; *synonyms* (*v*) alleviate, forward, befriend, further, amend, correct, gain, profit, promote, (*n*) assistant, remedy, advantage, prompt, servant, service; *antonyms* (*v*) worsen, (*n*) detriment, 6. succor; *synonyms* (*n*) ministration, consolation, alleviation, opitulation, redress, solace, stay, (*v*) succour, 7. protect; *synonyms* (*v*) defend, keep, cover, preserve, hide, conceal, conserve, maintain, safeguard, save, screen, vindicate, insure, (*n*) guard, ward; *antonyms* (*v*) attack, expose, neglect, risk, 8. strengthen; *synonyms* (*v*) consolidate, confirm, corroborate, brace, enhance, fortify, intensify, invigorate, bolster, buttress, harden, increase, stiffen, toughen, reenforce; *antonyms* (*v*) weaken, undermine.

buokaki 1. assisted; *synonym* (*adj*) aided, 2. aided; *synonyms* (*adj*) assisted, favored, countenanced, featured, 3. protected; *synonyms* (*v*) covert, disguised, hid, (*adj*) secure, immune, saved, secured, sheltered, covered, comfortable, confined, cosseted, dependable, good, guaranteed, 4. strengthened; *synonyms* (*adj*) reinforced, consolidated, built, equipped, sinewed, united.

buokanamarake partake; *synonyms* (*v*) deal, participate, share, touch, consume, taste, communicate, imbibe.

buokanibwai 1. share; *synonyms* (*n*) piece, portion, deal, dole, lot, allotment, (*v*) participate, allot, apportion, distribute, part, partake, dispense, divide, partition; *antonym* (*v*) control, 2. partake; *synonyms* (*v*) share, touch, consume, taste, communicate, imbibe.

buokanibwaiaki shared; *synonyms* (*adj*) communal, common, divided, joint, mutual, collective, community, cooperative, reciprocal; *antonyms* (*adj*) individual, private.

buoki 1. help; *synonyms* (*v*) aid, assist, avail, facilitate, favor, ease, alleviate, contribute, (*n*) assistance, benefit, support, assistant, cure, boost, encouragement; *antonyms* (*v*) hinder, worsen, (*n*) hindrance, detriment, 2. collaborate; *synonyms* (*v*) cooperate, unite, concur, combine, agree, assemble, bargain, confer, consult, discuss, interact, league, parley, settle, talk.

bura 1. as; *synonyms* (*conj*) qua, because, since, considering, while, whilst, (*prep*) during, like, (*adv*) equally, from, (*n*) arsenic, 2. like; *synonyms* (*v*) corresponding, enjoy, identical, care, desire, fancy, (*adj*) equal, equivalent, alike, analogous, comparable, same, parallel, (n) love, relish; *antonyms* (*prep*) unlike, (v) dislike, (*adj*) different.

burabeti prophet; *synonyms* (n) augur, oracle, diviner, predictor, seer, vaticinator, forecaster, visionary, clairvoyant, priest.

buraerae hairy; *synonyms* (*adj*) bearded, bushy, hirsute, dangerous, downy, woolly, bristly, fleecy, fuzzy, pilose, rough, shaggy, fimbriated; *antonyms* (*adj*) bald, hairless.

buraun brown; *synonyms* (*adj*) chocolate, swarthy, tanned, (n) brunette, brownness, tan, (v) sear, cook, fry; *antonym* (*adj*) pale.

bure 1. err; *synonyms* (v) blunder, stray, stumble, deviate, misjudge, mistake, sin, slip, trip, wander, fault, digress, swerve, trespass, depart, **2.** defective; *synonyms* (*adj*) deficient, bad, faulty, imperfect, broken, incomplete, lacking, unsound, vicious, inaccurate, rotten, erroneous, flawed, inadequate, incorrect; *antonym* (*adj*) perfect, **3.** faulty; *synonyms* (*adj*) defective, false, wrong, damaged, poor, amiss, tainted, blamable, insufficient, mistaken, illogical; *antonyms* (*adj*) correct, flawless, **4.** guilty; *synonyms* (*adj*) ashamed, culpable, criminal, hangdog, wicked, chargeable, condemned, delinquent, reprehensible, sinful, contrite, responsible, shamefaced, sheepish; *antonyms* (*adj*) innocent, blameless, **5.** criminal; *synonyms* (*adj*) guilty, illegal, condemnable, miscreant, unlawful, (n) convict, crook, culprit, hoodlum, malefactor, felon, gangster, lawbreaker, outlaw, thug; *antonyms* (*adj*) law-abiding, legal, **6.** wicked; *synonyms* (*adj*) atrocious, evil, depraved, immoral, mischievous, unholy, vile, corrupt, diabolical, foul, hellish, iniquitous, nasty, naughty, pernicious; *antonyms* (*adj*) good, kind, moral, pious, pure, **7.** sin; *synonyms* (n) iniquity, crime, error, guilt, misdeed, offense, wickedness, immorality, peccancy, transgression, vice, (v) offend, blame, err, misbehave; *antonyms* (n) virtue, piety, **8.** sinful; *synonyms* (*adj*) impious, ungodly, profane, unrighteous, fiendish, nefarious, abandoned, baneful, dishonest, hurtful, irreligious; *antonym* (*adj*) virtuous, **9.** violate; *synonyms* (v) break, contravene, transgress, desecrate, dishonor, disobey, infringe, ravish, assault, breach, outrage, rape, abuse, debauch, defile; *antonym* (v) obey, **10.** transgress; *synonyms* (v) overstep, violate, infract, pass, boob, goof, intrude, exceed, transcend, destroy, escape, fail, injure, interrupt, **11.** wrong; *synonyms* (*adj*) harm, ill, improper, inappropriate, unjust, untrue, awry, (*adv*) badly, (n) damage, injury, injustice, hurt, mischief, grievance, misuse; *antonyms* (*adj*) proper, honest, (*adv*) correctly, (v) right, (n) justice, **12.** offend; *synonyms* (v) irritate, affront, insult, disgust, anger, annoy, displease, wound, pique, revolt, shock, appall, nauseate, repel, infuriate; *antonym* (v) please.

bureaki 1. offended; *synonyms* (*adj*) hurt, angry, affronted, aggrieved, annoyed, pained, wronged, shocked, appalled, ashamed, averted, bitter, cool, disappointed, disgusted; *antonym* (*adj*) composed, **2.** violated; *synonyms* (v) apart, blighted, contrite, cracked, disconnected, disunited, fractured, (*adj*) broken, profaned, seduced, debauched, defiled, desecrated, despoiled, dishonored; *antonym* (*adj*) pure.

bureburea 1. mislead; *synonyms* (v) betray, deceive, cheat, beguile, con, fool, misinform, delude, dupe, hoodwink, lie, misdirect, misguide, trick, seduce, **2.** err; *synonyms* (v) blunder, stray, stumble, deviate, misjudge, mistake, sin, slip, trip, wander, fault, digress, swerve, trespass, depart, **3.** deceive; *synonyms* (v) bamboozle, circumvent, pretend, cozen, hoax, mislead, sell, swindle, befool, defraud, gull, humbug, cuckold, blind, (n) fraud.

burebureaki mislead; *synonyms* (v) betray, deceive, cheat, beguile, con, fool, misinform, delude, dupe, hoodwink, lie, misdirect, misguide, trick, seduce.

burenia plane; *synonyms* (n) airplane, face, aeroplane, aircraft, degree, stage, surface, (v) flatten, shave, (*adj*) level, even, flat, horizontal, smooth, flush.

bureniaki planned; *synonyms* (*adj*) deliberate, intended, intentional, calculated, designed, aforethought, plotted, premeditated, scheduled, fixed, future, prepared, studied; *antonyms* (*adj*) spontaneous, unplanned.

burenibai 1. exceptional; *synonyms* (*adj*) special, abnormal, excellent, extraordinary, particular, prodigious, singular, uncommon, exceeding, outstanding, rare, single, superior, unique, unusual; *antonyms* (*adj*) common, mediocre, ordinary, average, normal, usual, abysmal, inferior, poor, **2.** precious; *synonyms* (*adj*) dear, beloved, cherished, costly, valuable, invaluable, expensive, golden, choice, inestimable, exquisite, cute, rich, noble, (n) darling; *antonym* (*adj*) worthless, **3.** rare; *synonyms* (*adj*) exceptional, infrequent, precious, scarce, seldom, thin, few, curious, fine, odd, peculiar, novel, flimsy, occasional, priceless; *antonym* (*adj*) frequent, **4.** seldom; *synonyms* (*adv*) rarely, occasionally, infrequently, uncommonly, hardly, scarcely; *antonyms* (*adv*) frequently, often.

burenibaia wear; *synonyms* (v) dress, endure, bear, fatigue, tire, waste, fray, frazzle, (n) clothing, apparel, attire, clothes, garb, erosion, garment; *antonym* (v) refresh.

burenibaiaki worn; *synonyms* (v) decayed, (*adj*) haggard, shabby, tired, ragged, tattered, threadbare, drawn, jaded, exhausted, fatigued, careworn, decrepit, faded, frayed; *antonyms* (*adj*) fresh, new.

burenibwai 1. rare; *synonyms* (*adj*) extraordinary, uncommon, exceptional, infrequent, precious, scarce, seldom, thin, unusual, few, choice, curious, fine, odd, peculiar; *antonyms* (*adj*) common, frequent, ordinary, **2.** rarely; *synonyms* (*adv*) infrequently, hardly, uncommonly, unusually, little, exceptionally, scarcely; *antonyms* (*adv*) frequently, often, usually.

bureta disfigured; *synonyms* (*adj*) deformed, crooked, ugly, blemished, dishonest, flawed, hurt, imperfect, shabby, shapeless, stained, disgraced, dishonorable, dishonored, faithless.

buretata 1. faulty; *synonyms* (*adj*) erroneous, deficient, defective, false, vicious, bad, broken, inaccurate, incorrect, wrong, damaged, imperfect, poor, amiss, tainted; *antonyms* (*adj*) correct, perfect, flawless, **2.** imperfect; *synonyms* (*adj*) faulty, incomplete, unfinished, flawed, inadequate, partial, fallible, frail, impaired, half, immature, corrupt, insufficient, rough, (*v*) infirm, **3.** defective; *synonyms* (*adj*) lacking, unsound, rotten, lame, sketchy, wanting.

bureti 1. hideous; *synonyms* (*adj*) awful, dreadful, frightful, fearful, ghastly, appalling, grim, grisly, gruesome, horrible, horrid, lurid, repulsive, ugly, offensive; *antonyms* (*adj*) attractive, lovely, pleasant, **2.** awesome; *synonyms* (*adj*) terrific, formidable, majestic, amazing, eerie, impressive, tremendous, wonderful, marvelous, astounding, frightening, great, magnificent, stunning, terrible; *antonym* (*adj*) insignificant, **3.** ugly; *synonyms* (*adj*) nasty, disagreeable, forbidding, hideous, homely, surly, evil, atrocious, deformed, despicable, grotesque, monstrous, ominous, plain, shocking; *antonyms* (*adj*) beautiful, good-looking, flowing, ornamental, **4.** unsightly; *synonyms* (*adj*) unpleasant, unattractive, **5.** vile; *synonyms* (*adj*) foul, contemptible, low, ignoble, bad, disgusting, filthy, infamous, mean, revolting, sorry, sordid, vicious, (*n*) dirty, (*v*) base.

buretireti 1. nasty; *synonyms* (*adj*) dirty, loathsome, disgusting, filthy, foul, awful, mean, abominable, coarse, disagreeable, distasteful, evil, hurtful, obnoxious, raw; *antonyms* (*adj*) agreeable, kind, pleasant, nice, charitable, lovely, **2.** vile; *synonyms* (*adj*) contemptible, despicable, low, ignoble, bad, infamous, nasty, offensive, revolting, sorry, sordid, vicious, atrocious, beastly, (*v*) base; *antonym* (*adj*) attractive, **3.** obscene; *synonyms* (*adj*) indecent, gross, lewd, licentious, bawdy, ribald, immoral, lascivious, fulsome, improper, immodest, abhorrent, detestable, impure, smutty.

burimangaoa 1. grad; *synonyms* (*n*) alumnus, graduate, alum, alumna, degree, class, form, grade, student, gradient, level, mark, score, slope, tier, **2.** disorderly; *synonyms* (*adj*) confused, chaotic, disordered, wild, boisterous, disobedient, disorganized, irregular, jumbled, rowdy, tumultuous, turbulent, unruly, untidy, (*v*) lawless;

antonyms (*adj*) orderly, well-behaved, neat, arranged, **3.** disheveled; *synonyms* (*adj*) unkempt, sloppy, tousled, uncombed, dishevelled, messy, scruffy, slovenly, tangled, grubby; *antonyms* (*adj*) tidy, free, **4.** pull; *synonyms* (*v*) drag, draw, draught, pluck, attract, haul, jerk, tug, pick, make, force, hale, (*n*) wrench, attraction, effort; *antonyms* (*v*) push, repel, **5.** ruffled; *synonyms* (*adj*) disheveled, frilled, frilly, rippled, upset, crinkled, crinkly, disconcerted, excited, nervous, rough, shaggy, wavelike, wavy, windswept.

burimangaoaki 1. graded; *synonyms* (*adj*) ranked, alphabetical, bedded, dirt, graveled, passable, stratified, thoroughbred, gravel, **2.** pulled; *synonyms* (*adj*) moulting, pilled, plucked.

burimaunia tear; *synonyms* (*n*) split, rupture, rent, (*v*) break, rip, crack, pull, rend, lacerate, race, run, rush, slit, rive, cleave.

burita 1. jerk; *synonyms* (*n*) tug, heave, pull, fool, (*v*) jolt, jump, shake, yank, jar, twitch, fling, bump, flip, bob, bounce, **2.** pluck; *synonyms* (*v*) cull, jerk, fleece, gather, pick, grab, harvest, extract, draw, (*n*) courage, grit, boldness, backbone, bravery, (*adj*) nerve.

buritaki plucked; *synonyms* (*v*) ploughed, plowed, (*adj*) moulting, pilled, pulled.

buritoto 1. disgusting; *synonyms* (*adj*) abominable, detestable, disgustful, distasteful, execrable, foul, loathsome, nasty, odious, offensive, disagreeable, abhorrent, awful, dirty, hateful; *antonyms* (*adj*) attractive, pleasant, appealing, **2.** dirty; *synonyms* (*adj*) dirt, contemptible, bawdy, contaminated, dingy, impure, despicable, filthy, (*v*) muddy, corrupt, soil, contaminate, begrime, bemire, (*n*) defile; *antonyms* (*adj*) hygienic, pure, spotless, immaculate, (*v*) clean, **3.** repugnant; *synonyms* (*adj*) repulsive, contradictory, ugly, adverse, disgusting, hideous, inimical, obscene, opposite, antagonistic, gruesome, (*v*) hostile, (*n*) irreconcilable, discordant, contrary.

buro 1. froth; *synonyms* (*n*) foam, effervescence, bubbles, spindrift, spray, (*v*) bubble, fizz, spume, boil, suds, effervesce, sparkle, ferment, seethe, (*adj*) scum, **2.** boiled; *synonyms* (*adj*) done, intoxicated, poached, stewed, (*v*) sodden, saturated, seethed, soaked, **3.** bubble; *synonyms* (*n*) blister, bead, blob, cheat, fantasy, illusion, plant, (*v*) babble, burble, froth, gurgle, churn, simmer, murmur, ripple, **4.** ferment; *synonyms* (*n*) agitation, excitement, barm, tumult, unrest, disturbance, confusion, fermentation, fermenting, (*v*) stew, turn, brew, fester, agitate, (*adj*) pother, **5.** boil; *synonyms* (*v*) burn, fume, heat, anger, cook, roast, (*n*) abscess, furuncle, pimple, boiling, bump, eruption, pustule, (*adj*) sore, rave; *antonym* (*v*) freeze, **6.** swell; *synonyms* (*n*) wave, (*v*) surge, enlarge, expand, heave, increase, rise, puff, bloat, grow, billow, augment, balloon, *(adj)* dandy, swagger; *antonyms (v)* decrease, deflate, desiccate, **7**. ooze; *synonyms (n)* mire, muck, slime, *(v)* exude, leak, dribble, seep, drain, drop, bleed, emit, filter, secrete, sweat, *(adj)* mud.

buroaki 1. fermented; *synonyms (adj)* alcoholic, arduous, backbreaking, difficult, hard, sour, grueling, gruelling, heavy, knockout, laborious, labourious, punishing, severe, strong, **2**. boiled; *synonyms (adj)* done, intoxicated, poached, stewed, *(v)* sodden, saturated, seethed, soaked, **3**. swelled; *synonyms (adj)* big, inflated, bloated, adult, bad, bighearted, boastful, bombastic, bounteous, bountiful, braggy, crowing, distended, elder, emphysematous.

buroburo foam; *synonyms (n)* froth, spume, bubbles, lather, *(v)* boil, bubble, effervesce, seethe, fizz, suds, ferment, churn, gurgle, rage, *(adj)* fume.

buroungia sweep; *synonyms (n)* compass, expanse, range, scope, field, stretch, area, room, *(v)* brush, rake, reach, sail, sway, *(adj)* curve, comb.

buru 1. blue; *synonyms (adj)* azure, depressed, down, gloomy, low, cheerless, dejected, dispirited, downcast, downhearted, naughty, sad, sapphire, spicy, black, **2**. row; *synonyms (n)* altercation, line, file, rank, squabble, wrangle, clash, dispute, *(v)* quarrel, brawl, fight, argue, bicker, order, *(adj)* fracas; *antonyms (n)* agreement, *(v)* agree.

buruburu 1. hairy; *synonyms (adj)* bearded, bushy, hirsute, dangerous, downy, woolly, bristly, fleecy, fuzzy, pilose, rough, shaggy, fimbriated; *antonyms (adj)* bald, hairless, **2**. frayed; *synonyms (adj)* worn, ragged, shabby, threadbare, tattered, *(v)* dilapidated; *antonym (adj)* pristine, **3**. fibrous; *synonyms (adj)* stringy, tough, ropy, brawny, fibry, gossamer, hempen, muscular, nemaline, raw, rubbery, sinewy, unchewable, wiry, coarse; *antonym (adj)* tender, **4**. fray; *synonyms (n)* brawl, conflict, action, affray, combat, fight, battle, broil, contention, disturbance, fracas, scrap, *(v)* rub, chafe, fret.

buruburuaki frayed; *synonyms (adj)* worn, ragged, shabby, threadbare, tattered, *(v)* dilapidated; *antonym (adj)* pristine.

buruna sweep; *synonyms (n)* compass, expanse, range, scope, field, stretch, area, room, *(v)* brush, rake, reach, sail, sway, *(adj)* curve, comb.

burunna 1. row; *synonyms (n)* altercation, line, file, rank, squabble, wrangle, clash, dispute, *(v)* quarrel, brawl, fight, argue, bicker, order, *(adj)* fracas; *antonyms (n)* agreement, *(v)* agree, **2**. paddle; *synonyms (n)* blade, oar, vane, *(v)* dabble, dodder, row, pull, spank, toddle, totter, coggle, larrup.

bururu 1. moisten; *synonyms (v)* dampen, wash, water, dip, drench, soak, soften, sprinkle, wet, deaden, drizzle, *(n)* damp, **2**. spatter; *synonyms (n)* splatter, *(v)* splash, plash, dash, slop, scatter, smear,

bespatter, soil, spit, spray, sputter, squirt, patter, dabble, **3**. spray; *synonyms (n)* jet, mist, froth, aerosol, atomizer, foam, branch, spirt, bouquet, *(v)* shower, spout, spurt, dust, gush, spatter, **4**. wet; *synonyms (adj)* humid, drenched, moist, soaked, sodden, dank, rainy, saturated, soggy, watery, *(v)* moisten, douse, irrigate, *(n)* moisture, humidity; *antonyms (adj)* dehydrated, parched, *(v)* dry, **5**. sprinkle; *synonyms (n)* scattering, sprinkling, *(v)* cast, dot, rain, spill, spread, diffuse, intersperse, disperse, baptize, shed, distribute, powder, *(adj)* besprinkle, **6**. splash; *synonyms (n)* spot, dab, flash, spattering, blotch, splurge, splotch, splashing, *(v)* drop, slosh, lap, slush, swash, puddle, splosh, **7**. spurt; *synonyms (n)* run, burst, effort, exertion, spell, *(v)* flow, race, stream, erupt, flood, discharge, dart, issue, shoot, spew.

bururua 1. spurt; *synonyms (n)* jet, run, burst, dash, *(v)* spirt, flow, race, squirt, gush, stream, erupt, flood, discharge, spill, spout, **2**. spray; *synonyms (n)* mist, froth, aerosol, atomizer, foam, branch, bouquet, bubble, *(v)* shower, splash, spurt, dust, scatter, spatter, sprinkle.

bururuaki 1. splashed; *synonyms (adj)* bespattered, besplashed, dabbled, spattered, dotted, marked, showy, speckled, splashy, splattered, streaked, **2**. spattered; *synonyms (adj)* dirty, splashed, **3**. sprinkled; *synonyms (adj)* besprent, scattered, spotted, spread, strewn.

buta 1. navel; *synonyms (n)* bellybutton, center, umbilicus, nave, omphalos, omphalus, **2**. extract; *synonyms (n)* excerpt, essence, juice, quotation, quote, citation, *(v)* draw, abstract, derive, educe, elicit, distill, express, get, extort, **3**. universal; *synonyms (adj)* general, ecumenical, global, common, international, worldwide, public, ubiquitous, comprehensive, oecumenical, widespread, cosmopolitan, generic, ordinary, pervasive; *antonyms (adj)* local, specific, **4**. traveled; *synonyms (adj)* travelled, cultured, passable, experienced, knowing, **5**. remove; *synonyms (v)* oust, take, pull, eject, expel, deduct, discharge, strip, delete, erase, evacuate, extract, abolish, dislodge, *(adj)* clear; *antonyms (v)* insert, install, place, keep, **6**. spread; *synonyms (v)* scatter, reach, disperse, expand, extend, broadcast, circulate, diffuse, disseminate, increase, propagate, stretch, broaden, deploy, *(n)* span; *antonym (adj)* concentrated, **7**. take; *synonyms (v)* admit, hold, adopt, bear, carry, catch, clutch, obtain, return, borrow, pick, acquire, *(n)* seize, *(phr)* accept, receive; *antonyms (v)* give, refuse, abstain, add, lose, **8**. widespread; *synonyms (adj)* prevalent, extensive, popular, universal, vast, broad, prevailing, current, expansive, national, rampant, rife, *(v)* dispread, sparse, sporadic; *antonym (adj)* narrow, **9**. taken; *synonyms (adj)* occupied, full, interpreted, besotted, crazed, enamored, engaged, interested, lovesick, obsessed, overcome, preferred, rapt, reserved, unavailable.

bûtabut cough; *synonyms* (*n*) coughing, sneeze, (*v*) choke, convulse, vomit.

butae numb; *synonyms* (*adj*) asleep, benumbed, dead, dull, insensible, torpid, deadened, callous, impassive, comatose, inactive, inert, (*v*) benumb, deaden, (*n*) blunt; *antonym* (*adj*) sensitive.

butaki 1. taken; *synonyms* (*v*) take, (*adj*) occupied, full, interpreted, besotted, crazed, enamored, engaged, interested, lovesick, obsessed, overcome, preferred, rapt, reserved, **2.** removed; *synonyms* (*adj*) distant, remote, separate, far, detached, abstracted, absent, apart, aloof, outlying, separated, **3.** spread; *synonyms* (*v*) scatter, reach, disperse, expand, extend, broadcast, circulate, diffuse, disseminate, increase, propagate, stretch, broaden, deploy, (*n*) span; *antonym* (*adj*) concentrated.

butan root; *synonyms* (*n*) base, foundation, origin, basis, radical, radix, cause, derivation, reason, beginning, bottom, core, essence, (*v*) establish, dig.

butan-te-ni stump; *synonyms* (*n*) stub, end, pulpit, rostrum, (*v*) confuse, baffle, bewilder, mystify, nonplus, perplex, puzzle, stamp, campaign, confound, flummox.

bûtara black; *synonyms* (*adj*) dark, sable, blackamoor, bleak, darkie, dirty, ebony, evil, nigger, unclean, cheerless, squalid, (*v*) sinister, villainous, blacken; *antonym* (*n*) white.

buti 1. advance; *synonyms* (*n*) progress, improvement, (*v*) further, proceed, promote, approach, encourage, raise, rise, boost, contribute, cultivate, develop, forward, (*phr*) accelerate; *antonyms* (*n*) deterioration, (*v*) retreat, recede, delay, demote, regress, **2.** move; *synonyms* (*v*) act, affect, carry, excite, go, impel, instigate, maneuver, touch, travel, flow, bear, (*n*) motion, drive, transfer; *antonym* (*v*) stay, **3.** progressive; *synonyms* (*adj*) advanced, gradual, active, radical, consecutive, modern, revolutionary, positive, alphabetical, avant-garde, broad, broad-minded, chronological, (*n*) liberal, imperfect; *antonyms* (*adj*) old-fashioned, traditional, (*n*) conservative.

butia solicit; *synonyms* (*v*) beg, crave, request, petition, ask, court, pray, importune, apply, demand, implore, require, desire, claim, (*n*) canvass.

butika 1. encounter; *synonyms* (*n*) collision, combat, battle, conflict, contest, action, brush, confrontation, impact, (*v*) clash, confront, experience, face, find, rencounter; *antonym* (*v*) retreat, **2.** meet; *synonyms* (*v*) converge, assemble, congregate, encounter, fulfill, gather, answer, cross, intersect, abut, concur, adjoin, collect, convene, (*adj*) fit; *antonyms* (*v*) avoid, disperse, diverge.

butikaraoi timely; *synonyms* (*adj*) opportune, convenient, punctual, appropriate, early, apt, prompt, propitious, fit, pat, providential, auspicious, favorable, (*v*) seasonable, (*adv*) apropos; *antonyms* (*adj*) untimely, inopportune.

butimaea 1. meet; *synonyms* (*v*) converge, find, assemble, congregate, encounter, fulfill, gather, answer, cross, confront, intersect, abut, concur, adjoin, (*adj*) fit; *antonyms* (*v*) avoid, disperse, diverge, **2.** welcome; *synonyms* (*adj*) acceptable, pleasant, agreeable, pleasing, enjoyable, (*v*) accept, greet, invite, receive, hail, entertain, (*n*) salute, hospitality, reception, embrace; *antonyms* (*adj*) unwelcome, unwanted, (*v*) reject, **3.** receive; *synonyms* (*v*) admit, get, assume, adopt, bear, have, obtain, welcome, make, acknowledge, take, hear, earn, own, realize.

butimaeaki received; *synonyms* (*v*) receiving, ascertained, current, recognized, (*adj*) accepted, acknowledged, conventional, acceptable, canonical, orthodox, customary, established, inward, known, legitimate.

butimwaaea accept; *synonyms* (*v*) receive, acknowledge, admit, take, recognize, abide, accede, acquiesce, adopt, assume, believe, yield, agree, approve, assent; *antonyms* (*v*) refuse, reject, deny, snub, oppose, renounce, resist.

butimwaaeaki accepted; *synonyms* (*adj*) acceptable, conventional, acknowledged, assumed, established, orthodox, understood, approved, current, received, customary, habitual, known, popular, proper; *antonyms* (*adj*) concealed, unpopular, unusual.

butinaiwa 1. roam; *synonyms* (*v*) ramble, stray, wander, gallivant, meander, range, gad, drift, journey, rove, stroll, tramp, walk, prowl, (*adj*) err, **2.** wander; *synonyms* (*v*) digress, deviate, roam, travel, depart, divagate, swerve, vagabond, amble, straggle, slog, trudge, (*n*) saunter, promenade, (*adj*) rave.

butiroko cocky; *synonyms* (*adj*) arrogant, proud, conceited, supercilious, vain, brash, flippant, insolent, overbearing, impudent, boastful, brazen, familiar, jaunty, superior.

butokaurake budding; *synonyms* (*adj*) young, blossoming, emergent, green, juvenile, youthful.

butua jog; *synonyms* (*v*) run, jiggle, square, dig, joggle, (*n*) trot, hustle, jolt, jostle, shake, poke, canter, prompt, gallop, lope.

butubutu nuzzle; *synonyms* (*v*) nestle, cuddle, snuggle, caress, nose.

butuia shove; *synonyms* (*v*) elbow, impel, press, prod, shift, boost, hustle, stuff, nudge, bump, (*n*) push, thrust, jostle, poke, shoulder; *antonym* (*v*) pull.

buun spoon; *synonyms* (*n*) ladle, spoonful, shovel, trowel, (*v*) scoop, smooch, dip, snog.

buuta 1. hire; *synonyms* (*n*) wage, employment, fee, pay, salary, fare, (*v*) employ, engage, charter, enlist, rent, retain, take, commission, compensation; *antonym* (*v*) dismiss, **2.** dislodge; *synonyms* (*v*) displace, bump, shift, throw, banish, discharge, dislocate, eject, expel, free, move, oust, remove, transfer; *antonym* (*v*) lodge.

buutaki hired; *synonyms* (*v*) compensated, contented, paid, satisfied, (*adj*) employed, leased, chartered, hack, hackneyed, mercenary, hireling, selfish, sordid, venal.

bûwu throat; *synonyms* (*n*) gullet, orifice, pharynx, gorge, mouth, muzzle, chimney, flue, funnel, nostril, nozzle, quarl, shaft, sucker.

bwaai things; *synonyms* (*n*) gear, stuff, belongings, equipment, garb, garment, clothes, apparel, goods, life, luggage, palliament, possessions, property.

bwabwa 1. fool; *synonyms* (*n*) blockhead, dunce, clown, ass, buffoon, dolt, (*v*) dupe, deceive, bamboozle, befool, cheat, con, defraud, delude, gull, **2.** committee; *synonyms* (*n*) board, council, commission, consignee, trustee, cabinet, bureau, staff, group, team, administration, assembly, charge, class, commissioning, **3.** imbecile; *synonyms* (*adj*) foolish, idiotic, fatuous, imbecilic, simple, (*n*) fool, idiot, moron, cretin, oaf, changeling, **4.** panel; *synonyms* (*n*) jury, defendant, committee, plank, set, sheet, wall, accused, window, (*v*) empanel, impanel.

bwabwakoa fondle; *synonyms* (*v*) caress, dandle, pet, cuddle, stroke, cherish, pamper, pat, lick, touch.

bwaibwai inherit; *synonyms* (*v*) succeed, heir, get, own, receive, follow, obtain, ascend, attain, promote, prosper, pursue.

bwaibwaiaki inherited; *synonyms* (*adj*) hereditary, inborn, familial, genetic, ancestral, congenital, incarnate, inherent, transmissible.

bwain 1. like; *synonyms* (*v*) corresponding, enjoy, identical, care, desire, fancy, (*adj*) equal, equivalent, alike, analogous, comparable, same, parallel, (*n*) love, relish; *antonyms* (*prep*) unlike, (*v*) dislike, (*adj*) different, **2.** as; *synonyms* (*conj*) qua, because, since, considering, while, whilst, (*prep*) during, like, (*adv*) equally, from, (*n*) arsenic.

bwaina 1. appropriate; *synonyms* (*adj*) pertinent, proper, true, agreeable, apposite, apt, congruous, correct, particular, peculiar, right, (*v*) annex, allocate, adopt, seize; *antonyms* (*adj*) inappropriate, unsuitable, unrelated, untimely, wrong, (*v*) surrender, **2.** employ; *synonyms* (*v*) apply, use, consume, engage, exercise, exploit, hire, wield, busy, exert, occupy, ply, retain, (*n*) employment, service; *antonyms* (*v*) fire, dismiss, **3.** wield; *synonyms* (*v*) handle, wave, brandish, flourish, hold, manipulate, manage, swing, treat, control, maintain, shake, operate, govern, rule, **4.** possess; *synonyms* (*v*) have, bear, enjoy, keep, obsess,

feature, (*n*) hazard, (*adj*) own, **5.** worn; *synonyms* (*v*) decayed, (*adj*) haggard, shabby, tired, ragged, tattered, threadbare, drawn, jaded, exhausted, fatigued, careworn, decrepit, faded, frayed; *antonyms* (*adj*) fresh, new, **6.** use; *synonyms* (*n*) custom, practice, benefit, habit, application, function, avail, consumption, (*v*) employ, expend, profit, advantage, spend, need, (*adj*) usage; *antonym* (*v*) conserve, **7.** own; *synonyms* (*v*) acknowledge, admit, concede, allow, grant, possess, confess, get, accept, avow, recognize, profess, master, (*adj*) individual, private, **8.** wear; *synonyms* (*v*) dress, endure, fatigue, tire, waste, fray, frazzle, assume, (*n*) clothing, apparel, attire, clothes, garb, erosion, garment; *antonym* (*v*) refresh.

bwainaki 1. employed; *synonyms* (*adj*) busy, engaged, occupied, working, affianced, betrothed, earnest, rapt, active, gainfully, inked, involved, laboring, operating, pledged; *antonym* (*adj*) unemployed, **2.** appropriated; *synonyms* (*adj*) destined, condemned, confiscate, confiscated, reserved, seized, censured, convicted, forfeit, forfeited, **3.** used; *synonyms* (*adj*) secondhand, exploited, accustomed, decrepit, depleted, exhausted, faded, habituated, hand-me-down, spent, threadbare, tried, victimised, victimized, wont; *antonyms* (*adj*) pristine, new, spanking, unused, **4.** owned; *synonyms* (*v*) behoove, ought, owed, (*adj*) own, proprietary, **5.** worn; *synonyms* (*v*) decayed, rotten, (*adj*) haggard, shabby, tired, ragged, tattered, drawn, jaded, fatigued, careworn, frayed, raddled, seedy, wasted; *antonym* (*adj*) fresh.

bwairaoi expert; *synonyms* (*adj*) adept, adroit, dexterous, skillful, able, clever, experienced, accomplished, ace, apt, (*n*) professional, proficient, critic, authority, connoisseur; *antonyms* (*adj*) unskilled, inept, inferior, untrained, (*n*) amateur, beginner.

bwaka 1. impeach; *synonyms* (*v*) accuse, charge, blame, criminate, censure, denounce, query, challenge, indict, question, incriminate, appeach, (*n*) arraign, prosecute, sue, **2.** abate; *synonyms* (*v*) subside, allay, bate, decline, diminish, fade, flag, lessen, relax, relieve, remit, slack, slake, wane, (*adj*) slacken; *antonym* (*v*) increase, **3.** fallen; *synonyms* (*adj*) dead, prostrate, destroyed, flat, degenerate, absolute, clear, depressed, downfallen, downright, dull, extinct, collapsed, decayed, decreased, **4.** collapse; *synonyms* (*n*) crash, breakdown, fall, subsidence, bust, debacle, (*v*) break, slump, buckle, crack, crumble, crumple, faint, flop, burst, **5.** capsize; *synonyms* (*adj*) drown, shipwreck, swamp, (*v*) turn, upset, invert, overturn, reverse, topple, keel, subvert, tip, raze, sink, upend; *antonym* (*v*) right, **6.** fell; *synonyms* (*v*) chop, cut, drop, floor, ax, level, down, demolish, destroy, (*adj*)

barbarous, cruel, brutal, fierce, savage, (n) skin, **7.**
deceive; *synonyms* (v) betray, cheat, bamboozle,
circumvent, dupe, pretend, beguile, con, cozen,
fool, hoax, mislead, sell, swindle, (n) fraud, **8.** fall;
synonyms (v) dip, decrease, descend, dive, rain,
dwindle, alight, come, (n) descent, downfall,
plunge, pitch, cascade, collapse, decay; *antonyms*
(v) rise, ascend, climb, triumph, win, (n) ascent, **9.**
dupe; *synonyms* (n) gull, victim, cully, prey, tool,
butt, (v) defraud, deceive, kid, befool, cod, delude,
trap, trick, victimize, **10.** scandalize; *synonyms* (v)
outrage, defame, disgust, scandalise, shock,
slander, offend, malign, calumniate, libel, reproach,
appal, appall, **11.** pretend; *synonyms* (v) assume,
feign, dissimulate, counterfeit, act, affect,
dissemble, imagine, imitate, profess, mask, (adj)
sham, fake, play, (n) allege; *antonyms* (v) real, (adj)
genuine, natural, **12.** simulate; *synonyms* (v)
mimic, mock, copy, emulate, model, ape, pattern,
disguise, personate, fabricate, mold, resemble,
reenact, reproduce, **13.** ruin; *synonyms* (v) ravage,
consume, defeat, desolate, devastate, blast,
annihilate, (n) devastation, destruction, doom,
damage, desolation, havoc, death, finish; *antonyms*
(v) conserve, enhance, **14.** sink; *synonyms* (n) sag,
basin, (v) droop, set, fell, bury, founder, lower,
settle, ebb, languish, abate, die, (adj) immerse, bog;
antonym (v) float, **15.** stumble; *synonyms* (v) slip,
flounder, fumble, err, falter, hit, stammer, bumble,
(n) trip, lurch, misstep, stagger, (adj) blunder, botch,
fault, **16.** veto; *synonyms* (n) bar, negative,
prohibition, rejection, (v) ban, disallow, forbid,
prohibit, proscribe, reject, blackball, interdict,
outlaw, exclude, kill; *antonyms* (n) approval,
permission, (v) approve, permit, sanction, **17.**
tumble; *synonyms* (v) jumble, stumble, spill,
confuse, toss, roll, agitate, embroil, perturb,
plummet, trouble, comprehend, slide, apprehend,
convulse, **18.** wreck; *synonyms* (n) ruins, debris,
hulk, (v) ruin, smash, spoil, wrack, sabotage,
shatter, harm, rack, total, overwhelm, crush,
deface.

bwakaki 1. collapsed; *synonyms* (adj) bent, bowed,
broken, buckled, depleted, distorted, fallen, flat,
malformed, misshapen, warped, shrunken, **2.** felt;
synonyms (v) mat, snarl, tangle, braid, entangle,
(adj) perceived, sensed, conscious, **3.** ruined;
synonyms (v) lost, undone, (adj) destroyed,
dilapidated, broke, desolate, bankrupt, desolated,
devastated, finished, insolvent, ravaged, spoiled,
beaten, wasted; *antonyms* (adj) untarnished,
solvent, first-rate, pure, **4.** tumbled; *synonyms*
(adj) disordered, upset, **5.** wrecked; *synonyms* (v)
stranded, grounded, swamped, (adj) ruined,
disabled, anxious, beached, busted, decaying,
decrepit, doomed, kaput, ramshackle, rundown,
(adv) aground, **6.** simulated; *synonyms* (adj) fake,

false, imitation, sham, artificial, bogus, ersatz,
mock, assumed, fictitious, affected, feigned,
pretended, counterfeit, pseudo; *antonym* (adj)
genuine.

bwakanako ago; *synonyms* (adv) formerly, earlier,
erst, since, back, over, backwards, afterwards,
erewhile, syne, whilom, contrarily, reflexively, (adj)
past, agone.

bwana lubricate; *synonyms* (v) bribe, grease, lube,
buy, fix, lubricitate, overreach.

bwanabwana indifferent; *synonyms* (adj) apathetic,
callous, cold, cool, fair, impassive, insensible,
unconcerned, careless, dull, average, aloof, casual,
detached, disinterested; *antonyms* (adj) caring,
enthusiastic, fervent, keen, obsessive, eager,
energetic, involved, surprised.

bwanaki lubricated; *synonyms* (adj) greased, greasy,
tipsy.

bwaranako dismiss; *synonyms* (v) discharge, cashier,
cast, disband, discard, drop, bounce, can, cease,
dispatch, banish, disallow, discount, displace,
dissolve; *antonyms* (v) hire, employ.

bwaranakoaki dismissed; *synonyms* (adj) fired,
discharged, clear, convalescent, released.

bwarara trickle; *synonyms* (n) drip, distill, drivel,
drool, (v) drop, dribble, percolate, flow, leak, ooze,
seep, filter, leach, bleed, drain; *antonyms* (n)
throng, (v) gush.

bwaro surge; *synonyms* (n) wave, burst, ripple, spurt,
(v) billow, flood, rise, rush, stream, flow, gush,
heave, jet, swell, soar.

bwaroa swamp; *synonyms* (n) marsh, mire, bog,
morass, quagmire, (v) flood, inundate, overwhelm,
submerge, sink, deluge, drench, drown, overflow,
engulf; *antonym* (n) desert.

bwaroaki swamped; *synonyms* (v) grounded, (adj)
flooded, inundated, overcome, busy, engulfed,
overpowered, overwhelmed, (adv) aground.

bwarubwaru 1. resonant; *synonyms* (adj) ringing,
sonorous, vibrant, deep, full, melodious,
resounding, reverberating, reverberative, rich, bass,
booming, cavernous, echoing, loud; *antonym* (adj)
weak, **2.** resound; *synonyms* (v) echo, reverberate,
ring, boom, peal, roar, blare, reecho, resonate,
sound, clatter, vibrate, clash, rumble, thunder.

bwata sunburnt; *synonyms* (adj) sunburned, adust,
fiery, gloomy, sallow.

bwatika 1. bicycle; *synonyms* (n) machine, vehicle,
coach, rack, (v) bike, wheel, cycle, pedal,
motorcycle, drive, roll, **2.** cycle; *synonyms* (n)
bicycle, circle, round, ring, sequence, circuit,
period, turn, bout, beat, run, age, interval, orbit,
revolution, **3.** bike; *synonym* (n) motorbike.

bwatobwato relax; *synonyms* (v) loose, abate, give,
lounge, unbend, melt, debilitate, ease, relieve,

remit, rest, slack, (n) loosen, release, (adj) relent; *antonyms* (v) tighten, tense.

bwatobwatoaki relaxed; *synonyms* (adj) lax, loose, slack, calm, comfortable, composed, easy, cool, informal, easygoing, happy, serene, slow, tranquil, unhurried; *antonyms* (adj) tense, anxious, formal, nervous, prim, stiff, uncomfortable, strict, haggard, harassed, prudish, reserved, restless, taut.

bwatoka worthless; *synonyms* (adj) futile, vile, idle, cheap, empty, trifling, trivial, void, miserable, fruitless, ineffective, mean, null, (v) useless, vain; *antonyms* (adj) valuable, precious, useful, helpful, meaningful, priceless, worthwhile.

bwe steer; *synonyms* (v) guide, navigate, direct, drive, aim, conduct, manage, maneuver, run, tip, show, channel, (n) lead, point, bullock.

bweari scorched; *synonyms* (adj) parched, baked, adust, burnt, dry, seared; *antonym* (adj) wet.

bwebwe 1. moldy; *synonyms* (adj) musty, fusty, rancid, mouldy, bad, rank, rotten, (v) mildewed, rusty, decayed; *antonym* (adj) fresh, **2.** mildew; *synonyms* (n) mold, blight, fungus, mushroom, decay, helminth, (v) rust, must, cast, **3.** mildewed; *synonyms* (adj) trite, stale, stuffy, (v) moldy, seedy, spotted, corrupt, effete, flyblown, high, lentiginous, maggoty, mucid, reasty, tainted, **4.** sprout; *synonyms* (v) bud, bourgeon, germinate, grow, pullulate, vegetate, (n) shoot, germ, offshoot, sprit, scion, acrospire, chit, outgrowth, plumule, **5.** sprouting; *synonyms* (adj) budding, growing, developing, embryonic, emergent, evolving, germinant, green, nascent, surfacing, (n) germination, growth, **6.** twin; *synonyms* (adj) dual, matching, identical, similar, (n) match, counterpart, mate, pair, fellow, parallel, (v) double, duplicate, equal, couple, geminate.

bwebweaki 1. mildewed; *synonyms* (adj) musty, trite, (v) moldy, fusty, rusty, seedy, spotted, decayed, bad, corrupt, effete, flyblown, high, lentiginous, maggoty, **2.** sprouted.

bwena 1. divide; *synonyms* (v) cut, distribute, part, dissociate, apportion, detach, disconnect, dismember, dispense, separate, share, split, deal, distinguish, (n) break; *antonyms* (v) unite, join, **2.** separate; *synonyms* (adj) detached, individual, particular, single, (v) divorce, insulate, scatter, discrete, discriminate, disjoin, disperse, divide, isolate, demarcate, differentiate; *antonyms* (adj) connected, joined, simultaneous, (v) merge, mix, combine, fuse, link, associate, **3.** split; *synonyms* (v) crack, fracture, slit, burst, breach, cleave, division, fork, rift, (n) rip, rupture, tear, cleavage, cleft, parting.

bwenabwena split; *synonyms* (v) crack, cut, fracture, slit, burst, divide, separate, divorce, breach, cleave, (n) break, rip, rupture, tear, cleavage; *antonyms* (v) join, unite, merge.

bwenabwenaki split; *synonyms* (v) crack, cut, fracture, slit, burst, divide, separate, divorce, breach, cleave, (n) break, rip, rupture, tear, cleavage; *antonyms* (v) join, unite, merge.

bwenaki 1. divided; *synonyms* (adj) cleft, split, detached, forked, separate, separated, shared, disjointed, **2.** split; *synonyms* (v) crack, cut, fracture, slit, burst, divide, divorce, breach, cleave, division, (n) break, rip, rupture, tear, cleavage; *antonyms* (v) join, unite, merge, **3.** separated; *synonyms* (adj) disconnected, apart, divided, isolated, free, disjunct, removed, dislocated, independent, lone, single, (prep) disjoined, distinct.

bwenaua 1. halve; *synonyms* (v) bisect, divide, split, dimidiate, **2.** sunder; *synonyms* (v) part, separate, dissever, tear, share, cleave, detach, (n) sever, divorce, fragment, **3.** open; *synonyms* (adj) frank, obvious, artless, exposed, free, honest, bare, forthright, guileless, ingenuous, naked, (v) expand, give, (n) candid, clear; *antonyms* (adj) devious, secretive, concealed, furtive, hidden, limited, repressive, reserved, restricted, secret, blocked, cautious, (v) shut, end, (tr v) close.

bwenauaki 1. halved; *synonyms* (adj) half, dimidiate, **2.** opened; *synonyms* (v) blown, distended, exhausted, inflated, (adj) open, candid, exposed, assailable, blatant, blazing, clear, conspicuous, lawless, loose, through.

bwerea 1. decorate; *synonyms* (v) beautify, deck, adorn, bedeck, dress, embellish, grace, apparel, bedight, arrange, array, emblazon, embroider, enrich, garnish; *antonym* (v) strip, **2.** mark; *synonyms* (n) brand, evidence, score, character, heed, impression, imprint, sign, feature, (v) blemish, characterize, distinguish, grade, label, (adj) notice.

bwereaki 1. marked; *synonyms* (adj) distinct, conspicuous, noticeable, pronounced, remarkable, distinguished, apparent, definite, notable, obvious, signal, striking, strong, clear, appreciable; *antonyms* (adj) plain, unblemished, **2.** decorated; *synonyms* (adj) adorned, ornate, fancy, beautiful, bejeweled, adorn, dyed, elaborate, emblazoned, festive, inscribed, painted, purfled, tinted, celebrated.

bwerebwerea slice; *synonyms* (n) share, part, section, bit, chip, gash, morsel, piece, slab, chunk, portion, (v) cut, slash, carve, lacerate.

bwerebwereaki sliced; *synonyms* (adj) shredded, chopped, torn.

bwerengaki shy; *synonyms* (adj) diffident, fearful, timid, abashed, reserved, ashamed, coy, modest, nervous, reticent, self-conscious, backward, (v) fling, cast, (n) throw; *antonyms* (adj) brash, bold, confident, demonstrative, forward, outgoing.

bweretia print; *synonyms* (n) imprint, mark, impression, engraving, copy, lettering, picture, facsimile, letterpress, reproduction, (v) impress, photograph, issue, engrave, stamp.

bweretiaki printed; *synonyms* (adj) print, imprinted, stamped, embossed, marked.

bweta row; *synonyms* (n) altercation, line, file, rank, squabble, wrangle, clash, dispute, (v) quarrel, brawl, fight, argue, bicker, order, (adj) fracas; *antonyms* (n) agreement, (v) agree.

bwetua 1. row; *synonyms* (n) altercation, line, file, rank, squabble, wrangle, clash, dispute, (v) quarrel, brawl, fight, argue, bicker, order, (adj) fracas; *antonyms* (n) agreement, (v) agree, 2. paddle; *synonyms* (n) blade, oar, vane, (v) dabble, dodder, row, pull, spank, toddle, totter, coggle, larrup, 3. oar; *synonyms* (n) sail, screw.

D

de child; *synonyms* (n) baby, boy, babe, bairn, brat, girl, infant, juvenile, kid, minor, toddler, tot, youngster, innocent, imp; *antonym* (n) adult.

dibûg wash; *synonyms* (v) rinse, paint, bathe, clean, lave, moisten, mop, scour, scrub, color, tint, lap, (n) soak, ablution, washing; *antonym* (v) dirty.

diduarô 1. generous; *synonyms* (adj) ample, full, abundant, benevolent, copious, bountiful, charitable, fair, flush, kind, liberal, spacious, rich, benign, (n) free; *antonyms* (adj) stingy, meager, mean, measly, miserly, small, tightfisted, avaricious, greedy, ungenerous, 2. liberal; *synonyms* (adj) generous, handsome, big, large, bounteous, broad, giving, tolerant, lavish, easy, bighearted, enlightened, freehanded, munificent, noble; *antonyms* (adj) strict, oppressive, totalitarian, intolerant, (n) conservative.

djak-bain crippled; *synonyms* (v) drooping, flagging, (adj) lame, deformed, game, broken, exhausted, crooked, decrepit, halt, halting, impotent, prostrate, bedridden, damaged.

dokóv 1. truly; *synonyms* (adv) actually, really, sincerely, exactly, genuinely, indeed, right, certainly, honestly, precisely, very, legitimately, correctly, loyally, absolutely; *antonym* (adv) falsely, 2. surely; *synonyms* (adv) definitely, positively, sure, undoubtedly, confidently, clearly, firmly, securely, truly, unquestionably, yes, (adj) doubtless; *antonym* (adv) doubtfully.

dua 1. sacred; *synonyms* (adj) hallowed, holy, consecrated, dedicated, divine, religious, pious, blessed, inviolable, spiritual, consecrate, celestial, devoted, (v) solemn, majestic; *antonyms* (adj) secular, profane, 2. tabu; *synonyms* (n) taboo, (adj) forbidden, out, prohibited, proscribed, banned,

extinct, extinguished, kayoed, quenched, retired, stunned, verboten.

E

e 1. he; *synonyms* (pron) cestui, (n) male, man, helium, 2. lift; *synonyms* (n) elevator, boost, heave, (v) hoist, raise, rise, elevate, erect, filch, hike, advance, airlift, pilfer, pinch, rear, 3. raise; *synonyms* (v) lift, increase, build, enhance, foster, grow, promote, prefer, augment, cultivate, exalt, excite, heighten, levy, nurture; *antonym* (v) lower.

eai yes; *synonyms* (int) surely, (n) consent, acceptance, nod, (adv) ay, yea, certainly, positively, precisely, (v) acquiesce, agree, allow, grovel, (adj) obedient, submissive.

ebanako recoil; *synonyms* (n) reaction, backlash, repercussion, (v) bounce, kick, rebound, bound, cringe, flinch, quail, shrink, retreat, balk, cower, funk.

ebiebi 1. heir; *synonyms* (n) beneficiary, inheritor, offspring, successor, descendant, heritor, progeny, receiver, scion, 2. independent; *synonyms* (adj) free, autonomous, separate, substantive, impartial, nonpartisan, sovereign, unallied, self-sufficient, detached, distinct, individual, (n) freelance, mugwump, (adv) apart; *antonyms* (adj) dependent, simultaneous, 3. free; *synonyms* (adj) loose, frank, liberal, (v) clear, exempt, liberate, discharge, excuse, extricate, relieve, disentangle, acquit, deliver, disengage, ease; *antonyms* (adj) bound, restricted, compelled, confined, imprisoned, repressive, secure, strict, stuck, tangled, attached, busy, (v) confine, block, cage.

Ebikobo bishop; *synonyms* (n) archbishop, primate, clergyman, elder, eminence, episcopant, metropolitan, minister, (v) wassail, cup, flip, grog, negus, punch, purl.

ebiñoño fetid; *synonyms* (adj) foul, malodorous, noisome, putrid, smelly, rank, stinking, disgusting, rotten, foetid, rancid, decayed, dirty, unclean; *antonyms* (adj) fragrant, fresh.

ebu discouraged; *synonyms* (adj) disappointed, despondent, crestfallen, dejected, demoralized, disheartened, dispirited, downcast, downhearted, frustrated, pessimistic, depressed, baffled, balked; *antonym* (adj) optimistic.

eeng 1. aright; *synonyms* (adv) correctly, right, well, favorably, satisfactorily, completely, decent, decently, flop, immediately, mighty, powerful, precisely, 2. okay; *synonyms* (adv) fine, (adj) good, alright, fair, (int) yes, (n) approval, authorization, agreement, (v) approve, sanction, consent, endorse, authorize, countenance, accept; *antonyms* *(adj)* unsatisfactory, *(v)* forbid.

egêgi blind; *synonyms* *(adj)* sightless, undiscerning, *(v)* bedazzle, daze, dazzle, obscure, *(n)* screen, curtain, shutter, awning, drape, trick, veil, camouflage, cheat; *antonym* *(adj)* sighted.

egî-mata cross-eyed; *synonym* *(adj)* cockeyed.

egi-memau coward; *synonyms* *(n)* craven, cur, sneak, weakling, cocktail, coistril, niding, alarmist, baby, deserter, invertebrate, jellyfish, lily-liver, *(adj)* gutless, *(v)* frighten.

ei fire; *synonyms* *(n)* discharge, ardor, conflagration, explode, fervor, flame, *(v)* excite, eject, blaze, dismiss, ignite, kindle, expel, animate, arouse; *antonym* *(v)* hire.

eiei 1. lean; *synonyms* *(adj)* emaciated, gaunt, thin, bony, lank, lanky, *(v)* incline, bend, list, slant, bow, careen, pitch, *(n)* tilt, inclination; *antonyms* *(adj)* fat, plump, 2. tilt; *synonyms* *(n)* slope, joust, sway, canopy, argument, contention, contestation, controversy, dip, leaning, *(v)* lean, rock, cant, lurch, tip; *antonyms* *(v)* straighten, surrender, 3. sway; *synonyms* *(n)* influence, reign, authority, empire, power, *(v)* command, rule, oscillate, control, reel, stagger, bias, persuade, roll, shake.

eieiaki tilted; *synonyms* *(adj)* canted, leaning, slanting, oblique, crooked, slanted, atilt, askew, intolerant, lopsided, opinionated, tipped, uneven, twisted; *antonym* *(adj)* straight.

Eikuna rasp; *synonyms* *(v)* grate, scrape, abrade, chafe, file, grind, rub, scratch, grater, graze, groan, squeak, fray, screech, jar.

einako incline; *synonyms* *(n)* slope, bias, angle, ascent, dip, grade, gradient, inclination, slant, *(v)* cant, bend, dispose, lean, tilt, bank.

einakoaki inclined; *synonyms* *(adj)* prone, apt, oblique, willing, bowed, liable, likely, minded, predisposed, ready, bent, fain, susceptible, *(v)* given, *(prep)* disposed; *antonyms* *(adj)* level, reluctant, unwilling.

eirikia seduce; *synonyms* *(v)* attract, lure, allure, captivate, decoy, entice, inveigle, persuade, coax, defile, *(adj)* debauch, fascinate, bewitch, charm, *(n)* tempt.

eirioui porpoise; *synonyms* *(n)* dunter, pellack, porpesse, *(adj)* cachalot, whale.

eka 1. withstand; *synonyms* *(v)* endure, stand, bear, defy, resist, survive, weather, confront, sustain, brave, hold, suffer, take, abide, *(n)* oppose; *antonyms* *(v)* surrender, yield, 2. recover; *synonyms* *(v)* reclaim, recuperate, regain, retrieve, convalesce, find, heal, mend, rally, restore, improve, obtain, recall, recoup, redeem; *antonyms* *(v)* deteriorate, lose.

ekaki recovered; *synonyms* *(adj)* cured, healed, aged, better, corned, healthier, improved, whole, vulcanised, vulcanized.

ekan near; *synonyms* *(prep)* about, by, around, *(adv)* close, almost, towards, *(adj)* adjoining, adjacent, contiguous, imminent, impending, narrow, *(v)* familiar, approximate, approach; *antonym* *(adj)* distant.

ekara 1. contradict; *synonyms* *(v)* deny, oppose, belie, conflict, confute, contravene, controvert, disprove, dissent, impugn, invalidate, refute, disaffirm, disclaim, counteract; *antonyms* *(v)* confirm, agree, match, 2. reject; *synonyms* *(v)* refuse, decline, disapprove, discard, dismiss, eliminate, exclude, rebuff, abandon, disallow, disown, ignore, renounce, repel, *(n)* cull; *antonyms* *(v)* accept, approve, choose, select, acknowledge, grant, 3. oppose; *synonyms* *(v)* object, contest, contend, contradict, resist, fight, counter, disagree, combat, confront, defend, dispute, gainsay, hinder, thwart; *antonyms* *(v)* support, advocate, back, advise.

ekaraki 1. rejected; *synonyms* *(v)* forsaken, *(adj)* castaway, jilted, refused, reprobate, abandoned, disallowed, refuse, bare, cheerless, consume, depraved, desolate, destroy, devastate, 2. opposed; *synonyms* *(adj)* conflicting, contradictory, hostile, contrary, antagonistic, opposing, adverse, averse, contrasted, repugnant, incompatible, irreconcilable, counter, against, opposite.

Ekaretia clergy; *synonyms* *(n)* clericals, clerics, ecclesiastics, presbytery, canonicate, canonry, churchmen, conclave, deaconry, diaconate, learning, rabbinate; *antonym* *(n)* laity.

ekaria retort; *synonyms* *(n)* reply, answer, return, rejoinder, response, riposte, comeback, repartee, replication, counter, *(v)* respond, alembic, rejoin, repay, crucible.

eke 1. celebrated; *synonyms* *(adj)* famous, illustrious, renowned, distinguished, notable, noted, splendid, well-known, known, conspicuous, eminent, famed, great, notorious, *(n)* glorious; *antonym* *(adj)* unknown, 2. illustrious; *synonyms* *(adj)* celebrated, bright, excellent, brilliant, grand, lofty, proud, mighty, noble, prominent, recognized, redoubtable, shining, dignified, *(n)* boastful, 3. famous; *synonyms* *(adj)* capital, important, stunning, extraordinary, magnificent, outstanding, popular, proverbial, remarkable, signal, wonderful, memorable; *antonyms* *(adj)* infamous, ordinary, 4. renowned; *synonyms* *(adj)* reputable, acknowledged, familiar, legendary.

ekea excavate; *synonyms* *(v)* dig, burrow, hollow, unearth, quarry, grub, mine, tunnel, undermine, *(adj)* delve, gouge, *(n)* scoop.

ekimôtëta 1. low; *synonyms* (*adj*) contemptible, abject, humble, ignoble, base, blue, common, deep, dejected, depressed, down, downcast, downhearted, (*adv*) gentle, (*n*) depression; *antonyms* (*adj*) cheerful, happy, high-pitched, loud, important, piercing, (*n*) high, **2.** short; *synonyms* (*adj*) brief, concise, scarce, brusque, close, curt, sharp, compendious, laconic, abrupt, deficient, diminutive, inadequate, insufficient, lacking; *antonyms* (*adj*) long, tall, lengthy.

eko cane; *synonyms* (*n*) rod, scourge, stick, bat, (*v*) flog, whip, beat, birch, lash, thrash.

embera emperor; *synonyms* (*n*) sovereign, monarch, ruler, imperator, king, judge, majesty, potentate, president, protector, stadholder, crown, commander, queen.

ena 1. conduct; *synonyms* (*n*) behavior, administration, manage, demeanor, lead, performance, (*v*) act, bring, direct, administer, carriage, acquit, bearing, carry, comport, **2.** guide; *synonyms* (*n*) escort, directory, attendant, control, usher, chief, command, director, (*v*) conduct, govern, drive, channel, advise, cicerone, convey; *antonym* (*v*) follow, **3.** direct; *synonyms* (*adj*) straight, blunt, immediate, transparent, (*v*) aim, address, charge, dictate, head, guide, level, order, point, bend, boss; *antonyms* (*adj*) indirect, roundabout, circuitous, oblique, second-hand, sideways, unplanned, (*v*) request, **4.** coax; *synonyms* (*v*) wheedle, allure, cajole, entice, charm, blarney, inveigle, persuade, seduce, flatter, induce, (*n*) tempt, captivate, conciliate, fascinate, **5.** lead; *synonyms* (*v*) contribute, chair, conduce, go, give, dispose, run, show, take, captain, (*n*) clue, advantage, hint, leash, (*adj*) front.

enaki 1. led, **2.** directed; *synonyms* (*adj*) absorbed, concentrating, destined, focussed, formal, intent, prescript, subject, engaged, fixed, prescribed, rapt, (*adv*) under, **3.** guided; *synonym* (*adj*) conducted.

eng 1. yes; *synonyms* (*int*) surely, (*n*) consent, acceptance, nod, (*adv*) ay, yea, certainly, positively, precisely, (*v*) acquiesce, agree, allow, grovel, (*adj*) obedient, submissive, **2.** yea; *synonyms* (*adv*) yes, yeah, egregiously, eminently, especially, even, particularly, peculiarly, preeminently, principally, prominently, superlatively, supremely, surpassing, (*n*) vote.

erake ascend; *synonyms* (*v*) rise, arise, mount, climb, scale, uprise, increase, appear, escalate, jump, lift, soar; *antonyms* (*v*) descend, drop.

erarán leaky; *synonyms* (*adj*) leaking, leak, cracked, permeable, holey, porous, blabbermouthed, absorbent, bigmouthed, blabby, faulty, talebearing, tattling, spongy, talkative.

erea 1. lop; *synonyms* (*v*) cut, crop, hew, chop, dress, poll, prune, sever, trim, truncate, curtail, hack, amputate, (*adj*) clip, dock, **2.** cut; *synonyms* (*v*) carve, abbreviate, abridge, bite, condense, drop, fashion, reduce, (*n*) notch, slice, cutting, nick, blow, gash, shape; *antonyms* (*v*) increase, lengthen, (*n*) addition, extension, **3.** trim; *synonyms* (*adj*) tidy, neat, spruce, orderly, shipshape, smart, trig, (*v*) garnish, shave, adorn, embellish, lop, shorten, snip, (*n*) border; *antonym* (*adj*) fat.

ereaki 1. cut; *synonyms* (*v*) carve, chop, clip, abbreviate, abridge, bite, condense, crop, drop, fashion, (*n*) notch, slice, cutting, nick, blow; *antonyms* (*v*) increase, lengthen, (*n*) addition, extension, **2.** trimmed; *synonyms* (*adj*) cut, cunning, demure, down, emasculated, gashed, gelded, level, mown, neat, shortened, slashed, sly, smooth, snoD.

eri net; *synonyms* (*adj*) final, last, (*n*) network, bag, lace, earnings, cobweb, (*v*) mesh, clear, gain, make, trap, catch, earn, knit; *antonym* (*v*) gross.

eria scoop; *synonyms* (*n*) ladle, spade, exclusive, pocket, scoopful, shovel, article, report, (*v*) draw, dig, excavate, hollow, best, outdo, outflank.

eriake tack; *synonyms* (*n*) nail, pin, brad, tacking, (*v*) affix, baste, attach, shift, fasten, turn, append, fix, supplement, veer, (*adj*) sew.

eriaki netted; *synonyms* (*adj*) netlike, reticulated, lacy, meshy, lacelike, webbed, webby, weblike.

erieri fish; *synonyms* (*n*) bird, insect, mollusk, shellfish, worm, amphibian, beginner, blacktail, (*v*) angle, seek, hunt, pursue, grope, rummage, beg.

erigi side; *synonyms* (*n*) edge, rim, faction, border, brink, direction, face, part, hand, aspect, facet, margin, page, position, (*v*) party; *antonym* (*adj*) distant.

eta up; *synonyms* (*adv*) aloft, upward, upwardly, upwards, (*v*) raise, mount, rise, boost, advance, effervescent, filling, frothy, (*adj*) over, uphill, cheerful; *antonym* (*adj*) asleep.

ete decorate; *synonyms* (*v*) beautify, deck, adorn, bedeck, dress, embellish, grace, apparel, bedight, arrange, array, emblazon, embroider, enrich, garnish; *antonym* (*v*) strip.

eteaki decorated; *synonyms* (*adj*) adorned, ornate, fancy, beautiful, bejeweled, adorn, dyed, elaborate, emblazoned, festive, inscribed, painted, purfled, tinted, celebrated.

etei standing; *synonyms* (*v*) stand, (*n*) rank, fame, importance, position, prestige, place, reputation, footing, attitude, class, (*adj*) erect, motionless, continuance, permanent.

eti 1. just; *synonyms* (*adv*) exactly, hardly, newly, (*adj*) fair, right, correct, equitable, accurate, honest, impartial, barely, fit, good, reasonable, righteous; *antonyms* (*adj*) unfair, biased, wrong, **2.** correct; *synonyms* (*adj*) appropriate, becoming, nice, precise, proper, (*v*) adjust, amend, castigate, chastise, chasten, better, remedy, straighten, atone, (*n*) true;

antonyms (*adj*) incorrect, false, faulty, inappropriate, mistaken, improper, (*v*) spoil, **3.** accurate; *synonyms* (*adj*) exact, faithful, authentic, close, detailed, literal, meticulous, strict, truthful, scientific, careful, delicate, express, faultless, genuine; *antonym* (*adj*) inaccurate, **4.** fair; *synonyms* (*adj*) clear, beautiful, average, dispassionate, fine, sweet, candid, comely, considerable, decent, (*adv*) clean, (*n*) bazaar, blonde, carnival, (*v*) bright; *antonyms* (*adj*) dark, exceptional, unjust, partial, foul, imbalanced, mismatched, prejudiced, unwarranted, **5.** right; *synonyms* (*adj*) due, just, even, perfect, direct, ethical, fitting, (*adv*) correctly, (*n*) privilege, law, liberty, authority, claim, freedom, (*v*) rectify; *antonyms* (*adj*) unjustified, immoral, (*n*) left, **6.** upright; *synonyms* (*adj*) perpendicular, straight, erect, vertical, honorable, plumb, virtuous, pure, moral, noble, respectable, standing, (*n*) column, pillar, post; *antonyms* (*adv*) horizontally, (*adj*) disreputable, prone, upturned, degenerate, hanging, unwholesome, **7.** straight; *synonyms* (*adv*) level, directly, frankly, immediately, openly, (*adj*) flat, upright, immediate, consecutive, frank, neat, sincere, square, firsthand, plain; *antonyms* (*adv*) indirectly, (*adj*) curly, curved, diluted, winding, zigzag, askew, bent, curvy, knotted, twisted, twisting, wavy, circuitous, guarded.

etiraoi absolute; *synonyms* (*adj*) downright, peremptory, total, unconditional, categorical, full, real, unqualified, utter, actual, arbitrary, authoritative, certain, complete, (*n*) positive; *antonyms* (*adj*) partial, qualified.

etiruru 1. erect; *synonyms* (*v*) build, elevate, raise, construct, rear, assemble, lift, create, advance, arouse, dignify, (*adj*) upright, vertical, perpendicular, raised; *antonym* (*adj*) horizontal, **2.** exact; *synonyms* (*adj*) detailed, precise, actual, authentic, careful, definite, direct, (*v*) accurate, close, demand, require, claim, command, ask, (*n*) correct; *antonyms* (*adj*) inaccurate, imprecise, vague, wrong, approximate, inexact, **3.** strait; *synonyms* (*n*) inlet, need, pass, pinch, quandary, channel, crisis, difficulty, distress, poverty, straits, emergency, frith, (*adj*) narrow, (*v*) dilemma, **4.** upright; *synonyms* (*adj*) straight, erect, fair, good, just, righteous, honest, honorable, plumb, right, true, virtuous, pure, clean, (*n*) column; *antonyms* (*adv*) horizontally, (*adj*) disreputable, prone, upturned, degenerate, hanging, unwholesome, **5.** straight; *synonyms* (*adv*) level, directly, frankly, due, immediately, openly, (*adj*) even, flat, proper, immediate, consecutive, frank, neat, sincere, square; *antonyms* (*adv*) indirectly, (*adj*) curly, curved, diluted, winding, zigzag, askew, bent, curvy, knotted, twisted, twisting, wavy, circuitous, guarded.

etou hair; *synonyms* (*n*) fuzz, coat, down, fleece, fur, hairbreadth, haircloth, locks, pile, coiffure, (*adj*) brush, clipping, driblet.

euta 1. lift; *synonyms* (*n*) elevator, boost, heave, (*v*) hoist, raise, rise, elevate, erect, filch, hike, advance, airlift, pilfer, pinch, rear, **2.** raise; *synonyms* (*v*) lift, increase, build, enhance, foster, grow, promote, prefer, augment, cultivate, exalt, excite, heighten, levy, nurture; *antonym* (*v*) lower.

eutaki 1. lifted; *synonyms* (*adj*) elevated, lofty, steep, upraised, **2.** raised; *synonyms* (*v*) repousse, (*adj*) embossed, erect, convex, brocaded, high, alert, bold, confident, elate, elated, elative, exultant, mountant, (*prep*) above.

euto black; *synonyms* (*adj*) dark, sable, blackamoor, bleak, darkie, dirty, ebony, evil, nigger, unclean, cheerless, squalid, (*v*) sinister, villainous, blacken; *antonym* (*n*) white.

ewa 1. agitated; *synonyms* (*adj*) restless, excited, nervous, restive, tumultuous, upset, distressed, tense, alarmed, anxious, distraught, jumpy, overwrought, perturbed, shaken; *antonyms* (*adj*) calm, composed, lethargic, **2.** abundant; *synonyms* (*adj*) copious, generous, lush, luxuriant, thick, plenty, affluent, ample, fertile, fruitful, liberal, plentiful, prolific, rich, substantial; *antonyms* (*adj*) scarce, sparse, meager, **3.** much; *synonyms* (*adv*) greatly, frequently, almost, awfully, considerably, far, most, often, pretty, highly, (*n*) lot, heap, (*adj*) great, considerable, practically; *antonym* (*adv*) slightly, **4.** profuse; *synonyms* (*adj*) abundant, bounteous, exuberant, lavish, bountiful, excessive, full, opulent, prodigal, overflowing, extravagant, plenteous, diffuse, rife, dissipated, **5.** numerous; *synonyms* (*adj*) manifold, many, frequent, multiple, multitudinous, innumerable, populous, myriad, several, various, common, numberless, countless, incalculable, different; *antonym* (*adj*) few.

ewara 1. jab; *synonyms* (*n*) dig, poke, injection, thrust, blow, clip, lick, jabbing, (*v*) stab, prick, prod, nudge, puncture, shove, lunge, **2.** spear; *synonyms* (*n*) harpoon, lance, pike, fizgig, gig, shaft, barb, (*v*) impale, spike, pierce, skewer, stick, transfix, wound, enfilade, **3.** pierce; *synonyms* (*v*) cut, perforate, bore, enter, bite, drill, gore, penetrate, broach, pick, punch, riddle, break, insert, cleave, **4.** stab; *synonyms* (*n*) jab, try, shot, pang, attempt, crack, effort, go, endeavor, (*v*) pink, spear, spit, knife, push, poniard, **5.** sting; *synonyms* (*n*) hurt, con, pain, chafe, swindle, (*v*) goad, irritate, itch, prickle, provoke, burn, cheat, nettle, smart, tingle, **6.** stung; *synonyms* (*adj*) bitten, annoyed, bit, irritated, nettled, peeved, pissed, riled, roiled, besotted, blotto, churning, crocked, fuddled, harassed.

ewaraki 1. pierced; *synonyms* (*adj*) perforated, punctured, perforate, cleft, entered, **2.** stung;

synonyms (*adj*) bitten, annoyed, bit, irritated, nettled, peeved, pissed, riled, roiled, besotted, blotto, churning, crocked, fuddled, harassed, **3.** stabbed.

ewe 1. jump; *synonyms* (*v*) hop, spring, dive, hurdle, rise, skip, startle, clear, dance, (*n*) leap, bound, bounce, start, caper, curvet; *antonyms* (*v*) decrease, fall, **2.** arise; *synonyms* (*v*) appear, ascend, emerge, issue, mount, originate, proceed, result, awake, commence, develop, emanate, ensue, follow, grow, **3.** leap; *synonyms* (*n*) vault, jumping, lunge, lope, bouncing, fault, leaping, saltation, (*v*) jump, pounce, increase, ramp, buck, gambol, rear; *antonym* (*v*) plummet, **4.** spring; *synonyms* (*n*) fountain, source, jet, cause, font, fount, well, run, derivation, (*v*) recoil, arise, prance, rebound, stem, (*adj*) elastic.

eweaki raised; *synonyms* (*v*) repousse, (*adj*) elevated, embossed, erect, convex, brocaded, high, alert, bold, confident, elate, elated, elative, exultant, (*prep*) above.

eweka invade; *synonyms* (*v*) encroach, assail, assault, infringe, intrude, occupy, overrun, impinge, raid, infest, seize, penetrate, permeate, (*n*) attack, charge.

ewenako 1. dive; *synonyms* (*n*) dip, fall, drop, diving, header, bound, (*v*) plunge, jump, duck, crash, plummet, pounce, descend, plump, fly, **2.** develop; *synonyms* (*v*) advance, amplify, educate, expand, grow, breed, contract, acquire, bloom, blossom, break, bud, build, come, cultivate; *antonyms* (*v*) decrease, erupt, neglect, regress.

ewenakoaki developed; *synonyms* (*adj*) adult, mature, advanced, grown, sophisticated, complete, detailed, distinguished, educated, established, full, full-fledged, full-grown, grown-up, matured; *antonym* (*adj*) immature.

ewewe 1. skip; *synonyms* (*n*) jump, bound, hop, caper, omission, (*v*) leap, dance, bounce, prance, cut, gambol, skim, trip, decamp, frisk, **2.** plunge; *synonyms* (*n*) dive, drop, fall, (*v*) dip, douse, duck, immerse, submerge, crash, drown, dunk, launch, plummet, descend, lunge.

ewewerake 1. hop; *synonyms* (*n*) jump, leap, bound, hops, trip, flight, (*v*) dance, gambol, bounce, caper, skip, spring, limp, fly, hurdle, **2.** pounce; *synonyms* (*v*) dive, swoop, stoop, charge, attack, seize, alight, condescend, ambush, lunge, souse, strike, submit, surge, (*n*) descent.

É

éra why; *synonyms* (*adv*) so, (*n*) wherefore, reason, grounds, conundrum, enigma, mystery, proof, riddle, (*adj*) indeed.

Ê

ê 1. fire; *synonyms* (*n*) discharge, ardor, conflagration, explode, fervor, flame, (*v*) excite, eject, blaze, dismiss, ignite, kindle, expel, animate, arouse; *antonym* (*v*) hire, **2.** here; *synonyms* (*adv*) hither, in, about, arrived, available, indoors, inwards, (*n*) hair, (*adj*) present, there, near, nearby, (*pron*) her, their; *antonym* (*adv*) out.

êa where; *synonyms* (*adv*) there, here, wherever, whither, anywhere, wherein, anyplace, whereas, somewhere, (*conj*) but, while, (*pron*) everywhere, (*n*) point, spot, situation.

Ë

ëdai child; *synonyms* (*n*) baby, boy, babe, bairn, brat, girl, infant, juvenile, kid, minor, toddler, tot, youngster, innocent, imp; *antonym* (*n*) adult.

ënt spirit; *synonyms* (*n*) apparition, courage, ghost, life, mood, bravery, character, disposition, energy, enthusiasm, essence, heart, mind, phantom, (*adj*) animation; *antonyms* (*n*) lethargy, body.

ëran thus; *synonyms* (*adv*) therefore, then, consequently, so, hence, accordingly, thence, ergo, thusly.

G

gakak 1. sprout; *synonyms* (*v*) bud, bourgeon, germinate, grow, pullulate, vegetate, (*n*) shoot, germ, offshoot, sprit, scion, acrospire, chit, outgrowth, plumule, **2.** spathe; *synonym* (*n*) spatha.

gaña how; *synonyms* (*adv*) whereby, however, whence, nevertheless, nonetheless, notwithstanding, withal, yet.

gañga like; *synonyms* (*v*) corresponding, enjoy, identical, care, desire, fancy, (*adj*) equal, equivalent, alike, analogous, comparable, same, parallel, (n) love, relish; **antonyms** (prep) unlike, (v) dislike, (adj) different.

guri almost; **synonyms** (adv) nearly, approximately, just, around, most, practically, roughly, virtually, some, (prep) about, (adj) near, nigh, approaching, approximate, barely.

H

hang wind; **synonyms** (n) air, gust, (v) coil, twist, curl, meander, turn, bend, curve, twine, blow, crook, entwine, roll, weave.

headteacher principal; **synonyms** (adj) master, cardinal, capital, leading, primary, grand, first, foremost, prime, great, (n) chief, head, leader, main, manager; **antonym** (adj) minor.

hehi soon; **synonyms** (adv) shortly, early, presently, anon, immediately, directly, betimes, now, promptly, quickly, soonly, briefly, erelong, fast, quick.

houa 1. son; **synonyms** (n) offspring, boy, lad, child, descendant, logos, word, bible, countersign, discussion, intelligence, kid, news, parole, password, **2.** two; **synonyms** (n) deuce, pair, binary, demon, devil, duality, (adj) tway.

houanpoui twenty; **synonym** (adj) twice.

houaoupoui ninety; **synonym** (n) xc.

houaran water; **synonyms** (n) urine, moisture, juice, liquor, crystal, glass, lymph, pee, piddle, (v) irrigate, moisten, wet, soak, dampen, dilute.

houetia carry; **synonyms** (v) bear, bring, convey, conduct, take, acquit, behave, accept, comport, hold, pack, transport, load, assume, admit.

houhoua swim; **synonyms** (v) float, hover, drift, spin, plane, spire, (n) dip, swimming, (adj) rise.

I

i 1. grate; **synonyms** (n) lattice, (v) chafe, creak, grind, abrade, scrape, fret, gall, gnash, rub, aggravate, annoy, crunch, irritate, provoke, **2.** mutually; **synonyms** (adv) reciprocally, together, jointly, agreeably, both, equally, interchangeably, inversely, collectively, commonly, conjointly, cooperatively, **3.** grind; **synonyms** (v) labor, toil, comminute, drudge, grate, chew, crush, file, mash, sharpen, whet, bray, (n) mill, drudgery, struggle, **4.** mill; **synonyms** (n) factory, grinder, manufactory, machine, plant, engine, gin, notch, shop, implement, instrument, lathe, (v) pulverize, spar,

(adj) cent, **5.** at; **synonyms** (prep) in, a, (n) astatine, (adv) on, along, (prf) all, completely, wholly, (adj) entertainment, levee, party, reception, conversazione, home, soiree, **6.** fade; **synonyms** (v) disappear, decline, dissolve, evaporate, wither, die, discolor, droop, drop, languish, expire, decay, diminish, (n) disappearance, (adj) vanish; **antonyms** (v) grow, increase, strengthen, **7.** nationality; **synonyms** (n) nation, nationalism, patriotism, people, civism, race, folk, nationalness, birth, origin, residency, rights, **8.** diminish; **synonyms** (v) decrease, abate, lessen, abridge, deduct, detract, dwindle, fall, reduce, depreciate, belittle, contract, curtail, retrench, (adj) degrade, **9.** disappear; **synonyms** (v) melt, fade, depart, dematerialize, sink, go, pass, end, abscond, scram, disperse, escape, lift, perish, leave; **antonyms** (v) appear, stay, **10.** pulverize; **synonyms** (v) pound, powder, demolish, smash, bruise, disintegrate, pulverise, shatter, granulate, powderize, **11.** reciprocally; **synonyms** (adv) mutually, conversely, communally, **12.** sink; **synonyms** (n) sag, basin, (v) dip, set, descend, fell, bury, collapse, flag, founder, lower, settle, subside, ebb, (adj) immerse; **antonyms** (v) rise, float, **13.** people; **synonyms** (n) community, family, multitude, populace, clan, mob, flock, citizenry, crowd, inhabitants, kin, (v) inhabit, occupy, reside, dwell.

ia 1. grind; **synonyms** (v) labor, toil, comminute, crunch, drudge, grate, abrade, chew, crush, file, mash, scrape, sharpen, (n) mill, drudgery, **2.** where; **synonyms** (adv) there, here, wherever, whither, anywhere, wherein, anyplace, whereas, somewhere, (conj) but, while, (pron) everywhere, (n) point, spot, situation.

i-â below; **synonyms** (adv) beneath, under, down, infra, downstairs, (prep) underneath, (adj) low, after; **antonyms** (prep) above, over.

iaaki sweep; **synonyms** (n) compass, expanse, range, scope, field, stretch, area, room, (v) brush, rake, reach, sail, sway, (adj) curve, comb.

iai 1. have; **synonyms** (v) contain, gain, bear, carry, get, hold, possess, accept, acquire, eat, suffer, take, allow, bring, conduct, **2.** exist; **synonyms** (v) dwell, lie, be, endure, abide, consist, belong, continue, live, occur, subsist, survive, remain; **antonym** (v) die, **3.** at; **synonyms** (prep) in, a, (n) astatine, (adv) on, along, (prf) all, completely, wholly, (adj) entertainment, levee, party, reception, conversazione, home, soiree.

iaia gray; **synonyms** (adj) dull, bleak, dim, gloomy, grizzled, hoary, leaden, old, overcast, pale, dismal, murky, white, (n) grizzle, (v) grey; **antonym** (adj) bright.

iaí-nuk eastward; **synonyms** (adv) east, eastwards, (adj) eastbound.

iak not; *synonyms* (*adv*) no, nay, nor, nowise, never, (*adj*) shaven, shorn.

iakai 1. frigid; *synonyms* (*adj*) cold, chilly, chill, arctic, cool, freezing, icy, bleak, frosty, dead, chilling, frozen, gelid, (*n*) dull, distant; *antonym* (*adj*) warm, **2.** stark; *synonyms* (*adj*) austere, bare, desolate, mere, plain, severe, simple, bald, positive, absolute, barren, harsh, sheer, naked, nude, **3.** rigid; *synonyms* (*adj*) fixed, hard, inflexible, stiff, firm, set, strict, exacting, formal, rigorous, stern, tense, tight, tough, determined; *antonyms* (*adj*) flexible, elastic, soft, **4.** stiff; *synonyms* (*adj*) rigid, difficult, numb, solid, sturdy, arduous, awkward, buckram, ceremonious, potent, prim, (*n*) stark, cadaver, corpse, body; *antonyms* (*adj*) relaxed, floppy, supple, free, pliable.

iákaman already; *synonyms* (*adv*) beforehand, previously, before, formerly, once, earlier, finally, (*adj*) erewhile, present.

iaki 1. faded; *synonyms* (*v*) dilapidated, stale, (*adj*) dim, pale, bleached, dull, exhausted, faint, washy, withered, attenuate, attenuated, colorless, discoloured, **2.** clean; *synonyms* (*adj*) clear, fair, antiseptic, blank, pure, chaste, adroit, tidy, unblemished, (*v*) brush, cleanse, bathe, clarify, disinfect, sweep; *antonyms* (*adj*) filthy, unclean, muddy, unhygienic, full, syrupy, tainted, unwholesome, (*v*) dirty, soil, contaminate, pollute, **3.** milled; *synonyms* (*adj*) ground, crushed, pulverized, beaten, dressed, minced, polished, pounded, refined, svelte, urbane, **4.** ground; *synonyms* (*n*) base, cause, land, floor, reason, dirt, field, account, country, basis, footing, (*v*) bottom, found, establish, fix; *antonym* (*n*) ceiling, **5.** diminished; *synonyms* (*adj*) abated, lessened, weakened, atrophied, belittled, lower, cut, short, active, airy, backward, blasted, bony, cadaverous, clipped, **6.** pulverized; *synonyms* (*adj*) powdery, powdered, fine, pulverised, broken, minute, **7.** sweep; *synonyms* (*n*) compass, expanse, range, scope, stretch, area, room, (*v*) rake, reach, sail, sway, shot, broom, (*adj*) curve, comb.

iakiaki 1. cleaned; *synonyms* (*adj*) cleansed, spick-and-span, (*n*) curried, prepared, **2.** wallow; *synonyms* (*v*) revel, flounder, roll, welter, triumph, bask, billow, enjoy, exult, gloat, rejoice, splash, (*adj*) luxuriate, crouch, slouch, **3.** struggle; *synonyms* (*n*) contest, battle, combat, conflict, strain, effort, exertion, scramble, scuffle, (*v*) fight, attempt, dispute, endeavor, labor, quarrel; *antonyms* (*v*) flourish, glide, **4.** swept.

iakina 1. clean; *synonyms* (*adj*) clear, fair, antiseptic, blank, pure, chaste, adroit, tidy, unblemished, (*v*) brush, cleanse, bathe, clarify, disinfect, sweep; *antonyms* (*adj*) filthy, unclean, muddy, unhygienic, full, syrupy, tainted, unwholesome, (*v*) dirty, soil,

contaminate, pollute, **2.** sweep; *synonyms* (*n*) compass, expanse, range, scope, field, stretch, area, room, (*v*) rake, reach, sail, sway, shot, (*adj*) curve, comb, **3.** swept.

iakinaki 1. cleaned; *synonyms* (*adj*) cleansed, spick-and-span, (*n*) curried, prepared, **2.** swept.

iân 1. beneath; *synonyms* (*prep*) under, (*adv*) below, underneath, infra, (*adj*) low; *antonyms* (*prep*) above, over, **2.** under; *synonyms* (*adv*) beneath, downstairs, (*adj*) lower, down, nether, bottom, inferior, subject, subordinate, lowest.

ianena 1. foreign; *synonyms* (*adj*) alien, extraneous, extrinsic, exotic, exterior, external, strange, oversea, adventitious, outlandish, peregrine, remote, unfamiliar, unknown, different; *antonyms* (*adj*) native, familiar, domestic, internal, **2.** foreigner; *synonyms* (*n*) stranger, outlander, outsider, barbarian, immigrant, newcomer, **3.** alien; *synonyms* (*adj*) foreign, unusual, hostile, outside, (*n*) foreigner, emigrant, extraterrestrial, (*v*) alienate, estrange, disaffect; *antonym* (*n*) citizen, **4.** external; *synonyms* (*adj*) outward, outlying, peripheral, superficial, formal, objective, outdoor, outer, surface; *antonyms* (*adj*) inner, interior, inmost, inside, **5.** stranger; *antonyms* (*n*) associate, friend, pal.

iango 1. imagine; *synonyms* (*v*) think, believe, conjecture, assume, conceive, daydream, fancy, guess, consider, devise, envision, fantasize, see, (*conj*) suppose, (*n*) dream, **2.** mind; *synonyms* (*n*) intellect, brain, head, inclination, intelligence, psyche, regard, (*v*) care, look, attend, beware, keep, listen, notice, (*adj*) heed; *antonym* (*v*) forget, **3.** meditate; *synonyms* (*v*) deliberate, contemplate, cogitate, reflect, speculate, ponder, ruminate, wonder, brood, intend, mull, study, chew, design, (*n*) muse, **4.** solve; *synonyms* (*v*) resolve, interpret, answer, decipher, dissolve, crack, elucidate, explain, riddle, decide, loosen, figure, conclude, clarify, (*adj*) loose, **5.** speculate; *synonyms* (*v*) imagine, venture, hazard, hypothesize, meditate, presume, infer, job, risk, theorize, gamble, say, suspect, adventure, reckon, **6.** recollect; *synonyms* (*v*) recall, remember, recognize, remind, mind, reminisce, retrieve, review, **7.** thought; *synonyms* (*v*) observation, (*n*) notion, idea, opinion, conception, consideration, impression, belief, feeling, reflection, sentiment, concept, judgment, apprehension, attention; *antonym* (*n*) fact, **8.** suppose; *synonyms* (*v*) divine, estimate, calculate, expect, judge, hope, count, anticipate, deem, feel, gather, opine, postulate, presuppose, put, **9.** think; *synonyms* (*v*) hold, reason, envisage, esteem, recollect, repute, cerebrate, mean, understand, account, plan, call, make, apprehend, find.

iangoa 1. contemplate; *synonyms* (*v*) consider, cogitate, meditate, muse, speculate, deliberate, look, ponder, reflect, gaze, behold, entertain, intend, mull, reason, **2**. consider; *synonyms* (*v*) believe, regard, think, view, assume, calculate, conceive, contemplate, reckon, analyze, consult, debate, deem, esteem, (*n*) study; *antonym* (*v*) ignore, **3**. reason; *synonyms* (*n*) mind, account, intellect, occasion, argument, object, purpose, rationality, understanding, basis, (*v*) cause, argue, conclude, deduce, discuss, **4**. ponder; *synonyms* (*v*) brood, chew, examine, imagine, ruminate, wonder, digest, excogitate, see, weigh, cerebrate, judge, mean, puzzle, **5**. think; *synonyms* (*v*) estimate, guess, hold, suppose, conjecture, expect, suspect, envisage, feel, recollect, fancy, figure, repute, opine, presume; *antonym* (*v*) forget.

iangoaki 1. imagined; *synonyms* (*adj*) imaginary, fanciful, notional, unreal, fancied, fictitious, conceptional, conjectural, doubtful, dubious, feigned, hypothetical, ideational, nonexistent, unseen, **2**. considered; *synonyms* (*adj*) deliberate, reasoned, intentional, premeditated, sensible, sound, willful, studied, calculated, planned, reputed, adult, careful, designed, exact; *antonyms* (*adj*) impulsive, sudden, impetuous, ingenuous, swift, thoughtless, **3**. minded; *synonyms* (*adj*) willing, prone, ready, partial, predisposed, prepared, (*prep*) inclined, disposed, jolly, **4**. fabled; *synonyms* (*adj*) legendary, mythical, mythological, fabulous, enchanted, magic, magical, storybook, **5**. planned; *synonyms* (*adj*) intended, aforethought, plotted, scheduled, fixed, future; *antonyms* (*adj*) spontaneous, unplanned, **6**. reasoned; *synonyms* (*adj*) considered, coherent, rational, logical, reasonable, articulate, clear, cogent, consistent, critical, deducible, derivable, diagnostic, dogmatic, good; *antonyms* (*adj*) illogical, confused, **7**. supposed; *synonyms* (*adj*) alleged, assumed, putative, apparent, ostensible, suppositional, professed, supposititious, supposititious, pretended, theoretical; *antonyms* (*adj*) real, actual, **8**. solved; *synonyms* (*v*) undiscovered, unexplained, untraced, undeveloped, (*adj*) resolved, determined, exposed.

iangomaka 1. calculate; *synonyms* (*v*) count, estimate, account, add, appraise, cipher, compute, deem, enumerate, forecast, gauge, guess, make, reckon, consider, **2**. formulate; *synonyms* (*v*) devise, compose, contrive, develop, express, invent, form, enunciate, create, formularize, put, articulate, conceive, frame, phrase, **3**. plan; *synonyms* (*n*) aim, map, figure, chart, intent, outline, pattern, scheme, arrangement, blueprint, (*v*) design, intend, plot, arrange, draft, **4**. resolve; *synonyms* (*v*) determine, decide, solve, conclude, decompose, dissolve, settle, end, (*n*) purpose, determination, decision, firmness, resolution, answer, analyze; *antonyms* (*n*) indecision, weakness.

iangomakaki 1. calculated; *synonyms* (*v*) advised, designed, (*adj*) deliberate, conscious, intended, intentional, premeditated, purposeful, studied, measured, planned, strategic; *antonym* (*adj*) accidental, **2**. formulated; *synonym* (*adj*) devised, **3**. resolved; *synonyms* (*v*) resolute, (*adj*) determined, definite, firm, fixed, set, certain, decided, conclusive, intent, final, positive, solved, unyielding, bent, **4**. planned; *synonyms* (*adj*) calculated, aforethought, plotted, scheduled, future, prepared; *antonyms* (*adj*) spontaneous, unplanned.

iangororoko theorize; *synonyms* (*v*) conjecture, speculate, suppose, theorise, guess, hypothesize, assume, contemplate, hypothecate, imagine, meditate, postulate.

ianna stranger; *synonyms* (*n*) alien, foreigner, outsider, newcomer, outlander, unknown; *antonyms* (*n*) associate, friend, native, pal.

ibaba 1. impregnated; *synonyms* (*adj*) impregnate, fertilised, fertilized, full, adequate, ample, copious, inseminated, perfect, plenteous, supplied, surfeited, **2**. saturated; *synonyms* (*adj*) drenched, sodden, wet, concentrated, soaked, sopping, soggy, soppy, pure, soaking; *antonym* (*adj*) dry.

ibabakoi 1. hug; *synonyms* (*n*) embrace, hold, clinch, (*v*) clasp, cuddle, squeeze, cling, cherish, clutch, grasp, touch, adhere, gripe, clench, bosom, **2**. embrace; *synonyms* (*v*) comprise, hug, admit, adopt, comprehend, contain, cover, encompass, espouse, grip, include, caress, accept, embody, assume; *antonym* (*v*) reject.

ibabannang forgetful; *synonyms* (*adj*) careless, oblivious, inattentive, negligent, remiss, lax, absent-minded, casual, heedless, neglectful, unmindful, mindless, unaware; *antonym* (*adj*) attentive.

ibabu 1. strive; *synonyms* (*v*) endeavor, labor, attempt, contend, contest, fight, struggle, combat, aim, aspire, compete, strain, toil, work, exert, **2**. struggle; *synonyms* (*n*) battle, conflict, effort, exertion, scramble, scuffle, encounter, strife, war, warfare, wrestle, (*v*) dispute, quarrel, fighting, strive; *antonyms* (*v*) flourish, glide.

ibe 1. compact; *synonyms* (*adj*) close, dense, compendious, concise, hard, (*n*) agreement, arrangement, contract, covenant, bargain, engagement, (*v*) compress, condense, consolidate, pack; *antonyms* (*adj*) loose, sprawling, bulky, sparse, **2**. stuffed; *synonyms* (*v*) farctate, (*adj*) full, crammed, packed, congested, replete, loaded, chock-full, crowded, fraught, abounding, big, brimming, concentrated, distended; *antonyms* (*adj*) empty, hungry, **3**. numerous; *synonyms* (*adj*) manifold, many, abundant, frequent, multiple, multitudinous, copious, innumerable, plentiful, populous, great, myriad, rife, several, various; *antonym* (*adj*) few.

ibea 1. break; *synonyms* (*v*) split, crack, burst, fail, infringe, leak, (*n*) breach, fracture, pause, rupture, stop, collapse, interruption, respite, suspension; *antonyms* (*v*) repair, obey, honor, mend, (*n*) continuation, **2.** smash; *synonyms* (*v*) crash, bang, hit, break, crush, mash, shatter, defeat, demolish, pound, ruin, (*n*) clash, blast, collision, knock.

ibeabure embarrass; *synonyms* (*v*) confuse, baffle, block, bother, confound, disconcert, encumber, hinder, complicate, abash, discomfit, distress, hamper, impede, (*adj*) bewilder.

ibeabureaki embarrassed; *synonyms* (*adj*) ashamed, abashed, awkward, uncomfortable, disconcerted, bashful, shamefaced, sheepish, shy, chagrined, discomfited, humiliated, mortified; *antonyms* (*adj*) proud, relaxed.

ibeaki 1. broken; *synonyms* (*v*) broke, (*adj*) tame, torn, busted, imperfect, intermittent, rough, rugged, ruined, uneven, disjointed, incomplete, confused, cracked, crushed; *antonyms* (*adj*) constant, unbroken, intact, whole, wild, **2.** smashed; *synonyms* (*adj*) shattered, drunk, inebriated, intoxicated, broken, plastered, sloshed, blotto, tipsy, besotted, pissed, tight; *antonym* (*adj*) sober.

ibebure 1. intimidate; *synonyms* (*v*) daunt, browbeat, bully, discourage, frighten, bullyrag, deter, scare, alarm, dismay, cow, terrify, terrorize, threaten, (*n*) affright; *antonym* (*v*) encourage, **2.** daunt; *synonyms* (*v*) abash, appall, dash, dishearten, horrify, awe, deject, dispirit, overawe, depress, (*n*) intimidate, fright, **3.** threaten; *synonyms* (*v*) menace, endanger, loom, offer, imperil, jeopardize, peril, approach, foreshadow, portend, impend, coerce, augur, await, (*n*) threat; *antonym* (*v*) help.

ibebureaki 1. daunted; *synonyms* (*adj*) bothered, downcast, dispirited, discouraged, frightened, abashed, afraid, bashful, fazed, impressed, overcome, overwhelmed, timid, awed, fearful, **2.** intimidated; *synonyms* (*adj*) bullied, scared, browbeaten, cowed, hangdog, daunted, anxious, demoralized, guilty, nervy, panicky, shamed, shamefaced, unsettled, upset; *antonym* (*adj*) unimpressed.

ibeki 1. scuffle; *synonyms* (*n*) brawl, scrap, melee, battle, clash, combat, fighting, fray, (*v*) tussle, fight, grapple, shuffle, struggle, disturbance, encounter, **2.** stomp; *synonyms* (*n*) clump, (*v*) stamp, tramp, trample, pound, plod, storm, stump.

ibenano constipated; *synonyms* (*adj*) costive, bellybound, close, cold, formal, impermeable, reserved, unyielding, (*v*) bound, certain, destined, resolved.

ibengu mutter; *synonyms* (*v*) mumble, grumble, growl, maunder, grouch, complain, croak, snarl, gnarl, (*n*) murmur, whisper, complaint, grumbling, murmuration, murmuring.

iberoro indigestible; *synonyms* (*adj*) ungenial, filling, heavy, incocted, inedible, innutritious, starchy, tough, undigestible, bad, buttery, calorific, cloying, creamy, disgusting; *antonyms* (*adj*) edible, light.

ibetutu dense; *synonyms* (*adj*) compact, thick, close, crowded, deep, crass, dim, dull, heavy, impenetrable, solid, stupid, concentrated, dumb, firm; *antonyms* (*adj*) bright, insightful, loose, clever, intelligent, readable, simple, sparse.

ibewi 1. dispute; *synonyms* (*n*) brawl, quarrel, debate, conflict, wrangle, difference, question, combat, (*v*) argue, contest, controversy, discuss, fight, row, squabble; *antonyms* (*n*) agreement, (*v*) agree, **2.** squabble; *synonyms* (*n*) bicker, feud, scrap, contention, fuss, hassle, argument, broil, spat, strife, altercation, bickering, (*v*) dispute, tiff, brabble, **3.** quarrel; *synonyms* (*n*) dissension, clash, disagreement, fracas, misunderstanding, breach, fray, discord, dustup, (*v*) disagree, affray, altercate, disturbance, differ, contend, **4.** quarrelsome; *synonyms* (*adj*) argumentative, pugnacious, belligerent, contentious, combative, aggressive, cantankerous, disputatious, currish, ugly, contrary, termagant, arguing, factious, (*v*) fretful; *antonym* (*adj*) peaceable.

ibewiaki disputed; *synonyms* (*adj*) controversial, moot, disputable, debatable, doubtful, dubious, opposed, uncertain, problematic.

ibibiti 1. meet; *synonyms* (*v*) converge, find, assemble, congregate, encounter, fulfill, gather, answer, cross, confront, intersect, abut, concur, adjoin, (*adj*) fit; *antonyms* (*v*) avoid, disperse, diverge, **2.** pass; *synonyms* (*v*) flow, deliver, give, happen, lead, move, offer, overtake, live, advance, die, elapse, exceed, (*adj*) go, run; *antonym* (*v*) fail.

ibo stuffed; *synonyms* (*v*) farctate, (*adj*) full, crammed, packed, congested, replete, loaded, chock-full, crowded, fraught, abounding, big, brimming, concentrated, distended; *antonyms* (*adj*) empty, hungry.

ibonga sorcerer; *synonyms* (*n*) magician, enchanter, necromancer, conjurer, wizard, conjuror.

ibuobuoki 1. helpful; *synonyms* (*adj*) beneficial, favorable, advantageous, friendly, handy, useful, beneficent, convenient, accommodating, constructive, instrumental, kindly, obliging, (*n*) benevolent, (*v*) adjuvant; *antonyms* (*adj*) unhelpful, useless, uncooperative, worthless, **2.** beneficial; *synonyms* (*adj*) fruitful, profitable, expedient, gainful, good, healthy, productive, propitious, salutary, serviceable, wholesome, worthwhile, curative, genial, healing; *antonyms* (*adj*) disadvantageous, harmful, **3.** cooperate;

synonyms (*v*) collaborate, assist, concur, help, join, unite, interact, participate, **4.** volunteer; *synonyms* (*n*) voluntary, (*v*) offer, proffer, tender, extend, propose, submit, (*adj*) unpaid.

ibutubuto 1. bump; *synonyms* (*n*) bang, crash, blow, bulge, clash, hit, knock, blast, collision, concussion, jar, push, (*v*) bash, jolt, break, **2.** jar; *synonyms* (*n*) jangle, crock, container, jog, shake, amphora, bottle, pot, can, (*v*) creak, bump, collide, jounce, grate, agitate, **3.** jolt; *synonyms* (*n*) jerk, hustle, shock, shove, surprise, thrust, tremor, (*v*) hitch, impact, rock, bounce, convulse, jostle, toss, elbow.

ibutubutoaki jolted; *synonym* (*adj*) shaken.

iduai not; *synonyms* (*adv*) no, nay, nor, nowise, never, (*adj*) shaven, shorn.

ie sail; *synonyms* (*n*) float, voyage, canvas, sheet, plane, ship, (*v*) cruise, navigate, run, glide, cross, drift, sweep, travel, fly.

iea sail; *synonyms* (*n*) float, voyage, canvas, sheet, plane, ship, (*v*) cruise, navigate, run, glide, cross, drift, sweep, travel, fly.

ieanga 1. excite; *synonyms* (*v*) animate, arouse, disturb, enliven, agitate, energize, awaken, electrify, encourage, evoke, exasperate, incite, inspire, kindle, provoke; *antonyms* (*v*) calm, pacify, bore, **2.** call; *synonyms* (*v*) cry, bellow, name, shout, bid, summon, howl, address, baptize, cite, (*n*) appeal, yell, appoint, command, demand; *antonym* (*v*) dismiss.

ieangaki 1. called; *synonyms* (*v*) nempt, ycleped, (*adj*) named, chosen, qualified, **2.** excited; *synonyms* (*adj*) agitated, ablaze, emotional, enthusiastic, frantic, ardent, aroused, delirious, fervent, heated, impassioned, passionate, warm, elated, (*v*) animated; *antonyms* (*adj*) calm, cool, unexcited.

iebaba 1. hasten; *synonyms* (*v*) speed, expedite, further, forward, dispatch, advance, hurry, dash, hie, rush, bustle, dart, (*adj*) accelerate, quicken, (*n*) haste; *antonym* (*v*) delay, **2.** hurry; *synonyms* (*n*) flurry, celerity, hastiness, hurriedness, press, (*v*) hasten, scurry, fly, run, zip, drive, race, scamper, scuttle, flit; *antonyms* (*n*) slowness, (*v*) dawdle.

iebabaki hurried; *synonyms* (*adj*) hasty, fast, headlong, quick, rapid, speedy, sudden, swift, abrupt, cursory, careless, precipitate, prompt, rash, slapdash; *antonyms* (*adj*) slow, unhurried, leisurely.

ieie 1. navigate; *synonyms* (*v*) cruise, guide, sail, fly, pilot, voyage, cross, maneuver, **2.** sail; *synonyms* (*n*) float, canvas, sheet, plane, ship, vessel, canvass, (*v*) navigate, run, glide, drift, sweep, travel, soar, coast.

iein 1. marry; *synonyms* (*v*) join, link, conjoin, splice, tie, unite, wive, couple, combine, merge, connect, unify, match, (*n*) espouse, wed; *antonym* (*v*) divorce, **2.** married; *synonyms* (*adj*) marital, wedded, conjugal, matrimonial, connubial, nuptial;

antonyms (*adj*) single, unmarried, **3.** wed; *synonyms* (*v*) marry, married.

ieinaki married; *synonyms* (*adj*) marital, wedded, conjugal, matrimonial, connubial, nuptial; *antonyms* (*adj*) single, unmarried.

ieka 1. inundate; *synonyms* (*v*) flood, drench, deluge, drown, submerge, glut, engulf, overflow, swamp, overwhelm, flush, flow, overrun, saturate, (*adj*) irrigate, **2.** flood; *synonyms* (*n*) pour, torrent, stream, downpour, cataclysm, alluvion, avalanche, barrage, flooding, inundation, (*v*) inundate, gush, rush, cascade, (*prep*) tide; *antonyms* (*n*) drought, shortage, (*v*) trickle.

iekaki flooded; *synonyms* (*adj*) awash, swamped, inundated, afloat, engulfed, submerged, aimless, beaten, busy, conquered, directionless, drenched, enveloped, filled, floating; *antonym* (*adj*) dry.

ienaka agitated; *synonyms* (*adj*) restless, excited, nervous, restive, tumultuous, upset, distressed, tense, alarmed, anxious, distraught, jumpy, overwrought, perturbed, shaken; *antonyms* (*adj*) calm, composed, lethargic.

ientaka 1. frantic; *synonyms* (*adj*) delirious, desperate, crazy, frenzied, excited, furious, distraught, distracted, frenetic, raging, boisterous, despairing, feverish, fierce, (*v*) wild; *antonym* (*adj*) calm, **2.** excited; *synonyms* (*adj*) agitated, ablaze, emotional, enthusiastic, frantic, ardent, aroused, fervent, heated, impassioned, passionate, warm, elated, tense, (*v*) animated; *antonyms* (*adj*) cool, unexcited.

ieta 1. lift; *synonyms* (*n*) elevator, boost, heave, (*v*) hoist, raise, rise, elevate, erect, filch, hike, advance, airlift, pilfer, pinch, rear, **2.** hold; *synonyms* (*v*) keep, detain, endure, adhere, bear, comprise, contain, entertain, have, arrest, carry, (*n*) grasp, grip, clasp, clutch; *antonym* (*v*) release, **3.** raise; *synonyms* (*v*) lift, increase, build, enhance, foster, grow, promote, prefer, augment, cultivate, exalt, excite, heighten, levy, nurture; *antonym* (*v*) lower, **4.** up; *synonyms* (*adv*) aloft, upward, upwardly, upwards, (*v*) mount, effervescent, filling, frothy, mousseux, nappy, (*adj*) over, uphill, cheerful, happy, improving; *antonym* (*adj*) asleep.

iéta above; *synonyms* (*prep*) on, past, surpassing, (*adv*) over, beyond, aloft, supra, up, more, overhead, (*adj*) preceding, former, upper, foregoing, previous; *antonym* (*prep*) below.

ietaki 1. held; *synonyms* (*adj*) absorbed, confined, alleged, assumed, believed, bound, caged, captive, detained, fast, immersed, obsessed, occupied, protected, (*adv*) on, **2.** lifted; *synonyms* (*adj*) elevated, lofty, steep, upraised, **3.** raised; *synonyms* (*v*) repousse, (*adj*) embossed, erect, convex, brocaded, high, alert, bold, confident, elate, elated, elative, exultant, mountant, (*prep*) above.

ietât high; *synonyms* (*adj*) eminent, elevated, great, expensive, distinguished, exalted, lofty, tall, heavy, arrogant, costly, dear, (*v*) bad, fusty, rancid; *antonyms* (*adj*) deep, short, sober, (*n*) low.

ietia 1. complete; *synonyms* (*adj*) perfect, absolute, consummate, whole, full, stark, accomplished, all, (*v*) accomplish, achieve, close, finish, execute, act, attain; *antonyms* (*adj*) incomplete, partial, unfinished, abridged, shortened, sketchy, lacking, narrow, qualified, (*v*) neglect, **2.** finished; *synonyms* (*v*) done, (*adj*) complete, completed, ended, polished, ripe, ruined, spent, round, capable, decided, final, elegant, concluded, (*adv*) over; *antonyms* (*adj*) remaining, rough.

igagi proud; *synonyms* (*adj*) arrogant, dignified, disdainful, haughty, lofty, exalted, conceited, egotistical, gallant, lordly, majestic, overbearing, pompous, imperious, elated; *antonyms* (*adj*) humble, modest, ashamed, embarrassed.

ii 1. grind; *synonyms* (*v*) labor, toil, comminute, crunch, drudge, grate, abrade, chew, crush, file, mash, scrape, sharpen, (*n*) mill, drudgery, **2.** grate; *synonyms* (*n*) lattice, (*v*) chafe, creak, grind, fret, gall, gnash, rub, aggravate, annoy, irritate, provoke, scratch, grit, bother.

iiaki ground; *synonyms* (*n*) base, cause, land, floor, reason, dirt, field, soil, account, country, basis, (*v*) bottom, found, establish, fix; *antonym* (*n*) ceiling.

ika fish; *synonyms* (*n*) bird, insect, mollusk, shellfish, worm, amphibian, beginner, blacktail, (*v*) angle, seek, hunt, pursue, grope, rummage, beg.

ikai 1. here; *synonyms* (*adv*) hither, in, about, arrived, available, indoors, inwards, (*n*) hair, (*adj*) present, there, near, nearby, (*pron*) her, their; *antonym* (*adv*) out, **2.** present; *synonyms* (*adj*) grant, confer, (*n*) gift, donation, (*v*) bestow, display, give, introduce, prefer, deliver, donate, offer, perform, gratuity, award; *antonyms* (*adj*) missing, (*n*) past, future, history, (*v*) withdraw, (*adv*) absent.

i-kai here; *synonyms* (*adv*) hither, in, about, arrived, available, indoors, inwards, (*n*) hair, (*adj*) present, there, near, nearby, (*pron*) her, their; *antonym* (*adv*) out.

ikaika tickle; *synonyms* (*v*) itch, titillate, indulge, thrill, prickle, please, tingle, flatter, humor, (*n*) titillation.

ikaikai hasten; *synonyms* (*v*) speed, expedite, further, forward, dispatch, advance, hurry, dash, hie, rush, bustle, dart, (*adj*) accelerate, quicken, (*n*) haste; *antonym* (*v*) delay.

ikainapa lately; *synonyms* (*adv*) recently, late, freshly, latterly, newly, just, new, (*adj*) anew, afresh.

ikakai 1. date; *synonyms* (*n*) age, appointment, assignation, engagement, epoch, meeting, period, era, time, year, boyfriend, (*v*) escort, determine, register, accompany, **2.** accompany; *synonyms* (*v*)

attend, follow, associate, companion, company, guide, lead, walk, consort, bring, concur, conduct, convoy, join, take, **3.** quick; *synonyms* (*adj*) bright, prompt, active, agile, clever, hasty, intelligent, nimble, speedy, alert, alive, cursory, dexterous, expeditious, (*adv*) fast; *antonyms* (*adj*) slow, leisurely, dull.

ikakaiaki 1. dated; *synonyms* (*adj*) antiquated, archaic, obsolete, outdated, outmoded, old-fashioned, ancient, dowdy, unfashionable, old, **2.** accompanied; *synonym* (*adj*) attended.

ikakaiwi 1. squabble; *synonyms* (*n*) quarrel, bicker, brawl, feud, scrap, contention, fight, fuss, hassle, argument, broil, spat, (*v*) dispute, row, argue, **2.** wrangle; *synonyms* (*n*) squabble, altercation, tiff, controversy, affray, disagreement, skirmish, difference, (*v*) debate, contest, bickering, misunderstanding, disagree, altercate, clash; *antonyms* (*n*) agreement, (*v*) agree, **3.** quarrel; *synonyms* (*n*) dissension, conflict, fracas, breach, fray, discord, dustup, strife, variance, disputation, (*v*) wrangle, disturbance, differ, contend, jar.

ikakan near; *synonyms* (*prep*) about, by, around, (*adv*) close, almost, towards, (*adj*) adjoining, adjacent, contiguous, imminent, impending, narrow, (*v*) familiar, approximate, approach; *antonym* (*adj*) distant.

ikake 1. cocky; *synonyms* (*adj*) arrogant, proud, conceited, supercilious, vain, brash, flippant, insolent, overbearing, impudent, boastful, brazen, familiar, jaunty, superior, **2.** grasping; *synonyms* (*adj*) avaricious, covetous, acquisitive, greedy, avid, grabby, rapacious, voracious, mercenary, miserly, ravenous, sordid, stingy, envious, (*n*) seizing; *antonym* (*adj*) generous, **3.** arrogant; *synonyms* (*adj*) haughty, imperious, presumptuous, dogmatic, condescending, disdainful, domineering, egotistical, cavalier, chesty, cocky, contemptuous, high, lordly, masterful; *antonyms* (*adj*) modest, self-effacing, (*syn*) humble, **4.** dominating; *synonyms* (*adj*) commanding, autocratic, bossy, ascendant, ascendent, inextinguishable, unquenchable, predominant, authoritarian, authoritative, autocratical, dictatorial, leading, ascensive, despotic, **5.** insolent; *synonyms* (*adj*) abusive, audacious, disrespectful, impertinent, fresh, defiant, barefaced, bold, brassy, discourteous, impolite, offensive, forward, cheeky, flip; *antonyms* (*adj*) polite, respectful.

ikana 1. chastise; *synonyms* (*v*) castigate, chasten, correct, criticize, punish, reprimand, scourge, beat, scold, discipline, flog, lash, objurgate, penalize, strike; *antonym* (*v*) praise, **2.** punish; *synonyms* (*v*) chastise, avenge, pay, penalise, whip, condemn, kill, fine, smite, torment, retaliate, revenge, thrash, (*n*) pain; *antonym* (*v*) excuse.

ikanaki 1. chastised; *synonyms* *(adj)* corrected, disciplined, **2.** punished.

ikangui 1. quarrel; *synonyms* *(n)* brawl, feud, altercation, dissension, clash, conflict, difference, disagreement, *(v)* dispute, fight, argue, row, disagree, squabble, wrangle; *antonyms* *(n)* agreement, *(v)* agree, **2.** squabble; *synonyms* *(n)* quarrel, bicker, scrap, contention, fuss, hassle, argument, broil, spat, strife, bickering, *(v)* tiff, brabble, contend, debate, **3.** wrangle; *synonyms* *(n)* controversy, affray, skirmish, haggle, discord, wrangling, *(v)* contest, misunderstanding, altercate, jangle, jar, brangle, scuffle, discuss, spar.

ikao gnaw; *synonyms* *(v)* bite, chew, fret, crunch, corrode, eat, erode, nibble, masticate, munch, champ, fray, harass, devour, *(n)* chafe.

ikarikiriki shivering; *synonyms* *(n)* chill, cold, *(adj)* quivering, shaking, trembling, quaking, shaky, shuddering, tremulous, chilled; *antonym* *(adj)* composed.

ikaroubu box; *synonyms* *(n)* basket, cage, chest, package, booth, blow, carton, case, container, crate, envelope, *(v)* cuff, buffet, beat, fight; *antonym* *(v)* unbox.

ikaruoruo 1. alternate; *synonyms* *(adj)* reciprocal, secondary, *(v)* reciprocate, change, fluctuate, interchange, vary, swerve, alter, *(n)* substitute, alternative, surrogate, standby, replacement, deputy; *antonym* *(n)* original, **2.** replace; *synonyms* *(v)* exchange, supersede, supplant, reinstate, displace, restore, shift, deputize, renew, return, succeed, switch, deputise, follow, place.

ikatoatoa 1. complete; *synonyms* *(adj)* perfect, absolute, consummate, whole, full, stark, accomplished, all, *(v)* accomplish, achieve, close, finish, execute, act, attain; *antonyms* *(adj)* incomplete, partial, unfinished, abridged, shortened, sketchy, lacking, narrow, qualified, *(v)* neglect, **2.** correspond; *synonyms* *(v)* accord, coincide, conform, suit, consort, answer, check, concur, fit, harmonize, match, parallel, accede, communicate, *(adj)* agree; *antonyms* *(v)* differ, disagree.

ikatoatoaki completed; *synonyms* *(adj)* complete, done, accomplished, finished, ended, perfect, ready, through, whole, *(adv)* over.

ikawai 1. adolescent; *synonyms* *(adj)* immature, young, teen, youthful, boyish, childish, infantile, jejune, puerile, teenage, *(n)* juvenile, teenager, minor, stripling, youngster; *antonyms* *(n)* adult, infant, **2.** grand; *synonyms* *(adj)* excellent, gorgeous, dignified, elevated, eminent, exalted, important, majestic, superb, beautiful, high, massive, *(n)* glorious, noble, *(v)* great; *antonyms* *(adj)* unimpressive, humble, modest, **3.** adult; *synonyms* *(adj)* big, full-grown, mature, elder, developed, grown, older, ripe, responsible, *(n)*

grownup; *antonyms* *(n)* adolescent, child, **4.** grownup; *synonyms* *(adj)* bad, bighearted, boastful, bounteous, bountiful, braggy, crowing, enceinte, expectant, freehanded, giving, gravid, handsome, large, magnanimous, **5.** ancient; *synonyms* *(adj)* aged, old, antiquated, obsolete, former, past, antique, archaic, bygone, hoary, primitive, olden, antediluvian, dated, earlier; *antonym* *(adj)* modern, **6.** mature; *synonyms* *(adj)* complete, experienced, fledged, perfect, due, prime, *(v)* grow, ripen, develop, age, maturate, mellow, season, digest, elaborate; *antonyms* *(adj)* naive, unripe, sophomoric, **7.** developed; *synonyms* *(adj)* advanced, sophisticated, detailed, distinguished, educated, established, full, full-fledged, grown-up, matured, polished, precocious, ready, seasoned, secondary, **8.** old; *synonyms* *(adj)* ancient, elderly, outdated, veteran, decrepit, stale, disused, hackneyed, late, traditional, decayed, inveterate, auld, gray, musty; *antonyms* *(adj)* new, fresh, latest, novel, original.

ikawaiaki matured; *synonyms* *(adj)* mature, ripe, adult, developed, experienced, old; *antonym* *(adj)* immature.

ikawawa wander; *synonyms* *(v)* ramble, digress, stray, deviate, err, roam, travel, depart, divagate, gad, meander, *(n)* saunter, stroll, tramp, drift.

ike 1. breath; *synonyms* *(n)* spirit, wind, air, inspiration, puff, aspiration, breather, breeze, flash, flatus, gust, instant, jiffy, respite, *(adj)* whisper, **2.** respire; *synonyms* *(v)* breathe, exhale, inhale, sigh, *(adj)* live.

ikeaki breathed; *synonyms* *(adj)* voiceless, aphonic, surd.

ikei here; *synonyms* *(adv)* hither, in, about, arrived, available, indoors, inwards, *(n)* hair, *(adj)* present, there, near, nearby, *(pron)* her, their; *antonym* *(adv)* out.

ikeike 1. breathe; *synonyms* *(v)* blow, exhale, live, subsist, be, emit, exist, imply, rest, whisper, inspire, convey, heave, *(n)* respire, bespeak, **2.** breath; *synonyms* *(n)* spirit, wind, air, inspiration, puff, aspiration, breather, breeze, flash, flatus, gust, instant, jiffy, respite, trice, **3.** inhale; *synonyms* *(v)* breathe, absorb, imbibe, draw, suck, drag, drink, attract, receive, admit, import, ingest, *(n)* sniff, **4.** yonder; *synonyms* *(adv)* beyond, abroad, farther, further, *(adj)* yon, distant, **5.** pulsate; *synonyms* *(v)* beat, palpitate, pound, throb, pulse, quiver, shake, shudder, thump, vibrate, **6.** respire; *synonyms* *(v)* inhale, sigh.

ikeikeaki 1. breathed; *synonyms* *(adj)* voiceless, aphonic, surd, **2.** inhaled; *synonym* *(adj)* inspired, **3.** pulsated.

ikekei 1. far; *synonyms* *(adv)* wide, off, widely, well, astray, *(adj)* distant, aloof, faraway, remote, much, outlying, *(v)* considerably, abundantly; *antonyms* *(adv)* close, briefly, *(adj)* near, **2.** **there;** *synonyms* *(adv)* here, thither, present, thereat, apparent, convenient, visible, *(adj)* adept, competent, expert, professional, reliable, skillful, trustworthy, unfailing.

ikemoro 1. gasp; *synonyms (n)* pant, inhalation, breath, *(v)* puff, blow, breathe, heave, sigh, wheeze, gag, **2.** pant; *synonyms (n)* gasp, thrill, tingle, *(v)* huff, long, desire, *(adj)* fume.

ikena inhale; *synonyms (v)* breathe, absorb, imbibe, draw, suck, drag, drink, attract, inspire, receive, respire, admit, import, ingest, *(n)* sniff; *antonym (v)* exhale.

ikenaki inhaled; *synonym (adj)* inspired.

ikenrawn sigh; *synonyms (n)* suspire, breath, wail, suspiration, whimper, whine, sike, *(v)* moan, groan, breathe, languish, murmur, pine, whisper.

ikibekibe struggle; *synonyms (n)* contest, battle, combat, conflict, strain, effort, exertion, scramble, scuffle, *(v)* fight, attempt, dispute, endeavor, labor, quarrel; *antonyms (v)* flourish, glide.

ikikua rasp; *synonyms (v)* grate, scrape, abrade, chafe, file, grind, rub, scratch, grater, graze, groan, squeak, fray, screech, jar.

ikinako 1. empty; *synonyms (adj)* discharge, hollow, destitute, bare, blank, barren, abandoned, deserted, vain, *(v)* drain, clear, deplete, desolate, pour, spill; *antonyms (adj)* full, crowded, meaningful, packed, brimming, inhabited, occupied, swarming, cultivated, filled, laden, *(v)* fill, **2.** flow; *synonyms (n)* flood, current, abound, rush, *(v)* stream, course, flux, jet, run, surge, float, emanate, fall, gush, seep.

ikinakoaki emptied; *synonyms (adj)* void, voided, depleted, annulled, open, vacuous, evacuated, invalidated.

iko 1. here; *synonyms (adv)* hither, in, about, arrived, available, indoors, inwards, *(n)* hair, *(adj)* present, there, near, nearby, *(pron)* her, their; *antonym (adv)* out, **2.** assemble; *synonyms (v)* amass, accumulate, aggregate, convene, gather, meet, call, collect, compile, concentrate, converge, group, make, rally, edit; *antonyms (v)* dismantle, disperse, disband, disassemble, **3.** harvest; *synonyms (n)* crop, fruit, ingathering, produce, profit, yield, production, *(v)* gain, glean, garner, get, pick, reap, earn, assemble, **4.** gather; *synonyms (v)* deduce, congregate, flock, tuck, derive, extract, acquire, cluster, conclude, crease, cull, harvest, infer, marshal, *(n)* fold; *antonym (v)* scatter, **5.** pick; *synonyms (v)* clean, opt, break, choose, draw, *(n)* alternative, elite, best, choice, option, selection, *(adj)* cream, select, mattock, flower.

ikoa 1. far; *synonyms (adv)* wide, off, widely, well, astray, *(adj)* distant, aloof, faraway, remote, much, outlying, *(v)* considerably, abundantly; *antonyms*

(adv) close, briefly, *(adj)* near, **2.** bruise; *synonyms (n)* blow, contusion, break, buffet, swelling, blemish, *(v)* crush, hurt, wound, beat, bray, contuse, grind, mash, pound, **3.** thereabouts; *synonyms (adv)* thereabout, generally, hereabouts, nearly, approximately, around, almost, so, therefore, thus, very, whereabouts, *(adj)* about, **4.** wound; *synonyms (n)* bruise, harm, pain, injury, scratch, sore, *(v)* cut, damage, offend, injure, stab, sting, insult, maim, bite.

ikoaki 1. bruised; *synonyms (adj)* contused, wounded, hurt, raw, sore, contusioned, discolored, inflamed, lame, livid, painful, rotten, sensitive, surbet, tender, **2.** gathered; *synonyms (adj)* collected, deepened, accumulated, amassed, assembled, collective, congregate, equanimous, massed, poised, **3.** assembled; *synonyms (adj)* united, accrued, aggregate, built, fabricated, fancied, fictional, fictitious, invented, reinforced, **4.** wounded; *synonyms (adj)* bruised, bloody, *(n)* casualty, maimed; *antonym (adj)* composed.

ikoikota collect; *synonyms (v)* assemble, accumulate, amass, gather, pick, accrue, acquire, aggregate, cluster, collate, congregate, convene, cull, harvest, hoard; *antonyms (v)* disperse, distribute.

ikoikotaki 1. grouped; *synonyms (adj)* sorted, collective, **2.** collected; *synonyms (v)* composed, *(adj)* calm, accumulated, amassed, assembled, cool, sober, tranquil, poised, unflappable, dispassionate, gathered, imperturbable, peaceful, placid; *antonym (adj)* agitated.

ikota 1. muster; *synonyms (v)* assemble, congregate, gather, collect, convene, marshal, rally, accumulate, amass, aggregate, call, garner, *(n)* levy, draft, gathering, **2.** add; *synonyms (v)* calculate, include, join, total, figure, lend, mix, divide, subtract, adjoin, affix, annex, append, attach, *(n)* addition; *antonym (v)* detach.

ikotaki 1. added; *synonyms (adj)* additional, extra, further, more, supplementary, **2.** unite; *synonyms (v)* combine, associate, blend, coalesce, connect, join, link, meet, amalgamate, attach, fuse, merge, tie, unify, converge; *antonyms (v)* separate, divide.

ikotakiaki united; *synonyms (adj)* joined, joint, combined, cooperative, connected, allied, mutual, concerted, mixed, common, conjunctive, undivided, conjunct, unanimous, *(v)* consolidated; *antonyms (adj)* individual, separate, divided.

ikti x; *synonyms (n)* ten, decade, tenner, decennary, decennium, ecstasy, exaltation, go, methylenedioxymethamphetamine, position, rapture, raptus, *(v)* mark, kiss, *(adj)* nameless.

ikua 1. mash; *synonyms (n)* mush, *(v)* crush, grind, squash, beat, bray, comminute, crunch, flirt, press, pulp, squeeze, blend, bruise, *(adj)* mess, **2.** beat; *synonyms (v)* batter, flap, pulsate, throb, tick, trounce, whip, bat, baste, break, *(n)* pulse, thump,

knock, round, cadence; *antonym* (*v*) lose, **3**. batter;
synonyms (*n*) batsman, concoction, hitter, (*v*)
hammer, bash, buffet, club, hit, mangle, pound,
slam, drive, clobber, demolish, destroy, **4**. rasp;
synonyms (*n*) rasping, (*v*) grate, scrape, abrade,
chafe, file, rub, scratch, grater, graze, groan,
squeak, fray, screech, jar, **5**. punch; *synonyms* (*n*)
jab, drill, cuff, die, wallop, blow, dig, (*v*) poke,
prick, perforate, stab, thrust, puncture, push, slap,
6. pound; *synonyms* (*n*) cage, fold, enclosure,
hammering, lb, (*v*) pen, bang, maul, palpitate,
mash, ram, thrash, stamp, strike, tap.

ikuaki 1. battered; *synonyms* (*adj*) beaten, worn,
damaged, hurt, maltreated, ragged, tattered,
abused, aching, bruised, decrepit, dilapidated,
injured, (*v*) seedy, shattered, **2**. beaten; *synonyms*
(*v*) beat, (*adj*) battered, overpowered, conquered,
routed, overcome; *antonym* (*adj*) victorious.

ikuiku 1. batter; *synonyms* (*n*) batsman, concoction,
(*v*) baste, hammer, bash, beat, break, buffet, club,
hit, knock, mangle, pound, slam, bruise, **2**. beat;
synonyms (*v*) batter, flap, pulsate, throb, tick,
trounce, whip, bat, cheat, clobber, crush, (*n*) pulse,
thump, round, cadence; *antonym* (*v*) lose, **3**.
punch; *synonyms* (*n*) jab, drill, cuff, die, wallop,
blow, dig, (*v*) poke, prick, perforate, stab, thrust,
puncture, push, slap, **4**. pound; *synonyms* (*n*)
cage, fold, enclosure, hammering, (*v*) pen, bang,
grind, maul, palpitate, mash, grate, ram, thrash,
bray, drive.

ikuikuaki 1. beaten; *synonyms* (*v*) beat, (*adj*) battered,
overpowered, conquered, routed, overcome;
antonym (*adj*) victorious, **2**. battered; *synonyms*
(*adj*) beaten, worn, damaged, hurt, maltreated,
ragged, tattered, abused, aching, bruised, decrepit,
dilapidated, injured, (*v*) seedy, shattered.

ikuiraetero equilateral; *synonyms* (*adj*) square, (*n*)
lozenge, rhombus, shape.

ikutaba 1. cute; *synonyms* (*adj*) attractive, charming,
clever, smart, beautiful, adorable, amiable,
cunning, pretty, adroit, delightful, enchanting,
fetching, precious, sharp, **2**. shrewd; *synonyms*
(*adj*) astute, calculating, crafty, knowing, sagacious,
keen, piercing, bright, ingenious, cautious, acute,
artful, canny, discerning, (*v*) prudent; *antonyms*
(*adj*) stupid, foolish, gullible.

ima five; *synonyms* (*n*) cinque, quint, quintuplet, fin,
ace, eight, fins, fivesome, interim, intermission,
interval, jack, king, knave, (*adj*) quinary.

imainna before; *synonyms* (*prep*) fore, beyond, facing,
(*adv*) above, ahead, afore, ago, earlier, already,
forward, previously, beforehand, ere, (*adj*)
preceding, prior; *antonyms* (*prep*) later, behind,
after, afterward.

imamanu 1. familiar; *synonyms* (*adj*) close, common,
conversant, customary, everyday, intimate,
commonplace, easy, ordinary, usual, (*n*)

accustomed, companion, comrade, habitual, (*v*)
confidential; *antonyms* (*adj*) unfamiliar, foreign,
strange, new, unaccustomed, formal, ignorant,
unknown, **2**. adopted; *synonyms* (*adj*) adoptive,
elected, consecrated, converted, inspired, justified,
regenerated, sanctified, unearthly, adoptious,
popular, preferred, **3**. sympathetic; *synonyms*
(*adj*) kind, compassionate, kindly, congenial, tender,
merciful, humane, agreeable, favorable, friendly,
considerate, (*n*) gentle, caring, (*v*) affectionate,
pitiful; *antonyms* (*adj*) unsympathetic, hardhearted,
unfeeling.

imammane 1. befriend; *synonyms* (*v*) aid, friend,
favor, help, assist, promote, sustain; *antonym* (*v*)
shun, **2**. adopt; *synonyms* (*v*) accept, admit,
affiliate, assume, borrow, espouse, pass, take,
acquire, choose, embrace, follow, imitate,
naturalize, prefer; *antonym* (*v*) reject, **3**.
familiarize; *synonyms* (*v*) acquaint, accustom,
adapt, familiarise, habituate, introduce, present, **4**.
sympathize; *synonyms* (*v*) commiserate, pity,
understand, sympathise, empathize, see, align,
bleed, comfort, empathise, gather, infer, interpret,
read, realise.

imammaneaki 1. familiarized; *synonyms* (*adj*)
familiarised, adjusted, familiar, accustomed,
adapted, comfortable, habituated, **2**. adopted;
synonyms (*adj*) adoptive, elected, consecrated,
converted, inspired, justified, regenerated,
sanctified, unearthly, adoptious, foreign, popular,
preferred.

imana 1. shave; *synonyms* (*v*) prune, clip, pare,
reduce, scrape, cut, brush, chip, crop, shear,
whittle, graze, mow, peel, (*adj*) lop, **2**. scale;
synonyms (*n*) flake, gamut, degree, graduation,
measure, yardstick, rate, criterion, (*v*) ascend, climb,
gauge, mount, weigh, rise, (*adj*) balance; *antonym*
(*v*) descend.

imanaki scaled; *synonyms* (*adj*) scaly, lepidote,
leprose, scabrous, scaley, scurfy.

imanna shave; *synonyms* (*v*) prune, clip, pare,
reduce, scrape, cut, brush, chip, crop, shear,
whittle, graze, mow, peel, (*adj*) lop.

imanono 1. harass; *synonyms* (*v*) afflict, annoy,
distress, plague, fret, badger, beset, bug, disturb,
molest, persecute, pester, tease, worry, (*adj*) tire, **2**.
insist; *synonyms* (*v*) affirm, assert, contend, claim,
asseverate, declare, maintain, urge, importune,
press, argue, force, dwell, hold, persist, **3**.
torment; *synonyms* (*n*) harass, agony, anguish,
pain, suffering, curse, misery, harassment, (*v*)
torture, irritate, oppress, rack, bedevil, bother,
crucify.

imanonoaki 1. harassed; *synonyms* (*adj*) vexed,
annoyed, pestered, beleaguered, distraught,
distressed, drawn, harried, hurried, obsessed,
stressed, uneasy, agitated, anxious, besieged;

antonyms (*adj*) calm, relaxed, **2.** tormented;
synonyms (*adj*) anguished, tortured, worried,
hagridden, beset, cruciate, cruciform, miserable,
plagued, suffering, agonized, fearful, littered,
painful, sorrowful; *antonym* (*adj*) content.

imbo javelin; *synonyms* (*n*) lance, spear, pike, dart,
bayonet, fish, spike, spontoon, weapon, arrow, bolt,
boomerang, jereed, jerid, reed.

imita 1. act; *synonyms* (*n*) accomplishment, action,
move, play, statute, decree, do, feat, (*v*)
achievement, behave, deed, go, perform, acquit,
enact; *antonym* (*v*) refrain, **2.** rub; *synonyms* (*v*)
fray, grate, gall, chafe, abrade, caress, fret, furbish,
graze, irritate, massage, scrape, (*n*) check, brush,
hitch, **3.** pierce; *synonyms* (*v*) impale, cut,
perforate, bore, enter, stab, stick, bite, drill, gore,
penetrate, puncture, thrust, wound, (*n*) prick, **4.**
throw; *synonyms* (*v*) cast, fling, shed, hurl, chuck,
flip, heave, pass, deliver, drop, give, hurtle, (*n*)
pitch, push, shot.

imitaki 1. pierced; *synonyms* (*adj*) perforated,
punctured, perforate, cleft, entered, **2.** thrown;
synonyms (*adj*) confused, puzzled, addled, baffled,
bewildered, confounded, disconcerted, distraught,
dumbfounded, fearful, frightened, mystified,
terrified, unnerved, (*n*) reminder.

immakurata immaculate; *synonyms* (*adj*) chaste,
clean, clear, faultless, flawless, pure, spotless,
perfect, blameless, neat, guiltless, impeccable,
innocent, unblemished, virgin; *antonym* (*adj*) dirty.

imoa front; *synonyms* (*adj*) head, fore, anterior,
preceding, (*n*) countenance, forefront, appearance,
disguise, facade, frontage, brow, audacity, (*v*) face,
confront, look; *antonyms* (*n*) rear, end, (*v*) back.

imwina after; *synonyms* (*prep*) following, since, (*adv*)
later, beyond, next, subsequently, then, when,
afterward, afterwards, behind, (*adj*) back, posterior,
rear, subsequent.

in 1. bolted; *synonyms* (*adj*) locked, barred,
barricaded, blockaded, fast, firm, latched, secured,
tight, bonded, colorfast, debauched, degenerate,
degraded, dissipated, **2.** held; *synonyms* (*adj*)
absorbed, confined, alleged, assumed, believed,
bound, caged, captive, detained, immersed,
obsessed, occupied, protected, rapt, (*adv*) on, **3.** for;
synonyms (*prep*) because, behind, by, per, during,
toward, (*conj*) considering, since, (*adv*) against, as,
therefore, hence, **4.** at; *synonyms* (*prep*) in, a, (*n*)
astatine, (*adv*) along, (*prf*) all, completely, wholly,
(*adj*) entertainment, levee, party, reception,
conversazione, home, soiree, **5.** coral; *synonyms*
(*adj*) rosy, (*n*) orange, red, roe, **6.** closed; *synonyms*
(*v*) close, accurate, adjoining, attentive, (*adj*) blind,
blocked, finished, shut, congested, fastened,
exclusive, insular, stopped, airtight, benighted;
antonym (*adj*) open, **7.** locked; *synonyms* (*adj*)
bolted, closed, clocked, dissolute, fixed, flying,

guaranteed, immobile, inexorable, intractable,
libertine, safe, secure, uncompromising, loyal, **8.**
constipated; *synonyms* (*adj*) costive, bellybound,
cold, formal, impermeable, reserved, unyielding, (*v*)
certain, destined, resolved, **9.** imprisoned;
synonyms (*adj*) jailed, enraptured, incarcerate,
enslaved, inside, interned, penned; *antonym* (*adj*)
free, **10.** shut; *synonyms* (*v*) bar, seal, fasten,
exclude, lock, (*adj*) cut, (*n*) end, finish, confine.

ina 1. gentle; *synonyms* (*adj*) clement, calm, easy,
friendly, soft, affable, balmy, kind, mild, tame,
feeble, amiable, benign, bland, (*n*) benevolent;
antonyms (*adj*) caustic, cruel, fierce, harsh, loud,
violent, rough, abrupt, hardhearted, heavy,
sarcastic, sheer, steep, **2.** to; *synonyms* (*prep*) at, by,
in, about, before, against, into, near, toward,
towards, until, unto, (*adv*) versus, (*prf*) on, (*v*) till, **3.**
will; *synonyms* (*v*) bequeath, devise, wish, leave,
(*n*) volition, command, desire, inclination,
determination, pleasure, resolve, intent, mind,
courage, liking.

inaaine 1. gentle; *synonyms* (*adj*) clement, calm, easy,
friendly, soft, affable, balmy, kind, mild, tame,
feeble, amiable, benign, bland, (*n*) benevolent;
antonyms (*adj*) caustic, cruel, fierce, harsh, loud,
violent, rough, abrupt, hardhearted, heavy,
sarcastic, sheer, steep, **2.** graceful; *synonyms* (*adj*)
beautiful, delicate, elegant, fine, charming, fair,
airy, becoming, comely, dainty, handsome, lithe,
lovely, refined, supple; *antonyms* (*adj*) clumsy,
inelegant, stocky, **3.** amiable; *synonyms* (*adj*)
agreeable, complaisant, genial, cordial, gentle,
likable, nice, pleasant, sweet, adorable, considerate,
amicable, attractive, congenial, delightful;
antonyms (*adj*) unfriendly, disagreeable, aggressive,
argumentative.

inaaomata 1. free; *synonyms* (*adj*) loose, frank, liberal,
(*v*) clear, exempt, liberate, discharge, excuse,
extricate, relieve, disentangle, acquit, deliver,
disengage, ease; *antonyms* (*adj*) bound, restricted,
compelled, confined, imprisoned, repressive,
secure, strict, stuck, tangled, attached, busy, (*v*)
confine, block, cage, **2.** independent; *synonyms*
(*adj*) free, autonomous, separate, substantive,
impartial, nonpartisan, sovereign, unallied, self-
sufficient, detached, distinct, individual, (*n*)
freelance, mugwump, (*adv*) apart; *antonyms* (*adj*)
dependent, simultaneous, **3.** chief; *synonyms* (*adj*)
head, principal, cardinal, capital, arch, central,
essential, first, main, (*n*) administrator, boss,
captain, executive, leader, paramount; *antonyms*
(*adj*) minor, associate, secondary, **4.** proprietor;
synonyms (*n*) owner, manager, possessor, landlord,
holder, host, master, employer, landowner;
antonym (*n*) tenant.

inababaura handsome; *synonyms* (*adj*) elegant,
beautiful, fair, charming, fine, generous, attractive,

bountiful, comely, bonny, big, bounteous, exquisite, gorgeous, graceful; *antonyms* (*adj*) ugly, unattractive.

inaberu 1. afraid; *synonyms* (*adj*) fearful, timid, shy, anxious, apprehensive, frightened, nervous, scared, worried, horrified, terrified, uneasy, reluctant, (*adv*) cowardly; *antonyms* (*adj*) fearless, brave, **2.** cowardly; *synonyms* (*adj*) coward, afraid, craven, gutless, shrinking, sneaky, base, dastardly, faint, fainthearted, poltroon, pusillanimous, recreant, spineless, weak; *antonyms* (*adj*) intrepid, strong, (*adv*) bold, courageous, daring, **3.** fearful; *synonyms* (*adj*) dreadful, awful, terrible, dire, eerie, formidable, frightful, appalling, awesome, alarming, desperate, direful, frightening, horrendous, horrible; *antonyms* (*adj*) calm, rational, confident, unimpressed, **4.** timid; *synonyms* (*adj*) diffident, bashful, cautious, coy, modest, retiring, reserved, embarrassed, mousy, timorous, conservative, hesitant, humble, meek, tentative.

inaguinagu skilful; *synonyms* (*adj*) dexterous, cunning, expert, practised, adept, good, practiced, proficient, handy, artful, skillful.

inai 1. engage; *synonyms* (*v*) contract, attract, book, employ, absorb, betroth, charter, enlist, retain, draw, engross, hire, involve, lock, mesh; *antonyms* (*v*) fire, disengage, **2.** pit; *synonyms* (*n*) cavity, dent, hole, depression, grave, colliery, excavation, mine, stone, dig, (*v*) den, ditch, oppose, cave, (*adj*) hollow.

inaiaki engaged; *synonyms* (*adj*) busy, occupied, betrothed, affianced, employed, engrossed, reserved, absorbed, working, pledged, bespoken, booked, immersed, intent, rapt; *antonyms* (*adj*) available, free.

inaina 1. scaly; *synonyms* (*adj*) scabrous, scaled, scabby, rough, scurfy, lepidote, leprose, scaley, (*v*) cortical, cutaneous, cuticular, dermal, **2.** rough; *synonyms* (*adj*) coarse, hard, harsh, raw, crude, cruel, grating, gross, hoarse, jagged, approximate, gruff, inclement, (*n*) boisterous, draft; *antonyms* (*adj*) gentle, smooth, polished, precise, refined, silky, soft, sophisticated, even, exact, glossy, pleasant.

inaine 1. gentle; *synonyms* (*adj*) clement, calm, easy, friendly, soft, affable, balmy, kind, mild, tame, feeble, amiable, benign, bland, (*n*) benevolent; *antonyms* (*adj*) caustic, cruel, fierce, harsh, loud, violent, rough, abrupt, hardhearted, heavy, sarcastic, sheer, steep, **2.** feminine; *synonyms* (*adj*) female, womanly, maidenly, pistillate, wifely, feminal, feminate; *antonyms* (*adj*) masculine, male.

inaito 1. puny; *synonyms* (*adj*) little, feeble, frail, petty, weak, small, tiny, minute, measly, paltry, runty, trifling, trivial, exiguous, meager; *antonyms* (*adj*) brawny, muscular, **2.** sickly; *synonyms* (*adj*) infirm, sick, ailing, diseased, indisposed, morbid, pale, poorly, sallow, peaked, pasty, languid, pallid, (*n*) invalid, (*v*) faint; *antonyms* (*adj*) healthy, bitter,

3. stunted; *synonyms* (*adj*) scrubby, scrawny, diminutive, puny, short, spare, (*v*) strangulated.

inakai 1. fit; *synonyms* (*v*) agree, accommodate, meet, suit, adapt, correspond, square, accord, dress, (*adj*) decorous, apt, applicable, appropriate, (*n*) adjust, convulsion; *antonyms* (*adj*) unfit, inappropriate, unwell, **2.** slim; *synonyms* (*adj*) slender, narrow, slight, thin, lean, remote, fine, skinny, flimsy, lithe, meager, light, (*v*) reduce, slenderize, cut; *antonyms* (*adj*) fat, heavy, hefty, plump, stocky, wide, **3.** slender; *synonyms* (*adj*) little, delicate, faint, feeble, gaunt, lissom, scanty, slim, exiguous, minute, graceful, lissome, poor, (*v*) lank, scant.

inakewe bragger; *synonyms* (*n*) boaster, braggart, blowhard, vaunter, bighead.

inaki 1. shut; *synonyms* (*v*) close, bar, seal, fasten, exclude, lock, (*adj*) closed, cut, tight, (*n*) end, finish, confine; *antonym* (*v*) open, **2.** slim; *synonyms* (*adj*) slender, narrow, slight, thin, lean, remote, fine, skinny, flimsy, lithe, meager, light, feeble, (*v*) reduce, slenderize; *antonyms* (*adj*) fat, heavy, hefty, plump, stocky, wide.

inako 1. immerse; *synonyms* (*v*) dip, douse, plunge, absorb, drench, drown, dunk, bury, engross, engulf, steep, submerge, bathe, duck, sink, **2.** plunge; *synonyms* (*n*) dive, drop, fall, jump, leap, slump, (*v*) immerse, crash, launch, plummet, descend, lunge, drive, dash, decline.

inakoaki immersed; *synonyms* (*adj*) absorbed, submerged, engrossed, deep, underwater, attentive, bathed, buried, captivated, concentrated, covered, engaged, enthralled, fascinated, gripped.

inamatoa 1. implacable; *synonyms* (*adj*) inexorable, cruel, remorseless, grim, irreconcilable, merciless, pitiless, unappeasable, deadly, mortal, inflexible, relentless, ruthless, stern, unforgiving; *antonyms* (*adj*) charitable, placable, **2.** hard; *synonyms* (*adj*) austere, bad, difficult, grave, severe, strong, arduous, callous, grueling, knotty, tough, bitter, (*adv*) firm, (*v*) acute, (*n*) rough; *antonyms* (*adj*) easy, soft, kind, merciful, simple, soggy, tender, yielding, (*adv*) gently, lightly, **3.** impassable; *synonyms* (*adj*) impervious, insurmountable, impenetrable, insuperable, invincible, inaccessible, unpassable; *antonym* (*adj*) passable, **4.** obstinate; *synonyms* (*adj*) headstrong, obdurate, determined, intractable, inveterate, disobedient, contrary, dogged, stubborn, uncompromising, wayward, willful, contumacious, cussed, defiant; *antonyms* (*adj*) compliant, amenable, flexible, **5.** tenacious; *synonyms* (*adj*) adhesive, obstinate, persistent, resolute, sticky, glutinous, persevering, pertinacious, steadfast, stringy, unyielding, viscous, fast, (*v*) retentive, durable.

inamoimoto 1. coward; *synonyms* (*n*) craven, cur, sneak, weakling, cocktail, coistril, niding, alarmist, baby, deserter, invertebrate, jellyfish, lily-liver, (*adj*) gutless, (v) frighten, **2.** cowardly; *synonyms* (adj) coward, timid, afraid, scared, shrinking, sneaky, base, dastardly, faint, fainthearted, fearful, poltroon, pusillanimous, recreant, spineless; *antonyms* (adj) fearless, intrepid, strong, (adv) brave, bold, courageous, daring.

inaña 1. full; *synonyms* (adj) complete, absolute, abundant, broad, flush, ample, enough, extensive, total, detailed, comprehensive, copious, good, (n) entire, crowded; *antonyms* (adj) empty, lacking, starving, hungry, sketchy, incomplete, **2.** satisfied; *synonyms* (v) convinced, (adj) contented, happy, content, full, pleased, certain, confident, sure, complacent, persuaded, fulfilled, sated, satiated, easy; *antonyms* (adj) unhappy, frustrated, **3.** tired; *synonyms* (adj) exhausted, fatigued, hackneyed, weary, banal, commonplace, stale, threadbare, trite, beat, haggard, jaded, stock, worn, drowsy; *antonyms* (adj) fresh, invigorated, alert, refreshed, energetic, original, strong.

inánan within; *synonyms* (prep) into, (adv) inside, in, indoors, internally, inwardly, inly, (n) interior, (adj) inwards; *antonyms* (prep) outside, beyond.

inanikuau freckled; *synonyms* (adj) dappled, speckled, discolored, mottled, freckly, blemished, lentiginose, lentiginous, marked, pitted, spotted, spotty, dotted, red, (v) studded.

inanoinano 1. bottom; *synonyms* (n) base, basis, backside, bed, behind, foot, footing, back, arse, ass, bum, butt, buttocks, craft, floor; *antonyms* (n) top, pinnacle, (adj) highest, **2.** lowest; *synonyms* (adj) least, bottom, minimum, smallest, last, minimal, **3.** deep; *synonyms* (adj) thick, profound, absorbed, abstruse, broad, dark, rich, sound, strong, wide, esoteric, bright, large, abysmal, (v) intense; *antonyms* (adj) shallow, superficial, high, high-pitched, light, soft, weak.

inao 1. doer; *synonyms* (n) actor, agent, executor, cause, facient, worker, activist, architect, executioner, extrovert, histrion, player, prole, proletarian, success, **2.** mover; *synonyms* (n) author, originator, proposer, founder, generator, inventor, motive, transporter, carrier, hauler, shipper, agitator, carter, father, inducement, **3.** hyperactive; *synonyms* (adj) frantic, overactive, furious, harried, hysterical, mad, possessed, turbulent, **4.** goer; *synonyms* (n) departer, barb, beast, bidet, cattle, charger, cob, colt, courser, filly, foal, hack, horse, hunter, jade, **5.** lively; *synonyms* (adj) brisk, active, agile, cheerful, energetic, keen, busy, fresh, gay, jolly, jovial, alert, animated, bright, enthusiastic; *antonyms* (adj) dull, inactive, lethargic, listless, lifeless, unexciting, **6.** workaholic; *synonym* (n) drudge.

inataba 1. docile; *synonyms* (adj) gentle, compliant, dutiful, humble, meek, obedient, submissive, tame,

teachable, acquiescent, conformable, kind, subservient, amenable, (v) tractable; *antonyms* (adj) rebellious, stubborn, assertive, **2.** humble; *synonyms* (adj) base, docile, low, lowly, modest, unassuming, baseborn, (v) degrade, demean, disgrace, abase, debase, humiliate, mortify, conquer; *antonyms* (adj) grand, arrogant, conceited, haughty, imposing, impressive, pompous, snooty, **3.** meek; *synonyms* (adj) mild, quiet, retiring, patient, biddable, calm, soft, unobtrusive, diffident; *antonym* (adj) bossy, **4.** gentle; *synonyms* (adj) clement, easy, friendly, affable, balmy, feeble, amiable, benign, bland, compassionate, delicate, fine, fond, kindly, (n) benevolent; *antonyms* (adj) caustic, cruel, fierce, harsh, loud, violent, rough, abrupt, hardhearted, heavy, sarcastic, sheer, steep, **5.** submissive; *synonyms* (adj) passive, obsequious, resigned, subject, servile, subdued, slavish, yielding, subordinate, pliable, unresisting, deferential, inactive, inert, respectful; *antonyms* (adj) domineering, resistant, disobedient, (adv) bossily, **6.** obedient; *synonyms* (adj) good, orderly, manageable, duteous, willing; *antonym* (adj) defiant.

inawiu 1. after; *synonyms* (prep) following, since, (adv) later, beyond, next, subsequently, then, when, afterward, afterwards, behind, (adj) back, posterior, rear, subsequent, **2.** last; *synonyms* (v) endure, continue, hold, exist, live, dwell, (n) abide, conclusion, (adj) extreme, closing, final, ultimate, conclusive, concluding, farthest; *antonyms* (n) opening, (adj) first, **3.** behind; *synonyms* (prep) after, abaft, (adv) backward, backwards, late, aback, trailing, (n) backside, bottom, buttocks, can, rump, tail, arse, ass; *antonyms* (adv) ahead, early, fore.

inenei continual; *synonyms* (adj) constant, ceaseless, incessant, continuous, endless, everlasting, frequent, uninterrupted, eternal, lasting, perennial, permanent, perpetual, persistent, unending; *antonyms* (adj) intermittent, sporadic, temporary.

ing 1. loose; *synonyms* (adj) lax, liberal, dissolute, licentious, light, vague, detached, immoral, (v) disengage, liberate, relax, release, detach, (n) free, limp; *antonyms* (adj) tight, close, compressed, dense, taut, strict, compact, wedged, **2.** move; *synonyms* (v) act, affect, carry, excite, go, impel, instigate, maneuver, touch, travel, flow, bear, (n) motion, drive, transfer; *antonym* (v) stay, **3.** cracked; *synonyms* (adj) broken, nutty, batty, chapped, crazy, balmy, wacky, bats, crackers, crackled, crazed, deranged, dotty, insane, kookie, **4.** uplift; *synonyms* (n) lift, upheaval, upthrust, (v) elate, elevate, raise, exhilarate, hoist, intoxicate, regenerate, **5.** shake; *synonyms* (v) beat, agitate, jar, brandish, disturb, flutter, totter, wag, drop, (n) tremble, jolt, quiver, wave, trembling, (adj) quake.

inga 1. greet; *synonyms* (*v*) accost, address, acknowledge, cry, hail, salute, welcome, bid, meet, weep, approach, recognize, (*n*) receive, **2.** kiss; *synonyms* (*n*) buss, brush, osculation, touch, (*v*) caress, embrace, osculate, love, **3.** impatient; *synonyms* (*adj*) eager, hasty, anxious, petulant, fidgety, keen, edgy, quick, avid, enthusiastic, impetuous, irritable, restive, restless, testy; *antonyms* (*adj*) patient, enduring, **4.** motivated; *synonyms* (*adj*) stimulated, aggravated, ambitious, determined, encouraged, enthused, inspired, moved, obsessed, provoked, pushy, ruthless, stirred, striving, annoyed; *antonyms* (*adj*) uninspired, unprovoked, unmotivated, **5.** eager; *synonyms* (*adj*) desirous, ardent, earnest, agog, acute, zealous, industrious, studious, active, burning, craving, excited, fervent, forward, hot; *antonyms* (*adj*) indifferent, apathetic, disinterested, unconcerned, **6.** anxious; *synonyms* (*adj*) afraid, alarmed, nervous, tense, uneasy, agitated, apprehensive, concerned, distressed, fearful, frightened, thoughtful, thirsty, (*v*) jumpy, solicitous; *antonyms* (*adj*) calm, relaxed, carefree, confident, rational, undisturbed, untroubled, **7.** fervent; *synonyms* (*adj*) cordial, intense, passionate, emotional, animated, impassioned, strong, torrid, vehement, warm, devout, ablaze, dedicated, devoted, fervid; *antonym* (*adj*) unenthusiastic, **8.** gesture; *synonyms* (*n*) signal, gesticulation, indication, movement, (*v*) sign, beckon, gesticulate, motion, wave, **9.** driven; *synonyms* (*v*) drive, (*adj*) impelled, compulsive, bound, dictated, dynamic, goaded, hell-bent, successful, activist, efficient, energetic, incited, influential, pressed, **10.** enthusiastic; *synonyms* (*adj*) hearty, fiery, heated, fanatical, glowing, impatient, lively, spirited, vivacious, wholehearted, wild, cheerful, (*n*) buoyant, gushing, (*v*) fanatic; *antonyms* (*adj*) lukewarm, lethargic, **11.** welcome; *synonyms* (*adj*) acceptable, pleasant, agreeable, pleasing, enjoyable, grateful, gratifying, (*v*) accept, greet, invite, entertain, (*n*) hospitality, reception, greeting, salutation; *antonyms* (*adj*) unwelcome, unwanted, (*v*) reject, **12.** salute; *synonyms* (*n*) bow, compliment, salaam, recognition, bonfire, kowtow, (*v*) kiss, give, acclaim, nod, ball, drink, pledge, present, **13.** smile; *synonyms* (*n*) grin, grinning, smiling, expression, luck, (*v*) beam, laugh, chuckle, grimace, sneer, countenance, favor, propitiousness; *antonym* (*v*) frown, **14.** zealous; *synonyms* (*adj*) strenuous, enterprising, jealous, fierce, vigorous, firm, great, loving, violent, willing, (*n*) sincere, **15.** receive; *synonyms* (*v*) admit, get, assume, adopt, bear, have, obtain, make, gather, take, hear, earn, own, realize, derive.

ingabong 1. morning; *synonyms* (*n*) dawn, daybreak, sunrise, daylight, forenoon, morn, aurora, cockcrow, dawning, dayspring, sunup; *antonym* (*n*) dusk, **2.** morn; *synonyms* (*n*) morning, prime, light, **3.** dawn; *synonyms* (*n*) beginning, commencement, onset, origin, start, birth, genesis, inception, opening, (*v*) break, begin, appear, originate, rise, click; *antonyms* (*n*) sunset, twilight, (*v*) end, finish.

ingainga anxious; *synonyms* (*adj*) afraid, alarmed, nervous, tense, uneasy, agitated, apprehensive, concerned, distressed, fearful, frightened, keen, thoughtful, (*v*) jumpy, solicitous; *antonyms* (*adj*) calm, relaxed, carefree, confident, rational, unconcerned, undisturbed, untroubled.

ingaki 1. gestured, **2.** received; *synonyms* (*v*) receiving, ascertained, current, recognized, (*adj*) accepted, acknowledged, conventional, acceptable, canonical, orthodox, customary, established, inward, known, legitimate, **3.** shaken; *synonyms* (*v*) broken, lame, passe, shaky, threadbare, wilted, shattered, stale, (*adj*) jolted, dazed, disconcerted, fallen, scared, stunned, surprised, **4.** uplifted; *synonyms* (*adj*) elevated, high, raised, alert, animated, bold, confident, dignified, elate, eminent, erect, grand, haughty, lofty, noble.

ingaro early; *synonyms* (*adj*) initial, first, primitive, prompt, young, quick, embryonic, matutinal, old, original, past, precocious, (*adv*) betimes, soon, earlier; *antonyms* (*adj*) delayed, last-minute, slow, (*adv*) late.

inginingaina 1. dawn; *synonyms* (*n*) beginning, commencement, aurora, cockcrow, morning, onset, origin, prime, start, sunrise, birth, (*v*) break, begin, appear, (*adj*) daybreak; *antonyms* (*n*) dusk, sunset, twilight, (*v*) end, finish, **2.** daybreak; *synonyms* (*n*) dawn, dawning, daylight, dayspring, light, sunup.

ingira linger; *synonyms* (*v*) dally, delay, hover, loiter, hesitate, stay, procrastinate, dawdle, remain, saunter, tarry, abide, endure, continue, (*adv*) lag; *antonyms* (*v*) leave, hurry.

ingiraki spring; *synonyms* (*n*) jump, leap, bound, fountain, skip, source, dance, rise, (*v*) hop, caper, bounce, dive, originate, recoil, (*adj*) elastic.

ingongo snore; *synonyms* (*v*) snort, breathe, coma, doze, dream, hibernation, nap, siesta, snooze, (*n*) snoring, stertor.

inibao 1. lie; *synonyms* (*v*) consist, repose, falsify, belong, couch, (*n*) fabrication, falsehood, falsity, fib, fiction, rest, untruth, bluff, counterfeit, deceit; *antonyms* (*v*) stand, (*n*) truth, **2.** lying; *synonyms* (*adj*) deceitful, false, deceptive, mendacious, untrue, misleading, fraudulent, recumbent, deceiving, dishonest, (*n*) lie, dishonesty, duplicity, prevarication, equivocation; *antonyms* (*adj*) honest, (*n*) honesty.

inimaki 1. dash; *synonyms* (*n*) rush, sprint, animation, beat, bit, bolt, line, (*v*) dart, touch, strike, break, charge, crash, hurry, jog; *antonym* (n) lethargy, **2.** bound; *synonyms* (v) leap, border, bounce, limit, circumscribe, confine, pounce, rebound, (n) spring, jump, boundary, edge, barrier, compass, hop; *antonym* (adj) free, **3.** jump; *synonyms* (v) dive, hurdle, rise, skip, startle, clear, dance, go, increase, lunge, plunge, (n) bound, start, caper, curvet; *antonyms* (v) decrease, fall, **4.** struggle; *synonyms* (n) contest, battle, combat, conflict, strain, effort, exertion, scramble, scuffle, (v) fight, attempt, dispute, endeavor, labor, quarrel; *antonyms* (v) flourish, glide, **5.** turn; *synonyms* (v) revolve, deviate, get, revolution, (n) bend, curve, roll, coil, twist, bout, change, round, bent, circle, shift.

inimakiaki 1. bounded; *synonyms* (adj) finite, restricted, delimited, limited, encircled, enclosed, local, qualified, surrounded, belted, compassed, contiguous, defined, definite, determinate, **2.** dashed; *synonyms* (v) abashed, ashamed, sunk, (adj) dejected, discouraged, dotted, flecked, specked, speckled, stippled, **3.** turned; *synonyms* (adj) off, sour, curved, rancid, twisted, altered, askew, awry, bent, bowed, cancelled, crooked, dark, deflected, dour.

ininimaki 1. wriggle; *synonyms* (v) squirm, twist, wrench, worm, struggle, turn, writhe, wrestle, (n) wiggle, **2.** squirm; *synonyms* (v) wriggle, fidget, twitch, distort, **3.** struggle; *synonyms* (n) contest, battle, combat, conflict, strain, effort, exertion, scramble, scuffle, (v) fight, attempt, dispute, endeavor, labor, quarrel; *antonyms* (v) flourish, glide.

inneti strait; *synonyms* (n) inlet, need, pass, pinch, quandary, channel, crisis, difficulty, distress, poverty, straits, emergency, frith, (adj) narrow, (v) dilemma.

ino wormy; *synonyms* (adj) cringing, groveling, grovelling, vermiculate, wormlike, vermicular, vermicious, vermiculated, earthy.

inono meet; *synonyms* (v) converge, find, assemble, congregate, encounter, fulfill, gather, answer, cross, confront, intersect, abut, concur, adjoin, (adj) fit; *antonyms* (v) avoid, disperse, diverge.

inra 1. deviate; *synonyms* (v) depart, deflect, stray, vary, digress, diverge, swerve, warp, shift, turn, wander, bend, differ, divert, (adj) deviant; *antonym* (v) conform, **2.** askew; *synonyms* (adj) lopsided, wry, cockeyed, oblique, (v) awry, (adv) wrong, skew; *antonym* (adv) straight, **3.** haphazard; *synonyms* (adj) accidental, careless, contingent, fortuitous, random, casual, indiscriminate, slipshod, chaotic, aimless, (n) chance, accident, hap, (adv) helter-skelter, haphazardly; *antonym* (adj) systematic, **4.** sprawl; *synonyms* (n) sprawling, (v) lie, loll, lounge, spread, straggle, recline, slouch, **5.** turned;

synonyms (adj) off, sour, curved, rancid, twisted, altered, askew, bent, bowed, cancelled, crooked, dark, deflected, dour, dull.

inraki sprawled; *synonyms* (adj) sprawling, sprawly, straggling, straggly.

inroa 1. stretched; *synonyms* (adj) taut, extended, stiff, tense, tight, strained, expanded, outstretched, elongated, outspread, prolonged, protracted, assiduous, close, delayed; *antonym* (adj) brief, **2.** strewn; *synonyms* (adj) scattered, spread, distributed, disordered, circulated, confused, diffuse, disconnected, disjointed, dispersed, disseminated, dotted, garbled, illogical, isolated; *antonym* (adj) concentrated, **3.** straggle; *synonyms* (n) wander, hover, nomadize, saunter, (v) sprawl, stray, ramble, depart, deviate, digress, range, roam, lag, drag, rove.

intibua 1. fatten; *synonyms* (v) batten, fat, elaborate, feed, expand, (n) enrich, (adj) fructify, bloom, blossom, blow, **2.** cram; *synonyms* (v) stuff, pack, ram, fill, jam, compress, load, shove, compact, ingurgitate, overeat, englut, gormandise, gormandize, gourmandize, **3.** full; *synonyms* (adj) complete, absolute, abundant, broad, flush, ample, enough, extensive, total, detailed, comprehensive, copious, good, (n) entire, crowded; *antonyms* (adj) empty, lacking, starving, hungry, sketchy, incomplete, **4.** swollen; *synonyms* (adj) bloated, inflated, bombastic, puffed, puffy, turgid, egotistic, high, bulging, tumescent, tumid, conceited, (v) distended, blown, (prep) pompous.

intibuaki fattened; *synonyms* (adj) meated, fed.

intinebu 1. awkward; *synonyms* (adj) clumsy, inconvenient, crude, embarrassing, inept, sticky, uncomfortable, ungainly, untoward, left-handed, annoying, bungling, cumbersome, difficult, graceless; *antonyms* (adj) graceful, easy, adroit, manageable, straightforward, convenient, dexterous, helpful, rotund, simple, **2.** heavy; *synonyms* (adj) dull, deep, dark, dense, fat, full, grave, gross, hard, arduous, bulky, burdensome, grievous, oppressive, thick; *antonyms* (adj) light, slim, thin, slight, gentle, puny, skinny, **3.** clumsy; *synonyms* (adj) bumbling, unwieldy, gawky, inapt, maladroit, rude, unskilled, wooden, incompetent, lumbering, boorish, heavy, inexpert, (n) awkward, gauche; *antonyms* (adj) nimble, clever, skillful, deft.

io 1. flutter; *synonyms* (n) bustle, flap, wave, waver, agitation, excitement, quiver, (v) flicker, beat, flit, flitter, palpitate, fly, (adj) flurry, flutter, **2.** sift; *synonyms* (v) screen, filter, investigate, analyze, examine, riddle, sieve, sprinkle, bolt, separate, sort, strain, probe, (n) scrutinize, canvass, **3.** wave; *synonyms* (n) billow, gesture, motion, sign, surge, (v) brandish, flutter, curl, flourish, swell, swing, undulate, beckon, ripple, shake, **4.** shake; *synonyms* (v) agitate, jar, disturb, excite, totter, wag, drop, bump, convulse, jiggle, quail, (*n*) tremble, jolt, trembling, (*adj*) quake.

i-ô above; *synonyms* (*prep*) on, past, surpassing, (*adv*) over, beyond, aloft, supra, up, more, overhead, (*adj*) preceding, former, upper, foregoing, previous; *antonym* (*prep*) below.

ioa waggle; *synonyms* (*n*) shake, shiver, (*v*) wag, jiggle, wiggle, bob, reel, stagger.

ioaawa mean; *synonyms* (*v*) intend, design, imply, denote, involve, (*adj*) middle, base, common, hateful, ignoble, medium, miserly, (*n*) average, contemptible, low; *antonyms* (*adj*) generous, kind.

ioaki shaken; *synonyms* (*v*) broken, lame, passe, shaky, threadbare, wilted, shattered, stale, (*adj*) jolted, dazed, disconcerted, fallen, scared, stunned, surprised.

ioawa 1. naughty; *synonyms* (*adj*) bad, blue, impish, mischievous, improper, disobedient, insubordinate, wicked, evil, lewd, dark, defiant, racy, rebellious, risque; *antonyms* (*adj*) well-behaved, good, 2. violent; *synonyms* (*adj*) fierce, rough, tempestuous, intense, raging, severe, turbulent, vehement, sharp, passionate, powerful, savage, stormy, (*n*) furious, boisterous; *antonyms* (*adj*) gentle, peaceful, calm, nonviolent, 3. rude; *synonyms* (*adj*) gross, impudent, blunt, coarse, bold, brutal, crude, discourteous, impolite, mean, abusive, barbarous, churlish, crass, (*n*) abrupt; *antonyms* (*adj*) polite, respectful, chivalrous, courteous, refined, civil, decent, proper, well-mannered, 4. obnoxious; *synonyms* (*adj*) objectionable, disagreeable, offensive, detestable, distasteful, hateful, liable, horrid, repellent, disgusting, invidious, revolting, ugly, abhorrent, (*n*) unpleasant; *antonym* (*adj*) pleasant, 5. wicked; *synonyms* (*adj*) atrocious, sinful, vicious, depraved, immoral, unholy, vile, corrupt, criminal, diabolical, foul, hellish, iniquitous, nasty, naughty; *antonyms* (*adj*) innocent, kind, moral, pious, pure.

ioia riddle; *synonyms* (*n*) enigma, conundrum, mystery, puzzle, screen, poser, problem, sieve, cribble, brainteaser, strainer, (*v*) puncture, filter, sift, strain.

ioioa 1. waggle; *synonyms* (*n*) shake, shiver, (*v*) wag, jiggle, wiggle, bob, reel, stagger, 2. wag; *synonyms* (*n*) humorist, waggle, joker, wit, comedian, clown, zany, card, comic, (*v*) wave, swing, beat, flourish, move, vibratiuncle.

ioioia agitated; *synonyms* (*adj*) restless, excited, nervous, restive, tumultuous, upset, distressed, tense, alarmed, anxious, distraught, jumpy, overwrought, perturbed, shaken; *antonyms* (*adj*) calm, composed, lethargic.

ioki 1. exchange; *synonyms* (*n*) commutation, swap, switch, commerce, conversion, substitute, (*v*) change, barter, interchange, commute, counterchange, alternate, alter, cash, convert, 2.

reconcile; *synonyms* (*v*) appease, accommodate, accord, harmonize, pacify, placate, mediate, adjust, compose, harmonise, propitiate, settle, adapt, intercede, (*adj*) conciliate.

iokiaki 1. exchanged; *synonyms* (*adj*) counterchanged, substituted, 2. reconciled; *synonyms* (*v*) affriended, (*adj*) meet, resigned, serene, submissive, acquiescent.

iokina exchange; *synonyms* (*n*) commutation, swap, switch, commerce, conversion, substitute, (*v*) change, barter, interchange, commute, counterchange, alternate, alter, cash, convert.

iokinaki exchanged; *synonyms* (*adj*) counterchanged, substituted.

iowawa 1. misbehave; *synonyms* (*v*) misconduct, transgress, disobey, err, misbear, misdemean, sin, trespass, contravene, deviate, fail, lapse, malfunction, mishandle, (*adj*) misdo; *antonym* (*v*) behave, 2. mischievous; *synonyms* (*adj*) bad, evil, injurious, detrimental, hurtful, naughty, deleterious, harmful, impish, maleficent, playful, arch, baneful, sly, disobedient; *antonym* (*adj*) good, 3. refractory; *synonyms* (*adj*) intractable, obstinate, perverse, recalcitrant, contumacious, fractious, headstrong, stubborn, unruly, insubordinate, restive, turbulent, wayward, willful, pervicacious, 4. rascally; *synonyms* (*adj*) dirty, contemptible, abject, mean, mischievous, roguish, scabby, scoundrelly, scurvy, shabby, blackguardly, devilish, groveling, little, paltry.

ipi yard; *synonyms* (*n*) court, courtyard, garden, backyard, grounds, close, quadrangle, enclosure, beehive, bindery, chiliad, g, grand, m, nailery.

ira 1. hair; *synonyms* (*n*) fuzz, coat, down, fleece, fur, hairbreadth, haircloth, locks, pile, coiffure, (*adj*) brush, clipping, driblet, 2. accompany; *synonyms* (*v*) attend, follow, associate, companion, company, guide, lead, walk, consort, bring, concur, conduct, convoy, join, (*n*) escort, 3. follow; *synonyms* (*v*) chase, pursue, adhere, adopt, accompany, comprehend, continue, ensue, grasp, hunt, realize, succeed, track, emulate, (*adj*) catch; *antonyms* (*v*) precede, head, 4. steal; *synonyms* (*v*) abstract, lift, purloin, creep, filch, misappropriate, pilfer, pinch, plunder, rob, snatch, sneak, plagiarize, slip, (*n*) bargain, 5. stole; *synonyms* (*n*) scarf, wrap, stolon, robe, alb, cassock, chasuble, cope, dalmatic, gown, mozetta, pallium, scapulary, surplice, tunicle, 6. pilfer; *synonyms* (*v*) steal, cabbage, embezzle, hook, nobble, pocket, swipe, thieve, appropriate, cop, poach, rustle, defraud, nick, 7. rob; *synonyms* (*v*) deprive, pillage, rifle, pick, divest, despoil, loot, pluck, ransack, sack, strip, rape, bereave, swindle, assault.

iraaua 1. hesitate; *synonyms* (*v*) falter, pause, doubt, fluctuate, halt, waver, boggle, demur, vacillate, procrastinate, dither, scruple, stammer, (*adj*) linger, delay; *antonym* (v) continue, **2.** indecisive; *synonyms* (adj) doubtful, hesitant, inconclusive, undecided, unsure, weak, dubious, irresolute, precarious, vague, feeble; *antonyms* (adj) decisive, conclusive, resolute, **3.** pause; *synonyms* (n) break, intermission, interruption, rest, gap, interval, respite, stop, breather, cessation, (v) adjournment, hesitate, desist, cease, (adj) discontinue; *antonym* (n) decisiveness, **4.** perplexed; *synonyms* (v) bewildered, complicated, intricate, (adj) confused, involved, lost, baffled, confounded, puzzled, distracted, uneasy, bemused, questioning, quizzical, entangled; *antonym* (adj) enlightened, **5.** unsure; *synonyms* (adj) uncertain, insecure, diffident, tentative, unclear, incertain, indecisive, shy, suspicious, timid; *antonyms* (adj) certain, sure, decided.

irabai steal; *synonyms* (v) abstract, lift, purloin, creep, filch, misappropriate, pilfer, pinch, plunder, rob, snatch, sneak, plagiarize, slip, (n) bargain.

irabaiaki stolen; *synonyms* (adj) purloined, furtive, misbegotten, secret, sly, stealthy.

iraea 1. pilfer; *synonyms* (v) filch, steal, abstract, cabbage, lift, pinch, purloin, rob, embezzle, hook, nobble, pocket, swipe, thieve, appropriate, **2.** stole; *synonyms* (n) scarf, wrap, stolon, robe, alb, cassock, chasuble, cope, dalmatic, gown, mozetta, pallium, scapulary, surplice, tunicle, **3.** steal; *synonyms* (v) creep, misappropriate, pilfer, plunder, snatch, sneak, plagiarize, slip, poach, prowl, nim, slink, take, (n) bargain, theft, **4.** rob; *synonyms* (v) deprive, pillage, rifle, fleece, pick, divest, defraud, despoil, loot, pluck, ransack, sack, strip, rape, bereave.

iraeaki 1. stolen; *synonyms* (adj) purloined, furtive, misbegotten, secret, sly, stealthy, **2.** robed; *synonyms* (adj) appareled, attired, clothed, dressed, garbed, garmented, habilimented, fixed, polished, vested.

irakea hoist; *synonyms* (n) boost, elevator, winch, (v) elevate, haul, heave, lift, erect, raise, rear, uphold, exalt, wind.

iraki 1. accompanied; *synonym* (adj) attended, **2.** robed; *synonyms* (adj) appareled, attired, clothed, dressed, garbed, garmented, habilimented, fixed, polished, vested, **3.** stolen; *synonyms* (adj) purloined, furtive, misbegotten, secret, sly, stealthy.

irananga follow; *synonyms* (v) chase, pursue, adhere, adopt, accompany, comprehend, continue, ensue, grasp, hunt, realize, succeed, track, emulate, (adj) catch; *antonyms* (v) precede, guide, head, lead.

iranikai 1. gesture; *synonyms* (n) signal, gesticulation, indication, movement, (v) sign, beckon, gesticulate, motion, wave, **2.** dodge; *synonyms* (v) circumvent, avoid, evade, maneuver, duck, elude, escape, fudge, hedge, parry, (n) contrivance, stratagem, cheat, device, quibble, **3.** avoid; *synonyms* (v) shun, avert, abstain, annul, forbear, ignore, prevent, shirk, fly, beware, balk, debar, flee, help, (adj) eschew; *antonyms* (v) confront, associate, face, tackle, **4.** sign; *synonyms* (n) mark, portent, brand, emblem, imprint, manifestation, omen, poster, presage, forerunner, attribute, augury, (v) gesture, indicate, autograph.

iranikaiaki 1. gestured, **2.** signed; *synonyms* (adj) gestural, sign, employed, engaged, nonverbal.

irannano 1. mimic; *synonyms* (v) mock, imitate, copy, counterfeit, mime, emulate, impersonate, parody, echo, personate, (n) ape, imitator, mimicker, impersonator, (adj) imitative, **2.** follow; *synonyms* (v) chase, pursue, adhere, adopt, accompany, comprehend, continue, ensue, grasp, hunt, realize, succeed, track, (adj) catch, course; *antonyms* (v) precede, guide, head, lead, **3.** approve; *synonyms* (v) sanction, accept, acknowledge, allow, admit, agree, endorse, let, ratify, support, applaud, acquiesce, authorize, confirm, okay; *antonyms* (v) reject, censure, condemn, disapprove, forbid, veto.

irannanoaki approved; *synonyms* (adj) accepted, certified, sanctioned, allowed, authorized, accredited, agreed, conventional, regular, official, orthodox; *antonyms* (adj) informal, unofficial.

irantanga retaliate; *synonyms* (v) avenge, pay, repay, retort, revenge, reciprocate, reply, requite, answer, return, recompense, counter, defend, get, rebuke.

iraorao amicable; *synonyms* (adj) friendly, affable, kind, amiable, cordial, familiar, genial, gracious, peaceable, peaceful; *antonym* (adj) hostile.

irariki 1. lank; *synonyms* (v) barren, (adj) gaunt, lean, angular, emaciated, meager, thin, scrawny, skinny, spare, spindly, **2.** lanky; *synonyms* (adj) lank, rangy, tall, gangling, bony, gangly; *antonym* (adj) short, **3.** fine; *synonyms* (adj) delicate, agreeable, dainty, brave, capital, elegant, excellent, nice, delightful, acute, admirable, alright, (n) penalty, amercement, (v) punish; *antonyms* (adj) poor, thick, coarse, substantial, unsatisfactory, wide, **4.** slight; *synonyms* (adj) flimsy, slender, fragile, faint, feeble, fine, (n) scorn, disdain, (v) disregard, insult, neglect, ignore, affront, cut, (adv) light; *antonyms* (adj) considerable, major, fat, heavy, intense, obvious, severe, thickset, **5.** thin; *synonyms* (adj) slight, tenuous, rare, slim, sparse, narrow, gossamer, weak, (v) dilute, sheer, subtle, scanty, adulterate, reduce, pare; *antonyms* (adj) concentrated, chubby, plump, broad, (v) thicken, **6.** slender; *synonyms* (adj) little, lithe, lissom, exiguous, minute, graceful, lissome, remote, small, svelte, trim, refined, mean, frail, (v) scant; *antonym* (adj) stocky, **7.** slim; *synonyms* (adj) taper, trivial, outside, (v) slenderize, sly, wily, diet; *antonym* *(adj)* hefty, **8**. strait; *synonyms* *(n)* inlet, need, pass, pinch, quandary, channel, crisis, difficulty, distress, poverty, straits, emergency, frith, *(v)* dilemma, *(adj)* nonplus, **9**. skinny; *synonyms* *(adj)* scraggy, underweight, weedy, starving, *(v)* cortical, cutaneous, cuticular, dermal; *antonyms* *(adj)* brawny, well-built.

ire 1. file; *synonyms* *(n)* archive, document, list, procession, rank, record, roll, series, string, *(v)* order, rasp, register, scrape, abrade, arrange, **2**. furbish; *synonyms* *(v)* buff, burnish, scour, shine, flush, gloss, rub, gild, grain, lacquer, paint, whitewash, file, dress, rehabilitate, **3**. polish; *synonyms* *(n)* finish, gentility, cultivation, elegance, refinement, civilization, culture, *(v)* furbish, glaze, civilize, clean, cultivate, grind, improve, perfect, **4**. shine; *synonyms* *(n)* sheen, luster, radiance, *(v)* glow, light, gleam, blaze, flash, glitter, sparkle, excel, flame, glance, glisten, radiate; *antonym* *(n)* dullness, **5**. rub; *synonyms* *(v)* fray, grate, gall, chafe, caress, fret, graze, irritate, massage, scratch, wipe, *(n)* check, brush, hitch, cross.

irea 1. gloss; *synonyms* *(n)* burnish, annotation, brightness, shine, finish, explanation, glossary, sheen, commentary, *(v)* glaze, comment, annotate, veneer, color, varnish; *antonym* *(n)* dullness, **2**. glaze; *synonyms* *(n)* coating, enamel, glazing, gloss, luster, *(v)* glass, coat, calender, candy, **3**. shine; *synonyms* *(n)* radiance, rub, *(v)* glow, light, gleam, blaze, flash, glitter, sparkle, excel, flame, glance, glisten, radiate, reflect, **4**. rub; *synonyms* *(v)* fray, grate, gall, chafe, abrade, caress, fret, furbish, graze, irritate, massage, scrape, *(n)* check, brush, hitch, **5**. polish; *synonyms* *(n)* gentility, cultivation, elegance, refinement, civilization, culture, *(v)* civilize, clean, cultivate, grind, improve, perfect, refine, scour, scrub.

ireaki 1. glazed; *synonyms* *(adj)* glassy, glossy, glassed, glazen, bright, burnished, dead, drunk, enameled, glassen, glasslike, shiny, slippery, varnished, glistening, **2**. polished; *synonyms* *(adj)* elegant, courteous, cultured, finished, refined, civil, courtly, genteel, lustrous, polite, smooth, accomplished, graceful, sleek, slick; *antonyms* *(adj)* dull, rough.

ireirea rub; *synonyms* *(v)* fray, grate, gall, chafe, abrade, caress, fret, furbish, graze, irritate, massage, scrape, *(n)* check, brush, hitch.

ireiti continual; *synonyms* *(adj)* constant, ceaseless, incessant, continuous, endless, everlasting, frequent, uninterrupted, eternal, lasting, perennial, permanent, perpetual, persistent, unending; *antonyms* *(adj)* intermittent, sporadic, temporary.

irengan mixed; *synonyms* *(adj)* miscellaneous, assorted, composite, heterogeneous, integrated, medley, impure, amalgamated, diverse, intermingled, motley, varied, indiscriminate, *(v)* blended, mingled; *antonyms* *(adj)* homogeneous, insular, pure.

irenganan 1. mix; *synonyms* *(n)* mixture, concoction, *(v)* alloy, blend, intermingle, mingle, combine, compound, confound, intermix, join, meld, merge, aggregate, admix; *antonym* *(v)* separate, **2**. blend; *synonyms* *(n)* mix, amalgam, composite, amalgamation, brew, combination, fusion, harmony, mash, *(v)* amalgamate, commingle, fuse, incorporate, go, immingle; *antonym* *(v)* divide.

irengananaki 1. mixed; *synonyms* *(adj)* miscellaneous, assorted, composite, heterogeneous, integrated, medley, impure, amalgamated, diverse, intermingled, motley, varied, indiscriminate, *(v)* blended, mingled; *antonyms* *(adj)* homogeneous, insular, pure, **2**. blended; *synonyms* *(v)* blent, polluted, stained, *(adj)* mixed, adulterate, beaten, conglomerate.

irerei repeating; *synonyms* *(adj)* repetitious, iterating, iterative, repetitive, iterant, perpetual, verbose, *(n)* repeat, repetition.

iri follow; *synonyms* *(v)* chase, pursue, adhere, adopt, accompany, comprehend, continue, ensue, grasp, hunt, realize, succeed, track, emulate, *(adj)* catch; *antonyms* *(v)* precede, guide, head, lead.

irîrep football; *synonyms* *(n)* soccer, hockey, note, baseball, basketball, footie.

iro ignite; *synonyms* *(v)* light, kindle, arouse, enkindle, fire, heat, flame, agitate, burn, excite, inflame, detonate, incite, provoke, awaken; *antonym* *(v)* extinguish.

iroaki ignited; *synonyms* *(v)* burning, active, flowing, laving, live, lively, quickening, running, vigorous, *(adj)* kindled, enkindled, flaming, ablaze, fiery.

iroroto inexperienced; *synonyms* *(adj)* immature, naive, young, callow, raw, ignorant, new, unsophisticated, unexperienced, clumsy, strange, amateurish, awkward, inexpert, *(v)* green; *antonyms* *(adj)* experienced, trained, skilled, sophisticated.

irou by; *synonyms* *(prep)* beside, at, of, about, on, per, *(adv)* aside, away, past, through, apart, along, beyond, *(adv, prep)* alongside, *(adj)* over.

irua 1. foreigner; *synonyms* *(n)* alien, stranger, outlander, outsider, unknown, barbarian, immigrant, newcomer; *antonym* *(n)* native, **2**. newcomer; *synonyms* *(n)* beginner, freshman, foreigner, arrival, fledgeling, neophyte, novice, recruit, entrant, fledgling, greenhorn, apprentice, *(adj)* interloper, intruder, **3**. stranger; *antonyms* *(n)* associate, friend, pal.

iruwa 1. alien; *synonyms* *(adj)* foreign, strange, unknown, extrinsic, exotic, extraneous, remote, unfamiliar, unusual, *(n)* foreigner, outsider, stranger, emigrant, *(v)* alienate, estrange; *antonyms* *(adj)* familiar, *(n)* native, citizen, **2**. illegal;

synonyms (*adj*) criminal, forbidden, prohibited, unauthorized, unlawful, illegitimate, illicit, lawless, taboo, wrongful; *antonyms* (*adj*) legal, lawful, honest, legitimate, official, **3.** guest; *synonyms* (*n*) caller, alien, customer, visitor, client, visitant, **4.** foreign; *synonyms* (*adj*) exterior, external, oversea, adventitious, outlandish, peregrine, different, imported, irrelevant, outside, outward, tramontane; *antonyms* (*adj*) domestic, internal.

itabon neighbor; *synonyms* (*n*) acquaintance, national, inhabitant, bystander, (*adj*) neighbour, neighboring, neighbouring, (*v*) abut, adjoin, touch, border, butt, join, line, verge.

itangitangiri love; *synonyms* (*n*) desire, affection, dear, fondness, liking, benevolence, charity, attachment, beloved, darling, devotion, honey, (*v*) cherish, enjoy, like; *antonyms* (*n*) abhorrence, hatred, aversion, (*v*) hate, dislike, abhor.

itangitangiriaki loved; *synonyms* (*adj*) dear, beloved, cherished, pet, precious, appreciated, esteemed, prized, respected, treasured, valued, important, (*n*) darling.

itaobuki support; *synonyms* (*n*) help, stand, aid, keep, comfort, maintenance, patronage, (*v*) assist, prop, back, brace, encourage, maintain, bear, boost; *antonyms* (*n*) hindrance, (*v*) oppose, neglect, undermine, abandon, reject, weaken.

itaobukiaki supported; *synonyms* (*v*) borne, carried, conveyed, supporting, (*adj*) bolstered, based, (*adv*) on.

iteratera 1. unstable; *synonyms* (*adj*) changeable, precarious, insecure, shaky, unsettled, unsound, erratic, fickle, fluid, inconstant, unpredictable, irresolute, unreliable, capricious, changeful; *antonyms* (*adj*) stable, steady, constant, **2.** unpredictable; *synonyms* (*adj*) uncertain, unstable, irregular, chancy, hazardous, impulsive, incalculable, inconsistent, undependable, unforeseeable; *antonyms* (*adj*) predictable, consistent.

iteraua many; *synonyms* (*adj*) manifold, abundant, countless, frequent, various, innumerable, much, multiple, numerous, plentiful, several, different, numberless, (*n*) number; *antonym* (*n*) few.

iti 1. bankrupt; *synonyms* (*adj*) insolvent, broke, destitute, impoverished, poor, (*v*) ruin, break, impoverish, deprive, (*n*) failure; *antonyms* (*adj*) solvent, rich, **2.** clear; *synonyms* (*adj*) clean, certain, open, apparent, distinct, empty, (*v*) bright, acquit, absolute, free, net, absolve, clarify, definite, discharge; *antonyms* (*adj*) cloudy, opaque, unclear, dark, fuzzy, hazy, incomprehensible, obscure, uncertain, vague, ambiguous, blurry, confused, confusing, (*v*) convict, **3.** finished; *synonyms* (*v*) done, (*adj*) complete, completed, ended, perfect, consummate, accomplished, polished, ripe, ruined, spent, round, capable, decided, (*adv*) over;

antonyms (*adj*) unfinished, incomplete, remaining, rough, **4.** penniless; *synonyms* (*adj*) impecunious, indigent, needy, moneyless, miserable, penurious, dowerless, fortuneless, **5.** ruined; *synonyms* (*v*) lost, undone, (*adj*) destroyed, dilapidated, broken, desolate, bankrupt, desolated, devastated, finished, ravaged, spoiled, beaten, fallen, wasted; *antonyms* (*adj*) untarnished, first-rate, pure, **6.** seven; *synonyms* (*n*) heptad, septet, ace, eight, jack, king, knave, nine, queen, septette, ten, deuce, five, four, sevensome.

itia scoop; *synonyms* (*n*) ladle, spade, exclusive, pocket, scoopful, shovel, article, report, (*v*) draw, dig, excavate, hollow, best, outdo, outflank.

itiaki 1. clean; *synonyms* (*adj*) clear, fair, antiseptic, blank, pure, chaste, adroit, tidy, unblemished, (*v*) brush, cleanse, bathe, clarify, disinfect, sweep; *antonyms* (*adj*) filthy, unclean, muddy, unhygienic, full, syrupy, tainted, unwholesome, (*v*) dirty, soil, contaminate, pollute, **2.** righteous; *synonyms* (*adj*) right, good, moral, honest, just, virtuous, godly, pious, correct, honorable, upright, impartial, saintly, equitable, proper, **3.** pure; *synonyms* (*adj*) absolute, genuine, natural, artless, clean, faultless, fresh, guileless, immaculate, innocent, mere, perfect, devout, authentic, net; *antonyms* (*adj*) impure, contaminated, diluted, dishonored, wicked.

itibabang appear; *synonyms* (*v*) occur, rise, seem, sound, emerge, show, break, arise, arrive, begin, feel, happen, look, surface, (*n*) come; *antonyms* (*v*) disappear, vanish.

itibabu 1. active; *synonyms* (*adj*) energetic, alert, busy, diligent, effective, live, lively, nimble, strong, agile, alive, brisk, dynamic, forcible, healthy; *antonyms* (*adj*) dormant, inactive, sluggish, idle, latent, lethargic, sedentary, slow, extinct, passive, quiet, **2.** diligent; *synonyms* (*adj*) active, assiduous, careful, painstaking, earnest, attentive, industrious, laborious, studious, occupied, conscientious, indefatigable, meticulous, persevering, sedulous; *antonyms* (*adj*) lazy, careless, negligent, **3.** rapid; *synonyms* (*adj*) fast, quick, prompt, swift, fleet, hasty, speedy, cursory, expeditious, sudden, winged, express, hurried, immediate, instant; *antonym* (*adj*) gradual.

itibubua 1. hundred; *synonyms* (*n*) century, cent, centred, lathe, riding, soke, tithing, carbon, cocain, cocaine, coke, coulomb, snow, (*adj*) centigrade, **2.** seven; *synonyms* (*n*) heptad, septet, ace, eight, jack, king, knave, nine, queen, septette, ten, deuce, five, four, sevensome.

itikurere 1. quiver; *synonyms* (*n*) quake, tremble, palpitate, shake, quaver, thrill, tremor, vibration, (*v*) shiver, shudder, flicker, flutter, pulsate, vibrate, wave, **2.** vibrate; *synonyms* (*v*) oscillate, quiver, swing, wobble, throb, fluctuate, move, sway, undulate, jar, wag, beat, blow, ring, pulse, **3.** shake; *synonyms* (*v*) agitate, brandish, disturb, excite, totter, drop, bump, convulse, flourish, jiggle, quail, rattle, rock, (*n*) jolt, trembling, **4.** shudder; *synonyms* (*n*) quivering, shivering, chill, frisson, twitch, palpitation, tingle, (*v*) dither, shrink, fear, jerk, **5.** tremble; *synonyms* (*v*) falter, waver, cower, blench, cringe, didder, flinch, recoil, stir, (*n*) heave, pant, (*adj*) crumble, starve.

itikurereaki shaken; *synonyms* (*v*) broken, lame, passe, shaky, threadbare, wilted, shattered, stale, (*adj*) jolted, dazed, disconcerted, fallen, scared, stunned, surprised.

itimareare 1. gone; *synonyms* (*v*) extinct, (*adj*) dead, past, absent, deceased, exhausted, away, bygone, departed, desperate, bypast, foregone, hopeless, late, lost; *antonym* (*adj*) present, **2.** eaten, **3.** scattered; *synonyms* (*adj*) dispersed, dissipated, confused, disconnected, disordered, sparse, sporadic, thin, diffuse, distributed, rare, separate, spread, stray, strewn; *antonym* (*adj*) concentrated.

itina 1. hurry; *synonyms* (*n*) speed, haste, dispatch, flurry, (*v*) bustle, hasten, accelerate, dash, expedite, scurry, fly, run, rush, zip, hie; *antonyms* (*n*) slowness, (*v*) dawdle, **2.** electrify; *synonyms* (*v*) excite, stagger, galvanize, rouse, shock, stir, thrill, amaze, astound, surprise, (*adv*) startle, **3.** inject; *synonyms* (*v*) infuse, enter, insert, instill, introduce, shoot, interject, (*adj*) syringe, **4.** vaccinate; *synonyms* (*v*) immunize, inoculate, inject, immunise, nurse.

itinaki 1. hurried; *synonyms* (*adj*) hasty, fast, headlong, quick, rapid, speedy, sudden, swift, abrupt, cursory, careless, precipitate, prompt, rash, slapdash; *antonyms* (*adj*) slow, unhurried, leisurely, **2.** vaccinated; *synonyms* (*adj*) immunized, immunised.

itinaniku outcast; *synonyms* (*n*) exile, pariah, castaway, expatriate, outlaw, vagabond, loon, lown, refugee, (*adj*) derelict, homeless, friendless.

ititi 1. need; *synonyms* (*v*) lack, claim, require, destitution, indigence, involve, (*n*) demand, want, desire, deficiency, must, necessity, deprivation, requirement, absence; *antonym* (*n*) wealth, **2.** require; *synonyms* (*v*) need, charge, crave, ask, exact, entail, call, command, compel, force, necessitate, request, enjoin, expect, oblige.

ititiaki 1. needed; *synonyms* (*adj*) necessary, essential, required, needful, requisite, indispensable, wanted, wanting, compulsory, devoid, good, lacking, mandatory, perfect, vital, **2.** required; *synonyms* (*adj*) needed, obligatory, prerequisite, bound, desired, binding; *antonyms* (*adj*) optional, free, undesirable.

itiua seven; *synonyms* (*n*) heptad, septet, ace, eight, jack, king, knave, nine, queen, septette, ten, deuce, five, four, sevensome.

itiwewe 1. clean; *synonyms* (*adj*) clear, fair, antiseptic, blank, pure, chaste, adroit, tidy, unblemished, (*v*) brush, cleanse, bathe, clarify, disinfect, sweep; *antonyms* (*adj*) filthy, unclean, muddy, unhygienic, full, syrupy, tainted, unwholesome, (*v*) dirty, soil, contaminate, pollute, **2.** lucid; *synonyms* (*adj*) intelligible, transparent, coherent, limpid, distinct, evident, bright, crystalline, diaphanous, explicit, light, logical, articulate, vivid, comprehensible; *antonyms* (*adj*) muddled, opaque, unintelligible, **3.** clear; *synonyms* (*adj*) clean, certain, open, apparent, empty, plain, blameless, (*v*) acquit, absolute, free, net, absolve, definite, discharge, exculpate; *antonyms* (*adj*) cloudy, unclear, dark, fuzzy, hazy, incomprehensible, obscure, uncertain, vague, ambiguous, blurry, confused, confusing, dull, (*v*) convict, **4.** vivid; *synonyms* (*adj*) graphic, intense, brilliant, lifelike, rich, live, acute, animated, colorful, glowing, strong, picturesque, expressive, brisk, lively, **5.** spotless; *synonyms* (*adj*) faultless, immaculate, guiltless, innocent, flawless, impeccable, perfect, speckless, stainless, virtuous, untarnished, neat, sinless, irreproachable, bloodless, **6.** pure; *synonyms* (*adj*) just, genuine, natural, artless, fresh, good, guileless, mere, devout, authentic, holy, modest, simple, spotless, (*v*) sheer; *antonyms* (*adj*) impure, contaminated, diluted, dishonored, wicked, **7.** unblemished; *synonyms* (*adj*) unspotted, uninjured, complete, sound, untouched; *antonyms* (*adj*) blemished, flawed, marked.

itonginako 1. panicky; *synonyms* (*adj*) frightened, panicked, fearful, scared, terrified, alarmed, anxious, befuddled, bemused, confused, dazed, disorientated, edgy, gloomy, (*adv*) cowardly; *antonym* (*adj*) confident, **2.** panicked; *synonym* (*adj*) panicky.

itoua seven; *synonyms* (*n*) heptad, septet, ace, eight, jack, king, knave, nine, queen, septette, ten, deuce, five, four, sevensome.

itu 1. thread; *synonyms* (*n*) string, line, yarn, rope, twine, wire, cord, fiber, (*v*) file, range, penetrate, lace, pass, run, meander, **2.** sew; *synonyms* (*v*) patch, knit, mend, stitch, tack, tailor, retick, tick, weave, make, beat, click, create, customise, (*adj*) tie.

ituaki threaded; *synonym* (*adj*) screwed.

itutu 1. knit; *synonyms* (*v*) entwine, tie, plait, intertwine, bind, fasten, join, pucker, interlace, bond, purse, crease, interconnect, (*adj*) stitch, lace, **2.** sew; *synonyms* (*v*) patch, knit, mend, tack, tailor, retick, tick, weave, make, beat, click, create, customise, customize, cut, **3.** stitch; *synonyms* (*n*) twinge, pang, cramp, (*v*) sew, seam, baste, crick, embroider, suture, articulation, commissure, gore,

gusset, hinge, joining; *antonym* (v) unpick, **4.**
thread; *synonyms* (n) string, line, yarn, rope,
twine, wire, cord, fiber, (v) file, range, penetrate,
pass, run, meander, permeate, **5.** sewed;
synonyms (adj) sewn, stitched.

itutuaki 1. knitted, **2.** threaded; *synonym* (adj)
screwed, **3.** stitched; *synonyms* (adj) sewed, sewn.

iwai 1. clash; *synonyms* (n) bang, battle, brush, clang,
crash, discord, encounter, (v) jar, fight, impact,
brawl, clank, collide, conflict, dispute; *antonyms* (n)
agreement, (v) agree, **2.** contest; *synonyms* (n)
bout, competition, altercation, contention, race,
struggle, debate, feud, game, match, (v) compete,
combat, contend, argue, challenge, **3.** grapple;
synonyms (v) clutch, clasp, grip, tackle, grab, deal,
seize, wrestle, cope, snatch, (n) grapnel, grappling,
grasp, (adj) lock, hook, **4.** conflict; *synonyms* (n)
clash, contest, action, antagonism, collision,
difference, disagreement, engagement, fighting,
scuffle, strife, war, clashing, argument, (v) disagree;
antonyms (n) accord, harmony, peace, **5.**
encounter; *synonyms* (n) confrontation, meeting,
(v) confront, experience, face, find, rencounter,
detect, bump, chance, incur, meet, receive, see,
suffer; *antonym* (v) retreat, **6.** contend; *synonyms*
(v) assert, altercate, quarrel, strive, vie, affirm,
buffet, profess, declare, emulate, grapple, rival, run,
(n) allege, maintain, **7.** oppose; *synonyms* (v)
object, contradict, contravene, controvert,
counteract, resist, counter, dissent, defend, gainsay,
hinder, repel, thwart, withstand, differ; *antonyms*
(v) support, advocate, back, advise, **8.** skirmish;
synonyms (n) tussle, brushwood, (v) bicker, **9.**
squirm; *synonyms* (v) wiggle, wriggle, twist,
fidget, writhe, twitch, distort, worm, **10.** struggle;
synonyms (n) strain, effort, exertion, scramble,
warfare, pull, (v) attempt, endeavor, labor, aim,
essay, oppose, push, tug, clamber; *antonyms* (v)
flourish, glide.

iwaiaki 1. contested; *synonyms* (adj) contentious,
litigated, litigious, quarrelsome, **2.** opposed;
synonyms (adj) conflicting, contradictory, hostile,
contrary, antagonistic, opposing, adverse, averse,
contrasted, repugnant, incompatible, irreconcilable,
counter, against, opposite.

iwaka 1. hard; *synonyms* (adj) austere, bad, difficult,
grave, severe, strong, arduous, callous, cruel,
grueling, knotty, tough, (adv) firm, (v) acute, (n)
rough; *antonyms* (adj) easy, soft, kind, merciful,
simple, soggy, tender, yielding, (adv) gently, lightly,
2. fibrous; *synonyms* (adj) stringy, ropy, brawny,
fibry, gossamer, hempen, muscular, nemaline, raw,
rubbery, sinewy, unchewable, wiry, coarse, gristly,
3. tenacious; *synonyms* (adj) stubborn, adhesive,
dogged, obstinate, persistent, resolute, sticky,
determined, glutinous, persevering, pertinacious,

steadfast, unyielding, viscous, (v) retentive, **4.** taut;
synonyms (adj) close, tight, drawn, rigid, stiff, tense,
strained, stringent, inflexible, taught, (v) fast;
antonyms (adj) loose, limp, **5.** tough; *synonyms*
(adj) hard, tenacious, hardy, laborious, rugged,
stout, sturdy, durable, leathery, robust, heavy, (n)
bully, rowdy, hoodlum, hooligan; *antonyms* (adj)
weak, flimsy, feeble, lightweight.

Í

íniañai when; *synonyms* (adv) as, once, then, because,
than, since, equally, erst, erstwhile, formerly, (conj)
although, while, immediately, (prep) during, (adj)
following.

íninan low; *synonyms* (adj) contemptible, abject,
humble, ignoble, base, blue, common, deep,
dejected, depressed, down, downcast,
downhearted, (adv) gentle, (n) depression; *antonyms*
(adj) cheerful, happy, high-pitched, loud, important,
piercing, (n) high.

Î

îa where; *synonyms* (adv) there, here, wherever,
whither, anywhere, wherein, anyplace, whereas,
somewhere, (conj) but, while, (pron) everywhere, (n)
point, spot, situation.

îra thief; *synonyms* (n) robber, burglar, bandit, pirate,
plunderer, crook, filcher, stealer, despoiler,
freebooter, pillager, rifler.

îru yellow; *synonyms* (adj) jaundiced, amber, chicken,
chickenhearted, fearful, xanthous, craven,
spineless, yellowish, flavous, golden, (n) coward,
(adv) cowardly.

îrua foreigner; *synonyms* (n) alien, stranger,
outlander, outsider, unknown, barbarian,
immigrant, newcomer; *antonym* (n) native.

îti straight; *synonyms* (adv) level, right, directly, (adj)
erect, honest, even, flat, upright, fair, correct, just,
perpendicular, proper, accurate, (v) direct;
antonyms (adv) indirectly, (adj) curly, curved,
diluted, winding, zigzag, askew, bent, curvy,
knotted, twisted, twisting, wavy, circuitous,
guarded.

J

jetia door; *synonyms* (*n*) gate, threshold, access, doorway, entrance, entry, mouth, opening, entryway, exit, hatch, inlet, porch, portal, wicket.

jevenako throw; *synonyms* (*v*) cast, fling, shed, hurl, chuck, flip, heave, pass, deliver, drop, give, hurtle, (*n*) pitch, push, shot.

K

ka 1. indistinct; *synonyms* (*adj*) confused, dim, faint, inarticulate, indefinite, dull, fuzzy, hazy, indeterminate, dark, neutral, ambiguous, blurred, doubtful, (*n*) cloudy; *antonyms* (*adj*) distinct, clear, **2.** let; *synonyms* (*v*) allow, hire, admit, lease, leave, permit, charter, have, rent, grant, authorize, cause, countenance, demise, (*n*) check; *antonyms* (*v*) forbid, prevent, **3.** dim; *synonyms* (*adj*) obscure, bleak, dense, gloomy, indistinct, misty, opaque, shadowy, (*v*) blur, darken, cloud, pale, tarnish, blear, blind; *antonyms* (*adj*) bright, brilliant, intelligent, clever, strong, (*v*) brighten, **4.** sombre; *synonyms* (*adj*) somber, dismal, dreary, drab, sober, solemn, black, grave, **5.** tired; *synonyms* (*adj*) exhausted, fatigued, hackneyed, weary, banal, commonplace, stale, threadbare, trite, beat, haggard, jaded, stock, worn, drowsy; *antonyms* (*adj*) fresh, invigorated, alert, refreshed, energetic, original.

kaaioroa rival; *synonyms* (*adj*) competitive, (*n*) competitor, emulate, enemy, foe, adversary, antagonist, challenger, contender, contestant, (*v*) equal, contest, match, compete, contend; *antonyms* (*adj*) allied, (*n*) ally, friend, partner.

kaairua confound; *synonyms* (*v*) bewilder, baffle, confuse, astonish, nonplus, perplex, puzzle, amaze, astound, bamboozle, mistake, mystify, complicate, (*n*) surprise, (*adj*) stupefy; *antonym* (*v*) enlighten.

kaairuaki confounded; *synonyms* (*adj*) bemused, bewildered, accursed, abashed, baffled, befuddled, confused, cursed, execrable, puzzled, aghast, abominable.

kaaitao cover; *synonyms* (*v*) coat, conceal, top, bury, cloak, (*n*) blind, blanket, screen, binding, camouflage, cap, covering, lid, mask, shield; *antonyms* (*v*) reveal, expose, uncover.

kaaitaoaki covered; *synonyms* (*adj*) hidden, veiled, concealed, covert, coated, masked, obscured, secret,

shrouded, thick, wrapped, (*prep*) cloaked; *antonyms* (*adj*) bare, naked.

kaakaea disrupt; *synonyms* (*v*) break, disorder, disturb, heckle, interpose, interrupt, perturb, cut, dislocate, agitate, cease, dissociate, rupture, scatter, smash.

kaakaeaki disrupted; *synonyms* (*adj*) disrupt, severed.

kaakea negate; *synonyms* (*v*) contradict, invalidate, deny, annul, belie, contravene, confute, disprove, cancel, nullify, refute, counteract, neutralize, controvert, quash; *antonym* (*v*) confirm.

kaaki put; *synonyms* (*v*) place, fix, lay, position, set, impose, couch, locate, pose, charge, pitch, arrange, assign, commit, (*n*) deposit.

kaan 1. near; *synonyms* (*prep*) about, by, around, (*adv*) close, almost, towards, (*adj*) adjoining, adjacent, contiguous, imminent, impending, narrow, (*v*) familiar, approximate, approach; *antonym* (*adj*) distant, **2.** nearly; *synonyms* (*adv*) approximately, closely, virtually, intimately, nigh, practically, roughly, much, just, dear, halfway, (*adj*) near, most, thereabouts, approaching.

káan 1. ward; *synonyms* (*n*) guard, charge, custody, protection, care, district, neighborhood, quarter, defense, keep, area, region, division, (*v*) shelter, protect, **2.** village; *synonyms* (*n*) hamlet, city, community, settlement, kraal, (*adv*) town.

kaananaua lengthen; *synonyms* (*v*) elongate, enlarge, draw, increase, prolong, expand, protract, stretch, continue, delay, spread, amplify, (*adj*) extend, elongated; *antonym* (*v*) shorten.

kaananauaki lengthened; *synonyms* (*adj*) extended, elongated, prolonged, long, protracted, expanded, elongate, extensive, lengthy, lingering, delayed, stretched, wide; *antonym* (*adj*) brief.

kaangitannenea 1. disquiet; *synonyms* (*n*) alarm, anxiety, trouble, worry, apprehension, concern, discomfort, dismay, disorder, (*v*) discompose, perturb, agitate, bother, turmoil, upset; *antonyms* (*n*) quiet, reassurance, (*v*) calm, **2.** vary; *synonyms* (*v*) alter, change, differ, modify, alternate, deviate, diverge, diversify, modulate, depart, disagree, fluctuate, shift, variegate, contrast, **3.** torment; *synonyms* (*n*) harass, agony, anguish, annoy, pain, suffering, curse, (*v*) torture, tease, distress, afflict, persecute, badger, irritate, oppress.

kaangitanneneaki 1. disquieted; *synonyms* (*adj*) upset, disturbed, worried, disordered, uneasy, unsettled, agitated, anxious, confused, apprehensive, awkward, brainsick, broken, constrained, constraining, **2.** varied; *synonyms* (*adj*) assorted, diverse, miscellaneous, mixed, various, different, diversified, sundry, heterogeneous, manifold, motley, many, dissimilar, versatile, odd; *antonyms* (*adj*) boring, dull, homogeneous, uniform, **3.** tormented; *synonyms* (*adj*) anguished, tortured, hagridden, beleaguered, beset, besieged, cruciate, cruciform, distraught, distressed, miserable, obsessed, plagued, suffering, agonized; *antonym* (*adj*) content.

kaaontia adjoin; *synonyms* (*v*) abut, border, annex, touch, neighbor, edge, meet, append, contact, verge, butt, (*adj*) join.

kaata widen; *synonyms* (*v*) expand, extend, broaden, stretch, distend, enlarge, increase, spread, develop, dilate, amplify, flare, thicken, grow, impart; *antonym* (*v*) narrow.

kaataibaia instruct; *synonyms* (*v*) charge, advise, direct, educate, enlighten, teach, command, drill, indoctrinate, inform, apprise, bid, coach, discipline, edify; *antonym* (*v*) request.

kaataibaiaki instructed; *synonyms* (*v*) erudite, leaned, lettered, (*adj*) educated, taught, tutored, enlightened, arranged, experienced, furnished, instruct, intelligent, qualified, schooled, provided.

kaawarebwea widen; *synonyms* (*v*) expand, extend, broaden, stretch, distend, enlarge, increase, spread, develop, dilate, amplify, flare, thicken, grow, impart; *antonym* (*v*) narrow.

kababa flatter; *synonyms* (*v*) coax, fawn, court, adulate, cajole, wheedle, blandish, grovel, kowtow, soap, compliment, entice, indulge, persuade, (*n*) caress.

kabae 1. engage; *synonyms* (*v*) contract, attract, book, employ, absorb, betroth, charter, enlist, retain, draw, engross, hire, involve, lock, mesh; *antonyms* (*v*) fire, disengage, **2**. tie; *synonyms* (*n*) band, connection, lace, association, relationship, sleeper, strap, (*v*) link, bond, attach, bind, join, knot, connect, fasten; *antonyms* (*v*) disconnect, untie, undo.

kabaea 1. hitch; *synonyms* (*n*) catch, hindrance, limp, arrest, barrier, check, difficulty, drawback, handicap, snag, block, blockage, (*v*) fasten, attach, hobble; *antonym* (*adj*) unhitch, **2**. bind; *synonyms* (*v*) tie, bandage, bundle, combine, fetter, fix, lace, truss, affix, bond, cement, gird, hold, knot, (*n*) band; *antonyms* (*v*) untie, release, unbind, **3**. bound; *synonyms* (*v*) leap, border, bounce, limit, circumscribe, confine, pounce, rebound, (*n*) spring, jump, boundary, edge, compass, hop, recoil; *antonym* (*adj*) free, **4**. fasten; *synonyms* (*v*) bind, connect, anchor, append, brace, clasp, clinch, determine, pin, secure, stick, tack, chain, hang, bar; *antonyms* (*v*) unfasten, detach, undo, unlock, **5**. tie; *synonyms* (*n*) connection, draw, association, relationship, sleeper, strap, string, cord, deadlock, fastening, (*v*) link, join, leash, marry, tether; *antonym* (*v*) disconnect.

kabaeai borrow; *synonyms* (*v*) adopt, appropriate, assume, take, accept, acquire, plagiarize, cadge, obtain, sponge, usurp, charter, copy, imitate, (*n*) pledge; *antonym* (*v*) lend.

kabaeaiaki borrowed; *synonyms* (*adj*) foreign, rubato, secondary, rented, robbed.

kabaeaki 1. bound; *synonyms* (*v*) leap, border, bounce, limit, circumscribe, confine, pounce, rebound, (*n*) spring, jump, boundary, edge, barrier, compass, hop; *antonym* (*adj*) free, **2**. bounded; *synonyms* (*adj*) finite, restricted, delimited, limited, encircled, enclosed, local, qualified, surrounded, belted, compassed, contiguous, defined, definite, determinate, **3**. engaged; *synonyms* (*adj*) busy, occupied, betrothed, affianced, employed, engrossed, reserved, absorbed, working, pledged, bespoken, booked, immersed, intent, rapt; *antonym* (*adj*) available, **4**. fastened; *synonyms* (*adj*) fixed, tied, buttoned, closed, fast, tight, binding, empight, even, firm, flat, frozen, laced, reconditioned, repaired, **5**. tied; *synonyms* (*adj*) fastened, connected, united, attached, joined, legato, liable, mixed, powerless, responsible, spiked, trussed, coupled, together; *antonym* (*adj*) separate.

kabaia 1. content; *synonyms* (*n*) capacity, contentment, matter, meaning, subject, substance, contentedness, (*adj*) contented, happy, fulfilled, (*v*) appease, please, satisfy, suffice, delight; *antonyms* (*adj*) tormented, unhappy, discontented, dissatisfied, rebellious, (*v*) discontent, upset, **2**. blessed; *synonyms* (*adj*) blest, holy, blasted, cursed, damned, fortunate, hallowed, sacred, saintly, lucky, consecrated, deuced, divine, heavenly, infernal; *antonym* (*adj*) unlucky, **3**. happy; *synonyms* (*adj*) felicitous, gay, buoyant, content, gleeful, gratified, blithe, bright, carefree, cheerful, cheery, convivial, delightful, (*n*) auspicious, blessed; *antonyms* (*adj*) sad, dejected, depressed, miserable, sorrowful, **4**. fortunate; *synonyms* (*adj*) favorable, advantageous, favored, fortuitous, prosperous, successful, well, golden, good, propitious, providential, advantaged, desirable, hopeful; *antonym* (*adj*) unfortunate, **5**. satisfied; *synonyms* (*v*) convinced, (*adj*) full, pleased, certain, confident, sure, complacent, persuaded, sated, satiated, easy, positive, quenched; *antonym* (*adj*) frustrated.

kabaibai 1. endow; *synonyms* (*v*) invest, give, clothe, contribute, bless, dower, furnish, supply, vest, empower, enable, confer, award, bequeath, equip, **2**. inherit; *synonyms* (*v*) succeed, heir, get, own, receive, follow, obtain, ascend, attain, promote, prosper, pursue.

kabaibaiaki 1. inherited; *synonyms* (*adj*) hereditary, inborn, familial, genetic, ancestral, congenital, incarnate, inherent, transmissible, **2**. endowed; *synonyms* (*adj*) able, gifted, clever, cute, artistic, blessed, brilliant, competent, felicitous, ingenious, qualitied, talented, capable.

kabainrang 1. insult; *synonyms* (n) dishonor, abuse, affront, contumely, disgrace, indignity, outrage, contempt, wound, derision, harm, injury, (v) flout, taunt, cut; *antonyms* (v) compliment, praise, **2.** rape; *synonyms* (n) assault, violation, colza, rapine, ravishment, abduction, (v) pillage, plunder, ravish, foray, despoil, destroy, dishonour, violate, ransack.

kabainranga 1. despise; *synonyms* (v) scorn, contemn, disdain, loathe, depreciate, abhor, detest, dislike, hate, slight, condemn, defy, disregard, execrate, (n) deride; *antonyms* (v) admire, respect, **2.** seduce; *synonyms* (v) attract, lure, allure, captivate, decoy, entice, inveigle, persuade, coax, defile, (adj) debauch, fascinate, bewitch, charm, (n) tempt.

kabainrangaki 1. insulted; *synonyms* (adj) affronted, huffy, disrespected, hurt, slighted, snubbed, upset, **2.** despised; *synonyms* (adj) detested, scorned, despicable, hated, abject, abhorrent, contemptible, contemptuous, loathed, opprobrious, reviled, unpopular, infamous, insolent, insufferable, **3.** raped; *synonyms* (adj) assaulted, despoiled, molested, pillaged, plundered, blasted, desolate, desolated, devastated, looted, ransacked, ravaged, sacked, ruined, wasted.

kabaitata hustle; *synonyms* (n) hurry, haste, ado, cheat, commotion, con, fuss, (v) jostle, bustle, elbow, hasten, flurry, push, shove, work.

kabaka 1. gather; *synonyms* (v) deduce, convene, accumulate, amass, assemble, collect, compile, congregate, flock, garner, meet, tuck, earn, rally, (n) fold; *antonyms* (v) disperse, scatter, **2.** fall; *synonyms* (v) decline, dip, decrease, descend, dive, rain, diminish, dwindle, sink, alight, (n) drop, descent, downfall, plunge, pitch; *antonyms* (v) rise, increase, ascend, climb, triumph, win, (n) ascent, **3.** deceptive; *synonyms* (adj) deceitful, dishonest, deceiving, fallacious, false, insidious, lying, misleading, spurious, untrue, unfounded, counterfeit, delusive, delusory, erroneous; *antonyms* (adj) honest, real, truthful, **4.** discourage; *synonyms* (v) deter, daunt, demoralize, depress, dishearten, deject, dismay, intimidate, dampen, cow, discountenance, dispirit, frustrate, check, (n) abash; *antonyms* (v) encourage, promote, **5.** discouraging; *synonyms* (adj) depressing, chill, disheartening, bad, bleak, gloomy, sad; *antonym* (adj) encouraging, **6.** useless; *synonyms* (adj) futile, pointless, unnecessary, needless, abortive, fruitless, hopeless, worthless, idle, barren, superfluous, bootless, incompetent, ineffective, ineffectual; *antonyms* (adj) useful, helpful, competent, effective, convenient, necessary, valuable, **7.** scandalous; *synonyms* (adj) shameful, disgraceful, infamous, ignominious, opprobrious, outrageous, shocking, base, disreputable, foul, disgusting, dishonorable, notorious, monstrous, atrocious; *antonym* (adj) uninteresting.

kabakaki gathered; *synonyms* (adj) collected, deepened, accumulated, amassed, assembled, collective, congregate, equanimous, massed, poised.

kabakarurua starve; *synonyms* (v) famish, fast, crave, hunger, lust, pinch, thirst, benumb, bite, clem, (adj) begrudge, gripe, grudge, lack, screw.

kabakaruruaki starved; *synonyms* (adj) hungry, famished, starving, ravenous, meager, emaciated, esurient, malnourished, thin.

kabakeketea lighten; *synonyms* (v) ease, alleviate, assuage, light, brighten, illuminate, lessen, allay, clear, mitigate, relieve, soften, palliate, decrease, soothe; *antonym* (v) darken.

kabaketea 1. ease; *synonyms* (n) comfort, convenience, rest, aid, leisure, relief, repose, satisfaction, (v) alleviate, assuage, relieve, allay, facilitate, relax, (adj) smooth; *antonyms* (n) difficulty, discomfort, awkwardness, formality, (v) aggravate, worsen, **2.** lighten; *synonyms* (v) ease, light, brighten, illuminate, lessen, clear, mitigate, soften, palliate, decrease, soothe; *antonym* (v) darken, **3.** diminish; *synonyms* (v) abate, decline, abridge, deduct, detract, dwindle, fall, reduce, depreciate, belittle, contract, curtail, retrench, shrink, (adj) degrade; *antonyms* (v) increase, grow, **4.** alleviate; *synonyms* (v) appease, lighten, moderate, remit, assist, meliorate, deaden, help, mollify, quench, (adj) calm, still, compose, pacify, quell; *antonym* (v) exacerbate, **5.** soften; *synonyms* (v) dull, melt, mute, relent, break, cushion, damp, dampen, mellow, mince, qualify, temper, thaw, dissolve, muffle; *antonyms* (v) harden, set, solidify, congeal, **6.** temper; *synonyms* (n) mood, character, disposition, humor, nature, condition, anger, irritation, spirit, rage, (v) modify, season, anneal, restrain, restrict; *antonyms* (v) intensify, upset.

kabaketeaki 1. alleviated; *synonyms* (adj) eased, relieved, palliate, levigate, cloaked, disguised, **2.** eased; *synonym* (adj) alleviated, **3.** diminished; *synonyms* (adj) abated, lessened, weakened, atrophied, belittled, attenuate, lower, attenuated, cut, short, active, airy, backward, blasted, bony, **4.** tempered; *synonyms* (adj) hardened, attempered, attemperate, elastic, enured, inured, mild, proportioned, set, subdued, toughened, treated, tough, **5.** softened; *synonyms* (adj) dull, diffused, muffled, muted, boring, deadening, dense, dim, dumb, faint, gray, grey, hushed, intenerate, irksome.

kabakia starve; *synonyms* (v) famish, fast, crave, hunger, lust, pinch, thirst, benumb, bite, clem, (adj) begrudge, gripe, grudge, lack, screw.

kabakiaki starved; *synonyms* (*adj*) hungry, famished, starving, ravenous, meager, emaciated, esurient, malnourished, thin.

kabakua 1. behead; *synonyms* (*v*) decapitate, decollate, cut, bowstring, electrocute, head, execute, murder, unhead, direct, lead, oppose, **2.** decapitate; *synonyms* (*v*) behead, guillotine, top.

kabakuaki 1. decapitated; *synonyms* (*adj*) beheaded, decollated, **2.** beheaded; *synonyms* (*adj*) decapitated, headless, foolish, obstinate, rash.

kabana 1. incapable; *synonyms* (*adj*) impotent, incompetent, inadequate, unable, helpless, powerless, inept, insufficient, unqualified, ineffectual, inefficient, unfit, weak; *antonyms* (*adj*) capable, able, **2.** deceptive; *synonyms* (*adj*) deceitful, dishonest, deceiving, fallacious, false, insidious, lying, misleading, spurious, untrue, unfounded, counterfeit, delusive, delusory, erroneous; *antonyms* (*adj*) honest, real, truthful, **3.** hopeless; *synonyms* (*adj*) despairing, despondent, forlorn, incurable, disconsolate, abject, desperate, impossible, useless, dismal, desolate, futile, incorrigible, ineffective, irredeemable; *antonyms* (*adj*) hopeful, cheerful, competent, promising.

kabane last; *synonyms* (*v*) endure, continue, hold, exist, live, dwell, (*n*) abide, conclusion, (*adj*) extreme, closing, final, ultimate, conclusive, concluding, farthest; *antonyms* (*n*) opening, (*adj*) first.

kabanea 1. dismiss; *synonyms* (*v*) discharge, cashier, cast, disband, discard, drop, bounce, can, cease, dispatch, banish, disallow, discount, displace, dissolve; *antonyms* (*v*) hire, employ, **2.** last; *synonyms* (*v*) endure, continue, hold, exist, live, dwell, (*n*) abide, conclusion, (*adj*) extreme, closing, final, ultimate, conclusive, concluding, farthest; *antonyms* (*n*) opening, (*adj*) first, **3.** conclude; *synonyms* (*v*) close, complete, finish, gather, accomplish, assume, deduce, determine, end, resolve, settle, terminate, decide, derive, do; *antonyms* (*v*) start, begin, **4.** finish; *synonyms* (*v*) achieve, execute, discontinue, consume, stop, culminate, (*n*) consummate, death, conclude, ending, finale, glaze, accomplishment, coating, completion; *antonym* (*n*) beginning, **5.** spent; *synonyms* (*v*) dull, evanid, (*adj*) exhausted, prostrate, expended, fatigued, finished, gone, dead, effete, jaded, tired, drained, weary, worn; *antonym* (*adj*) remaining, **6.** terminate; *synonyms* (*v*) dismiss, halt, result, abort, bound, cancel, ax, extinguish, fire, go, sack, break, sever, expire, interrupt; *antonym* (*v*) establish, **7.** spend; *synonyms* (*v*) exhaust, expend, squander, blow, deplete, pass, wear, lead, invest, dissipate, draw, lavish, use, destroy, (*adj*) waste; *antonyms* (*v*) save, conserve.

kabaneaki 1. concluded; *synonyms* (*adj*) complete, finished, done, completed, over, closed, accomplished, terminated, (*adv*) ended, **2.** finished; *synonyms* (*adj*) perfect, consummate, absolute, polished, ripe, ruined, spent, round, capable, decided, final, elegant, concluded, exhausted, fitted; *antonyms* (*adj*) unfinished, incomplete, remaining, rough, **3.** dismissed; *synonyms* (*adj*) fired, discharged, clear, convalescent, released, **4.** spent; *synonyms* (*v*) dull, evanid, past, (*adj*) prostrate, expended, fatigued, gone, dead, effete, jaded, tired, drained, weary, worn, fagged, **5.** terminated; *synonym* (*adj*) extinct.

kabaneana finally; *synonyms* (*adv*) eventually, lastly, last, ultimately, definitely, completely, (*adj*) final, (*v*) definitively; *antonym* (*adv*) firstly.

kabao spread; *synonyms* (*v*) scatter, reach, disperse, expand, extend, broadcast, circulate, diffuse, disseminate, increase, propagate, stretch, broaden, deploy, (*n*) span; *antonym* (*adj*) concentrated.

kabaoa 1. bend; *synonyms* (*n*) bow, arch, arc, elbow, twist, angle, curvature, (*v*) curve, turn, crouch, stoop, crook, curl, flex, deflect; *antonyms* (*v*) straighten, square, **2.** inflect; *synonyms* (*v*) modulate, bend, incline, arcograph, chant, tone, vary, voice, prostrate, regulate, strengthen, subdue, **3.** mitigate; *synonyms* (*v*) alleviate, assuage, abate, lessen, moderate, palliate, relieve, appease, diminish, extenuate, lighten, (*n*) ease, calm, (*adj*) allay, soften; *antonym* (*v*) exacerbate, **4.** spread; *synonyms* (*v*) scatter, reach, disperse, expand, extend, broadcast, circulate, diffuse, disseminate, increase, propagate, stretch, broaden, deploy, (*n*) span; *antonym* (*adj*) concentrated.

kabaoaki 1. bent; *synonyms* (*adj*) arched, curved, bended, crooked, deformed, intent, (*n*) aptitude, inclination, propensity, fancy, ability, bias, flair, gift, leaning; *antonym* (*adj*) straight, **2.** mitigated; *synonyms* (*adj*) alleviated, eased, palliate, cloaked, disguised, **3.** inflected; *synonyms* (*adj*) deflected, inflective, turned, **4.** spread; *synonyms* (*v*) scatter, reach, disperse, expand, extend, broadcast, circulate, diffuse, disseminate, increase, propagate, stretch, broaden, deploy, (*n*) span; *antonym* (*adj*) concentrated.

kabara 1. loosen; *synonyms* (*v*) free, relax, loose, detach, undo, discharge, ravel, fluff, unbend, untie, liberate, slacken, (*adj*) disengage, (*n*) ease, release; *antonyms* (*v*) tighten, compress, fasten, **2.** forgive; *synonyms* (*v*) condone, absolve, excuse, acquit, pardon, remit, exonerate, justify, clear, overlook, **3.** unravel; *synonyms* (*v*) unfold, disentangle, solve, decipher, explain, resolve, extricate, uncoil, unpick, untangle, unwind, unknot, unbind, interpret, translate, **4.** pounce; *synonyms* (*v*) bounce, bound, leap, dive, swoop, stoop, charge, attack, seize, alight, condescend, ambush, lunge, (*n*) jump, descent, **5.** undo; *synonyms* (*v*) loosen, annul, open, cancel, reverse, separate, disconnect, nullify, unbrace, overturn, neutralize, quash, unlock, unravel, abrogate; *antonyms* (*v*) attach, close, do, wrap.

kabarabara 1. interpret; *synonyms* (*v*) clarify, construe, elucidate, illustrate, read, understand, comment, gloss, decipher, explain, explicate, render, depict, illuminate, consider, **2.** illustrate; *synonyms* (*v*) demonstrate, describe, adorn, cite, decorate, embellish, expound, represent, show, define, ornament, embody, indicate, instance, (*adj*) exemplify, **3.** demonstrate; *synonyms* (*v*) prove, authenticate, attest, display, establish, exhibit, present, argue, certify, confirm, evidence, manifest, verify, try, declare; *antonyms* (*v*) disprove, conceal, **4.** define; *synonyms* (*v*) specify, characterize, bound, interpret, limit, name, restrict, circumscribe, outline, delimit, delimitate, delineate, demarcate, designate, fix, **5.** expound; *synonyms* (*v*) expand, annotate, elaborate, expatiate, dilate, exposit, amplify, solve, state, unfold, enlarge, **6.** explain; *synonyms* (*v*) account, enlighten, excuse, denote, answer, resolve, reveal, develop, clear, disclose, plain, justify, tell, translate; *antonym* (*v*) confuse.

kabarabaraki 1. interpreted; *synonyms* (*adj*) accurate, confined, exact, strict, taken, precise, restricted, rigidly, rigorous, severe, strained, tense, tight, **2.** illustrated; *synonyms* (*adj*) illustrate, distinguished, graphic, illustrious, **3.** defined; *synonyms* (*adj*) definite, fixed, settled, certain, set, bounded, colonised, colonized, conceived, exposed, formed, limited, outlined, particular, special; *antonym* (*adj*) formless, **4.** demonstrated; *synonyms* (*adj*) confirmed, established, tried, verified.

kabaraka 1. upset; *synonyms* (*v*) overturn, agitate, disquiet, overthrow, bother, confuse, disturb, perturb, reverse, (*adj*) unsettled, hurt, (*n*) disorder, trouble, distress, disturbance; *antonyms* (*v*) calm, please, encourage, soothe, (*adj*) pleased, confident, **2.** overturn; *synonyms* (*v*) capsize, upset, overset, annul, destroy, overrule, subvert, topple, invert, nullify, cancel, defeat, demolish, invalidate, lift; *antonym* (*v*) validate.

kabarakaki 1. upset; *synonyms* (*v*) overturn, agitate, disquiet, overthrow, bother, confuse, disturb, perturb, reverse, (*adj*) unsettled, hurt, (*n*) disorder, trouble, distress, disturbance; *antonyms* (*v*) calm, please, encourage, soothe, (*adj*) pleased, confident, **2.** overturned; *synonyms* (*adj*) upset, upturned, broken, confused, disordered, disquieted, distressed, disturbed, topsy-turvy, retrousse, worried; *antonym* (*adj*) upright.

kabaraki 1. loosened; *synonyms* (*adj*) detached, disentangled, loose, disengaged, extricated, unsnarled, **2.** undone; *synonyms* (*v*) accursed, devoted, (*adj*) lost, ruined, sunk, unfinished,

doomed, behindhand, decayed, destroyed, finished.

kabarara hush; *synonyms* (*n*) quiet, still, lull, peace, (*v*) calm, soothe, gag, allay, assuage, deaden, muffle, mute, muzzle, (*adj*) silence, appease; *antonym* (*n*) noise.

kabararaki hushed; *synonyms* (*adj*) quiet, calm, silent, still, subdued, muffled, noiseless, placid, soft, soundless, tranquil, gentle, muted; *antonym* (*adj*) loud.

kabараria 1. talkative; *synonyms* (*adj*) loquacious, chatty, garrulous, gabby, verbose, gossipy, glib, communicative, talky, wordy, bigmouthed, blabbermouthed, blabby, effusive, expansive; *antonyms* (*adj*) taciturn, reserved, mute, quiet, shy, silent, **2.** verbose; *synonyms* (*adj*) prolix, tedious, redundant, lengthy, talkative, windy, copious, diffuse, boring, dull, fluent, rhetorical, slow, tiresome; *antonym* (*adj*) concise, **3.** spout; *synonyms* (*n*) jet, nozzle, squirt, pipe, outlet, flow, nose, fountain, opening, (*v*) gush, spurt, spirt, burst, pawn, roll.

kabareka 1. litter; *synonyms* (*n*) brood, bedding, stretcher, garbage, junk, mess, refuse, rubbish, trash, waste, issue, (*v*) clutter, (*adj*) jumble, disarray, huddle, **2.** dirty; *synonyms* (*adj*) foul, dirt, contemptible, bawdy, contaminated, dingy, impure, despicable, (*v*) muddy, corrupt, soil, contaminate, begrime, bemire, (*n*) defile; *antonyms* (*adj*) hygienic, pure, spotless, immaculate, (*v*) clean, **3.** soil; *synonyms* (*n*) ground, grime, land, dust, (*v*) smudge, blot, dirty, pollute, mire, blemish, mould, smear, smirch, smutch, (*adj*) blur, **4.** pollute; *synonyms* (*v*) debase, infect, taint, maculate, poison, befoul, debauch, desecrate, besmear, adulterate, besmirch, (*n*) deprave, (*adj*) profane, stain, sully; *antonym* (*v*) purify.

kabarekaki 1. littered; *synonyms* (*adj*) cluttered, untidy, beleaguered, beset, besieged, messy, plagued, topsy-turvy, tormented, **2.** polluted; *synonyms* (*adj*) impure, dirty, contaminated, foul, defiled, filthy, unclean, profane, soiled, stained, tainted, infected, nasty, (*v*) mixed; *antonym* (*adj*) pure, **3.** soiled; *synonyms* (*adj*) dingy, grubby, grimy, muddy, black, mucky, polluted, squalid, lousy; *antonym* (*adj*) clean.

kabarere scald; *synonyms* (*v*) burn, cook, scorch, boil, char, heat, sear, seethe, singe, stew, digest, (*n*) blister, (*adj*) bard, lyrist.

kabarikoa heap; *synonyms* (*n*) pile, stack, accumulation, collection, amass, group, lot, mass, mound, bulk, bunch, congeries, (*v*) aggregate, bank, collect.

kabarikoaki heaped; *synonyms* (*adj*) piled, coacervate, collective, cumulative, dense, thick, cumulous.

kabaroa 1. spill; *synonyms* (v) fall, shed, drop, empty, flow, pour, slop, stream, upset, cast, overrun, flood, disgorge, (n) overflow, discharge, **2.** pour; *synonyms* (v) gush, decant, pelt, scatter, emit, jet, run, spill, teem, effuse, deluge, funnel, swarm, tip, (n) rain; *antonym* (v) drizzle.

kabaroaki poured; *synonym* (adj) concrete.

kabarukurukua wrinkle; *synonyms* (n) crease, fold, furrow, pucker, gather, line, (v) crinkle, rumple, crumple, ruffle, curl, purse, cockle, corrugate, crush; *antonym* (v) smooth.

kabarukurukuaki wrinkled; *synonyms* (adj) furrowed, creased, crumpled, lined, puckered, wizened, wrinkly, gnarled, unironed, (n) rough, rugged; *antonym* (adj) smooth.

kabata 1. increase; *synonyms* (n) gain, addition, augmentation, boom, expansion, extension, (v) advance, accrue, extend, grow, aggrandize, expand, enhance, enlarge, (adj) augment; *antonyms* (n) reduction, contraction, decline, (v) decrease, reduce, diminish, drop, deteriorate, **2.** multiply; *synonyms* (v) breed, increase, propagate, duplicate, procreate, proliferate, reproduce, calculate, add, boost, amplify, manifold, raise, repeat, double.

kabataki 1. multiplied; *synonyms* (v) absorb, acquisition, attainment, engross, engulf, (adj) manifold, many, multitudinous, peopled, populous, studded, teeming, thick, complicated, divers, **2.** increased; *synonyms* (adj) additional, more, enlarged, greater, fresh, new, plus, puffy, ripe, amplified, better, bigger, improved, other, superior.

kabatata scorch; *synonyms* (n) scorching, (v) bake, burn, parch, sear, singe, blister, char, dry, grill, fry, heat, roast, scald, broil.

kabatataki scorched; *synonyms* (adj) parched, baked, adust, burnt, dry, seared; *antonym* (adj) wet.

kabatatata scald; *synonyms* (v) burn, cook, scorch, boil, char, heat, sear, seethe, singe, stew, digest, (n) blister, (adj) bard, lyrist.

kabatebai 1. dishonor; *synonyms* (n) disgrace, shame, affront, disrepute, abuse, degradation, infamy, taint, dishonesty, (v) degrade, discredit, defile, violate, debase, desecrate; *antonyms* (v) honor, respect, **2.** defame; *synonyms* (v) libel, malign, slander, vilify, calumniate, denigrate, smear, blacken, besmirch, dishonor, disparage, lampoon, slur, traduce, (adj) asperse; *antonym* (v) praise, **3.** disgrace; *synonyms* (n) blemish, stain, reproach, humiliation, defect, obloquy, (v) blot, attaint, defame, demean, humble, spot, abase, humiliate, mortify; *antonyms* (v) credit, esteem, **4.** scandalize; *synonyms* (v) outrage, disgust, scandalise, shock, offend, appal, appall.

kabatebaiaki 1. dishonored; *synonyms* (adj) disgraced, shamed, discredited, broken, corrupt, damaged, defiled, disfigured, dishonest, dishonorable, embarrassed, fallen, humiliated, (n) degraded, derogate; *antonyms* (adj) pure, untarnished, **2.** disgraced; *synonyms* (adj) dishonored, abashed, mortified, faithless, fraudulent, guilty, hangdog, indecent, knavish, lewd, shamefaced, shameful, unchaste, unjust.

kabatete 1. incline; *synonyms* (n) slope, bias, angle, ascent, dip, grade, gradient, inclination, slant, (v) cant, bend, dispose, lean, tilt, bank, **2.** sloping; *synonyms* (adj) oblique, slanting, aslant, aslope, inclined, slanted, diagonal, leaning, sloped, tilted, declivous, (adv) sideways; *antonym* (adj) level.

kabateteaki inclined; *synonyms* (adj) prone, apt, oblique, willing, bowed, liable, likely, minded, predisposed, ready, bent, fain, susceptible, (v) given, (prep) disposed; *antonyms* (adj) level, reluctant, unwilling.

kabatia 1. multiply; *synonyms* (v) breed, expand, increase, propagate, augment, duplicate, procreate, proliferate, reproduce, calculate, extend, enlarge, add, boost, amplify; *antonym* (v) decrease, **2.** augment; *synonyms* (v) enhance, aggrandize, reinforce, grow, improve, intensify, magnify, raise, mount, broaden, compound, develop, heighten, multiply, (n) accrue; *antonym* (v) reduce, **3.** lavish; *synonyms* (adj) extravagant, exuberant, generous, ample, copious, prodigal, abundant, bountiful, excessive, improvident, lush, munificent, plush, (v) dissipate, profuse; *antonym* (adj) meager.

kabatiaki 1. multiplied; *synonyms* (v) absorb, acquisition, attainment, engross, engulf, (adj) manifold, many, multitudinous, peopled, populous, studded, teeming, thick, complicated, divers, **2.** augmented; *synonyms* (adj) inflated, more, plus, better, bigger, improved.

kabatiatia wrinkle; *synonyms* (n) crease, fold, furrow, pucker, gather, line, (v) crinkle, rumple, crumple, ruffle, curl, purse, cockle, corrugate, crush; *antonym* (v) smooth.

kabatiatiaki wrinkled; *synonyms* (adj) furrowed, creased, crumpled, lined, puckered, wizened, wrinkly, gnarled, unironed, (n) rough, rugged; *antonym* (adj) smooth.

kabatutu 1. pleated, **2.** puckered; *synonyms* (adj) wrinkled, corrugated, bullate, cockled, creased, furrowed, inflated, wrinkly, **3.** wrinkled; *synonyms* (adj) crumpled, lined, puckered, wizened, gnarled, unironed, (n) rough, rugged; *antonym* (adj) smooth.

kabaubau 1. gobble; *synonyms* (v) bolt, devour, gulp, consume, gorge, guzzle, stuff, swallow, cram, (n) cry; *antonym* (v) nibble, **2.** devour; *synonyms* (v) eat, demolish, gobble, absorb, devastate, enjoy, relish, down, exhaust, feed, glut, gnaw, guttle, raven, ruin, **3.** swallow; *synonyms* (v) accept, bear, endure, stomach, brook, engulf, abide, bury, engross, imbibe, (n) drink, sip, swig, taste, deglutition; *antonym* (v) regurgitate.

kabaubauaki 1. devoured, **2**. swallowed; *synonyms* (adj) engulfed, enveloped, flooded, inundated, overcome, overpowered, overwhelmed, swamped.

kabe odious; *synonyms* (adj) hateful, detestable, hideous, obnoxious, nasty, abhorrent, abominable, disgusting, execrable, heinous, forbidding, loathsome, atrocious, damnable, invidious; *antonyms* (adj) delightful, pleasant.

kabeabea 1. hire; *synonyms* (n) wage, employment, fee, pay, salary, fare, (v) employ, engage, charter, enlist, rent, retain, take, commission, compensation; *antonym* (v) dismiss, **2**. employ; *synonyms* (v) apply, use, consume, exercise, exploit, hire, wield, busy, exert, occupy, ply, spend, utilize, work, (n) service; *antonym* (v) fire.

kabeabeaki 1. hired; *synonyms* (v) compensated, contented, paid, satisfied, (adj) employed, leased, chartered, hack, hackneyed, mercenary, hireling, selfish, sordid, venal, **2**. employed; *synonyms* (adj) busy, engaged, occupied, working, affianced, betrothed, earnest, rapt, active, gainfully, inked, involved, laboring, operating, pledged; *antonym* (adj) unemployed.

kabeakoa 1. jumble; *synonyms* (n) muddle, clutter, hodgepodge, disarray, disorder, confusion, blend, chaos, huddle, mess, (v) confuse, mix, embroil, disturb, litter; *antonym* (v) order, **2**. entangle; *synonyms* (v) embrangle, tangle, enmesh, complicate, involve, snarl, entwine, catch, ensnare, entrap, knot, mat, perplex, (adj) embarrass, bewilder; *antonym* (v) disentangle, **3**. tangle; *synonyms* (n) maze, twine, labyrinth, mesh, entanglement, jungle, twist, (v) entangle, jumble, ravel, ruffle, felt, mire, intertwine, tousle; *antonym* (v) unravel.

kabeakoaki 1. jumbled; *synonyms* (adj) confused, disorderly, disordered, disorganized, untidy, cluttered, mixed, muddled, chaotic, incoherent, topsy-turvy; *antonyms* (adj) neat, tidy, **2**. entangled; *synonyms* (adj) involved, complicated, intricate, embroiled, complex, foul, matted, tangled; *antonym* (adj) free, **3**. tangled; *synonyms* (adj) knotted, entangled, convoluted, knotty, difficult, disheveled, tousled, kinky, labyrinthine, perplexed, raveled, tortuous.

kabebetea 1. mitigate; *synonyms* (v) alleviate, assuage, abate, lessen, moderate, palliate, relieve, appease, diminish, extenuate, lighten, (n) ease, calm, (adj) allay, soften; *antonym* (v) exacerbate, **2**. lighten; *synonyms* (v) light, brighten, illuminate, clear, mitigate, decrease, soothe, aid; *antonym* (v) darken.

kabebeteaki mitigated; *synonyms* (adj) alleviated, eased, palliate, cloaked, disguised.

kabei 1. waver; *synonyms* (v) falter, vacillate, flicker, fluctuate, hesitate, quiver, hover, shake, totter, wave, pause, reel, tremble, (n) flutter, faltering, **2**. swing; *synonyms* (n) sweep, range, (v) sway, oscillate, dangle, hang, rock, beat, brandish, change, move, turn, vibrate, dance, drop, **3**. oscillate; *synonyms* (v) swing, wag, alternate, vary, waver, wobble.

kabekau whore; *synonyms* (n) prostitute, harlot, trollop, courtesan, strumpet, tart, bawd, cocotte, advoutress, slattern, verticil, (v) debauch.

kabekua thump; *synonyms* (n) beat, cuff, punch, strike, crack, crash, tap, (v) bang, bump, knock, thud, hit, pound, clump, pulsate.

kaben 1. chief; *synonyms* (adj) head, principal, cardinal, capital, arch, central, essential, first, main, (n) administrator, boss, captain, executive, leader, paramount; *antonyms* (adj) minor, associate, secondary, **2**. captain; *synonyms* (n) chief, master, chieftain, commander, commodore, guide, officer, pilot, skipper, ruler, (v) govern, manage.

kabenga widen; *synonyms* (v) expand, extend, broaden, stretch, distend, enlarge, increase, spread, develop, dilate, amplify, flare, thicken, grow, impart; *antonym* (v) narrow.

kabeoa tangle; *synonyms* (n) snarl, maze, confusion, knot, (v) entangle, jumble, embroil, muddle, enmesh, embrangle, entrap, involve, mat, ravel, ruffle; *antonyms* (n) order, (v) disentangle, unravel.

kabeoaki tangled; *synonyms* (adj) involved, complex, knotted, intricate, complicated, entangled, convoluted, knotty, difficult, disheveled, tousled, kinky, labyrinthine, muddled, perplexed; *antonym* (adj) free.

kaberetokoa 1. spurn; *synonyms* (v) despise, rebuff, scorn, repulse, disdain, refuse, reject, snub, slight, decline, kick, deny, dismiss, repudiate, contemn, **2**. object; *synonyms* (n) design, aim, cause, end, intent, intention, meaning, mark, matter, subject, substance, drift, (v) except, mind, complain; *antonym* (v) agree, **3**. thwart; *synonyms* (v) foil, frustrate, baffle, hinder, impede, obstruct, oppose, prevent, defeat, disappoint, bilk, block, resist, stop, (adv) cross, **4**. scorn; *synonyms* (n) contempt, neglect, derision, mockery, insult, disparagement, disrespect, (v) ridicule, deride, disregard, reproach, dislike, disparage, flout, hate; *antonyms* (n) approval, (v) respect, appreciate, praise, **5**. snub; *synonyms* (n) rebuke, rejection, indignity, reprimand, (v) cut, offend, ignore, check, humiliate, spurn, discount, repel, shun; *antonym* (v) accept.

kaberetokoaki 1. spurned; *synonyms* (adj) jilted, rejected, **2**. snubbed; *synonyms* (adj) affronted, hurt, insulted, offended, slighted, upset, **3**. scorned; *synonyms* (adj) despised, detested, hated, abject, neglected, contemptible, contemptuous, despicable, insolent, mean, undesirable, unpopular, scornful, vile, **4**. thwarted; *synonyms* (*adj*) frustrated, disappointed, defeated, discomfited, foiled, baffled, balked, beaten, discouraged, disenchanted, disillusioned, dissatisfied, embarrassed, saddened, blocked; *antonym* (*adj*) successful.

kabetanga 1. jam; *synonyms* (*n*) crush, crowd, fix, squeeze, congestion, conserve, dilemma, hole, (*v*) block, cram, bar, fill, force, gorge, hinder; *antonym* (*v*) free, **2**. wedge; *synonyms* (*n*) chock, slice, cuneus, stick, plug, bomber, (*v*) compress, jam, pack, ram, stuff, lodge, fasten, press, compact.

kabetangaki 1. jammed; *synonyms* (*v*) stuck, (*adj*) crowded, packed, congested, full; *antonym* (*adj*) empty, **2**. wedged; *synonyms* (*adj*) impacted, fast, blocked, caught, fixed, immovable, lodged, stiff, trapped; *antonym* (*adj*) loose.

kabetingaingaia soil; *synonyms* (*n*) ground, dirt, grime, land, dust, (*v*) smudge, blot, contaminate, dirty, pollute, mire, blemish, defile, foul, mould; *antonym* (*v*) clean.

kabetingaingaiaki soiled; *synonyms* (*adj*) dingy, dirty, grubby, nasty, grimy, filthy, unclean, muddy, black, foul, mucky, polluted, squalid, stained, contaminated; *antonyms* (*adj*) clean, pure.

kabetiwai 1. criticize; *synonyms* (*v*) attack, belittle, berate, blame, censure, chide, comment, denounce, rebuke, reprimand, scold, condemn, criticise, deplore, disparage; *antonyms* (*v*) praise, approve, commend, admire, **2**. scrutinize; *synonyms* (*v*) inspect, examine, review, analyze, audit, consider, explore, investigate, scan, search, check, observe, probe, study, (*n*) canvass.

kabi 1. dull; *synonyms* (*adj*) dim, blunt, dense, dreary, sluggish, bland, boring, cloudy, cold, dark, dismal, inactive, inert, (*v*) deaden, dampen; *antonyms* (*adj*) bright, lively, sharp, exciting, interesting, lustrous, stimulating, amusing, exhilarating, glittery, glossy, glowing, high-pitched, intense, luminous, **2**. ignorant; *synonyms* (*adj*) unconscious, illiterate, rude, uneducated, unwitting, blind, dull, innocent, naive, unaware, uninformed, unlearned, barbarous, crude, shallow; *antonyms* (*adj*) knowledgeable, conscious, **3**. dumb; *synonyms* (*adj*) mute, silent, speechless, inarticulate, obtuse, slow, stupid, idiotic, quiet, taciturn, thick, voiceless, aphonous, **4**. thoughtless; *synonyms* (*adj*) inconsiderate, heedless, inattentive, rash, reckless, hasty, improvident, unthinking, neglectful, negligent, imprudent, incautious, indiscreet, (*v*) careless, giddy; *antonyms* (*adj*) thoughtful, considerate, considered.

kabikôuea 1. beach; *synonyms* (*n*) bank, coast, foreshore, shore, strand, coastline, land, seashore, shoreline, **2**. strand; *synonyms* (*n*) rope, chain,

filament, line, string, thread, wisp, yarn, fibril, scar, (*v*) beach, maroon, desert, abandon.

kabikoukou intercourse; *synonyms* (*n*) communion, contact, acquaintance, coition, coitus, communication, conversation, dealings, converse, commerce, congress, copulation, fellowship, fucking, (*adj*) familiarity.

kabin bottom; *synonyms* (*n*) base, basis, backside, bed, behind, foot, footing, back, arse, ass, bum, butt, buttocks, craft, floor; *antonyms* (*n*) top, pinnacle, (*adj*) highest.

kabinano deep; *synonyms* (*adj*) thick, profound, absorbed, abstruse, broad, dark, rich, sound, strong, wide, esoteric, bright, large, abysmal, (*v*) intense; *antonyms* (*adj*) shallow, superficial, high, high-pitched, light, soft, weak.

kabinanonano dreamer; *synonyms* (*n*) idealist, romancer, visionary, academic, escapist, logician, philosopher, theorist, thinker, airhead, (*v*) musard; *antonym* (*n*) realist.

kabinanonanoa 1. desire; *synonyms* (*n*) ambition, hope, aspiration, will, wish, craving, dream, impulse, (*v*) fancy, aspire, seek, want, aim, choose, crave; *antonyms* (*n*) aversion, reality, (*v*) dislike, hate, **2**. wish; *synonyms* (*v*) desire, like, please, bid, care, prefer, intend, (*n*) need, inclination, longing, pleasure, purpose, mind, request, urge.

kabinanonanoaki desired; *synonyms* (*adj*) coveted, craved, desirable, chosen, favorite, wanted, needed, welcome, beloved, adored, appropriate, pet, preferred, (*v*) complying, consenting; *antonym* (*adj*) undesirable.

kabioa pout; *synonyms* (*n*) eelpout, face, hornpout, moue, (*v*) brood, sulk, glout, mop, mow, (*adj*) frown, lower, glower, scowl, bulge, gloam.

kabira 1. lubricate; *synonyms* (*v*) bribe, grease, lube, buy, fix, lubricitate, overreach, **2**. smudge; *synonyms* (*n*) blot, blotch, smirch, spot, (*v*) mark, daub, smear, blemish, blur, stain, slur, foul, besmear, besmirch, dirty, **3**. smear; *synonyms* (*n*) smudge, slander, aspersion, defamation, rub, grime, (*v*) libel, malign, anoint, lubricate, plaster, defame, apply, asperse, bedaub.

kabiraki 1. lubricated; *synonyms* (*adj*) greased, greasy, tipsy, **2**. smeared; *synonyms* (*adj*) dirty, smudged, unclean, grimy, grubby, messy, muddy, smirched, smudgy, filthy, tarnished, **3**. smudged; *synonyms* (*adj*) smeared, caked, encrusted, gritty, mucky, soiled.

kabitara 1. ironical; *synonyms* (*adj*) ironic, sarcastic, satirical, burlesque, dry, sardonic, wry, (*n*) humorous, **2**. contrary; *synonyms* (*adj*) opposite, contradictory, adverse, conflicting, reverse, unfavorable, alien, cross, different, disobedient, obstinate, perverse, averse, antagonistic, (*adv*) counter, **3**. contradict; *synonyms* (*v*) deny, oppose, belie, conflict, confute, contravene, controvert, disprove, dissent, impugn, invalidate, refute, disaffirm, disclaim, counteract; *antonyms* (*v*) confirm, agree, match, **4**. contradictory; *synonyms* (*adj*) incompatible, inconsistent, contrary, discordant, discrepant, incoherent, incongruous, opposed, opposing, repugnant, confounding, divergent, unlike, (*n*) disagreeing; *antonyms* (*adj*) consistent, similar, compatible, **5**. paradoxical; *synonyms* (*adj*) ambiguous, illegible, clashing, complex, differing, difficult, paradoxal, questionable, unexplained, odd, peculiar, poignant, weird, (*v*) enigmatic, problematical, **6**. oppose; *synonyms* (*v*) object, contest, contend, contradict, resist, fight, disagree, combat, confront, defend, dispute, gainsay, hinder, repel, thwart; *antonyms* (*v*) support, advocate, back, advise, **7**. opposite; *synonyms* (*adj*) diametric, hostile, diametrical, across, contra, (*n*) opponent, adversary, contradiction, antonym, inverse, negation, counterpart, antagonist, opposition, (*pron*) other.

kabitaraea 1. misquote; *synonyms* (*v*) exaggerate, falsify, garble, twist, (*adv*) misstate, miscite, misreport, misrepresent, **2**. misstate; *synonyms* (*v*) belie, color, invent, lie, misinform, pervert, **3**. misconstrue; *synonyms* (*v*) misapprehend, misunderstand, misconceive, misinterpret, misjudge, misread, mistake; *antonym* (*v*) understand.

kabitaraki opposed; *synonyms* (*adj*) conflicting, contradictory, hostile, contrary, antagonistic, opposing, adverse, averse, contrasted, repugnant, incompatible, irreconcilable, counter, against, opposite.

kabo 1. mix; *synonyms* (*n*) mixture, concoction, (*v*) alloy, blend, intermingle, mingle, combine, compound, confound, intermix, join, meld, merge, aggregate, admix; *antonym* (*v*) separate, **2**. accept; *synonyms* (*v*) receive, acknowledge, admit, take, recognize, abide, accede, acquiesce, adopt, assume, believe, yield, agree, approve, assent; *antonyms* (*v*) refuse, reject, deny, snub, oppose, renounce, resist, **3**. agree; *synonyms* (*v*) accord, adjust, bargain, concord, correspond, fit, harmonize, suit, compromise, align, check, concur, consent, consort, (*n*) coincide; *antonyms* (*v*) disagree, differ, argue, object, refute, **4**. meet; *synonyms* (*v*) converge, find, assemble, congregate, encounter, fulfill, gather, answer, cross, confront, intersect, abut, adjoin, collect, convene; *antonyms* (*v*) avoid, disperse, diverge, **5**. knead; *synonyms* (*v*) mix, rub, form, fashion, massage, mould, shape, work, (*adj*) mash, **6**. couple; *synonyms* (*n*) brace, yoke, duo, dyad, twosome, (*v*) pair, connect, associate, attach, copulate, tie, link, match, mate, (*adj*) hook; *antonym* (*v*) uncouple, **7**. assemble; *synonyms* (*v*) amass, accumulate, meet, call, compile, concentrate,

group, make, rally, edit, arrange, build, construct, erect, garner; *antonyms* (*v*) dismantle, disband, disassemble, **8**. blend; *synonyms* (*n*) amalgam, composite, amalgamation, brew, combination, fusion, harmony, (*v*) amalgamate, commingle, fuse, incorporate, go, immingle, melt, stir; *antonym* (*v*) divide, **9**. join; *synonyms* (*v*) unite, graft, affiliate, affix, annex, conjoin, couple, enroll, fasten, integrate, interconnect, knit, splice, articulate, (*n*) bond; *antonyms* (*v*) detach, secede, split, undo, **10**. unite; *synonyms* (*v*) coalesce, unify, league, consolidate, marry, band, confederate, consociate, cooperate, ally, adhere, wed, bind, close, piece, **11**. reunite; *synonyms* (*v*) reconcile, reunify, conciliate, appease, pacify, placate, propitiate, reannex, settle, square, resolve.

kaboa 1. buy; *synonyms* (*v*) acquire, bribe, take, shop, accept, believe, get, admit, attain, corrupt, hold, (*n*) bargain, purchase, acquisition, deal; *antonym* (*v*) sell, **2**. mingle; *synonyms* (*v*) blend, combine, compound, merge, amalgamate, intermix, mix, commingle, associate, confuse, intermingle, join, immingle, coalesce, meddle; *antonym* (*v*) separate, **3**. mix; *synonyms* (*n*) mixture, concoction, combination, miscellany, (*v*) alloy, mingle, confound, meld, aggregate, admix, consort, fuse, immix, incorporate, jumble, **4**. sponsor; *synonyms* (*n*) backer, benefactor, patron, financier, guardian, supporter, (*v*) patronize, support, back, champion, finance, promote, vouch, assist, fund, **5**. paid; *synonyms* (*v*) compensated, (*adj*) gainful, paying, salaried, nonrecreational, profitable, remunerated, remunerative, mercenary, apaid, compensable, hired, hireling, lucrative, rewarding; *antonyms* (*adj*) unpaid, due, owing, **6**. pay; *synonyms* (*v*) compensate, compensation, liquidate, yield, afford, clear, expend, give, (*n*) recompense, wage, earnings, fee, salary, allowance, devote; *antonym* (*v*) owe, **7**. redeem; *synonyms* (*v*) atone, deliver, recover, recoup, expiate, ransom, reclaim, save, free, extricate, refund, pay, regain, rescue, retrieve, **8**. stir; *synonyms* (*v*) arouse, budge, move, rouse, affect, agitate, excite, inspire, go, (*n*) movement, commotion, disturbance, excitement, agitation, (*adj*) bustle, **9**. recompense; *synonyms* (*n*) reward, amends, atonement, payment, redress, consideration, indemnification, reparation, gratification, damages, guerdon, (*v*) indemnify, reimburse, remunerate, return.

kaboaki 1. mixed; *synonyms* (*adj*) miscellaneous, assorted, composite, heterogeneous, integrated, medley, impure, amalgamated, diverse, intermingled, motley, varied, indiscriminate, (*v*) blended, mingled; *antonyms* (*adj*) homogeneous, insular, pure, **2**. assembled; *synonyms* (*adj*) accumulated, amassed, collected, collective, united, accrued, aggregate, built, congregate, massed, equanimous, fabricated, fancied, fictional, fictitious, **3**. blended; *synonyms* (*v*) blent, polluted, stained, (*adj*) mixed, adulterate, beaten, conglomerate, **4**. accepted; *synonyms* (*adj*) acceptable, conventional, acknowledged, assumed, established, orthodox, understood, approved, current, received, customary, habitual, known, popular, proper; *antonyms* (*adj*) concealed, unpopular, unusual, **5**. coupled; *synonyms* (*adj*) connected, conjugate, double, joined, linked, associated, conjugated; *antonyms* (*adj*) separate, unrelated, **6**. joined; *synonyms* (*adj*) combined, coupled, allied, joint, concerted, **7**. redeemed; *synonyms* (*adj*) ransomed, blessed, **8**. stirred; *synonyms* (*adj*) stimulated, excited, affected, aroused, emotional, aflame, ablaze, enthused, horny, inspired, interested, overwrought, randy, ruttish, susceptible; *antonym* (*adj*) uninspired, **9**. paid; *synonyms* (*v*) compensated, (*adj*) gainful, paying, salaried, nonrecreational, profitable, remunerated, remunerative, mercenary, apaid, compensable, hired, hireling, lucrative, rewarding; *antonyms* (*adj*) unpaid, due, owing, **10**. united; *synonyms* (*adj*) cooperative, mutual, common, conjunctive, undivided, conjunct, unanimous, conjoint, one, together, inseparable, solid, (*v*) consolidated, join, (*n*) harmonious; *antonyms* (*adj*) individual, divided.

kaboanako 1. market; *synonyms* (*n*) fair, shop, bazaar, marketplace, trade, mart, outlet, store, (*v*) demand, sell, commercialize, exchange, handle, merchandise, sale, **2**. sold; *synonyms* (*adj*) depleted, interested, (*n*) solary.

kaboanakoaki sold; *synonyms* (*adj*) depleted, interested, (*n*) solary.

kaboati 1. tiresome; *synonyms* (*adj*) boring, tedious, dull, laborious, irksome, monotonous, annoying, bothersome, difficult, dreary, fatiguing, slow, trying, (*v*) troublesome, wearisome; *antonym* (*adj*) interesting, **2**. tiring; *synonyms* (*adj*) exhausting, tiresome, hard, wearing, arduous, grueling, onerous, strenuous; *antonyms* (*adj*) easy, undemanding.

kabobirimaka race; *synonyms* (*n*) kind, dash, family, career, competition, people, kin, nation, (*v*) course, run, rush, fly, hasten, hurry, (*adj*) lineage.

kabobo 1. exchange; *synonyms* (*n*) commutation, swap, switch, commerce, conversion, substitute, (*v*) change, barter, interchange, commute, counterchange, alternate, alter, cash, convert, **2**. miscarry; *synonyms* (*v*) fail, founder, abort, fall, flop, backfire, flunk, blow; *antonym* (*v*) succeed, **3**. abort; *synonyms* (*v*) expel, terminate, cancel, destroy, drop, fizzle, disappoint, end, scrub, arrest, axe, can, check, scrap, (*n*) miscarry.

kaboboa 1. mix; *synonyms* (*n*) mixture, concoction, (*v*) alloy, blend, intermingle, mingle, combine, compound, confound, intermix, join, meld, merge, aggregate, admix; *antonym* (*v*) separate, **2**. knead; *synonyms* (*v*) mix, rub, form, fashion, massage, mould, shape, work, (*adj*) mash, **3**. stir; *synonyms* (*v*) arouse, budge, move, rouse, affect, agitate, excite, inspire, go, (*n*) movement, commotion, disturbance, excitement, agitation, (*adj*) bustle.

kaboboaki 1. mixed; *synonyms* (*adj*) miscellaneous, assorted, composite, heterogeneous, integrated, medley, impure, amalgamated, diverse, intermingled, motley, varied, indiscriminate, (*v*) blended, mingled; *antonyms* (*adj*) homogeneous, insular, pure, **2**. exchanged; *synonyms* (*adj*) counterchanged, substituted, **3**. stirred; *synonyms* (*adj*) stimulated, excited, affected, aroused, emotional, aflame, ablaze, beaten, enthused, horny, inspired, interested, overwrought, randy, ruttish; *antonym* (*adj*) uninspired.

kabobooa stir; *synonyms* (*v*) arouse, budge, move, rouse, affect, agitate, excite, inspire, go, (*n*) movement, commotion, disturbance, excitement, agitation, (*adj*) bustle.

kabobooaki stirred; *synonyms* (*adj*) stimulated, excited, affected, aroused, emotional, aflame, ablaze, beaten, enthused, horny, inspired, interested, overwrought, randy, ruttish; *antonym* (*adj*) uninspired.

kaboituta inopportune; *synonyms* (*adj*) inconvenient, inappropriate, awkward, improper, inexpedient, disadvantageous, unfitting, unfortunate, untimely, untoward, unpropitious, ill-timed, premature, unlucky, unsuitable; *antonym* (*adj*) opportune.

kabomaki graze; *synonyms* (*v*) browse, scratch, rub, scrape, chafe, eat, brush, crease, crop, feed, pasture, rake, shave, (*n*) touch, cut.

kabomakiaki grazed; *synonyms* (*adj*) hurt, raw.

kabonakoa sold; *synonyms* (*adj*) depleted, interested, (*n*) solary.

kabongana use; *synonyms* (*n*) custom, practice, benefit, habit, application, function, (*v*) exercise, employ, employment, expend, profit, advantage, exploit, occupy, (*adj*) usage; *antonym* (*v*) conserve.

kabonganaki used; *synonyms* (*adj*) secondhand, exploited, accustomed, decrepit, depleted, exhausted, faded, habituated, hand-me-down, spent, threadbare, tried, victimised, victimized, wont; *antonyms* (*adj*) pristine, new, spanking, unused.

kabononanoa provoke; *synonyms* (*v*) excite, incite, defy, offend, anger, arouse, enrage, inflame, invite, irritate, kindle, get, aggravate, annoy, awaken; *antonyms* (*v*) calm, mollify, please, soothe.

kabononanoaki provoked; *synonyms (adj)* angry, exasperated, irritated, aggravated, indignant, infuriated, irate, inflamed; *antonym (adj)* unprovoked.

kabonota patch; *synonyms (n)* darn, fleck, mend, plot, bed, blot, freckle, bit, blotch, dapple, field, maculation, *(v)* piece, botch, fix.

kabonotaki patched; *synonyms (adj)* besmirched, damaged, flyblown, mean, ragged, spotted, stained, sullied, tainted, tarnished.

kaborake up; *synonyms (adv)* aloft, upward, upwardly, upwards, *(v)* raise, mount, rise, boost, advance, effervescent, filling, frothy, *(adj)* over, uphill, cheerful; *antonym (adj)* asleep.

kaboraoa 1. flatten; *synonyms (v)* fell, demolish, level, press, even, drop, roll, squash, depress, destroy, ruin, smash, smooth, unfold, bulldoze; *antonyms (v)* build, crumple, 2. plane; *synonyms (n)* airplane, face, aeroplane, aircraft, degree, stage, surface, jet, craft, facet, *(v)* flatten, shave, *(adj)* flat, horizontal, flush.

kaboraoaki 1. flattened; *synonyms (adj)* compressed, depressed, planate, trodden, unconscious, compacted, firmed, trampled; *antonym (adj)* loose, 2. planned; *synonyms (adj)* deliberate, intended, intentional, calculated, designed, aforethought, plotted, premeditated, scheduled, fixed, future, prepared, studied; *antonyms (adj)* spontaneous, unplanned.

kaborarinano hypocrite; *synonyms (n)* dissembler, impostor, pretender, trickster, fraud, cheat, fake.

kaborere 1. allot; *synonyms (v)* allocate, assign, apportion, distribute, administer, allow, deal, dispense, grant, portion, set, split, destine, issue, appropriate, 2. mix; *synonyms (n)* mixture, concoction, *(v)* alloy, blend, intermingle, mingle, combine, compound, confound, intermix, join, meld, merge, aggregate, admix; *antonym (v)* separate, 3. distribute; *synonyms (v)* allot, spread, diffuse, disperse, disseminate, broadcast, circulate, dispose, dispel, propagate, scatter, share, arrange, bestow, classify; *antonyms (v)* accumulate, amass, collect, gather, 4. proportion; *synonyms (n)* balance, percentage, degree, ratio, slice, dimension, equilibrium, equipoise, fraction, measure, part, rate, correspondence, ration, *(v)* scale, 5. proportional; *synonyms (adj)* proportionate, commensurate, proportionable, relative, balanced, symmetrical, even, graduated.

kaborereaki 1. mixed; *synonyms (adj)* miscellaneous, assorted, composite, heterogeneous, integrated, medley, impure, amalgamated, diverse, intermingled, motley, varied, indiscriminate, *(v)* blended, mingled; *antonyms (adj)* homogeneous, insular, pure, 2. distributed; *synonyms (adj)* dispersed, divided, spread, strewn, thin, separate,

diffuse, disseminated, circulated, disunited; *antonym (adj)* concentrated.

kaboria kiss; *synonyms (n)* buss, brush, osculation, salute, touch, *(v)* caress, embrace, osculate, love.

kaboriba 1. compare; *synonyms (v)* collate, liken, confront, comparison, equate, associate, contrast, correlate, equal, equalize, parallel, resemble, *(n)* comparability, 2. contrast; *synonyms (n)* contrariety, antithesis, distinction, difference, variation, collation, opposite, dissimilarity, *(v)* differ, conflict, oppose, diverge, clash, counterpoint, differentiate; *antonym (n)* similarity.

kabotaba 1. embrace; *synonyms (v)* comprise, clasp, hug, admit, adopt, comprehend, contain, cover, encompass, espouse, grip, include, *(n)* bosom, clutch, cuddle; *antonym (v)* reject, 2. hug; *synonyms (n)* embrace, hold, clinch, caress, *(v)* squeeze, cling, cherish, grasp, touch, adhere, gripe, clench, lock, press, stick.

kabotaeka argue; *synonyms (v)* contend, oppose, quarrel, reason, altercate, assert, attest, contest, convince, debate, declare, discuss, expostulate, fight, *(n)* dispute; *antonyms (v)* agree, deny.

kabotau 1. compare; *synonyms (v)* collate, liken, confront, comparison, equate, associate, contrast, correlate, equal, equalize, parallel, resemble, *(n)* comparability, 2. equalize; *synonyms (v)* balance, compensate, even, compare, counterbalance, equalise, level, match, counteract, 3. confront; *synonyms (v)* face, front, oppose, challenge, approach, brave, defy, affront, play, dare, encounter, meet, resist, withstand, accost; *antonyms (v)* avoid, evade, 4. proportion; *synonyms (n)* percentage, degree, ratio, portion, slice, dimension, equilibrium, equipoise, fraction, measure, part, rate, share, correspondence, *(v)* scale.

kabotauaki equalized; *synonyms (adj)* equalised, coordinate, even, poised, secure, stable, steady.

kabotu tiring; *synonyms (adj)* exhausting, tedious, tiresome, hard, laborious, wearing, arduous, grueling, boring, wearisome, onerous, strenuous; *antonyms (adj)* easy, undemanding.

kaboua update; *synonyms (n)* updating, briefing, *(v)* inform, modernize, renovate, revise, instruct, refresh, improve, rationalize, restore, advise, alter, brief, change.

kaboubwa prone; *synonyms (adj)* liable, apt, disposed, inclined, flat, predisposed, subject, likely, procumbent, prostrate, susceptible, supine, given, ready, exposed; *antonym (adj)* upright.

kaboulina quoits; *synonym (n)* horseshoes.

kabu bud; *synonyms (n)* bloom, blossom, flower, germ, button, embryo, implant, nucleus, *(v)* graft, shoot, vegetate, develop, germinate, grow, ingraft.

kabua 1. lose; *synonyms (v)* drop, forfeit, mislay, sacrifice, fail, clear, hurt, regress, retrogress, destroy, misplace, recede, suffer, waste, escape;

antonyms (v) gain, find, acquire, earn, get, obtain, recover, secure, win, beat, defeat, keep, succeed, **2.** mislay; *synonyms* (v) lose, disorganize, displace, leave, retreat, **3.** bereave; *synonyms* (v) deprive, divest, rob, strip, despoil, oust, disinherit, widow, depose, dismantle, outstrip, pass, skin, uncover, **4.** lost; *synonyms* (v) gone, missing, abandoned, (adj) doomed, forlorn, extinct, hopeless, bewildered, disoriented, forgotten, helpless, broken, confused, irrecoverable, absent; *antonyms* (adj) present, found, existing, **5.** damage; *synonyms* (n) blemish, injury, wound, loss, cost, detriment, disadvantage, impairment, (v) harm, abuse, injure, afflict, disfigure, mar, (adj) impair; *antonyms* (n) service, (v) conserve, enhance, repair, bolster, **6.** waste; *synonyms* (n) desert, refuse, damage, trash, (adj) spoil, desolate, barren, (v) consume, exhaust, ruin, squander, ravage, destruction, devastate, dissipate; *antonym* (v) save.

kabuâ 1. sore; *synonyms* (adj) painful, sensitive, angry, raw, indignant, aching, (n) injury, boil, cut, lesion, canker, abscess, (v) hurt, acute, sharp; *antonym* (adj) painless, **2.** requite; *synonyms* (v) repay, pay, recompense, reciprocate, compensate, remunerate, reward, reimburse, gratify, return, indemnify, refund, quit, avenge, (adj) satisfy.

kabuabua round; *synonyms* (adv) about, around, (adj) circular, plump, entire, chubby, complete, (n) circle, bout, ring, beat, circuit, (v) compass, turn, gird; *antonyms* (adj) slim, sharp.

kabuabuaki rounded; *synonyms* (adj) round, curved, circular, orbicular, full, globular, rotund, spherical, bent, blunt, fat, obtuse; *antonyms* (adj) pointed, straight, sharp, bony, concave.

kabuakaka 1. blame; *synonyms* (v) accuse, arraign, censure, reprimand, charge, reproach, chide, fault, rebuke, attribute, (n) attack, rap, onus, accusation, allegation; *antonyms* (v) pardon, absolve, praise, **2.** insult; *synonyms* (n) dishonor, abuse, affront, contumely, disgrace, indignity, outrage, contempt, wound, derision, harm, injury, (v) flout, taunt, cut; *antonym* (v) compliment, **3.** defame; *synonyms* (v) libel, malign, slander, vilify, calumniate, denigrate, smear, blacken, besmirch, discredit, disparage, lampoon, slur, traduce, (adj) asperse, **4.** affront; *synonyms* (n) slight, offense, snub, discourtesy, humiliation, (v) insult, face, offend, confront, displease, injure, anger, sneer, **5.** mar; *synonyms* (v) disfigure, spoil, blemish, deface, impair, corrupt, hurt, deflower, maim, mutilate, botch, mangle, blight, bungle, (adj) damage; *antonym* (v) enhance, **6.** reproach; *synonyms* (n) blame, invective, condemnation, imputation, reprehension, scandal, stigma, disparagement, (v) condemn, criminate, dispraise, impeach, opprobrium, (adj) stain, brand; *antonym* (v) commend, **7.** spoil; *synonyms* (v)

plunder, rot, indulge, mar, sack, baby, coddle, deprave, despoil, frustrate, pamper, pillage, ravage, (n) ruin, prey; *antonyms* (v) improve, conserve.

kabuakakaki 1. blamed; *synonyms* (adj) damned, goddam, goddamn, goddamned, infernal, damnable, aeonian, ageless, answerable, beatified, blame, blasted, blessed, damn, darned, **2.** insulted; *synonyms* (adj) affronted, huffy, disrespected, hurt, slighted, snubbed, upset, **3.** marred; *synonyms* (adj) damaged, defaced, crippled, deficient, deformed, dilapidated, faulty, impaired, imperfect, scarred, **4.** affronted; *synonyms* insulted, offended, angry, annoyed, ashamed, embarrassed, horrified, humiliated, piqued, peeved, sensitive, sulky, touchy, vexed, **5.** spoiled; *synonyms* (adj) decayed, bad, rotten, stale, coddled, pampered, corrupt, spoilt; *antonyms* (adj) first-rate, pure.

kabuaki 1. lost; *synonyms* (v) gone, missing, abandoned, (adj) doomed, forlorn, extinct, hopeless, bewildered, disoriented, forgotten, helpless, broken, confused, irrecoverable, absent; *antonyms* (adj) present, found, existing, **2.** damaged; *synonyms* (adj) faulty, unsound, defective, dilapidated, hurt, impaired, besmirched, deficient, flyblown; *antonym* (adj) undamaged, **3.** mislaid; *synonyms* (adj) lost, misplaced, disordered, omitted, vanished, **4.** bereaved; *synonyms* (adj) bereft, grieving, mourning, orbate, sad, sorrowing, childless, fatherless, lovelorn, unbeloved, (v) minus, denuded, **5.** wasted; *synonyms* (v) rotten, effete, (adj) squandered, thin, cadaverous, emaciated, gaunt, devastated, decayed, haggard, pointless, skeletal, atrophied, blasted, bony; *antonyms* (adj) worthwhile, bloated.

kabuane steam; *synonyms* (n) mist, fog, haze, vapor, cloud, energy, (v) reek, evaporate, exhale, smoke, fume, cook, pull, boil, (adj) gas.

kabuaneaki steamed; *synonyms* (adj) annoyed, besotted, bit, bitten, blotto, churning, crocked, fuddled, furious, harassed, harried, incensed, indignant, irate, irritated.

kabuanibai 1. accidental; *synonyms* (adj) casual, fortuitous, adventitious, chance, incidental, unintended, unintentional, contingent, haphazard, inadvertent, involuntary, random, unexpected, unforeseen; *antonyms* (adj) intentional, deliberate, **2.** disastrous; *synonyms* (adj) calamitous, destructive, dire, fateful, deplorable, bad, catastrophic, fatal, sad, sinister, terrible, unfortunate, unlucky, untoward, (v) ruinous; *antonyms* (adj) fortunate, successful, **3.** destructive; *synonyms* (adj) baneful, deadly, hurtful, malign, baleful, evil, harmful, injurious, mischievous, noxious, pernicious, deleterious, negative, vicious, slaughterous; *antonyms* (adj) harmless, constructive, creative, **4**. cataclysmic; *synonyms* (*adj*) cataclysmal, disastrous, tragic.

kabuanibwai 1. harm; *synonyms* (*n*) evil, hurt, detriment, bruise, wound, disadvantage, injury, disservice, (*v*) damage, abuse, blemish, injure, maim, poison, ravage; *antonyms* (*v*) enhance, benefit, **2**. damage; *synonyms* (*n*) loss, cost, impairment, price, ruin, tear, wreck, wrong, (*v*) harm, afflict, disfigure, mar, mutilate, spoil, (*adj*) impair; *antonyms* (*n*) service, (*v*) conserve, repair, bolster.

kabuanibwaia harm; *synonyms* (*n*) evil, hurt, detriment, bruise, wound, disadvantage, injury, disservice, (*v*) damage, abuse, blemish, injure, maim, poison, ravage; *antonyms* (*v*) enhance, benefit.

kabuanibwaiaki 1. harmed; *synonyms* (*v*) harm, damage, (*adj*) hurt, aggrieved, impaired, injured, abused, battered, crippled, debilitated, incapacitated, maltreated, mistreated, molested, neglected, **2**. damaged; *synonyms* (*adj*) faulty, unsound, defective, broken, dilapidated, besmirched, deficient, flyblown; *antonym* (*adj*) undamaged.

kabuari round; *synonyms* (*adv*) about, around, (*adj*) circular, plump, entire, chubby, complete, (*n*) circle, bout, ring, beat, circuit, (*v*) compass, turn, gird; *antonyms* (*adj*) slim, sharp.

kábub 1. blunt; *synonyms* (*adj*) dull, bluff, candid, direct, forthright, frank, outspoken, plain, round, abrupt, brusque, downright, obtuse, (*v*) deaden, numb; *antonyms* (*adj*) sharp, devious, pointed, (*v*) hone, sharpen, **2**. dull; *synonyms* (*adj*) dim, blunt, dense, dreary, sluggish, bland, boring, cloudy, cold, dark, dismal, inactive, inert, slack, (*v*) dampen; *antonyms* (*adj*) bright, lively, exciting, interesting, lustrous, stimulating, amusing, exhilarating, glittery, glossy, glowing, high-pitched, intense, luminous, shiny.

kabubu 1. disappointed; *synonyms* (*adj*) defeated, disgruntled, regretful, depressed, dissatisfied, frustrated, sad, unhappy, disenchanted; *antonyms* (*adj*) delighted, pleased, composed, satisfied, **2**. deceive; *synonyms* (*v*) betray, cheat, bamboozle, circumvent, dupe, pretend, beguile, con, cozen, fool, hoax, mislead, sell, swindle, (*n*) fraud, **3**. discouraged; *synonyms* (*adj*) disappointed, despondent, crestfallen, dejected, demoralized, disheartened, dispirited, downcast, downhearted, pessimistic, baffled, balked; *antonym* (*adj*) optimistic, **4**. blunt; *synonyms* (*adj*) dull, bluff, candid, direct, forthright, frank, outspoken, plain, round, abrupt, brusque, downright, obtuse, (*v*) deaden, numb; *antonyms* (*adj*) sharp, devious, pointed, (*v*) hone, sharpen, **5**. disappoint; *synonyms* (*v*) deceive, fail, baffle, balk, defeat, disenchant, bilk, mock, delude, foil, frustrate,

thwart, (*n*) dissatisfy; *antonyms* (*v*) please, satisfy, **6**. dull; *synonyms* (*adj*) dim, blunt, dense, dreary, sluggish, bland, boring, cloudy, cold, dark, dismal, inactive, inert, slack, (*v*) dampen; *antonyms* (*adj*) bright, lively, exciting, interesting, lustrous, stimulating, amusing, exhilarating, glittery, glossy, glowing, high-pitched, intense, luminous, shiny, **7**. dupe; *synonyms* (*n*) gull, victim, cully, prey, tool, butt, (*v*) defraud, kid, befool, cod, trap, trick, victimize, cajole, gudgeon.

kabubua lose; *synonyms* (*v*) drop, forfeit, mislay, sacrifice, fail, clear, hurt, regress, retrogress, destroy, misplace, recede, suffer, waste, escape; *antonyms* (*v*) gain, find, acquire, earn, get, obtain, recover, secure, win, beat, defeat, keep, succeed.

kabubuaki 1. lost; *synonyms* (*v*) gone, missing, abandoned, (*adj*) doomed, forlorn, extinct, hopeless, bewildered, disoriented, forgotten, helpless, broken, confused, irrecoverable, absent; *antonyms* (*adj*) present, found, existing, **2**. disappointed; *synonyms* (*adj*) defeated, disgruntled, regretful, depressed, dissatisfied, frustrated, sad, unhappy, disenchanted; *antonyms* (*adj*) delighted, pleased, composed, satisfied.

kabuebue 1. feverish; *synonyms* (*adj*) hectic, febrile, feverous, hot, fiery, frenzied, excited, fanatical, flushed, sick, (*n*) hysterical; *antonym* (*adj*) cool, **2**. hot; *synonyms* (*adj*) warm, ardent, boiling, burning, feverish, flaming, fresh, blistering, eager, enthusiastic, fast, peppery, pungent, spicy, angry; *antonyms* (*adj*) mild, cold, freezing, airy, bland, chilly, **3**. torrid; *synonyms* (*adj*) impassioned, sultry, fervent, fervid, perfervid, sweltering, scorching, stifling, tropical, baking, broiling, sunny.

kabueka ignite; *synonyms* (*v*) light, kindle, arouse, enkindle, fire, heat, flame, agitate, burn, excite, inflame, detonate, incite, provoke, awaken; *antonym* (*v*) extinguish.

kabuekaki ignited; *synonyms* (*v*) burning, active, flowing, laving, live, lively, quickening, running, vigorous, (*adj*) kindled, enkindled, flaming, ablaze, fiery.

kabuingoingo 1. indifferent; *synonyms* (*adj*) apathetic, callous, cold, cool, fair, impassive, insensible, unconcerned, careless, dull, average, aloof, casual, detached, disinterested; *antonyms* (*adj*) caring, enthusiastic, fervent, keen, obsessive, eager, energetic, involved, surprised, **2**. apathetic; *synonyms* (*adj*) indifferent, uninterested, perfunctory, lazy, lethargic, lukewarm, nonchalant, sluggish, spiritless, indolent, inattentive, inert, lackadaisical, languid, listless; *antonym* (*adj*) inquisitive, **3**. passive; *synonyms* (*adj*) inactive, submissive, lifeless, nonviolent, resigned, dormant, slow, unresisting, meek, patient, static, torpid, yielding, acquiescent, compliant; *antonyms* (*adj*) active, assertive, spirited, working.

kabukuwi spin; *synonyms* (*n*) turn, twirl, whirl, revolution, roll, ride, eddy, (*v*) revolve, twist, run, drive, reel, fabricate, gyrate, invent.

kabun 1. choke; *synonyms* (*v*) asphyxiate, block, throttle, stifle, clog, foul, gag, obstruct, smother, strangle, suffocate, check, die, close, congest; *antonym* (*v*) unclog, **2.** disgusting; *synonyms* (*adj*) abominable, detestable, disgustful, distasteful, execrable, loathsome, nasty, odious, offensive, disagreeable, abhorrent, awful, dirty, hateful, horrible; *antonyms* (*adj*) attractive, pleasant, appealing, **3.** gag; *synonyms* (*n*) muzzle, joke, quip, jest, prank, crack, humor, (*v*) choke, heave, muffle, quiet, silence, puke, spew, hush, **4.** irksome; *synonyms* (*adj*) troublesome, boring, dull, tiresome, wearisome, annoying, tedious, burdensome, trying, galling, grating, irritating, pesky, prosaic, slow, **5.** repulsive; *synonyms* (*adj*) ugly, nauseous, disgusting, hideous, obnoxious, forbidding, horrid, objectionable, repellent, repugnant, noisome, ghastly, nauseating, obscene, revolting, **6.** repugnant; *synonyms* (*adj*) repulsive, contradictory, adverse, inimical, opposite, antagonistic, gruesome, incompatible, sickening, vile, (*v*) hostile, (*n*) irreconcilable, discordant, contrary, inconsistent, **7.** teem; *synonyms* (*n*) abound, exuberate, (*v*) swarm, flow, pour, crowd, pullulate, brim, flower, fructify, rain, stream.

kabunaki choked; *synonyms* (*adj*) clogged, suffocated, congested, anxious, high-strung, insecure, neurotic, strained, suffocate, tense, clotted.

kabunenea 1. abuse; *synonyms* (*n*) affront, misuse, harm, outrage, reproach, invective, (*v*) insult, mistreat, injure, assault, censure, damage, exploit, hurt, (*adj*) maltreat; *antonyms* (*v*) praise, respect, **2.** insult; *synonyms* (*n*) dishonor, abuse, contumely, disgrace, indignity, contempt, wound, derision, injury, (*v*) flout, taunt, cut, mock, offend, slight; *antonym* (*v*) compliment, **3.** reprimand; *synonyms* (*n*) blame, admonition, chastisement, reproof, castigation, reprehension, (*v*) rebuke, chide, lecture, castigate, admonish, chastise, discipline, scold, accuse; *antonym* (*v*) commend.

kabuneneaki 1. abused; *synonyms* (*adj*) maltreated, mistreated, downtrodden, dull, perverted, battered, harmed, injured, molested, neglected, **2.** insulted; *synonyms* (*adj*) affronted, huffy, disrespected, hurt, slighted, snubbed, upset, **3.** reprimanded; *synonyms* (*adj*) rebuked, reproved, admonished, chastened.

kabunga deliver; *synonyms* (*v*) consign, bear, carry, rescue, save, abandon, bring, liberate, pronounce, render, return, send, utter, drop, acquit.

kabunnaa 1. multiply; *synonyms* (*v*) breed, expand, increase, propagate, augment, duplicate, procreate, proliferate, reproduce, calculate, extend, enlarge,

add, boost, amplify; *antonym* (*v*) decrease, **2.** increase; *synonyms* (*n*) gain, addition, augmentation, boom, expansion, extension, growth, progress, rise, (*v*) advance, accrue, grow, aggrandize, enhance, deepen; *antonyms* (*n*) reduction, contraction, decline, (*v*) reduce, diminish, drop, deteriorate, **3.** augment; *synonyms* (*v*) reinforce, improve, intensify, magnify, raise, mount, broaden, compound, develop, heighten, multiply, supplement, swell, wax, inflate, **4.** amplify; *synonyms* (*v*) exaggerate, dilate, distend, overstate, embellish, embroider, elaborate, overdo, overdraw, spread, dramatize, pad, (*adj*) descant, expatiate; *antonym* (*v*) understate.

kabunnaaki 1. augmented; *synonyms* (*adj*) inflated, more, plus, better, bigger, improved, **2.** increased; *synonyms* (*adj*) additional, enlarged, greater, fresh, new, puffy, ripe, amplified, other, superior, **3.** multiplied; *synonyms* (*v*) absorb, acquisition, attainment, engross, engulf, (*adj*) manifold, many, multitudinous, peopled, populous, studded, teeming, thick, complicated, divers.

kabuoka 1. burn; *synonyms* (*v*) bite, glow, blaze, incinerate, scorch, sting, bake, beam, boil, cremate, flare, ignite, sunburn, (*n*) fire, (*adj*) flush; *antonym* (*v*) dawdle, **2.** burnt; *synonyms* (*v*) brent, (*adj*) burned, adust, baked, heated, sunburnt, adusted, arid, combust, dry, overcooked, overdone, consumed, dehydrated, desiccated; *antonym* (*adj*) underdone.

kabuokaki burnt; *synonyms* (*v*) brent, (*adj*) burned, adust, baked, heated, sunburnt, adusted, arid, combust, dry, overcooked, overdone, consumed, dehydrated, desiccated; *antonym* (*adj*) underdone.

kaburabura swaggering; *synonyms* (*v*) swagger, (*adj*) blustering, hectoring, arrogant, boastful, disdainful, haughty, lordly, prideful, roistering, sniffy, (*n*) boasting, bluster, bravado, ostentation.

kaburati 1. coarse; *synonyms* (*adj*) barbarous, boorish, brutal, crude, gross, rough, vulgar, bawdy, blunt, broad, common, earthy, harsh, rude, uncivilized; *antonyms* (*adj*) refined, smooth, sophisticated, **2.** deformed; *synonyms* (*adj*) crooked, bent, distorted, malformed, misshapen, ugly, crippled, contorted, deform, grotesque, shapeless, twisted, warped, (*v*) crump, **3.** disgusting; *synonyms* (*adj*) abominable, detestable, disgustful, distasteful, execrable, foul, loathsome, nasty, odious, offensive, disagreeable, abhorrent, awful, dirty, hateful; *antonyms* (*adj*) attractive, pleasant, appealing, **4.** impolite; *synonyms* (*adj*) coarse, discourteous, gruff, brusque, churlish, disrespectful, impertinent, improper, insolent, abrupt, unrefined, curt, indecorous, indelicate, insulting; *antonyms* (*adj*) polite, respectful, courteous, **5.** vulgar; *synonyms* (*adj*) uncouth, low, plebeian, vile, indecent, cheap, public, tasteless, vernacular, ignoble, impolite, base, ordinary, inelegant, *(n)* mean; *antonym (adj)* tasteful, **6**. surly; *synonyms (adj)* grumpy, sullen, peevish, crusty, grouchy, morose, crabby, dark, gloomy, grim, sour, glum, unfriendly, *(n)* crabbed, severe, **7**. ugly; *synonyms (adj)* forbidding, frightful, gruesome, hideous, homely, repulsive, surly, evil, atrocious, deformed, despicable, horrible, monstrous, ominous, plain; *antonyms (adj)* beautiful, good-looking, flowing, ornamental.

kaburea convict; *synonyms (n)* captive, felon, con, criminal, inmate, jailbird, prisoner, culprit, gaolbird, malefactor, offender, *(v)* condemn, convince, confute, damn; *antonym (v)* acquit.

kabureaki convicted; *synonyms (v)* convict, *(adj)* condemned, guilty, doomed, apparent, appropriated, censured, confiscate, confiscated, manifest, detected, plain, seized.

kaburinana 1. squash; *synonyms (v)* crush, mash, quell, compress, press, smash, squeeze, flatten, quash, oppress, crash, depress, cram, crowd, grind, **2**. squelch; *synonyms (n)* squelcher, muting, *(v)* squash, repress, quench, slosh, splash, muffle, smother, squish, stifle, subdue, censor, slop, splosh, **3**. squeeze; *synonyms (v)* hug, pinch, embrace, extort, force, jam, nip, pack, compact, condense, constrict, contract, cuddle, pressure, *(n)* grip; *antonym (v)* loosen.

kaburinanaki squashed; *synonyms (adj)* compacted, compressed, condensed, dense, solid.

kaburoa 1. boil; *synonyms (v)* seethe, bubble, churn, simmer, ferment, burn, effervesce, fume, heat, anger, *(n)* abscess, blister, furuncle, pimple, *(adj)* sore; *antonym (v)* freeze, **2**. seethe; *synonyms (v)* boil, foam, stew, cook, rage, froth, fizz, buzz, digest, hum, moil, roil, roll.

kaburoaki boiled; *synonyms (adj)* done, intoxicated, poached, stewed, *(v)* sodden, saturated, seethed, soaked.

kaburuburua fray; *synonyms (n)* brawl, conflict, action, affray, combat, fight, battle, broil, contention, disturbance, fracas, scrap, *(v)* rub, chafe, fret.

kaburuburuaki frayed; *synonyms (adj)* worn, ragged, shabby, threadbare, tattered, *(v)* dilapidated; *antonym (adj)* pristine.

kabururu 1. gargle; *synonyms (n)* mouthwash, bath, gargarism, gargoyle, *(v)* rinse, drink, gargalize, gargarize, warble, *(adj)* inject, syringe, **2**. wash; *synonyms (v)* paint, bathe, clean, lave, moisten, mop, scour, scrub, color, tint, lap, gargle, *(n)* soak, ablution, washing; *antonym (v)* dirty.

kabururuaki washed; *synonyms (adj)* clean, refined, watery.

kabuta 1. drive; *synonyms (n)* ride, force, campaign, crusade, thrust, cause, ambition, *(v)* push, actuate, chase, compel, urge, coerce, beat, carry; *antonyms (n)* apathy, inertia, **2**. conventional; *synonyms (adj)* formal, orthodox, accepted, common, customary, everyday, conservative, decorous, established, habitual, normal, ordinary, routine, *(v)* commonplace, familiar; *antonyms (adj)* unconventional, radical, relaxed, unusual, original, rebellious, unorthodox, **3**. driven; *synonyms (v)* drive, *(adj)* determined, impelled, compulsive, bound, dictated, dynamic, encouraged, goaded, hell-bent, provoked, successful, activist, efficient, energetic, **4**. general; *synonyms (adj)* comprehensive, national, universal, broad, current, ecumenical, public, average, communal, extensive, wide, conventional, *(n)* chief, commander, *(v)* frequent; *antonyms (adj)* specific, individual, narrow, *(n)* particular, **5**. common; *synonyms (adj)* coarse, cheap, mutual, usual, vulgar, accustomed, base, ignoble, mean, mediocre, plebeian, trivial, banal, prosaic, poor; *antonyms (adj)* uncommon, rare, characteristic, one-off, unique, aristocratic, exclusive, extraordinary, infrequent, **6**. commonplace; *synonyms (adj)* humdrum, dull, mundane, pedestrian, plain, threadbare, uninspired, uninteresting, unoriginal, *(n)* platitude, banality, bromide, cliche, *(v)* hackneyed, trite, **7**. embark; *synonyms (v)* ship, leave, enter, sail, start, undertake, venture, open, emplane, adventure, approach, imbark, inship, enrol, enroll; *antonym (v)* disembark, **8**. everyday; *synonyms (adj)* casual, daily, regular, informal, colloquial, undistinguished, household, quotidian, workaday, typical, unremarkable, *(v)* general, wonted; *antonym (adj)* exquisite, **9**. drove; *synonyms (n)* flock, herd, swarm, crowd, horde, covey, mob, multitude, throng, group, host, legion, *(adj)* bevy, shoal, cloud, **10**. usual; *synonyms (adj)* prevalent, natural, prevailing, stock, traditional, chronic, expected, set; *antonym (adj)* abnormal, **11**. spread; *synonyms (v)* scatter, reach, disperse, expand, extend, broadcast, circulate, diffuse, disseminate, increase, propagate, stretch, broaden, deploy, *(n)* span; *antonym (adj)* concentrated, **12**. routine; *synonyms (n)* round, habit, method, procedure, process, act, custom, practice, rule, precedent, chore, convention, scheme, tradition, *(adj)* mechanical, **13**. typical; *synonyms (adj)* classic, distinctive, model, figurative, distinguishing, emblematic, symbolic, peculiar, exemplary, ideal, typic, archetypal, catachrestical, *(v)* representative, diacritical; *antonyms (adj)* atypical, uncharacteristic, **14**. ride; *synonyms (n)* outing, run, lift, jaunt, voyage, driving, *(v)* bait, float, mount, rag, tease, harass, annoy, drift, *(adj)* bestride, **15**. ordinary; *synonyms (adj)* middling, indifferent, inferior, medium, fair, humble, moderate, characterless, passable, simple, unexceptional, modest, (v) inconspicuous, cuisine, menu; *antonyms* (adj) incredible, outstanding, strange, special, distinguished, famous.

kabutaki 1. driven; *synonyms* (v) drive, (adj) determined, impelled, compulsive, bound, dictated, dynamic, encouraged, goaded, hell-bent, provoked, successful, activist, efficient, energetic, **2.** spread; *synonyms* (v) scatter, reach, disperse, expand, extend, broadcast, circulate, diffuse, disseminate, increase, propagate, stretch, broaden, deploy, (n) span; *antonym* (adj) concentrated.

kabutewetewe grill; *synonyms* (n) grid, grille, grillroom, (v) fry, bake, broil, cook, examine, quiz, roast, burn, inflame, toast, ask, interrogate.

kabuteweteweaki grilled; *synonyms* (adj) barbecued, broiled, baked.

kabutia revolve; *synonyms* (v) reel, consider, deliberate, meditate, ponder, circle, circulate, contemplate, orbit, return, rotate, spin, wheel, (n) gyrate, roll.

kabutika poisonous; *synonyms* (adj) deadly, toxic, mortal, malicious, noxious, venomous, fatal, baneful, lethal, noisome, malignant, pernicious, toxiferous, evil, pestilential; *antonym* (adj) harmless.

kabutikeke 1. glide; *synonyms* (n) slip, gliding, sailing, (v) slide, coast, float, flow, fly, run, drift, lapse, move, skid, slink, slither; *antonym* (v) struggle, **2.** slide; *synonyms* (n) glide, chute, decline, transparency, recession, slider, (v) drop, fall, slump, descend, sag, cut, tumble, sneak, (adj) shift, **3.** soft; *synonyms* (adj) gentle, easy, light, limp, balmy, delicate, quiet, slack, loose, clement, faint, flabby, flaccid, (v) feeble, low; *antonyms* (adj) hard, firm, harsh, loud, hoarse, rough, solid, stiff, alcoholic, shrill, strong, **4.** slippery; *synonyms* (adj) cunning, crafty, glib, elusive, glossy, oily, shifty, slick, slippy, tricky, untrustworthy, wily, dishonest, (v) precarious, questionable.

kabutu pout; *synonyms* (n) eelpout, face, hornpout, moue, (v) brood, sulk, glout, mop, mow, (adj) frown, lower, glower, scowl, bulge, gloam.

kabwaka 1. launch; *synonyms* (n) boat, (v) initiate, begin, dart, found, fire, introduce, toss, commence, establish, hurl, inaugurate, institute, start, cast; *antonym* (v) end, **2.** drop; *synonyms* (v) fall, decrease, deposit, dribble, droop, abandon, dip, discard, dismiss, drip, ebb, jump, shed, (n) decline, collapse; *antonyms* (v) rise, increase, lift, (n) growth.

kabwakabwai 1. bet; *synonyms* (v) gamble, play, lay, risk, venture, (n) wager, stake, stakes, **2.** wager; *synonyms* (n) bet, chance, set, speculation, suit, vie, (v) hazard, pledge, pawn, gage.

kabwakaki dropped; *synonyms* (adj) fallen, decreased, abandoned, dead, degraded, prostrate, ruined.

kabwarabwara 1. explain; *synonyms* (v) comment, elucidate, interpret, account, clarify, decipher, define, describe, enlighten, excuse, explicate, expound, gloss, solve, denote; *antonym* (v) confuse, **2.** describe; *synonyms* (v) delineate, depict, outline, report, represent, state, draw, relate, qualify, characterize, designate, explain, name, narrate, recite, **3.** enunciate; *synonyms* (v) articulate, declare, vocalize, pronounce, voice, enounce, express, proclaim, say, speak, utter, (n) allege, propound, advance; *antonym* (v) mumble.

kabwarabwaraki described; *synonyms* (adj) alleged, detailed.

kabwarikorikoa stack; *synonyms* (n) pile, accumulation, mound, rick, mass, bunch, bundle, hill, mountain, shock, (v) heap, load, lot, pack, store.

kabwarikorikoaki stacked; *synonyms* (adj) buxom, curvaceous, prepared, shapely, voluptuous.

kabwaroa pour; *synonyms* (v) gush, shed, decant, flow, pelt, scatter, stream, discharge, emit, jet, run, spill, teem, (n) overflow, rain; *antonym* (v) drizzle.

kabwaroaki poured; *synonym* (adj) concrete.

kabwatuta squint; *synonyms* (n) glance, look, strabismus, cast, (v) leer, skew, blink, squinch, (adj) askant, sidelong, askance, asquint.

kabwatutua squint; *synonyms* (n) glance, look, strabismus, cast, (v) leer, skew, blink, squinch, (adj) askant, sidelong, askance, asquint.

kabwaubwau guzzle; *synonyms* (v) bolt, devour, drink, gobble, gulp, consume, gorge, swill, guttle, imbibe, quaff; *antonyms* (v) nibble, sip.

kabwauta gulp; *synonyms* (n) drink, gasp, draft, draught, gulping, (v) bolt, devour, gobble, swig, gorge, down, quaff, sip, swallow, consume; *antonym* (v) nibble.

kabwea 1. maneuver; *synonyms* (v) manoeuvre, guide, handle, control, manipulate, manoeuver, steer, (n) artifice, ruse, scheme, measure, device, act, ploy, stratagem, **2.** steer; *synonyms* (v) navigate, direct, drive, aim, conduct, manage, maneuver, run, tip, show, channel, govern, (n) lead, point, bullock.

kadamwa cat; *synonyms* (n) caterpillar, guy, lynx, bozo, hombre, puss, (v) disgorge, puke, regorge, regurgitate, retch, spew, spue, upchuck, vomit.

kaea 1. follow; *synonyms* (v) chase, pursue, adhere, adopt, accompany, comprehend, continue, ensue, grasp, hunt, realize, succeed, track, emulate, (adj) catch; *antonyms* (v) precede, guide, head, lead, **2.** hunt; *synonyms* (n) search, pursuit, quest, (v) course, follow, hound, forage, rummage, prey, dog, persecute, seek, stalk, trace, trail, **3.** seek;

synonyms (*v*) attempt, endeavor, look, inquire, aspire, beg, explore, investigate, research, demand, essay, ransack, request, strive, (*n*) ask, **4**. pursue; *synonyms* (*v*) prosecute, haunt, persist, tail, conduct, practice, court, keep, engage, harass, shadow, bother, plague, observe, persevere.

kaeaki 1. hunted; *synonyms* (*adj*) coursed, required, sought, wanted, (*n*) victim, **2**. chased; *synonyms* (*adj*) engraved, (*n*) pursued, **3**. pursued; *synonym* (*n*) chased.

kaeea chase; *synonyms* (*n*) game, search, quest, (*v*) hunt, pursue, expel, follow, stalk, track, trail, chamfer, pursuit, race, seek, evict.

kaeeaki chased; *synonyms* (*adj*) engraved, (*n*) pursued.

kaeia sway; *synonyms* (*n*) influence, reign, rock, authority, empire, (*v*) command, rule, oscillate, control, reel, stagger, bias, career, lurch, persuade.

kaeka 1. answer; *synonyms* (*n*) reply, respond, retort, return, solution, defense, echo, (*v*) counter, resolve, serve, acknowledge, agree, correspond, do, (*adj*) pay; *antonyms* (*v*) question, ask, **2**. rejoin; *synonyms* (*v*) answer, join, riposte, meet, rebut, **3**. receive; *synonyms* (*v*) accept, admit, get, assume, adopt, bear, have, obtain, welcome, make, embrace, gather, greet, take, hear, **4**. react; *synonyms* (*v*) act, oppose, recoil, behave; *antonym* (*v*) ignore, **5**. reply; *synonyms* (*n*) rejoinder, response, reaction, repay, replication, repartee, comeback, (*v*) react, rejoin, say, **6**. question; *synonyms* (*n*) inquiry, challenge, demand, matter, problem, (*v*) doubt, query, distrust, inquire, interrogate, investigate, contest, dispute, examine, enquire; *antonym* (*n*) certainty, **7**. respond; *synonym* (*adj*) tally.

kaekaki received; *synonyms* (*v*) receiving, ascertained, current, recognized, (*adj*) accepted, acknowledged, conventional, acceptable, canonical, orthodox, customary, established, inward, known, legitimate.

kaena 1. mock; *synonyms* (*adj*) counterfeit, (*v*) deride, ridicule, burlesque, gibe, ape, flout, mimic, scoff, scorn, sham, taunt, bemock, (*n*) jeer, derision; *antonyms* (*adj*) genuine, real, **2**. mimic; *synonyms* (*v*) mock, imitate, copy, mime, emulate, impersonate, parody, echo, personate, act, (*n*) imitator, mimicker, impersonator, actor, (*adj*) imitative, **3**. mime; *synonyms* (*n*) buffoon, clown, pantomime, mimer, mummer, acting, gesture, (*v*) monkey, simulate, cuckoo, **4**. taunt; *synonyms* (*v*) insult, sneer, bait, quip, rally, tease, twit, banter, rag, chaff, (*n*) hiss, dig, hoot, barrack, boo; *antonyms* (*v*) compliment, praise, respect, **5**. tease; *synonyms* (*v*) harass, annoy, molest, harry, kid, pester, plague, provoke, worry, badger, bother, bug, bully, irritate, joke, **6**. ridiculous; *synonyms* (*adj*) absurd, foolish, preposterous, funny, laughable, ludicrous, comical, farcical, inane,

nonsensical, amusing, comic, derisory, droll, irrational; *antonyms* (*adj*) sensible, inspiring, reasonable, **7**. ridicule; *synonyms* (*n*) irony, mockery, contempt, disdain, sarcasm, disparagement, jest, caricature, (*v*) rib, gird, belittle, blackguard, debunk, (*adj*) lampoon, satire.

kaenaena 1. tease; *synonyms* (*v*) harass, annoy, molest, harry, taunt, bait, kid, pester, plague, provoke, worry, badger, banter, bother, bug, **2**. rally; *synonyms* (*n*) assembly, meeting, convention, gathering, (*v*) gather, muster, congregate, convene, assemble, chaff, collect, converge, meet, mobilize, recover; *antonym* (*v*) demobilize.

kaenaenaki teased; *synonym* (*adj*) titillated.

kaenaki teased; *synonym* (*adj*) titillated.

kaeng 1. absolute; *synonyms* (*adj*) downright, peremptory, total, unconditional, categorical, full, real, unqualified, utter, actual, arbitrary, authoritative, certain, complete, (*n*) positive; *antonyms* (*adj*) partial, qualified, **2**. sure; *synonyms* (*adj*) reliable, secure, safe, firm, indisputable, dependable, assured, confident, definite, infallible, bound, absolute, (*adv*) certainly, (*v*) steady, convinced; *antonyms* (*adj*) doubtful, uncertain, unsure, hesitant, **3**. positive; *synonyms* (*adj*) affirmative, decisive, direct, explicit, favorable, incontrovertible, plus, sure, advantageous, clear, constructive, decided, perfect, plain, dogmatic; *antonyms* (*adj*) negative, derogatory, pessimistic, sad.

kaeta 1. correct; *synonyms* (*adj*) right, accurate, appropriate, becoming, nice, precise, proper, (*v*) adjust, amend, castigate, chastise, chasten, better, remedy, (*n*) true; *antonyms* (*adj*) incorrect, false, faulty, inappropriate, mistaken, improper, (*v*) wrong, spoil, **2**. interpret; *synonyms* (*v*) clarify, construe, elucidate, illustrate, read, understand, comment, gloss, decipher, explain, expound, render, depict, illuminate, consider, **3**. rectify; *synonyms* (*v*) correct, improve, refine, reform, mend, emend, redress, reclaim, fix, meliorate, regulate, repair, restore, discipline, (*adj*) straighten, **4**. straiten; *synonyms* (*v*) limit, distress, tighten, stint, constrain, squeeze, press, curtail, oppress, scant, bite, (*adj*) confine, restrain, crowd, coarctate, **5**. straighten; *synonyms* (*v*) tidy, unbend, neaten, extend, dress, stretch, unwind, straight, disentangle, comb, rear, rise; *antonyms* (*v*) bend, deform.

kaetaea rebuke; *synonyms* (*n*) blame, rebuff, reproach, admonition, reproof, (*v*) censure, reprimand, chide, berate, castigate, lecture, admonish, caution, check, scold; *antonyms* (*v*) praise, commend, compliment.

kaetaeaki rebuked; *synonyms* (*adj*) reprimanded, reproved, admonished, chastened.

kaetaki 1. interpreted; *synonyms* (*adj*) accurate, confined, exact, strict, taken, precise, restricted, rigidly, rigorous, severe, strained, tense, tight, **2.** corrected; *synonyms* (*adj*) chastised, amended, reformed, altered, chastened, disciplined, educated, refined, **3.** straitened; *synonyms* (*adj*) narrow, bigoted, circumscribed, close, contracted, covetous, illiberal, near, niggardly, parsimonious, pinching, (*n*) needy, distressed, necessitous, pinched, **4.** rectified, **5.** straightened.

kaeti 1. associated; *synonyms* (*adj*) connected, related, affiliated, allied, united, attendant, attached, confederate, joined, linked, alike; *antonym* (*adj*) unrelated, **2.** explain; *synonyms* (*v*) comment, elucidate, interpret, account, clarify, decipher, define, describe, enlighten, excuse, explicate, expound, gloss, solve, denote; *antonym* (*v*) confuse, **3.** affiliated; *synonym* (*v*) associated, **4.** direct; *synonyms* (*adj*) straight, blunt, immediate, (*v*) aim, channel, conduct, address, charge, control, dictate, head, administer, guide, lead, (*n*) command; *antonyms* (*adj*) indirect, roundabout, circuitous, oblique, second-hand, sideways, unplanned, (*v*) request.

kaetia straiten; *synonyms* (*v*) limit, distress, tighten, stint, constrain, squeeze, press, curtail, oppress, scant, bite, (*adj*) confine, restrain, crowd, coarctate.

kaetiaki straitened; *synonyms* (*adj*) narrow, accurate, bigoted, circumscribed, close, contracted, covetous, exact, illiberal, near, niggardly, (*n*) needy, distressed, necessitous, pinched.

kaetieti 1. instruct; *synonyms* (*v*) charge, advise, direct, educate, enlighten, teach, command, drill, indoctrinate, inform, apprise, bid, coach, discipline, edify; *antonym* (*v*) request, **2.** teach; *synonyms* (*v*) instruct, learn, lecture, school, form, tell, train, tutor, catechize, demonstrate, develop, discover, ground, (*adj*) guide, show.

kaetietiaki 1. instructed; *synonyms* (*adj*) erudite, leaned, lettered, (*adj*) educated, taught, tutored, enlightened, arranged, experienced, furnished, instruct, intelligent, qualified, schooled, provided, **2.** taught; *synonyms* (*v*) close, fast, firm, overwrought, taut, tense, tight, (*adj*) instructed, gentle, scholarly, well-bred, wise, skilled.

kaetiko straight; *synonyms* (*adv*) level, right, directly, (*adj*) erect, honest, even, flat, upright, fair, correct, just, perpendicular, proper, accurate, (*v*) direct; *antonyms* (*adv*) indirectly, (*adj*) curly, curved, diluted, winding, zigzag, askew, bent, curvy, knotted, twisted, twisting, wavy, circuitous, guarded.

kaeweananga tattle; *synonyms* (*n*) gabble, (*v*) blab, gossip, babble, chat, chatter, blather, blabber, prate, prattle, snitch, talk, blither, betray, chitchat.

kaewetaeka 1. report; *synonyms* (*n*) description, gossip, notice, name, fame, message, narration,

narrative, news, notification, recital, record, (*v*) account, describe, communicate; *antonym* (*n*) fact, **2.** tattle; *synonyms* (*n*) gabble, (*v*) blab, babble, chat, chatter, blather, blabber, prate, prattle, snitch, talk, blither, betray, chitchat, jaw.

kaewetaekaki reported; *synonyms* (*adj*) narrative, putative, reputed.

kai 1. easily; *synonyms* (*adv*) lightly, comfortably, readily, well, easy, handily, simply, smoothly, swimmingly, naturally; *antonyms* (*adv*) awkwardly, hardly, **2.** here; *synonyms* (*adv*) hither, in, about, arrived, available, indoors, inwards, (*n*) present, there, near, nearby, (*pron*) her, their; *antonym* (*adv*) out, **3.** readily; *synonyms* (*adv*) easily, promptly, soon, quick, freely, gladly, quickly, cheerfully, eagerly, pronto, willingly, commonly, openly, **4.** post; *synonyms* (*n*) place, function, office, position, pillar, stake, attitude, berth, column, job, (*v*) mail, locate, base, enter, lay, **5.** stiff; *synonyms* (*adj*) rigid, hard, difficult, formal, inflexible, firm, numb, rigorous, severe, solid, sturdy, (*adv*) tight, (*n*) stark, cadaver, corpse; *antonyms* (*adj*) relaxed, flexible, floppy, soft, supple, free, pliable, **6.** stick; *synonyms* (*n*) bar, club, (*v*) adhere, stab, attach, cling, fix, paste, staff, cohere, affix, bind, cleave, fasten, hold, **7.** promptly; *synonyms* (*adv*) immediately, forthwith, directly, exactly, instantly, now, fast, hastily, punctually, rapidly, swiftly, instantaneously, early, summarily, hurriedly; *antonyms* (*adv*) later, slowly, late, **8.** wood; *synonyms* (*n*) forest, timber, woods, tree, lumber, coppice, jungle, **9.** tree; *synonyms* (*n*) gallows, gibbet, stem, house, tribe, hierarchy, landmark, lentisk, ranking, trunk, filler, (*v*) corner, collar.

kaiaki 1. endeavor; *synonyms* (*n*) attempt, try, effort, essay, trial, enterprise, shot, work, endeavour, (*v*) struggle, strive, aim, labor, strain, offer; *antonym* (*v*) neglect, **2.** labor; *synonyms* (*n*) drudgery, endeavor, exertion, travail, childbirth, grind, birth, business, task, trouble, (*v*) toil, confinement, delivery, drudge, labour; *antonym* (*v*) rest, **3.** try; *synonyms* (*v*) test, prove, assay, examine, experiment, judge, sample, probe, seek, taste, adjudicate, hear, (*n*) chance, go, crack, **4.** struggle; *synonyms* (*n*) contest, battle, combat, conflict, scramble, scuffle, encounter, strife, war, warfare, (*v*) fight, dispute, quarrel, contend, fighting; *antonyms* (*v*) flourish, glide, **5.** strive; *synonyms* (*v*) aspire, compete, exert, reach, emulate, fag, force, slave, drive, tug, wrestle, moil, sweat.

kaiakiaki tried; *synonyms* (*adj*) reliable, tested, trustworthy, dependable, proved, experienced, baffled, beaten, believable, conquered, exhausted, faithful, just, practiced, qualified.

kaiakina 1. lodge; *synonyms* (*n*) house, club, cottage, hut, inn, (*v*) cabin, live, place, accommodate, deposit, fix, inhabit, quarter, (adj) abide, dwell, **2.** devoted; *synonyms* (adj) addicted, affectionate, ardent, consecrated, constant, faithful, fond, loyal, pious, committed, dutiful, eager, enthusiastic, keen, (prep) dedicated; *antonyms* (adj) uncommitted, disloyal, indifferent, **3.** committed; *synonyms* (v) compromised, (adj) attached, engaged, devoted, firm, involved, connected, active, affiliated, attentive, caring, confirmed, dependable, determined, established; *antonym* (adj) unattached, **4.** settle; *synonyms* (v) clarify, establish, pay, regulate, resolve, set, adjudicate, adjust, agree, conclude, decide, determine, drop, explain, (adj) confirm, **5.** quarter; *synonyms* (n) area, part, district, division, mercy, neighborhood, region, direction, portion, quart, (v) lodge, line, put, billet, canton, **6.** shelter; *synonyms* (n) guard, refuge, asylum, harbor, protect, protection, sanctuary, security, shield, covert, haven, (v) cover, screen, defend, (adj) defense; *antonym* (v) expose, **7.** station; *synonyms* (n) rank, position, seat, standing, base, depot, office, spot, condition, (v) locate, post, stand, lay, order, site.

kaiakinaki 1. settled; *synonyms* (adj) definite, fixed, set, firm, permanent, calm, certain, decided, established, defined, formed, confirmed, finished, sedate, standing; *antonym* (adj) uninhabited, **2.** sheltered; *synonyms* (adj) secure, comfortable, safe, screened, cozy, secluded, (v) protected, private; *antonym* (adj) desolate.

kaiba splint; *synonyms* (n) splinter, heel, shoe, sole, sprit, brace, fusee, stilts, stirrup.

kaibâba bamboo; *synonyms* (n) cane, stick, (adj) wicker, rush, woven.

kaibabaru 1. luscious; *synonyms* (adj) appetizing, delectable, delicious, juicy, rich, scrumptious, dulcet, delightful, succulent, sweet, tasty, voluptuous, yummy, delicate, lush; *antonym* (adj) dry, **2.** desirable; *synonyms* (adj) advisable, eligible, expedient, fitting, suitable, worthy, appropriate, alluring, charming, agreeable, covetable, enviable, fascinating, good, pleasant; *antonym* (adj) undesirable, **3.** lush; *synonyms* (adj) luscious, lavish, drunk, exuberant, green, plentiful, abundant, fertile, luxuriant, luxurious, profuse, rank, (n) alcoholic, (v) drunkard, sot; *antonym* (adj) infertile, **4.** lust; *synonyms* (n) appetite, craving, lecherousness, libido, cupidity, lechery, wantonness, (v) desire, hunger, itch, covet, crave, thirst, long, (adj) concupiscence, **5.** sensuous; *synonyms* (adj) sensible, sensitive, sensual, epicurean, carnal, sexy, exciting, fleshy, hedonistic, passionate, physical, pleasurable, pleasure-loving, pleasure-seeking, primrose.

kaibaea splint; *synonyms* (n) splinter, heel, shoe, sole, sprit, brace, fusee, stilts, stirrup.

kaibako 1. hollowed; *synonym* (adj) concave, **2.** smashed; *synonyms* (adj) shattered, drunk, inebriated, intoxicated, broken, plastered, sloshed, blotto, tipsy, besotted, pissed, tight; *antonym* (adj) sober.

kaibakoa 1. dint; *synonyms* (n) blow, indentation, depression, hollow, cavity, impression, (v) dent, indent, (adj) delve, dig, **2.** bash; *synonyms* (n) bang, knock, whack, crack, party, belt, (v) swipe, hit, punch, smash, strike, wallop, beat, slap, thump, **3.** hollow; *synonyms* (adj) blank, concave, empty, false, insincere, (n) hole, cave, groove, excavation, trench, gap, sinus, basin, (v) excavate, scoop; *antonyms* (adj) convex, (n) solid, hump, **4.** smash; *synonyms* (v) collapse, crash, break, crush, mash, shatter, defeat, demolish, pound, ruin, slam, fragment, (n) clash, blast, collision.

kaibakoaki 1. hollowed; *synonym* (adj) concave, **2.** smashed; *synonyms* (adj) shattered, drunk, inebriated, intoxicated, broken, plastered, sloshed, blotto, tipsy, besotted, pissed, tight; *antonym* (adj) sober.

kaibangaka cross; *synonyms* (n) crisscross, affliction, (v) intersect, baffle, cover, thwart, (adj) crabbed, crabby, angry, cantankerous, grouchy, grumpy, traverse, cranky, annoyed; *antonyms* (v) uncross, (adj) calm, good-tempered.

kaibangakaki crossed; *synonyms* (v) matted, unhinged, frustrated, (adj) across, crossbred, decussated, hybrid, interbred, intercrossed, mixed, intersected.

kaibea 1. stow; *synonyms* (v) pack, cram, charge, house, load, store, place, squeeze, deposit, crush, put, accommodate, compress, keep, stuff, **2.** stuff; *synonyms* (n) material, cloth, force, gear, matter, goods, stock, substance, (v) fill, jam, pad, ram, glut, gorge, shove; *antonym* (v) unstuff.

kaibeaki 1. stowed, **2.** stuffed; *synonyms* (v) farctate, (adj) full, crammed, packed, congested, replete, loaded, chock-full, crowded, fraught, abounding, big, brimming, concentrated, distended; *antonyms* (adj) empty, hungry.

kaibekua labor; *synonyms* (n) drudgery, effort, endeavor, exertion, travail, childbirth, grind, struggle, birth, business, (v) toil, confinement, delivery, drudge, labour; *antonym* (v) rest.

kaibekura overwork; *synonyms* (n) overworking, excess, load, (v) exhaust, strain, tax, exploit, overlabor, drive, abuse, wear, overdo, overplay, overply, (adj) overtask.

kaibibitia 1. exchange; *synonyms* (n) commutation, swap, switch, commerce, conversion, substitute, (v) change, barter, interchange, commute, counterchange, alternate, alter, cash, convert, **2.** interchange; *synonyms* (n) reciprocity, trade, traffic, interaction, alternation, intercourse, intersection, permutation, reciprocation, (v) exchange, reciprocate, transpose, bargain, permute, reverse, **3**. change; *synonyms* (*n*) shift, alteration, modification, variation, move, adjustment, amendment, development, (*v*) adapt, turn, twist, affect, adjust, amend, correct; *antonyms* (*v*) stay, leave, idle, maintain.

kaibibitiaki 1. changed; *synonyms* (*adj*) altered, transformed, varied, affected, changeling, different, disguised, distorted, inverse, malformed, misshapen, new, reformed, rehabilitated, tainted; *antonym* (*adj*) unchanged, **2**. exchanged; *synonyms* (*adj*) counterchanged, substituted.

kaibobua 1. enclose; *synonyms* (*v*) bound, confine, contain, circumscribe, corral, cover, encircle, encompass, enfold, envelop, beset, border, circle, embrace, (*adv*) compass; *antonyms* (*v*) expose, free, release, **2**. shut; *synonyms* (*v*) close, bar, seal, fasten, exclude, lock, (*adj*) closed, cut, tight, (*n*) end, finish; *antonym* (*v*) open.

kaibobuaki 1. enclosed; *synonyms* (*adj*) confined, surrounded, bounded, covered, limited, airtight, bordered, contained, controlled, delimited, inside, interior, internal, restricted, unexpressed, **2**. shut; *synonyms* (*v*) close, bar, seal, fasten, exclude, lock, (*adj*) closed, cut, tight, (*n*) end, finish, confine; *antonym* (*v*) open.

kaibuke ship; *synonyms* (*n*) boat, ferry, craft, bottom, (*v*) dispatch, send, forward, transport, consign, carry, embark, move, transfer, post, charge.

kaienikuria hustle; *synonyms* (*n*) hurry, haste, ado, cheat, commotion, con, fuss, (*v*) jostle, bustle, elbow, hasten, flurry, push, shove, work.

kaierake impatient; *synonyms* (*adj*) eager, hasty, anxious, petulant, fidgety, keen, edgy, quick, avid, enthusiastic, impetuous, irritable, restive, restless, testy; *antonyms* (*adj*) patient, enduring.

kaiewe 1. entangle; *synonyms* (*v*) embrangle, tangle, enmesh, complicate, confuse, involve, snarl, entwine, catch, ensnare, entrap, knot, (*n*) embroil, (*adj*) embarrass, bewilder; *antonym* (*v*) disentangle, **2**. jumble; *synonyms* (*n*) muddle, clutter, hodgepodge, disarray, disorder, confusion, blend, chaos, huddle, mess, miscellany, mixture, (*v*) mix, disturb, litter; *antonym* (*v*) order, **3**. complicate; *synonyms* (*v*) perplex, aggravate, entangle, puzzle, complexify, elaborate; *antonyms* (*v*) clarify, simplify.

kaiewea misstate; *synonyms* (*v*) falsify, misrepresent, twist, belie, color, garble, invent, lie, misinform, pervert, (*adv*) miscite, misreport.

kaieweaki 1. entangled; *synonyms* (*adj*) involved, complicated, intricate, embroiled, complex, foul, matted, tangled; *antonym* (*adj*) free, **2**. complicated; *synonyms* (*adj*) elaborate, hard, complicate, awkward, convoluted, deep, difficult, knotty, obscure, sophisticated, tortuous, tricky,

circuitous, detailed, indirect; *antonyms* (*adj*) simple, straightforward, clear, easy, **3**. jumbled; *synonyms* (*adj*) confused, disorderly, disordered, disorganized, untidy, cluttered, mixed, muddled, chaotic, incoherent, topsy-turvy; *antonyms* (*adj*) neat, tidy.

kaiia precipitate; *synonyms* (*v*) expedite, hurry, hasten, (*n*) deposit, accelerate, (*adj*) hasty, headlong, impetuous, sudden, immediate, instant, abrupt, hurried, precipitant, precipitous.

kaiiók friendship; *synonyms* (*n*) fellowship, association, affection, familiarity, amity, companionship, company, friendliness, intimacy, attachment, concord, comradeship, love, relationship, acquaintance; *antonyms* (*n*) enmity, hostility.

kaikai eat; *synonyms* (*v*) devour, consume, bite, dine, munch, corrode, deplete, drink, feed, finish, gnaw, gobble, gorge, graze, (*adj*) digest.

kaikeike 1. sigh; *synonyms* (*v*) suspire, breath, wail, suspiration, whimper, whine, sike, (*v*) moan, groan, breathe, languish, murmur, pine, whisper, **2**. sob; *synonyms* (*n*) cry, lament, sobbing, asshole, bastard, cocksucker, motherfucker, prick, shit, (*v*) weep, snivel, howl, sigh, pipe.

kaikewi snack; *synonyms* (*n*) bite, morsel, collation, meal, nibble, share, (*v*) nosh, bever, dejeuner, dinner, eat.

kaiki bail; *synonyms* (*n*) pledge, security, surety, bond, guarantee, handle, (*v*) deliver.

kaikoa 1. hoard; *synonyms* (*n*) store, bank, heap, stock, accumulation, fund, reserve, reservoir, (*v*) accumulate, amass, cache, collect, gather, garner, pile, **2**. save; *synonyms* (*v*) deliver, economize, rescue, conserve, free, hoard, keep, maintain, preserve, liberate, protect, redeem, retain, defend, (*prep*) except; *antonyms* (*v*) spend, squander, waste, **3**. store; *synonyms* (*n*) shop, market, business, emporium, supply, place, deposit, depository, depot, entrepot, memory, provision, repository, (*v*) save, pack.

kaikoaka 1. harm; *synonyms* (*n*) evil, hurt, detriment, bruise, wound, disadvantage, injury, disservice, (*v*) damage, abuse, blemish, injure, maim, poison, ravage; *antonyms* (*v*) enhance, benefit, **2**. maim; *synonyms* (*v*) mutilate, deform, mar, lacerate, deface, disable, disfigure, harm, impair, mangle, truncate, (*adj*) cripple, becripple, **3**. hurt; *synonyms* (*v*) pain, afflict, ail, cost, anguish, cut, grieve, offend, sting, (*adj*) upset, (*n*) ache, distress, lesion, agony, wrong; *antonyms* (*v*) encourage, (*adj*) uninjured, unhurt, **4**. wound; *synonyms* (*n*) scratch, sore, abrasion, graze, laceration, (*v*) stab, insult, bite, affront, contuse, pierce, slash, break, torture, pique.

kaikoakaki 1. hurt; *synonyms* (*v*) pain, wound, afflict, injure, ail, cost, (*adj*) evil, (*n*) harm, damage, detriment, ache, disadvantage, abuse, distress, lesion; *antonyms* (v) encourage, (adj) uninjured, unhurt, **2**. maimed; *synonyms* (adj) crippled, deformed, disabled, mutilated, faulty, game, truncated, mangled, (n) wounded, **3**. harmed; *synonyms* (adj) hurt, aggrieved, impaired, injured, abused, battered, debilitated, incapacitated, maltreated, mistreated, molested, neglected, **4**. wounded; *synonyms* (adj) bruised, bloody, (n) casualty, maimed; *antonym* (adj) composed.

kaikoaki 1. stored; *synonyms* (adj) charged, filled, fraught, freighted, laden, **2**. saved; *synonyms* (adj) protected, blessed, secure.

kaikonaka resemble; *synonyms* (v) imitate, seem, compare, correspond, agree, look, match, simulate, approximate, echo.

kaimaranga alternate; *synonyms* (adj) reciprocal, secondary, (v) reciprocate, change, fluctuate, interchange, vary, swerve, alter, (n) substitute, alternative, surrogate, standby, replacement, deputy; *antonym* (n) original.

kain inhabitant; *synonyms* (n) denizen, dweller, resident, citizen, occupant, occupier, tenant, indweller, native, (v) habitant.

kaina 1. day; *synonyms* (n) light, daylight, generation, age, daytime, epoch, time, crisis; *antonyms* (n) nighttime, night, **2**. close; *synonyms* (adj) near, adjacent, nearby, accurate, tight, approximate, narrow, (v) compact, stop, conclude, (adv) by, about, (n) end, finish, conclusion; *antonyms* (adj) distant, airy, fresh, loose, far, (v) open, start, **3**. latch; *synonyms* (n) catch, hasp, clasp, hook, (v) bar, bolt, lock, **4**. inhabit; *synonyms* (v) dwell, reside, abide, occupy, live, lodge, people, settle, be, bide, exist, roost, domicile, (n) habit, (adj) perch, **5**. populate; *synonym* (v) inhabit, **6**. shut; *synonyms* (v) close, seal, fasten, exclude, (adj) closed, cut, (n) confine.

kainababu 1. mute; *synonyms* (adj) dumb, silent, quiet, inarticulate, dummy, mum, speechless, tongueless, (v) muffle, dampen, deaden, dull, damp, hush, silence; *antonym* (adj) talkative, **2**. silent; *synonyms* (adj) motionless, mute, tacit, inaudible, incommunicative, noiseless, placid, reserved, reticent, still, taciturn, calm, implicit, soundless, dormant; *antonyms* (adj) noisy, spoken, loud, explicit, open, **3**. quiet; *synonyms* (adj) lull, pacify, cool, gentle, peaceful, tranquil, (v) appease, moderate, assuage, allay, easy, repose, (n) compose, ease, peace; *antonyms* (adj) vociferous, active, (n) noise.

kainabaea 1. cheat; *synonyms* (v) trick, beguile, betray, defraud, fake, beat, deceive, fleece, (n) swindle, con, fraud, bilk, impostor, sham, charlatan, **2**. sneak; *synonyms* (v) creep, lurk, crawl, fawn, filch, mouse, (n) cower, slink, informer, skulk, snitch, fink, (adj) coward, grovel, dastard.

kainabau bride; *synonyms* (n) wife, mate, woman, helpmate.

kainaki 1. closed; *synonyms* (v) close, tight, accurate, adjoining, attentive, (adj) blind, blocked, finished, shut, congested, fastened, exclusive, insular, stopped, airtight; *antonym* (adj) open, **2**. latched; *synonyms* (adj) locked, barred, bolted, fast, barricaded, blockaded, bonded, colorfast, debauched, degenerate, degraded, dissipated, dissolute, firm, flying, **3**. inhabited; *synonyms* (v) populous, accustomed, arrayed, clothed, dressed, habited, (adj) peopled, occupied, housing, colonized, suburban, uninhabited, uptown; *antonyms* (adj) empty, unoccupied, **4**. populated; *synonyms* (adj) thick, settled, **5**. shut; *synonyms* (v) bar, seal, fasten, exclude, lock, (adj) closed, cut, (n) end, finish, confine.

kainakoa 1. sink; *synonyms* (n) sag, basin, (v) decline, dip, droop, fall, set, descend, drop, fell, bury, collapse, decay, flag, founder; *antonyms* (v) rise, float, **2**. overwhelm; *synonyms* (v) defeat, flood, inundate, overcome, overpower, overthrow, crush, deluge, drown, engulf, astound, beat, overrun, overtake, overturn.

kainakoaki overwhelmed; *synonyms* (v) overborne, (adj) overcome, beaten, overpowered, vanquished, conquered, dumbfounded, engulfed, flooded, inundated, overthrown; *antonyms* (adj) victorious, unimpressed.

kainaoa propel; *synonyms* (v) drive, impel, launch, actuate, force, motivate, move, prompt, throw, carry, cast, fling, incite, push, shoot.

kainaomata 1. emancipate; *synonyms* (v) discharge, deliver, liberate, free, release, rescue, save, extricate, manumit, redeem, clear, (adj) exonerate, disburden, **2**. liberate; *synonyms* (v) emancipate, disengage, absolve, acquit, exempt, disentangle, excuse, disembarrass, turn, loose, loosen, rid, unfetter, unloose, issue; *antonyms* (v) confine, enslave, **3**. exempt; *synonyms* (adj) immune, released, privileged, (v) dispense, forgive, relieve, justify, except, spare; *antonyms* (adj) chargeable, liable, (v) nonexempt, **4**. rescue; *synonyms* (n) deliverance, delivery, salvage, liberation, salvation, extrication, redemption, recovery, relief, (v) ransom, recover, help, recapture, reclaim, retrieve; *antonyms* (n) involvement, loss, (v) abandon, **5**. release; *synonyms* (n) departure, exemption, disengagement, freedom, immunity, death, ease, emancipation, firing, freeing, liberty, (v) pardon, dismiss, allow, expel; *antonyms* (n) imprisonment, abduction, custody, preservation, (v) capture, imprison, arrest, catch.

kainaomataki 1. liberated; *synonyms* (adj) free, emancipated, loose, released, exempt, liberal, clear, disengaged, independent, charming, communicative, disentangled, dissevered, eager,

easy; *antonym* (*adj*) restricted, **2**. emancipated;
synonyms (*adj*) liberated, uncontrolled, boundless,
limitless, open, unbound, uninhibited, extricated,
3. rescued; *synonyms* (*adj*) reclaimed, saved,
protected, **4**. released; *synonym* (*adj*) discharged.

kainga 1. move; *synonyms* (*v*) act, affect, carry, excite,
go, impel, instigate, maneuver, touch, travel, flow,
bear, (*n*) motion, drive, transfer; *antonym* (*v*) stay,
2. heave; *synonyms* (*v*) cast, fling, chuck, gasp,
haul, toss, billow, drag, draw, elevate, gag, (*n*) tug,
raise, elevation, heaving.

kaingingnga loosen; *synonyms* (*v*) free, relax, loose,
detach, undo, discharge, ravel, fluff, unbend, untie,
liberate, slacken, (*adj*) disengage, (*n*) ease, release;
antonyms (*v*) tighten, compress, fasten.

kaingingngaki loosened; *synonyms* (*adj*) detached,
disentangled, loose, disengaged, extricated,
unsnarled.

kai-ni-kâbua spade; *synonyms* (*n*) coon, nigger,
jigaboo, nigra, spit, belch, eject, ringtail, saliva, (*v*)
dig, grub, delve, scoop, excavate, spay.

kainikatonga 1. haughty; *synonyms* (*adj*) disdainful,
arrogant, assuming, supercilious, contemptuous,
cavalier, lordly, proud, vain, contumelious, grand,
aloof, conceited, condescending, (*n*) boastful;
antonyms (*adj*) humble, modest, **2**. boastful;
synonyms (*adj*) big, braggart, pompous, vaunting,
thrasonical, vainglorious, ostentatious, **3**.
arrogant; *synonyms* (*adj*) haughty, imperious,
presumptuous, dogmatic, domineering, egotistical,
insolent, overbearing, chesty, cocky, high,
masterful, overconfident, overweening,
patronizing; *antonym* (*adj*) self-effacing, **4**.
insolent; *synonyms* (*adj*) abusive, audacious,
disrespectful, impertinent, brazen, fresh, impudent,
defiant, barefaced, bold, brassy, discourteous,
impolite, offensive, brash; *antonyms* (*adj*) polite,
respectful, **5**. conceited; *synonyms* (*adj*) egotistic,
smug, affected, complacent, narcissistic, priggish,
bigheaded, pretentious, swollen, (*v*) besotted, **6**.
proud; *synonyms* (*adj*) dignified, lofty, exalted,
gallant, majestic, elated, magnificent, noble,
sublime, superior, fine, eminent, glorious,
illustrious, (*v*) great; *antonyms* (*adj*) ashamed,
embarrassed.

kainnano 1. need; *synonyms* (*v*) lack, claim, require,
destitution, indigence, involve, (*n*) demand, want,
desire, deficiency, must, necessity, deprivation,
requirement, absence; *antonym* (*n*) wealth, **2**.
destitute; *synonyms* (*adj*) indigent, bankrupt,
broke, forlorn, impoverished, needy, poor, helpless,
impecunious, necessitous, penniless, void, wanting,
bare, (*v*) devoid; *antonym* (*adj*) rich, **3**. poor;
synonyms (*adj*) bad, low, miserable, paltry,
deplorable, destitute, evil, inadequate, insufficient,
pathetic, piteous, pitiful, meagre, (*v*) meager, (*n*)

mean; *antonyms* (*adj*) wealthy, excellent, first-rate,
privileged, well-off, admirable, good.

kainnanoa 1. need; *synonyms* (*v*) lack, claim, require,
destitution, indigence, involve, (*n*) demand, want,
desire, deficiency, must, necessity, deprivation,
requirement, absence; *antonym* (*n*) wealth, **2**.
needed; *synonyms* (*adj*) necessary, essential,
required, needful, requisite, indispensable, wanted,
wanting, compulsory, devoid, good, lacking,
mandatory, perfect, vital.

kainnanoaki needed; *synonyms* (*adj*) necessary,
essential, required, needful, requisite,
indispensable, wanted, wanting, compulsory,
devoid, good, lacking, mandatory, perfect, vital.

kainoki susceptible; *synonyms* (*adj*) impressionable,
receptive, responsive, sensitive, subject, liable,
delicate, pliable, susceptive, vulnerable, irritable,
open, amenable, exposed, impressible; *antonyms*
(*adj*) resistant, unsusceptible.

kainraea displace; *synonyms* (*v*) dislocate, dislodge,
dismiss, bump, depose, remove, shift, uproot,
cashier, discharge, disturb, eject, evacuate, expel,
move; *antonym* (*v*) replace.

kainraei displace; *synonyms* (*v*) dislocate, dislodge,
dismiss, bump, depose, remove, shift, uproot,
cashier, discharge, disturb, eject, evacuate, expel,
move; *antonym* (*v*) replace.

kainrou engaged; *synonyms* (*adj*) busy, occupied,
betrothed, affianced, employed, engrossed,
reserved, absorbed, working, pledged, bespoken,
booked, immersed, intent, rapt; *antonyms* (*adj*)
available, free.

kaintoka 1. disturb; *synonyms* (*v*) agitate, disconcert,
disorder, disquiet, distract, distress, perturb,
trouble, annoy, bother, commove, concern,
derange, disarrange, discompose; *antonyms* (*v*)
arrange, calm, please, smooth, soothe, **2**. interject;
synonyms (*v*) insert, interpose, inject, interfere,
intersperse, interpolate, interrupt, introduce, **3**.
interfere; *synonyms* (*v*) intercede, obstruct,
disturb, conflict, clash, hinder, impede, intervene,
meddle, tamper, contravene, encroach, jar, intrude,
(*adj*) intermeddle, **4**. interrupt; *synonyms* (*v*) break,
intermit, cut, pause, stop, arrest, check, disrupt,
heckle, bar, end, intercept, preclude, (*n*) suspend,
(*adj*) discontinue.

kaintokaki 1. interrupted; *synonyms* (*adj*)
discontinuous, fitful, intermittent, (*prep*) broken;
antonym (*adj*) constant, **2**. disturbed; *synonyms*
(*adj*) agitated, concerned, anxious, confused,
disquieted, restless, upset, worried, disordered,
bothered, deranged, disconcerted, distracted,
distressed, nervous; *antonyms* (*adj*) rational, calm,
relaxed.

kaintorua 1. reinforce; *synonyms* (*v*) bolster,
intensify, enhance, buttress, consolidate, fortify,
support, enforce, harden, recruit, reenforce,

strengthen, amplify, increase, assist; *antonym* (v) weaken, **2.** support; *synonyms* (n) help, stand, aid, keep, comfort, maintenance, patronage, (v) prop, back, brace, encourage, maintain, bear, boost, carry; *antonyms* (n) hindrance, (v) oppose, neglect, undermine, abandon, reject, **3.** straiten; *synonyms* (v) limit, distress, tighten, stint, constrain, squeeze, press, curtail, oppress, scant, bite, (adj) confine, restrain, crowd, coarctate, **4.** prop; *synonyms* (n) post, shore, fulcrum, property, mainstay, airscrew, column, pillar, stay, sustain, countenance, (v) hold, rest, uphold, buoy.

kaintoruaki 1. supported; *synonyms* (v) borne, carried, conveyed, supporting, (adj) bolstered, based, (adv) on, **2.** reinforced; *synonyms* (adj) strengthened, built, strong, assembled, resistant, shatterproof, toughened, unbreakable, armored, durable; *antonym* (adj) fragile, **3.** straitened; *synonyms* (adj) narrow, accurate, bigoted, circumscribed, close, contracted, covetous, exact, illiberal, near, niggardly, (n) needy, distressed, necessitous, pinched.

kainuano want; *synonyms* (v) need, desire, (n) lack, poverty, wish, deficiency, deprivation, famine, absence, dearth, demand, destitution, indigence, necessity, penury; *antonyms* (v) dislike, hate.

kainuanoaki wanted; *synonyms* (adj) required, cherished, invited, marketable, precious, treasured, welcome, necessary, comfortable, cute, essential, fugitive, notorious, urgent, (n) runaway; *antonym* (adj) undesirable.

kaira 1. direct; *synonyms* (adj) straight, blunt, immediate, (v) aim, channel, conduct, address, charge, control, dictate, head, administer, guide, lead, (n) command; *antonyms* (adj) indirect, roundabout, circuitous, oblique, second-hand, sideways, unplanned, (v) request, **2.** guide; *synonyms* (n) escort, directory, attendant, usher, chief, director, pilot, rule, (v) direct, govern, drive, bring, advise, cicerone, convey; *antonym* (v) follow, **3.** let; *synonyms* (v) allow, hire, admit, lease, leave, permit, charter, have, rent, grant, authorize, cause, countenance, demise; *antonyms* (v) forbid, prevent, **4.** man; *synonyms* (n) fellow, gentleman, guy, person, husband, homo, human, humanity, humankind, humans, individual, mankind, mortal, (obj) he, male; *antonym* (n) woman, **5.** led, **6.** lead; *synonyms* (v) contribute, chair, conduce, go, give, carry, dispose, run, show, take, (n) clue, advantage, hint, leash, (adj) front, **7.** conduct; *synonyms* (n) behavior, administration, manage, demeanor, performance, behaviour, deportment, (v) act, carriage, acquit, bearing, comport, accompany, bear, behave, **8.** control; *synonyms* (n) authority, care, hold, influence, sway, ascendancy, ascendency, dominance, regulation, (v) curb, bridle, handle, conquer, contain, order;

antonyms (n) freedom, weakness, (v) intensify, share, **9.** spearhead; *synonyms* (v) pioneer, (n) forefront, spearpoint.

kairakea hoist; *synonyms* (n) boost, elevator, winch, (v) elevate, haul, heave, lift, erect, raise, rear, uphold, exalt, wind.

kairaki 1. guided; *synonym* (adj) conducted, **2.** manned, **3.** let; *synonyms* (v) allow, hire, admit, lease, leave, permit, charter, have, rent, grant, authorize, cause, countenance, demise, (n) check; *antonyms* (v) forbid, prevent, **4.** directed; *synonyms* (adj) absorbed, concentrating, destined, focussed, formal, intent, prescript, subject, engaged, fixed, prescribed, rapt, (adv) under, **5.** led, **6.** controlled; *synonyms* (adj) limited, restrained, restricted, temperate, subdued, inhibited, banned, calm, chaste, composed, confidential, conscious, conservative, contained, deliberate; *antonym* (adj) spontaneous.

kairarika 1. reduce; *synonyms* (v) lower, pare, abbreviate, curtail, cut, debase, abate, condense, contract, diminish, shorten, concentrate, compress, (adj) abridge, lessen; *antonyms* (v) increase, bolster, expand, enlarge, exacerbate, intensify, **2.** thin; *synonyms* (adj) flimsy, gaunt, lean, light, slight, tenuous, emaciated, fine, rare, slim, sparse, (v) slender, dilute, meager, sheer; *antonyms* (adj) thick, fat, concentrated, chubby, plump, wide, broad, heavy, (v) thicken.

kairarikaki 1. thinned; *synonyms* (adj) cut, dilute, adulterate, attenuate, attenuated, diminished, down, emasculated, faded, gashed, gelded, hurt, lessened, mown, shortened, **2.** reduced; *synonyms* (adj) decreased, abridged, curtailed, miniature, cheap, limited, bated, inexpensive, low, lower, prostrate; *antonyms* (adj) expensive, complete.

kairariki 1. slim; *synonyms* (adj) slender, narrow, slight, thin, lean, remote, fine, skinny, flimsy, lithe, meager, light, (v) reduce, slenderize, cut; *antonyms* (adj) fat, heavy, hefty, plump, stocky, wide, **2.** thin; *synonyms* (adj) gaunt, tenuous, emaciated, rare, slim, sparse, bony, delicate, feeble, gossamer, (v) dilute, sheer, subtle, scanty, adulterate; *antonyms* (adj) thick, concentrated, chubby, broad, (v) thicken, **3.** skinny; *synonyms* (adj) scrawny, scraggy, underweight, weedy, lank, angular, spare, starving, (v) cortical, cutaneous, cuticular, dermal; *antonyms* (adj) brawny, well-built.

kairengarenga 1. intermix; *synonyms* (v) blend, intermingle, commingle, immix, amalgamate, commix, immingle, mingle, fuse, mix, **2.** blend; *synonyms* (n) alloy, amalgam, composite, amalgamation, brew, combination, compound, fusion, harmony, (v) combine, merge, incorporate, confound, go, join; *antonyms* (v) separate, divide,

3. intermingle; *synonyms* (*v*) confuse, intermix, interweave, knit, **4**. concoct; *synonyms* (*v*) hatch, invent, fabricate, contrive, create, devise, manufacture, plan, prepare, compose, conceive, cook, frame, make, ferment, **5**. mix; *synonyms* (*n*) mixture, concoction, miscellany, admixture, assortment, commixture, intermixture, (*v*) meld, aggregate, admix, associate, coalesce, consort, jumble, integrate.

kairengarengaki 1. mixed; *synonyms* (*adj*) miscellaneous, assorted, composite, heterogeneous, integrated, medley, impure, amalgamated, diverse, intermingled, motley, varied, indiscriminate, (*v*) blended, mingled; *antonyms* (*adj*) homogeneous, insular, pure, **2**. blended; *synonyms* (*v*) blent, polluted, stained, (*adj*) mixed, adulterate, beaten, conglomerate.

kairerebua 1. misconduct; *synonyms* (*n*) misbehavior, misdeed, crime, fault, misdemeanor, wrong, wrongdoing, sin, transgression, trespass, (*v*) misbehave, mishandle, (*adj*) mismanage, mismanagement, **2**. misrepresent; *synonyms* (*v*) distort, falsify, belie, garble, juggle, lie, pervert, warp, color, exaggerate, fake, fudge, overdraw, twist, cheat, **3**. delude; *synonyms* (*v*) deceive, betray, defraud, beguile, cozen, fool, mislead, trick, bamboozle, circumvent, cajole, disappoint, dupe, hoax, bluff, **4**. mislead; *synonyms* (*v*) con, misinform, delude, hoodwink, misdirect, misguide, seduce, entice, inveigle, outwit, swindle, decoy, **5**. dupe; *synonyms* (*n*) gull, victim, cully, prey, tool, butt, sap, (*v*) kid, befool, cod, trap, victimize, gudgeon, have, mock, **6**. misdirect; *synonyms* (*v*) abuse, corrupt, debase, debauch, demoralize, deprave, (*adj*) misconduct, **7**. deceive; *synonyms* (*v*) pretend, sell, humbug, cuckold, blind, double-cross, wile, bilk, fleece, mystify, ensnare, (*n*) fraud, (*adj*) dazzle.

kairerebuaki 1. misrepresented; *synonyms* (*adj*) distorted, twisted, changed, contorted, deformed, depraved, immoral, kinky, malformed, perverted, tainted, altered, misshapen, misused, perverse; *antonyms* (*adj*) unchanged, **2**. mislead; *synonyms* (*v*) betray, deceive, cheat, beguile, con, fool, misinform, delude, dupe, hoodwink, lie, misdirect, misguide, trick, seduce.

kairi 1. novice; *synonyms* (*n*) apprentice, beginner, fledgling, learner, amateur, greenhorn, neophyte, newcomer, freshman, initiate, novitiate, recruit, student, tyro, entrant, **2**. follower; *synonyms* (*n*) disciple, backer, devotee, fan, adherent, admirer, cohort, apostle, attendant, believer, partisan, proselyte, dependent, pupil, (*adj*) lover; *antonyms* (*n*) detractor, opponent, **3**. lank; *synonyms* (*v*) barren, (*adj*) gaunt, lean, angular, emaciated, meager, thin, scrawny, skinny, spare, spindly, **4**. bony; *synonyms* (*adj*) osseous, lanky, boney;

antonym (*adj*) rounded, **5**. disciple; *synonyms* (*n*) follower, scholar, supporter, convert, **6**. slim; *synonyms* (*adj*) slender, narrow, slight, remote, fine, flimsy, lithe, light, feeble, frail, small, (*v*) reduce, slenderize, cut, sly; *antonyms* (*adj*) fat, heavy, hefty, plump, stocky, wide, **7**. robust; *synonyms* (*adj*) healthy, firm, strong, athletic, brawny, muscular, powerful, vigorous, lusty, mighty, healthful, hearty, stout, (*n*) hardy, hard; *antonyms* (*adj*) weak, fragile, **8**. student; *synonyms* (*n*) novice, savant, trainee, educatee; *antonym* (*n*) teacher.

kairiri 1. guide; *synonyms* (*n*) escort, directory, attendant, control, usher, chief, (*v*) direct, conduct, govern, drive, channel, bring, advise, cicerone, convey; *antonym* (*v*) follow, **2**. conduct; *synonyms* (*n*) behavior, administration, manage, demeanor, lead, performance, (*v*) act, administer, carriage, acquit, bearing, carry, comport, show, accompany.

kaiririaki guided; *synonym* (*adj*) conducted.

kairiribai 1. foe; *synonyms* (*n*) adversary, enemy, antagonist, opponent, competitor, opposition, assailant, foeman, rival, challenger, contender; *antonym* (*n*) ally, **2**. enemy; *synonyms* (*n*) foe, hostile; *antonyms* (*n*) friend, supporter, **3**. rival; *synonyms* (*adj*) competitive, competing, (*v*) emulate, contestant, corrival, competition, outvie, (*v*) equal, contest, match, compete, contend, oppose, compare, meet; *antonyms* (*adj*) allied, (*n*) partner, **4**. thwart; *synonyms* (*v*) foil, frustrate, baffle, hinder, impede, obstruct, prevent, defeat, disappoint, bilk, block, resist, stop, elude, (*adv*) cross, **5**. opponent; *synonyms* (*n*) contrary, opposer, opposite, fighter, player, withstander, (*adj*) opposing; *antonym* (*n*) follower, **6**. spite; *synonyms* (*n*) resentment, malice, grudge, hatred, malevolence, pique, animosity, maliciousness, nastiness, rancor, venom, envy, bitterness, despite, hate; *antonym* (*n*) kindness.

kairiribaiaki thwarted; *synonyms* (*adj*) frustrated, disappointed, defeated, discomfited, foiled, baffled, balked, beaten, discouraged, disenchanted, disillusioned, dissatisfied, embarrassed, saddened, upset; *antonym* (*adj*) successful.

kairoa ignite; *synonyms* (*v*) light, kindle, arouse, enkindle, fire, heat, flame, agitate, burn, excite, inflame, detonate, incite, provoke, awaken; *antonym* (*v*) extinguish.

kairoaki ignited; *synonyms* (*v*) burning, active, flowing, laving, live, lively, quickening, running, vigorous, (*adj*) kindled, enkindled, flaming, ablaze, fiery.

kairoro 1. insist; *synonyms* (*v*) affirm, assert, contend, claim, asseverate, declare, maintain, urge, importune, press, argue, force, dwell, hold, persist, **2**. beseech; *synonyms* (*v*) entreat, beg, adjure, ask, crave, implore, pray, request, appeal, conjure, plead, solicit, sue, supplicate, bid, **3**. urge; *synonyms* (*n*) goad, spur, drive, impulse, (*v*) push, advocate, impel, incite, induce, inspire, instigate, persuade, prompt, promote, (*adj*) quicken; *antonym* (*v*) discourage.

kairoroa 1. force; *synonyms* (*n*) energy, strength, agency, effect, enforce, impetus, (*v*) drive, coerce, pressure, squeeze, thrust, compel, cram, impel, (*adj*) constrain; *antonyms* (*n*) weakness, persuasion, **2**. compel; *synonyms* (*v*) force, cause, command, make, necessitate, obligate, oblige, press, require, bind, impose, intimidate, push, urge, bend, **3**. persuade; *synonyms* (*v*) convince, inveigle, allure, assure, cajole, coax, entice, induce, influence, argue, exhort, lure, incite, get, tempt; *antonyms* (*v*) discourage, dissuade, **4**. urge; *synonyms* (*n*) goad, spur, impulse, (*v*) advocate, inspire, instigate, persuade, prompt, promote, entreat, expedite, advise, cheer, counsel, (*adj*) quicken.

kairoroaki forced; *synonyms* (*adj*) compulsory, compelled, bound, artificial, constrained, involuntary, unnatural, farfetched, false, labored, obligatory, obliged, strained; *antonyms* (*adj*) free, unprovoked, spontaneous, voluntary.

kairua 1. confound; *synonyms* (*v*) bewilder, baffle, confuse, astonish, nonplus, perplex, puzzle, amaze, astound, bamboozle, mistake, mystify, complicate, (*n*) surprise, (*adj*) stupefy; *antonym* (*v*) enlighten, **2**. error; *synonyms* (*n*) deviation, blunder, fault, wrong, delusion, lapse, oversight, crime, defect, demerit, guilt, misunderstanding, falsehood, confusion, erroneousness; *antonym* (*n*) correctness, **3**. err; *synonyms* (*v*) stray, stumble, deviate, misjudge, sin, slip, trip, wander, digress, swerve, trespass, depart, drift, **4**. amiss; *synonyms* (*adv*) badly, poorly, awry, wrongly, adrift, (*adj*) bad, haywire, astray, faulty; *antonyms* (*adv*) right, (*adj*) suitable, **5**. mistake; *synonyms* (*n*) error, failure, misapprehension, misconception, inaccuracy, misprint, foolishness, fallacy, fail, (*v*) err, misapprehend, misunderstand, misconstrue, confound, misinterpret, **6**. stumble; *synonyms* (*v*) fall, flounder, fumble, falter, hit, stammer, bumble, reel, totter, tumble, wobble, (*n*) lurch, misstep, stagger, (*adj*) botch.

kairuaki 1. confounded; *synonyms* (*adj*) bemused, bewildered, accursed, abashed, baffled, befuddled, confused, cursed, execrable, puzzled, aghast, abominable, **2**. mistaken; *synonyms* (*adj*) incorrect, erroneous, false, wrong, misguided, inaccurate, fallacious, untrue, misleading; *antonym* (*adj*) correct.

kairuwaea 1. lodge; *synonyms* (*n*) house, club, cottage, hut, inn, (*v*) cabin, live, place, accommodate, deposit, fix, inhabit, quarter, (*adj*) abide, dwell, **2**. harbor; *synonyms* (*n*) dock,

asylum, cover, harbour, port, shelter, haven, quay, wharf, (*v*) entertain, shield, contain, cherish, conceal, nurse, **3**. entertain; *synonyms* (*v*) amuse, divert, delight, bear, beguile, admit, harbor, hold, interest, distract, comfort, indulge, tickle, feast, (*n*) engage; *antonym* (*v*) bore.

kairuwaeaki entertained; *synonyms* (*adj*) amused, diverted.

kaita 1. empty; *synonyms* (*adj*) discharge, hollow, destitute, bare, blank, barren, abandoned, deserted, vain, (*v*) drain, clear, deplete, desolate, pour, spill; *antonyms* (*adj*) full, crowded, meaningful, packed, brimming, inhabited, occupied, swarming, cultivated, filled, laden, (*v*) fill, **2**. exhaust; *synonyms* (*v*) consume, spend, empty, tire, expend, sap, use, dry, debilitate, enervate, evacuate, finish, (*adj*) waste, dissipate, fatigue; *antonyms* (*v*) conserve, refresh, invigorate, **3**. clear; *synonyms* (*adj*) clean, certain, open, apparent, distinct, light, (*v*) bright, acquit, absolute, free, net, absolve, clarify, definite, exculpate; *antonyms* (*adj*) cloudy, opaque, unclear, dark, fuzzy, hazy, incomprehensible, obscure, uncertain, vague, ambiguous, blurry, confused, confusing, (*v*) convict, **4**. void; *synonyms* (*adj*) null, vacant, invalid, vacuous, devoid, (*n*) emptiness, vacancy, (*v*) nullify, quash, rescind, annul, avoid, cancel, invalidate, repeal; *antonyms* (*adj*) valid, (*v*) validate, **5**. vacate; *synonyms* (*v*) quit, abandon, resign, abdicate, leave, relinquish, renounce, desert, revoke, depart, reverse, withdraw, forsake, abrogate, (*adj*) void.

kaitaka purge; *synonyms* (*n*) purgation, purification, expulsion, cathartic, (*v*) cleanse, clean, expurgate, eradicate, clear, liquidate, purify, remove, scour, absolve, eliminate; *antonym* (*v*) binge.

kaitaki 1. emptied; *synonyms* (*adj*) void, voided, depleted, annulled, open, vacuous, evacuated, invalidated, **2**. cleared; *synonyms* (*adj*) clear, absolved, clean, blank, bleak, empty, exculpated, exempt, exonerated, innocent, official, vacant, vindicated, blameless, decipherable, **3**. exhausted; *synonyms* (*v*) weak, (*adj*) drained, fatigued, spent, tired, gone, dry, beat, enervated, faint, jaded, weary, expended, dead, finished; *antonyms* (*adj*) energetic, fresh, refreshed, strong.

kaitara 1. con; *synonyms* (*n*) swindle, bunko, captive, convict, deception, (*v*) cheat, trick, bunco, defraud, hoax, bamboozle, bilk, deceive, dupe, fleece; *antonym* (*n*) pro, **2**. confront; *synonyms* (*v*) face, front, oppose, challenge, approach, brave, defy, collate, affront, play, compare, dare, encounter, meet, resist; *antonyms* (*v*) avoid, evade, **3**. face; *synonyms* (*n*) look, aspect, countenance, expression, side, top, exterior, appearance, facade, surface, (*v*) confront, audacity, veneer, visage, breast; *antonym* (*v*) back, **4**. adverse; *synonyms* (*adj*) contrary, unfavorable, harmful, hostile, untoward, adversary, averse, counter, inimical, negative, repugnant, antagonistic, bad, contradictory, (n) opposite; *antonym* (adj) favorable, **5.** encounter; *synonyms* (n) collision, combat, battle, conflict, contest, action, brush, confrontation, impact, (v) clash, experience, find, rencounter, detect, bump; *antonym* (v) retreat, **6.** ultimate; *synonyms* (adj) last, conclusive, final, end, supreme, definitive, decisive, elemental, extreme, farthest, furthest, eventual, primary, ending, (n) maximum; *antonyms* (adj) opening, first.

kaitatan desire; *synonyms* (n) ambition, hope, aspiration, will, wish, craving, dream, impulse, (v) fancy, aspire, seek, want, aim, choose, crave; *antonyms* (n) aversion, reality, (v) dislike, hate.

kaitatanaki desired; *synonyms* (adj) coveted, craved, desirable, chosen, favorite, wanted, needed, welcome, beloved, adored, appropriate, pet, preferred, (v) complying, consenting; *antonym* (adj) undesirable.

kaitau thank; *synonyms* (v) acknowledge, bless, remercy, kiss, praise.

kaiti 1. clear; *synonyms* (adj) clean, certain, open, apparent, distinct, empty, (v) bright, acquit, absolute, free, net, absolve, clarify, definite, discharge; *antonyms* (adj) cloudy, opaque, unclear, dark, fuzzy, hazy, incomprehensible, obscure, uncertain, vague, ambiguous, blurry, confused, confusing, (v) convict, **2.** purify; *synonyms* (v) disinfect, purge, distill, refine, sanctify, depurate, chasten, lustrate, expurgate, filter, improve, bless, consecrate, (adj) clear, cleanse; *antonyms* (v) contaminate, pollute.

kaitiaka 1. clean; *synonyms* (adj) clear, fair, antiseptic, blank, pure, chaste, adroit, tidy, unblemished, (v) brush, cleanse, bathe, clarify, disinfect, sweep; *antonyms* (adj) filthy, unclean, muddy, unhygienic, full, syrupy, tainted, unwholesome, (v) dirty, soil, contaminate, pollute, **2.** purify; *synonyms* (v) clean, purge, distill, refine, sanctify, depurate, chasten, lustrate, expurgate, filter, improve, bless, consecrate, defecate, rinse, **3.** sweep; *synonyms* (n) compass, expanse, range, scope, field, stretch, area, room, (v) rake, reach, sail, sway, shot, (adj) curve, comb.

kaitiakaki 1. cleaned; *synonyms* (adj) cleansed, spick-and-span, (n) curried, prepared, **2.** purified; *synonyms* (adj) refined, clean, pure, corrected, chastened, defecate, disciplined, elegant, exalted, graceful, neat, polished, processed, pured, sanitary, **3.** swept.

kaitiaki 1. cleared; *synonyms* (adj) clear, absolved, clean, blank, bleak, empty, exculpated, exempt, exonerated, innocent, official, open, vacant, vindicated, blameless, **2.** purified; *synonyms* (adj) refined, pure, corrected, chastened, defecate,

disciplined, elegant, exalted, graceful, neat, polished, processed, pured, sanitary, sublimate.

kaitibo meet; *synonyms* (v) converge, find, assemble, congregate, encounter, fulfill, gather, answer, cross, confront, intersect, abut, concur, adjoin, (adj) fit; *antonyms* (v) avoid, disperse, diverge.

kaitiboa introduce; *synonyms* (v) insert, interject, inject, acquaint, advance, enter, exhibit, implant, inaugurate, infuse, initiate, precede, present, instill, interpose; *antonym* (v) end.

kaitiboaki introduced; *synonyms* (adj) exotic, familiar, imported, interpolated.

kaitira 1. final; *synonyms* (adj) conclusive, decisive, definite, extreme, latter, definitive, last, ultimate, irrevocable, decided, concluding, eventual, net, peremptory, firm; *antonyms* (adj) first, opening, preliminary, **2.** last; *synonyms* (v) endure, continue, hold, exist, live, dwell, go, (n) abide, conclusion, finale, finis, finish, (adj) closing, final, farthest, **3.** latest; *synonyms* (adj) fresh, current, modern, new, hot, contemporary, newest, fashionable, stylish, (n) vogue; *antonym* (adj) old.

kaitoan opposite; *synonyms* (adj) adverse, contradictory, diametric, different, hostile, opposing, opposed, antagonistic, (adv) counter, (n) contrary, opponent, adversary, contradiction, antonym, (pron) other; *antonym* (adj) similar.

kaitoana 1. counter; *synonyms* (n) buffet, bench, reverse, (v) reply, contradict, resist, answer, react, respond, retort, thwart, (adj) converse, antagonistic, contrary, opposite, **2.** oppose; *synonyms* (v) object, contest, contend, contravene, controvert, counteract, fight, counter, disagree, dissent, combat, confront, defend, dispute, gainsay; *antonyms* (v) support, advocate, agree, back, advise.

kaitoanaki opposed; *synonyms* (adj) conflicting, contradictory, hostile, contrary, antagonistic, opposing, adverse, averse, contrasted, repugnant, incompatible, irreconcilable, counter, against, opposite.

kaitonginakoa panic; *synonyms* (n) alarm, dismay, horror, scare, dread, fright, anxiety, fear, flap, hysteria, funk, (v) shock, (adj) consternation, terror, awe; *antonym* (n) composure.

kaitonginakoaki panicked; *synonyms* (adj) panicky, scared, frightened, terrified.

kaiwa 1. divination; *synonyms* (n) forecast, augury, prediction, foretelling, prophecy, soothsaying, sorcery, witchcraft, **2.** sorcery; *synonyms* (n) charm, incantation, enchantment, magic, necromancy, witchery, fascination, spell, wizardry, **3.** prognosticate; *synonyms* (v) augur, predict, foretell, portend, presage, anticipate, bode, divine, forebode, foreshow, prophesy, foresee, betoken, call, herald.

kaka 1. cast; *synonyms* (v) hurl, throw, form, shed, stamp, fling, shape, chuck, dump, figure, heave, mould, (n) appearance, casting, mold, **2.** fling; *synonyms* (n) crack, go, lob, (v) cast, toss, dash, pitch, shoot, discard, rush, slam, break, launch, project, propel; *antonym* (v) catch, **3.** eject; *synonyms* (v) discharge, dislodge, dismiss, displace, emit, evict, expel, banish, depose, empty, evacuate, spew, drop, ejaculate, disgorge, **4.** launch; *synonyms* (n) boat, inauguration, initiation, launching, (v) initiate, begin, dart, found, fire, introduce, commence, establish, inaugurate, institute, start; *antonym* (v) end, **5.** hurl; *synonyms* (v) pelt, send, bowl, hurtle, precipitate, vomit, drive, flip, force, jerk, shy, sling, thrust, contrive, deposit, **6.** toss; *synonyms* (n) pass, (v) agitate, shake, convulse, roll, churn, stir, thrash, dispose, tumble, flounder, huddle, lag, lurch, muddle, **7.** suppress; *synonyms* (v) repress, subdue, check, crush, curb, quell, restrain, silence, stifle, subjugate, strangle, conceal, control, inhibit, oppress; *antonym* (v) express.

kâkâ 1. noise; *synonyms* (n) clatter, clamor, hubbub, racket, sound, din, disturbance, echo, uproar, buzz, clang, commotion, crack, crash, (v) fame; *antonyms* (n) silence, quiet, **2.** outcry; *synonyms* (n) noise, call, exclaim, exclamation, protest, roar, bawl, tumult, yell, (v) cry, shout, vociferation, hollo.

kakaaua quadruple; *synonyms* (adj) fourfold, quadruplicate, quadrable, quadrumanous, (v) double.

kakaauba 1. majestic; *synonyms* (adj) grand, lofty, imposing, awesome, imperial, royal, stately, exalted, glorious, kingly, dignified, magnificent, solemn, grandiose, (adv) regal, **2.** awesome; *synonyms* (adj) terrific, formidable, majestic, amazing, frightful, eerie, impressive, tremendous, wonderful, marvelous, astounding, awful, frightening, great, stunning; *antonym* (adj) insignificant.

kakaauongo hark; *synonyms* (n) look, (v) harken, hear, hearken, listen, heed.

kakaautakia 1. loiter; *synonyms* (v) linger, dawdle, lag, loaf, dally, saunter, tarry, prowl, idle, loll, continue, (adj) delay, lounge, hesitate, (adv) crawl, **2.** linger; *synonyms* (v) hover, loiter, stay, procrastinate, remain, abide, endure, drag, dwell, stop, persist, stroll, trail, cling, (adv) creep; *antonyms* (v) leave, hurry, **3.** delay; *synonyms* (n) pause, arrest, deferment, wait, deferral, extension, holdup, (v) defer, check, postpone, reserve, adjourn, break, detain, hinder; *antonyms* (n) punctuality, decisiveness, (v) rush, advance, **4.** dwindle; *synonyms* (v) abate, decline, decrease, diminish, contract, fade, fall, lessen, recede, reduce, wane, decay, drop, ebb, fail; *antonym* (v) increase, **5.** drift; *synonyms* (n) stream, current, course, tendency, tone, bearing, design, gist, (v) aim, blow, float, ramble, cast, glide, (adj) flow, **6.** amble; *synonyms* (v) walk, mosey, wander, gallop, hike, (n) trot, promenade, run, **7.** dawdle; *synonyms* (v) amble, idler, **8.** loaf; *synonyms* (v) laze, lurk, (adj) block, lump, poke, **9.** stroll; *synonyms* (n) tramp, excursion, perambulation, turn, journey, nomadize, ride, (v) roam, range, jaunt, meander, trip, gad, rove, stray.

kakaautakiaki delayed; *synonyms* (adj) belated, late, tardy, protracted, deferred, slow, (adv) behind; *antonyms* (adj) brief, early.

kakae 1. desire; *synonyms* (n) ambition, hope, aspiration, will, wish, craving, dream, impulse, (v) fancy, aspire, seek, want, aim, choose, crave; *antonyms* (n) aversion, reality, (v) dislike, hate, **2.** look; *synonyms* (v) seem, appear, expect, figure, attend, (n) face, gaze, appearance, aspect, air, countenance, expression, glance, guise, view, **3.** covet; *synonyms* (v) begrudge, desire, envy, long, grudge, hanker, **4.** seek; *synonyms* (v) search, attempt, endeavor, hunt, look, inquire, beg, explore, pursue, quest, investigate, research, follow, demand, (n) ask, **5.** search; *synonyms* (n) pursuit, examination, exploration, inquiry, inspection, study, hunting, investigation, (v) grope, ransack, rummage, pry, examine, forage, inspect.

kakaea seek; *synonyms* (v) search, attempt, endeavor, hunt, look, inquire, aspire, beg, explore, pursue, quest, investigate, research, follow, (n) ask.

kakaeaki 1. coveted; *synonyms* (adj) desired, craved, exceptional, impressive, marketable, **2.** desired; *synonyms* (adj) coveted, desirable, chosen, favorite, wanted, needed, welcome, beloved, adored, appropriate, pet, preferred, proper, (v) complying, consenting; *antonym* (adj) undesirable.

kakaenaena mock; *synonyms* (adj) counterfeit, (v) deride, ridicule, burlesque, gibe, ape, flout, mimic, scoff, scorn, sham, taunt, bemock, (n) jeer, derision; *antonyms* (adj) genuine, real.

kakaero crow; *synonyms* (n) gasconade, crowing, bragging, (v) boast, brag, cackle, chuckle, cry, exult, triumph, bluster, giggle, gloat, (adj) raven, charcoal.

kakaeutakia 1. flaunt; *synonyms* (v) display, exhibit, flash, flourish, show, boast, brandish, parade, strut, swank, wave, expose, (n) glitter, **2.** strut; *synonyms* (n) buttress, brace, prop, splurge, beam, (v) prance, stalk, swagger, stride, support, cock, flaunt, brag, vaunt, bluster, **3.** pose; *synonyms* (v) attitudinize, masquerade, impersonate, lay, perplex, place, fix, (n) attitude, position, affectation, airs, bearing, posture, stand, manner, **4.** parade; *synonyms* (n) ostentation, pageant, ceremony, pomp, demonstration, file, procession, review, (v) demonstrate, array, troop, walk, process, promenade, demo.

kakai 1. inhabit; *synonyms* (*v*) dwell, reside, abide, occupy, live, lodge, people, settle, be, bide, exist, roost, domicile, (*n*) habit, (*adj*) perch, **2.** badger; *synonyms* (*v*) pester, annoy, tease, bother, harass, beleaguer, bug, harry, hassle, hound, molest, plague, worry, disturb, aggravate, **3.** inhabited; *synonyms* (*v*) populous, accustomed, arrayed, clothed, dressed, habited, (*adj*) peopled, occupied, housing, colonized, suburban, uninhabited, uptown; *antonyms* (*adj*) empty, unoccupied, **4.** disturb; *synonyms* (*v*) agitate, disconcert, disorder, disquiet, distract, distress, perturb, trouble, commove, concern, derange, disarrange, discompose, disrupt, upset; *antonyms* (*v*) arrange, calm, please, smooth, soothe, **5.** hound; *synonyms* (*n*) dog, blackguard, cad, cur, (*v*) bloodhound, chase, hunt, badger, course, hound, pursue, drive, haunt, persecute, **6.** irritate; *synonyms* (*v*) chafe, fret, gall, incense, anger, displease, enrage, goad, grate, infuriate, provoke, vex, exasperate, inflame, irk; *antonym* (*v*) pacify, **7.** annoy; *synonyms* (*v*) irritate, afflict, rile, torment, bore, devil, get, infest, madden, nag, nettle, offend, rankle, (*n*) annoyance, (*adj*) excite, **8.** harass; *synonyms* (*v*) beset, grind, besiege, fatigue, oppress, bully, chevy, chivvy, exhaust, jade, press, grieve, embarrass, (*adj*) tire, weary, **9.** bother; *synonyms* (*v*) bedevil, crucify, discommode, inconvenience, perplex, bewilder, ruffle, (*n*) fuss, pain, ado, nuisance, aggravation, disturbance, annoying, (*adj*) nonplus; *antonyms* (*v*) delight, (*n*) pleasure, **10.** nag; *synonyms* (*n*) hack, horse, hackney, nagger, plug, (*v*) complain, gripe, scold, grouse, carp, moan, (*adj*) bicker, wrangle, brangle, jangle, **11.** heckle; *synonyms* (*v*) hatchel, taunt, interrupt, (*adj*) hackle, **12.** easily; *synonyms* (*adv*) lightly, comfortably, readily, well, easy, handily, simply, smoothly, swimmingly, naturally; *antonyms* (*adv*) awkwardly, hardly, **13.** stiff; *synonyms* (*adj*) rigid, hard, difficult, formal, inflexible, firm, numb, rigorous, severe, solid, sturdy, (*adv*) tight, (*n*) stark, cadaver, corpse; *antonyms* (*adj*) relaxed, flexible, floppy, soft, supple, free, pliable, **14.** trouble; *synonyms* (*n*) anxiety, difficulty, care, hardship, load, misfortune, problem, grief, matter, adversity, (*v*) burden, confuse, incommode, anguish, (*adj*) affliction, **15.** torment; *synonyms* (*n*) agony, suffering, curse, misery, harassment, agonize, martyrdom, badgering, (*v*) torture, rack, martyr, tantalize, excruciate, hurt, wring, **16.** occupied; *synonyms* (*adj*) busy, engaged, employed, diligent, absorbed, active, engrossed, working, affianced, betrothed, concerned, industrious, involved; *antonyms* (*adj*) vacant, available, idle, **17.** worry; *synonyms* (*v*) fear, mind, stress, alarm, brood, (*n*) sorrow, apprehension, misgiving, vexation, unrest, irritation, agitation, trepidation, uneasiness, cark;

antonyms (*v*) reassure, (*n*) calmness, reassurance, **18.** pester; *synonyms* (*v*) heckle, importune, rag.

kakaiaki 1. annoyed; *synonyms* (*adj*) angry, irate, irritated, vexed, aggravated, angered, cross, disgruntled, displeased, exasperated, infuriated, offended, peeved, pestered, resentful; *antonyms* (*adj*) calm, pleased, unprovoked, smiling, **2.** harassed; *synonyms* (*adj*) annoyed, beleaguered, distraught, distressed, drawn, harried, hurried, obsessed, stressed, uneasy, agitated, anxious, besieged, careworn, fraught; *antonym* (*adj*) relaxed, **3.** irritated; *synonyms* (*adj*) enraged, furious, incensed, inflamed, nettled, provoked, sore, mad, riled, **4.** disturbed; *synonyms* (*adj*) concerned, confused, disquieted, restless, upset, worried, disordered, bothered, deranged, disconcerted, distracted, nervous, tumultuous, turbulent, unsettled; *antonym* (*adj*) rational, **5.** chafed; *synonyms* (*v*) fretted, variegated, (*adj*) galled, raw, uncomfortable, **6.** inhabited; *synonyms* (*v*) populous, accustomed, arrayed, clothed, dressed, habited, (*adj*) peopled, occupied, housing, colonized, suburban, uninhabited, uptown; *antonyms* (*adj*) empty, unoccupied, **7.** bothered; *synonyms* (*adj*) disturbed, troubled, **8.** troubled; *synonyms* (*adj*) solicitous, apprehensive, perturbed, disruptive, doubtful, riotous, unhappy; *antonyms* (*adj*) untroubled, composed, unconcerned, **9.** tormented; *synonyms* (*adj*) anguished, tortured, hagridden, beset, cruciate, cruciform, miserable, plagued, suffering, agonized, fearful, littered, painful, sorrowful; *antonym* (*adj*) content, **10.** pestered; *synonyms* (*adj*) harassed, miffed, pissed, roiled, steamed, stung, **11.** terminal; *synonyms* (*adj*) final, last, definitive, endmost, fatal, concluding, incurable, (*n*) depot, end, extremity, terminus, boundary, station, destination, **12.** worried; *synonyms* (*adj*) afraid, alarmed, fretful, tense, (*v*) afflicted, frightened, pained; *antonyms* (*adj*) carefree, reassured.

kakaianga 1. altruistic; *synonyms* (*adj*) selfless, unselfish, charitable, generous, benevolent, humanitarian, kind, magnanimous, philanthropic; *antonyms* (*adj*) self-centered, selfish, egoistic, **2.** charitable; *synonyms* (*adj*) merciful, clement, gentle, bountiful, humane, kindly, lenient, liberal, compassionate, forbearing, munificent, hospitable, large, altruistic, bighearted; *antonyms* (*adj*) unforgiving, mean, nasty, uncharitable, **3.** benevolent; *synonyms* (*adj*) good, gracious, loving, considerate, tender, affable, benign, eleemosynary, friendly, helpful, openhanded, propitious, (*n*) beneficent, nice, sympathetic; *antonyms* (*adj*) malevolent, malicious, unfeeling, **4.** generous; *synonyms* (*adj*) ample, full, abundant, copious, fair, flush, spacious, rich, bounteous, broad, considerable, handsome, noble, open, (n) free; *antonyms* (adj) stingy, meager, measly, miserly, small, tightfisted, avaricious, greedy, ungenerous, **5.** bountiful; *synonyms* (adj) plentiful, fruitful, luxuriant, profuse, lush, big, prolific, affluent, abounding, fertile, freehanded, lavish, many, plenteous, prodigal; *antonym* (adj) sparse, **6.** liberal; *synonyms* (adj) giving, tolerant, easy, enlightened, permissive, wide, left, frank, indulgent, advanced, capacious, gratuitous, great, plenty, (n) progressive; *antonyms* (adj) strict, oppressive, totalitarian, intolerant, (n) conservative, **7.** philanthropic.

kakaiewa impatient; *synonyms* (adj) eager, hasty, anxious, petulant, fidgety, keen, edgy, quick, avid, enthusiastic, impetuous, irritable, restive, restless, testy; *antonyms* (adj) patient, enduring.

kakainareke slim; *synonyms* (adj) slender, narrow, slight, thin, lean, remote, fine, skinny, flimsy, lithe, meager, light, (v) reduce, slenderize, cut; *antonyms* (adj) fat, heavy, hefty, plump, stocky, wide.

kakainroua 1. engage; *synonyms* (v) contract, attract, book, employ, absorb, betroth, charter, enlist, retain, draw, engross, hire, involve, lock, mesh; *antonyms* (v) fire, disengage, **2.** marry; *synonyms* (v) join, link, conjoin, splice, tie, unite, wive, couple, combine, merge, connect, unify, match, (n) espouse, wed; *antonym* (v) divorce.

kakainrouaki 1. engaged; *synonyms* (adj) busy, occupied, betrothed, affianced, employed, engrossed, reserved, absorbed, working, pledged, bespoken, booked, immersed, intent, rapt; *antonyms* (adj) available, free, **2.** married; *synonyms* (adj) marital, wedded, conjugal, matrimonial, connubial, nuptial; *antonyms* (adj) single, unmarried.

kakairi 1. emulate; *synonyms* (v) copy, compete, contend, imitate, rival, contest, echo, reproduce, ape, follow, mimic, reflect, (adj) vie, **2.** imitate; *synonyms* (v) duplicate, forge, emulate, feign, counterfeit, mock, act, assume, model, pattern, pretend, sham, simulate, adopt, parody.

kakairua mistake; *synonyms* (n) blunder, fault, defect, error, failure, misapprehension, misconception, demerit, inaccuracy, (v) err, misapprehend, slip, confuse, misjudge, misunderstand.

kakairuaki mistaken; *synonyms* (adj) incorrect, erroneous, false, wrong, misguided, inaccurate, fallacious, untrue, misleading; *antonym* (adj) correct.

kakaiun 1. irascible; *synonyms* (adj) fiery, angry, choleric, irritable, crabby, excitable, hot, hotheaded, passionate, testy, touchy, hasty, impatient, impetuous, edgy, **2.** quarrelsome; *synonyms* (adj) argumentative, pugnacious, belligerent, contentious, combative, aggressive, cantankerous,

disputatious, currish, ugly, contrary, termagant, arguing, factious, (v) fretful; *antonym* (adj) peaceable, **3.** resentful; *synonyms* (adj) bitter, indignant, malicious, rancorous, envious, jealous, offended, hurt, mad, raging, annoyed, cross, sore, wrathful, revengeful; *antonyms* (adj) charitable, resigned, **4.** tempered; *synonyms* (adj) hardened, attempered, attemperate, elastic, enured, inured, mild, proportioned, set, subdued, toughened, treated, tough, **5.** testy; *synonyms* (adj) peevish, petulant, cranky, fractious, irascible, grumpy, nettlesome, pettish, snappish, techy, tetchy, grouchy, huffy, querulous, crusty.

kakakao invite; *synonyms* (v) draw, allure, bid, call, tempt, ask, attract, entice, summon, beckon, court, encourage, receive, solicit, (n) invitation.

kakakaoaki invited; *synonyms* (adj) welcome, cherished, wanted, precious, treasured.

kakaki 1. cast; *synonyms* (v) hurl, throw, form, shed, stamp, fling, shape, chuck, dump, figure, heave, mould, (n) appearance, casting, mold, **2.** suppressed; *synonyms* (adj) smothered, stifled, strangled, downtrodden, buried, composed, concealed, covert, doomed, dormant, embryonic, forgotten, hidden, latent, (n) subordinate; *antonym* (adj) available.

kakamaku 1. dreadful; *synonyms* (adj) awful, bad, dire, dread, alarming, atrocious, fearful, terrible, abominable, appalling, direful, ghastly, grisly, hideous, horrible; *antonyms* (adj) pleasant, wonderful, **2.** grizzly; *synonyms* (adj) gray, grey, greyish, grayish, dull, (n) silvertip, **3.** horrible; *synonyms* (adj) frightful, dreadful, fearsome, formidable, cruel, dismal, monstrous, forbidding, fierce, hateful, frightening, grim, gruesome, (v) horrid, (adv) detestable; *antonyms* (adj) lovely, nice, **4.** horrid; *synonyms* (adj) ugly, disgusting, lurid, foul, horrendous, horrific, macabre, nasty, offensive, repulsive, vile, morbid, obnoxious, odious, outrageous, **5.** fearsome; *synonyms* (adj) awesome, terrifying, dreaded, **6.** horrifying; *synonyms* (adj) scary, shocking, heinous, **7.** monstrous; *synonyms* (adj) enormous, grotesque, huge, monster, immense, flagitious, gigantic, grievous, preposterous, fantastic, inordinate, exorbitant, abnormal, big, colossal; *antonym* (adj) tiny, **8.** formidable; *synonyms* (adj) arduous, difficult, heavy, onerous, redoubtable, stiff, tough, herculean, rugged, serious, hard, laborious, mighty, strong, terrific, **9.** appalling; *synonyms* (adj) revolting, unspeakable, woeful, dismaying, horrifying, tremendous, unearthly; *antonym* (adj) admirable, **10.** awful; *synonyms* (adj) amazing, deplorable, lousy, sickening, unpleasant, painful, unholy, disastrous, repellent, severe, (adv) beastly, highly, awfully, frightfully, (v) solemn; *antonyms* (adj) excellent, great, marvelous, **11.** fearful;

synonyms (*adj*) afraid, cowardly, anxious, apprehensive, craven, timid, eerie, dastardly, desperate, frightened, nervous, scared, shy, timorous, worried; *antonyms* (*adj*) brave, calm, rational, bold, confident, unimpressed, **12.** frightful, **13.** shocking; *synonyms* (*adj*) disgraceful, shameful, scandalous, repugnant, flagrant, astonishing, disreputable, evil, indecent, staggering, startling, surprising, crushing, disconcerting, distressing, **14.** tremendous; *synonyms* (*adj*) prodigious, vast, massive, rattling, howling, brilliant, devastating, intense, magnificent, marvellous, phenomenal, splendid, superb, wondrous, (*v*) thrilling; *antonym* (*adj*) insignificant, **15.** scary; *synonyms* (*adj*) scarey, uncanny, chilling, ghostly, creepy, intimidating; *antonyms* (*adj*) reassuring, soothing, **16.** terrible; *synonyms* (*adj*) extreme, wicked, dangerous, almighty, rotten, tragic, violent, calamitous, grave, indescribable, loathsome, **17.** scare; *synonyms* (*n*) fear, (*v*) alarm, dismay, fright, intimidate, daunt, frighten, awe, appall, affright, horrify, startle, (*adj*) panic, consternation, horror, **18.** terrifying.

kakamakuaki scared; *synonyms* (*adj*) afraid, frightened, fearful, anxious, horrified, intimidated, nervous, terrified, timid, panicky, (*adv*) cowardly; *antonyms* (*adj*) calm, confident, fearless.

kakamakuri fidget; *synonyms* (*v*) wriggle, squirm, wiggle, fiddle, (*n*) fidgetiness, restlessness, (*adj*) bustle, bother, fuss, hurry, stir, ado, drive.

kakamataku 1. interesting; *synonyms* (*adj*) entertaining, absorbing, amusing, attractive, charming, engaging, exciting, fascinating, readable, diverting, appealing, engrossing, gripping, captivating, provocative; *antonyms* (*adj*) uninteresting, boring, dull, **2.** absorbing; *synonyms* (*adj*) interesting, enthralling, riveting, **3.** intriguing; *synonyms* (*adj*) designing, scheming, challenging, enchanting, **4.** fascinating; *synonyms* (*adj*) delightful, alluring, bewitching, seductive, desirable, entrancing, fetching, magnetic, beautiful, tempting, compelling, exotic, glamorous, lovely, pleasing, **5.** amazing; *synonyms* (*adj*) astonishing, terrific, wonderful, astounding, awesome, breathtaking, extraordinary, fabulous, impressive, incredible, prodigious, spectacular, stupendous, surprising, tremendous; *antonyms* (*adj*) mundane, ordinary, **6.** remarkable; *synonyms* (*adj*) exceptional, notable, noteworthy, odd, distinguished, conspicuous, phenomenal, famous, illustrious, curious, great, noticeable, outstanding, rare, (*n*) memorable; *antonyms* (*adj*) insignificant, unremarkable, **7.** spectacular; *synonyms* (*adj*) dramatic, sensational, amazing, salient, striking, stunning, scenic, fantastic, magnificent, splendid, theatrical, prominent, (*n*) extravaganza; *antonym* (*adj*) modest.

kakammari 1. exalting; *synonyms* (*adj*) ennobling, abundant, benevolent, courageous, dignifying, exhilarating, generous, humane, highborn, honorable, human, humanizing, kind, magnanimous, munificent, **2.** rejoicing; *synonyms* (*n*) exultation, happiness, jubilation, joy, mirth, triumph, (*adj*) jubilant, exultant, exulting, heyday, prideful, triumphant.

kakamwakuri 1. move; *synonyms* (*v*) act, affect, carry, excite, go, impel, instigate, maneuver, touch, travel, flow, bear, (*n*) motion, drive, transfer; *antonym* (*v*) stay, **2.** agitate; *synonyms* (*v*) disturb, stir, toss, fan, bother, foment, perturb, rouse, shake, trouble, actuate, annoy, arouse, canvass, convulse; *antonyms* (*v*) calm, soothe, **3.** rouse; *synonyms* (*v*) awake, awaken, kindle, provoke, agitate, incite, move, fire, inflame, revive, heat, animate, encourage, induce, irritate; *antonym* (*v*) dampen, **4.** shake; *synonyms* (*v*) beat, jar, brandish, flutter, totter, wag, drop, bump, flourish, (*n*) tremble, jolt, quiver, wave, trembling, (*adj*) quake, **5.** stir; *synonyms* (*v*) budge, inspire, cause, shift, (*n*) movement, commotion, disturbance, excitement, agitation, fuss, riot, tumult, ferment, ado, (*adj*) bustle.

kakamwakuriaki 1. agitated; *synonyms* (*adj*) restless, excited, nervous, restive, tumultuous, upset, distressed, tense, alarmed, anxious, distraught, jumpy, overwrought, perturbed, shaken; *antonyms* (*adj*) calm, composed, lethargic, **2.** shaken; *synonyms* (*v*) broken, lame, passe, shaky, threadbare, wilted, shattered, stale, (*adj*) jolted, dazed, disconcerted, fallen, scared, stunned, surprised, **3.** stirred; *synonyms* (*adj*) stimulated, affected, aroused, emotional, aflame, ablaze, beaten, enthused, horny, inspired, interested, randy, ruttish, susceptible, touched; *antonym* (*adj*) uninspired.

kakamwarua steal; *synonyms* (*v*) abstract, lift, purloin, creep, filch, misappropriate, pilfer, pinch, plunder, rob, snatch, sneak, plagiarize, slip, (*n*) bargain.

kakamwaruaki stolen; *synonyms* (*adj*) purloined, furtive, misbegotten, secret, sly, stealthy.

kâkaña cannibal; *synonyms* (*n*) anthropophagite, savage, anthropophagus, barbarian, brute, aborigine, anthropophaginian, islander, native, ogress, primitive, ruffian, tribesman, (*adj*) anthropophagous, carnivorous.

käkaña 1. oppressive; *synonyms* (*adj*) heavy, burdensome, despotic, muggy, stuffy, sultry, tyrannical, dictatorial, gloomy, cruel, domineering, hard, harsh, (*v*) onerous, close; *antonyms* (*adj*) fresh, liberal, democratic, **2.** sharp; *synonyms* (*adj*) acute, bitter, intelligent, acid, acrid, incisive, intense, penetrating, piercing, pointed, pungent, quick, severe, (*n*) keen, (*v*) biting; *antonyms* (*adj*) blunt, dull, mild, gentle, rounded, sweet, bland, blurred, naive, round, smooth.

kakanaki edible; *synonyms* (*adj*) comestible, palatable, esculent, (*n*) eatable, food, pabulum, victual, victuals; *antonyms* (*adj*) inedible, indigestible.

kakanato 1. notable; *synonyms* (*adj*) distinguished, conspicuous, celebrated, eminent, illustrious, extraordinary, famous, memorable, remarkable, renowned, famed, great, important, (*n*) celebrity, luminary; *antonyms* (*adj*) insignificant, ordinary, **2.** great; *synonyms* (*adj*) gigantic, big, extensive, extreme, grand, large, chief, ample, capital, considerable, dignified, fantastic, fine, glorious, good; *antonyms* (*adj*) small, awful, tiny, mild, **3.** main; *synonyms* (*adj*) head, leading, essential, principal, basic, central, first, key, major, paramount, primary, prominent, (*n*) cardinal, ocean, sea; *antonyms* (*adj*) minor, auxiliary, secondary, supplementary, **4.** grand; *synonyms* (*adj*) excellent, gorgeous, elevated, exalted, majestic, superb, beautiful, high, massive, brilliant, heroic, huge, immense, impressive, (*n*) noble; *antonyms* (*adj*) unimpressive, humble, modest, **5.** famous; *synonyms* (*adj*) splendid, known, notable, notorious, stunning, magnificent, noted, outstanding, popular, proverbial, signal, wonderful; *antonyms* (*adj*) unknown, infamous, **6.** important; *synonyms* (*adj*) grave, fundamental, significant, crucial, serious, earnest, authoritative, consequential, critical, decisive, eventful, heavy, historic, influential, meaningful; *antonyms* (*adj*) unimportant, trivial, irrelevant, low, worthless, **7.** substantial; *synonyms* (*adj*) actual, solid, firm, real, strong, palpable, momentous, sturdy, sound, concrete, corporeal, durable, hearty, hefty, material; *antonyms* (*adj*) insubstantial, ethereal.

kakanaugaki 1. mysterious; *synonyms* (*adj*) hidden, inscrutable, deep, eerie, incomprehensible, inexplicable, abstruse, arcane, cryptic, dark, obscure, secret, clandestine, concealed, covert; *antonyms* (*adj*) known, straightforward, apparent, normal, **2.** fearsome; *synonyms* (*adj*) awful, dreadful, fearful, frightening, terrible, awesome, dire, direful, frightful, horrendous, horrific, terrifying, alarming, dreaded, **3.** eerie; *synonyms* (*adj*) grisly, ghostly, spooky, strange, uncanny, unearthly, weird, bizarre, creepy, eery, horrible, macabre, mysterious, supernatural, **4.** ghastly; *synonyms* (*adj*) cadaverous, appalling, ashen, atrocious, gruesome, hideous, offensive, deathly, dismal, grim, shocking, wan, sallow, disgusting, vile; *antonyms* (*adj*) pleasant, lovely, wonderful, **5.** supernatural; *synonyms* (*adj*) miraculous, mystical, preternatural, superhuman, unnatural, divine, hyperphysical, mystic, magic, magical,

marvelous, numinous, spiritual, celestial, (*n*) occult; *antonym* (*syn*) natural.

kakang 1. keen; *synonyms* (*adj*) acute, eager, sharp, intense, intelligent, biting, brisk, enthusiastic, exquisite, piercing, discriminating, clever, astute, (*v*) fresh, avid; *antonyms* (*adj*) dull, apathetic, indifferent, unenthusiastic, blunt, **2.** fierce; *synonyms* (*adj*) bitter, violent, cruel, ferocious, brutal, furious, grim, savage, nasty, angry, ardent, atrocious, barbarous, boisterous, fervent; *antonyms* (*adj*) gentle, mild, **3.** thorny; *synonyms* (*adj*) difficult, prickly, spiny, briery, awkward, barbed, burry, hard, knotty, tricky, tough, troublesome, trying, barbellate, briary; *antonyms* (*adj*) simple, smooth, easy, **4.** spiny; *synonyms* (*adj*) thorny, bristly, bristled, burred, **5.** pointed; *synonyms* (*adj*) penetrating, keen, poignant, piquant, cutting, marked, pithy, acuminate, pungent, short, meaningful, fine, angular, emphatic, acid; *antonym* (*adj*) rounded, **6.** sharpened; *synonyms* (*adj*) acuate, better, sensual, **7.** spiky; *synonyms* (*adj*) peaky, spiked, pointed, pointy, jagged, abrasive, argumentative, spikelike, **8.** spiked; *synonyms* (*adj*) laced, altered, firm, tied, **9.** sharp; *synonyms* (*adj*) acrid, harsh, incisive, quick, severe, alert, caustic, prompt, sarcastic, smart, hot, bright, discerning, distinct, (*v*) acrimonious; *antonyms* (*adj*) sweet, bland, blurred, naive, round, **10.** prickly; *synonyms* (*adj*) irritable, cantankerous, moody, scratchy, spiky, splenetic, tetchy, waspish.

kakangare 1. ludicrous; *synonyms* (*adj*) absurd, ridiculous, farcical, foolish, laughable, comical, grotesque, derisory, droll, jocular, preposterous, funny, humorous, amusing, comic; *antonym* (*adj*) sensible, **2.** outrageous; *synonyms* (*adj*) exorbitant, inordinate, atrocious, furious, monstrous, offensive, gross, excessive, extravagant, awful, disgusting, dreadful, extortionate, hideous, horrid; *antonym* (*adj*) acceptable.

kakangia 1. whet; *synonyms* (*v*) sharpen, excite, grind, quicken, stimulate, stir, hone, (*n*) goad, spur, fillip, provocative, stimulus, incentive, whip, (*adj*) point, **2.** sharpen; *synonyms* (*v*) focus, edge, intensify, sharp, increase, heighten, whet, improve, compound, taper, incite, kindle, (*n*) aim; *antonym* (*v*) cloud.

kakangiaki sharpened; *synonyms* (*adj*) sharp, acute, acuate, better, sensual.

kakanikoa 1. contempt; *synonyms* (*n*) disdain, scorn, derision, disrespect, disregard, mockery, ridicule, shame, slight, reproach, discourtesy, disrepute, arrogance, defiance, disgrace; *antonyms* (*n*) respect, approval, **2.** despise; *synonyms* (*v*) contemn, loathe, depreciate, abhor, detest, dislike, hate, condemn, defy, execrate, neglect, spurn, reject, (*n*) deride; *antonym* (*v*) admire, **3.** mock;

synonyms (*adj*) counterfeit, fake, false, fictitious, (*v*) burlesque, gibe, ape, flout, mimic, scoff, sham, taunt, bemock, imitate, (*n*) jeer; *antonyms* (*adj*) genuine, real, **4.** ridicule; *synonyms* (*n*) irony, insult, contempt, sarcasm, sneer, disparagement, (*v*) banter, mock, tease, rib, chaff, joke, gird, hoot, (*adj*) lampoon; *antonym* (*v*) praise, **5.** scoff; *synonyms* (*v*) quip, jest, barrack, (*n*) jibe, jeering, scoffing, hiss, (*adj*) blaspheme, desecrate, profane, revile.

kakanikoaki despised; *synonyms* (*adj*) detested, scorned, despicable, hated, abject, abhorrent, contemptible, contemptuous, loathed, opprobrious, reviled, unpopular, infamous, insolent, insufferable.

kakanimomoi whistle; *synonyms* (*n*) whistling, pennywhistle, (*v*) pipe, sing, twitter, hiss, cry, warble, cheep, tweet, chirp, wheeze.

kakannanton celebrated; *synonyms* (*adj*) famous, illustrious, renowned, distinguished, notable, noted, splendid, well-known, known, conspicuous, eminent, famed, great, notorious, (*n*) glorious; *antonym* (*adj*) unknown.

kakannato 1. distinguished; *synonyms* (*adj*) celebrated, dignified, eminent, conspicuous, illustrious, important, renowned, reputable, famous, great, high, noble, prominent, splendid, superior; *antonyms* (*adj*) unknown, ordinary, **2.** illustrious; *synonyms* (*adj*) glorious, bright, excellent, brilliant, distinguished, famed, grand, well-known, lofty, notable, noted, proud, mighty, recognized, redoubtable, **3.** glorious; *synonyms* (*adj*) magnificent, super, resplendent, superb, cool, regal, divine, gorgeous, heavenly, lustrous, marvelous, radiant, splendiferous, sublime, terrific, **4.** eminent; *synonyms* (*adj*) elevated, big, exalted, signal, first, chief, singular, imposing, leading, majestic, outstanding, paramount, principal, remarkable, towering, **5.** great; *synonyms* (*adj*) gigantic, extensive, extreme, large, ample, capital, considerable, fantastic, fine, good, massive, spacious, voluminous, stunning, vigorous; *antonyms* (*adj*) small, awful, insignificant, tiny, mild, **6.** renowned; *synonyms* (*adj*) notorious, known, acknowledged, familiar, legendary.

kakannatoa 1. glorify; *synonyms* (*v*) celebrate, exalt, extol, bless, eulogize, dignify, adore, commend, laud, praise, canonize, admire, aggrandize, magnify, (*n*) honor, **2.** applaud; *synonyms* (*v*) acclaim, cheer, hail, clap, approve, compliment, encourage, congratulate; *antonyms* (*v*) boo, criticize, **3.** emanate; *synonyms* (*v*) arise, emerge, effuse, discharge, breathe, exhale, proceed, radiate, spring, stem, exude, emit, flow, gush, issue, **4.** celebrate; *synonyms* (*v*) commemorate, keep, fete, solemnize, applaud, honour, distinguish, exult, glorify, hold, observe, rejoice, triumph, lionize; *antonym* (*v*) ignore, **5.** distinguish; *synonyms* (*v*)

discern, discriminate, describe, know, perceive, discover, descry, behold, characterize, classify, detect, difference, differentiate, identify, recognize; *antonym* (*v*) confuse, **6.** extol; *synonym* (*v*) proclaim, **7.** honor; *synonyms* (*n*) award, fame, glory, reputation, accolade, reverence, reward, deference, celebrity, credit, (*v*) esteem, respect, grace, worship, (*adj*) chastity; *antonyms* (*n*) shame, humiliation, (*v*) dishonor, disgrace, break, **8.** commend; *synonyms* (*v*) recommend, cite, endorse, entrust, give, assign, commit, confide, consign, trust, advert; *antonyms* (*v*) rebuke, censure, reproach.

kakannatoaki 1. glorified; *synonyms* (*adj*) canonized, blessed, canonised, haloed, holy, hyped, overestimated, overrated, overvalued, **2.** celebrated; *synonyms* (*adj*) famous, illustrious, renowned, distinguished, notable, noted, splendid, well-known, known, conspicuous, eminent, famed, great, notorious, (*n*) glorious; *antonym* (*adj*) unknown, **3.** distinguished; *synonyms* (*adj*) celebrated, dignified, important, reputable, high, noble, prominent, superior, considerable, distinct, ace, exalted, excellent, grand, lofty; *antonym* (*adj*) ordinary, **4.** honored; *synonyms* (*v*) completed, consummated, crowned, excessive, (*adj*) esteemed, honoured, respected, privileged, advantaged, estimable, fortunate, hallowed, lucky, prestigious, proud.

kakanno 1. lustrous; *synonyms* (*adj*) glossy, brilliant, lucid, light, luminous, shining, shiny, glowing, polished, radiant, sleek, splendent, glistening, effulgent, (*v*) bright; *antonym* (*adj*) dull, **2.** marvelous; *synonyms* (*adj*) fantastic, wonderful, astonishing, extraordinary, fabulous, grand, great, incredible, prodigious, terrific, tremendous, glorious, amazing, cool, excellent; *antonym* (*adj*) awful, **3.** gorgeous; *synonyms* (*adj*) beautiful, attractive, gaudy, luxurious, rich, gay, costly, delicious, delightful, fine, handsome, lovely, magnificent, opulent, pretty; *antonym* (*adj*) ugly, **4.** dazzling; *synonyms* (*adj*) blinding, glaring, splendid, vivid, fulgent, resplendent, sparkling, striking, stunning, blazing, flamboyant, garish, gorgeous, outstanding, shimmering, **5.** magnificent; *synonyms* (*adj*) imposing, illustrious, grandiose, elegant, superb, divine, exquisite, majestic, royal, stately, brave, impressive, awesome, marvelous, mighty, **6.** luxurious; *synonyms* (*adj*) voluptuous, deluxe, lavish, sumptuous, epicurean, luscious, comfortable, expensive, palatial, princely, sensual, sensuous, swanky, (*n*) lush, luxuriant; *antonym* (*adj*) cheap, **7.** splendid; *synonyms* (*adj*) noble, gallant, proud, admirable, good, lustrous, regal, spectacular, capital, relucent, dazzling, dignified, glittering, heroic, (*n*) ostentatious; *antonym* (*adj*) poor.

kakano twine; *synonyms* (*n*) coil, string, cord, rope, thread, (*v*) wind, entwine, lace, enlace, interlace, intertwine, meander, twist, weave, braid; *antonym* (*v*) untwist.

kakanoa 1. contain; *synonyms* (*v*) comprise, accommodate, comprehend, curb, include, admit, bear, carry, check, confine, control, embrace, hold, restrain, restrict; *antonyms* (*v*) exclude, express, **2.** capacious; *synonyms* (*adj*) large, spacious, big, ample, broad, extensive, roomy, vast, commodious, expansive, voluminous, wide; *antonyms* (*adj*) cramped, small.

kakanoaki 1. contained; *synonyms* (*adj*) implied, implicit, inside, latent, numbered, understood, unexpressed, unspoken, buried, confined, constrained, controlled, couched, cramped, embedded; *antonym* (*adj*) all-encompassing, **2.** twined; *synonyms* (*adj*) twisted, bent, contorted, distorted, misrepresented, perverted.

kakaokoroa 1. insulate; *synonyms* (*v*) isolate, segregate, cushion, sequester, protect, separate, wrap, cocoon, coat, cosset, cover, envelop, inlay, line, tape, **2.** segregate; *synonyms* (*v*) detach, discriminate, divide, dissociate, divorce, part, differentiate, distinguish, split, dispart, relegate, rescind, (*adj*) detached, **3.** vary; *synonyms* (*v*) alter, change, differ, modify, alternate, deviate, diverge, diversify, modulate, depart, disagree, fluctuate, shift, variegate, contrast.

kakaokoroaki 1. insulated; *synonyms* (*adj*) cloistered, (*prep*) separated, unconnected, **2.** varied; *synonyms* (*adj*) assorted, diverse, miscellaneous, mixed, various, different, diversified, sundry, heterogeneous, manifold, motley, many, dissimilar, versatile, odd; *antonyms* (*adj*) boring, dull, homogeneous, uniform, **3.** segregated; *synonyms* (*adj*) isolated, secluded, uncombined, exclusive, nonintegrated, unintegrated.

kakaonimaki 1. faithful; *synonyms* (*adj*) authentic, correct, close, constant, exact, dependable, devoted, sound, true, unfailing, devout, dutiful, fast, honest, (*n*) accurate; *antonyms* (*adj*) disloyal, false, inaccurate, unfaithful, unreliable, **2.** loyal; *synonyms* (*adj*) unwavering, reliable, steady, obedient, dedicated, liege, observant, patriotic, responsible, staunch, steadfast, trustworthy, (*n*) faithful, (*v*) firm, stanch, **3.** devoted; *synonyms* (*adj*) addicted, affectionate, ardent, consecrated, fond, loyal, pious, committed, eager, enthusiastic, keen, loving, passionate, religious, zealous; *antonyms* (*adj*) uncommitted, indifferent, **4.** punctual; *synonyms* (*adj*) prompt, punctilious, precise, regular, timely, nice, (*v*) lenten, paschal; *antonym* (*adj*) late, **5.** upright; *synonyms* (*adj*) perpendicular, straight, erect, vertical, fair, good, just, righteous, honorable, plumb, right, virtuous, pure, clean, (*n*) column; *antonyms* (*adv*)

horizontally, (*adj*) disreputable, prone, upturned, degenerate, hanging, unwholesome, **6.** staunch; *synonyms* (*v*) halt, stem, stop, (*adj*) solid, hardy, resolute, stalwart, secure, sturdy, stable, sure, dogged, stout, strong, tenacious, **7.** steadfast; *synonyms* (*adj*) permanent, immovable, determined, persistent, consistent, hard, inflexible, set, abiding, immobile, rigid, stubborn, unfaltering, (*v*) fixed, impregnable; *antonym* (*adj*) irresolute.

kakara grate; *synonyms* (*n*) lattice, (*v*) chafe, creak, grind, abrade, scrape, fret, gall, gnash, rub, aggravate, annoy, crunch, irritate, provoke.

kakarabakau 1. communicate; *synonyms* (*v*) deliver, express, impart, advertise, advise, announce, apprise, carry, commune, convey, intimate, relay, reveal, transmit, acquaint, **2.** chat; *synonyms* (*n*) gossip, talk, chatter, chitchat, conversation, causerie, confab, gab, rap, (*v*) converse, chaffer, confabulate, prattle, speak, tattle; *antonym* (*v*) listen, **3.** discuss; *synonyms* (*v*) argue, debate, agitate, consult, deliberate, canvass, discourse, dispute, mention, moot, negotiate, reason, weigh, controvert, address, **4.** deliberate; *synonyms* (*adj*) careful, calculated, circumspect, slow, thoughtful, conscious, considered, (*v*) consider, cogitate, think, confer, contemplate, ponder, reflect, discuss; *antonyms* (*adj*) accidental, chance, unintentional, hasty, ingenuous, involuntary, spontaneous, **5.** converse; *synonyms* (*n*) colloquy, contrast, reverse, antithesis, communication, communion, intercourse, (*v*) chat, communicate, articulate, (*adj*) contrary, opposite, counter, inverse, reversed; *antonyms* (*n*) equal, same, **6.** confabulate; *synonyms* (*v*) jaw, visit, blabber, claver, **7.** confer; *synonyms* (*v*) bestow, accord, give, afford, award, grant, present, allow, assign, show, pay, provide, contribute, donate, endow, **8.** conference; *synonyms* (*n*) assembly, meeting, council, consultation, interview, negotiation, congress, discussion, gathering, session, sitting, audience, conclave, association, convocation, **9.** interview; *synonyms* (*n*) conference, hearing, examination, appointment, parley, (*v*) question, interrogate, encounter, **10.** talk; *synonyms* (*v*) lecture, prate, babble, tongue, say, gabble, jabber, mouth, (*n*) language, dialogue, palaver, speech, parlance, idiom, natter.

kakarabakaua 1. gloat; *synonyms* (*v*) exult, brag, crow, vaunt, bluster, boast, revel, triumph, (*n*) gloating, glee, **2.** boast; *synonyms* (*v*) blow, gasconade, pride, rodomontade, bounce, exaggerate, flourish, sport, swagger, swash, avaunt, (*n*) arrogance, boasting, glory, jactitation, **3.** brag; *synonyms* (*v*) crack, (*n*) bragging, vapor, crowing, (*adj*) boss, **4.** talk; *synonyms* (*v*) gossip, converse, lecture, chatter, address, articulate, chat, prattle, speak, (*n*) discourse, language, colloquy, conversation, dialogue, palaver.

kakarako 1. little; *synonyms* *(adj)* small, diminutive, insignificant, brief, minute, petty, short, some, tiny, exiguous, light, baby, bantam, *(v)* dash, bit; *antonyms* *(adj)* big, enormous, large, important, **2**. tiny; *synonyms* *(adj)* little, infinitesimal, midget, petite, puny, slight, teeny, miniature, minor, trifling, trivial, cramped, stunted, *(phr)* minuscule; *antonyms* *(adj)* huge, gigantic, vast, **3**. small; *synonyms* *(adj)* narrow, fine, inadequate, low, remote, young, limited, faint, humble, modest, paltry, slender, scanty, ungenerous, outside; *antonyms* *(adj)* bulky, colossal, considerable, extra-large, great, sizeable, giant, major.

kakarakoa lessen; *synonyms* *(v)* diminish, decrease, abridge, abate, contract, curtail, decline, fall, allay, alleviate, assuage, cut, dwindle, mitigate, moderate; *antonyms* *(v)* increase, exacerbate.

kakarakoaki lessened; *synonyms* *(adj)* diminished, atrophied, attenuate, attenuated, belittled, conical, corrupted, cut, debased, depleted, faded, hurt, lower, pointed, short.

kakarau rainy; *synonyms* *(adj)* wet, moist, pluvial, damp, pluvious, showery, stormy; *antonym* *(adj)* dry.

kakaraurekana 1. diverge; *synonyms* *(v)* deflect, deviate, differ, digress, divaricate, fork, vary, depart, disagree, separate, split, change, wander, contrast, divide; *antonyms* *(v)* converge, conform, concur, meet, **2**. disunite; *synonyms* *(v)* detach, disjoin, disconnect, dissociate, disengage, disjoint, dissolve, sever, disassociate, dissever, divorce, part, disarticulate, cleave, break, **3**. disarrange; *synonyms* *(v)* confuse, derange, clutter, disorder, disorganize, muddle, muss, ruffle, perturb, discompose, disconcert, disturb, jumble, litter, shuffle.

kakaraurekanaki 1. disarranged; *synonyms* *(adj)* confused, disheveled, disorderly, deranged, untidy, delirious, disordered, mussy, topsy-turvy, tousled, unkempt, immethodical, lawless, rumpled, tumultuous; *antonym* *(adj)* arranged, **2**. disunited; *synonyms* *(adj)* divided, split, disjointed, abrupt, crumbled, cut, distinct, distributed, fragmented, *(v)* disconnected, apart, blighted, broken, contrite, cracked.

kakari thatch; *synonyms* *(n)* thatching, ceiling, roof, teach, tile, hair, mop.

kakaria 1. graze; *synonyms* *(v)* browse, scratch, rub, scrape, chafe, eat, brush, crease, crop, feed, pasture, rake, shave, *(n)* touch, cut, **2**. scratch; *synonyms* *(n)* score, mark, nick, scrabble, dent, abrasion, groove, scar, furrow, *(v)* graze, notch, grate, scrawl, tear, engrave.

kakariaki 1. grazed; *synonyms* *(adj)* hurt, raw, **2**. scratched; *synonyms* *(adj)* scraped, abraded, dented, injured, sgraffito, spoiled, broken, skinned, smashed.

kakariki 1. create; *synonyms* *(v)* cause, construct, make, constitute, produce, beget, breed, build, compose, do, establish, form, generate, institute, start; *antonyms* *(v)* destroy, terminate, **2**. breed; *synonyms* *(n)* kind, race, variety, ancestry, sort, order, class, genus, posterity, *(v)* engender, multiply, bear, brood, cultivate, hatch, **3**. beget; *synonyms* *(v)* father, get, create, procreate, sire, mother, propagate, acquire, **4**. procreate; *synonyms* *(v)* reproduce, fertilize, impregnate, originate.

kakarikiaki begotten; *synonyms* *(adj)* create, composed, created.

kakarine moralize; *synonyms* *(v)* sermonize, moralise, preach, lecture, moral, preachify, sermonise, urge.

kakaro 1. avoid; *synonyms* *(v)* shun, avert, parry, escape, evade, abstain, annul, circumvent, duck, elude, forbear, fudge, ignore, prevent, *(adj)* eschew; *antonyms* *(v)* confront, associate, face, tackle, **2**. elude; *synonyms* *(v)* avoid, dodge, skirt, baffle, defy, bilk, shirk, sidestep, frustrate, deflect, flee, hedge, neglect, equivocate, mystify, **3**. dodge; *synonyms* *(v)* maneuver, beat, lurch, blench, blink, *(n)* contrivance, stratagem, cheat, device, quibble, ruse, scheme, trick, wile, avoidance, **4**. duck; *synonyms* *(n)* darling, canvas, dear, *(v)* dip, douse, plunge, dive, souse, bob, crouch, dunk, stoop, submerge, cut, *(adj)* immerse, **5**. evade; *synonyms* *(v)* omit, prevaricate, block, fence, **6**. equivocate; *synonyms* *(v)* palter, lie, **7**. parry; *synonyms* *(n)* counterpunch, *(v)* counter, flinch, fend, repel, defeat, **8**. swerve; *synonyms* *(v)* deviate, depart, sheer, stray, turn, veer, wander, diverge, shift, bend, digress, slew, swing, warp, *(n)* curve, **9**. sidestep; *synonyms* *(v)* bypass, pussyfoot.

kakarua whoop; *synonyms* *(n)* shout, call, *(v)* cry, bellow, halloo, howl, roar, shriek, yell, cough, gasp, hack.

kakateke 1. graceful; *synonyms* *(adj)* beautiful, delicate, elegant, amiable, easy, fine, charming, fair, airy, becoming, comely, dainty, handsome, lithe, lovely; *antonyms* *(adj)* clumsy, inelegant, stocky, **2**. elegant; *synonyms* *(adj)* graceful, courtly, splendid, polite, refined, dressy, artistic, chic, classy, cultured, debonair, neat, pretty, smart, stately; *antonyms* *(adj)* scruffy, ugly, coarse, plain, tacky, **3**. neat; *synonyms* *(adj)* adroit, clear, natty, tidy, clean, clever, deft, dexterous, fresh, methodical, nifty, pure, straight, felicitous, *(v)* compact; *antonyms* *(adj)* untidy, messy, unkempt, disordered, **4**. pretty; *synonyms* *(adv)* very, fairly, jolly, quite, rather, somewhat, moderately, *(adj)* attractive, good-looking, picturesque, cute, pleasing, bonny, noble, *(n)* nice.

kakatika 1. beautiful; *synonyms (adj)* attractive, good-looking, bright, beauteous, fine, handsome, lovely, picturesque, pleasant, pretty, striking, sweet, adorned, ornate, dainty; *antonyms (adj)* ugly, unattractive, **2.** angelic; *synonyms (adj)* pure, angelical, beautiful, celestial, cherubic, heavenly, seraphic, virtuous, divine, good, holy, lovable, saintly, **3.** dazzling; *synonyms (adj)* brilliant, blinding, glaring, splendid, vivid, fulgent, resplendent, sparkling, stunning, blazing, flamboyant, garish, glorious, gorgeous, luminous; *antonym (adj)* dull, **4.** gorgeous; *synonyms (adj)* gaudy, luxurious, rich, wonderful, gay, costly, delicious, delightful, magnificent, opulent, showy, sumptuous, superb, delectable, **5.** radiant; *synonyms (adj)* beaming, beamy, effulgent, lucid, glowing, incandescent, refulgent, shining, shiny, sunny, glad, cheerful, *(v)* glittering, lustrous, illustrious, **6.** resplendent; *synonyms (adj)* radiant, dazzling, clear, silver.

kakatonga 1. exult; *synonyms (v)* delight, rejoice, cheer, triumph, chuckle, crow, glory, jubilate, boast, brag, celebrate, gloat, *(n)* joy, **2.** rejoice; *synonyms (v)* gladden, revel, gratify, exhilarate, please, recreate, enjoy, wallow, *(n)* exult; *antonyms (v)* lament, mourn.

kakau tiring; *synonyms (adj)* exhausting, tedious, tiresome, hard, laborious, wearing, arduous, grueling, boring, wearisome, onerous, strenuous; *antonyms (adj)* easy, undemanding.

kakauara 1. contemptible; *synonyms (adj)* abject, despicable, base, mean, pitiful, abominable, dishonorable, ignoble, little, miserable, paltry, ridiculous, shameful, unworthy, worthless; *antonym (adj)* admirable, **2.** infamous; *synonyms (adj)* disreputable, flagrant, disgraceful, notorious, contemptible, heinous, ignominious, degenerate, discreditable, *(n)* scandalous, *(v)* foul, scurvy, *(adv)* nefarious, detestable, atrocious; *antonym (adj)* unknown, **3.** mean; *synonyms (v)* intend, design, imply, denote, involve, *(adj)* middle, common, hateful, medium, miserly, beggarly, close, *(n)* average, low, cheap; *antonyms (adj)* generous, kind, **4.** despicable; *synonyms (adj)* vile, dirty, filthy, lousy, nasty, ugly, wicked, wretched, abhorrent, loathsome, rotten, scornful, servile, sordid, squalid, **5.** disgusting; *synonyms (adj)* disgustful, distasteful, execrable, odious, offensive, disagreeable, awful, horrible, noisome, obscene, rank, repellent, repugnant, repulsive, revolting; *antonyms (adj)* attractive, pleasant, appealing, **6.** course; *synonyms (n)* stream, flow, bearing, career, current, path, road, route, track, channel, circuit, class, method, *(v)* run, chase, **7.** nasty; *synonyms (adj)* disgusting, coarse, evil, hurtful, obnoxious, raw, unpleasant, impure, dangerous, gross, hideous, malicious, objectionable, sickening, *(adv)*

beastly; *antonyms (adj)* agreeable, nice, charitable, lovely, **8.** rude; *synonyms (adj)* rough, impudent, blunt, bold, brutal, crude, discourteous, impolite, abusive, barbarous, churlish, crass, curt, disrespectful, *(n)* abrupt; *antonyms (adj)* polite, respectful, chivalrous, courteous, refined, civil, decent, proper, well-mannered, **9.** vulgar; *synonyms (adj)* rude, uncouth, plebeian, indecent, public, tasteless, unrefined, vernacular, indelicate, boorish, earthy, ordinary, inelegant, loud, humble; *antonyms (adj)* sophisticated, tasteful, **10.** undignified; *synonyms (adj)* unseemly, debasing, degrading, demeaning, humiliating, improper, inappropriate, corrupting, mortifying, unbecoming; *antonym (adj)* dignified, **11.** shameless; *synonyms (adj)* brazen, immodest, graceless, depraved, profligate, audacious, blatant, barefaced, unscrupulous, abandoned, unblushing, dissolute, immoral, insolent, lewd, **12.** treacherous; *synonyms (adj)* deceitful, false, perfidious, unfaithful, disloyal, faithless, fraudulent, insidious, unreliable, unsafe, dishonest, deceptive, perilous, traitorous, tricky; *antonyms (adj)* faithful, honest, loyal.

kakaunongo 1. listen; *synonyms (v)* hark, hear, attend, hearken, heed, harken, list, mind, concentrate, incline, **2.** destined; *synonyms (v)* certain, fated, *(adj)* bound, predetermined, sure, inescapable, intended, predestined, inevitable, **3.** destine; *synonyms (v)* design, designate, doom, intend, mean, determine, devote, fate, ordain, specify, condemn, **4.** hearken; *synonym (v)* listen, **5.** head; *synonyms (n)* chief, captain, front, point, boss, foam, froth, crown, chieftain, executive, chair, brain, *(v)* capital, direct, lead; *antonyms (n)* end, subordinate, *(v)* follow, **6.** hark; *synonym (n)* look, **7.** attend; *synonyms (v)* accompany, assist, escort, serve, advert, aid, conduct, help, minister, see, keep, remain, *(n)* tend, doctor, nurse.

kakaunongoaki attended; *synonyms (adj)* accompanied, fraught.

kakauongo 1. listen; *synonyms (v)* hark, hear, attend, hearken, heed, harken, list, mind, concentrate, incline, **2.** overhear; *synonyms (v)* catch, eavesdrop, listen, absorb, accept, adopt, arrest, assimilate, attract, becharm, befool, beguile, bewitch, bug, captivate.

kakawaki 1. expensive; *synonyms (adj)* costly, sumptuous, dear, extravagant, luxurious, valuable, lavish, overpriced, exclusive, fine, high, precious, rich, exorbitant, invaluable; *antonyms (adj)* cheap, inexpensive, reasonable, worthless, **2.** incalculable; *synonyms (adj)* immeasurable, countless, innumerable, boundless, immense, inestimable, infinite, numberless, myriad, measureless, numerous, priceless, uncertain, unpredictable, untold; *antonym* (*adj*) calculable, **3.** dear; *synonyms* (*adj*) beloved, close, expensive, lovely, near, adorable, affectionate, cherished, familiar, intimate, loved, pet, (*n*) darling, love, honey, **4.** immeasurable; *synonyms* (*adj*) endless, huge, enormous, illimitable, immensurable, incalculable, interminable, limitless, unlimited, unmeasurable, vast, inexhaustible, bottomless, fathomless, prodigious; *antonyms* (*adj*) measurable, limited, **5.** costly; *synonyms* (*adj*) pricey, plush, pricy, splendid, **6.** invaluable, **7.** inestimable; *synonym* (*adj*) incomputable, **8.** precious; *synonyms* (*adj*) golden, choice, exquisite, cute, noble, good, goodly, sweet, valued, worthy, delicate, gorgeous, opulent, (*adv*) extremely, preciously, **9.** valuable; *synonyms* (*adj*) estimable, beneficial, helpful, useful, admirable, important, profitable, rewarding, serviceable, advantageous, worthwhile, constructive, efficient, excellent, (*n*) treasure; *antonym* (*adj*) useless, **10.** rare; *synonyms* (*adj*) extraordinary, uncommon, exceptional, infrequent, scarce, seldom, thin, unusual, few, curious, odd, peculiar, novel, flimsy, occasional; *antonyms* (*adj*) common, frequent, ordinary, **11.** striped; *synonyms* (*adj*) streaked, stripy, paled, virgated, zoned, hooped, zonate, **12.** priceless; *synonyms* (*adj*) rare, best, elect, picked.

kakawara haunt; *synonyms* (*v*) frequent, follow, pursue, stalk, obsess, plague, visit, (*n*) den, resort, ghost, hangout, home, (*adj*) harass, molest, worry.

kakawaraki haunted; *synonyms* (*adj*) obsessed, ghostly, bemused, crazed, infatuated, mad, magical, overcome, phantom, possessed, preoccupied, unearthly, ethereal, shadowlike, shadowy.

kakawibaea 1. brag; *synonyms* (*v*) boast, bluster, pride, blow, gasconade, crow, crack, exaggerate, flourish, rodomontade, swagger, (*n*) vaunt, boasting, bounce, bragging, **2.** boast; *synonyms* (*v*) brag, exult, sport, swash, avaunt, (*n*) arrogance, glory, jactitation, **3.** chaff; *synonyms* (*n*) banter, husk, quiz, raillery, shuck, straw, (*v*) tease, jest, ridicule, badinage, joke, jolly, kid, mock, rally, **4.** exaggerate; *synonyms* (*v*) aggravate, amplify, dramatize, overdo, overdraw, enhance, enlarge, magnify, overstate, embellish, heighten, hyperbolize, increase, inflate, overplay; *antonyms* (*v*) understate, minimize, **5.** complicate; *synonyms* (*v*) involve, confuse, perplex, entangle, muddle, puzzle, snarl, tangle, complexify, elaborate; *antonyms* (*v*) clarify, simplify, **6.** enlarge; *synonyms* (*v*) expand, aggrandize, augment, dilate, distend, widen, boost, broaden, develop, extend, grow, rise, swell, diffuse, (*adj*) expatiate; *antonyms* (*v*) reduce, shrink, contract, decrease, **7.** romance; *synonyms* (*n*) fiction, novel,

story, intrigue, affair, fable, romanticism, tale, vagary, (*v*) court, flirt, woo, coquet, coquette, dally.

kakawibaeaki 1. enlarged; *synonyms* (*adj*) exaggerated, extended, inflated, magnified, increased, puffy, augmented, amplified, distended, broad, clear, coarse, comprehensive, cross, dilated; *antonym* (*adj*) lesser, **2.** exaggerated; *synonyms* (*adj*) enlarged, extravagant, theatrical, immoderate, hypertrophied, affected, excessive, hyperbolic, overdone, overstated, pretentious, melodramatic; *antonyms* (*adj*) understated, restrained, **3.** complicated; *synonyms* (*adj*) complex, intricate, elaborate, hard, complicate, awkward, convoluted, deep, difficult, knotty, obscure, sophisticated, tortuous, tricky, (*v*) involved; *antonyms* (*adj*) simple, straightforward, easy.

kakea 1. impair; *synonyms* (*v*) blemish, damage, mar, degrade, corrupt, hurt, disfigure, deface, debase, destroy, deteriorate, diminish, enervate, harm, injure, **2.** abate; *synonyms* (*v*) subside, allay, bate, decline, fade, flag, lessen, relax, relieve, remit, slack, slake, wane, weaken, (*adj*) slacken; *antonym* (*v*) increase, **3.** dwindle; *synonyms* (*v*) abate, decrease, contract, fall, recede, reduce, decay, drop, ebb, fail, shrink, shrivel, waste, **4.** diminish; *synonyms* (*v*) abridge, deduct, detract, dwindle, depreciate, belittle, curtail, retrench, alleviate, deflate, cut, depress, impair, lower, moderate; *antonym* (*v*) grow, **5.** lessen; *synonyms* (*v*) assuage, mitigate, ease, shorten, lighten, minify, minimize, pare, sink, taper, limit, attenuate, dampen, break, cool; *antonym* (*v*) exacerbate, **6.** lower; *synonyms* (*adj*) inferior, less, secondary, subordinate, (*v*) frown, humble, dip, abase, descend, scowl, disgrace, demean, humiliate, deject, glare; *antonym* (*v*) raise, **7.** forsake; *synonyms* (*v*) abandon, desert, ditch, relinquish, abdicate, leave, quit, chuck, forgo, disclaim, depart, desolate, discard, maroon, renounce, **8.** abjure; *synonyms* (*v*) recant, retract, deny, disavow, forswear, disown, recall, reject, repudiate, revoke, withdraw, **9.** forgo; *synonyms* (*v*) forfeit, waive, forsake, resign, foreswear, **10.** abdicate; *synonyms* (*v*) cede, yield, **11.** disavow; *synonyms* (*v*) disallow, abjure, disaffirm, contradict; *antonym* (*v*) avow, **12.** decrease; *synonyms* (*n*) cutback, diminution, reduction, abatement, contraction, decrement, deduction, remission, shortening, discount, (*v*) slow, plummet, subtract, modify, devalue; *antonyms* (*n*) growth, extension, (*v*) rise, intensify, **13.** moderate; *synonyms* (*adj*) temperate, abstemious, middling, mild, easy, dull, fair, frugal, gentle, passable, (*v*) calm, curb, mince, restrict, (*adv*) check; *antonyms* (*adj*) extreme, immoderate, radical, **14.** deny; *synonyms* (*v*) controvert, rebuff, abnegate, gainsay, oppose, refuse, contravene, disprove, traverse, withhold, veto, dispute, forbid, negate, rebut; *antonyms* (*v*) admit, affirm, acknowledge, claim, declare, agree, maintain, **15.** abandon; *synonyms* (*v*) vacate, evacuate, scrap, surrender, strand, cancel, cease, deliver, discontinue, disregard, dump, forego, forget, (*n*) candor, abandonment; *antonyms* (*v*) keep, support, (*n*) restraint, **16.** renounce; *synonyms* (*v*) abstain, sacrifice, spare, stop, evade, neglect, **17.** reject; *synonyms* (*v*) disapprove, dismiss, eliminate, exclude, ignore, repel, spurn, eject, jettison, proscribe, reprobate, repulse, scorn, shun, (*n*) cull; *antonyms* (*v*) accept, approve, choose, select, grant, **18.** prospect; *synonyms* (*n*) expectancy, outlook, view, anticipation, aspect, hope, lookout, perspective, possibility, chance, expectation, future, likelihood, panorama, picture; *antonym* (*n*) past.

kakeaki 1. lessened; *synonyms* (*adj*) diminished, atrophied, attenuate, attenuated, belittled, conical, corrupted, cut, debased, depleted, faded, hurt, lower, pointed, short, **2.** impaired; *synonyms* (*adj*) afflicted, sick, damaged, crippled, defective, faulty, adulterate, affected, deficient, depressed, dilapidated, diluted, disgusted, dumb, ill, **3.** decreased; *synonyms* (*adj*) reduced, dead, fallen, degraded, prostrate, ruined, **4.** abandoned; *synonyms* (*adj*) forlorn, immoral, deserted, empty, profligate, shameless, stranded, wicked, lonely, corrupt, debauched, depraved, derelict, desolate, discarded; *antonyms* (*adj*) restrained, inhabited, orderly, overcrowded, **5.** lowered; *synonyms* (*adj*) abased, bated, cheap, humbled, **6.** moderated; *synonyms* (*adj*) subdued, certified, dependant, dependent, equal, graduated, limited, measured, qualified, restricted, uniform, **7.** forsaken; *synonyms* (*adj*) abandoned, desert, jilted, solitary, friendless, isolated, **8.** diminished; *synonyms* (*adj*) abated, lessened, weakened, airy, backward, blasted, bony, cadaverous, clipped, delicate, desolated, devastated, diminute, less, **9.** rejected; *synonyms* (*v*) forsaken, (*adj*) castaway, refused, reprobate, disallowed, refuse, bare, cheerless, consume, destroy, devastate, dismal, dreary, gloomy, hence.

kakeboa 1. cram; *synonyms* (*v*) stuff, pack, ram, fill, jam, compress, load, shove, compact, ingurgitate, overeat, englut, gormandise, gormandize, gourmandize, **2.** stuff; *synonyms* (*n*) material, cloth, force, gear, matter, goods, stock, substance, fabric, (*v*) cram, pad, squeeze, glut, gorge, (*adj*) rubbish; *antonym* (*v*) unstuff, **3.** swamp; *synonyms* (*n*) marsh, mire, bog, morass, quagmire, (*v*) flood, inundate, overwhelm, submerge, sink, deluge, drench, drown, overflow, engulf; *antonym* (*n*) desert, **4.** pack; *synonyms* (*n*) bundle, mob, bevy, bunch, company, herd, batch, backpack, box, gang, horde, package, knapsack, (*v*) crowd, heap; *antonym* (*v*) unpack.

kakeboaki 1. swamped; *synonyms* (*v*) grounded, (*adj*) flooded, inundated, overcome, busy, engulfed, overpowered, overwhelmed, (*adv*) aground, **2.** stuffed; *synonyms* (*v*) farctate, (*adj*) full, crammed, packed, congested, replete, loaded, chock-full, crowded, fraught, abounding, big, brimming, concentrated, distended; *antonyms* (*adj*) empty, hungry, **3.** packed; *synonyms* (*adj*) compact, filled, jammed, overcrowded, dense, thick, close, cramped, teeming; *antonym* (*adj*) deserted.

kakeiaka stimulate; *synonyms* (*v*) excite, incite, arouse, encourage, enliven, inspire, prompt, provoke, animate, awaken, drive, energize, exhilarate, goad, (*adj*) quicken; *antonym* (*v*) defuse.

kakeiakaki stimulated; *synonyms* (*adj*) excited, inspired, ablaze, aroused, intoxicated, affected, aflame, angry, desirous, emotional, enraged, enthused, fresh, horny, interested; *antonym* (*adj*) uninspired.

kakekea rattle; *synonyms* (*n*) roll, jangle, jingle, click, clack, clang, (*v*) clatter, bang, confuse, patter, shake, disconcert, clash, disturb, drum.

kakekeaki rattled; *synonyms* (*adj*) flustered, perturbed, upset, abashed, addled, afraid, bewildered, disconcerted, distraught, puzzled, unsettled.

kakenakoa 1. lessen; *synonyms* (*v*) diminish, decrease, abridge, abate, contract, curtail, decline, fall, allay, alleviate, assuage, cut, dwindle, mitigate, moderate; *antonyms* (*v*) increase, exacerbate, **2.** thrust; *synonyms* (*v*) jab, force, boost, punch, ram, dig, impel, squeeze, (*n*) push, poke, drive, stab, shove, cast, prod; *antonym* (*v*) pull, **3.** ram; *synonyms* (*n*) tup, (*v*) beat, cram, crash, jam, pack, fill, bump, pound, press, stuff, thrust, crowd, dash, butt, **4.** shove; *synonyms* (*v*) elbow, shift, hustle, nudge, jog, jolt, move, hurtle, put, joggle, crush, (*n*) jostle, shoulder, jerk, impulse, **5.** reduce; *synonyms* (*v*) lower, pare, abbreviate, debase, condense, shorten, concentrate, compress, conquer, detract, dilute, deflate, enfeeble, (*adj*) lessen, degrade; *antonyms* (*v*) bolster, expand, enlarge, intensify, **6.** push; *synonyms* (*n*) energy, (*v*) rush, fight, incite, labor, plug, pressure, promote, campaign, crusade, strain, work, advance, advertise, coerce; *antonyms* (*v*) drag, haul.

kakenakoaki 1. lessened; *synonyms* (*adj*) diminished, atrophied, attenuate, attenuated, belittled, conical, corrupted, cut, debased, depleted, faded, hurt, lower, pointed, short, **2.** reduced; *synonyms* (*adj*) decreased, abridged, curtailed, miniature, cheap, limited, bated, inexpensive, low, prostrate; *antonyms* (*adj*) expensive, complete.

kakenga clash; *synonyms* (*n*) bang, battle, brush, clang, crash, discord, encounter, (*v*) jar, fight, impact, brawl, clank, collide, conflict, dispute; *antonyms* (*n*) agreement, (*v*) agree.

kakera sought; *synonyms (adj)* required, popular, hunted.

kakerakea 1. expand; *synonyms (v)* amplify, enlarge, balloon, broaden, develop, distend, aggrandize, augment, extend, inflate, swell, explicate, bloat, elaborate, *(adj)* dilate; *antonyms (v)* contract, shorten, abbreviate, decrease, deflate, reduce, shrink, summarize, narrow, **2**. extend; *synonyms (v)* expand, widen, continue, elongate, go, spread, carry, increase, offer, contribute, advance, crane, cover, grow, *(adj)* stretch; *antonyms (v)* withdraw, limit, **3**. increase; *synonyms (n)* gain, addition, augmentation, boom, expansion, extension, growth, progress, rise, accretion, *(v)* accrue, enhance, deepen, accumulate, benefit; *antonyms (n)* reduction, contraction, decline, *(v)* diminish, drop, deteriorate.

kakerakeaki 1. increased; *synonyms (adj)* additional, more, enlarged, greater, fresh, new, plus, puffy, ripe, amplified, better, bigger, improved, other, superior, **2**. expanded; *synonyms (adj)* extended, extensive, open, wide, dilated, prolonged; *antonym (adj)* brief, **3**. extended; *synonyms (adj)* broad, expanded, ample, long, elongated, lengthened, lengthy, protracted, comprehensive, continued, outstretched, spacious, stretched, capacious, continuous; *antonyms (adj)* short, condensed, unextended.

kakeraki sought; *synonyms (adj)* required, popular, hunted.

kakerikaka 1. recede; *synonyms (v)* ebb, decline, retire, withdraw, abate, diminish, retreat, give, decrease, go, lose, disappear, back, fall, descend; *antonym (v)* advance, **2**. reduce; *synonyms (v)* lower, pare, abbreviate, curtail, cut, debase, condense, contract, shorten, concentrate, cómpress, conquer, *(adj)* abridge, lessen, degrade; *antonyms (v)* increase, bolster, expand, enlarge, exacerbate, intensify, **3**. retract; *synonyms (v)* recant, abjure, rescind, cancel, forswear, recall, recoil, renounce, repeal, repudiate, reverse, revoke, annul, disclaim, disavow, **4**. withdraw; *synonyms (v)* extract, remove, retract, abandon, disengage, draw, leave, recede, secede, depart, shrink, subtract, swallow, unsay, deduct; *antonyms (v)* extend, offer, present, propose, deposit, **5**. retreat; *synonyms (n)* refuge, resort, asylum, departure, den, lair, privacy, retirement, sanctuary, shelter, withdrawal, flight, haven, *(v)* return, exit; *antonym (n)* raid.

kakerikakaki 1. retreated; *synonym (adj)* withdrawn, **2**. reduced; *synonyms (adj)* decreased, abridged, curtailed, miniature, cheap, limited, bated, cut, inexpensive, low, lower, prostrate; *antonyms (adj)* expensive, complete, **3**. retracted; *synonym (adj)* broken, **4**. withdrawn; *synonyms (adj)* reserved, secluded, retiring, solitary, indrawn, cloistered, reclusive, uncommunicative, lonely,

taciturn, unsociable, introverted, reticent, shy, aloof; *antonym (adj)* outgoing.

kakerua munch; *synonyms (v)* bite, chew, crunch, champ, chomp, eat, gnaw, nibble, cranch, craunch.

kakerukeru rattle; *synonyms (n)* roll, jangle, jingle, click, clack, clang, *(v)* clatter, bang, confuse, patter, shake, disconcert, clash, disturb, drum.

kakerukerua munch; *synonyms (v)* bite, chew, crunch, champ, chomp, eat, gnaw, nibble, cranch, craunch.

kakerukeruaki rattled; *synonyms (adj)* flustered, perturbed, upset, abashed, addled, afraid, bewildered, disconcerted, distraught, puzzled, unsettled.

kaki 1. loosen; *synonyms (v)* free, relax, loose, detach, undo, discharge, ravel, fluff, unbend, untie, liberate, slacken, *(adj)* disengage, *(n)* ease, release; *antonyms (v)* tighten, compress, fasten, **2**. abandon; *synonyms (v)* quit, relinquish, renounce, resign, vacate, desert, evacuate, leave, waive, depart, abdicate, chuck, ditch, drop, forfeit; *antonyms (v)* keep, support, maintain, *(n)* restraint, **3**. forsake; *synonyms (v)* abandon, fail, forgo, disclaim, desolate, discard, maroon, abjure, betray, defect, deny, disown, reject, repudiate, die, **4**. let; *synonyms (v)* allow, hire, admit, lease, permit, charter, have, rent, grant, authorize, cause, countenance, demise, get, *(n)* check; *antonyms (v)* forbid, prevent, **5**. slacken; *synonyms (v)* loosen, abate, slack, remit, retard, douse, decrease, diminish, lessen, moderate, slow, dowse, lag, relent, delay, **6**. reject; *synonyms (v)* refuse, decline, disapprove, dismiss, eliminate, exclude, rebuff, disallow, ignore, repel, spurn, eject, jettison, discount, *(n)* cull; *antonyms (v)* accept, approve, choose, select, acknowledge, **7**. relinquish; *synonyms (v)* cede, concede, forsake, give, surrender, yield, deliver, pass, cease, desist, consign, forego, let, refrain, render; *antonym (v)* retain, **8**. put; *synonyms (v)* place, fix, lay, position, set, impose, couch, locate, pose, charge, pitch, arrange, assign, commit, *(n)* deposit, **9**. tamp; *synonyms (v)* pack, ram, compact, jam, cram.

kakiaki 1. forsaken; *synonyms (adj)* deserted, desolate, abandoned, lonely, forlorn, derelict, desert, jilted, empty, solitary, friendless, isolated, **2**. loosened; *synonyms (adj)* detached, disentangled, loose, disengaged, extricated, unsnarled, **3**. downed; *synonym (adj)* felled, **4**. abandoned; *synonyms (adj)* immoral, profligate, shameless, stranded, wicked, corrupt, debauched, depraved, discarded, dissipated, dissolute, licentious, neglected, reprobate, unprincipled; *antonyms (adj)* restrained, inhabited, orderly, overcrowded, **5**. rejected; *synonyms (v)* forsaken, *(adj)* castaway, refused, disallowed, refuse, bare, cheerless, consume, destroy, devastate, devastated, dismal, dreary, gloomy, hence, **6**. relinquished; *synonym* *(adj)* surrendered, **7**. stowed.

kakibea 1. agitate; *synonyms* *(v)* disturb, stir, toss, fan, bother, foment, perturb, rouse, shake, trouble, actuate, annoy, arouse, canvass, convulse; *antonyms* *(v)* calm, soothe, **2**. scratch; *synonyms* *(n)* score, mark, nick, scrabble, dent, abrasion, cut, groove, *(v)* graze, notch, rub, scrape, chafe, rake, grate, **3**. stir; *synonyms* *(v)* budge, move, affect, agitate, excite, inspire, go, cause, *(n)* movement, commotion, disturbance, excitement, agitation, fuss, *(adj)* bustle.

kakibeaki 1. agitated; *synonyms* *(adj)* restless, excited, nervous, restive, tumultuous, upset, distressed, tense, alarmed, anxious, distraught, jumpy, overwrought, perturbed, shaken; *antonyms* *(adj)* calm, composed, lethargic, **2**. stirred; *synonyms* *(adj)* stimulated, affected, aroused, emotional, aflame, ablaze, beaten, enthused, horny, inspired, interested, randy, ruttish, susceptible, touched; *antonym* *(adj)* uninspired, **3**. scratched; *synonyms* *(adj)* scraped, hurt, abraded, dented, injured, raw, sgraffito, spoiled, broken, skinned, smashed.

kakibekibe stir; *synonyms* *(v)* arouse, budge, move, rouse, affect, agitate, excite, inspire, go, *(n)* movement, commotion, disturbance, excitement, agitation, *(adj)* bustle.

kakibekibeaki stirred; *synonyms* *(adj)* stimulated, excited, affected, aroused, emotional, aflame, ablaze, beaten, enthused, horny, inspired, interested, overwrought, randy, ruttish; *antonym* *(adj)* uninspired.

kakibeuria stir; *synonyms* *(v)* arouse, budge, move, rouse, affect, agitate, excite, inspire, go, *(n)* movement, commotion, disturbance, excitement, agitation, *(adj)* bustle.

kakibeuriaki stirred; *synonyms* *(adj)* stimulated, excited, affected, aroused, emotional, aflame, ablaze, beaten, enthused, horny, inspired, interested, overwrought, randy, ruttish; *antonym* *(adj)* uninspired.

kakibotu 1. divert; *synonyms* *(v)* amuse, distract, entertain, beguile, deflect, delight, deviate, depart, disport, sidetrack, pervert, convert, relax, gratify, dissuade, **2**. amuse; *synonyms* *(v)* divert, absorb, please, charm, occupy, recreate, sport, interest; *antonym* *(v)* bore, **3**. thwarted; *synonyms* *(adj)* frustrated, disappointed, defeated, discomfited, foiled, baffled, balked, beaten, discouraged, disenchanted, disillusioned, dissatisfied, embarrassed, saddened, upset; *antonym* *(adj)* successful, **4**. recreate; *synonyms* *(v)* cheer, reconstruct, play, animate, refresh, renew, renovate, enliven, reanimate, rebuild, invigorate, solace, regenerate, restore, revive, **5**. unwind;

synonyms *(v)* disentangle, unbend, unroll, unfold, unravel, untangle, straighten, loose, rest, decompress, unfurl, unlax, unstrain; *antonym* *(v)* wind, **6**. sidetrack; *synonyms* *(v)* digress, arrest, cast, divagate, diverge, drift, err, go, leave, part, quit, ramble, range, redirect, *(n)* siding, **7**. relax; *synonyms* *(v)* abate, give, lounge, melt, debilitate, ease, relieve, remit, slack, soften, unbrace, weaken, *(n)* loosen, release, *(adj)* relent; *antonyms* *(v)* tighten, tense.

kakibotuaki 1. amused; *synonyms* *(adj)* entertained, diverted, smiling, **2**. diverted; *synonyms* *(adj)* amused, abstracted, inattentive, preoccupied, sidetracked, unfocused, **3**. relaxed; *synonyms* *(adj)* lax, loose, slack, calm, comfortable, composed, easy, cool, informal, easygoing, happy, serene, slow, tranquil, unhurried; *antonyms* *(adj)* tense, anxious, formal, nervous, prim, stiff, uncomfortable, strict, haggard, harassed, prudish, reserved, restless, taut, **4**. unwound.

kakimatoa stiffen; *synonyms* *(v)* harden, set, indurate, ossify, tighten, brace, congeal, reinforce, fortify, intensify, jell, strengthen, temper, thicken, constrain.

kakimotoa 1. curtail; *synonyms* *(v)* contract, abridge, clip, condense, abate, confine, crop, curb, diminish, trim, dock, abbreviate, cut, decrease, *(adj)* shorten; *antonyms* *(v)* extend, lengthen, **2**. abbreviate; *synonyms* *(v)* curtail, reduce, abstract, compress, foreshorten, truncate, *(adj)* abbreviated; *antonym* *(v)* expand, **3**. shorten; *synonyms* *(v)* lessen, prune, summarize, bowdlerise, bowdlerize, expurgate, narrow, restrict, shrink, commute, concentrate.

kakimotoaki 1. abbreviated; *synonyms* *(adj)* shortened, short, abbreviate, abridged, brief, condensed, truncated, compendious, edited, reduced, little, telescoped; *antonym* *(adj)* complete, **2**. shortened; *synonyms* *(adj)* abbreviated, cut, curtailed, down, emasculated, gashed, gelded, imperfect, less, mown, partial, runty, scarce, unfinished, deficient.

kakino tag; *synonyms* *(n)* tail, shred, tab, catch, *(v)* label, dog, mark, name, chase, pursue, earmark, brand, shadow, append, designate.

kakinoaki tagged; *synonyms* *(adj)* labeled, labelled.

kakinounou 1. abyssal; *synonyms* *(adj)* abysmal, deep, marine, nautical, limitless, **2**. deep; *synonyms* *(adj)* thick, profound, absorbed, abstruse, broad, dark, rich, sound, strong, wide, esoteric, bright, large, bass, *(v)* intense; *antonyms* *(adj)* shallow, superficial, high, high-pitched, light, soft, weak, **3**. unfathomable; *synonyms* *(adj)* impenetrable, incomprehensible, inexplicable, inscrutable, mysterious, unintelligible, immeasurable, unaccountable, enigmatic, fathomless, obscure, bottomless, abyssal, illimitable, innumerable; *antonym* *(adj)* fathomable.

kakinranga 1. love; *synonyms* (*n*) desire, affection, dear, fondness, liking, benevolence, charity, attachment, beloved, darling, devotion, honey, (*v*) cherish, enjoy, like; *antonyms* (*n*) abhorrence, hatred, aversion, (*v*) hate, dislike, abhor, **2.** desire; *synonyms* (*n*) ambition, hope, aspiration, will, wish, craving, dream, impulse, (*v*) fancy, aspire, seek, want, aim, choose, crave; *antonym* (*n*) reality.

kakinrangaki 1. loved; *synonyms* (*adj*) dear, beloved, cherished, pet, precious, appreciated, esteemed, prized, respected, treasured, valued, important, (*n*) darling, **2.** desired; *synonyms* (*adj*) coveted, craved, desirable, chosen, favorite, wanted, needed, welcome, adored, appropriate, preferred, proper, (*v*) complying, consenting, willing; *antonym* (*adj*) undesirable.

kakioa 1. chase; *synonyms* (*n*) game, search, quest, (*v*) hunt, pursue, expel, follow, stalk, track, trail, chamfer, pursuit, race, seek, evict, **2.** pursue; *synonyms* (*v*) chase, dog, prosecute, course, haunt, hound, persist, tail, conduct, practice, court, keep, continue, engage, harass.

kakioaki 1. chased; *synonyms* (*adj*) engraved, (*n*) pursued, **2.** pursued; *synonym* (*n*) chased.

kakiokioa expel; *synonyms* (*v*) banish, dismiss, eject, evict, exclude, exile, eliminate, deport, discharge, dispossess, excrete, chase, discard, emit, expatriate.

kakiraroa distant; *synonyms* (*adj*) cold, aloof, remote, chill, cool, detached, far, reserved, long, faraway, icy, indifferent, removed, (*adv*) apart, (*n*) chilly; *antonyms* (*adj*) close, adjacent, friendly, near, nearby, neighboring, warm, pending, alert, intimate, involved.

kakiriaria retard; *synonyms* (*v*) delay, check, hinder, arrest, detain, impede, lag, obstruct, slow, decelerate, procrastinate, curb, prevent, (*n*) defer, (*adj*) deaden; *antonym* (*v*) accelerate.

kakiriariaki retarded; *synonyms* (*adj*) backward, slow, tardy, imbecile, defective, deferred, dull, half-baked, leisurely, obtuse, simple, birdbrained, dim, dim-witted, dopey.

kakiribabaoua 1. curve; *synonyms* (*n*) bend, crook, bow, arc, curvature, kink, round, bender, (*v*) curl, turn, arch, hook, wind, distort, (*adj*) flex, **2.** meander; *synonyms* (*n*) amble, promenade, (*v*) curve, wander, ramble, range, roam, saunter, stray, twine, twist, walk, drift, rove, snake, **3.** bend; *synonyms* (*n*) elbow, angle, bending, buckle, flexure, (*v*) crouch, stoop, deflect, fold, loop, swerve, contort, cower, deform, hunch; *antonyms* (*v*) straighten, square, **4.** snake; *synonyms* (*n*) ophidian, serpent, hydra, (*v*) meander, coil, creep, sneak, weave, **5.** twist; *synonyms* (*n*) spin, twirl, entwine, braid, strain, tangle, (*v*) pervert, wrench, pull, roll, sprain, bias, entangle, intertwine, convolute; *antonym* (*v*) untwist, **6.** wind; *synonyms* (*n*) air, gust, clue, gale, intimation,

suggestion, breath, flatus, hint, jazz, lead, (*v*) blow, spiral, enlace, nose.

kakiribabaouaki 1. bent; *synonyms* (*adj*) arched, curved, bended, crooked, deformed, intent, (*n*) aptitude, inclination, propensity, fancy, ability, bias, flair, gift, leaning; *antonym* (*adj*) straight, **2.** curved; *synonyms* (*adj*) bent, curve, round, bend, curving, curvy, hooked, rounded, tortuous, twisted, (*v*) bowed; *antonym* (*adj*) concave, **3.** twisted; *synonyms* (*adj*) perverted, distorted, coiled, misshapen, contorted, twined, winding, wry, gnarled, awry, kinky, wrong, warped, askew, depraved; *antonym* (*adj*) tidy.

kakiribeubeua 1. lump; *synonyms* (*n*) heap, chunk, knot, block, clod, hunk, tumor, bit, bulge, clump, fragment, knob, (*v*) clot, (*adj*) mass, lout, **2.** rough; *synonyms* (*adj*) coarse, hard, harsh, raw, crude, cruel, grating, gross, hoarse, jagged, approximate, gruff, inclement, (*n*) boisterous, draft; *antonyms* (*adj*) gentle, smooth, polished, precise, refined, silky, soft, sophisticated, even, exact, glossy, pleasant.

kakiritongitong 1. daze; *synonyms* (*n*) fog, shock, stupor, trance, confusion, (*v*) astonish, astound, bedazzle, amaze, befuddle, bewilder, dazzle, stun, surprise, flabbergast, **2.** dumbfound; *synonyms* (*v*) stagger, confound, daze, perplex, puzzle, stupefy, baffle, discombobulate, nonplus, stump, **3.** stupefy; *synonyms* (*v*) paralyze, deaden, numb, bemuse, besot, confuse, drug, petrify, hebetate, muddle, dope, dumbfound, floor, (*n*) benumb, blunt, **4.** stun; *synonyms* (*v*) electrify, galvanize, overwhelm, flummox, mystify, shake, anesthetize, bedaze, overcome, sandbag, (*n*) obtund, (*adv*) startle, (*adj*) deafen.

kakiritongitonga stun; *synonyms* (*v*) amaze, astonish, astound, bewilder, shock, baffle, daze, flabbergast, stagger, deaden, numb, bemuse, (*adv*) startle, surprise, (*adj*) deafen.

kakiritongitongaki 1. dazed; *synonyms* (*adj*) confused, bewildered, stunned, dizzy, dumbfounded, muzzy, stupefied, amazed, astounded, bleary, groggy, stupid; *antonym* (*adj*) alert, **2.** dumbfounded; *synonyms* (*adj*) astonished, staggered, dazed, speechless, flabbergasted, **3.** stunned; *synonyms* (*adj*) astonied, shocked, surprised, kayoed, out, unconscious, **4.** stupefied; *synonym* (*adj*) dumfounded.

kakiriuatao 1. compact; *synonyms* (*adj*) close, dense, compendious, concise, hard, (*n*) agreement, arrangement, contract, covenant, bargain, engagement, (*v*) compress, condense, consolidate, pack; *antonyms* (*adj*) loose, sprawling, bulky, sparse, **2.** heap; *synonyms* (*n*) pile, stack, accumulation, collection, amass, group, lot, mass, mound, bulk, bunch, congeries, (*v*) aggregate, bank, collect, **3.** layer; *synonyms* (*n*) coat, course, coating, cover, film, level, ply, stratum, crust, covering, floor, mantle, row, tier, blanket, **4**. pile; *synonyms* (n) heap, bundle, hoard, jam, nap, wad, lump, multitude, fortune, edifice, batch, down, (v) accumulate, crowd, throng.

kakiriuataoaki 1. layered; *synonyms* (adj) lamellated, caked, coated, covered, encrusted, lamellar, lamelliform, superimposed, overlying, **2**. heaped; *synonyms* (adj) piled, coacervate, collective, cumulative, dense, thick, cumulous, **3**. piled; *synonyms* (adj) heaped, aggregate, pointed.

kakiriwea 1. excite; *synonyms* (v) animate, arouse, disturb, enliven, agitate, energize, awaken, electrify, encourage, evoke, exasperate, incite, inspire, kindle, provoke; *antonyms* (v) calm, pacify, bore, **2**. agitate; *synonyms* (v) stir, toss, fan, bother, foment, perturb, rouse, shake, trouble, actuate, annoy, canvass, convulse, discompose, disquiet; *antonym* (v) soothe.

kakiriweaki 1. agitated; *synonyms* (adj) restless, excited, nervous, restive, tumultuous, upset, distressed, tense, alarmed, anxious, distraught, jumpy, overwrought, perturbed, shaken; *antonyms* (adj) calm, composed, lethargic, **2**. excited; *synonyms* (adj) agitated, ablaze, emotional, enthusiastic, frantic, ardent, aroused, delirious, fervent, heated, impassioned, passionate, warm, elated, (v) animated; *antonyms* (adj) cool, unexcited.

kakiro 1. lengthy; *synonyms* (adj) extended, extensive, long, protracted, wordy, copious, elongated, exuberant, prolonged, verbose, largiloquent; *antonyms* (adj) short, brief, **2**. afar; *synonyms* (adv) away, off, distantly, apart, aside, (adj) outlying, far, (prep) outside, past, **3**. distant; *synonyms* (adj) cold, aloof, remote, chill, cool, detached, reserved, faraway, icy, indifferent, removed, standoffish, unfriendly, abstracted, (n) chilly; *antonyms* (adj) close, adjacent, friendly, near, nearby, neighboring, warm, pending, alert, intimate, involved, **4**. far; *synonyms* (adv) wide, widely, well, astray, (adj) distant, much, (v) considerably, abundantly; *antonym* (adv) briefly.

kakiroa 1. anesthetize; *synonyms* (v) anaesthetise, anaesthetize, deaden, drug, freeze, dull, stun, paralyze, dope, ease, entrance, hypnotize, blunt, bother, discommode, **2**. repulse; *synonyms* (v) rebuff, repel, nauseate, disgust, reject, revolt, refuse, dismiss, drive, rebut, snub, sicken, check, (n) defeat, refusal; *antonyms* (v) attract, welcome, **3**. repel; *synonyms* (v) repulse, decline, displease, parry, oppose, combat, dispel, push, resist, shock, withstand, antagonize, confront, (adj) alienate, (n) defend; *antonyms* (v) charm, draw, **4**. rebuff; *synonyms* (n) denial, rebuke, rejection, repulsion, censure, setback, correction, (v) cut, disallow, ignore, slight, deny, discard, spurn, veto; *antonyms* (n) acceptance, (v) accept, **5**. thwart; *synonyms* (v)

foil, frustrate, baffle, hinder, impede, obstruct, prevent, disappoint, bilk, block, stop, elude, dash, balk, (adv) cross.

kakiroaki 1. anesthetized; *synonyms* (adj) anaesthetized, insensitive, numb, anaesthetised, dead, frozen, insensate, numbed, unfeeling, deadened; *antonym* (adj) sensitive, **2**. thwarted; *synonyms* (adj) frustrated, disappointed, defeated, discomfited, foiled, baffled, balked, beaten, discouraged, disenchanted, disillusioned, dissatisfied, embarrassed, saddened, upset; *antonym* (adj) successful.

kakitaia stain; *synonyms* (n) spot, blemish, blot, mark, smear, dirt, brand, (v) color, dye, tarnish, disgrace, soil, defile, blur, contaminate.

kakitaiaki stained; *synonyms* (adj) besmirched, spotted, dirty, sullied, tainted, tarnished, black, damaged, discolored, flyblown, painted, (v) polluted; *antonyms* (adj) pure, unspoiled.

kakoa fasten; *synonyms* (v) attach, bind, connect, fix, tie, anchor, append, brace, clasp, clinch, determine, pin, secure, stick, (adj) affix; *antonyms* (v) unfasten, detach, undo, unlock.

kakoaki fastened; *synonyms* (adj) fixed, tied, buttoned, closed, fast, tight, binding, empight, even, firm, flat, frozen, intent, laced, reconditioned.

kakoaua 1. establish; *synonyms* (v) confirm, erect, prove, appoint, base, build, constitute, demonstrate, settle, arrange, ascertain, create, determine, fix, found; *antonyms* (v) disprove, abolish, terminate, **2**. accepting; *synonyms* (adj) tolerant, acceptant, agreeable, compliant, considerate, cooperative, credulous, defeatist, helpful, kind, lenient, (n) acceptance, assumption, confirmation, credence, **3**. found; *synonyms* (v) establish, form, construct, ground, institute, bottom, begin, cast, plant, start, imbed, introduce, father, launch, originate; *antonym* (adj) misplaced, **4**. ascertain; *synonyms* (v) see, check, discover, learn, control, detect, ensure, find, tell, understand, assure, decide, identify, insure, notice, **5**. acknowledged; *synonyms* (v) received, (adj) accepted, avowed, recognized, renowned, customary, known, **6**. certify; *synonyms* (v) authenticate, attest, accredit, affirm, endorse, warrant, corroborate, declare, guarantee, license, vouch, sanction, ratify, validate, recognize, **7**. accept; *synonyms* (v) receive, acknowledge, admit, take, abide, accede, acquiesce, adopt, assume, believe, yield, agree, approve, assent, bear; *antonyms* (v) refuse, reject, deny, snub, oppose, renounce, resist, **8**. acknowledge; *synonyms* (v) accept, avow, confess, own, profess, appreciate, concede, answer, grant, hail, know, observe, receipt, recognise, respect; *antonyms* (v) ignore, overlook, **9**. demonstrate; *synonyms* (v) display, exhibit, present, show, argue, certify, evidence, exemplify, explain, indicate, manifest, verify, try, proclaim, illustrate; *antonym* (v) conceal, **10.** confirm; *synonyms* (v) clinch, assert, authorize, justify, testify, uphold, seal, aver, fortify, strengthen, substantiate, sustain, back, comfort, (adj) firm; *antonym* (v) contradict, **11.** assure; *synonyms* (v) secure, persuade, promise, reassure, satisfy, convince, cover, swear, vow, **12.** base; *synonyms* (n) foundation, basis, leg, stand, (adj) abject, mean, dishonorable, ignoble, low, vile, bad, contemptible, despicable, foul, infamous; *antonyms* (n) summit, top, (adj) noble, **13.** affirm; *synonyms* (v) maintain, protest, allege, claim, say, state, announce, asseverate, contend, pronounce, support, emphasize, utter; *antonym* (v) negate, **14.** believe; *synonyms* (v) think, conceive, consider, guess, reckon, expect, hope, imagine, suppose, suspect, apprehend, trow, conjecture, (n) belief, trust; *antonyms* (v) disbelieve, distrust, **15.** proven; *synonyms* (adj) established, proved, irrefutable, acknowledged, authoritative, common, experimental, medical, quantifiable, scientific, sound, undeniable, valid, well-founded; *antonyms* (adj) unconfirmed, unproven, unverified, **16.** prove; *synonyms* (v) examine, essay, evince, test, attempt, adduce, assay, experience, raise, rise, vindicate, eject, leaven, (n) taste, **17.** proved; *synonyms* (adj) proven, tried, apparent, confirmed, demonstrable, faithful, genuine, qualified, reliable, trustworthy.

kakoauaki 1. established; *synonyms* (v) settled, (adj) conventional, accepted, firm, fixed, regular, set, decided, confirmed, secure, accomplished, customary, effected, orthodox, completed; *antonym* (adj) unproven, **2.** acknowledged; *synonyms* (v) received, (adj) avowed, recognized, renowned, known, **3.** founded; *synonyms* (v) cast, fusil, fusible, (adj) based, (prep) established, institute, organized, **4.** certified; *synonyms* (adj) qualified, accredited, official, guaranteed, authorized, approved, certifiable; *antonyms* (adj) informal, unofficial, **5.** affirmed; *synonyms* (adj) declared, stated, **6.** ascertained; *synonyms* (v) absolute, noted, notorious, categorical, clear, decisive, definite, determinate, positive, unequivocal, unmistakable, unqualified, (adj) discovered, certain, observed, **7.** demonstrated; *synonyms* (adj) tried, verified, **8.** confirmed; *synonyms* (adj) chronic, inveterate, assured, habitual, constant, affirmed, ingrained, valid, accustomed; *antonym* (adj) unconfirmed, **9.** assured; *synonyms* (adj) confident, sure, assertive, convinced, reliable, safe, surefire; *antonyms* (adj) insecure, uncertain, **10.** based; *synonyms* (adj) founded, supported, **11.** accepted; *synonyms* (adj) acceptable, acknowledged, assumed, understood, current, popular, proper, usual; *antonyms* (adj) concealed, unpopular, unusual, **12.** proven; *synonyms* (adj) proved, irrefutable, authoritative, common, experimental, medical, quantifiable, scientific, sound, undeniable, well-founded; *antonym* (adj) unverified.

kakokoea shrivel; *synonyms* (v) shrink, contract, wither, dwindle, fade, narrow, scorch, blight, blast, dry, parch, reduce, wilt, wrinkle, decrease.

kakora seed; *synonyms* (n) germ, issue, posterity, root, offspring, progeny, origin, nucleus, brood, embryo, source, beginning, (v) inseminate, plant, sow.

kakoraki seeded; *synonym* (adj) sown.

kakorakura industrious; *synonyms* (adj) active, diligent, assiduous, indefatigable, busy, energetic, hardworking, laborious, tireless, earnest, enterprising, careful, painstaking, sedulous, studious; *antonym* (adj) lazy.

kakorira wean; *synonyms* (v) estrange, alienate, disaffect, ablactate, clear, detach, disengage, disentangle, extricate, free, liberate, loose, raise, withdraw, (n) weanling.

kakoroa 1. complete; *synonyms* (adj) perfect, absolute, consummate, whole, full, stark, accomplished, all, (v) accomplish, achieve, close, finish, execute, act, attain; *antonyms* (adj) incomplete, partial, unfinished, abridged, shortened, sketchy, lacking, narrow, qualified, (v) neglect, **2.** finish; *synonyms* (v) end, complete, cease, determine, discontinue, consume, do, stop, (n) conclusion, death, conclude, ending, finale, glaze, accomplishment; *antonyms* (v) start, begin, continue, (n) beginning, **3.** gash; *synonyms* (n) cut, scratch, wound, crack, fissure, score, cleft, cutting, (v) slash, slit, tear, break, rip, slice, lacerate, **4.** notch; *synonyms* (n) gap, mark, nick, degree, grade, groove, hole, (v) dent, hack, indent, nock, hollow, jag, engrave, chip, **5.** perfect; *synonyms* (adj) exact, utter, entire, faultless, thorough, exquisite, integral, blameless, clean, correct, flawless, ideal, immaculate, (v) fulfill, mature; *antonyms* (adj) imperfect, faulty, flawed.

kakoroaki 1. notched; *synonyms* (adj) jagged, serrated, jaggy, serrate, toothed, erose, rough, uneven, **2.** finished; *synonyms* (adj) done, (adj) complete, completed, ended, perfect, consummate, absolute, accomplished, polished, ripe, ruined, spent, round, capable, (adv) over; *antonyms* (adj) unfinished, incomplete, remaining, **3.** completed; *synonyms* (adj) finished, ready, through, whole, **4.** perfected; *synonyms* (adj) elaborate, mature, mellow.

kakoroiku 1. bully; *synonyms* (n) browbeat, rowdy, tough, bravo, hooligan, ruffian, (v) bluster, bulldoze, ballyrag, coerce, intimidate, threaten, badger, swagger, (adj) domineer, **2.** threaten; *synonyms* (v) menace, bully, endanger, loom, offer, imperil, jeopardize, peril, approach, foreshadow, portend, impend, frighten, scare, (n) threat; *antonym* (v) help.

kakoroikuaki bullied; *synonyms* (adj) intimidated, browbeaten, cowed, hangdog, timid, guilty, shamed, shamefaced.

kakorone colonize; *synonyms* (v) colonise, people, inhabit, immigrate, pioneer, domesticate, fill, stay, crowd, (n) settle, balance, bench, calm, compose, depress.

kakoroneaki colonized; *synonyms* (adj) colonised, settled, inhabited, occupied, peopled, populated, defined, formed; *antonym* (adj) uninhabited.

kakuba 1. astound; *synonyms* (v) astonish, surprise, daze, shock, stun, frighten, baffle, confound, flabbergast, perplex, petrify, startle, electrify, (adj) amaze, **2.** stagger; *synonyms* (v) falter, lurch, flounder, hobble, reel, shake, pitch, dumbfound, totter, astound, limp, careen, distribute, flummox, (adj) bewilder, **3.** sudden; *synonyms* (adj) abrupt, hasty, precipitous, quick, rash, unexpected, steep, dramatic, headlong, immediate, precipitate, sharp, swift, unforeseen, impulsive; *antonyms* (adj) gradual, considered, **4.** startle; *synonyms* (v) alarm, jump, scare, dismay, rouse, stagger, terrify, disturb, panic, jolt, appall, daunt, agitate, (n) start, leap, **5.** surprise; *synonyms* (n) fright, amazement, astonishment, surprisal, wonder, admiration, consternation, miracle, stupefaction, (v) catch, overwhelm, overtake, capture, discover, ambush.

kakubaki 1. astounded; *synonyms* (adj) astonished, amazed, stunned, bewildered, dumbfounded, flabbergasted, staggered, surprised, astonied, **2.** surprised; *synonyms* (adj) astounded, shocked, startled, aghast, confused, curious, puzzled, questioning, quizzical, baffled, bemused, confounded, dazed, incredulous, inquiring; *antonym* (adj) indifferent, **3.** startled; *synonyms* (adj) scared, distressed, frightened, afraid, terrified, alarmed, anxious, troubled, upset, worried, horrified, panicky.

kakuia startle; *synonyms* (v) alarm, frighten, jump, scare, astonish, shock, astound, amaze, shake, dismay, electrify, rouse, stagger, (n) start, (adv) surprise.

kakuiaki startled; *synonyms* (adj) scared, dumbfounded, aghast, distressed, frightened, amazed, astonished, afraid, astounded, shocked, terrified, alarmed, anxious, bewildered, flabbergasted.

kakukua shrivel; *synonyms* (v) shrink, contract, wither, dwindle, fade, narrow, scorch, blight, blast, dry, parch, reduce, wilt, wrinkle, decrease.

kakukure gratify; *synonyms* (v) content, appease, delight, please, accommodate, humor, satisfy, amuse, cater, indulge, suit, divert, favor, feast, (adj) contented; *antonyms* (v) dissatisfy, displease.

kakukureaki gratified; *synonyms* (adj) contented, glad, delighted, pleased, happy, grateful, thankful.

kakukurei 1. exciting; *synonyms* (adj) excited, breathtaking, exhilarating, impressive, moving, provocative, rousing, stirring, dramatic, emotional, agitated, absorbing, arousing, electric, fascinating; *antonyms* (adj) boring, dull, bland, insipid, monotonous, uninteresting, unexciting, **2.** jolly; *synonyms* (adj) jovial, cheerful, gay, happy, festive, genial, bright, cheery, jocund, merry, convivial, jocular, gleeful, funny, (v) chaff; *antonym* (adj) sad.

kakukureia 1. enjoy; *synonyms* (v) appreciate, bask, have, hold, possess, relish, delight, experience, like, love, own, rejoice, revel, devour, take; *antonym* (v) dislike, **2.** please; *synonyms* (v) gratify, amuse, charm, entertain, oblige, enchant, enrapture, accommodate, divert, gladden, indulge, satisfy, suit, (adj) enjoy, content; *antonyms* (v) displease, annoy, anger, irritate, distress, **3.** thrill; *synonyms* (n) tingle, chill, excitement, flush, frisson, kick, shake, (v) excite, quiver, shiver, shudder, exhilarate, exalt, pierce, stir.

kakukureiaki 1. thrilled; *synonyms* (adj) delighted, jubilant, excited, happy, overjoyed, ecstatic, elated, pleased, **2.** pleased; *synonyms* (adj) contented, glad, content, gratified, joyful, thankful, appreciative, cheerful, comfortable, satisfied, grateful; *antonyms* (adj) displeased, angry, annoyed, unhappy, worried.

kakunainga 1. terrify; *synonyms* (v) alarm, fright, affright, panic, dismay, horrify, intimidate, startle, terrorize, daunt, dread, appall, petrify, (n) frighten, scare, **2.** terrible; *synonyms* (adj) atrocious, dreadful, horrible, horrid, monstrous, abominable, appalling, awful, dire, fearful, frightful, ghastly, hideous, alarming, bad; *antonyms* (adj) wonderful, lovely, pleasant, **3.** terrorize; *synonyms* (v) terrify, cow, terrorise, coerce, threaten, bully, menace, pressure.

kakunaingaki terrified; *synonyms* (adj) afraid, frightened, scared, fearful, aghast, panicked, panicky; *antonym* (adj) calm.

kakunna toast; *synonyms* (n) pledge, brown, plight, (v) drink, roast, burn, bake, wassail, cook, crisp, heat, inflame, salute.

kakunnaki toasted; *synonyms* (adj) baked, heated.

kakurere terrible; *synonyms* (adj) atrocious, dreadful, horrible, horrid, monstrous, abominable, appalling, awful, dire, fearful, frightful, ghastly, hideous, alarming, bad; *antonyms* (adj) wonderful, lovely, pleasant.

kakurerea 1. terrify; *synonyms* (v) alarm, fright, affright, panic, dismay, horrify, intimidate, startle, terrorize, daunt, dread, appall, petrify, (n) frighten, scare, **2.** terrorize; *synonyms* (v) terrify, cow, terrorise, coerce, threaten, bully, menace, pressure.

kakurereaki terrified; *synonyms* (*adj*) afraid, frightened, scared, fearful, aghast, panicked, panicky; *antonym* (*adj*) calm.

kama cook; *synonyms* (*n*) chef, (*v*) boil, bake, brew, make, prepare, concoct, falsify, grill, poach, roast, simmer, stew, coddle, heat.

kamabu 1. forbid; *synonyms* (*v*) debar, prohibit, ban, bar, disallow, exclude, deny, avert, frustrate, inhibit, interdict, outlaw, prevent, proscribe, veto; *antonyms* (*v*) permit, allow, let, approve, 2. bar; *synonyms* (*n*) barricade, band, stop, line, pub, snag, fence, (*v*) block, bolt, obstruct, arrest, balk, dam, foreclose, confine, 3. interdict; *synonyms* (*n*) embargo, prohibition, inhibition, curse, interdiction, proscription, restraint, taboo, exclusion, (*v*) enjoin, forbid, command, check, 4. ban; *synonyms* (*n*) anathema, banning, execration, forbiddance, forbidding, imprecation, malediction, restriction, (*v*) banish, expel, illegalize, reject, blackball, hinder, impede; *antonym* (*v*) sanction, 5. strike; *synonyms* (*n*) knock, assault, clap, (*v*) bang, beat, hit, impress, slap, move, affect, box, buffet, bump, clout, coin, 6. restrict; *synonyms* (*v*) limit, restrain, circumscribe, constrain, fetter, bound, curb, curtail, hamper, reduce, ration, bind, contain, cramp, modify, 7. prohibit; *synonyms* (*v*) preclude, deter, oppose, restrict, disqualify, negative, 8. repudiate; *synonyms* (*v*) discard, renounce, forswear, decline, recant, disavow, disown, refuse, relinquish, forsake, refute, abdicate, abjure, dismiss, ignore.

kamabuaki 1. barred; *synonyms* (*v*) striated, areolar, veined, cancellated, grated, (*adj*) prohibited, forbidden, barricaded, banned, blockaded, bolted, disallowed, disqualified, excluded, fast; *antonyms* (*adj*) admissible, legitimate, 2. banned; *synonyms* (*adj*) taboo, illegal, contraband, unlawful, 3. forbidden; *synonyms* (*adj*) illicit, proscribed, verboten; *antonym* (*adj*) acceptable, 4. prohibited; *synonyms* (*adj*) barred, out, 5. repudiated; *synonym* (*adj*) disowned, 6. restricted; *synonyms* (*v*) qualified, (*adj*) limited, confined, cramped, narrow, constrained, exclusive, local, controlled, finite, classified, secret, bounded, circumscribed, private; *antonyms* (*adj*) unrestricted, far-reaching, free, liberated, unimpeded, unlimited, open, wide.

kamaea smash; *synonyms* (*v*) collapse, crash, bang, hit, break, crush, mash, shatter, defeat, demolish, pound, (*n*) clash, blast, collision, knock.

kamaeaki smashed; *synonyms* (*adj*) shattered, drunk, inebriated, intoxicated, broken, plastered, sloshed, blotto, tipsy, besotted, pissed, tight; *antonym* (*adj*) sober.

kamaen supple; *synonyms* (*adj*) flexible, lithe, pliable, pliant, soft, elastic, graceful, lissom, lissome, lithesome, plastic, active, agile, ductile, (*v*) limber; *antonyms* (*adj*) stiff, rigid, inflexible.

kamaenikuna shatter; *synonyms* (*v*) break, fragment, burst, destroy, ruin, smash, dash, rupture, crash, blast, crack, demolish, batter, frustrate, disintegrate.

kamaenikunaki shattered; *synonyms* (*v*) exhausted, battered, lame, (*adj*) broken, destroyed, smashed, crazy, shaky.

kamaerikirikia shatter; *synonyms* (*v*) break, fragment, burst, destroy, ruin, smash, dash, rupture, crash, blast, crack, demolish, batter, frustrate, disintegrate.

kamaerikirikiaki shattered; *synonyms* (*v*) exhausted, battered, lame, (*adj*) broken, destroyed, smashed, crazy, shaky.

kamâg 1. fearful; *synonyms* (*adj*) afraid, cowardly, dreadful, anxious, apprehensive, awful, craven, terrible, timid, dire, eerie, formidable, frightful, appalling, awesome; *antonyms* (*adj*) brave, calm, rational, bold, confident, unimpressed, 2. dreadful; *synonyms* (*adj*) bad, dread, alarming, atrocious, fearful, abominable, direful, ghastly, grisly, hideous, horrible, monstrous, detestable, deplorable, disastrous; *antonyms* (*adj*) pleasant, wonderful.

kamai fetch; *synonyms* (*v*) carry, bring, convey, draw, elicit, attract, catch, get, retrieve, transport, conduct, extract, earn, bear, (*adj*) feint.

kamaimaia saturate; *synonyms* (*v*) drench, imbue, infuse, satiate, charge, fill, permeate, impregnate, sate, soak, steep, douse, infiltrate, imbrue, (*adj*) wet.

kamaimaiaki saturated; *synonyms* (*adj*) drenched, sodden, wet, concentrated, soaked, sopping, full, soggy, soppy, pure, soaking; *antonym* (*adj*) dry.

kamainaina 1. blanch; *synonyms* (*v*) whiten, pale, blench, fade, parboil, whitewash, (*adj*) bleach, decolorize, achromatize, 2. whiten; *synonyms* (*v*) white, dealbate, gloss, palliate, scour, veneer, chalk, dull, frost, grizzle, lighten, (*adj*) blanch; *antonym* (*v*) blacken.

kamainainaki 1. blanched; *synonyms* (*adj*) ashen, colorless, livid, white, bleached, achromatic, afraid, benevolent, bloodless, cadaverous, etiolate, etiolated, faded, fair, lightened, 2. whitened; *synonyms* (*adj*) blanched, blank, clean, snowy, unsullied.

kamainga move; *synonyms* (*v*) act, affect, carry, excite, go, impel, instigate, maneuver, touch, travel, flow, bear, (*n*) motion, drive, transfer; *antonym* (*v*) stay.

kamaioa wait; *synonyms* (*v*) expect, anticipate, stop, ambush, await, lurk, stay, linger, remain, abide, hesitate, (*n*) delay, pause, hold, (*adj*) tarry.

kamaira 1. nasty; *synonyms* (*adj*) dirty, loathsome, disgusting, filthy, foul, awful, mean, abominable, coarse, disagreeable, distasteful, evil, hurtful, obnoxious, raw; *antonyms* (*adj*) agreeable, kind, pleasant, nice, charitable, lovely, **2.** impure; *synonyms* (*adj*) defiled, bastard, sordid, squalid, unclean, immoral, profane, contaminated, indecent, lewd, libidinous, licentious, muddy, obscene, improper; *antonym* (*adj*) pure, **3.** filthy; *synonyms* (*adj*) dingy, nasty, bawdy, grimy, grubby, impure, ribald, smutty, vile, vulgar, despicable, lousy, low, messy, mucky; *antonyms* (*adj*) clean, decent, **4.** obscene; *synonyms* (*adj*) gross, lascivious, fulsome, immodest, abhorrent, detestable, naughty, loose, blue, indelicate, dissolute, repugnant, repulsive, revolting, salacious, **5.** squalid; *synonyms* (*adj*) seedy, abject, seamy, sleazy, mangy, shabby, miserable, base, black, scruffy, poor, wretched, flyblown, **6.** ugly; *synonyms* (*adj*) forbidding, frightful, gruesome, hideous, homely, surly, offensive, atrocious, deformed, grotesque, horrible, monstrous, ominous, plain, shocking; *antonyms* (*adj*) beautiful, attractive, good-looking, flowing, ornamental.

kamairatuatua 1. grotesque; *synonyms* (*adj*) fantastic, bizarre, funny, antic, baroque, droll, strange, fantastical, hideous, monstrous, ugly, weird, fanciful, outlandish, (*n*) freak, **2.** hideous; *synonyms* (*adj*) awful, dreadful, frightful, fearful, ghastly, appalling, grim, grisly, gruesome, horrible, horrid, lurid, repulsive, offensive, disgusting; *antonyms* (*adj*) attractive, lovely, pleasant, **3.** ugly; *synonyms* (*adj*) nasty, disagreeable, forbidding, homely, surly, evil, atrocious, deformed, despicable, grotesque, ominous, plain, shocking, sinister, vile; *antonyms* (*adj*) beautiful, good-looking, flowing, ornamental.

kamairia foul; *synonyms* (*adj*) base, disgusting, filthy, nasty, evil, dingy, putrid, unclean, abominable, (*n*) soil, (*v*) dirty, corrupt, coarse, defile, befoul; *antonyms* (*adj*) pleasant, fair, (*v*) clean, pure.

kamairiaki fouled; *synonyms* (*adj*) dirty, afoul, befouled, foul, polluted, contaminated, soiled, stained, dirtied, disgustful, disgusting, distasteful, fetid, filthy, foetid.

kamaita 1. lavish; *synonyms* (*adj*) extravagant, exuberant, generous, ample, copious, prodigal, abundant, bountiful, excessive, improvident, lush, munificent, plush, (*v*) dissipate, profuse; *antonym* (*adj*) meager, **2.** increase; *synonyms* (*n*) gain, addition, augmentation, boom, expansion, extension, (*v*) advance, accrue, extend, grow, aggrandize, expand, enhance, enlarge, (*adj*) augment; *antonyms* (*n*) reduction, contraction, decline, (*v*) decrease, reduce, diminish, drop, deteriorate, **3.** multiply; *synonyms* (*v*) breed, increase, propagate, duplicate, procreate, proliferate, reproduce, calculate, add, boost, amplify, manifold, raise, repeat, double, **4.**

augment; *synonyms* (*v*) reinforce, improve, intensify, magnify, mount, broaden, compound, develop, heighten, multiply, rise, supplement, swell, wax, inflate.

kamaitaki 1. increased; *synonyms* (*adj*) additional, more, enlarged, greater, fresh, new, plus, puffy, ripe, amplified, better, bigger, improved, other, superior, **2.** multiplied; *synonyms* (*v*) absorb, acquisition, attainment, engross, engulf, (*adj*) manifold, many, multitudinous, peopled, populous, studded, teeming, thick, complicated, divers, **3.** augmented; *synonym* (*adj*) inflated.

kamaitan multiply; *synonyms* (*v*) breed, expand, increase, propagate, augment, duplicate, procreate, proliferate, reproduce, calculate, extend, enlarge, add, boost, amplify; *antonym* (*v*) decrease.

kamaitanaki multiplied; *synonyms* (*v*) absorb, acquisition, attainment, engross, engulf, (*adj*) manifold, many, multitudinous, peopled, populous, studded, teeming, thick, complicated, divers.

kamaitoroa 1. cool; *synonyms* (*adj*) chilly, cold, collected, composed, fine, aloof, apathetic, lukewarm, (*v*) calm, chill, assuage, allay, pacify, (*n*) composure, poise; *antonyms* (*adj*) agitated, hot, excited, enthusiastic, feverish, friendly, temperate, tepid, (*v*) warm, heat, **2.** refresh; *synonyms* (*v*) freshen, air, enliven, invigorate, update, comfort, cool, recruit, regenerate, rejuvenate, renew, restore, revive, fan, quicken.

kamaitoroaki refreshed; *synonyms* (*adj*) fresh, invigorated, reinvigorated, new, novel, bracing, brisk, clean, energising, energizing, impertinent, impudent, overbold, recharged, refreshful; *antonyms* (*adj*) exhausted, tired.

kamaiu 1. energizing; *synonyms* (*adj*) bracing, energising, brisk, dynamic, invigorating, refreshing, (*n*) activating, activation, **2.** agreeable; *synonyms* (*adj*) acceptable, accordant, pleasant, pleasing, nice, affable, amusing, compatible, conformable, congenial, consistent, enjoyable, genial, grateful, (*v*) desirable; *antonyms* (*adj*) disagreeable, discordant, nasty, unpleasant, unwilling, aggressive, resistant, **3.** refreshing; *synonyms* (*adj*) fresh, refreshful, cool, crisp, tonic, clean, energizing, lively, new, novel, welcome; *antonyms* (*adj*) unwelcome, soporific.

kamaiua 1. save; *synonyms* (*v*) deliver, economize, rescue, conserve, free, hoard, keep, maintain, preserve, liberate, protect, redeem, retain, defend, (*prep*) except; *antonyms* (*v*) spend, squander, waste, **2.** refresh; *synonyms* (*v*) freshen, air, enliven, invigorate, update, comfort, cool, recruit, regenerate, rejuvenate, renew, restore, revive, fan, quicken, **3.** redeem; *synonyms* (*v*) atone, recover, recoup, expiate, ransom, reclaim, save, extricate, refund, pay, regain, retrieve, salvage, offset, recuperate.

kamaiuaki 1. saved; *synonyms* (*adj*) protected, blessed, secure, **2.** redeemed; *synonym* (*adj*) ransomed, **3.** refreshed; *synonyms* (*adj*) fresh, invigorated, reinvigorated, new, novel, bracing, brisk, clean, energising, energizing, impertinent, impudent, overbold, recharged, refreshful; *antonyms* (*adj*) exhausted, tired.

kamaka 1. frighten; *synonyms* (*v*) alarm, cow, dismay, daunt, terrify, appall, affright, intimidate, scare, terrorize, awe, deter, horrify, startle, (*n*) fright; *antonyms* (*n*) comfort, encourage, **2.** scare; *synonyms* (*n*) dread, fear, menace, anxiety, shock, start, (*v*) frighten, discourage, threaten, amaze, petrify, (*adj*) panic, consternation, horror, terror, **3.** spook; *synonyms* (*n*) apparition, phantom, ghost, shade, specter, spectre, wraith, spirit, spy, creep, schmuck, **4.** revive; *synonyms* (*v*) recover, animate, invigorate, quicken, refresh, renew, renovate, restore, resuscitate, awake, repair, reanimate, recreate, regenerate, reinstate, **5.** terrorize; *synonyms* (*v*) terrorise, coerce, bully, pressure, **6.** shock; *synonyms* (*n*) blow, daze, impact, collision, outrage, surprise, concussion, tremor, (*v*) jar, offend, revolt, clash, disgust, shake, agitate.

kamakaki 1. frightened; *synonyms* (*adj*) afraid, fearful, scared, terrified, timid, anxious, apprehensive, horrified, intimidated, restless, worried, (*adv*) cowardly; *antonyms* (*adj*) calm, confident, unimpressed, brave, fearless, **2.** shocked; *synonyms* (*adj*) dismayed, aghast, amazed, distressed, stunned, surprised, appalled, bewildered, dumbfounded, speechless, upset; *antonyms* (*adj*) delighted, indifferent, **3.** scared; *synonyms* (*adj*) frightened, nervous, panicky, **4.** revived; *synonyms* (*adj*) reanimated, fresh, refreshed, revitalized, invigorated, new, recharged, rejuvenated; *antonym* (*adj*) tired.

kamakanakana soften; *synonyms* (*v*) mitigate, moderate, assuage, dull, melt, mute, relent, relieve, alleviate, allay, pacify, break, cushion, (*adj*) mollify, palliate; *antonyms* (*v*) harden, set, solidify, congeal.

kamakanakanaki softened; *synonyms* (*adj*) dull, diffused, muffled, muted, boring, deadening, dense, dim, dumb, faint, gray, grey, hushed, intenerate, irksome.

kamakerua 1. bit; *synonyms* (*n*) crumb, morsel, piece, atom, drop, fleck, fragment, moment, part, portion, shred, snatch, (*v*) curb, scrap, scantling, **2.** masticate; *synonyms* (*v*) chew, crunch, munch, gnaw, manducate, eat, bite, champ, jaw, cranch, craunch, **3.** gnaw; *synonyms* (*v*) fret, corrode, erode, nibble, masticate, fray, harass, devour, rankle, rasp, tease, waste, curry, (*n*) chafe, sting, **4.**

bite; *synonyms* (*n*) taste, bit, cheat, pain, sample, tang, spice, try, catch, chomp, (*v*) nip, cut, pinch, burn, hurt, **5.** chomp, **6.** chaw; *synonyms* (*n*) quid, ballyhoo, batch, cud, plug, talk, wad, chewing, deal, fireplug, flock, (*v*) deliberate, mull, muse, consider, **7.** crunch; *synonyms* (*n*) squeeze, compaction, compression, (*v*) crush, crackle, scrunch, grind, shatter, crash, crinkle, mash, beat, bray, comminute, crump, **8.** rend; *synonyms* (*v*) cleave, pull, break, lacerate, split, divide, rive, tear, disrupt, slash, mangle, pluck, snap, dismember, (*n*) rip.

kamaki cooked; *synonyms* (*adj*) ripe, overcooked, altered, damaged, defiled, heated, spent, wanting.

kamakimakia saturate; *synonyms* (*v*) drench, imbue, infuse, satiate, charge, fill, permeate, impregnate, sate, soak, steep, douse, infiltrate, imbrue, (*adj*) wet.

kamakimakiaki saturated; *synonyms* (*adj*) drenched, sodden, wet, concentrated, soaked, sopping, full, soggy, soppy, pure, soaking; *antonym* (*adj*) dry.

kamakin intimidate; *synonyms* (*v*) daunt, browbeat, bully, discourage, frighten, bullyrag, deter, scare, alarm, dismay, cow, terrify, terrorize, threaten, (*n*) affright; *antonym* (*v*) encourage.

kamakinaki intimidated; *synonyms* (*adj*) bullied, frightened, scared, afraid, browbeaten, cowed, hangdog, timid, daunted, anxious, demoralized, fearful, guilty, impressed, nervy; *antonym* (*adj*) unimpressed.

kamakua 1. terrorize; *synonyms* (*v*) frighten, intimidate, scare, terrify, cow, terrorise, coerce, threaten, bully, menace, pressure, **2.** terrify; *synonyms* (*v*) alarm, fright, affright, panic, dismay, horrify, startle, terrorize, daunt, dread, appall, petrify, **3.** threaten; *synonyms* (*v*) endanger, loom, offer, imperil, jeopardize, peril, approach, foreshadow, portend, impend, augur, await, betoken, (*n*) threat; *antonym* (*v*) help, **4.** scare; *synonyms* (*n*) fear, anxiety, shock, start, (*v*) awe, discourage, deter, amaze, surprise, bother, dash, pall, (*adj*) consternation, horror, terror.

kamakuaki terrified; *synonyms* (*adj*) afraid, frightened, scared, fearful, aghast, panicked, panicky; *antonym* (*adj*) calm.

kamakuna immerse; *synonyms* (*v*) dip, douse, plunge, absorb, drench, drown, dunk, bury, engross, engulf, steep, submerge, bathe, duck, sink.

kamakunaki immersed; *synonyms* (*adj*) absorbed, submerged, engrossed, deep, underwater, attentive, bathed, buried, captivated, concentrated, covered, engaged, enthralled, fascinated, gripped.

kamakunakuna mar; *synonyms* (*v*) disfigure, spoil, blemish, deface, harm, impair, injure, corrupt, hurt, deflower, maim, mutilate, botch, mangle, (*adj*) damage; *antonym* (*v*) enhance.

kamakunakunaki marred; *synonyms* (*adj*) damaged, defaced, crippled, deficient, deformed, dilapidated, faulty, hurt, impaired, imperfect, scarred.

kamakura move; *synonyms* (*v*) act, affect, carry, excite, go, impel, instigate, maneuver, touch, travel, flow, bear, (*n*) motion, drive, transfer; *antonym* (*v*) stay.

kamama 1. confound; *synonyms* (*v*) bewilder, baffle, confuse, astonish, nonplus, perplex, puzzle, amaze, astound, bamboozle, mistake, mystify, complicate, (*n*) surprise, (*adj*) stupefy; *antonym* (*v*) enlighten, **2**. humiliate; *synonyms* (*v*) degrade, debase, disgrace, abase, demean, insult, mortify, embarrass, lower, shame, snub, chagrin, (*n*) humble, dishonor, disparage; *antonym* (*v*) respect, **3**. shame; *synonyms* (*n*) reproach, discredit, humiliation, modesty, pity, scandal, contempt, degradation, embarrassment, ignominy, infamy, mortification, opprobrium, (*v*) humiliate, abash; *antonym* (*v*) honor, **4**. shameful; *synonyms* (*adj*) disgraceful, dishonorable, scandalous, contemptible, degrading, despicable, disreputable, ignominious, inglorious, opprobrious, shocking, (*v*) base, foul, gross, black; *antonyms* (*adj*) honorable, dignified, noble, admirable.

kamamaea 1. shame; *synonyms* (*n*) reproach, disgrace, discredit, humiliation, chagrin, insult, modesty, pity, scandal, contempt, (*v*) dishonor, degrade, humiliate, abash, debase; *antonym* (*v*) honor, **2**. reproach; *synonyms* (*n*) blame, charge, abuse, invective, condemnation, imputation, (*v*) censure, rebuke, accuse, reprimand, chide, condemn, criminate, dispraise, impeach; *antonyms* (*v*) praise, commend.

kamamaeaki shamed; *synonyms* (*adj*) disgraced, dishonored, ashamed, discredited, guilty, hangdog, abashed, browbeaten, bullied, cowed, damaged, fallen, intimidated, shamefaced, mortified.

kamamaki 1. confounded; *synonyms* (*adj*) bemused, bewildered, accursed, abashed, baffled, befuddled, confused, cursed, execrable, puzzled, aghast, abominable, **2**. humiliated; *synonyms* (*adj*) ashamed, humbled, mortified, embarrassed, humble, broken, crushed; *antonym* (*adj*) proud, **3**. shamed; *synonyms* (*adj*) disgraced, dishonored, discredited, guilty, hangdog, browbeaten, bullied, cowed, damaged, fallen, intimidated, shamefaced.

kamamara relax; *synonyms* (*v*) loose, abate, give, lounge, unbend, melt, debilitate, ease, relieve, remit, rest, slack, (*n*) loosen, release, (*adj*) relent; *antonyms* (*v*) tighten, tense.

kamamaraea 1. impair; *synonyms* (*v*) blemish, damage, mar, degrade, corrupt, hurt, disfigure, deface, debase, destroy, deteriorate, diminish, enervate, harm, injure, **2**. debilitate; *synonyms* (*v*) enfeeble, weaken, exhaust, impair, waste, drain, depress, undermine, prostrate, sap, (*adj*) eviscerate;

antonym (*v*) enable, **3**. enfeeble; *synonyms* (*v*) debilitate, attenuate, unnerve, break, cripple, reduce, disable; *antonym* (*v*) fortify.

kamamaraeaki 1. impaired; *synonyms* (*adj*) afflicted, sick, damaged, crippled, corrupted, defective, faulty, adulterate, affected, deficient, depressed, dilapidated, diluted, disgusted, dumb, **2**. debilitated; *synonyms* (*adj*) enervated, feeble, infirm, enfeebled, adynamic, asthenic, (*v*) weak, **3**. enfeebled; *synonyms* (*adj*) debilitated, decrepit.

kamamaraki relaxed; *synonyms* (*adj*) lax, loose, slack, calm, comfortable, composed, easy, cool, informal, easygoing, happy, serene, slow, tranquil, unhurried; *antonyms* (*adj*) tense, anxious, formal, nervous, prim, stiff, uncomfortable, strict, haggard, harassed, prudish, reserved, restless, taut.

kamamate 1. fatal; *synonyms* (*adj*) calamitous, deadly, destructive, disastrous, lethal, pestilent, dangerous, deathly, fateful, mortal, grave, killing, malignant, noxious, pernicious; *antonym* (*adj*) nonfatal, **2**. grievous; *synonyms* (*adj*) bitter, deplorable, dolorous, dreadful, sad, tough, pitiful, atrocious, heavy, painful, plaintive, regrettable, serious, sorrowful, weighty, **3**. dodgy; *synonyms* (*adj*) crafty, dicey, chancy, cunning, unsafe, devious, dishonest, foxy, guileful, hazardous, risky, slick, sly, tricksy, tricky, **4**. noxious; *synonyms* (*adj*) detrimental, injurious, deleterious, harmful, evil, bad, baneful, inimical, malign, noisome, poisonous, venomous, damaging, nasty, adverse; *antonyms* (*adj*) harmless, innocuous, pleasant, **5**. killing; *synonyms* (*adj*) captivating, fascinating, (*n*) homicide, carnage, manslaughter, assassination, bloodshed, cleanup, kill, massacre, murder, execution, (*adj*) fatal, draining, murderous, **6**. dangerous; *synonyms* (*adj*) critical, severe, adventurous, unhealthy, hurtful, perilous, precarious, threatening, desperate, explosive, hard, parlous, reckless, terrible, unsound; *antonyms* (*adj*) safe, secure, stable, **7**. heavy; *synonyms* (*adj*) dull, deep, dark, dense, fat, full, gross, arduous, bulky, burdensome, grievous, oppressive, thick, compact, ample; *antonyms* (*adj*) light, easy, slim, thin, slight, gentle, puny, skinny, **8**. grave; *synonyms* (*adj*) austere, solemn, earnest, grand, important, sedate, sober, material, great, calm, (*n*) cemetery, death, (*v*) acute, engrave, carve; *antonyms* (*adj*) mild, frivolous, funny, **9**. mortal; *synonyms* (*adj*) human, earthly, implacable, dying, terminal, (*n*) individual, man, creature, person, being, body, soul, homo, life, party; *antonyms* (*adj*) eternal, (*n*) immortal, **10**. risky; *synonyms* (*adj*) insecure, daring, dodgy, uncertain, venturesome, audacious, awkward, speculative, treacherous, venturous, **11**. venomous; *synonyms* (*adj*) toxic, malicious, spiteful, virulent, caustic, vicious, corrosive, acrimonious, biting, maleficent, acid, rancorous, acerb, sharp; *antonym* (*adj*) kind, **12**. poisonous; *synonyms* (*adj*) toxiferous, pestilential, mischievous, toxicant, contagious, **13**. virulent; *synonyms* (*adj*) hostile, acerbic, acrid, infectious, envenomed, mordacious, (*v*) harsh, **14**. painful; *synonyms* (*adj*) difficult, sore, afflictive, harrowing, aching, excruciating, irritating, laborious, poignant, unpleasant, intolerable, galling, cruel, doleful, (*v*) distressing; *antonyms* (*adj*) painless, content.

kamamma suckle; *synonyms* (*v*) nurse, lactate, breastfeed, suck, foster, raise, nourish, draw, harbour, absorb, caress, cherish, entertain, harbor, (*n*) nurture.

kamammaki suckled; *synonym* (*adj*) nursed.

kaman already; *synonyms* (*adv*) beforehand, previously, before, formerly, once, earlier, finally, (*adj*) erewhile, present.

kamanamana 1. maul; *synonyms* (*n*) hammer, sledge, sledgehammer, (*v*) mall, mangle, beat, buffet, batter, molest, thrash, disfigure, (*adj*) bruise, **2**. squelch; *synonyms* (*n*) squelcher, (*v*) quell, crush, squash, repress, smash, mash, quench, slosh, splash, squeeze, crash, muffle, quash, smother.

kamanana 1. domesticate; *synonyms* (*v*) tame, cultivate, naturalize, chasten, school, tend, civilize, civilise, crop, discipline, domesticise, domesticize, domiciliate, domify, (*adj*) conquer, **2**. subdue; *synonyms* (*v*) crush, defeat, overpower, quash, quell, reduce, repress, curb, overcome, restrain, soften, subjugate, suppress, humble, (*adv*) control; *antonym* (*v*) surrender, **3**. tame; *synonyms* (*adj*) docile, meek, bland, boring, domestic, gentle, insipid, mild, slow, spiritless, (*v*) dull, break, subdue, domesticate, moderate; *antonyms* (*adj*) exciting, wild.

kamananaki 1. domesticated; *synonyms* (*adj*) domestic, tame, vernacular, subdued, gentle, crushed, depressed, naturalized, submissive, cultivated, disciplined, dull, flat, insipid, intestine, **2**. subdued; *synonyms* (*adj*) muffled, quiet, soft, muted, restrained, faint, resigned, repressed, low, meek, broken, delicate, sober, mild, unruffled; *antonyms* (*adj*) loud, enthusiastic, lively, **3**. tamed; *synonym* (*adj*) controlled.

kamanang 1. delete; *synonyms* (*v*) cancel, erase, clear, expunge, raze, cut, destroy, edit, excise, obliterate, remove, scratch, redact, annul, omit; *antonyms* (*v*) insert, record, **2**. erase; *synonyms* (*v*) delete, efface, annihilate, eradicate, eliminate, scrape, blot, extinguish, kill, rase, wipe, **3**. cancel; *synonyms* (*v*) abrogate, invalidate, remit, revoke, abate, avoid, repeal, counteract, drop, negate, neutralize, quash, recall, (*adj*) abolish, nullify; *antonym* (*v*) validate, **4**. omit; *synonyms* (*v*) fail, neglect, disregard, forget, except, exclude, ignore, leave, pretermit, lose, overlook, default, (*adj*) skip,

jump, (*n*) forsake; *antonym* (*v*) include, **5**. undo; *synonyms* (*v*) loosen, open, disentangle, reverse, separate, unfold, untie, disconnect, unbrace, overturn, detach, disengage, loose, release, unlock; *antonyms* (*v*) fasten, attach, close, do, wrap.

kamanangaki 1. cancelled; *synonyms* (*adj*) off, sour, turned, **2**. undone; *synonyms* (*v*) accursed, devoted, (*adj*) lost, ruined, sunk, unfinished, doomed, behindhand, decayed, destroyed, finished.

kamanatua mangle; *synonyms* (*n*) destroy, (*v*) deface, lacerate, blemish, disfigure, distort, murder, twist, batter, damage, maul, mutilate, hack, (*adj*) maim, cripple.

kamanatuaa crush; *synonyms* (*n*) squeeze, press, crowd, (*v*) beat, break, compress, conquer, crunch, stamp, bruise, jam, mash, overpower, overwhelm, quash.

kamanatuaaki crushed; *synonyms* (*v*) victimized, (*adj*) broken, beaten, low, subdued, conquered, flattened, dispirited, compressed, overwhelmed, abashed, abject, blue, brokenhearted, (*n*) crushing; *antonyms* (*adj*) loose, victorious.

kamanatuaki mangled; *synonyms* (*adj*) torn, lacerated, deformed, mutilated, disabled, lacerate, broken, blasted, crippled, distorted, maimed, confused, corrupted, jumbled, (*prep*) rent.

kamanea waylay; *synonyms* (*v*) ambush, ambuscade, lurk, accost, besiege, bushwhack, harass, scupper.

kamaneaka 1. safeguard; *synonyms* (*v*) preserve, ensure, cover, defend, protect, shelter, keep, (*n*) guard, protection, shield, care, defense, escort, precaution, security, **2**. secure; *synonyms* (*v*) close, fix, fasten, acquire, assure, attain, fast, gain, get, (*adj*) safe, firm, certain, confident, attach, bind; *antonyms* (*v*) lose, detach, (*adj*) insecure, vulnerable, loose, unsafe.

kamaneakaki secured; *synonyms* (*adj*) guaranteed, protected, barred, bolted, bonded, fast, firm, latched, locked.

kamaneanea 1. confuse; *synonyms* (*v*) bewilder, baffle, confound, muddle, agitate, blur, derange, disconcert, disturb, fluster, jumble, mystify, obscure, perplex, puzzle; *antonyms* (*v*) clarify, enlighten, elucidate, explain, **2**. abash; *synonyms* (*v*) confuse, embarrass, humble, intimidate, mortify, discountenance, dash, humiliate, discomfit, discourage, shame, cow, (*n*) deter, daunt, overawe, **3**. shame; *synonyms* (*n*) reproach, disgrace, discredit, humiliation, chagrin, insult, modesty, pity, scandal, contempt, degradation, (*v*) dishonor, degrade, abash, debase; *antonym* (*v*) honor.

kamaneaneaki 1. abashed; *synonyms* (*adj*) bashful, discomfited, mortified, ashamed, confused, embarrassed, sheepish; *antonym* (*adj*) brazen, **2**. confused; *synonyms* (*adj*) abashed, bewildered, baffled, befuddled, bemused, chaotic, confounded, disjointed, disordered, dizzy, incoherent, indistinct, ambiguous, (n) cloudy, (adv, adj) topsy-turvy; *antonyms* (adj) clear, enlightened, alert, clearheaded, clear-headed, orderly, **3**. shamed; *synonyms* (adj) disgraced, dishonored, discredited, guilty, hangdog, browbeaten, bullied, cowed, damaged, fallen, intimidated, shamefaced.

kamaneanikum 1. invincible; *synonyms* (adj) indomitable, insurmountable, impregnable, insuperable, irresistible, unbeatable, unconquerable; *antonym* (adj) vulnerable, **2**. impassable; *synonyms* (adj) impervious, impenetrable, invincible, inaccessible, unpassable; *antonym* (adj) passable, **3**. impregnable; *synonyms* (adj) fast, inexpugnable, invulnerable, secure, unassailable, safe, strong, unshakable, **4**. insurmountable; *synonyms* (adj) unsurmountable, impassable, impossible; *antonym* (adj) surmountable, **5**. invulnerable; *synonym* (v) defensible.

kamaneaua secure; *synonyms* (v) close, fix, preserve, fasten, acquire, assure, attain, ensure, fast, (adj) safe, firm, certain, confident, attach, bind; *antonyms* (v) lose, detach, (adj) insecure, vulnerable, loose, unsafe.

kamaneauaki secured; *synonyms* (adj) guaranteed, protected, barred, bolted, bonded, fast, firm, latched, locked.

kamaneka scar; *synonyms* (n) mark, cicatrix, blemish, seam, cicatrice, defect, scratch, stain, injury, line, disfigurement, (v) disfigure, brand, damage, mar.

kamanekaki scarred; *synonyms* (adj) marred, defaced, hurt.

kamanena 1. use; *synonyms* (n) custom, practice, benefit, habit, application, function, (v) exercise, employ, employment, expend, profit, advantage, exploit, occupy, (adj) usage; *antonym* (v) conserve, **2**. wear; *synonyms* (v) dress, endure, bear, fatigue, tire, waste, fray, frazzle, (n) clothing, apparel, attire, clothes, garb, erosion, garment; *antonym* (v) refresh, **3**. wield; *synonyms* (v) handle, ply, wave, brandish, exert, flourish, hold, manipulate, manage, use, swing, treat, control, maintain, shake.

kamanenaka 1. anoint; *synonyms* (v) anele, embrocate, oil, sanctify, consecrate, dedicate, bless, embalm, fragrance, freshen, imbue, inunct, lace, latch, noint, **2**. oil; *synonyms* (n) petroleum, fat, ointment, salve, cream, fuel, cerate, lotion, (v) lubricate, anoint, glycerine.

kamanenakaki oiled; *synonyms* (adj) drunk, intoxicated, oily.

kamanenaki 1. used; *synonyms* (adj) secondhand, exploited, accustomed, decrepit, depleted, exhausted, faded, habituated, hand-me-down, spent, threadbare, tried, victimised, victimized,

wont; *antonyms* (adj) pristine, new, spanking, unused, **2**. worn; *synonyms* (v) decayed, rotten, (adj) haggard, shabby, tired, ragged, tattered, drawn, jaded, fatigued, careworn, frayed, raddled, seedy, wasted; *antonym* (adj) fresh.

kamanenanti 1. attempt; *synonyms* (n) try, endeavor, assay, effort, essay, offer, trial, attack, assault, adventure, bid, (v) struggle, aim, chance, undertake, **2**. endeavor; *synonyms* (n) attempt, enterprise, shot, work, endeavour, exertion, go, action, venture, pursuit, stab, (v) strive, labor, strain, seek; *antonym* (v) neglect, **3**. essay; *synonyms* (n) dissertation, article, disquisition, composition, tentative, paper, taste, discourse, review, critique, experiment, study, (v) prove, test, examine, **4**. try; *synonyms* (v) judge, sample, probe, adjudicate, hear, render, afflict, demonstrate, exercise, hazard, risk, tempt, search, explore, (n) crack, **5**. strive; *synonyms* (v) contend, contest, fight, combat, aspire, compete, toil, exert, reach, scramble, battle, war, emulate, fag, force, **6**. risk; *synonyms* (n) peril, danger, gamble, jeopardy, bet, insecurity, menace, (v) endanger, wager, dare, imperil, jeopardize, stake, expose, jeopard; *antonyms* (n) safety, (v) protect.

kamanenantiaki 1. attempted, **2**. tried; *synonyms* (adj) reliable, tested, trustworthy, dependable, proved, experienced, baffled, beaten, believable, conquered, exhausted, faithful, just, practiced, qualified.

kamanga 1. misquote; *synonyms* (v) exaggerate, falsify, garble, twist, (adv) misstate, miscite, misreport, misrepresent, **2**. misstate; *synonyms* (v) belie, color, invent, lie, misinform, pervert, **3**. smother; *synonyms* (v) quench, choke, muffle, stifle, suffocate, extinguish, asphyxiate, suppress, gag, overwhelm, repress, douse, deaden, contain, cover, **4**. suffocate; *synonyms* (v) strangle, smother, throttle, drown, die, garrote, hang, kill.

kamangaki 1. suffocated; *synonyms* (v) asphyxied, (adj) choked, suffocate, **2**. smothered; *synonyms* (adj) stifled, strangled, suppressed, pent-up.

kamangaoa confuse; *synonyms* (v) bewilder, baffle, confound, muddle, agitate, blur, derange, disconcert, disturb, fluster, jumble, mystify, obscure, perplex, puzzle; *antonyms* (v) clarify, enlighten, elucidate, explain.

kamangaoaki confused; *synonyms* (adj) abashed, bewildered, baffled, befuddled, bemused, chaotic, confounded, disjointed, disordered, dizzy, incoherent, indistinct, ambiguous, (n) cloudy, (adv, adj) topsy-turvy; *antonyms* (adj) clear, enlightened, alert, clearheaded, clear-headed, orderly.

kamangaungauakina devour; *synonyms* (v) consume, bolt, eat, gulp, demolish, gobble, gorge, guzzle, swallow, absorb, devastate, enjoy, relish, down, exhaust.

kamangeange litter; *synonyms* (*n*) brood, bedding, stretcher, garbage, junk, mess, refuse, rubbish, trash, waste, issue, (*v*) clutter, (*adj*) jumble, disarray, huddle.

kamangeangeaki littered; *synonyms* (*adj*) cluttered, untidy, beleaguered, beset, besieged, messy, plagued, topsy-turvy, tormented.

kamanginga ferment; *synonyms* (*n*) agitation, excitement, barm, tumult, unrest, disturbance, confusion, (*v*) effervesce, stew, turn, brew, fester, foam, agitate, (*adj*) pother.

kamangingaki fermented; *synonyms* (*adj*) alcoholic, arduous, backbreaking, difficult, hard, sour, grueling, gruelling, heavy, knockout, laborious, labourious, punishing, severe, strong.

kamangingnga intoxicate; *synonyms* (*v*) fuddle, inebriate, befuddle, elate, disguise, apprehend, arrest, catch, collar, collect, cop, discover, disease, disorder, distemper.

kamangingngaki intoxicated; *synonyms* (*adj*) drunken, inebriated, drunk, inebriate, tipsy, elated; *antonym* (*adj*) sober.

kamangora 1. abase; *synonyms* (*v*) degrade, humble, debase, humiliate, mortify, demean, depress, sink, dishonor, lower, reduce, shame, (*n*) disgrace, (*adj*) abash, snub, 2. debase; *synonyms* (*v*) corrupt, adulterate, alloy, contaminate, debauch, defile, cheapen, bastardize, demoralize, deprave, impair, pervert, pollute, taint, (*n*) abase, 3. lower; *synonyms* (*adj*) inferior, less, (*v*) diminish, frown, dip, cut, descend, drop, scowl, decrease, fall, lessen, abate, depreciate, ebb; *antonyms* (*v*) increase, raise, 4. slight; *synonyms* (*adj*) flimsy, slender, thin, fragile, delicate, faint, feeble, (*n*) scorn, disdain, (*v*) disregard, insult, neglect, ignore, affront, (*adv*) light; *antonyms* (*adj*) considerable, major, fat, heavy, intense, obvious, severe, thickset, wide.

kamangoraki 1. debased; *synonyms* (*adj*) corrupt, adulterated, degraded, low, base, degenerate, depraved, adulterate, corrupted, debauched, decadent, impure, perverted; *antonym* (*adj*) pure, 2. lowered; *synonyms* (*adj*) abased, bated, cheap, humbled, restrained.

kamaniman bastard; *synonyms* (*n*) whoreson, scoundrel, cad, mongrel, (*adj*) illegitimate, spurious, fake, misbegotten, phony, adulterate, bastardly, bogus, false, natural, phoney; *antonym* (*n*) legitimate.

kamaninga mislead; *synonyms* (*v*) betray, deceive, cheat, beguile, con, fool, misinform, delude, dupe, hoodwink, lie, misdirect, misguide, trick, seduce.

kamaningaki mislead; *synonyms* (*v*) betray, deceive, cheat, beguile, con, fool, misinform, delude, dupe, hoodwink, lie, misdirect, misguide, trick, seduce.

kamanoa shelter; *synonyms* (*n*) guard, refuge, asylum, harbor, protect, protection, sanctuary, security, shield, hut, covert, (*v*) cover, screen, defend, (*adj*) defense; *antonym* (*v*) expose.

kamanoaki sheltered; *synonyms* (*adj*) secure, comfortable, safe, screened, cozy, secluded, (*v*) protected, private; *antonym* (*adj*) desolate.

kamanraoia praise; *synonyms* (*n*) compliment, acclaim, applause, commendation, glory, kudos, admiration, (*v*) applaud, approve, commend, extol, honor, flatter, celebrate, glorify; *antonyms* (*n*) criticism, disparagement, (*v*) criticize, belittle, disparage, rebuke, reprimand, reproach, scold, chastise, denigrate, sully.

kamantintia 1. batter; *synonyms* (*n*) batsman, concoction, (*v*) baste, hammer, bash, beat, break, buffet, club, hit, knock, mangle, pound, slam, bruise, 2. beat; *synonyms* (*v*) batter, flap, pulsate, throb, tick, trounce, whip, bat, cheat, clobber, crush, (*n*) pulse, thump, round, cadence; *antonym* (*v*) lose, 3. pound; *synonyms* (*n*) cage, fold, enclosure, hammering, (*v*) pen, bang, grind, maul, palpitate, mash, grate, ram, thrash, bray, drive, 4. punch; *synonyms* (*n*) jab, drill, cuff, die, wallop, blow, dig, (*v*) poke, prick, perforate, stab, thrust, puncture, push, slap.

kamantintiaki 1. battered; *synonyms* (*adj*) beaten, worn, damaged, hurt, maltreated, ragged, tattered, abused, aching, bruised, decrepit, dilapidated, injured, (*v*) seedy, shattered, 2. beaten; *synonyms* (*v*) beat, (*adj*) battered, overpowered, conquered, routed, overcome; *antonym* (*adj*) victorious.

kamantoa 1. assimilate; *synonyms* (*v*) absorb, compare, imbibe, incorporate, comprehend, conform, digest, engross, 2. acquire; *synonyms* (*v*) get, achieve, find, gain, take, accept, attain, buy, collect, contract, earn, obtain, purchase, receive, assume; *antonyms* (*v*) lose, sell, 3. pollute; *synonyms* (*v*) defile, corrupt, debase, foul, infect, taint, dirty, maculate, poison, befoul, debauch, desecrate, soil, besmear, (*n*) contaminate; *antonyms* (*v*) clean, purify, 4. seize; *synonyms* (*v*) capture, catch, grab, arrest, apprehend, clutch, grapple, annex, clasp, confiscate, conquer, grasp, grip, nail, carry; *antonym* (*v*) release.

kamantoaki 1. acquired; *synonyms* (*v*) acquiring, (*adj*) acquisite, acquisitive, derivative, extrinsic, 2. seized; *synonyms* (*adj*) confiscate, confiscated, appropriated, condemned, apprehended, detained, held, censured, convicted, forfeit, forfeited, obsessed, 3. polluted; *synonyms* (*adj*) impure, dirty, contaminated, foul, defiled, filthy, unclean, profane, soiled, stained, tainted, infected, nasty, (*v*) mixed; *antonym* (*adj*) pure.

kamanua relax; *synonyms* (*v*) loose, abate, give, lounge, unbend, melt, debilitate, ease, relieve, remit, rest, slack, (*n*) loosen, release, (*adj*) relent; *antonyms* (*v*) tighten, tense.

kamanuaki relaxed; *synonyms* (*adj*) lax, loose, slack, calm, comfortable, composed, easy, cool, informal, easygoing, happy, serene, slow, tranquil, unhurried; *antonyms* (*adj*) tense, anxious, formal, nervous, prim, stiff, uncomfortable, strict, haggard, harassed, prudish, reserved, restless, taut.

kamanunua 1. gather; *synonyms* (*v*) deduce, convene, accumulate, amass, assemble, collect, compile, congregate, flock, garner, meet, tuck, earn, rally, (*n*) fold; *antonyms* (*v*) disperse, scatter, 2. pleat; *synonyms* (*n*) plait, crease, wrinkle, ply, (*v*) crimp, crinkle, braid, plat, pucker, ruffle, 3. wrinkle; *synonyms* (*n*) furrow, gather, line, flexure, (*v*) rumple, crumple, curl, purse, cockle, corrugate, crush, crisp, scrunch, shrivel, groove; *antonym* (*v*) smooth.

kamanunuaki 1. corrugated; *synonyms* (*adj*) puckered, wrinkly, ridged, channelled, flexed, folded, ribbed, roughened, rumpled, uneven; *antonym* (*adj*) smooth, 2. gathered; *synonyms* (*adj*) collected, deepened, accumulated, amassed, assembled, collective, congregate, equanimous, massed, poised, 3. pleated, 4. wrinkled; *synonyms* (*adj*) furrowed, creased, crumpled, lined, wizened, gnarled, unironed, (*n*) rough, rugged.

kamaoa 1. heal; *synonyms* (*v*) cure, cicatrize, doctor, mend, recover, recuperate, fix, remedy, restore, help, physic, repair, treat, (*n*) correct, salve, 2. close; *synonyms* (*adj*) near, adjacent, nearby, accurate, tight, approximate, narrow, (*v*) compact, stop, conclude, (*adv*) by, about, (*n*) end, finish, conclusion; *antonyms* (*adj*) distant, airy, fresh, loose, far, (*v*) open, start, 3. cure; *synonyms* (*n*) antidote, medicine, curative, curing, healing, therapy, treatment, restorative, aid, drug, medication, (*v*) heal, pickle, preserve, keep, 4. recuperate; *synonyms* (*v*) convalesce, improve, rally, reclaim, recruit, recoup, regain, resume, revive; *antonym* (*v*) deteriorate, 5. remedy; *synonyms* (*n*) redress, relief, remediation, amendment, amends, prescription, assistance, correction, (*v*) amend, rectify, relieve, reform, resolve, right, solve.

kamaoaki 1. closed; *synonyms* (*v*) close, tight, accurate, adjoining, attentive, (*adj*) blind, blocked, finished, shut, congested, fastened, exclusive, insular, stopped, airtight; *antonym* (*adj*) open, 2. cured; *synonyms* (*adj*) healed, recovered, aged, corned, better, mellow, salted, vulcanised, vulcanized, whole, elderly, older, ripened, senior, 3. healed; *synonym* (*adj*) cured.

kamaoriori 1. disjoint; *synonyms* (*v*) dislocate, disarticulate, disjoin, separate, dismember, part, dissociate, disunite, divorce, 2. bend; *synonyms* (*n*) bow, arch, arc, elbow, twist, angle, curvature, (*v*)

curve, turn, crouch, stoop, crook, curl, flex, deflect; *antonyms* (*v*) straighten, square.

kamaorioriaki 1. disjointed; *synonyms* (*adj*) disconnected, incoherent, confused, broken, split, dislocated, rambling, unconnected, disordered, fragmentary; *antonyms* (*adj*) coherent, united, 2. bent; *synonyms* (*adj*) arched, curved, bended, crooked, deformed, intent, (*n*) aptitude, inclination, propensity, fancy, ability, bias, flair, gift, leaning; *antonym* (*adj*) straight.

kamara 1. melt; *synonyms* (*v*) fuse, dissolve, deliquesce, run, thaw, vanish, coalesce, combine, fade, heat, meld, mellow, relent, soften, (*adj*) liquefy; *antonyms* (*v*) freeze, cool, solidify, 2. liquefy; *synonyms* (*v*) melt, flux, liquidise, liquidize, liquify; *antonym* (*v*) set, 3. dissolve; *synonyms* (*v*) disappear, disperse, dissipate, disband, evaporate, resolve, dispel, cut, analyze, cancel, dismiss, end, terminate, disembody, withdraw; *antonyms* (*v*) appear, harden, 4. soak; *synonyms* (*v*) dip, drench, saturate, immerse, permeate, impregnate, drown, moisten, bathe, douse, fleece, imbue, infuse, steep, dowse; *antonym* (*v*) dry, 5. thaw; *synonyms* (*n*) melting, thawing, heating, (*v*) unfreeze, warm, 6. sow; *synonyms* (*n*) pig, hog, swine, bitch, (*v*) scatter, broadcast, inseminate, seed, disseminate, plant, sough, farm, distribute, propagate, spread, 7. saturate; *synonyms* (*v*) satiate, charge, fill, sate, soak, infiltrate, imbrue, penetrate, brew, pervade, satisfy, glut, suffuse, swamp, (*adj*) wet, 8. sop; *synonyms* (*n*) bribe, amends, baby, child, infant, innocent, milksop, reckoning, requital, (*v*) dunk, souse, bolus, gobbet, morsel, mouthful, 9. steep; *synonyms* (*adj*) high, abrupt, excessive, exorbitant, outrageous, sheer, extortionate, headlong, precipitous, unreasonable, immoderate, harsh, upright, (*v*) plunge, (*n*) bold; *antonyms* (*adj*) gentle, gradual.

kamarabea grow; *synonyms* (*v*) advance, augment, develop, enlarge, expand, come, emerge, become, farm, get, rise, spring, turn, breed, accrue; *antonyms* (*v*) decrease, weaken, shrink.

kamaraka 1. inflict; *synonyms* (*v*) impose, cause, enforce, force, wreak, deal, deliver, administer, land, put, send, visit, commit, 2. hurt; *synonyms* (*v*) pain, wound, afflict, injure, ail, cost, (*adj*) evil, (*n*) harm, damage, detriment, ache, disadvantage, abuse, distress, lesion; *antonyms* (*v*) encourage, (*adj*) uninjured, unhurt, 3. rack; *synonyms* (*n*) manger, wrack, bracket, cage, stand, boot, ledge, board, hob, (*v*) torture, excruciate, torment, agonize, bedevil, crucify, 4. pain; *synonyms* (*n*) bother, ill, agony, nuisance, harass, annoyance, discomfort, dolor, grief, plague, (*v*) hurt, anguish, grieve, trouble, inconvenience; *antonym* (*n*) pleasure, 5. torture; *synonyms* (*n*) suffering, excruciation, misery, martyrdom, distortion, ordeal, torturing, (v) rack, persecute, martyr, distort, wring, lacerate, worry, tease.

kamarakaki 1. hurt; *synonyms* (v) pain, wound, afflict, injure, ail, cost, (adj) evil, (n) harm, damage, detriment, ache, disadvantage, abuse, distress, lesion; *antonyms* (v) encourage, (adj) uninjured, unhurt, **2.** tortured; *synonyms* (adj) tormented, anguished, agonized, excruciate, excruciated, gnarled, hagridden, hurt, miserable, suffering, woeful, distressed, painful, sorrowful, **3.** pained; *synonyms* (adj) offended, aggrieved, sore, angry, lame, uncomfortable, unfortunate, upset, disapproving, disparaging, reproachful, weary, withering; *antonym* (adj) hopeful.

kamaraki 1. dissolved; *synonyms* (adj) liquid, adulterate, gone, **2.** melted; *synonyms* (adj) molten, fluid, liquified, liquefied, baked, flowing, fluent, limpid, sorry, touched, smooth, swimming, watery, yielding, **3.** liquefied; *synonyms* (adj) runny, (v) liquescent, **4.** victimize; *synonyms* (v) cheat, cozen, defraud, swindle, victimise, diddle, dupe, assassinate, butcher, murder, slaughter, **5.** soaked; *synonyms* (adj) saturated, wet, drenched, sodden, soaking, soggy, sopping, drunk, damp, plastered, sloshed, soppy, besotted; *antonym* (adj) dry, **6.** painful; *synonyms* (adj) difficult, hard, sore, afflictive, bad, grievous, harrowing, sharp, aching, arduous, bitter, dolorous, excruciating, harsh, (v) distressing; *antonyms* (adj) painless, content, **7.** thawed, **8.** traumatic; *synonyms* (adj) vulnerary, stabbing, (n) arquebusade, cataplasm, embrocation, epithem, liniment, sinapism, **9.** saturated; *synonyms* (adj) concentrated, soaked, full, pure.

kamaramara 1. compliment; *synonyms* (n) honor, eulogy, tribute, (v) commend, praise, flattery, laud, applaud, adulation, congratulate, greet, belaud; *antonyms* (n) criticism, (v) insult, libel, slander, **2.** coax; *synonyms* (v) wheedle, allure, cajole, entice, charm, blarney, inveigle, persuade, seduce, flatter, induce, (n) tempt, captivate, conciliate, fascinate, **3.** flatter; *synonyms* (v) coax, fawn, court, adulate, blandish, grovel, kowtow, soap, compliment, indulge, suit, become, puff, (n) caress, **4.** wheedle; *synonyms* (v) deceive, glaver, palaver, prate, (n) bewitch, overpersuade.

kamarana 1. smooth; *synonyms* (adj) easy, calm, level, oily, facile, flat, flowing, fluent, fluid, glossy, graceful, greasy, (v) quiet, facilitate, even; *antonyms* (adj) rough, uneven, abrasive, coarse, crumpled, flaking, harsh, jerky, lined, peeling, prickly, ridged, wrinkled, corrugated, (v) wrinkle, **2.** polish; *synonyms* (n) finish, gloss, burnish, gentility, cultivation, elegance, refinement, shine, civilization, (v) furbish, glaze, rub, civilize, clean, cultivate.

kamaranaki polished; *synonyms* (adj) elegant, courteous, cultured, finished, glossy, refined, civil, courtly, genteel, lustrous, polite, smooth, accomplished, graceful, bright; *antonyms* (adj) dull, rough.

kamaranea tickle; *synonyms* (v) itch, titillate, indulge, thrill, prickle, please, tingle, flatter, humor, (n) titillation.

kamaranga 1. disengage; *synonyms* (v) detach, discharge, disentangle, disconnect, extricate, free, release, loosen, undo, unlock, withdraw, ease, (adj) clear, disembarrass, disencumber; *antonyms* (v) fasten, engage, **2.** disassociate; *synonyms* (v) dissociate, disunite, divorce, disengage, disarticulate, disjoint, **3.** disjoin; *synonyms* (v) divide, sever, part, separate, uncouple, unyoke; *antonym* (v) join, **4.** disconnect; *synonyms* (v) abstract, deactivate, disjoin, stop, cleave, discontinue, isolate, segregate, unplug; *antonyms* (v) connect, attach, **5.** separate; *synonyms* (adj) detached, individual, particular, single, disjoined, (v) insulate, scatter, cut, discrete, discriminate, disperse, distinguish, demarcate, break, differentiate; *antonyms* (adj) connected, joined, simultaneous, (v) unite, merge, mix, combine, fuse, link, associate, **6.** segregate; *synonyms* (v) split, sequester, dispart, relegate, rescind.

kamarangaki 1. disjoined; *synonyms* (adj) detached, clear, conspicuous, different, disjunct, distinct, freestanding, independent, individual, obvious, plain, (prep) separate, disconnected, disembodied, (adv) asunder, **2.** disconnected; *synonyms* (adj) broken, abrupt, desultory, disjointed, fragmentary, confused, incoherent, unconnected, discontinuous, discrete, loose, scattered, scrappy, disordered, (adv) apart; *antonym* (adj) attached, **3.** disengaged; *synonyms* (adj) open, vacant, disentangled, free, unemployed, devoid, abandoned, accessible, apparent, bounteous, extricated, inactive, neutral, emancipated, expanded, **4.** segregated; *synonyms* (adj) isolated, secluded, uncombined, exclusive, nonintegrated, unintegrated, **5.** separated; *synonyms* (adj) divided, removed, dislocated, lone, single, (prep) disjoined.

kamarara 1. attenuate; *synonyms* (v) assuage, dilute, reduce, thin, lighten, diminish, enfeeble, extenuate, lessen, lower, pare, (adj) tenuous, fine, rare, attenuated; *antonym* (v) intensify, **2.** moderate; *synonyms* (adj) temperate, abstemious, middling, mild, easy, dull, fair, (v) calm, mitigate, allay, curb, ease, cool, abate, (adv) check; *antonyms* (adj) extreme, immoderate, radical, (v) increase.

kamararaki 1. attenuated; *synonyms* (adj) attenuate, weakened, barebone, marcid, rawboned, shriveled, tabid, adulterate, emaciated, faded, finespun, gaunt, lanky, narrow, rare, **2.** moderated; *synonyms* (adj) subdued, certified, dependant, dependent, equal, graduated, limited, measured, qualified, restricted, uniform.

kamaratiarati 1. grease; *synonyms* (n) fat, bribe, butter, grime, lard, lubricant, soil, stain, cream, dirt, (v) oil, boodle, anoint, graft, lubricate, **2.** saturate; *synonyms* (v) drench, imbue, infuse, satiate, charge, fill, permeate, impregnate, sate, soak, steep, douse, infiltrate, imbrue, (adj) wet, **3.** oil; *synonyms* (n) petroleum, ointment, salve, fuel, cerate, lotion, (v) anele, glycerine.

kamaratiaratiaki 1. greased; *synonyms* (adj) lubricated, greasy, **2.** saturated; *synonyms* (adj) drenched, sodden, wet, concentrated, soaked, sopping, full, soggy, soppy, pure, soaking; *antonym* (adj) dry, **3.** oiled; *synonyms* (adj) drunk, intoxicated, oily.

kamarauaka 1. mitigate; *synonyms* (v) alleviate, assuage, abate, lessen, moderate, palliate, relieve, appease, diminish, extenuate, lighten, (n) ease, calm, (adj) allay, soften; *antonym* (v) exacerbate, **2.** relieve; *synonyms* (v) comfort, mitigate, aid, assist, console, excuse, free, help, liberate, disengage, deliver, discharge, disembarrass, (n) redress, (adj) absolve; *antonyms* (v) worsen, burden, **3.** soften; *synonyms* (v) dull, melt, mute, relent, pacify, break, cushion, damp, dampen, mellow, mince, qualify, temper, (adj) mollify, smooth; *antonyms* (v) harden, set, solidify, congeal.

kamarauakaki 1. mitigated; *synonyms* (adj) alleviated, eased, palliate, cloaked, disguised, **2.** relieved; *synonyms* (adj) thankful, cheerful, comfortable, delighted, fresh, happy, joyful, pleased, prominent, **3.** softened; *synonyms* (adj) dull, diffused, muffled, muted, boring, deadening, dense, dim, dumb, faint, gray, grey, hushed, intenerate, irksome.

kamarauakina 1. appease; *synonyms* (v) allay, assuage, pacify, placate, alleviate, calm, conciliate, mollify, quiet, still, abate, content, ease, quell, reconcile; *antonyms* (v) aggravate, provoke, **2.** alleviate; *synonyms* (v) relieve, comfort, mitigate, soothe, appease, lighten, moderate, palliate, aid, remit, assist, meliorate, deaden, (adj) smooth, compose; *antonym* (v) exacerbate, **3.** soften; *synonyms* (v) dull, melt, mute, relent, break, cushion, damp, dampen, mellow, mince, qualify, temper, thaw, dissolve, muffle; *antonyms* (v) harden, set, solidify, congeal.

kamarauakinaki 1. alleviated; *synonyms* (adj) eased, relieved, palliate, levigate, cloaked, disguised, **2.** softened; *synonyms* (adj) dull, diffused, muffled, muted, boring, deadening, dense, dim, dumb, faint, gray, grey, hushed, intenerate, irksome.

kamareireia sift; *synonyms* (v) screen, filter, investigate, analyze, examine, riddle, sieve, sprinkle, bolt, separate, sort, strain, probe, (n) scrutinize, canvass.

kamarengau dissatisfy; *synonyms* (n) mortify, (v) displease, discontent, disappoint, disgruntle, chagrin, affront, anger, annoy, chafe, disaffect, disgust, mispay, dishearten, disillusion; *antonym* (v) satisfy.

kamarengauaki dissatisfied; *synonyms* (v) discontented, querulous, (adj) discontent, disgruntled, disappointed, malcontent, complaining, grumpy; *antonyms* (adj) satisfied, content, contented.

kamaria 1. abash; *synonyms* (v) confuse, disconcert, embarrass, confound, humble, intimidate, mortify, discountenance, dash, humiliate, discomfit, discourage, (n) deter, daunt, overawe, **2.** produce; *synonyms* (v) give, effect, cause, make, bring, present, procreate, breed, construct, create, form, frame, generate, fetch, (n) gain, **3.** output; *synonyms* (n) crop, harvest, turnout, yield, outturn, product, expenditure, (v) outcome.

kamariaki 1. abashed; *synonyms* (adj) bashful, discomfited, mortified, ashamed, confused, embarrassed, sheepish; *antonym* (adj) brazen, **2.** produced; *synonyms* (v) producing, (adj) created, formed, bent, fashioned, shaped, twisted, wrought.

kamariboa 1. supply; *synonyms* (n) provision, hoard, (v) furnish, stock, afford, fill, store, feed, offer, provide, cater, contribute, deliver, equip, give, **2.** procure; *synonyms* (v) acquire, buy, get, obtain, earn, gain, win, have, attain, derive, enlist, find, induce, purchase, engage, **3.** stock; *synonyms* (n) breed, lineage, goods, ancestry, descent, family, origin, race, backlog, birth, commodity, extraction, (adj) regular, (v) handle, supply, **4.** provide; *synonyms* (v) accommodate, administer, allow, fit, endow, outfit, nourish, nurture, arm, bestow, donate, ensure, extend, ply, prepare.

kamariboaki 1. stocked; *synonym* (adj) full, **2.** supplied; *synonyms* (adj) adequate, ample, available, complete, copious, fitted, impregnated, offered, perfect, plenteous, ready, sated, abounding, surfeited.

kamaribobo inventory; *synonyms* (n) list, catalogue, index, stock, catalog, account, enumeration, roll, schedule, bill, table, inventorying, listing, record, stocktaking.

kamarika 1. fatten; *synonyms* (v) batten, fat, elaborate, feed, expand, (n) enrich, (adj) fructify, bloom, blossom, blow, **2.** plump; *synonyms* (adj) chubby, corpulent, obese, overweight, round, stout, gross, buxom, pudgy, full, heavy, (v) fatten, drop, go, (n) fleshy; *antonyms* (adj) thin, emaciated, skinny, slim, slender.

kamarikaki fattened; *synonyms* (adj) meated, fed.

kamarinrinna loosen; *synonyms* (*v*) free, relax, loose, detach, undo, discharge, ravel, fluff, unbend, untie, liberate, slacken, (*adj*) disengage, (*n*) ease, release; *antonyms* (*v*) tighten, compress, fasten.

kamarinrinnaki loosened; *synonyms* (*adj*) detached, disentangled, loose, disengaged, extricated, unsnarled.

kamariri 1. frigid; *synonyms* (*adj*) cold, chilly, chill, arctic, cool, freezing, icy, bleak, frosty, dead, chilling, frozen, gelid, (*n*) dull, distant; *antonym* (*adj*) warm, **2.** cool; *synonyms* (*adj*) collected, composed, fine, aloof, apathetic, lukewarm, soothe, (*v*) calm, assuage, allay, pacify, quench, refrigerate, (*n*) composure, poise; *antonyms* (*adj*) agitated, hot, excited, enthusiastic, feverish, friendly, temperate, tepid, (*v*) heat.

kamariroa 1. move; *synonyms* (*v*) act, affect, carry, excite, go, impel, instigate, maneuver, touch, travel, flow, bear, (*n*) motion, drive, transfer; *antonym* (*v*) stay, **2.** shake; *synonyms* (*v*) beat, agitate, jar, brandish, disturb, flutter, totter, wag, drop, (*n*) tremble, jolt, quiver, wave, trembling, (*adj*) quake, **3.** rattle; *synonyms* (*n*) roll, jangle, jingle, click, clack, clang, rattling, (*v*) clatter, bang, confuse, patter, shake, disconcert, clash, drum.

kamariroaki 1. rattled; *synonyms* (*adj*) flustered, perturbed, upset, abashed, addled, afraid, bewildered, disconcerted, distraught, puzzled, unsettled, **2.** shaken; *synonyms* (*v*) broken, lame, passe, shaky, threadbare, wilted, shattered, stale, (*adj*) jolted, dazed, fallen, scared, stunned, surprised, uneasy.

kamaroa 1. confine; *synonyms* (*v*) bound, limit, bind, circumscribe, restrain, tie, hold, incarcerate, restrict, cage, abridge, (*n*) border, boundary, bounds, brim; *antonyms* (*v*) release, free, liberate, **2.** desolate; *synonyms* (*v*) waste, devastate, comfortless, destroy, (*adj*) bare, barren, desert, forlorn, alone, bleak, deserted, cheerless, disconsolate, sad, solitary; *antonyms* (*adj*) cheerful, inhabited, happy, sheltered, **3.** desolated; *synonyms* (*adj*) desolate, devastated, ravaged, ruined, blasted, atrophied, blame, blamed, blessed, bony, cadaverous, damn, damned, darned, wasted, **4.** disconnect; *synonyms* (*v*) detach, abstract, disengage, divide, separate, deactivate, disjoin, dissociate, divorce, sever, stop, uncouple, undo, cleave, discontinue; *antonyms* (*v*) connect, attach, **5.** segregate; *synonyms* (*v*) isolate, discriminate, part, differentiate, distinguish, split, sequester, dispart, relegate, rescind, (*adj*) detached.

kamaroaki 1. desolated; *synonyms* (*adj*) desolate, devastated, ravaged, ruined, blasted, atrophied, bare, barren, blame, blamed, bleak, blessed, bony, cadaverous, damn, **2.** confined; *synonyms* (*v*) accurate, (*adj*) captive, close, cramped, imprisoned, limited, bounded, invalided, constrained, narrow,

poky, qualified, restricted, strict, jailed; *antonym* (*adj*) free, **3.** disconnected; *synonyms* (*adj*) broken, abrupt, desultory, disjointed, fragmentary, confused, incoherent, separate, unconnected, discontinuous, discrete, detached, loose, scattered, scrappy; *antonym* (*adj*) attached, **4.** segregated; *synonyms* (*adj*) isolated, secluded, uncombined, exclusive, nonintegrated, unintegrated.

kamaroro 1. entertain; *synonyms* (*v*) amuse, divert, delight, bear, beguile, cherish, admit, accommodate, harbor, hold, interest, distract, comfort, indulge, (*n*) engage; *antonym* (*v*) bore, **2.** party; *synonyms* (*n*) gang, band, company, assembly, association, crew, gathering, group, affair, bevy, celebration, crowd, do, faction, meeting.

kamaroroaki entertained; *synonyms* (*adj*) amused, diverted.

kamarua 1. murder; *synonyms* (*n*) carnage, homicide, slaughter, butchery, bloodshed, (*v*) massacre, butcher, kill, slay, assassinate, destroy, dispatch, execute, hit, manslaughter, **2.** destroy; *synonyms* (*v*) break, demolish, blight, despoil, annihilate, blast, crush, dash, destruct, devastate, devour, dismantle, (*adj*) desolate, abolish, consume; *antonyms* (*v*) build, preserve, create, make, **3.** kill; *synonyms* (*v*) erase, eliminate, extinguish, finish, decimate, eradicate, behead, efface, defeat, liquidate, obliterate, quell, (*n*) murder, game, prey, **4.** execute; *synonyms* (*v*) do, achieve, complete, perform, accomplish, act, effect, enforce, carry, consummate, discharge, fulfill, practice, administer, commit, **5.** extinguish; *synonyms* (*v*) exterminate, quench, douse, end, suppress, quash, extirpate, ravage, stifle, subvert, choke, expunge, raze, (*adj*) allay, slake; *antonyms* (*v*) light, ignite, **6.** terminate; *synonyms* (*v*) close, cease, conclude, stop, drop, discontinue, dismiss, dissolve, halt, can, result, abort, bound, cancel, ax; *antonyms* (*v*) begin, start, establish, **7.** slay; *synonyms* (*v*) remove, mangle, **8.** slaughter; *synonyms* (*n*) drubbing, killing, thrashing, destruction, beating, butchering, annihilation, slaying, walloping, whipping, debacle, trouncing, (*v*) gore, thrash, trounce, **9.** waylay; *synonyms* (*v*) ambush, ambuscade, lurk, accost, besiege, bushwhack, harass, scupper, **10.** slain; *synonyms* (*adj*) dejected, fallen, mat, overthrown, **11.** rob; *synonyms* (*v*) filch, pinch, deprive, pilfer, pillage, plunder, rifle, fleece, lift, purloin, steal, pick, divest, defraud, hook, **12.** wound; *synonyms* (*n*) bruise, harm, pain, injury, scratch, (*v*) hurt, cut, damage, offend, injure, stab, sting, insult, maim, bite, **13.** ravage; *synonyms* (*v*) harry, loot, sack, forage, overrun, ruin, spoil, wreck, smash, (*n*) waste, havoc, loss, desolation, devastation, outrage, **14.** violate; *synonyms* (*v*) contravene, transgress, desecrate, dishonor, disobey, infringe, ravish, assault, breach, profane, rape, abuse, debauch, defile, force; *antonym* (*v*) obey.

kamaruaki 1. extinguished; *synonyms* (*adj*) extinct, out, dead, quenched, allayed, nonexistent, forbidden, inactive, kayoed, nonextant, prohibited, (*n*) defunctness, extermination, extinction, extinguishing, **2**. executed; *synonyms* (*v*) done, (*adj*) finished, fulfilled, complete, given, issued, **3**. killed; *synonyms* (*adj*) slain, fallen, (*n*) casualty, **4**. murdered, **5**. destroyed; *synonyms* (*adj*) lost, ruined, desolate, desolated, shattered, depressed, **6**. violated; *synonyms* (*v*) apart, blighted, contrite, cracked, disconnected, disunited, fractured, (*adj*) broken, profaned, seduced, debauched, defiled, desecrated, despoiled, dishonored; *antonym* (*adj*) pure, **7**. wounded; *synonyms* (*adj*) hurt, bruised, bloody, (*n*) maimed; *antonym* (*adj*) composed, **8**. ravaged; *synonyms* (*adj*) devastated, destroyed, blasted, pillaged, raped, assaulted, atrophied, bare, barren, blame, blamed, bleak, blessed, bony, cadaverous, **9**. terminated; *synonyms* (*adj*) concluded, ended, over, **10**. robed; *synonyms* (*adj*) appareled, attired, clothed, dressed, garbed, garmented, habilimented, fixed, polished, vested.

kamarurua muffle; *synonyms* (*v*) dampen, deaden, stifle, dull, curb, damp, gag, hush, muzzle, silence, smother, suppress, check, quieten, mute.

kamaruruaki muffled; *synonyms* (*adj*) dull, hushed, muted, faint, hollow, inarticulate, soft, subdued, deep, inaudible, indistinct, low, quiet, (*v*) allusive, covert; *antonyms* (*adj*) loud, high-pitched.

kamarurung 1. exercise; *synonyms* (*n*) practice, employment, application, discipline, play, movement, action, activity, (*v*) drill, apply, employ, use, exert, train, educate, **2**. strengthen; *synonyms* (*v*) consolidate, confirm, corroborate, brace, encourage, enhance, fortify, intensify, invigorate, bolster, buttress, harden, increase, stiffen, toughen; *antonyms* (*v*) weaken, undermine.

kamarurunga 1. fortify; *synonyms* (*v*) strengthen, confirm, consolidate, secure, buttress, encourage, reinforce, fort, harden, invigorate, support, arm, cheer, (*n*) brace, nerve; *antonym* (*v*) weaken, **2**. animate; *synonyms* (*adj*) alive, live, spirited, quick, vivacious, (*v*) enliven, inspire, actuate, exhilarate, hearten, inspirit, quicken, revive, stimulate, elevate; *antonyms* (*adj*) lifeless, (*v*) deaden.

kamarurungaki 1. fortified; *synonyms* (*adj*) bastioned, secure, castled, defended, equipped, fast, protected, safeguarded, secured, shielded, prepared, turreted, **2**. animated; *synonyms* (*adj*) active, alive, lively, animate, perky, brisk, cheerful, quick, spirited, sprightly, vivacious, airy, alert, bright, energetic; *antonyms* (*adj*) listless, lethargic, blank, dull, **3**. strengthened; *synonyms* (*adj*)

reinforced, consolidated, built, comfortable, sinewed, united.

kamataanoa 1. dazzle; *synonyms* (*n*) sparkle, brightness, (*v*) bedazzle, shine, blind, flash, glare, awe, captivate, gleam, (*adj*) daze, confuse, bewilder, hoodwink, perplex, **2**. blind; *synonyms* (*adj*) sightless, undiscerning, (*v*) dazzle, obscure, (*n*) screen, curtain, shutter, awning, drape, trick, veil, camouflage, cheat, cloak, concealment; *antonym* (*adj*) sighted.

kamataanoaki 1. dazzled; *synonyms* (*adj*) dizzy, bewildered, fascinated, **2**. blinded; *synonyms* (*adj*) blindfolded, blindfold.

kamataanoanoa 1. blur; *synonyms* (*n*) blot, blemish, smudge, brand, (*v*) smear, taint, blear, cloud, dim, obscure, slur, bedim, confuse, (*adj*) daub, stain; *antonym* (*v*) clarify, **2**. cloud; *synonyms* (*n*) mist, blur, haze, steam, cloak, (*v*) fog, becloud, befog, blacken, eclipse, overshadow, shadow, hide, impair, (*adj*) swarm; *antonym* (*v*) sharpen, **3**. dazzle; *synonyms* (*n*) sparkle, brightness, shimmer, (*v*) bedazzle, shine, blind, flash, glare, awe, captivate, gleam, (*adj*) daze, bewilder, hoodwink, perplex, **4**. obscure; *synonyms* (*adj*) cloudy, dark, gloomy, ambiguous, concealed, darken, hidden, incomprehensible, muddy, mysterious, clandestine, confused, (*v*) conceal, cover, (*n*) difficult; *antonyms* (*adj*) clear, noticeable, simple, obvious, distinct, mainstream, **5**. stupefy; *synonyms* (*v*) astonish, astound, amaze, paralyze, deaden, numb, bemuse, baffle, besot, drug, petrify, stagger, stump, (*adj*) stun, (*n*) benumb.

kamataanoanoaki 1. clouded; *synonyms* (*adj*) cloudy, gloomy, blurred, dark, foggy, obscure, overcast, misty, hazy, **2**. fogged; *synonyms* (*adj*) bleary, blurry, brumous, dazed, fuzzy, groggy, logy, muzzy, stuporous, **3**. dazzled; *synonyms* (*adj*) dizzy, bewildered, fascinated, **4**. blurred; *synonyms* (*adj*) indistinct, vague, blear, clouded, dim, unclear; *antonym* (*v*) clear, **5**. stupefied; *synonyms* (*adj*) stunned, amazed, astonished, astounded, dumbfounded, stupid, confused, dumfounded, flabbergasted.

kamatabaoa squint; *synonyms* (*n*) glance, look, strabismus, cast, (*v*) leer, skew, blink, squinch, (*adj*) askant, sidelong, askance, asquint.

kamataboua bewilder; *synonyms* (*v*) astonish, astound, amaze, perplex, baffle, bemuse, puzzle, befuddle, confound, nonplus, perturb, stump, stun, daze, (*adj*) confuse; *antonym* (*v*) clarify.

kamatabouaki bewildered; *synonyms* (*adj*) baffled, bemused, confused, lost, befuddled, confounded, perplexed, puzzled, dumbfounded, addled, amazed, blank, dazed, disconcerted, disoriented; *antonyms* (*adj*) enlightened, unimpressed.

kamatakia blind; *synonyms* (*adj*) sightless, undiscerning, (*v*) bedazzle, daze, dazzle, obscure, (*n*) screen, curtain, shutter, awning, drape, trick, veil, camouflage, cheat; *antonym* (*adj*) sighted.

kamatakiaki blinded; *synonyms* (*adj*) blindfolded, blindfold, dizzy.

kamatakiaua 1. disturb; *synonyms* (*v*) agitate, disconcert, disorder, disquiet, distract, distress, perturb, trouble, annoy, bother, commove, concern, derange, disarrange, discompose; *antonyms* (*v*) arrange, calm, please, smooth, soothe, **2**. disconcert; *synonyms* (*v*) confuse, baffle, discomfit, disappoint, abash, embarrass, throw, unsettle, upset, bewilder, confound, discombobulate, balk, defeat, faze, **3**. bewilder; *synonyms* (*v*) astonish, astound, amaze, perplex, bemuse, puzzle, befuddle, nonplus, stump, stun, daze, dumbfound, entangle, flummox, muddle; *antonym* (*v*) clarify, **4**. move; *synonyms* (*v*) act, affect, carry, excite, go, impel, instigate, maneuver, touch, travel, flow, bear, (*n*) motion, drive, transfer; *antonym* (*v*) stay, **5**. agitate; *synonyms* (*v*) disturb, stir, toss, fan, foment, rouse, shake, actuate, arouse, canvass, convulse, incite, jiggle, kindle, move, **6**. concern; *synonyms* (*n*) business, affair, regard, attention, anxiety, matter, company, apprehension, burden, fear, firm, (*v*) worry, care, interest, import; *antonym* (*v*) unconcern, **7**. aggravate; *synonyms* (*v*) exacerbate, exasperate, enrage, increase, irritate, provoke, worsen, anger, displease, inflame, infuriate, magnify, peeve, rile, (*adj*) embitter; *antonyms* (*v*) appease, pacify, ease, improve, **8**. abash; *synonyms* (*v*) humble, intimidate, mortify, discountenance, dash, humiliate, discourage, shame, cow, (*n*) deter, daunt, overawe, **9**. perturb; *synonyms* (*v*) fluster, harass, disarray, incommode, disorganize, embroil, discommode, ruffle, shock, unhinge, cark, depress, unnerve, **10**. perplex; *synonyms* (*v*) mystify, complicate, get, involve, stagger, bamboozle, beset, gravel, stupefy, beat, tease, afflict, tangle, (*n*) torment, (*adj*) pose, **11**. trouble; *synonyms* (*n*) pain, difficulty, fuss, hardship, load, misfortune, problem, grief, annoyance, disturbance, hassle, nuisance, (*v*) inconvenience, plague, (*adj*) affliction, **12**. upset; *synonyms* (*v*) overturn, overthrow, reverse, subvert, dislocate, disrupt, offend, turn, (*adj*) unsettled, hurt, agitated, confused, disordered, disturbed, (*n*) turnover; *antonyms* (*v*) encourage, (*adj*) pleased, confident.

kamatakiauaki 1. disconcerted; *synonyms* (*adj*) confused, upset, bewildered, blank, disturbed, embarrassed, troubled, worried, ashamed, discombobulated; *antonym* (*adj*) calm, **2**. bewildered; *synonyms* (*adj*) baffled, bemused, lost, befuddled, confounded, perplexed, puzzled, dumbfounded, addled, amazed, dazed, disconcerted, disoriented, muddled, mystified; *antonyms* (*adj*) enlightened, unimpressed, **3**.

abashed; *synonyms* (*adj*) bashful, discomfited, mortified, sheepish; *antonym* (*adj*) brazen, **4**. aggravated; *synonyms* (*adj*) irritated, angry, infuriated, afflictive, exasperated, grievous, provoked, bothered, discouraged, displeased, flagitious, forced, frustrated, goaded, harmful; *antonym* (*adj*) unprovoked, **5**. disturbed; *synonyms* (*adj*) agitated, concerned, anxious, disquieted, restless, disordered, deranged, distracted, distressed, nervous, tumultuous, turbulent, unsettled, unbalanced, mad; *antonyms* (*adj*) rational, relaxed, **6**. agitated; *synonyms* (*adj*) excited, restive, tense, alarmed, distraught, jumpy, overwrought, perturbed, shaken, uneasy, hysterical; *antonyms* (*adj*) composed, lethargic, **7**. troubled; *synonyms* (*adj*) solicitous, apprehensive, uncomfortable, vexed, disruptive, doubtful, riotous, unhappy; *antonyms* (*adj*) untroubled, unconcerned, **8**. perturbed; *synonym* (*adj*) flustered, **9**. perplexed; *synonyms* (*v*) complicated, intricate, (*adj*) involved, questioning, quizzical, entangled, knotted, **10**. upset; *synonyms* (*v*) overturn, agitate, disquiet, overthrow, bother, confuse, disturb, perturb, reverse, subvert, (*adj*) hurt, (*n*) disorder, trouble, distress, disturbance; *antonyms* (*v*) please, encourage, soothe, (*adj*) pleased, confident.

kamataku 1. captivating; *synonyms* (*adj*) attractive, enchanting, fascinating, absorbing, alluring, bewitching, appealing, delightful, engaging, engrossing, enthralling, entrancing, lovely, (*v*) charming, interesting, **2**. act; *synonyms* (*n*) accomplishment, action, move, play, statute, decree, do, feat, (*v*) achievement, behave, deed, go, perform, acquit, enact; *antonym* (*v*) refrain, **3**. curious; *synonyms* (*adj*) abnormal, funny, interested, odd, peculiar, strange, unusual, bizarre, extraordinary, inquiring, inquisitive, quaint, queer, quizzical, remarkable; *antonyms* (*adj*) normal, incurious, ordinary, **4**. intriguing; *synonyms* (*adj*) designing, scheming, challenging, provocative, **5**. interesting; *synonyms* (*adj*) entertaining, amusing, exciting, readable, diverting, gripping, captivating; *antonyms* (*adj*) uninteresting, boring, dull, **6**. fascinating; *synonyms* (*adj*) seductive, desirable, fetching, magnetic, riveting, beautiful, tempting, compelling, exotic, glamorous, pleasing, spellbinding, winning, amiable, (*v*) taking, **7**. consuming; *synonyms* (*v*) grating, grinding, racking, searching, (*n*) consumption, absumption, contraction, (*adj*) intense, blazing, overwhelming, burning, corrosive, afire, ardent, brilliant, **8**. enthralling; *synonym* (*adj*) enticing, **9**. engrossing, **10**. absorbing, **11**. perform; *synonyms* (*v*) execute, accomplish, fulfill, achieve, complete, appear, effect, make, function, administer, operate, produce, carry, fill, (n) act; *antonym* (v) neglect.

kamatakua 1. amaze; *synonyms* (v) astonish, astound, baffle, dazzle, dumbfound, puzzle, stagger, discombobulate, alarm, bewilder, confound, daze, flabbergast, mystify, (adj) surprise, **2**. entertain; *synonyms* (v) amuse, divert, delight, bear, beguile, cherish, admit, accommodate, harbor, hold, interest, distract, comfort, indulge, (n) engage; *antonym* (v) bore, **3**. amuse; *synonyms* (v) absorb, entertain, please, charm, disport, occupy, recreate, sport, **4**. astonish; *synonyms* (v) amaze, stun, confuse, nonplus, perplex, shock, startle, **5**. astound; *synonyms* (v) frighten, petrify, electrify, **6**. mesmerize; *synonyms* (v) entrance, hypnotize, captivate, enchant, fascinate, attract, bewitch, enthrall, magnetize, spellbind, hypnotise, mesmerise, grip, transfix, **7**. dumbfound; *synonyms* (v) stupefy, befuddle, stump.

kamatakuaki 1. dumbfounded; *synonyms* (adj) astonished, astounded, amazed, staggered, bewildered, dazed, speechless, stunned, stupefied, flabbergasted, **2**. astonished; *synonyms* (adj) astonish, dumbfounded, aghast, thunderstruck, astonied, **3**. astounded; *synonym* (adj) surprised, **4**. entertained; *synonyms* (adj) amused, diverted, **5**. amused; *synonyms* (adj) entertained, smiling, **6**. amazed; *synonym* (adj) shocked.

kamatamata 1. color; *synonyms* (n) blush, colour, stain, tinge, tint, complexion, guise, (v) dye, flush, paint, redden, disguise, distort, embellish, (adj) tone; *antonyms* (n) colorlessness, (v) discolor, **2**. dye; *synonyms* (n) color, hue, colorant, dyestuff, pigment, shade, (v) imbue, soil, blot, **3**. stain; *synonyms* (n) spot, blemish, mark, smear, dirt, brand, damage, discoloration, (v) tarnish, disgrace, defile, blur, contaminate, daub, dirty, **4**. tint; *synonyms* (n) tincture, cast, coloration, coloring, nuance, rinse, (v) tinct, touch, bepaint.

kamatamataki 1. colored; *synonyms* (adj) black, tinged, colorful, coloured, dyed, tinted, biased, bleached, dark, partial, **2**. tinted; *synonyms* (adj) bright, soft, painted, decorated, highlighted, **3**. stained; *synonyms* (adj) besmirched, spotted, dirty, sullied, tainted, tarnished, damaged, discolored, flyblown, (v) polluted; *antonyms* (adj) pure, unspoiled.

kamatana 1. coil; *synonyms* (n) spiral, roll, loop, reel, convolution, helix, kink, (v) curl, circle, round, twist, wind, tangle, curve, entwine; *antonym* (v) uncoil, **2**. plait; *synonyms* (n) fold, braid, pigtail, plat, pleat, tuck, plication, pucker, (v) lace, crease, double, interlace, intertwine, plight, ply, **3**. string; *synonyms* (n) chain, file, row, strand, twine, range, cord, filament, rank, series, thread, tie, sequence, (v) run, (adj) line, **4**. roll; *synonyms* (n) list, revolution,

catalogue, inventory, register, (v) coil, enfold, revolve, wheel, rock, turn, wallow, envelop, grumble, level, **5**. relax; *synonyms* (v) loose, abate, give, lounge, unbend, melt, debilitate, ease, relieve, remit, rest, slack, (n) loosen, release, (adj) relent; *antonyms* (v) tighten, tense.

kamatanaki 1. coiled; *synonyms* (adj) curled, spiral, curved, bent, bowed, curly, kinky, round, tortile, twisting, wavy, arched, corkscrew, rounded, (v) helical; *antonym* (adj) straight, **2**. rolled; *synonyms* (adj) rolling, furled, involute, beaten, billowing, level, resonant, resonating, resounding, reverberating, reverberative, trilled, tumbling, **3**. relaxed; *synonyms* (adj) lax, loose, slack, calm, comfortable, composed, easy, cool, informal, easygoing, happy, serene, slow, tranquil, unhurried; *antonyms* (adj) tense, anxious, formal, nervous, prim, stiff, uncomfortable, strict, haggard, harassed, prudish, reserved, restless, taut.

kamatanatana loosen; *synonyms* (v) free, relax, loose, detach, undo, discharge, ravel, fluff, unbend, untie, liberate, slacken, (adj) disengage, (n) ease, release; *antonyms* (v) tighten, compress, fasten.

kamatanatanaki loosened; *synonyms* (adj) detached, disentangled, loose, disengaged, extricated, unsnarled.

kamataniaia 1. blind; *synonyms* (adj) sightless, undiscerning, (v) bedazzle, daze, dazzle, obscure, (n) screen, curtain, shutter, awning, drape, trick, veil, camouflage, cheat; *antonym* (adj) sighted, **2**. dazzle; *synonyms* (n) sparkle, brightness, shimmer, (v) shine, blind, flash, glare, awe, captivate, gleam, (adj) confuse, bewilder, hoodwink, perplex, startle.

kamataniaiaki 1. blinded; *synonyms* (adj) blindfolded, blindfold, dizzy, **2**. dazzled; *synonyms* (adj) bewildered, fascinated.

kamatantana 1. loosen; *synonyms* (v) free, relax, loose, detach, undo, discharge, ravel, fluff, unbend, untie, liberate, slacken, (adj) disengage, (n) ease, release; *antonyms* (v) tighten, compress, fasten, **2**. slacken; *synonyms* (v) loosen, abate, slack, remit, retard, douse, decrease, diminish, lessen, moderate, slow, dowse, lag, relent, delay.

kamatantanaki loosened; *synonyms* (adj) detached, disentangled, loose, disengaged, extricated, unsnarled.

kamataraea 1. overcharge; *synonyms* (n) extortion, (v) surcharge, overburden, overload, fleece, burden, swindle, bleed, gazump, hook, ornament, **2**. overprice; *synonym* (v) cheat.

kamataraeaki overpriced; *synonyms* (adj) expensive, steep, dear, costly, exorbitant, extravagant, high, (adv) excessive, inflated, ridiculous.

kamatataua check; *synonyms* (*v*) bridle, stop, block, limit, agree, halt, restrain, bar, dampen, delay, (*n*) control, arrest, curb, bill, cheque.

kamatatauaki checked; *synonyms* (*adj*) checkered, chequered, plaid, backward, curbed, intermittent, limited, numbered, pent-up, safe, silent, tartan, temperate.

kamataua 1. capture; *synonyms* (*v*) bag, catch, take, apprehend, captivate, carry, ensnare, get, seize, bewitch, acquire, beguile, (*n*) arrest, seizure, apprehension; *antonyms* (*v*) release, surrender, 2. arrest; *synonyms* (*n*) stop, check, halt, custody, hold, detention, (*v*) capture, collar, delay, detain, hinder, inhibit, nail, obstruct, retard; *antonym* (*v*) discharge, 3. bag; *synonyms* (*n*) pocket, pouch, package, briefcase, purse, sack, case, container, knapsack, poke, (*v*) bulge, filch, hook, net, pilfer, 4. catch; *synonyms* (*v*) intercept, snatch, trap, attract, block, entangle, entrap, (*n*) haul, hitch, trick, bolt, clasp, grab, pawl, snap, 5. apprehend; *synonyms* (*v*) appreciate, comprehend, conceive, fathom, grasp, realize, understand, follow, sense, anticipate, dig, fear, believe, recognize, compass, 6. collar; *synonyms* (*n*) choker, pinch, ruff, chaplet, flange, neck, neckband, necklace, tie, yoke, (*v*) clutch, cop, nab, 7. control; *synonyms* (*n*) rule, authority, care, influence, sway, ascendancy, ascendency, dominance, (*v*) command, curb, bridle, conduct, handle, conquer, contain; *antonyms* (*n*) freedom, weakness, (*v*) intensify, share, 8. foil; *synonyms* (*n*) contrast, blade, sheet, (*v*) frustrate, baffle, balk, defeat, thwart, bilk, cross, elude, avert, prevent, ruin, scotch, 9. inspect; *synonyms* (*v*) examine, overhaul, overlook, survey, explore, inquire, look, review, scrutinize, view, watch, monitor, analyze, audit, consider, 10. seize; *synonyms* (*v*) grapple, receive, annex, assume, confiscate, grip, appropriate, commandeer, impound, perceive, tackle, kidnap, abduct, adopt, obtain.

kamatauaki 1. foiled; *synonyms* (*adj*) frustrated, thwarted, disappointed, defeated, discomfited, baffled, balked, discouraged, embarrassed, blocked, hindered, obstructed, stymied; *antonym* (*adj*) successful, 2. controlled; *synonyms* (*adj*) limited, restrained, restricted, temperate, subdued, inhibited, banned, calm, chaste, composed, confidential, conscious, conservative, contained, deliberate; *antonym* (*adj*) spontaneous, 3. apprehended; *synonyms* (*adj*) held, appreciated, comprehended, detained, gratifying, pleasing, satisfying, 4. arrested; *synonyms* (*adj*) backward, intermittent, 5. seized; *synonyms* (*adj*) confiscate, confiscated, appropriated, condemned, apprehended, censured, convicted, forfeit, forfeited, obsessed.

kamatauninga 1. disgrace; *synonyms* (*n*) shame, blemish, stain, degradation, reproach, slur, abuse, (*v*) dishonor, discredit, degrade, blot, debase, attaint, defame, defile; *antonyms* (*v*) honor, respect, credit, esteem, 2. disgraceful; *synonyms* (*adj*) dishonorable, shameful, degrading, disreputable, infamous, scandalous, shocking, base, black, despicable, discreditable, ignoble, ignominious, inglorious, outrageous; *antonyms* (*adj*) admirable, honorable, reputable, 3. affront; *synonyms* (*n*) outrage, slight, disgrace, indignity, offense, snub, discourtesy, contumely, (*v*) insult, face, offend, taunt, confront, displease, flout; *antonym* (*v*) compliment, 4. insolent; *synonyms* (*adj*) abusive, audacious, disrespectful, impertinent, arrogant, brazen, fresh, impudent, defiant, barefaced, bold, brassy, discourteous, impolite, offensive; *antonyms* (*adj*) polite, respectful, 5. insult; *synonyms* (*n*) affront, contempt, wound, derision, harm, injury, jeer, mockery, revilement, (*v*) cut, mock, insolence, damage, deride, injure; *antonym* (*v*) praise, 6. impudent; *synonyms* (*adj*) forward, daring, insolent, brash, cheeky, saucy, cool, flip, flippant, overbold, pert, shameless, brave, blatant, immodest, 7. slight; *synonyms* (*adj*) flimsy, slender, thin, fragile, delicate, faint, feeble, fine, lean, (*n*) scorn, disdain, (*v*) disregard, neglect, ignore, (*adv*) light; *antonyms* (*adj*) considerable, major, fat, heavy, intense, obvious, severe, thickset, wide.

kamatauningaki 1. affronted; *synonyms* (*adj*) insulted, offended, hurt, angry, annoyed, ashamed, embarrassed, horrified, humiliated, piqued, peeved, sensitive, snubbed, sulky, touchy, 2. insulted; *synonyms* (*adj*) affronted, huffy, disrespected, slighted, upset, 3. disgraced; *synonyms* (*adj*) discredited, shamed, dishonored, abashed, damaged, disfigured, dishonest, mortified, dishonorable, faithless, fraudulent, guilty, hangdog, indecent, knavish.

kamatawea 1. rapid; *synonyms* (*adj*) fast, quick, prompt, swift, agile, fleet, hasty, speedy, cursory, expeditious, sudden, nimble, winged, express, hurried; *antonyms* (*adj*) slow, gradual, 2. retard; *synonyms* (*v*) delay, check, hinder, arrest, detain, impede, lag, obstruct, decelerate, procrastinate, curb, prevent, (*n*) defer, moron, (*adj*) deaden; *antonym* (*v*) accelerate.

kamataweaki retarded; *synonyms* (*adj*) backward, slow, tardy, imbecile, defective, deferred, dull, half-baked, leisurely, obtuse, simple, birdbrained, dim, dim-witted, dopey.

kamatea 1. extinguish; *synonyms* (*v*) destroy, exterminate, quench, annihilate, douse, eradicate, consume, end, suppress, quash, devastate, crush, decimate, efface, (*adj*) allay; *antonyms* (*v*) light, ignite, 2. exterminate; *synonyms* (*v*) eliminate, obliterate, extirpate, liquidate, slay, extinguish, kill, massacre, slaughter, uproot, butcher, deracinate, assassinate, murder, **3**. kill; *synonyms* (*v*) erase, finish, blast, dispatch, execute, behead, defeat, quell, remove, shoot, smother, stop, impale, (*n*) game, prey, **4**. destroy; *synonyms* (*v*) break, demolish, blight, despoil, dash, destruct, devour, dismantle, raze, spoil, subvert, waste, wreck, (*adj*) desolate, abolish; *antonyms* (*v*) build, preserve, create, make, **5**. execute; *synonyms* (*v*) do, achieve, complete, perform, accomplish, act, effect, enforce, carry, consummate, discharge, fulfill, practice, administer, commit, **6**. dispatch; *synonyms* (*n*) despatch, speed, consignment, celerity, expedition, haste, hurry, letter, quickness, (*v*) accelerate, send, deliver, convey, forward, quicken; *antonyms* (*n*) receiving, receipt, **7**. negate; *synonyms* (*v*) contradict, invalidate, deny, annul, belie, contravene, confute, disprove, cancel, nullify, refute, counteract, neutralize, controvert, reverse; *antonym* (*v*) confirm, **8**. assassin; *synonyms* (*n*) murderer, assassinator, liquidator, bravo, cutthroat, killer, (*v*) slayer, **9**. assassinate; *synonym* (*v*) assassin, **10**. annihilate; *synonyms* (*v*) abrogate, expunge, undo, vitiate, overcome, ravage, rout, smash, **11**. killer; *synonyms* (*n*) grampus, poison, marauder, orca, playboy, demolisher, (*adj*) murderous, deadly, fatal, competitive, lethal, ruthless, virulent, bloodthirsty, dangerous, **12**. nix; *synonyms* (*n*) nothing, zero, zilch, nihil, rebuff, aught, cipher, naught, null, leprechaun, nichts, nixie, refusal, (*v*) veto, (*adj*) nil, **13**. quench; *synonyms* (*v*) appease, assuage, slake, calm, chill, cool, fill, satisfy, damp, choke, deaden, quiet, satiate, slack, (*n*) quenching, **14**. slain; *synonyms* (*adj*) dejected, fallen, mat, overthrown, **15**. terminate; *synonyms* (*v*) close, cease, conclude, drop, discontinue, dismiss, dissolve, halt, can, result, abort, bound, ax, culminate, fire; *antonyms* (*v*) begin, start, establish, **16**. slay; *synonyms* (*v*) mangle, hit.

kamateaki 1. assassinated, **2**. annihilated; *synonyms* (*v*) perished, (*adj*) annihilate, exterminated, lost, uncreated, broken, eternal, impoverished, **3**. executed; *synonyms* (*v*) done, (*adj*) finished, fulfilled, complete, given, issued, **4**. destroyed; *synonyms* (*adj*) ruined, desolate, desolated, shattered, dead, depressed, **5**. dispatched, **6**. exterminated; *synonyms* (*adj*) annihilated, extinct, **7**. killed; *synonyms* (*adj*) slain, fallen, (*n*) casualty, **8**. extinguished; *synonyms* (*adj*) out, quenched, allayed, nonexistent, forbidden, inactive, kayoed, nonextant, prohibited, proscribed, quelled, (*n*) defunctness, extermination, extinction, extinguishing, **9**. slain; *synonyms* (*adj*) dejected, mat, overthrown, **10**. quenched; *synonyms* (*adj*) extinguished, slaked, squelched, satisfied, retired, stunned, taboo, tabu, verboten, **11**. terminated; *synonyms* (*adj*) concluded, ended, over.

kamateanibai 1. hardened; *synonyms* (*adj*) hard, callous, confirmed, tough, indurated, tempered, unfeeling, enured, habitual, inured, veteran, **2**. insensible; *synonyms* (*adj*) imperceptible, numb, unconscious, apathetic, dull, impassive, indiscernible, unaware, comatose, inert, ignorant, oblivious, insensate, insensitive, senseless; *antonym* (*adj*) sensible, **3**. imperturbable; *synonyms* (*adj*) calm, dispassionate, composed, placid, cool, unflappable, equable, steady, sedate, serene, unruffled, nonchalant, **4**. impassable; *synonyms* (*adj*) impervious, insurmountable, impenetrable, insuperable, invincible, inaccessible, unpassable; *antonym* (*adj*) passable, **5**. intrepid; *synonyms* (*adj*) bold, brave, courageous, daring, fearless, audacious, dauntless, gallant, hardy, adventurous, heroic, confident, enterprising, doughty, undaunted; *antonym* (*adj*) cowardly, **6**. indifferent; *synonyms* (*adj*) cold, fair, insensible, unconcerned, careless, average, aloof, casual, detached, disinterested, frigid, mediocre, neutral, ordinary, uninterested; *antonyms* (*adj*) caring, enthusiastic, fervent, keen, obsessive, eager, energetic, involved, surprised.

kamatebwai 1. expect; *synonyms* (*v*) anticipate, assume, believe, demand, understand, abide, await, calculate, hope, suppose, think, conceive, call, mean, ask, **2**. cognize; *synonyms* (*v*) know, comprehend, fathom, grasp, acknowledge, bang, bed, bonk, cognise, eff, experience, fuck, hump, jazz, live, **3**. comprehend; *synonyms* (*v*) apprehend, catch, embrace, appreciate, comprise, feel, see, sense, apperceive, admit, compass, contain, cover, dig, digest, **4**. conceive; *synonyms* (*v*) imagine, design, realize, discover, cogitate, consider, create, fancy, invent, originate, coin, dream, suspect, concoct, deem, **5**. interpret; *synonyms* (*v*) clarify, construe, elucidate, illustrate, read, comment, gloss, decipher, explain, explicate, render, depict, illuminate, define, expound, **6**. corroborate; *synonyms* (*v*) confirm, validate, authenticate, establish, prove, substantiate, verify, affirm, demonstrate, support, attest, show, reassert, assert, bolster; *antonym* (*v*) refute, **7**. assume; *synonyms* (*v*) affect, accept, adopt, appropriate, arrogate, feign, take, presume, sham, simulate, usurp, acquire, conclude, conjecture, deduce, **8**. conclude; *synonyms* (*v*) close, complete, finish, gather, accomplish, cease, determine, end, resolve, settle, terminate, decide, derive, do, generalize; *antonyms* (*v*) start, begin, **9**. digest; *synonyms* (*n*) resume, brief, collection, compendium, compilation, condensation, epitome, abridgement, precis, (*v*) abstract, absorb, stomach, summarize, codify, (*adj*) brook, **10**. note; *synonyms* (*n*) mention, remark, annotation, heed, indication, mark, attention, bill, distinction, epistle, letter, (*v*) notice, mind, look, detect; *antonym* (*v*) ignore, **11**.

discern; *synonyms* (v) behold, differentiate, descry, distinguish, perceive, recognize, find, discriminate, judge, note, observe, spot, learn, espy, identify, **12**. distinguish; *synonyms* (v) discern, describe, characterize, classify, difference, separate, tell, contrast, honor, secern, signalize, dignify, severalize, celebrate, spy; *antonym* (v) confuse, **13**. learn; *synonyms* (v) get, ascertain, have, hear, con, study, assimilate, instruct, teach, follow, memorize, remember, check, condition, glean, **14**. confirm; *synonyms* (v) approve, corroborate, clinch, assure, authorize, certify, justify, sanction, testify, uphold, seal, aver, endorse, evidence, (adj) firm; *antonyms* (v) disprove, contradict, **15**. certify; *synonyms* (v) accredit, warrant, ensure, declare, guarantee, license, vouch, ratify, allow, licence, manifest, witness, **16**. appreciate; *synonyms* (v) esteem, prize, treasure, value, appraise, admire, apprize, cherish, enjoy, estimate, like, respect, apprise, enhance, praise; *antonyms* (v) depreciate, scorn, **17**. fathom; *synonyms* (v) sound, plumb, bottom, penetrate, measure, examine, solve, (n) gauge, probe, **18**. accept; *synonyms* (v) receive, accede, acquiesce, yield, agree, assent, bear, consent, espouse, reconcile, suffer, tolerate, undertake, welcome, swallow; *antonyms* (v) refuse, reject, deny, snub, oppose, renounce, resist, **19**. grasp; *synonyms* (n) grip, clasp, clutch, appreciation, apprehension, clutches, comprehension, reach, (v) hold, grapple, capture, cling, grab, clench, snatch; *antonym* (v) release, **20**. notice; *synonyms* (n) advertisement, declaration, information, caution, message, observation, admonition, announcement, bulletin, consideration, critique, eye, account, (v) attend, regard; *antonym* (v) disregard.

kamatebwaiaki 1. conceived; *synonyms* (adj) formed, defined, settled, **2**. confirmed; *synonyms* (adj) chronic, inveterate, assured, habitual, constant, affirmed, definite, established, fixed, ingrained, set, valid, accustomed; *antonyms* (adj) unconfirmed, unproven, **3**. digested; *synonyms* (adj) completed, mature, perfect, prepared, ready, ripe, **4**. assumed; *synonyms* (adj) false, sham, affected, counterfeit, fake, feigned, fictitious, pretended, reputed, artificial, alleged, assumptive, hypothetical, phony, spurious, **5**. noted; *synonyms* (v) notorious, (adj) distinguished, famous, illustrious, conspicuous, glorious, celebrated, eminent, famed, known, renowned, well-known, noble, marked, notable, **6**. distinguished; *synonyms* (adj) dignified, important, reputable, great, high, prominent, splendid, superior, considerable, distinct, ace, exalted, excellent, grand, lofty; *antonyms* (adj) unknown, ordinary, **7**. noticed, **8**. interpreted; *synonyms* (adj) accurate, confined, exact, strict, taken, precise, restricted, rigidly, rigorous, severe, strained, tense, tight, **9**.

concluded; *synonyms* (adj) complete, finished, done, over, closed, accomplished, terminated, (adv) ended, **10**. certified; *synonyms* (adj) qualified, accredited, official, guaranteed, authorized, approved, certifiable; *antonyms* (adj) informal, unofficial, **11**. comprehended; *synonyms* (adj) appreciated, apprehended, gratifying, pleasing, satisfying, **12**. learned; *synonyms* (v) knowing, (adj) erudite, educated, enlightened, knowledgeable, wise, academic, scholarly, bookish, cultured, intellectual, lettered, literary, studious, informed; *antonyms* (adj) ignorant, innate, **13**. appreciated; *synonyms* (adj) understood, comprehended, prized, respected, valued, welcome, aesthetic, esteemed, valuable, acceptable, artistic, cheering, cherished, comforting, dear; *antonym* (adj) unwelcome, **14**. expected; *synonyms* (adj) likely, anticipated, predictable, prospective, conventional, intended, usual, **15**. accepted; *synonyms* (adj) acknowledged, assumed, orthodox, current, received, customary, popular, proper, recognized; *antonyms* (adj) concealed, unpopular, unusual, **16**. verified; *synonyms* (adj) corroborated, substantiated, confirmed, actual, authoritative, demonstrated, hard, **17**. perceived; *synonyms* (adj) felt, sensed, apparent, ostensible, professed, supposed, seeming, superficial, **18**. sensed; *synonym* (adj) perceived, **19**. realized; *synonyms* (adj) realised, effected, fulfilled, caught, earned, **20**. understood; *synonyms* (v) admitted, (adj) implicit, tacit, implied, silent; *antonyms* (adj) explicit, spoken.

kamatenakoa annihilate; *synonyms* (v) abolish, eradicate, destroy, eliminate, exterminate, extinguish, quash, crush, defeat, demolish, extirpate, kill, obliterate, quench, suppress.

kamatenakoaki annihilated; *synonyms* (v) perished, (adj) annihilate, exterminated, lost, uncreated, broken, eternal, impoverished.

kamaterangaea paralyze; *synonyms* (v) palsy, cripple, disable, paralyse, deaden, petrify, prostrate, (n) benumb, numb, blunt, obtund, stun, (adj) anaesthetize, pall.

kamaterangaeaki paralyzed; *synonyms* (v) paralytic, (adj) palsied, crippled, dead, disabled, enervated, helpless, impotent, inert, motionless, numb, paralytical, powerless, prostrate, torpid.

kamateraoa profit; *synonyms* (n) gain, benefit, account, good, produce, earnings, increase, dividend, interest, (v) net, advance, avail, earn, help, (adj) advantage; *antonym* (v) lose.

kamaterea 1. advance; *synonyms* (n) progress, improvement, (v) further, proceed, promote, approach, encourage, raise, rise, boost, contribute, cultivate, develop, forward, (phr) accelerate; *antonyms* (n) deterioration, (v) retreat, recede, delay, demote, regress, **2**. excel; *synonyms* (*v*) surpass, top, cap, outdo, pass, eclipse, beat, transcend, lead, outshine, overshadow, (*adj*) exceed, better, **3**. exceed; *synonyms* (*v*) surmount, outweigh, overrun, excel, outgo, outmatch, outstrip, overstep, overtake, best, break, crown, **4**. beat; *synonyms* (*v*) batter, flap, pulsate, throb, tick, trounce, whip, bat, baste, cheat, (*n*) pulse, thump, knock, round, cadence; *antonym* (*v*) lose, **5**. better; *synonyms* (*adj*) superior, major, healthier, (*n*) bettor, (*v*) amend, improve, mend, recover, advance, ameliorate, emend, reform, enhance, refine, benefit; *antonyms* (*adj*) lesser, (*adv*) worse, (*n*) inferior, (*v*) worsen, **6**. outclass; *synonyms* (*v*) defeat, overcome, thrash, hammer, outdistance, overwhelm, shine, cream, slaughter, **7**. outdo; *synonyms* (*v*) outwit, circumvent, outrival, outrun, distance, **8**. surmount; *synonyms* (*v*) conquer, master, subdue, climb, vanquish, scale, overpower, negotiate, reduce, subjugate, hurdle, overbear, clamber, escalade, (*adj*) perch, **9**. overrun; *synonyms* (*v*) overflow, deluge, flood, infest, invade, occupy, inundate, rout, ravage, spill, distribute, makeup, mortise, (*n*) excess, (*adj*) infested.

kamatereaki 1. advanced; *synonyms* (*adj*) sophisticated, progressive, senior, higher, modern, new, precocious, late, cultured, developed, elevated, forward, liberal, ripe, superior; *antonyms* (*adj*) conservative, old-fashioned, inferior, **2**. beaten; *synonyms* (*v*) beat, (*adj*) battered, overpowered, conquered, routed, overcome; *antonym* (*adj*) victorious, **3**. overrun; *synonyms* (*v*) overflow, deluge, flood, infest, invade, occupy, inundate, overwhelm, conquer, rout, exceed, ravage, spill, distribute, (*n*) excess, **4**. surmounted; *synonym* (*adj*) beaten.

kamatibutibua 1. inflate; *synonyms* (*v*) enlarge, expand, dilate, distend, amplify, balloon, bloat, billow, blow, bulge, increase, heave, exaggerate, fill, magnify; *antonym* (*v*) deflate, **2**. ripen; *synonyms* (*v*) mature, grow, maturate, ripe, age, season, cultivate, develop, elaborate, fructify, (*adj*) perfect.

kamatibutibuaki 1. inflated; *synonyms* (*adj*) bombastic, grandiloquent, exaggerated, puffy, conceited, bloated, hyperbolic, swollen, vain, extravagant, flatulent, enlarged, overblown, pompous, (*v*) distended; *antonyms* (*adj*) understated, deflated, humble, **2**. ripened; *synonyms* (*adj*) ripe, mature, matured, aged, elderly, adult, cured, developed, full-grown, grown, mellow, old, older, ready, seasoned.

kamatiketikea 1. loosen; *synonyms* (*v*) free, relax, loose, detach, undo, discharge, ravel, fluff, unbend, untie, liberate, slacken, (*adj*) disengage, (*n*) ease, release; *antonyms* (*v*) tighten, compress, fasten, **2**.

soften; *synonyms* (*v*) mitigate, moderate, assuage, dull, melt, mute, relent, relieve, alleviate, allay, pacify, break, cushion, (*adj*) mollify, palliate; *antonyms* (*v*) harden, set, solidify, congeal, **3**. slacken; *synonyms* (*v*) loosen, abate, slack, remit, retard, douse, decrease, diminish, lessen, slow, dowse, lag, delay, lull, slake.

kamatiketikeaki 1. loosened; *synonyms* (*adj*) detached, disentangled, loose, disengaged, extricated, unsnarled, **2**. softened; *synonyms* (*adj*) dull, diffused, muffled, muted, boring, deadening, dense, dim, dumb, faint, gray, grey, hushed, intenerate, irksome.

kamatine 1. hanging; *synonyms* (*n*) dangling, execution, suspension, curtain, (*adj*) pendant, pendent, suspended, pending, pendulous; *antonym* (*adj*) upright, **2**. balancing; *synonyms* (*adj*) matching, libratory, corresponding, harmonizing, opposite, paired, (*n*) balance, adjustment, antilibration, audit, comparison, reconciliation, redress, rapprochement, trimming, **3**. perching; *synonym* (*adj*) insessorial.

kamatiratira 1. flatten; *synonyms* (*v*) fell, demolish, level, press, even, drop, roll, squash, depress, destroy, ruin, smash, smooth, unfold, bulldoze; *antonyms* (*v*) build, crumple, **2**. crush; *synonyms* (*n*) squeeze, crowd, (*v*) beat, break, compress, conquer, crunch, stamp, bruise, jam, mash, overpower, overwhelm, quash, subdue, **3**. squash; *synonyms* (*v*) crush, quell, flatten, oppress, crash, cram, grind, push, squelch, quench, trample, silence, muzzle, constrict, (*adj*) knead.

kamatiratiraki 1. flattened; *synonyms* (*adj*) compressed, depressed, planate, trodden, unconscious, compacted, firmed, trampled; *antonym* (*adj*) loose, **2**. crushed; *synonyms* (*v*) victimized, (*adj*) broken, beaten, low, subdued, conquered, flattened, dispirited, overwhelmed, abashed, abject, blue, brokenhearted, busted, (*n*) crushing; *antonym* (*adj*) victorious, **3**. squashed; *synonyms* (*adj*) condensed, dense, solid.

kamatiraua 1. crush; *synonyms* (*n*) squeeze, press, crowd, (*v*) beat, break, compress, conquer, crunch, stamp, bruise, jam, mash, overpower, overwhelm, quash, **2**. flatten; *synonyms* (*v*) fell, demolish, level, even, drop, roll, squash, depress, destroy, ruin, smash, smooth, unfold, bulldoze, deflate; *antonyms* (*v*) build, crumple, **3**. squash; *synonyms* (*v*) crush, quell, flatten, oppress, crash, cram, grind, push, squelch, quench, trample, silence, muzzle, constrict, (*adj*) knead.

kamatirauaki 1. flattened; *synonyms* (*adj*) compressed, depressed, planate, trodden, unconscious, compacted, firmed, trampled; *antonym* (*adj*) loose, **2**. crushed; *synonyms* (*v*) victimized, (*adj*) broken, beaten, low, subdued, conquered, flattened, dispirited, overwhelmed, abashed, abject, blue, brokenhearted, busted, (*n*) crushing; *antonym* (*adj*) victorious, **3.** squashed; *synonyms* (*adj*) condensed, dense, solid.

kamatoa 1. fortify; *synonyms* (*v*) strengthen, confirm, consolidate, secure, buttress, encourage, reinforce, fort, harden, invigorate, support, arm, cheer, (*n*) brace, nerve; *antonym* (*v*) weaken, **2.** found; *synonyms* (*v*) erect, establish, base, build, form, constitute, construct, appoint, create, ground, institute, bottom, begin, cast, plant; *antonym* (*adj*) misplaced, **3.** confirm; *synonyms* (*v*) affirm, approve, corroborate, prove, validate, verify, clinch, assert, assure, authenticate, authorize, certify, demonstrate, justify, sanction; *antonyms* (*v*) disprove, contradict, **4.** affirm; *synonyms* (*v*) declare, avow, maintain, protest, accept, allege, aver, claim, profess, promise, say, state, substantiate, swear, vow; *antonyms* (*v*) deny, negate, **5.** ascertain; *synonyms* (*v*) see, check, determine, discover, learn, control, detect, ensure, find, tell, understand, decide, identify, insure, notice, **6.** fix; *synonyms* (*v*) assign, fasten, settle, define, anchor, adjust, arrange, set, clamp, do, castrate, emasculate, (*n*) bind, (*adj*) ascertain, attach; *antonyms* (*v*) break, unfasten, **7.** demonstrate; *synonyms* (*v*) attest, display, exhibit, present, show, argue, evidence, exemplify, explain, indicate, manifest, try, proclaim, illustrate, mark; *antonym* (*v*) conceal, **8.** prove; *synonyms* (*v*) examine, essay, evince, test, attempt, adduce, bear, assay, uphold, experience, raise, rise, sustain, testify, (*n*) taste, **9.** strengthen; *synonyms* (*v*) enhance, fortify, intensify, bolster, increase, stiffen, toughen, reenforce, hearten, revive, deepen, gird, comfort, thicken, fix; *antonym* (*v*) undermine, **10.** secure; *synonyms* (*v*) close, preserve, acquire, attain, fast, gain, get, guarantee, guard, lock, obtain, (*adj*) safe, firm, certain, confident; *antonyms* (*v*) lose, detach, (*adj*) insecure, vulnerable, loose, unsafe.

kamatoaki 1. confirmed; *synonyms* (*adj*) chronic, inveterate, assured, habitual, constant, affirmed, definite, established, fixed, ingrained, set, valid, accustomed; *antonyms* (*adj*) unconfirmed, unproven, **2.** demonstrated; *synonyms* (*adj*) confirmed, tried, verified, **3.** ascertained; *synonyms* (*v*) absolute, noted, notorious, received, recognized, categorical, clear, decided, decisive, determinate, positive, (*adj*) discovered, certain, guaranteed, observed, **4.** affirmed; *synonyms* (*adj*) avowed, declared, stated, **5.** fortified; *synonyms* (*adj*) bastioned, secure, castled, defended, equipped, fast, protected, safeguarded, secured, shielded, prepared, turreted, **6.** fixed; *synonyms* (*adj*) determined, steady, durable, fastened, intent, permanent, resolute, rigid, standing, still, adamant, flat, (*v*) stable, (*adv*) firm, tight; *antonyms* (*adj*) flexible, adaptable, adjustable, changeable,

movable, separate, variable, compliant, loose, moveable, portable, removable, temporary, **7.** founded; *synonyms* (*v*) cast, fusil, fusible, (*adj*) based, (*prep*) institute, organized, **8.** secured; *synonyms* (*adj*) barred, bolted, bonded, latched, locked, **9.** strengthened; *synonyms* (*adj*) reinforced, consolidated, built, comfortable, sinewed, united, **10.** proven; *synonyms* (*adj*) proved, irrefutable, accepted, acknowledged, authoritative, common, experimental, medical, quantifiable, scientific, sound, undeniable, well-founded; *antonym* (*adj*) unverified.

kamatoatoa harden; *synonyms* (*v*) habituate, consolidate, inure, season, coagulate, congeal, freeze, petrify, solidify, anneal, ossify, (*n*) strengthen, brace, fortify, (*adj*) vitrify; *antonyms* (*v*) soften, liquefy.

kamatoatoaki hardened; *synonyms* (*adj*) hard, callous, confirmed, tough, indurated, tempered, unfeeling, enured, habitual, inured, veteran.

kamatoroa recycle; *synonyms* (*v*) reuse, salvage, reprocess.

kamatua 1. lull; *synonyms* (*n*) peace, rest, break, drop, (*v*) calm, quiet, hush, allay, pause, still, tranquilize, compose, (*adj*) appease, assuage, pacify; *antonym* (*v*) agitate, **2.** hypnotize; *synonyms* (*v*) entrance, mesmerize, captivate, charm, enchant, enthrall, hypnotise, bewitch, fascinate, mesmerise, **3.** anaesthetize; *synonyms* (*v*) anaesthetise, anesthetize, bother, discommode, disoblige, douse, extend, incommode, inconvenience, issue, publish, (*n*) chloroform, (*adj*) blunt, obtund, pall.

kamatuaki 1. anaesthetized; *synonyms* (*adj*) anaesthetised, anesthetized, **2.** hypnotized; *synonyms* (*adj*) hypnotised, mesmerized, fascinated, mesmerised, rapt, transfixed.

kamatutua numb; *synonyms* (*adj*) asleep, benumbed, dead, dull, insensible, torpid, deadened, callous, impassive, comatose, inactive, inert, (*v*) benumb, deaden, (*n*) blunt; *antonym* (*adj*) sensitive.

kamauanea bait; *synonyms* (*n*) bribe, decoy, snare, attraction, incentive, inducement, temptation, (*v*) badger, tease, harass, lure, molest, heckle, ride, (*adj*) harry.

kamauanta improbable; *synonyms* (*adj*) unlikely, implausible, impossible, incredible, unbelievable, fishy, marvelous, questionable, impractical, inconceivable, absurd, tall, unthinkable, dubious, fantastic; *antonyms* (*adj*) likely, probable.

kamaukua 1. disable; *synonyms* (*v*) maim, disqualify, incapacitate, cripple, disenable, paralyze, weaken, disarm, hamstring, injure, invalid, mutilate, unfit, dismantle; *antonym* (*v*) enable, **2.** maim; *synonyms* (*v*) deform, damage, mar, lacerate, deface, disable, disfigure, harm, hurt, impair, mangle, truncate, (*adj*) wound, becripple, **3.**

cripple; *synonyms* (*v*) lame, enfeeble, (*adj*) prostrate.

kamaukuaki 1. maimed; *synonyms* (*adj*) crippled, deformed, disabled, mutilated, faulty, game, truncated, mangled, (*n*) wounded, **2.** disabled; *synonyms* (*adj*) handicapped, helpless, incapacitated, invalid, weakened, wrecked, unavailable, paralytic, broken, cripply, exhausted, palsied, powerless, bedridden, (*adv*) aground, **3.** crippled; *synonyms* (*v*) drooping, flagging, (*adj*) lame, crooked, decrepit, halt, halting, impotent, prostrate, damaged, defective, feeble, gimp, gimpy, harmed.

kamauna 1. bleach; *synonyms* (*n*) whitener, peroxide, (*v*) blanch, whiten, decolor, decolorize, decolourize, fade, white, **2.** blank; *synonyms* (*adj*) bare, empty, unfilled, clean, vacant, deadpan, dull, expressionless, impassive, inexpressive, (*n*) space, form, emptiness, gap, hiatus; *antonyms* (*adj*) animated, full, expressive, **3.** cancel; *synonyms* (*v*) annul, abrogate, erase, expunge, invalidate, remit, revoke, abate, avoid, efface, eliminate, obliterate, repeal, (*adj*) abolish, nullify; *antonym* (*v*) validate, **4.** erase; *synonyms* (*v*) cancel, delete, annihilate, eradicate, clear, destroy, raze, remove, scrape, blot, extinguish, kill, rase, wipe; *antonym* (*v*) insert, **5.** blot; *synonyms* (*n*) blemish, spot, smudge, blotch, slur, daub, defect, fault, flaw, (*v*) stain, mark, taint, tarnish, blob, blur, **6.** expunge; *synonyms* (*v*) excise, strike, **7.** extinguish; *synonyms* (*v*) exterminate, quench, douse, consume, end, suppress, quash, devastate, crush, decimate, extirpate, ravage, stifle, subvert, (*adj*) allay; *antonyms* (*v*) light, ignite, **8.** overwhelm; *synonyms* (*v*) defeat, flood, inundate, overcome, overpower, overthrow, deluge, drown, engulf, astound, beat, overrun, overtake, overturn, swamp, **9.** obliterate; *synonyms* (*v*) demolish, obscure, hide.

kamaunaki 1. bleached; *synonyms* (*adj*) colorless, attenuate, attenuated, biased, coloured, dyed, faded, faint, fair, pale, wan, washy, white, colorful, (*n*) blonde, **2.** extinguished; *synonyms* (*adj*) extinct, out, dead, quenched, allayed, nonexistent, forbidden, inactive, kayoed, nonextant, prohibited, (*n*) defunctness, extermination, extinction, extinguishing, **3.** blanked, **4.** cancelled; *synonyms* (*adj*) off, sour, turned, **5.** overwhelmed; *synonyms* (*v*) overborne, (*adj*) overcome, beaten, overpowered, vanquished, conquered, dumbfounded, engulfed, flooded, inundated, overthrown; *antonyms* (*adj*) victorious, unimpressed, **6.** obliterated; *synonyms* (*v*) effaced, erased, (*adj*) obliterate, forgotten, invisible, lost.

kamaunea deafen; *synonyms* (*v*) deaf, muffle, blindfold, deave, envelop, inclose, muff, (*adj*) stun.

kamauneaki deafened; *synonyms* (*adj*) deaf, dead, deadened, stunned, decayed, regardless, stifled, tasteless.

kamaura 1. greet; *synonyms* (*v*) accost, address, acknowledge, cry, hail, salute, welcome, bid, meet, weep, approach, recognize, (*n*) receive, **2.** salute; *synonyms* (*n*) greeting, salutation, bow, compliment, salaam, recognition, bonfire, (*v*) greet, kiss, buss, give, acclaim, nod, ball, drink.

kamawa evacuate; *synonyms* (*v*) deplete, void, discharge, quit, clear, drain, abandon, displace, eject, eliminate, leave, pass, vacate, annul, (*adj*) empty.

kamawaki evacuated; *synonyms* (*adj*) empty, annulled, emptied, voided, invalidated.

kamba 1. inhale; *synonyms* (*v*) breathe, absorb, imbibe, draw, suck, drag, drink, attract, inspire, receive, respire, admit, import, ingest, (*n*) sniff; *antonym* (*v*) exhale, **2.** suck; *synonyms* (*v*) nurse, lactate, suckle, drain, puff, aspirate, pull, breastfeed, (*n*) sucking, suction, **3.** sniff; *synonyms* (*v*) scent, inhale, nose, smell, snuff, whiff, sniffle, smoke.

kambaki inhaled; *synonym* (*adj*) inspired.

kameamea stain; *synonyms* (*n*) spot, blemish, blot, mark, smear, dirt, brand, (*v*) color, dye, tarnish, disgrace, soil, defile, blur, contaminate.

kameameaki stained; *synonyms* (*adj*) besmirched, spotted, dirty, sullied, tainted, tarnished, black, damaged, discolored, flyblown, painted, (*v*) polluted; *antonyms* (*adj*) pure, unspoiled.

kamei give; *synonyms* (*v*) allow, bestow, extend, accord, commit, donate, contribute, convey, deliver, dispense, endow, grant, present, yield, administer; *antonyms* (*v*) withdraw, take, withhold.

kameio 1. boring; *synonyms* (*adj*) dull, tedious, tiresome, annoying, arid, bland, dreary, monotonous, prosaic, tame, uninteresting, wearisome, vapid, drab, (*n*) drilling; *antonyms* (*adj*) exciting, fascinating, interesting, gripping, original, thrilling, varied, **2.** annoying; *synonyms* (*adj*) galling, irritating, troublesome, vexatious, aggravating, awkward, bothersome, disagreeable, grating, inconvenient, offensive, pesky, trying, vexing, (*n*) annoyance; *antonyms* (*adj*) pleasing, soothing, **3.** odd; *synonyms* (*adj*) grotesque, exceptional, funny, abnormal, curious, droll, eccentric, extraordinary, singular, strange, chance, novel, anomalous, bizarre, fantastic; *antonyms* (*adj*) normal, ordinary, even, typical, **4.** vexatious; *synonyms* (*adj*) untoward, burdensome, thorny, pestiferous, heavy, mischievous, painful, peevish, pestering, petulant, plaguy, (*v*) invidious, unaccommodating, **5.** weird; *synonyms* (*adj*) supernatural, uncanny, unearthly, eerie, mysterious, odd, peculiar, unusual, ghostly, quaint, outlandish, mystic, uncommon, crazy, (*n*) destiny;

antonym (*adj*) real, **6.** troublesome; *synonyms* (*adj*) difficult, arduous, hard, onerous, laborious, tough, embarrassing, irksome, unpleasant, grievous, ponderous, taxing, importunate, niggling, (*v*) toilsome; *antonym* (*adj*) easy, **7.** queer; *synonyms* (*adj*) fishy, gay, comical, fanciful, (*v*) baffle, bilk, cross, endanger, expose, foil, frustrate, (*n*) fag, faggot, fagot, fairy, **8.** uncanny; *synonyms* (*adj*) weird, eldritch, unnatural, frightful, hideous, spooky, unco, odious; *antonym* (*adj*) natural.

kameme peevish; *synonyms* (*adj*) fractious, fretful, irritable, irascible, morose, testy, moody, cantankerous, captious, cross, petulant, touchy, crusty, grumpy, excitable.

kamemena 1. deposit; *synonyms* (*n*) charge, residue, guarantee, heap, hoard, lees, (*v*) bank, commit, store, fix, lay, repose, cast, file, leave; *antonym* (*v*) withdraw, **2.** leave; *synonyms* (*v*) depart, forsake, go, abandon, desert, quit, escape, flee, lead, (*n*) furlough, holiday, permission, permit, break, (*adj*) empty; *antonyms* (*v*) arrive, enter, stay, remain, approach, change, come, **3.** seat; *synonyms* (*n*) place, bench, base, backside, behind, bottom, buttocks, chair, position, post, posterior, (*v*) locate, put, contain, hold, **4.** put; *synonyms* (*v*) set, impose, couch, pose, pitch, arrange, assign, establish, express, install, make, plant, localize, (*n*) deposit, invest, **5.** place; *synonyms* (*n*) domicile, office, order, spot, attitude, job, location, situation, circumstance, center, abode, berth, (*v*) rank, station, lie; *antonym* (*v*) remove.

kamemenaki 1. placed; *synonyms* (*adj*) located, situated, laid, set, positioned, fixed, collocate, determined, dictated, hardened, residing, rigid, **2.** seated; *synonyms* (*adj*) sitting, sedentary.

kamena 1. deposit; *synonyms* (*n*) charge, residue, guarantee, heap, hoard, lees, (*v*) bank, commit, store, fix, lay, repose, cast, file, leave; *antonym* (*v*) withdraw, **2.** install; *synonyms* (*v*) establish, inaugurate, appoint, erect, crown, induct, instal, invest, lodge, place, plant, post, put, quarter, seat; *antonym* (*v*) overthrow, **3.** lodge; *synonyms* (*n*) house, club, cottage, hut, inn, (*v*) cabin, live, accommodate, deposit, inhabit, set, board, (*adj*) abide, dwell, reside, **4.** touch; *synonyms* (*n*) feel, tinge, feeling, hint, (*v*) affect, contact, hit, border, adjoin, strike, stroke, regard, brush, concern, handle, **5.** place; *synonyms* (*n*) position, domicile, office, order, spot, attitude, base, job, location, (*v*) arrange, locate, rank, station, install, pitch; *antonym* (*v*) remove, **6.** put; *synonyms* (*v*) impose, couch, pose, assign, express, make, localize, aim, frame, park, reckon, rest, settle, situate, stake.

kamenaiaki refreshed; *synonyms* (*adj*) fresh, invigorated, reinvigorated, new, novel, bracing, brisk, clean, energising, energizing, impertinent,

impudent, overbold, recharged, refreshful; *antonyms* (*adj*) exhausted, tired.

kamenaki 1. placed; *synonyms* (*adj*) located, situated, laid, set, positioned, fixed, collocate, determined, dictated, hardened, residing, rigid, **2.** *synonyms* (*v*) compassionate, pitiful, sympathetic, bad, decayed, lentiginous, mildewed, moldy, (*adj*) affected, cracked, crazy, daft, insane, tinged, interested; *antonym* (*adj*) untouched.

kamengoa 1. burden; *synonyms* (*n*) load, anxiety, pack, strain, bale, care, cargo, concern, core, (*v*) bother, weight, burthen, clog, trouble, afflict; *antonyms* (*v*) relieve, unburden, **2.** lade; *synonyms* (*v*) burden, charge, fill, dip, laden, ladle, scoop, **3.** encumber; *synonyms* (*v*) saddle, hamper, lumber, tax, bound, constrain, cumber, embarrass, hinder, fetter, limit, restrict, throttle, delay, handicap; *antonym* (*v*) free, **4.** load; *synonyms* (*n*) freight, stack, heap, consignment, lading, shipment, crowd, encumbrance, loading, (*v*) encumber, pile, lade, stow, glut, cram; *antonym* (*v*) unload, **5.** overload; *synonyms* (*n*) overburden, excess, (*v*) overcharge, oppress, surcharge, overlay, overwhelm, overdo, overdose, overfeed, overrun, swamp, **6.** oppress; *synonyms* (*v*) persecute, harass, press, pinch, depress, crush, repress, harry, harrow, distress, control, torture, bully, (*adj*) aggrieve, wrong.

kamengoaki 1. burdened; *synonyms* (*adj*) encumbered, loaded, oppressed, overburdened, beleaguered, drawn, full, gestant, haggard, heavy, (*prep*) laden, (*adv*) deceitfully, deceptively, dishonestly, falsely; *antonym* (*adj*) empty, **2.** encumbered; *synonyms* (*adj*) burdened, burdensome, clayey, cloggy, deep, forcible, gloomy, inactive, loud, oppressive, overloaded, ponderous, pregnant, slow, sluggish, **3.** loaded; *synonyms* (*adj*) flush, moneyed, wealthy, affluent, rich, tight, tipsy, intoxicated, pixilated, plastered, soused, wet, besotted, inebriated, ladened; *antonym* (*adj*) poor, **4.** oppressed; *synonyms* (*adj*) downtrodden, persecuted, broken, aggrieved, browbeaten, despairing, downcast, forlorn, subjugated, worried, demoralized, exploited, **5.** overloaded; *synonyms* (*adj*) overcrowded, overladen, busy, congested, overfull, packed, clogged, jammed, stuffed, swarming, teeming.

kamerea 1. bestrew; *synonyms* (*v*) scatter, spread, disperse, disseminate, broadcast, diffuse, shed, sow, disband, disembody, dismember, dispense, distribute, **2.** dissipate; *synonyms* (*v*) dispel, squander, waste, disappear, consume, break, evaporate, fritter, spend, part, separate, split, lose, dissolve, drain; *antonym* (*v*) save, **3.** disperse; *synonyms* (*v*) circulate, dissipate, dismiss, propagate, sprinkle, allot, adjourn, divide, dot, vanish, circularise, circularize, deal, fade; *antonyms* (*v*) assemble, gather, collect, **4.** cast;

synonyms (*v*) hurl, throw, form, stamp, fling, shape, chuck, dump, figure, heave, mould, pitch, (*n*) appearance, casting, mold, **5**. emit; *synonyms* (*v*) discharge, shoot, belch, eject, evolve, radiate, reek, emanate, disgorge, beam, breathe, exhale, exude, issue, (*n*) give; *antonym* (*v*) absorb, **6**. sprinkle; *synonyms* (*n*) dash, scattering, (*v*) drizzle, splash, moisten, cast, spatter, spray, rain, spill, intersperse, splatter, douse, dust, (*adj*) besprinkle, **7**. spatter; *synonyms* (*n*) spattering, splashing, splutter, (*v*) plash, slop, smear, bespatter, soil, spit, sputter, squirt, patter, dabble, slosh, smudge, **8**. scatter; *synonyms* (*v*) litter, rout, plant, lavish, disorder, disrupt, overspread, shower, strew, defeat, disunite, expand, (*n*) dispersion, sprinkling, strewing.

kamereaki 1. dissipated; *synonyms* (*adj*) debauched, dissolute, fast, immoral, abandoned, gay, prodigal, profligate, rakish, degenerate, squandered, libertine, licentious, loose, profuse, **2**. dispersed; *synonyms* (*adj*) diffuse, scattered, sparse, spread, diffused, detached, discrete, fractional, rare, thin, circulated, flowing, isolated, single, strewn; *antonym* (*adj*) concentrated, **3**. cast; *synonyms* (*v*) hurl, throw, form, shed, stamp, fling, shape, chuck, dump, figure, heave, mould, (*n*) appearance, casting, mold, **4**. scattered; *synonyms* (*adj*) dispersed, dissipated, confused, disconnected, disordered, sporadic, distributed, separate, stray, disjointed, disorderly, garbled, illogical, **5**. spattered; *synonyms* (*adj*) bespattered, besplashed, dabbled, dirty, showy, splashed, splashy, splattered, **6**. sprinkled; *synonyms* (*adj*) besprent, dotted, speckled, spotted.

kametebwai understood; *synonyms* (*v*) admitted, (*adj*) implicit, tacit, implied, silent, assumed; *antonyms* (*adj*) explicit, spoken.

kameterea outdo; *synonyms* (*v*) exceed, excel, beat, best, break, better, outgo, outstrip, outwit, surpass, overrun, circumvent, outdistance, outshine, overtake.

kamia 1. astonish; *synonyms* (*v*) amaze, astound, confound, daze, dazzle, flabbergast, stun, alarm, confuse, dumbfound, nonplus, perplex, shock, stagger, (*adj*) surprise, **2**. amaze; *synonyms* (*v*) astonish, baffle, puzzle, discombobulate, bewilder, mystify, startle, stupefy, excite.

kamiaki 1. astonished; *synonyms* (*adj*) amazed, astonish, dumbfounded, flabbergasted, stunned, aghast, astounded, bewildered, thunderstruck, astonied, **2**. amazed; *synonyms* (*adj*) astonished, speechless, shocked, staggered, surprised.

kamiakina 1. enrapture; *synonyms* (*v*) captivate, enchant, bewitch, delight, entrance, fascinate, ravish, enamor, enthrall, transport, please, beguile, rapture, (*adj*) charm, attract; *antonym* (*v*) disenchant, **2**. enchant; *synonyms* (*v*) allure,

capture, enrapture, thrill, witch, gratify, catch, enamour, glamour, hex, hypnotize, mesmerize, appeal, becharm, (*n*) conjure.

kamiakinaki 1. enchanted; *synonyms* (*adj*) bewitched, charmed, delighted, fascinated, rapt, blissful, elated, enamored, happy, magical, pleased, possessed, dreamlike, (*v*) entranced, overjoyed; *antonym* (*adj*) prosaic, **2**. enraptured; *synonyms* (*adj*) ecstatic, rapturous, captive, absorbed, confined, ecstasy, engrossed, infatuated, intoxicated, joyful, jubilant, rhapsodic, enwrapped, imprisoned, (*prep*) enrapt.

kamimi 1. heavenly; *synonyms* (*adj*) divine, celestial, blissful, delightful, ethereal, angelic, blessed, godlike, holy, lovely, sacred, supernal, unearthly, adorable, hallowed; *antonym* (*adj*) earthly, **2**. extraordinary; *synonyms* (*adj*) distinguished, curious, exceptional, odd, abnormal, amazing, astonishing, bizarre, extra, phenomenal, rare, special, strange, unusual, famous; *antonyms* (*adj*) ordinary, normal, everyday, **3**. fantastic; *synonyms* (*adj*) extraordinary, antic, extravagant, grotesque, marvelous, terrific, wonderful, capricious, chimerical, fabulous, fantastical, great, illusory, (*n*) fanciful, (*v*) fancy; *antonyms* (*adj*) awful, real, **4**. marvelous; *synonyms* (*adj*) fantastic, grand, incredible, prodigious, tremendous, glorious, brilliant, cool, excellent, magnificent, marvellous, miraculous, splendid, stupendous, super, **5**. astounding; *synonyms* (*adj*) spectacular, sensational, awesome, breathtaking, overwhelming, remarkable, staggering, stunning, stupefying, surprising, impressive, **6**. awesome; *synonyms* (*adj*) formidable, majestic, frightful, eerie, astounding, frightening, terrible; *antonym* (*adj*) insignificant, **7**. miraculous; *synonyms* (*adj*) supernatural, magical, preternatural, **8**. surprise; *synonyms* (*n*) fright, amazement, astonishment, surprisal, wonder, admiration, (*v*) astound, alarm, amaze, astonish, shock, startle, jolt, stun, catch, **9**. odd; *synonyms* (*adj*) funny, droll, eccentric, singular, chance, novel, anomalous, individual, irregular, peculiar, queer, laughable, erratic, particular, different; *antonyms* (*adj*) even, typical, **10**. sensational; *synonyms* (*adj*) exciting, lurid, melodramatic, sensory, thrilling, dramatic, emotional, startling, arresting, exaggerated, spicy, **11**. strange; *synonyms* (*adj*) extraneous, foreign, mysterious, new, outlandish, alien, exotic, quaint, uncommon, unfamiliar, unknown, inexplicable, crazy, monstrous, unaccountable; *antonym* (*adj*) familiar, **12**. wonderful; *synonyms* (*adj*) beautiful, superb, wondrous, striking, admirable, heavenly, rattling, charming, fine, good, outstanding, howling, unexpected, (*n*) improbable; *antonyms* (*adj*) unpleasant, dreadful.

kamimiaki surprised; *synonyms* (*adj*) astonished, amazed, astounded, dumbfounded, shocked, stunned, bewildered, startled, aghast, confused, curious, puzzled, questioning, quizzical, baffled; *antonym* (*adj*) indifferent.

kamimitoiaka rotate; *synonyms* (*v*) revolve, reel, roll, alternate, gyrate, spin, swing, wheel, orbit, pivot, turn, twirl, circulate, circle, twist.

kamimitoiakaki rotated; *synonym* (*adj*) revolved.

kamimitoiaki drawn; *synonyms* (*adj*) haggard, careworn, worn, gaunt, pinched, taut, cadaverous, tired.

kamimitonga glorify; *synonyms* (*v*) celebrate, exalt, extol, bless, eulogize, dignify, adore, commend, laud, praise, canonize, admire, aggrandize, magnify, (*n*) honor.

kamimitongaki glorified; *synonyms* (*adj*) canonized, blessed, canonised, haloed, holy, hyped, overestimated, overrated, overvalued.

kaminoa 1. confused; *synonyms* (*adj*) abashed, bewildered, baffled, befuddled, bemused, chaotic, confounded, disjointed, disordered, dizzy, incoherent, indistinct, ambiguous, (*n*) cloudy, (*adv, adj*) topsy-turvy; *antonyms* (*adj*) clear, enlightened, alert, clearheaded, clear-headed, orderly, **2.** disoriented; *synonyms* (*adj*) confused, lost, alienated, anomic, adrift, astray, broken, disconnected, neurotic, estranged, forgotten, garbled, helpless, illogical, irretrievable; *antonym* (*adj*) oriented, **3.** baffled; *synonyms* (*adj*) perplexed, puzzled, frustrated, beaten, **4.** spin; *synonyms* (*n*) turn, twirl, whirl, revolution, roll, ride, eddy, (*v*) revolve, twist, run, drive, reel, fabricate, gyrate, invent, **5.** turn; *synonyms* (*v*) deviate, get, spin, (*n*) bend, curve, coil, go, bout, change, round, bent, circle, shift, tour, curl, **6.** perplexed; *synonyms* (*v*) complicated, intricate, (*adj*) involved, doubtful, distracted, uneasy, questioning, quizzical, entangled, knotted, mystified.

kaminoaki turned; *synonyms* (*adj*) off, sour, curved, rancid, twisted, altered, askew, awry, bent, bowed, cancelled, crooked, dark, deflected, dour.

kaminominoa twirl; *synonyms* (*n*) spin, turn, whirl, eddy, (*v*) twist, roll, coil, curl, swirl, twiddle, wheel, pivot, bend, gyrate, reel.

kaminominotaka rotate; *synonyms* (*v*) revolve, reel, roll, alternate, gyrate, spin, swing, wheel, orbit, pivot, turn, twirl, circulate, circle, twist.

kaminominotakaki rotated; *synonym* (*adj*) revolved.

kamiroaroa 1. amaze; *synonyms* (*v*) astonish, astound, baffle, dazzle, dumbfound, puzzle, stagger, discombobulate, alarm, bewilder, confound, daze, flabbergast, mystify, (*adj*) surprise, **2.** astonish; *synonyms* (*v*) amaze, stun, confuse, nonplus, perplex, shock, startle.

kamiroaroaki 1. amazed; *synonyms* (*adj*) astonished, astounded, speechless, stunned, bewildered, dumbfounded, flabbergasted, shocked, staggered, surprised, thunderstruck, **2.** astonished; *synonyms* (*adj*) amazed, astonish, aghast, astonied.

kamitina commissioner; *synonyms* (*n*) commissary, delegate, agent, executive, official, representative, collector.

kammamma 1. breastfeed; *synonyms* (*v*) nurse, suckle, absorb, lactate, suck, draw, entertain, harbor, harbour, hold, imbibe, **2.** nurse; *synonyms* (*n*) nurture, doctor, amah, care, nanny, (*v*) nourish, attend, cherish, foster, cradle, cultivate, keep, raise, breastfeed, feed.

kammammaki nursed; *synonym* (*adj*) suckled.

kamoa 1. boast; *synonyms* (*v*) bluster, vaunt, blow, brag, crow, gasconade, pride, rodomontade, exult, bounce, exaggerate, flourish, (*n*) arrogance, boasting, glory, **2.** exalt; *synonyms* (*v*) animate, celebrate, dignify, glorify, raise, advance, elevate, promote, adore, ennoble, aggrandize, elate, extol, inspire, magnify; *antonym* (*v*) humiliate, **3.** glorify; *synonyms* (*v*) exalt, bless, eulogize, commend, laud, praise, canonize, admire, worship, applaud, acclaim, applause, proclaim, revere, (*n*) honor, **4.** dignify; *synonyms* (*v*) grace, accredit, adorn, crown, (*n*) reward; *antonym* (*v*) discredit, **5.** praise; *synonyms* (*n*) compliment, commendation, kudos, admiration, approval, encomium, eulogy, panegyric, credit, exaltation, (*v*) approve, flatter, congratulate, fame, appreciate; *antonyms* (*n*) criticism, disparagement, (*v*) criticize, belittle, disparage, rebuke, reprimand, reproach, scold, chastise, denigrate, sully.

kamoaki 1. glorified; *synonyms* (*adj*) canonized, blessed, canonised, haloed, holy, hyped, overestimated, overrated, overvalued, **2.** exalted; *synonyms* (*adj*) elevated, eminent, lofty, high, noble, elated, dignified, grand, great, sublime, celebrated, distinguished, elate, glorious, magnificent, **3.** dignified; *synonyms* (*adj*) exalted, majestic, respectable, imposing, lordly, proud, solemn, manly, courtly, grave, impressive, magisterial, sedate, splendid, stately; *antonyms* (*adj*) humiliating, undignified.

kamoamoa 1. boastful; *synonyms* (*adj*) big, braggart, pompous, arrogant, proud, vaunting, thrasonical, vain, vainglorious, ostentatious; *antonym* (*adj*) modest, **2.** admire; *synonyms* (*v*) love, revere, idolize, adore, appreciate, esteem, praise, wonder, worship, honor, like, laud, cherish, regard, commend; *antonyms* (*v*) criticize, despise, loathe, scorn, **3.** conceited; *synonyms* (*adj*) cocky, egotistic, boastful, smug, affected, assuming, egotistical, haughty, complacent, narcissistic, priggish, bigheaded, overbearing, overconfident, overweening; *antonym* (*adj*) humble, **4.** boast;

synonyms (*v*) bluster, vaunt, blow, brag, crow, gasconade, pride, rodomontade, exult, bounce, exaggerate, flourish, (*n*) arrogance, boasting, glory, **5**. pretentious; *synonyms* (*adj*) showy, stilted, presumptuous, grandiose, snobbish, ambitious, exaggerated, mannered, mincing, gaudy, lofty, flamboyant, overblown, precious, (*v*) conceited; *antonym* (*adj*) down-to-earth.

kamoamoaki admired; *synonyms* (*adj*) esteemed, respected, accepted, beloved, estimable, favorite, honored, pet, popular, revered, valuable, valued, cherished, fashionable, indulged.

kamona pamper; *synonyms* (*v*) indulge, baby, cocker, coddle, pet, spoil, cherish, cosset, mollycoddle, gratify, fondle, featherbed, mother.

kamonaki pampered; *synonyms* (*adj*) coddled, indulged, spoiled, bad, luxurious, soft, luxuriant, spoilt.

kamoriau 1. abashed; *synonyms* (*adj*) bashful, discomfited, mortified, ashamed, confused, embarrassed, sheepish; *antonym* (*adj*) brazen, **2**. embarrassed; *synonyms* (*adj*) abashed, awkward, uncomfortable, disconcerted, shamefaced, shy, chagrined, humiliated; *antonyms* (*adj*) proud, relaxed.

kamou 1. laborious; *synonyms* (*adj*) difficult, arduous, hard, backbreaking, diligent, heavy, industrious, grueling, assiduous, exhausting, formidable, painful, strenuous, tedious, toilsome; *antonym* (*adj*) easy, **2**. hard; *synonyms* (*adj*) austere, bad, grave, severe, strong, callous, cruel, knotty, tough, bitter, alcoholic, compact, (*adv*) firm, (*v*) acute, (*n*) rough; *antonyms* (*adj*) soft, kind, merciful, simple, soggy, tender, yielding, (*adv*) gently, lightly, **3**. languish; *synonyms* (*v*) decline, fail, die, ache, decay, ebb, faint, long, (*adj*) fade, flag, drop, (*n*) droop, pine, wither, yearn, **4**. exhausting; *synonyms* (*adj*) draining, tiresome, tiring, wearing, wearisome, wearying, demanding; *antonym* (*adj*) undemanding, **5**. arduous; *synonyms* (*adj*) laborious, onerous, uphill, troublesome, trying, precipitous, burdensome, challenging, exacting, fatiguing, harsh, labored, operose, sheer, stiff, **6**. difficult; *synonyms* (*adj*) awkward, complicated, delicate, fastidious, finicky, abstruse, ambitious, cantankerous, complex, contrary, crabby, disagreeable, fussy, inconvenient, intricate; *antonyms* (*adj*) straightforward, good-natured, rewarding, clear, **7**. burdensome; *synonyms* (*adj*) weighty, cumbrous, cumbersome, oppressive, unwieldy, distressing, irksome, ponderous, taxing, vexatious, **8**. oppressive; *synonyms* (*adj*) despotic, muggy, stuffy, sultry, tyrannical, dictatorial, gloomy, domineering, stifling, extortionate, grievous, humid, airless, dismal, (*v*) close; *antonyms* (*adj*) fresh, liberal, democratic, **9**. toilsome; *synonyms* (*adj*) gruelling, labourious,

punishing, **10**. onerous; *synonym* (*adj*) exigent, **11**. tiring; *synonym* (*adj*) boring, **12**. wither; *synonyms* (*v*) shrink, wilt, contract, languish, shrivel, dry, wane, waste, atrophy, blight, dwindle, sear, parch, collapse, (*adj*) scorch; *antonym* (*v*) bloom.

kamoua 1. bend; *synonyms* (*n*) bow, arch, arc, elbow, twist, angle, curvature, (*v*) curve, turn, crouch, stoop, crook, curl, flex, deflect; *antonyms* (*v*) straighten, square, **2**. droop; *synonyms* (*v*) bend, decline, dangle, wilt, flag, hang, sink, loll, slump, collapse, decrease, fade, (*n*) sag, pine, (*adj*) despond, **3**. sag; *synonyms* (*n*) dip, depression, drop, (*v*) droop, bag, tumble, lean, distort, flop, (*adj*) swag, sway; *antonym* (*v*) rise, **4**. slag; *synonyms* (*n*) cinder, clinker, dross, scoria, scum, residue, trash, bastard, impurities, impurity, rock, scoriae, (*adj*) recrement.

kamouaki 1. bent; *synonyms* (*adj*) arched, curved, bended, crooked, deformed, intent, (*n*) aptitude, inclination, propensity, fancy, ability, bias, flair, gift, leaning; *antonym* (*adj*) straight, **2**. withered; *synonyms* (*adj*) sere, wizened, sear, shriveled, shrunken, thin, dry, lean, parched, shrivelled, shrunk, wizen, (*v*) broken, lame.

kamrara spill; *synonyms* (*v*) fall, shed, drop, empty, flow, pour, slop, stream, upset, cast, overrun, flood, disgorge, (*n*) overflow, discharge.

kamronrona round; *synonyms* (*adv*) about, around, (*adj*) circular, plump, entire, chubby, complete, (*n*) circle, bout, ring, beat, circuit, (*v*) compass, turn, gird; *antonyms* (*adj*) slim, sharp.

kamronronaki rounded; *synonyms* (*adj*) round, curved, circular, orbicular, full, globular, rotund, spherical, bent, blunt, fat, obtuse; *antonyms* (*adj*) pointed, straight, sharp, bony, concave.

kamta carpenter; *synonyms* (*n*) joiner, builder, craftsman, laborer, mason, workman, (*v*) build.

kamumun 1. pleat; *synonyms* (*n*) plait, crease, wrinkle, ply, (*v*) fold, crimp, crinkle, braid, plat, pucker, ruffle, **2**. skirt; *synonyms* (*n*) border, edge, brim, flap, kilt, apron, margin, (*v*) fringe, circumvent, evade, hem, elude, sidestep, verge, dodge.

kamwa 1. grill; *synonyms* (*n*) grid, grille, grillroom, (*v*) fry, bake, broil, cook, examine, quiz, roast, burn, inflame, toast, ask, interrogate, **2**. broil; *synonyms* (*n*) brawl, quarrel, affray, feud, fight, fray, scuffle, clash, altercation, broiling, dispute, fracas, grilling, (*v*) scorch, grill, **3**. roast; *synonyms* (*adj*) roasted, (*n*) ridicule, joint, knock, parody, (*v*) joke, heat, tease, banter, chaff, slam, boil, twit, criticize, rally.

kamwaea move; *synonyms* (*v*) act, affect, carry, excite, go, impel, instigate, maneuver, touch, travel, flow, bear, (*n*) motion, drive, transfer; *antonym* (*v*) stay.

kamwaeieia jar; *synonyms* (*n*) jangle, blow, crock, container, jog, shake, amphora, bottle, crash, (*v*) jolt, clash, creak, bump, collide, jounce.

kamwaki 1. grilled; *synonyms* (*adj*) barbecued, broiled, baked, **2**. broiled; *synonyms* (*adj*) grilled, done, heated, **3**. roasted; *synonym* (*adj*) roast.

kamwanea 1. betray; *synonyms* (*v*) bewray, deceive, disclose, dupe, grass, mislead, reveal, sell, accuse, misinform, blab, cheat, cuckold, denounce, display, **2**. wile; *synonyms* (*n*) trick, ruse, artifice, deception, guile, dodge, deceit, fraud, stratagem, chicane, chicanery, feint, juggle, ploy, trickery.

kamwaneaua 1. confide; *synonyms* (*v*) commend, commit, trust, entrust, consign, intrust, rely, charge, depend, hope, lean, leave, whisper, admit, **2**. compose; *synonyms* (*v*) build, allay, compile, constitute, tranquilize, write, weave, adjust, arrange, compound, form, frame, (*adj*) assuage, appease, (*n*) calm, **3**. stabilize; *synonyms* (*v*) stabilise, poise, fix, consolidate, establish, support, balance, arouse, brace, control, crown, energise, energize, even, regularize, **4**. poise; *synonyms* (*n*) assurance, composure, equanimity, equilibrium, parity, bearing, aplomb, calmness, cool, confidence, dignity, tranquillity, (*v*) hover, stand, float.

kamwaneauaki 1. composed; *synonyms* (*adj*) collected, calm, cool, dispassionate, peaceable, easy, equable, impassive, imperturbable, peaceful, placid, sedate, serene, staid, temperate; *antonyms* (*adj*) agitated, distressed, trembling, nervous, **2**. stabilized; *synonyms* (*adj*) stabilised, balanced, **3**. poised; *synonyms* (*adj*) composed, steady, assured, equanimous, stable, urbane; *antonym* (*adj*) insecure.

kamwanua slacken; *synonyms* (*v*) relax, loosen, abate, slack, ease, remit, retard, loose, douse, decrease, diminish, lessen, moderate, slow, dowse; *antonym* (*v*) tighten.

kamwara 1. licentious; *synonyms* (*adj*) dissolute, immoral, lewd, filthy, abandoned, debauched, lascivious, depraved, lecherous, fast, loose, unchaste, wanton, wild, carnal, **2**. indecent; *synonyms* (*adj*) improper, indelicate, unseemly, dirty, gross, immodest, inappropriate, indecorous, shameful, unbecoming, bawdy, coarse, crude, impure, scurrilous; *antonyms* (*adj*) decent, proper, **3**. shameful; *synonyms* (*adj*) disgraceful, dishonorable, scandalous, contemptible, degrading, despicable, disreputable, ignominious, inglorious, opprobrious, shocking, nasty, (*v*) base, foul, black; *antonyms* (*adj*) honorable, dignified, noble, admirable, **4**. obscene; *synonyms* (*adj*) indecent, licentious, ribald, fulsome, abhorrent, detestable, smutty, naughty, libidinous, low, blue, repugnant, repulsive, revolting, salacious.

kamwaraea 1. litter; *synonyms* (*n*) brood, bedding, stretcher, garbage, junk, mess, refuse, rubbish, trash, waste, issue, (*v*) clutter, (*adj*) jumble, disarray, huddle, **2**. pollute; *synonyms* (*v*) defile, corrupt, debase, foul, infect, taint, dirty, maculate, poison, befoul, debauch, desecrate, soil, besmear, (*n*) contaminate; *antonyms* (*v*) clean, purify, **3**. violate; *synonyms* (*v*) break, contravene, transgress, dishonor, disobey, infringe, ravish, assault, breach, offend, outrage, profane, rape, abuse, force; *antonym* (*v*) obey.

kamwaraeaki 1. littered; *synonyms* (*adj*) cluttered, untidy, beleaguered, beset, besieged, messy, plagued, topsy-turvy, tormented, **2**. violated; *synonyms* (*v*) apart, blighted, contrite, cracked, disconnected, disunited, fractured, (*adj*) broken, profaned, seduced, debauched, defiled, desecrated, despoiled, dishonored; *antonym* (*adj*) pure, **3**. polluted; *synonyms* (*adj*) impure, dirty, contaminated, foul, filthy, unclean, profane, soiled, stained, tainted, infected, nasty, (*v*) mixed.

kamweau 1. hinder; *synonyms* (*adj*) posterior, hind, (*v*) block, bar, impede, check, hamper, obstruct, resist, curb, arrest, clog, counteract, delay, detain; *antonyms* (*v*) help, assist, facilitate, **2**. hamper; *synonyms* (*n*) basket, bond, disadvantage, (*v*) cramp, fetter, hinder, interfere, confine, embarrass, encumber, handicap, hobble, restrain, restrict, tie, **3**. retard; *synonyms* (*v*) lag, slow, decelerate, procrastinate, prevent, slacken, choke, (*n*) defer, moron, changeling, cretin, idiot, (*adj*) deaden, debar, waive; *antonym* (*v*) accelerate.

kamweauaki retarded; *synonyms* (*adj*) backward, slow, tardy, imbecile, defective, deferred, dull, half-baked, leisurely, obtuse, simple, birdbrained, dim, dim-witted, dopey.

kamweengaraoi comfortable; *synonyms* (*adj*) cozy, easy, agreeable, pleased, pleasing, prosperous, congenial, pleasurable, rich, enjoyable, commodious, content, contented, (*v*) snug, calm; *antonyms* (*adj*) uncomfortable, poor, formal, tense, unpleasant, intimidating, unaccustomed, unhappy.

kamwemwea 1. elevate; *synonyms* (*v*) raise, advance, lift, boost, erect, exalt, hoist, cheer, dignify, promote, rear, aggrandize, uphold, animate, ennoble; *antonyms* (*v*) demote, lower, **2**. lift; *synonyms* (*n*) elevator, heave, support, climb, (*v*) rise, elevate, filch, hike, airlift, pilfer, pinch, steal, swipe, enhance, heighten, **3**. heave; *synonyms* (*v*) cast, fling, chuck, gasp, haul, toss, billow, drag, draw, gag, jerk, pitch, (*n*) tug, elevation, heaving, **4**. jack; *synonyms* (*n*) knave, flag, jackass, mariner, ace, burgee, jackfruit, **5**. hoist; *synonyms* (*n*) winch, (*v*) wind, **6**. shift; *synonyms* (*n*) interchange, turn, move, switch, conversion, (*v*) change, exchange, remove, quibble, alter, budge, convert, displace, transfer, fluctuate, **7**. uplift; *synonyms* (*n*) upheaval, upthrust, (*v*) elate, exhilarate, intoxicate, regenerate, **8**. raise;

synonyms (*v*) increase, build, foster, grow, prefer, augment, cultivate, excite, levy, nurture, amplify, found, enlarge, breed, (*n*) mount.

kamwemweaki 1. elevated; *synonyms* (*adj*) high, exalted, lofty, noble, towering, grand, great, majestic, tall, elated, magnanimous, advanced, dignified, eminent, (*v*) steep; *antonym* (*adj*) short, **2**. lifted; *synonyms* (*adj*) elevated, upraised, **3**. uplifted; *synonyms* (*adj*) raised, alert, animated, bold, confident, elate, erect, haughty, proud, solemn, stately, sublime, undismayed, watchful, **4**. raised; *synonyms* (*v*) repousse, salient, (*adj*) embossed, convex, brocaded, elative, exultant, mountant, prominent, upright, (*prep*) above.

kamwi scar; *synonyms* (*n*) mark, cicatrix, blemish, seam, cicatrice, defect, scratch, stain, injury, line, disfigurement, (*v*) disfigure, brand, damage, mar.

kamwia 1. disparage; *synonyms* (*v*) denigrate, belittle, deprecate, depreciate, derogate, decry, defame, censure, condemn, criticize, detract, abuse, slur, (*n*) disgrace, discredit; *antonyms* (*v*) praise, compliment, flatter, **2**. slight; *synonyms* (*adj*) flimsy, slender, thin, fragile, delicate, faint, (*n*) scorn, disdain, (*v*) disregard, insult, neglect, ignore, affront, cut, (*adv*) light; *antonyms* (*adj*) considerable, major, fat, heavy, intense, obvious, severe, thickset, wide.

kan 1. abutting; *synonyms* (*adj*) adjoining, contiguous, adjacent, bordering, conterminous, near, next, **2**. nigh; *synonyms* (*adv*) almost, most, closely, around, approximately, approach, (*adj*) close, nearly, nearby, about, approximate, imminent, intimate, dear, (*prep*) by, **3**. about; *synonyms* (*prep*) encircling, for, encompassing, circa, concerning, of, regarding, respecting, round, throughout, (*adv*) roughly, in, nigh, (*adj*) some, practically; *antonyms* (*prep*) exactly, precisely, **4**. good; *synonyms* (*adj*) able, benefit, delicious, right, efficient, capable, excellent, fine, nice, superior, well, advantageous, (*n*) benign, advantage, gain; *antonyms* (*adj*) disobedient, poor, wicked, unpleasant, (*n*) evil, bad, **5**. nearby; *synonyms* (*adj*) nearest, immediate, neighboring, (*adv*) beside, (*prep*) alongside; *antonyms* (*adj*) distant, remote, (*adv*) faraway, **6**. attractive; *synonyms* (*adj*) alluring, amiable, appealing, charming, engaging, good-looking, tempting, adorable, delightful, enchanting, fascinating, glamorous, gorgeous, handsome, interesting; *antonyms* (*adj*) unattractive, ugly, unappealing, disgusting, repellent, revolting, repulsive, straight, **7**. fancy; *synonyms* (*v*) daydream, imagine, wish, consider, crotchet, envision, (*adj*) conceive, elaborate, extravagant, (*n*) desire, caprice, fantasy, dream, conceit, conception; *antonyms* (*adj*) plain, unadorned, (*n*) reality, **8**. elegant; *synonyms* (*adj*) graceful, courtly, delicate, splendid, beautiful, dainty, polite, refined, dressy,

artistic, chic, classy, cultured, debonair, neat; *antonyms* (*adj*) clumsy, inelegant, scruffy, coarse, tacky, **9**. likable; *synonyms* (*adj*) agreeable, likeable, pleasant, pleasing, lovable, sympathetic; *antonym* (*adj*) disagreeable, **10**. crave; *synonyms* (*v*) beg, ask, beseech, covet, implore, want, entreat, long, fancy, claim, adjure, demand, hunger, lust, need, **11**. close; *synonyms* (*adj*) accurate, tight, narrow, brief, airless, complete, (*v*) compact, stop, conclude, bar, block, (*n*) end, finish, conclusion, expiration; *antonyms* (*adj*) airy, fresh, loose, far, (*v*) open, start, **12**. near; *synonyms* (*adv*) towards, aside, (*adj*) impending, coming, closer, handy, stingy, mean, miserly, cheeseparing, ready, approaching, crowded, (*v*) familiar, come, **13**. aside; *synonyms* (*adv*) apart, away, off, abreast, (*n*) digression, divagation, parenthesis, statement, **14**. nearly; *synonyms* (*adv*) virtually, intimately, much, just, halfway, (*adj*) thereabouts, **15**. desire; *synonyms* (*n*) ambition, hope, aspiration, will, craving, impulse, liking, request, (*v*) aspire, seek, aim, choose, crave, like, care; *antonyms* (*n*) aversion, (*v*) dislike, hate, **16**. admirable; *synonyms* (*adj*) outstanding, commendable, creditable, good, grand, great, lovely, praiseworthy, worthy, valuable, exquisite, laudable, meritorious, noble, respectable; *antonyms* (*adj*) disgraceful, appalling, unworthy, **17**. adjacent; *synonyms* (*adj*) abutting, touching, **18**. fine; *synonyms* (*adj*) brave, capital, elegant, thin, acute, admirable, alright, choice, glorious, stunning, terrific, (*n*) penalty, amercement, (*v*) punish, mulct; *antonyms* (*adj*) thick, substantial, unsatisfactory, wide, **19**. nice; *synonyms* (*adj*) fastidious, kind, likable, correct, decent, difficult, enjoyable, exact, particular, precise, minute, suitable, discriminating, curious, comely; *antonym* (*adj*) horrible, **20**. covet; *synonyms* (*v*) begrudge, envy, grudge, hanker.

kân people; *synonyms* (*n*) nation, community, family, folk, multitude, populace, clan, mob, flock, citizenry, crowd, (*v*) inhabit, occupy, reside, dwell.

kana 1. deteriorate; *synonyms* (*v*) degenerate, degrade, decline, spoil, worsen, vitiate, descend, drop, fail, impair, lapse, rot, crumble, decrease, (*adj*) debase; *antonyms* (*v*) improve, convalesce, recover, **2**. feed; *synonyms* (*v*) eat, dine, nurture, browse, board, diet, encourage, nourish, fatten, consume, feast, (*n*) aliment, food, provender, fare; *antonym* (*v*) starve, **3**. devour; *synonyms* (*v*) bolt, gulp, demolish, gobble, gorge, guzzle, swallow, absorb, devastate, enjoy, relish, down, exhaust, feed, glut, **4**. fed; *synonyms* (*adj*) fattened, meated, (*n*) federal, detective, **5**. consume; *synonyms* (*v*) spend, dissipate, use, waste, burn, expend, fritter, squander, annihilate, corrode, destroy, devour, drain, drink, engross; *antonyms* (v) save, abstain, **6.** gnaw; *synonyms* (v) bite, chew, fret, crunch, erode, nibble, masticate, munch, champ, fray, harass, rankle, rasp, (n) chafe, sting, **7.** food; *synonyms* (n) edible, dish, nourishment, sustenance, eating, fodder, meat, nutriment, nutrition, pabulum, victual, bread, menu, feeding, foodstuffs, **8.** town; *synonyms* (n) city, borough, township, village, community, burgh, townspeople, civilization, metropolis, (adj) municipal, urban, local.

kanabuaka picnic; *synonyms* (n) excursion, junket, cinch, outing, pushover, snap, jaunt, coportion, expedition, feast, jollification, meal, (v) collation.

kanaeng 1. brood; *synonyms* (n) breed, issue, offspring, family, litter, posterity, progeny, young, flock, farrow, (v) hatch, sulk, think, incubate, (adj) herd, **2.** grieve; *synonyms* (v) distress, mourn, aggrieve, bemoan, deplore, lament, sorrow, trouble, annoy, fret, bewail, hurt, injure, pain, (n) afflict; *antonym* (v) please, **3.** muse; *synonyms* (n) study, (v) contemplate, meditate, cogitate, consider, deliberate, ponder, reflect, brood, ruminate, speculate, dream, mull, daydream, puzzle, **4.** fret; *synonyms* (n) anxiety, (v) agitate, chafe, gall, grate, irritate, worry, fray, rub, upset, anger, disquiet, concern, corrode, erode, **5.** offended; *synonyms* (adj) angry, affronted, aggrieved, annoyed, pained, wronged, shocked, appalled, ashamed, averted, bitter, cool, disappointed, disgusted, dismayed; *antonym* (adj) composed, **6.** sulk; *synonyms* (v) mope, pout, glower, grizzle, stew, (n) mood, temper, sulkiness.

kanaengai 1. irk; *synonyms* (v) tire, grate, annoy, bug, disturb, gall, weary, aggravate, anger, bore, bother, displease, exasperate, harass, irritate, **2.** displease; *synonyms* (v) disgust, affront, offend, rile, vex, fret, pique, trouble, discompose; *antonyms* (v) please, satisfy, **3.** vex; *synonyms* (v) plague, provoke, tease, torment, agitate, chafe, harry, worry, irk, excite, molest, perplex, afflict, nettle, peeve, **4.** offend; *synonyms* (v) insult, contravene, injure, infringe, abuse, break, wound, err, breach, hurt, infract, outrage, revolt, shock, violate.

kanaengaiaki 1. displeased; *synonyms* (v) pained, afflicted, (adj) discontented, disgruntled, angry, dissatisfied, annoyed, irritated, peeved, unhappy; *antonym* (adj) pleased, **2.** offended; *synonyms* (adj) hurt, affronted, aggrieved, wronged, shocked, appalled, ashamed, averted, bitter, cool, disappointed, disgusted, dismayed, distraught, distressed; *antonym* (adj) composed, **3.** vexed; *synonyms* (adj) troubled, harassed, harried, pestered, sore, uneasy.

kanai if; *synonyms* (conj) provided, although, providing, whether, though, and, so, an, gin, (n) but, conditionally, condition, stipulation, proviso, (adv) peradventure.

kanaiai stoke; *synonyms* (v) hit, paddle, tap, touch, stab, stick, thrust.

kanaki 1. devoured, **2.** desired; *synonyms* (adj) coveted, craved, desirable, chosen, favorite, wanted, needed, welcome, beloved, adored, appropriate, pet, preferred, (v) complying, consenting; *antonym* (adj) undesirable, **3.** coveted; *synonyms* (adj) desired, exceptional, impressive, marketable, **4.** fancied; *synonyms* (adj) imaginary, unreal, chimerical, fanciful, fictional, fictitious, fabricated, assumed, assembled, conjectural, doubtful, false, invented, nonexistent, illusive, **5.** craved, **6.** consumed; *synonyms* (adj) exhausted, spent, finished, worn, absorbed, burnt, combust, dissipated, engrossed, gone, immersed, lost, obsessed, possessed, tired, **7.** wanted; *synonyms* (adj) required, cherished, invited, precious, treasured, necessary, comfortable, cute, essential, fugitive, notorious, urgent, hunted, (n) runaway.

kanako attack; *synonyms* (n) incursion, thrust, aggression, fit, onset, onslaught, seizure, (v) assault, assail, attempt, aggress, charge, invade, raid, accuse; *antonyms* (n) defense, (v) defend, protect, retreat.

kanakoa 1. dispatch; *synonyms* (n) despatch, speed, consignment, celerity, expedition, haste, hurry, letter, (v) accelerate, send, deliver, convey, discharge, forward, murder; *antonyms* (n) receiving, receipt, **2.** chase; *synonyms* (n) game, search, quest, (v) hunt, pursue, expel, follow, stalk, track, trail, chamfer, pursuit, race, seek, evict, **3.** sent; *synonyms* (adj) blissful, ecstatic, fascinated, imported, intoxicated, **4.** send; *synonyms* (v) pass, dispatch, give, mail, post, carry, divert, project, beam, cast, channel, commit, consign, direct, place, **5.** push; *synonyms* (n) press, thrust, jolt, poke, (v) drive, impel, crowd, force, jab, jostle, nudge, prod, jam, rush, boost; *antonyms* (v) pull, drag, haul, **6.** release; *synonyms* (n) issue, liberation, departure, ransom, exemption, (v) exempt, free, liberate, pardon, absolve, acquit, dismiss, excuse, exonerate, (adj) disengage; *antonyms* (n) imprisonment, abduction, custody, involvement, preservation, (v) capture, confine, imprison, arrest, catch.

kanakoaki 1. dispatched; *synonyms* (adj) finished, fulfilled, **2.** chased; *synonyms* (adj) engraved, (n) pursued, **3.** released; *synonyms* (adj) free, loose, discharged, liberated, exempt, open; *antonym* (adj) restricted, **4.** sent; *synonyms* (adj) blissful, ecstatic, fascinated, imported, intoxicated.

kananama flavor; *synonyms* (n) savor, relish, taste, aroma, smack, smell, tang, salt, odor, sapidity, (v) flavour, season, spice, sauce, twang.

kananamaki flavored; *synonyms* (adj) flavoured, seasoned.

kanananga 1. graze; *synonyms* (v) browse, scratch, rub, scrape, chafe, eat, brush, crease, crop, feed, pasture, rake, shave, (n) touch, cut, **2**. scratch; *synonyms* (n) score, mark, nick, scrabble, dent, abrasion, groove, scar, furrow, (v) graze, notch, grate, scrawl, tear, engrave.

kananangaki 1. grazed; *synonyms* (adj) hurt, raw, **2**. scratched; *synonyms* (adj) scraped, abraded, dented, injured, sgraffito, spoiled, broken, skinned, smashed.

kananginang cloud; *synonyms* (n) mist, blur, haze, steam, (v) fog, becloud, obscure, befog, blacken, eclipse, overshadow, shadow, taint, hide, (adj) swarm; *antonym* (v) sharpen.

kananginangaki clouded; *synonyms* (adj) cloudy, gloomy, blurred, dark, foggy, obscure, overcast, misty, hazy.

kananoanga miserable; *synonyms* (adj) mean, poor, meager, abject, bad, deplorable, desolate, downcast, low, measly, unhappy, distressed, lamentable, (v) forlorn, wretched; *antonyms* (adj) happy, cheerful, generous.

kananobaba 1. flatter; *synonyms* (v) coax, fawn, court, adulate, cajole, wheedle, blandish, grovel, kowtow, soap, compliment, entice, indulge, persuade, (n) caress, **2**. stupefy; *synonyms* (v) astonish, astound, bewilder, daze, amaze, paralyze, deaden, numb, bemuse, baffle, besot, confuse, drug, (adj) stun, (n) benumb.

kananobabaki stupefied; *synonyms* (adj) dazed, stunned, amazed, astonished, bewildered, astounded, dumbfounded, stupid, confused, dumfounded, flabbergasted, groggy.

kananobaraka 1. deject; *synonyms* (v) depress, discourage, dishearten, chill, dampen, demoralize, dismay, dispirit, sink, daunt, sadden, appall, (adj) damp, lower, **2**. calumniate; *synonyms* (v) defame, slander, asperse, libel, backbite, besmirch, blacken, denigrate, malign, smear, traduce, vilify, charge, decry, (n) belie, **3**. disparage; *synonyms* (v) belittle, deprecate, depreciate, derogate, censure, condemn, criticize, detract, abuse, slur, degrade, dispraise, knock, (n) disgrace, discredit; *antonyms* (v) praise, compliment, flatter, **4**. discourage; *synonyms* (v) deter, deject, intimidate, cow, discountenance, frustrate, check, dissuade, inhibit, reject, scare, unnerve, admonish, (n) abash, terrorize; *antonyms* (v) encourage, promote, **5**. depress; *synonyms* (v) push, abase, reduce, deflate, burden, debase, decline, diminish, drop, flatten, humble, humiliate, lessen, mortify, oppress; *antonym* (v) cheer, **6**. prostrate; *synonyms* (adj) flat, prone, exhaust, fatigue, procumbent, tire, dull, (v) fell, level, overwhelm, overcome, floor, lie, overthrow, exhausted.

kananobarakaki 1. discouraged; *synonyms* (adj) disappointed, despondent, crestfallen, dejected, demoralized, disheartened, dispirited, downcast, downhearted, frustrated, pessimistic, depressed, baffled, balked; *antonym* (adj) optimistic, **2**. dejected; *synonyms* (adj) gloomy, low, sad, blue, desolate, despairing, down, melancholy, miserable, sorrowful, spiritless, unhappy, cheerless, damp, prostrate; *antonyms* (adj) cheerful, elated, happy, **3**. depressed; *synonyms* (adj) concave, hollow, discouraged, flat, forlorn, morose, dark, crushed, melancholic, disconsolate, dismal, doleful, dull, gaunt, glum; *antonym* (adj) convex.

kananobitaka 1. change; *synonyms* (n) shift, alteration, barter, modification, variation, move, (v) exchange, alter, adapt, alternate, cash, convert, switch, transpose, turn; *antonyms* (v) stay, leave, idle, maintain, **2**. disunite; *synonyms* (v) detach, disjoin, disconnect, dissociate, separate, disengage, disjoint, dissolve, divide, sever, split, disassociate, dissever, divorce, part.

kananobitakaki 1. changed; *synonyms* (adj) altered, transformed, varied, affected, changeling, different, disguised, distorted, inverse, malformed, misshapen, new, reformed, rehabilitated, tainted; *antonym* (adj) unchanged, **2**. disunited; *synonyms* (adj) divided, split, disjointed, abrupt, confused, crumbled, cut, disordered, distinct, (v) disconnected, apart, blighted, broken, contrite, cracked.

kananobu discourage; *synonyms* (v) deter, daunt, demoralize, depress, dishearten, deject, dismay, intimidate, dampen, cow, discountenance, dispirit, frustrate, check, (n) abash; *antonyms* (v) encourage, promote.

kananobuaka provoke; *synonyms* (v) excite, incite, defy, offend, anger, arouse, enrage, inflame, invite, irritate, kindle, get, aggravate, annoy, awaken; *antonyms* (v) calm, mollify, please, soothe.

kananobuakaki provoked; *synonyms* (adj) angry, exasperated, irritated, aggravated, indignant, infuriated, irate, inflamed; *antonym* (adj) unprovoked.

kananobuaki discouraged; *synonyms* (adj) disappointed, despondent, crestfallen, dejected, demoralized, disheartened, dispirited, downcast, downhearted, frustrated, pessimistic, depressed, baffled, balked; *antonym* (adj) optimistic.

kananobukibuki 1. excite; *synonyms* (v) animate, arouse, disturb, enliven, agitate, energize, awaken, electrify, encourage, evoke, exasperate, incite, inspire, kindle, provoke; *antonyms* (v) calm, pacify, bore, **2**. concern; *synonyms* (n) business, affair, regard, attention, anxiety, bother, matter, company, apprehension, burden, (v) worry, affect, care, interest, trouble; *antonym* (v) unconcern, **3**. move; *synonyms* (v) act, carry, excite, go, impel, instigate, maneuver, touch, travel, flow, bear, actuate, (n) motion, drive, transfer; *antonym* (v) stay, **4**.

enthuse; *synonyms* (v) drool, fire, thrill, fascinate, gush, impress, motivate, rave, send, stimulate, stir, enthrall, mesmerize, move, rivet, **5**. disturb; *synonyms* (v) disconcert, disorder, disquiet, distract, distress, perturb, annoy, commove, concern, derange, disarrange, discompose, disrupt, upset, alarm; *antonyms* (v) arrange, please, smooth, soothe, **6**. frighten; *synonyms* (v) cow, dismay, daunt, terrify, appall, affright, intimidate, scare, terrorize, awe, deter, horrify, startle, threaten, (n) fright; *antonym* (v) comfort.

kananobukibukiaki 1. frightened; *synonyms* (adj) afraid, fearful, scared, terrified, timid, anxious, apprehensive, horrified, intimidated, restless, worried, (adv) cowardly; *antonyms* (adj) calm, confident, unimpressed, brave, fearless, **2**. disturbed; *synonyms* (adj) agitated, concerned, confused, disquieted, upset, disordered, bothered, deranged, disconcerted, distracted, distressed, nervous, tumultuous, turbulent, unsettled; *antonyms* (adj) rational, relaxed, **3**. excited; *synonyms* (adj) ablaze, emotional, enthusiastic, frantic, ardent, aroused, delirious, fervent, heated, impassioned, passionate, warm, elated, tense, (v) animated; *antonyms* (adj) cool, unexcited.

kananokawaki 1. dishearten; *synonyms* (v) daunt, depress, deject, sadden, deter, intimidate, disappoint, dismay, dispirit, frustrate, unnerve, chill, cow, demoralize, (adj) discourage; *antonyms* (v) encourage, cheer, **2**. grievous; *synonyms* (adj) grave, bitter, deplorable, dolorous, dreadful, sad, tough, pitiful, atrocious, heavy, painful, plaintive, regrettable, serious, sorrowful, **3**. sadden; *synonyms* (v) aggrieve, distress, pain, grieve, afflict, hurt, oppress, trouble, dull.

kananokawakiaki disheartened; *synonyms* (v) discouraged, (adj) dejected, depressed, despondent, demoralized, dispirited, disappointed, downcast, sad, down, low; *antonym* (adj) optimistic.

kananokoraki 1. confuse; *synonyms* (v) bewilder, baffle, confound, muddle, agitate, blur, derange, disconcert, disturb, fluster, jumble, mystify, obscure, perplex, puzzle; *antonyms* (v) clarify, enlighten, elucidate, explain, **2**. confound; *synonyms* (v) confuse, astonish, nonplus, amaze, astound, bamboozle, mistake, complicate, dash, bedevil, befuddle, bemuse, (n) surprise, (adj) stupefy, checkmate, **3**. bewilder; *synonyms* (v) perturb, stump, stun, daze, dumbfound, entangle, flummox, stagger, throw, maze, bother, discombobulate, discompose, dismay, distract, **4**. mystify; *synonyms* (v) get, hoodwink, gravel, hoax, blindfold, (adj) equivocate, **5**. perplex; *synonyms* (v) discomfit, embarrass, involve, trouble, distress, embroil, beset, beat, tease, afflict, abash, (n) harass, annoy, torment, (adj) pose.

kananokorakiaki 1. mystified; *synonyms* (adj) bewildered, metagrabolized, metagrobolized, perplexed, puzzled, baffled, bemused, confused, flummoxed, metagrabolised, metagrobolised, stumped, thrown, unclear, absentminded; *antonym* (adj) enlightened, **2**. confounded; *synonyms* (adj) accursed, abashed, befuddled, cursed, execrable, aghast, abominable, **3**. confused; *synonyms* (adj) chaotic, confounded, disjointed, disordered, dizzy, incoherent, indistinct, ambiguous, broken, disconnected, disorderly, disorganized, indefinite, (n) cloudy, (adv, adj) topsy-turvy; *antonyms* (adj) clear, alert, clearheaded, clear-headed, orderly, **4**. bewildered; *synonyms* (adj) lost, dumbfounded, addled, amazed, blank, dazed, disconcerted, disoriented, muddled, mystified, stunned; *antonym* (adj) unimpressed, **5**. perplexed; *synonyms* (v) complicated, intricate, (adj) involved, doubtful, distracted, uneasy, questioning, quizzical, entangled, knotted.

kananomaraea dissuade; *synonyms* (v) discourage, deter, advise, remonstrate, divert, expostulate, dehort; *antonym* (v) persuade.

kananomaruru 1. disturb; *synonyms* (v) agitate, disconcert, disorder, disquiet, distract, distress, perturb, trouble, annoy, bother, commove, concern, derange, disarrange, discompose; *antonyms* (v) arrange, calm, please, smooth, soothe, **2**. agitate; *synonyms* (v) disturb, stir, toss, fan, foment, rouse, shake, actuate, arouse, canvass, convulse, excite, incite, jiggle, kindle, **3**. trouble; *synonyms* (n) pain, anxiety, difficulty, fuss, torment, care, harass, hardship, load, misfortune, (v) inconvenience, worry, afflict, burden, (adj) affliction.

kananomaruruaki 1. disturbed; *synonyms* (adj) agitated, concerned, anxious, confused, disquieted, restless, upset, worried, disordered, bothered, deranged, disconcerted, distracted, distressed, nervous; *antonyms* (adj) rational, calm, relaxed, **2**. agitated; *synonyms* (adj) excited, restive, tumultuous, tense, alarmed, distraught, jumpy, overwrought, perturbed, shaken, troubled, uneasy, unsettled, hysterical, turbulent; *antonyms* (adj) composed, lethargic, **3**. troubled; *synonyms* (adj) disturbed, solicitous, apprehensive, uncomfortable, vexed, disruptive, doubtful, riotous, unhappy; *antonyms* (adj) untroubled, unconcerned.

kananonibaia 1. attach; *synonyms* (v) add, adhere, append, affix, bind, link, associate, assign, annex, apply, fasten, fix, nail, stick, yoke; *antonyms* (v) detach, undo, disconnect, separate, unfasten, **2**. possess; *synonyms* (v) have, hold, occupy, wield, bear, enjoy, keep, maintain, obsess, retain, consume, feature, (n) hazard, (adj) own.

kananonibaiaki attached; *synonyms* (adj) connected, affectionate, affiliated, committed, associated, devoted, fond, loving, loyal, near; *antonyms* (adj) detached, separate, unmarried.

kananora 1. irritate; *synonyms* (v) chafe, fret, gall, incense, harass, aggravate, anger, annoy, bother, displease, enrage, goad, grate, infuriate, provoke; *antonyms* (v) soothe, pacify, please, **2**. aggravate; *synonyms* (v) exacerbate, exasperate, increase, irritate, worsen, inflame, magnify, peeve, rile, rankle, agitate, badger, compound, (adj) embitter, acerbate; *antonyms* (v) appease, ease, improve, **3**. agitate; *synonyms* (v) disturb, stir, toss, fan, foment, perturb, rouse, shake, trouble, actuate, arouse, canvass, convulse, discompose, disquiet; *antonym* (v) calm, **4**. disturb; *synonyms* (v) disconcert, disorder, distract, distress, commove, concern, derange, disarrange, disrupt, upset, alarm, displace, embroil, fluster, interrupt; *antonyms* (v) arrange, smooth, **5**. perturb; *synonyms* (v) confuse, unsettle, worry, disarray, incommode, disorganize, muddle, affect, discommode, ruffle, shock, unhinge, cark, depress, unnerve, **6**. upset; *synonyms* (v) overturn, overthrow, reverse, subvert, defeat, discomfit, dislocate, offend, (adj) unsettled, hurt, agitated, confused, disordered, disturbed, (n) disturbance; *antonyms* (v) encourage, (adj) pleased, confident.

kananoraki 1. irritated; *synonyms* (adj) angry, annoyed, exasperated, aggravated, enraged, furious, incensed, irate, displeased, inflamed, nettled, provoked, sore, disgruntled, infuriated; *antonyms* (adj) calm, unprovoked, pleased, **2**. disturbed; *synonyms* (adj) agitated, concerned, anxious, confused, disquieted, restless, upset, worried, disordered, bothered, deranged, disconcerted, distracted, distressed, nervous; *antonyms* (adj) rational, relaxed, **3**. aggravated; *synonyms* (adj) irritated, afflictive, grievous, discouraged, disturbed, flagitious, forced, frustrated, goaded, harmful, heinous, maddened, motivated, offensive, painful, **4**. agitated; *synonyms* (adj) excited, restive, tumultuous, tense, alarmed, distraught, jumpy, overwrought, perturbed, shaken, troubled, uneasy, unsettled, hysterical, turbulent; *antonyms* (adj) composed, lethargic, **5**. perturbed; *synonym* (adj) flustered, **6**. upset; *synonyms* (v) overturn, agitate, disquiet, overthrow, bother, confuse, disturb, perturb, reverse, subvert, (adj) hurt, (n) disorder, trouble, distress, disturbance; *antonyms* (v) please, encourage, soothe, (adj) confident.

kananoraoa quiet; *synonyms* (adj) still, lull, pacify, cool, gentle, motionless, peaceful, (v) appease, moderate, assuage, allay, (n) calm, hush, compose, ease; *antonyms* (adj) loud, noisy, talkative, vociferous, active, (n) noise.

kanebu 1. beat; *synonyms* (v) batter, flap, pulsate, throb, tick, trounce, whip, bat, baste, break, (n)

pulse, thump, knock, round, cadence; *antonym* (v) lose, **2**. flutter; *synonyms* (n) bustle, wave, waver, agitation, excitement, quiver, thrill, (v) flicker, beat, flit, flitter, palpitate, fly, (adj) flurry, fluster, **3**. palpitate; *synonyms* (v) flutter, shake, shiver, pant, pound, tremble, vibrate, (n) heave, tingle, **4**. undulate; *synonyms* (v) ripple, roll, surge, fluctuate, billow, cockle, ruffle, curl, alternate, riffle, sway, twine, **5**. vibrate; *synonyms* (v) oscillate, shudder, swing, wobble, move, quake, quaver, undulate, jar, wag, blow, ring, reverberate, **6**. vacillate; *synonyms* (v) hesitate, falter, hover, totter, stagger, scruple, waffle, demur, linger, pause, change, dither, doubt, shift, **7**. reverberate; *synonyms* (v) reflect, echo, rebound, resound, resonate, sound, boom, recoil, bounce, clank, repercuss.

kanebuaki beaten; *synonyms* (v) beat, (adj) battered, overpowered, conquered, routed, overcome; *antonym* (adj) victorious.

kaneheke bonito; *synonym* (n) bonetta.

kanene 1. obstinate; *synonyms* (adj) headstrong, obdurate, determined, inflexible, intractable, inveterate, disobedient, contrary, dogged, firm, stubborn, uncompromising, wayward, willful, contumacious; *antonyms* (adj) compliant, amenable, flexible, **2**. tenacious; *synonyms* (adj) adhesive, obstinate, persistent, resolute, tough, sticky, glutinous, persevering, pertinacious, steadfast, stringy, unyielding, viscous, (v) retentive, strong.

kanenea 1. fix; *synonyms* (v) establish, assign, determine, fasten, settle, define, anchor, adjust, arrange, set, clamp, (n) bind, (adj) ascertain, confirm, attach; *antonyms* (v) break, unfasten, **2**. coerce; *synonyms* (v) force, compel, drive, make, impose, bulldoze, bully, dragoon, necessitate, oblige, push, blackmail, extort, demand, constrain, **3**. enforce; *synonyms* (v) coerce, apply, execute, implement, dispense, effect, impress, accomplish, enjoin, inflict, perform, press, achieve, (n) assert, **4**. force; *synonyms* (n) energy, strength, agency, enforce, impetus, impulse, power, vigor, violence, (v) pressure, squeeze, thrust, cram, impel, ram; *antonyms* (n) weakness, persuasion, **5**. pressure; *synonyms* (n) compulsion, constraint, duress, exigency, influence, insistence, load, pinch, urge, weight, emergency, hardship, jam, coercion, (v) burden.

kaneneaki 1. enforced; *synonyms* (adj) forced, obligatory, required, applied, compulsory, binding, essential, implemented, lawful, legal, mandatory, necessary, requisite, unavoidable, **2**. forced; *synonyms* (adj) compelled, bound, artificial, constrained, involuntary, unnatural, farfetched, false, labored, obliged, strained; *antonyms* (adj) free, unprovoked, spontaneous, voluntary, **3**. fixed; *synonyms* (adj) determined, definite, steady, constant, durable, certain, decided, determinate, established, fast, fastened, intent, permanent, (v) stable, (adv) firm; antonyms (adj) flexible, adaptable, adjustable, changeable, movable, separate, variable, compliant, loose, moveable, portable, removable, temporary.

kanenei 1. decide; synonyms (v) choose, determine, adjudicate, conclude, resolve, judge, settle, try, arbitrate, arrange, decree, fix, purpose, rule, select; antonym (v) waver, **2**. determine; synonyms (v) ascertain, decide, define, appoint, measure, set, specify, designate, assign, assess, detect, estimate, provide, regulate, (adj) will, **3**. will; synonyms (v) bequeath, devise, wish, leave, shall, (n) volition, command, desire, inclination, determination, pleasure, intent, mind, courage, liking, **4**. resolve; synonyms (v) solve, decompose, dissolve, end, explain, melt, do, disentangle, (n) decision, firmness, resolution, answer, analyze, resoluteness, dissect; antonyms (n) indecision, weakness, **5**. onward; synonyms (adv) forward, ahead, forwards, on, before, forth, onwards, along, frontward, forrader.

kaneneiaki 1. decided; synonyms (v) absolute, clear, positive, categorical, emphatic, marked, (adj) decisive, definite, determined, distinct, resolute, unmistakable, conclusive, fixed, peremptory; antonym (adj) undecided, **2**. determined; synonyms (adj) constant, decided, certain, determinate, inflexible, resolved, stubborn, ambitious, adamant, bold, firm, obstinate, set, tenacious, unyielding; antonyms (adj) weak, irresolute, uncertain, feeble, unmotivated, **3**. resolved; synonyms (adj) intent, final, solved, bent.

kanenge unbalanced; synonyms (adj) lopsided, crazy, mad, wobbly, demented, disproportionate, imbalanced, unequal, asymmetrical, unsettled, unstable, unsteady, brainsick, distracted, disturbed; antonyms (adj) sane, balanced, even, well-balanced.

kang 1. consume; synonyms (v) absorb, exhaust, spend, dissipate, use, waste, burn, eat, expend, fritter, squander, swallow, annihilate, corrode, destroy; antonyms (v) save, abstain, **2**. devour; synonyms (v) consume, bolt, gulp, demolish, gobble, gorge, guzzle, devastate, enjoy, relish, down, feed, glut, gnaw, guttle.

kanga 1. how; synonyms (adv) whereby, however, whence, nevertheless, nonetheless, notwithstanding, withal, yet, **2**. quite; synonyms (adv) altogether, absolutely, all, completely, entirely, fully, sheer, exactly, enough, even, fairly, rather, right, stark, (adj) just; antonym (adv) extremely, **3**. so; synonyms (adv) accordingly, as, consequently, hence, thus, indeed, then, therefore, insomuch, also, wherefore, (n) sol, (pron) that, (adj) likewise.

kangai 1. thus; synonyms (adv) therefore, then, consequently, so, hence, accordingly, thence, ergo,

thusly, **2**. speak; synonyms (v) express, converse, pronounce, articulate, deliver, say, utter, discourse, recite, talk, lecture, address, emit, mouth, state.

kangaki 1. consumed; synonyms (adj) exhausted, spent, finished, worn, absorbed, burnt, combust, dissipated, engrossed, gone, immersed, lost, obsessed, possessed, tired, **2**. devoured.

kangana hard; synonyms (adj) austere, bad, difficult, grave, severe, strong, arduous, callous, cruel, grueling, knotty, tough, (adv) firm, (v) acute, (n) rough; antonyms (adj) easy, soft, kind, merciful, simple, soggy, tender, yielding, (adv) gently, lightly.

kanganga 1. laborious; synonyms (adj) difficult, arduous, hard, backbreaking, diligent, heavy, industrious, grueling, assiduous, exhausting, formidable, painful, strenuous, tedious, toilsome; antonym (adj) easy, **2**. complicated; synonyms (adj) complex, intricate, elaborate, complicate, awkward, convoluted, deep, knotty, obscure, sophisticated, tortuous, tricky, circuitous, detailed, (v) involved; antonyms (adj) simple, straightforward, clear, **3**. arduous; synonyms (adj) laborious, onerous, uphill, severe, tough, troublesome, trying, precipitous, burdensome, challenging, demanding, exacting, fatiguing, harsh, labored, **4**. hard; synonyms (adj) austere, bad, grave, strong, callous, cruel, bitter, alcoholic, compact, complicated, dour, dry, (adv) firm, (v) acute, (n) rough; antonyms (adj) soft, kind, merciful, soggy, tender, yielding, (adv) gently, lightly, **5**. complex; synonyms (adj) composite, abstruse, abstract, multifarious, compound, multiple, perplexing, thorny, (n) obsession, combination, syndrome, whole, character, system; antonyms (adj) basic, plain, **6**. difficult; synonyms (adj) delicate, fastidious, finicky, ambitious, cantankerous, contrary, crabby, disagreeable, fussy, inconvenient, strict, taxing, tiresome, uncomfortable, rebellious; antonyms (adj) good-natured, rewarding, **7**. painful; synonyms (adj) sore, afflictive, grievous, harrowing, sharp, aching, dolorous, excruciating, irritating, poignant, unpleasant, intolerable, galling, nasty, (v) distressing; antonyms (adj) painless, content, **8**. trying; synonyms (adj) annoying, bothersome, rugged, exasperating, maddening, wearing, wearisome, perverse, plaguy, refractory, stressful, (n) testing, **9**. strenuous; synonyms (adj) energetic, dynamic, eager, forward, intensive, aggressive, tiring, vigorous, gruelling, straining; antonyms (adj) undemanding, weak.

kangare ludicrous; synonyms (adj) absurd, ridiculous, farcical, foolish, laughable, comical, grotesque, derisory, droll, jocular, preposterous, funny, humorous, amusing, comic; antonym (adj) sensible.

kangata 1. dirty; synonyms (adj) foul, dirt, contemptible, bawdy, contaminated, dingy, impure, despicable, (v) muddy, corrupt, soil, contaminate, begrime, bemire, (n) defile; *antonyms* (*adj*) hygienic, pure, spotless, immaculate, (v) clean, **2.** soil; *synonyms* (n) ground, grime, land, dust, (v) smudge, blot, dirty, pollute, mire, blemish, mould, smear, smirch, smutch, (*adj*) blur.

kangataki soiled; *synonyms* (*adj*) dingy, dirty, grubby, nasty, grimy, filthy, unclean, muddy, black, foul, mucky, polluted, squalid, stained, contaminated; *antonyms* (*adj*) clean, pure.

kangera curl; *synonyms* (n) kink, lock, roll, frizzle, ringlet, (v) coil, crimp, loop, bow, wave, crinkle, fold, bend, curve, (*adj*) crisp; *antonym* (v) uncoil.

kangeraki curled; *synonyms* (*adj*) curly, curling, braided, round, bent, bowed, helicine, kinky, spiral, tressed, wreathy, arched, helicoid, rounded, serpentine.

kangibuea warm; *synonyms* (*adj*) hot, affectionate, tender, ardent, cordial, fervent, lively, fond, loving, earnest, caring, enthusiastic, genial, glowing, hearty; *antonyms* (*adj*) aloof, cold, unfriendly, reserved, hostile, (v) cool, chill.

kangibueaki warmed; *synonym* (*adj*) baked.

kangkai 1. insensible; *synonyms* (*adj*) callous, imperceptible, numb, unconscious, unfeeling, apathetic, dull, impassive, indiscernible, unaware, comatose, inert, ignorant, oblivious, insensate; *antonym* (*adj*) sensible, **2.** imperturbable; *synonyms* (*adj*) calm, dispassionate, composed, placid, cool, unflappable, equable, steady, sedate, serene, unruffled, nonchalant, **3.** vibrant; *synonyms* (*adj*) resonant, vivacious, sonorous, glowing, lively, vigorous, rich, **4.** virile; *synonyms* (*adj*) masculine, strong, male, manly, potent, forceful, manful, robust, mature, manlike; *antonym* (*adj*) impotent, **5.** robust; *synonyms* (*adj*) healthy, firm, athletic, brawny, muscular, powerful, lusty, mighty, healthful, hearty, stout, sturdy, forcible, (n) hardy, hard; *antonyms* (*adj*) weak, slight, fragile, frail, **6.** tough; *synonyms* (*adj*) difficult, tenacious, arduous, laborious, rugged, severe, rough, bad, durable, leathery, stubborn, (n) bully, rowdy, hoodlum, hooligan; *antonyms* (*adj*) tender, easy, flimsy, soft, feeble, lightweight, simple.

kangkang 1. good; *synonyms* (*adj*) able, benefit, delicious, right, efficient, capable, excellent, fine, nice, superior, well, advantageous, (n) benign, advantage, gain; *antonyms* (*adj*) disobedient, poor, wicked, unpleasant, (n) evil, bad, **2.** appetizing; *synonyms* (*adj*) appetising, delectable, luscious, tasty, tantalizing, palatable, savory, scrumptious, spicy; *antonyms* (*adj*) tasteless, unappetizing, **3.** luscious; *synonyms* (*adj*) appetizing, juicy, rich, dulcet, delightful, succulent, sweet, voluptuous, yummy, delicate, lush, luxurious, sumptuous, toothsome, candied; *antonym* (*adj*) dry, **4.** delicious; *synonyms* (*adj*) pleasing, agreeable,

charming, dainty, enjoyable, lovely, grateful, fragrant, exquisite, pleasant, wonderful, **5.** delectable; *synonyms* (*adj*) tasteful, good, lovable, **6.** yummy, **7.** scrumptious, **8.** palatable; *synonyms* (*adj*) eatable, edible; *antonym* (*adj*) unpalatable, **9.** tasty; *synonyms* (*adj*) savoury, flavorful, appreciate, criticise, cute, judge; *antonyms* (*adj*) bland, inedible, **10.** savory; *synonyms* (n) delicacy, (*adj*) piquant, aromatic, inoffensive, peppery.

kangongoa 1. interrogate; *synonyms* (v) inquire, question, ask, demand, examine, pump, catechize, investigate, probe, query, quiz, grill, **2.** query; *synonyms* (n) doubt, inquiry, interrogative, enquiry, interrogation, problem, dispute, uncertainty, (v) interrogate, challenge, wonder, impeach, suspect; *antonym* (v) answer, **3.** question; *synonyms* (n) matter, issue, doubtfulness, head, (v) distrust, contest, enquire, mistrust, argue, scruple, discredit, controvert, debate, disbelieve, impugn; *antonym* (n) certainty, **4.** request; *synonyms* (n) petition, bid, prayer, application, claim, entreaty, wish, (v) invite, order, pray, appeal, beg, call, desire, entreat; *antonym* (v) command.

kangorea 1. debilitate; *synonyms* (v) enfeeble, weaken, enervate, exhaust, impair, waste, drain, depress, injure, undermine, prostrate, sap, debase, (*adj*) eviscerate; *antonym* (v) enable, **2.** weaken; *synonyms* (v) dilute, lessen, attenuate, break, debilitate, diminish, relax, thin, dull, blunt, damp, deaden, decrease, emasculate, (*adj*) reduce; *antonyms* (v) strengthen, bolster, grow.

kangoreaki 1. debilitated; *synonyms* (*adj*) enervated, feeble, infirm, enfeebled, adynamic, asthenic, (v) weak, **2.** weakened; *synonyms* (*adj*) attenuate, attenuated, cut, damaged, diluted, diminished, disabled, faded, hurt, lessened, thinned, vitiated.

kanhai ask; *synonyms* (v) inquire, request, appeal, beg, demand, interrogate, question, take, beseech, call, charge, claim, consult, crave, invite; *antonym* (v) answer.

kania approach; *synonyms* (n) access, entry, advent, arrival, avenue, coming, entrance, means, method, adit, (v) advance, accost, address, near, approximate; *antonym* (v) leave.

kanibangabanga riddle; *synonyms* (n) enigma, conundrum, mystery, puzzle, screen, poser, problem, sieve, cribble, brainteaser, strainer, (v) puncture, filter, sift, strain.

kanibobotaki gregarious; *synonyms* (*adj*) companionable, outgoing, sociable, friendly, social, cordial, common, expansive, aggregative, collective, cosmopolitan, easy, gregarian, hospitable, neighborly.

kanibwaoua warp; *synonyms* (*n*) twist, buckle, distortion, deflection, deformation, (*v*) bend, distort, deform, contort, turn, bias, falsify, garble, misrepresent, pervert; *antonym* (*v*) straighten.

kanibwaouaki warped; *synonyms* (*adj*) bent, deformed, crooked, kinky, misshapen, perverted, (*n*) twisted; *antonym* (*adj*) straight.

kanikamate cramp; *synonyms* (*n*) convulsion, spasm, constraint, crick, pain, kink, restriction, (*v*) confine, constrict, restrict, bind, hamper, limit, pinch, tighten.

kanikamateaki cramped; *synonyms* (*adj*) confined, cramp, limited, close, constrained, contracted, crowded, narrow, poky, restricted, small, tight; *antonyms* (*adj*) roomy, spacious, open.

kanikan 1. neat; *synonyms* (*adj*) adroit, elegant, clear, natty, tidy, graceful, dainty, clean, clever, deft, dexterous, fresh, methodical, nifty, (*v*) compact; *antonyms* (*adj*) untidy, messy, scruffy, unkempt, clumsy, disordered, **2.** tidy; *synonyms* (*adj*) neat, trim, spruce, orderly, respectable, shipshape, goodish, sizable, nice, proper, (*v*) arrange, straighten, groom, neaten, order; *antonyms* (*adj*) disheveled, knotted, **3.** trim; *synonyms* (*adj*) smart, trig, (*v*) cut, dress, clip, garnish, shave, adorn, embellish, lop, prune, reduce, shorten, snip, (*n*) border; *antonym* (*adj*) fat.

kanikina 1. brand; *synonyms* (*n*) badge, blade, class, kind, stain, type, emblem, falchion, make, nature, slur, (*v*) mark, denounce, (*adj*) stigma, blot, **2.** mark; *synonyms* (*n*) brand, evidence, score, character, heed, impression, imprint, sign, feature, (*v*) blemish, characterize, distinguish, grade, label, (*adj*) notice, **3.** label; *synonyms* (*n*) name, tag, title, designation, earmark, docket, group, ticket, denomination, (*v*) call, classify, check, designate, identify, entitle, **4.** inscribe; *synonyms* (*v*) engrave, enroll, enter, dedicate, enlist, enrol, etch, grave, impress, register, autograph, list, describe, record, scribe, **5.** signal; *synonyms* (*n*) gesture, indication, presage, flag, alarm, motion, (*v*) omen, indicate, wave, alert, betoken, (*adj*) conspicuous, memorable, notable, prominent, **6.** sign; *synonyms* (*n*) signal, portent, manifestation, poster, forerunner, attribute, augury, banner, ensign, hint, indicator, premonition, prognostic, (*v*) bless, ratify.

kanikinaea denote; *synonyms* (*v*) express, imply, indicate, mean, point, mark, name, note, represent, spell, suggest, (*n*) declare, betoken, signify, announce.

kanikinaki 1. inscribed; *synonyms* (*adj*) engraved, etched, graven, incised, adorned, celebrated, decorated, extolled, sculpted, sculptured, **2.** marked; *synonyms* (*adj*) distinct, conspicuous, noticeable, pronounced, remarkable, distinguished, apparent, definite, notable, obvious, signal, striking, strong, clear, appreciable; *antonyms* (*adj*)

plain, unblemished, **3.** labelled; *synonyms* (*adj*) labeled, tagged, **4.** branded; *synonyms* (*adj*) acknowledged, identified, known, recognized, famous, notorious, renowned, **5.** signed; *synonyms* (*adj*) gestural, sign, employed, engaged, nonverbal.

kaniko pamper; *synonyms* (*v*) indulge, baby, cocker, coddle, pet, spoil, cherish, cosset, mollycoddle, gratify, fondle, featherbed, mother.

kanikoaki pampered; *synonyms* (*adj*) coddled, indulged, spoiled, bad, luxurious, soft, luxuriant, spoilt.

kanikua widen; *synonyms* (*v*) expand, extend, broaden, stretch, distend, enlarge, increase, spread, develop, dilate, amplify, flare, thicken, grow, impart; *antonym* (*v*) narrow.

kanikureirei rejoice; *synonyms* (*v*) cheer, delight, gladden, glory, joy, jubilate, revel, triumph, gratify, gloat, exhilarate, please, celebrate, recreate, (*n*) exult; *antonyms* (*v*) lament, mourn.

kanima 1. fasten; *synonyms* (*v*) attach, bind, connect, fix, tie, anchor, append, brace, clasp, clinch, determine, pin, secure, stick, (*adj*) affix; *antonyms* (*v*) unfasten, detach, undo, unlock, **2.** glue; *synonyms* (*n*) adhesive, gum, mucilage, (*v*) cement, adhere, fasten, bond, plaster, join, paste, **3.** adhere; *synonyms* (*v*) cohere, abide, accede, cleave, cling, hold, observe, unite, (*adj*) agree, **4.** cement; *synonyms* (*n*) glue, size, cementum, (*adj*) concrete, **5.** stick; *synonyms* (*n*) bar, club, rod, bat, cane, cudgel, (*v*) stab, staff, impale, persist, pink, spear, spike, put, poke, **6.** paste; *synonyms* (*n*) dough, cream, batter, pulp, spread, clinquant, finery, frippery, gewgaw, gimcrack, (*v*) hit, lute, **7.** tape; *synonyms* (*n*) band, ribbon, strip, rope, cassette, seal, (*v*) record, videotape, video.

kanimaki 1. glued; *synonyms* (*adj*) pasted, attentive, watchful, **2.** fastened; *synonyms* (*adj*) fixed, tied, buttoned, closed, fast, tight, binding, empight, even, firm, flat, frozen, intent, laced, reconditioned, **3.** taped, **4.** stuck; *synonyms* (*v*) sticked, (*adj*) stranded, aground, abandoned, absorbed, ashore, beached, delayed, deserted, dumbfounded, hindered, immovable, isolated, (*n*) thrust, sticking; *antonym* (*adj*) free.

kanimamate 1. decline; *synonyms* (*n*) decay, declension, decrease, dip, declination, (*v*) wane, drop, reject, fall, abate, ebb, fail, refuse, sink, deny; *antonyms* (*n*) improvement, recovery, development, growth, rebirth, (*v*) increase, rise, accept, flourish, improve, **2.** enfeeble; *synonyms* (*v*) debilitate, enervate, weaken, attenuate, impair, unnerve, waste, break, cripple, diminish, exhaust, reduce, sap, undermine, debase; *antonym* (*v*) fortify.

kanimamateaki enfeebled; *synonyms* (*adj*) debilitated, infirm, enervated, feeble, decrepit.

kanimanumuaki crumbled; *synonyms* (*adj*) broken, fragmented, rotten, disconnected, disunited, split.

kanimanunua 1. crease; *synonyms* (*n*) wrinkle, line, plait, pleat, pucker, bend, crimp, groove, (*v*) fold, crinkle, crumple, cockle, furrow, rumple, crush; *antonym* (*v*) smooth, **2**. crumple; *synonyms* (*v*) crease, collapse, buckle, ruffle, scrunch, break, corrugate, crumble, ruckle, double, tumble, (*n*) gather, crankle, (*adj*) crisp; *antonym* (*v*) flatten, **3**. wrinkle; *synonyms* (*n*) flexure, seam, (*v*) curl, purse, shrivel, crunch, knit, ridge.

kanimanunuaki 1. creased; *synonyms* (*adj*) crumpled, furrowed, lined, rumpled, wrinkled, wrinkly, corrugated, bent, craggy, crinkly, dented, disheveled, dishevelled, frowzled, puckered; *antonym* (*adj*) smooth, **2**. crumpled; *synonyms* (*adj*) creased, bended, bowed, corrugate, inclined, rutted, stooped, tousled, uneven, **3**. wrinkled; *synonyms* (*adj*) wizened, gnarled, unironed, (*n*) rough, rugged.

kanimarangrangaki 1. overjoyed; *synonyms* (*adj*) delighted, happy, joyful, jubilant, elated, ecstatic, transported, exultant, pleased, enchanted; *antonyms* (*adj*) despairing, heartbroken, **2**. overexcited; *synonyms* (*adj*) active, animated, anxious, delirious, distraught, emotional, energetic, high, lively, manic, nervous, noisy, rowdy, strained, (*v*) overwrought; *antonym* (*adj*) calm.

kanimatoaua enervate; *synonyms* (*v*) enfeeble, unnerve, weaken, exhaust, fatigue, break, impair, sap, weary, (*adj*) debilitate, relax, shake, unman.

kanimatoauaki enervated; *synonyms* (*adj*) debilitated, exhausted, limp, adynamic, asthenic, colorless, faint, languid, lethargic, tired, weak.

kanimiboi track; *synonyms* (*n*) course, path, line, racetrack, road, route, (*v*) trace, trail, hunt, tail, chase, pursue, dog, follow, footprint.

kanimma fix; *synonyms* (*v*) establish, assign, determine, fasten, settle, define, anchor, adjust, arrange, set, clamp, (*n*) bind, (*adj*) ascertain, confirm, attach; *antonyms* (*v*) break, unfasten.

kanimmaki fixed; *synonyms* (*adj*) determined, definite, steady, constant, durable, certain, decided, determinate, established, fast, fastened, intent, permanent, (*v*) stable, (*adv*) firm; *antonyms* (*adj*) flexible, adaptable, adjustable, changeable, movable, separate, variable, compliant, loose, moveable, portable, removable, temporary.

kanimoumoui whistle; *synonyms* (*n*) whistling, pennywhistle, (*v*) pipe, sing, twitter, hiss, cry, warble, cheep, tweet, chirp, wheeze.

kaningangata delay; *synonyms* (*n*) pause, arrest, deferment, wait, stay, deferral, extension, (*v*) defer, check, postpone, reserve, adjourn, break, detain, hesitate; *antonyms* (*n*) punctuality, decisiveness, (*v*) rush, advance.

kaningangataki delayed; *synonyms* (*adj*) belated, late, tardy, protracted, deferred, slow, (*adv*) behind; *antonyms* (*adj*) brief, early.

kaninganinga 1. pry; *synonyms* (*v*) peep, prize, inquire, jimmy, nose, peer, snoop, prise, poke, spy, (*n*) lever, crowbar, ransack, explore, rummage, **2**. peek; *synonyms* (*n*) glance, glimpse, (*v*) look, gaze, cheep, pry, see, glint.

kaniniraka rotate; *synonyms* (*v*) revolve, reel, roll, alternate, gyrate, spin, swing, wheel, orbit, pivot, turn, twirl, circulate, circle, twist.

kaninirakaki rotated; *synonym* (*adj*) revolved.

kaniwanga reward; *synonyms* (*n*) pay, return, guerdon, payment, wage, bribe, fee, premium, award, (*v*) recompense, compensation, meed, prize, repay, requite; *antonym* (*v*) punish.

kanna nourish; *synonyms* (*v*) breed, foster, keep, cradle, aliment, cherish, cultivate, feed, maintain, nurture, sustain, supply, entertain, encourage, help.

kannaki nourished; *synonym* (*adj*) fostered.

kanngea harden; *synonyms* (*v*) habituate, consolidate, inure, season, coagulate, congeal, freeze, petrify, solidify, anneal, ossify, (*n*) strengthen, brace, fortify, (*adj*) vitrify; *antonyms* (*v*) soften, liquefy.

kanngeaki hardened; *synonyms* (*adj*) hard, callous, confirmed, tough, indurated, tempered, unfeeling, enured, habitual, inured, veteran.

kannim 1. agreeable; *synonyms* (*adj*) acceptable, accordant, pleasant, pleasing, nice, affable, amusing, compatible, conformable, congenial, consistent, enjoyable, genial, grateful, (*v*) desirable; *antonyms* (*adj*) disagreeable, discordant, nasty, unpleasant, unwilling, aggressive, resistant, **2**. tasty; *synonyms* (*adj*) savory, tasteful, delicious, appetizing, dainty, delectable, spicy, luscious, palatable, savoury, scrumptious, rich, flavorful, appreciate, criticise; *antonyms* (*adj*) tasteless, bland, inedible, **3**. taste; *synonyms* (*n*) bit, flavor, liking, morsel, penchant, appetite, drink, drop, fondness, gusto, (*v*) relish, savor, sample, smack, discernment; *antonyms* (*n*) dislike, tastelessness.

kanoa fill; *synonyms* (*v*) block, clog, charge, line, stuff, accomplish, execute, complete, brim, close, cram, flood, fulfill, (*n*) crowd, filling; *antonyms* (*v*) empty, free.

kanoabo 1. acarpous; *synonyms* (*adj*) addled, inoperative, unfertile, unprolific, unproductive, infertile, **2**. fruitless; *synonyms* (*adj*) abortive, barren, vain, empty, futile, useless, bootless, idle, ineffective, pointless, sterile, ineffectual, poor, profitless, unfruitful; *antonym* (*adj*) fertile, **3**. infertile; *synonyms* (*adj*) fruitless, lean, childless;

antonym (*adj*) lush, **4.** barren; *synonyms* (*adj*) deserted, arid, dry, meagre, stark, void, bleak, dead, desert, desolate, devoid, effete, meager, (*v*) bare, (*n*) waste; *antonym* (*adj*) productive, **5.** arid; *synonyms* (*adj*) dull, boring, parched, tedious, acarpous, dehydrated, desiccated, droughty, humdrum, insipid, thirsty, waterless, (*v*) monotonous, uninteresting, bald; *antonyms* (*adj*) wet, verdant, **6.** sterile; *synonyms* (*adj*) antiseptic, aseptic, hygienic, unprofitable, inadequate, sanitary, uninspired; *antonym* (*adj*) unhygienic, **7.** unfruitful; *synonym* (*adj*) infecund.

kanoaki filled; *synonyms* (*adj*) replete, packed, crowded, fraught, teeming, (*adv*) full.

kanoan 1. blissful; *synonyms* (*adj*) blessed, happy, cheerful, delighted, delightful, glad, heavenly, joyful, merry, beatified, blest, ecstatic, elated, **2.** content; *synonyms* (*n*) capacity, contentment, matter, meaning, subject, substance, contentedness, (*adj*) contented, fulfilled, (*v*) appease, please, satisfy, suffice, delight, gratify; *antonyms* (*adj*) tormented, unhappy, discontented, dissatisfied, rebellious, (*v*) discontent, upset, **3.** satisfied; *synonyms* (*v*) convinced, (*adj*) content, full, pleased, certain, confident, sure, complacent, persuaded, sated, satiated, easy, positive, quenched; *antonym* (*adj*) frustrated.

kanotona 1. accuse; *synonyms* (*v*) impeach, charge, incriminate, arraign, criminate, defame, denounce, indict, fault, betray, accusation, admonish, censure, condemn, criticize, **2.** impute; *synonyms* (*v*) ascribe, assign, attribute, accuse, blame, attach, credit, lay, refer, tax, **3.** blame; *synonyms* (*v*) reprimand, reproach, chide, rebuke, knock, scold, (*n*) attack, rap, onus, allegation, condemnation, inculpation, responsibility, indictment, disapprobation; *antonyms* (*v*) pardon, absolve, praise, **4.** attribute; *synonyms* (*n*) quality, characteristic, emblem, feature, character, mark, peculiarity, dimension, qualification, temper, trait, (*v*) impute, (*adj*) property, faculty, **5.** charge; *synonyms* (*n*) burden, care, command, commission, bill, accusal, assail, demand, direction, mission, (*v*) bid, load, assault, cost, fill; *antonyms* (*v*) request, retreat.

kanotonaki 1. charged; *synonyms* (*adj*) fraught, laden, loaded, aerated, replete, abounding, deferred, electric, excited, explosive, invigorating, pregnant, supercharged, freighted, meaningful, **2.** accused; *synonyms* (*n*) panel, perpetrator, **3.** blamed; *synonyms* (*adj*) damned, goddam, goddamn, goddamned, infernal, damnable, aeonian, ageless, answerable, beatified, blame, blasted, blessed, damn, darned.

kanrairaia exhaust; *synonyms* (*v*) consume, drain, spend, empty, tire, deplete, expend, sap, use, dry,

debilitate, enervate, evacuate, (*adj*) waste, dissipate; *antonyms* (*v*) conserve, refresh, invigorate.

kanrairaiaki exhausted; *synonyms* (*v*) weak, (*adj*) drained, fatigued, spent, tired, gone, dry, beat, depleted, empty, enervated, faint, jaded, weary, expended; *antonyms* (*adj*) energetic, fresh, refreshed, strong.

kanroaroa 1. next; *synonyms* (*adj*) later, nearest, adjacent, contiguous, following, subsequent, future, coming, ensuing, after, close, near, adjoining, (*adv*) afterward, then; *antonyms* (*adj*) distant, outgoing, (*adv*) previous, preceding, previously, **2.** immediate; *synonyms* (*adj*) prompt, direct, sudden, present, quick, expeditious, fast, hasty, instant, proximate, speedy, express, firsthand, nearby, early; *antonyms* (*adj*) slow, gradual, consecutive, deliberate.

kanta 1. chew; *synonyms* (*v*) champ, munch, chomp, crunch, gnaw, manducate, masticate, mouth, eat, jaw, (*n*) bite, chaw, chewing, cud, mastication, **2.** masticate; *synonyms* (*v*) chew, cranch, craunch.

kantaninga 1. expect; *synonyms* (*v*) anticipate, assume, believe, demand, understand, abide, await, calculate, hope, suppose, think, conceive, call, mean, ask, **2.** anticipate; *synonyms* (*v*) antedate, expect, forecast, forestall, foretell, estimate, apprehend, divine, guess, predict, presume, prevent, intercept, trust, envision, **3.** hope; *synonyms* (*v*) confide, wish, look, (*n*) aspiration, belief, desire, expectation, faith, anticipation, confidence, expectancy, assurance, ambition, fancy, prospect; *antonyms* (*v*) despair, (*n*) reality, **4.** presume; *synonyms* (*v*) dare, consider, infer, esteem, conclude, conjecture, deduce, gather, imagine, presuppose, hazard, impose, accept, deem, hold, **5.** prospect; *synonyms* (*n*) outlook, view, aspect, lookout, perspective, possibility, chance, future, likelihood, panorama, picture, probability, scene, candidate, (*v*) explore; *antonym* (*n*) past, **6.** presumptuous; *synonyms* (*adj*) arrogant, assuming, audacious, forward, insolent, impertinent, assumptive, familiar, haughty, proud, daring, pert, conceited, (*n*) impudent, bold.

kantaningaki 1. anticipated; *synonyms* (*adj*) likely, expected, predictable, appointed, awaited, coming, forthcoming, future, natural, planned, probable, projected, proposed, scheduled, **2.** expected; *synonyms* (*adj*) anticipated, prospective, conventional, intended, usual, **3.** premeditated; *synonyms* (*adj*) deliberate, intentional, designed, calculated, conscious, studied, prearranged, premeditate, purposeful, willful, considered, express, (*v*) prepense, aforethought; *antonyms* (*adj*) accidental, ingenuous, **4.** premeditate; *synonyms* (*v*) predestine, predetermine, resolve, preconceived, preordain.

kantaningakiaki premeditated; *synonyms* *(adj)* deliberate, intentional, planned, designed, calculated, conscious, studied, intended, prearranged, premeditate, purposeful, willful, considered, *(v)* prepense, aforethought; *antonyms* *(adj)* accidental, ingenuous.

kantara neat; *synonyms* *(adj)* adroit, elegant, clear, natty, tidy, graceful, dainty, clean, clever, deft, dexterous, fresh, methodical, nifty, *(v)* compact; *antonyms* *(adj)* untidy, messy, scruffy, unkempt, clumsy, disordered.

kanua shade; *synonyms* *(n)* screen, tinge, color, ghost, hue, blind, cloud, apparition, conceal, darkness, dye, *(v)* darken, shadow, tint, cover; *antonyms* *(n)* light, brightness.

kanuai nutritional; *synonyms* *(adj)* alimentary, nutritionary, dietetic, food.

kanuaia satisfy; *synonyms* *(v)* please, content, fill, indulge, meet, persuade, sate, satiate, appease, answer, assuage, convince, delight, *(adj)* suffice, do; *antonyms* *(v)* dissatisfy, disappoint, displease, intensify.

kanuaiaki satisfied; *synonyms* *(v)* convinced, *(adj)* contented, happy, content, full, pleased, certain, confident, sure, complacent, persuaded, fulfilled, sated, satiated, easy; *antonyms* *(adj)* unhappy, frustrated.

kanuaki shaded; *synonyms* *(adj)* shady, dark, cheerless, darksome, gloomy, gray, leafy, obscure, soft, subdued, sunless, twilight, umbrageous, cool, dappled.

kanubebeoa 1. humble; *synonyms* *(adj)* base, docile, low, lowly, modest, unassuming, baseborn, *(v)* degrade, demean, disgrace, abase, debase, humiliate, mortify, conquer; *antonyms* *(adj)* grand, arrogant, conceited, haughty, imposing, impressive, pompous, snooty, **2.** degrade; *synonyms* *(v)* cheapen, debauch, corrupt, decrease, dishonor, disparage, lessen, reduce, abate, demote, deprave, depress, discredit, downgrade, *(n)* defame, **3.** disgrace; *synonyms* *(n)* shame, blemish, stain, degradation, reproach, slur, abuse, humiliation, taint, defect, *(v)* blot, attaint, defile, humble, spot; *antonyms* *(v)* honor, respect, credit, esteem, **4.** dishonor; *synonyms* *(n)* affront, disrepute, infamy, dishonesty, contumely, dishonour, disparagement, ignominy, disesteem, stigma, contempt, indignity, *(v)* violate, desecrate, insult, **5.** abase; *synonyms* *(v)* sink, lower, crush, *(adj)* abash, snub, **6.** confound; *synonyms* *(v)* bewilder, baffle, confuse, astonish, nonplus, perplex, puzzle, amaze, astound, bamboozle, mistake, mystify, complicate, *(n)* surprise, *(adj)* stupefy; *antonym* *(v)* enlighten, **7.** downgrade; *synonyms* *(v)* depreciate, relegate, *(n)* decline, downgrading, grade, slope; *antonyms* *(v)* upgrade, promote, *(n)* improvement, **8.** shame; *synonyms*

(n) chagrin, modesty, pity, scandal, embarrassment, mortification, opprobrium, odium, guilt, compunction, conscience, remorse, *(v)* embarrass, discountenance, confound.

kanubebeoaki 1. disgraced; *synonyms* *(adj)* discredited, shamed, dishonored, abashed, damaged, disfigured, dishonest, humiliated, mortified, dishonorable, embarrassed, faithless, fraudulent, guilty, hangdog, **2.** degraded; *synonyms* *(adj)* degenerate, debased, ignoble, low, debauched, depraved, abject, sordid, adulterate, base, contemptible, corrupted; *antonym* *(adj)* untarnished, **3.** confounded; *synonyms* *(adj)* bemused, bewildered, accursed, baffled, befuddled, confused, cursed, execrable, puzzled, aghast, abominable, **4.** humbled; *synonyms* *(adj)* broken, humble, crushed, depressed, dispirited, **5.** dishonored; *synonyms* *(adj)* disgraced, corrupt, defiled, fallen, tainted, besmirched, desecrated, despoiled, indecent, knavish, lewd, ruined, shamefaced, *(n)* degraded, derogate; *antonym* *(adj)* pure, **6.** shamed; *synonyms* *(adj)* ashamed, browbeaten, bullied, cowed, intimidated.

kanuka 1. mar; *synonyms* *(v)* disfigure, spoil, blemish, deface, harm, impair, injure, corrupt, hurt, deflower, maim, mutilate, botch, mangle, *(adj)* damage; *antonym* *(v)* enhance, **2.** humiliate; *synonyms* *(v)* degrade, debase, disgrace, abase, demean, insult, mortify, embarrass, lower, shame, snub, chagrin, *(n)* humble, dishonor, disparage; *antonym* *(v)* respect, **3.** shame; *synonyms* *(n)* reproach, discredit, humiliation, modesty, pity, scandal, contempt, degradation, embarrassment, ignominy, infamy, mortification, *(v)* humiliate, abash, confuse; *antonym* *(v)* honor.

kanukaki 1. humiliated; *synonyms* *(adj)* ashamed, humbled, mortified, embarrassed, humble, abashed, broken, crushed; *antonym* *(adj)* proud, **2.** marred; *synonyms* *(adj)* damaged, defaced, crippled, deficient, deformed, dilapidated, faulty, hurt, impaired, imperfect, scarred, **3.** shamed; *synonyms* *(adj)* disgraced, dishonored, discredited, guilty, hangdog, browbeaten, bullied, cowed, fallen, intimidated, shamefaced.

kao 1. lure; *synonyms* *(n)* allure, bait, enticement, seduce, attraction, *(v)* decoy, entice, bribe, charm, draw, invite, coax, inveigle, tempt, attract, **2.** entice; *synonyms* *(v)* lure, cajole, captivate, persuade, call, beguile, appeal, bewitch, entrap, wheedle, court, lead, pull, influence, enchant, **3.** bid; *synonyms* *(n)* offer, tender, attempt, proffer, suggestion, *(v)* ask, command, adjure, beseech, charge, direct, instruct, order, summon, tell, **4.** call; *synonyms* *(v)* cry, bellow, name, shout, bid, howl, address, baptize, cite, dub, entitle, *(n)* yell, appoint, demand, request; *antonym* *(v)* dismiss, **5.** antenna; *synonyms* *(n)* aerial, feeler, advance, finger, forefinger, hand, nose, paw, snout, thumb, trunk, approach, barbel, ears, hustler, **6**. invite; *synonyms* (*v*) beckon, encourage, receive, solicit, beg, crave, entreat, entertain, excite, incite, petition, pray, seek, sue, (*n*) invitation, **7**. request; *synonyms* (*n*) prayer, application, claim, entreaty, wish, asking, quest, requisition, inquiry, plea, (*v*) desire, inquire, need, query, implore, **8**. solicit; *synonyms* (*v*) importune, apply, require, plead, woo, lobby, accost, procure, invoke, move, supplicate, urge, proposition, question, (*n*) canvass, **9**. summon; *synonyms* (*v*) assemble, convene, convoke, evoke, muster, page, rally, challenge, collect, gather, raise, recall, summons, exhort, arraign.

kaoa 1. order; *synonyms* (*n*) command, decree, dictate, array, rank, sort, charge, class, condition, disposition, edict, (*v*) direct, commission, arrange, call; *antonyms* (*n*) anarchy, chaos, confusion, mayhem, mess, (*v*) disorder, request, **2**. wipe; *synonyms* (*v*) rub, clean, mop, towel, brush, scour, scrub, clear, dry, wash, cover, (*n*) fling, flout, (*adj*) sponge, flush, **3**. push; *synonyms* (*n*) press, thrust, jolt, poke, (*v*) drive, impel, crowd, force, jab, jostle, nudge, prod, jam, rush, boost; *antonyms* (*v*) pull, drag, haul.

kaoaki 1. called; *synonyms* (*v*) nempt, ycleped, (*adj*) named, chosen, qualified, **2**. invited; *synonyms* (*adj*) welcome, cherished, wanted, precious, treasured, **3**. ordered; *synonyms* (*adj*) tidy, regular, arranged, methodical, orderly, coherent, consistent, lawful, logical, **4**. solicited.

kaoanikai 1. imprudent; *synonyms* (*adj*) careless, foolish, foolhardy, hasty, improvident, indiscreet, heedless, impolitic, unadvised, ill-advised, injudicious, rash, reckless, silly, thoughtless; *antonyms* (*adj*) sensible, prudent, cautious, wise, deliberate, **2**. dangerous; *synonyms* (*adj*) critical, grave, serious, severe, adventurous, unhealthy, chancy, dicey, hazardous, hurtful, perilous, precarious, threatening, unsafe, poisonous; *antonyms* (*adj*) safe, secure, stable, **3**. perilous; *synonyms* (*adj*) dangerous, insecure, parlous, risky, treacherous, dodgy, shaky, uncertain, unstable, daring, menacing.

kaobainako 1. diligent; *synonyms* (*adj*) busy, active, assiduous, careful, painstaking, earnest, attentive, industrious, laborious, studious, occupied, brisk, conscientious, indefatigable, meticulous; *antonyms* (*adj*) lazy, careless, negligent, **2**. punctual; *synonyms* (*adj*) correct, accurate, exact, prompt, punctilious, precise, regular, timely, nice, (*v*) steady, lenten, paschal; *antonym* (*adj*) late, **3**. prompt; *synonyms* (*adj*) agile, quick, nimble, punctual, dexterous, expeditious, immediate, (*v*) actuate, incite, fleet, inspire, instigate, move, animate, cue; *antonym* (*adj*) slow.

kaoioia 1. thicken; *synonyms* (*v*) congeal, condense, clot, set, coagulate, stiffen, gel, gather, harden, incrassate, jell, reduce, (*n*) curdle; *antonym* (*v*) thin, **2**. set; *synonyms* (*v*) fix, place, lay, put, locate, position, regulate, define, adjust, arrange, (*n*) class, bent, (*adj*) fixed, fast, secure; *antonyms* (*v*) soften, liquefy, melt, (*n*) combing, comb-out, (*adj*) variable, flexible, liquid.

kaoioiaki 1. thickened; *synonyms* (*adj*) calloused, thick, concentrated, incrassated, inspissated, spissated, stiff, **2**. set; *synonyms* (*v*) fix, place, lay, put, locate, position, regulate, define, adjust, arrange, (*n*) class, bent, (*adj*) fixed, fast, secure; *antonyms* (*v*) soften, liquefy, melt, (*n*) combing, comb-out, (*adj*) variable, flexible, liquid.

kaoka 1. remit; *synonyms* (*v*) excuse, relax, acquit, defer, dispatch, forgive, loose, loosen, pardon, mitigate, forward, abate, absolve, postpone, (*adj*) exempt, **2**. repel; *synonyms* (*v*) nauseate, disgust, revolt, rebuff, repulse, sicken, decline, displease, refuse, reject, parry, drive, oppose, rebut, dismiss; *antonyms* (*v*) attract, charm, draw, **3**. render; *synonyms* (*v*) afford, interpret, explain, furnish, give, offer, pay, construe, depict, impart, make, provide, return, translate, yield, **4**. restore; *synonyms* (*v*) mend, refresh, reinstate, renew, renovate, fix, rehabilitate, rejuvenate, repay, replace, reimburse, heal, reconstruct, recover, (*adj*) repair; *antonym* (*v*) keep, **5**. return; *synonyms* (*n*) recompense, refund, restitution, proceeds, income, revenue, (*v*) recur, render, restoration, restore, retort, answer, reply, requite, revert; *antonyms* (*n*) departure, abolition, confiscation, recovery.

kaokaki restored; *synonyms* (*adj*) fresh, comfortable, convalescent, healthy, new.

kaokia 1. speak; *synonyms* (*v*) express, converse, pronounce, articulate, deliver, say, utter, discourse, recite, talk, lecture, address, emit, mouth, state, **2**. say; *synonyms* (*v*) remark, assert, enunciate, observe, maintain, order, read, speak, tell, guess, relate, dictate, command, (*n*) declare, voice, **3**. repeat; *synonyms* (*v*) copy, recapitulate, reduplicate, rehearse, reiterate, return, double, duplicate, iterate, recur, renew, reproduce, cite, multiply, echo.

kaokiaki repeated; *synonyms* (*adj*) continual, recurrent, frequent, persistent, double, habitual, chronic, common, continuous, perennial, perpetual; *antonym* (*adj*) intermittent.

kaokoro 1. disparate; *synonyms* (*adj*) different, dissimilar, unlike, divergent, heterogeneous, unequal, uneven, distinct, diverse, various, (*v*) separate; *antonym* (*adj*) similar, **2**. divergent; *synonyms* (*adj*) differing, conflicting, disparate, diverging, abnormal, variant, centrifugal, deviant; *antonym* (*adj*) convergent, **3**. different; *synonyms* (*adj*) another, assorted, unusual, alien, alternative, discrete, foreign, fresh, miscellaneous, new, opposite, several, strange, mixed, discrepant; *antonyms* (*adj*) corresponding, equal, identical, like, typical, **4.** differ; *synonyms* (*v*) dissent, disagree, contradict, clash, deviate, diverge, depart, conflict, vary, dispute, diversify, quarrel, ablude; *antonyms* (*v*) agree, concur, conform, correspond, **5.** diversified; *synonyms* (*adj*) manifold, varied, altered, **6.** vary; *synonyms* (*v*) alter, change, differ, modify, alternate, modulate, fluctuate, shift, variegate, contrast, exchange, turn, range, interchange, amend, **7.** sorted; *synonyms* (*adj*) grouped, fixed, straight, **8.** variable; *synonyms* (*adj*) unstable, changeable, fickle, inconstant, capricious, erratic, fitful, mutable, uncertain, unsettled, unsteady, fluctuating, inconsistent, shifting, versatile; *antonyms* (*adj*) constant, invariable, regular, set, smooth, **9.** queer; *synonyms* (*adj*) fantastic, eccentric, odd, curious, funny, fishy, gay, peculiar, quaint, outlandish, comical, fanciful, droll, (*v*) baffle, bilk, **10.** sort; *synonyms* (*n*) kind, type, assortment, breed, description, form, rank, variety, pattern, (*v*) class, group, arrange, classify, divide, (*adj*) manner, **11.** varied; *synonyms* (*adj*) diversified, sundry, motley, many; *antonyms* (*adj*) boring, dull, homogeneous, uniform.

kaokoroaki 1. apart; *synonyms* (*adv*) aside, asunder, away, independently, individually, (*adj*) aloof, alone, distant, separate, detached, isolated, only, individual, loose, (*v*) discrete, **2.** varied; *synonyms* (*adj*) assorted, diverse, miscellaneous, mixed, various, different, diversified, sundry, heterogeneous, manifold, motley, many, dissimilar, versatile, odd; *antonyms* (*adj*) boring, dull, homogeneous, uniform, **3.** sorted; *synonyms* (*adj*) grouped, fixed, straight.

kaomwaka throw; *synonyms* (*v*) cast, fling, shed, hurl, chuck, flip, heave, pass, deliver, drop, give, hurtle, (*n*) pitch, push, shot.

kaomwakaki thrown; *synonyms* (*adj*) confused, puzzled, addled, baffled, bewildered, confounded, disconcerted, distraught, dumbfounded, fearful, frightened, mystified, terrified, unnerved, (*n*) reminder.

kaona infest; *synonyms* (*v*) plague, disturb, overrun, beset, pester, annoy, invade.

kaonaki infested; *synonyms* (*adj*) plagued, contaminated, diseased, infected, malodorous, overrun, polluted, swarming, filled, flooded, swamped, teeming.

kaonako 1. diligent; *synonyms* (*adj*) busy, active, assiduous, careful, painstaking, earnest, attentive, industrious, laborious, studious, occupied, brisk, conscientious, indefatigable, meticulous; *antonyms* (*adj*) lazy, careless, negligent, **2.** scornful;

synonyms (*adj*) contemptuous, disdainful, haughty, arrogant, sarcastic, disparaging, derisive, mocking, abusive, insulting, opprobrious, scathing, derogatory, proud, cynical; *antonyms* (*adj*) respectful, approving, **3.** punctual; *synonyms* (*adj*) correct, accurate, exact, prompt, punctilious, precise, regular, timely, nice, (*v*) steady, lenten, paschal; *antonym* (*adj*) late, **4.** prompt; *synonyms* (*adj*) agile, quick, nimble, punctual, dexterous, expeditious, immediate, (*v*) actuate, incite, fleet, inspire, instigate, move, animate, cue; *antonym* (*adj*) slow.

kaonakoa 1. do; *synonyms* (*v*) act, cheat, commit, accomplish, complete, conduct, perform, achieve, make, practice, defraud, answer, arrange, (*n*) function, occasion; *antonyms* (*v*) neglect, unmake, **2.** push; *synonyms* (*n*) press, thrust, jolt, poke, (*v*) drive, impel, crowd, force, jab, jostle, nudge, prod, jam, rush, boost; *antonyms* (*v*) pull, drag, haul, **3.** shove; *synonyms* (*v*) elbow, shift, hustle, stuff, bump, cram, jog, move, squeeze, hurtle, put, joggle, (*n*) push, shoulder, jerk, **4.** scorn; *synonyms* (*n*) disdain, contempt, derision, mockery, insult, (*v*) despise, ridicule, contemn, deride, disregard, reject, slight, reproach, dislike, disparage; *antonyms* (*n*) approval, (*v*) respect, appreciate, praise, **5.** throw; *synonyms* (*v*) cast, fling, shed, hurl, chuck, flip, heave, pass, deliver, drop, give, project, (*n*) pitch, shot, shy.

kaonakoaki 1. done; *synonyms* (*adj*) finished, complete, completed, over, gone, through, (*adv*) ended; *antonym* (*adj*) unfinished, **2.** scorned; *synonyms* (*adj*) despised, detested, hated, abject, neglected, contemptible, contemptuous, despicable, insolent, mean, undesirable, unpopular, scornful, vile, **3.** thrown; *synonyms* (*adj*) confused, puzzled, addled, baffled, bewildered, confounded, disconcerted, distraught, dumbfounded, fearful, frightened, mystified, terrified, unnerved, (*n*) reminder.

kaongoa inform; *synonyms* (*v*) communicate, acquaint, advise, impart, announce, enlighten, tell, familiarize, explain, advertise, apprise, educate, instruct, state, warn.

kaongoaki informed; *synonyms* (*adj*) aware, cognizant, educated, conscious, knowledgeable, familiar, apprised, wise, conversant, experienced, (*adv*) abreast; *antonym* (*adj*) ignorant.

kaongora notify; *synonyms* (*v*) acquaint, advise, advertise, instruct, announce, inform, apprise, warn, alert, apprize, declare, enlighten, tell, counsel, promulgate.

kaongoraea inform; *synonyms* (*v*) communicate, acquaint, advise, impart, announce, enlighten, tell, familiarize, explain, advertise, apprise, educate, instruct, state, warn.

kaongoraeaki informed; *synonyms* (*adj*) aware, cognizant, educated, conscious, knowledgeable, familiar, apprised, wise, conversant, experienced, (*adv*) abreast; *antonym* (*adj*) ignorant.

kaonoa 1. grant; *synonyms* (*n*) concession, donation, permit, (*v*) give, allow, award, bestow, admit, afford, concede, confer, gift, acknowledge, accord, boon; *antonyms* (*v*) deny, reject, **2.** give; *synonyms* (*v*) extend, commit, donate, contribute, convey, deliver, dispense, endow, grant, present, yield, administer, apply, bequeath, bring; *antonyms* (*v*) withdraw, take, withhold, **3.** distribute; *synonyms* (*v*) allot, apportion, deal, spread, assign, diffuse, disperse, disseminate, broadcast, circulate, dispose, dispel, portion, propagate, scatter; *antonyms* (*v*) accumulate, amass, collect, gather, **4.** dispense; *synonyms* (*v*) distribute, issue, allocate, discharge, furnish, supply, provide, manage, treat, divide, exempt, release, relieve, share, spend, **5.** assign; *synonyms* (*v*) delegate, appoint, ascribe, consign, accredit, appropriate, attribute, dedicate, depute, place, put, cast, designate, detail, (*n*) adjudge, **6.** present; *synonyms* (*adj*) current, (*n*) offering, presentation, (*v*) display, introduce, prefer, offer, perform, gratuity, exhibit, serve, indicate, cede, largess, advance; *antonyms* (*adj*) missing, (*n*) past, future, history, (*adv*) absent, **7.** offer; *synonyms* (*v*) impart, propose, tender, lay, sacrifice, submit, suggest, (*n*) bid, proposal, go, proposition, approach, crack, fling, overture; *antonym* (*v*) refuse, **8.** relay; *synonyms* (*n*) relief, spell, (*v*) pass, transmit, transfer, send.

kaonoaki 1. given; *synonyms* (*adj*) apt, disposed, prone, liable, granted, inclined, set, (*n*) assumption, particular, presumption, fact, **2.** distributed; *synonyms* (*adj*) dispersed, divided, spread, strewn, thin, separate, diffuse, disseminated, circulated, disunited; *antonym* (*adj*) concentrated, **3.** dispensed, **4.** granted; *synonyms* (*adj*) given, assumed, fixed, approved, arranged, blessed, decided, legal, privileged, settled, contracted, established, (*adv*) yes, **5.** assigned; *synonyms* (*adj*) destined, definite, **6.** presented; *synonyms* (*adj*) bestowed, conferred, offered, existing, accessible, obtainable, free, open, unfilled, untaken, vacant.

kaonota 1. specify; *synonyms* (*v*) name, designate, signify, define, assign, describe, determine, fix, prescribe, set, enumerate, mark, (*n*) detail, particularize, appoint; *antonym* (*v*) simplify, **2.** restrict; *synonyms* (*v*) limit, restrain, circumscribe, confine, constrain, fetter, bound, curb, curtail, forbid, hamper, reduce, ration, bind, check.

kaonotaki 1. restricted; *synonyms* (*v*) qualified, (*adj*) limited, confined, cramped, narrow, constrained, exclusive, local, controlled, finite, prohibited, classified, secret, bounded, circumscribed; *antonyms* (*adj*) unrestricted, far-reaching, free,

liberated, unimpeded, unlimited, open, wide, **2.** specified; *synonyms* (*adj*) specific, certain, particular, set, individual, destined, distinct, precise, agreed, clear, detailed, different, distinguished, following, known.

kaooa order; *synonyms* (*n*) command, decree, dictate, array, rank, sort, charge, class, condition, disposition, edict, (*v*) direct, commission, arrange, call; *antonyms* (*n*) anarchy, chaos, confusion, mayhem, mess, (*v*) disorder, request.

kaooaki ordered; *synonyms* (*adj*) tidy, regular, arranged, methodical, orderly, coherent, consistent, lawful, logical.

kaoraba profit; *synonyms* (*n*) gain, benefit, account, good, produce, earnings, increase, dividend, interest, (*v*) net, advance, avail, earn, help, (*adj*) advantage; *antonym* (*v*) lose.

kaoraia prepare; *synonyms* (*v*) arrange, fix, form, plan, dress, coach, devise, lay, make, set, adjust, concoct, cook, equip, fit.

kaoraiaki prepared; *synonyms* (*adj*) disposed, fit, willing, fitted, fain, finished, ready, ripe, competent, inclined, primed, completed, efficient, mature, apt; *antonyms* (*adj*) unprepared, spontaneous.

kaorakora 1. loud; *synonyms* (*adj*) flashy, garish, gaudy, blatant, boisterous, brassy, forte, high, brazen, jazzy, clamorous, colorful, flash, meretricious, (*adv*) aloud; *antonyms* (*adj*) soft, gentle, quiet, tasteful, low, subdued, subtle, **2.** thunderous; *synonyms* (*adj*) thundery, deafening, earsplitting, loud, booming, roaring, flourishing, hollow, noisy, palmy, piercing, prospering, prosperous, resonant, shrill.

kaoro 1. swarming; *synonyms* (*v*) dense, serried, (*adj*) teeming, alive, crowded, full, packed, populous; *antonym* (*adj*) empty, **2.** swarm; *synonyms* (*n*) crowd, horde, host, mob, drove, multitude, assembly, cloud, gathering, herd, mass, (*v*) pour, teem, abound, flock.

kaota 1. demonstrate; *synonyms* (*v*) prove, authenticate, attest, display, establish, exhibit, present, show, argue, certify, confirm, evidence, exemplify, explain, indicate; *antonyms* (*v*) disprove, conceal, **2.** notify; *synonyms* (*v*) acquaint, advise, advertise, instruct, announce, inform, apprise, warn, alert, apprize, declare, enlighten, tell, counsel, promulgate, **3.** divulge; *synonyms* (*v*) disclose, betray, communicate, impart, reveal, leak, break, confess, expose, blab, convey, discover, unveil, utter, voice, **4.** irradiate; *synonyms* (*v*) illuminate, radiate, lighten, ray, shine, **5.** explain; *synonyms* (*v*) comment, elucidate, interpret, account, clarify, decipher, define, describe, excuse, explicate, expound, gloss, solve, denote, annotate; *antonym* (*v*) confuse, **6.** denote;

synonyms (*v*) express, imply, mean, point, mark, name, note, represent, spell, suggest, identify, characterize, (*n*) betoken, signify, brand, **7.** exposed; *synonyms* (*v*) vulnerable, (*adj*) bare, open, defenseless, liable, nude, obvious, subject, uncovered, unprotected, bald, bleak, public, undefended; *antonyms* (*adj*) concealed, covered, hidden, safe, **8.** indicate; *synonyms* (*v*) direct, augur, designate, foretell, foreshadow, bespeak, bode, demonstrate, evince, presage, finger, hint, intimate, portend, predict, **9.** illuminate; *synonyms* (*v*) brighten, illumine, adorn, clear, decorate, color, ignite, edify, illustrate, irradiate, paint, crystallize, dye, (*adj*) illume, (*n*) light, **10.** display; *synonyms* (*n*) array, presentation, appearance, screen, demonstration, exhibition, ostentation, scene, showing, spectacle, view, (*v*) parade, produce, brandish, flaunt, **11.** light; *synonyms* (*adj*) fair, facile, easy, faint, flimsy, (*n*) flame, brightness, daylight, illumination, dawn, (*v*) fire, kindle, inflame, glow, dismount; *antonyms* (*adj*) fattening, nauseating, (*n*) dark, darkness, gloom, shade, night, (*v*) extinguish, darken, (*alt sp*) heavy, **12.** manifest; *synonyms* (*adj*) apparent, evident, conspicuous, distinct, patent, plain, discernible, overt, marked, noticeable, transparent, bold, bright, (*n*) list, (*adv*) visible; *antonym* (*adj*) unclear, **13.** enlighten; *synonyms* (*v*) educate, notify, train, discipline; *antonym* (*v*) puzzle, **14.** exhibit; *synonyms* (*v*) perform, bear, manifest, offer, propound, develop, divulge, flash, proclaim, register, stage, confront, demo, (*n*) proof, **15.** present; *synonyms* (*adj*) grant, confer, current, (*n*) gift, donation, offering, (*v*) bestow, give, introduce, prefer, deliver, donate, gratuity, award, serve; *antonyms* (*adj*) missing, (*n*) past, future, history, (*v*) withdraw, (*adv*) absent, **16.** show; *synonyms* (*v*) broadcast, guide, figure, look, play, record, emerge, (*n*) pageant, picture, semblance, act, indication, performance, shew, sight; *antonym* (*v*) hide, **17.** represent; *synonyms* (*v*) depict, portray, be, embody, enact, make, impersonate, comprise, constitute, epitomize, personify, render, typify, form, correspond, **18.** reveal; *synonyms* (*v*) detect, uncover, find, publish, unearth, unfold, out, report, bewray, uncloak, ascertain, read, confide, descry, debunk; *antonym* (*v*) cover.

kaotabaea 1. idolize; *synonyms* (*v*) adore, worship, idolise, revere, admire, deify, glorify, **2.** cherish; *synonyms* (*v*) appreciate, entertain, foster, hug, nurture, treasure, cultivate, bosom, esteem, harbor, nourish, nurse, prize, bear, (*n*) embrace; *antonym* (*v*) hate, **3.** endear; *synonyms* (*v*) attract, enamor, dear, indear, (*adj*) attach, enrapture, fascinate, seduce, **4.** prize; *synonyms* (*n*) award, plunder, booty, premium, loot, price, trophy, honour, (*v*) cherish, honor, value, pry, evaluate, appraise, (*adj*)

choice, **5.** treasure; *synonyms* (*n*) gem, fortune, riches, funds, valuable, pearl, capital, treasury, valuables, wealth, (*v*) hoard, store, garner, (*adj*) jewel, bijou.

kaotabaeaki 1. idolized; *synonyms* (*adj*) idolised, adored, beloved, precious, worshipped, **2.** cherished; *synonyms* (*adj*) dear, loved, treasured, intimate, prized, valued, wanted, pet, **3.** treasured; *synonym* (*adj*) cherished.

kaotaki 1. demonstrated; *synonyms* (*adj*) confirmed, established, tried, verified, **2.** lighted; *synonyms* (*adj*) alight, illuminated, lit, ablaze, bright, airy, cheering, exhilarating, gay, lightsome, luminous, **3.** irradiated; *synonyms* (*adj*) exposed, irradiate, **4.** illuminated; *synonyms* (*adj*) lighted, enlightened, clear, brilliant, burning, intelligent, intelligible, **5.** enlightened; *synonyms* (*adj*) educated, liberal, disillusioned, progressive, aware, cultured, informed, learned, lettered, refined, (*v*) wise, savant, shrewd; *antonyms* (*adj*) mystified, puzzled, unenlightened, **6.** lit; *synonyms* (*n*) literature, (*adj*) drunk, intoxicated, tipsy, **7.** revealed; *synonyms* (*adj*) disclosed, discovered, open, naked; *antonym* (*adj*) hidden, **8.** presented; *synonyms* (*adj*) bestowed, conferred, offered, existing, accessible, obtainable, free, unfilled, untaken, vacant, **9.** represented; *synonyms* (*adj*) delineate, delineated.

kaotinakoa 1. eject; *synonyms* (*v*) discharge, dislodge, dismiss, displace, emit, evict, expel, banish, depose, empty, evacuate, spew, drop, ejaculate, disgorge, **2.** issue; *synonyms* (*n*) aftermath, egress, consequence, effect, event, exit, progeny, result, (*v*) flow, emanate, arise, emerge, release, gush, circulate.

kaotiota 1. represent; *synonyms* (*v*) depict, portray, act, be, describe, embody, exemplify, illustrate, play, enact, make, impersonate, comprise, constitute, (*adj*) express, **2.** profess; *synonyms* (*v*) assert, declare, feign, affirm, avow, claim, confess, pretend, protest, state, allege, aver, acknowledge, admit, affect, **3.** reveal; *synonyms* (*v*) disclose, divulge, expose, betray, convey, detect, discover, display, exhibit, impart, present, announce, communicate, indicate, show; *antonyms* (*v*) conceal, hide, cover.

kaotiotaki 1. represented; *synonyms* (*adj*) delineate, delineated, **2.** revealed; *synonyms* (*adj*) exposed, disclosed, discovered, open, naked; *antonym* (*adj*) hidden.

kaotioti 1. announce; *synonyms* (*v*) advertise, herald, declare, enunciate, proclaim, return, affirm, annunciate, broadcast, communicate, foretell, intimate, promulgate, publicize, publish, **2.** sermon; *synonyms* (*n*) discourse, lecture, oration, address, homily, speech, preachment, harangue, preaching, exhortation, predication, talk, delivery, disquisition, (v) lesson, **3**. testify; *synonyms* (v) attest, certify, evidence, protest, prove, demonstrate, manifest, express, show, vouch, indicate, assert, aver, tell, argue, **4**. witness; *synonyms* (n) spectator, testimony, bystander, eyewitness, onlooker, observer, testifier, beholder, proof, testify, (v) observe, notice, see, view, watch; *antonym* (n) participant, **5**. speak; *synonyms* (v) converse, pronounce, articulate, deliver, say, utter, recite, emit, mouth, state, vocalize, voice, mumble, prattle, declaim.

kaotiotiaki announced; *synonyms* (adj) proclaimed, spoken.

kaotirake raise; *synonyms* (v) boost, lift, erect, hoist, increase, build, elevate, enhance, foster, grow, promote, prefer, augment, cultivate, (n) advance; *antonym* (v) lower.

kaotirakeaki raised; *synonyms* (v) repousse, (adj) elevated, embossed, erect, convex, brocaded, high, alert, bold, confident, elate, elated, elative, exultant, (prep) above.

kaoura light; *synonyms* (adj) fair, clear, facile, easy, faint, flimsy, (n) flame, brightness, daylight, (v) fire, kindle, inflame, glow, ignite, dismount; *antonyms* (adj) fattening, nauseating, (n) dark, darkness, gloom, shade, night, (v) extinguish, darken, (alt sp) heavy.

kapanga penis; *synonyms* (n) member, phallus, appendage, extremity.

kapara detach; *synonyms* (v) disengage, divide, part, disconnect, disentangle, dissociate, remove, separate, unhook, isolate, abstract, cleave, disjoin, divorce, (n) detail; *antonyms* (v) attach, fasten, add, associate.

kara 1. abrade; *synonyms* (v) scrape, file, skin, chafe, rub, scour, graze, abrase, erode, gall, grate, grind, scratch, scrub, scuff, **2**. chase; *synonyms* (n) game, search, quest, (v) hunt, pursue, expel, follow, stalk, track, trail, chamfer, pursuit, race, seek, evict, **3**. carve; *synonyms* (v) sculpture, cut, mold, engrave, incise, inscribe, shape, whittle, slash, deal, divide, etch, forge, form, mangle, **4**. elderly; *synonyms* (adj) aged, old, elder, older, senior, antiquated, geriatric, ripened, antique, ancient, cured, matronly, declining, grave, mature; *antonym* (adj) young, **5**. graze; *synonyms* (v) browse, eat, brush, crease, crop, feed, pasture, rake, shave, fray, range, rasp, score, (n) touch, grazing, **6**. aged; *synonyms* (adj) senile, elderly, hoary, ripe, decrepit, venerable, **7**. scrape; *synonyms* (v) pare, mark, abrade, claw, squeak, dent, skimp, clean, scoop, (n) abrasion, predicament, difficulty, quagmire, dilemma, fix, **8**. pursue; *synonyms* (v) chase, dog, prosecute, course, haunt, hound, persist, tail, conduct, practice, court, keep, continue, engage, harass, **9**. scratch; *synonyms* (n) nick, scrabble, groove, scar,

furrow, excoriation, gash, line, rip, scraping, (v) notch, scrawl, tear, itch, (adj) bruise, **10**. old; *synonyms* (adj) obsolete, former, experienced, outdated, veteran, archaic, past, stale, disused, hackneyed, late, traditional, decayed, inveterate, auld; *antonyms* (adj) new, modern, fresh, latest, novel, original, youthful, **11**. peel; *synonyms* (n) hide, peeling, rind, scale, (v) hull, bark, flake, flay, decorticate, excoriate, husk, strip, disrobe, desquamate, slice.

karaba 1. conceal; *synonyms* (v) cover, disguise, hide, bury, cloak, mask, obscure, screen, shield, smother, suppress, cloud, ensconce, muffle, (n) veil; *antonyms* (v) reveal, show, expose, divulge, clarify, uncover, **2**. hold; *synonyms* (v) keep, detain, endure, adhere, bear, comprise, contain, entertain, have, arrest, carry, (n) grasp, grip, clasp, clutch; *antonym* (v) release, **3**. hide; *synonyms* (v) conceal, shelter, ambush, camouflage, dissemble, enshroud, envelop, (n) fur, coat, fell, skin, bark, fleece, pelt, (adj) darken; *antonym* (v) express, **4**. mask; *synonyms* (n) blind, guise, curtain, pretense, blanket, masque, facade, mantle, covering, pretext, shroud, (v) masquerade, dissimulate, feign, secrete; *antonym* (v) disclose, **5**. suppress; *synonyms* (v) repress, subdue, check, crush, curb, quell, restrain, silence, stifle, subjugate, strangle, control, inhibit, oppress, quash, **6**. seclude; *synonyms* (v) isolate, sequester, insulate, remove, separate, disengage, retreat, adjourn, attach, confiscate, crawfish, cushion, draw, impound, recall, **7**. reticent; *synonyms* (adj) reserved, quiet, restrained, close, distant, modest, retiring, shy, taciturn, uncommunicative, bashful, guarded, closemouthed, demure, inhibited, **8**. thank; *synonyms* (v) acknowledge, bless, remercy, kiss, praise, **9**. veil; *synonyms* (n) shade, film, garment, pall, gauze, caul, fog, shutter, (v) wrap, eclipse.

karababa 1. enlarge; *synonyms* (v) amplify, expand, aggrandize, augment, dilate, distend, elaborate, increase, widen, boost, broaden, develop, enhance, extend, grow; *antonyms* (v) reduce, shrink, contract, decrease, **2**. extend; *synonyms* (v) enlarge, continue, elongate, go, spread, carry, offer, contribute, advance, crane, cover, lengthen, proffer, project, (adj) stretch; *antonyms* (v) withdraw, shorten, limit, narrow, **3**. widen; *synonyms* (v) flare, thicken, impart, prolong.

karababaki 1. enlarged; *synonyms* (adj) exaggerated, extended, inflated, magnified, increased, puffy, augmented, amplified, distended, broad, clear, coarse, comprehensive, cross, dilated; *antonym* (adj) lesser, **2**. extended; *synonyms* (adj) expanded, ample, extensive, long, wide, elongated, enlarged, lengthened, lengthy, prolonged, protracted, open, continued, outstretched, spacious; *antonyms* (adj) brief, short, condensed, unextended.

karabakau 1. intellectual; *synonyms* (*adj*) cerebral, mental, rational, learned, spiritual, academic, ideal, cultured, brilliant, clever, (*n*) intellect, brain, scholar, thinker, mind, **2.** clever; *synonyms* (*adj*) adroit, capable, acute, able, apt, intelligent, smart, astute, cunning, expert, ingenious, quick, sharp, skillful, artful; *antonyms* (*adj*) stupid, clumsy, unintelligent, dim, dull, inept, **3.** slick; *synonyms* (*adj*) sleek, glib, crafty, foxy, glossy, silken, silky, smooth, dexterous, dodgy, greasy, oily, satiny, shiny, slippery, **4.** smart; *synonyms* (*adj*) bright, dapper, shrewd, sly, prompt, chic, jaunty, lively, natty, neat, saucy, fine, (*v*) ache, hurt, (*n*) pain; *antonyms* (*adj*) scruffy, shabby, unkempt, slow, **5.** sly; *synonyms* (*adj*) wily, furtive, secret, designing, arch, clandestine, deceitful, devious, guileful, insidious, scheming, slick, stealthy, tricky, canny; *antonyms* (*adj*) open, naive.

karabakaua boast; *synonyms* (*v*) bluster, vaunt, blow, brag, crow, gasconade, pride, rodomontade, exult, bounce, exaggerate, flourish, (*n*) arrogance, boasting, glory.

karabakauakina considered; *synonyms* (*adj*) deliberate, reasoned, intentional, premeditated, sensible, sound, willful, studied, calculated, planned, reputed, adult, careful, designed, exact; *antonyms* (*adj*) impulsive, sudden, impetuous, ingenuous, swift, thoughtless.

karabaki 1. held; *synonyms* (*adj*) absorbed, confined, alleged, assumed, believed, bound, caged, captive, detained, fast, immersed, obsessed, occupied, protected, (*adv*) on, **2.** masked; *synonyms* (*adj*) cloaked, disguised, covert, concealed, hidden, covered, camouflaged, **3.** concealed; *synonyms* (*adj*) clandestine, blind, buried, mysterious, obscure, occult, secret, invisible, secreted, surreptitious, underground, dark, latent, masked, privy; *antonyms* (*adj*) exposed, unconcealed, available, overt, **4.** covert; *synonyms* (*adj*) furtive, undercover, sly, secluded, stealthy, ulterior, (*n*) cover, concealment, covering, refuge, shelter, cloak, forest, (*v*) allusive; *antonym* (*adj*) open, **5.** secluded; *synonyms* (*adj*) private, remote, cloistered, isolated, lonely, reclusive, retired, sequestered, solitary, withdrawn, lone, quiet, close, distant, lonesome, **6.** veiled; *synonyms* (*adj*) unseen, cryptic, dusky, hazy, implicit, implied, masquerading, oblique, prophetic, roundabout, underlying, velate, shrouded, coded, hinted; *antonym* (*adj*) direct, **7.** suppressed; *synonyms* (*adj*) smothered, stifled, strangled, downtrodden, composed, doomed, dormant, embryonic, forgotten, muffled, pent-up, subconscious, unconscious, untold, (*n*) subordinate.

karabana 1. conceal; *synonyms* (*v*) cover, disguise, hide, bury, cloak, mask, obscure, screen, shield, smother, suppress, cloud, ensconce, muffle, (*n*) veil;

antonyms (*v*) reveal, show, expose, divulge, clarify, uncover, **2.** cover; *synonyms* (*v*) coat, conceal, top, wrap, comprise, bind, (*n*) blind, blanket, binding, camouflage, cap, covering, lid, spread, coating, **3.** hide; *synonyms* (*v*) shelter, ambush, dissemble, enshroud, envelop, shade, shroud, withhold, (*n*) fur, fell, skin, bark, fleece, pelt, (*adj*) darken; *antonym* (*v*) express.

karabanaki 1. covered; *synonyms* (*adj*) hidden, veiled, concealed, covert, coated, masked, obscured, secret, shrouded, thick, wrapped, (*prep*) cloaked; *antonyms* (*adj*) exposed, unconcealed, available, overt.

karabebe sloping; *synonyms* (*adj*) oblique, slanting, aslant, aslope, inclined, slanted, diagonal, leaning, sloped, slope, tilted, declivous, (*v*) slant, (*adv*) sideways; *antonym* (*adj*) level.

karabinobinoa roll; *synonyms* (*n*) list, revolution, catalogue, inventory, register, (*v*) coil, reel, curl, enfold, revolve, wheel, rock, turn, twist, wallow.

karabinobinoaki rolled; *synonyms* (*adj*) rolling, furled, involute, beaten, billowing, kinky, level, resonant, resonating, resounding, reverberating, reverberative, spiral, trilled, tumbling.

karae 1. zigzag; *synonyms* (*n*) ankle, astragal, crane, crotch, (*v*) meander, wind, bend, indirect, twist, crank, (*adj*) forked, furcated, meandering, winding, bifurcate; *antonym* (*adj*) straight, **2.** swerve; *synonyms* (*v*) deviate, depart, deflect, sheer, stray, turn, veer, wander, diverge, shift, digress, slew, swing, warp, (*n*) curve.

karaea 1. scatter; *synonyms* (*v*) disperse, dispel, disseminate, distribute, dissipate, spray, circulate, diffuse, disband, sprinkle, propagate, litter, rout, broadcast, (*n*) spread; *antonym* (*v*) gather, **2.** spread; *synonyms* (*v*) scatter, reach, expand, extend, increase, stretch, broaden, deploy, enlarge, dilate, (*n*) span, dissemination, expanse, expansion, feast; *antonym* (*adj*) concentrated, **3.** squint; *synonyms* (*n*) glance, look, strabismus, cast, (*v*) leer, skew, blink, squinch, (*adj*) askant, sidelong, askance, asquint.

karaeaki 1. spread; *synonyms* (*v*) scatter, reach, disperse, expand, extend, broadcast, circulate, diffuse, disseminate, increase, propagate, stretch, broaden, deploy, (*n*) span; *antonym* (*adj*) concentrated, **2.** scattered; *synonyms* (*adj*) dispersed, dissipated, confused, disconnected, disordered, sparse, sporadic, thin, distributed, rare, separate, spread, stray, strewn, disjointed.

karaia 1. fade; *synonyms* (*v*) disappear, decline, dissolve, evaporate, wither, die, discolor, droop, drop, languish, expire, decay, diminish, (*n*) disappearance, *(adj)* vanish; *antonyms (v)* grow, increase, strengthen, **2.** wind; *synonyms (n)* air, gust, *(v)* coil, twist, curl, meander, turn, bend, curve, twine, blow, crook, entwine, roll, weave, **3.** turn; *synonyms (v)* revolve, deviate, get, revolution, spin, become, *(n)* go, bout, change, round, bent, circle, shift, tour, bow, **4.** twist; *synonyms (n)* wind, twirl, braid, kink, loop, strain, tangle, *(v)* distort, contort, deform, pervert, wrench, pull, sprain, bias; *antonyms (v)* straighten, untwist, **5.** tangle; *synonyms (n)* snarl, maze, confusion, knot, *(v)* entangle, jumble, embroil, muddle, enmesh, embrangle, entrap, involve, mat, ravel, ruffle; *antonyms (n)* order, *(v)* disentangle, unravel, **6.** wither; *synonyms (v)* fade, shrink, wilt, contract, shrivel, dry, wane, waste, atrophy, blight, dwindle, sear, parch, flag, *(adj)* scorch; *antonym (v)* bloom.

karaiaki 1. faded; *synonyms (v)* dilapidated, stale, *(adj)* dim, pale, bleached, dull, exhausted, faint, washy, withered, attenuate, attenuated, colorless, discoloured, **2.** turned; *synonyms (adj)* off, sour, curved, rancid, twisted, altered, askew, awry, bent, bowed, cancelled, crooked, dark, deflected, dour, **3.** tangled; *synonyms (adj)* involved, complex, knotted, intricate, complicated, entangled, convoluted, knotty, difficult, disheveled, tousled, kinky, labyrinthine, muddled, perplexed; *antonym (adj)* free, **4.** withered; *synonyms (adj)* sere, wizened, sear, shriveled, shrunken, thin, dry, lean, parched, shrivelled, shrunk, wizen, *(v)* broken, lame, **5.** twisted; *synonyms (adj)* deformed, perverted, distorted, coiled, misshapen, contorted, twined, winding, wry, gnarled, tortuous, wrong, warped, depraved, malformed; *antonyms (adj)* straight, tidy.

karairaki 1. return; *synonyms (n)* yield, pay, recompense, refund, restitution, proceeds, income, *(v)* recur, reimburse, render, repay, restoration, restore, retort, answer; *antonyms (n)* departure, abolition, confiscation, recovery, *(v)* keep, **2.** revert; *synonyms (v)* return, lapse, relapse, regress, reverse, reflect, turn, meditate, recede, regrade, retreat, **3.** repeat; *synonyms (v)* recite, copy, recapitulate, reduplicate, rehearse, reiterate, double, duplicate, iterate, renew, reproduce, say, cite, multiply, echo, **4.** restore; *synonyms (v)* mend, refresh, reinstate, renovate, fix, rehabilitate, rejuvenate, replace, heal, reconstruct, recover, reestablish, refurbish, regenerate, *(adj)* repair.

karairakiaki 1. restored; *synonyms (adj)* fresh, comfortable, convalescent, healthy, new, **2.** repeated; *synonyms (adj)* continual, recurrent, frequent, persistent, double, habitual, chronic, common, continuous, perennial, perpetual; *antonym (adj)* intermittent.

karaka supplement; *synonyms (n)* accessory, annex, accompaniment, addendum, addition, adjunct, appendix, increment, continuation, appendage, appurtenance, *(v)* add, append, affix, *(adj)* complement; *antonym (v)* diminish.

karakara 1. hoarse; *synonyms (adj)* harsh, gruff, husky, grating, raucous, strident, guttural, rough, throaty, croaking, *(v)* coarse, hollow, sepulchral; *antonym (adj)* soft, **2.** harsh; *synonyms (adj)* sharp, austere, bitter, crude, cruel, discordant, grim, unkind, acrid, acute, biting, brutal, extreme, rigorous, *(v)* hard; *antonyms (adj)* smooth, gentle, harmonious, kind, lenient, pleasant, melodious, sweet, **3.** inclement; *synonyms (n)* rugged, *(adj)* bleak, boisterous, turbulent, wild, cold, keen, raw, rude, severe, stormy, unmerciful, unpitying, fresh; *antonyms (adj)* clement, mild, **4.** scrape; *synonyms (v)* scratch, graze, rub, pare, rake, grate, mark, abrade, chafe, grind, claw, engrave, *(n)* score, abrasion, predicament, **5.** rough; *synonyms (adj)* gross, hoarse, jagged, approximate, inclement, indelicate, rocky, uneven, impolite, robust, abrasive, bluff, blunt, boorish, *(n)* draft; *antonyms (adj)* polished, precise, refined, silky, sophisticated, even, exact, glossy, **6.** rasp; *synonyms (n)* rasping, *(v)* scrape, file, grater, groan, squeak, fray, screech, jar, scour, scrub, arrastra, gristmill, mill, **7.** raspy; *synonyms (adj)* gravelly, gravel, approximative, ballpark, croaky, dirt, fierce, graveled, noisy, pebbly, pugnacious, shingly, uncut, unsmooth.

karakaraka exaggerate; *synonyms (v)* boast, aggravate, amplify, dramatize, overdo, overdraw, enhance, enlarge, magnify, overstate, embellish, heighten, hyperbolize, increase, inflate; *antonyms (v)* understate, minimize.

karakarakaki exaggerated; *synonyms (adj)* enlarged, extravagant, theatrical, immoderate, hypertrophied, affected, excessive, hyperbolic, inflated, magnified, overdone, overstated, pretentious, melodramatic; *antonyms (adj)* understated, restrained.

karakarakea increase; *synonyms (n)* gain, addition, augmentation, boom, expansion, extension, *(v)* advance, accrue, extend, grow, aggrandize, expand, enhance, enlarge, *(adj)* augment; *antonyms (n)* reduction, contraction, decline, *(v)* decrease, reduce, diminish, drop, deteriorate.

karakarakeaki increased; *synonyms (adj)* additional, more, enlarged, greater, fresh, new, plus, puffy, ripe, amplified, better, bigger, improved, other, superior.

karakaraki scraped; *synonyms (adj)* abraded, scratched, frayed, hurt, raw, skinned, threadbare, worn, shabby, tattered.

karakarongorongo 1. exaggerate; *synonyms (v)* boast, aggravate, amplify, dramatize, overdo, overdraw, enhance, enlarge, magnify, overstate, embellish, heighten, hyperbolize, increase, inflate; *antonyms* (*v*) understate, minimize, **2.** exaggerated; *synonyms* (*adj*) enlarged, extravagant, theatrical, immoderate, hypertrophied, affected, excessive, hyperbolic, inflated, magnified, overdone, overstated, pretentious, melodramatic; *antonyms* (*adj*) understated, restrained.

karakarongorongoaki exaggerated; *synonyms* (*adj*) enlarged, extravagant, theatrical, immoderate, hypertrophied, affected, excessive, hyperbolic, inflated, magnified, overdone, overstated, pretentious, melodramatic; *antonyms* (*adj*) understated, restrained.

karakea 1. win; *synonyms* (*v*) acquire, gain, get, attain, obtain, conquer, achieve, earn, prevail, secure, take, succeed, carry, vanquish, (*n*) triumph; *antonyms* (*v*) lose, (*n*) defeat, **2.** won; *synonyms* (*v*) wan, (*n*) dwelling, wone.

karakeaki won; *synonyms* (*v*) wan, (*n*) dwelling, wone.

karaki 1. chased; *synonyms* (*adj*) engraved, (*n*) pursued, **2.** carved; *synonyms* (*adj*) carven, cut, incised, tipsy, (*v*) graven, fixed, imprinted, stamped, impressed, **3.** advance; *synonyms* (*n*) progress, improvement, (*v*) further, proceed, promote, approach, encourage, raise, rise, boost, contribute, cultivate, develop, forward, (*phr*) accelerate; *antonyms* (*n*) deterioration, (*v*) retreat, recede, delay, demote, regress, **4.** grazed; *synonyms* (*adj*) hurt, raw, **5.** hurry; *synonyms* (*n*) speed, haste, dispatch, flurry, celerity, (*v*) bustle, hasten, dash, expedite, scurry, fly, run, rush, zip, hie; *antonyms* (*n*) slowness, (*v*) dawdle, **6.** arrive; *synonyms* (*v*) come, mature, attain, fall, land, reach, succeed, show, derive, emerge, enter, get, happen, issue, (*n*) appear; *antonyms* (*v*) leave, depart, go, **7.** abraded; *synonyms* (*adj*) scraped, skinned, **8.** pursued; *synonym* (*n*) chased, **9.** scratched; *synonyms* (*adj*) abraded, dented, injured, sgraffito, spoiled, broken, smashed, **10.** scraped; *synonyms* (*adj*) scratched, frayed, threadbare, worn, shabby, tattered, **11.** peeled; *synonyms* (*adj*) naked, bare, bleak, crude, cutting, exposed, natural, new, nude, open, sore, unsanded.

karakiaki 1. hurried; *synonyms* (*adj*) hasty, fast, headlong, quick, rapid, speedy, sudden, swift, abrupt, cursory, careless, precipitate, prompt, rash, slapdash; *antonyms* (*adj*) slow, unhurried, leisurely, **2.** advanced; *synonyms* (*adj*) sophisticated, progressive, senior, higher, modern, new, precocious, late, cultured, developed, elevated, forward, liberal, ripe, superior; *antonyms* (*adj*) conservative, old-fashioned, inferior.

karakina 1. congregate; *synonyms* (*v*) collect, assemble, gather, concentrate, convene, meet,

crowd, amass, accumulate, compile, group, join, mass, muster, unite; *antonym* (*v*) disperse, **2.** huddle; *synonyms* (*n*) cluster, conference, meeting, discussion, clutter, disorder, (*v*) bunch, cower, crouch, flock, nestle, cuddle, stoop, snuggle, (*adj*) disarray, **3.** flock; *synonyms* (*n*) band, bevy, congregation, covey, gang, herd, horde, pack, troop, cloud, army, assembly, batch, (*v*) clump, (*adj*) swarm, **4.** narrate; *synonyms* (*v*) tell, relate, describe, recite, recount, report, express, inform, rehearse, state, detail, depict, explain, recapitulate, represent, **5.** gather; *synonyms* (*v*) deduce, congregate, garner, tuck, earn, rally, reap, derive, converge, extract, acquire, aggregate, conclude, crease, (*n*) fold; *antonym* (*v*) scatter, **6.** proportionate; *synonyms* (*adj*) commensurate, proportionable, proportional, equal, harmonious, comparable, balanced, adequate, appropriate, relative, sufficient, corresponding, equitable, (*n*) compatible, consistent, **7.** proportional; *synonyms* (*adj*) proportionate, symmetrical, even, graduated, **8.** recite; *synonyms* (*v*) enumerate, narrate, repeat, say, lecture, read, sing, cite, utter, announce, declare, deliver, pronounce, speak, (*n*) declaim, **9.** retail; *synonyms* (*adj*) commercial, (*v*) sell, issue, merchandise, trade, wholesale, vend, handle, market, (*n*) dispense, business, buying, exchange, export, import, **10.** relate; *synonyms* (*v*) connect, associate, link, appertain, apply, pertain, refer, concern, tie, affect, interrelate, convey, mention, involve, affiliate.

karakinaki 1. gathered; *synonyms* (*adj*) collected, deepened, accumulated, amassed, assembled, collective, congregate, equanimous, massed, poised, **2.** related; *synonyms* (*adj*) germane, kindred, cognate, relevant, similar, akin, allied, associated, collateral, connected, consanguineous, pertinent, like, near, analogous; *antonym* (*adj*) unrelated.

karako 1. minus; *synonyms* (*n*) negative, disadvantage, subtraction, (*v*) bereft, lack, bereaved, denuded, (*adj*) minor, less, lacking, deficient, lesser, short, (*adv*) without; *antonym* (*prep*) plus, **2.** less; *synonyms* (*adj*) inferior, wanting, lower, secondary, subordinate, minus; *antonyms* (*adv*) more, (*adj*) additional, **3.** little; *synonyms* (*adj*) small, diminutive, insignificant, brief, minute, petty, some, tiny, exiguous, light, baby, bantam, contemptible, (*v*) dash, bit; *antonyms* (*adj*) big, enormous, large, important, **4.** few; *synonyms* (*adj*) infrequent, rare, scarce, occasional, sporadic, uncommon, erratic, imperceptible, inconsequential, intermittent, middling, negligible, paltry, piddling, scattered; *antonyms* (*n*) plenty, (*adj*) many, countless, innumerable, various, **5.** meager; *synonyms* (*adj*) lean, emaciated, gaunt, feeble, inadequate, insufficient, spare, frugal, dry, jejune, measly, (*v*) bare, barren, lank, (*adv*) stingy;

antonyms (*adj*) abundant, generous, lavish, **6.** inferior; *synonyms* (*adj*) bad, humble, poor, cheap, junior, base, coarse, common, vulgar, ignoble, ordinary, second, shoddy, subaltern, (*prep*) below; *antonyms* (*adj*) better, choice, excellent, first-rate, high-class, premium, (*n*) superior, superscript, **7.** tiny; *synonyms* (*adj*) little, infinitesimal, midget, petite, puny, slight, teeny, miniature, trifling, trivial, cramped, stunted, (*phr*) minuscule; *antonyms* (*adj*) huge, gigantic, vast, **8.** scant; *synonyms* (*adj*) meager, scanty, skimpy, few, narrow, limited, slender, sparse, low, chary, parsimonious, (*v*) skimp, neglect, scrimp, stint, **9.** scarce; *synonyms* (*adj*) scant, exceptional, thin, unusual, (*adv*) just, barely, hardly, scarcely; *antonym* (*adj*) plentiful, **10.** sparse; *synonym* (*adj*) flimsy; *antonym* (*adj*) crowded, **11.** small; *synonyms* (*adj*) fine, remote, young, faint, modest, ungenerous, outside, lowly, mean, miserable, petit, diminished, microscopic, (*v*) frail, weak; *antonyms* (*adj*) bulky, colossal, considerable, extra-large, great, sizeable, giant, major.

karakoa 1. lower; *synonyms* (*adj*) debase, inferior, (*v*) degrade, diminish, frown, humble, dip, abase, cut, descend, drop, scowl, disgrace, decrease, (*n*) depress; *antonyms* (*v*) increase, raise, **2.** decrease; *synonyms* (*n*) decline, cutback, diminution, reduction, (*v*) abate, lessen, abridge, fall, curtail, lower, wane, contract, decay, detract, ebb; *antonyms* (*n*) growth, extension, (*v*) rise, grow, intensify, **3.** lessen; *synonyms* (*v*) allay, alleviate, assuage, dwindle, mitigate, moderate, depreciate, ease, impair, reduce, shorten, deduct, fade, lighten, minify; *antonym* (*v*) exacerbate, **4.** diminish; *synonyms* (*v*) belittle, retrench, shrink, deflate, narrow, qualify, recede, relieve, subside, weaken, break, dampen, taper, discount, flag, **5.** cut; *synonyms* (*v*) carve, chop, clip, abbreviate, bite, condense, crop, fashion, (*n*) notch, slice, cutting, nick, blow, gash, shape; *antonyms* (*v*) lengthen, (*n*) addition, **6.** curtail; *synonyms* (*v*) confine, curb, trim, dock, restrain, restrict, truncate, control, contain, slash, epitomize, limit, slow, check; *antonym* (*v*) extend, **7.** abbreviate; *synonyms* (*v*) abstract, compress, foreshorten, (*adj*) abbreviated; *antonym* (*v*) expand, **8.** shorten; *synonyms* (*v*) prune, summarize, bowdlerise, bowdlerize, expurgate, commute, concentrate.

karakoaea 1. abate; *synonyms* (*v*) subside, allay, bate, decline, diminish, fade, flag, lessen, relax, relieve, remit, slack, slake, wane, (*adj*) slacken; *antonym* (*v*) increase, **2.** allay; *synonyms* (*v*) assuage, abate, alleviate, calm, lay, mitigate, moderate, quell, quench, quiet, solace, (*n*) ease, (*adj*) still, appease, soothe.

karakoaki 1. decreased; *synonyms* (*adj*) reduced, dead, depleted, fallen, lower, short, degraded, prostrate, ruined, **2.** cut; *synonyms* (*v*) carve, chop, clip, abbreviate, abridge, bite, condense, crop, drop, fashion, (*n*) notch, slice, cutting, nick, blow; *antonyms* (*v*) increase, lengthen, (*n*) addition, extension, **3.** abbreviated; *synonyms* (*adj*) shortened, abridged, brief, condensed, truncated, compendious, edited, little, telescoped; *antonym* (*adj*) complete, **4.** lessened; *synonyms* (*adj*) diminished, atrophied, attenuate, attenuated, belittled, conical, corrupted, cut, debased, faded, hurt, pointed, tapering, vitiated, weakened, **5.** diminished; *synonyms* (*adj*) abated, lessened, active, airy, backward, blasted, bony, cadaverous, clipped, delicate, desolate, desolated, devastated, diminute, less, **6.** lowered; *synonyms* (*adj*) abased, bated, cheap, humbled, restrained, **7.** shortened; *synonyms* (*adj*) abbreviated, curtailed, down, emasculated, gashed, gelded, imperfect, mown, partial, runty, scarce, unfinished, deficient, slashed, split.

karamakina 1. foreshadow; *synonyms* (*v*) augur, betoken, bode, foretell, forebode, bespeak, foreshow, portend, prefigure, presage, prognosticate, signal, point, forecast, herald, **2.** indicate; *synonyms* (*v*) denote, direct, designate, imply, mark, show, foreshadow, argue, demonstrate, evince, exhibit, mean, suggest, express, finger, **3.** guess; *synonyms* (*v*) conjecture, surmise, believe, deem, divine, reckon, suppose, assume, calculate, feel, figure, gauge, (*n*) estimate, assumption, hypothesis, **4.** suppose; *synonyms* (*v*) guess, infer, consider, imagine, presume, speculate, conceive, expect, judge, regard, think, hope, fancy, count, anticipate, **5.** suspect; *synonyms* (*v*) doubt, distrust, mistrust, disbelieve, fear, query, question, (*adj*) fishy, questionable, shady, suspicious, dubious, funny, queer, doubtful; *antonyms* (*v*) trust, (*adj*) trustworthy, **6.** predict; *synonyms* (*v*) foresee, indicate, omen, prophesy, call, envision, announce, auspicate, envisage, soothsay, augurate, foreknow, promise.

karamakinaki 1. predicted; *synonyms* (*adj*) foretold, foreseen, **2.** suspected; *synonyms* (*adj*) suspect, supposed, distrusted, assumed, **3.** supposed; *synonyms* (*adj*) conjectural, alleged, hypothetical, reputed, imaginary, putative, apparent, ostensible, suppositional, professed, suppositious, supposititious, pretended, theoretical; *antonyms* (*adj*) real, actual.

karamwemmwe calm; *synonyms* (*adj*) quiet, peaceful, tranquil, (*v*) assuage, appease, cool, still, allay, pacify, easy, moderate, mollify, steady, (*n*) lull, equanimity; *antonyms* (*adj*) agitated, angry, nervous, stormy, wild, annoyed, anxious, enraged, frantic, frightened, intense, irritable, (v) agitate, upset, (n) agitation.

karan 1. lurk; *synonyms* (v) ambush, ambuscade, conceal, prowl, skulk, waylay, loiter, lurch, creep, slink, sneak, wait, bushwhack, linger, **2.** ambush; *synonyms* (n) trap, attack, (v) assault, intercept, catch, lurk, surprise, defeat, **3.** watch; *synonyms* (v) observe, clock, look, see, regard, wake, care, protect, defend, (n) guard, view, sentinel, sentry, surveillance, (adj) vigilance.

karanea 1. furbish; *synonyms* (v) buff, burnish, scour, shine, flush, gloss, rub, gild, grain, lacquer, paint, whitewash, file, dress, rehabilitate, **2.** file; *synonyms* (n) archive, document, list, procession, rank, record, roll, series, string, (v) order, rasp, register, scrape, abrade, arrange, **3.** dazzle; *synonyms* (n) sparkle, brightness, shimmer, (v) bedazzle, blind, flash, glare, awe, captivate, gleam, (adj) daze, confuse, bewilder, hoodwink, perplex, **4.** rub; *synonyms* (v) fray, grate, gall, chafe, caress, fret, furbish, graze, irritate, massage, scratch, wipe, (n) check, brush, hitch, **5.** polish; *synonyms* (n) finish, gentility, cultivation, elegance, refinement, civilization, culture, (v) glaze, civilize, clean, cultivate, grind, improve, perfect, refine, **6.** shine; *synonyms* (n) sheen, luster, radiance, (v) glow, light, blaze, glitter, excel, flame, glance, glisten, radiate, reflect, beam, flicker; *antonym* (n) dullness.

karaneaki 1. dazzled; *synonyms* (adj) dizzy, bewildered, fascinated, **2.** polished; *synonyms* (adj) elegant, courteous, cultured, finished, glossy, refined, civil, courtly, genteel, lustrous, polite, smooth, accomplished, graceful, bright; *antonyms* (adj) dull, rough.

karaneanea 1. glaze; *synonyms* (n) shine, coating, sheen, enamel, glazing, finish, gloss, luster, (v) burnish, glass, coat, varnish, calender, candy, **2.** gloss; *synonyms* (n) annotation, brightness, explanation, glossary, commentary, glossiness, note, (v) glaze, comment, annotate, veneer, color, rationalize, interpret, smooth; *antonym* (n) dullness, **3.** shine; *synonyms* (n) radiance, rub, (v) glow, light, gleam, blaze, flash, glitter, sparkle, excel, flame, glance, glisten, radiate, reflect, **4.** polish; *synonyms* (n) gentility, cultivation, elegance, refinement, civilization, culture, (v) furbish, civilize, clean, cultivate, grind, improve, perfect, refine, scour.

karaneaneaki 1. glazed; *synonyms* (adj) glassy, glossy, glassed, glazen, bright, burnished, dead, drunk, enameled, glassen, glasslike, shiny, slippery, varnished, glistening, **2.** polished; *synonyms* (adj) elegant, courteous, cultured, finished, refined, civil, courtly, genteel, lustrous, polite, smooth, accomplished, graceful, sleek, slick; *antonyms* (adj) dull, rough.

karaneboneboa 1. gloss; *synonyms* (n) burnish, annotation, brightness, shine, finish, explanation, glossary, sheen, commentary, (v) glaze, comment, annotate, veneer, color, varnish; *antonym* (n) dullness, **2.** glaze; *synonyms* (n) coating, enamel, glazing, gloss, luster, (v) glass, coat, calender, candy, **3.** polish; *synonyms* (n) gentility, cultivation, elegance, refinement, civilization, culture, (v) furbish, rub, civilize, clean, cultivate, grind, improve, perfect, refine, **4.** shine; *synonyms* (n) radiance, (v) glow, light, gleam, blaze, flash, glitter, sparkle, excel, flame, glance, glisten, radiate, reflect, beam, **5.** scour; *synonyms* (v) scrub, ransack, abrade, cleanse, flush, search, graze, buff, rake, hunt, rasp, scrape, scratch, (adj) mop, rinse.

karaneboneboaki 1. glazed; *synonyms* (adj) glassy, glossy, glassed, glazen, bright, burnished, dead, drunk, enameled, glassen, glasslike, shiny, slippery, varnished, glistening, **2.** scoured; *synonyms* (adj) eroded, worn, battered, craggy, gnarled, tough, weathered, windswept, wrinkled, lined, **3.** polished; *synonyms* (adj) elegant, courteous, cultured, finished, refined, civil, courtly, genteel, lustrous, polite, smooth, accomplished, graceful, sleek, slick; *antonyms* (adj) dull, rough.

karang falsify; *synonyms* (v) adulterate, counterfeit, garble, misrepresent, cook, distort, fake, forge, fudge, juggle, manipulate, twist, alter, doctor, (adv) belie; *antonym* (v) correct.

karanga 1. capsize; *synonyms* (adj) drown, shipwreck, swamp, (v) turn, upset, invert, overturn, reverse, topple, keel, subvert, tip, raze, sink, upend; *antonym* (v) right, **2.** pour; *synonyms* (v) gush, shed, decant, flow, pelt, scatter, stream, discharge, emit, jet, run, spill, teem, (n) overflow, rain; *antonym* (v) drizzle, **3.** overturn; *synonyms* (v) overthrow, capsize, overset, annul, destroy, overrule, nullify, cancel, defeat, demolish, invalidate, lift, overpower, ruin, (n) turnover; *antonym* (v) validate.

karangaki 1. overturned; *synonyms* (adj) upset, upturned, broken, confused, disordered, disquieted, distressed, disturbed, topsy-turvy, retrousse, worried; *antonym* (adj) upright, **2.** poured; *synonym* (adj) concrete.

karania waylay; *synonyms* (v) ambush, ambuscade, lurk, accost, besiege, bushwhack, harass, scupper.

karao 1. fix; *synonyms* (v) establish, assign, determine, fasten, settle, define, anchor, adjust, arrange, set, clamp, (n) bind, (adj) ascertain, confirm, attach; *antonyms* (v) break, unfasten, **2.** repair; *synonyms* (n) fix, overhaul, (v) remedy, mend, patch, redress, correct, cure, compensate, doctor, renovate, restore, heal, amend, go.

karaoa 1. frame; *synonyms* (n) design, border, build, fashion, anatomy, chassis, (v) form, construct, fabricate, draft, erect, make, forge, constitute, contrive, **2.** execute; *synonyms* (*v*) do, achieve, complete, perform, accomplish, act, effect, enforce, carry, consummate, discharge, dispatch, fulfill, practice, administer, **3.** fashion; *synonyms* (*n*) cut, mode, craze, fad, manner, method, way, custom, guise, style, wise, (*v*) cast, create, shape, compose, **4.** form; *synonyms* (*n*) figure, arrange, ceremony, class, conformation, appearance, frame, mould, type, (*v*) establish, carve, comprise, devise, generate, mold, **5.** do; *synonyms* (*v*) cheat, commit, conduct, defraud, answer, cause, execute, play, serve, be, (*n*) function, occasion, bash, (*adj*) suffice, avail; *antonyms* (*v*) neglect, unmake, **6.** act; *synonyms* (*n*) accomplishment, action, move, statute, decree, feat, law, (*v*) achievement, behave, deed, go, acquit, enact, feign, operate; *antonym* (*v*) refrain, **7.** commit; *synonyms* (*v*) commend, assign, charge, consign, apply, confide, dedicate, entrust, submit, deliver, devote, give, intrust, leave, send, **8.** make; *synonyms* (*v*) force, get, produce, let, compel, drive, fetch, gain, prepare, attain, bring, clear, earn, engender, (*n*) brand; *antonyms* (*v*) destroy, lose, **9.** effect; *synonyms* (*n*) consequence, product, result, sequel, aftermath, conclusion, impression, outgrowth, sense, core, corollary, (*v*) induce, use, win, implement; *antonym* (*n*) reason, **10.** made; *synonyms* (*adj*) finished, built, ready, constructed, formed, prepared, synthetic, bound, completed, ended, fictitious, rabid, through, **11.** negotiate; *synonyms* (*v*) bargain, treat, mediate, intercede, confer, discuss, arbitrate, trade, contract, manage, barter, consult, haggle, pass, settle, **12.** operate; *synonyms* (*v*) run, direct, employ, handle, proceed, work, maneuver, exercise, fly, control, engage, manipulate, manoeuvre, guide, influence, **13.** style; *synonyms* (*n*) name, kind, pattern, sort, designate, nature, panache, language, approach, chic, elegance, (*v*) call, entitle, denominate, (*adj*) character, **14.** perform; *synonyms* (*v*) appear, fill, comply, fulfil, keep, observe, perfect, represent, transact, declaim, display, portray, effectuate, obey, (*n*) manufacture.

karaoaki 1. framed; *synonyms* (*adj*) counterfeit, methodical, orderly, prepared, spurious, **2.** executed; *synonyms* (*v*) done, (*adj*) finished, fulfilled, complete, given, issued, **3.** fashioned; *synonyms* (*adj*) shaped, bent, featured, fictitious, wrought, created, produced, twisted, **4.** fixed; *synonyms* (*adj*) determined, definite, steady, constant, durable, certain, decided, determinate, established, fast, fastened, intent, permanent, (*v*) stable, (*adv*) firm; *antonyms* (*adj*) flexible, adaptable, adjustable, changeable, movable, separate, variable, compliant, loose, moveable, portable, removable, temporary, **5.** done; *synonyms* (*adj*) completed, over, gone, through, (*adv*) ended; *antonym* (*adj*) unfinished, **6.** made; *synonyms* (*adj*) built, ready,

constructed, formed, synthetic, bound, rabid, **7.** effected; *synonyms* (*adj*) accomplished, constituted, conventional, naturalized, realised, **8.** formed; *synonyms* (*adj*) settled, affected, characterized, conceived, defined, fashioned, adapted, adjusted, arranged, beaten, colonised, colonized, contrived, educated, formal, **9.** styled; *synonyms* (*v*) benempt, named, promised, vowed, **10.** repaired; *synonyms* (*adj*) fixed, reconditioned, maintained, flat, frozen, serviced, retained, rigid, set, **11.** wrought; *synonyms* (*adj*) molded, elaborated.

karaoakiaki wrought; *synonyms* (*adj*) molded, shaped, done, bent, created, elaborated, fashioned, produced, twisted.

karaoana 1. laborious; *synonyms* (*adj*) difficult, arduous, hard, backbreaking, diligent, heavy, industrious, grueling, assiduous, exhausting, formidable, painful, strenuous, tedious, toilsome; *antonym* (*adj*) easy, **2.** intricate; *synonyms* (*adj*) complex, complicated, involved, knotty, tricky, convoluted, elaborate, entangled, inextricable, obscure, tortuous, knotted, compound, dark, (*n*) composite; *antonyms* (*adj*) simple, straightforward.

karaoia 1. accomplish; *synonyms* (*v*) achieve, compass, do, perform, reach, attain, complete, execute, fulfill, make, perfect, realize, consummate, effect, finish, **2.** execute; *synonyms* (*v*) accomplish, act, enforce, carry, discharge, dispatch, practice, administer, commit, conduct, apply, effectuate, hang, kill, manage, **3.** commit; *synonyms* (*v*) commend, assign, charge, consign, confide, dedicate, entrust, submit, deliver, devote, give, intrust, leave, send, trust, **4.** act; *synonyms* (*n*) accomplishment, action, move, play, statute, decree, feat, law, (*v*) achievement, behave, deed, go, acquit, enact, feign; *antonym* (*v*) refrain.

karaoiaki 1. executed; *synonyms* (*v*) done, (*adj*) finished, fulfilled, complete, given, issued, **2.** accomplished; *synonyms* (*adj*) able, proficient, adept, completed, experienced, gifted, skillful, fine, capable, clever, competent, concluded, consummate, cultured, effected; *antonyms* (*adj*) inept, unfinished.

karaoiroia justify; *synonyms* (*v*) excuse, explain, absolve, confirm, defend, exonerate, vindicate, deserve, apologize, claim, exculpate, palliate, rationalize, exempt, (*n*) warrant.

karaoiroiaki justified; *synonyms* (*adj*) just, correct, proper, right, adopted, elected, due, righteous, regenerated, sanctified, unearthly, fair, acceptable, admirable, cogent; *antonym* (*adj*) unwarranted.

karaora craft; *synonyms* (*n*) boat, ability, art, cunning, trade, artfulness, guile, fraud, shift, artifice, business, deceit, job, occupation, profession.

karaoria run; *synonyms* (*v*) flow, rule, dash, gush, race, career, conduct, direct, function, go, (*n*) pass, campaign, course, drive, (*adj*) stream.

karaotua stake; *synonyms* (*n*) bet, chance, venture, post, wager, interest, shaft, adventure, column, deposit, (*v*) hazard, risk, gamble, back, gage.

karaou rain; *synonyms* (*n*) precipitation, wet, pelting, flow, rainfall, rainwater, abound, exuberate, mist, (*v*) pour, stream, hail, precipitate, shower, condense.

karapa hide; *synonyms* (*v*) conceal, disguise, obscure, bury, cloak, mask, shelter, (*n*) cover, fur, coat, fell, skin, veil, cloud, (*adj*) darken; *antonyms* (*v*) reveal, show, expose, express.

karara 1. cough; *synonyms* (*n*) coughing, sneeze, (*v*) choke, convulse, vomit, 2. croak; *synonyms* (*n*) croaking, (*v*) grumble, mutter, complain, conk, murmur, maunder, decease, die, expire, growl, perish, clamor, 3. cackle; *synonyms* (*n*) chuckle, laugh, laughter, yack, (*v*) giggle, snicker, chatter, crow, gaggle, chortle, snigger, squawk, titter, (*adj*) prate, prattle, 4. tilt; *synonyms* (*n*) slope, list, bend, inclination, joust, sway, (*v*) incline, lean, pitch, slant, careen, rock, cant, lurch, tip; *antonyms* (*v*) straighten, surrender.

kararaea rust; *synonyms* (*n*) decay, corrosion, (*v*) corrode, eat, tarnish, (*adj*) rusty.

kararaeaki rusted; *synonym* (*adj*) rusty.

kararaki tilted; *synonyms* (*adj*) canted, leaning, slanting, oblique, crooked, slanted, atilt, askew, intolerant, lopsided, opinionated, tipped, uneven, twisted; *antonym* (*adj*) straight.

kararaniman yawn; *synonyms* (*n*) yawning, nod, (*v*) gape, open, ope, yaw.

kararaoma disquieting; *synonyms* (*adj*) disconcerting, alarming, distressing, disturbing, troublesome, worrying, shocking, afflictive, amazing, arduous, astonishing, astounding, careful, difficult, frightening; *antonyms* (*adj*) reassuring, soothing.

kararati 1. filling; *synonyms* (*n*) fill, filler, weft, contents, loading, plug, pad, impletion, padding, stuffing, wadding, woof, 2. satisfying; *synonyms* (*adj*) pleasing, satisfactory, enjoyable, gratifying, pleasant, comforting, delightful, good, hearty, pleasurable, welcome, agreeable, comfortable, substantial, appreciated; *antonyms* (*adj*) unpleasant, unrewarding.

kararatia 1. gorge; *synonyms* (*n*) abyss, chasm, cleft, esophagus, ravine, canyon, (*v*) devour, glut, cram, fill, gobble, engorge, satiate, stuff, bolt; *antonyms* (*n*) hill, (*v*) nibble, fast, 2. saturate; *synonyms* (*v*) drench, imbue, infuse, charge, permeate, impregnate, sate, soak, steep, douse, infiltrate, imbrue, penetrate, (*adj*) wet, immerse, 3. satiate; *synonyms* (*v*) gorge, cloy, pall, satisfy, quench,

replete, slake, jam, fulfil, take, saturate, surfeit, (*adj*) satiated, 4. stretch; *synonyms* (*n*) extent, run, expanse, extension, range, (*v*) extend, reach, strain, elongate, lengthen, prolong, spread, draw, enlarge, broaden; *antonym* (*v*) shorten.

kararatiaki 1. gorged; *synonyms* (*adj*) satiated, sated, full, stuffed, bursting, congested, replete, satisfied, surfeited, glutted, 2. stretched; *synonyms* (*adj*) taut, extended, stiff, tense, tight, strained, expanded, outstretched, elongated, outspread, prolonged, protracted, assiduous, close, delayed; *antonym* (*adj*) brief, 3. saturated; *synonyms* (*adj*) drenched, sodden, wet, concentrated, soaked, sopping, soggy, soppy, pure, soaking; *antonym* (*adj*) dry, 4. satiated; *synonyms* (*adj*) satiate, jaded, blasé, corpulent, cropful, disgusted, fat, fleshed, initiated, sick; *antonym* (*adj*) hungry.

kararoa 1. hold; *synonyms* (*v*) keep, detain, endure, adhere, bear, comprise, contain, entertain, have, arrest, carry, (*n*) grasp, grip, clasp, clutch; *antonym* (*v*) release, 2. apart; *synonyms* (*adv*) aside, asunder, away, independently, individually, (*adj*) aloof, alone, distant, separate, detached, isolated, only, individual, loose, (*v*) discrete, 3. repel; *synonyms* (*v*) nauseate, disgust, revolt, rebuff, repulse, sicken, decline, displease, refuse, reject, parry, drive, oppose, rebut, dismiss; *antonyms* (*v*) attract, charm, draw.

kararoaki 1. held; *synonyms* (*adj*) absorbed, confined, alleged, assumed, believed, bound, caged, captive, detained, fast, immersed, obsessed, occupied, protected, (*adv*) on, 2. parted; *synonyms* (*adj*) cleft, divided, separate, distributed, disunited, dividable, divisible, devided.

karau 1. rain; *synonyms* (*n*) precipitation, wet, pelting, flow, rainfall, rainwater, abound, exuberate, mist, (*v*) pour, stream, hail, precipitate, shower, condense, 2. precipitate; *synonyms* (*v*) expedite, hurry, hasten, (*n*) deposit, accelerate, (*adj*) hasty, headlong, impetuous, sudden, immediate, instant, abrupt, hurried, precipitant, precipitous.

karaua 1. lull; *synonyms* (*n*) peace, rest, break, drop, (*v*) calm, quiet, hush, allay, pause, still, tranquilize, compose, (*adj*) appease, assuage, pacify; *antonym* (*v*) agitate, 2. pacify; *synonyms* (*v*) mollify, conciliate, placate, moderate, mitigate, reassure, gentle, reconcile, settle, (*n*) ease, alleviate, (*adj*) lull, soothe, quell, cool; *antonyms* (*v*) annoy, enrage, excite, infuriate, 3. quiet; *synonyms* (*adj*) motionless, peaceful, placid, tranquil, collected, composed, dull, harmonious, hushed, inactive, (*v*) silence, easy, repose, gag, (*n*) peacefulness; *antonyms* (*adj*) loud, noisy, talkative, vociferous, active, (*n*) noise, 4. still; *synonyms* (*adv*) however, but, nevertheless, yet, more, nonetheless, (*adj*) quiescent, serene, silent, mute, sedate, equable, immobile, noiseless, (v) even; *antonyms* (adj) moving, effervescent, fizzy, windy.

karauaka 1. content; *synonyms* (n) capacity, contentment, matter, meaning, subject, substance, contentedness, (adj) contented, happy, fulfilled, (v) appease, please, satisfy, suffice, delight; *antonyms* (adj) tormented, unhappy, discontented, dissatisfied, rebellious, (v) discontent, upset, **2**. satisfy; *synonyms* (v) content, fill, indulge, meet, persuade, sate, satiate, answer, assuage, convince, execute, fulfill, gratify, serve, (adj) do; *antonyms* (v) dissatisfy, disappoint, displease, intensify.

karauakaki 1. contented; *synonyms* (adj) content, comfortable, happy, cheerful, quiet, calm, complacent, delighted, easy, placid, pleased, proud, satisfied, smug; *antonyms* (adj) dissatisfied, discontented, unhappy, **2**. satisfied; *synonyms* (v) convinced, (adj) contented, full, certain, confident, sure, persuaded, fulfilled, sated, satiated, positive, quenched; *antonym* (adj) frustrated.

karaun fish; *synonyms* (n) bird, insect, mollusk, shellfish, worm, amphibian, beginner, blacktail, (v) angle, seek, hunt, pursue, grope, rummage, beg.

karaurau 1. gently; *synonyms* (adv) gradually, mildly, tenderly, soft, delicately, kindly, lightly, meekly, quietly, softly; *antonyms* (adv) abruptly, cruelly, fiercely, forcefully, harshly, severely, sharply, violently, intensely, roughly, **2**. moderately; *synonyms* (adv) fairly, pretty, reasonably, somewhat, partly, slightly, middling, partially, passably, quite, **3**. mindful; *synonyms* (adj) attentive, aware, careful, conscious, heedful, observant, considerate, cautious, cognizant, regardful, thoughtful; *antonyms* (adj) unaware, unmindful, **4**. beware; *synonyms* (v) mind, look, mistrust, consider, listen, worry, **5**. slow; *synonyms* (adj) dull, late, easy, sluggish, heavy, dense, dim, gradual, inactive, indolent, lazy, stupid, (v) slack, (adv) behind, behindhand; *antonyms* (adj) fast, intelligent, rapid, bright, alert, brisk, hasty, prompt, quick, speedy, hurried, rushed, (v) accelerate, **6**. slowly; *synonyms* (adv) tardily, deliberately, leisurely, unhurriedly, belatedly, hard, lethargically, (v) slow, (adj) lento, (adv, adj) piecemeal; *antonyms* (adv) quickly, hurriedly, immediately, promptly, rapidly, **7**. softly; *synonyms* (adv) gently, quiet, slowly, silently, light, piano; *antonyms* (adv) hoarsely, loudly, clearly.

karaurea sunder; *synonyms* (v) divide, part, separate, dissever, tear, share, cleave, detach, (n) sever, divorce, fragment.

karautaria shower; *synonyms* (n) rain, drizzle, barrage, rainfall, torrent, volley, (v) pour, bathe, hail, sprinkle, wash, shed, bath, scatter, spray.

karava 1. heaven; *synonyms* (n) paradise, bliss, glory, nirvana, sky, ecstasy, utopia; *antonym* (n) hell, **2**. sky; *synonyms* (n) air, heaven, atmosphere, heavens, space, (v) fling, flip, pitch, agitate, alternate, cant, chuck, convulse, deliver, discard.

karawawata 1. irritate; *synonyms* (v) chafe, fret, gall, incense, harass, aggravate, anger, annoy, bother, displease, enrage, goad, grate, infuriate, provoke; *antonyms* (v) soothe, pacify, please, **2**. chaff; *synonyms* (n) banter, husk, quiz, raillery, shuck, straw, (v) tease, jest, ridicule, badinage, joke, jolly, kid, mock, rally, **3**. harass; *synonyms* (v) afflict, distress, plague, badger, beset, bug, disturb, molest, persecute, pester, worry, distract, grind, besiege, (adj) tire, **4**. badger; *synonyms* (v) beleaguer, harry, hassle, hound, bait, heckle, importune, nag, torment, vex, intimidate, pursue, **5**. bother; *synonyms* (v) trouble, irk, irritate, bedevil, crucify, discommode, disquiet, (n) fuss, bore, pain, ado, annoyance, concern, nuisance, aggravation; *antonyms* (v) delight, (n) pleasure, **6**. nag; *synonyms* (n) hack, jade, horse, hackney, nagger, plug, (v) complain, gripe, scold, grouse, carp, (adj) bicker, wrangle, brangle, jangle, **7**. heckle; *synonyms* (v) hatchel, taunt, interrupt, (adj) hackle, **8**. disturb; *synonyms* (v) agitate, disconcert, disorder, perturb, commove, derange, disarrange, discompose, disrupt, upset, alarm, displace, embroil, fluster, ruffle; *antonyms* (v) arrange, calm, smooth, **9**. annoy; *synonyms* (v) rile, devil, exasperate, get, infest, madden, nettle, offend, rankle, hurt, haunt, embarrass, exercise, (adj) excite, incite, **10**. worry; *synonyms* (v) care, fear, mind, stress, perplex, oppress, (n) burden, sorrow, anxiety, apprehension, misgiving, vexation, load, unrest, irritation; *antonyms* (v) reassure, (n) calmness, reassurance, **11**. pester; *synonym* (v) rag, **12**. trouble; *synonyms* (n) difficulty, hardship, misfortune, problem, grief, disturbance, matter, adversity, (v) inconvenience, confuse, incommode, anguish, ail, disoblige, (adj) affliction, **13**. oppress; *synonyms* (v) press, pinch, depress, encumber, crush, repress, harrow, control, torture, bully, jam, overload, overpower, (adj) aggrieve, wrong.

karawawataki 1. irritated; *synonyms* (adj) angry, annoyed, exasperated, aggravated, enraged, furious, incensed, irate, displeased, inflamed, nettled, provoked, sore, disgruntled, infuriated; *antonyms* (adj) calm, unprovoked, pleased, **2**. chafed; *synonyms* (v) agitated, fretted, variegated, vexed, worried, (adj) galled, raw, uncomfortable, **3**. annoyed; *synonyms* (adj) irritated, angered, cross, offended, peeved, pestered, resentful, upset, dissatisfied, irritable, riled; *antonym* (adj) smiling, **4**. bothered; *synonyms* (adj) disturbed, troubled, concerned, distraught, nervous, uneasy, **5**.

disturbed; *synonyms* *(adj)* anxious, confused, disquieted, restless, disordered, bothered, deranged, disconcerted, distracted, distressed, tumultuous, turbulent, unsettled, unbalanced, mad; *antonyms* *(adj)* rational, relaxed, **6.** harassed; *synonyms* *(adj)* beleaguered, drawn, harried, hurried, obsessed, stressed, besieged, careworn, fraught, frazzled, hassled, miffed, pissed, roiled, steamed, **7.** oppressed; *synonyms* *(adj)* downtrodden, laden, persecuted, broken, burdened, aggrieved, browbeaten, despairing, downcast, forlorn, gloomy, haggard, heavy, ladened, loaded, **8.** troubled; *synonyms* *(adj)* solicitous, apprehensive, perturbed, disruptive, doubtful, riotous, unhappy; *antonyms* *(adj)* untroubled, composed, unconcerned, **9.** pestered; *synonyms* *(adj)* harassed, stung, **10.** worried; *synonyms* *(adj)* afraid, fearful, alarmed, fretful, tense, *(v)* afflicted, frightened, pained; *antonyms* *(adj)* carefree, reassured.

kare 1. fling; *synonyms* *(n)* throw, crack, hurl, go, heave, *(v)* cast, toss, chuck, dash, pitch, shoot, discard, rush, slam, break; *antonym* *(v)* catch, **2.** hurl; *synonyms* *(v)* fling, dart, pelt, send, drop, bowl, fire, hurtle, launch, precipitate, project, vomit, drive, flip, *(n)* casting, **3.** hit; *synonyms* *(v)* strike, attain, belt, blow, bump, collide, encounter, *(n)* knock, bang, smash, touch, chance, bash, beat, collision; *antonyms* *(n)* failure, flop, **4.** dash; *synonyms* *(n)* sprint, animation, bit, bolt, line, splash, tinge, energy, *(v)* charge, crash, hurry, jog, race, run, blast; *antonym* *(n)* lethargy, **5.** shy; *synonyms* *(adj)* diffident, fearful, timid, abashed, reserved, ashamed, coy, modest, nervous, reticent, self-conscious, backward, careful, bashful, *(n)* flinch; *antonyms* *(adj)* brash, bold, confident, demonstrative, forward, outgoing, **6.** thrown; *synonyms* *(adj)* confused, puzzled, addled, baffled, bewildered, confounded, disconcerted, distraught, dumbfounded, frightened, mystified, terrified, unnerved, unsettled, *(n)* reminder, **7.** throw; *synonyms* *(v)* shed, pass, deliver, give, jerk, make, bewilder, dumbfound, mystify, nonplus, amaze, *(n)* push, shot, shy, stroke, **8.** pitch; *synonyms* *(n)* degree, dip, slant, slope, measure, angle, delivery, grade, gradient, height, *(v)* lurch, tilt, careen, erect, fall, **9.** reject; *synonyms* *(v)* refuse, decline, deny, disapprove, dismiss, eliminate, exclude, rebuff, abandon, disallow, disown, ignore, renounce, repel, *(n)* cull; *antonyms* *(v)* accept, approve, choose, select, acknowledge, grant.

karea sacrifice; *synonyms* *(n)* immolation, loss, forfeiture, *(v)* offering, oblation, forfeit, immolate, offer, give, lose, relinquish, grant, propose, contribute, present.

kareaki 1. hit; *synonyms* *(v)* strike, attain, belt, blow, bump, collide, encounter, *(n)* knock, bang, smash,

touch, chance, bash, beat, collision; *antonyms* *(n)* failure, flop, **2.** dashed; *synonyms* *(v)* abashed, ashamed, sunk, *(adj)* dejected, discouraged, dotted, flecked, specked, speckled, stippled, **3.** pitched; *synonyms* *(v)* determined, fixed, pight, *(adj)* inclined, oblique, leaning, slanting, **4.** thrown; *synonyms* *(adj)* confused, puzzled, addled, baffled, bewildered, confounded, disconcerted, distraught, dumbfounded, fearful, frightened, mystified, terrified, unnerved, *(n)* reminder, **5.** rejected; *synonyms* *(v)* forsaken, *(adj)* castaway, jilted, refused, reprobate, abandoned, disallowed, refuse, bare, cheerless, consume, depraved, desolate, destroy, devastate.

karean sacrifice; *synonyms* *(n)* immolation, loss, forfeiture, *(v)* offering, oblation, forfeit, immolate, offer, give, lose, relinquish, grant, propose, contribute, present.

kareao 1. joke; *synonyms* *(n)* jest, banter, hoax, fun, caper, gag, game, quip, antic, farce, humor, jape, jocularity, pleasantry, *(v)* chaff; *antonym* *(n)* tragedy, **2.** exaggerate; *synonyms* *(v)* boast, aggravate, amplify, dramatize, overdo, overdraw, enhance, enlarge, magnify, overstate, embellish, heighten, hyperbolize, increase, inflate; *antonyms* *(v)* understate, minimize, **3.** chaff; *synonyms* *(n)* husk, quiz, raillery, shuck, straw, *(v)* tease, ridicule, badinage, joke, jolly, kid, mock, rally, **4.** jeer; *synonyms* *(v)* deride, hiss, taunt, barrack, insult, sneer, tantalize, *(n)* gibe, flout, scoff, mockery, boo, derision, hoot, scorn; *antonym* *(v)* cheer, **5.** jest; *synonyms* *(n)* pun, crack, laugh, play, sport, trick, wheeze, wit, witticism, yak, parody, *(v)* gird, jeer, clown, bourd, **6.** josh.

kareaoaki exaggerated; *synonyms* *(adj)* enlarged, extravagant, theatrical, immoderate, hypertrophied, affected, excessive, hyperbolic, inflated, magnified, overdone, overstated, pretentious, melodramatic; *antonyms* *(adj)* understated, restrained.

karebenakoa 1. displace; *synonyms* *(v)* dislocate, dislodge, dismiss, bump, depose, remove, shift, uproot, cashier, discharge, disturb, eject, evacuate, expel, move; *antonym* *(v)* replace, **2.** dislocate; *synonyms* *(v)* displace, disjoint, muddle, wrench, transfer, jumble, disorder, disorganize, slip, splay, unhinge, upset, dismember, **3.** disjoint; *synonyms* *(v)* disarticulate, disjoin, separate, part, dissociate, disunite, divorce.

karebenakoaki 1. disjointed; *synonyms* *(adj)* disconnected, incoherent, confused, broken, split, dislocated, rambling, unconnected, disordered, fragmentary; *antonyms* *(adj)* coherent, jointed, united, **2.** dislocated; *synonyms* *(adj)* disjointed, dislocate, disorderly, detached, separated, topsy-turvy, garbled, illogical, isolated, scattered, separate, spaced.

karebo 1. babble; *synonyms* (*n*) drivel, burble, gibberish, (*v*) murmur, chat, gab, gossip, ripple, talk, blab, blather, bubble, chatter, guggle, gurgle; *antonyms* (*v*) quietness, silence, stillness, **2**. intrude; *synonyms* (*v*) interfere, encroach, impose, infringe, trespass, disturb, impinge, interrupt, obtrude, disrupt, transgress, enter, interlope, interpose, invade, **3**. ramble; *synonyms* (*n*) journey, stroll, excursion, hike, promenade, walk, amble, (*v*) meander, roam, saunter, wander, range, rove, tramp, digress.

karebun 1. abundant; *synonyms* (*adj*) copious, generous, lush, luxuriant, thick, plenty, affluent, ample, fertile, fruitful, liberal, plentiful, prolific, rich, substantial; *antonyms* (*adj*) scarce, sparse, meager, **2**. infinite; *synonyms* (*adj*) absolute, boundless, countless, endless, eternal, immense, incalculable, immeasurable, innumerable, everlasting, enormous, illimitable, indefinite, multitudinous, myriad; *antonyms* (*adj*) finite, limited, restricted, **3**. abounding; *synonyms* (*adj*) abundant, full, rife, replete, wealthy; *antonym* (*adj*) lacking, **4**. swarming; *synonyms* (*v*) dense, serried, (*adj*) teeming, alive, crowded, packed, populous; *antonym* (*adj*) empty, **5**. promiscuous; *synonyms* (*adj*) indiscriminate, miscellaneous, mixed, random, confused, loose, wanton, disorderly, licentious, easy, light, **6**. numerous; *synonyms* (*adj*) manifold, many, frequent, multiple, great, several, various, common, numberless, different; *antonym* (*adj*) few.

karebutia 1. chase; *synonyms* (*n*) game, search, quest, (*v*) hunt, pursue, expel, follow, stalk, track, trail, chamfer, pursuit, race, seek, evict, **2**. expel; *synonyms* (*v*) banish, dismiss, eject, exclude, exile, eliminate, deport, discharge, dispossess, excrete, chase, discard, emit, expatriate, empty, **3**. repel; *synonyms* (*v*) nauseate, disgust, revolt, rebuff, repulse, sicken, decline, displease, refuse, reject, parry, drive, oppose, rebut, combat; *antonyms* (*v*) attract, charm, draw, **4**. push; *synonyms* (*n*) press, thrust, jolt, poke, elbow, (*v*) impel, crowd, force, jab, jostle, nudge, prod, jam, rush, boost; *antonyms* (*v*) pull, drag, haul.

karebutiaki chased; *synonyms* (*adj*) engraved, (*n*) pursued.

karebwe rap; *synonyms* (*n*) hit, blow, bang, bump, cuff, pat, strike, whack, knocking, (*v*) knock, tap, blame, chat, knap, beat.

karebwea knock; *synonyms* (*v*) hit, blow, bump, cuff, punch, strike, boot, clip, (*n*) rap, bang, tap, bash, crash, whack, clap; *antonym* (*v*) praise.

karebwerebwe 1. knock; *synonyms* (*v*) hit, blow, bump, cuff, punch, strike, boot, clip, (*n*) rap, bang, tap, bash, crash, whack, clap; *antonym* (*v*) praise, **2**. tap; *synonyms* (*n*) pat, dab, stroke, touch, faucet, hydrant, plug, slap, spigot, (*v*) knock, broach, bug, beat, eavesdrop, exploit, **3**. pop; *synonyms* (*n*) dad, daddy, father, pa, papa, shot, click, (*v*) burst, crack, shoot, protrude, pawn, appear, place, (*adv*) plump.

karebwerebweaki tapped; *synonyms* (*adj*) helpless, poor, powerless.

karebwetata crackle; *synonyms* (*n*) crackling, crepitation, (*v*) crack, crepitate, crunch, rustle, snap, sputter.

karebwetataki crackled; *synonyms* (*adj*) cracked, alligatored, balmy, barmy, bats, batty, bonkers, buggy, chapped, crackers, crazed, daft, deranged, dotty, fruity.

kareio joke; *synonyms* (*n*) jest, banter, hoax, fun, caper, gag, game, quip, antic, farce, humor, jape, jocularity, pleasantry, (*v*) chaff; *antonym* (*n*) tragedy.

kareite proud; *synonyms* (*adj*) arrogant, dignified, disdainful, haughty, lofty, exalted, conceited, egotistical, gallant, lordly, majestic, overbearing, pompous, imperious, elated; *antonyms* (*adj*) humble, modest, ashamed, embarrassed.

karekanano 1. captive; *synonyms* (*adj*) confined, imprisoned, rapt, amoroso, jailed, (*n*) prisoner, convict, slave, detainee, caitiff; *antonym* (*adj*) free, **2**. charismatic; *synonyms* (*adj*) magnetic, attractive, charming, glamorous, magical, alluring, amiable, appealing, captivating, compelling, delightful, dynamic, enchanting, fascinating, interesting, **3**. attractive; *synonyms* (*adj*) engaging, good-looking, tempting, adorable, gorgeous, handsome, inviting, lovable, lovely, pleasing, prepossessing, seductive, striking, sweet, dainty; *antonyms* (*adj*) unattractive, ugly, unappealing, disgusting, repellent, revolting, repulsive, straight, unpleasant, **4**. charming; *synonyms* (*adj*) beautiful, winning, nice, agreeable, amusing, bewitching, cute, delectable, exquisite, magic, pleasant, pretty, wizard, likable, delicious, **5**. seductive; *synonyms* (*adj*) enticing, seducing, desirable, sexy, irresistible, persuasive.

karekare 1. pitch; *synonyms* (*n*) degree, dip, slant, slope, (*v*) fling, cast, chuck, lurch, tilt, toss, heave, hurl, throw, careen, launch, **2**. throw; *synonyms* (*v*) shed, flip, pass, deliver, drop, give, hurtle, jerk, make, project, bewilder, (*n*) pitch, push, shot, shy.

karekareaki 1. pitched; *synonyms* (*v*) determined, fixed, pight, (*adj*) inclined, oblique, leaning, slanting, **2**. thrown; *synonyms* (*adj*) confused, puzzled, addled, baffled, bewildered, confounded, disconcerted, distraught, dumbfounded, fearful, frightened, mystified, terrified, unnerved, (*n*) reminder.

kareke 1. irregularly; *synonyms* (*adv*) erratically, abnormally, sporadically, unevenly, occasionally, fitfully, illegally, arbitrarily, asymmetrically, chaotically, confusedly, crookedly, dishonestly, disorderly, haphazardly; *antonym* (*adv*) regularly, **2**. charming; *synonyms* (*adj*) amiable, beautiful, attractive, captivating, delightful, enchanting, lovely, pleasing, winning, nice, adorable, agreeable, alluring, amusing, appealing; *antonyms* (*adj*) repellent, unappealing, unpleasant, **3**. infrequently; *synonyms* (*adv*) rarely, uncommonly, hardly, unfrequently, unoften, sometimes, intermittently, irregularly, off-and-on, scarcely, periodically; *antonym* (*adv*) frequently, **4**. fascinating; *synonyms* (*adj*) charming, absorbing, engaging, engrossing, bewitching, seductive, desirable, enthralling, entrancing, fetching, gripping, magnetic, riveting, tempting, (*v*) interesting; *antonyms* (*adj*) boring, uninteresting, dull, **5**. rarely; *synonyms* (*adv*) seldom, infrequently, unusually, little, exceptionally; *antonyms* (*adv*) often, usually, **6**. sometimes; *synonyms* (*adv*) once, formerly, sometime, otherwhiles, consistently, constantly, recurrently, (*n*) exemplar, meantime, meanwhile, specimen, (*adj*) former.

karekea 1. gain; *synonyms* (*v*) acquire, benefit, derive, attain, catch, earn, get, win, achieve, advance, make, (*n*) profit, earnings, acquisition, advantage; *antonyms* (*v*) lose, (*n*) loss, **2**. achieve; *synonyms* (*v*) accomplish, reach, complete, do, effect, execute, gain, perform, act, fulfill, manage, obtain, secure, strike, conclude, **3**. have; *synonyms* (*v*) contain, bear, carry, hold, possess, accept, eat, suffer, take, allow, bring, conduct, consume, embrace, find, **4**. inspect; *synonyms* (*v*) examine, overhaul, overlook, survey, explore, inquire, look, review, scrutinize, view, watch, monitor, analyze, audit, check, **5**. implement; *synonyms* (*v*) fulfil, apply, enforce, discharge, realize, (*n*) tool, apparatus, utensil, appliance, device, instrument, gadget, organ, contrivance, machine, **6**. contrive; *synonyms* (*v*) plan, concoct, design, invent, cast, concert, devise, excogitate, fabricate, formulate, frame, compose, conceive, conspire, construct, **7**. acquire; *synonyms* (*v*) buy, collect, contract, purchase, receive, assume, develop, harvest, have, accumulate, garner, adopt, conquer, form, gather; *antonym* (*v*) sell, **8**. get; *synonyms* (*v*) become, come, fall, fetch, beget, capture, cause, engage, extract, apprehend, contrive, arrest, comprehend, convey, draw; *antonyms* (*v*) give, leave, **9**. obtain; *synonyms* (*v*) prevail, procure, extort, compass, enlist, incur, reap, stand, can, raise, be, exist, keep, (*n*) breathe, live, **10**. ponder; *synonyms* (*v*) contemplate, consider, meditate, muse, cogitate, deliberate, reflect, think, mull, study, brood, chew, imagine, ruminate, speculate, **11**. receive; *synonyms* (*v*) admit, welcome, acknowledge, greet, hear, own, entertain, include, absorb, deliver, encounter, experience, grasp, imbibe, ingest, **12**.

scour; *synonyms* (*v*) rub, scrub, ransack, burnish, abrade, cleanse, flush, furbish, search, graze, buff, rake, hunt, clean, (*adj*) mop, **13**. procure; *synonyms* (*v*) induce, book, solicit, cater, pander, pimp, provide, seize, choose, employ, hire, recruit, **14**. own; *synonyms* (*v*) concede, grant, confess, avow, enjoy, occupy, recognize, retain, profess, master, control, (*adj*) individual, proper, private, personal, **15**. secure; *synonyms* (*v*) close, fix, preserve, fasten, assure, ensure, fast, guarantee, guard, (*adj*) safe, firm, certain, confident, attach, bind; *antonyms* (*v*) detach, (*adj*) insecure, vulnerable, loose, unsafe.

karekeaki 1. contrived; *synonyms* (*adj*) artificial, affected, unnatural, false, forced, labored; *antonym* (*adj*) natural, **2**. implemented; *synonyms* (*adj*) enforced, fitted, **3**. acquired; *synonyms* (*v*) acquiring, (*adj*) acquisite, acquisitive, derivative, extrinsic, **4**. owned; *synonyms* (*v*) behoove, ought, owed, (*adj*) own, proprietary, **5**. received; *synonyms* (*v*) receiving, ascertained, current, recognized, (*adj*) accepted, acknowledged, conventional, acceptable, canonical, orthodox, customary, established, inward, known, legitimate, **6**. scoured; *synonyms* (*adj*) eroded, worn, battered, craggy, gnarled, tough, weathered, windswept, wrinkled, lined, **7**. secured; *synonyms* (*adj*) guaranteed, protected, barred, bolted, bonded, fast, firm, latched, locked.

karekei 1. display; *synonyms* (*n*) array, presentation, appearance, screen, demonstration, exhibition, (*v*) exhibit, show, disclose, parade, expose, produce, brandish, flaunt, indicate; *antonym* (*v*) conceal, **2**. show; *synonyms* (*v*) present, broadcast, guide, demonstrate, evidence, give, manifest, perform, prove, reveal, (*n*) display, ostentation, pageant, picture, semblance; *antonyms* (*v*) disprove, hide.

karekenano 1. captivate; *synonyms* (*v*) attract, charm, allure, bewitch, enchant, enamor, engage, engross, hypnotize, lure, seduce, take, (*adj*) fascinate, (*n*) entice, tempt, **2**. charm; *synonyms* (*n*) amulet, appeal, spell, attraction, conjure, incantation, attractiveness, beauty, (*v*) captivate, entrance, beguile, capture, please, amuse, catch; *antonyms* (*n*) repulsion, ugliness, (*v*) repel, **3**. seduce; *synonyms* (*v*) decoy, inveigle, persuade, coax, defile, solicit, invite, deprave, induce, entrap, pervert, mislead, wheedle, (*adj*) debauch, attach.

karekenanoaki 1. captivated; *synonyms* (*adj*) fascinated, charmed, spellbound, absorbed, beguiled, delighted, enamored, engrossed, enthralled, rapt, **2**. charmed; *synonyms* (*adj*) captivated, enchanted, entranced, captive.

karekereke 1. catchy; *synonyms* (*adj*) tricky, fitful, memorable, arty, deceptive, misleading, treacherous, addictive, crafty, dodgy, foxy, guileful, haunting, knavish, popular, **2**. course; *synonyms*

(n) stream, flow, bearing, career, current, path, road, route, track, channel, circuit, class, method, (v) run, chase, **3**. bristly; *synonyms* (adj) barbed, prickly, thorny, rough, spiny, hairy, setaceous, stiff, barbellate, briary, briery, bristled; *antonym* (adj) smooth, **4**. rugose; *synonyms* (adj) rugged, rugous, **5**. rough; *synonyms* (adj) coarse, hard, harsh, raw, crude, cruel, grating, gross, hoarse, jagged, approximate, gruff, inclement, (n) boisterous, draft; *antonyms* (adj) gentle, polished, precise, refined, silky, soft, sophisticated, even, exact, glossy, pleasant.

karekeria 1. appetizing; *synonyms* (adj) appetising, delectable, delicious, luscious, tasty, tantalizing, palatable, savory, scrumptious, spicy; *antonyms* (adj) tasteless, unappetizing, **2**. tasty; *synonyms* (adj) tasteful, appetizing, dainty, nice, savoury, rich, flavorful, appreciate, criticise, cute, edible, judge; *antonyms* (adj) bland, inedible.

kareketara stare; *synonyms* (v) gaze, look, gape, glare, peer, squint, goggle, see, view, watch, leer, (n) regard.

kareketata obstruct; *synonyms* (v) bar, block, check, choke, clog, delay, encumber, hamper, impede, screen, intercept, debar, arrest, (n) hinder, barricade; *antonyms* (v) encourage, facilitate, free.

kareketataki obstructed; *synonyms* (adj) hindered, blind, blocked, congested, foiled, frustrated, impedite, stymied, thwarted, tight; *antonym* (adj) successful.

kareketatia retard; *synonyms* (v) delay, check, hinder, arrest, detain, impede, lag, obstruct, slow, decelerate, procrastinate, curb, prevent, (n) defer, (adj) deaden; *antonym* (v) accelerate.

kareketatiaki retarded; *synonyms* (adj) backward, slow, tardy, imbecile, defective, deferred, dull, half-baked, leisurely, obtuse, simple, birdbrained, dim, dim-witted, dopey.

karemaku cover; *synonyms* (v) coat, conceal, top, bury, cloak, (n) blind, blanket, screen, binding, camouflage, cap, covering, lid, mask, shield; *antonyms* (v) reveal, expose, uncover.

karemakuaki covered; *synonyms* (adj) hidden, veiled, concealed, covert, coated, masked, obscured, secret, shrouded, thick, wrapped, (prep) cloaked; *antonyms* (adj) bare, naked.

karemaranga 1. scarce; *synonyms* (adj) rare, insufficient, deficient, infrequent, scant, scanty, uncommon, few, inadequate, sparse, slender, lacking, (adv) just, barely, hardly; *antonyms* (adj) abundant, plentiful, **2**. scattered; *synonyms* (adj) dispersed, dissipated, confused, disconnected, disordered, sporadic, thin, diffuse, distributed, separate, spread, stray, strewn, disjointed, disorderly; *antonym* (adj) concentrated.

karemea 1. narrow; *synonyms* (adj) close, limited, insular, little, cramped, illiberal, mean, (v) confined, contract, limit, lessen, constrict, shrink, abridge, dwindle; *antonyms* (adj) wide, broad, comprehensive, extensive, (v) widen, extend, **2**. induct; *synonyms* (v) install, inaugurate, initiate, invest, instate, introduce, seat, call, crown.

karemeaki narrowed; *synonyms* (adj) angustate, conical, lessened, pointed, tapering.

karemereme 1. inconvenience; *synonyms* (n) bother, disadvantage, difficulty, nuisance, awkwardness, unsuitableness, encumbrance, ineptness, (v) trouble, discommode, incommode, disoblige, annoy, disquiet, disturb; *antonym* (n) convenience, **2**. meddle; *synonyms* (v) tamper, interfere, intervene, intrude, fiddle, monkey, pry, **3**. intrude; *synonyms* (v) encroach, impose, infringe, trespass, impinge, interrupt, obtrude, disrupt, transgress, enter, interlope, interpose, invade, irrupt, meddle, **4**. interfere; *synonyms* (v) intercede, obstruct, conflict, clash, hinder, impede, contravene, jar, mediate, make, (adj) intermeddle.

karemrem accumulate; *synonyms* (v) amass, collect, gather, pile, store, accrue, assemble, compile, cumulate, heap, hoard, drift, add, aggregate, concentrate; *antonyms* (v) disperse, distribute, dwindle.

karemremaki accumulated; *synonyms* (adj) accrued, amassed, assembled, collected, accumulate, aggregate, congregate, massed, store, upheaped, equanimous, poised.

karemwaewe scarce; *synonyms* (adj) rare, insufficient, deficient, infrequent, scant, scanty, uncommon, few, inadequate, sparse, slender, lacking, (adv) just, barely, hardly; *antonyms* (adj) abundant, plentiful.

karena stretch; *synonyms* (n) extent, run, expanse, extension, range, (v) extend, reach, strain, elongate, lengthen, prolong, spread, draw, enlarge, broaden; *antonym* (v) shorten.

karenaki stretched; *synonyms* (adj) taut, extended, stiff, tense, tight, strained, expanded, outstretched, elongated, outspread, prolonged, protracted, assiduous, close, delayed; *antonym* (adj) brief.

karenga precarious; *synonyms* (adj) dangerous, perilous, doubtful, hazardous, insecure, uncertain, unsafe, unstable, delicate, chancy, critical, debatable, disputable, parlous, risky; *antonyms* (adj) safe, stable.

karengaoa tangle; *synonyms* (n) snarl, maze, confusion, knot, (v) entangle, jumble, embroil, muddle, enmesh, embrangle, entrap, involve, mat, ravel, ruffle; *antonyms* (n) order, (v) disentangle, unravel.

karengaoaki tangled; *synonyms* (adj) involved, complex, knotted, intricate, complicated, entangled, convoluted, knotty, difficult, disheveled, tousled, kinky, labyrinthine, muddled, perplexed; *antonym* (*adj*) free.

karenoa 1. interfere; *synonyms* (*v*) intercede, obstruct, disturb, conflict, clash, hinder, impede, intervene, meddle, tamper, interrupt, contravene, encroach, (*n*) interpose, (*adj*) intermeddle, **2.** inconvenience; *synonyms* (*n*) bother, disadvantage, difficulty, nuisance, awkwardness, unsuitableness, encumbrance, ineptness, unwieldiness, (*v*) trouble, discommode, incommode, disoblige, annoy, disquiet; *antonym* (*n*) convenience, **3.** meddle; *synonyms* (*v*) interfere, intrude, fiddle, monkey, pry, **4.** intrude; *synonyms* (*v*) impose, infringe, trespass, impinge, obtrude, disrupt, transgress, enter, interlope, invade, irrupt, thrust.

karerea 1. excite; *synonyms* (*v*) animate, arouse, disturb, enliven, agitate, energize, awaken, electrify, encourage, evoke, exasperate, incite, inspire, kindle, provoke; *antonyms* (*v*) calm, pacify, bore, **2.** animate; *synonyms* (*adj*) alive, live, spirited, quick, vivacious, (*v*) actuate, cheer, exhilarate, hearten, inspirit, invigorate, quicken, revive, stimulate, elevate; *antonyms* (*adj*) lifeless, (*v*) deaden.

karereaki 1. animated; *synonyms* (*adj*) active, alive, lively, animate, perky, brisk, cheerful, quick, spirited, sprightly, vivacious, airy, alert, bright, energetic; *antonyms* (*adj*) listless, lethargic, blank, dull, **2.** excited; *synonyms* (*adj*) agitated, ablaze, emotional, enthusiastic, frantic, ardent, aroused, delirious, fervent, heated, impassioned, passionate, warm, elated, (*v*) animated; *antonyms* (*adj*) calm, cool, unexcited.

karereantia 1. imprecate; *synonyms* (*v*) curse, damn, execrate, beshrew, blaspheme, cuss, swear, anathematize, accurse, anathemize, bedamn, impetrate, **2.** curse; *synonyms* (*n*) bane, anathema, blasphemy, malediction, denunciation, condemnation, execration, expletive, (*v*) blight, ban, plague, vituperate, blast, excommunicate, imprecate.

karereantiaki cursed; *synonyms* (*v*) accurst, cursing, (*adj*) abominable, damned, doomed, execrable, blamed, blasted, blessed, curst, damnable, detestable, hateful, infernal, unlucky.

karerei 1. approve; *synonyms* (*v*) sanction, adopt, accept, acknowledge, allow, admit, agree, endorse, let, ratify, support, applaud, acquiesce, authorize, confirm; *antonyms* (*v*) reject, censure, condemn, disapprove, forbid, veto, **2.** praise; *synonyms* (*n*) compliment, acclaim, applause, commendation, glory, kudos, admiration, (*v*) approve, commend, extol, honor, flatter, celebrate, glorify, admire; *antonyms* (*n*) criticism, disparagement, (*v*) criticize,

belittle, disparage, rebuke, reprimand, reproach, scold, chastise, denigrate, sully.

karereiaki approved; *synonyms* (*adj*) accepted, certified, sanctioned, allowed, authorized, accredited, agreed, conventional, regular, official, orthodox; *antonyms* (*adj*) informal, unofficial.

karerema 1. agitated; *synonyms* (*adj*) restless, excited, nervous, restive, tumultuous, upset, distressed, tense, alarmed, anxious, distraught, jumpy, overwrought, perturbed, shaken; *antonyms* (*adj*) calm, composed, lethargic, **2.** restive; *synonyms* (*adj*) obstinate, edgy, fidgety, jittery, nervy, uptight, restiff, uneasy, unruly, overstrung, resty, (*v*) skittish; *antonym* (*adj*) relaxed, **3.** restless; *synonyms* (*adj*) unquiet, agitated, apprehensive, fretful, impatient, feverish, turbulent, disturbed, wakeful, eager, hasty, mercurial, frightened, hectic, (*n*) tremulous.

karetun hurt; *synonyms* (*v*) pain, wound, afflict, injure, ail, cost, (*adj*) evil, (*n*) harm, damage, detriment, ache, disadvantage, abuse, distress, lesion; *antonyms* (*v*) encourage, (*adj*) uninjured, unhurt.

karetunaki hurt; *synonyms* (*v*) pain, wound, afflict, injure, ail, cost, (*adj*) evil, (*n*) harm, damage, detriment, ache, disadvantage, abuse, distress, lesion; *antonyms* (*v*) encourage, (*adj*) uninjured, unhurt.

kareu turbulent; *synonyms* (*adj*) tempestuous, tumultuous, rough, furious, boisterous, disorderly, noisy, riotous, violent, wild, rude, troubled, unruly, agitated, (*n*) stormy; *antonym* (*adj*) calm.

kareua intervene; *synonyms* (*v*) interfere, intercede, interpose, mediate, arbitrate, meddle, interject, intermediate.

kareuatao 1. layer; *synonyms* (*n*) coat, course, coating, cover, film, level, ply, stratum, crust, covering, floor, mantle, row, tier, (*v*) pile, **2.** heap; *synonyms* (*n*) stack, accumulation, collection, amass, group, lot, mass, mound, bulk, bunch, congeries, (*v*) aggregate, bank, collect, gather, **3.** pile; *synonyms* (*n*) heap, bundle, hoard, jam, nap, wad, lump, multitude, fortune, edifice, batch, (*v*) pack, accumulate, crowd, throng.

kareuataoaki 1. layered; *synonyms* (*adj*) lamellated, caked, coated, covered, encrusted, lamellar, lamelliform, superimposed, overlying, **2.** heaped; *synonyms* (*adj*) piled, coacervate, collective, cumulative, dense, thick, cumulous, **3.** piled; *synonyms* (*adj*) heaped, aggregate, pointed.

kareuma gallivant; *synonyms* (*v*) gad, stroll, ramble, range, roam, stray, wander, drift, meander, cruise, jaunt.

kareureu turbulent; *synonyms* (*adj*) tempestuous, tumultuous, rough, furious, boisterous, disorderly, noisy, riotous, violent, wild, rude, troubled, unruly, agitated, (*n*) stormy; *antonym* (*adj*) calm.

karewe sweet; *synonyms* (*adj*) beloved, delicious, fresh, lovely, mellow, dear, lovable, melodious, musical, pleasant, pleasing, sugary, charming, delightful, (*n*) confection; *antonyms* (*adj*) sour, acid, bitter, discordant, acidic, pungent, sharp, salty.

karewena sweeten; *synonyms* (*v*) dulcify, edulcorate, sugar, dulcorate, mollify, appease, pacify, popularize; *antonym* (*v*) sour.

karewenaki sweetened; *synonyms* (*adj*) sweet, sugared, angelic, angelical, appetizing, cherubic, dulcet, dulcified, fresh, gratifying, honeyed, mellifluous, mellisonant, mollified, odoriferous.

karewerewe sweet; *synonyms* (*adj*) beloved, delicious, fresh, lovely, mellow, dear, lovable, melodious, musical, pleasant, pleasing, sugary, charming, delightful, (*n*) confection; *antonyms* (*adj*) sour, acid, bitter, discordant, acidic, pungent, sharp, salty.

karewi 1. sweeten; *synonyms* (*v*) dulcify, edulcorate, sugar, dulcorate, mollify, appease, pacify, popularize; *antonym* (*v*) sour, **2.** spoonfeed.

karewiaki sweetened; *synonyms* (*adj*) sweet, sugared, angelic, angelical, appetizing, cherubic, dulcet, dulcified, fresh, gratifying, honeyed, mellifluous, mellisonant, mollified, odoriferous.

karia 1. scratch; *synonyms* (*n*) score, mark, nick, scrabble, dent, abrasion, cut, groove, (*v*) graze, notch, rub, scrape, chafe, rake, grate, **2.** peel; *synonyms* (*n*) skin, hide, peeling, (*v*) hull, bark, flake, flay, pare, decorticate, excoriate, husk, shave, strip, disrobe, desquamate, **3.** plane; *synonyms* (*n*) airplane, face, aeroplane, aircraft, degree, stage, surface, jet, (*v*) flatten, (*adj*) level, even, flat, horizontal, smooth, flush.

kariaia 1. indulge; *synonyms* (*v*) gratify, coddle, baby, cosset, pamper, spoil, mollycoddle, please, satisfy, cocker, cherish, content, (*n*) humor, favor, accord, **2.** approve; *synonyms* (*v*) sanction, adopt, accept, acknowledge, allow, admit, agree, endorse, let, ratify, support, applaud, acquiesce, authorize, confirm; *antonyms* (*v*) reject, censure, condemn, disapprove, forbid, veto, **3.** let; *synonyms* (*v*) hire, lease, leave, permit, charter, have, rent, grant, cause, countenance, demise, get, give, (*n*) check, hindrance; *antonym* (*v*) prevent, **4.** allow; *synonyms* (*v*) accede, afford, bear, consent, enable, endure, own, recognize, stand, suffer, abide, appropriate, assent, brook, concede; *antonyms* (*v*) prohibit, deny, **5.** agree; *synonyms* (*v*) adjust, bargain, concord, correspond, fit, harmonize, suit, compromise, align, concur, consort, contract, jibe, match, (*n*) coincide; *antonyms* (*v*) disagree, oppose, differ, argue, object, refuse, refute, **6.** consent; *synonyms* (*n*) acquiescence, consensus, agreement, approval, approbation, compliance, concurrence, acceptance, permission, promise, confirmation, unity, (*v*) approve, comply, yield; *antonyms* (*n*)

opposition, refusal, **7.** accede; *synonyms* (*v*) defer, submit, adhere, receive, succumb.

kariaiakaki 1. allow; *synonyms* (*v*) acknowledge, accord, agree, give, grant, permit, accede, acquiesce, accept, afford, authorize, bear, consent, enable, (*adj*) admit; *antonyms* (*v*) forbid, prohibit, deny, reject, **2.** authorized; *synonyms* (*v*) allowed, (*adj*) authoritative, authorised, official, competent, lawful, legal, legitimate, permissible, privileged; *antonym* (*adj*) informal, **3.** approve; *synonyms* (*v*) sanction, adopt, allow, endorse, let, ratify, support, applaud, confirm, okay, sustain, approbate, recognize, esteem, (*adj*) like; *antonyms* (*v*) censure, condemn, disapprove, veto, **4.** consent; *synonyms* (*n*) acquiescence, consensus, agreement, approval, approbation, compliance, concurrence, acceptance, leave, permission, (*v*) assent, approve, concur, coincide, comply; *antonyms* (*n*) opposition, refusal, (*v*) disagree, refuse, **5.** approved; *synonyms* (*adj*) accepted, certified, sanctioned, authorized, accredited, agreed, conventional, regular, orthodox; *antonym* (*adj*) unofficial, **6.** agree; *synonyms* (*v*) adjust, bargain, concord, correspond, fit, harmonize, suit, compromise, align, check, consort, contract, jibe, match, parallel; *antonyms* (*v*) oppose, differ, argue, object, refute, **7.** permitted; *synonyms* (*adj*) allowable, admissible, free.

kariaiakakiaki approved; *synonyms* (*adj*) accepted, certified, sanctioned, allowed, authorized, accredited, agreed, conventional, regular, official, orthodox; *antonyms* (*adj*) informal, unofficial.

kariaiaki 1. approved; *synonyms* (*adj*) accepted, certified, sanctioned, allowed, authorized, accredited, agreed, conventional, regular, official, orthodox; *antonyms* (*adj*) informal, unofficial, **2.** let; *synonyms* (*v*) allow, hire, admit, lease, leave, permit, charter, have, rent, grant, authorize, cause, countenance, demise, (*n*) check; *antonyms* (*v*) forbid, prevent, **3.** authorized; *synonyms* (*adj*) authoritative, authorised, competent, lawful, legal, legitimate, permissible, privileged, **4.** permitted; *synonyms* (*adj*) allowable, admissible, free.

kariaki 1. planned; *synonyms* (*adj*) deliberate, intended, intentional, calculated, designed, aforethought, plotted, premeditated, scheduled, fixed, future, prepared, studied; *antonyms* (*adj*) spontaneous, unplanned, **2.** scratched; *synonyms* (*adj*) scraped, hurt, abraded, dented, injured, raw, sgraffito, spoiled, broken, skinned, smashed, **3.** peeled; *synonyms* (*adj*) naked, bare, bleak, crude, cutting, exposed, natural, new, nude, open, sore, unsanded.

karianako 1. many; *synonyms* (*adj*) manifold, abundant, countless, frequent, various, innumerable, much, multiple, numerous, plentiful, several, different, numberless, (*n*) number;

antonym (*n*) few, **2.** much; *synonyms* (*adv*) greatly, frequently, almost, awfully, considerably, far, most, often, pretty, highly, (*n*) lot, heap, (*adj*) great, considerable, practically; *antonym* (*adv*) slightly.

kariara 1. innumerable; *synonyms* (*adj*) countless, incalculable, numberless, infinite, innumerous, multitudinous, unnumbered, myriad, numerous, uncounted, untold, incommensurable, incommensurate, many, unnumerable; *antonym* (*adj*) few, **2.** countless; *synonyms* (*adj*) innumerable, endless, measureless, immeasurable, legion; *antonym* (*adj*) finite, **3.** exaggerate; *synonyms* (*v*) boast, aggravate, amplify, dramatize, overdo, overdraw, enhance, enlarge, magnify, overstate, embellish, heighten, hyperbolize, increase, inflate; *antonyms* (*v*) understate, minimize, **4.** plenty; *synonyms* (*n*) abundance, affluence, copiousness, much, plenteousness, exuberance, opulence, plenitude, galore, flood, multitude, heap, (*adj*) enough, adequate, ample; *antonym* (*adj*) insufficient, **5.** profuse; *synonyms* (*adj*) abundant, generous, plentiful, liberal, bounteous, copious, exuberant, lavish, bountiful, excessive, full, opulent, prodigal, overflowing, extravagant; *antonym* (*adj*) scarce.

kariaraki exaggerated; *synonyms* (*adj*) enlarged, extravagant, theatrical, immoderate, hypertrophied, affected, excessive, hyperbolic, inflated, magnified, overdone, overstated, pretentious, melodramatic; *antonyms* (*adj*) understated, restrained.

kariba 1. packed; *synonyms* (*adj*) crowded, compact, full, filled, jammed, overcrowded, congested, dense, thick, brimming, close, cramped, teeming; *antonyms* (*adj*) empty, deserted, **2.** on; *synonyms* (*prep*) at, about, concerning, in, by, into, upon, for, above, (*adv*) forth, ahead, (*adj*) forward, aboard, (*prf*) along, against; *antonym* (*adv*) off, **3.** tight; *synonyms* (*adj*) firm, mean, parsimonious, taut, secure, snug, tense, drunk, miserly, rigorous, sparing, (*v*) narrow, fast, stingy, near; *antonyms* (*adj*) loose, baggy, generous, slack, wide, (*adv*) loosely.

karibak 1. congest; *synonyms* (*v*) block, choke, clog, obstruct, stuff, crowd, fill, jam, occlude, plug, **2.** compress; *synonyms* (*v*) abridge, compact, press, squeeze, condense, contract, pack, abbreviate, concentrate, constrict, cram, crush, pinch, tighten, (*n*) bandage; *antonym* (*v*) loosen, **3.** crowd; *synonyms* (*n*) huddle, swarm, collection, crew, circle, cluster, army, assembly, concourse, congregation, gang, group, (*v*) bunch, flock, compress; *antonym* (*v*) disperse, **4.** tighten; *synonyms* (*v*) strain, brace, fasten, narrow, reduce, stiffen, stretch, screw, secure, constrain, frap, fix, confine, straiten, pucker; *antonym* (*v*) relax, **5.** press; *synonyms* (*n*) closet, newspaper, (*v*) force,

coerce, exhort, mash, push, urge, clasp, hug, pressure, squash, stress, entreat, (*adj*) weigh.

karibakaki 1. congested; *synonyms* (*adj*) packed, full, overcrowded, teeming, engorged, closed, stopped, close, overfull, busy, cramped, swarming, blocked, bunged, (*prep*) inflamed; *antonym* (*adj*) empty, **2.** compressed; *synonyms* (*adj*) compact, dense, flat, tight, pointed, concise, besotted, bland, blotto, categoric, categorical, concrete, firm, hard, narrow; *antonym* (*adj*) loose, **3.** crowded; *synonyms* (*adj*) congested, populous, jammed, thick, (*n*) thronged; *antonym* (*adj*) sparse, **4.** tightened, **5.** pressed; *synonyms* (*adj*) printed, pushed, stamped, bound, driven, embossed, encouraged, impelled, imprinted, incited, marked, provoked, prompted.

karibeua deform; *synonyms* (*v*) distort, deface, bend, contort, disfigure, twist, turn, warp, convolute, mangle, injure, mar, misshape, strain, wrest; *antonym* (*v*) straighten.

karibeuaki deformed; *synonyms* (*adj*) crooked, bent, distorted, malformed, misshapen, ugly, crippled, contorted, deform, grotesque, shapeless, twisted, warped, (*v*) crump.

karibonobonoa amass; *synonyms* (*v*) accumulate, aggregate, collect, gather, heap, hoard, pile, accrue, compile, save, stack, stock, store, drift, increase; *antonym* (*v*) disperse.

karibonobonoaki amassed; *synonyms* (*adj*) accumulated, assembled, collected, cumulative, aggregate, accrued, collective, combined, conglomerate, congregate, massed, more, total, comprehensive, equanimous.

karibua 1. drive; *synonyms* (*n*) ride, force, campaign, crusade, thrust, cause, ambition, (*v*) push, actuate, chase, compel, urge, coerce, beat, carry; *antonyms* (*n*) apathy, inertia, **2.** force; *synonyms* (*n*) energy, strength, agency, effect, enforce, impetus, impulse, power, (*v*) drive, pressure, squeeze, cram, impel, press, (*adj*) constrain; *antonyms* (*n*) weakness, persuasion, **3.** penetrate; *synonyms* (*v*) bore, imbue, fathom, infiltrate, permeate, pierce, cut, filter, interpenetrate, enter, drill, diffuse, percolate, perforate, probe.

karibuaki 1. driven; *synonyms* (*v*) drive, (*adj*) determined, impelled, compulsive, bound, dictated, dynamic, encouraged, goaded, hell-bent, provoked, successful, activist, efficient, energetic, **2.** forced; *synonyms* (*adj*) compulsory, compelled, artificial, constrained, involuntary, unnatural, farfetched, false, labored, obligatory, obliged, strained; *antonyms* (*adj*) free, unprovoked, spontaneous, voluntary.

karietata exalt; *synonyms* (*v*) animate, celebrate, dignify, glorify, raise, advance, elevate, promote, adore, ennoble, aggrandize, elate, extol, inspire, magnify; *antonym* (*v*) humiliate.

karietataki exalted; *synonyms* *(adj)* elevated, eminent, lofty, high, noble, elated, dignified, grand, great, sublime, celebrated, distinguished, elate, glorious, magnificent.

kariete 1. elated; *synonyms* *(adj)* elate, delighted, joyful, jubilant, exultant, gleeful, happy, overjoyed, proud, triumphant, ecstatic, euphoric, elevated, high, *(n)* buoyant; *antonyms* *(adj)* dejected, disappointed, **2.** conceited; *synonyms* *(adj)* arrogant, cocky, egotistic, vain, boastful, smug, affected, assuming, egotistical, haughty, pompous, complacent, narcissistic, priggish, bigheaded; *antonyms* *(adj)* humble, modest, **3.** proud; *synonyms* *(adj)* dignified, disdainful, lofty, exalted, conceited, gallant, lordly, majestic, overbearing, imperious, elated, grand, magnificent, noble, presumptuous; *antonyms* *(adj)* ashamed, embarrassed.

karika 1. create; *synonyms* *(v)* cause, construct, make, constitute, produce, beget, breed, build, compose, do, establish, form, generate, institute, start; *antonyms* *(v)* destroy, terminate, **2.** form; *synonyms* *(n)* figure, design, arrange, ceremony, shape, class, conformation, appearance, *(v)* cast, fashion, carve, create, comprise, contrive, devise, **3.** found; *synonyms* *(v)* erect, base, appoint, ground, bottom, begin, plant, imbed, introduce, father, launch, originate, predicate, rest, embed; *antonym* *(adj)* misplaced, **4.** generate; *synonyms* *(v)* develop, bear, engender, get, provoke, raise, reproduce, yield, propagate, effect, impregnate, afford, conceive, earn, *(adj)* procreate, **5.** conceive; *synonyms* *(v)* believe, imagine, think, apprehend, comprehend, realize, discover, cogitate, catch, consider, fancy, invent, see, coin, dream, **6.** imagine; *synonyms* *(v)* conjecture, assume, daydream, guess, envision, fantasize, visualize, calculate, image, divine, gather, deduce, envisage, expect, *(conj)* suppose, **7.** commence; *synonyms* *(v)* open, embark, initiate, arise, enter, inaugurate, approach, found, undertake; *antonyms* *(v)* end, finish, stop, **8.** beget; *synonyms* *(v)* sire, mother, acquire, **9.** invent; *synonyms* *(v)* fabricate, forge, concoct, excogitate, formulate, frame, hatch, feign, fake, mint, compile, manufacture, counterfeit, fib, *(n)* project, **10.** propagate; *synonyms* *(v)* circulate, disseminate, disperse, spread, broadcast, diffuse, distribute, multiply, sow, grow, extend, publicize, circularise, circularize, progenerate, **11.** procreate; *synonym* *(v)* fertilize.

karikaka disenchant; *synonyms* *(v)* disappoint, disillusion, disgust, dishearten, offend, repel, shock, decharm, disencharm, disillusionize, nauseate, revolt, sicken, sour, unbewitch; *antonym* *(v)* enchant.

karikakaki disenchanted; *synonyms* *(adj)* disillusioned, cynical, blasé, disappointed, dissatisfied, sophisticated, worldly, disenthralled, disentranced, disheartened, embittered, frustrated, indifferent, jaded, jaundiced; *antonym* *(adj)* enchanted.

karikaki 1. generated, **2.** imagined; *synonyms* *(adj)* imaginary, fanciful, notional, unreal, fancied, fictitious, conceptional, conjectural, doubtful, dubious, feigned, hypothetical, ideational, nonexistent, unseen, **3.** begotten; *synonyms* *(adj)* create, composed, created, **4.** formed; *synonyms* *(adj)* wrought, settled, shaped, affected, characterized, conceived, defined, fashioned, built, constructed, established, firm, adapted, adjusted, arranged, **5.** baked; *synonyms* *(adj)* dry, adust, parched, scorched, arid, burned, burnt, daft, done, heated, lunatic, seared, sunbaked, barren, broiled; *antonym* *(adj)* wet, **6.** founded; *synonyms* *(v)* cast, fusil, fusible, *(adj)* based, *(prep)* institute, organized, **7.** invented; *synonyms* *(adj)* fabricated, fictional, fake, fabulous, false, fictive, legendary, mythical; *antonym* *(adj)* real, **8.** conceived; *synonym* *(adj)* formed, **9.** refurbish; *synonyms* *(v)* renovate, restore, remodel, freshen, furbish, renew, revamp, fix, mend, repair, **10.** reconstructed, **11.** reconstruct; *synonyms* *(v)* rebuild, alter, build, rehabilitate, redo, regenerate, retrace, construct, doctor, make, recast, **12.** repair; *synonyms* *(n)* overhaul, renewal, renovation, *(v)* remedy, patch, redress, correct, cure, compensate, heal, amend, go, reclaim, recover, rectify; *antonym* *(v)* break.

karikakiaki repaired; *synonyms* *(adj)* fixed, reconditioned, maintained, fastened, flat, frozen, intent, serviced, retained, rigid, set.

karikamate numb; *synonyms* *(adj)* asleep, benumbed, dead, dull, insensible, torpid, deadened, callous, impassive, comatose, inactive, inert, *(v)* benumb, deaden, *(n)* blunt; *antonym* *(adj)* sensitive.

karikari 1. throb; *synonyms* *(n)* pulsation, thrill, pain, *(v)* beat, quiver, ache, pulsate, pulse, pound, flutter, palpitate, shudder, smart, tingle, pant, **2.** thrill; *synonyms* *(n)* delight, chill, excitement, flush, frisson, kick, shake, *(v)* excite, shiver, exhilarate, exalt, pierce, stir, electrify, charm, **3.** pulsate; *synonyms* *(v)* throb, thump, vibrate.

karikariaki 1. pulsated, **2.** thrilled; *synonyms* *(adj)* delighted, jubilant, excited, happy, overjoyed, ecstatic, elated, pleased.

karikaua 1. doubting; *synonyms* *(adj)* doubtful, distrustful, disbelieving, incredulous, skeptical, sceptical, suspicious, wary; *antonym* *(adj)* trusting, **2.** doubtful; *synonyms* *(adj)* ambiguous, debatable, dubious, disputable, queer, questionable, tentative, diffident, hesitant, indistinct, uncertain, undecided, unlikely, unsettled, unsure; *antonyms* *(adj)* certain, convinced, reliable, confident, persuaded, provable, sure, **3.** perplexed; *synonyms* *(v)* bewildered, complicated, intricate, (*adj*) confused, involved, lost, baffled, confounded, puzzled, distracted, uneasy, bemused, questioning, quizzical, entangled; *antonym* (*adj*) enlightened.

kariki 1. create; *synonyms* (*v*) cause, construct, make, constitute, produce, beget, breed, build, compose, do, establish, form, generate, institute, start; *antonyms* (*v*) destroy, terminate, **2**. conceive; *synonyms* (*v*) believe, imagine, think, apprehend, comprehend, design, realize, discover, cogitate, catch, consider, create, fancy, invent, originate, **3**. invent; *synonyms* (*v*) devise, fabricate, forge, coin, concoct, excogitate, contrive, formulate, frame, hatch, feign, fake, mint, fashion, (*n*) project, **4**. generate; *synonyms* (*v*) develop, bear, engender, get, provoke, father, raise, reproduce, yield, propagate, begin, effect, impregnate, afford, (*adj*) procreate, **5**. breed; *synonyms* (*n*) kind, race, variety, ancestry, sort, order, class, genus, posterity, progeny, species, (*v*) multiply, brood, cultivate, spawn, **6**. beget; *synonyms* (*v*) sire, mother, acquire, **7**. bread; *synonyms* (*n*) living, livelihood, cash, maintenance, currency, dough, food, kale, loot, money, pelf, sustenance, **8**. bake; *synonyms* (*v*) burn, broil, cook, fire, fry, roast, grill, heat, parch, scorch, singe, toast, **9**. manufacture; *synonyms* (*n*) construction, fabrication, formation, production, creation, industry, assembly, work, business, composition, making, manufacturing, output, (*v*) erect, operate, **10**. found; *synonyms* (*v*) base, appoint, ground, bottom, cast, plant, imbed, introduce, arrange, launch, predicate, rest, embed; *antonym* (*adj*) misplaced, **11**. reproduce; *synonyms* (*v*) imitate, repeat, regenerate, replicate, reflect, echo, mirror, iterate, reiterate, increase, manifold, proliferate, reconstruct, (*n*) copy, duplicate, **12**. procreate; *synonym* (*v*) fertilize, **13**. produce; *synonyms* (*v*) give, bring, present, fetch, prepare, grow, manufacture, product, elicit, have, deliver, (*n*) gain, crop, merchandise, proceeds.

karikiaki 1. breaded; *synonyms* (*adj*) braided, breadcrumbed, **2**. generated, **3**. baked; *synonyms* (*adj*) dry, adust, parched, scorched, arid, burned, burnt, daft, done, heated, lunatic, seared, sunbaked, barren, broiled; *antonym* (*adj*) wet, **4**. conceived; *synonyms* (*adj*) formed, defined, settled, **5**. founded; *synonyms* (*v*) cast, fusil, fusible, (*adj*) based, (*prep*) established, institute, organized, **6**. begotten; *synonyms* (*adj*) create, composed, created, **7**. invented; *synonyms* (*adj*) fictitious, fabricated, fictional, imaginary, unreal, fake, fabulous, false, fancied, fictive, legendary, mythical; *antonym* (*adj*) real, **8**. manufactured; *synonyms* (*adj*) artificial, industrial, affected, contrived, ersatz, feigned, insincere, man-made, pretend, synthetic, unnatural, fixed; *antonym* (*adj*)

natural, **9**. produced; *synonyms* (*v*) producing, (*adj*) bent, fashioned, shaped, twisted, wrought.

karikirakea propagate; *synonyms* (*v*) circulate, disseminate, disperse, procreate, spread, breed, broadcast, diffuse, distribute, beget, generate, multiply, produce, reproduce, sow.

karimoa front; *synonyms* (*adj*) head, fore, anterior, preceding, (*n*) countenance, forefront, appearance, disguise, facade, frontage, brow, audacity, (*v*) face, confront, look; *antonyms* (*n*) rear, end, (*v*) back.

karimwi 1. junior; *synonyms* (*adj*) subordinate, juvenile, minor, young, associate, puisne, lesser, lower, petty, secondary, younger, (*n*) inferior, boy, assistant; *antonyms* (*adj*) senior, chief, **2**. younger; *synonyms* (*adj*) junior, little, brief, fiddling, footling, lowercase, minuscule, niggling, picayune, piddling, piffling, puisny, small, trivial, unskilled.

karina 1. introduce; *synonyms* (*v*) insert, interject, inject, acquaint, advance, enter, exhibit, implant, inaugurate, infuse, initiate, precede, present, instill, interpose; *antonym* (*v*) end, **2**. enter; *synonyms* (*v*) enlist, embark, enroll, book, chronicle, record, input, arrive, come, accede, attack, begin, board, enrol, introduce; *antonyms* (*v*) leave, depart, delete, exit, **3**. drove; *synonyms* (*n*) flock, herd, swarm, crowd, horde, covey, mob, multitude, throng, group, host, legion, (*adj*) bevy, shoal, cloud, **4**. infuse; *synonyms* (*v*) inculcate, brew, imbue, impregnate, steep, indoctrinate, engraft, fill, inspire, saturate, soak, breathe, immerse, impress, inoculate, **5**. insert; *synonyms* (*v*) embed, put, enclose, graft, inclose, infix, plant, stick, inscribe, attach, include, interpolate, (*n*) inset, supplement, addition; *antonyms* (*v*) remove, erase, **6**. dress; *synonyms* (*n*) attire, costume, apparel, array, dressing, clothes, (*v*) clothe, clothing, garb, rig, trim, adjust, adorn, bandage, cover; *antonym* (*v*) undress, **7**. inject; *synonyms* (*v*) shoot, (*adj*) syringe, **8**. drive; *synonyms* (*n*) ride, force, campaign, crusade, thrust, cause, ambition, (*v*) push, actuate, chase, compel, urge, coerce, beat, carry; *antonyms* (*n*) apathy, inertia, **9**. clothe; *synonyms* (*v*) dress, clad, arrange, deck, invest, vest, wrap, fit, bedeck, drape, furnish, garment, habilitate, indue, (*n*) habit, **10**. act; *synonyms* (*n*) accomplishment, action, move, play, statute, decree, do, feat, (*v*) achievement, behave, deed, go, perform, acquit, enact; *antonym* (*v*) refrain, **11**. driven; *synonyms* (*v*) drive, (*adj*) determined, impelled, compulsive, bound, dictated, dynamic, encouraged, goaded, hell-bent, provoked, successful, activist, efficient, energetic, **12**. abrupt; *synonyms* (*adj*) sudden, brusque, sharp, precipitous, disconnected, discourteous, gruff, hasty, immediate, instant, instantaneous, swift, unexpected, bluff, (*n*) bold; *antonyms* (*adj*) civil, gentle, gradual, gracious, rambling, **13**. come; *synonyms* (*v*) approach, become, aggregate, appear, arise, fall, befall, amount, descend, get, hail, number, originate, reach, rise, **14**. penetrate; *synonyms* (*v*) bore, fathom, infiltrate, permeate, pierce, cut, filter, interpenetrate, drill, diffuse, percolate, perforate, probe, puncture, stab, **15**. sudden; *synonyms* (*adj*) abrupt, quick, rash, dramatic, headlong, precipitate, unforeseen, impulsive, impetuous, fleeting, hurried, rapid, speedy, surprising, (*adv*) suddenly; *antonym* (*adj*) considered, **16**. suddenly; *synonyms* (*adv*) abruptly, short, presto, dead, hastily, rapidly, fast, instantly, sharply, unawares, precipitously, (*adj*) quickly, immediately, instanter, subito; *antonyms* (*adv*) gradually, increasingly, predictably, slowly.

karinaki 1. inset; *synonyms* (*n*) insert, gusset, voider, (*v*) introduce, **2**. dressed; *synonyms* (*v*) clothed, accustomed, arrayed, habited, (*adj*) attired, clad, appareled, garbed, covered, garmented, habilimented, kerchieft, polished, raw, robed; *antonym* (*adj*) undressed, **3**. driven; *synonyms* (*v*) drive, (*adj*) determined, impelled, compulsive, bound, dictated, dynamic, encouraged, goaded, hell-bent, provoked, successful, activist, efficient, energetic, **4**. introduced; *synonyms* (*adj*) exotic, familiar, imported, interpolated, **5**. clothed; *synonyms* (*adj*) dressed, wrapped, cloaked, absorbed, decent, draped, mantled, vested, vestured, disguised, engrossed, enveloped, enwrapped, fixed, furnished.

karinakin divide; *synonyms* (*v*) cut, distribute, part, dissociate, apportion, detach, disconnect, dismember, dispense, separate, share, split, deal, distinguish, (*n*) break; *antonyms* (*v*) unite, join.

karinakinaki divided; *synonyms* (*adj*) cleft, split, detached, forked, separate, separated, shared, disjointed.

karinakoa penetrate; *synonyms* (*v*) bore, imbue, fathom, infiltrate, permeate, pierce, cut, filter, interpenetrate, enter, drill, diffuse, percolate, perforate, probe.

karinan range; *synonyms* (*n*) area, array, compass, reach, scope, domain, (*v*) line, arrange, order, rank, roam, group, ramble, wander, align.

karinanaki rung; *synonyms* (*n*) round, rundle, degree, grade, stage, stair, spoke, stave, step, tread.

karinanoa 1. lower; *synonyms* (*adj*) debase, inferior, (*v*) degrade, diminish, frown, humble, dip, abase, cut, descend, drop, scowl, disgrace, decrease, (*n*) depress; *antonyms* (*v*) increase, raise, **2**. abase; *synonyms* (*v*) humiliate, mortify, demean, sink, dishonor, lower, reduce, shame, crush, (*adj*) abash, snub, **3**. humiliate; *synonyms* (*v*) insult, embarrass, chagrin, ridicule, (*n*) disparage; *antonym* (*v*) respect.

karinanoaki 1. lowered; *synonyms* (*adj*) abased, bated, cheap, humbled, restrained, **2**. humiliated;

synonyms (*adj*) ashamed, mortified, embarrassed, humble, abashed, broken, crushed; *antonym* (*adj*) proud, **3**. downed; *synonym* (*adj*) felled.

karinea 1. adore; *synonyms* (*v*) revere, worship, idolize, admire, cherish, glorify, appreciate, deify, praise, respect, venerate, (*n*) honor; *antonyms* (*v*) hate, detest, **2**. honor; *synonyms* (*n*) award, fame, glory, reputation, accolade, compliment, reverence, reward, deference, celebrity, (*v*) esteem, celebrate, grace, dignify, adore; *antonyms* (*n*) shame, humiliation, (*v*) dishonor, disgrace, break, ignore, **3**. venerate; *synonyms* (*v*) fear, prize, consecrate, exalt, idolise, love, observe, value, **4**. respect; *synonyms* (*n*) homage, heed, notice, account, consideration, connection, obeisance, admiration, appreciation, attention, awe, (*v*) regard, estimation, keep, consider; *antonyms* (*n*) cheek, insolence, impudence, (*v*) disrespect, scorn, despise, disregard, humiliate.

karineaki 1. honored; *synonyms* (*v*) completed, consummated, crowned, excessive, (*adj*) esteemed, reputable, honoured, respected, privileged, distinguished, glorious, exalted, advantaged, estimable, famous, **2**. adored; *synonyms* (*adj*) worshipped, acclaimed, beloved, blessed, favorite, idolised, idolized, precious, venerated, chosen, darling, desired, established, preferred, recognized, **3**. respected; *synonyms* (*adj*) illustrious, respectable, appreciated, dear, honored, revered, valued, celebrated, prestigious, redoubtable, **4**. venerated; *synonyms* (*adj*) reverenced, reverend, sublime, venerable, admired, empyreal, empyrean, holy, adored.

karinerine 1. genteel; *synonyms* (*adj*) elegant, cultured, polite, courteous, courtly, fashionable, graceful, refined, civil, nice, ladylike, civilized, modest, prim, decorous; *antonym* (*adj*) coarse, **2**. polite; *synonyms* (*adj*) genteel, gentle, proper, attentive, kind, friendly, chivalrous, complaisant, considerate, cultivated, gracious, polished, good, gallant, affable; *antonyms* (*adj*) impolite, rude, bad-mannered, discourteous, boorish, **3**. respectful; *synonyms* (*adj*) deferential, mannerly, dutiful, obedient, regardful, reverent, reverential, humble, respectable, compliant, obsequious; *antonyms* (*adj*) disrespectful, cheeky, contemptuous, impudent, insolent, disobedient, scornful.

kario compose; *synonyms* (*v*) build, allay, compile, constitute, tranquilize, write, weave, adjust, arrange, compound, form, frame, (*adj*) assuage, appease, (*n*) calm.

karioaki composed; *synonyms* (*adj*) collected, calm, cool, dispassionate, peaceable, easy, equable, impassive, imperturbable, peaceful, placid, sedate, serene, staid, temperate; *antonyms* (*adj*) agitated, distressed, trembling, nervous.

kariraki 1. consistent; *synonyms* *(adj)* coherent, uniform, agreeable, compatible, congruous, constant, logical, conformable, consonant, regular, unchanging, concurrent, unvarying, accordant, equable; *antonyms* *(adj)* inconsistent, erratic, contradictory, illogical, unpredictable, unreliable, **2.** stiffen; *synonyms* *(v)* harden, set, indurate, ossify, tighten, brace, congeal, reinforce, fortify, intensify, jell, strengthen, temper, thicken, constrain, **3.** stretch; *synonyms* *(n)* extent, run, expanse, extension, range, *(v)* extend, reach, strain, elongate, lengthen, prolong, spread, draw, enlarge, broaden; *antonym* *(v)* shorten.

karirakiaki 1. stiffened, **2.** stretched; *synonyms* *(adj)* taut, extended, stiff, tense, tight, strained, expanded, outstretched, elongated, outspread, prolonged, protracted, assiduous, close, delayed; *antonym* *(adj)* brief.

kariri 1. impose; *synonyms* *(v)* force, dictate, charge, enforce, exact, prescribe, clamp, deceive, burden, enjoin, lay, levy, order, set, tax, **2.** intransigent; *synonyms* *(adj)* adamant, obstinate, adamantine, inexorable, uncompromising, die-hard, stubborn, irreconcilable, rigid, unrelenting, *(n)* reactionary; *antonym* *(n)* activist, **3.** entice; *synonyms* *(v)* attract, lure, bait, cajole, allure, charm, coax, draw, tempt, captivate, persuade, call, beguile, *(n)* decoy, seduce, **4.** tempt; *synonyms* *(v)* entice, inveigle, invite, fascinate, attempt, bewitch, incite, instigate, provoke, appeal, encourage, influence, interest, mislead, *(adj)* appetize.

kariria 1. lure; *synonyms* *(n)* allure, bait, enticement, seduce, attraction, *(v)* decoy, entice, bribe, charm, draw, invite, coax, inveigle, tempt, attract, **2.** temp; *synonyms* *(n)* substitute, assistant, *(adj)* temporary, makeshift, stopgap.

kaririaki imposed; *synonyms* *(adj)* compulsory, forced.

karitei 1. boycott; *synonyms* *(n)* ban, disapproval, exclusion, sanction, *(v)* ostracize, exclude, proscribe, strike, bar, blacklist, cut, denounce, picket, rebel, revolt; *antonym* *(v)* patronize, **2.** mutiny; *synonyms* *(n)* insurrection, disobedience, revolution, uprising, defiance, outbreak, rising, *(v)* rebellion, rise, **3.** mutinous; *synonyms* *(adj)* insubordinate, defiant, insurgent, lawless, rebellious, unruly, contumacious, disobedient, factious, riotous, radical, **4.** cantankerous; *synonyms* *(adj)* irascible, cranky, cross, crotchety, grumpy, irritable, moody, morose, peevish, quarrelsome, testy, touchy, prickly, stubborn, argumentative; *antonyms* *(adj)* good-humored, good-natured, **5.** abstain; *synonyms* *(v)* refrain, desist, avoid, forbear, cease, decline, eschew, withhold, fast; *antonym* *(v)* consume, **6.** resistant; *synonyms* *(adj)* immune, impervious, durable, tough, proof, hardy, solid, stable, strong, antagonistic, repellent, unbreakable, *(v)* resistive; *antonyms* *(adj)* fragile, permeable, submissive, agreeable, **7.** oppose; *synonyms* *(v)* object, contest, contend, contradict, contravene, controvert, counteract, resist, fight, counter, disagree, dissent, combat, confront, defend; *antonyms* *(v)* support, advocate, agree, back, advise, **8.** rebel; *synonyms* *(n)* nonconformist, anarchist, dissident, insurrectionist, traitor, revolutionist, subverter, *(v)* mutiny, renegade, arise, disobey, oppose, defect, originate, *(adj)* mutineer; *antonym* *(n)* conformist, **9.** rebellious; *synonyms* *(adj)* disaffected, mutinous, contrary, malcontent, recalcitrant, perverse, disorderly, naughty, revolutionary, seditious, wayward, insurrectionary, noncompliant, pugnacious, rebelling; *antonyms* *(adj)* compliant, docile, content, conventional, obedient, **10.** resist; *synonyms* *(v)* repel, defy, endure, balk, impede, protest, refuse, reject, withstand, rebuff, hold, demur, baulk, challenge, dare; *antonyms* *(v)* surrender, yield, assent, **11.** revolt; *synonyms* *(n)* repulsion, commotion, distaste, insurgence, sedition, unrest, *(v)* disgust, nauseate, sicken, offend, repulse, appall, riot, displease, *(adj)* shock, **12.** revolutionary; *synonyms* *(adj)* fanatic, militant, progressive, *(n)* extremist, subversive, activist; *antonym* *(adj)* old-fashioned, **13.** stay; *synonyms* *(v)* remain, reside, rest, prop, stop, abide, continue, pause, arrest, bide, dwell, *(n)* delay, halt, check, *(adj)* inhabit; *antonyms* *(v)* leave, change, abscond, depart.

kariteiaki opposed; *synonyms* *(adj)* conflicting, contradictory, hostile, contrary, antagonistic, opposing, adverse, averse, contrasted, repugnant, incompatible, irreconcilable, counter, against, opposite.

karitoa 1. steadfast; *synonyms* *(adj)* constant, firm, solid, permanent, fast, immovable, loyal, resolute, determined, steady, persistent, stable, consistent, *(v)* fixed, faithful; *antonym* *(adj)* irresolute, **2.** strong; *synonyms* *(adj)* intense, powerful, able, deep, cogent, durable, forcible, good, hard, influential, lusty, potent, rigid, robust, secure; *antonyms* *(adj)* weak, bland, delicate, faint, feeble, frail, mild, pale, slight, unconvincing, cowardly, diluted, dull, exhausted, flimsy, **3.** valiant; *synonyms* *(adj)* brave, courageous, fearless, intrepid, audacious, daring, gallant, heroic, dauntless, stout, doughty, stalwart, plucky, valorous, *(prep)* bold.

karo 1. daddy; *synonyms* *(n)* dad, father, papa, pappa, pater, pop, boyfriend, fellow, man, popping, soda, tonic, **2.** dad; *synonyms* *(n)* daddy, sire, paterfamilias, divinity, elder, idol, **3.** father; *synonyms* *(n)* begetter, creator, abba, beginner, forefather, founder, padre, patriarch, author, *(v)* beget, engender, create, generate, begin, breed; *antonym* *(n)* mother, **4.** pa; *synonym* *(n)* protactinium, **5.** pop; *synonyms (n)* pa, bang, shot, click, *(v)* burst, crack, shoot, protrude, pawn, appear, place, snap, bulge, *(adj)* popular, *(adv)* plump.

karoa obscure; *synonyms (adj)* cloudy, dim, dark, gloomy, ambiguous, concealed, darken, hidden, incomprehensible, muddy, mysterious, clandestine, *(v)* hide, blur, cloud; *antonyms (adj)* clear, noticeable, simple, obvious, distinct, mainstream, *(v)* clarify.

karokoa 1. adapt; *synonyms (v)* adjust, accommodate, acclimate, fashion, alter, arrange, assimilate, change, edit, familiarize, gear, modify, shape, suit, *(adj)* fit, **2.** adjust; *synonyms (v)* temper, adapt, align, acclimatize, balance, fix, reconcile, regulate, set, compose, conform, coordinate, dispose, *(adj)* dress, *(n)* square, **3.** come; *synonyms (v)* approach, become, aggregate, appear, arise, arrive, fall, befall, amount, descend, get, go, hail, number, originate; *antonym (v)* leave.

karokoaki 1. adjusted; *synonyms (adj)* adapted, altered, set, applied, even, familiarised, familiarized, prepared, ready, resigned, secure, associate, balanced, calm, equable, **2.** adapted; *synonyms (v)* convenient, *(adj)* fit, agreeable, appropriate, conformable, fitted; *antonyms (adj)* mass-produced, unaccustomed.

karongo 1. faded; *synonyms (v)* dilapidated, stale, *(adj)* dim, pale, bleached, dull, exhausted, faint, washy, withered, attenuate, attenuated, colorless, discoloured, **2.** rancid; *synonyms (adj)* bad, putrid, high, musty, rank, sour, fetid, rotten, tainted, offensive, reasty, foul, fulsome, *(v)* decayed, moldy; *antonym (adj)* fresh, **3.** old; *synonyms (adj)* antiquated, obsolete, ancient, former, aged, antique, elderly, experienced, outdated, veteran, archaic, decrepit, hoary, mature, past; *antonyms (adj)* new, young, modern, latest, novel, original, youthful, **4.** sour; *synonyms (adj)* morose, sharp, acid, bitter, rancid, severe, gruff, dour, glum, grim, pungent, *(v)* acidify, ferment, *(n)* harsh, acidity; *antonyms (adj)* sweet, kindly.

karongoa loud; *synonyms (adj)* flashy, garish, gaudy, blatant, boisterous, brassy, forte, high, brazen, jazzy, clamorous, colorful, flash, meretricious, *(adv)* aloud; *antonyms (adj)* soft, gentle, quiet, tasteful, low, subdued, subtle.

karoraoma 1. afflict; *synonyms (v)* grieve, pain, plague, trouble, distress, torment, aggrieve, bother, disturb, hurt, smite, strike, upset, vex, grind, **2.** worry; *synonyms (v)* tease, annoy, care, fear, molest, agitate, *(n)* concern, burden, harass, fuss, annoyance, sorrow, anxiety, apprehension, *(adj)* irritate; *antonyms (v)* soothe, reassure, *(n)* calmness, reassurance.

karoraomaki 1. afflicted; *synonyms (v)* afflict, displeased, *(adj)* distressed, miserable, pitiful,

sorrowful, stricken, ill, woeful, dejected, doleful, dolorous, sorry, aggrieved, affected, **2.** worried; *synonyms (adj)* apprehensive, nervous, uneasy, upset, anxious, afraid, bothered, concerned, disturbed, troubled, fearful, restless, unhappy, *(v)* afflicted, agitated; *antonyms (adj)* calm, carefree, reassured, relaxed, untroubled.

karoroa 1. navigate; *synonyms (v)* cruise, guide, sail, fly, pilot, voyage, cross, maneuver, **2.** pilot; *synonyms (n)* leader, aviator, captain, airman, cowcatcher, *(v)* manage, lead, conduct, direct, director, navigate, show, escort, control, *(adj)* experimental.

karota 1. dampen; *synonyms (v)* deaden, muffle, depress, dishearten, dull, moisten, mute, soften, wet, blunt, chill, cool, check, dash, *(n)* damp; *antonym (v)* stimulate, **2.** moisten; *synonyms (v)* dampen, wash, water, dip, drench, soak, sprinkle, drizzle, **3.** humidify; *synonyms (v)* moisturize, moisturise, **4.** wet; *synonyms (adj)* humid, drenched, moist, soaked, sodden, dank, rainy, saturated, soggy, watery, *(v)* douse, irrigate, bedew, *(n)* moisture, humidity; *antonyms (adj)* dehydrated, parched, *(v)* dry.

karotu 1. disobedient; *synonyms (adj)* contrary, insubordinate, intractable, defiant, disorderly, naughty, rebellious, unruly, wayward, headstrong, willful, contumacious, froward, perverse, refractory; *antonyms (adj)* obedient, compliant, good, well-behaved, orderly, **2.** indisposed; *synonyms (adj)* disinclined, ailing, ill, averse, loath, poorly, sick, reluctant, sickly, unwell, unwilling, diseased, loth, **3.** contrary; *synonyms (adj)* opposite, contradictory, adverse, conflicting, reverse, unfavorable, alien, cross, different, disobedient, obstinate, antagonistic, *(n)* antithesis, converse, *(adv)* counter, **4.** contradictory; *synonyms (adj)* incompatible, inconsistent, discordant, ironic, discrepant, incoherent, incongruous, opposed, opposing, repugnant, confounding, divergent, unlike, *(n)* disagreeing; *antonyms (adj)* consistent, similar, compatible, **5.** frustrate; *synonyms (v)* baffle, counteract, disappoint, fail, foil, thwart, balk, bilk, disconcert, prevent, elude, dash, bar, circumvent, confound; *antonym (v)* encourage, **6.** counteract; *synonyms (v)* antagonize, check, counterbalance, balance, cancel, contradict, hinder, neutralize, resist, compensate, contravene, kill, curb, block, countervail, **7.** contradict; *synonyms (v)* deny, oppose, belie, conflict, confute, controvert, disprove, dissent, impugn, invalidate, refute, disaffirm, disclaim, differ, disagree; *antonyms (v)* confirm, agree, match, **8.** thwart; *synonyms (v)* frustrate, impede, obstruct, defeat, stop, hamper, scotch, spoil, ruin, stymie, traverse, delay, evade, nonplus, perplex.

karotua 1. impede; *synonyms* (v) block, clog, hinder, bar, obstruct, barricade, check, delay, preclude, curb, debar, embarrass, encumber, forbid, hamper; *antonym* (v) facilitate, **2**. contradict; *synonyms* (v) deny, oppose, belie, conflict, confute, contravene, controvert, disprove, dissent, impugn, invalidate, refute, disaffirm, disclaim, counteract; *antonyms* (v) confirm, agree, match, **3**. counteract; *synonyms* (v) antagonize, counterbalance, balance, cancel, contradict, neutralize, resist, compensate, kill, baffle, countervail, frustrate, nullify, offset, prevent.

karotuaki 1. frustrated; *synonyms* (adj) disappointed, baffled, defeated, discouraged, foiled, thwarted, dissatisfied, balked, discomfited; *antonym* (adj) satisfied, **2**. impeded; *synonyms* (adj) disabled, crippled, slow, lame, lamed, **3**. thwarted; *synonyms* (adj) frustrated, beaten, disenchanted, disillusioned, embarrassed, saddened, upset, blocked, hindered, obstructed, stymied; *antonym* (adj) successful.

karotuang 1. arbitrate; *synonyms* (v) adjudicate, intercede, mediate, intervene, referee, determine, interfere, intermediate, judge, reconcile, umpire, negotiate, **2**. umpire; *synonyms* (n) arbitrator, arbiter, mediator, ump, (v) arbitrate, **3**. referee; *synonyms* (n) adjudicator, ref, moderator, intermediary, referendary.

karou turbulent; *synonyms* (adj) tempestuous, tumultuous, rough, furious, boisterous, disorderly, noisy, riotous, violent, wild, rude, troubled, unruly, agitated, (n) stormy; *antonym* (adj) calm.

karout king; *synonyms* (n) emperor, mogul, sovereign, chief, baron, crown, magnate, ruler, tycoon, majesty, rex, monarch, power, ace.

karua lost; *synonyms* (v) gone, missing, abandoned, (adj) doomed, forlorn, extinct, hopeless, bewildered, disoriented, forgotten, helpless, broken, confused, irrecoverable, absent; *antonyms* (adj) present, found, existing.

karuaiwa ninth; *synonym* (adj) ninefold.

karuanano 1. astonishing; *synonyms* (adj) amazing, astounding, prodigious, strange, stupendous, surprising, wonderful, breathtaking, incredible, striking, fabulous, extraordinary, fantastic, miraculous, (n) marvelous; *antonyms* (adj) unremarkable, ordinary, **2**. misleading; *synonyms* (adj) deceptive, false, delusive, fallacious, deceitful, dishonest, deceiving, erroneous, illusory, untrue, evasive, lying, equivocal, delusory, incorrect; *antonym* (adj) honest, **3**. surprising; *synonyms* (adj) astonishing, remarkable, startling, shocking, unusual, odd, stunning, uncommon, unexpected, unforeseen; *antonym* (adj) unsurprising, **4**. troubling; *synonyms* (adj) disturbing, worrying, disquieting, alarming, bad, disconcerting, distressful, distressing, perturbing.

karuanikai 1. hazardous; *synonyms* (adj) dangerous, risky, perilous, unsafe, critical, chancy, dicey, insecure, precarious, uncertain, awkward, explosive, treacherous, (n) daring, adventurous; *antonym* (adj) safe, **2**. dangerous; *synonyms* (adj) grave, serious, severe, unhealthy, hazardous, hurtful, threatening, poisonous, desperate, fatal, hard, nasty, parlous, pernicious, reckless; *antonyms* (adj) secure, stable.

karuanikaia 1. endanger; *synonyms* (v) imperil, hazard, menace, venture, chance, expose, jeopard, jeopardise, jeopardize, peril, queer, scupper, (n) compromise, risk, danger; *antonyms* (v) defend, protect, **2**. jeopardize; *synonyms* (v) endanger, gamble, adventure, stake, threaten.

karuanikaiaki endangered; *synonyms* (adj) defenseless, risky, exposed, helpless, susceptible, (n) tiger.

karuarua entrench; *synonyms* (v) encroach, fortify, impinge, infringe, intrench, trench, establish, invade, defend, ditch, fence, fix, implant, insert, intrude.

karuaruaki entrenched; *synonyms* (adj) confirmed, ingrained, inveterate, constant, set, steadfast, unwavering, chronic, embedded, hardened, inbuilt, incorrigible, incurable, inherent, innate; *antonym* (adj) superficial.

karuataoa 1. heap; *synonyms* (n) pile, stack, accumulation, collection, amass, group, lot, mass, mound, bulk, bunch, congeries, (v) aggregate, bank, collect, **2**. pile; *synonyms* (n) heap, bundle, hoard, jam, nap, wad, lump, multitude, fortune, edifice, batch, (v) pack, accumulate, crowd, throng.

karuataoaki 1. heaped; *synonyms* (adj) piled, coacervate, collective, cumulative, dense, thick, cumulous, **2**. piled; *synonyms* (adj) heaped, aggregate, pointed.

karuoa 1. lower; *synonyms* (adj) debase, inferior, (v) degrade, diminish, frown, humble, dip, abase, cut, descend, drop, scowl, disgrace, decrease, (n) depress; *antonyms* (v) increase, raise, **2**. descend; *synonyms* (v) alight, condescend, settle, deign, derive, dismount, down, subside, tumble, come, decline, fall, sink, slope, stoop; *antonyms* (v) rise, ascend, climb.

karuoaki 1. lowered; *synonyms* (adj) abased, bated, cheap, humbled, restrained, **2**. downed; *synonym* (adj) felled.

karuonako profuse; *synonyms* (adj) abundant, generous, plentiful, liberal, ample, bounteous, copious, exuberant, lavish, bountiful, excessive, full, opulent, prodigal, overflowing; *antonym* (adj) scarce.

karuoruo 1. alternate; *synonyms* (adj) reciprocal, secondary, (v) reciprocate, change, fluctuate, interchange, vary, swerve, alter, (n) substitute, alternative, surrogate, standby, replacement, deputy; *antonym* (*n*) original, **2.** replace; *synonyms* (*v*) exchange, supersede, supplant, reinstate, displace, restore, shift, deputize, renew, return, succeed, switch, deputise, follow, place.

karuotua 1. gamble; *synonyms* (*n*) bet, hazard, game, speculation, (*v*) chance, risk, wager, stake, adventure, venture, **2.** bet; *synonyms* (*v*) gamble, play, lay, (*n*) stakes, **3.** fine; *synonyms* (*adj*) delicate, agreeable, dainty, brave, capital, elegant, excellent, nice, thin, delightful, acute, admirable, alright, (*n*) penalty, (*v*) punish; *antonyms* (*adj*) poor, thick, coarse, substantial, unsatisfactory, wide, **4.** wager; *synonyms* (*n*) set, suit, vie, (*v*) pledge, pawn, gage.

karurua 1. gobble; *synonyms* (*v*) bolt, devour, gulp, consume, gorge, guzzle, stuff, swallow, cram, (*n*) cry; *antonym* (*v*) nibble, **2.** jar; *synonyms* (*n*) jangle, blow, crock, container, jog, shake, amphora, bottle, crash, (*v*) jolt, clash, creak, bump, collide, jounce, **3.** jolt; *synonyms* (*n*) jerk, jar, hustle, knock, shock, shove, surprise, thrust, (*v*) push, agitate, hitch, impact, rock, bounce, convulse.

karuruaki jolted; *synonym* (*adj*) shaken.

karurunginakoa stampede; *synonyms* (*v*) rush, panic, dash, charge, hurtle, (*n*) run, departure, exit, commotion.

karutua 1. knock; *synonyms* (*v*) hit, blow, bump, cuff, punch, strike, boot, clip, (*n*) rap, bang, tap, bash, crash, whack, clap; *antonym* (*v*) praise, **2.** bang; *synonyms* (*n*) beat, smack, knock, slap, smash, blast, thud, clang, (*v*) slam, boom, clatter, clink, thump, pat, clank.

kata 1. attempt; *synonyms* (*n*) try, endeavor, assay, effort, essay, offer, trial, attack, assault, adventure, bid, (*v*) struggle, aim, chance, undertake, **2.** experimental; *synonyms* (*adj*) empirical, tentative, scientific, observational, pilot, test, **3.** experiment; *synonyms* (*n*) attempt, examination, taste, experience, experimentation, (*v*) examine, venture, check, **4.** endeavor; *synonyms* (*n*) enterprise, shot, work, endeavour, exertion, go, action, pursuit, stab, plan, (*v*) strive, labor, strain, seek, intend; *antonym* (*v*) neglect, **5.** scientific; *synonyms* (*adj*) technical, mathematical, exact, punctual, accurate, artistic, objective, shipshape, learned, precise, scientifical, analytical, clinical, detached, disinterested; *antonym* (*adj*) theoretical, **6.** tentative; *synonyms* (*adj*) doubtful, experimental, provisional, probationary, exploratory, shy, cautious, conditional, hesitant, indecisive, indefinite, provisionary, undecided; *antonyms* (*adj*) definite, sure, **7.** trying; *synonyms* (*adj*) difficult, arduous, hard, taxing, annoying, bothersome, demanding, rugged, severe, thorny, tiresome, tough, painful, troublesome, irritating; *antonyms* (*adj*) easy, rewarding, **8.** try; *synonyms* (*v*) prove, experiment,

judge, sample, probe, adjudicate, hear, render, afflict, demonstrate, exercise, hazard, risk, tempt, (*n*) crack, **9.** tempt; *synonyms* (*v*) lure, allure, entice, decoy, charm, coax, inveigle, invite, seduce, fascinate, captivate, persuade, bewitch, cajole, (*adj*) attract.

katababaea 1. bristle; *synonyms* (*n*) fiber, hair, (*v*) abound, teem, arise, brustle, burn, rage, seethe, **2.** frizz; *synonyms* (*v*) curl, crimp, kink, frizzle, crape, crepe, curve, pinch, **3.** ruffle; *synonyms* (*v*) rumple, agitate, crumple, discompose, fret, crease, disturb, fluster, fold, wrinkle, (*n*) crinkle, ruff, perturbation, flounce, frill.

katababaeaki 1. bristled; *synonyms* (*adj*) barbed, barbellate, briary, briery, biting, bristly, burred, burry, echinated, horrent, prickly, spiny, thorny, mordacious, nipping, **2.** ruffled; *synonyms* (*adj*) disheveled, frilled, frilly, rippled, disordered, upset, crinkled, crinkly, disconcerted, excited, messy, nervous, rough, shaggy, tangled.

katabakurakura 1. encumber; *synonyms* (*v*) burden, saddle, clog, hamper, charge, lumber, tax, bound, constrain, cumber, embarrass, hinder, load, fetter, limit; *antonym* (*v*) free, **2.** embarrass; *synonyms* (*v*) confuse, baffle, block, bother, confound, disconcert, encumber, complicate, abash, discomfit, distress, impede, obstruct, (*adj*) bewilder, perplex, **3.** overload; *synonyms* (*n*) overburden, excess, (*v*) overcharge, oppress, surcharge, glut, overlay, overwhelm, overdo, overdose, overfeed, overrun, swamp.

katabakurakuraki 1. encumbered; *synonyms* (*adj*) laden, burdened, burdensome, clayey, cloggy, deep, heavy, forcible, full, gloomy, inactive, loud, oppressive, overloaded, ponderous, **2.** embarrassed; *synonyms* (*adj*) ashamed, abashed, awkward, uncomfortable, disconcerted, bashful, shamefaced, sheepish, shy, chagrined, discomfited, humiliated, mortified; *antonyms* (*adj*) proud, relaxed, **3.** overloaded; *synonyms* (*adj*) overcrowded, overladen, busy, congested, encumbered, loaded, overfull, packed, clogged, jammed, stuffed, swarming, teeming; *antonym* (*adj*) empty.

katabanina encircle; *synonyms* (*v*) beset, surround, besiege, circle, embrace, bound, circumvent, enclose, encompass, environ, hem, begird, circumscribe, beleaguer, (*adv*) compass.

katabaninaki encircled; *synonyms* (*adj*) surrounded, enclosed, bounded, annular, annulate, annulated, bordered, circinate, circular, delimited, ingirt, ringed, wreathed.

katabara 1. string; *synonyms* (*n*) chain, file, row, strand, twine, range, cord, filament, rank, series, thread, tie, sequence, (*v*) run, (*adj*) line, **2.** wind; *synonyms* (*n*) air, gust, clue, (*v*) coil, twist, curl, meander, turn, bend, curve, blow, crook, entwine, roll, weave.

katabaruarua 1. hinder; *synonyms* (*adj*) posterior, hind, (*v*) block, bar, impede, check, hamper, obstruct, resist, curb, arrest, clog, counteract, delay, detain; *antonyms* (*v*) help, assist, facilitate, **2.** embarrass; *synonyms* (*v*) confuse, baffle, bother, confound, disconcert, encumber, hinder, complicate, abash, discomfit, distress, puzzle, discountenance, (*adj*) bewilder, perplex, **3.** overburden; *synonyms* (*v*) drive, overcharge, load, overwhelm, surcharge, abuse, overdo, overdose, overfeed, overlade, overlay, overrun, (*n*) overload, (*adj*) overwork, overstrain.

katabaruaruaki 1. embarrassed; *synonyms* (*adj*) ashamed, abashed, awkward, uncomfortable, disconcerted, bashful, shamefaced, sheepish, shy, chagrined, discomfited, humiliated, mortified; *antonyms* (*adj*) proud, relaxed, **2.** overburdened; *synonyms* (*adj*) burdened, heavy.

katabatibutibua swell; *synonyms* (*n*) wave, (*v*) surge, enlarge, expand, heave, increase, rise, puff, bloat, grow, billow, augment, balloon, (*adj*) dandy, swagger; *antonyms* (*v*) decrease, deflate, desiccate.

katabaua confuse; *synonyms* (*v*) bewilder, baffle, confound, muddle, agitate, blur, derange, disconcert, disturb, fluster, jumble, mystify, obscure, perplex, puzzle; *antonyms* (*v*) clarify, enlighten, elucidate, explain.

katabauaki confused; *synonyms* (*adj*) abashed, bewildered, baffled, befuddled, bemused, chaotic, confounded, disjointed, disordered, dizzy, incoherent, indistinct, ambiguous, (*n*) cloudy, (*adv*, *adj*) topsy-turvy; *antonyms* (*adj*) clear, enlightened, alert, clearheaded, clear-headed, orderly.

katabea obstruct; *synonyms* (*v*) bar, block, check, choke, clog, delay, encumber, hamper, impede, screen, intercept, debar, arrest, (*n*) hinder, barricade; *antonyms* (*v*) encourage, facilitate, free.

katabeaianga 1. trouble; *synonyms* (*n*) distress, bother, pain, anxiety, difficulty, (*v*) inconvenience, annoy, disorder, disquiet, worry, afflict, agitate, burden, distract, disturb; *antonyms* (*v*) calm, please, **2.** worry; *synonyms* (*v*) torment, trouble, tease, care, fear, molest, vex, fret, (*n*) concern, harass, fuss, annoyance, sorrow, apprehension, (*adj*) irritate; *antonyms* (*v*) soothe, reassure, (*n*) calmness, reassurance.

katabeaiangaki 1. worried; *synonyms* (*adj*) apprehensive, distressed, nervous, uneasy, upset, anxious, afraid, bothered, concerned, disturbed, troubled, fearful, restless, unhappy, (*v*) afflicted; *antonyms* (*adj*) calm, carefree, reassured, relaxed, untroubled, **2.** troubled; *synonyms* (*adj*) solicitous, disconcerted, uncomfortable, worried, distraught, perturbed, tumultuous, turbulent, unsettled, vexed,

disruptive, doubtful, riotous; *antonyms* (*adj*) composed, unconcerned.

katabeaki obstructed; *synonyms* (*adj*) hindered, blind, blocked, congested, foiled, frustrated, impedite, stymied, thwarted, tight; *antonym* (*adj*) successful.

katabetabe bother; *synonyms* (*v*) trouble, annoy, torment, vex, worry, afflict, aggravate, (*n*) fuss, plague, bore, hassle, pain, ado, annoyance, concern; *antonyms* (*v*) delight, please, soothe, (*n*) pleasure.

katabetabea 1. disturb; *synonyms* (*v*) agitate, disconcert, disorder, disquiet, distract, distress, perturb, trouble, annoy, bother, commove, concern, derange, disarrange, discompose; *antonyms* (*v*) arrange, calm, please, smooth, soothe, **2.** distress; *synonyms* (*n*) agony, anguish, pain, anxiety, calamity, difficulty, grief, hurt, torture, adversity, (*v*) afflict, torment, upset, worry, discomfort; *antonym* (*v*) comfort, **3.** trouble; *synonyms* (*n*) fuss, care, harass, hardship, load, misfortune, problem, annoyance, disturbance, (*v*) inconvenience, burden, disturb, confuse, discommode, (*adj*) affliction.

katabetabeaki 1. distressed; *synonyms* (*adj*) upset, worried, anxious, distraught, disturbed, sad, downcast, hurt, distracted, miserable, mournful, shocked, sorrowful, troubled, (*n*) needy; *antonyms* (*adj*) calm, composed, content, euphoric, **2.** disturbed; *synonyms* (*adj*) agitated, concerned, confused, disquieted, restless, disordered, bothered, deranged, disconcerted, distressed, nervous, tumultuous, turbulent, unsettled, unbalanced; *antonyms* (*adj*) rational, relaxed, **3.** troubled; *synonyms* (*adj*) solicitous, apprehensive, uncomfortable, uneasy, perturbed, vexed, disruptive, doubtful, riotous, unhappy; *antonyms* (*adj*) untroubled, unconcerned.

katabiroa 1. twist; *synonyms* (*n*) twine, wind, spin, twirl, entwine, (*v*) turn, bend, distort, curl, coil, contort, deform, curve, pervert, wrench; *antonyms* (*v*) straighten, untwist, **2.** turn; *synonyms* (*v*) revolve, deviate, get, revolution, become, (*n*) roll, go, twist, bout, change, round, bent, circle, shift, tour.

katabiroaki 1. twisted; *synonyms* (*adj*) crooked, deformed, perverted, bent, distorted, coiled, misshapen, contorted, curved, twined, winding, wry, gnarled, tortuous, awry; *antonyms* (*adj*) straight, tidy, **2.** turned; *synonyms* (*adj*) off, sour, rancid, twisted, altered, askew, bowed, cancelled, dark, deflected, dour, dull, false, glowering, glum.

katabua 1. commit; *synonyms* (*v*) commend, assign, charge, consign, apply, confide, dedicate, entrust, submit, deliver, devote, give, intrust, leave, send, **2.** dedicate; *synonyms* (*v*) consecrate, commit, bless, render, addict, destine, inaugurate, pay, sanctify, vow, **3**. hallow; *synonyms* (*v*) venerate, commemorate, honor, **4**. forbid; *synonyms* (*v*) debar, prohibit, ban, bar, disallow, exclude, deny, avert, frustrate, inhibit, interdict, outlaw, prevent, proscribe, veto; *antonyms* (*v*) permit, allow, let, approve, **5**. bless; *synonyms* (*v*) celebrate, anoint, eulogize, exalt, glorify, grant, hallow, keep, laud, magnify, praise, sign, (*adj*) ordain; *antonyms* (*v*) desecrate, curse, condemn, **6**. consecrate; *synonyms* (*v*) canonize, enshrine, induct, call, (*adj*) consecrated, dedicated; *antonym* (*v*) despoil, **7**. ban; *synonyms* (*n*) anathema, restraint, command, embargo, prohibition, banning, exclusion, execration, (*v*) forbid, banish, expel, enjoin, illegalize, reject, blackball; *antonym* (*v*) sanction.

katabuaki 1. dedicated; *synonyms* (*adj*) consecrated, consecrate, committed, devoted, sacred, zealous, eager, fervent, holy, keen, loyal, passionate, addicted, steadfast, (*prep*) dedicate; *antonyms* (*adj*) indifferent, desecrated, **2**. forbidden; *synonyms* (*adj*) unlawful, banned, illegal, prohibited, taboo, contraband, illicit, proscribed, verboten; *antonym* (*adj*) acceptable, **3**. hallowed; *synonyms* (*adj*) blessed, divine, sanctified, **4**. consecrated; *synonyms* (*adj*) hallowed, dedicated, adopted, **5**. banned; *synonym* (*adj*) forbidden; *antonym* (*adj*) legitimate, **6**. blessed; *synonyms* (*adj*) blest, happy, blasted, cursed, damned, fortunate, saintly, lucky, deuced, heavenly, infernal, beatified; *antonym* (*adj*) unlucky.

katabuka heap; *synonyms* (*n*) pile, stack, accumulation, collection, amass, group, lot, mass, mound, bulk, bunch, congeries, (*v*) aggregate, bank, collect.

katabukaki heaped; *synonyms* (*adj*) piled, coacervate, collective, cumulative, dense, thick, cumulous.

katabuki elevated; *synonyms* (*adj*) high, exalted, lofty, noble, towering, grand, great, majestic, tall, elated, magnanimous, advanced, dignified, eminent, (*v*) steep; *antonym* (*adj*) short.

katabukirurunga obstruct; *synonyms* (*v*) bar, block, check, choke, clog, delay, encumber, hamper, impede, screen, intercept, debar, arrest, (*n*) hinder, barricade; *antonyms* (*v*) encourage, facilitate, free.

katabukirurungaki obstructed; *synonyms* (*adj*) hindered, blind, blocked, congested, foiled, frustrated, impedite, stymied, thwarted, tight; *antonym* (*adj*) successful.

katabun 1. leftover; *synonyms* (*adj*) excess, odd, spare, surplus, left, remaining, extra, (*n*) remainder, remnant, remains, scrap, end, **2**. outcast; *synonyms* (*n*) exile, pariah, castaway, expatriate, outlaw, vagabond, loon, lown, refugee, (*adj*) derelict, homeless, friendless.

kataburorokoa 1. forbid; *synonyms* (*v*) debar, prohibit, ban, bar, disallow, exclude, deny, avert, frustrate, inhibit, interdict, outlaw, prevent, proscribe, veto; *antonyms* (*v*) permit, allow, let, approve, **2**. prohibit; *synonyms* (*v*) enjoin, forbid, hinder, preclude, hamper, impede, check, deter, oppose, block, embargo, restrict, stop, (*n*) prohibition, obstruct.

kataburorokoaki 1. forbidden; *synonyms* (*adj*) unlawful, banned, illegal, prohibited, taboo, contraband, illicit, proscribed, verboten; *antonym* (*adj*) acceptable, **2**. prohibited; *synonyms* (*adj*) forbidden, barred, out; *antonym* (*adj*) admissible, legitimate.

katabwa forbidden; *synonyms* (*adj*) unlawful, banned, illegal, prohibited, taboo, contraband, illicit, proscribed, verboten; *antonym* (*adj*) acceptable.

katabwaki forbidden; *synonyms* (*adj*) unlawful, banned, illegal, prohibited, taboo, contraband, illicit, proscribed, verboten; *antonym* (*adj*) acceptable.

kataea 1. test; *synonyms* (*n*) trial, audition, experiment, examination, measure, (*v*) assay, essay, examine, prove, quiz, sample, check, try, analyze, attempt, **2**. split; *synonyms* (*v*) crack, cut, fracture, slit, burst, divide, separate, divorce, breach, cleave, (*n*) break, rip, rupture, tear, cleavage; *antonyms* (*v*) join, unite, merge, **3**. thrash; *synonyms* (*v*) flog, lash, beat, defeat, pound, whip, baste, clobber, drub, lam, lick, whack, batter, bang, bat, **4**. subdue; *synonyms* (*v*) conquer, crush, overpower, quash, quell, reduce, repress, chasten, curb, overcome, restrain, soften, subjugate, suppress, (*adv*) control; *antonym* (*v*) surrender, **5**. overpowering; *synonyms* (*adj*) irresistible, overwhelming, oppressive, resistless, heavy, intense, strong, **6**. overpower; *synonyms* (*v*) overwhelm, overmaster, rout, subdue, master, oppress, overthrow, vanquish, drown, frustrate, floor, kill, confound, dominate, (*adj*) overset.

kataeaki 1. subdued; *synonyms* (*adj*) muffled, quiet, soft, dull, muted, restrained, tame, faint, resigned, repressed, low, meek, broken, delicate, sober; *antonyms* (*adj*) loud, enthusiastic, lively, **2**. overpowered; *synonyms* (*adj*) beaten, overcome, conquered, engulfed, flooded, inundated; *antonym* (*adj*) victorious, **3**. tested; *synonyms* (*adj*) tried, experienced, applied, faithful, genuine, hardened, proved, qualified, valid, veteran, trustworthy, weathered, **4**. split; *synonyms* (*v*) crack, cut, fracture, slit, burst, divide, separate, divorce, breach, cleave, (*n*) break, rip, rupture, tear, cleavage; *antonyms* (*v*) join, unite, merge.

kataeare 1. wasted; *synonyms* (*v*) rotten, effete, (*adj*) lost, squandered, thin, cadaverous, emaciated, gaunt, devastated, decayed, haggard, pointless, skeletal, atrophied, blasted; *antonyms* (*adj*) worthwhile, bloated, **2.** **wasting;** *synonyms* (*adj*) consuming, consumptive, corrosive, destructive, drooping, (*n*) atrophy, homicide, murder, slaughter, abrasion, assassination, cachexia, cachexy, carnage, decay, **3.** **waste;** *synonyms* (*n*) desert, refuse, damage, trash, (*adj*) spoil, desolate, barren, (*v*) consume, exhaust, ruin, squander, ravage, destruction, devastate, dissipate; *antonyms* (*v*) conserve, save.

kataeareaki wasted; *synonyms* (*v*) rotten, effete, (*adj*) lost, squandered, thin, cadaverous, emaciated, gaunt, devastated, decayed, haggard, pointless, skeletal, atrophied, blasted; *antonyms* (*adj*) worthwhile, bloated.

kataeari 1. excoriate; *synonyms* (*v*) condemn, denounce, decorticate, chafe, castigate, gall, pare, peel, skin, damn, decry, scourge, **2.** hurt; *synonyms* (*v*) pain, wound, afflict, injure, ail, cost, (*adj*) evil, (*n*) harm, damage, detriment, ache, disadvantage, abuse, distress, lesion; *antonyms* (*v*) encourage, (*adj*) uninjured, unhurt, **3.** wound; *synonyms* (*n*) bruise, injury, scratch, sore, lacerate, (*v*) hurt, cut, offend, stab, sting, insult, maim, bite, affront, contuse.

kataeariaki 1. hurt; *synonyms* (*v*) pain, wound, afflict, injure, ail, cost, (*adj*) evil, (*n*) harm, damage, detriment, ache, disadvantage, abuse, distress, lesion; *antonyms* (*v*) encourage, (*adj*) uninjured, unhurt, **2.** wounded; *synonyms* (*adj*) hurt, bruised, bloody, (*n*) casualty, maimed; *antonym* (*adj*) composed.

kataeboa 1. intensify; *synonyms* (*v*) enhance, increase, aggravate, escalate, heighten, accelerate, augment, compound, deepen, raise, exacerbate, exaggerate, amplify, quicken, rise; *antonyms* (*v*) curb, decrease, moderate, lessen, reduce, satisfy, **2.** animate; *synonyms* (*adj*) alive, live, spirited, quick, (*v*) enliven, encourage, inspire, actuate, cheer, exhilarate, hearten, inspirit, invigorate, revive, stimulate; *antonyms* (*adj*) lifeless, (*v*) deaden, **3.** reanimate; *synonyms* (*v*) refresh, animate, regenerate, revivify, renew, restore, resurrect, resuscitate, vivify, arouse.

kataeboaki 1. animated; *synonyms* (*adj*) active, alive, lively, animate, perky, brisk, cheerful, quick, spirited, sprightly, vivacious, airy, alert, bright, energetic; *antonyms* (*adj*) listless, lethargic, blank, dull, **2.** intensified; *synonyms* (*adj*) high, intense, furious, resonant, **3.** reanimated; *synonym* (*adj*) revived.

kataenang 1. gear; *synonyms* (*n*) equipment, outfit, tackle, apparatus, device, dress, baggage, belongings, clothing, cogwheel, contrivance, kit, luggage, stuff, (*v*) harness, **2.** prepare; *synonyms*

(*v*) arrange, fix, form, plan, coach, devise, lay, make, set, adjust, concoct, cook, equip, fit, groom.

kataenangaki 1. geared, **2.** prepared; *synonyms* (*adj*) disposed, fit, willing, fitted, fain, finished, ready, ripe, competent, inclined, primed, completed, efficient, mature, apt; *antonyms* (*adj*) unprepared, spontaneous.

kataenano 1. disheartening; *synonyms* (*adj*) discouraging, depressing, dispiriting, demoralising, demoralizing, dismal, sad, **2.** depressing; *synonyms* (*adj*) cheerless, dark, gloomy, oppressive, bleak, blue, desolate, dreary, grim, black, chill, depressed, depressive, disconsolate, dour; *antonyms* (*adj*) cheerful, heartening, inspiring, bright, cheery, **3.** incorrigible; *synonyms* (*adj*) hopeless, incurable, inveterate, confirmed, irredeemable, irreparable, hardened, uncorrectable, insubordinate, unruly, abandoned, absolute, audacious, (*v*) obdurate, reprobate; *antonym* (*adj*) corrigible, **4.** discouraging; *synonyms* (*adj*) disheartening, bad; *antonym* (*adj*) encouraging.

kataenikaia 1. conquer; *synonyms* (*v*) beat, capture, subdue, overcome, overpower, quell, subjugate, suppress, surmount, vanquish, crush, defeat, overthrow, overturn, overwhelm; *antonyms* (*v*) surrender, lose, **2.** subdue; *synonyms* (*v*) conquer, quash, reduce, repress, chasten, curb, restrain, soften, humble, mitigate, domesticate, check, master, (*n*) impair, (*adv*) control.

kataenikaiaki subdued; *synonyms* (*adj*) muffled, quiet, soft, dull, muted, restrained, tame, faint, resigned, repressed, low, meek, broken, delicate, sober; *antonyms* (*adj*) loud, enthusiastic, lively.

kataere 1. beat; *synonyms* (*v*) batter, flap, pulsate, throb, tick, trounce, whip, bat, baste, break, (*n*) pulse, thump, knock, round, cadence; *antonym* (*v*) lose, **2.** flog; *synonyms* (*v*) beat, chastise, lash, lick, birch, flagellate, castigate, cane, lather, scourge, strap, wallop, sell, hit, lambaste, **3.** whip; *synonyms* (*n*) coachman, spur, thong, urge, (*v*) flog, goad, punish, stir, thrash, pip, slash, switch, thresh, welt, whisk.

kataerea 1. lash; *synonyms* (*n*) goad, scourge, hit, blow, eyelash, (*v*) whip, beat, flog, chastise, bind, lace, batter, castigate, (*adj*) strap, tie, **2.** lick; *synonyms* (*v*) lap, clobber, bat, drub, thrash, defeat, bang, trim, overcome, touch, (*n*) biff, jab, speed, dash, punch.

kataereaki 1. beaten; *synonyms* (*v*) beat, (*adj*) battered, overpowered, conquered, routed, overcome; *antonym* (*adj*) victorious, **2.** licked; *synonyms* (*adj*) beaten, dumbfounded.

kataeri 1. irritating; *synonyms* (*adj*) galling, annoying, bothersome, exasperating, infuriating, aggravating, irksome, irritative, troublesome, vexatious, irritant, exciting, maddening, nettlesome, (v) stinging; *antonym* (adj) pleasing, **2.** vexing; *synonyms* (adj) irritating, pestiferous, pesky, trying.

kataerina sudden; *synonyms* (adj) abrupt, hasty, precipitous, quick, rash, unexpected, steep, dramatic, headlong, immediate, precipitate, sharp, swift, unforeseen, impulsive; *antonyms* (adj) gradual, considered.

kataetae 1. interrogate; *synonyms* (v) inquire, question, ask, demand, examine, pump, catechize, investigate, probe, query, quiz, grill, **2.** question; *synonyms* (n) inquiry, challenge, matter, problem, interrogation, issue, (v) doubt, distrust, interrogate, contest, dispute, enquire, mistrust, argue, scruple; *antonyms* (n) certainty, (v) answer.

kataetaea 1. lecture; *synonyms* (n) address, discourse, harangue, reprimand, speech, talk, oration, censure, declaim, homily, (v) rebuke, sermon, chide, preach, instruct, **2.** rate; *synonyms* (n) price, worth, pace, value, percentage, (v) assess, estimate, evaluate, appreciate, appraise, compute, count, calculate, merit, put, **3.** scold; *synonyms* (v) berate, abuse, lecture, reproach, rail, admonish, castigate, grouch, grumble, jaw, reprove, rap, (n) nag, (adj) shrew, curse; *antonym* (v) praise, **4.** reprove; *synonyms* (v) blame, condemn, accuse, criticize, scold, warn, disapprove, punish, chasten, correct, chastise, caution, discipline, rebuff, (n) reprehend.

kataetaeaki 1. reproved; *synonyms* (adj) rebuked, reprimanded, admonished, chastened, **2.** rated; *synonym* (adj) nominal.

kataewa 1. chop; *synonyms* (v) ax, chip, cleave, cut, hack, hash, hew, mince, slash, slice, smite, crop, crunch, divide, grind, **2.** cut; *synonyms* (v) carve, chop, clip, abbreviate, abridge, bite, condense, drop, fashion, reduce, (n) notch, cutting, nick, blow, gash; *antonyms* (v) increase, lengthen, (n) addition, extension, **3.** quarter; *synonyms* (n) area, part, district, division, mercy, neighborhood, region, direction, portion, quart, (v) place, lodge, line, put, accommodate.

kataewaki 1. chopped; *synonyms* (adj) shredded, sliced, **2.** cut; *synonyms* (v) carve, chop, clip, abbreviate, abridge, bite, condense, crop, drop, fashion, (n) notch, slice, cutting, nick, blow; *antonyms* (v) increase, lengthen, (n) addition, extension, **3.** quartered.

kataia try; *synonyms* (v) attempt, test, struggle, prove, strive, assay, examine, experiment, judge, sample, (n) endeavor, essay, chance, effort, shot.

kataiaki tried; *synonyms* (adj) reliable, tested, trustworthy, dependable, proved, experienced, baffled, beaten, believable, conquered, exhausted, faithful, just, practiced, qualified.

katairo ignite; *synonyms* (v) light, kindle, arouse, enkindle, fire, heat, flame, agitate, burn, excite, inflame, detonate, incite, provoke, awaken; *antonym* (v) extinguish.

katairoa ignite; *synonyms* (v) light, kindle, arouse, enkindle, fire, heat, flame, agitate, burn, excite, inflame, detonate, incite, provoke, awaken; *antonym* (v) extinguish.

katairoaki ignited; *synonyms* (v) burning, active, flowing, laving, live, lively, quickening, running, vigorous, (adj) kindled, enkindled, flaming, ablaze, fiery.

kataka dry; *synonyms* (adj) thirsty, arid, barren, boring, dehydrated, dull, bald, hoarse, jejune, plain, (v) dehydrate, desiccate, drain, uninteresting, sardonic; *antonyms* (adj) wet, damp, moist, saturated, soaked, boggy, drenched, rainy, sodden, interesting, fresh, humid, juicy, succulent, (v) drench.

katakakaroa amuse; *synonyms* (v) divert, absorb, beguile, entertain, please, charm, delight, disport, distract, occupy, recreate, sport, interest; *antonym* (v) bore.

katakakaroaki amused; *synonyms* (adj) entertained, diverted, smiling.

katakaki dried; *synonyms* (adj) dry, arid, dehydrated, desiccated, shriveled, shrunken, torrid, baked, concrete, desiccate, stale, wizened, lifeless, weazen, (n) milk.

katakanakana 1. bedaub; *synonyms* (v) besmear, smear, daub, soil, asperse, beplaster, plaster, bemire, bespatter, calumniate, conceal, defame, denigrate, dirt, disguise, **2.** dirty; *synonyms* (adj) foul, contemptible, bawdy, contaminated, dingy, impure, despicable, filthy, nasty, (v) muddy, corrupt, contaminate, begrime, pollute, (n) defile; *antonyms* (adj) hygienic, pure, spotless, immaculate, (v) clean, **3.** besmirch; *synonyms* (v) malign, slander, sully, taint, disgrace, smirch, stain, **4.** smear; *synonyms* (n) blot, smudge, blotch, aspersion, spot, defamation, rub, grime, (v) slur, libel, blur, anoint, lubricate, besmirch, apply, **5.** soil; *synonyms* (n) ground, land, dust, tarnish, region, sand, clod, country, (v) dirty, mire, blemish, mould, smutch, bedaub, (adj) filth.

katakanakanaki 1. besmirched; *synonyms* (adj) stained, tarnished, grimy, tainted, defiled, begrimed, soiled, dirty, damaged, discolored, dishonored, flyblown, spotted, sullied, unclean; *antonym* (adj) untarnished, **2.** soiled; *synonyms* (adj) dingy, grubby, nasty, filthy, muddy, black, foul, mucky, polluted, squalid, contaminated, lousy; *antonyms* (adj) clean, pure, **3.** smeared; *synonyms* (adj) smudged, greasy, messy, smirched, smudgy.

katakarea 1. spread; *synonyms* (*v*) scatter, reach, disperse, expand, extend, broadcast, circulate, diffuse, disseminate, increase, propagate, stretch, broaden, deploy, (*n*) span; *antonym* (*adj*) concentrated, **2.** strew; *synonyms* (*v*) litter, spread, distribute, sow, sprinkle, dissipate, straw, **3.** scatter; *synonyms* (*v*) dispel, spray, disband, rout, dot, dust, squander, plant, intersperse, cast, lavish, disorder, (*n*) dispersion, splash, sprinkling; *antonym* (*v*) gather.

katakareaki 1. spread; *synonyms* (*v*) scatter, reach, disperse, expand, extend, broadcast, circulate, diffuse, disseminate, increase, propagate, stretch, broaden, deploy, (*n*) span; *antonym* (*adj*) concentrated, **2.** scattered; *synonyms* (*adj*) dispersed, dissipated, confused, disconnected, disordered, sparse, sporadic, thin, distributed, rare, separate, spread, stray, strewn, disjointed.

katakarebua 1. agitate; *synonyms* (*v*) disturb, stir, toss, fan, bother, foment, perturb, rouse, shake, trouble, actuate, annoy, arouse, canvass, convulse; *antonyms* (*v*) calm, soothe, **2.** shake; *synonyms* (*v*) beat, agitate, jar, brandish, excite, flutter, totter, wag, drop, (*n*) tremble, jolt, quiver, wave, trembling, (*adj*) quake.

katakarebuaki 1. agitated; *synonyms* (*adj*) restless, excited, nervous, restive, tumultuous, upset, distressed, tense, alarmed, anxious, distraught, jumpy, overwrought, perturbed, shaken; *antonyms* (*adj*) calm, composed, lethargic, **2.** shaken; *synonyms* (*v*) broken, lame, passe, shaky, threadbare, wilted, shattered, stale, (*adj*) jolted, dazed, disconcerted, fallen, scared, stunned, surprised.

katakea embarrass; *synonyms* (*v*) confuse, baffle, block, bother, confound, disconcert, encumber, hinder, complicate, abash, discomfit, distress, hamper, impede, (*adj*) bewilder.

katakeaki embarrassed; *synonyms* (*adj*) ashamed, abashed, awkward, uncomfortable, disconcerted, bashful, shamefaced, sheepish, shy, chagrined, discomfited, humiliated, mortified; *antonyms* (*adj*) proud, relaxed.

kataki 1. attempted, **2.** tried; *synonyms* (*adj*) reliable, tested, trustworthy, dependable, proved, experienced, baffled, beaten, believable, conquered, exhausted, faithful, just, practiced, qualified.

katakokoa burst; *synonyms* (*v*) break, crack, blast, rupture, belch, abound, erupt, open, (*n*) flash, explosion, (*adj*) split, explode, detonate, flare, splinter; *antonym* (*v*) implode.

katakokoaki burst; *synonyms* (*v*) break, crack, blast, rupture, belch, abound, erupt, open, (*n*) flash, explosion, (*adj*) split, explode, detonate, flare, splinter; *antonym* (*v*) implode.

katama cat; *synonyms* (*n*) caterpillar, guy, lynx, bozo, hombre, puss, (*v*) disgorge, puke, regorge, regurgitate, retch, spew, spue, upchuck, vomit.

katamanti wild; *synonyms* (*adj*) desert, waste, fierce, boisterous, violent, reckless, desolate, ferocious, furious, raging, rude, stormy, untamed, giddy, barbarous; *antonyms* (*adj*) calm, orderly, domestic, manageable, sane, cultivated, restrained, tame.

katamaroa 1. beautify; *synonyms* (*v*) adorn, ornament, embellish, decorate, deck, enhance, garnish, gild, trim, bead, embroider, improve, enrich, grace, prettify; *antonym* (*v*) spoil, **2.** garnish; *synonyms* (*v*) beautify, dress, apparel, bedeck, furnish, rig, garnishee, (*n*) adornment, decoration, fee, footing, **3.** adorn; *synonyms* (*v*) bedight, blazon, invest, crown, attire, equip, clothe, color, dignify, **4.** dress; *synonyms* (*n*) costume, array, dressing, clothes, frock, vest, covering, disguise, (*v*) clothing, garb, adjust, bandage, cover, align, arrange; *antonym* (*v*) undress, **5.** magnify; *synonyms* (*v*) amplify, exaggerate, aggrandize, enlarge, intensify, expand, glorify, increase, laud, extend, aggravate, augment, exalt, dilate, bless; *antonyms* (*v*) reduce, understate, **6.** decorate; *synonyms* (*v*) emblazon, hang, paint; *antonym* (*v*) strip.

katamaroaki 1. garnished; *synonym* (*adj*) elaborate, **2.** decorated; *synonyms* (*adj*) adorned, ornate, fancy, beautiful, bejeweled, adorn, dyed, emblazoned, festive, inscribed, painted, purfled, tinted, celebrated, extolled, **3.** dressed; *synonyms* (*v*) clothed, accustomed, arrayed, habited, (*adj*) attired, clad, appareled, garbed, covered, garmented, habilimented, kerchieft, polished, raw, robed; *antonym* (*adj*) undressed, **4.** adorned; *synonyms* (*adj*) decorated, bedecked, festooned, garlanded, **5.** magnified; *synonyms* (*adj*) exaggerated, enlarged, inflated, hyperbolic, hypertrophied, overblown, overstated, extravagant, overdone.

katana 1. defend; *synonyms* (*v*) cover, guard, assert, justify, protect, advocate, champion, maintain, shield, support, apologize, hold, preserve, safeguard, shelter; *antonyms* (*v*) attack, prosecute, **2.** guess; *synonyms* (*v*) conjecture, surmise, forecast, believe, deem, divine, reckon, suppose, assume, calculate, feel, figure, foretell, (*n*) estimate, assumption, **3.** cover; *synonyms* (*v*) coat, conceal, top, bury, cloak, (*n*) blind, blanket, screen, binding, camouflage, cap, covering, lid, mask, spread; *antonyms* (*v*) reveal, expose, uncover, **4.** shelter; *synonyms* (*n*) refuge, asylum, harbor, protection, sanctuary, security, hut, covert, haven, shade, lee, (*v*) defend, hide, keep, (*adj*) defense, **5.** shade; *synonyms* (*n*) tinge, color, ghost, hue, cloud, apparition, darkness, dye, nuance, phantom, (*v*) darken, shadow, tint, obscure, overshadow;

antonyms (*n*) light, brightness, **6.** screen; *synonyms* (*n*) riddle, disguise, partition, veil, curtain, drape, concealment, divider, mesh, hedge, (*v*) filter, sieve, examine, secrete, sort, **7.** safeguard; *synonyms* (*v*) ensure, convoy, save, conserve, secure, (*n*) care, escort, precaution, safety, cushion, barrier, buffer, bulwark, fortification, **8.** protect; *synonyms* (*v*) vindicate, insure, patronize, fence, guarantee, insulate, bless, assist, cherish, nurse, rescue, tend, uphold, watch, (*n*) ward; *antonyms* (*v*) neglect, risk.

katanaki 1. covered; *synonyms* (*adj*) hidden, veiled, concealed, covert, coated, masked, obscured, secret, shrouded, thick, wrapped, (*prep*) cloaked; *antonyms* (*adj*) bare, naked, **2.** sheltered; *synonyms* (*adj*) secure, comfortable, safe, screened, cozy, secluded, (*v*) protected, private; *antonym* (*adj*) desolate, **3.** shaded; *synonyms* (*adj*) shady, dark, cheerless, darksome, gloomy, gray, leafy, obscure, soft, subdued, sunless, twilight, umbrageous, cool, dappled, **4.** protected; *synonyms* (*v*) disguised, hid, (*adj*) immune, saved, secured, sheltered, covered, confined, cosseted, dependable, good, guaranteed, impregnable, inviolable, lawful, **5.** screened; *synonyms* (*adj*) hazy, invisible, isolated, select.

katanea 1. sear; *synonyms* (*n*) steel, (*v*) burn, scorch, char, dry, cauterize, parch, scald, brand, fry, broil, singe, blister, (*adj*) sere, withered, **2.** spot; *synonyms* (*n*) blot, place, speck, stain, dot, dapple, dirty, location, mark, (*v*) blemish, soil, fleck, speckle, daub, flaw.

kataneaki 1. seared; *synonyms* (*adj*) scorched, arid, parched, baked, cauterized; *antonym* (*adj*) wet, **2.** spotted; *synonyms* (*adj*) mottled, dappled, speckled, blotchy, dotted, flyblown, piebald, multicolored, dirty, spotty, stained, tainted, besmirched, damaged, freckled; *antonym* (*adj*) plain.

kataneiai 1. experiment; *synonyms* (*n*) test, attempt, essay, trial, tentative, try, examination, taste, experience, experimentation, (*v*) examine, venture, check, **2.** accustom; *synonyms* (*v*) familiarize, acquaint, adjust, habituate, season, teach, acclimate, adapt, assimilate, custom, train, **3.** exercise; *synonyms* (*n*) practice, employment, application, discipline, play, movement, action, activity, (*v*) drill, apply, employ, use, exert, educate, do, **4.** give; *synonyms* (*v*) allow, bestow, extend, accord, commit, donate, contribute, convey, deliver, dispense, endow, grant, present, yield, administer; *antonyms* (*v*) withdraw, take, withhold, **5.** practice; *synonyms* (*n*) exercise, fashion, convention, habit, form, observance, performance, process, rule, usage, work, behavior, manner, (*v*) act, rehearse, **6.** train; *synonyms* (*n*) chain, string,

caravan, (*v*) aim, coach, direct, trail, tail, tame, instruct, prepare, school, domesticate, drag, groom, **7.** practise; *synonyms* (*v*) execute, perform, answer, arrange, behave, bore, cause, coif, coiffe, coiffure, come, dress, fare, make, manage.

kataneiaiaki 1. accustomed; *synonyms* (*adj*) customary, habitual, familiar, normal, usual, wonted, natural, common, everyday, habituated, ordinary, traditional, hardened; *antonyms* (*adj*) unaccustomed, unusual, **2.** given; *synonyms* (*adj*) apt, disposed, prone, liable, granted, inclined, set, (*n*) assumption, particular, presumption, fact, **3.** practised; *synonyms* (*adj*) practiced, expert, adept, good, **4.** practiced; *synonyms* (*adj*) experienced, skillful, accomplished, proficient, versed, practised, skilful, skilled, trained, able, qualified; *antonym* (*adj*) amateur, **5.** trained; *synonyms* (*adj*) capable, competent, accustomed, educated, efficient, fit, fitted, professional; *antonyms* (*adj*) untrained, inexpert, untaught, untutored.

katanetanea score; *synonyms* (*n*) mark, bill, count, scratch, line, groove, scotch, account, check, debt, (*v*) notch, cut, tally, achieve, dash.

katanetaneaki scored; *synonym* (*adj*) serrated.

katang gossip; *synonyms* (*n*) rumor, chitchat, gab, chatterbox, conversation, babble, comment, talk, blabbermouth, (*v*) chat, chatter, natter, tattle, blab, chaffer; *antonym* (*n*) fact.

katanga 1. group; *synonyms* (*n*) bunch, brigade, collection, crowd, flock, gang, association, clump, company, gathering, (*v*) assemblage, class, cluster, rank, sort, **2.** team; *synonyms* (*n*) crew, squad, organization, party, side, troop, couple, faction, group, (*v*) pair, band, (*adj*) file, line, range, row, **3.** round; *synonyms* (*adv*) about, around, (*adj*) circular, plump, entire, chubby, complete, (*n*) circle, bout, ring, beat, circuit, (*v*) compass, turn, gird; *antonyms* (*adj*) slim, sharp, **4.** rung; *synonyms* (*n*) round, rundle, degree, grade, stage, stair, spoke, stave, step, tread, **5.** perform; *synonyms* (*v*) execute, accomplish, do, fulfill, achieve, appear, behave, effect, make, play, enact, function, administer, operate, (*n*) act; *antonym* (*v*) neglect.

katangaki 1. grouped; *synonyms* (*adj*) sorted, collective, **2.** rung; *synonyms* (*n*) round, rundle, degree, grade, stage, stair, spoke, stave, step, tread, **3.** rounded; *synonyms* (*adj*) curved, circular, orbicular, full, globular, rotund, spherical, bent, blunt, fat, obtuse; *antonyms* (*adj*) pointed, straight, sharp, bony, concave.

katangare funny; *synonyms* (*adj*) comical, amusing, droll, eccentric, facetious, fishy, peculiar, strange, diverting, comic, curious, entertaining, farcical, humorous, (*adv*) funnily; *antonyms* (*adj*) serious, grave.

katangaua perplex; *synonyms* (*v*) bewilder, amaze, confuse, mystify, astonish, complicate, confound, nonplus, disconcert, baffle, bemuse, bother, discomfit, distract, (*adj*) puzzle.

katangauaki perplexed; *synonyms* (*v*) bewildered, complicated, intricate, (*adj*) confused, involved, lost, baffled, confounded, doubtful, puzzled, distracted, uneasy, bemused, questioning, quizzical; *antonym* (*adj*) enlightened.

katangibu protruding; *synonyms* (*adj*) prominent, obtrusive, jutting, projecting, salient, projected, noticeable, proposed, sticking.

katangibwerei whistle; *synonyms* (*n*) whistling, pennywhistle, (*v*) pipe, sing, twitter, hiss, cry, warble, cheep, tweet, chirp, wheeze.

katangitang sing; *synonyms* (*v*) chant, hymn, chirp, hum, drone, pipe, twitter, vocalize, carol, snitch, betray, harmonize, poetize, squeal, (*n*) squeak.

katania shift; *synonyms* (*n*) interchange, turn, move, switch, conversion, (*v*) change, exchange, remove, quibble, alter, budge, convert, displace, transfer, fluctuate.

katanina 1. devote; *synonyms* (*v*) apply, consecrate, dedicate, commit, assign, give, appropriate, allot, bestow, addict, consign, pay, present, (*n*) destine, vow, **2.** detail; *synonyms* (*n*) report, point, feature, item, circumstance, respect, (*v*) describe, enumerate, relate, appoint, cast, itemize, recite, specify, define; *antonym* (*n*) generalization, **3.** cast; *synonyms* (*v*) hurl, throw, form, shed, stamp, fling, shape, chuck, dump, figure, heave, mould, (*n*) appearance, casting, mold, **4.** authorize; *synonyms* (*v*) approve, empower, certify, commission, delegate, license, pass, permit, sanction, allow, authorise, charter, entitle, legalize, (*n*) grant, **5.** commission; *synonyms* (*n*) board, mission, delegation, job, mandate, warrant, assignment, charge, committee, duty, errand, task, (*v*) accredit, designate, authorize, **6.** group; *synonyms* (*n*) bunch, brigade, collection, crowd, flock, gang, association, clump, company, gathering, (*v*) assemblage, class, cluster, rank, sort, **7.** designate; *synonyms* (*v*) call, denominate, allocate, note, denote, direct, mark, name, prescribe, characterize, dub, elect, indicate, intend, (*adj*) express, **8.** appoint; *synonyms* (*v*) nominate, set, create, choose, constitute, depute, fix, institute, make, ordain, hire, attach, command, detail, employ, **9.** assign; *synonyms* (*v*) apportion, ascribe, attribute, award, distribute, place, put, accord, administer, confer, contribute, devote, dispense, entrust, (*n*) adjudge, **10.** separate; *synonyms* (*adj*) detached, (*v*) detach, divorce, part, insulate, scatter, cut, dissociate, disconnect, discrete, discriminate, disjoin, disperse, distinguish, divide; *antonyms* (*adj*) connected, joined, simultaneous, (*v*) unite, merge, mix, combine, fuse, join, link, associate.

kataninaki 1. designated; *synonyms* (*v*) designate, appointed, chosen, indicate, show, (*adj*) special, destined, numbered, nominated, selected, voted, **2.** appointed; *synonyms* (*adj*) prescribed, ordained, fit, set, fitted, appointive, bound, decreed, due, expected, fated, preordained, scheduled, anticipated, appropriate, **3.** cast; *synonyms* (*v*) hurl, throw, form, shed, stamp, fling, shape, chuck, dump, figure, heave, mould, (*n*) appearance, casting, mold, **4.** detailed; *synonyms* (*adj*) circumstantial, close, careful, accurate, delicate, elaborate, meticulous, minute, thorough, scrupulous, complete, comprehensive, elaborated, exact, exhaustive, **5.** devoted; *synonyms* (*adj*) addicted, affectionate, ardent, consecrated, constant, faithful, fond, loyal, pious, committed, dutiful, eager, enthusiastic, keen, (*prep*) dedicated; *antonyms* (*adj*) uncommitted, disloyal, indifferent, **6.** commissioned; *synonyms* (*adj*) accredited, licenced, licensed, vicarious, bespoke, customized, **7.** authorized; *synonyms* (*v*) allowed, (*adj*) authoritative, authorised, official, competent, lawful, legal, legitimate, permissible, privileged; *antonym* (*adj*) informal, **8.** assigned; *synonym* (*adj*) definite, **9.** grouped; *synonyms* (*adj*) sorted, collective, **10.** separated; *synonyms* (*adj*) disconnected, separate, apart, detached, divided, isolated, disjointed, free, disjunct, removed, dislocated, independent, lone, (*prep*) disjoined, distinct.

kataninga mean; *synonyms* (*v*) intend, design, imply, denote, involve, (*adj*) middle, base, common, hateful, ignoble, medium, miserly, (*n*) average, contemptible, low; *antonyms* (*adj*) generous, kind.

katanoata notify; *synonyms* (*v*) acquaint, advise, advertise, instruct, announce, inform, apprise, warn, alert, apprize, declare, enlighten, tell, counsel, promulgate.

katantana 1. mark; *synonyms* (*n*) brand, evidence, score, character, heed, impression, imprint, sign, feature, (*v*) blemish, characterize, distinguish, grade, label, (*adj*) notice, **2.** speckle; *synonyms* (*n*) fleck, dapple, spot, freckle, point, blot, maculation, patch, daub, flake, (*v*) speck, mark, stain, stipple, (*adj*) bespeckle, **3.** spot; *synonyms* (*n*) place, dot, dirty, location, position, space, defect, site, smudge, (*v*) soil, speckle, flaw, mottle, blur, locate.

katantanaki 1. marked; *synonyms* (*adj*) distinct, conspicuous, noticeable, pronounced, remarkable, distinguished, apparent, definite, notable, obvious, signal, striking, strong, clear, appreciable; *antonyms* (*adj*) plain, unblemished, **2.** spotted; *synonyms* (*adj*) mottled, dappled, speckled, blotchy, dotted, flyblown, piebald, multicolored, dirty, spotty, stained, tainted, besmirched, damaged, freckled, **3.** speckled; *synonyms* (*adj*) specked, spotted, flecked.

kataoa 1. deduct; *synonyms* (v) deduce, subtract, abate, allow, curtail, derive, discount, withhold, cut, infer, reason, recoup, reduce, take; *antonym* (v) add, **2.** deductible; *synonyms* (adj) consequential, deducible, rebatable, (n) excess, **3.** overflow; *synonyms* (n) flood, deluge, inundation, flooding, outpouring, runoff, torrent, affluence, flowage, (v) inundate, flow, drown, fill, overrun, submerge, **4.** overfill; *synonyms* (v) satiate, glut, spill, cloy, cram, gorge, saturate, stuff, sate, satisfy, suffice, surcharge, surfeit.

kataoaki 1. deducted, **2.** wasted; *synonyms* (v) rotten, effete, (adj) lost, squandered, thin, cadaverous, emaciated, gaunt, devastated, decayed, haggard, pointless, skeletal, atrophied, blasted; *antonyms* (adj) worthwhile, bloated.

kataoati 1. pass; *synonyms* (v) flow, deliver, give, happen, lead, move, offer, overtake, live, advance, die, elapse, exceed, (adj) go, run; *antonym* (v) fail, **2.** skirt; *synonyms* (n) border, edge, brim, flap, kilt, apron, margin, (v) fringe, circumvent, evade, hem, elude, sidestep, verge, dodge.

kataoatia overflow; *synonyms* (n) flood, deluge, inundation, excess, flooding, outpouring, runoff, torrent, affluence, (v) inundate, flow, drown, fill, overrun, submerge.

kataomata nap; *synonyms* (n) catnap, rest, drowse, down, pile, grain, (v) snooze, sleep, slumber, nod, coma, dream, (adj) doze, velvet, wool.

kataonaba squander; *synonyms* (v) waste, fritter, dissipate, exhaust, lavish, spend, blow, expend, desolate, lose, scatter, trifle, deplete, devour, (adj) consume; *antonyms* (v) save, conserve.

kataonabaki squandered; *synonyms* (v) alienated, bewildered, (adj) lost, wasted, dissipated, atrophied, blasted, bony, cadaverous, desolate, desolated, devastated, diminished, dissolute, emaciated.

kataorababa spread; *synonyms* (v) scatter, reach, disperse, expand, extend, broadcast, circulate, diffuse, disseminate, increase, propagate, stretch, broaden, deploy, (n) span; *antonym* (adj) concentrated.

kataorababaki spread; *synonyms* (v) scatter, reach, disperse, expand, extend, broadcast, circulate, diffuse, disseminate, increase, propagate, stretch, broaden, deploy, (n) span; *antonym* (adj) concentrated.

katara 1. exhibit; *synonyms* (v) evince, demonstrate, evidence, expose, disclose, announce, flaunt, parade, perform, present, produce, show, bear, indicate, (n) display; *antonym* (v) conceal, **2.** display; *synonyms* (n) array, presentation, appearance, screen, demonstration, exhibition, ostentation, scene, showing, spectacle, view, performance, (v) exhibit, brandish, reveal, **3.** show; *synonyms* (v) broadcast, guide, give, manifest, prove, figure, attest, denote, establish, illustrate, (n) pageant, picture, semblance, act, (adj) direct; *antonyms* (v) disprove, hide.

kataratara show; *synonyms* (v) present, broadcast, expose, guide, indicate, parade, demonstrate, disclose, evidence, (n) display, appearance, exhibit, produce, ostentation, presentation; *antonyms* (v) conceal, disprove, hide.

kataribaba detach; *synonyms* (v) disengage, divide, part, disconnect, disentangle, dissociate, remove, separate, unhook, isolate, abstract, cleave, disjoin, divorce, (n) detail; *antonyms* (v) attach, fasten, add, associate.

kataribabaki detached; *synonyms* (adj) aloof, cool, isolated, separate, distinct, disconnected, disinterested, dispassionate, impartial, indifferent, neutral, objective, remote, separated, unconcerned; *antonyms* (adj) attached, involved, engrossed, warm.

kataribabua 1. calm; *synonyms* (adj) quiet, peaceful, tranquil, (v) assuage, appease, cool, still, allay, pacify, easy, moderate, mollify, steady, (n) lull, equanimity; *antonyms* (adj) agitated, angry, nervous, stormy, wild, annoyed, anxious, enraged, frantic, frightened, intense, irritable, (v) agitate, upset, (n) agitation, **2.** quiet; *synonyms* (adj) gentle, motionless, placid, tranquilize, collected, composed, (v) silence, repose, (n) calm, hush, compose, ease, peace, peacefulness, alleviate; *antonyms* (adj) loud, noisy, talkative, vociferous, active, (n) noise.

kataribia 1. granulate; *synonyms* (v) grain, triturate, comminute, grind, powder, corn, levigate, crumble, pound, crush, grate, kern, pulverize, refine, crystallize, **2.** fragment; *synonyms* (n) fraction, crumb, morsel, part, division, piece, portion, rag, remnant, (v) bit, chip, scrap, shiver, splinter, break.

kataribiaki 1. fragmented; *synonyms* (adj) broken, crumbled, disconnected, disjointed, disunited, abrupt, confused, cut, disordered, ragged, split, garbled, illogical, scattered, sketchy, **2.** granulated; *synonym* (adj) granulate.

kataribono constipating; *synonyms* (adj) binding, constricting.

kataribonoa constipate; *synonyms* (v) bind, adhere, attach, bandage, bond, choke, clog, clot, congest, stagnate, stifle, foul, hold, (adj) compress, squeeze.

kataribonoaki constipated; *synonyms* (adj) costive, bellybound, close, cold, formal, impermeable, reserved, unyielding, (v) bound, certain, destined, resolved.

katarimarima sharpen; *synonyms* (v) focus, edge, hone, intensify, point, sharp, increase, heighten, whet, improve, compound, stimulate, taper, incite, (n) aim; *antonym* (v) cloud.

katarimarimaki sharpened; *synonyms* (adj) sharp, acute, acuate, better, sensual.

katarina cut; *synonyms* (*v*) carve, chop, clip, abbreviate, abridge, bite, condense, crop, drop, fashion, (*n*) notch, slice, cutting, nick, blow; *antonyms* (*v*) increase, lengthen, (*n*) addition, extension.

katarinaki cut; *synonyms* (*v*) carve, chop, clip, abbreviate, abridge, bite, condense, crop, drop, fashion, (*n*) notch, slice, cutting, nick, blow; *antonyms* (*v*) increase, lengthen, (*n*) addition, extension.

katarou 1. strain; *synonyms* (*n*) stress, breed, effort, stretch, exertion, race, (*v*) filter, screen, sift, tax, endeavor, exert, extend, percolate, pull; *antonym* (*v*) relax, **2.** sprain; *synonyms* (*n*) strain, injury, (*v*) wrench, rick, twist, wrick, injure, (*adj*) cramp, adynamy, asthenia, cachexia, cachexy, decrepitude, delicacy, invalidation.

katarouaki strained; *synonyms* (*adj*) forced, labored, tense, intense, constrained, laboured, unnatural, taut, tight, agonistic, agonistical, combative, farfetched; *antonyms* (*adj*) relaxed, natural.

katata 1. bounce; *synonyms* (*v*) jump, leap, bound, discharge, glance, recoil, beat, sack, caper, bob, fire, (*n*) spring, impact, jolt, bouncing, **2.** dribble; *synonyms* (*n*) trickle, dribbling, (*v*) drip, drool, drop, drivel, slobber, distill, flow, ooze, spout, trill, leak, seep, slabber, **3.** rebound; *synonyms* (*n*) kick, backlash, repercussion, return, echo, reaction, (*v*) bounce, ricochet, rally, boomerang, backfire, recover, reflect, resile, reverberate.

katataia snare; *synonyms* (*n*) trap, lure, decoy, net, noose, (*v*) mesh, catch, gin, ambush, ensnare, entrap, hook, capture, enmesh, entangle.

kataua 1. fit; *synonyms* (*v*) agree, accommodate, meet, suit, adapt, correspond, square, accord, dress, (*adj*) decorous, apt, applicable, appropriate, (*n*) adjust, convulsion; *antonyms* (*adj*) unfit, inappropriate, unwell, **2.** approve; *synonyms* (*v*) sanction, adopt, accept, acknowledge, allow, admit, endorse, let, ratify, support, applaud, acquiesce, authorize, confirm, okay; *antonyms* (*v*) reject, censure, condemn, disapprove, forbid, veto, **3.** consent; *synonyms* (*n*) acquiescence, consensus, agreement, approval, approbation, compliance, concurrence, acceptance, (*v*) assent, approve, concur, accede, coincide, comply, grant; *antonyms* (*n*) opposition, refusal, (*v*) disagree, refuse, **4.** tolerate; *synonyms* (*v*) suffer, bear, endure, permit, take, abide, brook, stand, stomach, sustain, undergo, have, submit, bide, withstand, **5.** permit; *synonyms* (*v*) give, license, leave, legalize, enable, tolerate, warrant, countenance, (*n*) consent, licence, pass, permission, charter, authority, authorization; *antonyms* (*v*) ban, prevent, prohibit, stop.

katauaki approved; *synonyms* (*adj*) accepted, certified, sanctioned, allowed, authorized, accredited, agreed, conventional, regular, official, orthodox; *antonyms* (*adj*) informal, unofficial.

kataumangaoa disorder; *synonyms* (*n*) ailment, complaint, clutter, disease, jumble, muddle, chaos, commotion, confusion, disarrangement, disturbance, (*v*) derange, disarray, confuse, perturb; *antonyms* (*n*) orderliness, calm, peace, (*v*) order.

kataumangaoaki disordered; *synonyms* (*adj*) confused, chaotic, broken, deranged, disorganized, incoherent, messy, sick, upset, disconnected, disjointed, disorderly, ill, jumbled, mixed; *antonyms* (*adj*) neat, orderly, ordered.

kataunata compare; *synonyms* (*v*) collate, liken, confront, comparison, equate, associate, contrast, correlate, equal, equalize, parallel, resemble, (*n*) comparability.

katauraoa prepare; *synonyms* (*v*) arrange, fix, form, plan, dress, coach, devise, lay, make, set, adjust, concoct, cook, equip, fit.

katauraoaki prepared; *synonyms* (*adj*) disposed, fit, willing, fitted, fain, finished, ready, ripe, competent, inclined, primed, completed, efficient, mature, apt; *antonyms* (*adj*) unprepared, spontaneous.

katauraoi prepare; *synonyms* (*v*) arrange, fix, form, plan, dress, coach, devise, lay, make, set, adjust, concoct, cook, equip, fit.

katauraoiaki prepared; *synonyms* (*adj*) disposed, fit, willing, fitted, fain, finished, ready, ripe, competent, inclined, primed, completed, efficient, mature, apt; *antonyms* (*adj*) unprepared, spontaneous.

kataururoa reduce; *synonyms* (*v*) lower, pare, abbreviate, curtail, cut, debase, abate, condense, contract, diminish, shorten, concentrate, compress, (*adj*) abridge, lessen; *antonyms* (*v*) increase, bolster, expand, enlarge, exacerbate, intensify.

kataururoaki reduced; *synonyms* (*adj*) decreased, abridged, curtailed, miniature, cheap, limited, bated, cut, inexpensive, low, lower, prostrate; *antonyms* (*adj*) expensive, complete.

kataururua 1. crash; *synonyms* (*n*) clash, collision, smash, clank, clatter, fall, impact, (*v*) bang, collapse, break, clang, crack, dash, plunge, ram, **2.** smash; *synonyms* (*v*) crash, hit, crush, mash, shatter, defeat, demolish, pound, ruin, slam, fragment, batter, (*n*) blast, knock, bash.

kataururuaki smashed; *synonyms* (*adj*) shattered, drunk, inebriated, intoxicated, broken, plastered, sloshed, blotto, tipsy, besotted, pissed, tight; *antonym* (*adj*) sober.

katautau 1. estimate; *synonyms* (*n*) calculation, appraisal, assessment, (*v*) compute, consider, count, esteem, guess, weigh, account, appraise, assess, computation, conjecture, estimation; *antonym* (*v*) calculate, **2.** guess; *synonyms* (*v*) surmise, forecast, believe, deem, divine, reckon, suppose, assume, feel, figure, foretell, gauge, (n) estimate, assumption, hypothesis, **3**. suppose; *synonyms* (v) infer, imagine, presume, speculate, conceive, expect, judge, regard, think, hope, fancy, anticipate, gather, hypothesize, opine, **4**. reckon; *synonyms* (v) enumerate, hold, number, rate, tally, measure, make, cipher, plan, tell, view, cast, cypher, depend, evaluate.

katautauaki 1. estimated; *synonyms* (adj) approximate, rough, anticipated, expected, ballpark, likely, predictable, probable, projected, reputed, sketchy, theoretical, vague, academic, hypothetical; *antonym* (adj) exact, **2**. supposed; *synonyms* (adj) conjectural, alleged, assumed, imaginary, putative, apparent, ostensible, suppositional, professed, suppositious, supposititious, pretended; *antonyms* (adj) real, actual.

katawa 1. loud; *synonyms* (adj) flashy, garish, gaudy, blatant, boisterous, brassy, forte, high, brazen, jazzy, clamorous, colorful, flash, meretricious, (adv) aloud; *antonyms* (adj) soft, gentle, quiet, tasteful, low, subdued, subtle, **2**. noisy; *synonyms* (adj) disorderly, loud, vociferous, rowdy, shrill, strident, tumultuous, turbulent, vocal, bustling, confused, harsh, rambunctious, obstreperous, piercing; *antonyms* (adj) peaceful, silent, calm, tranquil.

katawaea 1. mature; *synonyms* (adj) ripe, complete, adult, aged, developed, experienced, fledged, old, perfect, (v) grow, ripen, develop, age, maturate, mellow; *antonyms* (adj) childish, naive, unripe, young, sophomoric, (v) immature, **2**. ripen; *synonyms* (v) mature, season, cultivate, elaborate, fructify.

katawaeaki 1. matured; *synonyms* (adj) mature, ripe, adult, developed, experienced, old; *antonym* (adj) immature, **2**. ripened; *synonyms* (adj) matured, aged, elderly, cured, full-grown, grown, mellow, older, ready, seasoned, senior.

katawe 1. filch; *synonyms* (v) pilfer, steal, pinch, purloin, rob, cabbage, lift, swipe, palm, poach, abstract, cop, embezzle, hook, nim, **2**. hasten; *synonyms* (v) speed, expedite, further, forward, dispatch, advance, hurry, dash, hie, rush, bustle, dart, (adj) accelerate, quicken, (n) haste; *antonym* (v) delay, **3**. hasty; *synonyms* (adj) fast, abrupt, cursory, fleet, careless, hurried, impetuous, quick, rash, speedy, sudden, brisk, brusque, eager, expeditious; *antonyms* (adj) slow, considered, deliberate, leisurely, sensible, **4**. loot; *synonyms* (n) plunder, booty, prey, prize, bread, kale, haul, pickings, (v) pillage, despoil, rifle, foray, ransack, sack, gut, **5**. pinch; *synonyms* (n) arrest, crisis, emergency, squeeze, twinge, exigency, (v) nip, compress, wring, bite, clip, constrict, filch, gripe, pass, **6**. pilfer; *synonyms* (v) nobble, pocket,

thieve, appropriate, rustle, sneak, defraud, nick, **7**. pirate; *synonyms* (n) buccaneer, corsair, bandit, freebooter, pillager, robber, picaroon, marauder, plagiarizer, (v) hijack, plagiarist, infringe, loot, ravage, rover.

kataweaki 1. looted; *synonyms* (adj) pillaged, plundered, despoiled, ransacked, raped, ravaged, sacked, **2**. pinched; *synonyms* (adj) gaunt, haggard, drawn, emaciated, cadaverous, necessitous, adenoidal, bony, careworn, destitute, impecunious, narrow, nasal, (n) distressed, needy.

katea 1. found; *synonyms* (v) erect, establish, base, build, form, constitute, construct, appoint, create, ground, institute, bottom, begin, cast, plant; *antonym* (adj) misplaced, **2**. lift; *synonyms* (n) elevator, boost, heave, (v) hoist, raise, rise, elevate, filch, hike, advance, airlift, pilfer, pinch, rear, steal, **3**. establish; *synonyms* (v) confirm, prove, demonstrate, settle, arrange, ascertain, determine, fix, found, certify, compose, corroborate, decide, enact, make; *antonyms* (v) disprove, abolish, terminate, **4**. built; *synonyms* (adj) buxom, curvaceous, heavy, reinforced, robust, shapely, timbered, contrived, shaped, strengthened, wooden, (n) shape, **5**. erect; *synonyms* (v) assemble, lift, arouse, dignify, enhance, exalt, fabricate, frame, produce, stand, (adj) upright, vertical, perpendicular, raised, plumb; *antonym* (adj) horizontal, **6**. build; *synonyms* (v) fashion, formulate, calculate, compile, edify, forge, increase, (n) construction, figure, built, conformation, constitution, cut, formation, physique; *antonyms* (v) demolish, destroy, **7**. raise; *synonyms* (v) foster, grow, promote, prefer, augment, cultivate, excite, heighten, levy, nurture, pitch, amplify, enlarge, breed, (n) mount; *antonym* (v) lower, **8**. station; *synonyms* (n) rank, position, seat, standing, depot, office, spot, (v) place, locate, post, lay, order, put, set, site.

kateaki 1. founded; *synonyms* (v) cast, fusil, fusible, (adj) based, (prep) established, institute, organized, **2**. established; *synonyms* (v) settled, (adj) conventional, accepted, firm, fixed, regular, set, decided, confirmed, secure, accomplished, customary, effected, orthodox, completed; *antonym* (adj) unproven, **3**. lifted; *synonyms* (adj) elevated, lofty, steep, upraised, **4**. erected, **5**. built; *synonyms* (adj) buxom, curvaceous, heavy, reinforced, robust, shapely, timbered, contrived, shaped, strengthened, wooden, (n) shape, **6**. raised; *synonyms* (v) repousse, (adj) embossed, erect, convex, brocaded, high, alert, bold, confident, elate, elated, elative, exultant, mountant, (prep) above.

kateba 1. flick; *synonyms* (n) film, movie, pic, picture, show, (v) click, flip, jerk, flicker, snap, **2**. snap;

synonyms (*v*) crack, bite, break, fracture, nip, clack, snarl, rap, rip, (*n*) photograph, catch, go, picnic, pushover, clasp, **3**. peck; *synonyms* (*n*) dab, mass, pile, plenty, flock, heap, lot, mint, slew, stack, batch, (*v*) nibble, beak, kiss, pick.

katebaki snapped; *synonyms* (*adj*) tight, torn.

katebe 1. construct; *synonyms* (*v*) make, build, compose, erect, fabricate, form, arrange, constitute, manufacture, produce, raise, rear, assemble, compile, (*n*) concept; *antonyms* (*v*) destroy, demolish, **2**. found; *synonyms* (*v*) establish, base, construct, appoint, create, ground, institute, bottom, begin, cast, plant, start, imbed, introduce, father; *antonym* (*adj*) misplaced, **3**. erect; *synonyms* (*v*) elevate, lift, advance, arouse, dignify, enhance, exalt, found, frame, heave, hoist, (*adj*) upright, vertical, perpendicular, raised; *antonym* (*adj*) horizontal, **4**. institute; *synonyms* (*n*) academy, association, establishment, foundation, institution, organization, society, (*v*) fix, bring, initiate, inaugurate, launch, ordain, originate, (*adj*) enact.

katebea shear; *synonyms* (*v*) clip, cut, fleece, lop, pare, prune, shave, chop, chip, crop, trim, poll, (*n*) shearing, shears, (*adj*) dock.

katebeaki 1. instituted, **2**. founded; *synonyms* (*v*) cast, fusil, fusible, (*adj*) based, (*prep*) established, institute, organized, **3**. erected.

katebetebe peck; *synonyms* (*n*) dab, mass, pile, plenty, flock, heap, lot, mint, slew, stack, batch, (*v*) nibble, beak, kiss, pick.

katebetebea 1. nibble; *synonyms* (*v*) eat, munch, chew, browse, gnaw, nip, pick, crunch, champ, taste, cranch, craunch, (*n*) bite, morsel, nybble; *antonyms* (*v*) gobble, guzzle, **2**. peck; *synonyms* (*n*) dab, mass, pile, plenty, flock, heap, lot, mint, slew, stack, batch, (*v*) nibble, beak, kiss, lick.

kateboa immerse; *synonyms* (*v*) dip, douse, plunge, absorb, drench, drown, dunk, bury, engross, engulf, steep, submerge, bathe, duck, sink.

kateboaki immersed; *synonyms* (*adj*) absorbed, submerged, engrossed, deep, underwater, attentive, bathed, buried, captivated, concentrated, covered, engaged, enthralled, fascinated, gripped.

katebwina tenth; *synonyms* (*n*) tithe, disme, (*adj*) decimal, decuple, denary, tenfold.

katei 1. erect; *synonyms* (*v*) build, elevate, raise, construct, rear, assemble, lift, create, advance, arouse, dignify, (*adj*) upright, vertical, perpendicular, raised; *antonym* (*adj*) horizontal, **2**. lift; *synonyms* (*n*) elevator, boost, heave, support, climb, (*v*) hoist, rise, erect, filch, hike, airlift, pilfer, pinch, steal, swipe, **3**. institute; *synonyms* (*n*) academy, association, establishment, foundation, (*v*) establish, found, constitute, appoint, form, fix, begin, bring, initiate, base, (*adj*) enact, **4**. found; *synonyms* (*v*) ground, institute, bottom, cast, plant,

start, imbed, introduce, arrange, father, launch, originate, predicate, rest, embed; *antonym* (*adj*) misplaced, **5**. instruct; *synonyms* (*v*) charge, advise, direct, educate, enlighten, teach, command, drill, indoctrinate, inform, apprise, bid, coach, discipline, edify; *antonym* (*v*) request, **6**. build; *synonyms* (*v*) make, fabricate, fashion, produce, formulate, calculate, compile, compose, (*n*) shape, frame, construction, figure, built, conformation, constitution; *antonyms* (*v*) demolish, destroy, **7**. plant; *synonyms* (*n*) manufactory, equipment, factory, herb, mill, bush, cheat, (*v*) place, graft, set, lay, bury, cultivate, nominate, engraft, **8**. sheer; *synonyms* (*adj*) absolute, pure, mere, bold, diaphanous, filmy, gauzy, gossamer, simple, steep, transparent, regular, (*n*) complete, perfect, entire; *antonyms* (*adj*) gentle, thick, **9**. train; *synonyms* (*n*) chain, string, caravan, (*v*) aim, exercise, trail, tail, tame, instruct, prepare, school, domesticate, practice, drag, groom.

kateibaba disorder; *synonyms* (*n*) ailment, complaint, clutter, disease, jumble, muddle, chaos, commotion, confusion, disarrangement, disturbance, (*v*) derange, disarray, confuse, perturb; *antonyms* (*n*) orderliness, calm, peace, (*v*) order.

kateibabaki disordered; *synonyms* (*adj*) confused, chaotic, broken, deranged, disorganized, incoherent, messy, sick, upset, disconnected, disjointed, disorderly, ill, jumbled, mixed; *antonyms* (*adj*) neat, orderly, ordered.

kateibai 1. build; *synonyms* (*v*) make, erect, establish, raise, rise, base, construct, create, fabricate, fashion, (*n*) form, shape, frame, construction, figure; *antonyms* (*v*) demolish, destroy, **2**. manufacture; *synonyms* (*n*) fabrication, formation, production, creation, industry, assembly, work, (*v*) produce, build, contrive, invent, forge, concoct, do, coin, **3**. form; *synonyms* (*n*) design, arrange, ceremony, class, conformation, appearance, manner, (*v*) cast, constitute, carve, compose, comprise, devise, generate, mold, **4**. construct; *synonyms* (*v*) manufacture, rear, assemble, compile, fabric, organize, cause, craft, found, model, originate, (*n*) concept, conception, notion, idea, **5**. erect; *synonyms* (*v*) elevate, lift, advance, arouse, dignify, enhance, exalt, heave, hoist, institute, (*adj*) upright, vertical, perpendicular, raised, plumb; *antonym* (*adj*) horizontal.

kateibaiaki 1. manufactured; *synonyms* (*adj*) artificial, industrial, affected, contrived, ersatz, false, feigned, insincere, man-made, pretend, synthetic, unnatural, fixed; *antonym* (*adj*) natural, **2**. erected, **3**. built; *synonyms* (*adj*) buxom, curvaceous, heavy, reinforced, robust, shapely, timbered, shaped, strengthened, wooden, (*n*) shape, **4**. formed; *synonyms* (*adj*) wrought, settled, characterized, conceived, defined, fashioned, built, constructed, established, firm, adapted, adjusted, arranged, beaten, bent.

kateibanaea 1. disorder; *synonyms* (*n*) ailment, complaint, clutter, disease, jumble, muddle, chaos, commotion, confusion, disarrangement, disturbance, (*v*) derange, disarray, confuse, perturb; *antonyms* (*n*) orderliness, calm, peace, (*v*) order, **2.** trash; *synonyms* (*n*) nonsense, rubbish, junk, litter, garbage, refuse, rubble, scum, debris, trumpery, waste, (*v*) scrap, destroy, stuff, wreck.

kateibanaeaki disordered; *synonyms* (*adj*) confused, chaotic, broken, deranged, disorganized, incoherent, messy, sick, upset, disconnected, disjointed, disorderly, ill, jumbled, mixed; *antonyms* (*adj*) neat, orderly, ordered.

kateibuaka ungrateful; *synonyms* (*adj*) thankless, unmindful, unappreciative, unthankful, unnatural, ingrate, distasteful, displeasing, unkind, childless, cruel, harsh, ingrateful, offensive, unacceptable; *antonyms* (*adj*) grateful, thankful.

kateikai 1. check; *synonyms* (*v*) bridle, stop, block, limit, agree, halt, restrain, bar, dampen, delay, (*n*) control, arrest, curb, bill, cheque, **2.** forbid; *synonyms* (*v*) debar, prohibit, ban, disallow, exclude, deny, avert, frustrate, inhibit, interdict, outlaw, prevent, proscribe, veto, check; *antonyms* (*v*) permit, allow, let, approve, **3.** prohibit; *synonyms* (*v*) enjoin, forbid, hinder, preclude, hamper, impede, deter, oppose, embargo, restrict, command, disqualify, negative, (*n*) prohibition, obstruct.

kateikaiaki 1. forbidden; *synonyms* (*adj*) unlawful, banned, illegal, prohibited, taboo, contraband, illicit, proscribed, verboten; *antonym* (*adj*) acceptable, **2.** checked; *synonyms* (*adj*) checkered, chequered, plaid, backward, curbed, intermittent, limited, numbered, pent-up, safe, silent, tartan, temperate, **3.** prohibited; *synonyms* (*adj*) forbidden, barred, out; *antonyms* (*adj*) admissible, legitimate.

kateimatoa 1. construct; *synonyms* (*v*) make, build, compose, erect, fabricate, form, arrange, constitute, manufacture, produce, raise, rear, assemble, compile, (*n*) concept; *antonyms* (*v*) destroy, demolish, **2.** erect; *synonyms* (*v*) elevate, construct, lift, create, advance, arouse, dignify, enhance, establish, exalt, found, (*adj*) upright, vertical, perpendicular, raised; *antonym* (*adj*) horizontal, **3.** consolidate; *synonyms* (*v*) combine, compact, amalgamate, fuse, coagulate, coalesce, concentrate, incorporate, merge, unite, fix, embody, (*n*) close, (*adj*) set, concrete, **4.** establish; *synonyms* (*v*) confirm, prove, appoint, base, demonstrate, settle, ascertain, determine, institute, begin, certify, corroborate, decide, enact, plant; *antonyms* (*v*) disprove, abolish, terminate, **5.** ratify; *synonyms* (*v*) approve, acknowledge, authorize, endorse,

sanction, affirm, attest, pass, adopt, sign, substantiate, sustain, (*n*) countersign, indorse, support.

kateimatoaki 1. erected, **2.** established; *synonyms* (*v*) settled, (*adj*) conventional, accepted, firm, fixed, regular, set, decided, confirmed, secure, accomplished, customary, effected, orthodox, completed; *antonym* (*adj*) unproven, **3.** consolidated; *synonyms* (*adj*) amalgamated, coalesced, united, amalgamate, consolidate, joint, solid, close, collective, concrete, entire, fused, hard, thick, intermingled, **4.** ratified; *synonyms* (*adj*) approved, canonic, canonical, sanctioned.

kateinang 1. frighten; *synonyms* (*v*) alarm, cow, dismay, daunt, terrify, appall, affright, intimidate, scare, terrorize, awe, deter, horrify, startle, (*n*) fright; *antonyms* (*v*) comfort, encourage, **2.** tiresome; *synonyms* (*adj*) boring, tedious, dull, laborious, irksome, monotonous, annoying, bothersome, difficult, dreary, fatiguing, slow, trying, (*v*) troublesome, wearisome; *antonym* (*adj*) interesting, **3.** overwhelming; *synonyms* (*adj*) overpowering, devastating, irresistible, insurmountable, crushing, monumental, amazing, astounding, tremendous, awesome, breathtaking, consuming, formidable, impossible, intense; *antonym* (*adj*) imperceptible, **4.** unapproachable; *synonyms* (*adj*) inaccessible, aloof, distant, remote, illimitable, immeasurable, incalculable, inexhaustible, innumerable, interminable, unreachable; *antonyms* (*adj*) approachable, accessible, **5.** opposed; *synonyms* (*adj*) conflicting, contradictory, hostile, contrary, antagonistic, opposing, adverse, averse, contrasted, repugnant, incompatible, irreconcilable, counter, against, opposite, **6.** tiring; *synonyms* (*adj*) exhausting, tiresome, hard, wearing, arduous, grueling, onerous, strenuous; *antonyms* (*adj*) easy, undemanding, **7.** overwhelmed; *synonyms* (*v*) overborne, (*adj*) overcome, beaten, overpowered, vanquished, conquered, dumbfounded, engulfed, flooded, inundated, overthrown; *antonyms* (*adj*) victorious, unimpressed, **8.** overwhelm; *synonyms* (*v*) defeat, flood, inundate, overpower, overthrow, crush, deluge, drown, engulf, astound, beat, overrun, overtake, overturn, swamp.

kateinangaki overwhelmed; *synonyms* (*v*) overborne, (*adj*) overcome, beaten, overpowered, vanquished, conquered, dumbfounded, engulfed, flooded, inundated, overthrown; *antonyms* (*adj*) victorious, unimpressed.

kateirakea 1. stir; *synonyms* (*v*) arouse, budge, move, rouse, affect, agitate, excite, inspire, go, (*n*) movement, commotion, disturbance, excitement, agitation, (*adj*) bustle, **2.** rouse; *synonyms* (*v*) awake, awaken, kindle, provoke, instigate, actuate, disturb, incite, fire, inflame, revive, heat, animate, encourage, induce; *antonyms* (v) calm, dampen, **3.** rise; *synonyms* (n) elevation, lift, ascent, progress, raise, swell, raising, advancement, (v) climb, mount, ascend, increase, heave, arise, jump; *antonyms* (n) reduction, (v) fall, decrease, drop, sink, descend, plummet, retire.

kateirakeaki stirred; *synonyms* (adj) stimulated, excited, affected, aroused, emotional, aflame, ablaze, beaten, enthused, horny, inspired, interested, overwrought, randy, ruttish; *antonym* (adj) uninspired.

kateka pierce; *synonyms* (v) impale, cut, perforate, bore, enter, stab, stick, bite, drill, gore, penetrate, puncture, thrust, wound, (n) prick.

katekaki pierced; *synonyms* (adj) perforated, punctured, perforate, cleft, entered.

kateke 1. natty; *synonyms* (adj) dapper, jaunty, smart, spruce, chic, dashing, neat, rakish, snappy, stylish, trim, elegant, prim, tidy, trig, **2.** elegant; *synonyms* (adj) graceful, courtly, delicate, splendid, beautiful, dainty, polite, refined, dressy, artistic, charming, classy, cultured, debonair, fine; *antonyms* (adj) clumsy, inelegant, scruffy, ugly, coarse, plain, tacky, **3.** incisive; *synonyms* (adj) sharp, acute, cutting, keen, penetrating, piercing, pungent, pointed, biting, discriminating, quick, trenchant, perceptive, crisp, barbed; *antonym* (adj) mild, **4.** keen; *synonyms* (adj) eager, intense, intelligent, brisk, enthusiastic, exquisite, clever, astute, desirous, ardent, bright, fervent, hungry, (v) fresh, avid; *antonyms* (adj) dull, apathetic, indifferent, unenthusiastic, blunt, **5.** nice; *synonyms* (adj) fastidious, good, kind, lovely, likable, delicious, agreeable, correct, decent, difficult, enjoyable, exact, particular, precise, right; *antonyms* (adj) unpleasant, horrible, **6.** agreeable; *synonyms* (adj) acceptable, accordant, pleasant, pleasing, nice, affable, amusing, compatible, conformable, congenial, consistent, genial, grateful, harmonious, (v) desirable; *antonyms* (adj) disagreeable, discordant, nasty, unwilling, aggressive, resistant, **7.** prim; *synonyms* (adj) formal, priggish, prudish, stiff, ceremonious, decorous, demure, mincing, prissy, squeamish, stilted, genteel, stuffy, conventional, proper; *antonyms* (adj) relaxed, brash, **8.** stylish; *synonyms* (adj) fashionable, cool, in, modern, popular, swanky, trendy, attractive, handsome, hip, polished, prevalent, swell, swish, (n) modish; *antonym* (adj) unfashionable, **9.** striking; *synonyms* (adj) impressive, dramatic, outstanding, salient, spectacular, imposing, astonishing, conspicuous, extraordinary, notable, noticeable, prominent, remarkable, (n) hit, strike; *antonyms* (adj) ordinary, unimpressive, **10.** pretty; *synonyms* (adv) very, fairly, jolly, quite, rather, somewhat, moderately, (adj) fair, good-looking, picturesque, cute, comely,

bonny, becoming, noble, **11.** smart; *synonyms* (adj) crafty, shrewd, sly, prompt, lively, natty, saucy, ready, alert, artful, cunning, knowing, (v) ache, hurt, (n) pain; *antonyms* (adj) stupid, dim, shabby, unkempt, slow.

katekea 1. impale; *synonyms* (v) transfix, empale, spike, kill, lance, spear, thrust, enfilade, (n) stick, **2.** irradiate; *synonyms* (v) illuminate, enlighten, radiate, lighten, ray, shine, **3.** pierce; *synonyms* (v) impale, cut, perforate, bore, enter, stab, bite, drill, gore, penetrate, puncture, wound, broach, pick, (n) prick, **4.** stab; *synonyms* (n) jab, pierce, dig, try, shot, pang, attempt, crack, effort, go, (v) poke, prod, pink, spit, knife, **5.** surpass; *synonyms* (v) pass, beat, exceed, outdo, better, excel, outstrip, surmount, overcome, overrun, best, outgo, outshine, outweigh, overstep, **6.** perforate; *synonyms* (v) punch, (adj) perforated, **7.** penetrate; *synonyms* (v) imbue, fathom, infiltrate, permeate, filter, interpenetrate, diffuse, percolate, probe, saturate, cross, move, break, strike, discern.

katekeaki 1. irradiated; *synonyms* (adj) illuminated, bright, exposed, irradiate, **2.** stabbed, **3.** pierced; *synonyms* (adj) perforated, punctured, perforate, cleft, entered, **4.** perforated; *synonyms* (adj) pierced, penetrated.

katekebotia inform; *synonyms* (v) communicate, acquaint, advise, impart, announce, enlighten, tell, familiarize, explain, advertise, apprise, educate, instruct, state, warn.

katekebotiaki informed; *synonyms* (adj) aware, cognizant, educated, conscious, knowledgeable, familiar, apprised, wise, conversant, experienced, (adv) abreast; *antonym* (adj) ignorant.

katekeria 1. charming; *synonyms* (adj) amiable, beautiful, attractive, captivating, delightful, enchanting, lovely, pleasing, winning, nice, adorable, agreeable, alluring, amusing, appealing; *antonyms* (adj) repellent, unappealing, unpleasant, **2.** appetizing; *synonyms* (adj) appetising, delectable, delicious, luscious, tasty, tantalizing, palatable, savory, scrumptious, spicy; *antonyms* (adj) tasteless, unappetizing, **3.** alluring; *synonyms* (adj) charming, enticing, seductive, tempting, beguiling, glamorous, magnetic, desirable, engaging, enthralling, fascinating, inviting, interesting, **4.** seductive; *synonyms* (adj) seducing, sexy, irresistible, persuasive, **5.** tasty; *synonyms* (adj) tasteful, appetizing, dainty, savoury, rich, flavorful, appreciate, criticise, cute, edible, judge; *antonyms* (adj) bland, inedible.

katemeteme squeak; *synonyms* (n) cry, screech, chirp, (v) shriek, scream, peep, creak, screak, yell, scrape, howl, cheep, wail, yelp, shrill.

katena 1. acidify; *synonyms* (v) acetify, sour, acidulate, turn, ferment, imbitter, work, (n) curdle,

2. cauterize; *synonyms* (*v*) burn, sear, brand, cauterise, fire, bite, bake, animate, blister, callous, clean, dress, combust, consume, cut, 3. burnt; *synonyms* (*v*) brent, (*adj*) burned, adust, baked, heated, sunburnt, adusted, arid, dry, overcooked, overdone, consumed, dehydrated, desiccated, parched; *antonym* (*adj*) underdone, 4. adjoin; *synonyms* (*v*) abut, border, annex, touch, neighbor, edge, meet, append, contact, verge, butt, (*adj*) join, 5. burn; *synonyms* (*v*) glow, blaze, incinerate, scorch, sting, beam, boil, cremate, flare, ignite, sunburn, seethe, smolder, (*adj*) flush, smoke; *antonym* (*v*) dawdle, 6. sear; *synonyms* (*n*) steel, caseharden, (*v*) char, cauterize, parch, scald, fry, broil, singe, heat, (*adj*) sere, withered, 7. sting; *synonyms* (*n*) hurt, con, pain, chafe, stab, (*v*) prick, goad, irritate, itch, prickle, provoke, cheat, nettle, prod, smart, 8. tighten; *synonyms* (*v*) contract, strain, brace, compress, constrict, fasten, narrow, reduce, squeeze, stiffen, stretch, screw, secure, constrain, frap; *antonyms* (*v*) loosen, relax.

katenaki 1. burnt; *synonyms* (*v*) brent, (*adj*) burned, adust, baked, heated, sunburnt, adusted, arid, combust, dry, overcooked, overdone, consumed, dehydrated, desiccated; *antonym* (*adj*) underdone, 2. tightened; *synonyms* (*adj*) tight, firm, 3. seared; *synonyms* (*adj*) scorched, parched, cauterized; *antonym* (*adj*) wet.

katengetengea 1. exhibit; *synonyms* (*v*) evince, demonstrate, evidence, expose, disclose, announce, flaunt, parade, perform, present, produce, show, bear, indicate, (*n*) display; *antonym* (*v*) conceal, 2. bare; *synonyms* (*adj*) naked, austere, bald, stark, bleak, desolate, devoid, exposed, mere, nude, plain, vacant, vacuous, barren, (*v*) empty; *antonyms* (*adj*) covered, cultivated, ornate, concealed, (*v*) cover.

katengetengeaki bore; *synonyms* (*v*) dig, bother, tire, annoy, drill, perforate, pierce, plague, tap, (*n*) caliber, diameter, nuisance, well, annoyance, (*adj*) pother; *antonyms* (*v*) interest, excite, fascinate.

kateniua third; *synonyms* (*n*) second, three, inquiry, leash, probe, question, terce, tercet, ternary, ternion, (*adj*) tertiary, least, tertial, (*adv*) thirdly, (*v*) interrogate.

katenua 1. correspond; *synonyms* (*v*) accord, coincide, conform, suit, consort, answer, check, concur, fit, harmonize, match, parallel, accede, communicate, (*adj*) agree; *antonyms* (*v*) differ, disagree, 2. enunciate; *synonyms* (*v*) articulate, declare, vocalize, pronounce, voice, enounce, express, proclaim, say, speak, state, utter, (*n*) allege, propound, advance; *antonym* (*v*) mumble, 3. adapt; *synonyms* (*v*) adjust, accommodate, acclimate, fashion, alter, arrange, assimilate, change, edit, familiarize, gear, modify, shape, tailor, accustom, 4. pronounce; *synonyms* (*v*) enunciate, affirm, assert, deliver, announce, decree,

judge, rule, pass, adjudicate, prolate, (*n*) give, maintain, adjudge, (*adj*) discharge.

katenuaki 1. adapted; *synonyms* (*v*) convenient, (*adj*) altered, fit, agreeable, appropriate, conformable, fitted, prepared; *antonyms* (*adj*) mass-produced, unaccustomed, 2. pronounced; *synonyms* (*adj*) marked, clear, emphatic, distinct, notable, prominent, definite, obvious, salient, bold, decided, demonstrative, outstanding, striking.

katerea 1. exhibit; *synonyms* (*v*) evince, demonstrate, evidence, expose, disclose, announce, flaunt, parade, perform, present, produce, show, bear, indicate, (*n*) display; *antonym* (*v*) conceal, 2. show; *synonyms* (*v*) broadcast, guide, give, manifest, prove, reveal, figure, (*n*) appearance, exhibit, ostentation, presentation, pageant, picture, semblance, act; *antonyms* (*v*) disprove, hide, 3. present; *synonyms* (*adj*) grant, confer, current, (*n*) gift, donation, offering, (*v*) bestow, introduce, prefer, deliver, donate, offer, gratuity, award, serve; *antonyms* (*adj*) missing, (*n*) past, future, history, (*v*) withdraw, (*adv*) absent.

katereaki presented; *synonyms* (*adj*) bestowed, conferred, offered, existing, accessible, obtainable, free, open, unfilled, untaken, vacant.

katereke 1. distinguished; *synonyms* (*adj*) celebrated, dignified, eminent, conspicuous, illustrious, important, renowned, reputable, famous, great, high, noble, prominent, splendid, superior; *antonyms* (*adj*) unknown, ordinary, 2. noble; *synonyms* (*adj*) imposing, magnificent, glorious, distinguished, elevated, exalted, generous, impressive, majestic, patrician, aristocratic, elegant, (*n*) grand, excellent, aristocrat; *antonyms* (*adj*) lower-class, selfish, shameful, humble, dishonorable, lowly, 3. handsome; *synonyms* (*adj*) beautiful, fair, charming, fine, attractive, bountiful, comely, bonny, big, bounteous, exquisite, gorgeous, graceful, liberal, lovely; *antonyms* (*adj*) ugly, unattractive.

kateretere 1. exhibit; *synonyms* (*v*) evince, demonstrate, evidence, expose, disclose, announce, flaunt, parade, perform, present, produce, show, bear, indicate, (*n*) display; *antonym* (*v*) conceal, 2. show; *synonyms* (*v*) broadcast, guide, give, manifest, prove, reveal, figure, (*n*) appearance, exhibit, ostentation, presentation, pageant, picture, semblance, act; *antonyms* (*v*) disprove, hide, 3. present; *synonyms* (*adj*) grant, confer, current, (*n*) gift, donation, offering, (*v*) bestow, introduce, prefer, deliver, donate, offer, gratuity, award, serve; *antonyms* (*adj*) missing, (*n*) past, future, history, (*v*) withdraw, (*adv*) absent.

katereterea 1. manifest; *synonyms* (*adj*) apparent, evident, clear, conspicuous, distinct, patent, plain, (*v*) demonstrate, display, evidence, exhibit, express, indicate, attest, (*n*) declare; *antonym* (*adj*) unclear, 2.

expose; *synonyms* (*v*) disclose, endanger, betray, detect, air, bare, debunk, discover, divulge, reveal, uncover, unfold, compromise, bewray, find; *antonyms* (*v*) conceal, protect, cover, enclose, **3.** explain; *synonyms* (*v*) comment, elucidate, interpret, account, clarify, decipher, define, describe, enlighten, excuse, explicate, expound, gloss, solve, denote; *antonym* (*v*) confuse, **4.** accentuate; *synonyms* (*v*) emphasize, accent, stress, underline, emphasise, punctuate, underscore, highlight; *antonym* (*v*) deaden, **5.** emphasize; *synonym* (*v*) accentuate, **6.** reveal; *synonyms* (*v*) expose, convey, impart, present, announce, communicate, show, proclaim, develop, instruct, break, confess, explain, leak, manifest; *antonym* (*v*) hide, **7.** represent; *synonyms* (*v*) depict, portray, act, be, embody, exemplify, illustrate, play, enact, make, impersonate, comprise, constitute, epitomize, introduce.

kateretereaki 1. exposed; *synonyms* (*v*) vulnerable, (*adj*) bare, open, defenseless, liable, naked, nude, obvious, subject, uncovered, unprotected, bald, bleak, public, undefended; *antonyms* (*adj*) concealed, covered, hidden, safe, **2.** emphasized; *synonyms* (*adj*) emphasised, emphatic, exclamatory, forceful, **3.** represented; *synonyms* (*adj*) delineate, delineated, **4.** revealed; *synonyms* (*adj*) exposed, disclosed, discovered, **5.** presented; *synonyms* (*adj*) bestowed, conferred, offered, existing, accessible, obtainable, free, unfilled, untaken, vacant.

katetea boil; *synonyms* (*v*) seethe, bubble, churn, simmer, ferment, burn, effervesce, fume, heat, anger, (*n*) abscess, blister, furuncle, pimple, (*adj*) sore; *antonym* (*v*) freeze.

kateteaki boiled; *synonyms* (*adj*) done, intoxicated, poached, stewed, (*v*) sodden, saturated, seethed, soaked.

kati 1. canon; *synonyms* (*n*) rule, doctrine, law, principle, regulation, code, criterion, formula, statute, creed, prebendary, **2.** gun; *synonyms* (*n*) artillery, gunman, handgun, ordnance, pistol, revolver, shooter, torpedo, accelerator, arrow, gas, (*v*) shoot, cracker, **3.** fire; *synonyms* (*n*) discharge, ardor, conflagration, explode, fervor, flame, (*v*) excite, eject, blaze, dismiss, ignite, kindle, expel, animate, arouse; *antonym* (*v*) hire, **4.** arms; *synonyms* (*n*) arm, armament, weaponry, shield, blazon, munition, order, weapons, (*v*) war, **5.** gush; *synonyms* (*n*) flow, spout, burst, jet, effusion, rush, stream, surge, (*v*) flood, spurt, course, emanate, cascade, emit, erupt; *antonym* (*v*) trickle, **6.** shot; *synonyms* (*n*) gunshot, injection, go, fling, ball, crack, picture, attempt, bang, bullet, chance, effort, endeavor, guess, (*adj*) iridescent, **7.** slick; *synonyms* (*adj*) sleek, clever, glib, adroit, crafty, cunning, foxy, glossy, silken, silky, smooth, artful,

dexterous, dodgy, greasy, **8.** squirt; *synonyms* (*n*) spirt, fountain, child, nobody, (*v*) spray, gush, splash, spill, **9.** shoot; *synonyms* (*v*) bud, dart, dash, drive, flash, hunt, send, fire, germinate, grow, inject, (*n*) scion, branch, sprout, chute, **10.** smooth; *synonyms* (*adj*) easy, calm, level, oily, facile, flat, flowing, fluent, fluid, graceful, liquid, mellow, (*v*) quiet, facilitate, even; *antonyms* (*adj*) rough, uneven, abrasive, coarse, crumpled, flaking, harsh, jerky, lined, peeling, prickly, ridged, wrinkled, corrugated, (*v*) wrinkle, **11.** spout; *synonyms* (*n*) nozzle, squirt, pipe, outlet, nose, opening, conduit, trough, lip, tap, (*v*) pawn, roll, vent, dribble, pour, **12.** slippery; *synonyms* (*adj*) elusive, shifty, slick, slippy, tricky, untrustworthy, wily, dishonest, icy, shady, insidious, shrewd, changeable, (*v*) precarious, questionable.

katia 1. hone; *synonyms* (*v*) sharpen, perfect, whet, refine, edge, coach, consummate, develop, drill, enhance, exercise, improve, practice, rehearse, (*adj*) sharpener, **2.** complete; *synonyms* (*adj*) absolute, whole, full, stark, accomplished, all, (*v*) accomplish, achieve, close, finish, execute, act, attain, cease, clear; *antonyms* (*adj*) incomplete, partial, unfinished, abridged, shortened, sketchy, lacking, narrow, qualified, (*v*) neglect, **3.** conclude; *synonyms* (*v*) complete, gather, assume, deduce, determine, end, resolve, settle, terminate, decide, derive, do, generalize, judge, reason; *antonyms* (*v*) start, begin, **4.** done; *synonyms* (*adj*) finished, completed, over, gone, through, (*adv*) ended, **5.** augment; *synonyms* (*v*) amplify, increase, add, enlarge, aggrandize, reinforce, boost, expand, grow, intensify, magnify, raise, mount, broaden, (*n*) accrue; *antonym* (*v*) reduce, **6.** concluded; *synonyms* (*adj*) done, closed, terminated, **7.** closed; *synonyms* (*v*) tight, accurate, adjoining, attentive, (*adj*) blind, blocked, shut, congested, fastened, exclusive, insular, stopped, airtight, benighted, black; *antonym* (*adj*) open, **8.** finished; *synonyms* (*adj*) polished, ripe, ruined, spent, round, capable, decided, final, elegant, concluded, exhausted, fitted, fulfilled, nice, past; *antonyms* (*adj*) remaining, rough, **9.** close; *synonyms* (*adj*) near, adjacent, nearby, approximate, brief, airless, (*v*) compact, stop, conclude, bar, block, (*adv*) by, about, (*n*) conclusion, expiration; *antonyms* (*adj*) distant, airy, fresh, loose, far, **10.** finish; *synonyms* (*v*) discontinue, consume, culminate, deplete, exhaust, expire, go, (*n*) death, ending, finale, glaze, accomplishment, coating, completion, last; *antonyms* (*v*) continue, (*n*) beginning, **11.** increase; *synonyms* (*n*) gain, addition, augmentation, boom, expansion, extension, growth, progress, rise, accretion, (*v*) advance, extend, deepen, accumulate, (*adj*) augment; *antonyms* (*n*) reduction, contraction, decline, (*v*) decrease, diminish, drop, deteriorate,

12. terminated; *synonym* (*adj*) extinct, **13**. terminate; *synonyms* (*v*) dismiss, dissolve, halt, can, result, abort, bound, cancel, ax, extinguish, fire, sack, break, sever, interrupt; *antonym* (*v*) establish, **14**. sharpen; *synonyms* (*v*) focus, hone, point, sharp, heighten, compound, stimulate, taper, incite, kindle, quicken, (*n*) aim; *antonym* (*v*) cloud.

katiaki 1. honed; *synonyms* (*adj*) keen, pithy, sharp, **2**. completed; *synonyms* (*adj*) complete, done, accomplished, finished, ended, perfect, ready, through, whole, (*adv*) over, **3**. augmented; *synonyms* (*adj*) inflated, more, plus, better, bigger, improved, **4**. fired; *synonyms* (*adj*) dismissed, discharged, unemployed, ablaze, enthusiastic, heated, interested, passionate, zealous, afire, excited, released, **5**. finished; *synonyms* (*adj*) completed, consummate, absolute, polished, ripe, ruined, spent, round, capable, decided, final, elegant, concluded, exhausted, fitted; *antonyms* (*adj*) unfinished, incomplete, remaining, rough, **6**. increased; *synonyms* (*adj*) additional, enlarged, greater, fresh, new, puffy, amplified, other, superior, **7**. closed; *synonyms* (*v*) close, tight, accurate, adjoining, attentive, (*adj*) blind, blocked, shut, congested, fastened, exclusive, insular, stopped, airtight, benighted; *antonym* (*adj*) open, **8**. concluded; *synonyms* (*adj*) closed, terminated, **9**. sharpened; *synonyms* (*adj*) acute, acuate, sensual, **10**. terminated; *synonym* (*adj*) extinct.

katiatia plead; *synonyms* (*v*) beseech, entreat, beg, implore, appeal, ask, petition, defend, invoke, solicit, sue, argue, importune, justify, (*n*) allege.

katiba 1. dislocate; *synonyms* (*v*) shift, displace, disjoint, disturb, move, muddle, wrench, transfer, jumble, dislodge, disorder, disorganize, slip, splay, unhinge, **2**. slip; *synonyms* (*n*) lapse, fault, mistake, cutting, error, escape, oversight, scion, trip, (*v*) fall, slide, drop, glide, skid, (*adj*) blunder; *antonym* (*v*) improve, **3**. unhook; *synonyms* (*v*) liberate, loosen, undo, disengage, unbolt, unbutton, unlock, untie; *antonym* (*v*) hook, **4**. untidy; *synonyms* (*adj*) slovenly, disheveled, disordered, disorderly, messy, sloppy, unkempt, confused, disorganized, frowzy, scruffy, sluttish, slipshod, dowdy, tousled; *antonyms* (*adj*) tidy, neat, elegant, **5**. upset; *synonyms* (*v*) overturn, agitate, disquiet, overthrow, bother, confuse, perturb, reverse, subvert, unsettle, (*adj*) unsettled, hurt, (*n*) trouble, distress, disturbance; *antonyms* (*v*) calm, please, encourage, soothe, (*adj*) pleased, confident.

katibaki 1. dislocated; *synonyms* (*adj*) disjointed, disordered, dislocate, disorderly, confused, detached, disconnected, separated, topsy-turvy, garbled, illogical, isolated, scattered, separate, spaced, **2**. upset; *synonyms* (*v*) overturn, agitate, disquiet, overthrow, bother, confuse, disturb, perturb, reverse, (*adj*) unsettled, hurt, (*n*) disorder,

trouble, distress, disturbance; *antonyms* (*v*) calm, please, encourage, soothe, (*adj*) pleased, confident.

katibanakoa pass; *synonyms* (*v*) flow, deliver, give, happen, lead, move, offer, overtake, live, advance, die, elapse, exceed, (*adj*) go, run; *antonym* (*v*) fail.

katibebe 1. unbalanced; *synonyms* (*adj*) lopsided, crazy, mad, wobbly, demented, disproportionate, imbalanced, unequal, asymmetrical, unsettled, unstable, unsteady, brainsick, distracted, disturbed; *antonyms* (*adj*) sane, balanced, even, well-balanced, **2**. unsteady; *synonyms* (*adj*) changeable, dizzy, insecure, rickety, shaky, unbalanced, unsound, precarious, uneven, irregular, erratic, fluctuating, inconstant, jerky, (*n*) uncertain; *antonym* (*adj*) steady.

katibetibeaki freed; *synonyms* (*adj*) free, disentangled, emancipated, disengaged, liberated, extricated, disillusioned, flowing, unsnarled; *antonym* (*adj*) secure.

katibua inflate; *synonyms* (*v*) enlarge, expand, dilate, distend, amplify, balloon, bloat, billow, blow, bulge, increase, heave, exaggerate, fill, magnify; *antonym* (*v*) deflate.

katibuaki inflated; *synonyms* (*adj*) bombastic, grandiloquent, exaggerated, puffy, conceited, bloated, hyperbolic, swollen, vain, extravagant, flatulent, enlarged, overblown, pompous, (*v*) distended; *antonyms* (*adj*) understated, deflated, humble.

katietiea swing; *synonyms* (*n*) sweep, range, (*v*) sway, fluctuate, oscillate, dangle, hang, rock, beat, brandish, change, move, shake, turn, vibrate.

katika 1. hail; *synonyms* (*n*) greet, call, greeting, rain, (*v*) address, cry, acclaim, applaud, summon, accost, cheer, come, fall, receive, salute, **2**. drag; *synonyms* (*v*) attract, haul, draw, puff, trail, cart, hale, heave, lug, tow, delay, (*n*) pull, bother, bore, hindrance; *antonym* (*v*) push, **3**. jerk; *synonyms* (*n*) tug, fool, dork, (*v*) jolt, jump, shake, yank, jar, twitch, fling, bump, flip, bob, bounce, convulse, **4**. heave; *synonyms* (*v*) cast, chuck, gasp, toss, billow, drag, elevate, gag, hoist, jerk, lift, pitch, (*n*) raise, elevation, heaving, **5**. tug; *synonyms* (*n*) strain, towboat, effort, exertion, tugboat, nip, (*v*) labor, fight, labour, pluck, strive, tote, move, wrench, drive, **6**. pull; *synonyms* (*v*) draught, pick, make, force, lure, get, appeal, arrest, commit, extract, (*n*) attraction, twist, influence, control, allure; *antonym* (*v*) repel, **7**. tow; *synonyms* (*n*) towage, (*v*) rake, taw.

katikaki 1. towed, **2**. pulled; *synonyms* (*adj*) moulting, pilled, plucked.

katikeke 1. coast; *synonyms* (*n*) bank, beach, seaside, shore, seashore, sand, seacoast, shoreline, (*v*) glide, slide, drift, cruise; *antonym* (*n*) interior, **2**. glide; *synonyms* (*n*) slip, gliding, sailing, soaring, (*v*) coast, float, flow, fly, run, lapse, move, skid, slink, slither, soar; *antonym* (*v*) struggle, **3**. slither; *synonyms* (*v*) crawl, creep, **4**. skate; *synonyms* (*v*) skim, jade, plug, rackabones, **5**. skim; *synonyms* (*v*) browse, skip, sweep, brush, graze, race, read, scan, shave, glance, remove, scum, (*n*) cream, review, (*adj*) skimmed, **6**. slide; *synonyms* (*n*) chute, decline, transparency, recession, slider, err, (*v*) drop, fall, slump, descend, sag, cut, tumble, sneak, (*adj*) shift, **7**. skid; *synonyms* (*n*) shoe, sideslip, stay, clog, (*v*) trig, scotch, **8**. slip; *synonyms* (*n*) fault, mistake, cutting, error, escape, oversight, scion, trip, ticket, band, dip, gaffe, strip, (*adj*) blunder, omission; *antonym* (*v*) improve.

katiki 1. stroll; *synonyms* (*n*) promenade, tramp, excursion, perambulation, turn, (*v*) ramble, saunter, walk, amble, roam, wander, hike, range, jaunt, meander, **2**. trawl; *synonyms* (*n*) dragnet, bultow, setline, shedder, trotline, (*v*) angle, fish, tow, haul, draw, lug, search, seek, probe, **3**. process; *synonyms* (*n*) operation, proceeding, method, procedure, act, course, formula, outgrowth, means, mode, practice, (*v*) action, function, refine, litigate.

katikia 1. hoist; *synonyms* (*n*) boost, elevator, winch, (*v*) elevate, haul, heave, lift, erect, raise, rear, uphold, exalt, wind, **2**. yank; *synonyms* (*n*) jerk, pull, squeeze, twist, (*v*) tug, draw, wrench, drag, lug, pluck, twitch, snatch, nip, pinch, tow.

katikiaki processed; *synonyms* (*adj*) prepared, refined, elegant, graceful, neat, polished, purified, sublimate, svelte, tasteful, urbane.

katikinono strain; *synonyms* (*n*) stress, breed, effort, stretch, exertion, race, (*v*) filter, screen, sift, tax, endeavor, exert, extend, percolate, pull; *antonym* (*v*) relax.

katikinonoaki strained; *synonyms* (*adj*) forced, labored, tense, intense, constrained, laboured, unnatural, taut, tight, agonistic, agonistical, combative, farfetched; *antonyms* (*adj*) relaxed, natural.

katikintakaea 1. dry; *synonyms* (*adj*) thirsty, arid, barren, boring, dehydrated, dull, bald, hoarse, jejune, plain, (*v*) dehydrate, desiccate, drain, uninteresting, sardonic; *antonyms* (*adj*) wet, damp, moist, saturated, soaked, boggy, drenched, rainy, sodden, interesting, fresh, humid, juicy, succulent, (*v*) drench, **2**. toughen; *synonyms* (*v*) harden, temper, season, reinforce, strengthen, anneal, brace, fortify, **3**. tighten; *synonyms* (*v*) contract, strain, compress, constrict, fasten, narrow, reduce, squeeze, stiffen, stretch, screw, secure, constrain, frap, fix; *antonyms* (*v*) loosen, relax, **4**. stiffen; *synonyms* (*v*) set, indurate, ossify, tighten, congeal, intensify, jell, thicken, restrain, restrict.

katikintakaeaki 1. dried; *synonyms* (*adj*) dry, arid, dehydrated, desiccated, shriveled, shrunken, torrid, baked, concrete, desiccate, stale, wizened,

lifeless, weazen, (*n*) milk, **2**. tightened; *synonyms* (*adj*) tight, firm, **3**. stiffened, **4**. toughened; *synonyms* (*adj*) hardened, tempered, tough, unbreakable, bad, callous, enured, hard, hardy, inured, resistant, ruffianly, rugged, set, shatterproof; *antonym* (*adj*) fragile.

katikiraoa trim; *synonyms* (*adj*) tidy, neat, spruce, orderly, shipshape, (*v*) cut, dress, clip, garnish, shave, adorn, embellish, lop, prune, reduce; *antonym* (*adj*) fat.

katikiraoaki trimmed; *synonyms* (*adj*) cut, cunning, demure, down, emasculated, gashed, gelded, level, mown, neat, shortened, slashed, sly, smooth, snoD.

katikitiki 1. convulse; *synonyms* (*v*) agitate, jolt, shake, jar, jerk, toss, shudder, (*adj*) accelerate, aggravate, **2**. twitch; *synonyms* (*n*) twinge, pull, tweak, start, twitching, vellication, (*v*) yank, pluck, tug, wrench, draw, nip, pinch, flinch, snatch, **3**. spasm; *synonyms* (*n*) seizure, fit, cramp, outburst, attack, convulsion, paroxysm, twitch, pain, pang, tic, ache, **4**. stiffen; *synonyms* (*v*) harden, set, indurate, ossify, tighten, brace, congeal, reinforce, fortify, intensify, jell, strengthen, temper, thicken, constrain.

katikua 1. retire; *synonyms* (*v*) recede, resign, leave, retreat, withdraw, abdicate, ebb, adjourn, depart, go, quit, remove, return, secede, regrade, **2**. set; *synonyms* (*v*) fix, place, lay, put, locate, position, regulate, define, adjust, arrange, (*n*) class, bent, (*adj*) fixed, fast, secure; *antonyms* (*v*) soften, liquefy, melt, (*n*) combing, comb-out, (*adj*) variable, flexible, liquid, **3**. omit; *synonyms* (*v*) fail, neglect, disregard, delete, forget, except, exclude, drop, ignore, pretermit, expunge, erase, (*adj*) skip, jump, (*n*) forsake; *antonym* (*v*) include, **4**. stow; *synonyms* (*v*) pack, cram, charge, house, load, store, squeeze, deposit, crush, accommodate, compress, keep, stuff, conceal, condense.

katikuaki 1. downed; *synonym* (*adj*) felled, **2**. set; *synonyms* (*v*) fix, place, lay, put, locate, position, regulate, define, adjust, arrange, (*n*) class, bent, (*adj*) fixed, fast, secure; *antonyms* (*v*) soften, liquefy, melt, (*n*) combing, comb-out, (*adj*) variable, flexible, liquid, **3**. stowed, **4**. retired; *synonyms* (*v*) covert, (*adj*) private, obscure, emeritus, secluded, secret, sequestered, solitary, lonely, withdrawn, close, superannuated, isolated, old, out.

katikurerea 1. lure; *synonyms* (*n*) allure, bait, enticement, seduce, attraction, (*v*) decoy, entice, bribe, charm, draw, invite, coax, inveigle, tempt, attract, **2**. entice; *synonyms* (*v*) lure, cajole, captivate, persuade, call, beguile, appeal, bewitch, entrap, wheedle, court, lead, pull, influence, enchant, **3**. seduce; *synonyms* (*v*) defile, solicit, deprave, induce, pervert, mislead, deflower, have, make, score, (*adj*) debauch, fascinate, attach, endear.

katimaran 1. glossy; *synonyms* (*adj*) shiny, sleek, bright, smooth, brilliant, glazed, flat, burnished, glassy, glistening, lustrous, resplendent, satiny, slick, silky; *antonyms* (*adj*) dull, rough, **2.** lustrous; *synonyms* (*adj*) glossy, lucid, light, luminous, shining, glowing, polished, radiant, splendent, effulgent, sheeny, splendid, beamy, (*v*) vivid, nitid, **3.** glazed; *synonyms* (*adj*) glassed, glazen, dead, drunk, enameled, glassen, glasslike, slippery, varnished, sunny, sunshiny, **4.** sleek; *synonyms* (*adj*) silken, satin, even, soft, silklike, (*v*) shine, **5.** polished; *synonyms* (*adj*) elegant, courteous, cultured, finished, refined, civil, courtly, genteel, polite, accomplished, graceful, stylish, urbane, exquisite, suave, **6.** smooth; *synonyms* (*adj*) easy, calm, level, oily, facile, flowing, fluent, fluid, greasy, liquid, mellow, peaceful, (*v*) quiet, facilitate, flatten; *antonyms* (*adj*) uneven, abrasive, coarse, crumpled, flaking, harsh, jerky, lined, peeling, prickly, ridged, wrinkled, corrugated, (*v*) wrinkle, crease, **7.** refined; *synonyms* (*adj*) delicate, gentle, pure, cultivated, dainty, chaste, fine, educated, nice, purified, tasteful, classical, beautiful, discerning, discriminating; *antonyms* (*adj*) unrefined, raw, uncouth.

katimarau hairless; *synonyms* (*adj*) bald, tonsured, shorn, depilous, smooth, baldheaded, clean-shaven, glabrate, glabrescent, receding, shaved, shaven, skinhead, smooth-faced, whiskerless; *antonym* (*adj*) hairy.

katimoia 1. lump; *synonyms* (*n*) heap, chunk, knot, block, clod, hunk, tumor, bit, bulge, clump, fragment, knob, (*v*) clot, (*adj*) mass, lout, **2.** knot; *synonyms* (*n*) bow, cluster, tie, loop, bunch, gang, joint, lump, tangle, band, burl, (*v*) entangle, knit, bind, fasten.

katimoiaki 1. lumped, **2.** knotted; *synonyms* (*adj*) intricate, gnarled, gnarly, knotty, entangled, involved, complicated, tangled, kinky, knobbed, matted; *antonyms* (*adj*) free, straight, tidy.

katimoimoi ball; *synonyms* (*n*) bulb, globe, shot, shell, bead, baseball, bullet, dance, football, lump, orb, party, pellet, projectile, sphere.

katimronrona 1. glob; *synonyms* (*n*) chunk, clot, ball, bead, clod, clump, drop, ballock, baseball, blob, bollock, bubble, bunch, clunk, cluster, **2.** round; *synonyms* (*adv*) about, around, (*adj*) circular, plump, entire, chubby, complete, (*n*) circle, bout, ring, beat, circuit, (*v*) compass, turn, gird; *antonyms* (*adj*) slim, sharp.

katimronronaki rounded; *synonyms* (*adj*) round, curved, circular, orbicular, full, globular, rotund, spherical, bent, blunt, fat, obtuse; *antonyms* (*adj*) pointed, straight, sharp, bony, concave.

katimtima 1. water; *synonyms* (*n*) urine, moisture, juice, liquor, crystal, glass, lymph, pee, piddle, (*v*) irrigate, moisten, wet, soak, dampen, dilute, **2.**

sprinkle; *synonyms* (*n*) dash, (*v*) scatter, drizzle, splash, cast, dot, spatter, spray, rain, spill, spread, diffuse, intersperse, splatter, (*adj*) besprinkle.

katimtimaki 1. sprinkled; *synonyms* (*adj*) besprent, scattered, dotted, speckled, spotted, spread, strewn, **2.** watered; *synonyms* (*adj*) moire, dewy, irriguous, moist, watery.

katinanikua 1. exclude; *synonyms* (*v*) banish, bar, eject, except, expel, discharge, ban, debar, shut, disallow, eliminate, forbid, omit, ostracize, (*adj*) excommunicate; *antonyms* (*v*) include, incorporate, admit, comprise, permit, **2.** shun; *synonyms* (*v*) avoid, evade, escape, elude, dodge, flee, refuse, shirk, parry, duck, reject, blackball, (*adj*) eschew.

katinanikuaki excluded; *synonyms* (*adj*) exempt, precluded, debarred, disqualified, alien, banned, barred, contraband, distant, foreign, prohibited, unwelcome, disallowed, exiled, (*adv*) apart; *antonym* (*adj*) admissible.

katinano deep; *synonyms* (*adj*) thick, profound, absorbed, abstruse, broad, dark, rich, sound, strong, wide, esoteric, bright, large, abysmal, (*v*) intense; *antonyms* (*adj*) shallow, superficial, high, high-pitched, light, soft, weak.

katinea 1. hang; *synonyms* (*v*) dangle, depend, drape, float, append, cling, decorate, execute, fall, flow, hover, swing, (*n*) suspend, delay, knack, **2.** swing; *synonyms* (*n*) sweep, range, (*v*) sway, fluctuate, oscillate, hang, rock, beat, brandish, change, move, shake, turn, vibrate, dance.

katinerua hang; *synonyms* (*v*) dangle, depend, drape, float, append, cling, decorate, execute, fall, flow, hover, swing, (*n*) suspend, delay, knack.

katingoa 1. drench; *synonyms* (*v*) soak, deluge, douse, steep, swamp, dip, drown, flush, immerse, moisten, souse, wash, imbue, (*adj*) splash, bathe; *antonym* (*v*) dry, **2.** soil; *synonyms* (*n*) ground, dirt, grime, land, dust, (*v*) smudge, blot, contaminate, dirty, pollute, mire, blemish, defile, foul, mould; *antonym* (*v*) clean, **3.** wet; *synonyms* (*adj*) damp, humid, drenched, moist, soaked, sodden, dank, rainy, saturated, soggy, watery, (*v*) water, dampen, irrigate, (*n*) moisture; *antonyms* (*adj*) dehydrated, parched.

katingoaki 1. drenched; *synonyms* (*adj*) wet, saturated, soaked, soaking, damp, soppy, sodden, sopping; *antonym* (*adj*) dry, **2.** soiled; *synonyms* (*adj*) dingy, dirty, grubby, nasty, grimy, filthy, unclean, muddy, black, foul, mucky, polluted, squalid, stained, contaminated; *antonyms* (*adj*) clean, pure.

katinono 1. insist; *synonyms* (*v*) affirm, assert, contend, claim, asseverate, declare, maintain, urge, importune, press, argue, force, dwell, hold, persist, **2.** insistent; *synonyms* (*adj*) exigent, stubborn, pressing, clamant, crying, emphatic, importunate, instant, persistent, imperative, adamant, assertive, dogged, forceful, obstinate; *antonym* (*adj*) halfhearted, **3**. harp; *synonyms* (*n*) harmonica, constellation, (*v*) belong, brood, consist, domicile, domiciliate, inhabit, lie, live, people, populate, reside, shack, worry, **4**. insisting; *synonyms* (*n*) insistence, imperativeness, insistency, instancy, pressure, (*adj*) incumbent, insistent, persevering, **5**. stubborn; *synonyms* (*adj*) contrary, hard, intractable, perverse, determined, obdurate, refractory, rigid, tenacious, inveterate, contumacious, difficult, firm, headstrong, inflexible; *antonyms* (*adj*) compliant, flexible, irresolute, amenable, **6**. persistent; *synonyms* (*adj*) durable, constant, continual, lasting, permanent, continuous, chronic, consistent, incessant, perpetual, relentless, unrelenting, habitual, indefatigable, (*n*) frequent; *antonyms* (*adj*) contained, occasional, **7**. persist; *synonyms* (*v*) continue, last, persevere, abide, endure, insist, remain, linger, follow, go, pursue, keep, extend, prevail, resist; *antonym* (*v*) stop.

katioa 1. swing; *synonyms* (*n*) sweep, range, (*v*) sway, fluctuate, oscillate, dangle, hang, rock, beat, brandish, change, move, shake, turn, vibrate, **2**. shake; *synonyms* (*v*) agitate, jar, disturb, excite, flutter, totter, wag, drop, bump, (*n*) tremble, jolt, quiver, wave, trembling, (*adj*) quake, **3**. wave; *synonyms* (*n*) billow, gesture, motion, sign, surge, signal, (*v*) flap, curl, flourish, swell, swing, undulate, beckon, ripple, roll.

katioaki shaken; *synonyms* (*v*) broken, lame, passe, shaky, threadbare, wilted, shattered, stale, (*adj*) jolted, dazed, disconcerted, fallen, scared, stunned, surprised.

katiobabaea 1. hang; *synonyms* (*v*) dangle, depend, drape, float, append, cling, decorate, execute, fall, flow, hover, swing, (*n*) suspend, delay, knack, **2**. dangle; *synonyms* (*v*) hang, droop, loll, drop, flop, sag, trail, **3**. suspend; *synonyms* (*v*) defer, adjourn, interrupt, postpone, stop, shelve, stay, break, debar, halt, freeze, discontinue, dismiss, exclude, bar; *antonym* (*v*) continue.

katiobabeaki suspended; *synonyms* (*adj*) hanging, pendent, dormant, pendulous, abeyant, dangling, inactive, pendant.

katiobuki 1. tumble; *synonyms* (*n*) fall, drop, (*v*) jumble, stumble, collapse, crumble, plunge, slip, spill, topple, confuse, downfall, toss, crash, crumple, **2**. somersault; *synonyms* (*n*) flip, somersaulting, vault, pass, (*v*) jump.

katiobukiaki tumbled; *synonyms* (*adj*) disordered, upset.

katiotioa 1. wave; *synonyms* (*n*) billow, gesture, motion, sign, surge, (*v*) brandish, flap, flutter, curl, flourish, swell, swing, undulate, beat, beckon, **2**. waggle; *synonyms* (*n*) shake, shiver, (*v*) wag, jiggle, wiggle, bob, reel, stagger, **3**. wag; *synonyms* (*n*) humorist, waggle, joker, wit, comedian, clown, zany, card, comic, (*v*) wave, move, vibratiuncle.

katira 1. flatten; *synonyms* (*v*) fell, demolish, level, press, even, drop, roll, squash, depress, destroy, ruin, smash, smooth, unfold, bulldoze; *antonyms* (*v*) build, crumple, **2**. iron; *synonyms* (*n*) chain, irons, chains, (*v*) firm, flatten, (*adj*) hard, adamant, inflexible, steel, tenacious.

katiraki 1. flattened; *synonyms* (*adj*) compressed, depressed, planate, trodden, unconscious, compacted, firmed, trampled; *antonym* (*adj*) loose, **2**. ironed.

katirea temper; *synonyms* (*n*) mood, character, disposition, humor, nature, condition, anger, (*v*) moderate, soften, harden, mitigate, modify, season, qualify, anneal; *antonyms* (*v*) intensify, upset.

katireaki tempered; *synonyms* (*adj*) hardened, attempered, attemperate, elastic, enured, inured, mild, proportioned, set, subdued, toughened, treated, tough.

katiribo 1. appropriate; *synonyms* (*adj*) pertinent, proper, true, agreeable, apposite, apt, congruous, correct, particular, peculiar, right, (*v*) annex, allocate, adopt, seize; *antonyms* (*adj*) inappropriate, unsuitable, unrelated, untimely, wrong, (*v*) surrender, **2**. take; *synonyms* (*v*) admit, get, hold, bear, carry, catch, clutch, obtain, return, borrow, pick, acquire, appropriate, (*phr*) accept, receive; *antonyms* (*v*) give, refuse, abstain, add, lose.

katiriboaki 1. appropriated; *synonyms* (*adj*) destined, condemned, confiscate, confiscated, reserved, seized, censured, convicted, forfeit, forfeited, **2**. taken; *synonyms* (*v*) take, (*adj*) occupied, full, interpreted, besotted, crazed, enamored, engaged, interested, lovesick, obsessed, overcome, preferred, rapt, unavailable.

katirironrona roll; *synonyms* (*n*) list, revolution, catalogue, inventory, register, (*v*) coil, reel, curl, enfold, revolve, wheel, rock, turn, twist, wallow.

katirironronaki rolled; *synonyms* (*adj*) rolling, furled, involute, beaten, billowing, kinky, level, resonant, resonating, resounding, reverberating, reverberative, spiral, trilled, tumbling.

katirorona round; *synonyms* (*adv*) about, around, (*adj*) circular, plump, entire, chubby, complete, (*n*) circle, bout, ring, beat, circuit, (*v*) compass, turn, gird; *antonyms* (*adj*) slim, sharp.

katiroronaki rounded; *synonyms* (*adj*) round, curved, circular, orbicular, full, globular, rotund, spherical, bent, blunt, fat, obtuse; *antonyms* (*adj*) pointed, straight, sharp, bony, concave.

katita soften; *synonyms* (*v*) mitigate, moderate, assuage, dull, melt, mute, relent, relieve, alleviate, allay, pacify, break, cushion, (*adj*) mollify, palliate; *antonyms* (*v*) harden, set, solidify, congeal.

katitaki softened; *synonyms* (*adj*) dull, diffused, muffled, muted, boring, deadening, dense, dim, dumb, faint, gray, grey, hushed, intenerate, irksome.

katiti 1. hiss; *synonyms* (*n*) buzz, hoot, jeer, taunt, hissing, ridicule, bird, (*v*) boo, fizz, spit, sibilate, whisper, whiz, whoosh, clamor, **2.** mush; *synonyms* (*n*) pulp, paste, batter, countenance, flattery, flesh, mouth, nostalgia, supawn, talk, treacle, blend, pottage, (*v*) kiss, (*adj*) oatmeal, **3.** mash; *synonyms* (*n*) mush, (*v*) crush, grind, squash, beat, bray, comminute, crunch, flirt, press, squeeze, bruise, philander, pulverize, (*adj*) mess.

katitibengaua swell; *synonyms* (*n*) wave, (*v*) surge, enlarge, expand, heave, increase, rise, puff, bloat, grow, billow, augment, balloon, (*adj*) dandy, swagger; *antonyms* (*v*) decrease, deflate, desiccate.

katitiro overseer; *synonyms* (*n*) foreman, superintendent, manager, inspector, supervisor, warden, controller, director, examiner, administrator, custodian, boss, governor, surveyor.

katitirou 1. eminent; *synonyms* (*adj*) distinguished, celebrated, high, elevated, brilliant, big, conspicuous, famous, illustrious, noble, renowned, dignified, exalted, grand, great; *antonym* (*adj*) unknown, **2.** remarkable; *synonyms* (*adj*) exceptional, extraordinary, notable, noteworthy, odd, phenomenal, curious, noticeable, outstanding, rare, signal, singular, uncommon, prominent, (*n*) memorable; *antonyms* (*adj*) ordinary, insignificant, unremarkable.

katitua 1. arouse; *synonyms* (*v*) animate, rouse, stir, wake, agitate, awaken, excite, stimulate, anger, kindle, provoke, raise, awake, call, evoke; *antonym* (*v*) calm, **2.** force; *synonyms* (*n*) energy, strength, agency, effect, enforce, impetus, (*v*) drive, coerce, pressure, squeeze, thrust, compel, cram, impel, (*adj*) constrain; *antonyms* (*n*) weakness, persuasion, **3.** manipulate; *synonyms* (*v*) handle, control, fiddle, influence, manage, operate, rig, wield, work, touch, cook, direct, fake, falsify, fix.

katituaki 1. forced; *synonyms* (*adj*) compulsory, compelled, bound, artificial, constrained, involuntary, unnatural, farfetched, false, labored, obligatory, obliged, strained; *antonyms* (*adj*) free, unprovoked, spontaneous, voluntary, **2.** aroused; *synonyms* (*adj*) excited, ablaze, aflame, passionate, hot, activated, afraid, awake, demonic, elated, emotional, fascinated, flaming, flushed, horny.

katitura 1. drag; *synonyms* (*v*) attract, haul, draw, puff, trail, cart, hale, heave, lug, tow, delay, (*n*) pull, bother, bore, hindrance; *antonym* (*v*) push, **2.** crawl; *synonyms* (*v*) creep, grovel, clamber, climb, cringe, fawn, scramble, sneak, swarm, teem, inch, lag, move, (*n*) crawling, creeping; *antonym* (*v*) race.

katoa 1. assist; *synonyms* (*v*) aid, support, abet, serve, contribute, boost, attend, avail, back, comfort, encourage, expedite, facilitate, (*n*) help, assistance; *antonym* (*v*) hinder, **2.** complete; *synonyms* (*adj*) perfect, absolute, consummate, whole, full, stark, accomplished, all, (*v*) accomplish, achieve, close, finish, execute, act, attain; *antonyms* (*adj*) incomplete, partial, unfinished, abridged, shortened, sketchy, lacking, narrow, qualified, (*v*) neglect, **3.** help; *synonyms* (*v*) assist, favor, ease, alleviate, forward, befriend, further, countenance, (*n*) benefit, assistant, cure, encouragement, backing, relief, remedy; *antonyms* (*v*) worsen, (*n*) hindrance, detriment, **4.** supply; *synonyms* (*n*) provision, hoard, issue, (*v*) furnish, stock, afford, fill, store, feed, offer, provide, cater, deliver, equip, give.

katoaki 1. completed; *synonyms* (*adj*) complete, done, accomplished, finished, ended, perfect, ready, through, whole, (*adv*) over, **2.** assisted; *synonym* (*adj*) aided, **3.** supplied; *synonyms* (*adj*) full, adequate, ample, available, copious, fitted, impregnated, offered, plenteous, sated, abounding, surfeited.

katoang square; *synonyms* (*adj*) right, even, rectangular, fair, quadrate, straight, equal, (*n*) area, foursquare, rectangle, quadrilateral, (*v*) settle, agree, correspond, (*adv*) just.

katoangaki squared; *synonyms* (*adj*) square, agree, balanced, correspond, correspondent, equal, even, exact, quadrate, suit, suited.

katoatoa square; *synonyms* (*adj*) right, even, rectangular, fair, quadrate, straight, equal, (*n*) area, foursquare, rectangle, quadrilateral, (*v*) settle, agree, correspond, (*adv*) just.

katoatoaki squared; *synonyms* (*adj*) square, agree, balanced, correspond, correspondent, equal, even, exact, quadrate, suit, suited.

katobibia 1. encompass; *synonyms* (*v*) embrace, comprehend, contain, comprise, cover, embody, besiege, circumscribe, enclose, include, circle, (*n*) encircle, (*adv*) beset, compass, surround, **2.** around; *synonyms* (*adv*) about, approximately, almost, round, roughly, nearly, some, somewhere, (*prep*) encompassing, encircling, circa, surrounding, (*adj*) near, nearby, (*n*) vicinity, **3.** surround; *synonyms* (*v*) gird, border, inclose, ring, skirt, circumvent, envelop, environ, entwine, bound, beleaguer, blockade, edge, encompass, enfold, **4.** skirt; *synonyms* (*n*) brim, flap, kilt, apron, margin, brink, dame, (*v*) fringe, evade, hem, elude, sidestep, verge, dodge, avoid.

katobibiaki surrounded; *synonyms* (*v*) beset, begone, furnished, (*adj*) encircled, bounded, circumstanced, conditioned, entrenched, fixed, ingirt, inside, ringed, rooted, bordered, delimited.

katoka 1. chief; *synonyms* (*adj*) head, principal, cardinal, capital, arch, central, essential, first, main, (*n*) administrator, boss, captain, executive, leader, paramount; *antonyms* (*adj*) minor, associate, secondary, **2**. discontinue; *synonyms* (v) cease, stop, break, abandon, desist, drop, terminate, interrupt, quit, adjourn, part, end, finish, pause, separate; *antonym* (v) continue, **3**. lord; *synonyms* (n) chief, master, noble, sir, seignior, almighty, creator, gentleman, maker, mistress, nobleman, overlord, ruler, impropriator, **4**. king; *synonyms* (n) emperor, mogul, sovereign, baron, crown, magnate, tycoon, majesty, rex, monarch, power, ace, **5**. succeed; *synonyms* (v) follow, replace, arrive, ensue, manage, prevail, prosper, supersede, supplant, do, achieve, flourish, displace, pursue, thrive; *antonyms* (v) fail, precede, lose, **6**. set; *synonyms* (v) fix, place, lay, put, locate, position, regulate, define, adjust, arrange, (n) class, bent, (adj) fixed, fast, secure; *antonyms* (v) soften, liquefy, melt, (n) combing, comb-out, (adj) variable, flexible, liquid, **7**. station; *synonyms* (n) rank, seat, standing, base, depot, office, spot, condition, dignity, (v) post, stand, order, set, site, establish, **8**. quench; *synonyms* (v) extinguish, allay, appease, quash, destroy, assuage, slake, annihilate, calm, chill, cool, douse, fill, quell, satisfy, **9**. overseer; *synonyms* (n) foreman, superintendent, manager, inspector, supervisor, warden, controller, director, examiner, custodian, governor, surveyor, **10**. terminate; *synonyms* (v) close, complete, conclude, discontinue, dismiss, dissolve, halt, can, result, abort, bound, cancel, ax, culminate, fire; *antonyms* (v) begin, start, **11**. win; *synonyms* (v) acquire, gain, get, attain, obtain, conquer, earn, take, succeed, carry, vanquish, procure, reach, score, (n) triumph; *antonym* (n) defeat, **12**. quell; *synonyms* (v) crush, overpower, pacify, suppress, compose, mollify, subjugate, abate, curb, kill, overcome, quench, repress, squelch, (adj) hush, **13**. suppress; *synonyms* (v) subdue, check, restrain, silence, stifle, strangle, conceal, control, inhibit, oppress, contain, hide, muffle, smother, confine; *antonym* (v) express, **14**. place; *synonyms* (n) domicile, attitude, job, location, situation, circumstance, center, abode, berth, (v) station, deposit, install, pitch, lie, commit; *antonym* (v) remove, **15**. position; *synonyms* (n) employment, opinion, placement, arrangement, bearing, posture, stance, status, case, disposition, belief, character, (v) grade, point, pose.

katokaki 1. discontinued; *antonym* (adj) continued, **2**. set; *synonyms* (v) fix, place, lay, put, locate, position, regulate, define, adjust, arrange, (n) class, bent, (adj) fixed, fast, secure; *antonyms* (v) soften, liquefy, melt, (n) combing, comb-out, (adj) variable, flexible, liquid, **3**. quelled; *synonyms* (adj) quenched, squelched, allayed, extinct, extinguished, satisfied, slaked, **4**. suppressed; *synonyms* (adj) smothered, stifled, strangled, downtrodden, buried, composed, concealed,

covert, doomed, dormant, embryonic, forgotten, hidden, latent, (n) subordinate; *antonym* (adj) available, **5**. terminated; *synonyms* (adj) complete, concluded, ended, finished, done, over, **6**. quenched; *synonyms* (adj) quelled, out, dead, forbidden, inactive, kayoed, nonextant, prohibited, proscribed, retired, stunned, taboo, tabu, verboten, **7**. placed; *synonyms* (adj) located, situated, laid, set, positioned, collocate, determined, dictated, hardened, residing, rigid.

katokiaki downed; *synonym* (adj) felled.

katokoaki ended; *synonyms* (adj) complete, concluded, finished, over, completed, done, closed, past, terminated, through, consummate.

katomam taste; *synonyms* (n) bit, flavor, liking, morsel, penchant, appetite, drink, drop, fondness, gusto, (v) relish, savor, sample, smack, discernment; *antonyms* (n) dislike, tastelessness.

katonga 1. flavor; *synonyms* (n) savor, relish, taste, aroma, smack, smell, tang, salt, odor, sapidity, (v) flavour, season, spice, sauce, twang, **2**. feast; *synonyms* (n) banquet, dinner, entertainment, binge, carousal, celebration, festival, meal, spread, (v) junket, fete, eat, feed, treat, entertain; *antonym* (v) fast, **3**. dine; *synonyms* (v) lunch, breakfast, consume, drink, touch, **4**. sample; *synonyms* (n) example, instance, specimen, model, pattern, assay, case, illustration, exemplar, design, (v) try, attempt, essay, prove, (adj) test, **5**. stun; *synonyms* (v) amaze, astonish, astound, bewilder, shock, baffle, daze, flabbergast, stagger, deaden, numb, bemuse, (adv) startle, surprise, (adj) deafen, **6**. taste; *synonyms* (n) bit, flavor, liking, morsel, penchant, appetite, drop, fondness, gusto, mouthful, predilection, preference, refinement, (v) sample, discernment; *antonyms* (n) dislike, tastelessness.

katongaki 1. flavored; *synonyms* (adj) flavoured, seasoned, **2**. stunned; *synonyms* (adj) astonished, astounded, dumbfounded, amazed, dazed, flabbergasted, bewildered, staggered, stupefied, astonied, confused, shocked, stupid, surprised, groggy.

katongatonga rejoice; *synonyms* (v) cheer, delight, gladden, glory, joy, jubilate, revel, triumph, gratify, gloat, exhilarate, please, celebrate, recreate, (n) exult; *antonyms* (v) lament, mourn.

katonginakoa 1. frighten; *synonyms* (v) alarm, cow, dismay, daunt, terrify, appall, affright, intimidate, scare, terrorize, awe, deter, horrify, startle, (n) fright; *antonyms* (v) comfort, encourage, **2**. shock; *synonyms* (n) blow, daze, impact, collision, outrage, surprise, concussion, tremor, (v) jar, offend, revolt, clash, disgust, frighten, shake, **3**. stun; *synonyms* (v) amaze, astonish, astound, bewilder, shock, baffle, flabbergast, stagger, deaden, numb, bemuse, dumbfound, floor, perplex, (adj) deafen, **4**.

terrorize; *synonyms* (*v*) terrorise, coerce, threaten, bully, menace, pressure.

katonginakoaki 1. frightened; *synonyms* (*adj*) afraid, fearful, scared, terrified, timid, anxious, apprehensive, horrified, intimidated, restless, worried, (*adv*) cowardly; *antonyms* (*adj*) calm, confident, unimpressed, brave, fearless, **2.** stunned; *synonyms* (*adj*) astonished, astounded, dumbfounded, amazed, dazed, flabbergasted, bewildered, staggered, stupefied, astonied, confused, shocked, stupid, surprised, groggy, **3.** shocked; *synonyms* (*adj*) dismayed, aghast, distressed, stunned, appalled, speechless, upset; *antonyms* (*adj*) delighted, indifferent.

katongiraraea 1. deafen; *synonyms* (*v*) deaf, muffle, blindfold, deave, envelop, inclose, muff, (*adj*) stun, **2.** stupefy; *synonyms* (*v*) astonish, astound, bewilder, daze, amaze, paralyze, deaden, numb, bemuse, baffle, besot, confuse, drug, perplex, (*n*) benumb, **3.** stun; *synonyms* (*v*) shock, flabbergast, stagger, dumbfound, floor, petrify, electrify, galvanize, overwhelm, dazzle, flummox, (*n*) stupefy, (*adv*) startle, surprise, (*adj*) deafen.

katongiraraeaki 1. deafened; *synonyms* (*adj*) deaf, dead, deadened, stunned, decayed, regardless, stifled, tasteless, **2.** stunned; *synonyms* (*adj*) astonished, astounded, dumbfounded, amazed, dazed, flabbergasted, bewildered, staggered, stupefied, astonied, confused, shocked, stupid, surprised, groggy, **3.** stupefied; *synonym* (*adj*) dumfounded.

katootoonga 1. follow; *synonyms* (*v*) chase, pursue, adhere, adopt, accompany, comprehend, continue, ensue, grasp, hunt, realize, succeed, track, emulate, (*adj*) catch; *antonyms* (*v*) precede, guide, head, lead, **2.** pursue; *synonyms* (*v*) follow, dog, prosecute, course, haunt, hound, persist, stalk, tail, conduct, practice, court, keep, engage, harass.

katootoongaki pursued; *synonym* (*n*) chased.

katorobubua kneel; *synonyms* (*v*) bow, cringe, bob, dip, duck, stoop, crouch, fawn, grovel, kowtow, curtsey, (*n*) kneeling, tolling.

katorotakanana dirty; *synonyms* (*adj*) foul, dirt, contemptible, bawdy, contaminated, dingy, impure, despicable, (*v*) muddy, corrupt, soil, contaminate, begrime, bemire, (*n*) defile; *antonyms* (*adj*) hygienic, pure, spotless, immaculate, (*v*) clean.

katorotoro humble; *synonyms* (*adj*) base, docile, low, lowly, modest, unassuming, baseborn, (*v*) degrade, demean, disgrace, abase, debase, humiliate, mortify, conquer; *antonyms* (*adj*) grand, arrogant, conceited, haughty, imposing, impressive, pompous, snooty.

katorotoroaki humbled; *synonyms* (*adj*) broken, humble, humiliated, crushed, depressed, dispirited.

katoto 1. apathetic; *synonyms* (*adj*) indifferent, cool, impassive, uninterested, perfunctory, casual, dull, lazy, lethargic, lukewarm, nonchalant, sluggish, spiritless, detached, indolent; *antonyms* (*adj*) energetic, enthusiastic, fervent, inquisitive, **2.** imitate; *synonyms* (*v*) copy, duplicate, forge, ape, emulate, follow, feign, counterfeit, mimic, mock, act, assume, echo, model, pattern, **3.** mimic; *synonyms* (*v*) imitate, mime, impersonate, parody, personate, simulate, (*n*) imitator, mimicker, impersonator, actor, clown, buffoon, (*adj*) imitative, **4.** duplicate; *synonyms* (*adj*) dual, matching, (*v*) double, twin, trace, redouble, reduplicate, repeat, replicate, (*n*) counterpart, equal, second, imitation, match, parallel; *antonym* (*n*) original, **5.** forge; *synonyms* (*v*) falsify, devise, fabricate, fake, fashion, coin, contrive, invent, mint, construct, excogitate, form, hammer, mold, mould, **6.** copy; *synonyms* (*n*) transcription, forgery, reproduction, cast, book, facsimile, image, likeness, picture, print, replica, sham, sketch, (*v*) record, reproduce, **7.** model; *synonyms* (*n*) example, dummy, figure, prototype, frame, lesson, archetype, design, epitome, exemplar, manikin, mannequin, paradigm, (*adj*) ideal, (*v*) shape; *antonym* (*adj*) atypical, **8.** trace; *synonyms* (*n*) line, shadow, spot, clue, dash, hint, indication, mark, shade, sign, suggestion, touch, (*v*) track, hunt, pursue, **9.** reproduce; *synonyms* (*v*) breed, generate, regenerate, multiply, procreate, reflect, mirror, produce, iterate, reiterate, increase, manifold, proliferate, reconstruct, depict, **10.** replicate; *synonym* (*v*) clone.

katotoa 1. rot; *synonyms* (*n*) decay, corruption, drivel, nonsense, blight, bullshit, decomposition, (*v*) decompose, canker, corrupt, disintegrate, fester, molder, perish, languish, **2.** tenderize; *synonyms* (*v*) tender, tenderise, soften, bid, offer, **3.** soften; *synonyms* (*v*) mitigate, moderate, assuage, dull, melt, mute, relent, relieve, alleviate, allay, pacify, break, cushion, (*adj*) mollify, palliate; *antonyms* (*v*) harden, set, solidify, congeal.

katotoaki 1. copied; *synonyms* (*adj*) traced, counterfeit, derivative, artificial, bogus, ersatz, fake, false, forged, imitative, mock, phony, sham, twin, banal; *antonyms* (*adj*) original, real, **2.** duplicated; *synonym* (*adj*) double, **3.** forged; *synonyms* (*adj*) fabricated, spurious, bad, fabulous; *antonym* (*adj*) genuine, **4.** softened; *synonyms* (*adj*) dull, diffused, muffled, muted, boring, deadening, dense, dim, dumb, faint, gray, grey, hushed, intenerate, irksome, **5.** traced; *synonyms* (*adj*) copied, graphic, **6.** tenderized; *synonym* (*adj*) tenderised.

katotonga 1. mimic; *synonyms* (*v*) mock, imitate, copy, counterfeit, mime, emulate, impersonate, parody, echo, personate, (*n*) ape, imitator, mimicker, impersonator, (*adj*) imitative, **2.** mirror;

synonyms (*n*) model, exemplar, (*v*) glass, reflect, represent, reproduce, lens, mimic, (*adj*) pattern, cynosure, **3**. imitate; *synonyms* (*v*) duplicate, forge, follow, feign, act, assume, pretend, sham, simulate, adopt, fake, mirror, replicate, resemble, apply, **4**. emulate; *synonyms* (*v*) compete, contend, rival, contest, (*adj*) vie, **5**. impersonate; *synonyms* (*v*) masquerade, personify, pose, portray, **6**. resemble; *synonyms* (*v*) seem, compare, correspond, agree, look, match, approximate.

katotoroa 1. displace; *synonyms* (*v*) dislocate, dislodge, dismiss, bump, depose, remove, shift, uproot, cashier, discharge, disturb, eject, evacuate, expel, move; *antonym* (*v*) replace, **2**. push; *synonyms* (*n*) press, thrust, jolt, poke, (*v*) drive, impel, crowd, force, jab, jostle, nudge, prod, jam, rush, boost; *antonyms* (*v*) pull, drag, haul.

katoua spear; *synonyms* (*n*) harpoon, lance, pike, fizgig, gig, prick, shaft, barb, (*v*) impale, spike, stab, pierce, skewer, stick, transfix.

katourakea startle; *synonyms* (*v*) alarm, frighten, jump, scare, astonish, shock, astound, amaze, shake, dismay, electrify, rouse, stagger, (*n*) start, (*adv*) surprise.

katourakeaki startled; *synonyms* (*adj*) scared, dumbfounded, aghast, distressed, frightened, amazed, astonished, afraid, astounded, shocked, terrified, alarmed, anxious, bewildered, flabbergasted.

katow nod; *synonyms* (*n*) bow, greeting, beck, sleep, motion, assent, fiat, agreement, behest, (*v*) nap, doze, signal, beckon, bob, stoop.

katua 1. miss; *synonyms* (*v*) lack, lose, fail, jump, omit, overlook, long, drop, escape, (*n*) maid, girl, want, fille, missy, (*adj*) fault; *antonym* (*v*) perceive, **2**. fine; *synonyms* (*adj*) delicate, agreeable, dainty, brave, capital, elegant, excellent, nice, thin, delightful, acute, admirable, alright, (*n*) penalty, (*v*) punish; *antonyms* (*adj*) poor, thick, coarse, substantial, unsatisfactory, wide, **3**. avoid; *synonyms* (*v*) shun, avert, parry, evade, abstain, annul, circumvent, duck, elude, forbear, fudge, ignore, prevent, shirk, (*adj*) eschew; *antonyms* (*v*) confront, associate, face, tackle, **4**. evade; *synonyms* (*v*) avoid, dodge, equivocate, hedge, sidestep, skirt, bilk, neglect, prevaricate, quibble, block, deflect, fence, flee, baffle, **5**. swerve; *synonyms* (*v*) deviate, depart, sheer, stray, turn, veer, wander, diverge, shift, bend, digress, slew, swing, warp, (*n*) curve, **6**. parry; *synonyms* (*n*) counterpunch, (*v*) counter, flinch, fend, repel, blench, blink, defeat.

katuaea 1. inflict; *synonyms* (*v*) impose, cause, enforce, force, wreak, deal, deliver, administer, land, put, send, visit, commit, **2**. fine; *synonyms* (*adj*) delicate, agreeable, dainty, brave, capital, elegant, excellent, nice, thin, delightful, acute, admirable, alright, (*n*) penalty, (*v*) punish; *antonyms* (*adj*) poor, thick, coarse, substantial, unsatisfactory, wide.

katuaeaki fined; *synonyms* (*adj*) penalized, penalised.

katuaki 1. missed; *synonyms* (*adj*) lost, baffled, befuddled, bemused, bewildered, confounded, confused, disoriented, forgotten, helpless, irretrievable, mazed, preoccupied, **2**. fined; *synonyms* (*adj*) penalized, penalised, **3**. parried.

katuatua 1. hop; *synonyms* (*n*) jump, leap, bound, hops, trip, flight, (*v*) dance, gambol, bounce, caper, skip, spring, limp, fly, hurdle, **2**. bounce; *synonyms* (*v*) discharge, glance, recoil, beat, sack, bob, fire, bump, dismiss, eject, expel, hop, (*n*) impact, jolt, bouncing, **3**. skim; *synonyms* (*v*) glide, slip, browse, sweep, brush, graze, race, read, scan, shave, remove, scum, (*n*) cream, slide, review, **4**. ricochet; *synonyms* (*n*) carom, (*v*) rebound, kick, reverberate, boom, echo, **5**. skitter; *synonyms* (*v*) skim, scamper, run, scurry, scuttle, bypass, cut, decamp, plane, rake, slink, vamoose, **6**. skip; *synonyms* (*n*) omission, (*v*) prance, frisk, omit, cross, abscond, bolt, ramp, escape, forget, pass, skitter, step, vault, (*adj*) pretermit.

katudaki excited; *synonyms* (*adj*) agitated, ablaze, emotional, enthusiastic, frantic, ardent, aroused, delirious, fervent, heated, impassioned, passionate, warm, elated, (*v*) animated; *antonyms* (*adj*) calm, cool, unexcited.

katuka 1. lower; *synonyms* (*adj*) debase, inferior, (*v*) degrade, diminish, frown, humble, dip, abase, cut, descend, drop, scowl, disgrace, decrease, (*n*) depress; *antonyms* (*v*) increase, raise, **2**. leave; *synonyms* (*v*) depart, forsake, go, abandon, desert, quit, escape, flee, lead, (*n*) furlough, holiday, permission, permit, break, (*adj*) empty; *antonyms* (*v*) arrive, enter, stay, remain, approach, change, come, **3**. abandon; *synonyms* (*v*) relinquish, renounce, resign, vacate, evacuate, leave, waive, abdicate, chuck, ditch, forfeit, forgo, maroon, scrap, surrender; *antonyms* (*v*) keep, support, maintain, (*n*) restraint, **4**. bequeath; *synonyms* (*v*) will, give, demise, entrust, devise, endow, transmit, bestow, contribute, donate; *antonym* (*v*) disinherit, **5**. forsake; *synonyms* (*v*) fail, disclaim, desolate, discard, abjure, betray, defect, deny, disown, reject, repudiate, die, **6**. maroon; *synonyms* (*adj*) banish, chestnut, ostracize, proscribe, auburn, bay, brown, castaneous, chocolate, cinnamon, (*v*) strand, (*n*) crimson, carmine, lake, red, **7**. deposit; *synonyms* (*n*) charge, residue, guarantee, heap, hoard, lees, lode, (*v*) bank, commit, store, fix, lay, repose, cast, file; *antonym* (*v*) withdraw, **8**. desert; *synonyms* (*n*) wilderness, desolation, solitude, basin, (*v*) abscond, fly, (*adj*) waste, barren, merit, wild, worth, bleak, excellence, arid, godforsaken; *antonym* (*n*) bog, **9**. put; *synonyms* (*v*) place, position, set, impose, couch, locate, pose, pitch, arrange, assign, establish, express, install, (n) deposit, invest, **10.** set; *synonyms* (v) put, regulate, define, adjust, congeal, posit, (n) class, bent, circle, lot, party, (adj) fixed, fast, secure, ready; *antonyms* (v) soften, liquefy, melt, (n) combing, comb-out, (adj) variable, flexible, liquid, **11.** seat; *synonyms* (n) bench, base, backside, behind, bottom, buttocks, chair, post, posterior, rear, rump, residence, berth, (v) contain, hold, **12.** place; *synonyms* (n) domicile, office, order, spot, attitude, job, location, situation, circumstance, center, abode, (v) rank, station, lie, dispose; *antonym* (v) remove.

katukaki 1. lowered; *synonyms* (adj) abased, bated, cheap, humbled, restrained, **2.** deserted; *synonyms* (adj) abandoned, desert, solitary, bleak, derelict, desolate, empty, forsaken, isolated, lonely, lonesome, vacant, alone, secluded, (v) forlorn; *antonyms* (adj) inhabited, occupied, packed, **3.** forsaken; *synonyms* (adj) deserted, jilted, friendless, **4.** abandoned; *synonyms* (adj) immoral, profligate, shameless, stranded, wicked, corrupt, debauched, depraved, discarded, dissipated, dissolute, licentious, loose, neglected, reprobate; *antonyms* (adj) orderly, overcrowded, **5.** seated; *synonyms* (adj) sitting, sedentary, **6.** placed; *synonyms* (adj) located, situated, laid, set, positioned, fixed, collocate, determined, dictated, hardened, residing, rigid, **7.** set; *synonyms* (v) fix, place, lay, put, locate, position, regulate, define, adjust, arrange, (n) class, bent, circle, (adj) fast, secure; *antonyms* (v) soften, liquefy, melt, (n) combing, comb-out, (adj) variable, flexible, liquid.

katumara bald; *synonyms* (adj) bare, hairless, simple, austere, meager, threadbare, raw, barefaced, dry, forthright, mere, naked, nude, plain, stark; *antonym* (adj) hairy.

katumaua 1. seep; *synonyms* (v) ooze, exude, percolate, filter, course, dribble, flow, leak, permeate, trickle, drop, drip, **2.** ooze; *synonyms* (n) mire, muck, slime, escape, oozing, (v) seep, drain, bleed, emit, secrete, sweat, release, discharge, perspire, (adj) mud.

katuna 1. join; *synonyms* (v) connect, unite, associate, combine, link, graft, assemble, affiliate, attach, meet, affix, annex, conjoin, converge, (n) bond; *antonyms* (v) detach, secede, separate, split, undo, **2.** combine; *synonyms* (v) amalgamate, blend, fuse, piece, aggregate, coalesce, incorporate, join, league, merge, mix, alloy, band, (n) cartel, combination, **3.** couple; *synonyms* (n) brace, yoke, duo, dyad, twosome, (v) pair, copulate, tie, match, mate, fasten, wed, bridge, add, (adj) hook; *antonym* (v) uncouple, **4.** connected; *synonyms* (v) related, (adj) associated, affiliated, allied, attached, linked, committed; *antonyms* (adj) unconnected, unrelated,

5. connect; *synonyms* (v) bind, relate, knit, adjoin, communicate, fix, interconnect, interlink, involve, articulate, consociate, close, implicate, append, concern; *antonym* (v) disconnect, **6.** stick; *synonyms* (n) bar, club, rod, bat, (v) adhere, stab, cling, paste, staff, cohere, cleave, hold, impale, persist, pink.

katunaki 1. connected; *synonyms* (v) related, (adj) associated, affiliated, allied, attached, linked, committed; *antonyms* (adj) unconnected, unrelated, separate, **2.** combined; *synonyms* (adj) joint, united, collective, aggregate, amalgamated, concerted, cooperative, incorporate, conjunct, conjunctive, connected, fused, joined, (adv) jointly, together; *antonyms* (adj) individual, simple, **3.** coupled; *synonyms* (adj) conjugate, double, conjugated, **4.** joined; *synonyms* (adj) combined, coupled, **5.** stuck; *synonyms* (v) sticked, (adj) stranded, aground, abandoned, absorbed, ashore, beached, delayed, deserted, dumbfounded, fast, hindered, immovable, (n) thrust, sticking; *antonym* (adj) free.

katura 1. drag; *synonyms* (v) attract, haul, draw, puff, trail, cart, hale, heave, lug, tow, delay, (n) pull, bother, bore, hindrance; *antonym* (v) push, **2.** drive; *synonyms* (n) ride, force, campaign, crusade, thrust, cause, ambition, (v) actuate, chase, compel, urge, coerce, beat, carry, constrain; *antonyms* (n) apathy, inertia, **3.** slip; *synonyms* (n) lapse, fault, mistake, cutting, error, escape, oversight, scion, trip, (v) fall, slide, drop, glide, skid, (adj) blunder; *antonym* (v) improve, **4.** slide; *synonyms* (n) chute, decline, transparency, gliding, recession, (v) slip, slither, run, slump, coast, descend, sag, cut, tumble, (adj) shift.

katurabeau 1. drag; *synonyms* (v) attract, haul, draw, puff, trail, cart, hale, heave, lug, tow, delay, (n) pull, bother, bore, hindrance; *antonym* (v) push, **2.** heave; *synonyms* (v) cast, fling, chuck, gasp, toss, billow, drag, elevate, gag, hoist, jerk, (n) tug, raise, elevation, heaving, **3.** hoist; *synonyms* (v) boost, elevator, winch, (v) lift, erect, rear, uphold, exalt, wind, **4.** pull; *synonyms* (v) draught, pluck, pick, make, force, lure, strain, get, (n) wrench, attraction, effort, twist, influence, control, allure; *antonym* (v) repel.

katurabeauaki pulled; *synonyms* (adj) moulting, pilled, plucked.

katuraki driven; *synonyms* (v) drive, (adj) determined, impelled, compulsive, bound, dictated, dynamic, encouraged, goaded, hell-bent, provoked, successful, activist, efficient, energetic.

katurara 1. blunder; *synonyms* (n) fault, mistake, error, gaffe, bloomer, blooper, botch, lapse, misstep, oversight, trip, (v) stumble, fail, slip, fumble, **2.** waste; *synonyms* (n) desert, refuse, damage, trash, (adj) spoil, desolate, barren, (v) consume, exhaust, ruin, squander, ravage, destruction, devastate, dissipate; antonyms (v) conserve, save, 3. squander; synonyms (v) waste, fritter, lavish, spend, blow, expend, lose, scatter, trifle, deplete, devour, eat, disperse, use, abuse.

katuraraki 1. squandered; synonyms (v) alienated, bewildered, (adj) lost, wasted, dissipated, atrophied, blasted, bony, cadaverous, desolate, desolated, devastated, diminished, dissolute, emaciated, 2. wasted; synonyms (v) rotten, effete, languishing, (adj) squandered, thin, gaunt, decayed, haggard, pointless, skeletal, depleted, destroyed, faded, futile, ineffectual; antonyms (adj) worthwhile, bloated.

katuru 1. crunch; synonyms (n) squeeze, (v) crush, munch, chew, crackle, scrunch, craunch, champ, bite, grind, shatter, cranch, crash, nibble, crinkle, 2. press; synonyms (n) jam, closet, newspaper, (v) crowd, force, pack, coerce, compress, exhort, mash, push, urge, clasp, hug, (adj) constrain, 3. stamp; synonyms (n) mark, seal, brand, impression, cachet, emblem, (v) imprint, print, cast, impress, trample, punch, characterize, shape, note.

katurua stamp; synonyms (n) mark, seal, brand, impression, cachet, emblem, (v) imprint, print, cast, impress, trample, punch, characterize, shape, note.

katuruaki 1. crunched, 2. stamped; synonyms (v) imprinted, engraved, fixed, carved, impressed, (adj) beaten, embossed, 3. pressed; synonyms (adj) compact, printed, pushed, stamped, bound, driven, encouraged, impelled, incited, marked, provoked, prompted.

katuruturu stamp; synonyms (n) mark, seal, brand, impression, cachet, emblem, (v) imprint, print, cast, impress, trample, punch, characterize, shape, note.

katuruturuaki stamped; synonyms (v) imprinted, engraved, fixed, carved, impressed, (adj) beaten, embossed.

katuta 1. fix; synonyms (v) establish, assign, determine, fasten, settle, define, anchor, adjust, arrange, set, clamp, (n) bind, (adj) ascertain, confirm, attach; antonyms (v) break, unfasten, 2. join; synonyms (v) connect, unite, associate, combine, link, graft, assemble, affiliate, meet, affix, annex, conjoin, converge, couple, (n) bond; antonyms (v) detach, secede, separate, split, undo.

katutaki 1. joined; synonyms (adj) combined, coupled, united, allied, connected, joint, amalgamated, associated, linked, concerted; antonym (adj) separate, 2. ended; synonyms (adj) complete, concluded, finished, over, completed, done, closed, past, terminated, through, consummate, 3. fixed; synonyms (adj) determined, definite, steady, constant, durable, certain, decided, determinate, established, fast, fastened, intent, permanent, (v) stable, (adv) firm; antonyms (adj)

flexible, adaptable, adjustable, changeable, movable, variable, compliant, loose, moveable, portable, removable, temporary.

katutua 1. flow; synonyms (n) flood, current, discharge, abound, (v) stream, course, flux, jet, run, surge, float, emanate, fall, gush, pour, 2. excite; synonyms (v) animate, arouse, disturb, enliven, agitate, energize, awaken, electrify, encourage, evoke, exasperate, incite, inspire, kindle, provoke; antonyms (v) calm, pacify, bore, 3. inspire; synonyms (v) cheer, excite, inhale, exhilarate, affect, infuse, hearten, actuate, impress, fire, cause, exalt, exhort, inbreathe, induce, 4. provoke; synonyms (v) defy, offend, anger, enrage, inflame, invite, irritate, get, aggravate, annoy, challenge, elicit, goad, ignite, infuriate; antonyms (v) mollify, please, soothe, 5. ooze; synonyms (n) mire, muck, slime, (v) exude, leak, dribble, seep, drain, drop, bleed, emit, filter, secrete, sweat, (adj) mud, 6. stimulate; synonyms (v) prompt, drive, hasten, instigate, invigorate, rouse, spur, stir, urge, accelerate, refresh, foment, impel, inspirit, (adj) quicken; antonym (v) defuse.

katutuaki 1. inspired; synonyms (adj) divine, ingenious, adopted, creative, elected, elysian, imaginative, inventive; antonym (adj) uninspired, 2. provoked; synonyms (adj) angry, exasperated, irritated, aggravated, indignant, infuriated, irate, inflamed; antonym (adj) unprovoked, 3. stimulated; synonyms (adj) excited, inspired, ablaze, aroused, intoxicated, affected, aflame, desirous, emotional, enraged, enthused, fresh, horny, interested, keen.

kau 1. leave; synonyms (v) depart, forsake, go, abandon, desert, quit, escape, flee, lead, (n) furlough, holiday, permission, permit, break, (adj) empty; antonyms (v) arrive, enter, stay, remain, approach, change, come, 2. exit; synonyms (n) departure, door, egress, outlet, gate, going, passage, vent, death, entrance, exodus, expiration, (v) leave, decease, die; antonyms (n) arrival, entry, 3. depart; synonyms (v) deviate, diverge, part, start, stray, vary, wander, deflect, digress, expire, move, pass, retire, withdraw, differ, 4. retreat; synonyms (n) refuge, resort, asylum, den, lair, privacy, retirement, sanctuary, shelter, withdrawal, (v) recede, ebb, return, exit, retract; antonyms (n) raid, (v) advance, 5. pass; synonyms (v) flow, deliver, give, happen, offer, overtake, live, elapse, exceed, extend, lapse, proceed, surpass, make, (adj) run; antonym (v) fail, 6. part; synonyms (n) constituent, piece, article, character, component, cut, division, portion, section, share, (v) branch, disjoin, divide, divorce, class; antonyms (n) whole, entirety, (adj) complete, 7. quit; synonyms (v) discharge, drop, cease, discontinue, end, evacuate, renounce, abdicate, desist, free, relinquish, resign, disclaim, halt, (n) release; *antonym* (v) continue, **8**. retire; *synonyms* (v) retreat, adjourn, remove, secede, regrade, back, pension, dismiss, flinch, recall, recoil, sequester, shrink.

kaua 1. double; *synonyms* (adj) duplicate, dual, duple, twofold, (v) fold, reduplicate, bend, geminate, plait, (n) twin, image, match, mate, substitute, alternate; *antonym* (n) single, **2.** fourth; *synonyms* (n) quarter, quartern, second, third, poop, stern, tail, (adv) fourthly, (adj) quaternary, quaternate, **3.** augment; *synonyms* (v) amplify, increase, add, enhance, enlarge, aggrandize, reinforce, boost, expand, grow, improve, intensify, magnify, raise, (n) accrue; *antonym* (v) reduce, **4.** rival; *synonyms* (adj) competitive, (n) competitor, emulate, enemy, foe, adversary, antagonist, challenger, contender, contestant, corrival, (v) equal, contest, compete, contend; *antonyms* (adj) allied, (n) ally, friend, partner, **5.** replenish; *synonyms* (v) renew, fill, refill, recruit, furnish, refresh, supply, (adj) load, charge; *antonym* (v) empty, **6.** restock; *synonyms* (v) replenish, reload, **7.** repeat; *synonyms* (v) recite, copy, recapitulate, rehearse, reiterate, return, double, iterate, recur, reproduce, say, cite, multiply, echo, ingeminate, **8.** regenerate; *synonyms* (v) reform, restore, revive, renovate, rejuvenate, reclaim, reconstruct, mend, resurrect, modernize, recommence, revitalize, (n) convert, beatify, edify, **9.** relapse; *synonyms* (n) lapse, recidivism, fall, regression, deterioration, relapsing, reversal, reversion, setback, (v) regress, decline, backslide, revert, deteriorate, retrogress; *antonym* (n) improvement, **10.** refurbish; *synonyms* (v) remodel, freshen, furbish, revamp, fix, repair, **11.** renew; *synonyms* (v) regenerate, refurbish, overhaul, reinstate, invigorate, recover, reanimate, recreate, repeat, update, revise, continue, enliven, heal, rebuild, **12.** seed; *synonyms* (n) germ, issue, posterity, root, offspring, progeny, origin, nucleus, brood, embryo, source, beginning, (v) inseminate, plant, sow.

kauabangaka cross; *synonyms* (n) crisscross, affliction, (v) intersect, baffle, cover, thwart, (adj) crabbed, crabby, angry, cantankerous, grouchy, grumpy, traverse, cranky, annoyed; *antonyms* (v) uncross, (adj) calm, good-tempered.

kauabangakaki crossed; *synonyms* (v) matted, unhinged, frustrated, (adj) across, crossbred, decussated, hybrid, interbred, intercrossed, mixed, intersected.

kauaka troll; *synonyms* (n) circle, imp, round, leprechaun, sprite, (v) sing, trundle, twirl, amble, circulate, fish, gallop.

kauaki 1. departed; *synonyms* (v) lost, (adj) dead, gone, bygone, bypast, defunct, extinct, former, late, past, left, foregone, lifeless, (n) deceased, decedent, **2.** doubled; *synonyms* (adj) double, twofold,

bivalent, reduplicate, duple, forked, reduplicative, threefold, treble, **3.** augmented; *synonyms* (adj) inflated, more, plus, better, bigger, improved, **4.** retreated; *synonym* (adj) withdrawn, **5.** renewed; *synonyms* (adj) changed, converted, fresh, new, redintegrate, reformed, regenerate, rehabilitated, transformed, **6.** retired; *synonyms* (v) covert, (adj) private, obscure, emeritus, secluded, secret, sequestered, solitary, lonely, close, superannuated, isolated, old, out, **7.** parted; *synonyms* (adj) cleft, divided, separate, distributed, disunited, dividable, divisible, devided, **8.** repeated; *synonyms* (adj) continual, recurrent, frequent, persistent, habitual, chronic, common, continuous, perennial, perpetual; *antonym* (adj) intermittent, **9.** regenerated; *synonyms* (adj) adopted, elected, justified, unearthly, sanctified, **10.** seeded; *synonym* (adj) sown.

kauakina 1. modulate; *synonyms* (v) moderate, modify, change, inflect, qualify, regulate, temper, **2.** moderate; *synonyms* (adj) temperate, abstemious, middling, mild, easy, (v) calm, mitigate, allay, curb, diminish, lessen, ease, cool, abate, (adv) check; *antonyms* (adj) extreme, immoderate, radical, (v) increase, intensify, **3.** restrain; *synonyms* (v) bridle, confine, control, hold, rein, bind, arrest, bound, contain, govern, inhibit, limit, prevent, repress, circumscribe.

kauakinaki 1. modulated; *synonym* (adj) vocal, **2.** moderated; *synonyms* (adj) subdued, certified, dependant, dependent, equal, graduated, limited, measured, qualified, restricted, uniform, **3.** restrained; *synonyms* (adj) moderate, quiet, reserved, modest, temperate, discreet, reasonable, reticent, unemotional, guarded, confined, mild, gentle, sober, understated; *antonyms* (adj) exaggerated, unrestrained, flashy, immoral, open, ostentatious, wild.

kauakonikona contract; *synonyms* (n) compact, charter, (v) covenant, bargain, concentrate, condense, narrow, catch, compress, constrict, shrink, wrinkle, abbreviate, (adj) abridge, shorten; *antonyms* (v) expand, widen, stretch.

kauakonikonaki contracted; *synonyms* (v) shrunk, (adj) narrow, insular, contract, constricted, tight, bound.

kauamaea 1. disperse; *synonyms* (v) dispel, spread, circulate, disband, dissipate, scatter, diffuse, dispense, disseminate, break, disappear, dismiss, broadcast, distribute, propagate; *antonyms* (v) assemble, gather, collect, **2.** disseminate; *synonyms* (v) disperse, popularize, sow, air, carry, promulgate, sprinkle, strew, transmit, circularise, circularize, continue, deal, **3.** scatter; *synonyms* (v) spray, litter, rout, dot, dust, squander, plant, intersperse, cast, lavish, disorder, spill, *(n)* dispersion, splash, sprinkling.

kauamaeaki 1. dispersed; *synonyms (adj)* diffuse, scattered, sparse, spread, diffused, detached, discrete, fractional, rare, thin, circulated, flowing, isolated, loose, single; *antonym (adj)* concentrated, **2**. disseminated; *synonyms (adj)* dispersed, distributed, strewn, **3**. scattered; *synonyms (adj)* dissipated, confused, disconnected, disordered, sporadic, separate, stray, disjointed, disorderly, garbled, illogical.

kauanakoa 1. choose; *synonyms (v)* adopt, elect, pick, prefer, select, appoint, take, assign, decide, desire, determine, draw, excerpt, like, vote; *antonyms (v)* reject, refuse, **2**. decide; *synonyms (v)* choose, adjudicate, conclude, resolve, judge, settle, try, arbitrate, arrange, decree, fix, purpose, rule, deem, define; *antonym (v)* waver, **3**. figure; *synonyms (n)* form, appearance, character, estimate, shape, cost, build, contour, emblem, fashion, *(v)* design, cast, count, calculate, cipher, **4**. weigh; *synonyms (v)* balance, press, study, consider, matter, measure, poise, deliberate, assess, contemplate, ponder, evaluate, load, tell, discuss.

kauanakoaki 1. chosen; *synonyms (v)* designate, *(adj)* picked, preferred, select, favored, *(n)* elect, **2**. decided; *synonyms (v)* absolute, clear, positive, categorical, emphatic, marked, *(adj)* decisive, definite, determined, distinct, resolute, unmistakable, conclusive, fixed, peremptory; *antonym (adj)* undecided.

kauanga 1. cunning; *synonyms (adj)* clever, crafty, adroit, canny, sly, wily, artful, astute, shrewd, tricky, *(n)* craft, craftiness, cleverness, guile, deception; *antonyms (adj)* naive, honest, simple, **2**. astute; *synonyms (adj)* acute, bright, sharp, quick, cunning, discerning, discriminating, intelligent, perceptive, quick-witted, sagacious, sensible, wise, apt, arch; *antonym (adj)* stupid, **3**. clever; *synonyms (adj)* capable, able, smart, expert, ingenious, skillful, learned, adept, brainy, cagey, cagy, competent, dexterous, *(v)* brilliant, brisk; *antonyms (adj)* clumsy, unintelligent, dim, dull, inept, **4**. foxy; *synonyms (adj)* russet, vulpine, dodgy, slick, shifty, subtle, guileful, slippery, tricksy, **5**. crafty; *synonyms (adj)* calculating, deceitful, designing, devious, foxy, fraudulent, furtive, insidious, scheming, deceptive, dishonest, insinuating, knavish, sneaky, subtile; *antonym (adj)* open, **6**. ingenious; *synonyms (adj)* creative, deft, imaginative, cute, inventive, handy, artistic, gifted, original, resourceful, inspired, neat, witty, elegant; *antonym (adj)* unimaginative.

kauanging 1. contract; *synonyms (n)* compact, charter, *(v)* covenant, bargain, concentrate, condense, narrow, catch, compress, constrict, shrink, wrinkle, abbreviate, *(adj)* abridge, shorten;

antonyms (v) expand, widen, stretch, **2**. shrivel; *synonyms (v)* contract, wither, dwindle, fade, scorch, blight, blast, dry, parch, reduce, wilt, decrease, diminish, **3**. reduce; *synonyms (v)* lower, pare, curtail, cut, debase, abate, conquer, detract, dilute, deflate, enfeeble, abase, overcome, *(adj)* lessen, degrade; *antonyms (v)* increase, bolster, enlarge, exacerbate, intensify, **4**. wane; *synonyms (n)* ebb, ebbing, *(v)* decline, fall, sink, fail, recede, decay, flag, subside, waste, weaken, subsidence, collapse, slump, **5**. shrink; *synonyms (v)* flinch, recoil, cower, quail, wince, cringe, shrivel, blench, funk, retreat, start, withdraw, jib, *(n)* analyst, psychiatrist.

kauangingaki 1. contracted; *synonyms (v)* shrunk, *(adj)* narrow, insular, contract, constricted, tight, bound, **2**. reduced; *synonyms (adj)* decreased, abridged, curtailed, miniature, cheap, limited, bated, cut, inexpensive, low, lower, prostrate; *antonyms (adj)* expensive, complete.

kauangingia 1. lessen; *synonyms (v)* diminish, decrease, abridge, abate, contract, curtail, decline, fall, allay, alleviate, assuage, cut, dwindle, mitigate, moderate; *antonyms (v)* increase, exacerbate, **2**. retract; *synonyms (v)* recant, abjure, rescind, cancel, forswear, recall, recoil, renounce, repeal, repudiate, reverse, revoke, annul, disclaim, disavow, **3**. shrink; *synonyms (v)* flinch, shorten, cower, lessen, quail, reduce, wince, cringe, narrow, shrivel, blench, condense, collapse, ebb, *(n)* analyst; *antonyms (v)* expand, enlarge.

kauangingiaki 1. lessened; *synonyms (adj)* diminished, atrophied, attenuate, attenuated, belittled, conical, corrupted, cut, debased, depleted, faded, hurt, lower, pointed, short, **2**. retracted; *synonym (adj)* broken.

kauara 1. embarrass; *synonyms (v)* confuse, baffle, block, bother, confound, disconcert, encumber, hinder, complicate, abash, discomfit, distress, hamper, impede, *(adj)* bewilder, **2**. instigate; *synonyms (v)* incite, agitate, goad, abet, actuate, encourage, impel, induce, inspire, prompt, provoke, influence, arouse, *(n)* foment, animate, **3**. fetter; *synonyms (v)* shackle, bind, chain, confine, handcuff, band, restrain, *(n)* bond, gyve, hobble, tether, irons, pinion, tie; *antonyms (v)* release, free.

kauaraki 1. fettered; *synonyms (adj)* shackled, responsible, **2**. embarrassed; *synonyms (adj)* ashamed, abashed, awkward, uncomfortable, disconcerted, bashful, shamefaced, sheepish, shy, chagrined, discomfited, humiliated, mortified; *antonyms (adj)* proud, relaxed.

kauarerekea 1. lessen; *synonyms (v)* diminish, decrease, abridge, abate, contract, curtail, decline, fall, allay, alleviate, assuage, cut, dwindle, mitigate, moderate; *antonyms (v)* increase, exacerbate, **2**. abridge; *synonyms (adj)* shorten, abstract, *(v)* abbreviate, condense, reduce, compress, summarize, brief, deprive, digest, lessen, restrain, simplify, truncate; *antonyms* (v) expand, lengthen, **3.** curtail; *synonyms* (v) clip, confine, crop, curb, trim, dock, restrict, retrench, control, contain, slash, epitomize, limit, slow, check; *antonym* (v) extend, **4.** condense; *synonyms* (v) compact, concentrate, congeal, set, centralize, foreshorten, coagulate, constrict, distill, pack, press, shrink, squeeze, (adj) liquefy, melt, **5.** diminish; *synonyms* (v) deduct, detract, depreciate, belittle, deflate, depress, fade, impair, lower, narrow, qualify, recede, relieve, subside, (adj) degrade; *antonym* (v) grow, **6.** reduce; *synonyms* (v) pare, debase, conquer, dilute, enfeeble, abase, overcome, demote, drop, humble, thin, prostrate, get, overpower, break; *antonyms* (v) bolster, enlarge, intensify, **7.** shorten; *synonyms* (v) prune, bowdlerise, bowdlerize, expurgate, commute.

kauarerekeaki 1. diminished; *synonyms* (adj) abated, lessened, weakened, atrophied, belittled, attenuate, lower, attenuated, cut, short, active, airy, backward, blasted, bony, **2.** lessened; *synonyms* (adj) diminished, conical, corrupted, debased, depleted, faded, hurt, pointed, tapering, vitiated, narrowed, small, thinned, wasted, **3.** abridged; *synonyms* (adj) abbreviated, condensed, shortened, concise, abbreviate, capsule, compendious, incomplete, pocket, tail, censored, compact, comprehensive, concentrated, (v) abrege; *antonym* (adj) complete, **4.** condensed; *synonyms* (adj) abridged, compressed, succinct, summary, brief, dense, terse, thick, (v) condense; *antonym* (adj) loose, **5.** reduced; *synonyms* (adj) decreased, curtailed, miniature, cheap, limited, bated, inexpensive, low, prostrate; *antonym* (adj) expensive, **6.** shortened; *synonyms* (adj) down, emasculated, gashed, gelded, imperfect, less, mown, partial, runty, scarce, telescoped, truncated, unfinished, deficient, edited.

kauatibu stony; *synonyms* (adj) hard, rocky, rough, callous, cold, flinty, obdurate, pitiless, unfeeling, icy, insensitive, unsympathetic, bouldered, bouldery, concrete.

kauba 1. frighten; *synonyms* (v) alarm, cow, dismay, daunt, terrify, appall, affright, intimidate, scare, terrorize, awe, deter, horrify, startle, (n) fright; *antonyms* (v) comfort, encourage, **2.** surprise; *synonyms* (n) amazement, astonishment, surprisal, wonder, admiration, (v) astound, amaze, astonish, shock, jolt, stun, catch, bewilder, confound, stagger, **3.** startle; *synonyms* (v) frighten, jump, shake, electrify, rouse, disturb, panic, dumbfound, agitate, fluster, galvanize, originate, (n) start, leap, (adv) surprise.

kaubai 1. opulent; *synonyms* (adj) rich, affluent, luxurious, deluxe, lush, sumptuous, wealthy,

copious, lavish, generous, costly, gorgeous, grand, luxuriant, moneyed, **2.** wealthy; *synonyms* (adj) flush, opulent, prosperous, loaded, substantial, abounding, abundant, ample, monied, successful, thriving; *antonyms* (adj) poor, impoverished.

kaubaki 1. frightened; *synonyms* (adj) afraid, fearful, scared, terrified, timid, anxious, apprehensive, horrified, intimidated, restless, worried, (adv) cowardly; *antonyms* (adj) calm, confident, unimpressed, brave, fearless, **2.** surprised; *synonyms* (adj) astonished, amazed, astounded, dumbfounded, shocked, stunned, bewildered, startled, aghast, confused, curious, puzzled, questioning, quizzical, baffled; *antonym* (adj) indifferent, **3.** startled; *synonyms* (adj) distressed, frightened, alarmed, flabbergasted, staggered, troubled, upset, panicky.

kaubata tackle; *synonyms* (v) handle, harness, undertake, attempt, stop, struggle, grapple, (n) gear, equipment, rigging, kit, paraphernalia, rig, apparatus, outfit; *antonym* (v) avoid.

kaubatial tenderize; *synonyms* (v) tender, tenderise, soften, bid, offer.

kaubatialaki tenderized; *synonym* (adj) tenderised.

kaubiroto 1. fat; *synonyms* (adj) stout, corpulent, dense, thick, bulky, fatty, fertile, fleshy, gainful, greasy, great, (n) avoirdupois, blubber, cream, (v) fatten; *antonyms* (adj) thin, slim, skinny, slender, **2.** husky; *synonyms* (adj) hoarse, gruff, burly, big, beefy, dry, raucous, strapping, brawny, hefty, muscular, robust, rough, strong, sturdy; *antonym* (adj) slight, **3.** corpulent; *synonyms* (adj) fat, obese, portly, overweight, plump, lusty, chubby, tubby, gross, rotund, round, weighty, heavy, **4.** portly; *synonyms* (adj) stately, large, **5.** paunchy; *synonyms* (adj) abdominous, potbellied, **6.** obese, **7.** plump; *synonyms* (adj) buxom, pudgy, full, squab, stocky, chunky, embonpoint, (v) drop, go, dive, plop, flump, plunk, plank, plonk; *antonym* (adj) emaciated, **8.** stout; *synonyms* (adj) bold, hardy, husky, fearless, hearty, mighty, gallant, brave, healthy, resolute, solid, stalwart, thickset, daring, forcible; *antonym* (adj) flimsy, **9.** pudgy; *synonyms* (adj) dumpy, podgy, **10.** stocky; *synonyms* (adj) heavyset, stubby, short, compact.

kaubuai bearded; *synonyms* (adj) awned, barbate, awny, hairy, whiskered, aristate, calamiform, coniform, echinate, gladiate, pilous, shagged, barbigerous, bewhiskered, bushy.

kaubunranga 1. devaluate; *synonyms* (v) depreciate, devalue, decrease, debase, belittle, deprecate, depress, detract, impair, lower, undervalue, underestimate, **2.** animalize; *synonyms* (v) animalise, brutalize, canker, corrupt, pervert, rot, stain, brutalise, sensualize, **3.** debase; *synonyms* (v) degrade, adulterate, alloy, contaminate, debauch, defile, demean, cheapen, bastardize, demoralize, deprave, humble, humiliate, (*n*) abase, disgrace, **4**. bastardize; *synonyms* (*v*) bastardise, embastardize, imbastardize, bastard, illegitimate, illegitimatize, warp, bestialize, **5**. befoul; *synonyms* (*v*) foul, pollute, soil, dirty, maculate, tarnish, violate, (*adj*) begrime, bemire, besmear, **6**. adulterate; *synonyms* (*v*) doctor, dilute, weaken, falsify, sophisticate, thin, taint, (*adj*) adulterated, spurious; *antonyms* (*v*) clean, purify, **7**. pervert; *synonyms* (*n*) bend, apostate, degenerate, deviant, deviate, (*v*) distort, misuse, abuse, misrepresent, twist, garble, misapply, convolute, profane, vitiate, **8**. shame; *synonyms* (*n*) reproach, discredit, humiliation, chagrin, insult, modesty, pity, scandal, contempt, degradation, embarrassment, ignominy, infamy, (*v*) dishonor, abash; *antonym* (*v*) honor, **9**. vilify; *synonyms* (*v*) malign, defame, slander, libel, disparage, revile, traduce, blacken, smear, decry, calumniate, denigrate, slur, vituperate, (*adj*) asperse; *antonyms* (*v*) praise, compliment.

kaubunrangaki 1. debased; *synonyms* (*adj*) corrupt, adulterated, degraded, low, base, degenerate, depraved, adulterate, corrupted, debauched, decadent, impure, perverted; *antonym* (*adj*) pure, **2**. befouled; *synonyms* (*adj*) unclean, fouled, foul, **3**. bastardized; *synonym* (*adj*) bastardised, **4**. adulterated; *synonyms* (*adj*) debased, dirty, bastard, contaminated, diluted, false, faulty, sham, sophisticated, watery, devalued, filthy, (*v*) contraband, illegitimate, surreptitious, **5**. shamed; *synonyms* (*adj*) disgraced, dishonored, ashamed, discredited, guilty, hangdog, abashed, browbeaten, bullied, cowed, damaged, fallen, intimidated, shamefaced, mortified, **6**. perverted; *synonyms* (*adj*) perverse, distorted, immoral, kinky, abnormal, twisted, deviant, reprobate, unnatural, contorted, contrary, misrepresented, (*v*) hardened.

kaubure councilman; *synonyms* (*n*) alderman, burgomaster, representative, seneschal, committeeman, constable, councilwoman, freeholder, portreeve, warden.

kaubwai 1. opulent; *synonyms* (*adj*) rich, affluent, luxurious, deluxe, lush, sumptuous, wealthy, copious, lavish, generous, costly, gorgeous, grand, luxuriant, moneyed, **2**. wealthy; *synonyms* (*adj*) flush, opulent, prosperous, loaded, substantial, abounding, abundant, ample, monied, successful, thriving; *antonyms* (*adj*) poor, impoverished, **3**. rich; *synonyms* (*adj*) fertile, productive, fruitful, full, deep, fat, plentiful, prolific, bright, liberal, heavy, fecund, magnificent, mellow, (*v*) ornate; *antonyms* (*adj*) broke, destitute, light.

ka'ue flowery; *synonyms* (*adj*) florid, ornate, bloomy, floral, blossomy, figurative, fancy, elaborate, rhetorical, verbose, (*v*) gay; *antonym* (*adj*) plain.

kauea enthrone; *synonyms* (*v*) crown, throne, invest, coronate, deify, adorn, clothe, commit, empower, endow, endue, inthronize, vest, (*n*) immortalize, signalize.

kauekea alert; *synonyms* (*adj*) active, agile, quick, aware, intelligent, lively, vigilant, clever, alive, animated, attentive, bright, (*v*) awake, (*n*) alarm, alarum; *antonyms* (*adj*) drowsy, inattentive, absentminded, dazed, sleepy, tired, asleep, slow, unalert, unconscious.

kauka 1. blab; *synonyms* (*v*) babble, chatter, tattle, mouth, blabber, chat, clack, disclose, divulge, gabble, gibber, gossip, palaver, piffle, prate, **2**. disclose; *synonyms* (*v*) betray, declare, impart, detect, discover, reveal, convey, announce, air, communicate, bare, break, expose, show, (*adj*) confess; *antonyms* (*v*) conceal, secrete, **3**. admit; *synonyms* (*v*) acknowledge, concede, accede, grant, affirm, include, permit, take, appreciate, welcome, accommodate, adjudge, avouch, (*n*) allow, (*phr*) accept; *antonyms* (*v*) deny, exclude, reject, **4**. inform; *synonyms* (*v*) acquaint, advise, enlighten, tell, familiarize, explain, advertise, apprise, educate, instruct, state, warn, describe, animate, notify, **5**. notify; *synonyms* (*v*) inform, alert, apprize, counsel, promulgate, report, call, **6**. open; *synonyms* (*adj*) frank, obvious, artless, exposed, free, honest, forthright, guileless, ingenuous, naked, direct, (*v*) expand, give, (*n*) candid, clear; *antonyms* (*adj*) devious, secretive, concealed, furtive, hidden, limited, repressive, reserved, restricted, secret, blocked, cautious, (*v*) shut, end, (*tr v*) close, **7**. reveal; *synonyms* (*v*) display, exhibit, express, present, indicate, uncover, proclaim, find, develop, leak, manifest, open, publish, unearth, unfold; *antonyms* (*v*) hide, cover.

kaukaki 1. disclosed; *synonyms* (*adj*) revealed, exposed, ascertained, detailed, discovered, manifest, naked, open, observed, **2**. informed; *synonyms* (*adj*) aware, cognizant, educated, conscious, knowledgeable, familiar, apprised, wise, conversant, experienced, (*adv*) abreast; *antonym* (*adj*) ignorant, **3**. revealed; *synonym* (*adj*) disclosed; *antonym* (*adj*) hidden, **4**. opened; *synonyms* (*v*) blown, distended, exhausted, inflated, stale, swollen, (*adj*) candid, assailable, blatant, blazing, clear, conspicuous, lawless, loose, through.

kaukau 1. bellow; *synonyms* (*n*) roar, shout, cry, yell, scream, bay, screech, (*v*) growl, bawl, snarl, call, howl, holler, shriek, whoop, **2**. yelp; *synonyms* (*n*) bark, whine, woof, (*v*) yap, squeal, bellow, yip.

kaukea 1. scrounge; *synonyms* (*v*) forage, cadge, beg, bum, filch, mooch, pilfer, grub, borrow, rob, schnorr, use, freeload, wheedle, **2**. scavenge; *synonyms* (*v*) clean, cleanse, salvage, houseclean, pick, prowl, relieve, salve, save, hunt, search.

kaukeuke scratch; *synonyms* (*n*) score, mark, nick, scrabble, dent, abrasion, cut, groove, (*v*) graze, notch, rub, scrape, chafe, rake, grate.

kaukeukeaki scratched; *synonyms* (*adj*) scraped, hurt, abraded, dented, injured, raw, sgraffito, spoiled, broken, skinned, smashed.

kaukintaea shame; *synonyms* (*n*) reproach, disgrace, discredit, humiliation, chagrin, insult, modesty, pity, scandal, contempt, (*v*) dishonor, degrade, humiliate, abash, debase; *antonym* (*v*) honor.

kaukintaeaki shamed; *synonyms* (*adj*) disgraced, dishonored, ashamed, discredited, guilty, hangdog, abashed, browbeaten, bullied, cowed, damaged, fallen, intimidated, shamefaced, mortified.

kauma 1. tired; *synonyms* (*adj*) exhausted, fatigued, hackneyed, weary, banal, commonplace, stale, threadbare, trite, beat, haggard, jaded, stock, worn, drowsy; *antonyms* (*adj*) fresh, invigorated, alert, refreshed, energetic, original, strong, 2. raise; *synonyms* (*v*) boost, lift, erect, hoist, increase, build, elevate, enhance, foster, grow, promote, prefer, augment, cultivate, (*n*) advance; *antonym* (*v*) lower.

kaumaka hurry; *synonyms* (*n*) speed, haste, dispatch, flurry, (*v*) bustle, hasten, accelerate, dash, expedite, scurry, fly, run, rush, zip, hie; *antonyms* (*n*) slowness, (*v*) dawdle.

kaumakaki hurried; *synonyms* (*adj*) hasty, fast, headlong, quick, rapid, speedy, sudden, swift, abrupt, cursory, careless, precipitate, prompt, rash, slapdash; *antonyms* (*adj*) slow, unhurried, leisurely.

kaumaki 1. fast; *synonyms* (*adj*) dissolute, firm, agile, debauched, fixed, hurried, instant, quick, rapid, staunch, brisk, (*adv*) soon, hard, close, (*n*) diet; *antonyms* (*adj*) sluggish, loose, (*adv*) slow, slowly, leisurely, (*v*) gorge, (*n*) binge, 2. breakneck; *synonyms* (*adj*) dangerous, fast, hasty, swift, 3. brisk; *synonyms* (*adj*) active, bracing, alive, bright, lively, acute, alert, energetic, nimble, smart, sprightly, adroit, animated, crisp, fresh; *antonym* (*adj*) soporific, 4. expedite; *synonyms* (*v*) accelerate, dispatch, advance, hasten, assist, hurry, quicken, speed, facilitate, forward, further, precipitate, rush, 5. dispatch; *synonyms* (*n*) despatch, consignment, celerity, expedition, haste, letter, quickness, rapidity, (*v*) send, deliver, convey, discharge, murder, slay, transmit; *antonyms* (*n*) receiving, receipt, 6. fleet; *synonyms* (*n*) armada, float, marine, navy, (*adj*) expeditious, speedy, (*v*) flit, fly, pass, dart, evanesce, fade, 7. expeditious; *synonyms* (*adj*) prompt, fleet, immediate, ready, punctual, 8. hasten; *synonyms* (*v*) expedite, dash, hie, bustle, race, run, gallop, sprint, drive, hotfoot, hustle, scurry, (*adj*) course, go, (*n*) promote; *antonym* (*v*) delay, 9. dispatched; *synonyms* (*adj*) finished, fulfilled, 10. accelerate; *synonyms* (*v*) heighten, increase, intensify, (*adj*) vivify; *antonyms*

(*v*) decelerate, stop, 11. accelerated; *synonyms* (*adj*) intensive, express, sudden, 12. rapid; *synonyms* (*adj*) cursory, winged, impetuous, precipitous, abrupt, rash, volant, instantaneous; *antonym* (*adj*) gradual, 13. raised; *synonyms* (*v*) repousse, (*adj*) elevated, embossed, erect, convex, brocaded, high, bold, confident, elate, elated, elative, exultant, lofty, (*prep*) above, 14. quick; *synonyms* (*adj*) clever, intelligent, dexterous, keen, brief, apt, ingenious, sharp, skillful, facile, expert, observant, cutting, deft, (*adv*) apace; *antonym* (*adj*) dull, 15. swift; *synonyms* (*adj*) unexpected, impulsive, meteoric, (*n*) cylinder, (*adv*) swiftly; *antonym* (*adj*) considered.

kaumakiaki 1. dispatched; *synonyms* (*adj*) finished, fulfilled, 2. expedited, 3. accelerated; *synonyms* (*adj*) fast, quick, intensive, rapid, speedy, express, sudden.

kauman 1. ingenious; *synonyms* (*adj*) adroit, artful, clever, cunning, creative, deft, expert, imaginative, cute, acute, able, inventive, canny, handy, bright; *antonym* (*adj*) unimaginative, 2. crafty; *synonyms* (*adj*) astute, sly, tricky, wily, shifty, calculating, deceitful, designing, devious, foxy, fraudulent, furtive, ingenious, insidious, scheming; *antonyms* (*adj*) naive, honest, open, 3. witty; *synonyms* (*adj*) humorous, amusing, funny, facetious, intelligent, jocular, brilliant, quick, comic, comical, poignant, waggish, (*v*) smart, sharp, keen; *antonym* (*adj*) serious, 4. smart; *synonyms* (*adj*) crafty, dapper, shrewd, prompt, chic, jaunty, lively, natty, neat, saucy, fine, fashionable, (*v*) ache, hurt, (*n*) pain; *antonyms* (*adj*) scruffy, stupid, dim, shabby, unkempt, slow, 5. resourceful; *synonym* (*adj*) original.

kaumata colorful; *synonyms* (*adj*) bright, flamboyant, vivid, gorgeous, brilliant, coloured, colourful, garish, gaudy, loud, picturesque, showy, expressive, graphic, vibrant; *antonyms* (*adj*) colorless, dull, monochrome, uncolored.

kaumau 1. hurried; *synonyms* (*adj*) hasty, fast, headlong, quick, rapid, speedy, sudden, swift, abrupt, cursory, careless, precipitate, prompt, rash, slapdash; *antonyms* (*adj*) slow, unhurried, leisurely, 2. hasten; *synonyms* (*v*) speed, expedite, further, forward, dispatch, advance, hurry, dash, hie, rush, bustle, dart, (*adj*) accelerate, quicken, (*n*) haste; *antonym* (*v*) delay, 3. hasty; *synonyms* (*adj*) fleet, hurried, impetuous, brisk, brusque, eager, expeditious, foolhardy, impatient, impulsive, inconsiderate, injudicious, precipitant, precipitous, reckless; *antonyms* (*adj*) considered, deliberate, sensible, 4. hurry; *synonyms* (*n*) flurry, celerity, hastiness, hurriedness, press, (*v*) hasten, scurry, fly, run, zip, drive, race, scamper, scuttle, flit; *antonyms* (*n*) slowness, (*v*) dawdle.

kaumauaki hurried; *synonyms* *(adj)* hasty, fast, headlong, quick, rapid, speedy, sudden, swift, abrupt, cursory, careless, precipitate, prompt, rash, slapdash; *antonyms* *(adj)* slow, unhurried, leisurely.

kaumwangai scold; *synonyms* *(v)* censure, berate, chide, rebuke, reprimand, abuse, lecture, reproach, rail, admonish, castigate, grouch, grumble, jaw, *(n)* nag; *antonym* *(v)* praise.

kauna 1. conflict; *synonyms* *(n)* clash, combat, fight, battle, contention, contest, dispute, encounter, action, antagonism, collision, difference, disagreement, engagement, *(v)* collide; *antonyms* *(n)* agreement, accord, harmony, peace, *(v)* agree, **2.** provoke; *synonyms* *(v)* excite, incite, defy, offend, anger, arouse, enrage, inflame, invite, irritate, kindle, get, aggravate, annoy, awaken; *antonyms* *(v)* calm, mollify, please, soothe, **3.** stem; *synonyms* *(n)* root, bow, branch, shank, stalk, stick, handle, axis, bough, *(v)* originate, block, arrest, halt, issue, proceed, **4.** taunt; *synonyms* *(v)* jeer, flout, deride, insult, sneer, bait, quip, rally, tease, twit, banter, *(n)* ridicule, gibe, mock, scoff; *antonyms* *(v)* compliment, praise, respect, **5.** oppose; *synonyms* *(v)* object, contend, contradict, contravene, controvert, counteract, resist, counter, disagree, dissent, confront, defend, gainsay, hinder, repel; *antonyms* *(v)* support, advocate, back, advise.

kaunainea respect; *synonyms* *(n)* honor, esteem, homage, worship, heed, notice, account, consideration, deference, *(v)* regard, observe, admire, appreciate, estimation, keep; *antonyms* *(n)* cheek, insolence, impudence, *(v)* disrespect, scorn, despise, dishonor, disregard, humiliate.

kaunaineaki respected; *synonyms* *(adj)* esteemed, illustrious, respectable, appreciated, dear, honored, revered, valued, celebrated, famous, glorious, prestigious, redoubtable.

kaunaki 1. stemmed; *synonyms* *(adj)* caulescent, cauline, **2.** provoked; *synonyms* *(adj)* angry, exasperated, irritated, aggravated, indignant, infuriated, irate, inflamed; *antonym* *(adj)* unprovoked, **3.** opposed; *synonyms* *(adj)* conflicting, contradictory, hostile, contrary, antagonistic, opposing, adverse, averse, contrasted, repugnant, incompatible, irreconcilable, counter, against, opposite.

kaunga 1. excite; *synonyms* *(v)* animate, arouse, disturb, enliven, agitate, energize, awaken, electrify, encourage, evoke, exasperate, incite, inspire, kindle, provoke; *antonyms* *(v)* calm, pacify, bore, **2.** invoke; *synonyms* *(v)* entreat, appeal, conjure, pray, beseech, cite, summon, name, beg, adjure, bid, wish, address, mention, implore, **3.** enslave; *synonyms* *(v)* bind, enthrall, captivate, slave, subjugate, tame, chain, confine; *antonym* *(v)* liberate, **4.** stimulate; *synonyms* *(v)* excite, prompt, drive, exhilarate, goad, hasten, instigate,

invigorate, rouse, spur, stir, urge, accelerate, refresh, *(adj)* quicken; *antonym* *(v)* defuse, **5.** rouse; *synonyms* *(v)* awake, actuate, move, fire, inflame, revive, heat, induce, irritate, wake, call, bestir, motivate, raise, rear; *antonym* *(v)* dampen.

kaungaki 1. excited; *synonyms* *(adj)* agitated, ablaze, emotional, enthusiastic, frantic, ardent, aroused, delirious, fervent, heated, impassioned, passionate, warm, elated, *(v)* animated; *antonyms* *(adj)* calm, cool, unexcited, **2.** enslaved; *synonyms* *(adj)* bond, captive, beguiled, bound, captivated, charmed, cringing, delighted, dependent, enthralled, imprisoned, incarcerated, obsequious, servile, subject; *antonym* *(adj)* free, **3.** stimulated; *synonyms* *(adj)* excited, inspired, intoxicated, affected, aflame, angry, desirous, enraged, enthused, fresh, horny, interested, keen, randy, red; *antonym* *(adj)* uninspired.

kauniben 1. firm; *synonyms* *(n)* company, *(adj)* constant, hard, stable, close, compact, determined, fixed, resolute, solid, steadfast, steady, strong, decisive, *(v)* faithful; *antonyms* *(adj)* irresolute, soft, weak, hesitant, limp, liquid, soggy, **2.** stable; *synonyms* *(adj)* firm, permanent, reliable, durable, fast, lasting, secure, stationary, enduring, persistent, sound, immovable, certain, set, immobile; *antonyms* *(adj)* unstable, shaky, wobbly, dangerous, precarious, rickety, volatile, **3.** sturdy; *synonyms* *(adj)* rugged, stout, burly, mighty, robust, hardy, healthy, hefty, muscular, stalwart, tight, tough, tenacious, husky, *(n)* brawny; *antonyms* *(adj)* flimsy, fragile, puny, **4.** resistant; *synonyms* *(adj)* immune, impervious, defiant, proof, rebellious, antagonistic, insubordinate, repellent, unbreakable, *(v)* resistive; *antonyms* *(adj)* permeable, submissive, agreeable, **5.** solid; *synonyms* *(adj)* dense, consistent, real, good, massive, substantial, hearty, heavy, material, potent, rigid, sturdy, thick, whole, fine; *antonyms* *(adj)* unreliable, loose, gaseous, runny, transparent, watery, **6.** sound; *synonyms* *(n)* echo, peal, audio, *(v)* ring, chime, blow, chirp, *(adj)* reasonable, complete, fit, just, rational, right, sane, sensible; *antonyms* *(n)* silence, *(adj)* illogical, unsound, confused.

kaunikai 1. combat; *synonyms* *(n)* fight, encounter, action, brawl, conflict, contest, fighting, fray, war, hostility, affray, contention, engagement, *(v)* battle, clash, **2.** compete; *synonyms* *(v)* emulate, race, rival, strive, participate, oppose, contend, struggle, vie, play, run, **3.** oppose; *synonyms* *(v)* object, contradict, contravene, controvert, counteract, resist, counter, disagree, dissent, combat, confront, defend, dispute, gainsay, hinder; *antonyms* *(v)* support, advocate, agree, back, advise.

kaunikaiaki opposed; *synonyms* *(adj)* conflicting, contradictory, hostile, contrary, antagonistic, opposing, adverse, averse, contrasted, repugnant, incompatible, irreconcilable, counter, against, opposite.

kaunrabakau 1. graduate; *synonyms* (n) alum, alumna, alumnus, grad, grade, connoisseur, file, licentiate, organize, sort, wrangler, (v) calibrate, catalogue, pass, divide, **2.** examine; *synonyms* (v) assay, audit, consider, overhaul, try, check, control, search, survey, ascertain, ask, contemplate, compare, analyze, canvass.

kaunrabakauaki graduated; *synonyms* (adj) gradational, progressive, gradatory, calibrated, equal, measured, proportional, limited, moderated, relative, tapered, uniform, (n) graduate.

kaunrabata 1. grapple; *synonyms* (v) clutch, clasp, grip, fight, tackle, contend, grab, deal, seize, struggle, (n) grapnel, grappling, grasp, (adj) lock, hook, **2.** wrestle; *synonyms* (v) grapple, scuffle, strive, battle, wrench, tussle, contest, scramble, clash, brawl, squirm, turn, twist, worm, (n) wrestling.

kaunta 1. distinguish; *synonyms* (v) discern, discriminate, describe, know, perceive, discover, descry, behold, characterize, classify, detect, difference, differentiate, identify, recognize; *antonym* (v) confuse, **2.** contrast; *synonyms* (n) contrariety, antithesis, comparison, distinction, variation, collation, opposite, dissimilarity, (v) differ, conflict, oppose, collate, diverge, clash, counterpoint; *antonym* (n) similarity.

kauntaba oppose; *synonyms* (v) object, contest, contend, contradict, contravene, controvert, counteract, resist, fight, counter, disagree, dissent, combat, confront, defend; *antonyms* (v) support, advocate, agree, back, advise.

kauntabaea provoke; *synonyms* (v) excite, incite, defy, offend, anger, arouse, enrage, inflame, invite, irritate, kindle, get, aggravate, annoy, awaken; *antonyms* (v) calm, mollify, please, soothe.

kauntabaeaki provoked; *synonyms* (adj) angry, exasperated, irritated, aggravated, indignant, infuriated, irate, inflamed; *antonym* (adj) unprovoked.

kauntabaki opposed; *synonyms* (adj) conflicting, contradictory, hostile, contrary, antagonistic, opposing, adverse, averse, contrasted, repugnant, incompatible, irreconcilable, counter, against, opposite.

kauntabama 1. contradict; *synonyms* (v) deny, oppose, belie, conflict, confute, contravene, controvert, disprove, dissent, impugn, invalidate, refute, disaffirm, disclaim, counteract; *antonyms* (v) confirm, agree, match, **2.** clash; *synonyms* (n) bang, battle, brush, clang, crash, discord, encounter, (v) jar, fight, impact, brawl, clank, collide, dispute, hit; *antonym* (n) agreement, **3.** collide; *synonyms* (v) bump, clash, strike, beat, hurtle, knock, smash, quarrel, **4.** oppose;

synonyms (v) object, contest, contend, contradict, resist, counter, disagree, combat, confront, defend, gainsay, hinder, repel, thwart, withstand; *antonyms* (v) support, advocate, back, advise.

kauntabamaki opposed; *synonyms* (adj) conflicting, contradictory, hostile, contrary, antagonistic, opposing, adverse, averse, contrasted, repugnant, incompatible, irreconcilable, counter, against, opposite.

kauntaeka 1. dispute; *synonyms* (n) brawl, quarrel, debate, conflict, wrangle, difference, question, combat, (v) argue, contest, controversy, discuss, fight, row, squabble; *antonyms* (n) agreement, (v) agree, **2.** argue; *synonyms* (v) contend, oppose, reason, altercate, assert, attest, convince, declare, expostulate, indicate, object, witness, defend, hassle, (n) dispute; *antonym* (v) deny, **3.** squabble; *synonyms* (n) bicker, feud, scrap, contention, fuss, argument, broil, spat, strife, altercation, bickering, disagreement, (v) tiff, brabble, brangle, **4.** quarrel; *synonyms* (n) dissension, clash, fracas, misunderstanding, breach, fray, discord, dustup, variance, disputation, (v) disagree, affray, disturbance, differ, jar, **5.** wrangle; *synonyms* (n) skirmish, haggle, wrangling, haggling, struggle, words, (v) jangle, scuffle, spar, clashing, dissent, quibble.

kauntaekaki disputed; *synonyms* (adj) controversial, moot, disputable, debatable, doubtful, dubious, opposed, uncertain, problematic.

kauntaki distinguished; *synonyms* (adj) celebrated, dignified, eminent, conspicuous, illustrious, important, renowned, reputable, famous, great, high, noble, prominent, splendid, superior; *antonyms* (adj) unknown, ordinary.

kaunun infuriate; *synonyms* (v) exasperate, aggravate, enrage, incense, anger, furious, irritate, outrage, provoke, rile, inflame, annoy, madden, vex, (adj) exacerbate; *antonyms* (v) pacify, please.

kaununaki infuriated; *synonyms* (adj) angry, enraged, furious, incensed, angered, mad, exasperated, provoked, boiling, livid, annoyed, maddened, raging, wrathful, fierce; *antonym* (adj) calm.

kauoman second; *synonyms* (n) instant, moment, flash, jiffy, minute, sec, (v) back, endorse, support, encourage, forward, help, (adj) latter, further, (pron) additional; *antonym* (adj) first.

kauongo listen; *synonyms* (v) hark, hear, attend, hearken, heed, harken, list, mind, concentrate, incline.

kauoua 1. dual; *synonyms* (adj) double, duplex, duple, twin, twofold, doubled, bivalent, combined, threefold, treble, bifold, binal, common, cooperative, double-dip; *antonyms* (adj) individual, single, **2.** second; *synonyms* (n) instant, moment, flash, jiffy, minute, sec, (v) back, endorse, support, encourage, forward, help, *(adj)* latter, further, *(pron)* additional; *antonym (adj)* first.

kaura 1. cremate; *synonyms (v)* burn, incremate, cook, destroy, **2**. kindle; *synonyms (v)* arouse, excite, fire, inflame, awaken, flame, animate, enkindle, heat, incite, provoke, stimulate, stir, *(n)* ignite, light, **3**. lit; *synonyms (n)* literature, *(adj)* illuminated, lighted, drunk, intoxicated, luminous, tipsy, **4**. brave; *synonyms (adj)* adventurous, bold, audacious, courageous, endure, fearless, hardy, intrepid, valiant, virile, confident, daring, dauntless, *(v)* defy, confront; *antonyms (adj)* cowardly, frightened, gutless, pathetic, *(n)* timid, **5**. fire; *synonyms (n)* discharge, ardor, conflagration, explode, fervor, bonfire, burning, enthusiasm, *(v)* eject, blaze, dismiss, kindle, expel, sack, shoot; *antonym (v)* hire, **6**. ignite; *synonyms (v)* agitate, detonate, erupt; *antonym (v)* extinguish, **7**. light; *synonyms (adj)* fair, clear, facile, easy, faint, flimsy, airy, *(n)* brightness, daylight, illumination, dawn, *(v)* glow, dismount, illuminate, alight; *antonyms (adj)* fattening, nauseating, *(n)* dark, darkness, gloom, shade, night, *(v)* darken, *(alt sp)* heavy, **8**. strong; *synonyms (adj)* intense, powerful, able, deep, firm, stable, steady, cogent, durable, forcible, good, hard, influential, lusty, potent; *antonyms (adj)* weak, bland, delicate, feeble, frail, mild, pale, slight, unconvincing, diluted, dull, exhausted, imperceptible, lightweight, soft, **9**. valiant; *synonyms (adj)* brave, gallant, heroic, stout, doughty, stalwart, plucky, valorous, resolute, strenuous, undaunted, strong, *(prep)* forward.

kaurakea toss; *synonyms (v)* fling, throw, agitate, cast, chuck, pitch, flip, hurl, shake, convulse, discard, project, roll, heave, jerk.

kauraki 1. lit; *synonyms (n)* literature, *(adj)* illuminated, lighted, drunk, intoxicated, luminous, tipsy, **2**. kindled; *synonyms (adj)* ignited, enkindled, burning, **3**. ignited; *synonyms (v)* active, flowing, laving, live, lively, quickening, running, vigorous, *(adj)* kindled, flaming, ablaze, fiery, **4**. fired; *synonyms (adj)* dismissed, discharged, unemployed, enthusiastic, heated, interested, passionate, zealous, afire, excited, released, **5**. lighted; *synonyms (adj)* alight, lit, bright, airy, cheering, exhilarating, gay, lightsome.

kaurama 1. encounter; *synonyms (n)* collision, combat, battle, conflict, contest, action, brush, confrontation, impact, *(v)* clash, confront, experience, face, find, rencounter; *antonym (v)* retreat, **2**. meet; *synonyms (v)* converge, assemble, congregate, encounter, fulfill, gather, answer, cross, intersect, abut, concur, adjoin, collect, convene, *(adj)* fit; *antonyms (v)* avoid, disperse, diverge.

kauramaka 1. inflame; *synonyms (v)* burn, fire, enkindle, arouse, heat, ignite, incense, incite, irritate, kindle, agitate, aggravate, anger, chafe,

enrage; *antonym (v)* calm, **2**. light; *synonyms (adj)* fair, clear, facile, easy, faint, flimsy, *(n)* flame, brightness, daylight, illumination, dawn, *(v)* inflame, glow, dismount, illuminate; *antonyms (adj)* fattening, nauseating, *(n)* dark, darkness, gloom, shade, night, *(v)* extinguish, darken, *(alt sp)* heavy.

kauramakaki 1. lit; *synonyms (n)* literature, *(adj)* illuminated, lighted, drunk, intoxicated, luminous, tipsy, **2**. lighted; *synonyms (adj)* alight, lit, ablaze, bright, airy, cheering, exhilarating, gay, lightsome, **3**. inflamed; *synonyms (adj)* sore, impassioned, excited, angry, flaming, hot, irritated, passionate, burning, painful, *(n)* red.

kauramara reduce; *synonyms (v)* lower, pare, abbreviate, curtail, cut, debase, abate, condense, contract, diminish, shorten, concentrate, compress, *(adj)* abridge, lessen; *antonyms (v)* increase, bolster, expand, enlarge, exacerbate, intensify.

kauramaraki reduced; *synonyms (adj)* decreased, abridged, curtailed, miniature, cheap, limited, bated, cut, inexpensive, low, lower, prostrate; *antonyms (adj)* expensive, complete.

kauraura redden; *synonyms (v)* flush, color, crimson, glow, rubify, *(adj)* blush, mantle.

kaurauraki reddened; *synonyms (adj)* ablaze, aflame, crimson, flushed, inflamed, red, aroused, blazing, blemished, blooming, blushful, burning, carmine, cerise, cherry.

kaure 1. divorce; *synonyms (n)* separation, divorcement, rupture, *(v)* detach, dissociate, disunite, separate, divide, isolate, disjoin, disjoint, disassociate, part, sever, split; *antonyms (n)* marriage, wedding, **2**. open; *synonyms (adj)* frank, obvious, artless, exposed, free, honest, bare, forthright, guileless, ingenuous, naked, *(v)* expand, give, *(n)* candid, clear; *antonyms (adj)* devious, secretive, concealed, furtive, hidden, limited, repressive, reserved, restricted, secret, blocked, cautious, *(v)* shut, end, *(tr v)* close, **3**. separate; *synonyms (adj)* detached, individual, particular, single, *(v)* divorce, insulate, scatter, cut, disconnect, discrete, discriminate, disperse, distinguish, demarcate, break; *antonyms (adj)* connected, joined, simultaneous, *(v)* unite, merge, mix, combine, fuse, join, link, associate.

kaurea 1. hatch; *synonyms (n)* brood, door, gate, *(v)* breed, contrive, concoct, brew, design, cook, cover, devise, invent, generate, engender, create, **2**. open; *synonyms (adj)* frank, obvious, artless, exposed, free, honest, bare, forthright, guileless, ingenuous, naked, *(v)* expand, give, *(n)* candid, clear; *antonyms (adj)* devious, secretive, concealed, furtive, hidden, limited, repressive, reserved, restricted, secret, blocked, cautious, *(v)* shut, end, *(tr v)* close.

kaureaki 1. divorced; *synonyms (adj)* separate, single, *(adv)* apart, **2**. hatched; *synonyms (adj)* crosshatched, ruled, **3**. separated; *synonyms (adj)* disconnected, detached, divided, isolated, disjointed, free, disjunct, removed, dislocated, independent, lone, *(prep)* disjoined, distinct, **4**. opened; *synonyms (v)* blown, distended, exhausted, inflated, *(adj)* open, candid, exposed, assailable, blatant, blazing, clear, conspicuous, lawless, loose, through.

kauri bony; *synonyms (adj)* osseous, gaunt, lean, thin, angular, emaciated, scrawny, skinny, lanky, meager, boney, spare; *antonym (adj)* rounded.

kauring 1. revise; *synonyms (v)* edit, amend, emend, alter, convert, correct, fix, retouch, reform, adapt, reconsider, *(n)* review, revisal, revision, proof, **2**. review; *synonyms (n)* examination, critique, inspection, retrospect, commentary, comment, parade, magazine, criticism, investigation, *(v)* check, survey, criticize, examine, inspect.

kauringa remind; *synonyms (v)* remember, recollect, prompt, recall, commemorate, hint, jog, think, consider, cue, *(n)* mind.

kauringaba flashback; *synonyms (n)* remembrance, memory, recurrence.

kauringaki revised; *synonym (adj)* altered.

kauriri hurry; *synonyms (n)* speed, haste, dispatch, flurry, *(v)* bustle, hasten, accelerate, dash, expedite, scurry, fly, run, rush, zip, hie; *antonyms (n)* slowness, *(v)* dawdle.

kauririaki hurried; *synonyms (adj)* hasty, fast, headlong, quick, rapid, speedy, sudden, swift, abrupt, cursory, careless, precipitate, prompt, rash, slapdash; *antonyms (adj)* slow, unhurried, leisurely.

kautikaikaia 1. frighten; *synonyms (v)* alarm, cow, dismay, daunt, terrify, appall, affright, intimidate, scare, terrorize, awe, deter, horrify, startle, *(n)* fright; *antonyms (v)* comfort, encourage, **2**. electrify; *synonyms (v)* excite, stagger, galvanize, rouse, shock, stir, thrill, amaze, astound, surprise, **3**. rapture; *synonyms (n)* joy, bliss, delight, enthusiasm, transport, elation, exaltation, happiness, enchantment, exultation, spirit, excitement, *(v)* ecstasy, passion, *(adj)* devotion.

kautikaikaiaki frightened; *synonyms (adj)* afraid, fearful, scared, terrified, timid, anxious, apprehensive, horrified, intimidated, restless, worried, *(adv)* cowardly; *antonyms (adj)* calm, confident, unimpressed, brave, fearless.

kautokoa support; *synonyms (n)* help, stand, aid, keep, comfort, maintenance, patronage, *(v)* assist, prop, back, brace, encourage, maintain, bear, boost; *antonyms (n)* hindrance, *(v)* oppose, neglect, undermine, abandon, reject, weaken.

kautokoaki supported; *synonyms (v)* borne, carried, conveyed, supporting, *(adj)* bolstered, based, *(adv)* on.

kautu 1. head; *synonyms (n)* chief, captain, front, point, boss, foam, froth, crown, chieftain, executive,

chair, brain, *(v)* capital, direct, lead; *antonyms (n)* end, subordinate, *(v)* follow, **2**. crest; *synonyms (n)* apex, peak, summit, top, brow, acme, pinnacle, height, hilltop, zenith, upside, edge, device, *(v)* cap, climax, **3**. preside; *synonyms (v)* manage, rule, moderate, act, hold, sit, celebrate, oversee, solemnize.

kautua 1. aggravate; *synonyms (v)* exacerbate, exasperate, enrage, increase, irritate, provoke, worsen, anger, annoy, bother, displease, inflame, infuriate, magnify, *(adj)* embitter; *antonyms (v)* appease, pacify, ease, improve, please, soothe, **2**. infect; *synonyms (v)* taint, contaminate, corrupt, affect, inspire, defile, foul, poison, pollute, touch, animate, impress, dirty, infest, move; *antonyms (v)* disinfect, purify.

kautuaka 1. infect; *synonyms (v)* taint, contaminate, corrupt, affect, inspire, defile, foul, poison, pollute, touch, animate, impress, dirty, infest, move; *antonyms (v)* disinfect, purify, **2**. aggravate; *synonyms (v)* exacerbate, exasperate, enrage, increase, irritate, provoke, worsen, anger, annoy, bother, displease, inflame, infuriate, magnify, *(adj)* embitter; *antonyms (v)* appease, pacify, ease, improve, please, soothe.

kautuakaki 1. aggravated; *synonyms (adj)* irritated, angry, infuriated, afflictive, exasperated, grievous, provoked, bothered, discouraged, displeased, disturbed, flagitious, forced, frustrated, goaded; *antonym (adj)* unprovoked, **2**. infected; *synonyms (adj)* contaminated, diseased, dirty, impure, tainted, corrupt, festering; *antonyms (adj)* pure, healthy.

kautuaki 1. infected; *synonyms (adj)* contaminated, diseased, dirty, impure, tainted, corrupt, festering; *antonyms (adj)* pure, healthy, **2**. aggravated; *synonyms (adj)* irritated, angry, infuriated, afflictive, exasperated, grievous, provoked, bothered, discouraged, displeased, disturbed, flagitious, forced, frustrated, goaded; *antonym (adj)* unprovoked, **3**. crested; *synonyms (adj)* tufted, cristate, caespitose, cespitose, conical, copped, plumed, topknotted, plumate, plumose, plumy, pointed.

kawa 1. craw; *synonyms (n)* crop, stomach, throat, gizzard, esophagus, paunch, venter, ventricle, harvest, **2**. doleful; *synonyms (adj)* dismal, mournful, sad, sorrowful, disconsolate, dolorous, melancholy, miserable, piteous, somber, woeful, dejected, downcast, dark, *(v)* dolesome; *antonym (adj)* cheerful, **3**. lurk; *synonyms (v)* ambush, ambuscade, conceal, prowl, skulk, waylay, loiter, lurch, creep, slink, sneak, wait, bushwhack, linger, **4**. disconsolate; *synonyms (adj)* desolate, inconsolable, blue, cheerless, depressed, crestfallen, depressing, downhearted, forlorn, gloomy, unhappy, despairing, distressed, brokenhearted, despondent, **5.** creep; *synonyms* (*v*) crawl, grovel, steal, fawn, lurk, cringe, sidle, slip, truckle, cower, edge, (*n*) crawling, creeping, sycophant, toady, **6.** destitute; *synonyms* (*adj*) indigent, bankrupt, broke, impoverished, needy, poor, helpless, impecunious, necessitous, penniless, void, wanting, bare, abandoned, (*v*) devoid; *antonym* (*adj*) rich, **7.** needy; *synonyms* (*adj*) destitute, underprivileged, deficient, deprived, poverty-stricken; *antonym* (*adj*) well-off, **8.** miserable; *synonyms* (*adj*) mean, meager, abject, bad, deplorable, low, measly, lamentable, contemptible, doleful, hapless, paltry, pitiful, shabby, (*v*) wretched; *antonyms* (*adj*) happy, generous, **9.** distressed; *synonyms* (*adj*) upset, worried, anxious, distraught, disturbed, hurt, distracted, shocked, troubled, concerned, confounded, disquieted, nervous, stressed; *antonyms* (*adj*) calm, composed, content, euphoric, **10.** forlorn; *synonyms* (*adj*) desperate, hopeless, deserted, comfortless, lorn, bleak, dreary, alone, down, forsaken, godforsaken, gone, lonely, lonesome; *antonym* (*adj*) hopeful, **11.** heartbroken; *synonym* (*adj*) heartsick; *antonym* (*adj*) overjoyed, **12.** uncomfortable; *synonyms* (*adj*) awkward, embarrassing, inconvenient, difficult, discomfited, uneasy, embarrassed, painful, (*v*) untoward; *antonyms* (*adj*) comfortable, relaxed, comfy, **13.** skulk; *synonyms* (*v*) malinger, shirk, (*adj*) hide, **14.** prowl; *synonyms* (*n*) rove, (*v*) range, roam, **15.** unhappy; *synonyms* (*adj*) unfortunate, infelicitous, disappointed, sorry, unlucky, unpleasant, adverse, discontented, joyless, calamitous, displeased, glum, regretful, unsuccessful, damned; *antonyms* (*adj*) pleased, satisfied, **16.** uneasy; *synonyms* (*adj*) uncomfortable, fidgety, restless, apprehensive, unquiet, fretful, restive, solicitous, agitated, jittery, impatient, clumsy, doubtful, fearful, stiff, **17.** sad; *synonyms* (*adj*) distressing, pitiable, funereal, grave, lugubrious, pensive, poignant, rueful, grievous, heavy, pathetic, drab, regrettable, dim, (*n*) plaintive; *antonyms* (*adj*) joyful, brave, cheery, **18.** slink; *synonyms* (*v*) glide, slide, (*n*) flinch, shy, **19.** sneak; *synonyms* (*v*) filch, mouse, pilfer, swipe, pussyfoot, nip, abstract, (*n*) informer, snitch, fink, prowler, reptile, (*adj*) coward, dastard, poltroon, **20.** poor; *synonyms* (*adj*) evil, inadequate, insufficient, meagre, feeble, lean, nasty, sordid, jejune, skimpy, barren, base, beggarly, cheap, flimsy; *antonyms* (*adj*) wealthy, excellent, first-rate, privileged, admirable, good.

kawaerakei land; *synonyms* (*n*) ground, country, soil, field, kingdom, domain, estate, nation, realm, state, (*v*) disembark, debark, alight, get, drop; *antonym* (*adj*) aquatic.

kawaeremwea retard; *synonyms* (*v*) delay, check, hinder, arrest, detain, impede, lag, obstruct, slow, decelerate, procrastinate, curb, prevent, (*n*) defer, (*adj*) deaden; *antonym* (*v*) accelerate.

kawaeremweaki retarded; *synonyms* (*adj*) backward, slow, tardy, imbecile, defective, deferred, dull, half-baked, leisurely, obtuse, simple, birdbrained, dim, dim-witted, dopey.

kawaeremwi retard; *synonyms* (*v*) delay, check, hinder, arrest, detain, impede, lag, obstruct, slow, decelerate, procrastinate, curb, prevent, (*n*) defer, (*adj*) deaden; *antonym* (*v*) accelerate.

kawaeremwiaki retarded; *synonyms* (*adj*) backward, slow, tardy, imbecile, defective, deferred, dull, half-baked, leisurely, obtuse, simple, birdbrained, dim, dim-witted, dopey.

kawaetata 1. hurry; *synonyms* (*n*) speed, haste, dispatch, flurry, (*v*) bustle, hasten, accelerate, dash, expedite, scurry, fly, run, rush, zip, hie; *antonyms* (*n*) slowness, (*v*) dawdle, **2.** rush; *synonyms* (*n*) hurry, charge, flood, flow, attack, (*v*) gush, race, dart, stream, quicken, jet, flush, hurtle, (*adj*) burst, spurt.

kawaetataia spur; *synonyms* (*n*) inducement, incentive, impulse, prick, impetus, (*v*) goad, incite, prod, prompt, provoke, animate, drive, encourage, impel, inspire.

kawaetataki 1. hurried; *synonyms* (*adj*) hasty, fast, headlong, quick, rapid, speedy, sudden, swift, abrupt, cursory, careless, precipitate, prompt, rash, slapdash; *antonyms* (*adj*) slow, unhurried, leisurely, **2.** rushed; *synonyms* (*adj*) hurried, rush, hassled, immediate, instant, instantaneous, unexpected, harried, pressurized, snatched.

kawaia use; *synonyms* (*n*) custom, practice, benefit, habit, application, function, (*v*) exercise, employ, employment, expend, profit, advantage, exploit, occupy, (*adj*) usage; *antonym* (*v*) conserve.

kawaiaki used; *synonyms* (*adj*) secondhand, exploited, accustomed, decrepit, depleted, exhausted, faded, habituated, hand-me-down, spent, threadbare, tried, victimised, victimized, wont; *antonyms* (*adj*) pristine, new, spanking, unused.

kawaina 1. mannered; *synonyms* (*adj*) artificial, affected, stiff, ponderous, assumed, camp, ceremonial, conscious, self-conscious, theatrical, thewed, wooden, airish, apish, artsy, **2.** use; *synonyms* (*n*) custom, practice, benefit, habit, application, function, (*v*) exercise, employ, employment, expend, profit, advantage, exploit, occupy, (*adj*) usage; *antonym* (*v*) conserve, **3.** way; *synonyms* (*n*) course, method, path, passage, road, route, track, direction, form, manner, means, style, fashion, mode, pathway.

kawainaki used; *synonyms* (*adj*) secondhand, exploited, accustomed, decrepit, depleted, exhausted, faded, habituated, hand-me-down, spent, threadbare, tried, victimised, victimized, wont; *antonyms* (*adj*) pristine, new, spanking, unused.

kawainimone sneak; *synonyms* (*v*) creep, lurk, crawl, fawn, filch, mouse, (*n*) cower, slink, informer, skulk, snitch, fink, (*adj*) coward, grovel, dastard.

kawairinan 1. arrange; *synonyms* (*v*) adjust, appoint, dress, order, set, settle, pack, adapt, agree, classify, compose, decorate, do, engineer, fix; *antonyms* (*v*) disturb, disarrange, **2.** arranged; *synonyms* (*adj*) settled, fixed, orderly, organized, prepared, ready, regular, neat, ordered, straight, tidy, **3.** processed; *synonyms* (*adj*) refined, elegant, graceful, polished, purified, sublimate, svelte, tasteful, urbane, **4.** ranked; *synonyms* (*adj*) graded, bedded, graveled, stratified.

kawairinana 1. streamline; *synonyms* (*v*) simplify, centralize, order, reorganize, shape, redistribute, reform, reshuffle, (*n*) streamlining, **2.** rank; *synonyms* (*n*) range, place, file, gradation, line, degree, quality, rate, (*v*) arrange, class, classify, grade, position, array, group; *antonym* (*adj*) fresh.

kawairinanaki 1. arranged; *synonyms* (*adj*) set, settled, fixed, orderly, organized, prepared, ready, regular, neat, ordered, straight, tidy, **2.** ranked; *synonyms* (*adj*) graded, bedded, graveled, stratified.

kawaka propel; *synonyms* (*v*) drive, impel, launch, actuate, force, motivate, move, prompt, throw, carry, cast, fling, incite, push, shoot.

kawakawa 1. crawl; *synonyms* (*v*) creep, grovel, clamber, climb, cringe, fawn, scramble, sneak, swarm, teem, inch, lag, move, (*n*) crawling, creeping; *antonym* (*v*) race, **2.** creep; *synonyms* (*v*) crawl, steal, lurk, sidle, slip, truckle, cower, edge, itch, pussyfoot, tingle, (*n*) sycophant, toady.

kawaki 1. valuable; *synonyms* (*adj*) costly, estimable, precious, beneficial, expensive, helpful, useful, worthy, admirable, important, dear, invaluable, priceless, profitable, rich; *antonyms* (*adj*) worthless, useless, **2.** precious; *synonyms* (*adj*) beloved, cherished, valuable, golden, choice, inestimable, exquisite, cute, noble, good, goodly, adorable, (*n*) darling, (*adv*) extremely, preciously.

kawakina 1. maintain; *synonyms* (*v*) continue, justify, affirm, allege, assert, aver, conserve, declare, defend, guard, hold, keep, preserve, bear, insist; *antonyms* (*v*) deny, change, **2.** defend; *synonyms* (*v*) cover, protect, advocate, champion, maintain, shield, support, apologize, safeguard, shelter, uphold, vindicate, back, claim, excuse; *antonyms* (*v*) attack, prosecute, **3.** keep; *synonyms* (*v*) retain, have, celebrate, confine, observe, reserve, save, commemorate, check, harbor, direct, rear, restrain, (*n*) custody, maintenance; *antonyms* (*v*) dump, lose, **4.** mind; *synonyms* (*n*) intellect, brain, head, inclination, intelligence, psyche, regard, mentality, (*v*) care, look, attend, beware, listen,

notice, (*adj*) heed; *antonym* (*v*) forget, **5.** protect; *synonyms* (*v*) hide, conceal, screen, insure, cushion, patronize, shade, ensure, fence, guarantee, insulate, bless, assist, cherish, (*n*) ward; *antonyms* (*v*) expose, neglect, risk, **6.** tend; *synonyms* (*v*) incline, lead, lean, nurse, contribute, nurture, run, go, gravitate, nourish, carry, conduce, mind, verge, watch, **7.** preserve; *synonyms* (*v*) cure, pickle, perpetuate, sustain, economise, economize, husband, deliver, rescue, (*n*) jam, jelly, conserves, marmalade, preserves, reservation; *antonym* (*v*) destroy, **8.** save; *synonyms* (*v*) free, hoard, liberate, redeem, accumulate, amass, spare, garner, deposit, cache, help, (*prep*) except, but, excepting, (*adv*) besides; *antonyms* (*v*) spend, squander, waste.

kawakinaki 1. kept; *synonyms* (*adj*) reserved, detained, intransitive, unbroken, unploughed, unplowed, **2.** minded; *synonyms* (*adj*) willing, prone, ready, partial, predisposed, prepared, (*prep*) inclined, disposed, jolly, **3.** maintained; *synonyms* (*adj*) retained, fixed, repaired, safe, serviced, reconditioned, shipshape, trim, **4.** saved; *synonyms* (*adj*) protected, blessed, secure, **5.** protected; *synonyms* (*v*) covert, disguised, hid, (*adj*) immune, saved, secured, sheltered, covered, comfortable, confined, cosseted, dependable, good, guaranteed, impregnable, **6.** preserved; *synonyms* (*adj*) condite, pickled, whole, potted, sealed.

kawakinibwai circumspect; *synonyms* (*adj*) chary, careful, cautious, guarded, prudent, alert, cagey, considerate, discreet, thoughtful, vigilant, wary, watchful, attentive, deliberate.

kawakiniko beware; *synonyms* (*v*) mind, look, mistrust, consider, listen, worry.

kawanakoa shed; *synonyms* (*v*) cast, discard, drop, moult, scatter, exuviate, molt, dismiss, disgorge, emit, fling, (*n*) hut, shack, cabin, booth.

kawanawana warn; *synonyms* (*v*) admonish, advise, caution, counsel, inform, alert, threaten, exhort, notify, reprove, tell, deter, discourage, dissuade, instruct.

kawanga tiring; *synonyms* (*adj*) exhausting, tedious, tiresome, hard, laborious, wearing, arduous, grueling, boring, wearisome, onerous, strenuous; *antonyms* (*adj*) easy, undemanding.

kawanra disagree; *synonyms* (*v*) differ, clash, argue, conflict, dissent, bicker, disaccord, discord, diverge, squabble, vary, collide, dispute, fight, jar; *antonyms* (*v*) agree, consent, match.

kawanrea 1. deteriorate; *synonyms* (*v*) degenerate, degrade, decline, spoil, worsen, vitiate, descend, drop, fail, impair, lapse, rot, crumble, decrease, (*adj*) debase; *antonyms* (*v*) improve, convalesce, recover, **2.** tarnish; *synonyms* (*v*) defile, taint, smear, stain, blur, foul, corrupt, dirty, (*adj*) sully, darken, (*n*) blemish, blot, soil, spot, disgrace; *antonym* (v) praise, **3.** spoil; *synonyms* (v) plunder, damage, deface, indulge, injure, mar, sack, baby, botch, bungle, coddle, deprave, despoil, (n) ruin, (adj) harm; *antonyms* (v) enhance, conserve.

kawanreaki 1. spoiled; *synonyms* (adj) decayed, bad, rotten, stale, coddled, pampered, corrupt, damaged, spoilt; *antonyms* (adj) first-rate, pure, **2.** tarnished; *synonyms* (adj) sullied, besmirched, dim, stained, tainted, flyblown, imperfect, spotted; *antonym* (adj) untarnished.

kawanta 1. discreditable; *synonyms* (adj) disreputable, disgraceful, dishonorable, scandalous, shameful, reprehensible; *antonym* (adj) honorable, **2.** discolor; *synonyms* (v) stain, colour, tarnish, tinge, color, discolour, fade, blot, damage, defile, soil, **3.** fault; *synonyms* (n) defect, blemish, error, failing, blame, crime, delinquency, flaw, blunder, break, demerit, weakness, default, (v) deficiency, culpability; *antonyms* (n) merit, strength, **4.** mark; *synonyms* (n) brand, evidence, score, character, heed, impression, imprint, sign, feature, badge, (v) characterize, distinguish, grade, label, (adj) notice, **5.** dishonorable; *synonyms* (adj) dishonest, base, ignoble, mean, degrading, infamous, unfair, unethical, wrong, abject, foul, contemptible, crooked, despicable, discreditable; *antonyms* (adj) honest, noble, **6.** blemish; *synonyms* (n) spot, scar, fault, imperfection, mark, stigma, maculation, bruise, disgrace, (v) deface, disfigure, slur, dent, harm, (adj) mangle; *antonym* (v) enhance, **7.** spot; *synonyms* (n) place, speck, dot, dapple, dirty, location, position, space, (v) fleck, speckle, daub, mottle, freckle, blur, locate, **8.** spoil; *synonyms* (v) plunder, corrupt, impair, rot, indulge, injure, mar, sack, baby, botch, bungle, coddle, deprave, despoil, (n) ruin; *antonyms* (v) improve, conserve, **9.** stain; *synonyms* (n) smear, dirt, discoloration, pollute, smudge, tint, blotch, filth, (v) dye, contaminate, paint, taint, discolor, maculate, (adj) splash, **10.** speckle; *synonyms* (n) point, patch, flake, (v) stipple, (adj) bespeckle.

kawantaki 1. discolored; *synonyms* (adj) discoloured, blemished, crusty, dappled, dark, dingy, dirty, dull, faded, flawed, flecked, freckled, gray, imperfect, livid, **2.** marked; *synonyms* (adj) distinct, conspicuous, noticeable, pronounced, remarkable, distinguished, apparent, definite, notable, obvious, signal, striking, strong, clear, appreciable; *antonyms* (adj) plain, unblemished, **3.** blemished; *synonyms* (adj) damaged, faulty, covered, defective, deformed, discolored, dotted, marked, mottled, patterned, speckled, spotty, stippled, disfigured, greasy; *antonym* (adj) unspoiled, **4.** spotted; *synonyms* (v) mildewed, moldy, rusty, (adj) blotchy, flyblown, piebald, multicolored, stained, tainted, besmirched,

patched, **5.** stained; *synonyms* (adj) spotted, sullied, tarnished, black, painted, (v) polluted; *antonym* (adj) pure, **6.** speckled; *synonym* (adj) specked, **7.** spoiled; *synonyms* (adj) decayed, bad, rotten, stale, coddled, pampered, corrupt, spoilt; *antonym* (adj) first-rate.

kawara 1. frequent; *synonyms* (adj) continual, everyday, familiar, many, ordinary, incessant, habitual, accustomed, commonplace, (v) common, customary, usual, haunt, patronize, attend; *antonyms* (adj) rare, infrequent, occasional, **2.** approach; *synonyms* (n) access, entry, advent, arrival, avenue, coming, entrance, means, method, adit, (v) advance, accost, address, near, approximate; *antonym* (v) leave, **3.** company; *synonyms* (n) companionship, society, association, band, business, cohort, collection, brigade, assemblage, bevy, caller, club, companion, corps, (v) accompany; *antonym* (n) solitude, **4.** call; *synonyms* (v) cry, bellow, name, shout, bid, summon, howl, baptize, cite, dub, (n) appeal, yell, appoint, command, demand; *antonym* (v) dismiss, **5.** visit; *synonyms* (n) chat, sojourn, (v) see, frequent, call, tour, view, gossip, inspect, jaw, impose, inflict, talk, understand, meet.

kawaraki 1. called; *synonyms* (v) nempt, ycleped, (adj) named, chosen, qualified, **2.** narrow; *synonyms* (adj) close, limited, insular, little, cramped, illiberal, mean, (v) confined, contract, limit, lessen, constrict, shrink, abridge, dwindle; *antonyms* (adj) wide, broad, comprehensive, extensive, (v) widen, extend, **3.** tight; *synonyms* (adj) compact, firm, parsimonious, taut, secure, snug, tense, drunk, miserly, rigorous, sparing, (v) narrow, fast, stingy, near; *antonyms* (adj) loose, baggy, generous, slack, (adv) loosely.

kawarakua dampen; *synonyms* (v) deaden, muffle, depress, dishearten, dull, moisten, mute, soften, wet, blunt, chill, cool, check, dash, (n) damp; *antonym* (v) stimulate.

kawarawara perforated; *synonyms* (adj) perforate, pierced, punctured, penetrated, entered.

kawarebwea 1. enlarge; *synonyms* (v) amplify, expand, aggrandize, augment, dilate, distend, elaborate, increase, widen, boost, broaden, develop, enhance, extend, grow; *antonyms* (v) reduce, shrink, contract, decrease, **2.** space; *synonyms* (n) length, gap, opening, period, place, scope, void, margin, distance, emptiness, extent, interval, latitude, location, range.

kawarebweaki enlarged; *synonyms* (adj) exaggerated, extended, inflated, magnified, increased, puffy, augmented, amplified, distended, broad, clear, coarse, comprehensive, cross, dilated; *antonym* (adj) lesser.

kawarika 1. narrow; *synonyms* (*adj*) close, limited, insular, little, cramped, illiberal, mean, (*v*) confined, contract, limit, lessen, constrict, shrink, abridge, dwindle; *antonyms* (*adj*) wide, broad, comprehensive, extensive, (*v*) widen, extend, **2.** confine; *synonyms* (*v*) bound, bind, circumscribe, restrain, tie, hold, incarcerate, restrict, cage, constrain, detain, (*n*) border, boundary, bounds, brim; *antonyms* (*v*) release, free, liberate, **3.** restrict; *synonyms* (*v*) confine, fetter, curb, curtail, forbid, hamper, reduce, ration, check, contain, cramp, modify, prohibit, qualify, regulate, **4.** straiten; *synonyms* (*v*) distress, tighten, stint, squeeze, press, oppress, scant, bite, compel, compress, enforce, force, grip, (*adj*) crowd, coarctate.

kawarikaki 1. narrowed; *synonyms* (*adj*) angustate, conical, lessened, pointed, tapering, **2.** confined; *synonyms* (*v*) accurate, (*adj*) captive, close, cramped, imprisoned, limited, bounded, invalided, constrained, narrow, poky, qualified, restricted, strict, jailed; *antonym* (*adj*) free, **3.** straitened; *synonyms* (*adj*) bigoted, circumscribed, contracted, covetous, exact, illiberal, near, niggardly, parsimonious, pinching, selfish, (*n*) needy, distressed, necessitous, pinched, **4.** restricted; *synonyms* (*adj*) confined, exclusive, local, controlled, finite, prohibited, classified, secret, private, reserved, tight, fixed, precise, special; *antonyms* (*adj*) unrestricted, far-reaching, liberated, unimpeded, unlimited, open, wide.

kawawa 1. circulate; *synonyms* (*v*) spread, broadcast, circle, disseminate, disperse, distribute, propagate, circularize, diffuse, issue, mobilize, proclaim, announce, flow, go, **2.** dunk; *synonyms* (*v*) dip, duck, douse, plunge, drench, bathe, immerse, soak, souse, steep, **3.** drain; *synonyms* (*n*) ditch, culvert, dike, channel, sewer, (*v*) deplete, waste, exhaust, bleed, leak, consume, finish, sap, (*adj*) cloaca, dissipate; *antonym* (*v*) bolster.

kawawaea 1. aggregate; *synonyms* (*adj*) sum, aggregative, all, collective, (*n*) total, agglomerate, whole, complex, pile, combination, compound, (*v*) accumulate, cluster, amount, collect; *antonyms* (*n*) individual, part, **2.** gather; *synonyms* (*v*) deduce, convene, amass, assemble, compile, congregate, flock, garner, meet, tuck, earn, rally, reap, derive, (*n*) fold; *antonyms* (*v*) disperse, scatter, **3.** collect; *synonyms* (*v*) gather, pick, accrue, acquire, aggregate, collate, cull, harvest, hoard, raise, accept, catch, gain, glean, group; *antonym* (*v*) distribute, **4.** convoke; *synonyms* (*v*) call, summon, muster, convocate, **5.** amass; *synonyms* (*v*) heap, save, stack, stock, store, drift, increase, bank, conglomerate, cumulate, integrate, mound, **6.** accumulate; *synonyms* (*v*) add, concentrate, multiply, stockpile, swell, keep; *antonym* (*v*)

dwindle, **7.** compile; *synonyms* (*v*) build, edit, compose, construct, invent, make, write, **8.** assemble; *synonyms* (*v*) converge, arrange, erect, piece, combine, form, convoke, create, fabricate, foregather, forgather, frame, join, marshal, mass; *antonyms* (*v*) dismantle, disband, disassemble.

kawawaeaki 1. accumulated; *synonyms* (*adj*) accrued, amassed, assembled, collected, accumulate, aggregate, congregate, massed, store, upheaped, equanimous, poised, **2.** aggregated; *synonym* (*adj*) cumulative, **3.** amassed; *synonyms* (*adj*) accumulated, collective, combined, conglomerate, more, total, comprehensive, summative, **4.** collected; *synonyms* (*v*) composed, (*adj*) calm, cool, sober, tranquil, unflappable, dispassionate, gathered, imperturbable, peaceful, placid, quiet, sedate, serene, staid; *antonym* (*adj*) agitated, **5.** assembled; *synonyms* (*adj*) united, built, fabricated, fancied, fictional, fictitious, invented, reinforced, **6.** gathered; *synonym* (*adj*) deepened.

kawawaki 1. drained; *synonyms* (*adj*) exhausted, tired, weary, spent, dead, dry, **2.** dunked; *synonyms* (*adj*) besotted, blotto, crocked, soused, fuddled, loaded, pissed, pixilated, plastered, potty, slopped, sloshed, smashed, soaked, sozzled.

kawe 1. trail; *synonyms* (*n*) track, trace, path, course, trudge, (*v*) haul, drag, hunt, tail, chase, pursue, train, draw, tow, dog, **2.** tail; *synonyms* (*n*) rear, shadow, behind, butt, posterior, rump, stub, backside, bottom, buttocks, stern, (*v*) follow, trail, tag, (*adj*) back; *antonyms* (*v*) head, front.

kawenea 1. lay; *synonyms* (*v*) place, put, fix, set, deposit, install, lie, rest, invest, bear, allay, arrange, (*adj*) secular, (*n*) ballad, pitch, **2.** laid; *synonyms* (*adj*) determined, dictated, fixed, hardened, located, rigid.

kaweneaki laid; *synonyms* (*adj*) set, determined, dictated, fixed, hardened, located, rigid.

kawete 1. top; *synonyms* (*adj*) maximum, (*n*) crown, peak, acme, apex, crest, cover, height, pinnacle, summit, (*v*) best, cap, exceed, head, outdo; *antonyms* (*adj*) worst, (*n*) bottom, base, nadir, **2.** pointed; *synonyms* (*adj*) penetrating, keen, poignant, acute, piquant, cutting, marked, pithy, biting, acuminate, barbed, prickly, pungent, sharp, short; *antonym* (*adj*) rounded, **3.** spear; *synonyms* (*n*) harpoon, lance, pike, fizgig, gig, prick, shaft, barb, (*v*) impale, spike, stab, pierce, skewer, stick, transfix.

kawikoa 1. hurry; *synonyms* (*n*) speed, haste, dispatch, flurry, (*v*) bustle, hasten, accelerate, dash, expedite, scurry, fly, run, rush, zip, hie; *antonyms* (*n*) slowness, (*v*) dawdle, **2.** hasten; *synonyms* (*v*) further, forward, advance, hurry, dart, facilitate, precipitate, race, gallop, sprint, drive, hotfoot, (adj) quicken, course, go; antonym (v) delay.

kawikoaki hurried; synonyms (adj) hasty, fast, headlong, quick, rapid, speedy, sudden, swift, abrupt, cursory, careless, precipitate, prompt, rash, slapdash; antonyms (adj) slow, unhurried, leisurely.

ke 1. let; synonyms (v) allow, hire, admit, lease, leave, permit, charter, have, rent, grant, authorize, cause, countenance, demise, (n) check; antonyms (v) forbid, prevent, **2.** okay; synonyms (adv) fine, (adj) good, alright, well, fair, (int) yes, (n) approval, authorization, agreement, blessing, (v) approve, sanction, consent, endorse, accept; antonym (adj) unsatisfactory, **3.** right; synonyms (adj) correct, appropriate, due, just, proper, decent, even, perfect, accurate, exact, faithful, fit, reasonable, (n) privilege, law; antonyms (adj) inappropriate, unjustified, immoral, incorrect, (n) left, (v) wrong, **4.** yes; synonyms (int) surely, (n) acceptance, nod, (adv) ay, yea, certainly, positively, precisely, ye, (v) acquiesce, agree, grovel, subscribe, (adj) obedient, submissive, **5.** or; synonyms (conj) otherwise, (n) operation, surgery, (prep) before, ere.

kea 1. beckon; synonyms (v) wave, attract, signal, summon, call, gesture, invite, motion, sign, **2.** bid; synonyms (n) offer, tender, attempt, proffer, suggestion, (v) ask, command, adjure, beseech, charge, direct, instruct, order, tell, allure, **3.** hail; synonyms (n) greet, greeting, rain, storm, barrage, (v) address, cry, acclaim, applaud, accost, cheer, come, fall, receive, salute, **4.** call; synonyms (v) bellow, name, shout, bid, howl, baptize, cite, dub, entitle, scream, (n) appeal, yell, appoint, demand, request; antonym (v) dismiss, **5.** squeal; synonyms (n) yelp, (v) shriek, screech, squeak, inform, confess, betray, whoop, bawl, shrill, sing, squall, tattle, blab, oink, **6.** summon; synonyms (v) assemble, convene, beckon, convoke, evoke, invoke, muster, page, rally, challenge, collect, gather, raise, recall, summons.

keaki 1. let; synonyms (v) allow, hire, admit, lease, leave, permit, charter, have, rent, grant, authorize, cause, countenance, demise, (n) check; antonyms (v) forbid, prevent, **2.** called; synonyms (v) nempt, ycleped, (adj) named, chosen, qualified.

kebo 1. full; synonyms (adj) complete, absolute, abundant, broad, flush, ample, enough, extensive, total, detailed, comprehensive, copious, good, (n) entire, crowded; antonyms (adj) empty, lacking, starving, hungry, sketchy, incomplete, **2.** congested; synonyms (adj) packed, full, overcrowded, teeming, engorged, closed, stopped, close, overfull, busy, cramped, swarming, blocked, bunged, (prep) inflamed, **3.** crowded; synonyms (adj) compact, congested, dense, populous, jammed, thick, tight, (n) thronged; antonym (adj) sparse.

kebutua 1. jostle; synonyms (v) jog, shove, joggle, bump, encounter, jolt, push, shoulder, thrust, drive, squeeze, (n) elbow, jostling, (adj) clash, jar, **2.** butt; synonyms (n) extremity, stump, grip, barrel, base, bottom, buttocks, can, cask, poke, posterior, (v) bunt, abut, border, edge, **3.** jar; synonyms (n) jangle, blow, crock, container, shake, amphora, bottle, crash, pot, canister, (v) creak, collide, jounce, grate, agitate, **4.** repel; synonyms (v) nauseate, disgust, revolt, rebuff, repulse, sicken, decline, displease, refuse, reject, parry, oppose, rebut, dismiss, combat; antonyms (v) attract, charm, draw, **5.** push; synonyms (n) press, energy, (v) impel, crowd, force, jab, jostle, nudge, prod, jam, rush, boost, fight, incite, labor; antonyms (v) pull, drag, haul.

keiakina strive; synonyms (v) endeavor, labor, attempt, contend, contest, fight, struggle, combat, aim, aspire, compete, strain, toil, work, exert.

keinano 1. preoccupied; synonyms (adj) obsessed, absorbed, abstracted, thoughtful, lost, distracted, faraway, rapt, inattentive, engrossed, pensive, absent, baffled, bemused, bewildered; antonym (adj) attentive, **2.** obsessed; synonyms (adj) preoccupied, possessed, infatuated, enthusiastic, haunted, gripped, hooked, addicted, ambitious, amok, amuck, anxious, berserk, besotted, captivated; antonym (adj) rational.

keinanoa 1. frigate; synonyms (n) gunboat, cruiser, destroyer, **2.** fuss; synonyms (n) bustle, commotion, flap, ado, bother, disturbance, fidget, excitement, bickering, (v) flurry, bicker, fret, hubbub, complain, (adj) stir, **3.** fret; synonyms (n) anxiety, (v) agitate, chafe, gall, grate, irritate, trouble, worry, annoy, fray, rub, upset, anger, disquiet, concern, **4.** head; synonyms (n) chief, captain, front, point, boss, foam, froth, crown, chieftain, executive, chair, brain, (v) capital, direct, lead; antonyms (n) end, subordinate, (v) follow, **5.** worry; synonyms (v) torment, distress, tease, care, disturb, fear, molest, vex, (n) burden, harass, pain, fuss, annoyance, sorrow, apprehension; antonyms (v) soothe, reassure, (n) calmness, reassurance.

keinanoaki worried; synonyms (adj) apprehensive, distressed, nervous, uneasy, upset, anxious, afraid, bothered, concerned, disturbed, troubled, fearful, restless, unhappy, (v) afflicted; antonyms (adj) calm, carefree, reassured, relaxed, untroubled.

keke 1. jingle; synonyms (n) jangle, chime, chink, tune, doggerel, gingle, (v) ring, ding, clang, clank, clink, peal, rattle, sound, tinkle, **2.** clink; synonyms (n) clash, click, jail, gaol, (v) jingle, twang, burr, **3.** cheer; synonyms (v) encourage, animate, applaud, amuse, comfort, hearten, inspire, lighten, barrack, console, elevate, (n) delight, cry, consolation, (adj) embolden; antonyms (v) dishearten, depress, (n) sadness, **4.** shout;

synonyms (v) clamor, scream, bellow, bawl, exclaim, hollo, howl, shriek, (n) call, roar, yell, cheer, halloo, outcry, screech; *antonym* (v) whisper, **5**. rattle; *synonyms* (n) roll, clack, rattling, harmonica, (v) clatter, bang, confuse, patter, shake, disconcert, disturb, drum, rumble, (adj) twaddle.

kekeaki rattled; *synonyms* (adj) flustered, perturbed, upset, abashed, addled, afraid, bewildered, disconcerted, distraught, puzzled, unsettled.

kekeia 1. applaud; *synonyms* (v) acclaim, cheer, eulogize, praise, extol, hail, admire, clap, commend, approve, compliment, encourage, exalt, laud, congratulate; *antonyms* (v) boo, criticize, **2**. cheer; *synonyms* (v) animate, applaud, amuse, comfort, hearten, inspire, lighten, barrack, console, elevate, enliven, (n) delight, cry, consolation, (adj) embolden; *antonyms* (v) dishearten, depress, (n) sadness.

kekeiaki 1. learn; *synonyms* (v) discover, get, know, find, ascertain, have, hear, determine, acquire, con, perceive, study, tell, understand, gather, **2**. endeavor; *synonyms* (n) attempt, try, effort, essay, trial, enterprise, shot, work, endeavour, (v) struggle, strive, aim, labor, strain, offer; *antonym* (v) neglect, **3**. essay; *synonyms* (n) dissertation, article, disquisition, composition, tentative, paper, taste, adventure, discourse, (v) endeavor, assay, prove, seek, test, bid, **4**. study; *synonyms* (n) survey, consideration, investigation, learning, (v) consider, examine, review, learn, research, check, analyze, contemplate, inquire, investigate, meditate, **5**. try; *synonyms* (v) experiment, judge, sample, probe, adjudicate, render, undertake, afflict, demonstrate, exercise, hazard, risk, (n) chance, go, crack.

kekeiakiaki 1. learned; *synonyms* (v) knowing, (adj) erudite, educated, enlightened, knowledgeable, wise, academic, scholarly, bookish, cultured, intellectual, lettered, literary, studious, informed; *antonyms* (adj) ignorant, innate, **2**. tried; *synonyms* (adj) reliable, tested, trustworthy, dependable, proved, experienced, baffled, beaten, believable, conquered, exhausted, faithful, just, practiced, qualified, **3**. studied; *synonyms* (v) advised, (adj) intentional, deliberate, calculated, conscious, premeditated, affected, elaborate, intended, learned, willful, labored, planned; *antonyms* (adj) natural, spontaneous.

kekera 1. check; *synonyms* (v) bridle, stop, block, limit, agree, halt, restrain, bar, dampen, delay, (n) control, arrest, curb, bill, cheque, **2**. investigate; *synonyms* (v) examine, explore, inquire, inspect, search, check, research, ask, hunt, analyze, enquire, interrogate, scrutinize, study, test, **3**. quest; *synonyms* (n) pursuit, investigation, inquiry, examination, chase, exploration, expedition, inquest, voyage, pursuance, seeking, (v) probe, demand, request, seek, **4**. seek; *synonyms* (v)

attempt, endeavor, look, aspire, beg, pursue, quest, investigate, follow, essay, ransack, strive, struggle, try, prospect, **5**. query; *synonyms* (n) question, doubt, interrogative, quiz, enquiry, interrogation, problem, dispute, uncertainty, (v) challenge, wonder, impeach, suspect; *antonym* (v) answer.

kekeraki 1. checked; *synonyms* (adj) checkered, chequered, plaid, backward, curbed, intermittent, limited, numbered, pent-up, safe, silent, tartan, temperate, **2**. desired; *synonyms* (adj) coveted, craved, desirable, chosen, favorite, wanted, needed, welcome, beloved, adored, appropriate, pet, preferred, (v) complying, consenting; *antonym* (adj) undesirable, **3**. wanted; *synonyms* (adj) required, cherished, invited, marketable, precious, treasured, necessary, comfortable, cute, essential, fugitive, notorious, urgent, hunted, (v) runaway.

kekerua shriek; *synonyms* (n) scream, cry, yell, (v) screech, shout, call, howl, bellow, yowl, caterwaul, screak, bawl, holler, pipe, roar.

kekeruatai 1. clink; *synonyms* (n) ring, clang, clash, click, jail, gaol, (v) clank, chink, jingle, tinkle, rattle, sound, jangle, twang, burr, **2**. clap; *synonyms* (v) blast, acclaim, applaud, slam, rumble, hit, (n) bang, boom, applause, gonorrhoea, blow, clack, crack, crash, gonorrhea; *antonym* (v) boo, **3**. crackle; *synonyms* (n) crackling, crepitation, (v) crepitate, crunch, rustle, snap, sputter, **4**. rustle; *synonyms* (n) whisper, rustling, (v) hiss, lift, buzz, pilfer, steal, whiz.

kekeruataiaki crackled; *synonyms* (adj) cracked, alligatored, balmy, barmy, bats, batty, bonkers, buggy, chapped, crackers, crazed, daft, deranged, dotty, fruity.

kekiaki tried; *synonyms* (adj) reliable, tested, trustworthy, dependable, proved, experienced, baffled, beaten, believable, conquered, exhausted, faithful, just, practiced, qualified.

kena 1. excavate; *synonyms* (v) dig, burrow, hollow, unearth, quarry, grub, mine, tunnel, undermine, (adj) delve, gouge, (n) scoop, **2**. burrow; *synonyms* (n) den, hole, lair, (v) excavate, nestle, nuzzle, root, bivouac, cuddle, **3**. dig; *synonyms* (v) jab, prod, comprehend, investigate, probe, apprehend, compass, drudge, (n) poke, excavation, gibe, punch, stab, taunt, crack; *antonym* (n) compliment, **4**. dug; *synonyms* (n) teat, breast, nipple, pap, papilla, tit, titty, boob, knocker, (adj) understood.

kenaki dug; *synonyms* (n) teat, breast, nipple, pap, papilla, tit, titty, boob, knocker, (adj) understood.

kenako wane; *synonyms* (n) ebb, (v) decline, fade, fall, sink, decrease, diminish, dwindle, fail, recede, wither, shrink, contract, decay, abate.

kennano 1. puzzle; *synonyms* (n) enigma, maze, mystery, riddle, (v) bewilder, perplex, nonplus, baffle, confound, mystify, bamboozle, entangle, (adj) confuse, embarrass, pose; *antonym* (v) enlighten, **2**.

worry; *synonyms* (*v*) torment, trouble, bother, distress, tease, annoy, care, disturb, fear, molest, (*n*) concern, burden, harass, pain, fuss; *antonyms* (*v*) soothe, reassure, (*n*) calmness, reassurance.

kennanoaki 1. puzzled; *synonyms* (*adj*) perplexed, bewildered, confused, baffled, nonplussed, doubtful, bemused, curious, mystified, nonplused; *antonym* (*adj*) enlightened, **2.** worried; *synonyms* (*adj*) apprehensive, distressed, nervous, uneasy, upset, anxious, afraid, bothered, concerned, disturbed, troubled, fearful, restless, unhappy, (*v*) afflicted; *antonyms* (*adj*) calm, carefree, reassured, relaxed, untroubled.

kerake advance; *synonyms* (*n*) progress, improvement, (*v*) further, proceed, promote, approach, encourage, raise, rise, boost, contribute, cultivate, develop, forward, (*phr*) accelerate; *antonyms* (*n*) deterioration, (*v*) retreat, recede, delay, demote, regress.

kerakeaki advanced; *synonyms* (*adj*) sophisticated, progressive, senior, higher, modern, new, precocious, late, cultured, developed, elevated, forward, liberal, ripe, superior; *antonyms* (*adj*) conservative, old-fashioned, inferior.

keria 1. disappoint; *synonyms* (*v*) deceive, fail, baffle, balk, defeat, disenchant, circumvent, bilk, mock, delude, foil, frustrate, thwart, (*n*) dissatisfy; *antonyms* (*v*) please, satisfy, **2.** deceive; *synonyms* (*v*) betray, cheat, bamboozle, dupe, pretend, beguile, con, cozen, fool, hoax, mislead, sell, swindle, trick, (*n*) fraud, **3.** disappointed; *synonyms* (*adj*) defeated, disgruntled, regretful, depressed, dissatisfied, frustrated, sad, unhappy, disenchanted; *antonyms* (*adj*) delighted, pleased, composed, satisfied.

keriaki disappointed; *synonyms* (*adj*) defeated, disgruntled, regretful, depressed, dissatisfied, frustrated, sad, unhappy, disenchanted; *antonyms* (*adj*) delighted, pleased, composed, satisfied.

kerikaki 1. lapse; *synonyms* (*n*) fall, error, fault, mistake, oversight, omission, (*v*) relapse, decline, expire, drop, elapse, collapse, degenerate, die, backslide, **2.** abdicate; *synonyms* (*v*) abandon, renounce, cede, desert, forgo, forsake, quit, relinquish, resign, yield, **3.** retreat; *synonyms* (*n*) refuge, resort, asylum, departure, den, lair, privacy, retirement, (*v*) recede, retire, withdraw, depart, ebb, leave, return; *antonyms* (*n*) raid, (*v*) advance, **4.** retire; *synonyms* (*v*) retreat, abdicate, adjourn, go, remove, secede, regrade, back, give, pension, dismiss, exit, flinch, recall, recoil, **5.** withdraw; *synonyms* (*v*) extract, retract, cancel, disengage, draw, repeal, rescind, revoke, shrink, subtract, swallow, unsay, deduct, sequester, recant; *antonyms* (*v*) extend, offer, present, propose, deposit, **6.** resign; *synonyms* (*v*) deliver, surrender, forego, submit, reconcile, release,

commit, render, cease, concede, consign, desist, disclaim, succumb, vacate, **7.** secede; *synonyms* (*v*) break, bunk, chip, flee, lam, rebel, retrocede, run, scarper, splinter, sliver; *antonym* (*v*) join.

kerikakiaki 1. retreated; *synonym* (*adj*) withdrawn, **2.** withdrawn; *synonyms* (*adj*) reserved, secluded, retiring, solitary, indrawn, cloistered, reclusive, uncommunicative, lonely, taciturn, unsociable, introverted, reticent, shy, aloof; *antonym* (*adj*) outgoing, **3.** resigned; *synonyms* (*v*) content, (*adj*) patient, submissive, subdued, yielding, abject, forbearing, passive, pessimistic; *antonyms* (*adj*) resentful, resistant, **4.** retired; *synonyms* (*v*) covert, (*adj*) private, obscure, emeritus, secret, sequestered, close, superannuated, isolated, old, out.

kerio 1. westbound; *synonyms* (*adj*) westward, westerly, western, **2.** westward; *synonyms* (*adv*) west, westwards, (*adj*) westbound.

keru 1. gnaw; *synonyms* (*v*) bite, chew, fret, crunch, corrode, eat, erode, nibble, masticate, munch, champ, fray, harass, devour, (*n*) chafe, **2.** clash; *synonyms* (*n*) bang, battle, brush, clang, crash, discord, encounter, (*v*) jar, fight, impact, brawl, clank, collide, conflict, dispute; *antonyms* (*n*) agreement, (*v*) agree, **3.** crack; *synonyms* (*n*) break, fracture, cleft, fissure, chip, (*v*) chink, crevice, split, breach, burst, snap, clap, check, cleave, rift; *antonyms* (*v*) repair, mend, **4.** crackle; *synonyms* (*n*) crackling, crepitation, (*v*) crack, crepitate, rustle, sputter, **5.** resound; *synonyms* (*v*) echo, reverberate, ring, boom, peal, roar, blare, reecho, resonate, sound, clatter, vibrate, clash, rumble, thunder.

kerua 1. shout; *synonyms* (*v*) cry, clamor, scream, bellow, bawl, exclaim, hollo, howl, (*n*) call, roar, yell, cheer, halloo, outcry, screech; *antonym* (*v*) whisper, **2.** scream; *synonyms* (*n*) shriek, wail, riot, exclamation, hum, screaming, screeching, (*v*) shout, holler, whoop, yelp, yowl, moan, laugh, ring.

keruaki 1. cracked; *synonyms* (*adj*) broken, nutty, batty, chapped, crazy, balmy, wacky, bats, crackers, crackled, crazed, deranged, dotty, insane, kookie, **2.** crackled; *synonyms* (*adj*) cracked, alligatored, barmy, bonkers, buggy, daft, fruity, haywire, kooky, loco, loony, loopy, nuts, roughened.

keta 1. envy; *synonyms* (*n*) desire, enviousness, resentment, hatred, discontent, emulation, (*v*) begrudge, covet, want, grudge, **2.** covet; *synonyms* (*v*) envy, long, aspire, crave, hanker, fancy, wish, **3.** desire; *synonyms* (*n*) ambition, hope, aspiration, will, craving, dream, impulse, liking, lust, request, (*v*) seek, aim, choose, like, care; *antonyms* (*n*) aversion, reality, (*v*) dislike, hate.

ketaki 1. desired; *synonyms* (*adj*) coveted, craved, desirable, chosen, favorite, wanted, needed, welcome, beloved, adored, appropriate, pet, preferred, (v) complying, consenting; *antonym* (adj) undesirable, **2**. coveted; *synonyms* (adj) desired, exceptional, impressive, marketable.

keuea shout; *synonyms* (v) cry, clamor, scream, bellow, bawl, exclaim, hollo, howl, (n) call, roar, yell, cheer, halloo, outcry, screech; *antonym* (v) whisper.

kewe 1. jest; *synonyms* (n) gag, gibe, jape, quip, game, caper, pleasantry, pun, antic, (v) joke, banter, gird, jeer, sneer, clown, **2**. con; *synonyms* (n) swindle, bunko, captive, convict, deception, (v) cheat, trick, bunco, defraud, hoax, bamboozle, bilk, deceive, dupe, fleece; *antonym* (n) pro, **3**. false; *synonyms* (adj) bastard, counterfeit, untrue, deceitful, dishonest, erroneous, artificial, assumed, deceptive, disloyal, faithless, fake, fictitious, sham, ersatz; *antonyms* (adj) true, real, correct, factual, faithful, genuine, natural, truthful, honest, valid, **4**. deceive; *synonyms* (v) betray, circumvent, pretend, beguile, con, cozen, fool, mislead, sell, befool, delude, gull, hoodwink, humbug, (n) fraud, **5**. lie; *synonyms* (v) consist, repose, falsify, belong, couch, dwell, (n) fabrication, falsehood, falsity, fib, fiction, rest, untruth, bluff, deceit; *antonyms* (v) stand, (n) truth, **6**. defraud; *synonyms* (v) rob, victimize, chouse, diddle, do, fiddle, gyp, mulct, nobble, outwit, rook, beat.

kewea 1. lie; *synonyms* (v) consist, repose, falsify, belong, couch, (n) fabrication, falsehood, falsity, fib, fiction, rest, untruth, bluff, counterfeit, deceit; *antonyms* (v) stand, (n) truth, **2**. dupe; *synonyms* (n) con, gull, victim, cully, (v) cheat, defraud, fool, bamboozle, beguile, deceive, kid, befool, betray, cod, delude, **3**. deceive; *synonyms* (v) circumvent, dupe, pretend, cozen, hoax, mislead, sell, swindle, trick, hoodwink, humbug, lie, cuckold, blind, (n) fraud.

kewena 1. lie; *synonyms* (v) consist, repose, falsify, belong, couch, (n) fabrication, falsehood, falsity, fib, fiction, rest, untruth, bluff, counterfeit, deceit; *antonyms* (v) stand, (n) truth, **2**. deceive; *synonyms* (v) betray, cheat, bamboozle, circumvent, dupe, pretend, beguile, con, cozen, fool, hoax, mislead, sell, swindle, (n) fraud.

kewenimakina lie; *synonyms* (v) consist, repose, falsify, belong, couch, (n) fabrication, falsehood, falsity, fib, fiction, rest, untruth, bluff, counterfeit, deceit; *antonyms* (v) stand, (n) truth.

kewetaia 1. lie; *synonyms* (v) consist, repose, falsify, belong, couch, (n) fabrication, falsehood, falsity, fib, fiction, rest, untruth, bluff, counterfeit, deceit; *antonyms* (v) stand, (n) truth, **2**. crooked; *synonyms* (adj) bent, awry, corrupt, irregular, askew, curved, deformed, dishonest, indirect, lopsided, unfair, unscrupulous, angular,

asymmetrical, (v) wry; *antonyms* (adj) straight, honest, even, principled.

ki anus; *synonyms* (n) arse, arsehole, asshole, bum, bastard, behind, buns, can, cocksucker, derriere, dickhead, fanny, hindquarters, hobo, homeless.

kia 1. dribble; *synonyms* (n) trickle, dribbling, (v) drip, drool, drop, drivel, slobber, distill, flow, ooze, spout, trill, leak, seep, slabber, **2**. bounce; *synonyms* (v) jump, leap, bound, discharge, glance, recoil, beat, sack, caper, bob, fire, (n) spring, impact, jolt, bouncing, **3**. throng; *synonyms* (n) crowd, herd, host, multitude, press, assembly, concourse, horde, mass, legion, gathering, (v) swarm, flock, mob, crush, **4**. reverberate; *synonyms* (v) reflect, echo, rebound, resound, ring, resonate, sound, boom, bounce, vibrate, clank, repercuss, **5**. spurt; *synonyms* (n) jet, run, burst, dash, effort, (v) spirt, race, squirt, gush, stream, erupt, flood, spill, sputter, dart, **6**. splash; *synonyms* (n) spot, dab, flash, spattering, (v) spatter, spray, plash, splatter, slop, slosh, moisten, lap, drench, slush, (adj) sprinkle.

kiaiai 1. fragile; *synonyms* (adj) dainty, delicate, frail, breakable, brittle, flimsy, weak, faint, feeble, fine, slim, frangible, insubstantial, shaky, slender; *antonyms* (adj) strong, unbreakable, substantial, sturdy, permanent, robust, **2**. green; *synonyms* (adj) fresh, callow, immature, emerald, jealous, raw, young, youthful, crude, envious, grassy, gullible, inexperienced, juvenile, (n) lawn; *antonym* (adj) experienced, **3**. juvenile; *synonyms* (adj) childish, puerile, babyish, boyish, green, infantile, jejune, infant, teenage, (n) adolescent, child, youngster, kid, teenager, youth; *antonym* (n) adult, **4**. immature; *synonyms* (adj) tender, unripe, childlike, early, unfledged, little, new, imperfect, premature, small, unfinished, unformed, unripened, baby, dependent; *antonyms* (adj) mature, developed, full-grown, grown-up, ripe, **5**. delicate; *synonyms* (adj) accurate, fragile, refined, beautiful, difficult, nice, sensitive, soft, agreeable, infirm, careful, decent, elegant, exquisite, gentle; *antonyms* (adj) inelegant, heavy, tough, **6**. adolescent; *synonyms* (adj) teen, (n) minor, stripling, **7**. youthful; *synonyms* (adj) vernal, beardless; *antonym* (adj) old, **8**. soft; *synonyms* (adj) easy, light, limp, balmy, quiet, slack, loose, clement, flabby, flaccid, lenient, mild, pliant, smooth, (v) low; *antonyms* (adj) hard, firm, harsh, loud, hoarse, rough, solid, stiff, alcoholic, shrill, **9**. tender; *synonyms* (adj) affectionate, painful, loving, sore, compassionate, fond, caring, kind, (v) proffer, present, propose, give, (n) offer, bid, overture; *antonyms* (adj) hardhearted, rubbery.

kiaki splashed; *synonyms* *(adj)* bespattered, besplashed, dabbled, spattered, dotted, marked, showy, speckled, splashy, splattered, streaked.

kiakia radiate; *synonyms* *(v)* gleam, beam, glow, glitter, shine, diverge, glisten, emanate, emit, flash, shed, coruscate, burn, *(adj)* radiant, dazzle.

kiakiaki radiated; *synonyms* *(adj)* radiate, diffuse, penciled, radial, stelliform, stellular.

kiakina 1. billet; *synonyms* *(n)* position, note, berth, job, bar, housing, office, post, quarters, spot, ticket, *(v)* accommodate, quarter, house, lodge, 2. house; *synonyms* *(n)* family, home, dwelling, firm, abode, domicile, building, edifice, habitation, establishment, structure, ancestry, company, address, audience.

kiangang 1. nimble; *synonyms* *(adj)* active, adroit, agile, lively, brisk, spry, alert, clever, energetic, expeditious, lithe, quick, deft, lissome, *(v)* light; *antonym* *(adj)* clumsy, 2. fiery; *synonyms* *(adj)* ardent, burning, fervent, ablaze, fierce, hot, passionate, fervid, flaming, glowing, impassioned, peppery, violent, excitable, combustible; *antonym* *(adj)* mild, 3. strong; *synonyms* *(adj)* intense, powerful, able, deep, firm, stable, steady, cogent, durable, forcible, good, hard, influential, lusty, potent; *antonyms* *(adj)* weak, bland, delicate, faint, feeble, frail, pale, slight, unconvincing, cowardly, diluted, dull, exhausted, flimsy, imperceptible, 4. quick; *synonyms* *(adj)* bright, prompt, hasty, intelligent, nimble, speedy, alive, cursory, dexterous, hurried, immediate, instant, keen, swift, *(adv)* fast; *antonyms* *(adj)* slow, leisurely.

kiara 1. cover; *synonyms* *(v)* coat, conceal, top, bury, cloak, *(n)* blind, blanket, screen, binding, camouflage, cap, covering, lid, mask, shield; *antonyms* *(v)* reveal, expose, uncover, 2. splash; *synonyms* *(n)* spot, dab, flash, *(v)* spatter, spray, spill, dash, drop, plash, splatter, slop, slosh, moisten, lap, drench.

kiaraki 1. covered; *synonyms* *(adj)* hidden, veiled, concealed, covert, coated, masked, obscured, secret, shrouded, thick, wrapped, *(prep)* cloaked; *antonyms* *(adj)* bare, naked, 2. splashed; *synonyms* *(adj)* bespattered, besplashed, dabbled, spattered, dotted, marked, showy, speckled, splashy, splattered, streaked.

kiba 1. flying; *synonyms* *(adj)* fast, fluttering, quick, rapid, swift, aflare, flaring, moving, *(n)* fly, flight, 2. jump; *synonyms* *(v)* hop, spring, dive, hurdle, rise, skip, startle, clear, dance, *(n)* leap, bound, bounce, start, caper, curvet; *antonyms* *(v)* decrease, fall, 3. fly; *synonyms* *(v)* escape, dash, drive, flee, glide, elope, aviate, dart, flutter, hover, hurry, *(n)* flap, *(adj)* break, flit, burst, 4. jumping; *synonyms* *(v)* bounding, salient, conspicuous, dancing, saltant, *(n)* jump, *(adj)* active, festive, industrious, lively, merry,

noisy, spirited, sprightly, tireless, 5. soaring; *synonyms* *(adj)* high, lofty, towering, flying, beetling, eminent, tall, *(n)* gliding, sailing, sailplaning; *antonym* *(adj)* short.

kibakibaki 1. hungry; *synonyms* *(adj)* avid, eager, esurient, famished, greedy, ravenous, starving, desirous, meager, starveling, barren, keen, peckish, *(v)* craving, *(adv)* empty; *antonyms* *(adj)* full, sated, satiated, 2. famished; *synonyms* *(adj)* hungry, starved, 3. voracious; *synonyms* *(adj)* gluttonous, rapacious, edacious, grasping, insatiable, ravening, predatory, avaricious, devouring, 4. starving; *synonyms* *(adj)* malnourished, *(n)* starvation, 5. ravenous; *synonyms* *(adj)* voracious, covetous, ferocious, wolfish.

kibana 1. inapt; *synonyms* *(adj)* inadequate, inappropriate, unbecoming, inapposite, awkward, clumsy, improper, inept, unsuitable, undue, unseemly, inapplicable, irrelevant, incongruous, unapt, 2. ineffectual; *synonyms* *(adj)* fruitless, futile, ineffective, useless, feeble, abortive, idle, pointless, powerless, unable, vain, void, weak, feckless, impotent; *antonyms* *(adj)* effective, effectual, strong, 3. useless; *synonyms* *(adj)* unnecessary, needless, hopeless, worthless, barren, superfluous, bootless, incompetent, ineffectual, inefficacious, inefficient, inutile, purposeless, unavailing, meaningless; *antonyms* *(adj)* useful, helpful, competent, convenient, necessary, valuable, 4. worthless; *synonyms* *(adj)* vile, cheap, empty, trifling, trivial, miserable, mean, null, trashy, valueless, abject, base, contemptible, despicable, poor; *antonyms* *(adj)* precious, meaningful, priceless, worthwhile.

kibangabanga perforated; *synonyms* *(adj)* perforate, pierced, punctured, penetrated, entered.

kibangebange 1. mean; *synonyms* *(v)* intend, design, imply, denote, involve, *(adj)* middle, base, common, hateful, ignoble, medium, miserly, *(n)* average, contemptible, low; *antonyms* *(adj)* generous, kind, 2. miserly; *synonyms* *(adj)* stingy, mean, close, parsimonious, closefisted, grasping, avaricious, measly, mingy, penurious, tight, greedy, cheap, covetous, *(adv)* ungenerous, 3. contrary; *synonyms* *(adj)* opposite, contradictory, adverse, conflicting, reverse, unfavorable, alien, cross, different, disobedient, obstinate, perverse, averse, antagonistic, *(adv)* counter, 4. vexing; *synonyms* *(adj)* irritating, annoying, infuriating, maddening, galling, troublesome, bothersome, aggravating, exasperating, pestiferous, vexatious, pesky, trying, 5. stingy; *synonyms* *(adj)* skimpy, niggard, frugal, niggardly, scanty, scarce, selfish, shabby, spare, sparing, thrifty, chary, economical, *(v)* narrow, near; *antonym* *(adj)* spendthrift, 6. selfish; *synonyms* *(adj)* mercenary, egocentric, egoistic, egotistic, egotistical, self-centered, inconsiderate, sordid, thoughtless, exclusive, worldly, (v) contracted; *antonyms* (adj) unselfish, selfless, altruistic.

kibao 1. crooked; *synonyms* (adj) bent, awry, corrupt, irregular, askew, curved, deformed, dishonest, indirect, lopsided, unfair, unscrupulous, angular, asymmetrical, (v) wry; *antonyms* (adj) straight, honest, even, principled, **2.** twisted; *synonyms* (adj) crooked, perverted, distorted, coiled, misshapen, contorted, twined, winding, gnarled, tortuous, kinky, wrong, warped, depraved, malformed; *antonym* (adj) tidy.

kibara 1. attack; *synonyms* (n) incursion, thrust, aggression, fit, onset, onslaught, seizure, (v) assault, assail, attempt, aggress, charge, invade, raid, accuse; *antonyms* (n) defense, (v) defend, protect, retreat, **2.** assail; *synonyms* (v) attack, bombard, molest, beset, besiege, hit, impugn, storm, strike, encounter, pelt, harass, shower, snipe, **3.** lethargic; *synonyms* (adj) drowsy, dozy, indolent, languid, comatose, dull, listless, sleepy, slow, torpid, lazy, inactive, lethargical, heavy, apathetic; *antonyms* (adj) energetic, alert, lively, playful, agitated, vigorous, **4.** encumbered; *synonyms* (adj) laden, burdened, burdensome, clayey, cloggy, deep, forcible, full, gloomy, loud, oppressive, overloaded, ponderous, pregnant, sluggish, **5.** rush; *synonyms* (n) hurry, flood, flow, (v) dash, gush, race, run, speed, dart, hasten, stream, quicken, jet, (adj) burst, spurt, **6.** sluggish; *synonyms* (adj) idle, inert, slack, slothful, lethargic, obtuse, dormant, dilatory, backward, lifeless, blunt, flat, leaden, stupid, weak; *antonyms* (adj) active, brisk, fast.

kibaraki rushed; *synonyms* (adj) hasty, hurried, rush, precipitate, rapid, hassled, immediate, instant, instantaneous, quick, speedy, sudden, swift, unexpected, abrupt; *antonym* (adj) leisurely.

kibaura 1. fiery; *synonyms* (adj) ardent, burning, fervent, ablaze, fierce, hot, passionate, fervid, flaming, glowing, impassioned, peppery, violent, excitable, combustible; *antonym* (adj) mild, **2.** irascible; *synonyms* (adj) fiery, angry, choleric, irritable, crabby, hotheaded, testy, touchy, hasty, impatient, impetuous, edgy, quarrelsome, acrimonious, inflammable, **3.** temperamental; *synonyms* (adj) fickle, erratic, moody, capricious, variable, emotional.

kibe fish; *synonyms* (n) bird, insect, mollusk, shellfish, worm, amphibian, beginner, blacktail, (v) angle, seek, hunt, pursue, grope, rummage, beg.

kibera till; *synonyms* (prep) until, unto, (n) drawer, tiller, cashbox, (v) cultivate, plow, hoe, farm, dig, turn.

kiberuberu timid; *synonyms* (adj) fearful, afraid, cowardly, diffident, shy, bashful, cautious, coy, nervous, apprehensive, frightened, modest,

retiring, craven, anxious; *antonyms* (adj) confident, bold, fearless, (n) brave.

kibono 1. obstructed; *synonyms* (adj) hindered, blind, blocked, congested, foiled, frustrated, impedite, stymied, thwarted, tight; *antonym* (adj) successful, **2.** virgin; *synonyms* (adj) pure, vestal, chaste, innocent, new, fresh, intact, untouched, unmixed, virginal, virtuous, unmarried, (n) maiden, maid, girl, **3.** stopped; *synonyms* (adj) halted, unmoving, finished, chinked, clogged, immobile, motionless, static, stationary, bunged, crashed, still.

kibubu cowardly; *synonyms* (adj) coward, timid, afraid, craven, gutless, scared, shrinking, sneaky, base, dastardly, faint, fainthearted, fearful, poltroon, pusillanimous; *antonyms* (adj) fearless, intrepid, strong, (adv) brave, bold, courageous, daring.

kibubura 1. avarice; *synonyms* (n) greed, cupidity, covetousness, avariciousness, rapacity, (adj) greediness; *antonym* (adj) generosity, **2.** greedy; *synonyms* (adj) eager, avid, gluttonous, covetous, desirous, acquisitive, glutton, grasping, piggish, esurient, grabby, hungry, insatiable, ravenous, (v) avaricious; *antonym* (adj) generous.

kie mat; *synonyms* (n) matte, rug, tangle, cushion, matt, matting, flatness, (adj) dull, flat, matted, (v) entangle, felt, knot, snarl, twist.

kiea 1. coast; *synonyms* (n) bank, beach, seaside, shore, seashore, sand, seacoast, shoreline, (v) glide, slide, drift, cruise; *antonym* (n) interior, **2.** heel; *synonyms* (n) blackguard, counter, dog, cad, scoundrel, shoe, sole, villain, bounder, (v) list, lean, **3.** skirt; *synonyms* (n) border, edge, brim, flap, kilt, apron, margin, (v) fringe, circumvent, evade, hem, elude, sidestep, verge, dodge.

kiengenenge 1. miserable; *synonyms* (adj) mean, poor, meager, abject, bad, deplorable, desolate, downcast, low, measly, unhappy, distressed, lamentable, (v) forlorn, wretched; *antonyms* (adj) happy, cheerful, generous, **2.** poor; *synonyms* (adj) miserable, paltry, destitute, evil, inadequate, insufficient, needy, pathetic, penniless, piteous, pitiful, meagre, deficient, feeble, impecunious; *antonyms* (adj) rich, wealthy, excellent, first-rate, privileged, well-off, admirable, good, **3.** thin; *synonyms* (adj) flimsy, gaunt, lean, light, slight, tenuous, emaciated, fine, rare, slim, sparse, (v) slender, dilute, sheer, subtle; *antonyms* (adj) thick, fat, concentrated, chubby, plump, wide, broad, heavy, (v) thicken.

kiimamaaku cowardly; *synonyms* (adj) coward, timid, afraid, craven, gutless, scared, shrinking, sneaky, base, dastardly, faint, fainthearted, fearful, poltroon, pusillanimous; *antonyms* (adj) fearless, intrepid, strong, (adv) brave, bold, courageous, daring.

kikaura 1. irascible; *synonyms* *(adj)* fiery, angry, choleric, irritable, crabby, excitable, hot, hotheaded, passionate, testy, touchy, hasty, impatient, impetuous, edgy, **2.** irritable; *synonyms* *(adj)* fractious, irascible, cantankerous, cross, disagreeable, grumpy, petulant, sensitive, huffy, cranky, difficult, fretful, grouchy, peevish, techy; *antonyms* *(adj)* calm, easygoing, good-humored, good-natured, even-tempered, good-tempered, **3.** sensitive; *synonyms* *(adj)* delicate, sensible, sore, tender, painful, impressionable, emotional, gentle, perceptive, receptive, susceptible, nice, nervous, exquisite, considerate; *antonyms* *(adj)* insensitive, numb, hardhearted, tactless, thick-skinned.

kikebokeboa fill; *synonyms* *(v)* block, clog, charge, line, stuff, accomplish, execute, complete, brim, close, cram, flood, fulfill, *(n)* crowd, filling; *antonyms* *(v)* empty, free.

kikebokeboaki filled; *synonyms* *(adj)* replete, packed, crowded, fraught, teeming, *(adv)* full.

kikekibe scratch; *synonyms* *(n)* score, mark, nick, scrabble, dent, abrasion, cut, groove, *(v)* graze, notch, rub, scrape, chafe, rake, grate.

kikekibeaki scratched; *synonyms* *(adj)* scraped, hurt, abraded, dented, injured, raw, sgraffito, spoiled, broken, skinned, smashed.

kiki scrape; *synonyms* *(v)* scratch, graze, rub, pare, rake, grate, mark, abrade, chafe, grind, claw, engrave, *(n)* score, abrasion, predicament.

kikiaki scraped; *synonyms* *(adj)* abraded, scratched, frayed, hurt, raw, skinned, threadbare, worn, shabby, tattered.

kikibokiboa heap; *synonyms* *(n)* pile, stack, accumulation, collection, amass, group, lot, mass, mound, bulk, bunch, congeries, *(v)* aggregate, bank, collect.

kikibokiboaki heaped; *synonyms* *(adj)* piled, coacervate, collective, cumulative, dense, thick, cumulous.

kikiman ingenious; *synonyms* *(adj)* adroit, artful, clever, cunning, creative, deft, expert, imaginative, cute, acute, able, inventive, canny, handy, bright; *antonym* *(adj)* unimaginative.

kikinto 1. careful; *synonyms* *(adj)* accurate, attentive, thrifty, alert, deliberate, economical, frugal, mindful, prudent, thoughtful, assiduous, aware, cagey, cautious, *(v)* anxious; *antonyms* *(adj)* careless, reckless, slapdash, neglectful, **2.** assiduous; *synonyms* *(adj)* diligent, industrious, active, busy, careful, painstaking, sedulous, thorough, devoted, conscientious, constant, indefatigable, laborious, persistent, studious; *antonym* *(adj)* lazy, **3.** diligent; *synonyms* *(adj)* earnest, occupied, brisk, meticulous, persevering, acting; *antonym* *(adj)* negligent, **4.** scrupulous; *synonyms* *(adj)* precise, punctilious, exact, particular, rigorous, finicky, nice, religious, squeamish, dainty, delicate, circumspect, correct, fastidious, fussy.

kikiriman 1. industrious; *synonyms* *(adj)* active, diligent, assiduous, indefatigable, busy, energetic, hardworking, laborious, tireless, earnest, enterprising, careful, painstaking, sedulous, studious; *antonym* *(adj)* lazy, **2.** smart; *synonyms* *(adj)* bright, crafty, dapper, quick, shrewd, sly, prompt, astute, chic, clever, intelligent, *(v)* ache, hurt, *(n)* pain, sharp; *antonyms* *(adj)* scruffy, stupid, dim, shabby, unkempt, slow.

kikitoa seek; *synonyms* *(v)* search, attempt, endeavor, hunt, look, inquire, aspire, beg, explore, pursue, quest, investigate, research, follow, *(n)* ask.

kiko 1. turn; *synonyms* *(v)* revolve, deviate, get, revolution, *(n)* bend, curve, roll, coil, go, twist, bout, change, round, bent, circle, **2.** whirl; *synonyms* *(n)* turn, wheel, crack, fling, vortex, commotion, pass, turmoil, *(v)* spin, twirl, eddy, reel, swirl, gyrate, rotate.

kikoaki turned; *synonyms* *(adj)* off, sour, curved, rancid, twisted, altered, askew, awry, bent, bowed, cancelled, crooked, dark, deflected, dour.

kima 1. keen; *synonyms* *(adj)* acute, eager, sharp, intense, intelligent, biting, brisk, enthusiastic, exquisite, piercing, discriminating, clever, astute, *(v)* fresh, avid; *antonyms* *(adj)* dull, apathetic, indifferent, unenthusiastic, blunt, **2.** sharp; *synonyms* *(adj)* bitter, acid, acrid, harsh, incisive, penetrating, pointed, pungent, quick, severe, alert, caustic, cutting, piquant, *(n)* keen; *antonyms* *(adj)* mild, gentle, rounded, sweet, bland, blurred, naive, round, smooth, **3.** steely; *synonyms* *(adj)* hard, stern, stony, icy, unbending, iron, stiff, inflexible, obdurate, pitiless, cruel, cold-blooded, merciless.

kimai 1. delicate; *synonyms* *(adj)* fine, accurate, breakable, dainty, fragile, refined, tender, beautiful, brittle, difficult, frail, nice, sensitive, soft, slim; *antonyms* *(adj)* strong, inelegant, robust, heavy, sturdy, tough, **2.** faint; *synonyms* *(adj)* collapse, dim, dizzy, feeble, indistinct, weak, dull, gentle, vague, delicate, distant, *(v)* languish, swoon, droop, conk; *antonyms* *(adj)* distinct, clear, obvious, considerable, loud, pungent, **3.** ailing; *synonyms* *(adj)* sick, sickly, ill, poorly, unwell, bad, indisposed, unhealthy, invalid, diseased, infirm, morbid, peaked, *(n)* illness; *antonyms* *(adj)* well, healthy, **4.** feeble; *synonyms* *(adj)* decrepit, ailing, helpless, lax, mild, poor, powerless, thin, enfeebled, flimsy, forceless, impotent, inadequate, *(v)* faint, debilitated; *antonyms* *(adj)* vigorous, hearty, **5.** approach; *synonyms* *(n)* access, entry, advent, arrival, avenue, coming, entrance, means, method, adit, *(v)* advance, accost, address, near, approximate; *antonym* *(v)* leave, **6.** frail; *synonyms* *(adj)* light, rickety, slender, puny, slight, fallible, flabby, brash, unsound, frangible, insubstantial, low, vulnerable, anemic, (v) shattery; *antonym* (adj) substantial, **7.** sickly; *synonyms* (adj) pale, sallow, pasty, languid, pallid, wan, bloodless, ashen, valetudinarian, (v) exhausted; *antonym* (adj) bitter, **8.** peaked; *synonyms* (adj) acute, pointed, sharp, spiky, ensiform, peaky, salient, gaunt, emaciated, cadaverous, drawn, peakish, piked, run-down, spiked.

kimamaku 1. coward; *synonyms* (n) craven, cur, sneak, weakling, cocktail, coistril, niding, alarmist, baby, deserter, invertebrate, jellyfish, lily-liver, (adj) gutless, (v) frighten, **2.** timid; *synonyms* (adj) fearful, afraid, cowardly, diffident, shy, bashful, cautious, coy, nervous, apprehensive, frightened, modest, retiring, anxious, faint; *antonyms* (adj) confident, bold, fearless, (n) brave.

kimangamanga disoriented; *synonyms* (adj) confused, lost, alienated, anomic, bewildered, adrift, astray, confounded, baffled, befuddled, bemused, broken, disconnected, disjointed, disordered; *antonym* (adj) oriented.

kimangare 1. homeless; *synonyms* (adj) houseless, roofless, dispossessed, destitute, friendless, itinerant, unhoused, stray, abandoned, broke, (n) anus, arse, ass, backside, bottom, **2.** migratory; *synonyms* (adj) migrant, nomadic, (v) ambulatory, rambling, roving, vagrant, discursive, gadding, **3.** nomadic; *synonyms* (adj) mobile, wandering, nomad, migratory, vagabond, drifting, erratic.

kimao thievish; *synonyms* (adj) thieving, furacious, pilfering, thiefly, sly, secret, thievishly.

kimareirei 1. jubilate; *synonyms* (v) exult, glory, triumph, crow, rejoice, celebrate, delight, gloat, joy, prevail, wallow, **2.** rejoice; *synonyms* (v) cheer, gladden, jubilate, revel, gratify, exhilarate, please, recreate, enjoy; *antonyms* (v) lament, mourn.

kimarimari 1. fertile; *synonyms* (adj) productive, fat, fecund, abundant, affluent, copious, exuberant, fruitful, creative, bountiful, inventive, luxuriant, prolific, rich, ample; *antonyms* (adj) infertile, sterile, **2.** fruitful; *synonyms* (adj) fertile, plentiful, profitable, good, lucrative, useful, fructiferous, gainful, lush, plenteous, pregnant, successful, frugiferous; *antonyms* (adj) unproductive, barren, unfruitful, **3.** abundant; *synonyms* (adj) generous, thick, plenty, liberal, substantial, teeming, abounding, considerable, enough, full, fulsome, great, heavy, large, lavish; *antonyms* (adj) scarce, sparse, meager, **4.** prolific; *synonyms* (adj) profuse, voluminous, opulent, **5.** producer; *synonyms* (n) director, creator, manufacturer, author, maker, manager, cause, entrepreneur, farmer, **6.** productive; *synonyms* (adj) generative, helpful, constructive, original, producing, efficient, economic, efficacious, imaginative, procreative, active, beneficial, effectual, positive, rewarding;

antonym (adj) unprofitable, **7.** plenteous; *synonyms* (adj) extensive, overflowing, **8.** spawning; *synonym* (n) generation.

kimaua 1. waste; *synonyms* (n) desert, refuse, damage, trash, (adj) spoil, desolate, barren, (v) consume, exhaust, ruin, squander, ravage, destruction, devastate, dissipate; *antonyms* (v) conserve, save, **2.** squanderer; *synonyms* (n) spendthrift, prodigal, profligate, wastrel, rip, blood, rake, roue, (v) losel, **3.** squander; *synonyms* (v) waste, fritter, lavish, spend, blow, expend, lose, scatter, trifle, deplete, devour, eat, disperse, use, abuse.

kimauaki 1. wasted; *synonyms* (v) rotten, effete, (adj) lost, squandered, thin, cadaverous, emaciated, gaunt, devastated, decayed, haggard, pointless, skeletal, atrophied, blasted; *antonyms* (adj) worthwhile, bloated, **2.** squandered; *synonyms* (v) alienated, bewildered, insensible, missing, (adj) wasted, dissipated, bony, desolate, desolated, diminished, dissolute, exhausted, intemperate, misspent, otiose.

kimaung 1. dilapidated; *synonyms* (adj) ramshackle, decayed, decrepit, derelict, ragged, rickety, shabby, damaged, faded, frayed, ruinous, scruffy, seedy, tattered, (v) bedraggled; *antonyms* (adj) pristine, elegant, **2.** neglectful; *synonyms* (adj) inattentive, negligent, heedless, careless, delinquent, forgetful, nonchalant, indifferent, lax, reckless, regardless, slapdash, dilatory, oblivious, (v) remiss; *antonyms* (adj) careful, attentive, **3.** negligent; *synonyms* (adj) neglectful, inadvertent, slack, slow, improvident, loose, neglect, incautious, mindless, disregardful, imprudent, unwary, inconsiderate, lazy, perfunctory; *antonym* (adj) strict, **4.** squandering; *synonyms* (v) waste, (n) extravagance, dissipation, damage, (adj) wasteful, prodigal, extravagant, profligate, **5.** wasteful; *synonyms* (adj) lavish, profuse, spendthrift, uneconomical, thriftless, destructive, excessive, squandering, uneconomic, losel, unthrifty; *antonyms* (adj) thrifty, economical.

kimautari 1. boatman; *synonyms* (n) waterman, boater, lighterman, longshoreman, boatsman, shipman, leghorn, skimmer, **2.** seafarer; *synonyms* (n) mariner, gob, sailor, seaman, navigator, jack, tar, hole, maw, pitch, traveler, trap, yap.

kimoa 1. stole; *synonyms* (n) scarf, wrap, stolon, robe, alb, cassock, chasuble, cope, dalmatic, gown, mozetta, pallium, scapulary, surplice, tunicle, **2.** rifle; *synonyms* (n) gun, firearm, (v) pillage, plunder, despoil, loot, ransack, steal, foray, reave, take, deprive, gut, rob, sack, **3.** pilfer; *synonyms* (v) filch, abstract, cabbage, lift, pinch, purloin, embezzle, hook, nobble, pocket, swipe, thieve, appropriate, cop, poach, **4.** steal; *synonyms* (v) creep, misappropriate, pilfer, snatch, sneak, plagiarize, slip, prowl, nim, slink, pussyfoot, (n) bargain, theft, buy, seize, **5.** rob; *synonyms* (v) rifle, fleece, pick, divest, defraud, pluck, strip, rape, bereave, swindle, assault, burgle, nick, raid, spoil.

kimoaki 1. stolen; *synonyms* (adj) purloined, furtive, misbegotten, secret, sly, stealthy, **2.** rifled, **3.** robed; *synonyms* (adj) appareled, attired, clothed, dressed, garbed, garmented, habilimented, fixed, polished, vested.

kimoiauea 1. cowardly; *synonyms* (adj) coward, timid, afraid, craven, gutless, scared, shrinking, sneaky, base, dastardly, faint, fainthearted, fearful, poltroon, pusillanimous; *antonyms* (adj) fearless, intrepid, strong, (adv) brave, bold, courageous, daring, **2.** rascal; *synonyms* (n) imp, knave, miscreant, monkey, rapscallion, rogue, scamp, scoundrel, villain, vagabond, varlet, brat, cad, crook, cheat, **3.** scoundrel; *synonyms* (n) rascal, blackguard, **4.** weasel; *synonyms* (n) informer, sneak, troublemaker, vare, whittret, (v) equivocate, evade, hedge, confess, dodge, pussyfoot.

kimotoitoi 1. dim; *synonyms* (adj) dark, obscure, cloudy, dull, bleak, dense, faint, gloomy, (v) blur, darken, cloud, pale, tarnish, blear, blind; *antonyms* (adj) bright, brilliant, intelligent, clever, strong, (v) clear, brighten, **2.** little; *synonyms* (adj) small, diminutive, insignificant, brief, minute, petty, short, some, tiny, exiguous, light, baby, bantam, (v) dash, bit; *antonyms* (adj) big, enormous, large, important, **3.** dwarfish; *synonyms* (adj) dwarf, stunted, dwarfed, puny, midget, miniature, pocket, pygmean, undershapen, **4.** undersized; *synonyms* (adj) little, undersize, dumpy, frail, immature, petite, scrawny, squat, underdeveloped, underweight, weak, unused, **5.** slight; *synonyms* (adj) flimsy, slender, thin, fragile, delicate, feeble, fine, (n) scorn, disdain, (v) disregard, insult, neglect, ignore, affront, cut; *antonyms* (adj) considerable, major, fat, heavy, intense, obvious, severe, thickset, wide, **6.** tiny; *synonyms* (adj) infinitesimal, slight, teeny, minor, trifling, trivial, cramped, (phr) minuscule; *antonyms* (adj) huge, gigantic, vast, **7.** short; *synonyms* (adj) concise, scarce, brusque, close, curt, sharp, compendious, laconic, abrupt, deficient, inadequate, insufficient, lacking, pithy, poor; *antonyms* (adj) long, tall, high, lengthy.

kimototo 1. brief; *synonyms* (adj) concise, short, abridge, little, summary, transient, short-lived, abrupt, abbreviated, brusque, compendious, curt, (n) abstract, digest, (v) compact; *antonyms* (adj) long, long-drawn-out, long-winded, permanent, lengthy, time-consuming, **2.** short; *synonyms* (adj) brief, scarce, close, sharp, laconic, deficient, diminutive, inadequate, insufficient, lacking, pithy, poor, scanty, small, blunt; *antonyms* (adj) tall, high.

kimra 1. compact; *synonyms* (adj) close, dense, compendious, concise, hard, (n) agreement,

arrangement, contract, covenant, bargain, engagement, (v) compress, condense, consolidate, pack; *antonyms* (adj) loose, sprawling, bulky, sparse, **2.** tighten; *synonyms* (v) strain, brace, constrict, fasten, narrow, reduce, squeeze, stiffen, stretch, screw, secure, constrain, frap, fix, pinch; *antonyms* (v) loosen, relax, **3.** pack; *synonyms* (n) bundle, mob, bevy, bunch, company, herd, batch, backpack, box, gang, horde, (v) crowd, heap, cram, fill; *antonym* (v) unpack, **4.** stuff; *synonyms* (n) material, cloth, force, gear, matter, goods, stock, substance, (v) jam, pad, ram, glut, gorge, load, shove; *antonym* (v) unstuff.

kimraki 1. tightened; *synonyms* (adj) tight, firm, **2.** packed; *synonyms* (adj) crowded, compact, full, filled, jammed, overcrowded, congested, dense, thick, brimming, close, cramped, teeming; *antonyms* (adj) empty, deserted, **3.** stuffed; *synonyms* (v) farctate, (adj) crammed, packed, replete, loaded, chock-full, fraught, abounding, big, concentrated, distended, overflowing, overfull, overloaded, plentiful; *antonym* (adj) hungry.

kimri 1. compact; *synonyms* (adj) close, dense, compendious, concise, hard, (n) agreement, arrangement, contract, covenant, bargain, engagement, (v) compress, condense, consolidate, pack; *antonyms* (adj) loose, sprawling, bulky, sparse, **2.** packed; *synonyms* (adj) crowded, compact, full, filled, jammed, overcrowded, congested, thick, brimming, cramped, teeming; *antonyms* (adj) empty, deserted, **3.** tight; *synonyms* (adj) firm, mean, parsimonious, taut, secure, snug, tense, drunk, miserly, rigorous, sparing, (v) narrow, fast, stingy, near; *antonyms* (adj) baggy, generous, slack, wide, (adv) loosely, **4.** stuffed; *synonyms* (v) farctate, (adj) crammed, packed, replete, loaded, chock-full, fraught, abounding, big, concentrated, distended, overflowing, overfull, overloaded, plentiful; *antonym* (adj) hungry.

kin pinch; *synonyms* (n) arrest, crisis, emergency, squeeze, twinge, exigency, (v) nip, compress, lift, wring, bite, clip, constrict, filch, gripe.

kina 1. comprehend; *synonyms* (v) apprehend, catch, embrace, grasp, understand, appreciate, comprise, feel, see, sense, apperceive, admit, compass, conceive, contain, **2.** aquatint; *synonyms* (n) aquatinta, mezzotint, lithotint, **3.** fathom; *synonyms* (v) sound, plumb, bottom, comprehend, penetrate, know, measure, examine, solve, (n) gauge, probe, **4.** discern; *synonyms* (v) behold, differentiate, descry, detect, distinguish, perceive, recognize, find, discover, discriminate, judge, note, notice, observe, realize, **5.** know; *synonyms* (v) discern, can, have, acknowledge, agnise, agnize, fathom, cognize, experience, get, endure, hear, interpret, place, (n) ken, **6.** perceive; *synonyms* (v) divine, espy, receive, taste, view, read, tell, regard, spy, witness, believe, **7.** saw; *synonyms* (*v*) cut, (*n*) adage, byword, proverb, dictum, maxim, saying, aphorism, axiom, motto, **8.** understand; *synonyms* (*v*) learn, assume, construe, deduce, gather, translate, suppose, consider, infer, absorb, dig, digest, accept, (*adj*) take, imply; *antonyms* (*v*) misinterpret, misconstrue, misunderstand, **9.** remark; *synonyms* (*n*) observation, mind, commentary, heed, observance, reflection, word, declaration, statement, quip, (*v*) comment, mention, mark, (*adj*) look, attend, **10.** see; *synonyms* (*v*) deem, ascertain, envision, inspect, call, check, contemplate, control, escort, figure, glimpse, identify, meet, picture, watch, **11.** recognize; *synonyms* (*v*) allow, confess, accredit, own, agree, hail, recognise, recognition, spot, greet, assent, avow, concede, grant, recollect, **12.** spy; *synonyms* (*n*) scout, detective, mole, patrol, emissary, bivouac, (*v*) snoop, investigate, sight, peek, pry, sleuth, stag, grass, mouchard, **13.** spot; *synonyms* (*n*) blot, speck, stain, dot, dapple, dirty, location, position, (*v*) blemish, soil, fleck, speckle, daub, flaw, mottle.

kinaki 1. comprehended; *synonyms* (*adj*) appreciated, apprehended, gratifying, pleasing, satisfying, **2.** known; *synonyms* (*adj*) well-known, familiar, conscious, certain, accepted, acknowledged, plain, published, understood, evident, recognized, apparent, aware, common, apprised; *antonyms* (*adj*) nameless, unknown, secret, unidentified, **3.** understood; *synonyms* (*v*) admitted, (*adj*) implicit, tacit, implied, silent, assumed; *antonyms* (*adj*) explicit, spoken, **4.** perceived; *synonyms* (*adj*) felt, sensed, ostensible, professed, supposed, alleged, seeming, superficial, **5.** recognized; *synonyms* (*v*) ascertained, (*adj*) established, noted, recognised, received, distinguished, illustrious, known, famous, notorious, official; *antonyms* (*adj*) unofficial, concealed, **6.** spotted; *synonyms* (*adj*) mottled, dappled, speckled, blotchy, dotted, flyblown, piebald, multicolored, dirty, spotty, stained, tainted, besmirched, damaged, freckled, **7.** pinched; *synonyms* (*adj*) gaunt, haggard, drawn, emaciated, cadaverous, necessitous, adenoidal, bony, careworn, destitute, impecunious, narrow, nasal, (*n*) distressed, needy.

kinako backup; *synonyms* (*n*) backing, substitute, surrogate, assistant, aid, congestion, jam, accompaniment, allayer, alleviation, (*adj*) alternate, spare, auxiliary, subsidiary, alternative.

kinano 1. extreme; *synonyms* (*adj*) deep, excessive, enormous, immoderate, intense, severe, supreme, terrible, ultimate, utmost, uttermost, drastic, extraordinary, (*n*) edge, end; *antonyms* (*adj*) middle, reasonable, near, (*n*) mild, moderate, slight, **2.** intense; *synonyms* (*adj*) bright, acute, ardent,

brilliant, fervent, fierce, burning, energetic, extreme, fiery, furious, heated, rich, sharp, (*v*) vivid; *antonyms* (*adj*) calm, dull, weak, imperceptible, **3.** deep; *synonyms* (*adj*) thick, profound, absorbed, abstruse, broad, dark, sound, strong, wide, esoteric, large, abysmal, bass, concentrated, (*n*) brine; *antonyms* (*adj*) shallow, superficial, high, high-pitched, light, soft, **4.** drastic; *synonyms* (*adj*) desperate, sweeping, ultra, thorough, escharotic, harsh, stiff, tough, dire, forcible, rough, essential, fundamental, exorbitant, extravagant, **5.** abstruse; *synonyms* (*adj*) recondite, obscure, abstract, cryptic, difficult, mysterious, occult, complex, intricate, puzzling, secret, **6.** mysterious; *synonyms* (*adj*) hidden, inscrutable, eerie, incomprehensible, inexplicable, arcane, clandestine, concealed, covert, cryptical, enigmatic, impenetrable, mystic, mystical, unknown; *antonyms* (*adj*) known, straightforward, apparent, normal, **7.** profound; *synonyms* (*adj*) heavy, bottomless, important, solid, grave, utter, complete, exhaustive, intimate, shrewd, good, penetrating, hard, crass, (*n*) impressive; *antonym* (*adj*) trivial, **8.** ultra; *synonyms* (*adv*) extremely, (*adj*) radical, extremist, (*v*) distinguished.

kinanoa 1. monitor; *synonyms* (*v*) check, regulate, control, eavesdrop, observe, supervise, (*n*) admonisher, dame, ironclad, moderator, **2.** inspect; *synonyms* (*v*) examine, overhaul, overlook, survey, explore, inquire, look, review, scrutinize, view, watch, monitor, analyze, audit, consider, **3.** assess; *synonyms* (*v*) appraise, evaluate, appreciate, value, estimate, gauge, mark, measure, tax, demand, regard, assay, calculate, compute, count, **4.** examine; *synonyms* (*v*) try, search, ascertain, ask, contemplate, compare, canvass, essay, investigate, probe, quiz, study, test, collate, browse, **5.** check; *synonyms* (*v*) bridle, stop, block, limit, agree, halt, restrain, bar, dampen, delay, hinder, (*n*) arrest, curb, bill, cheque, **6.** determine; *synonyms* (*v*) decide, define, resolve, appoint, adjudicate, conclude, set, specify, designate, assign, decree, arrange, assess, choose, detect, **7.** audit; *synonyms* (*n*) examination, scrutiny, (*v*) balance, inspect, prove, **8.** analyze; *synonyms* (*v*) analyse, anatomize, research, determine, dissect, diagnose, identify; *antonym* (*v*) synthesize, **9.** review; *synonyms* (*n*) critique, inspection, retrospect, commentary, comment, parade, magazine, criticism, investigation, notice, (*v*) criticize, judge, reexamine, revise, recapitulate.

kinanoaki 1. determined; *synonyms* (*adj*) constant, decided, definite, resolute, certain, decisive, determinate, inflexible, resolved, stubborn, ambitious, adamant, bold, firm, obstinate; *antonyms* (*adj*) weak, irresolute, uncertain, feeble, unmotivated, **2.** monitored, **3.** analyzed, **4.**

checked; *synonyms* *(adj)* checkered, chequered, plaid, backward, curbed, intermittent, limited, numbered, pent-up, safe, silent, tartan, temperate, **5.** assessed; *synonym* *(adj)* deferred.

kinanona 1. desire; *synonyms* *(n)* ambition, hope, aspiration, will, wish, craving, dream, impulse, *(v)* fancy, aspire, seek, want, aim, choose, crave; *antonyms* *(n)* aversion, reality, *(v)* dislike, hate, **2.** love; *synonyms* *(n)* desire, affection, dear, fondness, liking, benevolence, charity, attachment, beloved, darling, devotion, honey, *(v)* cherish, enjoy, like; *antonyms* *(n)* abhorrence, hatred, *(v)* abhor.

kinanonaki 1. desired; *synonyms* *(adj)* coveted, craved, desirable, chosen, favorite, wanted, needed, welcome, beloved, adored, appropriate, pet, preferred, *(v)* complying, consenting; *antonym* *(adj)* undesirable, **2.** loved; *synonyms* *(adj)* dear, cherished, precious, appreciated, esteemed, prized, respected, treasured, valued, important, *(n)* darling.

kinanonano 1. mysterious; *synonyms* *(adj)* hidden, inscrutable, deep, eerie, incomprehensible, inexplicable, abstruse, arcane, cryptic, dark, obscure, secret, clandestine, concealed, covert; *antonyms* *(adj)* known, straightforward, apparent, normal, **2.** apocalyptic; *synonyms* *(adj)* prophetic, apocalyptical, revelatory, oracular, direful, fateful, indicative, ominous, sinister, threatening, *(n)* apocalyptist, **3.** profound; *synonyms* *(adj)* intense, heavy, bottomless, important, solid, sound, grave, utter, abysmal, complete, exhaustive, intimate, recondite, shrewd, *(n)* impressive; *antonyms* *(adj)* superficial, shallow, trivial.

kinati 1. last; *synonyms* *(v)* endure, continue, hold, exist, live, dwell, *(n)* abide, conclusion, *(adj)* extreme, closing, final, ultimate, conclusive, concluding, farthest; *antonyms* *(n)* opening, *(adj)* first, **2.** smallest; *synonyms* *(adj)* least, minimal, littlest, lowest, bottom, last, negligible, nominal, token, *(n)* minimum.

kinauere 1. puny; *synonyms* *(adj)* little, feeble, frail, petty, weak, small, tiny, minute, measly, paltry, runty, trifling, trivial, exiguous, meager; *antonyms* *(adj)* brawny, muscular, **2.** sickly; *synonyms* *(adj)* infirm, sick, ailing, diseased, indisposed, morbid, pale, poorly, sallow, peaked, pasty, languid, pallid, *(n)* invalid, *(v)* faint; *antonyms* *(adj)* healthy, bitter.

kinawanawa 1. fleck; *synonyms* *(n)* spot, speck, speckle, stigma, bit, chip, dapple, flake, splotch, stain, *(v)* dot, blot, blob, daub, mark, **2.** marked; *synonyms* *(adj)* distinct, conspicuous, noticeable, pronounced, remarkable, distinguished, apparent, definite, notable, obvious, signal, striking, strong, clear, appreciable; *antonyms* *(adj)* plain, unblemished, **3.** dappled; *synonyms* *(adj)* mottled, motley, speckled, flecked, dotted, freckled, spotted, spotty, multicolored, **4.** mottled; *synonyms* *(adj)*

dappled, piebald, variegated, mixed, **5.** spotted; *synonyms* *(v)* mildewed, moldy, rusty, *(adj)* blotchy, flyblown, dirty, stained, tainted, besmirched, damaged, patched, **6.** speckled; *synonym* *(adj)* specked.

kinawanawaki flecked; *synonyms* *(adj)* dappled, dotted, speckled, spotted, mottled, multicolored, stippled.

kinawanawana spotted; *synonyms* *(adj)* mottled, dappled, speckled, blotchy, dotted, flyblown, piebald, multicolored, dirty, spotty, stained, tainted, besmirched, damaged, freckled; *antonym* *(adj)* plain.

kinene 1. puny; *synonyms* *(adj)* little, feeble, frail, petty, weak, small, tiny, minute, measly, paltry, runty, trifling, trivial, exiguous, meager; *antonyms* *(adj)* brawny, muscular, **2.** rickety; *synonyms* *(adj)* shaky, unstable, wobbly, decrepit, dilapidated, insecure, ramshackle, rachitic, flimsy, precarious, unsteady, wonky, awkward, clumsy, gross; *antonyms* *(adj)* stable, steady, **3.** stunted; *synonyms* *(adj)* scrubby, scrawny, diminutive, puny, short, spare, *(v)* strangulated.

kinerang 1. deformed; *synonyms* *(adj)* crooked, bent, distorted, malformed, misshapen, ugly, crippled, contorted, deform, grotesque, shapeless, twisted, warped, *(v)* crump, **2.** puny; *synonyms* *(adj)* little, feeble, frail, petty, weak, small, tiny, minute, measly, paltry, runty, trifling, trivial, exiguous, meager; *antonyms* *(adj)* brawny, muscular, **3.** rickety; *synonyms* *(adj)* shaky, unstable, wobbly, decrepit, dilapidated, insecure, ramshackle, rachitic, flimsy, precarious, unsteady, wonky, awkward, clumsy, gross; *antonyms* *(adj)* stable, steady, **4.** stunted; *synonyms* *(adj)* scrubby, scrawny, diminutive, puny, short, spare, *(v)* strangulated.

kingina lock; *synonyms* *(n)* curl, hook, padlock, *(v)* bolt, bar, close, latch, engage, fasten, hug, hold, interlock, secure, shut, *(adj)* hair; *antonyms* *(v)* unlock, open.

kinginaki locked; *synonyms* *(adj)* bolted, latched, closed, barred, fast, barricaded, blockaded, bonded, clocked, colorfast, debauched, degenerate, degraded, dissipated, dissolute.

kingking runty; *synonyms* *(adj)* puny, short, stunted, shrimpy, small, diminutive, mean, shortened.

kinika 1. nip; *synonyms* *(v)* bite, chill, drink, snip, squeeze, clip, dash, twitch, *(n)* pinch, cut, gulp, sip, sting, tang, *(adj)* dram, **2.** pluck; *synonyms* *(v)* cull, jerk, fleece, gather, pick, pull, grab, harvest, extract, *(n)* courage, grit, boldness, backbone, bravery, *(adj)* nerve, **3.** pick; *synonyms* *(v)* clean, opt, break, choose, collect, *(n)* alternative, elite, best, choice, option, selection, *(adj)* cream, select, mattock, flower, **4.** pinch; *synonyms* *(n)* arrest, crisis, emergency, twinge, exigency, (v) nip, compress, lift, wring, constrict, filch, gripe, pilfer, steal, pass.

kinikaki 1. plucked; *synonyms* (v) ploughed, plowed, (adj) moulting, pilled, pulled, **2**. pinched; *synonyms* (adj) gaunt, haggard, drawn, emaciated, cadaverous, necessitous, adenoidal, bony, careworn, destitute, impecunious, narrow, nasal, (n) distressed, needy.

kinikin nip; *synonyms* (v) bite, chill, drink, snip, squeeze, clip, dash, twitch, (n) pinch, cut, gulp, sip, sting, tang, (adj) dram.

kinikini pinch; *synonyms* (n) arrest, crisis, emergency, squeeze, twinge, exigency, (v) nip, compress, lift, wring, bite, clip, constrict, filch, gripe.

kinikon 1. shriveled; *synonyms* (adj) dry, wizened, shrivelled, shrunken, attenuated, dried, parched, sear, sere, thin, withered, **2**. wrinkled; *synonyms* (adj) furrowed, creased, crumpled, lined, puckered, wrinkly, gnarled, unironed, (n) rough, rugged; *antonym* (adj) smooth.

kinka pinch; *synonyms* (n) arrest, crisis, emergency, squeeze, twinge, exigency, (v) nip, compress, lift, wring, bite, clip, constrict, filch, gripe.

kinkaki pinched; *synonyms* (adj) gaunt, haggard, drawn, emaciated, cadaverous, necessitous, adenoidal, bony, careworn, destitute, impecunious, narrow, nasal, (n) distressed, needy.

kinnano 1. checker; *synonyms* (n) examiner, counter, block, director, (v) check, chequer, agree, arrest, ascertain, assure, break, counterchange, freak, freck, (adj) variegate, **2**. auditor; *synonyms* (n) accountant, hearer, listener, bookkeeper, attendant, attendee, attender, clerk, investigator, assessor, superintendent, tender, **3**. observer; *synonyms* (n) beholder, bystander, spectator, witness, eyewitness, onlooker, viewer, watcher, commentator, student.

kinoa quiet; *synonyms* (adj) still, lull, pacify, cool, gentle, motionless, peaceful, (v) appease, moderate, assuage, allay, (n) calm, hush, compose, ease; *antonyms* (adj) loud, noisy, talkative, vociferous, active, (n) noise.

kinokino 1. fairly; *synonyms* (adv) completely, moderately, somewhat, clean, equitably, fair, justly, passably, pretty, quite, rather, reasonably, enough, middling, relatively; *antonyms* (adv) unfairly, extremely, unjustly, **2**. far; *synonyms* (adv) wide, off, widely, well, astray, (adj) distant, aloof, faraway, remote, much, outlying, (v) considerably, abundantly; *antonyms* (adv) close, briefly, (adj) near, **3**. afar; *synonyms* (adv) away, distantly, apart, aside, (adj) far, (prep) outside, past, **4**. distant; *synonyms* (adj) cold, chill, cool, detached, reserved, long, icy, indifferent, removed, standoffish, unfriendly, abstracted, deep, dull, (n) chilly; *antonyms* (adj) adjacent, friendly, nearby,

neighboring, warm, pending, alert, intimate, involved, **5**. away; *synonyms* (adv) absent, by, forth, way, hence, elsewhere, (adj) abroad, gone, missing, (int) out, **6**. removed; *synonyms* (adj) separate, separated, **7**. rather; *synonyms* (adv) fairly, instead, kinda, preferably, comparatively, sooner, **8**. significantly; *synonyms* (adv) importantly, essentially, greatly, highly, meaningfully, noticeably, substantially; *antonyms* (adv) insignificantly, slightly, unimportantly, **9**. quite; *synonyms* (adv) altogether, absolutely, all, entirely, fully, sheer, exactly, even, right, stark, totally, wholly, awfully, (adj) just, outright.

kinokunoku 1. brooding; *synonyms* (adj) brood, pondering, contemplative, hatching, meditative, pensive, thoughtful, (v) batching, brewing, **2**. susceptible; *synonyms* (adj) impressionable, receptive, responsive, sensitive, subject, liable, delicate, pliable, susceptive, vulnerable, irritable, open, amenable, exposed, impressible; *antonyms* (adj) resistant, unsusceptible, **3**. sulky; *synonyms* (adj) gloomy, sullen, grouchy, morose, surly, moody, peevish, cross, petulant, angry, crabby, huffish, grim, dour, (v) glum, **4**. peevish; *synonyms* (adj) fractious, fretful, irascible, testy, cantankerous, captious, touchy, crusty, grumpy, excitable, crotchety, cranky, nettlesome, pettish, sour.

kinongo perforated; *synonyms* (adj) perforate, pierced, punctured, penetrated, entered.

kinono deep; *synonyms* (adj) thick, profound, absorbed, abstruse, broad, dark, rich, sound, strong, wide, esoteric, bright, large, abysmal, (v) intense; *antonyms* (adj) shallow, superficial, high, high-pitched, light, soft, weak.

kinounou abyssal; *synonyms* (adj) abysmal, deep, marine, nautical, limitless.

kinra 1. hint; *synonyms* (n) clue, intimation, suggestion, trace, allusion, cue, inkling, implication, (v) suggest, dash, tip, touch, allude, imply, (adj) intimate; *antonym* (n) overtone, **2**. banter; *synonyms* (n) ridicule, raillery, (v) badinage, chaff, jest, joke, kid, tease, deride, quiz, retort, twit, jeer, jolly, josh, **3**. chaff; *synonyms* (n) banter, husk, shuck, straw, (v) mock, rally, **4**. pinch; *synonyms* (n) arrest, crisis, emergency, squeeze, twinge, exigency, (v) nip, compress, lift, wring, bite, clip, constrict, filch, gripe, **5**. prick; *synonyms* (n) cock, pricking, spur, pang, asshole, (v) goad, puncture, impale, pierce, stab, needle, fret, pinch, bore, hurt.

kinraea insinuate; *synonyms* (v) allude, hint, imply, indicate, intimate, suggest, adumbrate, connote, ingratiate, signify, denote, impute, instill.

kinraki pinched; *synonyms* (adj) gaunt, haggard, drawn, emaciated, cadaverous, necessitous, adenoidal, bony, careworn, destitute, impecunious, narrow, nasal, (*n*) distressed, needy.

kinrangia 1. love; *synonyms* (*n*) desire, affection, dear, fondness, liking, benevolence, charity, attachment, beloved, darling, devotion, honey, (*v*) cherish, enjoy, like; *antonyms* (*n*) abhorrence, hatred, aversion, (*v*) hate, dislike, abhor, **2.** desire; *synonyms* (*n*) ambition, hope, aspiration, will, wish, craving, dream, impulse, (*v*) fancy, aspire, seek, want, aim, choose, crave; *antonym* (*n*) reality.

kinrangiaki 1. desired; *synonyms* (*adj*) coveted, craved, desirable, chosen, favorite, wanted, needed, welcome, beloved, adored, appropriate, pet, preferred, (*v*) complying, consenting; *antonym* (*adj*) undesirable, **2.** loved; *synonyms* (*adj*) dear, cherished, precious, appreciated, esteemed, prized, respected, treasured, valued, important, (*n*) darling.

kio 1. evade; *synonyms* (*v*) elude, avoid, escape, dodge, equivocate, parry, circumvent, duck, hedge, sidestep, skirt, bilk, fudge, neglect, omit; *antonym* (*v*) confront, **2.** escape; *synonyms* (*v*) break, evade, run, bolt, leave, abscond, desert, elope, (*n*) leak, avoidance, evasion, outlet, deliverance, egress, flight; *antonyms* (*v*) capture, return, **3.** avoid; *synonyms* (*v*) shun, avert, abstain, annul, forbear, ignore, prevent, shirk, fly, beware, balk, debar, flee, help, (*adj*) eschew; *antonyms* (*v*) associate, face, tackle, **4.** elude; *synonyms* (*v*) baffle, defy, frustrate, deflect, mystify.

kioaki escaped; *synonyms* (*v*) escaping, (*adj*) free, loose, easy, runaway, wild, fugitive, idle, informal, lax, liberal, light, open, promiscuous, slack.

kioi 1. detonate; *synonyms* (*v*) explode, blast, burst, fulminate, shoot, (*adj*) discharge, thunder, bounce; *antonym* (*v*) defuse, **2.** burst; *synonyms* (*v*) break, crack, rupture, belch, abound, erupt, open, (*n*) flash, explosion, bang, (*adj*) split, detonate, flare, splinter, broken; *antonym* (*v*) implode, **3.** blast; *synonyms* (*n*) slam, gust, clap, eruption, noise, (*v*) attack, blare, blight, bomb, boom, roar, smash, blow, bombard, shell, **4.** discharge; *synonyms* (*n*) release, dismissal, drain, (*v*) acquit, clear, absolve, complete, deliver, eject, cashier, disgorge, empty, exonerate, expel, flow; *antonyms* (*v*) capture, hire, **5.** explode; *synonyms* (*v*) disprove, fire, expand, discredit, shatter, disintegrate, overthrow, refute, belie, blaze, displode, **6.** blow; *synonyms* (*n*) beat, knock, shock, wallop, hit, jolt, rap, (*v*) puff, bloom, blossom, pant, play, slap, squander, (*adj*) gasp; *antonyms* (*v*) calm, save.

kioiaki 1. discharged; *synonyms* (*adj*) released, exempt, clear, convalescent, dead, deadened, defunct, dismissed, drained, finished, fired, idle, inactive, inanimate, lifeless, **2.** burst; *synonyms* (*v*) break, crack, blast, rupture, belch, abound, erupt, open, (*n*) flash, explosion, (*adj*) split, explode, detonate, flare, splinter; *antonym* (*v*) implode, **3.**

exploded; *synonyms* (*adj*) antebellum, antediluvian, elapsed, expired, extinct, lapsed, forgotten, irrecoverable, refuted, **4.** blasted; *synonyms* (*adj*) cursed, damned, infernal, blessed, damn, darned, deuced, goddamn, goddamned, blame, blamed, **5.** blown; *synonyms* (*v*) distended, (*adj*) breathless, puffy, panting, swollen, winded, dissipated, flushed, gasping, high, late, mighty, misspent, pursy, spent.

kioina 1. for; *synonyms* (*prep*) because, behind, by, per, during, on, toward, (*conj*) considering, since, (*adv*) against, as, therefore, hence, **2.** as; *synonyms* (*conj*) qua, while, whilst, (*prep*) like, (*adv*) equally, from, (*n*) arsenic.

kiraoki 1. intoxicate; *synonyms* (*v*) fuddle, inebriate, befuddle, elate, disguise, apprehend, arrest, catch, collar, collect, cop, discover, disease, disorder, distemper, **2.** drink; *synonyms* (*n*) beverage, alcohol, brew, potion, swallow, crapulence, intoxicant, nip, (*v*) draught, booze, carouse, bib, absorb, down, gulp, **3.** toast; *synonyms* (*n*) pledge, brown, plight, (*v*) drink, roast, burn, bake, wassail, cook, crisp, heat, inflame, salute.

kiraokiaki 1. intoxicated; *synonyms* (*adj*) drunken, inebriated, drunk, inebriate, tipsy, elated; *antonym* (*adj*) sober, **2.** toasted; *synonyms* (*adj*) baked, heated.

kirara sandy; *synonyms* (*adj*) gritty, light, granular, arenaceous, sabulous, dusty, farinaceous, loose, mealy, powdery, branny, creamy, flaxen, flocculent, floury.

kirarang 1. follower; *synonyms* (*n*) disciple, backer, devotee, fan, adherent, admirer, cohort, apostle, attendant, believer, partisan, proselyte, dependent, pupil, (*adj*) lover; *antonyms* (*n*) detractor, opponent, **2.** sheepish; *synonyms* (*adj*) ashamed, coy, diffident, bashful, shamefaced, shy, guilty, embarrassed, nervous, skittish.

kiraroa distant; *synonyms* (*adj*) cold, aloof, remote, chill, cool, detached, far, reserved, long, faraway, icy, indifferent, removed, (*adv*) apart, (*n*) chilly; *antonyms* (*adj*) close, adjacent, friendly, near, nearby, neighboring, warm, pending, alert, intimate, involved.

kire 1. frantic; *synonyms* (*adj*) delirious, desperate, crazy, frenzied, excited, furious, distraught, distracted, frenetic, raging, boisterous, despairing, feverish, fierce, (*v*) wild; *antonym* (*adj*) calm, **2.** feeble; *synonyms* (*adj*) delicate, weak, decrepit, ailing, dim, dull, frail, helpless, infirm, lax, mild, poor, powerless, (*v*) faint, debilitated; *antonyms* (*adj*) strong, vigorous, hearty, tough, **3.** frenzied; *synonyms* (*adj*) frantic, hectic, manic, fanatical, mad, passionate, phrenetic, rabid, agitated, ecstatic, **4.** furious; *synonyms* (*adj*) angry, violent, enraged, ferocious, vehement, infuriated, rampant, angered, cross, fiery, heated, hot, impetuous, incensed, irate,

5. weak; *synonyms* (*adj*) feeble, flat, flimsy, fragile, thin, watery, light, cowardly, diluted, exhausted, inadequate, nerveless, shaky, sickly, (*v*) loose; *antonyms* (*adj*) brave, concentrated, firm, safe, compelling, determined, effective, forceful, healthy, intense, powerful, resolute, robust, sturdy, able, **6.** wild; *synonyms* (*adj*) desert, waste, reckless, desolate, rude, stormy, untamed, giddy, barbarous, rough, vicious, wanton, barbarian, barbaric, barren; *antonyms* (*adj*) orderly, domestic, manageable, sane, cultivated, restrained, tame, **7.** puny; *synonyms* (*adj*) little, petty, small, tiny, minute, measly, paltry, runty, trifling, trivial, exiguous, meager; *antonyms* (*adj*) brawny, muscular, **8.** weakly; *synonyms* (*adv*) feebly, badly, faintly, softly, (*adj*) sapless; *antonyms* (*adv*) strongly, confidently, firmly, powerfully.

kirei 1. frolic; *synonyms* (*n*) play, romp, sport, caper, diversion, fun, joke, joy, merriment, mirth, (*v*) cavort, disport, frisk, gambol, lark, **2.** gamble; *synonyms* (*n*) bet, hazard, game, speculation, (*v*) chance, risk, wager, stake, adventure, venture, **3.** caper; *synonyms* (*n*) prank, skip, hop, antic, spring, trick, escapade, (*v*) bound, dance, frolic, leap, jump, prance, ramp, trip, **4.** frisk; *synonyms* (*n*) frisking, amble, canter, drive, (*v*) rollick, search, **5.** swaggering; *synonyms* (*v*) swagger, (*adj*) blustering, hectoring, arrogant, boastful, disdainful, haughty, lordly, prideful, roistering, sniffy, (*n*) boasting, bluster, bravado, ostentation, **6.** prance; *synonyms* (*n*) strut, (*v*) parade, curvet, bounce, cock, flop, flounce, flounder, **7.** romp; *synonyms* (*n*) hoyden, runaway, tomboy, walkaway, laugher, **8.** swagger; *synonyms* (*n*) arrogance, bragging, pride, (*v*) brag, boast, ruffle, flourish, sashay, stalk, swash, vaunt, walk, browbeat, (*adj*) bully, groovy, **9.** rollick.

kiri 1. especially; *synonyms* (*adv*) specially, chiefly, exceedingly, particularly, principally, namely, exceptionally, expressly, extra, extraordinarily, peculiarly, primarily, remarkably, specifically, very; *antonym* (*adv*) slightly, **2.** really; *synonyms* (*adv*) actually, honestly, absolutely, genuinely, certainly, real, truly, simply, authentically, practically, essentially, extremely, forsooth, (*adj*) indeed, sincerely, **3.** very; *synonyms* (*adv*) greatly, highly, really, completely, entirely, most, quite, too, awfully, excessively, (*adj*) much, identical, considerably, exact, (*n*) self; *antonyms* (*adv*) abysmally, somewhat, **4.** triple; *synonyms* (*adj*) treble, threefold, ternary, triplex, thribble.

kiria 1. go; *synonyms* (*v*) come, elapse, pass, break, crack, depart, disappear, drive, run, travel, fall, extend, function, (*n*) fare, (*adj*) follow, **2.** pass; *synonyms* (*v*) flow, deliver, give, happen, lead,

move, offer, overtake, live, advance, die, exceed, lapse, leave, (*adj*) go; *antonym* (*v*) fail.

kiriaria 1. lately; *synonyms* (*adv*) recently, late, freshly, latterly, newly, just, new, (*adj*) anew, afresh, **2.** future; *synonyms* (*adj*) unborn, coming, prospective, intended, potential, approaching, forthcoming, imminent, impending, later, (*n*) prospect, hereafter, fate, futurity, (*v*) horizon; *antonym* (*n*) past, **3.** after; *synonyms* (*prep*) following, since, (*adv*) beyond, next, subsequently, then, when, afterward, afterwards, behind, (*adj*) back, posterior, rear, subsequent, **4.** late; *synonyms* (*adj*) former, dead, deceased, behindhand, belated, delayed, modern, slow, tardy, dull, defunct, (*adv*) dilatory, fresh, backward, belatedly; *antonyms* (*adj*) ahead, (*adv*) early, punctually, promptly, punctual, **5.** distantly; *synonyms* (*adv*) remotely, vaguely, aloofly, coldly, coolly, formally, reservedly, apathetically, callously, dispassionately, frigidly, frostily, grimly, impassively, impersonally; *antonyms* (*adv*) closely, intimately, **6.** later; *synonyms* (*adv*) after, (*adj*) last, ensuing, future, latter, final, succeeding; *antonyms* (*adv*) earlier, immediately, before, prior, **7.** afterwards, **8.** afterward; *synonym* (*adv*) thereafter; *antonym* (*adv*) beforehand, **9.** following; *synonyms* (*adj*) consequent, consecutive, deducible, sequent, successive, (*v*) consequential, consectary, (*n*) entourage, chase, followers, pursuit, audience, train, clientele, (*adv*) under; *antonym* (*adj*) preceding, **10.** subsequent; *synonyms* (*adj*) second, sequential, postnate; *antonym* (*adj*) previous, **11.** posterior; *synonyms* (*adj*) caudal, hindmost, (*n*) backside, bottom, buttocks, can, rump, tail, arse, ass, bum, butt, fanny, fundament, hindquarters; *antonyms* (*adj*) fore, anterior, forward, **12.** procrastinate; *synonyms* (*v*) defer, delay, adjourn, linger, postpone, suspend, tarry, dawdle, protract, retard, stall, **13.** subsequently; *synonym* (*adv*) accordingly, **14.** ulterior; *synonyms* (*adj*) eventual, subterranean, covert, alien, extraneous, foreign.

kiribabaoua 1. bent; *synonyms* (*adj*) arched, curved, bended, crooked, deformed, intent, (*n*) aptitude, inclination, propensity, fancy, ability, bias, flair, gift, leaning; *antonym* (*adj*) straight, **2.** meandering; *synonyms* (*adj*) circuitous, indirect, tortuous, winding, zigzag, serpentine, sinuous, roundabout, snaky, windy; *antonym* (*adj*) direct, **3.** curved; *synonyms* (*adj*) bent, curve, round, bend, curving, curvy, hooked, rounded, twisted, (*v*) bowed; *antonym* (*adj*) concave, **4.** winding; *synonyms* (*adj*) twisting, meandering, twisty, wandering, devious, intricate, involved, oblique, rambling, (*n*) twist, wind, turn, coiling, breath, hoisting, **5.** twisted; *synonyms* (*adj*) perverted, distorted, coiled, misshapen, contorted, twined, wry, gnarled, awry, kinky, wrong, warped, askew, depraved, malformed; *antonym* (*adj*) tidy.

kiribambanta 1. encircle; *synonyms* (*v*) beset, surround, besiege, circle, embrace, bound, circumvent, enclose, encompass, environ, hem, begird, circumscribe, beleaguer, (*adv*) compass, **2**. overwhelm; *synonyms* (*v*) defeat, flood, inundate, overcome, overpower, overthrow, crush, deluge, drown, engulf, astound, beat, overrun, overtake, overturn, **3**. surround; *synonyms* (*v*) encircle, gird, border, inclose, ring, round, skirt, envelop, entwine, blockade, edge, enfold, fence, (*n*) environment, environs, **4**. overcome; *synonyms* (*v*) conquer, subdue, vanquish, master, hurdle, overwhelm, prevail, subjugate, surmount, demolish, affect, cross, exceed, (*adj*) beaten, conquered; *antonyms* (*v*) fail, (*adj*) victorious, unimpressed.

kiribambantaki 1. encircled; *synonyms* (*adj*) surrounded, enclosed, bounded, annular, annulate, annulated, bordered, circinate, circular, delimited, ingirt, ringed, wreathed, **2**. surrounded; *synonyms* (*v*) beset, begone, furnished, (*adj*) encircled, circumstanced, conditioned, entrenched, fixed, inside, rooted, implanted, **3**. overwhelmed; *synonyms* (*v*) overborne, (*adj*) overcome, beaten, overpowered, vanquished, conquered, dumbfounded, engulfed, flooded, inundated, overthrown; *antonyms* (*adj*) victorious, unimpressed, **4**. overcome; *synonyms* (*v*) conquer, beat, crush, subdue, vanquish, defeat, master, overpower, hurdle, overwhelm, prevail, subjugate, surmount, demolish, affect; *antonym* (*v*) fail.

kiribangabanga honeycombed; *synonyms* (*v*) porous, cribriform, follicular, infundibular, riddled, (*adj*) pitted, alveolate, cavitied, faveolate, cavernous, alveolar.

kiribanin 1. congealed; *synonyms* (*adj*) coagulated, firm, concrete, jelled, jellied, stiff, thick, hard, solid, **2**. clotted; *synonyms* (*adj*) clogged, grumous, bloody, choked, fleamy, concreted, foul, grumose, slimy, (*n*) amylaceous, clammy, gelatin, glutenous, mastic, ropy, **3**. coagulated; *synonyms* (*adj*) coagulate, curdled, viscous, crudy, curdy, gelatinous, glutinous, gooey, heavy, solidified, syrupy, raw, **4**. adhesive; *synonyms* (*adj*) tacky, clingy, gummy, tenacious, agglutinative, gluey, pasty, smeary, (*v*) cement, glue, paste, gum, (*v*) cohesive; *antonym* (*adj*) nonadhesive, **5**. curdled; *synonyms* (*adj*) rancid, sour, (*n*) succulent, uliginous, emulsive.

kiribare 1. alike; *synonyms* (*adv*) equally, likewise, (*adj*) like, corresponding, equal, equivalent, analogous, cognate, comparable, duplicate, even, identical, likely, parallel, similar; *antonyms* (*adv*) differently, (*adj*) different, dissimilar, **2**. identical; *synonyms* (*adj*) uniform, consistent, alike, selfsame,

very, synonymous, congruent, exact, tantamount, twin, indistinguishable, (*v*) same; *antonyms* (*adj*) incompatible, inconsistent, **3**. duplicate; *synonyms* (*adj*) dual, matching, (*v*) copy, double, trace, redouble, reduplicate, repeat, replicate, reproduce, fake, (*n*) counterpart, second, imitation, match; *antonym* (*n*) original, **4**. same; *synonyms* (*adj*) monotonous, self, interchangeable.

kiribebe 1. reel; *synonyms* (*n*) bobbin, coil, roll, spool, (*v*) lurch, rock, spin, stagger, totter, waver, teeter, falter, fluctuate, dance, gyrate, **2**. stagger; *synonyms* (*v*) astonish, startle, flabbergast, flounder, hobble, reel, shake, shock, pitch, amaze, dumbfound, stun, surprise, astound, (*adj*) bewilder.

kiribeubeu 1. jagged; *synonyms* (*adj*) rough, uneven, angular, irregular, crooked, craggy, bumpy, harsh, jaggy, notched, rugged, scraggy, zigzag, (*n*) ragged; *antonyms* (*adj*) smooth, even, **2**. craggy; *synonyms* (*adj*) cragged, rocky, cliffy, hilly, jagged, broken, **3**. bumpy; *synonyms* (*adj*) jolty, asymmetrical, bouncing, bouncy, coarse, eroded, furrowed, itchy, jarring, jolting, jumpy, lopsided, painful, pitted, potholed; *antonym* (*adj*) flat, **4**. lumpy; *synonyms* (*adj*) chunky, dull, dumpy, gawky, gritty, indolent, rude, squat, squatty, stumpy, (*v*) lumpish, (*n*) failure, **5**. cragged; *synonyms* (*adj*) mountainous, (*n*) austere, boisterous, crabbed, frowning, hard, inclement, severe, sour, stormy, surly, tempestuous, tumultuous, turbulent, violent, **6**. rough; *synonyms* (*adj*) raw, crude, cruel, grating, gross, hoarse, approximate, gruff, indelicate, impolite, robust, abrasive, bluff, blunt, (*n*) draft; *antonyms* (*adj*) gentle, polished, precise, refined, silky, soft, sophisticated, exact, glossy, pleasant, **7**. rugged; *synonyms* (*adj*) difficult, hardy, strong, sturdy, tough, firm, shaggy, perverse, refractory, bitter, knotty, rigorous, rigid, stalwart, abrupt; *antonym* (*adj*) delicate, **8**. uneven; *synonyms* (*adj*) unequal, erratic, patchy, spotty, disproportionate, unbalanced, variable, changeable, disparate, mismatched, partial, wobbly; *antonyms* (*adj*) straight, equal, symmetrical.

kiribwebwe 1. inseparable; *synonyms* (*adj*) indivisible, inherent, built-in, close, essential, inborn, inbred, indiscerptible, indispensable, innate, inseverable, tenacious, thick, (*v*) severable, united; *antonym* (*adj*) divisible, **2**. intimate; *synonyms* (*adj*) confidential, informal, inner, internal, bosom, (*v*) express, allude, hint, imply, indicate, insinuate, suggest, (*n*) familiar, confidante, (*adv*) dear; *antonym* (*adj*) distant, **3**. close; *synonyms* (*adj*) near, adjacent, nearby, accurate, tight, approximate, narrow, (*v*) compact, stop, conclude, (*adv*) by, about, (*n*) end, finish, conclusion; *antonyms* (*adj*) airy, fresh, loose, far, (*v*) open, start, **4**. confidential; *synonyms* (*adj*) classified, private, secret, clandestine, intimate, privileged, closet, hidden, inward, personal, privy, undercover; *antonym* (*adj*) public, **5.** together; *synonyms* (*adv*) jointly, conjointly, simultaneously, collectively, running, (*adj*) composed, stable, whole; *antonyms* (*adv*) individually, separately, independently, (*adj*) separate.

kiriin green; *synonyms* (*adj*) fresh, callow, immature, emerald, jealous, raw, young, youthful, crude, envious, grassy, gullible, inexperienced, juvenile, (*n*) lawn; *antonym* (*adj*) experienced.

kirikakang spiked; *synonyms* (*adj*) pointed, laced, thorny, sharp, acute, altered, firm, jagged, tied.

kirikaki 1. mend; *synonyms* (*v*) repair, improve, correct, cure, amend, better, doctor, heal, restore, convalesce, ameliorate, bushel, (*n*) fix, patch, botch; *antonym* (*v*) break, **2.** fix; *synonyms* (*v*) establish, assign, determine, fasten, settle, define, anchor, adjust, arrange, set, clamp, (*n*) bind, (*adj*) ascertain, confirm, attach; *antonym* (*v*) unfasten.

kirikakiaki fixed; *synonyms* (*adj*) determined, definite, steady, constant, durable, certain, decided, determinate, established, fast, fastened, intent, permanent, (*v*) stable, (*adv*) firm; *antonyms* (*adj*) flexible, adaptable, adjustable, changeable, movable, separate, variable, compliant, loose, moveable, portable, removable, temporary.

kiriman 1. industrious; *synonyms* (*adj*) active, diligent, assiduous, indefatigable, busy, energetic, hardworking, laborious, tireless, earnest, enterprising, careful, painstaking, sedulous, studious; *antonym* (*adj*) lazy, **2.** clever; *synonyms* (*adj*) adroit, capable, acute, able, apt, intelligent, smart, astute, cunning, expert, ingenious, quick, sharp, skillful, (*v*) brilliant; *antonyms* (*adj*) stupid, clumsy, unintelligent, dim, dull, inept, **3.** resourceful; *synonyms* (*adj*) inventive, clever, creative, imaginative, original; *antonym* (*adj*) unimaginative.

kirimanga 1. complex; *synonyms* (*adj*) composite, complicate, abstruse, difficult, elaborate, intricate, knotty, abstract, tricky, multifarious, complicated, compound, convoluted, (*n*) obsession, combination; *antonyms* (*adj*) simple, basic, straightforward, clear, plain, **2.** forked; *synonyms* (*adj*) bifurcate, branched, branching, bifurcated, biramous, double, furcated, tined, forky, anchored, angular, bivalent, cross, crotched, doubled, **3.** entangled; *synonyms* (*adj*) involved, embroiled, complex, foul, matted, tangled; *antonym* (*adj*) free, **4.** deep; *synonyms* (*adj*) thick, profound, absorbed, broad, dark, rich, sound, strong, wide, esoteric, bright, large, abysmal, bass, (*v*) intense; *antonyms* (*adj*) shallow, superficial, high, high-pitched, light, soft, weak, **5.** abstract; *synonyms* (*adj*) theoretical, academic, (*v*) abridge, filch, extract, lift, (*n*) synopsis, abridgement, digest, epitome, summary, abridgment, brief, outline,

precis; *antonym* (*adj*) concrete, **6.** branched; *synonyms* (*adj*) forked, ramose, ramous, divided, cleft, pronged, prongy, ramate, ramigerous, split, forficate, **7.** complicated; *synonyms* (*adj*) hard, awkward, deep, obscure, sophisticated, tortuous, circuitous, detailed, indirect; *antonym* (*adj*) easy.

kirimaruarua pitted; *synonyms* (*adj*) honeycombed, pockmarked, alveolate, cavitied, faveolate, hollow, bicched, foveate, notched, pecked, rutted, scrobiculated, bumpy, eroded, uneven.

kirimotimoti 1. lacerated; *synonyms* (*adj*) lacerate, torn, rent, blasted, hurt, mangled, mutilated, **2.** mangled; *synonyms* (*adj*) lacerated, deformed, disabled, broken, crippled, distorted, maimed, confused, corrupted, jumbled, muddled, ripped, **3.** broken; *synonyms* (*v*) broke, (*adj*) tame, busted, imperfect, intermittent, rough, rugged, ruined, uneven, disjointed, incomplete, cracked, crushed, disconnected, discontinuous; *antonyms* (*adj*) constant, unbroken, intact, whole, wild, **4.** mutilated; *synonyms* (*adj*) truncated, defective, mutilate, mutilous, shapeless, **5.** shredded; *synonyms* (*adj*) sliced, chopped, ragged, (*adv*) asunder, **6.** slashed; *synonyms* (*adj*) cut, gashed, cheap, down, emasculated, fringed, gelded, laciniated, low, mown, shortened, strikeout, laciniate, thinned, trimmed, **7.** torn; *synonym* (*adj*) tattered; *antonym* (*adj*) pristine.

kirimoumou 1. confused; *synonyms* (*adj*) abashed, bewildered, baffled, befuddled, bemused, chaotic, confounded, disjointed, disordered, dizzy, incoherent, indistinct, ambiguous, (*n*) cloudy, (*adv, adj*) topsy-turvy; *antonyms* (*adj*) clear, enlightened, alert, clearheaded, clear-headed, orderly, **2.** epileptic; *synonym* (*adj*) epileptical.

kirinaki 1. abundant; *synonyms* (*adj*) copious, generous, lush, luxuriant, thick, plenty, affluent, ample, fertile, fruitful, liberal, plentiful, prolific, rich, substantial; *antonyms* (*adj*) scarce, sparse, meager, **2.** copious; *synonyms* (*adj*) abundant, bountiful, plenteous, much, diffuse, full, large, lavish, many, profuse, voluminous, overflowing, big, great, diffusive; *antonym* (*adj*) small.

kirinikamate 1. headstrong; *synonyms* (*adj*) intractable, obstinate, stubborn, disobedient, froward, rash, unruly, wayward, willful, headlong, contumacious, heady, inflexible, mulish, (*v*) ungovernable; *antonym* (*adj*) biddable, **2.** furious; *synonyms* (*adj*) angry, fierce, violent, enraged, ferocious, frantic, vehement, wild, boisterous, frenzied, infuriated, raging, rampant, desperate, angered; *antonym* (*adj*) calm, **3.** obstinate; *synonyms* (*adj*) headstrong, obdurate, determined, inveterate, contrary, dogged, firm, uncompromising, cussed, defiant, insistent, persistent, perverse, refractory, resolute; *antonyms* (*adj*) compliant, amenable, flexible.

kiriongong 1. reel; *synonyms* (n) bobbin, coil, roll, spool, (v) lurch, rock, spin, stagger, totter, waver, teeter, falter, fluctuate, dance, gyrate, **2**. stagger; *synonyms* (v) astonish, startle, flabbergast, flounder, hobble, reel, shake, shock, pitch, amaze, dumbfound, stun, surprise, astound, (adj) bewilder, **3**. numb; *synonyms* (adj) asleep, benumbed, dead, dull, insensible, torpid, deadened, callous, impassive, comatose, inactive, inert, (v) benumb, deaden, (n) blunt; *antonym* (adj) sensitive, **4**. stupefied; *synonyms* (adj) dazed, stunned, amazed, astonished, bewildered, astounded, dumbfounded, stupid, confused, dumfounded, flabbergasted, groggy.

kiriringng 1. gamble; *synonyms* (n) bet, hazard, game, speculation, (v) chance, risk, wager, stake, adventure, venture, **2**. caper; *synonyms* (n) prank, skip, hop, joke, play, antic, gambol, spring, trick, (v) bound, dance, frolic, leap, romp, jump, **3**. frolic; *synonyms* (n) sport, caper, diversion, fun, joy, merriment, mirth, revel, entertainment, amusement, recreation, (v) cavort, disport, frisk, lark.

kirirnang 1. frolicsome; *synonyms* (adj) playful, frisky, frolic, waggish, coltish, gay, rollicking, frolicky, airy, gleeful, jocular, jolly, kittenish, lighthearted, lively, **2**. zany; *synonyms* (adj) wacky, foolish, silly, clownish, crazy, fool, ridiculous, daft, (n) buffoon, clown, fathead, jackass, joker, nincompoop, badaud, **3**. waggish; *synonyms* (adj) facetious, humorous, jocose, funny, comical, comic, droll, sportive, witty, arch.

kiritabaiore 1. stagger; *synonyms* (v) falter, astonish, lurch, startle, flabbergast, flounder, hobble, reel, shake, shock, pitch, amaze, dumbfound, stun, (adj) bewilder, **2**. zigzag; *synonyms* (n) ankle, astragal, crane, crotch, (v) meander, wind, bend, indirect, twist, crank, (adj) forked, furcated, meandering, winding, bifurcate; *antonym* (adj) straight, **3**. ramble; *synonyms* (n) journey, stroll, excursion, hike, promenade, walk, amble, (v) roam, saunter, wander, range, rove, tramp, digress, gad.

kiritabaniban preceding; *synonyms* (adj) antecedent, anterior, foregoing, former, previous, prior, past, precedent, prevenient, old, ancient, older, (adv) earlier, forward, (prep) before; *antonyms* (adj) subsequent, following.

kiritababa 1. deviate; *synonyms* (v) depart, deflect, stray, vary, digress, diverge, swerve, warp, shift, turn, wander, bend, differ, divert, (adj) deviant; *antonym* (v) conform, **2**. stagger; *synonyms* (v) falter, astonish, lurch, startle, flabbergast, flounder, hobble, reel, shake, shock, pitch, amaze, dumbfound, stun, (adj) bewilder, **3**. swerve; *synonyms* (v) deviate, sheer, veer, slew, swing, alternate, recoil, skid, slant, wind, chop, (n) curve, yaw, swerving, veering, **4**. sheer; *synonyms*

(adj) absolute, pure, mere, bold, diaphanous, filmy, gauzy, gossamer, simple, steep, transparent, regular, (n) complete, perfect, entire; *antonyms* (adj) gentle, thick.

kiritantan 1. lace; *synonyms* (n) edging, lacing, net, galloon, (v) braid, enlace, entwine, interlace, bind, rope, tie, knot, tat, knit, (adj) string, **2**. marked; *synonyms* (adj) distinct, conspicuous, noticeable, pronounced, remarkable, distinguished, apparent, definite, notable, obvious, signal, striking, strong, clear, appreciable; *antonyms* (adj) plain, unblemished, **3**. mottled; *synonyms* (adj) dappled, motley, speckled, multicolored, piebald, spotted, variegated, mixed, **4**. dotted; *synonyms* (adj) specked, dashed, stippled, scattered, flecked, freckled, freckly, marked, blemished, covered, patterned, splashed, spread, sprinkled, streaked, **5**. spotted; *synonyms* (v) mildewed, moldy, rusty, (adj) mottled, blotchy, dotted, flyblown, dirty, spotty, stained, tainted, besmirched, damaged, patched, **6**. speckled.

kiritantanaki laced; *synonyms* (adj) tied, drunk, even, fastened, spiked, trussed.

kiritibutibu 1. bloat; *synonyms* (v) balloon, bulge, distend, expand, inflate, swell, billow; *antonym* (v) deflate, **2**. bloated; *synonyms* (adj) puffy, swollen, distended, inflated, turgid, proud, pompous, puffed, tumescent, tumid; *antonym* (adj) wasted, **3**. puffed; *synonyms* (adj) bloated, puff, bepuffed, bombastic, bouffant, conceited, declamatory, egotistic, egotistical, erect, flooding, huffing, large, lordly, orotund, **4**. swollen; *synonyms* (adj) high, bulging, enlarged, expanded, mighty, overflowing, (v) blown.

kiritibutibuaki bloated; *synonyms* (adj) puffy, swollen, distended, inflated, turgid, proud, pompous, puffed, tumescent, tumid; *antonym* (adj) wasted.

kiritoatoa 1. multifaceted; *synonyms* (adj) versatile, complex, composite, multifarious, multiple, profound, compound, comprehensive, exceptional, intricate, meaningful, multilateral, multipart, multitalented, mysterious; *antonym* (adj) simple, **2**. polyhedral; *synonym* (adj) polyhedrous.

kiritongitong 1. dizzy; *synonyms* (adj) dazed, giddy, faint, frivolous, light, silly, vertiginous, featherbrained, flighty, muzzy, unsteady, airheaded, woozy, (v) daze; *antonyms* (adj) alert, clear-headed, **2**. dazed; *synonyms* (adj) confused, bewildered, stunned, dizzy, dumbfounded, stupefied, amazed, astounded, bleary, groggy, stupid, **3**. dumbfounded; *synonyms* (adj) astonished, staggered, speechless, flabbergasted, **4**. stunned; *synonyms* (adj) astonied, shocked, surprised, kayoed, out, unconscious, **5**. stupefied; *synonym* (adj) dumfounded.

kiriuatao 1. close; *synonyms* (*adj*) near, adjacent, nearby, accurate, tight, approximate, narrow, (*v*) compact, stop, conclude, (*adv*) by, about, (*n*) end, finish, conclusion; *antonyms* (*adj*) distant, airy, fresh, loose, far, (*v*) open, start, **2.** heaped; *synonyms* (*adj*) piled, coacervate, collective, cumulative, dense, thick, cumulous, **3.** compact; *synonyms* (*adj*) close, compendious, concise, hard, solid, (*n*) agreement, arrangement, contract, covenant, bargain, engagement, (*v*) compress, condense, consolidate, pack; *antonyms* (*adj*) sprawling, bulky, sparse, **4.** layered; *synonyms* (*adj*) lamellated, caked, coated, covered, encrusted, lamellar, lamelliform, superimposed, overlying, **5.** serried; *synonyms* (*adj*) packed, serrated, (*v*) swarming, teeming, thickset, **6.** piled; *synonyms* (*adj*) heaped, aggregate, pointed.

kiriuous paired; *synonyms* (*adj*) double, mated, opposite, dual, twin, complementary, matching.

kiriwaka 1. fibrous; *synonyms* (*adj*) stringy, tough, ropy, brawny, fibry, gossamer, hempen, muscular, nemaline, raw, rubbery, sinewy, unchewable, wiry, coarse; *antonym* (*adj*) tender, **2.** stringy; *synonyms* (*adj*) fibrous, glutinous, filamentous, tenacious, thready, lean, resisting, ropey, sequacious.

kiriwantanta spotted; *synonyms* (*adj*) mottled, dappled, speckled, blotchy, dotted, flyblown, piebald, multicolored, dirty, spotty, stained, tainted, besmirched, damaged, freckled; *antonym* (*adj*) plain.

kiriwea riot; *synonyms* (*n*) revolt, disturbance, commotion, disorder, insurrection, mutiny, sedition, tumult, rebellion, brawl, fight, (*v*) rebel, carouse, (*adj*) hubbub, uproar.

kiriweswe struggle; *synonyms* (*n*) contest, battle, combat, conflict, strain, effort, exertion, scramble, scuffle, (*v*) fight, attempt, dispute, endeavor, labor, quarrel; *antonyms* (*v*) flourish, glide.

kirmatamata 1. familiar; *synonyms* (*adj*) close, common, conversant, customary, everyday, intimate, commonplace, easy, ordinary, usual, (*n*) accustomed, companion, comrade, habitual, (*v*) confidential; *antonyms* (*adj*) unfamiliar, foreign, strange, new, unaccustomed, formal, ignorant, unknown, **2.** impudent; *synonyms* (*adj*) forward, audacious, brassy, disrespectful, impertinent, barefaced, daring, brazen, insolent, brash, cheeky, fresh, saucy, cool, (*n*) bold; *antonym* (*adj*) respectful, **3.** free; *synonyms* (*adj*) loose, frank, liberal, (*v*) clear, exempt, liberate, discharge, excuse, extricate, relieve, disentangle, acquit, deliver, disengage, ease; *antonyms* (*adj*) bound, restricted, compelled, confined, imprisoned, repressive, secure, strict, stuck, tangled, attached, busy, (*v*) confine, block, cage, **4.** shameless; *synonyms* (*adj*) immodest, graceless, depraved, profligate, blatant, unscrupulous, abandoned, impudent, indecent, obscene, unblushing, dissolute, immoral, lewd, reprobate.

kirmrim bunched; *synonyms* (*adj*) agglomerate, agglomerated, agglomerative, bunchy, clustered, compact.

kiro 1. faint; *synonyms* (*adj*) collapse, dim, dizzy, feeble, indistinct, weak, dull, gentle, soft, vague, delicate, distant, (*v*) languish, swoon, droop; *antonyms* (*adj*) distinct, strong, clear, obvious, considerable, loud, pungent, **2.** distant; *synonyms* (*adj*) cold, aloof, remote, chill, cool, detached, far, reserved, long, faraway, icy, indifferent, removed, (*adv*) apart, (*n*) chilly; *antonyms* (*adj*) close, adjacent, friendly, near, nearby, neighboring, warm, pending, alert, intimate, involved, **3.** insensible; *synonyms* (*adj*) callous, imperceptible, numb, unconscious, unfeeling, apathetic, impassive, indiscernible, unaware, comatose, inert, ignorant, oblivious, insensate, insensitive; *antonym* (*adj*) sensible, **4.** swoon; *synonyms* (*n*) fainting, syncope, deliquium, lipothymy, prostration, (*v*) faint, conk, die, (*adj*) blow, drop, gasp, pant, puff, **5.** slumber; *synonyms* (*n*) rest, doze, nap, snooze, catnap, siesta, (*v*) sleep, drowse, repose, kip.

kiruatao 1. heaped; *synonyms* (*adj*) piled, coacervate, collective, cumulative, dense, thick, cumulous, **2.** piled; *synonyms* (*adj*) heaped, aggregate, pointed, **3.** stacked; *synonyms* (*adj*) buxom, curvaceous, prepared, shapely, voluptuous.

kitaina stain; *synonyms* (*n*) spot, blemish, blot, mark, smear, dirt, brand, (*v*) color, dye, tarnish, disgrace, soil, defile, blur, contaminate.

kitainaki stained; *synonyms* (*adj*) besmirched, spotted, dirty, sullied, tainted, tarnished, black, damaged, discolored, flyblown, painted, (*v*) polluted; *antonyms* (*adj*) pure, unspoiled.

kitana 1. leave; *synonyms* (*v*) depart, forsake, go, abandon, desert, quit, escape, flee, lead, (*n*) furlough, holiday, permission, permit, break, (*adj*) empty; *antonyms* (*v*) arrive, enter, stay, remain, approach, change, come, **2.** desert; *synonyms* (*n*) wilderness, (*v*) defect, ditch, leave, relinquish, abscond, fail, maroon, (*adj*) waste, barren, desolate, merit, wild, worth, bleak; *antonym* (*n*) bog, **3.** abandon; *synonyms* (*v*) renounce, resign, vacate, evacuate, waive, abdicate, chuck, drop, forfeit, forgo, scrap, surrender, yield, strand, (*n*) candor; *antonyms* (*v*) keep, support, maintain, (*n*) restraint, **4.** left; *synonyms* (*adj*) gone, absent, odd, port, remaining, larboard, sinister, unexpended, abandoned, remainder, corrupt, deserted, disastrous, dishonest, evil; *antonym* (*n*) right, **5.** evacuate; *synonyms* (*v*) deplete, void, discharge, clear, drain, displace, eject, eliminate, pass, annul, nullify, excrete, exhaust, expel, (*adj*) emit, **6.** renounce; *synonyms* (*v*) abjure, disclaim, deny, disown, reject, decline, forego, forswear, recant, repudiate, discard, cede, disavow, refuse, retract, **7.** quit; *synonyms* (*v*) part, cease, discontinue, end, desist, exit, free, halt, stop, withdraw, move, finish, secede, (*n*) release, resignation; *antonym* (*v*) continue, **8.** relinquish; *synonyms* (*v*) concede, give, deliver, allow, grant, consign, let, refrain, render, retire, spare, submit, foreswear, reach; *antonym* (*v*) retain.

kitanaki 1. deserted; *synonyms* (*adj*) abandoned, desert, solitary, bleak, derelict, desolate, empty, forsaken, isolated, lonely, lonesome, vacant, alone, secluded, (*v*) forlorn; *antonyms* (*adj*) inhabited, occupied, packed, **2.** evacuated; *synonyms* (*adj*) annulled, emptied, voided, invalidated, **3.** forlorn; *synonyms* (*adj*) desperate, despairing, hopeless, deserted, disconsolate, miserable, unhappy, downcast, cheerless, abject, comfortless, dejected, despondent, gloomy, inconsolable; *antonyms* (*adj*) cheerful, happy, hopeful, **4.** abandoned; *synonyms* (*adj*) immoral, profligate, shameless, stranded, wicked, corrupt, debauched, depraved, discarded, dissipated, dissolute, licentious, loose, neglected, reprobate; *antonyms* (*adj*) restrained, orderly, overcrowded, **5.** relinquished; *synonym* (*adj*) surrendered.

kitangitang whimper; *synonyms* (*n*) whine, cry, moan, (*v*) wail, sob, weep, howl, pule, snivel, groan, blubber, complain, mewl, sigh, bleat.

kite 1. hunt; *synonyms* (*n*) search, pursuit, quest, (*v*) chase, course, follow, hound, forage, rummage, prey, dog, persecute, pursue, seek, stalk, **2.** pursue; *synonyms* (*v*) hunt, prosecute, haunt, persist, tail, conduct, practice, court, keep, continue, engage, harass, shadow, trace, track, **3.** search; *synonyms* (*n*) examination, exploration, inquire, inquiry, inspection, study, hunting, investigation, (*v*) grope, ransack, pry, examine, explore, inspect, look.

kiteaki 1. hunted; *synonyms* (*adj*) coursed, required, sought, wanted, (*n*) victim, **2.** pursued; *synonym* (*n*) chased.

kiube cubic; *synonyms* (*adj*) solid, compact, dense, firm, genuine, hard, impenetrable, just, sound, stable, strong, unanimous, united, unyielding, valid.

kiubu 1. cube; *synonyms* (*n*) block, rhomboid, blockage, blocking, closure, quadrangle, quadrantal, rectangle, tetragon, interference, (*v*) dice, chop, multiply, triplicate, (*adj*) unworldly, **2.** cubic; *synonyms* (*adj*) solid, compact, dense, firm, genuine, hard, impenetrable, just, sound, stable, strong, unanimous, united, unyielding, valid.

kiura 1. irritable; *synonyms* (*adj*) angry, fractious, irascible, edgy, cantankerous, cross, disagreeable, excitable, grumpy, petulant, sensitive, touchy,

huffy, crabby, cranky; *antonyms* (*adj*) calm, easygoing, good-humored, good-natured, even-tempered, good-tempered, **2.** cantankerous; *synonyms* (*adj*) crotchety, irritable, moody, morose, peevish, quarrelsome, testy, prickly, stubborn, argumentative, captious, crusty, difficult, grouchy, ornery, **3.** irascible; *synonyms* (*adj*) fiery, choleric, hot, hotheaded, passionate, hasty, impatient, impetuous, acrimonious, inflammable, peppery, waspish, short, **4.** atrabilious; *synonyms* (*adj*) bilious, dyspeptic, atrabiliar, atrabilarious, atrabiliary, dejected, despairing, liverish, biliary, (*v*) melancholic, saturnine, hypochondriacal, hypped, jaundiced, lachrymose, **5.** fiery; *synonyms* (*adj*) ardent, burning, fervent, ablaze, fierce, fervid, flaming, glowing, impassioned, violent, combustible, blazing, torrid, (*n*) enthusiastic, (*v*) vehement; *antonym* (*adj*) mild, **6.** cross; *synonyms* (*n*) crisscross, affliction, check, crossing, (*v*) intersect, baffle, cover, thwart, bilk, dash, divide, ford, (*adj*) crabbed, traverse, annoyed; *antonym* (*v*) uncross, **7.** cranky; *synonyms* (*adj*) crank, tetchy, fretful, pettish, techy, tender, tortuous, (*v*) rickety, **8.** petulant; *synonyms* (*adj*) nettlesome, sullen, quick-tempered, perverse, pert, querulous, peckish, **9.** tempered; *synonyms* (*adj*) hardened, attempered, attemperate, elastic, enured, inured, proportioned, set, subdued, toughened, treated, tough.

kiwarawara 1. transparent; *synonyms* (*adj*) diaphanous, lucid, obvious, plain, luminous, filmy, limpid, sheer, crystalline, gauzy, pellucid, gossamer, apparent, (*n*) clear, bright; *antonyms* (*adj*) opaque, solid, **2.** pale; *synonyms* (*adj*) ghastly, faint, wan, dull, light, pallid, weak, watery, cadaverous, (*v*) dim, blanch, (*n*) boundary, confine, border, bound; *antonyms* (*adj*) dark, rosy, strong, brown, **3.** sallow; *synonyms* (*adj*) pale, pasty, bloodless, ashen, sickly, fair.

ko 1. compact; *synonyms* (*adj*) close, dense, compendious, concise, hard, (*n*) agreement, arrangement, contract, covenant, bargain, engagement, (*v*) compress, condense, consolidate, pack; *antonyms* (*adj*) loose, sprawling, bulky, sparse, **2.** close; *synonyms* (*adj*) near, adjacent, nearby, accurate, tight, approximate, narrow, (*v*) compact, stop, conclude, (*adv*) by, about, (*n*) end, finish, conclusion; *antonyms* (*adj*) distant, airy, fresh, far, (*v*) open, start, **3.** despite; *synonyms* (*prep*) notwithstanding, (*conj*) although, (*n*) spite, contempt, scorn, disdain, malice, **4.** if; *synonyms* (*conj*) provided, providing, whether, though, and, so, an, gin, (*n*) but, conditionally, condition, stipulation, proviso, rider, (*adv*) peradventure, **5.** though; *synonyms* (*conj*) nevertheless, still, whereas, while, (*adv*) even, tho', (*adj*) however, **6.** serried; *synonyms* (*adj*) packed, serrated, (*v*) swarming, teeming, thickset, **7.** the; *synonyms* (*n*) queenliness, stateliness, (v) thee, **8.** while; *synonyms* (conj) as, (n) spell, time, period, moment, interval, space, bit, piece, (prep) during, (adv) when, whilst, because, **9.** whereas; *synonyms* (conj) whenas, where, (adv) then, **10.** tight; *synonyms* (adj) firm, mean, parsimonious, taut, secure, snug, tense, drunk, miserly, rigorous, sparing, stiff, strict, (v) fast, stingy; *antonyms* (adj) baggy, generous, slack, wide, (adv) loosely, **11.** suppose; *synonyms* (v) believe, guess, infer, assume, conjecture, consider, divine, estimate, imagine, presume, reckon, speculate, calculate, conceive, expect.

koa 1. hurry; *synonyms* (n) speed, haste, dispatch, flurry, (v) bustle, hasten, accelerate, dash, expedite, scurry, fly, run, rush, zip, hie; *antonyms* (n) slowness, (v) dawdle, **2.** hasten; *synonyms* (v) further, forward, advance, hurry, dart, facilitate, precipitate, race, gallop, sprint, drive, hotfoot, (adj) quicken, course, go; *antonym* (v) delay, **3.** sharp; *synonyms* (adj) acute, bitter, intelligent, acid, acrid, harsh, incisive, intense, penetrating, piercing, pointed, pungent, quick, (n) keen, (v) biting; *antonyms* (adj) blunt, dull, mild, gentle, rounded, sweet, bland, blurred, naive, round, smooth.

koaki hurried; *synonyms* (adj) hasty, fast, headlong, quick, rapid, speedy, sudden, swift, abrupt, cursory, careless, precipitate, prompt, rash, slapdash; *antonyms* (adj) slow, unhurried, leisurely.

koanoa hand; *synonyms* (n) deal, aid, applause, employee, paw, worker, (v) deliver, give, pass, commit, bestow, afford, communicate, reach, grant.

koaua 1. arch; *synonyms* (n) arc, acute, bend, curvature, dome, archway, (v) curve, bow, vault, (adj) shrewd, sly, wily, round, crafty, consummate; *antonym* (v) straightness, **2.** genuine; *synonyms* (adj) actual, authentic, sincere, true, unsophisticated, candid, faithful, artless, factual, hearty, real, unaffected, unfeigned, very, absolute; *antonyms* (adj) bogus, fake, insincere, affected, artificial, dishonest, false, pretend, hypocritical, replica, **3.** affirmative; *synonyms* (adj) affirmatory, optimistic, positive, assertive, declaratory, predicatory, (adv) yes; *antonym* (n) negative, **4.** certain; *synonyms* (adj) definite, sure, assured, dependable, indisputable, reliable, categorical, decisive, fixed, inevitable, infallible, particular, perfect, safe, (v) bound; *antonyms* (adj) uncertain, doubtful, unsure, questionable, **5.** authentic; *synonyms* (adj) genuine, accurate, right, straight, believable, trustworthy, valid, credible, honest, natural, original, pure, veritable, convincing, (v) authoritative; *antonym* (adj) unrealistic, **6.** flatly; *synonyms* (adv) categorically, directly, evenly, plainly, smoothly, flat, blankly, completely, downright, totally, utterly, bluntly, deeply, dully, insipidly, **7.** absolutely; *synonyms* (adv) surely, dead, decidedly, definitely, entirely, exactly, fully,

just, precisely, purely, simply, thoroughly, (int) positively, certainly, (adj) really; *antonyms* (adv) partially, doubtfully, partly, **8.** true; *synonyms* (adj) even, correct, exact, truthful, direct, literal, loyal, precise, proper, rightful, substantial, sound, lawful, legitimate, (v) square; *antonyms* (adj) inaccurate, untrue, **9.** positive; *synonyms* (adj) certain, affirmative, confident, explicit, favorable, incontrovertible, peremptory, plus, advantageous, arbitrary, clear, constructive, decided, plain, total; *antonyms* (adj) derogatory, pessimistic, sad, **10.** sure; *synonyms* (adj) secure, firm, fast, guaranteed, indubitable, stable, unerring, unfailing, unwavering, hard, resolute, steadfast, incontestable, (v) steady, convinced; *antonym* (adj) hesitant, **11.** real; *synonyms* (adj) material, physical, concrete, native, good, tangible, essential, cordial, corporeal, effective, existent, frank, realistic, (adv) actually, rattling; *antonyms* (adj) unreal, imaginary, apparent, deceptive, fantasy, imitation, insubstantial, mock, nominal.

kobakoba empty; *synonyms* (adj) discharge, hollow, destitute, bare, blank, barren, abandoned, deserted, vain, (v) drain, clear, deplete, desolate, pour, spill; *antonyms* (adj) full, crowded, meaningful, packed, brimming, inhabited, occupied, swarming, cultivated, filled, laden, (v) fill.

kobu 1. gush; *synonyms* (n) flow, spout, burst, jet, effusion, rush, stream, surge, (v) flood, spurt, discharge, course, emanate, cascade, emit; *antonym* (v) trickle, **2.** bubble; *synonyms* (n) blister, bead, blob, (v) boil, babble, foam, burble, effervesce, fizz, froth, gurgle, seethe, churn, spray, simmer.

koburake 1. enrage; *synonyms* (v) anger, incense, aggravate, inflame, infuriate, irritate, exasperate, madden, provoke, enchafe, chafe, tease, displease, annoy, rile; *antonyms* (v) pacify, placate, **2.** overflow; *synonyms* (n) flood, deluge, inundation, excess, flooding, outpouring, runoff, torrent, affluence, (v) inundate, flow, drown, fill, overrun, submerge.

koburakea 1. gush; *synonyms* (n) flow, spout, burst, jet, effusion, rush, stream, surge, (v) flood, spurt, discharge, course, emanate, cascade, emit; *antonym* (v) trickle, **2.** enrage; *synonyms* (v) anger, incense, aggravate, inflame, infuriate, irritate, exasperate, madden, provoke, enchafe, chafe, tease, displease, annoy, rile; *antonyms* (v) pacify, placate, **3.** overflow; *synonyms* (n) deluge, inundation, excess, flooding, outpouring, runoff, torrent, affluence, flowage, (v) inundate, drown, fill, overrun, submerge, brim.

koburakeaki enraged; *synonyms* (adj) angry, angered, furious, infuriated, irate, incensed, livid, mad, exasperated, irritated, raging, boiling; *antonym* (adj) calm.

koburaken overflowing; *synonyms* (*v*) inundation, deluge, (*adj*) abundant, full, copious, exuberant, flooding, bountiful, generous, brimming, profuse, superfluous, afloat, ample, (*n*) flood; *antonym* (*adj*) empty.

koi grate; *synonyms* (*n*) lattice, (*v*) chafe, creak, grind, abrade, scrape, fret, gall, gnash, rub, aggravate, annoy, crunch, irritate, provoke.

koikoi grate; *synonyms* (*n*) lattice, (*v*) chafe, creak, grind, abrade, scrape, fret, gall, gnash, rub, aggravate, annoy, crunch, irritate, provoke.

koka drag; *synonyms* (*v*) attract, haul, draw, puff, trail, cart, hale, heave, lug, tow, delay, (*n*) pull, bother, bore, hindrance; *antonym* (*v*) push.

koko 1. full; *synonyms* (*adj*) complete, absolute, abundant, broad, flush, ample, enough, extensive, total, detailed, comprehensive, copious, good, (*n*) entire, crowded; *antonyms* (*adj*) empty, lacking, starving, hungry, sketchy, incomplete, 2. crow; *synonyms* (*n*) gasconade, crowing, bragging, (*v*) boast, brag, cackle, chuckle, cry, exult, triumph, bluster, giggle, gloat, (*adj*) raven, charcoal, 3. jealous; *synonyms* (*adj*) covetous, distrustful, envious, suspicious, resentful, invidious, green, grudging, 4. redundant; *synonyms* (*adj*) excessive, extra, needless, superfluous, excess, unnecessary, pleonastic, spare, surplus, wordy, additional, repetitious, pointless, exuberant, superabundant; *antonym* (*adj*) necessary, 5. scrape; *synonyms* (*v*) scratch, graze, rub, pare, rake, grate, mark, abrade, chafe, grind, claw, engrave, (*n*) score, abrasion, predicament, 6. stocked; *synonym* (*adj*) full.

kokoa grate; *synonyms* (*n*) lattice, (*v*) chafe, creak, grind, abrade, scrape, fret, gall, gnash, rub, aggravate, annoy, crunch, irritate, provoke.

kokoaki scraped; *synonyms* (*adj*) abraded, scratched, frayed, hurt, raw, skinned, threadbare, worn, shabby, tattered.

kokoi shrink; *synonyms* (*v*) dwindle, flinch, recoil, contract, shorten, cower, decrease, diminish, lessen, quail, reduce, wince, decline, cringe, (*n*) analyst; *antonyms* (*v*) expand, increase, enlarge.

kokona prey; *synonyms* (*n*) chase, game, plunder, victim, quarry, raven, target, mark, capture, booty, (*v*) feed, eat, ravage, pasture; *antonym* (*n*) hunter.

kokoni 1. gathered; *synonyms* (*adj*) collected, deepened, accumulated, amassed, assembled, collective, congregate, equanimous, massed, poised, 2. shrivel; *synonyms* (*v*) shrink, contract, wither, dwindle, fade, narrow, scorch, blight, blast, dry, parch, reduce, wilt, wrinkle, decrease, 3. shrink; *synonyms* (*v*) flinch, recoil, shorten, cower, diminish, lessen, quail, wince, decline, cringe, shrivel, blench, condense, abridge, (*n*) analyst; *antonyms* (*v*) expand, increase, enlarge.

kokotaia miser; *synonyms* (*n*) churl, curmudgeon, hunks, muckworm, niggard, skinflint, accumulator, collector, magpie, muckerer, pickpenny, pinchfist, saver, scrapepenny, snudge.

kom 1. hide; *synonyms* (*v*) conceal, disguise, obscure, bury, cloak, mask, shelter, (*n*) cover, fur, coat, fell, skin, veil, cloud, (*adj*) darken; *antonyms* (*v*) reveal, show, expose, express, 2. cease; *synonyms* (*v*) end, break, quit, stop, terminate, abstain, close, conclude, discontinue, drop, desist, expire, halt, (*n*) finish, (*adj*) abate; *antonyms* (*v*) continue, begin, 3. miss; *synonyms* (*v*) lack, lose, fail, jump, omit, overlook, long, escape, neglect, (*n*) maid, girl, want, fille, missy, (*adj*) fault; *antonym* (*v*) perceive, 4. escape; *synonyms* (*v*) elude, dodge, avoid, evade, run, bolt, circumvent, leave, duck, bilk, abscond, (*n*) leak, avoidance, evasion, outlet; *antonyms* (*v*) capture, return, 5. shorten; *synonyms* (*v*) condense, abbreviate, reduce, abridge, clip, curtail, cut, contract, compress, dock, diminish, lessen, prune, summarize, trim; *antonyms* (*v*) lengthen, expand.

komaki 1. adhesive; *synonyms* (*adj*) tacky, clingy, gummy, sticky, tenacious, agglutinative, gluey, glutinous, gooey, pasty, (*n*) cement, glue, paste, gum, (*v*) cohesive; *antonym* (*adj*) nonadhesive, 2. missed; *synonyms* (*adj*) lost, baffled, befuddled, bemused, bewildered, confounded, confused, disoriented, forgotten, helpless, irretrievable, mazed, preoccupied, 3. escaped; *synonyms* (*v*) escaping, (*adj*) free, loose, easy, runaway, wild, fugitive, idle, informal, lax, liberal, light, open, promiscuous, slack, 4. shortened; *synonyms* (*adj*) abbreviated, abridged, cut, short, curtailed, abbreviate, brief, down, emasculated, gashed, gelded, imperfect, less, mown, partial; *antonym* (*adj*) complete.

komatangitang 1. miserly; *synonyms* (*adj*) stingy, mean, close, parsimonious, closefisted, grasping, avaricious, measly, mingy, penurious, tight, greedy, cheap, covetous, (*adv*) ungenerous; *antonym* (*adj*) generous, 2. excessive; *synonyms* (*adj*) inordinate, exaggerated, intense, enormous, exorbitant, extravagant, extreme, exuberant, immoderate, profuse, superfluous, undue, unreasonable, huge, lavish; *antonyms* (*adj*) reasonable, moderate, affordable.

komau 1. miserly; *synonyms* (*adj*) stingy, mean, close, parsimonious, closefisted, grasping, avaricious, measly, mingy, penurious, tight, greedy, cheap, covetous, (*adv*) ungenerous; *antonym* (*adj*) generous, 2. stringy; *synonyms* (*adj*) ropy, tough, wiry, muscular, fibrous, sinewy, glutinous, brawny, filamentous, tenacious, thready, lean, resisting, ropey, sequacious; *antonym* (*adj*) tender.

komua comb; *synonyms* (*n*) cockscomb, combing, crest, (*v*) brush, ransack, search, dress, groom, rake, scour, (*adj*) weed.

kon 1. contract; *synonyms* (*n*) compact, charter, (*v*) covenant, bargain, concentrate, condense, narrow, catch, compress, constrict, shrink, wrinkle, abbreviate, (*adj*) abridge, shorten; *antonyms* (*v*) expand, widen, stretch, **2**. contracted; *synonyms* (*v*) shrunk, (*adj*) insular, contract, constricted, tight, bound, **3**. disappointed; *synonyms* (*adj*) defeated, disgruntled, regretful, depressed, dissatisfied, frustrated, sad, unhappy, disenchanted; *antonyms* (*adj*) delighted, pleased, composed, satisfied, **4**. retire; *synonyms* (*v*) recede, resign, leave, retreat, withdraw, abdicate, ebb, adjourn, depart, go, quit, remove, return, secede, regrade, **5**. retired; *synonyms* (*v*) covert, (*adj*) private, obscure, emeritus, secluded, secret, sequestered, solitary, lonely, withdrawn, close, superannuated, isolated, old, out.

kona 1. able; *synonyms* (*adj*) capable, clever, competent, dexterous, accomplished, adroit, consummate, effective, expert, fit, gifted, ingenious, endowed, (*n*) efficient, talented; *antonyms* (*adj*) incapable, incompetent, inept, unable, untrained, weak, **2**. adapted; *synonyms* (*v*) convenient, (*adj*) altered, agreeable, appropriate, conformable, fitted, prepared; *antonyms* (*adj*) mass-produced, unaccustomed, **3**. fit; *synonyms* (*v*) agree, accommodate, meet, suit, adapt, correspond, square, accord, dress, (*adj*) decorous, apt, applicable, (*n*) adjust, convulsion, attack; *antonyms* (*adj*) unfit, inappropriate, unwell, **4**. can; *synonyms* (*v*) tin, dismiss, fire, might, pickle, pot, sack, (*n*) bathroom, behind, buttocks, container, lavatory, posterior, rump, jar; *antonym* (*v*) hire, **5**. may; *synonyms* (*v*) can, could, get, acquire, aim, amaze, arrest, arrive, baffle, beat, become, beget, begin, bewilder, bring, **6**. apt; *synonyms* (*adj*) apropos, apposite, intelligent, good, able, adequate, ready, smart, deft, disposed, fitting, happy, just, liable, likely, **7**. press; *synonyms* (*n*) jam, closet, (*v*) crush, crowd, force, squeeze, pack, coerce, compress, exhort, mash, push, urge, clasp, (*adj*) constrain, **8**. squeeze; *synonyms* (*v*) hug, pinch, embrace, extort, cram, nip, squash, compact, condense, constrict, oppress, contract, cuddle, (*n*) press, grip; *antonym* (*v*) loosen, **9**. worthy; *synonyms* (*adj*) noble, estimable, meritorious, respectable, valuable, deserving, honorable, suitable, virtuous, worthwhile, admirable, desirable, (*n*) celebrity, notable, personage; *antonym* (*adj*) unworthy, **10**. probably; *synonyms* (*adv*) presumably, maybe, perhaps, belike, believably, credibly, apparently, possibly, plausibly, (*adj*) doubtless, like, **11**. powerful; *synonyms* (*adj*) cogent, brawny, forcible, hard, mighty, muscular, potent, strong, energetic,

influential, intense, lusty, vigorous, hardy, full; *antonyms* (*adj*) powerless, mild, **12**. suited; *synonyms* (*adj*) proper, adapted, eligible, useful, seemly, **13**. spring; *synonyms* (*n*) jump, leap, bound, fountain, skip, source, dance, rise, (*v*) hop, caper, bounce, dive, originate, recoil, (*adj*) elastic.

konaaki surrender; *synonyms* (*n*) resign, resignation, capitulation, release, (*v*) concede, relinquish, abandon, render, capitulate, deliver, submit, forsake, forfeit, leave, cede; *antonyms* (*v*) conquer, resist, appropriate, fight, persevere, subdue, win.

konaakiaki surrendered; *synonym* (*adj*) relinquished.

konaki 1. contracted; *synonyms* (*v*) shrunk, (*adj*) narrow, insular, contract, constricted, tight, bound, **2**. potential; *synonyms* (*adj*) likely, possible, prospective, latent, virtual, dormant, (*n*) capability, potency, ability, capacity, possibility, prospect, faculty, potentiality, power, **3**. pressed; *synonyms* (*adj*) compact, printed, pushed, stamped, driven, embossed, encouraged, impelled, imprinted, incited, marked, provoked, prompted, **4**. retired; *synonyms* (*v*) covert, (*adj*) private, obscure, emeritus, secluded, secret, sequestered, solitary, lonely, withdrawn, close, superannuated, isolated, old, out, **5**. possible; *synonyms* (*adj*) conceivable, imaginable, feasible, practicable, earthly, maybe, potential, practical, probable, thinkable, workable, attainable, believable, credible, eventual; *antonyms* (*adj*) impossible, unlikely, compulsory.

konamaki 1. depress; *synonyms* (*v*) push, dampen, deject, discourage, dishearten, chill, abase, demoralize, dismay, dispirit, lower, reduce, sadden, (*adj*) damp, degrade; *antonyms* (*v*) encourage, cheer, **2**. aware; *synonyms* (*adj*) awake, attentive, conscious, heedful, mindful, vigilant, sentient, alert, enlightened, knowing, knowledgeable, observant, sensible, wary, watchful; *antonyms* (*adj*) unaware, unconscious, **3**. alive; *synonyms* (*adj*) active, live, living, vivacious, animated, lively, responsive, aware, eager, acute, energetic, animate, extant, keen, quick; *antonyms* (*adj*) dead, deceased, inanimate, **4**. alert; *synonyms* (*adj*) agile, intelligent, clever, alive, bright, brisk, careful, cautious, discreet, nimble, prompt, ready, (*v*) caution, (*n*) alarm, alarum; *antonyms* (*adj*) drowsy, inattentive, absentminded, dazed, sleepy, tired, asleep, slow, unalert, **5**. active; *synonyms* (*adj*) busy, diligent, effective, strong, dynamic, forcible, healthy, mercurial, spirited, sprightly, vigorous, vivid, operational, hearty, (*v*) smart; *antonyms* (*adj*) dormant, inactive, sluggish, idle, latent, lethargic, sedentary, extinct, passive, quiet, **6**. exhaust; *synonyms* (*v*) consume, drain, spend, empty, tire, deplete, expend, sap, use, dry, debilitate, enervate, evacuate, (*adj*) waste, dissipate; *antonyms* (*v*) conserve, refresh, invigorate.

konamakiaki 1. exhausted; *synonyms* (v) weak, (adj) drained, fatigued, spent, tired, gone, dry, beat, depleted, empty, enervated, faint, jaded, weary, expended; *antonyms* (adj) energetic, fresh, refreshed, strong, **2.** depressed; *synonyms* (adj) concave, low, blue, dejected, dispirited, down, downcast, downhearted, gloomy, hollow, sad, crestfallen, disappointed, discouraged, flat; *antonyms* (adj) cheerful, happy, convex.

konana 1. capture; *synonyms* (v) bag, catch, take, apprehend, captivate, carry, ensnare, get, seize, bewitch, acquire, beguile, (n) arrest, seizure, apprehension; *antonyms* (v) release, surrender, **2.** abduct; *synonyms* (v) kidnap, snatch, abduce, ravish, crimp, steal, collar, nobble, seduce, abstract, bunco, cabbage, capture, con, defraud, **3.** kidnap; *synonyms* (n) abduction, (v) abduct, hook, filch, spirit, diddle, encourage, excite, goldbrick, gyp, inspirit, coax, decoy, entice, hold, **4.** ravish; *synonyms* (v) outrage, charm, delight, enrapture, rape, violate, defile, deflower, assault, enchant, enthral, enthrall, entrance, force, transport.

konanaki 1. abducted; *synonyms* (adj) kidnaped, kidnapped, **2.** kidnapped; *synonym* (adj) abducted.

konin 1. callous; *synonyms* (adj) heartless, insensible, unfeeling, relentless, brutal, cruel, hard, hardened, hardhearted, indifferent, insensitive, merciless, obdurate, pitiless, remorseless; *antonyms* (adj) kind, caring, merciful, compassionate, **2.** harden; *synonyms* (v) habituate, consolidate, inure, season, coagulate, congeal, freeze, petrify, solidify, anneal, ossify, (n) strengthen, brace, fortify, (adj) vitrify; *antonyms* (v) soften, liquefy, **3.** contract; *synonyms* (n) compact, charter, (v) covenant, bargain, concentrate, condense, narrow, catch, compress, constrict, shrink, wrinkle, abbreviate, (adj) abridge, shorten; *antonyms* (v) expand, widen, stretch, **4.** shrink; *synonyms* (v) dwindle, flinch, recoil, contract, cower, decrease, diminish, lessen, quail, reduce, wince, decline, cringe, shrivel, (n) analyst; *antonyms* (v) increase, enlarge.

koninaki 1. hardened; *synonyms* (adj) hard, callous, confirmed, tough, indurated, tempered, unfeeling, enured, habitual, inured, veteran, **2.** contracted; *synonyms* (v) shrunk, (adj) narrow, insular, contract, constricted, tight, bound, **3.** calloused; *synonym* (adj) thickened.

kontano innumerable; *synonyms* (adj) countless, incalculable, numberless, infinite, innumerous, multitudinous, unnumbered, myriad, numerous, uncounted, untold, incommensurable, incommensurate, many, unnumerable; *antonym* (adj) few.

koomwia comb; *synonyms* (n) cockscomb, combing, crest, (v) brush, ransack, search, dress, groom, rake, scour, (adj) weed.

kora 1. golden; *synonyms* (adj) aureate, fortunate, gilded, auspicious, gilt, gold, lucky, advantageous, fair, favorable, favored, **2.** big; *synonyms* (adj) ample, major, heavy, important, significant, thick, sturdy, generous, adult, bad, burly, considerable, great, hefty, (adv) large; *antonyms* (adj) little, puny, (adv) small, (syn) tiny, **3.** strong; *synonyms* (adj) intense, powerful, able, deep, firm, stable, steady, cogent, durable, forcible, good, hard, influential, lusty, potent; *antonyms* (adj) weak, bland, delicate, faint, feeble, frail, mild, pale, slight, unconvincing, cowardly, diluted, dull, exhausted, flimsy, **4.** vigorous; *synonyms* (adj) robust, strong, energetic, hardy, lively, strenuous, active, athletic, hearty, mighty, healthy, smart, brawny, (n) brave, (v) brisk; *antonyms* (adj) lethargic, unenergetic.

korabaia 1. corpulent; *synonyms* (adj) fat, obese, portly, stout, fleshy, overweight, plump, lusty, chubby, tubby, bulky, gross, rotund, round, weighty; *antonym* (adj) skinny, **2.** immense; *synonyms* (adj) huge, vast, colossal, enormous, gigantic, great, immeasurable, big, boundless, giant, infinite, large, endless, extensive, extreme; *antonyms* (adj) small, tiny, **3.** enormous; *synonyms* (adj) immense, excessive, exorbitant, prodigious, tremendous, stupendous, gargantuan, massive, monumental, terrific, terrible, flagrant, mammoth, mighty, monstrous; *antonyms* (adj) minute, insignificant, miniature, **4.** mammoth; *synonyms* (adj) jumbo, monster, **5.** monstrous; *synonyms* (adj) atrocious, grotesque, heinous, dreadful, flagitious, grievous, preposterous, ugly, fantastic, inordinate, abnormal, evil, horrible, outrageous, frightful, **6.** gigantic; *synonyms* (adj) gigantean, whopping, brawny, high, **7.** huge; *synonyms* (adj) elephantine, ample, considerable, heavy, untold, cavernous, cosmic, hefty, mountainous, roomy, substantial, wide, **8.** colossal; *synonym* (adj) formidable, **9.** stout; *synonyms* (adj) sturdy, bold, corpulent, hardy, husky, robust, stocky, strong, fearless, hearty, gallant, brave, burly, healthy, resolute; *antonyms* (adj) slender, slim, thin, flimsy.

koraki 1. blood; *synonyms* (n) ancestry, birth, gore, descent, family, kindred, lineage, origin, beau, bloodshed, consanguinity, coxcomb, exquisite, extraction, (adj) humor, **2.** kindred; *synonyms* (adj) cognate, akin, similar, allied, congenial, related, analogous, (n) kin, folk, folks, relation, blood, clan, (v) genealogy, house; *antonym* (n) unrelated, **3.** kin; *synonyms* (n) gender, stock, tribe, connection, kinsmen, affinity, kinfolk, kinsfolk, kinsperson, people, race, relations, relatives, sex, **4.** party; *synonyms* (n) gang, band, company, assembly, association, crew, gathering, group, affair, bevy, celebration, crowd, do, faction, meeting, **5.** relative; *synonyms* (adj) comparative, proportionate, proportional, dependent, relevant, (*n*) brother, congenator, congener, (*v*) kinsman; *antonym* (*adj*) absolute.

korakina belong; *synonyms* (*v*) appertain, pertain, go, lie, consist, dwell, rank, become, stand, vest, retain, accord, agree, associate, (*adj*) long.

korakora 1. corpulent; *synonyms* (*adj*) fat, obese, portly, stout, fleshy, overweight, plump, lusty, chubby, tubby, bulky, gross, rotund, round, weighty; *antonym* (*adj*) skinny, **2.** great; *synonyms* (*adj*) eminent, famous, gigantic, big, distinguished, extensive, extreme, grand, large, chief, ample, capital, celebrated, considerable, dignified; *antonyms* (*adj*) small, awful, insignificant, tiny, mild, **3.** hardy; *synonyms* (*adj*) courageous, sturdy, audacious, brave, fearless, hard, manly, strong, gallant, robust, forcible, doughty, (*n*) bold, daring, rugged; *antonym* (*adj*) weak, **4.** big; *synonyms* (*adj*) major, heavy, important, significant, thick, generous, adult, bad, burly, great, hefty, high, liberal, magnanimous, momentous; *antonyms* (*adj*) little, puny, **5.** violent; *synonyms* (*adj*) fierce, rough, tempestuous, intense, raging, severe, turbulent, vehement, sharp, passionate, powerful, savage, stormy, (*n*) furious, boisterous; *antonyms* (*adj*) gentle, peaceful, calm, nonviolent, **6.** vigorous; *synonyms* (*adj*) energetic, hardy, lively, strenuous, active, athletic, hearty, mighty, healthy, smart, brawny, muscular, animated, (*v*) brisk, fresh; *antonyms* (*adj*) feeble, lethargic, dull, unenergetic, **7.** powerful; *synonyms* (*adj*) cogent, able, potent, effective, influential, vigorous, full, deep, dominant, formidable, stiff, valid, convincing, husky, fit; *antonym* (*adj*) powerless, **8.** robust; *synonyms* (*adj*) firm, healthful, masculine, rich, stalwart, strapping, tough, hale, forceful, robustious, able-bodied, handsome, stable, (*n*) enduring; *antonyms* (*adj*) slight, fragile, frail, **9.** super; *synonyms* (*adj*) crack, ace, fabulous, marvelous, remarkable, sensational, superb, terrific, wonderful, fine, brilliant, hot, fantastic, (*n*) superintendent, (*adv*) extremely, **10.** reek; *synonyms* (*n*) smoke, stench, fetor, malodor, malodour, vapor, fumes, (*v*) fume, stink, emit, exhale, fumigate, smack, smell, (*adj*) gas, **11.** strong; *synonyms* (*adj*) steady, durable, good, rigid, secure, solid, sound, loud, persuasive, staunch, quick, pungent, sure, fiery, (*v*) steadfast; *antonyms* (*adj*) bland, delicate, faint, pale, unconvincing, cowardly, diluted, exhausted, flimsy, imperceptible, lightweight, soft, tired, watery, **12.** strict; *synonyms* (*adj*) stern, correct, accurate, austere, harsh, precise, rigorous, scrupulous, exacting, inflexible, meticulous, cruel, grim, (*v*) exact, close; *antonyms* (*adj*) lenient, free, lax, flexible, imprecise, negligent, relaxed, **13.** stout; *synonyms* (*adj*) corpulent, stocky, resolute,

thickset, bouncing, chunky, substantial, intrepid, tenacious, adamantine, heroic, valiant, (*n*) obstinate, beefy; *antonyms* (*adj*) slender, slim, thin.

korana 1. hero; *synonyms* (*n*) champion, character, leader, protector, worthy, protagonist, warrior, bomber, celebrity, combatant, conqueror, defender, fighter, **2.** master; *synonyms* (*n*) captain, instructor, head, boss, gentleman, (*v*) conquer, control, command, defeat, dominate, (*adj*) chief, original, ace, expert, proficient, **3.** champion; *synonyms* (*n*) advocate, backer, partisan, hero, champ, exponent, paladin, patron, supporter, upholder, (*v*) defend, support, back, maintain, uphold; *antonym* (*v*) oppose, **4.** corpulent; *synonyms* (*adj*) fat, obese, portly, stout, fleshy, overweight, plump, lusty, chubby, tubby, bulky, gross, rotund, round, weighty; *antonym* (*adj*) skinny, **5.** victor; *synonyms* (*n*) winner, master, superior; *antonym* (*n*) loser.

koranaki mastered; *synonyms* (*adj*) down, beaten, blue, cut, declining, depressed, dispirited, downcast, downhearted, low, tame, shut.

korea 1. cut; *synonyms* (*v*) carve, chop, clip, abbreviate, abridge, bite, condense, crop, drop, fashion, (*n*) notch, slice, cutting, nick, blow; *antonyms* (*v*) increase, lengthen, (*n*) addition, extension, **2.** slit; *synonyms* (*n*) crevice, breach, crack, gap, split, chink, cranny, fissure, (*v*) cut, rip, score, slash, scratch, gash, (*adj*) cleft, **3.** sliced; *synonyms* (*adj*) shredded, chopped, torn, **4.** slice; *synonyms* (*n*) share, part, section, bit, chip, morsel, piece, slab, chunk, portion, scrap, parcel, (*v*) lacerate, slit, mangle.

koreaki 1. cut; *synonyms* (*v*) carve, chop, clip, abbreviate, abridge, bite, condense, crop, drop, fashion, (*n*) notch, slice, cutting, nick, blow; *antonyms* (*v*) increase, lengthen, (*n*) addition, extension, **2.** sliced; *synonyms* (*adj*) shredded, chopped, torn, **3.** slit; *synonyms* (*n*) crevice, breach, crack, gap, split, chink, cranny, fissure, (*v*) cut, rip, score, slash, scratch, gash, (*adj*) cleft.

kori scratch; *synonyms* (*n*) score, mark, nick, scrabble, dent, abrasion, cut, groove, (*v*) graze, notch, rub, scrape, chafe, rake, grate.

koria 1. carve; *synonyms* (*v*) sculpture, cut, mold, engrave, incise, inscribe, shape, whittle, slash, deal, divide, etch, forge, form, mangle, **2.** cut; *synonyms* (*v*) carve, chop, clip, abbreviate, abridge, bite, condense, crop, drop, fashion, (*n*) notch, slice, cutting, nick, blow; *antonyms* (*v*) increase, lengthen, (*n*) addition, extension, **3.** incise; *synonyms* (*v*) scrape, scratch, hack, slit, incide, pierce, **4.** type; *synonyms* (*n*) pattern, character, kind, nature, sort, breed, category, stamp, brand, emblem, font, manner, print, style, (*adj*) model, **5.** write; *synonyms* (*v*) compose, indite, pen, correspond, compile, draw, publish, record, spell, outline, type, construct, create, frame, (n) copy.

koriaki 1. carved; *synonyms* (adj) carven, cut, incised, tipsy, (v) engraved, graven, fixed, imprinted, stamped, impressed, **2**. cut; *synonyms* (v) carve, chop, clip, abbreviate, abridge, bite, condense, crop, drop, fashion, (n) notch, slice, cutting, nick, blow; *antonyms* (v) increase, lengthen, (n) addition, extension, **3**. incised; *synonyms* (adj) etched, inscribed, sculpted, sculptured, **4**. typed; *synonym* (adj) typewritten, **5**. scratched; *synonyms* (adj) scraped, hurt, abraded, dented, injured, raw, sgraffito, spoiled, broken, skinned, smashed.

korira 1. weaned, **2**. weaning; *synonym* (n) ablactation.

koriria 1. affiliate; *synonyms* (n) member, chapter, (v) associate, ally, unite, adopt, assort, band, consort, join, **2**. comrade; *synonyms* (n) colleague, companion, chum, buddy, brother, compeer, fellow, mate, partner, familiar, friend, pal, cohort, confidante, (adj) accomplice.

koririaki affiliated; *synonyms* (adj) connected, united, attached, allied, related, (v) associated.

koririra wean; *synonyms* (v) estrange, alienate, disaffect, ablactate, clear, detach, disengage, disentangle, extricate, free, liberate, loose, raise, withdraw, (n) weanling.

korita 1. claw; *synonyms* (n) chela, hook, nipper, pincer, unguis, (v) clutch, lacerate, rip, scratch, seize, tear, **2**. scratch; *synonyms* (n) score, mark, nick, scrabble, dent, abrasion, cut, groove, (v) graze, notch, rub, scrape, chafe, rake, grate.

koritaki 1. clawed; *synonym* (adj) taloned, **2**. scratched; *synonyms* (adj) scraped, hurt, abraded, dented, injured, raw, sgraffito, spoiled, broken, skinned, smashed.

koro 1. finished; *synonyms* (v) done, (adj) complete, completed, ended, perfect, consummate, absolute, accomplished, polished, ripe, ruined, spent, round, capable, (adv) over; *antonyms* (adj) unfinished, incomplete, remaining, rough, **2**. cut; *synonyms* (v) carve, chop, clip, abbreviate, abridge, bite, condense, crop, drop, fashion, (n) notch, slice, cutting, nick, blow; *antonyms* (v) increase, lengthen, (n) addition, extension, **3**. complete; *synonyms* (adj) whole, full, stark, all, (v) accomplish, achieve, close, finish, execute, act, attain, cease, clear, conclude, effect; *antonyms* (adj) partial, abridged, shortened, sketchy, lacking, narrow, qualified, (v) neglect, **4**. accomplished; *synonyms* (adj) able, proficient, adept, experienced, finished, gifted, skillful, fine, clever, competent, concluded, cultured, effected, efficient, excellent; *antonym* (adj) inept, **5**. grounded; *synonyms* (v) aground, nonsuited, shipwrecked, swamped, wrecked, (adj) stranded, ashore, aware, beached, bottomed,

cognizant, confined, familiar, learned, stuck, **6**. aground; *synonyms* (adv) foundered, grounded.

koroaki cut; *synonyms* (v) carve, chop, clip, abbreviate, abridge, bite, condense, crop, drop, fashion, (n) notch, slice, cutting, nick, blow; *antonyms* (v) increase, lengthen, (n) addition, extension.

korobaiaki limited; *synonyms* (adj) finite, circumscribed, moderate, qualified, special, insular, bounded, narrow, scanty, slender, particular, specific, definite, conditional, constricted; *antonyms* (adj) boundless, infinite, limitless, open, complete, never-ending, unlimited, wide.

korobitia mangle; *synonyms* (n) destroy, (v) deface, lacerate, blemish, disfigure, distort, murder, twist, batter, damage, maul, mutilate, hack, (adj) maim, cripple.

korobitiaki mangled; *synonyms* (adj) torn, lacerated, deformed, mutilated, disabled, lacerate, broken, blasted, crippled, distorted, maimed, confused, corrupted, jumbled, (prep) rent.

koroboki 1. inscribe; *synonyms* (v) engrave, enroll, enter, imprint, dedicate, enlist, enrol, etch, grave, impress, mark, register, autograph, list, character, **2**. writ; *synonyms* (n) command, edict, injunction, order, act, agreement, expression, indictment, law, (v) communicate, (adj) brief, common, concise, epitome, prevalent, **3**. write; *synonyms* (v) compose, indite, pen, correspond, compile, draw, publish, record, spell, outline, type, construct, create, frame, (n) copy, **4**. written; *synonyms* (adj) scripted, registered, clerical, conscript, enrolled, hard-and-fast, literal, (n) examination; *antonym* (adj) spoken.

korobokiaki inscribed; *synonyms* (adj) engraved, etched, graven, incised, adorned, celebrated, decorated, extolled, sculpted, sculptured.

korobuai shave; *synonyms* (v) prune, clip, pare, reduce, scrape, cut, brush, chip, crop, shear, whittle, graze, mow, peel, (adj) lop.

korobuaiaki shaved; *synonyms* (adj) shaven, bald, hairless, scalped.

koroheina white; *synonyms* (adj) fair, ashen, blank, clean, snowy, wan, achromatic, bloodless, livid, pallid, colorless, bright, good, (n) pale, (v) whiten; *antonyms* (adj) dark, rosy, (n) black.

korokoro mangle; *synonyms* (n) destroy, (v) deface, lacerate, blemish, disfigure, distort, murder, twist, batter, damage, maul, mutilate, hack, (adj) maim, cripple.

korokoroaki mangled; *synonyms* (adj) torn, lacerated, deformed, mutilated, disabled, lacerate, broken, blasted, crippled, distorted, maimed, confused, corrupted, jumbled, (prep) rent.

korokoroia incise; *synonyms* (*v*) carve, etch, cut, engrave, notch, scrape, scratch, slash, hack, slice, slit, incide, pierce.

korokoroiaki incised; *synonyms* (*adj*) engraved, graven, etched, inscribed, sculpted, sculptured.

koroma husk; *synonyms* (*n*) bark, crust, skin, cortex, chaff, coat, covering, peel, rind, shell, shuck, cod, cornhusk, (*v*) hull.

kororo 1. abbreviated; *synonyms* (*adj*) shortened, short, abbreviate, abridged, brief, condensed, truncated, compendious, edited, reduced, little, telescoped; *antonym* (*adj*) complete, 2. short; *synonyms* (*adj*) concise, scarce, brusque, close, curt, sharp, laconic, abrupt, deficient, diminutive, inadequate, insufficient, lacking, pithy, poor; *antonyms* (*adj*) long, tall, high, lengthy.

korouaia sunder; *synonyms* (*v*) divide, part, separate, dissever, tear, share, cleave, detach, (*n*) sever, divorce, fragment.

korouaiaki halved; *synonyms* (*adj*) half, dimidiate.

korouia 1. cut; *synonyms* (*v*) carve, chop, clip, abbreviate, abridge, bite, condense, crop, drop, fashion, (*n*) notch, slice, cutting, nick, blow; *antonyms* (*v*) increase, lengthen, (*n*) addition, extension, 2. fray; *synonyms* (*n*) brawl, conflict, action, affray, combat, fight, battle, broil, contention, disturbance, fracas, scrap, (*v*) rub, chafe, fret, 3. unravelling, 4. trim; *synonyms* (*adj*) tidy, neat, spruce, orderly, shipshape, (*v*) cut, dress, garnish, shave, adorn, embellish, lop, prune, reduce, shorten; *antonym* (*adj*) fat.

kotea 1. indicate; *synonyms* (*v*) denote, direct, augur, betoken, designate, imply, mark, show, foretell, foreshadow, argue, bespeak, bode, demonstrate, evince, 2. jab; *synonyms* (*n*) dig, poke, injection, thrust, blow, clip, lick, jabbing, (*v*) stab, prick, prod, nudge, puncture, shove, lunge, 3. point; *synonyms* (*n*) place, grade, peak, nib, edge, aim, article, degree, dot, spot, phase, apex, detail, (*v*) head, level.

koto point; *synonyms* (*n*) place, grade, peak, nib, edge, aim, article, degree, dot, mark, spot, phase, (*v*) head, direct, level.

koukou reach; *synonyms* (*v*) range, overtake, obtain, achieve, attain, extend, get, make, pass, accomplish, (*n*) fetch, compass, stretch, extent, gain.

kraoan prohibit; *synonyms* (*v*) prevent, bar, disallow, enjoin, exclude, forbid, hinder, ban, outlaw, preclude, proscribe, veto, debar, inhibit, interdict; *antonyms* (*v*) permit, allow.

kraoanaki prohibited; *synonyms* (*adj*) forbidden, illegal, illicit, banned, taboo, unlawful, contraband, barred, out, proscribed; *antonyms* (*adj*) admissible, legitimate.

ku shrivelled; *synonyms* (*adj*) shriveled, shrunken, withered, wizened, sear, sere, wizen.

kua 1. weary; *synonyms* (*adj*) tired, exhausted, fatigued, aweary, beat, languid, irksome, (*v*) fatigue, tire, exhaust, bore, dull, irk, wear, (*n*) jade; *antonyms* (*adj*) energetic, fresh, 2. tired; *synonyms* (*adj*) hackneyed, weary, banal, commonplace, stale, threadbare, trite, haggard, jaded, stock, worn, drowsy, sick, whacked, corny; *antonyms* (*adj*) invigorated, alert, refreshed, original, strong.

kuama weary; *synonyms* (*adj*) tired, exhausted, fatigued, aweary, beat, languid, irksome, (*v*) fatigue, tire, exhaust, bore, dull, irk, wear, (*n*) jade; *antonyms* (*adj*) energetic, fresh.

kuba 1. aback; *synonyms* (*adv*) abaft, aft, after, astern, backward, short, sternmost, suddenly, unawares, (*adj*) back, (*n*) abacus, 2. start; *synonyms* (*v*) begin, originate, commence, drive, launch, embark, spring, activate, arise, (*n*) jump, onset, origin, shock, beginning, commencement; *antonyms* (*v*) end, finish, stop, conclude, halt, (*n*) conclusion.

kui start; *synonyms* (*v*) begin, originate, commence, drive, launch, embark, spring, activate, arise, (*n*) jump, onset, origin, shock, beginning, commencement; *antonyms* (*v*) end, finish, stop, conclude, halt, (*n*) conclusion.

kuikui twitch; *synonyms* (*n*) twinge, pull, tweak, start, (*v*) jerk, yank, pluck, tug, wrench, draw, nip, pinch, flinch, jolt, snatch.

kuka cook; *synonyms* (*n*) chef, (*v*) boil, bake, brew, make, prepare, concoct, falsify, grill, poach, roast, simmer, stew, coddle, heat.

kukaki cooked; *synonyms* (*adj*) ripe, overcooked, altered, damaged, defiled, heated, spent, wanting.

kukume swoop; *synonyms* (*n*) descent, sweep, slide, (*v*) pounce, descend, raid, stoop, plunge, clutch.

kukunakuna 1. bruised; *synonyms* (*adj*) contused, wounded, hurt, raw, sore, contusioned, discolored, inflamed, lame, livid, painful, rotten, sensitive, surbet, tender, 2. scarred; *synonyms* (*adj*) marred, defaced.

kukurei 1. gay; *synonyms* (*adj*) cheerful, bright, convivial, festive, gaudy, airy, blithe, brave, buoyant, cheery, festal, flashy, frolicsome, (*n*) homosexual, gallant, 2. merry; *synonyms* (*adj*) gay, joyful, lively, glad, jolly, jovial, facetious, brisk, happy, jocund, lighthearted, gleeful, joyous, playful, rollicking; *antonym* (*adj*) sad, 3. blessed; *synonyms* (*adj*) blest, holy, blasted, cursed, damned, fortunate, hallowed, sacred, saintly, lucky, consecrated, deuced, divine, heavenly, infernal; *antonym* (*adj*) unlucky, 4. blissful; *synonyms* (*adj*) blessed, delighted, delightful, merry, beatified, ecstatic, elated, 5. blithe; *synonyms* (*adj*) breezy, carefree, animated, blissful, unconcerned, blithesome, jocular, light, lightsome, sprightly, sunny, vivacious, 6. chipper; *synonyms* (*adj*) spirited, debonair, jaunty, active, bubbly, bully, 7.

delectable; *synonyms* (adj) delicious, dainty, luscious, scrumptious, sweet, tasty, appetizing, charming, lovely, palatable, savory, yummy, tasteful, delicate, enjoyable, **8.** exhilarated; *synonyms* (adj) excited, exuberant, animating, cheering, ebullient, effervescent, elevated, enthusiastic, flushed, gladdened, high, hilarious, intoxicated, overjoyed, gratified, **9.** glad; *synonyms* (adj) contented, jubilant, content, genial, willing, beaming, proud, lief, pleased, radiant, **10.** delighted; *synonyms* (adj) charmed, captivated, exultant, entranced, rapt, beguiled, enthralled; *antonyms* (adj) disappointed, shocked, sorrowful, unhappy, **11.** elated; *synonyms* (adj) elate, triumphant, euphoric; *antonym* (adj) dejected, **12.** joyful; *synonyms* (adj) exhilarated, smiling, **13.** delightful; *synonyms* (adj) agreeable, delectable, pleasing, grateful, adorable, amiable, nice, captivating, congenial, cute, gorgeous, lovable, pleasant, pretty, welcome; *antonyms* (adj) unpleasant, hateful, unwelcome, **14.** exuberant; *synonyms* (adj) abundant, copious, ample, excessive, extravagant, opulent, profuse, bountiful, hearty, lavish, lush, luxuriant, rank, rampant, liberal, **15.** cheery; *synonym* (adj) upbeat; *antonyms* (adj) gloomy, depressing, miserable, **16.** happy; *synonyms* (adj) felicitous, favorable, appropriate, apt, comfortable, optimistic, providential, satisfied, successful, well, suitable, fitting, fortuitous, fit, (n) auspicious; *antonym* (adj) depressed, **17.** pleasant; *synonyms* (adj) acceptable, kindly, affable, attractive, clear, fair, fine, gentle, kind, mirthful, mild, suave, amusing, beautiful, clement; *antonyms* (adj) disagreeable, disgusting, foul, gruesome, harsh, horrible, nasty, repugnant, shocking, terrible, appalling, discordant, frosty, grisly, rough, **18.** rejoice; *synonyms* (v) cheer, delight, gladden, glory, joy, jubilate, revel, triumph, gratify, gloat, exhilarate, please, celebrate, recreate, (n) exult; *antonyms* (v) lament, mourn, **19.** pleased; *synonyms* (adj) thankful, appreciative; *antonyms* (adj) displeased, angry, annoyed, worried, **20.** pleasurable; *synonyms* (adj) entertaining, gratifying, satisfying.

kukuri hasty; *synonyms* (adj) fast, abrupt, cursory, fleet, careless, hurried, impetuous, quick, rash, speedy, sudden, brisk, brusque, eager, expeditious; *antonyms* (adj) slow, considered, deliberate, leisurely, sensible.

kun skinned; *synonyms* (adj) abraded, scraped, frustrated, painful, raw, scratched, sensitive, sore, tender, bleeding, bloody.

kunainga shudder; *synonyms* (n) shake, quake, quivering, shivering, chill, frisson, tremor, twitch, (v) shiver, quiver, tremble, dither, flicker, flutter, thrill.

kunea 1. find; *synonyms* (v) catch, discover, detect, encounter, acquire, ascertain, attain, feel, procure, gather, (n) detection, disclosure, discovery, search, breakthrough; *antonyms* (v) lose, misplace, **2.** found; *synonyms* (v) erect, establish, base, build, form, constitute, construct, appoint, create, ground, institute, bottom, begin, cast, plant; *antonym* (adj) misplaced, **3.** discover; *synonyms* (v) discern, disclose, see, find, perceive, determine, divulge, expose, hear, impart, observe, trace, descry, behold, betray.

kuneaki 1. founded; *synonyms* (v) cast, fusil, fusible, (adj) based, (prep) established, institute, organized, **2.** discovered; *synonyms* (adj) ascertained, revealed, disclosed, exposed, naked, bare, observed, open, seen, **3.** found; *synonyms* (v) erect, establish, base, build, form, constitute, construct, appoint, create, ground, bottom, begin, plant, start, imbed; *antonym* (adj) misplaced.

kungkung grunt; *synonyms* (n) cry, groan, (v) grumble, growl, croak, mutter, complain, moan, murmur, clamor.

kunnikaia 1. clothed; *synonyms* (v) accustomed, arrayed, habited, (adj) clad, dressed, wrapped, cloaked, robed, absorbed, decent, draped, mantled, vested, vestured, disguised; *antonym* (adj) undressed, **2.** clad; *synonyms* (v) costume, shod, dress, attire, face, garb, (adj) clothed, garbed, accomplished, appearing, beseen, seen, versed, (n) cladding, (prep) gowned, **3.** clothe; *synonyms* (v) array, apparel, cover, arrange, deck, invest, vest, wrap, adorn, fit, rig, bedeck, drape, furnish, (n) habit; *antonym* (v) undress.

kunnikaiaki 1. clothed; *synonyms* (v) accustomed, arrayed, habited, (adj) clad, dressed, wrapped, cloaked, robed, absorbed, decent, draped, mantled, vested, vestured, disguised; *antonym* (adj) undressed, **2.** clad; *synonyms* (v) costume, shod, dress, attire, face, garb, (adj) clothed, garbed, accomplished, appearing, beseen, seen, versed, (n) cladding, (prep) gowned.

kuokuo skin; *synonyms* (n) peel, hide, coating, fur, hull, rind, shell, crust, integument, pelt, (v) pare, bark, scrape, excoriate, flay.

kuokuoaki skinned; *synonyms* (adj) abraded, scraped, frustrated, painful, raw, scratched, sensitive, sore, tender, bleeding, bloody.

kuota 1. abrade; *synonyms* (v) scrape, file, skin, chafe, rub, scour, graze, abrase, erode, gall, grate, grind, scratch, scrub, scuff, **2.** flay; *synonyms* (v) excoriate, peel, decorticate, pare, lash, flog, castigate, scalp, **3.** skin; *synonyms* (n) hide, coating, fur, hull, rind, shell, crust, integument, pelt, case, coat, covering, (v) bark, flay, abrade.

kuotaki 1. abraded; *synonyms* (adj) scraped, skinned, raw, **2.** skinned; *synonyms* (adj) abraded, frustrated, painful, scratched, sensitive, sore, tender, bleeding, bloody.

kuri 1. almost; *synonyms* (*adv*) nearly, approximately, just, around, most, practically, roughly, virtually, some, (*prep*) about, (*adj*) near, nigh, approaching, approximate, barely, **2.** hasty; *synonyms* (*adj*) fast, abrupt, cursory, fleet, careless, hurried, impetuous, quick, rash, speedy, sudden, brisk, brusque, eager, expeditious; *antonyms* (*adj*) slow, considered, deliberate, leisurely, sensible, **3.** nearly; *synonyms* (*adv*) almost, close, closely, intimately, much, dear, halfway, (*adj*) thereabouts.

kuria snatch; *synonyms* (*v*) grab, pinch, abduct, clutch, kidnap, seize, snap, jerk, capture, grasp, grip, pluck, (*n*) catch, seizure, arrest.

kuribaia deprive; *synonyms* (*v*) strip, bereave, divest, abridge, despoil, curtail, denude, deny, dismantle, disrobe, rob, cheat, contract, disinherit, impoverish; *antonym* (*v*) enrich.

kuribaiaki deprived; *synonyms* (*adj*) disadvantaged, bereft, destitute, poor, depressed, bankrupt, broke, humble, impecunious, indigent, insolvent, rundown, underprivileged, void, wanting; *antonym* (*adj*) privileged.

kuribwaia 1. spoil; *synonyms* (*v*) plunder, corrupt, impair, rot, damage, deface, indulge, injure, mar, sack, baby, botch, bungle, (*n*) ruin, (*adj*) harm; *antonyms* (*v*) enhance, improve, conserve, **2.** sack; *synonyms* (*n*) pocket, pouch, sac, poke, (*v*) pillage, bag, discharge, dismiss, despoil, fire, ransack, rob, rifle, can, loot; *antonym* (*v*) hire, **3.** plunder; *synonyms* (*v*) harry, spoil, devastate, destroy, maraud, strip, divest, forage, foray, prey, raid, (*n*) booty, depredation, despoliation, prize.

kuribwaiaki 1. sacked; *synonyms* (*adj*) despoiled, pillaged, raped, ravaged, assaulted, blasted, desolate, desolated, devastated, looted, molested, plundered, ransacked, ruined, wasted, **2.** plundered; *synonyms* (*adj*) fleeced, sacked, **3.** spoiled; *synonyms* (*adj*) decayed, bad, rotten, stale, coddled, pampered, corrupt, damaged, spoilt; *antonyms* (*adj*) first-rate, pure.

L

lelei good; *synonyms* (*adj*) able, benefit, delicious, right, efficient, capable, excellent, fine, nice, superior, well, advantageous, (*n*) benign, advantage, gain; *antonyms* (*adj*) disobedient, poor, wicked, unpleasant, (*n*) evil, bad.

louachoua nine; *synonyms* (*n*) niner, club, ennead, ace, cabaret, clubhouse, gild, golfclub, guild, jack, king, knave, lodge, nightclub, nightspot.

M

ma 1. crumble; *synonyms* (*v*) decay, collapse, crush, decompose, disintegrate, fragment, perish, rust, fail, bust, chip, crumple, crunch, (*adj*) break, crack, **2.** but; *synonyms* (*conj*) while, (*adv*) alone, only, though, barely, however, merely, simply, yet, exclusively, if, just, (*prep*) besides, except, excluding, **3.** break; *synonyms* (*v*) split, burst, infringe, leak, tear, undo, beat, (*n*) breach, fracture, pause, rupture, stop, interruption, respite, suspension; *antonyms* (*v*) repair, obey, honor, mend, (*n*) continuation, **4.** and; *synonyms* (*conj*) with, (*adv*) also, additionally, (*prep*) plus, including, (*adj*) more, **5.** as; *synonyms* (*conj*) qua, because, since, considering, whilst, (*prep*) during, like, (*adv*) equally, from, (*n*) arsenic, **6.** yet; *synonyms* (*adv*) but, notwithstanding, even, nonetheless, further, hitherto, eventually, unless, always, finally, heretofore, (*conj*) nevertheless, (*n*) already, (*v*) still, (*adj*) erewhile, **7.** still; *synonyms* (*adj*) calm, pacify, peaceful, silence, quiescent, serene, silent, appease, (*n*) hush, (*v*) quiet, assuage, compose, lull, soothe, allay; *antonyms* (*adj*) moving, effervescent, fizzy, windy, (*n*) noisy, **8.** with; *synonyms* (*prep*) by, for, alongside, among, (*adv*) on, beside, (*n*) withe, **9.** rupture; *synonyms* (*n*) rift, breakage, hernia, rent, breaking, disruption, gap, puncture, detachment, discord, (*v*) division, rive, rip, rend, lacerate.

maae scattered; *synonyms* (*adj*) dispersed, dissipated, confused, disconnected, disordered, sparse, sporadic, thin, diffuse, distributed, rare, separate, spread, stray, strewn; *antonym* (*adj*) concentrated.

maama withdrawn; *synonyms* (*adj*) reserved, secluded, retiring, solitary, indrawn, cloistered, reclusive, uncommunicative, lonely, taciturn, unsociable, introverted, reticent, shy, aloof; *antonym* (*adj*) outgoing.

mabe chart; *synonyms* (*n*) plan, plot, table, graphic, diagram, drawing, schematic, figure, illustration, (*v*) map, graph, sketch, design, draw, list.

maborabora 1. flat; *synonyms* (*adj*) dull, bland, even, plain, insipid, level, plane, tasteless, dreary, boring, absolute, dead, downright, (*n*) apartment, (*v*) uninteresting; *antonyms* (*adj*) exciting, high-pitched, bumpy, **2.** glossy; *synonyms* (*adj*) shiny, sleek, bright, smooth, brilliant, glazed, flat, burnished, glassy, glistening, lustrous, resplendent, satiny, slick, silky; *antonym* (*adj*) rough, **3.** glassy; *synonyms* (*adj*) vitreous, glossy, clear, crystalline, hyaline, limpid, transparent, slippery, (*v*) glabrous, **4.** smooth; *synonyms* (*adj*) easy, calm, oily, facile, flowing, fluent, fluid, graceful, greasy, liquid, mellow, polished, peaceful, (v) quiet, facilitate; *antonyms* (adj) uneven, abrasive, coarse, crumpled, flaking, harsh, jerky, lined, peeling, prickly, ridged, wrinkled, corrugated, (v) wrinkle, crease, **5.** polished; *synonyms* (adj) elegant, courteous, cultured, finished, refined, civil, courtly, genteel, polite, accomplished, stylish, urbane, exquisite, suave, gentle.

mabu 1. illegal; *synonyms* (adj) criminal, forbidden, prohibited, unauthorized, unlawful, illegitimate, illicit, lawless, taboo, wrongful; *antonyms* (adj) legal, lawful, honest, legitimate, official, **2.** forbid; *synonyms* (v) debar, prohibit, ban, bar, disallow, exclude, deny, avert, frustrate, inhibit, interdict, outlaw, prevent, proscribe, veto; *antonyms* (v) permit, allow, let, approve, **3.** banned; *synonyms* (adj) illegal, contraband, **4.** forbidden; *synonyms* (adj) banned, proscribed, verboten; *antonym* (adj) acceptable, **5.** ban; *synonyms* (n) anathema, restraint, command, curse, embargo, prohibition, banning, exclusion, (v) forbid, banish, expel, enjoin, illegalize, reject, blackball; *antonym* (v) sanction, **6.** taboo; *synonyms* (adj) out, (n) tabu, **7.** prohibit; *synonyms* (v) hinder, preclude, hamper, impede, check, deter, oppose, block, restrict, stop, disqualify, negative, (n) obstruct, **8.** prohibited; *synonym* (adj) barred; *antonym* (adj) admissible, **9.** unauthorized; *synonyms* (adj) unauthorised, wildcat, unofficial, abnormal, dishonest, fierce, forcible, furious, groundless, impetuous, informal, outrageous, severe, surreptitious, unendorsed; *antonym* (adj) authorized.

mabuaki 1. forbidden; *synonyms* (adj) unlawful, banned, illegal, prohibited, taboo, contraband, illicit, proscribed, verboten; *antonym* (adj) acceptable, **2.** banned; *synonym* (adj) forbidden; *antonym* (adj) legitimate, **3.** prohibited; *synonyms* (adj) barred, out; *antonym* (adj) admissible.

mabubu hazy; *synonyms* (adj) cloudy, fuzzy, blurred, blurry, faint, foggy, indistinct, misty, nebulous, vague, ambiguous, dull, bleary, brumous, dim; *antonyms* (adj) clear, bright, distinct, precise.

maca rope; *synonyms* (n) cable, lasso, lariat, noose, cord, hawser, leash, line, string, tape, lace, tether, thread, (v) tie, bind.

mae 1. drag; *synonyms* (v) attract, haul, draw, puff, trail, cart, hale, heave, lug, tow, delay, (n) pull, bother, bore, hindrance; *antonym* (v) push, **2.** disperse; *synonyms* (v) dispel, spread, circulate, disband, dissipate, scatter, diffuse, dispense, disseminate, break, disappear, dismiss, broadcast, distribute, propagate; *antonyms* (v) assemble, gather, collect, **3.** dry; *synonyms* (adj) thirsty, arid, barren, boring, dehydrated, dull, bald, hoarse, jejune, plain, (v) dehydrate, desiccate, drain, uninteresting, sardonic; *antonyms* (adj) wet, damp,

moist, saturated, soaked, boggy, drenched, rainy, sodden, interesting, fresh, humid, juicy, succulent, (v) drench, **4.** dried; *synonyms* (adj) dry, desiccated, shriveled, shrunken, torrid, baked, concrete, stale, wizened, lifeless, weazen, (n) milk, **5.** break; *synonyms* (v) split, crack, burst, fail, infringe, leak, (n) breach, fracture, pause, rupture, stop, collapse, interruption, respite, suspension; *antonyms* (v) repair, obey, honor, mend, (n) continuation, **6.** move; *synonyms* (v) act, affect, carry, excite, go, impel, instigate, maneuver, touch, travel, flow, bear, (n) motion, drive, transfer; *antonym* (v) stay, **7.** roasted; *synonym* (adj) roast, **8.** scatter; *synonyms* (v) disperse, spray, sprinkle, litter, rout, dot, dust, squander, plant, intersperse, cast, lavish, (n) dispersion, splash, sprinkling.

maeae 1. frayed; *synonyms* (adj) worn, ragged, shabby, threadbare, tattered, (v) dilapidated; *antonym* (adj) pristine, **2.** torn; *synonyms* (adj) lacerated, ripped, mangled, rent, blasted, lacerate, **3.** tattered; *synonyms* (adj) scruffy, frayed, seedy, torn, shattered, (v) bedraggled; *antonym* (adj) elegant, **4.** shredded; *synonyms* (adj) sliced, chopped, broken, (adv) asunder.

maeaki 1. broken; *synonyms* (v) broke, (adj) tame, torn, busted, imperfect, intermittent, rough, rugged, ruined, uneven, disjointed, incomplete, confused, cracked, crushed; *antonyms* (adj) constant, unbroken, intact, whole, wild, **2.** dispersed; *synonyms* (adj) diffuse, scattered, sparse, spread, diffused, detached, discrete, fractional, rare, thin, circulated, flowing, isolated, loose, single; *antonym* (adj) concentrated, **3.** scattered; *synonyms* (adj) dispersed, dissipated, disconnected, disordered, sporadic, distributed, separate, stray, strewn, disorderly, garbled, illogical.

maeao westward; *synonyms* (adv) west, westwards, (adj) westerly, westbound, western.

maebwebu comfortable; *synonyms* (adj) cozy, easy, agreeable, pleased, pleasing, prosperous, congenial, pleasurable, rich, enjoyable, commodious, content, contented, (v) snug, calm; *antonyms* (adj) uncomfortable, poor, formal, tense, unpleasant, intimidating, unaccustomed, unhappy.

maeiei 1. agitate; *synonyms* (v) disturb, stir, toss, fan, bother, foment, perturb, rouse, shake, trouble, actuate, annoy, arouse, canvass, convulse; *antonyms* (v) calm, soothe, **2.** quake; *synonyms* (n) quiver, earthquake, tremble, tremor, (v) shiver, shudder, quail, flutter, flicker, vibrate, fluctuate, jar, palpitate, dance, rock, **3.** tremble; *synonyms* (v) thrill, quake, totter, falter, agitate, quaver, waver, cower, wave, fear, jolt, wobble, blench, (n) throb, tingle, **4.** wave; *synonyms* (n) billow, gesture, motion, sign, surge, (v) brandish, flap, curl, flourish, swell, swing, undulate, beat, beckon, ripple, **5.** shake; *synonyms* (v) excite, wag, drop, bump, jiggle, rattle, trill, jerk, jog, judder, push, (n) trembling, wiggle, sprinkle, handshake, **6.** worn; *synonyms* (v) decayed, (adj) haggard, shabby, tired, ragged, tattered, threadbare, drawn, jaded, exhausted, fatigued, careworn, decrepit, faded, frayed; *antonyms* (adj) fresh, new, **7.** wag; *synonyms* (n) humorist, waggle, joker, wit, comedian, clown, zany, card, comic, (v) reel, move, vibratiuncle.

maeieiaki 1. agitated; *synonyms* (adj) restless, excited, nervous, restive, tumultuous, upset, distressed, tense, alarmed, anxious, distraught, jumpy, overwrought, perturbed, shaken; *antonyms* (adj) calm, composed, lethargic, **2.** shaken; *synonyms* (v) broken, lame, passe, shaky, threadbare, wilted, shattered, stale, (adj) jolted, dazed, disconcerted, fallen, scared, stunned, surprised.

maeka 1. live; *synonyms* (v) exist, inhabit, reside, subsist, abide, be, dwell, endure, stay, survive, (adj) alive, active, animate, living, (n) go; *antonyms* (adj) dead, inanimate, **2.** dwell; *synonyms* (v) bide, live, lodge, belong, brood, continue, delay, occupy, remain, settle, consist, domicile, domiciliate, keep, (adj) roost, **3.** reside; *synonyms* (v) populate, lie, people, repose, rest, shack, last, perch, **4.** stay; *synonyms* (v) prop, stop, pause, arrest, support, linger, persist, sojourn, stand, wait, (n) halt, check, postponement, (adj) cease, tarry; *antonyms* (v) leave, change, abscond, depart, **5.** powder; *synonyms* (n) dust, gunpowder, explosive, (v) grind, crush, pound, pulverise, pulverize, sprinkle, bespangle, **6.** sojourn; *synonyms* (n) residence, abode, dwelling, habitation, (v) visit.

maekaki powdered; *synonyms* (adj) pulverized, powdery, fine, crushed, ground, milled, minced, pounded, pulverised, corned, salted, (n) milk, punctated.

maekana inhabit; *synonyms* (v) dwell, reside, abide, occupy, live, lodge, people, settle, be, bide, exist, roost, domicile, (n) habit, (adj) perch.

maekanaki 1. livable; *synonyms* (adj) bearable, endurable, habitable, inhabitable, liveable, tolerable, adequate, cozy, homey, lodgeable, satisfactory, snug, sustainable, worthwhile, **2.** inhabited; *synonyms* (v) populous, accustomed, arrayed, clothed, dressed, habited, (adj) peopled, occupied, housing, colonized, suburban, uninhabited, uptown; *antonyms* (adj) empty, unoccupied.

maeke 1. crunchy; *synonyms* (adj) crisp, crispy, brittle, crusty, crumbly, firm, hard, short, curt, established, fast, frizzly, frizzy, frosty, immobile; *antonym* (adj) soggy, **2.** dry; *synonyms* (adj) thirsty, arid, barren, boring, dehydrated, dull, bald, hoarse,

jejune, plain, (v) dehydrate, desiccate, drain, uninteresting, sardonic; *antonyms* (adj) wet, damp, moist, saturated, soaked, boggy, drenched, rainy, sodden, interesting, fresh, humid, juicy, succulent, (v) drench, **3.** crisp; *synonyms* (adj) terse, brisk, crunchy, curl, sharp, brief, curly, abrupt, biting, chilly, (n) chip, (v) wrinkle, crease, crinkle, crimp.

maem 1. gentle; *synonyms* (adj) clement, calm, easy, friendly, soft, affable, balmy, kind, mild, tame, feeble, amiable, benign, bland, (n) benevolent; *antonyms* (adj) caustic, cruel, fierce, harsh, loud, violent, rough, abrupt, hardhearted, heavy, sarcastic, sheer, steep, **2.** mellow; *synonyms* (adj) mature, ripe, gentle, luscious, mollify, smooth, juicy, perfect, mellowed, melodious, peaceful, relaxed, (v) melt, ripen, soften, **3.** mild; *synonyms* (adj) kindly, gracious, lenient, docile, humble, delicate, meek, sweet, fine, indulgent, moderate, temperate, compliant, light, flat; *antonyms* (adj) intense, extreme, pungent, severe, sharp, spicy, barbed, great, hot, incisive, passionate, powerful, scathing, wintry, **4.** calm; *synonyms* (adj) quiet, tranquil, (v) assuage, appease, cool, still, allay, pacify, steady, tranquilize, abate, alleviate, becalm, (n) lull, equanimity; *antonyms* (adj) agitated, angry, nervous, stormy, wild, annoyed, anxious, enraged, frantic, frightened, irritable, overexcited, (v) agitate, upset, (n) agitation, **5.** gracious; *synonyms* (adj) genial, courteous, good, compassionate, accommodating, congenial, benignant, civil, cordial, kindhearted, polite, propitious, beneficent, charitable, courtly; *antonyms* (adj) boorish, ungracious, **6.** composed; *synonyms* (adj) collected, dispassionate, peaceable, equable, impassive, imperturbable, placid, sedate, serene, staid, unflappable, easygoing, unmoved, even, nerveless; *antonyms* (adj) distressed, trembling, **7.** complacent; *synonyms* (adj) content, self-satisfied, contented, smug, comfortable, proud, arrogant, self-righteous, assured, bigheaded, bragging, companionable, complaisant, conceited, conciliatory, **8.** placid; *synonyms* (adj) composed, unruffled, hushed, leisurely, untroubled, tender, undisturbed, unperturbed, **9.** peaceful; *synonyms* (adj) peace, silent, amicable, halcyon, harmonious, restful, happy, idyllic, inactive, passive; *antonyms* (adj) aggressive, noisy, tense.

maen 1. flexible; *synonyms* (adj) elastic, adaptable, pliable, yielding, lissome, pliant, soft, supple, facile, adjustable, bendable, compliant, ductile, flexile, lithe; *antonyms* (adj) inflexible, rigid, fixed, obstinate, stiff, stubborn, **2.** plaint; *synonyms* (n) complaint, lament, mourning, lamentation, wail, moan, (v) chorus, clamor, hullabaloo, outcry, **3.** supple; *synonyms* (adj) flexible, graceful, lissom, lithesome, plastic, active, agile, malleable, nimble, tender, resilient, floppy, alert, limp, (v) limber.

maenikun 1. dismantled; *synonyms* *(adj)* demolished, razed, **2**. smashed; *synonyms* *(adj)* shattered, drunk, inebriated, intoxicated, broken, plastered, sloshed, blotto, tipsy, besotted, pissed, tight; *antonym* *(adj)* sober, **3**. undone; *synonyms* *(v)* accursed, devoted, *(adj)* lost, ruined, sunk, unfinished, doomed, behindhand, decayed, destroyed, finished.

maerere striped; *synonyms* *(adj)* streaked, stripy, paled, virgated, zoned, hooped, zonate.

maererua checkered; *synonyms* *(adj)* check, checked, chequered, dappled, mottled, multicolored, mutable, tessellated, variable, checky, curbed, diversified, patchwork, quilted, spotted.

maeretongitong streaked; *synonyms* *(v)* barred, areolar, cancellated, grated, *(adj)* veined, streaky, striped, brindled, lined, mottled, brinded, dotted, marbled, marked, *(n)* hairstyle.

maete 1. greasy; *synonyms* *(adj)* fat, fatty, dirty, oily, tallowy, oleaginous, sebaceous, slick, slippery, unctuous; *antonym* *(adj)* dry, **2**. slippery; *synonyms* *(adj)* cunning, crafty, glib, elusive, glossy, shifty, slippy, tricky, untrustworthy, wily, dishonest, greasy, icy, *(v)* precarious, questionable, **3**. slip; *synonyms* *(n)* lapse, fault, mistake, cutting, error, escape, oversight, scion, trip, *(v)* fall, slide, drop, glide, skid, *(adj)* blunder; *antonym* *(v)* improve, **4**. oily; *synonyms* *(adj)* buttery, fulsome, obsequious, rich, smarmy, *(v)* bland, soapy, glassy, glabrous, lubricous.

maetete slip; *synonyms* *(n)* lapse, fault, mistake, cutting, error, escape, oversight, scion, trip, *(v)* fall, slide, drop, glide, skid, *(adj)* blunder; *antonym* *(v)* improve.

maewe 1. indefinite; *synonyms* *(adj)* ambiguous, indeterminate, uncertain, vague, boundless, equivocal, hazy, unlimited, doubtful, dubious, confused, imprecise, indecisive, indistinct, general; *antonym* *(adj)* definite, **2**. murky; *synonyms* *(adj)* dismal, dark, gloomy, cloudy, dusky, dingy, misty, dim, muddy, opaque, dirty, black, dull, depressing, foggy; *antonyms* *(adj)* clear, bright, **3**. dimly; *synonyms* *(adv)* indistinctly, darkly, faintly, hazily, vaguely, palely, fuzzily, distantly, feebly, blankly, blindly, blurrily, confusedly, imprecisely, inanely; *antonyms* *(adv)* brightly, clearly, strongly, **4**. ambiguous; *synonyms* *(adj)* evasive, slippery, amphibolous, cryptic, enigmatic, indefinite, loose, misleading, nebulous, obscure, oracular, puzzling, questionable, unclear, undefined; *antonyms* *(adj)* unambiguous, unequivocal, **5**. indistinct; *synonyms* *(adj)* faint, inarticulate, fuzzy, neutral, blurred, formless, shady, thick, blurry, shadowy, unintelligible, wooly, bleary, muffled, shapeless; *antonym* *(adj)* distinct, **6**. dim; *synonyms* *(adj)* bleak, dense, slow, stupid, clouded, darkish, *(v)* blur, darken, cloud, pale, tarnish, blear, blind,

deaden, mist; *antonyms* *(adj)* brilliant, intelligent, clever, strong, *(v)* brighten, **7**. dusky; *synonyms* *(adj)* murky, somber, sooty, swarthy, tenebrous, dusk, sable, sombre, fuliginous, swart, *(n)* brunette; *antonym* *(adj)* light, **8**. dull; *synonyms* *(adj)* blunt, dreary, sluggish, bland, boring, cold, inactive, inert, obtuse, slack, torpid, uninteresting, deep, apathetic, *(v)* dampen; *antonyms* *(adj)* lively, sharp, exciting, interesting, lustrous, stimulating, amusing, exhilarating, glittery, glossy, glowing, high-pitched, intense, luminous, shiny, **9**. faded; *synonyms* *(v)* dilapidated, stale, *(adj)* bleached, exhausted, washy, withered, attenuate, attenuated, colorless, discoloured, **10**. gloomy; *synonyms* *(adj)* cheerless, dejected, desolate, disconsolate, downcast, downhearted, funereal, melancholy, sad, dispirited, blue, depressed, despondent, doleful, drab; *antonyms* *(adj)* cheerful, cheery, encouraging, happy, hopeful, **11**. obscure; *synonyms* *(adj)* concealed, hidden, incomprehensible, mysterious, clandestine, nameless, covert, *(v)* hide, conceal, confuse, cover, eclipse, becloud, bedim, *(n)* difficult; *antonyms* *(adj)* noticeable, simple, obvious, mainstream, *(v)* clarify, **12**. unclear; *synonyms* *(adj)* unsure, borderline, illegible, indecipherable, unsettled, **13**. vague; *synonyms* *(adj)* undetermined, feeble, lax, intangible, indefinable, flimsy, rough, poor, distracted, inexplicit, noncommittal, unfixed, approximate, impalpable, imperceptible; *antonyms* *(adj)* exact, particular, precise, specific, sure, **14**. pale; *synonyms* *(adj)* ghastly, wan, pallid, weak, watery, cadaverous, faded, fair, *(v)* blanch, *(n)* boundary, confine, border, bound, limit, picket; *antonyms* *(adj)* rosy, brown.

mahono sweat; *synonyms* *(n)* labor, perspiration, lather, sudor, effort, struggle, drudgery, fret, labour, *(v)* work, perspire, toil, drudge, exude, ooze.

mai 1. cooked; *synonyms* *(adj)* ripe, overcooked, altered, damaged, defiled, heated, spent, wanting, **2**. acidic; *synonyms* *(adj)* sour, acid, acidulent, acidulous, bitter, sharp, corrosive, astringent; *antonym* *(adj)* sweet, **3**. alive; *synonyms* *(adj)* active, live, living, sensible, vivacious, animated, lively, responsive, aware, eager, acute, energetic, animate, awake, extant; *antonyms* *(adj)* dead, deceased, inanimate, **4**. distasteful; *synonyms* *(adj)* disagreeable, disgusting, offensive, unwelcome, ugly, revolting, undesirable, dirty, disgustful, displeasing, foul, loathsome, nasty, objectionable, repellent; *antonyms* *(adj)* pleasant, attractive, tasteful, **5**. live; *synonyms* *(v)* exist, inhabit, reside, subsist, abide, be, dwell, endure, stay, survive, *(adj)* alive, brisk, bouncy, breathing, *(n)* go, **6**. disgusting; *synonyms* *(adj)* abominable, detestable, distasteful, execrable, odious, abhorrent, awful, hateful, horrible, noisome, obscene, rank, repugnant, repulsive, shocking; *antonym* (*adj*) appealing, **7**. grayish; *synonyms* (*adj*) gray, greyish, begrimed, besmirched, cinereous, dark, darkish, discolored, dull, grey, grimy, grizzled, shadowy, soiled, stained, **8**. insipid; *synonyms* (*adj*) flat, tasteless, bland, flavorless, uninteresting, vapid, watery, boring, flavourless, humdrum, savorless, tame, tedious, weak, dry; *antonyms* (*adj*) exciting, strong, tasty, **9**. whitish; *synonyms* (*adj*) milky, pale, fair, milk, milklike, ashen, colorless, light, pastel, pasty, soft, towheaded, white, insipid, **10**. pale; *synonyms* (*adj*) ghastly, faint, wan, pallid, cadaverous, faded, feeble, (*v*) dim, blanch, (*n*) boundary, confine, border, bound, limit, picket; *antonyms* (*adj*) rosy, brown, **11**. tart; *synonyms* (*n*) pie, pastry, prostitute, cake, (*adj*) pungent, keen, piquant, acerbic, acrid, crabbed, harsh, tangy, acrimonious, incisive, shrewd, **12**. off; *synonyms* (*adv*) by, forth, beyond, over, aside, gone, abreast, (*adj*) away, bad, putrid, remote, down, rotten, wide, (*int*) out; *antonyms* (*adj*) fresh, on, **13**. unripe; *synonyms* (*adj*) immature, green, raw, crude, premature, young, juvenile; *antonym* (*adj*) mature, **14**. sour; *synonyms* (*adj*) morose, rancid, severe, gruff, dour, glum, grim, sullen, off, rough, (*v*) acidify, ferment, turn, embitter, (*n*) acidity; *antonym* (*adj*) kindly, **15**. tasteless; *synonyms* (*adj*) flashy, gaudy, vulgar, garish, stale, diluted, indelicate, showy, tacky, tawdry, unsavory, gustless, inappropriate, lifeless, loud; *antonym* (*adj*) delicious.

maia 1. rope; *synonyms* (*n*) cable, lasso, lariat, noose, cord, hawser, leash, line, string, tape, lace, tether, thread, (*v*) tie, bind, **2**. whence; *synonyms* (*adv*) wherefrom, because, for, hence, then, therefore, whenceforth.

maiai therefrom; *synonyms* (*adv*) thence, therefore, hence, (*adj*) accurate, bestowed, coincidence, conformed, correct, correctness, deportment, detail, exact, expected, likeness, precise.

maiaki 1. southerly; *synonyms* (*adj*) southern, meridional, (*n*) austral, austrine, (*adv*) southly, **2**. southbound; *synonym* (*adj*) southward.

maibunia underdone; *synonyms* (*adj*) rare, raw, undercooked, bloody, crazy, dispersed, juicy, meshuga, meshugge, pink, red, screwball, softheaded, thin, uncooked; *antonyms* (*adj*) overcooked, overdone.

maii pale; *synonyms* (*adj*) ghastly, faint, wan, dull, light, pallid, weak, watery, cadaverous, (*v*) dim, blanch, (*n*) boundary, confine, border, bound; *antonyms* (*adj*) dark, rosy, strong, brown.

maikai hence; *synonyms* (*adv*) accordingly, consequently, therefore, away, because, for, then, thus, so, thence, whence.

maikanne therefrom; *synonyms* (*adv*) thence, therefore, hence, (*adj*) accurate, bestowed, coincidence, conformed, correct, correctness, deportment, detail, exact, expected, likeness, precise.

maikeike sob; *synonyms* (*n*) cry, moan, lament, groan, sobbing, asshole, bastard, cocksucker, (*v*) whine, wail, weep, snivel, whimper, howl, sigh.

maimai 1. damp; *synonyms* (*adj*) moist, muggy, clammy, cool, dank, humid, (*v*) break, check, chill, deaden, benumb, (*n*) wet, dampness, moisture, clamminess; *antonyms* (*adj*) dry, (*n*) dryness, **2**. wet; *synonyms* (*adj*) damp, drenched, soaked, sodden, rainy, saturated, soggy, watery, (*v*) moisten, water, dampen, wash, douse, irrigate, (*n*) humidity; *antonyms* (*adj*) dehydrated, parched, **3**. soaked; *synonyms* (*adj*) soaking, sopping, drunk, plastered, sloshed, soppy, besotted, **4**. pee; *synonyms* (*n*) piss, peeing, urine, (*v*) piddle, micturate, urinate, wee, make, **5**. urinate; *synonyms* (*v*) pee, excrete, addle, attain, build, cause, clear, constitute, construct, cook, crap, create, defecate, do, draw.

maina abreast; *synonyms* (*adj*) near, arow, contemporary, conversant, familiar, informed, knowledgeable, up-to-date, versed, (*adv*) acquainted, off, opposite, aside, (*prep*) against, facing.

mainaina white; *synonyms* (*adj*) fair, ashen, blank, clean, snowy, wan, achromatic, bloodless, livid, pallid, colorless, bright, good, (*n*) pale, (*v*) whiten; *antonyms* (*adj*) dark, rosy, (*n*) black.

mainarake wan; *synonyms* (*v*) pale, (*adj*) pallid, cadaverous, ghastly, sickly, faint, haggard, ashen, colorless, pasty, sallow, bloodless, lurid, weak, ashy; *antonym* (*adj*) strong.

maing 1. left; *synonyms* (*adj*) gone, absent, odd, port, remaining, larboard, sinister, unexpended, abandoned, remainder, corrupt, deserted, disastrous, dishonest, evil; *antonym* (*n*) right, **2**. move; *synonyms* (*v*) act, affect, carry, excite, go, impel, instigate, maneuver, touch, travel, flow, bear, (*n*) motion, drive, transfer; *antonym* (*v*) stay.

mainiku east; *synonyms* (*n*) orient, e, einsteinium, tocopherol, (*v*) orientate.

maio 1. assemble; *synonyms* (*v*) amass, accumulate, aggregate, convene, gather, meet, call, collect, compile, concentrate, converge, group, make, rally, edit; *antonyms* (*v*) dismantle, disperse, disband, disassemble, **2**. gather; *synonyms* (*v*) deduce, assemble, congregate, flock, garner, tuck, earn, reap, derive, extract, acquire, cluster, conclude, crease, (*n*) fold; *antonym* (*v*) scatter.

maioaki 1. gathered; *synonyms* (*adj*) collected, deepened, accumulated, amassed, assembled, collective, congregate, equanimous, massed, poised, **2**. assembled; *synonyms* (*adj*) united, accrued, aggregate, built, fabricated, fancied, fictional, fictitious, invented, reinforced.

maioraora underdone; *synonyms* (*adj*) rare, raw, undercooked, bloody, crazy, dispersed, juicy, meshuga, meshugge, pink, red, screwball, softheaded, thin, uncooked; *antonyms* (*adj*) overcooked, overdone.

mairiri mob; *synonyms* (*n*) crowd, gang, pack, mass, horde, crew, band, bunch, concourse, rabble, swarm, cluster, company, army, (*v*) throng.

mairoun therefrom; *synonyms* (*adv*) thence, therefore, hence, (*adj*) accurate, bestowed, coincidence, conformed, correct, correctness, deportment, detail, exact, expected, likeness, precise.

maiti numerous; *synonyms* (*adj*) manifold, many, abundant, frequent, multiple, multitudinous, copious, innumerable, plentiful, populous, great, myriad, rife, several, various; *antonym* (*adj*) few.

maitia unified; *synonyms* (*adj*) incorporated, integrated, united, amalgamated, coordinated, incorporate, interconnected, merged, allied, collective, combined, concurrent, conformable, corporate, entire.

maitiaki unified; *synonyms* (*adj*) incorporated, integrated, united, amalgamated, coordinated, incorporate, interconnected, merged, allied, collective, combined, concurrent, conformable, corporate, entire.

maitin 1. exact; *synonyms* (*adj*) detailed, precise, actual, authentic, careful, definite, direct, (*v*) accurate, close, demand, require, claim, command, ask, (*n*) correct; *antonyms* (*adj*) inaccurate, imprecise, vague, wrong, approximate, inexact, 2. exactly; *synonyms* (*adv*) precisely, correctly, right, truly, sharp, absolutely, just, accurately, certainly, closely, completely, directly, punctually, rightly, barely; *antonyms* (*adv*) approximately, inaccurately, (*prep*) about, 3. precisely; *synonyms* (*adv*) exactly, literally, meticulously, strictly, only, clearly, expressly, carefully, justly, faithfully, quite, specifically, delicately, (*adj*) even, really; *antonyms* (*adv*) clumsily, indistinctly, vaguely, 4. precise; *synonyms* (*adj*) exact, minute, certain, delicate, neat, particular, ceremonious, clear, distinct, faithful, fastidious, formal, meticulous, punctilious, specific; *antonym* (*adj*) rough.

maitoro 1. cold; *synonyms* (*adj*) chilly, frigid, aloof, callous, distant, icy, indifferent, apathetic, bleak, cool, dead, dull, freezing, (*n*) chilliness, chill; *antonyms* (*adj*) warm, friendly, hot, burning, prepared, affectionate, loving, soporific, (*n*) heat, warmth, 2. cool; *synonyms* (*adj*) cold, collected, composed, fine, lukewarm, soothe, nonchalant, (*v*) calm, assuage, allay, pacify, quench, refrigerate, (*n*) composure, poise; *antonyms* (*adj*) agitated, excited, enthusiastic, feverish, temperate, tepid, 3. freshen;

synonyms (*v*) air, invigorate, refresh, ventilate, fresh, aerate, renew, purify, complete, expose, fragrance, imbue, refill, refreshen, refuel, 4. frigid; *synonyms* (*adj*) arctic, frosty, chilling, frozen, gelid, glacial, wintry, stony, feeble, reserved, tame, unfriendly, vapid, bald, polar.

maitorotoro 1. biting; *synonyms* (*v*) acute, (*adj*) acrid, acid, acrimonious, sarcastic, sharp, bitter, cutting, pungent, severe, acerbic, barbed, hot, incisive, keen; *antonyms* (*adj*) gentle, mild, blunt, kind, 2. frozen; *synonyms* (*adj*) cold, frosty, arctic, frigid, glacial, wintry, freezing, icy, stiff, congealed, chilled, chilly, gelid, iced, set; *antonym* (*adj*) moving.

maiu 1. animate; *synonyms* (*adj*) alive, live, spirited, (*v*) enliven, encourage, inspire, actuate, cheer, exhilarate, hearten, inspirit, invigorate, quicken, revive, stimulate; *antonyms* (*adj*) lifeless, (*v*) deaden, 2. flourishing; *synonyms* (*adj*) prosperous, thriving, booming, healthy, luxuriant, palmy, successful, verdant, lush, auspicious, favorable, affluent, blooming, golden, growing; *antonym* (*adj*) failing, 3. alive; *synonyms* (*adj*) active, living, sensible, vivacious, animated, lively, responsive, aware, eager, acute, energetic, animate, awake, extant, keen; *antonyms* (*adj*) dead, deceased, inanimate, 4. existing; *synonyms* (*adj*) actual, current, existent, present, real, contemporary, instant, modern, (*v*) being; *antonym* (*adj*) lost, 5. exist; *synonyms* (*v*) dwell, lie, be, endure, abide, consist, belong, continue, occur, subsist, survive, hold, remain; *antonym* (*v*) die, 6. fresh; *synonyms* (*adj*) bracing, brisk, clean, novel, bright, original, recent, airy, bold, chilly, cool, forward, green, pure, (*adv*) new; *antonyms* (*adj*) old, stale, decayed, exhausted, hot, humid, muggy, musty, off, oppressive, rotten, tired, worn, dry, sweltering, 7. living; *synonyms* (*adj*) fresh, quick, vital, lifelike, (*n*) livelihood, life, aliveness, animation, benefice, existence, keep, maintenance, subsistence, support, lifetime; *antonym* (*n*) death, 8. prosperous; *synonyms* (*adj*) lucky, flourishing, opulent, advantageous, comfortable, easy, rich, well-off, propitious, happy, favourable, prospering, wealthy, (*n*) fortunate, good; *antonym* (*adj*) poor, 9. survive; *synonyms* (*v*) outlast, outlive, exist, last, resist, weather, withstand, brave, cope, go, overcome, prevail, (*adj*) exceed; *antonym* (*v*) succumb, 10. subsist; *synonyms* (*v*) reside, obtain, feed, maintain.

maiureirei 1. luxurious; *synonyms* (*adj*) voluptuous, costly, deluxe, lavish, sumptuous, epicurean, grand, luscious, comfortable, expensive, magnificent, opulent, rich, (*n*) lush, luxuriant; *antonym* (*adj*) cheap, 2. thrive; *synonyms* (*v*) prosper, flourish, grow, advance, blossom, succeed, bloom, increase, boom, expand, wax, develop, burgeon, extend, *(adj)* luxuriate; *antonym (v)* decline, **3**. vivid; *synonyms (adj)* graphic, intense, brilliant, lifelike, live, acute, animated, clear, colorful, glowing, strong, picturesque, expressive, brisk, *(v)* bright; *antonym (adj)* dull.

maiurerirei 1. flourishing; *synonyms (adj)* prosperous, thriving, booming, healthy, luxuriant, palmy, successful, verdant, lush, auspicious, favorable, affluent, blooming, golden, growing; *antonym (adj)* failing, **2**. thriving; *synonyms (adj)* flourishing, prospering, rich, easy, fortunate, lucky, roaring; *antonym (adj)* declining.

maiuroaroa 1. alive; *synonyms (adj)* active, live, living, sensible, vivacious, animated, lively, responsive, aware, eager, acute, energetic, animate, awake, extant; *antonyms (adj)* dead, deceased, inanimate, **2**. thriving; *synonyms (adj)* flourishing, prosperous, successful, booming, prospering, rich, affluent, auspicious, easy, favorable, fortunate, growing, healthy, lucky, lush; *antonyms (adj)* failing, declining.

maiutakoni 1. intelligent; *synonyms (adj)* clever, alert, astute, bright, intellectual, quick-witted, rational, sensible, cunning, brilliant, canny, gifted, knowing, knowledgeable, quick; *antonyms (adj)* unintelligent, dim, dull-witted, thick, slow, stupid, **2**. quick; *synonyms (adj)* prompt, active, agile, hasty, intelligent, nimble, speedy, alive, cursory, dexterous, expeditious, hurried, immediate, instant, *(adv)* fast; *antonyms (adj)* leisurely, dull, **3**. witty; *synonyms (adj)* humorous, amusing, funny, facetious, jocular, comic, comical, poignant, waggish, acute, lively, wise, *(v)* smart, sharp, keen; *antonym (adj)* serious, **4**. vivacious; *synonyms (adj)* animated, spirited, cheerful, sprightly, vibrant, brisk, buoyant, effervescent, energetic, gay, merry, spry, vigorous, exuberant, blithe; *antonyms (adj)* lethargic, listless.

maka apprehend; *synonyms (v)* appreciate, arrest, comprehend, catch, conceive, fathom, grasp, realize, understand, follow, sense, anticipate, capture, detain, dig; *antonym (v)* release.

makaiao 1. enormous; *synonyms (adj)* big, colossal, huge, immense, vast, excessive, exorbitant, great, large, prodigious, tremendous, stupendous, gargantuan, giant, gigantic; *antonyms (adj)* minute, small, tiny, insignificant, miniature, **2**. gigantic; *synonyms (adj)* enormous, mammoth, massive, monstrous, monumental, monster, terrific, gigantean, infinite, whopping, brawny, high, **3**. huge; *synonyms (adj)* extensive, elephantine, ample, considerable, jumbo, heavy, untold, bulky, cavernous, cosmic, extreme, hefty, mighty, mountainous, roomy.

makaki apprehended; *synonyms (adj)* held, appreciated, comprehended, detained, gratifying, pleasing, satisfying.

makana 1. delicate; *synonyms (adj)* fine, accurate, breakable, dainty, fragile, refined, tender, beautiful, brittle, difficult, frail, nice, sensitive, soft, slim; *antonyms (adj)* strong, inelegant, robust, heavy, sturdy, tough, **2**. brittle; *synonyms (adj)* crisp, crumbly, crispy, short, brickle, crunchy, delicate, flimsy, frangible, friable, insubstantial, shivery, brickly; *antonyms (adj)* soggy, solid, **3**. frail; *synonyms (adj)* light, rickety, slender, decrepit, puny, sick, slight, unhealthy, fallible, impotent, flabby, ailing, *(v)* weak, feeble, faint; *antonym (adj)* substantial, **4**. fragile; *synonyms (adj)* shaky, brash, infirm, thin; *antonyms (adj)* unbreakable, permanent, **5**. soft; *synonyms (adj)* gentle, easy, limp, balmy, quiet, slack, loose, clement, flaccid, lenient, mild, pliant, smooth, pleasant, *(v)* low; *antonyms (adj)* hard, firm, harsh, loud, hoarse, rough, stiff, alcoholic, shrill, **6**. weak; *synonyms (adj)* flat, watery, cowardly, diluted, exhausted, inadequate, lax, nerveless, poor, sickly, powerless, effeminate, bland, debilitated, *(n)* helpless; *antonyms (adj)* brave, concentrated, safe, compelling, determined, effective, forceful, healthy, intense, powerful, resolute, vigorous, able, fit, hard-wearing, **7**. tender; *synonyms (adj)* affectionate, painful, loving, sore, compassionate, fond, caring, immature, *(v)* proffer, present, propose, give, *(n)* offer, bid, overture; *antonyms (adj)* hardhearted, rubbery.

makanakana soft; *synonyms (adj)* gentle, easy, light, limp, balmy, delicate, quiet, slack, loose, clement, faint, flabby, flaccid, *(v)* feeble, low; *antonyms (adj)* hard, firm, harsh, loud, hoarse, rough, solid, stiff, alcoholic, shrill, strong.

makaoakao 1. tangled; *synonyms (adj)* involved, complex, knotted, intricate, complicated, entangled, convoluted, knotty, difficult, disheveled, tousled, kinky, labyrinthine, muddled, perplexed; *antonym (adj)* free, **2**. twisted; *synonyms (adj)* crooked, deformed, perverted, bent, distorted, coiled, misshapen, contorted, curved, twined, winding, wry, gnarled, tortuous, awry; *antonyms (adj)* straight, tidy.

makareirei ardent; *synonyms (adj)* burning, enthusiastic, fervent, passionate, eager, impassioned, keen, vehement, warm, acute, affectionate, avid, devoted, earnest, fervid; *antonyms (adj)* indifferent, apathetic.

makaro smoulder; *synonyms (v)* smolder, choke, suffocate.

makei 1. frolic; *synonyms (n)* play, romp, sport, caper, diversion, fun, joke, joy, merriment, mirth, *(v)* cavort, disport, frisk, gambol, lark, **2**.

frolicsome; *synonyms* (*adj*) playful, frisky, frolic, waggish, coltish, gay, rollicking, frolicky, airy, gleeful, jocular, jolly, kittenish, lighthearted, lively, **3.** sportive; *synonyms* (*adj*) frolicsome, cheerful, jocund, merry, blithe, facetious, jovial, mirthful, vivacious, hilarious, funny, gamesome, jaunty, sprightly, (*v*) wanton, **4.** playful; *synonyms* (*adj*) humorous, impish, mischievous, skittish, naughty, frivolous, amusing, spirited, whimsical, arch, joking, flippant, perky, sportive, wicked; *antonyms* (*adj*) serious, lethargic, solemn.

makeke wane; *synonyms* (*n*) ebb, (*v*) decline, fade, fall, sink, decrease, diminish, dwindle, fail, recede, wither, shrink, contract, decay, abate.

makerekere rough; *synonyms* (*adj*) coarse, hard, harsh, raw, crude, cruel, grating, gross, hoarse, jagged, approximate, gruff, inclement, (*n*) boisterous, draft; *antonyms* (*adj*) gentle, smooth, polished, precise, refined, silky, soft, sophisticated, even, exact, glossy, pleasant.

makerikaki 1. contract; *synonyms* (*n*) compact, charter, (*v*) covenant, bargain, concentrate, condense, narrow, catch, compress, constrict, shrink, wrinkle, abbreviate, (*adj*) abridge, shorten; *antonyms* (*v*) expand, widen, stretch, **2.** recoil; *synonyms* (*n*) reaction, backlash, repercussion, (*v*) bounce, kick, rebound, bound, cringe, flinch, quail, retreat, balk, cower, funk, react.

makerikakiaki contracted; *synonyms* (*v*) shrunk, (*adj*) narrow, insular, contract, constricted, tight, bound.

maki 1. broken; *synonyms* (*v*) broke, (*adj*) tame, torn, busted, imperfect, intermittent, rough, rugged, ruined, uneven, disjointed, incomplete, confused, cracked, crushed; *antonyms* (*adj*) constant, unbroken, intact, whole, wild, **2.** barely; *synonyms* (*adv*) hardly, just, scarcely, simply, merely, narrowly, purely, scantily, scarce, slightly, solely, absolutely, (*adj*) only; *antonym* (*adv*) almost, **3.** closed; *synonyms* (*v*) close, tight, accurate, adjoining, attentive, (*adj*) blind, blocked, finished, shut, congested, fastened, exclusive, insular, stopped, airtight; *antonym* (*adj*) open, **4.** crumbled; *synonyms* (*adj*) broken, fragmented, rotten, disconnected, disunited, split, **5.** ruptured; *synonyms* (*adj*) burst, cleft, **6.** sodden; *synonyms* (*adj*) soaked, soaking, damp, dripping, saturated, wet, muddy, soggy, sopping, drenched, moist, soppy, watery, (*v*) soft, molten; *antonym* (*adj*) dry, **7.** scarcely; *synonyms* (*adv*) barely, rarely, seldom, scantly, exactly, precisely.

makibora 1. dented; *synonyms* (*v*) indented, (*adj*) bent, crumpled, bended, bowed, concave, creased, hurt, injured, spoiled, broken, inclined, rumpled, scratched, smashed, **2.** battered; *synonyms* (*adj*) beaten, worn, damaged, maltreated, ragged, tattered, abused, aching, bruised, decrepit,

dilapidated, conquered, craggy, (*v*) seedy, shattered, **3.** squashed; *synonyms* (*adj*) compacted, compressed, condensed, dense, solid.

makiki grimace; *synonyms* (*n*) frown, face, mop, sneer, smile, mouth, expression, roar, (*v*) scowl, glower, cringe, glare, wince.

makimaki 1. saturated; *synonyms* (*adj*) drenched, sodden, wet, concentrated, soaked, sopping, full, soggy, soppy, pure, soaking; *antonym* (*adj*) dry, **2.** sodden; *synonyms* (*adj*) damp, dripping, saturated, muddy, moist, watery, (*v*) soft, molten, reeking.

makin little; *synonyms* (*adj*) small, diminutive, insignificant, brief, minute, petty, short, some, tiny, exiguous, light, baby, bantam, (*v*) dash, bit; *antonyms* (*adj*) big, enormous, large, important.

makina 1. doubt; *synonyms* (*n*) disbelief, misgiving, question, dispute, apprehension, incertitude, skepticism, uncertainty, diffidence, (*v*) distrust, query, suspicion, mistrust, suspect, demur; *antonyms* (*n*) certainty, confidence, conclusiveness, (*v*) trust, **2.** dread; *synonyms* (*n*) anxiety, awe, panic, alarm, consternation, dismay, foreboding, terror, trepidation, affright, doubt, fright, horror, (*v*) fear, worry; *antonym* (*n*) bravery, **3.** fear; *synonyms* (*n*) anguish, care, disquiet, fearfulness, intimidation, trouble, funk, phobia, respect, unease, (*v*) dread, concern, reverence, apprehend, revere; *antonyms* (*n*) fearlessness, reassurance, **4.** respect; *synonyms* (*n*) honor, esteem, homage, worship, heed, notice, account, consideration, deference, (*v*) regard, observe, admire, appreciate, estimation, keep; *antonyms* (*n*) cheek, insolence, impudence, (*v*) disrespect, scorn, despise, dishonor, disregard, humiliate.

makinaki 1. dreaded; *synonyms* (*adj*) dread, awful, terrible, abominable, amazing, atrocious, awed, awesome, awing, cowardly, desperate, dire, direful, dreadful, (*v*) drad, **2.** respected; *synonyms* (*adj*) esteemed, illustrious, respectable, appreciated, dear, honored, revered, valued, celebrated, famous, glorious, prestigious, redoubtable.

makinono 1. saturated; *synonyms* (*adj*) drenched, sodden, wet, concentrated, soaked, sopping, full, soggy, soppy, pure, soaking; *antonym* (*adj*) dry, **2.** wet; *synonyms* (*adj*) damp, humid, moist, dank, rainy, saturated, watery, (*v*) moisten, water, dampen, wash, douse, irrigate, (*n*) moisture, humidity; *antonyms* (*adj*) dehydrated, parched, **3.** soaked; *synonyms* (*adj*) drunk, plastered, sloshed, besotted.

makiro 1. gnaw; *synonyms* (*v*) bite, chew, fret, crunch, corrode, eat, erode, nibble, masticate, munch, champ, fray, harass, devour, (*n*) chafe, **2.** masticate; *synonyms* (*v*) gnaw, manducate, jaw, cranch, craunch, **3.** crunch; *synonyms* (*n*) squeeze, compaction, compression, (*v*) crush, crackle, scrunch, grind, shatter, crash, crinkle, mash, beat, bray, comminute, crump, **4**. chew; *synonyms* (*v*) chomp, mouth, berate, taste, (*n*) chaw, chewing, cud, mastication.

makoko 1. close; *synonyms* (*adj*) near, adjacent, nearby, accurate, tight, approximate, narrow, (*v*) compact, stop, conclude, (*adv*) by, about, (*n*) end, finish, conclusion; *antonyms* (*adj*) distant, airy, fresh, loose, far, (*v*) open, start, **2**. bunched; *synonyms* (*adj*) agglomerate, agglomerated, agglomerative, bunchy, clustered, **3**. stacked; *synonyms* (*adj*) buxom, curvaceous, prepared, shapely, voluptuous.

makone 1. tender; *synonyms* (*adj*) affectionate, painful, loving, sensitive, soft, sore, compassionate, delicate, fond, gentle, mild, (*v*) proffer, (*n*) offer, bid, overture; *antonyms* (*adj*) tough, hard, hardhearted, rubbery, rough, **2**. pliable; *synonyms* (*adj*) flexible, elastic, plastic, ductile, pliant, flexile, malleable, fictile, supple, yielding, docile, resilient, (*v*) lithe, limber; *antonyms* (*adj*) rigid, stiff, **3**. soft; *synonyms* (*adj*) easy, light, limp, balmy, quiet, slack, loose, clement, faint, flabby, flaccid, frail, lenient, (*v*) feeble, low; *antonyms* (*adj*) firm, harsh, loud, hoarse, solid, alcoholic, shrill, strong.

makoneua doubled; *synonyms* (*adj*) double, twofold, bivalent, reduplicate, duple, forked, reduplicative, threefold, treble.

makoro incise; *synonyms* (*v*) carve, etch, cut, engrave, notch, scrape, scratch, slash, hack, slice, slit, incide, pierce.

makoroaki incised; *synonyms* (*adj*) engraved, graven, etched, inscribed, sculpted, sculptured.

makoroua 1. half; *synonyms* (*n*) mediety, halve, piece, bisection, hemisphere, (*adv*) halfendeal, imperfectly, (*adj*) moiety, part, short, behalf, bisected, divided, even-steven, halved; *antonyms* (*n*) whole, all, **2**. halve; *synonyms* (*v*) bisect, divide, split, dimidiate, **3**. divided; *synonyms* (*adj*) cleft, detached, forked, separate, separated, shared, disjointed, **4**. split; *synonyms* (*v*) crack, cut, fracture, slit, burst, divorce, breach, cleave, division, fork, (*n*) break, rip, rupture, tear, cleavage; *antonyms* (*v*) join, unite, merge.

makorouaki 1. halved; *synonyms* (*adj*) half, dimidiate, **2**. split; *synonyms* (*v*) crack, cut, fracture, slit, burst, divide, separate, divorce, breach, cleave, (*n*) break, rip, rupture, tear, cleavage; *antonyms* (*v*) join, unite, merge.

makota 1. minor; *synonyms* (*adj*) little, inferior, insignificant, junior, lesser, lower, small, inconsequential, less, marginal, negligible, petty, secondary, (*n*) child, juvenile; *antonyms* (*adj*) major, important, significant, basic, chief, fundamental, leading, main, overriding, superseding, serious, considerable, extensive, greater, senior, **2**. mere; *synonyms* (*adj*) bare, entire, pure, simple, clear,

naked, (*n*) lake, loch, downright, tarn, absolute, boundary, pond, stark, (*v*) sheer, **3**. insignificant; *synonyms* (*adj*) minute, inconsiderable, humble, immaterial, infinitesimal, light, poor, trivial, unimportant, diminutive, inappreciable, meaningless, minor, paltry, slight; *antonyms* (*adj*) enormous, great, huge, substantial, colossal, influential, momentous, valuable, **4**. trifle; *synonyms* (*n*) nothing, bagatelle, detail, triviality, (*v*) play, dally, fiddle, flirt, fool, frivol, coquet, dawdle, (*adj*) toy, trinket, plaything.

maku 1. afraid; *synonyms* (*adj*) fearful, timid, shy, anxious, apprehensive, frightened, nervous, scared, worried, horrified, terrified, uneasy, reluctant, (*adv*) cowardly; *antonyms* (*adj*) fearless, brave, **2**. dismayed; *synonyms* (*adj*) appalled, aghast, shocked, startled, afraid, dejected, discouraged, disheartened, downcast, downhearted, upset; *antonym* (*adj*) delighted, **3**. dismay; *synonyms* (*n*) alarm, consternation, terror, awe, discouragement, dread, anxiety, (*v*) appall, depress, dishearten, daunt, affright, discourage, horrify, appal, **4**. dread; *synonyms* (*n*) apprehension, panic, dismay, foreboding, trepidation, doubt, fright, horror, phobia, reverence, (*v*) fear, worry, (*adj*) dreadful, frightful, terrible; *antonym* (*n*) bravery, **5**. frightened; *synonyms* (*adj*) intimidated, restless; *antonyms* (*adj*) calm, confident, unimpressed, **6**. apprehensive; *synonyms* (*adj*) alarmed, doubtful, insecure, jealous, concerned, discerning, distrustful, fidgety, hesitant, jumpy, knowing, solicitous, timorous, troubled, (*n*) tremulous, **7**. alarmed; *synonyms* (*adj*) disturbed, petrified, fretful, panicky, unnerved, **8**. fear; *synonyms* (*n*) anguish, care, disquiet, fearfulness, intimidation, trouble, diffidence, funk, misgiving, respect, unease, (*v*) concern, apprehend, revere, venerate; *antonyms* (*n*) confidence, fearlessness, reassurance, **9**. scared.

makuaki dreaded; *synonyms* (*adj*) dread, awful, terrible, abominable, amazing, atrocious, awed, awesome, awing, cowardly, desperate, dire, direful, dreadful, (*v*) drad.

makuna cover; *synonyms* (*v*) coat, conceal, top, bury, cloak, (*n*) blind, blanket, screen, binding, camouflage, cap, covering, lid, mask, shield; *antonyms* (*v*) reveal, expose, uncover.

makunaki covered; *synonyms* (*adj*) hidden, veiled, concealed, covert, coated, masked, obscured, secret, shrouded, thick, wrapped, (*prep*) cloaked; *antonyms* (*adj*) bare, naked.

makuriana laborious; *synonyms* (*adj*) difficult, arduous, hard, backbreaking, diligent, heavy, industrious, grueling, assiduous, exhausting, formidable, painful, strenuous, tedious, toilsome; *antonym* (*adj*) easy.

mama 1. breast; *synonyms* (*n*) bosom, boob, chest, knocker, tit, titty, mammilla, bust, heart, mamma, nipple, pap, soul, spirit, (v) front, **2.** bashful; *synonyms* (adj) timid, ashamed, coy, diffident, backward, modest, retiring, shy, shrinking, mousy, blate, demure, reserved, sheepish, (n) shamefaced; *antonym* (adj) brash, **3.** timid; *synonyms* (adj) fearful, afraid, cowardly, bashful, cautious, nervous, apprehensive, frightened, craven, anxious, faint, fainthearted, pusillanimous, scared, spineless; *antonyms* (adj) confident, bold, fearless, (n) brave.

mamaka 1. instrumental; *synonyms* (adj) conducive, helpful, implemental, useful, lyric, operatic, vocal, subservient, influential, profitable, inservient, instrumentary, organic, usable, active, **2.** effectual; *synonyms* (adj) effective, efficacious, efficient, telling, authoritative, operative, powerful, practical, sovereign, trenchant, (n) able, capable, competent; *antonym* (adj) ineffectual, **3.** ardent; *synonyms* (adj) burning, enthusiastic, fervent, passionate, eager, impassioned, keen, vehement, warm, acute, affectionate, avid, devoted, earnest, fervid; *antonyms* (adj) indifferent, apathetic, **4.** important; *synonyms* (adj) essential, grave, fundamental, significant, chief, crucial, key, remarkable, serious, big, central, consequential, considerable, critical, decisive; *antonyms* (adj) unimportant, insignificant, trivial, minor, irrelevant, low, worthless, **5.** influential; *synonyms* (adj) dominant, potent, cogent, forcible, impressive, predominant, prevailing, strong, eminent, energetic, prominent, convincing, dynamic, major, (v) important; *antonym* (adj) unconvincing, **6.** energetic; *synonyms* (adj) animated, brisk, busy, driving, agile, emphatic, aggressive, enterprising, forceful, hearty, industrious, lively, spirited, sprightly, spry; *antonyms* (adj) lethargic, lazy, sluggish, exhausted, inactive, indolent, languid, weary, dull, listless, **7.** substantial; *synonyms* (adj) actual, solid, firm, real, palpable, momentous, sturdy, sound, concrete, ample, corporeal, durable, heavy, hefty, large; *antonyms* (adj) insubstantial, small, ethereal, fine, **8.** strong; *synonyms* (adj) intense, deep, stable, steady, good, hard, lusty, rigid, robust, secure, fierce, athletic, high, loud, (v) steadfast; *antonyms* (adj) weak, bland, delicate, faint, feeble, frail, mild, pale, slight, cowardly, diluted, flimsy, imperceptible, lightweight, soft, **9.** significant; *synonyms* (adj) material, meaningful, expressive, indicative, pregnant, relevant, substantial, meaning, solemn, eloquent, historic, noteworthy, portentous, vital, appreciable, **10.** vigorous; *synonyms* (adj) hardy, strenuous, mighty, healthy, smart, brawny, muscular, stout, tough, valiant, (n) brave, rugged, courageous, (v) fresh, live; *antonym* (adj) unenergetic, **11.** prominent; *synonyms* (adj) notable, noted, great, celebrated, distinguished, famous, illustrious, leading, noticeable, obvious, outstanding, salient, striking, (n) bold, (v) conspicuous; *antonyms* (adj) inconspicuous, unknown.

mamaku 1. cowardly; *synonyms* (adj) coward, timid, afraid, craven, gutless, scared, shrinking, sneaky, base, dastardly, faint, fainthearted, fearful, poltroon, pusillanimous; *antonyms* (adj) fearless, intrepid, strong, (adv) brave, bold, courageous, daring, **2.** nervous; *synonyms* (adj) anxious, excitable, tense, cowardly, apprehensive, shy, uneasy, firm, edgy, fidgety, neurotic, restless, uncomfortable, (adv) excited, agitated; *antonyms* (adj) calm, relaxed, **3.** fearful; *synonyms* (adj) dreadful, awful, terrible, dire, eerie, formidable, frightful, appalling, awesome, alarming, desperate, direful, frightened, frightening, horrendous; *antonyms* (adj) rational, confident, unimpressed, **4.** apprehensive; *synonyms* (adj) nervous, alarmed, worried, doubtful, insecure, jealous, concerned, discerning, distrustful, hesitant, jumpy, knowing, solicitous, timorous, (n) tremulous, **5.** timorous; *synonyms* (adj) bashful, diffident, fearsome, retiring, terrified, weak.

mamakuri 1. fidget; *synonyms* (v) wriggle, squirm, wiggle, fiddle, (n) fidgetiness, restlessness, (adj) bustle, bother, fuss, hurry, stir, ado, drive, **2.** wobble; *synonyms* (v) totter, rock, sway, lurch, reel, swing, stagger, quake, oscillate, dodder, quiver, shift, tilt, (n) shake, tremor.

mamana 1. cheat; *synonyms* (v) trick, beguile, betray, defraud, fake, beat, deceive, fleece, (n) swindle, con, fraud, bilk, impostor, sham, charlatan, **2.** mislead; *synonyms* (v) cheat, fool, misinform, delude, dupe, hoodwink, lie, misdirect, misguide, seduce, bluff, circumvent, cajole, entice, inveigle, **3.** dupe; *synonyms* (n) gull, victim, cully, prey, tool, butt, (v) bamboozle, kid, befool, cod, mislead, trap, cozen, victimize, gudgeon, **4.** deceive; *synonyms* (v) pretend, hoax, sell, humbug, cuckold, blind, double-cross, wile, disappoint, falsify, mock, mystify, abuse, ensnare, (adj) dazzle, **5.** delude; *synonym* (v) decoy, **6.** trick; *synonyms* (n) deceit, deception, joke, prank, device, stratagem, knack, delusion, gimmick, illusion, ruse, shift, subterfuge, (v) fob, maneuver, **7.** swindle; *synonyms* (n) imposture, racket, cheating, (v) do, bunco, diddle, gyp, jockey, scam, fiddle, mulct, nobble, rook, rob, chouse.

mamanaki mislead; *synonyms* (v) betray, deceive, cheat, beguile, con, fool, misinform, delude, dupe, hoodwink, lie, misdirect, misguide, trick, seduce.

mamananga itinerant; *synonyms* (adj) errant, ambulatory, traveling, journeying, migratory, nomadic, wandering, (n) migrant, traveler, vagabond, wanderer, nomad, drifter, rover, vagrant.

mamangaingai nag; *synonyms* (*n*) hack, jade, worry, horse, hackney, (*v*) annoy, bother, complain, gripe, scold, badger, torment, fret, grouse, (*adj*) bicker.

mamaoriori 1. bending; *synonyms* (*n*) bend, bow, flexion, deflection, deflexion, crook, flexure, (*adj*) flexible, supple, pliant, winding, **2.** nerveless; *synonyms* (*adj*) cool, coolheaded, feeble, weak, flaccid, imperturbable, spineless, faint, impotent, nervous, infirm, lame, decrepit, fearful, (*v*) sinewless, **3.** sick; *synonyms* (*adj*) ill, queasy, ailing, indisposed, poorly, weary, invalid, diseased, morbid, sickly, nauseous, poor, crazy, disgusted, (*v*) unwell; *antonyms* (*adj*) well, healthy, **4.** soft; *synonyms* (*adj*) gentle, easy, light, limp, balmy, delicate, quiet, slack, loose, clement, flabby, frail, lenient, mild, (*v*) low; *antonyms* (*adj*) hard, firm, harsh, loud, hoarse, rough, solid, stiff, alcoholic, shrill, strong.

mamara 1. feeble; *synonyms* (*adj*) delicate, weak, decrepit, ailing, dim, dull, frail, helpless, infirm, lax, mild, poor, powerless, (*v*) faint, debilitated; *antonyms* (*adj*) strong, vigorous, hearty, tough, **2.** faint; *synonyms* (*adj*) collapse, dizzy, feeble, indistinct, gentle, soft, vague, distant, drop, fuzzy, (*v*) languish, swoon, droop, conk, exhausted; *antonyms* (*adj*) distinct, clear, obvious, considerable, loud, pungent, **3.** impaired; *synonyms* (*adj*) afflicted, sick, damaged, crippled, corrupted, defective, faulty, adulterate, affected, deficient, depressed, dilapidated, diluted, disgusted, dumb, **4.** slight; *synonyms* (*adj*) flimsy, slender, thin, fragile, fine, lean, (*n*) scorn, disdain, (*v*) disregard, insult, neglect, ignore, affront, cut, (*adv*) light; *antonyms* (*adj*) major, fat, heavy, intense, severe, thickset, wide, **5.** sickly; *synonyms* (*adj*) diseased, indisposed, morbid, pale, poorly, sallow, peaked, pasty, languid, pallid, unhealthy, unwell, wan, (*n*) invalid, (*v*) low; *antonyms* (*adj*) healthy, bitter, **6.** weak; *synonyms* (*adj*) flat, watery, cowardly, inadequate, nerveless, shaky, sickly, slack, slight, effeminate, impotent, bland, dilute, insipid, (*v*) loose; *antonyms* (*adj*) brave, concentrated, firm, safe, compelling, determined, effective, forceful, powerful, resolute, robust, sturdy, able, fit, hard-wearing, **7.** pining; *synonyms* (*n*) longing, hankering, ache, craving, desire, hunger, mourning, nostalgia, (*adj*) languishing, eager, heartless, infatuated, listless, marcid, mean.

mamarake 1. aspire; *synonyms* (*v*) aim, plan, hope, endeavor, long, purpose, rise, soar, want, wish, **2.** incline; *synonyms* (*n*) slope, bias, angle, ascent, dip, grade, gradient, inclination, slant, (*v*) cant, bend, dispose, lean, tilt, bank, **3.** yearn; *synonyms* (*v*) languish, pine, ache, aspire, hanker, yen, **4.** strive; *synonyms* (*v*) labor, attempt, contend, contest, fight, struggle, combat, compete, strain, toil, work, exert, endeavour, reach, scramble.

mamarakeaki inclined; *synonyms* (*adj*) prone, apt, oblique, willing, bowed, liable, likely, minded, predisposed, ready, bent, fain, susceptible, (*v*) given, (*prep*) disposed; *antonyms* (*adj*) level, reluctant, unwilling.

mamaroa solitary; *synonyms* (*adj*) lonesome, forlorn, alone, lone, lonely, only, single, sole, unaccompanied, isolated, secluded, separate, one, (*n*) hermit, recluse.

mamata 1. intuitive; *synonyms* (*adj*) instinctive, inborn, innate, automatic, impulsive, natural, perceptive, **2.** discerning; *synonyms* (*adj*) astute, acute, apprehensive, discriminating, shrewd, discreet, judicious, penetrating, refined, sharp, conscious, understanding, clever, clairvoyant, observant; *antonym* (*adj*) indiscriminate, **3.** foresight; *synonyms* (*n*) anticipation, prevision, forecast, caution, prospicience, calculation, foreknowledge, foreseeing, foresightedness, forethought, precaution, prediction, prescience, vision, (*v*) expectation, **4.** distinct; *synonyms* (*adj*) clear, articulate, different, discrete, apparent, definite, distinctive, palpable, decided, dissimilar, marked, plain, tangible, (*prep*) separate, (*adv*) apart; *antonyms* (*adj*) indistinct, similar, unclear, vague, inaudible, shapeless, **5.** clairvoyant; *synonyms* (*adj*) prophetic, mystic, intuitive, extrasensory, farsighted, magical, mental, oracular, (*n*) psychic, seer, soothsayer, medium, sibyl, astrologer, oracle, **6.** feed; *synonyms* (*v*) eat, dine, nurture, browse, board, diet, encourage, nourish, fatten, consume, feast, (*n*) aliment, food, provender, fare; *antonym* (*v*) starve, **7.** perspicacious; *synonyms* (*adj*) discerning, wise, keen, sagacious, incisive, intelligent, **8.** predict; *synonyms* (*v*) anticipate, augur, foresee, foretell, portend, bode, divine, forebode, foreshadow, foreshow, presage, expect, herald, betoken, calculate, **9.** sagacious; *synonyms* (*adj*) prudent, rational, knowing, perspicacious, politic, sapient, reasonable, sage, deep, provident, sane, canny, profound, knowledgeable, (*v*) crafty; *antonym* (*adj*) foolish.

mamataki 1. fed; *synonyms* (*adj*) fattened, meated, (*n*) federal, detective, **2.** predicted; *synonyms* (*adj*) foretold, foreseen, **3.** parasitic; *synonyms* (*adj*) parasitical, bloodsucking, leechlike, epenthetic, fawning, obsequious, parasital, sycophantical.

mamatam 1. diet; *synonyms* (*n*) congress, convocation, council, convention, nurture, food, assembly, dieting, fare, nourishment, sustenance, synod, cockpit, fast; *antonyms* (*v*) binge, (*adj*) fattening, **2.** fasting; *synonyms* (*n*) abstinence, flagellation, lustration, maceration, shrift, penance.

mamataro 1. unconscious; *synonyms* (*adj*) involuntary, unaware, ignorant, subconscious, unwitting, oblivious, automatic, insensible, instinctive, senseless, unintentional, spontaneous, innocent, unknowing, unacquainted; *antonyms* (*adj*) conscious, awake, deliberate, **2**. obscure; *synonyms* (*adj*) cloudy, dim, dark, gloomy, ambiguous, concealed, darken, hidden, incomprehensible, muddy, mysterious, clandestine, (*v*) hide, blur, cloud; *antonyms* (*adj*) clear, noticeable, simple, obvious, distinct, mainstream, (*v*) clarify.

mamataroro faint; *synonyms* (*adj*) collapse, dim, dizzy, feeble, indistinct, weak, dull, gentle, soft, vague, delicate, distant, (*v*) languish, swoon, droop; *antonyms* (*adj*) distinct, strong, clear, obvious, considerable, loud, pungent.

mamatauna shadow; *synonyms* (*n*) shade, ghost, tail, trace, darkness, hint, apparition, follower, gloom, phantom, reflection, (*v*) eclipse, follow, obscure, overshadow.

mamataunaki shadowed; *synonyms* (*adj*) shady, shaded, shadowy, dim, faint, fishy, funny, incensed, indignant, louche, outraged, queer, sunless, umbrageous, suspect.

mamaunga 1. elevated; *synonyms* (*adj*) high, exalted, lofty, noble, towering, grand, great, majestic, tall, elated, magnanimous, advanced, dignified, eminent, (*v*) steep; *antonym* (*adj*) short, **2**. hilly; *synonyms* (*adj*) craggy, mountainous, rugged, cragged, knobby, prominent, tumulous, precipitous, tumulose, **3**. mountainous; *synonyms* (*adj*) colossal, gargantuan, alpine, giant, hilly, huge, enormous, large, **4**. raised; *synonyms* (*v*) repousse, salient, (*adj*) elevated, embossed, erect, convex, brocaded, alert, bold, confident, elate, elative, exultant, mountant, (*prep*) above.

mambwea brackish; *synonyms* (*adj*) salt, salty, saline, bracky, briny, nauseous, stagnant, salted.

mamma 1. inhale; *synonyms* (*v*) breathe, absorb, imbibe, draw, suck, drag, drink, attract, inspire, receive, respire, admit, import, ingest, (*n*) sniff; *antonym* (*v*) exhale, **2**. suck; *synonyms* (*v*) nurse, lactate, suckle, drain, puff, aspirate, pull, breastfeed, (*n*) sucking, suction.

mammaki inhaled; *synonym* (*adj*) inspired.

mammam 1. mundane; *synonyms* (*adj*) earthly, everyday, terrestrial, worldly, commonplace, humdrum, ordinary, telluric, usual, banal, common, mediocre, pedestrian, prosaic, quotidian; *antonym* (*adj*) amazing, **2**. insipid; *synonyms* (*adj*) flat, tasteless, bland, dull, flavorless, uninteresting, vapid, watery, boring, flavourless, savorless, tame, tedious, weak, dry; *antonyms* (*adj*) exciting, strong, tasty, **3**. dull; *synonyms* (*adj*) dim, blunt, dense, dreary, sluggish, cloudy, cold, dark, dismal, inactive, inert, obtuse, slack, (*v*) deaden, dampen; *antonyms* (*adj*) bright, lively, sharp, interesting, lustrous, stimulating, amusing, exhilarating, glittery, glossy, glowing, high-pitched, intense, luminous, shiny, **4**. uninteresting; *synonyms* (*adj*)

insipid, monotonous, stupid, tiresome, prosy, stuffy, dead, nondescript, plane, pointless, prostrate, stale, unentertaining, (*n*) frigid, spiritless; *antonyms* (*adj*) fascinating, **5**. tasteless; *synonyms* (*adj*) flashy, gaudy, vulgar, garish, diluted, indelicate, showy, tacky, tawdry, unsavory, gustless, inappropriate, lifeless, loud, unbecoming; *antonyms* (*adj*) tasteful, delicious.

mamwakuri move; *synonyms* (*v*) act, affect, carry, excite, go, impel, instigate, maneuver, touch, travel, flow, bear, (*n*) motion, drive, transfer; *antonym* (*v*) stay.

mamwka powerful; *synonyms* (*adj*) cogent, able, brawny, forcible, hard, mighty, muscular, potent, strong, effective, energetic, influential, intense, lusty, vigorous; *antonyms* (*adj*) powerless, weak, mild.

man 1. ambassador; *synonyms* (*n*) agent, delegate, emissary, envoy, messenger, minister, deputy, embassador, herald, representative, diplomat, **2**. out; *synonyms* (*adv*) off, forward, beyond, forth, aside, abroad, by, outwards, (*v*) reveal, (*adj*) away, extinct, outside, absent, gone, outward; *antonyms* (*adv*) in, (*prep*) inside, **3**. off; *synonyms* (*adv*) over, abreast, (*adj*) bad, putrid, remote, down, rotten, wide, cancelled, decayed, sour, (*n*) murder, (*int*) out, begone; *antonyms* (*adj*) fresh, on.

mana sticky; *synonyms* (*adj*) adhesive, awkward, clammy, muggy, embarrassing, glutinous, gummy, humid, difficult, slimy, gluey, gooey, hard, mucilaginous, pasty; *antonyms* (*adj*) dry, fresh, easy.

manana 1. domesticated; *synonyms* (*adj*) domestic, tame, vernacular, subdued, gentle, crushed, depressed, naturalized, submissive, cultivated, disciplined, dull, flat, insipid, intestine, **2**. tame; *synonyms* (*adj*) docile, meek, bland, boring, mild, slow, spiritless, quiet, (*v*) break, subdue, chasten, discipline, domesticate, moderate, soften; *antonyms* (*adj*) exciting, wild.

manangia journey; *synonyms* (*n*) jaunt, excursion, expedition, passage, trip, way, course, flight, outing, pilgrimage, (*v*) go, travel, cruise, fare, navigate.

manango 1. slumber; *synonyms* (*n*) rest, doze, nap, snooze, catnap, siesta, (*v*) sleep, drowse, repose, kip, **2**. sleepy; *synonyms* (*adj*) lethargic, drowsy, dozy, lazy, slow, hypnotic, inactive, comatose, dreamy, dull, heavy, somnolent, tired, weary; *antonyms* (*adj*) alert, awake.

manawaia entrench; *synonyms* (*v*) encroach, fortify, impinge, infringe, intrench, trench, establish, invade, defend, ditch, fence, fix, implant, insert, intrude.

manawaiaki entrenched; *synonyms* (*adj*) confirmed, ingrained, inveterate, constant, set, steadfast, unwavering, chronic, embedded, hardened, inbuilt, incorrigible, incurable, inherent, innate; *antonym* (*adj*) superficial.

manawanawa hollow; *synonyms* (*adj*) blank, concave, empty, false, insincere, (*n*) cavity, hole, cave, depression, groove, excavation, (*v*) excavate, dent, scoop, dig; *antonyms* (*adj*) convex, (*n*) solid, hump.

mane 1. faded; *synonyms* (*v*) dilapidated, stale, (*adj*) dim, pale, bleached, dull, exhausted, faint, washy, withered, attenuate, attenuated, colorless, discoloured, **2**. shabby; *synonyms* (*adj*) abject, low, mangy, mean, poor, sorry, cheap, decrepit, paltry, ragged, sordid, worn, ignoble, grubby, (*v*) frayed; *antonyms* (*adj*) pristine, smart, **3**. used; *synonyms* (*adj*) secondhand, exploited, accustomed, depleted, faded, habituated, hand-me-down, spent, threadbare, tried, victimised, victimized, wont, recycled; *antonyms* (*adj*) new, spanking, unused, **4**. worn; *synonyms* (*v*) decayed, rotten, (*adj*) haggard, shabby, tired, tattered, drawn, jaded, fatigued, careworn, raddled, seedy, wasted; *antonyms* (*adj*) fresh, **5**. old; *synonyms* (*adj*) antiquated, obsolete, ancient, former, aged, antique, elderly, experienced, outdated, veteran, archaic, hoary, mature, past, disused; *antonyms* (*adj*) young, modern, latest, novel, original, youthful.

maneanea humiliated; *synonyms* (*adj*) ashamed, humbled, mortified, embarrassed, humble, abashed, broken, crushed; *antonym* (*adj*) proud.

maneaua 1. tied; *synonyms* (*adj*) fastened, connected, even, fixed, laced, united, attached, binding, buttoned, joined, legato, liable, mixed, powerless, responsible; *antonym* (*adj*) separate, **2**. surrounded; *synonyms* (*v*) beset, begone, furnished, (*adj*) encircled, bounded, circumstanced, conditioned, entrenched, ingirt, inside, ringed, rooted, bordered, delimited, implanted, **3**. taken; *synonyms* (*v*) take, (*adj*) occupied, full, interpreted, besotted, crazed, enamored, engaged, interested, lovesick, obsessed, overcome, preferred, rapt, reserved.

manebaeba 1. diligent; *synonyms* (*adj*) busy, active, assiduous, careful, painstaking, earnest, attentive, industrious, laborious, studious, occupied, brisk, conscientious, indefatigable, meticulous; *antonyms* (*adj*) lazy, careless, negligent, **2**. zealous; *synonyms* (*adj*) eager, enthusiastic, keen, passionate, fervent, ardent, avid, devoted, strenuous, vehement, burning, fiery, glowing, impassioned, (*n*) hearty; *antonym* (*adj*) indifferent, **3**. prompt; *synonyms* (*adj*) agile, quick, nimble, punctual, dexterous, expeditious, immediate, (*v*) actuate, incite, fleet, inspire, instigate, move, animate, cue; *antonyms* (*adj*) slow, late.

manebuaka worthless; *synonyms* (*adj*) futile, vile, idle, cheap, empty, trifling, trivial, void, miserable, fruitless, ineffective, mean, null, (*v*) useless, vain;

antonyms (*adj*) valuable, precious, useful, helpful, meaningful, priceless, worthwhile.

m'aneka 1. mark; *synonyms* (*n*) brand, evidence, score, character, heed, impression, imprint, sign, feature, (*v*) blemish, characterize, distinguish, grade, label, (*adj*) notice, **2**. gash; *synonyms* (*n*) cut, scratch, wound, crack, fissure, cleft, cutting, (*v*) slash, slit, tear, break, rip, slice, lacerate, split, **3**. trace; *synonyms* (*n*) line, shadow, spot, clue, dash, hint, indication, mark, shade, suggestion, touch, trail, (*v*) track, hunt, pursue.

m'anekaki traced; *synonyms* (*adj*) copied, graphic.

manekaneka scarred; *synonyms* (*adj*) marred, defaced, hurt.

manena 1. important; *synonyms* (*adj*) essential, grave, fundamental, significant, chief, crucial, key, remarkable, serious, earnest, authoritative, big, central, consequential, considerable; *antonyms* (*adj*) unimportant, insignificant, trivial, minor, irrelevant, low, worthless, **2**. advantageous; *synonyms* (*adj*) expedient, favorable, auspicious, useful, beneficial, convenient, fortunate, gainful, helpful, lucky, profitable, serviceable, worthwhile, handy, right; *antonym* (*adj*) useless, **3**. precious; *synonyms* (*adj*) dear, beloved, cherished, costly, valuable, invaluable, expensive, golden, choice, inestimable, exquisite, cute, rich, noble, (*n*) darling, **4**. useful; *synonyms* (*adj*) practical, advantageous, effective, functional, clever, constructive, efficient, usable, good, suitable, comfortable, important, lucrative, practicable, instrumental; *antonym* (*adj*) ineffective.

manenanti 1. abnormal; *synonyms* (*adj*) aberrant, anomalous, atypical, irregular, monstrous, odd, perverted, strange, uncommon, unnatural, unusual, perverse, improper, preternatural, grotesque; *antonyms* (*adj*) normal, typical, usual, **2**. chance; *synonyms* (*n*) hazard, fortune, opportunity, probability, venture, accident, break, contingency, fate, (*adj*) accidental, (*v*) gamble, adventure, risk, bet, befall; *antonyms* (*n*) predictability, (*adj*) deliberate, intentional, (*v*) design, plan, **3**. curious; *synonyms* (*adj*) abnormal, funny, interested, peculiar, bizarre, extraordinary, inquiring, inquisitive, quaint, queer, quizzical, remarkable, singular, weird, whimsical; *antonyms* (*adj*) incurious, ordinary, **4**. happening; *synonyms* (*n*) episode, incident, circumstance, affair, event, experience, fact, occasion, occurrence, eventuality, fortuity, chance, thing, business, matter, **5**. irregular; *synonyms* (*adj*) broken, eccentric, erratic, changeable, desultory, deviant, disorderly, guerilla, sporadic, unequal, uneven, indiscriminate, capricious, casual, (*n*) guerrilla; *antonyms* (*adj*) regular, constant, even, smooth, symmetrical, compact, cyclic, equal, steady, **6**. exceptional; *synonyms* (*adj*) special, excellent, particular, prodigious, exceeding, outstanding, rare, single, superior, unique, especial, infrequent, great, incomparable, individual; *antonyms* (*adj*) common, mediocre, average, abysmal, inferior, poor, **7.** rare; *synonyms* (*adj*) exceptional, precious, scarce, seldom, thin, few, choice, curious, fine, novel, exquisite, flimsy, occasional, priceless, raw; *antonym* (*adj*) frequent, **8.** odd; *synonyms* (*adj*) droll, fantastic, laughable, different, unaccountable, crazy, fanciful, comical, leftover, outlandish, rum, rummy, wacky, farcical, idiosyncratic, **9.** peculiar; *synonyms* (*adj*) characteristic, distinctive, personal, proper, appropriate, exclusive, specific, original, own, private, distinct, respective, separate, uncanny, inexplicable, **10.** surprising; *synonyms* (*adj*) astonishing, marvelous, amazing, startling, wonderful, shocking, striking, astounding, stunning, unexpected, unforeseen, (*n*) incredible; *antonym* (*adj*) unsurprising.

manenikai outcast; *synonyms* (*n*) exile, pariah, castaway, expatriate, outlaw, vagabond, loon, lown, refugee, (*adj*) derelict, homeless, friendless.

maneouna 1. brilliant; *synonyms* (*adj*) bright, splendid, glorious, illustrious, intelligent, luminous, magnificent, spectacular, sunny, vivid, brainy, diamond, gaudy, gifted, (*v*) smart; *antonyms* (*adj*) dull, dim, awful, dark, **2.** oiled; *synonyms* (*adj*) drunk, intoxicated, oily, **3.** soft; *synonyms* (*adj*) gentle, easy, light, limp, balmy, delicate, quiet, slack, loose, clement, faint, flabby, flaccid, (*v*) feeble, low; *antonyms* (*adj*) hard, firm, harsh, loud, hoarse, rough, solid, stiff, alcoholic, shrill, strong.

maneuna 1. important; *synonyms* (*adj*) essential, grave, fundamental, significant, chief, crucial, key, remarkable, serious, earnest, authoritative, big, central, consequential, considerable; *antonyms* (*adj*) unimportant, insignificant, trivial, minor, irrelevant, low, worthless, **2.** valuable; *synonyms* (*adj*) costly, estimable, precious, beneficial, expensive, helpful, useful, worthy, admirable, important, dear, invaluable, priceless, profitable, rich; *antonym* (*adj*) useless, **3.** practical; *synonyms* (*adj*) operative, practicable, efficient, feasible, functional, pragmatic, realistic, active, expedient, handy, positive, sensible, workable, working, constructive; *antonyms* (*adj*) impractical, theoretical, unrealistic, impossible, **4.** useful; *synonyms* (*adj*) practical, advantageous, convenient, effective, valuable, clever, gainful, serviceable, usable, good, suitable, comfortable, lucrative, instrumental, proper; *antonym* (*adj*) ineffective, **5.** profitable; *synonyms* (*adj*) productive, fruitful, desirable, economic, fat, salutary, edifying, fertile, commercial, healthy, moneymaking, rewarding, worthwhile; *antonyms* (*adj*) unprofitable, dependent.

manga 1. additionally; *synonyms* (*adv*) besides, also, too, furthermore, moreover, again, more, along, and, still, (*adj*) likewise, **2.** branching; *synonyms* (*adj*) branched, forked, ramose, (*n*) bifurcation, branch, forking, ramification, fork, arborescence, **3.** branchy; *synonyms* (*adj*) branching, ramifying, **4.** forked; *synonyms* (*adj*) bifurcate, bifurcated, biramous, double, furcated, tined, forky, anchored, angular, bivalent, cross, crotched, doubled, dual, duple, **5.** bother; *synonyms* (*v*) trouble, annoy, torment, vex, worry, afflict, aggravate, (*n*) fuss, plague, bore, hassle, pain, ado, annoyance, concern; *antonyms* (*v*) delight, please, soothe, (*n*) pleasure, **6.** again; *synonyms* (*adv*) afresh, anew, encore, repeatedly, then, further, often, **7.** complicated; *synonyms* (*adj*) complex, intricate, elaborate, hard, complicate, awkward, convoluted, deep, difficult, knotty, obscure, sophisticated, tortuous, tricky, (*v*) involved; *antonyms* (*adj*) simple, straightforward, clear, easy, **8.** inconvenience; *synonyms* (*n*) bother, disadvantage, difficulty, nuisance, awkwardness, unsuitableness, encumbrance, ineptness, unwieldiness, disturbance, (*v*) discommode, incommode, disoblige, disquiet, disturb; *antonym* (*n*) convenience, **9.** over; *synonyms* (*adv*) beyond, across, by, o'er, on, crosswise, (*prep*) above, during, (*n*) overs, (*adj*) finished, done, extra, odd, past, gone, **10.** redo; *synonyms* (*v*) recast, reconstruct, rebuild, refurbish, refashion, remake, repeat, revise, change, remodel, **11.** repeat; *synonyms* (*v*) recite, copy, recapitulate, reduplicate, rehearse, reiterate, return, duplicate, iterate, recur, renew, reproduce, say, cite, multiply.

mangainrang guzzle; *synonyms* (*v*) bolt, devour, drink, gobble, gulp, consume, gorge, swill, guttle, imbibe, quaff; *antonyms* (*v*) nibble, sip.

mangaki 1. bothered; *synonyms* (*adj*) worried, disturbed, troubled, concerned, distraught, nervous, uneasy, upset; *antonym* (*adj*) calm, **2.** repeated; *synonyms* (*adj*) continual, recurrent, frequent, persistent, double, habitual, chronic, common, continuous, perennial, perpetual; *antonym* (*adj*) intermittent.

mangamanga 1. embarrass; *synonyms* (*v*) confuse, baffle, block, bother, confound, disconcert, encumber, hinder, complicate, abash, discomfit, distress, hamper, impede, (*adj*) bewilder, **2.** complicate; *synonyms* (*v*) involve, perplex, aggravate, entangle, muddle, puzzle, snarl, tangle, complexify, elaborate; *antonyms* (*v*) clarify, simplify, **3.** thwart; *synonyms* (*v*) foil, frustrate, obstruct, oppose, prevent, defeat, disappoint, bilk, resist, stop, elude, dash, balk, contravene, (*adv*) cross, **4.** oppose; *synonyms* (*v*) object, contest, contend, contradict, controvert, counteract, fight, counter, disagree, dissent, combat, confront, defend, dispute, gainsay; *antonyms* (*v*) support, advocate, agree, back, advise.

mangamangaki 1. embarrassed; *synonyms* (*adj*) ashamed, abashed, awkward, uncomfortable, disconcerted, bashful, shamefaced, sheepish, shy, chagrined, discomfited, humiliated, mortified; *antonyms* (*adj*) proud, relaxed, **2**. complicated; *synonyms* (*adj*) complex, intricate, elaborate, hard, complicate, convoluted, deep, difficult, knotty, obscure, sophisticated, tortuous, tricky, circuitous, (*v*) involved; *antonyms* (*adj*) simple, straightforward, clear, easy, **3**. opposed; *synonyms* (*adj*) conflicting, contradictory, hostile, contrary, antagonistic, opposing, adverse, averse, contrasted, repugnant, incompatible, irreconcilable, counter, against, opposite, **4**. thwarted; *synonyms* (*adj*) frustrated, disappointed, defeated, foiled, baffled, balked, beaten, discouraged, disenchanted, disillusioned, dissatisfied, embarrassed, saddened, upset, blocked; *antonym* (*adj*) successful.

mangao 1. disorderly; *synonyms* (*adj*) confused, chaotic, disordered, wild, boisterous, disobedient, disorganized, irregular, jumbled, rowdy, tumultuous, turbulent, unruly, untidy, (*v*) lawless; *antonyms* (*adj*) orderly, well-behaved, neat, arranged, **2**. jumbled; *synonyms* (*adj*) disorderly, cluttered, mixed, muddled, incoherent, topsy-turvy; *antonym* (*adj*) tidy, **3**. disorganized; *synonyms* (*adj*) disorganised, messy, haphazard; *antonyms* (*adj*) organized, methodical, **4**. disharmonious; *synonyms* (*adj*) discordant, dissonant, inharmonic, unlike, nonmusical, unmusical, unresolved, **5**. disordered; *synonyms* (*adj*) broken, deranged, sick, upset, disconnected, disjointed, ill, scattered, complex, discontinuous; *antonym* (*adj*) ordered.

mangaoangao 1. chaotic; *synonyms* (*adj*) disorderly, confused, disorganized, hectic, messy, wild, topsy-turvy, turbulent, untidy, cluttered, disordered, haphazard, indiscriminate, muddled, lawless; *antonyms* (*adj*) neat, orderly, organized, **2**. inextricable; *synonyms* (*adj*) complicated, insoluble, intricate, involved, perplexed, entangled, impassable, impervious, inaccessible, (*v*) inseparable; *antonym* (*adj*) extricable.

mangaongao 1. jumbled; *synonyms* (*adj*) confused, disorderly, disordered, disorganized, untidy, cluttered, mixed, muddled, chaotic, incoherent, topsy-turvy; *antonyms* (*adj*) neat, tidy, **2**. untidy; *synonyms* (*adj*) slovenly, disheveled, messy, sloppy, unkempt, frowzy, scruffy, sluttish, slipshod, dowdy, tousled, dirty, ragged, slatternly, grubby; *antonym* (*adj*) elegant.

mangaungau 1. ravenous; *synonyms* (*adj*) greedy, hungry, avid, famished, gluttonous, voracious, edacious, insatiable, rapacious, covetous, predatory, avaricious, esurient, grasping, ravening;

antonym (*adj*) full, **2**. voracious; *synonyms* (*adj*) ravenous, devouring, eager, starved.

mangauti 1. awake; *synonyms* (*adj*) alive, alert, attentive, conscious, aware, intelligent, keen, sleepless, (*v*) arouse, wake, awaken, waken, rouse, stimulate, stir; *antonyms* (*adj*) asleep, unconscious, comatose, sleeping, sleepy, **2**. waken; *synonyms* (*v*) awake, excite, call, evoke, kindle, provoke, **3**. rouse; *synonyms* (*v*) instigate, actuate, agitate, disturb, incite, move, fire, inflame, revive, heat, animate, encourage, induce, irritate, enliven; *antonyms* (*v*) calm, dampen.

mange 1. chew; *synonyms* (*v*) champ, munch, chomp, crunch, gnaw, manducate, masticate, mouth, eat, jaw, (*n*) bite, chaw, chewing, cud, mastication, **2**. eat; *synonyms* (*v*) devour, consume, dine, corrode, deplete, drink, feed, finish, gobble, gorge, graze, nibble, swallow, down, (*adj*) digest, **3**. dependent; *synonyms* (*adj*) subject, subordinate, contingent, addicted, tributary, relative, secondary, (*n*) dependant, charge, adjective, attendant, follower, servant, slave, vassal; *antonyms* (*adj*) independent, self-governing, self-sufficient, **4**. panhandle; *synonyms* (*v*) beg, solicit.

mangeto dirty; *synonyms* (*adj*) foul, dirt, contemptible, bawdy, contaminated, dingy, impure, despicable, (*v*) muddy, corrupt, soil, contaminate, begrime, bemire, (*n*) defile; *antonyms* (*adj*) hygienic, pure, spotless, immaculate, (*v*) clean.

manging 1. inebriated; *synonyms* (*adj*) drunk, intoxicated, high, inebriate, tight, (*v*) drunken; *antonym* (*adj*) sober, **2**. drunk; *synonyms* (*adj*) tipsy, wet, inebriated, delirious, (*n*) drunkard, rummy, sot.

mangingi 1. faded; *synonyms* (*v*) dilapidated, stale, (*adj*) dim, pale, bleached, dull, exhausted, faint, washy, withered, attenuate, attenuated, colorless, discoloured, **2**. grimace; *synonyms* (*n*) frown, face, mop, sneer, smile, mouth, expression, roar, (*v*) scowl, glower, cringe, glare, wince, **3**. contracted; *synonyms* (*v*) shrunk, (*adj*) narrow, insular, contract, constricted, tight, bound, **4**. wrinkled; *synonyms* (*adj*) furrowed, creased, crumpled, lined, puckered, wizened, wrinkly, gnarled, unironed, (*n*) rough, rugged; *antonym* (*adj*) smooth, **5**. shrunk; *synonyms* (*adj*) shrunken, shriveled, shrivelled, insipid, wearish, tasteless, unsavory, weak, **6**. sour; *synonyms* (*adj*) morose, sharp, acid, bitter, rancid, severe, gruff, dour, glum, grim, pungent, (*v*) acidify, ferment, (*n*) harsh, acidity; *antonyms* (*adj*) sweet, kindly.

mangkana formerly; *synonyms* (*adv*) before, already, earlier, aforetime, first, erst, erstwhile, once, previously, afore, beforehand, originally, sometime, sometimes.

mangkongko 1. curved; *synonyms* (*adj*) bent, crooked, curve, round, bend, curving, curvy, deformed, hooked, rounded, tortuous, twisted, (*v*) bowed; *antonyms* (*adj*) straight, concave, **2.** concave; *synonyms* (*adj*) hollow, cavernous, crescent, biconcave, cupped, dipped, arched, depress, dishing, vaulted, vaulty, deceitful, deep, dented, (*v*) dig; *antonyms* (*adj*) convex, curved, **3.** hollow; *synonyms* (*adj*) blank, empty, false, insincere, (*n*) cavity, hole, cave, depression, groove, excavation, trench, gap, (*v*) excavate, dent, scoop; *antonyms* (*n*) solid, hump.

mango 1. howl; *synonyms* (*n*) bark, shout, yell, shriek, yap, (*v*) bellow, cry, bawl, roar, scream, growl, bay, snarl, wail, yawl, **2.** grieve; *synonyms* (*v*) distress, mourn, aggrieve, bemoan, deplore, lament, sorrow, trouble, annoy, fret, bewail, hurt, injure, pain, (*n*) afflict; *antonym* (*v*) please, **3.** doleful; *synonyms* (*adj*) dismal, mournful, sad, sorrowful, disconsolate, dolorous, melancholy, miserable, piteous, somber, woeful, dejected, downcast, dark, (*v*) dolesome; *antonym* (*adj*) cheerful, **4.** apologetic; *synonyms* (*adj*) contrite, penitent, regretful, remorseful, sorry, rueful, alleged, ashamed; *antonym* (*adj*) unrepentant, **5.** mournful; *synonyms* (*adj*) doleful, funereal, gloomy, lamentable, lugubrious, pensive, cheerless, grievous, unhappy, dreary, black, depressed, morose, (*n*) plaintive, (*v*) distressing, **6.** mourn; *synonyms* (*v*) grieve, regret, weep; *antonym* (*v*) rejoice, **7.** apologize; *synonyms* (*v*) apologise, justify, repent, absolve, atone, compensate, rationalise, rationalize, redress, (*n*) excuse, extenuate, palliate, gloze, slur, varnish, **8.** contrite; *synonyms* (*adj*) apologetic, repentant, bad, **9.** repent; *synonym* (*v*) rue, **10.** remorseful, **11.** sob; *synonyms* (*n*) moan, groan, sobbing, asshole, bastard, cocksucker, motherfucker, prick, shit, (*v*) whine, snivel, whimper, howl, sigh, pipe, **12.** penitent, **13.** regret; *synonyms* (*n*) grief, compunction, contrition, penitence, remorse, repentance, disappointment, woe, mourning, qualm, contriteness, dissatisfaction, bitterness, anguish, apology, **14.** regretful; *synonym* (*adj*) nostalgic, **15.** sorry; *synonyms* (*adj*) pathetic, paltry, pitiable, pitiful, base, deplorable, mean, low, abject, dingy, drab, poor, wretched, contemptible, (*v*) concerned.

mangoieta 1. elder; *synonyms* (*adj*) older, big, adult, (*n*) senior, ancient, patriarch, boss, chief, superior, **2.** venerable; *synonyms* (*adj*) old, reverend, estimable, respectable, aged, distinguished, sacred, worthy, considerable, grand, revered, reverenced, solemn, **3.** senior; *synonyms* (*adj*) elderly, major, predecessor, (*n*) elder, head, dean, ruler, sachem; *antonyms* (*adj*) subordinate, (*n*) junior, **4.** superior;

synonyms (*adj*) dominant, better, exceptional, predominant, great, arrogant, eminent, excellent, high, higher, lofty, proud, select, commanding, admirable; *antonyms* (*adj*) humble, worse, poor, (*n*) inferior, subscript.

mangori 1. insignificant; *synonyms* (*adj*) minute, inconsequential, inconsiderable, humble, immaterial, infinitesimal, light, little, poor, small, trivial, unimportant, diminutive, inappreciable, inferior; *antonyms* (*adj*) significant, considerable, enormous, great, huge, important, major, substantial, colossal, influential, momentous, valuable, **2.** lowly; *synonyms* (*adj*) base, low, lower, baseborn, modest, insignificant, ignoble, simple, mean, meek, menial, petty, plain, submissive, (*adv*) humbly, **3.** immaterial; *synonyms* (*adj*) bodiless, incorporeal, irrelevant, spiritual, extraneous, psychic, indifferent, insubstantial, minor, nonmaterial, trifling, airy, foreign; *antonym* (*adj*) relevant, **4.** inferior; *synonyms* (*adj*) bad, secondary, subordinate, cheap, junior, lesser, feeble, coarse, common, vulgar, contemptible, less, ordinary, second, (*prep*) below; *antonyms* (*adj*) better, choice, excellent, first-rate, high-class, premium, (*n*) superior, superscript, **5.** humble; *synonyms* (*adj*) docile, lowly, unassuming, obscure, reverent, (*v*) degrade, demean, disgrace, abase, debase, humiliate, mortify, conquer, depress, (*n*) dishonor; *antonyms* (*adj*) grand, arrogant, conceited, haughty, imposing, impressive, pompous, snooty, **6.** minuscule; *synonyms* (*n*) majuscule, (*adj*) miniscule, tiny, microscopic, lowercase, miniature, minuscular, teeny, **7.** vile; *synonyms* (*adj*) foul, despicable, evil, disgusting, filthy, infamous, nasty, offensive, revolting, sorry, sordid, vicious, atrocious, beastly, (*n*) dirty; *antonyms* (*adj*) pleasant, attractive, **8.** unimportant; *synonyms* (*adj*) frivolous, slight, negligible, paltry, futile, silly, peripheral, nonessential, meaningless, measly, vain; *antonym* (*adj*) crucial, **9.** squalid; *synonyms* (*adj*) seedy, abject, grimy, grubby, seamy, sleazy, mangy, shabby, impure, miserable, unclean, black, scruffy, wretched, flyblown, **10.** puny; *synonyms* (*adj*) frail, weak, runty, exiguous, meager; *antonyms* (*adj*) brawny, muscular, **11.** paltry; *synonyms* (*adj*) puny, piddling, pitiful, worthless, inadequate, pathetic, pettifogging, piteous, stingy, woeful, groveling; *antonym* (*adj*) generous.

mangung intoxicated; *synonyms* (*adj*) drunken, inebriated, drunk, inebriate, tipsy, elated; *antonym* (*adj*) sober.

manibuaka 1. mistreat; *synonyms* (*v*) abuse, maltreat, torture, harm, mishandle, misuse, wrong, manhandle, torment, injure, molest, outrage, assault, blackguard, clapperclaw, **2.** maltreat; *synonyms* (*v*) mistreat, damage, hurt, oppress, persecute, assail, **3.** ungrateful; *synonyms* (adj) thankless, unmindful, unappreciative, unthankful, unnatural, ingrate, distasteful, displeasing, unkind, childless, cruel, harsh, ingrateful, offensive, unacceptable; *antonyms* (adj) grateful, thankful, **4.** unkind; *synonyms* (adj) unfeeling, heartless, inconsiderate, pitiless, inhuman, hard, thoughtless, brutal, mean, merciless, nasty, rigorous, severe, ungracious, uncharitable; *antonym* (adj) kind.

manibuakaki 1. mistreated; *synonyms* (adj) abused, maltreated, battered, aggrieved, downtrodden, harmed, injured, neglected, wronged, ignored, offended, persecuted, victimized, **2.** maltreated; *synonym* (adj) mistreated.

manikangare 1. humor; *synonyms* (n) caprice, fancy, temper, disposition, mood, spirit, wit, freak, character, joke, nature, (v) indulge, gratify, humour, (adj) lymph; *antonym* (n) tragedy, **2.** banter; *synonyms* (n) ridicule, raillery, (v) badinage, chaff, jest, kid, tease, deride, quiz, retort, twit, jeer, jolly, josh, mock, **3.** jest; *synonyms* (n) gag, gibe, jape, quip, game, caper, pleasantry, pun, antic, derision, mockery, (v) banter, gird, sneer, clown, **4.** amuse; *synonyms* (v) divert, absorb, beguile, entertain, please, charm, delight, disport, distract, occupy, recreate, sport, interest; *antonym* (v) bore, **5.** joke; *synonyms* (n) hoax, fun, farce, humor, jocularity, prank, trick, frolic, amusement, epigram, laugh, teasing, wheeze, (v) play, rally.

manikangareaki amused; *synonyms* (adj) entertained, diverted, smiling.

manikonana 1. able; *synonyms* (adj) capable, clever, competent, dexterous, accomplished, adroit, consummate, effective, expert, fit, gifted, ingenious, endowed, (n) efficient, talented; *antonyms* (adj) incapable, incompetent, inept, unable, untrained, weak, **2.** capable; *synonyms* (adj) able, adequate, adept, proficient, qualified, trained, experienced, good, intelligent, powerful, skilled, skillful, strong, quick, resourceful, **3.** apt; *synonyms* (adj) appropriate, apropos, apposite, convenient, ready, smart, deft, disposed, fitting, happy, just, liable, likely, opportune, pertinent; *antonym* (adj) inappropriate, **4.** competent; *synonyms* (adj) sufficient, commensurate, enough, professional, apt, prepared, becoming, full, proper, responsible, satisfactory, suitable, versed, efficacious; *antonym* (adj) useless.

manikoraki 1. capable; *synonyms* (adj) able, competent, adequate, adept, accomplished, fit, gifted, proficient, qualified, trained, clever, consummate, effective, experienced, (n) efficient; *antonyms* (adj) incompetent, incapable, inept, unable, **2.** able; *synonyms* (adj) capable, dexterous, adroit, expert, ingenious, endowed, apt, cute, deft, good, handy, potent, powerful, professional, (n) talented; *antonyms* (adj) untrained, weak, **3.**

competent; *synonyms* (adj) sufficient, commensurate, appropriate, enough, skillful, prepared, becoming, full, proper, responsible, satisfactory, skilled, suitable, versed, efficacious; *antonym* (adj) useless, **4.** apt; *synonyms* (adj) apropos, apposite, intelligent, convenient, ready, smart, disposed, fitting, happy, just, liable, likely, opportune, pertinent, prompt; *antonym* (adj) inappropriate, **5.** qualify; *synonyms* (v) modify, prepare, moderate, capacitate, characterize, confine, define, designate, determine, condition, enable, entitle, equip, limit, modulate; *antonym* (v) disqualify, **6.** qualified; *synonyms* (adj) eligible, conditional, certified, limited, restricted, fitted, provisional, accredited, comparative, dependant, dependent, entitled, moderated; *antonyms* (adj) unqualified, total, unofficial, definite.

manikorakiaki qualified; *synonyms* (adj) competent, capable, eligible, efficient, conditional, fit, proficient, able, clever, expert, adequate, certified, limited, restricted, fitted; *antonyms* (adj) unqualified, total, unofficial, definite.

maniman keep; *synonyms* (v) hold, preserve, retain, defend, continue, guard, have, maintain, celebrate, confine, conserve, observe, reserve, save, commemorate; *antonyms* (v) dump, lose.

manimanaki kept; *synonyms* (adj) reserved, detained, intransitive, unbroken, unploughed, unplowed.

manimaninia 1. embroider; *synonyms* (v) adorn, embellish, decorate, broider, trim, hyperbolize, lard, ornament, stitch, aggrandize, amplify, beautify, dramatise, dramatize, (adv) color, **2.** illuminate; *synonyms* (v) brighten, clarify, elucidate, enlighten, illumine, shine, clear, explain, ignite, expound, edify, explicate, illustrate, (adj) illume, (n) light; *antonym* (v) confuse, **3.** decorate; *synonyms* (v) deck, bedeck, dress, grace, apparel, bedight, arrange, array, emblazon, embroider, enrich, garnish, hang, paint, clothe; *antonym* (v) strip, **4.** design; *synonyms* (n) aim, purpose, scheme, conception, drawing, arrangement, device, idea, intent, contrivance, (v) plan, conceive, contrive, sketch, construct; *antonym* (n) chance.

manimaniniaki 1. designed; *synonyms* (v) advised, (adj) deliberate, intended, intentional, studied, premeditated, willful, configured, **2.** illuminated; *synonyms* (adj) bright, lighted, lit, luminous, enlightened, clear, ablaze, brilliant, burning, irradiate, intelligent, intelligible, **3.** embroidered; *synonyms* (adj) bewrought, exaggerated, inflated, ornate, overstated, embellished, **4.** decorated; *synonyms* (adj) adorned, fancy, beautiful, bejeweled, adorn, dyed, elaborate, emblazoned, festive, inscribed, painted, purfled, tinted, celebrated, extolled.

manin 1. amiable; *synonyms* (adj) affable, agreeable, benign, complaisant, friendly, genial, charming, cordial, gentle, kind, likable, lovely, nice, pleasant, sweet; *antonyms* (*adj*) unfriendly, disagreeable, aggressive, argumentative, **2**. attractive; *synonyms* (*adj*) alluring, amiable, appealing, engaging, good-looking, tempting, adorable, delightful, enchanting, fascinating, glamorous, gorgeous, handsome, interesting, inviting; *antonyms* (*adj*) unattractive, ugly, unappealing, disgusting, repellent, revolting, repulsive, straight, unpleasant, **3**. charming; *synonyms* (*adj*) beautiful, attractive, captivating, pleasing, winning, amusing, bewitching, cute, delectable, exquisite, lovable, magic, magical, pretty, wizard, **4**. seductive; *synonyms* (*adj*) enticing, seducing, desirable, sexy, irresistible, persuasive.

manina standardize; *synonyms* (*v*) normalize, regulate, order, standardise, adjust, organize, regularize.

maninaki standardized; *synonyms* (*adj*) standardised, exchangeable, interchangeable, similar, complementary, consistent, constant, convertible, harmonized, like, mechanical, regular, stereotyped, systematic, titrated.

maninga 1. doting; *synonyms* (*adj*) adoring, affectionate, fond, loving, devoted, amorous, caring, delirious, **2**. distracted; *synonyms* (*adj*) frantic, demented, inattentive, abstracted, crazy, distraught, distressed, frenzied, mad, preoccupied, confused, disconcerted, forgetful, absentminded, distrait, **3**. forgetful; *synonyms* (*adj*) careless, oblivious, negligent, remiss, lax, absent-minded, casual, heedless, neglectful, unmindful, mindless, unaware; *antonym* (*adj*) attentive, **4**. omit; *synonyms* (*v*) fail, neglect, disregard, delete, forget, except, exclude, drop, ignore, leave, pretermit, expunge, erase, (*adj*) skip, jump; *antonym* (*v*) include, **5**. shudder; *synonyms* (*n*) shake, quake, quivering, shivering, chill, frisson, tremor, twitch, (*v*) shiver, quiver, tremble, dither, flicker, flutter, thrill, **6**. tremble; *synonyms* (*v*) totter, palpitate, quail, falter, agitate, quaver, vibrate, waver, cower, wave, rock, fear, (*n*) shudder, throb, tingle, **7**. shiver; *synonyms* (*n*) fragment, splinter, palpitation, vibration, fright, (*v*) shatter, crash, smash, dash, burst, quell, rupture, (*adj*) break, crack, split.

maningainga 1. hospitable; *synonyms* (*adj*) friendly, affable, cordial, gracious, receptive, generous, amiable, convivial, genial, pleasant, warm; *antonyms* (*adj*) unfriendly, inhospitable, unwelcoming, **2**. affable; *synonyms* (*adj*) civil, courteous, polite, approachable, congenial, nice, sociable, agreeable, amicable, bland, companionable, complaisant, courtly, familiar, gentle; *antonyms* (*adj*) disagreeable, hostile, reserved, **3**. sociable; *synonyms* (*adj*) outgoing, social, clubbable, conversable, gregarious, easy,

expansive, jovial, kind, chatty, (*n*) desobligeant, mixer; *antonym* (*adj*) unsociable.

maninganinga 1. humane; *synonyms* (*adj*) benevolent, compassionate, beneficent, clement, charitable, kind, merciful, good, benignant, tender, (*n*) gentle, gracious, kindly, sympathetic, caring; *antonyms* (*adj*) cruel, inhumane, **2**. civilized; *synonyms* (*adj*) civil, cultured, polite, refined, civilised, cultivated, educated, courteous, genteel, polished, urbane, **3**. cultivated; *synonyms* (*adj*) civilized, tame, elegant, sophisticated, accomplished, artistic, suave, tasteful; *antonyms* (*adj*) uncultivated, untamed, wild, **4**. civil; *synonyms* (*adj*) civic, affable, mannerly, municipal, obliging, public, attentive, complaisant, considerate, courtly, domestic, friendly, national, respectful, secular; *antonyms* (*adj*) rude, abrupt, **5**. elevated; *synonyms* (*adj*) high, exalted, lofty, noble, towering, grand, great, majestic, tall, elated, magnanimous, advanced, dignified, eminent, (*v*) steep; *antonym* (*adj*) short, **6**. educated; *synonyms* (*v*) instructed, (*adj*) erudite, enlightened, learned, lettered, trained, informed, taught; *antonyms* (*adj*) uneducated, ignorant, **7**. refined; *synonyms* (*adj*) delicate, graceful, pure, dainty, chaste, fine, exquisite, nice, purified, classical, beautiful, discerning, discriminating, keen, ladylike; *antonyms* (*adj*) coarse, unrefined, raw, uncouth, rough.

maningare dimpled; *synonyms* (*adj*) concave, dimply, hollow.

maninge dissatisfied; *synonyms* (*v*) discontented, querulous, (*adj*) discontent, disgruntled, disappointed, malcontent, complaining, grumpy; *antonyms* (*adj*) satisfied, content, contented.

maningenge 1. dissatisfy; *synonyms* (*n*) mortify, (*v*) displease, discontent, disappoint, disgruntle, chagrin, affront, anger, annoy, chafe, disaffect, disgust, mispay, dishearten, disillusion; *antonym* (*v*) satisfy, **2**. deceive; *synonyms* (*v*) betray, cheat, bamboozle, circumvent, dupe, pretend, beguile, con, cozen, fool, hoax, mislead, sell, swindle, (*n*) fraud, **3**. disappoint; *synonyms* (*v*) deceive, fail, baffle, balk, defeat, disenchant, bilk, mock, delude, foil, frustrate, thwart, (*n*) dissatisfy; *antonym* (*v*) please.

maningengeaki 1. dissatisfied; *synonyms* (*v*) discontented, querulous, (*adj*) discontent, disgruntled, disappointed, malcontent, complaining, grumpy; *antonyms* (*adj*) satisfied, content, contented, **2**. disappointed; *synonyms* (*adj*) defeated, regretful, depressed, dissatisfied, frustrated, sad, unhappy, disenchanted; *antonyms* (*adj*) delighted, pleased, composed.

maningongo whisper; *synonyms* (*n*) buzz, hum, rustle, breath, trace, undertone, rumor, (*v*) murmur, breathe, mumble, hint, suggestion, hiss, inkling, innuendo; *antonym* (v) shout.

maningongoaki whispered; *synonyms* (*adj*) low, soft, voiceless, aspirated, atonic, deaf, faint, irrational, muted, nonvocal, quiet, radical, sharp, supposed, surd.

maninrongorongo 1. exaggerate; *synonyms* (v) boast, aggravate, amplify, dramatize, overdo, overdraw, enhance, enlarge, magnify, overstate, embellish, heighten, hyperbolize, increase, inflate; *antonyms* (v) understate, minimize, **2.** overstate; *synonyms* (v) exaggerate, embroider, overcharge, pad.

maninrongorongoaki 1. exaggerated; *synonyms* (*adj*) enlarged, extravagant, theatrical, immoderate, hypertrophied, affected, excessive, hyperbolic, inflated, magnified, overdone, overstated, pretentious, melodramatic; *antonyms* (*adj*) understated, restrained, **2.** overstated; *synonyms* (*adj*) exaggerated, flashy, garish, gaudy, loud, showy, sweeping, vulgar, embellished, embroidered, ornate, overblown, profuse.

manintaeka report; *synonyms* (n) description, gossip, notice, name, fame, message, narration, narrative, news, notification, recital, record, (v) account, describe, communicate; *antonym* (n) fact.

manintaekaki reported; *synonyms* (*adj*) narrative, putative, reputed.

maninuto 1. accused; *synonyms* (n) panel, perpetrator, **2.** suspect; *synonyms* (v) doubt, distrust, mistrust, suppose, conjecture, guess, surmise, believe, disbelieve, divine, (*adj*) fishy, questionable, shady, suspicious, dubious; *antonyms* (v) trust, (*adj*) trustworthy.

maninutoa 1. accuse; *synonyms* (v) impeach, charge, incriminate, arraign, criminate, defame, denounce, indict, fault, betray, accusation, admonish, censure, condemn, criticize, **2.** allege; *synonyms* (v) affirm, maintain, plead, say, argue, assert, aver, claim, declare, pretend, accuse, lay, adduce, avow, (n) advance; *antonym* (v) deny, **3.** suspect; *synonyms* (v) doubt, distrust, mistrust, suppose, conjecture, guess, surmise, believe, disbelieve, divine, (*adj*) fishy, questionable, shady, suspicious, dubious; *antonyms* (v) trust, (*adj*) trustworthy.

maninutoaki 1. accused; *synonyms* (n) panel, perpetrator, **2.** alleged; *synonyms* (*adj*) reputed, apparent, assumed, ostensible, professed, supposed, apologetic, pretended, putative, so-called, believed, nominal, perceived, seeming, thought; *antonym* (*adj*) real, **3.** suspected; *synonyms* (*adj*) suspect, distrusted.

manio 1. inert; *synonyms* (*adj*) idle, dead, dull, inactive, indolent, sluggish, dormant, flat, inanimate, lifeless, passive, still, stationary, apathetic, heavy; *antonyms* (*adj*) moving, active, animate, **2.** indolent; *synonyms* (*adj*) lazy, slothful,

careless, drowsy, faineant, inert, listless, otiose, slow, torpid, lackadaisical, languid, lethargic, slack, (v) remiss; *antonym* (*adj*) energetic, **3.** sluggish; *synonyms* (*adj*) obtuse, dilatory, backward, blunt, leaden, stupid, weak, gradual, dim, phlegmatic, dense, deliberate, stagnant, supine, (n) sleepy; *antonyms* (*adj*) brisk, fast, **4.** numb; *synonyms* (*adj*) asleep, benumbed, insensible, deadened, callous, impassive, comatose, paralytic, frozen, unconscious, (v) benumb, deaden, paralyze, harden; *antonym* (*adj*) sensitive.

manionio 1. limp; *synonyms* (*adj*) flabby, flaccid, slack, flexible, drooping, flimsy, floppy, lax, loose, weak, (n) hobble, (v) halt, hitch, hop, shamble; *antonyms* (*adj*) taut, firm, (n) energetic, **2.** jaded; *synonyms* (*adj*) exhausted, tired, fatigued, wearied, weary, worn, bored, satiated, sick, sophisticated, blasé, clichéd, cynical, disenchanted, disillusioned; *antonym* (*adj*) fresh, **3.** flabby; *synonyms* (*adj*) feeble, baggy, limp, heavy, soft, chubby, fat; *antonym* (*adj*) slim, **4.** slack; *synonyms* (*adj*) idle, indolent, negligent, neglectful, dilatory, inattentive, lazy, backward, careless, (v) remiss, dull, slow, relax, abate, easy; *antonyms* (*adj*) tight, strict, thorough.

maniwaira 1. disparage; *synonyms* (v) denigrate, belittle, deprecate, depreciate, derogate, decry, defame, censure, condemn, criticize, detract, abuse, slur, (n) disgrace, discredit; *antonyms* (v) praise, compliment, flatter, **2.** vilify; *synonyms* (v) malign, slander, libel, disparage, revile, traduce, blacken, smear, calumniate, vituperate, bespatter, assail, attack, (*adj*) asperse, injure.

maniwia 1. fortunate; *synonyms* (*adj*) favorable, auspicious, lucky, advantageous, blessed, favored, fortuitous, happy, prosperous, successful, well, felicitous, golden, good, propitious; *antonyms* (*adj*) unfortunate, unlucky, **2.** lucky; *synonyms* (*adj*) favourable, flourishing, chance, providential, encouraging, promising, (v) fortunate; *antonyms* (*adj*) hapless, ill-fated.

mannanoa 1. heed; *synonyms* (n) care, consideration, concern, caution, regard, notice, note, charge, discretion, (v) attend, hear, attention, mind, beware, consider; *antonyms* (v) disregard, ignore, **2.** mind; *synonyms* (n) intellect, brain, head, inclination, intelligence, psyche, mentality, conscience, belief, brains, (v) look, keep, listen, guard, (*adj*) heed; *antonym* (v) forget, **3.** regard; *synonyms* (v) estimate, account, believe, count, hold, observe, reckon, appreciate, gaze, (n) respect, esteem, deference, value, admiration, estimation; *antonym* (n) disrespect, **4.** respect; *synonyms* (n) honor, homage, worship, connection, obeisance, appreciation, awe, courtesy, duty, relation, (v) admire, prize, reverence, reference, revere;

antonyms (*n*) cheek, insolence, impudence, (*v*) scorn, despise, dishonor, humiliate.

mannanoaki 1. minded; *synonyms* (*adj*) willing, prone, ready, partial, predisposed, prepared, (*prep*) inclined, disposed, jolly, **2**. respected; *synonyms* (*adj*) esteemed, illustrious, respectable, appreciated, dear, honored, revered, valued, celebrated, famous, glorious, prestigious, redoubtable.

mannaoka 1. joke; *synonyms* (*n*) jest, banter, hoax, fun, caper, gag, game, quip, antic, farce, humor, jape, jocularity, pleasantry, (*v*) chaff; *antonym* (*n*) tragedy, **2**. bully; *synonyms* (*n*) browbeat, rowdy, tough, bravo, hooligan, ruffian, (*v*) bluster, bulldoze, ballyrag, coerce, intimidate, threaten, badger, swagger, (*adj*) domineer, **3**. exploit; *synonyms* (*v*) act, exercise, apply, employ, use, abuse, harness, (*n*) deed, achievement, feat, accomplishment, action, adventure, effort, performance.

mannaoakaki 1. bullied; *synonyms* (*adj*) intimidated, browbeaten, cowed, hangdog, timid, guilty, shamed, shamefaced, **2**. exploited; *synonyms* (*adj*) used, downtrodden, broken, commercial, demoralized, oppressed, subjugated, victimised, victimized, secondhand.

mannawa turbid; *synonyms* (*adj*) muddy, thick, murky, opaque, cloudy, dirty, mirky.

mannei 1. apathetic; *synonyms* (*adj*) indifferent, cool, impassive, uninterested, perfunctory, casual, dull, lazy, lethargic, lukewarm, nonchalant, sluggish, spiritless, detached, indolent; *antonyms* (*adj*) energetic, enthusiastic, fervent, inquisitive, **2**. nonchalant; *synonyms* (*adj*) negligent, careless, insouciant, unconcerned, carefree, calm, offhand, easygoing; *antonym* (*adj*) anxious, **3**. feeble; *synonyms* (*adj*) delicate, weak, decrepit, ailing, dim, frail, helpless, infirm, lax, mild, poor, powerless, thin, (*v*) faint, debilitated; *antonyms* (*adj*) strong, vigorous, hearty, tough, **4**. lethargic; *synonyms* (*adj*) drowsy, dozy, languid, comatose, listless, sleepy, slow, torpid, inactive, lethargical, heavy, apathetic, lackadaisical, languorous, lifeless; *antonyms* (*adj*) alert, lively, playful, agitated.

manni 1. fine; *synonyms* (*adj*) delicate, agreeable, dainty, brave, capital, elegant, excellent, nice, thin, delightful, acute, admirable, alright, (*n*) penalty, (*v*) punish; *antonyms* (*adj*) poor, thick, coarse, substantial, unsatisfactory, wide, **2**. thin; *synonyms* (*adj*) flimsy, gaunt, lean, light, slight, tenuous, emaciated, fine, rare, slim, sparse, (*v*) slender, dilute, meager, sheer; *antonyms* (*adj*) fat, concentrated, chubby, plump, broad, heavy, (*v*) thicken.

mannibwerebwere skinny; *synonyms* (*adj*) lean, meager, emaciated, scrawny, thin, gaunt, scraggy, underweight, weedy, lank, angular, slender, slight,

spare, (*v*) cortical; *antonyms* (*adj*) fat, plump, brawny, well-built.

mannikiba bird; *synonyms* (*n*) birdie, chick, fowl, girl, wench, hiss, shuttlecock, insect, mollusk, reptile, shellfish, worm, person, biddy, (*v*) birdwatch.

mano 1. concave; *synonyms* (*adj*) hollow, cavernous, crescent, biconcave, cupped, dipped, arched, depress, dishing, vaulted, vaulty, deceitful, deep, (*v*) curve, dig; *antonyms* (*adj*) convex, curved, **2**. hollow; *synonyms* (*adj*) blank, concave, empty, false, insincere, (*n*) cavity, hole, cave, depression, groove, excavation, trench, (*v*) excavate, dent, scoop; *antonyms* (*n*) solid, hump, **3**. watertight; *synonyms* (*adj*) unassailable, waterproof, tight, firm, impregnable, ironclad, leakproof, unshakable; *antonyms* (*adj*) permeable, indefensible, **4**. safe; *synonyms* (*adj*) secure, reliable, cautious, dependable, good, harmless, innocuous, sound, correct, innocent, inoffensive, certain, stable, (*n*) closet, coffer; *antonyms* (*adj*) dangerous, unsafe, hurt, risky, unprotected, vulnerable, harmful, insecure, reckless, **5**. secure; *synonyms* (*v*) close, fix, preserve, fasten, acquire, assure, attain, ensure, fast, gain, get, (*adj*) safe, confident, attach, bind; *antonyms* (*v*) lose, detach, (*adj*) loose.

manoa oily; *synonyms* (*adj*) greasy, fat, fatty, oleaginous, unctuous, buttery, slick, fulsome, obsequious, rich, sebaceous, (*v*) bland, soapy, glassy, slippery.

manoanga feeling; *synonyms* (*n*) affection, feel, passion, emotion, atmosphere, belief, hunch, impression, intuition, mood, opinion, sense, sensitivity, sentiment, enthusiasm; *antonyms* (*n*) numbness, indifference.

manobotabota 1. ardent; *synonyms* (*adj*) burning, enthusiastic, fervent, passionate, eager, impassioned, keen, vehement, warm, acute, affectionate, avid, devoted, earnest, fervid; *antonyms* (*adj*) indifferent, apathetic, **2**. active; *synonyms* (*adj*) energetic, alert, busy, diligent, effective, live, lively, nimble, strong, agile, alive, brisk, dynamic, forcible, healthy; *antonyms* (*adj*) dormant, inactive, sluggish, idle, latent, lethargic, sedentary, slow, extinct, passive, quiet, **3**. zealous; *synonyms* (*adj*) ardent, strenuous, fiery, glowing, intense, dedicated, enterprising, fanatical, cordial, forward, solicitous, active, jealous, (*n*) hearty, sincere.

manono 1. hollow; *synonyms* (*adj*) blank, concave, empty, false, insincere, (*n*) cavity, hole, cave, depression, groove, excavation, (*v*) excavate, dent, scoop, dig; *antonyms* (*adj*) convex, (*n*) solid, hump, **2**. depressed; *synonyms* (*adj*) low, blue, dejected, dispirited, down, downcast, downhearted, gloomy, hollow, sad, crestfallen, disappointed, discouraged, flat, forlorn; *antonyms* (*adj*) cheerful, happy, **3**.

dented; *synonyms* (*v*) indented, (*adj*) bent,
crumpled, bended, bowed, creased, hurt, injured,
spoiled, broken, inclined, rumpled, scratched,
smashed, stooped, **4**. gorged; *synonyms* (*adj*)
satiated, sated, full, stuffed, bursting, congested,
replete, satisfied, surfeited, glutted.

manouna 1. futile; *synonyms* (*adj*) fruitless, useless,
empty, abortive, frivolous, idle, ineffective,
bootless, hollow, hopeless, ineffectual,
meaningless, pointless, vain, worthless; *antonym*
(*adj*) successful, **2**. ineffectual; *synonyms* (*adj*)
futile, feeble, powerless, unable, void, weak,
feckless, impotent, barren, inactive, incompetent,
impracticable, spineless, inefficient, inept;
antonyms (*adj*) effective, effectual, strong, **3**.
fruitless; *synonyms* (*adj*) sterile, unproductive,
infertile, poor, profitless, unfruitful, unprofitable,
unsuccessful, wasted, conceited; *antonym* (*adj*)
fertile, **4**. unavailing; *synonyms* (*adj*) inefficacious,
otiose, inutile, **5**. profitless; *synonym* (*adj*)
gainless.

manrea 1. traditional; *synonyms* (*adj*) orthodox,
conventional, customary, conservative, normal,
immemorial, ordinary, classic, habitual, legendary,
traditionary, usual, accepted, accustomed,
established; *antonyms* (*adj*) new, modern,
progressive, unconventional, unusual, **2**. stale;
synonyms (*adj*) musty, old, commonplace,
hackneyed, banal, corny, flat, insipid, moldy,
stagnant, trite, dull, obsolete, cold, (*v*) dry;
antonyms (*adj*) fresh, original, innovative.

manrerei 1. foolish; *synonyms* (*adj*) childish, crazy,
fool, daft, dopey, dull, dumb, fatuous,
preposterous, silly, stupid, unwise, anserine, dopy,
(*n*) absurd; *antonyms* (*adj*) wise, sensible, prudent,
shrewd, visionary, **2**. frivolous; *synonyms* (*adj*)
empty, foolish, dizzy, idle, petty, facetious, flighty,
flippant, light, shallow, superficial, trifling, trivial,
unimportant, fickle; *antonyms* (*adj*) serious,
important, **3**. childish; *synonyms* (*adj*) boyish,
childlike, babyish, immature, naive, frivolous,
infantile, juvenile, puerile, simple, young, innocent,
adolescent, peevish, youthful; *antonyms* (*adj*)
mature, grown-up, old, **4**. idle; *synonyms* (*adj*)
inactive, indolent, lazy, free, baseless, fruitless,
groundless, unfounded, disengaged, flimsy, barren,
dead, futile, jobless, (*v*) loaf; *antonyms* (*adj*) busy,
active, employed, (*v*) change, **5**. futile; *synonyms*
(*adj*) useless, abortive, ineffective, bootless, hollow,
hopeless, ineffectual, meaningless, pointless, vain,
worthless, unproductive, inane, inefficacious,
inefficient; *antonym* (*adj*) successful, **6**. puerile;
synonyms (*adj*) jejune, callow, **7**. vain; *synonyms*
(*adj*) proud, arrogant, conceited, egotistic,
egotistical, narcissistic, null, unavailing,
unsuccessful, void, nugatory, unprofitable, cocky,
feeble, profitless; *antonym* (*adj*) modest.

mantakarara 1. bolster; *synonyms* (*v*) encourage,
support, uphold, back, buttress, pad, prop,
reinforce, strengthen, help, advocate, aid, (*n*) brace,
cushion, sustain; *antonyms* (*v*) weaken, undermine,
reduce, **2**. informal; *synonyms* (*adj*) colloquial,
familiar, casual, easy, free, cozy, unofficial, chatty,
cosy, homely, wanton, comfortable, conversational,
everyday, intimate; *antonyms* (*adj*) formal,
authorized, official, **3**. familiar; *synonyms* (*adj*)
close, common, conversant, customary,
commonplace, ordinary, usual, acquainted,
chummy, (*n*) accustomed, companion, comrade,
habitual, associate, (*v*) confidential; *antonyms* (*adj*)
unfamiliar, foreign, strange, new, unaccustomed,
ignorant, unknown, **4**. unconstrained; *synonyms*
(*adj*) independent, informal, unobstructed,
unrestrained, voluntary, outgoing, spontaneous,
uncaught, unchecked, unconfined.

manti 1. crush; *synonyms* (*n*) squeeze, press, crowd,
(*v*) beat, break, compress, conquer, crunch, stamp,
bruise, jam, mash, overpower, overwhelm, quash,
2. flatten; *synonyms* (*v*) fell, demolish, level, even,
drop, roll, squash, depress, destroy, ruin, smash,
smooth, unfold, bulldoze, deflate; *antonyms* (*v*)
build, crumple, **3**. reduce; *synonyms* (*v*) lower,
pare, abbreviate, curtail, cut, debase, abate,
condense, contract, diminish, shorten, concentrate,
decrease, (*adj*) abridge, lessen; *antonyms* (*v*)
increase, bolster, expand, enlarge, exacerbate,
intensify.

mantiaki 1. flattened; *synonyms* (*adj*) compressed,
depressed, planate, trodden, unconscious,
compacted, firmed, trampled; *antonym* (*adj*) loose,
2. crushed; *synonyms* (*v*) victimized, (*adj*) broken,
beaten, low, subdued, conquered, flattened,
dispirited, overwhelmed, abashed, abject, blue,
brokenhearted, busted, (*n*) crushing; *antonym* (*adj*)
victorious, **3**. reduced; *synonyms* (*adj*) decreased,
abridged, curtailed, miniature, cheap, limited,
bated, cut, inexpensive, lower, prostrate; *antonyms*
(*adj*) expensive, complete.

manto 1. acquired; *synonyms* (*v*) acquiring, (*adj*)
acquisite, acquisitive, derivative, extrinsic, **2**.
taken; *synonyms* (*v*) take, (*adj*) occupied, full,
interpreted, besotted, crazed, enamored, engaged,
interested, lovesick, obsessed, overcome, preferred,
rapt, reserved.

mantoa 1. mystify; *synonyms* (*v*) baffle, bamboozle,
bewilder, confound, confuse, nonplus, perplex,
puzzle, stump, amaze, flummox, get, hoodwink,
bemuse, gravel, **2**. muddle; *synonyms* (*n*) jumble,
clutter, mess, disorder, chaos, confusion, disarray,
huddle, hash, maze, (*v*) blunder, addle, botch,
befuddle, (*adj*) fluster; *antonym* (*n*) order, **3**. dense;
synonyms (*adj*) compact, thick, close, crowded,
deep, crass, dim, dull, heavy, impenetrable, solid,
stupid, concentrated, dumb, firm; *antonyms* (*adj*)

bright, insightful, loose, clever, intelligent, readable, simple, sparse, **4**. ridicule; *synonyms* (*n*) derision, irony, mockery, insult, contempt, scoff, taunt, disdain, gibe, (*v*) banter, deride, jeer, flout, mock, scorn; *antonyms* (*v*) praise, respect, **5**. troubled; *synonyms* (*adj*) concerned, disturbed, anxious, distressed, solicitous, apprehensive, disconcerted, uncomfortable, uneasy, upset, worried, restless, distraught, bothered, perturbed; *antonyms* (*adj*) untroubled, composed, unconcerned, **6**. turbid; *synonyms* (*adj*) muddy, murky, opaque, cloudy, dirty, mirky, **7**. turbulent; *synonyms* (*adj*) tempestuous, tumultuous, rough, furious, boisterous, disorderly, noisy, riotous, violent, wild, rude, troubled, unruly, agitated, (*n*) stormy; *antonym* (*adj*) calm.

mantoaki 1. muddled; *synonyms* (*adj*) confused, bewildered, addled, disordered, disorganized, messy, incoherent, bemused, chaotic, jumbled, unintelligible, upset, befuddled, blank, (*n*) corned; *antonyms* (*adj*) neat, organized, **2**. mystified; *synonyms* (*adj*) metagrabolized, metagrobolized, perplexed, puzzled, baffled, flummoxed, metagrabolised, metagrobolised, stumped, thrown, unclear, absentminded, bamboozled, faraway, preoccupied; *antonym* (*adj*) enlightened.

mantokotoko 1. lazy; *synonyms* (*adj*) indolent, idle, inert, drowsy, inactive, shiftless, dull, faineant, remiss, slothful, slow, sluggish, leisurely, sluggard, tardy; *antonyms* (*adj*) energetic, diligent, active, **2**. shirker; *synonyms* (*n*) idler, loafer, malingerer, slacker, absentee, lazybones, dawdler, do-nothing, coward, deserter, laggard, slowcoach, straggler; *antonym* (*n*) leader.

manu 1. pleated, **2**. wrinkled; *synonyms* (*adj*) furrowed, creased, crumpled, lined, puckered, wizened, wrinkly, gnarled, unironed, (*n*) rough, rugged; *antonyms* (*adj*) smooth.

manuia 1. lucky; *synonyms* (*adj*) auspicious, favorable, propitious, prosperous, favourable, successful, flourishing, advantageous, blessed, chance, good, providential, (*n*) happy, favored, (*v*) fortunate; *antonyms* (*adj*) unlucky, hapless, ill-fated, unfortunate, **2**. fortunate; *synonyms* (*adj*) lucky, fortuitous, well, felicitous, golden, advantaged, desirable, hopeful.

manunu wrinkled; *synonyms* (*adj*) furrowed, creased, crumpled, lined, puckered, wizened, wrinkly, gnarled, unironed, (*n*) rough, rugged; *antonym* (*adj*) smooth.

manuoka 1. forget; *synonyms* (*v*) disregard, leave, bury, ignore, neglect, overlook, fail, abandon, lose, omit, slight, block; *antonym* (*v*) remember, **2**. omit; *synonyms* (*v*) delete, forget, except, exclude, drop, pretermit, expunge, erase, eliminate, default, sink, contract, (*adj*) skip, jump, (*n*) forsake; *antonym* (*v*) include, **3**. overlook; *synonyms* (*v*) excuse,

command, control, dominate, oversee, forgive, overleap, pardon, survey, face, connive, condone, check, (*n*) oversight, lookout.

manuokaki 1. forgotten; *synonyms* (*adj*) lost, disregarded, elapsed, past, abandoned, antebellum, antediluvian, baffled, befuddled, bemused, bewildered, beyond, bygone, confounded, confused, **2**. overlooked; *synonyms* (*adj*) unnoticed, ignored, unmarked, unnoted, unobserved, unseen.

manuokina 1. forget; *synonyms* (*v*) disregard, leave, bury, ignore, neglect, overlook, fail, abandon, lose, omit, slight, block; *antonym* (*v*) remember, **2**. overlook; *synonyms* (*v*) excuse, forget, command, control, dominate, oversee, forgive, drop, overleap, pardon, survey, face, connive, (*n*) oversight, lookout.

manuokinaki 1. forgotten; *synonyms* (*adj*) lost, disregarded, elapsed, past, abandoned, antebellum, antediluvian, baffled, befuddled, bemused, bewildered, beyond, bygone, confounded, confused, **2**. overlooked; *synonyms* (*adj*) unnoticed, ignored, unmarked, unnoted, unobserved, unseen.

mao 1. bitter; *synonyms* (*adj*) acrimonious, biting, acrid, sharp, acerbic, acid, caustic, keen, malicious, resentful, sour, virulent, acerb, cutting, (*n*) acerbity; *antonyms* (*adj*) mild, sweet, charitable, hot, kind, sugary, **2**. healed; *synonyms* (*adj*) cured, recovered, aged, corned, whole, vulcanised, vulcanized, **3**. diminishing; *synonyms* (*adj*) decreasing, abating, declining, dwindling, lessening, waning, ablatitious, deteriorating, extenuating, fading, failing, falling, flagging, (*n*) decrease, contraction; *antonym* (*adj*) increasing, **4**. decreasing; *synonyms* (*adj*) amortizing, decrescent, music; *antonym* (*adj*) rising, **5**. acid; *synonyms* (*adj*) acidic, bitter, pointed, sarcastic, astringent, blistering, corrosive, harsh, incisive, mordant, pungent, unkind, venomous, vitriolic, (*v*) tart, **6**. sour; *synonyms* (*adj*) morose, rancid, severe, gruff, dour, glum, grim, rotten, sullen, off, (*v*) acidify, ferment, turn, embitter, (*n*) acidity; *antonym* (*adj*) kindly, **7**. sharp; *synonyms* (*adj*) acute, intelligent, intense, penetrating, piercing, quick, alert, piquant, prompt, smart, astute, bright, discerning, (*v*) brisk, clever; *antonyms* (*adj*) blunt, dull, gentle, rounded, bland, blurred, naive, round, smooth.

maomoa feverish; *synonyms* (*adj*) hectic, febrile, feverous, hot, fiery, frenzied, excited, fanatical, flushed, sick, (*n*) hysterical; *antonym* (*adj*) cool.

maon 1. intermittent; *synonyms* (*adj*) broken, occasional, sporadic, discontinuous, fitful, irregular, periodic, spasmodic, recurrent, recurring, uneven, frequent, infrequent, restless; *antonyms* (*adj*) continuous, constant, continual, repeated, **2**.

rare; *synonyms* (*adj*) extraordinary, uncommon, exceptional, precious, scarce, seldom, thin, unusual, few, choice, curious, fine, odd, peculiar, novel; *antonyms* (*adj*) common, ordinary.

maong 1. exhausted; *synonyms* (*v*) weak, (*adj*) drained, fatigued, spent, tired, gone, dry, beat, depleted, empty, enervated, faint, jaded, weary, expended; *antonyms* (*adj*) energetic, fresh, refreshed, strong, **2.** wet; *synonyms* (*adj*) damp, humid, drenched, moist, soaked, sodden, dank, rainy, saturated, soggy, (*v*) moisten, water, dampen, wash, (*n*) moisture; *antonyms* (*adj*) dehydrated, parched, **3.** sweating; *synonyms* (*adj*) perspiring, sweaty, (*n*) perspiration, exudation, sweat, diaphoresis, hidrosis, extravasation, fermentation, sudation, **4.** perspiring; *synonyms* (*adj*) sweating, perspirable, sudatory, sweltering, warm, clammy, sticky, **5.** tired; *synonyms* (*adj*) exhausted, hackneyed, banal, commonplace, stale, threadbare, trite, haggard, stock, worn, drowsy, sick, whacked, corny, limp; *antonyms* (*adj*) invigorated, alert, original, **6.** soaked; *synonyms* (*adj*) wet, soaking, sopping, drunk, plastered, sloshed, soppy, besotted.

maono 1. clammy; *synonyms* (*adj*) wet, damp, humid, moist, muggy, sticky, sweaty, viscous, dank, sultry, viscid, soggy, (*n*) ropy, amylaceous; *antonym* (*adj*) dry, **2.** sweaty; *synonyms* (*adj*) clammy, perspiring, sweating, warm, **3.** perspiring; *synonyms* (*adj*) perspirable, sudatory, sweltering, **4.** sweat; *synonyms* (*n*) labor, perspiration, lather, sudor, effort, struggle, drudgery, fret, labour, (*v*) work, perspire, toil, drudge, exude, ooze, **5.** perspire; *synonyms* (*v*) sweat, transpire, excrete, emit, exhale, heat, secrete, sudate.

maonon 1. malleable; *synonyms* (*adj*) ductile, elastic, flexible, pliable, soft, pliant, supple, yielding, adaptable, plastic, tensile, tractable, bendable, **2.** limber; *synonyms* (*adj*) lithe, agile, lissom, lissome, lithesome, svelte, willowy, **3.** elastic; *synonyms* (*adj*) buoyant, limber, resilient, springy, stretchable, bouncy, expansive, malleable, bendy, spongy; *antonyms* (*adj*) rigid, stiff, inflexible, inelastic, **4.** flexible; *synonyms* (*adj*) facile, adjustable, compliant, flexile, variable, versatile, conciliatory, easy, bending, changeable, limp, movable, nimble, stretchy, compromising; *antonyms* (*adj*) fixed, obstinate, stubborn, **5.** pliable; *synonyms* (*adj*) fictile, susceptible, docile, tame, submissive.

maoria 1. disappointed; *synonyms* (*adj*) defeated, disgruntled, regretful, depressed, dissatisfied, frustrated, sad, unhappy, disenchanted; *antonyms* (*adj*) delighted, pleased, composed, satisfied, **2.** corrected; *synonyms* (*adj*) chastised, amended,

reformed, altered, chastened, disciplined, educated, refined.

maoriori 1. flexible; *synonyms* (*adj*) elastic, adaptable, pliable, yielding, lissome, pliant, soft, supple, facile, adjustable, bendable, compliant, ductile, flexile, lithe; *antonyms* (*adj*) inflexible, rigid, fixed, obstinate, stiff, stubborn, **2.** supple; *synonyms* (*adj*) flexible, graceful, lissom, lithesome, plastic, active, agile, malleable, nimble, tender, resilient, floppy, alert, limp, (*v*) limber.

maoto fracture; *synonyms* (*n*) break, breach, cleft, fissure, breaking, crevice, disruption, breakage, chap, cracking, (*v*) crack, rupture, burst, bust, smash.

maotoaki fractured; *synonyms* (*adj*) fissured, torn, splintered, split, (*v*) broken, cracked, apart, blighted, contrite, disconnected, disunited, humbled, rough, strained, subdued.

maotorikiriki smashed; *synonyms* (*adj*) shattered, drunk, inebriated, intoxicated, broken, plastered, sloshed, blotto, tipsy, besotted, pissed, tight; *antonym* (*adj*) sober.

maotorrikiriki 1. fulfill; *synonyms* (*v*) accomplish, achieve, execute, do, perform, attain, complete, effect, fill, meet, satisfy, consummate, discharge, answer, effectuate, **2.** perfect; *synonyms* (*adj*) exact, utter, entire, faultless, thorough, exquisite, integral, blameless, clean, correct, flawless, (*v*) finish, fulfill, (*n*) absolute, full; *antonyms* (*adj*) imperfect, faulty, flawed.

maotorrikirikiaki 1. fulfilled; *synonyms* (*adj*) content, complete, finished, done, satisfied, accomplished, completed, concluded, delighted, happy, pleased, whole, actualized, attained, compassed; *antonym* (*adj*) unfinished, **2.** perfected; *synonyms* (*adj*) consummate, elaborate, mature, mellow, ripe.

mara 1. feebleness; *synonyms* (*n*) frailty, infirmity, weakness, decrepitude, faintness, fragility, frailness, imbecility, languor, tenuity, defect, dotage, (*adj*) debility, disease; *antonyms* (*n*) strength, perseverance, **2.** feeble; *synonyms* (*adj*) delicate, weak, decrepit, ailing, dim, dull, frail, helpless, infirm, lax, mild, poor, powerless, (*v*) faint, debilitated; *antonyms* (*adj*) strong, vigorous, hearty, tough, **3.** bald; *synonyms* (*adj*) bare, hairless, simple, austere, meager, threadbare, raw, barefaced, dry, forthright, mere, naked, nude, plain, stark; *antonym* (*adj*) hairy, **4.** weak; *synonyms* (*adj*) feeble, flat, flimsy, fragile, thin, watery, light, cowardly, diluted, exhausted, inadequate, nerveless, shaky, sickly, (*v*) loose; *antonyms* (*adj*) brave, concentrated, firm, safe, compelling, determined, effective, forceful, healthy, intense, powerful, resolute, robust, sturdy, able, **5.** smooth; *synonyms* (*adj*) easy, calm, level, oily, facile, flowing, fluent, fluid, glossy, graceful, greasy, liquid, (v) quiet, facilitate, even; *antonyms* (adj) rough, uneven, abrasive, coarse, crumpled, flaking, harsh, jerky, lined, peeling, prickly, ridged, wrinkled, corrugated, (v) wrinkle, **6.** soaked; *synonyms* (adj) saturated, wet, drenched, sodden, soaking, soggy, sopping, drunk, damp, plastered, sloshed, soppy, besotted, **7.** softened; *synonyms* (adj) diffused, muffled, muted, boring, deadening, dense, dumb, gray, grey, hushed, intenerate, irksome, leaden, low-key, macerated, **8.** oiled; *synonym* (adj) intoxicated, **9.** separated; *synonyms* (adj) disconnected, separate, apart, detached, divided, isolated, disjointed, free, disjunct, removed, dislocated, independent, lone, (prep) disjoined, distinct.

marabe 1. flourishing; *synonyms* (adj) prosperous, thriving, booming, healthy, luxuriant, palmy, successful, verdant, lush, auspicious, favorable, affluent, blooming, golden, growing; *antonym* (adj) failing, **2.** healthy; *synonyms* (adj) healthful, fit, good, hale, salubrious, wholesome, beneficial, hearty, sound, well, whole, sane, abundant, nutritious, active; *antonyms* (adj) unhealthy, harmful, unwell, unfit, dependent, fattening, infected, soporific, unwholesome, weak, **3.** prosperous; *synonyms* (adj) lucky, flourishing, opulent, advantageous, comfortable, easy, rich, well-off, propitious, happy, favourable, prospering, wealthy, bright, (n) fortunate; *antonym* (adj) poor.

maraia 1. cursed; *synonyms* (v) accurst, cursing, (adj) abominable, damned, doomed, execrable, blamed, blasted, blessed, curst, damnable, detestable, hateful, infernal, unlucky, **2.** bewitched; *synonyms* (adj) spellbound, fascinated, captive, enamored, ensorcelled, infatuated, magical, obsessed, rapt, bugged, captivated, enraptured, entranced, hooked, mesmerized, **3.** unlucky; *synonyms* (adj) unfortunate, hapless, luckless, unhappy, untoward, inauspicious, sinister, adverse, disastrous, ominous, unsuccessful, unfavorable, poor, fatal, unblest; *antonyms* (adj) lucky, fortunate, **4.** spellbound; *synonyms* (adj) enchanted, bewitched, hypnotised, hypnotized, mesmerised.

marairai 1. lengthy; *synonyms* (adj) extended, extensive, long, protracted, wordy, copious, elongated, exuberant, prolonged, verbose, largiloquent; *antonyms* (adj) short, brief, **2.** long; *synonyms* (adj) lengthy, dragging, far, oblong, (v) aspire, desire, hanker, languish, yearn, ache, hunger, wish, crave, pine, (n) large.

maraka hurt; *synonyms* (v) pain, wound, afflict, injure, ail, cost, (adj) evil, (n) harm, damage, detriment, ache, disadvantage, abuse, distress, lesion; *antonyms* (v) encourage, (adj) uninjured, unhurt.

maraki 1. hurt; *synonyms* (v) pain, wound, afflict, injure, ail, cost, (adj) evil, (n) harm, damage, detriment, ache, disadvantage, abuse, distress, lesion; *antonyms* (v) encourage, (adj) uninjured, unhurt, **2.** painful; *synonyms* (adj) difficult, hard, sore, afflictive, bad, grievous, harrowing, sharp, aching, arduous, bitter, dolorous, excruciating, harsh, (v) distressing; *antonyms* (adj) painless, content, **3.** suffer; *synonyms* (v) bear, encounter, abide, accept, brook, endure, experience, have, stand, undergo, permit, receive, smart, sustain, (adj) allow, **4.** smart; *synonyms* (adj) bright, crafty, dapper, quick, shrewd, sly, prompt, astute, chic, clever, intelligent, jaunty, lively, natty, (v) hurt; *antonyms* (adj) scruffy, stupid, dim, shabby, unkempt, slow.

marakiaki hurt; *synonyms* (v) pain, wound, afflict, injure, ail, cost, (adj) evil, (n) harm, damage, detriment, ache, disadvantage, abuse, distress, lesion; *antonyms* (v) encourage, (adj) uninjured, unhurt.

marakiraki painful; *synonyms* (adj) difficult, hard, sore, afflictive, bad, grievous, harrowing, sharp, aching, arduous, bitter, dolorous, excruciating, harsh, (v) distressing; *antonyms* (adj) painless, content.

maramara 1. feeble; *synonyms* (adj) delicate, weak, decrepit, ailing, dim, dull, frail, helpless, infirm, lax, mild, poor, powerless, (v) faint, debilitated; *antonyms* (adj) strong, vigorous, hearty, tough, **2.** soft; *synonyms* (adj) gentle, easy, light, limp, balmy, quiet, slack, loose, clement, flabby, flaccid, lenient, pliant, (v) feeble, low; *antonyms* (adj) hard, firm, harsh, loud, hoarse, rough, solid, stiff, alcoholic, shrill.

maran 1. glossy; *synonyms* (adj) shiny, sleek, bright, smooth, brilliant, glazed, flat, burnished, glassy, glistening, lustrous, resplendent, satiny, slick, silky; *antonyms* (adj) dull, rough, **2.** polished; *synonyms* (adj) elegant, courteous, cultured, finished, glossy, refined, civil, courtly, genteel, polite, accomplished, graceful, stylish, urbane, exquisite, **3.** smooth; *synonyms* (adj) easy, calm, level, oily, facile, flowing, fluent, fluid, greasy, liquid, mellow, polished, (v) quiet, facilitate, even; *antonyms* (adj) uneven, abrasive, coarse, crumpled, flaking, harsh, jerky, lined, peeling, prickly, ridged, wrinkled, corrugated, (v) wrinkle, crease, **4.** slippery; *synonyms* (adj) cunning, crafty, glib, elusive, shifty, slippy, tricky, untrustworthy, wily, dishonest, icy, artful, shady, (v) precarious, questionable.

maranako slip; *synonyms* (n) lapse, fault, mistake, cutting, error, escape, oversight, scion, trip, (v) fall, slide, drop, glide, skid, (adj) blunder; *antonym* (v) improve.

maranea tickle; *synonyms* (*v*) itch, titillate, indulge, thrill, prickle, please, tingle, flatter, humor, (*n*) titillation.

maranga 1. sector; *synonyms* (*n*) department, area, branch, district, division, section, segment, region, arm, part, quadrant, domain, field, piece, quarter, **2.** section; *synonyms* (*n*) portion, compartment, percentage, class, chapter, clause, episode, partition, subdivision, article, fraction, lot, paragraph, passage, plot.

marangaki sectioned; *synonym* (*adj*) sectional.

maranoa 1. crafty; *synonyms* (*adj*) cunning, adroit, artful, astute, sly, clever, tricky, wily, shifty, calculating, deceitful, designing, devious, foxy, fraudulent; *antonyms* (*adj*) naive, honest, open, **2.** lurk; *synonyms* (*v*) ambush, ambuscade, conceal, prowl, skulk, waylay, loiter, lurch, creep, slink, sneak, wait, bushwhack, linger, **3.** creep; *synonyms* (*v*) crawl, grovel, steal, fawn, lurk, cringe, sidle, slip, truckle, cower, edge, (*n*) crawling, creeping, sycophant, toady, **4.** prowl; *synonyms* (*n*) rove, (*v*) range, roam, **5.** skulk; *synonyms* (*v*) malinger, shirk, (*adj*) hide, **6.** slink; *synonyms* (*v*) glide, slide, (*n*) flinch, shy, **7.** sneak; *synonyms* (*v*) filch, mouse, pilfer, swipe, pussyfoot, nip, abstract, (*n*) informer, snitch, fink, prowler, reptile, (*adj*) coward, dastard, poltroon.

maranran 1. slick; *synonyms* (*adj*) sleek, clever, glib, adroit, crafty, cunning, foxy, glossy, silken, silky, smooth, artful, dexterous, dodgy, greasy, **2.** smooth; *synonyms* (*adj*) easy, calm, level, oily, facile, flat, flowing, fluent, fluid, graceful, liquid, mellow, (*v*) quiet, facilitate, even; *antonyms* (*adj*) rough, uneven, abrasive, coarse, crumpled, flaking, harsh, jerky, lined, peeling, prickly, ridged, wrinkled, corrugated, (*v*) wrinkle, **3.** sleek; *synonyms* (*adj*) shiny, slippery, satiny, satin, lustrous, polished, soft, silklike, (*v*) slick, shine; *antonym* (*adj*) dull, **4.** slippery; *synonyms* (*adj*) elusive, shifty, slippy, tricky, untrustworthy, wily, dishonest, icy, shady, insidious, shrewd, changeable, inconstant, (*v*) precarious, questionable.

marara indistinct; *synonyms* (*adj*) confused, dim, faint, inarticulate, indefinite, dull, fuzzy, hazy, indeterminate, dark, neutral, ambiguous, blurred, doubtful, (*n*) cloudy; *antonyms* (*adj*) distinct, clear.

marati 1. flourishing; *synonyms* (*adj*) prosperous, thriving, booming, healthy, luxuriant, palmy, successful, verdant, lush, auspicious, favorable, affluent, blooming, golden, growing; *antonym* (*adj*) failing, **2.** healthy; *synonyms* (*adj*) healthful, fit, good, hale, salubrious, wholesome, beneficial, hearty, sound, well, whole, sane, abundant, nutritious, active; *antonyms* (*adj*) unhealthy, harmful, unwell, unfit, dependent, fattening, infected, soporific, unwholesome, weak, **3.**

saturated; *synonyms* (*adj*) drenched, sodden, wet, concentrated, soaked, sopping, full, soggy, soppy, pure, soaking; *antonym* (*adj*) dry, **4.** prosperous; *synonyms* (*adj*) lucky, flourishing, opulent, advantageous, comfortable, easy, rich, well-off, propitious, happy, favourable, prospering, wealthy, bright, (*n*) fortunate; *antonym* (*adj*) poor.

maratingo sodden; *synonyms* (*adj*) soaked, soaking, damp, dripping, saturated, wet, muddy, soggy, sopping, drenched, moist, soppy, watery, (*v*) soft, molten; *antonym* (*adj*) dry.

maratirati 1. greased; *synonyms* (*adj*) lubricated, greasy, **2.** polished; *synonyms* (*adj*) elegant, courteous, cultured, finished, glossy, refined, civil, courtly, genteel, lustrous, polite, smooth, accomplished, graceful, bright; *antonyms* (*adj*) dull, rough, **3.** oiled; *synonyms* (*adj*) drunk, intoxicated, oily, **4.** saturated; *synonyms* (*adj*) drenched, sodden, wet, concentrated, soaked, sopping, full, soggy, soppy, pure, soaking; *antonym* (*adj*) dry.

marau tender; *synonyms* (*adj*) affectionate, painful, loving, sensitive, soft, sore, compassionate, delicate, fond, gentle, mild, (*v*) proffer, (*n*) offer, bid, overture; *antonyms* (*adj*) tough, hard, hardhearted, rubbery, rough.

maraurau tender; *synonyms* (*adj*) affectionate, painful, loving, sensitive, soft, sore, compassionate, delicate, fond, gentle, mild, (*v*) proffer, (*n*) offer, bid, overture; *antonyms* (*adj*) tough, hard, hardhearted, rubbery, rough.

mare 1. marry; *synonyms* (*v*) join, link, conjoin, splice, tie, unite, wive, couple, combine, merge, connect, unify, match, (*n*) espouse, wed; *antonym* (*v*) divorce, **2.** dispersed; *synonyms* (*adj*) diffuse, scattered, sparse, spread, diffused, detached, discrete, fractional, rare, thin, circulated, flowing, isolated, loose, single; *antonym* (*adj*) concentrated, **3.** married; *synonyms* (*adj*) marital, wedded, conjugal, matrimonial, connubial, nuptial; *antonym* (*adj*) unmarried, **4.** disperse; *synonyms* (*v*) dispel, circulate, disband, dissipate, scatter, dispense, disseminate, break, disappear, dismiss, broadcast, distribute, propagate, sprinkle, allot; *antonyms* (*v*) assemble, gather, collect, **5.** wed; *synonyms* (*v*) marry, married, **6.** scatter; *synonyms* (*v*) disperse, spray, litter, rout, dot, dust, squander, plant, intersperse, cast, lavish, disorder, (*n*) dispersion, splash, sprinkling, **7.** scattered; *synonyms* (*adj*) dispersed, dissipated, confused, disconnected, disordered, sporadic, distributed, separate, stray, strewn, disjointed, disorderly, garbled, illogical.

mareaki 1. married; *synonyms* (*adj*) marital, wedded, conjugal, matrimonial, connubial, nuptial; *antonyms* (*adj*) single, unmarried, **2.** dispersed; *synonyms* (*adj*) diffuse, scattered, sparse, spread, diffused, detached, discrete, fractional, rare, thin, circulated, flowing, isolated, loose, strewn; *antonym* (*adj*) concentrated, **3.** scattered; *synonyms* (*adj*) dispersed, dissipated, confused, disconnected, disordered, sporadic, distributed, separate, stray, disjointed, disorderly, garbled, illogical.

marebu 1. agitated; *synonyms* (*adj*) restless, excited, nervous, restive, tumultuous, upset, distressed, tense, alarmed, anxious, distraught, jumpy, overwrought, perturbed, shaken; *antonyms* (*adj*) calm, composed, lethargic, **2.** tumultuous; *synonyms* (*adj*) disorderly, noisy, riotous, turbulent, furious, loud, agitated, disturbed, troubled, stormy, chaotic, fierce, (*n*) boisterous, tempestuous, (*v*) tumultuary, **3.** troubled; *synonyms* (*adj*) concerned, solicitous, apprehensive, disconcerted, uncomfortable, uneasy, worried, bothered, unsettled, vexed, disruptive, doubtful, unhappy; *antonyms* (*adj*) untroubled, unconcerned.

marei hiccup; *synonyms* (*n*) hiccough, anomaly, fault, hitch, malfunction, problem, singultus, (*v*) belch.

marena 1. interpose; *synonyms* (*v*) interject, insert, intercede, intermeddle, interpolate, intervene, meddle, intrude, tamper, interrupt, introduce, mediate, inject, (*adj*) interfere, **2.** intercalate; *synonyms* (*v*) interpose, interdigitate, interlard, interleave, interline, intersperse, interweave, enter, insinuate, **3.** space; *synonyms* (*n*) length, gap, opening, period, place, scope, void, margin, distance, emptiness, extent, interval, latitude, location, range.

marengau 1. discontented; *synonyms* (*adj*) discontent, disaffected, disgruntled, displeased, dissatisfied, malcontent, unsatisfied, miserable, (*v*) querulous, complaining; *antonyms* (*adj*) contented, pleased, happy, satisfied, **2.** dissatisfied; *synonyms* (*v*) discontented, (*adj*) disappointed, grumpy; *antonym* (*adj*) content, **3.** discontent; *synonyms* (*n*) dissatisfaction, disapproval, discontentment, disaffection, disappointment, discontentedness, displeasure, annoyance, unrest, (*adj*) melancholy; *antonyms* (*n*) satisfaction, contentment, **4.** insufficient; *synonyms* (*adj*) deficient, defective, inadequate, incompetent, scanty, imperfect, incapable, limited, meager, poor, small, unsatisfactory, feeble, faulty, few; *antonyms* (*adj*) sufficient, plentiful, **5.** parsimonious; *synonyms* (*adj*) frugal, mean, miserly, stingy, illiberal, avaricious, penurious, sparing, thrifty, tight, economical, (*v*) close, near, niggardly, chary; *antonyms* (*adj*) generous, extravagant, spendthrift.

mari abashed; *synonyms* (*adj*) bashful, discomfited, mortified, ashamed, confused, embarrassed, sheepish; *antonym* (*adj*) brazen.

maribo 1. clever; *synonyms* (*adj*) adroit, capable, acute, able, apt, intelligent, smart, astute, cunning,

expert, ingenious, quick, sharp, skillful, (*v*) brilliant; *antonyms* (*adj*) stupid, clumsy, unintelligent, dim, dull, inept, **2.** industrious; *synonyms* (*adj*) active, diligent, assiduous, indefatigable, busy, energetic, hardworking, laborious, tireless, earnest, enterprising, careful, painstaking, sedulous, studious; *antonym* (*adj*) lazy.

marika 1. fat; *synonyms* (*adj*) stout, corpulent, dense, thick, bulky, fatty, fertile, fleshy, gainful, greasy, great, (*n*) avoirdupois, blubber, cream, (*v*) fatten; *antonyms* (*adj*) thin, slim, skinny, slender, **2.** plump; *synonyms* (*adj*) fat, chubby, obese, overweight, round, gross, buxom, pudgy, full, heavy, squab, (*v*) drop, go, dive, plop; *antonym* (*adj*) emaciated, **3.** stoutness; *synonyms* (*n*) corpulence, fatness, strength, fleshiness, obesity, robustness, plumpness, brawniness, courage, force, sturdiness, toughness, adiposis, stalwartness; *antonyms* (*n*) slenderness, thinness.

marin 1. loose; *synonyms* (*adj*) lax, liberal, dissolute, licentious, light, vague, detached, immoral, (*v*) disengage, liberate, relax, release, detach, (*n*) free, limp; *antonyms* (*adj*) tight, close, compressed, dense, taut, strict, compact, wedged, **2.** shaky; *synonyms* (*adj*) rickety, precarious, insecure, ramshackle, unsafe, unstable, broken, quaking, shaking, trembling, unsound, unsteady, weak, wobbly, (*v*) crazy; *antonyms* (*adj*) stable, steady, strong, **3.** unstable; *synonyms* (*adj*) changeable, shaky, unsettled, erratic, fickle, fluid, inconstant, unpredictable, irresolute, unreliable, capricious, changeful, fluctuating, inconsistent, unbalanced; *antonym* (*adj*) constant.

marinrin loose; *synonyms* (*adj*) lax, liberal, dissolute, licentious, light, vague, detached, immoral, (*v*) disengage, liberate, relax, release, detach, (*n*) free, limp; *antonyms* (*adj*) tight, close, compressed, dense, taut, strict, compact, wedged.

mariri 1. cold; *synonyms* (*adj*) chilly, frigid, aloof, callous, distant, icy, indifferent, apathetic, bleak, cool, dead, dull, freezing, (*n*) chilliness, chill; *antonyms* (*adj*) warm, friendly, hot, burning, prepared, affectionate, loving, soporific, (*n*) heat, warmth, **2.** chilly; *synonyms* (*adj*) unfriendly, algid, frosty, frozen, raw, crisp, fresh, glacial, hostile, nippy, stiff, wintry, (*n*) cold, cayenne, chili, **3.** chilled; *synonyms* (*adj*) refrigerated, confined, iced, inhibited, restrained, shivering, quaking, quivering, shaking, shaky, trembling, **4.** frigid; *synonyms* (*adj*) arctic, chilling, gelid, stony, feeble, reserved, tame, vapid, bald, polar, **5.** cool; *synonyms* (*adj*) collected, composed, fine, lukewarm, soothe, nonchalant, (*v*) calm, assuage, allay, pacify, quench, refrigerate, (*n*) composure, poise, aplomb; *antonyms* (*adj*) agitated, excited, enthusiastic, feverish, temperate, tepid.

---

mariro 1. loose; *synonyms* *(adj)* lax, liberal, dissolute, licentious, light, vague, detached, immoral, *(v)* disengage, liberate, relax, release, detach, *(n)* free, limp; *antonyms* *(adj)* tight, close, compressed, dense, taut, strict, compact, wedged, **2.** wavering; *synonyms* *(adj)* vacillating, irresolute, indecisive, undecided, hesitant, uncertain, changeable, variable, dithering, inconstant, unstable, unsteady, *(n)* fluctuation, hesitation, vacillation; *antonyms* *(adj)* constant, decided, *(n)* decisiveness, **3.** rattling; *synonyms* *(adj)* brisk, lively, racy, snappy, spanking, zippy, crepitant, hilarious, merry, *(n)* rattle, *(adv)* real, very.

mariroriro loose; *synonyms* *(adj)* lax, liberal, dissolute, licentious, light, vague, detached, immoral, *(v)* disengage, liberate, relax, release, detach, *(n)* free, limp; *antonyms* *(adj)* tight, close, compressed, dense, taut, strict, compact, wedged.

maritata smart; *synonyms* *(adj)* bright, crafty, dapper, quick, shrewd, sly, prompt, astute, chic, clever, intelligent, *(v)* ache, hurt, *(n)* pain, sharp; *antonyms* *(adj)* scruffy, stupid, dim, shabby, unkempt, slow.

maro 1. burglarize; *synonyms* *(v)* burgle, rob, burglarise, loot, steal, thieve, heist, invade, rifle, **2.** intrude; *synonyms* *(v)* interfere, encroach, impose, infringe, trespass, disturb, impinge, interrupt, obtrude, disrupt, transgress, enter, interlope, interpose, irrupt, **3.** penetrate; *synonyms* *(v)* bore, imbue, fathom, infiltrate, permeate, pierce, cut, filter, interpenetrate, drill, diffuse, percolate, perforate, probe, puncture.

maroa 1. desolate; *synonyms* *(v)* waste, devastate, comfortless, destroy, *(adj)* bare, barren, desert, forlorn, alone, bleak, deserted, cheerless, disconsolate, sad, solitary; *antonyms* *(adj)* cheerful, inhabited, happy, sheltered, **2.** alone; *synonyms* *(adj)* individual, lonely, lonesome, all, unequalled, friendless, lone, *(adv)* only, solely, apart, entirely, exclusively, individually, separately, *(n)* isolated; *antonym* *(adv)* together, **3.** forlorn; *synonyms* *(adj)* desperate, desolate, despairing, hopeless, miserable, unhappy, downcast, abandoned, abject, dejected, despondent, gloomy, inconsolable, lorn, wretched; *antonym* *(adj)* hopeful, **4.** isolated; *synonyms* *(adj)* detached, separate, distant, insular, remote, separated, single, sporadic, unfrequented, disconnected, secluded, withdrawn, adrift, disjunct, *(prep)* insulated, **5.** disconnected; *synonyms* *(adj)* broken, abrupt, desultory, disjointed, fragmentary, confused, incoherent, unconnected, discontinuous, discrete, loose, scattered, scrappy, disordered, fragmented; *antonym* *(adj)* attached, **6.** detached; *synonyms* *(adj)* aloof, cool, distinct, disinterested, dispassionate, impartial, indifferent, neutral, objective, unconcerned, fair, clinical, reserved, casual, cold; *antonyms* *(adj)* involved, engrossed,

warm, **7.** lonely; *synonyms* *(adj)* dreary, forsaken, sequestered, odd, private; *antonym* *(adj)* sociable, **8.** confined; *synonyms* *(v)* accurate, *(adj)* captive, close, cramped, imprisoned, limited, bounded, invalided, constrained, narrow, poky, qualified, restricted, strict, jailed; *antonym* *(adj)* free, **9.** solitary; *synonyms* *(adj)* sole, unaccompanied, one, retired, unique, reclusive, cloistered, eremitical, quiet, singular, eremitic, *(n)* hermit, recluse, troglodyte, introvert, **10.** segregated; *synonyms* *(adj)* uncombined, exclusive, nonintegrated, unintegrated.

maroaka 1. evident; *synonyms* *(adj)* apparent, obvious, distinct, clear, conspicuous, discernible, manifest, patent, plain, noticeable, open, certain, bright, marked, palpable; *antonyms* *(adj)* unclear, concealed, obscure, unnoticed, hidden, inconspicuous, **2.** ascertain; *synonyms* *(v)* see, check, determine, discover, establish, learn, control, detect, ensure, find, tell, understand, assure, confirm, decide, **3.** determine; *synonyms* *(v)* ascertain, define, resolve, appoint, adjudicate, conclude, measure, set, specify, designate, assign, decree, arrange, assess, choose, **4.** locate; *synonyms* *(v)* base, lay, localize, situate, fix, deposit, identify, install, position, post, settle, unearth, localise, send, *(n)* place, **5.** contrive; *synonyms* *(v)* plan, concoct, design, invent, cast, concert, devise, excogitate, fabricate, formulate, frame, manage, compose, conceive, conspire, **6.** discover; *synonyms* *(v)* discern, disclose, perceive, catch, divulge, expose, hear, impart, observe, trace, descry, behold, betray, declare, locate, **7.** hit; *synonyms* *(v)* strike, attain, belt, blow, bump, collide, encounter, *(n)* knock, bang, smash, touch, chance, bash, beat, collision; *antonyms* *(n)* failure, flop, **8.** invent; *synonyms* *(v)* forge, form, coin, create, imagine, construct, contrive, hatch, feign, fake, mint, originate, fashion, build, *(n)* project, **9.** clear; *synonyms* *(adj)* clean, empty, light, pure, blameless, sure, *(v)* acquit, absolute, free, net, absolve, clarify, definite, discharge, exculpate; *antonyms* *(adj)* cloudy, opaque, dark, fuzzy, hazy, incomprehensible, uncertain, vague, ambiguous, blurry, confused, confusing, dull, illegible, *(v)* convict, **10.** detect; *synonyms* *(v)* notice, spot, distinguish, sniff, espy, note, uncover, **11.** originate; *synonyms* *(v)* arise, begin, initiate, commence, issue, come, develop, grow, make, rise, start, emanate, emerge, institute, breed, **12.** reveal; *synonyms* *(v)* convey, display, exhibit, express, present, announce, communicate, indicate, show, proclaim, instruct, break, confess, explain, leak; *antonyms* *(v)* conceal, hide, cover, **13.** palpable; *synonyms* *(adj)* tangible, evident, transparent, indubitable, perceptible, unmistakable, gross, sensible, substantial, visible, barefaced, material;

antonyms *(adj)* imaginary, intangible, **14.**
unmistakable; *synonyms (adj)* decided, decisive,
unambiguous, unquestionable, flat, simple, *(v)*
unequivocal, positive, unqualified, categorical,
determinate, **15.** obvious; *synonyms (adj)* flagrant,
blatant, glaring, undeniable, explicit, indisputable,
lucid, overt, prominent, salient, observable,
intelligible, luminous, broad, downright; *antonyms*
(adj) imperceptible, undetectable, slight, subtle, **16.**
perceive; *synonyms (v)* apprehend, comprehend,
feel, grasp, appreciate, know, sense, recognize,
apperceive, penetrate, divine, get, experience,
receive, taste, **17.** plain; *synonyms (adj)* ordinary,
comprehensible, easy, homely, humble, level,
perspicuous, outspoken, direct, even, natural,
naked, artless, bald, candid; *antonyms (adj)*
elaborate, fancy, mottled, multicolored, ornate,
attractive, fussy, two-colored, **18.** spot; *synonyms*
(n) blot, speck, stain, dot, dapple, dirty, location,
mark, *(v)* blemish, soil, fleck, speckle, daub, flaw,
mottle.

maroakaki 1. discovered; *synonyms (adj)*
ascertained, revealed, disclosed, exposed, naked,
bare, observed, open, seen, **2.** contrived;
synonyms (adj) artificial, affected, unnatural, false,
forced, labored; *antonym (adj)* natural, **3.** detected;
synonyms (adj) apparent, convicted, detect,
manifest, plain, **4.** invented; *synonyms (adj)*
fictitious, fabricated, fictional, imaginary, unreal,
fake, fabulous, fancied, fictive, legendary, mythical;
antonym (adj) real, **5.** located; *synonyms (adj)* set,
situated, placed, fixed, determined, dictated,
hardened, laid, residing, rigid, **6.** hit; *synonyms (v)*
strike, attain, belt, blow, bump, collide, encounter,
(n) knock, bang, smash, touch, chance, bash, beat,
collision; *antonyms (n)* failure, flop, **7.**
ascertained; *synonyms (v)* absolute, noted,
notorious, received, recognized, categorical, clear,
decided, decisive, definite, determinate, positive,
(adj) discovered, certain, guaranteed, **8.**
determined; *synonyms (adj)* constant, resolute,
inflexible, resolved, stubborn, ambitious, adamant,
bold, firm, obstinate, tenacious, unyielding,
definitive, earnest, brave; *antonyms (adj)* weak,
irresolute, uncertain, feeble, unmotivated, **9.**
perceived; *synonyms (adj)* felt, sensed, ostensible,
professed, supposed, alleged, seeming, superficial,
10. spotted; *synonyms (adj)* mottled, dappled,
speckled, blotchy, dotted, flyblown, piebald,
multicolored, dirty, spotty, stained, tainted,
besmirched, damaged, freckled, **11.** revealed;
antonym (adj) hidden.

marooro 1. chat; *synonyms (n)* gossip, talk, chatter,
chitchat, conversation, causerie, confab, gab, rap, *(v)*
converse, chaffer, confabulate, prattle, speak, tattle;
antonym (v) listen, **2.** speak; *synonyms (v)* express,
pronounce, articulate, deliver, say, utter, discourse,

recite, lecture, address, emit, mouth, state, vocalize,
voice, **3.** talk; *synonyms (v)* chat, prate, babble,
parley, tongue, jaw, *(n)* language, colloquy,
dialogue, palaver, speech, communication,
discussion, parlance, interview.

maroroakini discuss; *synonyms (v)* argue, debate,
agitate, consult, deliberate, canvass, discourse,
dispute, mention, moot, negotiate, reason,
converse, weigh, controvert.

maru 1. superimposed; *synonyms (v)*
superincumbent, supernatant, plated, *(adj)*
incumbent, overlying, layered, lying, obligatory,
reclining, recumbent, resting, **2.** thick; *synonyms*
(adj) dense, compact, stupid, crowded, dull, heavy,
opaque, slow, stocky, close, deep, dim, familiar, fat,
gross; *antonyms (adj)* thin, intelligent, bright,
sparse, clever, diluted, fine, slight, transparent, **3.**
piled; *synonyms (adj)* heaped, aggregate, collective,
cumulous, pointed.

marua 1. astray; *synonyms (adv)* adrift, wide, amiss,
(adj) lost, wrong, disoriented, **2.** lost; *synonyms (v)*
gone, missing, abandoned, *(adj)* doomed, forlorn,
extinct, hopeless, bewildered, forgotten, helpless,
broken, confused, irrecoverable, absent, astray;
antonyms (adj) present, found, existing.

maruaki lost; *synonyms (v)* gone, missing,
abandoned, *(adj)* doomed, forlorn, extinct, hopeless,
bewildered, disoriented, forgotten, helpless,
broken, confused, irrecoverable, absent; *antonyms*
(adj) present, found, existing.

marurung 1. fine; *synonyms (adj)* delicate, agreeable,
dainty, brave, capital, elegant, excellent, nice, thin,
delightful, acute, admirable, alright, *(n)* penalty, *(v)*
punish; *antonyms (adj)* poor, thick, coarse,
substantial, unsatisfactory, wide, **2.** fit; *synonyms*
(v) agree, accommodate, meet, suit, adapt,
correspond, square, accord, dress, *(adj)* decorous,
apt, applicable, appropriate, *(n)* adjust, convulsion;
antonyms (adj) unfit, inappropriate, unwell, **3.**
healthy; *synonyms (adj)* healthful, fit, good, hale,
salubrious, wholesome, beneficial, hearty, sound,
well, whole, sane, abundant, nutritious, active;
antonyms (adj) unhealthy, harmful, dependent,
fattening, infected, soporific, unwholesome, weak,
4. robust; *synonyms (adj)* healthy, firm, strong,
athletic, brawny, muscular, powerful, vigorous,
lusty, mighty, stout, sturdy, forcible, *(n)* hardy,
hard; *antonyms (adj)* slight, fragile, frail, **5.** well;
synonyms (adv) right, easily, thoroughly,
considerably, fully, correctly, amply, *(adj)* shaft,
robust, *(n)* fountain, spring, pit, hollow,
fountainhead, *(v)* gush; *antonyms (adv)* ill, badly,
poorly, *(adj)* sick, dying, nauseous, **6.** vigorous;
synonyms (adj) energetic, lively, strenuous, smart,
animated, dynamic, forceful, potent, spirited,
tough, *(v)* brisk, fresh, live, *(n)* rugged, courageous;
antonyms (adj) feeble, lethargic, dull, unenergetic,

7. strenuous; *synonyms* (*adj*) arduous, laborious, grueling, eager, forward, difficult, intensive, heavy, trying, aggressive, demanding, exhausting, onerous, severe, tiring; *antonyms* (*adj*) easy, undemanding.

mata 1. look; *synonyms* (*v*) seem, appear, expect, figure, attend, (*n*) face, gaze, appearance, aspect, air, countenance, expression, glance, guise, view, **2.** appear; *synonyms* (*v*) occur, rise, sound, emerge, show, break, arise, arrive, begin, feel, happen, look, surface, act, (*n*) come; *antonyms* (*v*) disappear, vanish, **3.** colored; *synonyms* (*adj*) black, tinged, colorful, coloured, dyed, tinted, biased, bleached, dark, partial, **4.** multicolored; *synonyms* (*adj*) motley, multicolor, multicolour, multicoloured, piebald, pied, varicolored, varicoloured; *antonym* (*adj*) plain, **5.** eyes; *synonyms* (*n*) sight, vision, eyen, guard, propensity, **6.** eye; *synonyms* (*n*) optic, opinion, peeper, ring, center, centre, oculus, (*v*) behold, see, stare, watch, glimpse, examine, eyeball, regard, **7.** motley; *synonyms* (*adj*) assorted, miscellaneous, mixed, mottled, heterogeneous, multicolored, checkered, indiscriminate, dappled, particoloured, (*n*) medley, assortment, miscellany, mixture, mix, **8.** dyed; *synonyms* (*adj*) decorated, faded, highlighted, plausible, slanted, specious, washy, **9.** underdone; *synonyms* (*adj*) rare, raw, undercooked, bloody, crazy, dispersed, juicy, meshuga, meshugge, pink, red, screwball, softheaded, thin, uncooked; *antonyms* (*adj*) overcooked, overdone, **10.** stained; *synonyms* (*adj*) besmirched, spotted, dirty, sullied, tainted, tarnished, damaged, discolored, flyblown, painted, (*v*) polluted; *antonyms* (*adj*) pure, unspoiled, **11.** seem; *synonyms* (*v*) beseem, front, **12.** streaked; *synonyms* (*v*) barred, areolar, cancellated, grated, (*adj*) veined, streaky, striped, brindled, lined, brinded, dotted, marbled, marked, patterned, (*n*) hairstyle, **13.** tinted; *synonyms* (*adj*) bright, soft.

matabae 1. absorb; *synonyms* (*v*) consume, drink, engross, imbibe, assimilate, engage, occupy, suck, swallow, amuse, digest, engulf, fascinate, ingest, (*adj*) immerse; *antonyms* (*v*) bore, emit, **2.** stop; *synonyms* (*v*) stand, block, close, delay, interrupt, obstruct, plug, (*n*) halt, hold, stay, check, end, arrest, bar, cease; *antonyms* (*v*) continue, start, begin, encourage, permit, prolong, **3.** sightsee; *synonyms* (*v*) visit, travel, explore, **4.** occupy; *synonyms* (*v*) have, fill, get, absorb, employ, inhabit, invade, possess, conquer, busy, capture, keep, take, (*n*) entertain, interest; *antonym* (*v*) leave.

matabaeaki 1. absorbed; *synonyms* (*adj*) engrossed, intent, rapt, immersed, fixed, deep, engaged, preoccupied, fascinated, pensive, **2.** stopped; *synonyms* (*adj*) halted, congested, unmoving, blocked, finished, chinked, clogged, immobile,

motionless, static, stationary, bunged, crashed, still, **3.** occupied; *synonyms* (*adj*) busy, employed, diligent, absorbed, active, working, affianced, betrothed, concerned, industrious, involved; *antonyms* (*adj*) empty, vacant, available, uninhabited, free, idle.

matabaiawa 1. launch; *synonyms* (*n*) boat, (*v*) initiate, begin, dart, found, fire, introduce, toss, commence, establish, hurl, inaugurate, institute, start, cast; *antonym* (*v*) end, **2.** embark; *synonyms* (*v*) ship, leave, enter, sail, undertake, venture, open, emplane, adventure, approach, imbark, inship, enrol, enroll, entrain; *antonym* (*v*) disembark.

matabao unsure; *synonyms* (*adj*) uncertain, doubtful, dubious, insecure, vague, diffident, precarious, tentative, unclear, hesitant, incertain, indecisive, shy, suspicious, timid; *antonyms* (*adj*) certain, sure, decided, decisive.

matabou 1. guileless; *synonyms* (*adj*) frank, artless, candid, forthright, honest, ingenuous, innocent, open, pure, simple, sincere, straightforward, transparent, genuine, childlike, **2.** embarrassed; *synonyms* (*adj*) ashamed, abashed, awkward, uncomfortable, disconcerted, bashful, shamefaced, sheepish, shy, chagrined, discomfited, humiliated, mortified; *antonyms* (*adj*) proud, relaxed, **3.** aboveboard; *synonyms* (*adj*) straight, undesigning, unreserved, square, upright, credible, moral, naive, true, trustworthy, (*adv*) honestly, openly, sincerely, honesty, truly; *antonyms* (*adj*) dishonest, suspicious, (*adv*) dishonestly, **4.** bewildered; *synonyms* (*adj*) baffled, bemused, confused, lost, befuddled, confounded, perplexed, puzzled, dumbfounded, addled, amazed, blank, dazed, disoriented, muddled; *antonyms* (*adj*) enlightened, unimpressed, **5.** honest; *synonyms* (*adj*) fair, equitable, good, clean, decent, dependable, faithful, guileless, heartfelt, just, reliable, righteous, virtuous, ethical, hearty; *antonyms* (*adj*) corrupt, guarded, lying, misleading, disloyal, unwholesome, **6.** intimidated; *synonyms* (*adj*) bullied, frightened, scared, afraid, browbeaten, cowed, hangdog, timid, daunted, anxious, demoralized, fearful, guilty, impressed, nervy, **7.** candid; *synonyms* (*adj*) blunt, direct, outspoken, plain, plainspoken, truthful, demonstrative, aboveboard, bluff, free, impartial, natural, round, unaffected, unguarded; *antonyms* (*adj*) devious, scheming, **8.** frank; *synonyms* (*adj*) downright, clear, exempt, evident, real, unfeigned, unvarnished, veracious, communicative, (*n*) frankfurter, **9.** raw; *synonyms* (*adj*) crude, fresh, immature, bleak, coarse, cutting, green, piercing, sore, cold, biting, chilly, inclement, inexperienced, naked; *antonyms* (*adj*) refined, cooked, **10.** unreserved; *synonyms* (*adj*) unqualified, complete, unconditional, expansive, absolute, total, familiar, outgoing, full, categorical, entire, unrestrained, unrestricted, abandoned, effusive; *antonyms* (*adj*) qualified, reserved.

matabuaka 1. hostile; *synonyms* (*adj*) unfriendly, aggressive, contrary, adverse, belligerent, warlike, averse, unfavorable, antagonistic, chilly, inhospitable, inimical, irreconcilable, opposed, opposite; *antonyms* (*adj*) friendly, soothing, warm, **2**. defiant; *synonyms* (*adj*) bold, insubordinate, rebellious, audacious, resistant, brazen, disobedient, mutinous, naughty, obstinate, recalcitrant, rude, stubborn, unruly; *antonyms* (*adj*) obedient, submissive.

matabubuaka 1. hostile; *synonyms* (*adj*) unfriendly, aggressive, contrary, adverse, belligerent, warlike, averse, unfavorable, antagonistic, chilly, inhospitable, inimical, irreconcilable, opposed, opposite; *antonyms* (*adj*) friendly, soothing, warm, **2**. scowling; *synonyms* (*adj*) frowning, angry, dark, dire, frowny, grim, threatening, ugly, sullen, surly, (*n*) growling, **3**. surly; *synonyms* (*adj*) grumpy, peevish, crusty, churlish, brusque, grouchy, gruff, morose, crabby, gloomy, rough, (*n*) harsh, rude, crabbed, severe.

matabubura 1. puckering, **2**. pucker; *synonyms* (*v*) crease, crinkle, crumple, wrinkle, furrow, gather, plait, knit, purse, rumple, cockle, crisp, ruck, (*n*) fold, ruckle.

matabuburaki puckered; *synonyms* (*adj*) wrinkled, corrugated, bullate, cockled, creased, furrowed, inflated, wrinkly.

mataena fertilize; *synonyms* (*v*) impregnate, enrich, fecundate, feed, fertilise, fructify, cultivate, inseminate.

mataenaki fertilized; *synonyms* (*adj*) fertilised, impregnated, inseminated.

mataiakina 1. covet; *synonyms* (*v*) begrudge, desire, envy, long, aspire, crave, grudge, hanker, want, fancy, wish, **2**. envy; *synonyms* (*n*) enviousness, resentment, hatred, discontent, emulation, (*v*) covet, **3**. desire; *synonyms* (*n*) ambition, hope, aspiration, will, craving, dream, impulse, liking, lust, request, (*v*) seek, aim, choose, like, care; *antonyms* (*n*) aversion, reality, (*v*) dislike, hate.

mataiakinaki 1. coveted; *synonyms* (*adj*) desired, craved, exceptional, impressive, marketable, **2**. desired; *synonyms* (*adj*) coveted, desirable, chosen, favorite, wanted, needed, welcome, beloved, adored, appropriate, pet, preferred, proper, (*v*) complying, consenting; *antonym* (*adj*) undesirable.

matairiki 1. acute; *synonyms* (*adj*) sharp, incisive, intense, keen, penetrating, critical, piercing, severe, shrewd, shrill, smart, strong, acrid, acuate, (*v*) high; *antonyms* (*adj*) dull, obtuse, **2**. lucid; *synonyms* (*adj*) clear, intelligible, transparent, coherent, limpid, distinct, evident, bright, crystalline, diaphanous,

explicit, light, logical, articulate, vivid; *antonyms* (*adj*) muddled, opaque, unintelligible, **3**. perspicuous; *synonyms* (*adj*) lucid, obvious, pellucid, luminous, luculent, apparent, **4**. sharpen; *synonyms* (*v*) focus, edge, hone, intensify, point, increase, heighten, whet, improve, compound, stimulate, taper, incite, kindle, (*n*) aim; *antonym* (*v*) cloud.

matairikiaki sharpened; *synonyms* (*adj*) sharp, acute, acuate, better, sensual.

matakanikan 1. noble; *synonyms* (*adj*) dignified, imposing, magnificent, glorious, distinguished, elevated, exalted, generous, high, impressive, majestic, patrician, (*n*) grand, excellent, (*v*) great; *antonyms* (*adj*) lower-class, selfish, shameful, humble, dishonorable, lowly, **2**. elegant; *synonyms* (*adj*) graceful, courtly, delicate, splendid, beautiful, dainty, polite, refined, dressy, artistic, charming, chic, classy, cultured, debonair; *antonyms* (*adj*) clumsy, inelegant, scruffy, ugly, coarse, plain, tacky, **3**. pretty; *synonyms* (*adv*) very, fairly, jolly, (*adj*) fair, lovely, attractive, handsome, good-looking, picturesque, cute, elegant, fine, neat, pleasing, (*n*) nice.

matakao 1. abstruse; *synonyms* (*adj*) recondite, esoteric, obscure, abstract, cryptic, deep, difficult, mysterious, occult, complex, dark, intricate, profound, puzzling, secret, **2**. deep; *synonyms* (*adj*) thick, absorbed, abstruse, broad, rich, sound, strong, wide, bright, large, abysmal, bass, concentrated, (*n*) brine, (*v*) intense; *antonyms* (*adj*) shallow, superficial, high, high-pitched, light, soft, weak, **3**. abstract; *synonyms* (*adj*) theoretical, academic, (*v*) abridge, filch, extract, lift, (*n*) synopsis, abridgement, digest, epitome, summary, abridgment, brief, outline, precis; *antonym* (*adj*) concrete, **4**. difficult; *synonyms* (*adj*) arduous, awkward, demanding, burdensome, complicated, delicate, fastidious, hard, knotty, uphill, finicky, ambitious, cantankerous, contrary, crabby; *antonyms* (*adj*) easy, simple, straightforward, good-natured, rewarding, clear, **5**. complex; *synonyms* (*adj*) composite, complicate, elaborate, tricky, multifarious, compound, convoluted, involved, multiple, perplexing, sophisticated, thorny, (*n*) obsession, combination, syndrome; *antonyms* (*adj*) basic, plain, **6**. complicated; *synonyms* (*adj*) tortuous, circuitous, detailed, indirect, **7**. tangled; *synonyms* (*adj*) knotted, entangled, disheveled, tousled, kinky, labyrinthine, muddled, perplexed, raveled; *antonym* (*adj*) free, **8**. obscure; *synonyms* (*adj*) cloudy, dim, gloomy, ambiguous, concealed, darken, hidden, incomprehensible, muddy, clandestine, (*v*) hide, blur, cloud, conceal, confuse; *antonyms* (*adj*) noticeable, obvious, distinct, mainstream, (*v*) clarify.

mataki 1. blind; *synonyms* *(adj)* sightless, undiscerning, *(v)* bedazzle, daze, dazzle, obscure, *(n)* screen, curtain, shutter, awning, drape, trick, veil, camouflage, cheat; *antonym* *(adj)* sighted, **2**. sightless; *synonyms* *(adj)* eyeless, unseeing, viewless, visionless, unobservant, unsightly.

matakiaua 1. abashed; *synonyms* *(adj)* bashful, discomfited, mortified, ashamed, confused, embarrassed, sheepish; *antonym* *(adj)* brazen, **2**. disconcerted; *synonyms* *(adj)* upset, bewildered, blank, disturbed, troubled, worried, discombobulated; *antonym* *(adj)* calm, **3**. aggravated; *synonyms* *(adj)* irritated, angry, infuriated, afflictive, exasperated, grievous, provoked, bothered, discouraged, displeased, flagitious, forced, frustrated, goaded, harmful; *antonym* *(adj)* unprovoked, **4**. agitated; *synonyms* *(adj)* restless, excited, nervous, restive, tumultuous, distressed, tense, alarmed, anxious, distraught, jumpy, overwrought, perturbed, shaken, uneasy; *antonyms* *(adj)* composed, lethargic, **5**. bewildered; *synonyms* *(adj)* baffled, bemused, lost, befuddled, confounded, perplexed, puzzled, dumbfounded, addled, amazed, dazed, disconcerted, disoriented, muddled, mystified; *antonyms* *(adj)* enlightened, unimpressed, **6**. disturbed; *synonyms* *(adj)* agitated, concerned, disquieted, disordered, deranged, distracted, turbulent, unsettled, unbalanced, mad, afraid, uncomfortable, unquiet, uptight, brainsick; *antonyms* *(adj)* rational, relaxed, **7**. concerned; *synonyms* *(adj)* careful, interested, involved, thoughtful, apprehensive, considerate, solicitous, affected, attentive, caring, fearful, paternal, sympathetic; *antonyms* *(adj)* unconcerned, uncaring, unfeeling, **8**. troubled; *synonyms* *(adj)* vexed, disruptive, doubtful, riotous, unhappy; *antonym* *(adj)* untroubled, **9**. perplexed; *synonyms* *(v)* complicated, intricate, *(adj)* questioning, quizzical, entangled, knotted, **10**. perturbed; *synonym* *(adj)* flustered, **11**. upset; *synonyms* *(v)* overturn, agitate, disquiet, overthrow, bother, confuse, disturb, perturb, reverse, subvert, *(adj)* hurt, *(n)* disorder, trouble, distress, disturbance; *antonyms* *(v)* please, encourage, soothe, *(adj)* pleased, confident, **12**. uneasy; *synonyms* *(adj)* fidgety, awkward, fretful, jittery, embarrassing, impatient, clumsy, difficult, stiff, edgy.

matam eat; *synonyms* *(v)* devour, consume, bite, dine, munch, corrode, deplete, drink, feed, finish, gnaw, gobble, gorge, graze, *(adj)* digest.

matamane prime; *synonyms* *(adj)* main, chief, first, head, early, essential, fundamental, paramount, primary, excellent, exquisite, *(n)* best, cardinal, flower, *(v)* ground; *antonym* *(adj)* minor.

matamata 1. colored; *synonyms* *(adj)* black, tinged, colorful, coloured, dyed, tinted, biased, bleached, dark, partial, **2**. select; *synonyms* *(v)* pick, extract, adopt, choose, elect, excellent, prefer, excerpt, assign, opt, appoint, *(adj)* choice, exclusive, chosen, best; *antonym* *(v)* reject.

matamataki selected; *synonyms* *(adj)* select, chosen, preferred, choice, elected, *(n)* best.

matamatana 1. color; *synonyms* *(n)* blush, colour, stain, tinge, tint, complexion, guise, *(v)* dye, flush, paint, redden, disguise, distort, embellish, *(adj)* tone; *antonyms* *(n)* colorlessness, *(v)* discolor, **2**. stripe; *synonyms* *(n)* strip, band, line, bar, stria, striation, chevron, mark, stroke, ribbon, scratch, score, slip, dash, *(v)* streak, **3**. stain; *synonyms* *(n)* spot, blemish, blot, smear, dirt, brand, damage, *(v)* color, tarnish, disgrace, soil, defile, blur, contaminate, daub.

matamatanaki 1. colored; *synonyms* *(adj)* black, tinged, colorful, coloured, dyed, tinted, biased, bleached, dark, partial, **2**. striped; *synonyms* *(adj)* streaked, stripy, paled, virgated, zoned, hooped, zonate, **3**. stained; *synonyms* *(adj)* besmirched, spotted, dirty, sullied, tainted, tarnished, damaged, discolored, flyblown, painted, *(v)* polluted; *antonyms* *(adj)* pure, unspoiled.

matamau stare; *synonyms* *(v)* gaze, look, gape, glare, peer, squint, goggle, see, view, watch, leer, *(n)* regard.

matamea lasso; *synonyms* *(n)* lariat, noose, cestus, garter, girdle, girth, halter, *(v)* rope, catch.

matamtam fast; *synonyms* *(adj)* dissolute, firm, agile, debauched, fixed, hurried, instant, quick, rapid, staunch, brisk, *(adv)* soon, hard, close, *(n)* diet; *antonyms* *(adj)* sluggish, loose, *(adv)* slow, slowly, leisurely, *(v)* gorge, *(n)* binge.

matamu eat; *synonyms* *(v)* devour, consume, bite, dine, munch, corrode, deplete, drink, feed, finish, gnaw, gobble, gorge, graze, *(adj)* digest.

matan 1. color; *synonyms* *(n)* blush, colour, stain, tinge, tint, complexion, guise, *(v)* dye, flush, paint, redden, disguise, distort, embellish, *(adj)* tone; *antonyms* *(n)* colorlessness, *(v)* discolor, **2**. coiled; *synonyms* *(adj)* curled, spiral, curved, bent, bowed, curly, kinky, round, tortile, twisting, wavy, arched, corkscrew, rounded, *(v)* helical; *antonym* *(adj)* straight, **3**. rolled; *synonyms* *(adj)* rolling, furled, involute, beaten, billowing, level, resonant, resonating, resounding, reverberating, reverberative, trilled, tumbling.

matana 1. escort; *synonyms* *(n)* chaperon, guard, guide, attendant, conduct, suite, accompaniment, bodyguard, companion, *(v)* attend, accompany, convoy, see, date, direct, **2**. guide; *synonyms* *(n)* escort, directory, control, usher, chief, command, director, *(v)* govern, drive, channel, bring, advise,

cicerone, convey, head; *antonym* (v) follow, **3.**
loose; *synonyms* (adj) lax, liberal, dissolute,
licentious, light, vague, detached, immoral, (v)
disengage, liberate, relax, release, detach, (n) free,
limp; *antonyms* (adj) tight, close, compressed,
dense, taut, strict, compact, wedged, **4.** lead;
synonyms (v) contribute, chair, conduce, go, give,
carry, dispose, run, show, take, (n) clue, advantage,
hint, leash, (adj) front, **5.** advise; *synonyms* (v)
admonish, acquaint, inform, propose, recommend,
suggest, warn, apprise, caution, exhort, forewarn,
instruct, notify, offer, tell; *antonym* (v) oppose, **6.**
patrol; *synonyms* (n) beat, protection, patrolman,
scout, sentinel, spy, detachment, force, (v) watch,
prowl, **7.** scout; *synonyms* (n) lookout, pathfinder,
picket, patrol, detective, vanguard, pioneer,
spotter, bivouac, discoverer, (v) explore,
reconnoiter, reconnoitre, investigate, repudiate, **8.**
put; *synonyms* (v) place, fix, lay, position, set,
impose, couch, locate, pose, charge, pitch, arrange,
assign, commit, (n) deposit, **9.** pilot; *synonyms* (n)
leader, aviator, captain, airman, cowcatcher, flier,
(v) manage, lead, fly, navigate, steer, conductor,
operate, (adj) experimental, trial.

matanaine womanly; *synonyms* (adj) feminine,
effeminate, ladylike, womanish, female,
womanlike, (v) feminate, soft.

matanaki 1. advised; *synonyms* (v) designed,
determinate, express, (adj) intentional, considered,
studied, deliberate, premeditated, intended, **2.** led,
3. colored; *synonyms* (adj) black, tinged, colorful,
coloured, dyed, tinted, biased, bleached, dark,
partial, **4.** guided; *synonym* (adj) conducted, **5.**
escorted.

matanatana 1. loose; *synonyms* (adj) lax, liberal,
dissolute, licentious, light, vague, detached,
immoral, (v) disengage, liberate, relax, release,
detach, (n) free, limp; *antonyms* (adj) tight, close,
compressed, dense, taut, strict, compact, wedged,
2. slack; *synonyms* (adj) loose, idle, indolent,
negligent, baggy, flaccid, flabby, neglectful,
dilatory, inattentive, lazy, (v) remiss, dull, slow,
abate; *antonym* (adj) thorough.

mataneai 1. dazzled; *synonyms* (adj) dizzy,
bewildered, fascinated, **2.** blinded; *synonyms* (adj)
blindfolded, blindfold, **3.** dazzle; *synonyms* (n)
sparkle, brightness, (v) bedazzle, shine, blind, flash,
glare, awe, captivate, gleam, (adj) daze, confuse,
bewilder, hoodwink, perplex.

mataneaiaki dazzled; *synonyms* (adj) dizzy,
bewildered, fascinated.

matangare 1. smile; *synonyms* (n) grin, grinning,
smiling, expression, luck, (v) beam, laugh, chuckle,
grimace, sneer, countenance, favor, propitiousness;
antonym (v) frown, **2.** smiling; *synonyms* (adj)
bright, cheerful, jolly, joyful, twinkly, fair, sunny,

beaming, cheery, good-humored, happy,
optimistic, positive, amused, (n) smile; *antonym*
(adj) annoyed.

matanikananoanga 1. depressing; *synonyms* (adj)
cheerless, dark, dismal, gloomy, sad, oppressive,
bleak, blue, desolate, dreary, grim, black, chill,
depressed, depressive; *antonyms* (adj) cheerful,
heartening, inspiring, bright, cheery, **2.** dismal;
synonyms (adj) dejected, depressing, disconsolate,
melancholy, dim, doleful, dull, funereal, gaunt,
sorry, cloudy, dingy, dour, down, drab; *antonym*
(adj) happy, **3.** pitiable; *synonyms* (adj) forlorn,
piteous, abject, miserable, pathetic, pitiful,
deplorable, lamentable, poor, wretched, paltry,
unfortunate, woeful, (v) mournful, distressing, **4.**
poor; *synonyms* (adj) bad, low, destitute, evil,
inadequate, insufficient, needy, penniless, meagre,
deficient, feeble, impecunious, indigent, (v) meager,
(n) mean; *antonyms* (adj) rich, wealthy, excellent,
first-rate, privileged, well-off, admirable, good, **5.**
pathetic; *synonyms* (adj) touching, affecting, tragic,
grievous, moving, poignant, measly, pitiable,
plaintive, contemptible, execrable, hapless,
laughable, misfortunate, ridiculous; *antonym* (adj)
brave, **6.** pitiful; *synonyms* (adj) compassionate,
despicable, merciful, heartbreaking, heartrending,
regrettable, small, base, tender, (n) beggarly,
scrubby, dirty, ignominious, **7.** piteous; *synonym*
(adj) sorrowful.

matanikanebu 1. gentle; *synonyms* (adj) clement,
calm, easy, friendly, soft, affable, balmy, kind, mild,
tame, feeble, amiable, benign, bland, (n) benevolent;
antonyms (adj) caustic, cruel, fierce, harsh, loud,
violent, rough, abrupt, hardhearted, heavy,
sarcastic, sheer, steep, **2.** frail; *synonyms* (adj)
brittle, fragile, delicate, flimsy, breakable, light,
rickety, slender, slim, dainty, decrepit, fine, puny,
(v) weak, faint; *antonyms* (adj) strong, substantial,
robust, **3.** feeble; *synonyms* (adj) ailing, dim, dull,
frail, helpless, infirm, lax, poor, powerless, thin,
enfeebled, forceless, impotent, inadequate, (v)
debilitated; *antonyms* (adj) vigorous, hearty, tough,
4. anemic; *synonyms* (adj) anaemic, colorless,
insipid, pallid, bloodless, antiseptic, ghastly,
inoffensive, neutral, pale, pasty, sallow, sickly,
tired, unexciting, **5.** modest; *synonyms* (adj)
humble, bashful, diffident, lowly, moderate, gentle,
chaste, decent, low, meek, small, unassuming,
unobtrusive, distant, coy; *antonyms* (adj) arrogant,
conceited, elaborate, pompous, pretentious, proud,
self-important, showy, spectacular, boastful,
conspicuous, grand, immodest, ostentatious.

matanikimoa 1. devious; *synonyms* (adj) crooked,
circuitous, shifty, crafty, fraudulent, indirect,
insincere, oblique, roundabout, sly, untrustworthy,
errant, remote, clever, cunning; *antonyms* (adj)
honest, open, straight, aboveboard,

straightforward, trustworthy, up-front, **2.**
underhanded; *synonyms* *(adj)* furtive, underhand,
stealthy, sneaky, secret, covert, clandestine,
surreptitious, corrupt, deceitful, devious,
dishonest, false, tricky, underarm, **3.** shifty;
synonyms *(adj)* evasive, slippery, unreliable,
elusive, dubious, fishy, suspicious, treacherous,
wily, shady, unfaithful.

matanikukurei jolly; *synonyms* *(adj)* jovial, cheerful,
gay, happy, festive, genial, bright, cheery, jocund,
merry, convivial, jocular, gleeful, funny, *(v)* chaff;
antonym *(adj)* sad.

mataningare jolly; *synonyms* *(adj)* jovial, cheerful,
gay, happy, festive, genial, bright, cheery, jocund,
merry, convivial, jocular, gleeful, funny, *(v)* chaff;
antonym *(adj)* sad.

mataniwi 1. boss; *synonyms* *(n)* chief, governor,
head, overseer, superior, ruler, administrator,
captain, director, executive, foreman, leader, *(v)*
administer, govern, direct, **2.** overseer; *synonyms*
(n) superintendent, manager, inspector, supervisor,
warden, controller, examiner, custodian, boss,
surveyor.

mataniwii chief; *synonyms* *(adj)* head, principal,
cardinal, capital, arch, central, essential, first, main,
(n) administrator, boss, captain, executive, leader,
paramount; *antonyms* *(adj)* minor, associate,
secondary.

matanoku 1. frown; *synonyms* *(n)* scowl, *(v)* lower,
pout, glower, grimace, glare; *antonym* *(v)* smile, **2.**
discontented; *synonyms* *(adj)* discontent,
disaffected, disgruntled, displeased, dissatisfied,
malcontent, unsatisfied, miserable, *(v)* querulous,
complaining; *antonyms* *(adj)* contented, pleased,
happy, satisfied, **3.** sullen; *synonyms* *(adj)* morose,
gloomy, gruff, cross, dark, glum, grim, moody,
sour, dismal, dour, lowering, peevish, surly, *(n)*
sulky; *antonym* *(adj)* cheerful, **4.** scowl; *synonyms*
(n) growl, *(v)* frown, sulk, roar, sneer, *(adj)* bouderie,
doldrums, dudgeon, dumps, mumps; *antonym* *(v)*
grin, **5.** sulky; *synonyms* *(adj)* sullen, grouchy,
petulant, angry, crabby, huffish, grumpy.

matantan 1. loose; *synonyms* *(adj)* lax, liberal,
dissolute, licentious, light, vague, detached,
immoral, *(v)* disengage, liberate, relax, release,
detach, *(n)* free, limp; *antonyms* *(adj)* tight, close,
compressed, dense, taut, strict, compact, wedged,
2. slack; *synonyms* *(adj)* loose, idle, indolent,
negligent, baggy, flaccid, flabby, neglectful,
dilatory, inattentive, lazy, *(v)* remiss, dull, slow,
abate; *antonym* *(adj)* thorough.

matantokomaung stagnate; *synonyms* *(v)* idle, laze,
drag, restagnate, slog, *(n)* be, halt, abide, pause,
stand, accord, agree, consist, endure, last.

matanun frown; *synonyms* *(n)* scowl, *(v)* lower, pout,
glower, grimace, glare; *antonym* *(v)* smile.

matao 1. outside; *synonyms* *(adj)* external, out,
outdoor, foreign, extraneous, outer, away,
outward, remote, slight, surface, distant, *(adv)*
outdoors, alfresco, *(n)* exterior; *antonyms* *(prep)*
inside, in, *(adj)* indoor, internal, *(adv)* indoors, **2.**
outer; *synonyms* *(adj)* outside, extrinsic, outlying,
peripheral, utter; *antonym* *(adj)* middle.

mataou fishhook; *synonyms* *(n)* angle, corner, nook.

matara 1. mortified; *synonyms* *(adj)* ashamed,
humiliated, abashed, embarrassed, chagrined,
gangrenous, sheepish, **2.** embarrassed; *synonyms*
(adj) awkward, uncomfortable, disconcerted,
bashful, shamefaced, shy, discomfited, mortified;
antonyms *(adj)* proud, relaxed.

mataraoi judicious; *synonyms* *(adj)* careful, discreet,
wise, discerning, prudent, rational, sensible,
cautious, reasonable, sagacious, sound, advisable,
circumspect, intelligent, *(n)* clever; *antonyms* *(adj)*
foolish, ill-advised.

matarere glance; *synonyms* *(n)* look, gaze, glimpse,
glitter, *(v)* peek, flash, bounce, glint, peep, ricochet,
allude, brush, burnish, gleam, hint; *antonym* *(v)*
study.

mataroa door; *synonyms* *(n)* gate, threshold, access,
doorway, entrance, entry, mouth, opening,
entryway, exit, hatch, inlet, porch, portal, wicket.

mataronron 1. abashed; *synonyms* *(adj)* bashful,
discomfited, mortified, ashamed, confused,
embarrassed, sheepish; *antonym* *(adj)* brazen, **2.**
reprimanded; *synonyms* *(adj)* rebuked, reproved,
admonished, chastened.

matararoro 1. attentive; *synonyms* *(adj)* thoughtful,
assiduous, diligent, heedful, observant, watchful,
advertent, alert, aware, careful, considerate,
mindful, vigilant, devoted; *antonyms* *(adj)*
inattentive, negligent, unfocused, forgetful,
neglectful, heedless, **2.** interested; *synonyms* *(adj)*
concerned, curious, involved, inquiring,
inquisitive, keen, attentive; *antonyms* *(adj)*
apathetic, uninterested, **3.** astonished; *synonyms*
(adj) amazed, astonish, dumbfounded,
flabbergasted, stunned, aghast, astounded,
bewildered, thunderstruck, astonied.

mataruberube 1. blink; *synonyms* *(v)* wink, flash,
twinkle, flicker, shirk, nictate, nictitate, shine,
flinch, *(n)* blinking, glimmer, instant, winking,
peek, **2.** wink; *synonyms* *(n)* twinkling, jiffy,
moment, trice, hint, second, signal, *(v)* blink,
sparkle, leer, flutter, scintillate, gleam, glisten,
winkle.

matata 1. evidently; *synonyms* *(adv)* apparently,
clearly, patently, obviously, plainly, palpably,
manifestly, markedly, noticeably, openly, plain,
visibly, **2.** evident; *synonyms* *(adj)* apparent,
obvious, distinct, clear, conspicuous, discernible,
manifest, patent, noticeable, open, certain, bright,

marked, palpable, perceptible; *antonyms* (*adj*) unclear, concealed, obscure, unnoticed, hidden, inconspicuous, **3.** barren; *synonyms* (*adj*) infertile, sterile, deserted, abortive, arid, dry, fruitless, meagre, stark, void, bleak, dead, desert, desolate, (*v*) bare; *antonyms* (*adj*) fertile, lush, productive, **4.** bare; *synonyms* (*adj*) naked, austere, bald, devoid, exposed, mere, nude, vacant, vacuous, barren, (*v*) empty, show, disclose, denude, expose; *antonyms* (*adj*) covered, cultivated, ornate, (*v*) cover, **5.** clear; *synonyms* (*adj*) clean, light, pure, blameless, sure, (*v*) acquit, absolute, free, net, absolve, clarify, definite, discharge, exculpate, bear; *antonyms* (*adj*) cloudy, opaque, dark, fuzzy, hazy, incomprehensible, uncertain, vague, ambiguous, blurry, confused, confusing, dull, illegible, (*v*) convict.

matatae 1. discolored; *synonyms* (*adj*) discoloured, blemished, crusty, dappled, dark, dingy, dirty, dull, faded, flawed, flecked, freckled, gray, imperfect, livid, **2.** faded; *synonyms* (*v*) dilapidated, stale, (*adj*) dim, pale, bleached, exhausted, faint, washy, withered, attenuate, attenuated, colorless.

matatoka 1. conscious; *synonyms* (*adj*) aware, alive, calculated, cognizant, deliberate, mindful, premeditated, intended, discerning, self-conscious, intentional, knowing, knowledgeable, known, purposeful; *antonyms* (*adj*) unconscious, unaware, ignorant, **2.** convinced; *synonyms* (*v*) positive, cocksure, assured, persuaded, satisfied, (*adj*) certain, confident, sure, clear; *antonym* (*adj*) unsure, **3.** clear; *synonyms* (*adj*) clean, open, apparent, distinct, empty, (*v*) bright, acquit, absolute, free, net, absolve, clarify, definite, discharge, exculpate; *antonyms* (*adj*) cloudy, opaque, unclear, dark, fuzzy, hazy, incomprehensible, obscure, uncertain, vague, ambiguous, blurry, confused, confusing, (*v*) convict, **4.** learned; *synonyms* (*adj*) erudite, educated, enlightened, wise, academic, scholarly, bookish, cultured, intellectual, lettered, literary, studious, informed, conversant, literate; *antonym* (*adj*) innate, **5.** confident; *synonyms* (*adj*) bold, brave, hopeful, sanguine, secure, fearless, forward, assertive, convinced, decisive, dogmatic, composed, optimistic, (*v*) emphatic; *antonyms* (*adj*) insecure, anxious, frightened, pessimistic, timid, hesitant, **6.** keen; *synonyms* (*adj*) acute, eager, sharp, intense, intelligent, biting, brisk, enthusiastic, exquisite, piercing, discriminating, clever, astute, (*v*) fresh, avid; *antonyms* (*adj*) dull, apathetic, indifferent, unenthusiastic, blunt, **7.** convincing; *synonyms* (*adj*) conclusive, cogent, compelling, forceful, persuasive, believable, impressive, likely, probable, credible, plausible, potent, strong, valid, authentic; *antonym* (*adj*) unconvincing, **8.** known; *synonyms* (*adj*) well-known, familiar, conscious, accepted,

acknowledged, plain, published, understood, evident, recognized, common, apprised, approved, broadcast, documented; *antonyms* (*adj*) nameless, unknown, secret, unidentified, **9.** identified; *synonyms* (*adj*) coherent, synonymous, branded, celebrated, famous, notorious, renowned, **10.** aware; *synonyms* (*adj*) awake, attentive, heedful, vigilant, sentient, alert, observant, sensible, wary, watchful, appreciative, perceptive, responsive, **11.** certain; *synonyms* (*adj*) actual, dependable, indisputable, reliable, categorical, fixed, inevitable, infallible, particular, perfect, safe, special, specific, unavoidable, (*v*) bound; *antonyms* (*adj*) doubtful, questionable, **12.** evident; *synonyms* (*adj*) obvious, conspicuous, discernible, manifest, patent, noticeable, marked, palpable, perceptible, tangible, unequivocal, unmistakable, visible, observable, broad; *antonyms* (*adj*) concealed, unnoticed, hidden, inconspicuous, **13.** absolute; *synonyms* (*adj*) downright, peremptory, total, unconditional, full, real, unqualified, utter, arbitrary, authoritative, complete, dictatorial, extreme, flat, great; *antonyms* (*adj*) partial, qualified, **14.** assured; *synonyms* (*adj*) guaranteed, surefire, **15.** cognizant; *synonym* (*adj*) cognisant, **16.** explicit; *synonyms* (*adj*) direct, exact, lucid, perspicuous, transparent, express, precise, clear-cut, trenchant, comprehensible, decided, detailed, unambiguous, denotative; *antonyms* (*adj*) tacit, unspoken, implicit, bland, **17.** unconditional; *synonyms* (*adj*) categoric, unlimited, consummate, outright, sheer, unconditioned, unmitigated, unreserved, unrestricted, entire, regular; *antonym* (*adj*) conditional, **18.** tangible; *synonyms* (*adj*) material, substantial, concrete, physical, corporeal, genuine, adequate, bodily, commensurate, competent, enough, (*n*) applicable, available, handy, ready; *antonym* (*adj*) intangible, **19.** sure; *synonyms* (*adj*) firm, fast, indubitable, stable, true, unerring, unfailing, unwavering, hard, resolute, steadfast, incontestable, (*adv*) certainly, (*v*) steady, (*int*) yes, **20.** unequivocal; *synonyms* (*adj*) explicit, definitive, determinate, straightforward, outspoken, stark, univocal, unquestionable; *antonym* (*adj*) equivocal.

matau 1. apprehended; *synonyms* (*adj*) held, appreciated, comprehended, detained, gratifying, pleasing, satisfying, **2.** foiled; *synonyms* (*adj*) frustrated, thwarted, disappointed, defeated, discomfited, baffled, balked, discouraged, embarrassed, blocked, hindered, obstructed, stymied; *antonym* (*adj*) successful, **3.** arrested; *synonyms* (*adj*) backward, intermittent, **4.** seized; *synonyms* (*adj*) confiscate, confiscated, appropriated, condemned, apprehended, censured, convicted, forfeit, forfeited, obsessed.

matauaki arrested; *synonyms* (*adj*) backward, intermittent.

matauakina 1. inspect; *synonyms* (*v*) examine, overhaul, overlook, survey, explore, inquire, look, review, scrutinize, view, watch, monitor, analyze, audit, check, **2.** observe; *synonyms* (*v*) celebrate, comment, notice, commemorate, mind, guard, behold, discover, follow, heed, keep, mark, mention, note, see; *antonyms* (*v*) ignore, feel, **3.** scrutinize; *synonyms* (*v*) inspect, consider, investigate, scan, search, observe, probe, study, spy, research, scrutinise, sift, debate, dissect, (*n*) canvass, **4.** regard; *synonyms* (*v*) attention, concern, estimate, attend, account, believe, count, hold, reckon, appreciate, (*n*) respect, esteem, deference, value, admiration; *antonym* (*n*) disrespect, **5.** witness; *synonyms* (*n*) spectator, testimony, bystander, eyewitness, onlooker, evidence, observer, testifier, beholder, proof, testify, attestant, confirmation, viewer, (*v*) attest; *antonym* (*n*) participant, **6.** view; *synonyms* (*n*) sight, judgment, opinion, scene, idea, outlook, prospect, thought, aspect, notion, position, show, spectacle, (*v*) regard, eye.

matauakinaki observed; *synonyms* (*adj*) seen, ascertained, discovered, empirical, disclosed, experiential, experimental, visual, practical, pragmatic, revealed.

mataukiro sly; *synonyms* (*adj*) crafty, cunning, wily, furtive, artful, clever, secret, shrewd, designing, arch, astute, clandestine, deceitful, devious, foxy; *antonyms* (*adj*) open, naive.

matauna 1. check; *synonyms* (*v*) bridle, stop, block, limit, agree, halt, restrain, bar, dampen, delay, (*n*) control, arrest, curb, bill, cheque, **2.** examine; *synonyms* (*v*) assay, audit, consider, overhaul, try, check, search, survey, ascertain, ask, contemplate, compare, analyze, canvass, essay, **3.** observe; *synonyms* (*v*) celebrate, comment, notice, commemorate, mind, guard, behold, discover, follow, heed, keep, look, mark, mention, note; *antonyms* (*v*) ignore, feel, **4.** watch; *synonyms* (*v*) observe, clock, see, regard, wake, care, protect, defend, (*n*) view, sentinel, sentry, surveillance, lookout, patrol, (*adj*) vigilance.

mataunaki 1. checked; *synonyms* (*adj*) checkered, chequered, plaid, backward, curbed, intermittent, limited, numbered, pent-up, safe, silent, tartan, temperate, **2.** observed; *synonyms* (*adj*) seen, ascertained, discovered, empirical, disclosed, experiential, experimental, visual, practical, pragmatic, revealed.

matauningananti 1. insulted; *synonyms* (*adj*) affronted, huffy, disrespected, hurt, slighted, snubbed, upset, **2.** offended; *synonyms* (*adj*) angry, aggrieved, annoyed, pained, wronged, shocked, appalled, ashamed, averted, bitter, cool, disappointed, disgusted, dismayed, dissatisfied; *antonym* (*adj*) composed.

matauraura reddened; *synonyms* (*adj*) ablaze, aflame, crimson, flushed, inflamed, red, aroused, blazing, blemished, blooming, blushful, burning, carmine, cerise, cherry.

matawe distant; *synonyms* (*adj*) cold, aloof, remote, chill, cool, detached, far, reserved, long, faraway, icy, indifferent, removed, (*adv*) apart, (*n*) chilly; *antonyms* (*adj*) close, adjacent, friendly, near, nearby, neighboring, warm, pending, alert, intimate, involved.

mate 1. dead; *synonyms* (*adj*) dull, lifeless, cold, defunct, inanimate, absolute, breathless, deceased, extinct, fallen, flat, gone, idle, (*adv*) right, absolutely; *antonyms* (*adj*) alive, animate, (*n*) living, **2.** die; *synonyms* (*v*) decease, dead, death, depart, expire, fall, go, pass, conk, croak, break, cease, fail, (*n*) dice, matrix, **3.** expired; *synonyms* (*adj*) lapsed, invalid, elapsed, out, antebellum, antediluvian, exploded, forgotten, irrecoverable, **4.** extenuating; *synonyms* (*adj*) justifying, palliatory, condoning, diminishing, excusing, explanatory, lessening, mitigating, moderating, palliating, qualifying, reducing, sanitizing, softening, varnishing, **5.** lost; *synonyms* (*v*) missing, abandoned, undone, (*adj*) doomed, forlorn, hopeless, bewildered, disoriented, helpless, broken, confused, absent, astray, missed, preoccupied; *antonyms* (*adj*) present, found, existing, **6.** late; *synonyms* (*adj*) former, behindhand, belated, delayed, modern, slow, tardy, bygone, posthumous, erstwhile, advanced, (*adv*) dilatory, fresh, backward, belatedly; *antonyms* (*adj*) ahead, (*adv*) early, punctually, promptly, punctual, **7.** defunct; *synonyms* (*adj*) departed, late, obsolete, dated, useless, deadened, demised, ended, finished, nonexistent, outmoded, ruined, (*n*) dust, relics, reliquiae, **8.** disappear; *synonyms* (*v*) die, vanish, melt, fade, dematerialize, sink, end, abscond, scram, disperse, dissolve, escape, evaporate, lift, perish; *antonyms* (*v*) appear, stay, **9.** departed; *synonyms* (*v*) lost, (*adj*) bypast, past, left, foregone, asleep, (*n*) decedent, **10.** block; *synonyms* (*n*) bar, barricade, pad, clog, cluster, (*v*) arrest, stop, hinder, encumber, halt, lock, obstruct, parry, plug, (*adj*) lump; *antonyms* (*v*) free, unblock, open, **11.** extinct; *synonyms* (*adj*) extinguished, quenched, inactive, **12.** expire; *synonyms* (*v*) conclude, elapse, exhale, exit, succumb, breathe, emit, finish, lapse, terminate; *antonyms* (*v*) inhale, live, **13.** perish; *synonyms* (*v*) decay, ruin, crumble, rot, starve, disappear, wither, decompose, putrefy, waste, extend, lead, leave; *antonym* (*v*) survive, **14.** succumb; *synonyms* (*v*) submit, defer, yield, bow, accede, faint, surrender, capitulate, give, cede, accept, (*adj*) blow, drop, gasp, pant; *antonyms* (*v*) endure, resist, **15.** tired; *synonyms* (*adj*) exhausted, fatigued, hackneyed, weary, banal, commonplace, stale, threadbare, trite, beat, haggard, jaded, stock, worn, drowsy; *antonyms* (*adj*) invigorated, alert, refreshed, energetic, original, strong, **16**. unconscious; *synonyms* (*adj*) involuntary, unaware, ignorant, subconscious, unwitting, oblivious, automatic, insensible, instinctive, senseless, unintentional, spontaneous, innocent, unknowing, unacquainted; *antonyms* (*adj*) conscious, awake, deliberate.

mateaki expired; *synonyms* (*adj*) defunct, lapsed, deceased, invalid, dead, elapsed, out, antebellum, antediluvian, exploded, forgotten, irrecoverable.

matebuaka fail; *synonyms* (*v*) abort, collapse, fade, cease, abandon, break, bust, default, deteriorate, die, disappoint, flag, want, (*v*) decline, drop; *antonyms* (*v*) succeed, triumph.

matebuakaki failed; *synonyms* (*adj*) unsuccessful, abortive, failing, bankrupt, declining, deteriorating, ineffective, insolvent, bungled, disastrous, erstwhile, former, inferior, poor, regressing; *antonym* (*adj*) first-rate.

maten thick; *synonyms* (*adj*) dense, compact, stupid, crowded, dull, heavy, opaque, slow, stocky, close, deep, dim, familiar, fat, gross; *antonyms* (*adj*) thin, intelligent, bright, sparse, clever, diluted, fine, slight, transparent.

matenibaki ravenous; *synonyms* (*adj*) greedy, hungry, avid, famished, gluttonous, voracious, edacious, insatiable, rapacious, covetous, predatory, avaricious, esurient, grasping, ravening; *antonym* (*adj*) full.

matenruarua 1. impassable; *synonyms* (*adj*) impervious, insurmountable, impenetrable, insuperable, invincible, inaccessible, unpassable; *antonym* (*adj*) passable, **2**. insensible; *synonyms* (*adj*) callous, imperceptible, numb, unconscious, unfeeling, apathetic, dull, impassive, indiscernible, unaware, comatose, inert, ignorant, oblivious, insensate; *antonym* (*adj*) sensible, **3**. numb; *synonyms* (*adj*) asleep, benumbed, dead, insensible, torpid, deadened, inactive, paralytic, frozen, (*v*) benumb, deaden, paralyze, harden, (*n*) blunt; *antonym* (*adj*) sensitive.

matenten 1. dense; *synonyms* (*adj*) compact, thick, close, crowded, deep, crass, dim, dull, heavy, impenetrable, solid, stupid, concentrated, dumb, firm; *antonyms* (*adj*) bright, insightful, loose, clever, intelligent, readable, simple, sparse, **2**. thick; *synonyms* (*adj*) dense, opaque, slow, stocky, familiar, fat, gross, intimate, muddy, obtuse, broad, populous, frequent, chummy, (*n*) midst; *antonyms* (*adj*) thin, diluted, fine, slight, transparent.

matera 1. costly; *synonyms* (*adj*) expensive, dear, precious, valuable, extravagant, high, luxurious, pricey, rich, sumptuous, invaluable, beloved, plush, priceless, pricy; *antonyms* (*adj*) cheap, worthless, **2**. expensive; *synonyms* (*adj*) costly, lavish, overpriced, exclusive, fine, exorbitant,

splendid; *antonyms* (*adj*) inexpensive, reasonable, **3**. overpriced; *synonyms* (*adj*) steep, (*adv*) excessive, inflated, ridiculous.

materaoi 1. fruitful; *synonyms* (*adj*) fertile, copious, abundant, fecund, plentiful, profitable, rich, good, fat, lucrative, productive, prolific, useful, fructiferous, bountiful; *antonyms* (*adj*) unproductive, barren, infertile, unfruitful, **2**. cheap; *synonyms* (*adj*) inexpensive, low, stingy, tacky, base, brassy, bum, cheesy, economical, flashy, mean, niggardly, reasonable, shabby, sleazy; *antonyms* (*adj*) expensive, costly, generous, tasteful, first-rate, luxurious, **3**. profitable; *synonyms* (*adj*) advantageous, beneficial, fruitful, helpful, gainful, desirable, economic, valuable, expedient, handy, salutary, edifying, commercial, healthy, moneymaking; *antonyms* (*adj*) unprofitable, dependent, **4**. worthwhile; *synonyms* (*adj*) worthy, rewarding, meaningful; *antonyms* (*adj*) pointless, wasted, worthless.

materetere 1. outstanding; *synonyms* (*adj*) eminent, due, conspicuous, great, owing, famous, distinguished, excellent, exceptional, notable, noteworthy, prominent, unpaid, major, brilliant; *antonyms* (*adj*) ordinary, paid, inferior, **2**. visible; *synonyms* (*adj*) obvious, perceptible, apparent, evident, open, clear, discernible, manifest, noticeable, observable, plain, appreciable, visual, transparent, palpable; *antonyms* (*adj*) invisible, imperceptible.

Mati march; *synonyms* (*n*) walk, hike, parade, demonstration, ramble, trek, course, (*v*) journey, tramp, advance, border, pace, process, stride, stroll.

matibu 1. ripe; *synonyms* (*adj*) mature, adult, ready, advanced, good, prepared, perfect, matured, consummate, right, (*v*) mellow; *antonym* (*adj*) green, **2**. swollen; *synonyms* (*adj*) bloated, inflated, bombastic, puffed, puffy, turgid, egotistic, high, bulging, tumescent, tumid, conceited, (*v*) distended, blown, (*prep*) pompous.

matie sneeze; *synonyms* (*v*) arrest, (*n*) sneezing, sternutation.

matiketike 1. loose; *synonyms* (*adj*) lax, liberal, dissolute, licentious, light, vague, detached, immoral, (*v*) disengage, liberate, relax, release, detach, (*n*) free, limp; *antonyms* (*adj*) tight, close, compressed, dense, taut, strict, compact, wedged, **2**. idle; *synonyms* (*adj*) inactive, indolent, lazy, baseless, frivolous, fruitless, groundless, unfounded, empty, disengaged, flimsy, barren, dead, futile, jobless; *antonyms* (*adj*) busy, active, employed, (*v*) change, **3**. soft; *synonyms* (*adj*) gentle, easy, balmy, delicate, quiet, slack, loose, clement, faint, flabby, flaccid, frail, lenient, (*v*) feeble, low; *antonyms* (*adj*) hard, firm, harsh, loud, hoarse, rough, solid, stiff, alcoholic, shrill, strong,

4. slack; *synonyms* *(adj)* idle, negligent, baggy, neglectful, dilatory, inattentive, backward, careless, flat, heavy, inert, *(v)* remiss, dull, slow, abate; *antonym* *(adj)* thorough.

matim 1. drip; *synonyms* *(n)* dribble, trickle, leak, leakage, escape, splash, *(v)* drop, distill, seep, weep, trill, drizzle, fall, ooze, percolate, **2**. down; *synonyms* *(adv)* below, *(adj)* cut, dejected, depressed, downward, despondent, dispirited, downcast, downhearted, *(n)* feather, fur, fuzz, *(v)* consume, devour, drink; *antonyms* *(adv)* up, *(adj)* cheerful, happy, upward, **3**. level; *synonyms* *(n)* grade, degree, *(adj)* even, equal, horizontal, *(v)* flat, flatten, floor, aim, demolish, destroy, dismantle, raze, bulldoze, balance; *antonyms* *(adj)* inclined, slanting, angled, unequal, *(v)* uneven, build, raise, **4**. drop; *synonyms* *(v)* decrease, deposit, droop, abandon, cast, dip, discard, dismiss, drip, ebb, jump, shed, sink, *(n)* decline, collapse; *antonyms* *(v)* rise, increase, lift, *(n)* growth, **5**. fell; *synonyms* *(v)* chop, ax, level, down, *(adj)* barbarous, cruel, prostrate, brutal, fierce, savage, murderous, ferocious, *(n)* skin, coat, fleece, **6**. fall; *synonyms* *(v)* descend, dive, rain, diminish, dwindle, alight, come, crash, *(n)* descent, downfall, plunge, pitch, cascade, decay, declivity; *antonyms* *(v)* ascend, climb, triumph, win, *(n)* ascent.

matimaki 1. dropped; *synonyms* *(adj)* fallen, decreased, abandoned, dead, degraded, prostrate, ruined, **2**. felt; *synonyms* *(v)* mat, snarl, tangle, braid, entangle, *(adj)* perceived, sensed, conscious, **3**. downed; *synonym* *(adj)* felled.

matinnao 1. flat; *synonyms* *(adj)* dull, bland, even, plain, insipid, level, plane, tasteless, dreary, boring, absolute, dead, downright, *(n)* apartment, *(v)* uninteresting; *antonyms* *(adj)* exciting, high-pitched, bumpy, **2**. level; *synonyms* *(n)* grade, degree, category, *(adj)* equal, horizontal, *(v)* flat, flatten, floor, aim, demolish, destroy, dismantle, raze, bulldoze, balance; *antonyms* *(adj)* inclined, slanting, angled, unequal, *(v)* uneven, build, raise, **3**. smooth; *synonyms* *(adj)* easy, calm, oily, facile, flowing, fluent, fluid, glossy, graceful, greasy, liquid, mellow, polished, *(v)* quiet, facilitate; *antonyms* *(adj)* rough, abrasive, coarse, crumpled, flaking, harsh, jerky, lined, peeling, prickly, ridged, wrinkled, corrugated, *(v)* wrinkle, crease.

matiratira 1. crushed; *synonyms* *(v)* victimized, *(adj)* broken, beaten, low, subdued, conquered, flattened, dispirited, compressed, overwhelmed, abashed, abject, blue, brokenhearted, *(n)* crushing; *antonyms* *(adj)* loose, victorious, **2**. flattened; *synonyms* *(adj)* depressed, planate, trodden, unconscious, compacted, firmed, trampled, **3**. squashed; *synonyms* *(adj)* condensed, dense, solid.

matiraua 1. squashed; *synonyms* *(adj)* compacted, compressed, condensed, dense, solid, **2**. reduced; *synonyms* *(adj)* decreased, abridged, curtailed, miniature, cheap, limited, bated, cut, inexpensive, low, lower, prostrate; *antonyms* *(adj)* expensive, complete, **3**. trodden; *synonyms* *(adj)* trampled, beaten, crushed, firmed, flattened; *antonym* *(adj)* loose.

matoa 1. brave; *synonyms* *(adj)* adventurous, bold, audacious, courageous, endure, fearless, hardy, intrepid, valiant, virile, confident, daring, dauntless, *(v)* defy, confront; *antonyms* *(adj)* cowardly, frightened, gutless, pathetic, *(n)* timid, **2**. hard; *synonyms* *(adj)* austere, bad, difficult, grave, severe, strong, arduous, callous, cruel, grueling, knotty, tough, *(adv)* firm, *(v)* acute, *(n)* rough; *antonyms* *(adj)* easy, soft, kind, merciful, simple, soggy, tender, yielding, *(adv)* gently, lightly, **3**. steady; *synonyms* *(adj)* even, secure, constant, continual, fixed, resolute, stable, cool, incessant, sedate, settled, consistent, *(v)* steadfast, calm, regular; *antonyms* *(adj)* unsteady, shaky, wobbly, intermittent, unreliable, **4**. strict; *synonyms* *(adj)* rigid, stern, correct, accurate, harsh, precise, rigorous, scrupulous, exacting, hard, inflexible, stiff, meticulous, *(v)* exact, close; *antonyms* *(adj)* lenient, free, lax, flexible, imprecise, negligent, relaxed.

matoanna starch; *synonyms* *(n)* amylum, vitality, stamina, mettle, vigor, durability, endurance, fire, fortitude, go, *(v)* stiffen, *(adj)* stiff, glair, commonplace, everyday.

matoatao austere; *synonyms* *(adj)* ascetic, stern, harsh, severe, abstemious, astringent, plain, rigid, rigorous, stark, stiff, strict, bare, bleak, firm; *antonym* *(adj)* ornate.

matoato hard; *synonyms* *(adj)* austere, bad, difficult, grave, severe, strong, arduous, callous, cruel, grueling, knotty, tough, *(adv)* firm, *(v)* acute, *(n)* rough; *antonyms* *(adj)* easy, soft, kind, merciful, simple, soggy, tender, yielding, *(adv)* gently, lightly.

matoatoa strong; *synonyms* *(adj)* intense, powerful, able, deep, firm, stable, steady, cogent, durable, forcible, good, hard, influential, lusty, potent; *antonyms* *(adj)* weak, bland, delicate, faint, feeble, frail, mild, pale, slight, unconvincing, cowardly, diluted, dull, exhausted, flimsy.

matoro 1. accepted; *synonyms* *(adj)* acceptable, conventional, acknowledged, assumed, established, orthodox, understood, approved, current, received, customary, habitual, known, popular, proper; *antonyms* *(adj)* concealed, unpopular, unusual, **2**. fortified; *synonyms* *(adj)* bastioned, secure, castled, defended, equipped, fast, protected, safeguarded, secured, shielded, prepared, turreted, **3**. established; *synonyms* *(v)* settled, *(adj)* accepted, firm, fixed, regular, set, decided, confirmed, accomplished, effected, completed, constituted, official, recognized, stable; *antonym* (*adj*) unproven.

matu 1. doze; *synonyms* (*n*) nap, drowse, slumber, (*v*) snooze, sleep, siesta, catnap, nod, coma, rest, **2.** nap; *synonyms* (*n*) down, pile, grain, lotto, monte, texture, (*v*) dream, hibernation, (*adj*) doze, velvet, wool, **3.** asleep; *synonyms* (*adj*) dead, deceased, dormant, inactive, numb, sleeping, sleepy, comatose, departed, gone, napping, slumbering, snoozing, lifeless, defunct; *antonyms* (*adj*) awake, up, **4.** slumber; *synonyms* (*v*) repose, kip, **5.** repose; *synonyms* (*n*) peace, calm, composure, ease, quiet, leisure, recreation, peacefulness, placidity, quietness, quietude, (*v*) recline, lay, lie, place; *antonym* (*v*) work, **6.** sleep; *synonyms* (*n*) quietus, relaxation, remainder, residue, stupor, (*v*) hibernate, lodge, couch, perch, settle, (*adj*) abide.

matunako 1. dawdle; *synonyms* (*v*) dally, linger, delay, lag, amble, procrastinate, hesitate, idler, loiter, lounge, saunter, drag; *antonyms* (*v*) hurry, rush, **2.** oversleep; *synonym* (*v*) sleep.

matutu 1. drowsy; *synonyms* (*adj*) dozy, comatose, lazy, lethargic, slow, somnolent, dull, indolent, listless, sluggish, soporific, dozing, drowsing, oscitant, (*n*) sleepy; *antonyms* (*adj*) alert, energetic, **2.** numb; *synonyms* (*adj*) asleep, benumbed, dead, insensible, torpid, deadened, callous, impassive, inactive, inert, paralytic, (*v*) benumb, deaden, paralyze, (*n*) blunt; *antonym* (*adj*) sensitive, **3.** sleepy; *synonyms* (*adj*) drowsy, hypnotic, dreamy, heavy, tired, weary; *antonym* (*adj*) awake.

mau dry; *synonyms* (*adj*) thirsty, arid, barren, boring, dehydrated, dull, bald, hoarse, jejune, plain, (*v*) dehydrate, desiccate, drain, uninteresting, sardonic; *antonyms* (*adj*) wet, damp, moist, saturated, soaked, boggy, drenched, rainy, sodden, interesting, fresh, humid, juicy, succulent, (*v*) drench.

mauku 1. lame; *synonyms* (*adj*) crippled, game, disabled, feeble, halt, halting, weak, becripple, paralytic, inadequate, infirm, (*v*) cripple, maim, paralyze, disable, **2.** disabled; *synonyms* (*adj*) handicapped, helpless, incapacitated, invalid, mangled, mutilated, weakened, wrecked, unavailable, broken, cripply, exhausted, palsied, powerless, (*adv*) aground.

mauna 1. efface; *synonyms* (*v*) cancel, delete, erase, obliterate, blur, destroy, expunge, raze, sponge, annihilate, eradicate, rase, remove, scratch, **2.** disappear; *synonyms* (*v*) die, vanish, melt, fade, depart, dematerialize, sink, go, pass, end, abscond, fall, scram, disperse, dissolve; *antonyms* (*v*) appear, stay, **3.** die; *synonyms* (*v*) decease, dead, death, expire, conk, croak, break, cease, fail, perish, starve, succumb, wither, (*n*) dice, matrix, **4.** eclipse; *synonyms* (*n*) disappearance, darkness, (*v*) darken,

cloud, outdo, overshadow, shade, surpass, dim, transcend, exceed, excel, obscure, outshine, outweigh, **5.** perish; *synonyms* (*v*) decay, ruin, crumble, exit, rot, disappear, decompose, putrefy, waste, extend, lead, leave; *antonym* (*v*) survive.

maunea 1. deafened; *synonyms* (*adj*) deaf, dead, deadened, stunned, decayed, regardless, stifled, tasteless, **2.** deafening; *synonyms* (*adj*) loud, earsplitting, thunderous, noisy, piercing, shrill, (*v*) thundering; *antonym* (*adj*) quiet.

maung 1. foul; *synonyms* (*adj*) base, disgusting, filthy, nasty, evil, dingy, putrid, unclean, abominable, (*n*) soil, (*v*) dirty, corrupt, coarse, defile, befoul; *antonyms* (*adj*) pleasant, fair, (*v*) clean, pure, **2.** decomposed; *synonyms* (*adj*) rotten, decayed, bad, decaying, malodorous, off, rotting, corroded, decomposing, disintegrating, fetid, fusty, moldy, musty, perished; *antonym* (*adj*) fresh, **3.** stinking; *synonyms* (*adj*) foul, loathsome, noisome, smelly, odorous, foetid, funky, lousy, sickening, offensive, smelling, rank, stinky, vile, crappy; *antonym* (*adj*) fragrant, **4.** putrid; *synonyms* (*adj*) putrefied, stinking, vicious, rancid, festering, infected, purulent, pussy.

maunganga incapable; *synonyms* (*adj*) impotent, incompetent, inadequate, unable, helpless, powerless, inept, insufficient, unqualified, ineffectual, inefficient, unfit, weak; *antonyms* (*adj*) capable, able.

maungaro gumming; *synonyms* (*n*) gluing, mumbling.

maunika forget; *synonyms* (*v*) disregard, leave, bury, ignore, neglect, overlook, fail, abandon, lose, omit, slight, block; *antonym* (*v*) remember.

maunikaki forgotten; *synonyms* (*adj*) lost, disregarded, elapsed, past, abandoned, antebellum, antediluvian, baffled, befuddled, bemused, bewildered, beyond, bygone, confounded, confused.

mauoti divulge; *synonyms* (*v*) announce, disclose, betray, communicate, declare, impart, reveal, leak, break, confess, expose, tell, blab, convey, discover; *antonym* (*v*) conceal.

maura 1. mishandle; *synonyms* (*v*) botch, abuse, mistreat, bungle, misconduct, fumble, maltreat, mismanage, grope, **2.** abuse; *synonyms* (*n*) affront, misuse, harm, outrage, reproach, invective, maltreatment, (*v*) insult, injure, assault, censure, damage, exploit, hurt, pervert; *antonyms* (*v*) praise, respect, **3.** harm; *synonyms* (*n*) evil, detriment, bruise, wound, disadvantage, injury, disservice, wrong, disaster, ill, (*v*) blemish, maim, poison, ravage, endamage; *antonyms* (*v*) enhance, benefit, **4.** maltreat; *synonyms* (*v*) mishandle, molest, oppress, persecute, assail, **5.** mistreat; *synonyms* (*v*) torture, manhandle, torment, blackguard, clapperclaw, corrupt, knock, manipulate, vilify, backbite, bash, chop, hose, hump, misappropriate, **6.** wrong; *synonyms* (*adj*) false, improper, bad, inappropriate, incorrect, criminal, inaccurate, iniquitous, unjust, untrue, vicious, wicked, (*v*) erroneous, (*n*) injustice, crime; *antonyms* (*adj*) correct, good, proper, honest, law-abiding, (*adv*) correctly, (*v*) right, (*n*) justice.

maurake 1. impudent; *synonyms* (*adj*) forward, audacious, brassy, disrespectful, impertinent, barefaced, daring, brazen, insolent, brash, cheeky, fresh, saucy, cool, (*n*) bold; *antonym* (*adj*) respectful, **2.** cheeky; *synonyms* (*adj*) impudent, nervy, presumptuous, rude, familiar, flippant, sassy, **3.** impertinent; *synonyms* (*adj*) pert, discourteous, extraneous, insulting, offensive, officious, immaterial, foreign, impolite, irrelevant, irreverent, abusive, brisk, cavalier, smart; *antonym* (*adj*) well-behaved, **4.** frontal; *synonyms* (*adj*) front, anterior, fore, candid, metopic, blunt, confrontational, (*n*) facade, frontlet, face, frontage, **5.** forward; *synonyms* (*adv*) onward, ahead, along, (*adj*) advanced, early, confident, eager, (*n*) further, (*v*) advance, expedite, promote, cultivate, consign, encourage, (*phr*) dispatch; *antonyms* (*adv*) backward, (*adj*) shy, posterior, **6.** assured; *synonyms* (*adj*) certain, secure, sure, assertive, definite, guaranteed, positive, convinced, reliable, safe, surefire; *antonyms* (*adj*) insecure, uncertain, **7.** confident; *synonyms* (*adj*) brave, hopeful, sanguine, fearless, decisive, dogmatic, composed, optimistic, (*v*) assured, cocksure, satisfied, absolute, emphatic; *antonyms* (*adj*) anxious, frightened, pessimistic, timid, hesitant, unsure, **8.** bold; *synonyms* (*adj*) adventurous, manly, resolute, arrogant, courageous, heroic, intrepid, spirited, stalwart, bluff, defiant, enterprising, gallant, obvious, shameless; *antonyms* (*adj*) cowardly, modest, **9.** cheek; *synonyms* (*n*) audacity, boldness, brass, impertinence, nerve, gall, impudence, insolence, lip, mouth, disrespect, effrontery, jowl, presumption, buttock; *antonym* (*n*) respect, **10.** insolent; *synonyms* (*adj*) flip, haughty, imperious, lordly, overbearing, contemptuous, magisterial, disdainful, opprobrious, presuming, proud, supercilious, uncivil, bodacious, dictatorial; *antonym* (*adj*) polite, **11.** audacious; *synonyms* (*adj*) blatant, gutsy, unabashed, valiant, venturesome, unashamed, risky, dauntless, foolhardy, plucky, rash, reckless, undaunted, venturous, **12.** brash; *synonyms* (*adj*) brittle, daredevil, hasty, impetuous, madcap, temerarious, thoughtless, bloodstroke, loud, overconfident; *antonym* (*adj*) prim, **13.** brassy; *synonyms* (*adj*) garish, showy, cheap, meretricious, tawdry, vulgar, aggressive, brasslike, flashy, gaudy, tasteless, **14.** brazen; *synonym* (*adj*) flagrant; *antonym* (*adj*) abashed, **15.** shameless; *synonyms* (*adj*)

immodest, graceless, depraved, profligate, unscrupulous, abandoned, indecent, obscene, unblushing, dissolute, immoral, lewd, reprobate, wicked, licentious, **16.** rude; *synonyms* (*adj*) gross, rough, coarse, brutal, crude, mean, barbarous, churlish, crass, curt, indelicate, plain, raw, (*n*) abrupt, robust; *antonyms* (*adj*) chivalrous, courteous, refined, civil, decent, proper, well-mannered.

mauraki 1. mistreated; *synonyms* (*adj*) abused, maltreated, battered, aggrieved, downtrodden, harmed, injured, neglected, wronged, ignored, offended, persecuted, victimized, **2.** harmed; *synonyms* (*v*) harm, damage, wound, (*adj*) hurt, impaired, crippled, debilitated, incapacitated, mistreated, molested, **3.** maltreated, **4.** abused; *synonyms* (*adj*) dull, perverted.

maurea rude; *synonyms* (*adj*) gross, rough, impudent, blunt, coarse, bold, brutal, crude, discourteous, impolite, mean, abusive, barbarous, churlish, (*n*) abrupt; *antonyms* (*adj*) polite, respectful, chivalrous, courteous, refined, civil, decent, proper, well-mannered.

maureka 1. impudent; *synonyms* (*adj*) forward, audacious, brassy, disrespectful, impertinent, barefaced, daring, brazen, insolent, brash, cheeky, fresh, saucy, cool, (*n*) bold; *antonym* (*adj*) respectful, **2.** rude; *synonyms* (*adj*) gross, rough, impudent, blunt, coarse, brutal, crude, discourteous, impolite, mean, abusive, barbarous, churlish, crass, (*n*) abrupt; *antonyms* (*adj*) polite, chivalrous, courteous, refined, civil, decent, proper, well-mannered.

mauri 1. hello; *synonyms* (*n*) greeting, hi, howdy, hullo, welcome, (*v*) hail, **2.** healthy; *synonyms* (*adj*) healthful, fit, good, hale, salubrious, wholesome, beneficial, hearty, sound, well, whole, sane, abundant, nutritious, active; *antonyms* (*adj*) unhealthy, harmful, unwell, unfit, dependent, fattening, infected, soporific, unwholesome, weak, **3.** well; *synonyms* (*adv*) right, easily, thoroughly, considerably, fully, correctly, amply, (*adj*) healthy, shaft, robust, (*n*) fountain, spring, pit, hollow, (*v*) gush; *antonyms* (*adv*) ill, badly, poorly, (*adj*) sick, dying, nauseous, **4.** safe; *synonyms* (*adj*) secure, reliable, cautious, dependable, harmless, innocuous, correct, innocent, inoffensive, certain, stable, steady, (*n*) closet, coffer, strongbox; *antonyms* (*adj*) dangerous, unsafe, hurt, risky, unprotected, vulnerable, insecure, reckless.

mauringa forget; *synonyms* (*v*) disregard, leave, bury, ignore, neglect, overlook, fail, abandon, lose, omit, slight, block; *antonym* (*v*) remember.

mauringaki forgotten; *synonyms* (*adj*) lost, disregarded, elapsed, past, abandoned, antebellum, antediluvian, baffled, befuddled, bemused, bewildered, beyond, bygone, confounded, confused.

maurouro 1. embodied; *synonyms (adj)* incarnate, corporate, bodied, corporal, corporeal, personified, alive, associated, bodily, collective, combined, incorporate, mixed, real, tangible, **2.** inclusive; *synonyms (adj)* broad, comprehensive, overall, sweeping, extensive, general, total, whole, *(adv)* including; *antonym (adj)* exclusive, **3.** included; *synonyms (adj)* numbered, confined, inclosed, integrated, *(adv)* under.

mautakaroro 1. dry; *synonyms (adj)* thirsty, arid, barren, boring, dehydrated, dull, bald, hoarse, jejune, plain, *(v)* dehydrate, desiccate, drain, uninteresting, sardonic; *antonyms (adj)* wet, damp, moist, saturated, soaked, boggy, drenched, rainy, sodden, interesting, fresh, humid, juicy, succulent, *(v)* drench, **2.** thirsty; *synonyms (adj)* dry, eager, parched, avid, keen, athirst, greedy, absorbent, ambitious, *(v)* craving, hungry, **3.** parched; *synonyms (adj)* adust, torrid, desiccated, scorched, baked.

mautara 1. aware; *synonyms (adj)* awake, attentive, conscious, heedful, mindful, vigilant, sentient, alert, enlightened, knowing, knowledgeable, observant, sensible, wary, watchful; *antonyms (adj)* unaware, unconscious, **2.** alert; *synonyms (adj)* active, agile, quick, aware, intelligent, lively, clever, alive, animated, bright, brisk, careful, *(v)* caution, *(n)* alarm, alarum; *antonyms (adj)* drowsy, inattentive, absentminded, dazed, sleepy, tired, asleep, slow, unalert, **3.** circumspect; *synonyms (adj)* chary, cautious, guarded, prudent, cagey, considerate, discreet, thoughtful, deliberate, judicious, cautelous, **4.** cautious; *synonyms (adj)* conservative, circumspect, provident, reserved, shy, moderate, canny, tactful, sly, economical, frugal, gingerly, scrupulous, sparing, subtle; *antonyms (adj)* rash, reckless, careless, impetuous, impulsive, open, incautious, irresponsible, wasteful, **5.** attentive; *synonyms (adj)* assiduous, diligent, advertent, devoted, friendly, studious, concerned, courteous, gallant, intent, kind, painstaking, polite, regardful, solicitous; *antonyms (adj)* negligent, unfocused, forgetful, neglectful, heedless, **6.** heedful, **7.** vigilant; *synonyms (adj)* wakeful, jealous, sleepless, nimble, **8.** wary; *synonyms (adj)* suspicious, leery, distrustful, mistrustful, safe, cunning, reluctant, sagacious, untrusting, wise, *(v)* calculating, crafty, shrewd, skillful; *antonyms (adj)* unwary, trusting.

mautete 1. nosy; *synonyms (adj)* curious, inquisitive, inquiring, nosey, prying, snoopy, meddlesome, meddling, intrusive; *antonym (adj)* apathetic, **2.** inquisitive; *synonyms (adj)* nosy, questioning, speculative, investigative, quizzical, **3.** bold; *synonyms (adj)* adventurous, audacious, manly,

resolute, arrogant, barefaced, courageous, daring, fearless, heroic, intrepid, spirited, stalwart, bluff, brave; *antonyms (adj)* cowardly, timid, modest, **4.** detested; *synonyms (adj)* despised, hated, unpopular, disliked, loathed, reviled, scorned, abhorrent, despicable, insufferable, ostracized; *antonym (adj)* popular, **5.** mean; *synonyms (v)* intend, design, imply, denote, involve, *(adj)* middle, base, common, hateful, ignoble, medium, miserly, *(n)* average, contemptible, low; *antonyms (adj)* generous, kind, **6.** curious; *synonyms (adj)* abnormal, funny, interested, odd, peculiar, strange, unusual, bizarre, extraordinary, quaint, queer, remarkable, singular, weird, whimsical; *antonyms (adj)* normal, incurious, ordinary, **7.** prying; *synonyms (adj)* busy, snooping, *(n)* curiosity, nosiness, inquisitiveness, **8.** ugly; *synonyms (adj)* nasty, disagreeable, forbidding, frightful, gruesome, hideous, homely, repulsive, surly, evil, offensive, atrocious, deformed, grotesque, horrible; *antonyms (adj)* beautiful, attractive, good-looking, flowing, ornamental.

mautoto lazy; *synonyms (adj)* indolent, idle, inert, drowsy, inactive, shiftless, dull, faineant, remiss, slothful, slow, sluggish, leisurely, sluggard, tardy; *antonyms (adj)* energetic, diligent, active.

mawa 1. ample; *synonyms (adj)* abundant, big, broad, copious, large, plentiful, affluent, considerable, full, heavy, liberal, rich, roomy, sizable, spacious; *antonyms (adj)* inadequate, small, meager, insufficient, scarce, **2.** breathless; *synonyms (adj)* dead, panting, breathtaking, inanimate, winded, choking, excited, exhausted, puffing, wheezing, puffed, *(v)* aghast, undistracted, *(n)* eager, urgent; *antonym (adj)* breathing, **3.** roomy; *synonyms (adj)* capacious, extensive, ample, commodious, expansive, voluminous, comprehensive, huge, open, wide, baggy, convenient; *antonym (adj)* cramped, **4.** winded; *synonyms (adj)* gasping, breathless, blown, pursy, wheezy, **5.** spacious; *synonyms (adj)* vast, extended, airy, comfortable; *antonym (adj)* narrow, **6.** vast; *synonyms (adj)* immense, boundless, colossal, enormous, gigantic, great, immeasurable, unlimited, gargantuan, giant, infinite, massive, monumental, unbounded, limitless; *antonyms (adj)* limited, tiny.

mawaki winded; *synonyms (adj)* gasping, panting, breathless, blown, pursy, puffed, puffing, wheezing, wheezy.

mawawa 1. blue; *synonyms (adj)* azure, depressed, down, gloomy, low, cheerless, dejected, dispirited, downcast, downhearted, naughty, sad, sapphire, spicy, black, **2.** verdant; *synonyms (adj)* green, lush, leafy, flourishing, fresh, raw, verdurous; *antonym (adj)* arid.

mbambaea 1. aspirate; *synonyms (v)* accentuate, articulate, deliver, mouth, enunciate, prolate, pronounce, vocalize, attract, curl, pull, retract, (adj) aspirated, **2**. inhale; *synonyms* (v) breathe, absorb, imbibe, draw, suck, drag, drink, inspire, receive, respire, admit, import, ingest, puff, (n) sniff; *antonym* (v) exhale, **3**. suck; *synonyms* (v) nurse, lactate, suckle, drain, aspirate, breastfeed, (n) sucking, suction.

mbambaeaki inhaled; *synonym* (adj) inspired.

mbwa kiss; *synonyms* (n) buss, brush, osculation, salute, touch, (v) caress, embrace, osculate, love.

me 1. bad; *synonyms* (adj) evil, adverse, harmful, immoral, naughty, poisonous, sad, sinister, wicked, malicious, infamous, appalling, awful, damaging, (v) decayed; *antonyms* (adj) fresh, pleasant, well, well-behaved, (n) good, **2**. crooked; *synonyms* (adj) bent, awry, corrupt, irregular, askew, curved, deformed, dishonest, indirect, lopsided, unfair, unscrupulous, angular, asymmetrical, (v) wry; *antonyms* (adj) straight, honest, even, principled, **3**. ugly; *synonyms* (adj) nasty, disagreeable, forbidding, frightful, gruesome, hideous, homely, repulsive, surly, offensive, atrocious, despicable, grotesque, horrible, monstrous; *antonyms* (adj) beautiful, attractive, good-looking, flowing, ornamental.

mea 1. complain; *synonyms* (v) beef, bemoan, bewail, protest, squawk, whine, grudge, accuse, carp, croak, gripe, grouse, grumble, mutter, object; *antonym* (v) compliment, **2**. recriminate; *synonyms* (v) remonstrate, expostulate, inveigh, scold.

meakina blurt; *synonyms* (v) ejaculate, babble, blunder, exclaim.

meamea gray; *synonyms* (adj) dull, bleak, dim, gloomy, grizzled, hoary, leaden, old, overcast, pale, dismal, murky, white, (n) grizzle, (v) grey; *antonym* (adj) bright.

meere slow; *synonyms* (adj) dull, late, easy, sluggish, heavy, dense, dim, gradual, inactive, indolent, lazy, stupid, (v) slack, (adv) behind, behindhand; *antonyms* (adj) fast, intelligent, rapid, bright, alert, brisk, hasty, prompt, quick, speedy, hurried, observant, rushed, (v) accelerate.

mehi breadfruit; *synonyms* (v) blackberry, blancmange, bloater, bouilli, bouillon.

Mei may; *synonyms* (v) can, could, get, might, acquire, aim, amaze, arrest, arrive, baffle, beat, become, beget, begin, bewilder.

meia scold; *synonyms* (v) censure, berate, chide, rebuke, reprimand, abuse, lecture, reproach, rail, admonish, castigate, grouch, grumble, jaw, (n) nag; *antonym* (v) praise.

meira urinate; *synonyms* (v) pee, piddle, micturate, piss, excrete, make, urine, addle, attain, build, cause, clear, constitute, construct, cook.

meme 1. moan; *synonyms* (n) groan, gripe, whine, complaint, lament, grievance, grouse, protest, (v) grumble, bewail, complain, cry, howl, mourn, bleat, **2**. fret; *synonyms* (n) anxiety, (v) agitate, chafe, gall, grate, irritate, trouble, worry, annoy, fray, rub, upset, anger, disquiet, concern, **3**. boring; *synonyms* (adj) dull, tedious, tiresome, annoying, arid, bland, dreary, monotonous, prosaic, tame, uninteresting, wearisome, vapid, drab, (n) drilling; *antonyms* (adj) exciting, fascinating, interesting, gripping, original, thrilling, varied, **4**. annoying; *synonyms* (adj) galling, irritating, troublesome, vexatious, aggravating, awkward, bothersome, disagreeable, grating, inconvenient, offensive, pesky, trying, vexing, (n) annoyance; *antonyms* (adj) pleasing, soothing, **5**. importunate; *synonyms* (adj) exigent, insistent, pressing, instant, demanding, earnest, pleading, urgent, appealing, imploring, (v) important; *antonym* (adj) halfhearted, **6**. cry; *synonyms* (n) shout, bark, scream, yell, clamor, roar, bay, crying, (v) call, bellow, shriek, weep, exclaim, moan, outcry; *antonyms* (v) laugh, whisper, **7**. complain; *synonyms* (v) beef, bemoan, squawk, grudge, accuse, carp, croak, mutter, object, plain, remonstrate, whimper, bellyache, rail, grieve; *antonym* (v) compliment, **8**. tiresome; *synonyms* (adj) boring, laborious, irksome, difficult, fatiguing, slow, dry, exhausting, humdrum, tiring, weary, deadening, exasperating, **9**. troublesome; *synonyms* (adj) arduous, hard, onerous, tough, heavy, embarrassing, burdensome, thorny, unpleasant, painful, grievous, ponderous, taxing, importunate, (v) toilsome; *antonym* (adj) easy, **10**. whine; *synonyms* (n) wail, drone, hum, sob, (v) sigh, squeal, buzz, grizzle, screech, snivel, bawl, blubber, yammer, kick, kvetch.

memeka 1. inhale; *synonyms* (v) breathe, absorb, imbibe, draw, suck, drag, drink, attract, inspire, receive, respire, admit, import, ingest, (n) sniff; *antonym* (v) exhale, **2**. suck; *synonyms* (v) nurse, lactate, suckle, drain, puff, aspirate, pull, breastfeed, (n) sucking, suction.

memekaki inhaled; *synonym* (adj) inspired.

memekia sip; *synonyms* (n) nip, gulp, swallow, taste, bite, drop, mouthful, shot, slurp, (v) drink, imbibe, sample, quaff, lap, (adj) sup.

memerake 1. constraining; *synonyms* (adj) confining, compelling, awkward, close, compulsory, compulsory, constrained, constrictive, exigent, forceful, limiting, (prep) cogent, conclusive, forcible, powerful, **2**. importunate; *synonyms* (adj) troublesome, annoying, insistent, pressing, instant, demanding, earnest, pleading, urgent, appealing, imploring, (v) important; *antonym* (adj) halfhearted, **3**. coerce; *synonyms* (v) force, compel, drive, make, impose, bulldoze, bully, dragoon, necessitate, oblige, push, blackmail, extort, demand, constrain, **4**. fawn; *synonyms* (*n*) dun, (*v*) crawl, creep, cringe, grovel, cower, crouch, bootlick, kowtow, flatter, sneak, toady, truckle, (*adj*) beige, **5**. constrain; *synonyms* (*v*) coerce, confine, bind, curb, bridle, obligate, bound, check, control, enforce, press, require, restrain, put, compress; *antonym* (*v*) liberate, **6**. cower; *synonyms* (*v*) flinch, shrink, squat, wince, blench, huddle, quail, recoil, stoop, bow, fawn, (*n*) skulk, funk, **7**. force; *synonyms* (*n*) energy, strength, agency, effect, impetus, impulse, power, vigor, violence, (*v*) pressure, squeeze, thrust, cram, impel, ram; *antonyms* (*n*) weakness, persuasion, **8**. bootlick; *synonyms* (*v*) absorb, cajole, court, ingratiate, kotow, draw, genuflect, imbibe, scrape, suck, (*n*) sycophant, **9**. oblige; *synonyms* (*v*) accommodate, hold, exact, indulge, pledge, assist, bond, favor, gratify, have, induce, please, serve, tie, (*n*) assign, **10**. urge; *synonyms* (*n*) goad, spur, (*v*) advocate, incite, inspire, instigate, persuade, prompt, promote, entreat, expedite, advise, cheer, counsel, (*adj*) quicken; *antonym* (*v*) discourage.

memerakeaki 1. forced; *synonyms* (*adj*) compulsory, compelled, bound, artificial, constrained, involuntary, unnatural, farfetched, false, labored, obligatory, obliged, strained; *antonyms* (*adj*) free, unprovoked, spontaneous, voluntary, **2**. constrained; *synonyms* (*adj*) uneasy, forced, stiff, awkward, limited, affected, confined, cramped, restricted, rigid, stilted; *antonym* (*adj*) unrestricted.

memeri 1. chubby; *synonyms* (*adj*) buxom, fat, fleshy, plump, round, chunky, heavy, pudgy, stout, tubby, overweight; *antonyms* (*adj*) thin, skinny, slim, **2**. fresh; *synonyms* (*adj*) bracing, brisk, clean, novel, bright, original, recent, airy, bold, alive, chilly, cool, forward, green, (*adv*) new; *antonyms* (*adj*) old, stale, decayed, exhausted, hot, humid, muggy, musty, off, oppressive, rotten, tired, worn, dry, sweltering, **3**. delicate; *synonyms* (*adj*) fine, accurate, breakable, dainty, fragile, refined, tender, beautiful, brittle, difficult, frail, nice, sensitive, soft, agreeable; *antonyms* (*adj*) strong, inelegant, robust, sturdy, tough, **4**. tender; *synonyms* (*adj*) affectionate, painful, loving, sore, compassionate, delicate, fond, gentle, mild, (*v*) proffer, present, propose, (*n*) offer, bid, overture; *antonyms* (*adj*) hard, hardhearted, rubbery, rough, **5**. rosy; *synonyms* (*adj*) blooming, hopeful, optimistic, auspicious, promising, roseate, ruddy, flushed, fortunate, pink, cheerful, reddish, blushing, encouraging, (*n*) red; *antonym* (*adj*) pale.

memeroa suck; *synonyms* (*v*) draw, drink, imbibe, nurse, absorb, lactate, suckle, drain, puff, aspirate, pull, breastfeed, (*n*) sucking, suction.

memeto 1. inquisitive; *synonyms* (*adj*) curious, inquiring, nosy, prying, questioning, speculative, meddling, investigative, meddlesome, quizzical;

antonym (*adj*) apathetic, **2**. importunate; *synonyms* (*adj*) troublesome, annoying, exigent, insistent, pressing, instant, demanding, earnest, pleading, urgent, appealing, imploring, (*v*) important; *antonym* (*adj*) halfhearted, **3**. annoying; *synonyms* (*adj*) galling, irritating, vexatious, aggravating, awkward, bothersome, disagreeable, grating, inconvenient, offensive, pesky, trying, vexing, worrying, (*n*) annoyance; *antonyms* (*adj*) pleasing, soothing, **4**. turbulent; *synonyms* (*adj*) tempestuous, tumultuous, rough, furious, boisterous, disorderly, noisy, riotous, violent, wild, rude, troubled, unruly, agitated, (*n*) stormy; *antonym* (*adj*) calm, **5**. tiresome; *synonyms* (*adj*) boring, tedious, dull, laborious, irksome, monotonous, difficult, dreary, fatiguing, slow, uninteresting, dry, exhausting, humdrum, (*v*) wearisome; *antonym* (*adj*) interesting, **6**. troublesome; *synonyms* (*adj*) arduous, hard, onerous, tough, heavy, embarrassing, burdensome, thorny, unpleasant, painful, grievous, ponderous, taxing, importunate, (*v*) toilsome; *antonym* (*adj*) easy.

men yet; *synonyms* (*adv*) however, but, notwithstanding, even, nonetheless, though, besides, further, hitherto, eventually, unless, always, (*conj*) nevertheless, (*n*) already, (*v*) still.

mena 1. hiatus; *synonyms* (*n*) blank, break, gap, chasm, recess, respite, suspension, intermission, interruption, interval, lacuna, pause, abatement, **2**. be; *synonyms* (*v*) exist, live, act, consist, constitute, represent, cost, follow, form, lie, remain, rest, stay, subsist, (*n*) stand, **3**. are, **4**. located; *synonyms* (*adj*) set, situated, placed, fixed, determined, dictated, hardened, laid, residing, rigid, **5**. reside; *synonyms* (*v*) inhabit, occupy, abide, belong, lodge, populate, people, repose, be, domicile, domiciliate, settle, shack, (*adj*) dwell, roost, **6**. stay; *synonyms* (*v*) reside, prop, stop, continue, endure, arrest, bide, support, linger, persist, sojourn, (*n*) delay, halt, check, (*adj*) cease; *antonyms* (*v*) leave, change, abscond, depart, **7**. remain; *synonyms* (*v*) keep, last, hold, persevere, stick, attend, detain, hang, retain, survive, tarry, prevail, wait.

menai 1. modern; *synonyms* (*adj*) fresh, new, fashionable, late, advanced, current, latest, recent, contemporary, novel, present, stylish, innovative, chic, latter; *antonyms* (*adj*) old-fashioned, ancient, antiquated, old, prehistoric, traditional, conservative, neurotic, old-time, primordial, **2**. late; *synonyms* (*adj*) former, dead, deceased, behindhand, belated, delayed, modern, slow, tardy, dull, defunct, bygone, (*adv*) dilatory, backward, belatedly; *antonyms* (*adj*) ahead, (*adv*) early, punctually, promptly, punctual, **3**. new; *synonyms* (*adj*) green, original, additional, inexperienced, raw, strange, unaccustomed, unprecedented, young, different, newfangled, unfamiliar, (*adv*) lately, freshly, recently; *antonyms* (*adj*) familiar, outgoing, second-hand, used, less, stale, (*adv*) past, **4.** current; *synonyms* (*adj*) common, instant, actual, popular, prevalent, rife, accepted, (*n*) flow, stream, run, afloat, movement, trend, (*prep*) course, tide; *antonyms* (*adj*) obsolete, previous, **5.** recent; *synonyms* (*adj*) last, final, immediate.

menga 1. deformed; *synonyms* (*adj*) crooked, bent, distorted, malformed, misshapen, ugly, crippled, contorted, deform, grotesque, shapeless, twisted, warped, (*v*) crump, **2.** crooked; *synonyms* (*adj*) awry, corrupt, irregular, askew, curved, deformed, dishonest, indirect, lopsided, unfair, unscrupulous, angular, asymmetrical, bowed, (*v*) wry; *antonyms* (*adj*) straight, honest, even, principled, **3.** arched; *synonyms* (*adj*) arcuate, vaulted, convex, arciform, arced, **4.** curved; *synonyms* (*adj*) curve, round, bend, curving, curvy, hooked, rounded, tortuous; *antonym* (*adj*) concave, **5.** twisted; *synonyms* (*adj*) perverted, coiled, twined, winding, gnarled, kinky, wrong, depraved, misrepresented, oblique; *antonym* (*adj*) tidy.

mengamenga 1. toil; *synonyms* (*n*) labor, drudge, work, drudgery, effort, grind, exertion, struggle, swink, (*v*) sweat, plod, labour, moil, slave, travail, **2.** slave; *synonyms* (*n*) serf, servant, bondman, inferior, thrall, bondsman, captive, vassal, dependent, (*v*) fag, toil.

mengo 1. exert; *synonyms* (*v*) exercise, act, employ, wield, strain, use, (*n*) energize, excite, **2.** grind; *synonyms* (*v*) labor, toil, comminute, crunch, drudge, grate, abrade, chew, crush, file, mash, scrape, sharpen, (*n*) mill, drudgery, **3.** drudge; *synonyms* (*n*) hack, laborer, drudger, plodder, (*v*) slave, fag, moil, work, dig, grind, grub, plod, sweat, labour, travail, **4.** overwork; *synonyms* (*n*) overworking, excess, load, (*v*) exhaust, tax, exploit, overlabor, drive, abuse, wear, overdo, overplay, overply, overtoil, (*adj*) overtask, **5.** work; *synonyms* (*n*) business, employment, function, task, action, book, composition, occupation, (*v*) operate, cultivate, ferment, form, manipulate, (*adj*) job, trade; *antonyms* (*v*) idle, malfunction, **6.** travail; *synonyms* (*n*) effort, confinement, exertion, birth, childbed, endeavor, journey, parturiency, parturition, (*v*) childbirth, delivery, accouchement, travel, **7.** toil; *synonyms* (*n*) struggle, swink, industry, fatigue, entanglement, slavery, tire, (*v*) strive, **8.** pain; *synonyms* (*n*) distress, ache, bother, ill, torment, agony, nuisance, harass, annoyance, (*v*) hurt, afflict, anguish, grieve, trouble, agonize; *antonym* (*n*) pleasure, **9.** slave; *synonyms* (*n*) serf, servant, bondman, inferior, thrall, bondsman, captive, vassal, dependent.

mengoaki 1. ground; *synonyms* (*n*) base, cause, land, floor, reason, dirt, field, soil, account, country, basis, (*v*) bottom, found, establish, fix; *antonym* (*n*) ceiling, **2.** pained; *synonyms* (*adj*) hurt, offended, aggrieved, distressed, sore, miserable, angry, lame, uncomfortable, unfortunate, upset, disapproving, disparaging, reproachful, weary; *antonym* (*adj*) hopeful.

mere 1. murmur; *synonyms* (*n*) mutter, babble, whine, complaint, (*v*) buzz, grumble, hum, mumble, whisper, bubble, complain, breathe, drone, croak, grouch, **2.** grumble; *synonyms* (*v*) murmur, gripe, growl, rumble, roar, gnarl, carp, (*n*) moan, groan, roll, protest, wail, beef, grievance, grumbling, **3.** growl; *synonyms* (*n*) snarl, bark, thunder, cry, growling, (*v*) howl, yap, grunt, bay, crash, frown, scowl, snap, woof, **4.** complain; *synonyms* (*v*) bemoan, bewail, squawk, grudge, accuse, grouse, object, plain, remonstrate, whimper, bellyache, rail, weep, grieve, kick; *antonym* (*v*) compliment.

merimeri 1. infant; *synonyms* (*n*) baby, babe, child, minor, nursling, kid, toddler, (*adj*) juvenile, young, **2.** toddler; *synonyms* (*n*) infant, tot, bambino, newborn, yearling, adolescent, teen, teenager.

meroa slurp; *synonyms* (*n*) gulp, mouthful, swig, taste, draft, glug, (*v*) sip, swallow, eat, down, drink, imbibe, investigate, pry.

meromero 1. suck; *synonyms* (*v*) draw, drink, imbibe, nurse, absorb, lactate, suckle, drain, puff, aspirate, pull, breastfeed, (*n*) sucking, suction, **2.** slurp; *synonyms* (*n*) gulp, mouthful, swig, taste, draft, glug, (*v*) sip, swallow, eat, down, investigate, pry, **3.** sip; *synonyms* (*n*) nip, bite, drop, shot, slurp, nibble, (*v*) sample, quaff, lap, test, try, (*adj*) sup, **4.** taste; *synonyms* (*n*) bit, flavor, liking, morsel, penchant, appetite, fondness, gusto, predilection, preference, refinement, (*v*) relish, savor, smack, discernment; *antonyms* (*n*) dislike, tastelessness.

mi dream; *synonyms* (*n*) daydream, aspiration, ambition, vision, desire, fantasy, figment, nightmare, reverie, sleep, coma, trance, notion, (*v*) imagine, muse; *antonym* (*n*) reality.

mia dream; *synonyms* (*n*) daydream, aspiration, ambition, vision, desire, fantasy, figment, nightmare, reverie, sleep, coma, trance, notion, (*v*) imagine, muse; *antonym* (*n*) reality.

miakina 1. enchanted; *synonyms* (*adj*) bewitched, charmed, delighted, fascinated, rapt, blissful, elated, enamored, happy, magical, pleased, possessed, dreamlike, (*v*) entranced, overjoyed; *antonym* (*adj*) prosaic, **2.** enraptured; *synonyms* (*adj*) ecstatic, rapturous, captive, absorbed, confined, ecstasy, engrossed, infatuated, intoxicated, joyful, jubilant, rhapsodic, enwrapped, imprisoned, (prep) enrapt.

mika 1. burning; *synonyms* (adj) ardent, ablaze, afire, blazing, boiling, flaming, hot, passionate, aflame, alight, (n) combustion, firing, glowing, zealous, burn; *antonyms* (adj) cold, cool, trivial, **2.** hot; *synonyms* (adj) warm, burning, feverish, fiery, fresh, blistering, eager, enthusiastic, fast, peppery, pungent, spicy, angry, new, acrid; *antonyms* (adj) mild, freezing, airy, bland, chilly.

mim 1. urinate; *synonyms* (v) pee, piddle, micturate, piss, excrete, make, urine, addle, build, cause, clear, constitute, construct, cook, **2.** pee; *synonyms* (n) peeing, (v) urinate, wee.

mimi 1. contemplate; *synonyms* (v) consider, cogitate, meditate, muse, speculate, deliberate, look, ponder, reflect, gaze, behold, entertain, intend, mull, reason, **2.** marvel; *synonyms* (n) wonder, prodigy, curiosity, phenomenon, amazement, miracle, portent, (v) admire, **3.** admire; *synonyms* (v) love, revere, idolize, adore, appreciate, esteem, praise, worship, honor, like, laud, cherish, regard, commend, eulogize; *antonyms* (v) criticize, despise, loathe, scorn, **4.** strange; *synonyms* (adj) extraneous, foreign, peculiar, abnormal, curious, extraordinary, irregular, mysterious, new, odd, outlandish, unusual, rare, alien, anomalous; *antonyms* (adj) normal, ordinary, familiar, typical, **5.** urinate; *synonyms* (v) pee, piddle, micturate, piss, excrete, make, urine, addle, attain, build, cause, clear, constitute, construct, cook, **6.** wonder; *synonyms* (v) query, question, gape, (n) marvel, admiration, astonishment, surprise, wonderment, appreciation, awe, oddity, disbelief, shock, approval, curio.

mimiaki admired; *synonyms* (adj) esteemed, respected, accepted, beloved, estimable, favorite, honored, pet, popular, revered, valuable, valued, cherished, fashionable, indulged.

miminota turn; *synonyms* (v) revolve, deviate, get, revolution, (n) bend, curve, roll, coil, go, twist, bout, change, round, bent, circle.

miminotaki turned; *synonyms* (adj) off, sour, curved, rancid, twisted, altered, askew, awry, bent, bowed, cancelled, crooked, dark, deflected, dour.

mimioua 1. coiled; *synonyms* (adj) curled, spiral, curved, bent, bowed, curly, kinky, round, tortile, twisting, wavy, arched, corkscrew, rounded, (v) helical; *antonym* (adj) straight, **2.** twisted; *synonyms* (adj) crooked, deformed, perverted, distorted, coiled, misshapen, contorted, twined, winding, wry, gnarled, tortuous, awry, wrong, warped; *antonym* (adj) tidy, **3.** twist; *synonyms* (n) twine, wind, spin, twirl, entwine, (v) turn, bend, distort, curl, coil, contort, deform, curve, pervert, wrench; *antonyms* (v) straighten, untwist.

mimiouaki twisted; *synonyms* (adj) crooked, deformed, perverted, bent, distorted, coiled, misshapen, contorted, curved, twined, winding, wry, gnarled, tortuous, awry; *antonyms* (adj) straight, tidy.

mimitang imposing; *synonyms* (v) impressive, (adj) grand, dignified, noble, grandiose, stately, distinguished, baronial, lofty, regal, awesome, exalted, (n) commanding, solemn, grave; *antonym* (adj) humble.

mimitoi 1. turning; *synonyms* (adj) revolving, rotating, rotary, spinning, wheeling, winding, (n) turn, revolution, bend, deviation, conversion, diversion, version, **2.** whirling; *synonyms* (adj) swirling, dizzy, giddy, lightheaded, (n) gyration, rotation, **3.** whirl; *synonyms* (n) wheel, twist, crack, fling, go, vortex, commotion, pass, (v) spin, twirl, eddy, roll, reel, swirl, gyrate, **4.** turn; *synonyms* (v) revolve, deviate, get, become, (n) curve, coil, bout, change, round, bent, circle, shift, tour, curl, bow, **5.** spinning; *synonyms* (adj) turning, whirling, gyratory, spiraling, (n) spinstry, circulation, **6.** spin; *synonyms* (n) whirl, ride, tailspin, (v) run, drive, fabricate, invent, narrate, pivot, recite, recount, rotate, tell, birl, pluck.

mimitoiaki 1. turned; *synonyms* (adj) off, sour, curved, rancid, twisted, altered, askew, awry, bent, bowed, cancelled, crooked, dark, deflected, dour, **2.** overwhelmed; *synonyms* (v) overborne, (adj) overcome, beaten, overpowered, vanquished, conquered, dumbfounded, engulfed, flooded, inundated, overthrown; *antonyms* (adj) victorious, unimpressed.

mimitong 1. impressive; *synonyms* (adj) forcible, effective, commanding, imposing, powerful, striking, awesome, efficacious, exciting, formidable, influential, massive, memorable, (n) grand, noble; *antonyms* (adj) unimpressive, humble, ordinary, weak, **2.** glorious; *synonyms* (adj) famous, distinguished, bright, brilliant, celebrated, illustrious, eminent, great, magnificent, splendid, super, proud, resplendent, superb, lofty, **3.** dignified; *synonyms* (adj) exalted, majestic, respectable, high, lordly, solemn, manly, courtly, elevated, grave, impressive, magisterial, sedate, stately, sublime; *antonyms* (adj) humiliating, undignified, **4.** grand; *synonyms* (adj) excellent, gorgeous, dignified, important, beautiful, big, chief, fine, heroic, huge, immense, vast, spectacular, (n) glorious, earnest; *antonym* (adj) modest, **5.** regal; *synonyms* (adj) imperial, purple, royal, kingly, princely, pompous, **6.** radiant; *synonyms* (adj) beaming, beamy, effulgent, luminous, lucid, glowing, incandescent, refulgent, shining, shiny, sunny, glad, cheerful, (v) glittering, lustrous; *antonym* (adj) dull, **7.** splendid; *synonyms* (adj) gallant, admirable, good, luxurious, costly, grandiose, exquisite, lovely, marvelous, regal, sumptuous, capital, palatial, relucent, sparkling; *antonym* (adj) poor, **8.** resplendent; *synonyms* (adj) radiant, flamboyant, dazzling, clear, showy, silver.

minita pastor; *synonyms* (n) clergyman, minister, ecclesiastic, cleric, divine, curate, parson, priest, churchman, chaplain, presbyter, rector, father, hierophant.

miniti minute; *synonyms* (n) instant, flash, jiffy, note, memorandum, moment, second, (adj) little, delicate, microscopic, atomic, careful, circumstantial, diminutive, elaborate; *antonyms* (adj) enormous, huge, big, gigantic.

mino 1. confuse; *synonyms* (v) bewilder, baffle, confound, muddle, agitate, blur, derange, disconcert, disturb, fluster, jumble, mystify, obscure, perplex, puzzle; *antonyms* (v) clarify, enlighten, elucidate, explain, **2.** embroiled; *synonyms* (adj) involved, entangled, **3.** embroil; *synonyms* (v) confuse, implicate, tangle, complicate, disorder, entangle, involve, snarl, drag, **4.** disorderly; *synonyms* (adj) confused, chaotic, disordered, wild, boisterous, disobedient, disorganized, irregular, jumbled, rowdy, tumultuous, turbulent, unruly, untidy, (v) lawless; *antonyms* (adj) orderly, well-behaved, neat, arranged, **5.** entangled; *synonyms* (adj) complicated, intricate, embroiled, complex, foul, matted, tangled; *antonym* (adj) free, **6.** disorder; *synonyms* (n) ailment, complaint, clutter, disease, chaos, commotion, confusion, disarrangement, disturbance, anarchy, derangement, (v) disarray, perturb, disarrange, discompose; *antonyms* (n) orderliness, calm, peace, (v) order, **7.** entangle; *synonyms* (v) embrangle, enmesh, entwine, catch, ensnare, entrap, knot, mat, ensnarl, distract, intertwine, (n) embroil, (adj) embarrass, encumber, ravel; *antonym* (v) disentangle, **8.** disordered; *synonyms* (adj) broken, deranged, incoherent, messy, sick, upset, disconnected, disjointed, disorderly, ill, mixed, muddled, scattered, discontinuous; *antonym* (adj) ordered, **9.** file; *synonyms* (n) archive, document, list, procession, rank, record, roll, series, string, (v) rasp, register, scrape, abrade, arrange, grind, **10.** revolve; *synonyms* (v) reel, consider, deliberate, meditate, ponder, circle, circulate, contemplate, orbit, return, rotate, spin, wheel, debate, (n) gyrate, **11.** rotate; *synonyms* (v) revolve, alternate, swing, pivot, turn, twirl, twist, **12.** rotated; *synonym* (adj) revolved, **13.** swivel; *synonyms* (n) hinge, axis, falconet, jingal, **14.** twist; *synonyms* (n) twine, wind, braid, kink, loop, (v) bend, distort, curl, coil, contort, deform, curve, pervert, wrench, pull; *antonyms* (v) straighten, untwist.

minoa file; *synonyms* (n) archive, document, list, procession, rank, record, roll, series, string, (v) order, rasp, register, scrape, abrade, arrange.

minoaki 1. embroiled; *synonyms* (adj) involved, entangled, **2.** confused; *synonyms* (adj) abashed, bewildered, baffled, befuddled, bemused, chaotic, confounded, disjointed, disordered, dizzy, incoherent, indistinct, ambiguous, (n) cloudy, (adv, adj) topsy-turvy; *antonyms* (adj) clear, enlightened, alert, clearheaded, clear-headed, orderly, **3.** entangled; *synonyms* (adj) complicated, intricate, embroiled, complex, foul, matted, tangled; *antonym* (adj) free, **4.** disordered; *synonyms* (adj) confused, broken, deranged, disorganized, messy, sick, upset, disconnected, disorderly, ill, jumbled, mixed, muddled, scattered, untidy; *antonyms* (adj) neat, ordered, **5.** revolved; *synonyms* (adj) rotated, disgusted, **6.** rotated; *synonym* (adj) revolved, **7.** twisted; *synonyms* (adj) crooked, deformed, perverted, bent, distorted, coiled, misshapen, contorted, curved, twined, winding, wry, gnarled, tortuous, awry; *antonyms* (adj) straight, tidy.

minomino 1. gyrate; *synonyms* (v) spin, whirl, circle, gyre, revolve, roll, turn, wheel, circulate, reel, rotate, spiral, twirl, coil, **2.** roll; *synonyms* (n) list, revolution, catalogue, inventory, register, (v) curl, enfold, rock, twist, wallow, wind, envelop, grumble, round, level, **3.** twirl; *synonyms* (n) eddy, rotation, loop, kink, (v) swirl, twiddle, pivot, bend, gyrate, circuit, swivel, birl, circumbendibus, flourish, (adj) twine.

minominoaki rolled; *synonyms* (adj) rolling, furled, involute, beaten, billowing, kinky, level, resonant, resonating, resounding, reverberating, reverberative, spiral, trilled, tumbling.

minominota revolve; *synonyms* (v) reel, consider, deliberate, meditate, ponder, circle, circulate, contemplate, orbit, return, rotate, spin, wheel, (n) gyrate, roll.

minominotaki revolved; *synonyms* (adj) rotated, disgusted.

minota 1. roll; *synonyms* (n) list, revolution, catalogue, inventory, register, (v) coil, reel, curl, enfold, revolve, wheel, rock, turn, twist, wallow, **2.** twist; *synonyms* (n) twine, wind, spin, twirl, entwine, braid, kink, loop, (v) bend, distort, contort, deform, curve, pervert, wrench; *antonyms* (v) straighten, untwist, **3.** spin; *synonyms* (n) whirl, roll, ride, eddy, rotation, (v) run, drive, fabricate, gyrate, invent, narrate, pivot, recite, recount, rotate, **4.** turn; *synonyms* (v) deviate, get, become, convert, deflect, (n) go, bout, change, round, bent, circle, shift, tour, bow, move.

minotaki 1. giddy; *synonyms* (adj) frivolous, flighty, dizzy, faint, silly, changeable, featherbrained, fickle, light, vertiginous, capricious, vacillating, bewildered, (adv) careless, rash, **2.** featherbrained; *synonyms* (adj) giddy, airheaded, harebrained, cockamamie, cockamamy, dizzily, empty-headed, lightheaded, scatterbrained, shallow, flippant, giddily, lightsomely, pathetic, ridiculous, **3.** fickle; *synonyms* (adj) erratic, volatile, inconsistent, mercurial, mobile, variable, changeful, inconstant, shifting, skittish, unfaithful, unstable, irresolute, unpredictable, faithless; *antonyms* (adj) resolute, untiring, **4.** flighty; *synonyms* (adj) irresponsible, flyaway, thoughtless, wild, **5.** eccentric; *synonyms* (adj) bizarre, odd, wacky, abnormal, anomalous, crazy, irregular, outlandish, peculiar, strange, droll, comical, kinky, (n) character, case; *antonyms* (adj) normal, ordinary, (n) conformist, **6.** capricious; *synonyms* (adj) arbitrary, fanciful, freakish, whimsical, fantastic, impulsive, moody, aimless, unreliable, eccentric, fitful, temperamental, uncertain, unsettled, wayward; *antonyms* (adj) constant, dependable, predictable, **7.** dizzy; *synonyms* (adj) dazed, muzzy, unsteady, woozy, (v) daze; *antonyms* (adj) alert, clear-headed, **8.** frivolous; *synonyms* (adj) empty, foolish, idle, petty, childish, facetious, superficial, trifling, trivial, unimportant, small, airy, inane, stupid, vacuous; *antonyms* (adj) serious, important, **9.** twisted; *synonyms* (adj) crooked, deformed, perverted, bent, distorted, coiled, misshapen, contorted, curved, twined, winding, wry, gnarled, tortuous, awry; *antonyms* (adj) straight, tidy, **10.** rolled; *synonyms* (adj) rolling, furled, involute, beaten, billowing, level, resonant, resonating, resounding, reverberating, reverberative, spiral, trilled, tumbling, **11.** unsettled; *synonyms* (adj) doubtful, undecided, unfixed, indefinite, uneasy, outstanding, disturbed, undetermined, unpaid, unresolved, restless, indecisive, dubious, open, roving; *antonyms* (adj) settled, confident, definite, **12.** reeling; *synonyms* (n) titubation, (adj) fuddled, groggy, intoxicated, queer, tipsy, **13.** turned; *synonyms* (adj) off, sour, rancid, twisted, altered, askew, bowed, cancelled, dark, deflected, dour, dull, false, glowering, glum.

minotia 1. involve; *synonyms* (v) imply, contain, affect, embrace, entail, implicate, comprise, complicate, demand, encompass, engage, envelop, include, tangle, (n) entangle; *antonym* (v) exclude, **2.** involving; *synonyms* (prep) between, connecting, linking, concerning, relating, **3.** twine; *synonyms* (n) coil, string, cord, rope, thread, (v) wind, entwine, lace, enlace, interlace, intertwine, meander, twist, weave, braid; *antonym* (v) untwist, **4.** turn; *synonyms* (v) revolve, deviate, get, revolution, spin, (n) bend, curve, roll, go, bout, change, round, bent, circle, shift, **5.** twirl; *synonyms* (n) turn, whirl, eddy, rotation, loop, (v) curl, swirl, twiddle, wheel, pivot, gyrate, reel,

rotate, circuit, (adj) twine, **6.** rotate; *synonyms* (v) alternate, swing, orbit, twirl, circulate, **7.** twist; *synonyms* (n) kink, strain, convolution, crook, (v) distort, contort, deform, pervert, wrench, pull, sprain, bias, convolute, garble, squirm; *antonym* (v) straighten.

minotiaki 1. involved; *synonyms* (adj) complex, intricate, complicated, convoluted, tortuous, confused, difficult, elaborate, engaged, entangled, interested, knotty, obscure, tangled, knotted; *antonyms* (adj) simple, aloof, detached, straightforward, **2.** rotated; *synonym* (adj) revolved, **3.** turned; *synonyms* (adj) off, sour, curved, rancid, twisted, altered, askew, awry, bent, bowed, cancelled, crooked, dark, deflected, dour, **4.** twisted; *synonyms* (adj) deformed, perverted, distorted, coiled, misshapen, contorted, twined, winding, wry, gnarled, kinky, wrong, warped, depraved, malformed; *antonyms* (adj) straight, tidy, **5.** twined; *synonym* (adj) misrepresented.

mirion million; *synonyms* (n) meg, myriad, heap, mint.

miroa 1. cherish; *synonyms* (v) appreciate, entertain, foster, hug, nurture, treasure, cultivate, bosom, adore, esteem, harbor, nourish, nurse, prize, (n) embrace; *antonym* (v) hate, **2.** admire; *synonyms* (v) love, revere, idolize, praise, wonder, worship, honor, like, laud, cherish, regard, commend, eulogize, look, marvel; *antonyms* (v) criticize, despise, loathe, scorn.

miroaki 1. cherished; *synonyms* (adj) beloved, dear, precious, loved, treasured, intimate, prized, valued, wanted, pet, **2.** admired; *synonyms* (adj) esteemed, respected, accepted, favorite, honored, popular, revered, valuable, cherished, fashionable, indulged, petted, trendy, venerated.

mitara 1. hallucinate; *synonyms* (v) dream, daydream, fantasize, envisage, fancy, imagine, visualize, blunder, err, think, wander, **2.** daydream; *synonyms* (n) fantasy, reverie, revery, vision, daydreaming, hope, (v) moon; *antonym* (n) reality, **3.** dream; *synonyms* (n) aspiration, ambition, desire, figment, nightmare, sleep, coma, trance, notion, delusion, dreaming, phantom, conceit, (v) muse, contemplate, **4.** muse; *synonyms* (n) study, (v) meditate, cogitate, consider, deliberate, ponder, reflect, brood, ruminate, speculate, mull, puzzle, mediate.

mka 1. corrupt; *synonyms* (adj) bad, rotten, canker, dishonest, evil, impure, (n) poison, (v) adulterate, contaminate, taint, bribe, debase, defile, infect, buy; *antonyms* (adj) honest, moral, principled, pure, **2.** decayed; *synonyms* (adj) corrupt, dilapidated, rank, wasted, decaying, old, putrid, rotted, rotting, rusty, behindhand, (v) stale; *antonym* (adj) fresh, **3.** decomposed; *synonyms* (adj) decayed, malodorous, off, corroded, decomposing, disintegrating, fetid, fusty, moldy, musty, perished, rancid, **4**. spoiled; *synonyms* (*adj*) coddled, pampered, damaged, spoilt; *antonym* (*adj*) first-rate, **5**. rotten; *synonyms* (*adj*) foul, poor, lousy, ill, shabby, crappy, decomposed, sour, stinking, terrible, mean, vicious, low, treacherous, (*v*) weak.

mmani thin; *synonyms* (*adj*) flimsy, gaunt, lean, light, slight, tenuous, emaciated, fine, rare, slim, sparse, (*v*) slender, dilute, meager, sheer; *antonyms* (*adj*) thick, fat, concentrated, chubby, plump, wide, broad, heavy, (*v*) thicken.

mmanibwerebwere skinny; *synonyms* (*adj*) lean, meager, emaciated, scrawny, thin, gaunt, scraggy, underweight, weedy, lank, angular, slender, slight, spare, (*v*) cortical; *antonyms* (*adj*) fat, plump, brawny, well-built.

moa 1. chicken; *synonyms* (*n*) chick, cock, coward, fowl, hen, crybaby, nestling, poultry, weakling, wimp, (*adj*) yellow, chickenhearted, **2**. chief; *synonyms* (*adj*) head, principal, cardinal, capital, arch, central, essential, first, main, (*n*) administrator, boss, captain, executive, leader, paramount; *antonyms* (*adj*) minor, associate, secondary, **3**. firstly; *synonyms* (*adv*) foremost, initially, originally, basically, formerly; *antonym* (*adv*) lastly, **4**. exceed; *synonyms* (*v*) beat, pass, surpass, outdo, surmount, transcend, cap, outshine, outweigh, overrun, top, excel, outgo, outmatch, (*adj*) better, **5**. better; *synonyms* (*adj*) superior, (*n*) bettor, (*v*) amend, improve, best, mend, recover, advance, ameliorate, emend, reform, enhance, exceed, refine, benefit; *antonyms* (*adj*) lesser, (*adv*) worse, (*n*) inferior, (*v*) worsen, **6**. initial; *synonyms* (*adj*) beginning, elementary, incipient, preliminary, primary, rudimentary, commencing, early, introductory, leading, opening, original, (*n*) alpha, (*v*) sign, **7**. first; *synonyms* (*adv*) before, rather, firstly, (*adj*) chief, primitive, former, forward, initial, maiden, premier, front, aboriginal, dominant, fundamental, (*n*) commencement; *antonyms* (*adj*) last, final, (*n*) end, **8**. initially; *synonym* (*adv*) primarily, **9**. central; *synonyms* (*adj*) basic, crucial, important, inner, key, pivotal, centrical, core, critical, focal, halfway, intermediate, major, (*n*) umbilical, exchange; *antonyms* (*adj*) peripheral, regional, tangential, **10**. excel; *synonyms* (*v*) eclipse, lead, overshadow, **11**. surmount; *synonyms* (*v*) overcome, conquer, defeat, master, subdue, climb, outstrip, vanquish, scale, overpower, negotiate, overwhelm, reduce, subjugate, hurdle, **12**. primary; *synonyms* (*adj*) primal, basal, primeval, primordial, highest, base, overriding, vital, direct, elemental, firsthand, staple, ultimate, (*n*) prime, radical, **13**. primarily; *synonyms* (*adv*) chiefly, mainly, principally, largely, especially, essentially, mostly, generally, **14**. start;

synonyms (*v*) begin, originate, commence, drive, launch, embark, spring, activate, arise, enter, (*n*) jump, onset, origin, shock, dawn; *antonyms* (*v*) finish, stop, conclude, halt, (*n*) conclusion, **15**. transcend; *synonyms* (*v*) overstep, hand, spend, (*adj*) soar, tower, **16**. prevalent; *synonyms* (*adj*) common, general, predominant, popular, rife, extensive, ascendant, epidemic, pervasive, ruling, widespread, rampant, regnant, (*n*) current, (*v*) prevailing, **17**. surpass; *synonyms* (*v*) break, overreach, go, outdistance, overtake, transgress, circumvent, outrank, rival, overhaul, outperform, die, elapse, happen, occur.

mo'aiine hen; *synonyms* (*n*) fowl, cock, chicken, biddy, rooster, poultry, mare, roe, sow, chick, partlet, capon, ruff.

moakakung 1. despised; *synonyms* (*adj*) detested, scorned, despicable, hated, abject, abhorrent, contemptible, contemptuous, loathed, opprobrious, reviled, unpopular, infamous, insolent, insufferable, **2**. detested; *synonyms* (*adj*) despised, disliked, ostracized; *antonym* (*adj*) popular, **3**. unwelcome; *synonyms* (*adj*) undesirable, unwanted, disagreeable, objectionable, unasked, unwished, unintroduced, uninvited, unvisited, (*n*) unsatisfactory; *antonyms* (*adj*) welcome, desirable, longed-for, **4**. unwanted; *synonyms* (*adj*) unwelcome, needless, superfluous, redundant, leftover; *antonym* (*adj*) wanted.

moaki surmounted; *synonym* (*adj*) beaten.

moakura ugly; *synonyms* (*adj*) nasty, disagreeable, forbidding, frightful, gruesome, hideous, homely, repulsive, surly, evil, offensive, atrocious, deformed, despicable, grotesque; *antonyms* (*adj*) beautiful, attractive, good-looking, flowing, ornamental.

moan incipient; *synonyms* (*adj*) inchoate, initial, introductory, budding, commencing, first, undeveloped, basic, fundamental, originating, (*v*) inceptive.

moana 1. enter; *synonyms* (*v*) enlist, embark, enroll, book, chronicle, record, input, arrive, come, accede, attack, begin, board, enrol, insert; *antonyms* (*v*) leave, depart, delete, exit, **2**. inaugurate; *synonyms* (*v*) commence, initiate, install, introduce, launch, enter, induct, institute, open, originate, start, create, establish, crown, found, **3**. embark; *synonyms* (*v*) ship, sail, undertake, venture, emplane, adventure, approach, imbark, inship, entrain, figure, guess, hazard, infix, inscribe; *antonym* (*v*) disembark, **4**. begin; *synonyms* (*v*) arise, become, rise, dawn, build, happen, induce, attempt, bring, broach, cause, develop, get, grow, instigate; *antonyms* (*v*) finish, end, stop, **5**. make; *synonyms* (*v*) construct, do, fashion, force, give, produce, let, compel, constitute, design, drive, erect, execute, fabricate, (*n*) form; *antonyms* (*v*) destroy, lose, **6.** cause; *synonyms* (*n*) case, action, occasion, account, basis, campaign, excuse, lawsuit, (*v*) make, breed, allow, arouse, beget, engender, inspire; *antonym* (*n*) consequence, **7.** continue; *synonyms* (*v*) abide, remain, endure, keep, persevere, sustain, bide, be, extend, last, maintain, persist, preserve, (*n*) hold, (*adj*) prolong; *antonyms* (*v*) cease, discontinue, **8.** launch; *synonyms* (*n*) boat, inauguration, initiation, launching, introduction, (*v*) dart, fire, toss, hurl, inaugurate, cast, fling, shoot, throw, discharge, **9.** start; *synonyms* (*v*) spring, activate, flinch, set, startle, actuate, break, (*n*) jump, onset, origin, shock, beginning, commencement, leap, source; *antonyms* (*v*) conclude, halt, (*n*) conclusion, **10.** open; *synonyms* (*adj*) frank, obvious, artless, exposed, free, honest, bare, forthright, guileless, ingenuous, naked, direct, (*v*) expand, (*n*) candid, clear; *antonyms* (*adj*) devious, secretive, concealed, furtive, hidden, limited, repressive, reserved, restricted, secret, blocked, cautious, closed, (*v*) shut, (*tr v*) close, **11.** resume; *synonyms* (*v*) recover, continue, regain, restart, summarize, outline, revert, adopt, renew, (*n*) digest, synopsis, abstract, summary, epitome, recapitulation.

moanaki 1. made; *synonyms* (*adj*) finished, built, ready, constructed, formed, prepared, synthetic, bound, complete, completed, ended, fictitious, rabid, through, **2.** continued; *synonyms* (*adj*) continuous, constant, continual, extended, unremitting, serial, continuate, eternal, long, perpetual, protracted, recurrent, solid, undivided, untiring, **3.** opened; *synonyms* (*v*) blown, distended, exhausted, inflated, stale, (*adj*) open, candid, exposed, assailable, blatant, blazing, clear, conspicuous, lawless, loose.

moanang 1. begin; *synonyms* (*v*) commence, start, arise, become, enter, initiate, originate, rise, create, dawn, embark, found, institute, introduce, open; *antonyms* (*v*) finish, end, stop, **2.** commence; *synonyms* (*v*) begin, inaugurate, launch, approach, develop, get, undertake, **3.** undertake; *synonyms* (*v*) attempt, try, accept, contract, covenant, guarantee, tackle, take, assume, assure, engage, promise, endeavor, seek, do.

moanangia 1. begin; *synonyms* (*v*) commence, start, arise, become, enter, initiate, originate, rise, create, dawn, embark, found, institute, introduce, open; *antonyms* (*v*) finish, end, stop, **2.** attempt; *synonyms* (*n*) try, endeavor, assay, effort, essay, offer, trial, attack, assault, adventure, bid, (*v*) struggle, aim, chance, undertake.

moangare smile; *synonyms* (*n*) grin, grinning, smiling, expression, luck, (*v*) beam, laugh, chuckle, grimace, sneer, countenance, favor, propitiousness; *antonym* (*v*) frown.

moaniba 1. cream; *synonyms* (*n*) pick, ointment, prime, balm, top, liniment, elite, fat, salve, unguent, (*adj*) flower, milk, (*v*) best, skim, ream, **2.** first; *synonyms* (*adv*) foremost, before, rather, early, (*adj*) beginning, chief, primitive, former, forward, head, initial, leading, maiden, opening, (*n*) commencement; *antonyms* (*adj*) last, final, (*n*) end, **3.** finest; *synonyms* (*adj*) excellent, select, classic, exclusive, greatest, optimal, paramount, preeminent, quality, superlative, unsurpassed, (*n*) cream; *antonym* (*adj*) worst, **4.** elite; *synonyms* (*n*) aristocracy, nobility, prize, (*adj*) elect, choice, **5.** best; *synonyms* (*adj*) better, superior, supreme, great, superb, extreme, first, (*v*) beat, outdo, overcome, outshine, conquer, defeat, (*n*) most, maximum, **6.** favorite; *synonyms* (*adj*) favored, favourite, beloved, dear, (*n*) darling, pet, preference, competitor, dearie, deary, ducky; *antonyms* (*n*) loser, indifference, **7.** flower; *synonyms* (*n*) bouquet, efflorescence, floret, florescence, ornament, nosegay, flush, heyday, (*v*) bloom, blossom, blow, flourish, (*adj*) floral, fructify, flowery, **8.** premium; *synonyms* (*n*) bonus, agio, bounty, payment, extra, price, reward, agiotage; *antonym* (*adj*) inferior, **9.** optimum; *synonyms* (*adj*) all-out, handpicked, premium, baddest, capital, deluxe, flawless, gilt-edge, highest, luxury, matchless, peerless, perfect, (*n*) acme, **10.** pick; *synonyms* (*v*) clean, gather, harvest, opt, break, choose, collect, cull, draw, nibble, peck, (*n*) alternative, option, selection, (*adj*) mattock, **11.** unequaled; *synonyms* (*adj*) unparalleled, incomparable, unique, unequalled, unmatched, unrivaled, alone, only, **12.** ranking; *synonyms* (*n*) rank, rating, position, place, eminence, footing, hierarchy, mark, reputation, repute, scale, (*adj*) commanding, dominating, overlooking, peremptory, **13.** originally; *synonyms* (*adv*) primarily, primitively, firstly, initially, earlier, formerly, essentially, creatively, naturally, alternatively, autonomously, connaturally, eccentrically, freely, fundamentally, **14.** superlative; *synonyms* (*adj*) outstanding, consummate, magnificent, splendid, brilliant, sterling, ultimate, (*n*) peak, elevation, height, pinnacle, point, summit, **15.** premiere; *synonym* (*v*) premier, **16.** prime; *synonyms* (*adj*) main, essential, fundamental, primary, exquisite, overriding, grand, central, eminent, original, principal, (*n*) cardinal, (*v*) ground, coach, prepare; *antonym* (*adj*) minor.

moaningaina dawn; *synonyms* (*n*) beginning, commencement, aurora, cockcrow, morning, onset, origin, prime, start, sunrise, birth, (*v*) break, begin, appear, (*adj*) daybreak; *antonyms* (*n*) dusk, sunset, twilight, (*v*) end, finish.

---

moanna 1. begin; *synonyms* (*v*) commence, start, arise, become, enter, initiate, originate, rise, create, dawn, embark, found, institute, introduce, open; *antonyms* (*v*) finish, end, stop, **2.** won; *synonyms* (*v*) wan, (*n*) dwelling, wone, **3.** win; *synonyms* (*v*) acquire, gain, get, attain, obtain, conquer, achieve, earn, prevail, secure, take, succeed, carry, vanquish, (*n*) triumph; *antonyms* (*v*) lose, (*n*) defeat, **4.** start; *synonyms* (*v*) begin, drive, launch, spring, activate, flinch, set, (*n*) jump, onset, origin, shock, beginning, commencement, leap, source; *antonyms* (*v*) conclude, halt, (*n*) conclusion.

moannaki won; *synonyms* (*v*) wan, (*n*) dwelling, wone.

moantaai early; *synonyms* (*adj*) initial, first, primitive, prompt, young, quick, embryonic, matutinal, old, original, past, precocious, (*adv*) betimes, soon, earlier; *antonyms* (*adj*) delayed, last-minute, slow, (*adv*) late.

moantaia 1. gather; *synonyms* (*v*) deduce, convene, accumulate, amass, assemble, collect, compile, congregate, flock, garner, meet, tuck, earn, rally, (*n*) fold; *antonyms* (*v*) disperse, scatter, **2.** harvest; *synonyms* (*n*) crop, fruit, ingathering, produce, profit, yield, production, harvesting, (*v*) gain, gather, glean, get, pick, reap, acquire.

moantaiaki gathered; *synonyms* (*adj*) collected, deepened, accumulated, amassed, assembled, collective, congregate, equanimous, massed, poised.

moaraoi 1. comely; *synonyms* (*adj*) becoming, beautiful, decent, fair, good-looking, attractive, bonny, decorous, handsome, personable, proper, seemly, shapely, elegant, agreeable, **2.** amiable; *synonyms* (*adj*) affable, benign, complaisant, friendly, genial, charming, cordial, gentle, kind, likable, lovely, nice, pleasant, sweet, adorable; *antonyms* (*adj*) unfriendly, disagreeable, aggressive, argumentative, **3.** pleasing; *synonyms* (*adj*) acceptable, amiable, lovable, amusing, delightful, gratifying, inviting, artistic, engaging, enjoyable, merry, palatable, fine, favorable, grateful; *antonyms* (*adj*) annoying, unpleasant, unwelcome, disappointing, hurtful, infuriating, straight.

moatoki 1. contrite; *synonyms* (*adj*) apologetic, penitent, remorseful, repentant, sorry, regretful, rueful, bad, ashamed; *antonym* (*adj*) unrepentant, **2.** crestfallen; *synonyms* (*adj*) chapfallen, dejected, depressed, disconsolate, discouraged, dispirited, downcast, gloomy, chopfallen, downhearted, low, miserable, unhappy, **3.** abashed; *synonyms* (*adj*) bashful, discomfited, mortified, confused, embarrassed, sheepish; *antonym* (*adj*) brazen, **4.** shamed; *synonyms* (*adj*) disgraced, dishonored, discredited, guilty, hangdog, abashed, browbeaten, bullied, cowed, damaged, fallen, intimidated,

shamefaced, **5.** sheepish; *synonyms* (*adj*) coy, diffident, shy, nervous, skittish.

môg dog; *synonyms* (*n*) cur, andiron, blackguard, click, detent, cad, cock, (*v*) chase, hound, beset, hunt, tail, track, trail, course.

môgur 1. labor; *synonyms* (*n*) drudgery, effort, endeavor, exertion, travail, childbirth, grind, struggle, birth, business, (*v*) toil, confinement, delivery, drudge, labour; *antonym* (*v*) rest, **2.** task; *synonyms* (*n*) job, assignment, charge, commission, duty, enterprise, labor, project, stint, occupation, activity, chore, function, (*v*) tax, exercise, **3.** work; *synonyms* (*n*) employment, task, action, act, book, composition, (*v*) operate, cultivate, exploit, ferment, form, manipulate, operation, run, (*adj*) trade; *antonyms* (*v*) idle, malfunction.

mohoko dog; *synonyms* (*n*) cur, andiron, blackguard, click, detent, cad, cock, (*v*) chase, hound, beset, hunt, tail, track, trail, course.

moi drink; *synonyms* (*n*) beverage, alcohol, brew, potion, swallow, crapulence, intoxicant, nip, (*v*) draught, booze, carouse, bib, absorb, down, gulp.

moimoti 1. damage; *synonyms* (*n*) blemish, injury, wound, loss, cost, detriment, disadvantage, impairment, (*v*) harm, hurt, abuse, injure, afflict, disfigure, (*adj*) impair; *antonyms* (*v*) service, (*v*) conserve, enhance, repair, bolster, **2.** destroyed; *synonyms* (*adj*) lost, ruined, desolate, desolated, shattered, dead, depressed, **3.** broken; *synonyms* (*v*) broke, (*adj*) tame, torn, busted, imperfect, intermittent, rough, rugged, uneven, disjointed, incomplete, confused, cracked, crushed, disconnected; *antonyms* (*adj*) constant, unbroken, intact, whole, wild.

moimotiaki damaged; *synonyms* (*adj*) faulty, unsound, defective, broken, dilapidated, hurt, impaired, besmirched, deficient, flyblown; *antonym* (*adj*) undamaged.

moimotikia 1. break; *synonyms* (*v*) split, crack, burst, fail, infringe, leak, (*n*) breach, fracture, pause, rupture, stop, collapse, interruption, respite, suspension; *antonyms* (*v*) repair, obey, honor, mend, (*n*) continuation, **2.** tear; *synonyms* (*n*) rent, hole, (*v*) break, rip, pull, rend, lacerate, race, run, rush, slit, rive, cleave, dash, fly.

moimotikiaki broken; *synonyms* (*v*) broke, (*adj*) tame, torn, busted, imperfect, intermittent, rough, rugged, ruined, uneven, disjointed, incomplete, confused, cracked, crushed; *antonyms* (*adj*) constant, unbroken, intact, whole, wild.

moko 1. smoke; *synonyms* (*n*) fumes, fog, mist, perfume, smoking, smoulder, (*v*) fume, reek, fumigate, puff, exhale, cure, burn, smolder, (*adj*) smudge, **2.** rotten; *synonyms* (*adj*) bad, foul, poor, fetid, lousy, musty, off, putrid, ill, shabby, corrupt, crappy, decomposed, (v) decayed, rancid; *antonym* (*adj*) fresh.

mona 1. filthy; *synonyms* (*adj*) dirty, dingy, foul, nasty, unclean, disgusting, squalid, bawdy, awful, grimy, grubby, impure, indecent, muddy, ribald; *antonyms* (*adj*) clean, decent, **2.** whimper; *synonyms* (*n*) whine, cry, moan, (v) wail, sob, weep, howl, pule, snivel, groan, blubber, complain, mewl, sigh, bleat, **3.** slimy; *synonyms* (*adj*) greasy, slippery, oily, oozy, ropy, viscous, slimed, **4.** wet; *synonyms* (*adj*) damp, humid, drenched, moist, soaked, sodden, dank, rainy, saturated, soggy, (v) moisten, water, dampen, wash, (*n*) moisture; *antonyms* (*adj*) dehydrated, parched, (v) dry, **5.** sticky; *synonyms* (*adj*) adhesive, awkward, clammy, muggy, embarrassing, glutinous, gummy, difficult, slimy, gluey, gooey, hard, mucilaginous, pasty, sultry; *antonyms* (*adj*) fresh, easy.

monamona slimy; *synonyms* (*adj*) greasy, slippery, muddy, squalid, oily, oozy, ropy, viscous, slimed.

monei iron; *synonyms* (*n*) chain, irons, chains, (v) firm, flatten, press, smooth, (*adj*) hard, adamant, inflexible, steel, tenacious.

monota revolve; *synonyms* (*v*) reel, consider, deliberate, meditate, ponder, circle, circulate, contemplate, orbit, return, rotate, spin, wheel, (*n*) gyrate, roll.

monotaki revolved; *synonyms* (*adj*) rotated, disgusted.

montaua whimper; *synonyms* (*n*) whine, cry, moan, (v) wail, sob, weep, howl, pule, snivel, groan, blubber, complain, mewl, sigh, bleat.

mooi 1. drunk; *synonyms* (*adj*) intoxicated, tipsy, tight, wet, inebriated, delirious, high, (*n*) inebriate, drunkard, rummy, sot; *antonym* (*adj*) sober, **2.** drink; *synonyms* (*n*) beverage, alcohol, brew, potion, swallow, crapulence, intoxicant, nip, (v) draught, booze, carouse, bib, absorb, down, gulp, **3.** imbibe; *synonyms* (*v*) drink, suck, engulf, assimilate, consume, draw, quaff, guzzle, adopt, engross, admit, have, ingest, receive, sip.

mori 1. bruised; *synonyms* (*adj*) contused, wounded, hurt, raw, sore, contusioned, discolored, inflamed, lame, livid, painful, rotten, sensitive, surbet, tender, **2.** bent; *synonyms* (*adj*) arched, curved, bended, crooked, deformed, intent, (*n*) aptitude, inclination, propensity, fancy, ability, bias, flair, gift, leaning; *antonym* (*adj*) straight, **3.** tender; *synonyms* (*adj*) affectionate, loving, soft, compassionate, delicate, fond, gentle, mild, frail, (v) proffer, present, propose, (*n*) offer, bid, overture; *antonyms* (*adj*) tough, hard, hardhearted, rubbery, rough, **4.** overripe; *synonyms* (*adj*) decadent, effete, decayed, degenerate, fracid, overmellow, **5.** soft; *synonyms* (*adj*) easy, light, limp, balmy, quiet, slack, loose, clement, faint, flabby, flaccid, lenient, pliant, (v)

feeble, low; *antonyms* (*adj*) firm, harsh, loud, hoarse, solid, stiff, alcoholic, shrill, strong.

moringa 1. amiable; *synonyms* (*adj*) affable, agreeable, benign, complaisant, friendly, genial, charming, cordial, gentle, kind, likable, lovely, nice, pleasant, sweet; *antonyms* (*adj*) unfriendly, disagreeable, aggressive, argumentative, **2.** charitable; *synonyms* (*adj*) merciful, benevolent, clement, bountiful, generous, humane, kindly, lenient, liberal, magnanimous, philanthropic, compassionate, forbearing, munificent, hospitable; *antonyms* (*adj*) unforgiving, mean, nasty, uncharitable, **3.** attentive; *synonyms* (*adj*) thoughtful, assiduous, diligent, heedful, observant, watchful, advertent, alert, aware, careful, considerate, mindful, vigilant, wary, devoted; *antonyms* (*adj*) inattentive, negligent, unfocused, forgetful, neglectful, heedless, **4.** nice; *synonyms* (*adj*) beautiful, dainty, fastidious, fine, good, neat, delicious, correct, decent, delicate, difficult, enjoyable, exact, particular, precise; *antonyms* (*adj*) unpleasant, horrible, **5.** kind; *synonyms* (*n*) form, helpful, sort, brand, breed, class, type, variety, description, manner, beneficent, (*adj*) affectionate, charitable, amiable, attentive; *antonyms* (*adj*) unkind, callous, cruel, hardhearted, merciless, spiteful, uncaring, upsetting, unfeeling, **6.** obliging; *synonyms* (*v*) civil, (*adj*) accommodating, compliant, courteous, gracious, cooperative, polite, good-natured, urbane, mild, neighborly, accommodative, caring, complying, docile; *antonyms* (*adj*) unhelpful, uncooperative, **7.** pleasant; *synonyms* (*adj*) bright, acceptable, jolly, facetious, attractive, cheerful, clear, comfortable, congenial, delightful, fair, joyful, joyous, mirthful, pleasing; *antonyms* (*adj*) disgusting, foul, gruesome, harsh, repugnant, shocking, terrible, unwelcome, appalling, discordant, frosty, grisly, rough.

morokaei immense; *synonyms* (*adj*) huge, vast, colossal, enormous, gigantic, great, immeasurable, big, boundless, giant, infinite, large, endless, extensive, extreme; *antonyms* (*adj*) small, tiny.

môt broken; *synonyms* (*v*) broke, (*adj*) tame, torn, busted, imperfect, intermittent, rough, rugged, ruined, uneven, disjointed, incomplete, confused, cracked, crushed; *antonyms* (*adj*) constant, unbroken, intact, whole, wild.

moti 1. interrupted; *synonyms* (*adj*) discontinuous, fitful, intermittent, (*prep*) broken; *antonym* (*adj*) constant, **2.** decided; *synonyms* (*v*) absolute, clear, positive, categorical, emphatic, marked, (*adj*) decisive, definite, determined, distinct, resolute, unmistakable, conclusive, fixed, peremptory; *antonym* (*adj*) undecided, **3.** finished; *synonyms* (*v*) done, (*adj*) complete, completed, ended, perfect, consummate, accomplished, polished, ripe, ruined, spent, round, capable, decided, (*adv*) over; *antonyms* (*adj*) unfinished, incomplete, remaining, rough, **4.** broken; *synonyms* (*v*) broke, (*adj*) tame, torn, busted, imperfect, rugged, uneven, disjointed, confused, cracked, crushed, disconnected, disordered, faulty, fractured; *antonyms* (*adj*) unbroken, intact, whole, wild, **5.** ended; *synonyms* (*adj*) concluded, finished, closed, past, terminated, through, **6.** terminated; *synonym* (*adj*) extinct, **7.** resolved; *synonyms* (*adj*) firm, set, certain, intent, final, solved, unyielding, bent, obstinate, **8.** regulated; *synonyms* (*adj*) orderly, ordered, arranged, consistent, lawful, logical, regular, regulatory, temperate, systematic, (*adv*) synchronized.

motibuaka misunderstood; *synonyms* (*adj*) confused, vague.

motika 1. break; *synonyms* (*v*) split, crack, burst, fail, infringe, leak, (*n*) breach, fracture, pause, rupture, stop, collapse, interruption, respite, suspension; *antonyms* (*v*) repair, obey, honor, mend, (*n*) continuation, **2.** determine; *synonyms* (*v*) ascertain, decide, define, resolve, appoint, adjudicate, conclude, measure, set, specify, designate, assign, decree, arrange, assess, **3.** decide; *synonyms* (*v*) choose, determine, judge, settle, try, arbitrate, fix, purpose, rule, select, deem, consider, adjust, end, figure; *antonym* (*v*) waver, **4.** snap; *synonyms* (*v*) bite, break, nip, clack, snarl, rap, rip, rive, bust, (*n*) photograph, catch, go, picnic, pushover, clasp, **5.** regulate; *synonyms* (*v*) manage, control, direct, order, govern, influence, modulate, regularize, align, check, correct, guide, organize, rectify, (*n*) form.

motikaki 1. determined; *synonyms* (*adj*) constant, decided, definite, resolute, certain, decisive, determinate, inflexible, resolved, stubborn, ambitious, adamant, bold, firm, obstinate; *antonyms* (*adj*) weak, irresolute, uncertain, feeble, unmotivated, **2.** broken; *synonyms* (*v*) broke, (*adj*) tame, torn, busted, imperfect, intermittent, rough, rugged, ruined, uneven, disjointed, incomplete, confused, cracked, crushed; *antonyms* (*adj*) unbroken, intact, whole, wild, **3.** decided; *synonyms* (*v*) absolute, clear, positive, categorical, emphatic, marked, (*adj*) determined, distinct, unmistakable, conclusive, fixed, peremptory, unequivocal, final, finished; *antonym* (*adj*) undecided, **4.** regulated; *synonyms* (*adj*) orderly, ordered, arranged, consistent, lawful, logical, regular, regulatory, temperate, systematic, (*adv*) synchronized, **5.** snapped; *synonym* (*adj*) tight.

motikana finally; *synonyms* (*adv*) eventually, lastly, last, ultimately, definitely, completely, (*adj*) final, (*v*) definitively; *antonym* (*adv*) firstly.

motikitaeka judge; *synonyms* (*n*) arbiter, arbitrator, referee, (*v*) consider, estimate, evaluate, think,

believe, condemn, assess, adjudicate, calculate, decide, guess, umpire.

motikoraki favor; *synonyms* (*n*) countenance, aid, advantage, grace, support, boon, approval, clemency, (*v*) befriend, benefit, encourage, favour, patronize, privilege, (*adj*) kindness; *antonym* (*v*) disfavor.

motikorakiaki favored; *synonyms* (*adj*) fortunate, advantaged, preferred, lucky, advantageous, blessed, favorite, pet, privileged.

motinnano 1. dealt, **2.** engage; *synonyms* (*v*) contract, attract, book, employ, absorb, betroth, charter, enlist, retain, draw, engross, hire, involve, lock, mesh; *antonyms* (*v*) fire, disengage, **3.** bound; *synonyms* (*v*) leap, border, bounce, limit, circumscribe, confine, pounce, rebound, (*n*) spring, jump, boundary, edge, barrier, compass, hop; *antonym* (*adj*) free, **4.** deal; *synonyms* (*n*) bargain, buy, agreement, arrangement, covenant, trade, convention, (*v*) administer, allot, apportion, conduct, cope, distribute, truck, assign; *antonym* (*n*) purchase, **5.** contract; *synonyms* (*n*) compact, agree, (*v*) concentrate, condense, narrow, catch, compress, constrict, shrink, wrinkle, abbreviate, diminish, lessen, (*adj*) abridge, shorten; *antonyms* (*v*) expand, widen, stretch, **6.** bond; *synonyms* (*n*) association, tie, alliance, deed, cement, attachment, bail, connection, joint, link, adhesion, (*v*) bind, band, adhere, attach, **7.** bind; *synonyms* (*v*) bandage, bundle, combine, fasten, fetter, fix, lace, truss, affix, bond, gird, hold, knot, obligate, oblige; *antonyms* (*v*) untie, release, unbind, **8.** pledge; *synonyms* (*n*) gage, assurance, engage, promise, plight, bet, oath, security, (*v*) pawn, wager, guarantee, assure, undertake, vow, warrant, **9.** obligate; *synonyms* (*v*) force, compel, accommodate, burden, command, cost, (*adj*) bound, compelled, constrained, forced, apprenticed, articled, bandaged, destined, indentured.

motinnanoaki 1. engaged; *synonyms* (*adj*) busy, occupied, betrothed, affianced, employed, engrossed, reserved, absorbed, working, pledged, bespoken, booked, immersed, intent, rapt; *antonyms* (*adj*) available, free, **2.** bonded; *synonyms* (*adj*) guaranteed, barred, bolted, responsible, secured, warranted, fast, latched, locked, **3.** bound; *synonyms* (*v*) leap, border, bounce, limit, circumscribe, confine, pounce, rebound, (*n*) spring, jump, boundary, edge, barrier, compass, hop, **4.** contracted; *synonyms* (*v*) shrunk, (*adj*) narrow, insular, contract, constricted, tight, bound, **5.** bounded; *synonyms* (*adj*) finite, restricted, delimited, limited, encircled, enclosed, local, qualified, surrounded, belted, compassed, contiguous, defined, definite, determinate, **6.** pledged; *synonym* (*adj*) engaged.

motiraran 1. decide; *synonyms* (*v*) choose, determine, adjudicate, conclude, resolve, judge, settle, try, arbitrate, arrange, decree, fix, purpose, rule, select; *antonym* (*v*) waver, **2.** judge; *synonyms* (*n*) arbiter, arbitrator, referee, (*v*) consider, estimate, evaluate, think, believe, condemn, assess, calculate, decide, guess, umpire, examine, **3.** regulate; *synonyms* (*v*) adjust, manage, control, direct, order, govern, influence, modulate, regularize, align, check, correct, guide, organize, (*n*) form.

motiraranaki 1. decided; *synonyms* (*v*) absolute, clear, positive, categorical, emphatic, marked, (*adj*) decisive, definite, determined, distinct, resolute, unmistakable, conclusive, fixed, peremptory; *antonym* (*adj*) undecided, **2.** regulated; *synonyms* (*adj*) orderly, ordered, arranged, consistent, lawful, logical, regular, regulatory, temperate, systematic, (*adv*) synchronized.

motirawa 1. hiatus; *synonyms* (*n*) blank, break, gap, chasm, recess, respite, suspension, intermission, interruption, interval, lacuna, pause, abatement, **2.** leisurely; *synonyms* (*adj*) easy, deliberate, easygoing, slow, leisure, measured, unhurried, (*adv*) deliberately, slowly; *antonyms* (*adj*) quick, rushed, hurried, **3.** retire; *synonyms* (*v*) recede, resign, leave, retreat, withdraw, abdicate, ebb, adjourn, depart, go, quit, remove, return, secede, regrade, **4.** rest; *synonyms* (*n*) remnant, repose, balance, relaxation, residue, quiet, halt, (*v*) nap, remain, sleep, ease, lie, perch, abide, (*adj*) remainder; *antonym* (*v*) work, **5.** pause; *synonyms* (*n*) rest, stop, breather, cessation, hesitation, abeyance, (*v*) adjournment, delay, hesitate, desist, cease, intermit, interrupt, waver, (*adj*) discontinue; *antonyms* (*n*) decisiveness, (*v*) continue, **6.** retired; *synonyms* (*v*) covert, (*adj*) private, obscure, emeritus, secluded, secret, sequestered, solitary, lonely, withdrawn, close, superannuated, isolated, old, out, **7.** repose; *synonyms* (*n*) peace, calm, composure, recreation, peacefulness, placidity, quietness, quietude, calmness, equanimity, (*v*) recline, lay, place, lean, relax.

motirawaki 1. retired; *synonyms* (*v*) covert, (*adj*) private, obscure, emeritus, secluded, secret, sequestered, solitary, lonely, withdrawn, close, superannuated, isolated, old, out, **2.** rested; *synonyms* (*adj*) fresh, comfortable.

moui teeth; *synonyms* (*n*) ivory, dentition, odontiasis, vice, hold, (*v*) arrastra, fangs, file, grater, gristmill, mill, rasp, tenaculum, tentacle, unguis.

mô'umân cock; *synonyms* (*n*) rooster, chicken, stack, fowl, hammer, hand, pecker, pointer, prick, shaft, stopcock, tool, turncock, vane, (*v*) ruffle.

mra 1. converge; *synonyms* (*v*) concentrate, approach, assemble, meet, congregate, collect, focus, gather, huddle, join, merge; *antonyms* (*v*) diverge, disperse, **2.** crowd; *synonyms* (*n*) swarm, collection, crew, press, circle, cluster, army, assembly, concourse, congregation, (*v*) bunch, flock, squeeze, compress, cram, **3.** acclaim; *synonyms* (*n*) applause, acclamation, approval, commendation, (*v*) praise, applaud, clap, commend, eulogize, extol, hail, laud, honor, compliment, cheer; *antonym* (*v*) boo, **4.** welcome; *synonyms* (*adj*) acceptable, pleasant, agreeable, pleasing, enjoyable, grateful, (*v*) accept, greet, invite, receive, entertain, (*n*) salute, hospitality, reception, embrace; *antonyms* (*adj*) unwelcome, unwanted, (*v*) reject.

mraki crowded; *synonyms* (*adj*) close, compact, congested, busy, dense, full, packed, populous, jammed, cramped, teeming, thick, tight, (*n*) thronged; *antonyms* (*adj*) empty, sparse.

mramra 1. importunate; *synonyms* (*adj*) troublesome, annoying, exigent, insistent, pressing, instant, demanding, earnest, pleading, urgent, appealing, imploring, (*v*) important; *antonym* (*adj*) halfhearted, **2.** eager; *synonyms* (*adj*) avid, desirous, ardent, agog, acute, ambitious, enthusiastic, keen, zealous, industrious, studious, active, burning, craving, excited; *antonyms* (*adj*) indifferent, apathetic, disinterested, unconcerned, **3.** anxious; *synonyms* (*adj*) afraid, alarmed, nervous, tense, uneasy, agitated, apprehensive, concerned, distressed, fearful, frightened, thoughtful, thirsty, (*v*) jumpy, solicitous; *antonyms* (*adj*) calm, relaxed, carefree, confident, rational, undisturbed, untroubled, **4.** insistent; *synonyms* (*adj*) stubborn, clamant, crying, emphatic, importunate, persistent, imperative, adamant, assertive, dogged, forceful, obstinate, unremitting, unyielding, **5.** urgent; *synonyms* (*adj*) immediate, quick, critical, serious, vital, hasty, compelling, eager, necessary, cogent, crucial, strong, (*v*) clamorous, forcible, (*n*) breathless; *antonym* (*adj*) trivial.

mrara fall; *synonyms* (*v*) decline, dip, decrease, descend, dive, rain, diminish, dwindle, sink, alight, (*n*) drop, descent, downfall, plunge, pitch; *antonyms* (*v*) rise, increase, ascend, climb, triumph, win, (*n*) ascent.

mron 1. circular; *synonyms* (*adj*) round, annular, circinate, globular, orbicular, rotund, rounded, spherical, (*n*) advertisement, bill, handbill, brochure, publication, bulletin, flier; *antonym* (*adj*) square, **2.** round; *synonyms* (*adv*) about, around, (*adj*) circular, plump, entire, chubby, complete, (*n*) circle, bout, ring, beat, circuit, (*v*) compass, turn, gird; *antonyms* (*adj*) slim, sharp, **3.** spherical; *synonyms* (*adj*) global, globose, spheric, orbiculate.

mronron 1. curve; *synonyms* (*n*) bend, crook, bow, arc, curvature, kink, round, bender, (*v*) curl, turn, arch, hook, wind, distort, (*adj*) flex, **2.** cooperative; *synonyms* (*adj*) combined, joint, accommodating, concerted, helpful, obliging, united, accommodative, communal, conjunct, conjunctive, (*n*) collective, association, commune; *antonyms* (*adj*) uncooperative, individual, **3.** circular; *synonyms* (*adj*) annular, circinate, globular, orbicular, rotund, rounded, spherical, (*n*) advertisement, bill, handbill, brochure, publication, bulletin, flier, flyer; *antonym* (*adj*) square, **4.** circle; *synonyms* (*n*) band, compass, ring, field, range, beat, circuit, company, gang, scope, set, league, area, (*v*) whirl, encircle, **5.** orbit; *synonyms* (*n*) circle, cycle, orb, domain, expanse, course, ambit, reach, realm, sphere, track, trajectory, (*v*) revolve, rotate, wheel, **6.** spherical; *synonyms* (*adj*) circular, global, globose, spheric, orbiculate, **7.** round; *synonyms* (*adv*) about, around, (*adj*) plump, entire, chubby, complete, fat, (*n*) bout, orbit, patrol, rung, sequence, loop, (*v*) gird, ball; *antonyms* (*adj*) slim, sharp, **8.** reciprocal; *synonyms* (*adj*) mutual, common, inverse, complementary, interchangeable, equivalent, bilateral, relative, alternate, reflexive, aliquot, commutative, commutual, divisible, numeral.

mronronaki 1. curved; *synonyms* (*adj*) bent, crooked, curve, round, bend, curving, curvy, deformed, hooked, rounded, tortuous, twisted, (*v*) bowed; *antonyms* (*adj*) straight, concave, **2.** rounded; *synonyms* (*adj*) curved, circular, orbicular, full, globular, rotund, spherical, blunt, fat, obtuse; *antonyms* (*adj*) pointed, sharp, bony.

mte 1. finite; *synonyms* (*adj*) bounded, limited, mortal, conditioned, demarcated; *antonyms* (*adj*) infinite, countless, endless, never-ending, **2.** fine; *synonyms* (*adj*) delicate, agreeable, dainty, brave, capital, elegant, excellent, nice, thin, delightful, acute, admirable, alright, (*n*) penalty, (*v*) punish; *antonyms* (*adj*) poor, thick, coarse, substantial, unsatisfactory, wide, **3.** small; *synonyms* (*adj*) little, minute, narrow, fine, inadequate, insignificant, low, minor, petty, slight, light, remote, cramped, young, diminutive; *antonyms* (*adj*) bulky, colossal, considerable, enormous, extra-large, great, huge, sizeable, giant, major, (*syn*) big, large.

mui after; *synonyms* (*prep*) following, since, (*adv*) later, beyond, next, subsequently, then, when, afterward, afterwards, behind, (*adj*) back, posterior, rear, subsequent.

mumun 1. retire; *synonyms* (*v*) recede, resign, leave, retreat, withdraw, abdicate, ebb, adjourn, depart, go, quit, remove, return, secede, regrade, **2.** retreat; *synonyms* (*n*) refuge, resort, asylum, departure, den, lair, privacy, retirement, sanctuary, shelter, withdrawal, flight, (*v*) retire, exit, retract; *antonyms* (*n*) raid, (*v*) advance.

mumunaki 1. retired; *synonyms* (*v*) covert, (*adj*) private, obscure, emeritus, secluded, secret, sequestered, solitary, lonely, withdrawn, close, superannuated, isolated, old, out, **2.** retreated.

mumuta 1. upchuck; *synonyms* (*v*) spew, vomit, puke, heave, regurgitate, cat, disgorge, sick, spue, chuck, gag, hurl, retch, **2.** vomit; *synonyms* (*n*) regurgitation, vomiting, emetic, emesis, vomitus, disgorgement, nauseant, puking, (*v*) cast, eject, barf, regorge, upchuck, honk, parbreak, **3.** regurgitate; *synonyms* (*v*) babble, bubble, ebb, guggle, murmur, purl, **4.** sick; *synonyms* (*adj*) ill, queasy, ailing, indisposed, poorly, weary, invalid, diseased, morbid, sickly, nauseous, poor, crazy, disgusted, (*v*) unwell; *antonyms* (*adj*) well, healthy, **5.** spew; *synonyms* (*v*) expel, spit, spurt, emit, discharge, gush, flow, ptyalize, (*n*) chunder.

mura 1. anxious; *synonyms* (*adj*) afraid, alarmed, nervous, tense, uneasy, agitated, apprehensive, concerned, distressed, fearful, frightened, keen, thoughtful, (*v*) jumpy, solicitous; *antonyms* (*adj*) calm, relaxed, carefree, confident, rational, unconcerned, undisturbed, untroubled, **2.** importunate; *synonyms* (*adj*) troublesome, annoying, exigent, insistent, pressing, instant, demanding, earnest, pleading, urgent, appealing, imploring, (*v*) important; *antonym* (*adj*) halfhearted, **3.** insistent; *synonyms* (*adj*) stubborn, clamant, crying, emphatic, importunate, persistent, imperative, adamant, assertive, dogged, forceful, obstinate, unremitting, unyielding, **4.** eager; *synonyms* (*adj*) avid, desirous, ardent, agog, acute, ambitious, enthusiastic, zealous, industrious, studious, active, burning, craving, excited, fervent; *antonyms* (*adj*) indifferent, apathetic, disinterested, **5.** urgent; *synonyms* (*adj*) immediate, quick, critical, serious, vital, hasty, compelling, eager, necessary, cogent, crucial, strong, (*v*) clamorous, forcible, (*n*) breathless; *antonym* (*adj*) trivial.

muramura 1. insistent; *synonyms* (*adj*) exigent, stubborn, pressing, clamant, crying, emphatic, importunate, instant, persistent, imperative, adamant, assertive, dogged, forceful, obstinate; *antonym* (*adj*) halfhearted, **2.** eager; *synonyms* (*adj*) avid, desirous, ardent, earnest, agog, acute, ambitious, enthusiastic, keen, zealous, industrious, studious, active, burning, craving; *antonyms* (*adj*) indifferent, apathetic, disinterested, unconcerned, **3.** anxious; *synonyms* (*adj*) afraid, alarmed, nervous, tense, uneasy, agitated, apprehensive, concerned, distressed, fearful, frightened, thoughtful, thirsty, (*v*) jumpy, solicitous; *antonyms* (*adj*) calm, relaxed, carefree, confident, rational, undisturbed, untroubled, **4.** importunate; *synonyms* (*adj*) troublesome, annoying, insistent, demanding, pleading, urgent, appealing, imploring, (*v*) important, **5.** urgent; *synonyms* (*adj*) immediate, quick, critical, serious, vital, hasty, compelling, eager, necessary, cogent, crucial, strong, (*v*) clamorous, forcible, (*n*) breathless; *antonym* (*adj*) trivial.

Reference: Webster's Online Dictionary (www.websters-online-dictionary.org)

murkuri labor; *synonyms* (*n*) drudgery, effort, endeavor, exertion, travail, childbirth, grind, struggle, birth, business, (*v*) toil, confinement, delivery, drudge, labour; *antonym* (*v*) rest.

muti 1. attentive; *synonyms* (*adj*) thoughtful, assiduous, diligent, heedful, observant, watchful, advertent, alert, aware, careful, considerate, mindful, vigilant, wary, devoted; *antonyms* (*adj*) inattentive, negligent, unfocused, forgetful, neglectful, heedless, 2. interested; *synonyms* (*adj*) concerned, curious, involved, inquiring, inquisitive, keen, attentive; *antonyms* (*adj*) apathetic, uninterested, 3. caring; *synonyms* (*adj*) affectionate, tender, fond, loving, compassionate, sympathetic, kind, kindly, obliging, solicitous, warm, adoring, benevolent, helpful, protective; *antonyms* (*adj*) uncaring, unfeeling, callous, flippant, 4. considerate; *synonyms* (*adj*) magnanimous, humane, caring, circumspect, courteous, delicate, discreet, polite, tactful, cautious, generous, civil, gracious, (*n*) gentle, nice; *antonyms* (*adj*) inconsiderate, tactless, thoughtless, 5. concerned; *synonyms* (*adj*) anxious, interested, apprehensive, nervous, worried, affected, fearful, troubled, uneasy, upset, distraught, paternal; *antonym* (*adj*) unconcerned.

mutiakina 1. mind; *synonyms* (*n*) intellect, brain, head, inclination, intelligence, psyche, regard, (*v*) care, look, attend, beware, keep, listen, notice, (*adj*) heed; *antonym* (*v*) forget, 2. heed; *synonyms* (*n*) consideration, concern, caution, note, charge, discretion, attentiveness, circumspection, deliberation, (*v*) hear, attention, mind, consider, esteem, observe; *antonyms* (*v*) disregard, ignore, 3. concerned; *synonyms* (*adj*) anxious, careful, interested, involved, thoughtful, apprehensive, considerate, nervous, solicitous, worried, affected, attentive, caring, fearful, troubled; *antonyms* (*adj*) unconcerned, uncaring, unfeeling, 4. busy; *synonyms* (*adj*) active, brisk, assiduous, engaged, occupied, agile, crowded, industrious, meddlesome, officious, live, diligent, earnest, (*v*) occupy, employ; *antonyms* (*adj*) idle, free, inactive, 5. notice; *synonyms* (*n*) advertisement, declaration, information, message, observation, admonition, announcement, (*v*) detect, discover, distinguish, find, mark, remark, see, acknowledge, 6. remark; *synonyms* (*n*) commentary, observance, reflection, word, statement, quip, annotate, reference, designate, expression, (*v*) comment, mention, perceive, discern, criticise.

mutiakinaki 1. minded; *synonyms* (*adj*) willing, prone, ready, partial, predisposed, prepared, (*prep*) inclined, disposed, jolly, 2. noticed.

mutigak 1. determine; *synonyms* (*v*) ascertain, decide, define, resolve, appoint, adjudicate, conclude, measure, set, specify, designate, assign, decree, arrange, assess, 2. resolve; *synonyms* (*v*) determine, solve, decompose, dissolve, settle, end, explain, melt, (*n*) purpose, determination, decision, firmness, resolution, answer, analyze; *antonyms* (*n*) indecision, weakness.

mwaamwanna 1. cheat; *synonyms* (*v*) trick, beguile, betray, defraud, fake, beat, deceive, fleece, (*n*) swindle, con, fraud, bilk, impostor, sham, charlatan, 2. deceive; *synonyms* (*v*) cheat, bamboozle, circumvent, dupe, pretend, cozen, fool, hoax, mislead, sell, befool, delude, gull, hoodwink, humbug.

mwaane man; *synonyms* (*n*) fellow, gentleman, guy, person, husband, homo, human, humanity, humankind, humans, individual, mankind, mortal, (*obj*) he, male; *antonym* (*n*) woman.

mwaaneu 1. cousin; *synonyms* (*n*) nephew, friend, companion, allied, 2. sister; *synonyms* (*n*) nun, nurse, brother, mate, twin, baby, counterpart, double, match, member, pair, pendant, sis.

mwaawa loose; *synonyms* (*adj*) lax, liberal, dissolute, licentious, light, vague, detached, immoral, (*v*) disengage, liberate, relax, release, detach, (*n*) free, limp; *antonyms* (*adj*) tight, close, compressed, dense, taut, strict, compact, wedged.

mwae sunburnt; *synonyms* (*adj*) sunburned, adust, fiery, gloomy, sallow.

mwai cooked; *synonyms* (*adj*) ripe, overcooked, altered, damaged, defiled, heated, spent, wanting.

mwaie dance; *synonyms* (*n*) dancing, party, (*v*) bound, caper, hop, bop, cavort, play, jump, shake, skip, step, beat, dandle, prance.

mwaimwai wet; *synonyms* (*adj*) damp, humid, drenched, moist, soaked, sodden, dank, rainy, saturated, soggy, (*v*) moisten, water, dampen, wash, (*n*) moisture; *antonyms* (*adj*) dehydrated, parched, (*v*) dry.

mwaka 1. defective; *synonyms* (*adj*) deficient, bad, faulty, imperfect, broken, incomplete, lacking, unsound, vicious, inaccurate, rotten, erroneous, flawed, inadequate, incorrect; *antonym* (*adj*) perfect, 2. decayed; *synonyms* (*adj*) corrupt, dilapidated, rank, wasted, decaying, old, putrid, rotted, rotting, rusty, behindhand, (*v*) stale; *antonym* (*adj*) fresh, 3. rapidly; *synonyms* (*adv*) promptly, quick, quickly, fast, soon, apace, hastily, speedily, swiftly, fleetly, readily, abruptly, hurriedly, shortly, (*adj*) immediately; *antonyms* (*adv*) slowly, permanently, 4. rapid; *synonyms* (*adj*) prompt, swift, agile, fleet, hasty, speedy, cursory, expeditious, sudden, nimble, winged, express, hurried, immediate, instant; *antonyms* (*adj*) slow, gradual, 5. sore; *synonyms* (*adj*) painful, sensitive, angry, raw, indignant, aching, (*n*) injury, boil, cut, lesion, canker, abscess, (*v*) hurt, acute, sharp; *antonym* (*adj*) painless, 6. swiftly; *synonyms* (*adv*) rapidly, nimbly, suddenly, **7.** swift; *synonyms* (*adj*) rapid, alert, lively, abrupt, ready, sprightly, impetuous, unexpected, active, brisk, keen, brief, impulsive, (*n*) cylinder, (*v*) dissolute; *antonyms* (*adj*) considered, leisurely, **8.** uncured.

mwakaikai rustle; *synonyms* (*n*) whisper, rustling, (*v*) hiss, lift, buzz, pilfer, steal, whiz.

mwakorokoro fraction; *synonyms* (*n*) divide, part, segment, bit, division, piece, proportion, section, share, faction, cut, fragment, portion, ratio, (*adj*) constituent.

mwakuri 1. labor; *synonyms* (*n*) drudgery, effort, endeavor, exertion, travail, childbirth, grind, struggle, birth, business, (*v*) toil, confinement, delivery, drudge, labour; *antonym* (*v*) rest, **2.** function; *synonyms* (*n*) position, office, place, role, service, work, agency, application, duty, employment, (*v*) act, exercise, run, serve, go, **3.** act; *synonyms* (*n*) accomplishment, action, move, play, statute, decree, do, feat, (*v*) achievement, behave, deed, perform, acquit, enact, feign; *antonym* (*v*) refrain, **4.** operate; *synonyms* (*v*) function, direct, employ, handle, manage, proceed, maneuver, fly, control, drive, engage, form, make, manipulate, manoeuvre, **5.** occupy; *synonyms* (*v*) hold, have, engross, fill, get, absorb, inhabit, invade, possess, conquer, busy, capture, keep, take, (*n*) entertain; *antonym* (*v*) leave, **6.** serve; *synonyms* (*v*) help, aid, assist, attend, benefit, operate, tend, answer, facilitate, provide, accommodate, minister, profit, (*n*) avail, officiate, **7.** work; *synonyms* (*n*) task, book, composition, occupation, writing, activity, (*v*) labor, cultivate, exploit, ferment, operation, use, produce, (*adj*) job, trade; *antonyms* (*v*) idle, malfunction.

mwakuria operate; *synonyms* (*v*) act, function, run, direct, employ, go, handle, manage, move, perform, proceed, work, maneuver, exercise, fly.

mwakuriaki 1. serviced; *synonyms* (*adj*) maintained, repaired, fixed, reconditioned, retained, **2.** occupied; *synonyms* (*adj*) busy, engaged, employed, diligent, absorbed, active, engrossed, working, affianced, betrothed, concerned, industrious, involved; *antonyms* (*adj*) empty, vacant, available, uninhabited, free, idle.

mwamwae move; *synonyms* (*v*) act, affect, carry, excite, go, impel, instigate, maneuver, touch, travel, flow, bear, (*n*) motion, drive, transfer; *antonym* (*v*) stay.

mwananga 1. travel; *synonyms* (*n*) journey, pass, stroke, passage, tour, (*v*) go, run, proceed, move, roam, ride, cruise, ramble, sail, (*adj*) course, **2.** voyage; *synonyms* (*n*) trip, expedition, flight, quest, excursion, outing, (*v*) travel, navigate, **3.** trek; *synonyms* (*n*) hike, slog, (*v*) tramp, voyage, migrate, trudge, walk, range, wander.

mwanangaki traveled; *synonyms* (*adj*) travelled, cultured, passable, experienced, knowing.

mwane 1. male; *synonyms* (*adj*) masculine, manly, virile, manful, manlike, (*n*) chap, guy, man, (*obj*) he; *antonyms* (*adj*) feminine, (*n*) female, woman, **2.** fellow; *synonyms* (*adj*) comrade, (*n*) companion, associate, boy, equal, brother, colleague, compeer, peer, buddy, dude, dog, counterpart, escort, (*v*) concomitant, **3.** guy; *synonyms* (*n*) lad, cat, fellow, bozo, hombre, male, person, rope, tether, band, (*v*) rib, blackguard.

mwanea receive; *synonyms* (*v*) accept, admit, get, assume, adopt, bear, have, obtain, welcome, make, acknowledge, embrace, gather, greet, take.

mwaneaki received; *synonyms* (*v*) receiving, ascertained, current, recognized, (*adj*) accepted, acknowledged, conventional, acceptable, canonical, orthodox, customary, established, inward, known, legitimate.

mwaneka scar; *synonyms* (*n*) mark, cicatrix, blemish, seam, cicatrice, defect, scratch, stain, injury, line, disfigurement, (*v*) disfigure, brand, damage, mar.

mwanekaki marked; *synonyms* (*adj*) distinct, conspicuous, noticeable, pronounced, remarkable, distinguished, apparent, definite, notable, obvious, signal, striking, strong, clear, appreciable; *antonyms* (*adj*) plain, unblemished.

mwanem brother; *synonyms* (*n*) fellow, pal, associate, buddy, chum, companion, compeer, comrade, counterpart, crony, friend, mate, monk, peer, sidekick; *antonym* (*n*) sister.

mwanena brother; *synonyms* (*n*) fellow, pal, associate, buddy, chum, companion, compeer, comrade, counterpart, crony, friend, mate, monk, peer, sidekick; *antonym* (*n*) sister.

mwaneu brother; *synonyms* (*n*) fellow, pal, associate, buddy, chum, companion, compeer, comrade, counterpart, crony, friend, mate, monk, peer, sidekick; *antonym* (*n*) sister.

mwanibuaka oppress; *synonyms* (*v*) persecute, afflict, harass, press, burden, pinch, depress, encumber, crush, repress, load, harry, harrow, (*adj*) aggrieve, wrong.

mwanibuakaki oppressed; *synonyms* (*adj*) downtrodden, laden, persecuted, broken, burdened, aggrieved, beleaguered, browbeaten, despairing, downcast, drawn, forlorn, gloomy, haggard, heavy.

mwanika 1. pace; *synonyms* (*n*) walk, rate, footstep, rapidity, speed, tempo, tread, celerity, fastness, run, beat, cadence, (*v*) step, gait, stride; *antonym* (*n*) slowness, **2.** step; *synonyms* (*n*) degree, measure, stage, gradation, level, rank, act, footprint, move, advance, phase, procedure, process, (*v*) pace, proceeding.

mwanikaki stepped; *synonyms* (*v*) advanced, gone, stopen.

mwaninga 1. forget; *synonyms* (*v*) disregard, leave, bury, ignore, neglect, overlook, fail, abandon, lose, omit, slight, block; *antonym* (*v*) remember, **2**. forgotten; *synonyms* (*adj*) lost, disregarded, elapsed, past, abandoned, antebellum, antediluvian, baffled, befuddled, bemused, bewildered, beyond, bygone, confounded, confused.

mwaningaki forgotten; *synonyms* (*adj*) lost, disregarded, elapsed, past, abandoned, antebellum, antediluvian, baffled, befuddled, bemused, bewildered, beyond, bygone, confounded, confused.

mwanu sag; *synonyms* (*n*) decline, dip, depression, drop, slump, collapse, (*v*) droop, flag, bag, bend, tumble, curve, loll, lean, (*adj*) swag; *antonym* (*v*) rise.

mwau humid; *synonyms* (*adj*) moist, wet, damp, dank, sultry, clammy, muggy, oppressive, soggy, steamy, sticky, watery, wettish, hot; *antonyms* (*adj*) dry, fresh.

mwawawa spacious; *synonyms* (*adj*) roomy, broad, extensive, large, ample, wide, capacious, commodious, vast, comprehensive, big, expansive, extended, liberal, open; *antonyms* (*adj*) cramped, narrow.

mwe 1. lift; *synonyms* (*n*) elevator, boost, heave, (*v*) hoist, raise, rise, elevate, erect, filch, hike, advance, airlift, pilfer, pinch, rear, **2**. heave; *synonyms* (*v*) cast, fling, chuck, gasp, haul, toss, billow, drag, draw, gag, jerk, lift, (*n*) tug, elevation, heaving, **3**. raise; *synonyms* (*v*) increase, build, enhance, foster, grow, promote, prefer, augment, cultivate, exalt, excite, heighten, levy, nurture, pitch; *antonym* (*v*) lower.

mweaka offer; *synonyms* (*v*) give, bestow, put, advance, extend, impart, introduce, perform, propose, tender, lay, (*n*) bid, proposal, go, proposition; *antonyms* (*v*) withdraw, refuse.

mweaki 1. lifted; *synonyms* (*adj*) elevated, lofty, steep, upraised, **2**. raised; *synonyms* (*v*) repousse, (*adj*) embossed, erect, convex, brocaded, high, alert, bold, confident, elate, elated, elative, exultant, mountant, (*prep*) above.

mweau slow; *synonyms* (*adj*) dull, late, easy, sluggish, heavy, dense, dim, gradual, inactive, indolent, lazy, stupid, (*v*) slack, (*adv*) behind, behindhand; *antonyms* (*adj*) fast, intelligent, rapid, bright, alert, brisk, hasty, prompt, quick, speedy, hurried, observant, rushed, (*v*) accelerate.

mwebuaka 1. insecure; *synonyms* (*adj*) dangerous, slippery, unsound, doubtful, bad, hazardous, precarious, rickety, risky, shaky, uncertain, unsafe, wobbly, diffident, (*v*) unstable; *antonyms* (*adj*) secure, confident, self-assured, self-confident, overconfident, safe, **2**. uncomfortable; *synonyms* (*adj*) awkward, embarrassing, troubled, inconvenient, difficult, discomfited, anxious, uneasy, cheerless, embarrassed, painful, (*v*) untoward; *antonyms* (*adj*) comfortable, relaxed, comfy, **3**. uneasy; *synonyms* (*adj*) uncomfortable, fidgety, restless, apprehensive, concerned, nervous, unquiet, fretful, restive, solicitous, agitated, jittery, worried, impatient, disturbed; *antonym* (*adj*) calm.

mwemekia raise; *synonyms* (*v*) boost, lift, erect, hoist, increase, build, elevate, enhance, foster, grow, promote, prefer, augment, cultivate, (*n*) advance; *antonym* (*v*) lower.

mwemekiaki raised; *synonyms* (*v*) repousse, (*adj*) elevated, embossed, erect, convex, brocaded, high, alert, bold, confident, elate, elated, elative, exultant, (*prep*) above.

mwemwe 1. featherweight; *synonyms* (*adj*) light, lightweight, thin, **2**. light; *synonyms* (*adj*) fair, clear, facile, easy, faint, flimsy, (*n*) flame, brightness, daylight, (*v*) fire, kindle, inflame, glow, ignite, dismount; *antonyms* (*adj*) fattening, nauseating, (*n*) dark, darkness, gloom, shade, night, (*v*) extinguish, darken, (*alt sp*) heavy, **3**. buoyant; *synonyms* (*adj*) cheerful, optimistic, sanguine, lighthearted, airy, blithe, bright, elastic, floaty, hopeful, lively, perky, resilient, animated, enthusiastic; *antonym* (*adj*) pessimistic, **4**. shift; *synonyms* (*n*) interchange, turn, move, switch, conversion, (*v*) change, exchange, remove, quibble, alter, budge, convert, displace, transfer, fluctuate, **5**. weightless; *synonyms* (*adj*) astatic, buoyant, feathery, fluffy, frothy, insubstantial, wispy.

mwemweaero nocturnal; *synonyms* (*adj*) nightly, vespertine, autumnal, late; *antonym* (*adj*) diurnal.

mwemwerake lifted; *synonyms* (*adj*) elevated, lofty, steep, upraised.

mwemwerakeaki lifted; *synonyms* (*adj*) elevated, lofty, steep, upraised.

mwemweraoi lightweight; *synonyms* (*adj*) light, fine, insignificant, shallow, sheer, superficial, thin, diaphanous, entertaining, gauzy, portable, (*n*) jackanapes, dunce, fool, nobody; *antonyms* (*adj*) hardwearing, heavy-duty.

mwenga 1. lodge; *synonyms* (*n*) house, club, cottage, hut, inn, (*v*) cabin, live, place, accommodate, deposit, fix, inhabit, quarter, (*adj*) abide, dwell, **2**. inhabit; *synonyms* (*v*) reside, occupy, lodge, people, settle, be, bide, exist, roost, domicile, populate, remain, shack, (*n*) habit, (*adj*) perch, **3**. dwell; *synonyms* (*v*) stay, belong, brood, continue, delay, consist, domiciliate, endure, keep, last, lie, ponder, tarry, aby, detain, **4**. reside; *synonyms* (*v*) repose, rest.

mwengaki inhabited; *synonyms* (*v*) populous, accustomed, arrayed, clothed, dressed, habited, (*adj*) peopled, occupied, housing, colonized, suburban, uninhabited, uptown; *antonyms* (*adj*) empty, unoccupied.

mweraoi 1. live; *synonyms* (*v*) exist, inhabit, reside, subsist, abide, be, dwell, endure, stay, survive, (*adj*) alive, active, animate, living, (*n*) go; *antonyms* (*adj*) dead, inanimate, **2.** dwell; *synonyms* (*v*) bide, live, lodge, belong, brood, continue, delay, occupy, remain, settle, consist, domicile, domiciliate, keep, (*adj*) roost, **3.** peaceful; *synonyms* (*adj*) calm, gentle, peaceable, quiet, even, meek, peace, placid, silent, amicable, composed, halcyon, mild, serene, tranquil; *antonyms* (*adj*) aggressive, noisy, tense, violent, **4.** secure; *synonyms* (*v*) close, fix, preserve, fasten, acquire, assure, attain, ensure, fast, (*adj*) safe, firm, certain, confident, attach, bind; *antonyms* (*v*) lose, detach, (*adj*) insecure, vulnerable, loose, unsafe, **5.** tranquil; *synonyms* (*adj*) still, unruffled, sedate, collected, equable, motionless, comfortable, cool, relaxed, untroubled, imperturbable, (*n*) peaceful, (*v*) smooth, easy, moderate.

mwere 1. late; *synonyms* (*adj*) former, dead, deceased, behindhand, belated, delayed, modern, slow, tardy, dull, defunct, (*adv*) dilatory, fresh, backward, belatedly; *antonyms* (*adj*) ahead, (*adv*) early, punctually, promptly, punctual, **2.** dawdling; *synonyms* (*adj*) deliberate, easygoing, hesitant, laggard, leisurely, measured, (*n*) delay, dalliance, coquetry, dithering, faltering, hesitation, idleness, indecision, pause; *antonym* (*n*) decisiveness, **3.** slow; *synonyms* (*adj*) late, easy, sluggish, heavy, dense, dim, gradual, inactive, indolent, lazy, stupid, boring, (*v*) slack, check, (*adv*) behind; *antonyms* (*adj*) fast, intelligent, rapid, bright, alert, brisk, hasty, prompt, quick, speedy, hurried, observant, rushed, (*v*) accelerate, **4.** tardy; *synonyms* (*adj*) remiss, overdue, lagging, reluctant, procrastinating, (*v*) recent.

mwerengau 1. embarrassed; *synonyms* (*adj*) ashamed, abashed, awkward, uncomfortable, disconcerted, bashful, shamefaced, sheepish, shy, chagrined, discomfited, humiliated, mortified; *antonyms* (*adj*) proud, relaxed, **2.** disturbed; *synonyms* (*adj*) agitated, concerned, anxious, confused, disquieted, restless, upset, worried, disordered, bothered, deranged, distracted, distressed, nervous, tumultuous; *antonyms* (*adj*) rational, calm, **3.** constrained; *synonyms* (*adj*) uneasy, bound, forced, stiff, strained, compelled, limited, affected, confined, cramped, restricted, rigid, stilted; *antonyms* (*adj*) free, unrestricted, **4.** offended; *synonyms* (*adj*) hurt, angry, affronted, aggrieved, annoyed, pained, wronged, shocked, appalled, averted, bitter, cool, disappointed,

disgusted, dismayed; *antonym* (*adj*) composed, **5.** uneasy; *synonyms* (*adj*) fidgety, apprehensive, unquiet, fretful, restive, solicitous, jittery, troubled, embarrassing, impatient, disturbed, clumsy, difficult, doubtful, fearful, **6.** shocked; *synonyms* (*adj*) aghast, amazed, stunned, surprised, afraid, bewildered, dumbfounded, speechless; *antonyms* (*adj*) delighted, indifferent.

mweuti sleepless; *synonyms* (*adj*) restless, insomniac, lidless, vigilant, wakeful, watchful, disturbed.

mwina result; *synonyms* (*n*) consequence, fruit, issue, outcome, aftermath, answer, conclusion, effect, end, produce, outgrowth, (*v*) ensue, follow, eventuate, arise; *antonym* (*v*) cause.

mwiniba 1. devaluate; *synonyms* (*v*) depreciate, devalue, decrease, debase, belittle, deprecate, depress, detract, impair, lower, undervalue, underestimate, **2.** bastardize; *synonyms* (*v*) bastardise, deprave, pervert, embastardize, imbastardize, bastard, corrupt, debauch, demoralize, illegitimate, illegitimatize, stain, warp, bestialize, brutalize, **3.** degrade; *synonyms* (*v*) cheapen, demean, dishonor, disparage, lessen, reduce, abate, demote, discredit, downgrade, humble, humiliate, (*n*) disgrace, defame, (*adj*) abase, **4.** abase; *synonyms* (*v*) degrade, mortify, sink, shame, crush, (*adj*) abash, snub, **5.** demean; *synonyms* (*v*) conduct, behave, **6.** debase; *synonyms* (*v*) adulterate, alloy, contaminate, defile, bastardize, pollute, taint, vitiate, profane, doctor, cut, deteriorate, dilute, sophisticate, spoil, **7.** befoul; *synonyms* (*v*) foul, soil, dirty, maculate, tarnish, violate, (*adj*) begrime, bemire, besmear, **8.** animalize; *synonyms* (*v*) animalise, canker, rot, brutalise, sensualize, **9.** disparage; *synonyms* (*v*) denigrate, derogate, decry, censure, condemn, criticize, abuse, slur, dispraise, knock, malign, minimize, despise, impeach, deride; *antonyms* (*v*) praise, compliment, flatter, **10.** cheapen; *synonyms* (*v*) diminish, chaffer, **11.** ignoble; *synonyms* (*adj*) contemptible, abject, base, beggarly, disgraceful, dishonorable, degraded, despicable, mean, ignominious, shabby, low, lowly, menial, plebeian; *antonym* (*adj*) noble, **12.** adulterate; *synonyms* (*v*) weaken, falsify, thin, (*adj*) adulterated, spurious; *antonyms* (*v*) clean, purify, **13.** inferior; *synonyms* (*adj*) bad, secondary, subordinate, poor, cheap, junior, lesser, petty, feeble, coarse, common, vulgar, ignoble, less, (*prep*) below; *antonyms* (*adj*) better, choice, excellent, first-rate, high-class, premium, (*n*) superior, superscript, **14.** last; *synonyms* (*v*) endure, continue, hold, exist, live, dwell, (*n*) abide, conclusion, (*adj*) extreme, closing, final, ultimate, conclusive, concluding, farthest; *antonyms* (*n*) opening, (*adj*) first, **15.** lower; *synonyms* (*adj*) inferior, damp, (*v*) frown, dip, descend, drop, scowl, fall, ebb, deject, glare, decline, bow, dash, (adv) underneath; *antonyms* (v) increase, raise, **16.** humble; *synonyms* (adj) docile, modest, unassuming, baseborn, meek, obscure, ordinary, reverent, simple, small, submissive, unpretentious, coy, (v) conquer, chasten; *antonyms* (adj) grand, arrogant, conceited, haughty, imposing, impressive, pompous, snooty, **17.** despise; *synonyms* (v) scorn, contemn, disdain, loathe, abhor, detest, dislike, hate, slight, defy, disregard, execrate, neglect, spurn, reject; *antonyms* (v) admire, respect, **18.** low; *synonyms* (adj) blue, deep, dejected, depressed, down, downcast, downhearted, despondent, dispirited, faint, gloomy, inexpensive, miserable, (adv) gentle, (n) depression; *antonyms* (adj) cheerful, happy, high-pitched, loud, important, piercing, (n) high.

mwinibaki 1. adulterated; *synonyms* (adj) adulterate, impure, debased, dirty, unclean, bastard, contaminated, corrupt, diluted, false, faulty, sham, sophisticated, (v) contraband, illegitimate, **2.** befouled; *synonyms* (adj) fouled, foul, **3.** debased; *synonyms* (adj) adulterated, degraded, low, base, degenerate, depraved, corrupted, debauched, decadent, perverted; *antonym* (adj) pure, **4.** degraded; *synonyms* (adj) ignoble, abject, dishonored, sordid, contemptible; *antonym* (adj) untarnished, **5.** lowered; *synonyms* (adj) abased, bated, cheap, humbled, restrained, **6.** bastardized; *synonym* (adj) bastardised, **7.** despised; *synonyms* (adj) detested, scorned, despicable, hated, abhorrent, contemptuous, loathed, opprobrious, reviled, unpopular, infamous, insolent, insufferable, neglected, reproachful.

mwinikai scarred; *synonyms* (adj) marred, defaced, hurt.

mwiokoa order; *synonyms* (n) command, decree, dictate, array, rank, sort, charge, class, condition, disposition, edict, (v) direct, commission, arrange, call; *antonyms* (n) anarchy, chaos, confusion, mayhem, mess, (v) disorder, request.

mwiokoaki ordered; *synonyms* (adj) tidy, regular, arranged, methodical, orderly, coherent, consistent, lawful, logical.

mwnanga depart; *synonyms* (v) quit, deviate, go, decease, die, diverge, leave, part, start, stray, vary, wander, deflect, digress, expire; *antonyms* (v) stay, arrive, enter, come.

mwnangaki departed; *synonyms* (v) lost, (adj) dead, gone, bygone, bypast, defunct, extinct, former, late, past, left, foregone, lifeless, (n) deceased, decedent.

N

n 1. by; *synonyms* (prep) beside, at, of, about, on, per, (adv) aside, away, past, through, apart, along, beyond, (adv, prep) alongside, (adj) over, **2.** in; *synonyms* (prep) during, between, by, inside, (adv) indoors, inward, (v) press, (n) inch, (adj) stylish, fashionable, inwards, trendy, within, modish, popular; *antonyms* (prep) out, outside, **3.** for; *synonyms* (prep) because, behind, toward, (conj) considering, since, (adv) against, as, therefore, hence, **4.** at; *synonyms* (prep) in, a, (n) astatine, (prf) all, completely, wholly, (adj) entertainment, levee, party, reception, conversazione, home, soiree, **5.** with; *synonyms* (prep) for, among, plus, (adj) including, (n) withe, **6.** to; *synonyms* (prep) before, into, near, towards, until, unto, (adv) versus, (v) till.

na 1. near; *synonyms* (prep) about, by, around, (adv) close, almost, towards, (adj) adjoining, adjacent, contiguous, imminent, impending, narrow, (v) familiar, approximate, approach; *antonym* (adj) distant, **2.** will; *synonyms* (v) bequeath, devise, wish, leave, (n) volition, command, desire, inclination, determination, pleasure, resolve, intent, mind, courage, liking.

naba 1. also; *synonyms* (adv) too, likewise, moreover, more, besides, withal, again, equally, further, item, similarly, so, (conj) and, furthermore, **2.** besides; *synonyms* (adv) also, additionally, anyway, else, therewithal, beyond, but, still, thereto, therewith, yet, (prep) except, on, beside, excepting, **3.** including; *synonyms* (prep) plus, (v) included, (adj) counting; *antonyms* (prep) excluding, without, **4.** indeed; *synonyms* (adv) actually, certainly, exactly, much, really, surely, greatly, absolutely, clearly, definitely, positively, precisely, truly, (int) forsooth, (adj) verily; *antonym* (adv) possibly, **5.** yet; *synonyms* (adv) however, notwithstanding, even, nonetheless, though, hitherto, eventually, unless, always, if, finally, heretofore, (conj) nevertheless, (n) already, (adj) erewhile.

nabangkai 1. lately; *synonyms* (adv) recently, late, freshly, latterly, newly, just, new, (adj) anew, afresh, **2.** certain; *synonyms* (adj) actual, definite, sure, absolute, assured, dependable, indisputable, reliable, categorical, decisive, fixed, inevitable, infallible, particular, (v) bound; *antonyms* (adj) uncertain, doubtful, unsure, questionable, **3.** fresh; *synonyms* (adj) bracing, brisk, clean, novel, bright, original, recent, airy, bold, alive, chilly, cool, forward, green, pure; *antonyms* (adj) old, stale, decayed, exhausted, hot, humid, muggy, musty, off, oppressive, rotten, tired, worn, dry, sweltering,

4. afresh; *synonyms* (*adv*) again, lately, often, repeatedly, (*adj*) repeated, **5**. new; *synonyms* (*adj*) modern, additional, inexperienced, innovative, raw, strange, unaccustomed, unprecedented, young, contemporary, current, different, newfangled, unfamiliar, (*adv*) fresh; *antonyms* (*adj*) familiar, outgoing, second-hand, traditional, used, less, old-fashioned, (*adv*) past, **6**. late; *synonyms* (*adj*) former, dead, deceased, behindhand, belated, delayed, slow, tardy, dull, defunct, bygone, posthumous, (*adv*) dilatory, backward, belatedly; *antonyms* (*adj*) ahead, (*adv*) early, punctually, promptly, punctual, **7**. existent; *synonyms* (*adj*) factual, real, instant, existing, extant, living, present, substantial, genuine, **8**. categorical; *synonyms* (*adj*) distinct, flat, categoric, dogmatic, downright, emphatic, explicit, positive, unconditional, certain, (*v*) definitive, unqualified, decided, unequivocal, clear; *antonym* (*adj*) qualified, **9**. decided; *synonyms* (*v*) marked, determinate, settled, (*adj*) determined, resolute, unmistakable, conclusive, peremptory, final, finished, firm, stark; *antonym* (*adj*) undecided, **10**. actual; *synonyms* (*adj*) true, authentic, existent, literal, precise, tangible, veritable, very, concrete, correct, direct, effective, exact, immediate, (*n*) accurate; *antonyms* (*adj*) false, hypothetical, supposed, **11**. newly, **12**. anew, **13**. freshly, **14**. factual; *synonyms* (*adj*) practical, right, truthful; *antonyms* (*adj*) untrue, legendary, **15**. absolute; *synonyms* (*adj*) total, full, sheer, arbitrary, authoritative, complete, dictatorial, extreme, great, outright, sheer, supreme, thorough, unconditioned, unlimited; *antonym* (*adj*) partial, **16**. contemporary; *synonyms* (*adj*) contemporaneous, up-to-date, topical, fashionable, simultaneous, coetaneous, cotemporary, (*n*) coeval, equal, **17**. extant; *synonym* (*adj*) surviving; *antonym* (*adj*) extinct, **18**. determinate; *synonyms* (*adj*) special, limited, specific, (*v*) express, advised, **19**. novel; *synonyms* (*n*) fiction, romance, book, narrative, story, tale, literature, (*adj*) curious, unique, extraordinary, abnormal, foreign, uncommon, **20**. modern; *synonyms* (*adj*) advanced, latest, stylish, chic, latter, modernistic, modish, groundbreaking, later, mod, progressive, (*n*) neoteric; *antonyms* (*adj*) ancient, antiquated, prehistoric, conservative, neurotic, old-time, primordial.

nabawe 1. bygone; *synonyms* (*adj*) past, ancient, former, gone, obsolete, outmoded, archaic, bypast, dead, departed, erstwhile, foregone, late, old, (*n*) antique, **2**. ancient; *synonyms* (*adj*) aged, antiquated, bygone, hoary, primitive, olden, antediluvian, dated, earlier, older, original, prehistoric, previous, primeval, (*n*) elder; *antonym* (*adj*) modern, **3**. hoary; *synonyms* (*adj*) gray, hoar, grey, white, elderly, musty, canescent, dull, **4**.

discontinued; *antonym* (*adj*) continued, **5**. fossilized; *synonyms* (*adj*) fossilised, ossified, **6**. archaic; *synonyms* (*adj*) old-fashioned, outdated, quaint, passé, extinct, medieval, **7**. aged; *synonyms* (*adj*) senile, ripe, decrepit, senior, venerable; *antonym* (*n*) young, **8**. antique; *synonyms* (*adj*) antiquarian, demode, passe, (*n*) relic, antiquity, (*v*) antiquate; *antonym* (*n*) new, **9**. prehistoric; *synonyms* (*adj*) primordial, prehistorical, **10**. old; *synonyms* (*adj*) experienced, veteran, mature, stale, disused, hackneyed, traditional, decayed, inveterate, auld, superannuated, worn, neglected, unoriginal; *antonyms* (*adj*) fresh, latest, novel, youthful, **11**. venerable; *synonyms* (*adj*) reverend, estimable, respectable, distinguished, sacred, worthy, considerable, grand, revered, reverenced, solemn.

nabe 1. fond; *synonyms* (*adj*) affectionate, amorous, caring, devoted, loving, tender, adoring, ardent, doting, attached, indulgent, kind, enamored; *antonym* (*adj*) uncaring, **2**. loving; *synonyms* (*adj*) fond, friendly, admiring, compassionate, fatherly, gentle, intimate, motherly, passionate, warm, (*v*) sympathetic; *antonym* (*adj*) cold, **3**. friendly; *synonyms* (*adj*) amiable, favorable, amicable, benevolent, companionable, convivial, decent, good-natured, complaisant, approachable, accommodating, affable, close, familiar, genial; *antonyms* (*adj*) hostile, unfriendly, aggressive, aloof, disagreeable, distant, formal, bad-tempered, belligerent, curt, frosty, reserved, **4**. attached; *synonyms* (*adj*) connected, affiliated, committed, associated, loyal, near; *antonyms* (*adj*) detached, separate, unmarried, **5**. devoted; *synonyms* (*adj*) addicted, consecrated, constant, faithful, pious, dutiful, eager, enthusiastic, keen, reliable, religious, zealous, assiduous, attentive, (*prep*) dedicated; *antonyms* (*adj*) uncommitted, disloyal, indifferent, **6**. tender; *synonyms* (*adj*) painful, sensitive, soft, sore, delicate, mild, frail, immature, (*v*) proffer, present, propose, give, (*n*) offer, bid, overture; *antonyms* (*adj*) tough, hard, hardhearted, rubbery, rough.

nabea 1. cherish; *synonyms* (*v*) appreciate, entertain, foster, hug, nurture, treasure, cultivate, bosom, adore, esteem, harbor, nourish, nurse, prize, (*n*) embrace; *antonym* (*v*) hate, **2**. foster; *synonyms* (*v*) encourage, advance, cherish, breed, boost, foment, further, rear, support, educate, tend, keep, feed, patronize, promote; *antonym* (*v*) neglect, **3**. pamper; *synonyms* (*v*) indulge, baby, cocker, coddle, pet, spoil, cosset, mollycoddle, gratify, fondle, featherbed, mother.

nabeaki 1. fostered; *synonyms* (*adj*) nourished, safe, **2**. cherished; *synonyms* (*adj*) beloved, dear, precious, loved, treasured, intimate, prized, valued, wanted, pet, **3**. pampered; *synonyms (adj)* coddled, indulged, spoiled, bad, luxurious, soft, luxuriant, spoilt.

nabenabea idolize; *synonyms (v)* adore, worship, idolise, revere, admire, deify, glorify.

nabenabeaki idolized; *synonyms (adj)* idolised, adored, beloved, precious, worshipped.

nainaina 1. circle; *synonyms (n)* round, association, band, compass, ring, field, range, beat, circuit, company, gang, scope, *(v)* turn, whirl, encircle, **2**. encircle; *synonyms (v)* beset, surround, besiege, circle, embrace, bound, circumvent, enclose, encompass, environ, hem, begird, circumscribe, beleaguer, border.

nainainaki encircled; *synonyms (adj)* surrounded, enclosed, bounded, annular, annulate, annulated, bordered, circinate, circular, delimited, ingirt, ringed, wreathed.

naip 1. bottle; *synonyms (n)* container, flask, jug, jar, pot, carboy, gourd, *(v)* preserve, can, **2**. flask; *synonyms (n)* bottle, flasket, carafe, cask, decanter, beaker, flaskful, tin, alembic, bag, caster, chalice, crock, cruel, crystal.

naka 1. gentlemen; *synonym (n)* messieurs, **2**. ladies.

nakibaina 1. limbless; *synonym (adj)* boughless, **2**. armless, **3**. legless, **4**. paralyzed; *synonyms (v)* paralytic, *(adj)* palsied, crippled, dead, disabled, enervated, helpless, impotent, inert, motionless, numb, paralytical, powerless, prostrate, torpid.

nakina tow; *synonyms (n)* towage, *(v)* pull, drag, draw, haul, lug, tug, heave, trail, rake, taw; *antonym (v)* push.

nako 1. gestate; *synonyms (v)* carry, bear, expect, extend, abide, accept, acquit, advance, anticipate, apply, ask, assume, avail, await, behave, **2**. away; *synonyms (adv)* apart, absent, aside, aloof, by, forth, way, hence, *(adj)* abroad, distant, wide, gone, missing, *(int)* out, off, **3**. depart; *synonyms (v)* quit, deviate, go, decease, die, diverge, leave, part, start, stray, vary, wander, deflect, digress, expire; *antonyms (v)* stay, arrive, enter, come, **4**. go; *synonyms (v)* elapse, pass, break, crack, depart, disappear, drive, run, travel, fall, function, operate, *(n)* fare, *(adj)* follow, move, **5**. forth; *synonyms (adv)* along, away, forward, ahead, onward, on, **6**. left; *synonyms (adj)* odd, port, remaining, larboard, sinister, unexpended, abandoned, remainder, corrupt, deserted, disastrous, dishonest, evil, inauspicious, injurious; *antonym (n)* right, **7**. leave; *synonyms (v)* forsake, abandon, desert, escape, flee, lead, lay, allow, bequeath, *(n)* furlough, holiday, permission, permit, consent, *(adj)* empty; *antonyms (v)* remain, approach, change, **8**. suction; *synonyms (n)* suck, sucking, aspiration, absorption, draft, leverage, traction, succion, **9**. to;

synonyms (prep) at, in, about, before, against, into, near, toward, towards, until, unto, *(adv)* versus, *(v)* till, **10**. out; *synonyms (adv)* beyond, outwards, *(v)* reveal, disclose, discover, impart, *(adj)* extinct, outside, outward; *antonym (prep)* inside, **11**. progress; *synonyms (n)* headway, improvement, furtherance, betterment, gain, course, advancement, development, growth, increase, movement, *(v)* proceed, continue, develop, grow; *antonyms (n)* decline, deterioration, *(v)* regress, **12**. proceed; *synonyms (v)* originate, ensue, flow, arise, emanate, happen, issue, progress, result, stem, do, hold, journey, act, keep.

nakoa approach; *synonyms (n)* access, entry, advent, arrival, avenue, coming, entrance, means, method, adit, *(v)* advance, accost, address, near, approximate; *antonym (v)* leave.

nakoaki departed; *synonyms (v)* lost, *(adj)* dead, gone, bygone, bypast, defunct, extinct, former, late, past, left, foregone, lifeless, *(n)* deceased, decedent.

nakomai 1. move; *synonyms (v)* act, affect, carry, excite, go, impel, instigate, maneuver, touch, travel, flow, bear, *(n)* motion, drive, transfer; *antonym (v)* stay, **2**. hike; *synonyms (n)* walk, raise, rise, advance, increase, saunter, trek, ascent, climb, journey, *(v)* boost, tramp, stroll, trudge, jump, **3**. march; *synonyms (n)* hike, parade, demonstration, ramble, course, protest, gait, *(v)* border, pace, process, stride, demo, demonstrate, bound, strut, **4**. displace; *synonyms (v)* dislocate, dislodge, dismiss, bump, depose, remove, shift, uproot, cashier, discharge, disturb, eject, evacuate, expel, move; *antonym (v)* replace, **5**. voyage; *synonyms (n)* cruise, tour, trip, expedition, passage, flight, quest, excursion, outing, *(v)* sail, navigate, **6**. publish; *synonyms (v)* declare, announce, disclose, circulate, divulge, issue, proclaim, communicate, notify, advertise, broadcast, print, promulgate, spread, expose, **7**. parade; *synonyms (n)* display, ostentation, show, pageant, ceremony, pomp, flourish, file, procession, *(v)* flaunt, exhibit, array, swagger, troop, flash, **8**. stroll; *synonyms (n)* promenade, perambulation, turn, nomadize, ride, *(v)* amble, roam, wander, range, jaunt, meander, loiter, linger, gad, dawdle, **9**. promenade; *synonyms (n)* ball, mall, prom, gala, *(v)* dance.

nakomaiaki published; *synonyms (adj)* edited, known, promulgated, divulgate, public, *(adv)* available.

nakon to; *synonyms (prep)* at, by, in, about, before, against, into, near, toward, towards, until, unto, *(adv)* versus, *(prf)* on, *(v)* till.

nakonako 1. march; *synonyms (n)* walk, hike, parade, demonstration, ramble, trek, course, *(v)* journey, tramp, advance, border, pace, process, stride, stroll, **2**. move; *synonyms (v)* act, affect, carry, excite, go, impel, instigate, maneuver, touch, travel, flow, bear, (*n*) motion, drive, transfer; *antonym* (*v*) stay, **3.** pace; *synonyms* (*n*) rate, footstep, rapidity, speed, tempo, tread, celerity, fastness, run, beat, cadence, carriage, footfall, (*v*) step, gait; *antonym* (*n*) slowness, **4.** tread; *synonyms* (*v*) trample, crush, plod, (*n*) rung, track, **5.** walk; *synonyms* (*v*) move, roam, promenade, foot, ambulate, ambulation, traverse, amble, (*n*) path, saunter, excursion, pass, turn, trip, constitutional.

nam 1. suck; *synonyms* (*v*) draw, drink, imbibe, nurse, absorb, lactate, suckle, drain, puff, aspirate, pull, breastfeed, (*n*) sucking, suction, **2.** taste; *synonyms* (*n*) bit, flavor, liking, morsel, penchant, appetite, drop, fondness, gusto, mouthful, (*v*) relish, savor, sample, smack, discernment; *antonyms* (*n*) dislike, tastelessness.

nama 1. agree; *synonyms* (*v*) accord, admit, acknowledge, acquiesce, adjust, accede, bargain, concord, correspond, fit, harmonize, suit, compromise, align, (*n*) coincide; *antonyms* (*v*) disagree, oppose, differ, argue, object, refuse, refute, **2.** attach; *synonyms* (*v*) add, adhere, append, affix, bind, link, associate, assign, annex, apply, fasten, fix, nail, stick, yoke; *antonyms* (*v*) detach, undo, disconnect, separate, unfasten, **3.** thread; *synonyms* (*n*) string, line, yarn, rope, twine, wire, cord, fiber, (*v*) file, range, penetrate, lace, pass, run, meander, **4.** pledge; *synonyms* (*n*) bond, gage, assurance, engage, promise, plight, bet, bail, oath, (*v*) pawn, wager, covenant, guarantee, contract, assure, **5.** understand; *synonyms* (*v*) interpret, recognize, catch, hear, learn, realize, see, appreciate, assume, believe, comprehend, construe, deduce, gather, grasp; *antonyms* (*v*) misinterpret, misconstrue, misunderstand, **6.** unite; *synonyms* (*v*) combine, blend, coalesce, connect, join, meet, amalgamate, attach, fuse, merge, tie, unify, converge, couple, agree; *antonym* (*v*) divide.

namaki 1. attached; *synonyms* (*adj*) connected, affectionate, affiliated, committed, associated, devoted, fond, loving, loyal, near; *antonyms* (*adj*) detached, separate, unmarried, **2.** understood; *synonyms* (*v*) admitted, (*adj*) implicit, tacit, implied, silent, assumed; *antonyms* (*adj*) explicit, spoken, **3.** pledged; *synonyms* (*adj*) engaged, affianced, betrothed, bespoken, bound, busy, occupied, **4.** threaded; *synonym* (*adj*) screwed, **5.** united; *synonyms* (*adj*) joined, joint, combined, cooperative, allied, mutual, concerted, mixed, common, conjunctive, undivided, conjunct, unanimous, conjoint, (*v*) consolidated; *antonyms* (*adj*) individual, divided.

namakin 1. note; *synonyms* (*n*) comment, mention, remark, annotation, heed, indication, mark, attention, bill, distinction, epistle, (*v*) notice, mind,

look, detect; *antonym* (*v*) ignore, **2.** mistrust; *synonyms* (*n*) doubt, suspicion, misgiving, disbelief, apprehension, wariness, hesitation, jealousy, scruple, (*v*) distrust, suspect, disbelieve, discredit, query, question; *antonym* (*v*) trust, **3.** distrust; *synonyms* (*n*) mistrust, uncertainty, incredulity, skepticism, cynicism, pessimism; *antonyms* (*n*) confidence, faith, (*v*) believe, **4.** doubt; *synonyms* (*n*) dispute, incertitude, diffidence, doubtfulness, dubiety, fear, qualm, quandary, reservation, suspense, anxiety, uncertainness, (*v*) demur, hesitate, contest; *antonyms* (*n*) certainty, conclusiveness, **5.** impress; *synonyms* (*v*) imprint, affect, move, print, inscribe, instill, touch, emboss, dent, inculcate, strike, amaze, (*n*) stamp, impression, press, **6.** conjecture; *synonyms* (*n*) guess, supposition, assumption, speculation, hypothesis, surmise, guesswork, (*v*) suppose, estimate, anticipate, assume, speculate, divine, expect, forecast; *antonym* (*n*) fact, **7.** guess; *synonyms* (*v*) conjecture, deem, reckon, calculate, feel, figure, foretell, gauge, infer, think, count, measure, consider, deduce, (*n*) belief, **8.** suppose; *synonyms* (*v*) imagine, presume, conceive, judge, regard, hope, fancy, gather, hypothesize, opine, postulate, presuppose, say, put, take, **9.** perceive; *synonyms* (*v*) apprehend, comprehend, discern, discover, grasp, see, find, appreciate, know, observe, sense, catch, behold, distinguish, note, **10.** sense; *synonyms* (*n*) intelligence, perception, meaning, sensation, logic, awareness, experience, feeling, idea, notion, reason, understanding, purport, (*v*) intellect, perceive; *antonyms* (*n*) garbage, ludicrousness, nonsense, stupidity, foolishness, gibberish, **11.** suspect; *synonyms* (*v*) affright, (*n*) dread, defendant, (*adj*) fishy, questionable, shady, suspicious, dubious, funny, queer, doubtful, implausible; *antonym* (*adj*) trustworthy, **12.** surmise; *synonyms* (*v*) understand, conclude, (*n*) opinion, presumption, shot, venture, theory, surmisal.

namakina 1. comprehend; *synonyms* (*v*) apprehend, catch, embrace, grasp, understand, appreciate, comprise, feel, see, sense, apperceive, admit, compass, conceive, contain, **2.** felt; *synonyms* (*v*) mat, snarl, tangle, braid, entangle, (*adj*) perceived, sensed, conscious, **3.** feel; *synonyms* (*v*) experience, consider, finger, handle, believe, deem, endure, find, hold, (*n*) touch, atmosphere, feeling, sound, texture, air; *antonym* (*v*) observe, **4.** perceive; *synonyms* (*v*) comprehend, discern, discover, know, notice, behold, detect, distinguish, note, recognize, penetrate, hear, divine, get, descry, **5.** understand; *synonyms* (*v*) interpret, learn, realize, assume, construe, deduce, gather, perceive, read, translate, suppose, infer, absorb, dig, (*adj*) take; *antonyms* (*v*) misinterpret, misconstrue, misunderstand, **6**. see; *synonyms* (*v*) look, ascertain, envision, inspect, regard, witness, attend, call, check, contemplate, control, escort, espy, figure, glimpse.

namakinaki 1. comprehended; *synonyms* (*adj*) appreciated, apprehended, gratifying, pleasing, satisfying, **2**. noted; *synonyms* (*v*) notorious, (*adj*) distinguished, famous, illustrious, conspicuous, glorious, celebrated, eminent, famed, known, renowned, well-known, noble, marked, notable, **3**. felt; *synonyms* (*v*) mat, snarl, tangle, braid, entangle, (*adj*) perceived, sensed, conscious, **4**. perceived; *synonyms* (*adj*) felt, apparent, ostensible, professed, supposed, alleged, seeming, superficial, **5**. sensed, **6**. understood; *synonyms* (*v*) admitted, (*adj*) implicit, tacit, implied, silent, assumed; *antonyms* (*adj*) explicit, spoken, **7**. suspected; *synonyms* (*adj*) suspect, distrusted, **8**. supposed; *synonyms* (*adj*) conjectural, hypothetical, reputed, imaginary, putative, suppositional, suppositious, supposititious, pretended, theoretical; *antonyms* (*adj*) real, actual.

namatoa stubborn; *synonyms* (*adj*) obstinate, contrary, hard, intractable, perverse, determined, obdurate, persistent, refractory, rigid, tenacious, inveterate, contumacious, difficult, firm; *antonyms* (*adj*) compliant, flexible, irresolute, amenable.

namomara 1. nauseous; *synonyms* (*adj*) distasteful, disgusting, loathsome, nasty, nauseating, sickening, filthy, noisome, offensive, revolting, ugly, vile, (*v*) fulsome, abhorrent, insufferable; *antonym* (*adj*) well, **2**. discouraged; *synonyms* (*adj*) disappointed, despondent, crestfallen, dejected, demoralized, disheartened, dispirited, downcast, downhearted, frustrated, pessimistic, depressed, baffled, balked; *antonym* (*adj*) optimistic, **3**. abhorrent; *synonyms* (*adj*) hateful, repulsive, detestable, repugnant, abominable, horrible, obnoxious, unpleasant, foul, forbidding, despicable, ghastly, heinous, (*v*) execrable, odious, **4**. disgusted; *synonyms* (*adj*) sick, ill, sickened, weary, aghast, appalled, brainsick, corrupted, crazy, demented, horrified, shocked, squeamish, abhorred, dismayed; *antonym* (*adj*) delighted, **5**. sick; *synonyms* (*adj*) queasy, ailing, indisposed, poorly, invalid, diseased, morbid, sickly, nauseous, poor, disgusted, nauseated, upset, (*v*) unwell, puke; *antonym* (*adj*) healthy.

namoro 1. dribble; *synonyms* (*n*) trickle, dribbling, (*v*) drip, drool, drop, drivel, slobber, distill, flow, ooze, spout, trill, leak, seep, slabber, **2**. drool; *synonyms* (*n*) bosh, humbug, tosh, twaddle, baloney, bilgewater, boloney, (*v*) dribble, salivate, slaver, spit.

namta 1. inhale; *synonyms* (*v*) breathe, absorb, imbibe, draw, suck, drag, drink, attract, inspire, receive, respire, admit, import, ingest, (*n*) sniff;

antonym (*v*) exhale, **2**. slurp; *synonyms* (*n*) gulp, mouthful, swig, taste, draft, glug, (*v*) sip, swallow, eat, down, investigate, pry, **3**. suck; *synonyms* (*v*) nurse, lactate, suckle, drain, puff, aspirate, pull, breastfeed, (*n*) sucking, suction, **4**. sip; *synonyms* (*n*) nip, bite, drop, shot, slurp, nibble, (*v*) sample, quaff, lap, test, try, (*adj*) sup, **5**. sample; *synonyms* (*n*) example, instance, specimen, model, pattern, assay, case, illustration, exemplar, design, piece, precedent, (*v*) attempt, essay, prove, **6**. taste; *synonyms* (*n*) bit, flavor, liking, morsel, penchant, appetite, fondness, gusto, predilection, preference, refinement, (*v*) relish, savor, smack, discernment; *antonyms* (*n*) dislike, tastelessness.

namtaki inhaled; *synonym* (*adj*) inspired.

namtete 1. greedy; *synonyms* (*adj*) eager, avid, gluttonous, covetous, desirous, acquisitive, glutton, grasping, piggish, esurient, grabby, hungry, insatiable, ravenous, (*v*) avaricious; *antonym* (*adj*) generous, **2**. insatiable; *synonyms* (*adj*) greedy, insatiate, voracious, unsatiable.

namwakaina moon; *synonyms* (*n*) lunation, moonlight, moonshine, satellite, epoch, bootleg, (*v*) daydream, dream, fantasize, bemuse, gaze, glare, meditate, (*adj*) quicksilver, weathercock.

nana accustomed; *synonyms* (*adj*) customary, habitual, familiar, normal, usual, wonted, natural, common, everyday, habituated, ordinary, traditional, hardened; *antonyms* (*adj*) unaccustomed, unusual.

nanai 1. mob; *synonyms* (*n*) crowd, gang, pack, mass, horde, crew, band, bunch, concourse, rabble, swarm, cluster, company, army, (*v*) throng, **2**. drove; *synonyms* (*n*) flock, herd, covey, mob, multitude, group, host, legion, school, troop, (*adj*) bevy, shoal, cloud, **3**. brood; *synonyms* (*n*) breed, issue, offspring, family, litter, posterity, progeny, young, farrow, (*v*) hatch, sulk, think, incubate, cover, (*adj*) brooding, **4**. appetizing; *synonyms* (*adj*) appetising, delectable, delicious, luscious, tasty, tantalizing, palatable, savory, scrumptious, spicy; *antonyms* (*adj*) tasteless, unappetizing, **5**. luscious; *synonyms* (*adj*) appetizing, juicy, rich, dulcet, delightful, succulent, sweet, voluptuous, yummy, delicate, lush, luxurious, sumptuous, toothsome, candied; *antonym* (*adj*) dry, **6**. crowd; *synonyms* (*n*) huddle, collection, press, circle, assembly, congregation, assemblage, audience, gathering, knot, (*v*) squeeze, compress, cram, jam, crush; *antonym* (*v*) disperse, **7**. herd; *synonyms* (*n*) drove, ruck, (*v*) drive, **8**. bevy; *synonyms* (*n*) party, array, set, **9**. crowded; *synonyms* (*adj*) close, compact, congested, busy, dense, full, packed, populous, jammed, cramped, teeming, thick, tight, (*n*) thronged; *antonyms* (*adj*) empty, sparse, **10**. delicious; *synonyms* (*adj*) pleasing, agreeable, charming, dainty, enjoyable, lovely, grateful, fragrant, exquisite, pleasant, wonderful, **11.** group; *synonyms* (n) brigade, association, clump, lump, muster, assortment, batch, category, clique, (v) class, rank, sort, arrange, assemble, classify, **12.** pack; *synonyms* (n) bundle, backpack, box, package, knapsack, bag, lot, (v) heap, fill, load, carry, pile, ram, stuff, wrap; *antonym* (v) unpack, **13.** palatable; *synonyms* (adj) eatable, edible, good; *antonym* (adj) unpalatable, **14.** tasty; *synonyms* (adj) tasteful, nice, savoury, flavorful, appreciate, criticise, cute, judge; *antonyms* (adj) bland, inedible, **15.** sweet; *synonyms* (adj) beloved, fresh, mellow, dear, lovable, melodious, musical, sugary, honeyed, odorous, aromatic, clean, amiable, (n) confection, confectionery; *antonyms* (adj) sour, acid, bitter, discordant, acidic, pungent, sharp, salty, **16.** swarm; *synonyms* (v) pour, teem, abound, stream, infest, gather, overrun, congregate, **17.** savory; *synonyms* (n) delicacy, (adj) piquant, inoffensive, peppery, **18.** packed; *synonyms* (adj) crowded, filled, overcrowded, brimming; *antonym* (adj) deserted.

nanaiaki 1. crowded; *synonyms* (adj) close, compact, congested, busy, dense, full, packed, populous, jammed, cramped, teeming, thick, tight, (n) thronged; *antonyms* (adj) empty, sparse, **2.** driven; *synonyms* (v) drive, (adj) determined, impelled, compulsive, bound, dictated, dynamic, encouraged, goaded, hell-bent, provoked, successful, activist, efficient, energetic, **3.** grouped; *synonyms* (adj) sorted, collective, **4.** packed; *synonyms* (adj) crowded, filled, overcrowded, brimming; *antonym* (adj) deserted.

nananga 1. stripped; *synonyms* (adj) bare, naked, nude, exposed, fleeced, undressed, desolate, stark, unclothed, **2.** skinned; *synonyms* (adj) abraded, scraped, frustrated, painful, raw, scratched, sensitive, sore, tender, bleeding, bloody.

nang 1. going; *synonyms* (v) go, course, (n) departure, exit, leaving, parting, disappearance, expiration, action, passing, (adj) running, working, **2.** near; *synonyms* (prep) about, by, around, (adv) close, almost, towards, (adj) adjoining, adjacent, contiguous, imminent, impending, narrow, (v) familiar, approximate, approach; *antonym* (adj) distant, **3.** leaving; *synonyms* (n) leave, desertion, going, farewell, abandonment, departing; *antonym* (n) arrival, **4.** nearly; *synonyms* (adv) approximately, closely, virtually, intimately, nigh, practically, roughly, much, just, dear, halfway, (adj) near, most, thereabouts, approaching, **5.** soon; *synonyms* (adv) shortly, early, presently, anon, immediately, directly, betimes, now, promptly, quickly, soonly, briefly, erelong, fast, quick, **6.** shortly; *synonyms* (adv) soon, abruptly, concisely, curtly, short, brusquely, rapidly, (adj) forthwith, summarily.

nanginang 1. hindering; *synonyms* (adj) impeding, clogging, obstructive, counter, discouraging, impedimental, meddlesome, obstruent, preclusive, impeditive, (n) impedition, **2.** veil; *synonyms* (n) cover, camouflage, shroud, blind, curtain, shade, (v) screen, hide, cloak, disguise, mask, cloud, conceal, obscure, secrete; *antonyms* (v) disclose, reveal, **3.** worry; *synonyms* (v) torment, trouble, bother, distress, tease, annoy, care, disturb, fear, molest, (n) concern, burden, harass, pain, fuss; *antonyms* (v) soothe, reassure, (n) calmness, reassurance.

nango 1. prop; *synonyms* (n) support, post, shore, fulcrum, property, mainstay, airscrew, column, pillar, stay, (v) buttress, brace, bolster, hold, rest, **2.** support; *synonyms* (n) help, stand, aid, keep, comfort, maintenance, patronage, (v) assist, prop, back, encourage, maintain, bear, boost, carry; *antonyms* (n) hindrance, (v) oppose, neglect, undermine, abandon, reject, weaken.

nangoa 1. prop; *synonyms* (n) support, post, shore, fulcrum, property, mainstay, airscrew, column, pillar, stay, (v) buttress, brace, bolster, hold, rest, **2.** support; *synonyms* (n) help, stand, aid, keep, comfort, maintenance, patronage, (v) assist, prop, back, encourage, maintain, bear, boost, carry; *antonyms* (n) hindrance, (v) oppose, neglect, undermine, abandon, reject, weaken.

nangoaki supported; *synonyms* (v) borne, carried, conveyed, supporting, (adj) bolstered, based, (adv) on.

nangoango listless; *synonyms* (adj) indifferent, lethargic, dull, careless, indolent, languid, inert, inattentive, dispirited, lackadaisical, slow, spiritless, uninterested, heavy, apathetic; *antonyms* (adj) lively, animated, energetic.

nangonango 1. indolent; *synonyms* (adj) idle, inactive, lazy, slothful, sluggish, careless, drowsy, dull, faineant, inert, listless, otiose, slow, torpid, lackadaisical; *antonyms* (adj) energetic, active, **2.** nonchalant; *synonyms* (adj) negligent, indifferent, insouciant, unconcerned, carefree, casual, calm, cool, offhand, easygoing; *antonym* (adj) anxious, **3.** listless; *synonyms* (adj) lethargic, indolent, languid, inattentive, dispirited, spiritless, uninterested, heavy, apathetic, feeble, heedless, impassive, phlegmatic, pococurante, regardless; *antonyms* (adj) lively, animated, **4.** feeble; *synonyms* (adj) delicate, weak, decrepit, ailing, dim, frail, helpless, infirm, lax, mild, poor, powerless, thin, (v) faint, debilitated; *antonyms* (adj) strong, vigorous, hearty, tough, **5.** weak; *synonyms* (adj) flat, flimsy, fragile, watery, light, cowardly, diluted, exhausted, inadequate, nerveless, shaky, sickly, slack, slight, (v) loose; *antonyms* (adj) brave, concentrated, firm, safe, compelling, determined, effective, forceful, healthy, intense, powerful, resolute, robust, sturdy, able.

nangora 1. miserable; *synonyms* *(adj)* mean, poor, meager, abject, bad, deplorable, desolate, downcast, low, measly, unhappy, distressed, lamentable, *(v)* forlorn, wretched; *antonyms* *(adj)* happy, cheerful, generous, **2.** restless; *synonyms* *(adj)* fidgety, nervous, uneasy, unquiet, agitated, apprehensive, fretful, impatient, restive, feverish, turbulent, jumpy, disturbed, edgy, *(v)* anxious; *antonyms* *(adj)* calm, relaxed, **3.** uncomfortable; *synonyms* *(adj)* awkward, embarrassing, troubled, inconvenient, difficult, discomfited, cheerless, embarrassed, painful, *(v)* untoward; *antonyms* *(adj)* comfortable, comfy.

nangoraoi 1. comfortable; *synonyms* *(adj)* cozy, easy, agreeable, pleased, pleasing, prosperous, congenial, pleasurable, rich, enjoyable, commodious, content, contented, *(v)* snug, calm; *antonyms* *(adj)* uncomfortable, poor, formal, tense, unpleasant, intimidating, unaccustomed, unhappy, **2.** aligned; *synonyms* *(adj)* level, alined, amalgamated, combined, horizontal, joined, united, parallel, partnered, **3.** restful; *synonyms* *(adj)* quiet, peaceful, comfortable, still, placid, soft, reposeful, tranquil, relaxing, peaceable, serene, soothing.

nano 1. apt; *synonyms* *(adj)* appropriate, adroit, apropos, apposite, intelligent, good, able, adequate, convenient, dexterous, efficient, fit, ready, smart, clever; *antonym* *(adj)* inappropriate, **2.** liable; *synonyms* *(adj)* amenable, accountable, answerable, apt, disposed, exposed, inclined, responsible, likely, subject, culpable, vulnerable, given, obnoxious, susceptible; *antonym* *(adj)* exempt, **3.** low; *synonyms* *(adj)* contemptible, abject, humble, ignoble, base, blue, common, deep, dejected, depressed, down, downcast, downhearted, *(adv)* gentle, *(n)* depression; *antonyms* *(adj)* cheerful, happy, high-pitched, loud, important, piercing, *(n)* high, **4.** astute; *synonyms* *(adj)* acute, shrewd, artful, bright, sharp, quick, crafty, cunning, discerning, discriminating, perceptive, quick-witted, sagacious, sensible, *(v)* canny; *antonyms* *(adj)* naive, stupid, **5.** discerning; *synonyms* *(adj)* astute, apprehensive, discreet, judicious, penetrating, refined, conscious, understanding, clairvoyant, observant, critical, knowledgeable, insightful, keen, knowing; *antonym* *(adj)* indiscriminate, **6.** deep; *synonyms* *(adj)* thick, profound, absorbed, abstruse, broad, dark, rich, sound, strong, wide, esoteric, large, abysmal, bass, *(v)* intense; *antonyms* *(adj)* shallow, superficial, light, soft, weak, **7.** extreme; *synonyms* *(adj)* excessive, enormous, immoderate, severe, supreme, terrible, ultimate, utmost, uttermost, drastic, extraordinary, exceeding, exorbitant, *(n)* edge, end;

antonyms *(adj)* middle, reasonable, near, *(n)* mild, moderate, slight, **8.** absorbed; *synonyms* *(adj)* engrossed, intent, rapt, immersed, fixed, engaged, preoccupied, fascinated, pensive, **9.** incisive; *synonyms* *(adj)* cutting, pungent, pointed, biting, trenchant, crisp, barbed, acerbic, caustic, exquisite, incisor, knifelike, penetrative, vivid, *(n)* lively, **10.** earnest; *synonyms* *(adj)* devout, serious, eager, solemn, ardent, diligent, heartfelt, sincere, studious, staid, cordial, enthusiastic, fervent, *(n)* guarantee, deposit; *antonyms* *(adj)* flippant, halfhearted, uncertain, **11.** heartfelt; *synonyms* *(adj)* earnest, dear, genuine, wholehearted, frank, honest, real, affectionate, hearty, straight, truthful, unfeigned, warm, costly, passionate, **12.** intense; *synonyms* *(adj)* brilliant, fierce, burning, energetic, extreme, fiery, furious, heated, impassioned, hot, grave, hard, excruciating, forceful, heavy; *antonyms* *(adj)* calm, dull, imperceptible, **13.** abstruse; *synonyms* *(adj)* recondite, obscure, abstract, cryptic, difficult, mysterious, occult, complex, intricate, puzzling, secret, **14.** abstract; *synonyms* *(adj)* theoretical, academic, *(v)* abridge, filch, extract, lift, *(n)* synopsis, abridgement, digest, epitome, summary, abridgment, brief, outline, precis; *antonym* *(adj)* concrete, **15.** likely; *synonyms* *(adj)* credible, believable, probable, expected, plausible, potential, conceivable, feasible, hopeful, possible, prospective, verisimilar, convincing, *(adv)* possibly, belike; *antonyms* *(adj)* improbable, *(adv)* unlikely, **16.** below; *synonyms* *(adv)* beneath, under, infra, downstairs, *(prep)* underneath, *(adj)* low, after; *antonyms* *(prep)* above, over, **17.** abysmal; *synonyms* *(adj)* abyssal, appalling, dreadful, unfathomable, awful, horrible, unending, dire, frightful, atrocious, unspeakable, defective, deficient, faulty, flawed; *antonyms* *(adj)* excellent, exceptional, **18.** inclined; *synonyms* *(adj)* prone, oblique, willing, bowed, liable, minded, predisposed, bent, fain, diagonal, slanting, sloping, favorable, game, glad; *antonyms* *(adj)* level, reluctant, unwilling, **19.** absorbing; *synonyms* *(v)* exciting, *(adj)* interesting, engrossing, fascinating, charming, captivating, enthralling, gripping, riveting, **20.** tending; *synonyms* *(n)* care, aid, attention, treatment, nurture, assist, assistance, attending, caution, charge, concern, *(adj)* conducive, boun, conducent, conducible.

nanoa 1. bother; *synonyms* *(v)* trouble, annoy, torment, vex, worry, afflict, aggravate, *(n)* fuss, plague, bore, hassle, pain, ado, annoyance, concern; *antonyms* *(v)* delight, please, soothe, *(n)* pleasure, **2.** think; *synonyms* *(v)* consider, believe, reckon, estimate, guess, hold, imagine, muse, ponder, reflect, regard, suppose, cogitate, conjecture, contemplate; *antonym* *(v)* forget, **3.** trouble; *synonyms* *(n)* distress, bother, anxiety, difficulty, care, harass, hardship, (v) inconvenience, disorder, disquiet, agitate, burden, distract, disturb, (adj) affliction; *antonym* (v) calm, **4.** worry; *synonyms* (v) tease, fear, molest, fret, harry, mind, nag, pester, stress, (n) sorrow, apprehension, misgiving, vexation, load, (adj) irritate; *antonyms* (v) reassure, (n) calmness, reassurance.

nanoaki 1. bothered; *synonyms* (adj) worried, disturbed, troubled, concerned, distraught, nervous, uneasy, upset; *antonym* (adj) calm, **2.** troubled; *synonyms* (adj) anxious, distressed, solicitous, apprehensive, disconcerted, uncomfortable, restless, bothered, perturbed, tumultuous, turbulent, unsettled, vexed, disruptive, doubtful; *antonyms* (adj) untroubled, composed, unconcerned, **3.** worried; *synonyms* (adj) afraid, fearful, unhappy, alarmed, disquieted, fretful, stressed, tense, (v) afflicted, agitated, frightened, pained; *antonyms* (adj) carefree, reassured, relaxed.

nanoanga 1. compassionate; *synonyms* (adj) benevolent, clement, merciful, gentle, kind, pitiful, caring, considerate, humane, tender, warm, (n) sympathetic, (v) commiserate, pity, sympathize; *antonyms* (adj) hardhearted, unfeeling, **2.** merciful; *synonyms* (adj) compassionate, gracious, lenient, benign, kindly, beneficent, forgiving, good, sparing, benignant, charitable, indulgent, mild, propitious, forbearing; *antonyms* (adj) cruel, pitiless, merciless, **3.** pitying; *synonyms* (adj) affectionate, bad, contrite, deplorable, dingy, dismal, distressing, drab, drear, dreary, gloomy, lamentable, meritless, soft, sorry, **4.** sympathise; *synonyms* (v) empathise, empathize, gather, infer, interpret, read, realise, realize, see, understand, translate, **5.** sympathetic; *synonyms* (adj) congenial, agreeable, favorable, friendly, likeable, pleasant, appreciative, brotherly, compatible, cordial, harmonious, helpful, likable, sensitive, sympathizing; *antonym* (adj) unsympathetic, **6.** pity; *synonyms* (n) compassion, commiseration, mercy, condolence, clemency, pathos, remorse, shame, sympathy, comfort, feeling, benevolence, forgiveness, kindness, (v) condole; *antonym* (n) blame.

nanoangaea sympathize; *synonyms* (v) commiserate, pity, understand, sympathise, empathize, see, align, bleed, comfort, empathise, gather, infer, interpret, read, realise.

nanoata 1. doubt; *synonyms* (n) disbelief, misgiving, question, dispute, apprehension, incertitude, skepticism, uncertainty, diffidence, (v) distrust, query, suspicion, mistrust, suspect, demur; *antonyms* (n) certainty, confidence, conclusiveness, (v) trust, **2.** conjecture; *synonyms* (n) guess, supposition, assumption, speculation, hypothesis, surmise, (v) suppose, estimate, believe, anticipate,

assume, speculate, divine, expect, forecast; *antonym* (n) fact, **3.** distrust; *synonyms* (n) hesitation, incredulity, cynicism, pessimism, (v) doubt, disbelieve, discredit; *antonym* (n) faith, **4.** feel; *synonyms* (v) experience, sense, consider, finger, handle, deem, endure, find, hold, (n) touch, atmosphere, feeling, sound, texture, air; *antonym* (v) observe, **5.** mistrust; *synonyms* (n) wariness, jealousy, scruple, distrustfulness, qualm, **6.** note; *synonyms* (n) comment, mention, remark, annotation, heed, indication, mark, attention, bill, distinction, epistle, (v) notice, mind, look, detect; *antonym* (v) ignore, **7.** impress; *synonyms* (v) imprint, affect, move, print, inscribe, instill, emboss, dent, inculcate, strike, amaze, dazzle, (n) stamp, impression, press, **8.** guess; *synonyms* (v) conjecture, reckon, calculate, feel, figure, foretell, gauge, infer, think, count, measure, deduce, imagine, (n) belief, estimation, **9.** suspect; *synonyms* (v) fear, presume, gather, conceive, affright, (n) dread, defendant, (adj) fishy, questionable, shady, suspicious, dubious, funny, queer, doubtful; *antonym* (adj) trustworthy, **10.** suppose; *synonyms* (v) judge, regard, hope, fancy, hypothesize, opine, postulate, presuppose, say, put, take, plan, hypothesise, make, reflect, **11.** surmise; *synonyms* (v) understand, conclude, (n) opinion, presumption, shot, venture, theory, surmisal, **12.** perceive; *synonyms* (v) apprehend, comprehend, discern, discover, grasp, see, appreciate, know, catch, behold, distinguish, note, recognize, apperceive, penetrate, **13.** sense; *synonyms* (n) intelligence, perception, meaning, sensation, logic, awareness, idea, notion, reason, understanding, purport, (v) intellect, perceive, scent, brains; *antonyms* (n) garbage, ludicrousness, nonsense, stupidity, foolishness, gibberish.

nanoataki 1. noted; *synonyms* (v) notorious, (adj) distinguished, famous, illustrious, conspicuous, glorious, celebrated, eminent, famed, known, renowned, well-known, noble, marked, notable, **2.** felt; *synonyms* (v) mat, snarl, tangle, braid, entangle, (adj) perceived, sensed, conscious, **3.** supposed; *synonyms* (adj) conjectural, alleged, assumed, hypothetical, reputed, imaginary, putative, apparent, ostensible, suppositional, professed, supposititious, suppositious, pretended, theoretical; *antonyms* (adj) real, actual, **4.** suspected; *synonyms* (adj) suspect, supposed, distrusted, **5.** perceived; *synonyms* (adj) felt, seeming, superficial, **6.** sensed.

nanoati 1. covet; *synonyms* (v) begrudge, desire, envy, long, aspire, crave, grudge, hanker, want, fancy, wish, **2.** crave; *synonyms* (v) beg, ask, beseech, covet, implore, entreat, claim, adjure, demand, hunger, lust, need, pine, pray, request, **3.**

need; *synonyms* (*v*) lack, require, destitution, indigence, involve, exact, (*n*) deficiency, must, necessity, deprivation, requirement, absence, beggary, distress, exigency; *antonym* (*n*) wealth, **4.** lack; *synonyms* (*n*) dearth, default, defect, deficit, famine, insufficiency, poverty, shortage, shortcoming, inadequacy, drought, vacancy, (*v*) fail, fault, failure; *antonyms* (*n*) abundance, excess, provision, (*v*) have, **5.** fancy; *synonyms* (*v*) daydream, imagine, consider, crotchet, envision, (*adj*) conceive, elaborate, extravagant, (*n*) caprice, fantasy, dream, conceit, conception, idea, imagination; *antonyms* (*adj*) plain, unadorned, (*n*) reality, **6.** desire; *synonyms* (*n*) ambition, hope, aspiration, will, craving, impulse, liking, goal, appetite, greed, (*v*) seek, aim, choose, like, care; *antonyms* (*n*) aversion, (*v*) dislike, hate, **7.** require; *synonyms* (*v*) charge, entail, call, command, compel, force, necessitate, enjoin, expect, oblige, order, take, make, insist, bid, **8.** want; *synonyms* (*v*) mean, (*n*) penury, privation, pauperism, essential, hardship, impoverishment, longing, necessary, neediness, requisite, wishing, loss, scarcity, scarceness, **9.** wish; *synonyms* (*v*) please, prefer, intend, trust, favor, decide, (*n*) inclination, pleasure, purpose, mind, urge, plan, thirst, petition, compliments.

nanoatiaki 1. desired; *synonyms* (*adj*) coveted, craved, desirable, chosen, favorite, wanted, needed, welcome, beloved, adored, appropriate, pet, preferred, (*v*) complying, consenting; *antonym* (*adj*) undesirable, **2.** needed; *synonyms* (*adj*) necessary, essential, required, needful, requisite, indispensable, wanting, compulsory, devoid, good, lacking, mandatory, perfect, vital, basic, **3.** fancied; *synonyms* (*adj*) imaginary, unreal, chimerical, fanciful, fictional, fictitious, fabricated, assumed, assembled, conjectural, doubtful, false, invented, nonexistent, illusive, **4.** coveted; *synonyms* (*adj*) desired, exceptional, impressive, marketable, **5.** craved, **6.** wanted; *synonyms* (*adj*) cherished, invited, precious, treasured, comfortable, cute, fugitive, notorious, urgent, hunted, (*n*) runaway, **7.** required; *synonyms* (*adj*) obligatory, prerequisite, bound, binding; *antonyms* (*adj*) optional, free.

nanobaba 1. jackass; *synonyms* (*n*) ass, jack, cuckoo, donkey, fathead, fool, goof, goose, dunce, jerk, idiot, zany, **2.** giddy; *synonyms* (*adj*) frivolous, flighty, dizzy, faint, silly, changeable, featherbrained, fickle, light, vertiginous, capricious, vacillating, bewildered, (*adv*) careless, rash, **3.** foolish; *synonyms* (*adj*) childish, crazy, daft, dopey, dull, dumb, fatuous, preposterous, stupid, unwise, anserine, dopy, dotty, idiotic, (*n*) absurd; *antonyms* (*adj*) wise, sensible, prudent, shrewd, visionary, **4.** imbecile; *synonyms* (*adj*) foolish, imbecilic, simple,

(*n*) moron, cretin, oaf, changeling, **5.** silly; *synonyms* (*adj*) ridiculous, irrational, unreasonable, ludicrous, nonsensical, sappy, senseless, wacky, insignificant, puerile, babyish, giddy, goofy, imprudent, (*n*) imbecile; *antonym* (*adj*) mature, **6.** simple; *synonyms* (*adj*) plain, homely, pure, elementary, humble, innocent, mere, natural, rustic, honest, bare, chaste, childlike, (*v*) clear, downright; *antonyms* (*adj*) complex, complicated, compound, elaborate, difficult, multiple, obscure, ornate, confused, confusing, cunning, multifaceted, problematical, sophisticated, **7.** stupid; *synonyms* (*adj*) crass, insane, dim, pointless, slow, booby, dense, doltish, heavy, insipid, obtuse, stolid, (*n*) dullard, dolt, (*adv*) thoughtless; *antonyms* (*adj*) bright, clever, intelligent.

nanobakobako 1. feeble; *synonyms* (*adj*) delicate, weak, decrepit, ailing, dim, dull, frail, helpless, infirm, lax, mild, poor, powerless, (*v*) faint, debilitated; *antonyms* (*adj*) strong, vigorous, hearty, tough, **2.** weak; *synonyms* (*adj*) feeble, flat, flimsy, fragile, thin, watery, light, cowardly, diluted, exhausted, inadequate, nerveless, shaky, sickly, (*v*) loose; *antonyms* (*adj*) brave, concentrated, firm, safe, compelling, determined, effective, forceful, healthy, intense, powerful, resolute, robust, sturdy, able.

nanobebebebe 1. involuntary; *synonyms* (*adj*) automatic, instinctive, forced, mechanical, unconscious, unintentional, unthinking, accidental, inadvertent, reluctant, unwilling, intuitive, perfunctory, unvoluntary; *antonyms* (*adj*) deliberate, voluntary, intentional, **2.** dicey; *synonyms* (*adj*) chancy, risky, dangerous, dodgy, hazardous, perilous, precarious, chanceful, unpredictable; *antonym* (*adj*) safe, **3.** doubtful; *synonyms* (*adj*) ambiguous, debatable, dubious, disputable, distrustful, queer, questionable, suspicious, tentative, diffident, hesitant, indistinct, skeptical, uncertain, undecided; *antonyms* (*adj*) certain, trusting, convinced, reliable, confident, persuaded, provable, sure, **4.** hesitate; *synonyms* (*v*) falter, pause, doubt, fluctuate, halt, waver, boggle, demur, vacillate, procrastinate, dither, scruple, stammer, (*adj*) linger, delay; *antonym* (*v*) continue, **5.** groping; *synonyms* (*adj*) blind, examining, exploratory, investigative, probing, hesitating, irresolute, **6.** delayed; *synonyms* (*adj*) belated, late, tardy, protracted, deferred, slow, (*adv*) behind; *antonyms* (*adj*) brief, early, **7.** hesitant; *synonyms* (*adj*) doubtful, indecisive, shy, unsure, backward, loath, apprehensive, insecure, timid, wavering, afraid, fearful, groping, inarticulate, nervous; *antonyms* (*adj*) decided, decisive, firm, resolute, **8.** dither; *synonyms* (*n*) flap, lather, commotion, fluster, state, (*v*) hesitate, shiver, shudder, shake, quiver, pother, **9.** falter; *synonyms* (*v*) stumble, stutter, bumble, hobble, lurch, reel, teeter, totter, wobble, (n) faltering, flounder, hesitation, limp, (adv) flag, **10.** doubt; *synonyms* (n) disbelief, misgiving, question, dispute, apprehension, incertitude, skepticism, uncertainty, diffidence, (v) distrust, query, suspicion, mistrust, suspect, disbelieve; *antonyms* (n) certainty, confidence, conclusiveness, (v) trust, **11.** hesitating, **12.** apprehensive; *synonyms* (adj) anxious, uneasy, alarmed, worried, jealous, concerned, discerning, fidgety, frightened, jumpy, knowing, solicitous, timorous, troubled, (n) tremulous, **13.** grope; *synonyms* (v) feel, finger, fumble, touch, grabble, search, handle, paw, scrabble, **14.** delay; *synonyms* (n) arrest, deferment, wait, stay, deferral, extension, holdup, (v) defer, check, postpone, reserve, adjourn, break, detain, hinder; *antonyms* (n) punctuality, decisiveness, (v) rush, advance, **15.** halt; *synonyms* (n) block, cessation, suspension, standstill, deadlock, (v) stop, cease, desist, discontinue, hold, freeze, end, stand, brake, finish; *antonym* (v) start, **16.** unintentional; *synonyms* (adj) involuntary, undesigned, unwitting, chance, coincidental, spontaneous, **17.** stammer, **18.** uncertain; *synonyms* (adj) changeable, vague, equivocal, unsafe, unsettled, variable, indeterminate, fitful, hazy, inconstant, problematic, shaky, unreliable, unstable, (v) indefinite; *antonyms* (adj) definite, clear, inevitable, strong-minded, unquestionable, **19.** wavering; *synonyms* (adj) vacillating, dithering, unsteady, vacillant, capricious, erratic, fickle, infirm, (n) fluctuation, vacillation, swinging, hesitancy, indecision, indecisiveness, instability; *antonym* (adj) constant, **20.** unwilling; *synonyms* (adj) disinclined, averse, recalcitrant, loth, adverse; *antonyms* (adj) willing, inclined.

nanobebebebeaki delayed; *synonyms* (adj) belated, late, tardy, protracted, deferred, slow, (adv) behind; *antonyms* (adj) brief, early.

nanobebete 1. joyful; *synonyms* (adj) gay, happy, glad, cheerful, elated, gleeful, blissful, cheery, delighted, jolly, joyous, blithe, festive, buoyant, frolicsome; *antonym* (adj) sad, **2.** relieved; *synonyms* (adj) alleviated, eased, thankful, comfortable, fresh, joyful, pleased, prominent, **3.** tranquil; *synonyms* (adj) calm, placid, serene, still, unruffled, sedate, collected, composed, equable, mild, motionless, cool, (v) quiet, smooth, (n) peaceful; *antonyms* (adj) noisy, tense.

nanobibitaki changeable; *synonyms* (adj) variable, capricious, erratic, inconsistent, irregular, fickle, giddy, mercurial, mobile, mutable, slippery, temperamental, uncertain, unsettled, unstable; *antonyms* (adj) constant, fixed, stable, unchangeable, consistent, dependable, predictable, regular.

nanobitaki 1. disunited; *synonyms* (adj) divided, split, disjointed, abrupt, confused, crumbled, cut, disordered, distinct, (v) disconnected, apart, blighted, broken, contrite, cracked, **2.** changing; *synonyms* (adj) changeable, shifting, unsettled, variable, dynamic, moving, choppy, uncertain, various, alterable, fluctuating, irresolute, migrant, (n) correction, motion; *antonym* (adj) smooth, **3.** inconsistent; *synonyms* (adj) incongruous, incoherent, incompatible, contrary, absurd, conflicting, inconsequent, discordant, discrepant, erratic, illogical, irreconcilable, abhorrent, opposite, (n) contradictory; *antonyms* (adj) consistent, constant, reliable, **4.** disharmonious; *synonyms* (adj) dissonant, inharmonic, unlike, nonmusical, unmusical, unresolved.

nanobu 1. afraid; *synonyms* (adj) fearful, timid, shy, anxious, apprehensive, frightened, nervous, scared, worried, horrified, terrified, uneasy, reluctant, (adv) cowardly; *antonyms* (adj) fearless, brave, **2.** faint; *synonyms* (adj) collapse, dim, dizzy, feeble, indistinct, weak, dull, gentle, soft, vague, delicate, distant, (v) languish, swoon, droop; *antonyms* (adj) distinct, strong, clear, obvious, considerable, loud, pungent, **3.** cowardly; *synonyms* (adj) coward, afraid, craven, gutless, shrinking, sneaky, base, dastardly, faint, fainthearted, poltroon, pusillanimous, recreant, spineless; *antonyms* (adj) intrepid, (adv) bold, courageous, daring, **4.** chicken; *synonyms* (n) chick, cock, fowl, hen, crybaby, nestling, poultry, weakling, wimp, (adj) yellow, chickenhearted, **5.** pusillanimous; *synonyms* (adj) timorous, unmanly, **6.** sniveling; *synonyms* (n) snivel, howling, weeping, (adj) crying, fawning, abased, bawling, cringing, groveling, oily, pliant, slavish, **7.** tame; *synonyms* (adj) docile, meek, bland, boring, domestic, insipid, mild, slow, (v) break, subdue, chasten, discipline, domesticate, moderate, soften; *antonyms* (adj) exciting, wild.

nanobuaka 1. bitter; *synonyms* (adj) acrimonious, biting, acrid, sharp, acerbic, acid, caustic, keen, malicious, resentful, sour, virulent, acerb, cutting, (n) acerbity; *antonyms* (adj) mild, sweet, charitable, hot, kind, sugary, **2.** hurt; *synonyms* (v) pain, wound, afflict, injure, ail, cost, (adj) evil, (n) harm, damage, detriment, ache, disadvantage, abuse, distress, lesion; *antonyms* (v) encourage, (adj) uninjured, unhurt, **3.** malicious; *synonyms* (adj) malevolent, spiteful, venomous, vicious, cruel, envious, mean, mischievous, nasty, pernicious, poisonous, unkind, harmful, wanton, bitter; *antonyms* (adj) benevolent, harmless, **4.** malevolent; *synonyms* (adj) malign, hateful, malefic, baleful, ill-natured, malignant, rancorous, sinister, wicked, hostile, **5.** discontented; *synonyms* (adj) discontent, disaffected, disgruntled, displeased, dissatisfied, malcontent, unsatisfied,

miserable, *(v)* querulous, complaining; *antonyms (adj)* contented, pleased, happy, satisfied, **6.**
malignant; *synonyms (adj)* fatal, deadly, detrimental, destructive, injurious, deleterious, hurtful, dangerous, mortal, noxious, **7.** offended; *synonyms (adj)* hurt, angry, affronted, aggrieved, annoyed, pained, wronged, shocked, appalled, ashamed, averted, cool, disappointed, disgusted, dismayed; *antonym (adj)* composed, **8.** resentful; *synonyms (adj)* indignant, jealous, offended, mad, raging, cross, irritable, sore, wrathful, revengeful, vindictive; *antonym (adj)* resigned, **9.** spiteful; *synonyms (adj)* despiteful, invidious, bad, ugly, unfriendly, vengeful, pitiless.

nanobuakaki hurt; *synonyms (v)* pain, wound, afflict, injure, ail, cost, *(adj)* evil, *(n)* harm, damage, detriment, ache, disadvantage, abuse, distress, lesion; *antonyms (v)* encourage, *(adj)* uninjured, unhurt.

nanobukibuki 1. anxious; *synonyms (adj)* afraid, alarmed, nervous, tense, uneasy, agitated, apprehensive, concerned, distressed, fearful, frightened, keen, thoughtful, *(v)* jumpy, solicitous; *antonyms (adj)* calm, relaxed, carefree, confident, rational, unconcerned, undisturbed, untroubled, **2.** concerned; *synonyms (adj)* anxious, careful, interested, involved, considerate, worried, affected, attentive, caring, troubled, upset, distraught, paternal, sympathetic; *antonyms (adj)* uncaring, unfeeling, **3.** dreading, **4.** eager; *synonyms (adj)* avid, desirous, ardent, earnest, agog, acute, ambitious, enthusiastic, zealous, industrious, studious, active, burning, craving, excited; *antonyms (adj)* indifferent, apathetic, disinterested, **5.** excited; *synonyms (adj)* ablaze, emotional, frantic, aroused, delirious, fervent, heated, impassioned, passionate, warm, elated, feverish, effervescent, aflame, *(v)* animated; *antonyms (adj)* cool, unexcited, **6.** disturbed; *synonyms (adj)* confused, disquieted, restless, disordered, bothered, deranged, disconcerted, distracted, tumultuous, turbulent, unsettled, unbalanced, mad, perturbed, uncomfortable, **7.** afraid; *synonyms (adj)* timid, shy, scared, horrified, terrified, reluctant, *(adv)* cowardly; *antonyms (adj)* fearless, brave, **8.** fervent; *synonyms (adj)* eager, cordial, hot, intense, strong, torrid, vehement, devout, dedicated, devoted, fervid, fierce, fiery, flaming, glowing; *antonym (adj)* unenthusiastic, **9.** desirous; *synonyms (adj)* wistful, covetous, greedy, hungry, longing, envious, *(v)* willing; *antonym (adj)* undesirous, **10.** apprehensive; *synonyms (adj)* doubtful, insecure, jealous, discerning, distrustful, fidgety, hesitant, knowing, timorous, uptight, *(n)* tremulous, coy, **11.** enthusiastic; *synonyms (adj)* hearty, dynamic, energetic, fanatical, impatient, lively, spirited, vivacious, wholehearted, wild,

cheerful, sanguine, *(n)* buoyant, gushing, *(v)* fanatic; *antonyms (adj)* lukewarm, lethargic, **12.** uneasy; *synonyms (adj)* awkward, unquiet, fretful, restive, jittery, embarrassing, disturbed, clumsy, difficult, stiff, edgy, **13.** solicitous; *synonyms (adj)* loving, *(v)* sedulous, **14.** troubled; *synonyms (adj)* vexed, disruptive, riotous, unhappy; *antonym (adj)* composed, **15.** zealous; *synonyms (adj)* strenuous, enterprising, forward, vigorous, firm, great, violent, *(n)* sincere, **16.** wild; *synonyms (adj)* desert, waste, boisterous, reckless, desolate, ferocious, furious, raging, rude, stormy, untamed, giddy, barbarous, rough, vicious; *antonyms (adj)* orderly, domestic, manageable, sane, cultivated, restrained, tame.

nanoibwai partial; *synonyms (adj)* incomplete, imperfect, fragmentary, unfair, sectional, inequitable, biased, part, unequal, halfway, partisan, prejudiced, unfinished, unjust, *(v)* party; *antonyms (adj)* complete, impartial, total, absolute, comprehensive, unbiased.

nanoingainga 1. impatient; *synonyms (adj)* eager, hasty, anxious, petulant, fidgety, keen, edgy, quick, avid, enthusiastic, impetuous, irritable, restive, restless, testy; *antonyms (adj)* patient, enduring, **2.** eager; *synonyms (adj)* desirous, ardent, earnest, agog, acute, ambitious, zealous, industrious, studious, active, burning, craving, excited, fervent, forward; *antonyms (adj)* indifferent, apathetic, disinterested, unconcerned, **3.** active; *synonyms (adj)* energetic, alert, busy, diligent, effective, live, lively, nimble, strong, agile, alive, brisk, dynamic, forcible, healthy; *antonyms (adj)* dormant, inactive, sluggish, idle, latent, lethargic, sedentary, slow, extinct, passive, quiet, **4.** enthusiastic; *synonyms (adj)* hearty, cordial, devoted, fiery, passionate, animated, vehement, heated, dedicated, fanatical, glowing, hot, *(n)* buoyant, gushing, *(v)* fanatic; *antonyms (adj)* unenthusiastic, lukewarm, **5.** excited; *synonyms (adj)* agitated, ablaze, emotional, frantic, aroused, delirious, impassioned, warm, elated, tense, feverish, effervescent, aflame, cheerful, ecstatic; *antonyms (adj)* calm, cool, unexcited, **6.** devoted; *synonyms (adj)* addicted, affectionate, consecrated, constant, faithful, fond, loyal, pious, committed, dutiful, loving, reliable, religious, assiduous, attentive; *antonyms (adj)* uncommitted, disloyal, **7.** rabid; *synonyms (adj)* furious, mad, wild, insane, frenzied, crazy, extreme, raging, hysterical, overzealous, *(v)* fierce, enrage, infuriate.

nanokabakoba 1. fragile; *synonyms (adj)* dainty, delicate, frail, breakable, brittle, flimsy, weak, faint, feeble, fine, slim, frangible, insubstantial, shaky, slender; *antonyms (adj)* strong, unbreakable, substantial, sturdy, permanent, robust, **2.** languid; *synonyms (adj)* lazy, dull, indolent, lackadaisical, lethargic, sluggish, torpid, apathetic, inert, infirm, listless, sickly, dreamy, remiss, insipid; *antonym* (*adj*) energetic, **3.** faint; *synonyms* (*adj*) collapse, dim, dizzy, indistinct, gentle, soft, vague, distant, drop, fuzzy, (*v*) languish, swoon, droop, conk, exhausted; *antonyms* (*adj*) distinct, clear, obvious, considerable, loud, pungent, **4.** bleary; *synonyms* (*adj*) hazy, blear, blurry, misty, filmy, blurred, foggy, muzzy, tired, **5.** faltering; *synonyms* (*adj*) tentative, vacillating, doubtful, hesitant, irresolute, uncertain, halting, hesitating, unsure, (*n*) falter, wavering, pause, hesitation, vacillation, waver; *antonym* (*n*) decisiveness, **6.** feeble; *synonyms* (*adj*) decrepit, ailing, helpless, lax, mild, poor, powerless, thin, enfeebled, forceless, fragile, impotent, inadequate, lame, (*v*) debilitated; *antonyms* (*adj*) vigorous, hearty, tough, **7.** fuzzy; *synonyms* (*adj*) indefinite, hairy, bleary, downy, curly, bushy, rough, imprecise, unclear, wooly, fuzzed, **8.** frail; *synonyms* (*adj*) light, rickety, puny, sick, slight, unhealthy, fallible, flabby, brash, unsound, low, tender, unwell, vulnerable, (*v*) shattery, **9.** droopy; *synonyms* (*adj*) drooping, limp, pendulous, downcast, baggy, bent, cernuous, dejected, fatigued, floppy, indifferent, joyless, languorous, leisurely, melancholy, **10.** weak; *synonyms* (*adj*) flat, watery, cowardly, diluted, nerveless, slack, effeminate, bland, dilute, invalid, pale, spineless, spiritless, tasteless, (*v*) loose; *antonyms* (*adj*) brave, concentrated, firm, safe, compelling, determined, effective, forceful, healthy, intense, powerful, resolute, able, fit, hard-wearing.

nanokanga singularity; *synonyms* (*n*) oddity, peculiarity, individuality, eccentricity, idiosyncrasy, oddness, abnormality, uniqueness, identity, irregularity.

nanokawa 1. dismal; *synonyms* (*adj*) cheerless, dark, dejected, depressing, desolate, disconsolate, dreary, gloomy, melancholy, black, dim, bleak, blue, depressed, doleful; *antonyms* (*adj*) cheerful, bright, happy, **2.** desolate; *synonyms* (*v*) waste, devastate, comfortless, destroy, abandon, depopulate, (*adj*) bare, barren, desert, forlorn, alone, deserted, sad, solitary, unhappy; *antonyms* (*adj*) inhabited, sheltered, **3.** dispirited; *synonyms* (*adj*) crestfallen, discouraged, downcast, dismal, disheartened, down, downhearted, despondent, spiritless, listless, low, crushed, **4.** despondent; *synonyms* (*adj*) desperate, hopeless, disappointed, despairing, miserable, brokenhearted, dispirited, glum, heartsick, sorrowful, wretched, pessimistic; *antonym* (*adj*) hopeful, **5.** dreary; *synonyms* (*adj*) drab, dull, drear, stuffy, boring, humdrum, monotonous, somber, tedious, uninteresting, dingy, ponderous, dour, overcast, distressing; *antonym* (*adj*) interesting, **6.** afflicted; *synonyms* (*v*) afflict, displeased, pained, (*adj*) distressed, pitiful,

stricken, ill, woeful, dolorous, sorry, aggrieved, affected, diseased, impaired, sore, **7.** gloomy; *synonyms* (*adj*) funereal, cloudy, dusky, forbidding, grim, morose, murky, sullen, heavy, lurid, moody, shadowy, surly, tenebrous, bad; *antonyms* (*adj*) cheery, encouraging, light, **8.** heavyhearted, **9.** dejected; *synonyms* (*adj*) damp, prostrate, deject, melancholic, woebegone, inconsolable; *antonym* (*adj*) elated, **10.** glum; *synonyms* (*adj*) mournful, grumpy, saturnine, sour, glowering, (*n*) sulky, **11.** doleful; *synonyms* (*adj*) piteous, joyless, lamentable, lugubrious, plaintive, (*v*) dolesome, **12.** oppressive; *synonyms* (*adj*) burdensome, despotic, muggy, sultry, tyrannical, dictatorial, cruel, domineering, hard, harsh, stifling, extortionate, grievous, (*v*) onerous, close; *antonyms* (*adj*) fresh, liberal, democratic, **13.** unhappy; *synonyms* (*adj*) unfortunate, infelicitous, poor, unlucky, unpleasant, hapless, adverse, discontented, calamitous, regretful, unsuccessful, worried, damned, dysphoric, unblest; *antonyms* (*adj*) pleased, satisfied, **14.** somber; *synonyms* (*adj*) grave, serious, sober, solemn, sable, leaden, obscure, sedate, dun, gray, severe, sombre, swarthy, ebon, inky.

nanokawaki 1. depressed; *synonyms* (*adj*) concave, low, blue, dejected, dispirited, down, downcast, downhearted, gloomy, hollow, sad, crestfallen, disappointed, discouraged, flat; *antonyms* (*adj*) cheerful, happy, convex, **2.** disheartened; *synonyms* (*adj*) depressed, despondent, demoralized; *antonym* (*adj*) optimistic, **3.** sad; *synonyms* (*adj*) dreary, dismal, distressing, miserable, mournful, pitiable, pitiful, bad, bleak, deplorable, depressing, disconsolate, doleful, dolorous, funereal; *antonyms* (*adj*) joyful, brave, cheery, composed, **4.** sorry; *synonyms* (*adj*) pathetic, contrite, paltry, penitent, piteous, remorseful, sorrowful, base, apologetic, mean, regretful, repentant, abject, dingy, drab; *antonym* (*adj*) unrepentant, **5.** unhappy; *synonyms* (*adj*) unfortunate, melancholy, distressed, infelicitous, poor, sorry, unlucky, unpleasant, hapless, adverse, cheerless, discontented, joyless, calamitous, displeased; *antonyms* (*adj*) pleased, satisfied, **6.** sorrowful; *synonyms* (*adj*) lugubrious, rueful, grievous, lamentable, unhappy, plaintive, dark, forlorn, painful, heavy, poignant, desolate, tearful, tragic, (*v*) sorrowing; *antonyms* (*adj*) content, successful.

nanokirokiro 1. abysmal; *synonyms* (*adj*) abyssal, deep, appalling, dreadful, profound, terrible, unfathomable, awful, horrible, unending, dire, frightful, atrocious, unspeakable, defective; *antonyms* (*adj*) excellent, exceptional, **2.** deep; *synonyms* (*adj*) thick, absorbed, abstruse, broad, dark, rich, sound, strong, wide, esoteric, bright, large, abysmal, bass, (v) intense; *antonyms* (adj) shallow, superficial, high, high-pitched, light, soft, weak, **3.** boundless; *synonyms* (adj) limitless, endless, infinite, unlimited, bottomless, immeasurable, immense, incalculable, interminable, unbounded, vast, never-ending, eternal, everlasting, illimitable; *antonyms* (adj) limited, restricted, **4.** infinite; *synonyms* (adj) absolute, boundless, countless, innumerable, enormous, indefinite, multitudinous, myriad, numerous, continual, fathomless, ceaseless, gigantic, great, huge; *antonym* (adj) finite, **5.** soundless; *synonyms* (adj) quiet, silent, dumb, noiseless, still, mute, hushed, inactive, motionless, **6.** unbelievable; *synonyms* (adj) improbable, incredible, implausible, inconceivable, unlikely, fabulous, impossible, unthinkable, marvellous, marvelous, tall, astounding, fantastic, questionable, (v) staggering; *antonyms* (adj) credible, plausible, believable, **7.** unfathomable; *synonyms* (adj) impenetrable, incomprehensible, inexplicable, inscrutable, mysterious, unintelligible, unaccountable, enigmatic, obscure, incommensurable, incommensurate, inexhaustible, puzzling, undecipherable, undiscoverable; *antonym* (adj) fathomable.

nanokiroro 1. boundless; *synonyms* (adj) limitless, endless, infinite, unlimited, bottomless, immeasurable, immense, incalculable, interminable, unbounded, vast, never-ending, eternal, everlasting, illimitable; *antonyms* (adj) limited, restricted, **2.** abysmal; *synonyms* (adj) abyssal, deep, appalling, dreadful, profound, terrible, unfathomable, awful, horrible, unending, dire, frightful, atrocious, unspeakable, defective; *antonyms* (adj) excellent, exceptional, **3.** infinite; *synonyms* (adj) absolute, boundless, countless, innumerable, enormous, indefinite, multitudinous, myriad, numerous, continual, fathomless, ceaseless, gigantic, great, huge; *antonym* (adj) finite, **4.** deep; *synonyms* (adj) thick, absorbed, abstruse, broad, dark, rich, sound, strong, wide, esoteric, bright, large, abysmal, bass, (v) intense; *antonyms* (adj) shallow, superficial, high, high-pitched, light, soft, weak, **5.** unbelievable; *synonyms* (adj) improbable, incredible, implausible, inconceivable, unlikely, fabulous, impossible, unthinkable, marvellous, marvelous, tall, astounding, fantastic, questionable, (v) staggering; *antonyms* (adj) credible, plausible, believable, **6.** soundless; *synonyms* (adj) quiet, silent, dumb, noiseless, still, mute, hushed, inactive, motionless, **7.** unfathomable; *synonyms* (adj) impenetrable, incomprehensible, inexplicable, inscrutable, mysterious, unintelligible, unaccountable, enigmatic, obscure, incommensurable, incommensurate, inexhaustible, puzzling,

undecipherable, undiscoverable; *antonym* (adj) fathomable.

nanokokoraki 1. doubt; *synonyms* (n) disbelief, misgiving, question, dispute, apprehension, incertitude, skepticism, uncertainty, diffidence, (v) distrust, query, suspicion, mistrust, suspect, demur; *antonyms* (n) certainty, confidence, conclusiveness, (v) trust, **2.** hesitate; *synonyms* (v) falter, pause, doubt, fluctuate, halt, waver, boggle, vacillate, procrastinate, dither, scruple, stammer, stutter, (adj) linger, delay; *antonym* (v) continue.

nanokoraki 1. confused; *synonyms* (adj) abashed, bewildered, baffled, befuddled, bemused, chaotic, confounded, disjointed, disordered, dizzy, incoherent, indistinct, ambiguous, (n) cloudy, (adv, adj) topsy-turvy; *antonyms* (adj) clear, enlightened, alert, clearheaded, clear-headed, orderly, **2.** bewildered; *synonyms* (adj) confused, lost, perplexed, puzzled, dumbfounded, addled, amazed, blank, dazed, disconcerted, disoriented, muddled, mystified, stunned; *antonym* (adj) unimpressed, **3.** confounded; *synonyms* (adj) accursed, cursed, execrable, aghast, abominable, **4.** hesitant; *synonyms* (adj) doubtful, indecisive, irresolute, uncertain, diffident, hesitating, reluctant, shy, undecided, unsure, backward, loath, apprehensive, insecure, tentative; *antonyms* (adj) certain, confident, decided, decisive, firm, resolute, sure, **5.** indecisive; *synonyms* (adj) hesitant, inconclusive, weak, dubious, precarious, vague, feeble; *antonym* (adj) conclusive, **6.** mystified; *synonyms* (adj) metagrabolized, metagrobolized, flummoxed, metagrabolised, metagrobolised, stumped, thrown, unclear, absentminded, bamboozled, faraway, preoccupied, **7.** undecided; *synonyms* (adj) unsettled, pending, unresolved, undetermined, debatable, indefinite, indeterminate, ambivalent, borderline, moot, open; *antonym* (adj) determined, **8.** perplexed; *synonyms* (v) complicated, intricate, (adj) involved, distracted, uneasy, questioning, quizzical, entangled, knotted.

nanomaiti 1. confuse; *synonyms* (v) bewilder, baffle, confound, muddle, agitate, blur, derange, disconcert, disturb, fluster, jumble, mystify, obscure, perplex, puzzle; *antonyms* (v) clarify, enlighten, elucidate, explain, **2.** confused; *synonyms* (adj) abashed, bewildered, baffled, befuddled, bemused, chaotic, confounded, disjointed, disordered, dizzy, incoherent, indistinct, ambiguous, (n) cloudy, (adv, adj) topsy-turvy; *antonyms* (adj) clear, enlightened, alert, clearheaded, clear-headed, orderly, **3.** mystified; *synonyms* (adj) metagrabolized, metagrobolized, perplexed, puzzled, confused, flummoxed, metagrabolised, metagrobolised, stumped, thrown, unclear, absentminded, bamboozled, faraway, preoccupied, **4.** indecisive; *synonyms* (*adj*) doubtful, hesitant, inconclusive, undecided, unsure, weak, dubious, irresolute, precarious, vague, feeble; *antonyms* (*adj*) decisive, conclusive, resolute, **5.** bewilder; *synonyms* (*v*) astonish, astound, amaze, bemuse, befuddle, nonplus, perturb, stump, stun, daze, dumbfound, entangle, flummox, stagger, (*adj*) confuse, **6.** hesitant; *synonyms* (*adj*) indecisive, uncertain, diffident, hesitating, reluctant, shy, backward, loath, apprehensive, insecure, tentative, timid, wavering, afraid, fearful; *antonyms* (*adj*) certain, confident, decided, firm, sure, **7.** confounded; *synonyms* (*adj*) accursed, cursed, execrable, aghast, abominable, **8.** mystify; *synonyms* (*v*) bamboozle, get, hoodwink, gravel, hoax, stupefy, blindfold, discombobulate, (*adj*) equivocate, **9.** bewildered; *synonyms* (*adj*) lost, dumbfounded, addled, amazed, blank, dazed, disconcerted, disoriented, muddled, mystified, stunned; *antonym* (*adj*) unimpressed, **10.** confound; *synonyms* (*v*) mistake, complicate, dash, bedevil, defeat, discomfit, distract, flabbergast, overwhelm, throw, compound, (*n*) surprise, (*adj*) checkmate, petrify, upset, **11.** perplex; *synonyms* (*v*) bother, embarrass, involve, trouble, distress, embroil, beset, beat, tease, afflict, discompose, abash, (*n*) harass, annoy, torment, **12.** perplexed; *synonyms* (*v*) complicated, intricate, (*adj*) involved, distracted, uneasy, questioning, quizzical, entangled, knotted, **13.** undecided; *synonyms* (*adj*) unsettled, pending, unresolved, undetermined, debatable, indefinite, indeterminate, ambivalent, borderline, moot, open; *antonym* (*adj*) determined.

nanomaitiaki 1. confused; *synonyms* (*adj*) abashed, bewildered, baffled, befuddled, bemused, chaotic, confounded, disjointed, disordered, dizzy, incoherent, indistinct, ambiguous, (*n*) cloudy, (*adv*, *adj*) topsy-turvy; *antonyms* (*adj*) clear, enlightened, alert, clearheaded, clear-headed, orderly, **2.** mystified; *synonyms* (*adj*) metagrabolized, metagrobolized, perplexed, puzzled, confused, flummoxed, metagrabolised, metagrobolised, stumped, thrown, unclear, absentminded, bamboozled, faraway, preoccupied, **3.** bewildered; *synonyms* (*adj*) lost, dumbfounded, addled, amazed, blank, dazed, disconcerted, disoriented, muddled, mystified, stunned; *antonym* (*adj*) unimpressed, **4.** confounded; *synonyms* (*adj*) accursed, cursed, execrable, aghast, abominable, **5.** perplexed; *synonyms* (*v*) complicated, intricate, (*adj*) involved, doubtful, distracted, uneasy, questioning, quizzical, entangled, knotted.

nanomaka 1. animated; *synonyms* (*adj*) active, alive, lively, animate, perky, brisk, cheerful, quick, spirited, sprightly, vivacious, airy, alert, bright,

energetic; *antonyms* (*adj*) listless, lethargic, blank, dull, **2.** energetic; *synonyms* (*adj*) animated, busy, driving, dynamic, effective, powerful, strong, agile, emphatic, aggressive, efficacious, efficient, enterprising, forceful, forcible; *antonyms* (*adj*) lazy, sluggish, exhausted, inactive, indolent, languid, weary, apathetic, indifferent, **3.** firm; *synonyms* (*n*) company, (*adj*) constant, hard, stable, close, compact, determined, fixed, resolute, solid, steadfast, steady, decisive, dense, (*v*) faithful; *antonyms* (*adj*) irresolute, soft, weak, hesitant, limp, liquid, soggy, **4.** inspired; *synonyms* (*adj*) divine, ingenious, adopted, creative, elected, elysian, imaginative, inventive; *antonym* (*adj*) uninspired, **5.** determined; *synonyms* (*adj*) decided, definite, certain, determinate, inflexible, resolved, stubborn, ambitious, adamant, bold, firm, obstinate, set, tenacious, unyielding; *antonyms* (*adj*) uncertain, feeble, unmotivated, **6.** fortified; *synonyms* (*adj*) bastioned, secure, castled, defended, equipped, fast, protected, safeguarded, secured, shielded, prepared, turreted, **7.** encouraging; *synonyms* (*adj*) favorable, cheering, promising, auspicious, comforting, favourable, heartening, hopeful, hortatory, reassuring, rosy, propitious, sympathetic; *antonyms* (*adj*) gloomy, upsetting, warning, disappointing, **8.** encouraged; *synonyms* (*adj*) optimistic, confident, enthused, expectant, inspired, moved, positive, stimulated, stirred, buoyant, driven, impelled, incited, motivated, pressed, **9.** persevering; *synonyms* (*adj*) patient, diligent, dogged, persistent, industrious, insistent, assiduous, indefatigable, sedulous, tireless, unremitting, untiring, laborious, **10.** persistent; *synonyms* (*adj*) durable, continual, lasting, permanent, continuous, chronic, consistent, incessant, perpetual, relentless, unrelenting, habitual, abiding, perennial, (*n*) frequent; *antonyms* (*adj*) contained, occasional, **11.** pertinacious; *synonyms* (*adj*) dour, headstrong, stiff, intractable, contumacious, willful, bulldog, **12.** resolving; *synonyms* (*adj*) conclusive, (*n*) resolution, resolve, answer, conversion, declaration, firmness, resoluteness, result, solvent, **13.** tenacious; *synonyms* (*adj*) adhesive, tough, sticky, glutinous, persevering, pertinacious, stringy, viscous, severe, tight, viscid, coherent, courageous, gritty, (*v*) retentive.

nanomakaki 1. fearful; *synonyms* (*adj*) afraid, cowardly, dreadful, anxious, apprehensive, awful, craven, terrible, timid, dire, eerie, formidable, frightful, appalling, awesome; *antonyms* (*adj*) brave, calm, rational, bold, confident, unimpressed, **2.** horrendous; *synonyms* (*adj*) fearful, hideous, lurid, atrocious, ghastly, horrible, horrific, monstrous, dread, direful, fearsome, gruesome, horrid, shocking, terrifying; *antonym* (*adj*) wonderful, **3**. dire; *synonyms* *(adj)* desperate, extreme, forbidding, calamitous, ominous, critical, mortal, deplorable, inauspicious, acute, disastrous, frightening, horrendous, severe, sinister, **4**. alarming; *synonyms* *(adj)* scary, disturbing, horrifying, threatening; *antonyms* *(adj)* reassuring, soothing, **5**. awful; *synonyms* *(adj)* abominable, bad, nasty, alarming, amazing, detestable, disgusting, hateful, lousy, serious, sickening, tremendous, unpleasant, unspeakable, *(adv)* beastly; *antonyms* *(adj)* excellent, great, marvelous, lovely, nice, pleasant, **6**. frightful; *synonyms* *(adj)* grim, morbid, grisly, terrific, ugly, heinous, **7**. excessive; *synonyms* *(adj)* inordinate, exaggerated, intense, enormous, exorbitant, extravagant, exuberant, immoderate, profuse, superfluous, undue, unreasonable, huge, lavish, radical; *antonyms* *(adj)* reasonable, moderate, affordable, **8**. gruesome; *synonyms* *(adj)* macabre, chilling, dismal, creepy, repugnant, grewsome, **9**. dreadful; *synonyms* *(adj)* grievous, woeful, offensive, arrant, execrable, foul, ill, odious, outrageous, portentous, repellent, scandalous, unholy, vile, wicked, **10**. distressing; *synonyms* *(adj)* disquieting, painful, pitiful, sorrowful, depressing, hurtful, lamentable, pathetic, perturbing, sad, sore, sorry, worrying, bothersome, *(v)* bitter; *antonym* *(adj)* heartwarming, **11**. hideous; *synonyms* *(adj)* repulsive, abhorrent, loathsome, obscene, revolting, unsightly; *antonym* *(adj)* attractive, **12**. appalling; *synonyms* *(adj)* dismaying, unearthly; *antonym* *(adj)* admirable, **13**. disturbing; *synonyms* *(adj)* distressing, disconcerting, troublesome, troubling, unsettling, upsetting, worrisome, discordant, distressful, poignant; *antonym* *(adj)* comforting, **14**. extreme; *synonyms* *(adj)* deep, excessive, supreme, ultimate, utmost, uttermost, drastic, extraordinary, exceeding, furthest, keen, *(n)* edge, end, extremity, *(adv)* farthest; *antonyms* *(adj)* middle, near, *(n)* mild, slight, **15**. severe; *synonyms* *(adj)* harsh, austere, rigid, biting, hard, inclement, rigorous, rough, arduous, cutting, heavy, strict, caustic, cruel, difficult; *antonyms* *(adj)* gentle, lenient, easy, lax, **16**. relentless; *synonyms* *(adj)* inexorable, implacable, inflexible, stern, pitiless, merciless, obdurate, persistent, unrelenting, determined, remorseless, ruthless, unbending, unyielding, continual; *antonym* *(adj)* intermittent, **17**. redoubtable; *synonyms* *(adj)* glorious, illustrious, resolute, strong, **18**. terrible; *synonyms* *(adj)* dangerous, almighty, evil, rotten, tough, tragic, violent, grave, indescribable.

nanomaki cowardice; *synonyms* *(n)* cowardliness, dastardliness, poltroonery, fear, pusillanimity, cowardship; *antonyms* *(n)* courage, bravery, daring, nerve.

nanomamara 1. indulging; *synonyms* *(n)* humoring, pampering, indulgence, folly, foolery, lenience, leniency, tomfoolery, **2**. indulgent; *synonyms* *(adj)* easy, forgiving, gentle, clement, gracious, kind, lenient, permissive, soft, tolerant, compassionate, merciful, lax, mild, fond; *antonym* *(adj)* strict, **3**. easy; *synonyms* *(adj)* comfortable, convenient, familiar, graceful, light, clear, contented, cozy, casual, comfy, cushy, easygoing, effortless, free, *(adv)* easily; *antonyms* *(adj)* difficult, arduous, demanding, hard, laborious, burdensome, particular, strenuous, tough, awkward, formal, testing, uneasy, **4**. condescending; *synonyms* *(adj)* cavalier, arrogant, snobbish, superior, haughty, patronizing, arch, supercilious; *antonyms* *(adj)* humble, down-to-earth, **5**. weak; *synonyms* *(adj)* feeble, frail, faint, flat, flimsy, fragile, thin, watery, ailing, cowardly, delicate, diluted, exhausted, inadequate, infirm; *antonyms* *(adj)* strong, brave, concentrated, firm, safe, compelling, determined, effective, forceful, healthy, intense, powerful, resolute, robust, sturdy.

nanomane 1. mighty; *synonyms* *(adj)* enormous, immense, huge, grand, powerful, intense, high, big, forcible, great, large, strong, mammoth, cogent, formidable, **2**. manly; *synonyms* *(adj)* male, manlike, brave, manful, masculine, virile, gallant, courageous, mature, *(adv)* manfully, **3**. masculine; *synonyms* *(adj)* manly, mankind, bold, cruel, adult, ape, beefcake, caveman, generative, hairy, honorable, hunk, jock, resolute, stallion; *antonyms* *(adj)* feminine, female, **4**. burly; *synonyms* *(adj)* rugged, beefy, brawny, strapping, hefty, husky, muscular, portly, stout, robust, solid, sturdy, thickset, buirdly; *antonyms* *(adj)* puny, slight, skinny, **5**. capable; *synonyms* *(adj)* able, competent, adequate, adept, accomplished, fit, gifted, proficient, qualified, trained, clever, consummate, effective, experienced, *(n)* efficient; *antonyms* *(adj)* incompetent, incapable, inept, unable, **6**. strong; *synonyms* *(adj)* deep, firm, stable, steady, durable, good, hard, influential, lusty, potent, rigid, secure, sound, fierce, *(v)* steadfast; *antonyms* *(adj)* weak, bland, delicate, faint, feeble, frail, mild, pale, unconvincing, cowardly, diluted, dull, exhausted, flimsy, imperceptible, **7**. vigorous; *synonyms* *(adj)* energetic, hardy, lively, strenuous, active, athletic, hearty, mighty, healthy, smart, animated, dynamic, forceful, *(v)* brisk, fresh; *antonyms* *(adj)* lethargic, unenergetic, **8**. virile; *synonym* *(adj)* vigorous; *antonym* *(adj)* impotent, **9**. powerful; *synonyms* *(adj)* full, dominant, important, stiff, valid, convincing, efficacious, herculean, impressive, nervous, noisy, puissant, significant, vehement,

violent; *antonym (adj)* powerless, **10**. potent;
synonyms (adj) persuasive, heady, telling,
adamantine, *(n)* effectual.

nanomanikoraki 1. disqualified; *synonyms (adj)*
unqualified, ineligible, disentitled, incapable,
incompetent, unable, banned, barred, deficient,
unentitled, unfit, debarred, disallowed, expelled,
improper, **2**. disqualify; *synonyms (v)* disable,
incapacitate, indispose, exclude, disincline, *(adj)*
disarm, disentitle, disfranchise, dismantle, dismast,
dismount; *antonym (v)* qualify.

nanomanikorakiaki disqualified; *synonyms (adj)*
unqualified, ineligible, disentitled, incapable,
incompetent, unable, banned, barred, deficient,
unentitled, unfit, debarred, disallowed, expelled,
improper.

nanomano 1. discreet; *synonyms (adj)* circumspect,
prudent, careful, cautious, chary, discerning,
tactful, wise, diplomatic, considerate, judicious,
modest, politic, sensible, thoughtful; *antonyms (adj)*
conspicuous, elaborate, tactless, careless, indiscreet,
2. deep; *synonyms (adj)* thick, profound, absorbed,
abstruse, broad, dark, rich, sound, strong, wide,
esoteric, bright, large, abysmal, *(v)* intense;
antonyms (adj) shallow, superficial, high, high-
pitched, light, soft, weak, **3**. careful; *synonyms
(adj)* accurate, attentive, thrifty, alert, deliberate,
economical, frugal, mindful, assiduous, aware,
cagey, conscientious, delicate, diligent, *(v)* anxious;
antonyms (adj) reckless, slapdash, neglectful, **4**.
cautious; *synonyms (adj)* conservative, guarded,
watchful, discreet, provident, reserved, shy, wary,
moderate, canny, sly, gingerly, heedful,
scrupulous, sparing; *antonyms (adj)* rash,
impetuous, impulsive, open, incautious,
irresponsible, wasteful, **5**. circumspect;
synonyms (adj) vigilant, cautelous, **6**. chary;
synonyms (adj) cagy, reluctant, safe, stingy, leery,
saving, scant, scanty, stealthy, distrustful, *(v)* spare,
7. discerning; *synonyms (adj)* astute, acute,
apprehensive, discriminating, perceptive, shrewd,
penetrating, refined, sharp, conscious,
understanding, clever, clairvoyant, observant,
critical; *antonym (adj)* indiscriminate, **8**. sullen;
synonyms (adj) morose, gloomy, gruff, cross, glum,
grim, moody, sour, dismal, dour, lowering,
peevish, surly, black, *(n)* sulky; *antonym (adj)*
cheerful, **9**. sly; *synonyms (adj)* crafty, cunning,
wily, furtive, artful, secret, designing, arch,
clandestine, deceitful, devious, foxy, guileful,
ingenious, insidious; *antonym (adj)* naive.

nanomara detestable; *synonyms (adj)* abominable,
abhorrent, hateful, damnable, despicable,
execrable, odious, offensive, accursed, disgusting,
horrible, infamous, loathsome, *(v)* cursed, *(adv)*
atrocious.

nanomaraki 1. repent; *synonyms (v)* regret, deplore,
bewail, rue, lament, atone, **2**. regret; *synonyms (v)*
grieve, bemoan, mourn, sorrow, repent, *(n)* grief,
compunction, contrition, penitence, remorse,
repentance, disappointment, woe, mourning,
qualm.

nanomaruru 1. disturbed; *synonyms (adj)* agitated,
concerned, anxious, confused, disquieted, restless,
upset, worried, disordered, bothered, deranged,
disconcerted, distracted, distressed, nervous;
antonyms (adj) rational, calm, relaxed, **2**.
apprehensive; *synonyms (adj)* afraid, fearful,
uneasy, alarmed, timid, doubtful, shy, insecure,
jealous, discerning, distrustful, fidgety, frightened,
hesitant, jumpy; *antonym (adj)* confident, **3**.
agitated; *synonyms (adj)* excited, restive,
tumultuous, tense, distraught, overwrought,
perturbed, shaken, troubled, unsettled, hysterical,
turbulent; *antonyms (adj)* composed, lethargic, **4**.
anxious; *synonyms (adj)* apprehensive, keen,
thoughtful, thirsty, careful, desirous, disturbed,
eager, edgy, enthusiastic, impatient, nervy,
uncomfortable, unquiet, *(v)* solicitous; *antonyms
(adj)* carefree, unconcerned, undisturbed,
untroubled, **5**. uneasy; *synonyms (adj)* awkward,
fretful, jittery, embarrassing, clumsy, difficult, stiff,
6. troubled; *synonyms (adj)* vexed, disruptive,
riotous, unhappy.

nanomatoa 1. obstinate; *synonyms (adj)* headstrong,
obdurate, determined, inflexible, intractable,
inveterate, disobedient, contrary, dogged, firm,
stubborn, uncompromising, wayward, willful,
contumacious; *antonyms (adj)* compliant, amenable,
flexible, **2**. resolute; *synonyms (adj)* constant,
decisive, brave, fixed, adamant, bold, courageous,
decided, persistent, stable, steadfast, unbending,
fast, bent, *(n)* steady; *antonyms (adj)* irresolute,
weak, uncertain, **3**. stubborn; *synonyms (adj)*
obstinate, hard, perverse, refractory, rigid,
tenacious, difficult, recalcitrant, resolute, stiff,
tough, opinionated, restive, strong, fractious.

nanomatoatoa 1. strict; *synonyms (adj)* rigid, severe,
stern, correct, accurate, austere, harsh, precise,
rigorous, scrupulous, exacting, hard, inflexible, *(v)*
exact, close; *antonyms (adj)* lenient, free, lax,
flexible, imprecise, negligent, relaxed, **2**. severe;
synonyms (adj) biting, inclement, rough, arduous,
bad, cutting, grim, heavy, intense, serious, strict,
acute, atrocious, bitter, *(v)* poignant; *antonyms (adj)*
gentle, mild, slight, easy, **3**. persevering;
synonyms (adj) patient, diligent, firm, determined,
constant, resolute, dogged, persistent, steadfast,
tenacious, industrious, insistent, stubborn,
assiduous, indefatigable.

nanomawa 1. generous; *synonyms (adj)* ample, full,
abundant, benevolent, copious, bountiful,
charitable, fair, flush, kind, liberal, spacious, rich,

benign, (n) free; *antonyms* (adj) stingy, meager, mean, measly, miserly, small, tightfisted, avaricious, greedy, ungenerous, **2.** liberal; *synonyms* (adj) generous, handsome, big, large, bounteous, broad, giving, tolerant, lavish, easy, bighearted, enlightened, freehanded, munificent, noble; *antonyms* (adj) strict, oppressive, totalitarian, intolerant, (n) conservative, **3.** honorable; *synonyms* (adj) good, honest, decent, estimable, exalted, reputable, respectable, ethical, honor, distinguished, commendable, creditable, grand, (v) great, dignified; *antonyms* (adj) dishonorable, disgraceful, shameful, corrupt, **4.** magnanimous; *synonyms* (adj) lofty, considerate, elevated, chivalrous, high, lenient, magnificent, unselfish, gallant, greathearted, **5.** amiable; *synonyms* (adj) affable, agreeable, complaisant, friendly, genial, charming, cordial, gentle, likable, lovely, nice, pleasant, sweet, adorable, amicable; *antonyms* (adj) unfriendly, disagreeable, aggressive, argumentative, **6.** tolerant; *synonyms* (adj) indulgent, patient, forbearing, forgiving, permissive, understanding, merciful, magnanimous, broadminded, uncomplaining, wide, loose, moderate, progressive, (v) meek; *antonyms* (adj) narrow-minded, impatient, **7.** understanding; *synonyms* (n) intellect, mind, reason, appreciation, comprehension, agreement, apprehension, bargain, deal, judgment, sense, sympathy, arrangement, (v) intelligence, discernment; *antonyms* (n) ignorance, bewilderment, disbelief.

nanomiakina disenchanted; *synonyms* (adj) disillusioned, cynical, blasé, disappointed, dissatisfied, sophisticated, worldly, disenthralled, disentranced, disheartened, embittered, frustrated, indifferent, jaded, jaundiced; *antonym* (adj) enchanted.

nanomwaka 1. indomitable; *synonyms* (adj) unconquerable, firm, dogged, inflexible, invincible, tough, gritty, dauntless, irresistible, undaunted, brave, fearless, impregnable, insurmountable, (v) iron; *antonym* (adj) vulnerable, **2.** willful; *synonyms* (adj) deliberate, headstrong, intentional, obstinate, perverse, voluntary, wayward, stubborn, disobedient, premeditated, wilful, froward, unruly, designed, studied; *antonym* (adj) flexible.

nanomwane 1. indomitable; *synonyms* (adj) unconquerable, firm, dogged, inflexible, invincible, tough, gritty, dauntless, irresistible, undaunted, brave, fearless, impregnable, insurmountable, (v) iron; *antonym* (adj) vulnerable, **2.** valiant; *synonyms* (adj) courageous, intrepid, audacious, daring, gallant, heroic, stout, doughty, stalwart, plucky, valorous, resolute, adventurous, strenuous, (prep) bold; *antonym* (adj) cowardly, **3.** strenuous; *synonyms* (adj) arduous, energetic, laborious, hard, grueling, dynamic, eager, forward, difficult,

intensive, heavy, trying, aggressive, demanding, exhausting; *antonyms* (adj) easy, undemanding, weak.

nanon 1. mean; *synonyms* (v) intend, design, imply, denote, involve, (adj) middle, base, common, hateful, ignoble, medium, miserly, (n) average, contemptible, low; *antonyms* (adj) generous, kind, **2.** means; *synonyms* (n) expedient, agency, instrument, assets, capital, channel, funds, income, manner, agent, contrivance, device, method, process, property.

nanona 1. craving; *synonyms* (n) aspiration, appetite, desire, longing, addiction, appetency, eagerness, hankering, hunger, passion, urge, yearning, yen, (adj) eager, hungry, **2.** infatuated; *synonyms* (adj) enamored, fanatical, crazy, dotty, gaga, mad, obsessed, smitten, foolish, loving, (v) besotted, confined, illiberal, **3.** import; *synonyms* (n) consequence, meaning, sense, effect, connotation, implication, importance, moment, purport, significance, value, betoken, (v) matter, denote, imply; *antonym* (v) export, **4.** desire; *synonyms* (n) ambition, hope, will, wish, craving, dream, impulse, (v) fancy, aspire, seek, want, aim, choose, crave, like; *antonyms* (n) aversion, reality, (v) dislike, hate, **5.** love; *synonyms* (n) affection, dear, fondness, liking, benevolence, charity, attachment, beloved, darling, devotion, honey, sweetheart, (v) cherish, enjoy, worship; *antonyms* (n) abhorrence, hatred, (v) abhor, **6.** will; *synonyms* (v) bequeath, devise, leave, shall, (n) volition, command, inclination, determination, pleasure, resolve, intent, mind, courage, purpose, testament, **7.** yearn; *synonyms* (v) long, languish, pine, ache, hanker.

nanonaki 1. desired; *synonyms* (adj) coveted, craved, desirable, chosen, favorite, wanted, needed, welcome, beloved, adored, appropriate, pet, preferred, (v) complying, consenting; *antonym* (adj) undesirable, **2.** loved; *synonyms* (adj) dear, cherished, precious, appreciated, esteemed, prized, respected, treasured, valued, important, (n) darling, **3.** imported; *synonyms* (adj) foreign, exotic, extrinsic, unaccustomed, alien, carried, choice, ferried, introduced, rare, sent, shipped, transported, trucked.

nanonibwi 1. covet; *synonyms* (v) begrudge, desire, envy, long, aspire, crave, grudge, hanker, want, fancy, wish, **2.** envy; *synonyms* (n) enviousness, resentment, hatred, discontent, emulation, (v) covet, **3.** rival; *synonyms* (adj) competitive, (n) competitor, emulate, enemy, foe, adversary, antagonist, challenger, contender, contestant, (v) equal, contest, match, compete, contend; *antonyms* (adj) allied, (n) ally, friend, partner.

nanonibwiaki coveted; *synonyms* (adj) desired, craved, exceptional, impressive, marketable.

nanora resent; *synonyms* (*v*) dislike, begrudge, envy, grudge, antagonize, brook, combat, covet, miff, mind, oppose, oppugn, repel, stomach, feel.

nanorake 1. impatient; *synonyms* (*adj*) eager, hasty, anxious, petulant, fidgety, keen, edgy, quick, avid, enthusiastic, impetuous, irritable, restive, restless, testy; *antonyms* (*adj*) patient, enduring, **2**. cross; *synonyms* (*n*) crisscross, affliction, (*v*) intersect, baffle, cover, thwart, (*adj*) crabbed, crabby, angry, cantankerous, grouchy, grumpy, traverse, cranky, annoyed; *antonyms* (*v*) uncross, (*adj*) calm, good-tempered, **3**. exposed; *synonyms* (*v*) vulnerable, (*adj*) bare, open, defenseless, liable, naked, nude, obvious, subject, uncovered, unprotected, bald, bleak, public, undefended; *antonyms* (*adj*) concealed, covered, hidden, safe, **4**. choleric; *synonyms* (*adj*) irascible, passionate, peppery, fiery, quick-tempered, cross, quarrelsome, hotheaded, snappish, waspish, **5**. defenseless; *synonyms* (*adj*) defenceless, helpless, exposed, unguarded, weak, (*v*) indefensible, unarmed, **6**. irritable; *synonyms* (*adj*) fractious, disagreeable, excitable, sensitive, touchy, huffy, difficult, fretful, impatient, peevish, techy, temperamental, tetchy, captious, morose; *antonyms* (*adj*) easygoing, good-humored, good-natured, even-tempered, **7**. irascible; *synonyms* (*adj*) choleric, hot, acrimonious, inflammable, moody, short, **8**. fiery; *synonyms* (*adj*) ardent, burning, fervent, ablaze, fierce, fervid, flaming, glowing, impassioned, violent, combustible, blazing, torrid, cordial, (*v*) vehement; *antonym* (*adj*) mild, **9**. cantankerous; *synonyms* (*adj*) crotchety, prickly, stubborn, argumentative, crusty, ornery, perverse, querulous, ugly, **10**. assailable; *synonyms* (*adj*) flimsy, undefendable, blatant, candid, clear, conspicuous, lawless, loose, opened, overt, undecided, undetermined, unfastened, unresolved, unstopped, **11**. peppery; *synonyms* (*adj*) spicy, poignant, gingery, piquant, pungent, racy, sharp, **12**. resentful; *synonyms* (*adj*) bitter, indignant, malicious, rancorous, envious, jealous, offended, hurt, mad, raging, sore, wrathful, revengeful, vindictive; *antonyms* (*adj*) charitable, resigned, **13**. susceptible; *synonyms* (*adj*) impressionable, receptive, responsive, delicate, pliable, susceptive, amenable, impressible, prone; *antonyms* (*adj*) resistant, unsusceptible, **14**. vulnerable; *synonyms* (*adj*) susceptible, tender, feeble, insecure, powerless, dependent, disadvantaged, (*v*) frail; *antonyms* (*adj*) impervious, invincible, invulnerable, unassailable, unbeatable, secure, untouchable, **15**. unguarded; *synonyms* (*adj*) unwary, incautious, careless, natural, (*v*) thoughtless, improvident, shiftless, thriftless, **16**. petulant; *synonyms* (*adj*) pettish, nettlesome, sullen, pert, peckish.

nanoraki 1. stealth; *synonyms* (*n*) secrecy, stealing, furtiveness, stealthiness, larceny, missile, secretiveness, caution, conspiracy, evasiveness, thieving, (*adj*) undercover; *antonym* (*n*) openness, **2**. visible; *synonyms* (*adj*) obvious, perceptible, conspicuous, apparent, evident, open, clear, discernible, manifest, noticeable, observable, plain, appreciable, visual, transparent; *antonyms* (*adj*) invisible, imperceptible, **3**. stealthy; *synonyms* (*adj*) furtive, clandestine, secret, sneaky, surreptitious, covert, private, backstairs, concealed, feline, catlike, noiseless, hidden, (*v*) sly, insidious.

nanoraoi 1. genial; *synonyms* (*adj*) benign, cheerful, bright, affable, amiable, cordial, friendly, nice, agreeable, convivial, warm, bland, suave, amicable, congenial; *antonyms* (*adj*) unfriendly, disagreeable, **2**. moderate; *synonyms* (*adj*) temperate, abstemious, middling, mild, easy, (*v*) calm, mitigate, allay, curb, diminish, lessen, ease, cool, abate, (*adv*) check; *antonyms* (*adj*) extreme, immoderate, radical, (*v*) increase, intensify, **3**. calm; *synonyms* (*adj*) quiet, peaceful, tranquil, (*v*) assuage, appease, still, pacify, moderate, mollify, steady, tranquilize, alleviate, becalm, (*n*) lull, equanimity; *antonyms* (*adj*) agitated, angry, nervous, stormy, wild, annoyed, anxious, enraged, frantic, frightened, intense, irritable, (*v*) agitate, upset, (*n*) agitation, **4**. easygoing; *synonyms* (*adj*) careless, leisurely, placid, carefree, genial, optimistic, casual, composed, gentle, insouciant, serene, unconcerned; *antonyms* (*adj*) bad-tempered, grumpy, severe, **5**. collected; *synonyms* (*adj*) accumulated, amassed, assembled, sober, poised, unflappable, dispassionate, gathered, imperturbable, sedate, staid, congregate, **6**. mild; *synonyms* (*adj*) kindly, gracious, lenient, docile, humble, balmy, clement, delicate, kind, meek, sweet, fine, indulgent, compliant, light; *antonyms* (*adj*) pungent, sharp, spicy, barbed, fierce, great, hot, incisive, passionate, powerful, scathing, wintry, **7**. composed; *synonyms* (*adj*) collected, peaceable, equable, impassive, easygoing, unmoved, even, nerveless, relaxed, unperturbed, unruffled, untroubled, nonchalant, patient; *antonyms* (*adj*) distressed, trembling, **8**. aloof; *synonyms* (*adj*) distant, reserved, indifferent, standoffish, frigid, arrogant, chill, cold, detached, disinterested, frosty, haughty, icy, remote, (*adv*) apart; *antonyms* (*adj*) approachable, involved, **9**. meek; *synonyms* (*adj*) lowly, tame, low, modest, submissive, retiring, unassuming, acquiescent, biddable, dutiful, obedient, soft, tractable, unobtrusive, diffident; *antonyms* (*adj*) assertive, bossy, **10**. even; *synonyms* (*adv*) yet, (*adj*) direct, equal, constant, equivalent, flat, horizontal, identical, plane, regular, clear, balanced, (*v*) level, balance, smooth; *antonyms* (*adj*) uneven, inconsistent, irregular, jagged, unequal, **11**. cool; *synonyms* *(adj)* chilly, aloof, apathetic, lukewarm, soothe, bracing, marvelous, offhand, stylish, *(v)* quench, refrigerate, refresh, *(n)* composure, poise, aplomb; *antonyms* *(adj)* excited, enthusiastic, feverish, tepid, *(v)* heat, **12**. placid; *synonyms* *(adj)* contented, hushed, tender, undisturbed, **13**. peaceful; *synonyms* *(adj)* peace, silent, halcyon, harmonious, restful, conciliatory, happy, idyllic, inactive, passive; *antonyms* *(adj)* aggressive, noisy, tense, violent, **14**. patient; *synonyms* *(adj)* invalid, forbearing, enduring, resigned, tolerant, uncomplaining, stoical, persistent, considerate, indefatigable; *antonym* *(adj)* impatient, **15**. pacific, **16**. quiet; *synonyms* *(adj)* motionless, dull, mute, muted, noiseless, *(v)* silence, repose, gag, quell, rest, slow, *(n)* hush, compose, peacefulness, leisure; *antonyms* *(adj)* loud, talkative, vociferous, active, *(n)* noise.

nanorau 1. peaceable; *synonyms* *(adj)* gentle, mild, calm, amicable, quiet, friendly, inoffensive, moderate, meek, placid, serene, soft, still, amiable, *(v)* peaceful; *antonyms* *(adj)* aggressive, argumentative, **2**. peaceful; *synonyms* *(adj)* peaceable, even, peace, silent, composed, halcyon, tranquil, untroubled, collected, bland, easy, harmonious, restful, sedate, smooth; *antonyms* *(adj)* noisy, tense, violent.

nanoriba 1. intolerant; *synonyms* *(adj)* impatient, bigoted, illiberal, dogmatic, racist, narrow-minded, contumelious, *(v)* confined; *antonyms* *(adj)* tolerant, broadminded, liberal, **2**. bigoted; *synonyms* *(adj)* intolerant, fanatical, narrow, opinionated, hidebound, insular, arbitrary, biased, unfair, **3**. selfish; *synonyms* *(adj)* mean, greedy, mercenary, egocentric, egoistic, egotistic, egotistical, self-centered, stingy, covetous, inconsiderate, sordid, thoughtless, exclusive, *(v)* contracted; *antonyms* *(adj)* unselfish, selfless, altruistic, generous.

nanorinano 1. humble; *synonyms* *(adj)* base, docile, low, lowly, modest, unassuming, baseborn, *(v)* degrade, demean, disgrace, abase, debase, humiliate, mortify, conquer; *antonyms* *(adj)* grand, arrogant, conceited, haughty, imposing, impressive, pompous, snooty, **2**. lowly; *synonyms* *(adj)* humble, lower, inferior, poor, insignificant, ignoble, simple, little, mean, meek, menial, petty, plain, small, *(adv)* humbly.

nanoro backward; *synonyms* *(adj)* back, late, behindhand, coy, dilatory, laggard, reluctant, retarded, slow, tardy, averse, bashful, *(adv)* behind, aback, backwards; *antonyms* *(adv)* forward, ahead.

nanotati cooperative; *synonyms* *(adj)* combined, joint, accommodating, concerted, helpful, obliging, united, accommodative, communal, conjunct, conjunctive, *(n)* collective, association, commune; *antonyms* *(adj)* uncooperative, individual.

nanotau 1. agreeable; *synonyms* *(adj)* acceptable, accordant, pleasant, pleasing, nice, affable, amusing, compatible, conformable, congenial, consistent, enjoyable, genial, grateful, *(v)* desirable; *antonyms* *(adj)* disagreeable, discordant, nasty, unpleasant, unwilling, aggressive, resistant, **2**. resigned; *synonyms* *(v)* content, *(adj)* patient, submissive, subdued, yielding, abject, forbearing, passive, pessimistic; *antonym* *(adj)* resentful, **3**. pliable; *synonyms* *(adj)* flexible, elastic, plastic, ductile, pliant, flexile, malleable, soft, fictile, supple, susceptible, docile, resilient, *(v)* lithe, limber; *antonyms* *(adj)* rigid, stiff.

nanoteuana agree; *synonyms* *(v)* accord, admit, acknowledge, acquiesce, adjust, accede, bargain, concord, correspond, fit, harmonize, suit, compromise, align, *(n)* coincide; *antonyms* *(v)* disagree, oppose, differ, argue, object, refuse, refute.

nanotiotio 1. changeable; *synonyms* *(adj)* variable, capricious, erratic, inconsistent, irregular, fickle, giddy, mercurial, mobile, mutable, slippery, temperamental, uncertain, unsettled, unstable; *antonyms* *(adj)* constant, fixed, stable, unchangeable, consistent, dependable, predictable, regular, **2**. heedless; *synonyms* *(adj)* careless, reckless, inattentive, neglectful, negligent, rash, thoughtless, blind, forgetful, inadvertent, incautious, inconsiderate, indifferent, listless, mindless; *antonym* *(adj)* heedful, **3**. distracted; *synonyms* *(adj)* frantic, demented, abstracted, crazy, distraught, distressed, frenzied, mad, preoccupied, confused, disconcerted, absentminded, distrait, disturbed, unbalanced, **4**. inadvertent; *synonyms* *(adj)* accidental, heedless, casual, chance, unintended, unintentional, imprudent, unplanned, adventitious, involuntary, regardless, unthinking, unwitting; *antonyms* *(adj)* intentional, deliberate, **5**. careless; *synonyms* *(adj)* cursory, haphazard, insouciant, hasty, lax, messy, nonchalant, oblivious, perfunctory, slack, sloppy, unaware, unconcerned, unwary, carefree; *antonyms* *(adj)* careful, cautious, prudent, attentive, diligent, meticulous, thorough, thoughtful, guarded, methodical, strict, wary, **6**. unstable; *synonyms* *(adj)* changeable, precarious, insecure, shaky, unsound, fluid, inconstant, unpredictable, irresolute, unreliable, changeful, fluctuating, rickety, unsteady, volatile; *antonym* *(adj)* steady, **7**. unmindful; *synonyms* *(adj)* ungrateful, remiss, unobservant, unconscious, **8**. regardless; *synonyms* *(adv)* anyhow, irregardless, irrespective, disregarding, disregardless.

nanouki 1. magnanimous; *synonyms* *(adj)* generous, liberal, great, noble, bountiful, exalted, big, handsome, lofty, charitable, considerate, large, elevated, chivalrous, high, **2**. amiable; *synonyms* *(adj)* affable, agreeable, benign, complaisant, friendly, genial, charming, cordial, gentle, kind, likable, lovely, nice, pleasant, sweet; *antonyms* (adj) unfriendly, disagreeable, aggressive, argumentative, **3.** cordial; *synonyms* (adj) hearty, warm, amiable, ardent, genuine, gracious, hospitable, neighborly, sociable, brotherly, harmonious, open, (n) liqueur, glowing, tonic; *antonyms* (adj) hostile, stern, **4.** generous; *synonyms* (adj) ample, full, abundant, benevolent, copious, fair, flush, spacious, rich, bounteous, broad, considerable, kindly, munificent, (n) free; *antonyms* (adj) stingy, meager, mean, measly, miserly, small, tightfisted, avaricious, greedy, ungenerous, **5.** liberal; *synonyms* (adj) giving, tolerant, lavish, easy, bighearted, enlightened, freehanded, permissive, plentiful, wide, left, frank, indulgent, lenient, (n) progressive; *antonyms* (adj) strict, oppressive, totalitarian, intolerant, (n) conservative, **6.** honorable; *synonyms* (adj) good, honest, decent, estimable, reputable, respectable, ethical, honor, distinguished, commendable, creditable, grand, just, praiseworthy, (v) dignified; *antonyms* (adj) dishonorable, disgraceful, shameful, corrupt, **7.** tolerant; *synonyms* (adj) patient, forbearing, forgiving, understanding, merciful, magnanimous, broadminded, uncomplaining, loose, moderate, resigned, thoughtful, (v) meek; *antonyms* (adj) narrow-minded, impatient, **8.** understanding; *synonyms* (n) intellect, mind, reason, appreciation, comprehension, agreement, apprehension, bargain, deal, judgment, sense, sympathy, arrangement, (v) intelligence, discernment; *antonyms* (n) ignorance, bewilderment, disbelief, **9.** sincere; *synonyms* (adj) devout, faithful, heartfelt, artless, candid, direct, real, serious, simple, downright, plain, guileless, ingenuous, unaffected, (v) earnest; *antonyms* (adj) insincere, dishonest, affected, flippant, guarded, **10.** respected; *synonyms* (adj) esteemed, illustrious, appreciated, dear, honored, revered, valued, celebrated, famous, glorious, prestigious, redoubtable.

nanoun 1. cross; *synonyms* (n) crisscross, affliction, (v) intersect, baffle, cover, thwart, (adj) crabbed, crabby, angry, cantankerous, grouchy, grumpy, traverse, cranky, annoyed; *antonyms* (v) uncross, (adj) calm, good-tempered, **2.** irascible; *synonyms* (adj) fiery, choleric, irritable, excitable, hot, hotheaded, passionate, testy, touchy, hasty, impatient, impetuous, edgy, quarrelsome, acrimonious, **3.** fiery; *synonyms* (adj) ardent, burning, fervent, ablaze, fierce, fervid, flaming, glowing, impassioned, peppery, violent, combustible, blazing, torrid, (n) enthusiastic; *antonym* (adj) mild, **4.** choleric; *synonyms* (adj) irascible, quick-tempered, cross, snappish, waspish, **5.** irritable; *synonyms* (adj) fractious,

disagreeable, petulant, sensitive, huffy, difficult, fretful, peevish, techy, temperamental, tetchy, captious, morose, inflammable, (n) sullen; *antonyms* (adj) easygoing, good-humored, good-natured, even-tempered, **6.** cantankerous; *synonyms* (adj) crotchety, moody, prickly, stubborn, argumentative, crusty, ornery, perverse, querulous, ugly, **7.** violent; *synonyms* (adj) rough, tempestuous, intense, raging, severe, turbulent, vehement, sharp, powerful, savage, stormy, strong, wild, (n) furious, boisterous; *antonyms* (adj) gentle, peaceful, nonviolent, **8.** peppery; *synonyms* (adj) spicy, poignant, gingery, piquant, pungent, racy, **9.** petulant; *synonyms* (adj) pettish, nettlesome, pert, peckish, **10.** peevish; *synonyms* (adj) sour, grumbling, spleeny, splenetic.

nanououa 1. mystified; *synonyms* (adj) bewildered, metagrabolized, metagrobolized, perplexed, puzzled, baffled, bemused, confused, flummoxed, metagrabolised, metagrobolised, stumped, thrown, unclear, absentminded; *antonym* (adj) enlightened, **2.** confused; *synonyms* (adj) abashed, befuddled, chaotic, confounded, disjointed, disordered, dizzy, incoherent, indistinct, ambiguous, broken, disconnected, disorderly, (n) cloudy, (adv, adj) topsy-turvy; *antonyms* (adj) clear, alert, clearheaded, clear-headed, orderly, **3.** bewildered; *synonyms* (adj) lost, dumbfounded, addled, amazed, blank, dazed, disconcerted, disoriented, muddled, mystified, stunned; *antonym* (adj) unimpressed, **4.** mystify; *synonyms* (v) baffle, bamboozle, bewilder, confound, confuse, nonplus, perplex, puzzle, stump, amaze, flummox, get, hoodwink, bemuse, gravel, **5.** confounded; *synonyms* (adj) accursed, cursed, execrable, aghast, abominable, **6.** falter; *synonyms* (v) hesitate, waver, stammer, stumble, stutter, halt, bumble, dither, doubt, hobble, lurch, (n) faltering, flounder, hesitation, (adv) flag; *antonym* (v) continue, **7.** confuse; *synonyms* (v) muddle, agitate, blur, derange, disconcert, disturb, fluster, jumble, mystify, obscure, unsettle, abash, bedevil, befuddle, daze; *antonyms* (v) clarify, enlighten, elucidate, explain, **8.** hesitant; *synonyms* (adj) doubtful, indecisive, irresolute, uncertain, diffident, hesitating, reluctant, shy, undecided, unsure, backward, loath, apprehensive, insecure, tentative; *antonyms* (adj) certain, confident, decided, decisive, firm, resolute, sure, **9.** confound; *synonyms* (v) astonish, astound, mistake, complicate, dash, defeat, discomfit, distract, dumbfound, flabbergast, overwhelm, (n) surprise, (adj) stupefy, checkmate, petrify, **10.** indecisive; *synonyms* (adj) hesitant, inconclusive, weak, dubious, precarious, vague, feeble; *antonym* (adj) conclusive, **11.** bewilder; *synonyms* (v) perturb, stun, entangle, stagger, throw, maze, bother, discombobulate, discompose, dismay,

embarrass, floor, fog, obfuscate, upset, **12.**
hesitate; *synonyms* (v) falter, pause, fluctuate,
boggle, demur, vacillate, procrastinate, scruple,
totter, (adj) linger, delay, alternate, sputter, demure,
dillydally, **13.** doubt; *synonyms* (n) disbelief,
misgiving, question, dispute, apprehension,
incertitude, skepticism, uncertainty, diffidence, (v)
distrust, query, suspicion, mistrust, suspect,
disbelieve; *antonyms* (n) certainty, confidence,
conclusiveness, (v) trust, **14.** undecided;
synonyms (adj) unsettled, pending, unresolved,
undetermined, debatable, indefinite, indeterminate,
ambivalent, borderline, moot, open; *antonym* (adj)
determined, **15.** perplexed; *synonyms* (v)
complicated, intricate, (adj) involved, distracted,
uneasy, questioning, quizzical, entangled, knotted,
16. perplex; *synonyms* (v) involve, trouble,
distress, embroil, beset, beat, tease, afflict, tangle,
vex, (n) harass, annoy, torment, calamity, (adj) pose.
nanououaki 1. confounded; *synonyms* (adj)
bemused, bewildered, accursed, abashed, baffled,
befuddled, confused, cursed, execrable, puzzled,
aghast, abominable, **2.** mystified; *synonyms* (adj)
metagrabolized, metagrobolized, perplexed,
flummoxed, metagrabolised, metagrobolised,
stumped, thrown, unclear, absentminded,
bamboozled, faraway, preoccupied; *antonym* (adj)
enlightened, **3.** bewildered; *synonyms* (adj) lost,
confounded, dumbfounded, addled, amazed,
blank, dazed, disconcerted, disoriented, muddled,
mystified, stunned; *antonym* (adj) unimpressed, **4.**
confused; *synonyms* (adj) chaotic, disjointed,
disordered, dizzy, incoherent, indistinct,
ambiguous, broken, disconnected, disorderly,
disorganized, indefinite, indiscriminate, (n) cloudy,
(adv, adj) topsy-turvy; *antonyms* (adj) clear, alert,
clearheaded, clear-headed, orderly, **5.** perplexed;
synonyms (v) complicated, intricate, (adj) involved,
doubtful, distracted, uneasy, questioning,
quizzical, entangled, knotted.
nanouti desire; *synonyms* (n) ambition, hope,
aspiration, will, wish, craving, dream, impulse, (v)
fancy, aspire, seek, want, aim, choose, crave;
antonyms (n) aversion, reality, (v) dislike, hate.
nanoutiaki desired; *synonyms* (adj) coveted, craved,
desirable, chosen, favorite, wanted, needed,
welcome, beloved, adored, appropriate, pet,
preferred, (v) complying, consenting; *antonym* (adj)
undesirable.
nanoutu 1. clannish; *synonyms* (adj) cliquish, clubby,
exclusive, ancestral, ethnic, family, sectarian,
snobbish, snobby, akin, alike, associative, close,
clubbish, insular, **2.** racial; *synonyms* (adj) cultural,
hereditary, lineal, paternal, patriarchical, phyletic,
phylogenetic, **3.** tribal; *synonyms* (adj) racial,
national, tribular.

nanowaki disconsolate; *synonyms* (adj) desolate,
inconsolable, blue, cheerless, melancholy, dejected,
depressed, crestfallen, dark, depressing,
downhearted, forlorn, gloomy, miserable, sad;
antonym (adj) cheerful.
nanowana 1. judicious; *synonyms* (adj) careful,
discreet, wise, discerning, prudent, rational,
sensible, cautious, reasonable, sagacious, sound,
advisable, circumspect, intelligent, (n) clever;
antonyms (adj) foolish, ill-advised, **2.** just;
synonyms (adv) exactly, hardly, newly, simply, (adj)
fair, right, correct, equitable, accurate, honest,
impartial, barely, fit, good, righteous; *antonyms*
(adj) unfair, biased, wrong, **3.** fair; *synonyms* (adj)
clear, beautiful, average, dispassionate, fine, sweet,
candid, comely, considerable, decent, (adv) clean, (n)
bazaar, blonde, carnival, (v) bright; *antonyms* (adj)
dark, exceptional, unjust, partial, foul, imbalanced,
mismatched, prejudiced, unwarranted, **4.**
equitable; *synonyms* (adj) just, even-handed,
objective, balanced, disinterested, due, even,
unbiased, unprejudiced, judicial, evenhanded,
indifferent, rightful, square, straight; *antonym* (adj)
inequitable, **5.** cognitive; *synonym* (adj)
psychological, **6.** coherent; *synonyms* (adj) logical,
consistent, lucid, tenacious, orderly,
comprehensible, connected; *antonyms* (adj)
incoherent, illogical, confused, disjointed,
rambling, **7.** impartial; *synonyms* (adj) detached,
impersonal, open, level, equal, independent,
neutral, upright, **8.** logical; *synonyms* (adj)
coherent, legitimate, justifiable, valid, arranged,
methodical, systematic; *antonyms* (adj) imaginative,
irrational, unintelligible, **9.** prudent; *synonyms*
(adj) judicious, chary, economical, frugal, deliberate,
canny, politic, provident, modest, sane, guarded,
shrewd, tactful, thoughtful, thrifty; *antonyms* (adj)
imprudent, reckless, spendthrift, careless, stupid,
10. sensible; *synonyms* (adj) aware, perceptible,
appreciable, sage, practical, conscious, sapient,
cognizant, palpable, sensitive, knowing, realistic,
susceptible, feeling, discernible; *antonyms* (adj)
absurd, crazy, idiotic, ludicrous, mad, outrageous,
ridiculous, silly, unreasonable, unwise,
harebrained, hasty, impractical, **11.** wise;
synonyms (adj) cunning, knowledgeable, sharp,
skillful, smart, diplomatic, perceptive, profound,
farsighted, astute, considered, erudite, (n) method,
manner, way, **12.** rational; *synonyms* (adj)
intellectual, mental, sober, philosophical, reasoned,
cerebral, convincing; *antonym* (adj) anxious, **13.**
objective; *synonyms* (adj) concrete, accusative, (n)
aim, mark, goal, object, ambition, design, end,
intent, intention, target, purport, point, purpose;
antonym (adj) subjective, **14.** sapient; *synonym*
(adj) perspicacious, **15.** reasonable; *synonyms* (adj)
moderate, admissible, appropriate, cheap,

inexpensive, plausible, temperate, acceptable, credible, respectable, suitable, normal, feasible, adequate, fitting; *antonyms* (*adj*) expensive, unsatisfactory, inadequate.

nao 1. boy; *synonyms* (*n*) lad, fellow, kid, male, man, minor, servant, son, youngster, youth, boots, **2.** man; *synonyms* (*n*) gentleman, guy, person, husband, homo, human, humanity, humankind, humans, individual, mankind, mortal, world, (*v*) equip, (*obj*) he; *antonym* (*n*) woman, **3.** sire; *synonyms* (*n*) father, forefather, patriarch, parent, founder, (*v*) beget, engender, generate, mother, procreate, get, make, create, breed, **4.** sir; *synonyms* (*n*) esquire, master, don, signior, buck, dominus, effendi, magister, signore.

naonao surge; *synonyms* (*n*) wave, burst, ripple, spurt, (*v*) billow, flood, rise, rush, stream, flow, gush, heave, jet, swell, soar.

naou wave; *synonyms* (*n*) billow, gesture, motion, sign, surge, (*v*) brandish, flap, flutter, curl, flourish, swell, swing, undulate, beat, beckon.

narei 1. after; *synonyms* (*prep*) following, since, (*adv*) later, beyond, next, subsequently, then, when, afterward, afterwards, behind, (*adj*) back, posterior, rear, subsequent, **2.** following; *synonyms* (*adj*) consequent, ensuing, consecutive, succeeding, deducible, latter, sequent, (*v*) consequential, (*n*) entourage, chase, followers, pursuit, audience, (*adv*) under, after; *antonym* (*adj*) preceding, **3.** later; *synonyms* (*adj*) last, future, final; *antonyms* (*adv*) earlier, immediately, before, prior, **4.** next; *synonyms* (*adj*) nearest, adjacent, contiguous, coming, close, near, adjoining, closest, neighboring, proximate, immediate, imminent, nearby, second, (*adv*) on; *antonyms* (*adj*) distant, outgoing, (*adv*) previous, previously, **5.** beyond; *synonyms* (*prep*) above, (*adv*) further, without, besides, away, by, farther, more, over, abroad, past, yonder, (*adj*) across; *antonym* (*prep*) within, **6.** afterward; *synonym* (*adv*) thereafter; *antonym* (*adv*) beforehand.

nariki narrow; *synonyms* (*adj*) close, limited, insular, little, cramped, illiberal, mean, (*v*) confined, contract, limit, lessen, constrict, shrink, abridge, dwindle; *antonyms* (*adj*) wide, broad, comprehensive, extensive, (*v*) widen, extend.

nata swarm; *synonyms* (*n*) crowd, horde, host, mob, drove, multitude, assembly, cloud, gathering, herd, mass, (*v*) pour, teem, abound, flock.

natao teem; *synonyms* (*n*) abound, exuberate, (*v*) swarm, flow, pour, crowd, pullulate, brim, flower, fructify, rain, stream.

nati 1. bastard; *synonyms* (*n*) whoreson, scoundrel, cad, mongrel, (*adj*) illegitimate, spurious, fake, misbegotten, phony, adulterate, bastardly, bogus, false, natural, phoney; *antonym* (*n*) legitimate, **2.**

child; *synonyms* (*n*) baby, boy, babe, bairn, brat, girl, infant, juvenile, kid, minor, toddler, tot, youngster, innocent, imp; *antonym* (*n*) adult, **3.** son; *synonyms* (*n*) offspring, lad, child, descendant, logos, word, bible, countersign, discussion, intelligence, news, parole, password, schoolboy, scripture.

natina 1. adopt; *synonyms* (*v*) accept, admit, affiliate, assume, borrow, espouse, pass, take, acquire, choose, embrace, follow, imitate, naturalize, prefer; *antonym* (*v*) reject, **2.** egg; *synonyms* (*n*) ball, rudiment, eggs, nut, testicle, testis, ballock, bollock, stock, bud, embryo, nucleus, addict, baseball, beginning, **3.** parent; *synonyms* (*n*) mother, origin, source, forefather, prototype, precursor, (*v*) father, foster, rear, nurture, generate, advance, advert, arouse, boot; *antonym* (*n*) child.

natinaki adopted; *synonyms* (*adj*) adoptive, elected, consecrated, converted, inspired, justified, regenerated, sanctified, unearthly, adoptious, foreign, popular, preferred.

natinati adopt; *synonyms* (*v*) accept, admit, affiliate, assume, borrow, espouse, pass, take, acquire, choose, embrace, follow, imitate, naturalize, prefer; *antonym* (*v*) reject.

natinatiaki adopted; *synonyms* (*adj*) adoptive, elected, consecrated, converted, inspired, justified, regenerated, sanctified, unearthly, adoptious, foreign, popular, preferred.

nawa 1. breathe; *synonyms* (*v*) blow, exhale, live, subsist, be, emit, exist, imply, rest, whisper, inspire, convey, heave, (*n*) respire, bespeak, **2.** inhale; *synonyms* (*v*) breathe, absorb, imbibe, draw, suck, drag, drink, attract, receive, admit, import, ingest, puff, (*n*) sniff, **3.** rest; *synonyms* (*n*) remnant, repose, balance, pause, recess, relaxation, residue, leisure, break, (*v*) nap, remain, sleep, ease, lie, (*adj*) remainder; *antonym* (*v*) work, **4.** pause; *synonyms* (*n*) intermission, interruption, gap, interval, respite, stop, breather, cessation, (*v*) halt, adjournment, delay, hesitate, desist, cease, (*adj*) discontinue; *antonyms* (*n*) decisiveness, (*v*) continue.

nawaki 1. breathed; *synonyms* (*adj*) voiceless, aphonic, surd, **2.** inhaled; *synonym* (*adj*) inspired, **3.** rested; *synonyms* (*adj*) fresh, comfortable.

nawanawa 1. motley; *synonyms* (*adj*) assorted, colorful, miscellaneous, mixed, mottled, heterogeneous, multicolored, checkered, indiscriminate, dappled, (*n*) medley, assortment, miscellany, mixture, mix, **2.** streaked; *synonyms* (*v*) barred, areolar, cancellated, grated, (*adj*) veined, streaky, striped, brindled, lined, brinded, dotted, marbled, marked, patterned, (*n*) hairstyle.

nea 1. confused; *synonyms* (*adj*) abashed, bewildered, baffled, befuddled, bemused, chaotic, confounded, disjointed, disordered, dizzy, incoherent, indistinct, ambiguous, (*n*) cloudy, (*adv, adj*) topsy-turvy;

antonyms (*adj*) clear, enlightened, alert, clearheaded, clear-headed, orderly, **2**. lay; *synonyms* (*v*) place, put, fix, set, deposit, install, lie, rest, invest, bear, allay, arrange, (*adj*) secular, (*n*) ballad, pitch, **3**. humiliated; *synonyms* (*adj*) ashamed, humbled, mortified, embarrassed, humble, broken, crushed; *antonym* (*adj*) proud, **4**. arrange; *synonyms* (*v*) adjust, appoint, dress, order, settle, pack, adapt, agree, classify, compose, decorate, do, engineer, provide, reconcile; *antonyms* (*v*) disturb, disarrange, **5**. abashed; *synonyms* (*adj*) bashful, discomfited, confused, sheepish; *antonym* (*adj*) brazen, **6**. deposit; *synonyms* (*n*) charge, residue, guarantee, heap, hoard, lees, lode, (*v*) bank, commit, store, lay, repose, cast, file, leave; *antonym* (*v*) withdraw, **7**. seat; *synonyms* (*n*) bench, base, backside, behind, bottom, buttocks, chair, position, post, posterior, rear, rump, (*v*) locate, contain, hold, **8**. shameful; *synonyms* (*adj*) disgraceful, dishonorable, scandalous, contemptible, degrading, despicable, disreputable, ignominious, inglorious, opprobrious, shocking, nasty, (*v*) foul, gross, black; *antonyms* (*adj*) honorable, dignified, noble, admirable, **9**. put; *synonyms* (*v*) impose, couch, pose, assign, establish, express, make, plant, localize, aim, frame, park, reckon, situate, stake, **10**. set; *synonyms* (*v*) regulate, define, congeal, posit, (*n*) class, bent, circle, lot, party, batch, battery, (*adj*) fixed, fast, secure, ready; *antonyms* (*v*) soften, liquefy, melt, (*n*) combing, comb-out, (*adj*) variable, flexible, liquid, **11**. place; *synonyms* (*n*) domicile, office, spot, attitude, job, location, situation, circumstance, center, abode, berth, dwelling, (*v*) rank, station, dispose; *antonym* (*v*) remove, **12**. settle; *synonyms* (*v*) clarify, pay, resolve, adjudicate, conclude, decide, determine, drop, explain, fall, subside, accommodate, negotiate, sit, (*adj*) confirm, **13**. snubbed; *synonyms* (*adj*) affronted, hurt, insulted, offended, slighted, upset.

neaki 1. laid; *synonyms* (*adj*) set, determined, dictated, fixed, hardened, located, rigid, **2**. arranged; *synonyms* (*adj*) settled, orderly, organized, prepared, ready, regular, neat, ordered, straight, tidy, **3**. settled; *synonyms* (*adj*) definite, firm, permanent, calm, certain, decided, established, defined, formed, confirmed, finished, sedate, standing, quiet, done; *antonym* (*adj*) uninhabited, **4**. placed; *synonyms* (*adj*) situated, laid, positioned, collocate, residing, **5**. seated; *synonyms* (*adj*) sitting, sedentary, **6**. set; *synonyms* (*v*) fix, place, lay, put, locate, position, regulate, define, adjust, arrange, (*n*) class, bent, circle, (*adj*) fast, secure; *antonyms* (*v*) soften, liquefy, melt, (*n*) combing, comb-out, (*adj*) variable, flexible, liquid.

neakina 1. shove; *synonyms* (*v*) elbow, impel, press, prod, shift, boost, hustle, stuff, nudge, bump, (*n*)

push, thrust, jostle, poke, shoulder; *antonym* (*v*) pull, **2**. push; *synonyms* (*n*) jolt, energy, (*v*) drive, crowd, force, jab, jam, rush, fight, incite, jog, labor, plug, pressure, promote; *antonyms* (*v*) drag, haul.

neboa 1. extol; *synonyms* (*v*) commend, exalt, acclaim, applaud, celebrate, eulogize, laud, glorify, praise, admire, compliment, magnify, proclaim; *antonym* (*v*) criticize, **2**. heave; *synonyms* (*v*) cast, fling, chuck, gasp, haul, toss, billow, drag, draw, elevate, gag, (*n*) tug, raise, elevation, heaving, **3**. celebrate; *synonyms* (*v*) commemorate, extol, keep, fete, honor, solemnize, honour, distinguish, exult, hold, observe, rejoice, triumph, lionize; *antonym* (*v*) ignore, **4**. glorify; *synonyms* (*v*) bless, dignify, adore, canonize, aggrandize, worship, applause, revere, accredit, idolize, (*n*) ennoble, **5**. exalt; *synonyms* (*v*) animate, advance, promote, elate, inspire, consecrate, enhance, encourage, improve, intensify, invigorate, lift, prefer, thrill, cheer; *antonym* (*v*) humiliate, **6**. praise; *synonyms* (*n*) commendation, glory, kudos, admiration, approval, encomium, eulogy, panegyric, credit, exaltation, (*v*) approve, flatter, congratulate, fame, appreciate; *antonyms* (*n*) criticism, disparagement, (*v*) belittle, disparage, rebuke, reprimand, reproach, scold, chastise, denigrate, sully, **7**. raise; *synonyms* (*v*) boost, erect, hoist, increase, build, foster, grow, augment, cultivate, excite, heave, heighten, levy, nurture, (*n*) hike; *antonym* (*v*) lower.

neboaki 1. celebrated; *synonyms* (*adj*) famous, illustrious, renowned, distinguished, notable, noted, splendid, well-known, known, conspicuous, eminent, famed, great, notorious, (*n*) glorious; *antonym* (*adj*) unknown, **2**. exalted; *synonyms* (*adj*) elevated, lofty, high, noble, elated, dignified, grand, sublime, celebrated, elate, magnificent, majestic, rarefied, **3**. glorified; *synonyms* (*adj*) canonized, blessed, canonised, haloed, holy, hyped, overestimated, overrated, overvalued, **4**. raised; *synonyms* (*v*) repousse, salient, (*adj*) embossed, erect, convex, brocaded, alert, bold, confident, elative, exultant, mountant, prominent, steep, (*prep*) above.

nebonebo 1. glorify; *synonyms* (*v*) celebrate, exalt, extol, bless, eulogize, dignify, adore, commend, laud, praise, canonize, admire, aggrandize, magnify, (*n*) honor, **2**. praise; *synonyms* (*n*) compliment, acclaim, applause, commendation, glory, kudos, admiration, approval, encomium, eulogy, panegyric, (*v*) applaud, approve, flatter, glorify; *antonyms* (*n*) criticism, disparagement, (*v*) criticize, belittle, disparage, rebuke, reprimand, reproach, scold, chastise, denigrate, sully.

neboneboaki glorified; *synonyms* (*adj*) canonized, blessed, canonised, haloed, holy, hyped, overestimated, overrated, overvalued.

nei 1. madame; *synonym* (*n*) dame, **2.** miss; *synonyms* (*v*) lack, lose, fail, jump, omit, overlook, long, drop, escape, (*n*) maid, girl, want, fille, missy, (*adj*) fault; *antonym* (*v*) perceive.

neiko woman; *synonyms* (*n*) wife, girl, maid, womanhood, char, charwoman, soul, (*obj*) female, she; *antonyms* (*n*) man, gentleman.

neinei 1. marshy; *synonyms* (*adj*) boggy, muddy, marsh, miry, quaggy, sloughy, swampy, paludal, moist, dirty, cloudy, coastal, dingy, moory, morassy, **2.** liquid; *synonyms* (*adj*) flowing, fluent, fluid, juicy, limpid, watery, sappy, succulent, mobile, smooth, (*n*) liquor, drink, juice, liquidness, sap; *antonyms* (*adj*) firm, (*n*) solid, gaseous, **3.** swampy; *synonyms* (*adj*) marshy, mucky.

neiranraoi 1. lucky; *synonyms* (*adj*) auspicious, favorable, propitious, prosperous, favourable, successful, flourishing, advantageous, blessed, chance, good, providential, (*n*) happy, favored, (*v*) fortunate; *antonyms* (*adj*) unlucky, hapless, ill-fated, unfortunate, **2.** fortunate; *synonyms* (*adj*) lucky, fortuitous, well, felicitous, golden, advantaged, desirable, hopeful, **3.** serendipitous; *synonyms* (*adj*) casual, helpful, opportune, unexpected, unanticipated, unforeseen.

nekea 1. needle; *synonyms* (*n*) injection, pointer, awl, plunger, probe, rudder, spike, (*v*) annoy, goad, irritate, sting, rile, aggravate, gall, nag, **2.** jab; *synonyms* (*n*) dig, poke, thrust, blow, clip, lick, jabbing, (*v*) stab, prick, prod, nudge, puncture, shove, lunge, pierce, **3.** nip; *synonyms* (*v*) bite, chill, drink, snip, squeeze, dash, twitch, check, (*n*) pinch, cut, gulp, sip, tang, drop, (*adj*) dram, **4.** puncture; *synonyms* (*n*) hole, break, leak, opening, nip, (*v*) bore, drill, penetrate, perforate, broach, impale, gore, punch, deflate, pink; *antonym* (*v*) inflate, **5.** stab; *synonyms* (*n*) jab, try, shot, pang, attempt, crack, effort, go, endeavor, (*v*) spear, stick, spit, knife, push, poniard, **6.** sting; *synonyms* (*n*) hurt, con, pain, chafe, swindle, bunco, (*v*) itch, prickle, provoke, burn, cheat, nettle, smart, tingle, ache, **7.** prick; *synonyms* (*n*) cock, pricking, spur, asshole, pecker, point, mark, shaft, tool, whip, bastard, (*v*) needle, twinge, fret, lance.

nekeaki 1. punctured; *synonyms* (*adj*) perforated, pierced, perforate, disillusioned, flat, **2.** stabbed.

nene 1. tight; *synonyms* (*adj*) close, compact, firm, mean, parsimonious, taut, secure, snug, tense, drunk, miserly, (*v*) narrow, fast, stingy, near; *antonyms* (*adj*) loose, baggy, generous, slack, wide, (*adv*) loosely, **2.** steady; *synonyms* (*adj*) even, constant, continual, fixed, resolute, stable, cool, incessant, sedate, settled, consistent, (*v*) steadfast, calm, regular, brace; *antonyms* (*adj*) unsteady, shaky, wobbly, intermittent, unreliable, **3.** steadfast; *synonyms* (*adj*) solid, permanent, immovable, loyal, determined, steady, persistent, hard, inflexible, reliable, set, staunch, unwavering, (*v*) faithful, impregnable; *antonym* (*adj*) irresolute, **4.** stiff; *synonyms* (*adj*) rigid, difficult, formal, numb, rigorous, severe, sturdy, arduous, austere, awkward, (*adv*) tight, (*n*) stark, cadaver, corpse, body; *antonyms* (*adj*) relaxed, flexible, floppy, soft, supple, free, pliable.

nenea 1. creamy; *synonyms* (*adj*) cream, greasy, buttery, pearly, sandy, oily, rich, smooth, soft, beaten, calorific, chalky, cloudy, cloying, fair, **2.** appetizing; *synonyms* (*adj*) appetising, delectable, delicious, luscious, tasty, tantalizing, palatable, savory, scrumptious, spicy; *antonyms* (*adj*) tasteless, unappetizing, **3.** fatty; *synonyms* (*adj*) fat, adipose, heavy, (*n*) fatso, **4.** greasy; *synonyms* (*adj*) fatty, dirty, tallowy, oleaginous, sebaceous, slick, slippery, unctuous; *antonym* (*adj*) dry, **5.** juicy; *synonyms* (*adj*) gamy, liquid, succulent, fluid, lush, mellow, moist, racy, sappy, blue, gamey, sensational.

neneboi 1. sniff; *synonyms* (*v*) scent, inhale, nose, smell, snuff, breathe, whiff, sniffle, smoke; *antonym* (*v*) exhale, **2.** track; *synonyms* (*n*) course, path, line, racetrack, road, route, (*v*) trace, trail, hunt, tail, chase, pursue, dog, follow, footprint, **3.** smell; *synonyms* (*n*) odor, fragrance, savor, aroma, bouquet, odour, savour, stench, flavor, smack, feel, flavour, (*v*) reek, perfume, stink, **4.** scent; *synonyms* (*n*) essence, redolence, incense, clue, relish, clew, key, hint, tang, track, wake, (*v*) wind, aromatize, sniff, (*adj*) suspect.

neneboiaki 1. tracked, **2.** scented; *synonyms* (*adj*) odorous, aromatic, fragrant, perfumed, balmy, odoriferous, redolent, sweet, spicy.

nenei fugitive; *synonyms* (*n*) escapee, absconder, deserter, emigrant, criminal, outlaw, refugee, renegade, (*adj*) runaway, ephemeral, fleeting, momentary, elusive, passing, (*v*) fugacious.

nenera 1. investigate; *synonyms* (*v*) examine, explore, inquire, inspect, search, check, research, ask, hunt, analyze, enquire, interrogate, scrutinize, study, test, **2.** explore; *synonyms* (*v*) delve, discover, investigate, plumb, probe, prospect, view, do, detect, spy, feel, ransack, rummage, (*n*) reconnoiter, scan, **3.** hunt; *synonyms* (*n*) pursuit, quest, (*v*) chase, course, follow, hound, forage, prey, dog, persecute, pursue, seek, stalk, trace, track, **4.** look; *synonyms* (*v*) seem, appear, expect, figure, attend, (*n*) face, gaze, appearance, aspect, air, countenance, expression, glance, guise, (*int*) behold, **5.** investigative; *synonyms* (*adj*) inquisitive, inquiring, investigatory, analytical, analytic, curious, indicative, logical, critical, diagnostic, examining, groping, methodical, pinpointing, probing, **6.** delve; *synonyms* (*v*) dig, burrow, excavate, grub, mine, root, tunnel, **7.** dig;

synonyms (v) jab, prod, comprehend, apprehend, compass, drudge, grasp, grind, (n) poke, excavation, gibe, punch, stab, taunt, crack; antonym (n) compliment, **8.** pry; synonyms (v) peep, prize, jimmy, nose, peer, snoop, prise, esteem, force, meddle, (n) lever, crowbar, **9.** research; synonyms (n) exploration, inquiry, examination, investigation, inquisition, question, enquiry, inspection, learning, query, (v) experiment, survey, **10.** search; synonyms (n) hunting, analysis, lookup, scrutiny, bust, (v) grope, pry, look, rake, fumble, attempt, **11.** query; synonyms (n) doubt, interrogative, quiz, interrogation, problem, dispute, uncertainty, (v) challenge, wonder, impeach, suspect; antonym (v) answer.

neneraki 1. hunted; synonyms (adj) coursed, required, sought, wanted, (n) victim, **2.** dug; synonyms (n) teat, breast, nipple, pap, papilla, tit, titty, boob, knocker, (adj) understood.

neneria 1. sift; synonyms (v) screen, filter, investigate, analyze, examine, riddle, sieve, sprinkle, bolt, separate, sort, strain, probe, (n) scrutinize, canvass, **2.** scrutinize; synonyms (v) inspect, review, audit, consider, explore, scan, search, check, observe, study, survey, inquire, view, spy, research.

nenge 1. lick; synonyms (v) lap, clobber, bat, beat, drub, thrash, defeat, bang, trim, overcome, (n) biff, jab, speed, dash, blow, **2.** suck; synonyms (v) draw, drink, imbibe, nurse, absorb, lactate, suckle, drain, puff, aspirate, pull, breastfeed, (n) sucking, suction.

nengeaki licked; synonyms (adj) beaten, dumbfounded.

nengenenge extremely; synonyms (adv) very, exceedingly, awfully, enormously, excessively, extraordinarily, much, badly, desperately, exceptionally, greatly, hugely, infinitely, terribly, (adj) highly; antonyms (adv) mildly, fairly, quite, slightly.

neve tongue; synonyms (n) language, dialect, idiom, lingua, speech, clapper, glossa, talk, knife, lingo, palate, (v) lick, (adj) flippancy, flowing, fluency.

newe tongue; synonyms (n) language, dialect, idiom, lingua, speech, clapper, glossa, talk, knife, lingo, palate, (v) lick, (adj) flippancy, flowing, fluency.

newea 1. lick; synonyms (v) lap, clobber, bat, beat, drub, thrash, defeat, bang, trim, overcome, (n) biff, jab, speed, dash, blow, **2.** lap; synonyms (n) circle, circuit, fold, coil, knee, orbit, (v) lick, overlap, bind, (adv) compass, encircle, encompass, embrace, enclose, beset.

neweaba 1. haunt; synonyms (v) frequent, follow, pursue, stalk, obsess, plague, visit, (n) den, resort, ghost, hangout, home, (adj) harass, molest, worry, **2.** frequent; synonyms (adj) continual, everyday, familiar, many, ordinary, incessant, habitual, accustomed, commonplace, (v) common,

customary, usual, haunt, patronize, attend; antonyms (adj) rare, infrequent, occasional, **3.** explore; synonyms (v) delve, examine, search, research, discover, hunt, investigate, plumb, probe, prospect, scrutinize, view, do, detect, spy, **4.** attend; synonyms (v) accompany, assist, escort, serve, advert, aid, conduct, hear, help, listen, look, minister, (n) tend, doctor, nurse, **5.** visit; synonyms (n) chat, sojourn, trip, (v) see, call, tour, gossip, inspect, jaw, impose, inflict, talk, understand, meet, travel.

neweabaki 1. attended; synonyms (adj) accompanied, fraught, **2.** haunted; synonyms (adj) obsessed, ghostly, bemused, crazed, infatuated, mad, magical, overcome, phantom, possessed, preoccupied, unearthly, ethereal, shadowlike, shadowy.

neweaki licked; synonyms (adj) beaten, dumbfounded.

newenewea lick; synonyms (v) lap, clobber, bat, beat, drub, thrash, defeat, bang, trim, overcome, (n) biff, jab, speed, dash, blow.

neweneweaki licked; synonyms (adj) beaten, dumbfounded.

nga thousand; synonyms (n) chiliad, grand, m, g, thou, curtilage, gee, gigabyte, gm, gram, gramme, green, grounds, heap, jet.

ngae 1. contented; synonyms (adj) content, comfortable, happy, cheerful, quiet, calm, complacent, delighted, easy, placid, pleased, proud, satisfied, smug; antonyms (adj) dissatisfied, discontented, unhappy, **2.** content; synonyms (n) capacity, contentment, matter, meaning, subject, substance, contentedness, (adj) contented, fulfilled, (v) appease, please, satisfy, suffice, delight, gratify; antonyms (adj) tormented, rebellious, (v) discontent, upset, **3.** complacent; synonyms (adj) self-satisfied, gracious, accommodating, arrogant, self-righteous, assured, bigheaded, bragging, companionable, complaisant, conceited, conciliatory, docile, immodest, imperturbable, **4.** satisfied; synonyms (v) convinced, (adj) full, certain, confident, sure, persuaded, sated, satiated, positive, quenched; antonym (adj) frustrated.

ngai me; synonym (n) myself.

ngaia 1. he; synonyms (pron) cestui, (n) male, man, helium, **2.** yes; synonyms (int) surely, (n) consent, acceptance, nod, (adv) ay, yea, certainly, positively, precisely, (v) acquiesce, agree, allow, grovel, (adj) obedient, submissive.

ngaiangaia 1. yea; synonyms (adv) yes, ay, yeah, egregiously, eminently, especially, even, particularly, peculiarly, preeminently, principally, prominently, superlatively, supremely, surpassing, **2.** surely; synonyms (adv) definitely, absolutely, positively, sure, undoubtedly, confidently, clearly, firmly, indeed, securely, truly, unquestionably, (*int*) certainly, (*adj*) really, doubtless; *antonym* (*adv*) doubtfully, **3**. undoubtedly; *synonyms* (*adv*) surely, indubitably, evidently; *antonym* (*adv*) questionably, **4**. positively; *synonyms* (*adv*) necessarily, expressly, decidedly, categorically, favorably; *antonyms* (*adv*) disapprovingly, negatively.

ngaina 1. daybreak; *synonyms* (*n*) dawn, sunrise, morning, prime, aurora, cockcrow, dawning, daylight, dayspring, light, sunup; *antonyms* (*n*) dusk, sunset, **2**. daytime; *synonyms* (*n*) day, sunshine; *antonym* (*n*) nighttime.

ngaira us; *synonyms* (*n*) aurochs, demigod, superman.

ngak particularly; *synonyms* (*adv*) especially, specially, only, chiefly, curiously, expressly, markedly, notably, peculiarly, principally, singly, very, individually, definitely, distinctly; *antonym* (*adv*) slightly.

nganga poisonous; *synonyms* (*adj*) deadly, toxic, mortal, malicious, noxious, venomous, fatal, baneful, lethal, noisome, malignant, pernicious, toxiferous, evil, pestilential; *antonym* (*adj*) harmless.

ngangarake snuffle; *synonyms* (*n*) snivel, cry, (*v*) sniff, sniffle, snuff, wheeze, blubber, inhale.

ngangau gluttonous; *synonyms* (*adj*) voracious, greedy, insatiable, ravenous, avid, edacious, hoggish.

ngangaua 1. cram; *synonyms* (*v*) stuff, pack, ram, fill, jam, compress, load, shove, compact, ingurgitate, overeat, englut, gormandise, gormandize, gourmandize, **2**. stuff; *synonyms* (*n*) material, cloth, force, gear, matter, goods, stock, substance, fabric, (*v*) cram, pad, squeeze, glut, gorge, (*adj*) rubbish; *antonym* (*v*) unstuff.

ngangauaki stuffed; *synonyms* (*v*) farctate, (*adj*) full, crammed, packed, congested, replete, loaded, chock-full, crowded, fraught, abounding, big, brimming, concentrated, distended; *antonyms* (*adj*) empty, hungry.

ngao 1. jumbled; *synonyms* (*adj*) confused, disorderly, disordered, disorganized, untidy, cluttered, mixed, muddled, chaotic, incoherent, topsy-turvy; *antonyms* (*adj*) neat, tidy, **2**. entangled; *synonyms* (*adj*) involved, complicated, intricate, embroiled, complex, foul, matted, tangled; *antonym* (*adj*) free.

ngare laugh; *synonyms* (*n*) chuckle, chortle, jest, gag, jape, laughter, cackle, sneer, scream, (*v*) joke, giggle, smile, titter, snicker, beam; *antonym* (*v*) cry.

ngareakina 1. mock; *synonyms* (*adj*) counterfeit, (*v*) deride, ridicule, burlesque, gibe, ape, flout, mimic, scoff, scorn, sham, taunt, bemock, (*n*) jeer, derision; *antonyms* (*adj*) genuine, real, **2**. rally; *synonyms* (*n*)

assembly, meeting, convention, gathering, (*v*) banter, gather, muster, congregate, convene, assemble, chaff, collect, converge, meet, mobilize; *antonym* (*v*) demobilize, **3**. ridicule; *synonyms* (*n*) irony, mockery, insult, contempt, disdain, sarcasm, sneer, disparagement, (*v*) mock, tease, rib, joke, gird, hoot, (*adj*) lampoon; *antonyms* (*v*) praise, respect.

ngareanina ridicule; *synonyms* (*n*) derision, irony, mockery, insult, contempt, scoff, taunt, disdain, gibe, (*v*) banter, deride, jeer, flout, mock, scorn; *antonyms* (*v*) praise, respect.

ngarengare titter; *synonyms* (*n*) chuckle, laugh, snigger, chortle, twitter, gurgle, laughter, (*v*) giggle, snicker.

ngarongaro toothless; *synonyms* (*adj*) dull, edentulous, immobilized, powerless.

ngaruru 1. thunderous; *synonyms* (*adj*) thundery, deafening, earsplitting, loud, booming, roaring, boisterous, flourishing, hollow, noisy, palmy, piercing, prospering, prosperous, resonant; *antonym* (*adj*) quiet, **2**. roll; *synonyms* (*n*) list, revolution, catalogue, inventory, register, (*v*) coil, reel, curl, enfold, revolve, wheel, rock, turn, twist, wallow, **3**. quake; *synonyms* (*n*) quiver, earthquake, tremble, tremor, (*v*) shake, shiver, shudder, quail, flutter, flicker, vibrate, fluctuate, jar, palpitate, dance.

ngaruruaki rolled; *synonyms* (*adj*) rolling, furled, involute, beaten, billowing, kinky, level, resonant, resonating, resounding, reverberating, reverberative, spiral, trilled, tumbling.

ngatingati 1. filthy; *synonyms* (*adj*) dirty, dingy, foul, nasty, unclean, disgusting, squalid, bawdy, awful, grimy, grubby, impure, indecent, muddy, ribald; *antonyms* (*adj*) clean, decent, **2**. dirty; *synonyms* (*adj*) dirt, contemptible, contaminated, despicable, filthy, shabby, sordid, (*v*) corrupt, soil, contaminate, begrime, bemire, pollute, spoil, (*n*) defile; *antonyms* (*adj*) hygienic, pure, spotless, immaculate, **3**. soiled; *synonyms* (*adj*) black, mucky, polluted, stained, lousy.

ngau 1. greedy; *synonyms* (*adj*) eager, avid, gluttonous, covetous, desirous, acquisitive, glutton, grasping, piggish, esurient, grabby, hungry, insatiable, ravenous, (*v*) avaricious; *antonym* (*adj*) generous, **2**. gluttonous; *synonyms* (*adj*) voracious, greedy, edacious, hoggish.

ngaungau 1. devour; *synonyms* (*v*) consume, bolt, eat, gulp, demolish, gobble, gorge, guzzle, swallow, absorb, devastate, enjoy, relish, down, exhaust, **2**. ingurgitate; *synonyms* (*v*) cram, fill, engorge, glut, gormandize, stuff, **3**. cram; *synonyms* (*v*) pack, ram, jam, compress, load, shove, compact, ingurgitate, overeat, englut, gormandise, gourmandize, overgorge, overindulge, inflate, **4**.

gulp; *synonyms* (n) drink, gasp, draft, draught, gulping, mouthful, (v) devour, swig, quaff, sip, imbibe, nip, raven, sup, deglutition; *antonym* (v) nibble.

ngauta 1. gulp; *synonyms* (n) drink, gasp, draft, draught, gulping, (v) bolt, devour, gobble, swig, gorge, down, quaff, sip, swallow, consume; *antonym* (v) nibble, **2.** devour; *synonyms* (v) eat, gulp, demolish, guzzle, absorb, devastate, enjoy, relish, exhaust, feed, glut, gnaw, guttle, raven, ruin, **3.** cram; *synonyms* (v) stuff, pack, ram, fill, jam, compress, load, shove, compact, ingurgitate, overeat, englut, gormandise, gormandize, gourmandize.

ngawa 1. asphyxiate; *synonyms* (v) choke, smother, suffocate, stifle, strangle, throttle, strangulate, garrote, **2.** choke; *synonyms* (v) asphyxiate, block, clog, foul, gag, obstruct, check, die, close, congest, conk, constrict, extinguish, occlude, plug; *antonym* (v) unclog, **3.** suffocate; *synonyms* (v) drown, quench, hang, kill.

ngawaki 1. asphyxiated; *synonym* (v) asphyxied, **2.** choked; *synonyms* (adj) clogged, suffocated, congested, anxious, high-strung, insecure, neurotic, strained, suffocate, tense, clotted, **3.** suffocated; *synonym* (adj) choked.

ngea taut; *synonyms* (adj) close, firm, tight, drawn, rigid, stiff, tense, strained, stringent, inflexible, taught, (v) fast; *antonyms* (adj) loose, limp.

ngearuru 1. hard; *synonyms* (adj) austere, bad, difficult, grave, severe, strong, arduous, callous, cruel, grueling, knotty, tough, (adv) firm, (v) acute, (n) rough; *antonyms* (adj) easy, soft, kind, merciful, simple, soggy, tender, yielding, (adv) gently, lightly, **2.** rigid; *synonyms* (adj) harsh, fixed, hard, inflexible, stiff, set, strict, exacting, formal, rigorous, stern, tense, tight, determined, resolute; *antonyms* (adj) flexible, elastic, **3.** stiff; *synonyms* (adj) rigid, numb, solid, sturdy, awkward, buckram, ceremonious, potent, prim, starchy, (n) stark, cadaver, corpse, body, remains; *antonyms* (adj) relaxed, floppy, supple, free, pliable.

ngengetaia 1. find; *synonyms* (v) catch, discover, detect, encounter, acquire, ascertain, attain, feel, procure, gather, (n) detection, disclosure, discovery, search, breakthrough; *antonyms* (v) lose, misplace, **2.** accuse; *synonyms* (v) impeach, charge, incriminate, arraign, criminate, defame, denounce, indict, fault, betray, accusation, admonish, censure, condemn, criticize, **3.** treat; *synonyms* (v) handle, deal, manage, process, heal, nurse, regale, operate, doctor, (n) feast, administer, delicacy, luxury, tidbit, banquet.

ngengetaiaki 1. accused; *synonyms* (n) panel, perpetrator, **2.** found; *synonyms* (v) erect, establish, base, build, form, constitute, construct,

appoint, create, ground, institute, bottom, begin, cast, plant; *antonym* (adj) misplaced, **3.** treated; *synonyms* (adj) hardened, tempered, toughened, considered, enured, inured, set, tough.

ngeri 1. curly; *synonyms* (adj) curled, kinky, crimped, frizzed, permed, curved, wiry, coiled, convoluted, corkscrew, crinkled, crinkling, looped, spiraled, waving; *antonym* (adj) straight, **2.** curled; *synonyms* (adj) curly, curling, braided, round, bent, bowed, helicine, spiral, tressed, wreathy, arched, helicoid, rounded, serpentine, sinuous.

ngeta 1. envious; *synonyms* (adj) covetous, jealous, invidious, jaundiced, malicious, greedy, resentful, green, grudging, begrudging, **2.** greedy; *synonyms* (adj) eager, avid, gluttonous, desirous, acquisitive, glutton, grasping, piggish, esurient, grabby, hungry, insatiable, ravenous, selfish, (v) avaricious; *antonym* (adj) generous, **3.** passionate; *synonyms* (adj) ardent, hot, angry, animated, burning, excited, fervent, fierce, earnest, amorous, enthusiastic, excitable, flaming, (adv) fiery, (v) impetuous; *antonyms* (adj) apathetic, indifferent, mild, passionless.

ngio 1. fail; *synonyms* (v) abort, collapse, fade, cease, abandon, break, bust, default, deteriorate, die, disappoint, flag, want, (adj) decline, drop; *antonyms* (v) succeed, triumph, **2.** dizzy; *synonyms* (adj) dazed, giddy, faint, frivolous, light, silly, vertiginous, featherbrained, flighty, muzzy, unsteady, airheaded, woozy, (v) daze; *antonyms* (adj) alert, clear-headed, **3.** faint; *synonyms* (adj) dim, dizzy, feeble, indistinct, weak, dull, gentle, soft, vague, delicate, distant, (v) languish, swoon, droop, conk; *antonyms* (adj) distinct, strong, clear, obvious, considerable, loud, pungent.

ngioaki failed; *synonyms* (adj) unsuccessful, abortive, failing, bankrupt, declining, deteriorating, ineffective, insolvent, bungled, disastrous, erstwhile, former, inferior, poor, regressing; *antonym* (adj) first-rate.

ngira 1. groan; *synonyms* (n) grumble, cry, rumble, complaint, wail, (v) moan, murmur, howl, mutter, sigh, complain, squeak, scrape, rasp, sough, **2.** moan; *synonyms* (n) groan, gripe, whine, lament, grievance, grouse, protest, sob, (v) bewail, mourn, bleat, weep, whimper, hum, regret.

ngirangira 1. groan; *synonyms* (n) grumble, cry, rumble, complaint, wail, (v) moan, murmur, howl, mutter, sigh, complain, squeak, scrape, rasp, sough, **2.** moan; *synonyms* (n) groan, gripe, whine, lament, grievance, grouse, protest, sob, (v) bewail, mourn, bleat, weep, whimper, hum, regret.

ngirataua groan; *synonyms* (n) grumble, cry, rumble, complaint, wail, (v) moan, murmur, howl, mutter, sigh, complain, squeak, scrape, rasp, sough.

ngka 1. give; *synonyms* (v) allow, bestow, extend, accord, commit, donate, contribute, convey, deliver, dispense, endow, grant, present, yield, administer; *antonyms* (*v*) withdraw, take, withhold, **2.** fetch; *synonyms* (*v*) carry, bring, draw, elicit, attract, catch, get, retrieve, transport, conduct, extract, earn, bear, cause, (*adj*) feint, **3.** pass; *synonyms* (*v*) flow, give, happen, lead, move, offer, overtake, live, advance, die, elapse, exceed, lapse, (*adj*) go, run; *antonym* (*v*) fail.

ngkae 1. despite; *synonyms* (*prep*) notwithstanding, (*conj*) although, (*n*) spite, contempt, scorn, disdain, malice, **2.** although; *synonyms* (*conj*) albeit, whereas, (*prep*) however, (*adv*) though, even, **3.** suppose; *synonyms* (*v*) believe, guess, infer, assume, conjecture, consider, divine, estimate, imagine, presume, reckon, speculate, calculate, conceive, expect, **4.** whereas; *synonyms* (*conj*) while, whenas, where, (*adv*) when, then, (*prep*) because, **5.** while; *synonyms* (*conj*) as, (*n*) spell, time, period, moment, interval, space, bit, piece, (*prep*) during, (*adv*) whilst.

ngkai 1. immediately; *synonyms* (*adv*) directly, forthwith, instantly, now, right, direct, readily, instantaneously, presently, rapidly, incontinently, momentarily, summarily, exactly, (*adj*) instanter; *antonyms* (*adv*) later, slowly, **2.** now; *synonyms* (*adv*) here, immediately, currently, already, nowadays, straight, today, just, promptly, straightaway, (*adj*) current, present, trendy, immediate, (*prep*) because; *antonym* (*adv*) soon, **3.** as; *synonyms* (*conj*) qua, since, considering, while, whilst, (*prep*) during, like, (*adv*) equally, from, (*n*) arsenic, **4.** present; *synonyms* (*adj*) grant, confer, (*n*) gift, donation, (*v*) bestow, display, give, introduce, prefer, deliver, donate, offer, perform, gratuity, award; *antonyms* (*adj*) missing, (*n*) past, future, history, (*v*) withdraw, (*adv*) absent, **5.** while; *synonyms* (*conj*) as, whereas, although, though, (*n*) spell, time, period, moment, interval, space, bit, piece, (*adv*) when, **6.** under; *synonyms* (*adv*) below, beneath, underneath, downstairs, infra, (*adj*) lower, down, nether, bottom, inferior, low, subject, subordinate, lowest; *antonym* (*prep*) over.

ngkainaba 1. new; *synonyms* (*adj*) green, modern, novel, original, additional, inexperienced, innovative, raw, recent, strange, unaccustomed, unprecedented, young, (*adv*) fresh, lately; *antonyms* (*adj*) old, familiar, outgoing, second-hand, traditional, used, less, old-fashioned, stale, (*adv*) past, **2.** away; *synonyms* (*adv*) apart, absent, aside, aloof, by, forth, way, hence, (*adj*) abroad, distant, wide, gone, missing, (*int*) out, off, **3.** instantaneously; *synonyms* (*adv*) directly, immediately, instantly, forthwith, outright, **4.** instant; *synonyms* (*adj*) immediate, present, exigent, prompt, clamant, crying, (*n*) moment, flash, jiffy, minute, point, second, tick, (*v*) pressing, urgent; *antonyms* (*adj*) gradual, long-term, **5.**

instantaneous; *synonyms* (*adj*) instant, precipitate, sudden, momentary; *antonym* (*adj*) consecutive, **6.** immediate; *synonyms* (*adj*) close, direct, near, quick, expeditious, fast, hasty, proximate, speedy, express, adjacent, firsthand, nearby, adjoining, early; *antonyms* (*adj*) slow, deliberate, **7.** directly; *synonyms* (*adv*) bluntly, frankly, straight, personally, sheer, flat, now, promptly, quickly, slap, rapidly, precisely, absolutely, exactly, (*adj*) forthright; *antonyms* (*adv*) indirectly, obliquely, later, **8.** instantly; *synonyms* (*adv*) instantaneously, momentarily, right, soon, straightaway, suddenly, (*adj*) instanter; *antonyms* (*adv*) eventually, slowly, **9.** immediately; *synonyms* (*adv*) readily, presently, incontinently, summarily, speedily, straightway, swiftly, completely, correctly, hastily, **10.** fresh; *synonyms* (*adj*) bracing, brisk, clean, bright, airy, bold, alive, chilly, cool, forward, pure, smart, sweet, flippant, (*adv*) new; *antonyms* (*adj*) decayed, exhausted, hot, humid, muggy, musty, oppressive, rotten, tired, worn, dry, sweltering, **11.** forthwith, **12.** recent; *synonyms* (*adj*) late, latest, contemporary, current, last, latter, final, **13.** present; *synonyms* (*adj*) grant, confer, (*n*) gift, donation, (*v*) bestow, display, give, introduce, prefer, deliver, donate, offer, perform, gratuity, award; *antonyms* (*n*) future, history, (*v*) withdraw, **14.** straight; *synonyms* (*adv*) level, due, openly, (*adj*) erect, honest, even, upright, fair, correct, just, perpendicular, proper, accurate, frank, neat; *antonyms* (*adj*) curly, curved, diluted, winding, zigzag, askew, bent, curvy, knotted, twisted, twisting, wavy, circuitous, guarded, lopsided, **15.** straightaway.

ngkaki given; *synonyms* (*adj*) apt, disposed, prone, liable, granted, inclined, set, (*n*) assumption, particular, presumption, fact.

ngkana 1. if; *synonyms* (*conj*) provided, although, providing, whether, though, and, so, an, gin, (*n*) but, conditionally, condition, stipulation, proviso, (*adv*) peradventure, **2.** while; *synonyms* (*conj*) as, whereas, (*n*) spell, time, period, moment, interval, space, bit, piece, (*prep*) during, (*adv*) when, whilst, because.

ngkanne thereupon; *synonyms* (*adv*) hereupon, thereafter, next, then, immediately, therefore, therewith, early.

ngke 1. as; *synonyms* (*conj*) qua, because, since, considering, while, whilst, (*prep*) during, like, (*adv*) equally, from, (*n*) arsenic, **2.** last; *synonyms* (*v*) endure, continue, hold, exist, live, dwell, (*n*) abide, conclusion, (*adj*) extreme, closing, final, ultimate, conclusive, concluding, farthest; *antonyms* (*n*) opening, (*adj*) first, **3.** during; *synonyms* (*prep*) within, on, by, for, of, pending, inside, about, amid, besides, concerning, adhering, meanwhile, mid, (*adj*) throughout, **4.** while; *synonyms* (*conj*) as, whereas, although, though, (n) spell, time, period, moment, interval, space, bit, piece, (adv) when, **5.** under; *synonyms* (adv) below, beneath, underneath, downstairs, infra, (adj) lower, down, nether, bottom, inferior, low, subject, subordinate, lowest; *antonym* (prep) over, **6.** then; *synonyms* (adv) so, accordingly, afterward, again, consequently, later, (conj) therefore.

ngkekei 1. beforehand; *synonyms* (adv) before, ahead, early, previously, aforehand, first, formerly, forward, (adj) advance, already, afore, **2.** past; *synonyms* (adj) beyond, bygone, former, old, back, earlier, gone, over, preceding, preterit, previous, prior, (n) history, (adv) by, (prf) along; *antonyms* (adj) contemporary, current, (prep) within, (n) future, present, prospect.

ngkoa 1. ago; *synonyms* (adv) formerly, earlier, erst, since, back, over, backwards, afterwards, erewhile, syne, whilom, contrarily, reflexively, (adj) past, agone, **2.** historically, **3.** previously; *synonyms* (adv) before, already, beforehand, antecedently, once, fore, ahead.

Ngkoananoa yesterday; *synonyms* (n) past, history, bygone, foretime, (adj) passé, stale; *antonym* (n) tomorrow.

ngkoangkoa yesterday; *synonyms* (n) past, history, bygone, foretime, (adj) passé, stale; *antonym* (n) tomorrow.

ngkoe lecture; *synonyms* (n) address, discourse, harangue, reprimand, speech, talk, oration, censure, declaim, homily, (v) rebuke, sermon, chide, preach, instruct.

ngo murmur; *synonyms* (n) mutter, babble, whine, complaint, (v) buzz, grumble, hum, mumble, whisper, bubble, complain, breathe, drone, croak, grouch.

ngoa scratch; *synonyms* (n) score, mark, nick, scrabble, dent, abrasion, cut, groove, (v) graze, notch, rub, scrape, chafe, rake, grate.

ngoaki scratched; *synonyms* (adj) scraped, hurt, abraded, dented, injured, raw, sgraffito, spoiled, broken, skinned, smashed.

ngongo itch; *synonyms* (n) desire, urge, impulse, scabies, wish, longing, craving, fancy, (v) irritate, tickle, prickle, scratch, tingle, chafe, (adj) herpes.

ngore 1. feeble; *synonyms* (adj) delicate, weak, decrepit, ailing, dim, dull, frail, helpless, infirm, lax, mild, poor, powerless, (v) faint, debilitated; *antonyms* (adj) strong, vigorous, hearty, tough, **2.** debilitated; *synonyms* (adj) enervated, feeble, enfeebled, adynamic, asthenic, **3.** puny; *synonyms* (adj) little, petty, small, tiny, minute, measly, paltry, runty, trifling, trivial, exiguous, meager; *antonyms* (adj) brawny, muscular, **4.** weak; *synonyms* (adj) flat, flimsy, fragile, thin, watery, light, cowardly, diluted, exhausted, inadequate, nerveless, shaky,

sickly, slack, (v) loose; *antonyms* (adj) brave, concentrated, firm, safe, compelling, determined, effective, forceful, healthy, intense, powerful, resolute, robust, sturdy, able, **5.** sick; *synonyms* (adj) ill, queasy, indisposed, poorly, weary, invalid, diseased, morbid, nauseous, crazy, disgusted, nauseated, upset, (v) unwell, puke; *antonym* (adj) well, **6.** sickly; *synonyms* (adj) sick, pale, sallow, peaked, pasty, languid, pallid, unhealthy, wan, bloodless, ashen, valetudinarian, (v) low; *antonym* (adj) bitter.

ngoro infant; *synonyms* (n) baby, babe, child, minor, nursling, kid, toddler, (adj) juvenile, young.

ngure 1. grouse; *synonyms* (n) bellyache, beef, groan, complaint, blackcock, duck, (v) gripe, complain, moan, grumble, whine, grouch, mutter, **2.** murmur; *synonyms* (n) babble, grumbling, murmuration, sound, croon, (v) buzz, hum, mumble, whisper, bubble, breathe, drone, croak, growl, maunder, **3.** complain; *synonyms* (v) bemoan, bewail, protest, squawk, grudge, accuse, carp, grouse, object, plain, remonstrate, whimper, rail, weep, cry; *antonym* (v) compliment.

ngurengure 1. grumble; *synonyms* (v) murmur, mutter, complain, gripe, growl, rumble, grouch, mumble, roar, croak, gnarl, (n) complaint, moan, groan, roll, **2.** complain; *synonyms* (v) beef, bemoan, bewail, protest, squawk, whine, grudge, accuse, carp, grouse, grumble, object, plain, remonstrate, whimper; *antonym* (v) compliment, **3.** murmur; *synonyms* (n) babble, grumbling, murmuration, sound, croon, murmuring, muttering, (v) buzz, hum, whisper, bubble, breathe, drone, maunder, repine, **4.** balk; *synonyms* (v) frustrate, prevent, retard, flinch, hamper, traverse, baffle, disappoint, foil, jib, recoil, thwart, (n) baulk, hindrance, disconcert.

ni 1. by; *synonyms* (prep) beside, at, of, about, on, per, (adv) aside, away, past, through, apart, along, beyond, (adv, prep) alongside, (adj) over, **2.** for; *synonyms* (prep) because, behind, by, during, toward, (conj) considering, since, (adv) against, as, therefore, hence, **3.** k; *synonyms* (n) m, chiliad, g, grand, kilobyte, curtilage, gee, gigabyte, gm, gram, gramme, grounds, kelvin, potassium, (adj) thousand, **4.** in; *synonyms* (prep) between, inside, (adv) indoors, inward, (v) press, (n) inch, (adj) stylish, fashionable, inwards, trendy, within, modish, popular; *antonyms* (prep) out, outside, **5.** at; *synonyms* (prep) in, a, (n) astatine, (prf) all, completely, wholly, (adj) entertainment, levee, party, reception, conversazione, home, soiree, **6.** m; *synonyms* (n) beat, cadence, green, jet, meter, metre, molarity, thou, yard, measure, pace, time, **7.** with; *synonyms* (prep) for, among, plus, (adj) including, (n) withe.

nî 1. whence; *synonyms* (*adv*) wherefrom, because, for, hence, then, therefore, whenceforth, **2.** tree; *synonyms* (*n*) gallows, gibbet, stem, house, tribe, hierarchy, landmark, lentisk, ranking, trunk, filler, (*v*) corner, collar, **3.** pond; *synonyms* (*n*) lake, mere, pool, loch, plash, reservoir, sea, tank, broad, lough.

niabuti navigable; *synonyms* (*adj*) passable, open, sailable, voyageable, crossable, traversable.

niau 1. awkward; *synonyms* (*adj*) clumsy, inconvenient, crude, embarrassing, inept, sticky, uncomfortable, ungainly, untoward, left-handed, annoying, bungling, cumbersome, difficult, graceless; *antonyms* (*adj*) graceful, easy, adroit, manageable, straightforward, convenient, dexterous, helpful, rotund, simple, **2.** indolent; *synonyms* (*adj*) idle, inactive, lazy, slothful, sluggish, careless, drowsy, dull, faineant, inert, listless, otiose, slow, torpid, lackadaisical; *antonyms* (*adj*) energetic, active, **3.** nonchalant; *synonyms* (*adj*) negligent, indifferent, insouciant, unconcerned, carefree, casual, calm, cool, offhand, easygoing; *antonym* (*adj*) anxious, **4.** idle; *synonyms* (*adj*) indolent, free, baseless, frivolous, fruitless, groundless, unfounded, empty, disengaged, flimsy, barren, dead, futile, jobless, light; *antonyms* (*adj*) busy, employed, (*v*) change, **5.** slow; *synonyms* (*adj*) late, heavy, dense, dim, gradual, stupid, belated, boring, dilatory, leisurely, (*v*) slack, check, delay, (*adv*) behind, behindhand; *antonyms* (*adj*) fast, intelligent, rapid, bright, alert, brisk, hasty, prompt, quick, speedy, hurried, observant, rushed, (*v*) accelerate.

niba 1. excavate; *synonyms* (*v*) dig, burrow, hollow, unearth, quarry, grub, mine, tunnel, undermine, (*adj*) delve, gouge, (*n*) scoop, **2.** gutter; *synonyms* (*n*) channel, groove, ditch, drain, trough, chute, canal, conduit, furrow, trench, waterway, aqueduct, culvert, kennel, adit, **3.** entrench; *synonyms* (*v*) encroach, fortify, impinge, infringe, intrench, establish, invade, defend, fence, fix, implant, insert, intrude, lodge, trespass, **4.** hollow; *synonyms* (*adj*) blank, concave, empty, false, insincere, (*n*) cavity, hole, cave, depression, excavation, gap, sinus, basin, (*v*) excavate, dent; *antonyms* (*adj*) convex, (*n*) solid, hump, **5.** nick; *synonyms* (*n*) notch, mark, cut, chip, incision, score, scratch, arrest, gash, indentation, (*v*) steal, hack, indent, slash, snick, **6.** notch; *synonyms* (*n*) nick, degree, grade, clove, gradation, gulch, line, breach, cleft, pass, slit, tick, (*v*) nock, jag, engrave, **7.** dig; *synonyms* (*v*) jab, prod, comprehend, investigate, probe, apprehend, compass, drudge, grasp, (*n*) poke, gibe, punch, stab, taunt, crack; *antonym* (*n*) compliment, **8.** scoop; *synonyms* (*n*) ladle, spade, exclusive, pocket, scoopful, shovel, article, report, (*v*) draw, best, outdo, outflank, **9.** trench;

synonyms (*n*) dike, gutter, dugout, foxhole, sewer, deep, (*v*) entrench.

nibaia indent; *synonyms* (*v*) dent, indenture, cut, impress, nick, score, hollow, (*n*) notch, impression, indentation, (*adj*) scollop, crimp.

nibaiaki indented; *synonyms* (*adj*) depressed, concave, hollow, jagged, serrated, crenelate, crenelated, crenellate, crenellated, embattled.

nibakabaka 1. stagger; *synonyms* (*v*) falter, astonish, lurch, startle, flabbergast, flounder, hobble, reel, shake, shock, pitch, amaze, dumbfound, stun, (*adj*) bewilder, **2.** unsteady; *synonyms* (*adj*) unstable, changeable, dizzy, insecure, rickety, shaky, unbalanced, unsettled, unsound, precarious, uneven, irregular, erratic, fluctuating, (*n*) uncertain; *antonym* (*adj*) steady, **3.** stumble; *synonyms* (*v*) slip, fall, fumble, err, hit, stammer, bumble, totter, tumble, (*n*) trip, misstep, stagger, (*adj*) blunder, botch, fault.

nibaki 1. entrenched; *synonyms* (*adj*) confirmed, ingrained, inveterate, constant, set, steadfast, unwavering, chronic, embedded, hardened, inbuilt, incorrigible, incurable, inherent, innate; *antonym* (*adj*) superficial, **2.** hollowed; *synonym* (*adj*) concave, **3.** dug; *synonyms* (*n*) teat, breast, nipple, pap, papilla, tit, titty, boob, knocker, (*adj*) understood, **4.** nicked; *synonym* (*adj*) hurt, **5.** notched; *synonyms* (*adj*) jagged, serrated, jaggy, serrate, toothed, erose, rough, uneven.

nibanaoraki sickly; *synonyms* (*adj*) feeble, infirm, sick, ailing, diseased, indisposed, morbid, pale, poorly, sallow, peaked, pasty, (*n*) invalid, (*v*) faint, frail; *antonyms* (*adj*) healthy, bitter.

nibanga perforated; *synonyms* (*adj*) perforate, pierced, punctured, penetrated, entered.

nibangabanga network; *synonyms* (*n*) net, grid, mesh, netting, reticulation, meshwork, web, grating, lattice, system, complex, (*v*) link, communicate, contact, exchange.

nibanibaia indent; *synonyms* (*v*) dent, indenture, cut, impress, nick, score, hollow, (*n*) notch, impression, indentation, (*adj*) scollop, crimp.

nibanibaiaki indented; *synonyms* (*adj*) depressed, concave, hollow, jagged, serrated, crenelate, crenelated, crenellate, crenellated, embattled.

nibara 1. uneasy; *synonyms* (*adj*) uncomfortable, anxious, fidgety, restless, apprehensive, concerned, nervous, awkward, unquiet, fretful, restive, solicitous, agitated, jittery, troubled; *antonym* (*adj*) calm, **2.** uncomfortable; *synonyms* (*adj*) embarrassing, inconvenient, difficult, discomfited, uneasy, cheerless, embarrassed, painful, (*v*) untoward; *antonyms* (*adj*) comfortable, relaxed, comfy.

nibarabara 1. undone; *synonyms* (*v*) accursed, devoted, (*adj*) lost, ruined, sunk, unfinished, doomed, behindhand, decayed, destroyed, finished, **2.** peeled; *synonyms* (adj) raw, naked, bare, bleak, crude, cutting, exposed, natural, new, nude, open, sore, unsanded.

nibiongong 1. drowsy; *synonyms* (adj) dozy, comatose, lazy, lethargic, slow, somnolent, dull, indolent, listless, sluggish, soporific, dozing, drowsing, oscitant, (n) sleepy; *antonyms* (adj) alert, energetic, **2.** torpid; *synonyms* (adj) inactive, inert, dormant, dead, lifeless, flat, benumbed, heavy, numb, supine, slack, apathetic, indifferent, callous, obtuse; *antonym* (adj) active.

nibunini 1. distended; *synonyms* (adj) swollen, bloated, inflated, puffy, puffed, turgid, bombastic, (v) bigswoln, blowzy, **2.** puffed; *synonyms* (adj) distended, puff, tumid, bepuffed, bouffant, conceited, declamatory, egotistic, egotistical, erect, flooding, huffing, large, lordly, orotund, **3.** swollen; *synonyms* (adj) high, bulging, tumescent, enlarged, expanded, mighty, overflowing, (v) blown, (prep) pompous.

nibwara 1. restless; *synonyms* (adj) fidgety, nervous, uneasy, unquiet, agitated, apprehensive, fretful, impatient, restive, feverish, turbulent, jumpy, disturbed, edgy, (v) anxious; *antonyms* (adj) calm, relaxed, **2.** restive; *synonyms* (adj) obstinate, jittery, nervy, restless, uptight, restiff, tense, unruly, overstrung, resty, (v) skittish.

nika 1. as; *synonyms* (conj) qua, because, since, considering, while, whilst, (prep) during, like, (adv) equally, from, (n) arsenic, **2.** like; *synonyms* (v) corresponding, enjoy, identical, care, desire, fancy, (adj) equal, equivalent, alike, analogous, comparable, same, parallel, (n) love, relish; *antonyms* (prep) unlike, (v) dislike, (adj) different.

nikabu covered; *synonyms* (adj) hidden, veiled, concealed, covert, coated, masked, obscured, secret, shrouded, thick, wrapped, (prep) cloaked; *antonyms* (adj) bare, naked.

nikamonmon 1. go; *synonyms* (v) come, elapse, pass, break, crack, depart, disappear, drive, run, travel, fall, extend, function, (n) fare, (adj) follow, **2.** gyrate; *synonyms* (v) spin, whirl, circle, gyre, revolve, roll, turn, wheel, circulate, reel, rotate, spiral, twirl, coil, **3.** roll; *synonyms* (n) list, revolution, catalogue, inventory, register, (v) curl, enfold, rock, twist, wallow, wind, envelop, grumble, round, level.

nikamonmonaki rolled; *synonyms* (adj) rolling, furled, involute, beaten, billowing, kinky, level, resonant, resonating, resounding, reverberating, reverberative, spiral, trilled, tumbling.

nikarara juggle; *synonyms* (v) beguile, conjure, hoodwink, catch, charm, handle, (n) cheat, trick, blind, bubble, chicane, feint, deception, imposture, juggling.

nikawai ancient; *synonyms* (adj) aged, old, antiquated, obsolete, former, past, antique, archaic, bygone, hoary, primitive, olden, antediluvian, dated, (n) elder; *antonym* (adj) modern.

nikebokebo full; *synonyms* (adj) complete, absolute, abundant, broad, flush, ample, enough, extensive, total, detailed, comprehensive, copious, good, (n) entire, crowded; *antonyms* (adj) empty, lacking, starving, hungry, sketchy, incomplete.

nikiari tingle; *synonyms* (n) thrill, tremble, twitter, tingling, chill, frisson, prickling, (v) itch, prickle, tickle, smart, sting, burn, creep, pain.

nikierere 1. jubilant; *synonyms* (adj) elated, exultant, joyful, delighted, gleeful, joyous, happy, overjoyed, triumphant, exulting, rejoicing, triumphal, euphoric, **2.** exult; *synonyms* (v) delight, rejoice, cheer, triumph, chuckle, crow, glory, jubilate, boast, brag, celebrate, gloat, (n) joy, **3.** celebrate; *synonyms* (v) commemorate, extol, keep, praise, acclaim, fete, honor, laud, solemnize, applaud, honour, distinguish, eulogize, exult, glorify; *antonym* (v) ignore, **4.** swaggering; *synonyms* (v) swagger, (adj) blustering, hectoring, arrogant, boastful, disdainful, haughty, lordly, prideful, roistering, sniffy, (n) boasting, bluster, bravado, ostentation, **5.** triumph; *synonyms* (n) conquest, exultation, victory, success, achievement, accomplishment, celebration, defeat, feat, mastery, (v) prevail, win, succeed, conquer, revel; *antonyms* (n) failure, sorrow, (v) fail, lose, **6.** rejoice; *synonyms* (v) gladden, gratify, exhilarate, please, recreate, enjoy, wallow; *antonyms* (v) lament, mourn.

nikierereaki celebrated; *synonyms* (adj) famous, illustrious, renowned, distinguished, notable, noted, splendid, well-known, known, conspicuous, eminent, famed, great, notorious, (n) glorious; *antonym* (adj) unknown.

nikira 1. bring; *synonyms* (v) convey, fetch, bear, carry, conduct, get, put, take, reduce, afford, bestow, deliver, land, move, provide, **2.** take; *synonyms* (v) admit, hold, adopt, catch, clutch, obtain, return, borrow, pick, acquire, appropriate, assume, (phr) accept, receive; *antonyms* (v) give, refuse, abstain, add, lose, **3.** repossess; *synonyms* (v) recover, regain, reclaim, recoup, retrieve, resume, recruit, **4.** put; *synonyms* (v) place, fix, lay, position, set, impose, couch, locate, pose, charge, pitch, arrange, assign, commit, (n) deposit.

nikiraki taken; *synonyms* (v) take, (adj) occupied, full, interpreted, besotted, crazed, enamored, engaged, interested, lovesick, obsessed, overcome, preferred, rapt, reserved.

niko 1. fit; *synonyms* (v) agree, accommodate, meet, suit, adapt, correspond, square, accord, dress, (adj) decorous, apt, applicable, appropriate, (n) adjust, convulsion; *antonyms* (*adj*) unfit, inappropriate, unwell, **2**. elegant; *synonyms* (*adj*) graceful, courtly, delicate, splendid, beautiful, dainty, polite, refined, dressy, artistic, charming, chic, classy, cultured, debonair; *antonyms* (*adj*) clumsy, inelegant, scruffy, ugly, coarse, plain, tacky, **3**. beautiful; *synonyms* (*adj*) attractive, good-looking, bright, beauteous, fine, handsome, lovely, picturesque, pleasant, pretty, striking, sweet, adorned, ornate, stylish; *antonym* (*adj*) unattractive, **4**. nice; *synonyms* (*adj*) fastidious, good, kind, neat, likable, delicious, agreeable, correct, decent, difficult, enjoyable, exact, particular, precise, right; *antonyms* (*adj*) unpleasant, horrible, **5**. firm; *synonyms* (*n*) company, (*adj*) constant, hard, stable, close, compact, determined, fixed, resolute, solid, steadfast, steady, strong, decisive, (*v*) faithful; *antonyms* (*adj*) irresolute, soft, weak, hesitant, limp, liquid, soggy, **6**. well; *synonyms* (*adv*) easily, thoroughly, considerably, fully, correctly, (*adj*) healthy, fit, shaft, sound, robust, (*n*) fountain, spring, pit, hollow, (*v*) gush; *antonyms* (*adv*) ill, badly, poorly, (*adj*) sick, dying, nauseous, **7**. tight; *synonyms* (*adj*) firm, mean, parsimonious, taut, secure, snug, tense, drunk, miserly, rigorous, sparing, (*v*) narrow, fast, stingy, near; *antonyms* (*adj*) loose, baggy, generous, slack, wide, (*adv*) loosely.

nikoa 1. make; *synonyms* (*v*) build, cause, construct, do, create, fashion, force, get, give, produce, let, compel, constitute, design, (*n*) form; *antonyms* (*v*) destroy, lose, **2**. build; *synonyms* (*v*) make, erect, establish, raise, rise, base, fabricate, found, rear, formulate, (*n*) shape, frame, construction, figure, built; *antonym* (*v*) demolish.

nikoaki 1. built; *synonyms* (*adj*) buxom, curvaceous, heavy, reinforced, robust, shapely, timbered, contrived, shaped, strengthened, wooden, (*n*) shape, **2**. made; *synonyms* (*adj*) finished, built, ready, constructed, formed, prepared, synthetic, bound, complete, completed, ended, fictitious, rabid, through.

nikoniko nice; *synonyms* (*adj*) beautiful, dainty, fastidious, fine, good, kind, lovely, neat, likable, delicious, agreeable, correct, decent, delicate, difficult; *antonyms* (*adj*) unpleasant, horrible.

nikora 1. bad; *synonyms* (*adj*) evil, adverse, harmful, immoral, naughty, poisonous, sad, sinister, wicked, malicious, infamous, appalling, awful, damaging, (*v*) decayed; *antonyms* (*adj*) fresh, pleasant, well, well-behaved, (*n*) good, **2**. weak; *synonyms* (*adj*) feeble, frail, faint, flat, flimsy, fragile, thin, watery, light, ailing, cowardly, delicate, diluted, exhausted, inadequate; *antonyms* (*adj*) strong, brave, concentrated, firm, safe, compelling, determined, effective, forceful, healthy, intense, powerful, resolute, robust, sturdy.

nikoraoi quiet; *synonyms* (*adj*) still, lull, pacify, cool, gentle, motionless, peaceful, (*v*) appease, moderate, assuage, allay, (*n*) calm, hush, compose, ease; *antonyms* (*adj*) loud, noisy, talkative, vociferous, active, (*n*) noise.

nikotatawa fast; *synonyms* (*adj*) dissolute, firm, agile, debauched, fixed, hurried, instant, quick, rapid, staunch, brisk, (*adv*) soon, hard, close, (*n*) diet; *antonyms* (*adj*) sluggish, loose, (*adv*) slow, slowly, leisurely, (*v*) gorge, (*n*) binge.

nikotaungaunga unbalanced; *synonyms* (*adj*) lopsided, crazy, mad, wobbly, demented, disproportionate, imbalanced, unequal, asymmetrical, unsettled, unstable, unsteady, brainsick, distracted, disturbed; *antonyms* (*adj*) sane, balanced, even, well-balanced.

niku wide; *synonyms* (*adj*) broad, spacious, roomy, comprehensive, extensive, large, ample, vast, capacious, expanded, extended, full, open, sweeping, big; *antonyms* (*adj*) narrow, thin, restricted.

nikuakua 1. fatigued; *synonyms* (*adj*) exhausted, tired, weary, beat, worn, jaded, spent, fagged; *antonyms* (*adj*) fresh, refreshed, **2**. tired; *synonyms* (*adj*) fatigued, hackneyed, banal, commonplace, stale, threadbare, trite, haggard, stock, drowsy, sick, whacked, corny, limp, weak; *antonyms* (*adj*) invigorated, alert, energetic, original, strong.

nikuma cover; *synonyms* (*v*) coat, conceal, top, bury, cloak, (*n*) blind, blanket, screen, binding, camouflage, cap, covering, lid, mask, shield; *antonyms* (*v*) reveal, expose, uncover.

nikumaki covered; *synonyms* (*adj*) hidden, veiled, concealed, covert, coated, masked, obscured, secret, shrouded, thick, wrapped, (*prep*) cloaked; *antonyms* (*adj*) bare, naked.

nikunakuna 1. bruised; *synonyms* (*adj*) contused, wounded, hurt, raw, sore, contusioned, discolored, inflamed, lame, livid, painful, rotten, sensitive, surbet, tender, **2**. wounded; *synonyms* (*adj*) bruised, bloody, (*n*) casualty, maimed; *antonym* (*adj*) composed.

nikunikun bruised; *synonyms* (*adj*) contused, wounded, hurt, raw, sore, contusioned, discolored, inflamed, lame, livid, painful, rotten, sensitive, surbet, tender.

nikutaro 1. embarrassed; *synonyms* (*adj*) ashamed, abashed, awkward, uncomfortable, disconcerted, bashful, shamefaced, sheepish, shy, chagrined, discomfited, humiliated, mortified; *antonyms* (*adj*) proud, relaxed, **2**. unbalanced; *synonyms* (*adj*) lopsided, crazy, mad, wobbly, demented, disproportionate, imbalanced, unequal, asymmetrical, unsettled, unstable, unsteady, brainsick, distracted, disturbed; *antonyms* (*adj*) sane, balanced, even, well-balanced.

nim 1. adhesive; *synonyms (adj)* tacky, clingy, gummy, sticky, tenacious, agglutinative, gluey, glutinous, gooey, pasty, *(n)* cement, glue, paste, gum, *(v)* cohesive; *antonym (adj)* nonadhesive, **2.** attach; *synonyms (v)* add, adhere, append, affix, bind, link, associate, assign, annex, apply, fasten, fix, nail, stick, yoke; *antonyms (v)* detach, undo, disconnect, separate, unfasten, **3.** cling; *synonyms (v)* cleave, cohere, hang, attach, clutch, grasp, grip, hold, hug, **4.** adhere; *synonyms (v)* abide, accede, bond, cling, join, observe, unite, *(adj)* agree, **5.** sticky; *synonyms (adj)* adhesive, awkward, clammy, muggy, embarrassing, humid, difficult, slimy, hard, mucilaginous, sultry, sweltering, troublesome, viscid, persistent; *antonyms (adj)* dry, fresh, easy, **6.** stick; *synonyms (n)* bar, club, rod, bat, cane, cudgel, *(v)* stab, staff, impale, persist, pink, spear, spike, put, poke.

nima 1. absorb; *synonyms (v)* consume, drink, engross, imbibe, assimilate, engage, occupy, suck, swallow, amuse, digest, engulf, fascinate, ingest, *(adj)* immerse; *antonyms (v)* bore, emit, **2.** five; *synonyms (n)* cinque, quint, quintuplet, fin, ace, eight, fins, fivesome, interim, intermission, interval, jack, king, knave, *(adj)* quinary, **3.** drink; *synonyms (n)* beverage, alcohol, brew, potion, crapulence, intoxicant, nip, *(v)* draught, booze, carouse, bib, absorb, down, gulp, pledge, **4.** swallow; *synonyms (v)* eat, bolt, devour, accept, bear, endure, stomach, brook, gobble, gorge, abide, bury, *(n)* sip, swig, taste; *antonym (v)* regurgitate.

nimábui fifty; *synonyms (n)* l, lambert, liter, litre.

nimabwi fifty; *synonyms (n)* l, lambert, liter, litre.

nimaenen 1. flexible; *synonyms (adj)* elastic, adaptable, pliable, yielding, lissome, pliant, soft, supple, facile, adjustable, bendable, compliant, ductile, flexile, lithe; *antonyms (adj)* inflexible, rigid, fixed, obstinate, stiff, stubborn, **2.** pliable; *synonyms (adj)* flexible, plastic, malleable, fictile, susceptible, docile, resilient, tame, submissive, limp, springy, tractable, bendy, *(v)* limber.

nimahoua five; *synonyms (n)* cinque, quint, quintuplet, fin, ace, eight, fins, fivesome, interim, intermission, interval, jack, king, knave, *(adj)* quinary.

nimaki 1. attached; *synonyms (adj)* connected, affectionate, affiliated, committed, associated, devoted, fond, loving, loyal, near; *antonyms (adj)* detached, separate, unmarried, **2.** absorbed; *synonyms (adj)* engrossed, intent, rapt, immersed, fixed, deep, engaged, preoccupied, fascinated, pensive, **3.** swallowed; *synonyms (adj)* engulfed, enveloped, flooded, inundated, overcome, overpowered, overwhelmed, swamped, **4.** stuck; *synonyms (v)* sticked, *(adj)* stranded, aground, abandoned, absorbed, ashore, beached, delayed,

deserted, dumbfounded, fast, hindered, immovable, *(n)* thrust, sticking; *antonym (adj)* free.

nimamanei 1. meek; *synonyms (adj)* humble, lowly, docile, gentle, tame, low, compliant, mild, modest, quiet, submissive, kind, retiring, unassuming, patient; *antonyms (adj)* assertive, bossy, **2.** gentle; *synonyms (adj)* clement, calm, easy, friendly, soft, affable, balmy, feeble, amiable, benign, bland, compassionate, delicate, fine, *(n)* benevolent; *antonyms (adj)* caustic, cruel, fierce, harsh, loud, violent, rough, abrupt, hardhearted, heavy, sarcastic, sheer, steep, **3.** inoffensive; *synonyms (adj)* harmless, innocuous, innoxious, safe, unoffending, euphemistic, *(n)* innocent; *antonym (adj)* offensive, **4.** peaceable; *synonyms (adj)* amicable, inoffensive, moderate, meek, placid, serene, still, conciliatory, obedient, orderly, *(v)* peaceful; *antonyms (adj)* aggressive, argumentative.

nimamano 1. whirl; *synonyms (n)* turn, wheel, twist, crack, fling, go, vortex, commotion, *(v)* spin, twirl, eddy, roll, reel, swirl, gyrate, **2.** spin; *synonyms (n)* whirl, revolution, ride, rotation, *(v)* revolve, run, drive, fabricate, invent, narrate, pivot, recite, recount, rotate, tell.

nimamate 1. exhausted; *synonyms (v)* weak, *(adj)* drained, fatigued, spent, tired, gone, dry, beat, depleted, empty, enervated, faint, jaded, weary, expended; *antonyms (adj)* energetic, fresh, refreshed, strong, **2.** avenge; *synonyms (v)* revenge, punish, retaliate, vindicate, wreak, repay, venge, chasten, chastise, claim, defend, deliver, inflict, justify, liberate, **3.** languid; *synonyms (adj)* lazy, dull, feeble, indolent, lackadaisical, lethargic, sluggish, torpid, apathetic, inert, infirm, listless, sickly, dreamy, remiss, **4.** sluggish; *synonyms (adj)* idle, inactive, slow, drowsy, languid, slack, slothful, obtuse, dormant, dilatory, backward, lifeless, blunt, *(n)* heavy, sleepy; *antonyms (adj)* active, brisk, fast.

nimana muddy; *synonyms (adj)* boggy, cloudy, filthy, turbid, foul, dark, dingy, dull, grimy, marshy, miry, murky, sloppy, *(v)* dirty, blur; *antonyms (adj)* clear, clean, dry.

nimanan 1. languid; *synonyms (adj)* lazy, dull, feeble, indolent, faint, lackadaisical, lethargic, sluggish, torpid, apathetic, inert, infirm, listless, sickly, dreamy; *antonym (adj)* energetic, **2.** indisposed; *synonyms (adj)* disinclined, ailing, ill, averse, loath, poorly, sick, reluctant, unwell, unwilling, diseased, loth, **3.** faint; *synonyms (adj)* collapse, dim, dizzy, indistinct, weak, gentle, soft, vague, delicate, distant, drop, *(v)* languish, swoon, droop, conk; *antonyms (adj)* distinct, strong, clear, obvious, considerable, loud, pungent, **4.** suffering; *synonyms (v)* pain, *(n)* affliction, agony, anguish, distress, hurt, grief, hardship, misery, ordeal, sorrow, torment, torture, adversity, (adj) miserable; *antonym* (n) content.

nimanana healthier; *synonyms* (adj) better, fitter, improved, recovered; *antonym* (adj) worse.

nimananginang 1. apart; *synonyms* (adv) aside, asunder, away, independently, individually, (adj) aloof, alone, distant, separate, detached, isolated, only, individual, loose, (v) discrete, **2.** dislocated; *synonyms* (adj) disjointed, disordered, dislocate, disorderly, confused, disconnected, separated, topsy-turvy, garbled, illogical, scattered, spaced, unconnected, **3.** tattered; *synonyms* (adj) ragged, scruffy, shabby, worn, dilapidated, frayed, threadbare, seedy, torn, shattered, (v) bedraggled; *antonyms* (adj) pristine, elegant.

nimanomano uneven; *synonyms* (adj) rough, unequal, irregular, jagged, erratic, patchy, rugged, spotty, disproportionate, ragged, craggy, crooked, unbalanced, (v) broken, (n) harsh; *antonyms* (adj) even, smooth, straight, equal, symmetrical.

nimanonganonga 1. much; *synonyms* (adv) greatly, frequently, almost, awfully, considerably, far, most, often, pretty, highly, (n) lot, heap, (adj) great, considerable, practically; *antonym* (adv) slightly, **2.** abundant; *synonyms* (adj) copious, generous, lush, luxuriant, thick, plenty, affluent, ample, fertile, fruitful, liberal, plentiful, prolific, rich, substantial; *antonyms* (adj) scarce, sparse, meager, **3.** many; *synonyms* (adj) manifold, abundant, countless, frequent, various, innumerable, much, multiple, numerous, several, different, numberless, (n) number; *antonym* (n) few.

nimanonginong fast; *synonyms* (adj) dissolute, firm, agile, debauched, fixed, hurried, instant, quick, rapid, staunch, brisk, (adv) soon, hard, close, (n) diet; *antonyms* (adj) sluggish, loose, (adv) slow, slowly, leisurely, (v) gorge, (n) binge.

nimanunu 1. crumpled; *synonyms* (adj) creased, rumpled, crinkly, wrinkled, bent, corrugated, bended, bowed, corrugate, dented, furrowed, lined, craggy, dishevelled, frowzled; *antonym* (adj) smooth, **2.** creased; *synonyms* (adj) crumpled, wrinkly, disheveled, puckered, rutted, tousled, uneven, **3.** rumpled; *synonyms* (adj) untidy, disordered, unkempt, **4.** wrinkled; *synonyms* (adj) wizened, gnarled, unironed, (n) rough, rugged.

nimaoraki sickly; *synonyms* (adj) feeble, infirm, sick, ailing, diseased, indisposed, morbid, pale, poorly, sallow, peaked, pasty, (n) invalid, (v) faint, frail; *antonyms* (adj) healthy, bitter.

nimaoriori 1. flabby; *synonyms* (adj) loose, feeble, flaccid, baggy, drooping, limp, heavy, lax, slack, soft, weak, chubby, fat; *antonyms* (adj) firm, slim, **2.** flaccid; *synonyms* (adj) flabby, floppy, (v) unstrung, weakly; *antonym* (adj) stiff, **3.** apathetic; *synonyms* (adj) indifferent, cool, impassive,

uninterested, perfunctory, casual, dull, lazy, lethargic, lukewarm, nonchalant, sluggish, spiritless, detached, indolent; *antonyms* (adj) energetic, enthusiastic, fervent, inquisitive, **4.** limp; *synonyms* (adj) flexible, flimsy, exhausted, enervated, languid, lame, crumble, drop, (n) hobble, (v) halt, hitch, hop, shamble, (adv) shuffle; *antonym* (adj) taut, **5.** slack; *synonyms* (adj) idle, negligent, neglectful, dilatory, inattentive, backward, careless, flat, inactive, inert, (v) remiss, slow, relax, abate, easy; *antonyms* (adj) tight, strict, thorough, **6.** spineless; *synonyms* (adj) gutless, timid, nerveless, craven, fearful, (adv) cowardly; *antonym* (adj) brave.

nimaoupoui fifty; *synonyms* (n) l, lambert, liter, litre.

nimarawarawa seasick; *synonyms* (adj) sick, airsick, carsick, ill, nauseous, unsettled.

nimareburebu innumerable; *synonyms* (adj) countless, incalculable, numberless, infinite, innumerous, multitudinous, unnumbered, myriad, numerous, uncounted, untold, incommensurable, incommensurate, many, unnumerable; *antonym* (adj) few.

nimatamata 1. flowered; *synonym* (adj) floral, **2.** striped; *synonyms* (adj) streaked, stripy, paled, virgated, zoned, hooped, zonate, **3.** scarred; *synonyms* (adj) marred, defaced, hurt, **4.** variegated; *synonyms* (adj) motley, mottled, dappled, piebald, varicolored, varicoloured, various, assorted, speckled, different, multicolored, **5.** pitted; *synonyms* (adj) honeycombed, pockmarked, alveolate, cavitied, faveolate, hollow, bicched, foveate, notched, pecked, rutted, scrobiculated, bumpy, eroded, uneven.

nimatenten 1. grouped; *synonyms* (adj) sorted, collective, **2.** gathered; *synonyms* (adj) collected, deepened, accumulated, amassed, assembled, congregate, equanimous, massed, poised.

nimatewetewe 1. move; *synonyms* (v) act, affect, carry, excite, go, impel, instigate, maneuver, touch, travel, flow, bear, (n) motion, drive, transfer; *antonym* (v) stay, **2.** advance; *synonyms* (n) progress, improvement, (v) further, proceed, promote, approach, encourage, raise, rise, boost, contribute, cultivate, develop, forward, (phr) accelerate; *antonyms* (n) deterioration, (v) retreat, recede, delay, demote, regress.

nimateweteweaki advanced; *synonyms* (adj) sophisticated, progressive, senior, higher, modern, new, precocious, late, cultured, developed, elevated, forward, liberal, ripe, superior; *antonyms* (adj) conservative, old-fashioned, inferior.

nimatoaua 1. feverish; *synonyms* (adj) hectic, febrile, feverous, hot, fiery, frenzied, excited, fanatical, flushed, sick, (n) hysterical; *antonym* (adj) cool, **2.** enervated; *synonyms* (adj) debilitated, exhausted, limp, adynamic, asthenic, colorless, faint, languid, lethargic, tired, weak, **3**. worried; *synonyms (adj)* apprehensive, distressed, nervous, uneasy, upset, anxious, afraid, bothered, concerned, disturbed, troubled, fearful, restless, unhappy, *(v)* afflicted; *antonyms (adj)* calm, carefree, reassured, relaxed, untroubled.

nimatutu 1. drowsy; *synonyms (adj)* dozy, comatose, lazy, lethargic, slow, somnolent, dull, indolent, listless, sluggish, soporific, dozing, drowsing, oscitant, *(n)* sleepy; *antonyms (adj)* alert, energetic, **2**. somnolent; *synonyms (adj)* slumberous, slumbrous, asleep, dreamy, slumbery, *(v)* drowsy.

nimaua five; *synonyms (n)* cinque, quint, quintuplet, fin, ace, eight, fins, fivesome, interim, intermission, interval, jack, king, knave, *(adj)* quinary.

nimaukuku 1. hobble; *synonyms (v)* limp, fetter, hamper, hitch, hopple, handcuff, bridle, manacle, shamble, gag, *(adv)* halt, shuffle, toddle, *(adj)* scrape, **2**. lame; *synonyms (adj)* crippled, game, disabled, feeble, halting, weak, becripple, paralytic, inadequate, infirm, *(v)* cripple, maim, paralyze, disable, broken, **3**. limp; *synonyms (adj)* flabby, flaccid, slack, flexible, drooping, flimsy, floppy, lax, loose, exhausted, enervated, languid, lame, *(n)* hobble, *(v)* hop; *antonyms (adj)* taut, firm, *(n)* energetic.

nimibwaoua warp; *synonyms (n)* twist, buckle, distortion, deflection, deformation, *(v)* bend, distort, deform, contort, turn, bias, falsify, garble, misrepresent, pervert; *antonym (v)* straighten.

nimibwaouaki warped; *synonyms (adj)* bent, deformed, crooked, kinky, misshapen, perverted, *(n)* twisted; *antonym (adj)* straight.

nimimarea 1. abut; *synonyms (v)* adjoin, border, butt, neighbor, touch, join, meet, verge, **2**. border; *synonyms (n)* margin, brink, extremity, fringe, bed, boundary, brim, limit, skirt, limits, barrier, *(v)* edge, abut, hem, surround; *antonyms (n)* middle, *(v)* center, **3**. append; *synonyms (v)* add, affix, annex, attach, include, suffix, suspend, tack, conjoin, connect, fasten, insert, supplement, supply, *(adj)* hang, **4**. adjoin; *synonyms (v)* append, contact.

nimimareaki bordered; *synonyms (adj)* bounded, surrounded, encircled, enclosed.

nimnana 1. dirty; *synonyms (adj)* foul, dirt, contemptible, bawdy, contaminated, dingy, impure, despicable, *(v)* muddy, corrupt, soil, contaminate, begrime, bemire, *(n)* defile; *antonyms (adj)* hygienic, pure, spotless, immaculate, *(v)* clean, **2**. sticky; *synonyms (adj)* adhesive, awkward, clammy, muggy, embarrassing, glutinous, gummy, humid, difficult, slimy, gluey, gooey, hard, mucilaginous, pasty; *antonyms (adj)* dry, fresh, easy.

nimnim 1. adhesive; *synonyms (adj)* tacky, clingy, gummy, sticky, tenacious, agglutinative, gluey,

glutinous, gooey, pasty, *(n)* cement, glue, paste, gum, *(v)* cohesive; *antonym (adj)* nonadhesive, **2**. gummy; *synonyms (adj)* adhesive, viscous, thick, mucilaginous, viscid, gelatinous, **3**. sticky; *synonyms (adj)* awkward, clammy, muggy, embarrassing, humid, difficult, slimy, hard, sultry, sweltering, troublesome, persistent, oppressive, tricky, damp; *antonyms (adj)* dry, fresh, easy.

nimorimori 1. exhausted; *synonyms (v)* weak, *(adj)* drained, fatigued, spent, tired, gone, dry, beat, depleted, empty, enervated, faint, jaded, weary, expended; *antonyms (adj)* energetic, fresh, refreshed, strong, **2**. tired; *synonyms (adj)* exhausted, hackneyed, banal, commonplace, stale, threadbare, trite, haggard, stock, worn, drowsy, sick, whacked, corny, limp; *antonyms (adj)* invigorated, alert, original.

nimoti 1. broken; *synonyms (v)* broke, *(adj)* tame, torn, busted, imperfect, intermittent, rough, rugged, ruined, uneven, disjointed, incomplete, confused, cracked, crushed; *antonyms (adj)* constant, unbroken, intact, whole, wild, **2**. smashed; *synonyms (adj)* shattered, drunk, inebriated, intoxicated, broken, plastered, sloshed, blotto, tipsy, besotted, pissed, tight; *antonym (adj)* sober.

nimroa 1. attached; *synonyms (adj)* connected, affectionate, affiliated, committed, associated, devoted, fond, loving, loyal, near; *antonyms (adj)* detached, separate, unmarried, **2**. coat; *synonyms (n)* cover, coating, crust, film, fur, jacket, layer, bark, case, casing, *(v)* cloak, sheath, blanket, plaster, glaze, **3**. cling; *synonyms (v)* adhere, cleave, stick, cohere, hang, attach, clutch, grasp, grip, hold, hug.

nimroaki 1. coated; *synonyms (adj)* covered, bloomed, laminated, crusted, encrusted, layered, thick, **2**. attached; *synonyms (adj)* connected, affectionate, affiliated, committed, associated, devoted, fond, loving, loyal, near; *antonyms (adj)* detached, separate, unmarried.

nimroroko 1. importunate; *synonyms (adj)* troublesome, annoying, exigent, insistent, pressing, instant, demanding, earnest, pleading, urgent, appealing, imploring, *(v)* important; *antonym (adj)* halfhearted, **2**. persistent; *synonyms (adj)* durable, constant, continual, lasting, obstinate, permanent, continuous, chronic, consistent, dogged, firm, incessant, perpetual, relentless, stubborn; *antonyms (adj)* contained, occasional.

nimta 1. adhere; *synonyms (v)* cohere, abide, accede, attach, bond, cleave, cling, stick, bind, fasten, fix, hold, join, observe, *(adj)* agree, **2**. entwine; *synonyms (v)* intertwine, twine, coil, wind, curl, enlace, fold, interlace, knit, lace, tangle, braid, interlock, *(n)* wreathe, embrace, **3**. clasp; *synonyms (n)* grasp, grip, hug, buckle, clutch, brooch, clamp, cuddle, clench, clinch, *(v)* squeeze, catch, grapple, gripe, *(adj)* pin, **4**. stick; *synonyms* (*n*) bar, club, rod, bat, cane, (*v*) adhere, stab, paste, staff, affix, impale, persist, pink, spear, spike.

nimtaki stuck; *synonyms* (*v*) sticked, (*adj*) stranded, aground, abandoned, absorbed, ashore, beached, delayed, deserted, dumbfounded, fast, hindered, immovable, (*n*) thrust, sticking; *antonym* (*adj*) free.

nimtangira 1. love; *synonyms* (*n*) desire, affection, dear, fondness, liking, benevolence, charity, attachment, beloved, darling, devotion, honey, (*v*) cherish, enjoy, like; *antonyms* (*n*) abhorrence, hatred, aversion, (*v*) hate, dislike, abhor, **2.** attach; *synonyms* (*v*) add, adhere, append, affix, bind, link, associate, assign, annex, apply, fasten, fix, nail, stick, yoke; *antonyms* (*v*) detach, undo, disconnect, separate, unfasten.

nimtangiraki 1. attached; *synonyms* (*adj*) connected, affectionate, affiliated, committed, associated, devoted, fond, loving, loyal, near; *antonyms* (*adj*) detached, separate, unmarried, **2.** loved; *synonyms* (*adj*) dear, beloved, cherished, pet, precious, appreciated, esteemed, prized, respected, treasured, valued, important, (*n*) darling.

nimwamwano eddy; *synonyms* (*n*) spin, twirl, vortex, gurge, twist, whir, undercurrent, (*v*) whirl, purl, whirlpool, swirl, turn.

nimwatoaua 1. restless; *synonyms* (*adj*) fidgety, nervous, uneasy, unquiet, agitated, apprehensive, fretful, impatient, restive, feverish, turbulent, jumpy, disturbed, edgy, (*v*) anxious; *antonyms* (*adj*) calm, relaxed, **2.** restive; *synonyms* (*adj*) obstinate, jittery, nervy, restless, uptight, restiff, tense, unruly, overstrung, resty, (*v*) skittish.

ninamate exhausting; *synonyms* (*adj*) arduous, difficult, draining, grueling, strenuous, tiresome, tiring, wearing, hard, wearisome, wearying, demanding, tough; *antonym* (*adj*) undemanding.

ningai when; *synonyms* (*adv*) as, once, then, because, than, since, equally, erst, erstwhile, formerly, (*conj*) although, while, immediately, (*prep*) during, (*adj*) following.

ningangabong tomorrow; *synonyms* (*adv*) kal, never.

ninga'ngata 1. dawdling; *synonyms* (*adj*) slow, dilatory, tardy, deliberate, easygoing, hesitant, laggard, (*n*) delay, dalliance, coquetry, dithering, faltering, hesitation, idleness, indecision; *antonym* (*n*) decisiveness, **2.** late; *synonyms* (*adj*) former, dead, deceased, behindhand, belated, delayed, modern, dull, defunct, bygone, posthumous, erstwhile, (*adv*) fresh, backward, belatedly; *antonyms* (*adj*) ahead, (*adv*) early, punctually, promptly, punctual, **3.** dawdle; *synonyms* (*v*) dally, linger, lag, amble, procrastinate, hesitate, idler, loiter, lounge, saunter, drag; *antonyms* (*v*) hurry, rush, **4.** delay; *synonyms* (*n*) pause, arrest, deferment, wait, stay, deferral, extension, (*v*) defer, check, postpone, reserve, adjourn, break, detain, hinder; *antonyms* (*n*) punctuality, (*v*) advance.

ninga'ngataki delayed; *synonyms* (*adj*) belated, late, tardy, protracted, deferred, slow, (*adv*) behind; *antonyms* (*adj*) brief, early.

ningiongio 1. move; *synonyms* (*v*) act, affect, carry, excite, go, impel, instigate, maneuver, touch, travel, flow, bear, (*n*) motion, drive, transfer; *antonym* (*v*) stay, **2.** withdraw; *synonyms* (*v*) extract, remove, retire, retract, retreat, abandon, cancel, disengage, draw, leave, recall, recede, secede, depart, repeal; *antonyms* (*v*) advance, extend, give, offer, present, propose, deposit.

ningiongioaki withdrawn; *synonyms* (*adj*) reserved, secluded, retiring, solitary, indrawn, cloistered, reclusive, uncommunicative, lonely, taciturn, unsociable, introverted, reticent, shy, aloof; *antonym* (*adj*) outgoing.

ningorengore 1. small; *synonyms* (*adj*) little, minute, narrow, fine, inadequate, insignificant, low, minor, petty, slight, light, remote, cramped, young, limited; *antonyms* (*adj*) bulky, colossal, considerable, enormous, extra-large, great, huge, sizeable, giant, major, (*syn*) big, large, **2.** puny; *synonyms* (*adj*) feeble, frail, weak, small, tiny, measly, paltry, runty, trifling, trivial, exiguous, meager; *antonyms* (*adj*) brawny, muscular, **3.** sick; *synonyms* (*adj*) ill, queasy, ailing, indisposed, poorly, weary, invalid, diseased, morbid, sickly, nauseous, poor, crazy, disgusted, (*v*) unwell; *antonyms* (*adj*) well, healthy.

nini 1. all; *synonyms* (*adv*) whole, purely, altogether, entirely, totally, wholly, apiece, (*adj*) universal, each, every, gross, complete, alone, (*det*) aggregate, (*det*) any; *antonyms* (*pron*) none, (*det*) some, **2.** completely; *synonyms* (*adv*) all, thoroughly, stark, bodily, absolutely, exactly, fully, perfectly, simply, solely, roundly, right, (*adj*) out, throughout, quite; *antonyms* (*adv*) partly, partially, hardly, **3.** continually; *synonyms* (*adv*) ceaselessly, constantly, ever, forever, perpetually, continuously, endlessly, frequently, incessantly, persistently, regularly, unceasingly, eternally, (*adj*) always, **4.** extremely; *synonyms* (*adv*) very, exceedingly, awfully, enormously, excessively, extraordinarily, much, badly, desperately, exceptionally, greatly, hugely, infinitely, terribly, (*adj*) highly; *antonyms* (*adv*) mildly, fairly, slightly, **5.** always; *synonyms* (*adv*) whenever, consistently, continually, e'er, everlastingly, evermore, hourly, (*adj*) still, eternal; *antonyms* (*adv*) never, erratically, **6.** altogether; *synonyms* (*adv*) completely, ensemble, utterly, generally.

ninia penetrating; *synonyms* (*adj*) acute, astute, sharp, cutting, discerning, incisive, piercing, discriminating, perceptive, trenchant, intense, high, harsh, (*v*) keen, biting.

niniakai 1. indolent; *synonyms* (*adj*) idle, inactive, lazy, slothful, sluggish, careless, drowsy, dull, faineant, inert, listless, otiose, slow, torpid, lackadaisical; *antonyms* (*adj*) energetic, active, **2**. slow; *synonyms* (*adj*) late, easy, heavy, dense, dim, gradual, indolent, stupid, belated, boring, (*v*) slack, check, delay, (*adv*) behind, behindhand; *antonyms* (*adj*) fast, intelligent, rapid, bright, alert, brisk, hasty, prompt, quick, speedy, hurried, observant, rushed, (*v*) accelerate.

ninibaoua 1. crooked; *synonyms* (*adj*) bent, awry, corrupt, irregular, askew, curved, deformed, dishonest, indirect, lopsided, unfair, unscrupulous, angular, asymmetrical, (*v*) wry; *antonyms* (*adj*) straight, honest, even, principled, **2**. twisted; *synonyms* (*adj*) crooked, perverted, distorted, coiled, misshapen, contorted, twined, winding, gnarled, tortuous, kinky, wrong, warped, depraved, malformed; *antonym* (*adj*) tidy, **3**. warped; *synonym* (*n*) twisted.

ninibete 1. agile; *synonyms* (*adj*) active, nimble, adroit, quick, spry, deft, lively, brisk, lithe, sprightly, supple, quick-witted, alert, dexterous, fast; *antonym* (*adj*) clumsy, **2**. nimble; *synonyms* (*adj*) agile, clever, energetic, expeditious, lissome, fleet, dapper, diligent, flexible, lissom, smart, speedy, tripping, busy, (*v*) light, **3**. light; *synonyms* (*adj*) fair, clear, facile, easy, faint, flimsy, (*n*) flame, brightness, daylight, (*v*) fire, kindle, inflame, glow, ignite, dismount; *antonyms* (*adj*) fattening, nauseating, (*n*) dark, darkness, gloom, shade, night, (*v*) extinguish, darken, (*alt sp*) heavy.

niniboi 1. seek; *synonyms* (*v*) search, attempt, endeavor, hunt, look, inquire, aspire, beg, explore, pursue, quest, investigate, research, follow, (*n*) ask, **2**. scent; *synonyms* (*n*) perfume, fragrance, smell, aroma, bouquet, essence, redolence, odour, savor, flavor, flavour, incense, clue, (*v*) odor, nose, **3**. track; *synonyms* (*n*) course, path, line, racetrack, road, route, circuit, (*v*) trace, trail, tail, chase, dog, footprint, stalk, mark.

niniboiaki 1. scented; *synonyms* (*adj*) odorous, aromatic, fragrant, perfumed, balmy, odoriferous, redolent, sweet, spicy, **2**. tracked.

ninibwaoua warped; *synonyms* (*adj*) bent, deformed, crooked, kinky, misshapen, perverted, (*n*) twisted; *antonym* (*adj*) straight.

ninikoa 1. dauntless; *synonyms* (*adj*) brave, courageous, bold, audacious, daring, fearless, intrepid, heroic, stout, valiant, confident, gallant, game, undaunted, **2**. bold; *synonyms* (*adj*) adventurous, manly, resolute, arrogant, barefaced, spirited, stalwart, bluff, brazen, cheeky, defiant, disrespectful, enterprising, forward, impudent; *antonyms* (*adj*) cowardly, timid, modest, **3**. brave; *synonyms* (*adj*) endure, hardy, virile, dauntless, gay, martial, colorful, braw, chivalrous, (*v*) defy,

confront, face, challenge, dare, (*n*) abrupt; *antonyms* (*adj*) frightened, gutless, pathetic, **4**. courageous; *synonyms* (*adj*) gritty, plucky, valorous, gutsy, strong, **5**. fearless; *synonyms* (*adj*) doughty, indomitable, dashing, unafraid, venturesome, dreadless, (*n*) venturous; *antonyms* (*adj*) afraid, scared, **6**. daring; *synonyms* (*adj*) adventuresome, spirit, foolhardy, (*n*) audacity, boldness, bravery, courage, adventurousness, gallantry, guts, heroism, temerity, cheek, fearlessness, hardihood; *antonyms* (*adj*) cautious, dull, (*n*) cowardice, **7**. valiant; *synonym* (*adj*) strenuous.

ninikoria 1. hardy; *synonyms* (*adj*) courageous, sturdy, audacious, brave, fearless, hard, manly, strong, gallant, robust, stout, forcible, (*n*) bold, daring, rugged; *antonym* (*adj*) weak, **2**. distant; *synonyms* (*adj*) cold, aloof, remote, chill, cool, detached, far, reserved, long, faraway, icy, indifferent, removed, (*adv*) apart, (*n*) chilly; *antonyms* (*adj*) close, adjacent, friendly, near, nearby, neighboring, warm, pending, alert, intimate, involved, **3**. intrepid; *synonyms* (*adj*) dauntless, hardy, adventurous, heroic, confident, enterprising, doughty, undaunted, game, spirited, plucky, tough, valiant, valorous, venturesome; *antonym* (*adj*) cowardly, **4**. gallant; *synonyms* (*adj*) chivalrous, courteous, dashing, fine, stately, courtly, intrepid, attentive, gay, (*n*) beau, fop, cavalier, dandy, dude, spark; *antonym* (*adj*) boorish, **5**. brave; *synonyms* (*adj*) endure, virile, martial, impudent, colorful, braw, determined, masculine, (*v*) defy, confront, face, challenge, dare, (*n*) abrupt, florid; *antonyms* (*adj*) frightened, gutless, pathetic, (*n*) timid, **6**. timid; *synonyms* (*adj*) fearful, afraid, diffident, shy, bashful, cautious, coy, nervous, apprehensive, modest, retiring, craven, anxious, faint, fainthearted, **7**. shy; *synonyms* (*adj*) abashed, ashamed, reticent, self-conscious, backward, careful, hesitant, quiet, (*v*) fling, cast, chuck, pitch, jib, (*n*) throw, flinch; *antonyms* (*adj*) brash, demonstrative, forward, outgoing, **8**. valiant; *synonyms* (*adj*) stalwart, resolute, strenuous.

niniku 1. embarrass; *synonyms* (*v*) confuse, baffle, block, bother, confound, disconcert, encumber, hinder, complicate, abash, discomfit, distress, hamper, impede, (*adj*) bewilder, **2**. shame; *synonyms* (*n*) reproach, disgrace, discredit, humiliation, chagrin, insult, modesty, pity, scandal, contempt, degradation, (*v*) dishonor, degrade, humiliate, debase; *antonym* (*v*) honor.

ninikuaki 1. embarrassed; *synonyms* (*adj*) ashamed, abashed, awkward, uncomfortable, disconcerted, bashful, shamefaced, sheepish, shy, chagrined, discomfited, humiliated, mortified; *antonyms* (*adj*) proud, relaxed, **2**. shamed; *synonyms* (*adj*) disgraced, dishonored, discredited, guilty, hangdog, browbeaten, bullied, cowed, damaged, fallen, intimidated.

ninikuraroa unsociable; *synonyms* (*adj*) aloof, antisocial, distant, unfriendly, uncommunicative, inhospitable, solitary, cool, hostile, reserved, retiring; *antonyms* (*adj*) sociable, friendly.

ninimakoro 1. carved; *synonyms* (*adj*) carven, cut, incised, tipsy, (*v*) engraved, graven, fixed, imprinted, stamped, impressed, **2.** cut; *synonyms* (*v*) carve, chop, clip, abbreviate, abridge, bite, condense, crop, drop, fashion, (*n*) notch, slice, cutting, nick, blow; *antonyms* (*v*) increase, lengthen, (*n*) addition, extension, **3.** slashed; *synonyms* (*adj*) gashed, torn, cheap, down, emasculated, fringed, gelded, laciniated, low, mown, shortened, strikeout, laciniate, thinned, trimmed.

ninimarea 1. accompany; *synonyms* (*v*) attend, follow, associate, companion, company, guide, lead, walk, consort, bring, concur, conduct, convoy, join, (*n*) escort, **2.** convoy; *synonyms* (*n*) guard, column, fleet, procession, safeguard, train, (*v*) accompany, **3.** follow; *synonyms* (*v*) chase, pursue, adhere, adopt, comprehend, continue, ensue, grasp, hunt, realize, succeed, track, emulate, (*adj*) catch, course; *antonyms* (*v*) precede, head.

ninimareaki accompanied; *synonym* (*adj*) attended.

ninimoti 1. broken; *synonyms* (*v*) broke, (*adj*) tame, torn, busted, imperfect, intermittent, tough, rugged, ruined, uneven, disjointed, incomplete, confused, cracked, crushed; *antonyms* (*adj*) constant, unbroken, intact, whole, wild, **2.** tattered; *synonyms* (*adj*) ragged, scruffy, shabby, worn, dilapidated, frayed, threadbare, seedy, shattered, (*v*) bedraggled; *antonyms* (*adj*) pristine, elegant.

niningaina 1. daybreak; *synonyms* (*n*) dawn, sunrise, morning, prime, aurora, cockcrow, dawning, daylight, dayspring, light, sunup; *antonyms* (*n*) dusk, sunset, **2.** dawn; *synonyms* (*n*) beginning, commencement, onset, origin, start, birth, genesis, inception, opening, (*v*) break, begin, appear, originate, rise, (*adj*) daybreak; *antonyms* (*n*) twilight, (*v*) end, finish.

ninira 1. drape; *synonyms* (*v*) clothe, attire, array, cover, envelop, hang, wrap, adorn, enfold, swathe, (*n*) dress, curtain, blanket, drapery, mantle; *antonym* (*v*) undrape, **2.** involve; *synonyms* (*v*) imply, contain, affect, embrace, entail, implicate, comprise, complicate, demand, encompass, engage, include, tangle, comprehend, (*n*) entangle; *antonym* (*v*) exclude, **3.** pack; *synonyms* (*n*) bundle, mob, bevy, bunch, company, herd, batch, backpack, box, gang, (*v*) crowd, compress, heap, cram, fill; *antonym* (*v*) unpack, **4.** wind; *synonyms* (*n*) air, gust, (*v*) coil, twist, curl, meander, turn, bend,

curve, twine, blow, crook, entwine, roll, weave, **5.** wound; *synonyms* (*n*) bruise, harm, pain, injury, scratch, (*v*) hurt, cut, damage, offend, injure, stab, sting, insult, maim, bite, **6.** parcel; *synonyms* (*n*) lot, bale, pack, division, package, packet, section, plot, patch, allotment, group, (*v*) portion, distribute, apportion, divide, **7.** wrap; *synonyms* (*v*) cloak, shroud, wind, enclose, bind, drape, enwrap, hide, involve, muffle, surround, cocoon, (*n*) coat, wrapping, cape; *antonyms* (*v*) unwrap, uncover.

niniraki 1. draped; *synonyms* (*adj*) mantled, wrapped, cloaked, clothed, covered, absorbed, clad, disguised, engrossed, enwrapped, hooded, intent, masked, rapt, **2.** involved; *synonyms* (*adj*) complex, intricate, complicated, convoluted, tortuous, confused, difficult, elaborate, engaged, entangled, interested, knotty, obscure, tangled, knotted; *antonyms* (*adj*) simple, aloof, detached, straightforward, **3.** dizzy; *synonyms* (*adj*) dazed, giddy, faint, frivolous, light, silly, vertiginous, featherbrained, flighty, muzzy, unsteady, airheaded, woozy, (*v*) daze; *antonyms* (*adj*) alert, clear-headed, **4.** packed; *synonyms* (*adj*) crowded, compact, full, filled, jammed, overcrowded, congested, dense, thick, brimming, close, cramped, teeming; *antonyms* (*adj*) empty, deserted, **5.** wounded; *synonyms* (*adj*) hurt, bruised, bloody, (*n*) casualty, maimed; *antonym* (*adj*) composed, **6.** wrapped; *synonym* (*adj*) draped.

niniwana 1. keen; *synonyms* (*adj*) acute, eager, sharp, intense, intelligent, biting, brisk, enthusiastic, exquisite, piercing, discriminating, clever, astute, (*v*) fresh, avid; *antonyms* (*adj*) dull, apathetic, indifferent, unenthusiastic, blunt, **2.** insightful; *synonyms* (*adj*) perceptive, discerning, keen, smart, shrewd, aware, deep, knowing, knowledgeable, philosophical, receptive, reflective, responsive, sagacious, sensitive; *antonym* (*adj*) dense, **3.** brilliant; *synonyms* (*adj*) bright, splendid, glorious, illustrious, luminous, magnificent, spectacular, sunny, vivid, brainy, diamond, gaudy, gifted, impressive, incandescent; *antonyms* (*adj*) dim, awful, dark, **4.** momentary; *synonyms* (*adj*) fleeting, brief, fugitive, short, transient, instantaneous, ephemeral, momentaneous, passing, temporary, impermanent, temporal, transitory, meteoric; *antonyms* (*adj*) permanent, lasting, **5.** intellectual; *synonyms* (*adj*) cerebral, mental, rational, learned, spiritual, academic, ideal, cultured, brilliant, noetic, (*n*) intellect, brain, scholar, thinker, mind, **6.** beaming; *synonyms* (*adj*) effulgent, beamy, glad, glowing, radiant, cheerful, refulgent; *antonym* (*adj*) unhappy, **7.** intelligent; *synonyms* (*adj*) alert, intellectual, quick-witted, sensible, cunning, canny, quick, wise, witty, ingenious, artful, capable, discreet, apt, judicious; *antonyms* (*adj*) unintelligent, dull-witted, thick, slow, stupid, **8.** bright; *synonyms* (*adj*) clear, alive, beaming, light, lustrous, shining, shiny, gorgeous, nimble, auspicious, blithe, airy, buoyant, cheering, cloudless; *antonyms* (*adj*) cloudy, dreary, gloomy, overcast, shadowy, leaden, **9.** resourceful; *synonyms* (*adj*) inventive, creative, imaginative, original; *antonym* (*adj*) unimaginative, **10.** understanding; *synonyms* (*n*) reason, appreciation, comprehension, agreement, apprehension, bargain, deal, judgment, sense, sympathy, arrangement, contract, grasp, (*v*) intelligence, discernment; *antonyms* (*n*) ignorance, bewilderment, disbelief, **11.** smart; *synonyms* (*adj*) crafty, dapper, sly, prompt, chic, jaunty, lively, natty, neat, saucy, fine, fashionable, (*v*) ache, hurt, (*n*) pain; *antonyms* (*adj*) scruffy, shabby, unkempt, **12.** quick; *synonyms* (*adj*) active, agile, hasty, speedy, cursory, dexterous, expeditious, hurried, immediate, instant, swift, abrupt, animated, (*adv*) fast, (*v*) fleet; *antonym* (*adj*) leisurely, **13.** sharp; *synonyms* (*adj*) bitter, acid, acrid, harsh, incisive, penetrating, pointed, pungent, severe, caustic, cutting, piquant, sarcastic, hot, (*v*) acrimonious; *antonyms* (*adj*) mild, gentle, rounded, sweet, bland, blurred, naive, round, smooth.

nion 1. twisted; *synonyms* (*adj*) crooked, deformed, perverted, bent, distorted, coiled, misshapen, contorted, curved, twined, winding, wry, gnarled, tortuous, awry; *antonyms* (*adj*) straight, tidy, **2.** write; *synonyms* (*v*) compose, indite, pen, correspond, compile, draw, publish, record, spell, outline, type, construct, create, frame, (*n*) copy, **3.** twist; *synonyms* (*n*) twine, wind, spin, twirl, entwine, (*v*) turn, bend, distort, curl, coil, contort, deform, curve, pervert, wrench; *antonyms* (*v*) straighten, untwist.

nionaki twisted; *synonyms* (*adj*) crooked, deformed, perverted, bent, distorted, coiled, misshapen, contorted, curved, twined, winding, wry, gnarled, tortuous, awry; *antonyms* (*adj*) straight, tidy.

nira 1. lap; *synonyms* (*n*) circle, circuit, fold, coil, knee, orbit, (*v*) lick, overlap, bind, (*adv*) compass, encircle, encompass, embrace, enclose, beset, **2.** bind; *synonyms* (*v*) attach, tie, bandage, bundle, combine, fasten, fetter, fix, lace, truss, affix, bond, cement, gird, (*n*) band; *antonyms* (*v*) untie, release, unbind.

niraki bound; *synonyms* (*v*) leap, border, bounce, limit, circumscribe, confine, pounce, rebound, (*n*) spring, jump, boundary, edge, barrier, compass, hop; *antonym* (*adj*) free.

niria 1. fold; *synonyms* (*n*) crease, bend, pucker, wrinkle, flock, crimp, (*v*) crinkle, collapse, crumple, double, lap, roll, close, enfold, fail, **2.** wrap; *synonyms* (*v*) cloak, cover, envelop, shroud, swathe, wind, enclose, bind, drape, enwrap, hide, involve,

muffle, surround, (*n*) coat; *antonyms* (*v*) unwrap, uncover.

niriaki wrapped; *synonyms* (*adj*) clothed, draped, enwrapped, absorbed, cloaked, intent, rapt, engrossed, mantled, (*prep*) covered.

niwaewae 1. far; *synonyms* (*adv*) wide, off, widely, well, astray, (*adj*) distant, aloof, faraway, remote, much, outlying, (*v*) considerably, abundantly; *antonyms* (*adv*) close, briefly, (*adj*) near, **2.** distant; *synonyms* (*adj*) cold, chill, cool, detached, far, reserved, long, icy, indifferent, removed, standoffish, unfriendly, abstracted, (*adv*) apart, (*n*) chilly; *antonyms* (*adj*) adjacent, friendly, nearby, neighboring, warm, pending, alert, intimate, involved.

nkona 1. left; *synonyms* (*adj*) gone, absent, odd, port, remaining, larboard, sinister, unexpended, abandoned, remainder, corrupt, deserted, disastrous, dishonest, evil; *antonym* (*n*) right, **2.** gone; *synonyms* (*v*) extinct, (*adj*) dead, past, deceased, exhausted, away, bygone, departed, desperate, bypast, foregone, hopeless, late, lost, missing; *antonym* (*adj*) present.

nna 1. lower; *synonyms* (*adj*) debase, inferior, (*v*) degrade, diminish, frown, humble, dip, abase, cut, descend, drop, scowl, disgrace, decrease, (*n*) depress; *antonyms* (*v*) increase, raise, **2.** give; *synonyms* (*v*) allow, bestow, extend, accord, commit, donate, contribute, convey, deliver, dispense, endow, grant, present, yield, administer; *antonyms* (*v*) withdraw, take, withhold, **3.** dispense; *synonyms* (*v*) allot, distribute, apportion, assign, deal, give, issue, diffuse, allocate, discharge, furnish, portion, spread, supply, provide.

nnaki 1. dispensed, **2.** lowered; *synonyms* (*adj*) abased, bated, cheap, humbled, restrained, **3.** given; *synonyms* (*adj*) apt, disposed, prone, liable, granted, inclined, set, (*n*) assumption, particular, presumption, fact.

nnea stow; *synonyms* (*v*) pack, cram, charge, house, load, store, place, squeeze, deposit, crush, put, accommodate, compress, keep, stuff.

no 1. notice; *synonyms* (*n*) advertisement, attention, declaration, information, mind, caution, heed, (*v*) note, look, attend, detect, discover, distinguish, find, mark; *antonyms* (*v*) disregard, ignore, **2.** look; *synonyms* (*v*) seem, appear, expect, figure, (*n*) face, gaze, appearance, aspect, air, countenance, expression, glance, guise, view, (*int*) behold, **3.** watch; *synonyms* (*n*) observe, clock, see, regard, wake, care, protect, defend, check, follow, (*n*) guard, sentinel, sentry, surveillance, (*adj*) vigilance, **4.** see; *synonyms* (*v*) feel, appreciate, consider, deem, discern, know, notice, recognize, apprehend, ascertain, catch, envision, hear, inspect, (*adj*) perceive, **5.** surf; *synonyms* (*n*) breakers, foam, breaker, spray, surge, swell, wave, bubble, froth, head, lather, spume, (*v*) browse, riffle, rollers, **6.** witness; *synonyms* (*n*) spectator, testimony, bystander, eyewitness, onlooker, evidence, observer, testifier, beholder, proof, testify, attestant, confirmation, (*v*) attest, watch; *antonym* (*n*) participant, **7.** view; *synonyms* (*n*) sight, judgment, opinion, scene, idea, outlook, prospect, thought, notion, position, show, spectacle, survey, belief, (*v*) eye, **8.** observe; *synonyms* (*v*) celebrate, comment, commemorate, keep, mention, fulfill, comply, maintain, obey, remark, honor, hold, contemplate, acknowledge, espy.

noaki 1. noticed, **2.** observed; *synonyms* (*adj*) seen, ascertained, discovered, empirical, disclosed, experiential, experimental, visual, practical, pragmatic, revealed.

noakinak 1. look; *synonyms* (*v*) seem, appear, expect, figure, attend, (*n*) face, gaze, appearance, aspect, air, countenance, expression, glance, guise, view, **2.** admire; *synonyms* (*v*) love, revere, idolize, adore, appreciate, esteem, praise, wonder, worship, honor, like, laud, cherish, regard, commend; *antonyms* (*v*) criticize, despise, loathe, scorn, **3.** oversee; *synonyms* (*v*) manage, inspect, control, direct, monitor, administer, head, regulate, run, supervise, guide, govern, handle, observe, overlook, **4.** overlook; *synonyms* (*v*) disregard, neglect, excuse, forget, ignore, omit, fail, command, dominate, oversee, forgive, drop, lose, (*n*) oversight, lookout; *antonym* (*v*) remember.

noakinakaki 1. admired; *synonyms* (*adj*) esteemed, respected, accepted, beloved, estimable, favorite, honored, pet, popular, revered, valuable, valued, cherished, fashionable, indulged, **2.** overlooked; *synonyms* (*adj*) unnoticed, ignored, unmarked, unnoted, unobserved, disregarded, unseen.

nok breakers; *synonyms* (*n*) breaker, surf, flat, shallows, shelf, shoals, waves, ledgeman, side, top, (*v*) whitecaps, riffle, rollers.

nokangkang taste; *synonyms* (*n*) bit, flavor, liking, morsel, penchant, appetite, drink, drop, fondness, gusto, (*v*) relish, savor, sample, smack, discernment; *antonyms* (*n*) dislike, tastelessness.

noku 1. peevish; *synonyms* (*adj*) fractious, fretful, irritable, irascible, morose, testy, moody, cantankerous, captious, cross, petulant, touchy, crusty, grumpy, excitable, **2.** surly; *synonyms* (*adj*) sullen, peevish, churlish, brusque, grouchy, gruff, crabby, dark, gloomy, grim, rough, (*n*) harsh, rude, crabbed, severe, **3.** resentful; *synonyms* (*adj*) angry, bitter, indignant, malicious, rancorous, envious, jealous, offended, hurt, mad, raging, annoyed, sore, wrathful, revengeful; *antonyms* (*adj*) charitable, resigned, **4.** resent; *synonyms* (*v*) dislike, begrudge, envy, grudge, antagonize, brook,

combat, covet, miff, mind, oppose, oppugn, repel, stomach, feel, **5.** sulky; *synonyms* (*adj*) surly, huffish, dour, sour, (*v*) glum, **6.** sullen; *synonyms* (*adj*) dismal, lowering, black, cloudy, cheerless, heavy, saturnine, blue, depressed, sad, forbidding, rusty, (*n*) sulky, obstinate, splenetic; *antonym* (*adj*) cheerful.

nokua 1. spite; *synonyms* (*n*) resentment, malice, grudge, hatred, malevolence, pique, animosity, maliciousness, nastiness, rancor, venom, envy, bitterness, despite, hate; *antonym* (*n*) kindness, **2.** scorn; *synonyms* (*n*) disdain, contempt, neglect, derision, mockery, insult, (*v*) despise, ridicule, contemn, deride, disregard, reject, slight, reproach, dislike; *antonyms* (*n*) approval, (*v*) respect, appreciate, praise, **3.** offend; *synonyms* (*v*) irritate, affront, contravene, injure, disgust, infringe, abuse, anger, annoy, break, displease, wound, err, breach, hurt; *antonym* (*v*) please.

nokuaki 1. offended; *synonyms* (*adj*) hurt, angry, affronted, aggrieved, annoyed, pained, wronged, shocked, appalled, ashamed, averted, bitter, cool, disappointed, disgusted; *antonym* (*adj*) composed, **2.** scorned; *synonyms* (*adj*) despised, detested, hated, abject, neglected, contemptible, contemptuous, despicable, insolent, mean, undesirable, unpopular, scornful, vile.

non tough; *synonyms* (*adj*) hard, difficult, tenacious, strong, arduous, firm, hardy, laborious, rugged, severe, stout, sturdy, rough, (*n*) bully, rowdy; *antonyms* (*adj*) tender, easy, weak, flimsy, soft, feeble, lightweight, simple.

nonga 1. much; *synonyms* (*adv*) greatly, frequently, almost, awfully, considerably, far, most, often, pretty, highly, (*n*) lot, heap, (*adj*) great, considerable, practically; *antonym* (*adv*) slightly, **2.** abundant; *synonyms* (*adj*) copious, generous, lush, luxuriant, thick, plenty, affluent, ample, fertile, fruitful, liberal, plentiful, prolific, rich, substantial; *antonyms* (*adj*) scarce, sparse, meager, **3.** many; *synonyms* (*adj*) manifold, abundant, countless, frequent, various, innumerable, much, multiple, numerous, several, different, numberless, (*n*) number; *antonym* (*n*) few, **4.** full; *synonyms* (*adj*) complete, absolute, broad, flush, enough, extensive, total, detailed, comprehensive, good, plump, undivided, whole, (*n*) entire, crowded; *antonyms* (*adj*) empty, lacking, starving, hungry, sketchy, incomplete, **5.** bountiful; *synonyms* (*adj*) bounteous, profuse, benevolent, big, bighearted, charitable, handsome, munificent, openhanded, abounding, beneficent, philanthropic, free, freehanded, lavish, **6.** wealthy; *synonyms* (*adj*) moneyed, opulent, prosperous, loaded, monied, successful, thriving; *antonyms* (*adj*) poor, impoverished, **7.** rich; *synonyms* (*adj*) productive, full, deep, fat, luxurious, bright, heavy, fecund, grand, magnificent, mellow, plenteous, wealthy, well-off, (v) ornate; *antonyms* (adj) broke, destitute, light, **8.** plenty; *synonyms* (n) abundance, affluence, copiousness, many, plenteousness, exuberance, opulence, plenitude, galore, flood, multitude, plentifulness, plentitude, (adj) adequate, riches; *antonym* (adj) insufficient.

nonginong altogether; *synonyms* (adv) absolutely, all, wholly, completely, entirely, perfectly, purely, simply, totally, ensemble, fully, utterly, generally, quite, thoroughly; *antonym* (adv) partly.

nongoa 1. cork; *synonyms* (n) bung, stopper, phellem, bob, bobber, bobfloat, (v) plug, cap, stop, close, (adj) cobweb, **2.** obstruct; *synonyms* (v) bar, block, check, choke, clog, delay, encumber, hamper, impede, screen, intercept, debar, arrest, (n) hinder, barricade; *antonyms* (v) encourage, facilitate, free.

nongoaki 1. corked; *synonym* (adj) corky, **2.** obstructed; *synonyms* (adj) hindered, blind, blocked, congested, foiled, frustrated, impedite, stymied, thwarted, tight; *antonym* (adj) successful.

nôno surf; *synonyms* (n) breakers, foam, breaker, spray, surge, swell, wave, bubble, froth, head, lather, spume, (v) browse, riffle, rollers.

nonoa 1. fortify; *synonyms* (v) strengthen, confirm, consolidate, secure, buttress, encourage, reinforce, fort, harden, invigorate, support, arm, cheer, (n) brace, nerve; *antonym* (v) weaken, **2.** protect; *synonyms* (v) defend, keep, cover, preserve, hide, conceal, conserve, maintain, safeguard, save, screen, vindicate, insure, (n) guard, ward; *antonyms* (v) attack, expose, neglect, risk, **3.** strengthen; *synonyms* (v) corroborate, enhance, fortify, intensify, bolster, increase, stiffen, toughen, reenforce, hearten, revive, deepen, establish, gird, substantiate; *antonym* (v) undermine, **4.** secure; *synonyms* (v) close, fix, fasten, acquire, assure, attain, ensure, fast, gain, (adj) safe, firm, certain, confident, attach, bind; *antonyms* (v) lose, detach, (adj) insecure, vulnerable, loose, unsafe, **5.** safeguard; *synonyms* (v) protect, shelter, convoy, (n) protection, shield, care, defense, escort, precaution, security, safety, cushion, barrier, buffer, bulwark.

nonoaba 1. heaped; *synonyms* (adj) piled, coacervate, collective, cumulative, dense, thick, cumulous, **2.** piled; *synonyms* (adj) heaped, aggregate, pointed.

nonoaki 1. fortified; *synonyms* (adj) bastioned, secure, castled, defended, equipped, fast, protected, safeguarded, secured, shielded, prepared, turreted, **2.** strengthened; *synonyms* (adj) reinforced, consolidated, built, comfortable, sinewed, united, **3.** secured; *synonyms* (adj) guaranteed, barred, bolted, bonded, firm, latched, locked, **4.** protected; *synonyms* (v) covert, disguised, hid, (adj) immune, saved, sheltered, covered, confined,

cosseted, dependable, good, impregnable, inviolable, lawful, legal.

nonon tough; *synonyms* (adj) hard, difficult, tenacious, strong, arduous, firm, hardy, laborious, rugged, severe, stout, sturdy, rough, (n) bully, rowdy; *antonyms* (adj) tender, easy, weak, flimsy, soft, feeble, lightweight, simple.

nonoro 1. benighted; *synonyms* (adj) ignorant, belated, dark, illiterate, uneducated, nighted, blue, closed, coloured, depressing, disconsolate, dismal, dispiriting, dour, glowering, **2.** ignorant; *synonyms* (adj) unconscious, rude, unwitting, blind, dull, innocent, naive, unaware, uninformed, unlearned, barbarous, crude, shallow, coarse, foolish; *antonyms* (adj) knowledgeable, conscious, **3.** illiterate; *synonyms* (adj) unschooled, untaught, empty, green, (n) analphabetic; *antonym* (adj) literate, **4.** uncultured; *synonyms* (adj) uncultivated, boorish, artless, rough, unrefined; *antonym* (adj) sophisticated, **5.** unenlightened; *synonyms* (adj) nescient, undiscerning, uninstructed; *antonym* (adj) enlightened.

nonoua 1. fortify; *synonyms* (v) strengthen, confirm, consolidate, secure, buttress, encourage, reinforce, fort, harden, invigorate, support, arm, cheer, (n) brace, nerve; *antonym* (v) weaken, **2.** surround; *synonyms* (v) encircle, circle, gird, border, compass, inclose, ring, round, skirt, beset, besiege, circumvent, embrace, enclose, envelop.

nonouaki 1. fortified; *synonyms* (adj) bastioned, secure, castled, defended, equipped, fast, protected, safeguarded, secured, shielded, prepared, turreted, **2.** surrounded; *synonyms* (v) beset, begone, furnished, (adj) encircled, bounded, circumstanced, conditioned, entrenched, fixed, ingirt, inside, ringed, rooted, bordered, delimited.

nora 1. learn; *synonyms* (v) discover, get, know, find, ascertain, have, hear, determine, acquire, con, perceive, study, tell, understand, gather, **2.** comprehend; *synonyms* (v) apprehend, catch, embrace, grasp, appreciate, comprise, feel, see, sense, apperceive, admit, compass, conceive, contain, cover, **3.** interpret; *synonyms* (v) clarify, construe, elucidate, illustrate, read, comment, gloss, decipher, explain, explicate, render, depict, illuminate, consider, define, **4.** conceive; *synonyms* (v) believe, imagine, think, comprehend, design, realize, cogitate, create, fancy, invent, originate, coin, dream, suspect, concoct, **5.** accept; *synonyms* (v) receive, acknowledge, take, recognize, abide, accede, acquiesce, adopt, assume, yield, agree, approve, assent, bear, consent; *antonyms* (v) refuse, reject, deny, snub, oppose, renounce, resist, **6.** conclude; *synonyms* (v) close, complete, finish, accomplish, cease, deduce, end, resolve, settle, terminate, decide, derive, do, generalize, judge; *antonyms* (v) start, begin, **7.**

behold; *synonyms* (*v*) view, contemplate, look, observe, regard, descry, discern, notice, watch, witness, (*n*) aspect, **8.** expect; *synonyms* (*v*) anticipate, demand, await, calculate, hope, suppose, call, mean, ask, carry, conjecture, foresee, guess, presume, reckon, **9.** notice; *synonyms* (*n*) advertisement, attention, declaration, information, mind, caution, heed, message, observation, (*v*) note, attend, detect, distinguish, mark, remark; *antonyms* (*v*) disregard, ignore, **10.** confirm; *synonyms* (*v*) affirm, corroborate, establish, prove, validate, verify, clinch, assert, assure, authenticate, authorize, certify, demonstrate, justify, sanction; *antonyms* (*v*) disprove, contradict, **11.** corroborate; *synonyms* (*v*) confirm, substantiate, support, attest, show, reassert, bolster, ratify, strengthen, sustain, underpin, (*n*) indorse; *antonym* (*v*) refute, **12.** note; *synonyms* (*n*) mention, annotation, indication, bill, distinction, epistle, letter, memorandum, report, importance, line, minute, ticket, (*v*) record, label, **13.** appreciate; *synonyms* (*v*) esteem, prize, treasure, value, appraise, fathom, admire, apprize, cherish, enjoy, estimate, like, respect, apprise, enhance; *antonyms* (*v*) depreciate, scorn, **14.** certify; *synonyms* (*v*) accredit, endorse, warrant, ensure, declare, guarantee, license, vouch, allow, evidence, licence, manifest, testify, **15.** gape; *synonyms* (*n*) gaze, (*v*) gawk, open, yawn, glare, goggle, split, dehisce, (*adj*) stare, **16.** identify; *synonyms* (*v*) name, pinpoint, place, spot, describe, differentiate, associate, characterize, key, link, locate, match, enumerate, **17.** fathom; *synonyms* (*v*) sound, plumb, bottom, penetrate, measure, examine, solve, (*n*) gauge, probe, **18.** cognize; *synonyms* (*v*) bang, bed, bonk, cognise, eff, experience, fuck, hump, jazz, live, love, screw, **19.** distinguish; *synonyms* (*v*) discriminate, behold, classify, difference, identify, separate, contrast, honor, secern, signalize, dignify, severalize, celebrate, spy, diagnose; *antonym* (*v*) confuse, **20.** assume; *synonyms* (*v*) affect, accept, appropriate, arrogate, feign, sham, simulate, usurp, conclude, don, expect, fake, infer, postulate, presuppose.

noraki 1. concluded; *synonyms* (*adj*) complete, finished, done, completed, over, closed, accomplished, terminated, (*adv*) ended, **2.** certified; *synonyms* (*adj*) qualified, accredited, official, guaranteed, authorized, approved, certifiable; *antonyms* (*adj*) informal, unofficial, **3.** confirmed; *synonyms* (*adj*) chronic, inveterate, assured, habitual, constant, affirmed, definite, established, fixed, ingrained, set, valid, accustomed; *antonyms* (*adj*) unconfirmed, unproven, **4.** interpreted; *synonyms* (*adj*) accurate, confined, exact, strict, taken, precise, restricted, rigidly, rigorous, severe, strained, tense, tight, **5.**

accepted; *synonyms* (*adj*) acceptable, conventional, acknowledged, assumed, orthodox, understood, current, received, customary, known, popular, proper, recognized, usual; *antonyms* (*adj*) concealed, unpopular, unusual, **6.** appreciated; *synonyms* (*adj*) comprehended, prized, respected, valued, welcome, aesthetic, apprehended, esteemed, gratifying, pleasing, satisfying, valuable, artistic, cheering, cherished; *antonym* (*adj*) unwelcome, **7.** noticed, **8.** identified; *synonyms* (*adj*) coherent, synonymous, branded, celebrated, famous, notorious, renowned, **9.** learned; *synonyms* (*v*) knowing, (*adj*) erudite, educated, enlightened, knowledgeable, wise, academic, scholarly, bookish, cultured, intellectual, lettered, literary, studious, informed; *antonyms* (*adj*) ignorant, innate, **10.** distinguished; *synonyms* (*adj*) dignified, eminent, conspicuous, illustrious, important, reputable, great, high, noble, prominent, splendid, superior, considerable, distinct, ace; *antonyms* (*adj*) unknown, ordinary, **11.** comprehended; *synonym* (*adj*) appreciated, **12.** assumed; *synonyms* (*adj*) false, sham, affected, counterfeit, fake, feigned, fictitious, pretended, reputed, artificial, alleged, assumptive, hypothetical, phony, spurious, **13.** expected; *synonyms* (*adj*) likely, anticipated, predictable, prospective, intended, **14.** appear; *synonyms* (*v*) occur, rise, seem, sound, emerge, show, break, arise, arrive, begin, feel, happen, look, surface, (*n*) come; *antonyms* (*v*) disappear, vanish, **15.** conceived; *synonyms* (*adj*) formed, defined, settled, **16.** noted; *synonyms* (*v*) ascertained, (*adj*) distinguished, glorious, famed, well-known, marked, notable, excellent, distingue, **17.** sensed; *synonyms* (*adj*) felt, perceived, **18.** verified; *synonyms* (*adj*) corroborated, substantiated, confirmed, actual, authoritative, demonstrated, hard, **19.** realized; *synonyms* (*adj*) realised, effected, fulfilled, caught, earned, **20.** understood; *synonyms* (*v*) admitted, (*adj*) implicit, tacit, implied, silent; *antonyms* (*adj*) explicit, spoken.

noria see; *synonyms* (*v*) look, feel, discover, appreciate, behold, consider, deem, discern, distinguish, know, notice, recognize, apprehend, (*adj*) observe, perceive.

notua 1. jerk; *synonyms* (*n*) tug, heave, pull, fool, (*v*) jolt, jump, shake, yank, jar, twitch, fling, bump, flip, bob, bounce, **2.** jog; *synonyms* (*v*) run, jiggle, square, dig, joggle, prod, (*n*) trot, hustle, jostle, poke, canter, prompt, gallop, lope, nudge, **3.** discount; *synonyms* (*n*) deduction, rebate, allowance, bargain, decrease, reduction, (*v*) reduce, disregard, ignore, neglect, deduct, depreciate, cut, dismiss, reject; *antonym* (*v*) increase, **4.** repel; *synonyms* (*v*) nauseate, disgust, revolt, rebuff, repulse, sicken, decline, displease, refuse, parry, drive, oppose, rebut, combat, dispel; *antonyms* (*v*) attract, charm, draw, **5.** push; *synonyms* (*n*) press, thrust, elbow, energy, (*v*) impel, crowd, force, jab, jam, rush, boost, fight, incite, jog, labor; *antonyms* (*v*) drag, haul, **6.** shove; *synonyms* (*v*) shift, stuff, cram, move, squeeze, hurtle, put, crush, lunge, ram, squash, (*n*) push, shoulder, jerk, impulse, **7.** reject; *synonyms* (*v*) deny, disapprove, discard, eliminate, exclude, abandon, disallow, disown, renounce, repel, repudiate, spurn, eject, jettison, (*n*) cull; *antonyms* (*v*) accept, approve, choose, select, acknowledge, grant, **8.** thrust; *synonyms* (*v*) punch, throw, stick, plunge, hurl, intrude, (*n*) stab, shove, cast, blow, impetus, impulsion, brunt, hit, jabbing, **9.** rebuff; *synonyms* (*n*) denial, defeat, rebuke, refusal, rejection, repulsion, censure, setback, correction, (*v*) snub, check, slight, veto; *antonym* (*n*) acceptance, **10.** nudge; *synonyms* (*n*) touch, bother, glance, leer.

notuaki 1. discounted; *synonyms* (*adj*) economical, inexpensive, reduced; *antonym* (*adj*) expensive, **2.** rejected; *synonyms* (*v*) forsaken, (*adj*) castaway, jilted, refused, reprobate, abandoned, disallowed, refuse, bare, cheerless, consume, depraved, desolate, destroy, devastate.

notunotu 1. thrust; *synonyms* (*v*) jab, force, boost, punch, ram, dig, impel, squeeze, (*n*) push, poke, drive, stab, shove, cast, prod; *antonym* (*v*) pull, **2.** shove; *synonyms* (*v*) elbow, press, shift, hustle, stuff, nudge, bump, cram, jog, jolt, move, hurtle, (*n*) thrust, jostle, shoulder.

nou blister; *synonyms* (*n*) bleb, boil, bubble, bulla, abscess, pimple, pustule, growth, (*v*) scorch, burn, scald, swell, vesicate, assail, attack.

nouaki blistered; *synonyms* (*adj*) raw, scalded, scorched.

noumangang 1. idle; *synonyms* (*adj*) inactive, indolent, lazy, free, baseless, frivolous, fruitless, groundless, unfounded, empty, disengaged, flimsy, barren, dead, futile; *antonyms* (*adj*) busy, active, employed, (*v*) change, **2.** indolent; *synonyms* (*adj*) idle, slothful, sluggish, careless, drowsy, dull, faineant, inert, listless, otiose, slow, torpid, lackadaisical, languid, lethargic; *antonym* (*adj*) energetic, **3.** inactive; *synonyms* (*adj*) dormant, passive, fixed, heavy, immobile, inanimate, latent, motionless, quiet, sedentary, silent, slack, stagnant, static, still; *antonyms* (*adj*) lively, moving, **4.** soft; *synonyms* (*adj*) gentle, easy, light, limp, balmy, delicate, loose, clement, faint, flabby, flaccid, frail, lenient, (*v*) feeble, low; *antonyms* (*adj*) hard, firm, harsh, loud, hoarse, rough, solid, stiff, alcoholic, shrill, strong, **5.** unoccupied; *synonyms* (*adj*) vacant, desolate, unemployed, uninhabited, void, deserted, abandoned, open, spare, thoughtless,

unfurnished, unideal, unintellectual, untenanted; *antonyms* (*adj*) occupied, full, inhabited.

noumaninganinga 1. inattentive; *synonyms* (*adj*) heedless, forgetful, neglectful, negligent, careless, reckless, remiss, unaware, inadvertent, inconsiderate, indifferent, mindless, regardless, slack, thoughtless; *antonyms* (*adj*) attentive, alert, observant, **2.** heedless; *synonyms* (*adj*) inattentive, rash, blind, incautious, listless, unwary, wanton, hasty, insouciant, foolhardy, unadvised, improvident, imprudent, indiscreet, loose; *antonym* (*adj*) heedful, **3.** forgetful; *synonyms* (*adj*) oblivious, lax, absent-minded, casual, unmindful.

nrairai 1. exhausted; *synonyms* (*v*) weak, (*adj*) drained, fatigued, spent, tired, gone, dry, beat, depleted, empty, enervated, faint, jaded, weary, expended; *antonyms* (*adj*) energetic, fresh, refreshed, strong, **2.** listless; *synonyms* (*adj*) indifferent, lethargic, dull, careless, indolent, languid, inert, inattentive, dispirited, lackadaisical, slow, spiritless, uninterested, heavy, apathetic; *antonyms* (*adj*) lively, animated, **3.** weary; *synonyms* (*adj*) exhausted, aweary, irksome, wearisome, (*v*) fatigue, tire, exhaust, bore, irk, wear, depress, drain, harass, pall, (*n*) jade.

ntakuakua 1. exhausted; *synonyms* (*v*) weak, (*adj*) drained, fatigued, spent, tired, gone, dry, beat, depleted, empty, enervated, faint, jaded, weary, expended; *antonyms* (*adj*) energetic, fresh, refreshed, strong, **2.** tired; *synonyms* (*adj*) exhausted, hackneyed, banal, commonplace, stale, threadbare, trite, haggard, stock, worn, drowsy, sick, whacked, corny, limp; *antonyms* (*adj*) invigorated, alert, original.

ntangaingai 1. inert; *synonyms* (*adj*) idle, dead, dull, inactive, indolent, sluggish, dormant, flat, inanimate, lifeless, passive, still, stationary, apathetic, heavy; *antonyms* (*adj*) moving, active, animate, **2.** flabby; *synonyms* (*adj*) loose, feeble, flaccid, baggy, drooping, limp, lax, slack, soft, weak, chubby, fat; *antonyms* (*adj*) firm, slim, **3.** apathetic; *synonyms* (*adj*) indifferent, cool, impassive, uninterested, perfunctory, casual, lazy, lethargic, lukewarm, nonchalant, spiritless, detached, callous, cold, inattentive; *antonyms* (*adj*) energetic, enthusiastic, fervent, inquisitive, **4.** indolent; *synonyms* (*adj*) slothful, careless, drowsy, faineant, inert, listless, otiose, slow, torpid, lackadaisical, languid, supine, futile, (*v*) remiss, **5.** slovenly; *synonyms* (*adj*) slipshod, untidy, sloppy, frowzy, dowdy, frowsy, messy, negligent, unkempt, disheveled, disorderly, inefficient.

ntangana swarm; *synonyms* (*n*) crowd, horde, host, mob, drove, multitude, assembly, cloud, gathering, herd, mass, (*v*) pour, teem, abound, flock.

ntanganga 1. mob; *synonyms* (*n*) crowd, gang, pack, mass, horde, crew, band, bunch, concourse, rabble, swarm, cluster, company, army, (*v*) throng, **2.** weak; *synonyms* (*adj*) feeble, frail, faint, flat, flimsy, fragile, thin, watery, light, ailing, cowardly, delicate, diluted, exhausted, inadequate; *antonyms* (*adj*) strong, brave, concentrated, firm, safe, compelling, determined, effective, forceful, healthy, intense, powerful, resolute, robust, sturdy.

ntangianga swarm; *synonyms* (*n*) crowd, horde, host, mob, drove, multitude, assembly, cloud, gathering, herd, mass, (*v*) pour, teem, abound, flock.

ntangorengore 1. debilitated; *synonyms* (*adj*) enervated, feeble, infirm, enfeebled, adynamic, asthenic, (*v*) weak, **2.** languid; *synonyms* (*adj*) lazy, dull, indolent, faint, lackadaisical, lethargic, sluggish, torpid, apathetic, inert, listless, sickly, dreamy, remiss, insipid; *antonym* (*adj*) energetic, **3.** weak; *synonyms* (*adj*) frail, flat, flimsy, fragile, thin, watery, light, ailing, cowardly, delicate, diluted, exhausted, inadequate, lax, (*v*) loose; *antonyms* (*adj*) strong, brave, concentrated, firm, safe, compelling, determined, effective, forceful, healthy, intense, powerful, resolute, robust, sturdy, **4.** puny; *synonyms* (*adj*) little, petty, small, tiny, minute, measly, paltry, runty, trifling, trivial, exiguous, meager; *antonyms* (*adj*) brawny, muscular, **5.** sickly; *synonyms* (*adj*) sick, diseased, indisposed, morbid, pale, poorly, sallow, peaked, pasty, languid, pallid, unhealthy, unwell, wan, (*n*) invalid; *antonym* (*adj*) bitter, **6.** stunted; *synonyms* (*adj*) scrubby, scrawny, diminutive, puny, short, spare, (*v*) strangulated.

ntaninin 1. concentrated; *synonyms* (*adj*) strong, intense, compact, condensed, deep, heavy, solid, dense, intensive, intent, saturated, thick; *antonyms* (*adj*) dispersed, weak, uncondensed, unsaturated, **2.** assembled; *synonyms* (*adj*) accumulated, amassed, collected, collective, united, accrued, aggregate, built, congregate, massed, equanimous, fabricated, fancied, fictional, fictitious, **3.** coagulated; *synonyms* (*adj*) coagulate, curdled, viscous, crudy, curdy, gelatinous, glutinous, gooey, grumose, grumous, solidified, syrupy, raw, **4.** congested; *synonyms* (*adj*) packed, full, overcrowded, teeming, engorged, closed, stopped, close, overfull, busy, cramped, swarming, blocked, bunged, (*prep*) inflamed; *antonym* (*adj*) empty, **5.** united; *synonyms* (*adj*) joined, joint, combined, cooperative, connected, allied, mutual, concerted, mixed, common, conjunctive, undivided, conjunct, unanimous, (*v*) consolidated; *antonyms* (*adj*) individual, separate, divided.

ntarie 1. violent; *synonyms* (*adj*) fierce, rough, tempestuous, intense, raging, severe, turbulent, vehement, sharp, passionate, powerful, savage, stormy, (*n*) furious, boisterous; *antonyms* (*adj*) gentle, peaceful, calm, nonviolent, **2.** wicked; *synonyms* (*adj*) atrocious, bad, evil, sinful, vicious, depraved, immoral, mischievous, unholy, vile, corrupt, criminal, diabolical, foul, hellish; *antonyms* (*adj*) good, innocent, kind, moral, pious, pure.

ntarierie 1. contrary; *synonyms* (*adj*) opposite, contradictory, adverse, conflicting, reverse, unfavorable, alien, cross, different, disobedient, obstinate, perverse, averse, antagonistic, (*adv*) counter, **2.** rascally; *synonyms* (*adj*) dirty, contemptible, abject, mean, mischievous, roguish, scabby, scoundrelly, scurvy, shabby, blackguardly, devilish, groveling, little, paltry, **3.** quarrelsome; *synonyms* (*adj*) argumentative, pugnacious, belligerent, contentious, combative, aggressive, cantankerous, disputatious, currish, ugly, contrary, termagant, arguing, factious, (*v*) fretful; *antonym* (*adj*) peaceable.

ntinebu 1. heavy; *synonyms* (*adj*) dull, deep, dark, dense, fat, full, grave, gross, hard, arduous, bulky, burdensome, grievous, oppressive, thick; *antonyms* (*adj*) light, easy, slim, thin, slight, gentle, puny, skinny, **2.** dropsy; *synonyms* (*n*) edema, hydrops, oedema, intumescence, tumefaction, tumor.

ntokotoko 1. incompetent; *synonyms* (*adj*) impotent, incapable, inadequate, inapt, unable, awkward, clumsy, feeble, inept, insufficient, powerless, unprofessional, unskilled, useless, (*n*) bungler; *antonyms* (*adj*) competent, capable, skillful, **2.** incapacitated; *synonyms* (*adj*) disabled, handicapped, helpless, unfit, incompetent, crippled, decrepit, enervated, game, paralytic, prostrate, suffering, harmed, injured, lost, **3.** impotent; *synonyms* (*adj*) barren, ineffective, weak, frigid; *antonym* (*adj*) potent, **4.** incapable; *synonyms* (*adj*) unqualified, ineffectual, inefficient; *antonym* (*adj*) able, **5.** disability; *synonyms* (*n*) handicap, inability, disablement, disqualification, drawback, impairment, incapacity, disadvantage, damage, deadening, deterioration, deterrent, detriment, illness, trouble.

ntongitong stunned; *synonyms* (*adj*) astonished, astounded, dumbfounded, amazed, dazed, flabbergasted, bewildered, staggered, stupefied, astonied, confused, shocked, stupid, surprised, groggy.

ntorotoro 1. inactive; *synonyms* (*adj*) idle, dead, dormant, dull, inert, passive, slow, sluggish, fixed, heavy, immobile, inanimate, indolent, latent, lazy; *antonyms* (*adj*) active, lively, moving, **2.** lazy; *synonyms* (*adj*) drowsy, inactive, shiftless, faineant, remiss, slothful, leisurely, sluggard, tardy, apathetic, careless, easygoing, languid, listless, negligent; *antonyms* (*adj*) energetic, diligent.

ntungaungau 1. fatigued; *synonyms (adj)* exhausted, tired, weary, beat, worn, jaded, spent, fagged; *antonyms (adj)* fresh, refreshed, **2.** tired; *synonyms (adj)* fatigued, hackneyed, banal, commonplace, stale, threadbare, trite, haggard, stock, drowsy, sick, whacked, corny, limp, weak; *antonyms (adj)* invigorated, alert, energetic, original, strong.

nu 1. framed; *synonyms (adj)* counterfeit, methodical, orderly, prepared, spurious, **2.** contour; *synonyms (n)* form, outline, profile, shape, configuration, line, silhouette, circuit, curve, edge, figure, perimeter, periphery, ambit, **3.** frame; *synonyms (n)* design, border, build, fashion, anatomy, chassis, *(v)* construct, fabricate, draft, erect, make, forge, constitute, contrive, fabric, **4.** delineated; *synonyms (adj)* delineate, portrayed, graphic, lineal, represented, hereditary, linear, **5.** delineate; *synonyms (v)* define, draw, describe, represent, sketch, characterize, delimit, paint, trace, circumscribe, attract, depict, limn, picture, *(n)* show, **6.** sombre; *synonyms (adj)* somber, dismal, dreary, dark, drab, dull, gloomy, sober, solemn, black, obscure, grave, **7.** shadow; *synonyms (n)* shade, ghost, tail, darkness, hint, apparition, follower, gloom, phantom, reflection, umbrage, *(v)* eclipse, follow, overshadow, track, **8.** shadowed; *synonyms (adj)* shady, shaded, shadowy, dim, faint, fishy, funny, incensed, indignant, louche, outraged, queer, sunless, umbrageous, suspect, **9.** shade; *synonyms (n)* screen, tinge, color, hue, blind, cloud, conceal, dye, nuance, tone, look, *(v)* darken, shadow, tint, cover; *antonyms (n)* light, brightness, **10.** silhouette; *synonym (n)* contour, **11.** shady; *synonyms (adj)* questionable, doubtful, suspicious, uncertain, disreputable, dishonest, dubious, shadowed, corrupt, untrustworthy, illegal, crooked, cloudy, devious, iffy; *antonyms (adj)* honest, bright, reputable, sunny, trustworthy, **12.** shadowy; *synonyms (adj)* indistinct, misty, dusky, hazy, insubstantial, vague, foggy, nebulous, fuzzy, dreamy, indefinite, muddy, murky, impalpable, ghostly; *antonym (adj)* clear.

nuai satisfied; *synonyms (v)* convinced, *(adj)* contented, happy, content, full, pleased, certain, confident, sure, complacent, persuaded, fulfilled, sated, satiated, easy; *antonyms (adj)* unhappy, frustrated.

nuaki 1. delineated; *synonyms (adj)* delineate, portrayed, graphic, lineal, represented, hereditary, linear, **2.** framed; *synonyms (adj)* counterfeit, methodical, orderly, prepared, spurious, **3.** shaded; *synonyms (adj)* shady, dark, cheerless, darksome, gloomy, gray, leafy, obscure, soft, subdued, sunless, twilight, umbrageous, cool, dappled, **4.** shadowed; *synonyms (adj)* shaded, shadowy, dim, faint, fishy, funny, incensed,

indignant, louche, outraged, queer, suspect, suspicious, vague, wispy.

nubono 1. covered; *synonyms (adj)* hidden, veiled, concealed, covert, coated, masked, obscured, secret, shrouded, thick, wrapped, *(prep)* cloaked; *antonyms (adj)* bare, naked, **2.** cloudy; *synonyms (adj)* dull, gloomy, murky, nebulous, opaque, dark, foggy, misty, muddy, turbid, sunless, vaporous, dim, dismal, dusky; *antonyms (adj)* clear, bright, cloudless, sunny, **3.** dull; *synonyms (adj)* blunt, dense, dreary, sluggish, bland, boring, cloudy, cold, inactive, inert, obtuse, slack, slow, *(v)* deaden, dampen; *antonyms (adj)* lively, sharp, exciting, interesting, lustrous, stimulating, amusing, exhilarating, glittery, glossy, glowing, high-pitched, intense, luminous, shiny, **4.** overcast; *synonyms (adj)* heavy, clouded, depressing, gray, hazy, leaden, *(n)* cloud, overcasting, cloudiness, *(v)* obscure, darken, fog, becloud, overshadow, befog.

nûk 1. middle; *synonyms (adj)* intermediate, central, halfway, median, mediate, mid, inner, inside, *(n)* average, heart, hub, mean, center, core, centre; *antonyms (adj)* extreme, outer, *(n)* edge, outside, **2.** waist; *synonyms (n)* waistline, shank, middle, belly, blouse, cannon, stem, arch, *(adj)* neck, stricture, wasp.

nuka 1. central; *synonyms (adj)* basic, capital, cardinal, fundamental, chief, crucial, important, inner, key, main, pivotal, primary, centrical, core, *(n)* umbilical; *antonyms (adj)* peripheral, minor, regional, tangential, **2.** marred; *synonyms (adj)* damaged, defaced, crippled, deficient, deformed, dilapidated, faulty, hurt, impaired, imperfect, scarred.

nukabebeo 1. ignoble; *synonyms (adj)* contemptible, abject, base, beggarly, disgraceful, dishonorable, degraded, despicable, humble, mean, ignominious, shabby, low, lowly, menial; *antonym (adj)* noble, **2.** notorious; *synonyms (adj)* famous, infamous, known, illustrious, disreputable, egregious, flagrant, celebrated, noted, prominent, famed, familiar, well-known, *(v)* notable, *(n)* errant; *antonym (adj)* unknown, **3.** degraded; *synonyms (adj)* degenerate, debased, ignoble, debauched, depraved, dishonored, sordid, adulterate, corrupted; *antonym (adj)* untarnished, **4.** infamous; *synonyms (adj)* notorious, shameful, heinous, discreditable, opprobrious, reproachful, distinguished, *(n)* scandalous, *(v)* foul, scurvy, vile, *(adv)* nefarious, detestable, atrocious, **5.** dishonored; *synonyms (adj)* disgraced, shamed, discredited, broken, corrupt, damaged, defiled, disfigured, dishonest, embarrassed, fallen, humiliated, mortified, tainted, *(n)* derogate; *antonym (adj)* pure, **6.** disgraced; *synonyms (adj)* abashed, faithless, fraudulent, guilty, hangdog, indecent, knavish, lewd, shamefaced, unchaste, unjust, **7**. disreputable; *synonyms* (adj) doubtful, seedy, sleazy, wicked; *antonyms* (adj) reputable, honorable, respected, **8**. humble; *synonyms* (adj) docile, modest, unassuming, baseborn, (v) degrade, demean, disgrace, abase, debase, humiliate, mortify, conquer, depress, lower, (n) dishonor; *antonyms* (adj) grand, arrogant, conceited, haughty, imposing, impressive, pompous, snooty, **9**. shameful; *synonyms* (adj) degrading, inglorious, shocking, nasty, embarrassing, humiliating, immoral, outrageous, improper, scurrilous, miserable, indecorous, disgusting, (v) gross, black; *antonyms* (adj) dignified, admirable.

nukama 1. arrange; *synonyms* (v) adjust, appoint, dress, order, set, settle, pack, adapt, agree, classify, compose, decorate, do, engineer, fix; *antonyms* (v) disturb, disarrange, **2**. fold; *synonyms* (n) crease, bend, pucker, wrinkle, flock, crimp, (v) crinkle, collapse, crumple, double, lap, roll, close, enfold, fail.

nukamaki 1. arranged; *synonyms* (adj) set, settled, fixed, orderly, organized, prepared, ready, regular, neat, ordered, straight, tidy, **2**. folded; *synonyms* (adj) closed, plaited, artful, braided, corrugated, intricate.

nuku 1. broad; *synonyms* (adj) wide, ample, comprehensive, extensive, general, large, sweeping, vast, free, big, blanket, capacious, deep, full, (n) female; *antonyms* (adj) narrow, specific, thin, **2**. large; *synonyms* (adj) generous, broad, bulky, considerable, handsome, high, heavy, abundant, great, gross, hefty, huge, important, roomy, stout; *antonyms* (adj) small, cramped, insignificant, **3**. extensive; *synonyms* (adj) commodious, extended, copious, major, long, enormous, detailed, expanded, expansive, immense, massive, spacious, voluminous, widespread, universal; *antonyms* (adj) restricted, limited, minor, partial, short, **4**. big; *synonyms* (adj) significant, thick, sturdy, adult, bad, burly, liberal, magnanimous, momentous, noble, substantial, loud, meaningful, boastful, bountiful; *antonyms* (adj) little, puny, (syn) tiny, **5**. enormous; *synonyms* (adj) colossal, excessive, exorbitant, prodigious, tremendous, stupendous, gargantuan, giant, gigantic, infinite, monumental, terrific, terrible, flagrant, immeasurable; *antonyms* (adj) minute, miniature, **6**. fat; *synonyms* (adj) corpulent, dense, fatty, fertile, fleshy, gainful, greasy, obese, overweight, plump, rich, (n) avoirdupois, blubber, cream, (v) fatten; *antonyms* (adj) slim, skinny, slender.

num folded; *synonyms* (adj) closed, plaited, artful, braided, corrugated, intricate.

numa fold; *synonyms* (n) crease, bend, pucker, wrinkle, flock, crimp, (v) crinkle, collapse, crumple, double, lap, roll, close, enfold, fail.

numaki folded; *synonyms* (adj) closed, plaited, artful, braided, corrugated, intricate.

nuna 1. blur; *synonyms* (n) blot, blemish, smudge, brand, (v) smear, taint, blear, cloud, dim, obscure, slur, bedim, confuse, (adj) daub, stain; *antonym* (v) clarify, **2**. curtain; *synonyms* (n) veil, cover, barrier, blind, drapery, screen, drape, mantle, mask, pall, shade, shroud, blanket, (v) hide, banquette, **3**. cover; *synonyms* (v) coat, conceal, top, bury, cloak, wrap, comprise, (n) binding, camouflage, cap, covering, lid, shield, spread, coating; *antonyms* (v) reveal, expose, uncover, **4**. tint; *synonyms* (n) color, tinge, hue, dye, tincture, tone, cast, coloration, coloring, complexion, nuance, (v) tinct, colour, imbue, paint, **5**. screen; *synonyms* (n) riddle, disguise, partition, guard, curtain, protection, covert, concealment, (v) protect, shelter, filter, safeguard, sieve, defend, harbor, **6**. shade; *synonyms* (n) ghost, apparition, darkness, phantom, look, gloom, obscurity, umbrage, awning, dark, dimness, (v) darken, shadow, tint, overshadow; *antonyms* (n) light, brightness, **7**. veil; *synonyms* (n) film, garment, gauze, pretense, caul, fog, shutter, (v) secrete, envelop, eclipse, masquerade; *antonym* (v) disclose.

nunaki 1. blurred; *synonyms* (adj) fuzzy, hazy, indistinct, bleary, blurry, foggy, vague, blear, clouded, cloudy, dim, misty, muzzy, obscure, unclear; *antonym* (adj) clear, **2**. covered; *synonyms* (adj) hidden, veiled, concealed, covert, coated, masked, obscured, secret, shrouded, thick, wrapped, (prep) cloaked; *antonyms* (adj) bare, naked, **3**. screened; *synonyms* (adj) covered, invisible, isolated, secluded, select, shady, **4**. shaded; *synonyms* (adj) dark, cheerless, darksome, gloomy, gray, leafy, soft, subdued, sunless, twilight, umbrageous, cool, dappled, suspicious, **5**. veiled; *synonyms* (adj) unseen, disguised, cryptic, camouflaged, dusky, implicit, implied, latent, masquerading, mysterious, oblique, occult, prophetic, roundabout, secreted; *antonym* (adj) direct, **6**. tinted; *synonyms* (adj) dyed, coloured, bleached, bright, painted, decorated, highlighted.

nunu 1. cover; *synonyms* (v) coat, conceal, top, bury, cloak, (n) blind, blanket, screen, binding, camouflage, cap, covering, lid, mask, shield; *antonyms* (v) reveal, expose, uncover, **2**. shade; *synonyms* (n) tinge, color, ghost, hue, cloud, apparition, darkness, dye, nuance, (v) darken, shadow, tint, cover, obscure, overshadow; *antonyms* (n) light, brightness.

nunuaki 1. covered; *synonyms* (adj) hidden, veiled, concealed, covert, coated, masked, obscured, secret, shrouded, thick, wrapped, (*prep*) cloaked; *antonyms* (*adj*) bare, naked, **2.** shaded; *synonyms* (*adj*) shady, dark, cheerless, darksome, gloomy, gray, leafy, obscure, soft, subdued, sunless, twilight, umbrageous, cool, dappled.

nuo 1. billow; *synonyms* (*v*) surge, balloon, heave, zoom, bloat, inflate, roll, (*n*) wave, sea, swell, cloud, **2.** wave; *synonyms* (*n*) billow, gesture, motion, sign, (*v*) brandish, flap, flutter, curl, flourish, swing, undulate, beat, beckon, ripple, shake.

nuraka sprinkled; *synonyms* (*adj*) besprent, scattered, dotted, speckled, spotted, spread, strewn.

nuraki 1. pour; *synonyms* (*v*) gush, shed, decant, flow, pelt, scatter, stream, discharge, emit, jet, run, spill, teem, (*n*) overflow, rain; *antonym* (*v*) drizzle, **2.** sprinkle; *synonyms* (*n*) dash, (*v*) splash, moisten, cast, dot, spatter, spray, spread, diffuse, intersperse, splatter, disperse, douse, dust, (*adj*) besprinkle.

nurakiaki 1. sprinkled; *synonyms* (*adj*) besprent, scattered, dotted, speckled, spotted, spread, strewn, **2.** poured; *synonym* (*adj*) concrete.

nurakina 1. lavish; *synonyms* (*adj*) extravagant, exuberant, generous, ample, copious, prodigal, abundant, bountiful, excessive, improvident, lush, munificent, plush, (*v*) dissipate, profuse; *antonym* (*adj*) meager, **2.** pour; *synonyms* (*v*) gush, shed, decant, flow, pelt, scatter, stream, discharge, emit, jet, run, spill, teem, (*n*) overflow, rain; *antonym* (*v*) drizzle, **3.** spill; *synonyms* (*v*) fall, drop, empty, pour, slop, upset, cast, overrun, flood, disgorge, drain, slosh, (*n*) release, spillage, tumble.

nurakinaki poured; *synonym* (*adj*) concrete.

Ñ

ñâ fathom; *synonyms* (*v*) sound, plumb, bottom, comprehend, penetrate, understand, know, measure, examine, solve, (*n*) gauge, probe.

ñaboñiboñi tomorrow; *synonyms* (*adv*) kal, never.

ñai day; *synonyms* (*n*) light, daylight, generation, age, daytime, epoch, time, crisis; *antonyms* (*n*) nighttime, night.

ñgôe thou; *synonyms* (*n*) chiliad, g, grand, m, curtilage, gee, gigabyte, gm, gram, gramme, green, grounds, jet, kelvin, kilobyte.

ñieta 1. horn; *synonyms* (*n*) hooter, cornet, klaxon, alarm, trumpet, aparejo, arm, faldstool, ophicleide, trombone, cup, beak, nose, basin, (*v*) butt, **2.** spine; *synonyms* (*n*) backbone, thorn, point, prickle, quill, spike, back, barb, rachis, pricker, ridge, spur, sticker.

ñkan then; *synonyms* (*adv*) so, accordingly, afterward, again, consequently, later, (*conj*) therefore.

O

o paddle; *synonyms* (*n*) blade, oar, vane, (*v*) dabble, dodder, row, pull, spank, toddle, totter, coggle, larrup.

oa overtake; *synonyms* (*v*) catch, overhaul, attain, exceed, overcome, overpower, gain, outstrip, beat, capture, outdo, overstep, overwhelm, pass, reach.

oaníbui eighty; *synonym* (*n*) fourscore.

oánu eight; *synonyms* (*n*) eighter, eleven, ace, jack, king, knave, nine, octad, octet, octonary, ogdoad, queen, team, ten, (*adj*) octave.

oin proper; *synonyms* (*adj*) appropriate, correct, due, decent, fit, just, agreeable, apt, becoming, befitting, decorous, fitting, legitimate, modest, right; *antonyms* (*adj*) improper, inappropriate, unseemly, wrong, rude.

oki 1. back; *synonyms* (*adv*) before, backward, (*n*) rear, (*adj*) assist, (*v*) support, advocate, endorse, recede, second, stake, vouch, guarantee, aid, champion, encourage; *antonyms* (*n*) face, (*v*) front, oppose, advance, **2.** return; *synonyms* (*n*) yield, pay, recompense, refund, restitution, proceeds, income, (*v*) recur, reimburse, render, repay, restoration, restore, retort, answer; *antonyms* (*n*) departure, abolition, confiscation, recovery, (*v*) keep.

okioki 1. global; *synonyms* (*adj*) general, international, overall, cosmopolitan, universal, worldwide, comprehensive, earthly, ecumenical, total, globose, globular, inclusive, orbicular, planetary; *antonyms* (*adj*) local, national, **2.** common; *synonyms* (*adj*) ordinary, coarse, cheap, mutual, usual, vulgar, accustomed, base, ignoble, mean, mediocre, plebeian, public, trivial, (*n*) habitual; *antonyms* (*adj*) individual, uncommon, rare, unusual, characteristic, one-off, specific, unique, aristocratic, exclusive, extraordinary, infrequent, **3.** conventional; *synonyms* (*adj*) formal, orthodox, accepted, common, customary, everyday, conservative, decorous, established, normal, routine, traditional, typical, (*v*) commonplace, familiar; *antonyms* (*adj*) unconventional, radical, relaxed, original, rebellious, unorthodox, **4.** shared; *synonyms* (*adj*) communal, divided, joint, collective, community, cooperative, reciprocal; *antonym* (*adj*) private, **5.** routine; *synonyms* (*n*) round, habit, method, procedure, process, act, custom, practice, rule, (*adj*) regular, mundane, conventional, dull, mechanical, quotidian.

okoro 1. distinct; *synonyms* (*adj*) clear, articulate, different, discrete, apparent, definite, distinctive, palpable, decided, dissimilar, marked, plain, tangible, (*prep*) separate, (*adv*) apart; *antonyms* (*adj*) indistinct, similar, unclear, vague, inaudible, shapeless, **2.** especially; *synonyms* (*adv*) specially, chiefly, exceedingly, particularly, principally, namely, exceptionally, expressly, extra, extraordinarily, peculiarly, primarily, remarkably, specifically, very; *antonym* (*adv*) slightly, **3.** chiefly; *synonyms* (*adv*) mainly, mostly, especially, largely, generally, (*adj*) notably, **4.** apart; *synonyms* (*adv*) aside, asunder, away, independently, individually, separately, (*adj*) aloof, alone, distant, detached, isolated, only, individual, loose, remote, **5.** namely; *synonyms* (*adv*) videlicet, viz, scilicet, nominately, explicitly, i.e, viz, wit, **6.** accurately; *synonyms* (*adv*) truly, correctly, exactly, precisely, closely, faithfully, (*adj*) justly; *antonyms* (*adv*) inaccurately, falsely, **7.** explicitly; *synonyms* (*adv*) definitely, clearly, purposely, **8.** exact; *synonyms* (*adj*) detailed, precise, actual, authentic, careful, direct, faithful, (*v*) accurate, close, demand, require, claim, command, ask, (*n*) correct; *antonyms* (*adj*) inaccurate, imprecise, wrong, approximate, inexact, **9.** exactly; *synonyms* (*adv*) right, sharp, absolutely, just, accurately, certainly, completely, directly, punctually, rightly, barely, full, due, minutely, literally; *antonyms* (*adv*) approximately, (*prep*) about, **10.** definite; *synonyms* (*adj*) absolute, certain, categorical, conclusive, concrete, decisive, distinct, exact, specific, reliable, assured, defined, explicit, particular, (*v*) determinate; *antonyms* (*adj*) uncertain, doubtful, undefined, indeterminate, evasive, indefinite, indescribable, qualified, **11.** explicit; *synonyms* (*adj*) unmistakable, broad, lucid, manifest, perspicuous, emphatic, transparent, express, obvious, clear-cut, flat, trenchant, comprehensible, evident, positive; *antonyms* (*adj*) tacit, understood, unspoken, implicit, bland, **12.** correctly; *synonyms* (*adv*) aright, appropriately, duly, properly, rightfully, strictly, suitably, well, actually; *antonyms* (*adv*) incorrectly, wrongly, **13.** definitely; *synonyms* (*adv*) decidedly, surely, undoubtedly, unquestionably, determinately, distinctly, emphatically, finally, firmly, indeed, indubitably, plainly, positively, resolutely; *antonyms* (*adv*) perhaps, doubtfully, maybe, possibly, vaguely, **14.** unequivocally; *synonym* (*adv*) unambiguously, **15.** strictly; *synonyms* (*adv*) rigorously, severely, purely, rigidly, sternly, harshly, narrowly, stringently, thoroughly; *antonym* (*adv*) gently, **16.** specifically, **17.** precise; *synonyms* (*adj*) minute, delicate, neat, ceremonious, fastidious, formal, meticulous, punctilious, methodical, fixed, fine, orderly, perfect, prim, (*v*) narrow; *antonym* (*adj*)

rough, **18.** specific; *synonyms* (*adj*) special, peculiar, especial, single, characteristic, personal, proper, unique, set, appropriate, exceptional, several, singular, unambiguous, (*n*) detail; *antonyms* (*adj*) universal, (*n*) general, **19.** particular; *synonyms* (*adj*) finicky, fussy, choosy, circumstantial, critical, extraordinary, finical, nice, painstaking, own, curious, dainty, exclusive, (*n*) item, circumstance; *antonyms* (*adj*) careless, easy, ordinary, **20.** special; *synonyms* (*adj*) limited, rare, distinguished, private, outstanding, uncommon, unusual, technical, quaint, select, additional, impressive, noteworthy, preferential, (*n*) specialty.

omaoma pliable; *synonyms* (*adj*) flexible, elastic, plastic, ductile, pliant, flexile, malleable, soft, fictile, supple, susceptible, yielding, docile, (*v*) lithe, limber; *antonyms* (*adj*) rigid, stiff.

on 1. dew; *synonyms* (*n*) condensation, mist, freshness, humidity, moisture, dag, dagger, prime, vapor, poniard, (*adj*) madefaction, **2.** tortoise; *synonyms* (*n*) snail, testudo, (*v*) lingerer, loiterer, sluggard.

onea 1. alter; *synonyms* (*v*) adapt, change, move, adjust, affect, amend, castrate, convert, correct, shift, transform, turn, vary, alternate, distort; *antonym* (*v*) maintain, **2.** vary; *synonyms* (*v*) alter, differ, modify, deviate, diverge, diversify, modulate, depart, disagree, fluctuate, variegate, contrast, exchange, dissent, range.

oneaki 1. altered; *synonyms* (*v*) battered, (*adj*) adapted, transformed, changed, diversified, distorted, varied, affected, corrupt, different, malformed, misrepresented, misshapen, misused, neutered; *antonyms* (*adj*) unchanged, unaltered, **2.** varied; *synonyms* (*adj*) assorted, diverse, miscellaneous, mixed, various, sundry, heterogeneous, manifold, motley, many, dissimilar, versatile, odd; *antonyms* (*adj*) boring, dull, homogeneous, uniform.

onga swallow; *synonyms* (*v*) eat, bolt, gulp, consume, devour, accept, absorb, bear, endure, stomach, brook, (*n*) drink, sip, swig, taste; *antonym* (*v*) regurgitate.

ongaki swallowed; *synonyms* (*adj*) engulfed, enveloped, flooded, inundated, overcome, overpowered, overwhelmed, swamped.

ongeaba 1. obey; *synonyms* (*v*) follow, comply, mind, heed, listen, keep, fulfill, hear, conform, serve, mark, observe, respect, submit; *antonyms* (*v*) disobey, break, defy, **2.** obedient; *synonyms* (*adj*) docile, compliant, submissive, good, acquiescent, amenable, biddable, conformable, dutiful, meek, tame, subservient, humble, orderly, manageable; *antonyms* (*adj*) disobedient, defiant, assertive.

ongira 1. wring; *synonyms* (*v*) extort, squeeze, twist, distort, torment, torture, wrench, wrest, extract, contort, rack, twine, milk, turn, exact, **2.** squeeze; *synonyms* (*v*) hug, compress, pinch, embrace, cram, crush, force, jam, nip, pack, squash, compact, condense, constrict, (*n*) press; *antonym* (*v*) loosen.

ongo 1. hear; *synonyms* (*v*) attend, discover, apprehend, understand, catch, examine, learn, listen, overhear, see, try, find, get, comprehend, gather, **2.** head; *synonyms* (*n*) chief, captain, front, point, boss, foam, froth, crown, chieftain, executive, chair, brain, (*v*) capital, direct, lead; *antonyms* (*n*) end, subordinate, (*v*) follow, **3.** hark; *synonyms* (*n*) look, (*v*) harken, hear, hearken, heed, **4.** heard, **5.** hearken; *synonym* (*v*) hark, **6.** listen; *synonyms* (*v*) list, mind, concentrate, incline, **7.** attend; *synonyms* (*v*) accompany, assist, escort, serve, advert, aid, conduct, help, minister, keep, remain, view, (*n*) tend, doctor, nurse.

ongoaki attended; *synonyms* (*adj*) accompanied, fraught.

ongong wring; *synonyms* (*v*) extort, squeeze, twist, distort, torment, torture, wrench, wrest, extract, contort, rack, twine, milk, turn, exact.

ongora listen; *synonyms* (*v*) hark, hear, attend, hearken, heed, harken, list, mind, concentrate, incline.

onika 1. change; *synonyms* (*n*) shift, alteration, barter, modification, variation, move, (*v*) exchange, alter, adapt, alternate, cash, convert, switch, transpose, turn; *antonyms* (*v*) stay, leave, idle, maintain, **2.** alter; *synonyms* (*v*) change, adjust, affect, amend, castrate, correct, transform, vary, distort, diversify, edit, emasculate, fluctuate, invert, neuter, **3.** vary; *synonyms* (*v*) differ, modify, deviate, diverge, modulate, depart, disagree, variegate, contrast, dissent, range, interchange, digress, go, motley, **4.** transform; *synonyms* (*v*) metamorphose, translate, become, transfigure, transmute, process, reform, transmogrify, interpret, mold, shape.

onikaki 1. altered; *synonyms* (*v*) battered, (*adj*) adapted, transformed, changed, diversified, distorted, varied, affected, corrupt, different, malformed, misrepresented, misshapen, misused, neutered; *antonyms* (*adj*) unchanged, unaltered, **2.** changed; *synonyms* (*adj*) altered, changeling, disguised, inverse, new, reformed, rehabilitated, tainted, improved, inconstant, renewed, untouched, various, **3.** transformed; *synonyms* (*adj*) bewitched, converted, **4.** varied; *synonyms* (*adj*) assorted, diverse, miscellaneous, mixed, sundry, heterogeneous, manifold, motley, many, dissimilar, versatile, odd; *antonyms* (*adj*) boring, dull, homogeneous, uniform.

onikia transform; *synonyms* (*v*) change, alter, convert, metamorphose, modify, translate, turn, become, transfigure, transmute, process, vary, reform, transmogrify, adapt.

onikiaki transformed; *synonyms* (*adj*) altered, bewitched, distorted, malformed, misshapen, reformed, rehabilitated, converted, improved, new, renewed.

onimakina 1. trusting; *synonyms* (*adj*) trustful, credulous, unsuspecting, naive, confident, gullible, innocent, simple; *antonyms* (*adj*) distrustful, doubtful, suspicious, **2.** trust; *synonyms* (*n*) charge, confidence, credit, faith, reliance, rely, assurance, belief, cartel, responsibility, dependence, care, (*v*) believe, hope, confide; *antonyms* (*v*) distrust, doubt, disbelieve, mistrust.

onimakinaki trusted; *synonyms* (*adj*) confidential, intimate, sure, beloved, bosom, certain, cherished, familiar, indisputable.

onionikaki vary; *synonyms* (*v*) alter, change, differ, modify, alternate, deviate, diverge, diversify, modulate, depart, disagree, fluctuate, shift, variegate, contrast.

onionikakiaki varied; *synonyms* (*adj*) assorted, diverse, miscellaneous, mixed, various, different, diversified, sundry, heterogeneous, manifold, motley, many, dissimilar, versatile, odd; *antonyms* (*adj*) boring, dull, homogeneous, uniform.

ono six; *synonyms* (*n*) sise, sixer, hexad, sestet, sextet, sextuplet, ace, assize, bigness, bulk, eight, jack, king, knave, magnitude.

onobwi sixty; *synonyms* (*adj*) lx, threescore, (*n*) lux.

onohoua six; *synonyms* (*n*) sise, sixer, hexad, sestet, sextet, sextuplet, ace, assize, bigness, bulk, eight, jack, king, knave, magnitude.

onon 1. beseech; *synonyms* (*v*) entreat, beg, adjure, ask, crave, implore, pray, request, appeal, conjure, importune, plead, solicit, sue, supplicate, **2.** implore; *synonyms* (*v*) beseech, demand, invoke, petition, require, seek, urge, **3.** entreat; *synonyms* (*v*) bid, call, invite, woo, desire, press, **4.** crave; *synonyms* (*v*) covet, want, long, wish, fancy, claim, hunger, lust, need, pine, starve, thirst, yearn, **5.** plead; *synonyms* (*v*) defend, argue, justify, (*n*) allege, **6.** solicit; *synonyms* (*v*) court, apply, entice, attract, lobby, accost, procure, inquire, move, allure, tempt, proposition, question, romance, (*n*) canvass, **7.** supplicate; *synonym* (*v*) obtest, **8.** request; *synonyms* (*n*) prayer, application, entreaty, invitation, asking, command, quest, requisition, inquiry, offer, plea, bidding, (*v*) order, query, summon.

ononaki 1. craved; *synonyms* (*adj*) desired, coveted, **2.** solicited.

onopoui sixty; *synonyms* (*adj*) lx, threescore, (*n*) lux.

onoua 1. eight; *synonyms* (*n*) eighter, eleven, ace, jack, king, knave, nine, octad, octet, octonary, ogdoad, queen, team, ten, (*adj*) octave, **2.** six; *synonyms* (*n*) sise, sixer, hexad, sestet, sextet, sextuplet, assize, bigness, bulk, eight, magnitude, seven, sextette, size, deuce.

onton all; *synonyms* (*adv*) whole, purely, altogether, entirely, totally, wholly, apiece, (*adj*) universal, each, every, gross, complete, alone, (*n*) aggregate, (*det*) any; *antonyms* (*pron*) none, (*det*) some.

oota clear; *synonyms* (*adj*) clean, certain, open, apparent, distinct, empty, (*v*) bright, acquit, absolute, free, net, absolve, clarify, definite, discharge; *antonyms* (*adj*) cloudy, opaque, unclear, dark, fuzzy, hazy, incomprehensible, obscure, uncertain, vague, ambiguous, blurry, confused, confusing, (*v*) convict.

ootana order; *synonyms* (*n*) command, decree, dictate, array, rank, sort, charge, class, condition, disposition, edict, (*v*) direct, commission, arrange, call; *antonyms* (*n*) anarchy, chaos, confusion, mayhem, mess, (*v*) disorder, request.

ootanaki ordered; *synonyms* (*adj*) tidy, regular, arranged, methodical, orderly, coherent, consistent, lawful, logical.

ooua spear; *synonyms* (*n*) harpoon, lance, pike, fizgig, gig, prick, shaft, barb, (*v*) impale, spike, stab, pierce, skewer, stick, transfix.

ora shallow; *synonyms* (*adj*) shoal, superficial, low, cursory, petty, little, sketchy, flimsy, frivolous, simple, surface, dull, mean, airy, facile; *antonyms* (*adj*) deep, bottomless.

orak 1. disease; *synonyms* (*n*) ailment, condition, illness, sickness, complaint, infirmity, affection, affliction, bug, disorder, ill, evil, infection, malady, (*v*) distemper, **2.** illness; *synonyms* (*n*) disease, attack, pain, trouble.

oraora 1. uncooked; *synonyms* (*adj*) raw, unblown, unpolished, tough, unfashioned, unformed, unhewn, unlabored, unwrought, pink, rare, red, underdone, **2.** raw; *synonyms* (*adj*) crude, fresh, immature, bleak, coarse, cutting, green, piercing, sore, cold, biting, chilly, inclement, inexperienced, naked; *antonyms* (*adj*) refined, cooked.

orea 1. bean; *synonyms* (*n*) dome, attic, bead, head, bonce, choke, noggin, noodle, garret, loft, (*v*) attack, strike, **2.** lash; *synonyms* (*n*) goad, scourge, hit, blow, eyelash, (*v*) whip, beat, flog, chastise, bind, lace, batter, castigate, (*adj*) strap, tie, **3.** maul; *synonyms* (*n*) hammer, sledge, sledgehammer, (*v*) mall, mangle, buffet, molest, thrash, disfigure, (*adj*) bruise, **4.** lick; *synonyms* (*v*) lap, clobber, bat, drub, defeat, bang, trim, overcome, touch, trounce, (*n*) biff, jab, speed, dash, punch, **5.** bang; *synonyms* (*n*) clap, smack, knock, slap, smash, blast, bump, rap, thud, (*v*) slam, bash, boom, clatter, clink, thump, **6.** hit; *synonyms* (*v*) attain, belt, collide, encounter, clash, club, contact, do, lick, (*n*) chance, collision, play, clout, crack, cuff; *antonyms* (*n*) failure, flop, **7.** whack; *synonyms* (*n*) wallop, thrust, thwack, whang, (*v*) swipe, spank, bop,

pound, sock, wham, whop, clip, **8.** strike; *synonyms* (*n*) assault, tap, dab, (*v*) impress, move, affect, box, coin, mint, whack, lash, hew, afflict, find, impact, **9.** struck; *synonyms* (*v*) stroke, wounded, (*adj*) smitten, stricken, afflicted, crazy, doting, dotty, enamored, gaga, hurt, infatuated, interested, **10.** whop; *synonyms* (*v*) whap, bonk, **11.** smite; *synonyms* (*v*) cut, punish, animate, excite, impassion, inspire, interest, **12.** trounce; *synonyms* (*v*) rout, overpower, baste, slash, crush, reprimand, thresh, pummel, pip, lambaste, scold, vanquish, best, cheat, lather; *antonym* (*v*) lose, **13.** stricken; *synonyms* (*adj*) struck, low, impaired, unfortunate, (*v*) victimized, entire, whole.

oreaki 1. hit; *synonyms* (*v*) strike, attain, belt, blow, bump, collide, encounter, (*n*) knock, bang, smash, touch, chance, bash, beat, collision; *antonyms* (*n*) failure, flop, **2.** licked; *synonyms* (*adj*) beaten, dumbfounded, **3.** struck; *synonyms* (*v*) stroke, wounded, (*adj*) smitten, stricken, afflicted, crazy, doting, dotty, enamored, gaga, hurt, infatuated, interested, **4.** whacked; *synonyms* (*adj*) tired, exhausted, fatigued, shattered, spent, weary.

ori see; *synonyms* (*v*) look, feel, discover, appreciate, behold, consider, deem, discern, distinguish, know, notice, recognize, apprehend, (*adj*) observe, perceive.

oro 1. blown; *synonyms* (*v*) distended, (*adj*) breathless, puffy, panting, swollen, winded, dissipated, flushed, gasping, high, late, mighty, misspent, pursy, spent, **2.** blow; *synonyms* (*n*) bang, beat, blast, knock, shock, wallop, gust, hit, jolt, (*v*) puff, bloom, blossom, pant, play, (*adj*) gasp; *antonyms* (*v*) calm, save, **3.** batter; *synonyms* (*n*) batsman, concoction, (*v*) baste, hammer, bash, break, buffet, club, mangle, pound, slam, bruise, drive, clobber, demolish, **4.** assault; *synonyms* (*n*) attack, aggression, rush, violence, charge, onset, raid, rape, thrust, battery, offensive, (*v*) assail, storm, invade, violate; *antonyms* (*n*) defense, (*v*) defend, **5.** hit; *synonyms* (*v*) strike, attain, belt, blow, bump, collide, encounter, clash, contact, (*n*) smash, touch, chance, collision, clout, crack; *antonyms* (*n*) failure, flop, **6.** knock; *synonyms* (*v*) cuff, punch, boot, clip, condemn, criticize, knap, smack, (*n*) rap, tap, crash, whack, clap, criticism, stroke; *antonym* (*v*) praise, **7.** punch; *synonyms* (*n*) jab, drill, die, dig, nudge, buffoon, (*v*) poke, prick, perforate, stab, puncture, push, slap, bore, prod, **8.** trounce; *synonyms* (*v*) thrash, castigate, defeat, flog, lash, whip, rout, drub, chastise, overpower, slash, crush, reprimand, thresh, lick; *antonym* (*v*) lose, **9.** whack; *synonyms* (*n*) thump, thwack, whang, (*v*) swipe, spank, bop, batter, sock, wham, whop, bat, **10.** smite; *synonyms* (*v*) afflict, affect, cut, impress, punish, animate, excite, impassion, inspire, interest, move, **11**. pelt; *synonyms* (*n*) fur, hide, skin, fell, coat, chignon, dowse, (*v*) bombard, hurry, pepper, pour, stone, throw, lapidate, patter, **12**. strike; *synonyms* (*n*) assault, dab, pat, (*v*) box, coin, mint, hew, find, impact, pick, reach, get, imprint, peck, chime.

oroaki 1. hit; *synonyms* (*v*) strike, attain, belt, blow, bump, collide, encounter, (*n*) knock, bang, smash, touch, chance, bash, beat, collision; *antonyms* (*n*) failure, flop, **2**. blown; *synonyms* (*v*) distended, (*adj*) breathless, puffy, panting, swollen, winded, dissipated, flushed, gasping, high, late, mighty, misspent, pursy, spent, **3**. assaulted; *synonyms* (*adj*) beaten, molested, raped, despoiled, pillaged, ravaged, sacked, **4**. battered; *synonyms* (*adj*) worn, damaged, hurt, maltreated, ragged, tattered, abused, aching, bruised, decrepit, dilapidated, injured, conquered, (*v*) seedy, shattered, **5**. whacked; *synonyms* (*adj*) tired, exhausted, fatigued, weary.

oroia thrash; *synonyms* (*v*) flog, lash, beat, defeat, pound, whip, baste, clobber, drub, lam, lick, whack, batter, bang, bat.

orôra raw; *synonyms* (*adj*) crude, fresh, immature, bleak, coarse, cutting, green, piercing, sore, cold, biting, chilly, inclement, inexperienced, naked; *antonyms* (*adj*) refined, cooked.

oruak 1. lost; *synonyms* (*v*) gone, missing, abandoned, (*adj*) doomed, forlorn, extinct, hopeless, bewildered, disoriented, forgotten, helpless, broken, confused, irrecoverable, absent; *antonyms* (*adj*) present, found, existing, **2**. destroyed; *synonyms* (*adj*) lost, ruined, desolate, desolated, shattered, dead, depressed.

ota 1. comprehend; *synonyms* (*v*) apprehend, catch, embrace, grasp, understand, appreciate, comprise, feel, see, sense, apperceive, admit, compass, conceive, contain, **2**. know; *synonyms* (*v*) discern, comprehend, can, distinguish, have, recognize, acknowledge, agnise, agnize, fathom, cognize, experience, get, perceive, (*n*) ken, **3**. realize; *synonyms* (*v*) fulfill, achieve, perform, discover, attain, accomplish, complete, execute, know, make, obtain, effect, discharge, learn, clear, **4**. shine; *synonyms* (*n*) sheen, luster, (*v*) glow, light, burnish, gleam, blaze, flash, glitter, sparkle, excel, flame, glance, glisten, gloss; *antonym* (*n*) dullness, **5**. understand; *synonyms* (*v*) interpret, hear, realize, assume, believe, construe, deduce, gather, read, translate, suppose, consider, infer, penetrate, (*adj*) take; *antonyms* (*v*) misinterpret, misconstrue, misunderstand.

otabanini wrap; *synonyms* (*v*) cloak, cover, envelop, enfold, roll, shroud, swathe, wind, enclose, bind, drape, enwrap, hide, involve, (*n*) coat; *antonyms* (*v*) unwrap, uncover.

otabaninia surround; *synonyms* (*v*) encircle, circle, gird, border, compass, inclose, ring, round, skirt, beset, besiege, circumvent, embrace, enclose, envelop.

otabaniniaki surrounded; *synonyms* (*v*) beset, begone, furnished, (*adj*) encircled, bounded, circumstanced, conditioned, entrenched, fixed, ingirt, inside, ringed, rooted, bordered, delimited.

otabininiaki wrapped; *synonyms* (*adj*) clothed, draped, enwrapped, absorbed, cloaked, intent, rapt, engrossed, mantled, (*prep*) covered.

otaki 1. known; *synonyms* (*adj*) well-known, familiar, conscious, certain, accepted, acknowledged, plain, published, understood, evident, recognized, apparent, aware, common, apprised; *antonyms* (*adj*) nameless, unknown, secret, unidentified, **2**. comprehended; *synonyms* (*adj*) appreciated, apprehended, gratifying, pleasing, satisfying, **3**. realized; *synonyms* (*adj*) complete, accomplished, realised, completed, effected, fulfilled, caught, done, established, finished, earned, **4**. understood; *synonyms* (*v*) admitted, (*adj*) implicit, tacit, implied, silent, assumed; *antonyms* (*adj*) explicit, spoken.

otanga defend; *synonyms* (*v*) cover, guard, assert, justify, protect, advocate, champion, maintain, shield, support, apologize, hold, preserve, safeguard, shelter; *antonyms* (*v*) attack, prosecute.

otangana shelter; *synonyms* (*n*) guard, refuge, asylum, harbor, protect, protection, sanctuary, security, shield, hut, covert, (*v*) cover, screen, defend, (*adj*) defense; *antonym* (*v*) expose.

otanganaki sheltered; *synonyms* (*v*) secure, comfortable, safe, screened, cozy, secluded, (*v*) protected, private; *antonym* (*adj*) desolate.

otaotanga 1. guard; *synonyms* (*n*) defend, defense, bulwark, care, cover, escort, protection, watchman, custody, convoy, defence, fender, guardsman, (*v*) shield, keep, **2**. defend; *synonyms* (*v*) guard, assert, justify, protect, advocate, champion, maintain, support, apologize, hold, preserve, safeguard, shelter, uphold, vindicate; *antonyms* (*v*) attack, prosecute, **3**. protect; *synonyms* (*v*) hide, conceal, conserve, save, screen, insure, cushion, patronize, shade, ensure, fence, guarantee, insulate, bless, (*n*) ward; *antonyms* (*v*) expose, neglect, risk, **4**. shield; *synonyms* (*n*) buffer, armor, security, shell, covering, arms, casing, blind, covert, (*v*) secure, buckler, harbor, harbour, mask, shadow.

otaotangaki 1. guarded; *synonyms* (*adj*) cautious, careful, wary, chary, circumspect, cagey, vigilant, watchful, conditional, discreet, gingerly, conservative, prudent, reserved, safe; *antonyms* (*adj*) frank, honest, **2**. protected; *synonyms* (*v*) covert, disguised, hid, (*adj*) secure, immune, saved, secured, sheltered, covered, comfortable, confined, cosseted, dependable, good, guaranteed, **3.** shielded; *synonyms* *(adj)* protected, safeguarded, defended, cloistered, enshield, enshielded, sacred, fortified.

otea 1. broken; *synonyms* *(v)* broke, *(adj)* tame, torn, busted, imperfect, intermittent, rough, rugged, ruined, uneven, disjointed, incomplete, confused, cracked, crushed; *antonyms* *(adj)* constant, unbroken, intact, whole, wild, **2.** broke; *synonyms* *(adj)* bankrupt, poor, impecunious, impoverished, insolvent, penniless, bust, destitute, skint, strapped; *antonyms* *(adj)* rich, solvent, **3.** break; *synonyms* *(v)* split, crack, burst, fail, infringe, leak, *(n)* breach, fracture, pause, rupture, stop, collapse, interruption, respite, suspension; *antonyms* *(v)* repair, obey, honor, mend, *(n)* continuation.

oteaki 1. broken; *synonyms* *(v)* broke, *(adj)* tame, torn, busted, imperfect, intermittent, rough, rugged, ruined, uneven, disjointed, incomplete, confused, cracked, crushed; *antonyms* *(adj)* constant, unbroken, intact, whole, wild, **2.** folded; *synonyms* *(adj)* closed, plaited, artful, braided, corrugated, intricate.

oti appear; *synonyms* *(v)* occur, rise, seem, sound, emerge, show, break, arise, arrive, begin, feel, happen, look, surface, *(n)* come; *antonyms* *(v)* disappear, vanish.

otinako 1. exposed; *synonyms* *(v)* vulnerable, *(adj)* bare, open, defenseless, liable, naked, nude, obvious, subject, uncovered, unprotected, bald, bleak, public, undefended; *antonyms* *(adj)* concealed, covered, hidden, safe, **2.** revealed; *synonyms* *(adj)* exposed, disclosed, discovered.

otioro round; *synonyms* *(adv)* about, around, *(adj)* circular, plump, entire, chubby, complete, *(n)* circle, bout, ring, beat, circuit, *(v)* compass, turn, gird; *antonyms* *(adj)* slim, sharp.

oto 1. bend; *synonyms* *(n)* bow, arch, arc, elbow, twist, angle, curvature, *(v)* curve, turn, crouch, stoop, crook, curl, flex, deflect; *antonyms* *(v)* straighten, square, **2.** break; *synonyms* *(v)* split, crack, burst, fail, infringe, leak, *(n)* breach, fracture, pause, rupture, stop, collapse, interruption, respite, suspension; *antonyms* *(v)* repair, obey, honor, mend, *(n)* continuation, **3.** shatter; *synonyms* *(v)* break, fragment, destroy, ruin, smash, dash, crash, blast, demolish, batter, frustrate, disintegrate, scatter, confound, quell.

otoaki 1. broken; *synonyms* *(v)* broke, *(adj)* tame, torn, busted, imperfect, intermittent, rough, rugged, ruined, uneven, disjointed, incomplete, confused, cracked, crushed; *antonyms* *(adj)* constant, unbroken, intact, whole, wild, **2.** bent; *synonyms* *(adj)* arched, curved, bended, crooked, deformed, intent, *(n)* aptitude, inclination, propensity, fancy, ability, bias, flair, gift, leaning; *antonym* *(adj)*

straight, **3.** taken; *synonyms* *(v)* take, *(adj)* occupied, full, interpreted, besotted, crazed, enamored, engaged, interested, lovesick, obsessed, overcome, preferred, rapt, reserved, **4.** shattered; *synonyms* *(v)* exhausted, battered, lame, *(adj)* broken, destroyed, smashed, crazy, shaky.

otobebe garble; *synonyms* *(v)* distort, falsify, contort, misrepresent, twist, pervert, warp, alter, belie, color, cook.

otobebeaki garbled; *synonyms* *(adj)* disconnected, indistinct, unintelligible, confused, disjointed, disordered, incoherent, lopped, truncated, inarticulate, abrupt, baffled, befuddled, bemused, bewildered; *antonym* *(adj)* clear.

otonga shield; *synonyms* *(n)* screen, shelter, buffer, armor, protection, shade, *(v)* cover, guard, safeguard, preserve, secure, defend, hide, protect, buckler; *antonym* *(v)* expose.

otongaki shielded; *synonyms* *(adj)* protected, secure, safeguarded, defended, cloistered, enshield, enshielded, sacred, safe, secured, fortified.

otooto tuck; *synonyms* *(n)* crease, pleat, wrinkle, rapier, *(v)* fold, insert, pucker, enclose, gather, inclose, ruck.

otorao slander; *synonyms* *(n)* insult, scandal, aspersion, defamation, obloquy, disparagement, backbiting, calumny, *(v)* libel, defame, calumniate, denigrate, *(adj)* abuse, asperse, malign; *antonym* *(v)* praise.

otouia break; *synonyms* *(v)* split, crack, burst, fail, infringe, leak, *(n)* breach, fracture, pause, rupture, stop, collapse, interruption, respite, suspension; *antonyms* *(v)* repair, obey, honor, mend, *(n)* continuation.

ou 1. mad; *synonyms* *(adj)* frantic, frenzied, demented, foolish, insane, delirious, angry, crazy, distracted, frenetic, lunatic, wild, irate, *(n)* furious, anger; *antonyms* *(adj)* sane, calm, sensible, **2.** moonstruck; *synonyms* *(v)* awestruck, thunderstruck, *(adj)* deranged, maddened, sentimental, **3.** imbecile; *synonyms* *(adj)* idiotic, fatuous, imbecilic, simple, *(n)* fool, idiot, moron, cretin, ass, oaf, changeling, **4.** insane; *synonyms* *(adj)* daft, mad, nutty, irrational, possessed, psychotic, rabid, harebrained, **5.** lunatic; *synonyms* *(n)* mental, moonstruck, *(n)* madman, madcap, maniac, nut, daredevil, hothead, **6.** idiot; *synonyms* *(n)* dolt, dunce, dimwit, imbecile, dumbbell, half-wit, innocent, jerk, natural.

ouena brother; *synonyms* *(n)* fellow, pal, associate, buddy, chum, companion, compeer, comrade, counterpart, crony, friend, mate, monk, peer, sidekick; *antonym* *(n)* sister.

ouiponi eighty; *synonym* *(n)* fourscore.

oukia extinguish; *synonyms* *(v)* destroy, exterminate, quench, annihilate, douse, eradicate, consume, end, suppress, quash, devastate, crush, decimate, efface, *(adj)* allay; *antonyms (v)* light, ignite.

oukoumi skin; *synonyms (n)* peel, hide, coating, fur, hull, rind, shell, crust, integument, pelt, *(v)* pare, bark, scrape, excoriate, flay.

ourouake 1. tear; *synonyms (n)* split, rupture, rent, *(v)* break, rip, crack, pull, rend, lacerate, race, run, rush, slit, rive, cleave, **2.** rip; *synonyms (v)* cut, gash, scratch, claw, charge, hack, pluck, *(n)* tear, bust, rake, slash, debauchee, profligate, roue, scamp.

outi 1. carry; *synonyms (v)* bear, bring, convey, conduct, take, acquit, behave, accept, comport, hold, pack, transport, load, assume, admit, **2.** day; *synonyms (n)* light, daylight, generation, age, daytime, epoch, time, crisis; *antonyms (n)* nighttime, night.

Ô

ôgua tired; *synonyms (adj)* exhausted, fatigued, hackneyed, weary, banal, commonplace, stale, threadbare, trite, beat, haggard, jaded, stock, worn, drowsy; *antonyms (adj)* fresh, invigorated, alert, refreshed, energetic, original, strong.

ôkua whale; *synonyms (n)* giant, monster, behemoth, heavyweight, hulk, *(v)* thrash, beat, *(adj)* cachalot.

ôn full; *synonyms (adj)* complete, absolute, abundant, broad, flush, ample, enough, extensive, total, detailed, comprehensive, copious, good, *(n)* entire, crowded; *antonyms (adj)* empty, lacking, starving, hungry, sketchy, incomplete.

ôra shallow; *synonyms (adj)* shoal, superficial, low, cursory, petty, little, sketchy, flimsy, frivolous, simple, surface, dull, mean, airy, facile; *antonyms (adj)* deep, bottomless.

ôrara 1. tired; *synonyms (adj)* exhausted, fatigued, hackneyed, weary, banal, commonplace, stale, threadbare, trite, beat, haggard, jaded, stock, worn, drowsy; *antonyms (adj)* fresh, invigorated, alert, refreshed, energetic, original, strong, **2.** wearied; *synonyms (v)* awearied, *(adj)* spent, tired, dead, limp, prostrate.

ôt thither; *synonyms (adv)* there, hither, whither, *(adj)* further, remoter, succeeding, ulterior, farther.

P

paha thunder; *synonyms (n)* boom, bang, roll, bellow, clap, *(v)* roar, howl, rumble, fulminate, blast, storm, growl, *(adj)* peal, explode, detonate.

pahia lamp; *synonyms (n)* light, look, beacon, view, glance, alfalfa, glimpse, lucern, *(v)* behold, regard, perceive, gape, gaze, inspect, observe.

pake hunger; *synonyms (n)* desire, thirst, appetite, craving, wish, itch, eagerness, famine, longing, starvation, *(v)* crave, want, ache, long, lust; *antonym (n)* moderation.

pakenge box; *synonyms (n)* basket, cage, chest, package, booth, blow, carton, case, container, crate, envelope, *(v)* cuff, buffet, beat, fight; *antonym (v)* unbox.

pakoa shark; *synonyms (n)* cheat, fraud, swindler, charlatan, crook, harpy, trickster, thug, predator, wizard, expert, master, professional, scavenger, *(v)* lend.

panga reef; *synonyms (n)* ledge, rock, ait, eyot, isle, islet, bank, rand, *(v)* slow.

pange chin; *synonyms (n)* talk, jaw, jawbone, rap, mentum, button, cheek, chops, mouth, point, *(v)* speak, confer, utter.

pañi chin; *synonyms (n)* talk, jaw, jawbone, rap, mentum, button, cheek, chops, mouth, point, *(v)* speak, confer, utter.

paouare 1. spit; *synonyms (n)* broach, saliva, cape, expectoration, spittle, *(v)* drizzle, impale, expectorate, skewer, spew, sprinkle, drool, spike, hiss, spatter, **2.** saliva; *synonyms (n)* spit, sputum, slabber, belch, dig, eject, spade, spadeful, spital, spitting, tongue.

papa cheek; *synonyms (n)* audacity, boldness, brass, face, impertinence, nerve, gall, impudence, insolence, lip, mouth, daring, disrespect, effrontery, jowl; *antonym (n)* respect.

para 1. helmet; *synonyms (n)* casque, helm, hood, cowl, hat, *(v)* headpiece, pickelhaube, armor, aegis, apron, backplate, brains, breastplate, brigandine, buckler, **2.** hat; *synonyms (n)* cap, chapeau, lid, sou'wester, bonus, eyelid, palpebra, *(adj)* hot, **3.** cap; *synonyms (n)* cover, bonnet, capital, base, ceiling, crest, detonator, tip, closure, coif, *(v)* top, beat, limit, surpass, better, **4.** hairdo; *synonyms (n)* coiffure, hairstyle, style, **5.** shell; *synonyms (n)* peel, rind, bullet, case, casing, sheath, bark, carcass, crust, shot, *(v)* bomb, bombard, husk, pod, blast.

pare dirty; *synonyms (adj)* foul, dirt, contemptible, bawdy, contaminated, dingy, impure, despicable, *(v)* muddy, corrupt, soil, contaminate, begrime, bemire, (n) defile; *antonyms* (adj) hygienic, pure, spotless, immaculate, (v) clean.

pari nose; *synonyms* (n) beak, hooter, nozzle, proboscis, honker, bow, (v) pry, scent, sniff, wind, nuzzle, search, smell, snoop, poke.

paro inside; *synonyms* (adv) indoors, inwardly, within, (n) interior, middle, center, stomach, bosom, contents, (adj) inner, internal, indoor, inland, inward, private; *antonyms* (prep) outside, (n) exterior, (adj) free.

pei arm; *synonyms* (n) branch, wing, bay, department, division, limb, might, offshoot, power, section, sleeve, (v) equip, furnish, outfit, provide; *antonym* (v) disarm.

peka defecate; *synonyms* (v) clarify, dung, shit, crap, clear, excrete, refine, stool, attain, betray, bricks, build, cause, constitute, construct.

pekanikai ejaculate; *synonyms* (n) cum, seed, semen, (v) blurt, discharge, cry, exclaim, come, jaculate, excrete, blunder, climax, expel, utter, dart.

pen coconut; *synonyms* (n) coco, cocoanut, head.

penoua 1. island; *synonyms* (n) reef, aisle, egg, inch, (v) isle, insulate, isolate, segregate, sequester, separate, **2.** land; *synonyms* (n) ground, country, soil, field, kingdom, domain, estate, nation, realm, state, (v) disembark, debark, alight, get, drop; *antonym* (adj) aquatic.

piloto abdomen; *synonyms* (n) belly, stomach, venter, gut, breadbasket, guts, corporation, intestines, middle, midsection, pot, potbelly.

piroto 1. stomach; *synonyms* (n) abdomen, appetite, belly, breadbasket, inclination, (v) accept, brook, abide, bear, endure, stand, suffer, take, tolerate, (adj) digest, **2.** belly; *synonyms* (n) stomach, inside, bowels, intestines, waist, entrails, gut, paunch, venter, (v) balloon, swell, billow, bloat, bulge.

po close; *synonyms* (adj) near, adjacent, nearby, accurate, tight, approximate, narrow, (v) compact, stop, conclude, (adv) by, about, (n) end, finish, conclusion; *antonyms* (adj) distant, airy, fresh, loose, far, (v) open, start.

poenatma paddle; *synonyms* (n) blade, oar, vane, (v) dabble, dodder, row, pull, spank, toddle, totter, coggle, larrup.

poêtua 1. rudder; *synonyms* (n) helm, wheel, guide, tail, controls, **2.** paddle; *synonyms* (n) blade, oar, vane, (v) dabble, dodder, row, pull, spank, toddle, totter, coggle, larrup.

pong night; *synonyms* (n) dark, evening, dusk, darkness, nighttime, twilight, (adj) nocturnal; *antonyms* (n) day, light.

popihi sing; *synonyms* (v) chant, hymn, chirp, hum, drone, pipe, twitter, vocalize, carol, snitch, betray, harmonize, poetize, squeal, (n) squeak.

poua mouth; *synonyms* (n) jaw, lip, aperture, lips, edge, entrance, brim, (v) grimace, articulate, pronounce, speak, utter, vocalize, blab, deliver.

pouai favorite; *synonyms* (adj) favored, favourite, beloved, dear, (n) darling, choice, pet, pick, preference, competitor, dearie, deary, ducky; *antonyms* (n) loser, indifference.

poue rudder; *synonyms* (n) helm, wheel, guide, tail, controls.

pouki buttocks; *synonyms* (n) backside, bottom, arse, ass, bum, behind, butt, nates, posterior, rear, rump, tail, anus, base, can.

pouno deaf; *synonyms* (adj) earless, blind, indifferent, unhearing, aspirated, atonic, deve, inattentive, oblivious, regardless, surd, thoughtless, unaware, unconcerned, (v) deafen; *antonym* (adj) hearing.

pourai feather; *synonyms* (n) pen, pinion, plume, feathering, kind, plumage, spline, (v) fringe, cover, fledge, (adj) bulrush.

poutahi excrement; *synonyms* (n) dejection, faeces, dirt, evacuation, dung, excretion, ordure, excreta, (adj) feces.

pouto navel; *synonyms* (n) bellybutton, center, umbilicus, nave, omphalos, omphalus.

pü only; *synonyms* (adv) alone, but, exclusively, just, merely, barely, entirely, simply, however, (adj) exclusive, individual, lone, one, sole, all.

pumping 1. muscular; *synonyms* (adj) athletic, brawny, strong, burly, hefty, powerful, robust, husky, stalwart, stout, sturdy, manly, cogent, hardy, rugged; *antonyms* (adj) puny, slight, **2.** strong; *synonyms* (adj) intense, able, deep, firm, stable, steady, durable, forcible, good, hard, influential, lusty, potent, rigid, secure; *antonyms* (adj) weak, bland, delicate, faint, feeble, frail, mild, pale, unconvincing, cowardly, diluted, dull, exhausted, flimsy, imperceptible.

pün merely; *synonyms* (adv) just, only, but, simply, barely, exclusively, purely, alone, exactly, absolutely, solely, hardly.

punâ voice; *synonyms* (n) speech, sound, language, part, suffrage, vote, (v) enunciate, express, pronounce, say, speak, utter, vocalize, articulate, state.

R

r l; *synonyms* (n) litre, angle, ell, lambert, liter, wing, (adj) fifty.

ra 1. denuded; *synonyms* (adj) bare, naked, bald, denudate, exposed, barefaced, barren, bleak, devoid, desolate, marginal, nude, scanty, spare, (v) minus, **2.** inauspicious; *synonyms* (adj) ominous, unlucky, adverse, ill, sinister, untoward, unfavorable, unfortunate, bad, evil, fateful, ill-fated, threatening, harmful, inopportune; *antonyms* (*adj*) auspicious, favorable, **3.** naked; *synonyms* (*adj*) open, raw, unclothed, defenseless, defenceless, undraped, alone, denuded, destitute, mere, simple, stark, unaided, unvarnished; *antonyms* (*adj*) covered, concealed, **4.** deserted; *synonyms* (*adj*) abandoned, desert, solitary, derelict, empty, forsaken, isolated, lonely, lonesome, vacant, secluded, disused, uninhabited, unoccupied, (*v*) forlorn; *antonyms* (*adj*) inhabited, occupied, packed, **5.** nearly; *synonyms* (*adv*) almost, about, close, approximately, closely, virtually, around, intimately, nigh, practically, roughly, much, (*adj*) near, most, thereabouts, **6.** disagreeable; *synonyms* (*adj*) difficult, distasteful, nasty, offensive, uncomfortable, cantankerous, cross, ungrateful, abhorrent, bitter, horrible, objectionable, obnoxious, painful, sour; *antonyms* (*adj*) agreeable, friendly, pleasant, good-natured, amiable, **7.** bad; *synonyms* (*adj*) immoral, naughty, poisonous, sad, wicked, malicious, infamous, appalling, awful, damaging, devilish, disagreeable, dreadful, hurtful, (*v*) decayed; *antonyms* (*adj*) fresh, well, well-behaved, (*n*) good, **8.** impure; *synonyms* (*adj*) defiled, dirty, bastard, filthy, foul, sordid, squalid, unclean, profane, contaminated, indecent, lewd, libidinous, licentious, muddy; *antonym* (*adj*) pure, **9.** incomplete; *synonyms* (*adj*) defective, deficient, faulty, imperfect, inadequate, halfway, lacking, short, unfinished, half, insufficient, fragmentary, sketchy, scarce, (*n*) rough; *antonyms* (*adj*) complete, finished, whole, **10.** barren; *synonyms* (*adj*) infertile, sterile, deserted, abortive, arid, dry, fruitless, meagre, void, dead, effete, idle, meager, poor, (*v*) lean; *antonyms* (*adj*) fertile, lush, productive, **11.** improper; *synonyms* (*adj*) false, inappropriate, illicit, illegitimate, coarse, indecorous, unsuitable, wrong, amiss, undue, gross, impolite, inapt, incongruous, incorrect; *antonyms* (*adj*) proper, suitable, fitting, polite, **12.** constrained; *synonyms* (*adj*) uneasy, bound, forced, stiff, strained, awkward, compelled, limited, affected, confined, cramped, restricted, rigid, stilted; *antonyms* (*adj*) free, unrestricted, **13.** defective; *synonyms* (*adj*) broken, incomplete, unsound, vicious, inaccurate, rotten, erroneous, flawed, lame, wanting; *antonym* (*adj*) perfect, **14.** destitute; *synonyms* (*adj*) indigent, bankrupt, broke, impoverished, needy, helpless, impecunious, necessitous, penniless, depressed, deprived, miserable, abject, disadvantaged, underprivileged; *antonym* (*adj*) rich, **15.** sail; *synonyms* (*n*) float, voyage, canvas, sheet, plane, ship, (*v*) cruise, navigate, run, glide, drift, sweep, travel, fly, soar, **16.** unfavorable; *synonyms* (*adj*)

inauspicious, detrimental, disadvantageous, inimical, contrary, hostile, unfavourable, unfriendly, calamitous, conflicting, discouraging, infelicitous, intrusive, prejudicial, timeless, **17.** stripped; *synonyms* (*adj*) fleeced, undressed.

raa bad; *synonyms* (*adj*) evil, adverse, harmful, immoral, naughty, poisonous, sad, sinister, wicked, malicious, infamous, appalling, awful, damaging, (*v*) decayed; *antonyms* (*adj*) fresh, pleasant, well, well-behaved, (*n*) good.

raba 1. agreeable; *synonyms* (*adj*) acceptable, accordant, pleasant, pleasing, nice, affable, amusing, compatible, conformable, congenial, consistent, enjoyable, genial, grateful, (*v*) desirable; *antonyms* (*adj*) disagreeable, discordant, nasty, unpleasant, unwilling, aggressive, resistant, **2.** excellent; *synonyms* (*adj*) choice, estimable, admirable, superior, capital, beautiful, distinctive, brilliant, fantastic, fine, good, great, magnificent, marvelous, (*n*) worthy; *antonyms* (*adj*) inferior, poor, abysmal, awful, mediocre, **3.** good; *synonyms* (*adj*) able, benefit, delicious, right, efficient, capable, excellent, well, advantageous, agreeable, generous, gentle, (*n*) benign, advantage, gain; *antonyms* (*adj*) disobedient, wicked, (*n*) evil, bad, **4.** appreciated; *synonyms* (*adj*) understood, comprehended, prized, respected, valued, welcome, aesthetic, apprehended, esteemed, gratifying, satisfying, valuable, artistic, cheering, cherished; *antonym* (*adj*) unwelcome, **5.** pleasant; *synonyms* (*adj*) bright, amiable, charming, jolly, kindly, facetious, attractive, cheerful, clear, comfortable, delightful, fair, joyful, joyous, kind; *antonyms* (*adj*) disgusting, foul, gruesome, harsh, horrible, repugnant, shocking, terrible, appalling, frosty, grisly, rough.

rababa 1. broad; *synonyms* (*adj*) wide, ample, comprehensive, extensive, general, large, sweeping, vast, free, big, blanket, capacious, deep, full, (*n*) female; *antonyms* (*adj*) narrow, specific, thin, **2.** spacious; *synonyms* (*adj*) roomy, broad, commodious, expansive, extended, liberal, open, airy, comfortable, sizable, voluminous, convenient; *antonym* (*adj*) cramped.

rababaua 1. flatten; *synonyms* (*v*) fell, demolish, level, press, even, drop, roll, squash, depress, destroy, ruin, smash, smooth, unfold, bulldoze; *antonyms* (*v*) build, crumple, **2.** flat; *synonyms* (*adj*) dull, bland, plain, insipid, plane, tasteless, dreary, boring, absolute, dead, downright, equal, fixed, (*n*) apartment, (*v*) uninteresting; *antonyms* (*adj*) exciting, high-pitched, bumpy.

rababauaki flattened; *synonyms* (*adj*) compressed, depressed, planate, trodden, unconscious, compacted, firmed, trampled; *antonym* (*adj*) loose.

rabakai 1. artistic; *synonyms* (*adj*) esthetic, aesthetic, elegant, ingenious, pleasing, attic, creative,

imaginative, inventive, tasteful, **2.** competent;
synonyms *(adj)* able, capable, adequate, clever,
effective, efficient, fit, sufficient, commensurate,
accomplished, adept, appropriate, enough,
experienced, good; *antonyms* *(adj)* incompetent,
useless, inept, **3.** ingenious; *synonyms* *(adj)* adroit,
artful, cunning, deft, expert, cute, acute, canny,
handy, bright, artistic, crafty, gifted, original,
resourceful; *antonym* *(adj)* unimaginative, **4.**
smart; *synonyms* *(adj)* dapper, quick, shrewd, sly,
prompt, astute, chic, intelligent, jaunty, lively,
natty, *(v)* ache, hurt, *(n)* pain, sharp; *antonyms* *(adj)*
scruffy, stupid, dim, shabby, unkempt, slow, **5.**
quick; *synonyms* *(adj)* active, agile, hasty, nimble,
speedy, alert, alive, cursory, dexterous,
expeditious, hurried, immediate, instant, keen, *(adv)*
fast; *antonyms* *(adj)* leisurely, dull, **6.** tricky;
synonyms *(adj)* deceitful, delicate, difficult, foxy,
shifty, slippery, wily, complicated, designing,
dodgy, guileful, hard, scheming, slick, ticklish;
antonyms *(adj)* easy, straightforward, honest, **7.**
skillful; *synonyms* *(adj)* proficient, knowing, apt,
practiced, ready, skilled, nice, competent, skilful,
fine, practised, gracious, sagacious, *(v)* judicious, *(n)*
neat; *antonym* *(adj)* clumsy.

rabakau 1. informed; *synonyms* *(adj)* aware,
cognizant, educated, conscious, knowledgeable,
familiar, apprised, wise, conversant, experienced,
(adv) abreast; *antonym* *(adj)* ignorant, **2.**
competent; *synonyms* *(adj)* able, capable,
adequate, clever, effective, efficient, fit, sufficient,
commensurate, accomplished, adept, appropriate,
enough, good, professional; *antonyms* *(adj)*
incompetent, useless, inept, **3.** knowing;
synonyms *(v)* canny, *(adj)* astute, crafty, bright,
ingenious, intelligent, smart, understanding,
erudite, foxy, deliberate, intentional, sagacious,
sharp, *(n)* cunning, **4.** learned; *synonyms* *(v)*
knowing, *(adj)* enlightened, academic, scholarly,
bookish, cultured, intellectual, lettered, literary,
studious, informed, literate, sage, skilled, skillful;
antonym *(adj)* innate, **5.** clever; *synonyms* *(adj)*
adroit, acute, apt, expert, quick, artful, learned,
brainy, cagey, cagy, competent, dexterous, gifted,
(v) brilliant, brisk; *antonyms* *(adj)* stupid, clumsy,
unintelligent, dim, dull, **6.** bright; *synonyms* *(adj)*
clear, alive, vivid, beaming, light, luminous,
lustrous, shining, shiny, sunny, gorgeous, nimble,
auspicious, blithe, airy; *antonyms* *(adj)* cloudy,
dark, dreary, gloomy, overcast, shadowy, leaden,
slow, thick, **7.** enlightened; *synonyms* *(adj)* liberal,
disillusioned, progressive, refined, *(v)* savant,
shrewd; *antonyms* *(adj)* mystified, puzzled,
unenlightened, **8.** ingenious; *synonyms* *(adj)*
creative, deft, imaginative, cute, inventive, handy,
artistic, original, resourceful, sly, subtle, inspired,
neat, witty, discerning; *antonym* *(adj)*

unimaginative, **9.** apt; *synonyms* *(adj)* apropos,
apposite, convenient, ready, disposed, fitting,
happy, just, liable, likely, opportune, pertinent,
prompt, proper, suitable; *antonym* *(adj)*
inappropriate, **10.** capable; *synonyms* *(adj)*
proficient, qualified, trained, consummate,
powerful, strong, talented; *antonyms* *(adj)*
incapable, unable, **11.** expert; *synonyms* *(adj)* ace,
practiced, veteran, specialist, facile, *(n)* critic,
authority, connoisseur, dab, whiz, wizard, arbiter,
genius, dabster, *(v)* judge; *antonyms* *(adj)* unskilled,
inferior, untrained, *(n)* amateur, beginner, **12.**
talented; *synonyms* *(adj)* versatile, promising,
felicitous, **13.** skillful; *synonyms* *(adj)* nice, slick,
skilful, fine, practised, gracious, workmanlike,
benevolent, discreet, excellent, full, honorable,
prudent, *(v)* judicious, cautious, **14.** sagacious;
synonyms *(adj)* rational, keen, perspicacious, politic,
sapient, perceptive, reasonable, deep, farsighted,
provident, sane, penetrating, profound, sensible,
wily; *antonym* *(adj)* foolish, **15.** wise; *synonyms*
(adj) sound, thoughtful, diplomatic, logical, tactful,
considered, philosophical, sensitive, *(n)* method,
manner, way; *antonym* *(adj)* unwise, **16.** skilled;
synonyms *(adj)* old, sophisticated, versed, perfect,
masterly, crack, masterful; *antonym* *(adj)*
inexperienced, **17.** proficient; *synonyms* *(adj)*
finished, *(n)* master.

rabakei learn; *synonyms* *(v)* discover, get, know, find,
ascertain, have, hear, determine, acquire, con,
perceive, study, tell, understand, gather.

rabakeiaki learned; *synonyms* *(v)* knowing, *(adj)*
erudite, educated, enlightened, knowledgeable,
wise, academic, scholarly, bookish, cultured,
intellectual, lettered, literary, studious, informed;
antonyms *(adj)* ignorant, innate.

rabana huge; *synonyms* *(adj)* big, enormous, gigantic,
immense, large, vast, colossal, extensive, great,
elephantine, ample, considerable, excessive,
gargantuan, giant; *antonyms* *(adj)* tiny,
insignificant, miniature, small.

rabanako elude; *synonyms* *(v)* evade, circumvent,
avoid, dodge, duck, escape, skirt, baffle, defy, bilk,
parry, shirk, sidestep, frustrate, deflect.

rabane 1. maintain; *synonyms* *(v)* continue, justify,
affirm, allege, assert, aver, conserve, declare,
defend, guard, hold, keep, preserve, bear, insist;
antonyms *(v)* deny, change, **2.** guard; *synonyms*
(n) defense, bulwark, care, cover, escort, protection,
watchman, custody, convoy, defence, fender,
guardsman, safeguard, vigilance, *(v)* shield, **3.**
hold; *synonyms* *(v)* detain, endure, adhere,
comprise, contain, entertain, have, arrest, carry,
confine, delay, *(n)* grasp, grip, clasp, clutch;
antonym *(v)* release, **4.** keep; *synonyms* *(v)* retain,
maintain, celebrate, observe, reserve, save,

commemorate, check, harbor, direct, rear, restrain, store, (*n*) maintenance, subsistence; *antonyms* (*v*) dump, lose, **5.** preserve; *synonyms* (*v*) cure, pickle, protect, uphold, perpetuate, sustain, economise, economize, husband, deliver, (*n*) jam, jelly, conserves, marmalade, shelter; *antonym* (*v*) destroy.

rabaneaki 1. held; *synonyms* (*adj*) absorbed, confined, alleged, assumed, believed, bound, caged, captive, detained, fast, immersed, obsessed, occupied, protected, (*adv*) on, **2.** maintained; *synonyms* (*adj*) retained, fixed, repaired, safe, serviced, reconditioned, shipshape, trim, **3.** guarded; *synonyms* (*adj*) cautious, careful, wary, chary, circumspect, cagey, vigilant, watchful, conditional, discreet, gingerly, conservative, prudent, reserved, inhibited; *antonyms* (*adj*) frank, honest, **4.** preserved; *synonyms* (*adj*) condite, pickled, whole, potted, sealed.

rabaraba 1. completing; *synonyms* (*adj*) complementary, complemental, final, consummative, definitive, interchangeable, reciprocal, (*n*) implementation, effecting, **2.** finishing; *synonyms* (*adj*) ending, closing, last, ultimate, (*n*) finish, completion, close, conclusion, end, coating.

rabaroa covered; *synonyms* (*adj*) hidden, veiled, concealed, covert, coated, masked, obscured, secret, shrouded, thick, wrapped, (*prep*) cloaked; *antonyms* (*adj*) bare, naked.

rabata principal; *synonyms* (*adj*) master, cardinal, capital, leading, primary, grand, first, foremost, prime, great, (*n*) chief, head, leader, main, manager; *antonym* (*adj*) minor.

rabáta body; *synonyms* (*n*) cadaver, corpse, matter, organization, carcass, cluster, consistency, figure, mass, set, aggregate, association, entity, amount, bulk; *antonym* (*n*) spirit.

rabati hug; *synonyms* (*n*) embrace, hold, clinch, (*v*) clasp, cuddle, squeeze, cling, cherish, clutch, grasp, touch, adhere, gripe, clench, bosom.

rabatia 1. embrace; *synonyms* (*v*) comprise, clasp, hug, admit, adopt, comprehend, contain, cover, encompass, espouse, grip, include, (*n*) bosom, clutch, cuddle; *antonym* (*v*) reject, **2.** hug; *synonyms* (*n*) embrace, hold, clinch, caress, (*v*) squeeze, cling, cherish, grasp, touch, adhere, gripe, clench, lock, press, stick, **3.** grapple; *synonyms* (*v*) fight, tackle, contend, grab, deal, seize, struggle, wrestle, cope, snatch, (*n*) grapnel, grappling, grappler, (*adj*) hook, latch.

rabe 1. abrupt; *synonyms* (*adj*) sudden, brusque, sharp, precipitous, steep, disconnected, discourteous, gruff, hasty, immediate, instant, instantaneous, swift, unexpected, (*n*) bold; *antonyms* (*adj*) civil, gentle, gradual, gracious, rambling, **2.** beveled; *synonyms* (*adj*) bevel, cant,

diagonal, **3.** italic, **4.** hilly; *synonyms* (*adj*) craggy, mountainous, rugged, cragged, knobby, prominent, tumulous, high, tumulose, **5.** sloping; *synonyms* (*adj*) oblique, slanting, aslant, aslope, inclined, slanted, leaning, sloped, slope, tilted, declivous, (*v*) slant, (*adv*) sideways; *antonym* (*adj*) level, **6.** sloped; *synonyms* (*adj*) sloping, biased, coloured, **7.** slanting; *synonyms* (*adj*) askew, awry, indirect, **8.** sheer; *synonyms* (*adj*) absolute, pure, mere, diaphanous, filmy, gauzy, gossamer, simple, transparent, regular, perpendicular, flimsy, (*n*) complete, perfect, entire; *antonym* (*adj*) thick.

raben 1. lean; *synonyms* (*adj*) emaciated, gaunt, thin, bony, lank, lanky, (*v*) incline, bend, list, slant, bow, careen, pitch, (*n*) tilt, inclination; *antonyms* (*adj*) fat, plump, **2.** veer; *synonyms* (*v*) turn, shift, swerve, deviate, curve, change, sheer, slew, trend, slide, deflect, swing, wander, bear, cut.

rabeniben 1. tilt; *synonyms* (*n*) slope, list, bend, inclination, joust, sway, (*v*) incline, lean, pitch, slant, careen, rock, cant, lurch, tip; *antonyms* (*v*) straighten, surrender, **2.** oscillate; *synonyms* (*v*) fluctuate, swing, vibrate, hesitate, wag, alternate, quiver, shake, tremble, vacillate, vary, wave, waver, wobble.

rabenibenaki tilted; *synonyms* (*adj*) canted, leaning, slanting, oblique, crooked, slanted, atilt, askew, intolerant, lopsided, opinionated, tipped, uneven, twisted; *antonym* (*adj*) straight.

rabete dim; *synonyms* (*adj*) dark, obscure, cloudy, dull, bleak, dense, faint, gloomy, (*v*) blur, darken, cloud, pale, tarnish, blear, blind; *antonyms* (*adj*) bright, brilliant, intelligent, clever, strong, (*v*) clear, brighten.

rabi 1. curved; *synonyms* (*adj*) bent, crooked, curve, round, bend, curving, curvy, deformed, hooked, rounded, tortuous, twisted, (*v*) bowed; *antonyms* (*adj*) straight, concave, **2.** coiled; *synonyms* (*adj*) curled, spiral, curved, curly, kinky, tortile, twisting, wavy, arched, corkscrew, warped, wreathed, (*v*) helical, **3.** bent; *synonyms* (*adj*) bended, intent, set, (*n*) aptitude, inclination, propensity, fancy, ability, bias, flair, gift, leaning, mind, proclivity, endowment, **4.** concave; *synonyms* (*adj*) hollow, cavernous, crescent, biconcave, cupped, dipped, depress, dishing, vaulted, vaulty, deceitful, deep, dented, dimpled, (*v*) dig; *antonym* (*adj*) convex, **5.** arched; *synonyms* (*adj*) arcuate, arciform, arced, **6.** wavy; *synonyms* (*adj*) crinkled, crinkly, corrugated, undulating, waved, rippled, wavelike; *antonym* (*adj*) smooth.

rabino 1. tumble; *synonyms* (*n*) fall, drop, (*v*) jumble, stumble, collapse, crumble, plunge, slip, spill, topple, confuse, downfall, toss, crash, crumple, **2.** roll; *synonyms* (*n*) list, revolution, catalogue, inventory, register, (v) coil, reel, curl, enfold, revolve, wheel, rock, turn, twist, wallow.

rabinoaki 1. rolled; *synonyms* (*adj*) rolling, furled, involute, beaten, billowing, kinky, level, resonant, resonating, resounding, reverberating, reverberative, spiral, trilled, tumbling, **2**. tumbled; *synonyms* (*adj*) disordered, upset.

rabinobina revolve; *synonyms* (*v*) reel, consider, deliberate, meditate, ponder, circle, circulate, contemplate, orbit, return, rotate, spin, wheel, (*n*) gyrate, roll.

rabinobinaki revolved; *synonyms* (*adj*) rotated, disgusted.

rabinobino roll; *synonyms* (*n*) list, revolution, catalogue, inventory, register, (*v*) coil, reel, curl, enfold, revolve, wheel, rock, turn, twist, wallow.

rabinobinoaki rolled; *synonyms* (*adj*) rolling, furled, involute, beaten, billowing, kinky, level, resonant, resonating, resounding, reverberating, reverberative, spiral, trilled, tumbling.

rabirabi 1. bent; *synonyms* (*adj*) arched, curved, bended, crooked, deformed, intent, (*n*) aptitude, inclination, propensity, fancy, ability, bias, flair, gift, leaning; *antonym* (*adj*) straight, **2**. concave; *synonyms* (*adj*) hollow, cavernous, crescent, biconcave, cupped, dipped, depress, dishing, vaulted, vaulty, deceitful, deep, dented, (*v*) curve, dig; *antonym* (*adj*) convex, **3**. curved; *synonyms* (*adj*) bent, round, bend, curving, curvy, hooked, rounded, tortuous, twisted, (*v*) bowed; *antonym* (*adj*) concave, **4**. coiled; *synonyms* (*adj*) curled, spiral, curly, kinky, tortile, twisting, wavy, corkscrew, warped, wreathed, (*v*) helical, **5**. arched; *synonyms* (*adj*) arcuate, arciform, arced, **6**. wavy; *synonyms* (*adj*) crinkled, crinkly, corrugated, undulating, waved, rippled, wavelike; *antonym* (*adj*) smooth.

rabóna eel; *synonyms* (*n*) yeel, (*v*) labyrinth, maze, serpent.

rabu 1. forbidden; *synonyms* (*adj*) unlawful, banned, illegal, prohibited, taboo, contraband, illicit, proscribed, verboten; *antonym* (*adj*) acceptable, **2**. booked; *synonyms* (*adj*) reserved, affianced, bespoken, betrothed, destined, engaged, future, intermeshed, meshed, occupied, pledged, **3**. covered; *synonyms* (*adj*) hidden, veiled, concealed, covert, coated, masked, obscured, secret, shrouded, thick, wrapped, (*prep*) cloaked; *antonyms* (*adj*) bare, naked, **4**. reserved; *synonyms* (*adj*) modest, distant, coy, diffident, reticent, bashful, aloof, frigid, quiet, retiring, shy, formal, humble, moderate, (*n*) cold; *antonyms* (*adj*) outgoing, open, forthcoming, relaxed, uninhibited, warm, **5**. protected; *synonyms* (*v*) disguised, hid, (*adj*) secure, immune, saved, secured, sheltered,

covered, comfortable, confined, cosseted, dependable, good, guaranteed, impregnable.

rabua reserve; *synonyms* (*n*) backup, modesty, reservation, substitute, bank, cache, diffidence, hoard, (*v*) keep, save, book, maintain, appropriate, engage, hold; *antonyms* (*n*) openness, friendliness, informality, warmth.

rabuaki reserved; *synonyms* (*adj*) modest, distant, coy, diffident, reticent, bashful, aloof, frigid, quiet, retiring, shy, formal, humble, moderate, (*n*) cold; *antonyms* (*adj*) outgoing, open, forthcoming, relaxed, uninhibited, warm.

rabuna 1. clothe; *synonyms* (*v*) array, dress, apparel, cover, garb, clad, arrange, deck, invest, vest, wrap, adorn, fit, rig, (*n*) attire; *antonym* (*v*) undress, **2**. mask; *synonyms* (*n*) conceal, veil, camouflage, screen, blind, guise, curtain, pretense, blanket, masque, (*v*) cloak, disguise, hide, dissemble, masquerade; *antonym* (*v*) disclose, **3**. forbid; *synonyms* (*v*) debar, prohibit, ban, bar, disallow, exclude, deny, avert, frustrate, inhibit, interdict, outlaw, prevent, proscribe, veto; *antonyms* (*v*) permit, allow, let, approve, **4**. cover; *synonyms* (*v*) coat, top, bury, comprise, bind, (*n*) binding, cap, covering, lid, mask, shield, spread, coating, canopy, case; *antonyms* (*v*) reveal, expose, uncover, **5**. shelter; *synonyms* (*n*) guard, refuge, asylum, harbor, protect, protection, sanctuary, security, hut, covert, haven, shade, (*v*) defend, keep, (*adj*) defense, **6**. protect; *synonyms* (*v*) preserve, conserve, maintain, safeguard, save, vindicate, insure, hold, cushion, patronize, shelter, ensure, fence, guarantee, (*n*) ward; *antonyms* (*v*) attack, neglect, risk, **7**. stifle; *synonyms* (*v*) choke, repress, smother, suffocate, dampen, extinguish, muffle, quell, strangle, asphyxiate, check, contain, gag, silence, suppress, **8**. wrap; *synonyms* (*v*) envelop, enfold, roll, shroud, swathe, wind, enclose, drape, enwrap, involve, surround, twine, cocoon, (*n*) wrapping, cape; *antonym* (*v*) unwrap.

rabunaki 1. clothed; *synonyms* (*v*) accustomed, arrayed, habited, (*adj*) clad, dressed, wrapped, cloaked, robed, absorbed, decent, draped, mantled, vested, vestured, disguised; *antonym* (*adj*) undressed, **2**. forbidden; *synonyms* (*adj*) unlawful, banned, illegal, prohibited, taboo, contraband, illicit, proscribed, verboten; *antonym* (*adj*) acceptable, **3**. covered; *synonyms* (*adj*) hidden, veiled, concealed, covert, coated, masked, obscured, secret, shrouded, thick; *antonyms* (*adj*) bare, naked, **4**. masked; *synonyms* (*adj*) covered, camouflaged, **5**. sheltered; *synonyms* (*adj*) secure, comfortable, safe, screened, cozy, secluded, (*v*) protected, private; *antonym* (*adj*) desolate, **6**. wrapped; *synonyms* (*adj*) clothed, enwrapped, intent, rapt, engrossed, **7**. protected; *synonyms* (*v*) hid, *(adj)* immune, saved, secured, sheltered, confined, cosseted, dependable, good, guaranteed, impregnable, inviolable, lawful, legal, obtected, **8.** stifled; *synonyms (adj)* smothered, strangled, suppressed, muffled, dead, deadened, deaf, deafened, decayed, faint, pent-up, quiet, regardless, weak, hushed.

rabungaoa 1. hiss; *synonyms (n)* buzz, hoot, jeer, taunt, hissing, ridicule, bird, *(v)* boo, fizz, spit, sibilate, whisper, whiz, whoosh, clamor, **2.** censure; *synonyms (n)* reprimand, animadversion, attack, accusation, condemnation, criticism, *(v)* blame, accuse, abuse, reproach, berate, carp, condemn, knock, admonish; *antonyms (n)* approval, *(v)* praise, approve, commend, **3.** condemn; *synonyms (v)* censure, castigate, criticize, decry, deplore, doom, excoriate, sentence, upbraid, chide, adjudge, convict, damn, denounce, deprecate; *antonyms (v)* free, pardon, **4.** boo; *synonym (v)* hiss; *antonym (v)* applaud, **5.** disapprove; *synonyms (v)* object, deny, disallow, discountenance, refuse, reject, repudiate, decline, dislike, demur, spurn; *antonym (v)* endorse, **6.** ridicule; *synonyms (n)* derision, irony, mockery, insult, contempt, scoff, disdain, gibe, sarcasm, sneer, *(v)* banter, deride, flout, mock, scorn; *antonym (v)* respect.

rabungaoaki 1. censured; *synonyms (adj)* condemned, appropriated, guilty, confiscate, confiscated, convicted, seized, **2.** condemned; *synonyms (adj)* damned, censured, doomed, destined, **3.** disapproved; *synonyms (adj)* contraband, old-fashioned, taboo; *antonym (adj)* approved.

rabwana preserve; *synonyms (v)* maintain, keep, defend, guard, hold, save, cure, pickle, protect, uphold, *(n)* conserve, jam, jelly, conserves, marmalade; *antonym (v)* destroy.

rabwanaki preserved; *synonyms (adj)* condite, pickled, safe, whole, potted, sealed.

rae 1. inclined; *synonyms (adj)* prone, apt, oblique, willing, bowed, liable, likely, minded, predisposed, ready, bent, fain, susceptible, *(v)* given, *(prep)* disposed; *antonyms (adj)* level, reluctant, unwilling, **2.** diverted; *synonyms (adj)* amused, abstracted, entertained, inattentive, preoccupied, sidetracked, unfocused, **3.** crooked; *synonyms (adj)* awry, corrupt, irregular, askew, curved, deformed, dishonest, indirect, lopsided, unfair, unscrupulous, angular, asymmetrical, dishonorable, *(v)* wry; *antonyms (adj)* straight, honest, even, principled, **4.** rip; *synonyms (v)* cut, cleave, pull, gash, rend, scratch, *(n)* tear, bust, rake, slash, slit, split, debauchee, profligate, rent, **5.** squinting; *synonyms (adj)* squinched, *(n)* strabismus, **6.** tear; *synonyms (n)* rupture, hole, *(v)* break, rip, crack,

lacerate, race, run, rush, rive, dash, fly, pluck, shred, snap, **7.** slash; *synonyms (n)* slice, cleft, diagonal, *(v)* reduce, hack, clip, hew, wound, fell, chop, flog, lash, whip, pare, strike.

raea 1. dispersed; *synonyms (adj)* diffuse, scattered, sparse, spread, diffused, detached, discrete, fractional, rare, thin, circulated, flowing, isolated, loose, single; *antonym (adj)* concentrated, **2.** disordered; *synonyms (adj)* confused, chaotic, broken, deranged, disorganized, incoherent, messy, sick, upset, disconnected, disjointed, disorderly, ill, jumbled, mixed; *antonyms (adj)* neat, orderly, ordered, **3.** denude; *synonyms (v)* bare, strip, denudate, deprive, despoil, dismantle, disrobe, divest, expose, uncover, undress, **4.** disorganized; *synonyms (adj)* disordered, disorganised, muddled, untidy, haphazard; *antonyms (adj)* organized, methodical, **5.** rend; *synonyms (v)* cleave, pull, break, lacerate, split, divide, rive, tear, disrupt, slash, mangle, part, pluck, snap, *(n)* rip, **6.** slash; *synonyms (n)* cut, gash, slice, cleft, diagonal, scratch, *(v)* reduce, hack, clip, hew, wound, fell, chop, flog, lash, **7.** rip; *synonyms (v)* rend, claw, charge, shred, snag, wrench, *(n)* bust, rake, slit, debauchee, profligate, rent, roue, scamp, scapegrace, **8.** strip; *synonyms (n)* band, slip, ribbon, zone, *(v)* peel, plunder, rifle, denude, ransack, pillage, pare, sack, bereave, fleece, skin; *antonyms (v)* dress, decorate, **9.** torn; *synonyms (adj)* lacerated, ragged, ripped, mangled, tattered, blasted; *antonym (adj)* pristine, **10.** scattered; *synonyms (adj)* dispersed, dissipated, sporadic, distributed, separate, stray, strewn, garbled, illogical, **11.** tore; *synonyms (v)* tare, *(n)* torus, toroid, **12.** tear; *synonyms (n)* rupture, hole, laceration, rage, drop, *(v)* crack, race, run, rush, dash, fly, strain, agitate, burst, dart.

raeaeaki stripped; *synonyms (adj)* bare, naked, nude, exposed, fleeced, undressed, desolate, stark, unclothed.

raeaki 1. denuded; *synonyms (adj)* bare, naked, bald, denudate, exposed, barefaced, barren, bleak, devoid, desolate, marginal, nude, scanty, spare, *(v)* minus, **2.** torn; *synonyms (adj)* lacerated, ragged, ripped, mangled, rent, tattered, blasted, lacerate; *antonym (adj)* pristine, **3.** slashed; *synonyms (adj)* cut, gashed, torn, cheap, down, emasculated, fringed, gelded, laciniated, low, mown, shortened, strikeout, laciniate, thinned.

raeakina 1. divide; *synonyms (v)* cut, distribute, part, dissociate, apportion, detach, disconnect, dismember, dispense, separate, share, split, deal, distinguish, *(n)* break; *antonyms (v)* unite, join, **2.** portion; *synonyms (n)* division, piece, constituent, allot, component, fragment, parcel, section, dole, allowance, *(v)* lot, dividend, divide, allotment, assign, **3.** separate; *synonyms (adj)* detached, individual, particular, single, (*v*) divorce, insulate, scatter, discrete, discriminate, disjoin, disperse, isolate, demarcate, differentiate, disengage; *antonyms* (*adj*) connected, joined, simultaneous, (*v*) merge, mix, combine, fuse, link, associate, **4.** share; *synonyms* (*n*) portion, interest, proportion, ration, participation, contingent, helping, percentage, quota, dispensation, apportionment, (*v*) participate, partake, partition, allocate; *antonym* (*v*) control.

raeakinaki 1. divided; *synonyms* (*adj*) cleft, split, detached, forked, separate, separated, shared, disjointed, **2.** separated; *synonyms* (*adj*) disconnected, apart, divided, isolated, free, disjunct, removed, dislocated, independent, lone, single, (*prep*) disjoined, distinct, **3.** shared; *synonyms* (*adj*) communal, common, joint, mutual, collective, community, cooperative, reciprocal; *antonyms* (*adj*) individual, private.

raeaua 1. tear; *synonyms* (*n*) split, rupture, rent, (*v*) break, rip, crack, pull, rend, lacerate, race, run, rush, slit, rive, cleave, **2.** slash; *synonyms* (*n*) cut, gash, slice, cleft, diagonal, (*v*) reduce, hack, clip, hew, tear, wound, fell, chop, flog, lash, **3.** rip; *synonyms* (*v*) scratch, claw, charge, pluck, shred, snag, wrench, (*n*) bust, rake, slash, debauchee, profligate, roue, scamp, scapegrace.

raeauaki slashed; *synonyms* (*adj*) cut, gashed, torn, cheap, down, emasculated, fringed, gelded, laciniated, low, mown, shortened, strikeout, laciniate, thinned.

raebai dismember; *synonyms* (*v*) divide, disintegrate, dismantle, dissect, mutilate, quarter, disband, dislocate, amputate, analyse, disassemble, analyze, dispense, bestrew, broadcast.

raebaia mangle; *synonyms* (*n*) destroy, (*v*) deface, lacerate, blemish, disfigure, distort, murder, twist, batter, damage, maul, mutilate, hack, (*adj*) maim, cripple.

raebaiaki mangled; *synonyms* (*adj*) torn, lacerated, deformed, mutilated, disabled, lacerate, broken, blasted, crippled, distorted, maimed, confused, corrupted, jumbled, (*prep*) rent.

raebitia 1. mangle; *synonyms* (*n*) destroy, (*v*) deface, lacerate, blemish, disfigure, distort, murder, twist, batter, damage, maul, mutilate, hack, (*adj*) maim, cripple, **2.** lacerate; *synonyms* (*v*) rip, cut, gash, slash, mangle, tear, claw, rend, slice, torture, wound, discind, hackle, haggle, (*adj*) lacerated, **3.** tear; *synonyms* (*n*) split, rupture, rent, hole, (*v*) break, crack, pull, race, run, rush, slit, rive, cleave, dash, fly.

raebitiaki 1. mangled; *synonyms* (*adj*) torn, lacerated, deformed, mutilated, disabled, lacerate, broken, blasted, crippled, distorted, maimed, confused, corrupted, jumbled, (*prep*) rent, **2.** lacerated; *synonyms* (*adj*) hurt, mangled.

raee wry; *synonyms* (*adj*) ironic, ironical, twisted, dry, sardonic, twist, writhe, another, cynical, deadpan, erroneous, (*v*) awry, irregular, unsymmetric, asymmetric.

raeing 1. cracking; *synonyms* (*adj*) bully, corking, great, keen, neat, nifty, peachy, smashing, swell, (*n*) breaking, crack, break, fracture; *antonym* (*adj*) smooth, **2.** cracked; *synonyms* (*adj*) broken, nutty, batty, chapped, crazy, balmy, wacky, bats, crackers, crackled, crazed, deranged, dotty, insane, kookie, **3.** splitting; *synonyms* (*n*) partition, breakup, (*adj*) rending, ripping, rich.

raemangoa lacerate; *synonyms* (*v*) rip, cut, gash, slash, mangle, tear, claw, mutilate, rend, slice, torture, wound, discind, hackle, (*adj*) lacerated.

raemangoaki lacerated; *synonyms* (*adj*) lacerate, torn, rent, blasted, hurt, mangled, mutilated.

raemenga 1. dismantled; *synonyms* (*adj*) demolished, razed, **2.** dismantle; *synonyms* (*v*) demolish, destroy, strip, deprive, disassemble, disintegrate, dismember, disrobe, divest, level, raze, undress; *antonyms* (*v*) assemble, erect, raise, **3.** dislocated; *synonyms* (*adj*) disjointed, disordered, dislocate, disorderly, confused, detached, disconnected, separated, topsy-turvy, garbled, illogical, isolated, scattered, separate, spaced, **4.** break; *synonyms* (*v*) split, crack, burst, fail, infringe, leak, (*n*) breach, fracture, pause, rupture, stop, collapse, interruption, respite, suspension; *antonyms* (*v*) repair, obey, honor, mend, (*n*) continuation, **5.** broken; *synonyms* (*v*) broke, (*adj*) tame, torn, busted, imperfect, intermittent, rough, rugged, ruined, uneven, incomplete, cracked, crushed, discontinuous, faulty; *antonyms* (*adj*) constant, unbroken, intact, whole, wild, **6.** dislocate; *synonyms* (*v*) shift, displace, disjoint, disturb, move, muddle, wrench, transfer, jumble, dislodge, disorder, disorganize, slip, splay, unhinge, **7.** torn; *synonyms* (*adj*) lacerated, ragged, ripped, mangled, rent, tattered, blasted, lacerate; *antonym* (*adj*) pristine, **8.** tear; *synonyms* (*n*) hole, (*v*) break, rip, pull, rend, race, run, rush, slit, rive, cleave, dash, fly, pluck, shred.

raemengaki 1. dislocated; *synonyms* (*adj*) disjointed, disordered, dislocate, disorderly, confused, detached, disconnected, separated, topsy-turvy, garbled, illogical, isolated, scattered, separate, spaced, **2.** dismantled; *synonyms* (*adj*) demolished, razed, **3.** broken; *synonyms* (*v*) broke, (*adj*) tame, torn, busted, imperfect, intermittent, rough, rugged, ruined, uneven, incomplete, cracked, crushed, discontinuous, faulty; *antonyms* (*adj*) constant, unbroken, intact, whole, wild.

raena rip; *synonyms* (*v*) cut, cleave, pull, gash, rend, scratch, (*n*) tear, bust, rake, slash, slit, split, debauchee, profligate, rent.

raenen 1. flexible; *synonyms (adj)* elastic, adaptable, pliable, yielding, lissome, pliant, soft, supple, facile, adjustable, bendable, compliant, ductile, flexile, lithe; *antonyms (adj)* inflexible, rigid, fixed, obstinate, stiff, stubborn, **2**. pliable; *synonyms (adj)* flexible, plastic, malleable, fictile, susceptible, docile, resilient, tame, submissive, limp, springy, tractable, bendy, *(v)* limber, **3**. slim; *synonyms (adj)* slender, narrow, slight, thin, lean, remote, fine, skinny, flimsy, meager, light, feeble, *(v)* reduce, slenderize, cut; *antonyms (adj)* fat, heavy, hefty, plump, stocky, wide.

raerae 1. slash; *synonyms (n)* cut, gash, rip, slice, split, cleft, diagonal, *(v)* reduce, hack, clip, hew, tear, wound, fell, chop, **2**. rip; *synonyms (v)* cleave, pull, rend, scratch, claw, charge, lacerate, pluck, *(n)* bust, rake, slash, slit, debauchee, profligate, rent, **3**. tear; *synonyms (n)* rupture, hole, laceration, *(v)* break, crack, race, run, rush, rive, dash, fly, shred, snap, mangle, strain, **4**. strip; *synonyms (n)* band, slip, *(v)* deprive, despoil, divest, peel, plunder, rifle, denude, ransack, pillage, pare, sack, bare, bereave; *antonyms (v)* dress, decorate.

raeraea 1. lacerate; *synonyms (v)* rip, cut, gash, slash, mangle, tear, claw, mutilate, rend, slice, torture, wound, discind, hackle, *(adj)* lacerated, **2**. slash; *synonyms (n)* split, cleft, diagonal, scratch, *(v)* reduce, hack, clip, hew, fell, chop, flog, lash, slit, whip, pare, **3**. shred; *synonyms (n)* fragment, rag, scrap, bit, iota, piece, scintilla, strip, remnant, sliver, snatch, splinter, tatter, tittle, whit, **4**. rip; *synonyms (v)* cleave, pull, charge, lacerate, pluck, rive, shred, *(n)* bust, rake, debauchee, profligate, rent, roue, scamp, scapegrace, **5**. tear; *synonyms (n)* rupture, hole, laceration, rage, *(v)* break, crack, race, run, rush, dash, fly, snap, strain, agitate, burst.

raeraeaki 1. furrowed; *synonyms (adj)* creased, lined, wrinkled, wrinkly, crumpled, corrugated, corrugate, furrowy, porcate, rugged, uneven, bumpy, craggy, crinkly, potholed; *antonym (adj)* smooth, **2**. fissured; *synonyms (adj)* broken, clifted, fractured, **3**. lacerated; *synonyms (adj)* lacerate, torn, rent, blasted, hurt, mangled, mutilated, **4**. shredded; *synonyms (adj)* sliced, chopped, ragged, *(adv)* asunder, **5**. slashed; *synonyms (adj)* cut, gashed, cheap, down, emasculated, fringed, gelded, laciniated, low, mown, shortened, strikeout, laciniate, thinned, trimmed, **6**. stripped; *synonyms (adj)* bare, naked, nude, exposed, fleeced, undressed, desolate, stark, unclothed, **7**. ragged; *synonyms (adj)* seedy, threadbare, worn, hoarse, jagged, scruffy, dilapidated, shaggy, tattered, unkempt, untidy, *(v)* bald, *(n)* shabby, harsh, rough; *antonyms (adj)* pristine, smart, elegant, **8**. split; *synonyms (v)* crack, fracture, slit, burst, divide, separate, divorce,

breach, cleave, *(n)* break, rip, rupture, tear, cleavage, cleft; *antonyms (v)* join, unite, merge.

raerua wonder; *synonyms (v)* admire, query, question, reflect, speculate, *(n)* marvel, prodigy, admiration, amazement, astonishment, miracle, surprise, muse, phenomenon, wonderment.

raeten 1. tear; *synonyms (n)* split, rupture, rent, *(v)* break, rip, crack, pull, rend, lacerate, race, run, rush, slit, rive, cleave, **2**. rip; *synonyms (v)* cut, gash, scratch, claw, charge, hack, pluck, *(n)* tear, bust, rake, slash, debauchee, profligate, roue, scamp, **3**. slash; *synonyms (n)* slice, cleft, diagonal, *(v)* reduce, clip, hew, wound, fell, chop, flog, lash, whip, pare, strike, abridge.

raetenaki slashed; *synonyms (adj)* cut, gashed, torn, cheap, down, emasculated, fringed, gelded, laciniated, low, mown, shortened, strikeout, laciniate, thinned.

raeua 1. torn; *synonyms (adj)* lacerated, ragged, ripped, mangled, rent, tattered, blasted, lacerate; *antonym (adj)* pristine, **2**. split; *synonyms (v)* crack, cut, fracture, slit, burst, divide, separate, divorce, breach, cleave, *(n)* break, rip, rupture, tear, cleavage; *antonyms (v)* join, unite, merge, **3**. rend; *synonyms (v)* pull, split, rive, disrupt, slash, mangle, part, pluck, snap, dismember, sever, **4**. tear; *synonyms (n)* hole, bust, laceration, rage, drop, *(v)* rend, race, run, rush, dash, fly, shred, strain, agitate, dart.

raeuaki split; *synonyms (v)* crack, cut, fracture, slit, burst, divide, separate, divorce, breach, cleave, *(n)* break, rip, rupture, tear, cleavage; *antonyms (v)* join, unite, merge.

raewa 1. cracked; *synonyms (adj)* broken, nutty, batty, chapped, crazy, balmy, wacky, bats, crackers, crackled, crazed, deranged, dotty, insane, kookie, **2**. split; *synonyms (v)* crack, cut, fracture, slit, burst, divide, separate, divorce, breach, cleave, *(n)* break, rip, rupture, tear, cleavage; *antonyms (v)* join, unite, merge.

rai 1. flip; *synonyms (n)* pass, *(v)* fling, throw, toss, chuck, flick, jerk, pitch, tumble, *(adj)* impudent, insolent, flippant, frivolous, fresh, impertinent, **2**. exchange; *synonyms (n)* commutation, swap, switch, commerce, conversion, substitute, *(v)* change, barter, interchange, commute, counterchange, alternate, alter, cash, convert, **3**. dried; *synonyms (adj)* dry, arid, dehydrated, desiccated, shriveled, shrunken, torrid, baked, concrete, desiccate, stale, wizened, lifeless, weazen, *(n)* milk, **4**. faded; *synonyms (v)* dilapidated, *(adj)* dim, pale, bleached, dull, exhausted, faint, washy, withered, attenuate, attenuated, colorless, discoloured, **5**. change; *synonyms (n)* shift, alteration, modification, variation, move, adjustment, alternation, *(v)* exchange, adapt, transpose, turn, twist, affect, adjust, amend;

antonyms (*v*) stay, leave, idle, maintain, **6.**
withered; *synonyms* (*adj*) sere, sear, thin, lean,
parched, shrivelled, shrunk, wizen, (*v*) broken,
lame, **7.** plank; *synonyms* (*n*) board, beam, timber,
girder, panel, slat, bridge, footbridge, parachute,
planch, (*v*) flump, **8.** untwisted, **9.** wry;
synonyms (*adj*) ironic, ironical, twisted, sardonic,
writhe, another, cynical, deadpan, erroneous, error,
facetious, (*v*) awry, irregular, unsymmetric,
asymmetric, **10.** turn; *synonyms* (*v*) revolve,
deviate, get, revolution, spin, (*n*) bend, curve, roll,
coil, go, bout, round, bent, circle, tour, **11.** turned;
synonyms (*adj*) off, sour, curved, rancid, altered,
askew, bowed, cancelled, crooked, dark, deflected,
dour, false, glowering, glum, **12.** switch;
synonyms (*n*) cane, replacement, whip, cut,
permutation, substitution, rod, break, stick, (*v*) flip,
replace, swop, trade, jump, lash, **13.** wither;
synonyms (*v*) fade, shrink, wilt, contract, languish,
shrivel, droop, wane, waste, atrophy, blight, decay,
die, dwindle, (*adj*) scorch; *antonym* (*v*) bloom.

raiaki 1. changed; *synonyms* (*adj*) altered,
transformed, varied, affected, changeling, different,
disguised, distorted, inverse, malformed,
misshapen, new, reformed, rehabilitated, tainted;
antonym (*adj*) unchanged, **2.** exchanged;
synonyms (*adj*) counterchanged, substituted, **3.**
turned; *synonyms* (*adj*) off, sour, curved, rancid,
twisted, askew, awry, bent, bowed, cancelled,
crooked, dark, deflected, dour, dull, **4.** withered;
synonyms (*adj*) sere, wizened, sear, shriveled,
shrunken, thin, dry, lean, parched, shrivelled,
shrunk, wizen, (*v*) broken, lame.

raibanta 1. cover; *synonyms* (*v*) coat, conceal, top,
bury, cloak, (*n*) blind, blanket, screen, binding,
camouflage, cap, covering, lid, mask, shield;
antonyms (*v*) reveal, expose, uncover, **2.** covered;
synonyms (*adj*) hidden, veiled, concealed, covert,
coated, masked, obscured, secret, shrouded, thick,
wrapped, (*prep*) cloaked; *antonyms* (*adj*) bare, naked,
3. encircled; *synonyms* (*adj*) surrounded, enclosed,
bounded, annular, annulate, annulated, bordered,
circinate, circular, delimited, ingirt, ringed,
wreathed.

raibantaki covered; *synonyms* (*adj*) hidden, veiled,
concealed, covert, coated, masked, obscured, secret,
shrouded, thick, wrapped, (*prep*) cloaked; *antonyms*
(*adj*) bare, naked.

raiboro fiendish; *synonyms* (*adj*) devilish, diabolic,
demonic, diabolical, cruel, atrocious, hellish,
inhuman, wicked, brutal, evil, sinful, (*v*) infernal,
satanic, demoniacal.

raimenga 1. faded; *synonyms* (*v*) dilapidated, stale,
(*adj*) dim, pale, bleached, dull, exhausted, faint,
washy, withered, attenuate, attenuated, colorless,
discoloured, **2.** use; *synonyms* (*n*) custom, practice,
benefit, habit, application, function, (*v*) exercise,

employ, employment, expend, profit, advantage,
exploit, occupy, (*adj*) usage; *antonym* (*v*) conserve,
3. shabby; *synonyms* (*adj*) abject, low, mangy,
mean, poor, sorry, cheap, decrepit, paltry, ragged,
sordid, worn, ignoble, grubby, (*v*) frayed;
antonyms (*adj*) pristine, smart, **4.** wear; *synonyms*
(*v*) dress, endure, bear, fatigue, tire, waste, fray,
frazzle, (*n*) clothing, apparel, attire, clothes, garb,
erosion, garment; *antonym* (*v*) refresh, **5.** worn;
synonyms (*v*) decayed, rotten, (*adj*) haggard, shabby,
tired, tattered, threadbare, drawn, jaded, fatigued,
careworn, faded, raddled, seedy, wasted;
antonyms (*adj*) fresh, new.

raimengaki 1. used; *synonyms* (*adj*) secondhand,
exploited, accustomed, decrepit, depleted,
exhausted, faded, habituated, hand-me-down,
spent, threadbare, tried, victimised, victimized,
wont; *antonyms* (*adj*) pristine, new, spanking,
unused, **2.** worn; *synonyms* (*v*) decayed, rotten,
(*adj*) haggard, shabby, tired, ragged, tattered,
drawn, jaded, fatigued, careworn, frayed, raddled,
seedy, wasted; *antonym* (*adj*) fresh.

rain lined; *synonyms* (*adj*) furrowed, creased,
wrinkled, wrinkly, striped, banded, battered,
cemented, covered, craggy, crumpled, eroded,
gnarled, hooped, marbled; *antonym* (*adj*) smooth.

rainanoanga 1. afflicted; *synonyms* (*v*) afflict,
displeased, (*adj*) distressed, miserable, pitiful,
sorrowful, stricken, ill, woeful, dejected, doleful,
dolorous, sorry, aggrieved, affected, **2.** agonize;
synonyms (*v*) agonise, fret, hurt, worry, distress,
grieve, suffer, torment, torture, (*n*) pain, rack, **3.**
grieve; *synonyms* (*v*) mourn, aggrieve, bemoan,
deplore, lament, sorrow, trouble, annoy, bewail,
injure, regret, sadden, disturb, complain, sigh;
antonym (*v*) please, **4.** miserable; *synonyms* (*adj*)
mean, poor, meager, abject, bad, deplorable,
desolate, downcast, low, measly, unhappy,
lamentable, cheerless, (*v*) forlorn, wretched;
antonyms (*adj*) happy, cheerful, generous, **5.**
anguish; *synonyms* (*n*) agony, ache, misery,
affliction, desolation, despair, grief, pang, sadness,
suffering, bitterness, dolor, wretchedness,
despondency, gloom; *antonyms* (*n*) joy, pleasure, **6.**
anguished; *synonyms* (*adj*) tormented, tortured,
distressing, uneasy, inconsolable, tragic,
uncomfortable, anxious, brokenhearted,
despairing, fearful, hagridden, heartbreaking,
heartrending, mournful, **7.** agonizing; *synonyms*
(*adj*) excruciating, painful, harrowing, poignant,
grievous, agonising, torturous, **8.** woeful;
synonyms (*adj*) sad, pitiable, woebegone, piteous,
regrettable, dire, pathetic, rueful, execrable, paltry,
baleful, calamitous, hapless, melancholy, dreadful,
9. sorry; *synonyms* (*adj*) contrite, penitent,
remorseful, base, apologetic, regretful, repentant,

dingy, dismal, drab, dreary, gloomy, contemptible, glum, (v) concerned; *antonym* (adj) unrepentant.

rainanoangaki 1. anguished; *synonyms* (adj) miserable, suffering, tormented, tortured, distressing, dolorous, uneasy, woeful, inconsolable, sorrowful, tragic, uncomfortable, anxious, brokenhearted, despairing, **2**. agonized; *synonyms* (adj) agonised, hurt.

rainging 1. stumble; *synonyms* (v) slip, fall, flounder, fumble, err, falter, hit, stammer, (n) trip, lurch, misstep, stagger, (adj) blunder, botch, fault, **2**. stagger; *synonyms* (v) astonish, startle, flabbergast, hobble, reel, shake, shock, pitch, amaze, dumbfound, stun, surprise, totter, astound, (adj) bewilder.

rainia 1. line; *synonyms* (n) cord, file, house, breed, course, family, lineage, field, ancestry, border, boundary, cable, crease, row, (v) order, **2**. file; *synonyms* (n) archive, document, list, procession, rank, record, roll, series, string, (v) rasp, register, scrape, abrade, arrange, grind, **3**. stroke; *synonyms* (n) touch, beat, caress, hit, mark, apoplexy, attack, bang, impact, knock, line, (v) buffet, lick, fondle, (adj) blow, **4**. rank; *synonyms* (n) range, place, gradation, degree, quality, rate, post, (adj) putrid, (v) class, classify, grade, position, array, group, estimate; *antonym* (adj) fresh.

rainiaki 1. lined; *synonyms* (adj) furrowed, creased, wrinkled, wrinkly, striped, banded, battered, cemented, covered, craggy, crumpled, eroded, gnarled, hooped, marbled; *antonym* (adj) smooth, **2**. ranked; *synonyms* (adj) graded, bedded, graveled, stratified.

raira 1. incline; *synonyms* (n) slope, bias, angle, ascent, dip, grade, gradient, inclination, slant, (v) cant, bend, dispose, lean, tilt, bank, **2**. convert; *synonyms* (v) alter, change, adapt, reform, commute, invert, exchange, modify, switch, transform, turn, become, (n) proselyte, neophyte, (adj) believer, **3**. countless; *synonyms* (adj) numberless, innumerable, endless, many, multitudinous, myriad, measureless, immeasurable, infinite, legion, numerous, uncounted, unnumbered, untold; *antonyms* (adj) few, finite, **4**. turn; *synonyms* (v) revolve, deviate, get, revolution, spin, (n) curve, roll, coil, go, twist, bout, round, bent, circle, shift, **5**. translate; *synonyms* (v) interpret, construe, decipher, explain, read, render, convert, define, decode, transfer, understand, metamorphose, represent, elucidate, transmit.

rairake 1. twisting; *synonyms* (adj) tortuous, winding, sinuous, crooked, meandering, snaky, squirming, (n) distortion, twist, spin, torsion, turn, falsification, overrefinement, straining; *antonym* (adj) straight, **2**. turning; *synonyms* (adj) revolving,

rotating, rotary, spinning, wheeling, (n) revolution, bend, deviation, conversion, diversion, version.

rairaki 1. inclined; *synonyms* (adj) prone, apt, oblique, willing, bowed, liable, likely, minded, predisposed, ready, bent, fain, susceptible, (v) given, (prep) disposed; *antonyms* (adj) level, reluctant, unwilling, **2**. converted; *synonyms* (adj) adopted, consecrated, unearthly, altered, changed, convinced, elected, influenced, inspired, invert, justified, persuaded, reborn, reformed, regenerated; *antonym* (adj) doubtful, **3**. turn; *synonyms* (v) revolve, deviate, get, revolution, (n) bend, curve, roll, coil, go, twist, bout, change, round, circle, shift, **4**. turned; *synonyms* (adj) off, sour, curved, rancid, twisted, askew, awry, cancelled, crooked, dark, deflected, dour, dull, false, glowering, **5**. twist; *synonyms* (n) twine, wind, spin, twirl, entwine, braid, kink, loop, (v) turn, distort, curl, contort, deform, pervert, wrench; *antonyms* (v) straighten, untwist, **6**. rotate; *synonyms* (v) reel, alternate, gyrate, swing, wheel, orbit, pivot, circulate.

rairakiaki 1. rotated; *synonym* (adj) revolved, **2**. twisted; *synonyms* (adj) crooked, deformed, perverted, bent, distorted, coiled, misshapen, contorted, curved, twined, winding, wry, gnarled, tortuous, awry; *antonyms* (adj) straight, tidy, **3**. turned; *synonyms* (adj) off, sour, rancid, twisted, altered, askew, bowed, cancelled, dark, deflected, dour, dull, false, glowering, glum.

raiti 1. dazzling; *synonyms* (adj) bright, brilliant, blinding, glaring, splendid, vivid, fulgent, resplendent, sparkling, striking, stunning, blazing, beautiful, flamboyant, garish; *antonym* (adj) dull, **2**. flash; *synonyms* (n) sparkle, blaze, shimmer, glitter, instant, coruscation, (v) flicker, twinkle, blink, flame, gleam, glimmer, coruscate, dazzle, lighten, **3**. fleeting; *synonyms* (adj) brief, ephemeral, evanescent, fugitive, momentary, passing, short, transient, cursory, rapid, short-lived, temporal, transitory, vanishing, elusive; *antonyms* (adj) lasting, permanent, **4**. flashy; *synonyms* (adj) showy, cheap, gaudy, loud, brassy, flash, jazzy, tasteless, tawdry, colorful, blatant, conspicuous, prominent, swanky, gay; *antonyms* (adj) tasteful, restrained, **5**. dazzle; *synonyms* (n) brightness, (v) bedazzle, shine, blind, glare, awe, captivate, (adj) daze, confuse, bewilder, hoodwink, perplex, startle, **6**. shine; *synonyms* (n) sheen, luster, radiance, rub, (v) glow, light, burnish, excel, glance, glisten, gloss, radiate, reflect, beam, buff; *antonym* (n) dullness, **7**. shiny; *synonyms* (adj) lustrous, glossy, clear, glistening, sheeny, shining, sleek, slick, smooth, sunny, glassy, silken, burnished, (v) nitid, splendent; *antonym* (adj) rough, **8**. rapid; *synonyms* (adj) fast, quick, prompt, swift, agile, fleet, hasty, speedy, expeditious, sudden, nimble, winged, express, hurried, immediate; *antonyms* (*adj*) slow, gradual.

raitiaki dazzled; *synonyms* (*adj*) dizzy, bewildered, fascinated.

raititi sparkle; *synonyms* (*n*) flash, flicker, spark, blaze, glitter, beam, glance, brightness, (*v*) glimmer, shimmer, blink, fizz, gleam, shine, glare; *antonym* (*n*) lethargy.

raka 1. increase; *synonyms* (*n*) gain, addition, augmentation, boom, expansion, extension, (*v*) advance, accrue, extend, grow, aggrandize, expand, enhance, enlarge, (*adj*) augment; *antonyms* (*n*) reduction, contraction, decline, (*v*) decrease, reduce, diminish, drop, deteriorate, **2.** damned; *synonyms* (*adj*) cursed, doomed, blasted, condemned, damn, blamed, blessed, bloody, darned, deuced, fated, goddam, goddamn, goddamned, (*adv*) damnably, **3.** augment; *synonyms* (*v*) amplify, increase, add, reinforce, boost, improve, intensify, magnify, raise, mount, broaden, compound, develop, heighten, multiply, **4.** more; *synonyms* (*adv*) also, further, besides, beyond, over, (*adj*) additional, better, extra, larger, exceed, greater, other, (*pron*) another, (*prep*) above; *antonyms* (*adv*) fewer, less, (*adj*) inferior, **5.** bewitched; *synonyms* (*adj*) spellbound, fascinated, captive, enamored, ensorcelled, infatuated, magical, obsessed, rapt, bugged, captivated, enraptured, entranced, hooked, mesmerized, **6.** infringe; *synonyms* (*v*) encroach, break, contravene, impinge, violate, disobey, intrude, entrench, invade, trespass, infract, pirate, destroy, interrupt, conflict; *antonym* (*v*) obey, **7.** doomed; *synonyms* (*v*) destined, undone, (*adj*) damned, unfortunate, unlucky, inevitable, predetermined, (*n*) lost; *antonym* (*adj*) lucky, **8.** exceed; *synonyms* (*v*) beat, pass, surpass, outdo, surmount, transcend, cap, outshine, outweigh, overrun, top, excel, outgo, outmatch, outstrip, **9.** exaggerate; *synonyms* (*v*) boast, aggravate, dramatize, overdo, overdraw, overstate, embellish, hyperbolize, inflate, overplay, distort, falsify, lie, misrepresent, pad; *antonyms* (*v*) understate, minimize, **10.** above; *synonyms* (*prep*) on, past, surpassing, under, (*adv*) aloft, supra, up, more, overhead, (*adj*) preceding, former, upper, foregoing, previous; *antonym* (*prep*) below, **11.** condemned; *synonyms* (*adj*) censured, guilty, convicted, appropriated, **12.** greater; *synonyms* (*adj*) higher, major, superior, most, great, best, considerable, high, sizeable, advanced, copious, enhanced, finer, generous, huge; *antonyms* (*adj*) lesser, smaller, **13.** cursed; *synonyms* (*v*) accurst, cursing, (*adj*) abominable, execrable, curst, damnable, detestable, hateful, infernal, **14.** stride; *synonyms* (*n*) step, pace, footstep, gait, stalk, walk, progress, rate, stump, toddle, span, footfall, reach, (*v*) tread, strut, **15.** trespass; *synonyms* (*n*) offense,

breach, invasion, encroachment, infringement, transgression, crime, fault, intrusion, violation, (*v*) offend, sin, infringe, transgress, (*adj*) error; *antonym* (*v*) retreat, **16.** surpass; *synonyms* (*v*) overcome, overstep, overshadow, overreach, go, outdistance, overtake, circumvent, outrank, rival, lead, spend, overhaul, outperform, die, **17.** transgress; *synonyms* (*v*) blunder, boob, goof, dishonor, escape, fail, injure, misbehave, profane, (*adj*) err, **18.** straddle; *synonyms* (*v*) range, stride, coquet, ramble, shuffle, bestride, sprawl, array, browse, cast, crop, (*n*) brace, bridge, couple, couplet.

rakaia stride; *synonyms* (*n*) step, pace, footstep, gait, stalk, walk, progress, rate, stump, toddle, span, footfall, reach, (*v*) tread, strut.

rakaki 1. augmented; *synonyms* (*adj*) inflated, more, plus, better, bigger, improved, **2.** exaggerated; *synonyms* (*adj*) enlarged, extravagant, theatrical, immoderate, hypertrophied, affected, excessive, hyperbolic, magnified, overdone, overstated, pretentious, melodramatic; *antonyms* (*adj*) understated, restrained, **3.** increased; *synonyms* (*adj*) additional, greater, fresh, new, puffy, ripe, amplified, other, superior.

rakata pace; *synonyms* (*n*) walk, rate, footstep, rapidity, speed, tempo, tread, celerity, fastness, run, beat, cadence, (*v*) step, gait, stride; *antonym* (*n*) slowness.

rakatua transgress; *synonyms* (*v*) sin, break, infringe, offend, contravene, overstep, trespass, violate, breach, disobey, infract, pass, blunder, boob, (*adj*) err.

rakaua adulterate; *synonyms* (*v*) doctor, corrupt, defile, dilute, pollute, weaken, contaminate, debase, falsify, pervert, sophisticate, (*adj*) alloy, adulterated, spurious, (*n*) bastard; *antonyms* (*v*) clean, purify.

rakauaki adulterated; *synonyms* (*adj*) adulterate, impure, debased, dirty, unclean, bastard, contaminated, corrupt, diluted, false, faulty, sham, sophisticated, (*v*) contraband, illegitimate.

rake 1. eastward; *synonyms* (*adv*) east, eastwards, (*adj*) eastbound, **2.** eastwards; *synonym* (*adv*) eastward, **3.** hoist; *synonyms* (*n*) boost, elevator, winch, (*v*) elevate, haul, heave, lift, erect, raise, rear, uphold, exalt, wind, **4.** diminishing; *synonyms* (*adj*) decreasing, abating, declining, dwindling, lessening, waning, ablatitious, deteriorating, extenuating, fading, failing, falling, flagging, (*n*) decrease, contraction; *antonym* (*adj*) increasing, **5.** upward; *synonyms* (*adj*) up, overhead, rising, upper, improving, mounting, open, upright, vertical, budding, developing, (*adv*) upwardly, upwards, aloft, airwards; *antonym* (*adj*) descending, **6.** up; *synonyms* (*adv*) upward, (*v*) mount, rise, advance, effervescent, filling, frothy, mousseux, nappy, sparkling, (*adj*) over, uphill, cheerful, happy; *antonym* (*adj*) asleep.

rakea 1. awaken; *synonyms* (*v*) arouse, awake, wake, call, rouse, stir, kindle, provoke, raise, revive, waken, evoke, excite, incite, move, **2.** excite; *synonyms* (*v*) animate, disturb, enliven, agitate, energize, awaken, electrify, encourage, exasperate, inspire, quicken, stimulate, whet, enthuse, engender; *antonyms* (*v*) calm, pacify, bore.

rakeaki 1. excited; *synonyms* (*adj*) agitated, ablaze, emotional, enthusiastic, frantic, ardent, aroused, delirious, fervent, heated, impassioned, passionate, warm, elated, (*v*) animated; *antonyms* (*adj*) calm, cool, unexcited, **2.** awakened; *synonyms* (*adj*) awake, excited, interested.

rako 1. amiable; *synonyms* (*adj*) affable, agreeable, benign, complaisant, friendly, genial, charming, cordial, gentle, kind, likable, lovely, nice, pleasant, sweet; *antonyms* (*adj*) unfriendly, disagreeable, aggressive, argumentative, **2.** careful; *synonyms* (*adj*) accurate, attentive, thrifty, alert, deliberate, economical, frugal, mindful, prudent, thoughtful, assiduous, aware, cagey, cautious, (*v*) anxious; *antonyms* (*adj*) careless, reckless, slapdash, neglectful, **3.** care; *synonyms* (*n*) attention, bother, caution, concern, aid, apprehension, custody, keep, maintenance, worry, attendance, affection, (*v*) anxiety, charge, administer; *antonyms* (*n*) carelessness, recklessness, rashness, thoughtlessness, (*v*) neglect, disregard, **4.** thrifty; *synonyms* (*adj*) careful, provident, sparing, stingy, chary; *antonyms* (*adj*) spendthrift, wasteful, profligate.

rakoroa graze; *synonyms* (*v*) browse, scratch, rub, scrape, chafe, eat, brush, crease, crop, feed, pasture, rake, shave, (*n*) touch, cut.

rakoroaki grazed; *synonyms* (*adj*) hurt, raw.

rama 1. forehead; *synonyms* (*n*) brow, front, foreland, mut, phiz, physiognomy, visage, eyebrow, assurance, hilltop, supercilium, (*adv*) foremost, **2.** outrigger; *synonyms* (*n*) boom, bar, heel, lap, rod, shoe, sole, splint, sprit, stabilizer, stilts, stirrup.

ramanea 1. bound; *synonyms* (*v*) leap, border, bounce, limit, circumscribe, confine, pounce, rebound, (*n*) spring, jump, boundary, edge, barrier, compass, hop; *antonym* (*adj*) free, **2.** bind; *synonyms* (*v*) attach, tie, bandage, bundle, combine, fasten, fetter, fix, lace, truss, affix, bond, cement, gird, (*n*) band; *antonyms* (*v*) untie, release, unbind, **3.** tie; *synonyms* (*n*) connection, draw, association, relationship, sleeper, strap, string, cord, deadlock, (*v*) link, bind, join, knot, connect, leash; *antonyms* (*v*) disconnect, undo.

ramaneaki 1. bound; *synonyms* (*v*) leap, border, bounce, limit, circumscribe, confine, pounce, rebound, (*n*) spring, jump, boundary, edge, barrier,

compass, hop; *antonym* (*adj*) free, **2.** bounded; *synonyms* (*adj*) finite, restricted, delimited, limited, encircled, enclosed, local, qualified, surrounded, belted, compassed, contiguous, defined, definite, determinate, **3.** tied; *synonyms* (*adj*) fastened, connected, even, fixed, laced, united, attached, binding, buttoned, joined, legato, liable, mixed, powerless, responsible; *antonym* (*adj*) separate.

ramauna 1. fading; *synonyms* (*adj*) dying, disappearing, paling, weakening, (*n*) attenuation, bleaching, disappearance, evaporation; *antonym* (*n*) appearance, **2.** disappearing; *synonyms* (*adj*) vanishing, fading, declining, diminishing, failing, (*n*) departing, leaving, fade, (*adv*) off.

ran 1. water; *synonyms* (*n*) urine, moisture, juice, liquor, crystal, glass, lymph, pee, piddle, (*v*) irrigate, moisten, wet, soak, dampen, dilute, **2.** juicy; *synonyms* (*adj*) delicious, fat, gamy, liquid, luscious, succulent, fluid, lush, mellow, moist, racy, rich, sappy, spicy, blue; *antonym* (*adj*) dry, **3.** liquid; *synonyms* (*adj*) flowing, fluent, juicy, limpid, watery, mobile, smooth, liquefied, liquified, (*n*) drink, liquidness, sap; *antonyms* (*adj*) firm, (*n*) solid, gaseous, **4.** watery; *synonyms* (*adj*) diluted, washy, thin, damp, aqueous, hydrous, insipid, tearful, weak, dripping, humid, soggy, soft, aquatic, dull; *antonyms* (*adj*) concentrated, strong.

rañ 1. cloud; *synonyms* (*n*) mist, blur, haze, steam, (*v*) fog, becloud, obscure, befog, blacken, eclipse, overshadow, shadow, taint, hide, (*adj*) swarm; *antonym* (*v*) sharpen, **2.** slave; *synonyms* (*n*) serf, servant, bondman, inferior, thrall, bondsman, captive, vassal, dependent, (*v*) labor, drudge, fag, toil, work, moil.

rananoa desire; *synonyms* (*n*) ambition, hope, aspiration, will, wish, craving, dream, impulse, (*v*) fancy, aspire, seek, want, aim, choose, crave; *antonyms* (*n*) aversion, reality, (*v*) dislike, hate.

rananoaki desired; *synonyms* (*adj*) coveted, craved, desirable, chosen, favorite, wanted, needed, welcome, beloved, adored, appropriate, pet, preferred, (*v*) complying, consenting; *antonym* (*adj*) undesirable.

ranea 1. oscillate; *synonyms* (*v*) fluctuate, swing, vibrate, hesitate, wag, alternate, quiver, shake, sway, tremble, vacillate, vary, wave, waver, wobble, **2.** unstable; *synonyms* (*adj*) changeable, precarious, insecure, shaky, unsettled, unsound, erratic, fickle, fluid, inconstant, unpredictable, irresolute, unreliable, capricious, changeful; *antonyms* (*adj*) stable, steady, constant, **3.** oscillating; *synonyms* (*adj*) oscillatory, vibrant, zigzag, vibratory, **4.** shine; *synonyms* (*n*) sheen, luster, (*v*) glow, light, burnish, gleam, blaze, flash, glitter, sparkle, excel, flame, glance, glisten, gloss; *antonym* (*n*) dullness.

raneanea 1. clear; *synonyms* (*adj*) clean, certain, open, apparent, distinct, empty, (*v*) bright, acquit, absolute, free, net, absolve, clarify, definite, discharge; *antonyms* (*adj*) cloudy, opaque, unclear, dark, fuzzy, hazy, incomprehensible, obscure, uncertain, vague, ambiguous, blurry, confused, confusing, (*v*) convict, **2.** bright; *synonyms* (*adj*) clear, alive, apt, intelligent, vivid, beaming, brainy, brilliant, light, luminous, lustrous, shining, shiny, smart, sunny; *antonyms* (*adj*) dull, dim, dreary, gloomy, stupid, unintelligent, overcast, shadowy, leaden, slow, thick, **3.** splendid; *synonyms* (*adj*) fine, gorgeous, illustrious, magnificent, beautiful, grand, noble, royal, gallant, proud, admirable, good, impressive, (*v*) glorious, (*n*) excellent; *antonym* (*adj*) poor, **4.** shiny; *synonyms* (*adj*) glossy, glistening, sheeny, sleek, slick, smooth, glassy, resplendent, silken, burnished, glazed, (*v*) nitid, splendent; *antonym* (*adj*) rough.

ranebonebo 1. glossy; *synonyms* (*adj*) shiny, sleek, bright, smooth, brilliant, glazed, flat, burnished, glassy, glistening, lustrous, resplendent, satiny, slick, silky; *antonyms* (*adj*) dull, rough, **2.** glaze; *synonyms* (*n*) shine, coating, sheen, enamel, glazing, finish, gloss, luster, (*v*) burnish, glass, coat, varnish, calender, candy, **3.** glisten; *synonyms* (*v*) gleam, glimmer, beam, coruscate, glint, flare, glare, glow, (*n*) flash, sparkle, glance, glitter, shimmer, glister, twinkle, **4.** glistening; *synonyms* (*adj*) glossy, shining, beaming, **5.** gloss; *synonyms* (*n*) annotation, brightness, explanation, glossary, commentary, glossiness, note, (*v*) glaze, comment, annotate, veneer, color, rationalize, interpret, translate; *antonym* (*n*) dullness, **6.** varnished; *synonyms* (*adj*) stained, besmirched, buffed, damaged, finished, flyblown, polished, spotted, sullied, tainted, tarnished, glossed, planed, **7.** shiny; *synonyms* (*adj*) clear, sheeny, sunny, silken, (*v*) nitid, splendent, vivid, **8.** shining; *synonyms* (*adj*) luminous, radiant, glorious, effulgent, glittering, glowing, dazzling, distinguished, gleaming, illustrious, shimmering, sparkling, gay, (*n*) lucid, polishing, **9.** polish; *synonyms* (*n*) gentility, cultivation, elegance, refinement, civilization, culture, (*v*) furbish, rub, civilize, clean, cultivate, grind, improve, perfect, refine, **10.** shine; *synonyms* (*n*) radiance, brilliance, (*v*) light, blaze, excel, flame, glisten, radiate, reflect, buff, flicker, ray, burn, irradiate, scintillate.

ranebonéboaki 1. glazed; *synonyms* (*adj*) glassy, glossy, glassed, glazen, bright, burnished, dead, drunk, enameled, glassen, glasslike, shiny, slippery, varnished, glistening, **2.** polished; *synonyms* (*adj*) elegant, courteous, cultured, finished, refined, civil, courtly, genteel, lustrous, polite, smooth, accomplished, graceful, sleek, slick; *antonyms* (*adj*) dull, rough.

ranene 1. infiltrate; *synonyms* (*v*) soak, enter, penetrate, permeate, inculcate, indoctrinate, instill, **2.** intrude; *synonyms* (*v*) interfere, encroach, impose, infringe, trespass, disturb, impinge, interrupt, obtrude, disrupt, transgress, interlope, interpose, invade, irrupt, **3.** escape; *synonyms* (*v*) elude, break, dodge, avoid, evade, run, bolt, circumvent, leave, duck, bilk, (*n*) leak, avoidance, evasion, outlet; *antonyms* (*v*) capture, return.

raneneaki escaped; *synonyms* (*v*) escaping, (*adj*) free, loose, easy, runaway, wild, fugitive, idle, informal, lax, liberal, light, open, promiscuous, slack.

rang 1. much; *synonyms* (*adv*) greatly, frequently, almost, awfully, considerably, far, most, often, pretty, highly, (*n*) lot, heap, (*adj*) great, considerable, practically; *antonym* (*adv*) slightly, **2.** considerable; *synonyms* (*adj*) big, large, ample, momentous, significant, sizable, substantial, consequential, influential, meaningful, extensive, fair, generous, good, (*v*) important; *antonyms* (*adj*) small, insignificant, faint, trivial, **3.** excessively; *synonyms* (*adv*) exceedingly, very, extremely, immoderately, extravagantly, overly, too, (*adj*) exorbitant, inordinately, unduly; *antonym* (*adv*) justifiably, **4.** too; *synonyms* (*adv*) also, likewise, besides, excessively, over, further, furthermore, moreover, equally, and, similarly, **5.** very; *synonyms* (*adv*) really, completely, entirely, quite, truly, actually, intensely, rattling, real, thoroughly, (*adj*) much, identical, exact, indeed, (*n*) self; *antonyms* (*adv*) abysmally, somewhat.

ranga 1. acutely; *synonyms* (*adv*) extremely, intensely, severely, critically, deeply, keenly, sharply, badly, clearly, gravely, seriously, **2.** lean; *synonyms* (*adj*) emaciated, gaunt, thin, bony, lank, lanky, (*v*) incline, bend, list, slant, bow, careen, pitch, (*n*) tilt, inclination; *antonyms* (*adj*) fat, plump, **3.** flowing; *synonyms* (*v*) loose, (*adj*) easy, fluent, running, graceful, fluid, liquid, smooth, soft, copious, gentle, streaming, (*n*) current, flow, flux; *antonyms* (*adj*) secure, tight, ugly, **4.** flow; *synonyms* (*n*) flood, discharge, abound, rush, (*v*) stream, course, jet, run, surge, float, emanate, fall, gush, pour, seep, **5.** capsize; *synonyms* (*adj*) drown, shipwreck, swamp, (*v*) turn, upset, invert, overturn, reverse, topple, keel, subvert, tip, raze, sink, upend; *antonym* (*v*) right, **6.** upset; *synonyms* (*v*) agitate, disquiet, overthrow, bother, confuse, disturb, perturb, unsettle, (*adj*) unsettled, hurt, agitated, (*n*) disorder, trouble, distress, disturbance; *antonyms* (*v*) calm, please, encourage, soothe, (*adj*) pleased, confident, **7.** overturn; *synonyms* (*v*) capsize, overset, annul, destroy, overrule, nullify, cancel, defeat, demolish, invalidate, lift, overpower, ruin, spill, (*n*) turnover; *antonym* (*v*) validate.

rangaie 1. incline; *synonyms* (*n*) slope, bias, angle, ascent, dip, grade, gradient, inclination, slant, (*v*) cant, bend, dispose, lean, tilt, bank, **2.** lean; *synonyms* (*adj*) emaciated, gaunt, thin, bony, lank, lanky, scrawny, flimsy, angular, (*v*) incline, list, bow, careen, pitch, tip; *antonyms* (*adj*) fat, plump.

rangaieaki inclined; *synonyms* (*adj*) prone, apt, oblique, willing, bowed, liable, likely, minded, predisposed, ready, bent, fain, susceptible, (*v*) given, (*prep*) disposed; *antonyms* (*adj*) level, reluctant, unwilling.

rangaki 1. great; *synonyms* (*adj*) eminent, famous, gigantic, big, distinguished, extensive, extreme, grand, large, chief, ample, capital, celebrated, considerable, dignified; *antonyms* (*adj*) small, awful, insignificant, tiny, mild, **2.** upset; *synonyms* (*v*) overturn, agitate, disquiet, overthrow, bother, confuse, disturb, perturb, reverse, (*adj*) unsettled, hurt, (*n*) disorder, trouble, distress, disturbance; *antonyms* (*v*) calm, please, encourage, soothe, (*adj*) pleased, confident, **3.** overturned; *synonyms* (*adj*) upset, upturned, broken, confused, disordered, disquieted, distressed, disturbed, topsy-turvy, retrousse, worried; *antonym* (*adj*) upright.

rangaranga 1. lurch; *synonyms* (*v*) careen, stumble, pitch, reel, stagger, tilt, cant, rock, shake, sway, swing, teeter, totter, wobble, flounder, **2.** shimmy; *synonyms* (*n*) chemise, shift, vibration, berth, break, case, cutting, displacement, eluding, elusion, fault, fracture, gaffe, (*v*) dance, coggle, **3.** vacillate; *synonyms* (*v*) fluctuate, hesitate, waver, falter, oscillate, hover, wave, flutter, flicker, scruple, waffle, demur, linger, pause, change, **4.** wobble; *synonyms* (*v*) lurch, quake, dodder, quiver, waddle, tremble, roll, shiver, shudder, bob, shimmy, toddle, (*n*) tremor, **5.** roll; *synonyms* (*n*) list, revolution, catalogue, inventory, register, (*v*) coil, curl, enfold, revolve, wheel, turn, twist, wallow, wind, envelop, **6.** shake; *synonyms* (*v*) beat, agitate, jar, brandish, disturb, excite, wag, drop, bump, convulse, flourish, jiggle, quail, (*n*) jolt, trembling.

rangarangaki 1. shaken; *synonyms* (*v*) broken, lame, passe, shaky, threadbare, wilted, shattered, stale, (*adj*) jolted, dazed, disconcerted, fallen, scared, stunned, surprised, **2.** rolled; *synonyms* (*adj*) rolling, furled, involute, beaten, billowing, kinky, level, resonant, resonating, resounding, reverberating, reverberative, spiral, trilled, tumbling.

rangarangataki 1. tremble; *synonyms* (*v*) shake, thrill, quake, totter, flutter, palpitate, quail, falter, agitate, flicker, quaver, (*n*) quiver, shiver, shudder, throb, **2.** quiver; *synonyms* (*n*) tremble, tremor, vibration, chill, jolt, palpitation, tingle, beat, shock, (*v*) pulsate, vibrate, wave, waver, wobble, bob.

rangarangatau 1. active; *synonyms* (*adj*) energetic, alert, busy, diligent, effective, live, lively, nimble, strong, agile, alive, brisk, dynamic, forcible, healthy; *antonyms* (*adj*) dormant, inactive, sluggish, idle, latent, lethargic, sedentary, slow, extinct, passive, quiet, **2.** employed; *synonyms* (*adj*) engaged, occupied, working, affianced, betrothed, earnest, rapt, active, gainfully, inked, involved, laboring, operating, pledged, promised; *antonym* (*adj*) unemployed, **3.** hustle; *synonyms* (*n*) hurry, haste, ado, cheat, commotion, con, fuss, (*v*) jostle, bustle, elbow, hasten, flurry, push, shove, work, **4.** agitate; *synonyms* (*v*) disturb, stir, toss, fan, bother, foment, perturb, rouse, shake, trouble, actuate, annoy, arouse, canvass, convulse; *antonyms* (*v*) calm, soothe, **5.** bustling; *synonyms* (*adj*) buzzing, vibrant, perky, restless, spoffish, agitated, (*v*) stirring, eventful, **6.** diligent; *synonyms* (*adj*) assiduous, careful, painstaking, attentive, industrious, laborious, studious, conscientious, indefatigable, meticulous, persevering, sedulous, acting; *antonyms* (*adj*) lazy, careless, negligent, **7.** busy; *synonyms* (*adj*) crowded, meddlesome, officious, employed, full, fussy, (*v*) occupy, employ, engage, engross; *antonym* (*adj*) free, **8.** employ; *synonyms* (*v*) apply, use, consume, exercise, exploit, hire, wield, exert, ply, retain, spend, take, utilize, (*n*) employment, service; *antonyms* (*v*) fire, dismiss, **9.** bustle; *synonyms* (*n*) disorder, movement, activity, agitation, confusion, pother, ruckus, (*v*) hustle, clutter, fidget, hubbub, move, rush, (*adj*) scramble, speed; *antonym* (*n*) tranquillity, **10.** engaged; *synonyms* (*adj*) engrossed, reserved, absorbed, bespoken, booked, immersed, intent; *antonym* (*adj*) available, **11.** brisk; *synonyms* (*adj*) bracing, bright, quick, acute, smart, sprightly, adroit, animated, crisp, fast, fresh, hasty, invigorating, pert, sharp; *antonym* (*adj*) soporific, **12.** assiduous; *synonyms* (*adj*) thorough, devoted, constant, persistent, untiring, **13.** agitated; *synonyms* (*adj*) excited, nervous, restive, tumultuous, upset, distressed, tense, alarmed, anxious, distraught, jumpy, overwrought, perturbed, shaken, troubled; *antonym* (*adj*) composed, **14.** struggle; *synonyms* (*n*) contest, battle, combat, conflict, strain, effort, exertion, scuffle, (*v*) fight, attempt, dispute, endeavor, labor, quarrel, contend; *antonyms* (*v*) flourish, glide, **15.** work; *synonyms* (*n*) business, function, task, action, act, book, composition, (*v*) operate, toil, cultivate, ferment, form, manipulate, (*adj*) job, trade; *antonym* (*v*) malfunction, **16.** struggling; *synonyms* (*adj*) aggressive, agonizing, belligerent, careworn, disadvantaged, fraught, harassed, hostile, pugnacious, rebellious, stressed, besieged, (*n*) contention, colluctation, **17.** rash; *synonyms* (*adj*) foolhardy, imprudent, heedless, impetuous, precipitate, reckless, audacious, headlong, heady, impulsive, incautious, inconsiderate, indiscreet, sudden, (*n*) eruption; *antonyms* (*adj*) cautious, sensible, considered, deliberate, wise, **18**. occupied; *synonym* (*adj*) concerned; *antonyms* (*adj*) empty, vacant, uninhabited, **19**. working; *synonyms* (*adj*) operative, practical, operational, functional, transitive, (*n*) operation, running, functioning, play, agency, performance, go, workings, force.

rangarangatauaki 1. agitated; *synonyms* (*adj*) restless, excited, nervous, restive, tumultuous, upset, distressed, tense, alarmed, anxious, distraught, jumpy, overwrought, perturbed, shaken; *antonyms* (*adj*) calm, composed, lethargic, **2**. employed; *synonyms* (*adj*) busy, engaged, occupied, working, affianced, betrothed, earnest, rapt, active, gainfully, inked, involved, laboring, operating, pledged; *antonym* (*adj*) unemployed.

rangata 1. hurry; *synonyms* (*n*) speed, haste, dispatch, flurry, (*v*) bustle, hasten, accelerate, dash, expedite, scurry, fly, run, rush, zip, hie; *antonyms* (*n*) slowness, (*v*) dawdle, **2**. pace; *synonyms* (*n*) walk, rate, footstep, rapidity, tempo, tread, celerity, fastness, beat, cadence, carriage, footfall, (*v*) step, gait, stride, **3**. step; *synonyms* (*n*) degree, measure, stage, gradation, level, rank, act, footprint, move, advance, phase, procedure, process, (*v*) pace, proceeding, **4**. quickstep.

rangataki 1. hurried; *synonyms* (*adj*) hasty, fast, headlong, quick, rapid, speedy, sudden, swift, abrupt, cursory, careless, precipitate, prompt, rash, slapdash; *antonyms* (*adj*) slow, unhurried, leisurely, **2**. hurry; *synonyms* (*n*) speed, haste, dispatch, flurry, (*v*) bustle, hasten, accelerate, dash, expedite, scurry, fly, run, rush, zip, hie; *antonyms* (*n*) slowness, (*v*) dawdle, **3**. twitching; *synonyms* (*n*) twitch, tic, vellication, **4**. stepped; *synonyms* (*v*) advanced, gone, stopen.

rangatakiaki hurried; *synonyms* (*adj*) hasty, fast, headlong, quick, rapid, speedy, sudden, swift, abrupt, cursory, careless, precipitate, prompt, rash, slapdash; *antonyms* (*adj*) slow, unhurried, leisurely.

rangatia stride; *synonyms* (*n*) step, pace, footstep, gait, stalk, walk, progress, rate, stump, toddle, span, footfall, reach, (*v*) tread, strut.

rangi 1. most; *synonyms* (*adv*) nearly, greatly, nigh, virtually, (*adj*) almost, about, best, utmost, indeed, much, near, very, well, (*n*) majority, maximum; *antonym* (*adv*) least, **2**. madly; *synonyms* (*adv*) crazily, insanely, deadly, devilishly, furiously, dementedly, deucedly, hard, devilish, fiercely, foolishly, violently, amuck, amok, blindly; *antonym* (*adv*) sensibly, **3**. very; *synonyms* (*adv*) extremely, highly, really, completely, entirely, most, quite, truly, actually, too, awfully, (*adj*) identical, considerably, exact, (*n*) self; *antonyms*

(*adv*) abysmally, slightly, somewhat, **4**. pretty; *synonyms* (*adv*) fairly, (*adj*) beautiful, fair, graceful, lovely, attractive, charming, handsome, good-looking, picturesque, dainty, cute, elegant, fine, (*n*) nice; *antonym* (*adj*) ugly.

rangin quite; *synonyms* (*adv*) altogether, absolutely, all, completely, entirely, fully, sheer, exactly, enough, even, fairly, rather, right, stark, (*adj*) just; *antonym* (*adv*) extremely.

rangirang 1. lunatic; *synonyms* (*adj*) crazy, insane, foolish, mad, mental, moonstruck, deranged, demented, idiotic, nutty, psychotic, (*n*) madman, madcap, maniac, nut, **2**. drunk; *synonyms* (*adj*) intoxicated, tipsy, tight, wet, inebriated, delirious, high, (*n*) inebriate, drunkard, rummy, sot; *antonym* (*adj*) sober, **3**. crazy; *synonyms* (*adj*) wild, absurd, brainsick, cracked, crazed, eccentric, ludicrous, preposterous, silly, wacky, balmy, bonkers, outrageous, barmy, batty; *antonyms* (*adj*) sane, sensible, **4**. mad; *synonyms* (*adj*) frantic, frenzied, angry, distracted, frenetic, lunatic, irate, distraught, cross, enraged, infatuated, livid, possessed, (*n*) furious, anger; *antonym* (*adj*) calm, **5**. idiot; *synonyms* (*n*) fool, dolt, dunce, dimwit, moron, ass, cretin, imbecile, oaf, changeling, dumbbell, half-wit, innocent, jerk, natural, **6**. inebriated; *synonyms* (*adj*) drunk, (*v*) drunken.

rannake scummy; *synonyms* (*adj*) contemptible, foamy, abject, dirty, low, miserable, pitiful, execrable, blue, broken, crushed, depleted, deplorable, depressed, dispirited.

ran-ni-mata tears; *synonyms* (*n*) cry, crying, brine, lacerations, lament, moan, pickle, snuffle, weeping.

ranran 1. inconsistent; *synonyms* (*adj*) incongruous, incoherent, incompatible, contrary, absurd, conflicting, inconsequent, discordant, discrepant, erratic, illogical, irreconcilable, abhorrent, changeable, (*n*) contradictory; *antonyms* (*adj*) consistent, constant, reliable, **2**. leak; *synonyms* (*n*) leakage, crevice, breach, disclosure, chink, escape, fissure, hole, (*v*) dribble, reveal, release, disclose, drip, drop, ooze, **3**. juicy; *synonyms* (*adj*) delicious, fat, gamy, liquid, luscious, succulent, fluid, lush, mellow, moist, racy, rich, sappy, spicy, blue; *antonym* (*adj*) dry, **4**. liquid; *synonyms* (*adj*) flowing, fluent, juicy, limpid, watery, mobile, smooth, liquefied, liquified, (*n*) liquor, drink, juice, liquidness, sap; *antonyms* (*adj*) firm, (*n*) solid, gaseous, **5**. watery; *synonyms* (*adj*) dilute, diluted, washy, wet, thin, damp, aqueous, hydrous, insipid, tearful, weak, dripping, humid, soggy, soft; *antonyms* (*adj*) concentrated, strong.

rantia 1. desire; *synonyms* (*n*) ambition, hope, aspiration, will, wish, craving, dream, impulse, (*v*) fancy, aspire, seek, want, aim, choose, crave; *antonyms* (*n*) aversion, reality, (*v*) dislike, hate, **2**.

despise; *synonyms* (*v*) scorn, contemn, disdain, loathe, depreciate, abhor, detest, slight, condemn, defy, disregard, execrate, neglect, spurn, (*n*) deride; *antonyms* (*v*) admire, respect, **3.** love; *synonyms* (*n*) desire, affection, dear, fondness, liking, benevolence, charity, attachment, beloved, darling, devotion, honey, (*v*) cherish, enjoy, like; *antonyms* (*n*) abhorrence, hatred, **4.** hate; *synonyms* (*v*) abominate, despise, (*n*) enmity, animosity, detestation, abomination, antipathy, distaste, execration, hostility, loathing, odium, revulsion, spite, disgust; *antonyms* (*v*) love, adore.

rantiaki 1. loved; *synonyms* (*adj*) dear, beloved, cherished, pet, precious, appreciated, esteemed, prized, respected, treasured, valued, important, (*n*) darling, **2.** desired; *synonyms* (*adj*) coveted, craved, desirable, chosen, favorite, wanted, needed, welcome, adored, appropriate, preferred, proper, (*v*) complying, consenting, willing; *antonym* (*adj*) undesirable, **3.** hated; *synonyms* (*adj*) detested, despised, disliked, reviled, scorned, unpopular, abhorrent, despicable, insufferable, loathed, ostracized; *antonym* (*adj*) popular, **4.** despised; *synonyms* (*adj*) hated, abject, contemptible, contemptuous, opprobrious, infamous, insolent, neglected, reproachful, scornful, scurrilous, vile.

rao 1. neighbor; *synonyms* (*n*) acquaintance, national, inhabitant, bystander, (*adj*) neighbour, neighboring, neighbouring, (*v*) abut, adjoin, touch, border, butt, join, line, verge, **2.** friend; *synonyms* (*n*) fellow, ally, colleague, crony, advocate, assistant, booster, buddy, mate, connection, wellwisher, attendant, (*adj*) associate, companion, comrade; *antonyms* (*n*) enemy, foe, stranger, rival, **3.** mate; *synonyms* (*n*) match, partner, compeer, consort, friend, spouse, husband, wife, brother, chum, (*v*) equal, copulate, couple, pair, checkmate, **4.** partner; *synonyms* (*n*) copartner, accomplice, collaborator, pal, confederate, accessory, cooperator, pardner, helper, man, teammate, partaker, participator, coadjutor, (*v*) escort, **5.** pal; *synonyms* (*n*) sidekick, confidant, intimate.

raoi 1. just; *synonyms* (*adv*) exactly, hardly, newly, (*adj*) fair, right, correct, equitable, accurate, honest, impartial, barely, fit, good, reasonable, righteous; *antonyms* (*adj*) unfair, biased, wrong, **2.** appropriate; *synonyms* (*adj*) pertinent, proper, true, agreeable, apposite, apt, congruous, particular, peculiar, special, suitable, (*v*) annex, allocate, adopt, seize; *antonyms* (*adj*) inappropriate, unsuitable, unrelated, untimely, (*v*) surrender, **3.** applicable; *synonyms* (*adj*) relevant, germane, applicative, applicatory, appropriate, apropos, available, fitting, relative, admissible, (*n*) felicitous, happy; *antonym* (*adj*) irrelevant, **4.** agreeable; *synonyms* (*adj*) acceptable, accordant, pleasant, pleasing, nice, affable, amusing, compatible, conformable, congenial, consistent, enjoyable, genial, grateful, (*v*) desirable; *antonyms* (*adj*) disagreeable, discordant, nasty, unpleasant, unwilling, aggressive, resistant, **5.** justly; *synonyms* (*adv*) correctly, fairly, accurately, equitably, honestly, rightly, deservedly, duly, equally, lawfully, justifiedly, **6.** ethical; *synonyms* (*adj*) ethic, decent, just, moral, upright, virtuous, honorable; *antonyms* (*adj*) immoral, unethical, **7.** agreeably; *synonyms* (*adv*) enjoyably, kindly, pleasantly, pleasingly, suitably, well, (*v*) happily; *antonyms* (*adv*) disagreeably, unpleasantly, **8.** decently; *synonyms* (*adv*) properly, becomingly, appropriately, genially, courteously, justly; *antonyms* (*adv*) indecently, rudely, **9.** decent; *synonyms* (*adj*) adequate, becoming, comely, decorous, modest, respectable, seemly, sufficient, chaste, ethical, satisfactory, straight, convenient, fine, tolerable; *antonyms* (*adj*) unwholesome, disreputable, filthy, inadequate, indecent, **10.** fitting; *synonyms* (*adj*) applicable, expedient, advisable, befitting, feasible, opportune, due, competent, matched, (*n*) adaptation, adjustment, accommodation, appointment, installation, attachment; *antonym* (*adj*) improper, **11.** advantageous; *synonyms* (*adj*) favorable, auspicious, useful, beneficial, fortunate, gainful, helpful, lucky, profitable, serviceable, worthwhile, handy, effective, lucrative, positive; *antonym* (*adj*) useless, **12.** appropriately; *synonyms* (*adv*) fittingly, befittingly, fitly, accordingly; *antonyms* (*adv*) inappropriately, unsuitably, **13.** becomingly; *synonyms* (*adv*) honorably, thriftily, worthily, carefully, excellently, **14.** fine; *synonyms* (*adj*) delicate, dainty, brave, capital, elegant, excellent, thin, delightful, acute, admirable, alright, beautiful, (*n*) penalty, amercement, (*v*) punish; *antonyms* (*adj*) poor, thick, coarse, substantial, unsatisfactory, wide, **15.** good; *synonyms* (*adj*) able, benefit, delicious, efficient, capable, superior, advantageous, generous, gentle, beneficent, benevolent, estimable, (*n*) benign, advantage, gain; *antonyms* (*adj*) disobedient, wicked, (*n*) evil, bad, **16.** fittingly, **17.** becoming; *synonyms* (*v*) meet, (*adj*) eligible, handsome, attractive, graceful; *antonym* (*adj*) unbecoming, **18.** reasonable; *synonyms* (*adj*) moderate, rational, legitimate, judicious, sensible, cheap, inexpensive, intelligent, plausible, sane, temperate, credible, logical, sober, (*n*) clear; *antonyms* (*adj*) illogical, unreasonable, expensive, **19.** right; *synonyms* (*adj*) even, perfect, exact, faithful, direct, full, (*n*) privilege, law, liberty, authority, claim, freedom, interest, justice, (*v*) rectify; *antonyms* (*adj*) unjustified, incorrect, (*n*) left, **20.** seemly; *synonym* (*adj*) personable.

raoiakina 1. mediate; *synonyms* (*v*) arbitrate, intercede, intervene, interfere, intermediate, referee, interpose, moderate, negotiate, reconcile, adjudicate, decide, judge, liaise, *(adj)* middle, **2**. intercede; *synonym (v)* mediate, **3**. amend; *synonyms (v)* ameliorate, improve, mend, rectify, alter, better, correct, emend, fix, reform, adjust, help, redress, remedy, repair; *antonym (v)* worsen, **4**. reconcile; *synonyms (v)* appease, accommodate, accord, harmonize, pacify, placate, compose, harmonise, propitiate, settle, adapt, agree, conform, square, *(adj)* conciliate.

raoiakinaki 1. mediated; *synonym (adj)* considered, **2**. amended; *synonyms (adj)* altered, reformed, **3**. reconciled; *synonyms (v)* affriended, *(adj)* meet, resigned, serene, submissive, acquiescent.

raoiroi 1. beneficent; *synonyms (adj)* charitable, benevolent, good, kind, philanthropic, gracious, benefic, bounteous, eleemosynary, generous, merciful, munificent, altruistic, liberal, *(n)* kindly, **2**. nice; *synonyms (adj)* beautiful, dainty, fastidious, fine, lovely, neat, likable, delicious, agreeable, correct, decent, delicate, difficult, enjoyable, exact; *antonyms (adj)* unpleasant, horrible, **3**. good; *synonyms (adj)* able, benefit, right, efficient, capable, excellent, nice, superior, well, advantageous, desirable, gentle, *(n)* benign, advantage, gain; *antonyms (adj)* disobedient, poor, wicked, *(n)* evil, bad, **4**. well; *synonyms (adv)* easily, thoroughly, considerably, fully, correctly, *(adj)* healthy, fit, shaft, sound, robust, *(n)* fountain, spring, pit, hollow, *(v)* gush; *antonyms (adv)* ill, badly, poorly, *(adj)* sick, unwell, dying, nauseous, **5**. righteous; *synonyms (adj)* fair, moral, honest, just, virtuous, godly, pious, honorable, pure, upright, impartial, saintly, equitable, proper, rightful.

raom 1. companion; *synonyms (n)* colleague, buddy, mate, peer, chum, comrade, fellow, partner, assistant, brother, acquaintance, attendant, *(adj)* associate, ally, *(v)* accompany; *antonym (n)* enemy, **2**. acquaintance; *synonyms (n)* connection, familiarity, friend, acquaintanceship, awareness, companion, contact, conversance, conversancy, experience, friendship, information, intercourse, pal, *(v)* knowledge; *antonyms (n)* ignorance, stranger, **3**. adjutant; *synonyms (n)* aide-de-camp, aide, adjuvant, auxiliary, help, brigadier, captain, centurion, lieutenant, major, officer, skipper, sublieutenant, cadet, *(adj)* acting, **4**. comrade; *synonyms (n)* compeer, familiar, cohort, confidante, confrere, crony, equal, coadjutor, *(adj)* accomplice, **5**. assistant; *synonyms (adj)* ancillary, adjunct, helpful, *(n)* accessory, assist, subordinate, acolyte, assistance, helper, adjutant, deputy, second, subsidiary, servant, *(v)* aid, **6**. mate; *synonyms (n)* match, consort, spouse, husband, wife, counterpart, double, twin, woman, *(v)* copulate, couple, pair, checkmate, correspond, join, **7**. associate; *synonyms (v)* affiliate, connect, company, link,

relate, unite, coalesce, mingle, mix, socialize, amalgamate, *(n)* member, collaborator, consociate, participant; *antonyms (v)* avoid, dissociate, distance, *(adj)* chief, **8**. chum; *synonyms (n)* intimate, playmate, sidekick, **9**. buddy.

raona 1. associate; *synonyms (v)* affiliate, connect, company, link, relate, consort, *(n)* ally, assistant, companion, fellow, partner, accomplice, adjunct, acquaintance, colleague; *antonyms (v)* avoid, dissociate, distance, *(adj)* chief, *(n)* stranger, **2**. companion; *synonyms (n)* buddy, mate, peer, chum, comrade, brother, attendant, escort, familiar, friend, pal, playmate, boyfriend, *(adj)* associate, *(v)* accompany; *antonym (n)* enemy, **3**. associated; *synonyms (adj)* connected, related, affiliated, allied, united, attached, confederate, joined, linked, alike; *antonym (adj)* unrelated, **4**. convoy; *synonyms (n)* guard, column, fleet, procession, safeguard, train, *(v)* conduct, guide, attend, bring, lead, **5**. accompany; *synonyms (v)* follow, walk, concur, convoy, join, take, **6**. chaperone; *synonyms (v)* chaperon, entertain, matronize, superintend, **7**. uphold; *synonyms (v)* sustain, defend, maintain, preserve, continue, back, bolster, confirm, countenance, encourage, endorse, assert, buttress, advocate, *(n)* support.

raonaki 1. accompanied; *synonym (adj)* attended, **2**. associated; *synonyms (adj)* connected, related, affiliated, allied, united, attendant, attached, confederate, joined, linked, alike; *antonym (adj)* unrelated.

raonna ally; *synonyms (n)* confederate, accomplice, companion, friend, colleague, partner, accessory, adherent, assistant, auxiliary, *(v)* affiliate, align, support, *(adj)* associate, coadjutor; *antonyms (n)* adversary, foe, opponent.

raonnaki allied; *synonyms (adj)* akin, related, confederate, cognate, connected, united, joined, associated, confederative, kindred, linked, near, relative; *antonyms (adj)* rival, unrelated.

raoroa far; *synonyms (adv)* wide, off, widely, well, astray, *(adj)* distant, aloof, faraway, remote, much, outlying, *(v)* considerably, abundantly; *antonyms (adv)* close, briefly, *(adj)* near.

raou 1. fiance; *synonyms (v)* affiance, betroth, **2**. fiancee; *synonyms (adj)* betrothed, affianced.

râpape 1. broad; *synonyms (adj)* wide, ample, comprehensive, extensive, general, large, sweeping, vast, free, big, blanket, capacious, deep, full, *(n)* female; *antonyms (adj)* narrow, specific, thin, **2**. wide; *synonyms (adj)* broad, spacious, roomy, expanded, extended, open, expansive, liberal, thick, tolerant, huge, cavernous, *(adv)* far, widely, astray; *antonym (adj)* restricted.

rara 1. lean; *synonyms (adj)* emaciated, gaunt, thin, bony, lank, lanky, *(v)* incline, bend, list, slant, bow, careen, pitch, (*n*) tilt, inclination; *antonyms* (*adj*) fat, plump, **2**. incline; *synonyms* (*n*) slope, bias, angle, ascent, dip, grade, gradient, decline, descent, hill, (*v*) cant, dispose, lean, bank, influence, **3**. inclined; *synonyms* (*adj*) prone, apt, oblique, willing, bowed, liable, likely, minded, predisposed, ready, bent, fain, susceptible, (*v*) given, (*prep*) disposed; *antonyms* (*adj*) level, reluctant, unwilling, **4**. blood; *synonyms* (*n*) ancestry, birth, gore, family, kindred, lineage, origin, beau, bloodshed, consanguinity, coxcomb, exquisite, extraction, (*adj*) humor, juice, **5**. rust; *synonyms* (*n*) decay, corrosion, (*v*) corrode, eat, tarnish, (*adj*) rusty.

râra blood; *synonyms* (*n*) ancestry, birth, gore, descent, family, kindred, lineage, origin, beau, bloodshed, consanguinity, coxcomb, exquisite, extraction, (*adj*) humor.

rarabuareare 1. arouse; *synonyms* (*v*) animate, rouse, stir, wake, agitate, awaken, excite, stimulate, anger, kindle, provoke, raise, awake, call, evoke; *antonym* (*v*) calm, **2**. anger; *synonyms* (*n*) displeasure, fury, rage, indignation, resentment, annoyance, (*v*) enrage, incense, aggravate, displease, exasperate, irritate, offend, wrath, fume; *antonyms* (*n*) pleasure, composure, (*v*) please, placate, pacify, **3**. boil; *synonyms* (*v*) seethe, bubble, churn, simmer, ferment, burn, effervesce, heat, gurgle, (*n*) abscess, blister, furuncle, pimple, (*adj*) sore, rave; *antonym* (*v*) freeze.

rarabuareareaki 1. boiled; *synonyms* (*adj*) done, intoxicated, poached, stewed, (*v*) sodden, saturated, seethed, soaked, **2**. aroused; *synonyms* (*adj*) excited, ablaze, aflame, passionate, hot, activated, afraid, awake, demonic, elated, emotional, fascinated, flaming, flushed, horny, **3**. angered; *synonyms* (*adj*) infuriated, annoyed, enraged, furious, incensed, huffy, irate, maddened, spleened, ferocious, fierce, frustrated, savage, tempestuous, wild.

rarae scatter; *synonyms* (*v*) disperse, dispel, disseminate, distribute, dissipate, spray, circulate, diffuse, disband, sprinkle, propagate, litter, rout, broadcast, (*n*) spread; *antonym* (*v*) gather.

raraea tear; *synonyms* (*n*) split, rupture, rent, (*v*) break, rip, crack, pull, rend, lacerate, race, run, rush, slit, rive, cleave.

raraeaki scattered; *synonyms* (*adj*) dispersed, dissipated, confused, disconnected, disordered, sparse, sporadic, thin, diffuse, distributed, rare, separate, spread, stray, strewn; *antonym* (*adj*) concentrated.

raraeua 1. agitated; *synonyms* (*adj*) restless, excited, nervous, restive, tumultuous, upset, distressed, tense, alarmed, anxious, distraught, jumpy, overwrought, perturbed, shaken; *antonyms* (*adj*) calm, composed, lethargic, **2**. restless; *synonyms* (*adj*) fidgety, uneasy, unquiet, agitated,

apprehensive, fretful, impatient, feverish, turbulent, disturbed, edgy, wakeful, eager, hasty, mercurial; *antonym* (*adj*) relaxed.

rarai 1. rung; *synonyms* (*n*) round, rundle, degree, grade, stage, stair, spoke, stave, step, tread, **2**. sway; *synonyms* (*n*) influence, reign, rock, authority, empire, (*v*) command, rule, oscillate, control, reel, stagger, bias, careen, lurch, persuade, **3**. surly; *synonyms* (*adj*) grumpy, sullen, peevish, crusty, churlish, brusque, grouchy, gruff, morose, crabby, dark, gloomy, (*n*) harsh, rude, crabbed, **4**. sullen; *synonyms* (*adj*) cross, glum, grim, moody, sour, dismal, dour, lowering, surly, black, cloudy, cheerless, heavy, (*n*) sulky, obstinate; *antonym* (*adj*) cheerful, **5**. ring; *synonyms* (*n*) encircle, band, gang, jingle, loop, rim, circuit, annulus, (*v*) circle, call, peal, echo, resound, reverberate, gird.

raraiaki rung; *synonyms* (*n*) round, rundle, degree, grade, stage, stair, spoke, stave, step, tread.

raraikumea 1. badger; *synonyms* (*v*) pester, annoy, tease, bother, harass, beleaguer, bug, harry, hassle, hound, molest, plague, worry, disturb, aggravate, **2**. abrade; *synonyms* (*v*) scrape, file, skin, chafe, rub, scour, graze, abrase, erode, gall, grate, grind, scratch, scrub, scuff, **3**. annoy; *synonyms* (*v*) anger, displease, irritate, afflict, perturb, provoke, rile, torment, vex, badger, bore, devil, exasperate, (*n*) annoyance, (*adj*) excite; *antonyms* (*v*) please, pacify, soothe, **4**. bug; *synonyms* (*n*) beetle, disease, germ, illness, insect, microbe, microorganism, ailment, sickness, blemish, defect, (*v*) irk, beset, distress, (*adj*) louse, **5**. bother; *synonyms* (*v*) trouble, bedevil, bait, crucify, discommode, disquiet, fret, inconvenience, (*n*) fuss, pain, ado, concern, nuisance, aggravation, disturbance; *antonyms* (*v*) delight, (*n*) pleasure.

raraikumeaki 1. bugged; *synonyms* (*adj*) abashed, anxious, bewitched, distressed, engrossed, enthusiastic, fanatical, incensed, indignant, obsessed, preoccupied, rabid, tense, **2**. annoyed; *synonyms* (*adj*) angry, irate, irritated, vexed, aggravated, angered, cross, disgruntled, displeased, exasperated, infuriated, offended, peeved, pestered, resentful; *antonyms* (*adj*) calm, pleased, unprovoked, smiling, **3**. bothered; *synonyms* (*adj*) worried, disturbed, troubled, concerned, distraught, nervous, uneasy, upset, **4**. abraded; *synonyms* (*adj*) scraped, skinned, raw.

raraki 1. inclined; *synonyms* (*adj*) prone, apt, oblique, willing, bowed, liable, likely, minded, predisposed, ready, bent, fain, susceptible, (*v*) given, (*prep*) disposed; *antonyms* (*adj*) level, reluctant, unwilling, **2**. rusted; *synonym* (*adj*) rusty.

rarako conserve; *synonyms* (*v*) economize, embalm, husband, keep, protect, save, defend, hoard, maintain, safeguard, economise, (*n*) preserve, conserves, jam, preserves; *antonyms* (*v*) spend, use, waste, expend, damage.

rarakoaki conserved; *synonyms* (*adj*) preserved, potted, sealed.

raran 1. leak; *synonyms* (*n*) leakage, crevice, breach, disclosure, chink, escape, fissure, hole, (*v*) dribble, reveal, release, disclose, drip, drop, ooze, **2.** drip; *synonyms* (*n*) trickle, leak, splash, (*v*) distill, seep, weep, trill, drizzle, fall, percolate, **3.** trickle; *synonyms* (*n*) drivel, drool, (*v*) flow, filter, leach, bleed, drain, plash, pour, slobber, spirtle; *antonyms* (*n*) throng, (*v*) gush, **4.** percolate; *synonyms* (*v*) infiltrate, penetrate, diffuse, filtrate, permeate, soak, strain, exude, perk, **5.** seep; *synonym* (*v*) course.

raranga weave; *synonyms* (*v*) twine, twist, braid, knit, entwine, interweave, wind, waver, plait, fabricate, tissue, lurch, interlace, reel, (*n*) texture.

raranginako 1. flow; *synonyms* (*n*) flood, current, discharge, abound, (*v*) stream, course, flux, jet, run, surge, float, emanate, fall, gush, pour, **2.** seep; *synonyms* (*v*) ooze, exude, percolate, filter, dribble, flow, leak, permeate, trickle, drop, drip, **3.** pass; *synonyms* (*v*) deliver, give, happen, lead, move, offer, overtake, live, advance, die, elapse, exceed, extend, lapse, (*adj*) go; *antonym* (*v*) fail.

rarango 1. continued; *synonyms* (*adj*) continuous, constant, extended, unremitting, serial, continuate, eternal, long, perpetual, protracted, recurrent, solid, undivided, untiring, **2.** persistent; *synonyms* (*adj*) durable, insistent, lasting, obstinate, permanent, chronic, consistent, dogged, firm, incessant, relentless, stubborn, unrelenting, habitual, (*n*) frequent; *antonyms* (*adj*) contained, occasional, **3.** steady; *synonyms* (*adj*) even, secure, fixed, resolute, stable, cool, sedate, settled, certain, determined, (*v*) steadfast, calm, regular, brace, loyal; *antonyms* (*adj*) unsteady, shaky, wobbly, intermittent, unreliable.

raraoma 1. repent; *synonyms* (*v*) regret, deplore, bewail, rue, lament, atone, **2.** sorrowful; *synonyms* (*adj*) miserable, melancholy, doleful, lugubrious, rueful, sad, gloomy, dismal, dreary, grievous, lamentable, mournful, piteous, unhappy, dolorous; *antonyms* (*adj*) happy, cheerful, content, joyful, successful, **3.** penitent; *synonyms* (*adj*) repentant, apologetic, contrite, regretful, remorseful, sorry; *antonym* (*adj*) unrepentant.

raraomaeakin worry; *synonyms* (*v*) torment, trouble, bother, distress, tease, annoy, care, disturb, fear, molest, (*n*) concern, burden, harass, pain, fuss; *antonyms* (*v*) soothe, reassure, (*n*) calmness, reassurance.

raraomaeakina 1. regret; *synonyms* (*v*) bewail, grieve, bemoan, deplore, lament, mourn, sorrow, repent, (*n*) grief, compunction, contrition,

penitence, remorse, repentance, disappointment, **2.** worry; *synonyms* (*v*) torment, trouble, bother, distress, tease, annoy, care, disturb, fear, molest, (*n*) concern, burden, harass, pain, fuss; *antonyms* (*v*) soothe, reassure, (*n*) calmness, reassurance.

raraomaeakinaki worried; *synonyms* (*adj*) apprehensive, distressed, nervous, uneasy, upset, anxious, afraid, bothered, concerned, disturbed, troubled, fearful, restless, unhappy, (*v*) afflicted; *antonyms* (*adj*) calm, carefree, reassured, relaxed, untroubled.

rarati 1. full; *synonyms* (*adj*) complete, absolute, abundant, broad, flush, ample, enough, extensive, total, detailed, comprehensive, copious, good, (*n*) entire, crowded; *antonyms* (*adj*) empty, lacking, starving, hungry, sketchy, incomplete, **2.** gorged; *synonyms* (*adj*) satiated, sated, full, stuffed, bursting, congested, replete, satisfied, surfeited, glutted, **3.** saturated; *synonyms* (*adj*) drenched, sodden, wet, concentrated, soaked, sopping, soggy, soppy, pure, soaking; *antonym* (*adj*) dry, **4.** stretched; *synonyms* (*adj*) taut, extended, stiff, tense, tight, strained, expanded, outstretched, elongated, outspread, prolonged, protracted, assiduous, close, delayed; *antonym* (*adj*) brief, **5.** taught; *synonyms* (*v*) fast, firm, overwrought, (*adj*) instructed, educated, schooled, instruct, arranged, enlightened, furnished, gentle, provided, scholarly, tutored, well-bred, **6.** satiated; *synonyms* (*adj*) satiate, jaded, blasé, corpulent, cropful, disgusted, fat, fleshed, initiated, sick.

rarau 1. jealous; *synonyms* (*adj*) covetous, distrustful, envious, suspicious, resentful, invidious, green, grudging, **2.** faint; *synonyms* (*adj*) collapse, dim, dizzy, feeble, indistinct, weak, dull, gentle, soft, vague, delicate, distant, (*v*) languish, swoon, droop; *antonyms* (*adj*) distinct, strong, clear, obvious, considerable, loud, pungent, **3.** tired; *synonyms* (*adj*) exhausted, fatigued, hackneyed, weary, banal, commonplace, stale, threadbare, trite, beat, haggard, jaded, stock, worn, drowsy; *antonyms* (*adj*) fresh, invigorated, alert, refreshed, energetic, original, **4.** swoon; *synonyms* (*n*) fainting, syncope, deliquium, lipothymy, prostration, (*v*) faint, conk, die, (*adj*) blow, drop, gasp, pant, puff.

raraure 1. detach; *synonyms* (*v*) disengage, divide, part, disconnect, disentangle, dissociate, remove, separate, unhook, isolate, abstract, cleave, disjoin, divorce, (*n*) detail; *antonyms* (*v*) attach, fasten, add, associate, **2.** divorce; *synonyms* (*n*) separation, divorcement, rupture, (*v*) detach, disunite, disjoint, disassociate, sever, split, break; *antonyms* (*n*) marriage, wedding, **3.** disunite; *synonyms* (*v*) dissolve, dissever, disarticulate, cut, dislocate, embroil, **4.** separate; *synonyms* (*adj*) detached, individual, particular, single, disjoined, distinct, diverse, (*v*) insulate, scatter, discrete, discriminate, disperse, distinguish, demarcate, differentiate; *antonyms* (*adj*) connected, joined, simultaneous, (*v*) unite, merge, mix, combine, fuse, join, link.

raraureaki 1. disunited; *synonyms* (*adj*) divided, split, disjointed, abrupt, confused, crumbled, cut, disordered, distinct, (*v*) disconnected, apart, blighted, broken, contrite, cracked, **2**. detached; *synonyms* (*adj*) aloof, cool, isolated, separate, disinterested, dispassionate, impartial, indifferent, neutral, objective, remote, separated, unconcerned, unconnected, discrete; *antonyms* (*adj*) attached, involved, engrossed, warm, **3**. divorced; *synonym* (*adj*) single, **4**. separated; *synonyms* (*adj*) detached, free, disjunct, removed, dislocated, independent, lone, (*prep*) disjoined.

rarikin 1. heroine; *synonyms* (*n*) hero, adventurer, champion, heroess, part, protagonist, role, angel, conqueror, demigod, idol, seraph, **2**. indigent; *synonyms* (*adj*) destitute, poor, impoverished, needy, impecunious, penniless, miserable, necessitous, underprivileged, broke, (*n*) pauper; *antonym* (*adj*) rich, **3**. hero; *synonyms* (*n*) character, leader, protector, worthy, warrior, bomber, celebrity, combatant, defender, fighter, **4**. poor; *synonyms* (*adj*) bad, low, paltry, deplorable, evil, inadequate, insufficient, pathetic, piteous, pitiful, meagre, deficient, feeble, (*v*) meager, (*n*) mean; *antonyms* (*adj*) wealthy, excellent, first-rate, privileged, well-off, admirable, good.

rarikina trim; *synonyms* (*adj*) tidy, neat, spruce, orderly, shipshape, (*v*) cut, dress, clip, garnish, shave, adorn, embellish, lop, prune, reduce; *antonym* (*adj*) fat.

rarikinaki trimmed; *synonyms* (*adj*) cut, cunning, demure, down, emasculated, gashed, gelded, level, mown, neat, shortened, slashed, sly, smooth, snoD.

rarikiriki recline; *synonyms* (*v*) lie, lean, loll, lounge, repose, rest, couch, slant, lay, tilt, recumb, relax, sprawl.

raro far; *synonyms* (*adv*) wide, off, widely, well, astray, (*adj*) distant, aloof, faraway, remote, much, outlying, (*v*) considerably, abundantly; *antonyms* (*adv*) close, briefly, (*adj*) near.

raroa 1. afar; *synonyms* (*adv*) away, off, distantly, apart, aside, (*adj*) outlying, far, (*prep*) outside, past, **2**. far; *synonyms* (*adv*) wide, widely, well, astray, (*adj*) distant, aloof, faraway, remote, much, (*v*) considerably, abundantly; *antonyms* (*adv*) close, briefly, (*adj*) near, **3**. distant; *synonyms* (*adj*) cold, chill, cool, detached, reserved, long, icy, indifferent, removed, standoffish, unfriendly, abstracted, deep, dull, (*n*) chilly; *antonyms* (*adj*) adjacent, friendly, nearby, neighboring, warm, pending, alert, intimate, involved, **4**. remote; *synonyms* (*adj*) inaccessible, faint, alien, foreign, isolated, lonely, secluded, unapproachable, extraneous, slender,

slight, solitary, unlikely, obscure, quiet; *antonym* (*adj*) accessible.

raroi 1. good; *synonyms* (*adj*) able, benefit, delicious, right, efficient, capable, excellent, fine, nice, superior, well, advantageous, (*n*) benign, advantage, gain; *antonyms* (*adj*) disobedient, poor, wicked, unpleasant, (*n*) evil, bad, **2**. useful; *synonyms* (*adj*) profitable, beneficial, handy, helpful, practical, convenient, effective, valuable, functional, clever, constructive, gainful, serviceable, usable, good; *antonyms* (*adj*) useless, worthless, ineffective.

rarua scratch; *synonyms* (*n*) score, mark, nick, scrabble, dent, abrasion, cut, groove, (*v*) graze, notch, rub, scrape, chafe, rake, grate.

raruaki scratched; *synonyms* (*adj*) scraped, hurt, abraded, dented, injured, raw, sgraffito, spoiled, broken, skinned, smashed.

ratau 1. almost; *synonyms* (*adv*) nearly, approximately, just, around, most, practically, roughly, virtually, some, (*prep*) about, (*adj*) near, nigh, approaching, approximate, barely, **2**. nearly; *synonyms* (*adv*) almost, close, closely, intimately, much, dear, halfway, (*adj*) thereabouts, **3**. enough; *synonyms* (*adv*) rather, plenty, amply, adequately, satisfaction, fairly, fully, (*n*) adequacy, fill, sufficiency, (*adj*) ample, sufficient, adequate, competent, decent; *antonym* (*adj*) inadequate.

rau 1. thatch; *synonyms* (*n*) thatching, ceiling, roof, teach, tile, hair, mop, **2**. mellow; *synonyms* (*adj*) mature, ripe, gentle, luscious, mild, mollify, smooth, soft, juicy, perfect, mellowed, melodious, (*v*) melt, ripen, soften, **3**. impassive; *synonyms* (*adj*) apathetic, expressionless, calm, cool, stoic, stolid, callous, impervious, blank, dull, emotionless, immovable, unaffected, unconcerned, unemotional; *antonyms* (*adj*) emotional, expressive, involved, mobile, **4**. flexible; *synonyms* (*adj*) elastic, adaptable, pliable, yielding, lissome, pliant, supple, facile, adjustable, bendable, compliant, ductile, flexile, lithe, malleable; *antonyms* (*adj*) inflexible, rigid, fixed, obstinate, stiff, stubborn, **5**. harmonious; *synonyms* (*adj*) congruous, congenial, consonant, musical, amicable, peaceful, consistent, compatible, friendly, agreeable, congruent, harmonical, sweet, unanimous, concordant; *antonyms* (*adj*) discordant, dissonant, harsh, **6**. flask; *synonyms* (*n*) bottle, flasket, carafe, cask, container, decanter, jar, beaker, can, flaskful, tin, alembic, bag, carboy, caster, **7**. jealous; *synonyms* (*adj*) covetous, distrustful, envious, suspicious, resentful, invidious, green, grudging, **8**. calm; *synonyms* (*adj*) quiet, tranquil, bland, (*v*) assuage, appease, still, allay, pacify, easy, moderate, steady, tranquilize, abate, (*n*) lull, equanimity; *antonyms* (*adj*) agitated, angry, nervous, stormy, wild, annoyed, anxious, enraged, frantic, frightened, intense, irritable, (*v*) agitate, upset, (*n*) agitation, **9.** imperturbable; *synonyms* (*adj*) dispassionate, composed, impassive, placid, unflappable, equable, sedate, serene, unruffled, nonchalant, **10.** tranquil; *synonyms* (*adj*) collected, motionless, comfortable, relaxed, silent, untroubled, imperturbable, peaceable, easygoing, even, inactive, soothing; *antonyms* (*adj*) noisy, tense, **11.** still; *synonyms* (*adv*) however, but, nevertheless, yet, more, (*adj*) silence, quiescent, mute, peace, hushed, immobile, (*n*) hush, (*v*) compose, soothe, ease; *antonyms* (*adj*) moving, effervescent, fizzy, windy, **12.** silent; *synonyms* (*adj*) dumb, tacit, inarticulate, inaudible, incommunicative, mum, noiseless, reserved, reticent, taciturn, implicit, soundless, speechless, dormant, unpronounced; *antonyms* (*adj*) spoken, loud, talkative, explicit, open, **13.** placid; *synonyms* (*adj*) meek, contented, leisurely, kind, docile, tender, undisturbed, unperturbed, **14.** tender; *synonyms* (*adj*) affectionate, painful, loving, sensitive, sore, compassionate, delicate, fond, frail, (*v*) proffer, present, propose, (*n*) offer, bid, overture; *antonyms* (*adj*) tough, hard, hardhearted, rubbery, rough, **15.** quiet; *synonyms* (*adj*) harmonious, low, modest, muted, private, (*v*) repose, gag, quell, rest, slow, conciliate, mitigate, (*n*) peacefulness, alleviate, leisure; *antonyms* (*adj*) vociferous, active, (*n*) noise, **16.** unruffled; *synonyms* (*adj*) sober, unimpassioned, unexcited, unflustered, patient, serious, unflurried, (*v*) unmoved, **17.** serene; *synonyms* (*adj*) clear, lucid, limpid, bright, evident, light, perspicuous, plain, **18.** sedate; *synonyms* (*adj*) solemn, staid, earnest, heavy, decorous, severe, thoughtful, momentous, weighty, (*v*) grave, demure, important, tranquillize, wistful, contemplative; *antonym* (*adj*) exciting, **19.** soft; *synonyms* (*adj*) limp, balmy, slack, loose, clement, faint, flabby, flaccid, lenient, pleasant, temperate, amiable, downy, effeminate, (*v*) feeble; *antonyms* (*adj*) firm, hoarse, solid, alcoholic, shrill, strong, **20.** peaceful; *synonyms* (*adj*) halcyon, restful, conciliatory, happy, idyllic, passive; *antonyms* (*adj*) aggressive, violent.

rauakina 1. jealous; *synonyms* (*adj*) covetous, distrustful, envious, suspicious, resentful, invidious, green, grudging, **2.** content; *synonyms* (*n*) capacity, contentment, matter, meaning, subject, substance, contentedness, (*adj*) contented, happy, fulfilled, (*v*) appease, please, satisfy, suffice, delight; *antonyms* (*adj*) tormented, unhappy, discontented, dissatisfied, rebellious, (*v*) discontent, upset, **3.** satisfied; *synonyms* (*v*) convinced, (*adj*) content, full, pleased, certain, confident, sure, complacent, persuaded, sated, satiated, easy, positive, quenched; *antonym* (*adj*) frustrated.

raumea 1. filter; *synonyms* (*n*) strainer, (*v*) percolate, sieve, drip, leak, filtrate, ooze, purify, refine, screen, strain, dribble, drop, clean, permeate; *antonym* (*v*) contaminate, **2.** strain; *synonyms* (*n*) stress, breed, effort, stretch, exertion, race, reach, song, (*v*) filter, sift, tax, endeavor, exert, extend, pull; *antonym* (*v*) relax, **3.** sift; *synonyms* (*v*) investigate, analyze, examine, riddle, sprinkle, bolt, separate, sort, probe, scatter, explore, inquire, (*n*) scrutinize, canvass, search.

raumeaki strained; *synonyms* (*adj*) forced, labored, tense, intense, constrained, laboured, unnatural, taut, tight, agonistic, agonistical, combative, farfetched; *antonyms* (*adj*) relaxed, natural.

rauna thatch; *synonyms* (*n*) thatching, ceiling, roof, teach, tile, hair, mop.

raure 1. detached; *synonyms* (*adj*) aloof, cool, isolated, separate, distinct, disconnected, disinterested, dispassionate, impartial, indifferent, neutral, objective, remote, separated, unconcerned; *antonyms* (*adj*) attached, involved, engrossed, warm, **2.** disunited; *synonyms* (*adj*) divided, split, disjointed, abrupt, confused, crumbled, cut, disordered, distributed, fragmented, (*v*) apart, blighted, broken, contrite, cracked, **3.** divorced; *synonym* (*adj*) single, **4.** separated; *synonyms* (*adj*) detached, free, disjunct, removed, dislocated, independent, lone, (*prep*) disjoined.

raureure separable; *synonyms* (*adj*) divisible, dissociable, partible, severable, detachable, discernible, distinguishable, isolatable, movable, removable, attachable, dividable, (*v*) discerptible, scissile.

rourounoe foot; *synonyms* (*n*) bottom, base, feet, foundation, basis, footing, measure, paw, pes, bed, butt, floor, (*v*) hoof, pay, hand; *antonym* (*n*) top.

rautaria 1. shower; *synonyms* (*n*) rain, drizzle, barrage, rainfall, torrent, volley, (*v*) pour, bathe, hail, sprinkle, wash, shed, bath, scatter, spray, **2.** rinse; *synonyms* (*n*) clean, tint, rinsing, (*v*) cleanse, flush, gargle, launder, lave, swab, dampen, dip, moisten, wet, (*adj*) mundify.

rava channel; *synonyms* (*n*) canal, conduit, groove, drain, duct, line, passage, trough, waterway, aqueduct, link, hollow, (*v*) carry, conduct, convey.

rawa 1. abstain; *synonyms* (*v*) refrain, desist, avoid, forbear, cease, decline, eschew, withhold, fast; *antonym* (*v*) consume, **2.** refuse; *synonyms* (*v*) deny, reject, disallow, dross, rebuff, disdain, dismiss, balk, (*n*) garbage, trash, waste, offal, debris, litter, leavings; *antonym* (*v*) accept, **3.** sulk; *synonyms* (*v*) brood, mope, pout, glower, grizzle, stew, (*n*) mood, temper, sulkiness, **4.** oppose; *synonyms* (*v*) object, contest, contend, contradict, contravene, controvert, counteract, resist, fight, counter, disagree, dissent, combat, confront, defend; *antonyms* (v) support, advocate, agree, back, advise.

rawaki 1. refused; *synonyms* (adj) forbidden, hence, prohibited, refuse, worthless, **2**. opposed; *synonyms* (adj) conflicting, contradictory, hostile, contrary, antagonistic, opposing, adverse, averse, contrasted, repugnant, incompatible, irreconcilable, counter, against, opposite.

rawana 1. bore; *synonyms* (v) dig, bother, tire, annoy, drill, perforate, pierce, plague, tap, (n) caliber, diameter, nuisance, well, annoyance, (adj) pother; *antonyms* (v) interest, excite, fascinate, **2**. drill; *synonyms* (n) exercise, discipline, practice, auger, borer, rehearsal, gimlet, preparation, (v) bore, coach, educate, inculcate, instruct, train, habituate, **3**. puncture; *synonyms* (n) prick, cut, hole, sting, break, leak, opening, (v) penetrate, stab, broach, impale, gore, punch, deflate, pink; *antonym* (v) inflate, **4**. penetrate; *synonyms* (v) imbue, fathom, infiltrate, permeate, filter, interpenetrate, enter, diffuse, percolate, probe, puncture, saturate, cross, move, strike, **5**. perforate; *synonym* (adj) perforated, **6**. pierce; *synonyms* (v) stick, bite, thrust, wound, pick, riddle, spike, insert, cleave, nip, hurt, knife, burst, slit, spear, **7**. stab; *synonyms* (n) jab, try, shot, pang, attempt, crack, effort, go, endeavor, (v) poke, prod, spit, push, poniard, lunge.

rawanaki 1. bored; *synonyms* (adj) tired, weary, uninterested, jaded, listless, sick, blasé, discontented, droopy, inattentive, indifferent, lazy, lethargic, sophisticated, unconcerned, **2**. drilled; *synonym* (adj) proficient, **3**. pierced; *synonyms* (adj) perforated, punctured, perforate, cleft, entered, **4**. punctured; *synonyms* (adj) pierced, disillusioned, flat, **5**. stabbed, **6**. perforated; *synonym* (adj) penetrated.

rawata heavy; *synonyms* (adj) dull, deep, dark, dense, fat, full, grave, gross, hard, arduous, bulky, burdensome, grievous, oppressive, thick; *antonyms* (adj) light, easy, slim, thin, slight, gentle, puny, skinny.

rawatakaei ponderous; *synonyms* (adj) cumbersome, heavy, grave, onerous, burdensome, massive, unwieldy, bulky, dull, hard, stodgy, weighty, lumbering, laborious, ungainly.

rawawaa grievous; *synonyms* (adj) grave, bitter, deplorable, dolorous, dreadful, sad, tough, pitiful, atrocious, heavy, painful, plaintive, regrettable, serious, sorrowful.

rawawata 1. heavy; *synonyms* (adj) dull, deep, dark, dense, fat, full, grave, gross, hard, arduous, bulky, burdensome, grievous, oppressive, thick; *antonyms* (adj) light, easy, slim, thin, slight, gentle, puny, skinny, **2**. laborious; *synonyms* (adj) difficult, backbreaking, diligent, heavy, industrious, grueling, assiduous, exhausting, formidable, painful, strenuous, tedious, toilsome, tough, active, **3**. depressed; *synonyms* (adj) concave, low, blue, dejected, dispirited, down, downcast, downhearted, gloomy, hollow, sad, crestfallen, disappointed, discouraged, flat; *antonyms* (adj) cheerful, happy, convex, **4**. ponderous; *synonyms* (adj) cumbersome, onerous, massive, unwieldy, stodgy, weighty, lumbering, laborious, ungainly, clumsy, hefty, slow, artificial, clayey, cloggy, **5**. sad; *synonyms* (adj) dreary, dismal, distressing, miserable, mournful, pitiable, pitiful, bad, bleak, deplorable, depressed, depressing, disconsolate, doleful, dolorous; *antonyms* (adj) joyful, brave, cheery, composed.

rawea 1. grab; *synonyms* (v) capture, get, snatch, appropriate, clasp, clutch, fascinate, grapple, rob, seize, assume, attract, (n) arrest, catch, seizure, **2**. grip; *synonyms* (n) handle, bag, clench, clinch, clutches, clamp, compass, (v) grasp, hold, cling, apprehend, embrace, grab, gripe, captivate; *antonyms* (v) bore, release, **3**. grasp; *synonyms* (n) grip, appreciation, apprehension, comprehension, reach, (v) comprehend, conceive, dig, sense, understand, digest, fathom, gather, absorb, appreciate, **4**. gain; *synonyms* (v) acquire, benefit, derive, attain, earn, win, achieve, advance, make, find, accomplish, (n) profit, earnings, acquisition, advantage; *antonyms* (v) lose, (n) loss, **5**. nab; *synonyms* (v) collar, pinch, take, hook, cop, nail, bust, detain, steal, **6**. clasp; *synonyms* (n) hug, buckle, brooch, cuddle, lock, button, fastener, (v) squeeze, stick, enfold, adhere, link, clip, fasten, (adj) pin, **7**. catch; *synonyms* (v) ensnare, intercept, trap, block, entangle, entrap, hear, net, (n) haul, hitch, trick, bolt, pawl, snap, hasp, **8**. seize; *synonyms* (v) receive, annex, confiscate, conquer, carry, commandeer, impound, perceive, tackle, kidnap, abduct, adopt, obtain, affect, attach, **9**. snatch; *synonyms* (v) jerk, pluck, pilfer, plunder, lift, nobble, pull, twitch, filch, abstract, (n) bit, piece, scrap, bite, (adj) snack, **10**. rob; *synonyms* (v) deprive, pillage, rifle, fleece, purloin, pick, divest, defraud, despoil, loot, ransack, sack, strip, thieve, rape, **11**. take; *synonyms* (v) admit, bear, return, borrow, bring, claim, convey, demand, have, interpret, require, select, swallow, eat, (phr) accept; *antonyms* (v) give, refuse, abstain, add, **12**. tackle; *synonyms* (v) harness, undertake, attempt, stop, struggle, attack, (n) gear, equipment, rigging, kit, paraphernalia, rig, apparatus, outfit, tools; *antonym* (v) avoid, **13**. procure; *synonyms* (v) buy, gain, enlist, induce, purchase, engage, effect, secure, book, solicit, reap, cater, cause, fetch, pander.

raweaki 1. taken; *synonyms* (v) take, (adj) occupied, full, interpreted, besotted, crazed, enamored, engaged, interested, lovesick, obsessed, overcome, preferred, rapt, reserved, **2.** seized; *synonyms* (*adj*) confiscate, confiscated, appropriated, condemned, apprehended, detained, held, censured, convicted, forfeit, forfeited, **3.** robed; *synonyms* (*adj*) appareled, attired, clothed, dressed, garbed, garmented, habilimented, fixed, polished, vested.

rawebai 1. procure; *synonyms* (*v*) acquire, buy, get, obtain, earn, gain, win, have, attain, derive, enlist, find, induce, purchase, engage, **2.** seize; *synonyms* (*v*) capture, catch, grab, arrest, apprehend, clutch, grapple, receive, annex, assume, clasp, confiscate, conquer, grasp, grip; *antonym* (*v*) release, **3.** seek; *synonyms* (*v*) search, attempt, endeavor, hunt, look, inquire, aspire, beg, explore, pursue, quest, investigate, research, follow, (*n*) ask.

rawebaia 1. hoard; *synonyms* (*n*) store, bank, heap, stock, accumulation, fund, reserve, reservoir, (*v*) accumulate, amass, cache, collect, gather, garner, pile, **2.** monopolize; *synonyms* (*v*) engross, control, forestall, absorb, consume, monopolise, occupy, **3.** pilfer; *synonyms* (*v*) filch, steal, abstract, cabbage, lift, pinch, purloin, rob, embezzle, hook, nobble, pocket, swipe, thieve, appropriate, **4.** supply; *synonyms* (*n*) provision, hoard, issue, (*v*) furnish, afford, fill, feed, offer, provide, cater, contribute, deliver, equip, give, outfit, **5.** provide; *synonyms* (*v*) accommodate, administer, supply, allow, fit, endow, nourish, nurture, arm, bestow, donate, ensure, extend, ply, prepare, **6.** procure; *synonyms* (*v*) acquire, buy, get, obtain, earn, gain, win, have, attain, derive, enlist, find, induce, purchase, engage.

rawebaiaki 1. supplied; *synonyms* (*adj*) full, adequate, ample, available, complete, copious, fitted, impregnated, offered, perfect, plenteous, ready, sated, abounding, surfeited, **2.** seized; *synonyms* (*adj*) confiscate, confiscated, appropriated, condemned, apprehended, detained, held, censured, convicted, forfeit, forfeited, obsessed.

rawekai agile; *synonyms* (*adj*) active, nimble, adroit, quick, spry, deft, lively, brisk, lithe, sprightly, supple, quick-witted, alert, dexterous, fast; *antonym* (*adj*) clumsy.

rawekaia snatch; *synonyms* (*v*) grab, pinch, abduct, clutch, kidnap, seize, snap, jerk, capture, grasp, grip, pluck, (*n*) catch, seizure, arrest.

raweraweaba 1. grope; *synonyms* (*v*) feel, finger, fumble, touch, grabble, search, handle, paw, scrabble, **2.** finger; *synonyms* (*n*) digit, dactyl, (*v*) hand, thumb, grope, indicate, point, accuse, **3.** feel; *synonyms* (*v*) experience, sense, consider, believe, deem, endure, find, hold, perceive, (*n*) atmosphere, feeling, sound, texture, air, impression; *antonym* (*v*) observe, **4.** fumble; *synonyms* (*v*) blunder, botch,

muff, flounder, bobble, fluff, bumble, mishandle, (*adj*) bungle, boggle.

raweraweabaki 1. fingered, **2.** felt; *synonyms* (*v*) mat, snarl, tangle, braid, entangle, (*adj*) perceived, sensed, conscious.

rea intermingle; *synonyms* (*v*) commingle, blend, fuse, combine, confuse, immingle, intermix, merge, mingle, mix, interweave, knit.

rebe 1. dislocate; *synonyms* (*v*) shift, displace, disjoint, disturb, move, muddle, wrench, transfer, jumble, dislodge, disorder, disorganize, slip, splay, unhinge, **2.** jut; *synonyms* (*n*) projection, bump, excrescence, extrusion, gibbosity, hump, protuberance, jutting, prominence, protrusion, (*v*) bulge, project, overhang, protrude, butt, **3.** bulge; *synonyms* (*n*) swelling, bilge, knob, lump, nub, convexity, (*v*) belly, bag, balloon, bulk, jut, swell, rise, billow, distend, **4.** project; *synonyms* (*n*) design, device, scheme, idea, enterprise, venture, (*v*) plan, hurl, contrive, shoot, cast, devise, extend, forecast, throw, **5.** surpass; *synonyms* (*v*) pass, beat, exceed, outdo, better, excel, outstrip, surmount, overcome, overrun, best, outgo, outshine, outweigh, overstep.

rebeaki 1. dislocated; *synonyms* (*adj*) disjointed, disordered, dislocate, disorderly, confused, detached, disconnected, separated, topsy-turvy, garbled, illogical, isolated, scattered, separate, spaced, **2.** projected; *synonyms* (*adj*) projecting, jutting, proposed, planned, anticipated, deliberate, expected, future, likely, predictable, probable, protruding, sticking, estimated.

rebera leper; *synonyms* (*n*) lazar, outcast, derelict, invalid, measle, mesel, refugee.

reberake 1. inquisitive; *synonyms* (*adj*) curious, inquiring, nosy, prying, questioning, speculative, meddling, investigative, meddlesome, quizzical; *antonym* (*adj*) apathetic, **2.** importunate; *synonyms* (*adj*) troublesome, annoying, exigent, insistent, pressing, instant, demanding, earnest, pleading, urgent, appealing, imploring, (*v*) important; *antonym* (*adj*) halfhearted, **3.** curious; *synonyms* (*adj*) abnormal, funny, interested, odd, peculiar, strange, unusual, bizarre, extraordinary, inquisitive, quaint, queer, remarkable, singular, weird; *antonyms* (*adj*) normal, incurious, ordinary, **4.** erupt; *synonyms* (*v*) burst, belch, break, eruct, eject, emit, explode, flare, gush, spout, bubble; *antonym* (*v*) develop, **5.** petulant; *synonyms* (*adj*) irritable, peevish, cross, testy, irascible, cranky, fractious, fretful, pettish, choleric, touchy, cantankerous, crabby, grouchy, grumpy; *antonym* (*adj*) easygoing, **6.** vexing; *synonyms* (*adj*) irritating, infuriating, maddening, galling, bothersome, aggravating, exasperating, pestiferous, vexatious, pesky, trying, **7.** saucy; *synonyms* (*adj*) pert, bold, impudent, audacious, forward, fresh, impertinent, insolent, flippant, rude, brazen, irreverent, malapert, sassy, smart, **8.** turbulent; *synonyms* (*adj*) tempestuous, tumultuous, rough, furious, boisterous, disorderly, noisy, riotous, violent, wild, troubled, unruly, agitated, angry, (*n*) stormy; *antonym* (*adj*) calm.

rebetoko 1. irritating; *synonyms* (*adj*) galling, annoying, bothersome, exasperating, infuriating, aggravating, irksome, irritative, troublesome, vexatious, irritant, exciting, maddening, nettlesome, (*v*) stinging; *antonym* (*adj*) pleasing, **2.** vexing; *synonyms* (*adj*) irritating, pestiferous, pesky, trying.

rebetunga 1. meddlesome; *synonyms* (*adj*) intrusive, busy, inquisitive, interfering, officious, obtrusive, nosy, curious, pragmatical, prying, busybodied, impertinent, meddling, **2.** irritating; *synonyms* (*adj*) galling, annoying, bothersome, exasperating, infuriating, aggravating, irksome, irritative, troublesome, vexatious, irritant, exciting, maddening, nettlesome, (*v*) stinging; *antonym* (*adj*) pleasing, **3.** meddling; *synonyms* (*adj*) meddlesome, dabbling, **4.** annoying; *synonyms* (*adj*) irritating, awkward, disagreeable, grating, inconvenient, offensive, pesky, trying, vexing, worrying, undesirable, abrasive, incommodious, niggling, (*n*) annoyance; *antonym* (*adj*) soothing, **5.** meddle; *synonyms* (*v*) tamper, interfere, intervene, intrude, fiddle, monkey, pry, **6.** menacing; *synonyms* (*adj*) forbidding, ominous, sinister, threatening, imminent, impending, frightening, minacious, minatory, ugly, dangerous, formidable, intimidating, baleful, black.

rebu 1. gallivant; *synonyms* (*v*) gad, stroll, ramble, range, roam, stray, wander, drift, meander, cruise, jaunt, **2.** roam; *synonyms* (*v*) gallivant, journey, rove, tramp, walk, prowl, travel, divagate, roll, migrate, saunter, swan, traverse, trek, (*adj*) err.

rebua 1. daub; *synonyms* (*n*) smear, splotch, blot, spot, (*v*) spread, besmear, bedaub, blur, coat, plaster, smudge, stain, dab, apply, (*adj*) smutch, **2.** plaster; *synonyms* (*n*) mortar, cement, paste, gum, glue, bandage, cataplasm, attend, (*v*) daub, stucco, paint, affix, poultice, face, whitewash, **3.** paint; *synonyms* (*n*) painting, tint, coating, pigment, (*v*) color, dye, decorate, depict, varnish, enamel, lacquer, describe, draw, cover, gild.

rebuaki 1. daubed; *synonyms* (*adj*) besmeared, beplastered, greasy, **2.** painted; *synonyms* (*v*) depaint, (*adj*) dyed, motley, stained, tinted, assorted, calico, cosmetic, graphic, miscellaneous, mixed, multicolor, multicolored, multicolour, multicoloured, **3.** plastered; *synonyms* (*adj*) drunk, tight, intoxicated, loaded, pixilated, sloshed, smashed, soaked, wet, besotted, inebriated, pissed.

rebutata 1. agitated; *synonyms* (*adj*) restless, excited, nervous, restive, tumultuous, upset, distressed,

tense, alarmed, anxious, distraught, jumpy, overwrought, perturbed, shaken; *antonyms* (*adj*) calm, composed, lethargic, **2.** struggle; *synonyms* (*n*) contest, battle, combat, conflict, strain, effort, exertion, scramble, scuffle, (*v*) fight, attempt, dispute, endeavor, labor, quarrel; *antonyms* (*v*) flourish, glide, **3.** struggling; *synonyms* (*adj*) aggressive, agonizing, belligerent, careworn, disadvantaged, fraught, harassed, hostile, pugnacious, rebellious, stressed, besieged, (*n*) contention, colluctation.

rebutonga gallivant; *synonyms* (*v*) gad, stroll, ramble, range, roam, stray, wander, drift, meander, cruise, jaunt.

rebwe 1. rumble; *synonyms* (*n*) boom, roll, roar, peal, mutter, bang, brawl, noise, (*v*) murmur, growl, grumble, clatter, sound, thunder, mumble, **2.** pop; *synonyms* (*n*) dad, daddy, father, pa, papa, shot, click, (*v*) burst, crack, shoot, protrude, pawn, appear, place, (*adv*) plump, **3.** smack; *synonyms* (*n*) slap, knock, hit, blow, flavor, wallop, clout, cuff, (*v*) savor, kiss, buss, bash, beat, punch, (*adj*) dash, **4.** tick; *synonyms* (*n*) credit, score, minute, moment, second, instant, ticking, trust, line, (*v*) mark, check, tally, ticktack, clack, retick.

rebwetau explode; *synonyms* (*v*) erupt, detonate, crack, discharge, break, fulminate, blast, disprove, fire, shoot, expand, discredit, shatter, (*n*) burst, flare; *antonym* (*v*) implode.

rebwetauaki exploded; *synonyms* (*adj*) antebellum, antediluvian, elapsed, expired, extinct, lapsed, forgotten, irrecoverable, refuted.

rei 1. befriend; *synonyms* (*v*) aid, friend, favor, help, assist, promote, sustain; *antonym* (*v*) shun, **2.** friend; *synonyms* (*n*) fellow, acquaintance, ally, colleague, crony, advocate, assistant, booster, buddy, mate, connection, wellwisher, (*adj*) associate, companion, comrade; *antonyms* (*n*) enemy, foe, stranger, rival.

reimaurua 1. frolic; *synonyms* (*n*) play, romp, sport, caper, diversion, fun, joke, joy, merriment, mirth, (*v*) cavort, disport, frisk, gambol, lark, **2.** romp; *synonyms* (*n*) hoyden, runaway, tomboy, walkaway, antic, laugher, (*v*) frolic, prance, rollick.

reirei 1. charmingly; *synonyms* (*adv*) delightfully, alluringly, attractively, pleasingly, prettily, temptingly, beautifully, enchantingly, pleasantly, agreeably, appealingly, charismatically, delectably, elegantly, engagingly; *antonym* (*adv*) repulsively, **2.** learn; *synonyms* (*v*) discover, get, know, find, ascertain, have, hear, determine, acquire, con, perceive, study, tell, understand, gather, **3.** train; *synonyms* (*n*) chain, string, (*v*) aim, coach, direct, educate, exercise, trail, tail, tame, discipline, drill, instruct, prepare, school, **4.** well; *synonyms* (*adv*) right, easily, thoroughly, considerably, fully, good, (*adj*) healthy, fit, shaft, sound, robust, (*n*) fountain, spring, pit, (v) gush; *antonyms* (adv) ill, badly, poorly, (adj) sick, unwell, dying, nauseous, **5.** study; *synonyms* (n) survey, consideration, investigation, learning, (v) consider, examine, review, learn, research, check, analyze, contemplate, inquire, investigate, meditate, **6.** prettily; *synonyms* (adv) nicely, charmingly, gracefully, well, purely, adorably, daintily, delicately, deliciously, exquisitely, fastidiously, picturesquely, quaintly, captivatingly, deftly.

reireia 1. educate; *synonyms* (v) civilize, cultivate, instruct, train, breed, coach, discipline, drill, develop, enlighten, groom, inform, nurture, rear, school, **2.** instruct; *synonyms* (v) charge, advise, direct, educate, teach, command, indoctrinate, apprise, bid, edify, enjoin, form, guide, tutor, ground; *antonym* (v) request, **3.** teach; *synonyms* (v) learn, lecture, tell, catechize, demonstrate, discover, improve, inculcate, prepare, (adj) show, **4.** taught; *synonyms* (v) close, fast, firm, overwrought, taut, tense, (adj) instructed, educated, schooled, arranged, enlightened, furnished, gentle, provided, scholarly, **5.** rebuke; *synonyms* (n) blame, rebuff, reproach, admonition, reproof, admonishment, (v) censure, reprimand, chide, berate, castigate, admonish, caution, check, scold; *antonyms* (v) praise, commend, compliment.

reireiaki 1. instructed; *synonyms* (v) erudite, leaned, lettered, (adj) educated, taught, tutored, enlightened, arranged, experienced, furnished, instruct, intelligent, qualified, schooled, provided, **2.** educated; *synonyms* (v) instructed, (adj) cultured, learned, trained, informed, refined; *antonyms* (adj) uneducated, ignorant, **3.** learned; *synonyms* (v) knowing, (adj) knowledgeable, wise, academic, scholarly, bookish, intellectual, literary, studious, conversant, literate, sagacious, sage, skilled, skillful; *antonym* (adj) innate, **4.** taught; *synonyms* (v) close, fast, firm, overwrought, taut, tense, tight, (adj) gentle, well-bred, **5.** rebuked; *synonyms* (adj) reprimanded, reproved, admonished, chastened, **6.** studied; *synonyms* (v) advised, (adj) intentional, deliberate, calculated, conscious, premeditated, affected, elaborate, intended, willful, labored, planned; *antonyms* (adj) natural, spontaneous, **7.** trained; *synonyms* (adj) capable, competent, expert, accustomed, able, efficient, fit, fitted, professional, proficient; *antonyms* (adj) untrained, inexpert, untaught, untutored.

reireinai learn; *synonyms* (v) discover, get, know, find, ascertain, have, hear, determine, acquire, con, perceive, study, tell, understand, gather.

reireinaiaki learned; *synonyms* (v) knowing, (adj) erudite, educated, enlightened, knowledgeable, wise, academic, scholarly, bookish, cultured,

intellectual, lettered, literary, studious, informed; *antonyms* (adj) ignorant, innate.

reita 1. append; *synonyms* (v) adjoin, add, affix, annex, attach, join, include, suffix, suspend, tack, conjoin, connect, fasten, insert, (adj) hang, **2.** lengthen; *synonyms* (v) elongate, enlarge, draw, increase, prolong, expand, protract, stretch, continue, delay, spread, amplify, (adj) extend, elongated; *antonym* (v) shorten, **3.** interface; *synonyms* (n) link, port, boundary, junction, border, circumference, communication, display, edging, (v) contact, combine, merge, amalgamate, collaborate, communicate, **4.** continue; *synonyms* (v) abide, remain, endure, keep, persevere, sustain, bide, be, last, maintain, persist, preserve, proceed, resume, (n) hold; *antonyms* (v) stop, end, cease, discontinue, **5.** join; *synonyms* (v) unite, associate, graft, assemble, affiliate, meet, converge, couple, enroll, integrate, interconnect, knit, mix, pair, (n) bond; *antonyms* (v) detach, secede, separate, split, undo, **6.** link; *synonyms* (n) connection, joint, concatenation, association, attachment, liaison, (v) tie, bridge, relate, yoke, bind, fix, (adj) correlation, lock, hook, **7.** prolong; *synonyms* (v) lengthen, procrastinate, defer, postpone, produce, prolongate, renew, offer, **8.** unite; *synonyms* (v) blend, coalesce, fuse, unify, agree, league, concentrate, consolidate, gather, incorporate, marry, concur, band, compound, confederate; *antonym* (v) divide.

reitaki 1. continued; *synonyms* (adj) continuous, constant, continual, extended, unremitting, serial, continuate, eternal, long, perpetual, protracted, recurrent, solid, undivided, untiring, **2.** lengthened; *synonyms* (adj) elongated, prolonged, expanded, elongate, extensive, lengthy, lingering, delayed, stretched, wide; *antonym* (adj) brief, **3.** linked; *synonyms* (adj) connected, allied, coupled, joined, related, associated, correlated, united; *antonym* (adj) unrelated, **4.** joined; *synonyms* (adj) combined, joint, amalgamated, linked, concerted; *antonym* (adj) separate, **5.** united; *synonyms* (adj) cooperative, mutual, mixed, common, conjunctive, conjunct, unanimous, conjoint, collective, one, together, inseparable, (v) consolidated, join, (n) harmonious; *antonyms* (adj) individual, divided, **6.** prolonged; *synonyms* (adj) chronic, lengthened, continued, sustained, slow; *antonym* (adj) quick.

reitata tall; *synonyms* (adj) lofty, elevated, high, exalted, big, lanky, towering, eminent, unbelievable, strapping, long, exaggerated, gangling, grandiloquent, magniloquent; *antonyms* (adj) short, low, small.

reiti couple; *synonyms* (n) brace, yoke, duo, dyad, (v) pair, connect, associate, combine, attach, copulate, join, tie, link, match, *(adj)* hook; *antonym (v)* uncouple.

reitia 1. merge; *synonyms (v)* amalgamate, blend, combine, melt, coalesce, fuse, commingle, integrate, meld, unite, absorb, aggregate, consolidate, incorporate, *(adj)* immerse; *antonyms (v)* separate, split, **2.** splice; *synonyms (n)* joint, junction, splicing, *(v)* link, conjoin, join, marry, wed, inosculate, twine, anastomose, calk, careen, *(adj)* tie, braid.

reitiaki coupled; *synonyms (adj)* connected, conjugate, double, joined, linked, united, associated, conjugated; *antonyms (adj)* separate, unrelated.

reka 1. bony; *synonyms (adj)* osseous, gaunt, lean, thin, angular, emaciated, scrawny, skinny, lanky, meager, boney, spare; *antonym (adj)* rounded, **2.** stumpy; *synonyms (adj)* pudgy, squat, podgy, stocky, short, chunky, dumpy, squatty, stubby, thick, **3.** tart; *synonyms (n)* pie, pastry, prostitute, *(adj)* sharp, acid, pungent, sour, bitter, keen, piquant, acerbic, acrid, astringent, crabbed, harsh; *antonym (adj)* sweet, **4.** spicy; *synonyms (adj)* aromatic, fragrant, racy, salty, blue, hot, juicy, peppery, savory, redolent, balmy, gamy, gingery, naughty, risque; *antonyms (adj)* bland, mild, **5.** rugged; *synonyms (adj)* hard, difficult, rocky, broken, craggy, hardy, hilly, robust, strong, sturdy, tough, blunt, *(n)* rough, jagged, ragged; *antonym (adj)* delicate, **6.** rough; *synonyms (adj)* coarse, raw, crude, cruel, grating, gross, hoarse, approximate, gruff, inclement, indelicate, uneven, impolite, *(n)* boisterous, draft; *antonyms (adj)* gentle, smooth, polished, precise, refined, silky, soft, sophisticated, even, exact, glossy, pleasant, **7.** pointed; *synonyms (adj)* penetrating, poignant, acute, cutting, marked, pithy, biting, acuminate, barbed, prickly, meaningful, fine, piercing, thorny, emphatic, **8.** sharp; *synonyms (adj)* intelligent, incisive, intense, pointed, quick, severe, alert, caustic, prompt, sarcastic, smart, astute, *(v)* brisk, clever, acrimonious; *antonyms (adj)* dull, blurred, naive, round.

reke 1. catch; *synonyms (v)* arrest, capture, hook, apprehend, get, acquire, ensnare, intercept, *(n)* haul, hitch, trick, bolt, clasp, grab, pawl; *antonym (v)* release, **2.** hook; *synonyms (n)* crook, claw, crotchet, draw, lure, trap, anchor, *(v)* catch, bend, fasten, button, attach, bag, cop, crochet, **3.** acquire; *synonyms (v)* achieve, find, gain, take, accept, attain, buy, collect, contract, earn, obtain, purchase, receive, assume, derive; *antonyms (v)* lose, sell, **4.** arise; *synonyms (v)* rise, appear, ascend, emerge, issue, mount, originate, proceed, result, awake, commence, develop, emanate, ensue, follow, **5.** kidnap; *synonyms (n)* abduction, *(v)* abduct, snatch, steal, filch, spirit, abstract, bunco,

cabbage, con, defraud, diddle, encourage, excite, goldbrick, **6.** emanate; *synonyms (v)* arise, effuse, discharge, breathe, exhale, radiate, spring, stem, exude, emit, flow, gush, **7.** hooked; *synonyms (adj)* crooked, bent, curved, aquiline, addicted, infatuated, dependant, dependent, enamored, engrossed, obsessed, **8.** discover; *synonyms (v)* ascertain, discern, disclose, see, perceive, detect, determine, divulge, expose, hear, impart, observe, trace, descry, behold, **9.** answer; *synonyms (n)* reply, respond, retort, return, solution, defense, echo, *(v)* counter, resolve, serve, acknowledge, agree, correspond, do, *(adj)* pay; *antonyms (v)* question, ask, **10.** found; *synonyms (v)* erect, establish, base, build, form, constitute, construct, appoint, create, ground, institute, bottom, begin, cast, plant; *antonym (adj)* misplaced, **11.** acquired; *synonyms (v)* acquiring, *(adj)* acquisite, acquisitive, derivative, extrinsic, **12.** obtain; *synonyms (v)* have, accomplish, effect, extract, gather, make, prevail, procure, extort, compass, fetch, carry, enlist, hold, incur, **13.** seized; *synonyms (adj)* confiscate, confiscated, appropriated, condemned, apprehended, detained, held, censured, convicted, forfeit, forfeited, **14.** received; *synonyms (v)* receiving, ascertained, current, recognized, *(adj)* accepted, acknowledged, conventional, acceptable, canonical, orthodox, customary, established, inward, known, legitimate.

rekeaki 1. discovered; *synonyms (adj)* ascertained, revealed, disclosed, exposed, naked, bare, observed, open, seen, **2.** acquired; *synonyms (v)* acquiring, *(adj)* acquisite, acquisitive, derivative, extrinsic, **3.** hooked; *synonyms (adj)* crooked, bent, curved, aquiline, addicted, infatuated, dependant, dependent, enamored, engrossed, obsessed, **4.** kidnapped; *synonyms (adj)* abducted, kidnaped, **5.** raised; *synonyms (v)* repousse, *(adj)* elevated, embossed, erect, convex, brocaded, high, alert, bold, confident, elate, elated, elative, exultant, *(prep)* above.

rekebuta 1. hesitating; *synonyms (adj)* hesitant, indecisive, irresolute, doubtful, undecided, faltering, reluctant, unwilling, backward, **2.** dawdling; *synonyms (adj)* slow, dilatory, tardy, deliberate, easygoing, laggard, leisurely, measured, *(n)* delay, dalliance, coquetry, dithering, hesitation, idleness, indecision; *antonym (n)* decisiveness, **3.** stalling; *synonyms (n)* stall, arrest, booth, carrel, carrell, cubicle, kiosk, stabling.

rekereke rough; *synonyms (adj)* coarse, hard, harsh, raw, crude, cruel, grating, gross, hoarse, jagged, approximate, gruff, inclement, *(n)* boisterous, draft; *antonyms (adj)* gentle, smooth, polished, precise, refined, silky, soft, sophisticated, even, exact, glossy, pleasant.

rekerua matted; *synonyms* (*adj*) mat, entangled, tangled, flat, knotted, matt, matte, knotty, bland, categoric, categorical, compressed, fixed, flavorless, (*v*) crossed; *antonym* (*adj*) tidy.

reketa 1. recollect; *synonyms* (*v*) recall, remember, recognize, remind, mind, think, reminisce, retrieve, consider, review; *antonym* (*v*) forget, **2**. recall; *synonyms* (*v*) countermand, recollect, repeal, rescind, retract, reverse, revoke, cancel, recant, (*n*) anamnesis, memory, return, annulment, recollection, reminiscence.

reketangkoro rectangular; *synonyms* (*adj*) orthogonal, oblong, square, rectangled, rectangle.

reme 1. narrow; *synonyms* (*adj*) close, limited, insular, little, cramped, illiberal, mean, (*v*) confined, contract, limit, lessen, constrict, shrink, abridge, dwindle; *antonyms* (*adj*) wide, broad, comprehensive, extensive, (*v*) widen, extend, **2**. limited; *synonyms* (*adj*) finite, circumscribed, moderate, qualified, special, bounded, narrow, scanty, slender, particular, specific, definite, conditional, constricted, insufficient; *antonyms* (*adj*) boundless, infinite, limitless, open, complete, never-ending, unlimited.

remereme 1. heedless; *synonyms* (*adj*) careless, reckless, inattentive, neglectful, negligent, rash, thoughtless, blind, forgetful, inadvertent, incautious, inconsiderate, indifferent, listless, mindless; *antonym* (*adj*) heedful, **2**. thoughtless; *synonyms* (*adj*) heedless, hasty, improvident, unthinking, imprudent, indiscreet, regardless, vacant, dizzy, flighty, casual, foolish, injudicious, (*v*) giddy, remiss; *antonyms* (*adj*) thoughtful, considerate, considered, **3**. presumptuous; *synonyms* (*adj*) arrogant, assuming, audacious, forward, insolent, impertinent, assumptive, familiar, haughty, proud, daring, pert, conceited, (*n*) impudent, bold.

remoa before; *synonyms* (*prep*) fore, beyond, facing, (*adv*) above, ahead, afore, ago, earlier, already, forward, previously, beforehand, ere, (*adj*) preceding, prior; *antonyms* (*prep*) later, behind, after, afterward.

remrem 1. extract; *synonyms* (*n*) excerpt, essence, juice, quotation, quote, citation, (*v*) draw, abstract, derive, educe, elicit, distill, express, get, extort, **2**. gather; *synonyms* (*v*) deduce, convene, accumulate, amass, assemble, collect, compile, congregate, flock, garner, meet, tuck, earn, rally, (*n*) fold; *antonyms* (*v*) disperse, scatter, **3**. glean; *synonyms* (*v*) cull, gather, harvest, reap, extract, winnow.

remremaki gathered; *synonyms* (*adj*) collected, deepened, accumulated, amassed, assembled, collective, congregate, equanimous, massed, poised.

remwe late; *synonyms* (*adj*) former, dead, deceased, behindhand, belated, delayed, modern, slow, tardy, dull, defunct, (*adv*) dilatory, fresh, backward, belatedly; *antonyms* (*adj*) ahead, (*adv*) early, punctually, promptly, punctual.

rena 1. familiar; *synonyms* (*adj*) close, common, conversant, customary, everyday, intimate, commonplace, easy, ordinary, usual, (*n*) accustomed, companion, comrade, habitual, (*v*) confidential; *antonyms* (*adj*) unfamiliar, foreign, strange, new, unaccustomed, formal, ignorant, unknown, **2**. elastic; *synonyms* (*adj*) flexible, buoyant, ductile, limber, pliable, pliant, resilient, soft, springy, supple, yielding, lissom, stretchable, bouncy, expansive; *antonyms* (*adj*) rigid, stiff, inflexible, inelastic, **3**. duration; *synonyms* (*n*) length, continuation, continuance, period, standing, stretch, time, distance, age, permanency, span, continuity, endurance, course, space, **4**. adaptable; *synonyms* (*adj*) versatile, compliant, convertible, variable, adjustable, compatible, elastic, malleable; *antonyms* (*adj*) fixed, unadaptable, **5**. intermediate; *synonyms* (*adj*) average, medium, mean, mediate, mid, middle, moderate, central, halfway, median, mediocre, (*v*) intercede, interjacent, intercurrent, (*n*) intermediary, **6**. adjustable; *synonyms* (*adj*) adaptable, movable, changeable, alterable, fluid, mutable, amendable, bendable, erratic, fluctuating, inconsistent, regulating, **7**. stretched; *synonyms* (*adj*) taut, extended, tense, tight, strained, expanded, outstretched, elongated, outspread, prolonged, protracted, assiduous, delayed, extensive, firm; *antonym* (*adj*) brief, **8**. stretchable; *synonyms* (*adj*) stretchy, extendable.

renaua transect; *synonym* (*v*) cut.

renga 1. red; *synonyms* (*adj*) crimson, flushed, carmine, glowing, rosy, ruby, sanguine, cherry, pink, radical, ruddy, scarlet, cerise, bloody, inflamed, **2**. pink; *synonyms* (*adj*) flower, pinkish, (*n*) red, rose, (*v*) knock, gore, impale, prick, punch, spear, spike, stab, enfilade.

rengana 1. mingle; *synonyms* (*v*) blend, combine, compound, merge, amalgamate, intermix, mix, commingle, associate, confuse, intermingle, join, immingle, coalesce, meddle; *antonym* (*v*) separate, **2**. blend; *synonyms* (*n*) alloy, amalgam, composite, amalgamation, brew, combination, fusion, harmony, mash, (*v*) fuse, incorporate, confound, go, meld, melt; *antonym* (*v*) divide, **3**. amalgamate; *synonyms* (*v*) unite, affiliate, mingle, commix, connect, consolidate, embody, integrate, pool, unify, adulterate, (*adj*) amalgamated, **4**. involve; *synonyms* (*v*) imply, contain, affect, embrace, entail, implicate, comprise, complicate, demand, encompass, engage, envelop, include, tangle, (*n*) entangle; *antonym* (*v*) exclude, **5**. mix; *synonyms*

(n) mixture, concoction, miscellany, admixture, assortment, commixture, intermixture, mixing, (v) aggregate, admix, consort, immix, jumble, socialize, (adj) mishmash, **6.** combine; *synonyms* (v) attach, piece, league, band, bond, add, concur, cement, wed, adjoin, concentrate, (n) cartel, pair, trust, junction, **7.** intermingle; *synonyms* (v) interweave, knit.

renganaki 1. amalgamated; *synonyms* (adj) amalgamate, united, fused, mixed, coalesced, combined, consolidated, integrated, joined, merged; *antonym* (adj) simple, **2.** involved; *synonyms* (adj) complex, intricate, complicated, convoluted, tortuous, confused, difficult, elaborate, engaged, entangled, interested, knotty, obscure, tangled, knotted; *antonyms* (adj) aloof, detached, straightforward, **3.** blended; *synonyms* (v) blent, polluted, stained, (adj) composite, adulterate, beaten, conglomerate, **4.** mixed; *synonyms* (adj) miscellaneous, assorted, heterogeneous, medley, impure, amalgamated, diverse, intermingled, motley, varied, indiscriminate, different, pied, (v) blended, mingled; *antonyms* (adj) homogeneous, insular, pure, **5.** combined; *synonyms* (adj) joint, collective, aggregate, concerted, cooperative, incorporate, conjunct, conjunctive, connected, (adv) jointly, together; *antonym* (adj) individual, **6.** promiscuous; *synonyms* (adj) random, loose, wanton, disorderly, licentious, easy, light.

reraera stutter; *synonyms* (n) stammer, (v) falter, hesitate, stumble, bumble.

rerarera stammer; *synonyms* (v) stutter, falter, hesitate, bumble, stumble.

rere 1. flee; *synonyms* (v) escape, bolt, desert, fly, break, abscond, elope, elude, go, leave, run, avoid, evade, depart, lam, **2.** go; *synonyms* (v) come, elapse, pass, crack, disappear, drive, travel, fall, extend, function, operate, ride, (n) fare, (adj) follow, move, **3.** rapid; *synonyms* (adj) fast, quick, prompt, swift, agile, fleet, hasty, speedy, cursory, expeditious, sudden, nimble, winged, express, hurried; *antonyms* (adj) slow, gradual, **4.** pass; *synonyms* (v) flow, deliver, give, happen, lead, offer, overtake, live, advance, die, exceed, lapse, proceed, surpass, make; *antonym* (v) fail.

rerea 1. avoid; *synonyms* (v) shun, avert, parry, escape, evade, abstain, annul, circumvent, duck, elude, forbear, fudge, ignore, prevent, (adj) eschew; *antonyms* (v) confront, associate, face, tackle, **2.** bolt; *synonyms* (n) arrow, dash, pin, catch, (v) bar, abscond, gobble, latch, lock, decamp, devour, fasten, gulp, guzzle, (adv) bang; *antonyms* (v) nibble, unbolt, unlock, **3.** evade; *synonyms* (v) avoid, dodge, equivocate, hedge, sidestep, skirt, bilk, neglect, omit, prevaricate, quibble, block, deflect, fence, flee, **4.** dash; *synonyms* (n) rush, sprint, animation, beat, bit, bolt, line, (v) dart, touch,

strike, break, charge, crash, hurry, jog; *antonym* (n) lethargy, **5.** dart; *synonyms* (n) rocket, shot, barb, (v) bound, flash, run, shoot, flit, fly, gallop, race, scurry, spring, tear, fling, **6.** thrust; *synonyms* (v) jab, force, boost, punch, ram, dig, impel, squeeze, (n) push, poke, drive, stab, shove, cast, prod; *antonym* (v) pull, **7.** speed; *synonyms* (n) rapidity, velocity, celerity, fastness, haste, pace, promptness, quickness, (v) hasten, quicken, accelerate, dispatch, expedite, promote, hurtle; *antonym* (n) slowness, **8.** plunge; *synonyms* (n) dive, drop, fall, jump, leap, (v) dip, douse, immerse, submerge, drown, dunk, launch, plummet, descend, lunge, **9.** parry; *synonyms* (n) counterpunch, (v) counter, shirk, flinch, fend, repel, blench, blink, defeat, **10.** rush; *synonyms* (n) flood, flow, attack, surge, press, scramble, (v) gush, speed, stream, jet, flush, plunge, hustle, (adj) burst, spurt.

rereaki 1. bolted; *synonyms* (adj) locked, barred, barricaded, blockaded, fast, firm, latched, secured, tight, bonded, colorfast, debauched, degenerate, degraded, dissipated, **2.** dashed; *synonyms* (v) abashed, ashamed, sunk, (adj) dejected, discouraged, dotted, flecked, specked, speckled, stippled, **3.** rushed; *synonyms* (adj) hasty, hurried, rush, precipitate, rapid, hassled, immediate, instant, instantaneous, quick, speedy, sudden, swift, unexpected, abrupt; *antonym* (adj) leisurely, **4.** parried.

rerebakara pounce; *synonyms* (v) bounce, bound, leap, dive, swoop, stoop, charge, attack, seize, alight, condescend, ambush, lunge, (n) jump, descent.

rerebaua rush; *synonyms* (n) hurry, charge, flood, flow, attack, (v) dash, gush, race, run, speed, dart, hasten, stream, (adj) burst, spurt.

rerebauaki rushed; *synonyms* (adj) hasty, hurried, rush, precipitate, rapid, hassled, immediate, instant, instantaneous, quick, speedy, sudden, swift, unexpected, abrupt; *antonym* (adj) leisurely.

rerebetunga 1. annoy; *synonyms* (v) anger, displease, harass, irritate, pester, afflict, aggravate, bother, grate, harry, hassle, molest, perturb, plague, (n) annoyance; *antonyms* (v) please, pacify, soothe, **2.** disorder; *synonyms* (n) ailment, complaint, clutter, disease, jumble, muddle, chaos, commotion, confusion, disarrangement, disturbance, anarchy, (v) derange, disarray, confuse; *antonyms* (n) orderliness, calm, peace, (v) order, **3.** upset; *synonyms* (v) overturn, agitate, disquiet, overthrow, disturb, reverse, subvert, unsettle, (adj) unsettled, hurt, agitated, confused, (n) disorder, trouble, distress; *antonyms* (v) encourage, (adj) pleased, confident.

rerebetungaki 1. annoyed; *synonyms* (adj) angry, irate, irritated, vexed, aggravated, angered, cross, disgruntled, displeased, exasperated, infuriated, offended, peeved, pestered, resentful; *antonyms* (*adj*) calm, pleased, unprovoked, smiling, **2.** disordered; *synonyms* (*adj*) confused, chaotic, broken, deranged, disorganized, incoherent, messy, sick, upset, disconnected, disjointed, disorderly, ill, jumbled, mixed; *antonyms* (*adj*) neat, orderly, ordered, **3.** upset; *synonyms* (*v*) overturn, agitate, disquiet, overthrow, bother, confuse, disturb, perturb, reverse, (*adj*) unsettled, hurt, (*n*) disorder, trouble, distress, disturbance; *antonyms* (*v*) please, encourage, soothe, (*adj*) confident.

rerebu rush; *synonyms* (*n*) hurry, charge, flood, flow, attack, (*v*) dash, gush, race, run, speed, dart, hasten, stream, (*adj*) burst, spurt.

rerebuaki rushed; *synonyms* (*adj*) hasty, hurried, rush, precipitate, rapid, hassled, immediate, instant, instantaneous, quick, speedy, sudden, swift, unexpected, abrupt; *antonym* (*adj*) leisurely.

rerei 1. beautiful; *synonyms* (*adj*) attractive, good-looking, bright, beauteous, fine, handsome, lovely, picturesque, pleasant, pretty, striking, sweet, adorned, ornate, dainty; *antonyms* (*adj*) ugly, unattractive, **2.** excellent; *synonyms* (*adj*) choice, estimable, admirable, superior, capital, beautiful, distinctive, brilliant, fantastic, good, great, magnificent, marvelous, outstanding, (*n*) worthy; *antonyms* (*adj*) inferior, poor, abysmal, awful, mediocre, **3.** fine; *synonyms* (*adj*) delicate, agreeable, brave, elegant, excellent, nice, thin, delightful, acute, alright, exquisite, glorious, (*n*) penalty, amercement, (*v*) punish; *antonyms* (*adj*) thick, coarse, substantial, unsatisfactory, wide, **4.** perfect; *synonyms* (*adj*) consummate, complete, exact, utter, entire, faultless, thorough, integral, blameless, clean, correct, (*v*) achieve, accomplish, (*n*) absolute, full; *antonyms* (*adj*) imperfect, faulty, flawed.

rerek 1. narrow; *synonyms* (*adj*) close, limited, insular, little, cramped, illiberal, mean, (*v*) confined, contract, limit, lessen, constrict, shrink, abridge, dwindle; *antonyms* (*adj*) wide, broad, comprehensive, extensive, (*v*) widen, extend, **2.** thin; *synonyms* (*adj*) flimsy, gaunt, lean, light, slight, tenuous, emaciated, fine, rare, slim, sparse, (*v*) slender, dilute, meager, sheer; *antonyms* (*adj*) thick, fat, concentrated, chubby, plump, heavy, (*v*) thicken.

rereka swollen; *synonyms* (*adj*) bloated, inflated, bombastic, puffed, puffy, turgid, egotistic, high, bulging, tumescent, tumid, conceited, (*v*) distended, blown, (*prep*) pompous.

rerena file; *synonyms* (*n*) archive, document, list, procession, rank, record, roll, series, string, (*v*) order, rasp, register, scrape, abrade, arrange.

rereta 1. bloated; *synonyms* (*adj*) puffy, swollen, distended, inflated, turgid, proud, pompous,

puffed, tumescent, tumid; *antonym* (*adj*) wasted, **2.** swollen; *synonyms* (*adj*) bloated, bombastic, egotistic, high, bulging, conceited, egotistical, enlarged, expanded, flooding, mighty, overflowing, (*v*) blown, **3.** swell; *synonyms* (*n*) wave, (*v*) surge, enlarge, expand, heave, increase, rise, puff, bloat, grow, billow, augment, balloon, (*adj*) dandy, swagger; *antonyms* (*v*) decrease, deflate, desiccate.

rereti 1. suspect; *synonyms* (*v*) doubt, distrust, mistrust, suppose, conjecture, guess, surmise, believe, disbelieve, divine, (*adj*) fishy, questionable, shady, suspicious, dubious; *antonyms* (*v*) trust, (*adj*) trustworthy, **2.** surmise; *synonyms* (*v*) presume, suspect, imagine, infer, assume, deduce, think, speculate, gather, (*n*) hypothesis, supposition, assumption, speculation, estimate, opinion.

reretiaki suspected; *synonyms* (*adj*) suspect, supposed, distrusted, assumed.

rereua 1. desert; *synonyms* (*n*) wilderness, (*v*) abandon, escape, defect, ditch, forsake, leave, relinquish, abscond, (*adj*) waste, barren, desolate, merit, wild, worth; *antonyms* (*n*) bog, (*v*) stay, **2.** deserted; *synonyms* (*adj*) abandoned, desert, solitary, bleak, derelict, empty, forsaken, isolated, lonely, lonesome, vacant, alone, secluded, disused, (*v*) forlorn; *antonyms* (*adj*) inhabited, occupied, packed, **3.** uninhabited; *synonyms* (*adj*) deserted, unoccupied, unpopulated, uninhabitable, untenanted, **4.** retreat; *synonyms* (*n*) refuge, resort, asylum, departure, den, lair, privacy, retirement, sanctuary, (*v*) recede, retire, withdraw, depart, ebb, return; *antonyms* (*n*) raid, (*v*) advance.

rereuaki 1. deserted; *synonyms* (*adj*) abandoned, desert, solitary, bleak, derelict, desolate, empty, forsaken, isolated, lonely, lonesome, vacant, alone, secluded, (*v*) forlorn; *antonyms* (*adj*) inhabited, occupied, packed, **2.** retreated; *synonym* (*adj*) withdrawn.

reta extend; *synonyms* (*v*) expand, enlarge, amplify, broaden, dilate, widen, augment, continue, elongate, go, spread, carry, develop, increase, (*adj*) stretch; *antonyms* (*v*) withdraw, shorten, limit, narrow, shrink.

retaki extended; *synonyms* (*adj*) broad, expanded, ample, extensive, long, wide, elongated, enlarged, lengthened, lengthy, prolonged, protracted, open, comprehensive, continued; *antonyms* (*adj*) brief, short, condensed, unextended.

retát high; *synonyms* (*adj*) eminent, elevated, great, expensive, distinguished, exalted, lofty, tall, heavy, arrogant, costly, dear, (*v*) bad, fusty, rancid; *antonyms* (*adj*) deep, short, sober, (*n*) low.

revata heavy; *synonyms* (*adj*) dull, deep, dark, dense, fat, full, grave, gross, hard, arduous, bulky, burdensome, grievous, oppressive, thick;

antonyms (*adj*) light, easy, slim, thin, slight, gentle, puny, skinny.

rewák split; *synonyms* (*v*) crack, cut, fracture, slit, burst, divide, separate, divorce, breach, cleave, (*n*) break, rip, rupture, tear, cleavage; *antonyms* (*v*) join, unite, merge.

ri 1. need; *synonyms* (*v*) lack, claim, require, destitution, indigence, involve, (*n*) demand, want, desire, deficiency, must, necessity, deprivation, requirement, absence; *antonym* (*n*) wealth, **2.** desire; *synonyms* (*n*) ambition, hope, aspiration, will, wish, craving, dream, impulse, (*v*) fancy, aspire, seek, aim, choose, crave, like; *antonyms* (*n*) aversion, reality, (*v*) dislike, hate, **3.** bone; *synonyms* (*n*) os, ivory, mouth, osmium, argument, bead, block, (*v*) cartilage, swot, gristle, prepare, arise, attire, beat, bill, **4.** fascinated; *synonyms* (*adj*) spellbound, captivated, absorbed, gripped, attentive, engrossed, interested, preoccupied, **5.** pass; *synonyms* (*v*) flow, deliver, give, happen, lead, move, offer, overtake, live, advance, die, elapse, exceed, (*adj*) go, run; *antonym* (*v*) fail.

rî bone; *synonyms* (*n*) os, ivory, mouth, osmium, argument, bead, block, (*v*) cartilage, swot, gristle, prepare, arise, attire, beat, bill.

ria 1. appear; *synonyms* (*v*) occur, rise, seem, sound, emerge, show, break, arise, arrive, begin, feel, happen, look, surface, (*n*) come; *antonyms* (*v*) disappear, vanish, **2.** greedy; *synonyms* (*adj*) eager, avid, gluttonous, covetous, desirous, acquisitive, glutton, grasping, piggish, esurient, grabby, hungry, insatiable, ravenous, (*v*) avaricious; *antonym* (*adj*) generous, **3.** lip; *synonyms* (*n*) border, brim, cheek, edge, impertinence, mouth, rim, brink, verge, flange, impudence, backtalk, effrontery, insolence, circumference.

riaboro fiend; *synonyms* (*n*) demon, devil, fanatic, monster, brute, daemon, deuce, enthusiast, incubus, ogre, addict, devotee, beast, maniac, buff; *antonym* (*n*) angel.

riai 1. better; *synonyms* (*adj*) superior, (*n*) bettor, (*v*) amend, improve, best, mend, recover, advance, ameliorate, emend, reform, enhance, exceed, excel, refine; *antonyms* (*adj*) lesser, (*adv*) worse, (*n*) inferior, (*v*) worsen, **2.** good; *synonyms* (*adj*) able, benefit, delicious, right, efficient, capable, excellent, fine, nice, well, advantageous, agreeable, (*n*) benign, advantage, gain; *antonyms* (*adj*) disobedient, poor, wicked, unpleasant, (*n*) evil, bad, **3.** expedient; *synonyms* (*adj*) fit, adequate, advisable, becoming, desirable, apt, appropriate, convenient, suitable, handy, (*n*) contrivance, makeshift, artifice, device, resource, **4.** must; *synonyms* (*v*) have, need, mold, demand, ought, shall, should, (*n*) essential, necessity, requirement, obligation, necessary, mustiness, requisite, want; *antonym* (*n*) option, **5.** just; *synonyms* (*adv*) exactly, hardly, newly, simply, (*adj*) fair, correct, equitable, accurate, honest, impartial, barely, good, reasonable, righteous, upright; *antonyms* (*adj*) unfair, biased, wrong, **6.** needy; *synonyms* (*adj*) destitute, indigent, impoverished, necessitous, impecunious, penniless, underprivileged, deficient, miserable, deprived, poverty-stricken, wanting, broke; *antonym* (*adj*) well-off, **7.** proper; *synonyms* (*adj*) due, decent, just, befitting, decorous, fitting, legitimate, modest, neat, exact, formal, individual, meet, moral, peculiar; *antonyms* (*adj*) improper, inappropriate, unseemly, rude, **8.** right; *synonyms* (*adj*) proper, even, perfect, faithful, direct, ethical, full, (*adv*) correctly, (*n*) privilege, law, liberty, authority, claim, freedom, (*v*) rectify; *antonyms* (*adj*) unjustified, immoral, incorrect, (*n*) left.

rîak mixed; *synonyms* (*adj*) miscellaneous, assorted, composite, heterogeneous, integrated, medley, impure, amalgamated, diverse, intermingled, motley, varied, indiscriminate, (*v*) blended, mingled; *antonyms* (*adj*) homogeneous, insular, pure.

riaki 1. needed; *synonyms* (*adj*) necessary, essential, required, needful, requisite, indispensable, wanted, wanting, compulsory, devoid, good, lacking, mandatory, perfect, vital, **2.** desired; *synonyms* (*adj*) coveted, craved, desirable, chosen, favorite, needed, welcome, beloved, adored, appropriate, pet, preferred, proper, (*v*) complying, consenting; *antonym* (*adj*) undesirable.

riakina jib; *synonyms* (*n*) boom, beak, bow, (*v*) balk, baulk, gybe, jibe, check.

rianako 1. surpass; *synonyms* (*v*) pass, beat, exceed, outdo, better, excel, outstrip, surmount, overcome, overrun, best, outgo, outshine, outweigh, overstep, **2.** quality; *synonyms* (*n*) nature, character, characteristic, class, condition, feature, grade, distinction, faculty, description, mark, attribute, caliber, part, peculiarity; *antonym* (*adj*) shoddy, **3.** surpassing; *synonyms* (*adj*) exceeding, excellent, superior, exceptional, prodigious, transcendent, fine, extraordinary, towering, unequaled, (*prep*) above.

rianibwai happening; *synonyms* (*n*) accident, episode, incident, circumstance, affair, contingency, event, experience, fact, occasion, occurrence, eventuality, fortuity, chance, thing.

rianna foot; *synonyms* (*n*) bottom, base, feet, foundation, basis, footing, measure, paw, pes, bed, butt, floor, (*v*) hoof, pay, hand; *antonym* (*n*) top.

riao 1. surpassing; *synonyms* (*adj*) exceeding, excellent, superior, exceptional, prodigious, transcendent, fine, extraordinary, towering, unequaled, (*prep*) above, **2.** transgress; *synonyms* (*v*) sin, break, infringe, offend, contravene, overstep, trespass, violate, breach, disobey, infract, pass, blunder, boob, (*adj*) err.

riaoa 1. clear; *synonyms* *(adj)* clean, certain, open, apparent, distinct, empty, *(v)* bright, acquit, absolute, free, net, absolve, clarify, definite, discharge; *antonyms* *(adj)* cloudy, opaque, unclear, dark, fuzzy, hazy, incomprehensible, obscure, uncertain, vague, ambiguous, blurry, confused, confusing, *(v)* convict, **2.** transgress; *synonyms* *(v)* sin, break, infringe, offend, contravene, overstep, trespass, violate, breach, disobey, infract, pass, blunder, boob, *(adj)* err, **3.** surpass; *synonyms* *(v)* beat, exceed, outdo, better, excel, outstrip, surmount, overcome, overrun, best, outgo, outshine, outweigh, top, overshadow, **4.** overstep; *synonyms* *(v)* encroach, surpass, transcend, overtake, transgress, intrude.

riaoaki cleared; *synonyms* *(adj)* clear, absolved, clean, blank, bleak, empty, exculpated, exempt, exonerated, innocent, official, open, vacant, vindicated, blameless.

riaon over; *synonyms* *(adv)* beyond, across, more, by, o'er, on, too, *(prep)* above, during, *(n)* overs, *(adj)* finished, done, extra, odd, past.

riaonikai 1. conquer; *synonyms* *(v)* beat, capture, subdue, overcome, overpower, quell, subjugate, suppress, surmount, vanquish, crush, defeat, overthrow, overturn, overwhelm; *antonyms* *(v)* surrender, lose, **2.** win; *synonyms* *(v)* acquire, gain, get, attain, obtain, conquer, achieve, earn, prevail, secure, take, succeed, carry, procure, *(n)* triumph, **3.** surmount; *synonyms* *(v)* exceed, master, excel, climb, outdo, outmatch, outstrip, surpass, transcend, outgo, scale, negotiate, pass, reduce, hurdle, **4.** overcome; *synonyms* *(v)* demolish, affect, cross, overbear, overtake, repress, trounce, whelm, win, drown, seize, *(adj)* beaten, conquered, overwhelmed, prostrate; *antonyms* *(v)* fail, *(adj)* victorious, unimpressed.

riaonikaiaki 1. overcome; *synonyms* *(v)* conquer, beat, crush, subdue, vanquish, defeat, master, overpower, hurdle, overwhelm, prevail, subjugate, surmount, demolish, *(adj)* beaten; *antonyms* *(v)* fail, *(adj)* victorious, unimpressed, **2.** surmounted.

riara 1. excessive; *synonyms* *(adj)* inordinate, exaggerated, intense, enormous, exorbitant, extravagant, extreme, exuberant, immoderate, profuse, superfluous, undue, unreasonable, huge, lavish; *antonyms* *(adj)* reasonable, moderate, affordable, **2.** innumerable; *synonyms* *(adj)* countless, incalculable, numberless, infinite, innumerous, multitudinous, unnumbered, myriad, numerous, uncounted, untold, incommensurable, incommensurate, many, unnumerable; *antonym* *(adj)* few, **3.** enormous; *synonyms* *(adj)* big, colossal, immense, vast, excessive, great, large, prodigious, tremendous, stupendous, gargantuan, giant, gigantic, massive, monumental; *antonyms* *(adj)* minute, small, tiny, insignificant, miniature.

riba 1. dislike; *synonyms* *(n)* disgust, aversion, disapproval, hate, antipathy, disaffection, disdain, disfavor, disfavour, displeasure, dissatisfaction, *(v)* disinclination, distaste, detest, abhor; *antonyms* *(n)* liking, fondness, taste, attraction, enjoyment, *(v)* love, like, enjoy, **2.** loathe; *synonyms* *(v)* abominate, despise, execrate, dislike, nauseate, **3.** execrate; *synonyms* *(v)* anathematize, curse, loathe, beshrew, swear, damn, anathemize, **4.** disapprove; *synonyms* *(v)* condemn, object, blame, censure, deny, disallow, discountenance, refuse, reject, repudiate, decline, demur, spurn; *antonyms* *(v)* approve, endorse, **5.** detest; *antonym* *(v)* adore, **6.** congested; *synonyms* *(adj)* packed, full, overcrowded, teeming, engorged, closed, stopped, close, overfull, busy, cramped, swarming, blocked, bunged, *(prep)* inflamed; *antonym* *(adj)* empty, **7.** close; *synonyms* *(adj)* near, adjacent, nearby, accurate, tight, approximate, narrow, *(v)* compact, stop, conclude, *(adv)* by, about, *(n)* end, finish, conclusion; *antonyms* *(adj)* distant, airy, fresh, loose, far, *(v)* open, start, **8.** compact; *synonyms* *(adj)* dense, compendious, concise, hard, solid, *(n)* agreement, arrangement, contract, covenant, bargain, engagement, *(v)* compress, condense, consolidate, pack; *antonyms* *(adj)* sprawling, bulky, sparse, **9.** crowded; *synonyms* *(adj)* congested, populous, jammed, thick, *(n)* thronged, **10.** hate; *synonyms* *(v)* scorn, *(n)* enmity, abhorrence, animosity, detestation, hatred, abomination, execration, hostility, loathing, odium, revulsion, spite, grudge, rancor, **11.** abhor, **12.** perplexed; *synonyms* *(v)* bewildered, complicated, intricate, *(adj)* confused, involved, lost, baffled, confounded, doubtful, puzzled, distracted, uneasy, bemused, questioning, quizzical; *antonym* *(adj)* enlightened, **13.** shun; *synonyms* *(v)* avoid, evade, escape, elude, dodge, flee, shirk, banish, ostracize, parry, duck, ban, blackball, *(adj)* eschew, **14.** resent; *synonyms* *(v)* begrudge, envy, antagonize, brook, combat, covet, miff, mind, oppose, oppugn, repel, stomach, feel, recognize, resist, **15.** pressed; *synonyms* *(adj)* printed, pushed, stamped, bound, driven, embossed, encouraged, impelled, imprinted, incited, marked, provoked, prompted.

ribaba 1. agglomerated; *synonyms* *(adj)* agglomerate, agglomerative, clustered, bunched, bunchy, **2.** crowded; *synonyms* *(adj)* close, compact, congested, busy, dense, full, packed, populous, jammed, cramped, teeming, thick, tight, *(n)* thronged; *antonyms* *(adj)* empty, sparse, **3.** collected; *synonyms* *(v)* composed, *(adj)* calm, accumulated, amassed, assembled, cool, sober, tranquil, poised, unflappable, dispassionate, gathered, imperturbable, peaceful, placid; *antonym* *(adj)* agitated, **4.** accumulated; *synonyms* *(adj)* accrued, collected, accumulate, aggregate, congregate, massed, store, upheaped, equanimous, **5**. packed; *synonyms* *(adj)* crowded, filled, overcrowded, brimming; *antonym* *(adj)* deserted.

ribabati accumulation; *synonyms* *(n)* store, stock, accretion, mass, accrual, accruement, batch, hoard, pile, reserve, deposit, addition, aggregation, assemblage, *(v)* gain; *antonym* *(n)* shortage.

ribabetanga 1. crowded; *synonyms* *(adj)* close, compact, congested, busy, dense, full, packed, populous, jammed, cramped, teeming, thick, tight, *(n)* thronged; *antonyms* *(adj)* empty, sparse, **2**. compressed; *synonyms* *(adj)* flat, pointed, concise, besotted, bland, blotto, categoric, categorical, concrete, firm, hard, narrow, short, solid, crocked; *antonym* *(adj)* loose, **3**. wedged; *synonyms* *(adj)* impacted, fast, stuck, blocked, caught, fixed, immovable, lodged, stiff, trapped.

ribaki 1. hated; *synonyms* *(adj)* detested, despised, disliked, reviled, scorned, unpopular, abhorrent, despicable, insufferable, loathed, ostracized; *antonym* *(adj)* popular, **2**. detested; *synonym* *(adj)* hated, **3**. disapproved; *synonyms* *(adj)* contraband, old-fashioned, taboo; *antonym* *(adj)* approved, **4**. disliked; *synonyms* *(adj)* averse, companionless, loath, lousy, undesirable, hateful, ignored, odious, reluctant, unwilling; *antonym* *(adj)* liked.

ribana 1. farm; *synonyms* *(n)* property, grange, dairy, estate, farmhouse, *(v)* cultivate, raise, grow, hire, plant, produce, rear, rent, **2**. garden; *synonyms* *(n)* field, bed, orchard, grounds, park, patch, plaisance, plot, garth, lawn, backyard, court, *(v)* farm, *(adj)* commonplace, familiar, **3**. fertilize; *synonyms* *(v)* impregnate, enrich, fecundate, feed, fertilise, fructify, inseminate, **4**. cultivate; *synonyms* *(v)* civilize, educate, train, advance, breed, crop, develop, domesticate, improve, refine, prepare, dig, cherish, discipline, *(adj)* promote; *antonym* *(v)* neglect, **5**. dig; *synonyms* *(v)* jab, delve, prod, burrow, comprehend, excavate, investigate, probe, apprehend, *(n)* poke, excavation, gibe, punch, stab, taunt; *antonym* *(n)* compliment, **6**. till; *synonyms* *(prep)* until, unto, *(n)* drawer, tiller, cashbox, *(v)* plow, hoe, turn.

ribanaia cultivating; *synonyms* *(adj)* calming, educating, humanizing, taming, enlightening, refining.

ribanaki 1. fertilized; *synonyms* *(adj)* fertilised, impregnated, inseminated, **2**. cultivated; *synonyms* *(adj)* civilized, cultured, refined, tame, educated, elegant, polished, sophisticated, urbane, accomplished, civil, polite, artistic, courteous, genteel; *antonyms* *(adj)* uncultivated, untamed, wild, **3**. dug; *synonyms* *(n)* teat, breast, nipple, pap, papilla, tit, titty, boob, knocker, *(adj)* understood, **4**. tilled.

ribanono crowded; *synonyms* *(adj)* close, compact, congested, busy, dense, full, packed, populous, jammed, cramped, teeming, thick, tight, *(n)* thronged; *antonyms* *(adj)* empty, sparse.

ribata 1. bound; *synonyms* *(v)* leap, border, bounce, limit, circumscribe, confine, pounce, rebound, *(n)* spring, jump, boundary, edge, barrier, compass, hop; *antonym* *(adj)* free, **2**. bind; *synonyms* *(v)* attach, tie, bandage, bundle, combine, fasten, fetter, fix, lace, truss, affix, bond, cement, gird, *(n)* band; *antonyms* *(v)* untie, release, unbind, **3**. mend; *synonyms* *(v)* repair, improve, correct, cure, amend, better, doctor, heal, restore, convalesce, ameliorate, bushel, emend, *(n)* patch, botch; *antonym* *(v)* break, **4**. patch; *synonyms* *(n)* darn, fleck, mend, plot, bed, blot, freckle, bit, blotch, dapple, field, maculation, clout, *(v)* piece, cobble, **5**. splint; *synonyms* *(n)* splinter, heel, shoe, sole, sprit, brace, fusee, stilts, stirrup, **6**. readjust; *synonyms* *(v)* adapt, adjust, regulate, reset, readapt, suit, balance, redispose, *(adj)* dress.

ribataki 1. bound; *synonyms* *(v)* leap, border, bounce, limit, circumscribe, confine, pounce, rebound, *(n)* spring, jump, boundary, edge, barrier, compass, hop; *antonym* *(adj)* free, **2**. bounded; *synonyms* *(adj)* finite, restricted, delimited, limited, encircled, enclosed, local, qualified, surrounded, belted, compassed, contiguous, defined, definite, determinate, **3**. patched; *synonyms* *(adj)* besmirched, damaged, flyblown, mean, ragged, spotted, stained, sullied, tainted, tarnished.

ribeu 1. humped; *synonyms* *(adj)* humpbacked, gibbous, hunchbacked, crookback, crookbacked, gibbose, humpy, bent, curved, hunchback, kyphotic, protuberant, **2**. deformed; *synonyms* *(adj)* crooked, distorted, malformed, misshapen, ugly, crippled, contorted, deform, grotesque, shapeless, twisted, warped, *(v)* crump, **3**. misshapen; *synonym* *(adj)* deformed, **4**. knotty; *synonyms* *(adj)* knotted, complex, difficult, gnarled, intricate, involved, convoluted, gnarly, elaborate, troublesome, baffling, hard, nodose, problematic, complicated; *antonyms* *(adj)* simple, straight, straightforward.

ribeubeu 1. deformed; *synonyms* *(adj)* crooked, bent, distorted, malformed, misshapen, ugly, crippled, contorted, deform, grotesque, shapeless, twisted, warped, *(v)* crump, **2**. misshapen; *synonym* *(adj)* deformed.

ribinano 1. reach; *synonyms* *(v)* range, overtake, obtain, achieve, attain, extend, get, make, pass, accomplish, *(n)* fetch, compass, stretch, extent, gain, **2**. win; *synonyms* *(v)* acquire, conquer, earn, prevail, secure, take, succeed, carry, vanquish, procure, reach, score, hit, receive, *(n)* triumph; *antonyms* *(v)* lose, *(n)* defeat.

ribinanoa 1. attract; *synonyms* (*v*) fascinate, charm, beguile, captivate, draw, enamor, entice, invite, tempt, arrest, absorb, appeal, attach, beckon, (*adj*) allure; *antonyms* (*v*) repel, disgust, **2.** incite; *synonyms* (*v*) animate, excite, goad, impel, abet, actuate, agitate, arouse, encourage, foment, quicken, cheer, awaken, cause, induce; *antonym* (*v*) suppress.

ribita 1. hook; *synonyms* (*n*) clasp, crook, claw, crotchet, draw, lure, trap, anchor, (*v*) catch, bend, fasten, hitch, button, ensnare, attach, **2.** catch; *synonyms* (*v*) arrest, capture, hook, apprehend, get, acquire, intercept, snatch, take, (*n*) haul, trick, bolt, grab, pawl, snap; *antonym* (*v*) release.

ribitaki hooked; *synonyms* (*adj*) crooked, bent, curved, aquiline, addicted, infatuated, dependant, dependent, enamored, engrossed, obsessed.

ribono 1. crowded; *synonyms* (*adj*) close, compact, congested, busy, dense, full, packed, populous, jammed, cramped, teeming, thick, tight, (*n*) thronged; *antonyms* (*adj*) empty, sparse, **2.** congested; *synonyms* (*adj*) overcrowded, engorged, closed, stopped, overfull, swarming, blocked, bunged, crammed, glutted, gorged, gridlocked, (*prep*) inflamed, enkindled, exasperated, **3.** touching; *synonyms* (*v*) affecting, sad, (*adj*) moving, poignant, pathetic, pitiful, adjacent, adjoining, emotional, contiguous, near, (*prep*) concerning, about, (*n*) touch, contact.

riborika pacify; *synonyms* (*v*) allay, compose, mollify, conciliate, placate, moderate, mitigate, (*adj*) assuage, appease, lull, soothe, quell, (*n*) calm, ease, alleviate; *antonyms* (*v*) annoy, enrage, excite, infuriate.

riboriki 1. appease; *synonyms* (*v*) allay, assuage, pacify, placate, alleviate, calm, conciliate, mollify, quiet, still, abate, content, ease, quell, reconcile; *antonyms* (*v*) aggravate, provoke, **2.** calm; *synonyms* (*adj*) peaceful, tranquil, bland, composed, gentle, (*v*) appease, cool, easy, moderate, steady, tranquilize, becalm, compose, (*n*) lull, equanimity; *antonyms* (*adj*) agitated, angry, nervous, stormy, wild, annoyed, anxious, enraged, frantic, frightened, intense, irritable, (*v*) agitate, upset, (*n*) agitation, **3.** redress; *synonyms* (*n*) remedy, indemnification, help, amends, atonement, (*v*) cure, compensate, correct, recompense, indemnify, expiate, atone, rectify, mend, adjust.

ribu sink; *synonyms* (*n*) sag, basin, (*v*) decline, dip, droop, fall, set, descend, drop, fell, bury, collapse, decay, flag, founder; *antonyms* (*v*) rise, float.

ribuaka 1. bad; *synonyms* (*adj*) evil, adverse, harmful, immoral, naughty, poisonous, sad, sinister, wicked, malicious, infamous, appalling, awful, damaging, (*v*) decayed; *antonyms* (*adj*) fresh, pleasant, well, well-behaved, (*n*) good, **2.** disobliging; *synonyms* (*adj*) unaccommodating, harsh, uncooperative,

unwilling, awkward, contrary, disagreeable, ill-natured, obstructive, unhelpful, annoying, difficult, displeasing, ill-disposed, obstinate, **3.** ungrateful; *synonyms* (*adj*) thankless, unmindful, unappreciative, unthankful, unnatural, ingrate, distasteful, unkind, childless, cruel, ingrateful, offensive, unacceptable, unappreciated, careless; *antonyms* (*adj*) grateful, thankful, **4.** unjust; *synonyms* (*adj*) unfair, partial, injurious, foul, inequitable, unrighteous, wrong, wrongful, improper, unjustified, unmerited, dishonest, iniquitous, undue, unreasonable; *antonyms* (*adj*) fair, just, equitable, reasonable, rightful, **5.** wicked; *synonyms* (*adj*) atrocious, bad, sinful, vicious, depraved, mischievous, unholy, vile, corrupt, criminal, diabolical, hellish, nasty, pernicious, ungodly; *antonyms* (*adj*) innocent, kind, moral, pious, pure.

rierake 1. ascend; *synonyms* (*v*) rise, arise, mount, climb, scale, uprise, increase, appear, escalate, jump, lift, soar; *antonyms* (*v*) descend, drop, **2.** climb; *synonyms* (*v*) ascend, clamber, scramble, bestride, fly, (*n*) ascent, acclivity, advance, ascending, ascension, climbing, hike, mounting, raise, upgrade, **3.** soar; *synonyms* (*v*) hover, glide, leap, billow, tower, float, sail, expand, surge, swell, loom, sailplane, (*n*) zoom; *antonym* (*v*) plummet.

rieta 1. high; *synonyms* (*adj*) eminent, elevated, great, expensive, distinguished, exalted, lofty, tall, heavy, arrogant, costly, dear, (*v*) bad, fusty, rancid; *antonyms* (*adj*) deep, short, sober, (*n*) low, **2.** lofty; *synonyms* (*adj*) high, grand, haughty, gallant, majestic, noble, dignified, illustrious, proud, soaring, stately, steep, sublime, superior, towering; *antonym* (*adj*) lowly, **3.** elevated; *synonyms* (*adj*) elated, magnanimous, advanced, magnificent, (*n*) fresh, mellow, merry, boozy, cut.

rietata 1. arrogant; *synonyms* (*adj*) haughty, imperious, presumptuous, proud, dogmatic, boastful, conceited, condescending, disdainful, domineering, egotistical, insolent, overbearing, supercilious, vain; *antonyms* (*adj*) modest, self-effacing, (*syn*) humble, **2.** high; *synonyms* (*adj*) eminent, elevated, great, expensive, distinguished, exalted, lofty, tall, heavy, arrogant, costly, dear, (*v*) bad, fusty, rancid; *antonyms* (*adj*) deep, short, sober, (*n*) low, **3.** lofty; *synonyms* (*adj*) high, grand, gallant, majestic, noble, dignified, illustrious, soaring, stately, steep, sublime, superior, towering, big, cavalier; *antonym* (*adj*) lowly, **4.** elevated; *synonyms* (*adj*) elated, magnanimous, advanced, magnificent, (*n*) fresh, mellow, merry, boozy, cut, **5.** egotistic; *synonyms* (*adj*) selfish, egocentric, egoistic, narcissistic; *antonym* (*adj*) altruistic, **6.** flamboyant; *synonyms* (*adj*) loud, extravagant, pretentious, aureate, colorful, florid, ostentatious, showy, brilliant, elaborate, gay, vivid, flashy,

garish, gaudy; *antonym* (*adj*) restrained, **7.**
haughty; *synonyms* (*adj*) assuming, contemptuous, lordly, contumelious, aloof, prideful, snobbish, dictatorial, magisterial, patronizing, pompous, sniffy, snooty, authoritative, commanding, **8.** egotistical; *synonym* (*adj*) egotistic, **9.** swank; *synonyms* (*n*) smartness, chicness, modishness, stylishness, (*v*) flash, flaunt, boast, brag, swagger, (*adj*) chic, swanky, fashionable, posh, stylish, **10.** pretentious; *synonyms* (*adj*) affected, stilted, grandiose, ambitious, exaggerated, mannered, mincing, flamboyant, overblown, precious, dashing, imposing, (*v*) braggart, flaming, gasconading; *antonym* (*adj*) down-to-earth, **11.** proud; *synonyms* (*adj*) fine, bigheaded, glorious, inflated, regal, splendid, uppish, honorable, overjoyed, triumphant; *antonyms* (*adj*) ashamed, embarrassed, **12.** ostentatious; *synonyms* (*adj*) conspicuous, impressive, kitsch, luxurious, pedantic, tasteless, **13.** showy; *synonyms* (*adj*) striking, rich, fancy, ornate, superb, brassy, shining, theatrical, jaunty, meretricious, dazzling, resplendent, glitzy, (*v*) bright, (*n*) gorgeous; *antonym* (*adj*) tasteful.

rikaaki backward; *synonyms* (*adj*) back, late, behindhand, coy, dilatory, laggard, reluctant, retarded, slow, tardy, averse, bashful, (*adv*) behind, aback, backwards; *antonyms* (*adv*) forward, ahead.

rikaki 1. down; *synonyms* (*adv*) below, (*adj*) cut, dejected, depressed, downward, despondent, dispirited, downcast, downhearted, (*n*) feather, fur, fuzz, (*v*) consume, devour, drink; *antonyms* (*adv*) up, (*adj*) cheerful, happy, upward, **2.** retreat; *synonyms* (*n*) refuge, resort, asylum, departure, den, lair, privacy, retirement, (*v*) recede, retire, withdraw, depart, ebb, leave, return; *antonyms* (*n*) raid, (*v*) advance, **3.** retire; *synonyms* (*v*) resign, retreat, abdicate, adjourn, go, quit, remove, secede, regrade, back, give, pension, dismiss, exit, flinch, **4.** withdraw; *synonyms* (*v*) extract, retract, abandon, cancel, disengage, draw, recall, repeal, rescind, revoke, shrink, subtract, swallow, unsay, deduct; *antonyms* (*v*) extend, offer, present, propose, deposit.

rikakiaki 1. retired; *synonyms* (*v*) covert, (*adj*) private, obscure, emeritus, secluded, secret, sequestered, solitary, lonely, withdrawn, close, superannuated, isolated, old, out, **2.** retreated, **3.** withdrawn; *synonyms* (*adj*) reserved, retiring, indrawn, cloistered, reclusive, uncommunicative, taciturn, unsociable, introverted, reticent, shy, aloof, detached, distant, recluse; *antonym* (*adj*) outgoing.

rikakina return; *synonyms* (*n*) yield, pay, recompense, refund, restitution, proceeds, income, (*v*) recur, reimburse, render, repay, restoration,

restore, retort, answer; *antonyms* (*n*) departure, abolition, confiscation, recovery, (*v*) keep.

rikan deacon; *synonyms* (*n*) minister, warden, (*v*) fast, disguise, doctor, falsify, gloss.

riki 1. more; *synonyms* (*adv*) also, further, besides, beyond, over, (*adj*) additional, better, extra, larger, exceed, greater, other, (*pron*) another, (*prep*) above; *antonyms* (*adv*) fewer, less, (*adj*) inferior, **2.** emerge; *synonyms* (*v*) appear, arise, emanate, spring, transpire, develop, issue, occur, rise, surface, begin, escape, loom, materialize, originate, **3.** afoot; *synonyms* (*adv*) walking, abroach, broached, (*adj*) current, itinerant, (*n*) afloat, prevalent, (*v*) agoing, **4.** anew; *synonyms* (*adv*) afresh, again, newly, lately, recently, **5.** instead; *synonyms* (*adv*) rather, alternatively, otherwise, preferably, sooner, equivalent, kinda, quite, (*adj*) before, earlier, former, prior, somewhat, **6.** better; *synonyms* (*adj*) superior, (*n*) bettor, (*v*) amend, improve, best, mend, recover, advance, ameliorate, emend, reform, enhance, excel, refine, surpass; *antonyms* (*adj*) lesser, (*adv*) worse, (*v*) worsen, **7.** extra; *synonyms* (*adj*) odd, auxiliary, redundant, spare, (*adv*) more, especially, (*n*) supplement, accessory, excess, plus, supernumerary, addendum, addition, duplicate, (*v*) additive; *antonyms* (*adj*) basic, (*n*) lack, **8.** less; *synonyms* (*adj*) wanting, lower, minor, secondary, subordinate, minus, **9.** become; *synonyms* (*v*) be, grow, suit, get, match, sit, come, fall, fit, go, make, turn, wax, change, result, **10.** again; *synonyms* (*adv*) anew, encore, repeatedly, then, often, **11.** be; *synonyms* (*v*) exist, live, act, consist, constitute, represent, cost, follow, form, lie, remain, rest, stay, subsist, (*n*) stand, **12.** develop; *synonyms* (*v*) amplify, educate, expand, breed, contract, acquire, bloom, blossom, break, bud, build, cultivate, elaborate, evolve, extend; *antonyms* (*v*) decrease, erupt, neglect, regress, **13.** grown; *synonyms* (*adj*) adult, mature, big, grown-up, developed, grownup, ripe; *antonym* (*adj*) immature, **14.** happen; *synonyms* (*v*) befall, chance, bechance, hap, pass, arrive, encounter, find, proceed, supervene, fare, eventuate, elapse, become, (*n*) betide, **15.** are, **16.** grow; *synonyms* (*v*) augment, enlarge, emerge, farm, accrue, flourish, germinate, increase, raise, sprout, thrive, cause, climb, escalate, gain; *antonyms* (*v*) weaken, shrink, **17.** any; *synonyms* (*adj*) all, either, whichever, every, several, some, alone, few, ony, quantitative, only, (*n*) aught, part, (*pron*) who, **18.** else; *synonyms* (*adv*) moreover, (*n*) threat, (*adj*) new, fresh, **19.** occur; *synonyms* (*v*) happen, ensue, continue, start, ascend, die, fell, give, **20.** rather; *synonyms* (*adv*) enough, fairly, pretty, moderately, considerably, instead, relatively, comparatively, reasonably; *antonym* (*adv*) extremely.

rikiaki developed; *synonyms* *(adj)* adult, mature, advanced, grown, sophisticated, complete, detailed, distinguished, educated, established, full, full-fledged, full-grown, grown-up, matured; *antonym* *(adj)* immature.

rikibuaka 1. deformed; *synonyms* *(adj)* crooked, bent, distorted, malformed, misshapen, ugly, crippled, contorted, deform, grotesque, shapeless, twisted, warped, *(v)* crump, **2.** unwelcome; *synonyms* *(adj)* undesirable, unwanted, disagreeable, objectionable, unpopular, unasked, unwished, unintroduced, uninvited, unvisited, *(n)* unsatisfactory; *antonyms* *(adj)* welcome, desirable, longed-for.

rikimate stillborn; *synonyms* *(adj)* abortive, unsuccessful, deadborn, *(v)* addle.

rikirake 1. develop; *synonyms* *(v)* advance, amplify, educate, expand, grow, breed, contract, acquire, bloom, blossom, break, bud, build, come, cultivate; *antonyms* *(v)* decrease, erupt, neglect, regress, **2.** grown; *synonyms* *(adj)* adult, mature, big, grown-up, developed, grownup, ripe; *antonym* *(adj)* immature, **3.** increase; *synonyms* *(n)* gain, addition, augmentation, boom, expansion, extension, growth, progress, rise, *(v)* accrue, extend, aggrandize, enhance, enlarge, *(adj)* augment; *antonyms* *(n)* reduction, contraction, decline, *(v)* reduce, diminish, drop, deteriorate, **4.** accrue; *synonyms* *(v)* accumulate, collect, fall, result, yield, accresce, hoard, make, stockpile, adhere, contribute, devolve, flourish, hang, interfere, **5.** grow; *synonyms* *(v)* develop, emerge, become, farm, get, spring, turn, arise, evolve, germinate, increase, raise, sprout, thrive, go; *antonyms* *(v)* weaken, shrink, **6.** progress; *synonyms* *(n)* headway, improvement, furtherance, betterment, course, advancement, development, movement, *(v)* proceed, continue, move, improve, pass, prosper, way; *antonym* *(n)* deterioration, **7.** prosper; *synonyms* *(v)* flower, fare, succeed, arrive, burgeon, *(adj)* luxuriate.

rikirakeaki 1. developed; *synonyms* *(adj)* adult, mature, advanced, grown, sophisticated, complete, detailed, distinguished, educated, established, full, full-fledged, full-grown, grown-up, matured; *antonym* *(adj)* immature, **2.** accrued; *synonyms* *(adj)* accumulated, amassed, assembled, collected, congregate, massed, **3.** increased; *synonyms* *(adj)* additional, more, enlarged, greater, fresh, new, plus, puffy, ripe, amplified, better, bigger, improved, other, superior.

riko 1. collect; *synonyms* *(v)* assemble, accumulate, amass, gather, pick, accrue, acquire, aggregate, cluster, collate, congregate, convene, cull, harvest, hoard; *antonyms* *(v)* disperse, distribute, **2.** gather; *synonyms* *(v)* deduce, collect, compile, flock, garner, meet, tuck, earn, rally, reap, derive,

converge, extract, conclude, *(n)* fold; *antonym* *(v)* scatter, **3.** provide; *synonyms* *(v)* give, contribute, furnish, offer, accommodate, administer, afford, cater, equip, supply, allow, fit, endow, outfit, nourish.

rikoa 1. collect; *synonyms* *(v)* assemble, accumulate, amass, gather, pick, accrue, acquire, aggregate, cluster, collate, congregate, convene, cull, harvest, hoard; *antonyms* *(v)* disperse, distribute, **2.** gather; *synonyms* *(v)* deduce, collect, compile, flock, garner, meet, tuck, earn, rally, reap, derive, converge, extract, conclude, *(n)* fold; *antonym* *(v)* scatter.

rikoaki 1. gathered; *synonyms* *(adj)* collected, deepened, accumulated, amassed, assembled, collective, congregate, equanimous, massed, poised, **2.** collected; *synonyms* *(v)* composed, *(adj)* calm, cool, sober, tranquil, unflappable, dispassionate, gathered, imperturbable, peaceful, placid, quiet, sedate, serene, staid; *antonym* *(adj)* agitated.

rikoia 1. gather; *synonyms* *(v)* deduce, convene, accumulate, amass, assemble, collect, compile, congregate, flock, garner, meet, tuck, earn, rally, *(n)* fold; *antonyms* *(v)* disperse, scatter, **2.** collect; *synonyms* *(v)* gather, pick, accrue, acquire, aggregate, cluster, collate, cull, harvest, hoard, raise, accept, catch, derive, gain; *antonym* *(v)* distribute.

rikoiaki 1. collected; *synonyms* *(v)* composed, *(adj)* calm, accumulated, amassed, assembled, cool, sober, tranquil, poised, unflappable, dispassionate, gathered, imperturbable, peaceful, placid; *antonym* *(adj)* agitated, **2.** gathered; *synonyms* *(adj)* collected, deepened, collective, congregate, equanimous, massed.

rikuma 1. fold; *synonyms* *(n)* crease, bend, pucker, wrinkle, flock, crimp, *(v)* crinkle, collapse, crumple, double, lap, roll, close, enfold, fail, **2.** close; *synonyms* *(adj)* near, adjacent, nearby, accurate, tight, approximate, narrow, *(v)* compact, stop, conclude, *(adv)* by, about, *(n)* end, finish, conclusion; *antonyms* *(adj)* distant, airy, fresh, loose, far, *(v)* open, start, **3.** roll; *synonyms* *(n)* list, revolution, catalogue, inventory, register, *(v)* coil, reel, curl, revolve, wheel, rock, turn, twist, wallow, wind, **4.** wrap; *synonyms* *(v)* cloak, cover, envelop, shroud, swathe, enclose, bind, drape, enwrap, hide, involve, muffle, surround, twine, *(n)* coat; *antonyms* *(v)* unwrap, uncover.

rikumaki 1. closed; *synonyms* *(v)* close, tight, accurate, adjoining, attentive, *(adj)* blind, blocked, finished, shut, congested, fastened, exclusive, insular, stopped, airtight; *antonym* *(adj)* open, **2.** folded; *synonyms* *(adj)* closed, plaited, artful, braided, corrugated, intricate, **3.** wrapped;

synonyms (*adj*) clothed, draped, enwrapped, absorbed, cloaked, intent, rapt, engrossed, mantled, (*prep*) covered, **4**. rolled; *synonyms* (*adj*) rolling, furled, involute, beaten, billowing, kinky, level, resonant, resonating, resounding, reverberating, reverberative, spiral, trilled, tumbling.

rimoa 1. ancient; *synonyms* (*adj*) aged, old, antiquated, obsolete, former, past, antique, archaic, bygone, hoary, primitive, olden, antediluvian, dated, (*n*) elder; *antonym* (*adj*) modern, **2**. supersede; *synonyms* (*v*) substitute, supplant, displace, replace, succeed, annul, follow, overrule, (*n*) remove, **3**. precede; *synonyms* (*v*) lead, head, antecede, antedate, forego, anticipate, forerun, introduce, pass, preface, direct, go.

rimwi 1. lately; *synonyms* (*adv*) recently, late, freshly, latterly, newly, just, new, (*adj*) anew, afresh, **2**. go; *synonyms* (*v*) come, elapse, pass, break, crack, depart, disappear, drive, run, travel, fall, extend, function, (*n*) fare, (*adj*) follow, **3**. after; *synonyms* (*prep*) following, since, (*adv*) later, beyond, next, subsequently, then, when, afterward, afterwards, behind, (*adj*) back, posterior, rear, subsequent, **4**. later; *synonyms* (*adv*) after, (*adj*) last, ensuing, future, latter, final, succeeding; *antonyms* (*adv*) earlier, immediately, before, prior, **5**. late; *synonyms* (*adj*) former, dead, deceased, behindhand, belated, delayed, modern, slow, tardy, dull, defunct, (*adv*) dilatory, fresh, backward, belatedly; *antonyms* (*adj*) ahead, (*adv*) early, punctually, promptly, punctual, **6**. afterward; *synonym* (*adv*) thereafter; *antonym* (*adv*) beforehand, **7**. afterwards, **8**. following; *synonyms* (*adj*) consequent, consecutive, deducible, sequent, successive, (*v*) consequential, consectary, (*n*) entourage, chase, followers, pursuit, audience, train, clientele, (*adv*) under; *antonym* (*adj*) preceding, **9**. future; *synonyms* (*adj*) unborn, coming, prospective, intended, potential, approaching, forthcoming, imminent, impending, (*n*) prospect, hereafter, fate, futurity, time, (*v*) horizon; *antonym* (*n*) past, **10**. ulterior; *synonyms* (*adj*) eventual, subterranean, covert, alien, extraneous, foreign, **11**. pass; *synonyms* (*v*) flow, deliver, give, happen, lead, move, offer, overtake, live, advance, die, exceed, lapse, leave, (*adj*) go; *antonym* (*v*) fail, **12**. posterior; *synonyms* (*adj*) caudal, hindmost, (*n*) backside, bottom, buttocks, can, rump, tail, arse, ass, bum, butt, fanny, fundament, hindquarters; *antonyms* (*adj*) fore, anterior, forward, **13**. subsequent; *synonyms* (*adj*) second, sequential, postnate; *antonym* (*adj*) previous, **14**. subsequently; *synonym* (*adv*) accordingly.

rin 1. introduce; *synonyms* (*v*) insert, interject, inject, acquaint, advance, enter, exhibit, implant, inaugurate, infuse, initiate, precede, present, instill,

interpose; *antonym* (*v*) end, **2**. enter; *synonyms* (*v*) enlist, embark, enroll, book, chronicle, record, input, arrive, come, accede, attack, begin, board, enrol, introduce; *antonyms* (*v*) leave, depart, delete, exit, **3**. intrude; *synonyms* (*v*) interfere, encroach, impose, infringe, trespass, disturb, impinge, interrupt, obtrude, disrupt, transgress, interlope, invade, irrupt, meddle, **4**. wane; *synonyms* (*n*) ebb, (*v*) decline, fade, fall, sink, decrease, diminish, dwindle, fail, recede, wither, shrink, contract, decay, abate, **5**. penetrate; *synonyms* (*v*) bore, imbue, fathom, infiltrate, permeate, pierce, cut, filter, interpenetrate, drill, diffuse, percolate, perforate, probe, puncture, **6**. pierce; *synonyms* (*v*) impale, stab, stick, bite, gore, penetrate, thrust, wound, broach, pick, punch, riddle, spike, break, (*n*) prick.

rina 1. sudden; *synonyms* (*adj*) abrupt, hasty, precipitous, quick, rash, unexpected, steep, dramatic, headlong, immediate, precipitate, sharp, swift, unforeseen, impulsive; *antonyms* (*adj*) gradual, considered, **2**. unexpected; *synonyms* (*adj*) sudden, surprising, casual, unanticipated, unpredicted, accidental, strange, abnormal, astonishing, curious, forced, startling, unintentional, unusual, (*n*) surprise; *antonym* (*adj*) expected, **3**. suddenly; *synonyms* (*adv*) abruptly, short, presto, dead, hastily, rapidly, fast, instantly, sharply, unawares, precipitously, (*adj*) quickly, immediately, instanter, subito; *antonyms* (*adv*) gradually, increasingly, predictably, slowly.

rinaki 1. introduced; *synonyms* (*adj*) exotic, familiar, imported, interpolated, **2**. pierced; *synonyms* (*adj*) perforated, punctured, perforate, cleft, entered.

rinano 1. lower; *synonyms* (*adj*) debase, inferior, (*v*) degrade, diminish, frown, humble, dip, abase, cut, descend, drop, scowl, disgrace, decrease, (*n*) depress; *antonyms* (*v*) increase, raise, **2**. low; *synonyms* (*adj*) contemptible, abject, ignoble, base, blue, common, deep, dejected, depressed, down, downcast, downhearted, feeble, (*adv*) gentle, (*n*) depression; *antonyms* (*adj*) cheerful, happy, high-pitched, loud, important, piercing, (*n*) high, **3**. go; *synonyms* (*v*) come, elapse, pass, break, crack, depart, disappear, drive, run, travel, fall, extend, function, (*n*) fare, (*adj*) follow, **4**. humble; *synonyms* (*adj*) docile, low, lowly, modest, unassuming, baseborn, mean, meek, menial, (*v*) demean, humiliate, mortify, conquer, lower, (*n*) dishonor; *antonyms* (*adj*) grand, arrogant, conceited, haughty, imposing, impressive, pompous, snooty.

rinanoa 1. compare; *synonyms* (*v*) collate, liken, confront, comparison, equate, associate, contrast, correlate, equal, equalize, parallel, resemble, (*n*) comparability, **2**. edit; *synonyms* (*v*) delete, compile, cut, redact, revise, contract, correct,

emend, emit, prune, censor, (*n*) editing, **3.** check;
synonyms (*v*) bridle, stop, block, limit, agree, halt,
restrain, bar, dampen, delay, (*n*) control, arrest,
curb, bill, cheque, **4.** audit; *synonyms* (*n*) survey,
examination, review, scrutiny, (*v*) check, balance,
inspect, examine, prove, scrutinize, **5.** amend;
synonyms (*v*) ameliorate, improve, mend, rectify,
alter, better, fix, reform, adjust, help, redress,
remedy, repair, advance, change; *antonym* (*v*)
worsen, **6.** correct; *synonyms* (*adj*) right, accurate,
appropriate, becoming, nice, precise, proper, apt,
(*v*) amend, castigate, chastise, chasten, straighten,
atone, (*n*) true; *antonyms* (*adj*) incorrect, false,
faulty, inappropriate, mistaken, improper, (*v*)
wrong, spoil, **7.** rework; *synonyms* (*v*) repeat,
rehash, modify, retread, **8.** revise; *synonyms* (*v*)
edit, convert, retouch, adapt, reconsider, update,
vary, redraft, rework, rewrite, (*n*) revisal, revision,
proof, copy, (*adj*) overhaul, **9.** revamp; *synonyms*
(*v*) doctor, refurbish, renew, renovate, restore,
reconstruct, vamp, modernize, **10.** redraft;
synonyms (*v*) redraw, rephrase, reshape, reword, (*n*)
alteration, amendment, modification, **11.** redraw;
synonym (*n*) redrawing, **12.** reconsider;
synonyms (*v*) reassess, redeliberate, retrace, return,
rearrange, recheck, re-evaluate, re-examine, replan,
revisit, reweigh, rub, (*n*) criticism, critique,
reexamination.

rinanoaki 1. amended; *synonyms* (*adj*) altered,
reformed, **2.** edited; *synonyms* (*adj*) published,
abridged, emended, formatted, shortened,
abbreviated, condensed, reduced, **3.** corrected;
synonyms (*adj*) chastised, amended, chastened,
disciplined, educated, refined, **4.** checked;
synonyms (*adj*) checkered, chequered, plaid,
backward, curbed, intermittent, limited, numbered,
pent-up, safe, silent, tartan, temperate, **5.** revised.

rinanon through; *synonyms* (*prep*) for, per, along,
because, throughout, (*adv*) by, thorough, via, (*adj*)
finished, done, direct, straight, completed,
complete, (*prf*) past.

rine 1. distinctive; *synonyms* (*adj*) characteristic,
distinguishing, excellent, discriminating,
individual, special, typical, exceptional, separate,
unusual, different, distinct, idiosyncratic, (*v*)
discriminative, dioristic; *antonym* (*adj*) common, **2.**
choose; *synonyms* (*v*) adopt, elect, pick, prefer,
select, appoint, take, assign, decide, desire,
determine, draw, excerpt, like, vote; *antonyms* (*v*)
reject, refuse, **3.** eminent; *synonyms* (*adj*)
distinguished, celebrated, high, elevated, brilliant,
big, conspicuous, famous, illustrious, noble,
renowned, dignified, exalted, grand, great;
antonym (*adj*) unknown, **4.** illustrious; *synonyms*
(*adj*) glorious, bright, eminent, famed, well-known,
lofty, notable, noted, proud, mighty, prominent,
recognized, redoubtable, shining, splendid, **5.**

excellent; *synonyms* (*adj*) choice, estimable,
admirable, superior, capital, beautiful, distinctive,
fantastic, fine, good, magnificent, marvelous,
outstanding, perfect, (*n*) worthy; *antonyms* (*adj*)
inferior, poor, abysmal, awful, mediocre, **6.** prefer;
synonyms (*v*) choose, advance, elevate, favor, opt,
favour, promote, want, dignify, fancy, exalt, love,
relish, wish, **7.** opt, **8.** surpassing; *synonyms* (*adj*)
exceeding, prodigious, transcendent, extraordinary,
towering, unequaled, (*prep*) above, **9.** pick;
synonyms (*v*) clean, gather, harvest, break, collect,
cull, nibble, (*n*) alternative, elite, best, option,
selection, (*adj*) cream, mattock, flower, **10.**
superior; *synonyms* (*adj*) senior, dominant, better,
predominant, elder, arrogant, chief, higher,
commanding, important, paramount, haughty,
major, (*n*) boss, master; *antonyms* (*adj*) humble,
worse, (*n*) subordinate, subscript, **11.** venerable;
synonyms (*adj*) old, ancient, reverend, respectable,
aged, sacred, considerable, revered, reverenced,
solemn, **12.** project; *synonyms* (*n*) design, device,
scheme, idea, enterprise, (*v*) plan, hurl, contrive, jut,
overhang, protrude, shoot, bulge, cast, devise, **13.**
select; *synonyms* (*v*) extract, nominate, sort, hire,
indicate, designate, examine, mark, (*adj*) exclusive,
chosen, rare, selective, exquisite, prime, quality.

rinea 1. choose; *synonyms* (*v*) adopt, elect, pick,
prefer, select, appoint, take, assign, decide, desire,
determine, draw, excerpt, like, vote; *antonyms* (*v*)
reject, refuse, **2.** chosen; *synonyms* (*v*) designate,
(*adj*) picked, preferred, favored, **3.** decide;
synonyms (*v*) choose, adjudicate, conclude, resolve,
judge, settle, try, arbitrate, arrange, decree, fix,
purpose, rule, deem, define; *antonym* (*v*) waver, **4.**
apportion; *synonyms* (*v*) allot, allocate, distribute,
share, administer, award, deal, dispense, divide,
ration, partition, portion, split, (*n*) part, **5.** pick;
synonyms (*v*) clean, gather, harvest, opt, break,
collect, (*n*) alternative, elite, best, choice, option,
selection, (*adj*) cream, mattock, flower.

rineaki 1. apportioned; *synonyms* (*adj*) fractional,
separate, **2.** decided; *synonyms* (*v*) absolute, clear,
positive, categorical, emphatic, marked, (*adj*)
decisive, definite, determined, distinct, resolute,
unmistakable, conclusive, fixed, peremptory;
antonym (*adj*) undecided, **3.** chosen; *synonyms* (*v*)
designate, (*adj*) picked, preferred, select, favored, (*n*)
elect, **4.** selected; *synonyms* (*adj*) chosen, choice,
elected, (*n*) best, **5.** projected; *synonyms* (*adj*)
projecting, jutting, proposed, planned, anticipated,
deliberate, expected, future, likely, predictable,
probable, protruding, sticking, estimated, **6.**
preferred; *synonyms* (*adj*) favorite, pet, favourite,
selected, preferable.

ringa 1. affect; *synonyms* (*v*) touch, move, act, fake,
feign, impress, pretend, strike, concern, dispose,

dissemble, hit, influence, involve, lead, **2**. move; *synonyms* (*v*) affect, carry, excite, go, impel, instigate, maneuver, travel, flow, bear, disturb, actuate, (*n*) motion, drive, transfer; *antonym* (*v*) stay, **3**. feel; *synonyms* (*v*) experience, sense, consider, finger, handle, believe, deem, endure, find, hold, (*n*) atmosphere, feeling, sound, texture, air; *antonym* (*v*) observe, **4**. felt; *synonyms* (*v*) mat, snarl, tangle, braid, entangle, (*adj*) perceived, sensed, conscious, **5**. touch; *synonyms* (*n*) feel, tinge, hint, tap, (*v*) contact, border, adjoin, stroke, regard, brush, interest, meet, reach, taste, tint.

ringaki 1. affected; *synonyms* (*adj*) artificial, unnatural, pompous, pretentious, stilted, pedantic, assumed, concerned, contrived, exaggerated, feigned, forced, pretended, snobbish, strained; *antonyms* (*adj*) unaffected, down-to-earth, natural, unchanged, **2**. felt; *synonyms* (*v*) mat, snarl, tangle, braid, entangle, (*adj*) perceived, sensed, conscious, **3**. touched; *synonyms* (*v*) compassionate, pitiful, sympathetic, bad, decayed, lentiginous, mildewed, moldy, (*adj*) affected, cracked, crazy, daft, insane, tinged, interested; *antonym* (*adj*) untouched.

ringongo snore; *synonyms* (*v*) snort, breathe, coma, doze, dream, hibernation, nap, siesta, snooze, (*n*) snoring, stertor.

ringongoraki snort; *synonyms* (*n*) hoot, snicker, bird, boo, hiss, raspberry, razzing, sneer, snigger, (*v*) sniff, snore, huff, inhale, chuckle, giggle.

ringoungou 1. insatiable; *synonyms* (*adj*) greedy, gluttonous, insatiate, ravenous, voracious, avaricious, avid, unsatiable, **2**. ravenous; *synonyms* (*adj*) hungry, famished, edacious, insatiable, rapacious, covetous, predatory, esurient, grasping, ravening, starving, ferocious, eager, wolfish; *antonym* (*adj*) full.

rino 1. finicky; *synonyms* (*adj*) fastidious, finical, fussy, choosy, dainty, exacting, particular, picky, squeamish, demanding, meticulous, nice, persnickety, scrupulous, selective; *antonym* (*adj*) easy, **2**. meticulous; *synonyms* (*adj*) detailed, accurate, careful, conscientious, exact, finicky, precise, punctilious, rigorous, thorough, methodical, delicate, correct, close, comprehensive; *antonyms* (*adj*) careless, sloppy, **3**. particular; *synonyms* (*adj*) special, definite, individual, certain, circumstantial, critical, distinct, especial, exceptional, extra, extraordinary, minute, painstaking, (*n*) detail, item; *antonyms* (*adj*) vague, ordinary, (*n*) general.

rio 1. downward; *synonyms* (*adj*) downcast, absolute, downright, declivous, dejected, positive, sliding, (*adv*) down, below, under, downwardly, downwards, adown, **2**. westward; *synonyms* (*adv*) west, westwards, (*adj*) westerly, westbound, western.

rionako dip; *synonyms* (*n*) plunge, depression, tilt, (*v*) duck, bathe, drop, fall, bow, decline, dive, douse, immerse, sink, bend, declivity; *antonyms* (*n*) hump, mountain.

rionakoaki dipped; *synonyms* (*adj*) concave, lordotic, swayback, swaybacked, dished, hollow; *antonym* (*adj*) convex.

riri bony; *synonyms* (*adj*) osseous, gaunt, lean, thin, angular, emaciated, scrawny, skinny, lanky, meager, boney, spare; *antonym* (*adj*) rounded.

ririba hate; *synonyms* (*v*) abhor, detest, abominate, loathe, despise, scorn, (*n*) dislike, enmity, abhorrence, animosity, detestation, hatred, abomination, antipathy, aversion; *antonyms* (*v*) love, like, adore.

riribai hostile; *synonyms* (*adj*) unfriendly, aggressive, contrary, adverse, belligerent, warlike, averse, unfavorable, antagonistic, chilly, inhospitable, inimical, irreconcilable, opposed, opposite; *antonyms* (*adj*) friendly, soothing, warm.

riribaki hated; *synonyms* (*adj*) detested, despised, disliked, reviled, scorned, unpopular, abhorrent, despicable, insufferable, loathed, ostracized; *antonym* (*adj*) popular.

riribwa rocky; *synonyms* (*adj*) hard, unstable, rough, shaky, craggy, flinty, stony, wobbly, unsteady, harsh, insecure, obdurate, rugged, bouldered, bouldery.

ririere 1. arrogant; *synonyms* (*adj*) haughty, imperious, presumptuous, proud, dogmatic, boastful, conceited, condescending, disdainful, domineering, egotistical, insolent, overbearing, supercilious, vain; *antonyms* (*adj*) modest, self-effacing, (*syn*) humble, **2**. pretentious; *synonyms* (*adj*) ostentatious, affected, pompous, showy, stilted, arrogant, grandiose, snobbish, ambitious, exaggerated, mannered, mincing, gaudy, lofty, assuming; *antonym* (*adj*) down-to-earth.

ririka 1. charmed; *synonyms* (*adj*) captivated, delighted, enchanted, fascinated, entranced, spellbound, beguiled, captive, **2**. infatuated; *synonyms* (*adj*) enamored, fanatical, crazy, dotty, gaga, mad, obsessed, smitten, foolish, loving, (*v*) besotted, confined, illiberal, **3**. obsessed; *synonyms* (*adj*) preoccupied, possessed, infatuated, enthusiastic, haunted, gripped, hooked, absorbed, addicted, ambitious, amok, amuck, anxious, bemused, berserk; *antonym* (*adj*) rational.

ririkana indulge; *synonyms* (*v*) gratify, coddle, baby, cosset, pamper, spoil, mollycoddle, please, satisfy, cocker, cherish, content, (*n*) humor, favor, accord.

ririmoa 1. anterior; *synonyms* (*adj*) antecedent, prior, fore, former, forward, preceding, previous, foregoing, precedent, (*n*) front; *antonym* (*adj*) posterior, **2**. antecedent; *synonyms* (*adj*) anterior, past, first, (*n*) ancestor, forerunner, precursor, forebear, forefather, predecessor, ancestry, origin; *antonyms* (adj) subsequent, (n) descendant, successor, **3**. first; *synonyms* (adv) foremost, before, rather, early, (adj) best, beginning, chief, primitive, head, initial, leading, maiden, opening, preliminary, (n) commencement; *antonyms* (adj) last, final, (n) end, **4**. older; *synonyms* (adj) elder, old, aged, elderly, senior, adult, ancient, big, earlier.

rîriña 1. hot; *synonyms* (adj) warm, ardent, boiling, burning, feverish, fiery, flaming, fresh, blistering, eager, enthusiastic, fast, peppery, pungent, spicy; *antonyms* (adj) mild, cool, cold, freezing, airy, bland, chilly, **2**. heat; *synonyms* (n) glow, fervor, summer, warmth, ardor, caloric, estrus, fire, (v) bake, burn, anger, chafe, (adj) fever, excitement, passion; *antonym* (n) chill.

riringa 1. handle; *synonyms* (v) administer, conduct, feel, wield, control, deal, direct, finger, manage, manipulate, touch, treat, (n) grip, clutch, grasp, **2**. arrange; *synonyms* (v) adjust, appoint, dress, order, set, settle, pack, adapt, agree, classify, compose, decorate, do, engineer, fix; *antonyms* (v) disturb, disarrange, **3**. disturb; *synonyms* (v) agitate, disconcert, disorder, disquiet, distract, distress, perturb, trouble, annoy, bother, commove, concern, derange, discompose, disrupt; *antonyms* (v) arrange, calm, please, smooth, soothe, **4**. disarrange; *synonyms* (v) confuse, clutter, disorganize, muddle, muss, ruffle, jumble, litter, shuffle, unsettle, displace, **5**. feel; *synonyms* (v) experience, sense, consider, handle, believe, deem, endure, find, hold, (n) atmosphere, feeling, sound, texture, air, impression; *antonym* (v) observe, **6**. massage; *synonyms* (n) manipulation, friction, (v) rub, knead, press, caress, abrade, abrase, apply, cajole, corrade, daub, edit, fawn, fiddle, **7**. sunny; *synonyms* (adj) bright, cheerful, clear, gay, merry, blithe, brilliant, fair, radiant, shining, shiny, happy, jovial, beaming, jolly; *antonyms* (adj) dark, overcast, **8**. touch; *synonyms* (n) tinge, hint, (v) affect, contact, hit, border, adjoin, strike, stroke, regard, brush, interest, meet, move, reach.

riringaki 1. arranged; *synonyms* (adj) set, settled, fixed, orderly, organized, prepared, ready, regular, neat, ordered, straight, tidy, **2**. disturbed; *synonyms* (adj) agitated, concerned, anxious, confused, disquieted, restless, upset, worried, disordered, bothered, deranged, disconcerted, distracted, distressed, nervous; *antonyms* (adj) rational, calm, relaxed, **3**. handled, **4**. felt; *synonyms* (v) mat, snarl, tangle, braid, entangle, (adj) perceived, sensed, conscious, **5**. disarranged; *synonyms* (adj) disheveled, disorderly, untidy, delirious, mussy, topsy-turvy, tousled, unkempt, immethodical, lawless, rumpled, tumultuous, turbulent, unruly; *antonym* (adj) arranged, **6**.

touched; *synonyms* (v) compassionate, pitiful, sympathetic, bad, decayed, lentiginous, mildewed, moldy, (adj) affected, cracked, crazy, daft, insane, tinged, interested; *antonym* (adj) untouched.

riripia spoil; *synonyms* (v) plunder, corrupt, impair, rot, damage, deface, indulge, injure, mar, sack, baby, botch, bungle, (n) ruin, (adj) harm; *antonyms* (v) enhance, improve, conserve.

ritangia 1. deplore; *synonyms* (v) bemoan, lament, bewail, regret, mourn, moan, wail, weep, censure, condemn, criticize, deprecate, grieve, complain, repent; *antonym* (v) approve, **2**. lament; *synonyms* (n) cry, dirge, complaint, elegy, plaint, requiem, lamentation, (v) deplore, keen, howl, whine, groan, plain, rue, sigh; *antonyms* (n) celebration, (v) revel, **3**. regret; *synonyms* (v) sorrow, (n) grief, compunction, contrition, penitence, remorse, repentance, disappointment, woe, mourning, qualm, contriteness, dissatisfaction, bitterness, anguish.

ro 1. night; *synonyms* (n) dark, evening, dusk, darkness, nighttime, twilight, (adj) nocturnal; *antonyms* (n) day, light, **2**. dark; *synonyms* (adj) black, dismal, cheerless, dim, obscure, blind, blue, deep, gloomy, murky, mysterious, sable, (n) cloudy, night, shadow; *antonyms* (adj) bright, sunny, fair, clear, pale, pallid, sunlit, **3**. obscure; *synonyms* (adj) ambiguous, concealed, darken, hidden, incomprehensible, muddy, clandestine, confused, (v) hide, blur, cloud, conceal, confuse, cover, (n) difficult; *antonyms* (adj) noticeable, simple, obvious, distinct, mainstream, (v) clarify.

rô 1. peace; *synonyms* (n) calm, harmony, serenity, hush, repose, ease, agreement, amity, accord, composure, concord, coolness, heartsease, order, (adj) quiet; *antonyms* (n) noise, chaos, conflict, uproar, commotion, **2**. quietness; *synonyms* (n) peace, calmness, peacefulness, quietude, silence, stillness, tranquility, tranquillity, placidity, modesty, rest, still, reserve; *antonyms* (n) harshness, volume.

rö famine; *synonyms* (n) dearth, scarcity, deficiency, deficit, drought, hunger, shortage, starvation, poverty, lack, paucity, want.

roana join; *synonyms* (v) connect, unite, associate, combine, link, graft, assemble, affiliate, attach, meet, affix, annex, conjoin, converge, (n) bond; *antonyms* (v) detach, secede, separate, split, undo.

roanaki joined; *synonyms* (adj) combined, coupled, united, allied, connected, joint, amalgamated, associated, linked, concerted; *antonym* (adj) separate.

roba 1. balance; *synonyms* (n) poise, symmetry, excess, remainder, account, complement, counterpoise, credit, (v) counterbalance, adjust, offset, compensate, contrast, settle, audit;

antonyms (*n*) imbalance, (*v*) unbalance, **2.** flap; *synonyms* (*n*) fuss, slap, disturbance, pother, commotion, alarm, flapping, (*v*) flop, beat, wave, brandish, flutter, shake, dither, agitate, **3.** shiver; *synonyms* (*n*) quiver, fragment, splinter, thrill, chill, frisson, (*v*) tremble, quake, shudder, palpitate, shatter, tingle, crash, (*adj*) break, crack, **4.** shake; *synonyms* (*v*) jar, disturb, excite, totter, wag, drop, bump, convulse, flourish, jiggle, quail, quaver, rattle, (*n*) jolt, trembling.

robaki 1. balanced; *synonyms* (*adj*) equal, even, firm, regular, stable, steady, harmonious, impartial, steadfast, symmetrical, uniform, fast, fixed, secure, unprejudiced; *antonyms* (*adj*) biased, unbalanced, unfair, **2.** shaken; *synonyms* (*v*) broken, lame, passe, shaky, threadbare, wilted, shattered, stale, (*adj*) jolted, dazed, disconcerted, fallen, scared, stunned, surprised.

robuna 1. lash; *synonyms* (*n*) goad, scourge, hit, blow, eyelash, (*v*) whip, beat, flog, chastise, bind, lace, batter, castigate, (*adj*) strap, tie, **2.** flog; *synonyms* (*v*) lash, lick, birch, flagellate, trounce, cane, lather, wallop, sell, lambaste, punish, slash, thrash, welt, **3.** whip; *synonyms* (*n*) coachman, spur, thong, urge, incentive, stimulus, driver, (*v*) stir, pip, switch, thresh, whisk, churn, hustle, buffet.

robung 1. darkening; *synonyms* (*adj*) dark, blue, gloomy, depressing, depressive, dingy, disconsolate, dismal, dispiriting, drab, drear, dreary, (*n*) blackening, eclipse, gloaming, **2.** dark; *synonyms* (*adj*) black, cheerless, dim, obscure, blind, deep, murky, mysterious, sable, abstruse, (*n*) cloudy, darkness, evening, night, shadow; *antonyms* (*adj*) bright, sunny, fair, clear, pale, pallid, sunlit, (*n*) light, day.

robungia darken; *synonyms* (*v*) cloud, blur, blind, confuse, dim, conceal, fog, overcast, shade, shadow, overshadow, blacken, deepen, (*adj*) obscure, (*n*) adumbrate; *antonym* (*v*) brighten.

robungiaki darkened; *synonyms* (*adj*) dark, cloudy, murky, obfuscate, opaque, overcast, dim, gloomy, obfuscated.

roio counselor; *synonyms* (*n*) counsel, advisor, advocate, counsellor, adviser, attorney, consultant, lawyer, guide.

rokia enclose; *synonyms* (*v*) bound, confine, contain, circumscribe, corral, cover, encircle, encompass, enfold, envelop, beset, border, circle, embrace, (*adv*) compass; *antonyms* (*v*) expose, free, release.

rokiaki enclosed; *synonyms* (*adj*) confined, surrounded, bounded, covered, limited, airtight, bordered, contained, controlled, delimited, inside, interior, internal, restricted, unexpressed.

roko 1. came, **2.** arrive; *synonyms* (*v*) come, mature, attain, fall, land, reach, succeed, show, derive, emerge, enter, get, happen, issue, (*n*) appear;

antonyms (*v*) leave, depart, go, **3.** come; *synonyms* (*v*) approach, become, aggregate, arise, arrive, befall, amount, descend, hail, number, originate, rise, spring, total, advance, **4.** attained; *synonyms* (*adj*) complete, fulfilled, **5.** shoot; *synonyms* (*v*) bud, discharge, dart, dash, drive, flash, hunt, send, fire, germinate, grow, (*n*) scion, branch, sprout, chute, **6.** sapling; *synonyms* (*n*) youngster, plant, artifice, engender, establish, fix, generate, install, instate, plan, settle, swindle, trick, vegetable, **7.** return; *synonyms* (*n*) yield, pay, recompense, refund, restitution, proceeds, income, (*v*) recur, reimburse, render, repay, restoration, restore, retort, answer; *antonyms* (*n*) departure, abolition, confiscation, recovery, (*v*) keep, **8.** sprout; *synonyms* (*v*) bourgeon, pullulate, vegetate, bloom, (*n*) shoot, germ, offshoot, sprit, acrospire, chit, outgrowth, plumule.

rokona come; *synonyms* (*v*) approach, become, aggregate, appear, arise, arrive, fall, befall, amount, descend, get, go, hail, number, originate; *antonym* (*v*) leave.

romatoa 1. fixed; *synonyms* (*adj*) determined, definite, steady, constant, durable, certain, decided, determinate, established, fast, fastened, intent, permanent, (*v*) stable, (*adv*) firm; *antonyms* (*adj*) flexible, adaptable, adjustable, changeable, movable, separate, variable, compliant, loose, moveable, portable, removable, temporary, **2.** economical; *synonyms* (*adj*) cheap, economic, frugal, prudent, thrifty, careful, inexpensive, provident, sparing, cautious, saving, spare, stingy, chary, efficient; *antonyms* (*adj*) expensive, extravagant, spendthrift, wasteful, **3.** loiter; *synonyms* (*v*) linger, dawdle, lag, loaf, dally, saunter, tarry, prowl, idle, loll, continue, (*adj*) delay, lounge, hesitate, (*adv*) crawl, **4.** preserving; *synonyms* (*adj*) conserving, economical, rescuing, (*n*) conservation, continuation.

rona 1. sustain; *synonyms* (*v*) support, bear, carry, keep, continue, hold, maintain, preserve, endure, suffer, abide, have, prop, relieve, stand, **2.** pay; *synonyms* (*v*) compensate, compensation, liquidate, yield, afford, clear, expend, give, (*n*) recompense, wage, earnings, fee, salary, allowance, devote; *antonym* (*v*) owe.

ronaki 1. paid; *synonyms* (*v*) compensated, (*adj*) gainful, paying, salaried, nonrecreational, profitable, remunerated, remunerative, mercenary, apaid, compensable, hired, hireling, lucrative, rewarding; *antonyms* (*adj*) unpaid, due, owing, **2.** sustained; *synonyms* (*adj*) prolonged, uninterrupted, long, chronic, constant, perennial, sostenuto, protracted, continuing, continuant, lengthy, lingering, relentless, slow, nonstop.

ronna lessen; *synonyms* (*v*) diminish, decrease, abridge, abate, contract, curtail, decline, fall, allay, alleviate, assuage, cut, dwindle, mitigate, moderate; *antonyms* (*v*) increase, exacerbate.

ronnaki lessened; *synonyms* (*adj*) diminished, atrophied, attenuate, attenuated, belittled, corrupted, cut, debased, depleted, faded, hurt, lower, pointed, short.

ronorino particular; *synonyms* (*adj*) special, fastidious, careful, definite, delicate, exact, finicky, fussy, individual, detailed, certain, choosy, circumstantial, (*n*) detail, item; *antonyms* (*adj*) careless, easy, vague, ordinary, (*n*) general.

roro 1. black; *synonyms* (*adj*) dark, sable, blackamoor, bleak, darkie, dirty, ebony, evil, nigger, unclean, cheerless, squalid, (*v*) sinister, villainous, blacken; *antonym* (*n*) white, **2.** anchor; *synonyms* (*n*) mainstay, (*v*) tie, fasten, secure, fix, (*adj*) refuge, rest, **3.** far; *synonyms* (*adv*) wide, off, widely, well, astray, (*adj*) distant, aloof, faraway, remote, much, outlying, (*v*) considerably, abundantly; *antonyms* (*adv*) close, briefly, (*adj*) near.

roroa neck; *synonyms* (*n*) throat, cervix, neckline, lapel, beard, (*v*) pet, cut, love, manage, kiss, behead, bang, bed, (*adj*) stricture, wasp.

roroka 1. excite; *synonyms* (*v*) animate, arouse, disturb, enliven, agitate, energize, awaken, electrify, encourage, evoke, exasperate, incite, inspire, kindle, provoke; *antonyms* (*v*) calm, pacify, bore, **2.** convoke; *synonyms* (*v*) convene, call, assemble, summon, collect, muster, convocate, **3.** stimulate; *synonyms* (*v*) excite, prompt, drive, exhilarate, goad, hasten, instigate, invigorate, rouse, spur, stir, urge, accelerate, refresh, (*adj*) quicken; *antonym* (*v*) defuse.

rorokaki 1. excited; *synonyms* (*adj*) agitated, ablaze, emotional, enthusiastic, frantic, ardent, aroused, delirious, fervent, heated, impassioned, passionate, warm, elated, (*v*) animated; *antonyms* (*adj*) calm, cool, unexcited, **2.** stimulated; *synonyms* (*adj*) excited, inspired, intoxicated, affected, aflame, angry, desirous, enraged, enthused, fresh, horny, interested, keen, randy, red; *antonym* (*adj*) uninspired.

roromi massage; *synonyms* (*n*) manipulation, friction, (*v*) rub, knead, manipulate, press, caress, touch, abrade, abrase, apply, arrange, cajole, corrade, daub.

roronranairake 1. teenage; *synonyms* (*adj*) adolescent, juvenile, teen, jejune, puerile, teenaged, pubertal, pubescent, (*n*) adolescence; *antonym* (*adj*) adult, **2.** teenager; *synonyms* (*n*) youngster, kid, boy, child, girl, minor, schoolgirl, stripling.

rorouba 1. boast; *synonyms* (*v*) bluster, vaunt, blow, brag, crow, gasconade, pride, rodomontade, exult, bounce, exaggerate, flourish, (*n*) arrogance, boasting, glory, **2.** strut; *synonyms* (*n*) buttress, brace, prop, splurge, beam, (*v*) prance, stalk,

swagger, parade, boast, stride, support, cock, flaunt, crack.

roroutake 1. boastful; *synonyms* (*adj*) big, braggart, pompous, arrogant, proud, vaunting, thrasonical, vain, vainglorious, ostentatious; *antonym* (*adj*) modest, **2.** boasting; *synonyms* (*v*) brag, (*n*) boast, bluster, bravado, swagger, ostentation, (*adj*) swaggering, vaporing, **3.** pretentious; *synonyms* (*adj*) affected, showy, boastful, stilted, presumptuous, grandiose, snobbish, ambitious, exaggerated, mannered, mincing, gaudy, lofty, assuming, (*v*) conceited; *antonym* (*adj*) down-to-earth.

rota 1. equal; *synonyms* (*adj*) agree, comparable, adequate, balanced, commensurate, equivalent, (*v*) match, compare, correspond, even, parallel, rival, equalize, (*n*) compeer, peer; *antonyms* (*adj*) unequal, different, repressive, disproportionate, inconsistent, uneven, unlike, (*v*) differ, **2.** attain; *synonyms* (*v*) accomplish, achieve, make, reach, acquire, gain, catch, find, obtain, strike, arrive, compass, earn, get, hit; *antonyms* (*v*) lose, fail, **3.** sodden; *synonyms* (*adj*) soaked, soaking, damp, dripping, saturated, wet, muddy, soggy, sopping, drenched, moist, soppy, watery, (*v*) soft, molten; *antonym* (*adj*) dry, **4.** obtainable; *synonyms* (*adj*) attainable, available, accessible, gettable, procurable, ready, approachable, getable.

rotaki attained; *synonyms* (*adj*) complete, fulfilled.

roto 1. humid; *synonyms* (*adj*) moist, wet, damp, dank, sultry, clammy, muggy, oppressive, soggy, steamy, sticky, watery, wettish, hot; *antonyms* (*adj*) dry, fresh, **2.** damp; *synonyms* (*adj*) cool, humid, dampish, (*v*) break, check, chill, deaden, benumb, cut, dampen, depress, discourage, (*n*) dampness, moisture, clamminess; *antonym* (*n*) dryness, **3.** wet; *synonyms* (*adj*) drenched, soaked, sodden, rainy, saturated, (*v*) moisten, water, wash, douse, irrigate, drench, bedew, splash, humidify, (*n*) humidity; *antonyms* (*adj*) dehydrated, parched.

rotu 1. dull; *synonyms* (*adj*) dim, blunt, dense, dreary, sluggish, bland, boring, cloudy, cold, dark, dismal, inactive, inert, (*v*) deaden, dampen; *antonyms* (*adj*) bright, lively, sharp, exciting, interesting, lustrous, stimulating, amusing, exhilarating, glittery, glossy, glowing, high-pitched, intense, luminous, **2.** blunt; *synonyms* (*adj*) dull, bluff, candid, direct, forthright, frank, outspoken, plain, round, abrupt, brusque, downright, obtuse, plainspoken, (*v*) numb; *antonyms* (*adj*) devious, pointed, (*v*) hone, sharpen, **3.** round; *synonyms* (*adv*) about, around, (*adj*) circular, plump, entire, chubby, complete, (*n*) circle, bout, ring, beat, circuit, (*v*) compass, turn, gird; *antonym* (*adj*) slim.

rotuaki 1. dulled; *synonyms* (*adj*) dull, blunted, benumbed, grayed, jaded, rounded, numb, **2.**

rounded; *synonyms* (*adj*) round, curved, circular, orbicular, full, globular, rotund, spherical, bent, blunt, fat, obtuse; *antonyms* (*adj*) pointed, straight, sharp, bony, concave.

roue dance; *synonyms* (*n*) dancing, party, (*v*) bound, caper, hop, bop, cavort, play, jump, shake, skip, step, beat, dandle, prance.

routa 1. extract; *synonyms* (*n*) excerpt, essence, juice, quotation, quote, citation, (*v*) draw, abstract, derive, educe, elicit, distill, express, get, extort, **2.** extirpate; *synonyms* (*v*) annihilate, eradicate, exterminate, uproot, deracinate, destroy, extinguish, root, excise, raze, displace, (*adj*) obliterate, **3.** uproot; *synonyms* (*v*) extirpate, remove, dislodge, move, eliminate, pull, grub, transplant; *antonym* (*v*) plant.

rreretaki fated; *synonyms* (*adj*) doomed, destined, inevitable, certain, damned, predestined, unavoidable.

rua 1. nine; *synonyms* (*n*) niner, club, ennead, ace, cabaret, clubhouse, gild, golfclub, guild, jack, king, knave, lodge, nightclub, nightspot, **2.** confusion; *synonyms* (*n*) bewilderment, chaos, commotion, disarray, agitation, bedlam, clutter, disorder, distraction, disturbance, pandemonium, tumult, bustle, huddle, upset; *antonyms* (*n*) clarity, order, **3.** disorder; *synonyms* (*n*) ailment, complaint, disease, jumble, muddle, confusion, disarrangement, anarchy, derangement, litter, (*v*) derange, confuse, perturb, disarrange, discompose; *antonyms* (*n*) orderliness, calm, peace, **4.** error; *synonyms* (*n*) deviation, blunder, fault, mistake, wrong, delusion, lapse, oversight, crime, defect, demerit, guilt, misunderstanding, falsehood, erroneousness; *antonym* (*n*) correctness.

ruabwi ninety; *synonym* (*n*) xc.

ruamakana 1. diluted; *synonyms* (*adj*) dilute, thin, watery, weak, bland, insipid, tasteless; *antonyms* (*adj*) straight, strong, concentrated, **2.** liquefy; *synonyms* (*v*) fuse, dissolve, melt, thaw, flux, liquidise, liquidize, liquify, run; *antonym* (*v*) set, **3.** thin; *synonyms* (*adj*) flimsy, gaunt, lean, light, slight, tenuous, emaciated, fine, rare, slim, sparse, (*v*) slender, meager, sheer, subtle; *antonyms* (*adj*) thick, fat, chubby, plump, wide, broad, heavy, (*v*) thicken, **4.** watery; *synonyms* (*adj*) liquid, moist, diluted, washy, wet, damp, fluid, aqueous, hydrous, tearful, dripping, humid, soggy, soft, aquatic; *antonyms* (*adj*) solid, dry.

ruamakanaki liquefied; *synonyms* (*adj*) liquified, liquid, flowing, fluid, molten, runny, watery, (*v*) liquescent.

ruamwi 1. substitute; *synonyms* (*adj*) replacement, alternative, ersatz, makeshift, (*n*) deputy, backup, delegate, (*v*) alternate, shift, change, replace, surrogate, exchange, sub, cover, **2.** succeed; *synonyms* (*v*) follow, arrive, ensue, manage,

prevail, prosper, supersede, supplant, do, achieve, flourish, displace, pursue, thrive, triumph; *antonyms* (*v*) fail, precede, lose, **3.** replace; *synonyms* (*v*) substitute, reinstate, restore, deputize, renew, return, succeed, switch, deputise, place, put, refund, repay, trade, reestablish.

ruannano 1. frivolous; *synonyms* (*adj*) empty, foolish, dizzy, idle, petty, childish, facetious, flighty, flippant, light, shallow, silly, superficial, trifling, trivial; *antonyms* (*adj*) serious, important, **2.** changeable; *synonyms* (*adj*) variable, capricious, erratic, inconsistent, irregular, fickle, giddy, mercurial, mobile, mutable, slippery, temperamental, uncertain, unsettled, unstable; *antonyms* (*adj*) constant, fixed, stable, unchangeable, consistent, dependable, predictable, regular, **3.** inconsistent; *synonyms* (*adj*) incongruous, incoherent, incompatible, contrary, absurd, conflicting, inconsequent, discordant, discrepant, illogical, irreconcilable, abhorrent, changeable, opposite, (*n*) contradictory; *antonym* (*adj*) reliable, **4.** inconstant; *synonyms* (*adj*) faithless, fitful, changeful, untrue, unreliable, false, irresolute, unfaithful, unsteady, versatile, volatile, wanton, wayward, **5.** unfaithful; *synonyms* (*adj*) disloyal, inaccurate, traitorous, treacherous, untrustworthy, recreant, apostate, deceitful, dishonest; *antonyms* (*adj*) faithful, loyal, **6.** whimsical; *synonyms* (*adj*) fanciful, fantastic, eccentric, freakish, humorous, odd, arbitrary, bizarre, crotchety, grotesque, quaint, skittish, imaginary, impulsive, playful.

ruatatara 1. disharmonious; *synonyms* (*adj*) discordant, dissonant, inharmonic, unlike, nonmusical, unmusical, unresolved, **2.** asymmetrical; *synonyms* (*adj*) asymmetric, unbalanced, cockeyed, crooked, irregular, lopsided, unequal, uneven; *antonyms* (*adj*) symmetrical, equal, regular.

ruatu chief; *synonyms* (*adj*) head, principal, cardinal, capital, arch, central, essential, first, main, (*n*) administrator, boss, captain, executive, leader, paramount; *antonyms* (*adj*) minor, associate, secondary.

rubea pulse; *synonyms* (*n*) beat, impulse, pulsation, heartbeat, legume, rhythm, pounding, cadence, measure, pulsing, (*v*) pulsate, throb, palpitate, pound, vibrate.

ruberube 1. blink; *synonyms* (*v*) wink, flash, twinkle, flicker, shirk, nictate, nictitate, shine, flinch, (*n*) blinking, glimmer, instant, winking, peek, **2.** beat; *synonyms* (*v*) batter, flap, pulsate, throb, tick, trounce, whip, bat, baste, break, (*n*) pulse, thump, knock, round, cadence; *antonym* (*v*) lose, **3.** wink; *synonyms* (*n*) twinkling, jiffy, moment, trice, hint, second, signal, (*v*) blink, sparkle, leer, flutter, scintillate, gleam, glisten, winkle, **4.** throb;

synonyms (*n*) pulsation, thrill, pain, pounding, throbbing, (*v*) beat, quiver, ache, pound, palpitate, shudder, smart, tingle, pant, shiver, **5.** twinkle; *synonyms* (*n*) scintillation, sparkling, beam, spark, luster, flare, brilliancy, (*v*) glitter, shimmer, glow, glance, glint, radiate, coruscate, dazzle, **6.** sparkle; *synonyms* (*n*) blaze, brightness, coruscation, gloss, light, sheen, animation, flame, (*v*) fizz, glare, effervesce, froth, glister, bubble, foam; *antonym* (*n*) lethargy, **7.** palpitate; *synonyms* (*v*) shake, tremble, vibrate, (*n*) heave, **8.** pulsate.

ruberubeaki 1. beaten; *synonyms* (*v*) beat, (*adj*) battered, overpowered, conquered, routed, overcome; *antonym* (*adj*) victorious, **2.** pulsated.

ruiwa nine; *synonyms* (*n*) niner, club, ennead, ace, cabaret, clubhouse, gild, golfclub, guild, jack, king, knave, lodge, nightclub, nightspot.

rukuma folded; *synonyms* (*adj*) closed, plaited, artful, braided, corrugated, intricate.

rumangai 1. shiver; *synonyms* (*n*) quiver, fragment, splinter, thrill, chill, (*v*) shake, tremble, quake, shudder, palpitate, shatter, tingle, crash, (*adj*) break, crack, **2.** tremble; *synonyms* (*v*) totter, flutter, quail, falter, agitate, flicker, quaver, vibrate, waver, cower, wave, rock, (*n*) shiver, throb, tremor.

rume 1. changeable; *synonyms* (*adj*) variable, capricious, erratic, inconsistent, irregular, fickle, giddy, mercurial, mobile, mutable, slippery, temperamental, uncertain, unsettled, unstable; *antonyms* (*adj*) constant, fixed, stable, unchangeable, consistent, dependable, predictable, regular, **2.** variable; *synonyms* (*adj*) changeable, inconstant, fitful, unsteady, fluctuating, shifting, variant, versatile, volatile, adaptable, immethodical, uneven, wavering, fluid, adjustable; *antonyms* (*adj*) invariable, set, smooth.

rumwi 1. later; *synonyms* (*adv*) after, afterward, subsequently, afterwards, next, then, since, (*adj*) following, last, ensuing, future, latter, posterior, subsequent, final; *antonyms* (*adv*) earlier, immediately, before, prior, **2.** then; *synonyms* (*adv*) so, accordingly, again, consequently, later, (*conj*) therefore.

rung 1. flourishing; *synonyms* (*adj*) prosperous, thriving, booming, healthy, luxuriant, palmy, successful, verdant, lush, auspicious, favorable, affluent, blooming, golden, growing; *antonym* (*adj*) failing, **2.** lively; *synonyms* (*adj*) brisk, active, agile, cheerful, energetic, keen, busy, fresh, gay, jolly, jovial, alert, animated, bright, enthusiastic; *antonyms* (*adj*) dull, inactive, lethargic, listless, lifeless, unexciting, **3.** agreeable; *synonyms* (*adj*) acceptable, accordant, pleasant, pleasing, nice, affable, amusing, compatible, conformable, congenial, consistent, enjoyable, genial, grateful, (*v*) desirable; *antonyms* (*adj*) disagreeable, discordant, nasty, unpleasant, unwilling, aggressive, resistant,

4. prosperous; *synonyms* (*adj*) lucky, flourishing, opulent, advantageous, comfortable, easy, rich, well-off, propitious, happy, favourable, prospering, wealthy, (*n*) fortunate, good; *antonym* (*adj*) poor.

runga assembling; *synonyms* (*n*) assemblage, assembly, collection, collecting, compilation, meeting, aggregation, accumulation, appeal, appearance, assemblance, manufacturing, organization, compendium, (*adj*) gathering.

ruo 1. fall; *synonyms* (*v*) decline, dip, decrease, descend, dive, rain, diminish, dwindle, sink, alight, (*n*) drop, descent, downfall, plunge, pitch; *antonyms* (*v*) rise, increase, ascend, climb, triumph, win, (*n*) ascent, **2.** descend; *synonyms* (*v*) condescend, settle, deign, derive, dismount, down, subside, tumble, come, fall, slope, stoop, cascade, degenerate, crash, **3.** lose; *synonyms* (*v*) forfeit, mislay, sacrifice, fail, clear, hurt, regress, retrogress, destroy, misplace, recede, suffer, waste, escape; *antonyms* (*v*) gain, find, acquire, earn, get, obtain, recover, secure, beat, defeat, keep, succeed, **4.** decline; *synonyms* (*n*) decay, declension, declination, deterioration, diminution, (*v*) wane, reject, abate, ebb, refuse, deny, deteriorate, spurn, (*adj*) fade, languish; *antonyms* (*n*) improvement, recovery, development, growth, rebirth, (*v*) accept, flourish, improve.

ruoa hollow; *synonyms* (*adj*) blank, concave, empty, false, insincere, (*n*) cavity, hole, cave, depression, groove, excavation, (*v*) excavate, dent, scoop, dig; *antonyms* (*adj*) convex, (*n*) solid, hump.

ruoaki 1. hollowed; *synonym* (*adj*) concave, **2.** lost; *synonyms* (*v*) gone, missing, abandoned, (*adj*) doomed, forlorn, extinct, hopeless, bewildered, disoriented, forgotten, helpless, broken, confused, irrecoverable, absent; *antonyms* (*adj*) present, found, existing.

ruomatoa thickening; *synonyms* (*n*) thickener, growth, inspissation, boss, client, coagulation, guest, knob, node, pommel, (*v*) gelation.

ruona 1. attack; *synonyms* (*n*) incursion, thrust, aggression, fit, onset, onslaught, seizure, (*v*) assault, assail, attempt, aggress, charge, invade, raid, accuse; *antonyms* (*n*) defense, (*v*) defend, protect, retreat, **2.** rush; *synonyms* (*n*) hurry, flood, flow, attack, (*v*) dash, gush, race, run, speed, dart, hasten, stream, quicken, (*adj*) burst, spurt.

ruonaki rushed; *synonyms* (*adj*) hasty, hurried, rush, precipitate, rapid, hassled, immediate, instant, instantaneous, quick, speedy, sudden, swift, unexpected, abrupt; *antonym* (*adj*) leisurely.

ruonako 1. disproportionate; *synonyms* (*adj*) disproportional, incommensurate, undue, unequal, uneven, unsymmetrical, excessive, lopsided; *antonyms* (*adj*) equal, proportionate, **2.** immoderate; *synonyms* (*adj*) extravagant, exorbitant, extreme, inordinate, intemperate, unreasonable, fanatical, unrestrained, fulsome, outrageous, profuse, steep, ultra, unconscionable, violent; *antonym* (*adj*) moderate, **3.** extreme; *synonyms* (*adj*) deep, enormous, immoderate, intense, severe, supreme, terrible, ultimate, utmost, uttermost, drastic, extraordinary, exceeding, (*n*) edge, end; *antonyms* (*adj*) middle, reasonable, near, (*n*) mild, slight, **4.** inordinate; *synonyms* (*adj*) exuberant, irregular, preposterous, disorderly, lavish, wild, **5.** excessive; *synonyms* (*adj*) exaggerated, superfluous, huge, radical, redundant, over, disproportionate, monstrous, overly, high, rank, superabundant, unnecessary, wasteful, expensive; *antonym* (*adj*) affordable, **6.** extravagant; *synonyms* (*adj*) luxurious, prodigal, costly, profligate, egregious, fantastic, improvident, spendthrift, romantic, absurd, baroque, inflated, effusive, bizarre, (*v*) fabulous; *antonyms* (*adj*) economical, restrained, frugal, parsimonious, plain, stingy, understated, **7.** exorbitant; *synonyms* (*adj*) extortionate, usurious, **8.** massed; *synonyms* (*adj*) accumulated, amassed, assembled, collected, congregate, accrued, collective, congested, conglomerate, crowded, dense, equanimous, gathered, more, solid.

ruoruo 1. burst; *synonyms* (*v*) break, crack, blast, rupture, belch, abound, erupt, open, (*n*) flash, explosion, (*adj*) split, explode, detonate, flare, splinter; *antonym* (*v*) implode, **2.** explode; *synonyms* (*v*) discharge, fulminate, disprove, fire, shoot, expand, discredit, shatter, disintegrate, overthrow, refute, belie, blaze, (*n*) burst, (*adj*) bounce.

ruoruoaki 1. exploded; *synonyms* (*adj*) antebellum, antediluvian, elapsed, expired, extinct, lapsed, forgotten, irrecoverable, refuted, **2.** burst; *synonyms* (*v*) break, crack, blast, rupture, belch, abound, erupt, open, (*n*) flash, explosion, (*adj*) split, explode, detonate, flare, splinter; *antonym* (*v*) implode.

ruru 1. quiver; *synonyms* (*n*) quake, tremble, palpitate, shake, quaver, thrill, tremor, vibration, (*v*) shiver, shudder, flicker, flutter, pulsate, vibrate, wave, **2.** quaver; *synonyms* (*n*) quiver, wobble, breve, crotchet, minim, roll, (*v*) warble, trill, falter, waver, chirp, **3.** shake; *synonyms* (*v*) beat, agitate, jar, brandish, disturb, excite, totter, wag, drop, bump, convulse, flourish, jiggle, (*n*) jolt, trembling, **4.** tremulous; *synonyms* (*adj*) shaky, shaking, fearful, fidgety, quavering, shivering, (*n*) nervous, coy, diffident, **5.** quake; *synonyms* (*n*) earthquake, temblor, (*v*) quail, fluctuate, dance, rock, reel, curvet, **6.** shiver; *synonyms* (*n*) fragment, splinter, chill, frisson, palpitation, (*v*) shatter, tingle, crash, dither, smash, dash, throb, (*adj*) break, crack, split, **7.** vibrate; *synonyms* (*v*) oscillate, swing, move, sway, undulate, blow, ring, pulse, reverberate, **8.**

tremble; *synonyms* (*v*) cower, fear, blench, cringe, didder, flinch, recoil, shrink, stir, (*n*) heave, pant, (*adj*) crumble, starve.

ruruaki shaken; *synonyms* (*v*) broken, lame, passe, shaky, threadbare, wilted, shattered, stale, (*adj*) jolted, dazed, disconcerted, fallen, scared, stunned, surprised.

rurubenebene quiver; *synonyms* (*n*) quake, tremble, palpitate, shake, quaver, thrill, tremor, vibration, (*v*) shiver, shudder, flicker, flutter, pulsate, vibrate, wave.

rurung 1. flock; *synonyms* (*n*) bunch, crowd, cluster, band, bevy, congregation, covey, gang, herd, horde, pack, troop, (*v*) assemble, mass, (*adj*) swarm, **2.** herd; *synonyms* (*n*) flock, drove, crew, mob, multitude, company, ruck, school, throng, (*v*) drive, (*adj*) shoal, **3.** move; *synonyms* (*v*) act, affect, carry, excite, go, impel, instigate, maneuver, touch, travel, flow, bear, disturb, (*n*) motion, transfer; *antonym* (*v*) stay.

rurunga 1. resound; *synonyms* (*v*) echo, reverberate, ring, boom, peal, roar, blare, reecho, resonate, sound, clatter, vibrate, clash, rumble, thunder, **2.** rumble; *synonyms* (*n*) roll, mutter, bang, brawl, noise, buzz, report, riot, (*v*) murmur, growl, grumble, mumble, drone, howl, resound.

rutiakina regard; *synonyms* (*v*) attention, concern, estimate, heed, attend, account, believe, consider, count, hold, (*n*) notice, respect, esteem, deference, look; *antonym* (*n*) disrespect.

T

taari sea; *synonyms* (*n*) ocean, water, waves, (*adj*) marine, maritime, array, nautical, seagoing, army.

taba 1. choke; *synonyms* (*v*) asphyxiate, block, throttle, stifle, clog, foul, gag, obstruct, smother, strangle, suffocate, check, die, close, congest; *antonym* (*v*) unclog, **2.** deviate; *synonyms* (*v*) depart, deflect, stray, vary, digress, diverge, swerve, warp, shift, turn, wander, bend, differ, divert, (*adj*) deviant; *antonym* (*v*) conform, **3.** cut; *synonyms* (*v*) carve, chop, clip, abbreviate, abridge, bite, condense, crop, drop, fashion, (*n*) notch, slice, cutting, nick, blow; *antonyms* (*v*) increase, lengthen, (*n*) addition, extension, **4.** split; *synonyms* (*v*) crack, cut, fracture, slit, burst, divide, separate, divorce, breach, cleave, (*n*) break, rip, rupture, tear, cleavage; *antonyms* (*v*) join, unite, merge.

tababu 1. economical; *synonyms* (*adj*) cheap, economic, frugal, prudent, thrifty, careful, inexpensive, provident, sparing, cautious, saving, spare, stingy, chary, efficient; *antonyms* (*adj*) expensive, extravagant, spendthrift, wasteful, **2.** thrifty; *synonym* (*adj*) economical; *antonym* (*adj*) profligate, **3.** sparing; *synonyms* (*v*) meager, moderate, lean, scrimp, (*adj*) scanty, poor, parsimonious, niggardly, scant, miserly, tight, abstemious, scarce, penurious, sober, **4.** saving; *synonyms* (*n*) economy, conservation, preservation, rescue, cut, deliverance, delivery, thrift, frugality, discount, (*adj*) save, except, excepting, reserving, reserve; *antonym* (*n*) extravagance.

tabaitera 1. bias; *synonyms* (*n*) penchant, drift, influence, turn, twist, favor, slope, angle, bigotry, (*v*) prejudice, bent, slant, dispose, (*adj*) partiality, diagonal; *antonyms* (*n*) impartiality, neutrality, fairness, **2.** partial; *synonyms* (*adj*) incomplete, imperfect, fragmentary, unfair, sectional, inequitable, biased, part, unequal, halfway, partisan, prejudiced, unfinished, unjust, (*v*) party; *antonyms* (*adj*) complete, impartial, total, absolute, comprehensive, unbiased.

tabaka 1. bite; *synonyms* (*n*) taste, bit, cheat, morsel, (*v*) sting, nip, chew, cut, pinch, burn, eat, erode, gnaw, hurt, munch, **2.** seize; *synonyms* (*v*) capture, catch, grab, arrest, apprehend, clutch, get, grapple, receive, annex, assume, clasp, confiscate, conquer, grasp; *antonym* (*v*) release, **3.** surprise; *synonyms* (*n*) fright, amazement, astonishment, surprisal, wonder, admiration, (*v*) astound, alarm, amaze, astonish, shock, startle, jolt, stun, bewilder.

tabakaki 1. surprised; *synonyms* (*adj*) astonished, amazed, astounded, dumbfounded, shocked, stunned, bewildered, startled, aghast, confused, curious, puzzled, questioning, quizzical, baffled; *antonym* (*adj*) indifferent, **2.** seized; *synonyms* (*adj*) confiscate, confiscated, appropriated, condemned, apprehended, detained, held, censured, convicted, forfeit, forfeited, obsessed.

tabaki 1. choked; *synonyms* (*adj*) clogged, suffocated, congested, anxious, high-strung, insecure, neurotic, strained, suffocate, tense, clotted, **2.** cut; *synonyms* (*v*) carve, chop, clip, abbreviate, abridge, bite, condense, crop, drop, fashion, (*n*) notch, slice, cutting, nick, blow; *antonyms* (*v*) increase, lengthen, (*n*) addition, extension, **3.** split; *synonyms* (*v*) crack, cut, fracture, slit, burst, divide, separate, divorce, breach, cleave, (*n*) break, rip, rupture, tear, cleavage; *antonyms* (*v*) join, unite, merge.

tabakurakura 1. bushy; *synonyms* (*adj*) dense, shagged, hairy, shaggy, bearded, furry, hispid, pappous, pilous, villous, rough, profuse, disheveled, hirsute, queachy; *antonym* (*adj*) bald, **2.** encumbered; *synonyms* (*adj*) laden, burdened, burdensome, clayey, cloggy, deep, heavy, forcible, full, gloomy, inactive, loud, oppressive, overloaded, ponderous, **3.** overloaded; *synonyms* (*adj*) overcrowded, overladen, busy, congested,

encumbered, loaded, overfull, packed, clogged, jammed, stuffed, swarming, teeming; *antonym* (*adj*) empty, **4.** overflowing; *synonyms* (*v*) inundation, deluge, (*adj*) abundant, copious, exuberant, flooding, bountiful, generous, brimming, superfluous, afloat, ample, awash, crowded, (*n*) flood, **5.** puffed; *synonyms* (*adj*) bloated, distended, puff, swollen, puffy, tumid, turgid, bepuffed, bombastic, bouffant, conceited, declamatory, egotistic, egotistical, erect.

tabanga publicized; *synonyms* (*adj*) publicised, exposed, revealed.

tabangaea 1. display; *synonyms* (*n*) array, presentation, appearance, screen, demonstration, exhibition, (*v*) exhibit, show, disclose, parade, expose, produce, brandish, flaunt, indicate; *antonym* (*v*) conceal, **2.** exhibit; *synonyms* (*v*) evince, demonstrate, evidence, announce, perform, present, bear, manifest, reveal, attest, discover, argue, (*n*) display, proof, (*adj*) represent, **3.** parade; *synonyms* (*n*) ostentation, pageant, ceremony, pomp, flourish, file, procession, review, (*v*) strut, swagger, troop, walk, process, flash, promenade, **4.** publicize; *synonyms* (*v*) air, advertise, advertize, broadcast, promote, propagate, disseminate, declare, publicise, publish, push, circulate, promulgate, bare, beam.

tabangaeaki publicized; *synonyms* (*adj*) publicised, exposed, revealed.

tabanikai armed; *synonyms* (*adj*) equipped, military, fitted, aggressive, compulsory, fit, forcible, prepared, ready, violent, weaponed, martial, organized; *antonyms* (*adj*) unarmed, unprotected.

tabanin 1. all; *synonyms* (*adv*) whole, purely, altogether, entirely, totally, wholly, apiece, (*adj*) universal, each, every, gross, complete, alone, (*n*) aggregate, (*det*) any; *antonyms* (*pron*) none, (*det*) some, **2.** complete; *synonyms* (*adj*) perfect, absolute, consummate, full, stark, accomplished, all, (*v*) accomplish, achieve, close, finish, execute, act, attain, cease; *antonyms* (*adj*) incomplete, partial, unfinished, abridged, shortened, sketchy, lacking, narrow, qualified, (*v*) neglect, **3.** continuous; *synonyms* (*adj*) constant, continual, ceaseless, endless, perpetual, running, chronic, consecutive, continued, eternal, everlasting, incessant, unbroken, unending, uninterrupted; *antonyms* (*adj*) intermittent, temporary, discontinuous, sporadic, **4.** entire; *synonyms* (*adj*) total, integral, utter, clean, intact, mere, undivided, radical, dead, livelong, undiminished, implicit, main, (*n*) stallion, unabridged, **5.** intact; *synonyms* (*adj*) entire, undamaged, uninjured, untouched, sound, inviolate, pure, safe, unharmed, unhurt, unscathed, virgin, unblemished; *antonym* (*adj*) broken, **6.** whole; *synonyms* (*adj*) healthy, well, natural, round, unqualified, general, (*n*) sum, hale, unit, mass, amount, entirety, everything, ensemble, *(adv)* completely; *antonyms (adj)* imperfect, *(n)* part, **7.** visible; *synonyms (adj)* obvious, perceptible, conspicuous, apparent, evident, open, clear, discernible, manifest, noticeable, observable, plain, appreciable, visual, transparent; *antonyms (adj)* invisible, imperceptible, **8.** undiminished; *synonyms (adj)* unreduced, unrestricted, undying, faithful, interior, internal, unfalcated, unrelieved, utmost, **9.** unbroken; *synonyms (adj)* continuous, solid, steady, nonstop, unceasing, direct, even, immediate, kept, relentless, unrelenting, wild, **10.** square; *synonyms (adj)* right, rectangular, fair, quadrate, straight, equal, equitable, *(n)* area, foursquare, rectangle, quadrilateral, *(v)* settle, agree, correspond, *(adv)* just, **11.** perfect; *synonyms (adj)* exact, faultless, thorough, exquisite, blameless, correct, flawless, ideal, immaculate, irreproachable, great, infallible, *(v)* fulfill, mature, crown; *antonyms (adj)* faulty, flawed, **12.** undivided; *synonyms (adj)* single, united, exclusive, common, concentrated, individual, uncut; *antonym (adj)* divided.

tabara 1. hesitate; *synonyms (v)* falter, pause, doubt, fluctuate, halt, waver, boggle, demur, vacillate, procrastinate, dither, scruple, stammer, *(adj)* linger, delay; *antonym (v)* continue, **2.** misunderstand; *synonyms (v)* misapprehend, misconceive, misconstrue, misinterpret, mistake, misjudge, misread, miscalculate, miscomprehend; *antonym (v)* understand, **3.** grope; *synonyms (v)* feel, finger, fumble, touch, grabble, search, handle, paw, scrabble, **4.** aside; *synonyms (adv)* apart, by, away, beside, alongside, off, abreast, *(n)* digression, divagation, parenthesis, statement, **5.** loiter; *synonyms (v)* dawdle, lag, loaf, dally, saunter, tarry, prowl, idle, loll, drag, *(adj)* lounge, hesitate, *(adv)* crawl, creep, drawl, **6.** separated; *synonyms (adj)* disconnected, separate, detached, divided, isolated, disjointed, free, disjunct, removed, dislocated, independent, lone, single, *(prep)* disjoined, distinct, **7.** remote; *synonyms (adj)* distant, aloof, inaccessible, outside, faint, alien, far, foreign, lonely, outlying, secluded, unapproachable, extraneous, slender, slight; *antonyms (adj)* near, nearby, accessible, **8.** sidestep; *synonyms (v)* avoid, dodge, evade, circumvent, duck, elude, parry, skirt, hedge, escape, equivocate, fudge, shirk, bypass, pussyfoot, **9.** pussyfoot; *synonyms (v)* mouse, sneak, steal, sidestep, slip, abstract, cabbage, cower, cringe, dissemble, fawn, filch, grovel, hook, *(adj)* cautious.

tabarabara 1. discordant; *synonyms (adj)* contrary, conflicting, dissonant, discrepant, disharmonious, harsh, incompatible, inconsistent, jarring, raucous, hoarse, cacophonous, contradictory, disagreeing, grating; *antonyms (adj)* harmonious, musical, pleasant-sounding, melodic, **2.** asymmetrical;

synonyms (adj) asymmetric, unbalanced, cockeyed, crooked, irregular, lopsided, unequal, uneven; *antonyms (adj)* symmetrical, equal, regular.

tabaraki misunderstood; *synonyms (adj)* confused, vague.

tabarangaea trip; *synonyms (n)* excursion, expedition, tour, flight, jaunt, travel, lapse, run, drive, misstep, *(v)* journey, slip, stumble, fall, *(adj)* blunder; *antonym (v)* fix.

tabare 1. linger; *synonyms (v)* dally, delay, hover, loiter, hesitate, stay, procrastinate, dawdle, remain, saunter, tarry, abide, endure, continue, *(adv)* lag; *antonyms (v)* leave, hurry, **2.** mischievous; *synonyms (adj)* bad, evil, injurious, detrimental, hurtful, naughty, deleterious, harmful, impish, maleficent, playful, arch, baneful, sly, disobedient; *antonym (adj)* good, **3.** misbehave; *synonyms (v)* misconduct, transgress, disobey, err, misbear, misdemean, sin, trespass, contravene, deviate, fail, lapse, malfunction, mishandle, *(adj)* misdo; *antonym (v)* behave, **4.** meddling; *synonyms (adj)* interfering, busy, curious, inquisitive, intrusive, meddlesome, officious, prying, nosy, busybodied, dabbling, impertinent, **5.** importunate; *synonyms (adj)* troublesome, annoying, exigent, insistent, pressing, instant, demanding, earnest, pleading, urgent, appealing, imploring, *(v)* important; *antonym (adj)* halfhearted, **6.** disturbing; *synonyms (adj)* distressing, alarming, disconcerting, disquieting, worrying, bothersome, troubling, unsettling, upsetting, worrisome, discordant, distressful, perturbing, poignant; *antonyms (adj)* reassuring, soothing, comforting, **7.** meddlesome; *synonyms (adj)* obtrusive, pragmatical, meddling, **8.** turbulent; *synonyms (adj)* tempestuous, tumultuous, rough, furious, boisterous, disorderly, noisy, riotous, violent, wild, rude, troubled, unruly, agitated, *(n)* stormy; *antonym (adj)* calm, **9.** obnoxious; *synonyms (adj)* objectionable, disagreeable, offensive, detestable, distasteful, hateful, liable, horrid, repellent, disgusting, invidious, revolting, ugly, abhorrent, *(n)* unpleasant; *antonym (adj)* pleasant, **10.** upsetting; *synonyms (adj)* disturbing, sad.

tabarea 1. disorder; *synonyms (n)* ailment, complaint, clutter, disease, jumble, muddle, chaos, commotion, confusion, disarrangement, disturbance, *(v)* derange, disarray, confuse, perturb; *antonyms (n)* orderliness, calm, peace, *(v)* order, **2.** meddle; *synonyms (v)* tamper, interfere, intervene, intrude, fiddle, monkey, pry, **3.** annoy; *synonyms (v)* anger, displease, harass, irritate, pester, afflict, aggravate, bother, grate, harry, hassle, molest, plague, provoke, *(n)* annoyance; *antonyms (v)* please, pacify, soothe, **4.** interfere; *synonyms (v)* intercede, obstruct, disturb, conflict, clash, hinder, impede, meddle, interrupt, contravene, encroach,

jar, mediate, (n) interpose, (adj) intermeddle, **5.**
bother; *synonyms* (v) trouble, annoy, torment, vex,
worry, irk, tease, bedevil, (n) fuss, bore, pain, ado,
concern, nuisance, aggravation; *antonyms* (v)
delight, (n) pleasure, **6.** vex; *synonyms* (v) fret,
agitate, chafe, exasperate, gall, excite, perplex, tire,
bug, nettle, peeve, rankle, rile, offend, distress.

tabareaki 1. annoyed; *synonyms* (adj) angry, irate,
irritated, vexed, aggravated, angered, cross,
disgruntled, displeased, exasperated, infuriated,
offended, peeved, pestered, resentful; *antonyms*
(adj) calm, pleased, unprovoked, smiling, **2.**
bothered; *synonyms* (adj) worried, disturbed,
troubled, concerned, distraught, nervous, uneasy,
upset, **3.** disordered; *synonyms* (adj) confused,
chaotic, broken, deranged, disorganized,
incoherent, messy, sick, disconnected, disjointed,
disorderly, ill, jumbled, mixed, muddled;
antonyms (adj) neat, orderly, ordered, **4.** vexed;
synonyms (adj) annoyed, harassed, harried, sore.

tabarebare 1. active; *synonyms* (adj) energetic, alert,
busy, diligent, effective, live, lively, nimble, strong,
agile, alive, brisk, dynamic, forcible, healthy;
antonyms (adj) dormant, inactive, sluggish, idle,
latent, lethargic, sedentary, slow, extinct, passive,
quiet, **2.** meddling; *synonyms* (adj) interfering,
curious, inquisitive, intrusive, meddlesome,
officious, prying, nosy, busybodied, dabbling,
impertinent, **3.** mischievous; *synonyms* (adj) bad,
evil, injurious, detrimental, hurtful, naughty,
deleterious, harmful, impish, maleficent, playful,
arch, baneful, sly, disobedient; *antonym* (adj) good,
4. ardent; *synonyms* (adj) burning, enthusiastic,
fervent, passionate, eager, impassioned, keen,
vehement, warm, acute, affectionate, avid, devoted,
earnest, fervid; *antonyms* (adj) indifferent,
apathetic, **5.** enterprising; *synonyms* (adj)
adventurous, bold, active, aggressive, courageous,
daring, vigorous, ambitious, audacious, brave, go-
ahead, pushing, driving, pushful, venturesome, **6.**
enthusiastic; *synonyms* (adj) ardent, hearty,
cordial, anxious, excited, fiery, animated, heated,
dedicated, fanatical, glowing, hot, (n) buoyant,
gushing, (v) fanatic; *antonyms* (adj) unenthusiastic,
lukewarm, **7.** eager; *synonyms* (adj) desirous, agog,
zealous, industrious, studious, craving, forward,
hungry, impatient, longing, ready, willing, athirst,
biting, (n) hasty; *antonyms* (adj) disinterested,
unconcerned, **8.** fervent; *synonyms* (adj) intense,
emotional, torrid, devout, ablaze, fierce, flaming,
perfervid, excitable, heartfelt.

tabarekai 1. diligent; *synonyms* (adj) busy, active,
assiduous, careful, painstaking, earnest, attentive,
industrious, laborious, studious, occupied, brisk,
conscientious, indefatigable, meticulous; *antonyms*
(adj) lazy, careless, negligent, **2.** agile; *synonyms*
(adj) nimble, adroit, quick, spry, deft, lively, lithe,

sprightly, supple, quick-witted, alert, dexterous,
fast, fleet, flexible; *antonym* (adj) clumsy, **3.**
nimble; *synonyms* (adj) agile, clever, energetic,
expeditious, lissome, dapper, diligent, lissom,
smart, speedy, tripping, nifty, handy, limber, (v)
light, **4.** brisk; *synonyms* (adj) bracing, alive,
bright, acute, animated, crisp, fresh, hasty,
invigorating, pert, sharp, vigorous, perky, abrupt,
breezy; *antonyms* (adj) slow, soporific, **5.** prompt;
synonyms (adj) punctual, immediate, instant, (v)
actuate, incite, inspire, instigate, move, animate,
cue, goad, impel, induce, motivate, prod; *antonym*
(adj) late.

tabaretua meddle; *synonyms* (v) tamper, interfere,
intervene, intrude, fiddle, monkey, pry.

tabaronikarawa 1. gloomy; *synonyms* (adj) dark,
black, cheerless, dejected, depressing, desolate,
disconsolate, dismal, downcast, dim, dingy,
downhearted, dull, funereal, melancholy;
antonyms (adj) bright, cheerful, cheery,
encouraging, happy, hopeful, light, **2.** dark;
synonyms (adj) obscure, blind, blue, deep, gloomy,
murky, mysterious, sable, abstruse, cryptic, (n)
cloudy, darkness, evening, night, shadow;
antonyms (adj) sunny, fair, clear, pale, pallid, sunlit,
(n) day.

tabarua 1. bristling; *synonyms* (adj) thorny,
muricated, pectinated, studded, thistly, bristled,
bushy, fraught, horrent, horrid, teeming, thick,
dreadful, hideous, rough, **2.** overburdened;
synonyms (adj) burdened, heavy.

tabataba zigzag; *synonyms* (n) ankle, astragal, crane,
crotch, (v) meander, wind, bend, indirect, twist,
crank, (adj) forked, furcated, meandering, winding,
bifurcate; *antonym* (adj) straight.

tabati 1. huge; *synonyms* (adj) big, enormous,
gigantic, immense, large, vast, colossal, extensive,
great, elephantine, ample, considerable, excessive,
gargantuan, giant; *antonyms* (adj) tiny,
insignificant, miniature, small, **2.** enormous;
synonyms (adj) huge, exorbitant, prodigious,
tremendous, stupendous, infinite, massive,
monumental, terrific, terrible, flagrant,
immeasurable, mammoth, mighty, monstrous;
antonym (adj) minute, **3.** voluminous; *synonyms*
(adj) bulky, roomy, spacious, capacious, full,
copious; *antonyms* (adj) tight, cramped.

tabatibutibu 1. bumpy; *synonyms* (adj) rough,
uneven, jagged, jolty, asymmetrical, bouncing,
bouncy, coarse, crooked, eroded, furrowed, itchy,
jarring, jolting, jumpy; *antonym* (adj) flat, **2.**
swelled; *synonyms* (adj) big, inflated, bloated,
adult, bad, bighearted, boastful, bombastic,
bounteous, bountiful, braggy, crowing, distended,
elder, emphysematous, **3.** uneven; *synonyms* (adj)
unequal, irregular, erratic, patchy, rugged, spotty,
disproportionate, ragged, craggy, unbalanced,

variable, changeable, disparate, (v) broken, (n) harsh; *antonyms* (adj) even, smooth, straight, equal, symmetrical.

tabatoatoa 1. knobby; *synonyms* (adj) knobbly, hilly, rough, knotty, bent, crooked, knappy, knotted, (v) hubbly, hubby, papillose, selliform, subclavate, ventricose, verrucose, **2**. lumpy; *synonyms* (adj) chunky, coarse, dull, dumpy, gawky, gritty, indolent, rude, squat, squatty, stumpy, (v) lumpish, (n) failure, **3**. knotty; *synonyms* (adj) complex, difficult, gnarled, intricate, involved, convoluted, gnarly, elaborate, troublesome, baffling, hard, nodose, problematic, complicated, tricky; *antonyms* (adj) simple, straight, straightforward.

tabatoutou toss; *synonyms* (v) fling, throw, agitate, cast, chuck, pitch, flip, hurl, shake, convulse, discard, project, roll, heave, jerk.

tabaua 1. crazy; *synonyms* (adj) deranged, mad, madcap, wild, absurd, brainsick, cracked, crazed, demented, eccentric, foolish, ludicrous, preposterous, silly, wacky; *antonyms* (adj) sane, sensible, **2**. imbecile; *synonyms* (adj) idiotic, fatuous, imbecilic, simple, (n) fool, idiot, moron, cretin, ass, oaf, changeling, **3**. mad; *synonyms* (adj) frantic, frenzied, insane, delirious, angry, crazy, distracted, frenetic, lunatic, irate, maniac, distraught, cross, (n) furious, anger; *antonym* (adj) calm, **4**. moonstruck; *synonyms* (v) awestruck, thunderstruck, (adj) maddened, sentimental, **5**. idiot; *synonyms* (n) dolt, dunce, dimwit, imbecile, dumbbell, half-wit, innocent, jerk, natural, **6**. lunatic; *synonyms* (adj) mental, moonstruck, nutty, psychotic, (n) madman, nut, daredevil, hothead, **7**. unbalanced; *synonyms* (adj) lopsided, wobbly, disproportionate, imbalanced, unequal, asymmetrical, unsettled, unstable, unsteady, disturbed, immoderate, irregular, sick, uneven; *antonyms* (adj) balanced, even, well-balanced, **8**. unstable; *synonyms* (adj) changeable, precarious, insecure, shaky, unsound, erratic, fickle, fluid, inconstant, unpredictable, irresolute, unreliable, capricious, changeful, fluctuating; *antonyms* (adj) stable, steady, constant.

tabe 1. engaged; *synonyms* (adj) busy, occupied, betrothed, affianced, employed, engrossed, reserved, absorbed, working, pledged, bespoken, booked, immersed, intent, rapt; *antonyms* (adj) available, free, **2**. few; *synonyms* (adj) infrequent, rare, scarce, occasional, sporadic, uncommon, erratic, imperceptible, inconsequential, intermittent, middling, negligible, paltry, piddling, scattered; *antonyms* (n) plenty, (adj) many, countless, innumerable, various, **3**. busy; *synonyms* (adj) active, brisk, assiduous, engaged, agile, crowded, industrious, meddlesome, officious, live, diligent, earnest, energetic, (v) occupy, employ;

antonyms (adj) idle, inactive, **4**. occupied; *synonyms* (adj) concerned, involved; *antonyms* (adj) empty, vacant, uninhabited, **5**. some; *synonyms* (adv) nearly, rather, somewhat, about, approximately, around, roughly, round, almost, near, (adj) few, certain, several, (det) any, (n) one, **6**. several; *synonyms* (v) diverse, divers, sundry, (adj) different, individual, numerous, particular, separate, special, manifold, respective, proper, specific, discrete, (n) some, **7**. still; *synonyms* (adv) however, but, nevertheless, (adj) calm, pacify, peaceful, silence, quiescent, serene, silent, (n) hush, (v) quiet, assuage, compose, lull; *antonyms* (adj) moving, effervescent, fizzy, windy, (n) noisy, **8**. working; *synonyms* (adj) operative, practical, acting, effective, operating, operational, (n) operation, running, functioning, play, agency, movement, performance, go, workings; *antonyms* (adj) passive, unemployed.

tabea 1. confused; *synonyms* (adj) abashed, bewildered, baffled, befuddled, bemused, chaotic, confounded, disjointed, disordered, dizzy, incoherent, indistinct, ambiguous, (n) cloudy, (adv, adj) topsy-turvy; *antonyms* (adj) clear, enlightened, alert, clearheaded, clear-headed, orderly, **2**. endangered; *synonyms* (adj) defenseless, risky, exposed, helpless, susceptible, (n) tiger, **3**. stray; *synonyms* (v) roam, digress, ramble, range, wander, depart, deviate, drift, err, meander, rove, straggle, gad, (n) vagabond, waif.

tabeaki 1. lost; *synonyms* (v) gone, missing, abandoned, (adj) doomed, forlorn, extinct, hopeless, bewildered, disoriented, forgotten, helpless, broken, confused, irrecoverable, absent; *antonyms* (adj) present, found, existing, **2**. engaged; *synonyms* (adj) busy, occupied, betrothed, affianced, employed, engrossed, reserved, absorbed, working, pledged, bespoken, booked, immersed, intent, rapt; *antonyms* (adj) available, free.

tabeitera 1. bias; *synonyms* (n) penchant, drift, influence, turn, twist, favor, slope, angle, bigotry, (v) prejudice, bent, slant, dispose, (adj) partiality, diagonal; *antonyms* (n) impartiality, neutrality, fairness, **2**. supporting; *synonyms* (adj) auxiliary, collateral, encouraging, secondary, (n) support, backing, (prep) behind, **3**. unbalanced; *synonyms* (adj) lopsided, crazy, mad, wobbly, demented, disproportionate, imbalanced, unequal, asymmetrical, unsettled, unstable, unsteady, brainsick, distracted, disturbed; *antonyms* (adj) sane, balanced, even, well-balanced, **4**. partial; *synonyms* (adj) incomplete, imperfect, fragmentary, unfair, sectional, inequitable, biased, part, halfway, partisan, prejudiced, unfinished, unjust, disparate, (v) party; *antonyms* (adj) complete, impartial, total, absolute, comprehensive, unbiased.

tabeka 1. elevate; *synonyms* (*v*) raise, advance, lift, boost, erect, exalt, hoist, cheer, dignify, promote, rear, aggrandize, uphold, animate, ennoble; *antonyms* (*v*) demote, lower, **2.** lift; *synonyms* (*n*) elevator, heave, support, climb, (*v*) rise, elevate, filch, hike, airlift, pilfer, pinch, steal, swipe, enhance, heighten, **3.** heave; *synonyms* (*v*) cast, fling, chuck, gasp, haul, toss, billow, drag, draw, gag, jerk, pitch, (*n*) tug, elevation, heaving, **4.** carry; *synonyms* (*v*) bear, bring, convey, conduct, take, acquit, behave, accept, comport, hold, pack, transport, load, assume, admit, **5.** raise; *synonyms* (*v*) increase, build, foster, grow, prefer, augment, cultivate, excite, levy, nurture, amplify, found, enlarge, breed, (*n*) mount, **6.** show; *synonyms* (*v*) present, broadcast, expose, guide, indicate, parade, demonstrate, disclose, evidence, (*n*) display, appearance, exhibit, produce, ostentation, presentation; *antonyms* (*v*) conceal, disprove, hide, **7.** truck; *synonyms* (*n*) traffic, car, cart, trade, van, bogie, automobile, cap, crest, motortruck, tub, (*v*) exchange, barter, swap, swop.

tabekaki 1. elevated; *synonyms* (*adj*) high, exalted, lofty, noble, towering, grand, great, majestic, tall, elated, magnanimous, advanced, dignified, eminent, (*v*) steep; *antonym* (*adj*) short, **2.** lifted; *synonyms* (*adj*) elevated, upraised, **3.** raised; *synonyms* (*v*) repousse, salient, (*adj*) embossed, erect, convex, brocaded, alert, bold, confident, elate, elative, exultant, mountant, prominent, (*prep*) above.

tabeman 1. several; *synonyms* (*adj*) many, different, individual, various, numerous, particular, separate, special, manifold, respective, (*v*) diverse, divers, sundry, (*n*) some, (*det*) any; *antonym* (*adj*) few, **2.** some; *synonyms* (*adv*) nearly, rather, somewhat, about, approximately, around, roughly, round, almost, near, (*adj*) certain, several, extraordinary, quantitative, (*n*) one.

tabemoa beginner; *synonyms* (*n*) apprentice, novice, entrant, learner, founder, freshman, greenhorn, newcomer, recruit, tenderfoot, father, tiro, trainee, tyro, amateur; *antonym* (*n*) expert.

taberamate 1. dying; *synonyms* (*adj*) vanishing, last, moribund, (*n*) death, demise, decease; *antonyms* (*adj*) thriving, opening, well, **2.** withering; *synonyms* (*adj*) devastating, annihilating, annihilative, extortionate, grinding, (*v*) biting, cutting, cynical, desolating, dry, sarcastic, sardonic, satirical, severe, (*n*) atrophy.

taberua preoccupied; *synonyms* (*adj*) obsessed, absorbed, abstracted, thoughtful, lost, distracted, faraway, rapt, inattentive, engrossed, pensive, absent, baffled, bemused, bewildered; *antonym* (*adj*) attentive.

taberuarua strained; *synonyms* (*adj*) forced, labored, tense, intense, constrained, laboured, unnatural, taut, tight, agonistic, agonistical, combative, farfetched; *antonyms* (*adj*) relaxed, natural.

taberuru spatter; *synonyms* (*n*) splatter, (*v*) splash, plash, dash, slop, scatter, smear, bespatter, soil, spit, spray, sputter, squirt, patter, dabble.

taberuruaki spattered; *synonyms* (*adj*) bespattered, besplashed, dabbled, dirty, showy, splashed, splashy, splattered.

tabetabe 1. indisposed; *synonyms* (*adj*) disinclined, ailing, ill, averse, loath, poorly, sick, reluctant, sickly, unwell, unwilling, diseased, loth, **2.** surge; *synonyms* (*n*) wave, burst, ripple, spurt, (*v*) billow, flood, rise, rush, stream, flow, gush, heave, jet, swell, soar.

tabetai 1. hardly; *synonyms* (*adv*) scarcely, just, rarely, seldom, hard, little, narrowly, scarce, severely, slightly, (*adj*) barely; *antonym* (*adv*) completely, **2.** sometimes; *synonyms* (*adv*) occasionally, once, formerly, sometime, periodically, off-and-on, otherwhiles, usually, consistently, constantly, intermittently, (*n*) exemplar, meantime, meanwhile, (*adj*) former, **3.** occasionally; *synonyms* (*adv*) sometimes, irregularly, infrequently, uncommonly; *antonyms* (*adv*) frequently, regularly, **4.** occasional; *synonyms* (*adj*) accidental, casual, incidental, irregular, infrequent, episodic, intermittent, fortuitous, adventitious, contingent, odd, rare, periodic, sporadic, uncommon; *antonyms* (*adj*) frequent, recurrent, **5.** seldom; *synonyms* (*adv*) hardly, (*adj*) few; *antonym* (*adv*) often.

tabetea 1. skim; *synonyms* (*v*) glide, slip, browse, skip, sweep, brush, fly, graze, race, read, scan, shave, glance, (*n*) cream, slide, **2.** touch; *synonyms* (*n*) feel, tinge, feeling, hint, (*v*) affect, contact, hit, border, adjoin, strike, stroke, regard, concern, handle, interest, **3.** work; *synonyms* (*n*) exercise, business, employment, function, task, action, act, book, composition, (*v*) labor, operate, toil, cultivate, (*adj*) job, trade; *antonyms* (*v*) idle, malfunction.

tabeteaki touched; *synonyms* (*v*) compassionate, pitiful, sympathetic, bad, decayed, lentiginous, mildewed, moldy, (*adj*) affected, cracked, crazy, daft, insane, tinged, interested; *antonym* (*adj*) untouched.

tabetirake 1. ascend; *synonyms* (*v*) rise, arise, mount, climb, scale, uprise, increase, appear, escalate, jump, lift, soar; *antonyms* (*v*) descend, drop, **2.** float; *synonyms* (*n*) buoy, raft, bob, fleet, (*v*) drift, swim, blow, hover, ride, waft, fly, glide, hang, range, sail; *antonym* (*v*) sink.

tabeua 1. few; *synonyms* (*adj*) infrequent, rare, scarce, occasional, sporadic, uncommon, erratic, imperceptible, inconsequential, intermittent, middling, negligible, paltry, piddling, scattered; *antonyms* (*n*) plenty, (*adj*) many, countless, innumerable, various, **2**. several; *synonyms* (*v*) diverse, divers, sundry, (*adj*) different, individual, numerous, particular, separate, special, manifold, respective, certain, one, (*n*) some, (*det*) any; *antonym* (*adj*) few.

tabeuta 1. few; *synonyms* (*adj*) infrequent, rare, scarce, occasional, sporadic, uncommon, erratic, imperceptible, inconsequential, intermittent, middling, negligible, paltry, piddling, scattered; *antonyms* (*n*) plenty, (*adj*) many, countless, innumerable, various, **2**. portion; *synonyms* (*n*) part, division, piece, constituent, allot, component, fragment, parcel, section, dole, allowance, (*v*) lot, dividend, divide, allotment.

tabiria mince; *synonyms* (*v*) chop, hash, dice, moderate, slice, soften, fricassee, grate.

tabiriaki minced; *synonyms* (*adj*) crushed, ground, pulverized, milled, pounded, powdered.

tabiro 1. entangled; *synonyms* (*adj*) involved, complicated, intricate, embroiled, complex, foul, matted, tangled; *antonym* (*adj*) free, **2**. entangle; *synonyms* (*v*) embrangle, tangle, enmesh, complicate, confuse, involve, snarl, entwine, catch, ensnare, entrap, knot, (*n*) embroil, (*adj*) embarrass, bewilder; *antonym* (*v*) disentangle, **3**. hinder; *synonyms* (*adj*) posterior, hind, (*v*) block, bar, impede, check, hamper, obstruct, resist, curb, arrest, clog, counteract, delay, detain; *antonyms* (*v*) help, assist, facilitate, **4**. twisted; *synonyms* (*adj*) crooked, deformed, perverted, bent, distorted, coiled, misshapen, contorted, curved, twined, winding, wry, gnarled, tortuous, awry; *antonyms* (*adj*) straight, tidy, **5**. twist; *synonyms* (*n*) twine, wind, spin, twirl, braid, (*v*) turn, bend, distort, curl, coil, contort, deform, curve, pervert, wrench; *antonyms* (*v*) straighten, untwist, **6**. sprain; *synonyms* (*n*) strain, injury, (*v*) rick, twist, pull, wrick, injure, (*adj*) cramp, adynamy, asthenia, cachexia, cachexy, decrepitude, delicacy, invalidation.

tabiroaki 1. entangled; *synonyms* (*adj*) involved, complicated, intricate, embroiled, complex, foul, matted, tangled; *antonym* (*adj*) free, **2**. twisted; *synonyms* (*adj*) crooked, deformed, perverted, bent, distorted, coiled, misshapen, contorted, curved, twined, winding, wry, gnarled, tortuous, awry; *antonyms* (*adj*) straight, tidy.

tabitabitabita 1. excuse; *synonyms* (*n*) apology, alibi, evasion, palliate, pretext, color, (*v*) pardon, absolve, acquit, condone, exculpate, forgive, justify, apologise, apologize; *antonym* (*v*) punish, **2**. exonerate; *synonyms* (*v*) clear, discharge, excuse, exempt, liberate, purge, release, vindicate, whitewash, free, relieve, assoil, defend, (*adj*) disburden; *antonym* (*v*) convict, **3**. exculpate; *synonyms* (*v*) exonerate, disculpate, **4**. clear; *synonyms* (*adj*) clean, certain, open, apparent,

distinct, empty, light, plain, pure, blameless, (*v*) bright, absolute, net, clarify, definite; *antonyms* (*adj*) cloudy, opaque, unclear, dark, fuzzy, hazy, incomprehensible, obscure, uncertain, vague, ambiguous, blurry, confused, confusing, dull, **5**. absolve; *synonyms* (*v*) remit, redeem, dispense; *antonyms* (*v*) blame, condemn, **6**. discharge; *synonyms* (*n*) dismissal, drain, explosion, ooze, (*v*) complete, deliver, eject, cashier, burst, blast, bounce, detonate, disgorge, expel, flow; *antonyms* (*v*) capture, hire, **7**. acquit; *synonyms* (*v*) conduct, hold, bear, behave, carry, comport, (*adj*) quit.

tabitabitabitaki 1. exculpated; *synonyms* (*adj*) clear, exonerated, absolved, cleared, clean, decipherable, vindicated, light, open, percipient, readable, unclouded, unmortgaged, **2**. discharged; *synonyms* (*adj*) released, exempt, convalescent, dead, deadened, defunct, dismissed, drained, finished, fired, idle, inactive, inanimate, lifeless, nonliving, **3**. exonerated; *synonym* (*adj*) exculpated, **4**. excused; *synonyms* (*adj*) immune, privileged, excepted, **5**. absolved; *synonyms* (*v*) quit, acquitted, free, **6**. cleared; *synonyms* (*adj*) blank, bleak, empty, innocent, official, vacant, blameless, unfurnished, unoccupied.

taboa 1. attack; *synonyms* (*n*) incursion, thrust, aggression, fit, onset, onslaught, seizure, (*v*) assault, assail, attempt, aggress, charge, invade, raid, accuse; *antonyms* (*n*) defense, (*v*) defend, protect, retreat, **2**. invoke; *synonyms* (*v*) entreat, appeal, conjure, evoke, pray, beseech, arouse, cite, summon, name, beg, adjure, bid, wish, address, **3**. challenge; *synonyms* (*n*) question, defiance, protest, contest, (*v*) defy, dare, brave, dispute, ask, call, contradict, demur, deny, doubt, impeach; *antonym* (*v*) obey, **4**. defy; *synonyms* (*v*) challenge, confront, ignore, resist, revolt, disobey, oppose, withstand, rebel, mutiny, decline, break, contravene, face, flout.

taboang 1. enterprising; *synonyms* (*adj*) adventurous, bold, active, aggressive, energetic, courageous, daring, vigorous, ambitious, audacious, brave, go-ahead, pushing, driving, pushful, **2**. ardent; *synonyms* (*adj*) burning, enthusiastic, fervent, passionate, eager, impassioned, keen, vehement, warm, acute, affectionate, avid, devoted, earnest, fervid; *antonyms* (*adj*) indifferent, apathetic, **3**. vigorous; *synonyms* (*adj*) robust, strong, hardy, lively, powerful, strenuous, athletic, hearty, mighty, healthy, smart, brawny, muscular, (*v*) brisk, fresh; *antonyms* (*adj*) feeble, lethargic, weak, dull, unenergetic, **4**. strong; *synonyms* (*adj*) intense, able, deep, firm, stable, steady, cogent, durable, forcible, good, hard, influential, lusty, potent, rigid; *antonyms* (*adj*) bland, delicate, faint, frail, mild, pale, slight, unconvincing, cowardly, diluted, exhausted, flimsy, imperceptible, lightweight, soft, **5**. zealous; *synonyms* (*adj*) ardent, fiery, glowing, dedicated, enterprising, fanatical, cordial, forward, solicitous, jealous, devout, fierce, spirited, animated, (*n*) sincere, **6**. strapping; *synonyms* (*adj*) burly, beefy, hefty, husky, stout, stalwart, sturdy, sinewy, full, plump, rugged, big, heavy, tough, (*n*) strap; *antonym* (*adj*) puny.

tabobai rich; *synonyms* (*adj*) abundant, copious, fertile, productive, fruitful, full, affluent, ample, deep, fat, luxurious, opulent, plentiful, prolific, bright; *antonyms* (*adj*) poor, broke, destitute, impoverished, light.

tabobe 1. drifter; *synonyms* (*n*) tramp, vagabond, vagrant, wanderer, bum, floater, itinerant, nomad, rover, traveler; *antonym* (*n*) resident, **2**. transient; *synonyms* (*adj*) brief, fleeting, passing, temporary, transitory, ephemeral, fugacious, momentary, fugitive, temporal, impermanent, provisional, cursory, meteoric, migrant; *antonyms* (*adj*) permanent, enduring, **3**. vagabond; *synonyms* (*n*) outcast, hobo, beggar, derelict, loon, drifter, (*v*) roam, stray, ramble, range, rove, wander, unsettled, (*adj*) transient, aimless, **4**. scoundrel; *synonyms* (*n*) knave, rascal, rogue, blackguard, cad, crook, miscreant, villain, varlet, cheat.

tabokaikai 1. fearless; *synonyms* (*adj*) bold, daring, brave, courageous, dauntless, audacious, heroic, intrepid, undaunted, confident, doughty, gallant, valiant, manly, game; *antonyms* (*adj*) cowardly, afraid, frightened, scared, **2**. formidable; *synonyms* (*adj*) arduous, appalling, grim, awful, difficult, dreadful, fearful, forbidding, heavy, dread, onerous, redoubtable, stiff, tough, herculean.

tabomane 1. energetic; *synonyms* (*adj*) active, animated, brisk, busy, driving, dynamic, effective, powerful, strong, agile, emphatic, aggressive, efficacious, efficient, enterprising; *antonyms* (*adj*) lethargic, lazy, sluggish, exhausted, inactive, indolent, languid, weary, apathetic, dull, indifferent, listless, **2**. virile; *synonyms* (*adj*) masculine, male, manly, potent, forceful, manful, vigorous, robust, mature, manlike; *antonym* (*adj*) impotent.

tabonako 1. anywhere; *synonyms* (*adv*) anyplace, everyplace, **2**. anyplace; *synonyms* (*adv*) wherever, anywhere, where, (*n*) place, **3**. wherever; *synonyms* (*adv*) everywhere, wheresoever, where'er, someplace.

tabonang strong; *synonyms* (*adj*) intense, powerful, able, deep, firm, stable, steady, cogent, durable, forcible, good, hard, influential, lusty, potent; *antonyms* (*adj*) weak, bland, delicate, faint, feeble, frail, mild, pale, slight, unconvincing, cowardly, diluted, dull, exhausted, flimsy.

tabonao surge; *synonyms* (*n*) wave, burst, ripple, spurt, (*v*) billow, flood, rise, rush, stream, flow, gush, heave, jet, swell, soar.

tabonibainrang 1. clumsy; *synonyms* (*adj*) bumbling, bungling, cumbersome, unwieldy, gawky, inapt, inept, maladroit, rude, ungainly, unskilled, wooden, incompetent, lumbering, (*n*) awkward; *antonyms* (*adj*) graceful, nimble, clever, dexterous, skillful, adroit, deft, **2**. awkward; *synonyms* (*adj*) clumsy, inconvenient, crude, embarrassing, sticky, uncomfortable, untoward, left-handed, annoying, difficult, graceless, heavy, inelegant, rough, rustic; *antonyms* (*adj*) easy, manageable, straightforward, convenient, helpful, rotund, simple.

taboniwia 1. consult; *synonyms* (*v*) confer, consider, negotiate, advise, deliberate, refer, discuss, reason, canvass, confab, confabulate, (*n*) talk, **2**. plan; *synonyms* (*n*) aim, map, figure, chart, intent, outline, pattern, scheme, invent, form, (*v*) design, devise, intend, plot, arrange.

taboniwiaki planned; *synonyms* (*adj*) deliberate, intended, intentional, calculated, designed, aforethought, plotted, premeditated, scheduled, fixed, future, prepared, studied; *antonyms* (*adj*) spontaneous, unplanned.

tabora 1. insult; *synonyms* (*n*) dishonor, abuse, affront, contumely, disgrace, indignity, outrage, contempt, wound, derision, harm, injury, (*v*) flout, taunt, cut; *antonyms* (*v*) compliment, praise, **2**. curse; *synonyms* (*n*) bane, anathema, blasphemy, malediction, denunciation, (*v*) beshrew, blight, ban, damn, plague, swear, vituperate, anathematize, blaspheme, blast, **3**. threaten; *synonyms* (*v*) menace, bully, endanger, intimidate, loom, offer, imperil, jeopardize, peril, approach, foreshadow, portend, browbeat, impend, (*n*) threat; *antonym* (*v*) help.

taboraki 1. insulted; *synonyms* (*adj*) affronted, huffy, disrespected, hurt, slighted, snubbed, upset, **2**. cursed; *synonyms* (*v*) accurst, cursing, (*adj*) abominable, damned, doomed, execrable, blamed, blasted, blessed, curst, damnable, detestable, hateful, infernal, unlucky.

taborang 1. crackers; *synonyms* (*adj*) cracked, nuts, mad, barmy, bats, batty, bonkers, crazy, dotty, haywire, kookie, kooky, loony, nutty, balmy; *antonym* (*adj*) sane, **2**. crazy; *synonyms* (*adj*) deranged, madcap, wild, absurd, brainsick, crazed, demented, eccentric, foolish, ludicrous, preposterous, silly, wacky, outrageous, crackers; *antonym* (*adj*) sensible.

tabotua bored; *synonyms* (*adj*) tired, weary, uninterested, jaded, listless, sick, blasé, discontented, droopy, inattentive, indifferent, lazy, lethargic, sophisticated, unconcerned.

tabu 1. forbidden; *synonyms* (*adj*) unlawful, banned, illegal, prohibited, taboo, contraband, illicit, proscribed, verboten; *antonym* (*adj*) acceptable, **2.** illegal; *synonyms* (*adj*) criminal, forbidden, unauthorized, illegitimate, lawless, wrongful; *antonyms* (*adj*) legal, lawful, honest, legitimate, official, **3.** illicit; *synonyms* (*adj*) wrong, immoral, shady, adulterous, clandestine, outlawed; *antonym* (*adj*) licit, **4.** consecrated; *synonyms* (*adj*) sacred, blessed, consecrate, sanctified, hallowed, holy, dedicated, devoted, divine, adopted, (*prep*) dedicate, **5.** solemn; *synonyms* (*adj*) grave, serious, earnest, heavy, important, sedate, devout, formal, demure, dignified, (*v*) sober, imposing, reverent, (*n*) grand, noble; *antonym* (*adj*) frivolous, **6.** taboo; *synonyms* (*adj*) out, (*n*) tabu, prohibition, embargo, (*v*) ban, interdict, forbid, outlaw, enjoin, **7.** prohibited; *synonym* (*adj*) barred; *antonym* (*adj*) admissible, **8.** restricted; *synonyms* (*v*) qualified, (*adj*) limited, confined, cramped, narrow, constrained, exclusive, local, controlled, finite, classified, secret, bounded, circumscribed, private; *antonyms* (*adj*) unrestricted, far-reaching, free, liberated, unimpeded, unlimited, open, wide.

tabua 1. forbid; *synonyms* (*v*) debar, prohibit, ban, bar, disallow, exclude, deny, avert, frustrate, inhibit, interdict, outlaw, prevent, proscribe, veto; *antonyms* (*v*) permit, allow, let, approve, **2.** hallow; *synonyms* (*v*) consecrate, bless, sanctify, dedicate, venerate, commemorate, honor, **3.** interdict; *synonyms* (*n*) embargo, prohibition, inhibition, curse, interdiction, proscription, restraint, taboo, exclusion, (*v*) enjoin, forbid, command, check, **4.** prohibit; *synonyms* (*v*) hinder, preclude, hamper, impede, deter, oppose, block, restrict, stop, disqualify, negative, (*n*) obstruct.

tabuaetia 1. awkward; *synonyms* (*adj*) clumsy, inconvenient, crude, embarrassing, inept, sticky, uncomfortable, ungainly, untoward, left-handed, annoying, bungling, cumbersome, difficult, graceless; *antonyms* (*adj*) graceful, easy, adroit, manageable, straightforward, convenient, dexterous, helpful, rotund, simple, **2.** damage; *synonyms* (*n*) blemish, injury, wound, loss, cost, detriment, disadvantage, impairment, (*v*) harm, hurt, abuse, injure, afflict, disfigure, (*adj*) impair; *antonyms* (*v*) service, (*v*) conserve, enhance, repair, bolster, **3.** obtain; *synonyms* (*v*) gain, acquire, get, have, achieve, attain, earn, accomplish, derive, effect, buy, collect, extract, find, gather; *antonym* (*v*) lose.

tabuaetiaki damaged; *synonyms* (*adj*) faulty, unsound, defective, broken, dilapidated, hurt, impaired, besmirched, deficient, flyblown; *antonym* (*adj*) undamaged.

tabuaiaka vague; *synonyms* (*adj*) indeterminate, indistinct, obscure, ambiguous, faint, indefinite, uncertain, undefined, undetermined, feeble, dim, fuzzy, hazy, (*v*) loose, equivocal; *antonyms* (*adj*) clear, definite, distinct, exact, particular, precise, specific, sure.

tabuaki 1. forbidden; *synonyms* (*adj*) unlawful, banned, illegal, prohibited, taboo, contraband, illicit, proscribed, verboten; *antonym* (*adj*) acceptable, **2.** hallowed; *synonyms* (*adj*) holy, blessed, consecrated, sacred, divine, sanctified, **3.** prohibited; *synonyms* (*adj*) forbidden, barred, out; *antonyms* (*adj*) admissible, legitimate.

tabuarikia 1. brutalize; *synonyms* (*v*) brutalise, brutify, demoralize, bastardize, bestialize, debauch, deprave, harden, mistreat, misuse, stain, toughen, vitiate, (*adj*) pervert, prostitute, **2.** bungle; *synonyms* (*n*) blooper, gaffe, trip, bloomer, error, (*v*) blunder, botch, fumble, mishandle, mistake, flub, fluff, muddle, muff, blow, **3.** spoil; *synonyms* (*v*) plunder, corrupt, impair, rot, damage, deface, indulge, injure, mar, sack, baby, bungle, coddle, (*n*) ruin, (*adj*) harm; *antonyms* (*v*) enhance, improve, conserve.

tabuarikiaki 1. bungled; *synonyms* (*adj*) botched, failed, fruitless, futile, inferior, poor, ruined, spoiled, substandard, unproductive, unsuccessful, slipshod, **2.** spoiled; *synonyms* (*adj*) decayed, bad, rotten, stale, coddled, pampered, corrupt, damaged, spoilt; *antonyms* (*adj*) first-rate, pure.

tabuea other; *synonyms* (*adj*) additional, another, different, extra, further, more, new, second, distinct, dissimilar, fresh, else, opposite, added; *antonym* (*adj*) same.

tabuenga matted; *synonyms* (*adj*) mat, entangled, tangled, flat, knotted, matt, matte, knotty, bland, categoric, categorical, compressed, fixed, flavorless, (*v*) crossed; *antonym* (*adj*) tidy.

tabuki 1. elevated; *synonyms* (*adj*) high, exalted, lofty, noble, towering, grand, great, majestic, tall, elated, magnanimous, advanced, dignified, eminent, (*v*) steep; *antonym* (*adj*) short, **2.** hilly; *synonyms* (*adj*) craggy, mountainous, rugged, cragged, knobby, prominent, tumulous, precipitous, tumulose, **3.** uneven; *synonyms* (*adj*) rough, unequal, irregular, jagged, erratic, patchy, spotty, disproportionate, ragged, crooked, unbalanced, variable, (*v*) broken, (*n*) harsh, coarse; *antonyms* (*adj*) even, smooth, straight, equal, symmetrical.

tabukibuki rough; *synonyms* (*adj*) coarse, hard, harsh, raw, crude, cruel, grating, gross, hoarse, jagged, approximate, gruff, inclement, (*n*) boisterous, draft; *antonyms* (*adj*) gentle, smooth, polished, precise, refined, silky, soft, sophisticated, even, exact, glossy, pleasant.

tabukirurunga 1. hilly; *synonyms* (*adj*) craggy, mountainous, rugged, steep, cragged, knobby, prominent, tumulous, high, precipitous, tumulose,

2. rough; *synonyms* (*adj*) coarse, hard, harsh, raw, crude, cruel, grating, gross, hoarse, jagged, approximate, gruff, inclement, (*n*) boisterous, draft; *antonyms* (*adj*) gentle, smooth, polished, precise, refined, silky, soft, sophisticated, even, exact, glossy, pleasant, **3.** obstructed; *synonyms* (*adj*) hindered, blind, blocked, congested, foiled, frustrated, impedite, stymied, thwarted, tight; *antonym* (*adj*) successful, **4.** uneven; *synonyms* (*adj*) rough, unequal, irregular, erratic, patchy, spotty, disproportionate, ragged, crooked, unbalanced, variable, asymmetrical, changeable, disparate, (*v*) broken; *antonyms* (*adj*) straight, equal, symmetrical.

tabuna forbid; *synonyms* (*v*) debar, prohibit, ban, bar, disallow, exclude, deny, avert, frustrate, inhibit, interdict, outlaw, prevent, proscribe, veto; *antonyms* (*v*) permit, allow, let, approve.

tabunaák intercession; *synonyms* (*n*) interference, intervention, arbitration, interposition, invocation, prayer, supplication, atonement, (*adj*) mediation.

tabunak round; *synonyms* (*adv*) about, around, (*adj*) circular, plump, entire, chubby, complete, (*n*) circle, bout, ring, beat, circuit, (*v*) compass, turn, gird; *antonyms* (*adj*) slim, sharp.

tabunaki forbidden; *synonyms* (*adj*) unlawful, banned, illegal, prohibited, taboo, contraband, illicit, proscribed, verboten; *antonym* (*adj*) acceptable.

tabunimatea 1. idolize; *synonyms* (*v*) adore, worship, idolise, revere, admire, deify, glorify, **2.** hate; *synonyms* (*v*) abhor, detest, abominate, loathe, despise, scorn, (*n*) dislike, enmity, abhorrence, animosity, detestation, hatred, abomination, antipathy, aversion; *antonyms* (*v*) love, like, **3.** detest; *synonyms* (*v*) hate, execrate, nauseate, **4.** cherish; *synonyms* (*v*) appreciate, entertain, foster, hug, nurture, treasure, cultivate, bosom, esteem, harbor, nourish, nurse, prize, bear, (*n*) embrace, **5.** love; *synonyms* (*n*) desire, affection, dear, fondness, liking, benevolence, charity, attachment, beloved, darling, devotion, honey, sweetheart, (*v*) cherish, enjoy.

tabunimateaki 1. cherished; *synonyms* (*adj*) beloved, dear, precious, loved, treasured, intimate, prized, valued, wanted, pet, **2.** hated; *synonyms* (*adj*) detested, despised, disliked, reviled, scorned, unpopular, abhorrent, despicable, insufferable, loathed, ostracized; *antonym* (*adj*) popular, **3.** detested; *synonym* (*adj*) hated, **4.** idolized; *synonyms* (*adj*) idolised, adored, worshipped, **5.** loved; *synonyms* (*adj*) cherished, appreciated, esteemed, respected, important, (*n*) darling.

tabura 1. damned; *synonyms* (*adj*) cursed, doomed, blasted, condemned, damn, blamed, blessed, bloody, darned, deuced, fated, goddam, goddamn,

goddamned, (*adv*) damnably, **2.** damning; *synonyms* (*adj*) damnatory, derogatory, offensive, damnable, disparaging, negative, pejorative, unflattering, (*n*) curse, denunciation, malediction.

taburaka 1. constrict; *synonyms* (*v*) compress, condense, contract, choke, bind, compact, constringe, limit, narrow, press, restrict, squeeze, astringe, constrain, confine; *antonym* (*v*) loosen, **2.** exacting; *synonyms* (*adj*) demanding, fastidious, austere, difficult, exigent, stern, strict, trying, hard, finicky, harsh, nice, rigorous, severe, (*n*) exact; *antonym* (*adj*) easy.

taburakaki constricted; *synonyms* (*adj*) contracted, narrow, tense, tight, bound, caged, captive, confined, fine, held, knotted, restrained, slender, slight, slim; *antonym* (*adj*) baggy.

tabureka 1. bungle; *synonyms* (*n*) blooper, gaffe, trip, bloomer, error, (*v*) blunder, botch, fumble, mishandle, mistake, flub, fluff, muddle, muff, blow, **2.** bumpy; *synonyms* (*adj*) rough, uneven, jagged, jolty, asymmetrical, bouncing, bouncy, coarse, crooked, eroded, furrowed, itchy, jarring, jolting, jumpy; *antonym* (*adj*) flat, **3.** churlish; *synonyms* (*adj*) boorish, curt, gruff, impolite, loutish, rude, abrupt, blunt, brusque, clownish, crass, crude, disagreeable, discourteous, (*v*) illiberal, **4.** knotty; *synonyms* (*adj*) knotted, complex, difficult, gnarled, intricate, involved, convoluted, gnarly, elaborate, troublesome, baffling, hard, nodose, problematic, complicated; *antonyms* (*adj*) simple, straight, straightforward, **5.** rough; *synonyms* (*adj*) harsh, raw, cruel, grating, gross, hoarse, approximate, inclement, indelicate, rocky, robust, abrasive, austere, (*n*) boisterous, draft; *antonyms* (*adj*) gentle, smooth, polished, precise, refined, silky, soft, sophisticated, even, exact, glossy, pleasant, **6.** rugged; *synonyms* (*adj*) broken, craggy, hardy, hilly, strong, sturdy, tough, cragged, firm, shaggy, perverse, refractory, bitter, knotty, (*n*) ragged; *antonym* (*adj*) delicate, **7.** peevish; *synonyms* (*adj*) fractious, fretful, irritable, irascible, morose, testy, moody, cantankerous, captious, cross, petulant, touchy, crusty, grumpy, excitable, **8.** uneven; *synonyms* (*adj*) unequal, irregular, erratic, patchy, rugged, spotty, disproportionate, unbalanced, variable, changeable, disparate, lopsided, mismatched, partial, wobbly; *antonyms* (*adj*) equal, symmetrical, **9.** spoil; *synonyms* (*v*) plunder, corrupt, impair, rot, damage, deface, indulge, injure, mar, sack, baby, bungle, coddle, (*n*) ruin, (*adj*) harm; *antonyms* (*v*) enhance, improve, conserve, **10.** rude; *synonyms* (*adj*) impudent, bold, brutal, mean, abusive, barbarous, churlish, disrespectful, impertinent, insolent, plain, forward, audacious, awkward, brazen; *antonyms* (*adj*) polite, respectful, chivalrous, courteous, civil, decent, proper, well-mannered.

taburekaki 1. bungled; *synonyms* (*adj*) botched, failed, fruitless, futile, inferior, poor, ruined, spoiled, substandard, unproductive, unsuccessful, slipshod, **2**. spoiled; *synonyms* (*adj*) decayed, bad, rotten, stale, coddled, pampered, corrupt, damaged, spoilt; *antonyms* (*adj*) first-rate, pure.

tabuterang 1. forbidden; *synonyms* (*adj*) unlawful, banned, illegal, prohibited, taboo, contraband, illicit, proscribed, verboten; *antonym* (*adj*) acceptable, **2**. untouchable; *synonyms* (*adj*) inaccessible, unassailable, sacred, inviolable, invulnerable, unobtainable, unprocurable, (*n*) outcast; *antonym* (*adj*) vulnerable, **3**. sacred; *synonyms* (*adj*) hallowed, holy, consecrated, dedicated, divine, religious, pious, blessed, spiritual, consecrate, celestial, devoted, heavenly, (*v*) solemn, majestic; *antonyms* (*adj*) secular, profane.

tabwaia plunder; *synonyms* (*v*) loot, pillage, despoil, harry, spoil, devastate, destroy, maraud, ransack, strip, divest, forage, (*n*) booty, depredation, despoliation.

tabwaiaki plundered; *synonyms* (*adj*) looted, pillaged, despoiled, fleeced, ransacked, ravaged, sacked.

tabweang stupid; *synonyms* (*adj*) foolish, silly, dull, fatuous, idiotic, ridiculous, senseless, crass, insane, childish, dim, (*n*) simple, absurd, dullard, idiot; *antonyms* (*adj*) sensible, bright, clever, intelligent, shrewd, wise.

tabwenaua 1. asunder; *synonyms* (*adv*) apart, aside, (*adj*) separate, loose, adrift, distant, (*v*) discrete, **2**. split; *synonyms* (*v*) crack, cut, fracture, slit, burst, divide, divorce, breach, cleave, (*n*) break, rip, rupture, tear, cleavage, cleft; *antonyms* (*v*) join, unite, merge.

tabwenauaki split; *synonyms* (*v*) crack, cut, fracture, slit, burst, divide, separate, divorce, breach, cleave, (*n*) break, rip, rupture, tear, cleavage; *antonyms* (*v*) join, unite, merge.

tae face; *synonyms* (*n*) look, aspect, countenance, expression, side, top, exterior, appearance, facade, surface, (*v*) confront, audacity, veneer, visage, (*adj*) front; *antonyms* (*v*) avoid, back.

taea 1. clean; *synonyms* (*adj*) clear, fair, antiseptic, blank, pure, chaste, adroit, tidy, unblemished, (*v*) brush, cleanse, bathe, clarify, disinfect, sweep; *antonyms* (*adj*) filthy, unclean, muddy, unhygienic, full, syrupy, tainted, unwholesome, (*v*) dirty, soil, contaminate, pollute, **2**. dust; *synonyms* (*n*) powder, dirt, grit, relics, remains, rhino, blunt, debris, defunct, (*v*) clean, sprinkle, spray, wipe, spread, scatter, **3**. brush; *synonyms* (*n*) brushwood, clash, collision, conflict, copse, encounter, undergrowth, beard, (*v*) broom, graze,

touch, kiss, rub, scour, (*adj*) rake, **4**. shake; *synonyms* (*v*) beat, agitate, jar, brandish, disturb, excite, flutter, totter, wag, (*n*) tremble, jolt, quiver, wave, trembling, (*adj*) quake, **5**. sweep; *synonyms* (*n*) compass, expanse, range, scope, field, stretch, area, room, (*v*) reach, sail, sway, shot, cross, (*adj*) curve, comb, **6**. wipe; *synonyms* (*v*) mop, towel, scrub, dry, wash, cover, (*n*) fling, flout, gibe, gleek, hiss, hoot, jeer, (*adj*) sponge, flush.

taeaki 1. brushed; *synonyms* (*adj*) fleecy, napped, **2**. cleaned; *synonyms* (*adj*) cleansed, spick-and-span, (*n*) curried, prepared, **3**. faced, **4**. swept, **5**. shaken; *synonyms* (*v*) broken, lame, passe, shaky, threadbare, wilted, shattered, stale, (*adj*) jolted, dazed, disconcerted, fallen, scared, stunned, surprised.

taeare 1. exhausted; *synonyms* (*v*) weak, (*adj*) drained, fatigued, spent, tired, gone, dry, beat, depleted, empty, enervated, faint, jaded, weary, expended; *antonyms* (*adj*) energetic, fresh, refreshed, strong, **2**. ruined; *synonyms* (*v*) lost, undone, (*adj*) destroyed, dilapidated, broke, broken, desolate, bankrupt, desolated, devastated, finished, insolvent, ravaged, spoiled, beaten; *antonyms* (*adj*) untarnished, solvent, first-rate, pure.

taeba undress; *synonyms* (*v*) disrobe, strip, unclothe, discase, divest, doff, unrobe, uncase, (*n*) dishabille, disarray; *antonym* (*v*) dress.

taebai 1. hijack; *synonyms* (*v*) kidnap, highjack, seize, commandeer, abduct, capture, pirate, snatch, expropriate, (*n*) abduction, **2**. loot; *synonyms* (*n*) plunder, booty, prey, prize, bread, kale, haul, (*v*) pillage, despoil, rifle, foray, ransack, rob, sack, steal, **3**. rob; *synonyms* (*v*) filch, pinch, deprive, pilfer, fleece, lift, purloin, pick, divest, defraud, hook, loot, pluck, strip, thieve, **4**. rifle; *synonyms* (*n*) gun, firearm, (*v*) reave, take, gut, search, go, **5**. pillage; *synonyms* (*n*) depredation, despoliation, spoil, devastation, rape, despoilment, rapine, robbery, (*v*) harry, devastate, maraud, raid, ravage, spoliation, destroy, **6**. shoplift; *synonym* (*v*) burgle, **7**. plunder; *synonyms* (*v*) forage, desolate, poach, spoliate, desecrate, dismantle, (*n*) swag, pillaging, havoc, raven, spoils, theft, damage.

taebaiaki 1. looted; *synonyms* (*adj*) pillaged, plundered, despoiled, ransacked, raped, ravaged, sacked, **2**. pillaged; *synonyms* (*adj*) looted, assaulted, blasted, desolate, desolated, devastated, molested, unpeeled, ruined, wasted, **3**. robed; *synonyms* (*adj*) appareled, attired, clothed, dressed, garbed, garmented, habilimented, fixed, polished, vested, **4**. rifled, **5**. plundered; *synonym* (*adj*) fleeced.

taebaki undressed; *synonyms* (*adj*) nude, naked, unclad, unclothed, bare, raw, unappareled, unattired; *antonyms* (*adj*) dressed, covered.

taebo 1. eager; *synonyms* *(adj)* avid, desirous, ardent, earnest, agog, acute, ambitious, enthusiastic, keen, zealous, industrious, studious, active, burning, craving; *antonyms* *(adj)* indifferent, apathetic, disinterested, unconcerned, **2**. alert; *synonyms* *(adj)* agile, quick, aware, intelligent, lively, vigilant, clever, alive, animated, attentive, bright, brisk, *(v)* awake, *(n)* alarm, alarum; *antonyms* *(adj)* drowsy, inattentive, absentminded, dazed, sleepy, tired, asleep, slow, unalert, unconscious, **3**. hasty; *synonyms* *(adj)* fast, abrupt, cursory, fleet, careless, hurried, impetuous, rash, speedy, sudden, brusque, eager, expeditious, foolhardy, headlong; *antonyms* *(adj)* considered, deliberate, leisurely, sensible, **4**. ardent; *synonyms* *(adj)* fervent, passionate, impassioned, vehement, warm, affectionate, devoted, fervid, fiery, flaming, glowing, heated, hot, intense, perfervid.

taebu vivid; *synonyms* *(adj)* graphic, intense, brilliant, lifelike, rich, live, acute, animated, clear, colorful, glowing, strong, picturesque, expressive, *(v)* bright; *antonym* *(adj)* dull.

taeka 1. detach; *synonyms* *(v)* disengage, divide, part, disconnect, disentangle, dissociate, remove, separate, unhook, isolate, abstract, cleave, disjoin, divorce, *(n)* detail; *antonyms* *(v)* attach, fasten, add, associate, **2**. partake; *synonyms* *(v)* deal, participate, share, touch, consume, taste, communicate, imbibe, **3**. uproot; *synonyms* *(v)* eradicate, extirpate, deracinate, exterminate, dislodge, displace, move, eliminate, pull, grub, transplant; *antonym* *(v)* plant, **4**. separate; *synonyms* *(adj)* detached, individual, particular, single, *(v)* detach, insulate, scatter, cut, discrete, discriminate, disperse, distinguish, demarcate, break, differentiate; *antonyms* *(adj)* connected, joined, simultaneous, *(v)* unite, merge, mix, combine, fuse, join, link.

taekai tie; *synonyms* *(n)* band, connection, draw, lace, association, relationship, sleeper, *(v)* link, bond, attach, bind, join, knot, connect, fasten; *antonyms* *(v)* disconnect, untie, undo.

taekaiaki tied; *synonyms* *(adj)* fastened, connected, even, fixed, laced, united, attached, binding, buttoned, joined, legato, liable, mixed, powerless, responsible; *antonym* *(adj)* separate.

taekaki 1. detached; *synonyms* *(adj)* aloof, cool, isolated, separate, distinct, disconnected, disinterested, dispassionate, impartial, indifferent, neutral, objective, remote, separated, unconcerned; *antonyms* *(adj)* attached, involved, engrossed, warm, **2**. separated; *synonyms* *(adj)* apart, detached, divided, disjointed, free, disjunct, removed, dislocated, independent, lone, single, *(prep)* disjoined.

taekeke shrill; *synonyms* *(adj)* piercing, sharp, penetrating, strident, keen, shrewd, grating,

vociferous, *(v)* acute, high, screech, shriek, scream, yell, screak; *antonyms* *(adj)* soft, low.

taekina 1. narrate; *synonyms* *(v)* tell, relate, describe, recite, recount, report, express, inform, rehearse, state, detail, depict, explain, recapitulate, represent, **2**. mention; *synonyms* *(v)* cite, name, hint, observe, commend, adduce, advert, note, notice, *(n)* comment, allusion, citation, remark, call, reference, **3**. tell; *synonyms* *(v)* declare, divulge, impart, reveal, announce, command, communicate, distinguish, enumerate, instruct, notify, order, *(n)* disclose, count, number; *antonym* *(v)* request, **4**. relate; *synonyms* *(v)* connect, narrate, associate, link, appertain, apply, pertain, refer, concern, repeat, tie, affect, interrelate, convey, mention, **5**. predicate; *synonyms* *(n)* say, *(v)* affirm, assert, allege, base, connote, found, imply, establish, ground, proclaim, preach, *(adj)* predicative.

taekinaki related; *synonyms* *(adj)* germane, kindred, cognate, relevant, similar, akin, allied, associated, collateral, connected, consanguineous, pertinent, like, near, analogous; *antonym* *(adj)* unrelated.

taenako detached; *synonyms* *(adj)* aloof, cool, isolated, separate, distinct, disconnected, disinterested, dispassionate, impartial, indifferent, neutral, objective, remote, separated, unconcerned; *antonyms* *(adj)* attached, involved, engrossed, warm.

taenakoa chase; *synonyms* *(n)* game, search, quest, *(v)* hunt, pursue, expel, follow, stalk, track, trail, chamfer, pursuit, race, seek, evict.

taenakoaki chased; *synonyms* *(adj)* engraved, *(n)* pursued.

taenananga 1. crumbling; *synonyms* *(adj)* moldering, dilapidated, ramshackle, rotten, aging, blistering, *(v)* tainted, waterlogged, *(n)* collapse, ruin, decay, disintegration, fragmentation, breakdown, breakup, **2**. peeling; *synonyms* *(adj)* flaking, cracking, crumbling, crusty, detaching, encrusted, rough, *(n)* peel, desquamation, shelling, hull, skiving, bark, shedding, scalping; *antonym* *(adj)* smooth, **3**. shredded; *synonyms* *(adj)* sliced, chopped, ragged, broken, *(adv)* asunder.

taenang 1. relieved; *synonyms* *(adj)* alleviated, eased, thankful, cheerful, comfortable, delighted, fresh, happy, joyful, pleased, prominent, **2**. uplifted; *synonyms* *(adj)* elevated, high, raised, alert, animated, bold, confident, dignified, elate, eminent, erect, grand, haughty, lofty, noble, **3**. unburdened; *synonyms* *(adj)* disburdened, burdenless, clear, devoid, empty, free, hollow, open, unembarrassed, unfruitful, unsatisfactory, unsubstantial, vain; *antonym* *(adj)* burdened.

taenangina ready; *synonyms* *(adj)* fit, prompt, quick, nimble, apt, deft, disposed, finished, handy, *(v)* prepare, fix, willing, (n) available, dexterous, eager; *antonyms* (adj) unprepared, unwilling.

taenikai 1. defeat; *synonyms* (n) frustration, ruin, beating, (v) crush, overcome, beat, conquer, abolish, baffle, foil, overpower, repulse, rout, subdue, (adj) rebuff; *antonyms* (n) victory, success, win, (v) lose, surrender, **2**. vanquish; *synonyms* (v) defeat, subjugate, overthrow, thrash, surmount, trounce, drub, lick, overmaster, overwhelm, discomfit, whip, triumph, master, get.

taenikaia 1. disarm; *synonyms* (v) unarm, disable, disqualify, invalidate, demilitarise, demilitarize, (n) propitiate, (adj) conciliate; *antonym* (v) arm, **2**. defeat; *synonyms* (n) frustration, ruin, beating, (v) crush, overcome, beat, conquer, abolish, baffle, foil, overpower, repulse, rout, subdue, (adj) rebuff; *antonyms* (n) victory, success, win, (v) lose, surrender, **3**. conquest; *synonyms* (n) conquering, defeat, triumph, achievement, reduction, coup, mastery, occupation, overthrow, subjection, subjugation, expugnation, **4**. vanquish; *synonyms* (v) subjugate, thrash, surmount, trounce, drub, lick, overmaster, overwhelm, discomfit, whip, master, get, quell, reduce, tame.

taenikaiaki 1. defeated; *synonyms* (adj) disappointed, frustrated, beaten, discomfited, broken, overcome, baffled, balked, bested, down-and-out, failing, foiled, thwarted, worsted, (n) loser, **2**. succumb; *synonyms* (v) submit, defer, yield, bow, accede, faint, decease, die, go, perish, surrender, capitulate, give, fall, cede; *antonyms* (v) endure, resist.

taenoa 1. hurry; *synonyms* (n) speed, haste, dispatch, flurry, (v) bustle, hasten, accelerate, dash, expedite, scurry, fly, run, rush, zip, hie; *antonyms* (n) slowness, (v) dawdle, **2**. hasten; *synonyms* (v) further, forward, advance, hurry, dart, facilitate, precipitate, race, gallop, sprint, drive, hotfoot, (adj) quicken, course, go; *antonym* (v) delay, **3**. urgent; *synonyms* (adj) pressing, importunate, imperative, instant, immediate, quick, earnest, critical, serious, vital, hasty, insistent, compelling, (v) important, clamorous; *antonym* (adj) trivial.

taenoaki hurried; *synonyms* (adj) hasty, fast, headlong, quick, rapid, speedy, sudden, swift, abrupt, cursory, careless, precipitate, prompt, rash, slapdash; *antonyms* (adj) slow, unhurried, leisurely.

taera 1. lop; *synonyms* (v) cut, crop, hew, chop, dress, poll, prune, sever, trim, truncate, curtail, hack, amputate, (adj) clip, dock, **2**. correct; *synonyms* (adj) right, accurate, appropriate, becoming, nice, precise, proper, (v) adjust, amend, castigate, chastise, chasten, better, remedy, (n) true; *antonyms* (adj) incorrect, false, faulty, inappropriate, mistaken, improper, (v) wrong, spoil, **3**. trim; *synonyms* (adj) tidy, neat, spruce, orderly, shipshape, smart, trig, (v) garnish, shave,

adorn, embellish, lop, reduce, shorten, snip; *antonym* (adj) fat, **4**. prune; *synonyms* (v) pare, abbreviate, shear, abridge, edit, lower, thin, top, **5**. remove; *synonyms* (v) oust, take, pull, eject, expel, deduct, discharge, strip, delete, erase, evacuate, extract, abolish, get, (adj) clear; *antonyms* (v) insert, install, place.

taerake 1. denude; *synonyms* (v) bare, strip, denudate, deprive, despoil, dismantle, disrobe, divest, expose, uncover, undress, **2**. strand; *synonyms* (n) coast, shore, rope, chain, filament, line, string, bank, thread, wisp, yarn, (v) beach, maroon, desert, abandon.

taerakeaki 1. denuded; *synonyms* (adj) bare, naked, bald, denudate, exposed, barefaced, barren, bleak, devoid, desolate, marginal, nude, scanty, spare, (v) minus, **2**. stranded; *synonyms* (adj) abandoned, isolated, marooned, wrecked, stuck, (v) aground, beached, accursed, devoted, doomed, grounded, lost, (n) graveled, nonplussed.

taeraki 1. corrected; *synonyms* (adj) chastised, amended, reformed, altered, chastened, disciplined, educated, refined, **2**. depicted; *synonyms* (v) depict, (adj) pictured, portrayed, graphic, envisioned, visualised, visualized, **3**. removed; *synonyms* (adj) distant, remote, separate, far, detached, abstracted, absent, apart, aloof, outlying, separated, **4**. pruned, **5**. trimmed; *synonyms* (adj) cut, cunning, demure, down, emasculated, gashed, gelded, level, mown, neat, shortened, slashed, sly, smooth, snoD.

taeremea 1. aimless; *synonyms* (adj) purposeless, random, capricious, desultory, meaningless, pointless, afloat, empty, haphazard, vagabond, (adv) adrift, **2**. nonchalant; *synonyms* (adj) negligent, careless, indifferent, insouciant, unconcerned, carefree, casual, calm, cool, offhand, easygoing; *antonym* (adj) anxious, **3**. casual; *synonyms* (adj) accidental, adventitious, chance, irregular, nonchalant, occasional, coincidental, contingent, cursory, easy, fortuitous, lax, passing, temporary, light; *antonyms* (adj) deliberate, formal, thorough, **4**. insouciant; *synonyms* (adj) pococurante, lackadaisical, phlegmatic, happy-go-lucky, effortless, everyday, fooling, gay, lighthearted, listless, airy, buoyant, jaunty, light-hearted, perfunctory, **5**. incidental; *synonyms* (adj) collateral, attendant, concomitant, episodic, incident, extraneous, odd, side, causeless, indirect, secondary, subsidiary, accompanying; *antonym* (adj) concrete, **6**. offhand; *synonyms* (adj) curt, extemporaneous, impromptu, extemporary, cavalier, brusque, abrupt, improvised, rude, offhanded, short, brisk, gruff, (adv) extempore, offhandedly, **7**. purposeless; *synonyms* (adj) senseless, useless, driftless, directionless, objectless, designless, (adv) aimless; *antonym* (adj) purposeful,

8. unpremeditated; *synonyms* *(adj)* inadvertent, spontaneous, involuntary, unintentional, impulsive; *antonym* *(adj)* premeditated.

taerieri 1. smart; *synonyms* *(adj)* bright, crafty, dapper, quick, shrewd, sly, prompt, astute, chic, clever, intelligent, *(v)* ache, hurt, *(n)* pain, sharp; *antonyms* *(adj)* scruffy, stupid, dim, shabby, unkempt, slow, **2**. tingle; *synonyms* *(n)* thrill, tremble, twitter, tingling, chill, frisson, prickling, quiver, *(v)* itch, prickle, tickle, smart, sting, burn, creep.

taerina 1. sudden; *synonyms* *(adj)* abrupt, hasty, precipitous, quick, rash, unexpected, steep, dramatic, headlong, immediate, precipitate, sharp, swift, unforeseen, impulsive; *antonyms* *(adj)* gradual, considered, **2**. rapid; *synonyms* *(adj)* fast, prompt, agile, fleet, speedy, cursory, expeditious, sudden, nimble, winged, express, hurried, instant, brisk, impetuous; *antonym* *(adj)* slow.

taeririaki hurried; *synonyms* *(adj)* hasty, fast, headlong, quick, rapid, speedy, sudden, swift, abrupt, cursory, careless, precipitate, prompt, rash, slapdash; *antonyms* *(adj)* slow, unhurried, leisurely.

taetae 1. exclaim; *synonyms* *(v)* cry, call, shout, clamor, outcry, scream, speak, vociferate, yell, declare, utter, **2**. address; *synonyms* *(n)* accost, lecture, abode, discourse, residence, skill, speech, allocution, greeting, oration, sermon, talk, *(v)* greet, harangue, aim; *antonym* *(v)* ignore, **3**. talk; *synonyms* *(v)* gossip, converse, chatter, address, articulate, chat, prattle, prate, rap, babble, *(n)* language, colloquy, conversation, dialogue, palaver, **4**. speak; *synonyms* *(v)* express, pronounce, deliver, say, recite, emit, mouth, state, vocalize, voice, mumble, declaim, read, reason, *(adj)* disclose, **5**. spoke; *synonyms* *(n)* bar, radius, rung, clog, line, rule, rundle, shoe, skid, **6**. say; *synonyms* *(v)* remark, assert, enunciate, observe, maintain, order, tell, guess, relate, dictate, command, narrate, affirm, allege, aver, **7**. spoken; *synonyms* *(adj)* oral, verbal, expressed, speaking, unwritten, vocal, voiced; *antonyms* *(adj)* written, unspoken, tacit.

taetaebuaka swear; *synonyms* *(v)* affirm, assert, assure, curse, declare, avow, depone, depose, pledge, attest, asseverate, insist, *(n)* promise, aver, avouch.

taetaeraia threaten; *synonyms* *(v)* menace, bully, endanger, intimidate, loom, offer, imperil, jeopardize, peril, approach, foreshadow, portend, browbeat, impend, *(n)* threat; *antonym* *(v)* help.

taetoa smooth; *synonyms* *(adj)* easy, calm, level, oily, facile, flat, flowing, fluent, fluid, glossy, graceful, greasy, *(v)* quiet, facilitate, even; *antonyms* *(adj)* rough, uneven, abrasive, coarse, crumpled, flaking, harsh, jerky, lined, peeling, prickly, ridged, wrinkled, corrugated, *(v)* wrinkle.

taetoba 1. blanched; *synonyms* *(adj)* ashen, colorless, livid, white, bleached, achromatic, afraid, benevolent, bloodless, cadaverous, etiolate, etiolated, faded, fair, lightened, **2**. pale; *synonyms* *(adj)* ghastly, faint, wan, dull, light, pallid, weak, watery, feeble, *(v)* dim, blanch, *(n)* boundary, confine, border, bound; *antonyms* *(adj)* dark, rosy, strong, brown, **3**. wan; *synonyms* *(v)* pale, rueful, *(adj)* sickly, haggard, pasty, sallow, lurid, ashy, thin, deathly, **4**. sickly; *synonyms* *(adj)* infirm, sick, ailing, diseased, indisposed, morbid, poorly, peaked, languid, unhealthy, unwell, valetudinarian, *(n)* invalid, *(v)* frail, low; *antonyms* *(adj)* healthy, bitter, **5**. peaked; *synonyms* *(adj)* acute, pointed, sharp, spiky, ensiform, peaky, salient, gaunt, emaciated, drawn, ill, peakish, piked, run-down, spiked, **6**. sallow.

tagerame 1. disperse; *synonyms* *(v)* dispel, spread, circulate, disband, dissipate, scatter, diffuse, dispense, disseminate, break, disappear, dismiss, broadcast, distribute, propagate; *antonyms* *(v)* assemble, gather, collect, **2**. separate; *synonyms* *(adj)* detached, individual, *(v)* detach, divorce, part, insulate, cut, dissociate, disconnect, discrete, discriminate, disjoin, disperse, distinguish, divide; *antonyms* *(adj)* connected, joined, simultaneous, *(v)* unite, merge, mix, combine, fuse, join, link, associate.

tagerameaki 1. dispersed; *synonyms* *(adj)* diffuse, scattered, sparse, spread, diffused, detached, discrete, fractional, rare, thin, circulated, flowing, isolated, loose, single; *antonym* *(adj)* concentrated, **2**. separated; *synonyms* *(adj)* disconnected, separate, apart, divided, disjointed, free, disjunct, removed, dislocated, independent, lone, *(prep)* disjoined, distinct.

tahahi sun; *synonyms* *(n)* light, sunlight, sunshine, sunn, temperateness, *(adj)* star, *(v)* bask, sunbathe, heat, solarise, solarize.

tahari sea; *synonyms* *(n)* ocean, water, waves, *(adj)* marine, maritime, array, nautical, seagoing, army.

taheia wipe; *synonyms* *(v)* rub, clean, mop, towel, brush, scour, scrub, clear, dry, wash, cover, *(n)* fling, flout, *(adj)* sponge, flush.

tahete understand; *synonyms* *(v)* interpret, recognize, catch, hear, learn, realize, see, appreciate, assume, believe, comprehend, construe, deduce, gather, grasp; *antonyms* *(v)* misinterpret, misconstrue, misunderstand.

tahina 1. sharp; *synonyms* *(adj)* acute, bitter, intelligent, acid, acrid, harsh, incisive, intense, penetrating, piercing, pointed, pungent, quick, *(n)* keen, *(v)* biting; *antonyms* *(adj)* blunt, dull, mild, gentle, rounded, sweet, bland, blurred, naive, round, smooth, **2**. pointed; *synonyms* *(adj)* poignant, piquant, cutting, marked, pithy, acuminate, barbed, prickly, sharp, short, meaningful, fine, thorny, angular, emphatic.

tai 1. not; *synonyms* (*adv*) no, nay, nor, nowise, never, (*adj*) shaven, shorn, **2.** cease; *synonyms* (*v*) end, break, quit, stop, terminate, abstain, close, conclude, discontinue, drop, desist, expire, halt, (*n*) finish, (*adj*) abate; *antonyms* (*v*) continue, begin, **3.** age; *synonyms* (*n*) period, aeon, day, era, time, cycle, years, antiquity, epoch, eternity, generation, (*v*) mature, grow, ripen, develop, **4.** time; *synonyms* (*n*) hour, moment, duration, measure, season, spell, age, instant, interval, space, tempo, sentence, beat, occasion, course; *antonym* (*n*) death, **5.** timed, **6.** stop; *synonyms* (*v*) stand, block, delay, interrupt, obstruct, plug, catch, disrupt, (*n*) hold, stay, check, arrest, bar, cease, curb; *antonyms* (*v*) start, encourage, permit, prolong, **7.** sun; *synonyms* (*n*) light, sunlight, sunshine, sunn, temperateness, (*adj*) star, (*v*) bask, sunbathe, heat, solarise, solarize.

taia 1. harvest; *synonyms* (*n*) crop, fruit, ingathering, produce, profit, yield, (*v*) gain, gather, glean, amass, collect, garner, get, pick, reap, **2.** chip; *synonyms* (*n*) splinter, bit, flake, chipping, fleck, fragment, microchip, part, scrap, shaving, check, (*v*) crack, cut, nick, peel, **3.** reap; *synonyms* (*v*) harvest, obtain, receive, earn, acquire, draw, pluck, attain, achieve, make, win, (*adj*) mow, clip, prune, lop.

taiaganoro 1. lean; *synonyms* (*adj*) emaciated, gaunt, thin, bony, lank, lanky, (*v*) incline, bend, list, slant, bow, careen, pitch, (*n*) tilt, inclination; *antonyms* (*adj*) fat, plump, **2.** diagonal; *synonyms* (*adj*) oblique, aslant, slanting, sloping, aslope, (*n*) bias, slash, solidus, stroke, virgule; *antonym* (*adj*) level, **3.** slant; *synonyms* (*n*) angle, slope, lurch, grade, prejudice, bent, (*v*) lean, bevel, cant, dip, distort, tip, bank, decline, (*adj*) obliquity, **4.** slanted; *synonyms* (*adj*) biased, diagonal, lopsided, skewed, sloped, tilted, askew, **5.** tilt; *synonyms* (*n*) joust, sway, canopy, argument, contention, contestation, controversy, leaning, tilting, inclining, competition, propensity, tournament, (*v*) rock, recline; *antonyms* (*v*) straighten, surrender.

taiaganoroaki 1. slanted; *synonyms* (*adj*) biased, slanting, diagonal, lopsided, oblique, skewed, sloped, sloping, tilted, askew, aslant, aslope, **2.** tilted; *synonyms* (*adj*) canted, leaning, crooked, slanted, atilt, intolerant, opinionated, tipped, uneven, twisted; *antonym* (*adj*) straight.

taiaoka please; *synonyms* (*v*) delight, gratify, amuse, charm, entertain, like, oblige, enchant, enrapture, accommodate, divert, gladden, indulge, (*adj*) enjoy, content; *antonyms* (*v*) displease, annoy, anger, irritate, distress.

taiborana shovel; *synonyms* (*n*) digger, excavator, shovelful, poker, (*v*) dig, scoop, rake, besom, broom, delve, mop.

taie 1. mutate; *synonyms* (*v*) change, alter, transform, vary, modify, turn, metamorphose, adapt, adjust, amend, revise, **2.** importune; *synonyms* (*v*) beg, beseech, implore, entreat, badger, besiege, pester, press, tease, worry, bother, harass, beset, molest, persecute.

taim 1. whet; *synonyms* (*v*) sharpen, excite, grind, quicken, stimulate, stir, hone, (*n*) goad, spur, fillip, provocative, stimulus, incentive, whip, (*adj*) point, **2.** sharpen; *synonyms* (*v*) focus, edge, intensify, sharp, increase, heighten, whet, improve, compound, taper, incite, kindle, (*n*) aim; *antonym* (*v*) cloud.

taima 1. point; *synonyms* (*n*) place, grade, peak, nib, edge, aim, article, degree, dot, mark, spot, phase, (*v*) head, direct, level, **2.** whet; *synonyms* (*v*) sharpen, excite, grind, quicken, stimulate, stir, hone, (*n*) goad, spur, fillip, provocative, stimulus, incentive, whip, (*adj*) point, **3.** sharpen; *synonyms* (*v*) focus, intensify, sharp, increase, heighten, whet, improve, compound, taper, incite, kindle; *antonym* (*v*) cloud.

taimaki sharpened; *synonyms* (*adj*) sharp, acute, acuate, better, sensual.

taina 1. once; *synonyms* (*adv*) formerly, before, erstwhile, previously, already, erst, sometime, when, (*n*) whilom, (*adj*) former, **2.** regulate; *synonyms* (*v*) adjust, arrange, manage, control, direct, order, determine, fix, govern, influence, modulate, regularize, align, check, correct.

tainaki regulated; *synonyms* (*adj*) orderly, ordered, arranged, consistent, lawful, logical, regular, regulatory, temperate, systematic, (*adv*) synchronized.

tairaoi 1. for; *synonyms* (*prep*) because, behind, by, per, during, on, toward, (*conj*) considering, since, (*adv*) against, as, therefore, hence, **2.** pro; *synonyms* (*adj*) veteran, (*n*) expert, professional, specialist, authority, master, (*prep*) for; *antonyms* (*n*) disadvantage, con.

tairik evening; *synonyms* (*n*) even, dusk, dark, eve, eventide, nightfall, sunset, twilight, night, sundown; *antonyms* (*n*) dawn, daybreak.

tairiki 1. eve; *synonyms* (*n*) evening, eventide, apex, cover, nightfall, sunset, top, lid, point, summit, verge, vertex, **2.** evening; *synonyms* (*n*) even, dusk, dark, eve, twilight, night, sundown; *antonyms* (*n*) dawn, daybreak.

tairo blazing; *synonyms* (*adj*) ablaze, afire, burning, flaming, ardent, aflame, alight, blatant, bright, glaring, blistering, conspicuous, fervent, fierce, (*n*) blaze.

taitai 1. cut; *synonyms* (*v*) carve, chop, clip, abbreviate, abridge, bite, condense, crop, drop, fashion, (n) notch, slice, cutting, nick, blow; *antonyms* (v) increase, lengthen, (n) addition, extension, **2**. tattoo; *synonym* (v) drumroll.

taitaiaki cut; *synonyms* (v) carve, chop, clip, abbreviate, abridge, bite, condense, crop, drop, fashion, (n) notch, slice, cutting, nick, blow; *antonyms* (v) increase, lengthen, (n) addition, extension.

taitaim sharpen; *synonyms* (v) focus, edge, hone, intensify, point, sharp, increase, heighten, whet, improve, compound, stimulate, taper, incite, (n) aim; *antonym* (v) cloud.

taitaima whet; *synonyms* (v) sharpen, excite, grind, quicken, stimulate, stir, hone, (n) goad, spur, fillip, provocative, stimulus, incentive, whip, (adj) point.

taitaimaki sharpened; *synonyms* (adj) sharp, acute, acuate, better, sensual.

tak 1. speech; *synonyms* (n) address, delivery, expression, lecture, conversation, discourse, language, sermon, diction, communication, discussion, elocution, converse, (v) say, saying, **2**. talk; *synonyms* (v) gossip, chatter, articulate, chat, prattle, speak, prate, rap, babble, parley, (n) colloquy, dialogue, palaver, speech, parlance, **3**. saying; *synonyms* (v) proverb, (n) maxim, axiom, adage, saw, phrase, aphorism, byword, dictum, idiom, motto, locution, apothegm, declaration, cliché.

taka 1. dry; *synonyms* (adj) thirsty, arid, barren, boring, dehydrated, dull, bald, hoarse, jejune, plain, (v) dehydrate, desiccate, drain, uninteresting, sardonic; *antonyms* (adj) wet, damp, moist, saturated, soaked, boggy, drenched, rainy, sodden, interesting, fresh, humid, juicy, succulent, (v) drench, **2**. arid; *synonyms* (adj) dry, parched, sterile, tedious, unproductive, acarpous, desert, desiccated, droughty, humdrum, infertile, insipid, unfruitful, waterless, (v) monotonous; *antonym* (adj) verdant, **3**. very; *synonyms* (adv) extremely, greatly, highly, really, completely, entirely, most, quite, truly, actually, too, awfully, (adj) much, identical, (n) self; *antonyms* (adv) abysmally, slightly, somewhat, **4**. thirsty; *synonyms* (adj) eager, avid, keen, athirst, greedy, absorbent, ambitious, (v) craving, hungry.

takaarua 1. yell; *synonyms* (n) shout, roar, scream, call, outcry, screech, exclamation, (v) cry, howl, bellow, whoop, shriek, bawl, exclaim, holler, **2**. scream; *synonyms* (n) wail, riot, hum, screaming, screeching, shrieking, (v) yell, hollo, halloo, yelp, yowl, moan, laugh, ring, squall; *antonym* (v) whisper, **3**. shout; *synonyms* (v) clamor, hail, bark, hoop, proclaim, chant, acclaim, abuse, blackguard, clapperclaw, (n) cheer, crow, vociferation, chuckle, giggle.

takabea chatterbox; *synonyms* (n) chatterer, babbler, gossip, talker, cackler, busybody, communicator, conversationalist, spouter, cotinga, mouth, raconteur.

takaburi 1. ooze; *synonyms* (n) mire, muck, slime, (v) exude, leak, dribble, seep, drain, drop, bleed, emit, filter, secrete, sweat, (adj) mud, **2**. overflow; *synonyms* (n) flood, deluge, inundation, excess, flooding, outpouring, runoff, torrent, affluence, (v) inundate, flow, drown, fill, overrun, submerge.

takabwewebwere 1. comfortable; *synonyms* (adj) cozy, easy, agreeable, pleased, pleasing, prosperous, congenial, pleasurable, rich, enjoyable, commodious, content, contented, (v) snug, calm; *antonyms* (adj) uncomfortable, poor, formal, tense, unpleasant, intimidating, unaccustomed, unhappy, **2**. content; *synonyms* (n) capacity, contentment, matter, meaning, subject, substance, contentedness, (adj) happy, fulfilled, (v) appease, please, satisfy, suffice, delight, gratify; *antonyms* (adj) tormented, discontented, dissatisfied, rebellious, (v) discontent, upset, **3**. prosperous; *synonyms* (adj) lucky, auspicious, flourishing, favorable, opulent, advantageous, affluent, comfortable, palmy, successful, thriving, well-off, propitious, booming, (n) fortunate.

takaeakina 1. bellow; *synonyms* (n) roar, shout, cry, yell, scream, bay, screech, (v) growl, bawl, snarl, call, howl, holler, shriek, whoop, **2**. bark; *synonyms* (n) yelp, rind, crust, peel, boat, barque, coat, cortex, covering, shell, (v) yap, skin, bellow, cough, scrape; *antonyms* (v) mutter, whisper, **3**. shout; *synonyms* (v) clamor, exclaim, hollo, hail, bark, hoop, proclaim, chant, acclaim, (n) cheer, halloo, outcry, exclamation, wail, crow, **4**. proclaim; *synonyms* (v) announce, assert, declare, advertise, broadcast, enunciate, herald, promulgate, decree, divulge, notify, celebrate, avow, circulate, demonstrate.

takaeakinaki proclaimed; *synonyms* (adj) declared, announced, indictive, public.

takaere 1. hit; *synonyms* (v) strike, attain, belt, blow, bump, collide, encounter, (n) knock, bang, smash, touch, chance, bash, beat, collision; *antonyms* (n) failure, flop, **2**. cut; *synonyms* (v) carve, chop, clip, abbreviate, abridge, bite, condense, crop, drop, fashion, (n) notch, slice, cutting, nick, gash; *antonyms* (v) increase, lengthen, (n) addition, extension, **3**. struggle; *synonyms* (n) contest, battle, combat, conflict, strain, effort, exertion, scramble, scuffle, (v) fight, attempt, dispute, endeavor, labor, quarrel; *antonyms* (v) flourish, glide.

takaereaki 1. cut; *synonyms* (v) carve, chop, clip, abbreviate, abridge, bite, condense, crop, drop, fashion, (n) notch, slice, cutting, nick, blow; *antonyms* (v) increase, lengthen, (n) addition, extension, **2**. hit; *synonyms* (*v*) strike, attain, belt, bump, collide, encounter, (*n*) knock, bang, smash, touch, chance, bash, beat, collision, play; *antonyms* (*n*) failure, flop.

takaerere 1. nimble; *synonyms* (*adj*) active, adroit, agile, lively, brisk, spry, alert, clever, energetic, expeditious, lithe, quick, deft, lissome, (*v*) light; *antonym* (*adj*) clumsy, **2**. expeditious; *synonyms* (*adj*) prompt, swift, fast, hasty, rapid, speedy, fleet, immediate, nimble, ready, punctual; *antonym* (*adj*) slow, **3**. quick; *synonyms* (*adj*) bright, intelligent, alive, cursory, dexterous, hurried, instant, keen, brief, abrupt, acute, animated, apt, ingenious, sharp; *antonyms* (*adj*) leisurely, dull, **4**. violent; *synonyms* (*adj*) fierce, rough, tempestuous, intense, raging, severe, turbulent, vehement, passionate, powerful, savage, stormy, strong, (*n*) furious, boisterous; *antonyms* (*adj*) gentle, peaceful, calm, nonviolent, **5**. sudden; *synonyms* (*adj*) precipitous, rash, unexpected, steep, dramatic, headlong, precipitate, unforeseen, impulsive, instantaneous, impetuous, fleeting, surprising, momentary, (*adv*) suddenly; *antonyms* (*adj*) gradual, considered, **6**. rapid; *synonyms* (*adj*) sudden, winged, express, volant, **7**. thrash; *synonyms* (*v*) flog, lash, beat, defeat, pound, whip, baste, clobber, drub, lam, lick, whack, batter, bang, bat.

takaka 1. bark; *synonyms* (*n*) snarl, yelp, rind, bay, crust, peel, shout, boat, (*v*) yap, skin, cry, growl, roar, bellow, cough; *antonyms* (*v*) mutter, whisper, **2**. clamor; *synonyms* (*n*) din, noise, exclamation, hubbub, racket, uproar, clamoring, demand, disturbance, exclaim, (*v*) outcry, clamour, hullabaloo, blare, bawl, **3**. proclaim; *synonyms* (*v*) announce, assert, declare, advertise, broadcast, enunciate, herald, promulgate, decree, divulge, notify, call, celebrate, avow, circulate, **4**. shout; *synonyms* (*v*) clamor, scream, hollo, howl, shriek, hail, bark, holler, hoop, whoop, (*n*) yell, cheer, halloo, screech, wail.

takakaki proclaimed; *synonyms* (*adj*) declared, announced, indictive, public.

takanakana dirty; *synonyms* (*adj*) foul, dirt, contemptible, bawdy, contaminated, dingy, impure, despicable, (*v*) muddy, corrupt, soil, contaminate, begrime, bemire, (*n*) defile; *antonyms* (*adj*) hygienic, pure, spotless, immaculate, (*v*) clean.

takanana slimy; *synonyms* (*adj*) greasy, slippery, muddy, squalid, oily, oozy, ropy, viscous, slimed.

takaneanea 1. dazzling; *synonyms* (*adj*) bright, brilliant, blinding, glaring, splendid, vivid, fulgent, resplendent, sparkling, striking, stunning, blazing, beautiful, flamboyant, garish; *antonym* (*adj*) dull, **2**. brilliant; *synonyms* (*adj*) glorious, illustrious, intelligent, luminous, magnificent, spectacular, sunny, brainy, diamond, gaudy, gifted, impressive, incandescent, (*v*) smart, (*n*) jewel; *antonyms* (*adj*)

dim, awful, dark, **3**. sparkling; *synonyms* (*adj*) lively, effervescent, radiant, bubbly, glittering, glittery, scintillant, scintillating, shining, bubbling, dazzling, fizzy, (*n*) sparkle, scintillation, glitter; *antonym* (*adj*) still, **4**. resplendent; *synonyms* (*adj*) gorgeous, effulgent, glowing, lustrous, refulgent, clear, showy, silver, (*n*) lucid.

takarea 1. spread; *synonyms* (*v*) scatter, reach, disperse, expand, extend, broadcast, circulate, diffuse, disseminate, increase, propagate, stretch, broaden, deploy, (*n*) span; *antonym* (*adj*) concentrated, **2**. scattered; *synonyms* (*adj*) dispersed, dissipated, confused, disconnected, disordered, sparse, sporadic, thin, distributed, rare, separate, spread, stray, strewn, disjointed.

takareau webbed; *synonyms* (*adj*) lacy, netlike, netted, keld, lacelike, palmated, webby, weblike.

takarebu 1. agitated; *synonyms* (*adj*) restless, excited, nervous, restive, tumultuous, upset, distressed, tense, alarmed, anxious, distraught, jumpy, overwrought, perturbed, shaken; *antonyms* (*adj*) calm, composed, lethargic, **2**. restless; *synonyms* (*adj*) fidgety, uneasy, unquiet, agitated, apprehensive, fretful, impatient, feverish, turbulent, disturbed, edgy, wakeful, eager, hasty, mercurial; *antonym* (*adj*) relaxed, **3**. shaken; *synonyms* (*v*) broken, lame, passe, shaky, threadbare, wilted, shattered, stale, (*adj*) jolted, dazed, disconcerted, fallen, scared, stunned, surprised.

takareburebu slop; *synonyms* (*n*) pigwash, swill, slops, pigswill, (*v*) overflow, spill, splash, slosh, smudge, splatter, (*adj*) filth, dabble, dirt, soil.

takareburebuaki slopped; *synonyms* (*adj*) besotted, addlebrained, addlepated, affluent, annoyed, blotto, buckram, close, cockeyed, compressed, crocked, drenched, dunked, flush, fuddled.

takarebutata 1. agitate; *synonyms* (*v*) disturb, stir, toss, fan, bother, foment, perturb, rouse, shake, trouble, actuate, annoy, arouse, canvass, convulse; *antonyms* (*v*) calm, soothe, **2**. stir; *synonyms* (*v*) budge, move, affect, agitate, excite, inspire, go, cause, (*n*) movement, commotion, disturbance, excitement, agitation, fuss, (*adj*) bustle, **3**. struggle; *synonyms* (*n*) contest, battle, combat, conflict, strain, effort, exertion, scramble, scuffle, (*v*) fight, attempt, dispute, endeavor, labor, quarrel; *antonyms* (*v*) flourish, glide.

takarebutataki 1. agitated; *synonyms* (*adj*) restless, excited, nervous, restive, tumultuous, upset, distressed, tense, alarmed, anxious, distraught, jumpy, overwrought, perturbed, shaken; *antonyms* (*adj*) calm, composed, lethargic, **2**. stirred; *synonyms* (*adj*) stimulated, affected, aroused, emotional, aflame, ablaze, beaten, enthused, horny, inspired, interested, randy, ruttish, susceptible, touched; *antonym* (*adj*) uninspired.

takarebwetata 1. crepitate; *synonyms* (*v*) crackle, rump, creak, rustle, scranch, scraunch, snap, **2.** crackle; *synonyms* (*n*) crackling, crepitation, (*v*) crack, crepitate, crunch, sputter.

takarebwetataki crackled; *synonyms* (*adj*) cracked, alligatored, balmy, barmy, bats, batty, bonkers, buggy, chapped, crackers, crazed, daft, deranged, dotty, fruity.

takarema 1. flutter; *synonyms* (*n*) bustle, flap, wave, waver, agitation, excitement, quiver, (*v*) flicker, beat, flit, flitter, palpitate, fly, (*adj*) flurry, fluster, **2.** struggle; *synonyms* (*n*) contest, battle, combat, conflict, strain, effort, exertion, scramble, scuffle, (*v*) fight, attempt, dispute, endeavor, labor, quarrel; *antonyms* (*v*) flourish, glide.

takaremwaremwa fidget; *synonyms* (*v*) wriggle, squirm, wiggle, fiddle, (*n*) fidgetiness, restlessness, (*adj*) bustle, bother, fuss, hurry, stir, ado, drive.

takaremwermwe 1. slow; *synonyms* (*adj*) dull, late, easy, sluggish, heavy, dense, dim, gradual, inactive, indolent, lazy, stupid, (*v*) slack, (*adv*) behind, behindhand; *antonyms* (*adj*) fast, intelligent, rapid, bright, alert, brisk, hasty, prompt, quick, speedy, hurried, observant, rushed, (*v*) accelerate, **2.** tardy; *synonyms* (*adj*) backward, belated, dilatory, remiss, overdue, delayed, lagging, reluctant, procrastinating, (*v*) slow, recent.

takarere 1. famous; *synonyms* (*adj*) celebrated, eminent, splendid, distinguished, famed, illustrious, renowned, capital, conspicuous, important, known, notable, notorious, prominent, stunning; *antonyms* (*adj*) unknown, infamous, ordinary, **2.** eminent; *synonyms* (*adj*) high, elevated, brilliant, big, famous, noble, dignified, exalted, grand, great, noted, signal, sublime, first, chief, **3.** leading; *synonyms* (*adj*) main, outstanding, head, dominant, foremost, principal, best, central, major, paramount, (*n*) cardinal, lead, leadership, primary, (*adv*) ahead; *antonym* (*adj*) minor, **4.** conspicuous; *synonyms* (*adj*) clear, apparent, blatant, manifest, marked, obvious, visible, blazing, bold, distinct, evident, flagrant, glaring, noticeable, open; *antonyms* (*adj*) inconspicuous, unobtrusive, **5.** isolated; *synonyms* (*adj*) detached, apart, deserted, separate, distant, desolate, insular, lone, lonely, lonesome, remote, separated, single, solitary, sporadic; *antonym* (*adj*) inhabited, **6.** notable; *synonyms* (*adj*) extraordinary, memorable, remarkable, noteworthy, salient, significant, striking, worthy, impressive, momentous, glorious, excellent, (*n*) celebrity, luminary, notability; *antonym* (*adj*) insignificant, **7.** evident; *synonyms* (*adj*) discernible, patent, plain, certain, bright, palpable, perceptible, tangible, unequivocal, unmistakable, observable, broad, demonstrable, candid, pronounced; *antonyms* (*adj*) unclear, concealed,

obscure, unnoticed, hidden, **8.** distinguished; *synonyms* (*adj*) reputable, superior, considerable, ace, lofty, majestic, preeminent, recognized, shining, swell, unusual, **9.** known; *synonyms* (*adj*) well-known, familiar, conscious, accepted, acknowledged, published, understood, aware, common, apprised, approved, assured, broadcast, documented, felt; *antonyms* (*adj*) nameless, secret, unidentified, **10.** obvious; *synonyms* (*adj*) undeniable, definite, explicit, gross, indisputable, indubitable, lucid, overt, barefaced, intelligible, luminous, downright, absolute, axiomatic, exposed; *antonyms* (*adj*) imperceptible, undetectable, slight, subtle, **11.** prominent; *synonyms* (*adj*) leading, predominant, influential, obtrusive, handsome, star, popular, demonstrative, (*n*) brave, abrupt, courageous, daring, impudent, (*v*) projecting, convex, **12.** outstanding; *synonyms* (*adj*) due, owing, exceptional, unpaid, magnificent, overdue, superb, superlative, wonderful, dazzling, phenomenal, singular, special, terrific, top; *antonyms* (*adj*) paid, inferior, **13.** solitary; *synonyms* (*adj*) forlorn, alone, only, sole, unaccompanied, isolated, secluded, one, forsaken, private, individual, retired, unique, (*n*) hermit, recluse.

takariri 1. jitter; *synonyms* (*n*) flicker, (*v*) fidget, quiver, tremble, shudder, dance, quake, **2.** shudder; *synonyms* (*n*) shake, quivering, shivering, chill, frisson, tremor, twitch, palpitation, (*v*) shiver, dither, flutter, thrill, jolt, shrink, pulsate.

takariroriro 1. frisky; *synonyms* (*adj*) brisk, playful, lively, coltish, perky, frolicsome, kittenish, tricksy, **2.** fidgety; *synonyms* (*adj*) restless, fretful, fussy, unquiet, anxious, hasty, jumpy, mercurial, restive, skittish, tense, uneasy, (*n*) nervous, apprehensive, tremulous, **3.** wriggling; *synonyms* (*adj*) squirming, wiggling, writhing, twisting, wiggly, wriggle, flexible, frisky, pliant, sinuate, sinuous, tortuous, twisty, winding, wriggly.

takariuriu thrash; *synonyms* (*v*) flog, lash, beat, defeat, pound, whip, baste, clobber, drub, lam, lick, whack, batter, bang, bat.

takaro 1. inflame; *synonyms* (*v*) burn, fire, enkindle, arouse, heat, ignite, incense, incite, irritate, kindle, agitate, aggravate, anger, chafe, enrage; *antonym* (*v*) calm, **2.** kindle; *synonyms* (*v*) excite, inflame, awaken, flame, animate, provoke, stimulate, stir, glow, cause, illuminate, elicit, evoke, raise, (*n*) light, **3.** smoulder; *synonyms* (*v*) smolder, choke, suffocate, **4.** spark; *synonyms* (*n*) flicker, glimmer, arc, blaze, scintilla, scintillation, shimmer, (*v*) flash, sparkle, gleam, glint, glitter, activate, glisten, trigger.

takaroaki 1. inflamed; *synonyms* (*adj*) sore, impassioned, excited, angry, ablaze, flaming, hot, irritated, passionate, burning, painful, (n) red, **2.** kindled; *synonyms* (adj) ignited, enkindled.

takarokaro glow; *synonyms* (n) beam, color, glare, sparkle, blaze, flash, (v) blush, flush, gleam, glimmer, shine, burn, flare, fire, flame; *antonym* (n) dullness.

takaroro 1. dry; *synonyms* (adj) thirsty, arid, barren, boring, dehydrated, dull, bald, hoarse, jejune, plain, (v) dehydrate, desiccate, drain, uninteresting, sardonic; *antonyms* (adj) wet, damp, moist, saturated, soaked, boggy, drenched, rainy, sodden, interesting, fresh, humid, juicy, succulent, (v) drench, **2.** arid; *synonyms* (adj) dry, parched, sterile, tedious, unproductive, acarpous, desert, desiccated, droughty, humdrum, infertile, insipid, unfruitful, waterless, (v) monotonous; *antonym* (adj) verdant, **3.** thirsty; *synonyms* (adj) eager, avid, keen, athirst, greedy, absorbent, ambitious, (v) craving, hungry.

takarua 1. manageable; *synonyms* (adj) easy, docile, flexible, malleable, ductile, handy, gentle, controllable, pliable, tame, portable, wieldy, (v) governable, tractable; *antonyms* (adj) unwieldy, awkward, unbearable, uncontrollable, unmanageable, fixed, **2.** flexible; *synonyms* (adj) elastic, adaptable, yielding, lissome, pliant, soft, supple, facile, adjustable, bendable, compliant, flexile, lithe, variable, versatile; *antonyms* (adj) inflexible, rigid, obstinate, stiff, stubborn, **3.** changeable; *synonyms* (adj) capricious, erratic, inconsistent, irregular, fickle, giddy, mercurial, mobile, mutable, slippery, temperamental, uncertain, unsettled, unstable, volatile; *antonyms* (adj) constant, stable, unchangeable, consistent, dependable, predictable, regular, **4.** adaptable; *synonyms* (adj) convertible, compatible; *antonym* (adj) unadaptable, **5.** exclaim; *synonyms* (v) cry, call, shout, clamor, outcry, scream, speak, vociferate, yell, declare, utter, **6.** announce; *synonyms* (v) advertise, herald, enunciate, proclaim, return, affirm, annunciate, broadcast, communicate, foretell, intimate, promulgate, publicize, publish, report, **7.** shout; *synonyms* (v) bellow, bawl, exclaim, hollo, howl, shriek, hail, bark, holler, hoop, (n) roar, cheer, halloo, screech, exclamation; *antonym* (v) whisper, **8.** versatile; *synonyms* (adj) changeable, various, inconstant, unsteady, clever, **9.** yielding; *synonyms* (adj) submissive, obedient, complying, complaisant, meek, acquiescent, fertile, flowing, (v) limber, smooth, (n) submission, concession, surrender, capitulation, compliance; *antonyms* (adj) hard, resistant, **10.** signal; *synonyms* (n) sign, gesture, indication, presage, flag, alarm, mark, motion, (v) omen, indicate, wave, alert, betoken, (adj) conspicuous, memorable.

takaruaki announced; *synonyms* (adj) proclaimed, spoken.

takaruru 1. shake; *synonyms* (v) beat, agitate, jar, brandish, disturb, excite, flutter, totter, wag, (n) tremble, jolt, quiver, wave, trembling, (adj) quake, **2.** rattle; *synonyms* (n) roll, jangle, jingle, click, clack, clang, rattling, (v) clatter, bang, confuse, patter, shake, disconcert, clash, drum.

takaruruaki 1. rattled; *synonyms* (adj) flustered, perturbed, upset, abashed, addled, afraid, bewildered, disconcerted, distraught, puzzled, unsettled, **2.** shaken; *synonyms* (v) broken, lame, passe, shaky, threadbare, wilted, shattered, stale, (adj) jolted, dazed, fallen, scared, stunned, surprised, uneasy.

takataka song; *synonyms* (n) melody, air, strain, cry, warble, poem, tune, call, chanson, canticle, (v) ditty, chant, sing, (adj) lay, ballad.

takatau beads; *synonyms* (n) rosary, censer, cross, crucifix, host, patera, pax, pyx, reliquary, rood, thurible, jewelry, lot, relics.

take 1. dominating; *synonyms* (adj) commanding, autocratic, bossy, ascendant, ascendent, inextinguishable, unquenchable, predominant, authoritarian, authoritative, autocratical, dictatorial, leading, ascensive, despotic, **2.** dumbfounded; *synonyms* (adj) astonished, astounded, amazed, staggered, bewildered, dazed, speechless, stunned, stupefied, flabbergasted, **3.** exceeding; *synonyms* (adj) exceptional, prodigious, surpassing, transcendent, more, undue, superior, colossal, odd, passing, better, (prep) above, beyond, after, (adv) besides, **4.** duck; *synonyms* (n) darling, canvas, (v) dip, douse, plunge, dodge, circumvent, dive, evade, souse, bob, avoid, crouch, dunk, elude, **5.** abashed; *synonyms* (adj) bashful, discomfited, mortified, ashamed, confused, embarrassed, sheepish; *antonym* (adj) brazen, **6.** sheepish; *synonyms* (adj) coy, diffident, shamefaced, shy, guilty, nervous, skittish, **7.** surprised; *synonyms* (adj) dumbfounded, shocked, startled, aghast, curious, puzzled, questioning, quizzical, baffled, bemused, confounded, incredulous, inquiring, overcome, overwhelmed; *antonym* (adj) indifferent.

takebono 1. contrary; *synonyms* (adj) opposite, contradictory, adverse, conflicting, reverse, unfavorable, alien, cross, different, disobedient, obstinate, perverse, averse, antagonistic, (adv) counter, **2.** contradict; *synonyms* (v) deny, oppose, belie, conflict, confute, contravene, controvert, disprove, dissent, impugn, invalidate, refute, disaffirm, disclaim, counteract; *antonyms* (v) confirm, agree, match, **3.** irreducible; *synonyms* (adj) net, (v) incommutable, indefeasible, inextinguishable, intransmutable, uncommensurable, irresoluble, irretrievable, irreversible, irrevocable, reverseless, unaccommodating, incommensurable; *antonym* (*adj*) reducible, **4**. intractable; *synonyms* (*adj*) headstrong, inflexible, fractious, stubborn, contumacious, contrary, insubordinate, froward, obdurate, recalcitrant, unruly, wayward, mulish, incorrigible, indocile; *antonyms* (*adj*) biddable, flexible, tractable, **5**. defiant; *synonyms* (*adj*) bold, rebellious, audacious, resistant, brazen, mutinous, naughty, rude; *antonyms* (*adj*) obedient, submissive, **6**. naughty; *synonyms* (*adj*) bad, blue, impish, mischievous, improper, wicked, evil, lewd, dark, defiant, racy, risque, spicy, unmanageable, vulgar; *antonyms* (*adj*) well-behaved, good, **7**. disobedient; *synonyms* (*adj*) intractable, disorderly, willful, refractory, boisterous; *antonyms* (*adj*) compliant, orderly, **8**. disobey; *synonyms* (*v*) break, defy, disregard, infringe, violate, ignore, breach, rebel, transgress; *antonym* (*v*) obey, **9**. defy; *synonyms* (*v*) challenge, dare, brave, confront, resist, revolt, disobey, withstand, contradict, mutiny, decline, face, flout, hold, (*n*) defiance, **10**. immutable; *synonyms* (*adj*) constant, unchangeable, changeless, permanent, eternal, fixed, invariable, stable, unalterable, unchanging; *antonym* (*adj*) mutable.

taki wood; *synonyms* (*n*) forest, timber, woods, tree, lumber, coppice, jungle.

takibaba bamboo; *synonyms* (*n*) cane, stick, (*adj*) wicker, rush, woven.

takina unfold; *synonyms* (*v*) expand, explain, extend, open, spread, develop, display, reveal, stretch, evolve, show, splay, disentangle, solve, (*adj*) expound; *antonym* (*v*) fold.

takinaki unfolded; *synonyms* (*adj*) open, extended, detailed, displayed, evolved, expanded, explicate, outspread, outstretched, stretched; *antonym* (*adj*) folded.

takirara 1. reddish; *synonyms* (*adj*) ruddy, crimson, rosy, cherry, rufescent, rufous, carmine, cerise, erythroid, flushed, reddened, rubedinous, ruby, scarlet, (*n*) red, **2**. russet; *synonyms* (*adj*) tan, dingy, drab, dun, leaden, livid, pearly, (*n*) brown, auburn.

takiria drum; *synonyms* (*n*) barrel, cask, tympan, vat, drumfish, (*v*) beat, roll, bang, knock, pound, ram, thrum, thump, bone, cram.

takitaki 1. excited; *synonyms* (*adj*) agitated, ablaze, emotional, enthusiastic, frantic, ardent, aroused, delirious, fervent, heated, impassioned, passionate, warm, elated, (*v*) animated; *antonyms* (*adj*) calm, cool, unexcited, **2**. ecstatic; *synonyms* (*adj*) rapturous, delighted, excited, rapt, rhapsodic, blissful, exultant, happy, joyful, (*v*) thrilling; *antonyms* (*adj*) disappointed, depressed, **3**. affected; *synonyms* (*adj*) artificial, unnatural, pompous, pretentious, stilted, pedantic, assumed,

concerned, contrived, exaggerated, feigned, forced, pretended, snobbish, strained; *antonyms* (*adj*) unaffected, down-to-earth, natural, unchanged, **4**. anxious; *synonyms* (*adj*) afraid, alarmed, nervous, tense, uneasy, apprehensive, distressed, fearful, frightened, keen, thoughtful, thirsty, insecure, (*v*) jumpy, solicitous; *antonyms* (*adj*) relaxed, carefree, confident, rational, unconcerned, undisturbed, untroubled, **5**. click; *synonyms* (*n*) catch, chink, tick, clap, clink, detent, dog, pawl, (*v*) clack, snap, chatter, beat, cluck, flick, go, **6**. jingle; *synonyms* (*n*) jangle, chime, tune, doggerel, gingle, (*v*) ring, ding, clang, clank, peal, rattle, sound, tinkle, **7**. clack; *synonyms* (*n*) gossip, (*v*) clatter, cackle, babble, bang, prate, jaw, talk, blab, blabber, click, gabble, gibber, (*adj*) palaver, prattle.

takoko 1. compressed; *synonyms* (*adj*) compact, dense, flat, tight, pointed, concise, packed, close, besotted, bland, blotto, categoric, categorical, concrete, firm; *antonym* (*adj*) loose, **2**. close; *synonyms* (*adj*) near, adjacent, nearby, accurate, approximate, narrow, brief, (*v*) stop, conclude, (*adv*) by, about, (*n*) end, finish, conclusion, expiration; *antonyms* (*adj*) distant, airy, fresh, far, (*v*) open, start, **3**. tight; *synonyms* (*adj*) mean, parsimonious, taut, secure, snug, tense, drunk, miserly, rigorous, sparing, stiff, strict, stringent, (*v*) fast, stingy; *antonyms* (*adj*) baggy, generous, slack, wide, (*adv*) loosely, **4**. packed; *synonyms* (*adj*) crowded, full, filled, jammed, overcrowded, congested, thick, brimming, cramped, teeming; *antonyms* (*adj*) empty, deserted, **5**. together; *synonyms* (*adv*) jointly, conjointly, simultaneously, collectively, running, (*adj*) united, composed, stable, whole; *antonyms* (*adv*) individually, separately, independently, (*adj*) separate.

takomkom barely; *synonyms* (*adv*) hardly, just, scarcely, simply, merely, narrowly, purely, scantily, scarce, slightly, solely, absolutely, (*adj*) only; *antonym* (*adv*) almost.

takoro 1. notch; *synonyms* (*n*) cut, gap, mark, nick, score, scratch, degree, grade, groove, (*v*) dent, hack, indent, nock, hollow, jag, **2**. snip; *synonyms* (*n*) clipping, cutting, bit, snippet, snipping, (*v*) clip, crop, slice, nip, prune, trim, pare, pinch, lop, sever.

takoroaki notched; *synonyms* (*adj*) jagged, serrated, jaggy, serrate, toothed, erose, rough, uneven.

taku 1. look; *synonyms* (*v*) seem, appear, expect, figure, attend, (*n*) face, gaze, appearance, aspect, air, countenance, expression, glance, guise, view, **2**. conjugate; *synonyms* (*v*) join, couple, link, marry, copulate, yoke, cohabit, (*adj*) united, conjugated, coupled, paronymous, **3**. deliberate; *synonyms* (*adj*) careful, calculated, circumspect, slow, thoughtful, conscious, (*v*) consider, cogitate, consult, debate, think, confer, contemplate, ponder, reflect; *antonyms* (*adj*) accidental, chance, unintentional, hasty, ingenuous, involuntary, spontaneous, **4.** examine; *synonyms* (*v*) assay, audit, overhaul, try, check, control, search, survey, ascertain, ask, compare, analyze, canvass, essay, investigate, **5.** notice; *synonyms* (*n*) advertisement, attention, declaration, information, mind, caution, heed, message, (*v*) note, look, detect, discover, distinguish, find, mark; *antonyms* (*v*) disregard, ignore, **6.** contemplate; *synonyms* (*v*) meditate, muse, speculate, deliberate, behold, entertain, intend, mull, reason, study, see, watch, wonder, design, digest, **7.** muse; *synonyms* (*v*) brood, ruminate, dream, daydream, puzzle, mediate, **8.** consider; *synonyms* (*v*) believe, regard, assume, calculate, conceive, reckon, deem, esteem, feel, hold, suppose, account, call, (*n*) examine, (*adj*) scrutinize, **9.** gaze; *synonyms* (*v*) stare, gape, pry, glare, peer, gawk, **10.** meditate; *synonyms* (*v*) chew, imagine, plan, purpose, weigh, **11.** think; *synonyms* (*v*) estimate, guess, conjecture, suspect, envisage, recollect, fancy, repute, cerebrate, judge, mean, opine, presume, recall, remember; *antonym* (*v*) forget, **12.** speculate; *synonyms* (*v*) venture, hazard, hypothesize, infer, job, risk, theorize, gamble, say, adventure, bet, hypothecate, postulate, **13.** scan; *synonyms* (*n*) examination, inspection, review, scrutiny, recording, (*v*) inspect, rake, read, peruse, browse, ransack, ken, interpret, know, poetize, **14.** reflect; *synonyms* (*v*) mirror, bethink, echo, excogitate, shine, copy, imitate, repeat, flash, glint, pause, rebound, reproduce, gleam, hesitate, **15.** observe; *synonyms* (*v*) celebrate, comment, notice, commemorate, guard, follow, keep, mention, fulfill, comply, discern, maintain, obey, perceive, remark, **16.** suppose; *synonyms* (*v*) divine, hope, count, anticipate, gather, presuppose, put, take, hypothesise, make, picture, compute, accept, understand, (*n*) supposition, **17.** state; *synonyms* (*n*) nation, position, country, kingdom, show, place, (*v*) declare, expound, express, affirm, allege, announce, articulate, assert, (*adj*) national; *antonyms* (*v*) deny, (*adj*) private, **18.** weigh; *synonyms* (*v*) balance, press, matter, measure, poise, assess, evaluate, load, tell, discuss, gauge, revolve, (*adj*) gravitate, **19.** reckon; *synonyms* (*v*) enumerate, number, rate, tally, cipher, cast, cypher, depend, forecast, approximate, determine, total, add, prize, rely, **20.** say; *synonyms* (*v*) pronounce, enunciate, observe, order, speak, state, relate, dictate, command, narrate, aver, deliver, enjoin, enounce, (*n*) voice.

takua 1. chide; *synonyms* (*v*) censure, admonish, blame, rebuke, reprimand, chasten, lecture, reproach, scold, chastise, berate, correct, criticize, objurgate, reprehend; *antonym* (*v*) praise, **2.** lecture; *synonyms* (*n*) address, discourse, harangue, speech, talk, oration, declaim, homily, lesson, reproof, delivery, (*v*) sermon, chide, preach, instruct, **3.** rebuke; *synonyms* (*n*) rebuff, admonition, admonishment, rap, discipline, scolding, (*v*) castigate, caution, check, attack, accuse, jaw, lambaste, reprove, upbraid; *antonyms* (*v*) commend, compliment, **4.** reprove; *synonyms* (*v*) condemn, warn, disapprove, punish, **5.** rate; *synonyms* (*n*) price, worth, pace, value, percentage, (*v*) assess, estimate, evaluate, appreciate, appraise, compute, count, calculate, merit, put, **6.** scold; *synonyms* (*v*) abuse, rail, grouch, grumble, lash, vituperate, rate, remonstrate, slate, revile, (*n*) nag, nagger, (*adj*) shrew, curse, beshrew, **7.** reprimand; *synonyms* (*n*) chastisement, castigation, reprehension, chiding, accusation, condemnation, criticism, punishment, reproval, (*v*) criminate, denounce, snub, trounce, impeach, sneap.

takuaki 1. noticed, **2.** conjugated; *synonyms* (*adj*) conjugate, coupled, joined, linked, **3.** given; *synonyms* (*adj*) apt, disposed, prone, liable, granted, inclined, set, (*n*) assumption, particular, presumption, fact, **4.** considered; *synonyms* (*adj*) deliberate, reasoned, intentional, premeditated, sensible, sound, willful, studied, calculated, planned, reputed, adult, careful, designed, exact; *antonyms* (*adj*) impulsive, sudden, impetuous, ingenuous, swift, thoughtless, **5.** supposed; *synonyms* (*adj*) conjectural, alleged, assumed, hypothetical, imaginary, putative, apparent, ostensible, suppositional, professed, suppositious, supposititious, pretended, theoretical; *antonyms* (*adj*) real, actual, **6.** reflected; *synonyms* (*adj*) reverberate, reflectent, reflexed, **7.** observed; *synonyms* (*adj*) seen, ascertained, discovered, empirical, disclosed, experiential, experimental, visual, practical, pragmatic, revealed, **8.** reproved; *synonyms* (*adj*) rebuked, reprimanded, admonished, chastened, **9.** reprimanded; *synonym* (*adj*) reproved, **10.** rated; *synonym* (*adj*) nominal, **11.** stated; *synonyms* (*adj*) declared, explicit, regular, certain, settled, (*adv*) fixed, given, **12.** rebuked.

takuakua charmed; *synonyms* (*adj*) captivated, delighted, enchanted, fascinated, entranced, spellbound, beguiled, captive.

takuanganga worthless; *synonyms* (*adj*) futile, vile, idle, cheap, empty, trifling, trivial, void, miserable, fruitless, ineffective, mean, null, (*v*) useless, vain; *antonyms* (*adj*) valuable, precious, useful, helpful, meaningful, priceless, worthwhile.

takuarara 1. loquacious; *synonyms* (*adj*) garrulous, chatty, talkative, gabby, wordy, glib, talky, verbose, expansive, linguacious; *antonym* (*adj*) taciturn, **2.** blab; *synonyms* (*v*) babble, chatter, tattle, mouth, blabber, chat, clack, disclose, divulge, gabble, gibber, gossip, palaver, piffle, prate, **3.** babble;

synonyms (*n*) drivel, burble, gibberish, (*v*) murmur, gab, ripple, talk, blab, blather, bubble, guggle, gurgle, prattle, smatter, (*adj*) jabber; *antonyms* (*v*) quietness, silence, stillness, **4.** talkative; *synonyms* (*adj*) loquacious, gossipy, communicative, bigmouthed, blabbermouthed, blabby, effusive, fluent; *antonyms* (*adj*) reserved, mute, quiet, shy, silent.

takurara 1. grumble; *synonyms* (*v*) murmur, mutter, complain, gripe, growl, rumble, grouch, mumble, roar, croak, gnarl, (*n*) complaint, moan, groan, roll, **2.** growl; *synonyms* (*n*) snarl, bark, thunder, cry, growling, (*v*) grumble, howl, yap, grunt, bay, crash, frown, scowl, snap, woof, **3.** rave; *synonyms* (*n*) rage, rant, (*v*) fume, jabber, wander, gush, bluster, storm, tear, acclaim, babble, (*adj*) foam, boil, flame, seethe, **4.** storm; *synonyms* (*n*) tempest, attack, shower, blizzard, burst, gust, hurricane, explosion, blast, (*v*) rush, assault, hail, charge, invade, raid, **5.** ranting; *synonyms* (*adj*) bombastic, inflated, vociferous, (*n*) harangue, declamation, tirade, blah, bombast, claptrap, fustian, nonsense, **6.** rant; *synonyms* (*n*) spout, rodomontade, ranting, lecture, (*v*) rave, declaim, mouth, gag.

takurere 1. browbeat; *synonyms* (*v*) bully, domineer, intimidate, terrorize, bluster, bulldoze, frighten, bullyrag, cow, daunt, threaten, ballyrag, coerce, push, **2.** stutter; *synonyms* (*n*) stammer, (*v*) falter, hesitate, stumble, bumble, **3.** rebuke; *synonyms* (*n*) blame, rebuff, reproach, admonition, reproof, (*v*) censure, reprimand, chide, berate, castigate, lecture, admonish, caution, check, scold; *antonyms* (*v*) praise, commend, compliment, **4.** rail; *synonyms* (*n*) bar, balustrade, handrail, railing, fence, banister, track, path, pale, paling, bolt, barrier, (*v*) inveigh, vituperate, fulminate.

takurereaki rebuked; *synonyms* (*adj*) reprimanded, reproved, admonished, chastened.

takutaku 1. gibber; *synonyms* (*v*) jabber, chatter, gabble, babble, blab, clack, piffle, prate, prattle, tattle, (*n*) gibberish, **2.** jabber; *synonyms* (*n*) drivel, chat, twaddle, (*v*) rave, utter, gush, rant, (*adj*) palaver, **3.** dumb; *synonyms* (*adj*) mute, dense, dim, dull, silent, speechless, inarticulate, obtuse, slow, stupid, idiotic, quiet, taciturn, thick, voiceless, **4.** stutter; *synonyms* (*n*) stammer, (*v*) falter, hesitate, stumble, bumble, **5.** stammer; *synonym* (*v*) stutter.

tama 1. father; *synonyms* (*n*) begetter, dad, sire, creator, abba, beginner, forefather, founder, padre, patriarch, author, (*v*) beget, engender, create, generate; *antonym* (*adj*) mother, **2.** climb; *synonyms* (*v*) ascend, arise, clamber, escalate, increase, scale, scramble, (*n*) rise, mount, ascent, acclivity, advance, ascending, jump, ascension; *antonyms* (*v*) descend, drop, **3.** monk; *synonyms* (*n*) monastic, hermit, conventual, priest, cenobite, abbot, monkey,

palmer, pilgrim, cleric, justice, minister, nun, parson, preacher, **4.** ascend; *synonyms* (*v*) climb, uprise, appear, lift, soar, **5.** priest; *synonyms* (*n*) clergyman, ecclesiastic, churchman, pastor, presbyter, chaplain, monk, (*adj*) divine, **6.** spread; *synonyms* (*v*) scatter, reach, disperse, expand, extend, broadcast, circulate, diffuse, disseminate, propagate, stretch, broaden, deploy, enlarge, (*n*) span; *antonym* (*adj*) concentrated.

tamaewe coming; *synonyms* (*v*) instant, (*adj*) approaching, forthcoming, future, imminent, impending, following, (*n*) access, advent, approach, appearance, arrival, return, arrive, come; *antonym* (*n*) departure.

tamaka climb; *synonyms* (*v*) ascend, arise, clamber, escalate, increase, scale, scramble, (*n*) rise, mount, ascent, acclivity, advance, ascending, jump, ascension; *antonyms* (*v*) descend, drop.

tamakai 1. diligence; *synonyms* (*n*) care, assiduity, application, attention, industry, activity, perseverance, carefulness, industriousness, determination, (*adj*) painstaking; *antonym* (*n*) laziness, **2.** agile; *synonyms* (*adj*) active, nimble, adroit, quick, spry, deft, lively, brisk, lithe, sprightly, supple, quick-witted, alert, dexterous, fast; *antonym* (*adj*) clumsy.

tamaki spread; *synonyms* (*v*) scatter, reach, disperse, expand, extend, broadcast, circulate, diffuse, disseminate, increase, propagate, stretch, broaden, deploy, (*n*) span; *antonym* (*adj*) concentrated.

taman 1. line; *synonyms* (*n*) cord, file, house, breed, course, family, lineage, field, ancestry, border, boundary, cable, crease, row, (*v*) order, **2.** mark; *synonyms* (*n*) brand, evidence, score, character, heed, impression, imprint, sign, feature, (*v*) blemish, characterize, distinguish, grade, label, (*adj*) notice, **3.** trace; *synonyms* (*n*) line, shadow, spot, clue, dash, hint, indication, mark, shade, suggestion, touch, trail, (*v*) track, hunt, pursue.

tamanaki 1. marked; *synonyms* (*adj*) distinct, conspicuous, noticeable, pronounced, remarkable, distinguished, apparent, definite, notable, obvious, signal, striking, strong, clear, appreciable; *antonyms* (*adj*) plain, unblemished, **2.** lined; *synonyms* (*adj*) furrowed, creased, wrinkled, wrinkly, striped, banded, battered, cemented, covered, craggy, crumpled, eroded, gnarled, hooped, marbled; *antonym* (*adj*) smooth, **3.** traced; *synonyms* (*adj*) copied, graphic.

tamania 1. delineate; *synonyms* (*v*) define, draw, describe, line, represent, sketch, characterize, delimit, draft, outline, paint, trace, circumscribe, (*n*) design, show, **2.** mark; *synonyms* (*n*) brand, evidence, score, character, heed, impression, imprint, sign, feature, badge, (*v*) blemish, distinguish, grade, label, (*adj*) notice.

tamaniaki 1. delineated; *synonyms* *(adj)* delineate, portrayed, graphic, lineal, represented, hereditary, linear, **2.** marked; *synonyms* *(adj)* distinct, conspicuous, noticeable, pronounced, remarkable, distinguished, apparent, definite, notable, obvious, signal, striking, strong, clear, appreciable; *antonyms* *(adj)* plain, unblemished.

tamanna 1. someone; *synonyms* *(pron)* somebody, anybody, anyone, *(n)* individual, person, human, self, man, party, one, soul, homo, mortal, **2.** one; *synonyms* *(pron)* any, *(n)* single, ace, unit, unity, *(adj)* certain, lone, only, unique, some, singular, particular, sole, united, *(adv)* once.

tamaomao 1. familiar; *synonyms* *(adj)* close, common, conversant, customary, everyday, intimate, commonplace, easy, ordinary, usual, *(n)* accustomed, companion, comrade, habitual, *(v)* confidential; *antonyms* *(adj)* unfamiliar, foreign, strange, new, unaccustomed, formal, ignorant, unknown, **2.** united; *synonyms* *(adj)* joined, joint, combined, cooperative, connected, allied, mutual, concerted, mixed, conjunctive, undivided, conjunct, unanimous, conjoint, *(v)* consolidated; *antonyms* *(adj)* individual, separate, divided.

tamarake 1. ascend; *synonyms* *(v)* rise, arise, mount, climb, scale, uprise, increase, appear, escalate, jump, lift, soar; *antonyms* *(v)* descend, drop, **2.** climb; *synonyms* *(v)* ascend, clamber, scramble, bestride, fly, *(n)* ascent, acclivity, advance, ascending, ascension, climbing, hike, mounting, raise, upgrade, **3.** scale; *synonyms* *(n)* flake, gamut, degree, graduation, measure, yardstick, rate, chip, criterion, fur, gradation, *(v)* gauge, weigh, peel, *(adj)* balance.

tamarakea scale; *synonyms* *(n)* flake, gamut, degree, graduation, measure, yardstick, rate, chip, *(v)* ascend, climb, gauge, mount, weigh, rise, *(adj)* balance; *antonym* *(v)* descend.

tamarakeaki scaled; *synonyms* *(adj)* scaly, lepidote, leprose, scabrous, scaley, scurfy.

tamaroa 1. beautiful; *synonyms* *(adj)* attractive, good-looking, bright, beauteous, fine, handsome, lovely, picturesque, pleasant, pretty, striking, sweet, adorned, ornate, dainty; *antonyms* *(adj)* ugly, unattractive, **2.** lovely; *synonyms* *(adj)* beautiful, charming, delightful, enchanting, lovable, alluring, adorable, elegant, endearing, exquisite, fair, gorgeous, graceful, gracious, cute; *antonyms* *(adj)* hideous, terrible, unpleasant, **3.** nice; *synonyms* *(adj)* fastidious, good, kind, neat, likable, delicious, agreeable, correct, decent, delicate, difficult, enjoyable, exact, particular, precise; *antonym* *(adj)* horrible, **4.** grand; *synonyms* *(adj)* excellent, dignified, elevated, eminent, exalted, important, majestic, superb, high, massive, big, brilliant, *(n)* glorious, noble, *(v)* great; *antonyms* *(adj)* unimpressive, humble, modest, **5.** fair; *synonyms*

(adj) equitable, clear, average, dispassionate, impartial, reasonable, candid, comely, considerable, disinterested, evenhanded, *(adv)* clean, *(n)* bazaar, blonde, carnival; *antonyms* *(adj)* unfair, biased, dark, exceptional, unjust, partial, foul, imbalanced, mismatched, prejudiced, unwarranted, **6.** graceful; *synonyms* *(adj)* amiable, easy, airy, becoming, lithe, refined, supple, svelte, sophisticated, tripping, courtly, slim, genteel, lissom, shapely; *antonyms* *(adj)* clumsy, inelegant, stocky, **7.** pretty; *synonyms* *(adv)* very, fairly, jolly, quite, rather, somewhat, moderately, slightly, *(adj)* pleasing, smart, bonny, just, prepossessing, *(n)* nice, **8.** splendid; *synonyms* *(adj)* illustrious, magnificent, grand, royal, gallant, proud, admirable, impressive, luxurious, resplendent, shining, imposing, lustrous, costly, grandiose; *antonym* *(adj)* poor.

tamârua handsome; *synonyms* *(adj)* elegant, beautiful, fair, charming, fine, generous, attractive, bountiful, comely, bonny, big, bounteous, exquisite, gorgeous, graceful; *antonyms* *(adj)* ugly, unattractive.

tamatama 1. climb; *synonyms* *(v)* ascend, arise, clamber, escalate, increase, scale, scramble, *(n)* rise, mount, ascent, acclivity, advance, ascending, jump, ascension; *antonyms* *(v)* descend, drop, **2.** scale; *synonyms* *(n)* flake, gamut, degree, graduation, measure, yardstick, rate, chip, criterion, fur, gradation, *(v)* climb, gauge, weigh, *(adj)* balance.

tamatamaki scaled; *synonyms* *(adj)* scaly, lepidote, leprose, scabrous, scaley, scurfy.

tamatua acrobat; *synonyms* *(n)* tumbler, clown, charlatan, harlequin, mountebank, punch, scaramouch, buffoon, farceur, funambulist, mime, ropedancer, dancer, *(adj)* athlete, gymnast.

tamau dad; *synonyms* *(n)* father, daddy, papa, pappa, pater, pop, sire, paterfamilias, divinity, elder, idol, popping, soda, tonic.

tamruru 1. crumbled; *synonyms* *(adj)* broken, fragmented, rotten, disconnected, disunited, split, **2.** parted; *synonyms* *(adj)* cleft, divided, separate, distributed, dividable, divisible, devided.

tamwarake climb; *synonyms* *(v)* ascend, arise, clamber, escalate, increase, scale, scramble, *(n)* rise, mount, ascent, acclivity, advance, ascending, jump, ascension; *antonyms* *(v)* descend, drop.

tamwere 1. late; *synonyms* *(adj)* former, dead, deceased, behindhand, belated, delayed, modern, slow, tardy, dull, defunct, *(adv)* dilatory, fresh, backward, belatedly; *antonyms* *(adj)* ahead, *(adv)* early, punctually, promptly, punctual, **2.** behind; *synonyms* *(prep)* after, abaft, *(adv)* backwards, late, later, aback, beyond, *(n)* backside, bottom, buttocks, can, posterior, rump, *(adj)* back, rear; *antonym* *(adv)* fore.

tamweremwere 1. loaf; *synonyms* (*v*) dawdle, lounge, laze, linger, loiter, loll, lurk, (*adj*) block, lump, poke, **2.** dawdle; *synonyms* (*v*) dally, delay, lag, amble, procrastinate, hesitate, idler, saunter, drag; *antonyms* (*v*) hurry, rush, **3.** stroll; *synonyms* (*n*) promenade, tramp, excursion, perambulation, turn, (*v*) ramble, walk, roam, wander, hike, range, jaunt, meander, trip, gad, **4.** saunter; *synonyms* (*n*) stroll, constitutional, journey, nomadize, (*adv*) crawl, creep, drawl.

tan the; *synonyms* (*n*) queenliness, stateliness, (*v*) thee.

tana 1. executed; *synonyms* (*v*) done, (*adj*) finished, fulfilled, complete, given, issued, **2.** engaged; *synonyms* (*adj*) busy, occupied, betrothed, affianced, employed, engrossed, reserved, absorbed, working, pledged, bespoken, booked, immersed, intent, rapt; *antonyms* (*adj*) available, free, **3.** stung; *synonyms* (*adj*) bitten, annoyed, bit, irritated, nettled, peeved, pissed, riled, roiled, besotted, blotto, churning, crocked, fuddled, harassed, **4.** paint; *synonyms* (*n*) painting, tint, coating, (*v*) color, dye, daub, coat, decorate, depict, varnish, enamel, apply, lacquer, describe, draw, **5.** occupied; *synonyms* (*adj*) engaged, diligent, active, concerned, industrious, involved; *antonyms* (*adj*) empty, vacant, uninhabited, idle.

tanaki 1. stung; *synonyms* (*adj*) bitten, annoyed, bit, irritated, nettled, peeved, pissed, riled, roiled, besotted, blotto, churning, crocked, fuddled, harassed, **2.** painted; *synonyms* (*v*) depaint, (*adj*) dyed, motley, stained, tinted, assorted, calico, cosmetic, graphic, miscellaneous, mixed, multicolor, multicolored, multicolour, multicoloured.

tanako 1. lessening; *synonyms* (*n*) decrease, diminution, cutback, alleviation, contraction, mitigation, reduction, cut; *antonyms* (*n*) increase, growth, (*adj*) increasing, **2.** diminishing; *synonyms* (*adj*) decreasing, abating, declining, dwindling, lessening, waning, ablatitious, deteriorating, extenuating, fading, failing, falling, flagging, receding, retreating.

tanan 1. mottled; *synonyms* (*adj*) dappled, motley, speckled, multicolored, piebald, spotted, variegated, mixed; *antonym* (*adj*) plain, **2.** dappled; *synonyms* (*adj*) mottled, flecked, dapple, dotted, freckled, spotty, **3.** speckled; *synonym* (*adj*) specked, **4.** spotted; *synonyms* (*v*) mildewed, moldy, rusty, (*adj*) blotchy, flyblown, dirty, stained, tainted, besmirched, damaged, patched.

tanara 1. undo; *synonyms* (*v*) loosen, annul, open, cancel, disentangle, reverse, separate, unfold, untie, disconnect, nullify, unbrace, overturn, detach, disengage; *antonyms* (*v*) fasten, attach, close, do, wrap, **2.** untangle; *synonyms* (*v*) unravel, unscramble, undo, unwind, extricate, unknot,

unpick, ravel, solve, resolve, comb, disencumber, unsnarl, **3.** unwind; *synonyms* (*v*) relax, unbend, unroll, untangle, straighten, loose, rest, decompress, unfurl, unlax, unstrain; *antonym* (*v*) wind, **4.** unwrap; *synonyms* (*v*) uncover, (*adj*) uncurl, **5.** relinquish; *synonyms* (*v*) abandon, abdicate, cede, leave, quit, renounce, discard, disclaim, concede, desert, forgo, forsake, give, surrender, waive; *antonym* (*v*) retain.

tanaraki 1. unwound, **2.** relinquished; *synonyms* (*adj*) abandoned, deserted, derelict, surrendered, **3.** untangled; *synonym* (*adj*) intricate; *antonym* (*adj*) tangled, **4.** undone; *synonyms* (*v*) accursed, devoted, (*adj*) lost, ruined, sunk, unfinished, doomed, behindhand, decayed, destroyed, finished.

tañata 1. desire; *synonyms* (*n*) ambition, hope, aspiration, will, wish, craving, dream, impulse, (*v*) fancy, aspire, seek, want, aim, choose, crave; *antonyms* (*n*) aversion, reality, (*v*) dislike, hate, **2.** like; *synonyms* (*v*) corresponding, enjoy, identical, care, desire, (*adj*) equal, equivalent, alike, analogous, comparable, same, parallel, similar, (*n*) love, relish; *antonyms* (*prep*) unlike, (*adj*) different, **3.** wish; *synonyms* (*v*) like, please, bid, prefer, intend, mean, (*n*) need, inclination, longing, pleasure, purpose, mind, request, urge, plan.

tañáun ten; *synonyms* (*n*) tenner, decade, ace, break, breath, decennary, decennium, ecstasy, female, (*adj*) perfect, comely, desirable, faultless, glamorous, good-looking.

tanbwaia rob; *synonyms* (*v*) filch, pinch, deprive, pilfer, pillage, plunder, rifle, fleece, lift, purloin, steal, pick, divest, defraud, despoil.

tanbwaiaki robed; *synonyms* (*adj*) appareled, attired, clothed, dressed, garbed, garmented, habilimented, fixed, polished, vested.

taneiai proficient; *synonyms* (*adj*) adept, expert, able, accomplished, adroit, capable, competent, good, practiced, professional, skillful, deft, crack, qualified, dexterous; *antonyms* (*adj*) incompetent, inept.

tanewea 1. mention; *synonyms* (*v*) cite, name, hint, observe, commend, adduce, advert, note, notice, (*n*) comment, allusion, citation, remark, call, reference, **2.** name; *synonyms* (*n*) title, epithet, address, appellation, (*v*) appoint, baptize, describe, designate, entitle, enumerate, identify, list, mention, constitute, denominate, **3.** say; *synonyms* (*v*) articulate, express, pronounce, assert, enunciate, maintain, order, read, speak, state, tell, guess, relate, (*n*) declare, voice.

taneweaki named; *synonyms* (*v*) benempt, nempt, ycleped, promised, styled, vowed, (*adj*) called, nominative, chosen, nominal, nominated, preferred, titular, tokenish.

tang 1. howl; *synonyms* (*n*) bark, shout, yell, shriek, yap, (*v*) bellow, cry, bawl, roar, scream, growl, bay, snarl, wail, yawl, **2.** crack; *synonyms* (*n*) break, fracture, cleft, fissure, chip, (*v*) chink, crevice, split, breach, burst, snap, clap, bang, check, cleave; *antonyms* (*v*) repair, mend, **3.** complain; *synonyms* (*v*) beef, bemoan, bewail, protest, squawk, whine, grudge, accuse, carp, croak, gripe, grouse, grumble, mutter, object; *antonym* (*v*) compliment, **4.** claim; *synonyms* (*n*) call, charge, allegation, privilege, right, title, (*v*) demand, ask, assert, exact, arrogate, contend, need, require, requisition; *antonyms* (*v*) deny, disclaim, forfeit, **5.** mourn; *synonyms* (*v*) lament, deplore, grieve, regret, sorrow, weep; *antonym* (*v*) rejoice, **6.** ball; *synonyms* (*n*) bulb, globe, shot, shell, bead, baseball, bullet, dance, football, lump, orb, party, pellet, projectile, sphere, **7.** grind; *synonyms* (*v*) labor, toil, comminute, crunch, drudge, grate, abrade, chew, crush, file, mash, scrape, sharpen, (*n*) mill, drudgery, **8.** cry; *synonyms* (*n*) clamor, crying, buzz, exclamation, groan, hearsay, (*v*) exclaim, howl, moan, outcry, screech, yelp, yowl, holler, hollo; *antonyms* (*v*) laugh, whisper, **9.** lament; *synonyms* (*n*) dirge, complaint, elegy, plaint, requiem, lamentation, threnody, coronach, (*v*) complain, keen, mourn, plain, repent, rue, sigh; *antonyms* (*n*) celebration, (*v*) revel, **10.** whistle; *synonyms* (*n*) whistling, pennywhistle, (*v*) pipe, sing, twitter, hiss, warble, cheep, tweet, chirp, wheeze, hollo; *antonyms* (*v*) blubber, sob, drip, greet, whimper, ooze, (*n*) tear, **12.** sob; *synonyms* (*n*) sobbing, asshole, bastard, cocksucker, motherfucker, prick, shit, (*v*) snivel, **13.** ululate; *synonyms* (*v*) mewl, pule, thunder, wrawl, yammer, **14.** reclaim; *synonyms* (*v*) domesticate, recover, reform, cultivate, claim, correct, recycle, redeem, regain, repossess, retrieve, salvage, reprocess, improve, (*n*) revendicate; *antonym* (*v*) lose, **15.** rung; *synonyms* (*n*) round, rundle, degree, grade, stage, stair, spoke, stave, step, tread, **16.** squeak; *synonyms* (*n*) squeaker, (*v*) peep, creak, screak, shrill, skreak, skreigh, **17.** ring; *synonyms* (*n*) encircle, band, gang, jingle, loop, rim, circuit, annulus, arena, (*v*) circle, peal, echo, resound, reverberate, gird, **18.** peal; *synonyms* (*n*) ding, clang, noise, dingdong, blast, pealing, roll, rolling, (*v*) ring, chime, knell, toll, blare, (*adj*) swell, **19.** whimper; *synonyms* (*v*) bleat, bibber, grunt, **20.** wail; *synonyms* (*v*) ululate, squall, caterwaul, waul, woof.

tanga 1. extend; *synonyms* (*v*) expand, enlarge, amplify, broaden, dilate, widen, augment, continue, elongate, go, spread, carry, develop, increase, (*adj*) stretch; *antonyms* (*v*) withdraw, shorten, limit, narrow, shrink, **2.** develop; *synonyms* (*v*) advance, educate, grow, breed, contract, acquire, bloom, blossom, break, bud, build, come, cultivate, elaborate, evolve; *antonyms* (*v*) decrease, erupt, neglect, regress, **3.** diffuse; *synonyms* (*adj*) prolix, profuse, widespread, diffusive, copious, (*v*) circulate, disperse, disseminate, broadcast, propagate, scatter, distribute, permeate, shed, dissolve, **4.** spread; *synonyms* (*v*) reach, extend, diffuse, deploy, open, range, smear, splay, (*n*) span, dissemination, expanse, expansion, feast, propagation, scattering; *antonym* (*adj*) concentrated.

tangaina open; *synonyms* (*adj*) frank, obvious, artless, exposed, free, honest, bare, forthright, guileless, ingenuous, naked, (*v*) expand, give, (*n*) candid, clear; *antonyms* (*adj*) devious, secretive, concealed, furtive, hidden, limited, repressive, reserved, restricted, secret, blocked, cautious, (*v*) shut, end, (*tr v*) close.

tangaki 1. lamented, **2.** extended; *synonyms* (*adj*) broad, expanded, ample, extensive, long, wide, elongated, enlarged, lengthened, lengthy, prolonged, protracted, open, comprehensive, continued; *antonyms* (*adj*) brief, short, condensed, unextended, **3.** cracked; *synonyms* (*adj*) broken, nutty, batty, chapped, crazy, balmy, wacky, bats, crackers, crackled, crazed, deranged, dotty, insane, kookie, **4.** ground; *synonyms* (*n*) base, cause, land, floor, reason, dirt, field, soil, account, country, basis, (*v*) bottom, found, establish, fix; *antonym* (*n*) ceiling, **5.** diffused; *synonyms* (*adj*) dim, softened, dull, flowing, gentle, loose, mellow, muffled, muted, subtle, **6.** developed; *synonyms* (*adj*) adult, mature, advanced, grown, sophisticated, complete, detailed, distinguished, educated, established, full, full-fledged, full-grown, grown-up, matured; *antonym* (*adj*) immature, **7.** rung; *synonyms* (*n*) round, rundle, degree, grade, stage, stair, spoke, stave, step, tread, **8.** spread; *synonyms* (*v*) scatter, reach, disperse, expand, extend, broadcast, circulate, diffuse, disseminate, increase, propagate, stretch, broaden, deploy, (*n*) span; *antonym* (*adj*) concentrated, **9.** reclaimed; *synonyms* (*v*) reborn, (*adj*) cultivated, disciplined, domestic, domesticated, rescued, tame.

tangako 1. dirty; *synonyms* (*adj*) foul, dirt, contemptible, bawdy, contaminated, dingy, impure, despicable, (*v*) muddy, corrupt, soil, contaminate, begrime, bemire, (*n*) defile; *antonyms* (*adj*) hygienic, pure, spotless, immaculate, (*v*) clean, **2.** slimy; *synonyms* (*adj*) greasy, slippery, squalid, oily, oozy, ropy, viscous, slimed, **3.** untidy; *synonyms* (*adj*) slovenly, disheveled, disordered, disorderly, messy, sloppy, unkempt, confused, disorganized, frowzy, scruffy, sluttish, slipshod, dowdy, tousled; *antonyms* (*adj*) tidy, neat, elegant, **4.** slovenly; *synonyms* (*adj*) careless, untidy, frowsy, negligent, perfunctory, inefficient.

tangana 1. blend; *synonyms* (*n*) alloy, mix, amalgam, composite, amalgamation, brew, combination, compound, (*v*) amalgamate, combine, commingle, fuse, merge, incorporate, confound; *antonyms* (*v*) separate, divide, **2**. mix; *synonyms* (*n*) mixture, concoction, (*v*) blend, intermingle, mingle, intermix, join, meld, aggregate, admix, immingle, associate, coalesce, confuse, consort, **3**. knead; *synonyms* (*v*) rub, form, fashion, massage, mould, shape, work, (*adj*) mash.

tanganaki 1. blended; *synonyms* (*v*) blent, polluted, stained, (*adj*) mixed, composite, adulterate, beaten, conglomerate, **2**. mixed; *synonyms* (*adj*) miscellaneous, assorted, heterogeneous, integrated, medley, impure, amalgamated, diverse, intermingled, motley, varied, indiscriminate, different, (*v*) blended, mingled; *antonyms* (*adj*) homogeneous, insular, pure.

tangare perfect; *synonyms* (*adj*) consummate, complete, exact, utter, entire, faultless, thorough, exquisite, integral, blameless, clean, (*v*) achieve, accomplish, (*n*) absolute, full; *antonyms* (*adj*) imperfect, faulty, flawed.

tangaua 1. indecisive; *synonyms* (*adj*) doubtful, hesitant, inconclusive, undecided, unsure, weak, dubious, irresolute, precarious, vague, feeble; *antonyms* (*adj*) decisive, conclusive, resolute, **2**. perplexed; *synonyms* (*v*) bewildered, complicated, intricate, (*adj*) confused, involved, lost, baffled, confounded, puzzled, distracted, uneasy, bemused, questioning, quizzical, entangled; *antonym* (*adj*) enlightened.

tangauriuri 1. inconsistent; *synonyms* (*adj*) incongruous, incoherent, incompatible, contrary, absurd, conflicting, inconsequent, discordant, discrepant, erratic, illogical, irreconcilable, abhorrent, changeable, (*n*) contradictory; *antonyms* (*adj*) consistent, constant, reliable, **2**. friable; *synonyms* (*adj*) crumbly, fragile, crisp, brittle, breakable, powdery, short, arenaceous, dusty, light, **3**. apathetic; *synonyms* (*adj*) indifferent, cool, impassive, uninterested, perfunctory, casual, dull, lazy, lethargic, lukewarm, nonchalant, sluggish, spiritless, detached, indolent; *antonyms* (*adj*) energetic, enthusiastic, fervent, inquisitive, **4**. frail; *synonyms* (*adj*) delicate, flimsy, rickety, slender, slim, dainty, decrepit, fine, puny, sick, slight, unhealthy, (*v*) weak, feeble, faint; *antonyms* (*adj*) strong, substantial, robust, **5**. soft; *synonyms* (*adj*) gentle, easy, limp, balmy, quiet, slack, loose, clement, flabby, flaccid, frail, lenient, mild, pliant, (*v*) low; *antonyms* (*adj*) hard, firm, harsh, loud, hoarse, rough, solid, stiff, alcoholic, shrill, **6**. spineless; *synonyms* (*adj*) gutless, timid, soft, nerveless, craven, fearful, (*adv*) cowardly; *antonym* (*adj*) brave.

tangenge 1. bare; *synonyms* (*adj*) naked, austere, bald, stark, bleak, desolate, devoid, exposed, mere, nude, plain, vacant, vacuous, (*v*) empty, show; *antonyms* (*adj*) covered, cultivated, ornate, concealed, (*v*) cover, **2**. uncovered; *synonyms* (*adj*) open, bare, unclothed, **3**. open; *synonyms* (*adj*) frank, obvious, artless, free, honest, forthright, guileless, ingenuous, direct, explicit, downright, (*v*) expand, give, (*n*) candid, clear; *antonyms* (*adj*) devious, secretive, furtive, hidden, limited, repressive, reserved, restricted, secret, blocked, cautious, closed, (*v*) shut, end, (*tr v*) close.

tangibuaka 1. jar; *synonyms* (*n*) jangle, blow, crock, container, jog, shake, amphora, bottle, crash, (*v*) jolt, clash, creak, bump, collide, jounce, **2**. discordant; *synonyms* (*adj*) contrary, conflicting, dissonant, discrepant, disharmonious, harsh, incompatible, inconsistent, jarring, raucous, hoarse, cacophonous, contradictory, disagreeing, grating; *antonyms* (*adj*) harmonious, musical, pleasant-sounding, melodic.

tangibururu 1. buzz; *synonyms* (*n*) hum, rumor, hearsay, hiss, report, bell, whirr, (*v*) call, drone, ring, gossip, purr, murmur, sound, whine.

tangimwaka 1. resonant; *synonyms* (*adj*) ringing, sonorous, vibrant, deep, full, melodious, resounding, reverberating, reverberative, rich, bass, booming, cavernous, echoing, loud; *antonym* (*adj*) weak, **2**. resound; *synonyms* (*v*) echo, reverberate, ring, boom, peal, roar, blare, reecho, resonate, sound, clatter, vibrate, clash, rumble, thunder.

tanginiwenei wail; *synonyms* (*n*) lament, moan, scream, complaint, lamentation, plaint, (*v*) howl, cry, ululate, bellow, bawl, bewail, mewl, roar, sob.

tangio fading; *synonyms* (*adj*) dying, disappearing, paling, weakening, (*n*) attenuation, bleaching, disappearance, evaporation; *antonym* (*n*) appearance.

tangira 1. like; *synonyms* (*v*) corresponding, enjoy, identical, care, desire, fancy, (*adj*) equal, equivalent, alike, analogous, comparable, same, parallel, (*n*) love, relish; *antonyms* (*prep*) unlike, (*v*) dislike, (*adj*) different, **2**. love; *synonyms* (*n*) affection, dear, fondness, liking, benevolence, charity, attachment, beloved, darling, devotion, honey, sweetheart, (*v*) cherish, like, worship; *antonyms* (*n*) abhorrence, hatred, aversion, (*v*) hate, abhor, **3**. cherish; *synonyms* (*v*) appreciate, entertain, foster, hug, nurture, treasure, cultivate, bosom, adore, esteem, harbor, nourish, nurse, prize, (*n*) embrace, **4**. affectionate; *synonyms* (*adj*) fond, loving, ardent, caring, cordial, devoted, kind, tender, warm, brotherly, amorous, friendly, gentle, lovesome, (*adv*) fatherly; *antonyms* (*adj*) cold, uncaring, **5**. kind; *synonyms* (*n*) form, helpful, sort, benign, brand, breed, class, type, variety, benevolent, (*adj*) generous, good, humane, affectionate, charitable; *antonyms* (*adj*) unkind, callous, cruel, hardhearted, mean, merciless, nasty, spiteful, upsetting, disagreeable, unfeeling, **6**. desire; *synonyms (n)* ambition, hope, aspiration, will, wish, craving, dream, impulse, lust, *(v)* aspire, seek, want, aim, choose, crave; *antonym (n)* reality, **7**. covet; *synonyms (v)* begrudge, envy, long, grudge, hanker, **8**. wish; *synonyms (v)* please, bid, prefer, intend, trust, *(n)* need, inclination, longing, pleasure, purpose, mind, request, urge, plan, thirst, **9**. want; *synonyms (v)* require, *(n)* lack, poverty, deficiency, deprivation, famine, absence, dearth, demand, destitution, indigence, necessity, penury, privation, shortage.

tangiraki 1. coveted; *synonyms (adj)* desired, craved, exceptional, impressive, marketable, **2**. cherished; *synonyms (adj)* beloved, dear, precious, loved, treasured, intimate, prized, valued, wanted, pet, **3**. liked; *synonyms (adj)* popular, favorite, preferred, **4**. adored; *synonyms (adj)* worshipped, respected, acclaimed, blessed, idolised, idolized, venerated, chosen, darling, established, recognized, **5**. desired; *synonyms (adj)* coveted, desirable, needed, welcome, adored, appropriate, proper, *(v)* complying, consenting, willing, desirous, disposed, ready, spontaneous; *antonym (adj)* undesirable, **6**. loved; *synonyms (adj)* cherished, appreciated, esteemed, important, **7**. wanted; *synonyms (adj)* required, invited, necessary, comfortable, cute, essential, fugitive, notorious, urgent, hunted, *(n)* runaway.

tangirarae 1. twang; *synonyms (n)* accent, intonation, piquancy, pungency, *(v)* pluck, flavor, jar, play, strum, burr, creak, grate, pipe, savor, smack, **2**. tinkle; *synonyms (n)* chink, ring, chime, sound, clang, *(v)* jingle, clink, tink, ting, clank, buzz.

tangirariki prefer; *synonyms (v)* choose, pick, advance, elect, elevate, favor, like, opt, favour, promote, select, want, dignify, fancy, desire.

tangirarikiaki preferred; *synonyms (adj)* favored, favorite, chosen, pet, select, favourite, selected, choice, preferable.

tangiroa 1. bewail; *synonyms (v)* bemoan, lament, deplore, mourn, complain, grieve, regret, wail, weep, cry, moan, plain, repent, sorrow, **2**. bemoan; *synonym (v)* bewail.

tangiroro 1. demand; *synonyms (n)* claim, request, requirement, requisition, sale, call, *(v)* ask, command, need, require, appeal, beg, charge, expect, involve; *antonym (v)* supply, **2**. scream; *synonyms (n)* cry, shriek, wail, *(v)* howl, shout, screech, yell, bellow, roar, hollo, halloo, bawl, exclaim, holler, outcry; *antonym (v)* whisper.

tangitang 1. complain; *synonyms (v)* beef, bemoan, bewail, protest, squawk, whine, grudge, accuse, carp, croak, gripe, grouse, grumble, mutter, object; *antonym (v)* compliment, **2**. grieve; *synonyms (v)*

distress, mourn, aggrieve, deplore, lament, sorrow, trouble, annoy, fret, hurt, injure, pain, regret, sadden, *(n)* afflict; *antonym (v)* please, **3**. moan; *synonyms (n)* groan, complaint, grievance, sob, wail, murmur, grunt, *(v)* complain, cry, howl, bleat, weep, whimper, hum, growl, **4**. cry; *synonyms (n)* shout, bark, scream, yell, clamor, roar, bay, crying, *(v)* call, bellow, shriek, exclaim, moan, outcry, screech; *antonyms (v)* laugh, whisper, **5**. jingle; *synonyms (n)* jangle, chime, chink, tune, doggerel, gingle, *(v)* ring, ding, clang, clank, clink, peal, rattle, sound, tinkle, **6**. whine; *synonyms (n)* drone, *(v)* sigh, squeal, buzz, grizzle, snivel, bawl, blubber, yammer, kick, kvetch, **7**. peal; *synonyms (n)* noise, dingdong, blast, pealing, roll, rolling, thunder, *(v)* knell, toll, bang, blare, echo, *(adj)* swell, **8**. rung; *synonyms (n)* round, rundle, degree, grade, stage, stair, spoke, stave, step, tread, **9**. ring; *synonyms (n)* encircle, band, gang, jingle, loop, rim, circuit, annulus, arena, clique, hoop, *(v)* circle, resound, reverberate, gird.

tangitangaki rung; *synonyms (n)* round, rundle, degree, grade, stage, stair, spoke, stave, step, tread.

tangkongkoa gather; *synonyms (v)* deduce, convene, accumulate, amass, assemble, collect, compile, congregate, flock, garner, meet, tuck, earn, rally, *(n)* fold; *antonyms (v)* disperse, scatter.

tangkongkoaki gathered; *synonyms (adj)* collected, deepened, accumulated, amassed, assembled, collective, congregate, equanimous, massed, poised.

tangoa borrow; *synonyms (v)* adopt, appropriate, assume, take, accept, acquire, plagiarize, cadge, obtain, sponge, usurp, charter, copy, imitate, *(n)* pledge; *antonym (v)* lend.

tangoaki borrowed; *synonyms (adj)* foreign, rubato, secondary, rented, robbed.

tangoingoi darken; *synonyms (v)* cloud, blur, blind, confuse, dim, conceal, fog, overcast, shade, shadow, overshadow, blacken, deepen, *(adj)* obscure, *(n)* adumbrate; *antonym (v)* brighten.

tangorake 1. groan; *synonyms (n)* grumble, cry, rumble, complaint, wail, *(v)* moan, murmur, howl, mutter, sigh, complain, squeak, scrape, rasp, sough, **2**. wail; *synonyms (n)* lament, scream, lamentation, plaint, shriek, *(v)* ululate, bellow, bawl, bewail, mewl, roar, sob, weep, whimper, whine.

tania 1. declare; *synonyms (v)* announce, advertise, affirm, allege, assert, say, attest, acknowledge, admit, aver, avow, proclaim, call, divulge, *(adj)* communicate; *antonym (v)* deny, **2**. claim; *synonyms (n)* charge, allegation, privilege, right, title, application, *(v)* demand, ask, exact, arrogate, contend, need, require, requisition, want; *antonyms (v)* disclaim, forfeit, **3**. penetrate; *synonyms (v)* bore, imbue, fathom, infiltrate, permeate, pierce, cut, filter, interpenetrate, enter, drill, diffuse, percolate, perforate, probe, **4**. shift; *synonyms* (*n*) interchange, turn, move, switch, conversion, (*v*) change, exchange, remove, quibble, alter, budge, convert, displace, transfer, fluctuate.

taniaki declared; *synonyms* (*adj*) avowed, stated, apparent, affirmed, alleged, confirmed, indictive, ostensible, acknowledged, exhibited.

tanibaba 1. encumbered; *synonyms* (*adj*) laden, burdened, burdensome, clayey, cloggy, deep, heavy, forcible, full, gloomy, inactive, loud, oppressive, overloaded, ponderous, **2**. obstructed; *synonyms* (*adj*) hindered, blind, blocked, congested, foiled, frustrated, impedite, stymied, thwarted, tight; *antonym* (*adj*) successful.

tanibabu 1. dark; *synonyms* (*adj*) black, dismal, cheerless, dim, obscure, blind, blue, deep, gloomy, murky, mysterious, (*n*) cloudy, darkness, evening, night; *antonyms* (*adj*) bright, sunny, fair, clear, pale, pallid, sunlit, (*n*) light, day, **2**. cloudy; *synonyms* (*adj*) dull, nebulous, opaque, dark, foggy, misty, muddy, turbid, sunless, vaporous, dusky, hazy, heavy, overcast, shady; *antonym* (*adj*) cloudless, **3**. overcast; *synonyms* (*adj*) clouded, depressing, gray, leaden, obnubilated, (*n*) cloud, overcasting, cloudiness, (*v*) darken, fog, becloud, overshadow, befog, mist.

taniberoro 1. stifling; *synonyms* (*adj*) close, sultry, oppressive, stuffy, sweltering, heavy, hot, airless, muggy, sticky, torrid, humid, (*n*) crushing, quelling, suppression; *antonym* (*adj*) fresh, **2**. stale; *synonyms* (*adj*) musty, old, commonplace, hackneyed, banal, corny, flat, insipid, moldy, stagnant, trite, dull, obsolete, cold, (*v*) dry; *antonyms* (*adj*) original, innovative.

tanimaeao westward; *synonyms* (*adv*) west, westwards, (*adj*) westerly, westbound, western.

tanin grouped; *synonyms* (*adj*) sorted, collective.

taninga wait; *synonyms* (*v*) expect, anticipate, stop, ambush, await, lurk, stay, linger, remain, abide, hesitate, (*n*) delay, pause, hold, (*adj*) tarry.

taningaia wait; *synonyms* (*v*) expect, anticipate, stop, ambush, await, lurk, stay, linger, remain, abide, hesitate, (*n*) delay, pause, hold, (*adj*) tarry.

taningamarau 1. diligent; *synonyms* (*adj*) busy, active, assiduous, careful, painstaking, earnest, attentive, industrious, laborious, studious, occupied, brisk, conscientious, indefatigable, meticulous; *antonyms* (*adj*) lazy, careless, negligent, **2**. docile; *synonyms* (*adj*) gentle, compliant, dutiful, humble, meek, obedient, submissive, tame, teachable, acquiescent, conformable, kind, subservient, amenable, (*v*) tractable; *antonyms* (*adj*) rebellious, stubborn, assertive, **3**. dutiful; *synonyms* (*adj*) duteous, deferential, devoted, docile, faithful, good, loyal, pious, constant, respectful, stanch, devout; *antonym* (*adj*)

disobedient, **4**. obedient; *synonyms* (*adj*) biddable, orderly, manageable, subject, obsequious, pliable, quiet, servile, willing, yielding; *antonym* (*adj*) defiant.

taninganinga 1. idle; *synonyms* (*adj*) inactive, indolent, lazy, free, baseless, frivolous, fruitless, groundless, unfounded, empty, disengaged, flimsy, barren, dead, futile; *antonyms* (*adj*) busy, active, employed, (*v*) change, **2**. apathetic; *synonyms* (*adj*) indifferent, cool, impassive, uninterested, perfunctory, casual, dull, lethargic, lukewarm, nonchalant, sluggish, spiritless, detached, callous, cold; *antonyms* (*adj*) energetic, enthusiastic, fervent, inquisitive, **3**. careless; *synonyms* (*adj*) inconsiderate, cursory, forgetful, haphazard, inattentive, insouciant, reckless, hasty, imprudent, inadvertent, incautious, lax, listless, (*v*) heedless, (*adv*) thoughtless; *antonyms* (*adj*) careful, cautious, prudent, attentive, diligent, meticulous, thorough, thoughtful, guarded, methodical, strict, wary.

taningaroti 1. lazy; *synonyms* (*adj*) indolent, idle, inert, drowsy, inactive, shiftless, dull, faineant, remiss, slothful, slow, sluggish, leisurely, sluggard, tardy; *antonyms* (*adj*) energetic, diligent, active, **2**. indolent; *synonyms* (*adj*) lazy, careless, listless, otiose, torpid, lackadaisical, languid, lethargic, passive, slack, supine, futile, **3**. inert; *synonyms* (*adj*) dead, dormant, flat, inanimate, lifeless, still, stationary, apathetic, heavy, immobile, indifferent, motionless, neutral, static, fixed; *antonyms* (*adj*) moving, animate, **4**. idle; *synonyms* (*adj*) free, baseless, frivolous, fruitless, groundless, unfounded, empty, disengaged, flimsy, barren, jobless, light, unemployed, (*v*) loaf, moon; *antonyms* (*adj*) busy, employed, (*v*) change, **5**. sluggish; *synonyms* (*adj*) obtuse, dilatory, backward, blunt, leaden, stupid, weak, gradual, dim, phlegmatic, dense, deliberate, stagnant, glacial, (*n*) sleepy; *antonyms* (*adj*) brisk, fast, **6**. slothful; *synonym* (*adj*) ineffectual.

taningato 1. faithless; *synonyms* (*adj*) disloyal, dishonest, deceitful, false, traitorous, treacherous, unfaithful, untrue, untrustworthy, fickle, incredulous, mendacious, perfidious, truthless, fraudulent; *antonym* (*adj*) faithful, **2**. disloyal; *synonyms* (*adj*) faithless, treasonable, disaffected, rebellious; *antonyms* (*adj*) loyal, honest, **3**. subversive; *synonyms* (*adj*) seditious, incendiary, insurgent, (*n*) revolutionary, destructive, radical, revolutionist.

taningo 1. distant; *synonyms* (*adj*) cold, aloof, remote, chill, cool, detached, far, reserved, long, faraway, icy, indifferent, removed, (*adv*) apart, (*n*) chilly; *antonyms* (*adj*) close, adjacent, friendly, near, nearby, neighboring, warm, pending, alert, intimate, involved, **2**. fleeting; *synonyms* (*adj*) brief, ephemeral, evanescent, fugitive, momentary, passing, short, transient, cursory, rapid, short-lived, temporal, transitory, vanishing, elusive; *antonyms* (*adj*) lasting, permanent, **3.** untouchable; *synonyms* (*adj*) inaccessible, unassailable, sacred, inviolable, invulnerable, unobtainable, unprocurable, (*n*) outcast; *antonym* (*adj*) vulnerable.

tanitoko sedentary; *synonyms* (*adj*) inactive, lazy, sluggish, domestic, calm, desk, deskbound, desk-bound, idle, indolent, slothful, torpid, tranquil, (*v*) untraveled; *antonym* (*adj*) active.

tanna relish; *synonyms* (*v*) enjoy, bask, delight, like, (*n*) flavor, gusto, fancy, liking, love, palate, appetizer, enjoyment, enthusiasm, spice, (*adj*) savor; *antonym* (*v*) dislike.

tannaba roll; *synonyms* (*n*) list, revolution, catalogue, inventory, register, (*v*) coil, reel, curl, enfold, revolve, wheel, rock, turn, twist, wallow.

tannabaki rolled; *synonyms* (*adj*) rolling, furled, involute, beaten, billowing, kinky, level, resonant, resonating, resounding, reverberating, reverberative, spiral, trilled, tumbling.

tannaki diffused; *synonyms* (*adj*) dim, softened, dull, flowing, gentle, loose, mellow, muffled, muted, subtle.

tannene 1. fickle; *synonyms* (*adj*) erratic, capricious, volatile, inconsistent, mercurial, mobile, variable, changeful, giddy, inconstant, shifting, skittish, unfaithful, unstable, (*v*) changeable; *antonyms* (*adj*) resolute, untiring, **2.** variable; *synonyms* (*adj*) fickle, fitful, mutable, uncertain, unsettled, unsteady, fluctuating, variant, versatile, adaptable, immethodical, irregular, uneven, wavering, fluid; *antonyms* (*adj*) constant, fixed, invariable, regular, set, smooth, **3.** unsteady; *synonyms* (*adj*) dizzy, insecure, rickety, shaky, unbalanced, unsound, precarious, jerky, wobbly, irresolute, ramshackle, flighty, ticklish, loose, (*n*) doubtful; *antonym* (*adj*) steady, **4.** unstable; *synonyms* (*adj*) unpredictable, unreliable, neurotic, perilous, unsafe, uneasy, infirm, slippery, disturbed, rocky, weak, dangerous, flowing, fugitive, (*v*) perishable; *antonym* (*adj*) stable.

tano sand; *synonyms* (*n*) grit, guts, dust, beach, coast, seaside, backbone, dirt, gumption, shore, (*v*) sandpaper, rub, smooth, (*adj*) powder.

tanoata 1. known; *synonyms* (*adj*) well-known, familiar, conscious, certain, accepted, acknowledged, plain, published, understood, evident, recognized, apparent, aware, common, apprised; *antonyms* (*adj*) nameless, unknown, secret, unidentified, **2.** manifest; *synonyms* (*adj*) clear, conspicuous, distinct, patent, discernible, obvious, (*v*) demonstrate, display, evidence, exhibit, express, indicate, attest, certify, (*n*) declare; *antonym* (*adj*) unclear, **3.** public; *synonyms* (*adj*) national, overt, civic, general, communal, mutual,

popular, ordinary, (*n*) folk, community, people, populace, audience, (*v*) open, plebeian; *antonyms* (*adj*) private, confidential, personal, **4.** spread; *synonyms* (*v*) scatter, reach, disperse, expand, extend, broadcast, circulate, diffuse, disseminate, increase, propagate, stretch, broaden, deploy, (*n*) span; *antonym* (*adj*) concentrated.

tanoataki spread; *synonyms* (*v*) scatter, reach, disperse, expand, extend, broadcast, circulate, diffuse, disseminate, increase, propagate, stretch, broaden, deploy, (*n*) span; *antonym* (*adj*) concentrated.

tanoi 1. dizzy; *synonyms* (*adj*) dazed, giddy, faint, frivolous, light, silly, vertiginous, featherbrained, flighty, muzzy, unsteady, airheaded, woozy, (*v*) daze; *antonyms* (*adj*) alert, clear-headed, **2.** giddy; *synonyms* (*adj*) dizzy, changeable, fickle, capricious, vacillating, bewildered, flippant, unstable, volatile, gay, (*adv*) careless, rash, thoughtless.

tanomaki 1. confuse; *synonyms* (*v*) bewilder, baffle, confound, muddle, agitate, blur, derange, disconcert, disturb, fluster, jumble, mystify, obscure, perplex, puzzle; *antonyms* (*v*) clarify, enlighten, elucidate, explain, **2.** excited; *synonyms* (*adj*) agitated, ablaze, emotional, enthusiastic, frantic, ardent, aroused, delirious, fervent, heated, impassioned, passionate, warm, elated, (*v*) animated; *antonyms* (*adj*) calm, cool, unexcited, **3.** excite; *synonyms* (*v*) animate, arouse, enliven, energize, awaken, electrify, encourage, evoke, exasperate, incite, inspire, kindle, provoke, quicken, rouse; *antonyms* (*v*) pacify, bore, **4.** agitated; *synonyms* (*adj*) restless, excited, nervous, restive, tumultuous, upset, distressed, tense, alarmed, anxious, distraught, jumpy, overwrought, perturbed, shaken; *antonyms* (*adj*) composed, lethargic, **5.** panic; *synonyms* (*n*) alarm, dismay, horror, scare, dread, fright, anxiety, fear, flap, hysteria, funk, (*v*) shock, (*adj*) consternation, terror, awe; *antonym* (*n*) composure.

tanomakiaki 1. confused; *synonyms* (*adj*) abashed, bewildered, baffled, befuddled, bemused, chaotic, confounded, disjointed, disordered, dizzy, incoherent, indistinct, ambiguous, (*n*) cloudy, (*adv*, *adj*) topsy-turvy; *antonyms* (*adj*) clear, enlightened, alert, clearheaded, clear-headed, orderly, **2.** excited; *synonyms* (*adj*) agitated, ablaze, emotional, enthusiastic, frantic, ardent, aroused, delirious, fervent, heated, impassioned, passionate, warm, elated, (*v*) animated; *antonyms* (*adj*) calm, cool, unexcited, **3.** panicked; *synonyms* (*adj*) panicky, scared, frightened, terrified.

tanotano 1. gritty; *synonyms* (*adj*) courageous, fearless, game, grainy, granular, spirited, brave, gravelly, mettlesome, resolute, rough, sandy, spunky, farinaceous, (*v*) firm; *antonym* (*adj*) smooth, **2.** sandy; *synonyms* (*adj*) gritty, light, arenaceous, sabulous, dusty, loose, mealy, powdery, branny, creamy, flaxen, flocculent, floury, friable, furfuraceous.

tantan spotted; *synonyms* (*adj*) mottled, dappled, speckled, blotchy, dotted, flyblown, piebald, multicolored, dirty, spotty, stained, tainted, besmirched, damaged, freckled; *antonym* (*adj*) plain.

tantani 1. guard; *synonyms* (*n*) defend, defense, bulwark, care, cover, escort, protection, watchman, custody, convoy, defence, fender, guardsman, (*v*) shield, keep, 2. watch; *synonyms* (*v*) observe, clock, look, see, regard, wake, protect, check, follow, (*n*) guard, view, sentinel, sentry, surveillance, (*adj*) vigilance, 3. supervise; *synonyms* (*v*) administer, manage, superintend, control, direct, monitor, oversee, run, conduct, handle, inspect, administrate, command, head, lead.

tantaniaki 1. guarded; *synonyms* (*adj*) cautious, careful, wary, chary, circumspect, cagey, vigilant, watchful, conditional, discreet, gingerly, conservative, prudent, reserved, safe; *antonyms* (*adj*) frank, honest, 2. supervised.

tantano 1. soiled; *synonyms* (*adj*) dingy, dirty, grubby, nasty, grimy, filthy, unclean, muddy, black, foul, mucky, polluted, squalid, stained, contaminated; *antonyms* (*adj*) clean, pure, 2. soil; *synonyms* (*n*) ground, dirt, grime, land, dust, (*v*) smudge, blot, contaminate, pollute, mire, blemish, defile, mould, smear, (*adj*) blur, 3. sandy; *synonyms* (*adj*) gritty, light, granular, arenaceous, sabulous, dusty, farinaceous, loose, mealy, powdery, branny, creamy, flaxen, flocculent, floury.

tantanoaki soiled; *synonyms* (*adj*) dingy, dirty, grubby, nasty, grimy, filthy, unclean, muddy, black, foul, mucky, polluted, squalid, stained, contaminated; *antonyms* (*adj*) clean, pure.

tanua approximate; *synonyms* (*adj*) approximative, near, rough, general, inexact, (*v*) approach, approaching, estimate, judge, place, reckon; *antonyms* (*v*) exact, precise.

tao 1. about; *synonyms* (*prep*) encircling, for, encompassing, circa, concerning, (*adv*) around, approximately, almost, nearly, most, roughly, in, nearby, (*adj*) some, near; *antonyms* (*prep*) exactly, precisely, 2. full; *synonyms* (*adj*) complete, absolute, abundant, broad, flush, ample, enough, extensive, total, detailed, comprehensive, copious, good, (*n*) entire, crowded; *antonyms* (*adj*) empty, lacking, starving, hungry, sketchy, incomplete, 3. conceivably; *synonyms* (*adv*) perhaps, possibly, maybe, perchance, believably, credibly, probably, reasonably, 4. enough; *synonyms* (*adv*) rather, plenty, amply, adequately, satisfaction, fairly, fully, only, (*n*) adequacy, fill, sufficiency, (*adj*) sufficient,

adequate, competent, decent; *antonym* (*adj*) inadequate, 5. maybe; *synonyms* (*adv*) peradventure, debatably, questionably, conceivable, credible, feasible, imaginably, obtainable, potentially, (*n*) uncertainty; *antonym* (*adv*) definitely, 6. might; *synonyms* (*v*) can, could, (*n*) force, energy, power, ability, influence, brawn, intensity, puissance, strength, vehemence, authority, capability, efficacy; *antonym* (*n*) weakness, 7. possibly; *synonym* (*adv*) conceivably; *antonyms* (*adv*) impossibly, unimaginably, 8. perchance; *synonyms* (*adv*) accidentally, incidentally, mayhap, chance, 9. overabundant; *synonyms* (*adj*) overmuch, plethoric, rank, rife, prevailing, prevalent, 10. perhaps, 11. overflowing; *synonyms* (*v*) inundation, deluge, drenched, (*adj*) full, exuberant, flooding, bountiful, generous, brimming, profuse, superfluous, afloat, awash, flooded, (*n*) flood.

taoakai 1. press; *synonyms* (*n*) jam, closet, (*v*) crush, crowd, force, squeeze, pack, coerce, compress, exhort, mash, push, urge, clasp, (*adj*) constrain, 2. squeeze; *synonyms* (*v*) hug, pinch, embrace, extort, cram, nip, squash, compact, condense, constrict, oppress, contract, cuddle, (*n*) press, grip; *antonym* (*v*) loosen.

taoakaiaki pressed; *synonyms* (*adj*) compact, printed, pushed, stamped, bound, driven, embossed, encouraged, impelled, imprinted, incited, marked, provoked, prompted.

taobukia 1. aid; *synonyms* (*n*) assist, help, assistance, encouragement, relief, backing, boost, care, (*v*) support, benefit, abet, ease, facilitate, minister, serve; *antonyms* (*n*) hindrance, (*v*) hinder, 2. annotate; *synonyms* (*v*) gloss, comment, explain, expound, footnote, interpret, illustrate, edit, elucidate, unfold, (*n*) note, account, billet, brand, character.

taobukiaki 1. aided; *synonyms* (*adj*) assisted, favored, countenanced, featured, 2. annotated.

taobura observe; *synonyms* (*v*) celebrate, comment, notice, commemorate, mind, guard, behold, discover, follow, heed, keep, look, mark, mention, note; *antonyms* (*v*) ignore, feel.

taoburaki observed; *synonyms* (*adj*) seen, ascertained, discovered, empirical, disclosed, experiential, experimental, visual, practical, pragmatic, revealed.

taoburoburo skim; *synonyms* (*v*) glide, slip, browse, skip, sweep, brush, fly, graze, race, read, scan, shave, glance, (*n*) cream, slide.

taokabia 1. forestall; *synonyms* (*v*) avert, forbid, prevent, foreclose, obviate, preclude, stop, engross, avoid, frustrate, counter, expect, foresee, (*adv*) anticipate, (*adj*) monopolize, 2. block; *synonyms* (*n*) bar, barricade, pad, clog, cluster, barrier, (*v*) arrest, hinder, encumber, halt, lock, obstruct, parry, plug, (adj) lump; *antonyms* (v) free, unblock, open, **3.** intercept; *synonyms* (v) block, break, check, waylay, cease, grab, discontinue, tap, bug, (n) interrupt, **4.** preclude; *synonyms* (v) exclude, forestall, debar, prohibit, thwart, interdict, deter, disqualify, foil, eliminate, **5.** trap; *synonyms* (n) snare, net, ambush, gin, mesh, noose, entanglement, ambuscade, bait, (v) catch, entrap, ensnare, trick, entangle, capture, **6.** snare; *synonyms* (n) trap, lure, decoy, pitfall, temptation, trapan, (v) hook, enmesh, seize, allurement, springe, pilfer.

taokabiaki 1. blocked; *synonyms* (adj) jammed, clogged, locked, barren, blind, congested, foiled, fruitless, frustrated, infertile, lodged, plugged, sterile, stiff, stuck; *antonyms* (adj) successful, free, **2.** trapped; *synonyms* (adj) cornered, attentive, captive, confined, ensnared, entangled, fascinated, fixed, intent, rapt, restrained, spellbound, treed, wedged, abandoned.

taokai 1. climb; *synonyms* (v) ascend, arise, clamber, escalate, increase, scale, scramble, (n) rise, mount, ascent, acclivity, advance, ascending, jump, ascension; *antonyms* (v) descend, drop, **2.** press; *synonyms* (n) jam, closet, (v) crush, crowd, force, squeeze, pack, coerce, compress, exhort, mash, push, urge, clasp, (adj) constrain, **3.** scale; *synonyms* (n) flake, gamut, degree, graduation, measure, yardstick, rate, chip, criterion, fur, gradation, (v) climb, gauge, weigh, (adj) balance.

taokaiaki 1. pressed; *synonyms* (adj) compact, printed, pushed, stamped, bound, driven, embossed, encouraged, impelled, imprinted, incited, marked, provoked, prompted, **2.** scaled; *synonyms* (adj) scaly, lepidote, leprose, scabrous, scaley, scurfy.

taokitana 1. doctor; *synonyms* (n) physician, doc, medico, (v) cure, adulterate, attend, fix, heal, mend, remedy, repair, cook, debase, falsify, leech; *antonym* (v) break, **2.** treat; *synonyms* (v) handle, deal, manage, process, nurse, regale, operate, doctor, (n) feast, administer, delicacy, luxury, tidbit, banquet, entertainment.

taokitanaki treated; *synonyms* (adj) hardened, tempered, toughened, considered, enured, inured, set, tough.

taoman 1. compute; *synonyms* (v) calculate, cipher, account, measure, cast, add, count, enumerate, gauge, reckon, assess, estimate, figure, sum, tally, **2.** reckon; *synonyms* (v) deem, judge, hold, compute, guess, number, consider, rate, make, believe, esteem, expect, plan, regard, suppose.

taomaneka scent; *synonyms* (n) perfume, fragrance, smell, aroma, bouquet, essence, redolence, odour, savor, flavor, flavour, incense, clue, (v) odor, nose.

taomanekaki scented; *synonyms* (adj) odorous, aromatic, fragrant, perfumed, balmy, odoriferous, redolent, sweet, spicy.

taomaoma attract; *synonyms* (v) fascinate, charm, beguile, captivate, draw, enamor, entice, invite, tempt, arrest, absorb, appeal, attach, beckon, (adj) allure; *antonyms* (v) repel, disgust.

taomoa 1. abundant; *synonyms* (adj) copious, generous, lush, luxuriant, thick, plenty, affluent, ample, fertile, fruitful, liberal, plentiful, prolific, rich, substantial; *antonyms* (adj) scarce, sparse, meager, **2.** excessive; *synonyms* (adj) inordinate, exaggerated, intense, enormous, exorbitant, extravagant, extreme, exuberant, immoderate, profuse, superfluous, undue, unreasonable, huge, lavish; *antonyms* (adj) reasonable, moderate, affordable.

taon 1. curb; *synonyms* (v) check, control, limit, restrict, confine, conquer, contain, restrain, suppress, gag, repress, (n) bridle, kerb, restraint, (adv) moderate; *antonym* (v) intensify, **2.** restrain; *synonyms* (v) curb, hold, rein, bind, arrest, bound, govern, inhibit, prevent, circumscribe, constrain, detain, impede, keep, qualify.

taona 1. infest; *synonyms* (v) plague, disturb, overrun, beset, pester, annoy, invade, **2.** crush; *synonyms* (n) squeeze, press, crowd, (v) beat, break, compress, conquer, crunch, stamp, bruise, jam, mash, overpower, overwhelm, quash, **3.** lower; *synonyms* (adj) debase, inferior, (v) degrade, diminish, frown, humble, dip, abase, cut, descend, drop, scowl, disgrace, decrease, (n) depress; *antonyms* (v) increase, raise, **4.** lean; *synonyms* (adj) emaciated, gaunt, thin, bony, lank, lanky, (v) incline, bend, list, slant, bow, careen, pitch, (n) tilt, inclination; *antonyms* (adj) fat, plump, **5.** curb; *synonyms* (v) check, control, limit, restrict, confine, contain, restrain, suppress, gag, repress, stifle, (n) bridle, kerb, restraint, (adv) moderate; *antonym* (v) intensify, **6.** immerse; *synonyms* (v) douse, plunge, absorb, drench, drown, dunk, bury, engross, engulf, steep, submerge, bathe, duck, sink, soak, **7.** compress; *synonyms* (v) abridge, compact, condense, contract, pack, abbreviate, concentrate, constrict, cram, crush, pinch, stuff, tighten, (n) bandage, pledget; *antonym* (v) loosen, **8.** hold; *synonyms* (v) keep, detain, endure, adhere, bear, comprise, entertain, have, arrest, carry, delay, (n) grasp, grip, clasp, clutch; *antonym* (v) release, **9.** smother; *synonyms* (v) quench, choke, muffle, suffocate, extinguish, asphyxiate, deaden, cover, inhibit, curb, kill, strangle, strangulate, throttle, (n) clutter, **10.** overcome; *synonyms* (v) subdue, vanquish, defeat, master, hurdle, prevail, subjugate, surmount, demolish, affect, cross, exceed, outdo, (adj) beaten, conquered; *antonyms* (v) fail, (adj) victorious, unimpressed, **11.** suppress;

synonyms (v) quell, silence, conceal, oppress, stop, hide, overcome, smother, squash, hush, seize, lay, reduce, hold, mortify; *antonym* (v) express, **12.** overwhelm; *synonyms* (v) flood, inundate, overthrow, deluge, astound, overtake, overturn, swamp, astonish, overlay, confuse, daze, destroy, overload, overmaster, **13.** subdue; *synonyms* (v) chasten, soften, mitigate, domesticate, abate, allay, capture, daunt, pacify, still, dominate, intimidate, (n) impair, (adj) tame, mollify; *antonym* (v) surrender, **14.** press; *synonyms* (n) closet, newspaper, (v) force, coerce, exhort, push, urge, hug, pressure, stress, entreat, drive, hasten, (adj) constrain, weigh, **15.** trample; *synonyms* (v) tramp, tread, flatten, (n) trampling.

taonaba spread; *synonyms* (v) scatter, reach, disperse, expand, extend, broadcast, circulate, diffuse, disseminate, increase, propagate, stretch, broaden, deploy, (n) span; *antonym* (adj) concentrated.

taonabaki spread; *synonyms* (v) scatter, reach, disperse, expand, extend, broadcast, circulate, diffuse, disseminate, increase, propagate, stretch, broaden, deploy, (n) span; *antonym* (adj) concentrated.

taonaki 1. immersed; *synonyms* (adj) absorbed, submerged, engrossed, deep, underwater, attentive, bathed, buried, captivated, concentrated, covered, engaged, enthralled, fascinated, gripped, **2.** crushed; *synonyms* (v) victimized, (adj) broken, beaten, low, subdued, conquered, flattened, dispirited, compressed, overwhelmed, abashed, abject, blue, brokenhearted, (n) crushing; *antonyms* (adj) loose, victorious, **3.** downed; *synonym* (adj) felled, **4.** curbed; *synonyms* (adj) checked, limited, checkered, chequered, continent, cramped, pent-up, restricted, silent, small, temperate, **5.** lowered; *synonyms* (adj) abased, bated, cheap, humbled, restrained, **6.** compressed; *synonyms* (adj) compact, dense, flat, tight, pointed, concise, packed, close, besotted, bland, blotto, categoric, categorical, concrete, firm, **7.** held; *synonyms* (adj) confined, alleged, assumed, believed, bound, caged, captive, detained, fast, immersed, obsessed, occupied, protected, rapt, (adv) on, **8.** infested; *synonyms* (adj) plagued, contaminated, diseased, infected, malodorous, overrun, polluted, swarming, filled, flooded, swamped, teeming, **9.** pressed; *synonyms* (adj) printed, pushed, stamped, driven, embossed, encouraged, impelled, imprinted, incited, marked, provoked, prompted, **10.** subdued; *synonyms* (adj) muffled, quiet, soft, dull, muted, tame, faint, resigned, repressed, meek, delicate, sober, crushed, gentle, mild; *antonyms* (adj) loud, enthusiastic, lively, **11.** restrained; *synonyms* (adj) moderate, reserved, modest, discreet, reasonable, reticent, unemotional,

guarded, understated, calm, cautious, chaste, noncommittal, tasteful, unobtrusive; *antonyms* (adj) exaggerated, unrestrained, flashy, immoral, open, ostentatious, wild, **12.** overwhelmed; *synonyms* (v) overborne, (adj) overcome, overpowered, vanquished, dumbfounded, engulfed, inundated, overthrown; *antonym* (adj) unimpressed, **13.** suppressed; *synonyms* (adj) smothered, stifled, strangled, downtrodden, composed, concealed, covert, doomed, dormant, embryonic, forgotten, hidden, latent, subconscious, (n) subordinate; *antonym* (adj) available, **14.** overcome; *synonyms* (v) conquer, beat, crush, subdue, vanquish, defeat, master, overpower, hurdle, overwhelm, prevail, subjugate, surmount, demolish, affect; *antonym* (v) fail, **15.** smothered; *synonym* (adj) suppressed, **16.** trampled; *synonyms* (adj) trodden, compacted, firmed.

taonakia press; *synonyms* (n) jam, closet, (v) crush, crowd, force, squeeze, pack, coerce, compress, exhort, mash, push, urge, clasp, (adj) constrain.

taonakiaki pressed; *synonyms* (adj) compact, printed, pushed, stamped, bound, driven, embossed, encouraged, impelled, imprinted, incited, marked, provoked, prompted.

taonanoa 1. force; *synonyms* (n) energy, strength, agency, effect, enforce, impetus, (v) drive, coerce, pressure, squeeze, thrust, compel, cram, impel, (adj) constrain; *antonyms* (n) weakness, persuasion, **2.** press; *synonyms* (n) jam, closet, newspaper, (v) crush, crowd, force, pack, compress, exhort, mash, push, urge, clasp, hug, pinch.

taonanoaki 1. forced; *synonyms* (adj) compulsory, compelled, bound, artificial, constrained, involuntary, unnatural, farfetched, false, labored, obligatory, obliged, strained; *antonyms* (adj) free, unprovoked, spontaneous, voluntary, **2.** pressed; *synonyms* (adj) compact, printed, pushed, stamped, driven, embossed, encouraged, impelled, imprinted, incited, marked, provoked, prompted.

taonikai 1. enslaved; *synonyms* (adj) bond, captive, beguiled, bound, captivated, charmed, cringing, delighted, dependent, enthralled, imprisoned, incarcerated, obsequious, servile, subject; *antonym* (adj) free, **2.** bonded; *synonyms* (adj) guaranteed, barred, bolted, responsible, secured, warranted, fast, latched, locked, **3.** subjugated; *synonyms* (v) subdued, apart, blighted, broken, contrite, cracked, disconnected, disunited, fractured, (adj) beaten, downtrodden, overpowered, browbeaten, conquered, crushed; *antonyms* (adj) victorious, liberated, **4.** subdued; *synonyms* (adj) muffled, quiet, soft, dull, muted, restrained, tame, faint, resigned, repressed, low, meek, delicate, sober, gentle; *antonyms* (adj) loud, enthusiastic, lively.

taorababa 1. covering; *synonyms* (n) coating, cover, clothing, blanket, coat, casing, apparel, case, concealment, wrapper, awning, canopy, crust, envelope, film, **2**. spread; *synonyms* (*v*) scatter, reach, disperse, expand, extend, broadcast, circulate, diffuse, disseminate, increase, propagate, stretch, broaden, deploy, (*n*) span; *antonym* (*adj*) concentrated, **3**. spreading; *synonyms* (*adj*) scattering, diffusing, contagious, diffusive, dispersive, (*n*) diffusion, dissemination, propagation, dispersion, circulation, spread, dispersal, extension, distribution, airing.

taorona salt; *synonyms* (*n*) salinity, sal, blunt, cream, dust, mopus, (*adj*) salty, saline, briny, spice, pungent, season, (*v*) cure, pickle, embalm.

taoronaki salted; *synonyms* (*adj*) salt, salty, corned, saline, brackish, powdered, (*n*) antiseptic, bitter, corrective, flavor, leap, lecherous, lustful, pungent, sailor.

taoru preserve; *synonyms* (*v*) maintain, keep, defend, guard, hold, save, cure, pickle, protect, uphold, (*n*) conserve, jam, jelly, conserves, marmalade; *antonym* (*v*) destroy.

taoruaki preserved; *synonyms* (*adj*) condite, pickled, safe, whole, potted, sealed.

taotabo 1. lean; *synonyms* (*adj*) emaciated, gaunt, thin, bony, lank, lanky, (*v*) incline, bend, list, slant, bow, careen, pitch, (*n*) tilt, inclination; *antonyms* (*adj*) fat, plump, **2**. overload; *synonyms* (*n*) overburden, excess, (*v*) burden, overcharge, encumber, oppress, surcharge, glut, load, clog, overlay, overwhelm, overdo, overdose, overfeed.

taotaboaki overloaded; *synonyms* (*adj*) overcrowded, overladen, burdened, busy, congested, encumbered, laden, loaded, overfull, packed, clogged, jammed, stuffed, swarming, teeming; *antonym* (*adj*) empty.

taotebe submerge; *synonyms* (*v*) deluge, dive, drown, inundate, overwhelm, engulf, flood, cover, dip, douse, overflow, plunge, sink, soak, swamp.

taotebeaki submerged; *synonyms* (*adj*) immersed, subaqueous, submersed, sunken, underwater, subaquatic, submarine, covered, bathed, deep, engrossed, recessed, semiaquatic, suffused, (*pron*) drowned.

taotira 1. abundantly; *synonyms* (*adv*) freely, copiously, profusely, amply, generously, greatly, largely, plentifully, richly, adequately, fully, (*v*) well; *antonym* (*adv*) poorly, **2**. spread; *synonyms* (*v*) scatter, reach, disperse, expand, extend, broadcast, circulate, diffuse, disseminate, increase, propagate, stretch, broaden, deploy, (*n*) span; *antonym* (*adj*) concentrated, **3**. spreading; *synonyms* (*adj*) scattering, diffusing, contagious, diffusive, dispersive, (*n*) diffusion, dissemination, propagation, dispersion, circulation, spread, dispersal, extension, distribution, airing, **4**. superabundant; *synonyms* (*adj*) exuberant, excessive, profuse, plentiful, copious, redundant,

superfluous, inordinate, lavish, prodigal, **5**. plenty; *synonyms* (*n*) abundance, affluence, copiousness, many, much, plenteousness, exuberance, opulence, plenitude, galore, flood, multitude, (*adj*) enough, adequate, ample; *antonyms* (*n*) few, (*adj*) insufficient.

taotiraki spread; *synonyms* (*v*) scatter, reach, disperse, expand, extend, broadcast, circulate, diffuse, disseminate, increase, propagate, stretch, broaden, deploy, (*n*) span; *antonym* (*adj*) concentrated.

taoua take; *synonyms* (*v*) admit, get, hold, adopt, bear, carry, catch, clutch, obtain, return, borrow, pick, (*n*) seize, (*phr*) accept, receive; *antonyms* (*v*) give, refuse, abstain, add, lose.

taouanouk noon; *synonyms* (*n*) midday, noonday, noontide, crest, lunchtime, (*adj*) meridian, culmination, meridional.

taoumene shade; *synonyms* (*n*) screen, tinge, color, ghost, hue, blind, cloud, apparition, conceal, darkness, dye, (*v*) darken, shadow, tint, cover; *antonyms* (*n*) light, brightness.

tapa cheek; *synonyms* (*n*) audacity, boldness, brass, face, impertinence, nerve, gall, impudence, insolence, lip, mouth, daring, disrespect, effrontery, jowl; *antonym* (*n*) respect.

tapanou head; *synonyms* (*n*) chief, captain, front, point, boss, foam, froth, crown, chieftain, executive, chair, brain, (*v*) capital, direct, lead; *antonyms* (*n*) end, subordinate, (*v*) follow.

tapouanga shoulders; *synonym* (*n*) athlete.

tara 1. look; *synonyms* (*v*) seem, appear, expect, figure, attend, (*n*) face, gaze, appearance, aspect, air, countenance, expression, glance, guise, view, **2**. aspect; *synonyms* (*n*) look, surface, bearing, manner, prospect, side, angle, facet, feature, quality, respect, scene, vista, shape, (*v*) regard, **3**. behold; *synonyms* (*v*) see, contemplate, observe, perceive, consider, descry, discern, notice, watch, witness, **4**. appearance; *synonyms* (*n*) semblance, show, advent, apparition, form, image, impression, arrival, color, complexion, emergence, entrance, manifestation, performance, phenomenon; *antonyms* (*n*) disappearance, departure, vanishing, **5**. air; *synonyms* (*n*) tune, atmosphere, melody, strain, attitude, breeze, cast, feel, (*v*) ventilate, broadcast, transmit, vent, weather, aerate, beam, **6**. sprinkle; *synonyms* (*n*) dash, (*v*) scatter, drizzle, splash, moisten, dot, spatter, spray, rain, spill, spread, diffuse, intersperse, splatter, (*adj*) besprinkle, **7**. observe; *synonyms* (*v*) celebrate, comment, commemorate, mind, guard, behold, discover, follow, heed, keep, mark, mention, note, fulfill, comply; *antonym* (*v*) ignore, **8**. sight; *synonyms* (*n*) vision, glimpse, eye, eyesight, outlook, spectacle, ken, opinion, perception, perspective, (v) aim, spot, detect, find, (adj) eyesore, **9.** wipe; *synonyms* (v) rub, clean, mop, towel, brush, scour, scrub, clear, dry, wash, cover, (n) fling, flout, (adj) sponge, flush, **10.** saw; *synonyms* (v) cut, (n) adage, byword, proverb, dictum, maxim, saying, aphorism, axiom, motto.

tarabai 1. inspect; *synonyms* (v) examine, overhaul, overlook, survey, explore, inquire, look, review, scrutinize, view, watch, monitor, analyze, audit, check, **2.** check; *synonyms* (v) bridle, stop, block, limit, agree, halt, restrain, bar, dampen, delay, (n) control, arrest, curb, bill, cheque, **3.** examine; *synonyms* (v) assay, consider, try, search, ascertain, ask, contemplate, compare, canvass, essay, investigate, probe, quiz, study, test, **4.** supervise; *synonyms* (v) administer, manage, superintend, direct, oversee, run, conduct, handle, inspect, administrate, command, head, lead, observe, regulate.

tarabaiaki 1. checked; *synonyms* (adj) checkered, chequered, plaid, backward, curbed, intermittent, limited, numbered, pent-up, safe, silent, tartan, temperate, **2.** supervised.

tarabu 1. indolent; *synonyms* (adj) idle, inactive, lazy, slothful, sluggish, careless, drowsy, dull, faineant, inert, listless, otiose, slow, torpid, lackadaisical; *antonyms* (adj) energetic, active, **2.** apathetic; *synonyms* (adj) indifferent, cool, impassive, uninterested, perfunctory, casual, lethargic, lukewarm, nonchalant, spiritless, detached, indolent, callous, cold, inattentive; *antonyms* (adj) enthusiastic, fervent, inquisitive, **3.** dull; *synonyms* (adj) dim, blunt, dense, dreary, bland, boring, cloudy, dark, dismal, obtuse, slack, stupid, uninteresting, (v) deaden, dampen; *antonyms* (adj) bright, lively, sharp, exciting, interesting, lustrous, stimulating, amusing, exhilarating, glittery, glossy, glowing, high-pitched, intense, luminous, **4.** discouraging; *synonyms* (adj) depressing, chill, disheartening, bad, bleak, gloomy, sad; *antonym* (adj) encouraging.

tarabuaka 1. disproportion; *synonyms* (n) disparity, inequality, discrepancy, difference; *antonyms* (n) equality, proportion, symmetry, **2.** disproportionate; *synonyms* (adj) disproportional, incommensurate, undue, unequal, uneven, unsymmetrical, excessive, lopsided; *antonyms* (adj) equal, proportionate, **3.** asymmetrical; *synonyms* (adj) asymmetric, unbalanced, cockeyed, crooked, irregular; *antonyms* (adj) symmetrical, regular, **4.** bad; *synonyms* (adj) evil, adverse, harmful, immoral, naughty, poisonous, sad, sinister, wicked, malicious, infamous, appalling, awful, damaging, (v) decayed; *antonyms* (adj) fresh, pleasant, well, well-behaved, (n) good, **5.** ugly; *synonyms* (adj)

nasty, disagreeable, forbidding, frightful, gruesome, hideous, homely, repulsive, surly, offensive, atrocious, deformed, despicable, grotesque, horrible; *antonyms* (adj) beautiful, attractive, good-looking, flowing, ornamental.

tarae 1. allude; *synonyms* (v) advert, hint, refer, glance, intimate, suggest, touch, **2.** insinuate; *synonyms* (v) allude, imply, indicate, adumbrate, connote, ingratiate, signify, denote, impute, instill, **3.** metaphoric; *synonyms* (adj) metaphorical, figurative, symbolic, illustrative, abstract, allegorical, **4.** imply; *synonyms* (v) involve, entail, mean, argue, betoken, convey, implicate, carry, conceive, comprise, embody, import, infer, insinuate, (n) express.

taraeaki implied; *synonyms* (adj) implicit, understood, tacit, indirect, oblique, silent; *antonyms* (adj) direct, explicit.

taraki 1. observed; *synonyms* (adj) seen, ascertained, discovered, empirical, disclosed, experiential, experimental, visual, practical, pragmatic, revealed, **2.** sprinkled; *synonyms* (adj) besprent, scattered, dotted, speckled, spotted, spread, strewn.

taramangurea begrudge; *synonyms* (v) grudge, covet, envy, resent, pinch, stint.

taramata facing; *synonyms* (n) face, revetment, cladding, coating, lining, veneer, front, insert, (prep) opposite, against, before, (adj) fronting, diametric.

taramau 1. haggard; *synonyms* (adj) cadaverous, drawn, emaciated, gaunt, careworn, lean, tired, worn, thin, pinched, squalid, wan, wasted, bony; *antonyms* (adj) fresh, relaxed, **2.** ghostly; *synonyms* (adj) eerie, uncanny, ghostlike, spectral, spiritual, weird, supernatural, macabre, creepy, ghastly, phantasmal, spooky, unearthly, apparitional, **3.** gaunt; *synonyms* (adj) bleak, desolate, meager, angular, haggard, lanky, scrawny, skinny, spare, barren, hollow, depressed, skeletal; *antonym* (adj) plump.

tarao 1. missed; *synonyms* (adj) lost, baffled, befuddled, bemused, bewildered, confounded, confused, disoriented, forgotten, helpless, irretrievable, mazed, preoccupied, **2.** gone; *synonyms* (v) extinct, (adj) dead, past, absent, deceased, exhausted, away, bygone, departed, desperate, bypast, foregone, hopeless, late, missing; *antonym* (adj) present, **3.** past; *synonyms* (adj) beyond, former, old, back, earlier, gone, over, preceding, preterit, previous, prior, (n) history, (adv) by, before, (prf) along; *antonyms* (adj) contemporary, current, (prep) within, (n) future, prospect.

tarariao 1. glimpse; *synonyms* (n) glance, look, peek, peep, view, (v) blink, see, espy, notice, spot, spy, discover, **2.** glance; *synonyms* (n) gaze, glimpse, glitter, looking, regard, (v) flash, bounce, glint, ricochet, allude, brush, burnish, gleam, hint, refer; *antonym* (*v*) study.

tararuaia 1. control; *synonyms* (*n*) rule, authority, care, hold, influence, sway, ascendancy, ascendency, (*v*) command, check, curb, bridle, conduct, handle, conquer; *antonyms* (*n*) freedom, weakness, (*v*) intensify, share, **2**. supervisory; *synonyms* (*adj*) administrative, executive, managerial, predominant, supervisive, **3**. superintend; *synonyms* (*v*) manage, oversee, direct, administer, control, run, supervise, govern, overlook, inspect, observe, watch, **4**. oversee; *synonyms* (*v*) monitor, head, regulate, guide, superintend, deal, **5**. supervise; *synonyms* (*v*) administrate, lead, boss.

tararuaiaki 1. controlled; *synonyms* (*adj*) limited, restrained, restricted, temperate, subdued, inhibited, banned, calm, chaste, composed, confidential, conscious, conservative, contained, deliberate; *antonym* (*adj*) spontaneous, **2**. supervised.

taratara 1. looking; *synonyms* (*adj*) alert, sounding, (*n*) look, face, aspect, expression, feel, feeling, flavor, flavour, gaze, countenance, smell, (*prep*) appearing, liking, **2**. awake; *synonyms* (*adj*) alive, attentive, conscious, aware, intelligent, keen, sleepless, acute, (*v*) arouse, wake, awaken, waken, rouse, stimulate, stir; *antonyms* (*adj*) asleep, unconscious, comatose, sleeping, sleepy, **3**. boss; *synonyms* (*n*) chief, governor, head, overseer, superior, ruler, administrator, captain, director, executive, foreman, leader, (*v*) administer, govern, direct, **4**. bossy; *synonyms* (*adj*) authoritarian, domineering, autocratic, commanding, overbearing, dictatorial, dominating, lordly, magisterial, arrogant, peremptory, (*v*) bossed; *antonym* (*adj*) meek, **5**. supervise; *synonyms* (*v*) manage, superintend, check, control, monitor, oversee, run, conduct, handle, inspect, administrate, command, lead, observe, regulate, **6**. remark; *synonyms* (*n*) observation, regard, mind, commentary, heed, observance, reflection, (*v*) comment, notice, note, mention, perceive, mark, discern, see, **7**. watch; *synonyms* (*v*) clock, care, protect, defend, follow, (*n*) guard, view, sentinel, sentry, surveillance, lookout, patrol, timepiece, vigil, (*adj*) vigilance, **8**. spy; *synonyms* (*n*) scout, detective, mole, emissary, (*v*) espy, snoop, discover, descry, behold, investigate, recognize, sight, spot, distinguish, detect, **9**. superintend; *synonyms* (*v*) supervise, overlook, watch, **10**. regard; *synonyms* (*v*) attention, concern, estimate, attend, account, believe, consider, count, hold, reckon, appreciate, (*n*) respect, esteem, deference, value; *antonym* (*n*) disrespect, **11**. observe; *synonyms* (*v*) celebrate, commemorate, keep, fulfill, comply, find, maintain, obey, remark, honor, eye, contemplate,

acknowledge, examine, honour; *antonym* (*v*) ignore.

tarataraki 1. supervised, **2**. observed; *synonyms* (*adj*) seen, ascertained, discovered, empirical, disclosed, experiential, experimental, visual, practical, pragmatic, revealed.

tarau borrow; *synonyms* (*v*) adopt, appropriate, assume, take, accept, acquire, plagiarize, cadge, obtain, sponge, usurp, charter, copy, imitate, (*n*) pledge; *antonym* (*v*) lend.

tarauaki borrowed; *synonyms* (*adj*) foreign, rubato, secondary, rented, robbed.

tarauakina charge; *synonyms* (*n*) accusation, burden, care, command, commission, bill, tax, accusal, assail, (*v*) accuse, blame, attack, bid, load, arraign; *antonyms* (*v*) request, absolve, retreat.

tarauakinaki charged; *synonyms* (*adj*) fraught, laden, loaded, aerated, replete, abounding, deferred, electric, excited, explosive, invigorating, pregnant, supercharged, freighted, meaningful.

tare 1. meager; *synonyms* (*adj*) lean, emaciated, gaunt, feeble, inadequate, insufficient, spare, frugal, deficient, dry, exiguous, insignificant, (*v*) bare, barren, (*adv*) stingy; *antonyms* (*adj*) abundant, generous, lavish, **2**. infrequent; *synonyms* (*adj*) uncommon, few, rare, scarce, seldom, exceptional, occasional, sparse, sporadic, unusual, unwonted, intermittent, irregular, unfrequent; *antonyms* (*adj*) frequent, common, **3**. limited; *synonyms* (*adj*) finite, circumscribed, moderate, qualified, special, insular, bounded, narrow, scanty, slender, particular, specific, definite, conditional, constricted; *antonyms* (*adj*) boundless, infinite, limitless, open, complete, never-ending, unlimited, wide, **4**. uncommon; *synonyms* (*adj*) extraordinary, infrequent, odd, peculiar, singular, strange, unaccustomed, abnormal, remarkable, queer, different, unfamiliar, distinctive, eccentric, phenomenal; *antonym* (*adj*) typical, **5**. rare; *synonyms* (*adj*) precious, thin, choice, curious, fine, novel, exquisite, excellent, flimsy, priceless, raw, select, tenuous, unique, elegant; *antonym* (*adj*) ordinary, **6**. scarce; *synonyms* (*adj*) scant, lacking, meager, poor, short, wanting, (*adv*) barely, hardly, scarcely; *antonym* (*adj*) plentiful, **7**. sparse; *synonyms* (*adj*) limited, little, slight, light; *antonym* (*adj*) crowded, **8**. unconventional; *synonyms* (*adj*) improper, original, extreme, kinky, offbeat, wrong, (*n*) bohemian; *antonyms* (*adj*) conventional, usual, normal, orthodox.

tarere 1. restive; *synonyms* (*adj*) obstinate, edgy, fidgety, jittery, jumpy, nervy, restless, uptight, restiff, nervous, tense, uneasy, unruly, overstrung, (*v*) skittish; *antonym* (*adj*) relaxed, **2**. restless; *synonyms* (*adj*) unquiet, agitated, apprehensive, fretful, impatient, restive, feverish, turbulent, disturbed, wakeful, eager, hasty, mercurial, frightened, (v) anxious; *antonym* (adj) calm.

tari 1. juice; *synonyms* (n) extract, water, blood, gravy, liquid, succus, fluid, liquor, fuel, gasoline, current, oil, (adj) humor, serum, lymph, **2**. air; *synonyms* (n) tune, appearance, manner, atmosphere, look, melody, strain, face, (v) ventilate, broadcast, show, transmit, vent, weather, aerate, **3**. juicy; *synonyms* (adj) delicious, fat, gamy, luscious, succulent, lush, mellow, moist, racy, rich, sappy, spicy, blue, gamey, sensational; *antonym* (adj) dry, **4**. brethren; *synonyms* (n) assembly, congregation, people, family, flock, fold, laity, **5**. ocean; *synonyms* (n) sea, deep, brine, waves, multitude, lot, heap, pile, puddle, seaway, sink, splash, (adj) oceanic, marine, subaquatic, **6**. trace; *synonyms* (n) line, shadow, spot, clue, dash, hint, indication, mark, shade, sign, suggestion, touch, (v) track, hunt, pursue, **7**. salty; *synonyms* (adj) saline, salt, piquant, pungent, salted.

tári 1. brother; *synonyms* (n) fellow, pal, associate, buddy, chum, companion, compeer, comrade, counterpart, crony, friend, mate, monk, peer, sidekick; *antonym* (n) sister, **2**. sister; *synonyms* (n) nun, nurse, brother, twin, baby, double, match, member, pair, pendant, sis.

taribaba 1. imbecile; *synonyms* (adj) foolish, idiotic, fatuous, imbecilic, simple, (n) fool, idiot, moron, cretin, ass, oaf, changeling, **2**. senile; *synonyms* (adj) old, doddering, gaga, geriatric, elderly, doddery, decrepit, crazy, disabled, dotty, dull, enamored, infatuated, weak, enfeebled.

taribabu 1. calm; *synonyms* (adj) quiet, peaceful, tranquil, (v) assuage, appease, cool, still, allay, pacify, easy, moderate, mollify, steady, (n) lull, equanimity; *antonyms* (adj) agitated, angry, nervous, stormy, wild, annoyed, anxious, enraged, frantic, frightened, intense, irritable, (v) agitate, upset, (n) agitation, **2**. still; *synonyms* (adv) however, but, nevertheless, (adj) calm, silence, quiescent, serene, silent, inactive, motionless, mute, (n) hush, (v) compose, soothe, ease; *antonyms* (adj) moving, effervescent, fizzy, windy, (n) noisy, **3**. quiet; *synonyms* (adj) gentle, placid, tranquilize, collected, composed, dull, harmonious, hushed, low, (v) repose, gag, (n) peace, peacefulness, alleviate, leisure; *antonyms* (adj) loud, talkative, vociferous, active, (n) noise.

taribi 1. fragmented; *synonyms* (adj) broken, crumbled, disconnected, disjointed, disunited, abrupt, confused, cut, disordered, ragged, split, garbled, illogical, scattered, sketchy, **2**. granulated; *synonym* (adj) granulate.

taribo yellowish; *synonyms* (adj) yellow, sallow, chicken, chickenhearted, flavescent, jaundiced, luteous, saffrony, scandalmongering, sensationalistic, xanthous, yellowed, (n) buff.

taribobo pink; *synonyms* (adj) flower, pinkish, (n) red, crimson, rose, carmine, (v) knock, gore, impale, prick, punch, spear, spike, stab, enfilade.

taribono 1. constipated; *synonyms* (adj) costive, bellybound, close, cold, formal, impermeable, reserved, unyielding, (v) bound, certain, destined, resolved, **2**. blocked; *synonyms* (adj) jammed, clogged, locked, barren, blind, congested, foiled, fruitless, frustrated, infertile, lodged, plugged, sterile, stiff, stuck; *antonyms* (adj) successful, free.

taribubu 1. hazy; *synonyms* (adj) cloudy, fuzzy, blurred, blurry, faint, foggy, indistinct, misty, nebulous, vague, ambiguous, dull, bleary, brumous, dim; *antonyms* (adj) clear, bright, distinct, precise, **2**. misty; *synonyms* (adj) hazy, dark, wet, gloomy, damp, clouded, muddy, murky, obscure, opaque, steamy, thick, turbid, unclear, cloud, **3**. steamy; *synonyms* (adj) humid, torrid, muggy, hot, sultry, tropical.

tarie 1. evil; *synonyms* (adj) bad, corrupt, criminal, ill, wicked, depraved, destructive, harmful, malign, (n) damage, adversity, detriment, disaster, depravity, malice; *antonyms* (adj) kindhearted, (n) good, goodness, righteousness, **2**. bold; *synonyms* (adj) adventurous, audacious, manly, resolute, arrogant, barefaced, courageous, daring, fearless, heroic, intrepid, spirited, stalwart, bluff, brave; *antonyms* (adj) cowardly, timid, modest, **3**. wicked; *synonyms* (adj) atrocious, evil, sinful, vicious, immoral, mischievous, unholy, vile, diabolical, foul, hellish, iniquitous, nasty, naughty, pernicious; *antonyms* (adj) innocent, kind, moral, pious, pure, **4**. shameless; *synonyms* (adj) brazen, bold, immodest, graceless, profligate, blatant, unscrupulous, abandoned, impudent, indecent, obscene, unblushing, dissolute, insolent, lewd.

tarika brackish; *synonyms* (adj) salt, salty, saline, bracky, briny, nauseous, stagnant, salted.

tarikabana 1. awkward; *synonyms* (adj) clumsy, inconvenient, crude, embarrassing, inept, sticky, uncomfortable, ungainly, untoward, left-handed, annoying, bungling, cumbersome, difficult, graceless; *antonyms* (adj) graceful, easy, adroit, manageable, straightforward, convenient, dexterous, helpful, rotund, simple, **2**. weak; *synonyms* (adj) feeble, frail, faint, flat, flimsy, fragile, thin, watery, light, ailing, cowardly, delicate, diluted, exhausted, inadequate; *antonyms* (adj) strong, brave, concentrated, firm, safe, compelling, determined, effective, forceful, healthy, intense, powerful, resolute, robust, sturdy.

tarim sister; *synonyms* (n) nun, nurse, brother, mate, twin, baby, counterpart, double, match, member, pair, pendant, sis.

tarimarima 1. sharp; *synonyms* (adj) acute, bitter, intelligent, acid, acrid, harsh, incisive, intense, penetrating, piercing, pointed, pungent, quick, (n) keen, (v) biting; *antonyms* (*adj*) blunt, dull, mild, gentle, rounded, sweet, bland, blurred, naive, round, smooth, **2.** pointed; *synonyms* (*adj*) poignant, piquant, cutting, marked, pithy, acuminate, barbed, prickly, sharp, short, meaningful, fine, thorny, angular, emphatic.

tarina 1. salt; *synonyms* (*n*) salinity, sal, blunt, cream, dust, mopus, (*adj*) salty, saline, briny, spice, pungent, season, (v) cure, pickle, embalm, **2.** sister; *synonyms* (*n*) nun, nurse, brother, mate, twin, baby, counterpart, double, match, member, pair, pendant, sis.

tarinaki salted; *synonyms* (*adj*) salt, salty, corned, saline, brackish, powdered, (*n*) antiseptic, bitter, corrective, flavor, leap, lecherous, lustful, pungent, sailor.

taringa ear; *synonyms* (*n*) auricle, handle, hearing, lug, spike, capitulum, heed, earing, notice, crown, pinna, appreciation, discrimination, favor, (v) cultivate.

tariu 1. brother; *synonyms* (*n*) fellow, pal, associate, buddy, chum, companion, compeer, comrade, counterpart, crony, friend, mate, monk, peer, sidekick; *antonym* (*n*) sister, **2.** sister; *synonyms* (*n*) nun, nurse, brother, twin, baby, double, match, member, pair, pendant, sis.

taromauri adore; *synonyms* (v) revere, worship, idolize, admire, cherish, glorify, appreciate, deify, praise, respect, venerate, (*n*) honor; *antonyms* (v) hate, detest.

taromauria worship; *synonyms* (*n*) adoration, respect, adulation, veneration, cult, admiration, devotion, exaltation, homage, (v) praise, honor, revere, reverence, adore, glorify; *antonym* (v) hate.

taromauriaki adored; *synonyms* (*adj*) worshipped, respected, acclaimed, beloved, blessed, favorite, idolised, idolized, precious, venerated, chosen, darling, desired, established, preferred.

tarotu blunt; *synonyms* (*adj*) dull, bluff, candid, direct, forthright, frank, outspoken, plain, round, abrupt, brusque, downright, obtuse, (v) deaden, numb; *antonyms* (*adj*) sharp, devious, pointed, (v) hone, sharpen.

tarou 1. strain; *synonyms* (*n*) stress, breed, effort, stretch, exertion, race, (v) filter, screen, sift, tax, endeavor, exert, extend, percolate, pull; *antonym* (v) relax, **2.** sprint; *synonyms* (*n*) dash, (v) run, gallop, scurry, dart, hasten, jog, rush, bolt, speed, fly, trot.

tarouaki strained; *synonyms* (*adj*) forced, labored, tense, intense, constrained, laboured, unnatural, taut, tight, agonistic, agonistical, combative, farfetched; *antonyms* (*adj*) relaxed, natural.

tata 1. cut; *synonyms* (v) carve, chop, clip, abbreviate, abridge, bite, condense, crop, drop, fashion, (*n*) notch, slice, cutting, nick, blow; *antonyms* (v) increase, lengthen, (*n*) addition, extension, **2.** fast;

synonyms (*adj*) dissolute, firm, agile, debauched, fixed, hurried, instant, quick, rapid, staunch, brisk, (*adv*) soon, hard, close, (*n*) diet; *antonyms* (*adj*) sluggish, loose, (*adv*) slow, slowly, leisurely, (v) gorge, (*n*) binge, **3.** carve; *synonyms* (v) sculpture, cut, mold, engrave, incise, inscribe, shape, whittle, slash, deal, divide, etch, forge, form, mangle, **4.** notch; *synonyms* (*n*) gap, mark, score, scratch, degree, grade, groove, hole, (v) dent, hack, indent, nock, hollow, jag, chip, **5.** falter; *synonyms* (v) hesitate, waver, stammer, stumble, stutter, halt, bumble, dither, doubt, hobble, lurch, (*n*) faltering, flounder, hesitation, (*adv*) flag; *antonym* (v) continue, **6.** skim; *synonyms* (v) glide, slip, browse, skip, sweep, brush, fly, graze, race, read, scan, shave, glance, (*n*) cream, slide, **7.** stumble; *synonyms* (v) fall, fumble, err, falter, hit, reel, totter, tumble, wobble, (*n*) trip, misstep, stagger, (*adj*) blunder, botch, fault, **8.** skip; *synonyms* (*n*) jump, bound, hop, caper, omission, spring, (v) leap, dance, bounce, prance, gambol, skim, decamp, frisk, omit, **9.** throb; *synonyms* (*n*) pulsation, thrill, pain, (v) beat, quiver, ache, pulsate, pulse, pound, flutter, palpitate, shudder, smart, tingle, pant, **10.** trip; *synonyms* (*n*) excursion, expedition, tour, flight, jaunt, travel, lapse, run, drive, ride, outing, passage, voyage, break, (v) journey; *antonym* (v) fix, **11.** reel; *synonyms* (*n*) bobbin, coil, roll, spool, (v) rock, spin, teeter, fluctuate, gyrate, quake, shake, whirl, wind, sway, swing, **12.** pulsate; *synonyms* (v) throb, thump, vibrate.

tatabeua 1. each; *synonyms* (*adv*) apiece, (*adj*) every, any, singular, distinct, eche, ilk, eminent, exceptional, extraordinary, odd, same, strange, uncommon, unique, **2.** individually; *synonyms* (*adv*) apart, independently, personally, alone, separately, severally, singly, particularly, peculiarly; *antonym* (*adv*) together, **3.** apiece; *synonyms* (*adv*) each, aside, successively, (*pron*) all, both, **4.** any; *synonyms* (*adj*) either, whichever, several, some, few, ony, quantitative, only, (*n*) aught, part, (*pron*) who, **5.** singly; *synonyms* (*adv*) individually, solely, respectively, merely, (*adj*) single.

tatabuia 1. economize; *synonyms* (v) conserve, economise, save, preserve, husband, deliver, housewive, pinch, downscale, limit, maintain, rationalize, redeem, reduce, relieve; *antonym* (v) waste, **2.** keep; *synonyms* (v) hold, retain, defend, continue, guard, have, celebrate, confine, observe, reserve, commemorate, check, harbor, direct, (*n*) custody; *antonyms* (v) dump, lose, **3.** spare; *synonyms* (*adj*) slender, excess, slight, additional, lean, slim, thin, bare, (v) free, meager, exempt, economize, excuse, (*n*) extra, backup, **4.** save; *synonyms* (v) rescue, hoard, keep, liberate, protect, accumulate, amass, safeguard, spare, garner, deposit, (*prep*) except, but, excepting, (*adv*) besides; *antonyms* (*v*) spend, squander.

tatabuiaki 1. kept; *synonyms* (*adj*) reserved, detained, intransitive, unbroken, unploughed, unplowed, **2**. saved; *synonyms* (*adj*) protected, blessed, secure.

tatabwi 1. frugal; *synonyms* (*adj*) economical, chary, thrifty, abstemious, sparing, austere, careful, moderate, parsimonious, provident, prudent, slender, economic, scarce, (*v*) spare; *antonyms* (*adj*) spendthrift, extravagant, **2**. thrifty; *synonyms* (*adj*) frugal, stingy; *antonyms* (*adj*) wasteful, profligate, **3**. provident; *synonyms* (*adj*) circumspect, cautious, farsighted, sagacious, wise, discreet, wary, (*v*) precautionary; *antonym* (*adj*) improvident.

tatae sliver; *synonyms* (*n*) splinter, shred, fragment, bit, shaving, scrap, shiver, part, crumb, slip, (*v*) chip, flake, slice, shave, cut.

tataeanibai detach; *synonyms* (*v*) disengage, divide, part, disconnect, disentangle, dissociate, remove, separate, unhook, isolate, abstract, cleave, disjoin, divorce, (*n*) detail; *antonyms* (*v*) attach, fasten, add, associate.

tataeanibaiaki detached; *synonyms* (*adj*) aloof, cool, isolated, separate, distinct, disconnected, disinterested, dispassionate, impartial, indifferent, neutral, objective, remote, separated, unconcerned; *antonyms* (*adj*) attached, involved, engrossed, warm.

tataenoa 1. hasten; *synonyms* (*v*) speed, expedite, further, forward, dispatch, advance, hurry, dash, hie, rush, bustle, dart, (*adj*) accelerate, quicken, (*n*) haste; *antonym* (*v*) delay, **2**. urge; *synonyms* (*n*) goad, spur, drive, impulse, (*v*) push, advocate, press, force, impel, incite, induce, inspire, instigate, persuade, prompt; *antonym* (*v*) discourage.

tataki 1. carved; *synonyms* (*adj*) carven, cut, incised, tipsy, (*v*) engraved, graven, fixed, imprinted, stamped, impressed, **2**. notched; *synonyms* (*adj*) jagged, serrated, jaggy, serrate, toothed, erose, rough, uneven, **3**. cut; *synonyms* (*v*) carve, chop, clip, abbreviate, abridge, bite, condense, crop, drop, fashion, (*n*) notch, slice, cutting, nick, blow; *antonyms* (*v*) increase, lengthen, (*n*) addition, extension, **4**. pulsated.

tataneiai 1. frequently; *synonyms* (*adv*) often, commonly, continually, oft, oftentimes, ofttimes, repeatedly, usually, always, hourly, mostly, much, ordinarily, regularly, customarily; *antonyms* (*adv*) rarely, infrequently, unusually, **2**. habitually; *synonyms* (*adv*) generally, normally, frequently, **3**. customarily; *synonyms* (*adv*) habitually, typically, **4**. generally; *synonyms* (*adv*) altogether, broadly, chiefly, approximately, largely, mainly, principally, completely, overall, primarily; *antonyms* (*adv*) narrowly, specifically, **5**. commonly; *synonyms* (*adv*) currently, cheaply; *antonym* (*adv*)

uncommonly, **6**. regularly; *synonyms* (*adv*) evenly, ever, methodically, routinely, steadily, uniformly, recurrently; *antonyms* (*adv*) inconsistently, constantly, **7**. usually; *synonyms* (*adv*) readily, unremarkably; *antonym* (*adv*) exceptionally, **8**. ordinarily; *antonym* (*adv*) strangely.

tataninga 1. await; *synonyms* (*v*) expect, anticipate, abide, bide, tarry, wait, attend, look, hope, approach, loom, **2**. bide; *synonyms* (*v*) endure, bear, dwell, last, remain, (*adj*) stay, stand, suffer, tolerate, **3**. tarry; *synonyms* (*v*) linger, loiter, delay, lag, dally, dawdle, rest, hesitate, persist, saunter, stop, (*adj*) pitchy, resinous, resiny, **4**. wait; *synonyms* (*v*) ambush, await, lurk, watch, keep, defer, cease, depend, halt, (*n*) pause, hold, holdup, break, waiting, hesitation.

tataningamarau industrious; *synonyms* (*adj*) active, diligent, assiduous, indefatigable, busy, energetic, hardworking, laborious, tireless, earnest, enterprising, careful, painstaking, sedulous, studious; *antonym* (*adj*) lazy.

tatao 1. diffuse; *synonyms* (*adj*) prolix, profuse, widespread, diffusive, (*v*) circulate, disperse, disseminate, spread, broadcast, propagate, scatter, distribute, expand, permeate, shed, **2**. spread; *synonyms* (*v*) reach, extend, diffuse, increase, stretch, broaden, deploy, enlarge, dilate, open, (*n*) span, dissemination, expanse, expansion, feast; *antonym* (*adj*) concentrated, **3**. overflow; *synonyms* (*n*) flood, deluge, inundation, excess, flooding, outpouring, runoff, torrent, affluence, (*v*) inundate, flow, drown, fill, overrun, submerge.

tataoaki 1. diffused; *synonyms* (*adj*) dim, softened, dull, flowing, gentle, loose, mellow, muffled, muted, subtle, **2**. spread; *synonyms* (*v*) scatter, reach, disperse, expand, extend, broadcast, circulate, diffuse, disseminate, increase, propagate, stretch, broaden, deploy, (*n*) span; *antonym* (*adj*) concentrated.

tatara 1. examine; *synonyms* (*v*) assay, audit, consider, overhaul, try, check, control, search, survey, ascertain, ask, contemplate, compare, analyze, canvass, **2**. consider; *synonyms* (*v*) believe, regard, think, cogitate, view, assume, calculate, conceive, deliberate, reckon, reflect, consult, debate, deem, (*n*) study; *antonym* (*v*) ignore, **3**. look; *synonyms* (*v*) seem, appear, expect, figure, attend, (*n*) face, gaze, appearance, aspect, air, countenance, expression, glance, guise, (*int*) behold, **4**. regard; *synonyms* (*v*) attention, concern, estimate, heed, account, count, hold, observe, (*n*) notice, respect, esteem, deference, look, note, value; *antonym* (*n*) disrespect.

tataraki considered; *synonyms* (*adj*) deliberate, reasoned, intentional, premeditated, sensible, sound, willful, studied, calculated, planned, reputed, adult, careful, designed, exact; *antonyms* *(adj)* impulsive, sudden, impetuous, ingenuous, swift, thoughtless.

tatarara survey; *synonyms (n)* poll, review, measurement, inspection, digest, examination, *(v)* study, measure, view, appraise, canvass, prospect, assess, observe, evaluate; *antonym (v)* neglect.

tatarere singular; *synonyms (adj)* extraordinary, individual, odd, exceptional, particular, peculiar, phenomenal, quaint, queer, rare, single, separate, curious, one, outlandish; *antonym (n)* plural.

tataro 1. pray; *synonyms (v)* beg, implore, entreat, crave, appeal, beseech, invite, plead, importune, ask, invoke, petition, supplicate, bid, *(adv)* please, **2.** stumble; *synonyms (v)* slip, fall, flounder, fumble, err, falter, hit, stammer, *(n)* trip, lurch, misstep, stagger, *(adj)* blunder, botch, fault.

tatata hack; *synonyms (n)* drudge, cab, hacker, jade, nag, *(v)* cut, chop, ax, fell, gash, mutilate, rip, slash, slice, cleave.

tatatata 1. falter; *synonyms (v)* hesitate, waver, stammer, stumble, stutter, halt, bumble, dither, doubt, hobble, lurch, *(n)* faltering, flounder, hesitation, *(adv)* flag; *antonym (v)* continue, **2.** stagger; *synonyms (v)* falter, astonish, startle, flabbergast, reel, shake, shock, pitch, amaze, dumbfound, stun, surprise, totter, astound, *(adj)* bewilder, **3.** pulsate; *synonyms (v)* beat, palpitate, pound, throb, pulse, quiver, shudder, thump, vibrate, **4.** stumble; *synonyms (v)* slip, fall, fumble, err, hit, tumble, wobble, sin, *(n)* trip, misstep, stagger, *(adj)* blunder, botch, fault, bungle, **5.** patter; *synonyms (n)* jargon, vernacular, cant, slang, lingo, *(v)* babble, clatter, rattle, roll, rumble, drum, scuttle, skip, tiptoe, bespatter, **6.** totter; *synonyms (v)* rock, teeter, toddle, waddle, shamble, dodder, sway, tremble, limp, quake, walk, coggle, dance, *(adj)* crumble, drop, **7.** throb; *synonyms (n)* pulsation, thrill, pain, pounding, throbbing, heave, twinge, *(v)* ache, pulsate, flutter, smart, tingle, pant, shiver, hurt, **8.** thrill; *synonyms (n)* delight, chill, excitement, flush, frisson, kick, *(v)* excite, exhilarate, exalt, pierce, stir, electrify, charm, creep, titillate.

tatatataki 1. pulsated, **2.** thrilled; *synonyms (adj)* delighted, jubilant, excited, happy, overjoyed, ecstatic, elated, pleased.

tataumanta 1. discern; *synonyms (v)* behold, differentiate, comprehend, see, descry, detect, distinguish, perceive, recognize, find, discover, discriminate, feel, judge, note, **2.** examine; *synonyms (v)* assay, audit, consider, overhaul, try, check, control, search, survey, ascertain, ask, contemplate, compare, analyze, canvass, **3.** observe; *synonyms (v)* celebrate, comment, notice, commemorate, mind, guard, follow, heed, keep, look, mark, mention, fulfill, comply, attend; *antonym (v)* ignore, **4.** remark; *synonyms (n)* observation, regard, commentary, observance,

reflection, word, declaration, statement, quip, annotate, reference, designate, *(v)* observe, discern, criticise.

tataumantaki observed; *synonyms (adj)* seen, ascertained, discovered, empirical, disclosed, experiential, experimental, visual, practical, pragmatic, revealed.

tatauti 1. mean; *synonyms (v)* intend, design, imply, denote, involve, *(adj)* middle, base, common, hateful, ignoble, medium, miserly, *(n)* average, contemptible, low; *antonyms (adj)* generous, kind, **2.** stingy; *synonyms (adj)* parsimonious, avaricious, mean, penurious, skimpy, greedy, niggard, frugal, cheap, closefisted, measly, niggardly, *(v)* narrow, close, near; *antonym (adj)* spendthrift.

tatika haul; *synonyms (n)* freight, heave, catch, jerk, take, *(v)* draw, drag, pull, tow, carry, cart, lug, draught, hale, transport; *antonym (v)* push.

tau 1. enough; *synonyms (adv)* rather, plenty, amply, adequately, satisfaction, fairly, fully, *(n)* adequacy, fill, sufficiency, *(adj)* ample, sufficient, adequate, competent, decent; *antonym (adj)* inadequate, **2.** adequate; *synonyms (adj)* acceptable, enough, right, condign, effectual, passable, satisfactory, agreeable, equal, fair, fit, full, good, qualified, able; *antonyms (adj)* insufficient, unsatisfactory, **3.** fit; *synonyms (v)* agree, accommodate, meet, suit, adapt, correspond, square, accord, dress, *(adj)* decorous, apt, applicable, appropriate, *(n)* adjust, convulsion; *antonyms (adj)* unfit, inappropriate, unwell, **4.** apt; *synonyms (adj)* adroit, apropos, apposite, intelligent, convenient, dexterous, efficient, ready, smart, clever, deft, disposed, expert, fitting, happy, **5.** becoming; *synonyms (v)* proper, correct, *(adj)* seemly, befitting, due, relevant, comely, eligible, suitable, handsome, attractive, congruous, graceful, modest, nice; *antonym (adj)* unbecoming, **6.** hold; *synonyms (v)* keep, detain, endure, adhere, bear, comprise, contain, entertain, have, arrest, carry, *(n)* grasp, grip, clasp, clutch; *antonym (v)* release, **7.** keep; *synonyms (v)* hold, preserve, retain, defend, continue, guard, maintain, celebrate, confine, conserve, observe, reserve, save, commemorate, check; *antonyms (v)* dump, lose, **8.** suit; *synonyms (n)* lawsuit, plea, action, case, petition, cause, courtship, prayer, *(v)* answer, become, match, please, satisfy, befit, harmonize, **9.** retain; *synonyms (v)* employ, engage, hire, own, possess, occupy, remember, restrain, withhold, control, prevent, remain, sustain, uphold, admit, **10.** ready; *synonyms (adj)* prompt, quick, nimble, finished, handy, present, instant, agile, alert, facile, *(v)* prepare, fix, willing, *(n)* available, eager; *antonyms (adj)* unprepared, unwilling, **11.** suitable; *synonyms (adj)* desirable, pertinent, respectable, fitted, compatible, expedient, opportune, comfortable, congenial, harmonious, pleasing, timely, sortable, (*n*) seasonable, (*v*) becoming; *antonyms* (*adj*) unsuitable, wrong, improper, **12.** satisfied; *synonyms* (*v*) convinced, (*adj*) contented, content, pleased, certain, confident, sure, complacent, persuaded, fulfilled, sated, satiated, easy, positive, quenched; *antonyms* (*adj*) unhappy, frustrated.

taua 1. hold; *synonyms* (*v*) keep, detain, endure, adhere, bear, comprise, contain, entertain, have, arrest, carry, (*n*) grasp, grip, clasp, clutch; *antonym* (*v*) release, **2.** conserve; *synonyms* (*v*) economize, embalm, husband, protect, save, defend, hoard, maintain, safeguard, economise, (*n*) preserve, conserves, jam, preserves; *antonyms* (*v*) spend, use, waste, expend, damage, **3.** grasp; *synonyms* (*n*) catch, clinch, appreciation, apprehension, clutches, (*v*) comprehend, embrace, hold, apprehend, grapple, conceive, capture, cling, grab, clench, **4.** maintain; *synonyms* (*v*) continue, justify, affirm, allege, assert, aver, conserve, declare, guard, insist, support, sustain, uphold, argue, asseverate; *antonyms* (*v*) deny, change, **5.** held; *synonyms* (*adj*) absorbed, confined, alleged, assumed, believed, bound, caged, captive, detained, fast, immersed, obsessed, occupied, protected, (*adv*) on, **6.** grip; *synonyms* (*n*) handle, bag, clamp, compass, suitcase, mastery, (*v*) fascinate, gripe, captivate, nip, pinch, seize, snatch, squeeze, engage; *antonym* (*v*) bore, **7.** apprehend; *synonyms* (*v*) appreciate, fathom, realize, understand, follow, sense, anticipate, dig, fear, nail, believe, recognize, collar, cop, dread, **8.** keep; *synonyms* (*v*) retain, celebrate, confine, observe, reserve, commemorate, check, harbor, direct, rear, restrain, store, (*n*) custody, maintenance, subsistence; *antonyms* (*v*) dump, lose, **9.** restrain; *synonyms* (*v*) bridle, control, curb, rein, bind, govern, inhibit, limit, prevent, repress, circumscribe, constrain, impede, suppress, qualify, **10.** reserve; *synonyms* (*n*) backup, modesty, reservation, substitute, bank, cache, diffidence, order, provision, bashfulness, (*v*) book, appropriate, stock, withhold, allow; *antonyms* (*n*) openness, friendliness, informality, warmth, **11.** obtain; *synonyms* (*v*) gain, acquire, get, achieve, attain, earn, accomplish, derive, effect, buy, collect, extract, find, gather, make, **12.** secure; *synonyms* (*v*) close, fix, fasten, assure, ensure, guarantee, lock, obtain, procure, (*adj*) safe, firm, certain, confident, attach, reliable; *antonyms* (*v*) detach, (*adj*) insecure, vulnerable, loose, unsafe, **13.** wield; *synonyms* (*v*) ply, wave, brandish, exercise, exert, flourish, manipulate, manage, swing, treat, shake, operate, rule, sway, work, **14.** withhold; *synonyms* (*v*) abstain, stint, refrain, deduct, refuse, stifle, subtract, smother, suspend, forbear, cohibit, delay, estrange, (*adj*) begrudge, grudge, **15.** tackle; *synonyms* (*v*) harness, undertake, attempt, stop, struggle, attack,

(*n*) gear, equipment, rigging, kit, paraphernalia, rig, apparatus, outfit, tools; *antonym* (*v*) avoid, **16.** retain; *synonyms* (*v*) employ, hire, own, possess, occupy, remember, remain, admit, recall, recollect.

tauaki 1. kept; *synonyms* (*adj*) reserved, detained, intransitive, unbroken, unploughed, unplowed, **2.** conserved; *synonyms* (*adj*) preserved, potted, sealed, **3.** apprehended; *synonyms* (*adj*) held, appreciated, comprehended, gratifying, pleasing, satisfying, **4.** maintained; *synonyms* (*adj*) retained, fixed, repaired, safe, serviced, reconditioned, shipshape, trim, **5.** held; *synonyms* (*adj*) absorbed, confined, alleged, assumed, believed, bound, caged, captive, fast, immersed, obsessed, occupied, protected, rapt, (*adv*) on, **6.** restrained; *synonyms* (*adj*) moderate, quiet, modest, temperate, discreet, limited, reasonable, reticent, subdued, unemotional, guarded, mild, gentle, sober, understated; *antonyms* (*adj*) exaggerated, unrestrained, flashy, immoral, open, ostentatious, wild, **7.** secured; *synonyms* (*adj*) guaranteed, barred, bolted, bonded, firm, latched, locked, **8.** retained; *synonyms* (*adj*) maintained, aeonian, durable, eonian, eternal, everlasting, haunting, lasting, permanent, persistent, relentless, unrelenting, **9.** reserved; *synonyms* (*adj*) distant, coy, diffident, bashful, aloof, frigid, retiring, shy, formal, humble, unapproachable, cautious, cool, inhibited, (*n*) cold; *antonyms* (*adj*) outgoing, forthcoming, relaxed, uninhibited, warm, **10.** suited; *synonyms* (*v*) fit, convenient, (*adj*) suitable, proper, appropriate, fitted, adapted, apt, good, capable, eligible, useful, desirable, seemly.

tauantaboa 1. alternate; *synonyms* (*adj*) reciprocal, secondary, (*v*) reciprocate, change, fluctuate, interchange, vary, swerve, alter, (*n*) substitute, alternative, surrogate, standby, replacement, deputy; *antonym* (*n*) original, **2.** proxy; *synonyms* (*n*) attorney, agent, alternate, delegate, procurator, procuration, representative, vice, **3.** substitute; *synonyms* (*adj*) ersatz, makeshift, imitation, (*n*) backup, double, proxy, relief, (*v*) shift, replace, exchange, sub, cover, commute, deputise, deputize, **4.** understudy; *synonyms* (*n*) actor, attendant, reserve, substitution, supply, (*v*) flip, jump, switch, **5.** temp; *synonyms* (*n*) assistant, (*adj*) temporary, stopgap, **6.** replace; *synonyms* (*v*) supersede, supplant, reinstate, displace, restore, renew, return, succeed, follow, place, put, refund, repay, trade, reestablish, **7.** represent; *synonyms* (*v*) depict, portray, act, be, describe, embody, exemplify, illustrate, play, enact, make, impersonate, comprise, constitute, (*adj*) express.

tauantaboaki represented; *synonyms* (*adj*) delineate, delineated.

taubang 1. frugal; *synonyms (adj)* economical, chary, thrifty, abstemious, sparing, austere, careful, moderate, parsimonious, provident, prudent, slender, economic, scarce, *(v)* spare; *antonyms (adj)* spendthrift, extravagant, **2.** temperate; *synonyms (adj)* mild, sober, calm, reasonable, restrained, balmy, gentle, abstinent, composed, equable, frugal, cool, dispassionate, modest, clement; *antonym (adj)* intemperate.

taubank 1. moderate; *synonyms (adj)* temperate, abstemious, middling, mild, easy, *(v)* calm, mitigate, allay, curb, diminish, lessen, ease, cool, abate, *(adv)* check; *antonyms (adj)* extreme, immoderate, radical, *(v)* increase, intensify, **2.** restrain; *synonyms (v)* bridle, confine, control, hold, rein, bind, arrest, bound, contain, govern, inhibit, limit, prevent, repress, circumscribe, **3.** restrained; *synonyms (adj)* moderate, quiet, reserved, modest, discreet, limited, reasonable, reticent, subdued, unemotional, guarded, confined, gentle, sober, understated; *antonyms (adj)* exaggerated, unrestrained, flashy, immoral, open, ostentatious, wild, **4.** sober; *synonyms (adj)* serious, grave, sedate, sane, earnest, solemn, demure, dull, serene, somber, staid, severe, composed, rational, sad; *antonym (adj)* intoxicated, **5.** tempered; *synonyms (adj)* hardened, attempered, attemperate, elastic, enured, inured, proportioned, set, toughened, treated, tough, **6.** temper; *synonyms (n)* mood, character, disposition, humor, nature, condition, anger, irritation, *(v)* soften, harden, modify, season, qualify, anneal, *(adj)* mollify; *antonym (v)* upset.

taubankaki 1. moderated; *synonyms (adj)* subdued, certified, dependant, dependent, equal, graduated, limited, measured, qualified, restricted, uniform, **2.** tempered; *synonyms (adj)* hardened, attempered, attemperate, elastic, enured, inured, mild, proportioned, set, toughened, treated, tough, **3.** restrained; *synonyms (adj)* moderate, quiet, reserved, modest, temperate, discreet, reasonable, reticent, unemotional, guarded, confined, gentle, sober, understated, calm; *antonyms (adj)* exaggerated, unrestrained, flashy, immoral, open, ostentatious, wild.

taubarea 1. swipe; *synonyms (n)* hit, stroke, blow, knock, *(v)* pinch, steal, filch, lift, pilfer, rob, abstract, nobble, purloin, snatch, sneak, **2.** swish; *synonyms (v)* lap, rustle, sizzle, *(adj)* posh, classy, fashionable, swanky, smart, stylish.

taubea 1. chaperon; *synonyms (n)* escort, companion, *(v)* chaperone, accompany, attend, matronize, guide, *(adj)* duenna, **2.** escort; *synonyms (n)* chaperon, guard, attendant, conduct, suite, accompaniment, bodyguard, guardian, safeguard, usher, beau, *(v)* convoy, see, date, direct.

taubeakina guard; *synonyms (n)* defend, defense, bulwark, care, cover, escort, protection, watchman, custody, convoy, defence, fender, guardsman, *(v)* shield, keep.

taubeakinaki guarded; *synonyms (adj)* cautious, careful, wary, chary, circumspect, cagey, vigilant, watchful, conditional, discreet, gingerly, conservative, prudent, reserved, safe; *antonyms (adj)* frank, honest.

taubobonga 1. exact; *synonyms (adj)* detailed, precise, actual, authentic, careful, definite, direct, *(v)* accurate, close, demand, require, claim, command, ask, *(n)* correct; *antonyms (adj)* inaccurate, imprecise, vague, wrong, approximate, inexact, **2.** prompt; *synonyms (adj)* agile, quick, nimble, punctual, dexterous, expeditious, immediate, *(v)* actuate, incite, fleet, inspire, instigate, move, animate, cue; *antonyms (adj)* slow, late.

taubuaka unprepared; *synonyms (adj)* impromptu, offhand, extemporaneous, raw, unrehearsed, crude, improvised; *antonyms (adj)* prepared, ready.

taubuki 1. top; *synonyms (adj)* maximum, *(n)* crown, peak, acme, apex, crest, cover, height, pinnacle, summit, *(v)* best, cap, exceed, head, outdo; *antonyms (adj)* worst, *(n)* bottom, base, nadir, **2.** support; *synonyms (n)* help, stand, aid, keep, comfort, maintenance, patronage, *(v)* assist, prop, back, brace, encourage, maintain, bear, boost; *antonyms (n)* hindrance, *(v)* oppose, neglect, undermine, abandon, reject, weaken, **3.** roof; *synonyms (n)* ceiling, housing, dome, shelter, house, *(v)* top, **4.** ridge; *synonyms (n)* ledge, bank, hill, shelf, dune, swelling, projection, ridgepole, wrinkle, button, peg, *(v)* crease, fold, **5.** uphold; *synonyms (v)* sustain, defend, preserve, continue, bolster, confirm, countenance, endorse, assert, buttress, advocate, corroborate, hold, sanction, *(n)* support.

taubukiaki supported; *synonyms (v)* borne, carried, conveyed, supporting, *(adj)* bolstered, based, *(adv)* on.

tauburea 1. note; *synonyms (n)* comment, mention, remark, annotation, heed, indication, mark, attention, bill, distinction, epistle, *(v)* notice, mind, look, detect; *antonym (v)* ignore, **2.** criticize; *synonyms (v)* attack, belittle, berate, blame, censure, chide, denounce, rebuke, reprimand, scold, condemn, criticise, deplore, disparage, reproach; *antonyms (v)* praise, approve, commend, admire, **3.** correct; *synonyms (adj)* right, accurate, appropriate, becoming, nice, precise, proper, *(v)* adjust, amend, castigate, chastise, chasten, better, remedy, *(n)* true; *antonyms (adj)* incorrect, false, faulty, inappropriate, mistaken, improper, *(v)* wrong, spoil, **4.** censor; *synonyms (n)* censurer, critic, conscience, detractor, enemy, *(v)* ban, suppress, squelch, expurgate, muzzle, banish, blackball, disallow, edit, forbid, **5.** judge; *synonyms* (*n*) arbiter, arbitrator, referee, (*v*) consider, estimate, evaluate, think, believe, assess, adjudicate, calculate, decide, guess, umpire, examine, **6.** revise; *synonyms* (*v*) emend, alter, convert, correct, fix, retouch, reform, adapt, reconsider, modify, (*n*) review, revisal, revision, proof, (*adj*) overhaul.

taubureaki 1. noted; *synonyms* (*v*) notorious, (*adj*) distinguished, famous, illustrious, conspicuous, glorious, celebrated, eminent, famed, known, renowned, well-known, noble, marked, notable, **2.** censored; *synonyms* (*adj*) abridged, concealed, suppressed, cut; *antonym* (*adj*) available, **3.** corrected; *synonyms* (*adj*) chastised, amended, reformed, altered, chastened, disciplined, educated, refined, **4.** revised.

taubururu 1. skimp; *synonyms* (*v*) pinch, economize, save, scant, scrimp, stint, scrape, spare, conserve, neglect, penny-pinch, withhold, (*adj*) meager, **2.** spoil; *synonyms* (*v*) plunder, corrupt, impair, rot, damage, deface, indulge, injure, mar, sack, baby, botch, bungle, (*n*) ruin, (*adj*) harm; *antonyms* (*v*) enhance, improve, **3.** scamp; *synonyms* (*n*) knave, rascal, imp, miscreant, monkey, rogue, scalawag, villain, rapscallion, scallywag, devil, scoundrel, (*v*) skimp.

taubururuaki spoiled; *synonyms* (*adj*) decayed, bad, rotten, stale, coddled, pampered, corrupt, damaged, spoilt; *antonyms* (*adj*) first-rate, pure.

taubwe 1. command; *synonyms* (*n*) control, instruction, behest, bidding, decree, direction, administration, ascendancy, authority, (*v*) charge, order, rule, call, commission, direct; *antonym* (*v*) request, **2.** direct; *synonyms* (*adj*) straight, blunt, immediate, (*v*) aim, channel, conduct, address, dictate, head, administer, guide, lead, level, point, (*n*) command; *antonyms* (*adj*) indirect, roundabout, circuitous, oblique, second-hand, sideways, unplanned, **3.** steer; *synonyms* (*v*) navigate, drive, manage, maneuver, run, tip, show, govern, operate, sail, shepherd, regulate, (*n*) bullock, hint, ox.

taubweaki 1. directed; *synonyms* (*adj*) absorbed, concentrating, destined, focussed, formal, intent, prescript, subject, engaged, fixed, prescribed, rapt, (*adv*) under, **2.** steered.

taugara cinder; *synonyms* (*n*) scoriae, clinker, charcoal, scoria, scum, bastard, chark, impurities, residue, spark, (*v*) soot.

taukaro 1. glimmer; *synonyms* (*n*) flicker, flash, gleaming, glow, twinkle, glitter, glance, hint, (*v*) gleam, shimmer, blink, sparkle, beam, shine, glare, **2.** glitter; *synonyms* (*n*) glimmer, glisten, blaze, glister, radiance, coruscation, effulgence, brightness, brilliancy, dash, flourish, gaiety, light, (*v*) coruscate, glint, **3.** spark; *synonyms* (*n*) arc, fire,

flame, scintilla, scintillation, trace, discharge, gaillard, jester, joker, luminosity, (*v*) activate, trigger, stir, actuate.

taukirikiri 1. forecast; *synonyms* (*n*) calculation, forecasting, forethought, (*v*) presage, anticipate, augur, calculate, portend, bode, estimate, figure, forebode, foretell, predict, prognosticate, **2.** anticipate; *synonyms* (*v*) antedate, expect, forecast, forestall, think, apprehend, divine, guess, presume, prevent, intercept, trust, await, envision, foreknow, **3.** estimate; *synonyms* (*n*) appraisal, assessment, (*v*) compute, consider, count, esteem, weigh, account, appraise, assess, computation, conjecture, estimation, gauge, reckon, **4.** calculate; *synonyms* (*v*) add, cipher, deem, enumerate, make, measure, number, budget, determine, cast, cypher, depend, evaluate, plan, program, **5.** divine; *synonyms* (*adj*) beautiful, sacred, wonderful, almighty, blessed, holy, exquisite, splendid, hallowed, celestial, godlike, godly, (*n*) clergyman, churchman, cleric, **6.** count; *synonyms* (*n*) total, amount, reckoning, counting, enumeration, mark, numeration, point, (*v*) tally, matter, appreciate, include, tell, look, rely, **7.** preconceive; *synonym* (*n*) foreconceive.

taukirikiriaki 1. anticipated; *synonyms* (*adj*) likely, expected, predictable, appointed, awaited, coming, forthcoming, future, natural, planned, probable, projected, proposed, scheduled, **2.** estimated; *synonyms* (*adj*) approximate, rough, anticipated, ballpark, reputed, sketchy, theoretical, vague, academic, hypothetical, imprecise, inexact, near, speculative; *antonym* (*adj*) exact, **3.** calculated; *synonyms* (*v*) advised, designed, (*adj*) deliberate, conscious, intended, intentional, premeditated, purposeful, studied, measured, strategic; *antonym* (*adj*) accidental, **4.** preconceived; *synonyms* (*adj*) jaundiced, (*v*) aforethought, prepense, premeditate.

taukiro 1. spy; *synonyms* (*n*) scout, detective, mole, notice, patrol, emissary, (*v*) see, espy, snoop, discern, discover, observe, perceive, descry, behold, **2.** survey; *synonyms* (*n*) poll, review, measurement, inspection, digest, examination, (*v*) study, measure, view, appraise, canvass, prospect, assess, evaluate, examine; *antonym* (*v*) neglect, **3.** watch; *synonyms* (*v*) clock, look, regard, wake, care, protect, defend, check, follow, (*n*) guard, sentinel, sentry, surveillance, lookout, (*adj*) vigilance.

taumangang loafing; *synonyms* (*adj*) lazy, unemployed, (*n*) idling, idleness, dalliance, faineance.

taumangao disorderly; *synonyms* (*adj*) confused, chaotic, disordered, wild, boisterous, disobedient, disorganized, irregular, jumbled, rowdy, tumultuous, turbulent, unruly, untidy, (*v*) lawless; *antonyms* (*adj*) orderly, well-behaved, neat, arranged.

taumata fish; *synonyms* (*n*) bird, insect, mollusk, shellfish, worm, amphibian, beginner, blacktail, (*v*) angle, seek, hunt, pursue, grope, rummage, beg.

taumate bury; *synonyms* (*v*) immerse, inter, overwhelm, cloak, conceal, entomb, hide, mask, secrete, cache, cover, embed, engulf, forget, (*n*) grave; *antonyms* (*v*) exhume, unearth.

taumateaki buried; *synonyms* (*adj*) concealed, hidden, covert, inhumed, interred, underground, profound.

taumoa precede; *synonyms* (*v*) lead, head, antecede, antedate, forego, anticipate, forerun, introduce, pass, preface, direct, go; *antonyms* (*v*) follow, succeed.

taumwere loiter; *synonyms* (*v*) linger, dawdle, lag, loaf, dally, saunter, tarry, prowl, idle, loll, continue, (*adj*) delay, lounge, hesitate, (*adv*) crawl.

taun bury; *synonyms* (*v*) immerse, inter, overwhelm, cloak, conceal, entomb, hide, mask, secrete, cache, cover, embed, engulf, forget, (*n*) grave; *antonyms* (*v*) exhume, unearth.

tauna bury; *synonyms* (*v*) immerse, inter, overwhelm, cloak, conceal, entomb, hide, mask, secrete, cache, cover, embed, engulf, forget, (*n*) grave; *antonyms* (*v*) exhume, unearth.

taunaki buried; *synonyms* (*adj*) concealed, hidden, covert, inhumed, interred, underground, profound.

taunari 1. compare; *synonyms* (*v*) collate, liken, confront, comparison, equate, associate, contrast, correlate, equal, equalize, parallel, resemble, (*n*) comparability, 2. measure; *synonyms* (*n*) amount, criterion, extent, beat, benchmark, degree, estimate, measurement, meter, quantity, act, allotment, action, (*v*) grade, appraise, 3. differentiate; *synonyms* (*v*) characterize, distinguish, discriminate, separate, tell, know, identify, classify, discern, mark, secern, severalize; *antonym* (*v*) integrate.

taunariaki 1. measured; *synonyms* (*adj*) careful, deliberate, moderate, calculated, reasonable, temperate, regular, leisurely, metrical, sober, cool, slow, 2. differentiated.

taunga fluctuate; *synonyms* (*v*) waver, falter, change, vacillate, alternate, hesitate, oscillate, swing, vary, vibrate, wave, range, alter, quake, shake.

taungatangata 1. activate; *synonyms* (*v*) actuate, start, trigger, aerate, animate, incite, initiate, prompt, quicken, spark, stimulate, 2. hasten; *synonyms* (*v*) speed, expedite, further, forward, dispatch, advance, hurry, dash, hie, rush, bustle, dart, facilitate, (*adj*) accelerate, (*n*) haste; *antonym* (*v*) delay, 3. hurry; *synonyms* (*n*) flurry, celerity, hastiness, hurriedness, press, (*v*) hasten, scurry, fly, run, zip, drive, race, scamper, scuttle, flit; *antonyms* (*n*) slowness, (*v*) dawdle.

taungatangataki 1. hurried; *synonyms* (*adj*) hasty, fast, headlong, quick, rapid, speedy, sudden, swift, abrupt, cursory, careless, precipitate, prompt, rash, slapdash; *antonyms* (*adj*) slow, unhurried, leisurely, 2. activated; *synonyms* (*adj*) animate, animated, applied, excited, aroused, delirious, emotional, frantic, mad, unrestrained.

tauoa 1. keep; *synonyms* (*v*) hold, preserve, retain, defend, continue, guard, have, maintain, celebrate, confine, conserve, observe, reserve, save, commemorate; *antonyms* (*v*) dump, lose, 2. watch; *synonyms* (*v*) clock, look, see, regard, wake, care, protect, check, follow, (*n*) view, sentinel, sentry, surveillance, lookout, (*adj*) vigilance, 3. supervise; *synonyms* (*v*) administer, manage, superintend, control, direct, monitor, oversee, run, conduct, handle, inspect, administrate, command, head, lead.

tauoaki 1. kept; *synonyms* (*adj*) reserved, detained, intransitive, unbroken, unploughed, unplowed, 2. supervised.

taura 1. lift; *synonyms* (*n*) elevator, boost, heave, (*v*) hoist, raise, rise, elevate, erect, filch, hike, advance, airlift, pilfer, pinch, rear, 2. sprinkle; *synonyms* (*n*) dash, (*v*) scatter, drizzle, splash, moisten, cast, dot, spatter, spray, rain, spill, spread, diffuse, intersperse, (*adj*) besprinkle, 3. raise; *synonyms* (*v*) lift, increase, build, enhance, foster, grow, promote, prefer, augment, cultivate, exalt, excite, heighten, levy, nurture; *antonym* (*v*) lower.

tauraba 1. fortunate; *synonyms* (*adj*) favorable, auspicious, lucky, advantageous, blessed, favored, fortuitous, happy, prosperous, successful, well, felicitous, golden, good, propitious; *antonyms* (*adj*) unfortunate, unlucky, 2. lucky; *synonyms* (*adj*) favourable, flourishing, chance, providential, encouraging, promising, (*v*) fortunate; *antonyms* (*adj*) hapless, ill-fated.

tauraki 1. lifted; *synonyms* (*adj*) elevated, lofty, steep, upraised, 2. raised; *synonyms* (*v*) repousse, (*adj*) embossed, erect, convex, brocaded, high, alert, bold, confident, elate, elated, elative, exultant, mountant, (*prep*) above, 3. sprinkled; *synonyms* (*adj*) besprent, scattered, dotted, speckled, spotted, spread, strewn.

taurangaranga 1. totter; *synonyms* (*v*) reel, shake, stumble, falter, lurch, rock, stagger, teeter, toddle, waddle, waver, shamble, dodder, sway, tremble, 2. swing; *synonyms* (*n*) sweep, range, lilt, (*v*) fluctuate, oscillate, dangle, hang, beat, brandish, change, move, turn, vibrate, dance, drop, 3. waver; *synonyms* (*v*) vacillate, flicker, hesitate, quiver, hover, totter, wave, pause, scruple, wobble, doubt, quaver, (*n*) flutter, faltering, hesitation, 4. rock; *synonyms* (*n*) boulder, calculus, pillar, gem, (*v*) jar, cradle, jolt, toss, quake, pitch, roll, swing, careen, (adj) pebble, stone, **5**. roll; *synonyms* (n) list, revolution, catalogue, inventory, register, (v) coil, curl, enfold, revolve, wheel, twist, wallow, wind, envelop, grumble.

taurangarangaki rolled; *synonyms* (adj) rolling, furled, involute, beaten, billowing, kinky, level, resonant, resonating, resounding, reverberating, reverberative, spiral, trilled, tumbling.

tauraoi 1. equipped; *synonyms* (adj) prepared, armed, equipt, fitted, furnished, ready, weaponed, complete, able, fit, qualified, set, sinewed, arranged, fortified, **2**. furnished; *synonyms* (v) begone, beset, surrounded, (adj) equipped, clothed, enlightened, instruct, privileged, instructed, taught, **3**. dressed; *synonyms* (v) accustomed, arrayed, habited, (adj) attired, clad, appareled, garbed, covered, garmented, habilimented, kerchieft, polished, raw, robed, hooded; *antonym* (adj) undressed, **4**. available; *synonyms* (adj) accessible, free, possible, attainable, convenient, handy, obtainable, open, uncommitted, usable, vacant, valid, (adv) present, (n) applicable; *antonyms* (adj) unavailable, occupied, suppressed, concealed, engaged, **5**. ready; *synonyms* (adj) prompt, quick, nimble, apt, deft, disposed, finished, instant, adroit, (v) prepare, fix, willing, (n) available, dexterous, eager; *antonyms* (adj) unprepared, unwilling, **6**. prepared; *synonyms* (adj) fain, ripe, competent, inclined, primed, completed, efficient, mature, capable, destined, initiated, watchful; *antonym* (adj) spontaneous.

taurere wander; *synonyms* (v) ramble, digress, stray, deviate, err, roam, travel, depart, divagate, gad, meander, (n) saunter, stroll, tramp, drift.

taururu 1. formidable; *synonyms* (adj) arduous, appalling, grim, awful, difficult, dreadful, fearful, forbidding, heavy, dread, onerous, redoubtable, stiff, tough, herculean, **2**. forced; *synonyms* (adj) compulsory, compelled, bound, artificial, constrained, involuntary, unnatural, farfetched, false, labored, obligatory, obliged, strained; *antonyms* (adj) free, unprovoked, spontaneous, voluntary, **3**. animation; *synonyms* (n) life, liveliness, vitality, activity, dash, exhilaration, spirit, vivacity, buoyancy, energy, excitement, cartoon, liveness, airiness, (adj) alacrity; *antonym* (n) lethargy.

taut 1. stingy; *synonyms* (adj) parsimonious, avaricious, mean, miserly, low, penurious, skimpy, greedy, niggard, frugal, cheap, closefisted, measly, (v) narrow, close; *antonyms* (adj) generous, spendthrift, **2**. penurious; *synonyms* (adj) impecunious, niggardly, penniless, stingy, needy, illiberal, poor, chary, grudging, scanty, tight, (v) covetous.

tautaeka 1. govern; *synonyms* (v) administer, control, dictate, dominate, manage, check, bridle, command, conduct, determine, regulate, reign, rule, oversee, (n) direct, **2**. executive; *synonyms* (n) administrator, manager, director, administration, boss, officer, official, supervisor, commissioner, governor, head, management, (adj) administrative, managerial, (v) authoritative, **3**. legislate; *synonyms* (v) enact, constitute, establish, authorise, authorize, clear, communicate, decease, devolve, die, draw, egest, elapse, eliminate, evanesce, **4**. command; *synonyms* (n) instruction, behest, bidding, decree, direction, ascendancy, authority, claim, demand, (v) charge, order, call, commission, bid, instruct; *antonym* (v) request, **5**. administrate; *synonyms* (v) deal, govern, lead, run, **6**. rule; *synonyms* (n) dominion, law, ordinance, principle, government, line, precept, regulation, sway, code, constitution, custom, formula, (v) influence, measure.

tautaekaki 1. governed; *synonyms* (adj) subject, (adv) under, **2**. ruled; *synonyms* (adj) lined, lawful, feint, hatched.

tautaekana rule; *synonyms* (n) govern, order, decree, dominion, law, ordinance, principle, regulate, reign, authority, dictate, (v) command, control, influence, direct.

tautaekanaki ruled; *synonyms* (adj) lined, lawful, subject, feint, hatched.

tautata 1. kind; *synonyms* (n) form, helpful, sort, benign, brand, breed, class, gentle, type, variety, (adj) friendly, generous, good, humane, affectionate; *antonyms* (adj) unkind, callous, cruel, hardhearted, mean, merciless, nasty, spiteful, uncaring, upsetting, disagreeable, unfeeling, **2**. hospitable; *synonyms* (adj) affable, cordial, gracious, receptive, amiable, convivial, genial, pleasant, warm; *antonyms* (adj) unfriendly, inhospitable, unwelcoming, **3**. oblige; *synonyms* (v) coerce, compel, force, bind, constrain, drive, make, accommodate, enforce, necessitate, obligate, impel, impose, require, (n) assign, **4**. obliging; *synonyms* (v) complaisant, civil, (adj) accommodating, kind, compliant, considerate, courteous, attentive, charitable, cooperative, polite, thoughtful, good-natured, urbane, mild; *antonyms* (adj) unhelpful, uncooperative, **5**. pleasure; *synonyms* (n) delight, contentment, delectation, enjoyment, fun, gratification, joy, content, comfort, happiness, mirth, inclination, amusement, bliss, entertainment; *antonyms* (n) anger, irritation, ache, boredom, nuisance.

tauteaka administrative; *synonyms* (adj) departmental, official, managerial, authoritative, (v) executive.

tauti stingy; *synonyms* (adj) parsimonious, avaricious, mean, miserly, low, penurious, skimpy, greedy, niggard, frugal, cheap, closefisted, measly, (v) narrow, close; *antonyms* (adj) generous, spendthrift.

tautia soldier; *synonyms* (*n*) fighter, warrior, champion, swordsman, adventurer, assassin, bottle, cutthroat, fencer, gangster, murderer, recruit, sworder, warfarer, airman.

tautikoko stingy; *synonyms* (*adj*) parsimonious, avaricious, mean, miserly, low, penurious, skimpy, greedy, niggard, frugal, cheap, closefisted, measly, (*v*) narrow, close; *antonyms* (*adj*) generous, spendthrift.

tautoka 1. reinforce; *synonyms* (*v*) bolster, intensify, enhance, buttress, consolidate, fortify, support, enforce, harden, recruit, reenforce, strengthen, amplify, increase, assist; *antonym* (*v*) weaken, **2**. prop; *synonyms* (*n*) post, shore, fulcrum, property, mainstay, airscrew, column, pillar, stay, sustain, (*v*) brace, hold, rest, uphold, help, **3**. support; *synonyms* (*n*) stand, aid, keep, comfort, maintenance, patronage, (*v*) prop, back, encourage, maintain, bear, boost, carry, confirm, corroborate; *antonyms* (*n*) hindrance, (*v*) oppose, neglect, undermine, abandon, reject.

tautokaki 1. reinforced; *synonyms* (*adj*) strengthened, built, strong, assembled, resistant, shatterproof, toughened, unbreakable, armored, durable; *antonym* (*adj*) fragile, **2**. supported; *synonyms* (*v*) borne, carried, conveyed, supporting, (*adj*) bolstered, based, (*adv*) on.

tautooa dominate; *synonyms* (*v*) command, control, prevail, reign, rule, direct, manage, overlook, possess, predominate, crush, domineer, govern, hold, (*adj*) preponderate.

tautooaki dominated; *synonyms* (*adj*) conquered, henpecked, obsessed, occupied, subject, subjugated; *antonym* (*adj*) liberated.

tautorona 1. direct; *synonyms* (*adj*) straight, blunt, immediate, (*v*) aim, channel, conduct, address, charge, control, dictate, head, administer, guide, lead, (*n*) command; *antonyms* (*adj*) indirect, roundabout, circuitous, oblique, second-hand, sideways, unplanned, (*v*) request, **2**. lead; *synonyms* (*v*) contribute, direct, chair, conduce, go, govern, bring, convey, give, carry, dispose, (*n*) clue, advantage, hint, (*adj*) front; *antonym* (*v*) follow, **3**. domineer; *synonyms* (*v*) bully, browbeat, dominate, intimidate, tyrannize, bluster, **4**. rule; *synonyms* (*n*) order, decree, dominion, law, ordinance, principle, regulate, reign, authority, government, line, precept, regulation, (*v*) influence, measure, **5**. subject; *synonyms* (*n*) matter, citizen, affair, dependent, inferior, issue, motif, question, point, area, content, discipline, field, (*adj*) liable, exposed; *antonym* (*adj*) liberated.

tautoronaki 1. led, **2**. directed; *synonyms* (*adj*) absorbed, concentrating, destined, focussed, formal, intent, prescript, subject, engaged, fixed, prescribed, rapt, (*adv*) under, **3**. ruled; *synonyms* (*adj*) lined, lawful, feint, hatched.

tawa 1. ripe; *synonyms* (*adj*) mature, adult, ready, advanced, good, prepared, perfect, matured, consummate, right, (*v*) mellow; *antonym* (*adj*) green, **2**. dry; *synonyms* (*adj*) thirsty, arid, barren, boring, dehydrated, dull, bald, hoarse, jejune, plain, (*v*) dehydrate, desiccate, drain, uninteresting, sardonic; *antonyms* (*adj*) wet, damp, moist, saturated, soaked, boggy, drenched, rainy, sodden, interesting, fresh, humid, juicy, succulent, (*v*) drench, **3**. mature; *synonyms* (*adj*) ripe, complete, aged, developed, experienced, fledged, old, due, (*v*) grow, ripen, develop, age, maturate, season, digest; *antonyms* (*adj*) childish, naive, unripe, young, sophomoric, (*v*) immature.

tawaewae distant; *synonyms* (*adj*) cold, aloof, remote, chill, cool, detached, far, reserved, long, faraway, icy, indifferent, removed, (*adv*) apart, (*n*) chilly; *antonyms* (*adj*) close, adjacent, friendly, near, nearby, neighboring, warm, pending, alert, intimate, involved.

tawaki dried; *synonyms* (*adj*) dry, arid, dehydrated, desiccated, shriveled, shrunken, torrid, baked, concrete, desiccate, stale, wizened, lifeless, weazen, (*n*) milk.

tawanang bare; *synonyms* (*adj*) naked, austere, bald, stark, bleak, desolate, devoid, exposed, mere, nude, plain, vacant, vacuous, (*v*) empty, show; *antonyms* (*adj*) covered, cultivated, ornate, concealed, (*v*) cover.

taware snare; *synonyms* (*n*) trap, lure, decoy, net, noose, (*v*) mesh, catch, gin, ambush, ensnare, entrap, hook, capture, enmesh, entangle.

tawarea 1. catch; *synonyms* (*v*) arrest, capture, hook, apprehend, get, acquire, ensnare, intercept, (*n*) haul, hitch, trick, bolt, clasp, grab, pawl; *antonym* (*v*) release, **2**. ensnare; *synonyms* (*v*) entrap, trap, catch, enmesh, entangle, lure, snare, deceive, decoy, tangle, net, ambush.

tawe 1. rapid; *synonyms* (*adj*) fast, quick, prompt, swift, agile, fleet, hasty, speedy, cursory, expeditious, sudden, nimble, winged, express, hurried; *antonyms* (*adj*) slow, gradual, **2**. soon; *synonyms* (*adv*) shortly, early, presently, anon, immediately, directly, betimes, now, promptly, quickly, soonly, briefly, erelong, speedily, afterward.

tawere 1. blush; *synonyms* (*n*) flush, bloom, color, red, rosiness, redness, ruddiness, (*v*) glow, redden, crimson; *antonym* (*n*) pallor, **2**. ghastly; *synonyms* (*adj*) frightful, awful, cadaverous, dreadful, fearful, grisly, appalling, ashen, atrocious, gruesome, hideous, macabre, offensive, deathly, dismal; *antonyms* (*adj*) pleasant, lovely, wonderful, **3**. pale; *synonyms* (*adj*) ghastly, faint, wan, dull, light, pallid, weak, watery, colorless, (*v*) dim, blanch, (*n*) boundary, confine, border, bound; *antonyms* (*adj*) dark, rosy, strong, brown, **4**. wan; *synonyms* (*v*) pale, rueful, *(adj)* sickly, haggard, pasty, sallow, bloodless, lurid, ashy, thin, white, **5.** sallow; *synonym (adj)* fair.

tawira mince; *synonyms (v)* chop, hash, dice, moderate, slice, soften, fricassee, grate.

tawiraki minced; *synonyms (adj)* crushed, ground, pulverized, milled, pounded, powdered.

te 1. the; *synonyms (n)* queenliness, stateliness, *(v)* thee, **2.** an; *synonym (conj)* if, **3.** a; *synonyms (n)* amp, ampere, angstrom, axerophthol, forenoon, morn, morning, *(v)* grammar, initiation, *(adj)* cream, elite, flower, masterpiece, pick, prime, **4.** one; *synonyms (pron)* any, man, *(n)* anybody, single, somebody, person, ace, *(adj)* certain, individual, lone, only, unique, some, singular, *(adv)* once, **5.** ferment; *synonyms (n)* agitation, excitement, barm, tumult, unrest, disturbance, confusion, *(v)* effervesce, stew, turn, brew, fester, foam, agitate, *(adj)* pother, **6.** bubble; *synonyms (n)* blister, bead, blob, cheat, fantasy, *(v)* boil, babble, burble, fizz, froth, gurgle, seethe, churn, spray, simmer, **7.** fizz; *synonyms (n)* fizzle, sizzle, *(v)* bubble, buzz, lather, sparkle, hiss, **8.** froth; *synonyms (n)* effervescence, bubbles, spindrift, *(v)* spume, suds, ferment, *(adj)* scum.

tea 1. thin; *synonyms (adj)* flimsy, gaunt, lean, light, slight, tenuous, emaciated, fine, rare, slim, sparse, *(v)* slender, dilute, meager, sheer; *antonyms (adj)* thick, fat, concentrated, chubby, plump, wide, broad, heavy, *(v)* thicken, **2.** smooth; *synonyms (adj)* easy, calm, level, oily, facile, flat, flowing, fluent, fluid, glossy, graceful, greasy, *(v)* quiet, facilitate, even; *antonyms (adj)* rough, uneven, abrasive, coarse, crumpled, flaking, harsh, jerky, lined, peeling, prickly, ridged, wrinkled, corrugated, *(v)* wrinkle, **3.** trim; *synonyms (adj)* tidy, neat, spruce, orderly, shipshape, *(v)* cut, dress, clip, garnish, shave, adorn, embellish, lop, prune, reduce, **4.** pare; *synonyms (v)* peel, trim, truncate, skin, whittle, crop, scalp, abbreviate, scrape, shear, slice, flake.

teaki 1. fermented; *synonyms (adj)* alcoholic, arduous, backbreaking, difficult, hard, sour, grueling, gruelling, heavy, knockout, laborious, labourious, punishing, severe, strong, **2.** trimmed; *synonyms (adj)* cut, cunning, demure, down, emasculated, gashed, gelded, level, mown, neat, shortened, slashed, sly, smooth, snoD, **3.** thinned; *synonyms (adj)* dilute, adulterate, attenuate, attenuated, diminished, faded, hurt, lessened, split, weak, weakened, insipid, trimmed, vitiated, watery.

tebararairai sizzle; *synonyms (v)* hiss, fry, fizz, fizzle, sear, cook, libel, storm, bubble, buzz, effervesce, sparkle, spit.

tebe 1. burst; *synonyms (v)* break, crack, blast, rupture, belch, abound, erupt, open, *(n)* flash,

explosion, *(adj)* split, explode, detonate, flare, splinter; *antonym (v)* implode, **2.** dart; *synonyms (n)* bolt, arrow, rocket, *(v)* dash, bound, run, shoot, flit, fly, gallop, race, rush, scurry, spring, tear, **3.** snap; *synonyms (v)* bite, fracture, nip, clack, snarl, rap, rip, rive, burst, *(n)* photograph, catch, go, picnic, pushover, clasp, **4.** pop; *synonyms (n)* dad, daddy, father, pa, papa, bang, shot, click, popping, *(v)* protrude, pawn, appear, place, *(adj)* popular, *(adv)* plump, **5.** spring; *synonyms (n)* jump, leap, fountain, skip, source, dance, rise, *(v)* hop, caper, bounce, dive, originate, recoil, proceed, *(adj)* elastic.

tebeaki 1. burst; *synonyms (v)* break, crack, blast, rupture, belch, abound, erupt, open, *(n)* flash, explosion, *(adj)* split, explode, detonate, flare, splinter; *antonym (v)* implode, **2.** snapped; *synonyms (adj)* tight, torn.

tebeka splash; *synonyms (n)* spot, dab, flash, *(v)* spatter, spray, spill, dash, drop, plash, splatter, slop, slosh, moisten, lap, drench.

tebekaki splashed; *synonyms (adj)* bespattered, besplashed, dabbled, spattered, dotted, marked, showy, speckled, splashy, splattered, streaked.

tebetebe 1. halt; *synonyms (n)* stay, block, cessation, suspension, *(v)* stop, arrest, cease, check, limp, desist, discontinue, hold, pause, freeze, break; *antonyms (v)* start, continue, **2.** swagger; *synonyms (n)* arrogance, boasting, bragging, *(v)* brag, strut, bluster, boast, parade, prance, ruffle, flourish, cock, sashay, *(adj)* bully, groovy.

tebo 1. dive; *synonyms (n)* dip, fall, drop, diving, header, bound, *(v)* plunge, jump, duck, crash, plummet, pounce, descend, plump, fly, **2.** plunge; *synonyms (v)* dive, leap, slump, *(v)* douse, immerse, submerge, drown, dunk, launch, lunge, drive, dash, decline, sink, steep, **3.** submerge; *synonyms (v)* deluge, inundate, overwhelm, engulf, flood, cover, overflow, soak, swamp, drench, saturate, bathe, scuttle, submerse, fell.

teboaki submerged; *synonyms (adj)* immersed, subaqueous, submersed, sunken, underwater, subaquatic, submarine, covered, bathed, deep, engrossed, recessed, semiaquatic, suffused, *(pron)* drowned.

teboakina endeavor; *synonyms (n)* attempt, try, effort, essay, trial, enterprise, shot, work, endeavour, *(v)* struggle, strive, aim, labor, strain, offer; *antonym (v)* neglect.

teboka 1. cleanse; *synonyms (v)* bathe, wash, clarify, wipe, clear, disinfect, purify, refine, rinse, scour, scrub, expurgate, rub, flush, *(adj)* clean; *antonyms (v)* contaminate, dirty, **2.** bathe; *synonyms (v)* steep, tub, bath, immerse, soak, plunge, water, dip, douse, dunk, imbathe, wet, saturate, *(n)* swim, *(adj)* lave, **3.** disinfect; *synonyms (v)* cleanse, sterilize, antisepticize, bleach, distil, filter, neutralize, *(adj)* ventilate; *antonym (v)* infect, **4.** wash; *synonyms*

(v) paint, moisten, mop, color, tint, lap, gargle, dampen, launder, (n) ablution, washing, swamp, laundry, lotion, marsh, **5**. water; *synonyms* (n) urine, moisture, juice, liquor, crystal, glass, lymph, pee, piddle, piss, vitrite, (v) irrigate, dilute, (adj) soundings.

tebokaki 1. cleansed; *synonyms* (adj) cleaned, clean, depurate, refined, depurated, **2**. watered; *synonyms* (adj) moire, dewy, irriguous, moist, watery, **3**. washed.

tebomaurua 1. furious; *synonyms* (adj) angry, fierce, violent, enraged, ferocious, frantic, vehement, wild, boisterous, frenzied, infuriated, raging, rampant, desperate, angered; *antonym* (adj) calm, **2**. intent; *synonyms* (adj) attentive, absorbed, engrossed, earnest, bent, (n) aim, idea, design, intention, goal, import, meaning, purpose, spirit, drift, **3**. insist; *synonyms* (v) affirm, assert, contend, claim, asseverate, declare, maintain, urge, importune, press, argue, force, dwell, hold, persist, **4**. tenacious; *synonyms* (adj) stubborn, adhesive, dogged, obstinate, firm, persistent, resolute, tough, sticky, determined, glutinous, persevering, pertinacious, (v) retentive, strong.

tebona 1. dive; *synonyms* (n) dip, fall, drop, diving, header, bound, (v) plunge, jump, duck, crash, plummet, pounce, descend, plump, fly, **2**. plunge; *synonyms* (n) dive, leap, slump, (v) douse, immerse, submerge, drown, dunk, launch, lunge, drive, dash, decline, sink, steep, **3**. urge; *synonyms* (n) goad, spur, impulse, (v) push, advocate, press, force, impel, incite, induce, inspire, instigate, persuade, prompt, promote; *antonym* (v) discourage.

tebonengenenge persevere; *synonyms* (v) continue, persist, endure, abide, keep, pursue, remain, apply; *antonyms* (v) stop, surrender, yield.

teborake advance; *synonyms* (n) progress, improvement, (v) further, proceed, promote, approach, encourage, raise, rise, boost, contribute, cultivate, develop, forward, (phr) accelerate; *antonyms* (n) deterioration, (v) retreat, recede, delay, demote, regress.

teborakeaki advanced; *synonyms* (adj) sophisticated, progressive, senior, higher, modern, new, precocious, late, cultured, developed, elevated, forward, liberal, ripe, superior; *antonyms* (adj) conservative, old-fashioned, inferior.

teboran 1. drench; *synonyms* (v) soak, deluge, douse, steep, swamp, dip, drown, flush, immerse, moisten, souse, wash, imbue, (adj) splash, bathe; *antonym* (v) dry, **2**. splash; *synonyms* (n) spot, dab, flash, (v) spatter, spray, spill, dash, drop, plash, splatter, slop, slosh, lap, drench, slush.

teboranaki 1. drenched; *synonyms* (adj) wet, saturated, soaked, soaking, damp, soppy, sodden, sopping; *antonym* (adj) dry, **2**. splashed;

synonyms (adj) bespattered, besplashed, dabbled, spattered, dotted, marked, showy, speckled, splashy, splattered, streaked.

tebotebo 1. bathe; *synonyms* (v) wash, steep, tub, bath, clean, immerse, rinse, soak, plunge, water, dip, douse, dunk, (n) swim, (adj) lave, **2**. wash; *synonyms* (v) paint, bathe, moisten, mop, scour, scrub, color, tint, lap, gargle, dampen, launder, (n) ablution, washing, swamp; *antonym* (v) dirty.

teboteboaki washed; *synonyms* (adj) clean, refined, watery.

tebû grandparent; *synonyms* (n) ancestor, antecedent, forerunner, precursor, predecessor.

tebuina ten; *synonyms* (n) tenner, decade, ace, break, breath, decennary, decennium, ecstasy, female, (adj) perfect, comely, desirable, faultless, glamorous, good-looking.

tebwina ten; *synonyms* (n) tenner, decade, ace, break, breath, decennary, decennium, ecstasy, female, (adj) perfect, comely, desirable, faultless, glamorous, good-looking.

teei baby; *synonyms* (n) babe, child, darling, young, (v) coddle, indulge, pamper, cosset, mollycoddle, spoil, (adj) infant, miniature, small, babyish, dear; *antonym* (adj) giant.

teha yawn; *synonyms* (n) yawning, nod, (v) gape, open, ope, yaw.

tehiti lightning; *synonyms* (n) bolt, levin, bolter, dart, fetter, enlightenment, quarrel, shackle, (v) lightening, luminary, (adj) wind.

tei 1. child; *synonyms* (n) baby, boy, babe, bairn, brat, girl, infant, juvenile, kid, minor, toddler, tot, youngster, innocent, imp; *antonym* (n) adult, **2**. hesitate; *synonyms* (v) falter, pause, doubt, fluctuate, halt, waver, boggle, demur, vacillate, procrastinate, dither, scruple, stammer, (adj) linger, delay; *antonym* (v) continue, **3**. halt; *synonyms* (n) stay, block, cessation, suspension, (v) stop, arrest, cease, check, limp, desist, discontinue, hold, freeze, break, end; *antonym* (v) start, **4**. wait; *synonyms* (v) expect, anticipate, ambush, await, lurk, remain, abide, hesitate, watch, loiter, attend, keep, (n) rest, holdup, (adj) tarry, **5**. stationary; *synonyms* (adj) immovable, fixed, motionless, immobile, static, still, unmoving, sedentary, firm, stable, stagnant; *antonym* (adj) moving, **6**. park; *synonyms* (n) garden, common, green, parkland, arena, field, lawn, ballpark, commons, (v) deposit, locate, place, put, set, position, **7**. stop; *synonyms* (v) stand, close, interrupt, obstruct, plug, catch, disrupt, dwell, finish, hinder, impede, intercept, (n) bar, curb, (adj) quit; *antonyms* (v) begin, encourage, permit, prolong, **8**. undecided; *synonyms* (adj) unsettled, doubtful, dubious, indecisive, irresolute, pending, uncertain, unresolved, hesitant, undetermined, debatable, indefinite, indeterminate, ambivalent, borderline; *antonyms* (adj) decided,

certain, determined, **9. stand;** *synonyms* (v)
endure, stall, undergo, live, suffer, tolerate, prop,
erect, accept, bear, (n) attitude, booth, rack, base,
pedestal; *antonyms* (v) sit, lie.

teiaki 1. stopped; *synonyms* (adj) halted, congested,
unmoving, blocked, finished, chinked, clogged,
immobile, motionless, static, stationary, bunged,
crashed, still, **2.** parked.

teiakina 1. guard; *synonyms* (n) defend, defense,
bulwark, care, cover, escort, protection, watchman,
custody, convoy, defence, fender, guardsman, (v)
shield, keep, **2.** watch; *synonyms* (v) observe,
clock, look, see, regard, wake, protect, check,
follow, (n) guard, view, sentinel, sentry,
surveillance, (adj) vigilance.

teiakinaki guarded; *synonyms* (adj) cautious, careful,
wary, chary, circumspect, cagey, vigilant, watchful,
conditional, discreet, gingerly, conservative,
prudent, reserved, safe; *antonyms* (adj) frank,
honest.

teiao menstruate; *synonyms* (v) flow, course, fall,
flux, hang, run, (adj) menstruous.

teibaba disordered; *synonyms* (adj) confused,
chaotic, broken, deranged, disorganized,
incoherent, messy, sick, upset, disconnected,
disjointed, disorderly, ill, jumbled, mixed;
antonyms (adj) neat, orderly, ordered.

teibaka 1. unbalanced; *synonyms* (adj) lopsided,
crazy, mad, wobbly, demented, disproportionate,
imbalanced, unequal, asymmetrical, unsettled,
unstable, unsteady, brainsick, distracted, disturbed;
antonyms (adj) sane, balanced, even, well-balanced,
2. staggering; *synonyms* (adj) astonishing,
astounding, amazing, incredible, inconceivable,
prodigious, marvelous, startling, extraordinary,
ghastly, remarkable, shocking, lurching,
miraculous, stupefying, **3.** tottering; *synonyms* (v)
drooping, (adj) shaky, ramshackle, broken, cracked,
decrepit, doddering, quivering, rickety, rocky,
shaking, sick, tottery, trembling, (n) convulsion.

teibanae 1. disordered; *synonyms* (adj) confused,
chaotic, broken, deranged, disorganized,
incoherent, messy, sick, upset, disconnected,
disjointed, disorderly, ill, jumbled, mixed;
antonyms (adj) neat, orderly, ordered, **2.** strewn;
synonyms (adj) scattered, spread, distributed,
disordered, circulated, diffuse, dispersed,
disseminated, dotted, garbled, illogical, isolated,
rambling, speckled, spotted; *antonym* (adj)
concentrated.

teibanea 1. crowd; *synonyms* (n) huddle, swarm,
collection, crew, press, circle, cluster, army,
assembly, concourse, congregation, (v) bunch, flock,
squeeze, compress; *antonym* (v) disperse, **2.**
surround; *synonyms* (v) encircle, gird, border,
compass, inclose, ring, round, skirt, beset, besiege,
circumvent, embrace, enclose, envelop, environ.

teibaneaki 1. crowded; *synonyms* (adj) close,
compact, congested, busy, dense, full, packed,
populous, jammed, cramped, teeming, thick, tight,
(n) thronged; *antonyms* (adj) empty, sparse, **2.**
surrounded; *synonyms* (v) beset, begone,
furnished, (adj) encircled, bounded, circumstanced,
conditioned, entrenched, fixed, ingirt, inside,
ringed, rooted, bordered, delimited.

teimatoa 1. last; *synonyms* (v) endure, continue, hold,
exist, live, dwell, (n) abide, conclusion, (adj) extreme,
closing, final, ultimate, conclusive, concluding,
farthest; *antonyms* (n) opening, (adj) first, **2.**
consistent; *synonyms* (adj) coherent, uniform,
agreeable, compatible, congruous, constant, logical,
conformable, consonant, regular, unchanging,
concurrent, unvarying, accordant, equable;
antonyms (adj) inconsistent, erratic, contradictory,
illogical, unpredictable, unreliable, **3.** constant;
synonyms (adj) ceaseless, incessant, perpetual,
steady, continual, abiding, changeless, consistent,
continuous, eternal, faithful, frequent, loyal,
resolute, (n) invariable; *antonyms* (adj) changeable,
intermittent, irregular, sporadic, variable, episodic,
inconstant, disloyal, fickle, occasional, temporary,
4. firm; *synonyms* (n) company, (adj) hard, stable,
close, compact, determined, fixed, solid, steadfast,
strong, decisive, dense, fast, rigid, (v) durable;
antonyms (adj) irresolute, soft, weak, hesitant, limp,
liquid, soggy, **5.** staunch; *synonyms* (v) stanch,
halt, stem, stop, (adj) firm, hardy, devoted, stalwart,
secure, sturdy, reliable, sure, unfailing, dogged,
stout, **6.** stable; *synonyms* (adj) permanent, lasting,
stationary, enduring, persistent, sound, immovable,
certain, set, immobile, immutable, responsible, safe,
static, tight; *antonyms* (adj) unstable, shaky,
wobbly, dangerous, precarious, rickety, volatile, **7.**
steadfast; *synonyms* (adj) inflexible, staunch,
unwavering, stubborn, tenacious, unfaltering,
unshakable, dependable, obstinate, decided, gritty,
intent, staid, tireless, (v) impregnable, **8.** solid;
synonyms (adj) real, good, massive, substantial,
hearty, heavy, material, potent, thick, whole, fine,
concrete, full, convincing, muscular; *antonyms* (adj)
loose, gaseous, permeable, runny, transparent,
watery.

teirake 1. commence; *synonyms* (v) begin, start,
open, embark, initiate, arise, enter, inaugurate,
institute, introduce, launch, approach, develop,
found, get; *antonyms* (v) end, finish, stop, **2.**
begin; *synonyms* (v) commence, become, originate,
rise, create, dawn, undertake, build, happen,
induce, attack, attempt, bring, broach, cause, **3.**
stand; *synonyms* (v) endure, stall, undergo, live,
suffer, tolerate, prop, erect, hold, (n) attitude, booth,
rack, base, pedestal, position; *antonyms* (v) sit, lie.

teirakea undertake; *synonyms* (v) attempt, try,
accept, contract, covenant, guarantee, tackle, take,

assume, assure, begin, engage, promise, endeavor, seek.

teiraoi 1. firm; *synonyms* (*n*) company, (*adj*) constant, hard, stable, close, compact, determined, fixed, resolute, solid, steadfast, steady, strong, decisive, (*v*) faithful; *antonyms* (*adj*) irresolute, soft, weak, hesitant, limp, liquid, soggy, **2.** erect; *synonyms* (*v*) build, elevate, raise, construct, rear, assemble, lift, create, advance, arouse, dignify, (*adj*) upright, vertical, perpendicular, raised; *antonym* (*adj*) horizontal, **3.** upright; *synonyms* (*adj*) straight, erect, fair, good, just, righteous, honest, honorable, plumb, right, true, virtuous, pure, clean, (*n*) column; *antonyms* (*adv*) horizontally, (*adj*) disreputable, prone, upturned, degenerate, hanging, unwholesome, **4.** strait; *synonyms* (*n*) inlet, need, pass, pinch, quandary, channel, crisis, difficulty, distress, poverty, straits, emergency, frith, (*adj*) narrow, (*v*) dilemma.

teirobaroba 1. loose; *synonyms* (*adj*) lax, liberal, dissolute, licentious, light, vague, detached, immoral, (*v*) disengage, liberate, relax, release, detach, (*n*) free, limp; *antonyms* (*adj*) tight, close, compressed, dense, taut, strict, compact, wedged, **2.** hesitating; *synonyms* (*adj*) hesitant, indecisive, irresolute, doubtful, undecided, faltering, reluctant, unwilling, backward, **3.** flapping; *synonyms* (*adj*) loose, baggy, streaming, flying, incoherent, loquacious, relaxed, slack, (*n*) flap, flutter, fluttering, commotion, disruption, disturbance, dither, **4.** wavering; *synonyms* (*adj*) vacillating, uncertain, changeable, variable, dithering, inconstant, unstable, unsteady, vacillant, hesitating, shaky, (*n*) fluctuation, hesitation, vacillation, swinging; *antonyms* (*adj*) constant, decided, (*n*) decisiveness.

teiruarua 1. lost; *synonyms* (*v*) gone, missing, abandoned, (*adj*) doomed, forlorn, extinct, hopeless, bewildered, disoriented, forgotten, helpless, broken, confused, irrecoverable, absent; *antonyms* (*adj*) present, found, existing, **2.** bewildered; *synonyms* (*adj*) baffled, bemused, lost, befuddled, confounded, perplexed, puzzled, dumbfounded, addled, amazed, blank, dazed, disconcerted, muddled, mystified; *antonyms* (*adj*) enlightened, unimpressed, **3.** strange; *synonyms* (*adj*) extraneous, foreign, peculiar, abnormal, curious, extraordinary, irregular, mysterious, new, odd, outlandish, unusual, rare, alien, anomalous; *antonyms* (*adj*) normal, ordinary, familiar, typical.

teitei 1. loiter; *synonyms* (*v*) linger, dawdle, lag, loaf, dally, saunter, tarry, prowl, idle, loll, continue, (*adj*) delay, lounge, hesitate, (*adv*) crawl, **2.** linger; *synonyms* (*v*) hover, loiter, stay, procrastinate, remain, abide, endure, drag, dwell, stop, persist, stroll, trail, cling, (*adv*) creep; *antonyms* (*v*) leave, hurry, **3.** tarry; *synonyms* (*v*) bide, rest, wait, (*adj*)

pitchy, stand, resinous, resiny, **4.** posture; *synonyms* (*n*) position, attitude, pose, condition, deportment, stance, aspect, circumstance, figure, manner, mien, bearing, carriage, (*v*) place, model, **5.** stationary; *synonyms* (*adj*) immovable, fixed, motionless, immobile, static, still, unmoving, sedentary, firm, stable, stagnant; *antonym* (*adj*) moving.

teiuomania group; *synonyms* (*n*) bunch, brigade, collection, crowd, flock, gang, association, clump, company, gathering, (*v*) assemblage, class, cluster, rank, sort.

teiuomaniaki grouped; *synonyms* (*adj*) sorted, collective.

teka 1. hooked; *synonyms* (*adj*) crooked, bent, curved, aquiline, addicted, infatuated, dependant, dependent, enamored, engrossed, obsessed, **2.** beaten; *synonyms* (*v*) beat, (*adj*) battered, overpowered, conquered, routed, overcome; *antonym* (*adj*) victorious, **3.** hit; *synonyms* (*v*) strike, attain, belt, blow, bump, collide, encounter, (*n*) knock, bang, smash, touch, chance, bash, collision, play; *antonyms* (*n*) failure, flop, **4.** pierced; *synonyms* (*adj*) perforated, punctured, perforate, cleft, entered, **5.** punctured; *synonyms* (*adj*) pierced, disillusioned, flat, **6.** wounded; *synonyms* (*adj*) hurt, bruised, bloody, (*n*) casualty, maimed; *antonym* (*adj*) composed, **7.** shot; *synonyms* (*n*) gunshot, injection, go, fling, ball, crack, shoot, picture, attempt, bullet, discharge, effort, endeavor, guess, (*adj*) iridescent, **8.** struck; *synonyms* (*v*) stroke, wounded, (*adj*) smitten, stricken, afflicted, crazy, doting, dotty, gaga, interested, **9.** stabbed, **10.** touched; *synonyms* (*v*) compassionate, pitiful, sympathetic, bad, decayed, lentiginous, mildewed, moldy, mucid, musty, (*adj*) affected, cracked, daft, insane, tinged; *antonym* (*adj*) untouched.

tekai wood; *synonyms* (*n*) forest, timber, woods, tree, lumber, coppice, jungle.

tekaraoi 1. lucky; *synonyms* (*adj*) auspicious, favorable, propitious, prosperous, favourable, successful, flourishing, advantageous, blessed, chance, good, providential, (*n*) happy, favored, (*v*) fortunate; *antonyms* (*adj*) unlucky, hapless, ill-fated, unfortunate, **2.** fortunate; *synonyms* (*adj*) lucky, fortuitous, well, felicitous, golden, advantaged, desirable, hopeful, **3.** successful; *synonyms* (*adj*) effective, effectual, fruitful, efficacious, prevalent, efficient, thriving, triumphant, profitable, winning; *antonyms* (*adj*) unsuccessful, thwarted, dependent, failing, ineffective, sorrowful.

tekateka 1. sat; *synonym* (*v*) seet, **2.** sit; *synonyms* (*v*) model, pose, rest, ride, place, posture, put, seat, set, squat, meet, hold, convene, locate, mount;

antonyms (v) stand, rise, **3.** seated; *synonyms* (adj) sitting, sedentary.

teke pierced; *synonyms* (adj) perforated, punctured, perforate, cleft, entered.

tekeboti spread; *synonyms* (v) scatter, reach, disperse, expand, extend, broadcast, circulate, diffuse, disseminate, increase, propagate, stretch, broaden, deploy, (n) span; *antonym* (adj) concentrated.

tekebuaka 1. fail; *synonyms* (v) abort, collapse, fade, cease, abandon, break, bust, default, deteriorate, die, disappoint, flag, want, (adj) decline, drop; *antonyms* (v) succeed, triumph, **2.** unfortunate; *synonyms* (adj) inauspicious, poor, sad, bad, disastrous, hapless, inopportune, adverse, calamitous, deplorable, infelicitous, lamentable, unlucky, untoward, ill; *antonyms* (adj) fortunate, lucky, **3.** unlucky; *synonyms* (adj) unfortunate, luckless, unhappy, sinister, ominous, unsuccessful, doomed, unfavorable, fatal, unblest, damned, intrusive, timeless.

tekebuakaki failed; *synonyms* (adj) unsuccessful, abortive, failing, bankrupt, declining, deteriorating, ineffective, insolvent, bungled, disastrous, erstwhile, former, inferior, poor, regressing; *antonym* (adj) first-rate.

tekemangongo stinking; *synonyms* (adj) rotten, fetid, foul, malodorous, putrid, loathsome, noisome, smelly, odorous, disgusting, foetid, funky, lousy, sickening, nasty; *antonym* (adj) fragrant.

tekena 1. beat; *synonyms* (v) batter, flap, pulsate, throb, tick, trounce, whip, bat, baste, break, (n) pulse, thump, knock, round, cadence; *antonym* (v) lose, **2.** catch; *synonyms* (v) arrest, capture, hook, apprehend, get, acquire, ensnare, intercept, (n) haul, hitch, trick, bolt, clasp, grab, pawl; *antonym* (v) release, **3.** defeat; *synonyms* (n) frustration, ruin, beating, (v) crush, overcome, beat, conquer, abolish, baffle, foil, overpower, repulse, rout, subdue, (adj) rebuff; *antonyms* (n) victory, success, win, (v) surrender, **4.** pass; *synonyms* (v) flow, deliver, give, happen, lead, move, offer, overtake, live, advance, die, elapse, exceed, (adj) go, run; *antonym* (v) fail.

tekenaki 1. defeated; *synonyms* (adj) disappointed, frustrated, beaten, discomfited, broken, overcome, baffled, balked, bested, down-and-out, failing, foiled, thwarted, worsted, (n) loser, **2.** beaten; *synonyms* (v) beat, (adj) battered, overpowered, conquered, routed; *antonym* (adj) victorious.

tekera 1. failed; *synonyms* (adj) unsuccessful, abortive, failing, bankrupt, declining, deteriorating, ineffective, insolvent, bungled, disastrous, erstwhile, former, inferior, poor, regressing; *antonym* (adj) first-rate, **2.** adverse; *synonyms* (adj) contrary, unfavorable, harmful, hostile, untoward,

adversary, averse, counter, inimical, negative, repugnant, antagonistic, bad, contradictory, (n) opposite; *antonym* (adj) favorable, **3.** unfortunate; *synonyms* (adj) inauspicious, sad, hapless, inopportune, adverse, calamitous, deplorable, infelicitous, lamentable, unlucky, ill, luckless, miserable, ominous, pathetic; *antonyms* (adj) fortunate, lucky, **4.** unlucky; *synonyms* (adj) unfortunate, unhappy, sinister, doomed, fatal, unblest, damned, intrusive, timeless.

tekeraoi blessed; *synonyms* (adj) blest, happy, holy, blasted, cursed, damned, fortunate, hallowed, sacred, saintly, lucky, consecrated, deuced, divine, heavenly; *antonym* (adj) unlucky.

tekeria 1. disappointed; *synonyms* (adj) defeated, disgruntled, regretful, depressed, dissatisfied, frustrated, sad, unhappy, disenchanted; *antonyms* (adj) delighted, pleased, composed, satisfied, **2.** burned; *synonyms* (v) burnished, (adj) burnt, baked, adust, bleak, heated, hurt, parched, sore, sunbaked, **3.** punished.

tekinini 1. little; *synonyms* (adj) small, diminutive, insignificant, brief, minute, petty, short, some, tiny, exiguous, light, baby, bantam, (v) dash, bit; *antonyms* (adj) big, enormous, large, important, **2.** small; *synonyms* (adj) little, narrow, fine, inadequate, low, minor, slight, remote, cramped, young, limited, faint, humble, miniature, minuscule; *antonyms* (adj) bulky, colossal, considerable, extra-large, great, huge, sizeable, giant, major.

téköe elder; *synonyms* (adj) older, big, adult, (n) senior, ancient, patriarch, boss, chief, superior.

temanna single; *synonyms* (adj) only, celibate, one, odd, particular, distinct, individual, isolated, lone, lonely, separate, simple, sole, solitary, exclusive; *antonyms* (adj) married, double, multiple.

temant father; *synonyms* (n) begetter, dad, sire, creator, abba, beginner, forefather, founder, padre, patriarch, author, (v) beget, engender, create, generate; *antonym* (n) mother.

teme 1. drink; *synonyms* (n) beverage, alcohol, brew, potion, swallow, crapulence, intoxicant, nip, (v) draught, booze, carouse, bib, absorb, down, gulp, **2.** smoke; *synonyms* (n) fumes, fog, mist, perfume, smoking, smoulder, (v) fume, reek, fumigate, puff, exhale, cure, burn, smolder, (adj) smudge, **3.** taste; *synonyms* (n) bit, flavor, liking, morsel, penchant, appetite, drink, drop, fondness, gusto, (v) relish, savor, sample, smack, discernment; *antonyms* (n) dislike, tastelessness.

temeka 1. inhale; *synonyms* (v) breathe, absorb, imbibe, draw, suck, drag, drink, attract, inspire, receive, respire, admit, import, ingest, (n) sniff; *antonym* (v) exhale, **2.** sip; *synonyms* (n) nip, gulp, swallow, taste, bite, drop, mouthful, shot, slurp, swig, nibble, (v) sample, quaff, lap, (adj) sup, **3.** suck; *synonyms* (v) nurse, lactate, suckle, drain, puff, aspirate, pull, breastfeed, (n) sucking, suction.

temekaki inhaled; *synonym* (adj) inspired.

temekia sip; *synonyms* (n) nip, gulp, swallow, taste, bite, drop, mouthful, shot, slurp, (v) drink, imbibe, sample, quaff, lap, (adj) sup.

ten three; *synonyms* (n) leash, triplet, tercet, ternary, ternion, terzetto, third, lead, terce, tether, threesome, tierce, trey, triad, trine.

tena 1. bite; *synonyms* (n) taste, bit, cheat, morsel, (v) sting, nip, chew, cut, pinch, burn, eat, erode, gnaw, hurt, munch, **2.** bit; *synonyms* (n) crumb, piece, atom, drop, fleck, fragment, moment, part, portion, shred, snatch, trace, (v) curb, scrap, scantling, **3.** bitter; *synonyms* (adj) acrimonious, biting, acrid, sharp, acerbic, acid, caustic, keen, malicious, resentful, sour, virulent, acerb, cutting, (n) acerbity; *antonyms* (adj) mild, sweet, charitable, hot, kind, sugary, **4.** crowd; *synonyms* (n) huddle, swarm, collection, crew, press, circle, cluster, army, assembly, concourse, congregation, (v) bunch, flock, squeeze, compress; *antonym* (v) disperse, **5.** join; *synonyms* (v) connect, unite, associate, combine, link, graft, assemble, affiliate, attach, meet, affix, annex, conjoin, converge, (n) bond; *antonyms* (v) detach, secede, separate, split, undo, **6.** acid; *synonyms* (adj) acidic, bitter, pointed, sarcastic, astringent, blistering, corrosive, harsh, incisive, mordant, pungent, unkind, venomous, vitriolic, (v) tart, **7.** wedge; *synonyms* (n) chock, slice, cuneus, stick, plug, bomber, (v) jam, pack, ram, stuff, lodge, crowd, crush, fasten, fix, **8.** piquant; *synonyms* (adj) peppery, spicy, racy, engaging, salty, strong, tasty, trenchant, gamy, juicy, poignant, rough, savoury, stinging, zesty; *antonym* (adj) bland, **9.** smart; *synonyms* (adj) bright, crafty, dapper, quick, shrewd, sly, prompt, astute, chic, clever, intelligent, jaunty, lively, (v) ache, (n) pain; *antonyms* (adj) scruffy, stupid, dim, shabby, unkempt, slow, **10.** press; *synonyms* (n) closet, newspaper, (v) force, coerce, exhort, mash, push, urge, clasp, hug, pressure, squash, stress, (adj) constrain, weigh, **11.** stinging; *synonyms* (adj) piercing, piquant, prickling, painful, stabbing, burning, edged, raw, severe, (v) irritating, penetrating, provoking, **12.** pungent; *synonyms* (adj) brisk, acute, barbed, fiery, nipping, smart, aromatic, intense, mordacious, rank, fragrant, graveolent, lecherous, lustful, nidorous; *antonym* (adj) faint, **13.** sting; *synonyms* (n) bite, con, chafe, stab, swindle, bunco, (v) prick, goad, irritate, itch, prickle, provoke, nettle, prod, tingle, **14.** sour; *synonyms* (adj) morose, rancid, gruff, dour, glum, grim, rotten, sullen, off, bad, (v) acidify, ferment, turn, embitter, (n) acidity; *antonym* (adj) kindly.

tenabiti held; *synonyms* (adj) absorbed, confined, alleged, assumed, believed, bound, caged, captive, detained, fast, immersed, obsessed, occupied, protected, (adv) on.

tenaki 1. joined; *synonyms* (adj) combined, coupled, united, allied, connected, joint, amalgamated, associated, linked, concerted; *antonym* (adj) separate, **2.** crowded; *synonyms* (adj) close, compact, congested, busy, dense, full, packed, populous, jammed, cramped, teeming, thick, tight, (n) thronged; *antonyms* (adj) empty, sparse, **3.** wedged; *synonyms* (adj) impacted, fast, stuck, blocked, caught, fixed, immovable, lodged, stiff, trapped; *antonym* (adj) loose, **4.** pressed; *synonyms* (adj) printed, pushed, stamped, bound, driven, embossed, encouraged, impelled, imprinted, incited, marked, provoked, prompted.

tenana one; *synonyms* (pron) any, man, (n) anybody, single, somebody, person, ace, (adj) certain, individual, lone, only, unique, some, singular, (adv) once.

tenarua 1. hack; *synonyms* (n) drudge, cab, hacker, jade, nag, (v) cut, chop, ax, fell, gash, mutilate, rip, slash, slice, cleave, **2.** bite; *synonyms* (n) taste, bit, cheat, morsel, nibble, (v) sting, nip, chew, pinch, burn, eat, erode, gnaw, hurt, munch, **3.** devour; *synonyms* (v) consume, bolt, gulp, demolish, gobble, gorge, guzzle, swallow, absorb, devastate, enjoy, relish, down, exhaust, feed, **4.** tear; *synonyms* (n) split, rupture, rent, (v) break, crack, pull, rend, lacerate, race, run, rush, slit, rive, dash, fly.

tenatenaia nibble; *synonyms* (v) eat, munch, chew, browse, gnaw, nip, pick, crunch, champ, taste, cranch, craunch, (n) bite, morsel, nybble; *antonyms* (v) gobble, guzzle.

teñaun ten; *synonyms* (n) tenner, decade, ace, break, breath, decennary, decennium, ecstasy, female, (adj) perfect, comely, desirable, faultless, glamorous, good-looking.

teng the; *synonyms* (n) queenliness, stateliness, (v) thee.

tenga thousand; *synonyms* (n) chiliad, grand, m, g, thou, curtilage, gee, gigabyte, gm, gram, gramme, green, grounds, heap, jet.

tengetenge 1. exhibit; *synonyms* (v) evince, demonstrate, evidence, expose, disclose, announce, flaunt, parade, perform, present, produce, show, bear, indicate, (n) display; *antonym* (v) conceal, **2.** show; *synonyms* (v) broadcast, guide, give, manifest, prove, reveal, figure, (n) appearance, exhibit, ostentation, presentation, pageant, picture, semblance, act; *antonyms* (v) disprove, hide.

teni three; *synonyms* (n) leash, triplet, tercet, ternary, ternion, terzetto, third, lead, terce, tether, threesome, tierce, trey, triad, trine.

tenibwi thirty; *synonyms* (*n*) xxx, termination, dash, (*adj*) thretty.

tenikadaradara beads; *synonyms* (*n*) rosary, censer, cross, crucifix, host, patera, pax, pyx, reliquary, rood, thurible, jewelry, lot, relics.

tennai three; *synonyms* (*n*) leash, triplet, tercet, ternary, ternion, terzetto, third, lead, terce, tether, threesome, tierce, trey, triad, trine.

tennanoa 1. enraged; *synonyms* (*adj*) angry, angered, furious, infuriated, irate, incensed, livid, mad, exasperated, irritated, raging, boiling; *antonym* (*adj*) calm, 2. hateful; *synonyms* (*adj*) detestable, disgusting, abominable, execrable, nasty, obnoxious, odious, hideous, despicable, distasteful, foul, heinous, repugnant, repulsive, cursed; *antonyms* (*adj*) lovable, delightful, 3. furious; *synonyms* (*adj*) fierce, violent, enraged, ferocious, frantic, vehement, wild, boisterous, frenzied, rampant, desperate, cross, fiery, heated, hot.

tenoua three; *synonyms* (*n*) leash, triplet, tercet, ternary, ternion, terzetto, third, lead, terce, tether, threesome, tierce, trey, triad, trine.

tenu 1. grammatical; *synonym* (*adj*) grammatic, 2. expressive; *synonyms* (*adj*) eloquent, meaningful, significant, descriptive, mobile, revelatory, articulate, graphic, indicative, suggestive, vivid, enthusiastic, loving, 3. fitting; *synonyms* (*adj*) fit, applicable, appropriate, apt, felicitous, just, decorous, becoming, compatible, correct, (*n*) adaptation, adjustment, accommodation, appointment, installation; *antonyms* (*adj*) inappropriate, improper, wrong, 4. euphonic; *synonyms* (*adj*) euphonious, euphonical, melodious, sweet, 5. becoming; *synonyms* (*v*) proper, (*adj*) seemly, adequate, decent, agreeable, apposite, befitting, due, relevant, comely, eligible, right, suitable, handsome, attractive; *antonym* (*adj*) unbecoming, 6. good; *synonyms* (*adj*) able, benefit, delicious, efficient, capable, excellent, fine, nice, superior, well, advantageous, desirable, (*n*) benign, advantage, gain; *antonyms* (*adj*) disobedient, poor, wicked, unpleasant, (*n*) evil, bad, 7. suitable; *synonyms* (*adj*) good, convenient, fitting, pertinent, respectable, fitted, competent, expedient, opportune, comfortable, qualified, satisfactory, congenial, harmonious, (*n*) seasonable; *antonym* (*adj*) unsuitable, 8. seemly; *synonyms* (*adj*) modest, fair, apropos, personable, (*v*) meet, 9. pronounced; *synonyms* (*adj*) marked, clear, emphatic, distinct, notable, prominent, definite, obvious, salient, bold, decided, demonstrative, outstanding, striking.

tenua three; *synonyms* (*n*) leash, triplet, tercet, ternary, ternion, terzetto, third, lead, terce, tether, threesome, tierce, trey, triad, trine.

tepouina ten; *synonyms* (*n*) tenner, decade, ace, break, breath, decennary, decennium, ecstasy, female, (*adj*) perfect, comely, desirable, faultless, glamorous, good-looking.

tepouno virgin; *synonyms* (*adj*) pure, vestal, chaste, innocent, new, fresh, intact, untouched, unmixed, virginal, virtuous, unmarried, (*n*) maiden, maid, girl.

tere 1. distinct; *synonyms* (*adj*) clear, articulate, different, discrete, apparent, definite, distinctive, palpable, decided, dissimilar, marked, plain, tangible, (*prep*) separate, (*adv*) apart; *antonyms* (*adj*) indistinct, similar, unclear, vague, inaudible, shapeless, 2. apparent; *synonyms* (*adj*) manifest, discernible, patent, evident, obvious, open, ostensible, perceptible, conspicuous, noticeable, outward, overt, specious, superficial, (*adv*) visible; *antonyms* (*adj*) real, mysterious, obscure, 3. distinctive; *synonyms* (*adj*) characteristic, distinguishing, excellent, discriminating, individual, special, typical, exceptional, unusual, distinct, idiosyncratic, particular, peculiar, (*v*) discriminative, dioristic; *antonym* (*adj*) common, 4. visible; *synonyms* (*adj*) observable, appreciable, visual, transparent, glaring, external, physical, seeable; *antonyms* (*adj*) invisible, imperceptible, 5. plain; *synonyms* (*adj*) ordinary, comprehensible, intelligible, downright, easy, homely, humble, level, simple, perspicuous, outspoken, direct, dull, even, (*n*) flat; *antonyms* (*adj*) elaborate, fancy, mottled, multicolored, ornate, attractive, concealed, confused, fussy, two-colored.

teretere obvious; *synonyms* (*adj*) clear, visible, apparent, conspicuous, distinct, evident, flagrant, open, blatant, discernible, glaring, manifest, marked, noticeable, perceptible; *antonyms* (*adj*) inconspicuous, obscure, hidden, imperceptible, unclear, undetectable, concealed, slight, subtle.

teri 1. erection; *synonyms* (*n*) building, edifice, assembly, construction, structure, erecting, architecture, creation, composition, fabrication, (*adj*) elevation, (*v*) fabric, 2. bone; *synonyms* (*n*) os, ivory, mouth, osmium, argument, bead, block, (*v*) cartilage, swot, gristle, prepare, arise, attire, beat, bill.

teroa 1. rasp; *synonyms* (*v*) grate, scrape, abrade, chafe, file, grind, rub, scratch, grater, graze, groan, squeak, fray, screech, jar, 2. smooth; *synonyms* (*adj*) easy, calm, level, oily, facile, flat, flowing, fluent, fluid, glossy, graceful, greasy, (*v*) quiet, facilitate, even; *antonyms* (*adj*) rough, uneven, abrasive, coarse, crumpled, flaking, harsh, jerky, lined, peeling, prickly, ridged, wrinkled, corrugated, (*v*) wrinkle.

terona 1. enslave; *synonyms* (*v*) bind, enthrall, captivate, slave, subjugate, tame, chain, confine; *antonym* (*v*) liberate, 2. subdue; *synonyms* (*v*) conquer, crush, defeat, overpower, quash, quell, reduce, repress, chasten, curb, overcome, restrain, soften, suppress, (adv) control; antonym (v) surrender, **3.** subject; synonyms (n) matter, citizen, affair, dependent, inferior, issue, motif, question, point, area, content, discipline, field, (adj) liable, exposed; antonym (adj) liberated.

teronaki 1. enslaved; synonyms (adj) bond, captive, beguiled, bound, captivated, charmed, cringing, delighted, dependent, enthralled, imprisoned, incarcerated, obsequious, servile, subject; antonym (adj) free, **2.** subdued; synonyms (adj) muffled, quiet, soft, dull, muted, restrained, tame, faint, resigned, repressed, low, meek, broken, delicate, sober; antonyms (adj) loud, enthusiastic, lively.

tete 1. curious; synonyms (adj) abnormal, funny, interested, odd, peculiar, strange, unusual, bizarre, extraordinary, inquiring, inquisitive, quaint, queer, quizzical, remarkable; antonyms (adj) normal, incurious, ordinary, **2.** impolite; synonyms (adj) coarse, discourteous, gruff, brusque, churlish, disrespectful, impertinent, improper, insolent, rude, uncivilized, blunt, abrupt, brutal, unrefined; antonyms (adj) polite, respectful, courteous, **3.** importunate; synonyms (adj) troublesome, annoying, exigent, insistent, pressing, instant, demanding, earnest, pleading, urgent, appealing, imploring, (v) important; antonym (adj) halfhearted, **4.** bold; synonyms (adj) adventurous, audacious, manly, resolute, arrogant, barefaced, courageous, daring, fearless, heroic, intrepid, spirited, stalwart, bluff, brave; antonyms (adj) cowardly, timid, modest, **5.** detested; synonyms (adj) despised, hated, unpopular, disliked, loathed, reviled, scorned, abhorrent, despicable, insufferable, ostracized; antonym (adj) popular, **6.** pretentious; synonyms (adj) ostentatious, affected, pompous, showy, boastful, stilted, presumptuous, grandiose, snobbish, ambitious, exaggerated, mannered, mincing, gaudy, (v) conceited; antonym (adj) down-to-earth, **7.** sizzle; synonyms (v) hiss, fry, fizz, fizzle, sear, cook, libel, storm, bubble, buzz, effervesce, sparkle, spit, **8.** rude; synonyms (adj) gross, rough, impudent, bold, crude, impolite, mean, abusive, barbarous, crass, curt, indelicate, plain, raw, forward; antonyms (adj) chivalrous, refined, civil, decent, proper, well-mannered.

tetere advance; synonyms (n) progress, improvement, (v) further, proceed, promote, approach, encourage, raise, rise, boost, contribute, cultivate, develop, forward, (phr) accelerate; antonyms (n) deterioration, (v) retreat, recede, delay, demote, regress.

tetereaki advanced; synonyms (adj) sophisticated, progressive, senior, higher, modern, new, precocious, late, cultured, developed, elevated, forward, liberal, ripe, superior; antonyms (adj) conservative, old-fashioned, inferior.

teuana 1. a; synonyms (n) amp, ampere, angstrom, axerophthol, forenoon, morn, morning, (v) grammar, initiation, (adj) cream, elite, flower, masterpiece, pick, prime, **2.** sole; synonyms (adj) lone, single, singular, one, alone, exclusive, individual, only, solitary, particular, separate, (n) bottom, base, flounder, (v) resole, **3.** the; synonyms (n) queenliness, stateliness, (v) thee, **4.** single; synonyms (adj) celibate, odd, distinct, isolated, lonely, simple, sole, several, common, discrete, different, free, sincere, unmarried, (n) bachelor; antonyms (adj) married, double, multiple, **5.** one; synonyms (pron) any, man, (n) anybody, somebody, person, ace, anyone, unit, unity, (adj) certain, unique, some, united, ane, (adv) once.

teumaririe itching; synonyms (n) itch, pruritus, prickle, cupidity, itchiness, quiver, shiver, sting, prickling, (adj) anxious, creepy, enterprising, prurient, thirsty, lustful.

teutana 1. mediocre; synonyms (adj) average, middling, ordinary, commonplace, fair, indifferent, passable, common, inferior, intermediate, medium, tolerable, normal, everyday, (n) mean; antonyms (adj) exceptional, first-rate, excellent, impressive, **2.** little; synonyms (adj) small, diminutive, insignificant, brief, minute, petty, short, some, tiny, exiguous, light, baby, bantam, (v) dash, bit; antonyms (adj) big, enormous, large, important, **3.** insignificant; synonyms (adj) inconsequential, inconsiderable, humble, immaterial, infinitesimal, little, poor, trivial, unimportant, inappreciable, lesser, meaningless, minor, negligible, paltry; antonyms (adj) significant, considerable, great, huge, major, substantial, colossal, influential, momentous, valuable, **4.** minor; synonyms (adj) junior, lower, less, marginal, secondary, slight, subordinate, incidental, low, lowly, (n) child, juvenile, youngster, adolescent, youth; antonyms (adj) basic, chief, fundamental, leading, main, overriding, superseding, serious, extensive, greater, senior, **5.** inconsequential; synonyms (adj) inconsequent, frivolous, irrelevant, trifling, **6.** miniature; synonyms (adj) model, wee, midget, dwarf, teeny, petite, (n) toy, copy, illumination; antonyms (adj) extra-large, full-scale, full-size, **7.** paltry; synonyms (adj) miserable, abject, contemptible, measly, puny, despicable, dirty, piddling, pitiful, shabby, worthless, wretched, meager, base, cheap; antonym (adj) generous, **8.** tiny; synonyms (adj) miniature, cramped, stunted, (phr) minuscule; antonyms (adj) gigantic, vast, **9.** unessential; synonyms (adj) inessential, unnecessary, dispensable, extrinsic, disposable, external, extra, extraneous, gratuitous, outward, redundant, superfluous, surplus, excessive, unneeded; *antonym* (*adj*) essential, **10.** small; *synonyms* (*adj*) narrow, fine, inadequate, remote, young, limited, faint, modest, slender, scanty, ungenerous, outside, feeble, insufficient, (*v*) frail; *antonyms* (*adj*) bulky, sizeable, giant, **11.** pygmy; *synonym* (*n*) manikin, **12.** shallow; *synonyms* (*adj*) shoal, superficial, cursory, sketchy, flimsy, simple, surface, dull, airy, facile, ignorant, plain, thin, (*n*) flat, silly; *antonyms* (*adj*) deep, bottomless, **13.** slight; *synonyms* (*adj*) fragile, delicate, lean, tenuous, easy, shallow, (*n*) scorn, disdain, rebuff, (*v*) disregard, insult, neglect, ignore, affront, cut; *antonyms* (*adj*) fat, heavy, intense, obvious, severe, thickset, wide, **14.** rather; *synonyms* (*adv*) quite, enough, fairly, pretty, moderately, considerably, instead, kinda, preferably, relatively, somewhat, comparatively, reasonably, sooner; *antonym* (*adv*) extremely.

tewâk broken; *synonyms* (*v*) broke, (*adj*) tame, torn, busted, imperfect, intermittent, rough, rugged, ruined, uneven, disjointed, incomplete, confused, cracked, crushed; *antonyms* (*adj*) constant, unbroken, intact, whole, wild.

tewe 1. project; *synonyms* (*n*) design, device, scheme, idea, enterprise, (*v*) plan, hurl, contrive, jut, overhang, protrude, shoot, bulge, cast, devise, **2.** thrown; *synonyms* (*adj*) confused, puzzled, addled, baffled, bewildered, confounded, disconcerted, distraught, dumbfounded, fearful, frightened, mystified, terrified, unnerved, (*n*) reminder, **3.** throw; *synonyms* (*v*) fling, shed, chuck, flip, heave, pass, deliver, drop, give, hurtle, jerk, make, (*n*) pitch, push, shot.

tewea 1. fling; *synonyms* (*n*) throw, crack, hurl, go, heave, (*v*) cast, toss, chuck, dash, pitch, shoot, discard, rush, slam, break; *antonym* (*v*) catch, **2.** project; *synonyms* (*n*) design, device, scheme, idea, enterprise, venture, (*v*) plan, contrive, jut, overhang, protrude, bulge, devise, extend, forecast, **3.** throw; *synonyms* (*v*) fling, shed, flip, pass, deliver, drop, give, hurtle, jerk, make, project, bewilder, (*n*) push, shot, shy.

teweaki 1. thrown; *synonyms* (*adj*) confused, puzzled, addled, baffled, bewildered, confounded, disconcerted, distraught, dumbfounded, fearful, frightened, mystified, terrified, unnerved, (*n*) reminder, **2.** projected; *synonyms* (*adj*) projecting, jutting, proposed, planned, anticipated, deliberate, expected, future, likely, predictable, probable, protruding, sticking, estimated.

tewearaki windward; *synonyms* (*adj*) airy, boisterous, empty, flatulent, tempestuous, windy, (*adv*) downwind, (*n*) upwind, luff; *antonym* (*n*) leeward.

ti 1. but; *synonyms* (*conj*) while, (*adv*) alone, only, though, barely, however, merely, simply, yet,

exclusively, if, just, (*prep*) besides, except, excluding, **2.** gush; *synonyms* (*n*) flow, spout, burst, jet, effusion, rush, stream, surge, (*v*) flood, spurt, discharge, course, emanate, cascade, emit; *antonym* (*v*) trickle, **3.** mere; *synonyms* (*adj*) bare, entire, pure, simple, clear, naked, (*n*) lake, loch, downright, tarn, absolute, boundary, pond, stark, (*v*) sheer, **4.** j; *synonyms* (*n*) joule, psi, **5.** f; *synonyms* (*n*) farad, fluorine, (*v*) d, e, (*adj*) fine, good, okay, **6.** just; *synonyms* (*adv*) exactly, hardly, newly, (*adj*) fair, right, correct, equitable, accurate, honest, impartial, fit, reasonable, righteous, upright, appropriate; *antonyms* (*adj*) unfair, biased, wrong, **7.** jet; *synonyms* (*n*) squirt, fountain, spray, airplane, current, outpouring, nozzle, spirt, plane, (*v*) gush, fly, pour, erupt, (*adj*) raven, black, **8.** merely; *synonyms* (*adv*) but, purely, absolutely, solely, **9.** spout; *synonyms* (*n*) pipe, outlet, nose, opening, conduit, trough, lip, tap, well, aorta, (*v*) pawn, roll, vent, dribble, eject, **10.** s; *synonyms* (*n*) mho, arcsecond, bit, confederacy, dalliance, endorsement, indorsement, instant, irregular, minute, moment, sec, second, siemens, south, **11.** spurt; *synonyms* (*n*) run, dash, effort, exertion, flash, spell, strain, (*v*) race, spill, sputter, dart, spatter, issue, shoot, spew, **12.** squirt; *synonyms* (*n*) child, nobody, (*v*) splash, **13.** only; *synonyms* (*adv*) entirely, nevertheless, singly, (*adj*) exclusive, individual, lone, one, sole, all, solitary, matchless, single, singular, solo, unequaled, **14.** sheer; *synonyms* (*adj*) mere, bold, diaphanous, filmy, gauzy, gossamer, steep, transparent, regular, perpendicular, flimsy, rank, blatant, (*n*) complete, perfect; *antonyms* (*adj*) gentle, thick.

tia 1. finished; *synonyms* (*v*) done, (*adj*) complete, completed, ended, perfect, consummate, absolute, accomplished, polished, ripe, ruined, spent, round, capable, (*adv*) over; *antonyms* (*adj*) unfinished, incomplete, remaining, rough, **2.** done; *synonyms* (*adj*) finished, gone, through, **3.** accomplished; *synonyms* (*adj*) able, proficient, adept, experienced, gifted, skillful, fine, clever, competent, concluded, cultured, effected, efficient, excellent, expert; *antonym* (*adj*) inept, **4.** complete; *synonyms* (*adj*) whole, full, stark, all, (*v*) accomplish, achieve, close, finish, execute, act, attain, cease, clear, conclude, effect; *antonyms* (*adj*) partial, abridged, shortened, sketchy, lacking, narrow, qualified, (*v*) neglect, **5.** terminated; *synonym* (*adj*) extinct.

tiaaina sign; *synonyms* (*n*) signal, indication, mark, motion, portent, brand, emblem, imprint, manifestation, omen, poster, presage, wave, (*v*) gesture, indicate.

tiaainaki signed; *synonyms* (*adj*) gestural, sign, employed, engaged, nonverbal.

tiaka fool; *synonyms* (*n*) blockhead, dunce, clown, ass, buffoon, dolt, (*v*) dupe, deceive, bamboozle, befool, cheat, con, defraud, delude, gull.

tiakai 1. magician; *synonyms* (*n*) conjurer, enchanter, sorcerer, conjuror, illusionist, wizard, thaumaturge, performer, necromancer, prestidigitator, **2.** acrobat; *synonyms* (*n*) tumbler, clown, charlatan, harlequin, mountebank, punch, scaramouch, buffoon, farceur, funambulist, mime, ropedancer, dancer, (*adj*) athlete, gymnast, **3.** conjurer; *synonyms* (*n*) magician, juggler, **4.** prestidigitator; *synonyms* (*n*) legerdemainist, prestigiator, trickster, jockey, seer, visionary, **5.** sorcerer, **6.** wizard; *synonyms* (*n*) expert, genius, ace, whiz, warlock, prodigy, hotshot, star, virtuoso, whizz, wiz, (*adj*) adept.

tiaki 1. no; *synonyms* (*n*) refusal, rejection, denial, number, nix, rebuff, nobelium, ordinal, (*adv*) nay, (*adj*) zero, naught, none, non, nul, **2.** not; *synonyms* (*adv*) no, nor, nowise, never, (*adj*) shaven, shorn.

tianakiana 1. have; *synonyms* (*v*) contain, gain, bear, carry, get, hold, possess, accept, acquire, eat, suffer, take, allow, bring, conduct, **2.** take; *synonyms* (*v*) admit, adopt, catch, clutch, obtain, return, borrow, pick, appropriate, assume, capture, claim, convey, (*n*) seize, (*phr*) receive; *antonyms* (*v*) give, refuse, abstain, add, lose.

tianakianaki taken; *synonyms* (*v*) take, (*adj*) occupied, full, interpreted, besotted, crazed, enamored, engaged, interested, lovesick, obsessed, overcome, preferred, rapt, reserved.

tianna limiting; *synonyms* (*adj*) restrictive, confining, constrictive, restricting, constraining, definitive, limited, definite, determinative, binding, restraining, terminal, (*n*) modification, adjustment, alteration; *antonym* (*adj*) encouraging.

tiatianna limited; *synonyms* (*adj*) finite, circumscribed, moderate, qualified, special, insular, bounded, narrow, scanty, slender, particular, specific, definite, conditional, constricted; *antonyms* (*adj*) boundless, infinite, limitless, open, complete, never-ending, unlimited, wide.

tiatip coral; *synonyms* (*adj*) rosy, (*n*) orange, red, roe.

tiba 1. just; *synonyms* (*adv*) exactly, hardly, newly, (*adj*) fair, right, correct, equitable, accurate, honest, impartial, barely, fit, good, reasonable, righteous; *antonyms* (*adj*) unfair, biased, wrong, **2.** lately; *synonyms* (*adv*) recently, late, freshly, latterly, just, new, (*adj*) anew, afresh, **3.** misstep; *synonyms* (*n*) trip, blunder, mistake, slip, error, stumble, failure, **4.** ration; *synonyms* (*n*) portion, allowance, helping, part, share, serving, measure, percentage, quota, lot, (*v*) allocate, apportion, feed, provision, limit, **5.** slip; *synonyms* (*n*) lapse, fault, cutting, escape, oversight, scion, ticket, band, dip, (*v*) fall, slide, drop, glide, skid, sag; *antonym* (*v*) improve,

6. recently; *synonyms* (*adv*) lately, fresh, (*n*) yesterday, **7.** share; *synonyms* (*n*) piece, deal, dole, allotment, division, interest, proportion, (*v*) participate, allot, distribute, partake, dispense, divide, partition, assign; *antonym* (*v*) control, **8.** rearrange; *synonyms* (*v*) reform, shift, alter, change, reorder, reorganize, restructure, edit, reverse, switch, transpose.

tibaki 1. rationed, **2.** shared; *synonyms* (*adj*) communal, common, divided, joint, mutual, collective, community, cooperative, reciprocal; *antonyms* (*adj*) individual, private.

tibara miss; *synonyms* (*v*) lack, lose, fail, jump, omit, overlook, long, drop, escape, (*n*) maid, girl, want, fille, missy, (*adj*) fault; *antonym* (*v*) perceive.

tibaraki missed; *synonyms* (*adj*) lost, baffled, befuddled, bemused, bewildered, confounded, confused, disoriented, forgotten, helpless, irretrievable, mazed, preoccupied.

tibatiba 1. ration; *synonyms* (*n*) portion, allowance, helping, part, share, serving, measure, percentage, quota, lot, (*v*) allocate, apportion, feed, provision, limit, **2.** share; *synonyms* (*n*) piece, deal, dole, allotment, division, interest, proportion, (*v*) participate, allot, distribute, partake, dispense, divide, partition, assign; *antonym* (*v*) control.

tibatibaki 1. shared; *synonyms* (*adj*) communal, common, divided, joint, mutual, collective, community, cooperative, reciprocal; *antonyms* (*adj*) individual, private, **2.** rationed.

tibe unravel; *synonyms* (*v*) unfold, disentangle, solve, undo, decipher, explain, resolve, extricate, ravel, uncoil, unpick, untangle, unwind, unknot, unbind; *antonym* (*v*) fasten.

tibia spherical; *synonyms* (*adj*) round, circular, global, globose, globular, orbicular, rotund, rounded, spheric, orbiculate.

tibitibi lame; *synonyms* (*adj*) crippled, game, disabled, feeble, halt, halting, weak, becripple, paralytic, inadequate, infirm, (*v*) cripple, maim, paralyze, disable.

tiboña priest; *synonyms* (*n*) clergyman, minister, ecclesiastic, churchman, cleric, parson, pastor, presbyter, chaplain, monk, (*adj*) divine.

tibu 1. puffed; *synonyms* (*adj*) bloated, distended, puff, swollen, puffy, tumid, turgid, bepuffed, bombastic, bouffant, conceited, declamatory, egotistic, egotistical, erect, **2.** swelled; *synonyms* (*adj*) big, inflated, adult, bad, bighearted, boastful, bounteous, bountiful, braggy, crowing, elder, emphysematous, enceinte, expectant, freehanded, **3.** swell; *synonyms* (*n*) wave, (*v*) surge, enlarge, expand, heave, increase, rise, bloat, grow, billow, augment, balloon, bulge, (*adj*) dandy, swagger; *antonyms* (*v*) decrease, deflate, desiccate, **4.** puff; *synonyms* (*n*) gasp, whiff, drag, breath, (*v*) pant, blow, boast, gust, brag, huff, inflate, breathe, distend, plug, draw.

tibuaki puffed; *synonyms* (*adj*) bloated, distended, puff, swollen, puffy, tumid, turgid, bepuffed, bombastic, bouffant, conceited, declamatory, egotistic, egotistical, erect.

tibuatau convex; *synonyms* (*adj*) bulging, gibbous, biconvex, hunched, bulgy, bellied, bellying, bent, bulbous, curved, deformed, outbowed, (*n*) crescent, (*v*) projecting, curve; *antonym* (*adj*) concave.

tibuna adopt; *synonyms* (*v*) accept, admit, affiliate, assume, borrow, espouse, pass, take, acquire, choose, embrace, follow, imitate, naturalize, prefer; *antonym* (*v*) reject.

tibunaki adopted; *synonyms* (*adj*) adoptive, elected, consecrated, converted, inspired, justified, regenerated, sanctified, unearthly, adoptious, foreign, popular, preferred.

tiburake swelling; *synonyms* (*n*) growth, intumescence, lump, protuberance, swell, bulge, projection, prominence, dropsy, bump, expansion, increase, knob, (*v*) inflated, (*adj*) growing.

tiburere swollen; *synonyms* (*adj*) bloated, inflated, bombastic, puffed, puffy, turgid, egotistic, high, bulging, tumescent, tumid, conceited, (*v*) distended, blown, (*prep*) pompous.

tibutau 1. turgid; *synonyms* (*adj*) bombastic, swollen, inflated, puffy, tumid, declamatory, large, orotund, tumescent, distended, (*prep*) pompous, (*v*) bloated, dropsical, exaggerated, fat, 2. swollen; *synonyms* (*adj*) puffed, turgid, egotistic, high, bulging, conceited, egotistical, enlarged, expanded, flooding, mighty, overflowing, (*v*) blown, 3. tumid; *synonyms* (*adj*) swelling, rhetorical, erect, (*v*) overgrown.

tibutaua 1. full; *synonyms* (*adj*) complete, absolute, abundant, broad, flush, ample, enough, extensive, total, detailed, comprehensive, copious, good, (*n*) entire, crowded; *antonyms* (*adj*) empty, lacking, starving, hungry, sketchy, incomplete, 2. booked; *synonyms* (*adj*) reserved, affianced, bespoken, betrothed, destined, engaged, future, intermeshed, meshed, occupied, pledged, 3. stuffed; *synonyms* (*v*) farctate, (*adj*) full, crammed, packed, congested, replete, loaded, chock-full, fraught, abounding, big, brimming, concentrated, distended, overcrowded.

tibwa 1. just; *synonyms* (*adv*) exactly, hardly, newly, (*adj*) fair, right, correct, equitable, accurate, honest, impartial, barely, fit, good, reasonable, righteous; *antonyms* (*adj*) unfair, biased, wrong, 2. try; *synonyms* (*v*) attempt, test, struggle, prove, strive, assay, examine, experiment, judge, sample, (*n*) endeavor, essay, chance, effort, shot, 3. share; *synonyms* (*n*) piece, portion, deal, dole, lot, allotment, (*v*) participate, allot, apportion, distribute, part, partake, dispense, divide, partition; *antonym* (*v*) control.

tibwaki 1. tried; *synonyms* (*adj*) reliable, tested, trustworthy, dependable, proved, experienced, baffled, beaten, believable, conquered, exhausted, faithful, just, practiced, qualified, 2. shared; *synonyms* (*adj*) communal, common, divided, joint, mutual, collective, community, cooperative, reciprocal; *antonyms* (*adj*) individual, private.

tie 1. balance; *synonyms* (*n*) poise, symmetry, excess, remainder, account, complement, counterpoise, credit, (*v*) counterbalance, adjust, offset, compensate, contrast, settle, audit; *antonyms* (*n*) imbalance, (*v*) unbalance, 2. swing; *synonyms* (*n*) sweep, range, (*v*) sway, fluctuate, oscillate, dangle, hang, rock, beat, brandish, change, move, shake, turn, vibrate, 3. oscillate; *synonyms* (*v*) swing, hesitate, wag, alternate, quiver, tremble, vacillate, vary, wave, waver, wobble.

tieaki balanced; *synonyms* (*adj*) equal, even, firm, regular, stable, steady, harmonious, impartial, steadfast, symmetrical, uniform, fast, fixed, secure, unprejudiced; *antonyms* (*adj*) biased, unbalanced, unfair.

tiebba suspend; *synonyms* (*v*) defer, delay, adjourn, hang, interrupt, postpone, stop, dangle, shelve, stay, break, debar, halt, swing, freeze; *antonym* (*v*) continue.

tiebbaki suspended; *synonyms* (*adj*) hanging, pendent, dormant, pendulous, abeyant, dangling, inactive, pendant.

tiemanea 1. net; *synonyms* (*adj*) final, last, (*n*) network, bag, lace, earnings, cobweb, (*v*) mesh, clear, gain, make, trap, catch, earn, knit; *antonym* (*v*) gross, 2. catch; *synonyms* (*v*) arrest, capture, hook, apprehend, get, acquire, ensnare, intercept, (*n*) haul, hitch, trick, bolt, clasp, grab, pawl; *antonym* (*v*) release.

tiemaneaki netted; *synonyms* (*adj*) netlike, reticulated, lacy, meshy, lacelike, webbed, webby, weblike.

tiera 1. envelop; *synonyms* (*v*) cover, enfold, fold, encase, enclose, wrap, encircle, conceal, embrace, cloak, drape, hide, muffle, shroud, (*n*) envelope, 2. balance; *synonyms* (*n*) poise, symmetry, excess, remainder, account, complement, counterpoise, credit, (*v*) counterbalance, adjust, offset, compensate, contrast, settle, audit; *antonyms* (*n*) imbalance, (*v*) unbalance, 3. surround; *synonyms* (*v*) circle, gird, border, compass, inclose, ring, round, skirt, beset, besiege, circumvent, envelop, environ, circumscribe, entwine, 4. wrap; *synonyms* (*v*) roll, swathe, wind, bind, enwrap, involve, surround, twine, cocoon, bundle, twist, veil, (*n*) coat, wrapping, cape; *antonyms* (*v*) unwrap, uncover, 5. scoop; *synonyms* (*n*) ladle, spade, exclusive, pocket, scoopful, shovel, article, report, (*v*) draw, dig, excavate, hollow, best, outdo, outflank, **6.** over; *synonyms* *(adv)* beyond, across, more, by, o'er, on, too, *(prep)* above, during, *(n)* overs, *(adj)* finished, done, extra, odd, past.

tieraki 1. enveloped; *synonyms* *(adj)* engulfed, convoluted, bounded, clothed, involved, misty, swallowed, vestured, flooded, intricate, inundated, knotty, labyrinthine, mired, overcome, **2.** balanced; *synonyms* *(adj)* equal, even, firm, regular, stable, steady, harmonious, impartial, steadfast, symmetrical, uniform, fast, fixed, secure, unprejudiced; *antonyms* *(adj)* biased, unbalanced, unfair, **3.** wrapped; *synonyms* *(adj)* draped, enwrapped, absorbed, cloaked, intent, rapt, engrossed, mantled, *(prep)* covered, **4.** surrounded; *synonyms* *(v)* beset, begone, furnished, *(adj)* encircled, circumstanced, conditioned, entrenched, ingirt, inside, ringed, rooted, bordered, delimited, implanted, wreathed.

tietie oscillate; *synonyms* *(v)* fluctuate, swing, vibrate, hesitate, wag, alternate, quiver, shake, sway, tremble, vacillate, vary, wave, waver, wobble.

tiitebo 1. like; *synonyms* *(v)* corresponding, enjoy, identical, care, desire, fancy, *(adj)* equal, equivalent, alike, analogous, comparable, same, parallel, *(n)* love, relish; *antonyms* *(prep)* unlike, *(v)* dislike, *(adj)* different, **2.** as; *synonyms* *(conj)* qua, because, since, considering, while, whilst, *(prep)* during, like, *(adv)* equally, from, *(n)* arsenic, **3.** alike; *synonyms* *(adv)* likewise, *(adj)* cognate, duplicate, even, likely, similar; *antonyms* *(adv)* differently, *(adj)* dissimilar, **4.** similar; *synonyms* *(adj)* related, akin, correspondent, conformable, resembling, kindred, such, twin, uniform, exchangeable, interchangeable, matching, synonymous; *antonyms* *(adj)* incompatible, opposing, opposite, **5.** same; *synonyms* *(adj)* consistent, monotonous, self, very, indistinguishable.

tika 1. admirable; *synonyms* *(adj)* beautiful, excellent, fine, outstanding, commendable, creditable, good, grand, great, lovely, praiseworthy, worthy, valuable, exquisite, handsome; *antonyms* *(adj)* disgraceful, appalling, poor, unworthy, **2.** beautiful; *synonyms* *(adj)* attractive, good-looking, bright, beauteous, picturesque, pleasant, pretty, striking, sweet, adorned, ornate, dainty, stylish, bonny, charming; *antonyms* *(adj)* ugly, unattractive, **3.** gracious; *synonyms* *(adj)* amiable, benign, genial, courteous, compassionate, benevolent, kind, accommodating, congenial, affable, benignant, civil, cordial, friendly, *(n)* gentle; *antonyms* *(adj)* boorish, ungracious, **4.** magnificent; *synonyms* *(adj)* imposing, brilliant, splendid, gorgeous, illustrious, grandiose, elegant, glorious, superb, divine, fabulous, luxurious, majestic, rich, royal, **5.** marvelous; *synonyms* *(adj)* fantastic, wonderful, astonishing, extraordinary, incredible, prodigious, terrific, tremendous, amazing, cool, magnificent,

marvellous, miraculous, phenomenal, strange; *antonym* *(adj)* awful, **6.** pretty; *synonyms* *(adv)* very, fairly, jolly, quite, rather, somewhat, moderately, *(adj)* fair, graceful, cute, neat, pleasing, smart, comely, *(n)* nice.

tikaraoi good; *synonyms* *(adj)* able, benefit, delicious, right, efficient, capable, excellent, fine, nice, superior, well, advantageous, *(n)* benign, advantage, gain; *antonyms* *(adj)* disobedient, poor, wicked, unpleasant, *(n)* evil, bad.

tikaua 1. marvelous; *synonyms* *(adj)* fantastic, wonderful, astonishing, extraordinary, fabulous, grand, great, incredible, prodigious, terrific, tremendous, glorious, amazing, brilliant, cool; *antonym* *(adj)* awful, **2.** magnificent; *synonyms* *(adj)* fine, imposing, excellent, splendid, gorgeous, illustrious, grandiose, elegant, superb, beautiful, divine, exquisite, luxurious, majestic, rich, **3.** beautiful; *synonyms* *(adj)* attractive, good-looking, bright, beauteous, handsome, lovely, picturesque, pleasant, pretty, striking, sweet, adorned, ornate, dainty, stylish; *antonyms* *(adj)* ugly, unattractive, **4.** admirable; *synonyms* *(adj)* outstanding, commendable, creditable, good, praiseworthy, worthy, valuable, laudable, meritorious, noble, respectable, superior, estimable; *antonyms* *(adj)* disgraceful, appalling, poor, unworthy.

tikeke 1. glide; *synonyms* *(n)* slip, gliding, sailing, *(v)* slide, coast, float, flow, fly, run, drift, lapse, move, skid, slink, slither; *antonym* *(v)* struggle, **2.** slide; *synonyms* *(n)* glide, chute, decline, transparency, recession, slider, *(v)* drop, fall, slump, descend, sag, cut, tumble, sneak, *(adj)* shift, **3.** slip; *synonyms* *(n)* fault, mistake, cutting, error, escape, oversight, scion, trip, ticket, band, dip, gaffe, strip, *(adj)* blunder, omission; *antonym* *(v)* improve.

tikera 1. slide; *synonyms* *(n)* glide, chute, decline, transparency, gliding, *(v)* drop, slip, fall, slither, run, slump, coast, skid, descend, *(adj)* shift, **2.** skate; *synonyms* *(v)* skim, slide, jade, plug, rackabones.

tiketi ticket; *synonyms* *(n)* pass, card, label, certificate, ballot, check, slate, tag, warrant, mark, slip, voucher, plank, platform, *(v)* fine.

tikeuea square; *synonyms* *(adj)* right, even, rectangular, fair, quadrate, straight, equal, *(n)* area, foursquare, rectangle, quadrilateral, *(v)* settle, agree, correspond, *(adv)* just.

tiki 1. hurt; *synonyms* *(v)* pain, wound, afflict, injure, ail, cost, *(adj)* evil, *(n)* harm, damage, detriment, ache, disadvantage, abuse, distress, lesion; *antonyms* *(v)* encourage, *(adj)* uninjured, unhurt, **2.** gristly; *synonyms* *(adj)* cartilaginous, stringy, rubbery, tough, chewy, fibrous, hard, leathery, sinewy, stiff, rubberlike; *antonym* *(adj)* tender, **3.** stretched; *synonyms* *(adj)* taut, extended, tense, tight, strained, expanded, outstretched, elongated, outspread, prolonged, protracted, assiduous, close, delayed, extensive; *antonym* (*adj*) brief, **4**. twitch; *synonyms* (*n*) twinge, pull, tweak, start, (*v*) jerk, yank, pluck, tug, wrench, draw, nip, pinch, flinch, jolt, snatch, **5**. taut; *synonyms* (*adj*) firm, drawn, rigid, stringent, inflexible, taught, (*v*) fast; *antonyms* (*adj*) loose, limp, **6**. tight; *synonyms* (*adj*) compact, mean, parsimonious, secure, snug, drunk, miserly, rigorous, sparing, strict, impervious, (*adv*) closely, (*v*) narrow, stingy, near; *antonyms* (*adj*) baggy, generous, slack, wide, (*adv*) loosely, **7**. pierced; *synonyms* (*adj*) perforated, punctured, perforate, cleft, entered.

tikibuaka loose; *synonyms* (*adj*) lax, liberal, dissolute, licentious, light, vague, detached, immoral, (*v*) disengage, liberate, relax, release, detach, (*n*) free, limp; *antonyms* (*adj*) tight, close, compressed, dense, taut, strict, compact, wedged.

tikimaurekati undecided; *synonyms* (*adj*) unsettled, doubtful, dubious, indecisive, irresolute, pending, uncertain, unresolved, hesitant, undetermined, debatable, indefinite, indeterminate, ambivalent, borderline; *antonyms* (*adj*) decided, certain, determined.

tikinene stretched; *synonyms* (*adj*) taut, extended, stiff, tense, tight, strained, expanded, outstretched, elongated, outspread, prolonged, protracted, assiduous, close, delayed; *antonym* (*adj*) brief.

tikinono 1. hard; *synonyms* (*adj*) austere, bad, difficult, grave, severe, strong, arduous, callous, cruel, grueling, knotty, tough, (*adv*) firm, (*v*) acute, (*n*) rough; *antonyms* (*adj*) easy, soft, kind, merciful, simple, soggy, tender, yielding, (*adv*) gently, lightly, **2**. stretched; *synonyms* (*adj*) taut, extended, stiff, tense, tight, strained, expanded, outstretched, elongated, outspread, prolonged, protracted, assiduous, close, delayed; *antonym* (*adj*) brief, **3**. stiff; *synonyms* (*adj*) rigid, hard, formal, inflexible, numb, rigorous, solid, sturdy, awkward, buckram, ceremonious, (*n*) stark, cadaver, corpse, body; *antonyms* (*adj*) relaxed, flexible, floppy, supple, free, pliable, **4**. tight; *synonyms* (*adj*) compact, mean, parsimonious, secure, snug, drunk, miserly, sparing, strict, stringent, impervious, (*v*) narrow, fast, stingy, near; *antonyms* (*adj*) loose, baggy, generous, slack, wide, (*adv*) loosely, **5**. taut; *synonyms* (*adj*) drawn, taught; *antonym* (*adj*) limp, **6**. tough; *synonyms* (*adj*) tenacious, hardy, laborious, rugged, stout, durable, leathery, robust, stubborn, heavy, enduring, (*n*) bully, rowdy, hoodlum, hooligan; *antonyms* (*adj*) weak, flimsy, feeble, lightweight.

tikintaka 1. taut; *synonyms* (*adj*) close, firm, tight, drawn, rigid, stiff, tense, strained, stringent, inflexible, taught, (*v*) fast; *antonyms* (*adj*) loose,

limp, **2**. stiff; *synonyms* (*adj*) hard, difficult, formal, numb, rigorous, severe, solid, sturdy, arduous, austere, awkward, (*n*) stark, cadaver, corpse, body; *antonyms* (*adj*) relaxed, flexible, floppy, soft, supple, free, pliable.

tikiraoi 1. beautiful; *synonyms* (*adj*) attractive, good-looking, bright, beauteous, fine, handsome, lovely, picturesque, pleasant, pretty, striking, sweet, adorned, ornate, dainty; *antonyms* (*adj*) ugly, unattractive, **2**. nice; *synonyms* (*adj*) beautiful, fastidious, good, kind, neat, likable, delicious, agreeable, correct, decent, delicate, difficult, enjoyable, exact, particular; *antonyms* (*adj*) unpleasant, horrible, **3**. trim; *synonyms* (*adj*) tidy, spruce, orderly, shipshape, (*v*) cut, dress, clip, garnish, shave, adorn, embellish, lop, prune, reduce, shorten; *antonym* (*adj*) fat.

tikitiki 1. gristly; *synonyms* (*adj*) cartilaginous, stringy, rubbery, tough, chewy, fibrous, hard, leathery, sinewy, stiff, rubberlike; *antonym* (*adj*) tender, **2**. stiffen; *synonyms* (*v*) harden, set, indurate, ossify, tighten, brace, congeal, reinforce, fortify, intensify, jell, strengthen, temper, thicken, constrain.

tiko 1. little; *synonyms* (*adj*) small, diminutive, insignificant, brief, minute, petty, short, some, tiny, exiguous, light, baby, bantam, (*v*) dash, bit; *antonyms* (*adj*) big, enormous, large, important, **2**. fine; *synonyms* (*adj*) delicate, agreeable, dainty, brave, capital, elegant, excellent, nice, thin, delightful, acute, admirable, alright, (*n*) penalty, (*v*) punish; *antonyms* (*adj*) poor, thick, coarse, substantial, unsatisfactory, wide, **3**. graceful; *synonyms* (*adj*) beautiful, amiable, easy, fine, charming, fair, airy, becoming, comely, handsome, lithe, lovely, refined, supple, svelte; *antonyms* (*adj*) clumsy, inelegant, stocky, **4**. dainty; *synonyms* (*adj*) fastidious, savory, tidbit, delectable, delicious, exquisite, finicky, graceful, mincing, particular, squeamish, tasty, (*n*) delicacy, luxury, (*v*) sweet, **5**. pretty; *synonyms* (*adv*) very, fairly, jolly, quite, rather, somewhat, moderately, (*adj*) attractive, good-looking, picturesque, cute, neat, pleasing, smart, bonny; *antonym* (*adj*) ugly, **6**. small; *synonyms* (*adj*) little, narrow, inadequate, low, minor, slight, remote, cramped, young, limited, faint, humble, miniature, minuscule, modest; *antonyms* (*adj*) bulky, colossal, considerable, extra-large, great, huge, sizeable, giant, major, **7**. slim; *synonyms* (*adj*) slender, lean, skinny, flimsy, meager, feeble, frail, spare, taper, tenuous, trim, (*v*) reduce, slenderize, cut, sly; *antonyms* (*adj*) fat, heavy, hefty, plump, **8**. slender; *synonyms* (*adj*) gaunt, lissom, scanty, slim, lissome, mean, inconsiderable, lanky, lithesome, (*v*) lank, scant.

tikona 1. measure; *synonyms* (*n*) amount, criterion, extent, beat, benchmark, degree, estimate, measurement, meter, quantity, act, allotment, action, (v) grade, appraise, **2**. ration; *synonyms* (n) portion, allowance, helping, part, share, serving, measure, percentage, quota, lot, (v) allocate, apportion, feed, provision, limit, **3**. restrict; *synonyms* (v) restrain, circumscribe, confine, constrain, fetter, bound, curb, curtail, forbid, hamper, reduce, ration, bind, check, contain.

tikonaki 1. measured; *synonyms* (adj) careful, deliberate, moderate, calculated, reasonable, temperate, regular, leisurely, metrical, sober, cool, slow, **2**. rationed, **3**. restricted; *synonyms* (v) qualified, (adj) limited, confined, cramped, narrow, constrained, exclusive, local, controlled, finite, prohibited, classified, secret, bounded, circumscribed; *antonyms* (adj) unrestricted, far-reaching, free, liberated, unimpeded, unlimited, open, wide.

tiku 1. bide; *synonyms* (v) abide, endure, tarry, bear, dwell, last, remain, (adj) stay, wait, stand, suffer, tolerate, **2**. last; *synonyms* (v) continue, hold, exist, live, (n) conclusion, finale, finis, finish, (adj) extreme, closing, final, ultimate, conclusive, concluding, farthest; *antonyms* (n) opening, (adj) first, **3**. homestead; *synonyms* (n) abode, home, farmhouse, farmstead, homestall, house, farmery, habitat, (v) farm, **4**. dwell; *synonyms* (v) inhabit, reside, bide, lodge, be, belong, brood, delay, occupy, settle, consist, domicile, domiciliate, keep, (adj) roost, **5**. pause; *synonyms* (v) break, intermission, interruption, rest, gap, interval, respite, stop, breather, (v) halt, adjournment, hesitate, desist, cease, (adj) discontinue; *antonym* (n) decisiveness, **6**. stop; *synonyms* (v) block, close, interrupt, obstruct, plug, catch, disrupt, hinder, impede, intercept, (n) check, end, arrest, bar, curb; *antonyms* (v) start, begin, encourage, permit, prolong, **7**. remain; *synonyms* (v) linger, persist, persevere, stick, attend, lie, detain, hang, retain, subsist, survive, prevail; *antonym* (v) leave, **8**. sojourn; *synonyms* (n) residence, dwelling, habitation, (v) visit, **9**. perch; *synonyms* (n) rod, covert, (v) light, alight, land, sit, squat, balance, (adj) nestle, **10**. settle; *synonyms* (v) fix, place, clarify, establish, pay, regulate, resolve, set, adjudicate, adjust, agree, conclude, decide, determine, (adj) confirm, **11**. stay; *synonyms* (v) prop, pause, support, sojourn, await, suspend, adjourn, help, defer, (n) postponement, reprieve, cessation, quell, deferment, column; *antonyms* (v) change, abscond, depart.

tikua 1. lower; *synonyms* (adj) debase, inferior, (v) degrade, diminish, frown, humble, dip, abase, cut, descend, drop, scowl, disgrace, decrease, (n) depress; *antonyms* (v) increase, raise, **2**. leave; *synonyms* (v) depart, forsake, go, abandon, desert, quit, escape, flee, lead, (n) furlough, holiday,

permission, permit, break, (adj) empty; *antonyms* (v) arrive, enter, stay, remain, approach, change, come.

tikuaki 1. lowered; *synonyms* (adj) abased, bated, cheap, humbled, restrained, **2**. placed; *synonyms* (adj) located, situated, laid, set, positioned, fixed, collocate, determined, dictated, hardened, residing, rigid, **3**. settled; *synonyms* (adj) definite, firm, permanent, calm, certain, decided, established, defined, formed, confirmed, finished, sedate, standing, quiet, done; *antonym* (adj) uninhabited, **4**. stopped; *synonyms* (adj) halted, congested, unmoving, blocked, chinked, clogged, immobile, motionless, static, stationary, crashed, still.

tikubara invade; *synonyms* (v) encroach, assail, assault, infringe, intrude, occupy, overrun, impinge, raid, infest, seize, penetrate, permeate, (n) attack, charge.

tikumaurekaki stagnate; *synonyms* (v) idle, laze, drag, restagnate, slog, (n) be, halt, abide, pause, stand, accord, agree, consist, endure, last.

tikumenga flop; *synonyms* (n) bomb, collapse, dud, failure, disaster, bust, fiasco, nonstarter, (v) crash, fail, flounder, drop, dangle, droop, fall; *antonyms* (n) success, winner.

tikumoro stunted; *synonyms* (adj) small, scrubby, little, scrawny, diminutive, puny, short, spare, (v) strangulated.

tikura perch; *synonyms* (v) roost, light, abide, lodge, alight, land, rest, settle, sit, squat, stay, inhabit, lie, (adj) dwell, live.

tikurabirabi 1. crumpled; *synonyms* (adj) creased, rumpled, crinkly, wrinkled, bent, corrugated, bended, bowed, corrugate, dented, furrowed, lined, craggy, dishevelled, frowzled; *antonym* (adj) smooth, **2**. hang; *synonyms* (v) dangle, depend, drape, float, append, cling, decorate, execute, fall, flow, hover, swing, (n) suspend, delay, knack, **3**. wrinkled; *synonyms* (adj) crumpled, puckered, wizened, wrinkly, gnarled, unironed, (n) rough, rugged.

tikurerea 1. desire; *synonyms* (n) ambition, hope, aspiration, will, wish, craving, dream, impulse, (v) fancy, aspire, seek, want, aim, choose, crave; *antonyms* (n) aversion, reality, (v) dislike, hate, **2**. love; *synonyms* (n) desire, affection, dear, fondness, liking, benevolence, charity, attachment, beloved, darling, devotion, honey, (v) cherish, enjoy, like; *antonyms* (n) abhorrence, hatred, (v) abhor.

tikurereaki 1. desired; *synonyms* (adj) coveted, craved, desirable, chosen, favorite, wanted, needed, welcome, beloved, adored, appropriate, pet, preferred, (v) complying, consenting; *antonym* (adj) undesirable, **2**. loved; *synonyms* (adj) dear, cherished, precious, appreciated, esteemed, prized, respected, treasured, valued, important, (n) darling.

tikuroaroa overstay; *synonym* (*v*) outstay.

tikuruna screw; *synonyms* (*n*) fuck, propeller, fucking, gaoler, jailer, (*v*) cheat, fasten, wind, pin, bonk, jockey, turn, (*adj*) bolt, nail, stint.

tima 1. favored; *synonyms* (*adj*) fortunate, advantaged, preferred, lucky, advantageous, blessed, favorite, pet, privileged, **2.** ideal; *synonyms* (*adj*) fanciful, perfect, consummate, abstract, classic, imaginary, typical, (*n*) model, paragon, example, apotheosis, archetype, epitome, perfection, prototype.

timamwi roasted; *synonyms* (*adj*) roast, baked.

timina roast; *synonyms* (*n*) ridicule, joint, knock, (*v*) broil, burn, bake, grill, joke, heat, quiz, cook, fry, scorch, tease, banter.

timinaki roasted; *synonyms* (*adj*) roast, baked.

timinene 1. appetizing; *synonyms* (*adj*) appetising, delectable, delicious, luscious, tasty, tantalizing, palatable, savory, scrumptious, spicy; *antonyms* (*adj*) tasteless, unappetizing, **2.** enticing; *synonyms* (*adj*) alluring, tempting, attractive, beguiling, inviting, seductive, engaging, fetching, appealing, captivating, charming, enthralling, fascinating, **3.** greasy; *synonyms* (*adj*) fat, fatty, dirty, oily, tallowy, oleaginous, sebaceous, slick, slippery, unctuous; *antonym* (*adj*) dry, **4.** fatty; *synonyms* (*adj*) adipose, greasy, rich, heavy, (*n*) fatso.

timít pumice; *synonyms* (*v*) scour, buff.

timoi 1. knotty; *synonyms* (*adj*) knotted, complex, difficult, gnarled, intricate, involved, convoluted, gnarly, elaborate, troublesome, baffling, hard, nodose, problematic, complicated; *antonyms* (*adj*) simple, straight, straightforward, **2.** forsaken; *synonyms* (*adj*) deserted, desolate, abandoned, lonely, forlorn, derelict, desert, jilted, empty, solitary, friendless, isolated, **3.** abandoned; *synonyms* (*adj*) immoral, profligate, shameless, stranded, wicked, corrupt, debauched, depraved, discarded, dissipated, dissolute, licentious, loose, neglected, reprobate; *antonyms* (*adj*) restrained, inhabited, orderly, overcrowded, **4.** nodular; *synonyms* (*adj*) nodulated, noduled, rough, (*v*) bossed, bossy, embossed.

timron 1. globular; *synonyms* (*adj*) round, circular, global, globose, spheric, spherical, orbicular, rotund, rounded, bulging, **2.** rounded; *synonyms* (*adj*) curved, full, globular, bent, blunt, fat, obtuse; *antonyms* (*adj*) pointed, straight, sharp, bony, concave, **3.** round; *synonyms* (*adv*) about, around, (*adj*) plump, entire, chubby, complete, (*n*) circle, bout, ring, beat, circuit, cycle, (*v*) compass, turn, gird; *antonym* (*adj*) slim, **4.** rotund; *synonyms* (*adj*) obese, corpulent, orotund, overweight, stout, chunky, heavy, large, (*n*) fleshy; *antonym* (*adj*) gangling.

timtim drip; *synonyms* (*n*) dribble, trickle, leak, leakage, escape, splash, (*v*) drop, distill, seep, weep, trill, drizzle, fall, ooze, percolate.

timu 1. beautiful; *synonyms* (*adj*) attractive, good-looking, bright, beauteous, fine, handsome, lovely, picturesque, pleasant, pretty, striking, sweet, adorned, ornate, dainty; *antonyms* (*adj*) ugly, unattractive, **2.** decorated; *synonyms* (*adj*) fancy, beautiful, bejeweled, adorn, dyed, elaborate, emblazoned, festive, inscribed, painted, purfled, tinted, celebrated, extolled, festooned, **3.** adorned; *synonyms* (*adj*) decorated, bedecked, garlanded, **4.** embellished; *synonyms* (*adj*) ornamented, rhetorical, florid, baroque, embroidered, empurpled, exaggerated, flowery, inflated, overstated, purple, rich, tall, imperial, (*prep*) beautied, **5.** painted; *synonyms* (*v*) depaint, (*adj*) motley, stained, assorted, calico, cosmetic, graphic, miscellaneous, mixed, multicolor, multicolored, multicolour, multicoloured, particolored, particoloured.

timua 1. decorate; *synonyms* (*v*) beautify, deck, adorn, bedeck, dress, embellish, grace, apparel, bedight, arrange, array, emblazon, embroider, enrich, garnish; *antonym* (*v*) strip, **2.** paint; *synonyms* (*n*) painting, tint, coating, (*v*) color, dye, daub, coat, decorate, depict, varnish, enamel, apply, lacquer, describe, draw.

timuaki 1. decorated; *synonyms* (*adj*) adorned, ornate, fancy, beautiful, bejeweled, adorn, dyed, elaborate, emblazoned, festive, inscribed, painted, purfled, tinted, celebrated, **2.** painted; *synonyms* (*v*) depaint, (*adj*) motley, stained, assorted, calico, cosmetic, graphic, miscellaneous, mixed, multicolor, multicolored, multicolour, multicoloured, particolored, particoloured.

timurua 1. lounger; *synonyms* (*v*) bummer, goldbrick, (*n*) loafer, dallier, dillydallier, do-nothing, armchair, delinquent, derelict, flaneur, mope, recliner, **2.** loiter; *synonyms* (*v*) linger, dawdle, lag, loaf, dally, saunter, tarry, prowl, idle, loll, continue, (*adj*) delay, lounge, hesitate, (*adv*) crawl, **3.** dawdle; *synonyms* (*v*) amble, procrastinate, idler, loiter, drag; *antonyms* (*v*) hurry, rush, **4.** loaf; *synonyms* (*v*) laze, lurk, (*adj*) block, lump, poke, **5.** lounge; *synonyms* (*n*) couch, sofa, bar, (*v*) recline, rest, relax, sprawl, bask, lie.

tina 1. mother; *synonyms* (*n*) mamma, parent, (*v*) father, beget, engender, generate, care, sire, fuss, get, **2.** mommy; *synonyms* (*n*) mama, mammy, mom, momma, mother, mum, mummy, mater, am, milliampere, secrecy, **3.** mummy; *synonyms* (*n*) mommy, skeleton, (*v*) shrivel, **4.** mom, **5.** ma, **6.** nun; *synonyms* (*n*) postulant, religious, sister, cleric, cloistress, monk, parson, preacher, priest, rector, religieuse, religieux, reverend, vicar, abbess.

tínaba bottle; *synonyms* (*n*) container, flask, jug, jar, pot, carboy, gourd, (*v*) preserve, can.

tinaniku 1. external; *synonyms* (*adj*) exterior, outside, extraneous, extrinsic, outward, foreign, outlying, peripheral, superficial, formal, exotic, objective, outdoor, outer, surface; *antonyms* (*adj*) inner, interior, internal, domestic, inmost, inside, **2**. outdoors; *synonyms* (*adv*) alfresco, out, without, (*n*) open, nature, clear, country, countryside, environment, garden, hill, mountain, patio, woods, yard; *antonym* (*n*) indoors.

tinanikua disdain; *synonyms* (*n*) contempt, slight, arrogance, derision, haughtiness, disregard, mockery, pride, (*v*) scorn, despise, contemn, ridicule, scoff, disparage, neglect; *antonyms* (*n*) admiration, humility, (*v*) respect.

tinara 1. abuse; *synonyms* (*n*) affront, misuse, harm, outrage, reproach, invective, (*v*) insult, mistreat, injure, assault, censure, damage, exploit, hurt, (*adj*) maltreat; *antonyms* (*v*) praise, respect, **2**. insult; *synonyms* (*n*) dishonor, abuse, contumely, disgrace, indignity, contempt, wound, derision, injury, (*v*) flout, taunt, cut, mock, offend, slight; *antonym* (*v*) compliment, **3**. mock; *synonyms* (*adj*) counterfeit, fake, false, fictitious, (*v*) deride, ridicule, burlesque, gibe, ape, mimic, scoff, scorn, sham, bemock, (*n*) jeer; *antonyms* (*adj*) genuine, real, **4**. offend; *synonyms* (*v*) irritate, contravene, disgust, infringe, anger, annoy, break, displease, err, breach, infract, pique, revolt, shock, violate; *antonym* (*v*) please.

tinaraea threaten; *synonyms* (*v*) menace, bully, endanger, intimidate, loom, offer, imperil, jeopardize, peril, approach, foreshadow, portend, browbeat, impend, (*n*) threat; *antonym* (*v*) help.

tinaraki 1. abused; *synonyms* (*adj*) maltreated, mistreated, downtrodden, dull, perverted, battered, harmed, injured, molested, neglected, **2**. insulted; *synonyms* (*adj*) affronted, huffy, disrespected, hurt, slighted, snubbed, upset, **3**. offended; *synonyms* (*adj*) angry, aggrieved, annoyed, pained, wronged, shocked, appalled, ashamed, averted, bitter, cool, disappointed, disgusted, dismayed, dissatisfied; *antonym* (*adj*) composed.

tinaubati 1. brawny; *synonyms* (*adj*) muscular, athletic, burly, hefty, strong, beefy, powerful, robust, stalwart, strapping, sturdy, mighty, stocky, lusty, hardy; *antonyms* (*adj*) slight, puny, skinny, weak, **2**. opposing; *synonyms* (*adj*) conflicting, opposed, adverse, antagonistic, contrary, hostile, opponent, antithetical, anti, contradictory, opposite, rival, antipodean, contrasted, (*n*) clashing; *antonyms* (*adj*) similar, compatible, **3**. stout; *synonyms* (*adj*) fat, bold, corpulent, husky, obese, fleshy, fearless, hearty, gallant, brave, bulky, chubby, healthy, heavy, overweight; *antonyms* (*adj*) slender, slim, thin, flimsy.

tinauere 1. sickly; *synonyms* (*adj*) feeble, infirm, sick, ailing, diseased, indisposed, morbid, pale, poorly, sallow, peaked, pasty, (*n*) invalid, (*v*) faint, frail; *antonyms* (*adj*) healthy, bitter, **2**. puny; *synonyms* (*adj*) little, petty, weak, small, tiny, minute, measly, paltry, runty, trifling, trivial, exiguous, meager; *antonyms* (*adj*) brawny, muscular, **3**. runty; *synonyms* (*adj*) puny, short, stunted, shrimpy, diminutive, mean, shortened, **4**. stunted; *synonyms* (*adj*) scrubby, scrawny, spare, (*v*) strangulated.

tine 1. indecisive; *synonyms* (*adj*) doubtful, hesitant, inconclusive, undecided, unsure, weak, dubious, irresolute, precarious, vague, feeble; *antonyms* (*adj*) decisive, conclusive, resolute, **2**. hung; *synonyms* (*adj*) fatigued, puzzled, **3**. hang; *synonyms* (*v*) dangle, depend, drape, float, append, cling, decorate, execute, fall, flow, hover, swing, (*n*) suspend, delay, knack, **4**. hanging; *synonyms* (*n*) dangling, execution, suspension, curtain, (*adj*) pendant, pendent, suspended, pending, pendulous; *antonym* (*adj*) upright, **5**. weigh; *synonyms* (*v*) balance, press, study, consider, count, matter, measure, poise, deliberate, assess, contemplate, ponder, evaluate, load, tell, **6**. undecided; *synonyms* (*adj*) unsettled, indecisive, uncertain, unresolved, undetermined, debatable, indefinite, indeterminate, ambivalent, borderline, moot, open, tentative; *antonyms* (*adj*) decided, certain, determined.

tinebu 1. chubby; *synonyms* (*adj*) buxom, fat, fleshy, plump, round, chunky, heavy, pudgy, stout, tubby, overweight; *antonyms* (*adj*) thin, skinny, slim, **2**. heavy; *synonyms* (*adj*) dull, deep, dark, dense, full, grave, gross, hard, arduous, bulky, burdensome, grievous, oppressive, thick, compact; *antonyms* (*adj*) light, easy, slight, gentle, puny, **3**. fat; *synonyms* (*adj*) corpulent, fatty, fertile, gainful, greasy, great, obese, rich, stocky, big, (*n*) avoirdupois, blubber, cream, (*v*) fatten, bloated; *antonym* (*adj*) slender, **4**. obese; *synonyms* (*adj*) chubby, portly, weighty, rotund.

tinerua 1. hanging; *synonyms* (*n*) dangling, execution, suspension, curtain, (*adj*) pendant, pendent, suspended, pending, pendulous; *antonym* (*adj*) upright, **2**. dangling; *synonyms* (*adj*) floppy, limp, baggy, flaccid, lifeless, (*n*) hanging, abatement, abeyance, break, hiatus, intermission, interruption, pause, reprieve, (*adv*) adangle, **3**. impede; *synonyms* (*v*) block, clog, hinder, bar, obstruct, barricade, check, delay, preclude, curb, debar, embarrass, encumber, forbid, hamper; *antonym* (*v*) facilitate, **4**. retard; *synonyms* (*v*) arrest, detain, impede, lag, slow, decelerate, procrastinate, prevent, handicap, slacken, (*n*) defer, moron, changeling, *(adj)* deaden, waive; *antonym* *(v)* accelerate.

tineruaki 1. impeded; *synonyms (adj)* disabled, crippled, slow, lame, lamed, **2**. retarded; *synonyms (adj)* backward, tardy, imbecile, defective, deferred, dull, half-baked, leisurely, obtuse, simple, birdbrained, dim, dim-witted, dopey, dumbbell.

ting fart; *synonyms (n)* flatus, wind, breath, farting, hint, jazz, lead, nothingness, steer, tip, twist, winding.

tingaro dawn; *synonyms (n)* beginning, commencement, aurora, cockcrow, morning, onset, origin, prime, start, sunrise, birth, *(v)* break, begin, appear, *(adj)* daybreak; *antonyms (n)* dusk, sunset, twilight, *(v)* end, finish.

tingingi 1. infinitesimal; *synonyms (adj)* minute, microscopic, insignificant, tiny, little, evanescent, atomic, minuscule, inappreciable; *antonym (adj)* gigantic, **2**. minute; *synonyms (n)* instant, flash, jiffy, note, memorandum, moment, second, *(adj)* delicate, careful, circumstantial, diminutive, elaborate, fine, infinitesimal, miniature; *antonyms (adj)* enormous, huge, big, **3**. tiny; *synonyms (adj)* midget, petite, petty, puny, slight, teeny, exiguous, baby, bantam, short, minor, trifling, trivial, cramped, *(phr)* small; *antonyms (adj)* vast, large.

tingo 1. drenched; *synonyms (adj)* wet, saturated, soaked, soaking, damp, soppy, sodden, sopping; *antonym (adj)* dry, **2**. dripping; *synonyms (n)* drip, *(adj)* drenched, reeking, soggy, **3**. soaked; *synonyms (adj)* drunk, plastered, sloshed, besotted.

tinima 1. grill; *synonyms (n)* grid, grille, grillroom, *(v)* fry, bake, broil, cook, examine, quiz, roast, burn, inflame, toast, ask, interrogate, **2**. fry; *synonyms (n)* chicken, child, chrysalis, cub, nestling, *(v)* singe, grill, electrocute, heat.

tinimaki 1. grilled; *synonyms (adj)* barbecued, broiled, baked, **2**. fried; *synonyms (adj)* daft, deranged, done, inebriated, intoxicated.

tininanikua ostracize; *synonyms (v)* boycott, blackball, exile, exclude, expel, ostracise, proscribe, relegate, transport, ban, bar, blacklist, clamor, *(adj)* banish, outlaw.

tink fart; *synonyms (n)* flatus, wind, breath, farting, hint, jazz, lead, nothingness, steer, tip, twist, winding.

tinnim grill; *synonyms (n)* grid, grille, grillroom, *(v)* fry, bake, broil, cook, examine, quiz, roast, burn, inflame, toast, ask, interrogate.

tinnimaki grilled; *synonyms (adj)* barbecued, broiled, baked.

tintin roast; *synonyms (n)* ridicule, joint, knock, *(v)* broil, burn, bake, grill, joke, heat, quiz, cook, fry, scorch, tease, banter.

tintinaki roasted; *synonyms (adj)* roast, baked.

tio 1. flap; *synonyms (n)* fuss, slap, disturbance, pother, commotion, alarm, flapping, *(v)* flop, beat, wave, brandish, flutter, shake, dither, agitate, **2**. float; *synonyms (n)* buoy, raft, bob, fleet, *(v)* drift, swim, blow, hover, ride, waft, fly, glide, hang, range, sail; *antonym (v)* sink, **3**. hover; *synonyms (v)* float, hesitate, brood, poise, vacillate, cover, levitate, linger, loiter, waver, *(n)* ramble, stroll, wander, *(adj)* boggle, dillydally, **4**. oscillate; *synonyms (v)* fluctuate, swing, vibrate, wag, alternate, quiver, sway, tremble, vary, wobble, **5**. swing; *synonyms (n)* sweep, lilt, motion, play, *(v)* oscillate, dangle, rock, change, move, turn, dance, drop, lurch, suspend, swerve.

tiotio 1. wave; *synonyms (n)* billow, gesture, motion, sign, surge, *(v)* brandish, flap, flutter, curl, flourish, swell, swing, undulate, beat, beckon, **2**. oscillate; *synonyms (v)* fluctuate, vibrate, hesitate, wag, alternate, quiver, shake, sway, tremble, vacillate, vary, wave, waver, wobble, **3**. wander; *synonyms (v)* ramble, digress, stray, deviate, err, roam, travel, depart, divagate, gad, meander, *(n)* saunter, stroll, tramp, drift, **4**. wag; *synonyms (n)* humorist, waggle, joker, wit, comedian, clown, zany, card, comic, *(v)* wiggle, reel, move, shiver, vibratiuncle, **5**. wobble; *synonyms (v)* totter, rock, lurch, stagger, quake, oscillate, dodder, shift, tilt, waddle, falter, roll, shudder, bob, *(n)* tremor.

tip mallet; *synonyms (n)* hammer, maul, club, mall, beetle.

tira 1. flatten; *synonyms (v)* fell, demolish, level, press, even, drop, roll, squash, depress, destroy, ruin, smash, smooth, unfold, bulldoze; *antonyms (v)* build, crumple, **2**. fly; *synonyms (v)* escape, dash, drive, flee, glide, elope, aviate, dart, flutter, hop, hover, *(n)* flap, *(adj)* break, flit, burst, **3**. squash; *synonyms (v)* crush, mash, quell, compress, squeeze, flatten, quash, oppress, crash, cram, crowd, grind, jam, push, squelch, **4**. wipe; *synonyms (v)* rub, clean, mop, towel, brush, scour, scrub, clear, dry, wash, cover, *(n)* fling, flout, *(adj)* sponge, flush.

tiraka 1. smooth; *synonyms (adj)* easy, calm, level, oily, facile, flat, flowing, fluent, fluid, glossy, graceful, greasy, *(v)* quiet, facilitate, even; *antonyms (adj)* rough, uneven, abrasive, coarse, crumpled, flaking, harsh, jerky, lined, peeling, prickly, ridged, wrinkled, corrugated, *(v)* wrinkle, **2**. spread; *synonyms (v)* scatter, reach, disperse, expand, extend, broadcast, circulate, diffuse, disseminate, increase, propagate, stretch, broaden, deploy, *(n)* span; *antonym (adj)* concentrated.

tirakaki spread; *synonyms (v)* scatter, reach, disperse, expand, extend, broadcast, circulate, diffuse, disseminate, increase, propagate, stretch, broaden, deploy, (*n*) span; *antonym* (*adj*) concentrated.

tiraki 1. flattened; *synonyms* (*adj*) compressed, depressed, planate, trodden, unconscious, compacted, firmed, trampled; *antonym* (*adj*) loose, **2**. squashed; *synonyms* (*adj*) condensed, dense, solid.

tiri 1. kill; *synonyms* (*v*) assassinate, destroy, erase, annihilate, eliminate, extinguish, finish, blast, butcher, decimate, dispatch, eradicate, execute, (*n*) murder, game, **2**. fall; *synonyms* (*v*) decline, dip, decrease, descend, dive, rain, diminish, dwindle, sink, alight, (*n*) drop, descent, downfall, plunge, pitch; *antonyms* (*v*) rise, increase, ascend, climb, triumph, win, (*n*) ascent, **3**. beat; *synonyms* (*v*) batter, flap, pulsate, throb, tick, trounce, whip, bat, baste, break, (*n*) pulse, thump, knock, round, cadence; *antonym* (*v*) lose, **4**. cruel; *synonyms* (*adj*) barbarous, brutal, hard, harsh, heartless, unkind, bitter, bloody, atrocious, biting, fierce, inhuman, merciless, ruthless, savage; *antonyms* (*adj*) gentle, kind, merciful, humane, liberal, sympathetic, **5**. knock; *synonyms* (*v*) hit, blow, bump, cuff, punch, strike, boot, clip, (*n*) rap, bang, tap, bash, crash, whack, clap; *antonym* (*v*) praise, **6**. lop; *synonyms* (*v*) cut, crop, hew, chop, dress, poll, prune, sever, trim, truncate, curtail, hack, amputate, pare, (*adj*) dock, **7**. slaughter; *synonyms* (*n*) massacre, carnage, bloodshed, butchery, drubbing, homicide, killing, thrashing, destruction, beating, butchering, (*v*) defeat, kill, slay, exterminate, **8**. suppress; *synonyms* (*v*) repress, subdue, check, crush, curb, quell, restrain, silence, stifle, subjugate, strangle, conceal, control, inhibit, oppress; *antonym* (*v*) express, **9**. purely; *synonyms* (*adv*) only, just, merely, simply, utterly, absolutely, quite, all, solely, strictly, decidedly; *antonym* (*adv*) artificially, **10**. simply; *synonyms* (*adv*) alone, directly, exclusively, easily, plainly, purely, but, plain, honestly, manifestly, obviously, openly, clearly, entirely, (*adj*) barely; *antonym* (*adv*) elaborately.

tiriaki 1. beaten; *synonyms* (*v*) beat, (*adj*) battered, overpowered, conquered, routed, overcome; *antonym* (*adj*) victorious, **2**. suppressed; *synonyms* (*adj*) smothered, stifled, strangled, downtrodden, buried, composed, concealed, covert, doomed, dormant, embryonic, forgotten, hidden, latent, (*n*) subordinate; *antonym* (*adj*) available.

tiribaea 1. amend; *synonyms* (*v*) ameliorate, improve, mend, rectify, alter, better, correct, emend, fix, reform, adjust, help, redress, remedy, repair; *antonym* (*v*) worsen, **2**. reprimand; *synonyms* (*n*) blame, admonition, chastisement, reproof, castigation, reprehension, (*v*) rebuke, censure, chide, lecture, reproach, castigate,

admonish, chastise, discipline; *antonyms* (*v*) praise, commend.

tiribaeaki 1. amended; *synonyms* (*adj*) altered, reformed, **2**. reprimanded; *synonyms* (*adj*) rebuked, reproved, admonished, chastened.

tiribaonoa 1. fine; *synonyms* (*adj*) delicate, agreeable, dainty, brave, capital, elegant, excellent, nice, thin, delightful, acute, admirable, alright, (*n*) penalty, (*v*) punish; *antonyms* (*adj*) poor, thick, coarse, substantial, unsatisfactory, wide, **2**. trounce; *synonyms* (*v*) thrash, beat, castigate, defeat, flog, lash, whip, rout, drub, chastise, overpower, baste, slash, crush, reprimand; *antonym* (*v*) lose.

tiribaonoaki fined; *synonyms* (*adj*) penalized, penalised.

tiribo 1. chastise; *synonyms* (*v*) castigate, chasten, correct, criticize, punish, reprimand, scourge, beat, scold, discipline, flog, lash, objurgate, penalize, strike; *antonym* (*v*) praise, **2**. thrash; *synonyms* (*v*) defeat, pound, whip, baste, clobber, drub, lam, lick, whack, batter, bang, bat, belabor, crush, flail.

tiriboaki chastised; *synonyms* (*adj*) corrected, disciplined.

tiribure correct; *synonyms* (*adj*) right, accurate, appropriate, becoming, nice, precise, proper, (*v*) adjust, amend, castigate, chastise, chasten, better, remedy, (*n*) true; *antonyms* (*adj*) incorrect, false, faulty, inappropriate, mistaken, improper, (*v*) wrong, spoil.

tiribureaki corrected; *synonyms* (*adj*) chastised, amended, reformed, altered, chastened, disciplined, educated, refined.

tirigo 1. meat; *synonyms* (*n*) flesh, core, essence, food, gist, heart, kernel, marrow, substance, crux, matter, beef, brawn, stuff, content, **2**. flesh; *synonyms* (*n*) mortality, anatomy, chassis, figure, form, frame, humanity, mankind, meat, muscle, pulp, shape, (*adj*) carnality, concupiscence, lust.

tirikai 1. plane; *synonyms* (*n*) airplane, face, aeroplane, aircraft, degree, stage, surface, (*v*) flatten, shave, (*adj*) level, even, flat, horizontal, smooth, flush, **2**. trim; *synonyms* (*adj*) tidy, neat, spruce, orderly, shipshape, (*v*) cut, dress, clip, garnish, adorn, embellish, lop, prune, reduce, shorten; *antonym* (*adj*) fat.

tirikaiaki 1. trimmed; *synonyms* (*adj*) cut, cunning, demure, down, emasculated, gashed, gelded, level, mown, neat, shortened, slashed, sly, smooth, snoD, **2**. planned; *synonyms* (*adj*) deliberate, intended, intentional, calculated, designed, aforethought, plotted, premeditated, scheduled, fixed, future, prepared, studied; *antonyms* (*adj*) spontaneous, unplanned.

tirimataere 1. flog; *synonyms* (*v*) beat, chastise, lash, whip, lick, birch, flagellate, trounce, castigate, cane, lather, scourge, strap, wallop, sell, **2**. lash;

synonyms (n) goad, hit, blow, eyelash, (v) flog, bind, lace, batter, secure, slash, hitch, fasten, swish, (adj) tie, incite, **3**. thrash; synonyms (v) defeat, pound, baste, clobber, drub, lam, whack, bang, bat, belabor, crush, flail, hammer, overwhelm, slam.

tiring 1. abuse; synonyms (n) affront, misuse, harm, outrage, reproach, invective, (v) insult, mistreat, injure, assault, censure, damage, exploit, hurt, (adj) maltreat; antonyms (v) praise, respect, **2**. scold; synonyms (v) berate, chide, rebuke, reprimand, abuse, lecture, rail, admonish, castigate, grouch, grumble, jaw, reprove, (n) nag, (adj) shrew.

tiringa 1. beat; synonyms (v) batter, flap, pulsate, throb, tick, trounce, whip, bat, baste, break, (n) pulse, thump, knock, round, cadence; antonym (v) lose, **2**. kill; synonyms (v) assassinate, destroy, erase, annihilate, eliminate, extinguish, finish, blast, butcher, decimate, dispatch, eradicate, execute, (n) murder, game, **3**. immolate; synonyms (v) sacrifice, victimize, offer, kill, atone, attempt, bid, endeavor, essay, slaughter, move, proffer, propose, propound, suggest, **4**. assassinate; synonyms (v) slay, assassin, exterminate, massacre, **5**. massacre; synonyms (n) carnage, butchery, bloodshed, killing, defeat, destruction, (v) havoc, **6**. hit; synonyms (v) strike, attain, belt, blow, bump, collide, encounter, (n) bang, smash, touch, chance, bash, beat, collision, play; antonyms (n) failure, flop, **7**. lecture; synonyms (n) address, discourse, harangue, reprimand, speech, talk, oration, censure, declaim, homily, (v) rebuke, sermon, chide, preach, instruct, **8**. cane; synonyms (n) rod, scourge, stick, (v) flog, birch, lash, thrash, **9**. reprimand; synonyms (n) blame, admonition, chastisement, reproof, castigation, reprehension, rap, (v) lecture, reproach, castigate, admonish, chastise, discipline, scold, accuse; antonyms (v) praise, commend, **10**. scold; synonyms (v) berate, abuse, rail, grouch, grumble, jaw, reprove, vituperate, rate, remonstrate, slate, (n) nag, nagger, (adj) shrew, curse.

tiringaki 1. assassinated, **2**. abused; synonyms (adj) maltreated, mistreated, downtrodden, dull, perverted, battered, harmed, injured, molested, neglected, **3**. hit; synonyms (v) strike, attain, belt, blow, bump, collide, encounter, (n) knock, bang, smash, touch, chance, bash, beat, collision; antonyms (n) failure, flop, **4**. killed; synonyms (adj) slain, fallen, (n) casualty, **5**. beaten; synonyms (adj) overpowered, conquered, routed, overcome; antonym (adj) victorious, **6**. reprimanded; synonyms (adj) rebuked, reproved, admonished, chastened.

tirinta cylindrical; synonyms (adj) cylindric, cylinder, round, bulging, circular, complete, cylindroid, tubelike, vasiform, fair, finished, free, full, generous, globular.

tiriobora 1. devastate; synonyms (v) desolate, consume, demolish, destroy, spoil, havoc, ruin, waste, annihilate, ravage, sack, wreck, despoil, damage, harry; antonym (v) build, **2**. sack; synonyms (n) pocket, pouch, sac, poke, (v) pillage, bag, plunder, discharge, dismiss, fire, ransack, rob, rifle, can, loot; antonym (v) hire, **3**. plunder; synonyms (v) devastate, maraud, strip, divest, forage, foray, prey, raid, steal, (n) booty, depredation, despoliation, prize, rape, rapine.

tirioboraki 1. devastated; synonyms (adj) desolate, destroyed, desolated, ruined, ravaged, wasted, bare, blasted, **2**. sacked; synonyms (adj) despoiled, pillaged, raped, assaulted, devastated, looted, molested, plundered, ransacked, **3**. plundered; synonyms (adj) fleeced, sacked.

tiriou 1. crazy; synonyms (adj) deranged, mad, madcap, wild, absurd, brainsick, cracked, crazed, demented, eccentric, foolish, ludicrous, preposterous, silly, wacky; antonyms (adj) sane, sensible, **2**. cracked; synonyms (adj) broken, nutty, batty, chapped, crazy, balmy, bats, crackers, crackled, dotty, insane, kookie, kooky, loony, alligatored, **3**. insane; synonyms (adj) daft, delirious, lunatic, frantic, idiotic, furious, irrational, possessed, psychotic, rabid, harebrained.

tirireke cut; synonyms (v) carve, chop, clip, abbreviate, abridge, bite, condense, crop, drop, fashion, (n) notch, slice, cutting, nick, blow; antonyms (v) increase, lengthen, (n) addition, extension.

tirirekeaki cut; synonyms (v) carve, chop, clip, abbreviate, abridge, bite, condense, crop, drop, fashion, (n) notch, slice, cutting, nick, blow; antonyms (v) increase, lengthen, (n) addition, extension.

tiritabuki 1. craze; synonyms (n) fad, cult, enthusiasm, fashion, frenzy, furor, furore, mania, rage, style, trend, thing, (v) madden, crack, derange, **2**. flatten; synonyms (v) fell, demolish, level, press, even, drop, roll, squash, depress, destroy, ruin, smash, smooth, unfold, bulldoze; antonyms (v) build, crumple, **3**. touch; synonyms (n) feel, tinge, feeling, hint, (v) affect, contact, hit, border, adjoin, strike, stroke, regard, brush, concern, handle.

tiritabukiaki 1. flattened; synonyms (adj) compressed, depressed, planate, trodden, unconscious, compacted, firmed, trampled; antonym (adj) loose, **2**. crazed; synonyms (adj) cracked, crazy, deranged, wild, insane, mad, crackled, **3**. touched; synonyms (v) compassionate, pitiful, sympathetic, bad, decayed, lentiginous, mildewed, moldy, mucid, musty, (adj) affected, daft, tinged, interested, nutty; antonym (adj) untouched.

tiritiri 1. fierce; *synonyms (adj)* bitter, violent, acute, cruel, ferocious, brutal, furious, grim, savage, nasty, angry, ardent, atrocious, barbarous, boisterous; *antonyms (adj)* gentle, mild, **2.** brutal; *synonyms (adj)* beastly, barbaric, bestial, hard, harsh, truculent, unkind, vicious, barbarian, boarish, rugged, tough, fierce, inhuman, oppressive; *antonyms (adj)* kind, merciful, liberal, **3.** heartless; *synonyms (adj)* callous, hardhearted, ruthless, insensitive, merciless, obdurate, pitiless, stony, unfeeling, cold, unmerciful, unsympathetic, indifferent, spiritless, wicked, **4.** hard; *synonyms (adj)* austere, bad, difficult, grave, severe, strong, arduous, grueling, knotty, alcoholic, backbreaking, compact, complicated, *(adv)* firm, *(n)* rough; *antonyms (adj)* easy, soft, simple, soggy, tender, yielding, *(adv)* gently, lightly, **5.** bloodthirsty; *synonyms (adj)* bloody, murderous, sanguinary, **6.** ferocious; *synonyms (adj)* feral, fell, brutish, wild, ferine, ravenous, **7.** inhuman; *synonyms (adj)* heartless, remorseless, relentless, unhuman, insensate, **8.** cruel; *synonyms (adj)* biting, sharp, stern, tyrannical, unrelenting, bloodthirsty, deadly, monstrous, coldhearted, cutting, evil, horrible, implacable, malicious, mean; *antonyms (adj)* humane, sympathetic, **9.** barbarous; *synonyms (adj)* heathen, rude, uncivilized, tramontane, ignorant, untamed, outlandish, uncivil, **10.** severe; *synonyms (adj)* rigid, inclement, rigorous, heavy, intense, serious, strict, caustic, critical, exacting, extreme, painful, piercing, plain, *(v)* poignant; *antonyms (adj)* lenient, slight, lax.

tiritoa 1. even; *synonyms (adv)* yet, *(adj)* direct, equal, constant, equable, equivalent, flat, horizontal, identical, plane, regular, steady, *(v)* level, balance, smooth; *antonyms (adj)* uneven, inconsistent, irregular, jagged, unequal, **2.** level; *synonyms (n)* grade, degree, category, class, *(adj)* even, *(v)* flatten, floor, aim, demolish, destroy, dismantle, raze, bulldoze, equalize, fell; *antonyms (adj)* inclined, slanting, angled, *(v)* build, raise, **3.** smooth; *synonyms (adj)* easy, calm, oily, facile, flowing, fluent, fluid, glossy, graceful, greasy, liquid, mellow, polished, *(v)* quiet, facilitate; *antonyms (adj)* rough, abrasive, coarse, crumpled, flaking, harsh, jerky, lined, peeling, prickly, ridged, wrinkled, corrugated, *(v)* wrinkle, crease.

tiro stare; *synonyms (v)* gaze, look, gape, glare, peer, squint, goggle, see, view, watch, leer, *(n)* regard.

tiroa 1. look; *synonyms (v)* seem, appear, expect, figure, attend, *(n)* face, gaze, appearance, aspect, air, countenance, expression, glance, guise, view, **2.** stare; *synonyms (v)* look, gape, glare, peer, squint, goggle, see, watch, leer, *(n)* regard, **3.** observe; *synonyms (v)* celebrate, comment, notice, commemorate, mind, guard, behold, discover, follow, heed, keep, mark, mention, note, fulfill;

antonyms (v) ignore, feel, **4.** scrutinize; *synonyms (v)* inspect, examine, review, analyze, audit, consider, explore, investigate, scan, search, check, observe, probe, study, *(n)* canvass.

tiroaki observed; *synonyms (adj)* seen, ascertained, discovered, empirical, disclosed, experiential, experimental, visual, practical, pragmatic, revealed.

tiroakina 1. contemplate; *synonyms (v)* consider, cogitate, meditate, muse, speculate, deliberate, look, ponder, reflect, gaze, behold, entertain, intend, mull, reason, **2.** examine; *synonyms (v)* assay, audit, overhaul, try, check, control, search, survey, ascertain, ask, contemplate, compare, analyze, canvass, essay, **3.** scrutinize; *synonyms (v)* inspect, examine, review, explore, investigate, scan, observe, probe, study, inquire, view, spy, research, scrutinise, see.

tironron 1. round; *synonyms (adv)* about, around, *(adj)* circular, plump, entire, chubby, complete, *(n)* circle, bout, ring, beat, circuit, *(v)* compass, turn, gird; *antonyms (adj)* slim, sharp, **2.** spherical; *synonyms (adj)* round, global, globose, globular, orbicular, rotund, rounded, spheric, orbiculate.

tirotiroa scrutinize; *synonyms (v)* inspect, examine, review, analyze, audit, consider, explore, investigate, scan, search, check, observe, probe, study, *(n)* canvass.

titaou 1. hit; *synonyms (v)* strike, attain, belt, blow, bump, collide, encounter, *(n)* knock, bang, smash, touch, chance, bash, beat, collision; *antonyms (n)* failure, flop, **2.** threaten; *synonyms (v)* menace, bully, endanger, intimidate, loom, offer, imperil, jeopardize, peril, approach, foreshadow, portend, browbeat, impend, *(n)* threat; *antonym (v)* help.

titaoutana 1. little; *synonyms (adj)* small, diminutive, insignificant, brief, minute, petty, short, some, tiny, exiguous, light, baby, bantam, *(v)* dash, bit; *antonyms (adj)* big, enormous, large, important, **2.** small; *synonyms (adj)* little, narrow, fine, inadequate, low, minor, slight, remote, cramped, young, limited, faint, humble, miniature, minuscule; *antonyms (adj)* bulky, colossal, considerable, extra-large, great, huge, sizeable, giant, major.

titebo 1. congruent; *synonyms (adj)* congruous, harmonious, similar, compatible, fitting, coinciding, relevant, matching, harmonizing, logical, united, agreeing, concurring; *antonym (adj)* incongruent, **2.** equal; *synonyms (adj)* agree, comparable, adequate, balanced, commensurate, equivalent, *(v)* match, compare, correspond, even, parallel, rival, equalize, *(n)* compeer, peer; *antonyms (adj)* unequal, different, repressive, disproportionate, inconsistent, uneven, unlike, *(v)* differ.

tî-te-eran 1. equal; *synonyms (adj)* agree, comparable, adequate, balanced, commensurate, equivalent, *(v)* match, compare, correspond, even, parallel, rival, equalize, (*n*) compeer, peer; *antonyms* (*adj*) unequal, different, repressive, disproportionate, inconsistent, uneven, unlike, (*v*) differ, **2.** similar; *synonyms* (*adj*) corresponding, alike, like, same, related, akin, analogous, cognate, correspondent, equal, conformable, resembling, kindred, such, (*v*) identical; *antonyms* (*adj*) dissimilar, incompatible, opposing, opposite.

titerau half; *synonyms* (*n*) mediety, halve, piece, bisection, hemisphere, (*adv*) halfendeal, imperfectly, (*adj*) moiety, part, short, behalf, bisected, divided, even-steven, halved; *antonyms* (*n*) whole, all.

titi 1. soft; *synonyms* (*adj*) gentle, easy, light, limp, balmy, delicate, quiet, slack, loose, clement, faint, flabby, flaccid, (*v*) feeble, low; *antonyms* (*adj*) hard, firm, harsh, loud, hoarse, rough, solid, stiff, alcoholic, shrill, strong, **2.** watery; *synonyms* (*adj*) liquid, moist, dilute, diluted, washy, wet, thin, damp, fluid, aqueous, hydrous, insipid, tearful, weak, dripping; *antonyms* (*adj*) concentrated, dry.

titibengaua swelled; *synonyms* (*adj*) big, inflated, bloated, adult, bad, bighearted, boastful, bombastic, bounteous, bountiful, braggy, crowing, distended, elder, emphysematous.

titibo commensurate; *synonyms* (*adj*) adequate, commensurable, equal, sufficient, comparable, equivalent, proportionate; *antonym* (*adj*) disproportionate.

titiku 1. dwell; *synonyms* (*v*) abide, inhabit, reside, bide, live, stay, lodge, be, belong, brood, continue, delay, occupy, remain, settle, **2.** stay; *synonyms* (*v*) rest, prop, stop, endure, pause, arrest, dwell, support, linger, persist, sojourn, stand, (*n*) halt, check, (*adj*) cease; *antonyms* (*v*) leave, change, abscond, depart, **3.** tarry; *synonyms* (*v*) loiter, lag, dally, dawdle, hesitate, wait, saunter, (*adj*) pitchy, resinous, resiny, **4.** sojourn; *synonyms* (*n*) residence, abode, dwelling, habitation, (*v*) domicile, tarry, visit.

titiraki 1. ask; *synonyms* (*v*) inquire, request, appeal, beg, demand, interrogate, question, take, beseech, call, charge, claim, consult, crave, invite; *antonym* (*v*) answer, **2.** request; *synonyms* (*n*) petition, bid, prayer, application, entreaty, wish, invitation, asking, command, quest, (*v*) ask, order, pray, desire, entreat, **3.** question; *synonyms* (*n*) inquiry, challenge, matter, problem, interrogation, (*v*) doubt, query, distrust, investigate, contest, dispute, examine, enquire, mistrust, argue; *antonym* (*n*) certainty.

titirakina question; *synonyms* (*n*) inquiry, challenge, demand, matter, problem, (*v*) doubt, query, distrust, inquire, interrogate, investigate, contest, dispute, examine, enquire; *antonyms* (*n*) certainty, (*v*) answer.

titirakinia ask; *synonyms* (*v*) inquire, request, appeal, beg, demand, interrogate, question, take, beseech, call, charge, claim, consult, crave, invite; *antonym* (*v*) answer.

titirou sneeze; *synonyms* (*v*) arrest, (*n*) sneezing, sternutation.

tituaraoi 1. liberal; *synonyms* (*adj*) generous, bountiful, free, handsome, abundant, benevolent, big, large, kind, ample, bounteous, broad, charitable, giving, tolerant; *antonyms* (*adj*) strict, oppressive, totalitarian, intolerant, (*n*) conservative, **2.** generous; *synonyms* (*adj*) full, copious, fair, flush, liberal, spacious, rich, benign, considerable, kindly, munificent, noble, open, philanthropic, plentiful; *antonyms* (*adj*) stingy, meager, mean, measly, miserly, small, tightfisted, avaricious, greedy, ungenerous.

toa 1. enormous; *synonyms* (*adj*) big, colossal, huge, immense, vast, excessive, exorbitant, great, large, prodigious, tremendous, stupendous, gargantuan, giant, gigantic; *antonyms* (*adj*) minute, small, tiny, insignificant, miniature, **2.** gigantic; *synonyms* (*adj*) enormous, mammoth, massive, monstrous, monumental, monster, terrific, gigantean, infinite, whopping, brawny, high, **3.** monumental; *synonyms* (*adj*) grand, majestic, monolithic, memorable, towering, impressive, **4.** colossal; *synonyms* (*adj*) mighty, bulky, formidable, **5.** swollen; *synonyms* (*adj*) bloated, inflated, bombastic, puffed, puffy, turgid, egotistic, bulging, tumescent, tumid, conceited, egotistical, (*v*) distended, blown, (*prep*) pompous.

toabara 1. extinguish; *synonyms* (*v*) destroy, exterminate, quench, annihilate, douse, eradicate, consume, end, suppress, quash, devastate, crush, decimate, efface, (*adj*) allay; *antonyms* (*v*) light, ignite, **2.** moderate; *synonyms* (*adj*) temperate, abstemious, middling, mild, easy, (*v*) calm, mitigate, curb, diminish, lessen, ease, cool, abate, assuage, (*adv*) check; *antonyms* (*v*) extreme, immoderate, radical, (*v*) increase, intensify, **3.** stifle; *synonyms* (*v*) choke, repress, smother, suffocate, dampen, extinguish, muffle, quell, strangle, asphyxiate, contain, gag, silence, squash, damp, **4.** restrain; *synonyms* (*v*) bridle, confine, control, hold, rein, bind, arrest, bound, govern, inhibit, limit, prevent, circumscribe, constrain, detain, **5.** suppress; *synonyms* (*v*) subdue, restrain, stifle, subjugate, conceal, oppress, stop, conquer, hide, overcome, overpower, hush, seize, sink, lay; *antonym* (*v*) express, **6.** quell; *synonyms* (*v*) appease, pacify, defeat, compose, mollify, kill, squelch, crash, alleviate, deaden, dominate, overwhelm, (*adj*) lull, tranquilize, quiet, **7.** subdue; *synonyms* (*v*) reduce, chasten, soften, humble, domesticate, master, mortify, overthrow, surmount, bend, bow, break, capture, (n) impair, (adj) tame; *antonym* (v) surrender.

toabaraki 1. moderated; *synonyms* (adj) subdued, certified, dependant, dependent, equal, graduated, limited, measured, qualified, restricted, uniform, **2**. extinguished; *synonyms* (adj) extinct, out, dead, quenched, allayed, nonexistent, forbidden, inactive, kayoed, nonextant, prohibited, (n) defunctness, extermination, extinction, extinguishing, **3**. ended; *synonyms* (adj) complete, concluded, finished, over, completed, done, closed, past, terminated, through, consummate, **4**. stifled; *synonyms* (adj) smothered, strangled, suppressed, muffled, deadened, deaf, deafened, decayed, faint, pent-up, quiet, regardless, weak, hushed, muted, **5**. restrained; *synonyms* (adj) moderate, reserved, modest, temperate, discreet, reasonable, reticent, unemotional, guarded, confined, mild, gentle, sober, understated, calm; *antonyms* (adj) exaggerated, unrestrained, flashy, immoral, open, ostentatious, wild, **6**. suppressed; *synonyms* (adj) stifled, downtrodden, buried, composed, concealed, covert, doomed, dormant, embryonic, forgotten, hidden, latent, subconscious, unconscious, (n) subordinate; *antonym* (adj) available, **7**. quelled; *synonyms* (adj) squelched, extinguished, satisfied, slaked, **8**. subdued; *synonyms* (adj) soft, dull, restrained, tame, resigned, repressed, low, meek, broken, delicate, crushed, submissive, unruffled, (v) chastened, content; *antonyms* (adj) loud, enthusiastic, lively.

toae thigh; *synonym* (n) drumstick.

toang square; *synonyms* (adj) right, even, rectangular, fair, quadrate, straight, equal, (n) area, foursquare, rectangle, quadrilateral, (v) settle, agree, correspond, (adv) just.

toara odd; *synonyms* (adj) grotesque, exceptional, funny, abnormal, curious, droll, eccentric, extraordinary, singular, strange, chance, novel, anomalous, bizarre, fantastic; *antonyms* (adj) normal, ordinary, even, typical.

toari 1. stupendous; *synonyms* (adj) huge, prodigious, terrific, immense, tremendous, fantastic, mighty, mammoth, miraculous, enormous, astonishing, colossal, extraordinary, marvelous, (v) monstrous, **2**. titanic; *synonyms* (adj) gigantic, giant, massive, vast, stupendous, **3**. tremendous; *synonyms* (adj) dreadful, wonderful, formidable, fearful, awful, great, terrible, rattling, howling, awesome, brilliant, devastating, excellent, frightful, horrible; *antonym* (adj) insignificant.

toatoa 1. cubical; *synonyms* (adj) cubic, cubelike, cubiform, cuboid, cuboidal, **2**. square; *synonyms* (adj) right, even, rectangular, fair, quadrate, straight, equal, (n) area, foursquare, rectangle, quadrilateral, (v) settle, agree, correspond, (adv) just.

toatoana 1. cube; *synonyms* (n) block, rhomboid, blockage, blocking, closure, quadrangle, quadrantal, rectangle, tetragon, interference, (v) dice, chop, multiply, triplicate, (adj) unworldly, **2**. square; *synonyms* (adj) right, even, rectangular, fair, quadrate, straight, equal, equitable, (n) area, foursquare, quadrilateral, (v) settle, agree, correspond, (adv) just.

toatoanaki squared; *synonyms* (adj) square, agree, balanced, correspond, correspondent, equal, even, exact, quadrate, suit, suited.

toba 1. feed; *synonyms* (v) eat, dine, nurture, browse, board, diet, encourage, nourish, fatten, consume, feast, (n) aliment, food, provender, fare; *antonym* (v) starve, **2**. foster; *synonyms* (v) cultivate, advance, cherish, breed, boost, foment, further, rear, support, educate, entertain, tend, keep, feed, nurse; *antonym* (v) neglect, **3**. nurse; *synonyms* (n) doctor, amah, care, nanny, (v) attend, foster, harbor, lactate, cradle, raise, breastfeed, harbour, hold, suckle, minister.

tobaki 1. fostered; *synonyms* (adj) nourished, safe, **2**. nursed; *synonym* (adj) suckled.

tobi 1. caress; *synonyms* (n) rub, touch, endearment, (v) fondle, stroke, pat, pet, tickle, coddle, cuddle, kiss, **2**. massage; *synonyms* (n) manipulation, friction, (v) knead, manipulate, press, caress, abrade, abrase, apply, arrange, cajole, corrade, daub, edit, fawn, **3**. rub; *synonyms* (v) fray, grate, gall, chafe, fret, furbish, graze, irritate, massage, scrape, scratch, shine, (n) check, brush, hitch.

tobibi 1. circular; *synonyms* (adj) round, annular, circinate, globular, orbicular, rotund, rounded, spherical, (n) advertisement, bill, handbill, brochure, publication, bulletin, flier; *antonym* (adj) square, **2**. round; *synonyms* (adv) about, around, (adj) circular, plump, entire, chubby, complete, (n) circle, bout, ring, beat, circuit, (v) compass, turn, gird; *antonyms* (adj) slim, sharp.

tobu soap; *synonyms* (n) cleanser, run, (v) lather, bribe, grease, oil, wheedle, cajole, bathe, clean, flog, inveigle, lash, (adj) episodic, maudlin.

tohaine woman; *synonyms* (n) wife, girl, maid, womanhood, char, charwoman, soul, (obj) female, she; *antonyms* (n) man, gentleman.

tohount turtle; *synonyms* (n) turkle, (adj) game, venison, (v) capsize.

tohoupe steer; *synonyms* (v) guide, navigate, direct, drive, aim, conduct, manage, maneuver, run, tip, show, channel, (n) lead, point, bullock.

toitio 1. lost; *synonyms* (v) gone, missing, abandoned, (adj) doomed, forlorn, extinct, hopeless, bewildered, disoriented, forgotten, helpless, broken, confused, irrecoverable, absent; *antonyms* (adj) present, found, existing, **2**. fickle; *synonyms* (adj) erratic, capricious, volatile, inconsistent, mercurial, mobile, variable, changeful, giddy, inconstant, shifting, skittish, unfaithful, unstable, (v) changeable; *antonyms* (adj) resolute, untiring, **3**. vagrant; *synonyms* (n) tramp, drifter, hobo, wanderer, bum, nomad, (adj) vagabond, roving, itinerant, aimless, rambling, nomadic, (v) stray, unsettled, ambulatory; *antonym* (n) resident, **4**. roving; *synonyms* (adj) migratory, peregrine, errant, traveling, roaming, discursive, drifting, loose, restless, (n) wandering, ramble, rove, vagabondage, **5**. wandering; *synonyms* (adj) vagrant, lost, aberrant, delirious, incoherent, planetary, fugitive, migrant, devious, (n) peregrination, travel, roam, aberration, digression, (adv) astray.

toitioa rove; *synonyms* (v) gad, ramble, roam, range, wander, gallivant, drift, stray, stroll, tramp, err, meander, prowl, travel, walk.

toka 1. bottom; *synonyms* (n) base, basis, backside, bed, behind, foot, footing, back, arse, ass, bum, butt, buttocks, craft, floor; *antonyms* (n) top, pinnacle, (adj) highest, **2**. master; *synonyms* (n) captain, instructor, head, boss, leader, gentleman, (v) conquer, control, command, defeat, dominate, (adj) chief, original, ace, expert, **3**. mount; *synonyms* (v) ascend, rise, climb, board, arise, advance, jump, bestride, grow, increase, ride, scale, (n) hill, frame, mountain; *antonyms* (v) descend, drop, (n) valley, **4**. chief; *synonyms* (adj) principal, cardinal, capital, arch, central, essential, first, main, primary, sovereign, basic, (n) administrator, executive, paramount, superior; *antonyms* (adj) minor, associate, secondary, **5**. lord; *synonyms* (n) master, noble, sir, seignior, almighty, creator, maker, mistress, nobleman, overlord, ruler, impropriator, **6**. crush; *synonyms* (n) squeeze, press, crowd, (v) beat, break, compress, crunch, stamp, bruise, jam, mash, overpower, overwhelm, quash, squash, **7**. dominate; *synonyms* (v) prevail, reign, rule, direct, manage, overlook, possess, predominate, crush, domineer, govern, hold, influence, overrule, (adj) preponderate, **8**. dominating; *synonyms* (adj) commanding, autocratic, bossy, ascendant, ascendent, inextinguishable, unquenchable, predominant, authoritarian, authoritative, autocratical, dictatorial, leading, ascensive, despotic, **9**. overcome; *synonyms* (v) subdue, vanquish, hurdle, subjugate, surmount, demolish, affect, cross, exceed, outdo, overbear, overtake, overthrow, (adj) beaten, conquered; *antonyms* (v) fail, (adj) victorious, unimpressed, **10**. sit; *synonyms* (v) model, pose, rest, place, posture, put, seat, set, squat, meet, convene, locate, mount, stand, settle, **11**. vanquish; *synonyms* (v) overcome, rout, thrash, trounce, drub, lick, overmaster, discomfit, whip, triumph, get, quell, reduce, tame, confound; *antonym* (v) lose, **12**. top; *synonyms* (adj) maximum, superlative, (n) crown, peak, acme, apex, crest, cover, height, summit, surface, (v) best, cap, surpass, better; *antonyms* (adj) worst, (n) bottom, nadir, **13**. succeed; *synonyms* (v) follow, replace, arrive, ensue, prosper, supersede, supplant, do, achieve, flourish, displace, pursue, thrive, come, complete; *antonym* (v) precede, **14**. summit; *synonyms* (n) point, climax, tip, culmination, vertex, zenith, prime, heyday, altitude, elevation, meeting, **15**. prevail; *synonyms* (v) obtain, outweigh, persist, carry, succeed, win, endure, exist, live, take, be, continue, lead, remain, (adj) avail, **16**. prevailing; *synonyms* (adj) dominant, prevalent, rife, common, current, overriding, general, popular, epidemic, influential, powerful, usual, customary, ordinary, regular.

tokabeti 1. comfortable; *synonyms* (adj) cozy, easy, agreeable, pleased, pleasing, prosperous, congenial, pleasurable, rich, enjoyable, commodious, content, contented, (v) snug, calm; *antonyms* (adj) uncomfortable, poor, formal, tense, unpleasant, intimidating, unaccustomed, unhappy, **2**. survive; *synonyms* (v) live, outlast, outlive, subsist, endure, exist, remain, continue, last, be, abide, resist, weather, withstand, brave; *antonyms* (v) die, succumb.

tokaki 1. dominated; *synonyms* (adj) conquered, henpecked, obsessed, occupied, subject, subjugated; *antonym* (adj) liberated, **2**. crushed; *synonyms* (v) victimized, (adj) broken, beaten, low, subdued, flattened, dispirited, compressed, overwhelmed, abashed, abject, blue, brokenhearted, busted, (n) crushing; *antonyms* (adj) loose, victorious, **3**. mounted; *synonyms* (adj) equestrian, firm, **4**. bottomed; *synonym* (adj) grounded, **5**. overcome; *synonyms* (v) conquer, beat, crush, subdue, vanquish, defeat, master, overpower, hurdle, overwhelm, prevail, subjugate, surmount, demolish, affect; *antonyms* (v) fail, (adj) unimpressed, **6**. stuffed; *synonyms* (v) farctate, (adj) full, crammed, packed, congested, replete, loaded, chock-full, crowded, fraught, abounding, big, brimming, concentrated, distended; *antonyms* (adj) empty, hungry.

tokanikai 1. conquer; *synonyms* (v) beat, capture, subdue, overcome, overpower, quell, subjugate, suppress, surmount, vanquish, crush, defeat, overthrow, overturn, overwhelm; *antonyms* (v) surrender, lose, **2**. triumphant; *synonyms* (adj) jubilant, victorious, successful, triumphal, exulting, winning, conquering, elated, gleeful, joyful, prideful, rejoicing, (v) exultant; *antonym* (adj) unsuccessful, **3**. win; *synonyms* (v) acquire, gain, get, attain, obtain, conquer, achieve, earn, prevail, secure, take, succeed, carry, procure, (n) triumph, **4**. won; *synonyms* (v) wan, (n) dwelling, wone, **5**. victorious; *synonyms* (adj) triumphant, (v) triumphing; *antonym* (adj) beaten.

tokanikaia 1. dominate; *synonyms* (*v*) command, control, prevail, reign, rule, direct, manage, overlook, possess, predominate, crush, domineer, govern, hold, (*adj*) preponderate, **2.** vanquish; *synonyms* (*v*) beat, conquer, defeat, overcome, overpower, rout, subjugate, overthrow, thrash, subdue, surmount, trounce, drub, lick, overmaster; *antonym* (*v*) lose.

tokanikaiaki 1. dominated; *synonyms* (*adj*) conquered, henpecked, obsessed, occupied, subject, subjugated; *antonym* (*adj*) liberated, **2.** won; *synonyms* (*v*) wan, (*n*) dwelling, wone.

tokara ride; *synonyms* (*n*) outing, run, lift, jaunt, voyage, (*v*) drive, bait, float, mount, rag, tease, harass, annoy, drift, (*adj*) bestride.

tokarake 1. dominate; *synonyms* (*v*) command, control, prevail, reign, rule, direct, manage, overlook, possess, predominate, crush, domineer, govern, hold, (*adj*) preponderate, **2.** elevate; *synonyms* (*v*) raise, advance, lift, boost, erect, exalt, hoist, cheer, dignify, promote, rear, aggrandize, uphold, animate, ennoble; *antonyms* (*v*) demote, lower, **3.** overcome; *synonyms* (*v*) conquer, beat, subdue, vanquish, defeat, master, overpower, hurdle, overwhelm, subjugate, surmount, demolish, affect, cross, (*adj*) beaten; *antonyms* (*v*) fail, (*adj*) victorious, unimpressed.

tokarakeaki 1. dominated; *synonyms* (*adj*) conquered, henpecked, obsessed, occupied, subject, subjugated; *antonym* (*adj*) liberated, **2.** elevated; *synonyms* (*adj*) high, exalted, lofty, noble, towering, grand, great, majestic, tall, elated, magnanimous, advanced, dignified, eminent, (*v*) steep; *antonym* (*adj*) short, **3.** overcome; *synonyms* (*v*) conquer, beat, crush, subdue, vanquish, defeat, master, overpower, hurdle, overwhelm, prevail, subjugate, surmount, demolish, (*adj*) beaten; *antonyms* (*v*) fail, (*adj*) victorious, unimpressed.

tokatake chief; *synonyms* (*adj*) head, principal, cardinal, capital, arch, central, essential, first, main, (*n*) administrator, boss, captain, executive, leader, paramount; *antonyms* (*adj*) minor, associate, secondary.

toki 1. end; *synonyms* (*n*) close, aim, closure, destination, conclusion, death, cause, demise, object, (*v*) cease, complete, finish, discontinue, conclude, (*prep*) consequence; *antonyms* (*n*) beginning, maintenance, opening, middle, (*v*) start, begin, continue, **2.** discontinue; *synonyms* (*v*) stop, break, abandon, desist, drop, terminate, interrupt, quit, adjourn, part, end, pause, separate, stay, suspend, **3.** conclude; *synonyms* (*v*) gather, accomplish, assume, deduce, determine, resolve, settle, decide, derive, do, generalize, judge, reason, understand, suppose, **4.** lapse; *synonyms* (*n*) fall, error, fault, mistake, oversight, omission, blunder, (*v*) relapse, decline, expire, elapse, collapse,

degenerate, die, backslide, **5.** arrest; *synonyms* (*n*) check, halt, apprehension, custody, hold, detention, (*v*) capture, catch, apprehend, collar, delay, detain, get, hinder, inhibit; *antonyms* (*v*) release, discharge, **6.** abate; *synonyms* (*v*) subside, allay, bate, diminish, fade, flag, lessen, relax, relieve, remit, slack, slake, wane, weaken, (*adj*) slacken; *antonym* (*v*) increase, **7.** cease; *synonyms* (*v*) abstain, lapse, leave, block, cut, perish, refrain, stint, disappear, vanish, (*n*) termination, cessation, (*adj*) abate, **8.** final; *synonyms* (*adj*) conclusive, decisive, definite, extreme, latter, definitive, last, ultimate, irrevocable, decided, concluding, eventual, net, peremptory, firm; *antonyms* (*adj*) first, preliminary, **9.** terminate; *synonyms* (*v*) dismiss, dissolve, can, result, abort, bound, cancel, ax, culminate, extinguish, fire, go, sack, sever, consummate; *antonym* (*v*) establish, **10.** stop; *synonyms* (*v*) stand, obstruct, plug, disrupt, dwell, impede, intercept, prevent, (*n*) arrest, bar, curb, recess, obstruction, point, rest; *antonyms* (*v*) encourage, permit, prolong.

tokia stow; *synonyms* (*v*) pack, cram, charge, house, load, store, place, squeeze, deposit, crush, put, accommodate, compress, keep, stuff.

tokiaki 1. arrested; *synonyms* (*adj*) backward, intermittent, **2.** ended; *synonyms* (*adj*) complete, concluded, finished, over, completed, done, closed, past, terminated, through, consummate, **3.** discontinued; *antonym* (*adj*) continued, **4.** concluded; *synonyms* (*adj*) accomplished, (*adv*) ended, **5.** stowed, **6.** terminated; *synonym* (*adj*) extinct, **7.** stopped; *synonyms* (*adj*) halted, congested, unmoving, blocked, chinked, clogged, immobile, motionless, static, stationary, bunged, crashed, still.

tokina 1. end; *synonyms* (*n*) close, aim, closure, destination, conclusion, death, cause, demise, object, (*v*) cease, complete, finish, discontinue, conclude, (*prep*) consequence; *antonyms* (*n*) beginning, maintenance, opening, middle, (*v*) start, begin, continue, **2.** finish; *synonyms* (*v*) end, achieve, execute, accomplish, determine, consume, do, stop, (*n*) consummate, ending, finale, glaze, accomplishment, coating, completion, **3.** finite; *synonyms* (*adj*) bounded, limited, mortal, conditioned, demarcated; *antonyms* (*adj*) infinite, countless, endless, never-ending.

tokinaki 1. ended; *synonyms* (*adj*) complete, concluded, finished, over, completed, done, closed, past, terminated, through, consummate, **2.** finished; *synonyms* (*adj*) ended, perfect, absolute, accomplished, polished, ripe, ruined, spent, round, capable, decided, final, elegant, exhausted, fitted; *antonyms* (*adj*) unfinished, incomplete, remaining, rough.

tokira 1. weakly; *synonyms (adv)* feebly, badly, faintly, softly, *(adj)* feeble, infirm, weak, decrepit, faint, frail, sapless; *antonyms (adv)* strongly, confidently, firmly, powerfully, **2.** stunted; *synonyms (adj)* small, scrubby, little, scrawny, diminutive, puny, short, spare, *(v)* strangulated, **3.** undeveloped; *synonyms (adj)* backward, rudimentary, immature, embryonic, latent, fallow, crude, early, potential, premature, young; *antonyms (adj)* developed, mature, active, considered.

tokitoki 1. intermittent; *synonyms (adj)* broken, occasional, sporadic, discontinuous, fitful, irregular, periodic, spasmodic, recurrent, recurring, uneven, frequent, infrequent, restless; *antonyms (adj)* continuous, constant, continual, repeated, **2.** sporadic; *synonyms (adj)* intermittent, rare, sparse, few, scarce, episodic, uncommon, *(v)* broadcast, dispread; *antonyms (adj)* nonstop, regular.

toko 1. extremely; *synonyms (adv)* very, exceedingly, awfully, enormously, excessively, extraordinarily, much, badly, desperately, exceptionally, greatly, hugely, infinitely, terribly, *(adj)* highly; *antonyms (adv)* mildly, fairly, quite, slightly, **2.** altogether; *synonyms (adv)* absolutely, all, wholly, completely, entirely, perfectly, purely, simply, totally, ensemble, fully, utterly, generally, thoroughly, whole; *antonym (adv)* partly.

tokobeka 1. importunate; *synonyms (adj)* troublesome, annoying, exigent, insistent, pressing, instant, demanding, earnest, pleading, urgent, appealing, imploring, *(v)* important; *antonym (adj)* halfhearted, **2.** annoying; *synonyms (adj)* galling, irritating, vexatious, aggravating, awkward, bothersome, disagreeable, grating, inconvenient, offensive, pesky, trying, vexing, worrying, *(n)* annoyance; *antonyms (adj)* pleasing, soothing, **3.** upsetting; *synonyms (adj)* disconcerting, disturbing, distressing, poignant, sad; *antonyms (adj)* comforting, reassuring.

tokobito 1. importunate; *synonyms (adj)* troublesome, annoying, exigent, insistent, pressing, instant, demanding, earnest, pleading, urgent, appealing, imploring, *(v)* important; *antonym (adj)* halfhearted, **2.** annoying; *synonyms (adj)* galling, irritating, vexatious, aggravating, awkward, bothersome, disagreeable, grating, inconvenient, offensive, pesky, trying, vexing, worrying, *(n)* annoyance; *antonyms (adj)* pleasing, soothing, **3.** vexing; *synonyms (adj)* infuriating, maddening, exasperating, pestiferous, **4.** upsetting; *synonyms (adj)* disconcerting, disturbing, distressing, poignant, sad; *antonyms (adj)* comforting, reassuring.

tokobuakoako 1. jumbled; *synonyms (adj)* confused, disorderly, disordered, disorganized, untidy, cluttered, mixed, muddled, chaotic, incoherent, topsy-turvy; *antonyms (adj)* neat, tidy, **2.** bushy; *synonyms (adj)* dense, shagged, hairy, shaggy, bearded, furry, hispid, pappous, pilous, villous, rough, profuse, disheveled, hirsute, queachy; *antonym (adj)* bald, **3.** wooded; *synonyms (adj)* forested, leafy.

tokoie 1. annoying; *synonyms (adj)* galling, irritating, troublesome, vexatious, aggravating, awkward, bothersome, disagreeable, grating, inconvenient, offensive, pesky, trying, vexing, *(n)* annoyance; *antonyms (adj)* pleasing, soothing, **2.** importunate; *synonyms (adj)* annoying, exigent, insistent, pressing, instant, demanding, earnest, pleading, urgent, appealing, imploring, *(v)* important; *antonym (adj)* halfhearted, **3.** senseless; *synonyms (adj)* foolish, meaningless, absurd, insensible, irrational, mindless, pointless, preposterous, stupid, idiotic, fatuous, inane, insane, purposeless, silly; *antonym (adj)* sensible.

tokomangaongao encumbered; *synonyms (adj)* laden, burdened, burdensome, clayey, cloggy, deep, heavy, forcible, full, gloomy, inactive, loud, oppressive, overloaded, ponderous.

tokomeme verbose; *synonyms (adj)* wordy, prolix, tedious, redundant, garrulous, lengthy, talkative, windy, copious, diffuse, loquacious, boring, dull, fluent, rhetorical; *antonym (adj)* concise.

tokora cut; *synonyms (v)* carve, chop, clip, abbreviate, abridge, bite, condense, crop, drop, fashion, *(n)* notch, slice, cutting, nick, blow; *antonyms (v)* increase, lengthen, *(n)* addition, extension.

tokoran 1. braid; *synonyms (n)* plait, pigtail, tress, band, braiding, *(v)* plat, twine, entwine, intertwine, mat, *(adj)* knit, string, embroider, lace, tie; *antonym (v)* unbraid, **2.** cord; *synonyms (n)* bond, tape, rope, thread, whipcord, yarn, leash, fiber, cable, corduroy, strand, tether, twist, wire, *(v)* knot.

tokouki breath; *synonyms (n)* spirit, wind, air, inspiration, puff, aspiration, breather, breeze, flash, flatus, gust, instant, jiffy, respite, *(adj)* whisper.

toma 1. interface; *synonyms (n)* link, port, boundary, junction, border, circumference, communication, display, *(v)* contact, combine, connect, merge, amalgamate, collaborate, communicate, **2.** adjoin; *synonyms (v)* abut, annex, touch, neighbor, edge, meet, append, verge, butt, *(adj)* join, **3.** join; *synonyms (v)* unite, associate, graft, assemble, affiliate, attach, affix, conjoin, converge, couple, enroll, fasten, integrate, interconnect, *(n)* bond; *antonyms (v)* detach, secede, separate, split, undo, **4.** inhale; *synonyms (v)* breathe, absorb, imbibe, draw, suck, drag, drink, attract, inspire, receive, respire, admit, import, ingest, *(n)* sniff; *antonym (v)* exhale, **5.** link; *synonyms (n)* connection, joint, concatenation, association, attachment, liaison, *(v)* tie, bridge, relate, yoke, bind, fix, *(adj)* correlation, lock, hook, **6**. append; *synonyms* (*v*) adjoin, add, include, suffix, suspend, tack, insert, supplement, supply, (*adj*) hang, **7**. couple; *synonyms* (*n*) brace, duo, dyad, twosome, couplet, deuce, duad, duet, (*v*) pair, copulate, match, mate, wed, hitch, marry; *antonym* (*v*) uncouple, **8**. splice; *synonyms* (*n*) splicing, (*v*) inosculate, twine, anastomose, calk, careen, caulk, dovetail, (*adj*) braid, lace, **9**. unite; *synonyms* (*v*) blend, coalesce, fuse, unify, agree, league, mix, concentrate, consolidate, gather, incorporate, concur, band, compound, confederate; *antonym* (*v*) divide, **10**. seam; *synonyms* (*n*) layer, bed, furrow, line, juncture, crease, ridge, stratum, (*v*) crinkle, joining, articulation, wrinkle, commissure, sew, stitch, **11**. suck; *synonyms* (*v*) nurse, lactate, suckle, drain, puff, aspirate, pull, breastfeed, (*n*) sucking, suction, **12**. readjust; *synonyms* (*v*) adapt, adjust, regulate, reset, readapt, suit, balance, redispose, (*adj*) dress, **13**. sip; *synonyms* (*n*) nip, gulp, swallow, taste, bite, drop, mouthful, shot, slurp, swig, nibble, (*v*) sample, quaff, lap, (*adj*) sup.

tomaki 1. linked; *synonyms* (*adj*) connected, allied, coupled, joined, related, associated, correlated, united; *antonym* (*adj*) unrelated, **2**. joined; *synonyms* (*adj*) combined, joint, amalgamated, linked, concerted; *antonym* (*adj*) separate, **3**. coupled; *synonyms* (*adj*) conjugate, double, conjugated, **4**. inhaled; *synonym* (*adj*) inspired, **5**. united; *synonyms* (*adj*) cooperative, mutual, mixed, common, conjunctive, undivided, conjunct, unanimous, conjoint, collective, one, together, (*v*) consolidated, join, (*n*) harmonious; *antonyms* (*adj*) individual, divided.

tong 1. faint; *synonyms* (*adj*) collapse, dim, dizzy, feeble, indistinct, weak, dull, gentle, soft, vague, delicate, distant, (*v*) languish, swoon, droop; *antonyms* (*adj*) distinct, strong, clear, obvious, considerable, loud, pungent, **2**. the; *synonyms* (*n*) queenliness, stateliness, (*v*) thee, **3**. swoon; *synonyms* (*n*) fainting, syncope, deliquium, lipothymy, prostration, (*v*) faint, conk, die, (*adj*) blow, drop, gasp, pant, puff.

tonga 1. instruct; *synonyms* (*v*) charge, advise, direct, educate, enlighten, teach, command, drill, indoctrinate, inform, apprise, bid, coach, discipline, edify; *antonym* (*v*) request, **2**. cram; *synonyms* (*v*) stuff, pack, ram, fill, jam, compress, load, shove, compact, ingurgitate, overeat, englut, gormandise, gormandize, gourmandize, **3**. nourish; *synonyms* (*v*) breed, foster, keep, cradle, aliment, cherish, cultivate, feed, maintain, nurture, sustain, supply, entertain, encourage, help, **4**. educate; *synonyms* (*v*) civilize, instruct, train, develop, groom, rear, school, condition, refine, guide, nourish, tutor, prepare.

tongaki 1. instructed; *synonyms* (*v*) erudite, leaned, lettered, (*adj*) educated, taught, tutored, enlightened, arranged, experienced, furnished, instruct, intelligent, qualified, schooled, provided, **2**. nourished; *synonym* (*adj*) fostered, **3**. educated; *synonyms* (*v*) instructed, (*adj*) cultured, learned, trained, informed, refined; *antonyms* (*adj*) uneducated, ignorant.

tonginako 1. horrified; *synonyms* (*v*) chagrined, (*adj*) afraid, aghast, alarmed, dismayed, frightened, scared, terrified, ashamed, crushed, devastated, embarrassed, humiliated, petrified, shocked, **2**. stunned; *synonyms* (*adj*) astonished, astounded, dumbfounded, amazed, dazed, flabbergasted, bewildered, staggered, stupefied, astonied, confused, stupid, surprised, groggy, kayoed, **3**. stupefied; *synonyms* (*adj*) stunned, dumfounded.

toninta gravel; *synonyms* (*n*) grit, (*v*) bedevil, get, nonplus, rag, baffle, bewilder, flummox, mystify, perplex, puzzle, (*adj*) bother, dirt, grating, gravelly.

tonu 1. grammatical; *synonym* (*adj*) grammatic, **2**. euphonic; *synonyms* (*adj*) euphonious, euphonical, melodious, sweet, **3**. noon; *synonyms* (*n*) midday, noonday, noontide, crest, lunchtime, (*adj*) meridian, culmination, meridional.

too 1. broom; *synonyms* (*n*) besom, brush, heather, ling, burbot, cusk, (*v*) sweep, filter, rake, riddle, screen, shovel, sieve, bream, cross, **2**. paddler; *synonym* (*n*) canoeist.

toouk blow; *synonyms* (*n*) bang, beat, blast, knock, shock, wallop, gust, hit, jolt, (*v*) puff, bloom, blossom, pant, play, (*adj*) gasp; *antonyms* (*v*) calm, save.

tooun wrestle; *synonyms* (*v*) struggle, fight, grapple, scuffle, strive, battle, wrench, tussle, contest, scramble, clash, brawl, squirm, (*n*) wrestling, grappling.

torara 1. gnash; *synonyms* (*v*) grind, grate, frown, gnarl, clench, snap, rasp, cheerful, chirk, growl, lower, pout, scowl, snarl, groan, **2**. groan; *synonyms* (*n*) grumble, cry, rumble, complaint, wail, gripe, (*v*) moan, murmur, howl, mutter, sigh, complain, squeak, scrape, sough, **3**. grind; *synonyms* (*v*) labor, toil, comminute, crunch, drudge, abrade, chew, crush, file, mash, sharpen, whet, (*n*) mill, drudgery, struggle, **4**. squeak; *synonyms* (*n*) screech, chirp, squeaker, (*v*) shriek, scream, peep, creak, screak, yell, cheep, yelp, shrill, pipe, sing, tweet.

toraraki ground; *synonyms* (*n*) base, cause, land, floor, reason, dirt, field, soil, account, country, basis, (*v*) bottom, found, establish, fix; *antonym* (*n*) ceiling.

torea sip; *synonyms* (*n*) nip, gulp, swallow, taste, bite, drop, mouthful, shot, slurp, (*v*) drink, imbibe, sample, quaff, lap, (*adj*) sup.

toro squat; *synonyms* (*adj*) dumpy, short, chunky, squatty, stumpy, thick, low, squab, (*v*) crouch, perch, sit, bend, settle, couch, cower.

toroa rasp; *synonyms* (*v*) grate, scrape, abrade, chafe, file, grind, rub, scratch, grater, graze, groan, squeak, fray, screech, jar.

toroba 1. coax; *synonyms* (*v*) wheedle, allure, cajole, entice, charm, blarney, inveigle, persuade, seduce, flatter, induce, (*n*) tempt, captivate, conciliate, fascinate, **2.** flatter; *synonyms* (*v*) coax, fawn, court, adulate, blandish, grovel, kowtow, soap, compliment, indulge, praise, suit, become, puff, (*n*) caress, **3.** cajole; *synonyms* (*v*) palaver, beguile, delude, humbug, lure, **4.** caress; *synonyms* (*n*) rub, touch, endearment, (*v*) fondle, stroke, pat, pet, tickle, coddle, cuddle, kiss, **5.** rub; *synonyms* (*v*) fray, grate, gall, chafe, abrade, fret, furbish, graze, irritate, massage, scrape, scratch, (*n*) check, brush, hitch.

torobakara untidy; *synonyms* (*adj*) slovenly, disheveled, disordered, disorderly, messy, sloppy, unkempt, confused, disorganized, frowzy, scruffy, sluttish, slipshod, dowdy, tousled; *antonyms* (*adj*) tidy, neat, elegant.

torokaran lurk; *synonyms* (*v*) ambush, ambuscade, conceal, prowl, skulk, waylay, loiter, lurch, creep, slink, sneak, wait, bushwhack, linger.

torokarana waylay; *synonyms* (*v*) ambush, ambuscade, lurk, accost, besiege, bushwhack, harass, scupper.

torona 1. enslave; *synonyms* (*v*) bind, enthrall, captivate, slave, subjugate, tame, chain, confine; *antonym* (*v*) liberate, **2.** subject; *synonyms* (*n*) matter, citizen, affair, dependent, inferior, issue, motif, question, point, area, content, discipline, field, (*adj*) liable, exposed; *antonym* (*adj*) liberated.

toronaki enslaved; *synonyms* (*adj*) bond, captive, beguiled, bound, captivated, charmed, cringing, delighted, dependent, enthralled, imprisoned, incarcerated, obsequious, servile, subject; *antonym* (*adj*) free.

toronibai 1. established; *synonyms* (*v*) settled, (*adj*) conventional, accepted, firm, fixed, regular, set, decided, confirmed, secure, accomplished, customary, effected, orthodox, completed; *antonym* (*adj*) unproven, **2.** stable; *synonyms* (*adj*) permanent, reliable, constant, durable, fast, lasting, stationary, enduring, hard, persistent, solid, sound, steady, immovable, certain; *antonyms* (*adj*) unstable, shaky, wobbly, dangerous, precarious, rickety, volatile.

toronibwai 1. real; *synonyms* (*adj*) genuine, material, physical, true, concrete, literal, natural, positive, pure, native, right, good, absolute, (*n*) authentic, (*v*) actual; *antonyms* (*adj*) unreal, imaginary, apparent, artificial, fake, bogus, deceptive, false, fantasy,

imitation, insubstantial, mock, nominal, (*v*) pretend, **2.** wealthy; *synonyms* (*adj*) rich, moneyed, affluent, flush, opulent, prosperous, loaded, substantial, generous, abounding, abundant, ample, monied, successful, thriving; *antonyms* (*adj*) poor, impoverished, **3.** rich; *synonyms* (*adj*) copious, fertile, productive, fruitful, full, deep, fat, luxurious, plentiful, prolific, bright, liberal, heavy, fecund, (*v*) ornate; *antonyms* (*adj*) broke, destitute, light.

toronrang 1. neglected; *synonyms* (*adj*) abandoned, dilapidated, disregarded, ignored, derelict, deserted, ancient, antiquated, antique, disused, forsaken, obsolete, shabby, unnoticed, **2.** beggarly; *synonyms* (*adj*) abject, base, mean, miserable, poor, scrubby, sorry, humble, cheap, ignoble, meager, paltry, pitiful, wretched, (*n*) vile, **3.** destitute; *synonyms* (*adj*) indigent, bankrupt, broke, forlorn, impoverished, needy, helpless, impecunious, necessitous, penniless, void, wanting, bare, deficient, (*v*) devoid; *antonym* (*adj*) rich, **4.** poor; *synonyms* (*adj*) bad, low, deplorable, destitute, evil, inadequate, insufficient, pathetic, piteous, meagre, feeble, lean, nasty, pitiable, poverty-stricken; *antonyms* (*adj*) wealthy, excellent, first-rate, privileged, well-off, admirable, good, **5.** wretched; *synonyms* (*adj*) unfortunate, unhappy, sad, lamentable, woeful, contemptible, desolate, despicable, hapless, desperate, abominable, woebegone, grievous, squalid, wicked; *antonym* (*adj*) happy.

tororo fan; *synonyms* (*n*) admirer, buff, devotee, enthusiast, addict, adherent, afficionado, fiend, follower, advocate, disciple, (*v*) air, winnow, refresh, blow; *antonym* (*n*) detractor.

torotakanana 1. dirty; *synonyms* (*adj*) foul, dirt, contemptible, bawdy, contaminated, dingy, impure, despicable, (*v*) muddy, corrupt, soil, contaminate, begrime, bemire, (*n*) defile; *antonyms* (*adj*) hygienic, pure, spotless, immaculate, (*v*) clean, **2.** filthy; *synonyms* (*adj*) dirty, nasty, unclean, disgusting, squalid, awful, grimy, grubby, indecent, ribald, smutty, sordid, vile, vulgar, distasteful; *antonym* (*adj*) decent.

torotangako 1. dirty; *synonyms* (*adj*) foul, dirt, contemptible, bawdy, contaminated, dingy, impure, despicable, (*v*) muddy, corrupt, soil, contaminate, begrime, bemire, (*n*) defile; *antonyms* (*adj*) hygienic, pure, spotless, immaculate, (*v*) clean, **2.** untidy; *synonyms* (*adj*) slovenly, disheveled, disordered, disorderly, messy, sloppy, unkempt, confused, disorganized, frowzy, scruffy, sluttish, slipshod, dowdy, tousled; *antonyms* (*adj*) tidy, neat, elegant.

torotoroba rub; *synonyms* (*v*) fray, grate, gall, chafe, abrade, caress, fret, furbish, graze, irritate, massage, scrape, (*n*) check, brush, hitch.

toto 1. decomposing; *synonyms* (*adj*) rotten, moldering, rotting, crumbling, decayed, decaying, decomposed, moldy, mouldering, putrefying, rancid, bad, fetid, putrid, rank, **2.** groan; *synonyms* (*n*) grumble, cry, rumble, complaint, wail, (*v*) moan, murmur, howl, mutter, sigh, complain, squeak, scrape, rasp, sough, **3.** decomposed; *synonyms* (*adj*) malodorous, off, corroded, decomposing, disintegrating, fusty, musty, perished, stale; *antonym* (*adj*) fresh, **4.** indolent; *synonyms* (*adj*) idle, inactive, lazy, slothful, sluggish, careless, drowsy, dull, faineant, inert, listless, otiose, slow, torpid, lackadaisical; *antonyms* (*adj*) energetic, active, **5.** impotent; *synonyms* (*adj*) powerless, helpless, feeble, barren, inadequate, incapable, ineffective, unable, weak, frigid; *antonym* (*adj*) potent, **6.** moan; *synonyms* (*n*) groan, gripe, whine, lament, grievance, grouse, protest, sob, (*v*) bewail, mourn, bleat, weep, whimper, hum, regret, **7.** stole; *synonyms* (*n*) scarf, wrap, stolon, robe, alb, cassock, chasuble, cope, dalmatic, gown, mozetta, pallium, scapulary, surplice, tunicle, **8.** tender; *synonyms* (*adj*) affectionate, painful, loving, sensitive, soft, sore, compassionate, delicate, fond, gentle, mild, (*v*) proffer, (*n*) offer, bid, overture; *antonyms* (*adj*) tough, hard, hardhearted, rubbery, rough, **9.** slimy; *synonyms* (*adj*) greasy, slippery, muddy, squalid, oily, oozy, ropy, viscous, slimed, **10.** soft; *synonyms* (*adj*) easy, light, limp, balmy, quiet, slack, loose, clement, faint, flabby, flaccid, frail, lenient, pliant, (*v*) low; *antonyms* (*adj*) firm, harsh, loud, hoarse, solid, stiff, alcoholic, shrill, strong, **11.** whine; *synonyms* (*n*) drone, (*v*) squeal, buzz, grizzle, screech, snivel, bawl, blubber, yammer, kick, kvetch, **12.** steal; *synonyms* (*v*) abstract, lift, purloin, creep, filch, misappropriate, pilfer, pinch, plunder, rob, snatch, sneak, plagiarize, slip, (*n*) bargain.

totoaki stolen; *synonyms* (*adj*) purloined, furtive, misbegotten, secret, sly, stealthy.

totoka 1. evade; *synonyms* (*v*) elude, avoid, escape, dodge, equivocate, parry, circumvent, duck, hedge, sidestep, skirt, bilk, fudge, neglect, omit; *antonym* (*v*) confront, **2.** avoid; *synonyms* (*v*) shun, avert, evade, abstain, annul, forbear, ignore, prevent, shirk, fly, beware, balk, debar, flee, (*adj*) eschew; *antonyms* (*v*) associate, face, tackle, **3.** parry; *synonyms* (*n*) counterpunch, (*v*) counter, deflect, block, fence, flinch, fend, repel, blench, blink, defeat.

totoki ending; *synonyms* (*n*) conclusion, end, close, closure, closing, completion, finish, termination, dissolution, death, stop, demise, (*adj*) last,

concluding, dying; *antonyms* (*n*) start, beginning, middle.

totokoa 1. prop; *synonyms* (*n*) support, post, shore, fulcrum, property, mainstay, airscrew, column, pillar, stay, (*v*) buttress, brace, bolster, hold, rest, **2.** support; *synonyms* (*n*) help, stand, aid, keep, comfort, maintenance, patronage, (*v*) assist, prop, back, encourage, maintain, bear, boost, carry; *antonyms* (*n*) hindrance, (*v*) oppose, neglect, undermine, abandon, reject, weaken, **3.** stay; *synonyms* (*v*) remain, reside, stop, abide, continue, endure, pause, arrest, bide, dwell, (*n*) delay, halt, check, (*adj*) cease, inhabit; *antonyms* (*v*) leave, change, abscond, depart.

totokoaki supported; *synonyms* (*v*) borne, carried, conveyed, supporting, (*adj*) bolstered, based, (*adv*) on.

tou 1. trample; *synonyms* (*v*) tramp, oppress, crush, squash, stamp, tread, defeat, flatten, (*n*) trampling, **2.** pandanus.

touaki trampled; *synonyms* (*adj*) trodden, crushed, compressed, flattened, compacted, firmed; *antonym* (*adj*) loose.

touan stone; *synonyms* (*n*) jewel, rock, calculus, gem, pebble, concretion, gemstone, kernel, bullet, granite, (*v*) pit, lapidate, pelt, cake, clot.

touariki pound; *synonyms* (*v*) beat, pen, bang, crush, flap, grind, hammer, maul, palpitate, thump, mash, buffet, grate, baste, bruise.

toubeka 1. crush; *synonyms* (*n*) squeeze, press, crowd, (*v*) beat, break, compress, conquer, crunch, stamp, bruise, jam, mash, overpower, overwhelm, quash, **2.** tread; *synonyms* (*v*) step, pace, walk, trample, crush, plod, (*n*) gait, rate, stride, tramp, footstep, rung, track.

toubekaki crushed; *synonyms* (*v*) victimized, (*adj*) broken, beaten, low, subdued, conquered, flattened, dispirited, compressed, overwhelmed, abashed, abject, blue, brokenhearted, (*n*) crushing; *antonyms* (*adj*) loose, victorious.

toue chief; *synonyms* (*adj*) head, principal, cardinal, capital, arch, central, essential, first, main, (*n*) administrator, boss, captain, executive, leader, paramount; *antonyms* (*adj*) minor, associate, secondary.

touhana one; *synonyms* (*pron*) any, man, (*n*) anybody, single, somebody, person, ace, (*adj*) certain, individual, lone, only, unique, some, singular, (*adv*) once.

touma shed; *synonyms* (*v*) cast, discard, drop, moult, scatter, exuviate, molt, dismiss, disgorge, emit, fling, (*n*) hut, shack, cabin, booth.

tounene 1. resistant; *synonyms* (*adj*) immune, impervious, durable, tough, defiant, proof, rebellious, hardy, fast, solid, stable, strong, antagonistic, insubordinate, (*v*) resistive; *antonyms* *(adj)* fragile, permeable, submissive, agreeable, **2.** stubborn; *synonyms (adj)* obstinate, contrary, hard, intractable, perverse, determined, obdurate, persistent, refractory, rigid, tenacious, inveterate, contumacious, difficult, firm; *antonyms (adj)* compliant, flexible, irresolute, amenable.

tourake 1. chained; *synonym (adj)* enchained, **2.** linked; *synonyms (adj)* connected, allied, coupled, joined, related, associated, correlated, united; *antonym (adj)* unrelated, **3.** start; *synonyms (v)* begin, originate, commence, drive, launch, embark, spring, activate, arise, *(n)* jump, onset, origin, shock, beginning, commencement; *antonyms (v)* end, finish, stop, conclude, halt, *(n)* conclusion.

tourika 1. crush; *synonyms (n)* squeeze, press, crowd, *(v)* beat, break, compress, conquer, crunch, stamp, bruise, jam, mash, overpower, overwhelm, quash, **2.** beat; *synonyms (v)* batter, flap, pulsate, throb, tick, trounce, whip, bat, baste, cheat, *(n)* pulse, thump, knock, round, cadence; *antonym (v)* lose, **3.** powder; *synonyms (n)* dust, gunpowder, explosive, *(v)* grind, crush, pound, pulverise, pulverize, sprinkle, bespangle, **4.** splinter; *synonyms (n)* sliver, fragment, part, shaving, shred, fracture, piece, flinders, *(v)* split, chip, crack, shiver, smash, burst, *(adj)* scrap.

tourikaki 1. beaten; *synonyms (v)* beat, *(adj)* battered, overpowered, conquered, routed, overcome; *antonym (adj)* victorious, **2.** crushed; *synonyms (v)* victimized, *(adj)* broken, beaten, low, subdued, flattened, dispirited, compressed, overwhelmed, abashed, abject, blue, brokenhearted, busted, *(n)* crushing; *antonym (adj)* loose, **3.** splintered; *synonyms (adj)* shattered, smashed, besotted, blotto, cracked, crocked, fractured, fuddled, loaded, pissed, pixilated, plastered, potty, slopped, sloshed, **4.** powdered; *synonyms (adj)* pulverized, powdery, fine, crushed, ground, milled, minced, pounded, pulverised, corned, salted, *(n)* milk, punctated.

touru 1. strain; *synonyms (n)* stress, breed, effort, stretch, exertion, race, *(v)* filter, screen, sift, tax, endeavor, exert, extend, percolate, pull; *antonym (v)* relax, **2.** wrench; *synonyms (n)* spanner, turn, twist, yank, *(v)* sprain, jerk, strain, tug, distort, contort, force, snatch, tear, wrestle, hurt, **3.** sprain; *synonyms (n)* injury, *(v)* wrench, rick, wrick, injure, pervert, *(adj)* cramp, adynamy, asthenia, cachexia, cachexy, decrepitude, delicacy, invalidation, ratten.

touruaki strained; *synonyms (adj)* forced, labored, tense, intense, constrained, laboured, unnatural, taut, tight, agonistic, agonistical, combative, farfetched; *antonyms (adj)* relaxed, natural.

touti louse; *synonyms (n)* worm, insect, cad, miscreant, morpion, nuisance, scoundrel, sneak, mite, rascal, rogue, tick, *(adj)* vermin.

tu 1. bet; *synonyms (v)* gamble, play, lay, risk, venture, *(n)* wager, stake, stakes, **2.** flow; *synonyms (n)* flood, current, discharge, abound, *(v)* stream, course, flux, jet, run, surge, float, emanate, fall, gush, pour, **3.** ooze; *synonyms (n)* mire, muck, slime, *(v)* exude, leak, dribble, seep, drain, drop, bleed, emit, filter, secrete, sweat, *(adj)* mud.

tua 1. deviate; *synonyms (v)* depart, deflect, stray, vary, digress, diverge, swerve, warp, shift, turn, wander, bend, differ, divert, *(adj)* deviant; *antonym (v)* conform, **2.** inform; *synonyms (v)* communicate, acquaint, advise, impart, announce, enlighten, tell, familiarize, explain, advertise, apprise, educate, instruct, state, warn, **3.** miss; *synonyms (v)* lack, lose, fail, jump, omit, overlook, long, drop, escape, *(n)* maid, girl, want, fille, missy, *(adj)* fault; *antonym (v)* perceive, **4.** denounce; *synonyms (v)* condemn, censure, accuse, brand, criticize, decry, damn, reproach, arraign, betray, excoriate, fulminate, impeach, scold, charge; *antonym (v)* praise, **5.** bid; *synonyms (n)* offer, tender, attempt, proffer, suggestion, *(v)* ask, call, command, invite, adjure, beseech, direct, order, summon, allure, **6.** order; *synonyms (n)* decree, dictate, array, rank, sort, class, condition, disposition, edict, injunction, instruction, kind, *(v)* commission, arrange, ordain; *antonyms (n)* anarchy, chaos, confusion, mayhem, mess, *(v)* disorder, request, **7.** snitch; *synonyms (n)* fink, *(v)* sneak, rat, tattle, pinch, lift, cop, denounce, grass, hook, peach, squeal, steal, swipe, tattletale, **8.** squeal; *synonyms (n)* scream, shout, cry, *(v)* shriek, screech, yell, howl, squeak, inform, confess, whoop, bawl, shrill, sing, squall, **9.** tell; *synonyms (v)* relate, declare, divulge, express, recount, reveal, describe, distinguish, enumerate, notify, recite, say, *(n)* disclose, count, number, **10.** report; *synonyms (n)* description, gossip, notice, name, fame, message, narration, narrative, news, notification, recital, record, story, intelligence, *(v)* account; *antonym (n)* fact, **11.** prescribe; *synonyms (v)* enjoin, assign, determine, fix, appoint, establish, impose, recommend, require, set, define, place, *(n)* legalize, **12.** ricochet; *synonyms (n)* carom, *(v)* bounce, rebound, recoil, bound, glance, kick, reverberate, skip, boom, echo, leap, **13.** testify; *synonyms (v)* attest, certify, affirm, evidence, protest, prove, demonstrate, manifest, show, vouch, indicate, assert, aver, argue, witness, **14.** tattle; *synonyms (n)* gabble, *(v)* blab, babble, chat, chatter, blather, blabber, prate, prattle, snitch, talk, blither, chitchat, jaw, natter, **15.** rebound; *synonyms (n)* backlash, repercussion, return, reaction, *(v)* ricochet, rally, boomerang, backfire, recover, reflect, resile, spring, confine, limit.

tuabebeku 1. chubby; *synonyms (adj)* buxom, fat, fleshy, plump, round, chunky, heavy, pudgy, stout, tubby, overweight; *antonyms* (*adj*) thin, skinny, slim, **2**. corpulent; *synonyms* (*adj*) obese, portly, lusty, chubby, bulky, gross, rotund, weighty, **3**. round; *synonyms* (*adv*) about, around, (*adj*) circular, entire, complete, (*n*) circle, bout, ring, beat, circuit, cycle, orbit, (*v*) compass, turn, gird; *antonym* (*adj*) sharp, **4**. plump; *synonyms* (*adj*) corpulent, full, squab, stocky, fertile, thick, embonpoint, (*v*) fatten, drop, go, dive, plop, flump, plunk, plank; *antonyms* (*adj*) emaciated, slender.

tuai never; *synonyms* (*adv*) ne'er, nevermore, nor, tomorrow; *antonym* (*adv*) always.

tuaiaia muscular; *synonyms* (*adj*) athletic, brawny, strong, burly, hefty, powerful, robust, husky, stalwart, stout, sturdy, manly, cogent, hardy, rugged; *antonyms* (*adj*) puny, slight.

tuaira steal; *synonyms* (*v*) abstract, lift, purloin, creep, filch, misappropriate, pilfer, pinch, plunder, rob, snatch, sneak, plagiarize, slip, (*n*) bargain.

tuairaki stolen; *synonyms* (*adj*) purloined, furtive, misbegotten, secret, sly, stealthy.

tuairoa grate; *synonyms* (*n*) lattice, (*v*) chafe, creak, grind, abrade, scrape, fret, gall, gnash, rub, aggravate, annoy, crunch, irritate, provoke.

tuakaei large; *synonyms* (*adj*) big, ample, extensive, generous, broad, bulky, considerable, handsome, high, heavy, abundant, capacious, great, gross, hefty; *antonyms* (*adj*) small, cramped, insignificant.

tuaki 1. missed; *synonyms* (*adj*) lost, baffled, befuddled, bemused, bewildered, confounded, confused, disoriented, forgotten, helpless, irretrievable, mazed, preoccupied, **2**. informed; *synonyms* (*adj*) aware, cognizant, educated, conscious, knowledgeable, familiar, apprised, wise, conversant, experienced, (*adv*) abreast; *antonym* (*adj*) ignorant, **3**. ordered; *synonyms* (*adj*) tidy, regular, arranged, methodical, orderly, coherent, consistent, lawful, logical, **4**. reported; *synonyms* (*adj*) narrative, putative, reputed, **5**. prescribed; *synonyms* (*adj*) ordained, appointed, set, formal, official, decreed, positive.

tuana 1. keep; *synonyms* (*v*) hold, preserve, retain, defend, continue, guard, have, maintain, celebrate, confine, conserve, observe, reserve, save, commemorate; *antonyms* (*v*) dump, lose, **2**. govern; *synonyms* (*v*) administer, control, dictate, dominate, manage, check, bridle, command, conduct, determine, regulate, reign, rule, oversee, (*n*) direct, **3**. have; *synonyms* (*v*) contain, gain, bear, carry, get, possess, accept, acquire, eat, suffer, take, allow, bring, attain, catch, **4**. rule; *synonyms* (*n*) govern, order, decree, dominion, law, ordinance, principle, authority, government, line, precept, regulation, sway, (*v*) influence, measure, **5**. take; *synonyms* (*v*) admit, adopt, clutch, obtain, return, borrow, pick, appropriate, assume, capture, claim,

convey, demand, (*n*) seize, (*phr*) receive; *antonyms* (*v*) give, refuse, abstain, add, **6**. regulate; *synonyms* (*v*) adjust, arrange, fix, modulate, regularize, align, correct, decide, guide, organize, rectify, shape, accommodate, frame, (*n*) form.

tuanaki 1. kept; *synonyms* (*adj*) reserved, detained, intransitive, unbroken, unploughed, unplowed, **2**. governed; *synonyms* (*adj*) subject, (*adv*) under, **3**. ruled; *synonyms* (*adj*) lined, lawful, feint, hatched, **4**. regulated; *synonyms* (*adj*) orderly, ordered, arranged, consistent, logical, regular, regulatory, temperate, systematic, (*adv*) synchronized, **5**. taken; *synonyms* (*v*) take, (*adj*) occupied, full, interpreted, besotted, crazed, enamored, engaged, interested, lovesick, obsessed, overcome, preferred, rapt, unavailable.

tuanga 1. demonstrate; *synonyms* (*v*) prove, authenticate, attest, display, establish, exhibit, present, show, argue, certify, confirm, evidence, exemplify, explain, indicate; *antonyms* (*v*) disprove, conceal, **2**. command; *synonyms* (*n*) control, instruction, behest, bidding, decree, direction, administration, ascendancy, authority, (*v*) charge, order, rule, call, commission, direct; *antonym* (*v*) request, **3**. inform; *synonyms* (*v*) communicate, acquaint, advise, impart, announce, enlighten, tell, familiarize, advertise, apprise, educate, instruct, state, warn, describe, **4**. counsel; *synonyms* (*n*) caution, advocate, advisement, admonition, attorney, consultation, counselor, exhortation, guidance, recommendation, (*v*) advice, consult, admonish, confer, exhort, **5**. barn; *synonyms* (*n*) shed, store, stable, bawn, auditorium, bacilli, bacillus, lathe, bel, boron, shelter, (*adj*) foul, unclean, **6**. warn; *synonyms* (*v*) counsel, inform, alert, threaten, notify, reprove, deter, discourage, dissuade, bid, dehort, expostulate, menace, monish, previse, **7**. show; *synonyms* (*v*) broadcast, expose, guide, parade, demonstrate, disclose, give, manifest, perform, (*n*) appearance, produce, ostentation, presentation, pageant, picture; *antonym* (*v*) hide.

tuangaki 1. demonstrated; *synonyms* (*adj*) confirmed, established, tried, verified, **2**. informed; *synonyms* (*adj*) aware, cognizant, educated, conscious, knowledgeable, familiar, apprised, wise, conversant, experienced, (*adv*) abreast; *antonym* (*adj*) ignorant.

tuangia tell; *synonyms* (*v*) relate, declare, divulge, express, impart, recount, reveal, explain, announce, command, communicate, describe, distinguish, (*n*) disclose, count; *antonym* (*v*) request.

tuanokunoku 1. grazed; *synonyms* (*adj*) hurt, raw, **2**. skimmed; *synonyms* (*adj*) skim, (*v*) flet, flotten.

tuanonoku 1. bulky; *synonyms* (*adj*) big, large, unwieldy, ample, corpulent, cumbersome, fat, great, gross, heavy, huge, stout, substantial, awkward, (adv) portly; **antonyms** (adj) small, compact, manageable, **2.** stocky; **synonyms** (adj) thick, chunky, heavyset, stubby, thickset, dumpy, short, husky, robust, bulky, sturdy, (n) burly; **antonym** (adj) slim, **3.** squat; **synonyms** (adj) squatty, stumpy, low, squab, podgy, stocky, (v) crouch, perch, sit, bend, settle, couch, cower, bow, (n) squatting.

tuarere 1. restive; **synonyms** (adj) obstinate, edgy, fidgety, jittery, jumpy, nervy, restless, uptight, restiff, nervous, tense, uneasy, unruly, overstrung, (v) skittish; **antonym** (adj) relaxed, **2.** restless; **synonyms** (adj) unquiet, agitated, apprehensive, fretful, impatient, restive, feverish, turbulent, disturbed, wakeful, eager, hasty, mercurial, frightened, (v) anxious; **antonym** (adj) calm.

tuariri 1. bony; **synonyms** (adj) osseous, gaunt, lean, thin, angular, emaciated, scrawny, skinny, lanky, meager, boney, spare; **antonym** (adj) rounded, **2.** robust; **synonyms** (adj) healthy, firm, strong, athletic, brawny, muscular, powerful, vigorous, lusty, mighty, healthful, hearty, stout, (n) hardy, hard; **antonyms** (adj) weak, slight, fragile, frail.

tuea 1. promise; **synonyms** (n) engagement, assurance, bargain, engage, hope, plight, word, (v) pledge, covenant, guarantee, contract, vow, augur, assure, undertake, **2.** pledge; **synonyms** (n) bond, gage, promise, bet, bail, oath, security, collateral, commitment, (v) pawn, wager, warrant, ensure, drink, hock.

tueaki 1. promised; **synonyms** (v) benempt, named, (adj) engaged, pledged, affianced, betrothed, busy, devoted, earnest, employed, intended, involved, occupied, prospective, votary, **2.** pledged; **synonyms** (adj) bespoken, bound.

tuitui star; **synonyms** (n) asterisk, celebrity, ace, principal, headliner, leading, luminary, personality, champion, idol, lead, world, bigwig, (adj) asteriated, (v) feature; **antonym** (n) nobody.

tuka 1. avoid; **synonyms** (v) shun, avert, parry, escape, evade, abstain, annul, circumvent, duck, elude, forbear, fudge, ignore, prevent, (adj) eschew; **antonyms** (v) confront, associate, face, tackle, **2.** abandon; **synonyms** (v) quit, relinquish, renounce, resign, vacate, desert, evacuate, leave, waive, depart, abdicate, chuck, ditch, drop, forfeit; **antonyms** (v) keep, support, maintain, (n) restraint, **3.** circumvent; **synonyms** (v) baffle, avoid, besiege, surround, cheat, beat, beleaguer, bypass, circumnavigate, compass, dodge, outwit, sidestep, skirt, (adv) beset, **4.** lower; **synonyms** (adj) debase, inferior, (v) degrade, diminish, frown, humble, dip, abase, cut, descend, scowl, disgrace, decrease, demean, (n) depress; **antonyms** (v) increase, raise, **5.** impede; **synonyms** (v) block, clog, hinder, bar, obstruct, barricade, check, delay, preclude, curb, debar, embarrass, encumber, forbid, hamper;

antonym (v) facilitate, **6.** evade; **synonyms** (v) equivocate, hedge, bilk, neglect, omit, prevaricate, quibble, deflect, fence, flee, shirk, **7.** descend; **synonyms** (v) alight, condescend, settle, deign, derive, dismount, down, subside, tumble, come, decline, fall, sink, slope, stoop; **antonyms** (v) rise, ascend, climb, **8.** block; **synonyms** (n) pad, cluster, barrier, blocking, chock, chunk, (v) arrest, stop, halt, lock, plug, blockade, choke, close, (adj) lump; **antonyms** (v) free, unblock, open, **9.** resist; **synonyms** (v) repel, rebel, defy, revolt, endure, balk, combat, disobey, impede, protest, refuse, reject, withstand, rebuff, (n) oppose; **antonyms** (v) surrender, yield, assent, **10.** withstand; **synonyms** (v) stand, bear, resist, survive, weather, sustain, brave, hold, suffer, take, abide, defend, undergo, brook, tolerate, **11.** preclude; **synonyms** (v) exclude, forestall, obviate, foreclose, anticipate, prohibit, thwart, interdict, deter, disqualify, frustrate, foil, eliminate, **12.** repress; **synonyms** (v) control, crush, inhibit, quash, suppress, bridle, quell, reduce, restrain, subdue, mortify, coerce, confine, destroy, (adj) conquer, **13.** prevent; **synonyms** (v) interfere, counteract, discourage, ban, intercept, stymie, interrupt, dissuade, preserve, retain, stay, stifle, spoil, (adj) save, except; **antonym** (v) encourage, **14.** object; **synonyms** (n) design, aim, cause, end, intent, intention, meaning, mark, matter, subject, substance, drift, (v) mind, complain, demur; **antonym** (v) agree, **15.** obstruct; **synonyms** (v) screen, dam, jam, cross, detain, handicap, occlude, retard, traverse, disrupt, defeat, cramp, fill, obturate, restrict, **16.** prohibit; **synonyms** (v) disallow, enjoin, outlaw, proscribe, veto, embargo, command, negative, (n) prohibition; **antonyms** (v) permit, allow, **17.** parry; **synonyms** (n) counterpunch, (v) counter, flinch, fend, blench, blink.

tukaki 1. abandoned; **synonyms** (adj) forlorn, immoral, deserted, empty, profligate, shameless, stranded, wicked, lonely, corrupt, debauched, depraved, derelict, desolate, discarded; **antonyms** (adj) restrained, inhabited, orderly, overcrowded, **2.** blocked; **synonyms** (adj) jammed, clogged, locked, barren, blind, congested, foiled, fruitless, frustrated, infertile, lodged, plugged, sterile, stiff, stuck; **antonyms** (adj) successful, free, **3.** downed; **synonym** (adj) felled, **4.** impeded; **synonyms** (adj) disabled, crippled, slow, lame, lamed, **5.** lowered; **synonyms** (adj) abased, bated, cheap, humbled, **6.** repressed; **synonyms** (adj) subdued, inhibited, composed, forgotten, inner, pent-up, reserved, subconscious, unconscious, introverted, reticent, shy, withdrawn, **7.** parried, **8.** obstructed; **synonyms** (adj) hindered, blocked, impedite, stymied, thwarted, tight, **9.** prohibited; **synonyms** (adj) forbidden, illegal, illicit, banned, taboo, unlawful, contraband, barred, out, proscribed; *antonyms* (adj) admissible, legitimate.

tukuroro 1. ignorant; *synonyms* (adj) unconscious, illiterate, rude, uneducated, unwitting, blind, dull, innocent, naive, unaware, uninformed, unlearned, barbarous, crude, shallow; *antonyms* (adj) knowledgeable, conscious, **2.** retarded; *synonyms* (adj) backward, slow, tardy, imbecile, defective, deferred, half-baked, leisurely, obtuse, simple, birdbrained, dim, dim-witted, dopey, dumbbell.

tumoa excessive; *synonyms* (adj) inordinate, exaggerated, intense, enormous, exorbitant, extravagant, extreme, exuberant, immoderate, profuse, superfluous, undue, unreasonable, huge, lavish; *antonyms* (adj) reasonable, moderate, affordable.

tunga 1. faint; *synonyms* (adj) collapse, dim, dizzy, feeble, indistinct, weak, dull, gentle, soft, vague, delicate, distant, (v) languish, swoon, droop; *antonyms* (adj) distinct, strong, clear, obvious, considerable, loud, pungent, **2.** swoon; *synonyms* (n) fainting, syncope, deliquium, lipothymy, prostration, (v) faint, conk, die, (adj) blow, drop, gasp, pant, puff.

tungana plug; *synonyms* (n) hype, stopper, bung, fireplug, hack, hydrant, nag, (v) advertise, block, close, jade, occlude, advertize, fill, obstruct.

tunganaki plugged; *synonyms* (adj) congested, blocked, tight.

tungatunga 1. irregular; *synonyms* (adj) abnormal, atypical, anomalous, broken, eccentric, erratic, changeable, desultory, deviant, disorderly, guerilla, sporadic, strange, unequal, (n) guerrilla; *antonyms* (adj) regular, constant, even, normal, smooth, symmetrical, compact, cyclic, equal, steady, **2.** lumpy; *synonyms* (adj) chunky, coarse, dull, dumpy, gawky, gritty, indolent, rude, squat, squatty, stumpy, (v) lumpish, (n) failure, **3.** knotty; *synonyms* (adj) knotted, complex, difficult, gnarled, intricate, involved, convoluted, gnarly, elaborate, troublesome, baffling, hard, nodose, problematic, complicated; *antonyms* (adj) simple, straight, straightforward, **4.** faulty; *synonyms* (adj) erroneous, deficient, defective, false, vicious, bad, inaccurate, incorrect, wrong, damaged, imperfect, poor, amiss, tainted, blamable; *antonyms* (adj) correct, perfect, flawless, **5.** deformed; *synonyms* (adj) crooked, bent, distorted, malformed, misshapen, ugly, crippled, contorted, deform, grotesque, shapeless, twisted, warped, (v) crump.

tuoa 1. check; *synonyms* (v) bridle, stop, block, limit, agree, halt, restrain, bar, dampen, delay, (n) control, arrest, curb, bill, cheque, **2.** inspect; *synonyms* (v) examine, overhaul, overlook, survey, explore, inquire, look, review, scrutinize, view, watch, monitor, analyze, audit, check, **3.** examine; *synonyms* (v) assay, consider, try, search, ascertain, ask, contemplate, compare, canvass, essay, investigate, probe, quiz, study, test, **4.** reconnoiter; *synonyms* (v) scout, reconnoitre, pry, flout, range, recognize, reexamine, (n) scan, rummage, sound.

tuoaki checked; *synonyms* (adj) checkered, chequered, plaid, backward, curbed, intermittent, limited, numbered, pent-up, safe, silent, tartan, temperate.

tura 1. crawl; *synonyms* (v) creep, grovel, clamber, climb, cringe, fawn, scramble, sneak, swarm, teem, inch, lag, move, (n) crawling, creeping; *antonym* (v) race, **2.** slide; *synonyms* (n) glide, chute, decline, transparency, gliding, (v) drop, slip, fall, slither, run, slump, coast, skid, descend, (adj) shift, **3.** skid; *synonyms* (n) shoe, sideslip, stay, clog, shore, (v) slide, trig, scotch.

turabeau 1. dragging; *synonyms* (adj) long, slow, drained, exhausted, forlorn, interminable, lagging, lazy, lengthy, negligent, remiss, sickly, slack, sluggish, (n) stemming, **2.** moving; *synonyms* (adj) active, affecting, emotional, exciting, impressive, mobile, pitiful, poignant, touching, inspiring, movable, (n) movement, transport, advance, transfer; *antonyms* (adj) motionless, still, depressing, stationary, unemotional.

turabwi overbid; *synonym* (n) overcall.

turabwiaki overbid; *synonym* (n) overcall.

turaiangkor triangular; *synonyms* (adj) trigonal, trilateral, tripartite, deltoid, triangled.

turaki truck; *synonyms* (n) traffic, car, cart, trade, van, bogie, automobile, cap, crest, motortruck, (v) exchange, barter, swap, swop, transport.

turana prop; *synonyms* (n) support, post, shore, fulcrum, property, mainstay, airscrew, column, pillar, stay, (v) buttress, brace, bolster, hold, rest.

turatura 1. limp; *synonyms* (adj) flabby, flaccid, slack, flexible, drooping, flimsy, floppy, lax, loose, weak, (n) hobble, (v) halt, hitch, hop, shamble; *antonyms* (adj) taut, firm, (n) energetic, **2.** halt; *synonyms* (n) stay, block, cessation, suspension, (v) stop, arrest, cease, check, limp, desist, discontinue, hold, pause, freeze, break; *antonyms* (v) start, continue.

turu 1. hitting; *synonyms* (adj) convincing, (n) hit, striking, collision, smash, beating, bang, contact, drumming, defeat, hiding, impinging, smasher, trouncing, **2.** distinct; *synonyms* (adj) clear, articulate, different, discrete, apparent, definite, distinctive, palpable, decided, dissimilar, marked, plain, tangible, (prep) separate, (adv) apart; *antonyms* (adj) indistinct, similar, unclear, vague, inaudible, shapeless, **3.** stumbling; *synonyms* (n) lurching, staggering, astonishing, astounding, awkward, clumsy, halting, hesitant, maladroit, tentative, uncertain, weaving, faltering, stupefying, (n) hesitation.

turuna force; *synonyms* (*n*) energy, strength, agency, effect, enforce, impetus, (*v*) drive, coerce, pressure, squeeze, thrust, compel, cram, impel, (*adj*) constrain; *antonyms* (*n*) weakness, persuasion.

turunaki forced; *synonyms* (*adj*) compulsory, compelled, bound, artificial, constrained, involuntary, unnatural, farfetched, false, labored, obligatory, obliged, strained; *antonyms* (*adj*) free, unprovoked, spontaneous, voluntary.

tutari salty; *synonyms* (*adj*) saline, salt, piquant, pungent, salted, racy, spicy.

tutu 1. clambake; *synonyms* (*n*) bat, bum, bust, jamboree, kantikoy, nautch, randy, tear, assembly, blowout, colloquy, conclave, consultation, convention, convocation, 2. trickle; *synonyms* (*n*) drip, distill, drivel, drool, (*v*) drop, dribble, percolate, flow, leak, ooze, seep, filter, leach, bleed, drain; *antonyms* (*n*) throng, (*v*) gush.

tutuki adverse; *synonyms* (*adj*) contrary, unfavorable, harmful, hostile, untoward, adversary, averse, counter, inimical, negative, repugnant, antagonistic, bad, contradictory, (*n*) opposite; *antonym* (*adj*) favorable.

tutuneang 1. eager; *synonyms* (*adj*) avid, desirous, ardent, earnest, agog, acute, ambitious, enthusiastic, keen, zealous, industrious, studious, active, burning, craving; *antonyms* (*adj*) indifferent, apathetic, disinterested, unconcerned, 2. joyful; *synonyms* (*adj*) gay, happy, glad, cheerful, elated, gleeful, blissful, cheery, delighted, jolly, joyous, blithe, festive, buoyant, frolicsome; *antonym* (*adj*) sad.

tutuo 1. inspect; *synonyms* (*v*) examine, overhaul, overlook, survey, explore, inquire, look, review, scrutinize, view, watch, monitor, analyze, audit, check, 2. spy; *synonyms* (*n*) scout, detective, mole, notice, patrol, emissary, (*v*) see, espy, snoop, discern, discover, observe, perceive, descry, behold.

tuunga swoon; *synonyms* (*n*) fainting, syncope, deliquium, lipothymy, prostration, (*v*) faint, conk, die, (*adj*) collapse, blow, drop, gasp, pant, puff.

twake wry; *synonyms* (*adj*) ironic, ironical, twisted, dry, sardonic, twist, writhe, another, cynical, deadpan, erroneous, (*v*) awry, irregular, unsymmetric, asymmetric.

U

ua two; *synonyms* (*n*) deuce, pair, binary, demon, devil, duality, (*adj*) tway.

uabai 1. carry; *synonyms* (*v*) bear, bring, convey, conduct, take, acquit, behave, accept, comport, hold, pack, transport, load, assume, admit, 2.

have; *synonyms* (*v*) contain, gain, carry, get, possess, acquire, eat, suffer, allow, attain, catch, consume, do, embrace, find.

uabangaki 1. crooked; *synonyms* (*adj*) bent, awry, corrupt, irregular, askew, curved, deformed, dishonest, indirect, lopsided, unfair, unscrupulous, angular, asymmetrical, (*v*) wry; *antonyms* (*adj*) straight, honest, even, principled, 2. sideways; *synonyms* (*adv*) obliquely, laterally, sidelong, sideway, sidewise, (*adj*) oblique, side, crabwise, crosswise, aslant, slanting; *antonyms* (*adj*) direct, level.

uabuaka sneak; *synonyms* (*v*) creep, lurk, crawl, fawn, filch, mouse, (*n*) cower, slink, informer, skulk, snitch, fink, (*adj*) coward, grovel, dastard.

uabwi twenty; *synonym* (*adj*) twice.

uaereti 1. wire; *synonyms* (*n*) cable, telegram, line, rope, cord, string, thread, flex, guy, halser, hawser, marconigram, moorings, (*v*) telegraph, electrify, 2. telegram; *synonyms* (*n*) wire, news, report, flash, radiogram, buzzer, call, signal, summons, 3. radio; *synonyms* (*n*) wireless, broadcasting, radiotelegram, radiocommunication, tuner, television, (*v*) broadcast, transmit, notify.

uaeretiaki wired; *synonyms* (*adj*) tense, anxious, nervous, agitated, alert, distressed, done, fidgety, frantic, frenetic, high-strung, hyper, intoxicated, neurotic, on-line.

uakai armed; *synonyms* (*adj*) equipped, military, fitted, aggressive, compulsory, fit, forcible, prepared, ready, violent, weaponed, martial, organized; *antonyms* (*adj*) unarmed, unprotected.

uakaka 1. hairy; *synonyms* (*adj*) bearded, bushy, hirsute, dangerous, downy, woolly, bristly, fleecy, fuzzy, pilose, rough, shaggy, fimbriated; *antonyms* (*adj*) bald, hairless, 2. embarrassed; *synonyms* (*adj*) ashamed, abashed, awkward, uncomfortable, disconcerted, bashful, shamefaced, sheepish, shy, chagrined, discomfited, humiliated, mortified; *antonyms* (*adj*) proud, relaxed, 3. entangled; *synonyms* (*adj*) involved, complicated, intricate, embroiled, complex, foul, matted, tangled; *antonym* (*adj*) free, 4. bristling; *synonyms* (*adj*) thorny, muricated, pectinated, studded, thistly, bristled, fraught, horrent, horrid, teeming, thick, dreadful, hideous, rugged, shocking, 5. bristle; *synonyms* (*n*) fiber, hair, (*v*) abound, teem, arise, brustle, burn, rage, seethe, 6. worried; *synonyms* (*adj*) apprehensive, distressed, nervous, uneasy, upset, anxious, afraid, bothered, concerned, disturbed, troubled, fearful, restless, unhappy, (*v*) afflicted; *antonyms* (*adj*) calm, carefree, reassured, untroubled.

uakakaki bristled; *synonyms* (*adj*) barbed, barbellate, briary, briery, biting, bristly, burred, burry, echinated, horrent, prickly, spiny, thorny, mordacious, nipping.

uakana have; *synonyms* (v) contain, gain, bear, carry, get, hold, possess, accept, acquire, eat, suffer, take, allow, bring, conduct.

uakiua haul; *synonyms* (n) freight, heave, catch, jerk, take, (v) draw, drag, pull, tow, carry, cart, lug, draught, hale, transport; *antonym* (v) push.

uakonikon elastic; *synonyms* (adj) flexible, buoyant, ductile, limber, pliable, pliant, resilient, soft, springy, supple, yielding, lissom, stretchable, bouncy, expansive; *antonyms* (adj) rigid, stiff, inflexible, inelastic.

uakunikun fat; *synonyms* (adj) stout, corpulent, dense, thick, bulky, fatty, fertile, fleshy, gainful, greasy, great, (n) avoirdupois, blubber, cream, (v) fatten; *antonyms* (adj) thin, slim, skinny, slender.

uakurikuri countless; *synonyms* (adj) numberless, innumerable, endless, many, multitudinous, myriad, measureless, immeasurable, infinite, legion, numerous, uncounted, unnumbered, untold; *antonyms* (adj) few, finite.

uamane maneuver; *synonyms* (v) manoeuvre, guide, handle, control, manipulate, manoeuver, steer, (n) artifice, ruse, scheme, measure, device, act, ploy, stratagem.

uamanea 1. catch; *synonyms* (v) arrest, capture, hook, apprehend, get, acquire, ensnare, intercept, (n) haul, hitch, trick, bolt, clasp, grab, pawl; *antonym* (v) release, 2. encircle; *synonyms* (v) beset, surround, besiege, circle, embrace, bound, circumvent, enclose, encompass, environ, hem, begird, circumscribe, beleaguer, (adv) compass, 3. surround; *synonyms* (v) encircle, gird, border, inclose, ring, round, skirt, envelop, entwine, blockade, edge, enfold, fence, (n) environment, environs.

uamaneaki 1. encircled; *synonyms* (adj) surrounded, enclosed, bounded, annular, annulate, annulated, bordered, circinate, circular, delimited, ingirt, ringed, wreathed, 2. surrounded; *synonyms* (v) beset, begone, furnished, (adj) encircled, circumstanced, conditioned, entrenched, fixed, inside, rooted, implanted.

uamania measure; *synonyms* (n) amount, criterion, extent, beat, benchmark, degree, estimate, measurement, meter, quantity, act, allotment, action, (v) grade, appraise.

uamaniaki measured; *synonyms* (adj) careful, deliberate, moderate, calculated, reasonable, temperate, regular, leisurely, metrical, sober, cool, slow.

uamoa 1. earnest; *synonyms* (adj) devout, serious, eager, solemn, ardent, diligent, heartfelt, intense, sincere, studious, staid, cordial, enthusiastic, (n) guarantee, deposit; *antonyms* (adj) flippant, halfhearted, uncertain, 2. eager; *synonyms* (adj)

avid, desirous, earnest, agog, acute, ambitious, keen, zealous, industrious, active, burning, craving, excited, fervent, forward; *antonyms* (adj) indifferent, apathetic, disinterested, unconcerned, 3. intent; *synonyms* (adj) attentive, absorbed, engrossed, bent, (n) aim, idea, design, intention, goal, import, meaning, purpose, spirit, drift, end, 4. hopeful; *synonyms* (adj) cheerful, confident, auspicious, bright, optimistic, buoyant, expectant, likely, probable, rosy, sanguine, upbeat, (n) candidate, applicant, aspirant; *antonyms* (adj) hopeless, desperate, pessimistic, gloomy, pained, 5. determined; *synonyms* (adj) constant, decided, definite, resolute, certain, decisive, determinate, inflexible, resolved, stubborn, adamant, bold, firm, obstinate, set; *antonyms* (adj) weak, irresolute, feeble, unmotivated, 6. inspired; *synonyms* (adj) divine, ingenious, adopted, creative, elected, elysian, imaginative, inventive; *antonym* (adj) uninspired, 7. desirous; *synonyms* (adj) anxious, wistful, covetous, greedy, hungry, longing, envious, (v) willing; *antonym* (adj) undesirous, 8. excel; *synonyms* (v) surpass, top, cap, outdo, pass, eclipse, beat, transcend, lead, outshine, overshadow, (adj) exceed, better, 9. hankering; *synonyms* (n) desire, eagerness, thirst, wish, yen, appetite, urge, yearning, 10. emulous; *synonyms* (adj) competitive, rival, corrival, emulate, imitative, jealous, rivalrous, rivaling, 11. enterprising; *synonyms* (adj) adventurous, aggressive, energetic, courageous, daring, vigorous, audacious, brave, go-ahead, pushing, driving, pushful, venturesome, 12. industrious; *synonyms* (adj) assiduous, indefatigable, busy, hardworking, laborious, tireless, enterprising, careful, painstaking, sedulous, apt, gumptious, untiring; *antonym* (adj) lazy, 13. ambitious; *synonyms* (adj) aspiring, difficult, vaulting, challenging, grandiose, pushy, 14. contend; *synonyms* (v) assert, compete, wrestle, conflict, argue, combat, war, clash, altercate, battle, contest, fight, quarrel, (n) allege, maintain, 15. impudent; *synonyms* (adj) brassy, disrespectful, impertinent, barefaced, brazen, insolent, brash, cheeky, fresh, saucy, cool, flip, overbold, pert, shameless; *antonym* (adj) respectful, 16. strive; *synonyms* (v) endeavor, labor, attempt, contend, struggle, aspire, strain, toil, work, exert, endeavour, reach, scramble, seek, try, 17. saucy; *synonyms* (adj) impudent, rude, irreverent, malapert, sassy, smart, brisk, cavalier, rakish, obtrusive, sprightly, novel, 18. optimistic; *synonyms* (adj) affirmative, positive, carefree, happy, lighthearted; *antonyms* (adj) negative, disheartened.

uamumun 1. move; *synonyms* (v) act, affect, carry, excite, go, impel, instigate, maneuver, touch, travel, flow, bear, (n) motion, drive, transfer; *antonym* (v) stay, **2**. transmigrate; *synonyms* (*v*) migrate, emigrate, reincarnate, renew, transcorporate.

uamwi 1. impersonate; *synonyms* (*v*) ape, imitate, mimic, act, masquerade, mock, personify, pose, simulate, emulate, copy, personate, portray, represent, parody, **2**. mirror; *synonyms* (*n*) echo, model, exemplar, (*v*) glass, reflect, reproduce, lens, (*adj*) pattern, cynosure, **3**. copy; *synonyms* (*n*) imitation, trace, transcription, forgery, reproduction, cast, book, counterpart, double, facsimile, (*v*) counterfeit, duplicate, follow, fake, record; *antonym* (*n*) original, **4**. imitate; *synonyms* (*v*) forge, feign, assume, pretend, sham, adopt, impersonate, mirror, replicate, resemble, apply, appropriate, parallel, repeat.

uamwiaki 1. copied; *synonyms* (*adj*) traced, counterfeit, derivative, artificial, bogus, ersatz, fake, false, forged, imitative, mock, phony, sham, twin, banal; *antonyms* (*adj*) original, real, **2**. mirrored.

uana along; *synonyms* (*adv*) ahead, forward, lengthwise, on, onward, endlong, (*prep*) beside, (*prf*) by; *antonym* (*adv*) across.

uananti deformed; *synonyms* (*adj*) crooked, bent, distorted, malformed, misshapen, ugly, crippled, contorted, deform, grotesque, shapeless, twisted, warped, (*v*) crump.

uanao numerous; *synonyms* (*adj*) manifold, many, abundant, frequent, multiple, multitudinous, copious, innumerable, plentiful, populous, great, myriad, rife, several, various; *antonym* (*adj*) few.

uangingi 1. inconsiderable; *synonyms* (*adj*) insignificant, inconsequential, immaterial, negligible, petty, slight, small, trivial, fractional, minute, imperceptible, inappreciable, little, slender, trifling, **2**. small; *synonyms* (*adj*) narrow, fine, inadequate, low, minor, light, remote, cramped, young, limited, diminutive, faint, humble, miniature, minuscule; *antonyms* (*adj*) bulky, colossal, considerable, enormous, extra-large, great, huge, sizeable, giant, major, (*syn*) big, large, **3**. tiny; *synonyms* (*adj*) infinitesimal, midget, petite, puny, teeny, exiguous, baby, bantam, short, stunted; *antonyms* (*adj*) gigantic, vast.

uangini 1. minute; *synonyms* (*n*) instant, flash, jiffy, note, memorandum, moment, second, (*adj*) little, delicate, microscopic, atomic, careful, circumstantial, diminutive, elaborate; *antonyms* (*adj*) enormous, huge, big, gigantic, **2**. little; *synonyms* (*adj*) small, insignificant, brief, minute, petty, short, some, tiny, exiguous, light, baby, bantam, contemptible, (*v*) dash, bit; *antonyms* (*adj*) large, important, **3**. tiny; *synonyms* (*adj*) infinitesimal, midget, petite, puny, slight, teeny, miniature, minor, trifling, trivial, cramped, stunted, (*phr*) minuscule; *antonym* (*adj*) vast.

uara 1. insecure; *synonyms* (*adj*) dangerous, slippery, unsound, doubtful, bad, hazardous, precarious, rickety, risky, shaky, uncertain, unsafe, wobbly, diffident, (*v*) unstable; *antonyms* (*adj*) secure, confident, self-assured, self-confident, overconfident, safe, **2**. gawky; *synonyms* (*adj*) awkward, clumsy, gauche, ungainly, bungling, inelegant, inept, maladroit, uncouth, unwieldy, clownish, clunky, graceless, lumbering; *antonym* (*adj*) graceful, **3**. awkward; *synonyms* (*adj*) inconvenient, crude, embarrassing, sticky, uncomfortable, untoward, left-handed, annoying, cumbersome, difficult, heavy, inapt, rough, rustic, thorny; *antonyms* (*adj*) easy, adroit, manageable, straightforward, convenient, dexterous, helpful, rotund, simple, **4**. embarrassed; *synonyms* (*adj*) ashamed, abashed, disconcerted, bashful, shamefaced, sheepish, shy, chagrined, discomfited, humiliated, mortified; *antonyms* (*adj*) proud, relaxed, **5**. uncertain; *synonyms* (*adj*) ambiguous, changeable, dubious, questionable, vague, chancy, equivocal, indistinct, suspicious, unsettled, unsure, variable, debatable, indeterminate, (*v*) indefinite; *antonyms* (*adj*) certain, definite, clear, decisive, sure, decided, inevitable, strong-minded, unquestionable, **6**. slow; *synonyms* (*adj*) dull, late, sluggish, dense, dim, gradual, inactive, indolent, lazy, stupid, belated, boring, (*v*) slack, (*adv*) behind, behindhand; *antonyms* (*adj*) fast, intelligent, rapid, bright, alert, brisk, hasty, prompt, quick, speedy, hurried, observant, rushed, (*v*) accelerate.

uaran juicy; *synonyms* (*adj*) delicious, fat, gamy, liquid, luscious, succulent, fluid, lush, mellow, moist, racy, rich, sappy, spicy, blue; *antonym* (*adj*) dry.

uarao 1. impostor; *synonyms* (*n*) fraud, humbug, cheat, fake, hypocrite, charlatan, cheater, deceiver, faker, imposter, pretender, sham, counterfeit, hoax, shammer, **2**. defraud; *synonyms* (*v*) con, bamboozle, deceive, swindle, trick, mislead, rob, victimize, circumvent, bluff, bilk, chouse, cozen, diddle, do, **3**. cheat; *synonyms* (*v*) beguile, betray, defraud, beat, fleece, fob, jockey, rook, bite, chisel, (*n*) impostor, rogue, swindler, artifice, deception.

uaraoa 1. lie; *synonyms* (*v*) consist, repose, falsify, belong, couch, (*n*) fabrication, falsehood, falsity, fib, fiction, rest, untruth, bluff, counterfeit, deceit; *antonyms* (*v*) stand, (*n*) truth, **2**. cheat; *synonyms* (*v*) trick, beguile, betray, defraud, fake, beat, deceive, fleece, (*n*) swindle, con, fraud, bilk, impostor, sham, charlatan.

uareereke 1. little; *synonyms* (*adj*) small, diminutive, insignificant, brief, minute, petty, short, some, tiny, exiguous, light, baby, bantam, (*v*) dash, bit; *antonyms* (*adj*) big, enormous, large, important, **2**. thin; *synonyms* (*adj*) flimsy, gaunt, lean, slight, tenuous, emaciated, fine, rare, slim, sparse, (*v*) slender, dilute, meager, sheer, subtle; *antonyms* (*adj*) thick, fat, concentrated, chubby, plump, wide, broad, heavy, (*v*) thicken.

uarereke 1. short; *synonyms* (*adj*) brief, concise, scarce, brusque, close, curt, sharp, compendious, laconic, abrupt, deficient, diminutive, inadequate, insufficient, lacking; *antonyms* (*adj*) long, tall, high, lengthy, **2.** youthful; *synonyms* (*adj*) young, immature, fresh, green, juvenile, adolescent, vernal, childish, new, tender, beardless; *antonyms* (*adj*) old, adult, **3.** slight; *synonyms* (*adj*) flimsy, slender, thin, fragile, delicate, faint, (*n*) scorn, disdain, (*v*) disregard, insult, neglect, ignore, affront, cut, (*adv*) light; *antonyms* (*adj*) considerable, major, fat, heavy, intense, obvious, severe, thickset, wide, **4.** small; *synonyms* (*adj*) little, minute, narrow, fine, insignificant, low, minor, petty, slight, remote, cramped, limited, humble, miniature, minuscule; *antonyms* (*adj*) bulky, colossal, enormous, extralarge, great, huge, sizeable, giant, (*syn*) big, large, **5.** puny; *synonyms* (*adj*) feeble, frail, weak, small, tiny, measly, paltry, runty, trifling, trivial, exiguous, meager; *antonyms* (*adj*) brawny, muscular, **6.** young; *synonyms* (*adj*) raw, baby, boyish, callow, early, unripe, youthful, recent, childlike, inexperienced, infantile, (*n*) offspring, progeny, issue, child; *antonyms* (*adj*) mature, (*n*) aged.

uarurung 1. herd; *synonyms* (*n*) flock, swarm, drove, gang, crew, covey, mob, multitude, band, company, (*v*) crowd, cluster, drive, (*adj*) bevy, shoal, **2.** fluctuate; *synonyms* (*v*) waver, falter, change, vacillate, alternate, hesitate, oscillate, swing, vary, vibrate, wave, range, alter, quake, shake, **3.** drift; *synonyms* (*n*) stream, current, course, tendency, tone, bearing, design, gist, (*v*) aim, blow, float, ramble, cast, glide, (*adj*) flow.

uatao manifold; *synonyms* (*adj*) multiple, diverse, different, many, multiplex, various, multiplied, frequent, multifarious, multifold, multitudinous, (*v*) duplicate, copy, multiply, reproduce.

uati 1. launder; *synonyms* (*v*) wash, cleanse, clean, bathe, rinse, scour, fence, (*adj*) lave, **2.** wash; *synonyms* (*v*) paint, moisten, mop, scrub, color, tint, lap, gargle, dampen, launder, (*n*) soak, ablution, washing, swamp, bath; *antonym* (*v*) dirty.

uatiaki washed; *synonyms* (*adj*) clean, refined, watery.

uatingotingo minute; *synonyms* (*n*) instant, flash, jiffy, note, memorandum, moment, second, (*adj*) little, delicate, microscopic, atomic, careful, circumstantial, diminutive, elaborate; *antonyms* (*adj*) enormous, huge, big, gigantic.

uaua swim; *synonyms* (*v*) float, hover, drift, spin, plane, spire, (*n*) dip, swimming, (*adj*) rise.

ubararake float; *synonyms* (*n*) buoy, raft, bob, fleet, (*v*) drift, swim, blow, hover, ride, waft, fly, glide, hang, range, sail; *antonym* (*v*) sink.

ubati corpulent; *synonyms* (*adj*) fat, obese, portly, stout, fleshy, overweight, plump, lusty, chubby, tubby, bulky, gross, rotund, round, weighty; *antonym* (*adj*) skinny.

uburake rude; *synonyms* (*adj*) gross, rough, impudent, blunt, coarse, bold, brutal, crude, discourteous, impolite, mean, abusive, barbarous, churlish, (*n*) abrupt; *antonyms* (*adj*) polite, respectful, chivalrous, courteous, refined, civil, decent, proper, well-mannered.

uea 1. king; *synonyms* (*n*) emperor, mogul, sovereign, chief, baron, crown, magnate, ruler, tycoon, majesty, rex, monarch, power, ace, **2.** lord; *synonyms* (*n*) master, noble, sir, seignior, almighty, creator, gentleman, maker, mistress, nobleman, overlord, captain, impropriator, **3.** reign; *synonyms* (*n*) dominance, control, dominion, government, administration, kingdom, lead, regime, (*v*) rule, command, govern, dominate, predominate, prevail, manage.

uêa chief; *synonyms* (*adj*) head, principal, cardinal, capital, arch, central, essential, first, main, (*n*) administrator, boss, captain, executive, leader, paramount; *antonyms* (*adj*) minor, associate, secondary.

uêa flower; *synonyms* (*n*) bouquet, cream, efflorescence, elite, floret, florescence, ornament, nosegay, (*v*) bloom, blossom, blow, flourish, (*adj*) prime, floral, fructify.

ueana reign; *synonyms* (*n*) dominance, control, dominion, government, administration, kingdom, lead, power, (*v*) rule, command, govern, dominate, predominate, prevail, manage.

ueba skip; *synonyms* (*n*) jump, bound, hop, caper, omission, (*v*) leap, dance, bounce, prance, cut, gambol, skim, trip, decamp, frisk.

ueka 1. go; *synonyms* (*v*) come, elapse, pass, break, crack, depart, disappear, drive, run, travel, fall, extend, function, (*n*) fare, (*adj*) follow, **2.** visit; *synonyms* (*n*) chat, sojourn, (*v*) see, frequent, attend, call, tour, view, gossip, haunt, inspect, jaw, impose, inflict, talk.

ueke 1. brisk; *synonyms* (*adj*) active, agile, bracing, alive, bright, lively, quick, acute, alert, energetic, nimble, smart, sprightly, adroit, animated; *antonyms* (*adj*) slow, soporific, **2.** animated; *synonyms* (*adj*) animate, perky, brisk, cheerful, spirited, vivacious, airy, excited, fervent, keen, passionate, vivid, breezy, hot, ardent; *antonyms* (*adj*) listless, lethargic, blank, dull, **3.** excited; *synonyms* (*adj*) agitated, ablaze, emotional, enthusiastic, frantic, aroused, delirious, heated, impassioned, warm, elated, tense, feverish, effervescent, aflame; *antonyms* (*adj*) calm, cool, unexcited, **4.** alert; *synonyms* *(adj)* aware, intelligent, vigilant, clever, attentive, careful, cautious, discreet, prompt, ready, sharp, *(v)* awake, caution, *(n)* alarm, alarum; *antonyms* *(adj)* drowsy, inattentive, absentminded, dazed, sleepy, tired, asleep, unalert, unconscious, **5.** smart; *synonyms* *(adj)* crafty, dapper, shrewd, sly, astute, chic, jaunty, natty, neat, saucy, fine, fashionable, *(v)* ache, hurt, *(n)* pain; *antonyms* *(adj)* scruffy, stupid, dim, shabby, unkempt, **6.** quick; *synonyms* *(adj)* hasty, speedy, cursory, dexterous, expeditious, hurried, immediate, instant, swift, brief, abrupt, apt, ingenious, *(adv)* fast, *(v)* fleet; *antonym* *(adj)* leisurely, **7.** petulant; *synonyms* *(adj)* irritable, peevish, cross, testy, irascible, cranky, fractious, fretful, pettish, choleric, touchy, cantankerous, crabby, grouchy, grumpy; *antonym* *(adj)* easygoing.

uere 1. affected; *synonyms* *(adj)* artificial, unnatural, pompous, pretentious, stilted, pedantic, assumed, concerned, contrived, exaggerated, feigned, forced, pretended, snobbish, strained; *antonyms* *(adj)* unaffected, down-to-earth, natural, unchanged, **2.** shudder; *synonyms* *(n)* shake, quake, quivering, shivering, chill, frisson, tremor, twitch, *(v)* shiver, quiver, tremble, dither, flicker, flutter, thrill, **3.** touched; *synonyms* *(v)* compassionate, pitiful, sympathetic, bad, decayed, lentiginous, mildewed, moldy, *(adj)* affected, cracked, crazy, daft, insane, tinged, interested; *antonym* *(adj)* untouched.

ui place; *synonyms* *(n)* position, domicile, office, order, spot, attitude, *(v)* post, arrange, fix, lay, locate, rank, station, deposit, install; *antonym* *(v)* remove.

ui-katík sarcastic; *synonyms* *(adj)* cutting, sharp, acid, acrimonious, biting, bitter, caustic, poignant, pungent, satirical, acrid, cynical, incisive, ironic, *(v)* derisive; *antonym* *(adj)* gentle.

ui-n'anti slander; *synonyms* *(n)* insult, scandal, aspersion, defamation, obloquy, disparagement, backbiting, calumny, *(v)* libel, defame, calumniate, denigrate, *(adj)* abuse, asperse, malign; *antonym* *(v)* praise.

uka 1. blown; *synonyms* *(v)* distended, *(adj)* breathless, puffy, panting, swollen, winded, dissipated, flushed, gasping, high, late, mighty, misspent, pursy, spent, **2.** blow; *synonyms* *(n)* bang, beat, blast, knock, shock, wallop, gust, hit, jolt, *(v)* puff, bloom, blossom, pant, play, *(adj)* gasp; *antonyms* *(v)* calm, save, **3.** uncover; *synonyms* *(v)* disclose, expose, unveil, discover, reveal, find, show, divulge, strip, bare, detect, unearth, unfold, open, locate; *antonyms* *(v)* cover, conceal, **4.** open; *synonyms* *(adj)* frank, obvious, artless, exposed, free, honest, forthright, guileless, ingenuous, naked, direct, *(v)* expand, give, *(n)* candid, clear; *antonyms* *(adj)* devious, secretive, concealed, furtive, hidden, limited, repressive, reserved,

restricted, secret, blocked, cautious, *(v)* shut, end, *(tr v)* close.

ukaki 1. blown; *synonyms* *(v)* distended, *(adj)* breathless, puffy, panting, swollen, winded, dissipated, flushed, gasping, high, late, mighty, misspent, pursy, spent, **2.** opened; *synonyms* *(v)* blown, exhausted, inflated, stale, *(adj)* open, candid, exposed, assailable, blatant, blazing, clear, conspicuous, lawless, loose, through, **3.** uncovered; *synonyms* *(adj)* naked, bare, nude, unclothed; *antonym* *(adj)* covered.

uke 1. exhaust; *synonyms* *(v)* consume, drain, spend, empty, tire, deplete, expend, sap, use, dry, debilitate, enervate, evacuate, *(adj)* waste, dissipate; *antonyms* *(v)* conserve, refresh, invigorate, **2.** finish; *synonyms* *(v)* end, complete, achieve, execute, accomplish, cease, determine, discontinue, do, *(n)* close, consummate, conclusion, death, conclude, ending; *antonyms* *(v)* start, begin, continue, *(n)* beginning, **3.** exhausted; *synonyms* *(v)* weak, *(adj)* drained, fatigued, spent, tired, gone, beat, depleted, enervated, faint, jaded, weary, expended, dead, finished; *antonyms* *(adj)* energetic, fresh, refreshed, strong.

ukeaki 1. exhausted; *synonyms* *(v)* weak, *(adj)* drained, fatigued, spent, tired, gone, dry, beat, depleted, empty, enervated, faint, jaded, weary, expended; *antonyms* *(adj)* energetic, fresh, refreshed, strong, **2.** finished; *synonyms* *(v)* done, *(adj)* complete, completed, ended, perfect, consummate, absolute, accomplished, polished, ripe, ruined, round, capable, decided, *(adv)* over; *antonyms* *(adj)* unfinished, incomplete, remaining, rough.

ukera 1. examine; *synonyms* *(v)* assay, audit, consider, overhaul, try, check, control, search, survey, canvass, ascertain, ask, contemplate, compare, analyze, canvass, **2.** seek; *synonyms* *(v)* attempt, endeavor, hunt, look, inquire, aspire, beg, explore, pursue, quest, investigate, research, follow, demand, essay.

ukeroa 1. rummage; *synonyms* *(n)* search, explore, trash, scan, clutter, ransacking, reconnoiter, *(v)* hunt, jumble, ransack, root, delve, forage, rifle, seek, **2.** search; *synonyms* *(n)* pursuit, examination, exploration, inquire, inquiry, inspection, study, hunting, investigation, *(v)* grope, rummage, pry, examine, inspect, look.

ukeuke 1. evaluate; *synonyms* *(v)* appraise, assess, calculate, gauge, estimate, value, grade, measure, rank, reckon, review, weigh, assay, esteem, regard, **2.** test; *synonyms* *(n)* trial, audition, experiment, examination, criterion, *(v)* essay, examine, prove, quiz, sample, check, try, analyze, attempt, *(adj)* experimental, **3.** search; *synonyms* *(n)* hunt, pursuit, exploration, inquire, inquiry, inspection, study, hunting, *(v)* grope, ransack, rummage, pry, explore, forage, inspect, **4**. seek; *synonyms* (*v*) search, endeavor, look, aspire, beg, pursue, quest, investigate, research, follow, demand, request, strive, struggle, (*n*) ask, **5**. research; *synonyms* (*n*) investigation, inquisition, probe, question, enquiry, learning, query, (*v*) test, dig, scrutinize, survey.

ukeukeaki tested; *synonyms* (*adj*) tried, experienced, applied, faithful, genuine, hardened, proved, qualified, valid, veteran, trustworthy, weathered.

uki 1. gape; *synonyms* (*n*) gaze, (*v*) gawk, open, yawn, glare, goggle, split, dehisce, look, (*adj*) stare, **2**. nail; *synonyms* (*n*) arrest, pin, (*v*) catch, apprehend, collar, hook, strike, capture, cop, fasten, hit, nab, secure, spike, (*adj*) tack, **3**. gaping; *synonyms* (*adj*) agape, vast, yawning, cavernous, discontinuous, oscitant, **4**. breached, **5**. claw; *synonyms* (*n*) chela, nipper, pincer, unguis, (*v*) clutch, lacerate, rip, scratch, seize, tear, **6**. breach; *synonyms* (*n*) aperture, chink, crack, crevice, fracture, gap, infringement, opening, rift, trespass, (*v*) break, rupture, contravene, fissure, violate; *antonym* (*n*) observance, **7**. cleave; *synonyms* (*v*) adhere, cohere, burst, divide, stick, chop, cling, cut, hold, rive, sever, part, separate, share, (*n*) abide, **8**. space; *synonyms* (*n*) length, period, place, scope, void, margin, distance, emptiness, extent, interval, latitude, location, range, room, field, **9**. spaced; *synonyms* (*adj*) separated, detached, disjointed, dislocated, drugged, isolated, **10**. open; *synonyms* (*adj*) frank, obvious, artless, exposed, free, honest, bare, forthright, guileless, ingenuous, naked, (*v*) expand, give, (*n*) candid, clear; *antonyms* (*adj*) devious, secretive, concealed, furtive, hidden, limited, repressive, reserved, restricted, secret, blocked, cautious, (*v*) shut, end, (*tr v*) close.

ukiaki 1. breached, **2**. opened; *synonyms* (*v*) blown, distended, exhausted, inflated, (*adj*) open, candid, exposed, assailable, blatant, blazing, clear, conspicuous, lawless, loose, through.

uki-ni-bai fingernail; *synonym* (*n*) claw.

ukinta 1. involuntary; *synonyms* (*adj*) automatic, instinctive, forced, mechanical, unconscious, unintentional, unthinking, accidental, inadvertent, reluctant, unwilling, intuitive, perfunctory, unvoluntary; *antonyms* (*adj*) deliberate, voluntary, intentional, **2**. guilty; *synonyms* (*adj*) ashamed, culpable, criminal, faulty, hangdog, wicked, chargeable, condemned, delinquent, reprehensible, sinful, contrite, responsible, shamefaced, sheepish; *antonyms* (*adj*) innocent, blameless, **3**. confused; *synonyms* (*adj*) abashed, bewildered, baffled, befuddled, bemused, chaotic, confounded, disjointed, disordered, dizzy, incoherent, indistinct, ambiguous, (*n*) cloudy, (*adv, adj*) topsy-turvy; *antonyms* (*adj*) clear, enlightened, alert, clearheaded, clear-headed, orderly.

ukora 1. research; *synonyms* (*n*) exploration, inquiry, search, examination, investigation, hunt, inquisition, probe, quest, (*v*) check, explore, examine, investigate, study, experiment, **2**. seek; *synonyms* (*v*) attempt, endeavor, look, inquire, aspire, beg, pursue, research, follow, demand, essay, ransack, request, strive, (*n*) ask, **3**. search; *synonyms* (*n*) pursuit, inspection, hunting, scrutinize, analysis, chase, (*v*) grope, rummage, pry, forage, inspect, nose, scan, prospect, rake.

ukouko 1. investigate; *synonyms* (*v*) examine, explore, inquire, inspect, search, check, research, ask, hunt, analyze, enquire, interrogate, scrutinize, study, test, **2**. research; *synonyms* (*n*) exploration, inquiry, examination, investigation, inquisition, probe, quest, question, enquiry, inspection, pursuit, learning, query, (*v*) investigate, experiment.

ukoukora 1. sought; *synonyms* (*adj*) required, popular, hunted, **2**. seek; *synonyms* (*v*) search, attempt, endeavor, hunt, look, inquire, aspire, beg, explore, pursue, quest, investigate, research, follow, (*n*) ask.

ukoukoraki sought; *synonyms* (*adj*) required, popular, hunted.

ukuni snipe; *synonyms* (*n*) blackcock, duck, grouse, plover, rail, (*v*) assail, attack, assault, round, sharpshoot.

uma married; *synonyms* (*adj*) marital, wedded, conjugal, matrimonial, connubial, nuptial; *antonyms* (*adj*) single, unmarried.

umaki 1. expedite; *synonyms* (*v*) accelerate, dispatch, advance, hasten, assist, hurry, quicken, speed, facilitate, forward, further, precipitate, rush, **2**. hurry; *synonyms* (*n*) haste, flurry, celerity, hastiness, hurriedness, press, (*v*) bustle, dash, expedite, scurry, fly, run, zip, hie, drive; *antonyms* (*n*) slowness, (*v*) dawdle, **3**. hasten; *synonyms* (*v*) dart, race, gallop, sprint, hotfoot, hustle, stimulate, urge, (*adj*) course, go, (*n*) promote; *antonym* (*v*) delay.

umakiaki 1. hurried; *synonyms* (*adj*) hasty, fast, headlong, quick, rapid, speedy, sudden, swift, abrupt, cursory, careless, precipitate, prompt, rash, slapdash; *antonyms* (*adj*) slow, unhurried, leisurely, **2**. expedited.

umana dwell; *synonyms* (*v*) abide, inhabit, reside, bide, live, stay, lodge, be, belong, brood, continue, delay, occupy, remain, settle.

un 1. fight; *synonyms* (*v*) combat, contest, quarrel, feud, argue, bicker, campaign, clash, contend, (*n*) battle, dispute, engagement, conflict, contention, (*adj*) brawl; *antonyms* (*v*) agree, retreat, withdrawal, **2**. annoyed; *synonyms* (*adj*) angry, irate, irritated, vexed, aggravated, angered, cross, disgruntled, displeased, exasperated, infuriated, offended, peeved, pestered, resentful; *antonyms* (*adj*) calm, pleased, unprovoked, smiling, **3**. angry; *synonyms (adj)* furious, incensed, provoked, fierce, raging, vehement, maddened, fuming, outraged, piqued, splenetic, annoyed, boiling, choleric, enraged; *antonym (adj)* gentle, **4**. bothered; *synonyms (adj)* worried, disturbed, troubled, concerned, distraught, nervous, uneasy, upset, **5**. disturbed; *synonyms (adj)* agitated, anxious, confused, disquieted, restless, disordered, bothered, deranged, disconcerted, distracted, distressed, tumultuous, turbulent, unsettled, unbalanced; *antonyms (adj)* rational, relaxed, **6**. quarrel; *synonyms (n)* altercation, dissension, difference, disagreement, argument, controversy, debate, *(v)* fight, row, disagree, squabble, wrangle, affray, altercate, disturbance; *antonym (n)* agreement.

una 1. charge; *synonyms (n)* accusation, burden, care, command, commission, bill, tax, accusal, assail, *(v)* accuse, blame, attack, bid, load, arraign; *antonyms (v)* request, absolve, retreat, **2**. force; *synonyms (n)* energy, strength, agency, effect, enforce, impetus, *(v)* drive, coerce, pressure, squeeze, thrust, compel, cram, impel, *(adj)* constrain; *antonyms (n)* weakness, persuasion, **3**. pierce; *synonyms (v)* impale, cut, perforate, bore, enter, stab, stick, bite, drill, gore, penetrate, puncture, wound, broach, *(n)* prick, **4**. perforate; *synonyms (v)* pierce, punch, *(adj)* perforated.

unaenae 1. fleece; *synonyms (n)* skin, wool, coat, leather, *(v)* cheat, extort, bilk, bleed, deceive, pigeon, pluck, shear, strip, swindle, overcharge, **2**. despoil; *synonyms (v)* plunder, deprive, spoil, loot, pillage, ransack, rifle, sack, desecrate, ravage, reave, rob, spoliate, destroy, *(adj)* damage; *antonyms (v)* consecrate, respect, **3**. ransack; *synonyms (v)* comb, despoil, seek, rake, raid, foray, maraud, pry, search, delve, steal, forage, gut, *(n)* rummage, explore, **4**. strip; *synonyms (n)* band, slip, ribbon, shred, zone, *(v)* divest, peel, denude, pare, bare, bereave, dismantle, disrobe, fleece, undress; *antonyms (v)* dress, decorate.

unaenaeaki 1. despoiled; *synonyms (adj)* ruined, assaulted, besmirched, blasted, corrupted, defiled, desecrated, desolate, desolated, dishonored, empty, pillaged, raped, ravaged, sacked; *antonyms (adj)* pure, untarnished, **2**. stripped; *synonyms (adj)* bare, naked, nude, exposed, fleeced, undressed, stark, unclothed, **3**. ransacked; *synonyms (adj)* looted, plundered, despoiled.

unaine matron; *synonyms (n)* lady, wife, woman, matriarch, female, companion, administrator, biddy, mother, superintendent, *(v)* matronage, matronhood.

unaki 1. charged; *synonyms (adj)* fraught, laden, loaded, aerated, replete, abounding, deferred, electric, excited, explosive, invigorating, pregnant, supercharged, freighted, meaningful, **2**. forced; *synonyms (adj)* compulsory, compelled, bound, artificial, constrained, involuntary, unnatural, farfetched, false, labored, obligatory, obliged, strained; *antonyms (adj)* free, unprovoked, spontaneous, voluntary, **3**. pierced; *synonyms (adj)* perforated, punctured, perforate, cleft, entered, **4**. perforated; *synonyms (adj)* pierced, penetrated.

unarira 1. jerk; *synonyms (n)* tug, heave, pull, fool, *(v)* jolt, jump, shake, yank, jar, twitch, fling, bump, flip, bob, bounce, **2**. strip; *synonyms (n)* band, slip, *(v)* deprive, despoil, divest, peel, plunder, rifle, denude, ransack, pillage, pluck, pare, sack, bare; *antonyms (v)* dress, decorate.

unariraki stripped; *synonyms (adj)* bare, naked, nude, exposed, fleeced, undressed, desolate, stark, unclothed.

unauna 1. array; *synonyms (n)* arrangement, line, garment, *(v)* attire, dress, adorn, apparel, arrange, clothe, deck, display, garb, range, ornament, align; *antonym (v)* disarray, **2**. embellish; *synonyms (v)* beautify, decorate, embroider, bedeck, garnish, gild, trim, array, bedight, blazon, aggrandize, color, grace, broider, dramatize; *antonym (v)* strip, **3**. decorate; *synonyms (v)* embellish, emblazon, enrich, hang, paint, **4**. beautify; *synonyms (v)* enhance, bead, improve, prettify, adonize; *antonym (v)* spoil.

unaunaki 1. embellished; *synonyms (adj)* ornamented, ornate, rhetorical, fancy, florid, baroque, elaborate, embroidered, empurpled, exaggerated, flowery, inflated, overstated, *(prep)* beautied, beautiful, **2**. decorated; *synonyms (adj)* adorned, bejeweled, adorn, dyed, emblazoned, festive, inscribed, painted, purfled, tinted, celebrated, extolled, festooned, garlanded, highlighted.

uneakina 1. contest; *synonyms (n)* bout, competition, conflict, fight, altercation, contention, race, struggle, *(v)* battle, compete, combat, contend, dispute, argue, challenge, **2**. dispute; *synonyms (n)* brawl, quarrel, debate, wrangle, difference, question, argument, discussion, disputation, *(v)* contest, controversy, discuss, row, squabble, contradict; *antonyms (v)* agreement, agree, **3**. claim; *synonyms (n)* call, charge, allegation, privilege, right, title, *(v)* demand, ask, assert, exact, arrogate, need, require, requisition, want; *antonyms (v)* deny, disclaim, forfeit.

uneakinaki 1. contested; *synonyms (adj)* contentious, litigated, litigious, quarrelsome, **2**. disputed; *synonyms (adj)* controversial, moot, disputable, debatable, doubtful, dubious, opposed, uncertain, problematic.

unekea 1. decorate; *synonyms (v)* beautify, deck, adorn, bedeck, dress, embellish, grace, apparel, bedight, arrange, array, emblazon, embroider, enrich, garnish; *antonym* (v) strip, **2**. adorn; *synonyms* (v) decorate, ornament, trim, gild, blazon, invest, crown, attire, enhance, equip, clothe, color, dignify.

unekeaki 1. decorated; *synonyms* (adj) adorned, ornate, fancy, beautiful, bejeweled, adorn, dyed, elaborate, emblazoned, festive, inscribed, painted, purfled, tinted, celebrated, **2**. adorned; *synonyms* (adj) decorated, bedecked, festooned, extolled, garlanded.

unga 1. arduous; *synonyms* (adj) hard, difficult, laborious, heavy, onerous, strenuous, uphill, painful, severe, tough, troublesome, trying, grueling, precipitous, backbreaking; *antonym* (adj) easy, **2**. animated; *synonyms* (adj) active, alive, lively, animate, perky, brisk, cheerful, quick, spirited, sprightly, vivacious, airy, alert, bright, energetic; *antonyms* (adj) listless, lethargic, blank, dull, **3**. active; *synonyms* (adj) busy, diligent, effective, live, nimble, strong, agile, dynamic, forcible, healthy, mercurial, vigorous, vivid, operational, (v) smart; *antonyms* (adj) dormant, inactive, sluggish, idle, latent, sedentary, slow, extinct, passive, quiet, **4**. enthusiastic; *synonyms* (adj) ardent, eager, hearty, cordial, anxious, avid, devoted, excited, fiery, passionate, animated, vehement, heated, dedicated, (n) buoyant; *antonyms* (adj) unenthusiastic, apathetic, indifferent, lukewarm.

ungara 1. encourage; *synonyms* (v) cheer, abet, advance, aid, back, boost, comfort, foster, further, promote, urge, advocate, cherish, advise, animate; *antonyms* (v) discourage, dishearten, prevent, deter, hurt, obstruct, stop, **2**. accomplish; *synonyms* (v) achieve, compass, do, perform, reach, attain, complete, execute, fulfill, make, perfect, realize, consummate, effect, finish, **3**. excite; *synonyms* (v) arouse, disturb, enliven, agitate, energize, awaken, electrify, encourage, evoke, exasperate, incite, inspire, kindle, provoke, quicken; *antonyms* (v) calm, pacify, bore.

ungaraki 1. excited; *synonyms* (adj) agitated, ablaze, emotional, enthusiastic, frantic, ardent, aroused, delirious, fervent, heated, impassioned, passionate, warm, elated, (v) animated; *antonyms* (adj) calm, cool, unexcited, **2**. done; *synonyms* (adj) finished, complete, completed, over, gone, through, (adv) ended; *antonym* (adj) unfinished, **3**. accomplished; *synonyms* (adj) able, proficient, adept, experienced, gifted, skillful, fine, capable, clever, competent, concluded, consummate, cultured, done, effected; *antonym* (adj) inept, **4**. encouraged; *synonyms* (adj) optimistic, confident, enthused, expectant, inspired, moved, positive, stimulated, stirred, buoyant, driven, impelled,

incited, motivated, pressed; *antonym* (adj) uninspired.

uñgô thou; *synonyms* (n) chiliad, g, grand, m, curtilage, gee, gigabyte, gm, gram, gramme, green, grounds, jet, kelvin, kilobyte.

unika 1. establish; *synonyms* (v) confirm, erect, prove, appoint, base, build, constitute, demonstrate, settle, arrange, ascertain, create, determine, fix, found; *antonyms* (v) disprove, abolish, terminate, **2**. implant; *synonyms* (v) graft, embed, engraft, plant, establish, bury, bud, imbed, impregnate, imbue, lodge, inculcate, infuse, ingraft, insert, **3**. sow; *synonyms* (n) pig, hog, swine, bitch, (v) scatter, disperse, broadcast, inseminate, seed, disseminate, sough, farm, distribute, propagate, spread, **4**. plant; *synonyms* (n) manufactory, equipment, factory, herb, mill, bush, cheat, flora, (v) place, set, lay, cultivate, nominate, implant, install.

unikaikai 1. bump; *synonyms* (n) bang, crash, blow, bulge, clash, hit, knock, blast, collision, concussion, jar, push, (v) bash, jolt, break, **2**. knock; *synonyms* (v) bump, cuff, punch, strike, boot, clip, beat, condemn, (n) rap, tap, whack, clap, belt, clout, criticism; *antonym* (v) praise.

unikaki 1. established; *synonyms* (v) settled, (adj) conventional, accepted, firm, fixed, regular, set, decided, confirmed, secure, accomplished, customary, effected, orthodox, completed; *antonym* (adj) unproven, **2**. implanted; *synonyms* (adj) planted, ingrained, ingrafted, inherent, entrenched, native, rooted, surrounded, essential, natural, **3**. planted; *synonyms* (adj) implanted, concealed.

unikitero anchor; *synonyms* (n) mainstay, (v) tie, fasten, secure, fix, (adj) refuge, rest.

unin 1. irascible; *synonyms* (adj) fiery, angry, choleric, irritable, crabby, excitable, hot, hotheaded, passionate, testy, touchy, hasty, impatient, impetuous, edgy, **2**. moody; *synonyms* (adj) gloomy, dark, capricious, glum, morose, grumpy, dour, melancholy, sullen, temperamental, downcast, dismal, blue, depressed, erratic, **3**. harsh; *synonyms* (adj) grating, sharp, austere, bitter, coarse, crude, cruel, discordant, grim, unkind, acrid, acute, biting, brutal, (v) hard; *antonyms* (adj) smooth, gentle, harmonious, kind, lenient, pleasant, soft, melodious, sweet, **4**. fiery; *synonyms* (adj) ardent, burning, fervent, ablaze, fierce, fervid, flaming, glowing, impassioned, peppery, violent, combustible, blazing, torrid, (n) enthusiastic; *antonym* (adj) mild, **5**. cross; *synonyms* (n) crisscross, affliction, check, crossing, (v) intersect, baffle, cover, thwart, bilk, (adj) crabbed, cantankerous, grouchy, traverse, cranky, annoyed; *antonyms* (v) uncross, (adj) calm, good-tempered, **6**. disputatious; *synonyms* (adj) argumentative, controversial, contentious, quarrelsome, disputative, litigious, polemical, pugnacious, (v) polemic, **7.** choleric; *synonyms* (adj) irascible, quick-tempered, cross, snappish, waspish, **8.** passionate; *synonyms* (adj) animated, excited, earnest, amorous, eager, heated, intense, keen, loving, fond, devoted, emotional, furious, lustful, (v) impulsive; *antonyms* (adj) apathetic, indifferent, passionless, **9.** quarrelsome; *synonyms* (adj) belligerent, combative, aggressive, disputatious, currish, ugly, contrary, termagant, arguing, factious, fighting, unruly, warlike, (v) fretful; *antonym* (adj) peaceable, **10.** peevish; *synonyms* (adj) fractious, moody, captious, petulant, crusty, crotchety, nettlesome, pettish, sour, techy, tetchy, acrimonious, disagreeable, grumbling, querulous, **11.** pugnacious; *synonyms* (adj) bellicose, hostile, martial, peevish, militant, tough, **12.** violent; *synonyms* (adj) rough, tempestuous, raging, severe, turbulent, vehement, powerful, savage, stormy, strong, wild, tumultuous, rude, extreme, (n) boisterous; *antonyms* (adj) peaceful, nonviolent.

unknown absolved; *synonyms* (v) quit, acquitted, free, (adj) clear, cleared, exculpated, exempt, exonerated, vindicated, clean, decipherable, light, open, percipient, readable.

unobauta 1. detach; *synonyms* (v) disengage, divide, part, disconnect, disentangle, dissociate, remove, separate, unhook, isolate, abstract, cleave, disjoin, divorce, (n) detail; *antonyms* (v) attach, fasten, add, associate, **2.** break; *synonyms* (v) split, crack, burst, fail, infringe, leak, (n) breach, fracture, pause, rupture, stop, collapse, interruption, respite, suspension; *antonyms* (v) repair, obey, honor, mend, (n) continuation, **3.** unbind; *synonyms* (v) loose, undo, loosen, release, liberate, free, unfasten, unloose, untie, unbar; *antonym* (v) bind.

unobautaki 1. broken; *synonyms* (v) broke, (adj) tame, torn, busted, imperfect, intermittent, rough, rugged, ruined, uneven, disjointed, incomplete, confused, cracked, crushed; *antonyms* (adj) constant, unbroken, intact, whole, wild, **2.** detached; *synonyms* (adj) aloof, cool, isolated, separate, distinct, disconnected, disinterested, dispassionate, impartial, indifferent, neutral, objective, remote, separated, unconcerned; *antonyms* (adj) attached, involved, engrossed, warm, **3.** unbound; *synonyms* (adj) loose, uncontrolled, unconstrained, open, untied, untrammeled, exempt, dissolute, indeterminate, interminable, lax, liberated, rambling, unbuttoned, (v) unencumbered; *antonym* (adj) bound.

unora 1. twist; *synonyms* (n) twine, wind, spin, twirl, entwine, (v) turn, bend, distort, curl, coil, contort, deform, curve, pervert, wrench; *antonyms* (v) straighten, untwist, **2.** turn; *synonyms* (v) revolve, deviate, get, revolution, become, (n) roll, go, twist, bout, change, round, bent, circle, shift, tour, **3.**

wring; *synonyms* (v) extort, squeeze, torment, torture, wrest, extract, rack, milk, exact, force, pinch, writhe, (n) prick, fret, (adj) crimp.

unoraki 1. turned; *synonyms* (adj) off, sour, curved, rancid, twisted, altered, askew, awry, bent, bowed, cancelled, crooked, dark, deflected, dour, **2.** twisted; *synonyms* (adj) deformed, perverted, distorted, coiled, misshapen, contorted, twined, winding, wry, gnarled, tortuous, kinky, wrong, warped, depraved; *antonyms* (adj) straight, tidy.

unrake 1. contrary; *synonyms* (adj) opposite, contradictory, adverse, conflicting, reverse, unfavorable, alien, cross, different, disobedient, obstinate, perverse, averse, antagonistic, (adv) counter, **2.** contradictory; *synonyms* (adj) incompatible, inconsistent, contrary, discordant, ironic, discrepant, incoherent, incongruous, opposed, opposing, repugnant, confounding, divergent, unlike, (n) disagreeing; *antonyms* (adj) consistent, similar, compatible, **3.** contradict; *synonyms* (v) deny, oppose, belie, conflict, confute, contravene, controvert, disprove, dissent, impugn, invalidate, refute, disaffirm, disclaim, counteract; *antonyms* (v) confirm, agree, match, **4.** refuse; *synonyms* (v) reject, decline, disallow, dross, rebuff, disdain, dismiss, balk, (n) garbage, trash, waste, offal, debris, litter, leavings; *antonym* (v) accept, **5.** rebel; *synonyms* (n) insurgent, nonconformist, anarchist, dissident, insurrectionist, traitor, revolutionist, (v) mutiny, renegade, arise, disobey, revolt, rise, (adj) mutineer, rebellious; *antonym* (n) conformist, **6.** rebellious; *synonyms* (adj) insubordinate, defiant, disaffected, mutinous, contumacious, malcontent, recalcitrant, stubborn, unruly, disorderly, factious, naughty, revolutionary, riotous, (v) rebel; *antonyms* (adj) compliant, docile, content, conventional, obedient.

unrakeaki refused; *synonyms* (adj) forbidden, hence, prohibited, refuse, worthless.

untaba 1. contradict; *synonyms* (v) deny, oppose, belie, conflict, confute, contravene, controvert, disprove, dissent, impugn, invalidate, refute, disaffirm, disclaim, counteract; *antonyms* (v) confirm, agree, match, **2.** clash; *synonyms* (n) bang, battle, brush, clang, crash, discord, encounter, (v) jar, fight, impact, brawl, clank, collide, dispute, hit; *antonym* (n) agreement, **3.** collide; *synonyms* (v) bump, clash, strike, beat, hurtle, knock, smash, quarrel, **4.** impact; *synonyms* (n) shock, blow, collision, force, effect, impingement, impression, influence, touch, concussion, consequence, jolt, (v) affect, contact, ram, **5.** oppose; *synonyms* (v) object, contest, contend, contradict, resist, counter, disagree, combat, confront, defend, gainsay, hinder, repel, thwart, withstand; *antonyms* (v) support, advocate, back, advise.

Reference: Webster's Online Dictionary (www.websters-online-dictionary.org)

untabaki opposed; *synonyms* (adj) conflicting, contradictory, hostile, contrary, antagonistic, opposing, adverse, averse, contrasted, repugnant, incompatible, irreconcilable, counter, against, opposite.

unuana 1. direct; *synonyms* (adj) straight, blunt, immediate, (v) aim, channel, conduct, address, charge, control, dictate, head, administer, guide, lead, (n) command; *antonyms* (adj) indirect, roundabout, circuitous, oblique, second-hand, sideways, unplanned, (v) request, **2.** lead; *synonyms* (v) contribute, direct, chair, conduce, go, govern, bring, convey, give, carry, dispose, (n) clue, advantage, hint, (adj) front; *antonym* (v) follow, **3.** conduct; *synonyms* (n) behavior, administration, manage, demeanor, performance, behaviour, (v) act, carriage, acquit, bearing, comport, show, accompany, bear, behave.

unuanaki 1. led, **2.** directed; *synonyms* (adj) absorbed, concentrating, destined, focussed, formal, intent, prescript, subject, engaged, fixed, prescribed, rapt, (adv) under.

unuara 1. cross; *synonyms* (n) crisscross, affliction, (v) intersect, baffle, cover, thwart, (adj) crabbed, crabby, angry, cantankerous, grouchy, grumpy, traverse, cranky, annoyed; *antonyms* (v) uncross, (adj) calm, good-tempered, **2.** angry; *synonyms* (adj) furious, incensed, provoked, fierce, irate, raging, vehement, maddened, fuming, outraged, piqued, splenetic, angered, boiling, choleric; *antonyms* (adj) pleased, gentle, **3.** discontented; *synonyms* (adj) discontent, disaffected, disgruntled, displeased, dissatisfied, malcontent, unsatisfied, miserable, (v) querulous, complaining; *antonyms* (adj) contented, happy, satisfied, **4.** scorned; *synonyms* (adj) despised, detested, hated, abject, neglected, contemptible, contemptuous, despicable, insolent, mean, undesirable, unpopular, scornful, vile, **5.** offended; *synonyms* (adj) hurt, affronted, aggrieved, pained, wronged, shocked, appalled, ashamed, averted, bitter, cool, disappointed, disgusted, dismayed, distraught; *antonym* (adj) composed, **6.** vexed; *synonyms* (adj) troubled, irritated, harassed, harried, peeved, pestered, sore, uneasy, **7.** scorn; *synonyms* (n) disdain, contempt, neglect, derision, mockery, insult, (v) despise, ridicule, contemn, deride, disregard, reject, slight, reproach, dislike; *antonyms* (n) approval, (v) respect, appreciate, praise.

unuaraki scorned; *synonyms* (adj) despised, detested, hated, abject, neglected, contemptible, contemptuous, despicable, insolent, mean, undesirable, unpopular, scornful, vile.

unum fierce; *synonyms* (adj) bitter, violent, acute, cruel, ferocious, brutal, furious, grim, savage, nasty, angry, ardent, atrocious, barbarous, boisterous; *antonyms* (adj) gentle, mild.

unun 1. angry; *synonyms* (adj) furious, incensed, provoked, fierce, irate, raging, vehement, maddened, fuming, outraged, piqued, splenetic, angered, annoyed, boiling; *antonyms* (adj) calm, pleased, gentle, **2.** anger; *synonyms* (n) displeasure, fury, rage, indignation, resentment, annoyance, (v) enrage, incense, aggravate, displease, exasperate, irritate, offend, wrath, fume; *antonyms* (n) pleasure, composure, (v) please, placate, pacify, **3.** irate; *synonyms* (adj) angry, indignant, enraged, infuriated, exasperated, heated, ireful, livid, mad, wrathful.

ununaki angered; *synonyms* (adj) infuriated, annoyed, enraged, furious, incensed, huffy, irate, maddened, spleened, ferocious, fierce, frustrated, savage, tempestuous, wild.

ununiki sow; *synonyms* (n) pig, hog, swine, (v) scatter, disperse, broadcast, inseminate, seed, disseminate, plant, sough, farm, distribute, propagate, spread.

uo rock; *synonyms* (n) boulder, calculus, pillar, (v) jar, sway, cradle, jolt, shake, toss, waver, quake, pitch, reel, (adj) pebble, stone.

uomania 1. transpose; *synonyms* (v) exchange, change, shift, transfer, transplant, interchange, commute, convert, displace, bandy, counterchange, invert, permute, (adj) chime, harmonize, **2.** transport; *synonyms* (n) rapture, transportation, (v) transmit, bear, carry, delight, enrapture, exile, banish, convey, enchant, ferry, ravish, send, take; *antonyms* (v) disenchant, remain.

uomaniaki transposed; *synonyms* (adj) converse, inverse, reversed, hyperbatic, inverted.

uota 1. bring; *synonyms* (v) convey, fetch, bear, carry, conduct, get, put, take, reduce, afford, bestow, deliver, land, move, provide, **2.** carry; *synonyms* (v) bring, acquit, behave, accept, comport, hold, pack, transport, load, assume, admit, adopt, act, capture, cart, **3.** port; *synonyms* (n) harbor, haven, asylum, carriage, demeanor, pier, mien, bearing, deportment, dock, embrasure, gate, harbour, (adj) larboard, left; *antonym* (n) starboard.

uoua two; *synonyms* (n) deuce, pair, binary, demon, devil, duality, (adj) tway.

ura 1. break; *synonyms* (v) split, crack, burst, fail, infringe, leak, (n) breach, fracture, pause, rupture, stop, collapse, interruption, respite, suspension; *antonyms* (v) repair, obey, honor, mend, (n) continuation, **2.** destroy; *synonyms* (v) break, demolish, blight, despoil, annihilate, blast, crush, dash, destruct, devastate, devour, dismantle, (adj) desolate, abolish, consume; *antonyms* (v) build, preserve, create, make, **3.** smash; *synonyms* (v) crash, bang, hit, mash, shatter, defeat, pound, ruin, slam, fragment, batter, (n) clash, collision, knock, bash, **4.** shatter; *synonyms* (v) destroy, smash, frustrate, disintegrate, scatter, confound, quell, stagger, shiver, splinter, squelch, wreck, **5.** red;

synonyms (*adj*) crimson, flushed, carmine, glowing, rosy, ruby, sanguine, cherry, pink, radical, ruddy, scarlet, cerise, bloody, inflamed.

uraba 1. devastate; *synonyms* (*v*) desolate, consume, demolish, destroy, spoil, havoc, ruin, waste, annihilate, ravage, sack, wreck, despoil, damage, harry; *antonym* (*v*) build, **2**. waste; *synonyms* (*n*) desert, refuse, trash, dissipation, garbage, loss, rubbish, (*adj*) barren, lavish, (*v*) exhaust, squander, destruction, devastate, dissipate, languish; *antonyms* (*v*) conserve, save.

urabaki 1. devastated; *synonyms* (*adj*) desolate, destroyed, desolated, ruined, ravaged, wasted, bare, blasted, **2**. wasted; *synonyms* (*v*) rotten, effete, (*adj*) lost, squandered, thin, cadaverous, emaciated, gaunt, devastated, decayed, haggard, pointless, skeletal, atrophied, bony; *antonyms* (*adj*) worthwhile, bloated, **3**. waisted; *synonym* (*adj*) fitted.

urabo 1. discolored; *synonyms* (*adj*) discoloured, blemished, crusty, dappled, dark, dingy, dirty, dull, faded, flawed, flecked, freckled, gray, imperfect, livid, **2**. faded; *synonyms* (*v*) dilapidated, stale, (*adj*) dim, pale, bleached, exhausted, faint, washy, withered, attenuate, attenuated, colorless.

uraka 1. destroy; *synonyms* (*v*) break, demolish, blight, despoil, annihilate, blast, crush, dash, destruct, devastate, devour, dismantle, (*adj*) desolate, abolish, consume; *antonyms* (*v*) build, preserve, create, make, **2**. break; *synonyms* (*v*) split, crack, burst, fail, infringe, leak, (*n*) breach, fracture, pause, rupture, stop, collapse, interruption, respite, suspension; *antonyms* (*v*) repair, obey, honor, mend, (*n*) continuation, **3**. demolish; *synonyms* (*v*) defeat, batter, destroy, raze, level, overthrow, ruin, shatter, smash, spoil, wreck, overcome, beat, deface, eradicate; *antonym* (*v*) construct, **4**. smash; *synonyms* (*v*) crash, bang, hit, mash, pound, slam, fragment, impact, punch, (*n*) clash, collision, knock, bash, blow, bump, **5**. upset; *synonyms* (*v*) overturn, agitate, disquiet, bother, confuse, disturb, perturb, reverse, subvert, (*adj*) unsettled, hurt, (*n*) disorder, trouble, distress, disturbance; *antonyms* (*v*) calm, please, encourage, soothe, (*adj*) pleased, confident.

urakaki 1. broken; *synonyms* (*v*) broke, (*adj*) tame, torn, busted, imperfect, intermittent, rough, rugged, ruined, uneven, disjointed, incomplete, confused, cracked, crushed; *antonyms* (*adj*) constant, unbroken, intact, whole, wild, **2**. destroyed; *synonyms* (*adj*) lost, desolate, desolated, shattered, dead, depressed, **3**. demolished; *synonyms* (*adj*) broken, baneful, decayed, dismantled, razed, ruinous, destructive, dilapidated, mischievous, pernicious, wasteful, **4**.

upset; *synonyms* (*v*) overturn, agitate, disquiet, overthrow, bother, confuse, disturb, perturb, reverse, (*adj*) unsettled, hurt, (*n*) disorder, trouble, distress, disturbance; *antonyms* (*v*) calm, please, encourage, soothe, (*adj*) pleased, confident, **5**. smashed; *synonyms* (*adj*) drunk, inebriated, intoxicated, plastered, sloshed, blotto, tipsy, besotted, pissed, tight; *antonym* (*adj*) sober.

urake 1. load; *synonyms* (*n*) charge, cargo, freight, stack, heap, pack, weight, consignment, lading, shipment, (*v*) burden, fill, encumber, pile, lade; *antonym* (*v*) unload, **2**. convey; *synonyms* (*v*) carry, communicate, bring, channel, conduct, bear, express, fetch, transfer, transmit, impart, take, transport, mean, cause, **3**. flare; *synonyms* (*n*) flash, blaze, fire, signal, beacon, (*v*) burn, flame, burst, glint, erupt, flicker, glare, (*adj*) detonate, explode, fly, **4**. port; *synonyms* (*n*) harbor, haven, asylum, carriage, demeanor, pier, mien, bearing, deportment, dock, embrasure, gate, harbour, (*adj*) larboard, left; *antonym* (*n*) starboard, **5**. ship; *synonyms* (*n*) boat, ferry, craft, bottom, (*v*) dispatch, send, forward, consign, embark, move, post, mail, convey, **6**. transport; *synonyms* (*n*) rapture, transportation, conveyance, shipping, (*v*) delight, enrapture, exile, banish, enchant, ravish, entrance, run, haul, remove, ship; *antonyms* (*v*) disenchant, remain, **7**. unload; *synonyms* (*v*) discharge, drop, empty, unlade, clear, tip, unburden, exonerate, free, dump, relieve, offload, acquit, deliver, (*adj*) disburden; *antonym* (*v*) load.

urakeaki 1. conveyed; *synonyms* (*v*) carried, borne, supported, **2**. flared; *synonyms* (*adj*) flaring, aflare, fluttering, flying, waving, **3**. loaded; *synonyms* (*adj*) laden, full, burdened, flush, moneyed, wealthy, affluent, rich, tight, tipsy, intoxicated, heavy, pixilated, plastered, soused; *antonym* (*adj*) poor, **4**. unloaded; *synonyms* (*adj*) unobstructed, untrammeled, unfraught; *antonym* (*adj*) loaded.

uraki 1. broken; *synonyms* (*v*) broke, (*adj*) tame, torn, busted, imperfect, intermittent, rough, rugged, ruined, uneven, disjointed, incomplete, confused, cracked, crushed; *antonyms* (*adj*) constant, unbroken, intact, whole, wild, **2**. destroyed; *synonyms* (*adj*) lost, desolate, desolated, shattered, dead, depressed, **3**. smashed; *synonyms* (*adj*) drunk, inebriated, intoxicated, broken, plastered, sloshed, blotto, tipsy, besotted, pissed, tight; *antonym* (*adj*) sober, **4**. shattered; *synonyms* (*v*) exhausted, battered, lame, (*adj*) destroyed, smashed, crazy, shaky.

urakina 1. convey; *synonyms* (*v*) carry, communicate, bring, channel, conduct, bear, express, fetch, transfer, transmit, impart, take, transport, mean, cause, **2**. carry; *synonyms* (*v*) convey, acquit, behave, accept, comport, hold, pack, load, assume, admit, adopt, act, capture, cart, contain, **3.** load; *synonyms* (*n*) charge, cargo, freight, stack, heap, weight, consignment, lading, shipment, (*v*) burden, fill, encumber, pile, lade, stow; *antonym* (*v*) unload, **4.** unload; *synonyms* (*v*) discharge, drop, empty, unlade, clear, tip, unburden, exonerate, free, dump, relieve, offload, deliver, disencumber, (*adj*) disburden, **5.** ship; *synonyms* (*n*) boat, ferry, craft, bottom, (*v*) dispatch, send, forward, consign, embark, move, post, mail, **6.** transport; *synonyms* (*n*) rapture, transportation, conveyance, shipping, (*v*) delight, enrapture, exile, banish, enchant, ravish, entrance, run, haul, remove, ship; *antonyms* (*v*) disenchant, remain.

urakinaki 1. loaded; *synonyms* (*adj*) laden, full, burdened, flush, moneyed, wealthy, affluent, rich, tight, tipsy, intoxicated, heavy, pixilated, plastered, soused; *antonym* (*adj*) poor, **2.** conveyed; *synonyms* (*v*) carried, borne, supported, **3.** unloaded; *synonyms* (*adj*) unobstructed, untrammeled, unfraught; *antonym* (*adj*) loaded.

uramai 1. critical; *synonyms* (*adj*) acute, decisive, delicate, important, pressing, severe, ticklish, urgent, vital, crucial, dangerous, fastidious, grave, imperative, (*v*) censorious; *antonyms* (*adj*) complimentary, trivial, positive, flattering, insignificant, approving, unimportant, **2.** impending; *synonyms* (*adj*) imminent, forthcoming, close, coming, future, approaching, near, pending, prospective, menacing, nearing, threatening, upcoming; *antonym* (*adj*) distant, **3.** imminent; *synonyms* (*adj*) impending, oncoming; *antonym* (*adj*) far-off, **4.** near; *synonyms* (*prep*) about, by, around, (*adv*) almost, towards, approximately, (*adj*) adjoining, adjacent, contiguous, narrow, closer, handy, (*v*) familiar, approximate, approach, **5.** pink; *synonyms* (*adj*) flower, pinkish, (*n*) red, crimson, rose, carmine, (*v*) knock, gore, impale, prick, punch, spear, spike, stab, enfilade, **6.** serious; *synonyms* (*adj*) heavy, sedate, austere, great, hard, considerable, critical, earnest, grievous, sad, sober, bad, big, deep, (*v*) momentous; *antonyms* (*adj*) frivolous, lighthearted, cheerful, flippant, humorous, mild, minor, playful, slight.

uramaka blazing; *synonyms* (*adj*) ablaze, afire, burning, flaming, ardent, aflame, alight, blatant, bright, glaring, blistering, conspicuous, fervent, fierce, (*n*) blaze.

uramaki smoulder; *synonyms* (*v*) smolder, choke, suffocate.

uramate smoulder; *synonyms* (*v*) smolder, choke, suffocate.

uramwaka 1. glow; *synonyms* (*n*) beam, color, glare, sparkle, blaze, flash, (*v*) blush, flush, gleam, glimmer, shine, burn, flare, fire, flame; *antonym* (*n*) dullness, **2.** flare; *synonyms* (*n*) signal, beacon, (*v*)

burst, glint, erupt, flicker, glow, twinkle, combust, (*adj*) detonate, explode, fly, bounce, displode.

uramwakaki flared; *synonyms* (*adj*) flaring, aflare, fluttering, flying, waving.

urarakea blaze; *synonyms* (*n*) glare, flame, burning, fire, light, hell, scintillation, combustion, (*v*) flash, beam, flicker, mark, shimmer, (*adj*) burn, glow.

uraro purple; *synonyms* (*adj*) mauve, violet, imperial, lilac, regal, royal, embellished, majestic, (*n*) empurpled, magenta, purpleness, damask, ermine, mantle, (*v*) empurple.

uraura red; *synonyms* (*adj*) crimson, flushed, carmine, glowing, rosy, ruby, sanguine, cherry, pink, radical, ruddy, scarlet, cerise, bloody, inflamed.

ure 1. expand; *synonyms* (*v*) amplify, enlarge, balloon, broaden, develop, distend, aggrandize, augment, extend, inflate, swell, explicate, bloat, elaborate, (*adj*) dilate; *antonyms* (*v*) contract, shorten, abbreviate, decrease, deflate, reduce, shrink, summarize, narrow, **2.** burst; *synonyms* (*v*) break, crack, blast, rupture, belch, abound, erupt, open, (*n*) flash, explosion, (*adj*) split, explode, detonate, flare, splinter; *antonym* (*v*) implode, **3.** separate; *synonyms* (*adj*) detached, (*v*) detach, divorce, part, insulate, scatter, cut, dissociate, disconnect, discrete, discriminate, disjoin, disperse, distinguish, divide; *antonyms* (*adj*) connected, joined, simultaneous, (*v*) unite, merge, mix, combine, fuse, join, link, associate, **4.** open; *synonyms* (*adj*) frank, obvious, artless, exposed, free, honest, bare, forthright, guileless, ingenuous, naked, (*v*) expand, give, (*n*) candid, clear; *antonyms* (*adj*) devious, secretive, concealed, furtive, hidden, limited, repressive, reserved, restricted, secret, blocked, cautious, (*v*) shut, end, (*tr v*) close.

ureaki 1. burst; *synonyms* (*v*) break, crack, blast, rupture, belch, abound, erupt, open, (*n*) flash, explosion, (*adj*) split, explode, detonate, flare, splinter; *antonym* (*v*) implode, **2.** expanded; *synonyms* (*adj*) extended, extensive, wide, dilated, enlarged, prolonged; *antonym* (*adj*) brief, **3.** opened; *synonyms* (*v*) blown, distended, exhausted, inflated, stale, (*adj*) candid, exposed, assailable, blatant, blazing, clear, conspicuous, lawless, loose, through, **4.** separated; *synonyms* (*adj*) disconnected, separate, apart, detached, divided, isolated, disjointed, free, disjunct, removed, dislocated, independent, lone, (*prep*) disjoined, distinct.

uretatanga 1. expanded; *synonyms* (*adj*) extended, extensive, open, wide, dilated, enlarged, prolonged; *antonym* (*adj*) brief, **2.** open; *synonyms* (*adj*) frank, obvious, artless, exposed, free, honest, bare, forthright, guileless, ingenuous, naked, (*v*) expand, give, (*n*) candid, clear; *antonyms* (*adj*) devious, secretive, concealed, furtive, hidden, limited, repressive, reserved, restricted, secret, blocked, cautious, (*v*) shut, end, (*tr v*) close.

uri 1. baptize; *synonyms* (*v*) call, christen, dub, entitle, name, baptise, term, style, **2.** open; *synonyms* (*adj*) frank, obvious, artless, exposed, free, honest, bare, forthright, guileless, ingenuous, naked, (*v*) expand, give, (*n*) candid, clear; *antonyms* (*adj*) devious, secretive, concealed, furtive, hidden, limited, repressive, reserved, restricted, secret, blocked, cautious, (*v*) shut, end, (*tr v*) close.

uria sprinkle; *synonyms* (*n*) dash, (*v*) scatter, drizzle, splash, moisten, cast, dot, spatter, spray, rain, spill, spread, diffuse, intersperse, (*adj*) besprinkle.

uriaki 1. baptized, **2.** sprinkled; *synonyms* (*adj*) besprent, scattered, dotted, speckled, spotted, spread, strewn.

uring recollect; *synonyms* (*v*) recall, remember, recognize, remind, mind, think, reminisce, retrieve, consider, review; *antonym* (*v*) forget.

uringa 1. remember; *synonyms* (*v*) commemorate, recognize, recall, recollect, consider, record, remind, retain, think, review, ponder, mark, imagine, refresh, cite; *antonym* (*v*) forget, **2.** recollect; *synonyms* (*v*) remember, mind, reminisce, retrieve, **3.** recall; *synonyms* (*v*) countermand, repeal, rescind, retract, reverse, revoke, cancel, recant, withdraw, (*n*) anamnesis, memory, return, annulment, recollection, reminiscence.

uringaki remembered; *synonym* (*v*) remembering.

uringnga remember; *synonyms* (*v*) commemorate, recognize, recall, recollect, consider, record, remind, retain, think, review, ponder, mark, imagine, refresh, cite; *antonym* (*v*) forget.

uringngaki remembered; *synonym* (*v*) remembering.

uriri hasten; *synonyms* (*v*) speed, expedite, further, forward, dispatch, advance, hurry, dash, hie, rush, bustle, dart, (*adj*) accelerate, quicken, (*n*) haste; *antonym* (*v*) delay.

uru destroy; *synonyms* (*v*) break, demolish, blight, despoil, annihilate, blast, crush, dash, destruct, devastate, devour, dismantle, (*adj*) desolate, abolish, consume; *antonyms* (*v*) build, preserve, create, make.

urua 1. blot; *synonyms* (*n*) blemish, spot, smudge, blotch, slur, daub, defect, fault, flaw, (*v*) stain, mark, taint, tarnish, blob, blur, **2.** destroy; *synonyms* (*v*) break, demolish, blight, despoil, annihilate, blast, crush, dash, destruct, devastate, devour, dismantle, (*adj*) desolate, abolish, consume; *antonyms* (*v*) build, preserve, create, make, **3.** break; *synonyms* (*v*) split, crack, burst, fail, infringe, leak, (*n*) breach, fracture, pause, rupture, stop, collapse, interruption, respite, suspension; *antonyms* (*v*) repair, obey, honor, mend, (*n*) continuation, **4.**

damage; *synonyms* (*n*) injury, wound, loss, cost, detriment, disadvantage, impairment, (*v*) harm, hurt, abuse, injure, afflict, disfigure, mar, (*adj*) impair; *antonyms* (*n*) service, (*v*) conserve, enhance, bolster, **5.** smash; *synonyms* (*v*) crash, bang, hit, mash, shatter, defeat, pound, ruin, slam, fragment, batter, (*n*) clash, collision, knock, bash, **6.** plunder; *synonyms* (*v*) loot, pillage, harry, spoil, destroy, maraud, ransack, strip, divest, forage, foray, prey, (*n*) booty, depredation, despoliation, **7.** sack; *synonyms* (*n*) pocket, pouch, sac, poke, purse, rape, (*v*) bag, plunder, discharge, dismiss, fire, rob, rifle, can, eject; *antonym* (*v*) hire, **8.** violate; *synonyms* (*v*) contravene, transgress, desecrate, dishonor, disobey, ravish, assault, offend, outrage, profane, debauch, defile, force, pollute, trespass.

uruabai demolish; *synonyms* (*v*) consume, annihilate, break, defeat, batter, crush, destroy, devastate, raze, blast, dismantle, level, overthrow, ruin, shatter; *antonyms* (*v*) build, construct.

uruabaiaki demolished; *synonyms* (*adj*) broken, baneful, decayed, dismantled, lost, razed, ruinous, destructive, dilapidated, mischievous, pernicious, wasteful.

uruaki 1. damaged; *synonyms* (*adj*) faulty, unsound, defective, broken, dilapidated, hurt, impaired, besmirched, deficient, flyblown; *antonym* (*adj*) undamaged, **2.** destroyed; *synonyms* (*adj*) lost, ruined, desolate, desolated, shattered, dead, depressed, **3.** broken; *synonyms* (*v*) broke, (*adj*) tame, torn, busted, imperfect, intermittent, rough, rugged, uneven, disjointed, incomplete, confused, cracked, crushed, disconnected; *antonyms* (*adj*) constant, unbroken, intact, whole, wild, **4.** smashed; *synonyms* (*adj*) drunk, inebriated, intoxicated, plastered, sloshed, blotto, tipsy, besotted, pissed, tight; *antonym* (*adj*) sober, **5.** sacked; *synonyms* (*adj*) despoiled, pillaged, raped, ravaged, assaulted, blasted, devastated, looted, molested, plundered, ransacked, wasted, **6.** plundered; *synonyms* (*adj*) fleeced, sacked, **7.** violated; *synonyms* (*v*) apart, blighted, contrite, disunited, fractured, humbled, strained, subdued, subjugated, (*adj*) profaned, seduced, debauched, defiled, desecrated, dishonored; *antonym* (*adj*) pure.

urubeke break; *synonyms* (*v*) split, crack, burst, fail, infringe, leak, (*n*) breach, fracture, pause, rupture, stop, collapse, interruption, respite, suspension; *antonyms* (*v*) repair, obey, honor, mend, (*n*) continuation.

urubekeaki broken; *synonyms* (*v*) broke, (*adj*) tame, torn, busted, imperfect, intermittent, rough, rugged, ruined, uneven, disjointed, incomplete, confused, cracked, crushed; *antonyms* (*adj*) constant, unbroken, intact, whole, wild.

urukau 1. chief; *synonyms* (*adj*) head, principal, cardinal, capital, arch, central, essential, first, main, (*n*) administrator, boss, captain, executive, leader, paramount; *antonyms* (*adj*) minor, associate, secondary, **2.** superior; *synonyms* (*adj*) senior, dominant, better, exceptional, predominant, elder, great, arrogant, chief, eminent, excellent, high, higher, lofty, proud; *antonyms* (*adj*) humble, worse, poor, (*n*) inferior, subordinate, subscript.

urukauna 1. lead; *synonyms* (*v*) head, guide, conduct, contribute, direct, chair, conduce, control, go, govern, bring, convey, give, (*n*) clue, advantage; *antonym* (*v*) follow, **2.** direct; *synonyms* (*adj*) straight, blunt, immediate, transparent, (*v*) aim, channel, address, charge, dictate, administer, lead, level, order, point, (*n*) command; *antonyms* (*adj*) indirect, roundabout, circuitous, oblique, second-hand, sideways, unplanned, (*v*) request, **3.** head; *synonyms* (*n*) chief, captain, front, boss, foam, froth, crown, chieftain, executive, brain, commander, director, end, forefront, (*v*) capital; *antonym* (*n*) subordinate, **4.** organize; *synonyms* (*v*) establish, coordinate, constitute, devise, fix, form, institute, regulate, compose, engineer, found, make, orchestrate, organise, (*n*) arrange; *antonym* (*v*) disorganize.

urukaunaki 1. led, **2.** directed; *synonyms* (*adj*) absorbed, concentrating, destined, focussed, formal, intent, prescript, subject, engaged, fixed, prescribed, rapt, (*adv*) under, **3.** organized; *synonyms* (*adj*) organised, organic, systematic, regular, arranged, methodical, orderly, shipshape, efficient, ready; *antonyms* (*adj*) untidy, disorganized, muddled.

urunga 1. maneuver; *synonyms* (*v*) manoeuvre, guide, handle, control, manipulate, manoeuver, steer, (*n*) artifice, ruse, scheme, measure, device, act, ploy, stratagem, **2.** steer; *synonyms* (*v*) navigate, direct, drive, aim, conduct, manage, maneuver, run, tip, show, channel, govern, (*n*) lead, point, bullock.

ururinga recollect; *synonyms* (*v*) recall, remember, recognize, remind, mind, think, reminisce, retrieve, consider, review; *antonym* (*v*) forget.

uta some; *synonyms* (*adv*) nearly, rather, somewhat, about, approximately, around, roughly, round, almost, near, (*adj*) few, certain, several, (*det*) any, (*n*) one.

utakiaki aggravated; *synonyms* (*adj*) irritated, angry, infuriated, afflictive, exasperated, grievous, provoked, bothered, discouraged, displeased, disturbed, flagitious, forced, frustrated, goaded; *antonym* (*adj*) unprovoked.

uteute grass; *synonyms* (*n*) cannabis, forage, marijuana, pasture, dope, feed, ganja, herb, herbage, informer, (*v*) betray, denounce, (*adj*) pot, green, hemp.

uti 1. awake; *synonyms* (*adj*) alive, alert, attentive, conscious, aware, intelligent, keen, sleepless, (*v*) arouse, wake, awaken, waken, rouse, stimulate, stir; *antonyms* (*adj*) asleep, unconscious, comatose, sleeping, sleepy, **2.** conscious; *synonyms* (*adj*) calculated, cognizant, deliberate, mindful, premeditated, intended, discerning, self-conscious, intentional, knowing, knowledgeable, known, purposeful, sensible, studied; *antonyms* (*adj*) unaware, ignorant, **3.** awaken; *synonyms* (*v*) awake, call, kindle, provoke, raise, revive, evoke, excite, incite, move, advise, apprise, **4.** wake; *synonyms* (*v*) vigil, watch, (*n*) train, trail, backwash, track, wave, aftermath, consequence, funeral, jollification, junket, queue, tail, viewing; *antonym* (*v*) sleep.

utiaki awakened; *synonyms* (*adj*) awake, excited, interested.

utibaba 1. erect; *synonyms* (*v*) build, elevate, raise, construct, rear, assemble, lift, create, advance, arouse, dignify, (*adj*) upright, vertical, perpendicular, raised; *antonym* (*adj*) horizontal, **2.** raise; *synonyms* (*v*) boost, erect, hoist, increase, enhance, foster, grow, promote, prefer, augment, cultivate, exalt, excite, heave, heighten; *antonym* (*v*) lower.

utibabaki 1. erected, **2.** raised; *synonyms* (*v*) repousse, (*adj*) elevated, embossed, erect, convex, brocaded, high, alert, bold, confident, elate, elated, elative, exultant, (*prep*) above.

utikun jittery; *synonyms* (*adj*) fidgety, edgy, jumpy, tense, anxious, restive, uneasy, nervy, overstrung, uptight, (*v*) nervous, twitchy; *antonym* (*adj*) relaxed.

uton 1. incriminate; *synonyms* (*v*) arraign, accuse, charge, impeach, denounce, criminate, indict, involve, implicate, inculpate, censure, imply, **2.** inculpate; *synonyms* (*v*) incriminate, connote, entail, inculp, mean.

utowa 1. fidgety; *synonyms* (*adj*) restless, fretful, fussy, unquiet, anxious, hasty, jumpy, mercurial, restive, skittish, tense, uneasy, (*v*) nervous, apprehensive, tremulous, **2.** hyperactive; *synonyms* (*adj*) frantic, overactive, furious, harried, hysterical, mad, possessed, turbulent.

utu 1. kindred; *synonyms* (*adj*) cognate, akin, similar, allied, congenial, related, (*n*) family, kin, consanguinity, folk, folks, relation, blood, clan, (*v*) genealogy; *antonym* (*n*) unrelated, **2.** kin; *synonyms* (*n*) kindred, house, gender, stock, tribe, connection, kinsmen, affinity, kinfolk, kinsfolk, kinsperson, lineage, people, race, relations.

Û

ûi tooth; *synonyms* (*n*) palate, grain, nap, saw, stomach, tongue, liking, fiber, point, spicule, wire, apophysis, bulb, (*adj*) nib, (*v*) bite.

V

vaeiei sway; *synonyms* (*n*) influence, reign, rock, authority, empire, (*v*) command, rule, oscillate, control, reel, stagger, bias, careen, lurch, persuade.

vetea 1. convoke; *synonyms* (*v*) convene, call, assemble, summon, collect, muster, convocate, **2**. call; *synonyms* (*v*) cry, bellow, name, shout, bid, howl, address, baptize, cite, dub, (*n*) appeal, yell, appoint, command, demand; *antonym* (*v*) dismiss.

veteaki called; *synonyms* (*v*) nempt, ycleped, (*adj*) named, chosen, qualified.

W

w v; *synonyms* (*prep*) against, (*n*) five, cinque, fin, fins, fivesome, flipper, flippers, (*v*) clasp, comprehend, contain, display, embrace, encompass, (*adj*) doubtful.

wa 1. canoe; *synonyms* (*n*) boat, caique, felucca, (*adj*) self-sufficient, **2**. fruit; *synonyms* (*n*) effect, crop, outgrowth, product, consequence, issue, produce, production, yield, development, (*v*) result, return, building, edifice, erection.

waa boat; *synonyms* (*n*) yacht, scull, craft, dinghy, ship, vessel, vehicle, shallop, schooner, sailboat, bateau, bowl, sauceboat, truck, (*v*) cruise.

wae 1. feet; *synonyms* (*n*) fete, meter, rescue, arm, fact, performance, (*v*) legs, pegs, pins, trotters, **2**. foot; *synonyms* (*n*) bottom, base, feet, foundation, basis, footing, measure, paw, pes, bed, butt, floor, (*v*) hoof, pay, hand; *antonym* (*n*) top.

waea 1. pierce; *synonyms* (*v*) impale, cut, perforate, bore, enter, stab, stick, bite, drill, gore, penetrate, puncture, thrust, wound, (*n*) prick, **2**. thread; *synonyms* (*n*) string, line, yarn, rope, twine, wire, cord, fiber, (*v*) file, range, lace, pass, run, meander, permeate, **3**. skewer; *synonyms* (*n*) pin, brad, nail, staple, bolt, bundle, (*v*) spit, spike, spear, pierce, transfix, bayonet, goad, point, degree, **4**. prick; *synonyms* (*n*) cock, pricking, spur, pang, asshole,

pecker, (*v*) needle, twinge, nip, fret, pinch, hurt, prickle, smart, sting.

waeai 1. new; *synonyms* (*adj*) green, modern, novel, original, additional, inexperienced, innovative, raw, recent, strange, unaccustomed, unprecedented, young, (*adv*) fresh, lately; *antonyms* (*adj*) old, familiar, outgoing, second-hand, traditional, used, less, old-fashioned, stale, (*adv*) past, **2**. fresh; *synonyms* (*adj*) bracing, brisk, clean, bright, airy, bold, alive, chilly, cool, forward, pure, smart, sweet, flippant, (*adv*) new; *antonyms* (*adj*) decayed, exhausted, hot, humid, muggy, musty, off, oppressive, rotten, tired, worn, dry, sweltering, **3**. tender; *synonyms* (*adj*) affectionate, painful, loving, sensitive, soft, sore, compassionate, delicate, fond, gentle, mild, (*v*) proffer, (*n*) offer, bid, overture; *antonyms* (*adj*) tough, hard, hardhearted, rubbery, rough, **4**. recent; *synonyms* (*adj*) late, latest, contemporary, current, last, latter, final, immediate, present, **5**. young; *synonyms* (*adj*) juvenile, immature, adolescent, baby, boyish, callow, childish, early, tender, unripe, youthful, childlike, (*n*) offspring, progeny, issue; *antonyms* (*adj*) mature, adult, (*n*) aged.

waeaki 1. threaded; *synonym* (*adj*) screwed, **2**. pierced; *synonyms* (*adj*) perforated, punctured, perforate, cleft, entered.

waebaka 1. needy; *synonyms* (*adj*) destitute, indigent, impoverished, poor, necessitous, impecunious, penniless, underprivileged, deficient, miserable, deprived, poverty-stricken, wanting, broke; *antonym* (*adj*) well-off, **2**. destitute; *synonyms* (*adj*) bankrupt, forlorn, needy, helpless, void, bare, abandoned, depressed, empty, forsaken, naked, abject, disadvantaged, (*v*) devoid; *antonym* (*adj*) rich, **3**. impoverished; *synonyms* (*adj*) barren, broken, strapped; *antonym* (*adj*) wealthy, **4**. indigent; *synonym* (*n*) pauper, **5**. miserable; *synonyms* (*adj*) mean, meager, bad, deplorable, desolate, downcast, low, measly, unhappy, distressed, lamentable, cheerless, contemptible, dejected, (*v*) wretched; *antonyms* (*adj*) happy, cheerful, generous, **6**. penniless; *synonyms* (*adj*) moneyless, insolvent, penurious, dowerless, fortuneless; *antonym* (*adj*) solvent, **7**. poor; *synonyms* (*adj*) paltry, evil, inadequate, insufficient, pathetic, piteous, pitiful, meagre, feeble, lean, nasty, pitiable, shabby, sordid, unfortunate; *antonyms* (*adj*) excellent, first-rate, privileged, admirable, good.

waekirere hop; *synonyms* (*n*) jump, leap, bound, hops, trip, flight, (*v*) dance, gambol, bounce, caper, skip, spring, limp, fly, hurdle.

waekoa 1. hasten; *synonyms* (*v*) speed, expedite, further, forward, dispatch, advance, hurry, dash, hie, rush, bustle, dart, (*adj*) accelerate, quicken, (*n*) haste; *antonym* (*v*) delay, **2**. hurry; *synonyms* (*n*) flurry, celerity, hastiness, hurriedness, press, (v) hasten, scurry, fly, run, zip, drive, race, scamper, scuttle, flit; *antonyms* (n) slowness, (v) dawdle.

waekoaki hurried; *synonyms* (adj) hasty, fast, headlong, quick, rapid, speedy, sudden, swift, abrupt, cursory, careless, precipitate, prompt, rash, slapdash; *antonyms* (adj) slow, unhurried, leisurely.

waerake land; *synonyms* (n) ground, country, soil, field, kingdom, domain, estate, nation, realm, state, (v) disembark, debark, alight, get, drop; *antonym* (adj) aquatic.

waerebutata 1. restive; *synonyms* (adj) obstinate, edgy, fidgety, jittery, jumpy, nervy, restless, uptight, restiff, nervous, tense, uneasy, unruly, overstrung, (v) skittish; *antonym* (adj) relaxed, **2.** restless; *synonyms* (adj) unquiet, agitated, apprehensive, fretful, impatient, restive, feverish, turbulent, disturbed, wakeful, eager, hasty, mercurial, frightened, (v) anxious; *antonym* (adj) calm.

waeremwe 1. lag; *synonyms* (n) backwardness, interim, interval, (v) dawdle, delay, linger, dally, drag, gaol, immure, imprison, incarcerate, jail, jug, loiter, **2.** dawdle; *synonyms* (v) lag, amble, procrastinate, hesitate, idler, lounge, saunter; *antonyms* (v) hurry, rush, **3.** slow; *synonyms* (adj) dull, late, easy, sluggish, heavy, dense, dim, gradual, inactive, indolent, lazy, stupid, (v) slack, (adv) behind, behindhand; *antonyms* (adj) fast, intelligent, rapid, bright, alert, brisk, hasty, prompt, quick, speedy, hurried, observant, rushed, (v) accelerate, **4.** saunter; *synonyms* (v) roam, meander, (n) stroll, ramble, walk, promenade, wander, hike, perambulation, turn, constitutional, journey, (adv) crawl, creep, drawl.

waerikiriki prow; *synonyms* (n) bow, fore, stem, beak, nose, arc, base, bowing, bowknot, obeisance, rostrum, (adj) advantage, benefit, brave, courageous.

waero nocturnal; *synonyms* (adj) nightly, vespertine, autumnal, late; *antonym* (adj) diurnal.

waetata 1. fast; *synonyms* (adj) dissolute, firm, agile, debauched, fixed, hurried, instant, quick, rapid, staunch, brisk, (adv) soon, hard, close, (n) diet; *antonyms* (adj) sluggish, loose, (adv) slow, slowly, leisurely, (v) gorge, (n) binge, **2.** accelerated; *synonyms* (adj) fast, intensive, speedy, express, sudden, **3.** hurry; *synonyms* (n) speed, haste, dispatch, flurry, (v) bustle, hasten, accelerate, dash, expedite, scurry, fly, run, rush, zip, hie; *antonyms* (n) slowness, (v) dawdle, **4.** swift; *synonyms* (adj) fleet, alert, hasty, nimble, prompt, expeditious, lively, abrupt, ready, sprightly, impetuous, unexpected, active, immediate, (n) cylinder; *antonym* (adj) considered, **5.** rapid; *synonyms* (adj) swift, cursory, winged, precipitous, precipitate, rash, volant, instantaneous; *antonym* (adj) gradual,

6. quick; *synonyms* (adj) bright, clever, intelligent, alive, dexterous, keen, brief, acute, animated, apt, ingenious, sharp, skillful, smart, facile; *antonym* (adj) dull, **7.** swiftly; *synonyms* (adv) rapidly, promptly, speedily, fleetly, readily, nimbly, immediately, hastily, suddenly, (adj) quickly.

waetataki hurried; *synonyms* (adj) hasty, fast, headlong, quick, rapid, speedy, sudden, swift, abrupt, cursory, careless, precipitate, prompt, rash, slapdash; *antonyms* (adj) slow, unhurried, leisurely.

waetebetebe hop; *synonyms* (n) jump, leap, bound, hops, trip, flight, (v) dance, gambol, bounce, caper, skip, spring, limp, fly, hurdle.

waetoka 1. fast; *synonyms* (adj) dissolute, firm, agile, debauched, fixed, hurried, instant, quick, rapid, staunch, brisk, (adv) soon, hard, close, (n) diet; *antonyms* (adj) sluggish, loose, (adv) slow, slowly, leisurely, (v) gorge, (n) binge, **2.** agile; *synonyms* (adj) active, nimble, adroit, spry, deft, lively, lithe, sprightly, supple, quick-witted, alert, dexterous, fast, fleet, flexible; *antonym* (adj) clumsy.

waewae 1. criticize; *synonyms* (v) attack, belittle, berate, blame, censure, chide, comment, denounce, rebuke, reprimand, scold, condemn, criticise, deplore, disparage; *antonyms* (v) praise, approve, commend, admire, **2.** legged, **3.** footed; *synonym* (adj) established, **4.** contradict; *synonyms* (v) deny, oppose, belie, conflict, confute, contravene, controvert, disprove, dissent, impugn, invalidate, refute, disaffirm, disclaim, counteract; *antonyms* (v) confirm, agree, match, **5.** oppose; *synonyms* (v) object, contest, contend, contradict, resist, fight, counter, disagree, combat, confront, defend, dispute, gainsay, hinder, repel; *antonyms* (v) support, advocate, back, advise, **6.** stitch; *synonyms* (n) twinge, pang, cramp, (v) sew, seam, baste, crick, embroider, suture, tack, articulation, commissure, gore, gusset, (adj) tie; *antonym* (v) unpick.

waewaeaki 1. footed; *synonym* (adj) established, **2.** opposed; *synonyms* (adj) conflicting, contradictory, hostile, contrary, antagonistic, opposing, adverse, averse, contrasted, repugnant, incompatible, irreconcilable, counter, against, opposite, **3.** stitched; *synonyms* (adj) sewed, sewn.

wai 1. elongated; *synonyms* (adj) elongate, extended, long, lengthened, lengthy, prolonged, oblong, lengthen, extensive, oval, expanded, extend, linear, stretch, wide, **2.** leg; *synonyms* (n) stage, blackleg, branch, peg, post, arm, column, limb, member, phase, rook, shank, support, fork, **3.** long; *synonyms* (adj) dragging, far, diffuse, (v) aspire, desire, hanker, languish, yearn, ache, hunger, wish, crave, pine, yen, (n) large; *antonyms* (adj) short, brief, **4.** foot; *synonyms* (n) bottom, base, feet, foundation, basis, footing, measure, paw, pes, bed, butt, floor, (v) hoof, pay, hand; *antonym* (n) top, **5.**

harpoon; *synonyms* (*n*) dart, javelin, lance, spear, striker, arrow, bolt, boomerang, jereed, jerid, pike, reed, shaft, spontoon, wencher, **6.** thread; *synonyms* (*n*) string, line, yarn, rope, twine, wire, cord, fiber, (*v*) file, range, penetrate, lace, pass, run, meander, **7.** pierce; *synonyms* (*v*) impale, cut, perforate, bore, enter, stab, stick, bite, drill, gore, puncture, thrust, wound, broach, (*n*) prick, **8.** skewer; *synonyms* (*n*) pin, brad, nail, staple, bundle, hang, knife, (*v*) spit, spike, pierce, transfix, bayonet, goad, point, degree, **9.** prick; *synonyms* (*n*) cock, pricking, spur, pang, asshole, pecker, (*v*) needle, twinge, nip, fret, pinch, hurt, prickle, smart, sting, **10.** tapering; *synonyms* (*adj*) tapered, narrow, narrowing, angustation, coarctation, conical, dwindling, constricting, constrictive, sharp, lessened, narrowed, (*n*) crowning, contraction, lessening, **11.** oblong; *synonyms* (*adj*) elliptical, ellipsoidal, ovaliform, ovaloid, ovate, ovated, ovopyriform, (*n*) rectangle, block, quadrangle, diamond, lozenge, parallelogram, quadrilateral, (*v*) longitudinal, **12.** pointed; *synonyms* (*adj*) penetrating, keen, poignant, acute, piquant, cutting, marked, pithy, biting, acuminate, barbed, prickly, pungent, meaningful, fine; *antonym* (*adj*) rounded.

waiaki 1. threaded; *synonym* (*adj*) screwed, **2.** pierced; *synonyms* (*adj*) perforated, punctured, perforate, cleft, entered.

waibora 1. sew; *synonyms* (*v*) patch, knit, mend, stitch, tack, tailor, retick, tick, weave, make, beat, click, create, customise, (*adj*) tie, **2.** pierce; *synonyms* (*v*) impale, cut, perforate, bore, enter, stab, stick, bite, drill, gore, penetrate, puncture, thrust, wound, (*n*) prick.

waiboraki pierced; *synonyms* (*adj*) perforated, punctured, perforate, cleft, entered.

waikakang pointed; *synonyms* (*adj*) penetrating, keen, poignant, acute, piquant, cutting, marked, pithy, biting, acuminate, barbed, prickly, pungent, sharp, short; *antonym* (*adj*) rounded.

waira disparage; *synonyms* (*v*) denigrate, belittle, deprecate, depreciate, derogate, decry, defame, censure, condemn, criticize, detract, abuse, slur, (*n*) disgrace, discredit; *antonyms* (*v*) praise, compliment, flatter.

waitekea 1. prick; *synonyms* (*n*) cock, pricking, spur, pang, (*v*) goad, puncture, impale, pierce, stab, needle, bite, twinge, nip, fret, pinch, **2.** skewer; *synonyms* (*n*) pin, brad, nail, staple, bolt, bundle, hang, (*v*) spit, spike, spear, transfix, bayonet, point, prick, degree.

waiteketeke 1. marked; *synonyms* (*adj*) distinct, conspicuous, noticeable, pronounced, remarkable, distinguished, apparent, definite, notable, obvious, signal, striking, strong, clear, appreciable; *antonyms* (*adj*) plain, unblemished, **2.** mottled;

synonyms (*adj*) dappled, motley, speckled, multicolored, piebald, spotted, variegated, mixed, **3.** speckled; *synonyms* (*adj*) dotted, mottled, specked, spotty, flecked, **4.** spotted; *synonyms* (*v*) mildewed, moldy, rusty, (*adj*) blotchy, flyblown, dirty, stained, tainted, besmirched, damaged, freckled, patched.

waiteketekea 1. mark; *synonyms* (*n*) brand, evidence, score, character, heed, impression, imprint, sign, feature, (*v*) blemish, characterize, distinguish, grade, label, (*adj*) notice, **2.** speckle; *synonyms* (*n*) fleck, dapple, spot, freckle, point, blot, maculation, patch, daub, flake, (*v*) speck, mark, stain, stipple, (*adj*) bespeckle, **3.** spot; *synonyms* (*n*) place, dot, dirty, location, position, space, defect, site, smudge, (*v*) soil, speckle, flaw, mottle, blur, locate.

waiteketekeaki 1. marked; *synonyms* (*adj*) distinct, conspicuous, noticeable, pronounced, remarkable, distinguished, apparent, definite, notable, obvious, signal, striking, strong, clear, appreciable; *antonyms* (*adj*) plain, unblemished, **2.** speckled; *synonyms* (*adj*) dappled, dotted, mottled, piebald, specked, spotty, spotted, flecked, multicolored, **3.** spotted; *synonyms* (*v*) mildewed, moldy, rusty, (*adj*) speckled, blotchy, flyblown, dirty, stained, tainted, besmirched, damaged, freckled, patched.

waitotokoa 1. hinder; *synonyms* (*adj*) posterior, hind, (*v*) block, bar, impede, check, hamper, obstruct, resist, curb, arrest, clog, counteract, delay, detain; *antonyms* (*v*) help, assist, facilitate, **2.** counteract; *synonyms* (*v*) antagonize, counterbalance, balance, cancel, contradict, hinder, neutralize, compensate, contravene, kill, baffle, countervail, frustrate, nullify, offset, **3.** stop; *synonyms* (*v*) stand, close, interrupt, plug, catch, disrupt, dwell, finish, intercept, pause, (*n*) halt, hold, stay, end, cease; *antonyms* (*v*) continue, start, begin, encourage, permit, prolong, **4.** oppose; *synonyms* (*v*) object, contest, contend, controvert, fight, counter, disagree, dissent, combat, confront, defend, dispute, gainsay, repel, thwart; *antonyms* (*v*) support, advocate, agree, back, advise.

waitotokoaki 1. opposed; *synonyms* (*adj*) conflicting, contradictory, hostile, contrary, antagonistic, opposing, adverse, averse, contrasted, repugnant, incompatible, irreconcilable, counter, against, opposite, **2.** stopped; *synonyms* (*adj*) halted, congested, unmoving, blocked, finished, chinked, clogged, immobile, motionless, static, stationary, bunged, crashed, still.

waiwai reef; *synonyms* (*n*) ledge, rock, ait, eyot, isle, islet, bank, rand, (*v*) slow.

waka 1. fibrous; *synonyms* (*adj*) stringy, tough, ropy, brawny, fibry, gossamer, hempen, muscular, nemaline, raw, rubbery, sinewy, unchewable, wiry, coarse; *antonym* (*adj*) tender, **2.** stringy; *synonyms* (*adj*) fibrous, glutinous, filamentous, tenacious, thready, lean, resisting, ropey, sequacious, **3**. tough; *synonyms* (*adj*) hard, difficult, strong, arduous, firm, hardy, laborious, rugged, severe, stout, sturdy, rough, bad, (*n*) bully, rowdy; *antonyms* (*adj*) easy, weak, flimsy, soft, feeble, lightweight, simple, **4**. undercooked; *synonyms* (*adj*) rare, bloody, pink, **5**. threaded; *synonym* (*adj*) screwed.

wakâ root; *synonyms* (*n*) base, foundation, origin, basis, radical, radix, cause, derivation, reason, beginning, bottom, core, essence, (*v*) establish, dig.

wakaraoi 1. integrated; *synonyms* (*adj*) amalgamated, incorporated, combined, united, unified, entire, fused, merged, mixed, incorporate, **2**. adopted; *synonyms* (*adj*) adoptive, elected, consecrated, converted, inspired, justified, regenerated, sanctified, unearthly, adoptious, foreign, popular, preferred.

wakariri 1. fibrous; *synonyms* (*adj*) stringy, tough, ropy, brawny, fibry, gossamer, hempen, muscular, nemaline, raw, rubbery, sinewy, unchewable, wiry, coarse; *antonym* (*adj*) tender, **2**. stringy; *synonyms* (*adj*) fibrous, glutinous, filamentous, tenacious, thready, lean, resisting, ropey, sequacious, **3**. tough; *synonyms* (*adj*) hard, difficult, strong, arduous, firm, hardy, laborious, rugged, severe, stout, sturdy, rough, bad, (*n*) bully, rowdy; *antonyms* (*adj*) easy, weak, flimsy, soft, feeble, lightweight, simple.

wakawaka 1. fibrous; *synonyms* (*adj*) stringy, tough, ropy, brawny, fibry, gossamer, hempen, muscular, nemaline, raw, rubbery, sinewy, unchewable, wiry, coarse; *antonym* (*adj*) tender, **2**. stringy; *synonyms* (*adj*) fibrous, glutinous, filamentous, tenacious, thready, lean, resisting, ropey, sequacious.

waki 1. move; *synonyms* (*v*) act, affect, carry, excite, go, impel, instigate, maneuver, touch, travel, flow, bear, (*n*) motion, drive, transfer; *antonym* (*v*) stay, **2**. advance; *synonyms* (*n*) progress, improvement, (*v*) further, proceed, promote, approach, encourage, raise, rise, boost, contribute, cultivate, develop, forward, (*phr*) accelerate; *antonyms* (*n*) deterioration, (*v*) retreat, recede, delay, demote, regress, **3**. proceed; *synonyms* (*v*) advance, move, pass, originate, ensue, run, extend, arise, continue, emanate, happen, issue, operate, result, stem, **4**. progress; *synonyms* (*n*) headway, furtherance, betterment, gain, course, advancement, development, growth, increase, movement, passage, (*v*) grow, improve, prosper, way; *antonym* (*n*) decline, **5**. produce; *synonyms* (*v*) give, effect, cause, make, bring, present, procreate, breed, construct, form, frame, generate, fetch, prepare, **6**. onward; *synonyms* (*adv*) ahead, forwards, on, before, forth, onwards, along, frontward, forrader.

wakiaki 1. advanced; *synonyms* (*adj*) sophisticated, progressive, senior, higher, modern, new, precocious, late, cultured, developed, elevated, forward, liberal, ripe, superior; *antonyms* (*adj*) conservative, old-fashioned, inferior, **2**. produced; *synonyms* (*v*) producing, (*adj*) created, formed, bent, fashioned, shaped, twisted, wrought.

wakina 1. impel; *synonyms* (*v*) drive, coerce, constrain, force, carry, actuate, compel, goad, stimulate, urge, animate, encourage, incite, instigate, make, **2**. tug; *synonyms* (*n*) strain, towboat, effort, (*v*) drag, jerk, lug, pull, draw, haul, tow, labor, push, fight, labour, pluck, **3**. shove; *synonyms* (*v*) elbow, impel, press, prod, shift, boost, hustle, stuff, nudge, bump, cram, (*n*) thrust, jostle, poke, shoulder, **4**. propel; *synonyms* (*v*) launch, motivate, move, prompt, throw, cast, fling, shoot, shove, hurl, project, advance, displace, run, send, **5**. proceed; *synonyms* (*v*) go, pass, originate, ensue, flow, extend, arise, continue, emanate, happen, issue, operate, progress, result, stem, **6**. pursue; *synonyms* (*v*) chase, follow, dog, hunt, prosecute, course, haunt, hound, persist, stalk, tail, conduct, practice, court, keep.

wakinaki pursued; *synonym* (*n*) chased.

wana 1. intelligent; *synonyms* (*adj*) clever, alert, astute, bright, intellectual, quick-witted, rational, sensible, cunning, brilliant, canny, gifted, knowing, knowledgeable, quick; *antonyms* (*adj*) unintelligent, dim, dull-witted, thick, slow, stupid, **2**. sensible; *synonyms* (*adj*) reasonable, aware, judicious, perceptible, prudent, sagacious, intelligent, sane, wise, appreciable, sage, logical, practical, conscious, sapient; *antonyms* (*adj*) foolish, absurd, crazy, idiotic, imprudent, ludicrous, mad, outrageous, reckless, ridiculous, silly, unreasonable, unwise, harebrained, hasty, **3**. wise; *synonyms* (*adj*) sound, discreet, shrewd, discerning, thoughtful, sharp, skillful, smart, diplomatic, perceptive, provident, politic, (*n*) method, manner, way, **4**. reasonable; *synonyms* (*adj*) just, moderate, fair, legitimate, admissible, appropriate, cheap, due, equitable, impartial, inexpensive, plausible, temperate, acceptable, (*n*) clear; *antonyms* (*adj*) illogical, expensive, unfair, unsatisfactory, inadequate, **5**. prudent; *synonyms* (*adj*) cautious, circumspect, careful, chary, economical, frugal, deliberate, advisable, modest, guarded, tactful, thrifty, cautelous, expedient, (*v*) erudite; *antonyms* (*adj*) spendthrift, careless.

wanara 1. disentangle; *synonyms* (*v*) unravel, untangle, clear, disengage, ravel, detach, disembroil, extricate, unwind, comb, decipher, loosen, resolve, (*adj*) disembarrass, disencumber; *antonyms* (*v*) entangle, tangle, **2**. denude; *synonyms* (*v*) bare, strip, denudate, deprive, despoil, dismantle, disrobe, divest, expose, uncover, undress, **3**. separate; *synonyms* (*adj*) detached, individual, (*v*) divorce, part, insulate, scatter, cut, dissociate, disconnect, discrete, discriminate, disjoin, disperse, distinguish, divide; *antonyms* (*adj*) connected, joined, simultaneous, (*v*) unite, merge, mix, combine, fuse, join, link, associate.

wanaraki 1. denuded; *synonyms* (*adj*) bare, naked, bald, denudate, exposed, barefaced, barren, bleak, devoid, desolate, marginal, nude, scanty, spare, (*v*) minus, **2**. disentangled; *synonyms* (*adj*) disengaged, extricated, loosened, unsnarled, emancipated, liberated, **3**. separated; *synonyms* (*adj*) disconnected, separate, apart, detached, divided, isolated, disjointed, free, disjunct, removed, dislocated, independent, lone, (*prep*) disjoined, distinct.

wanawana 1. clever; *synonyms* (*adj*) adroit, capable, acute, able, apt, intelligent, smart, astute, cunning, expert, ingenious, quick, sharp, skillful, (*v*) brilliant; *antonyms* (*adj*) stupid, clumsy, unintelligent, dim, dull, inept, **2**. creative; *synonyms* (*adj*) original, productive, imaginative, inventive, resourceful, fertile, originative, artistic; *antonyms* (*adj*) unimaginative, uncreative, **3**. handy; *synonyms* (*adj*) available, convenient, clever, deft, dexterous, good, accessible, easy, commodious, functional, near, nearby, practical, useful, (*n*) ready; *antonyms* (*adj*) useless, fixed, **4**. clairvoyant; *synonyms* (*adj*) prophetic, mystic, perceptive, intuitive, extrasensory, farsighted, magical, mental, (*n*) psychic, seer, soothsayer, medium, sibyl, astrologer, oracle, **5**. intelligent; *synonyms* (*adj*) alert, bright, intellectual, quick-witted, rational, sensible, canny, gifted, knowing, knowledgeable, wise, witty, discerning, artful, discreet; *antonyms* (*adj*) dull-witted, thick, slow, **6**. ingenious; *synonyms* (*adj*) creative, cute, handy, crafty, sly, subtle, inspired, neat, shrewd, elegant, **7**. rational; *synonyms* (*adj*) reasonable, judicious, logical, sane, just, sagacious, sober, sound, lucid, fair, philosophical, coherent, equitable, justifiable, prudent; *antonyms* (*adj*) irrational, illogical, anxious, **8**. sagacious; *synonyms* (*adj*) keen, perspicacious, politic, sapient, sage, deep, provident, penetrating, profound, wily, farseeing, (*v*) learned; *antonym* (*adj*) foolish, **9**. sage; *synonyms* (*n*) philosopher, scholar, salvia, guru, master, rosemary, (*adj*) grave, **10**. sane; *synonyms* (*adj*) right, normal, wholesome; *antonyms* (*adj*) crazy, unbalanced, insane, **11**. sensible; *synonyms* (*adj*) aware, perceptible, appreciable, conscious, advisable, careful, cognizant, palpable, sensitive, realistic, susceptible, feeling, discernible, legitimate, physical; *antonyms* (*adj*) absurd, idiotic, imprudent, ludicrous, mad, outrageous, reckless, ridiculous, silly, unreasonable, unwise, harebrained, hasty,

impractical, **12**. reasonable; *synonyms* (*adj*) moderate, admissible, appropriate, cheap, due, impartial, inexpensive, plausible, temperate, acceptable, credible, decent, respectable, suitable, (*n*) clear; *antonyms* (*adj*) expensive, unfair, unsatisfactory, inadequate, **13**. sly; *synonyms* (*adj*) furtive, secret, designing, arch, clandestine, deceitful, devious, foxy, guileful, insidious, scheming, slick, stealthy, tricky, mischievous; *antonyms* (*adj*) open, naive, **14**. wise; *synonyms* (*adj*) thoughtful, diplomatic, tactful, considered, erudite, experienced, (*n*) method, manner, way, **15**. perspicuous; *synonyms* (*adj*) distinct, explicit, limpid, obvious, pellucid, luminous, evident, luculent, apparent, transparent, **16**. prudent; *synonyms* (*adj*) cautious, circumspect, chary, economical, frugal, deliberate, modest, guarded, thrifty, cautelous, expedient, conservative, considerate, parsimonious, prudential; *antonyms* (*adj*) spendthrift, careless, **17**. shrewd; *synonyms* (*adj*) calculating, piercing, poignant, shifty, pointed, discriminating, bitter, prompt, harsh, incisive, serious, abrupt, (*v*) nimble, enlightened, pawky; *antonym* (*adj*) gullible, **18**. smart; *synonyms* (*adj*) dapper, chic, jaunty, lively, natty, saucy, fine, fashionable, brisk, dashing, fresh, rakish, (*v*) ache, hurt, (*n*) pain; *antonyms* (*adj*) scruffy, shabby, unkempt.

waneinei 1. saturated; *synonyms* (*adj*) drenched, sodden, wet, concentrated, soaked, sopping, full, soggy, soppy, pure, soaking; *antonym* (*adj*) dry, **2**. soaked; *synonyms* (*adj*) saturated, drunk, damp, plastered, sloshed, besotted, **3**. watery; *synonyms* (*adj*) liquid, moist, dilute, diluted, washy, thin, fluid, aqueous, hydrous, insipid, tearful, weak, dripping, humid, soft; *antonyms* (*adj*) solid, strong.

wang 1. push; *synonyms* (*n*) press, thrust, jolt, poke, (*v*) drive, impel, crowd, force, jab, jostle, nudge, prod, jam, rush, boost; *antonyms* (*v*) pull, drag, haul, **2**. shove; *synonyms* (*v*) elbow, shift, hustle, stuff, bump, cram, jog, move, squeeze, hurtle, put, joggle, (*n*) push, shoulder, jerk.

wanga 1. meddling; *synonyms* (*adj*) interfering, busy, curious, inquisitive, intrusive, meddlesome, officious, prying, nosy, busybodied, dabbling, impertinent, **2**. baffling; *synonyms* (*adj*) mysterious, incomprehensible, inexplicable, knotty, puzzling, unaccountable, unfathomable, bewildering, confusing, perplexing, difficult; *antonym* (*adj*) clear, **3**. confusing; *synonyms* (*adj*) baffling, embarrassing, misleading, ambiguous, uncertain, obscure, disturbing, alarming, confusive, deceptive, devious, disruptive, indefinite, involved, mazy; *antonyms* (*adj*) enlightening, simple, **4**. bustling; *synonyms* (*adj*) active, lively, buzzing, alive, brisk, vibrant, agile, energetic, perky, restless, spoffish, agitated, (*v*) stirring, eventful, **5**. tire;

synonyms (*v*) bore, fatigue, exhaust, fag, harass, weary, pall, prostrate, wear, disturb, annoy, molest, tease, (*n*) jade, tyre; *antonym* (*v*) refresh, **6.** weary; *synonyms* (*adj*) tired, exhausted, fatigued, aweary, beat, languid, irksome, wearisome, spent, jaded, (*v*) tire, dull, irk, depress, drain; *antonym* (*adj*) fresh, **7.** shove; *synonyms* (*v*) elbow, impel, press, prod, shift, boost, hustle, stuff, nudge, bump, (*n*) push, thrust, jostle, poke, shoulder; *antonym* (*v*) pull, **8.** vexing; *synonyms* (*adj*) irritating, annoying, infuriating, maddening, galling, troublesome, bothersome, aggravating, exasperating, pestiferous, vexatious, pesky, trying, **9.** tired; *synonyms* (*adj*) hackneyed, banal, commonplace, stale, threadbare, trite, haggard, stock, worn, drowsy, sick, whacked, corny, limp, weak; *antonyms* (*adj*) invigorated, alert, refreshed, original, strong.

wangaki troubled; *synonyms* (*adj*) concerned, disturbed, anxious, distressed, solicitous, apprehensive, disconcerted, uncomfortable, uneasy, upset, worried, restless, distraught, bothered, perturbed; *antonyms* (*adj*) untroubled, composed, unconcerned.

wangaroro weary; *synonyms* (*adj*) tired, exhausted, fatigued, aweary, beat, languid, irksome, (*v*) fatigue, tire, exhaust, bore, dull, irk, wear, (*n*) jade; *antonyms* (*adj*) energetic, fresh.

wanibwi eighty; *synonym* (*n*) fourscore.

wanikangarea amuse; *synonyms* (*v*) divert, absorb, beguile, entertain, please, charm, delight, disport, distract, occupy, recreate, sport, interest; *antonym* (*v*) bore.

wanikangareaki amused; *synonyms* (*adj*) entertained, diverted, smiling.

wa-ni-matañ ship; *synonyms* (*n*) boat, ferry, craft, bottom, (*v*) dispatch, send, forward, transport, consign, carry, embark, move, transfer, post, charge.

wanin mend; *synonyms* (*v*) repair, improve, correct, cure, amend, better, doctor, heal, restore, convalesce, ameliorate, bushel, (*n*) fix, patch, botch; *antonym* (*v*) break.

wanina mend; *synonyms* (*v*) repair, improve, correct, cure, amend, better, doctor, heal, restore, convalesce, ameliorate, bushel, (*n*) fix, patch, botch; *antonym* (*v*) break.

waningarea joke; *synonyms* (*n*) jest, banter, hoax, fun, caper, gag, game, quip, antic, farce, humor, jape, jocularity, pleasantry, (*v*) chaff; *antonym* (*n*) tragedy.

wanua eight; *synonyms* (*n*) eighter, eleven, ace, jack, king, knave, nine, octad, octet, octonary, ogdoad, queen, team, ten, (*adj*) octave.

wara 1. detested; *synonyms* (*adj*) despised, hated, unpopular, disliked, loathed, reviled, scorned, abhorrent, despicable, insufferable, ostracized;

antonym (*adj*) popular, **2.** treeless; *synonym* (*adj*) unwooded.

waraku 1. moist; *synonyms* (*adj*) humid, damp, wet, clammy, dank, muggy, dampish, soggy, wettish, juicy, sodden, sticky, watery, dripping, marshy; *antonym* (*adj*) dry, **2.** damp; *synonyms* (*adj*) moist, cool, (*v*) break, check, chill, deaden, benumb, cut, dampen, depress, discourage, dishearten, (*n*) dampness, moisture, clamminess; *antonym* (*n*) dryness.

waranran 1. wet; *synonyms* (*adj*) damp, humid, drenched, moist, soaked, sodden, dank, rainy, saturated, soggy, (*v*) moisten, water, dampen, wash, (*n*) moisture; *antonyms* (*adj*) dehydrated, parched, (*v*) dry, **2.** watery; *synonyms* (*adj*) liquid, dilute, diluted, washy, wet, thin, fluid, aqueous, hydrous, insipid, tearful, weak, dripping, soft, aquatic; *antonyms* (*adj*) concentrated, solid, strong.

ware 1. count; *synonyms* (*n*) number, calculation, computation, total, (*v*) calculate, compute, tally, account, cipher, consider, estimate, matter, reckon, weigh, add, **2.** calculate; *synonyms* (*v*) count, appraise, deem, enumerate, forecast, gauge, guess, make, expect, figure, measure, budget, determine, assess, cast, **3.** enumerate; *synonyms* (*v*) detail, list, recount, tell, recapitulate, cite, quantify, recite, specify, amount, itemize, state, **4.** read; *synonyms* (*v*) interpret, construe, decipher, gather, indicate, learn, perceive, say, understand, demonstrate, comprehend, display, examine, explain, peruse, **5.** spell; *synonyms* (*n*) magic, fascination, bout, conjuration, incantation, period, sorcery, enchantment, turn, span, bewitchment, space, captivation, attack, (*v*) charm.

warea 1. dull; *synonyms* (*adj*) dim, blunt, dense, dreary, sluggish, bland, boring, cloudy, cold, dark, dismal, inactive, inert, (*v*) deaden, dampen; *antonyms* (*adj*) bright, lively, sharp, exciting, interesting, lustrous, stimulating, amusing, exhilarating, glittery, glossy, glowing, high-pitched, intense, luminous, **2.** lusterless; *synonyms* (*adj*) dull, lackluster, lustreless, flat, lacklustre, cheerless, complete, dead, deadly, deathlike, drab, expressionless, faded, fixed, inanimate, **3.** disreputable; *synonyms* (*adj*) disgraceful, base, dishonorable, doubtful, infamous, shameful, sordid, dishonest, despicable, notorious, seedy, sleazy, wicked, low, (*n*) discreditable; *antonyms* (*adj*) reputable, honorable, respected, **4.** tarnished; *synonyms* (*adj*) sullied, besmirched, stained, tainted, damaged, flyblown, imperfect, spotted; *antonym* (*adj*) untarnished.

wareaki 1. calculated; *synonyms* (*v*) advised, designed, (*adj*) deliberate, conscious, intended, intentional, premeditated, purposeful, studied, measured, planned, strategic; *antonym* (*adj*) accidental, **2.** read; *synonyms* (*v*) interpret, construe, decipher, gather, indicate, learn, perceive, say, understand, demonstrate, comprehend, display, examine, explain, peruse.

warebai calculate; *synonyms* (*v*) count, estimate, account, add, appraise, cipher, compute, deem, enumerate, forecast, gauge, guess, make, reckon, consider.

warebaia calculate; *synonyms* (*v*) count, estimate, account, add, appraise, cipher, compute, deem, enumerate, forecast, gauge, guess, make, reckon, consider.

warebaiaki calculated; *synonyms* (*v*) advised, designed, (*adj*) deliberate, conscious, intended, intentional, premeditated, purposeful, studied, measured, planned, strategic; *antonym* (*adj*) accidental.

wareboki read; *synonyms* (*v*) interpret, construe, decipher, gather, indicate, learn, perceive, say, understand, demonstrate, comprehend, display, examine, explain, peruse.

warebokiaki read; *synonyms* (*v*) interpret, construe, decipher, gather, indicate, learn, perceive, say, understand, demonstrate, comprehend, display, examine, explain, peruse.

warebwai count; *synonyms* (*n*) number, calculation, computation, total, (*v*) calculate, compute, tally, account, cipher, consider, estimate, matter, reckon, weigh, add.

warebwe 1. large; *synonyms* (*adj*) big, ample, extensive, generous, broad, bulky, considerable, handsome, high, heavy, abundant, capacious, great, gross, hefty; *antonyms* (*adj*) small, cramped, insignificant, 2. wide; *synonyms* (*adj*) spacious, roomy, comprehensive, large, vast, expanded, extended, full, open, sweeping, deep, expansive, liberal, thick, blanket; *antonyms* (*adj*) narrow, thin, restricted, 3. spacious; *synonyms* (*adj*) wide, commodious, airy, comfortable, sizable, voluminous, convenient.

wareka 1. enumerate; *synonyms* (*v*) count, detail, list, recount, compute, reckon, tally, tell, recapitulate, cite, figure, quantify, recite, (*n*) calculate, number, 2. number; *synonyms* (*n*) amount, score, act, issue, volume, character, company, digit, multitude, (*v*) aggregate, enumerate, total, come, add, account, 3. spell; *synonyms* (*n*) magic, fascination, bout, conjuration, incantation, period, sorcery, enchantment, turn, span, bewitchment, space, captivation, attack, (*v*) charm, 4. reckon; *synonyms* (*v*) deem, estimate, judge, hold, guess, consider, gauge, rate, measure, make, assess, believe, cipher, esteem, expect.

warekia number; *synonyms* (*n*) count, amount, score, act, issue, volume, character, (*v*) calculate, aggregate, enumerate, figure, total, come, add, account.

wareriri enumerate; *synonyms* (*v*) count, detail, list, recount, compute, reckon, tally, tell, recapitulate, cite, figure, quantify, recite, (*n*) calculate, number.

wareware read; *synonyms* (*v*) interpret, construe, decipher, gather, indicate, learn, perceive, say, understand, demonstrate, comprehend, display, examine, explain, peruse.

warewareaki read; *synonyms* (*v*) interpret, construe, decipher, gather, indicate, learn, perceive, say, understand, demonstrate, comprehend, display, examine, explain, peruse.

wari 1. gigantic; *synonyms* (*adj*) colossal, enormous, mammoth, giant, huge, large, stupendous, big, gargantuan, immense, massive, monstrous, vast, monumental, monster; *antonyms* (*adj*) small, tiny, 2. enormous; *synonyms* (*adj*) excessive, exorbitant, great, prodigious, tremendous, gigantic, infinite, terrific, terrible, flagrant, immeasurable, mighty, amazing, astonishing, incalculable; *antonyms* (*adj*) minute, insignificant, miniature, 3. big; *synonyms* (*adj*) ample, major, heavy, important, significant, thick, sturdy, generous, adult, bad, burly, considerable, hefty, high, liberal; *antonyms* (*adj*) little, puny, 4. large; *synonyms* (*adj*) extensive, broad, bulky, handsome, abundant, capacious, gross, roomy, stout, fat, bountiful, commodious, comprehensive, copious, expansive; *antonym* (*adj*) cramped, 5. monstrous; *synonyms* (*adj*) atrocious, grotesque, heinous, dreadful, flagitious, grievous, preposterous, ugly, fantastic, inordinate, abnormal, evil, horrible, outrageous, frightful, 6. titanic.

wariki 1. narrow; *synonyms* (*adj*) close, limited, insular, little, cramped, illiberal, mean, (*v*) confined, contract, limit, lessen, constrict, shrink, abridge, dwindle; *antonyms* (*adj*) wide, broad, comprehensive, extensive, (*v*) widen, extend, 2. confining; *synonyms* (*adj*) limiting, restricting, narrow, airless, cheeseparing, claudent, closelipped, closemouthed, constraining, constrictive, oppressive, stringent, constricting, crowded, (*n*) contraction, 3. restricted; *synonyms* (*v*) qualified, (*adj*) constrained, exclusive, local, controlled, finite, prohibited, classified, secret, bounded, circumscribed, private, reserved, tight, captive; *antonyms* (*adj*) unrestricted, far-reaching, free, liberated, unimpeded, unlimited, open, 4. strait; *synonyms* (*n*) inlet, need, pass, pinch, quandary, channel, crisis, difficulty, distress, poverty, straits, emergency, frith, (*v*) dilemma, (*adj*) nonplus.

warona knot; *synonyms* (*n*) bow, cluster, tie, loop, bunch, gang, joint, lump, tangle, band, burl, (*v*) entangle, knit, bind, fasten.

waronaki knotted; *synonyms* (*adj*) intricate, gnarled, gnarly, knotty, entangled, involved, complicated, tangled, kinky, knobbed, matted; *antonyms* (*adj*) free, straight, tidy.

waru 1. annoy; *synonyms* (*v*) anger, displease, harass, irritate, pester, afflict, aggravate, bother, grate, harry, hassle, molest, perturb, plague, (*n*) annoyance; *antonyms* (*v*) please, pacify, soothe, **2.** pull; *synonyms* (*v*) drag, draw, draught, pluck, attract, haul, jerk, tug, pick, make, force, hale, (*n*) wrench, attraction, effort; *antonyms* (*v*) push, repel.

waruaki 1. annoyed; *synonyms* (*adj*) angry, irate, irritated, vexed, aggravated, angered, cross, disgruntled, displeased, exasperated, infuriated, offended, peeved, pestered, resentful; *antonyms* (*adj*) calm, pleased, unprovoked, smiling, **2.** pulled; *synonyms* (*adj*) moulting, pilled, plucked.

wau 1. becoming; *synonyms* (*v*) proper, correct, (*adj*) appropriate, seemly, adequate, decent, decorous, agreeable, apposite, apt, befitting, due, fit, relevant, comely; *antonym* (*adj*) unbecoming, **2.** good; *synonyms* (*adj*) able, benefit, delicious, right, efficient, capable, excellent, fine, nice, superior, well, advantageous, (*n*) benign, advantage, gain; *antonyms* (*adj*) disobedient, poor, wicked, unpleasant, (*n*) evil, bad, **3.** fitting; *synonyms* (*adj*) applicable, felicitous, just, becoming, compatible, suitable, expedient, advisable, feasible, (*n*) adaptation, adjustment, accommodation, appointment, installation, attachment; *antonyms* (*adj*) inappropriate, improper, wrong, **4.** seemly; *synonyms* (*adj*) respectable, fitting, modest, fair, eligible, apropos, personable, (*v*) meet, **5.** well; *synonyms* (*adv*) easily, thoroughly, considerably, fully, good, correctly, (*adj*) healthy, shaft, sound, robust, (*n*) fountain, spring, pit, hollow, (*v*) gush; *antonyms* (*adv*) ill, badly, poorly, (*adj*) sick, unwell, dying, nauseous.

waua 1. embroider; *synonyms* (*v*) adorn, embellish, decorate, broider, trim, hyperbolize, lard, ornament, stitch, aggrandize, amplify, beautify, dramatise, dramatize, (*adv*) color, **2.** weave; *synonyms* (*v*) twine, twist, braid, knit, entwine, interweave, wind, waver, plait, fabricate, tissue, lurch, interlace, reel, (*n*) texture.

wauaki embroidered; *synonyms* (*adj*) bewrought, exaggerated, inflated, ornate, overstated, embellished.

wauna 1. bewitch; *synonyms* (*v*) fascinate, charm, enchant, attract, entrance, beguile, enamor, enrapture, spell, witch, influence, catch, conjure, (*n*) captivate, allure, **2.** curse; *synonyms* (*n*) bane, anathema, blasphemy, malediction, denunciation, (*v*) beshrew, blight, ban, damn, plague, swear, vituperate, anathematize, blaspheme, blast.

waunaki 1. bewitched; *synonyms* (*adj*) spellbound, fascinated, captive, doomed, enamored, ensorcelled, infatuated, magical, obsessed, rapt, bugged, captivated, enraptured, entranced, hooked, **2.** cursed; *synonyms* (*v*) accurst, cursing, (*adj*) abominable, damned, execrable, blamed, blasted, blessed, curst, damnable, detestable, hateful, infernal, unlucky.

wauwau 1. sneak; *synonyms* (*v*) creep, lurk, crawl, fawn, filch, mouse, (*n*) cower, slink, informer, skulk, snitch, fink, (*adj*) coward, grovel, dastard, **2.** slink; *synonyms* (*v*) prowl, slip, steal, glide, slide, (*n*) sneak, flinch, shy.

wauwi 1. blaspheme; *synonyms* (*v*) curse, desecrate, profane, swear, cuss, damn, defile, imprecate, **2.** curse; *synonyms* (*n*) bane, anathema, blasphemy, malediction, denunciation, condemnation, (*v*) beshrew, blight, ban, plague, vituperate, anathematize, blaspheme, blast, excommunicate, **3.** imprecate; *synonyms* (*v*) execrate, accurse, anathemize, bedamn, impetrate, **4.** hex; *synonyms* (*n*) spell, (*v*) enchant, jinx, bewitch, charm, glamour, witch, becharm, (*adj*) hexadecimal, **5.** swear; *synonyms* (*v*) affirm, assert, assure, declare, avow, depone, depose, pledge, attest, asseverate, insist, guarantee, (*n*) promise, aver, avouch.

wauwiaki cursed; *synonyms* (*v*) accurst, cursing, (*adj*) abominable, damned, doomed, execrable, blamed, blasted, blessed, curst, damnable, detestable, hateful, infernal, unlucky.

wawa trickle; *synonyms* (*n*) drip, distill, drivel, drool, (*v*) drop, dribble, percolate, flow, leak, ooze, seep, filter, leach, bleed, drain; *antonyms* (*n*) throng, (*v*) gush.

wawaikakang jagged; *synonyms* (*adj*) rough, uneven, angular, irregular, crooked, craggy, bumpy, harsh, jaggy, notched, rugged, scraggy, toothed, zigzag, (*n*) ragged; *antonyms* (*adj*) smooth, even.

wawaitai interrupt; *synonyms* (*v*) break, disturb, hinder, intermit, cut, pause, stop, arrest, check, disrupt, impede, heckle, bar, (*n*) suspend, (*adj*) discontinue.

wawaitaiaki interrupted; *synonyms* (*adj*) discontinuous, fitful, intermittent, (*prep*) broken; *antonym* (*adj*) constant.

wene lie; *synonyms* (*v*) consist, repose, falsify, belong, couch, (*n*) fabrication, falsehood, falsity, fib, fiction, rest, untruth, bluff, counterfeit, deceit; *antonyms* (*v*) stand, (*n*) truth.

weta summon; *synonyms* (*v*) cite, assemble, convene, demand, ask, beckon, bid, call, convoke, evoke, invite, invoke, muster, page, rally.

wetea 1. call; *synonyms* (*v*) cry, bellow, name, shout, bid, summon, howl, address, baptize, cite, (*n*) appeal, yell, appoint, command, demand; *antonym* (*v*) dismiss, **2.** invite; *synonyms* (*v*) draw, allure, call, tempt, ask, attract, entice, beckon, court, encourage, receive, solicit, beg, crave, (*n*) invitation, **3.** summon; *synonyms* (*v*) assemble, convene, convoke, evoke, invite, invoke, muster, page, rally, challenge, collect, gather, raise, recall, summons.

weteaki 1. called; *synonyms* (*v*) nempt, ycleped, (*adj*) named, chosen, qualified, **2.** invited; *synonyms* (*adj*) welcome, cherished, wanted, precious, treasured.

wew 1. bound; *synonyms* (*v*) leap, border, bounce, limit, circumscribe, confine, pounce, rebound, (*n*) spring, jump, boundary, edge, barrier, compass, hop; *antonym* (*adj*) free, **2.** bounce; *synonyms* (*v*) bound, discharge, glance, recoil, beat, sack, caper, bob, fire, bump, dismiss, eject, (*n*) impact, jolt, bouncing, **3.** jump; *synonyms* (*v*) dive, hurdle, rise, skip, startle, clear, dance, go, increase, lunge, plunge, twitch, (*n*) start, curvet, saltation; *antonyms* (*v*) decrease, fall.

wewaki bounded; *synonyms* (*adj*) finite, restricted, delimited, limited, encircled, enclosed, local, qualified, surrounded, belted, compassed, contiguous, defined, definite, determinate.

wewete call; *synonyms* (*v*) cry, bellow, name, shout, bid, summon, howl, address, baptize, cite, (*n*) appeal, yell, appoint, command, demand; *antonym* (*v*) dismiss.

weweteaki called; *synonyms* (*v*) nempt, ycleped, (*adj*) named, chosen, qualified.

wi 1. teeth; *synonyms* (*n*) ivory, dentition, odontiasis, vice, hold, (*v*) arrastra, fangs, file, grater, gristmill, mill, rasp, tenaculum, tentacle, unguis, **2.** tooth; *synonyms* (*n*) palate, grain, nap, saw, stomach, tongue, liking, fiber, point, spicule, wire, apophysis, bulb, (*adj*) nib, (*v*) bite.

wia 1. meet; *synonyms* (*v*) converge, find, assemble, congregate, encounter, fulfill, gather, answer, cross, confront, intersect, abut, concur, adjoin, (*adj*) fit; *antonyms* (*v*) avoid, disperse, diverge, **2.** face; *synonyms* (*n*) look, aspect, countenance, expression, side, top, exterior, appearance, facade, surface, (*v*) audacity, veneer, visage, affront, (*adj*) front; *antonym* (*v*) back.

wiba 1. shout; *synonyms* (*v*) cry, clamor, scream, bellow, bawl, exclaim, hollo, howl, (*n*) call, roar, yell, cheer, halloo, outcry, screech; *antonym* (*v*) whisper, **2.** roar; *synonyms* (*n*) boom, thunder, shout, bark, noise, peal, roll, bang, bellowing, (*v*) clatter, blare, holler, rave, (*adj*) bluster, rage.

wibarubaru toothless; *synonyms* (*adj*) dull, edentulous, immobilized, powerless.

wibeka 1. exaggerate; *synonyms* (*v*) boast, aggravate, amplify, dramatize, overdo, overdraw, enhance, enlarge, magnify, overstate, embellish, heighten, hyperbolize, increase, inflate; *antonyms* (*v*) understate, minimize, **2.** braggart; *synonyms* (*n*) boaster, blowhard, braggadocio, bragger, vaunter, swaggerer, talker, babbler, rodomont, (*v*) magniloquent, pretentious, flaming, gasconading, (*adj*) braggy, crowing, **3.** brag; *synonyms* (*v*) bluster, pride, blow, gasconade, crow, crack,

exaggerate, flourish, rodomontade, swagger, (*n*) vaunt, boasting, bounce, bragging, vapor, **4.** boaster; *synonyms* (*n*) braggart, bouncer, huff, pretension, rage, **5.** flirt; *synonyms* (*v*) coquette, dally, coquet, romance, toy, mash, philander, play, spoon, (*n*) dalliance, vamp, flirtation, flirting, minx, tease, **6.** romance; *synonyms* (*n*) fiction, novel, story, intrigue, affair, fable, romanticism, tale, vagary, exaggeration, rhapsody, (*adj*) extravagance, (*v*) court, flirt, woo.

wibekaki exaggerated; *synonyms* (*adj*) enlarged, extravagant, theatrical, immoderate, hypertrophied, affected, excessive, hyperbolic, inflated, magnified, overdone, overstated, pretentious, melodramatic; *antonyms* (*adj*) understated, restrained.

wibine 1. murmur; *synonyms* (*n*) mutter, babble, whine, complaint, (*v*) buzz, grumble, hum, mumble, whisper, bubble, complain, breathe, drone, croak, grouch, **2.** whisper; *synonyms* (*n*) rustle, breath, trace, undertone, rumor, susurration, whispering, rustling, (*v*) murmur, hint, suggestion, hiss, inkling, innuendo, confide; *antonym* (*v*) shout.

wibineaki whispered; *synonyms* (*adj*) low, soft, voiceless, aspirated, atonic, deaf, faint, irrational, muted, nonvocal, quiet, radical, sharp, supposed, surd.

wibino 1. babble; *synonyms* (*n*) drivel, burble, gibberish, (*v*) murmur, chat, gab, gossip, ripple, talk, blab, blather, bubble, chatter, guggle, gurgle; *antonyms* (*v*) quietness, silence, stillness, **2.** chatter; *synonyms* (*n*) prattle, chattering, chaffer, jangle, cry, (*v*) babble, jabber, cackle, blabber, natter, patter, tattle, chitchat, (*adj*) prate, palaver, **3.** prattle; *synonyms* (*v*) clack, gabble, gibber, jaw, twaddle, confabulate, speak, maunder, piffle, click, (*n*) blether, nonsense, claver, locution, parlance.

wibuakaia threaten; *synonyms* (*v*) menace, bully, endanger, intimidate, loom, offer, imperil, jeopardize, peril, approach, foreshadow, portend, browbeat, impend, (*n*) threat; *antonym* (*v*) help.

wibunai braggart; *synonyms* (*n*) boaster, blowhard, braggadocio, bragger, vaunter, swaggerer, talker, babbler, rodomont, (*v*) magniloquent, pretentious, flaming, gasconading, (*adj*) braggy, crowing.

wikabwea exaggerate; *synonyms* (*v*) boast, aggravate, amplify, dramatize, overdo, overdraw, enhance, enlarge, magnify, overstate, embellish, heighten, hyperbolize, increase, inflate; *antonyms* (*v*) understate, minimize.

wikabweaki exaggerated; *synonyms* (*adj*) enlarged, extravagant, theatrical, immoderate, hypertrophied, affected, excessive, hyperbolic, inflated, magnified, overdone, overstated, pretentious, melodramatic; *antonyms* (*adj*) understated, restrained.

wikakang incisive; *synonyms* (*adj*) sharp, acute, cutting, keen, penetrating, piercing, pungent, pointed, biting, discriminating, quick, smart, trenchant, perceptive, crisp; *antonym* (*adj*) mild.

wiki week; *synonyms* (*n*) hebdomad, day, hour, minute, second, year, sennight, sevennight, time, workweek.

wikotaua braggart; *synonyms* (*n*) boaster, blowhard, braggadocio, bragger, vaunter, swaggerer, talker, babbler, rodomont, (*v*) magniloquent, pretentious, flaming, gasconading, (*adj*) braggy, crowing.

wimamuai 1. flatter; *synonyms* (*v*) coax, fawn, court, adulate, cajole, wheedle, blandish, grovel, kowtow, soap, compliment, entice, indulge, persuade, (*n*) caress, **2.** pleasure; *synonyms* (*n*) delight, contentment, delectation, enjoyment, fun, gratification, joy, content, comfort, happiness, mirth, inclination, amusement, bliss, entertainment; *antonyms* (*n*) anger, irritation, ache, boredom, nuisance.

wina 1. inspire; *synonyms* (*v*) animate, cheer, encourage, enliven, excite, incite, inhale, exhilarate, affect, infuse, hearten, actuate, impress, fire, cause, **2.** counsel; *synonyms* (*n*) caution, advocate, advisement, admonition, attorney, consultation, counselor, exhortation, guidance, (*v*) advice, advise, consult, admonish, confer, exhort, **3.** tempt; *synonyms* (*v*) lure, allure, entice, decoy, charm, coax, inveigle, invite, seduce, fascinate, attempt, captivate, persuade, bewitch, (*adj*) attract, **4.** suggest; *synonyms* (*v*) allude, imply, indicate, offer, hint, intimate, propose, submit, counsel, proffer, point, connote, insinuate, mean, move; *antonym* (*v*) withdraw, **5.** recommend; *synonyms* (*v*) commend, suggest, praise, urge, endorse, promote, introduce, approve, nominate, warn, prompt.

winaki 1. inspired; *synonyms* (*adj*) divine, ingenious, adopted, creative, elected, elysian, imaginative, inventive; *antonym* (*adj*) uninspired, **2.** suggested; *synonyms* (*adj*) recommended, advisable, implied, nominal, optional, tacit, **3.** recommended; *synonyms* (*adj*) suggested, favored, required.

winanti 1. invisible; *synonyms* (*adj*) imperceptible, hidden, inconspicuous, obscure, intangible, sightless, concealed, impalpable, occult, unseeable, unseen, evanescent; *antonyms* (*adj*) obvious, visible, conspicuous, **2.** fugitive; *synonyms* (*n*) escapee, absconder, deserter, emigrant, criminal, outlaw, refugee, renegade, (*adj*) runaway, ephemeral, fleeting, momentary, elusive, passing, (*v*) fugacious, **3.** unreal; *synonyms* (*adj*) false, illusory, artificial, fanciful, fantastic, imaginary, insubstantial, fictitious, fake, mythical, shadowy, untrue, visionary, (*v*) ideal, fancied; *antonyms* (*adj*) real, genuine, **4.** transient; *synonyms* (*adj*) brief, temporary, transitory, fugitive, temporal, impermanent, provisional, cursory, meteoric, migrant, mortal, restless, transeunt, (*n*) vagabond; *antonyms* (*adj*) permanent, enduring.

wingare 1. grin; *synonyms* (*n*) smile, grinning, smirk, simper, (*v*) beam, laugh, sneer, leer, **2.** smile; *synonyms* (*n*) grin, smiling, expression, luck, (*v*) chuckle, grimace, countenance, favor, propitiousness; *antonym* (*v*) frown.

wingarongaro toothless; *synonyms* (*adj*) dull, edentulous, immobilized, powerless.

winikibwia transfix; *synonyms* (*v*) impale, pierce, spike, fascinate, thrust, spellbind, stab, stick, empale, grip.

winikibwiaki transfixed; *synonyms* (*v*) absorbed, rapt, riveted, (*adj*) fascinated, spellbound, hypnotised, hypnotized, mesmerised, mesmerized, motionless.

wira 1. avert; *synonyms* (*v*) avoid, deflect, obviate, preclude, prevent, deter, stop, debar, deviate, distract, divert, forestall, inhibit, repel, **2.** repulse; *synonyms* (*v*) rebuff, nauseate, disgust, reject, revolt, refuse, dismiss, drive, rebut, snub, sicken, check, (*n*) defeat, refusal, denial; *antonyms* (*v*) attract, welcome.

wirara rainbow; *synonyms* (*n*) iris, tulip, sunbow, chimera, dream, fantasy, illusion, spectrum, (*adj*) colorful, motley, multicolored, dappled, flecked, mottled.

wirebwerebwe 1. chatter; *synonyms* (*n*) prattle, gab, chattering, (*v*) babble, chat, gossip, jabber, cackle, blab, blabber, natter, patter, tattle, (*adj*) prate, palaver, **2.** chatterbox; *synonyms* (*n*) chatterer, babbler, talker, cackler, busybody, communicator, conversationalist, spouter, cotinga, mouth, raconteur, **3.** talkative; *synonyms* (*adj*) loquacious, chatty, garrulous, gabby, verbose, gossipy, glib, communicative, talky, wordy, bigmouthed, blabbermouthed, blabby, effusive, expansive; *antonyms* (*adj*) taciturn, reserved, mute, quiet, shy, silent.

wiremwe slow; *synonyms* (*adj*) dull, late, easy, sluggish, heavy, dense, dim, gradual, inactive, indolent, lazy, stupid, (*v*) slack, (*adv*) behind, behindhand; *antonyms* (*adj*) fast, intelligent, rapid, bright, alert, brisk, hasty, prompt, quick, speedy, hurried, observant, rushed, (*v*) accelerate.

wirikiriki 1. mutter; *synonyms* (*v*) mumble, grumble, growl, maunder, grouch, complain, croak, snarl, gnarl, (*n*) murmur, whisper, complaint, grumbling, murmuration, murmuring, **2.** whisper; *synonyms* (*n*) buzz, hum, rustle, breath, trace, undertone, rumor, susurration, (*v*) breathe, hint, suggestion, hiss, inkling, innuendo, mutter; *antonym* (*v*) shout.

wirikirikia 1. mumble; *synonyms* (*v*) grumble, maunder, murmur, whisper, hum, chew, mutter, jabber, rumble, talk, utter, verbalize, babble, munch, bite, **2.** whisper; *synonyms* (*n*) buzz, rustle, breath, trace, undertone, rumor, susurration, whispering, (v) breathe, mumble, hint, suggestion, hiss, inkling, innuendo; *antonym* (v) shout.

wirikirikiaki whispered; *synonyms* (adj) low, soft, voiceless, aspirated, atonic, deaf, faint, irrational, muted, nonvocal, quiet, radical, sharp, supposed, surd.

witakanana 1. indiscreet; *synonyms* (adj) foolish, careless, imprudent, incautious, ill-advised, rash, unadvised, unwise, impolitic, hasty, inadvisable, inconsiderate, tactless, thoughtless, heedless; *antonym* (adj) discreet, **2.** tactless; *synonyms* (adj) clumsy, tasteless, blunt, awkward, inept, insensitive; *antonyms* (adj) tactful, diplomatic, thoughtful.

witata 1. fast; *synonyms* (adj) dissolute, firm, agile, debauched, fixed, hurried, instant, quick, rapid, staunch, brisk, (adv) soon, hard, close, (n) diet; *antonyms* (adj) sluggish, loose, (adv) slow, slowly, leisurely, (v) gorge, (n) binge, **2.** patter; *synonyms* (n) jargon, vernacular, cant, slang, lingo, (v) babble, clatter, rattle, roll, rumble, drum, scuttle, skip, tiptoe, bespatter.

witeke incisive; *synonyms* (adj) sharp, acute, cutting, keen, penetrating, piercing, pungent, pointed, biting, discriminating, quick, smart, trenchant, perceptive, crisp; *antonym* (adj) mild.

witoko obstruct; *synonyms* (v) bar, block, check, choke, clog, delay, encumber, hamper, impede, screen, intercept, debar, arrest, (n) hinder, barricade; *antonyms* (v) encourage, facilitate, free.

witokoaki obstructed; *synonyms* (adj) hindered, blind, blocked, congested, foiled, frustrated, impedite, stymied, thwarted, tight; *antonym* (adj) successful.

witokonaua 1. protract; *synonyms* (v) prolong, extend, delay, lengthen, defer, procrastinate, continue, postpone, elongate, draw, linger, drag, stretch, (adj) produce, digress, **2.** prolong; *synonyms* (v) protract, expand, maintain, keep, sustain, prolongate, renew, offer, preserve; *antonyms* (v) shorten, stop.

witokonauaki 1. prolonged; *synonyms* (adj) long, lengthy, chronic, extended, lingering, elongated, lengthened, continuous, continued, expanded, sustained, extensive, slow, (v) protracted; *antonyms* (adj) brief, quick, **2.** protracted; *synonyms* (adj) prolonged, prolix.

wiwi 1. hint; *synonyms* (n) clue, intimation, suggestion, trace, allusion, cue, inkling, implication, (v) suggest, dash, tip, touch, allude, imply, (adj) intimate; *antonym* (n) overtone, **2.** counsel; *synonyms* (n) caution, advocate, advisement, admonition, attorney, consultation, counselor, exhortation, guidance, (v) advice, advise, consult, admonish, confer, exhort, **3.** inspire; *synonyms* (v) animate, cheer, encourage, enliven,

excite, incite, inhale, exhilarate, affect, infuse, hearten, actuate, impress, fire, cause, **4.** insinuate; *synonyms* (v) hint, indicate, adumbrate, connote, ingratiate, signify, denote, impute, instill, **5.** incite; *synonyms* (v) goad, impel, abet, agitate, arouse, foment, quicken, awaken, induce, instigate, motivate, move, prod, provoke, stimulate; *antonym* (v) suppress, **6.** suggest; *synonyms* (v) offer, propose, submit, counsel, proffer, point, insinuate, mean, present, prompt, recommend, advance, nominate, bid, proposition; *antonym* (v) withdraw, **7.** tempt; *synonyms* (v) lure, allure, entice, decoy, charm, coax, inveigle, invite, seduce, fascinate, attempt, captivate, persuade, bewitch, (adj) attract.

wiwiaki 1. inspired; *synonyms* (adj) divine, ingenious, adopted, creative, elected, elysian, imaginative, inventive; *antonym* (adj) uninspired, **2.** suggested; *synonyms* (adj) recommended, advisable, implied, nominal, optional, tacit.

wiwina tempt; *synonyms* (v) lure, allure, entice, decoy, charm, coax, inveigle, invite, seduce, fascinate, attempt, captivate, persuade, bewitch, (adj) attract.

Z

zentz spirit; *synonyms* (n) apparition, courage, ghost, life, mood, bravery, character, disposition, energy, enthusiasm, essence, heart, mind, phantom, (adj) animation; *antonyms* (n) lethargy, body.

Index of English Subjects to Kiribati Subjects

A

a *see* 1. te, 2. teuana, 3. aki.
aback *see* kuba.
abandon *see* 1. tuka, 2. biritana, 3. kakea, 4. kaki, 5. katuka, 6. kitana.
abandoned *see* 1. tukaki, 2. timoi, 3. kitanaki, 4. katukaki, 5. kakiaki, 6. kakeaki, 7. atutarere, 8. biritanaki.
abase *see* 1. mwiniba, 2. kamangora, 3. kanubebeoa, 4. karinanoa.
abash *see* 1. kamaneanea, 2. kamaria, 3. kamatakiaua.
abashed *see* 1. kamoriau, 2. take, 3. nea, 4. moatoki, 5. mataronron, 6. mari, 7. kamatakiauaki, 8. kamariaki, 9. kamaneaneaki, 10. matakiaua.
abate *see* 1. kakea, 2. toki, 3. bwaka, 4. bao, 5. baka, 6. karakoaea.
abbreviate *see* 1. kakimotoa, 2. karakoa.
abbreviated *see* 1. kakimotoaki, 2. karakoaki, 3. kororo.
abdicate *see* 1. kakea, 2. kerikaki.
abdomen *see* piloto.
abduct *see* konana.
abducted *see* konanaki.
abhor *see* riba.
abhorrent *see* namomara.
abjure *see* kakea.
able *see* 1. manikoraki, 2. kona, 3. manikonana.
abnormal *see* 1. bainanti, 2. manenanti.
aboriginal *see* 1. abo, 2. aboabo.
abort *see* kabobo.
abounding *see* karebun.
about *see* 1. tao, 2. aki, 3. aron, 4. kan.
above *see* 1. raka, 2. iéta, 3. i-ô.
aboveboard *see* matabou.
abrade *see* 1. kara, 2. kuota, 3. raraikumea.
abraded *see* 1. raraikumeaki, 2. karaki, 3. kuotaki.
abreast *see* maina.
abridge *see* kauarerekea.
abridged *see* 1. atake, 2. kauarerekeaki.
abrupt *see* 1. karina, 2. rabe.
absent *see* akea.
absolute *see* 1. matatoka, 2. nabangkai, 3. kaeng, 4. etiraoi.

absolutely *see* koaua.
absolve *see* tabitabitabita.
absolved *see* 1. tabitabitabitaki, 2. unknown.
absorb *see* 1. matabae, 2. nima.
absorbed *see* 1. nimaki, 2. matabaeaki, 3. nano.
absorbing *see* 1. nano, 2. kakamataku, 3. kamataku.
abstain *see* 1. karitei, 2. rawa.
abstract *see* 1. kirimanga, 2. matakao, 3. nano.
abstruse *see* 1. nano, 2. kinano, 3. matakao.
abundant *see* 1. taomoa, 2. nonga, 3. nimanonganonga, 4. kirinaki, 5. kimarimari, 6. ewa, 7. karebun.
abundantly *see* taotira.
abuse *see* 1. tiring, 2. tinara, 3. baebaeta, 4. kabunenea, 5. maura.
abused *see* 1. baebaetaki, 2. kabuneneaki, 3. mauraki, 4. tinaraki, 5. tiringaki.
abut *see* nimimarea.
abutting *see* kan.
abysmal *see* 1. nanokirokiro, 2. nanokiroro, 3. nano.
abyssal *see* 1. kakinounou, 2. kinounou.
acarpous *see* kanoabo.
accede *see* kariaia.
accelerate *see* 1. bareka, 2. kaumaki.
accelerated *see* 1. barekaki, 2. kaumaki, 3. kaumakiaki, 4. waetata.
accentuate *see* katatererea.
accept *see* 1. kakoaua, 2. kamatebwai, 3. kabo, 4. butimwaaea, 5. nora.
accepted *see* 1. butimwaaeaki, 2. kaboaki, 3. kakoauaki, 4. kamatebwaiaki, 5. matoro, 6. noraki.
accepting *see* kakoaua.
accidental *see* kabuanibai.
acclaim *see* mra.
accompanied *see* 1. airiaki, 2. ikakaiaki, 3. iraki, 4. ninimareaki, 5. raonaki.
accompany *see* 1. ira, 2. ninimarea, 3. ikakai, 4. airi, 5. raona.
accomplish *see* 1. karaoia, 2. ungara.
accomplished *see* 1. karaoiaki, 2. koro, 3. tia, 4. ungaraki.
accord *see* bo.
accrue *see* rikirake.
accrued *see* rikirakeaki.
accumulate *see* 1. ai, 2. karemrem, 3. kawawaea.
accumulated *see* 1. kawawaeaki, 2. ribaba, 3. karemremaki, 4. baki, 5. aiaki.
accumulation *see* ribabati.
accurate *see* eti.
accurately *see* okoro.
accuse *see* 1. bukina, 2. kanotona, 3. maninutoa, 4. ngengetaia.
accused *see* 1. ngengetaiaki, 2. kanotonaki, 3. bukinaki, 4. maninuto, 5. maninutoaki.

accustom *see* kataneiai.
accustomed *see* 1. kataneiaiaki, 2. nana.
achieve *see* karekea.
acid *see* 1. mao, 2. tena.
acidic *see* mai.
acidify *see* katena.
acknowledge *see* kakoaua.
acknowledged *see* 1. kakoaua, 2. kakoauaki.
acquaintance *see* raom.
acquire *see* 1. kamantoa, 2. karekea, 3. reke.
acquired *see* 1. kamantoaki, 2. rekeaki, 3. reke, 4.
   karekeaki, 5. manto.
acquit *see* tabitabitabita.
acrobat *see* 1. tamatua, 2. tiakai.
across *see* bangaki.
act *see* 1. kamataku, 2. mwakuri, 3. karina, 4. karaoa,
   5. imita, 6. karaoia.
activate *see* taungatangata.
activated *see* taungatangataki.
active *see* 1. tabarebare, 2. unga, 3. rangarangatau, 4.
   manobotabota, 5. konamaki, 6. itibabu, 7.
   nanoingainga.
actual *see* nabangkai.
actually *see* bon.
acute *see* matairiki.
acutely *see* ranga.
adapt *see* 1. karokoa, 2. katenua, 3. babako.
adaptable *see* 1. takarua, 2. rena.
adapted *see* 1. babakoaki, 2. karokoaki, 3.
   katenuaki, 4. kona.
add *see* ikota.
added *see* ikotaki.
additionally *see* manga.
address *see* taetae.
addressed *see* taetaeaki.
adequate *see* 1. areare, 2. tau.
adhere *see* 1. kanima, 2. nim, 3. nimta.
adhesive *see* 1. nim, 2. nimnim, 3. komaki, 4.
   kiribanin.
adjacent *see* kan.
adjoin *see* 1. kaaontia, 2. katena, 3. nimimarea, 4.
   toma.
adjust *see* 1. boraoi, 2. karokoa.
adjustable *see* rena.
adjusted *see* 1. boraoiaki, 2. karokoaki.
adjutant *see* raom.
administer *see* anga.
administrate *see* tautaeka.
administrative *see* tauteaka.
admirable *see* 1. bakitoutou, 2. kan, 3. tika, 4.
   tikaua.
admire *see* 1. kamoamoa, 2. noakinak, 3. mimi, 4.
   miroa.
admired *see* 1. kamoamoaki, 2. mimiaki, 3. miroaki,
   4. noakinakaki.

admit *see* kauka.
admonish *see* boa.
admonished *see* boaki.
adolescent *see* 1. kiaiai, 2. ikawai.
adopt *see* 1. imammane, 2. natina, 3. natinati, 4.
   tibuna.
adopted *see* 1. natinatiaki, 2. tibunaki, 3. natinaki, 4.
   imammaneaki, 5. imamanu, 6. wakaraoi.
adore *see* 1. karinea, 2. taromauri.
adored *see* 1. karineaki, 2. tangiraki, 3.
   taromauriaki.
adorn *see* 1. katamaroa, 2. unekea.
adorned *see* 1. unekeaki, 2. timu, 3. katamaroaki.
adrift *see* betinako.
adroit *see* bati.
adult *see* ikawai.
adulterate *see* 1. kaubunranga, 2. mwiniba, 3.
   rakaua.
adulterated *see* 1. kaubunrangaki, 2. mwinibaki, 3.
   rakauaki.
advance *see* 1. buti, 2. waki, 3. tetere, 4. teborake, 5.
   nimatewetewe, 6. kerake, 7. kamaterea, 8. karaki.
advanced *see* 1. teborakeaki, 2. wakiaki, 3.
   tetereaki, 4. bou, 5. kerakeaki, 6. kamatereaki, 7.
   karakiaki, 8. nimateweteweaki.
advantageous *see* 1. manena, 2. raoi.
adverse *see* 1. tekera, 2. tutuki, 3. kaitara.
advise *see* matana.
advised *see* matanaki.
afar *see* 1. kakiro, 2. kinokino, 3. raroa.
affable *see* maningainga.
affect *see* ringa.
affected *see* 1. uere, 2. takitaki, 3. ringaki.
affectionate *see* tangira.
affiliate *see* 1. botaki, 2. koriria.
affiliated *see* 1. botakiaki, 2. kaeti, 3. koririaki.
affirm *see* 1. kakoaua, 2. kamatoa.
affirmative *see* koaua.
affirmed *see* 1. kakoauaki, 2. kamatoaki.
afflict *see* karoraoma.
afflicted *see* 1. karoraomaki, 2. nanokawa, 3.
   rainanoanga.
affront *see* 1. kamatauninga, 2. kabuakaka.
affronted *see* 1. kamatauningaki, 2. kabuakakaki.
aflame *see* bue.
afloat *see* beibeti.
afoot *see* riki.
afraid *see* 1. nanobukibuki, 2. inaberu, 3. maku, 4.
   nanobu.
afresh *see* nabangkai.
after *see* 1. inawiu, 2. kiriaria, 3. mui, 4. narei, 5.
   rimwi, 6. imwina.
afterward *see* 1. rimwi, 2. kiriaria, 3. narei.
afterwards *see* 1. rimwi, 2. kiriaria.
again *see* 1. manga, 2. riki.

age *see* tai.
aged *see* 1. kara, 2. nabawe.
agglomerated *see* ribaba.
aggravate *see* 1. kautua, 2. kautuaka, 3. kananora, 4. kamatakiaua.
aggravated *see* 1. kananoraki, 2. kautuakaki, 3. kautuaki, 4. matakiaua, 5. utakiaki, 6. kamatakiauaki.
aggregate *see* kawawaea.
aggregated *see* kawawaeaki.
agile *see* 1. rawekai, 2. tabarekai, 3. waetoka, 4. baitata, 5. ninibete, 6. tamakai.
agitate *see* 1. rangarangatau, 2. takarebutata, 3. maeiei, 4. katakarebua, 5. kananora, 6. kamatakiaua, 7. kakiriwea, 8. kakibea, 9. kakamwakuri, 10. kananomaruru.
agitated *see* 1. marebu, 2. matakiaua, 3. nanomaruru, 4. rangarangatau, 5. rangarangatauaki, 6. raraeua, 7. takarebutataki, 8. rebutata, 9. takarebu, 10. ioioia, 11. tanomaki, 12. katakarebuaki, 13. karerema, 14. kananoraki, 15. kananomaruruaki, 16. kamatakiauaki, 17. kakiriweaki, 18. kakamwakuriaki, 19. ienaka, 20. ewa.
ago *see* 1. bwakanako, 2. ngkoa.
agonize *see* rainanoanga.
agonized *see* rainanoangaki.
agonizing *see* rainanoanga.
agree *see* 1. nama, 2. anibana, 3. nanoteuana, 4. kariaiakaki, 5. kariaia, 6. kabo, 7. boraoi, 8. bonnano.
agreeable *see* 1. rung, 2. kannim, 3. kateke, 4. nanotau, 5. raba, 6. raoi, 7. kamaiu.
agreeably *see* raoi.
aground *see* koro.
aid *see* 1. buoka, 2. taobukia.
aided *see* 1. buokaki, 2. taobukiaki.
ail *see* aoraki.
ailing *see* kimai.
aimless *see* taeremea.
air *see* 1. tara, 2. tari.
alarmed *see* maku.
alarming *see* nanomakaki.
alert *see* 1. kauekea, 2. konamaki, 3. mautara, 4. taebo, 5. ueke.
alien *see* 1. ianena, 2. iruwa.
aligned *see* nangoraoi.
alike *see* 1. kiribare, 2. tiitebo.
alive *see* 1. konamaki, 2. mai, 3. maiu, 4. maiuroaroa.
all *see* 1. onton, 2. tabanin, 3. nini.
allay *see* karakoaea.
allege *see* maninutoa.
alleged *see* maninutoaki.
alleviate *see* 1. kabaketea, 2. kamarauakina.

alleviated *see* 1. kabaketeaki, 2. kamarauakinaki.
allied *see* raonnaki.
allot *see* kaborere.
allow *see* 1. kariaiakaki, 2. kariaia.
allude *see* tarae.
alluring *see* katekeria.
ally *see* raonna.
almost *see* 1. guri, 2. kuri, 3. ratau.
alone *see* maroa.
along *see* uana.
aloof *see* nanoraoi.
already *see* 1. kaman, 2. atia, 3. iákaman.
also *see* naba.
alter *see* 1. onea, 2. onika.
altered *see* 1. oneaki, 2. onikaki, 3. bitabao.
alternate *see* 1. batoara, 2. ikaruoruo, 3. kaimaranga, 4. karuoruo, 5. tauantaboa.
although *see* ngkae.
altogether *see* 1. toko, 2. nini, 3. nonginong.
altruistic *see* kakaianga.
always *see* nini.
am *see* bon.
amalgamate *see* rengana.
amalgamated *see* renganaki.
amass *see* 1. karibonobonoa, 2. kawawaea.
amassed *see* 1. karibonobonoaki, 2. kawawaeaki.
amaze *see* 1. kamatakua, 2. kamiroaroa, 3. kamia.
amazed *see* 1. kamatakuaki, 2. kamiaki, 3. kamiroaroaki.
amazing *see* kakamataku.
ambassador *see* man.
ambiguous *see* maewe.
ambitious *see* uamoa.
amble *see* kakaautakia.
ambush *see* karan.
amend *see* 1. rinanoa, 2. tiribaea, 3. raoiakina.
amended *see* 1. raoiakinaki, 2. rinanoaki, 3. tiribaeaki.
amiable *see* 1. manin, 2. rako, 3. nanouki, 4. nanomawa, 5. inaaine, 6. moringa, 7. moaraoi.
amicable *see* iraorao.
amiss *see* kairua.
ample *see* mawa.
amplify *see* kabunnaa.
amuse *see* 1. kamatakua, 2. wanikangarea, 3. katakakaroa, 4. kakibotu, 5. manikangare.
amused *see* 1. kakibotuaki, 2. kamatakuaki, 3. katakakaroaki, 4. manikangareaki, 5. wanikangareaki.
amusing *see* aokangare.
an *see* te.
anaesthetize *see* kamatua.
anaesthetized *see* kamatuaki.
analyze *see* kinanoa.
analyzed *see* kinanoaki.

anchor *see* 1. roro, 2. unikitero.
ancient *see* 1. nikawai, 2. rimoa, 3. nabawe, 4. ikawai.
and *see* 1. ma, 2. ao.
anemic *see* matanikanebu.
anesthetize *see* kakiroa.
anesthetized *see* kakiroaki.
anew *see* 1. nabangkai, 2. riki.
angelic *see* kakatika.
anger *see* 1. unun, 2. rarabuareare, 3. bononano.
angered *see* 1. bononanoaki, 2. rarabuareareaki, 3. ununaki.
angle *see* angkoro.
angled *see* angkoroaki.
angry *see* 1. un, 2. unuara, 3. bononano, 4. unun.
anguish *see* rainanoanga.
anguished *see* 1. rainanoanga, 2. rainanoangaki.
angular *see* angkoro.
animalize *see* 1. kaubunranga, 2. mwiniba.
animate *see* 1. karerea, 2. kataeboa, 3. kamarurunga, 4. maiu.
animated *see* 1. unga, 2. kamarurungaki, 3. karereaki, 4. kataeboaki, 5. nanomaka, 6. ueke.
animation *see* taururu.
annihilate *see* 1. kamatenakoa, 2. kamatea.
annihilated *see* 1. kamateaki, 2. kamatenakoaki.
annotate *see* taobukia.
annotated *see* taobukiaki.
announce *see* 1. takarua, 2. kaotioti.
announced *see* 1. kaotiotiaki, 2. takaruaki.
annoy *see* 1. kakai, 2. karawawata, 3. raraikumea, 4. rerebetunga, 5. tabarea, 6. waru.
annoyed *see* 1. kakaiaki, 2. waruaki, 3. un, 4. tabareaki, 5. rerebetungaki, 6. karawawataki, 7. raraikumeaki.
annoying *see* 1. rebetunga, 2. tokobeka, 3. tokobito, 4. kameio, 5. meme, 6. tokoie, 7. memeto.
anoint *see* kamanenaka.
answer *see* 1. reke, 2. bo, 3. boa, 4. kaeka.
antecedent *see* ririmoa.
antenna *see* kao.
anterior *see* ririmoa.
anticipate *see* 1. biririmoa, 2. kantaninga, 3. taukirikiri.
anticipated *see* 1. biririmoaki, 2. kantaningaki, 3. taukirikiriaki.
antique *see* nabawe.
anus *see* ki.
anxious *see* 1. inga, 2. ingainga, 3. mramra, 4. mura, 5. muramura, 6. nanobukibuki, 7. nanomaruru, 8. takitaki.
any *see* 1. riki, 2. tatabeua.
anyplace *see* tabonako.
anywhere *see* tabonako.

apart *see* 1. kaokoroaki, 2. kararoa, 3. nimananginang, 4. okoro.
apathetic *see* 1. ntangaingai, 2. tangauriuri, 3. taninganinga, 4. mannei, 5. kabuingoingo, 6. katoto, 7. tarabu, 8. nimaoriori.
apiece *see* tatabeua.
apocalyptic *see* kinanonano.
apologetic *see* mango.
apologize *see* mango.
apostle *see* Abotoro.
appalling *see* 1. kakamaku, 2. nanomakaki.
apparent *see* tere.
appear *see* 1. bina, 2. itibabang, 3. mata, 4. noraki, 5. oti, 6. ria.
appearance *see* tara.
appease *see* 1. riboriki, 2. kamarauakina.
append *see* 1. nimimarea, 2. reita, 3. toma.
appetizing *see* 1. nenea, 2. timinene, 3. nanai, 4. katekeria, 5. karekeria, 6. kangkang.
applaud *see* 1. kekeia, 2. kakannatoa.
applicable *see* raoi.
applied *see* bubutiaki.
apply *see* bubuti.
appoint *see* katanina.
appointed *see* kataninaki.
apportion *see* rinea.
apportioned *see* rineaki.
appreciate *see* 1. nora, 2. kamatebwai.
appreciated *see* 1. kamatebwaiaki, 2. noraki, 3. raba.
apprehend *see* 1. kamataua, 2. maka, 3. taua.
apprehended *see* 1. kamatauaki, 2. tauaki, 3. makaki, 4. matau.
apprehensive *see* 1. maku, 2. mamaku, 3. nanobebebe, 4. nanobukibuki, 5. nanomaruru.
approach *see* 1. kimai, 2. nakoa, 3. kania, 4. kawara.
appropriate *see* 1. arokana, 2. babaina, 3. baina, 4. bwaina, 5. katiribo, 6. raoi.
appropriated *see* 1. bainaki, 2. bwainaki, 3. babainaki, 4. arokanaki, 5. katiriboaki.
appropriately *see* raoi.
approve *see* 1. irannano, 2. karerei, 3. kariaia, 4. kariaiakaki, 5. kataua.
approved *see* 1. kariaiakakiaki, 2. katauaki, 3. kariaiakaki, 4. karereiaki, 5. irannanoaki, 6. kariaiaki.
approximate *see* tanua.
apt *see* 1. nano, 2. rabakau, 3. manikoraki, 4. manikonana, 5. kona, 6. bairaoi, 7. tau.
aquatint *see* kina.
arbitrate *see* karotuang.
arbitrated *see* karotuangaki.
arch *see* 1. aokua, 2. koaua.
archaic *see* nabawe.

arched *see* 1. aokuaki, 2. rabirabi, 3. aokua, 4. menga, 5. rabi.
ardent *see* 1. taebo, 2. angang, 3. makareirei, 4. mamaka, 5. manobotabota, 6. tabarebare, 7. taboang.
arduous *see* 1. unga, 2. kamou, 3. kanganga.
are *see* 1. a, 2. bon, 3. mena, 4. riki.
argue *see* 1. kabotaeka, 2. kauntaeka.
arid *see* 1. kanoabo, 2. takaroro, 3. taka.
aright *see* eeng.
arise *see* 1. ewe, 2. reke.
arm *see* pei.
armed *see* 1. uakai, 2. tabanikai.
armless *see* nakibaina.
arms *see* kati.
around *see* katobibia.
arouse *see* 1. katitua, 2. rarabuareare.
aroused *see* 1. katituaki, 2. rarabuareareaki.
arrange *see* 1. nea, 2. nukama, 3. batia, 4. baire, 5. riringa, 6. kawairinan.
arranged *see* 1. riringaki, 2. baireaki, 3. batiaki, 4. kawairinan, 5. kawairinanaki, 6. neaki, 7. nukamaki.
array *see* unauna.
arrest *see* 1. toki, 2. kamataua.
arrested *see* 1. kamatauaki, 2. matau, 3. matauaki, 4. tokiaki.
arrive *see* 1. karaki, 2. roko.
arrogant *see* 1. rietata, 2. kainikatonga, 3. ikake, 4. ririere.
artistic *see* rabakai.
as *see* 1. ma, 2. tiitebo, 3. nika, 4. ngkai, 5. kioina, 6. bwain, 7. bura, 8. ba, 9. ngke.
ascend *see* 1. tama, 2. rierake, 3. tamarake, 4. tabetirake, 5. borake, 6. betirake, 7. ararake, 8. erake.
ascending *see* betirake.
ascertain *see* 1. kakoaua, 2. kamatoa, 3. maroaka.
ascertained *see* 1. maroakaki, 2. kakoauaki, 3. kamatoaki.
aside *see* 1. kan, 2. tabara.
ask *see* 1. kanhai, 2. titiraki, 3. titirakinia.
askew *see* inra.
asleep *see* matu.
aspect *see* tara.
asphyxiate *see* ngawa.
asphyxiated *see* ngawaki.
aspirate *see* mbambaea.
aspire *see* mamarake.
assail *see* kibara.
assailable *see* nanorake.
assassin *see* kamatea.
assassinate *see* 1. kamatea, 2. tiringa.
assassinated *see* 1. kamateaki, 2. tiringaki.
assault *see* oro.

assaulted *see* oroaki.
assemble *see* 1. maio, 2. kawawaea, 3. kabo, 4. iko, 5. baronga, 6. botaki.
assembled *see* 1. botakiaki, 2. maioaki, 3. kawawaeaki, 4. ntaninin, 5. botaki, 6. bau, 7. barongaki, 8. kaboaki, 9. ikoaki.
assembling *see* runga.
assert *see* biririmoa.
asserted *see* biririmoaki.
assess *see* kinanoa.
assessed *see* kinanoaki.
assiduous *see* 1. kikinto, 2. rangarangatau.
assign *see* 1. anga, 2. kaonoa, 3. katanina.
assigned *see* 1. angaki, 2. kaonoaki, 3. kataninaki.
assimilate *see* kamantoa.
assist *see* 1. buoka, 2. katoa.
assistant *see* raom.
assisted *see* 1. buokaki, 2. katoaki.
associate *see* 1. boibuako, 2. raom, 3. raona.
associated *see* 1. raona, 2. raonaki, 3. kaeti, 4. boibuakoaki.
assorted *see* aeka.
assume *see* 1. anua, 2. kamatebwai, 3. nora.
assumed *see* 1. anuaki, 2. kamatebwaiaki, 3. noraki.
assure *see* kakoaua.
assured *see* 1. maurake, 2. matatoka, 3. kakoauaki.
astonish *see* 1. kamatakua, 2. kamia, 3. kamiroaroa.
astonished *see* 1. kamiroaroaki, 2. mataroro, 3. kamiaki, 4. kamatakuaki, 5. bobouro.
astonishing *see* karuanano.
astound *see* 1. kakuba, 2. kamatakua.
astounded *see* 1. kakubaki, 2. kamatakuaki.
astounding *see* kamimi.
astray *see* marua.
astute *see* 1. kauanga, 2. nano.
asunder *see* tabwenaua.
asymmetrical *see* 1. ruatatara, 2. tabarabara, 3. tarabuaka.
at *see* 1. n, 2. ni, 3. in, 4. iai, 5. i.
atrabilious *see* kiura.
attach *see* 1. kananonibaia, 2. nama, 3. nim, 4. nimtangira.
attached *see* 1. nimaki, 2. nimtangiraki, 3. nimroa, 4. nabe, 5. kananonibaiaki, 6. nimroaki, 7. namaki.
attack *see* 1. buakana, 2. kanako, 3. kibara, 4. ruona, 5. taboa.
attain *see* rota.
attained *see* 1. roko, 2. rotaki.
attempt *see* 1. kamanenanti, 2. kata, 3. moanangia.
attempted *see* 1. kamanenantiaki, 2. kataki, 3. moanangiaki.
attend *see* 1. ongo, 2. neweaba, 3. kakaunongo.
attended *see* 1. neweabaki, 2. ongoaki, 3. kakaunongoaki.

attentive *see* **1.** mataroro, **2.** mautara, **3.** moringa, **4.** muti.
attenuate *see* kamarara.
attenuated *see* kamararaki.
attract *see* **1.** taomaoma, **2.** ribinanoa.
attractive *see* **1.** kan, **2.** karekanano, **3.** manin.
attribute *see* kanotona.
audacious *see* maurake.
audit *see* **1.** rinanoa, **2.** kinanoa.
auditor *see* kinnano.
augment *see* **1.** kabunnaa, **2.** kamaita, **3.** katia, **4.** kaua, **5.** raka, **6.** kabatia.
augmented *see* **1.** kabunnaaki, **2.** rakaki, **3.** kauaki, **4.** kamaitaki, **5.** kabatiaki, **6.** katiaki.
austere *see* matoatao.
authentic *see* koaua.
authorize *see* katanina.
authorized *see* **1.** kataninaki, **2.** kariaiakaki, **3.** kariaiaki.
available *see* tauraoi.
avarice *see* kibubura.
avenge *see* nimamate.
avenged *see* nimamateaki.
avert *see* wira.
avoid *see* **1.** kio, **2.** tuka, **3.** rerea, **4.** katua, **5.** kakaro, **6.** iranikai, **7.** totoka.
await *see* **1.** aurama, **2.** tataninga.
awake *see* **1.** mangauti, **2.** taratara, **3.** uti.
awaken *see* **1.** uti, **2.** rakea.
awakened *see* **1.** rakeaki, **2.** utiaki.
aware *see* **1.** ataki, **2.** konamaki, **3.** matatoka, **4.** mautara.
away *see* **1.** ngkainaba, **2.** kinokino, **3.** nako.
awesome *see* **1.** kamimi, **2.** bureti, **3.** kakaauba.
awful *see* **1.** kakamaku, **2.** nanomakaki.
awkward *see* **1.** tabuaetia, **2.** tarikabana, **3.** intinebu, **4.** tabonibainrang, **5.** niau, **6.** bake, **7.** baira, **8.** baibuaka, **9.** antibuaka, **10.** uara, **11.** beu.
axe *see* áñara.

B

babble *see* **1.** wibino, **2.** arenang, **3.** karebo, **4.** takuarara.
baby *see* teei.
back *see* **1.** oki, **2.** aukou.
backup *see* kinako.
backward *see* **1.** nanoro, **2.** rikaaki.
bad *see* **1.** nikora, **2.** tarabuaka, **3.** ribuaka, **4.** raa, **5.** buaakaka, **6.** ra, **7.** bubuaka, **8.** buaka, **9.** buakaka, **10.** be, **11.** me.
badger *see* **1.** raraikumea, **2.** kakai, **3.** karawawata.
baffled *see* kaminoa.

baffling *see* wanga.
bag *see* kamataua.
bail *see* kaiki.
bait *see* kamauanea.
bake *see* **1.** aumua, **2.** kariki.
baked *see* **1.** karikaki, **2.** karikiaki.
balance *see* **1.** roba, **2.** tie, **3.** tiera, **4.** boraoi.
balanced *see* **1.** tieraki, **2.** boraoi, **3.** boraoiaki, **4.** robaki, **5.** tieaki.
balancing *see* kamatine.
bald *see* **1.** katumara, **2.** mara, **3.** atumara.
balk *see* ngurengure.
ball *see* **1.** katimoimoi, **2.** tang.
bamboo *see* **1.** takibaba, **2.** kaibâba.
ban *see* **1.** mabu, **2.** katabua, **3.** kamabu.
bandage *see* bauta.
bandaged *see* bautaki.
bang *see* **1.** karutua, **2.** orea.
bankrupt *see* iti.
banned *see* **1.** katabuaki, **2.** mabu, **3.** kamabuaki, **4.** mabuaki.
banter *see* **1.** kinra, **2.** manikangare.
baptize *see* uri.
baptized *see* uriaki.
bar *see* kamabu.
barbarous *see* tiritiri.
bare *see* **1.** tangenge, **2.** tawanang, **3.** katengetengea, **4.** aomatata, **5.** matata.
barely *see* **1.** maki, **2.** takomkom.
bargain *see* bobai.
bark *see* **1.** anni, **2.** takaeakina, **3.** takaka.
barn *see* tuanga.
barred *see* kamabuaki.
barren *see* **1.** matata, **2.** ra, **3.** kanoabo.
base *see* kakoaua.
based *see* kakoauaki.
bash *see* kaibakoa.
bashful *see* mama.
basic *see* boto.
basket *see* **1.** apéi, **2.** baiene.
bastard *see* **1.** nati, **2.** kamaniman.
bastardize *see* **1.** kaubunranga, **2.** mwiniba.
bastardized *see* **1.** kaubunrangaki, **2.** mwinibaki.
bathe *see* **1.** teboka, **2.** tebotebo.
batter *see* **1.** ikua, **2.** oro, **3.** ikuiku, **4.** kamantintia.
battered *see* **1.** bakibora, **2.** ikuaki, **3.** ikuikuaki, **4.** kamantintiaki, **5.** makibora, **6.** oroaki.
battle *see* **1.** buaka, **2.** bo.
be *see* **1.** mena, **2.** riki.
beach *see* kabikôuea.
beads *see* **1.** bâmuti, **2.** takatau, **3.** tenikadaradara.
beaming *see* niniwana.
bean *see* orea.
beard *see* buai.
bearded *see* kaubuai.

beat see **1**. kanebu, **2**. tekena, **3**. tiri, **4**. tourika, **5**. ruberube, **6**. kataere, **7**. kamantintia, **8**. ikuiku, **9**. ikua, **10**. bukibuki, **11**. batiboa, **12**. kamaterea, **13**. tiringa.

beaten see **1**. kamantintiaki, **2**. tourikaki, **3**. tiringaki, **4**. tiriaki, **5**. tekenaki, **6**. teka, **7**. ruberubeaki, **8**. kataereaki, **9**. kamatereaki, **10**. ikuikuaki, **11**. ikuaki, **12**. bukibukiaki, **13**. batiboaki, **14**. kanebuaki.

beautiful see **1**. tika, **2**. timu, **3**. tamaroa, **4**. tikaua, **5**. tikiraoi, **6**. niko, **7**. kakatika, **8**. bakitoutou, **9**. rerei.

beautify see **1**. katamaroa, **2**. unauna.

beckon see **1**. kea, **2**. anoa, **3**. anoano.

become see riki.

becoming see **1**. tau, **2**. tenu, **3**. wau, **4**. raoi.

becomingly see raoi.

bedaub see katakanakana.

before see **1**. imainna, **2**. remoa.

beforehand see ngkekei.

befoul see **1**. mwiniba, **2**. kaubunranga.

befouled see **1**. kaubunrangaki, **2**. mwinibaki.

befriend see **1**. imammane, **2**. rei.

beg see bubuti.

beget see **1**. kariki, **2**. kakariki, **3**. karika.

beggarly see toronrang.

begin see **1**. moana, **2**. moanang, **3**. moanangia, **4**. moanna, **5**. teirake, **6**. aboka.

beginner see tabemoa.

begotten see **1**. karikiaki, **2**. kakarikiaki, **3**. karikaki.

begrudge see taramangurea.

behead see **1**. kabakua, **2**. baku.

beheaded see **1**. bakuaki, **2**. kabakuaki.

behind see **1**. inawiu, **2**. tamwere.

behold see **1**. nora, **2**. tara.

being see aomata.

belated see aubeabea.

believe see kakoaua.

bellow see **1**. takaeakina, **2**. kaukau.

belly see piroto.

belong see korakina.

below see **1**. ana, **2**. i-â, **3**. nano.

bemoan see tangiroa.

bend see **1**. baoua, **2**. oto, **3**. kamoua, **4**. kabaoa, **5**. kakiribabaoua, **6**. kamaoriori.

bending see mamaoriori.

beneath see iân.

beneficent see raoiroi.

beneficial see ibuobuoki.

benevolent see **1**. baiati, **2**. kakaianga, **3**. atataiaomata.

benighted see nonoro.

bent see **1**. kamaorioriaki, **2**. rabirabi, **3**. rabi, **4**. otoaki, **5**. bake, **6**. mori, **7**. kiribabaoua, **8**. kamouaki, **9**. kabaoaki, **10**. beuakora, **11**. baouaki, **12**. baoua, **13**. bako, **14**. kakiribabaouaki, **15**. babako, **16**. baokoko.

bequeath see katuka.

bereave see **1**. ana, **2**. kabua.

bereaved see **1**. anaki, **2**. kabuaki.

beseech see **1**. bubuti, **2**. kairoro, **3**. onon.

besides see naba.

besmirch see katakanakana.

besmirched see katakanakanaki.

best see moaniba.

bestrew see kamerea.

bet see **1**. beta, **2**. kabwakabwai, **3**. karuotua, **4**. tu.

betray see kamwanea.

better see **1**. moa, **2**. riai, **3**. kamaterea, **4**. riki.

beveled see rabe.

bevy see nanai.

bewail see tangiroa.

beware see **1**. karaurau, **2**. kawakiniko.

bewilder see **1**. kamataboua, **2**. nanououa, **3**. nanomaiti, **4**. kananokoraki, **5**. kamatakiaua.

bewildered see **1**. nanokoraki, **2**. teiruarua, **3**. nanououaki, **4**. nanououa, **5**. nanomaiti, **6**. matakiaua, **7**. matabou, **8**. kananokorakiaki, **9**. kamatakiauaki, **10**. kamatabouaki, **11**. nanomaitiaki.

bewitch see wauna.

bewitched see **1**. waunaki, **2**. maraia, **3**. raka.

beyond see narei.

bias see **1**. tabaitera, **2**. tabeitera.

bicycle see bwatika.

bid see **1**. tua, **2**. beta, **3**. kao, **4**. kea.

bide see **1**. tataninga, **2**. tiku.

big see **1**. bubura, **2**. ababaki, **3**. kora, **4**. korakora, **5**. nuku, **6**. wari.

bigoted see nanoriba.

bike see bwatika.

billet see kiakina.

billow see nuo.

bind see **1**. bauta, **2**. kabaea, **3**. motinnano, **4**. nira, **5**. ramanea, **6**. ribata.

bird see mannikiba.

birth see bungia.

bishop see Ebikobo.

bit see **1**. kamakerua, **2**. tena.

bite see **1**. tena, **2**. kamakerua, **3**. tabaka, **4**. tenarua.

biting see maitorotoro.

bitter see **1**. tena, **2**. nanobuaka, **3**. mao, **4**. ari.

blab see **1**. kauka, **2**. takuarara.

black see **1**. roro, **2**. bûtara, **3**. euto.

blame see **1**. bukina, **2**. kabuakaka, **3**. boa, **4**. kanotona.

blamed see **1**. boaki, **2**. bukinaki, **3**. kabuakakaki, **4**. kanotonaki.

blanch see kamainaina.

blanched see **1**. taetoba, **2**. kamainainaki.

blank *see* kamauna.
blanked *see* kamaunaki.
blaspheme *see* wauwi.
blast *see* kioi.
blasted *see* kioiaki.
blaze *see* urarakea.
blazing *see* 1. tairo, 2. uramaka.
bleach *see* kamauna.
bleached *see* kamaunaki.
bleary *see* nanokabakoba.
blemish *see* kawanta.
blemished *see* kawantaki.
blend *see* 1. irenganan, 2. kabo, 3. kairengarenga, 4. rengana, 5. tangana.
blended *see* 1. irengananaki, 2. tanganaki, 3. renganaki, 4. kairengarengaki, 5. kaboaki.
bless *see* katabua.
blessed *see* 1. kabaia, 2. katabuaki, 3. kukurei, 4. tekeraoi.
blind *see* 1. kamataanoa, 2. mataki, 3. kamatakia, 4. egêgi, 5. kamataniaia.
blinded *see* 1. kamataanoaki, 2. kamatakiaki, 3. kamataniaiaki, 4. mataneai.
blink *see* 1. ruberube, 2. mataruberube.
blissful *see* 1. kukurei, 2. kanoan.
blister *see* nou.
blistered *see* nouaki.
blithe *see* kukurei.
bloat *see* kiritibutibu.
bloated *see* 1. kiritibutibu, 2. kiritibutibuaki, 3. rereta.
block *see* 1. bonota, 2. tuka, 3. mate, 4. taokabia.
blocked *see* 1. bonotaki, 2. taokabiaki, 3. taribono, 4. tukaki.
blockhead *see* bobono.
blonde *see* atumeamea.
blood *see* 1. râra, 2. rara, 3. koraki.
bloodthirsty *see* tiritiri.
blot *see* 1. kamauna, 2. urua.
blow *see* 1. toouk, 2. uka, 3. oro, 4. kioi, 5. bo.
blown *see* 1. kioiaki, 2. oro, 3. oroaki, 4. uka, 5. ukaki, 6. boaki.
blue *see* 1. buru, 2. mawawa.
bluff *see* birikewe.
blunder *see* 1. katurara, 2. airua.
blunt *see* 1. bubu, 2. kábub, 3. kabubu, 4. rotu, 5. tarotu.
blur *see* 1. nuna, 2. kamataanoanoa.
blurred *see* 1. kamataanoanoaki, 2. nunaki.
blurt *see* meakina.
blush *see* tawere.
boast *see* 1. rorouba, 2. kakarabakaua, 3. kakawibaea, 4. kamoa, 5. kamoamoa, 6. karabakaua.
boaster *see* 1. bakamoamoa, 2. wibeka.

boastful *see* 1. kainikatonga, 2. kamoamoa, 3. roroutake.
boasting *see* roroutake.
boat *see* waa.
boatman *see* kimautari.
body *see* rabáta.
boil *see* 1. buro, 2. rarabuareare, 3. kaburoa, 4. katetea.
boiled *see* 1. buro, 2. buroaki, 3. kaburoaki, 4. kateteaki, 5. rarabuareareaki.
bold *see* 1. tarie, 2. ninikoa, 3. mautete, 4. maurake, 5. tete.
bolster *see* mantakarara.
bolt *see* rerea.
bolted *see* 1. in, 2. rereaki.
bond *see* motinnano.
bonded *see* 1. motinnanoaki, 2. taonikai.
bone *see* 1. rî, 2. teri, 3. ri.
bonito *see* kaneheke.
bony *see* 1. tuariri, 2. kairi, 3. kauri, 4. reka, 5. riri.
boo *see* rabungaoa.
book *see* boki.
booked *see* 1. rabu, 2. tibutaua.
bootlick *see* memerake.
border *see* nimimarea.
bordered *see* nimimareaki.
bore *see* 1. rawana, 2. botu, 3. katengetengeaki.
bored *see* 1. tabotua, 2. rawanaki, 3. botu, 4. botuaki.
boring *see* 1. botu, 2. kameio, 3. meme.
born *see* bungiaki.
borrow *see* 1. tarau, 2. tangoa, 3. kabaeai, 4. bubuti.
borrowed *see* 1. kabaeaiaki, 2. tangoaki, 3. tarauaki, 4. bubutiaki.
boss *see* 1. botia, 2. mataniwi, 3. taratara.
bossy *see* taratara.
bother *see* 1. tabarea, 2. raraikumea, 3. nanoa, 4. manga, 5. katabetabe, 6. kakai, 7. karawawata.
bothered *see* 1. raraikumeaki, 2. un, 3. nanoaki, 4. mangaki, 5. karawawataki, 6. kakaiaki, 7. tabareaki.
bottle *see* 1. naip, 2. tínaba.
bottom *see* 1. ana, 2. inanoinano, 3. kabin, 4. toka.
bottomed *see* tokaki.
bounce *see* 1. wew, 2. kia, 3. katata, 4. katuatua.
bound *see* 1. kabaeaki, 2. wew, 3. ribataki, 4. ribata, 5. ramaneaki, 6. ramanea, 7. niraki, 8. motinnanoaki, 9. kabaea, 10. inimaki, 11. buata, 12. bautaki, 13. motinnano.
bounded *see* 1. kabaeaki, 2. wewaki, 3. ribataki, 4. motinnanoaki, 5. inimakiaki, 6. buataki, 7. ramaneaki.
boundless *see* 1. nanokirokiro, 2. nanokiroro.
bountiful *see* 1. kakaianga, 2. nonga.
bow *see* bobaraki.

bowed *see* bobarakiaki.
box *see* 1. pakenge, 2. ikaroubu.
boxed *see* ikaroubuaki.
boy *see* nao.
boycott *see* karitei.
brackish *see* 1. mambwea, 2. tarika.
brag *see* 1. kakawibaea, 2. wibeka, 3. kakarabakaua.
braggart *see* 1. wibeka, 2. wibunai, 3. wikotaua, 4. bakamoamoa.
bragger *see* inakewe.
bragging *see* bakaunun.
braid *see* 1. bira, 2. tokoran.
braided *see* biraki.
branched *see* kirimanga.
branching *see* manga.
branchy *see* manga.
brand *see* kanikina.
branded *see* kanikinaki.
brash *see* maurake.
brassy *see* maurake.
brave *see* 1. matoa, 2. ninikoa, 3. kaura, 4. ninikoria.
brawny *see* tinaubati.
brazen *see* maurake.
breach *see* uki.
breached *see* 1. bangabanga, 2. uki, 3. ukiaki.
bread *see* kariki.
breaded *see* karikiaki.
breadfruit *see* mehi.
break *see* 1. raemenga, 2. urubeke, 3. urua, 4. uraka, 5. ibea, 6. unobauta, 7. otouia, 8. oto, 9. otea, 10. motika, 11. moimotikia, 12. mae, 13. ma, 14. ura.
breakers *see* nok.
breakneck *see* kaumaki.
breast *see* mama.
breastfeed *see* kammamma.
breath *see* 1. tokouki, 2. ike, 3. ikeike.
breathe *see* 1. ikeike, 2. nawa.
breathed *see* 1. ikeaki, 2. ikeikeaki, 3. nawaki.
breathless *see* mawa.
breed *see* 1. kariki, 2. kakariki.
brethren *see* tari.
bride *see* kainabau.
brief *see* kimototo.
bright *see* 1. niniwana, 2. rabakau, 3. raneanea.
brilliant *see* 1. maneouna, 2. niniwana, 3. takaneanea.
bring *see* 1. ana, 2. uota, 3. nikira.
brisk *see* 1. baitata, 2. kaumaki, 3. rangarangatau, 4. tabarekai, 5. ueke.
bristle *see* 1. katababaea, 2. uakaka.
bristled *see* 1. katababaeaki, 2. uakakaki.
bristling *see* 1. uakaka, 2. tabarua.
bristly *see* karekereke.
brittle *see* makana.
broad *see* 1. bubura, 2. nuku, 3. rababa, 4. rāpape.

broil *see* kamwa.
broiled *see* kamwaki.
broke *see* otea.
broken *see* 1. unobautaki, 2. urubekeaki, 3. uruaki, 4. urakaki, 5. tewâk, 6. raemengaki, 7. raemenga, 8. otoaki, 9. oteaki, 10. otea, 11. nimoti, 12. motikaki, 13. moti, 14. môt, 15. moimotikiaki, 16. moimoti, 17. maki, 18. maeaki, 19. kirimotimoti, 20. ibeaki.
brood *see* 1. nanai, 2. kanaeng.
brooding *see* kinokunoku.
broom *see* too.
brother *see* 1. mwanem, 2. mwanena, 3. mwaneu, 4. ouena, 5. tári, 6. tariu.
browbeat *see* takurere.
brown *see* buraun.
bruise *see* ikoa.
bruised *see* 1. ikoaki, 2. nikunikun, 3. nikunakuna, 4. mori, 5. kukunakuna.
brush *see* taea.
brushed *see* taeaki.
brutal *see* tiritiri.
brutalize *see* tabuarikia.
bubble *see* 1. buro, 2. kobu, 3. te.
bud *see* kabu.
budding *see* 1. bu, 2. butokaurake.
buddy *see* raom.
bug *see* raraikumea.
bugged *see* raraikumeaki.
build *see* 1. nikoa, 2. katea, 3. katei, 4. kateibai.
built *see* 1. nikoaki, 2. kateibaiaki, 3. kateaki, 4. katea.
bulge *see* rebe.
bulky *see* 1. bubura, 2. tuanonoku.
bullied *see* 1. kakoroikuaki, 2. mannaokaki.
bully *see* 1. kakoroiku, 2. mannaoka.
bump *see* 1. ibutubuto, 2. unikaikai, 3. airo.
bumpy *see* 1. kiribeubeu, 2. tabatibutibu, 3. tabureka.
bunched *see* 1. makoko, 2. kirmrim.
bundle *see* 1. batia, 2. atu.
bungle *see* 1. tabuarikia, 2. tabureka.
bungled *see* 1. tabuarikiaki, 2. taburekaki.
buoyant *see* mwemwe.
burden *see* kamengoa.
burdened *see* kamengoaki.
burdensome *see* kamou.
burglarize *see* maro.
buried *see* 1. taumateaki, 2. taunaki.
burly *see* nanomane.
burn *see* 1. bue, 2. kabuoka, 3. katena.
burned *see* tekeria.
burning *see* 1. bue, 2. mika.
burnt *see* 1. bueaki, 2. kabuoka, 3. kabuokaki, 4. katena, 5. katenaki, 6. bue.

burrow *see* kena.
burst *see* **1**. katakokoa, **2**. ureaki, **3**. ure, **4**. tebeaki, **5**. tebe, **6**. ruoruoaki, **7**. ruoruo, **8**. kioiaki, **9**. katakokoaki, **10**. kioi.
bury *see* **1**. taumate, **2**. tauna, **3**. taun.
bushy *see* **1**. tabakurakura, **2**. tokobuakoako.
bustle *see* rangarangatau.
bustling *see* **1**. rangarangatau, **2**. wanga.
busy *see* **1**. mutiakina, **2**. rangarangatau, **3**. baraki, **4**. tabe.
but *see* **1**. ba, **2**. bü, **3**. ma, **4**. ti.
butt *see* kebutua.
buttocks *see* pouki.
buy *see* **1**. kaboa, **2**. bobai.
buzz *see* tangibururu.
by *see* **1**. irou, **2**. n, **3**. ni.
bygone *see* nabawe.

C

cackle *see* karara.
cajole *see* toroba.
calculate *see* **1**. ware, **2**. warebai, **3**. taukirikiri, **4**. iangomaka, **5**. warebaia.
calculated *see* **1**. iangomakaki, **2**. taukirikiriaki, **3**. wareaki, **4**. warebaiaki.
call *see* **1**. kao, **2**. wewete, **3**. wetea, **4**. vetea, **5**. kea, **6**. ieanga, **7**. arana, **8**. anoano, **9**. kawara.
called *see* **1**. kawaraki, **2**. weweteaki, **3**. weteaki, **4**. keaki, **5**. kaoaki, **6**. ieangaki, **7**. aranaki, **8**. anoanoaki, **9**. veteaki.
callous *see* konin.
calloused *see* koninaki.
calm *see* **1**. kataribabua, **2**. riboriki, **3**. rau, **4**. taribabu, **5**. karamwemmwe, **6**. babu, **7**. aria, **8**. nanoraoi, **9**. maem.
calumniate *see* kananobaraka.
came *see* roko.
can *see* kona.
cancel *see* **1**. kamauna, **2**. kamanang.
cancelled *see* **1**. kamanangaki, **2**. kamaunaki.
candid *see* matabou.
cane *see* **1**. eko, **2**. tiringa.
cannibal *see* kâkaña.
canoe *see* wa.
canon *see* kati.
cantankerous *see* **1**. nanoun, **2**. nanorake, **3**. karitei, **4**. kiura.
cap *see* para.
capable *see* **1**. manikonana, **2**. manikoraki, **3**. nanomane, **4**. rabakau.
capacious *see* kakanoa.
caper *see* **1**. kiriringng, **2**. kirei.

capricious *see* **1**. atubitaki, **2**. minotaki.
capsize *see* **1**. bwaka, **2**. karanga, **3**. ranga.
captain *see* kaben.
captivate *see* karekenano.
captivated *see* karekenanoaki.
captivating *see* kamataku.
captive *see* karekanano.
capture *see* **1**. konana, **2**. kamataua.
card *see* ake.
carded *see* akeaki.
care *see* rako.
careful *see* **1**. ako, **2**. kikinto, **3**. nanomano, **4**. rako.
careless *see* **1**. arei, **2**. nanotiotio, **3**. taninganinga.
caress *see* **1**. botam, **2**. tobi, **3**. toroba.
caring *see* muti.
carpenter *see* kamta.
carry *see* **1**. houetia, **2**. urakina, **3**. uota, **4**. outi, **5**. tabeka, **6**. uabai.
carve *see* **1**. kara, **2**. koria, **3**. tata.
carved *see* **1**. ninimakoro, **2**. tataki, **3**. koriaki, **4**. karaki.
cast *see* **1**. kakaki, **2**. kamerea, **3**. kamereaki, **4**. katanina, **5**. kataninaki, **6**. kaka.
casual *see* taeremea.
casualty *see* bua.
cat *see* **1**. katama, **2**. kadamwa.
cataclysmic *see* kabuanibai.
catch *see* **1**. ribita, **2**. uamanea, **3**. tiemanea, **4**. tawarea, **5**. reke, **6**. rawea, **7**. kamataua, **8**. baua, **9**. bairekereke, **10**. tekena.
catchy *see* karekereke.
categorical *see* nabangkai.
caulked *see* au.
cause *see* moana.
cauterize *see* katena.
cautious *see* **1**. nanomano, **2**. mautara.
cease *see* **1**. kom, **2**. tai, **3**. toki.
celebrate *see* **1**. kakannatoa, **2**. neboa, **3**. nikierere.
celebrated *see* **1**. eke, **2**. nikierereaki, **3**. neboaki, **4**. kakannanton, **5**. kakannatoaki.
cement *see* kanima.
censor *see* tauburea.
censored *see* taubureaki.
censure *see* rabungaoa.
censured *see* rabungaoaki.
central *see* **1**. moa, **2**. nuka.
certain *see* **1**. koaua, **2**. matatoka, **3**. nabangkai.
certainly *see* bon.
certified *see* **1**. kakoauaki, **2**. kamatebwaiaki, **3**. noraki.
certify *see* **1**. kamatebwai, **2**. nora, **3**. kakoaua.
chafed *see* **1**. karawawataki, **2**. kakaiaki.
chaff *see* **1**. kakawibaea, **2**. karawawata, **3**. kareao, **4**. kinra.
chained *see* tourake.

challenge *see* taboa.
champion *see* 1. bakora, 2. korana.
chance *see* manenanti.
change *see* 1. bita, 2. kaibibitia, 3. kananobitaka, 4. onika, 5. rai.
changeable *see* 1. atubitaki, 2. takarua, 3. rume, 4. ruannano, 5. nanobibitaki, 6. angitannene, 7. nanotiotio.
changed *see* 1. raiaki, 2. bitaki, 3. kaibibitiaki, 4. kananobitakaki, 5. onikaki.
changing *see* nanobitaki.
channel *see* rava.
chaotic *see* mangaoangao.
chaperon *see* taubea.
chaperone *see* raona.
charge *see* 1. kanotona, 2. tarauakina, 3. una.
charged *see* 1. tarauakinaki, 2. unaki, 3. kanotonaki.
charismatic *see* karekanano.
charitable *see* 1. kakaianga, 2. moringa.
charm *see* karekenano.
charmed *see* 1. karekenanoaki, 2. ririka, 3. takuakua.
charming *see* 1. kareke, 2. katekeria, 3. manin, 4. karekanano.
charmingly *see* reirei.
chart *see* mabe.
chary *see* nanomano.
chase *see* 1. kara, 2. karebutia, 3. kanakoa, 4. kakioa, 5. kaeea, 6. taenakoa.
chased *see* 1. taenakoaki, 2. kaeaki, 3. kaeeaki, 4. kakioaki, 5. kanakoaki, 6. karaki, 7. karebutiaki.
chastise *see* 1. ikana, 2. tiribo.
chastised *see* 1. ikanaki, 2. tiriboaki.
chat *see* 1. kakarabakau, 2. marooro.
chatter *see* 1. wirebwerebwe, 2. babarantiko, 3. wibino.
chatterbox *see* 1. wirebwerebwe, 2. babarantiko, 3. takabea.
chaw *see* kamakerua.
cheap *see* materaoi.
cheapen *see* mwiniba.
cheat *see* 1. mwaamwanna, 2. uaraoa, 3. uarao, 4. kainabaea, 5. boba, 6. babakanikawai, 7. mamana.
check *see* 1. rinanoa, 2. tarabai, 3. matauna, 4. kinanoa, 5. kekera, 6. kateikai, 7. kamatataua, 8. tuoa.
checked *see* 1. kamatatauaki, 2. kateikaiaki, 3. kekeraki, 4. kinanoaki, 5. mataunaki, 6. rinanoaki, 7. tarabaiaki, 8. tuoaki.
checker *see* kinnano.
checkered *see* maererua.
cheek *see* 1. papa, 2. tapa, 3. maurake.
cheeked *see* maurakeaki.
cheeky *see* maurake.

cheer *see* 1. keke, 2. kekeia.
cheery *see* kukurei.
cherish *see* 1. kaotabaea, 2. tangira, 3. tabunimatea, 4. miroa, 5. nabea.
cherished *see* 1. kaotabaeaki, 2. miroaki, 3. nabeaki, 4. tabunimateaki, 5. tangiraki.
chew *see* 1. makiro, 2. mange, 3. baronria, 4. kanta.
chicken *see* 1. moa, 2. nanobu.
chide *see* takua.
chief *see* 1. moa, 2. urukau, 3. uêa, 4. toue, 5. tokatake, 6. ruatu, 7. mataniwii, 8. katoka, 9. kaben, 10. inaaomata, 11. toka.
chiefly *see* okoro.
child *see* 1. ëdai, 2. de, 3. tei, 4. ataei, 5. ati, 6. nati.
childish *see* 1. ataei, 2. manrerei.
chilled *see* mariri.
chilly *see* mariri.
chin *see* 1. pañi, 2. buña, 3. pange.
chip *see* taia.
chipper *see* kukurei.
choke *see* 1. bonoike, 2. kabun, 3. ngawa, 4. taba.
choked *see* 1. tabaki, 2. bonoikeaki, 3. kabunaki, 4. ngawaki.
choleric *see* 1. unin, 2. nanorake, 3. nanoun.
chomp *see* kamakerua.
choose *see* 1. kauanakoa, 2. rine, 3. rinea.
chop *see* 1. bouaia, 2. kataewa.
chopped *see* 1. bouaiaki, 2. kataewaki.
chosen *see* 1. rinea, 2. rineaki, 3. kauanakoaki.
christen *see* babetitoa.
chubby *see* 1. bubura, 2. memeri, 3. tinebu, 4. tuabebeku.
chum *see* raom.
churlish *see* tabureka.
cinder *see* taugara.
circle *see* 1. baua, 2. mronron, 3. nainaina.
circular *see* 1. mron, 2. mronron, 3. tobibi.
circulate *see* kawawa.
circumspect *see* 1. kawakinibwai, 2. mautara, 3. nanomano.
circumvent *see* tuka.
civil *see* maninganinga.
civilized *see* maninganinga.
clack *see* takitaki.
clad *see* 1. kunnikaia, 2. kunnikaiaki.
claim *see* 1. uneakina, 2. tania, 3. tang.
clairvoyant *see* 1. wanawana, 2. mamata.
clambake *see* tutu.
clammy *see* maono.
clamor *see* takaka.
clannish *see* nanoutu.
clap *see* kekeruatai.
clash *see* 1. aioro, 2. untaba, 3. keru, 4. kauntabama, 5. iwai, 6. kakenga.
clasp *see* 1. nimta, 2. rawea.

classified *see* aekaki.
classify *see* aeka.
claw *see* 1. korita, 2. uki.
clawed *see* koritaki.
clean *see* 1. iaki, 2. iakina, 3. itiaki, 4. itiwewe, 5. kaitiaka, 6. taea.
cleaned *see* 1. iakinaki, 2. kaitiakaki, 3. iakiaki, 4. taeaki.
cleanse *see* teboka.
cleansed *see* tebokaki.
clear *see* 1. matata, 2. tabitabitabita, 3. riaoa, 4. raneanea, 5. oota, 6. maroaka, 7. kaiti, 8. kaita, 9. itiwewe, 10. iti, 11. aomatata, 12. ainga, 13. matatoka.
cleared *see* 1. kaitaki, 2. tabitabitabitaki, 3. kaitiaki, 4. riaoaki.
cleave *see* uki.
clergy *see* Ekaretia.
clever *see* 1. kiriman, 2. rabakau, 3. wanawana, 4. maribo, 5. karabakau, 6. bairaoi, 7. atataibai, 8. ataibai, 9. kauanga.
click *see* takitaki.
climb *see* 1. tamatama, 2. tamwarake, 3. tamarake, 4. tama, 5. rierake, 6. ararake, 7. taokai, 8. tamaka.
cling *see* 1. nim, 2. nimroa.
clink *see* 1. keke, 2. kekeruatai.
close *see* 1. kaina, 2. riba, 3. ko, 4. po, 5. takoko, 6. makoko, 7. rikuma, 8. kiribwebwe, 9. katia, 10. kamaoa, 11. bonota, 12. beroro, 13. kan, 14. kiriuatao.
closed *see* 1. in, 2. rikumaki, 3. maki, 4. katiaki, 5. katia, 6. kainaki, 7. bonotaki, 8. bono, 9. kamaoaki.
clothe *see* 1. rabuna, 2. karina, 3. kunnikaia.
clothed *see* 1. rabunaki, 2. kunnikaiaki, 3. kunnikaia, 4. karinaki.
clotted *see* kiribanin.
cloud *see* 1. kamataanoanoa, 2. kananginang, 3. rañ.
clouded *see* 1. kamataanoanoaki, 2. kananginangaki.
cloudy *see* 1. nubono, 2. tanibabu.
club *see* baba.
clumsy *see* 1. antibuaka, 2. baibuaka, 3. baira, 4. intinebu, 5. tabonibainrang.
coagulated *see* 1. ntaninin, 2. kiribanin.
coarse *see* kaburati.
coast *see* 1. katikeke, 2. kiea.
coat *see* nimroa.
coated *see* nimroaki.
coax *see* 1. binenea, 2. ena, 3. kamaramara, 4. toroba.
cock *see* mô'umân.
cockroach *see* bebádoa.
cocky *see* 1. ikake, 2. butiroko.

coconut *see* 1. ben, 2. pen.
coerce *see* 1. kanenea, 2. memerake.
cognitive *see* nanowana.
cognizant *see* matatoka.
cognize *see* 1. kamatebwai, 2. nora.
coherent *see* nanowana.
coil *see* kamatana.
coiled *see* 1. kamatanaki, 2. matan, 3. mimioua, 4. rabi, 5. rabirabi.
cold *see* 1. mariri, 2. maitoro.
collaborate *see* 1. buoka, 2. buoki.
collapse *see* 1. baka, 2. bwaka.
collapsed *see* 1. bato, 2. bwakaki.
collar *see* kamataua.
collect *see* 1. riko, 2. rikoa, 3. rikoia, 4. boota, 5. ikoikota, 6. kawawaea.
collected *see* 1. rikoiaki, 2. bootaki, 3. ikoikotaki, 4. kawawaeaki, 5. nanoraoi, 6. ribaba, 7. rikoaki.
collide *see* 1. untaba, 2. aioro, 3. kauntabama.
colonize *see* kakorone.
colonized *see* kakoroneaki.
color *see* 1. matan, 2. kamatamata, 3. matamatana.
colored *see* 1. matanaki, 2. matamatanaki, 3. kamatamataki, 4. mata, 5. matamata.
colorful *see* kaumata.
colossal *see* 1. korabaia, 2. toa.
comb *see* 1. komua, 2. koomwia, 3. ake.
combat *see* 1. buaka, 2. buakana, 3. kaunikai, 4. bo.
combed *see* 1. akeaki, 2. komuaki, 3. koomwiaki.
combine *see* 1. katuna, 2. rengana.
combined *see* 1. renganaki, 2. katunaki.
come *see* 1. karina, 2. karokoa, 3. roko, 4. rokona.
comely *see* moaraoi.
comfortable *see* 1. maebwebu, 2. tokabeti, 3. nangoraoi, 4. kamweengaraoi, 5. takabwewebwere.
comical *see* aokangare.
coming *see* tamaewe.
command *see* 1. tuanga, 2. taubwe, 3. tautaeka.
commence *see* 1. teirake, 2. moanang, 3. aboka, 4. karika.
commend *see* kakannatoa.
commensurate *see* titibo.
commission *see* katanina.
commissioned *see* kataninaki.
commissioner *see* kamitina.
commit *see* 1. berita, 2. katabua, 3. karaoa, 4. karaoia.
committed *see* kaiakina.
committee *see* bwabwa.
common *see* 1. kabuta, 2. okioki.
commonly *see* tataneiai.
commonplace *see* kabuta.
communicate *see* kakarabakau.

compact *see* 1. ibe, 2. kakiriuatao, 3. kimra, 4. kimri, 5. kiriuatao, 6. ko, 7. riba.
companion *see* 1. raona, 2. raom.
company *see* kawara.
comparative *see* baikonaki.
compare *see* 1. kaboriba, 2. kabotau, 3. kataunata, 4. rinanoa, 5. taunari.
compassionate *see* nanoanga.
compel *see* kairoroa.
compensate *see* bo.
compensated *see* boaki.
compete *see* kaunikai.
competent *see* 1. manikonana, 2. manikoraki, 3. rabakai, 4. rabakau, 5. ataibai.
compile *see* kawawaea.
complacent *see* 1. maem, 2. ngae.
complain *see* 1. mea, 2. tangitang, 3. tang, 4. ngurengure, 5. ngure, 6. meme, 7. mere.
complete *see* 1. katoa, 2. aron, 3. tia, 4. tabanin, 5. koro, 6. kakoroa, 7. ikatoatoa, 8. ietia, 9. bobonga, 10. katia.
completed *see* 1. kakoroaki, 2. katiaki, 3. ikatoatoaki, 4. aronaki, 5. katoaki.
completely *see* nini.
completing *see* rabaraba.
complex *see* 1. kanganga, 2. kirimanga, 3. matakao.
complicate *see* 1. kakawibaea, 2. mangamanga, 3. kaiewe.
complicated *see* 1. matakao, 2. kaieweaki, 3. kakawibaeaki, 4. kanganga, 5. kirimanga, 6. manga, 7. mangamangaki.
compliment *see* kamaramara.
compose *see* 1. kario, 2. kamwaneaua.
composed *see* 1. kamwaneauaki, 2. karioaki, 3. maem, 4. nanoraoi.
comprehend *see* 1. ota, 2. nora, 3. kina, 4. kamatebwai, 5. namakina.
comprehended *see* 1. kamatebwaiaki, 2. kinaki, 3. namakinaki, 4. noraki, 5. otaki.
compress *see* 1. taona, 2. karibak.
compressed *see* 1. taonaki, 2. takoko, 3. karibakaki, 4. ribabetanga.
compute *see* taoman.
comrade *see* 1. koriria, 2. raom.
con *see* 1. kaitara, 2. kewe.
concave *see* 1. mangkongko, 2. rabirabi, 3. rabi, 4. mano.
conceal *see* 1. karaba, 2. karabana.
concealed *see* 1. karabaki, 2. karabanaki.
conceited *see* 1. kamoamoa, 2. kariete, 3. kainikatonga, 4. be.
conceivably *see* tao.
conceive *see* 1. kamatebwai, 2. karika, 3. kariki, 4. nora.

conceived *see* 1. noraki, 2. kamatebwaiaki, 3. karikaki, 4. karikiaki.
concentrated *see* ntaninin.
concern *see* 1. kamatakiaua, 2. kananobukibuki.
concerned *see* 1. matakiaua, 2. muti, 3. mutiakina, 4. nanobukibuki.
conclude *see* 1. katia, 2. nora, 3. kamatebwai, 4. kabanea, 5. toki.
concluded *see* 1. kabaneaki, 2. kamatebwaiaki, 3. katia, 4. katiaki, 5. noraki, 6. tokiaki.
concoct *see* kairengarenga.
condemn *see* 1. bukinna, 2. rabungaoa.
condemned *see* 1. rabungaoaki, 2. raka, 3. bukinnaki.
condense *see* kauarerekea.
condensed *see* kauarerekeaki.
condescending *see* nanomamara.
conduct *see* 1. ena, 2. unuana, 3. kaira, 4. atuna, 5. arona, 6. kairiri.
confabulate *see* kakarabakau.
confer *see* kakarabakau.
conference *see* kakarabakau.
confide *see* kamwaneaua.
confident *see* 1. matatoka, 2. maurake.
confidential *see* kiribwebwe.
confine *see* 1. kawarika, 2. kamaroa.
confined *see* 1. kamaroaki, 2. kawarikaki, 3. maroa.
confining *see* wariki.
confirm *see* 1. nora, 2. kakoaua, 3. kamatebwai, 4. kamatoa.
confirmed *see* 1. noraki, 2. kamatoaki, 3. kakoauaki, 4. kamatebwaiaki.
conflict *see* 1. iwai, 2. kauna.
conform *see* boraoi.
confound *see* 1. kamama, 2. nanououa, 3. nanomaiti, 4. kairua, 5. kaairua, 6. kanubebeoa, 7. kananokoraki.
confounded *see* 1. nanokoraki, 2. nanououaki, 3. nanououa, 4. nanomaiti, 5. kanubebeoaki, 6. kananokorakiaki, 7. kamamaki, 8. kairuaki, 9. kaairuaki, 10. nanomaitiaki.
confront *see* 1. kabotau, 2. kaitara.
confuse *see* 1. kananokoraki, 2. tanomaki, 3. nanououa, 4. nanomaiti, 5. mino, 6. kamangaoa, 7. kamaneanea, 8. katabaua.
confused *see* 1. tabea, 2. tanomakiaki, 3. nea, 4. nanououaki, 5. nanououa, 6. nanomaitiaki, 7. nanomaiti, 8. nanokoraki, 9. kirimoumou, 10. katabauaki, 11. kananokorakiaki, 12. kaminoa, 13. kamangaoaki, 14. kamaneaneaki, 15. angama, 16. minoaki, 17. ukinta.
confusing *see* wanga.
confusion *see* rua.
congealed *see* kiribanin.
congest *see* karibak.

congested *see* 1. ribono, 2. riba, 3. ntaninin, 4. karibakaki, 5. kebo.
congregate *see* karakina.
congruent *see* titebo.
conjecture *see* 1. namakin, 2. nanoata.
conjugate *see* taku.
conjugated *see* takuaki.
conjurer *see* tiakai.
connect *see* katuna.
connected *see* 1. katunaki, 2. katuna.
conquer *see* 1. kataenikaia, 2. riaonikai, 3. tokanikai.
conquest *see* taenikaia.
conscious *see* 1. matatoka, 2. uti.
consecrate *see* katabua.
consecrated *see* 1. katabuaki, 2. tabu.
consent *see* 1. kariaia, 2. kariaiakaki, 3. kataua.
conserve *see* 1. rarako, 2. taua.
conserved *see* 1. rarakoaki, 2. tauaki.
consider *see* 1. iangoa, 2. tatara, 3. taku.
considerable *see* rang.
considerate *see* muti.
considered *see* 1. iangoaki, 2. karabakauakina, 3. takuaki, 4. tataraki.
consistent *see* 1. kariraki, 2. teimatoa, 3. botuakina.
consolidate *see* kateimatoa.
consolidated *see* kateimatoaki.
conspicuous *see* takarere.
conspire *see* baka.
constable *see* boreitiman.
constant *see* teimatoa.
constipate *see* kataribonoa.
constipated *see* 1. ibenano, 2. taribono, 3. bono, 4. kataribonoaki, 5. in.
constipating *see* kataribono.
constrain *see* memerake.
constrained *see* 1. betuntun, 2. memerakeaki, 3. mwerengau, 4. ra.
constraining *see* memerake.
constrict *see* taburaka.
constricted *see* taburakaki.
construct *see* 1. katebe, 2. kateibai, 3. kateimatoa.
consult *see* taboniwia.
consume *see* 1. kana, 2. kang.
consumed *see* 1. kangaki, 2. kanaki.
consuming *see* kamataku.
contact *see* 1. aitibo, 2. bo.
contain *see* kakanoa.
contained *see* kakanoaki.
contemplate *see* 1. iangoa, 2. mimi, 3. taku, 4. tiroakina.
contemporary *see* nabangkai.
contempt *see* kakanikoa.
contemptible *see* kakauara.
contend *see* 1. iwai, 2. uamoa.

content *see* 1. takabwewebwere, 2. kabaia, 3. kanoan, 4. karauaka, 5. ngae, 6. rauakina.
contented *see* 1. ngae, 2. karauakaki.
contest *see* 1. iwai, 2. uneakina.
contested *see* 1. iwaiaki, 2. uneakinaki.
continual *see* 1. inenei, 2. ireiti.
continually *see* nini.
continue *see* 1. moana, 2. reita.
continued *see* 1. rarango, 2. reitaki, 3. moanaki.
continuous *see* tabanin.
contour *see* nu.
contract *see* 1. konin, 2. kauakonikona, 3. motinnano, 4. makerikaki, 5. kauanging, 6. bonnano, 7. kon.
contracted *see* 1. konaki, 2. motinnanoaki, 3. mangingi, 4. koninaki, 5. kon, 6. kauangingaki, 7. kauakonikonaki, 8. bonnanoaki, 9. makerikakiaki.
contradict *see* 1. kauntabama, 2. waewae, 3. takebono, 4. unrake, 5. karotu, 6. untaba, 7. kabitara, 8. ekara, 9. bitara, 10. karotua.
contradictory *see* 1. unrake, 2. bitara, 3. kabitara, 4. karotu.
contrary *see* 1. unrake, 2. takebono, 3. ntarierie, 4. kibangebange, 5. karotu, 6. bitara, 7. kabitara.
contrast *see* 1. kaboriba, 2. kaunta.
contribute *see* anga.
contrite *see* 1. mango, 2. moatoki.
contrive *see* 1. maroaka, 2. karekea.
contrived *see* 1. karekeaki, 2. maroakaki.
control *see* 1. babaireia, 2. kaira, 3. kamataua, 4. tararuaia.
controlled *see* 1. babaireiaki, 2. tararuaiaki, 3. kairaki, 4. kamatauaki.
controlling *see* baekeke.
conventional *see* 1. kabuta, 2. okioki.
converge *see* mra.
converse *see* kakarabakau.
convert *see* raira.
converted *see* rairaki.
convex *see* 1. aokua, 2. tibuatau.
convey *see* 1. urake, 2. urakina.
conveyed *see* 1. urakeaki, 2. urakinaki.
convict *see* kaburea.
convicted *see* kabureaki.
convinced *see* matatoka.
convincing *see* matatoka.
convoke *see* 1. vetea, 2. kawawaea, 3. roroka.
convoy *see* 1. ninimarea, 2. raona.
convulse *see* katikitiki.
cook *see* 1. kama, 2. kuka.
cooked *see* 1. mai, 2. kukaki, 3. kamaki, 4. mwai.
cool *see* 1. kamaitoroa, 2. kamariri, 3. maitoro, 4. mariri, 5. nanoraoi.
cooperate *see* 1. buoka, 2. ibuobuoki.
cooperative *see* 1. mronron, 2. nanotati.

coordinated *see* baiteke.
copied *see* 1. katotoaki, 2. uamwiaki.
copious *see* kirinaki.
copy *see* 1. katoto, 2. uamwi.
coral *see* 1. in, 2. tiatip.
cord *see* tokoran.
cordial *see* nanouki.
cork *see* nongoa.
corked *see* nongoaki.
corny *see* arobaba.
corpulent *see* 1. tuabebeku, 2. ubati, 3. korana, 4.
   korakora, 5. korabaia, 6. kaubiroto.
correct *see* 1. kaeta, 2. rinanoa, 3. taera, 4. tauburea,
   5. tiribure, 6. eti.
corrected *see* 1. taeraki, 2. taubureaki, 3. maoria, 4.
   kaetaki, 5. tiribureaki, 6. rinanoaki.
correctly *see* okoro.
correspond *see* 1. ikatoatoa, 2. katenua.
correspondingly *see* boo.
corroborate *see* 1. kamatebwai, 2. nora.
corrugated *see* kamanunuaki.
corrupt *see* 1. buakaka, 2. mka.
costly *see* 1. bobuaka, 2. kakawaki, 3. matera.
cough *see* 1. bekobeko, 2. bûtabut, 3. karara.
councilman *see* kaubure.
counsel *see* 1. wina, 2. wiwi, 3. tuanga.
counselor *see* roio.
count *see* 1. taukirikiri, 2. ware, 3. warebwai.
counter *see* kaitoana.
counteract *see* 1. karotu, 2. karotua, 3. waitotokoa.
countless *see* 1. raira, 2. uakurikuri, 3. kariara.
country *see* aba.
couple *see* 1. kabo, 2. katuna, 3. reiti, 4. toma.
coupled *see* 1. kaboaki, 2. katunaki, 3. reitiaki, 4.
   tomaki.
courageous *see* ninikoa.
course *see* 1. kakauara, 2. karekereke.
cousin *see* mwaaneu.
cover *see* 1. nuna, 2. raibanta, 3. nunu, 4. nikuma, 5.
   makuna, 6. katana, 7. karemaku, 8. karabana, 9.
   kaaitao, 10. atamana, 11. kiara, 12. rabuna.
covered *see* 1. raibantaki, 2. nunaki, 3. nunuaki, 4.
   rabaroa, 5. rabu, 6. atamanaki, 7. raibanta, 8.
   nubono, 9. rabunaki, 10. nikabu, 11. makunaki,
   12. kiaraki, 13. katanaki, 14. karemakuaki, 15.
   kaaitaoaki, 16. aitao, 17. karabanaki, 18.
   nikumaki.
covering *see* taorababa.
covert *see* karabaki.
covet *see* 1. mataiakina, 2. tangira, 3. nanoati, 4. kan,
   5. kakae, 6. bukinimata, 7. nanonibwi, 8. keta.
coveted *see* 1. ketaki, 2. tangiraki, 3. nanonibwiaki,
   4. mataiakinaki, 5. kanaki, 6. kakaeaki, 7.
   bukinimataki, 8. nanoatiaki.
covetous *see* bakantang.

coward *see* 1. kimamaku, 2. bato, 3. egi-memau, 4.
   inamoimoto.
cowardice *see* nanomaki.
cowardly *see* 1. inaberu, 2. inamoimoto, 3. kibubu,
   4. kiimamaaku, 5. kimoiauea, 6. mamaku, 7.
   nanobu.
cower *see* memerake.
crack *see* 1. keru, 2. tang.
cracked *see* 1. tiriou, 2. baba, 3. ing, 4. keruaki, 5.
   raeing, 6. raewa, 7. tangaki.
crackers *see* taborang.
cracking *see* raeing.
crackle *see* 1. karebwetata, 2. kekeruatai, 3. keru, 4.
   takarebwetata.
crackled *see* 1. keruaki, 2. takarebwetataki, 3.
   kekeruataiaki, 4. karebwetataki.
craft *see* karaora.
crafty *see* 1. kauanga, 2. kauman, 3. maranoa.
cragged *see* kiribeubeu.
craggy *see* kiribeubeu.
cram *see* 1. ngaungau, 2. tonga, 3. ngauta, 4.
   kakeboa, 5. intibua, 6. ngangaua.
cramp *see* kanikamate.
cramped *see* kanikamateaki.
cranky *see* kiura.
crash *see* 1. bukitaua, 2. kataururua.
crave *see* 1. kan, 2. nanoati, 3. baru, 4. onon.
craved *see* 1. baruaki, 2. kanaki, 3. nanoatiaki, 4.
   ononaki.
craving *see* nanona.
craw *see* kawa.
crawl *see* 1. tura, 2. katitura, 3. kawakawa.
craze *see* tiritabuki.
crazed *see* tiritabukiaki.
crazy *see* 1. baba, 2. rangirang, 3. tabaua, 4.
   taborang, 5. tiriou.
creak *see* aini.
cream *see* moaniba.
creamy *see* nenea.
crease *see* 1. kanimanunua, 2. batia, 3. borabi.
creased *see* 1. batia, 2. batiaki, 3. borabiaki, 4.
   kanimanunuaki, 5. nimanunu.
create *see* 1. kariki, 2. kakariki, 3. karika.
creative *see* wanawana.
creep *see* 1. kawa, 2. kawakawa, 3. maranoa.
cremate *see* kaura.
crepitate *see* takarebwetata.
crest *see* kautu.
crested *see* kautuaki.
crestfallen *see* moatoki.
criminal *see* bure.
cripple *see* kamaukua.
crippled *see* 1. djak-bain, 2. kamaukuaki.
crisp *see* maeke.
critical *see* uramai.

criticize see 1. waewae, 2. betunga, 3. kabetiwai, 4. tauburea.
croak see karara.
crooked see 1. uabangaki, 2. baoua, 3. kewetaia, 4. kibao, 5. me, 6. menga, 7. ninibaoua, 8. rae, 9. bake.
cross see 1. unuara, 2. unin, 3. nanoun, 4. nanorake, 5. kiura, 6. kauabangaka, 7. bononano, 8. kaibangaka.
crossed see 1. kauabangakaki, 2. kaibangakaki, 3. bononanoaki, 4. bangaki.
cross-eyed see egî-mata.
crossing see babangaki.
crosswise see 1. babangaki, 2. bangaki.
crow see 1. kakaero, 2. koko.
crowd see 1. karibak, 2. tena, 3. teibanea, 4. mra, 5. baroakina, 6. baki, 7. nanai.
crowded see 1. mraki, 2. tenaki, 3. teibaneaki, 4. ribono, 5. ribanono, 6. ribabetanga, 7. ribaba, 8. nanai, 9. nanaiaki, 10. kebo, 11. karibakaki, 12. baroakinaki, 13. baoua, 14. riba.
cruel see 1. tiri, 2. tiritiri, 3. bangaaomata.
crumble see ma.
crumbled see 1. batia, 2. kanimanumuaki, 3. maki, 4. tamruru.
crumbling see taenananga.
crumple see kanimanunua.
crumpled see 1. nimanunu, 2. tikurabirabi, 3. kanimanunuaki.
crunch see 1. katuru, 2. makiro, 3. kamakerua.
crunched see 1. kamakeruaki, 2. katuruaki, 3. makiroaki.
crunchy see maeke.
crush see 1. kamatiratira, 2. tourika, 3. toubeka, 4. toka, 5. taona, 6. kamatiraua, 7. kamanatuaa, 8. manti.
crushed see 1. mantiaki, 2. tourikaki, 3. toubekaki, 4. tokaki, 5. taonaki, 6. kamatirauaki, 7. kamatiratiraki, 8. kamanatuaaki, 9. matiratira.
cry see 1. tangitang, 2. ao, 3. baebaeta, 4. meme, 5. tang.
cube see 1. kiubu, 2. toatoana.
cubic see 1. kiube, 2. kiubu.
cubical see toatoa.
cuddle see 1. babako, 2. babakoa.
cultivate see ribana.
cultivated see 1. ribanaki, 2. maninganinga.
cultivating see ribanaia.
cunning see kauanga.
curb see 1. taon, 2. taona.
curbed see taonaki.
curdled see kiribanin.
cure see kamaoa.
cured see kamaoaki.

curious see 1. manenanti, 2. tete, 3. mautete, 4. kamataku, 5. reberake.
curl see kangera.
curled see 1. kangeraki, 2. ngeri.
curly see ngeri.
current see 1. bou, 2. menai.
curse see 1. karereantia, 2. wauwi, 3. wauna, 4. tabora.
cursed see 1. karereantiaki, 2. maraia, 3. raka, 4. taboraki, 5. waunaki, 6. wauwiaki.
curtail see 1. kakimotoa, 2. karakoa, 3. kauarerekea.
curtain see nuna.
curve see 1. kakiribabaoua, 2. mronron.
curved see 1. baoua, 2. rabirabi, 3. rabi, 4. menga, 5. mronronaki, 6. kiribabaoua, 7. kakiribabaouaki, 8. bari, 9. benono, 10. mangkongko.
customarily see tataneiai.
cut see 1. tirireke, 2. ninimakoro, 3. taba, 4. tabaki, 5. taitai, 6. taitaiaki, 7. takaere, 8. takaereaki, 9. tataki, 10. koro, 11. tirirekeaki, 12. tokora, 13. tata, 14. kataewaki, 15. erea, 16. ereaki, 17. karakoa, 18. korouia, 19. kataewa, 20. koroaki.
cute see ikutaba.
cycle see bwatika.
cycled see bwatikaki.
cylindrical see tirinta.

D

d see b.
dad see 1. tamau, 2. karo.
daddy see karo.
dainty see tiko.
damage see 1. urua, 2. kabua, 3. kabuanibwai, 4. moimoti, 5. tabuaetia.
damaged see 1. uruaki, 2. tabuaetiaki, 3. moimotiaki, 4. kabuaki, 5. kabuanibwaiaki.
damned see 1. raka, 2. tabura.
damning see tabura.
damp see 1. maimai, 2. roto, 3. aoi, 4. waraku.
dampen see 1. aoka, 2. karota, 3. kawarakua.
damsel see ataeinaine.
dance see 1. mwaie, 2. roue.
dangerous see 1. aomara, 2. karuanikai, 3. kamamate, 4. kaoanikai.
dangle see katiobabaea.
dangling see tinerua.
dappled see 1. kinawanawa, 2. tanan.
daring see ninikoa.
dark see 1. ro, 2. tanibabu, 3. bong, 4. tabaronikarawa, 5. robung.
darken see 1. robungia, 2. tangoingoi.
darkened see robungiaki.

darkening see robung.
dart see 1. tebe, 2. rerea.
dash see 1. rerea, 2. kare, 3. birimaka, 4. inimaki.
dashed see 1. birimakaki, 2. inimakiaki, 3. kareaki, 4. rereaki.
date see ikakai.
dated see ikakaiaki.
daub see rebua.
daubed see rebuaki.
daughter-in-law see tinêp.
daunt see ibebure.
daunted see ibebureaki.
dauntless see ninikoa.
dawdle see 1. matunako, 2. waeremwe, 3. timurua, 4. ninga'ngata, 5. kakaautakia, 6. aua, 7. tamweremwere.
dawdling see 1. mwere, 2. ninga'ngata, 3. rekebuta.
dawn see 1. inginingaina, 2. tingaro, 3. moaningaina, 4. aiota, 5. ingabong, 6. niningaina.
day see 1. bong, 2. kaina, 3. ñai, 4. outi.
daybreak see 1. ngaina, 2. niningaina, 3. inginingaina, 4. aiota.
daydream see mitara.
daytime see ngaina.
daze see 1. angitoi, 2. kakiritongitong.
dazed see 1. angitoiaki, 2. kakiritongitongaki, 3. kiritongitong.
dazzle see 1. kamataanoa, 2. raiti, 3. mataneai, 4. kamataanoanoa, 5. kamataniaia, 6. karanea.
dazzled see 1. mataneaiaki, 2. raitiaki, 3. mataneai, 4. karaneaki, 5. kamataniaiaki, 6. kamataanoanoaki, 7. kamataanoaki.
dazzling see 1. kakatika, 2. raiti, 3. takaneanea, 4. kakanno.
deacon see rikan.
dead see mate.
deaf see 1. buna, 2. pouno, 3. bonotaninga.
deafen see 1. kamaunea, 2. katongiraraea.
deafened see 1. kamauneaki, 2. katongiraraeaki, 3. maunea.
deafening see maunea.
deal see motinnano.
dealt see motinnano.
dear see kakawaki.
debase see 1. kamangora, 2. kaubunranga, 3. mwiniba.
debased see 1. mwinibaki, 2. kamangoraki, 3. kaubunrangaki.
debilitate see 1. kangorea, 2. kamamaraea.
debilitated see 1. kamamaraeaki, 2. kangoreaki, 3. ngore, 4. ntangorengore.
decapitate see 1. kabakua, 2. baku.
decapitated see 1. bakuaki, 2. kabakuaki.
decayed see 1. mka, 2. mwaka.

deceive see 1. kewe, 2. mamana, 3. maningenge, 4. kewena, 5. kewea, 6. kairerebua, 7. kabubu, 8. bureburea, 9. bwaka, 10. mwaamwanna, 11. keria.
decent see raoi.
decently see raoi.
deceptive see 1. kabaka, 2. kabana.
decide see 1. kauanakoa, 2. motika, 3. motiraran, 4. rinea, 5. kanenei.
decided see 1. motiraranaki, 2. rineaki, 3. nabangkai, 4. moti, 5. kauanakoaki, 6. kaneneiaki, 7. motikaki.
declare see tania.
declared see taniaki.
decline see 1. batete, 2. kanimamate, 3. ruo.
decomposed see 1. toto, 2. maung, 3. mka.
decomposing see toto.
decorate see 1. ete, 2. katamaroa, 3. manimaninia, 4. timua, 5. unauna, 6. unekea, 7. bwerea.
decorated see 1. timu, 2. unaunaki, 3. unekeaki, 4. timuaki, 5. katamaroaki, 6. manimaniniaki, 7. eteaki, 8. bwereaki.
decrease see 1. karakoa, 2. kakea.
decreased see 1. kakeaki, 2. karakoaki.
decreasing see mao.
dedicate see katabua.
dedicated see katabuaki.
deduct see kataoa.
deducted see kataoaki.
deductible see kataoa.
deep see 1. kakinounou, 2. nanomano, 3. nanokiroro, 4. nanokirokiro, 5. nano, 6. matakao, 7. kirimanga, 8. kinono, 9. kinano, 10. kabinano, 11. inanoinano, 12. bûbuti, 13. atamaumau, 14. aotaningo, 15. akideria, 16. katinano.
deepen see atamaumau.
deepened see atamaumauaki.
defame see 1. kabatebai, 2. kabuakaka.
defeat see 1. taenikai, 2. taenikaia, 3. tekena.
defeated see 1. taenikaiaki, 2. tekenaki.
defecate see 1. peka, 2. beka.
defective see 1. ra, 2. mwaka, 3. buretata, 4. bure.
defend see 1. katana, 2. kawakina, 3. otanga, 4. otatanga.
defenseless see nanorake.
defiant see 1. matabuaka, 2. takebono.
define see kabarabara.
defined see kabarabaraki.
definite see 1. nabangkai, 2. okoro.
definitely see 1. bon, 2. okoro.
deform see karibeua.
deformed see 1. ribeu, 2. tungatunga, 3. rikibuaka, 4. bitabao, 5. ribeubeu, 6. uananti, 7. kinerang, 8. kaburati, 9. bakibora, 10. baibainanti, 11. karibeuaki, 12. menga.

defraud see 1. kewe, 2. uarao, 3. babakanikawai.
defunct see mate.
defy see 1. taboa, 2. takebono.
degrade see 1. kanubebeoa, 2. mwiniba.
degraded see 1. nukabebeo, 2. kanubebeoaki, 3. mwinibaki.
deject see kananobaraka.
dejected see 1. nanokawa, 2. kananobarakaki.
delay see 1. baenikai, 2. kakaautakia, 3. kaningangata, 4. nanobebebebe, 5. ninga'ngata.
delayed see 1. baenikai, 2. ninga'ngataki, 3. nanobebebebeaki, 4. nanobebebebe, 5. kaningangataki, 6. baenikaiaki, 7. aubeabea, 8. kakaautakiaki.
delectable see 1. kangkang, 2. kukurei.
delete see kamanang.
deliberate see 1. taku, 2. kakarabakau, 3. bowi.
delicate see 1. kiaiai, 2. kimai, 3. makana, 4. memeri.
delicious see 1. kangkang, 2. nanai.
delighted see kukurei.
delightful see kukurei.
delineate see 1. tamania, 2. nu.
delineated see 1. nu, 2. nuaki, 3. tamaniaki.
delirious see aiwau.
deliver see 1. anga, 2. kabunga.
delivered see 1. angaki, 2. kabungaki.
delouse see 1. kateira, 2. kinuti.
delude see 1. kairerebua, 2. mamana.
delve see nenera.
demand see 1. bubuti, 2. tangiroro.
demean see mwiniba.
demolish see 1. uraka, 2. uruabai.
demolished see 1. uruabaiaki, 2. urakaki.
demonstrate see 1. kabarabara, 2. kakoaua, 3. kamatoa, 4. kaota, 5. tuanga.
demonstrated see 1. kakoauaki, 2. tuangaki, 3. kabarabaraki, 4. kaotaki, 5. kamatoaki.
denote see 1. kanikinaea, 2. kaota.
denounce see 1. bukina, 2. bukuna, 3. tua.
dense see 1. ibetutu, 2. mantoa, 3. buakoako, 4. matenten.
dented see 1. bakibora, 2. makibora, 3. manono.
denude see 1. raea, 2. taerake, 3. wanara.
denuded see 1. ra, 2. wanaraki, 3. raeaki, 4. taerakeaki.
deny see kakea.
depart see 1. kau, 2. mwnanga, 3. nako.
departed see 1. kauaki, 2. mate, 3. mwnangaki, 4. nakoaki.
dependent see mange.
depicted see taeraki.
deplore see ritangia.
deposit see 1. kamemena, 2. kamena, 3. katuka, 4. nea.

depress see 1. kananobaraka, 2. konamaki.
depressed see 1. kananobarakaki, 2. rawawata, 3. nanokawaki, 4. manono, 5. konamakiaki.
depressing see 1. kataenano, 2. matanikananoanga.
deprive see kuribaia.
deprived see kuribaiaki.
descend see 1. ruo, 2. tuka, 3. karuoa, 4. bung.
describe see 1. kabwarabwara, 2. aeka.
described see 1. aekaki, 2. kabwarabwaraki.
desert see 1. rereua, 2. katuka, 3. kitana.
deserted see 1. rereuaki, 2. rereua, 3. katukaki, 4. kitanaki, 5. ra.
design see manimaninia.
designate see katanina.
designated see kataninaki.
designed see manimaniniaki.
desirable see kaibabaru.
desire see 1. nanoati, 2. nanouti, 3. rananoa, 4. rantia, 5. ri, 6. tangira, 7. mataiakina, 8. tikurerea, 9. tañata, 10. kinanona, 11. keta, 12. kan, 13. kakinranga, 14. kakae, 15. kaitatan, 16. kabinanonanoa, 17. bakantang, 18. kinrangia, 19. nanona.
desired see 1. mataiakinaki, 2. nanoatiaki, 3. nanonaki, 4. nanoutiaki, 5. tikurereaki, 6. rananoaki, 7. kakaeaki, 8. rantiaki, 9. tangiraki, 10. riaki, 11. kinanonaki, 12. ketaki, 13. kekeraki, 14. kakinrangaki, 15. kaitatanaki, 16. kabinanonanoaki, 17. bakantangaki, 18. kinrangiaki, 19. kanaki.
desirous see 1. nanobukibuki, 2. uamoa.
desist see antai.
desolate see 1. kamaroa, 2. maroa, 3. nanokawa.
desolated see 1. kamaroa, 2. kamaroaki.
despicable see kakauara.
despise see 1. mwiniba, 2. rantia, 3. kabainranga, 4. kakanikoa.
despised see 1. kabainrangaki, 2. kakanikoaki, 3. moakakung, 4. mwinibaki, 5. rantiaki.
despite see 1. ko, 2. ngkae.
despoil see unaenae.
despoiled see unaenaeaki.
despondent see nanokawa.
destine see kakaunongo.
destined see kakaunongo.
destitute see 1. toronrang, 2. ra, 3. akikaubwai, 4. kainnano, 5. kawa, 6. waebaka.
destroy see 1. urua, 2. kamarua, 3. kamatea, 4. ura, 5. uraka, 6. uru.
destroyed see 1. uruaki, 2. uraki, 3. urakaki, 4. oruak, 5. moimoti, 6. kamaruaki, 7. kamateaki.
destructive see kabuanibai.
detach see 1. kataribaba, 2. tataeanibai, 3. unobauta, 4. kapara, 5. taeka, 6. raraure.

detached *see* 1. tataeanibaiaki, 2. unobautaki, 3. taenako, 4. taekaki, 5. raure, 6. raraureaki, 7. maroa, 8. kataribabaki.
detail *see* katanina.
detailed *see* kataninaki.
detect *see* maroaka.
detected *see* maroakaki.
deteriorate *see* 1. kana, 2. kawanrea.
determinate *see* nabangkai.
determine *see* 1. motika, 2. maroaka, 3. kinanoa, 4. kanenei, 5. mutigak.
determined *see* 1. uamoa, 2. kaneneiaki, 3. kinanoaki, 4. maroakaki, 5. motikaki, 6. nanomaka.
detest *see* 1. riba, 2. tabunimatea.
detestable *see* nanomara.
detested *see* 1. mautete, 2. moakakung, 3. ribaki, 4. tabunimateaki, 5. tete, 6. wara.
detonate *see* 1. baurana, 2. kioi.
devaluate *see* 1. kaubunranga, 2. mwiniba.
devastate *see* 1. tiriobora, 2. uraba.
devastated *see* 1. tirioboraki, 2. urabaki.
develop *see* 1. rikirake, 2. tanga, 3. riki, 4. ewenako.
developed *see* 1. ikawai, 2. rikiaki, 3. rikirakeaki, 4. tangaki, 5. ewenakoaki.
deviate *see* 1. tua, 2. inra, 3. kiritabataba, 4. taba.
devil *see* auderia.
devious *see* matanikimoa.
devote *see* katanina.
devoted *see* 1. kaiakina, 2. kakaonimaki, 3. kataninaki, 4. nabe, 5. nanoingainga.
devour *see* 1. kabaubau, 2. tenarua, 3. ngauta, 4. ngaungau, 5. kang, 6. kamangaungauakina, 7. kana.
devoured *see* 1. kangaki, 2. ngautaki, 3. ngaungauaki, 4. kamangaungauakinaki, 5. kabaubauaki, 6. tenaruaki, 7. kanaki.
dew *see* on.
dewy *see* aoi.
dexterous *see* baiteke.
diagonal *see* taiaganoro.
dicey *see* nanobebebe.
die *see* 1. mauna, 2. mate.
diet *see* mamatam.
differ *see* kaokoro.
different *see* kaokoro.
differentiate *see* taunari.
differentiated *see* taunariaki.
difficult *see* 1. kamou, 2. kanganga, 3. matakao.
diffuse *see* 1. tanga, 2. tatao.
diffused *see* 1. tangaki, 2. tataoaki, 3. tannaki.
dig *see* 1. kena, 2. nenera, 3. niba, 4. ribana.
digest *see* kamatebwai.
digested *see* kamatebwaiaki.
dignified *see* 1. kamoaki, 2. mimitong.

dignify *see* kamoa.
dilapidated *see* kimaung.
diligence *see* tamakai.
diligent *see* 1. manebaeba, 2. rangarangatau, 3. tabarekai, 4. kaonako, 5. itibabu, 6. kaobainako, 7. kikinto, 8. taningamarau.
diluted *see* ruamakana.
dim *see* 1. ka, 2. kimotoitoi, 3. maewe, 4. rabete.
diminish *see* 1. i, 2. kauarerekea, 3. karakoa, 4. kabaketea, 5. kakea.
diminished *see* 1. iaki, 2. kabaketeaki, 3. kakeaki, 4. karakoaki, 5. kauarerekeaki.
diminishing *see* 1. tanako, 2. rake, 3. mao.
dimly *see* maewe.
dimpled *see* maningare.
dine *see* 1. amarake, 2. katonga.
dint *see* kaibakoa.
dip *see* rionako.
dipped *see* rionakoaki.
dire *see* nanomakaki.
direct *see* 1. atuna, 2. urukauna, 3. unuana, 4. tautorona, 5. taubwe, 6. kaira, 7. ena, 8. arona, 9. kaeti.
directed *see* 1. tautoronaki, 2. aronaki, 3. urukaunaki, 4. unuanaki, 5. kairaki, 6. atunaki, 7. taubweaki, 8. enaki.
direction *see* ang.
directly *see* 1. abanaba, 2. ngkainaba.
dirt *see* bara.
dirty *see* 1. mangeto, 2. torotangako, 3. nimnana, 4. pare, 5. takanakana, 6. torotakanana, 7. katorotakanana, 8. tangako, 9. ngatingati, 10. kangata, 11. kabareka, 12. buritoto, 13. betiti, 14. barik, 15. barekareka, 16. bareka, 17. bara, 18. katakanakana.
disability *see* ntokotoko.
disable *see* kamaukua.
disabled *see* 1. kamaukuaki, 2. mauku.
disagree *see* kawanra.
disagreeable *see* 1. buakaka, 2. ra.
disappear *see* 1. mauna, 2. i, 3. mate.
disappearing *see* ramauna.
disappoint *see* 1. kabubu, 2. keria, 3. maningenge.
disappointed *see* 1. maningengeaki, 2. maoria, 3. kon, 4. keriaki, 5. keria, 6. kabubuaki, 7. kabubu, 8. tekeria.
disapprove *see* 1. rabungaoa, 2. riba.
disapproved *see* 1. rabungaoaki, 2. ribaki.
disarm *see* taenikaia.
disarrange *see* 1. kakaraurekana, 2. riringa.
disarranged *see* 1. kakaraurekanaki, 2. riringaki.
disassociate *see* kamaranga.
disastrous *see* kabuanibai.
disavow *see* kakea.

discern *see* 1. kamatebwai, 2. kina, 3. nora, 4. tataumanta.
discerning *see* 1. nano, 2. nanomano, 3. mamata.
discharge *see* 1. tabitabitabita, 2. kioi.
discharged *see* 1. kioiaki, 2. tabitabitabitaki.
disciple *see* kairi.
disclose *see* kauka.
disclosed *see* kaukaki.
discolor *see* kawanta.
discolored *see* 1. kawantaki, 2. urabo, 3. matatae.
disconcert *see* kamatakiaua.
disconcerted *see* 1. kamatakiauaki, 2. matakiaua.
disconnect *see* 1. kamaranga, 2. kamaroa.
disconnected *see* 1. maroa, 2. kamarangaki, 3. kamaroaki.
disconsolate *see* 1. kawa, 2. nanowaki.
discontent *see* marengau.
discontented *see* 1. marengau, 2. matanoku, 3. nanobuaka, 4. unuara.
discontinue *see* 1. toki, 2. katoka.
discontinued *see* 1. tokiaki, 2. nabawe, 3. katokaki.
discordant *see* 1. tabarabara, 2. tangibuaka.
discount *see* notua.
discounted *see* notuaki.
discourage *see* 1. kananobu, 2. kabaka, 3. kananobaraka.
discouraged *see* 1. namomara, 2. kananobuaki, 3. kananobarakaki, 4. ebu, 5. kabubu.
discouraging *see* 1. kabaka, 2. kataenano, 3. tarabu.
discover *see* 1. reke, 2. maroaka, 3. kunea.
discovered *see* 1. maroakaki, 2. rekeaki, 3. kuneaki.
discredit *see* baebaeta.
discreditable *see* kawanta.
discredited *see* baebaetaki.
discreet *see* 1. nanomano, 2. aotaningo.
discuss *see* 1. kakarabakau, 2. maroroakini.
disdain *see* tinanikua.
disease *see* orak.
diseased *see* aoraki.
disenchant *see* karikaka.
disenchanted *see* 1. karikakaki, 2. nanomiakina.
disengage *see* kamaranga.
disengaged *see* kamarangaki.
disentangle *see* wanara.
disentangled *see* wanaraki.
disfigured *see* bureta.
disgrace *see* 1. kabatebai, 2. kamatauninga, 3. kanubebeoa.
disgraced *see* 1. nukabebeo, 2. kabatebaiaki, 3. kamataauningaki, 4. kanubebeoaki.
disgraceful *see* kamatauninga.
disgusted *see* 1. namomara, 2. bararai.
disgusting *see* 1. buritoto, 2. kabun, 3. kaburati, 4. kakauara, 5. mai.
dish *see* anga.

disharmonious *see* 1. ruatatara, 2. nanobitaki, 3. mangao.
dishearten *see* kananokawaki.
disheartened *see* 1. kananokawakiaki, 2. nanokawaki.
disheartening *see* kataenano.
dished *see* angaki.
disheveled *see* 1. burimangaoa, 2. atutababa.
dishonor *see* 1. kabatebai, 2. kanubebeoa.
dishonorable *see* kawanta.
dishonored *see* 1. kabatebaiaki, 2. kanubebeoaki, 3. nukabebeo.
disinfect *see* teboka.
disjoin *see* kamaranga.
disjoined *see* kamarangaki.
disjoint *see* 1. kamaoriori, 2. karebenakoa.
disjointed *see* 1. kamaoririoriaki, 2. karebenakoaki.
dislike *see* riba.
disliked *see* ribaki.
dislocate *see* 1. rebe, 2. karebenakoa, 3. katiba, 4. raemenga.
dislocated *see* 1. rebeaki, 2. raemengaki, 3. raemenga, 4. nimananginang, 5. karebenakoaki, 6. katibaki.
dislodge *see* buuta.
disloyal *see* taningato.
dismal *see* 1. nanokawa, 2. matanikananoanga.
dismantle *see* raemenga.
dismantled *see* 1. maenikun, 2. raemenga, 3. raemengaki.
dismay *see* maku.
dismayed *see* maku.
dismember *see* raebai.
dismiss *see* 1. kabanea, 2. bwaranako.
dismissed *see* 1. bwaranakoaki, 2. kabaneaki.
disobedient *see* 1. bonotaninga, 2. karotu, 3. takebono.
disobey *see* takebono.
disobliging *see* ribuaka.
disorder *see* 1. mino, 2. tabarea, 3. rerebetunga, 4. kateibaba, 5. kataumangaoa, 6. rua, 7. kateibanaea.
disordered *see* 1. mino, 2. teibanae, 3. teibaba, 4. tabareaki, 5. rerebetungaki, 6. minoaki, 7. mangao, 8. kateibanaeaki, 9. kateibabaki, 10. kataumangaoaki, 11. bakarae, 12. raea.
disorderly *see* 1. taumangao, 2. burimangaoa, 3. mangao, 4. mino.
disorganized *see* 1. mangao, 2. raea.
disoriented *see* 1. kaminoa, 2. kimangamanga.
disparage *see* 1. kamwia, 2. kananobaraka, 3. maniwaira, 4. mwiniba, 5. waira.
disparate *see* kaokoro.
dispatch *see* 1. kaumaki, 2. kamatea, 3. kanakoa.

dispatched *see* 1. kamateaki, 2. kanakoaki, 3. kaumaki, 4. kaumakiaki.

dispense *see* 1. kaonoa, 2. nna.

dispensed *see* 1. kaonoaki, 2. nnaki.

disperse *see* 1. kamerea, 2. kauamaea, 3. mae, 4. mare, 5. tagerame.

dispersed *see* 1. mare, 2. tagerameaki, 3. mareaki, 4. maeaki, 5. kauamaeaki, 6. kamereaki, 7. raea.

dispirited *see* nanokawa.

displace *see* 1. nakomai, 2. kainraea, 3. kainraei, 4. karebenakoa, 5. katotoroa.

display *see* 1. tabangaea, 2. katara, 3. karekei, 4. kaota.

displease *see* 1. bononano, 2. kanaengai.

displeased *see* 1. bononano, 2. bononanoaki, 3. kanaengaiaki.

disproportion *see* tarabuaka.

disproportionate *see* 1. ruonako, 2. tarabuaka.

disputatious *see* unin.

dispute *see* 1. ibewi, 2. kauntaeka, 3. uneakina.

disputed *see* 1. ibewiaki, 2. kauntaekaki, 3. uneakinaki.

disqualified *see* 1. nanomanikoraki, 2. nanomanikorakiaki.

disqualify *see* nanomanikoraki.

disquiet *see* kaangitannenea.

disquieted *see* kaangitanneneaki.

disquieting *see* kararaoma.

disreputable *see* 1. nukabebeo, 2. warea.

disrupt *see* kaakaea.

disrupted *see* kaakaeaki.

dissatisfied *see* 1. marengau, 2. maningengeaki, 3. kamarengauaki, 4. maninge.

dissatisfy *see* 1. kamarengau, 2. maningenge.

disseminate *see* kauamaea.

disseminated *see* kauamaeaki.

dissipate *see* kamerea.

dissipated *see* kamereaki.

dissolve *see* kamara.

dissolved *see* kamaraki.

dissuade *see* kananomaraea.

distant *see* 1. matawe, 2. tawaewae, 3. taningo, 4. raroa, 5. ninikoria, 6. kiro, 7. kiraroa, 8. kinokino, 9. kakiro, 10. kakiraroa, 11. aotaningo, 12. niwaewae.

distantly *see* kiriaria.

distasteful *see* mai.

distended *see* nibunini.

distinct *see* 1. okoro, 2. tere, 3. turu, 4. mamata.

distinctive *see* 1. rine, 2. tere.

distinguish *see* 1. kakannatoa, 2. kamatebwai, 3. kaunta, 4. nora.

distinguished *see* 1. kakannatoaki, 2. takarere, 3. noraki, 4. kauntaki, 5. kamatebwaiaki, 6. kakannato, 7. atongaki, 8. katereke.

distorted *see* bitabao.

distracted *see* 1. maninga, 2. nanotiotio.

distress *see* katabetabea.

distressed *see* 1. katabetabeaki, 2. kawa.

distressing *see* nanomakaki.

distribute *see* 1. kaonoa, 2. kaborere.

distributed *see* 1. kaborereaki, 2. kaonoaki.

distrust *see* 1. namakin, 2. nanoata.

disturb *see* 1. kananomaruru, 2. riringa, 3. katabetabea, 4. kananora, 5. kananobukibuki, 6. kamatakiaua, 7. kakai, 8. kaintoka, 9. karawawata.

disturbed *see* 1. katabetabeaki, 2. baba, 3. riringaki, 4. un, 5. nanomaruru, 6. nanobukibuki, 7. mwerengau, 8. matakiaua, 9. kananoraki, 10. kananomaruruaki, 11. kananobukibukiaki, 12. kamatakiauaki, 13. kaintokaki, 14. kakaiaki, 15. karawawataki.

disturbing *see* 1. nanomakaki, 2. tabare.

disunite *see* 1. kakaraurekana, 2. kananobitaka, 3. raraure.

disunited *see* 1. raraureaki, 2. raure, 3. kananobitakaki, 4. kakaraurekanaki, 5. nanobitaki.

dither *see* nanobebebe.

dive *see* 1. ewenako, 2. tebo, 3. tebona.

diverge *see* kakaraurekana.

divergent *see* kaokoro.

diversified *see* kaokoro.

divert *see* kakibotu.

diverted *see* 1. kakibotuaki, 2. rae.

divide *see* 1. raeakina, 2. bwena, 3. karinakin.

divided *see* 1. raeakinaki, 2. makoroua, 3. karinakinaki, 4. bwenaki.

divination *see* kaiwa.

divine *see* 1. atua, 2. taukirikiri.

divorce *see* 1. kaure, 2. raraure.

divorced *see* 1. raraureaki, 2. raure, 3. kaureaki.

divulge *see* 1. mauoti, 2. kaota.

dizzy *see* 1. tanoi, 2. atubitaki, 3. kiritongitong, 4. minotaki, 5. ngio, 6. niniraki.

do *see* 1. karaoa, 2. kaonakoa, 3. bon.

docile *see* 1. inataba, 2. taningamarau.

doctor *see* 1. aorek, 2. taokitana.

dodge *see* 1. kakaro, 2. bitanikai, 3. iranikai.

dodgy *see* kamamate.

doer *see* inao.

dog *see* 1. môg, 2. mohoko.

doleful *see* 1. kawa, 2. mango, 3. nanokawa.

domesticate *see* kamanana.

domesticated *see* 1. kamananaki, 2. manana.

dominate *see* 1. tautooa, 2. toka, 3. tokanikaia, 4. tokarake.

dominated *see* 1. tautooaki, 2. tokaki, 3. tokanikaiaki, 4. tokarakeaki.

dominating *see* **1.** ikake, **2.** take, **3.** baekeke, **4.** toka.
domineer *see* tautorona.
domineering *see* baekeke.
donate *see* anga.
donated *see* angaki.
done *see* **1.** tia, **2.** aeraki, **3.** karaoaki, **4.** katia, **5.** ungaraki, **6.** bonaki, **7.** bane, **8.** aera, **9.** bon, **10.** kaonakoaki.
doomed *see* raka.
door *see* **1.** mataroa, **2.** jetia.
dote *see* babana.
doting *see* maninga.
dotted *see* kiritantan.
double *see* kaua.
doubled *see* **1.** kauaki, **2.** makoneua.
doubt *see* **1.** nanokokoraki, **2.** nanobebebebe, **3.** nanououa, **4.** namakin, **5.** makina, **6.** nanoata.
doubtful *see* **1.** karikaua, **2.** nanobebebebe.
doubting *see* karikaua.
down *see* **1.** matim, **2.** rikaki, **3.** bung.
downed *see* **1.** karinanoaki, **2.** karuoaki, **3.** katikuaki, **4.** katokiaki, **5.** matimaki, **6.** taonaki, **7.** tukaki, **8.** kakiaki.
downgrade *see* kanubebeoa.
downward *see* rio.
doze *see* matu.
drag *see* **1.** katika, **2.** katitura, **3.** katura, **4.** katurabeau, **5.** koka, **6.** mae.
dragging *see* turabeau.
drain *see* kawawa.
drained *see* kawawaki.
drape *see* ninira.
draped *see* niniraki.
drastic *see* kinano.
drawn *see* kamimitoiaki.
dread *see* **1.** makina, **2.** maku.
dreaded *see* **1.** makinaki, **2.** makuaki.
dreadful *see* **1.** kakamaku, **2.** nanomakaki, **3.** kamâg.
dreading *see* nanobukibuki.
dream *see* **1.** mi, **2.** mia, **3.** mitara.
dreamer *see* kabinanonano.
dreary *see* nanokawa.
drench *see* **1.** teboran, **2.** katingoa.
drenched *see* **1.** tingo, **2.** katingoaki, **3.** teboranaki.
dress *see* **1.** karina, **2.** katamaroa.
dressed *see* **1.** karinaki, **2.** katamaroaki, **3.** tauraoi.
dribble *see* **1.** katata, **2.** kia, **3.** namoro, **4.** baware.
dried *see* **1.** katakaki, **2.** katikintakeaki, **3.** mae, **4.** rai, **5.** tawaki.
drift *see* **1.** kakaautakia, **2.** uarurung.
drifter *see* tabobe.
drill *see* rawana.
drilled *see* rawanaki.

drink *see* **1.** kiraoki, **2.** moi, **3.** mooi, **4.** nima, **5.** teme.
drip *see* **1.** timtim, **2.** matim, **3.** raran.
dripping *see* tingo.
drive *see* **1.** kabuta, **2.** karibua, **3.** karina, **4.** katura.
driven *see* **1.** karina, **2.** nanaiaki, **3.** karinaki, **4.** karibuaki, **5.** kabutaki, **6.** kabuta, **7.** inga, **8.** katuraki.
drool *see* **1.** baware, **2.** namoro.
droop *see* kamoua.
droopy *see* nanokabakoba.
drop *see* **1.** kabwaka, **2.** matim.
dropped *see* **1.** kabwakaki, **2.** matimaki.
dropsy *see* ntinebu.
drove *see* **1.** kabuta, **2.** karina, **3.** nanai.
drown *see* baba.
drowned *see* babaki.
drowsy *see* **1.** nimatutu, **2.** matutu, **3.** nibiongong.
drudge *see* mengo.
drum *see* takiria.
drunk *see* **1.** batete, **2.** manging, **3.** mooi, **4.** rangirang.
dry *see* **1.** mautakaroro, **2.** tawa, **3.** takaroro, **4.** taka, **5.** kataka, **6.** maeke, **7.** katikintakaea, **8.** mae, **9.** bataka, **10.** mau.
dual *see* kauoua.
duck *see* **1.** kakaro, **2.** take.
dug *see* **1.** kena, **2.** ribanaki, **3.** nibaki, **4.** kenaki, **5.** neneraki.
dull *see* **1.** maewe, **2.** tarabu, **3.** rotu, **4.** warea, **5.** mammam, **6.** kábub, **7.** kabi, **8.** bono, **9.** nubono, **10.** kabubu.
dulled *see* rotuaki.
dumb *see* **1.** atubibitaki, **2.** kabi, **3.** arobaba, **4.** aretau, **5.** takutaku.
dumbfound *see* **1.** kakiritongitong, **2.** kamatakua.
dumbfounded *see* **1.** take, **2.** auba, **3.** kakiritongitongaki, **4.** kamatakuaki, **5.** kiritongitong.
dunce *see* bangabwai.
dunk *see* kawawa.
dunked *see* kawawaki.
dupe *see* **1.** bwaka, **2.** kabubu, **3.** kairerebua, **4.** kewea, **5.** mamana.
duplicate *see* **1.** katoto, **2.** kiribare.
duplicated *see* katotoaki.
durable *see* bongata.
duration *see* rena.
during *see* ngke.
dusk *see* airo.
dusky *see* maewe.
dust *see* taea.
dusty *see* bubu.
dutiful *see* taningamarau.
dwarfish *see* kimotoitoi.

dwell *see* 1. mweraoi, 2. umana, 3. titiku, 4. tiku, 5. maeka, 6. auti, 7. batana, 8. mwenga.
dwindle *see* 1. aua, 2. kakaautakia, 3. kakea.
dye *see* kamatamata.
dyed *see* mata.
dying *see* taberamate.

E

each *see* tatabeua.
eager *see* 1. muramura, 2. tutuneang, 3. taebo, 4. tabarebare, 5. uamoa, 6. mura, 7. mramra, 8. inga, 9. nanoingainga, 10. nanobukibuki.
ear *see* taringa.
early *see* 1. ingaro, 2. moantaai.
earnest *see* 1. nano, 2. uamoa.
earth *see* 1. Buînai, 2. Aba.
ease *see* kabaketea.
eased *see* kabaketeaki.
easily *see* 1. kai, 2. kakai.
east *see* mainiku.
eastward *see* 1. rake, 2. iaí-nuk.
eastwards *see* rake.
easy *see* 1. bebete, 2. beebete, 3. nanomamara.
easygoing *see* nanoraoi.
eat *see* 1. amarake, 2. matam, 3. matamu, 4. mange, 5. kaikai.
eaten *see* 1. itimareare, 2. kanák, 3. mangeaki, 4. matamaki, 5. matamuaki, 6. amarakeaki.
ebbtide *see* pike.
eccentric *see* minotaki.
eclipse *see* mauna.
economical *see* 1. romatoa, 2. tababu.
economize *see* tatabuia.
ecstatic *see* takitaki.
eddy *see* nimwamwano.
edible *see* kakanaki.
edit *see* rinanoa.
edited *see* rinanoaki.
educate *see* 1. reireia, 2. tonga, 3. beireina.
educated *see* 1. maninganinga, 2. reireiaki, 3. tongaki, 4. beireinaki.
eel *see* rabóna.
eerie *see* kakanaugaki.
efface *see* mauna.
effect *see* karaoa.
effected *see* karaoaki.
effective *see* bati.
effectual *see* mamaka.
egg *see* natina.
egotistic *see* rietata.
egotistical *see* rietata.

eight *see* 1. oánu, 2. onoua, 3. wanua.
eighth *see* kawaniua.
eighty *see* 1. oaníbui, 2. ouiponi, 3. wanibwi.
ejaculate *see* pekanikai.
eject *see* 1. kaka, 2. kaotinakoa.
elastic *see* 1. maonon, 2. rena, 3. uakonikon.
elated *see* 1. kukurei, 2. kariete.
elbow *see* 1. bukinibaia, 2. bubuônibai.
elder *see* 1. mangoieta, 2. téköe.
elderly *see* kara.
electrify *see* 1. itina, 2. kautikaikaia.
elegant *see* 1. kan, 2. niko, 3. kateke, 4. kakateke, 5. matakanikan.
elevate *see* 1. kamwemwea, 2. tabeka, 3. tokarake.
elevated *see* 1. rieta, 2. tabuki, 3. tokarakeaki, 4. rietata, 5. mamaunga, 6. katabuki, 7. kamwemweaki, 8. tabekaki, 9. maninganinga.
elite *see* moaniba.
elongated *see* wai.
elope *see* biriakinnako.
else *see* riki.
elude *see* 1. kakaro, 2. kio, 3. rabanako.
emaciate *see* bakikangenge.
emaciated *see* 1. bakikangengeaki, 2. bukimake.
emanate *see* 1. kakannatoa, 2. reke.
emancipate *see* kainaomata.
emancipated *see* kainaomataki.
embark *see* 1. moana, 2. matabaiawa, 3. kabuta, 4. borauakina.
embarrass *see* 1. mangamanga, 2. niniku, 3. kauara, 4. katakea, 5. katabaruarua, 6. katabakurakura, 7. ibeabure.
embarrassed *see* 1. matara, 2. mangamangaki, 3. uakaka, 4. ninikuaki, 5. mwerengau, 6. matabou, 7. uara, 8. katakeaki, 9. nikutaro, 10. katabaruaruaki, 11. katabakurakuraki, 12. kamoriau, 13. ibeabureaki, 14. angama, 15. kauaraki.
embattled *see* 1. boaki, 2. buakaki.
embellish *see* unauna.
embellished *see* 1. timu, 2. unaunaki.
embodied *see* maurouro.
embrace *see* 1. ibabakoi, 2. kabotaba, 3. rabatia.
embroider *see* 1. manimaninia, 2. waua.
embroidered *see* 1. manimaniniaki, 2. wauaki.
embroil *see* mino.
embroiled *see* 1. minoaki, 2. mino.
emerge *see* 1. bu, 2. riki.
eminent *see* 1. takarere, 2. atongaki, 3. kakannato, 4. katitirou, 5. rine.
emit *see* kamerea.
emperor *see* embera.
emphasize *see* katereterea.
emphasized *see* kateretereaki.

employ *see* 1. bwaina, 2. kabeabea, 3. rangarangatau.
employed *see* 1. rangarangatau, 2. rangarangatauaki, 3. bwainaki, 4. kabeabeaki.
emptied *see* 1. babaroaki, 2. ikinakoaki, 3. kaitaki.
emptiness *see* akea.
empty *see* 1. kaita, 2. kobakoba, 3. ikinako, 4. babaro, 5. akea.
emulate *see* 1. katotonga, 2. kakairi.
emulous *see* uamoa.
enchant *see* kamiakina.
enchanted *see* 1. kamiakinaki, 2. miakina.
encircle *see* 1. bomanea, 2. nainaina, 3. uamanea, 4. baua, 5. katabanina, 6. kiribambanta.
encircled *see* 1. uamaneaki, 2. bauaki, 3. bomaneaki, 4. katabaninaki, 5. kiribambantaki, 6. nainainaki, 7. raibanta.
enclose *see* 1. kaibobua, 2. rokia.
enclosed *see* 1. kaibobuaki, 2. rokiaki.
encompass *see* katobibia.
encounter *see* 1. butika, 2. iwai, 3. kaitara, 4. kaurama.
encourage *see* ungara.
encouraged *see* 1. ungaraki, 2. nanomaka.
encouraging *see* nanomaka.
encumber *see* 1. kamengoa, 2. katabakurakura.
encumbered *see* 1. tanibaba, 2. tokomangaongao, 3. tabakurakura, 4. kibara, 5. katabakurakuraki, 6. kamengoaki.
end *see* 1. toki, 2. tokina, 3. abu.
endanger *see* karuanikaia.
endangered *see* 1. karuanikaiaki, 2. tabea.
endear *see* kaotabaea.
endeavor *see* 1. barakia, 2. teboakina, 3. kekeiaki, 4. kaiaki, 5. kamanenanti, 6. kata.
ended *see* 1. tokinaki, 2. katokoaki, 3. katutaki, 4. moti, 5. toabaraki, 6. tokiaki.
ending *see* totoki.
endow *see* kabaibai.
endowed *see* kabaibaiaki.
endure *see* botuakina.
enemy *see* 1. aoun, 2. kairiribai.
energetic *see* 1. tabomane, 2. mamaka, 3. nanomaka.
energizing *see* kamaiu.
enervate *see* kanimatoaua.
enervated *see* 1. kanimatoauaki, 2. nimatoaua.
enfeeble *see* 1. kamamaraea, 2. kanimamate.
enfeebled *see* 1. kamamaraeaki, 2. kanimamateaki.
enforce *see* kanenea.
enforced *see* kaneneaki.
engage *see* 1. kabae, 2. kakainroua, 3. motinnano, 4. inai.

engaged *see* 1. kainrou, 2. tabeaki, 3. tabe, 4. rangarangatau, 5. tana, 6. kabaeaki, 7. inaiaki, 8. bae, 9. motinnanoaki, 10. kakainrouaki.
engrossing *see* kamataku.
enjoy *see* kakukureia.
enlarge *see* 1. kakawibaea, 2. karababa, 3. kawarebwea.
enlarged *see* 1. kakawibaeaki, 2. karababaki, 3. kawarebweaki.
enlighten *see* 1. ainga, 2. kaota.
enlightened *see* 1. aingaki, 2. kaotaki, 3. rabakau.
enormous *see* 1. tabati, 2. wari, 3. toa, 4. korabaia, 5. makaiao, 6. nuku, 7. riara.
enough *see* 1. tau, 2. areare, 3. ratau, 4. tao.
enrage *see* 1. koburake, 2. koburakea.
enraged *see* 1. tennanoa, 2. koburakeaki.
enrapture *see* kamiakina.
enraptured *see* 1. kamiakinaki, 2. miakina.
enslave *see* 1. terona, 2. torona, 3. kaunga.
enslaved *see* 1. kaungaki, 2. taonikai, 3. teronaki, 4. toronaki.
ensnare *see* tawarea.
entangle *see* 1. kabeakoa, 2. kaiewe, 3. mino, 4. tabiro.
entangled *see* 1. tabiroaki, 2. uakaka, 3. tabiro, 4. ngao, 5. minoaki, 6. kirimanga, 7. kaieweaki, 8. kabeakoaki, 9. beako, 10. mino.
enter *see* 1. moana, 2. rin, 3. karina.
enterprising *see* 1. uamoa, 2. tabarebare, 3. taboang.
entertain *see* 1. kamatakua, 2. kairuwaea, 3. kamaroro.
entertained *see* 1. kairuwaeaki, 2. kamaroroaki, 3. kamatakuaki.
enthralling *see* kamataku.
enthrone *see* kauea.
enthuse *see* kananobukibuki.
enthusiastic *see* 1. unga, 2. inga, 3. nanobukibuki, 4. nanoingainga, 5. tabarebare.
entice *see* 1. kao, 2. kariri, 3. katikurerea.
enticing *see* timinene.
entire *see* tabanin.
entirely *see* bane.
entrap *see* bomanea.
entreat *see* onon.
entrench *see* 1. niba, 2. karuarua, 3. manawaia.
entrenched *see* 1. karuaruaki, 2. manawaiaki, 3. nibaki.
entwine *see* nimta.
enumerate *see* 1. wareriri, 2. ware, 3. wareka.
enunciate *see* 1. kabwarabwara, 2. katenua.
envelop *see* tiera.
enveloped *see* tieraki.
envious *see* 1. bakantang, 2. ngeta.
envy *see* 1. keta, 2. mataiakina, 3. nanonibwi.

epileptic *see* kirimoumou.
equal *see* 1. tî-te-eran, 2. titebo, 3. rota, 4. botau, 5. bare, 6. boraoi.
equalize *see* 1. bo, 2. boraoi, 3. kabotau.
equalized *see* 1. boraoiaki, 2. kabotauaki.
equilateral *see* ikuiraetero.
equipped *see* tauraoi.
equitable *see* nanowana.
equivalent *see* boraoi.
equivocate *see* kakaro.
erase *see* 1. kamanang, 2. kamauna.
erect *see* 1. etiruru, 2. utibaba, 3. teiraoi, 4. kateimatoa, 5. kateibai, 6. katei, 7. katea, 8. katebe.
erected *see* 1. kateimatoaki, 2. utibabaki, 3. katebeaki, 4. kateaki, 5. kateibaiaki.
erection *see* teri.
err *see* 1. bure, 2. bureburea, 3. kairua.
error *see* 1. rua, 2. airua, 3. buír, 4. kairua.
erupt *see* reberake.
erupted *see* reberakeaki.
escape *see* 1. birinako, 2. kio, 3. kom, 4. ranene.
escaped *see* 1. birinakoaki, 2. kioaki, 3. komaki, 4. raneneaki.
escort *see* 1. matana, 2. taubea.
escorted *see* 1. matanaki, 2. taubeaki.
especially *see* 1. kiri, 2. okoro.
essay *see* 1. kamanenanti, 2. kekeiaki.
essential *see* boto.
establish *see* 1. katea, 2. kateimatoa, 3. kakoaua, 4. unika.
established *see* 1. kakoauaki, 2. kateaki, 3. kateimatoaki, 4. matoro, 5. toronibai, 6. unikaki.
estimate *see* 1. taukirikiri, 2. katautau.
estimated *see* 1. taukirikiriaki, 2. katautauaki.
ethical *see* raoi.
euphonic *see* 1. tenu, 2. tonu.
evacuate *see* 1. birinako, 2. kamawa, 3. kitana.
evacuated *see* 1. kamawaki, 2. kitanaki, 3. birinakoaki.
evade *see* 1. kakaro, 2. katua, 3. kio, 4. rerea, 5. totoka, 6. tuka, 7. birinako.
evaluate *see* ukeuke.
eve *see* 1. airo, 2. tairiki.
even *see* 1. aoraoi, 2. boraoi, 3. nanoraoi, 4. tiritoa.
evening *see* 1. boraoi, 2. tairik, 3. tairiki.
everyday *see* kabuta.
evident *see* 1. takarere, 2. matatoka, 3. maroaka, 4. matata.
evidently *see* matata.
evil *see* 1. be, 2. buakaka, 3. tarie.
exact *see* 1. okoro, 2. taubobonga, 3. etiruru, 4. maitin.
exacting *see* taburaka.
exactly *see* 1. maitin, 2. okoro.

exaggerate *see* 1. kareao, 2. wikabwea, 3. wibeka, 4. raka, 5. kariara, 6. karakarongorongo, 7. karakaraka, 8. kakawibaea, 9. betanna, 10. maninrongorongo.
exaggerated *see* 1. kariaraki, 2. betannaki, 3. wikabweaki, 4. wibekaki, 5. rakaki, 6. maninrongorongoaki, 7. karakarongorongoaki, 8. karakarongorongo, 9. betanna, 10. kakawibaeaki, 11. karakarakaki, 12. kareaoaki.
exalt *see* 1. neboa, 2. kamoa, 3. karietata.
exalted *see* 1. neboaki, 2. kamoaki, 3. karietataki.
exalting *see* kakammari.
examine *see* 1. tatara, 2. ukera, 3. tuoa, 4. tiroakina, 5. tarabai, 6. taku, 7. matauna, 8. kinanoa, 9. kaunrabakau, 10. tataumanta.
excavate *see* 1. ekea, 2. kena, 3. niba.
exceed *see* 1. kamaterea, 2. moa, 3. raka.
exceeding *see* take.
excel *see* 1. kamaterea, 2. moa, 3. uamoa.
excellent *see* 1. raba, 2. rerei, 3. rine.
exceptional *see* 1. bainanti, 2. manenanti, 3. burenibai.
excessive *see* 1. tumoa, 2. komatangitang, 3. nanomakaki, 4. riara, 5. ruonako, 6. taomoa.
excessively *see* rang.
exchange *see* 1. ioki, 2. iokina, 3. kabobo, 4. kaibibitia, 5. rai, 6. bô.
exchanged *see* 1. kaibibitiaki, 2. raiaki, 3. iokinaki, 4. iokiaki, 5. kaboboaki.
excite *see* 1. rakea, 2. ungara, 3. ieanga, 4. roroka, 5. kaunga, 6. katutua, 7. karerea, 8. kananobukibuki, 9. kakiriwea, 10. tanomaki.
excited *see* 1. nanobukibuki, 2. ueke, 3. tanomakiaki, 4. tanomaki, 5. takitaki, 6. rorokaki, 7. ungaraki, 8. nanoingainga, 9. katudaki, 10. karereaki, 11. kananobukibukiaki, 12. kakiriweaki, 13. ientaka, 14. ieangaki, 15. aibiko, 16. kaungaki, 17. rakeaki.
exciting *see* kakukurei.
exclaim *see* 1. taetae, 2. takarua.
exclude *see* katinanikua.
excluded *see* katinanikuaki.
excoriate *see* kataeari.
excrement *see* poutahi.
excrete *see* beka.
exculpate *see* tabitabitabita.
exculpated *see* tabitabitabitaki.
excuse *see* 1. aona, 2. tabitabitabita.
excused *see* 1. tabitabitabitaki, 2. aonaki.
execrate *see* riba.
execute *see* 1. kamarua, 2. kamatea, 3. karaoa, 4. karaoia.
executed *see* 1. kamateaki, 2. tana, 3. karaoaki, 4. kamaruaki, 5. karaoiaki.
executive *see* tautaeka.
exempt *see* kainaomata.

exercise *see* 1. kamarurung, 2. kataneiai.
exert *see* mengo.
exhaust *see* 1. uke, 2. konamaki, 3. kaita, 4. kanrairaia.
exhausted *see* 1. nrairai, 2. ukeaki, 3. uke, 4. ntakuakua, 5. nimorimori, 6. nimamate, 7. maong, 8. konamakiaki, 9. kanrairaiaki, 10. kaitaki, 11. bane, 12. taeare.
exhausting *see* 1. kamou, 2. ninamate.
exhibit *see* 1. katara, 2. tabangaea, 3. tengetenge, 4. kateretere, 5. kaota, 6. katerea, 7. katengetengea.
exhilarated *see* kukurei.
exist *see* 1. iai, 2. maiu.
existent *see* nabangkai.
existing *see* maiu.
exit *see* kau.
exonerate *see* tabitabitabita.
exonerated *see* tabitabitabitaki.
exorbitant *see* 1. bora, 2. ruonako.
expand *see* 1. kakerakea, 2. ure.
expanded *see* 1. ureaki, 2. uretatanga, 3. kakerakeaki.
expect *see* 1. kantaninga, 2. nora, 3. kamatebwai.
expected *see* 1. kamatebwaiaki, 2. kantaningaki, 3. noraki.
expedient *see* 1. riai, 2. aitau.
expedite *see* 1. umaki, 2. bareka, 3. kaumaki.
expedited *see* 1. barekaki, 2. kaumakiaki, 3. umakiaki.
expeditious *see* 1. baitata, 2. kaumaki, 3. takaerere.
expel *see* 1. kakiokioa, 2. karebutia.
expensive *see* 1. bobuaka, 2. bomatoa, 3. bora, 4. kakawaki, 5. matera.
experienced *see* atataibai.
experiment *see* 1. kataneiai, 2. kata.
experimental *see* kata.
expert *see* 1. bati, 2. bwairaoi, 3. rabakau, 4. atataibai.
expire *see* mate.
expired *see* 1. mate, 2. mateaki.
explain *see* 1. kaota, 2. kaeti, 3. kabwarabwara, 4. kabarabara, 5. katereterea.
explicit *see* 1. matatoka, 2. okoro.
explicitly *see* okoro.
explode *see* 1. ruoruo, 2. baurana, 3. kioi, 4. rebwetau.
exploded *see* 1. ruoruoaki, 2. rebwetauaki, 3. bauranaki, 4. kioiaki.
exploit *see* mannaoka.
exploited *see* mannaokaki.
explore *see* 1. nenera, 2. neweaba.
expose *see* katereterea.
exposed *see* 1. kaota, 2. otinako, 3. nanorake, 4. kateretereaki.
expound *see* kabarabara.

expressive *see* tenu.
expunge *see* kamauna.
extant *see* nabangkai.
extend *see* 1. kakerakea, 2. tanga, 3. karababa, 4. arora, 5. anga, 6. reta.
extended *see* 1. angaki, 2. aroraki, 3. kakerakeaki, 4. karababaki, 5. retaki, 6. tangaki.
extensive *see* nuku.
extenuating *see* mate.
exterminate *see* kamatea.
exterminated *see* kamateaki.
external *see* 1. ianena, 2. tinaniku.
extinct *see* mate.
extinguish *see* 1. oukia, 2. toabara, 3. kamauna, 4. kamatea, 5. kamarua.
extinguished *see* 1. kamateaki, 2. kamaunaki, 3. toabaraki, 4. kamaruaki.
extirpate *see* routa.
extol *see* 1. kakannatoa, 2. neboa.
extra *see* riki.
extract *see* 1. routa, 2. remrem, 3. buta, 4. au.
extraordinary *see* 1. bainanti, 2. kamimi.
extravagant *see* 1. bakatae, 2. ruonako.
extreme *see* 1. nanomakaki, 2. ruonako, 3. nano, 4. kinano.
extremely *see* 1. nini, 2. toko, 3. nengenenge.
extremity *see* abu.
exuberant *see* kukurei.
exult *see* 1. kakatonga, 2. nikierere.
eye *see* mata.
eyebrow *see* ari.
eyes *see* mata.

F

f *see* ti.
fabled *see* iangoaki.
face *see* 1. kaitara, 2. tae, 3. wia.
faced *see* 1. taeaki, 2. wiaki, 3. kaitaraki.
facing *see* taramata.
factual *see* nabangkai.
fade *see* 1. i, 2. karaia.
faded *see* 1. mane, 2. raimenga, 3. rai, 4. urabo, 5. mangingi, 6. karongo, 7. karaiaki, 8. iaki, 9. maewe, 10. matatae.
fading *see* 1. ramauna, 2. tangio.
fail *see* 1. tekebuaka, 2. matebuaka, 3. ngio.
failed *see* 1. tekera, 2. tekebuakaki, 3. matebuakaki, 4. ngioaki.
faint *see* 1. nanokabakoba, 2. tunga, 3. tong, 4. rarau, 5. nimanan, 6. nanobu, 7. mamataroro, 8. mamara, 9. kiro, 10. kimai, 11. bakoa, 12. ngio.

fair see 1. booraoi, 2. tamaroa, 3. eti, 4. arotau, 5. nanowana.
fairly see kinokino.
faithful see kakaonimaki.
faithless see taningato.
fall see 1. mrara, 2. ruo, 3. tiri, 4. kabaka, 5. bwaka, 6. buki, 7. matim.
fallen see bwaka.
false see 1. buaka, 2. kewe.
falsify see karang.
falter see 1. tatatata, 2. nanobebebe, 3. nanououa, 4. tata.
faltering see nanokabakoba.
familiar see 1. kirmatamata, 2. mantakarara, 3. rena, 4. tamaomao, 5. imamanu.
familiarize see imammane.
familiarized see imammaneaki.
famine see rö.
famished see kibakibaki.
famous see 1. takarere, 2. kakanato, 3. eke, 4. atongaki.
fan see tororo.
fancied see 1. kanaki, 2. nanoatiaki.
fancy see 1. kan, 2. nanoati.
fantastic see kamimi.
far see 1. ikekei, 2. roro, 3. raroa, 4. raro, 5. raoroa, 6. niwaewae, 7. kinokino, 8. ikoa, 9. kakiro.
farm see ribana.
fart see 1. ting, 2. tink.
fascinated see ri.
fascinating see 1. kakamataku, 2. kamataku, 3. kareke.
fashion see karaoa.
fashioned see karaoaki.
fast see 1. baitata, 2. witata, 3. waetoka, 4. waetata, 5. tata, 6. nimanonginong, 7. nikotatawa, 8. matamtam, 9. birimaka, 10. kaumaki.
fasten see 1. kabaea, 2. kanima, 3. kakoa.
fastened see 1. kabaeaki, 2. kakoaki, 3. kanimaki.
fasting see mamatam.
fat see 1. marika, 2. uakunikun, 3. nuku, 4. kaubiroto, 5. bubura, 6. tinebu.
fatal see kamamate.
fated see rreretaki.
father see 1. tama, 2. karo, 3. temant.
fathom see 1. kina, 2. ñâ, 3. kamatebwai, 4. nora.
fatigue see botu.
fatigued see 1. bakaruru, 2. botu, 3. botuaki, 4. nikuakua, 5. ntungaungau.
fatten see 1. kamarika, 2. intibua.
fattened see 1. intibuaki, 2. kamarikaki.
fatty see 1. nenea, 2. timinene.
fault see 1. buír, 2. kawanta.
faulty see 1. bure, 2. buretata, 3. tungatunga.
favor see motikoraki.

favored see 1. tima, 2. motikorakiaki.
favorite see 1. moaniba, 2. pouai.
fawn see memerake.
fear see 1. makina, 2. maku.
fearful see 1. kakamaku, 2. nanomakaki, 3. kamâg, 4. inaberu, 5. angama, 6. mamaku.
fearless see 1. ninikoa, 2. tabokaikai.
fearsome see 1. kakamaku, 2. kakanaugaki.
feast see katonga.
feather see pourai.
featherbrained see minotaki.
featherweight see mwemwe.
fed see 1. mamataki, 2. kana.
feeble see 1. matanikanebu, 2. ngore, 3. nanokabakoba, 4. nangonango, 5. maramara, 6. mara, 7. mannei, 8. mamara, 9. kire, 10. kimai, 11. nanobakobako.
feebleness see mara.
feed see 1. kana, 2. mamata, 3. toba.
feel see 1. nanoata, 2. riringa, 3. ringa, 4. namakina, 5. raweraweaba.
feeling see manoanga.
feet see 1. berurare, 2. wae.
feign see baka.
feigned see bakaki.
fell see 1. bwaka, 2. matim.
fellow see mwane.
felt see 1. ringa, 2. ringaki, 3. raweraweabaki, 4. nanoataki, 5. namakina, 6. riringaki, 7. matimaki, 8. bwakaki, 9. namakinaki.
female see aine.
feminine see inaine.
ferment see 1. buro, 2. kamanginga, 3. te.
fermented see 1. buroaki, 2. kamangingaki, 3. teaki.
ferocious see tiritiri.
fertile see kimarimari.
fertilize see 1. bon, 2. mataena, 3. ribana.
fertilized see 1. bonaki, 2. mataenaki, 3. ribanaki.
fervent see 1. inga, 2. tabarebare, 3. nanobukibuki.
fetch see 1. anganai, 2. kamai, 3. ngka.
fetid see 1. buíra, 2. ebiñoño.
fetter see kauara.
fettered see kauaraki.
feverish see 1. kabuebue, 2. maomoa, 3. biwa, 4. nimatoaua.
few see 1. karako, 2. tabe, 3. tabeua, 4. tabeuta.
fiance see raou.
fiancee see raou.
fibrous see 1. waka, 2. wakariri, 3. wakawaka, 4. buruburu, 5. iwaka, 6. kiriwaka.
fickle see 1. atubitaki, 2. minotaki, 3. tannene, 4. toitio.
fidget see 1. kakamakuri, 2. mamakuri, 3. takaremwaremwa.
fidgety see 1. takariroriro, 2. utowa.

fiend *see* riaboro.
fiendish *see* raiboro.
fierce *see* 1. unum, 2. tiritiri, 3. kakang.
fiery *see* 1. kibaura, 2. kiura, 3. nanorake, 4. nanoun, 5. unin, 6. kiangang.
fifth *see* kanimaua.
fifty *see* 1. nimabwi, 2. nimaoupoui, 3. nimábui.
fight *see* 1. bobuaka, 2. buaka, 3. buakana, 4. un, 5. bo.
figure *see* kauanakoa.
filch *see* katawe.
file *see* 1. ire, 2. rerena, 3. rainia, 4. karanea, 5. mino, 6. minoa.
fill *see* 1. atoa, 2. kanoa, 3. kikebokeboa.
filled *see* 1. kanoaki, 2. kikebokeboaki, 3. atoaki.
filling *see* kararati.
filter *see* raumea.
filthy *see* 1. betiti, 2. kamaira, 3. mona, 4. ngatingati, 5. torotakanana.
final *see* 1. kaitira, 2. toki.
finally *see* 1. kabaneana, 2. motikana.
find *see* 1. kunea, 2. ngengetaia.
fine *see* 1. katua, 2. tiribaonoa, 3. tiko, 4. rerei, 5. raoi, 6. mte, 7. marurung, 8. katuaea, 9. karuotua, 10. kan, 11. irariki, 12. manni.
fined *see* 1. katuaki, 2. tiribaonoaki, 3. katuaeaki.
finest *see* moaniba.
finger *see* raweraweaba.
fingered *see* raweraweabaki.
fingernail *see* uki-ni-bai.
finicky *see* 1. barino, 2. rino.
finish *see* 1. kabanea, 2. uke, 3. tokina, 4. kakoroa, 5. aron, 6. katia.
finished *see* 1. tia, 2. katia, 3. tokinaki, 4. moti, 5. koro, 6. katiaki, 7. kabaneaki, 8. iti, 9. ietia, 10. ukeaki, 11. bane, 12. aronaki, 13. kakoroaki.
finishing *see* rabaraba.
finite *see* 1. tokina, 2. mte.
fire *see* 1. kaura, 2. kati, 3. ei, 4. ai, 5. ê.
fired *see* 1. katiaki, 2. kauraki.
fireplace *see* ati.
firm *see* 1. teimatoa, 2. kauniben, 3. teiraoi, 4. nanomaka, 5. ba, 6. niko.
first *see* 1. moa, 2. moaniba, 3. ririmoa.
firstly *see* moa.
fish *see* 1. ika, 2. taumata, 3. kibe, 4. erieri, 5. akawa, 6. karaun.
fishhook *see* mataou.
fissured *see* raeraeaki.
fit *see* 1. kona, 2. tau, 3. niko, 4. kataua, 5. inakai, 6. bumbing, 7. boraoi, 8. marurung.
fitting *see* 1. raoi, 2. tenu, 3. wau.
fittingly *see* raoi.
five *see* 1. nimahoua, 2. nimaua, 3. nima, 4. ima.

fix *see* 1. kanenea, 2. kanimma, 3. karao, 4. katuta, 5. kirikaki, 6. kamatoa.
fixed *see* 1. kaneneaki, 2. romatoa, 3. kirikakiaki, 4. katutaki, 5. karaoaki, 6. kamatoaki, 7. kanimmaki.
fizz *see* te.
fizzle *see* barairai.
flabby *see* 1. manionio, 2. nimaoriori, 3. ntangaingai.
flaccid *see* nimaoriori.
flamboyant *see* rietata.
flap *see* 1. tio, 2. roba.
flapping *see* teirobaroba.
flare *see* 1. urake, 2. uramwaka.
flared *see* 1. urakeaki, 2. uramwakaki.
flash *see* raiti.
flashback *see* kauringaba.
flashy *see* raiti.
flask *see* 1. naip, 2. rau.
flat *see* 1. borata, 2. rababaua, 3. maborabora, 4. boraoi, 5. bato, 6. aoraoi, 7. matinnao.
flatly *see* koaua.
flatten *see* 1. tira, 2. manti, 3. tiritabuki, 4. rababaua, 5. kamatiraua, 6. kamatiratira, 7. kaboraoa, 8. boraoi, 9. katira.
flattened *see* 1. matiratira, 2. tiritabukiaki, 3. boraoiaki, 4. rababauaki, 5. mantiaki, 6. katiraki, 7. kamatirauaki, 8. kamatiratiraki, 9. kaboraoaki, 10. tiraki.
flatter *see* 1. kababa, 2. kamaramara, 3. kananobaba, 4. toroba, 5. wimamuai.
flaunt *see* kakaeutakia.
flavor *see* 1. kananama, 2. katonga.
flavored *see* 1. kananamaki, 2. katongaki.
flay *see* kuota.
fleck *see* kinawanawa.
flecked *see* kinawanawaki.
flee *see* rere.
fleece *see* unaenae.
fleet *see* kaumaki.
fleeting *see* 1. raiti, 2. taningo.
flesh *see* tirigo.
flexible *see* 1. takarua, 2. rau, 3. raenen, 4. nimaenen, 5. maoriori, 6. maen, 7. maonon.
flick *see* kateba.
flighty *see* minotaki.
fling *see* 1. kaka, 2. tewea, 3. kare.
flip *see* rai.
flirt *see* wibeka.
flirtatious *see* be.
float *see* 1. ubararake, 2. beibeti, 3. betirake, 4. tabetirake, 5. tio.
floating *see* betirake.
flock *see* 1. rurung, 2. karakina.
flog *see* 1. kataere, 2. robuna, 3. tirimataere.

flood *see* ieka.
flooded *see* iekaki.
flop *see* tikumenga.
flourishing *see* 1. maiurerirei, 2. rung, 3. maiu, 4. marati, 5. marabe.
flow *see* 1. ikinako, 2. katutua, 3. ranga, 4. raranginako, 5. tu.
flower *see* 1. moaniba, 2. uëa.
flowered *see* nimatamata.
flowery *see* ka'ue.
flowing *see* ranga.
fluctuate *see* 1. taunga, 2. uarurung.
flutter *see* 1. takarema, 2. io, 3. kanebu.
fly *see* 1. tira, 2. kiba.
flying *see* kiba.
foam *see* buroburo.
foe *see* kairiribai.
fogged *see* 1. bubuteiaki, 2. kamataanoanoaki.
foggy *see* 1. bubutei, 2. bubu.
foil *see* kamataua.
foiled *see* 1. matau, 2. kamatauaki.
fold *see* 1. niria, 2. nukama, 3. numa, 4. rikuma.
folded *see* 1. oteaki, 2. rikumaki, 3. rukuma, 4. num, 5. nukamaki, 6. numaki.
follow *see* 1. ninimarea, 2. ira, 3. irananga, 4. irannano, 5. iri, 6. kaea, 7. katootoonga.
follower *see* 1. kairi, 2. kirarang.
following *see* 1. kiriaria, 2. narei, 3. rimwi.
fond *see* nabe.
fondle *see* bwabwakoa.
food *see* kana.
fool *see* 1. bwabwa, 2. tiaka, 3. aoua, 4. baba.
foolish *see* 1. baba, 2. manrerei, 3. nanobaba.
foot *see* 1. raurounoue, 2. rianna, 3. wae, 4. wai.
football *see* irîrep.
footed *see* 1. waewae, 2. waewaeaki.
for *see* 1. kioina, 2. n, 3. ni, 4. tairaoi, 5. in.
forbear *see* antai.
forbid *see* 1. kataburorokoa, 2. tabuna, 3. tabua, 4. rabuna, 5. mabu, 6. katabua, 7. kamabu, 8. kateikai.
forbidden *see* 1. mabu, 2. tabuterang, 3. tabunaki, 4. tabuaki, 5. tabu, 6. rabunaki, 7. mabuaki, 8. kateikaiaki, 9. katabwaki, 10. katabwa, 11. kataburorokoaki, 12. katabuaki, 13. kamabuaki, 14. rabu.
force *see* 1. kairoroa, 2. taonanoa, 3. una, 4. turuna, 5. katitua, 6. kanenea, 7. karibua, 8. memerake.
forced *see* 1. katituaki, 2. unaki, 3. turunaki, 4. tauuru, 5. memerakeaki, 6. karibuaki, 7. kaneneaki, 8. kairoroaki, 9. taonanoaki.
forceful *see* buburamaiu.
forebode *see* bukinanganga.
forecast *see* taukirikiri.
forehead *see* rama.

foreign *see* 1. ianena, 2. iruwa, 3. anena.
foreigner *see* 1. ianena, 2. irua, 3. îrua.
foresee *see* biririmoa.
foreseen *see* 1. biririmoaki, 2. biririmoa.
foreshadow *see* karamakina.
foresight *see* mamata.
forestall *see* taokabia.
foretell *see* biritaetae.
foretold *see* 1. biritaetae, 2. biritaetaeaki.
forge *see* katoto.
forged *see* katotoaki.
forget *see* 1. manuoka, 2. mwaninga, 3. mauringa, 4. manuokina, 5. maunika.
forgetful *see* 1. ibabannang, 2. maninga, 3. noumaninganinga.
forgive *see* kabara.
forgiving *see* atataiaomata.
forgo *see* kakea.
forgotten *see* 1. manuokaki, 2. mwaningaki, 3. mwaninga, 4. mauringaki, 5. manuokinaki, 6. maunikaki.
forked *see* 1. kirimanga, 2. manga.
forlorn *see* 1. kitanaki, 2. maroa, 3. kawa.
form *see* 1. beireina, 2. karaoa, 3. karika, 4. kateibai.
formed *see* 1. beireinaki, 2. karaoaki, 3. karikaki, 4. kateibaiaki.
formerly *see* mangkana.
formidable *see* 1. tauuru, 2. kakamaku, 3. tabokaikai.
formulate *see* iangomaka.
formulated *see* iangomakaki.
forsake *see* 1. kakea, 2. kaki, 3. katuka.
forsaken *see* 1. kakeaki, 2. timoi, 3. katukaki, 4. bakarae, 5. kakiaki.
forth *see* nako.
forthwith *see* 1. abanaba, 2. ngkainaba.
fortified *see* 1. nanomaka, 2. nonoaki, 3. matoro, 4. kamatoaki, 5. kamarurungaki, 6. nonouaki.
fortify *see* 1. kamarurunga, 2. kamatoa, 3. nonoa, 4. nonoua.
fortunate *see* 1. kabaia, 2. tekaraoi, 3. tauraba, 4. neiranraoi, 5. manuia, 6. aoraba, 7. maniwia.
forty *see* 1. abwi, 2. aupoui.
forward *see* maurake.
fossilized *see* nabawe.
foster *see* 1. nabea, 2. toba.
fostered *see* 1. tobaki, 2. nabeaki.
foul *see* 1. maung, 2. kamairia, 3. îtingaingai, 4. bewawa.
fouled *see* kamairiaki.
found *see* 1. katei, 2. ngengetaiaki, 3. kamatoa, 4. kuneaki, 5. reke, 6. kunea, 7. katebe, 8. katea, 9. karika, 10. kakoaua, 11. kariki.
founded *see* 1. kakoauaki, 2. kamatoaki, 3. karikaki, 4. karikiaki, 5. kateaki, 6. katebeaki, 7. kuneaki.

four *see* 1. aua, 2. âua, 3. aai, 4. â, 5. ahoua.
fourth *see* kaua.
foxy *see* kauanga.
fraction *see* mwakorokoro.
fracture *see* maoto.
fractured *see* maotoaki.
fragile *see* 1. kiaiai, 2. makana, 3. nanokabakoba.
fragment *see* kataribia.
fragmented *see* 1. kataribiaki, 2. taribi.
fragrant *see* buiérar.
frail *see* 1. matanikanebu, 2. nanokabakoba, 3. tangauriuri, 4. kimai, 5. bakitaia, 6. makana.
frame *see* 1. karaoa, 2. nu.
framed *see* 1. karaoaki, 2. nu, 3. nuaki.
frank *see* matabou.
frantic *see* 1. kire, 2. ientaka.
fraudulent *see* babakanikawai.
fray *see* 1. kaburuburua, 2. korouia, 3. buruburu.
frayed *see* 1. buruburu, 2. buruburuaki, 3. kaburuburuaki, 4. maeae.
freak *see* baibainanti.
freckled *see* inanikuau.
free *see* 1. ebiebi, 2. kirmatamata, 3. inaaomata.
freed *see* katibetibeaki.
frenzied *see* kire.
frequent *see* 1. beroro, 2. kawara, 3. neweaba.
frequently *see* tataneiai.
fresh *see* 1. memeri, 2. waeai, 3. nabangkai, 4. maiu, 5. ngkainaba.
freshen *see* maitoro.
freshly *see* nabangkai.
fret *see* 1. kanaeng, 2. keinanoa, 3. meme.
friable *see* tangauriuri.
fried *see* 1. baniaki, 2. baniiaki, 3. tinimaki.
friend *see* 1. ara, 2. rao, 3. rei.
friendly *see* nabe.
friendship *see* kaiiók.
frigate *see* keinanoa.
frighten *see* 1. kananobukibuki, 2. kautikaikaia, 3. kauba, 4. kateinang, 5. kamaka, 6. katonginakoa.
frightened *see* 1. maku, 2. auba, 3. kamakaki, 4. kananobukibukiaki, 5. katonginakoaki, 6. kaubaki, 7. kautikaikaiaki.
frightful *see* 1. nanomakaki, 2. kakamaku.
frigid *see* 1. iakai, 2. kamariri, 3. maitoro, 4. mariri.
frisk *see* kirei.
frisky *see* takariroriro.
frivolous *see* 1. manrerei, 2. minotaki, 3. ruannano.
frizz *see* katababaea.
frolic *see* 1. kirei, 2. kiriringng, 3. makei, 4. reimaurua.
frolicsome *see* 1. kirirnang, 2. makei.
front *see* 1. imoa, 2. karimoa.
frontal *see* maurake.
froth *see* 1. buírābuir, 2. buro, 3. te.

frown *see* 1. matanoku, 2. matanun.
frozen *see* 1. maitorotoro, 2. brok.
frugal *see* 1. taubang, 2. akibakatae, 3. tatabwi.
fruit *see* wa.
fruitful *see* 1. kimarimari, 2. materaoi.
fruitless *see* 1. kanoabo, 2. manouna.
frustrate *see* karotu.
frustrated *see* karotuaki.
fry *see* 1. tinima, 2. baniia.
fuck *see* buno.
fugitive *see* 1. nenei, 2. winanti.
fulfill *see* maotorrikiriki.
fulfilled *see* maotorrikirikiaki.
full *see* 1. intibua, 2. tibutaua, 3. tao, 4. rarati, 5. ôn, 6. nonga, 7. nikebokebo, 8. kebo, 9. inaña, 10. koko.
fully *see* bane.
fumble *see* raweraweaba.
function *see* mwakuri.
funny *see* 1. aokangare, 2. katangare.
furbish *see* 1. ire, 2. karanea.
furious *see* 1. kire, 2. kirinikamate, 3. tebomaurua, 4. tennanoa.
furnished *see* tauraoi.
furrowed *see* raeraeaki.
fuss *see* keinanoa.
fussy *see* beberino.
futile *see* 1. manouna, 2. manrerei.
future *see* 1. kiriaria, 2. rimwi.
fuzzy *see* nanokabakoba.

G

gag *see* kabun.
gain *see* 1. karekea, 2. rawea.
gallant *see* ninikoria.
gallivant *see* 1. kareuma, 2. rebu, 3. rebutonga.
gamble *see* 1. karuotua, 2. kirei, 3. kiriringng.
gannet *see* kepoui.
gape *see* 1. a, 2. nora, 3. uki.
gaping *see* uki.
garble *see* otobebe.
garbled *see* otobebeaki.
garden *see* ribana.
gargle *see* kabururu.
garnish *see* katamaroa.
garnished *see* katamaroaki.
gash *see* 1. kakoroa, 2. m'aneka.
gasp *see* ikemoro.
gather *see* 1. maio, 2. tangkongkoa, 3. rikoia, 4. rikoa, 5. riko, 6. remrem, 7. moantaia, 8. batia, 9.

karakina, **10**. kamanunua, **11**. kabaka, **12**. iko, **13**.
botaki, **14**. kawawaea, **15**. boota.
gathered *see* **1**. moantaiaki, **2**. nimatenten, **3**.
remremaki, **4**. tangkongkoaki, **5**. rikoaki, **6**.
rikoiaki, **7**. maioaki, **8**. bootaki, **9**. ikoaki, **10**.
kawawaeaki, **11**. karakinaki, **12**. kamanunuaki,
13. kabakaki, **14**. botakiaki, **15**. batiaki, **16**.
kokoni.
gauge *see* baire.
gaunt *see* taramau.
gawky *see* uara.
gay *see* kukurei.
gaze *see* taku.
gear *see* kataenang.
geared *see* kataenangaki.
general *see* kabuta.
generally *see* tataneiai.
generate *see* **1**. kariki, **2**. karika.
generated *see* **1**. karikaki, **2**. karikiaki.
generous *see* **1**. diduarô, **2**. tituaraoi, **3**. nanouki, **4**.
kakaianga, **5**. bairaoi, **6**. baiati, **7**. nanomawa.
genial *see* nanoraoi.
genteel *see* karinerine.
gentle *see* **1**. maem, **2**. nimamanei, **3**. inataba, **4**.
inaine, **5**. inaaine, **6**. ina, **7**. matanikanebu.
gentlemen *see* naka.
gently *see* karaurau.
genuine *see* koaua.
gestate *see* nako.
gesture *see* **1**. inga, **2**. iranikai.
gestured *see* **1**. iranikaiaki, **2**. ingaki.
get *see* **1**. ana, **2**. karekea.
ghastly *see* **1**. kakanaugaki, **2**. tawere.
ghostly *see* taramau.
giant *see* bakora.
gibber *see* takutaku.
giddy *see* **1**. minotaki, **2**. nanobaba, **3**. tanoi.
gigantic *see* **1**. wari, **2**. bubura, **3**. korabaia, **4**.
makaiao, **5**. toa.
girl *see* ahine.
give *see* **1**. kamei, **2**. kaonoa, **3**. kataneiai, **4**. ngka, **5**.
nna, **6**. anga.
given *see* **1**. ngkaki, **2**. takuaki, **3**. kataneiaiaki, **4**.
nnaki, **5**. angaki, **6**. angaangaki, **7**. anga, **8**.
kaonoaki.
giving *see* baiati.
glad *see* kukurei.
glance *see* **1**. matarere, **2**. tarariao.
glassy *see* maborabora.
glaze *see* **1**. ranebonebo, **2**. karaneboneboa, **3**. irea,
4. karaneanea.
glazed *see* **1**. ireaki, **2**. karaneaneaki, **3**.
karaneboneboaki, **4**. katimaran, **5**. raneboneboaki.
glean *see* remrem.
glide *see* **1**. kabutikeke, **2**. tikeke, **3**. katikeke.

glimmer *see* taukaro.
glimpse *see* tarariao.
glisten *see* ranebonebo.
glistening *see* ranebonebo.
glitter *see* taukaro.
gloat *see* kakarabakaua.
glob *see* katimronrona.
global *see* okioki.
globular *see* timron.
gloomy *see* **1**. nanokawa, **2**. tabaronikarawa, **3**.
maewe.
glorified *see* **1**. kakannatoaki, **2**. kamimitongaki, **3**.
kamoaki, **4**. neboaki, **5**. neboneboaki.
glorify *see* **1**. kamimitonga, **2**. nebonebo, **3**. neboa,
4. kakannatoa, **5**. kamoa.
glorious *see* **1**. kakannato, **2**. mimitong.
gloss *see* **1**. ranebonebo, **2**. irea, **3**. karaneanea, **4**.
karaneboneboa.
glossy *see* **1**. ranebonebo, **2**. maran, **3**. katimaran, **4**.
maborabora.
glow *see* **1**. aimaka, **2**. bue, **3**. takarokaro, **4**.
uramwaka.
glue *see* kanima.
glued *see* kanimaki.
glum *see* nanokawa.
glutton *see* buabeka.
gluttonous *see* **1**. buabeka, **2**. ngangau, **3**. ngau.
gnash *see* torara.
gnaw *see* **1**. keru, **2**. makiro, **3**. kana, **4**. kamakerua,
5. ikao.
go *see* **1**. nako, **2**. nikamonmon, **3**. rere, **4**. rimwi, **5**.
rinano, **6**. ueka, **7**. kiria.
gobble *see* **1**. karurua, **2**. kabaubau.
goer *see* inao.
going *see* nang.
golden *see* **1**. baun, **2**. kora.
gone *see* **1**. boê, **2**. itimareare, **3**. nkona, **4**. tarao.
good *see* **1**. tikaraoi, **2**. wau, **3**. tenu, **4**. riai, **5**. raroi,
6. raoiroi, **7**. raba, **8**. lelei, **9**. kangkang, **10**. kan,
11. buni, **12**. atataiaomata, **13**. raoi.
gorge *see* **1**. atoa, **2**. kararatia.
gorged *see* **1**. rarati, **2**. atoaki, **3**. kararatiaki, **4**.
manono.
gorgeous *see* **1**. kakanno, **2**. kakatika.
gossip *see* **1**. babarantiko, **2**. katang.
gouge *see* auta.
gouged *see* autaki.
govern *see* **1**. tautaeka, **2**. tuana.
governed *see* **1**. tautaekaki, **2**. tuanaki.
grab *see* rawea.
graceful *see* **1**. inaaine, **2**. tiko, **3**. tamaroa, **4**.
kakateke.
gracious *see* **1**. maem, **2**. tika.
grad *see* burimangaoa.
graded *see* burimangaoaki.

graduate see kaunrabakau.
graduated see kaunrabakauaki.
grammatical see 1. tenu, 2. tonu.
grand see 1. ikawai, 2. kakanato, 3. mimitong, 4. tamaroa, 5. bubura.
grandparent see tebû.
grant see 1. kaonoa, 2. anga.
granted see 1. angaki, 2. kaonoaki.
granular see atiati.
granulate see kataribia.
granulated see 1. kataribiaki, 2. taribi.
grapple see 1. rabatia, 2. iwai, 3. kaunrabata.
grasp see 1. taua, 2. rawea, 3. kamatebwai, 4. nora.
grasping see 1. babakanikawai, 2. ikake.
grass see uteute.
grate see 1. koikoi, 2. tuairoa, 3. koi, 4. kakara, 5. ii, 6. i, 7. kokoa.
gratified see kakukureaki.
gratify see kakukure.
grating see anikai.
grave see kamamate.
gravel see toninta.
gray see 1. iaia, 2. meamea.
grayish see mai.
graze see 1. kabomaki, 2. kakaria, 3. kanananga, 4. kara, 5. rakoroa.
grazed see 1. kakariaki, 2. tuanokunoku, 3. rakoroaki, 4. kabomakiaki, 5. bomaki, 6. kananangaki, 7. karaki.
grease see kamaratiarati.
greased see 1. kamaratiaratiaki, 2. maratirati.
greasy see 1. timinene, 2. maete, 3. nenea.
great see 1. rangaki, 2. korakora, 3. kakannato, 4. kakanato, 5. bubura, 6. bâbaki, 7. ababaki, 8. apâpaki.
greater see 1. raka, 2. angi.
greatness see 1. böki, 2. bakin.
greedy see 1. ria, 2. buabeka, 3. buariki, 4. kibubura, 5. namtete, 6. ngau, 7. ngeta.
green see 1. kiaiai, 2. kiriin.
greet see 1. inga, 2. kamaura.
gregarious see kanibobotaki.
grieve see 1. kanaeng, 2. mango, 3. rainanoanga, 4. tangitang.
grievous see 1. rawawaa, 2. kamamate, 3. kananokawaki.
grill see 1. kabutewetewe, 2. kamwa, 3. tinima, 4. tinnim.
grilled see 1. kamwaki, 2. tinimaki, 3. kabuteweteweaki, 4. tinnimaki.
grimace see 1. makiki, 2. mangingi.
grin see wingare.
grind see 1. ii, 2. torara, 3. tang, 4. mengo, 5. i, 6. bubua, 7. bing, 8. ia.
grip see 1. rawea, 2. taua.

gristly see 1. baia, 2. tiki, 3. tikitiki.
gritty see 1. atiati, 2. tanotano.
grizzly see kakamaku.
groan see 1. ngira, 2. ngirangira, 3. ngirataua, 4. tangorake, 5. torara, 6. toto.
grope see 1. tabara, 2. nanobebebebe, 3. raweraweaba.
groping see nanobebebebe.
grotesque see kamairatuatua.
ground see 1. toraraki, 2. bing, 3. bingaki, 4. bubuaki, 5. iaki, 6. iiaki, 7. mengoaki, 8. tangaki.
grounded see koro.
group see 1. katanga, 2. katanina, 3. nanai, 4. teiuomania, 5. botaki.
grouped see 1. katangaki, 2. tanin, 3. nimatenten, 4. teiuomaniaki, 5. kataninaki, 6. botakiaki, 7. botaki, 8. bau, 9. baki, 10. nanaiaki, 11. ikoikotaki.
grouse see ngure.
grow see 1. rikirake, 2. kamarabea, 3. riki.
growl see 1. takurara, 2. bekorara, 3. mere.
grown see 1. riki, 2. rikirake.
grownup see ikawai.
grubby see barekareka.
gruesome see nanomakaki.
grumble see 1. takurara, 2. ngurengure, 3. mere.
grunt see kungkung.
guard see 1. otaotanga, 2. rabane, 3. tantani, 4. taubeakina, 5. teiakina.
guarded see 1. tantaniaki, 2. taubeakinaki, 3. rabaneaki, 4. otaotangaki, 5. teiakinaki.
guess see 1. karamakina, 2. katana, 3. katautau, 4. namakin, 5. nanoata.
guest see iruwa.
guide see 1. arona, 2. matana, 3. kairiri, 4. kaira, 5. ena.
guided see 1. aronaki, 2. enaki, 3. kairaki, 4. kaiririaki, 5. matanaki.
guileless see matabou.
guilty see 1. bure, 2. ukinta.
gulp see 1. ngaungau, 2. ngauta, 3. kabwauta.
gumming see maungaro.
gummy see nimnim.
gun see kati.
gush see 1. kobu, 2. koburakea, 3. ti, 4. kati.
gusty see 1. aboabo, 2. angitannenne.
gutter see niba.
guy see mwane.
guzzle see 1. kabwaubwau, 2. mangainrang.
gyrate see 1. minomino, 2. nikamonmon.

H

h see au.
habitually see tataneiai.
hack see 1. tatata, 2. tenarua.
hackle see ake.
haggard see taramau.
hail see 1. katika, 2. kea.
hair see 1. ira, 2. etou.
hairdo see para.
hairless see katimarau.
hairy see 1. buraerae, 2. buruburu, 3. uakaka.
half see 1. makoroua, 2. titerau.
hallow see 1. tabua, 2. katabua.
hallowed see 1. katabuaki, 2. tabuaki.
hallucinate see mitara.
halt see 1. nanobebebe, 2. tebetebe, 3. tei, 4. turatura.
halve see makoroua, 2. bwenaua.
halved see 1. makorouaki, 2. korouaiaki, 3. bwenauaki.
hammer see bobo.
hammered see boboaki.
hamper see 1. baenikai, 2. kamweau.
hand see 1. koanoa, 2. angana, 3. angangana.
handed see koanoaki.
handle see 1. riringa, 2. aebai.
handled see 1. aebaiaki, 2. riringaki.
handsome see 1. botonimwaane, 2. inababaura, 3. katereke, 4. tamârua.
handy see 1. antibuaka, 2. bairaoi, 3. wanawana.
hang see 1. katinea, 2. katinerua, 3. katiobabaea, 4. tikurabirabi, 5. tine.
hanging see 1. tinerua, 2. kamatine, 3. tine.
hankering see uamoa.
haphazard see inra.
happen see riki.
happening see 1. manenanti, 2. rianibwai.
happy see 1. kabaia, 2. kukurei.
harass see 1. karawawata, 2. imanono, 3. kakai.
harassed see 1. karawawataki, 2. kakaiaki, 3. imanonoaki.
harbor see kairuwaea.
hard see 1. kanganga, 2. tiritiri, 3. tikinono, 4. ngearuru, 5. matoa, 6. kangana, 7. kamou, 8. iwaka, 9. inamatoa, 10. ba, 11. matoato.
harden see 1. kamatoatoa, 2. kanngea, 3. konin.
hardened see 1. kamatoatoaki, 2. kanngeaki, 3. koninaki, 4. kamateanibai.
hardly see tabetai.
hardy see 1. korakora, 2. ninikoria.

hark see 1. kakaauongo, 2. kakaunongo, 3. ongo.
harm see 1. kabuanibwaia, 2. kaikoaka, 3. kabuanibwai, 4. maura.
harmed see 1. kabuanibwaiaki, 2. kaikoakaki, 3. mauraki.
harmonious see rau.
harp see katinono.
harpoon see wai.
harsh see 1. unin, 2. karakara.
harvest see 1. taia, 2. iko, 3. moantaia.
hasten see 1. kaumau, 2. waekoa, 3. uriri, 4. umaki, 5. taungatangata, 6. tataenoa, 7. taenoa, 8. kawikoa, 9. kaumaki, 10. katawe, 11. ikaikai, 12. iebaba, 13. bareka, 14. bare, 15. koa.
hasty see 1. taebo, 2. kaumau, 3. katawe, 4. kuri, 5. kukuri.
hat see para.
hatch see kaurea.
hatched see kaureaki.
hate see 1. tabunimatea, 2. rantia, 3. riba, 4. ririba.
hated see 1. tabunimateaki, 2. riribaki, 3. rantiaki, 4. ribaki.
hateful see tennanoa.
haughty see 1. kainikatonga, 2. rietata.
haul see 1. tatika, 2. uakiua.
haunt see 1. kakawara, 2. neweaba.
haunted see 1. kakawaraki, 2. neweabaki.
have see 1. uakana, 2. bon, 3. iai, 4. karekea, 5. tianakiana, 6. tuana, 7. uabai.
hazardous see 1. aomara, 2. karuanikai.
hazy see 1. bubutei, 2. mabubu, 3. taribubu.
he see 1. e, 2. ngaia.
head see 1. atuna, 2. ongo, 3. urukauna, 4. tapanou, 5. kautu, 6. kakaunongo, 7. atuu, 8. keinanoa.
headed see 1. atuna, 2. nakea.
headstrong see 1. buburamaiu, 2. kirinikamate.
heal see kamaoa.
healed see 1. kamaoaki, 2. mao.
healthier see nimanana.
healthy see 1. marabe, 2. marati, 3. marurung, 4. mauri.
heap see 1. kabarikoa, 2. kikibokiboa, 3. katabuka, 4. karuataoa, 5. ai, 6. kareuatao, 7. kakiriuatao.
heaped see 1. karuataoaki, 2. nonoaba, 3. kiruatao, 4. ratuatao, 5. katabukaki, 6. kareuataoaki, 7. kakiriuataoaki, 8. kabarikoaki, 9. aiaki, 10. kikibokiboaki.
hear see ongo.
heard see ongo.
hearken see 1. ongo, 2. kakaunongo.
heartbroken see kawa.
heartfelt see tiritiri.
heartless see nano.
heat see rîriña.

heave *see* **1**. katurabeau, **2**. tabeka, **3**. mwe, **4**. katika, **5**. kamwemwea, **6**. kainga, **7**. neboa.

heaven *see* karava.

heavenly *see* kamimi.

heavy *see* **1**. revata, **2**. rawawata, **3**. tinebu, **4**. ntinebu, **5**. kamamate, **6**. intinebu, **7**. rawata.

heavyhearted *see* nanokawa.

heckle *see* **1**. kakai, **2**. karawawata.

heed *see* **1**. mannanoa, **2**. mutiakina.

heedful *see* mautara.

heedless *see* **1**. nanotiotio, **2**. noumaninganinga, **3**. remereme.

heel *see* **1**. bukiniwae, **2**. buki-ni-wai, **3**. kiea.

heir *see* ebiebi.

held *see* **1**. rabaneaki, **2**. tenabiti, **3**. tauaki, **4**. taua, **5**. kararoaki, **6**. karabaki, **7**. in, **8**. ietaki, **9**. antingoaki, **10**. taonaki.

hello *see* mauri.

helmet *see* para.

help *see* **1**. buoki, **2**. katoa, **3**. buoka.

helpful *see* ibuobuoki.

hen *see* mo'aiine.

hence *see* maikai.

herd *see* **1**. nanai, **2**. rurung, **3**. uarurung.

here *see* **1**. iko, **2**. ikei, **3**. kai, **4**. ikai, **5**. ê, **6**. i-kai.

hero *see* **1**. korana, **2**. rarikin, **3**. bakora.

heroine *see* rarikin.

hesitant *see* **1**. nanououa, **2**. nanobebebe, **3**. nanokoraki, **4**. nanomaiti.

hesitate *see* **1**. tei, **2**. tabara, **3**. nanououa, **4**. nanokokoraki, **5**. iraaua, **6**. nanobebebe.

hesitating *see* **1**. nanobebebe, **2**. rekebuta, **3**. teirobaroba.

hex *see* wauwi.

hiatus *see* **1**. motirawa, **2**. mena.

hiccup *see* marei.

hide *see* **1**. karaba, **2**. karabana, **3**. karapa, **4**. kom.

hideous *see* **1**. bureti, **2**. kamairatuatua, **3**. nanomakaki.

high *see* **1**. retát, **2**. rieta, **3**. ietât, **4**. rietata.

hijack *see* taebai.

hike *see* nakomai.

hilly *see* **1**. aontabuki, **2**. mamaunga, **3**. rabe, **4**. tabuki, **5**. tabukirurunga.

hinder *see* **1**. kamweau, **2**. waitotokoa, **3**. baenikai, **4**. tabiro, **5**. katabaruarua.

hindering *see* nanginang.

hint *see* **1**. kinra, **2**. wiwi.

hire *see* **1**. buuta, **2**. kabeabea.

hired *see* **1**. buutaki, **2**. kabeabeaki.

hiss *see* **1**. katiti, **2**. rabungaoa.

historically *see* ngkoa.

hit *see* **1**. oro, **2**. titaou, **3**. tiringaki, **4**. tiringa, **5**. boaki, **6**. teka, **7**. takaereaki, **8**. takaere, **9**. oroaki, **10**. orea, **11**. maroakaki, **12**. maroaka, **13**.

kareaki, **14**. kare, **15**. bobo, **16**. boboaki, **17**. bo, **18**. oreaki.

hitch *see* kabaea.

hitting *see* turu.

hoard *see* **1**. rawebaia, **2**. kaikoa.

hoarse *see* **1**. bakabua, **2**. karakara.

hoary *see* nabawe.

hobble *see* nimaukuku.

hoist *see* **1**. katikia, **2**. rake, **3**. katurabeau, **4**. kamwemwea, **5**. irakea, **6**. kairakea.

hold *see* **1**. antingoa, **2**. ieta, **3**. karaba, **4**. kararoa, **5**. rabane, **6**. taona, **7**. tau, **8**. taua.

hollow *see* **1**. mangkongko, **2**. niba, **3**. ruoa, **4**. mano, **5**. kaibakoa, **6**. binibing, **7**. bangabanga, **8**. manono, **9**. manawanawa.

hollowed *see* **1**. ruoaki, **2**. kaibako, **3**. kaibakoaki, **4**. nibaki.

homeless *see* kimangare.

homestead *see* tiku.

hone *see* katia.

honed *see* katiaki.

honest *see* matabou.

honeycombed *see* kiribangabanga.

honor *see* **1**. kakannatoa, **2**. karinea.

honorable *see* **1**. nanomawa, **2**. nanouki.

honored *see* **1**. bainaka, **2**. kakannatoaki, **3**. karineaki.

hood *see* baba.

hook *see* **1**. reke, **2**. ribita.

hooked *see* **1**. rekeaki, **2**. ribitaki, **3**. reke, **4**. teka.

hop *see* **1**. ewewerake, **2**. katuatua, **3**. waekirere, **4**. waetebetebe.

hope *see* kantaninga.

hopeful *see* uamoa.

hopeless *see* kabana.

horn *see* ñîeta.

horrendous *see* nanomakaki.

horrible *see* kakamaku.

horrid *see* kakamaku.

horrified *see* tonginako.

horrifying *see* kakamaku.

hospitable *see* **1**. maningainga, **2**. tautata.

hostile *see* **1**. riribai, **2**. matabuaka, **3**. matabubuaka.

hot *see* **1**. rîriña, **2**. mika, **3**. bue, **4**. kabuebue.

hound *see* kakai.

house *see* **1**. auti, **2**. kiakina.

hover *see* tio.

how *see* **1**. kanga, **2**. gaña.

howl *see* **1**. tang, **2**. mango.

huddle *see* karakina.

hug *see* **1**. ibabakoi, **2**. kabotaba, **3**. rabati, **4**. rabatia.

huge *see* **1**. korabaia, **2**. tabati, **3**. makaiao, **4**. bubura, **5**. abakae, **6**. rabana.

human *see* aomata.

humane *see* **1**. aboabonaomata, **2**. maninganinga.

humble see **1**. mwiniba, **2**. nukabebeo, **3**. rinano, **4**. nanorinano, **5**. katorotoro, **6**. inataba, **7**. kanubebeoa, **8**. mangori.

humbled see **1**. kanubebeoaki, **2**. katorotoroaki.

humid see **1**. aoi, **2**. aomwaimwai, **3**. mwau, **4**. roto.

humidify see karota.

humiliate see **1**. karinanoa, **2**. kamama, **3**. kanuka.

humiliated see **1**. kamamaki, **2**. kanukaki, **3**. karinanoaki, **4**. maneanea, **5**. nea.

humor see manikangare.

humorous see aokangare.

humped see ribeu.

hundred see itibubua.

hung see tine.

hunger see **1**. baki, **2**. pake.

hungry see **1**. baki, **2**. bakaruru, **3**. kibakibaki.

hunt see **1**. kaea, **2**. kite, **3**. nenera.

hunted see **1**. neneraki, **2**. kaeaki, **3**. kiteaki.

hurl see **1**. kaka, **2**. kare.

hurried see **1**. koaki, **2**. waetataki, **3**. waekoaki, **4**. bareaki, **5**. umakiaki, **6**. taungatangataki, **7**. taeririaki, **8**. taenoaki, **9**. rangatakiaki, **10**. rangataki, **11**. barekaki, **12**. iebabaki, **13**. kawikoaki, **14**. itinaki, **15**. karakiaki, **16**. kaumakaki, **17**. kaumau, **18**. kaumauaki, **19**. kauririaki, **20**. kawaetataki.

hurry see **1**. kauriri, **2**. waekoa, **3**. umaki, **4**. taungatangata, **5**. taenoa, **6**. rangataki, **7**. rangata, **8**. koa, **9**. waetata, **10**. bareka, **11**. kawikoa, **12**. bare, **13**. kawaetata, **14**. iebaba, **15**. itina, **16**. karaki, **17**. kaumaka, **18**. kaumau.

hurt see **1**. kamarakaki, **2**. nanobuaka, **3**. marakiaki, **4**. maraki, **5**. maraka, **6**. tiki, **7**. kataeariaki, **8**. nanobuakaki, **9**. karetun, **10**. kamaraka, **11**. kaikoakaki, **12**. kaikoaka, **13**. boaki, **14**. bo, **15**. karetunaki, **16**. kataeari.

hurtful see buakaka.

hush see kabarara.

hushed see kabararaki.

husk see koroma.

husky see kaubiroto.

hustle see **1**. kaienikuria, **2**. rangarangatau, **3**. barekia, **4**. kabaitata.

hyperactive see **1**. inao, **2**. utowa.

hypnotize see kamatua.

hypnotized see kamatuaki.

hypocrite see **1**. bakamoamoa, **2**. kaborarinano.

hypocritical see atutekonaua.

I

ideal see tima.

identical see kiribare.

identified see **1**. ataiaki, **2**. matatoka, **3**. noraki.

identify see **1**. ataia, **2**. nora.

idiot see **1**. ou, **2**. rangirang, **3**. baba, **4**. tabaua.

idle see **1**. manrerei, **2**. matiketike, **3**. niau, **4**. noumangang, **5**. taninganinga, **6**. taningaroti.

idolize see **1**. nabenabea, **2**. tabunimatea, **3**. kaotabaea.

idolized see **1**. nabenabeaki, **2**. tabunimateaki, **3**. kaotabaeaki.

if see **1**. bain-ganai, **2**. kanai, **3**. ko, **4**. ngkana.

ignite see **1**. iro, **2**. katairoa, **3**. kaura, **4**. kairoa, **5**. kabueka, **6**. katairo.

ignited see **1**. iroaki, **2**. kabuekaki, **3**. kairoaki, **4**. katairoaki, **5**. kauraki.

ignoble see **1**. mwiniba, **2**. nukabebeo.

ignorant see **1**. bangabwai, **2**. kabi, **3**. nonoro, **4**. tukuroro, **5**. babanga.

ill see aoraki.

illegal see **1**. tabu, **2**. mabu, **3**. iruwa.

illicit see tabu.

illiterate see nonoro.

illness see orak.

illuminate see **1**. kaota, **2**. manimaninia.

illuminated see **1**. ainga, **2**. aokabu, **3**. kaotaki, **4**. manimaniniaki.

illustrate see kabarabara.

illustrated see kabarabaraki.

illustrious see **1**. kakannato, **2**. rine, **3**. eke.

imagine see **1**. iango, **2**. karika.

imagined see **1**. iangoaki, **2**. karikaki.

imbecile see **1**. bwabwa, **2**. taribaba, **3**. tabaua, **4**. ou, **5**. nanobaba.

imbibe see mooi.

imitate see **1**. kakairi, **2**. katoto, **3**. katotonga, **4**. uamwi.

immaculate see immakurata.

immaterial see mangori.

immature see kiaiai.

immeasurable see kakawaki.

immediate see **1**. kanroaroa, **2**. ngkainaba.

immediately see **1**. abanaba, **2**. ngkai, **3**. ngkainaba.

immense see **1**. abakaei, **2**. morokaei, **3**. korabaia, **4**. buburakaei.

immerse see **1**. inako, **2**. kamakuna, **3**. kateboa, **4**. taona.

immersed see **1**. kateboaki, **2**. taonaki, **3**. kamakunaki, **4**. inakoaki.

imminent see uramai.

immoderate see ruonako.

immolate see tiringa.

immutable see takebono.

impact see untaba.

impair see **1**. kakea, **2**. kamamaraea.

impaired see **1**. kamamaraeaki, **2**. mamara, **3**. kakeaki.

impale *see* katekea.
impart *see* anga.
impartial *see* 1. bairaoi, 2. nanowana.
impassable *see* 1. inamatoa, 2. kamaneanikum, 3. kamateanibai, 4. matenruarua.
impassive *see* rau.
impatient *see* 1. nanorake, 2. nanoingainga, 3. kakaiewa, 4. inga, 5. kaierake.
impeach *see* bwaka.
impede *see* 1. karotua, 2. tinerua, 3. tuka.
impeded *see* 1. karotuaki, 2. tukaki, 3. tineruaki.
impeding *see* angitaba.
impel *see* wakina.
impending *see* uramai.
impenetrable *see* aotaningo.
imperative *see* aori.
imperfect *see* buretata.
impersonate *see* 1. katotonga, 2. uamwi.
impertinent *see* maurake.
imperturbable *see* 1. kamateanibai, 2. kangkai, 3. rau.
impetuous *see* baibati.
implacable *see* inamatoa.
implant *see* unika.
implanted *see* unikaki.
implement *see* karekea.
implemented *see* karekeaki.
implied *see* taraeaki.
implore *see* onon.
imply *see* tarae.
impolite *see* 1. kaburati, 2. tete.
import *see* nanona.
important *see* 1. mamaka, 2. manena, 3. kakanato, 4. bongana, 5. maneuna.
imported *see* nanonaki.
importunate *see* 1. reberake, 2. tokobito, 3. memerake, 4. tokobeka, 5. tokoie, 6. tete, 7. tabare, 8. muramura, 9. mura, 10. memeto, 11. meme, 12. mramra, 13. nimroroko.
importune *see* 1. bubuti, 2. taie.
impose *see* kariri.
imposed *see* kaririaki.
imposing *see* mimitang.
impostor *see* uarao.
impotent *see* 1. ntokotoko, 2. toto.
impoverished *see* waebaka.
imprecate *see* 1. bukinna, 2. karereantia, 3. wauwi.
impregnable *see* kamaneanikum.
impregnated *see* ibaba.
impress *see* 1. namakin, 2. nanoata.
impressive *see* mimitong.
imprint *see* baiturua.
imprisoned *see* in.
improbable *see* kamauanta.
improper *see* 1. ra, 2. buaka.

improved *see* boou.
imprudent *see* kaoanikai.
impudent *see* 1. kamatauninga, 2. kirmatamata, 3. maurake, 4. maureka, 5. uamoa.
impulsive *see* aotakaka.
impure *see* 1. kamaira, 2. buakaka, 3. bareka, 4. ra.
impute *see* kanotona.
in *see* 1. n, 2. ni.
inactive *see* 1. noumangang, 2. ntorotoro.
inadequate *see* areare.
inadvertent *see* nanotiotio.
inane *see* arobaba.
inapt *see* 1. kibana, 2. babanga.
inattentive *see* 1. arei, 2. noumaninganinga.
inaugurate *see* moana.
inauspicious *see* ra.
incalculable *see* kakawaki.
incapable *see* 1. ntokotoko, 2. maunganga, 3. kabana.
incapacitated *see* ntokotoko.
incidental *see* taeremea.
incipient *see* moan.
incise *see* 1. koria, 2. korokoroia, 3. makoro.
incised *see* 1. makoroaki, 2. koriaki, 3. korokoroiaki.
incisive *see* 1. witeke, 2. wikakang, 3. kateke, 4. nano.
incite *see* 1. ribinanoa, 2. wiwi.
inclement *see* karakara.
incline *see* 1. mamarake, 2. rara, 3. raira, 4. kabatete, 5. einako, 6. rangaie.
inclined *see* 1. rara, 2. raraki, 3. rangaieaki, 4. rairaki, 5. rae, 6. nano, 7. mamarakeaki, 8. kabateteaki, 9. einakoaki.
included *see* maurouro.
including *see* naba.
inclusive *see* maurouro.
incompetent *see* 1. babanga, 2. ntokotoko.
incomplete *see* ra.
inconsequential *see* teutana.
inconsiderable *see* uangingi.
inconsistent *see* 1. nanobitaki, 2. tangauriuri, 3. ranran, 4. ruannano.
inconstant *see* ruannano.
inconvenience *see* 1. angabuaka, 2. karemereme, 3. karenoa, 4. manga.
incorrigible *see* kataenano.
increase *see* 1. kabunnaa, 2. rikirake, 3. raka, 4. katia, 5. karakarakea, 6. kakerakea, 7. kabata, 8. kamaita.
increased *see* 1. katiaki, 2. rikirakeaki, 3. rakaki, 4. kabataki, 5. kamaitaki, 6. kabunnaaki, 7. kakerakeaki, 8. karakarakeaki.
incriminate *see* 1. bukina, 2. uton.
inculpate *see* uton.

indebted *see* 1. bae, 2. banebane, 3. babae.
indecent *see* kamwara.
indecisive *see* 1. iraaua, 2. nanokoraki, 3. nanomaiti, 4. nanououa, 5. tangaua, 6. tine.
indeed *see* 1. bon, 2. naba.
indefinite *see* maewe.
indent *see* 1. nibaia, 2. nibanibaia.
indented *see* 1. nibaiaki, 2. nibanibaiaki.
independent *see* 1. ebiebi, 2. inaaomata.
indicate *see* 1. kaota, 2. karamakina, 3. kotea.
indict *see* bukina.
indifferent *see* 1. bwanabwana, 2. kabuingoingo, 3. kamateanibai.
indigent *see* 1. rarikin, 2. waebaka.
indigestible *see* iberoro.
indiscreet *see* 1. witakanana, 2. aouki.
indisposed *see* 1. karotu, 2. nimanan, 3. tabetabe.
indistinct *see* 1. bang, 2. ka, 3. maewe, 4. marara.
individually *see* tatabeua.
indocile *see* bonotaninga.
indolent *see* 1. tarabu, 2. toto, 3. taningaroti, 4. ntangaingai, 5. niniakai, 6. niau, 7. nangonango, 8. manio, 9. noumangang.
indomitable *see* 1. nanomwane, 2. nanomwaka.
induct *see* karemea.
indulge *see* 1. kariaia, 2. ririkana.
indulgent *see* nanomamara.
indulging *see* nanomamara.
industrious *see* 1. uamoa, 2. tataningamarau, 3. maribo, 4. kiriman, 5. kakorakura, 6. kikiriman.
inebriated *see* 1. manging, 2. rangirang.
ineffectual *see* 1. kibana, 2. manouna.
inelegant *see* baikiaro.
inert *see* 1. manio, 2. taningaroti, 3. ntangaingai.
inestimable *see* kakawaki.
inexperienced *see* iroroto.
inexpert *see* babanga.
inextricable *see* mangaoangao.
infamous *see* 1. kakauara, 2. nukabebeo.
infant *see* 1. merimeri, 2. ngoro.
infatuate *see* babanaine.
infatuated *see* 1. babanaineaki, 2. nanona, 3. ririka.
infect *see* 1. kautua, 2. kautuaka.
infected *see* 1. kautuakaki, 2. kautuaki.
inferior *see* 1. karako, 2. mangori, 3. mwiniba.
infertile *see* kanoabo.
infest *see* 1. kaona, 2. taona.
infested *see* 1. kaonaki, 2. taonaki.
infidel *see* bekan.
infiltrate *see* 1. ranene, 2. aeae.
infinite *see* 1. nanokiroro, 2. karebun, 3. nanokirokiro.
infinitesimal *see* tingingi.
inflame *see* 1. kauramaka, 2. takaro.
inflamed *see* 1. kauramakaki, 2. takaroaki.

inflate *see* 1. katibua, 2. kamatibutibua.
inflated *see* 1. katibuaki, 2. kamatibutibuaki.
inflect *see* kabaoa.
inflected *see* kabaoaki.
inflict *see* 1. kamaraka, 2. katuaea.
influential *see* mamaka.
inform *see* 1. kaongoa, 2. tuanga, 3. tua, 4. kauka, 5. kaongoraea, 6. beireina, 7. katekebotia.
informal *see* mantakarara.
informed *see* 1. kaukaki, 2. katekebotiaki, 3. tuangaki, 4. tuaki, 5. kaongoraeaki, 6. kaongoaki, 7. beireinaki, 8. rabakau.
infrequent *see* tare.
infrequently *see* kareke.
infringe *see* raka.
infuriate *see* kaunun.
infuriated *see* kaununaki.
infuse *see* karina.
ingenious *see* 1. kauman, 2. kikiman, 3. rabakai, 4. rabakau, 5. wanawana, 6. kauanga.
ingurgitate *see* ngaungau.
inhabit *see* 1. kakai, 2. maekana, 3. batana, 4. mwenga, 5. kaina.
inhabitant *see* kain.
inhabited *see* 1. batanaki, 2. kainaki, 3. kakai, 4. kakaiaki, 5. maekanaki, 6. mwengaki.
inhale *see* 1. ikena, 2. temeka, 3. nawa, 4. namta, 5. memeka, 6. mbambaea, 7. kamba, 8. toma, 9. ikeike, 10. mamma.
inhaled *see* 1. memekaki, 2. temekaki, 3. tomaki, 4. nawaki, 5. namtaki, 6. mbambaeaki, 7. mammaki, 8. kambaki, 9. ikeikeaki, 10. ikenaki.
inherit *see* 1. ababa, 2. bwaibwai, 3. kabaibai.
inherited *see* 1. ababaki, 2. bwaibwaiaki, 3. kabaibaiaki.
inhuman *see* tiritiri.
inhumane *see* bangaaomata.
iniquitous *see* babakanikawai.
initial *see* moa.
initially *see* moa.
initiate *see* 1. aboka, 2. bumoa.
inject *see* 1. itina, 2. karina.
innumerable *see* 1. riara, 2. kariara, 3. kontano, 4. nimareburebu.
inoffensive *see* nimamanei.
inopportune *see* kaboituta.
inordinate *see* ruonako.
inquisitive *see* 1. mautete, 2. memeto, 3. reberake.
insane *see* 1. tiriou, 2. baba, 3. ou.
insatiable *see* 1. ringoungou, 2. buabeka, 3. namtete.
inscribe *see* 1. kanikina, 2. koroboki.
inscribed *see* 1. kanikinaki, 2. korobokiaki.
inscrutable *see* aotaningo.
insecure *see* 1. uara, 2. mwebuaka.

insensible *see* 1. matenruarua, 2. kiro, 3. kamateanibai, 4. kangkai.
inseparable *see* 1. airi, 2. kiribwebwe.
insert *see* karina.
inset *see* karinaki.
inside *see* 1. ano, 2. paro.
insightful *see* niniwana.
insignificant *see* 1. makota, 2. mangori, 3. teutana.
insinuate *see* 1. wiwi, 2. kinraea, 3. tarae.
insipid *see* 1. mai, 2. mammam.
insist *see* 1. buburamaiu, 2. imanono, 3. kairoro, 4. katinono, 5. tebomaurua.
insistent *see* 1. mura, 2. muramura, 3. katinono, 4. buburamaiu, 5. mramra.
insisting *see* katinono.
insolent *see* 1. ikake, 2. kainikatonga, 3. kamatauninga, 4. maurake.
insouciant *see* taeremea.
inspect *see* 1. kamataua, 2. tutuo, 3. tuoa, 4. tarabai, 5. matauakina, 6. karekea, 7. kinanoa.
inspire *see* 1. katutua, 2. wina, 3. wiwi.
inspired *see* 1. wiwiaki, 2. winaki, 3. uamoa, 4. nanomaka, 5. katutuaki.
install *see* kamena.
instant *see* ngkainaba.
instantaneous *see* ngkainaba.
instantaneously *see* 1. abanaba, 2. ngkainaba.
instantly *see* 1. abanaba, 2. ngkainaba.
instead *see* riki.
instigate *see* kauara.
institute *see* 1. katei, 2. katebe.
instituted *see* katebeaki.
instruct *see* 1. tonga, 2. beireina, 3. kaataibaia, 4. kaetieti, 5. katei, 6. reireia.
instructed *see* 1. tongaki, 2. reireiaki, 3. beireinaki, 4. kaetietiaki, 5. kaataibaiaki.
instrumental *see* mamaka.
insufficient *see* marengau.
insulate *see* kakaokoroa.
insulated *see* kakaokoroaki.
insult *see* 1. bainraraea, 2. tinara, 3. tabora, 4. kamatauninga, 5. kabunenea, 6. kabainrang, 7. angabaibuaka, 8. kabuakaka.
insulted *see* 1. kabainrangaki, 2. taboraki, 3. tinaraki, 4. matauningananti, 5. kabuakakaki, 6. bainraraeaki, 7. kabuneneaki, 8. kamatauningaki.
insurmountable *see* kamaneanikum.
intact *see* tabanin.
integrated *see* wakaraoi.
intellectual *see* 1. niniwana, 2. karabakau.
intelligent *see* 1. wanawana, 2. wana, 3. maiutakoni, 4. niniwana.
intense *see* 1. kinano, 2. nano.
intensified *see* kataeboaki.
intensify *see* kataeboa.

intent *see* 1. uamoa, 2. tebomaurua.
intercalate *see* marena.
intercede *see* raoiakina.
intercept *see* taokabia.
intercession *see* tabunaák.
interchange *see* kaibibitia.
intercourse *see* 1. buno, 2. kabikoukou.
interdict *see* 1. tabua, 2. kamabu.
interested *see* 1. mataroro, 2. muti.
interesting *see* 1. kakamataku, 2. kamataku.
interface *see* 1. reita, 2. toma.
interfere *see* 1. tabarea, 2. kaintoka, 3. karemereme, 4. karenoa.
interject *see* kaintoka.
interlace *see* ata.
interlaced *see* ataki.
intermediate *see* rena.
intermingle *see* 1. kairengarenga, 2. rea, 3. rengana.
intermittent *see* 1. tokitoki, 2. maon.
intermix *see* kairengarenga.
interpose *see* marena.
interpret *see* 1. kabarabara, 2. kaeta, 3. kamatebwai, 4. nora.
interpreted *see* 1. noraki, 2. kabarabaraki, 3. kaetaki, 4. kamatebwaiaki.
interrogate *see* 1. kataetae, 2. kangongoa.
interrupt *see* 1. kaintoka, 2. wawaitai.
interrupted *see* 1. kaintokaki, 2. moti, 3. wawaitaiaki.
intervene *see* kareua.
interview *see* kakarabakau.
intimate *see* kiribwebwe.
intimidate *see* 1. ibebure, 2. kamakin.
intimidated *see* 1. ibebureaki, 2. kamakinaki, 3. matabou.
intolerant *see* nanoriba.
intoxicate *see* 1. kamangingnga, 2. kiraoki.
intoxicated *see* 1. mangung, 2. kiraokiaki, 3. kamangingngaki.
intractable *see* takebono.
intransigent *see* kariri.
intrepid *see* 1. kamateanibai, 2. ninikoria.
intricate *see* karaoana.
intriguing *see* 1. kamataku, 2. kakamataku.
introduce *see* 1. rin, 2. kaitiboa, 3. karina.
introduced *see* 1. kaitiboaki, 2. karinaki, 3. rinaki.
intrude *see* 1. maro, 2. ranene, 3. rin, 4. karemereme, 5. karebo, 6. karenoa.
intuitive *see* mamata.
inundate *see* ieka.
invade *see* 1. baroakina, 2. eweka, 3. tikubara.
invaluable *see* kakawaki.
invent *see* 1. kariki, 2. maroaka, 3. karika.
invented *see* 1. karikiaki, 2. maroakaki, 3. karikaki.
inventory *see* kamaribobo.

invert *see* **1.** bita, **2.** bitara.
inverted *see* **1.** bitaki, **2.** bitaraki.
investigate *see* **1.** nenera, **2.** ukouko, **3.** kekera.
investigative *see* nenera.
invincible *see* kamaneanikum.
invisible *see* winanti.
invite *see* **1.** kakakao, **2.** kao, **3.** wetea.
invited *see* **1.** kaoaki, **2.** weteaki, **3.** kakakaoaki.
invoke *see* **1.** taboa, **2.** kaunga.
involuntary *see* **1.** nanobebebe, **2.** ukinta.
involve *see* **1.** minotia, **2.** ninira, **3.** rengana.
involved *see* **1.** niniraki, **2.** renganaki, **3.** minotiaki.
involving *see* minotia.
invulnerable *see* kamaneanikum.
irascible *see* **1.** unin, **2.** kakaiun, **3.** kibaura, **4.** kikaura, **5.** kiura, **6.** nanorake, **7.** nanoun.
irate *see* unun.
irk *see* kanaengai.
irksome *see* kabun.
iron *see* **1.** biti, **2.** katira, **3.** monei.
ironed *see* katiraki.
ironical *see* kabitara.
irradiate *see* **1.** katekea, **2.** kaota.
irradiated *see* **1.** kaotaki, **2.** katekeaki.
irreducible *see* takebono.
irregular *see* **1.** manenanti, **2.** tungatunga.
irregularly *see* kareke.
irritable *see* **1.** nanoun, **2.** kikaura, **3.** kiura, **4.** nanorake.
irritate *see* **1.** karawawata, **2.** kananora, **3.** bononano, **4.** kakai.
irritated *see* **1.** karawawataki, **2.** bononano, **3.** bononanoaki, **4.** kakaiaki, **5.** kananoraki.
irritating *see* **1.** rebetunga, **2.** rebetoko, **3.** kataeri.
island *see* penoua.
isolated *see* **1.** maroa, **2.** takarere.
isosceles *see* aitiotiriti.
issue *see* kaotinakoa.
italic *see* rabe.
itch *see* ngongo.
itching *see* teumaririe.
itinerant *see* mamananga.

J

j *see* ti.
jab *see* **1.** ewara, **2.** kotea, **3.** nekea.
jabber *see* takutaku.
jack *see* kamwemwea.
jackass *see* nanobaba.
jaded *see* manionio.
jagged *see* **1.** kiribeubeu, **2.** wawaikakang.

jam *see* kabetanga.
jammed *see* kabetangaki.
jar *see* **1.** tangibuaka, **2.** bobuaka, **3.** ibutubuto, **4.** kamwaeieia, **5.** karurua, **6.** kebutua.
javelin *see* imbo.
jealous *see* **1.** koko, **2.** rarau, **3.** rau, **4.** rauakina, **5.** bakantang.
jeer *see* **1.** bukinimata, **2.** kareao.
jeopardize *see* karuanikaia.
jerk *see* **1.** notua, **2.** unarira, **3.** burita, **4.** katika.
jest *see* **1.** kareao, **2.** kewe, **3.** manikangare.
jet *see* ti.
jib *see* riakina.
jingle *see* **1.** keke, **2.** takitaki, **3.** tangitang.
jitter *see* takariri.
jittery *see* utikun.
jog *see* **1.** butua, **2.** notua.
join *see* **1.** reita, **2.** roana, **3.** tena, **4.** toma, **5.** katuna, **6.** kabo, **7.** katuta.
joined *see* **1.** tenaki, **2.** tomaki, **3.** roanaki, **4.** reitaki, **5.** katutaki, **6.** katunaki, **7.** kaboaki.
joke *see* **1.** kareio, **2.** manikangare, **3.** mannaoka, **4.** waningarea, **5.** kareao.
jolly *see* **1.** kakukurei, **2.** matanikukurei, **3.** mataningare.
jolt *see* **1.** karurua, **2.** ibutubuto.
jolted *see* **1.** karuruaki, **2.** ibutubutoaki.
josh *see* kareao.
jostle *see* **1.** bukinibaia, **2.** kebutua.
journey *see* **1.** borauakina, **2.** manangia.
joyful *see* **1.** tutuneang, **2.** kukurei, **3.** nanobebete.
jubilant *see* nikierere.
jubilate *see* kimareirei.
judge *see* **1.** motikitaeka, **2.** motiraran, **3.** tauburea.
judicious *see* **1.** mataraoi, **2.** nanowana.
juggle *see* nikarara.
juice *see* tari.
juicy *see* **1.** uaran, **2.** tari, **3.** nenea, **4.** ran, **5.** ranran.
jumble *see* **1.** kabeakoa, **2.** kaiewe.
jumbled *see* **1.** ngao, **2.** tokobuakoako, **3.** mangaongao, **4.** mangao, **5.** kaieweaki, **6.** kabeakoaki, **7.** beako.
jump *see* **1.** inimaki, **2.** kiba, **3.** wew, **4.** ewe.
jumping *see* kiba.
junior *see* karimwi.
just *see* **1.** raoi, **2.** tibwa, **3.** tiba, **4.** ti, **5.** riai, **6.** nanowana, **7.** eti, **8.** bün, **9.** a, **10.** booraoi.
justified *see* karaoiroiaki.
justify *see* karaoiroia.
justly *see* raoi.
jut *see* rebe.
juvenile *see* kiaiai.

K

k *see* ni.
keen *see* 1. matatoka, 2. niniwana, 3. kateke, 4. kakang, 5. kima.
keep *see* 1. tauoa, 2. tuana, 3. taua, 4. tau, 5. tatabuia, 6. rabane, 7. maniman, 8. kawakina.
kept *see* 1. manimanaki, 2. tatabuiaki, 3. tauaki, 4. tauoaki, 5. tuanaki, 6. kawakinaki.
kid *see* ataei.
kidnap *see* 1. reke, 2. konana.
kidnapped *see* 1. rekeaki, 2. konanaki.
kill *see* 1. kamarua, 2. kamatea, 3. tiri, 4. tiringa.
killed *see* 1. kamaruaki, 2. kamateaki, 3. tiringaki.
killer *see* kamatea.
killing *see* kamamate.
kin *see* 1. utu, 2. koraki.
kind *see* 1. akoi, 2. aro, 3. atataiaomata, 4. moringa, 5. tangira, 6. tautata.
kindle *see* 1. kaura, 2. takaro.
kindled *see* 1. takaroaki, 2. kauraki.
kindred *see* 1. koraki, 2. utu.
king *see* 1. karout, 2. katoka, 3. uea.
kiss *see* 1. inga, 2. kaboria, 3. mbwa.
knead *see* 1. kabo, 2. kaboboa, 3. tangana.
knee *see* bubuôniwai.
kneel *see* katorobubua.
knife *see* biti.
knit *see* itutu.
knitted *see* itutuaki.
knives *see* biti.
knobby *see* tabatoatoa.
knock *see* 1. bo, 2. karebwea, 3. karebwerebwe, 4. karutua, 5. oro, 6. tiri, 7. unikaikai.
knot *see* 1. katimoia, 2. warona.
knotted *see* 1. waronaki, 2. katimoiaki.
knotty *see* 1. ribeu, 2. tabatoatoa, 3. tabureka, 4. timoi, 5. tungatunga.
know *see* 1. kina, 2. ataia, 3. ata, 4. ota.
knowing *see* rabakau.
knowledgeable *see* 1. atabai, 2. atataibai.
known *see* 1. takarere, 2. tanoata, 3. otaki, 4. matatoka, 5. kinaki, 6. ataki, 7. ataiaki.

L

l *see* r.
label *see* kanikina.
labelled *see* kanikinaki.

labor *see* 1. mwakuri, 2. kaiaki, 3. kaibekua, 4. môgur, 5. murkuri.
laborious *see* 1. rawawata, 2. makuriana, 3. kamou, 4. karaoana, 5. kanganga.
lace *see* kiritantan.
laced *see* kiritantanaki.
lacerate *see* 1. raebitia, 2. raemangoa, 3. raeraea.
lacerated *see* 1. kirimotimoti, 2. raeraeaki, 3. raebitiaki, 4. raemangoaki.
lack *see* nanoati.
lad *see* ataeinimwani.
laddie *see* ataeinimwane.
lade *see* kamengoa.
ladies *see* naka.
lag *see* 1. waeremwe, 2. babaiwae, 3. aua.
laid *see* 1. kawenea, 2. kaweneaki, 3. neaki.
lame *see* 1. tibitibi, 2. mauku, 3. nimaukuku.
lament *see* 1. tang, 2. ao, 3. ritangia.
lamented *see* 1. ritangiaki, 2. tangaki.
lamp *see* pahia.
land *see* 1. penoua, 2. kawaerakei, 3. aerake, 4. aba, 5. waerake.
languid *see* 1. nanokabakoba, 2. nimamate, 3. nimanan, 4. ntangorengore.
languish *see* kamou.
lank *see* 1. irariki, 2. kairi.
lanky *see* irariki.
lap *see* 1. newea, 2. nira.
lapse *see* 1. kerikaki, 2. toki.
large *see* 1. warebwe, 2. wari, 3. nuku, 4. tuakaei, 5. bâbaki, 6. ati, 7. atamaumau, 8. bûbura.
lash *see* 1. tirimataere, 2. kataerea, 3. orea, 4. robuna.
lass *see* ataeinaine.
lassie *see* ataeinaine.
lasso *see* 1. baua, 2. bauna, 3. matamea.
last *see* 1. mwiniba, 2. tiku, 3. teimatoa, 4. ngke, 5. kaitira, 6. kabanea, 7. kabane, 8. inawiu, 9. kinati.
lasting *see* bongata.
latch *see* kaina.
latched *see* kainaki.
late *see* 1. menai, 2. tamwere, 3. rimwi, 4. remwe, 5. ninga'ngata, 6. mwere, 7. mate, 8. kiriaria, 9. baenikai, 10. nabangkai.
lately *see* 1. ikainapa, 2. kiriaria, 3. nabangkai, 4. rimwi, 5. tiba.
later *see* 1. kiriaria, 2. rumwi, 3. narei, 4. rimwi.
latest *see* 1. bou, 2. kaitira.
laugh *see* ngare.
laughable *see* 1. aokangare, 2. bainingare.
launch *see* 1. kabwaka, 2. moana, 3. kaka, 4. bumoa, 5. matabaiawa.
launder *see* uati.
lavish *see* 1. nurakina, 2. areare, 3. atatainimari, 4. bakatae, 5. kabatia, 6. kamaita.

lay *see* 1. nea, 2. kawenea.

layer *see* 1. kakiriuatao, 2. kareuatao.

layered *see* 1. kakiriuataoaki, 2. kareuataoaki, 3. kiriuatao.

lazy *see* 1. ntorotoro, 2. taningaroti, 3. mautoto, 4. mantokotoko.

lead *see* 1. bumoa, 2. ena, 3. kaira, 4. matana, 5. tautorona, 6. unuana, 7. urukauna, 8. arona.

leading *see* takarere.

leaf *see* banikai.

leak *see* 1. bunong, 2. ranran, 3. raran.

leaky *see* erarán.

lean *see* 1. ranga, 2. taotabo, 3. taona, 4. taiaganoro, 5. rangaie, 6. raben, 7. eiei, 8. rara.

leap *see* ewe.

learn *see* 1. rabakei, 2. reirei, 3. reireinai, 4. kekeiaki, 5. kamatebwai, 6. nora.

learned *see* 1. reireinaiaki, 2. kekeiakiaki, 3. matatoka, 4. noraki, 5. rabakau, 6. rabakeiaki, 7. reireiaki, 8. kamatebwaiaki.

leave *see* 1. tikua, 2. nako, 3. kitana, 4. kau, 5. katuka, 6. biritana, 7. kamemena.

leaves *see* banikai.

leaving *see* nang.

lecture *see* 1. kataetaea, 2. tiringa, 3. takua, 4. boaia, 5. ngkoe.

led *see* 1. kairaki, 2. urukaunaki, 3. unuanaki, 4. matanaki, 5. kaira, 6. irona, 7. enaki, 8. bumoaki, 9. aronaki, 10. tautoronaki.

left *see* 1. kitana, 2. maing, 3. nako, 4. nkona.

leftover *see* katabun.

leg *see* wai.

legged *see* waewae.

legislate *see* tautaeka.

legless *see* nakibaina.

leisurely *see* motirawa.

lend *see* anganako.

lengthen *see* 1. kaananaua, 2. reita.

lengthened *see* 1. reitaki, 2. kaananauaki.

lengthy *see* 1. kakiro, 2. marairai.

lent *see* 1. anganako, 2. anganakoaki.

leper *see* rebera.

less *see* 1. karako, 2. riki.

lessen *see* 1. karakoa, 2. ronna, 3. kauangingia, 4. kakea, 5. kakarakoa, 6. kauarerekea, 7. kakenakoa.

lessened *see* 1. kauarerekeaki, 2. ronnaki, 3. kauangingiaki, 4. karakoaki, 5. kakenakoaki, 6. kakeaki, 7. kakarakoaki.

lessening *see* tanako.

let *see* 1. keaki, 2. ka, 3. kaira, 4. kairaki, 5. kaki, 6. kariaia, 7. kariaiaki, 8. ke.

lethargic *see* 1. mannei, 2. kibara.

level *see* 1. aoraoi, 2. matim, 3. matinnao, 4. tiritoa.

liable *see* nano.

liberal *see* 1. diduarô, 2. tituaraoi, 3. nanouki, 4. kakaianga, 5. atatainimari, 6. akoi, 7. nanomawa.

liberate *see* kainaomata.

liberated *see* kainaomataki.

licentious *see* 1. baitangako, 2. kamwara.

lick *see* 1. kataerea, 2. orea, 3. newenewea, 4. nenge, 5. newea.

licked *see* 1. kataereaki, 2. nengeaki, 3. neweaki, 4. neweneweaki, 5. oreaki.

lie *see* 1. kewea, 2. wene, 3. uaraoa, 4. kewetaia, 5. kewena, 6. kewe, 7. inibao, 8. kewenimakina.

lift *see* 1. katei, 2. ieta, 3. taura, 4. tabeka, 5. mwe, 6. kamwemwea, 7. e, 8. euta, 9. katea.

lifted *see* 1. kateaki, 2. tauraki, 3. tabekaki, 4. mwemwerakeaki, 5. mweaki, 6. kamwemweaki, 7. ietaki, 8. eutaki, 9. mwemwerake.

light *see* 1. kaoura, 2. ninibete, 3. kaura, 4. kauramaka, 5. mwemwe, 6. bete, 7. bebete, 8. bakete, 9. kaota.

lighted *see* 1. kaotaki, 2. kauraki, 3. kauramakaki.

lighten *see* 1. kabakeketea, 2. kabaketea, 3. kabebetea.

lightning *see* tehiti.

lightweight *see* mwemweraoi.

likable *see* kan.

like *see* 1. nika, 2. tiitebo, 3. tangira, 4. tañata, 5. bwain, 6. bura, 7. aiûri, 8. gañga.

liked *see* tangiraki.

likely *see* nano.

limber *see* maonon.

limbless *see* nakibaina.

limited *see* 1. tiatianna, 2. korobaiaki, 3. reme, 4. tare.

limiting *see* tianna.

limp *see* 1. nimaoriori, 2. nimaukuku, 3. turatura, 4. manionio.

line *see* 1. rainia, 2. taman.

lined *see* 1. tamanaki, 2. rain, 3. rainiaki.

linger *see* 1. teitei, 2. tabare, 3. babaenikai, 4. kakaautakia, 5. ingira.

link *see* 1. reita, 2. toma.

linked *see* 1. reitaki, 2. tomaki, 3. tourake.

lip *see* ria.

liquefied *see* 1. kamaraki, 2. ruamakanaki.

liquefy *see* 1. kamara, 2. ruamakana.

liquid *see* 1. neinei, 2. ran, 3. ranran.

listen *see* 1. ongo, 2. kauongo, 3. kakauongo, 4. kakaunongo, 5. ongora.

listless *see* 1. nangoango, 2. nangonango, 3. nrairai.

lit *see* 1. kauramakaki, 2. kaotaki, 3. kaura, 4. kauraki.

litter *see* 1. kamwaraea, 2. kabareka, 3. kamangeange.

littered *see* 1. kabarekaki, 2. kamangeangeaki, 3. kamwaraeaki.

little see **1.** kimotoitoi, **2.** uangini, **3.** titaoutana, **4.** uareereke, **5.** tiko, **6.** makin, **7.** karako, **8.** kakarako, **9.** teutana, **10.** tekinini.
livable see maekanaki.
live see **1.** mweraoi, **2.** maeka, **3.** mai.
lively see **1.** rung, **2.** angang, **3.** inao.
liver see at.
living see maiu.
lizard see bïr.
load see **1.** urakina, **2.** kamengoa, **3.** urake.
loaded see **1.** urakinaki, **2.** urakeaki, **3.** kamengoaki.
loaf see **1.** kakaautakia, **2.** tamweremwere, **3.** timurua.
loafing see taumangang.
loam see buînai.
loathe see riba.
lobster see ûr.
locate see maroaka.
located see **1.** maroakaki, **2.** mena.
lock see kingina.
locked see **1.** in, **2.** kinginaki.
lodge see **1.** kairuwaea, **2.** kamena, **3.** mwenga, **4.** kaiakina.
lofty see **1.** rieta, **2.** rietata.
logical see nanowana.
loiter see **1.** babaenikai, **2.** kakaautakia, **3.** romatoa, **4.** tabara, **5.** taumwere, **6.** teitei, **7.** timurua.
lonely see maroa.
long see **1.** annanau, **2.** marairai, **3.** abwabwaki, **4.** ananau, **5.** wai, **6.** anânau.
look see **1.** noakinak, **2.** tiroa, **3.** tatara, **4.** taku, **5.** no, **6.** nenera, **7.** mata, **8.** kakae, **9.** tara.
looking see taratara.
loose see **1.** matanatana, **2.** matiketike, **3.** tikibuaka, **4.** mwaawa, **5.** matantan, **6.** mariroriro, **7.** mariro, **8.** ing, **9.** marinrin, **10.** teirobaroba, **11.** marin, **12.** matana.
loosen see **1.** kaki, **2.** kamatiketikea, **3.** kamatantana, **4.** kamarinrinna, **5.** kaingingnga, **6.** kabara, **7.** kamatanatana.
loosened see **1.** kamatiketikeaki, **2.** kabaraki, **3.** kaingingngaki, **4.** kakiaki, **5.** kamarinrinnaki, **6.** kamatanatanaki, **7.** kamatantanaki.
loot see **1.** katawe, **2.** taebai.
looted see **1.** kataweaki, **2.** taebaiaki.
lop see **1.** erea, **2.** taera, **3.** tiri.
loquacious see takuarara.
lord see **1.** uea, **2.** katoka, **3.** toka.
lose see **1.** ruo, **2.** kabubua, **3.** kabua, **4.** aiewe, **5.** baka.
lost see **1.** mate, **2.** toitio, **3.** teiruarua, **4.** tabeaki, **5.** ruoaki, **6.** maruaki, **7.** marua, **8.** karua, **9.** kabubuaki, **10.** kabuaki, **11.** kabua, **12.** baka, **13.** aieweaki, **14.** oruak.
loud see **1.** karongoa, **2.** katawa, **3.** kaorakora.

lounge see **1.** timurua, **2.** aoaoria.
lounger see timurua.
louse see touti.
love see **1.** nanona, **2.** nimtangira, **3.** tikurerea, **4.** tangira, **5.** tabunimatea, **6.** kinrangia, **7.** kinanona, **8.** kakinranga, **9.** itangitangiri, **10.** babana, **11.** rantia.
loved see **1.** kinrangiaki, **2.** tikurereaki, **3.** tangiraki, **4.** tabunimateaki, **5.** rantiaki, **6.** nanonaki, **7.** kinanonaki, **8.** kakinrangaki, **9.** itangitangiriaki, **10.** babanaki, **11.** nimtangiraki.
lovely see tamaroa.
loving see nabe.
low see **1.** barara, **2.** rinano, **3.** nano, **4.** ekimôtëta, **5.** mwiniba, **6.** ìninan.
lower see **1.** mwiniba, **2.** tuka, **3.** tikua, **4.** taona, **5.** nna, **6.** katuka, **7.** karuoa, **8.** karinanoa, **9.** karakoa, **10.** kamangora, **11.** kakea, **12.** rinano.
lowered see **1.** karinanoaki, **2.** tikuaki, **3.** taonaki, **4.** nnaki, **5.** tukaki, **6.** mwinibaki, **7.** karakoaki, **8.** kamangoraki, **9.** kakeaki, **10.** katukaki, **11.** karuoaki.
lowest see inanoinano.
lowly see **1.** mangori, **2.** nanorinano.
loyal see kakaonimaki.
lubricate see **1.** bwana, **2.** kabira.
lubricated see **1.** bwanaki, **2.** kabiraki.
lucid see **1.** itiwewe, **2.** matairiki.
lucky see **1.** aoraba, **2.** tekaraoi, **3.** tauraba, **4.** maniwia, **5.** manuia, **6.** neiranraoi.
ludicrous see **1.** kakangare, **2.** kangare.
lukewarm see **1.** abue, **2.** angibue.
lull see **1.** karaua, **2.** kamatua.
lump see **1.** kakiribeubeua, **2.** katimoia.
lumped see **1.** kakiribeubeuaki, **2.** katimoiaki.
lumpy see **1.** buabua, **2.** kiribeubeu, **3.** tabatoatoa, **4.** tungatunga.
lunatic see **1.** tabaua, **2.** rangirang, **3.** ou.
lurch see **1.** rangaranga, **2.** bebei.
lure see **1.** kao, **2.** kariria, **3.** katikurerea.
lurk see **1.** maranoa, **2.** torokaran, **3.** kawa, **4.** karan.
luscious see **1.** kangkang, **2.** nanai, **3.** kaibabaru.
lush see kaibabaru.
lust see **1.** babana, **2.** kaibabaru.
lusterless see warea.
lustrous see **1.** katimaran, **2.** kakanno.
luxurious see **1.** maiureirei, **2.** kakanno.
lye see bokewe.
lying see inibao.

M

m *see* ni.
ma *see* tina.
mad *see* 1. rangirang, 2. tabaua, 3. ou, 4. bononano.
madame *see* nei.
made *see* 1. karaoa, 2. karaoaki, 3. moanaki, 4. nikoaki.
madly *see* rangi.
magician *see* tiakai.
magnanimous *see* 1. nanomawa, 2. nanouki, 3. atainimari.
magnificent *see* 1. bakitoutou, 2. kakanno, 3. tika, 4. tikaua.
magnified *see* katamaroaki.
magnify *see* katamaroa.
maid *see* ataeinaine.
maiden *see* ataeinaine.
maim *see* 1. kaikoaka, 2. kamaukua.
maimed *see* 1. kamaukuaki, 2. kaikoakaki.
main *see* kakanato.
maintain *see* 1. kawakina, 2. rabane, 3. taua.
maintained *see* 1. tauaki, 2. kawakinaki, 3. rabaneaki.
majestic *see* kakaauba.
make *see* 1. karaoa, 2. moana, 3. nikoa.
male *see* mwane.
malevolent *see* nanobuaka.
malformed *see* beu.
malicious *see* 1. buakaka, 2. nanobuaka.
malignant *see* nanobuaka.
malleable *see* maonon.
mallet *see* tip.
maltreat *see* 1. bainikirina, 2. manibuaka, 3. maura.
maltreated *see* 1. bainikirinaki, 2. manibuakaki, 3. mauraki.
mammoth *see* korabaia.
man *see* 1. nao, 2. mwaane, 3. kaira.
manageable *see* takarua.
maneuver *see* 1. kabwea, 2. uamane, 3. urunga.
mangle *see* 1. korokoro, 2. raebaia, 3. korobitia, 4. kamanatua, 5. raebitia.
mangled *see* 1. kamanatuaki, 2. kirimotimoti, 3. korobitiaki, 4. korokoroaki, 5. raebaiaki, 6. raebitiaki.
manifest *see* 1. katereterea, 2. tanoata, 3. kaota.
manifold *see* uatao.
manipulate *see* katitua.
manly *see* nanomane.
manned *see* kairaki.
mannered *see* kawaina.

manufacture *see* 1. kariki, 2. kateibai.
manufactured *see* 1. karikiaki, 2. kateibaiaki.
many *see* 1. auáta, 2. bati, 3. betanga, 4. iteraua, 5. karianako, 6. nimanonganonga, 7. nonga, 8. angi.
mar *see* 1. kabuakaka, 2. kanuka, 3. kamakunakuna.
march *see* 1. Mati, 2. nakomai, 3. nakonako.
mark *see* 1. kawanta, 2. waiteketekea, 3. tamania, 4. m'aneka, 5. katantana, 6. kanikina, 7. bwerea, 8. baiturua, 9. taman.
marked *see* 1. katantanaki, 2. waiteketekeaki, 3. waiteketeke, 4. tamaniaki, 5. tamanaki, 6. mwanekaki, 7. kawantaki, 8. kinawanawa, 9. kanikinaki, 10. bwereaki, 11. baituruaki, 12. kiritantan.
market *see* kaboanako.
maroon *see* katuka.
marred *see* 1. kamakunakunaki, 2. kanukaki, 3. kabuakakaki, 4. nuka.
married *see* 1. bunaki, 2. iein, 3. ieinaki, 4. kakainrouaki, 5. mare, 6. mareaki, 7. uma.
marry *see* 1. buna, 2. mare, 3. kakainroua, 4. iein.
marshy *see* 1. aoneiney, 2. neinei.
marvel *see* mimi.
marvelous *see* 1. tikaua, 2. kakanno, 3. kamimi, 4. tika.
masculine *see* nanomane.
mash *see* 1. katiti, 2. ikua.
mask *see* 1. karaba, 2. rabuna.
masked *see* 1. karabaki, 2. rabunaki.
massacre *see* tiringa.
massage *see* 1. tobi, 2. roromi, 3. riringa, 4. abuabu.
massed *see* ruonako.
massive *see* abakaei.
mast *see* aneang.
master *see* 1. toka, 2. aonikaia, 3. article, 4. korana.
mastered *see* 1. aonikaiaki, 2. koranaki.
masticate *see* 1. kamakerua, 2. kanta, 3. makiro.
mat *see* kie.
match *see* 1. boraoi, 2. botau.
matched *see* 1. boraoi, 2. botauaki, 3. boraoiaki.
mate *see* 1. bu, 2. rao, 3. raom.
matron *see* 1. ainenuma, 2. unaine.
matted *see* 1. beo, 2. rekerua, 3. beako, 4. tabuenga.
mature *see* 1. ikawai, 2. katawaea, 3. tawa.
matured *see* 1. ikawaiaki, 2. katawaeaki.
maul *see* 1. kamanamana, 2. orea.
may *see* 1. kona, 2. Mei.
maybe *see* tao.
me *see* 1. ai, 2. ngai.
meager *see* 1. bakitaia, 2. karako, 3. tare.
mean *see* 1. nanon, 2. tatauti, 3. mautete, 4. kibangebange, 5. kataninga, 6. kakauara, 7. barantauti, 8. bangantauti, 9. banganikou, 10. bakoko, 11. babakanikawai, 12. ioaawa.
meander *see* kakiribabaoua.

meandering *see* kiribabaoua.
means *see* nanon.
measure *see* 1. bataua, 2. uamania, 3. taunari, 4. bairean, 5. bairea, 6. tikona.
measured *see* 1. baireaki, 2. baireanaki, 3. batauaki, 4. taunariaki, 5. tikonaki, 6. uamaniaki.
meat *see* tirigo.
meddle *see* 1. tabarea, 2. tabaretua, 3. karenoa, 4. karemereme, 5. rebetunga.
meddlesome *see* 1. baitabare, 2. banganuaru, 3. rebetunga, 4. tabare.
meddling *see* 1. rebetunga, 2. wanga, 3. tabare, 4. baotabare, 5. banganuaru, 6. tabarebare.
mediate *see* raoiakina.
mediated *see* raoiakinaki.
mediocre *see* teutana.
meditate *see* 1. iango, 2. taku.
meek *see* 1. nanoraoi, 2. nimamanei, 3. inataba.
meet *see* 1. butika, 2. butimaea, 3. ibibiti, 4. inono, 5. kabo, 6. kaitibo, 7. kaurama, 8. wia.
mellow *see* 1. maem, 2. rau.
melt *see* kamara.
melted *see* kamaraki.
menacing *see* rebetunga.
mend *see* 1. bonota, 2. kirikaki, 3. ribata, 4. wanin, 5. wanina.
menstruate *see* teiao.
mention *see* 1. taekina, 2. tanewea.
merciful *see* 1. atataiaomata, 2. nanoanga.
mere *see* 1. makota, 2. ti.
merely *see* 1. pün, 2. ti.
merge *see* 1. reitia, 2. boti.
merry *see* kukurei.
mesmerize *see* kamatakua.
messy *see* bakarae.
metaphoric *see* tarae.
meticulous *see* rino.
middle *see* nûk.
might *see* tao.
mighty *see* nanomane.
migratory *see* kimangare.
mild *see* 1. bebete, 2. maem, 3. nanoraoi.
mildew *see* bwebwe.
mildewed *see* 1. bwebwe, 2. bwebweaki.
mill *see* i.
milled *see* iaki.
million *see* mirion.
mime *see* kaena.
mimic *see* 1. katotonga, 2. katoto, 3. irannano, 4. kaena.
mince *see* 1. tabiria, 2. tawira.
minced *see* 1. tabiriaki, 2. tawiraki.
mind *see* 1. iango, 2. mutiakina, 3. mannanoa, 4. anneanea, 5. kawakina.

minded *see* 1. anneaneaki, 2. iangoaki, 3. kawakinaki, 4. mannanoaki, 5. mutiakinaki.
mindful *see* karaurau.
mingle *see* 1. kaboa, 2. rengana.
miniature *see* teutana.
minister *see* akoa.
minor *see* 1. makota, 2. teutana.
minus *see* karako.
minuscule *see* mangori.
minute *see* 1. miniti, 2. uatingotingo, 3. bingingi, 4. uangini, 5. tingingi.
miraculous *see* kamimi.
mirror *see* 1. katotonga, 2. uamwi.
mirrored *see* 1. katotongaki, 2. uamwiaki.
misbehave *see* 1. tabare, 2. iowawa.
miscarry *see* kabobo.
mischievous *see* 1. benoinoi, 2. iowawa, 3. tabare, 4. tabarebare, 5. be.
misconduct *see* kairerebua.
misconstrue *see* 1. bitabao, 2. kabitaraea.
misdirect *see* kairerebua.
miser *see* 1. kokotaia, 2. bakoko.
miserable *see* 1. kananoanga, 2. kawa, 3. kiengenenge, 4. nangora, 5. rainanoanga, 6. waebaka.
miserly *see* 1. bakoko, 2. komau, 3. kibangebange, 4. komatangitang.
mishandle *see* maura.
mislaid *see* kabuaki.
mislay *see* kabua.
mislead *see* 1. kamaningaki, 2. burebureaki, 3. mamanaki, 4. mamana, 5. bureburea, 6. kairerebua, 7. kairerebuaki, 8. kamaninga.
misleading *see* karuanano.
misplace *see* aiewe.
misplaced *see* aieweaki.
misquote *see* 1. kabitaraea, 2. kamanga.
misrepresent *see* kairerebua.
misrepresented *see* kairerebuaki.
miss *see* 1. nei, 2. tibara, 3. bobaranako, 4. kom, 5. katua, 6. baka, 7. baibao, 8. baibake, 9. aona, 10. tua, 11. biririmwi.
missed *see* 1. baka, 2. tuaki, 3. tibaraki, 4. tarao, 5. komaki, 6. katuaki, 7. biririmwiaki, 8. baibaoaki, 9. baibakeaki, 10. aonaki, 11. bobaranakoaki.
misshapen *see* 1. ribeu, 2. ribeubeu.
missing *see* bua.
misstate *see* 1. kabitaraea, 2. kamanga, 3. kaiewea.
misstep *see* tiba.
mistake *see* 1. airua, 2. kairua, 3. kakairua.
mistaken *see* 1. airuaki, 2. kairuaki, 3. kakairuaki.
mistreat *see* 1. manibuaka, 2. maura, 3. bainikirina.
mistreated *see* 1. manibuakaki, 2. mauraki, 3. bainikirinaki.
mistrust *see* 1. namakin, 2. nanoata.

misty *see* 1. bubu, 2. bubutei, 3. taribubu.
misunderstand *see* 1. ataki, 2. tabara, 3. ataia.
misunderstood *see* 1. ataia, 2. ataiaki, 3. ataki, 4. atakiaki, 5. motibuaka, 6. tabaraki.
mitigate *see* 1. kabaoa, 2. kabebetea, 3. kamarauaka.
mitigated *see* 1. kabaoaki, 2. kabebeteaki, 3. kamarauakaki.
mix *see* 1. kaborere, 2. kairengarenga, 3. rengana, 4. kaboa, 5. kabo, 6. irenganan, 7. tangana, 8. kaboboa.
mixed *see* 1. kaborereaki, 2. tanganaki, 3. rîak, 4. kairengarengaki, 5. kaboboaki, 6. kaboaki, 7. irengananaki, 8. irengan, 9. botau, 10. renganaki.
moan *see* 1. ao, 2. meme, 3. ngira, 4. ngirangira, 5. tangitang, 6. toto.
mob *see* 1. mairiri, 2. nanai, 3. ntanganga.
mock *see* 1. bainikirina, 2. bainingareakina, 3. kaena, 4. kakaenaena, 5. kakanikoa, 6. ngareakina, 7. tinara.
model *see* katoto.
moderate *see* 1. toabara, 2. taubank, 3. nanoraoi, 4. kauakina, 5. kamarara, 6. bao, 7. kakea.
moderated *see* 1. kakeaki, 2. taubankaki, 3. toabaraki, 4. baoaki, 5. kauakinaki, 6. kamararaki.
moderately *see* karaurau.
modern *see* 1. bou, 2. menai, 3. nabangkai.
modest *see* matanikanebu.
modified *see* bitaki.
modify *see* bita.
modulate *see* kauakina.
modulated *see* kauakinaki.
moist *see* waraku.
moisten *see* 1. bururu, 2. karota.
mold *see* aoi.
molded *see* aoiaki.
moldy *see* 1. bwebwe, 2. aoi.
mom *see* tina.
momentary *see* niniwana.
momentous *see* bonganga.
mommy *see* tina.
monitor *see* kinanoa.
monitored *see* kinanoaki.
monk *see* tama.
monopolize *see* 1. baurawata, 2. rawebaia, 3. aonikai.
monotone *see* arara.
monstrous *see* 1. bubura, 2. kakamaku, 3. korabaia, 4. wari.
month *see* aman.
monumental *see* toa.
moody *see* unin.
moon *see* namwakaina.
moonstruck *see* 1. ou, 2. tabaua.
moralize *see* kakarine.
more *see* 1. raka, 2. riki.

morn *see* ingabong.
morning *see* ingabong.
mortal *see* 1. aomata, 2. kamamate.
mortified *see* matara.
most *see* rangi.
mother *see* 1. tina, 2. atsina.
motivated *see* inga.
motley *see* 1. mata, 2. nawanawa.
mottled *see* 1. tanan, 2. waiteketeke, 3. kinawanawa, 4. kiritantan.
mount *see* 1. bumoa, 2. toka.
mountainous *see* mamaunga.
mounted *see* 1. bumoaki, 2. tokaki.
mourn *see* 1. mango, 2. tang.
mournful *see* mango.
mouth *see* 1. bua, 2. poua.
move *see* 1. mamwakuri, 2. rurung, 3. ringa, 4. ningiongio, 5. nimatewetewe, 6. nakonako, 7. nakomai, 8. kamatakiaua, 9. mwamwae, 10. waki, 11. uamumun, 12. kainga, 13. kananobukibuki, 14. ing, 15. maing, 16. kakamwakuri, 17. kamainga, 18. kamakura, 19. kamariroa, 20. kamwaea.
mover *see* inao.
moving *see* turabeau.
much *see* 1. karianako, 2. rang, 3. nonga, 4. ewa, 5. betanga, 6. bati, 7. ati, 8. angi, 9. nimanonganonga.
muddle *see* mantoa.
muddled *see* mantoaki.
muddy *see* 1. bareka, 2. nimana.
muffle *see* kamarurua.
muffled *see* kamaruruaki.
mullet *see* béniaka.
multicolored *see* mata.
multifaceted *see* kiritoatoa.
multiple *see* beroro.
multiplied *see* 1. kamaitanaki, 2. kamaitaki, 3. kabatiaki, 4. kabataki, 5. kabunnaaki.
multiply *see* 1. kabata, 2. kabatia, 3. kabunnaa, 4. kamaita, 5. kamaitan.
mumble *see* wirikirikia.
mummy *see* tina.
munch *see* 1. kakerua, 2. kakerukerua.
mundane *see* mammam.
murder *see* kamarua.
murdered *see* kamaruaki.
murky *see* maewe.
murmur *see* 1. mere, 2. ngo, 3. ngure, 4. ngurengure, 5. wibine.
muscular *see* 1. bumbing, 2. tuaiaia, 3. pumping.
muse *see* 1. kanaeng, 2. mitara, 3. taku.
mush *see* katiti.
must *see* riai.
muster *see* 1. boti, 2. ikota, 3. bobota.

musty *see* 1. buaraku, 2. bukarakara, 3. boibarabara.
mutate *see* taie.
mute *see* kainababu.
mutilated *see* kirimotimoti.
mutinous *see* karitei.
mutiny *see* karitei.
mutter *see* 1. ibengu, 2. wirikiriki.
mutually *see* i.
mysterious *see* 1. kakanaugaki, 2. kinano, 3. kinanonano.
mystified *see* 1. nanomaitiaki, 2. nanououa, 3. nanomaiti, 4. nanokoraki, 5. mantoaki, 6. kananokorakiaki, 7. nanououaki.
mystify *see* 1. kananokoraki, 2. mantoa, 3. nanomaiti, 4. nanououa.

N

nab *see* rawea.
nag *see* 1. mamangaingai, 2. kakai, 3. karawawata.
nail *see* 1. uki, 2. bobitia.
naked *see* 1. bekan, 2. ra.
name *see* 1. ara, 2. arana, 3. tanewea.
named *see* 1. aranaki, 2. taneweaki.
namely *see* okoro.
nap *see* 1. kataomata, 2. matu.
narrate *see* 1. karakina, 2. taekina.
narrow *see* 1. nariki, 2. reme, 3. rerek, 4. wariki, 5. kawaraki, 6. karemea, 7. kawarika.
narrowed *see* 1. karemeaki, 2. kawarikaki.
nasty *see* 1. kamaira, 2. betingaingai, 3. bewawa, 4. buretireti, 5. kakauara.
nationality *see* i.
natty *see* kateke.
naughty *see* 1. be, 2. ioawa, 3. takebono.
nauseous *see* namomara.
navel *see* 1. buta, 2. pouto.
navigable *see* niabuti.
navigate *see* 1. borauakina, 2. ieie, 3. borau, 4. karoroa.
near *see* 1. ekan, 2. ikakan, 3. kaan, 4. kan, 5. na, 6. nang, 7. uramai.
nearby *see* kan.
nearly *see* 1. kaan, 2. ratau, 3. ra, 4. nang, 5. kan, 6. kuri.
neat *see* 1. kakateke, 2. kanikan, 3. kantara.
neck *see* roroa.
need *see* 1. ri, 2. nanoati, 3. ititi, 4. kainnanoa, 5. kainnano.
needed *see* 1. ititiaki, 2. kainnanoa, 3. kainnanoaki, 4. nanoatiaki, 5. riaki.
needle *see* nekea.
needy *see* 1. waebaka, 2. kawa, 3. riai.

negate *see* 1. kaakea, 2. kamatea.
neglect *see* babakaine.
neglected *see* 1. babakaineaki, 2. toronrang.
neglectful *see* kimaung.
negligent *see* kimaung.
negotiate *see* karaoa.
neighbor *see* 1. itabon, 2. rao.
nerveless *see* mamaoriori.
nervous *see* mamaku.
net *see* 1. eri, 2. tiemanea.
netted *see* 1. tiemaneaki, 2. eriaki.
network *see* nibangabanga.
never *see* 1. tuai, 2. aikoa.
new *see* 1. boou, 2. bou, 3. menai, 4. nabangkai, 5. ngkainaba, 6. waeai.
newcomer *see* irua.
newly *see* nabangkai.
next *see* 1. narei, 2. kanroaroa.
nibble *see* 1. katebetebea, 2. tenatenaia.
nice *see* 1. raoiroi, 2. tamaroa, 3. nikoniko, 4. niko, 5. moringa, 6. kateke, 7. kan, 8. tikiraoi.
nick *see* niba.
nicked *see* nibaki.
nigh *see* kan.
night *see* 1. boñ, 2. pong, 3. ro.
nimble *see* 1. babane, 2. takaerere, 3. tabarekai, 4. ninibete, 5. kiangang.
nine *see* 1. louachoua, 2. rua, 3. ruiwa.
ninety *see* 1. houaoupoui, 2. ruabwi.
ninth *see* karuaiwa.
nip *see* 1. kinika, 2. kinikin, 3. nekea.
nix *see* kamatea.
no *see* 1. akea, 2. tiaki, 3. akêa.
noble *see* 1. banuea, 2. katereke, 3. matakanikan.
nocturnal *see* 1. mwemweaero, 2. waero.
nod *see* katow.
nodular *see* timoi.
noise *see* kâkâ.
noisy *see* katawa.
nomadic *see* kimangare.
nonchalant *see* 1. niau, 2. taeremea, 3. nangonango, 4. mannei.
none *see* akea.
noon *see* 1. taouanouk, 2. tonu.
nose *see* pari.
nosy *see* mautete.
not *see* 1. aki, 2. tiaki, 3. tai, 4. iduai, 5. akî, 6. akêa, 7. iak.
notable *see* 1. kakanato, 2. takarere.
notch *see* 1. niba, 2. takoro, 3. kakoroa, 4. boniba, 5. tata.
notched *see* 1. bonibaki, 2. kakoroaki, 3. nibaki, 4. takoroaki, 5. tataki.
note *see* 1. nora, 2. tauburea, 3. namakin, 4. kamatebwai, 5. nanoata.

noted *see* 1. namakinaki, 2. nanoataki, 3. noraki, 4. taubureaki, 5. kamatebwaiaki.
noteworthy *see* atongaki.
nothing *see* akea.
notice *see* 1. kamatebwai, 2. taku, 3. nora, 4. mutiakina, 5. no.
noticed *see* 1. kamatebwaiaki, 2. mutiakinaki, 3. noaki, 4. noraki, 5. takuaki.
notify *see* 1. kaongora, 2. kauka, 3. kaota, 4. katanoata.
notorious *see* nukabebeo.
nourish *see* 1. kanna, 2. tonga.
nourished *see* 1. kannaki, 2. tongaki.
novel *see* 1. bou, 2. nabangkai.
novice *see* kairi.
now *see* ngkai.
noxious *see* 1. kamamate, 2. buakaka.
nude *see* bekan.
nudge *see* 1. bukinibaia, 2. notua.
numb *see* 1. kamatutua, 2. matenruarua, 3. matutu, 4. manio, 5. butae, 6. karikamate, 7. kiriongong.
number *see* 1. wareka, 2. warekia.
numerous *see* 1. bekoko, 2. uanao, 3. maiti, 4. karebun, 5. ibe, 6. ewa, 7. beroro, 8. bati, 9. angi, 10. betuntun.
nun *see* tina.
nurse *see* 1. babako, 2. kammamma, 3. toba.
nursed *see* 1. babakoaki, 2. kammammaki, 3. tobaki.
nutritional *see* kanuai.
nuzzle *see* butubutu.

O

oar *see* bwetua.
obedient *see* 1. ongeaba, 2. taningamarau, 3. inataba.
obese *see* 1. tinebu, 2. kaubiroto.
obey *see* 1. anibana, 2. ongeaba.
object *see* 1. kaberetokoa, 2. tuka.
objective *see* nanowana.
obligate *see* motinnano.
oblige *see* 1. tautata, 2. memerake.
obliging *see* 1. moringa, 2. tautata.
obliterate *see* kamauna.
obliterated *see* kamaunaki.
oblong *see* wai.
obnoxious *see* 1. ioawa, 2. tabare.
obscene *see* 1. kamwara, 2. buretireti, 3. kamaira.
obscure *see* 1. ro, 2. matakao, 3. mamataro, 4. maewe, 5. kamataanoanoa, 6. karoa.

observe *see* 1. tara, 2. matauakina, 3. tiroa, 4. tataumanta, 5. taratara, 6. taku, 7. taobura, 8. matauna, 9. no.
observed *see* 1. taoburaki, 2. tiroaki, 3. tataumantaki, 4. taraki, 5. takuaki, 6. noaki, 7. mataunaki, 8. matauakinaki, 9. tarataraki.
observer *see* kinnano.
obsessed *see* 1. keinano, 2. ririka.
obstinate *see* 1. bobono, 2. nanomatoa, 3. kirinikamate, 4. kanene, 5. buburamaiu, 6. inamatoa.
obstruct *see* 1. bonota, 2. kareketata, 3. katabea, 4. katabukirurunga, 5. nongoa, 6. tuka, 7. witoko.
obstructed *see* 1. kibono, 2. tukaki, 3. nongoaki, 4. tabukirurunga, 5. witokoaki, 6. katabeaki, 7. kareketataki, 8. bonotaki, 9. bono, 10. katabukirurungaki, 11. tanibaba.
obtain *see* 1. karekea, 2. reke, 3. tabuaetia, 4. taua.
obtainable *see* rota.
obtrusive *see* baekeke.
obtuse *see* botitibaua.
obvious *see* 1. maroaka, 2. takarere, 3. teretere.
occasional *see* tabetai.
occasionally *see* tabetai.
occupied *see* 1. kakai, 2. tana, 3. tabe, 4. rangarangatau, 5. biriaki, 6. matabaeaki, 7. mwakuriaki.
occupy *see* 1. biria, 2. matabae, 3. mwakuri.
occur *see* riki.
ocean *see* tari.
odd *see* 1. baikoraki, 2. toara, 3. manenanti, 4. kamimi, 5. bobuaka, 6. kameio.
odious *see* kabe.
off *see* 1. mai, 2. man.
offend *see* 1. bure, 2. tinara, 3. nokua, 4. kanaengai.
offended *see* 1. nokuaki, 2. tinaraki, 3. nanobuaka, 4. mwerengau, 5. matauningananti, 6. kanaengaiaki, 7. kanaeng, 8. bureaki, 9. unuara.
offensive *see* buaka.
offer *see* 1. anga, 2. angaanga, 3. kaonoa, 4. mweaka.
offhand *see* taeremea.
offspring *see* ataei.
oil *see* 1. bâ, 2. kamaratiarati, 3. kamanenaka.
oiled *see* 1. kamanenakaki, 2. kamaratiaratiaki, 3. maneouna, 4. mara, 5. maratirati.
oily *see* 1. maete, 2. manoa.
okay *see* 1. eeng, 2. ke.
old *see* 1. kara, 2. karongo, 3. mane, 4. nabawe, 5. ikawai.
older *see* ririmoa.
omit *see* 1. katikua, 2. aona, 3. kamanang, 4. manuoka, 5. maninga.
on *see* kariba.
once *see* taina.

one *see* 1. te, 2. tamanna, 3. tenana, 4. teuana, 5. touhana.

onerous *see* kamou.

only *see* 1. pü, 2. ti.

onward *see* 1. kanenei, 2. waki.

ooze *see* 1. katumaua, 2. katutua, 3. takaburi, 4. tu, 5. buro.

open *see* 1. moana, 2. tangaina, 3. uri, 4. uretatanga, 5. ure, 6. uki, 7. tangenge, 8. anaia, 9. kaure, 10. kauka, 11. bwenaua, 12. boua, 13. benga, 14. uka, 15. kaurea.

opened *see* 1. kaureaki, 2. ureaki, 3. ukiaki, 4. moanaki, 5. kaukaki, 6. bouaki, 7. bengaki, 8. benga, 9. bangabanga, 10. ukaki, 11. bwenauaki.

operate *see* 1. mwakuri, 2. mwakuria, 3. karaoa.

opponent *see* kairiribai.

oppose *see* 1. kauntabama, 2. kauna, 3. waitotokoa, 4. waewae, 5. untaba, 6. rawa, 7. mangamanga, 8. ekara, 9. bitara, 10. kaunikai, 11. karitei, 12. kaitoana, 13. kabitara, 14. iwai, 15. kauntaba.

opposed *see* 1. kauntabaki, 2. kauntabamaki, 3. mangamangaki, 4. rawaki, 5. untabaki, 6. waitotokoaki, 7. kateinang, 8. waewaeaki, 9. kaunaki, 10. kariteiaki, 11. kaitoanaki, 12. kabitaraki, 13. iwaiaki, 14. ekaraki, 15. bitaraki, 16. kaunikaiaki.

opposing *see* tinaubati.

opposite *see* 1. kaitoan, 2. bitara, 3. kabitara.

oppress *see* 1. mwanibuaka, 2. karawawata, 3. aonikaia, 4. bainikirina, 5. kamengoa.

oppressed *see* 1. aonikaiaki, 2. bainikirinaki, 3. kamengoaki, 4. karawawataki, 5. mwanibuakaki.

oppressive *see* 1. käkaña, 2. kamou, 3. nanokawa.

opt *see* rine.

optimistic *see* uamoa.

optimum *see* moaniba.

opulent *see* 1. kaubwai, 2. kaubai.

or *see* ke.

orange *see* aoranti.

orbit *see* mronron.

order *see* 1. kaoa, 2. kaooa, 3. mwiokoa, 4. ootana, 5. tua.

ordered *see* 1. ootanaki, 2. tuaki, 3. kaoaki, 4. kaooaki, 5. mwiokoaki.

ordinarily *see* tataneiai.

ordinary *see* kabuta.

organize *see* 1. baire, 2. urukauna.

organized *see* 1. baireaki, 2. urukaunaki.

originally *see* moaniba.

originate *see* maroaka.

oscillate *see* 1. tietie, 2. tio, 3. tie, 4. tiotio, 5. rabeniben, 6. kabei, 7. ranea.

oscillating *see* ranea.

ostentatious *see* rietata.

ostracize *see* tininanikua.

other *see* tabuea.

out *see* 1. man, 2. nako.

outbid *see* 1. ruomaraterakeaki, 2. ruomaraterake.

outcast *see* 1. itinaniku, 2. katabun, 3. manenikai.

outclass *see* kamaterea.

outcry *see* kâkâ.

outdo *see* 1. kameterea, 2. kamaterea.

outdoors *see* tinaniku.

outer *see* matao.

output *see* kamaria.

outrageous *see* kakangare.

outrigger *see* rama.

outright *see* nabangkai.

outside *see* matao.

outstanding *see* 1. bakora, 2. materetere, 3. takarere.

over *see* 1. ao, 2. manga, 3. riaon, 4. tiera.

overabundant *see* tao.

overbid *see* 1. turabwi, 2. turabwiaki.

overburden *see* katabaruarua.

overburdened *see* 1. katabaruaruaki, 2. tabarua.

overcast *see* 1. nubono, 2. tanibabu.

overcharge *see* 1. bora, 2. kamataraea, 3. bomatoa.

overcome *see* 1. riaonikai, 2. tokarakeaki, 3. tokaki, 4. toka, 5. taonaki, 6. taona, 7. riaonikaiaki, 8. tokarake, 9. kiribambanta, 10. baimatoaki, 11. baimatoa, 12. aonikaiaki, 13. aonikaia, 14. aona, 15. aonaki, 16. kiribambantaki.

overeat *see* buabeka.

overexcited *see* kanimarangrangaki.

overfill *see* kataoa.

overflow *see* 1. babaro, 2. tatao, 3. takaburi, 4. koburakea, 5. koburake, 6. kataoa, 7. kataoatia.

overflowing *see* 1. aitao, 2. koburaken, 3. tabakurakura, 4. tao.

overhear *see* kakauongo.

overjoyed *see* kanimarangrangaki.

overload *see* 1. kamengoa, 2. taotabo, 3. katabakurakura.

overloaded *see* 1. kamengoaki, 2. katabakurakuraki, 3. tabakurakura, 4. taotaboaki.

overlook *see* 1. manuoka, 2. manuokina, 3. noakinak.

overlooked *see* 1. manuokaki, 2. manuokinaki, 3. noakinakaki.

overpower *see* kataea.

overpowered *see* kataeaki.

overpowering *see* kataea.

overprice *see* 1. bomatoa, 2. bora, 3. kamataraea.

overpriced *see* 1. bomatoaki, 2. boraki, 3. kamataraeaki, 4. matera.

overripe *see* 1. baka, 2. mori.

overrun *see* 1. kamaterea, 2. kamatereaki, 3. baroakina, 4. baroakinaki.

oversee *see* 1. noakinak, 2. tararuaia.

overseer *see* 1. katitiro, 2. katoka, 3. mataniwi.

oversleep *see* matunako.
overstate *see* maninrongorongo.
overstated *see* maninrongorongoaki.
overstay *see* tikuroaroa.
overstep *see* 1. biriao, 2. riaoa.
overtake *see* oa.
overturn *see* 1. kabaraka, 2. karanga, 3. ranga.
overturned *see* 1. kabarakaki, 2. karangaki, 3. rangaki.
overwhelm *see* 1. baroa, 2. kainakoa, 3. kamauna, 4. kateinang, 5. kiribambanta, 6. taona.
overwhelmed *see* 1. kamaunaki, 2. taonaki, 3. mimitoiaki, 4. kiribambantaki, 5. kainakoaki, 6. baroaki, 7. kateinangaki, 8. kateinang.
overwhelming *see* kateinang.
overwork *see* 1. kaibekura, 2. mengo.
own *see* 1. babaina, 2. baibai, 3. baina, 4. bwaina, 5. karekea.
owned *see* 1. baibaiaki, 2. karekeaki, 3. bainaki, 4. babainaki, 5. bwainaki.

P

pa *see* karo.
pace *see* 1. mwanika, 2. nakonako, 3. rakata, 4. rangata.
pacific *see* nanoraoi.
pacify *see* 1. karaua, 2. riborika.
pack *see* 1. batia, 2. ninira, 3. nanai, 4. kimra, 5. kakeboa.
packed *see* 1. batiaki, 2. kakeboaki, 3. kariba, 4. kimraki, 5. kimri, 6. nanai, 7. nanaiaki, 8. niniraki, 9. ribaba, 10. takoko.
paddle *see* 1. bukibuki, 2. poêtua, 3. poenatma, 4. o, 5. burunna, 6. bwetua.
paddler *see* too.
pagan *see* bekan.
page *see* anoano.
paged *see* anoanoaki.
paid *see* 1. kaboa, 2. kaboaki, 3. ronaki.
pain *see* 1. mengo, 2. kamaraka.
pained *see* 1. mengoaki, 2. kamarakaki.
painful *see* 1. kamamate, 2. kamaraki, 3. kanganga, 4. maraki, 5. marakiraki.
paint *see* 1. rebua, 2. tana, 3. timua.
painted *see* 1. timuaki, 2. rebuaki, 3. tanaki, 4. timu.
painting *see* ben.
paired *see* kiriuous.
pal *see* rao.
palatable *see* 1. kangkang, 2. nanai.
pale *see* 1. baang, 2. kiwarawara, 3. maewe, 4. mai, 5. maii, 6. taetoba, 7. tawere.
palpable *see* maroaka.

palpitate *see* 1. bukibuki, 2. ruberube, 3. kanebu.
paltry *see* 1. mangori, 2. teutana.
pamper *see* 1. kamona, 2. kaniko, 3. nabea.
pampered *see* 1. kamonaki, 2. kanikoaki, 3. nabeaki.
pandanus *see* tou.
panel *see* bwabwa.
panhandle *see* mange.
panic *see* 1. kaitonginakoa, 2. tanomaki.
panicked *see* 1. kaitonginakoaki, 2. tanomakiaki, 3. itonginako.
panicky *see* itonginako.
pant *see* ikemoro.
parade *see* 1. kakaeutakia, 2. nakomai, 3. tabangaea.
paradoxical *see* kabitara.
paralyze *see* kamaterangaea.
paralyzed *see* 1. kamaterangaeaki, 2. nakibaina.
parasitic *see* mamataki.
parcel *see* ninira.
parched *see* 1. mautakaroro, 2. bataka.
pare *see* tea.
parent *see* natina.
park *see* tei.
parked *see* teiaki.
parried *see* 1. kakaroaki, 2. katuaki, 3. rereaki, 4. totokaki, 5. tukaki.
parry *see* 1. totoka, 2. tuka, 3. katua, 4. kakaro, 5. rerea.
parsimonious *see* marengau.
part *see* kau.
partake *see* 1. taeka, 2. buokanamarake, 3. buokanibwai.
parted *see* 1. tamruru, 2. kararoaki, 3. kauaki.
partial *see* 1. nanoibwai, 2. tabaitera, 3. tabeitera.
particular *see* 1. okoro, 2. rino, 3. ronorino, 4. banganrino, 5. beberino, 6. berino.
particularly *see* 1. ngak, 2. okoro.
partner *see* 1. bu, 2. rao.
party *see* 1. aomata, 2. koraki, 3. botaki, 4. kamaroro.
pass *see* 1. raranginako, 2. tekena, 3. rimwi, 4. ri, 5. ibibiti, 6. rere, 7. ngka, 8. kiria, 9. kau, 10. kataoati, 11. bobaranako, 12. katibanakoa.
passionate *see* 1. ngeta, 2. unin.
passive *see* kabuingoingo.
past *see* 1. ngkekei, 2. tarao.
paste *see* anoano.
pastor *see* minita.
patch *see* 1. bonota, 2. kabonota, 3. ribata.
patched *see* 1. bonotaki, 2. kabonotaki, 3. ribataki.
pathetic *see* matanikananoanga.
patient *see* 1. aoraki, 2. nanoraoi.
patrol *see* matana.
patter *see* 1. tatatata, 2. witata.
paunchy *see* kaubiroto.

pause *see* **1.** iraaua, **2.** motirawa, **3.** nawa, **4.** tiku.
pay *see* **1.** kaboa, **2.** rona.
peace *see* rô.
peaceable *see* **1.** nanorau, **2.** nimamanei.
peaceful *see* **1.** rau, **2.** nanorau, **3.** maem, **4.** mweraoi, **5.** nanoraoi.
peaked *see* **1.** kimai, **2.** taetoba.
peal *see* **1.** tang, **2.** tangitang.
pebbles *see* atama.
peck *see* **1.** kateba, **2.** katebetebe, **3.** katebetebea.
peculiar *see* manenanti.
pee *see* **1.** maimai, **2.** mim.
peek *see* kaninganinga.
peel *see* **1.** kara, **2.** karia.
peeled *see* **1.** karaki, **2.** kariaki, **3.** nibarabara.
peeling *see* taenananga.
peevish *see* **1.** noku, **2.** tabureka, **3.** unin, **4.** kameme, **5.** kinokunoku, **6.** nanoun.
pelt *see* oro.
penetrate *see* **1.** karibua, **2.** karina, **3.** karinakoa, **4.** katekea, **5.** maro, **6.** rawana, **7.** rin, **8.** tania.
penetrating *see* **1.** ninia, **2.** nano.
penis *see* kapanga.
penitent *see* **1.** raraoma, **2.** mango.
penniless *see* **1.** iti, **2.** waebaka.
penurious *see* taut.
people *see* **1.** aomata, **2.** I, **3.** kân.
peppery *see* **1.** nanorake, **2.** nanoun.
perceive *see* **1.** namakina, **2.** nanoata, **3.** nora, **4.** maroaka, **5.** kamatebwai, **6.** kina, **7.** namakin.
perceived *see* **1.** namakinaki, **2.** kamatebwaiaki, **3.** nanoataki, **4.** maroakaki, **5.** kinaki, **6.** noraki.
perch *see* **1.** tiku, **2.** tikura.
perchance *see* tao.
perching *see* kamatine.
percolate *see* raran.
perfect *see* **1.** tangare, **2.** tabanin, **3.** rerei, **4.** kakoroa, **5.** maotorrikiriki.
perfected *see* **1.** kakoroaki, **2.** maotorrikirikiaki.
perfectly *see* bon.
perforate *see* **1.** katekea, **2.** rawana, **3.** una.
perforated *see* **1.** kawarawara, **2.** rawanaki, **3.** nibanga, **4.** unaki, **5.** katekeaki, **6.** bangabanga, **7.** kinongo, **8.** kibangabanga.
perform *see* **1.** kamataku, **2.** karaoa, **3.** katanga.
perhaps *see* tao.
perilous *see* kaoanikai.
perish *see* **1.** mate, **2.** mauna.
permit *see* kataua.
permitted *see* **1.** kariaiaki, **2.** kariaiakaki.
pernicious *see* buakaka.
perpendicular *see* bebentekura.
perplex *see* **1.** kamatakiaua, **2.** kananokoraki, **3.** katangaua, **4.** nanomaiti, **5.** nanououa.

perplexed *see* **1.** matakiaua, **2.** tangaua, **3.** nanououa, **4.** nanououaki, **5.** nanomaitiaki, **6.** nanomaiti, **7.** nanokoraki, **8.** auba, **9.** karikaua, **10.** kananokorakiaki, **11.** kaminoa, **12.** riba, **13.** kamatakiauaki, **14.** iraaua, **15.** katangauaki.
persecute *see* bainikirina.
persevere *see* **1.** tebonengenenge, **2.** botuakina.
persevering *see* **1.** nanomaka, **2.** nanomatoatoa.
persist *see* katinono.
persistent *see* **1.** rarango, **2.** nimroroko, **3.** nanomaka, **4.** botuakina, **5.** katinono.
perspicacious *see* mamata.
perspicuous *see* **1.** matairiki, **2.** wanawana.
perspire *see* maono.
perspiring *see* **1.** barara, **2.** maong, **3.** maono.
persuade *see* kairoroa.
pertinacious *see* nanomaka.
pertinent *see* bonganga.
perturb *see* **1.** kananora, **2.** kamatakiaua.
perturbed *see* **1.** kamatakiauaki, **2.** kananoraki, **3.** matakiaua.
pervert *see* kaubunranga.
perverted *see* kaubunrangaki.
pester *see* **1.** kakai, **2.** karawawata.
pestered *see* **1.** kakaiaki, **2.** karawawataki.
petition *see* bubuti.
petulant *see* **1.** nanorake, **2.** ueke, **3.** nanoun, **4.** kiura, **5.** reberake.
philanthropic *see* kakaianga.
pick *see* **1.** anai, **2.** iko, **3.** kinika, **4.** moaniba, **5.** rine, **6.** rinea.
picnic *see* kanabuaka.
pierce *see* **1.** rin, **2.** wai, **3.** waibora, **4.** una, **5.** katekea, **6.** kateka, **7.** imita, **8.** ewara, **9.** waea, **10.** rawana.
pierced *see* **1.** teka, **2.** waiboraki, **3.** waiaki, **4.** waeaki, **5.** unaki, **6.** teke, **7.** ewaraki, **8.** bangabanga, **9.** rawanaki, **10.** katekeaki, **11.** katekaki, **12.** imitaki, **13.** rinaki, **14.** tiki.
pile *see* **1.** karuataoa, **2.** kareuatao, **3.** baobao, **4.** kakiriuatao.
piled *see* **1.** kiriuatao, **2.** nonoaba, **3.** maru, **4.** kiruatao, **5.** kareuataoaki, **6.** kakiriuataoaki, **7.** baki, **8.** karuataoaki.
pilfer *see* **1.** ira, **2.** iraea, **3.** katawe, **4.** kimoa, **5.** rawebaia.
pillage *see* taebai.
pillaged *see* taebaiaki.
pilot *see* **1.** karoroa, **2.** matana.
pinch *see* **1.** kinikini, **2.** kinka, **3.** kin, **4.** katawe, **5.** kinra, **6.** kinika.
pinched *see* **1.** kinraki, **2.** kataweaki, **3.** kinaki, **4.** kinikaki, **5.** kinkaki.
pining *see* mamara.
pink *see* **1.** taribobo, **2.** uramai, **3.** renga.

piquant *see* tena.
pirate *see* katawe.
pit *see* inai.
pitch *see* 1. kare, 2. karekare.
pitched *see* 1. kareaki, 2. karekareaki.
piteous *see* matanikananoanga.
pitiable *see* matanikananoanga.
pitiful *see* matanikananoanga.
pitted *see* 1. kirimaruarua, 2. nimatamata.
pity *see* nanoanga.
pitying *see* nanoanga.
place *see* 1. nea, 2. ui, 3. katuka, 4. kamemena, 5. kamena, 6. katoka.
placed *see* 1. neaki, 2. kamemenaki, 3. tikuaki, 4. katukaki, 5. katokaki, 6. kamenaki.
placid *see* 1. maem, 2. nanoraoi, 3. rau, 4. ariki.
plain *see* 1. boraoi, 2. maroaka, 3. tere, 4. aomatata, 5. aoraoi, 6. borababaua.
plaint *see* maen.
plait *see* kamatana.
plan *see* 1. buata, 2. iangomaka, 3. taboniwia.
plane *see* 1. boraitia, 2. tirikai, 3. karia, 4. burenia, 5. kaboraoa.
plank *see* rai.
planned *see* 1. kaboraoaki, 2. boraitiaki, 3. taboniwiaki, 4. tirikaiaki, 5. kariaki, 6. iangomakaki, 7. iangoaki, 8. buataki, 9. bureniaki.
plant *see* 1. katei, 2. unika.
planted *see* unikaki.
plaster *see* rebua.
plastered *see* rebuaki.
playful *see* makei.
plead *see* 1. onon, 2. katiatia, 3. bubuti.
pleasant *see* 1. kukurei, 2. moringa, 3. raba, 4. kan.
please *see* 1. kakukureia, 2. taiaoka.
pleased *see* 1. kakukureiaki, 2. kukurei.
pleasing *see* 1. kan, 2. moaraoi.
pleasurable *see* kukurei.
pleasure *see* 1. wimamuai, 2. tautata.
pleat *see* 1. kamanunua, 2. kamumun.
pleated *see* 1. kabatutu, 2. kamanunuaki, 3. kamumunaki, 4. manu.
pledge *see* 1. motinnano, 2. nama, 3. tuea.
pledged *see* 1. motinnanoaki, 2. namaki, 3. tueaki.
plenteous *see* kimarimari.
plenty *see* 1. nonga, 2. kariara, 3. areare, 4. taotira.
pliable *see* 1. benono, 2. makone, 3. maonon, 4. nanotau, 5. nimaenen, 6. omaoma, 7. raenen.
plight *see* berita.
pluck *see* 1. burita, 2. kinika.
plucked *see* 1. kinikaki, 2. buritaki.
plug *see* tungana.
plugged *see* tunganaki.

plump *see* 1. kamarika, 2. kaubiroto, 3. marika, 4. tuabebeku.
plunder *see* 1. bubai, 2. kuribwaia, 3. tabwaia, 4. taebai, 5. tiriobora, 6. urua.
plundered *see* 1. kuribwaiaki, 2. tirioboraki, 3. uruaki, 4. bubaiaki, 5. taebaiaki, 6. tabwaiaki.
plunge *see* 1. tebona, 2. ewewe, 3. inako, 4. rerea, 5. tebo.
plural *see* berurare.
point *see* 1. koto, 2. taima, 3. kotea.
pointed *see* 1. tarimarima, 2. kakang, 3. waikakang, 4. wai, 5. tahina, 6. kawete, 7. aweawe, 8. reka.
poise *see* kamwaneaua.
poised *see* kamwaneauaki.
poisonous *see* 1. kabutika, 2. kamamate, 3. nganga.
policeman *see* boreitiman.
polish *see* 1. karaneanea, 2. karanea, 3. ranebonebo, 4. kamarana, 5. ire, 6. irea, 7. karaneboneboa.
polished *see* 1. karaneaneaki, 2. raneboneboaki, 3. maratirati, 4. maran, 5. maborabora, 6. karaneboneboaki, 7. karaneaki, 8. kamaranaki, 9. ireaki, 10. katimaran.
polite *see* 1. karinerine, 2. aboabo.
pollute *see* 1. kamwaraea, 2. kabareka, 3. kamantoa.
polluted *see* 1. kabarekaki, 2. kamantoaki, 3. kamwaraeaki.
polyhedral *see* kiritoatoa.
pond *see* ni.
ponder *see* 1. iangoa, 2. karekea.
ponderous *see* 1. rawawata, 2. rawatakaei.
poor *see* 1. matanikananoanga, 2. toronrang, 3. waebaka, 4. rarikin, 5. kawa, 6. akikaubwai, 7. kainnano, 8. kiengenenge.
pop *see* 1. karebwerebwe, 2. karo, 3. rebwe, 4. tebe.
populate *see* kaina.
populated *see* kainaki.
population *see* aomata.
populous *see* aomata.
porpoise *see* eirioui.
port *see* 1. urake, 2. uota.
portion *see* 1. raeakina, 2. tabeuta.
portly *see* kaubiroto.
pose *see* kakaeutakia.
position *see* katoka.
positive *see* 1. kaeng, 2. koaua.
positively *see* ngaiangaia.
possess *see* 1. bwaina, 2. kananonibaia, 3. babaina, 4. baibai.
possible *see* konaki.
possibly *see* tao.
post *see* kai.
posterior *see* 1. kiriaria, 2. rimwi.
posture *see* teitei.
potent *see* nanomane.
potential *see* konaki.

pounce *see* 1. ewewerake, 2. kabara, 3. rerebakara.
pound *see* 1. ikua, 2. touariki, 3. ikuiku, 4. kamantintia.
pour *see* 1. atoa, 2. babaro, 3. baroakina, 4. kabaroa, 5. kabwaroa, 6. karanga, 7. nuraki, 8. nurakina.
poured *see* 1. karangaki, 2. kabwaroaki, 3. nurakinaki, 4. atoaki, 5. baroakinaki, 6. nurakiaki, 7. babaroaki, 8. kabaroaki.
pout *see* 1. kabioa, 2. kabutu.
powder *see* 1. maeka, 2. tourika.
powdered *see* 1. maekaki, 2. tourikaki.
powdery *see* bubu.
powerful *see* 1. mamwka, 2. nanomane, 3. korakora, 4. kona.
practical *see* maneuna.
practice *see* 1. atakin, 2. kataneiai.
practiced *see* 1. atakinaki, 2. kataneiaiaki.
practise *see* kataneiai.
practised *see* kataneiaiaki.
pragmatic *see* banganuaru.
praise *see* 1. kamanraoia, 2. kamoa, 3. karerei, 4. neboa, 5. nebonebo.
prance *see* kirei.
prattle *see* wibino.
pray *see* tataro.
precarious *see* karenga.
precede *see* 1. biririmoa, 2. rimoa, 3. taumoa.
preceding *see* kiritabaniban.
precious *see* 1. burenibai, 2. kakawaki, 3. kawaki, 4. manena.
precipitate *see* 1. kaiia, 2. karau.
precipitated *see* 1. karauaki, 2. kaiiaki.
precise *see* 1. maitin, 2. okoro.
precisely *see* 1. maitin, 2. okoro.
preclude *see* 1. taokabia, 2. tuka.
preconceive *see* taukirikiri.
preconceived *see* taukirikiriaki.
predicate *see* taekina.
predict *see* 1. karamakina, 2. mamata.
predicted *see* 1. karamakinaki, 2. mamataki.
predominate *see* arona.
prefer *see* 1. tangirariki, 2. binenga, 3. rine.
preferred *see* 1. rineaki, 2. tangirarikiaki.
pregnant *see* 1. bigúgu, 2. bikoukou.
prehistoric *see* nabawe.
premeditate *see* kantaningaki.
premeditated *see* 1. kantaningaki, 2. kantaningakiaki.
premiere *see* moaniba.
premium *see* moaniba.
preoccupied *see* 1. keinano, 2. taberua.
prepare *see* 1. katauraoi, 2. kaoraia, 3. abina, 4. katauraoa, 5. kataenang.

prepared *see* 1. katauraoiaki, 2. tauraoi, 3. katauraoaki, 4. kataenangaki, 5. kaoraiaki, 6. abinaki.
prescribe *see* tua.
prescribed *see* tuaki.
present *see* 1. angangana, 2. ngkainaba, 3. ngkai, 4. kateretere, 5. katerea, 6. ikai, 7. kaonoa, 8. angana, 9. kaota.
presented *see* 1. kaonoaki, 2. kaotaki, 3. katereaki, 4. kateretereaki.
presently *see* abanaba.
preserve *see* 1. rabwana, 2. taoru, 3. rabane, 4. kawakina, 5. botuakina.
preserved *see* 1. kawakinaki, 2. rabaneaki, 3. rabwanaki, 4. taoruaki, 5. botuakinaki.
preserving *see* romatoa.
preside *see* 1. atuna, 2. kautu.
press *see* 1. taona, 2. tena, 3. taonanoa, 4. taonakia, 5. taoakai, 6. kona, 7. karibak, 8. katuru, 9. taokai.
pressed *see* 1. taonakiaki, 2. taonanoaki, 3. taonaki, 4. taokaiaki, 5. riba, 6. konaki, 7. karibakaki, 8. katuruaki, 9. tenaki, 10. taoakaiaki.
pressure *see* kanenea.
prestidigitator *see* tiakai.
presume *see* kantaninga.
presumptuous *see* 1. remereme, 2. kantaninga.
pretend *see* 1. baka, 2. bakaea, 3. bitanikai, 4. bwaka.
pretentious *see* 1. roroutake, 2. ririere, 3. rietata, 4. kamoamoa, 5. tete.
prettily *see* reirei.
pretty *see* 1. botonaine, 2. kakateke, 3. kateke, 4. matakanikan, 5. rangi, 6. tamaroa, 7. tika, 8. tiko.
prevail *see* 1. toka, 2. aonikai.
prevailing *see* toka.
prevalent *see* moa.
prevent *see* tuka.
previously *see* ngkoa.
prey *see* kokona.
priceless *see* kakawaki.
prick *see* 1. kinra, 2. nekea, 3. waea, 4. wai, 5. waitekea.
prickly *see* kakang.
priest *see* 1. tîboña, 2. berebitero, 3. tama.
prim *see* kateke.
primarily *see* moa.
primary *see* moa.
prime *see* 1. matamane, 2. moaniba.
princely *see* banuea.
principal *see* 1. headteacher, 2. rabata.
principled *see* boto.
print *see* 1. boretia, 2. bweretia.
printed *see* 1. boretiaki, 2. bweretiaki.
prize *see* kaotabaea.

pro *see* tairaoi.
probable *see* nano.
probably *see* kona.
proceed *see* **1.** nako, **2.** waki, **3.** wakina.
process *see* katiki.
processed *see* **1.** katikiaki, **2.** kawairinan.
proclaim *see* **1.** takaeakina, **2.** takaka.
proclaimed *see* **1.** takaeakinaki, **2.** takakaki.
procrastinate *see* kiriaria.
procreate *see* **1.** kariki, **2.** karika, **3.** kakariki.
procure *see* **1.** kamariboa, **2.** karekea, **3.** rawea, **4.** rawebai, **5.** rawebaia.
prodigal *see* bakatae.
produce *see* **1.** kamaria, **2.** kariki, **3.** waki.
produced *see* **1.** karikiaki, **2.** wakiaki, **3.** kamariaki.
producer *see* kimarimari.
productive *see* kimarimari.
profess *see* kaotiota.
professional *see* bati.
proficient *see* **1.** bairaoi, **2.** rabakau, **3.** taneiai.
profit *see* **1.** kamateraoa, **2.** kaoraba.
profitable *see* **1.** maneuna, **2.** materaoi.
profitless *see* manouna.
profound *see* **1.** kinano, **2.** kinanonano.
profuse *see* **1.** ewa, **2.** kariara, **3.** karuonako.
prognosticate *see* **1.** bukinanganga, **2.** kaiwa.
progress *see* **1.** nako, **2.** rikirake, **3.** waki.
progressive *see* buti.
prohibit *see* **1.** kraoan, **2.** tuka, **3.** mabu, **4.** kateikai, **5.** kataburorokoa, **6.** kamabu, **7.** tabua.
prohibited *see* **1.** kamabuaki, **2.** kataburorokoaki, **3.** kateikaiaki, **4.** kraoanaki, **5.** mabu, **6.** mabuaki, **7.** tabu, **8.** tabuaki, **9.** tukaki.
project *see* **1.** rine, **2.** tewe, **3.** rebe, **4.** tewea.
projected *see* **1.** rebeaki, **2.** rineaki, **3.** teweaki.
prolific *see* kimarimari.
prolong *see* **1.** reita, **2.** witokonaua.
prolonged *see* **1.** reitaki, **2.** witokonauaki.
promenade *see* nakomai.
prominent *see* **1.** mamaka, **2.** takarere.
promiscuous *see* **1.** karebun, **2.** renganaki.
promise *see* **1.** berita, **2.** tuea, **3.** bauarira.
promised *see* **1.** bauariraki, **2.** beritaki, **3.** tueaki.
promising *see* berita.
prompt *see* **1.** kaobainako, **2.** kaonako, **3.** manebaeba, **4.** tabarekai, **5.** taubobonga.
promptly *see* kai.
prone *see* **1.** nano, **2.** kaboubwa.
pronounce *see* **1.** atonga, **2.** katenua.
pronounced *see* **1.** atongaki, **2.** katenuaki, **3.** tenu.
prop *see* **1.** kaintorua, **2.** nango, **3.** nangoa, **4.** tautoka, **5.** totokoa, **6.** turana.
propagate *see* **1.** karika, **2.** karikirakea.
propel *see* **1.** kawaka, **2.** wakina, **3.** kainaoa.
proper *see* **1.** oin, **2.** raoi, **3.** riai.

properly *see* raoi.
property *see* boi.
prophet *see* burabeti.
proportion *see* **1.** kaborere, **2.** kabotau.
proportional *see* **1.** karakina, **2.** kaborere.
proportionate *see* karakina.
proprietor *see* inaaomata.
prospect *see* **1.** kakea, **2.** kantaninga.
prosper *see* rikirake.
prosperous *see* **1.** maiu, **2.** marabe, **3.** marati, **4.** rung, **5.** takabwewebwere.
prostrate *see* kananobaraka.
protect *see* **1.** kawakina, **2.** rabuna, **3.** nonoa, **4.** katana, **5.** buoka, **6.** otaotanga.
protected *see* **1.** buokaki, **2.** katanaki, **3.** kawakinaki, **4.** nonoaki, **5.** otaotangaki, **6.** rabu, **7.** rabunaki.
protract *see* witokonaua.
protracted *see* witokonauaki.
protruding *see* katangibu.
proud *see* **1.** kariete, **2.** rietata, **3.** kainikatonga, **4.** igagi, **5.** kareite.
prove *see* **1.** kakoaua, **2.** kamatoa.
proved *see* kakoaua.
proven *see* **1.** kakoauaki, **2.** kamatoaki, **3.** kakoaua.
provide *see* **1.** rawebaia, **2.** riko, **3.** kamariboa.
provident *see* **1.** banganibai, **2.** tatabwi.
provoke *see* **1.** kabononanoa, **2.** kauntabaea, **3.** kauna, **4.** kananobuaka, **5.** katutua.
provoked *see* **1.** kabononanoaki, **2.** kananobuakaki, **3.** katutuaki, **4.** kaunaki, **5.** kauntabaeaki.
prow *see* waerikiriki.
prowl *see* **1.** kawa, **2.** maranoa.
proximal *see* kan.
proxy *see* tauantaboa.
prudent *see* **1.** wanawana, **2.** wana, **3.** nanowana.
prune *see* taera.
pruned *see* taeraki.
pry *see* **1.** kaninganinga, **2.** nenera.
prying *see* mautete.
public *see* tanoata.
publicize *see* tabangaea.
publicized *see* **1.** tabanga, **2.** tabangaeaki.
publish *see* nakomai.
published *see* nakomaiaki.
pucker *see* matabubura.
puckered *see* **1.** kabatutu, **2.** matabuburaki.
puckering *see* matabubura.
pudgy *see* kaubiroto.
puerile *see* manrerei.
puff *see* tibu.
puffed *see* **1.** kiritibutibu, **2.** nibunini, **3.** tabakurakura, **4.** tibu, **5.** tibuaki.
pugnacious *see* unin.

pull *see* 1. katika, 2. katurabeau, 3. waru, 4. burimangaoa.
pulled *see* 1. burimangaoaki, 2. katikaki, 3. katurabeauaki, 4. waruaki.
pulsate *see* 1. bukibuki, 2. ikeike, 3. karikari, 4. ruberube, 5. tata, 6. tatatata.
pulsated *see* 1. ikeikeaki, 2. tatatataki, 3. tataki, 4. karikariaki, 5. bukibukiaki, 6. ruberubeaki.
pulse *see* rubea.
pulverize *see* 1. bubua, 2. i.
pulverized *see* 1. bubu, 2. bubuaki, 3. iaki.
pumice *see* timit.
pump *see* bam.
pumped *see* bamaki.
punch *see* 1. ikuiku, 2. kamantintia, 3. oro, 4. ikua.
punctual *see* 1. kakaonimaki, 2. kaobainako, 3. kaonako.
puncture *see* 1. nekea, 2. rawana.
punctured *see* 1. teka, 2. nekeaki, 3. rawanaki.
pungent *see* tena.
punish *see* ikana.
punished *see* 1. ikanaki, 2. tekeria.
puny *see* 1. ngore, 2. bingore, 3. tinauere, 4. uarereke, 5. ntangorengore, 6. ningorengore, 7. mangori, 8. kire, 9. kinerang, 10. kinene, 11. inaito, 12. kinauere.
pure *see* 1. itiaki, 2. itiwewe.
purely *see* tiri.
purge *see* kaitaka.
purified *see* 1. kaitiaki, 2. kaitiakaki.
purify *see* 1. kaiti, 2. kaitiaka.
purple *see* 1. beeboro, 2. uraro.
purposeless *see* taeremea.
pursue *see* 1. katootoonga, 2. kite, 3. kara, 4. kakioa, 5. kaea, 6. wakina.
pursued *see* 1. kaeaki, 2. kakioaki, 3. karaki, 4. katootoongaki, 5. kiteaki, 6. wakinaki.
push *see* 1. neakina, 2. katotoroa, 3. notua, 4. kebutua, 5. kaonakoa, 6. kaoa, 7. kakenakoa, 8. kanakoa, 9. wang, 10. karebutia.
pusillanimous *see* nanobu.
pussyfoot *see* tabara.
put *see* 1. nea, 2. matana, 3. katuka, 4. kamena, 5. kamemena, 6. kaaki, 7. nikira, 8. kaki.
putrid *see* maung.
puzzle *see* kennano.
puzzled *see* kennanoaki.
pygmy *see* teutana.

Q

quadruple *see* kakaaua.
quaint *see* baikoraki.

quake *see* 1. ngaruru, 2. ruru, 3. maeiei.
qualified *see* 1. manikorakiaki, 2. manikoraki.
qualify *see* manikoraki.
quality *see* rianako.
quantify *see* boraoi.
quarrel *see* 1. un, 2. kauntaeka, 3. ibewi, 4. ikakaiwi, 5. ikangui.
quarrelsome *see* 1. ibewi, 2. kakaiun, 3. ntarierie, 4. unin, 5. banganun.
quarter *see* 1. kaiakina, 2. kataewa.
quartered *see* 1. kataewaki, 2. taewa.
quaver *see* ruru.
queer *see* 1. kameio, 2. kaokoro, 3. aeka.
quell *see* 1. toabara, 2. katoka.
quelled *see* 1. katokaki, 2. toabaraki.
quench *see* 1. kamatea, 2. katoka.
quenched *see* 1. kamateaki, 2. katokaki.
query *see* 1. kekera, 2. nenera, 3. kangongoa.
quest *see* kekera.
question *see* 1. kaeka, 2. titirakina, 3. titiraki, 4. kataetae, 5. kangongoa.
quick *see* 1. niniwana, 2. waetata, 3. ueke, 4. rabakai, 5. maiutakoni, 6. kiangang, 7. kaumaki, 8. ikakai, 9. birimaka, 10. bareka, 11. takaerere.
quickstep *see* rangata.
quiet *see* 1. nanoraoi, 2. rau, 3. taribabu, 4. nikoraoi, 5. kinoa, 6. kataribabua, 7. karaua, 8. kainababu, 9. kananoraoa.
quietness *see* rô.
quit *see* 1. kau, 2. kitana.
quite *see* 1. kinokino, 2. kanga, 3. boni, 4. bon, 5. rangin.
quiver *see* 1. bakaruru, 2. itikurere, 3. rangarangataki, 4. ruru, 5. rurubenebene.
quoits *see* kaboulina.

R

rabid *see* nanoingainga.
race *see* kabobirimaka.
racial *see* nanoutu.
rack *see* kamaraka.
radiant *see* 1. mimitong, 2. kakatika.
radiate *see* kiakia.
radiated *see* kiakiaki.
radio *see* uaereti.
ragged *see* raeraeaki.
rail *see* takurere.
rain *see* 1. karaou, 2. karau.
rainbow *see* wírara.
rainy *see* kakarau.

raise *see* 1. kaotirake, 2. taura, 3. tabeka, 4. neboa, 5. mwemekia, 6. mwe, 7. utibaba, 8. kamwemwea, 9. ieta, 10. euta, 11. e, 12. kauma, 13. katea.
raised *see* 1. mamaunga, 2. utibabaki, 3. tauraki, 4. tabekaki, 5. rekeaki, 6. neboaki, 7. mweaki, 8. kaumaki, 9. kateaki, 10. kaotirakeaki, 11. kamwemweaki, 12. ietaki, 13. eweaki, 14. eutaki, 15. mwemekiaki.
rally *see* 1. kaenaena, 2. ngareakina.
ram *see* kakenakoa.
ramble *see* 1. kiritabaiore, 2. birianena, 3. karebo.
rancid *see* 1. karongo, 2. buakaka, 3. boongata.
range *see* karinan.
rank *see* 1. aeka, 2. bungata, 3. kawairinana, 4. rainia.
ranked *see* 1. aekaki, 2. kawairinan, 3. kawairinanaki, 4. rainiaki.
ranking *see* moaniba.
ransack *see* unaenae.
ransacked *see* unaenaeaki.
rant *see* takurara.
ranting *see* takurara.
rap *see* karebwe.
rapacious *see* babakanikoroa.
rape *see* kabainrang.
raped *see* kabainrangaki.
rapid *see* 1. rere, 2. tawe, 3. takaerere, 4. taerina, 5. mwaka, 6. kaumaki, 7. kamatawea, 8. itibabu, 9. waetata, 10. raiti.
rapidly *see* mwaka.
rapture *see* kautikaikaia.
rare *see* 1. tare, 2. maon, 3. manenanti, 4. kakawaki, 5. burenibai, 6. burenibwai.
rarely *see* 1. kareke, 2. burenibwai.
rascal *see* kimoiauea.
rascally *see* 1. iowawa, 2. ntarierie, 3. aonikai.
rash *see* rangarangatau.
rasp *see* 1. ikua, 2. toroa, 3. karakara, 4. ikikua, 5. Eikuna, 6. teroa.
raspy *see* karakara.
rate *see* 1. boa, 2. kataetaea, 3. takua.
rated *see* 1. kataetaeaki, 2. takuaki, 3. boaki.
rather *see* 1. kinokino, 2. riki, 3. teutana.
ratified *see* kateimatoaki.
ratify *see* kateimatoa.
ration *see* 1. tibatiba, 2. tikona, 3. tiba.
rational *see* 1. wanawana, 2. nanowana.
rationed *see* 1. tikonaki, 2. tibaki, 3. tibatibaki.
rattle *see* 1. takaruru, 2. keke, 3. kamariroa, 4. kakekea, 5. kakerukeru.
rattled *see* 1. kakekeaki, 2. kakerukeruaki, 3. kamariroaki, 4. kekeaki, 5. takaruruaki.
rattling *see* mariro.
ravage *see* kamarua.
ravaged *see* kamaruaki.

rave *see* 1. aiwau, 2. takurara.
ravel *see* 1. binoka, 2. btaona.
ravenous *see* 1. babakanikoroa, 2. kibakibaki, 3. mangaungau, 4. matenibaki, 5. ringoungou.
ravish *see* konana.
raw *see* 1. matabou, 2. oraora, 3. orôra.
reach *see* 1. ribinano, 2. koukou.
react *see* kaeka.
read *see* 1. wareaki, 2. wareboki, 3. warebokiaki, 4. wareware, 5. warewareaki, 6. ware.
readily *see* kai.
readjust *see* 1. ribata, 2. toma.
ready *see* 1. taenangina, 2. tau, 3. tauraoi.
real *see* 1. toronibwai, 2. koaua, 3. bon.
realize *see* 1. nora, 2. ota, 3. kamatebwai.
realized *see* 1. kamatebwaiaki, 2. noraki, 3. otaki.
really *see* 1. bon, 2. kiri.
reanimate *see* kataeboa.
reanimated *see* kataeboaki.
reap *see* taia.
rearrange *see* tiba.
reason *see* iangoa.
reasonable *see* 1. nanowana, 2. wanawana, 3. raoi, 4. wana.
reasoned *see* iangoaki.
rebel *see* 1. karitei, 2. unrake.
rebellious *see* 1. karitei, 2. unrake.
rebound *see* 1. bakannaioro, 2. katata, 3. tua.
rebuff *see* 1. kakiroa, 2. notua.
rebuke *see* 1. boa, 2. takurere, 3. takua, 4. kaetaea, 5. reireia.
rebuked *see* 1. boaki, 2. kaetaeaki, 3. reireiaki, 4. takuaki, 5. takurereaki.
recall *see* 1. reketa, 2. uringa.
recede *see* kakerikaka.
receive *see* 1. ana, 2. butimaea, 3. mwanea, 4. karekea, 5. inga, 6. anangaki, 7. kaeka.
received *see* 1. anaki, 2. anangakiaki, 3. butimaeaki, 4. ingaki, 5. kaekaki, 6. karekeaki, 7. mwaneaki, 8. reke.
recent *see* 1. menai, 2. waeai, 3. bou, 4. ngkainaba, 5. nabangkai.
recently *see* 1. atia, 2. nabangkai, 3. tiba.
reciprocal *see* mronron.
reciprocally *see* i.
recite *see* 1. ana, 2. karakina.
reckon *see* 1. taoman, 2. wareka, 3. taku, 4. katautau.
reclaim *see* tang.
reclaimed *see* tangaki.
recline *see* rarikiriki.
recognize *see* 1. ataia, 2. atakin, 3. kina.
recognized *see* 1. ataiaki, 2. atinkinaki, 3. kinaki.
recoil *see* 1. ebanako, 2. makerikaki.

recollect *see* 1. uring, 2. uringa, 3. reketa, 4. iango, 5. ururinga.
recommend *see* wina.
recommended *see* winaki.
recompense *see* kaboa.
reconcile *see* 1. ioki, 2. raoiakina.
reconciled *see* 1. iokiaki, 2. raoiakinaki.
reconnoiter *see* tuoa.
reconsider *see* rinanoa.
reconstruct *see* karikaki.
reconstructed *see* karikaki.
recover *see* eka.
recovered *see* ekaki.
recreate *see* kakibotu.
recriminate *see* mea.
rectangular *see* reketangkoro.
rectified *see* kaetaki.
rectify *see* kaeta.
recuperate *see* kamaoa.
recycle *see* kamatoroa.
red *see* 1. renga, 2. ura, 3. uraura.
redden *see* kauraura.
reddened *see* 1. kaurauraki, 2. matauraura.
reddish *see* takirara.
redeem *see* 1. kamaiua, 2. kaboa.
redeemed *see* 1. kaboaki, 2. kamaiuaki.
redo *see* manga.
redoubtable *see* nanomakaki.
redraft *see* rinanoa.
redraw *see* rinanoa.
redress *see* riboriki.
reduce *see* 1. kauanging, 2. manti, 3. kauarerekea, 4. kakerikaka, 5. kakenakoa, 6. kairarika, 7. katauururoa, 8. kauramara.
reduced *see* 1. kakerikakaki, 2. matiraua, 3. mantiaki, 4. kauramaraki, 5. kauarerekeaki, 6. katauururoaki, 7. kakenakoaki, 8. kairarikaki, 9. kauangingaki.
redundant *see* koko.
reef *see* 1. waiwai, 2. panga.
reek *see* 1. korakora, 2. bimaung.
reel *see* 1. bebe, 2. bebebebe, 3. kiribebe, 4. kiriongong, 5. tata.
reeling *see* minotaki.
referee *see* karotuang.
refined *see* 1. katimaran, 2. maninganinga.
reflect *see* taku.
reflected *see* takuaki.
refractory *see* iowawa.
refresh *see* 1. kamaitoroa, 2. kamaiua.
refreshed *see* 1. kamaitoroaki, 2. kamaiuaki, 3. kamenaiaki.
refreshing *see* kamaiu.
refurbish *see* 1. karikaki, 2. kaua.
refuse *see* 1. rawa, 2. unrake.

refused *see* 1. rawaki, 2. unrakeaki.
regal *see* mimitong.
regard *see* 1. taratara, 2. rutiakina, 3. matauakina, 4. mannanoa, 5. tatara.
regardless *see* nanotiotio.
regenerate *see* kaua.
regenerated *see* kauaki.
regret *see* 1. ao, 2. aoao, 3. mango, 4. nanomaraki, 5. raraomaeakina, 6. ritangia.
regretful *see* mango.
regular *see* boraoi.
regularly *see* tataneiai.
regulate *see* 1. motika, 2. motiraran, 3. taina, 4. tuana, 5. baire.
regulated *see* 1. baireaki, 2. moti, 3. motikaki, 4. motiraranaki, 5. tainaki, 6. tuanaki.
regurgitate *see* mumuta.
reign *see* 1. uea, 2. ueana.
reinforce *see* 1. kaintorua, 2. tautoka.
reinforced *see* 1. kaintoruaki, 2. tautokaki.
reject *see* 1. aobaki, 2. ekara, 3. kakea, 4. kaki, 5. kare, 6. notua.
rejected *see* 1. kakiaki, 2. kareaki, 3. ekaraki, 4. notuaki, 5. kakeaki.
rejoice *see* 1. kimareirei, 2. kukurei, 3. katongatonga, 4. kanikureirei, 5. kakatonga, 6. barekatia, 7. nikierere.
rejoicing *see* kakammari.
rejoin *see* kaeka.
relapse *see* kaua.
relate *see* 1. karakina, 2. taekina.
related *see* 1. karakinaki, 2. taekinaki.
relative *see* koraki.
relax *see* 1. bwatobwato, 2. kakibotu, 3. kamamara, 4. kamanua, 5. kamatana.
relaxed *see* 1. bwatobwatoaki, 2. kakibotuaki, 3. kamamaraki, 4. kamanuaki, 5. kamatanaki.
relay *see* kaonoa.
release *see* 1. kainaomata, 2. kanakoa.
released *see* 1. kanakoaki, 2. kainaomataki.
relentless *see* nanomakaki.
relieve *see* 1. bakuaku, 2. kamarauaka.
relieved *see* 1. kamarauakaki, 2. nanobebete, 3. taenang.
relinquish *see* 1. bunra, 2. kaki, 3. kitana, 4. tanara.
relinquished *see* 1. bunraki, 2. tanaraki, 3. kitanaki, 4. kakiaki.
relish *see* tanna.
remain *see* 1. mena, 2. tiku.
remark *see* 1. atonga, 2. kina, 3. mutiakina, 4. taratara, 5. tataumanta.
remarkable *see* 1. kakamataku, 2. katitirou.
remedy *see* kamaoa.
remember *see* 1. uringa, 2. uringnga.
remembered *see* 1. uringngaki, 2. uringaki.

remind *see* kauringa.
remit *see* kaoka.
remorseful *see* mango.
remote *see* 1. raroa, 2. tabara.
remove *see* 1. buta, 2. taera.
removed *see* 1. butaki, 2. kinokino, 3. taeraki.
rend *see* 1. kamakerua, 2. raeua, 3. raea.
render *see* kaoka.
renew *see* kaua.
renewed *see* kauaki.
renounce *see* 1. kakea, 2. kitana.
renowned *see* 1. atongaki, 2. eke, 3. kakannato.
repair *see* 1. karao, 2. karikaki.
repaired *see* 1. karaoaki, 2. karikakiaki.
repeat *see* 1. karairaki, 2. kaua, 3. manga, 4. kaokia.
repeated *see* 1. kaokiaki, 2. karairakiaki, 3. kauaki, 4. mangaki.
repeating *see* irerei.
repel *see* 1. karebutia, 2. kebutua, 3. notua, 4. kaoka, 5. kakiroa, 6. kararoa.
repent *see* 1. mango, 2. nanomaraki, 3. raraoma.
replace *see* 1. ikaruoruo, 2. karuoruo, 3. ruamwi, 4. tauantaboa.
replenish *see* kaua.
replicate *see* katoto.
reply *see* kaeka.
report *see* 1. manintaeka, 2. tua, 3. kaewetaeka.
reported *see* 1. manintaekaki, 2. tuaki, 3. kaewetaekaki.
repose *see* 1. matu, 2. motirawa.
repossess *see* nikira.
represent *see* 1. kaota, 2. tauantaboa, 3. kaotiota, 4. katereterea.
represented *see* 1. kaotaki, 2. kaotiotaki, 3. kateretereaki, 4. tauantaboaki.
repress *see* tuka.
repressed *see* tukaki.
reprimand *see* 1. boa, 2. kabunenea, 3. takua, 4. tiribaea, 5. tiringa.
reprimanded *see* 1. boaki, 2. kabuneneaki, 3. mataronron, 4. takuaki, 5. tiribaeaki, 6. tiringaki.
reproach *see* 1. kamamaea, 2. kabuakaka.
reproduce *see* 1. kariki, 2. katoto.
reprove *see* 1. boa, 2. kataetaea, 3. takua.
reproved *see* 1. boaki, 2. kataetaeaki, 3. takuaki.
repudiate *see* kamabu.
repudiated *see* kamabuaki.
repugnant *see* 1. ba, 2. buritoto, 3. kabun.
repulse *see* 1. kakiroa, 2. wira.
repulsive *see* 1. ba, 2. kabun.
request *see* 1. bubuti, 2. kangongoa, 3. kao, 4. onon, 5. titiraki.
require *see* 1. ititi, 2. nanoati.
required *see* 1. ititiaki, 2. nanoatiaki.
requite *see* kabuâ.

rescue *see* kainaomata.
rescued *see* kainaomataki.
research *see* 1. ukeuke, 2. ukora, 3. ukouko, 4. nenera.
resemble *see* 1. kaikonaka, 2. katotonga.
resent *see* 1. nanora, 2. noku, 3. riba.
resentful *see* 1. kakaiun, 2. nanobuaka, 3. nanorake, 4. noku.
reserve *see* 1. rabua, 2. taua.
reserved *see* 1. rabu, 2. rabuaki, 3. tauaki.
reside *see* 1. auti, 2. maeka, 3. mena, 4. mwenga.
resign *see* kerikaki.
resigned *see* 1. kerikakiaki, 2. nanotau.
resist *see* 1. karitei, 2. tuka.
resistant *see* 1. kauniben, 2. tounene, 3. karitei.
resolute *see* nanomatoa.
resolve *see* 1. iangomaka, 2. kanenei, 3. mutigak.
resolved *see* 1. iangomakaki, 2. kaneneiaki, 3. moti.
resolving *see* nanomaka.
resonant *see* 1. bing, 2. bingibing, 3. bwarubwaru, 4. tangimwaka.
resound *see* 1. bwarubwaru, 2. tangimwaka, 3. keru, 4. rurunga.
resourceful *see* 1. kauman, 2. kiriman, 3. niniwana.
respect *see* 1. karinea, 2. kaunainea, 3. makina, 4. mannanoa.
respected *see* 1. nanouki, 2. karineaki, 3. kaunaineaki, 4. makinaki, 5. mannanoaki.
respectful *see* karinerine.
respire *see* 1. ikeike, 2. ike.
resplendent *see* 1. kakatika, 2. mimitong, 3. takaneanea.
respond *see* kaeka.
rest *see* 1. motirawa, 2. nawa.
rested *see* 1. motirawaki, 2. nawaki.
restful *see* nangoraoi.
restive *see* 1. tarere, 2. nimwatoaua, 3. waerebutata, 4. karerema, 5. nibwara, 6. tuarere.
restless *see* 1. karerema, 2. nangora, 3. nibwara, 4. nimwatoaua, 5. raraeua, 6. takarebu, 7. tarere, 8. tuarere, 9. waerebutata.
restock *see* kaua.
restore *see* 1. karairaki, 2. kaoka.
restored *see* 1. kaokaki, 2. karairakiaki.
restrain *see* 1. kauakina, 2. taon, 3. taua, 4. taubank, 5. toabara.
restrained *see* 1. kauakinaki, 2. taonaki, 3. tauaki, 4. taubank, 5. taubankaki, 6. toabaraki.
restrict *see* 1. kamabu, 2. tikona, 3. kawarika, 4. kaonota.
restricted *see* 1. kamabuaki, 2. kaonotaki, 3. kawarikaki, 4. tabu, 5. tikonaki, 6. wariki.
result *see* mwina.
resume *see* moana.
retail *see* karakina.

retain *see* **1.** taua, **2.** antingoa, **3.** tau.

retained *see* **1.** antingoaki, **2.** tauaki.

retaliate *see* irantanga.

retard *see* **1.** tinerua, **2.** antingoa, **3.** kakiriaria, **4.** kamatawea, **5.** kamweau, **6.** kareketatia, **7.** kawaeremwea, **8.** kawaeremwi.

retarded *see* **1.** kawaeremweaki, **2.** tineruaki, **3.** tukuroro, **4.** kawaeremwiaki, **5.** kamweauaki, **6.** kamataweaki, **7.** antingoaki, **8.** kareketatiaki, **9.** kakiriariaki.

reticent *see* karaba.

retire *see* **1.** kerikaki, **2.** rikaki, **3.** mumun, **4.** kon, **5.** kau, **6.** katikua, **7.** motirawa.

retired *see* **1.** motirawa, **2.** kauaki, **3.** rikakiaki, **4.** mumunaki, **5.** motirawaki, **6.** konaki, **7.** kerikakiaki, **8.** katikuaki, **9.** kon.

retort *see* ekaria.

retract *see* **1.** kakerikaka, **2.** kauangingia.

retracted *see* **1.** kakerikakaki, **2.** kauangingiaki.

retreat *see* **1.** kakerikaka, **2.** rikaki, **3.** rereua, **4.** kau, **5.** kerikaki, **6.** mumun.

retreated *see* **1.** kakerikakaki, **2.** kauaki, **3.** kerikakiaki, **4.** mumunaki, **5.** rereuaki, **6.** rikakiaki.

retrieve *see* anaia.

return *see* **1.** oki, **2.** rikakina, **3.** karairaki, **4.** kaoka, **5.** roko.

reunite *see* **1.** botaki, **2.** kabo.

revamp *see* rinanoa.

reveal *see* **1.** kaota, **2.** kaotiota, **3.** katereterea, **4.** kauka, **5.** maroaka.

revealed *see* **1.** kaotiotaki, **2.** maroakaki, **3.** otinako, **4.** kaotaki, **5.** kaukaki, **6.** kateretereaki.

reverberate *see* **1.** kanebu, **2.** kia.

reverse *see* bitia.

reversed *see* bitiaki.

revert *see* karairaki.

review *see* **1.** kauring, **2.** kinanoa.

revise *see* **1.** tauburea, **2.** kauring, **3.** rinanoa.

revised *see* **1.** taubureaki, **2.** kauringaki, **3.** rinanoaki.

revive *see* kamaka.

revived *see* kamakaki.

revolt *see* karitei.

revolutionary *see* karitei.

revolve *see* **1.** kabutia, **2.** mino, **3.** minominota, **4.** monota, **5.** rabinobina.

revolved *see* **1.** minominotaki, **2.** monotaki, **3.** rabinobinaki, **4.** minoaki.

reward *see* **1.** bo, **2.** kaniwanga.

rework *see* rinanoa.

rich *see* **1.** kaubwai, **2.** nonga, **3.** tabobai, **4.** toronibwai.

rickety *see* **1.** bakitaia, **2.** kinene, **3.** kinerang.

ricochet *see* **1.** tua, **2.** katuatua.

riddle *see* **1.** ioia, **2.** kanibangabanga.

ride *see* **1.** aeka, **2.** kabuta, **3.** tokara.

ridge *see* taubuki.

ridicule *see* **1.** bainingareakina, **2.** kaena, **3.** kakanikoa, **4.** mantoa, **5.** ngareakina, **6.** ngareanina, **7.** rabungaoa.

ridiculous *see* **1.** bainingare, **2.** kaena.

rifle *see* **1.** kimoa, **2.** taebai.

rifled *see* **1.** kimoaki, **2.** taebaiaki.

right *see* **1.** ke, **2.** raoi, **3.** eti, **4.** atai, **5.** riai.

righteous *see* **1.** itiaki, **2.** raoiroi.

rigid *see* **1.** ngearuru, **2.** aotiki, **3.** iakai.

ring *see* **1.** tangitang, **2.** rarai, **3.** tang.

rinse *see* rautaria.

riot *see* kiriwea.

rip *see* **1.** ourouake, **2.** rae, **3.** raea, **4.** raeaua, **5.** raena, **6.** raerae, **7.** raeraea, **8.** raeten.

ripe *see* **1.** tawa, **2.** matibu.

ripen *see* **1.** katawaea, **2.** kamatibutibua.

ripened *see* **1.** kamatibutibuaki, **2.** katawaeaki.

rise *see* kateirakea.

rising *see* betirake.

risk *see* kamanenanti.

risky *see* kamamate.

rival *see* **1.** kaaioroa, **2.** kairiribai, **3.** kaua, **4.** nanonibwi.

roam *see* **1.** rebu, **2.** bukitiotio, **3.** butinaiwa.

roar *see* **1.** bekorara, **2.** wiba.

roast *see* **1.** kamwa, **2.** timina, **3.** tintin.

roasted *see* **1.** kamwaki, **2.** mae, **3.** timamwi, **4.** timinaki, **5.** tintinaki.

rob *see* **1.** kimoa, **2.** tanbwaia, **3.** taebai, **4.** rawea, **5.** bubai, **6.** ira, **7.** iraea, **8.** aubanga, **9.** kamarua.

robber *see* **1.** baikimoa, **2.** bairawata.

robed *see* **1.** bubaiaki, **2.** taebaiaki, **3.** raweaki, **4.** kimoaki, **5.** kamaruaki, **6.** iraeaki, **7.** tanbwaiaki, **8.** aubangaki, **9.** iraki.

robust *see* **1.** marurung, **2.** tuariri, **3.** korakora, **4.** kairi, **5.** kangkai.

rock *see* **1.** bâ, **2.** taurangaranga, **3.** uo.

rocky *see* riribwa.

roll *see* **1.** rabino, **2.** tannaba, **3.** rikuma, **4.** katirironrona, **5.** rangaranga, **6.** taurangaranga, **7.** rabinobino, **8.** ngaruru, **9.** minomino, **10.** karabinobinoa, **11.** kamatana, **12.** nikamonmon, **13.** minota.

rolled *see* **1.** minominoaki, **2.** taurangarangaki, **3.** tannabaki, **4.** rikumaki, **5.** rangarangaki, **6.** rabinobinoaki, **7.** rabinoaki, **8.** nikamonmonaki, **9.** minotaki, **10.** matan, **11.** katirironronaki, **12.** karabinobinoaki, **13.** kamatanaki, **14.** ngaruruaki.

rollick *see* kirei.

romance *see* **1.** wibeka, **2.** kakawibaea.

romp *see* **1.** reimaurua, **2.** kirei.

roof *see* taubuki.

roomy *see* mawa.
root *see* **1.** butan, **2.** wakâ.
rope *see* **1.** maca, **2.** maia.
rosy *see* memeri.
rot *see* katotoa.
rotate *see* **1.** kaminominotaka, **2.** kaniniraka, **3.** mino, **4.** minotia, **5.** rairaki, **6.** kamimitoiaka.
rotated *see* **1.** minoaki, **2.** rairakiaki, **3.** minotiaki, **4.** mino, **5.** kaninirakaki, **6.** kamimitoiakaki, **7.** kaminominotakaki.
rotten *see* **1.** mka, **2.** moko.
rotund *see* timron.
rough *see* **1.** makerekere, **2.** kakiribeubeua, **3.** tabureka, **4.** tabukirurunga, **5.** tabukibuki, **6.** rekereke, **7.** reka, **8.** aontabuki, **9.** karakara, **10.** inaina, **11.** aouti, **12.** kiribeubeu, **13.** karekereke.
round *see* **1.** katimronrona, **2.** tuabebeku, **3.** tobibi, **4.** tironron, **5.** timron, **6.** tabunak, **7.** rotu, **8.** otioro, **9.** mronron, **10.** katirorora, **11.** katanga, **12.** kamronrona, **13.** kabuari, **14.** kabuabua, **15.** bunin, **16.** buburatautau, **17.** mron.
rounded *see* **1.** kabuabuaki, **2.** mronronaki, **3.** rotuaki, **4.** timron, **5.** katimronronaki, **6.** kamronronaki, **7.** katangaki, **8.** katiroronaki.
rouse *see* **1.** kakamwakuri, **2.** kateirakea, **3.** kaunga, **4.** mangauti.
routine *see* **1.** kabuta, **2.** okioki.
rove *see* toitioa.
roving *see* toitio.
row *see* **1.** buru, **2.** bwetua, **3.** burunna, **4.** bweta.
royal *see* banuea.
rub *see* **1.** bubua, **2.** imita, **3.** ire, **4.** irea, **5.** ireirea, **6.** karanea, **7.** tobi, **8.** toroba, **9.** torotoroba.
rudder *see* **1.** poêtua, **2.** poue.
rude *see* **1.** be, **2.** betoto, **3.** ioawa, **4.** kakauara, **5.** maurake, **6.** maurea, **7.** maureka, **8.** tabureka, **9.** tete, **10.** uburake, **11.** akiako.
ruffle *see* katababaea.
ruffled *see* **1.** katababaeaki, **2.** atutababa, **3.** burimangaoa.
rugged *see* **1.** kiribeubeu, **2.** reka, **3.** tabureka.
rugose *see* karekereke.
ruin *see* bwaka.
ruined *see* **1.** bwakaki, **2.** iti, **3.** taeare.
rule *see* **1.** tautaeka, **2.** tuana, **3.** tautaekana, **4.** arona, **5.** tautorona, **6.** baire.
ruled *see* **1.** tuanaki, **2.** aronaki, **3.** baireaki, **4.** tautaekaki, **5.** tautaekanaki, **6.** tautoronaki.
rumble *see* **1.** rebwe, **2.** rurunga.
rummage *see* ukeroa.
rumpled *see* nimanunu.
run *see* **1.** biri, **2.** karaoria.
rung *see* **1.** tang, **2.** tangitangaki, **3.** tangitang, **4.** tangaki, **5.** raraiaki, **6.** rarai, **7.** katangaki, **8.** karinanaki, **9.** katanga.

runty *see* **1.** kingking, **2.** tinauere.
rupture *see* ma.
ruptured *see* maki.
rush *see* **1.** rerebu, **2.** kibara, **3.** ruona, **4.** rerea, **5.** kawaetata, **6.** rerebaua.
rushed *see* **1.** kawaetataki, **2.** kibaraki, **3.** rereaki, **4.** rerebauaki, **5.** rerebuaki, **6.** ruonaki.
russet *see* takirara.
rust *see* **1.** kararaea, **2.** rara.
rusted *see* **1.** raraki, **2.** kararaeaki.
rustle *see* **1.** kekeruatai, **2.** mwakaikai.

S

s *see* ti.
sack *see* **1.** kuribwaia, **2.** tiriobora, **3.** urua.
sacked *see* **1.** kuribwaiaki, **2.** tirioboraki, **3.** uruaki.
sacred *see* **1.** bainaka, **2.** dua, **3.** tabuterang.
sacrifice *see* **1.** karea, **2.** karean.
sad *see* **1.** rawawata, **2.** kawa, **3.** nanokawaki.
sadden *see* kananokawaki.
safe *see* **1.** mano, **2.** mauri.
safeguard *see* **1.** nonoa, **2.** kamaneaka, **3.** katana.
sag *see* **1.** kamoua, **2.** mwanu.
sagacious *see* **1.** mamata, **2.** rabakau, **3.** wanawana.
sage *see* wanawana.
sail *see* **1.** ra, **2.** ieie, **3.** ie, **4.** iea.
saliva *see* paouare.
salivate *see* **1.** baroa, **2.** baware.
sallow *see* **1.** kiwarawara, **2.** taetoba, **3.** tawere.
salt *see* **1.** taorona, **2.** tarina.
salted *see* **1.** taoronaki, **2.** tarinaki.
salty *see* **1.** tari, **2.** tutari.
salute *see* **1.** inga, **2.** kamaura.
same *see* **1.** anua, **2.** bare, **3.** boraoi, **4.** kiribare, **5.** tiitebo.
sample *see* **1.** katonga, **2.** namta.
sand *see* tano.
sandy *see* **1.** tanotano, **2.** tantano, **3.** atiati, **4.** kirara.
sane *see* wanawana.
sap *see* ana.
sapient *see* nanowana.
sapling *see* roko.
sarcastic *see* ui-katík.
sat *see* tekateka.
satiate *see* kararatia.
satiated *see* **1.** rarati, **2.** kararatiaki.
satisfied *see* **1.** ngae, **2.** inaña, **3.** rauakina, **4.** tau, **5.** nuai, **6.** kanuaiaki, **7.** kabaia, **8.** karauakaki, **9.** kanoan.
satisfy *see* **1.** kanuaia, **2.** karauaka.
satisfying *see* kararati.

saturate *see* 1. kamakimakia, 2. kararatia, 3. kamara, 4. kamaimaia, 5. kamaratiarati.
saturated *see* 1. makinono, 2. kamakimakiaki, 3. waneinei, 4. rarati, 5. maratirati, 6. marati, 7. makimaki, 8. kararatiaki, 9. kamaraki, 10. kamaimaiaki, 11. ibaba, 12. kamaratiaratiaki.
saucy *see* 1. reberake, 2. uamoa.
saunter *see* 1. waeremwe, 2. tamweremwere.
save *see* 1. tatabuia, 2. kawakina, 3. aoraia, 4. kaikoa, 5. kamaiua.
saved *see* 1. aoraiaki, 2. kaikoaki, 3. kamaiuaki, 4. kawakinaki, 5. tatabuiaki.
saving *see* tababu.
savory *see* 1. kangkang, 2. nanai.
saw *see* 1. kina, 2. nora, 3. kamatebwai, 4. tara.
say *see* 1. atonga, 2. kaokia, 3. taetae, 4. taku, 5. tanewea.
saying *see* tak.
scald *see* 1. kabarere, 2. kabatatata.
scale *see* 1. imana, 2. tamatama, 3. taokai, 4. ararakea, 5. tamarake, 6. tamarakea.
scaled *see* 1. ararakeaki, 2. imanaki, 3. tamarakeaki, 4. tamatamaki, 5. taokaiaki.
scalene *see* tikairin.
scaly *see* inaina.
scamp *see* taubururu.
scan *see* taku.
scandalize *see* 1. bwaka, 2. kabatebai, 3. baka.
scandalous *see* kabaka.
scant *see* karako.
scapula *see* rî-n'aña.
scar *see* 1. kamaneka, 2. kamwi, 3. mwaneka.
scarce *see* 1. karako, 2. karemaranga, 3. karemwaewe, 4. tare.
scarcely *see* maki.
scare *see* 1. bakara, 2. kamakua, 3. kamaka, 4. kakamaku.
scared *see* 1. aotakaka, 2. auba, 3. bakaraki, 4. kakamakuaki, 5. kamakaki, 6. maku.
scarred *see* 1. nimatamata, 2. kamanekaki, 3. kukunakuna, 4. manekaneka, 5. mwinikai.
scary *see* kakamaku.
scatter *see* 1. karaea, 2. katakarea, 3. kauamaea, 4. mae, 5. mare, 6. rarae, 7. kamerea.
scattered *see* 1. maae, 2. takarea, 3. raraeaki, 4. mare, 5. mareaki, 6. maeaki, 7. katakareaki, 8. karemaranga, 9. kauamaeaki, 10. karaeaki, 11. kamereaki, 12. itimareare, 13. bakarae, 14. raea.
scavenge *see* kaukea.
scent *see* 1. neneboi, 2. niniboi, 3. taomaneka.
scented *see* 1. taomanekaki, 2. neneboiaki, 3. niniboiaki.
scientific *see* kata.
scoff *see* 1. kakanikoa, 2. bainingareakina.

scold *see* 1. boa, 2. kataetaea, 3. kaumwangai, 4. meia, 5. takua, 6. tiring, 7. tiringa.
scoop *see* 1. anima, 2. tiera, 3. niba, 4. itia, 5. eria, 6. annan, 7. abuta, 8. abuabu, 9. animana.
scorch *see* kabatata.
scorched *see* 1. batata, 2. bweari, 3. kabatataki.
score *see* katanetanea.
scored *see* katanetaneaki.
scorn *see* 1. nokua, 2. unuara, 3. kaonakoa, 4. kaberetokoa.
scorned *see* 1. kaonakoaki, 2. nokuaki, 3. unuara, 4. unuaraki, 5. kaberetokoaki.
scornful *see* kaonako.
scoundrel *see* 1. kimoiauea, 2. tabobe.
scour *see* 1. karaneboneboa, 2. karekea.
scoured *see* 1. karaneboneboaki, 2. karekeaki.
scout *see* matana.
scowl *see* matanoku.
scowling *see* matabubuaka.
scrape *see* 1. kara, 2. karakara, 3. kiki, 4. koko.
scraped *see* 1. karaki, 2. kikiaki, 3. karakaraki, 4. kokoaki.
scratch *see* 1. kakibea, 2. kikekibe, 3. rarua, 4. ngoa, 5. korita, 6. kori, 7. kaukeuke, 8. karia, 9. kanananga, 10. kakaria, 11. angoa, 12. kara.
scratched *see* 1. kaukeukeaki, 2. ngoaki, 3. koritaki, 4. raruaki, 5. kikekibeaki, 6. karaki, 7. kananangaki, 8. kakibeaki, 9. kakariaki, 10. angoaki, 11. koriaki, 12. kariaki.
scream *see* 1. kerua, 2. takaarua, 3. tangiroro.
screen *see* 1. buibuina, 2. katana, 3. nuna.
screened *see* 1. katanaki, 2. nunaki, 3. buibuinaki.
screw *see* 1. tikuruna, 2. biroa.
scrounge *see* kaukea.
scrumptious *see* kangkang.
scrupulous *see* kikinto.
scrutinize *see* 1. kabetiwai, 2. tirotiroa, 3. tiroakina, 4. tiroa, 5. matauakina, 6. betunga, 7. neneria.
scuffle *see* ibeki.
scummy *see* rannake.
sea *see* 1. taari, 2. tahari.
seafarer *see* kimautari.
seal *see* au.
sealed *see* 1. au, 2. auaki.
seam *see* toma.
sear *see* 1. katanea, 2. katena.
search *see* 1. ukora, 2. kakae, 3. kite, 4. nenera, 5. ukeroa, 6. ukeuke.
seared *see* 1. kataneaki, 2. katenaki.
seasick *see* nimarawarawa.
seat *see* 1. kamemena, 2. katuka, 3. nea.
seated *see* 1. kamemenaki, 2. katukaki, 3. neaki, 4. tekateka.
secede *see* kerikaki.
seclude *see* karaba.

secluded *see* karabaki.
second *see* 1. kauoua, 2. kauoman.
section *see* maranga.
sectioned *see* marangaki.
sector *see* maranga.
secure *see* 1. kamaneaka, 2. kamaneaua, 3. kamatoa, 4. karekea, 5. mano, 6. mweraoi, 7. nonoa, 8. taua.
secured *see* 1. kamatoaki, 2. tauaki, 3. karekeaki, 4. kamaneauaki, 5. kamaneakaki, 6. nonoaki.
sedate *see* rau.
sedentary *see* tanitoko.
seduce *see* 1. eirikia, 2. kabainranga, 3. karekenano, 4. katikurerea.
seductive *see* 1. karekanano, 2. katekeria, 3. manin.
see *see* 1. namakina, 2. noria, 3. ori, 4. kina, 5. kamatebwai, 6. no, 7. nora.
seed *see* 1. kakora, 2. kaua.
seeded *see* 1. kakoraki, 2. kauaki.
seek *see* 1. rawebai, 2. ukoukora, 3. ukora, 4. ukera, 5. niniboi, 6. kekera, 7. kakaea, 8. kakae, 9. kaea, 10. kikitoa, 11. ukeuke.
seem *see* mata.
seemingly *see* raoi.
seemly *see* 1. wau, 2. raoi, 3. tenu.
seep *see* 1. katumaua, 2. raran, 3. raranginako.
seethe *see* 1. kaburoa, 2. awa.
segregate *see* 1. kamaroa, 2. kamaranga, 3. kakaokoroa.
segregated *see* 1. kakaokoroaki, 2. kamarangaki, 3. kamaroaki, 4. maroa.
seize *see* 1. biria, 2. rawebai, 3. rawea, 4. kamantoa, 5. tabaka, 6. aonikaia, 7. abuabu, 8. kamataua.
seized *see* 1. matau, 2. reke, 3. tabakaki, 4. rawebaiaki, 5. raweaki, 6. kamatauaki, 7. kamantoaki, 8. biriaki, 9. abuabuaki, 10. aonikaiaki.
seldom *see* 1. burenibai, 2. tabetai.
select *see* 1. rine, 2. matamata.
selected *see* 1. rineaki, 2. matamataki.
selfish *see* 1. bangaaomata, 2. kibangebange, 3. nanoriba.
send *see* kanakoa.
senile *see* taribaba.
senior *see* mangoieta.
sensational *see* kamimi.
sense *see* 1. kamatebwai, 2. namakin, 3. nanoata, 4. nora.
sensed *see* 1. nanoataki, 2. noraki, 3. namakinaki, 4. kamatebwaiaki.
senseless *see* tokoie.
sensible *see* 1. nanowana, 2. wana, 3. wanawana.
sensitive *see* 1. binainga, 2. kikaura.
sensuous *see* kaibabaru.
sent *see* 1. kanakoa, 2. kanakoaki.

separable *see* raureure.
separate *see* 1. kamaranga, 2. wanara, 3. ure, 4. tagerame, 5. taeka, 6. raraure, 7. katanina, 8. bwena, 9. benga, 10. kaure, 11. raeakina.
separated *see* 1. raraureaki, 2. wanaraki, 3. ureaki, 4. tagerameaki, 5. taekaki, 6. raure, 7. raeakinaki, 8. kaureaki, 9. kataninaki, 10. kamarangaki, 11. bwenaki, 12. bengaki, 13. benga, 14. mara, 15. tabara.
serenade *see* bino.
serendipitous *see* neiranraoi.
serene *see* rau.
serious *see* uramai.
sermon *see* kaotioti.
serried *see* 1. kiriuatao, 2. ko.
serve *see* 1. arobaia, 2. mwakuri.
serviced *see* mwakuriaki.
set *see* 1. katokaki, 2. neaki, 3. nea, 4. katuka, 5. katoka, 6. katikuaki, 7. katikua, 8. kaoioiaki, 9. kaoioia, 10. katukaki.
settle *see* 1. kaiakina, 2. nea, 3. tiku.
settled *see* 1. kaiakinaki, 2. tikuaki, 3. neaki.
seven *see* 1. iti, 2. itibubua, 3. itiua, 4. itoua.
seventh *see* kaitiua.
seventy *see* 1. itibwi, 2. itipoui.
several *see* 1. tabeman, 2. tabeua, 3. tabe.
severe *see* 1. tiritiri, 2. nanomakaki, 3. nanomatoatoa.
sew *see* 1. waibora, 2. itutu, 3. itu.
sewed *see* itutu.
shabby *see* 1. mane, 2. raimenga.
shade *see* 1. kanua, 2. katana, 3. nu, 4. nuna, 5. nunu, 6. taoumene.
shaded *see* 1. nunaki, 2. nunuaki, 3. katanaki, 4. kanuaki, 5. nuaki.
shadow *see* 1. mamatauna, 2. nu.
shadowed *see* 1. nuaki, 2. mamataunaki, 3. nu.
shadowy *see* nu.
shady *see* nu.
shake *see* 1. katioa, 2. taea, 3. takaruru, 4. ruru, 5. roba, 6. rangaranga, 7. maeiei, 8. kamariroa, 9. kakamwukuri, 10. itikurere, 11. io, 12. bakaruru, 13. ing, 14. katakarebua.
shaken *see* 1. katioaki, 2. takaruruaki, 3. takarebu, 4. taeaki, 5. ruruaki, 6. robaki, 7. maeieiaki, 8. ingaki, 9. katakarebuaki, 10. bakaruruaki, 11. kamariroaki, 12. kakamwukuriaki, 13. itikurereaki, 14. ioaki, 15. rangarangaki.
shaky *see* 1. bakaruru, 2. marin.
shallow *see* 1. teutana, 2. ora, 3. ôra.
shame *see* 1. niniku, 2. kaukintaea, 3. kanuka, 4. kaubunranga, 5. kamaneanea, 6. kamama, 7. kamamaea, 8. kanubebeoa.
shamed *see* 1. kaukintaeaki, 2. moatoki, 3. kaubunrangaki, 4. kanukaki, 5. kanubebeoaki, 6.

kamaneaneaki, **7**. kamamaki, **8**. kamamaeaki, **9**. ninikuaki.

shameful *see* **1**. kamama, **2**. kamwara, **3**. nea, **4**. nukabebeo.

shameless *see* **1**. kakauara, **2**. kirmatamata, **3**. maurake, **4**. tarie.

share *see* **1**. raeakina, **2**. tibwa, **3**. buokanibwai, **4**. tibatiba, **5**. tiba.

shared *see* **1**. tibatibaki, **2**. tibwaki, **3**. tibaki, **4**. raeakinaki, **5**. okioki, **6**. buokanibwaiaki.

shark *see* **1**. pakoa, **2**. bákoa.

sharp *see* **1**. antibuaka, **2**. niniwana, **3**. tarimarima, **4**. tahina, **5**. reka, **6**. mao, **7**. koa, **8**. kima, **9**. käkaña, **10**. kakang.

sharpen *see* **1**. taim, **2**. taitaim, **3**. taima, **4**. katia, **5**. katarimarima, **6**. kakangia, **7**. matairiki.

sharpened *see* **1**. katiaki, **2**. taitaimaki, **3**. kakang, **4**. matairikiaki, **5**. katarimarimaki, **6**. kakangiaki, **7**. taimaki.

shatter *see* **1**. ura, **2**. kamaenikuna, **3**. kamaerikirikia, **4**. oto.

shattered *see* **1**. uraki, **2**. otoaki, **3**. kamaenikunaki, **4**. kamaerikirikiaki.

shave *see* **1**. imana, **2**. imanna, **3**. korobuai.

shaved *see* korobuaiaki.

shear *see* katebea.

shed *see* **1**. kawanakoa, **2**. touma.

sheepish *see* **1**. take, **2**. kirarang, **3**. moatoki.

sheer *see* **1**. ti, **2**. rabe, **3**. bon, **4**. katei, **5**. kiritabataba.

shelf *see* **1**. bao, **2**. baobao, **3**. bora, **4**. buia.

shell *see* para.

shelter *see* **1**. otangana, **2**. katana, **3**. kamanoa, **4**. buibuina, **5**. rabuna, **6**. kaiakina.

sheltered *see* **1**. katanaki, **2**. rabunaki, **3**. otanganaki, **4**. kamanoaki, **5**. buibuinaki, **6**. kaiakinaki.

shelves *see* **1**. bao, **2**. baobao.

shield *see* **1**. otaotanga, **2**. otonga.

shielded *see* **1**. otaotangaki, **2**. otongaki.

shift *see* **1**. tania, **2**. mwemwe, **3**. katania, **4**. kamwemwea.

shifty *see* matanikimoa.

shimmy *see* rangaranga.

shine *see* **1**. ire, **2**. irea, **3**. karanea, **4**. karaneanea, **5**. karaneboneboa, **6**. ota, **7**. raiti, **8**. ranea, **9**. ranebonebo.

shining *see* ranebonebo.

shiny *see* **1**. raiti, **2**. raneanea, **3**. ranebonebo.

ship *see* **1**. kaibuke, **2**. urake, **3**. urakina, **4**. wa-ni-matañ.

shirker *see* mantokotoko.

shit *see* beka.

shiver *see* **1**. maninga, **2**. roba, **3**. rumangai, **4**. ruru.

shivering *see* ikarikiriki.

shock *see* **1**. angitoi, **2**. katonginakoa, **3**. kamaka, **4**. bakara.

shocked *see* **1**. angitoiaki, **2**. bakaraki, **3**. kamakaki, **4**. katonginakoaki, **5**. mwerengau.

shocking *see* kakamaku.

shoot *see* **1**. kati, **2**. roko.

shoplift *see* taebai.

short *see* **1**. kimototo, **2**. kororo, **3**. kimotoitoi, **4**. ekimôtëta, **5**. uarereke.

shorten *see* **1**. kakimotoa, **2**. karakoa, **3**. kauarerekea, **4**. kom.

shortened *see* **1**. kakimotoaki, **2**. karakoaki, **3**. kauarerekeaki, **4**. komaki.

shortly *see* **1**. kan, **2**. nang.

shot *see* **1**. teka, **2**. kati.

shoulder *see* **1**. aña, **2**. abunaña.

shouldered *see* **1**. aonangaki, **2**. roaki, **3**. tabonangaki.

shoulders *see* tapouanga.

shout *see* **1**. keuea, **2**. takarua, **3**. takaka, **4**. takaarua, **5**. wiba, **6**. kerua, **7**. keke, **8**. takaeakina.

shove *see* **1**. notunotu, **2**. wang, **3**. wanga, **4**. wakina, **5**. notua, **6**. neakina, **7**. kaonakoa, **8**. butuia, **9**. kakenakoa.

shovel *see* taiborana.

show *see* **1**. kataratara, **2**. tuanga, **3**. tengetenge, **4**. tabeka, **5**. kateretere, **6**. katara, **7**. karekei, **8**. kaota, **9**. katerea.

shower *see* **1**. karautaria, **2**. rautaria.

showy *see* rietata.

shred *see* raeraea.

shredded *see* **1**. kirimotimoti, **2**. maeae, **3**. raeraeaki, **4**. taenananga.

shrewd *see* **1**. baikoraki, **2**. ikutaba, **3**. wanawana.

shriek *see* kekerua.

shrill *see* taekeke.

shrink *see* **1**. kauanging, **2**. kauangingia, **3**. kokoi, **4**. kokoni, **5**. konin.

shrinking *see* buburerei.

shrivel *see* **1**. kokoni, **2**. kakokoea, **3**. kakukua, **4**. kauanging.

shriveled *see* kinikon.

shrivelled *see* ku.

shrunk *see* mangingi.

shudder *see* **1**. itikurere, **2**. kunainga, **3**. maninga, **4**. takariri, **5**. uere.

shun *see* **1**. katinanikua, **2**. riba.

shut *see* **1**. bonotakiaki, **2**. kainaki, **3**. kaina, **4**. kaibobuaki, **5**. kaibobua, **6**. in, **7**. bonotaki, **8**. bonota, **9**. bono, **10**. inaki.

shy *see* **1**. auba, **2**. bwerengaki, **3**. kare, **4**. ninikoria.

shyster *see* baikimoa.

sick *see* **1**. mamaoriori, **2**. ngore, **3**. ningorengore, **4**. mumuta, **5**. aorakina, **6**. aoraki, **7**. namomara, **8**. auoumaraki.

sickly *see* 1. nimaoraki, 2. tinauere, 3. ntangorengore, 4. nibanaoraki, 5. ngore, 6. mamara, 7. kimai, 8. inaito, 9. taetoba, 10. bingore, 11. aorakiaki, 12. aoaoraki, 13. kinauere.
side *see* erigi.
sidestep *see* 1. kakaro, 2. tabara.
sidetrack *see* kakibotu.
sideways *see* uabangaki.
sift *see* 1. io, 2. kamareireia, 3. neneria, 4. raumea.
sigh *see* 1. kaikeike, 2. ao, 3. ikenrawn.
sight *see* tara.
sightless *see* mataki.
sightsee *see* matabae.
sign *see* 1. iranikai, 2. kanikina, 3. tiaaina.
signal *see* 1. kanikina, 2. takarua.
signed *see* 1. iranikaiaki, 2. kanikinaki, 3. tiaainaki.
significant *see* mamaka.
significantly *see* kinokino.
silent *see* 1. kainababu, 2. rau.
silhouette *see* nu.
silly *see* 1. arobaba, 2. baba, 3. nanobaba.
similar *see* 1. tiitebo, 2. tî-te-eran.
simple *see* 1. aretau, 2. arobaba, 3. bebete, 4. beebete, 5. nanobaba.
simply *see* tiri.
simulate *see* bwaka.
simulated *see* bwakaki.
sin *see* 1. buír, 2. bure.
sincere *see* nanouki.
sinful *see* bure.
sing *see* 1. anene, 2. katangitang, 3. popihi.
single *see* 1. temanna, 2. teuana.
singly *see* tatabeua.
singular *see* 1. bainanti, 2. tatarere.
singularity *see* nanokanga.
sink *see* 1. bwaka, 2. ribu, 3. i, 4. kainakoa.
sip *see* 1. memekia, 2. meromero, 3. namta, 4. temeka, 5. temekia, 6. toma, 7. torea.
sir *see* Nao.
sire *see* Nao.
sister *see* 1. tariu, 2. tári, 3. mwaaneu, 4. tarina, 5. tarim.
sit *see* 1. tekateka, 2. toka.
six *see* 1. ono, 2. onohoua, 3. onoua.
sixth *see* kaonoua.
sixty *see* 1. onobwi, 2. onopoui.
size *see* böki.
sizzle *see* 1. tete, 2. tebarairai.
skate *see* 1. katikeke, 2. tikera.
skeptical *see* nanobebebebe.
sketch *see* bonua.
skewer *see* 1. waea, 2. wai, 3. waitekea.
skid *see* 1. katikeke, 2. tura.
skilful *see* inaguínagu.
skilled *see* 1. bati, 2. rabakau.

skillful *see* 1. rabakai, 2. rabakau, 3. bati, 4. bairaoi, 5. antibuaka.
skim *see* 1. taoburoburo, 2. bei, 3. tata, 4. tabetea, 5. katuatua, 6. katikeke.
skimmed *see* tuanokunoku.
skimp *see* taubururu.
skin *see* 1. kuokuo, 2. kuota, 3. oukoumi.
skinned *see* 1. kun, 2. nananga, 3. kuokuoaki, 4. kuotaki.
skinny *see* 1. bakikangenge, 2. bakitaia, 3. irariki, 4. kairariki, 5. mannibwerebwere, 6. mmanibwerebwere.
skip *see* 1. ewewe, 2. katuatua, 3. tata, 4. ueba.
skirmish *see* iwai.
skirt *see* 1. kamumun, 2. kiea, 3. katobibia, 4. kataoati.
skitter *see* katuatua.
skulk *see* 1. kawa, 2. maranoa.
sky *see* karava.
slack *see* 1. botumara, 2. manionio, 3. matanatana, 4. matantan, 5. matiketike, 6. nimaoriori.
slacken *see* 1. kamatantana, 2. kamatiketikea, 3. kaki, 4. kamwanua.
slag *see* kamoua.
slain *see* 1. kamarua, 2. kamatea, 3. kamateaki.
slander *see* 1. otorao, 2. ui-n'anti.
slant *see* taiaganoro.
slanted *see* 1. taiaganoro, 2. taiaganoroaki.
slanting *see* rabe.
slash *see* 1. raea, 2. raeraea, 3. raeten, 4. rae, 5. raerae, 6. raeaua.
slashed *see* 1. kirimotimoti, 2. ninimakoro, 3. raeaki, 4. raeauaki, 5. raeraeaki, 6. raetenaki.
slaughter *see* 1. kamarua, 2. tiri.
slave *see* 1. mengamenga, 2. mengo, 3. anákara, 4. rañ.
slay *see* 1. kamarua, 2. kamatea.
sleek *see* 1. katimaran, 2. maranran.
sleep *see* matu.
sleepless *see* mweuti.
sleepy *see* 1. manango, 2. matutu.
slender *see* 1. tiko, 2. aweawe, 3. inakai, 4. irariki.
slice *see* 1. korea, 2. bwerebwerea.
sliced *see* 1. bwerebwereaki, 2. korea, 3. koreaki.
slick *see* 1. karabakau, 2. kati, 3. maranran.
slide *see* 1. tikeke, 2. tikera, 3. katura, 4. kabutikeke, 5. batua, 6. tura, 7. katikeke.
slight *see* 1. kamwia, 2. uarereke, 3. teutana, 4. kimotoitoi, 5. kamatauninga, 6. kamangora, 7. irariki, 8. mamara.
slightly *see* aki.
slim *see* 1. kairi, 2. raenen, 3. kakainareke, 4. irariki, 5. inaki, 6. inakai, 7. tiko, 8. kairariki.
slimy *see* 1. tangako, 2. toto, 3. takanana, 4. monamona, 5. mona.

sling *see* bana.
slink *see* 1. kawa, 2. maranoa, 3. wauwau.
slip *see* 1. katiba, 2. maranako, 3. tikeke, 4. tiba, 5.
maetete, 6. maete, 7. katikeke, 8. katura.
slippery *see* 1. angamaran, 2. aomara, 3.
kabutikeke, 4. kati, 5. maete, 6. maran, 7.
maranran.
slit *see* 1. korea, 2. koreaki.
slither *see* katikeke.
sliver *see* 1. aea, 2. tatae.
slop *see* takareburebu.
slope *see* batete.
sloped *see* 1. bateteaki, 2. rabe.
sloping *see* 1. angamaran, 2. kabatete, 3. karabebe,
4. rabe.
slopped *see* takareburebuaki.
sloppy *see* arei.
slothful *see* taningaroti.
slovenly *see* 1. ntangaingai, 2. tangako.
slow *see* 1. wiremwe, 2. au, 3. bairemwe, 4.
birimara, 5. karaurau, 6. meere, 7. mweau, 8.
mwere, 9. niau, 10. niniakai, 11.
takaremwermwe, 12. uara, 13. waeremwe.
slowly *see* karaurau.
sluggish *see* 1. kibara, 2. manio, 3. nimamate, 4.
taningaroti.
slumber *see* 1. kiro, 2. manango, 3. matu.
slurp *see* 1. namta, 2. meroa, 3. meromero.
sly *see* 1. wanawana, 2. nanomano, 3. mataukiro, 4.
atutekonaua, 5. karabakau.
smack *see* 1. boa, 2. rebwe.
small *see* 1. teutana, 2. uangingi, 3. uarereke, 4.
titaoutana, 5. tiko, 6. ningorengore, 7. mte, 8.
kakarako, 9. karako, 10. tekinini.
smallest *see* kinati.
smart *see* 1. rabakai, 2. wanawana, 3. ueke, 4.
taerieri, 5. niniwana, 6. maritata, 7. kikiriman, 8.
kauman, 9. kateke, 10. karabakau, 11. baitata, 12.
maraki, 13. tena.
smash *see* 1. kaibakoa, 2. urua, 3. uraka, 4. ura, 5.
kamaea, 6. ibea, 7. kataururua.
smashed *see* 1. maenikun, 2. nimoti, 3. uruaki, 4.
urakaki, 5. maotorikiriki, 6. kamaeaki, 7.
kaibakoaki, 8. bakibora, 9. kaibako, 10. uraki, 11.
ibeaki, 12. kataururuaki.
smear *see* 1. katakanakana, 2. kabira.
smeared *see* 1. kabiraki, 2. katakanakanaki.
smell *see* 1. aroboi, 2. aroka, 3. aroki, 4. boi, 5.
neneboi.
smile *see* 1. wingare, 2. moangare, 3. matangare, 4.
inga.
smiling *see* matangare.
smite *see* 1. batiboa, 2. boa, 3. orea, 4. oro.
smoke *see* 1. moko, 2. teme.
smoked *see* 1. mokoaki, 2. temeaki.
smoky *see* 1. bubu, 2. buaiai.

smooth *see* 1. maranran, 2. tiraka, 3. tiritoa, 4. teroa,
5. tea, 6. taetoa, 7. matinnao, 8. mara, 9.
maborabora, 10. katimaran, 11. kati, 12. aomara,
13. maran, 14. kamarana.
smother *see* 1. kamanga, 2. taona.
smothered *see* 1. kamangaki, 2. taonaki.
smoulder *see* 1. makaro, 2. uramate, 3. takaro, 4.
uramaki.
smudge *see* kabira.
smudged *see* kabiraki.
snack *see* kaikewi.
snake *see* kakiribabaoua.
snap *see* 1. kateba, 2. motika, 3. tebe.
snapped *see* 1. tebeaki, 2. motikaki, 3. katebaki.
snare *see* 1. katataia, 2. taokabia, 3. taware, 4.
bauna.
snatch *see* 1. kuria, 2. rawea, 3. rawekaia.
sneak *see* 1. kainabaea, 2. kawa, 3. kawainimone, 4.
maranoa, 5. uabuaka, 6. wauwau.
sneer *see* bukinimata.
sneeze *see* 1. matie, 2. titirou.
sniff *see* 1. aroboi, 2. kamba, 3. neneboi.
snip *see* takoro.
snipe *see* ukuni.
snitch *see* tua.
sniveling *see* nanobu.
snore *see* 1. ringongo, 2. ingongo.
snort *see* ringongoraki.
snub *see* kaberetokoa.
snubbed *see* 1. kaberetokoaki, 2. nea.
snuffle *see* ngangarake.
so *see* kanga.
soak *see* kamara.
soaked *see* 1. kamaraki, 2. maimai, 3. makinono, 4.
maong, 5. mara, 6. tingo, 7. waneinei.
soap *see* tobu.
soar *see* rierake.
soaring *see* kiba.
sob *see* 1. mango, 2. tang, 3. kaikeike, 4. maikeike.
sober *see* taubank.
sociable *see* 1. boibuako, 2. maningainga.
sodden *see* 1. maratingo, 2. rota, 3. makimaki, 4.
maki.
soft *see* 1. matiketike, 2. titi, 3. tangauriuri, 4. rau, 5.
noumangang, 6. makana, 7. mori, 8. toto, 9.
maneouna, 10. mamaoriori, 11. makanakana, 12.
makone, 13. kiaiai, 14. kabutikeke, 15. baubau,
16. maramara.
soften *see* 1. kamatiketikea, 2. katita, 3.
kamarauakina, 4. kamakanakana, 5. kabaketea, 6.
katotoa, 7. kamarauaka.
softened *see* 1. kamarauakinaki, 2. mara, 3.
katotoaki, 4. kamatiketikeaki, 5. kamarauakaki, 6.
kamakanakanaki, 7. kabaketeaki, 8. katitaki.
softly *see* karaurau.

soil *see* **1.** kangata, **2.** tantano, **3.** katakanakana, **4.** kabareka, **5.** katingoa, **6.** kabetingaingaia.

soiled *see* **1.** betingaingai, **2.** kabarekaki, **3.** kabetingaingaiaki, **4.** kangataki, **5.** katakanakanaki, **6.** katingoaki, **7.** ngatingati, **8.** tantano, **9.** tantanoaki.

sojourn *see* **1.** maeka, **2.** tiku, **3.** titiku.

sold *see* **1.** kaboanako, **2.** kaboanakoaki, **3.** kabonakoa.

soldier *see* tautia.

sole *see* teuana.

solemn *see* tabu.

solicit *see* **1.** bubuti, **2.** butia, **3.** kao, **4.** onon.

solicited *see* **1.** butiaki, **2.** kaoaki, **3.** bubutiaki, **4.** ononaki.

solicitous *see* nanobukibuki.

solid *see* **1.** ba, **2.** banin, **3.** bua, **4.** kauniben, **5.** teimatoa.

solitary *see* **1.** atutarere, **2.** mamaroa, **3.** maroa, **4.** takarere.

solve *see* iango.

solved *see* iangoaki.

somber *see* nanokawa.

sombre *see* **1.** ka, **2.** nu.

some *see* **1.** tabe, **2.** tabeman, **3.** uta.

someone *see* tamanna.

somersault *see* katiobuki.

sometimes *see* **1.** kareke, **2.** tabetai.

somnolent *see* nimatutu.

son *see* **1.** houa, **2.** nati.

song *see* takataka.

soon *see* **1.** nang, **2.** kan, **3.** hehi, **4.** tawe.

sop *see* kamara.

sorcerer *see* **1.** ibonga, **2.** tiakai.

sorcery *see* kaiwa.

sore *see* **1.** mwaka, **2.** kabuâ.

sorrowful *see* **1.** nanokawaki, **2.** raraoma.

sorry *see* **1.** mango, **2.** nanokawaki, **3.** rainanoanga.

sort *see* **1.** kaokoro, **2.** aeka.

sorted *see* **1.** kaokoroaki, **2.** aekaki, **3.** kaokoro.

sought *see* **1.** kakera, **2.** kakeraki, **3.** ukoukora, **4.** ukoukoraki.

sound *see* **1.** baibait, **2.** banin, **3.** kauniben.

soundless *see* **1.** nanokirokiro, **2.** nanokiroro.

sour *see* **1.** boongata, **2.** tena, **3.** mao, **4.** karongo, **5.** mai, **6.** mangingi.

southbound *see* maiaki.

southerly *see* maiaki.

sow *see* **1.** ununiki, **2.** kamara, **3.** unika.

space *see* **1.** uki, **2.** marena, **3.** akea, **4.** kawarebwea.

spaced *see* uki.

spacious *see* **1.** ababaki, **2.** warebwe, **3.** rababa, **4.** mawa, **5.** mwawawa.

spade *see* kai-ni-kâbua.

span *see* binoka.

spare *see* tatabuia.

sparing *see* tababu.

spark *see* **1.** takaro, **2.** taukaro.

sparkle *see* **1.** raititi, **2.** ruberube.

sparkling *see* **1.** takaneanea, **2.** buburerei.

sparse *see* **1.** tare, **2.** karako.

spasm *see* katikitiki.

spat *see* **1.** baroa, **2.** baroaki, **3.** baware, **4.** bawareaki.

spathe *see* gakak.

spatter *see* **1.** bururu, **2.** kamerea, **3.** taberuru.

spattered *see* **1.** taberuruaki, **2.** bururuaki, **3.** kamereaki.

spawn *see* bung.

spawning *see* kimarimari.

speak *see* **1.** kangai, **2.** kaokia, **3.** kaotioti, **4.** marooro, **5.** taetae.

spear *see* **1.** ewara, **2.** katoua, **3.** kawete, **4.** ooua.

spearhead *see* kaira.

special *see* okoro.

specific *see* okoro.

specifically *see* okoro.

specified *see* kaonotaki.

specify *see* kaonota.

speckle *see* **1.** katantana, **2.** kawanta, **3.** waiteketekea.

speckled *see* **1.** katantanaki, **2.** kawantaki, **3.** kinawanawa, **4.** kiritantan, **5.** tanan, **6.** waiteketeke, **7.** waiteketekeaki.

spectacular *see* kakamataku.

speculate *see* **1.** iango, **2.** taku.

speech *see* tak.

speed *see* rerea.

spell *see* **1.** ware, **2.** wareka.

spellbound *see* maraia.

spend *see* kabanea.

spent *see* **1.** kabanea, **2.** kabaneaki.

spew *see* mumuta.

spherical *see* **1.** tironron, **2.** mron, **3.** mronron, **4.** tibia.

spicy *see* reka.

spike *see* boua.

spiked *see* **1.** bouaki, **2.** kakang, **3.** kirikakang.

spiky *see* kakang.

spill *see* **1.** baro, **2.** baroakina, **3.** kabaroa, **4.** kamrara, **5.** nurakina.

spin *see* **1.** kaminoa, **2.** nimamano, **3.** mimitoi, **4.** kabukuwi, **5.** binoka, **6.** minota.

spine *see* ñîeta.

spineless *see* **1.** nimaoriori, **2.** tangauriuri.

spinning *see* mimitoi.

spiny *see* kakang.

spirit *see* **1.** ënt, **2.** zentz.

spirited *see* kukurei.

spit *see* **1.** baroa, **2.** baware, **3.** paouare.

spite *see* 1. kairiribai, 2. nokua.
spiteful *see* nanobuaka.
spittle *see* bauwar.
splash *see* 1. teboran, 2. bururu, 3. kia, 4. kiara, 5. tebeka.
splashed *see* 1. teboranaki, 2. tebekaki, 3. kiaraki, 4. bururuaki, 5. kiaki.
splendid *see* 1. tamaroa, 2. kakanno, 3. mimitong, 4. raneanea.
splice *see* 1. reitia, 2. toma.
splint *see* 1. kaiba, 2. kaibaea, 3. ribata.
splinter *see* tourika.
splintered *see* tourikaki.
split *see* 1. tabaki, 2. raeraeaki, 3. raeua, 4. raeuaki, 5. tabwenauaki, 6. raewa, 7. bwena, 8. taba, 9. tabwenaua, 10. makorouaki, 11. rewák, 12. kataeaki, 13. kataea, 14. bwenaki, 15. bwenabwena, 16. bouaki, 17. boua, 18. aeaki, 19. aea, 20. makoroua.
splitting *see* raeing.
spoil *see* 1. taubururu, 2. tabureka, 3. tabuarikia, 4. riripia, 5. kuribwaia, 6. kawanta, 7. kabuakaka, 8. kawanrea.
spoiled *see* 1. kabuakakaki, 2. tabuarikiaki, 3. taubururuaki, 4. taburekaki, 5. kuribwaiaki, 6. mka, 7. kawanreaki, 8. kawantaki.
spoke *see* taetae.
spoken *see* taetae.
sponsor *see* kaboa.
spook *see* kamaka.
spoon *see* buun.
spoonfeed *see* karewi.
sporadic *see* tokitoki.
sportive *see* makei.
spot *see* 1. katanea, 2. waiteketekea, 3. maroaka, 4. kina, 5. katantana, 6. kawanta.
spotless *see* itiwewe.
spotted *see* 1. kinawanawana, 2. tanan, 3. waiteketekeaki, 4. tantan, 5. maroakaki, 6. kiriwantanta, 7. kiritantan, 8. kinaki, 9. kawantaki, 10. katantanaki, 11. bareka, 12. kataneaki, 13. kinawanawa, 14. borengarenga, 15. waiteketeke.
spouse *see* 1. bu, 2. bû.
spout *see* 1. kati, 2. ti, 3. kabararia.
sprain *see* 1. katarou, 2. tabiro, 3. touru.
sprawl *see* inra.
sprawled *see* inraki.
spray *see* 1. bururua, 2. bururu, 3. bunong.
spread *see* 1. taotira, 2. tanga, 3. tangaki, 4. karaeaki, 5. tanoata, 6. tanoataki, 7. taonaba, 8. taorababa, 9. taotiraki, 10. tatao, 11. tataoaki, 12. tekeboti, 13. tiraka, 14. tirakaki, 15. tamaki, 16. taonabaki, 17. kabao, 18. katakareaki, 19. arora, 20. aroraki.
spreading *see* 1. taorababa, 2. taotira.

spring *see* 1. ewe, 2. ingiraki, 3. kona, 4. tebe.
sprinkle *see* 1. uria, 2. nuraki, 3. tara, 4. kamerea, 5. bururu, 6. katimtima, 7. taura.
sprinkled *see* 1. bururuaki, 2. kamereaki, 3. katimtimaki, 4. nuraka, 5. nurakiaki, 6. taraki, 7. tauraki, 8. uriaki.
sprint *see* 1. tarou, 2. birimaka.
sprout *see* 1. roko, 2. bwebwe, 3. gakak.
sprouted *see* bwebweaki.
sprouting *see* bwebwe.
spur *see* kawaetataia.
spurn *see* kaberetokoa.
spurned *see* kaberetokoaki.
spurt *see* 1. bururu, 2. bururua, 3. kia, 4. ti.
spy *see* 1. kina, 2. tutuo, 3. taukiro, 4. taratara.
squabble *see* 1. ibewi, 2. ikakaiwi, 3. ikangui, 4. kauntaeka.
squalid *see* 1. bewawa, 2. kamaira, 3. mangori.
squander *see* 1. bakataea, 2. kataonaba, 3. katurara, 4. kimaua.
squandered *see* 1. bakataeaki, 2. kimauaki, 3. kataonabaki, 4. katuraraki.
squanderer *see* kimaua.
squandering *see* kimaung.
square *see* 1. katoang, 2. katoatoa, 3. tabanin, 4. tikeuea, 5. toang, 6. toatoa, 7. toatoana.
squared *see* 1. toatoanaki, 2. katoatoaki, 3. katoangaki.
squash *see* 1. kamatiratira, 2. kamatiraua, 3. tira, 4. kaburinana.
squashed *see* 1. kaburinanaki, 2. kamatiratiraki, 3. kamatirauaki, 4. makibora, 5. matiratira, 6. matiraua, 7. tiraki.
squat *see* 1. toro, 2. tuanonoku, 3. bakurakura.
squeak *see* 1. katemeteme, 2. tang, 3. torara, 4. ainikai.
squeal *see* 1. kea, 2. tua.
squeeze *see* 1. kaburinana, 2. kona, 3. ongira, 4. taoakai.
squelch *see* 1. kaburinana, 2. kamanamana.
squint *see* 1. kabwatutua, 2. kamatabaoa, 3. karaea, 4. kabwatuta.
squinting *see* rae.
squirm *see* 1. ininimaki, 2. iwai.
squirt *see* 1. bakati, 2. bunong, 3. kati, 4. ti.
stab *see* 1. ewara, 2. katekea, 3. nekea, 4. rawana.
stabbed *see* 1. nekeaki, 2. rawanaki, 3. katekeaki, 4. ewaraki, 5. teka.
stabilize *see* kamwaneaua.
stabilized *see* kamwaneauaki.
stable *see* 1. kauniben, 2. teimatoa, 3. toronibai.
stack *see* kabwarikorikoa.
stacked *see* 1. makoko, 2. kabwarikorikoaki, 3. kiruatao.

stagger *see* 1. bebe, 2. kiritabaiore, 3. rainging, 4. tatatata, 5. nibakabaka, 6. kiritabataba, 7. kiribebe, 8. kakuba, 9. bebebebe, 10. bebei, 11. kiriongong.

staggering *see* teibaka.

stagnate *see* 1. matantokomaung, 2. tikumaurekaki.

stain *see* 1. kawanta, 2. kitaina, 3. kameamea, 4. kamatamata, 5. kakitaia, 6. matamatana.

stained *see* 1. bareka, 2. kakitaiaki, 3. kamatamataki, 4. kameameaki, 5. kawantaki, 6. kitainaki, 7. mata, 8. matamatanaki.

stake *see* karaotua.

stale *see* 1. taniberoro, 2. manrea, 3. boongata.

stalling *see* rekebuta.

stammer *see* 1. nanobebebe, 2. rerarera, 3. takutaku.

stamp *see* 1. baiturua, 2. katuru, 3. katurua, 4. katuruturu.

stamped *see* 1. baituruaki, 2. katuruaki, 3. katuruturuaki.

stampede *see* karurunginakoa.

stand *see* 1. tei, 2. teirake.

standardize *see* manina.

standardized *see* maninaki.

standing *see* etei.

star *see* tuitui.

starch *see* matoanna.

stare *see* 1. matamau, 2. tiro, 3. kareketara, 4. tiroa.

stark *see* 1. banin, 2. bon, 3. iakai.

start *see* 1. moana, 2. tourake, 3. moanna, 4. kui, 5. aboka, 6. kuba, 7. moa.

starting *see* aboka.

startle *see* 1. bakara, 2. kakuba, 3. kakuia, 4. katourakea, 5. kauba.

startled *see* 1. kakubaki, 2. kaubaki, 3. kakuiaki, 4. bakaraki, 5. auba, 6. katourakeaki.

starve *see* 1. bakaruru, 2. bakiriro, 3. bakiruru, 4. kabakarurua, 5. kabakia.

starved *see* 1. kabakiaki, 2. bakaruruaki, 3. bakiriroaki, 4. bakiruruaki, 5. kabakaruruaki.

starving *see* kibakibaki.

state *see* taku.

stated *see* takuaki.

station *see* 1. kaiakina, 2. katea, 3. katoka.

stationary *see* 1. tei, 2. teitei.

staunch *see* 1. kakaonimaki, 2. teimatoa.

stay *see* 1. mena, 2. totokoa, 3. tiku, 4. maeka, 5. karitei, 6. titiku.

steadfast *see* 1. kakaonimaki, 2. karitoa, 3. nene, 4. teimatoa.

steady *see* 1. matoa, 2. nene, 3. rarango.

steal *see* 1. iraea, 2. toto, 3. tuaira, 4. kakamwarua, 5. ira, 6. baito, 7. aubanga, 8. kimoa, 9. irabai.

stealth *see* nanoraki.

stealthy *see* nanoraki.

steam *see* kabuane.

steamed *see* kabuaneaki.

steamy *see* taribubu.

steely *see* kima.

steep *see* kamara.

steer *see* 1. taubwe, 2. tohoupe, 3. bwe, 4. urunga, 5. kabwea.

steered *see* 1. bweaki, 2. kabweaki, 3. taubweaki, 4. urungaki.

stem *see* kauna.

stemmed *see* kaunaki.

step *see* 1. rangata, 2. mwanika.

stepped *see* 1. mwanikaki, 2. rangataki.

sterile *see* kanoabo.

stick *see* 1. kanima, 2. nimta, 3. kai, 4. nim, 5. katuna.

sticky *see* 1. bewawa, 2. mana, 3. mona, 4. nim, 5. nimnana, 6. nimnim.

stiff *see* 1. kakai, 2. tikintaka, 3. tikinono, 4. nene, 5. kai, 6. iakai, 7. aotiki, 8. ngeraruru.

stiffen *see* 1. kakimatoa, 2. kariraki, 3. katikintakaea, 4. katikitiki, 5. tikitiki.

stiffened *see* 1. tikitikiaki, 2. kakimatoaki, 3. karirakiaki, 4. katikintakaeaki, 5. katikitikiaki.

stifle *see* 1. toabara, 2. rabuna.

stifled *see* 1. rabunaki, 2. toabaraki.

stifling *see* taniberoro.

still *see* 1. karaua, 2. ma, 3. rau, 4. tabe, 5. taribabu.

stillborn *see* rikimate.

stimulate *see* 1. katutua, 2. kaunga, 3. kakeiaka, 4. angita, 5. roroka.

stimulated *see* 1. kakeiakaki, 2. katutuaki, 3. kaungaki, 4. rorokaki.

sting *see* 1. ewara, 2. katena, 3. nekea, 4. tena.

stinging *see* tena.

stingy *see* 1. taut, 2. tautikoko, 3. tauti, 4. kibangebange, 5. banganikoko, 6. tatauti.

stink *see* bimaung.

stinking *see* 1. maung, 2. tekemangongo.

stir *see* 1. kateirakea, 2. takarebutata, 3. kakibeuria, 4. kakibekibe, 5. kakamwakuri, 6. kabobooa, 7. kaboboa, 8. kaboa, 9. kakibea.

stirred *see* 1. kakamwakuriaki, 2. takarebutataki, 3. kateirakeaki, 4. kakibeuriaki, 5. kaboaki, 6. kakibeaki, 7. kabobooaki, 8. kaboboaki, 9. kakibekibeaki.

stitch *see* 1. itutu, 2. waewae.

stitched *see* 1. itutuaki, 2. waewaeaki.

stock *see* kamariboa.

stocked *see* 1. koko, 2. kamariboaki.

stocky *see* 1. kaubiroto, 2. tuanonoku.

stoke *see* 1. aerona, 2. kanaiai.

stole *see* 1. baito, 2. ira, 3. iraea, 4. kimoa, 5. toto.

stolen see 1. iraeaki, 2. tuairaki, 3. totoaki, 4. kimoaki, 5. iraki, 6. irabaiaki, 7. baitoaki, 8. aubangaki, 9. kakamwaruaki.

stomach see piroto.

stomp see ibeki.

stone see touan.

stony see kauatibu.

stoop see bobaraki.

stooped see 1. baokoko, 2. beuakora.

stop see 1. tiku, 2. waitotokoa, 3. toki, 4. tai, 5. matabae, 6. bonota, 7. tei.

stopped see 1. matabaeaki, 2. waitotokoaki, 3. tokiaki, 4. teiaki, 5. kibono, 6. bonotaki, 7. bono, 8. tikuaki.

store see kaikoa.

stored see kaikoaki.

storm see takurara.

stout see 1. tinaubati, 2. korakora, 3. korabaia, 4. bubura, 5. kaubiroto.

stoutness see marika.

stow see 1. kaibea, 2. katikua, 3. nnea, 4. tokia.

stowed see 1. tokiaki, 2. kaibeaki, 3. kakiaki, 4. katikuaki, 5. nneaki.

straddle see raka.

straggle see 1. aua, 2. inroa.

straight see 1. aweawe, 2. eti, 3. etiruru, 4. îti, 5. kaetiko, 6. ngkainaba.

straightaway see ngkainaba.

straighten see kaeta.

straightened see kaetaki.

strain see 1. raumea, 2. tarou, 3. katarou, 4. touru, 5. katikinono.

strained see 1. tarouaki, 2. touruaki, 3. taberuarua, 4. raumeaki, 5. katikinonoaki, 6. katarouaki.

strait see 1. inneti, 2. irariki, 3. teiraoi, 4. wariki, 5. etiruru.

straiten see 1. kaintorua, 2. kawarika, 3. kaeta, 4. kaetia.

straitened see 1. kaetaki, 2. kaetiaki, 3. kaintoruaki, 4. kawarikaki.

strand see 1. kabikôuea, 2. taerake.

stranded see taerakeaki.

strange see 1. antena, 2. kamimi, 3. mimi, 4. teiruarua.

stranger see 1. ianena, 2. ianna, 3. irua.

strapping see taboang.

stray see 1. batirae, 2. tabea.

streaked see 1. maeretongitong, 2. mata, 3. nawanawa.

streamline see kawairinana.

strengthen see 1. buoka, 2. kamarurung, 3. kamatoa, 4. nonoa.

strengthened see 1. buokaki, 2. nonoaki, 3. kamarurungaki, 4. kamatoaki.

strenuous see 1. kanganga, 2. marurung, 3. nanomwane.

stretch see 1. karena, 2. kariraki, 3. kararatia, 4. arora.

stretchable see rena.

stretched see 1. inroa, 2. tikinene, 3. tiki, 4. rena, 5. tikinono, 6. rarati, 7. karirakiaki, 8. kararatiaki, 9. borababaua, 10. aroraki, 11. anaukaei, 12. karenaki.

strew see katakarea.

strewn see 1. inroa, 2. teibanae.

stricken see orea.

strict see 1. nanomatoatoa, 2. matoa, 3. korakora.

strictly see okoro.

stride see 1. raka, 2. rakaia, 3. rangatia.

strike see 1. bobo, 2. oro, 3. kamabu, 4. boa, 5. batiboa, 6. orea.

striking see kateke.

string see 1. katabara, 2. kamatana.

stringy see 1. wakariri, 2. wakawaka, 3. waka, 4. kiriwaka, 5. komau.

strip see 1. ake, 2. bubai, 3. raea, 4. raerae, 5. unaenae, 6. unarira.

stripe see matamatana.

striped see 1. nimatamata, 2. matamatanaki, 3. aeae, 4. kakawaki, 5. maerere.

stripped see 1. akeaki, 2. bubaiaki, 3. nananga, 4. ra, 5. raeaeaki, 6. raeraeaki, 7. unaenaeaki, 8. unariraki.

strive see 1. mamarake, 2. uamoa, 3. keiakina, 4. kaiaki, 5. ibabu, 6. kamanenanti.

stroke see 1. bo, 2. botam, 3. rainia.

stroll see 1. nakomai, 2. tamweremwere, 3. katiki, 4. kakaautakia.

strong see 1. kora, 2. taboang, 3. pumping, 4. nanomane, 5. matoatoa, 6. mamaka, 7. korakora, 8. bumbing, 9. tabonang, 10. karitoa, 11. kaura, 12. batikora, 13. baibati, 14. baibait, 15. angamatoa, 16. aintoa, 17. kiangang.

struck see 1. orea, 2. oreaki, 3. teka.

struggle see 1. kiriweswe, 2. takarema, 3. takarebutata, 4. takaere, 5. rebutata, 6. ibabu, 7. rangarangatau, 8. kaiaki, 9. iwai, 10. ininimaki, 11. ikibekibe, 12. iakiaki, 13. buaka, 14. inimaki.

struggling see 1. rangarangatau, 2. rebutata.

strut see 1. kakaeutakia, 2. rorouba.

stubborn see 1. bakatoki, 2. bobono, 3. buburamaiu, 4. katinono, 5. namatoa, 6. nanomatoa, 7. tounene.

stuck see 1. kanimaki, 2. katunaki, 3. nimaki, 4. nimtaki.

student see kairi.

studied see 1. kekeiakiaki, 2. reireiaki.

study see 1. reirei, 2. kekeiaki.

stuff see 1. atoa, 2. kaibea, 3. kakeboa, 4. kimra, 5. ngangaua.

stuffed *see* **1.** atoaki, **2.** tokaki, **3.** tibutaua, **4.** kimraki, **5.** ngangauaki, **6.** kimri, **7.** kaibeaki, **8.** ibo, **9.** baki, **10.** ibe, **11.** kakeboaki.

stumble *see* **1.** bwaka, **2.** kairua, **3.** nibakabaka, **4.** rainging, **5.** tata, **6.** tataro, **7.** tatatata.

stumbling *see* turu.

stump *see* butan-te-ni.

stumpy *see* reka.

stun *see* **1.** kakiritongitong, **2.** kakiritongitonga, **3.** katonga, **4.** katonginakoa, **5.** katongiraraea, **6.** angitoi.

stung *see* **1.** ewara, **2.** ewaraki, **3.** tana, **4.** tanaki.

stunned *see* **1.** katongaki, **2.** tonginako, **3.** ntongitong, **4.** kiritongitong, **5.** katongiraraeaki, **6.** kakiritongitongaki, **7.** angitoiaki, **8.** katonginakoaki.

stunted *see* **1.** kinerang, **2.** tokira, **3.** tinauere, **4.** ntangorengore, **5.** kinene, **6.** inaito, **7.** bingore, **8.** tikumoro.

stupefied *see* **1.** kakiritongitongaki, **2.** kiriongong, **3.** kiritongitong, **4.** tonginako, **5.** katongiraraeaki, **6.** kamataanoanoaki, **7.** kananobabaki.

stupefy *see* **1.** kakiritongitong, **2.** kamataanoanoa, **3.** kananobaba, **4.** katongiraraea.

stupendous *see* **1.** abakaei, **2.** toari.

stupid *see* **1.** bobono, **2.** tabweang, **3.** nanobaba, **4.** baba, **5.** bono.

sturdy *see* kauniben.

stutter *see* **1.** reraera, **2.** takurere, **3.** takutaku.

style *see* karaoa.

styled *see* karaoaki.

stylish *see* kateke.

subdue *see* **1.** kataea, **2.** toabara, **3.** terona, **4.** kataenikaia, **5.** kamanana, **6.** baimatoa, **7.** aonkaia, **8.** taona.

subdued *see* **1.** aonkaiaki, **2.** baimatoaki, **3.** kamananaki, **4.** kataeaki, **5.** kataenikaiaki, **6.** taonaki, **7.** taonikai, **8.** teronaki, **9.** toabaraki.

subject *see* **1.** tautorona, **2.** torona, **3.** terona.

subjugated *see* taonikai.

sublime *see* nano.

submerge *see* **1.** taotebe, **2.** tebo.

submerged *see* **1.** aitao, **2.** taotebeaki, **3.** teboaki.

submissive *see* inataba.

submit *see* anibana.

subordinate *see* anibange.

subsequent *see* **1.** rimwi, **2.** kiriaria.

subsequently *see* **1.** kiriaria, **2.** rimwi.

subsist *see* maiu.

substantial *see* **1.** bongana, **2.** kakanato, **3.** mamaka.

substitute *see* **1.** ruamwi, **2.** tauantaboa.

subtract *see* **1.** ana, **2.** anai.

subtracted *see* **1.** anaiaki, **2.** anaki.

subversive *see* taningato.

succeed *see* **1.** katoka, **2.** toka, **3.** ruamwi.

successful *see* tekaraoi.

succor *see* **1.** bakuaku, **2.** buoka.

succumb *see* **1.** baka, **2.** mate, **3.** taenikaiaki.

such *see* aeka.

suck *see* **1.** mbambaea, **2.** toma, **3.** temeka, **4.** nenge, **5.** namta, **6.** nam, **7.** meromero, **8.** memeka, **9.** mamma, **10.** kamba, **11.** baronria, **12.** memeroa.

suckle *see* kamamma.

suckled *see* kamammaki.

suction *see* nako.

sudden *see* **1.** taerina, **2.** rina, **3.** takaerere, **4.** karina, **5.** kakuba, **6.** kataerina.

suddenly *see* **1.** karina, **2.** rina.

suffer *see* maraki.

suffering *see* nimanan.

sufficient *see* botau.

suffocate *see* **1.** bonoike, **2.** kamanga, **3.** ngawa.

suffocated *see* **1.** ngawaki, **2.** bonoikeaki, **3.** kamangaki.

suggest *see* **1.** wina, **2.** wiwi.

suggested *see* **1.** winaki, **2.** wiwiaki.

suit *see* **1.** botau, **2.** tau.

suitable *see* **1.** boraoi, **2.** botau, **3.** kan, **4.** raoi, **5.** tau, **6.** tenu.

suitably *see* raoi.

suited *see* **1.** kona, **2.** tauaki, **3.** botauaki.

sulk *see* **1.** kanaeng, **2.** rawa.

sulky *see* **1.** kinokunoku, **2.** matanoku, **3.** noku.

sullen *see* **1.** aotaningo, **2.** matanoku, **3.** nanomano, **4.** noku, **5.** rarai.

summit *see* toka.

summon *see* **1.** kea, **2.** weta, **3.** kao, **4.** wetea.

sun *see* **1.** tahahi, **2.** tai.

sunburnt *see* **1.** bwata, **2.** mwae.

sunder *see* **1.** boua, **2.** bwenaua, **3.** karaurea, **4.** korouaia.

sunny *see* riringa.

sunset *see* bungintaai.

super *see* korakora.

superabundant *see* taotira.

superficially *see* aki.

superimposed *see* maru.

superintend *see* **1.** tararuaia, **2.** taratara.

superior *see* **1.** mangoieta, **2.** rine, **3.** urukau.

superlative *see* moaniba.

supernatural *see* kakanaugaki.

supersede *see* rimoa.

supervise *see* **1.** taratara, **2.** tauoa, **3.** tarabai, **4.** tantani, **5.** tararuaia.

supervised *see* **1.** tauoaki, **2.** tantaniaki, **3.** tarabaiaki, **4.** tararuaiaki, **5.** tarataraki.

supervisory *see* tararuaia.

supplant *see* aonikaia.

supple *see* **1.** kamaen, **2.** maen, **3.** maoriori.

supplement *see* karaka.

supplicate *see* onon.
supplied *see* 1. kamariboaki, 2. rawebaiaki, 3. katoaki.
supply *see* 1. kamariboa, 2. katoa, 3. rawebaia.
support *see* 1. tautoka, 2. totokoa, 3. taubuki, 4. nangoa, 5. kautokoa, 6. kaintorua, 7. botuakina, 8. itaobuki, 9. nango.
supported *see* 1. kaintoruaki, 2. totokoaki, 3. tautokaki, 4. taubukiaki, 5. botuakinaki, 6. kautokoaki, 7. itaobukiaki, 8. nangoaki.
supporting *see* tabeitera.
suppose *see* 1. namakin, 2. nanoata, 3. ngkae, 4. katautau, 5. taku, 6. karamakina, 7. iango, 8. ko.
supposed *see* 1. iangoaki, 2. karamakinaki, 3. katautauaki, 4. namakinaki, 5. nanoataki, 6. takuaki.
suppress *see* 1. tiri, 2. toabara, 3. taona, 4. karaba, 5. kaka, 6. katoka.
suppressed *see* 1. toabaraki, 2. karabaki, 3. katokaki, 4. taonaki, 5. tiriaki, 6. kakaki.
sure *see* 1. matatoka, 2. koaua, 3. ataia, 4. kaeng.
surely *see* 1. ane, 2. bon, 3. dokóv, 4. ngaiangaia.
surf *see* 1. no, 2. nôno.
surge *see* 1. naonao, 2. tabetabe, 3. tabonao, 4. bwaro.
surly *see* 1. noku, 2. rarai, 3. matabubuaka, 4. kaburati.
surmise *see* 1. nanoata, 2. rereti, 3. namakin.
surmount *see* 1. riaonikai, 2. kamaterea, 3. moa.
surmounted *see* 1. riaonikaiaki, 2. kamatereaki, 3. moaki.
surpass *see* 1. aona, 2. katekea, 3. moa, 4. raka, 5. rebe, 6. rianako, 7. riaoa.
surpassing *see* 1. rianako, 2. riao, 3. rine.
surprise *see* 1. bakara, 2. tabaka, 3. kauba, 4. kamimi, 5. kakuba.
surprised *see* 1. tabakaki, 2. take, 3. kaubaki, 4. kamimiaki, 5. kakubaki, 6. bobouro, 7. bakaraki.
surprising *see* 1. manenanti, 2. karuanano.
surrender *see* konaaki.
surrendered *see* konaakiaki.
surround *see* 1. otabaninia, 2. tiera, 3. uamanea, 4. teibanea, 5. nonoua, 6. kiribambanta, 7. katobibia, 8. baua, 9. bomanea.
surrounded *see* 1. katobibiaki, 2. uamaneaki, 3. tieraki, 4. teibaneaki, 5. otabaniniaki, 6. kiribambantaki, 7. maneaua, 8. bomaneaki, 9. bauaki, 10. nonouaki.
survey *see* 1. tatarara, 2. taukiro.
survive *see* 1. maiu, 2. tokabeti.
susceptible *see* 1. kinokunoku, 2. nanorake, 3. kainoki.
suspect *see* 1. namakin, 2. rereti, 3. nanoata, 4. bukina, 5. maninutoa, 6. karamakina, 7. maninuto.

suspected *see* 1. bukunaki, 2. karamakinaki, 3. maninutoaki, 4. namakinaki, 5. nanoataki, 6. reretiaki.
suspend *see* 1. tiebba, 2. katiobabaea.
suspended *see* 1. katiobabaeaki, 2. tiebbaki.
sustain *see* rona.
sustained *see* ronaki.
swagger *see* 1. kirei, 2. tebetebe.
swaggering *see* 1. bakaunun, 2. kaburabura, 3. kirei, 4. nikierere.
swallow *see* 1. onga, 2. kabaubau, 3. nima.
swallowed *see* 1. ongaki, 2. kabaubauaki, 3. nimaki.
swamp *see* 1. baoti, 2. bwaroa, 3. kakeboa.
swamped *see* 1. baotiaki, 2. bwaroaki, 3. kakeboaki.
swampy *see* 1. aoneiney, 2. neinei.
swank *see* rietata.
swarm *see* 1. ntangana, 2. ntangianga, 3. nanai, 4. kaoro, 5. nata.
swarming *see* 1. kaoro, 2. karebun.
sway *see* 1. bebe, 2. eiei, 3. kaeia, 4. rarai, 5. vaeiei.
swear *see* 1. taetaebuaka, 2. wauwi.
sweat *see* 1. maono, 2. mahono.
sweating *see* 1. barara, 2. maong.
sweaty *see* maono.
sweep *see* 1. buroungia, 2. buruna, 3. iaaki, 4. iaki, 5. iakina, 6. kaitiaka, 7. taea.
sweet *see* 1. karewe, 2. karewerewe, 3. nanai.
sweeten *see* 1. karewi, 2. karewena.
sweetened *see* 1. karewenaki, 2. karewiaki.
swell *see* 1. buro, 2. katabatibutibua, 3. katitibengaua, 4. rereta, 5. tibu.
swelled *see* 1. buroaki, 2. titibengaua, 3. tabatibutibu, 4. tibu.
swelling *see* tiburake.
swept *see* 1. iaakiaki, 2. kaitiakaki, 3. iakinaki, 4. taeaki, 5. iakiaki, 6. burunaki, 7. buroungiaki, 8. iakina.
swerve *see* 1. kakaro, 2. karae, 3. katua, 4. kiritbataba.
swift *see* 1. birimaka, 2. kaumaki, 3. mwaka, 4. waetata.
swiftly *see* 1. waetata, 2. mwaka.
swim *see* 1. uaua, 2. houhoua.
swindle *see* 1. aubanga, 2. mamana.
swing *see* 1. kabei, 2. katietiea, 3. katinea, 4. katioa, 5. taurangaranga, 6. tie, 7. tio.
swipe *see* taubarea.
swish *see* taubarea.
switch *see* rai.
swivel *see* mino.
swollen *see* 1. babangaki, 2. intibua, 3. kiritibutibu, 4. matibu, 5. nibunini, 6. rereka, 7. rereta, 8. tiburere, 9. tibutau, 10. toa, 11. aouti.

swoon *see* **1**. tunga, **2**. kiro, **3**. tuunga, **4**. rarau, **5**. tong.

swoop *see* kukume.

sympathetic *see* **1**. imamanu, **2**. nanoanga.

sympathise *see* nanoanga.

sympathize *see* **1**. imammane, **2**. nanoangaea.

T

taboo *see* **1**. mabu, **2**. tabu.

tabu *see* dua.

tack *see* eriake.

tackle *see* **1**. kaubata, **2**. rawea, **3**. taua.

tactless *see* witakanana.

tag *see* kakino.

tagged *see* kakinoaki.

tail *see* kawe.

tailed *see* **1**. bukikakang, **2**. kaweaki.

tainted *see* **1**. boria, **2**. bunau.

take *see* **1**. taoua, **2**. tuana, **3**. rawea, **4**. tianakiana, **5**. katiribo, **6**. buta, **7**. ana, **8**. nikira.

taken *see* **1**. otoaki, **2**. tuanaki, **3**. raweaki, **4**. nikiraki, **5**. manto, **6**. katiriboaki, **7**. butaki, **8**. buta, **9**. anaki, **10**. ana, **11**. maneaua, **12**. tianakianaki.

talented *see* rabakau.

talk *see* **1**. kakarabakau, **2**. tak, **3**. taetae, **4**. kakarabakaua, **5**. marooro.

talkative *see* **1**. babarantiko, **2**. kabararia, **3**. takuarara, **4**. wirebwerebwe.

tall *see* **1**. anânau, **2**. reitata, **3**. ananau.

tame *see* **1**. manana, **2**. nanobu, **3**. kamanana.

tamed *see* kamananaki.

tamp *see* kaki.

tangible *see* matatoka.

tangle *see* **1**. kabeakoa, **2**. kabeoa, **3**. karaia, **4**. karengaoa.

tangled *see* **1**. kabeoaki, **2**. matakao, **3**. makaoakao, **4**. karaiaki, **5**. kabeakoaki, **6**. bewa, **7**. beako, **8**. karengaoaki.

tap *see* karebwerebwe.

tape *see* kanima.

taped *see* kanimaki.

tapering *see* wai.

tapped *see* karebwerebweaki.

tardy *see* **1**. mwere, **2**. takaremwermwe.

tarnish *see* kawanrea.

tarnished *see* **1**. kawanreaki, **2**. warea.

tarry *see* **1**. tataninga, **2**. teitei, **3**. titiku.

tart *see* **1**. mai, **2**. reka.

task *see* môgur.

taste *see* **1**. teme, **2**. kannim, **3**. katomam, **4**. katonga, **5**. meromero, **6**. nam, **7**. namta, **8**. nokangkang.

tasteless *see* **1**. mammam, **2**. ba, **3**. mai.

tasty *see* **1**. kangkang, **2**. kannim, **3**. karekeria, **4**. katekeria, **5**. nanai.

tattered *see* **1**. maeae, **2**. nimananginang, **3**. ninimoti.

tattle *see* **1**. tua, **2**. kaewetaeka, **3**. kaeweananga, **4**. babarantiko.

tattoo *see* **1**. taitai, **2**. bonu.

tattooing *see* tahite.

taught *see* **1**. beireinaki, **2**. kaetietiaki, **3**. rarati, **4**. reireia, **5**. reireiaki.

taunt *see* **1**. kaena, **2**. kauna.

taut *see* **1**. iwaka, **2**. tikintaka, **3**. tikinono, **4**. ngea, **5**. ariraki, **6**. tiki.

teach *see* **1**. beireina, **2**. kaetieti, **3**. reireia.

team *see* katanga.

tear *see* **1**. raerae, **2**. raraea, **3**. raeua, **4**. raemenga, **5**. raeraea, **6**. tenarua, **7**. raeaua, **8**. raea, **9**. rae, **10**. ourouake, **11**. moimotikia, **12**. burimaunia, **13**. raeten, **14**. raebitia.

tears *see* ran-ni-mata.

tease *see* **1**. kaena, **2**. kaenaena.

teased *see* **1**. kaenaenaki, **2**. kaenaki.

technically *see* okoro.

teem *see* **1**. kabun, **2**. natao.

teenage *see* roronranairake.

teenager *see* roronranairake.

teeth *see* **1**. moui, **2**. wi.

telegram *see* uaereti.

tell *see* **1**. taekina, **2**. tua, **3**. tuangia.

temp *see* **1**. kariria, **2**. tauantaboa.

temper *see* **1**. kabaketea, **2**. katirea, **3**. taubank.

temperamental *see* kibaura.

temperate *see* taubang.

tempered *see* **1**. kakaiun, **2**. katireaki, **3**. kiura, **4**. taubank, **5**. taubankaki, **6**. kabaketeaki.

temple *see* ba-ni-mata.

tempt *see* **1**. kariri, **2**. kata, **3**. wina, **4**. wiwi, **5**. wiwina.

ten *see* **1**. tebuina, **2**. tepouina, **3**. tañáun, **4**. teñaun, **5**. tebwina.

tenacious *see* **1**. nanomaka, **2**. tebomaurua, **3**. kanene, **4**. iwaka, **5**. inamatoa, **6**. botuakina.

tend *see* kawakina.

tender *see* **1**. mori, **2**. toto, **3**. rau, **4**. makone, **5**. nabe, **6**. waeai, **7**. marau, **8**. makana, **9**. kiaiai, **10**. maraurau, **11**. memeri.

tenderize *see* **1**. katotoa, **2**. kaubatial.

tenderized *see* **1**. kaubatialaki, **2**. katotoaki.

tending *see* nano.

tentative *see* kata.

tenth *see* katebwina.

tepid *see* **1**. ang, **2**. angibue.

terminal *see* kakaiaki.

terminate *see* **1**. kabanea, **2**. toki, **3**. katoka, **4**. katia, **5**. kamarua, **6**. kamatea.

terminated *see* **1**. tokiaki, **2**. kabaneaki, **3**. kamaruaki, **4**. kamateaki, **5**. katia, **6**. katiaki, **7**. katokaki, **8**. moti, **9**. tia.

terrible *see* **1**. nanomakaki, **2**. kakurere, **3**. kakunainga, **4**. kakamaku.

terrific *see* **1**. abakaei, **2**. buburakaei.

terrified *see* **1**. kakunaingaki, **2**. kakurereaki, **3**. kamakuaki.

terrify *see* **1**. kakunainga, **2**. kakurerea, **3**. kamakua.

terrifying *see* kakamaku.

terrorize *see* **1**. kamaka, **2**. kamakua, **3**. kakurerea, **4**. kakunainga, **5**. katonginakoa.

test *see* **1**. kataea, **2**. ukeuke.

tested *see* **1**. kataeaki, **2**. ukeukeaki.

testify *see* **1**. kaotioti, **2**. tua.

testy *see* kakaiun.

thank *see* **1**. kaitau, **2**. karaba.

thatch *see* **1**. rau, **2**. ati, **3**. rauna, **4**. kakari, **5**. ato.

thaw *see* kamara.

thawed *see* kamaraki.

the *see* **1**. te, **2**. ko, **3**. tan, **4**. teng, **5**. teuana, **6**. tong.

then *see* **1**. ñkan, **2**. rumwi, **3**. ngke, **4**. ao.

theorize *see* iangororoko.

there *see* **1**. âio, **2**. arei, **3**. ari, **4**. ikekei.

thereabouts *see* ikoa.

therefrom *see* **1**. maiai, **2**. maikanne, **3**. mairoun.

thereupon *see* ngkanne.

thick *see* **1**. bubura, **2**. matenten, **3**. maru, **4**. bua, **5**. atamaumau, **6**. maten, **7**. buabua.

thicken *see* **1**. atamaumau, **2**. kaoioia.

thickened *see* **1**. atamaumauaki, **2**. kaoioiaki.

thickening *see* ruomatoa.

thief *see* **1**. baikimoa, **2**. îra, **3**. bairawata, **4**. baitabare.

thievish *see* kimao.

thigh *see* toae.

thin *see* **1**. manni, **2**. tea, **3**. uareereke, **4**. ruamakana, **5**. rerek, **6**. mmani, **7**. kiengenenge, **8**. kairariki, **9**. kairarika, **10**. irariki, **11**. bakikangenge, **12**. bukimake.

things *see* bwaai.

think *see* **1**. taku, **2**. nanoa, **3**. iangoa, **4**. iango.

thinned *see* **1**. bakikangengeaki, **2**. kairarikaki, **3**. teaki.

third *see* kateniua.

thirsty *see* **1**. mautakaroro, **2**. taka, **3**. takaroro.

thirty *see* tenibwi.

thither *see* ôt.

thorny *see* kakang.

thou *see* **1**. ñgôe, **2**. uñgô.

though *see* ko.

thought *see* iango.

thoughtless *see* **1**. remereme, **2**. kabi.

thousand *see* **1**. nga, **2**. tenga.

thrash *see* **1**. batiboa, **2**. kataea, **3**. oroia, **4**. takaerere, **5**. takariuriu, **6**. tiribo, **7**. tirimataere.

thread *see* **1**. ararâ, **2**. wai, **3**. waea, **4**. itu, **5**. itutu, **6**. nama.

threaded *see* **1**. ituaki, **2**. itutuaki, **3**. namaki, **4**. waeaki, **5**. waiaki, **6**. waka.

threaten *see* **1**. tabora, **2**. wibuakaia, **3**. titaou, **4**. taetaeraia, **5**. kamakua, **6**. kakoroiku, **7**. ibebure, **8**. tinaraea.

three *see* **1**. ten, **2**. teni, **3**. tennai, **4**. tenoua, **5**. tenua.

thrifty *see* **1**. rako, **2**. tababu, **3**. tatabwi.

thrill *see* **1**. karikari, **2**. tatatata, **3**. kakukureia.

thrilled *see* **1**. kakukureiaki, **2**. karikariaki, **3**. tatatataki.

thrive *see* maiureirei.

thriving *see* **1**. maiurerirei, **2**. maiuroaroa.

throat *see* bûwu.

throb *see* **1**. tatatata, **2**. bukibuki, **3**. karikari, **4**. ruberube, **5**. tata.

throng *see* kia.

through *see* rinanon.

throw *see* **1**. imita, **2**. jevenako, **3**. kaomwaka, **4**. kaonakoa, **5**. kare, **6**. karekare, **7**. tewe, **8**. tewea.

thrown *see* **1**. kareaki, **2**. teweaki, **3**. karekareaki, **4**. kaonakoaki, **5**. kaomwakaki, **6**. imitaki, **7**. tewe, **8**. kare.

thrust *see* **1**. kakenakoa, **2**. notua, **3**. notunotu, **4**. rerea.

thud *see* **1**. buki, **2**. bukibuki, **3**. bukirurunga, **4**. bukitau.

thump *see* **1**. bekua, **2**. bo, **3**. batiboa, **4**. kabekua.

thunder *see* **1**. bä, **2**. paha.

thunderous *see* **1**. kaorakora, **2**. ngaruru.

thus *see* **1**. kangai, **2**. ëran.

thwart *see* **1**. mangamanga, **2**. karotu, **3**. kakiroa, **4**. kaberetokoa, **5**. kairiribai.

thwarted *see* **1**. kaberetokoaki, **2**. mangamangaki, **3**. karotuaki, **4**. kairiribaiaki, **5**. kakibotu, **6**. kakiroaki.

tick *see* rebwe.

ticket *see* tiketi.

tickle *see* **1**. ikaika, **2**. kamaranea, **3**. maranea.

tidy *see* kanikan.

tie *see* **1**. kabae, **2**. taekai, **3**. kabaea, **4**. bauta, **5**. arena, **6**. are, **7**. ramanea.

tied *see* **1**. areaki, **2**. arenaki, **3**. bautaki, **4**. kabaeaki, **5**. maneaua, **6**. ramaneaki, **7**. taekaiaki.

tight *see* **1**. nene, **2**. niko, **3**. tikinono, **4**. tiki, **5**. ko, **6**. kimri, **7**. kawaraki, **8**. kariba, **9**. takoko.

tighten *see* **1**. arira, **2**. biroa, **3**. karibak, **4**. katena, **5**. katikintakaea, **6**. kimra.

tightened *see* **1**. katenaki, **2**. katikintakaeaki, **3**. biroaki, **4**. ariraki, **5**. karibakaki, **6**. kimraki.

till *see* **1**. kibera, **2**. ribana.

tilled *see* **1**. ribanaki, **2**. kiberaki.

tilt *see* 1. taiaganoro, 2. rabeniben, 3. eiei, 4. karara.
tilted *see* 1. eieiaki, 2. kararaki, 3. rabenibenaki, 4. taiaganoroaki.
time *see* tai.
timed *see* 1. taiaki, 2. tai.
timely *see* 1. aitau, 2. butikaraoi.
timid *see* 1. angama, 2. binainga, 3. inaberu, 4. kiberuberu, 5. kimamaku, 6. mama, 7. ninikoria.
timorous *see* mamaku.
tingle *see* 1. nikiari, 2. taerieri.
tinkle *see* 1. bing, 2. tangirarae.
tint *see* 1. kamatamata, 2. nuna.
tinted *see* 1. kamatamataki, 2. mata, 3. nunaki.
tiny *see* 1. teutana, 2. uangini, 3. uangingi, 4. tingingi, 5. karako, 6. kakarako, 7. bingingi, 8. kimotoitoi.
tire *see* 1. wanga, 2. botu.
tired *see* 1. nimorimori, 2. wanga, 3. rarau, 4. ôrara, 5. ôgua, 6. ntakuakua, 7. nikuakua, 8. maong, 9. kua, 10. kauma, 11. ka, 12. inaña, 13. boubu, 14. botu, 15. mate, 16. ntungaungau.
tiresome *see* 1. kaboati, 2. memeto, 3. meme, 4. kateinang.
tiring *see* 1. kaboati, 2. kabotu, 3. kakau, 4. kamou, 5. kateinang, 6. kawanga.
titan *see* aintoa.
titanic *see* 1. abakaei, 2. buburakaei, 3. toari, 4. wari.
title *see* aranna.
titled *see* arannaki.
titter *see* ngarengare.
to *see* 1. ina, 2. n, 3. nako, 4. nakon.
to abdicate *see* 1. kakea, 2. kerikaki.
to abduct *see* konana.
to abhor *see* riba.
to abjure *see* kakea.
to abrade *see* 1. kara, 2. kuota, 3. raraikumea.
to abut *see* nimimarea.
to accede *see* kariaia.
to accomplish *see* 1. karaoia, 2. ungara.
to achieve *see* karekea.
to activate *see* taungatangata.
to administrate *see* tautaeka.
to admire *see* 1. kamoamoa, 2. noakinak, 3. mimi, 4. miroa.
to admonish *see* boa.
to adopt *see* 1. imammane, 2. natina, 3. natinati, 4. tibuna.
to advise *see* matana.
to allude *see* tarae.
to amass *see* 1. karibonobonoa, 2. kawawaea.
to amuse *see* 1. kamatakua, 2. wanikangarea, 3. katakakaroa, 4. kakibotu, 5. manikangare.
to anesthetize *see* kakiroa.
to animalize *see* 1. kaubunranga, 2. mwiniba.

to anoint *see* kamanenaka.
to applaud *see* 1. kekeia, 2. kakannatoa.
to arbitrate *see* karotuang.
to asphyxiate *see* ngawa.
to asphyxiated *see* ngawaki.
to aspire *see* mamarake.
to assemble *see* 1. maio, 2. kawawaea, 3. kabo, 4. iko, 5. baronga, 6. botaki.
to assess *see* kinanoa.
to attain *see* rota.
to avenge *see* nimamate.
to avert *see* wira.
to awaken *see* 1. uti, 2. rakea.
to bake *see* 1. aumua, 2. kariki.
to bastardize *see* 1. kaubunranga, 2. mwiniba.
to beautify *see* 1. katamaroa, 2. unauna.
to bedaub *see* katakanakana.
to behead *see* 1. kabakua, 2. baku.
to bemoan *see* tangiroa.
to bereave *see* 1. ana, 2. kabua.
to beseech *see* 1. bubuti, 2. kairoro, 3. onon.
to besmirch *see* katakanakana.
to bestrew *see* kamerea.
to bewail *see* tangiroa.
to beware *see* 1. karaurau, 2. kawakiniko.
to bloat *see* kiritibutibu.
to blurt *see* meakina.
to breastfeed *see* kammamma.
to bring *see* 1. ana, 2. uota, 3. nikira.
to burglarize *see* maro.
to cajole *see* toroba.
to celebrate *see* 1. kakannatoa, 2. neboa, 3. nikierere.
to cheapen *see* mwiniba.
to circulate *see* kawawa.
to cognize *see* 1. kamatebwai, 2. nora.
to collaborate *see* 1. buoka, 2. buoki.
to come *see* 1. karina, 2. karokoa, 3. roko, 4. rokona.
to commence *see* 1. teirake, 2. moanang, 3. aboka, 4. karika.
to compel *see* kairoroa.
to compensate *see* bo.
to compete *see* kaunikai.
to compile *see* kawawaea.
to complain *see* 1. mea, 2. tangitang, 3. tang, 4. ngurengure, 5. ngure, 6. meme, 7. mere.
to complicate *see* 1. kakawibaea, 2. mangamanga, 3. kaiewe.
to compute *see* taoman.
to condemn *see* 1. bukinna, 2. rabungaoa.
to confabulate *see* kakarabakau.
to congest *see* karibak.
to connect *see* katuna.
to conspire *see* baka.
to constrict *see* taburaka.

to **contemplate** *see* 1. iangoa, 2. mimi, 3. taku, 4. tiroakina.
to **contradict** *see* 1. kauntabama, 2. waewae, 3. takebono, 4. unrake, 5. karotu, 6. untaba, 7. kabitara, 8. ekara, 9. bitara, 10. karotua.
to **converge** *see* mra.
to **convey** *see* 1. urake, 2. urakina.
to **conveyed** *see* 1. urakeaki, 2. urakinaki.
to **convoke** *see* 1. vetea, 2. kawawaea, 3. roroka.
to **cooperate** *see* 1. buoka, 2. ibuobuoki.
to **covet** *see* 1. mataiakina, 2. tangira, 3. nanoati, 4. kan, 5. kakae, 6. bukinimata, 7. nanonibwi, 8. keta.
to **cram** *see* 1. ngaungau, 2. tonga, 3. ngauta, 4. kakeboa, 5. intibua, 6. ngangaua.
to **crave** *see* 1. kan, 2. nanoati, 3. baru, 4. onon.
to **create** *see* 1. kariki, 2. kakariki, 3. karika.
to **cremate** *see* kaura.
to **crepitate** *see* takarebwetata.
to **criticize** *see* 1. waewae, 2. betunga, 3. kabetiwai, 4. tauburea.
to **decapitate** *see* 1. kabakua, 2. baku.
to **decorate** *see* 1. ete, 2. katamaroa, 3. manimaninia, 4. timua, 5. unauna, 6. unekea, 7. bwerea.
to **deepen** *see* atamaumau.
to **defraud** *see* 1. kewe, 2. uarao, 3. babakanikawai.
to **delete** *see* kamanang.
to **delude** *see* 1. kairerebua, 2. mamana.
to **demolish** *see* 1. uraka, 2. uruabai.
to **denounce** *see* 1. bukina, 2. bukuna, 3. tua.
to **denude** *see* 1. raea, 2. taerake, 3. wanara.
to **deny** *see* kakea.
to **deplore** *see* ritangia.
to **descend** *see* 1. ruo, 2. tuka, 3. karuoa, 4. bung.
to **describe** *see* 1. kabwarabwara, 2. aeka.
to **destine** *see* kakaunongo.
to **devaluate** *see* 1. kaubunranga, 2. mwiniba.
to **develop** *see* 1. rikirake, 2. tanga, 3. riki, 4. ewenako.
to **devour** *see* 1. kabaubau, 2. tenarua, 3. ngauta, 4. ngaungau, 5. kang, 6. kamangaungauakina, 7. kana.
to **differ** *see* kaokoro.
to **differentiate** *see* taunari.
to **dine** *see* 1. amarake, 2. katonga.
to **disapprove** *see* 1. rabungaoa, 2. riba.
to **disarrange** *see* 1. kakakaurekana, 2. riringa.
to **disassociate** *see* kamaranga.
to **disavow** *see* kakea.
to **discover** *see* 1. reke, 2. maroaka, 3. kunea.
to **disenchant** *see* karikaka.
to **disjoin** *see* kamaranga.
to **dislocate** *see* 1. rebe, 2. karebenakoa, 3. katiba, 4. raemenga.

to **dismember** *see* raebai.
to **disobey** *see* takebono.
to **disperse** *see* 1. kamerea, 2. kauamaea, 3. mae, 4. mare, 5. tagerame.
to **displease** *see* 1. bononano, 2. kanaengai.
to **disseminate** *see* kauamaea.
to **dissuade** *see* kananomaraea.
to **disturb** *see* 1. kananomaruru, 2. riringa, 3. katabetabea, 4. kananora, 5. kananobukibuki, 6. kamatakiaua, 7. kakai, 8. kaintoka, 9. karawawata.
to **diverge** *see* kakaraurekana.
to **domineer** *see* tautorona.
to **donate** *see* anga.
to **dumbfound** *see* 1. kakiritongitong, 2. kamatakua.
to **economize** *see* tatabuia.
to **educate** *see* 1. reireia, 2. tonga, 3. beireina.
to **elope** *see* biriakinnako.
to **emaciate** *see* bakikangenge.
to **emerge** *see* 1. bu, 2. riki.
to **ensnare** *see* tawarea.
to **enthuse** *see* kananobukibuki.
to **entreat** *see* onon.
to **entrench** *see* 1. niba, 2. karuarua, 3. manawaia.
to **erupt** *see* reberake.
to **evaluate** *see* ukeuke.
to **exaggerate** *see* 1. kareao, 2. wikabwea, 3. wibeka, 4. raka, 5. kariara, 6. karakarongorongo, 7. karakaraka, 8. kakawibaea, 9. betanna, 10. maninrongorongo.
to **exclaim** *see* 1. taetae, 2. takarua.
to **excoriate** *see* kataeari.
to **excrete** *see* beka.
to **execrate** *see* riba.
to **execute** *see* 1. kamarua, 2. kamatea, 3. karaoa, 4. karaoia.
to **exist** *see* 1. iai, 2. maiu.
to **expect** *see* 1. kantaninga, 2. nora, 3. kamatebwai.
to **expire** *see* mate.
to **expunge** *see* kamauna.
to **exterminate** *see* kamatea.
to **extol** *see* 1. kakannatoa, 2. neboa.
to **fiance** *see* raou.
to **flay** *see* kuota.
to **flee** *see* rere.
to **flog** *see* 1. kataere, 2. robuna, 3. tirimataere.
to **fluctuate** *see* 1. taunga, 2. uarurung.
to **foresee** *see* biririmoa.
to **foretell** *see* biritaetae.
to **forgo** *see* kakea.
to **formulate** *see* iangomaka.
to **freshen** *see* maitoro.
to **fulfill** *see* maotorrikiriki.
to **furbish** *see* 1. ire, 2. karanea.

to gallivant *see* 1. kareuma, 2. rebu, 3. rebutonga.
to gestate *see* nako.
to gnash *see* torara.
to gyrate *see* 1. minomino, 2. nikamonmon.
to hallow *see* 1. tabua, 2. katabua.
to hallucinate *see* mitara.
to halve *see* 1. makoroua, 2. bwenaua.
to hearken *see* 1. ongo, 2. kakaunongo.
to humidify *see* karota.
to hypnotize *see* kamatua.
to identify *see* 1. ataia, 2. nora.
to imbibe *see* mooi.
to immolate *see* tiringa.
to impart *see* anga.
to impede *see* 1. karotua, 2. tinerua, 3. tuka.
to impel *see* wakina.
to implore *see* onon.
to imprecate *see* 1. bukinna, 2. karereantia, 3. wauwi.
to impute *see* kanotona.
to inaugurate *see* moana.
to incise *see* 1. koria, 2. korokoroia, 3. makoro.
to incriminate *see* 1. bukina, 2. uton.
to inculpate *see* uton.
to induct *see* karemea.
to infest *see* 1. kaona, 2. taona.
to infiltrate *see* 1. ranene, 2. aeae.
to inflect *see* kabaoa.
to infuse *see* karina.
to ingurgitate *see* ngaungau.
to inherit *see* 1. ababa, 2. bwaibwai, 3. kabaibai.
to insinuate *see* 1. wiwi, 2. kinraea, 3. tarae.
to insist *see* 1. buburamaiu, 2. imanono, 3. kairoro, 4. katinono, 5. tebomaurua.
to insulate *see* kakaokoroa.
to intercalate *see* marena.
to intercede *see* raoiakina.
to interject *see* kaintoka.
to intermingle *see* 1. kairengarenga, 2. rea, 3. rengana.
to intermix *see* kairengarenga.
to introduce *see* 1. rin, 2. kaitiboa, 3. karina.
to investigate *see* 1. nenera, 2. ukouko, 3. kekera.
to invoke *see* 1. taboa, 2. kaunga.
to josh *see* kareao.
to jubilate *see* kimareirei.
to lade *see* kamengoa.
to legislate *see* tautaeka.
to liquefy *see* 1. kamara, 2. ruamakana.
to listen *see* 1. ongo, 2. kauongo, 3. kakaunongo, 4. kakaunongo, 5. ongora.
to loathe *see* riba.
to lubricate *see* 1. bwana, 2. kabira.
to magnify *see* katamaroa.

to maltreat *see* 1. bainikirina, 2. manibuaka, 3. maura.
to masticate *see* 1. kamakerua, 2. kanta, 3. makiro.
to misconstrue *see* 1. bitabao, 2. kabitaraea.
to mishandle *see* maura.
to mislay *see* kabua.
to mislead *see* 1. kamaningaki, 2. burebureaki, 3. mamanaki, 4. mamana, 5. bureburea, 6. kairerebua, 7. kairerebuaki, 8. kamaninga.
to misplace *see* aiewe.
to mistreat *see* 1. manibuaka, 2. maura, 3. bainikirina.
to modify *see* bita.
to modulate *see* kauakina.
to moralize *see* kakarine.
to mourn *see* 1. mango, 2. tang.
to mutate *see* taie.
to narrate *see* 1. karakina, 2. taekina.
to navigate *see* 1. borauakina, 2. ieie, 3. borau, 4. karoroa.
to negate *see* 1. kaakea, 2. kamatea.
to notify *see* 1. kaongora, 2. kauka, 3. kaota, 4. katanoata.
to nuzzle *see* butubutu.
to occur *see* riki.
to opt *see* rine.
to originate *see* maroaka.
to oscillate *see* 1. tietie, 2. tio, 3. tie, 4. tiotio, 5. rabeniben, 6. kabei, 7. ranea.
to outclass *see* kamaterea.
to overeat *see* buabeka.
to overfill *see* kataoa.
to overhear *see* kakauongo.
to overprice *see* 1. bomatoa, 2. bora, 3. kamataraea.
to oversee *see* 1. noakinak, 2. tararuaia.
to oversleep *see* matunako.
to overstate *see* maninrongorongo.
to overstay *see* tikuroaroa.
to overstep *see* 1. biriao, 2. riaoa.
to overwhelm *see* 1. baroa, 2. kainakoa, 3. kamauna, 4. kateinang, 5. kiribambanta, 6. taona.
to pamper *see* 1. kamona, 2. kaniko, 3. nabea.
to panhandle *see* mange.
to pare *see* tea.
to partake *see* 1. taeka, 2. buokanamarake, 3. buokanibwai.
to penetrate *see* 1. karibua, 2. karina, 3. karinakoa, 4. katekea, 5. maro, 6. rawana, 7. rin, 8. tania.
to perish *see* 1. mate, 2. mauna.
to persevere *see* 1. tebonengenenge, 2. botuakina.
to perspire *see* maono.
to persuade *see* kairoroa.
to perturb *see* 1. kananora, 2. kamatakiaua.
to pilfer *see* 1. ira, 2. iraea, 3. katawe, 4. kimoa, 5. rawebaia.

to **practise** see kataneiai.
to **precede** see 1. biririmoa, 2. rimoa, 3. taumoa.
to **preclude** see 1. taokabia, 2. tuka.
to **preconceive** see taukirikiri.
to **predict** see 1. karamakina, 2. mamata.
to **prefer** see 1. tangirariki, 2. binenga, 3. rine.
to **premeditate** see kantaningaki.
to **preside** see 1. atuna, 2. kautu.
to **proclaim** see 1. takaeakina, 2. takaka.
to **procreate** see 1. kariki, 2. karika, 3. kakariki.
to **procure** see 1. kamariboa, 2. karekea, 3. rawea, 4. rawebai, 5. rawebaia.
to **prognosticate** see 1. bukinanganga, 2. kaiwa.
to **prolong** see 1. reita, 2. witokonaua.
to **propagate** see 1. karika, 2. karikirakea.
to **propel** see 1. kawaka, 2. wakina, 3. kainaoa.
to **provide** see 1. rawebaia, 2. riko, 3. kamariboa.
to **publicize** see tabangaea.
to **pulsate** see 1. bukibuki, 2. ikeike, 3. karikari, 4. ruberube, 5. tata, 6. tatatata.
to **pulverize** see 1. bubua, 2. i.
to **pursue** see 1. katootoonga, 2. kite, 3. kara, 4. kakioa, 5. kaea, 6. wakina.
to **qualify** see manikoraki.
to **quantify** see boraoi.
to **ravish** see konana.
to **react** see kaeka.
to **rearrange** see tiba.
to **recede** see kakerikaka.
to **recollect** see 1. uring, 2. uringa, 3. reketa, 4. iango, 5. ururinga.
to **recommend** see wina.
to **reconstruct** see karikaki.
to **recover** see eka.
to **recriminate** see mea.
to **recuperate** see kamaoa.
to **recycle** see kamatoroa.
to **redeem** see 1. kamaiua, 2. kaboa.
to **redo** see manga.
to **refurbish** see 1. karikaki, 2. kaua.
to **regurgitate** see mumuta.
to **reinforce** see 1. kaintorua, 2. tautoka.
to **rejoin** see kaeka.
to **relate** see 1. karakina, 2. taekina.
to **remember** see 1. uringa, 2. uringnga.
to **remembered** see 1. uringngaki, 2. uringaki.
to **renew** see kaua.
to **renounce** see 1. kakea, 2. kitana.
to **repent** see 1. mango, 2. nanomaraki, 3. raraoma.
to **replace** see 1. ikaruoruo, 2. karuoruo, 3. ruamwi, 4. tauantaboa.
to **repossess** see nikira.
to **repudiate** see kamabu.
to **resent** see 1. nanora, 2. noku, 3. riba.
to **resign** see kerikaki.

to **resound** see 1. bwarubwaru, 2. tangimwaka, 3. keru, 4. rurunga.
to **restock** see kaua.
to **restrict** see 1. kamabu, 2. tikona, 3. kawarika, 4. kaonota.
to **retain** see 1. taua, 2. antingoa, 3. tau.
to **retaliate** see irantanga.
to **retract** see 1. kakerikaka, 2. kauangingia.
to **reunite** see 1. botaki, 2. kabo.
to **revert** see karairaki.
to **revive** see kamaka.
to **sadden** see kananokawaki.
to **salivate** see 1. baroa, 2. baware.
to **scavenge** see kaukea.
to **scrounge** see kaukea.
to **secede** see kerikaki.
to **seclude** see karaba.
to **seem** see mata.
to **seep** see 1. katumaua, 2. raran, 3. raranginako.
to **send** see kanakoa.
to **shoplift** see taebai.
to **shrivel** see 1. kokoni, 2. kakokoea, 3. kakukua, 4. kauanging.
to **sightsee** see matabae.
to **sizzle** see 1. tete, 2. tebarairai.
to **skitter** see katuatua.
to **slither** see katikeke.
to **smite** see 1. batiboa, 2. boa, 3. orea, 4. oro.
to **speculate** see 1. iango, 2. taku.
to **stabilize** see kamwaneaua.
to **stepped** see 1. mwanikaki, 2. rangataki.
to **stoke** see 1. aerona, 2. kanaiai.
to **stow** see 1. kaibea, 2. katikua, 3. nnea, 4. tokia.
to **strew** see katakarea.
to **styled** see karaoaki.
to **subsist** see maiu.
to **subtract** see 1. ana, 2. anai.
to **summon** see 1. kea, 2. weta, 3. kao, 4. wetea.
to **superintend** see 1. tararuaia, 2. taratara.
to **supplicate** see onon.
to **suppress** see 1. tiri, 2. toabara, 3. taona, 4. karaba, 5. kaka, 6. katoka.
to **sweeten** see 1. karewi, 2. karewena.
to **sympathise** see nanoanga.
to **sympathize** see 1. imammane, 2. nanoangaea.
to **tend** see kawakina.
to **tenderize** see 1. katotoa, 2. kaubatial.
to **terminate** see 1. kabanea, 2. toki, 3. katoka, 4. katia, 5. kamarua, 6. kamatea.
to **terrorize** see 1. kamaka, 2. kamakua, 3. kakurerea, 4. kakunainga, 5. katonginakoa.
to **thank** see 1. kaitau, 2. karaba.
to **theorize** see iangororoko.
to **thrash** see 1. batiboa, 2. kataea, 3. oroia, 4. takaerere, 5. takariuriu, 6. tiribo, 7. tirimataere.

to **tighten** *see* 1. arira, 2. biroa, 3. karibak, 4. katena, 5. katikintakaea, 6. kimra.
to **toughen** *see* katikintakaea.
to **transect** *see* renaua.
to **transfix** *see* 1. bakarerea, 2. winikibwia.
to **transform** *see* 1. onika, 2. onikia.
to **translate** *see* raira.
to **transmigrate** *see* uamumun.
to **trisect** *see* korotenia.
to **trounce** *see* 1. tiribaonoa, 2. oro, 3. batiboa, 4. orea.
to **unbind** *see* unobauta.
to **uncover** *see* uka.
to **undertake** *see* 1. teirakea, 2. moanang.
to **undo** *see* 1. tanara, 2. kabara, 3. kamanang.
to **unhook** *see* katiba.
to **unify** *see* boraoi.
to **untangle** *see* tanara.
to **upchuck** *see* mumuta.
to **uproot** *see* 1. routa, 2. taeka.
to **urinate** *see* 1. maimai, 2. mimi, 3. meira, 4. mim.
to **vaccinate** *see* itina.
to **vacillate** *see* 1. kanebu, 2. rangaranga.
to **venerate** *see* karinea.
to **vibrate** *see* 1. itikurere, 2. ruru, 3. kanebu.
to **waken** *see* mangauti.
to **warn** *see* 1. kawanawana, 2. tuanga.
to **wield** *see* 1. bwaina, 2. kamanena, 3. taua.
to **yearn** *see* 1. mamarake, 2. nanona.
toast *see* 1. kiraoki, 2. kakunna.
toasted *see* 1. kakunnaki, 2. kiraokiaki.
toddler *see* merimeri.
together *see* 1. kiribwebwe, 2. takoko.
toil *see* 1. mengamenga, 2. mengo.
toilsome *see* kamou.
tolerant *see* 1. nanomawa, 2. nanouki.
tolerate *see* kataua.
tomorrow *see* 1. ñaboñiboñi, 2. ningangabong.
tongue *see* 1. neve, 2. newe.
too *see* rang.
tooth *see* 1. ûi, 2. wi.
toothless *see* 1. ngarongaro, 2. wibarubaru, 3. wingarongaro.
top *see* 1. abu, 2. kawete, 3. taubuki, 4. toka.
topped *see* kaweteaki.
tore *see* raea.
torment *see* 1. bainikirina, 2. kakai, 3. imanono, 4. kaangitannenea.
tormented *see* 1. bainikirinaki, 2. imanonoaki, 3. kaangitanneneaki, 4. kakaiaki.
torn *see* 1. kirimotimoti, 2. maeae, 3. raea, 4. raeaki, 5. raemenga, 6. raeua.
torpid *see* nibiongong.
torrid *see* kabuebue.
tortoise *see* on.

torture *see* kamaraka.
tortured *see* kamarakaki.
toss *see* 1. kaka, 2. kaurakea, 3. tabatoutou.
totter *see* 1. bebebebe, 2. tatatata, 3. taurangaranga.
tottering *see* teibaka.
touch *see* 1. riringa, 2. tabetea, 3. kamena, 4. bo, 5. tiritabuki, 6. ringa.
touched *see* 1. riringaki, 2. uere, 3. tiritabukiaki, 4. tabeteaki, 5. ringaki, 6. kamenaki, 7. boaki, 8. teka.
touching *see* ribono.
tough *see* 1. non, 2. waka, 3. wakariri, 4. kangkai, 5. iwaka, 6. nonon, 7. tikinono.
toughen *see* katikintakaea.
toughened *see* katikintakaeaki.
tow *see* 1. katika, 2. nakina, 3. aeaea.
towed *see* 1. katikaki, 2. nakinaki, 3. aeaeaki.
towering *see* ananau.
town *see* kana.
trace *see* 1. tari, 2. taman, 3. katoto, 4. m'aneka.
traced *see* 1. katotoaki, 2. m'anekaki, 3. tamanaki.
track *see* 1. kanimiboi, 2. neneboi, 3. niniboi.
tracked *see* 1. neneboiaki, 2. niniboiaki.
trade *see* bobai.
traded *see* bobaiaki.
traditional *see* manrea.
trail *see* kawe.
trailed *see* kaweaki.
train *see* 1. kataneiai, 2. katei, 3. reirei.
trained *see* 1. kataneiaiaki, 2. reireiaki.
trample *see* 1. taona, 2. tou.
trampled *see* 1. taonaki, 2. touaki.
tranquil *see* 1. nanobebete, 2. rau, 3. mweraoi.
transcend *see* moa.
transect *see* renaua.
transfix *see* 1. bakarerea, 2. winikibwia.
transfixed *see* 1. bakarereaki, 2. winikibwiaki.
transform *see* 1. onika, 2. onikia.
transformed *see* 1. onikaki, 2. onikiaki.
transgress *see* 1. riao, 2. riaoa, 3. raka, 4. bure, 5. rakatua.
transient *see* 1. tabobe, 2. winanti.
translate *see* raira.
transmigrate *see* uamumun.
transparent *see* kiwarawara.
transport *see* 1. uomania, 2. urake, 3. urakina.
transpose *see* uomania.
transposed *see* uomaniaki.
trap *see* taokabia.
trapped *see* taokabiaki.
trash *see* kateibanaea.
traumatic *see* kamaraki.
travail *see* mengo.
travel *see* mwananga.
traveled *see* 1. buta, 2. mwanangaki.

trawl *see* katiki.
treacherous *see* 1. babakanikawai, 2. kakauara.
tread *see* 1. toubeka, 2. nakonako.
treasure *see* kaotabaea.
treasured *see* kaotabaeaki.
treat *see* 1. ngengetaia, 2. taokitana.
treated *see* 1. ngengetaiaki, 2. taokitanaki.
tree *see* 1. nî, 2. kai.
treeless *see* wara.
trek *see* mwananga.
tremble *see* 1. itikurere, 2. maeiei, 3. maninga, 4. rangarangataki, 5. rumangai, 6. ruru.
tremendous *see* 1. abakaei, 2. kakamaku, 3. toari.
tremulous *see* ruru.
trench *see* niba.
trendy *see* bou.
trespass *see* raka.
triangular *see* turaiangkor.
tribal *see* nanoutu.
trick *see* 1. bitanikai, 2. mamana.
trickle *see* 1. bwarara, 2. wawa, 3. raran, 4. tutu.
tricky *see* rabakai.
tried *see* 1. kamanenantiaki, 2. kekiaki, 3. tibwaki, 4. kekeiakiaki, 5. kaiakiaki, 6. kataki, 7. kataiaki.
trifle *see* makota.
trim *see* 1. tikiraoi, 2. tirikai, 3. tea, 4. taera, 5. rarikina, 6. katikiraoa, 7. kanikan, 8. erea, 9. bukina, 10. korouia.
trimmed *see* 1. rarikinaki, 2. tirikaiaki, 3. bukinaki, 4. taeraki, 5. katikiraoaki, 6. ereaki, 7. teaki.
trip *see* 1. tabarangaea, 2. tata.
triple *see* kiri.
trisect *see* korotenia.
triumph *see* 1. nikierere, 2. aonikai.
triumphant *see* tokanikai.
trodden *see* matiraua.
troll *see* kauaka.
trouble *see* 1. katabeaianga, 2. katabetabea, 3. karawawata, 4. kananomaruru, 5. kamatakiaua, 6. kakai, 7. angabuaka, 8. nanoa.
troubled *see* 1. karawawataki, 2. marebu, 3. wangaki, 4. nanomaruru, 5. nanobukibuki, 6. nanoaki, 7. matakiaua, 8. mantoa, 9. katabeaiangaki, 10. kananomaruruaki, 11. kamatakiauaki, 12. kakaiaki, 13. katabetabeaki.
troublesome *see* 1. kameio, 2. meme, 3. memeto.
troubling *see* karuanano.
trounce *see* 1. tiribaonoa, 2. oro, 3. batiboa, 4. orea.
truck *see* 1. tabeka, 2. turaki.
true *see* koaua.
truly *see* 1. bon, 2. dokóv.
truncate *see* baku.
truncated *see* bakuaki.
trust *see* onimakina.
trusted *see* onimakinaki.

trusting *see* onimakina.
try *see* 1. kaiaki, 2. tibwa, 3. kekeiaki, 4. kataia, 5. kamanenanti, 6. kata.
trying *see* 1. kanganga, 2. kata.
tuck *see* otooto.
tucked *see* otootoaki.
tug *see* 1. katika, 2. wakina.
tumble *see* 1. bukitau, 2. rabino, 3. bwaka, 4. bukiruru, 5. bukirurunga, 6. katiobuki.
tumbled *see* 1. rabinoaki, 2. bukiruruaki, 3. bukirurungaki, 4. bukitauaki, 5. bwakaki, 6. katiobukiaki.
tumid *see* tibutau.
tumultuous *see* marebu.
turbid *see* 1. mannawa, 2. mantoa.
turbulent *see* 1. mantoa, 2. tabare, 3. reberake, 4. memeto, 5. banei, 6. karou, 7. kareu, 8. banaonao, 9. kareureu.
turgid *see* tibutau.
turn *see* 1. kiko, 2. rairaki, 3. raira, 4. rai, 5. minotia, 6. minota, 7. unora, 8. katabiroa, 9. karaia, 10. kaminoa, 11. inimaki, 12. bita, 13. miminota, 14. mimitoi.
turned *see* 1. kikoaki, 2. unoraki, 3. rairakiaki, 4. rairaki, 5. raiaki, 6. rai, 7. minotiaki, 8. minotaki, 9. miminotaki, 10. katabiroaki, 11. karaiaki, 12. kaminoaki, 13. inra, 14. inimakiaki, 15. bitaki, 16. mimitoiaki.
turning *see* 1. mimitoi, 2. rairake.
turtle *see* tohount.
twang *see* 1. tangirarae, 2. tang.
twenty *see* 1. uabwi, 2. houanpoui.
twilight *see* airo.
twin *see* bwebwe.
twine *see* 1. binoka, 2. binokaia, 3. kakano, 4. minotia.
twined *see* 1. kakanoaki, 2. minotiaki, 3. binokaki, 4. binokaiaki.
twinkle *see* ruberube.
twirl *see* 1. kaminominoa, 2. minomino, 3. minotia.
twist *see* 1. kakiribabaoua, 2. minota, 3. tabiro, 4. rairaki, 5. nion, 6. minotia, 7. binoka, 8. mimioua, 9. karaia, 10. unora, 11. biroa, 12. mino, 13. katabiroa.
twisted *see* 1. minotaki, 2. minotiaki, 3. ninibaoua, 4. nion, 5. nionaki, 6. rairakiaki, 7. tabiroaki, 8. unoraki, 9. minoaki, 10. tabiro, 11. binokaki, 12. mimioua, 13. menga, 14. makaokao, 15. kiribabaoua, 16. kibao, 17. katabiroaki, 18. karaiaki, 19. kakiribabaouaki, 20. mimiouaki.
twisting *see* rairake.
twitch *see* 1. katikitiki, 2. kuikui, 3. tiki.
twitching *see* rangataki.
two *see* 1. ua, 2. houa, 3. uoua.
type *see* koria.
typed *see* koriaki.

typical *see* kabuta.

U

ugly *see* 1. be, 2. bureti, 3. kaburati, 4. kamaira, 5. kamairatuatua, 6. mautete, 7. me, 8. moakura, 9. tarabuaka.
ulterior *see* 1. kiriaria, 2. rimwi.
ultimate *see* kaitara.
ultra *see* kinano.
ululate *see* tang.
umpire *see* karotuang.
un *see* aki.
unapproachable *see* kateinang.
unauthorized *see* mabu.
unavailing *see* manouna.
unbalanced *see* 1. kanenge, 2. katibebe, 3. nikotaungaunga, 4. nikutaro, 5. tabaua, 6. tabeitera, 7. teibaka.
unbecoming *see* buaka.
unbelievable *see* 1. nanokiroro, 2. nanokirokiro.
unbind *see* unobauta.
unblemished *see* itiwewe.
unbound *see* unobautaki.
unbroken *see* tabanin.
unburdened *see* taenang.
uncanny *see* kameio.
uncertain *see* 1. nanobebebe, 2. uara.
unclear *see* maewe.
uncomfortable *see* 1. nibara, 2. kawa, 3. mwebuaka, 4. nangora.
uncommon *see* tare.
unconditional *see* matatoka.
unconscious *see* 1. mamataro, 2. mate.
unconstrained *see* mantakarara.
unconventional *see* tare.
uncooked *see* oraora.
uncover *see* uka.
uncovered *see* 1. tangenge, 2. ukaki.
uncultured *see* nonoro.
uncured *see* mwaka.
undecided *see* 1. tei, 2. tikimaurekati, 3. tine, 4. nanokoraki, 5. nanououa, 6. nanomaiti.
under *see* 1. iân, 2. ngkai, 3. ngke.
undercooked *see* waka.
underdone *see* 1. maibunia, 2. maioraora, 3. mata.
underhanded *see* matanikimoa.
undermine *see* anra.
undersized *see* kimotoitoi.
understand *see* 1. nora, 2. ata, 3. tahete, 4. ota, 5. namakina, 6. nama, 7. kamatebwai, 8. kina.

understanding *see* 1. nanomawa, 2. nanouki, 3. niniwana.
understood *see* 1. namakinaki, 2. otaki, 3. noraki, 4. namaki, 5. kinaki, 6. kametebwai, 7. kamatebwaiaki, 8. ataki, 9. nora.
understudy *see* tauantaboa.
undertake *see* 1. teirakea, 2. moanang.
undeveloped *see* tokira.
undignified *see* kakauara.
undiminished *see* tabanin.
undivided *see* tabanin.
undo *see* 1. tanara, 2. kabara, 3. kamanang.
undone *see* 1. tanaraki, 2. nibarabara, 3. maenikun, 4. kabaraki, 5. kamanangaki.
undoubtedly *see* ngaiangaia.
undress *see* 1. bubai, 2. taeba.
undressed *see* 1. bubaiaki, 2. taebaki.
undulate *see* kanebu.
uneasy *see* 1. matakiaua, 2. nanomaruru, 3. nibara, 4. nanobukibuki, 5. kawa, 6. mwerengau, 7. mwebuaka.
unenlightened *see* nonoro.
unequal *see* 1. bari, 2. bobuaka.
unequaled *see* moaniba.
unequivocal *see* matatoka.
unequivocally *see* okoro.
unessential *see* teutana.
uneven *see* 1. nimanomano, 2. tabureka, 3. tabukirurunga, 4. tabatibutibu, 5. kiribeubeu, 6. aontabuki, 7. tabuki.
unexpected *see* rina.
unfaithful *see* ruannano.
unfathomable *see* 1. kakinounou, 2. nano, 3. nanokirokiro, 4. nanokiroro.
unfavorable *see* ra.
unfold *see* takina.
unfolded *see* takinaki.
unfortunate *see* 1. tekebuaka, 2. tekera.
unfruitful *see* 1. kanoabo, 2. aomate.
ungrateful *see* 1. angabe, 2. bangaomata, 3. kateibuaka, 4. manibuaka, 5. ribuaka.
unguarded *see* nanorake.
unhappy *see* 1. kawa, 2. nanokawa, 3. nanokawaki.
unhook *see* katiba.
unified *see* 1. maitiaki, 2. boraoiaki, 3. maitia.
uniform *see* boraoi.
unify *see* boraoi.
unimportant *see* mangori.
uninhabited *see* rereua.
unintelligent *see* anua.
unintentional *see* nanobebebe.
uninteresting *see* mammam.
unite *see* 1. nama, 2. baronga, 3. reita, 4. toma, 5. botaki, 6. ikotaki, 7. kabo.

united *see* 1. barongaki, 2. botakiaki, 3. ikotakiaki, 4. kaboaki, 5. namaki, 6. ntaninin, 7. reitaki, 8. tamaomao, 9. tomaki.
universal *see* buta.
unjust *see* 1. ribuaka, 2. babakanikawai, 3. buaka.
unkept *see* bakarae.
unkind *see* manibuaka.
unload *see* 1. urake, 2. urakina.
unloaded *see* 1. urakeaki, 2. urakinaki.
unlucky *see* 1. boituta, 2. maraia, 3. tekebuaka, 4. tekera.
unmindful *see* nanotiotio.
unmistakable *see* maroaka.
unoccupied *see* noumangang.
unpleasant *see* be.
unpredictable *see* iteratera.
unpremeditated *see* taeremea.
unprepared *see* taubuaka.
unqualified *see* babanga.
unravel *see* 1. kabara, 2. tibe.
unravelling *see* korouia.
unreal *see* winanti.
unreserved *see* matabou.
unripe *see* mai.
unruffled *see* rau.
unsettled *see* minotaki.
unsightly *see* bureti.
unskillful *see* babanga.
unsociable *see* ninikuraroa.
unstable *see* 1. atubitaki, 2. iteratera, 3. marin, 4. nanotiotio, 5. ranea, 6. tabaua, 7. tannene.
unsteady *see* 1. tannene, 2. bebe, 3. katibebe, 4. nibakabaka.
unsure *see* 1. iraaua, 2. matabao.
untangle *see* tanara.
untangled *see* tanaraki.
untidy *see* 1. torotangako, 2. baitangako, 3. bakarae, 4. katiba, 5. mangaongao, 6. tangako, 7. torobakara.
untouchable *see* 1. tabuterang, 2. taningo.
untrustworthy *see* atutekonaua.
untwisted *see* rai.
unusual *see* bainataei.
unwanted *see* moakakung.
unwelcome *see* 1. moakakung, 2. rikibuaka.
unwilling *see* nanobebebebe.
unwind *see* 1. kakibotu, 2. tanara.
unwound *see* 1. tanaraki, 2. kakibotuaki.
unwrap *see* tanara.
up *see* 1. eta, 2. ieta, 3. kaborake, 4. rake.
upchuck *see* mumuta.
update *see* kaboua.
uphold *see* 1. raona, 2. taubuki.
uplift *see* 1. ing, 2. kamwemwea.
uplifted *see* 1. kamwemweaki, 2. taenang, 3. ingaki.

upright *see* 1. etiruru, 2. kakaonimaki, 3. teiraoi, 4. eti.
uproot *see* 1. routa, 2. taeka.
upset *see* 1. katibaki, 2. rerebetungaki, 3. uraka, 4. rerebetunga, 5. rangaki, 6. ranga, 7. matakiaua, 8. kabaraka, 9. katiba, 10. babaraki, 11. urakaki, 12. kabarakaki, 13. kamatakiaua, 14. kamatakiauaki, 15. kananora, 16. kananoraki.
upsetting *see* 1. tokobeka, 2. tokobito, 3. tabare.
upward *see* rake.
urge *see* 1. kairoroa, 2. memerake, 3. tebona, 4. kairoro, 5. binenea, 6. tataenoa.
urgent *see* 1. mramra, 2. mura, 3. muramura, 4. taenoa.
urinate *see* 1. maimai, 2. mimi, 3. meira, 4. mim.
us *see* ngaira.
use *see* 1. baibai, 2. raimenga, 3. kawaina, 4. kawaia, 5. bwaina, 6. babaina, 7. kamanena, 8. kabongana.
used *see* 1. babainaki, 2. baibaiaki, 3. bwainaki, 4. kabonganaki, 5. kamanenaki, 6. kawaiaki, 7. kawainaki, 8. mane, 9. raimengaki.
useful *see* 1. bongana, 2. raroi, 3. manena, 4. maneuna.
useless *see* 1. bubuaka, 2. kabaka, 3. kibana.
usual *see* kabuta.
usually *see* tataneiai.
usurp *see* aonikaia.
usurped *see* aonikaiaki.
utter *see* atonga.

V

v *see* w.
vacate *see* kaita.
vaccinate *see* itina.
vaccinated *see* itinaki.
vacillate *see* 1. kanebu, 2. rangaranga.
vagabond *see* tabobe.
vagina *see* kere.
vagrant *see* toitio.
vague *see* 1. tabuaiaka, 2. maewe.
vain *see* manrerei.
valiant *see* 1. ninikoria, 2. kaura, 3. nanomwane, 4. ninikoa, 5. karitoa.
valuable *see* 1. maneuna, 2. kawaki, 3. bongana, 4. kakawaki.
vanquish *see* 1. taenikai, 2. taenikaia, 3. toka, 4. tokanikaia.
variable *see* 1. kaokoro, 2. rume, 3. tannene.
varied *see* 1. kaokoroaki, 2. onionikakiaki, 3. oneaki, 4. kakaokoroaki, 5. kaangitanneneaki, 6. aekaki, 7. onikaki, 8. kaokoro.

variegated *see* nimatamata.
varnished *see* ranebonebo.
vary *see* 1. aeka, 2. onionikaki, 3. onika, 4. onea, 5. kaokoro, 6. kaangitannenea, 7. kakaokoroa.
vast *see* 1. mawa, 2. abakaei.
veer *see* raben.
veil *see* 1. karaba, 2. nanginang, 3. nuna.
veiled *see* 1. karabaki, 2. nunaki.
venerable *see* 1. nabawe, 2. rine, 3. mangoieta.
venerate *see* karinea.
venerated *see* karineaki.
venomous *see* kamamate.
verbose *see* 1. kabararia, 2. tokomeme.
verdant *see* 1. mawawa, 2. bamaiu, 3. baroro.
verified *see* 1. noraki, 2. kamatebwaiaki.
verify *see* 1. kamatebwai, 2. nora.
versatile *see* takarua.
vertical *see* aetorake.
very *see* 1. ara, 2. bai, 3. kiri, 4. rang, 5. rangi, 6. taka.
veto *see* bwaka.
vex *see* 1. kanaengai, 2. tabarea.
vexatious *see* kameio.
vexed *see* 1. kanaengaiaki, 2. tabareaki, 3. unuara.
vexing *see* 1. kataeri, 2. kibangebange, 3. reberake, 4. rebetoko, 5. tokobito, 6. wanga.
vibrant *see* kangkai.
vibrate *see* 1. itikurere, 2. ruru, 3. kanebu.
vicious *see* buakaka.
victimize *see* kamaraki.
victor *see* korana.
victorious *see* tokanikai.
view *see* 1. matauakina, 2. no.
vigilant *see* mautara.
vigorous *see* 1. marurung, 2. nanomane, 3. mamaka, 4. kora, 5. batikora, 6. taboang, 7. korakora.
vile *see* 1. buretireti, 2. mangori, 3. bureti, 4. buakaka, 5. be.
vilify *see* 1. maniwaira, 2. kaubunranga.
village *see* káan.
villainous *see* 1. aonikai, 2. babakanikawai.
violate *see* 1. urua, 2. kamwaraea, 3. kamarua, 4. bure.
violated *see* 1. kamaruaki, 2. kamwaraeaki, 3. uruaki, 4. bureaki.
violent *see* 1. ioawa, 2. korakora, 3. nanoun, 4. ntarie, 5. takaerere, 6. unin.
virgin *see* 1. tepouno, 2. kibono.
virile *see* 1. tabomane, 2. kangkai, 3. nanomane.
virulent *see* kamamate.
visible *see* 1. materetere, 2. nanoraki, 3. tabanin, 4. tere.
visit *see* 1. kawara, 2. neweaba, 3. ueka.
vivacious *see* 1. buburamaiu, 2. maiutakoni.
vivid *see* 1. itiwewe, 2. taebu, 3. maiureirei.

voice *see* punâ.
void *see* kaita.
voluminous *see* tabati.
volunteer *see* ibuobuoki.
vomit *see* mumuta.
voracious *see* 1. babakanikora, 2. buabeka, 3. kibakibaki, 4. mangaungau.
vow *see* bauarira.
voyage *see* 1. nakomai, 2. mwananga.
vulgar *see* 1. kaburati, 2. kakauara.
vulnerable *see* nanorake.

W

wag *see* 1. ioioa, 2. katiotioa, 3. maeiei, 4. tiotio.
wager *see* 1. kabwakabwai, 2. karuotua.
waggish *see* kirirnang.
waggle *see* 1. ioa, 2. ioioa, 3. katiotioa.
wail *see* 1. tang, 2. tanginiwenei, 3. baebaeti, 4. baebaeta, 5. tangorake, 6. baebaetia.
waist *see* nûk.
waisted *see* urabaki.
wait *see* 1. aurama, 2. kamaioa, 3. taninga, 4. taningaia, 5. tataninga, 6. tei.
wake *see* uti.
waken *see* mangauti.
walk *see* nakonako.
wallow *see* iakiaki.
wan *see* 1. bang, 2. mainarake, 3. taetoba, 4. tawere.
wander *see* 1. batirae, 2. butinaiwa, 3. ikawawa, 4. taurere, 5. tiotio.
wandering *see* toitio.
wane *see* 1. makeke, 2. kenako, 3. kauanging, 4. rin.
want *see* 1. kainuano, 2. kan, 3. nanoati, 4. tangira.
wanted *see* 1. kainuanoaki, 2. kanaki, 3. kekeraki, 4. nanoatiaki, 5. tangiraki.
ward *see* káan.
warm *see* 1. angibue, 2. bue, 3. ang, 4. kangibuea.
warmed *see* kangibueaki.
warn *see* 1. kawanawana, 2. tuanga.
warp *see* 1. kanibwaoua, 2. nimibwaoua.
warped *see* 1. kanibwaouaki, 2. nimibwaouaki, 3. ninibaoua, 4. ninibwaoua.
warrior *see* aintoa.
wary *see* mautara.
wash *see* 1. teboka, 2. tebotebo, 3. dibûg, 4. uati, 5. kabururu.
washed *see* 1. kabururuaki, 2. tebokaki, 3. teboteboaki, 4. uatiaki.
waste *see* 1. bakataea, 2. kimaua, 3. katurara, 4. kabua, 5. uraba, 6. kataeare.

wasted *see* 1. kataoaki, 2. urabaki, 3. kimauaki, 4. katuraraki, 5. kataeareaki, 6. kataeare, 7. bakataeaki, 8. kabuaki.
wasteful *see* kimaung.
wasting *see* kataeare.
watch *see* 1. taratara, 2. teiakina, 3. tauoa, 4. taukiro, 5. no, 6. matauna, 7. karan, 8. tantani.
water *see* 1. ran, 2. teboka, 3. houaran, 4. katimtima.
watered *see* 1. katimtimaki, 2. tebokaki.
waterproof *see* au.
watertight *see* 1. au, 2. mano.
watery *see* 1. ruamakana, 2. waranran, 3. titi, 4. ran, 5. waneinei, 6. ranran.
wave *see* 1. naou, 2. nuo, 3. maeiei, 4. katiotioa, 5. katioa, 6. io, 7. tiotio.
waver *see* 1. bebe, 2. kabei, 3. nanobebebebe, 4. taurangaranga.
wavering *see* 1. teirobaroba, 2. mariro, 3. nanobebebebe.
wavy *see* 1. rabi, 2. rabirabi.
way *see* kawaina.
waylay *see* 1. kamanea, 2. kamarua, 3. karania, 4. torokarana.
weak *see* 1. nanokabakoba, 2. tarikabana, 3. ntangorengore, 4. ntanganga, 5. nikora, 6. nanomamara, 7. nanobakobako, 8. nangonango, 9. mara, 10. mamara, 11. makana, 12. kire, 13. ngore.
weaken *see* kangorea.
weakened *see* kangoreaki.
weakly *see* 1. kire, 2. tokira.
wealthy *see* 1. toronibwai, 2. kaubai, 3. kaubwai, 4. nonga.
wean *see* 1. koririra, 2. kakorira.
weaned *see* 1. kakoriraki, 2. korira, 3. koriri, 4. koririraki.
weaning *see* korira.
wear *see* 1. baranna, 2. raimenga, 3. kamanena, 4. bwaina, 5. botu, 6. burenibaia.
wearied *see* ôrara.
weary *see* 1. nrairai, 2. wanga, 3. wangaroro, 4. kuama, 5. botu, 6. kua.
weasel *see* kimoiauea.
weave *see* 1. ata, 2. ato, 3. raranga, 4. waua.
webbed *see* takareau.
wed *see* 1. mare, 2. buna, 3. iein.
wedge *see* 1. tena, 2. kabetanga.
wedged *see* 1. kabetangaki, 2. ribabetanga, 3. tenaki.
week *see* wiki.
weep *see* tang.
weigh *see* 1. taku, 2. tine, 3. kauanakoa.
weightless *see* mwemwe.
weird *see* kameio.
welcome *see* 1. mra, 2. akoa, 3. butimaea, 4. inga.

well *see* 1. raoiroi, 2. wau, 3. reirei, 4. raoi, 5. niko, 6. marurung, 7. mauri.
westbound *see* kerio.
westward *see* 1. kerio, 2. maeao, 3. rio, 4. tanimaeao.
wet *see* 1. maong, 2. roto, 3. waranran, 4. mwaimwai, 5. mona, 6. maimai, 7. katingoa, 8. karota, 9. aoi, 10. bururu, 11. makinono.
whack *see* 1. orea, 2. oro.
whacked *see* 1. oreaki, 2. oroaki.
whale *see* ôkua.
wheedle *see* kamaramara.
when *see* 1. íniañai, 2. ningai.
whence *see* 1. maia, 2. nî.
where *see* 1. êa, 2. ia, 3. îa.
whereas *see* 1. ko, 2. ngkae.
wherever *see* tabonako.
whet *see* 1. taitaima, 2. taima, 3. taim, 4. kakangia.
while *see* 1. ngkae, 2. ngkai, 3. ngkana, 4. ngke, 5. ko.
whimper *see* 1. antingoa, 2. kitangitang, 3. mona, 4. montaua, 5. tang.
whimsical *see* ruannano.
whine *see* 1. antingoa, 2. toto, 3. meme, 4. tangitang.
whip *see* 1. kataere, 2. robuna.
whirl *see* 1. kiko, 2. mimitoi, 3. nimamano.
whirling *see* mimitoi.
whisper *see* 1. maningongo, 2. wibine, 3. wirikiriki, 4. wirikirikia.
whispered *see* 1. wirikirikiaki, 2. wibineaki, 3. maningongoaki.
whistle *see* 1. kakanimomoi, 2. kanimoumoui, 3. katangibwerei, 4. tang, 5. bira.
white *see* 1. koroheina, 2. mainaina.
whiten *see* kamainaina.
whitened *see* kamainainaki.
whitish *see* mai.
who *see* 1. atai, 2. aika, 3. antai.
whole *see* tabanin.
wholly *see* bane.
whoop *see* kakarua.
whop *see* 1. batiboa, 2. orea.
whore *see* kabekau.
why *see* éra.
wicked *see* 1. benoinoi, 2. buakaka, 3. bure, 4. ioawa, 5. ntarie, 6. ribuaka, 7. tarie.
wide *see* 1. niku, 2. râpape, 3. warebwe.
widen *see* 1. kaata, 2. kaawarebwea, 3. kabenga, 4. kanikua, 5. karababa.
widespread *see* buta.
wield *see* 1. bwaina, 2. kamanena, 3. taua.
wild *see* 1. nanobukibuki, 2. anti, 3. katamanti, 4. kire.
wile *see* kamwanea.

will see 1. kan, 2. kanenei, 3. na, 4. nanona, 5. ina.
willful see nanomwaka.
win see 1. karakea, 2. tokanikai, 3. ribinano, 4. riaonikai, 5. katoka, 6. moanna.
wind see 1. añ, 2. ninira, 3. katabara, 4. hang, 5. kakiribabaoua, 6. karaia.
winded see 1. mawa, 2. mawaki.
winding see kiribabaoua.
windward see tewearaki.
wink see 1. mataruberube, 2. ruberube.
wipe see 1. tara, 2. tira, 3. taea, 4. kaoa, 5. taheia.
wire see uaereti.
wired see uaeretiaki.
wise see 1. wana, 2. wanawana, 3. rabakau, 4. nanowana.
wish see 1. tangira, 2. kan, 3. nanoati, 4. tañata, 5. kabinanonanoa.
with see 1. ni, 2. n, 3. ma, 4. aika.
withdraw see 1. aeka, 2. ana, 3. kakerikaka, 4. kerikaki, 5. ningiongio, 6. rikaki.
withdrawn see 1. ningiongioaki, 2. rikakiaki, 3. maama, 4. kakerikakaki, 5. aekaki, 6. anaki, 7. kerikakiaki.
wither see 1. kamou, 2. karaia, 3. rai.
withered see 1. karaiaki, 2. rai, 3. kamouaki, 4. raiaki.
withering see taberamate.
withhold see taua.
within see inánan.
withstand see 1. eka, 2. tuka.
witness see 1. nora, 2. kaotioti, 3. matauakina, 4. no.
witty see 1. kauman, 2. maiutakoni.
wizard see tiakai.
wobble see 1. mamakuri, 2. rangaranga, 3. tiotio.
woeful see rainanoanga.
woman see 1. neiko, 2. tohaine.
womanly see matanaine.
won see 1. karakeaki, 2. tokanikaiaki, 3. tokanikai, 4. moanna, 5. karakea, 6. moannaki.
wonder see 1. mimi, 2. raerua.
wonderful see kamimi.
wood see 1. kai, 2. taki, 3. tekai.
wooded see tokobuakoako.
woods see buoguínyikai.
work see 1. rangarangatau, 2. tabetea, 3. môgur, 4. mengo, 5. mwakuri.
workaholic see inao.
working see 1. baraki, 2. rangarangatau, 3. tabe.
wormy see ino.
worn see 1. burenibaiaki, 2. raimengaki, 3. raimenga, 4. mane, 5. maeiei, 6. kamanenaki, 7. bwaina, 8. botuaki, 9. barannaki, 10. bwainaki.
worried see 1. kennanoaki, 2. raraomaeakinaki, 3. uakaka, 4. nimatoaua, 5. nanoaki, 6.

katabeaiangaki, 7. karoraomaki, 8. karawawataki, 9. kakaiaki, 10. keinanoaki.
worry see 1. raraomaeakina, 2. kakai, 3. karawawata, 4. karoraoma, 5. katabeaianga, 6. keinanoa, 7. kennano, 8. nanginang, 9. nanoa, 10. raraomaeakin.
worship see taromauria.
worth see bonanga.
worthless see 1. bwatoka, 2. kibana, 3. manebuaka, 4. takuanganga.
worthwhile see materaoi.
worthy see kona.
wound see 1. ninira, 2. kataeari, 3. kamarua, 4. ikoa, 5. kaikoaka.
wounded see 1. kataeariaki, 2. niniraki, 3. nikunakuna, 4. kaikoakaki, 5. ikoaki, 6. teka, 7. kamaruaki.
wrangle see 1. ikakaiwi, 2. ikangui, 3. kauntaeka.
wrap see 1. batia, 2. rikuma, 3. rabuna, 4. otabanini, 5. ninira, 6. tiera, 7. niria.
wrapped see 1. rabunaki, 2. tieraki, 3. rikumaki, 4. otabininiaki, 5. niriaki, 6. batiaki, 7. niniraki.
wreathe see biria.
wreathed see biriaki.
wreck see bwaka.
wrecked see bwakaki.
wrench see touru.
wrestle see 1. kaunrabata, 2. tooun.
wretched see toronrang.
wriggle see ininimaki.
wriggling see takariroriro.
wring see 1. ongira, 2. ongong, 3. unora.
wrinkle see 1. kamanunua, 2. kanimanunua, 3. kabatiatia, 4. kabarukurukua.
wrinkled see 1. kabatutu, 2. manunu, 3. manu, 4. mangingi, 5. tikurabirabi, 6. kinikon, 7. nimanunu, 8. kamanunuaki, 9. kabatiatiaki, 10. kabarukurukuaki, 11. batiatia, 12. barukuruku, 13. kanimanunuaki.
wrist see atunipai.
writ see koroboki.
write see 1. koria, 2. koroboki, 3. nion.
written see koroboki.
wrong see 1. buaka, 2. maura, 3. bure.
wrought see 1. karaoaki, 2. karaoakiaki.
wry see 1. raee, 2. rai, 3. twake.

X

x *see* ikti.

Y

yank *see* katikia.
yard *see* ipi.
yawn *see* **1.** teha, **2.** a, **3.** aa, **4.** kararaniman.
yea *see* **1.** eng, **2.** ngaiangaia.
yearn *see* **1.** mamarake, **2.** nanona.
yell *see* takaarua.
yellow *see* **1.** babobo, **2.** îru.
yellowish *see* taribo.
yelp *see* kaukau.
yes *see* **1.** aia, **2.** eai, **3.** eng, **4.** ke, **5.** ngaia.
yesterday *see* **1.** Ngkoananoa, **2.** ngkoangkoa.
yet *see* **1.** men, **2.** naba, **3.** riki, **4.** ma.
yield *see* anibana.
yielding *see* takarua.
yonder *see* **1.** ari, **2.** ikeike.
young *see* **1.** ataei, **2.** uarereke, **3.** waeai.
younger *see* karimwi.
youth *see* ataei.
youthful *see* **1.** uarereke, **2.** ataei, **3.** kiaiai.
yummy *see* kangkang.

Z

zany *see* kirirnang.
zealous *see* **1.** inga, **2.** manebaeba, **3.** manobotabota,
    4. nanobukibuki, **5.** taboang.
zero *see* akea.
zigzag *see* **1.** karae, **2.** kiritabaiore, **3.** tabataba.
zilch *see* akea.

Vocabulary Study Lists

Verbs (Kiribati - English)

ababa	inherit
aboka	begin
abuabu	seize
aeae	infiltrate
aeka	vary
aerona	stoke
ai	accumulate
aiewe	misplace
ainga	enlighten
aioro	collide
airi	accompany
amarake	dine
ana	withdraw
anai	subtract
anaia	retrieve
anangaki	receive
anga	impart
anganako	lend
anibana	submit
antingoa	retain
anua	assume
aobaki	reject
aona	surpass
aonikaia	seize
arira	tighten
ata	interlace
ataia	identify
atamaumau	deepen
atuna	preside
aua	dwindle
aubanga	rob
aumua	bake
babakanikawai	defraud

babako	adapt
bainikirina	maltreat
baka	conspire
bakarerea	transfix
bakikangenge	emaciate
baku	behead
bao	abate
baroa	overwhelm
baronga	assemble
baru	crave
batiboa	smite
baware	salivate
beireina	educate
beka	excrete
betanna	exaggerate
betunga	criticize
bina	appear
binenga	prefer
biria	seize
biriakinnako	elope
biriao	overstep
birinako	evade
biririmoa	foresee
biritaetae	foretell
biroa	tighten
bita	modify
bitabao	misconstrue
bitara	contradict
bo	compensate
boa	admonish
bomanea	entrap
bomatoa	overprice
bon	have
bonoike	suffocate
bononano	displease
boota	collect
bora	overprice
boraoi	quantify
borau	navigate
borauakina	navigate
botaki	reunite
boti	merge
botuakina	persevere
bu	emerge
buabeka	overeat
bubai	rob

Reference: Webster's Online Dictionary (www.websters-online-dictionary.org)

kaboboa	knead	kakea	deny
kabononanoa	provoke	kakeboa	cram
kaborere	distribute	kakerikaka	withdraw
kabua	bereave	kakerua	munch
kabubu	disappoint	kakerukerua	munch
kabunnaa	multiply	kaki	relinquish
kabwarabwara	describe	kakibea	agitate
kaea	pursue	kakibotu	unwind
kaeka	receive	kakimotoa	shorten
kaeta	straighten	kakioa	pursue
kaeti	explain	kakiokioa	expel
kaetieti	instruct	kakiritongitong	dumbfound
kaibea	stow	kakiriwea	agitate
kaiewe	complicate	kakiroa	anesthetize
kaikai	eat	kakoaua	accept
kaina	populate	kakokoea	shrivel
kainakoa	overwhelm	kakoroiku	threaten
kainaoa	propel	kakukua	shrivel
kaintoka	interrupt	kakunainga	terrorize
kaintorua	reinforce	kakurerea	terrorize
kairengarenga	intermingle	kamabu	repudiate
kairerebua	delude	kamaenikuna	shatter
kairerebuaki	mislead	kamaerikirikia	shatter
kairoro	insist	kamaimaia	saturate
kairoroa	persuade	kamaita	multiply
kaitau	thank	kamaitan	multiply
kaitiboa	introduce	kamaitoroa	refresh
kaitoana	oppose	kamaiua	refresh
kaiwa	prognosticate	kamaka	frighten
kaka	suppress	kamakerua	masticate
kakaautakia	dwindle	kamakimakia	saturate
kakae	covet	kamakua	threaten
kakaea	seek	kamanang	undo
kakai	disturb	kamanea	waylay
kakakao	invite	kamanena	wield
kakamwakuri	rouse	kamanenaka	anoint
kakannatoa	commend	kamanga	suffocate
kakaokoroa	segregate	kamangaungauakina	devour
kakarabakau	confabulate	kamaninga	mislead
kakaurekana	disarrange	kamaningaki	mislead
kakariki	beget	kamantoa	seize
kakarine	moralize	kamaoa	recuperate
kakaro	avoid	kamara	saturate
kakaunongo	hearken	kamarabea	grow
kakauongo	overhear	kamaranga	disassociate
kakawibaea	exaggerate	kamaratiarati	saturate

Reference: Webster's Online Dictionary (www.websters-online-dictionary.org)

kamariboa	provide	kanna	nourish
kamaroa	disconnect	kanotona	impute
kamarua	execute	kanta	masticate
kamarurung	strengthen	kantaninga	anticipate
kamatakiaua	perturb	kantaningaki	premeditate
kamatakua	amaze	kao	summon
kamataraea	overprice	kaoka	restore
kamataua	seize	kaokoro	vary
kamatea	execute	kaona	infest
kamatebwai	verify	kaongora	notify
kamatenakoa	annihilate	kaonoa	distribute
kamaterea	outclass	kaonota	restrict
kamatoa	demonstrate	kaota	demonstrate
kamatoroa	recycle	kaotiota	profess
kamatua	hypnotize	kapara	detach
kamauna	expunge	kara	abrade
kamengoa	lade	karaba	thank
kamerea	bestrew	karababa	widen
kamia	amaze	karairaki	revert
kamimitoiaka	rotate	karakaraka	exaggerate
kaminominotaka	rotate	karakarongorongo	exaggerate
kamiroaroa	amaze	karaki	arrive
kammamma	breastfeed	karakina	narrate
kamoamoa	admire	karakoa	shorten
kamona	pamper	karakoaea	abate
kamwaneaua	stabilize	karamakina	predict
kamwemwea	elevate	karanea	furbish
kan	crave	karania	waylay
kana	devour	karaoa	execute
kanaengai	displease	karaoaki	styled
kanaiai	stoke	karaoia	accomplish
kanakoa	send	kararatia	saturate
kananobuaka	provoke	karaurau	beware
kananobukibuki	enthuse	karawawata	pester
kananokawaki	dishearten	kare	reject
kananokoraki	mystify	kareao	josh
kananomaraea	dissuade	karebenakoa	dislocate
kananomaruru	disturb	karebo	intrude
kananora	perturb	karebutia	expel
kanebu	undulate	karekea	ponder
kanenei	determine	karemea	induct
kang	devour	karemereme	interfere
kanhai	ask	karemrem	accumulate
kaniko	pamper	karenoa	intrude
kanikua	widen	karereantia	imprecate
kaniniraka	rotate	kareuma	gallivant

karewena	sweeten	katawe	pilfer
karewi	sweeten	katei	instruct
kariaia	accede	kateikai	forbid
kariara	exaggerate	kateinang	frighten
karibak	congest	kateirakea	rouse
karibonobonoa	amass	katekea	surpass
karibua	penetrate	katena	tighten
karika	beget	katenua	adapt
karikaka	disenchant	katereterea	reveal
karikaki	reconstruct	katia	terminate
karikari	pulsate	katiatia	plead
kariki	create	katiba	unhook
karikirakea	propagate	katikeke	slither
karina	penetrate	katikintakaea	tighten
karinakoa	penetrate	katikua	stow
karinea	venerate	katinanikua	exclude
kariri	impose	katinono	insist
karitei	oppose	katiobabaea	suspend
karokoa	adapt	katitua	manipulate
karoroa	navigate	katoka	suppress
karota	humidify	katonga	dine
karotu	frustrate	katonginakoa	frighten
karotua	impede	katootoonga	pursue
karotuang	arbitrate	katoto	replicate
karuanikaia	jeopardize	katotoa	tenderize
karuarua	entrench	katotonga	impersonate
karuoa	descend	katua	avoid
karuoruo	replace	katuatua	skitter
katabetabea	disturb	katumaua	seep
katabua	hallow	katuna	connect
kataburorokoa	forbid	katutua	provoke
kataea	thrash	kau	retire
kataeari	excoriate	kaua	renew
kataeboa	intensify	kauakina	modulate
kataere	flog	kauamaea	disseminate
katakakaroa	amuse	kauanakoa	decide
katakanakana	besmirch	kauanging	shrivel
katakarea	strew	kauangingia	retract
katakarebua	agitate	kauara	instigate
katamaroa	magnify	kauarerekea	shorten
kataneiai	practise	kauba	frighten
katanoata	notify	kaubatial	tenderize
kataoa	overfill	kaubunranga	animalize
kataribaba	detach	kauka	notify
kataua	tolerate	kaukea	scrounge
katautau	suppose	kauna	provoke

Reference: Webster's Online Dictionary (www.websters-online-dictionary.org)

kaunga	rouse	ko	suppose
kaunikai	compete	kokoni	shrivel
kaunrabakau	examine	kom	shorten
kaunta	distinguish	kon	retire
kautaba	oppose	konana	ravish
kauntabaea	provoke	korakina	belong
kauntabama	collide	koria	incise
kauongo	listen	korokoroia	incise
kaura	cremate	korotenia	trisect
kauramaka	inflame	kunea	discover
kautikaikaia	frighten	kuota	flay
kautu	preside	mabu	forbid
kautua	infect	mae	disperse
kautuaka	infect	maeiei	agitate
kawaka	propel	maimai	urinate
kawakina	tend	maio	assemble
kawakiniko	beware	maitoro	freshen
kawanawana	warn	maiu	subsist
kawanra	disagree	maiureirei	thrive
kawanta	discolor	makiro	masticate
kawarebwea	enlarge	makoro	incise
kawarika	restrict	makoroua	halve
kawawa	circulate	mamana	mislead
kawawaea	convoke	mamanaki	mislead
kea	summon	mamarake	aspire
kekeia	applaud	mamata	predict
kekeiaki	learn	manawaia	entrench
kekera	investigate	manga	redo
keria	disappoint	mangamanga	complicate
kerikaki	retire	mangauti	waken
keru	resound	mange	eat
keta	covet	mango	mourn
kewe	defraud	manibuaka	mistreat
kia	reverberate	manikangare	amuse
kikitoa	seek	manikoraki	qualify
kimareirei	jubilate	manimaninia	decorate
kimoa	rob	maningenge	disappoint
kimra	tighten	maninrongorongo	overstate
kina	discern	maninutoa	accuse
kinanoa	assess	mantoa	mystify
kinraea	insinuate	manuoka	overlook
kio	evade	manuokina	forget
kiribambanta	overwhelm	maono	perspire
kiritibutibu	bloat	maotorrikiriki	fulfill
kitana	relinquish	maraki	suffer
kite	pursue	mare	disperse

marena	intercalate	mwiniba	devaluate
maro	penetrate	mwnanga	depart
maroaka	perceive	nabea	pamper
mata	appear	nako	gestate
matabae	absorb	namakin	suppose
mataiakina	covet	namakina	perceive
matam	eat	nanoa	think
matamu	eat	nanoanga	sympathise
matana	advise	nanoangaea	sympathize
matauakina	inspect	nanoata	perceive
matauna	examine	nanoati	covet
mate	perish	nanobebebe	grope
matunako	oversleep	nanomaiti	mystify
mauna	perish	nanomaraki	repent
maunika	forget	nanona	yearn
mauoti	divulge	nanonibwi	covet
maura	maltreat	nanora	resent
mauringa	forget	nanououa	mystify
mea	recriminate	natina	adopt
meakina	blurt	natinati	adopt
meira	urinate	neboa	extol
meme	complain	nenera	investigate
mere	complain	ngangaua	cram
mim	urinate	ngaungau	ingurgitate
mimi	contemplate	ngauta	cram
mino	embroil	ngawa	asphyxiate
minomino	gyrate	ngawaki	asphyxiated
minotia	rotate	ngengetaia	accuse
miroa	admire	ngkae	suppose
mitara	hallucinate	ngure	complain
moa	surpass	ngurengure	complain
moana	inaugurate	niba	entrench
moanang	commence	nikamonmon	gyrate
moanangia	begin	nikierere	celebrate
moanna	begin	nikira	repossess
mooi	imbibe	nima	absorb
motika	decide	nimamate	avenge
motiraran	decide	nimimarea	abut
motirawa	retire	ningiongio	withdraw
mra	converge	niniboi	seek
mumun	retire	ninimarea	accompany
mumuta	regurgitate	nnea	stow
mutigak	determine	noakinak	overlook
mwanea	receive	noku	resent
mwanikaki	stepped	nokua	offend
mwaninga	forget	nonoa	strengthen

Reference: Webster's Online Dictionary (www.websters-online-dictionary.org)

nora	accept	rawana	penetrate
noraki	appear	rawea	seize
notua	reject	rawebai	procure
oa	overtake	rawebaia	pilfer
onea	vary	raweraweaba	grope
ongo	hear	rea	intermingle
ongora	listen	rebe	dislocate
onika	transform	reberake	erupt
onikia	transform	rebu	gallivant
onionikaki	vary	rebutonga	gallivant
onon	entreat	reirei	learn
orea	smite	reireia	educate
oro	smite	reireinai	learn
oroia	thrash	reita	prolong
ota	realize	reitia	merge
oti	appear	reke	obtain
oto	shatter	reketa	recollect
oukia	extinguish	renaua	transect
outi	carry	rengana	intermingle
rabakei	learn	rere	flee
raben	veer	rerea	avoid
rabeniben	oscillate	ria	appear
rabuna	forbid	rianako	surpass
rabungaoa	condemn	riaoa	overstep
raea	denude	riaonikai	surmount
raebai	dismember	riba	abhor
raemenga	dismantle	rikaki	retire
raira	translate	riki	grow
rairaki	rotate	rikirake	develop
raka	infringe	riko	collect
rakea	awaken	rikoa	collect
ranea	oscillate	rikoia	collect
ranene	infiltrate	rimoa	precede
rangaranga	vacillate	rin	intrude
rangarangatau	agitate	rinanoa	rework
rangataki	stepped	rine	opt
raoiakina	reconcile	rinea	choose
raona	accompany	riringa	disarrange
raou	fiance	ritangia	deplore
rarabuareare	arouse	robuna	flog
raraikumea	abrade	roko	arrive
raran	seep	rokona	come
raranginako	seep	roroka	convoke
raraoma	repent	rota	attain
raraure	detach	routa	uproot
rawa	oppose	ruamakana	liquefy

ruamwi	replace	tangiroa	bemoan
ruberube	pulsate	tangitang	complain
ruo	descend	tania	penetrate
ruru	vibrate	tantani	supervise
rurunga	resound	taokabia	intercept
tabaka	seize	taoman	compute
tabangaea	publicize	taon	restrain
tabara	grope	taona	trample
tabare	misbehave	taotebe	submerge
tabarea	interfere	tarabai	examine
tabeka	carry	tarae	insinuate
taboa	invoke	tararuaia	superintend
tabora	threaten	taratara	superintend
tabua	forbid	tata	pulsate
tabuaetia	obtain	tatabuia	economize
tabuna	forbid	tataeanibai	detach
taburaka	constrict	tatara	examine
taebai	shoplift	tatatata	pulsate
taeka	detach	tataumanta	discern
taekina	narrate	tau	retain
taenikai	vanquish	taua	wield
taenikaia	vanquish	tauantaboa	replace
taerake	denude	taubank	restrain
taetae	exclaim	tauburea	criticize
taetaeraia	threaten	taukirikiri	calculate
tagerame	disperse	taumoa	precede
taie	mutate	taunari	differentiate
takaeakina	proclaim	taunga	fluctuate
takaerere	thrash	taungatangata	activate
takaka	proclaim	tauoa	supervise
takarebutata	agitate	tautaeka	legislate
takarebwetata	crepitate	tautoka	reinforce
takariuriu	thrash	tautorona	domineer
takaro	inflame	tawarea	ensnare
takarua	exclaim	tea	pare
takebono	disobey	tebarairai	sizzle
taku	suppose	tebo	submerge
takua	chide	tebomaurua	insist
tanara	unwind	tebonengenenge	persevere
tanbwaia	rob	teirake	commence
tang	complain	teirakea	undertake
tanga	develop	tekateka	sit
tangana	knead	tenarua	devour
tangimwaka	resound	tete	sizzle
tangira	covet	tianakiana	have
tangirariki	prefer	tiba	rearrange

Reference: Webster's Online Dictionary (www.websters-online-dictionary.org)

tibuna	adopt	uka	uncover
tie	oscillate	ukera	seek
tiebba	suspend	ukeuke	seek
tietie	oscillate	ukora	seek
tikona	restrict	ukouko	investigate
tikuroaroa	overstay	ukoukora	seek
timua	decorate	unauna	beautify
tinara	offend	unekea	decorate
tinaraea	threaten	ungara	accomplish
tinerua	impede	unobauta	unbind
tio	oscillate	unrake	contradict
tiotio	oscillate	untaba	oppose
tiri	suppress	uota	bring
tiribaonoa	trounce	ura	shatter
tiribo	chastise	uraka	demolish
tirimataere	flog	urake	convey
tiringa	immolate	urakeaki	conveyed
tiroakina	examine	urakina	convey
titaou	threaten	urakinaki	conveyed
titiraki	ask	uri	baptize
titirakinia	ask	uring	recollect
toabara	extinguish	uringa	recollect
toka	sit	uringaki	remembered
tokabeti	survive	uringnga	remember
tokanikaia	vanquish	uringngaki	remembered
tokarake	elevate	uruabai	demolish
toki	abate	ururinga	recollect
tokia	stow	uti	awaken
tonga	instruct	uton	inculpate
torara	gnash	vetea	convoke
toroba	cajole	waewae	contradict
torokarana	waylay	waitotokoa	oppose
totoka	avoid	wakina	pursue
tou	trample	wanara	denude
tua	denounce	wanikangarea	amuse
tuana	have	ware	calculate
tuanga	demonstrate	wareaki	read
tuka	repress	warebai	calculate
tuoa	examine	warebaia	calculate
tutuo	inspect	wareboki	read
uabai	have	warebokiaki	read
uakana	have	wareware	read
uamumun	transmigrate	warewareaki	read
uamwi	impersonate	wauwi	imprecate
uarao	defraud	wawaitai	interrupt
uarurung	fluctuate	weta	summon

wetea	summon	amass	kawawaea
wibeka	exaggerate	amaze	kamiroaroa
wibuakaia	threaten	amuse	kakibotu
wikabwea	exaggerate	analyze	kinanoa
wina	recommend	anesthetize	kakiroa
winikibwia	transfix	animalize	mwiniba
wira	avert	annihilate	kamatea
witokonaua	prolong	anoint	kamanenaka
wiwi	suggest	anticipate	biririmoa
		appear	mata
		applaud	kakannatoa
		arbitrate	karotuang
		arouse	katitua
		arrive	karaki

Verbs (English - Kiribati)

		ascertain	kakoaua
		ask	kanhai
		asphyxiate	ngawa
abate	bao	asphyxiated	ngawaki
abdicate	kakea	aspire	mamarake
abduct	konana	assassinate	kamatea
abhor	riba	assemble	baronga
abjure	kakea	assess	kinanoa
abrade	kuota	assume	anua
absorb	matabae	attain	rota
abut	nimimarea	avenge	nimamate
accede	kariaia	avert	wira
accentuate	katereterea	avoid	iranikai
accept	nora	awaken	rakea
accompany	airi	bake	kariki
accomplish	karaoia	baptize	uri
accrue	rikirake	bastardize	mwiniba
accumulate	kawawaea	beautify	katamaroa
accuse	bukina	become	riki
achieve	karekea	bedaub	katakanakana
acknowledge	kakoaua	beget	kakariki
acquire	karekea	begin	moanangia
activate	taungatangata	behead	baku
adapt	babako	belong	korakina
administrate	tautaeka	bemoan	tangiroa
admire	kamoamoa	bereave	kabua
admit	kauka	beseech	onon
admonish	boa	besmirch	katakanakana
adopt	tibuna	bestrew	kamerea
advise	matana	bewail	tangiroa
affirm	kakoaua	beware	karaurau
agitate	kakiriwea	bloat	kiritibutibu
allude	tarae	blurt	meakina
alter	onea		

breastfeed	kammamma	cremate	kaura
bring	nikira	crepitate	takarebwetata
burglarize	maro	criticize	tauburea
cajole	toroba	decapitate	baku
calculate	warebai	decide	kanenei
carry	outi	decorate	ete
celebrate	kakannatoa	deduct	kataoa
chastise	ikana	deepen	atamaumau
cheapen	mwiniba	define	kabarabara
chide	takua	defraud	babakanikawai
choose	kauanakoa	delete	kamanang
circulate	kawawa	delude	kairerebua
cognize	kamatebwai	demolish	uraka
collaborate	buoki	demonstrate	kabarabara
collect	rikoia	denounce	tua
collide	aioro	denude	wanara
come	rokona	deny	kakea
commence	aboka	depart	kau
commend	kakannatoa	deplore	ritangia
compel	kairoroa	descend	tuka
compensate	bo	describe	kabwarabwara
compete	kaunikai	destine	kakaunongo
compile	kawawaea	detach	kapara
complain	meme	detect	maroaka
complicate	mangamanga	determine	kinanoa
compute	taoman	devaluate	kaubunranga
condemn	bukinna	develop	ewenako
confabulate	kakarabakau	devour	ngaungau
confide	kamwaneaua	differ	kaokoro
conform	boraoi	differentiate	taunari
congest	karibak	dine	amarake
connect	katuna	disagree	kawanra
consider	taku	disappear	mauna
conspire	baka	disappoint	maningenge
constrict	taburaka	disapprove	rabungaoa
contemplate	iangoa	disarrange	kakaraurekana
contradict	kauntabama	disassociate	kamaranga
contribute	anga	disavow	kakea
contrive	karekea	discern	nora
converge	mra	discolor	kawanta
convey	urake	disconnect	kamaranga
conveyed	urakinaki	discover	kunea
convoke	kawawaea	disenchant	karikaka
cooperate	buoka	disentangle	wanara
covet	kan	dishearten	kananokawaki
cram	tonga	disjoin	kamaranga
crave	onon	dislocate	karebenakoa
create	kakariki	dislodge	buuta

dismantle	raemenga	excrete	beka
dismember	raebai	execrate	riba
dismiss	kabanea	execute	kamarua
disobey	takebono	exist	iai
disperse	kauamaea	expect	kantaninga
displease	bononano	expel	karebutia
disseminate	kauamaea	expire	mate
dissolve	kamara	explain	kabarabara
dissuade	kananomaraea	expunge	kamauna
distinguish	nora	exterminate	kamatea
distribute	kaborere	extinguish	kamarua
disturb	kananora	extirpate	routa
diverge	kakaraurekana	extol	kakannatoa
divulge	kaota	familiarize	imammane
domineer	tautorona	fiance	raou
donate	anga	flay	kuota
dumbfound	kamatakua	flee	rere
dwindle	kakea	flog	kataere
eat	amarake	fluctuate	taunga
economize	tatabuia	forbid	mabu
edit	rinanoa	forebode	bukinanganga
educate	tonga	foresee	biririmoa
efface	mauna	foreshadow	karamakina
elevate	kamwemwea	foretell	biritaetae
elope	biriakinnako	forget	manuoka
emaciate	bakikangenge	forgive	kabara
embroil	mino	forgo	kakea
emerge	bu	formulate	iangomaka
emphasize	katereterea	freshen	maitoro
enlarge	kakawibaea	frighten	katonginakoa
enlighten	ainga	frustrate	karotu
ensnare	tawarea	fulfill	maotorrikiriki
enter	moana	furbish	ire
enthuse	kananobukibuki	gallivant	kareuma
entrap	bomanea	gestate	nako
entreat	onon	get	karekea
entrench	karuarua	gnash	torara
equivocate	kakaro	grope	raweraweaba
erase	kamanang	grow	kamarabea
erupt	reberake	gyrate	minomino
evade	birinako	hallow	katabua
evaluate	ukeuke	hallucinate	mitara
exaggerate	maninrongorongo	halve	bwenaua
examine	taku	happen	riki
exclaim	taetae	have	bon
exclude	katinanikua	hear	ongo
excoriate	kataeari	hearken	kakaunongo

humidify	karota	investigate	ukouko
hypnotize	kamatua	invite	kakakao
identify	ataia	invoke	kaunga
imagine	iango	jeopardize	karuanikaia
imbibe	mooi	josh	kareao
immolate	tiringa	jubilate	kimareirei
impart	anga	knead	tangana
impede	karotua	lade	kamengoa
impel	wakina	learn	kamatebwai
impersonate	katotonga	legislate	tautaeka
implore	onon	lend	anganako
impose	kariri	lighten	kabakeketea
imprecate	bukinna	liquefy	kamara
impute	kanotona	listen	ongora
inaugurate	moana	loathe	riba
incise	korokoroia	lubricate	kabira
incriminate	bukina	magnify	katamaroa
inculpate	uton	maltreat	bainikirina
induct	karemea	manipulate	katitua
infect	kautua	masticate	makiro
infest	kaona	merge	boti
infiltrate	aeae	mesmerize	kamatakua
inflame	kauramaka	misbehave	iowawa
inflect	kabaoa	misconstrue	bitabao
infringe	raka	mishandle	maura
infuse	karina	mislay	kabua
ingurgitate	ngaungau	mislead	burebureaki
inherit	kabaibai	misplace	aiewe
inject	itina	mistreat	bainikirina
insinuate	kinraea	modify	bita
insist	buburamaiu	modulate	kauakina
inspect	tarabai	moralize	kakarine
instigate	kauara	mourn	mango
instruct	katei	multiply	kabata
insulate	kakaokoroa	munch	kakerua
intensify	kataeboa	mutate	taie
intercalate	marena	mystify	kananokoraki
intercede	raoiakina	narrate	karakina
intercept	taokabia	navigate	borau
interfere	karenoa	negate	kaakea
interject	kaintoka	notify	katanoata
interlace	ata	nourish	kanna
intermingle	kairengarenga	nuzzle	butubutu
intermix	kairengarenga	obtain	karekea
interpret	nora	occur	riki
interrupt	kaintoka	offend	bure
introduce	kaitiboa	oppose	kauntaba
intrude	rin	opt	rine

originate	maroaka	propagate	karikirakea
oscillate	kabei	propel	kainaoa
outclass	kamaterea	provide	kamariboa
overeat	buabeka	provoke	kauna
overfill	kataoa	publicize	tabangaea
overhear	kakauongo	pulsate	bukibuki
overlook	noakinak	pulverize	i
overprice	bomatoa	pursue	wakina
oversee	noakinak	qualify	manikoraki
oversleep	matunako	quantify	boraoi
overstate	maninrongorongo	ravish	konana
overstay	tikuroaroa	react	kaeka
overstep	biriao	read	warebokiaki
overtake	oa	realize	kamatebwai
overwhelm	taona	rearrange	tiba
pamper	nabea	recede	kakerikaka
panhandle	mange	receive	anangaki
pare	tea	recollect	ururinga
partake	buokanamarake	recommend	wina
penetrate	karina	reconcile	ioki
perceive	namakina	reconstruct	karikaki
percolate	raran	recover	eka
perish	mate	recriminate	mea
persevere	botuakina	rectify	kaeta
perspire	maono	recuperate	kamaoa
persuade	kairoroa	recycle	kamatoroa
perturb	kamatakiaua	redeem	kamaiua
pester	karawawata	redo	manga
pilfer	ira	refresh	kamaiua
plead	bubuti	refurbish	karikaki
ponder	iangoa	regurgitate	mumuta
populate	kaina	reinforce	kaintorua
practise	kataneiai	reject	kakea
precede	biririmoa	rejoin	kaeka
preclude	taokabia	relate	karakina
preconceive	taukirikiri	relinquish	bunra
predict	karamakina	remember	uringa
prefer	rine	remembered	uringngaki
premeditate	kantaningaki	render	kaoka
preside	atuna	renew	kaua
presume	kantaninga	renounce	kakea
proclaim	takaeakina	repent	mango
procreate	kakariki	replace	ikaruoruo
procure	kamariboa	replicate	katoto
profess	kaotiota	repossess	nikira
prognosticate	bukinanganga	repress	tuka
prolong	reita	repudiate	kamabu

require	ititi	smite	batiboa
resent	riba	solicit	bubuti
resign	kerikaki	speculate	iango
resist	tuka	stabilize	kamwaneaua
resound	bwarubwaru	stepped	mwanikaki
restock	kaua	stoke	kanaiai
restore	kaoka	stow	tokia
restrain	taubank	straighten	kaeta
restrict	kamabu	strengthen	buoka
retain	antingoa	strew	katakarea
retaliate	irantanga	styled	karaoaki
retire	katikua	submerge	taotebe
retract	kakerikaka	submit	anibana
retrieve	anaia	subsist	maiu
reunite	kabo	subtract	ana
reveal	kauka	suffer	maraki
reverberate	kanebu	suffocate	ngawa
revert	karairaki	suggest	wiwi
revive	kamaka	summon	kao
rework	rinanoa	superintend	tararuaia
rob	bubai	supervise	tantani
rotate	mino	supplicate	onon
rouse	kateirakea	suppose	namakin
sadden	kananokawaki	suppress	kaka
salivate	baroa	surmount	moa
saturate	kamakimakia	surpass	katekea
scavenge	kaukea	survive	maiu
scrounge	kaukea	suspend	katiobabaea
secede	kerikaki	sweeten	karewena
seclude	karaba	sympathise	nanoanga
seek	rawebai	sympathize	imammane
seem	mata	tend	kawakina
seep	katumaua	tenderize	katotoa
segregate	kakaokoroa	terminate	katia
seize	kamataua	terrorize	kakunainga
send	kanakoa	thank	kaitau
shatter	kamaenikuna	theorize	iangororoko
shoplift	taebai	think	iango
shorten	karakoa	thrash	batiboa
shrivel	kakokoea	threaten	ibebure
sidestep	kakaro	thrive	maiureirei
sightsee	matabae	tighten	karibak
simulate	bwaka	tolerate	kataua
sit	toka	toughen	katikintakaea
sizzle	tebarairai	trample	taona
skitter	katuatua	transect	renaua
slay	kamarua	transfix	bakarerea
slither	katikeke	transform	onika

translate	raira	aintoa	warrior
transmigrate	uamumun	airo	eve
trisect	korotenia	akea	emptiness
trounce	batiboa	aman	month
unbind	unobauta	aneang	mast
uncover	uka	aomata	population
undertake	moanang	apéi	basket
undo	kabara	ari	eyebrow
undulate	kanebu	at	liver
unhook	katiba	ataei	child
unify	boraoi	ataeinaine	damsel
unload	urake	ataeinimwane	laddie
untangle	tanara	ataeinimwani	lad
unwind	kakibotu	atama	pebbles
upchuck	mumuta	ati	fireplace
uproot	routa	ato	thatch
urinate	maimai	au	h
usurp	aonikaia	baba	hood
vaccinate	itina	baiene	basket
vacillate	kanebu	baikimoa	robber
vanquish	taenikaia	bairawata	robber
vary	onionikaki	baito	stole
veer	raben	bakamoamoa	hypocrite
venerate	karinea	bakin	greatness
verify	kamatebwai	bâmuti	beads
vibrate	itikurere	banikai	leaves
waken	mangauti	ba-ni-mata	temple
warn	tuanga	bao	shelves
waylay	torokarana	baobao	shelves
widen	kaata	bauwar	spittle
wield	taua	bebádoa	cockroach
withdraw	rikaki	ben	coconut
withstand	eka	béniaka	mullet
yearn	nanona	bïr	lizard
		bokewe	lye
		böki	greatness
		bon	are
		bong	day

Nouns (Kiribati - English)

		bora	shelf
		boreitiman	constable
		bubuôniwai	knee
a	are	buia	shelf
Aba	earth	buînai	loam
Abotoro	apostle	bukinaki	accused
abu	extremity	bungintaai	sunset
ahine	girl	burabeti	prophet
ai	me		

nanomaki	cowardice	tabobe	drifter
nanomamara	indulging	taenikaia	conquest
nanon	means	tairiki	eve
nao	boy	takatau	beads
nati	son	tama	monk
natina	egg	tamau	dad
nei	madame	tapouanga	shoulders
ngai	me	tari	brethren
ngaina	daytime	tári	brother
ngaira	us	tarim	sister
ngengetaiaki	accused	tarina	sister
ntinebu	dropsy	tariu	sister
ntokotoko	disability	tautia	soldier
nu	contour	tebû	grandparent
ouena	brother	tei	child
outi	day	tenikadaradara	beads
paouare	saliva	ti	j
para	hairdo	tiakai	magician
pen	coconut	tina	nun
piloto	abdomen	tip	mallet
poêtua	rudder	tirigo	meat
poue	rudder	toae	thigh
pouki	buttocks	toka	summit
pouto	navel	tokouki	breath
rabe	italic	too	paddler
rama	outrigger	toto	stole
rangata	quickstep	tou	pandanus
rangataki	twitching	turabwi	overbid
ran-ni-mata	tears	turabwiaki	overbid
raom	buddy	tutu	clambake
rarikin	heroine	uaereti	telegram
rau	flask	uarao	impostor
rauna	thatch	uea	lord
rebera	leper	uki-ni-bai	fingernail
rekebuta	stalling	ûr	lobster
riaboro	fiend	wai	harpoon
ribata	splint	wakinaki	pursued
riki	are	wiki	week
rî-n'aña	scapula		
rô	quietness		
rö	famine		
roio	counselor		
roko	sapling	**Nouns (English - Kiribati)**	
roronranairake	teenager		
rua	confusion		
tabemoa	beginner	abdomen	piloto

accused	bukinaki	doer	inao
ambassador	man	door	jetia
antenna	kao	drifter	tabobe
anus	ki	dropsy	ntinebu
apostle	Abotoro	earth	Buînai
aquatint	kina	egg	natina
are	a	emperor	embera
basket	apéi	emptiness	akea
beads	bâmuti	eve	airo
beginner	tabemoa	extremity	abu
boatman	kimautari	eyebrow	ari
bonito	kaneheke	eyes	mata
boy	nao	famine	rö
bragger	inakewe	fiend	riaboro
breath	ikeike	fifth	kanimaua
brethren	tari	fingernail	uki-ni-bai
bride	kainabau	fireplace	ati
brother	mwanena	fishhook	mataou
buddy	raom	flashback	kauringaba
buttocks	pouki	flask	naip
canon	kati	foe	kairiribai
child	ati	football	irîrep
chum	raom	frigate	keinanoa
clambake	tutu	gentlemen	naka
clergy	Ekaretia	girl	ahine
cockroach	bebádoa	glob	katimronrona
coconut	pen	goer	inao
commissioner	kamitina	grad	burimangaoa
committee	bwabwa	grandparent	tebû
conference	kakarabakau	greatness	bakin
confusion	rua	guest	iruwa
conjurer	tiakai	gumming	maungaro
conquest	taenikaia	h	au
constable	boreitiman	hairdo	para
contempt	kakanikoa	harpoon	wai
contour	nu	heaven	karava
councilman	kaubure	heir	ebiebi
counselor	roio	hen	mo'aiíne
cousin	mwaaneu	heroine	rarikin
cowardice	nanomaki	hiatus	mena
craw	kawa	hood	baba
dad	tamau	hypocrite	bakamoamoa
daddy	karo	impostor	uarao
damsel	ataeinaine	indulging	nanomamara
day	outi	italic	rabe
daytime	ngaina	j	ti
disability	ntokotoko	javelin	imbo
divination	kaiwa	knee	bubuôniwai

lad	ataeinimwani	quickstep	rangata
laddie	ataeinimwane	quietness	rô
lass	ataeinaine	quoits	kaboulina
lassie	ataeinaine	robber	bairawata
leaves	banikai	rudder	poêtua
leaving	nang	s	ti
leper	rebera	saliva	paouare
liver	at	sapling	roko
lizard	bïr	scapula	rî-n'aña
loam	buînai	seafarer	kimautari
lobster	ûr	sector	maranga
lord	katoka	shelf	buia
lye	bokewe	shelves	bao
madame	nei	shirker	mantokotoko
magician	tiakai	shoulders	tapouanga
maid	ataeinaine	shyster	baikimoa
mallet	tip	singularity	nanokanga
mast	aneang	sir	Nao
me	ai	sister	mwaaneu
means	nanon	soldier	tautia
meat	tirigo	son	houa
mom	tina	sorcerer	ibonga
mommy	tina	sorcery	kaiwa
monk	tama	spasm	katikitiki
month	aman	spathe	gakak
morn	ingabong	spittle	bauwar
mover	inao	splint	ribata
mullet	béniaka	stalling	rekebuta
nationality	i	stole	toto
navel	buta	stoutness	marika
nun	tina	student	kairi
opponent	kairiribai	suction	nako
outrigger	rama	summit	toka
overbid	turabwiaki	sunset	bungintaai
overseer	mataniwi	tears	ran-ni-mata
pa	karo	teenager	roronranairake
paddler	too	telegram	uaereti
pandanus	tou	temple	ba-ni-mata
pastor	minita	thatch	ati
pebbles	atama	thigh	toae
penis	kapanga	things	bwaai
population	aomata	toddler	merimeri
prestidigitator	tiakai	twitching	rangataki
producer	kimarimari	us	ngaira
prophet	burabeti	victor	korana
proprietor	inaaomata	warrior	aintoa
pursued	kakioaki	weaning	korira

| week | wiki |
| workaholic | inao |

Adverbs (English - Kiribati)

Adverbs (Kiribati - English)

abanaba	instantaneously
aikoa	never
aki	slightly
bon	actually
eeng	aright
gaña	how
i	mutually
kai	easily
kakai	easily
kanga	how
karaurau	softly
kinokino	significantly
kiriaria	distantly
koaua	flatly
maia	whence
maitin	exactly
maki	scarcely
matata	evidently
moa	firstly
moaniba	originally
nabangkai	freshly
ngkainaba	instantaneously
ngkanne	thereupon
ngkoa	historically
nî	whence
okoro	exactly
rake	eastwards
rang	too
raoi	decently
reirei	prettily
tabetai	occasionally
tao	conceivably
tatabeua	individually
tataneiai	customarily
tuai	never

actually	bon
agreeably	raoi
appropriately	raoi
aright	eeng
charmingly	reirei
commonly	tataneiai
conceivably	tao
correctly	okoro
customarily	tataneiai
decently	raoi
definitely	bon
distantly	kiriaria
easily	kakai
eastwards	rake
evidently	matata
exactly	maitin
firstly	moa
fittingly	raoi
flatly	koaua
frequently	tataneiai
freshly	nabangkai
gently	karaurau
habitually	tataneiai
historically	ngkoa
how	gaña
individually	tatabeua
initially	moa
instantaneously	ngkainaba
moderately	karaurau
mutually	i
never	aikoa
occasionally	tabetai
ordinarily	tataneiai
originally	moaniba
perchance	tao
possibly	tao
presently	abanaba
prettily	reirei
previously	ngkoa
primarily	moa
promptly	kai

Reference: Webster's Online Dictionary (www.websters-online-dictionary.org)

properly	raoi	angaki	extended
reciprocally	i	angama	timid
scarcely	maki	angi	numerous
significantly	kinokino	angibue	lukewarm
slightly	aki	angitannene	changeable
softly	karaurau	angitoiaki	dazed
specifically	okoro	angkoro	angular
superficially	aki	angkoroaki	angled
technically	okoro	angoaki	scratched
thereupon	ngkanne	antibuaka	awkward
too	rang	antingoaki	retarded
unequivocally	okoro	anua	unintelligent
usually	tataneiai	aoi	dewy
whence	nî	aoiaki	molded
		aokabu	illuminated
		aokangare	comical
		aomate	unfruitful
		aomwaimwai	humid

Adjectives (Kiribati - English)

		aonaki	missed
		aonangaki	shouldered
		aoneiney	swampy
ababaki	spacious	aonikai	rascally
abakae	huge	aonikaiaki	oppressed
abakaei	titanic	aontabuki	hilly
abinaki	prepared	aoraiaki	saved
aboabo	polite	aoraki	diseased
abuabuaki	seized	aotakaka	scared
abue	lukewarm	aotaningo	impenetrable
aeae	striped	ararakeaki	scaled
aeka	assorted	areaki	tied
aekaki	withdrawn	areare	adequate
aiaki	heaped	arei	inattentive
ainga	illuminated	arenaki	tied
airiaki	accompanied	aretau	dumb
airuaki	mistaken	ariki	placid
aitiotiriti	isosceles	ariraki	tightened
aiwau	delirious	arobaba	inane
akea	none	arokanaki	appropriated
akeaki	stripped	aronaki	guided
anaiaki	subtracted	aroraki	stretched
anaki	withdrawn	atabai	knowledgeable
ananau	tall	ataei	childish
anânau	tall	ataia	misunderstood
anaukaei	stretched	ataiaki	identified
anena	foreign	atainimari	magnanimous
angabe	ungrateful	ataki	known

Reference: Webster's Online Dictionary (www.websters-online-dictionary.org)

atakiaki	misunderstood	baireanaki	measured
atakinaki	practiced	baitabare	meddlesome
atamaumauaki	thickened	baitangako	untidy
atataiaomata	forgiving	baitata	agile
atataibai	experienced	baiteke	coordinated
atiati	granular	baitoaki	stolen
atoaki	poured	baka	missed
atongaki	famous	bakantang	envious
atubibitaki	dumb	bakarae	untidy
atubitaki	dizzy	bakaraki	surprised
atutababa	disheveled	bakaruru	fatigued
au	sealed	bakaruruaki	starved
auaki	sealed	bakatoki	stubborn
auba	dumbfounded	bake	awkward
aubangaki	robed	baki	piled
ba	tasteless	bakibora	smashed
baba	silly	bakikangengeaki	emaciated
babainaki	appropriated	bakiriroaki	starved
babaireiaki	controlled	bakiruruaki	starved
babakaineaki	neglected	bakitoutou	admirable
babakanikawai	treacherous	bakora	outstanding
babakanikora	voracious	bakuaki	beheaded
babakanikoroa	ravenous	bamaiu	verdant
babakoaki	nursed	bamaki	pumped
babanga	incompetent	bang	indistinct
babaroaki	emptied	bangaaomata	ungrateful
bae	engaged	bangabanga	pierced
baebaetaki	discredited	bangabwai	ignorant
baekeke	domineering	banganibai	provident
baia	gristly	banganuaru	meddlesome
baibaiaki	used	baniaki	fried
baibakeaki	missed	baniiaki	fried
baibaoaki	missed	banin	stark
baibati	impetuous	baoaki	moderated
baibuaka	awkward	baokoko	stooped
baikiaro	inelegant	barara	perspiring
baikoraki	odd	bararai	disgusted
bainaki	appropriated	bare	same
bainanti	abnormal	bareaki	hurried
bainataei	unusual	bareka	impure
bainikirinaki	maltreated	barekaki	hurried
bainingare	laughable	barekareka	grubby
bainraraeaki	insulted	bari	unequal
baira	awkward	barino	finicky
bairaoi	impartial	baroaki	overwhelmed
baireaki	ruled	baroakinaki	poured

barongaki	assembled	bobaiaki	traded
baroro	verdant	bobaranakoaki	missed
baruaki	craved	boboaki	hammered
batata	scorched	bobono	stubborn
batauaki	measured	bobouro	surprised
bateteaki	sloped	bobuaka	costly
bati	numerous	boibuakoaki	associated
batia	creased	boituta	unlucky
batiaki	gathered	bomaki	grazed
batiboaki	beaten	bomaneaki	encircled
bato	collapsed	bomatoa	expensive
bau	assembled	bon	stark
bauaki	encircled	bonaki	fertilized
baun	golden	bongana	useful
bautaki	bandaged	bonibaki	notched
be	mischievous	bono	stopped
beako	matted	bonoikeaki	choked
bebe	unsteady	bononano	angry
beberino	fussy	bononanoaki	angered
beireinaki	informed	bonotaki	obstructed
bekan	naked	bonotaninga	indocile
bekoko	numerous	bootaki	gathered
benoinoi	mischievous	bora	exorbitant
beo	matted	borababaua	stretched
berita	promising	borabiaki	creased
beroro	numerous	boraitiaki	planned
betanna	exaggerated	boraoi	same
betannaki	exaggerated	boraoiaki	unified
betingaingai	soiled	boretiaki	printed
betiti	filthy	botaki	assembled
betuntun	constrained	botakiaki	grouped
beu	malformed	botauaki	matched
beuakora	stooped	botitibaua	obtuse
bewa	tangled	boto	principled
bewawa	squalid	botonimwaane	handsome
binainga	sensitive	botu	bored
binokaiaki	twined	botuaki	fatigued
binokaki	twined	botuakinaki	preserved
biriaki	seized	bouaiaki	chopped
birinakoaki	evacuated	bouaki	spiked
biririmoaki	anticipated	brok	frozen
biririmwiaki	missed	buabeka	voracious
biroaki	tightened	buaka	unbecoming
bitaki	turned	buakaka	impure
bitaraki	opposed	buataki	bounded
boaki	blamed	bubaiaki	robed

bubu	pulverized	bwaibwaiaki	inherited
bubuaki	pulverized	bwainaki	used
bubura	huge	bwaka	fallen
buburakaei	titanic	bwakaki	tumbled
buburamaiu	stubborn	bwanabwana	indifferent
bubutei	hazy	bwanaki	lubricated
bubuteiaki	fogged	bwaranakoaki	dismissed
bubutiaki	borrowed	bwata	sunburnt
buibuinaki	screened	bweari	scorched
buiérar	fragrant	bwenauaki	halved
buíra	fetid	bwereaki	decorated
bukibukiaki	beaten	bwerebwereaki	sliced
bukimake	emaciated	bweretiaki	printed
bukinaki	trimmed	ebiñoño	fetid
bukinimataki	coveted	ebu	discouraged
bukiruruaki	tumbled	egî-mata	cross-eyed
bukirurungaki	tumbled	eieiaki	tilted
bukitauaki	tumbled	ekaki	recovered
bukunaki	suspected	ekaraki	opposed
bumbing	muscular	eke	famous
bumoaki	mounted	enaki	guided
bunaki	married	erarán	leaky
bunraki	relinquished	ereaki	trimmed
buokaki	assisted	eriaki	netted
buokanibwaiaki	shared	eteaki	decorated
buraerae	hairy	eutaki	lifted
bure	sinful	ewa	numerous
bureaki	offended	ewara	stung
bureniaki	planned	ewaraki	stung
burenibai	rare	ewenakoaki	developed
burenibwai	rare	iaakiaki	swept
bureta	disfigured	iakai	stark
buretata	faulty	iaki	diminished
bureti	unsightly	iakiaki	swept
buretireti	obscene	iakina	swept
burimangaoa	disheveled	iakinaki	swept
burimangaoaki	graded	ianena	foreign
buritoto	disgusting	iangoaki	fabled
buroaki	fermented	iangomakaki	formulated
buroungiaki	swept	ibaba	impregnated
buruburu	hairy	ibabannang	forgetful
burunaki	swept	ibe	numerous
bururuaki	splashed	ibeabureaki	embarrassed
buta	traveled	ibeaki	smashed
butimwaaeaki	accepted	ibebureaki	daunted
butiroko	cocky	iberoro	indigestible

ibewiaki	disputed	inroa	strewn
ibuobuoki	beneficial	intibuaki	fattened
ibutubutoaki	jolted	intinebu	awkward
iebabaki	hurried	ioawa	wicked
iein	married	iokiaki	exchanged
ieinaki	married	iokinaki	exchanged
iekaki	flooded	iowawa	refractory
ietaki	lifted	iraaua	indecisive
igagi	proud	irabaiaki	stolen
ikakaiaki	dated	iraeaki	stolen
ikake	cocky	iraki	stolen
ikanaki	chastised	iranikaiaki	signed
ikaroubuaki	boxed	irannanoaki	approved
ikawai	developed	iraorao	amicable
ikawaiaki	matured	irariki	lanky
ikeaki	breathed	ireaki	glazed
ikeikeaki	breathed	iruwa	foreign
ikenaki	inhaled	iteratera	unpredictable
ikinakoaki	emptied	iti	penniless
ikoaki	gathered	itibabu	diligent
ikoikotaki	collected	itimareare	scattered
ikuaki	beaten	itinaki	vaccinated
ikuikuaki	beaten	ititiaki	required
ikutaba	cute	itiwewe	unblemished
imamanu	adopted	itonginako	panicked
imammaneaki	familiarized	ituaki	threaded
imanaki	scaled	itutu	sewed
imanonoaki	harassed	itutuaki	stitched
imitaki	pierced	iwaiaki	opposed
immakurata	immaculate	iwaka	fibrous
in	locked	ka	indistinct
inaaine	graceful	kaakaeaki	disrupted
inababaura	handsome	kaananauaki	lengthened
inaberu	timid	kaangitanneneaki	disquieted
inaguínagu	skilful	kabaeaiaki	borrowed
inaiaki	engaged	kabaeaki	bounded
inaine	feminine	kabaibaiaki	inherited
inamatoa	impassable	kabainrangaki	insulted
inao	hyperactive	kabaka	discouraging
inataba	submissive	kabakaki	gathered
inga	motivated	kabakaruruaki	starved
ingaki	uplifted	kabaketeaki	softened
inimakiaki	bounded	kabakiaki	starved
ino	wormy	kabakuaki	beheaded
inra	turned	kabana	hopeless
inraki	sprawled	kabaneaki	dismissed

Reference: Webster's Online Dictionary (www.websters-online-dictionary.org)

kabaoaki	inflected	kabubuaki	disappointed
kabarabaraki	demonstrated	kabuebue	torrid
kabarakaki	overturned	kabuingoingo	indifferent
kabaraki	loosened	kabun	disgusting
kabararaki	hushed	kabunaki	choked
kabararia	verbose	kabuneneaki	reprimanded
kabarekaki	soiled	kabunnaaki	increased
kabarikoaki	heaped	kaburati	disgusting
kabaroaki	poured	kaburinanaki	squashed
kabataki	increased	kabururuaki	washed
kabatataki	scorched	kabuta	conventional
kabatebaiaki	disgraced	kabuteweteweaki	grilled
kabatiaki	augmented	kabutika	poisonous
kabatutu	puckered	kabwakaki	dropped
kabaubauaki	swallowed	kabwarabwaraki	described
kabe	odious	kabwarikorikoaki	stacked
kabeabeaki	employed	kabwaroaki	poured
kabeakoaki	tangled	kaenaenaki	teased
kabebeteaki	mitigated	kaenaki	teased
kabeoaki	tangled	kaetaeaki	rebuked
kaberetokoaki	spurned	kaetaki	corrected
kabetangaki	wedged	kaeti	associated
kabetingaingaiaki	soiled	kaewetaekaki	reported
kabi	ignorant	kaiakiaki	tried
kabiraki	smeared	kaiakina	committed
kabitaraki	opposed	kaiakinaki	settled
kaboaki	stirred	kaibabaru	sensuous
kaboati	tiresome	kaibako	hollowed
kaboboaki	stirred	kaibakoaki	smashed
kabobooaki	stirred	kaibibitiaki	exchanged
kaboituta	inopportune	kaierake	impatient
kabomakiaki	grazed	kaikoaki	saved
kabonganaki	used	kainaki	populated
kabonotaki	patched	kainakoaki	overwhelmed
kaboraoaki	planned	kainaomataki	liberated
kaborere	proportional	kaingingngaki	loosened
kaborereaki	distributed	kainikatonga	proud
kabotauaki	equalized	kainnanoa	needed
kabotu	tiring	kainnanoaki	needed
kabuabuaki	rounded	kainoki	susceptible
kabuakakaki	affronted	kainrou	engaged
kabuaki	damaged	kaintokaki	disturbed
kabuaneaki	steamed	kaintoruaki	reinforced
kabuanibai	disastrous	kairaki	controlled
kabuanibwaiaki	damaged	kairarikaki	thinned
kabubu	discouraged	kairerebuaki	misrepresented

kairi	bony	kakau	tiring
kaiririaki	guided	kakauara	treacherous
kairiribaiaki	thwarted	kakaunongoaki	attended
kairoroaki	forced	kakawaki	incalculable
kairuaki	mistaken	kakawaraki	haunted
kairuwaeaki	entertained	kakawibaeaki	enlarged
kaitaki	cleared	kakeaki	diminished
kaitiakaki	swept	kakeboaki	packed
kaitiaki	cleared	kakeiakaki	stimulated
kaitiboaki	introduced	kakekeaki	rattled
kaitoanaki	opposed	kakenakoaki	lessened
kaitonginakoaki	panicked	kakera	sought
kakaauba	awesome	kakerakeaki	extended
kakaeaki	coveted	kakeraki	sought
kakai	occupied	kakerikakaki	retracted
kakaiaki	tormented	kakerukeruaki	rattled
kakaianga	charitable	kakiaki	loosened
kakaiewa	impatient	kakibeaki	stirred
kakainrouaki	married	kakibekibeaki	stirred
kakairuaki	mistaken	kakibeuriaki	stirred
kakaiun	testy	kakibotu	thwarted
kakakaoaki	invited	kakibotuaki	diverted
kakamaku	terrifying	kakimotoaki	shortened
kakamakuaki	scared	kakinounou	unfathomable
kakamataku	amazing	kakiriariaki	retarded
kakammari	exalting	kakiritongitongaki	dazed
kakamwakuriaki	stirred	kakiriuataoaki	piled
kakamwaruaki	stolen	kakiro	lengthy
kakanato	famous	kakiroaki	thwarted
kakanaugaki	ghastly	kakoaki	fastened
kakang	thorny	kakoaua	proven
kakangare	ludicrous	kakoauaki	affirmed
kakangiaki	sharpened	kakoraki	seeded
kakanikoaki	despised	kakorakura	industrious
kakannato	distinguished	kakoroaki	notched
kakannatoaki	distinguished	kakoroikuaki	bullied
kakanno	dazzling	kakoroneaki	colonized
kakanoa	capacious	kakubaki	surprised
kakanoaki	contained	kakuiaki	startled
kakaokoroaki	varied	kakukureaki	gratified
kakarakoaki	lessened	kakukureiaki	thrilled
kakaraurekanaki	disarranged	kakunainga	terrible
kakariaki	scratched	kakunaingaki	terrified
kakarikiaki	begotten	kakunnaki	toasted
kakateke	graceful	kakurere	terrible
kakatika	gorgeous	kakurereaki	terrified

kamabuaki	repudiated	kamarangaki	disengaged
kamaeaki	smashed	kamararaki	attenuated
kamâg	dreadful	kamaratiaratiaki	oiled
kamainainaki	blanched	kamarauakaki	softened
kamaira	ugly	kamarauakinaki	alleviated
kamairatuatua	ugly	kamariboaki	stocked
kamairiaki	fouled	kamarikaki	fattened
kamaitaki	augmented	kamarinrinnaki	loosened
kamaitoroaki	refreshed	kamariroaki	rattled
kamaiu	refreshing	kamaroa	desolated
kamaiuaki	saved	kamaroaki	segregated
kamakaki	scared	kamaroroaki	entertained
kamakanakanaki	softened	kamarua	slain
kamaki	cooked	kamaruaki	robed
kamakinaki	intimidated	kamaruruaki	muffled
kamakuaki	terrified	kamarurungaki	fortified
kamakunakunaki	marred	kamataanoaki	blinded
kamamaeaki	shamed	kamataanoanoaki	blurred
kamamaki	humiliated	kamatakiaki	blinded
kamamaraeaki	impaired	kamatakiauaki	troubled
kamamate	grievous	kamataku	enthralling
kamammaki	suckled	kamatakuaki	astounded
kamananaki	domesticated	kamatamataki	colored
kamanangaki	cancelled	kamatanaki	rolled
kamaneakaki	secured	kamatanatanaki	loosened
kamaneaneaki	shamed	kamataniaiaki	dazzled
kamaneanikum	invincible	kamatantanaki	loosened
kamaneauaki	secured	kamatatauaki	checked
kamanekaki	scarred	kamatauaki	controlled
kamanenakaki	oiled	kamatauninga	insolent
kamanenaki	used	kamatauningaki	insulted
kamanenantiaki	attempted	kamataweaki	retarded
kamangaki	smothered	kamatea	slain
kamangaoaki	confused	kamateaki	quenched
kamangaungauakinaki	devoured	kamateanibai	hardened
kamangeangeaki	littered	kamatebwaiaki	interpreted
kamangingaki	fermented	kamatereaki	surmounted
kamangingngaki	intoxicated	kamatibutibuaki	ripened
kamangoraki	debased	kamatiketikeaki	loosened
kamantintiaki	beaten	kamatiratiraki	squashed
kamantoaki	seized	kamatirauaki	flattened
kamanunuaki	corrugated	kamatoaki	confirmed
kamaoaki	cured	kamatoatoaki	hardened
kamaorioriaki	disjointed	kamatuaki	anaesthetized
kamarakaki	tortured	kamaunaki	cancelled
kamaraki	dissolved	kamauneaki	deafened

Reference: Webster's Online Dictionary (www.websters-online-dictionary.org)

kamawaki	evacuated	kananomaruruaki	troubled
kambaki	inhaled	kananoraki	aggravated
kameio	uncanny	kanebuaki	beaten
kameme	peevish	kaneneaki	enforced
kamemenaki	placed	kanenge	unbalanced
kamenaiaki	refreshed	kangaki	consumed
kamenaki	placed	kanganga	arduous
kamengoaki	encumbered	kangare	ludicrous
kamereaki	sprinkled	kangataki	soiled
kamimi	awesome	kangeraki	curled
kamimiaki	surprised	kangibueaki	warmed
kamimitoiakaki	rotated	kangkai	imperturbable
kamimitoiaki	drawn	kangkang	yummy
kamimitongaki	glorified	kangoreaki	weakened
kaminoa	confused	kanibobotaki	gregarious
kaminoaki	turned	kanikinaki	labelled
kaminominotakaki	rotated	kanikoaki	pampered
kammammaki	nursed	kanimaki	glued
kamoaki	exalted	kanimanumuaki	crumbled
kamoamoaki	admired	kanimanunuaki	creased
kamonaki	pampered	kanimarangrangaki	overjoyed
kamoriau	embarrassed	kanimatoauaki	enervated
kamou	arduous	kaninirakaki	rotated
kamronronaki	rounded	kannaki	nourished
kamwaki	grilled	kanngeaki	hardened
kamwaneauaki	stabilized	kannim	tasty
kamwara	indecent	kanoabo	acarpous
kamwaraeaki	littered	kanoan	blissful
kamweauaki	retarded	kanotonaki	charged
kamwemweaki	uplifted	kanroaroa	immediate
kan	admirable	kantaningaki	anticipated
kanaeng	offended	kanuai	nutritional
kanaengaiaki	offended	kanuaki	shaded
kanaki	devoured	kanubebeoaki	disgraced
kanakoa	sent	kanukaki	marred
kanakoaki	sent	kaoaki	ordered
kananamaki	flavored	kaoanikai	imprudent
kananangaki	grazed	kaobainako	diligent
kananobabaki	stupefied	kaoioiaki	thickened
kananobarakaki	dejected	kaokaki	restored
kananobitakaki	~	changed	kaokiaki	repeated
kananobuaki	discouraged	kaokoro	sorted
kananobukibukiaki	disturbed	kaokoroaki	varied
kananokawaki	grievous	kaonaki	infested
kananokawakiaki	disheartened	kaonako	diligent
kananokorakiaki	confused	kaonakoaki	scorned

kaongoaki	informed	kararatiaki	satiated
kaongoraeaki	informed	kararoaki	parted
kaonoaki	assigned	karawawataki	oppressed
kaonotaki	specified	kareaoaki	exaggerated
kaooaki	ordered	karebenakoaki	dislocated
kaoraiaki	prepared	karebun	promiscuous
kaorakora	thunderous	karebwerebweaki	tapped
kaotabaeaki	treasured	karebwetataki	crackled
kaotaki	irradiated	kareite	proud
kaotiotaki	revealed	karekanano	charismatic
kaotiotiaki	announced	kareke	charming
kara	elderly	karekeaki	scoured
karababaki	enlarged	karekenanoaki	captivated
karabakauakina	considered	karekereke	bristly
karabaki	masked	karekeria	tasty
karabanaki	concealed	kareketataki	obstructed
karabinobinoaki	rolled	kareketatiaki	retarded
karaeaki	scattered	karemaranga	scattered
karaiaki	tangled	karemeaki	narrowed
karairakiaki	restored	karemremaki	accumulated
karakara	raspy	karenaki	stretched
karakarakaki	exaggerated	karengaoaki	tangled
karakarakeaki	increased	karereaki	animated
karakaraki	scraped	karereiaki	approved
karakarongorongo	exaggerated	kareuataoaki	heaped
karakarongorongoaki	exaggerated	karewenaki	sweetened
karaki	peeled	karewiaki	sweetened
karakiaki	hurried	kariaiakaki	permitted
karakina	proportional	kariaiakakiaki	approved
karakinaki	related	kariaiaki	approved
karako	few	kariaki	peeled
karakoaki	shortened	kariara	innumerable
karamakinaki	supposed	kariaraki	exaggerated
karaneaki	dazzled	kariba	packed
karaneaneaki	glazed	karibakaki	pressed
karaneboneboaki	glazed	karibonobonoaki	amassed
karangaki	poured	karibuaki	forced
karaoaki	formed	karietataki	exalted
karaoakiaki	wrought	kariete	proud
karaoana	laborious	karikakaki	disenchanted
karaoiaki	accomplished	karikaki	begotten
karaoiroiaki	justified	karikakiaki	repaired
kararaeaki	rusted	karikariaki	thrilled
kararaki	tilted	karikaua	doubting
kararaoma	disquieting	karikiaki	begotten
kararati	satisfying	karimwi	younger

karinaki	introduced	katakareaki	scattered
karinanoaki	lowered	katakeaki	embarrassed
karineaki	venerated	kataki	attempted
karinerine	polite	katamaroaki	decorated
karioaki	composed	katanaki	shaded
karirakiaki	stretched	kataneaki	seared
kaririaki	imposed	kataneiaiaki	practiced
karitei	cantankerous	katanetaneaki	scored
kariteiaki	opposed	katangaki	rounded
karokoaki	adjusted	katangibu	protruding
karongo	old	kataninaki	detailed
karotu	indisposed	katantanaki	speckled
karotuaki	thwarted	kataribabaki	detached
karuaiwa	ninth	kataribiaki	granulated
karuanano	astonishing	kataribono	constipating
karuaruaki	entrenched	katarimarimaki	sharpened
karuataoaki	heaped	katauaki	approved
karuoaki	lowered	katauraoaki	prepared
karuruaki	jolted	katauraoiaki	prepared
kata	scientific	katauuroaki	reduced
katababaeaki	bristled	kataururuaki	smashed
katabakurakuraki	encumbered	katautauaki	supposed
katabaninaki	encircled	katawa	noisy
katabaruaruaki	embarrassed	katawaeaki	matured
katabauaki	confused	katawe	hasty
katabeaiangaki	troubled	kataweaki	looted
katabeaki	obstructed	kateaki	lifted
katabetabeaki	troubled	katebaki	snapped
katabiroaki	turned	kateibaiaki	formed
katabuaki	hallowed	kateibuaka	ungrateful
katabukaki	heaped	kateikaiaki	prohibited
katabukirurungaki	obstructed	kateimatoaki	ratified
kataburorokoaki	forbidden	kateinang	unapproachable
katabwa	forbidden	kateinangaki	overwhelmed
katabwaki	forbidden	kateirakeaki	stirred
kataea	overpowering	katekaki	pierced
kataeaki	tested	kateke	natty
kataeboaki	intensified	katekeaki	pierced
kataenangaki	prepared	katekebotiaki	informed
kataenano	discouraging	katekeria	alluring
kataereaki	licked	katenaki	seared
kataetaeaki	rated	katenuaki	pronounced
kataewaki	chopped	katereaki	presented
kataiaki	tried	katereke	distinguished
katakakaroaki	amused	kateretereaki	presented
katakanakanaki	smeared	katiaki	honed

katiba	untidy	kauanga	foxy
katibaki	dislocated	kauangingaki	reduced
katibebe	unsteady	kauangingiaki	retracted
katibetibeaki	freed	kauaraki	fettered
katikiaki	processed	kauarerekeaki	lessened
katikintakaeaki	tightened	kauatibu	stony
katikiraoaki	trimmed	kaubai	opulent
katikuaki	downed	kaubaki	surprised
katimaran	glazed	kaubatialaki	tenderized
katimarau	hairless	kaubiroto	stocky
katimoiaki	knotted	kaubuai	bearded
katimronronaki	rounded	kaubunrangaki	debased
katimtimaki	sprinkled	kaubwai	opulent
katingoaki	soiled	kaukaki	disclosed
katinono	stubborn	kaukeukeaki	scratched
katiobabaeaki	suspended	kaukintaeaki	shamed
katiobukiaki	tumbled	kaumakaki	hurried
katiraki	flattened	kaumaki	expeditious
katireaki	tempered	kaumakiaki	dispatched
katiriboaki	appropriated	kauman	ingenious
katirironronaki	rolled	kaumata	colorful
katiroronaki	rounded	kaumau	hurried
katitaki	softened	kaumauaki	hurried
katitirou	eminent	kaunaineaki	respected
katituaki	aroused	kaunaki	opposed
katoaki	supplied	kaungaki	stimulated
katoangaki	squared	kauniben	resistant
katoatoaki	squared	kaunikaiaki	opposed
katokaki	quenched	kauntabaki	opposed
katokiaki	downed	kauntabamaki	opposed
katongaki	flavored	kauntaekaki	disputed
katonginakoaki	shocked	kauntaki	distinguished
katongiraraeaki	deafened	kauoua	dual
katoto	apathetic	kauraki	fired
katotoaki	forged	kauramakaki	lighted
katourakeaki	startled	kauramaraki	reduced
katuaeaki	fined	kaurauraki	reddened
katuaki	missed	kaureaki	hatched
katukaki	seated	kauri	bony
katuna	connected	kauringaki	revised
katunaki	coupled	kauririaki	hurried
katuruaki	pressed	kautuakaki	aggravated
katutuaki	inspired	kautuaki	aggravated
kauaki	seeded	kawa	disconsolate
kauakinaki	restrained	kawaeremweaki	retarded
kauamaeaki	dispersed	kawaeremwiaki	retarded

kawaetataki	rushed	kikekibeaki	scratched
kawaiaki	used	kikiaki	scraped
kawaina	mannered	kikibokiboaki	heaped
kawainaki	used	kikiman	ingenious
kawairinan	processed	kikinto	diligent
kawairinanaki	ranked	kikiriman	industrious
kawakinaki	saved	kikoaki	turned
kawakinibwai	circumspect	kima	steely
kawanga	tiring	kimai	peaked
kawanreaki	tarnished	kimamaku	timid
kawanta	dishonorable	kimangamanga	disoriented
kawantaki	spoiled	kimangare	nomadic
kawarawara	perforated	kimao	thievish
kawarebweaki	enlarged	kimarimari	plenteous
kawarikaki	narrowed	kimoaki	stolen
kawawaeaki	assembled	kimotoitoi	undersized
kawawaki	dunked	kimraki	packed
kawenea	laid	kimri	packed
kaweneaki	laid	kinaki	comprehended
kawikoaki	hurried	kinano	abstruse
keinano	obsessed	kinanoaki	checked
kekeaki	rattled	kinanonano	mysterious
kekeiakiaki	studied	kinawanawa	speckled
kekeraki	checked	kinginaki	locked
kekeruataiaki	crackled	kingking	runty
kekiaki	tried	kinikon	shriveled
kennanoaki	puzzled	kinokunoku	peevish
keria	disappointed	kinongo	perforated
keriaki	disappointed	kinounou	abyssal
kerikakiaki	retreated	kioiaki	discharged
keruaki	crackled	kiraokiaki	intoxicated
ketaki	coveted	kirara	sandy
kiaiai	immature	kirarang	sheepish
kiaki	splashed	kire	frenzied
kiakiaki	radiated	kiriaria	ulterior
kiaraki	splashed	kiribambantaki	encircled
kibakibaki	ravenous	kiribanin	congealed
kibana	ineffectual	kiribare	same
kibangabanga	perforated	kiribeubeu	bumpy
kibangebange	selfish	kirikakang	spiked
kibara	encumbered	kiriman	industrious
kibaraki	rushed	kirimanga	forked
kibaura	temperamental	kirimaruarua	pitted
kiberuberu	timid	kirimotimoti	mutilated
kibono	stopped	kirimoumou	confused
kikaura	sensitive	kiriongong	stupefied

kirirnang	frolicsome	kororo	abbreviated
kiritantan	dotted	korouaiaki	halved
kiritantanaki	laced	kraoanaki	prohibited
kiritibutibu	puffed	ku	shrivelled
kiritoatoa	polyhedral	kukaki	cooked
kiritongitong	dazed	kukunakuna	scarred
kiriuatao	heaped	kukurei	blissful
kiriuous	paired	kukuri	hasty
kiriwaka	stringy	kun	skinned
kirmatamata	shameless	kuneaki	discovered
kirmrim	bunched	kuokuoaki	skinned
kiruatao	piled	kuotaki	abraded
kitanaki	evacuated	kuri	hasty
kiube	cubic	kuribaiaki	deprived
kiubu	cubic	kuribwaiaki	sacked
kiura	tempered	maae	scattered
koaki	hurried	maama	withdrawn
koaua	certain	mabu	forbidden
koko	stocked	mabuaki	prohibited
kokoaki	scraped	mabubu	hazy
kokoni	gathered	mae	roasted
komaki	shortened	maeae	tattered
komau	stringy	maeaki	dispersed
kon	disappointed	maekanaki	livable
konaakiaki	surrendered	maeke	crunchy
konaki	pressed	maem	complacent
konamaki	aware	maen	flexible
konamakiaki	depressed	maenikun	smashed
konanaki	abducted	maerere	striped
konin	callous	maererua	checkered
koninaki	hardened	maete	greasy
kontano	innumerable	maewe	indistinct
kora	golden	mai	alive
korabaia	huge	maiaki	southbound
korakora	corpulent	maibunia	underdone
korana	corpulent	maioaki	gathered
koranaki	mastered	maioraora	underdone
korea	sliced	maiti	numerous
koreaki	sliced	maitia	unified
koriaki	typed	maitiaki	unified
koritaki	scratched	maitorotoro	frozen
koro	accomplished	maiu	alive
korobaiaki	limited	maiureirei	vivid
korobokiaki	inscribed	maiurerirei	thriving
korobuaiaki	shaved	maiuroaroa	alive
korokoroiaki	incised	maiutakoni	intelligent

makaiao	enormous	mangaongao	untidy
makaki	apprehended	mangaungau	voracious
makana	brittle	mangingi	shrunk
makaoakao	tangled	mango	remorseful
makei	frolicsome	mangoieta	venerable
maki	ruptured	mangori	insignificant
makibora	squashed	mangung	intoxicated
makinaki	respected	manibuaka	unkind
makoko	bunched	manibuakaki	maltreated
makoneua	doubled	manikangareaki	amused
makoroaki	incised	manikoraki	qualified
makorouaki	halved	manikorakiaki	qualified
makota	insignificant	manimanaki	kept
maku	scared	manimaniniaki	illuminated
makuriana	laborious	manin	charming
mama	timid	maninaki	standardized
mamaka	substantial	maninga	forgetful
mamaku	fearful	maningainga	affable
mamara	impaired	maninganinga	civil
mamata	discerning	maningare	dimpled
mamataki	parasitic	maningengeaki	disappointed
mamataro	unconscious	maningongoaki	whispered
mamataunaki	shadowed	maninrongorongoaki	overstated
mamaunga	hilly	manintaekaki	reported
mambwea	brackish	maninutoaki	alleged
mammaki	inhaled	manio	indolent
mammam	mundane	manionio	flabby
mana	sticky	mannanoaki	respected
manana	domesticated	mannaokaki	bullied
manango	sleepy	mannei	nonchalant
manawaiaki	entrenched	mano	watertight
mane	old	manono	depressed
maneanea	humiliated	manouna	profitless
maneaua	tied	manrea	traditional
manebaeba	diligent	manrerei	childish
m'anekaki	traced	mantiaki	flattened
manekaneka	scarred	mantoa	troubled
manena	useful	mantoaki	mystified
manenanti	abnormal	manuokaki	overlooked
maneouna	oiled	manuokinaki	forgotten
maneuna	practical	mao	healed
manga	forked	maon	rare
mangaki	repeated	maong	perspiring
mangamangaki	embarrassed	maono	perspiring
mangao	disharmonious	maonon	malleable
mangaoangao	chaotic	maoria	corrected

maoriori	flexible	matara	embarrassed
maotorikiriki	smashed	mataronron	reprimanded
maotorrikirikiaki	fulfilled	mataroro	interested
mara	softened	matata	evident
marabe	flourishing	matatae	discolored
maraia	unlucky	matatoka	evident
marairai	lengthy	matau	foiled
marangaki	sectioned	matauaki	arrested
marara	indistinct	matauakinaki	observed
marati	flourishing	mataunaki	observed
maratirati	greased	matauningananti	offended
mare	scattered	matauraura	reddened
mareaki	married	mate	unconscious
marebu	troubled	mateaki	expired
marengau	insufficient	matebuakaki	failed
maribo	industrious	matenibaki	ravenous
maririri	chilled	matenruarua	impassable
maroa	detached	matera	costly
maroaka	evident	materaoi	profitable
maroakaki	located	materetere	outstanding
maru	piled	matibu	ripe
marurung	strenuous	matimaki	downed
mata	multicolored	matiratira	flattened
matabaeaki	occupied	matiraua	reduced
matabao	unsure	matoro	accepted
matabou	guileless	matutu	sleepy
matabuaka	hostile	maunea	deafened
matabubuaka	hostile	maung	putrid
matabuburaki	puckered	maunikaki	forgotten
mataenaki	fertilized	maurake	brazen
mataiakinaki	coveted	mauraki	mistreated
matairiki	perspicuous	mauringaki	forgotten
matairikiaki	sharpened	maurouro	embodied
matakanikan	elegant	mautara	circumspect
matakao	abstruse	mautete	curious
mataki	sightless	mawa	spacious
matakiaua	perturbed	mawawa	verdant
matamata	colored	mbambaeaki	inhaled
matamatanaki	striped	me	ugly
matan	rolled	meme	tiresome
matanaki	colored	memekaki	inhaled
mataneai	dazzled	memerakeaki	forced
mataneaiaki	dazzled	memeri	delicate
matanikananoanga	pathetic	memeto	inquisitive
matanikanebu	modest	mena	located
matanikimoa	shifty	mengoaki	pained

Reference: Webster's Online Dictionary (www.websters-online-dictionary.org)

mimiaki	admired	mwanangaki	traveled
miminotaki	turned	mwanibuakaki	oppressed
mimitoiaki	overwhelmed	mwaninga	forgotten
mimitong	dignified	mwaningaki	forgotten
mino	rotated	mwau	humid
minoaki	revolved	mwawawa	spacious
minominoaki	rolled	mweaki	lifted
minominotaki	revolved	mwebuaka	uneasy
minotaki	capricious	mwemwe	weightless
minotiaki	turned	mwemweaero	nocturnal
miroaki	admired	mwemwerake	lifted
mka	decomposed	mwemwerakeaki	lifted
moakakung	detested	mwerengau	constrained
moaki	surmounted	mweuti	sleepless
moakura	ugly	mwiniba	ignoble
moanaki	continued	mwinibaki	lowered
moanangiaki	attempted	mwinikai	scarred
moaniba	unequaled	mwiokoaki	ordered
moantaiaki	gathered	nabangkai	certain
moaraoi	comely	nabawe	prehistoric
moatoki	crestfallen	nabeaki	pampered
moimoti	destroyed	nabenabeaki	idolized
moimotiaki	damaged	nainainaki	encircled
mona	filthy	nakibaina	limbless
monamona	slimy	namaki	threaded
monotaki	revolved	namakinaki	perceived
mori	overripe	namatoa	stubborn
moringa	pleasant	namomara	disgusted
morokaei	immense	namtaki	inhaled
motibuaka	misunderstood	namtete	insatiable
motikaki	snapped	nanai	luscious
motinnanoaki	bonded	nanaiaki	packed
motirawaki	rested	nananga	stripped
mramra	insistent	nangoango	listless
mron	spherical	nangonango	nonchalant
mronron	spherical	nangoraoi	restful
mronronaki	rounded	nano	abysmal
mte	finite	nanoaki	troubled
mumunaki	retreated	nanoanga	pitying
mura	insistent	nanoataki	perceived
muramura	insistent	nanoatiaki	fancied
muti	interested	nanobaba	silly
mwae	sunburnt	nanobebebebe	involuntary
mwai	cooked	nanobebete	relieved
mwaka	uncured	nanobibitaki	changeable
mwakuriaki	serviced	nanobitaki	disharmonious

nanobuaka	resentful	neinei	swampy
nanobukibuki	uneasy	neiranraoi	serendipitous
nanoingainga	impatient	nekeaki	punctured
nanokabakoba	fragile	nenea	creamy
nanokawa	dismal	neneboiaki	scented
nanokawaki	unhappy	nenera	investigative
nanokirokiro	soundless	nengeaki	licked
nanokiroro	infinite	neweabaki	haunted
nanokoraki	mystified	neweaki	licked
nanomaiti	indecisive	neweneweaki	licked
nanomaitiaki	mystified	ngae	complacent
nanomaka	energetic	nganga	poisonous
nanomakaki	horrendous	ngarongaro	toothless
nanomamara	condescending	ngaruru	thunderous
nanomane	virile	ngaruruaki	rolled
nanomano	discerning	ngatingati	filthy
nanomaruru	disturbed	ngaungauaki	devoured
nanomatoa	stubborn	ngautaki	devoured
nanomatoatoa	persevering	ngawaki	choked
nanomawa	tolerant	ngengetaiaki	treated
nanomiakina	disenchanted	ngeri	curled
nanomwaka	willful	ngeta	envious
nanomwane	strenuous	ngio	dizzy
nanonaki	imported	ngioaki	failed
nanonibwiaki	coveted	ngkainaba	instantaneous
nanorake	choleric	ngoaki	scratched
nanoraoi	pacific	niabuti	navigable
nanorau	peaceable	niau	awkward
nanoriba	bigoted	nibakabaka	unsteady
nanorinano	lowly	nibaki	hollowed
nanotau	agreeable	nibanga	perforated
nanotiotio	changeable	nibara	uneasy
nanouki	amiable	nibarabara	peeled
nanoun	choleric	nibiongong	torpid
nanououa	mystified	nibunini	puffed
nanouououaki	mystified	nikamonmonaki	rolled
nanoutu	tribal	nikierere	jubilant
nanowaki	disconsolate	niko	elegant
nanowana	reasonable	nikotaungaunga	unbalanced
natinaki	adopted	nikuakua	fatigued
natinatiaki	adopted	nikutaro	embarrassed
nawaki	breathed	nim	sticky
nea	confused	nimaenen	flexible
neaki	placed	nimaki	swallowed
neboaki	glorified	nimamanei	peaceable
neboneboaki	glorified	nimamate	languid

ra	defective	rako	thrifty
raba	agreeable	rakoroaki	grazed
rababa	spacious	ramaneaki	tied
rababauaki	flattened	ran	juicy
rabakai	ingenious	ranea	oscillating
rabakau	ingenious	ranebonebo	glistening
rabana	huge	raneboneboaki	glazed
rabaneaki	maintained	rang	considerable
rabe	beveled	rangaki	overturned
rabenibenaki	tilted	rangarangaki	rolled
rabi	wavy	rangarangatau	engaged
rabinoaki	rolled	rangarangatauaki	employed
rabinobinaki	revolved	rangataki	hurried
rabinobinoaki	rolled	rangatakiaki	hurried
rabirabi	wavy	rannake	scummy
rabu	forbidden	ranran	juicy
rabunaki	stifled	rantiaki	despised
rabungaoaki	disapproved	raoi	reasonable
rabwanaki	preserved	raoiakinaki	mediated
rae	diverted	raona	associated
raea	scattered	raonaki	associated
raeaeaki	stripped	raou	fiancee
raeaki	slashed	rarabuareareaki	aroused
raeakinaki	shared	raraeaki	scattered
raeauaki	slashed	raraikumeaki	annoyed
raemenga	dismantled	raraki	rusted
raemengaki	dislocated	rarakoaki	conserved
raenen	flexible	rarango	continued
raeraeaki	stripped	raraoma	sorrowful
raetenaki	slashed	rarati	satiated
rai	untwisted	rarau	jealous
raiaki	exchanged	raraureaki	detached
raibanta	encircled	rarikin	indigent
raimengaki	used	rarikinaki	trimmed
rain	lined	raroa	remote
rainanoanga	anguished	raroi	useful
rainanoangaki	agonized	raruaki	scratched
rainiaki	lined	rau	jealous
raira	countless	rauakina	jealous
rairaki	converted	raure	detached
rairakiaki	rotated	rawaki	opposed
raiti	dazzling	rawanaki	drilled
raitiaki	dazzled	rawatakaei	ponderous
raka	bewitched	rawawaa	grievous
rakaki	augmented	rawawata	depressed
rakeaki	awakened	raweaki	robed

rawebaiaki	supplied	riki	grown
rawekai	agile	rikiaki	developed
raweraweabaki	fingered	rikirake	grown
rebeaki	projected	rikirakeaki	accrued
reberake	saucy	rikoaki	collected
rebetunga	meddlesome	rikoiaki	collected
rebuaki	plastered	rikumaki	folded
reireiaki	trained	rimwi	ulterior
reitaki	continued	rinaki	introduced
reitata	tall	rinanoaki	checked
reitiaki	coupled	rine	eminent
reka	spicy	rineaki	apportioned
reke	seized	ringoungou	ravenous
rekeaki	kidnapped	rino	meticulous
rekebuta	hesitating	rionakoaki	dipped
rekerua	matted	riri	bony
reme	limited	riribai	hostile
remremaki	gathered	riribaki	hated
rena	adjustable	riribwa	rocky
renganaki	promiscuous	ririere	arrogant
rereaki	rushed	ririka	obsessed
rerebauaki	rushed	ririmoa	older
rerebetungaki	annoyed	riringaki	disturbed
rerebuaki	rushed	ritangiaki	lamented
reretiaki	suspected	roaki	shouldered
rereua	uninhabited	robaki	balanced
rereuaki	retreated	robungiaki	darkened
retaki	extended	roko	attained
ri	fascinated	romatoa	economical
riai	needy	ronaki	sustained
riaki	needed	ronnaki	lessened
riaoaki	cleared	rorokaki	stimulated
riaonikaiaki	surmounted	rota	obtainable
riara	innumerable	rotaki	attained
riba	pressed	roto	humid
ribaba	accumulated	rotuaki	rounded
ribabetanga	compressed	rreretaki	fated
ribaki	disliked	ruamakana	watery
ribanaia	cultivating	ruannano	frivolous
ribanaki	fertilized	ruatatara	asymmetrical
ribataki	patched	ruberubeaki	beaten
ribeu	humped	rukuma	folded
ribeubeu	misshapen	rume	changeable
ribuaka	disobliging	rung	agreeable
rietata	arrogant	ruoaki	hollowed
rikakiaki	withdrawn	ruonaki	rushed

ruonako	immoderate	tabuenga	matted
tababu	economical	tabuki	hilly
tabakaki	surprised	tabukirurunga	obstructed
tabaki	choked	tabunaki	forbidden
tabakurakura	bushy	tabunimateaki	cherished
tabanga	publicized	taburakaki	constricted
tabangaeaki	publicized	tabureka	bumpy
tabanin	undivided	taburekaki	spoiled
tabara	remote	tabuterang	forbidden
tabarabara	discordant	tabwaiaki	plundered
tabaraki	misunderstood	taeaki	brushed
tabare	meddlesome	taeare	ruined
tabareaki	annoyed	taebaiaki	looted
tabarebare	fervent	taebaki	undressed
tabarekai	agile	taebo	hasty
tabaronikarawa	gloomy	taebu	vivid
tabarua	overburdened	taekaiaki	tied
tabati	enormous	taekaki	detached
tabatibutibu	swelled	taekinaki	related
tabaua	unbalanced	taenako	detached
tabe	few	taenang	unburdened
tabea	confused	taenoaki	hurried
tabeaki	engaged	taeraki	trimmed
tabeitera	unbalanced	taeremea	unpremeditated
tabekaki	lifted	taeririaki	hurried
taberua	preoccupied	taetae	spoken
taberuruaki	spattered	taetoba	blanched
tabetabe	indisposed	tagerameaki	dispersed
tabetai	occasional	taiaganoro	slanted
tabeua	few	taiaganoroaki	slanted
tabeuta	few	taimaki	sharpened
tabiriaki	minced	taitaimaki	sharpened
tabitabitabitaki	cleared	takaeakinaki	proclaimed
tabokaikai	formidable	takaerere	expeditious
tabomane	virile	takakaki	proclaimed
tabonangaki	shouldered	takanana	slimy
tabonibainrang	awkward	takaneanea	dazzling
taboniwiaki	planned	takarea	scattered
taboraki	insulted	takareau	webbed
taborang	crackers	takareburebuaki	slopped
tabotua	bored	takarebutataki	stirred
tabu	illegal	takarebwetataki	crackled
tabuaetia	awkward	takarere	distinguished
tabuaetiaki	damaged	takariroriro	wriggling
tabuaki	hallowed	takaroaki	kindled
tabuarikiaki	bungled	takarua	changeable

takaruaki	announced	tanoata	known
takaruruaki	rattled	tanoi	dizzy
take	surprised	tanomakiaki	confused
takebono	defiant	tanotano	sandy
takinaki	unfolded	tantaniaki	guarded
takoko	packed	tantano	sandy
takoroaki	notched	tantanoaki	soiled
takuaki	rated	tao	overabundant
takurereaki	rebuked	taoakaiaki	pressed
takutaku	dumb	taobukiaki	aided
tamakai	agile	taoburaki	observed
tamanaki	lined	taokabiaki	blocked
tamaniaki	delineated	taokaiaki	scaled
tamarakeaki	scaled	taokitanaki	treated
tamaroa	graceful	taomanekaki	scented
tamârua	handsome	taonaki	curbed
tamatamaki	scaled	taonakiaki	pressed
tamruru	parted	taonanoaki	pressed
tana	occupied	taonikai	bonded
tanaki	stung	taoruaki	preserved
tanan	speckled	taotira	superabundant
tanaraki	untangled	tarabaiaki	checked
tanbwaiaki	robed	tarabu	discouraging
tangaki	lamented	tarabuaka	disproportionate
tangako	slimy	tarae	metaphoric
tangaua	indecisive	taraeaki	implied
tangauriuri	friable	taraki	sprinkled
tangenge	uncovered	tarao	missed
tangibuaka	discordant	tararuaia	supervisory
tangira	affectionate	tararuaiaki	controlled
tangiraki	cherished	tarataraki	observed
tangirarikiaki	preferred	tarauaki	borrowed
tangkongkoaki	gathered	tarauakinaki	charged
tangoaki	borrowed	tare	unconventional
taniaki	declared	tari	juicy
tanibaba	obstructed	taribaba	senile
tanibabu	cloudy	taribi	granulated
tanin	grouped	taribono	blocked
taningamarau	diligent	taribubu	hazy
taninganinga	apathetic	tarie	wicked
taningaroti	slothful	tarika	brackish
taningato	faithless	tarikabana	awkward
taningo	fleeting	taromauriaki	adored
tannabaki	rolled	tatabuiaki	kept
tannaki	diffused	tatabwi	thrifty
tannene	unsteady	tataeanibaiaki	detached

tataki	notched	teitei	stationary
tataningamarau	industrious	teiuomaniaki	grouped
tataoaki	diffused	teka	punctured
tataraki	considered	tekateka	seated
tatarere	singular	teke	pierced
tatatataki	thrilled	tekebuaka	unlucky
tataumantaki	observed	tekebuakaki	failed
tau	adequate	tekemangongo	stinking
tauaki	conserved	tekenaki	beaten
tauantaboaki	represented	tekera	unfortunate
taubank	restrained	tekeria	disappointed
taubankaki	moderated	temekaki	inhaled
taubeakinaki	guarded	tenaki	wedged
taubureaki	censored	tenaruaki	devoured
taubururuaki	spoiled	tennanoa	hateful
taukirikiriaki	estimated	tenu	grammatical
taumateaki	buried	tete	impolite
taunaki	buried	teutana	paltry
taunariaki	measured	teweaki	projected
taungatangataki	hurried	tia	accomplished
tauoaki	kept	tiaainaki	signed
tauraki	lifted	tiatianna	limited
taurangarangaki	rolled	tibaki	shared
tauraoi	equipped	tibaraki	missed
taururu	forced	tibatibaki	shared
tautaekaki	ruled	tibia	spherical
tautaekanaki	ruled	tibu	puffed
tautata	hospitable	tibuaki	puffed
tautokaki	reinforced	tibunaki	adopted
tautooaki	dominated	tibwaki	tried
tautoronaki	ruled	tieaki	balanced
tawa	ripe	tiebbaki	suspended
tawere	ghastly	tiemaneaki	netted
tawiraki	minced	tieraki	balanced
teaki	trimmed	tiitebo	same
tebeaki	snapped	tika	marvelous
tebekaki	splashed	tikaua	marvelous
tebokaki	washed	tiki	stretched
teboranaki	splashed	tikimaurekati	undecided
teboteboaki	washed	tikinene	stretched
tei	undecided	tikinono	stretched
teiaki	stopped	tikitiki	gristly
teiakinaki	guarded	tiko	graceful
teibaka	unbalanced	tikonaki	measured
teibanae	strewn	tikuaki	placed
teirobaroba	hesitating	tikurabirabi	crumpled

timamwi	roasted	tokoie	senseless
timinaki	roasted	tokomangaongao	encumbered
timinene	greasy	tokomeme	verbose
timron	globular	tomaki	linked
timu	adorned	tongaki	nourished
timuaki	decorated	tonginako	stupefied
tinaraki	insulted	tonu	grammatical
tinauere	runty	torobakara	untidy
tine	undecided	toronrang	neglected
tinebu	chubby	torotakanana	filthy
tineruaki	retarded	torotangako	untidy
tinimaki	fried	toto	indolent
tinnimaki	grilled	totoaki	stolen
tintinaki	roasted	touaki	trampled
tiraki	flattened	tounene	resistant
tiriaki	beaten	tourake	chained
tiribaeaki	amended	tourikaki	beaten
tiribaonoaki	fined	tuabebeku	corpulent
tiriboaki	chastised	tuaiaia	muscular
tiribureaki	corrected	tuairaki	stolen
tirikaiaki	planned	tuaki	reported
tiringaki	reprimanded	tuanaki	kept
tirinta	cylindrical	tuangaki	informed
tirioboraki	sacked	tuanokunoku	grazed
tiriou	insane	tuanonoku	bulky
tiritabukiaki	crazed	tuariri	bony
tiritiri	brutal	tukaki	blocked
tiroaki	observed	tukuroro	retarded
tironron	spherical	tunganaki	plugged
titebo	congruent	tungatunga	faulty
titi	watery	tuoaki	checked
titibengaua	swelled	turaiangkor	triangular
toa	monumental	turunaki	forced
toabaraki	restrained	tutari	salty
toara	odd	tutuneang	joyful
toari	titanic	uakaka	hairy
toatoa	cubical	uakakaki	bristled
toatoanaki	squared	uakurikuri	countless
tobaki	nursed	uamaneaki	encircled
toka	dominating	uamaniaki	measured
tokaki	bottomed	uamoa	optimistic
tokanikaiaki	dominated	uamwiaki	copied
tokarakeaki	dominated	uanao	numerous
tokiaki	arrested	uara	embarrassed
tokina	finite	uaran	juicy
tokobuakoako	wooded	uarereke	youthful

uatiaki	washed	utakiaki	aggravated
ubati	corpulent	uti	conscious
ueke	petulant	utiaki	awakened
ui-katík	sarcastic	utowa	hyperactive
ukaki	uncovered	waeaki	threaded
ukeukeaki	tested	waebaka	needy
uki	spaced	waekoaki	hurried
ukinta	confused	waero	nocturnal
ukoukora	sought	waetata	accelerated
ukoukoraki	sought	waetataki	hurried
uma	married	waetoka	agile
umakiaki	hurried	waewae	footed
un	angry	waewaeaki	opposed
unaenaeaki	despoiled	wai	elongated
unaki	forced	waiaki	pierced
unariraki	stripped	waiboraki	pierced
unaunaki	decorated	waiteketeke	mottled
uneakinaki	disputed	waiteketekeaki	speckled
unekeaki	adorned	waitotokoaki	stopped
unga	arduous	waka	threaded
ungaraki	accomplished	wakaraoi	integrated
unikaki	implanted	wakariri	stringy
unin	irascible	wakawaka	stringy
unobautaki	detached	wana	reasonable
unoraki	turned	wanaraki	disentangled
unrake	rebellious	wanawana	sensible
unrakeaki	refused	waneinei	watery
untabaki	opposed	wanga	confusing
unuara	scorned	wangaki	troubled
unuaraki	scorned	wanikangareaki	amused
unun	irate	wara	treeless
ununaki	angered	waraku	moist
uomaniaki	transposed	waranran	watery
urabaki	devastated	warea	lusterless
urabo	discolored	warebwe	spacious
urakaki	destroyed	wari	gigantic
urakeaki	flared	waronaki	knotted
uraki	destroyed	waruaki	annoyed
urakinaki	unloaded	wauaki	embroidered
uramai	impending	waunaki	bewitched
uramwakaki	flared	weteaki	invited
ureaki	expanded	wewaki	bounded
uretatanga	expanded	wibarubaru	toothless
uriaki	sprinkled	wibekaki	exaggerated
uruabaiaki	demolished	wibineaki	whispered
uruaki	sacked	wikabweaki	exaggerated

winaki	inspired	affronted	kabuakakaki
winanti	unreal	aged	kara
wingarongaro	toothless	agglomerated	ribaba
wirikirikiaki	whispered	aggravated	kautuaki
witakanana	tactless	aggregated	kawawaeaki
witokoaki	obstructed	agile	waetoka
wiwiaki	suggested	agonized	rainanoangaki
		agreeable	kannim
		aided	taobukiaki
		alarmed	maku
		alarming	nanomakaki
		alive	konamaki

Adjectives (English - Kiribati)

		alleged	maninutoaki
		alleviated	kabaketeaki
		alluring	katekeria
abbreviated	karakoaki	altruistic	kakaianga
abducted	konanaki	amalgamated	renganaki
abnormal	bainanti	amassed	karibonobonoaki
abounding	karebun	amazing	kakamataku
abraded	karaki	amended	raoiakinaki
abstruse	nano	amiable	moringa
abused	tiringaki	amicable	iraorao
abysmal	nano	ample	mawa
abyssal	kakinounou	amused	wanikangareaki
acarpous	kanoabo	anaesthetized	kamatuaki
accelerated	kaumakiaki	anemic	matanikanebu
accepted	butimwaaeaki	angelic	kakatika
accidental	kabuanibai	angered	bononanoaki
accompanied	ikakaiaki	angled	angkoroaki
accomplished	karaoiaki	angry	bononano
accrued	rikirakeaki	anguished	rainanoanga
accumulated	kawawaeaki	angular	angkoro
acidic	mai	animated	kamarurungaki
activated	taungatangataki	announced	kaotiotiaki
adaptable	rena	annoyed	kakaiaki
adequate	areare	anticipated	biririmoaki
adjustable	rena	apathetic	ntangaingai
adjusted	karokoaki	apologetic	mango
admirable	tikaua	applied	bubutiaki
admired	kamoamoaki	apportioned	rineaki
admonished	boaki	appreciated	raba
adopted	imammaneaki	apprehended	tauaki
adored	karineaki	appropriated	arokanaki
adorned	katamaroaki	approved	kariaiaki
adroit	bati	archaic	nabawe
affable	maningainga	arduous	kamou
affectionate	tangira	aroused	katituaki
affirmed	kamatoaki		

arrested	matauaki	blasted	kioiaki
arrogant	kainikatonga	bleary	nanokabakoba
artistic	rabakai	blemished	kawantaki
assailable	nanorake	blinded	mataneai
assaulted	oroaki	blissful	kanoan
assembled	botaki	blistered	nouaki
assessed	kinanoaki	blithe	kukurei
assiduous	kikinto	blocked	bonotaki
assigned	angaki	bloodthirsty	tiritiri
assisted	buokaki	blurred	kamataanoanoaki
associated	kaeti	bolted	in
assorted	aeka	bonded	motinnanoaki
astonishing	karuanano	bony	tuariri
astounded	kakubaki	bordered	nimimareaki
astounding	kamimi	bored	botu
asymmetrical	ruatatara	borrowed	bubutiaki
attained	roko	bothered	kakaiaki
attempted	kamanenantiaki	bottomed	tokaki
attended	kakaunongoaki	bounded	ramaneaki
attenuated	kamararaki	boundless	nanokirokiro
audacious	maurake	boxed	ikaroubuaki
augmented	kabunnaaki	brackish	mambwea
awakened	rakeaki	branched	kirimanga
aware	matatoka	branchy	manga
awesome	bureti	branded	kanikinaki
awkward	intinebu	brash	maurake
baffled	kaminoa	brassy	maurake
baffling	wanga	brazen	maurake
baked	karikaki	breaded	karikiaki
balanced	robaki	breathed	ikeaki
bandaged	bautaki	bristled	katababaeaki
barbarous	tiritiri	bristling	tabarua
based	kakoauaki	bristly	karekereke
bashful	mama	brittle	makana
bastardized	kaubunrangaki	broiled	kamwaki
bearded	kaubuai	brushed	taeaki
beaten	ruberubeaki	brutal	tiritiri
befouled	kaubunrangaki	bugged	raraikumeaki
begotten	karikaki	bulky	bubura
beheaded	bakuaki	bullied	kakoroikuaki
beneficial	ibuobuoki	bumpy	kiribeubeu
benighted	nonoro	bunched	makoko
besmirched	katakanakanaki	bungled	tabuarikiaki
beveled	rabe	buried	taumateaki
bewitched	raka	burly	nanomane
bigoted	nanoriba	bushy	tabakurakura
blamed	boaki	callous	konin
blanched	kamainainaki	calloused	koninaki

cancelled	kamaunaki	collapsed	bato
cantankerous	nanoun	collected	bootaki
capacious	kakanoa	colonized	kakoroneaki
capricious	atubitaki	colored	matamatanaki
captivated	karekenanoaki	colorful	kaumata
casual	taeremea	colossal	korabaia
cataclysmic	kabuanibai	comely	moaraoi
catchy	karekereke	comical	aokangare
censored	taubureaki	commissioned	kataninaki
censured	rabungaoaki	committed	kaiakina
certain	nabangkai	complacent	maem
certified	kakoauaki	composed	karioaki
chained	tourake	comprehended	kamatebwaiaki
changeable	ruannano	compressed	taonaki
changed	bitaki	concealed	karabaki
chaotic	mangaoangao	conceived	kamatebwaiaki
charged	kanotonaki	concentrated	ntaninin
charismatic	karekanano	condescending	nanomamara
charitable	kakaianga	confirmed	kakoauaki
charming	karekanano	confused	nanokoraki
chastised	tiriboaki	confusing	wanga
cheap	materaoi	congealed	kiribanin
checked	kamatatauaki	congruent	titebo
checkered	maererua	conjugated	takuaki
cheeky	maurake	connected	katunaki
cheery	kukurei	conscious	matatoka
cherished	miroaki	conserved	rarakoaki
childish	ataei	considerable	rang
chilled	mariri	considered	iangoaki
choked	ngawaki	consolidated	kateimatoaki
choleric	nanorake	constipating	kataribono
chopped	bouaiaki	constrained	memerakeaki
chubby	tinebu	constricted	taburakaki
circumspect	mautara	consumed	kanaki
civil	maninganinga	contained	kakanoaki
civilized	maninganinga	contemptible	kakauara
clannish	nanoutu	contested	uneakinaki
clawed	koritaki	continued	reitaki
cleansed	tebokaki	controlled	babaireiaki
cleared	riaoaki	conventional	kabuta
cloudy	nubono	converted	rairaki
coagulated	kiribanin	convincing	matatoka
coated	nimroaki	cooked	mwai
cocky	butiroko	coordinated	baiteke
cognitive	nanowana	copied	katotoaki
cognizant	matatoka	corked	nongoaki
coherent	nanowana	corny	arobaba

corpulent	tuabebeku	decreased	kakeaki
corrected	maoria	deepened	atamaumauaki
corrugated	kamanunuaki	defective	buretata
costly	matera	defiant	matabuaka
countless	uakurikuri	defined	kabarabaraki
coupled	kaboaki	degraded	kanubebeoaki
coveted	mataiakinaki	dejected	kananobarakaki
crackers	taborang	delectable	kangkang
crackled	karebwetataki	delicate	kimai
craggy	kiribeubeu	delicious	kangkang
craved	baruaki	delightful	kukurei
crazed	tiritabukiaki	delineated	nu
creamy	nenea	delirious	aiwau
creased	batia	demolished	uruabaiaki
crested	kautuaki	demonstrated	kabarabaraki
crestfallen	moatoki	depressed	nanokawaki
cross-eyed	egî-mata	depressing	matanikananoanga
crumbled	kanimanumuaki	deprived	kuribaiaki
crumpled	kanimanunuaki	described	aekaki
crunchy	maeke	desirable	kaibabaru
cubic	kiubu	desolated	kamaroa
cubical	toatoa	despicable	kakauara
cultivated	maninganinga	despised	kakanikoaki
cultivating	ribanaia	despoiled	unaenaeaki
curbed	taonaki	despondent	nanokawa
cured	kamaoaki	destroyed	moimoti
curious	tete	destructive	kabuanibai
curled	kangeraki	detached	taekaki
curly	ngeri	detailed	kataninaki
cute	ikutaba	detected	maroakaki
cylindrical	tirinta	detested	tabunimateaki
damaged	kabuaki	devastated	tirioboraki
darkened	robungiaki	developed	tangaki
dated	ikakaiaki	devious	matanikimoa
daubed	rebuaki	devoured	kamangaungauakinaki
daunted	ibebureaki	dewy	aoi
dauntless	ninikoa	dicey	nanobebebebe
dazed	angitoiaki	different	kaokoro
dazzled	mataneai	diffused	tangaki
dazzling	kakanno	digested	kamatebwaiaki
deafened	kamauneaki	dignified	kamoaki
debased	kaubunrangaki	diligent	rangarangatau
decapitated	kabakuaki	diminished	kakeaki
deceptive	kabaka	dimpled	maningare
declared	taniaki	dipped	rionakoaki
decomposed	maung	dire	nanomakaki
decomposing	toto	disappointed	kon
decorated	bwereaki	disapproved	rabungaoaki

disarranged	kakaraurekanaki	disseminated	kauamaeaki
disastrous	kabuanibai	dissolved	kamaraki
discerning	nanomano	distasteful	mai
discharged	kioiaki	distinguished	takarere
disclosed	kaukaki	distressed	katabetabeaki
discolored	kawantaki	distributed	kaborereaki
disconcerted	kamatakiauaki	disturbed	karawawataki
disconsolate	kawa	disturbing	nanomakaki
discordant	tabarabara	diversified	kaokoro
discounted	notuaki	diverted	kakibotuaki
discouraged	namomara	dizzy	ngio
discouraging	tarabu	dodgy	kamamate
discovered	kuneaki	doleful	kawa
discredited	baebaetaki	domesticated	manana
diseased	aoraki	dominated	tokarakeaki
disenchanted	karikakaki	dominating	baekeke
disengaged	kamarangaki	domineering	baekeke
disentangled	wanaraki	donated	angaki
disfigured	bureta	doting	maninga
disgraced	kabatebaiaki	dotted	kiritantan
disgraceful	kamatauninga	doubled	makoneua
disgusted	bararai	doubtful	karikaua
disgusting	kabun	doubting	karikaua
disharmonious	mangao	downed	katokiaki
disheartened	kananokawakiaki	drained	kawawaki
disheveled	atutababa	draped	niniraki
dishonorable	kawanta	drastic	kinano
disjointed	kamaorioriaki	drawn	kamimitoiaki
disliked	ribaki	dreadful	kakamaku
dislocated	karebenakoaki	dreary	nanokawa
disloyal	taningato	drilled	rawanaki
dismal	nanokawa	droopy	nanokabakoba
dismantled	raemengaki	dropped	kabwakaki
dismayed	maku	dual	kauoua
dismissed	bwaranakoaki	dulled	rotuaki
disobedient	bonotaninga	dumb	aretau
disobliging	ribuaka	dumbfounded	kamatakuaki
disorganized	raea	dunked	kawawaki
disoriented	kimangamanga	duplicated	katotoaki
dispatched	kamateaki	dusky	maewe
dispersed	mareaki	dutiful	taningamarau
dispirited	nanokawa	dwarfish	kimotoitoi
disproportionate	ruonako	dyed	mata
disputed	ibewiaki	eased	kabaketeaki
disquieted	kaangitanneneaki	economical	tababu
disquieting	kararaoma	edited	rinanoaki
disrupted	kaakaeaki	eerie	kakanaugaki

Reference: Webster's Online Dictionary (www.websters-online-dictionary.org)

effected	karaoaki	exorbitant	bora
egotistic	rietata	expanded	ureaki
egotistical	rietata	expected	kantaningaki
elderly	kara	expeditious	baitata
elegant	kakateke	expensive	matera
elongated	wai	experienced	atataibai
emaciated	bakikangengeaki	experimental	kata
emancipated	kainaomataki	expired	mate
embarrassed	matabou	explicit	matatoka
embodied	maurouro	exploited	mannaokaki
embroidered	manimaniniaki	expressive	tenu
eminent	takarere	extant	nabangkai
emphasized	kateretereaki	extended	kakerakeaki
employed	bwainaki	extensive	nuku
emptied	babaroaki	extenuating	mate
encircled	bauaki	exterminated	kamateaki
encouraged	nanomaka	extinct	mate
encouraging	nanomaka	extraordinary	kamimi
encumbered	tokomangaongao	fabled	iangoaki
endowed	kabaibaiaki	factual	nabangkai
energetic	mamaka	failed	tekebuakaki
enervated	kanimatoauaki	faithless	taningato
enforced	kaneneaki	fallen	bwaka
engaged	rangarangatau	familiarized	imammaneaki
enlarged	kakawibaeaki	famous	atongaki
enormous	riara	fancied	kanaki
entertained	kairuwaeaki	fascinated	ri
enthralling	kamataku	fashioned	karaoaki
enticing	timinene	fastened	kabaeaki
entrenched	karuaruaki	fatal	kamamate
enveloped	tieraki	fated	rreretaki
envious	bakantang	fatigued	nikuakua
epileptic	kirimoumou	fattened	intibuaki
equalized	boraoiaki	faulty	bure
equipped	tauraoi	fearful	kamâg
equitable	nanowana	fearsome	kakamaku
estimated	katautauaki	featherbrained	minotaki
evacuated	birinakoaki	featherweight	mwemwe
evident	maroaka	feminine	inaine
exaggerated	rakaki	fermented	buroaki
exalted	karietataki	fertilized	mataenaki
exalting	kakammari	fervent	nanobukibuki
exceptional	bainanti	fetid	buíra
exchanged	iokinaki	fettered	kauaraki
exculpated	tabitabitabitaki	few	tabe
excused	aonaki	fiancee	raou
exhausting	kamou	fibrous	buruburu
exhilarated	kukurei	filthy	mona

fined	katuaeaki	frivolous	manrerei
fingered	raweraweabaki	frolicsome	kirirnang
finicky	barino	frozen	brok
finite	mte	fruitful	materaoi
fired	katiaki	frustrated	karotuaki
fissured	raeraeaki	fulfilled	maotorrikirikiaki
flabby	manionio	furrowed	raeraeaki
flared	urakeaki	fussy	beberino
flattened	tiritabukiaki	garbled	otobebeaki
flavored	kananamaki	garnished	katamaroaki
fleeting	raiti	gathered	kokoni
flexible	maen	genial	nanoraoi
flirtatious	be	genteel	karinerine
flooded	iekaki	ghastly	kakanaugaki
flourishing	rung	gigantic	bubura
flowered	nimatamata	glad	kukurei
fogged	bubuteiaki	glazed	ireaki
foggy	bubu	glistening	ranebonebo
foiled	kamatauaki	global	okioki
folded	num	globular	timron
footed	waewae	gloomy	maewe
forbidden	rabu	glorified	kakannatoaki
forced	kaneneaki	glued	kanimaki
forceful	buburamaiu	golden	baun
foreign	ianena	gorgeous	kakanno
forged	katotoaki	graceful	inaaine
forgetful	ibabannang	graded	burimangaoaki
forgiving	atataiaomata	grammatical	tenu
forgotten	manuokaki	granular	atiati
forked	manga	granulated	kataribiaki
formed	karikaki	gratified	kakukureaki
formidable	tabokaikai	grayish	mai
formulated	iangomakaki	grazed	kakariaki
fortified	kamarurungaki	greased	kamaratiaratiaki
fossilized	nabawe	greasy	maete
fostered	nabeaki	gregarious	kanibobotaki
fouled	kamairiaki	grievous	rawawaa
foxy	kauanga	grilled	tinnimaki
fragile	makana	gristly	baia
fragmented	kataribiaki	groping	nanobebebe
fragrant	buiérar	grotesque	kamairatuatua
framed	karaoaki	grouped	ikoikotaki
freed	katibetibeaki	grown	riki
frenzied	kire	grubby	barekareka
friable	tangauriuri	gruesome	nanomakaki
fried	baniaki	guarded	tantaniaki
frightful	kakamaku	guided	aronaki

guileless	matabou	ignorant	tukuroro
guilty	bure	illegal	tabu
hairless	katimarau	illicit	tabu
hairy	uakaka	illuminated	manimaniniaki
hallowed	tabuaki	illustrated	kabarabaraki
halved	bwenauaki	imagined	karikaki
hammered	boboaki	immaculate	immakurata
handsome	botonimwaane	immaterial	mangori
harassed	karawawataki	immature	kiaiai
hardened	koninaki	immeasurable	kakawaki
harmonious	rau	immediate	ngkainaba
hasty	katawe	immense	abakaei
hatched	kaureaki	imminent	uramai
hated	riribaki	immoderate	ruonako
hateful	tennanoa	immutable	takebono
haunted	kakawaraki	impaired	kakeaki
hazy	taribubu	impartial	bairaoi
healed	kamaoaki	impassable	kamateanibai
healthier	nimanana	impassive	rau
heaped	kakiriuataoaki	impatient	nanorake
heartbroken	kawa	impeded	tukaki
heavenly	kamimi	impending	uramai
heavyhearted	nanokawa	impenetrable	aotaningo
hesitant	nanououa	impertinent	maurake
hesitating	rekebuta	imperturbable	kamateanibai
hideous	bureti	impetuous	baibati
hilly	tabukirurunga	implacable	inamatoa
hoary	nabawe	implanted	unikaki
hollowed	kaibako	implemented	karekeaki
honed	katiaki	implied	taraeaki
honest	matabou	impolite	kaburati
honorable	nanomawa	imported	nanonaki
hopeless	kabana	imposed	kaririaki
horrendous	nanomakaki	impotent	ntokotoko
horrid	kakamaku	impoverished	waebaka
hospitable	tautata	impregnated	ibaba
hostile	riribai	imprudent	kaoanikai
huge	abakae	impulsive	aotakaka
humid	roto	impure	buakaka
humiliated	karinanoaki	inactive	noumangang
humped	ribeu	inadequate	areare
hurried	kaumauaki	inadvertent	nanotiotio
hushed	kabararaki	inane	arobaba
husky	kaubiroto	inapt	babanga
hyperactive	utowa	inattentive	noumaninganinga
identified	matatoka	inauspicious	ra
idolized	nabenabeaki	incalculable	kakawaki
ignoble	nukabebeo	incapacitated	ntokotoko

Reference: Webster's Online Dictionary (www.websters-online-dictionary.org)

lanky	irariki	married	uma
latched	kainaki	marshy	aoneiney
laughable	aokangare	marvelous	kakanno
layered	kiriuatao	masked	karabaki
leaky	erarán	massed	ruonako
lengthened	reitaki	mastered	aonikaiaki
lengthy	kakiro	matched	boraoi
lessened	kakenakoaki	matted	rekerua
liable	nano	matured	ikawaiaki
liberated	kainaomataki	measured	tikonaki
licked	oreaki	meddlesome	tabare
lifted	tabekaki	mediated	raoiakinaki
lighted	kaotaki	meek	inataba
likable	kan	melted	kamaraki
liked	tangiraki	menacing	rebetunga
limbless	nakibaina	merciful	nanoanga
limited	tiatianna	metaphoric	tarae
lined	rainiaki	meticulous	rino
linked	reitaki	milled	iaki
listless	nangonango	minced	tabiriaki
littered	kabarekaki	miraculous	kamimi
livable	maekanaki	mischievous	be
loaded	urakinaki	mislaid	kabuaki
located	maroakaki	misrepresented	kairerebuaki
locked	in	missed	katuaki
loosened	kaingingngaki	misshapen	ribeu
looted	taebaiaki	mistaken	airuaki
lowered	katukaki	mistreated	bainikirinaki
lowly	nanorinano	misty	bubu
lubricated	kabiraki	misunderstood	motibuaka
ludicrous	kakangare	mitigated	kabebeteaki
lukewarm	abue	moderated	toabaraki
luscious	kaibabaru	modest	matanikanebu
lusterless	warea	modulated	kauakinaki
luxurious	kakanno	moist	waraku
magnanimous	nanomawa	molded	aoiaki
magnified	katamaroaki	momentary	niniwana
maintained	kawakinaki	monumental	toa
malevolent	nanobuaka	mortified	matara
malformed	beu	motivated	inga
malicious	nanobuaka	mottled	kiritantan
malignant	nanobuaka	mountainous	mamaunga
malleable	maonon	mounted	tokaki
maltreated	bainikirinaki	muffled	kamaruruaki
manly	nanomane	multicolored	mata
mannered	kawaina	multifaceted	kiritoatoa
manufactured	kateibaiaki	mundane	mammam
marred	kamakunakunaki	murdered	kamaruaki

perspicacious	mamata	prickly	kakang
perspicuous	wanawana	principled	boto
perspiring	maono	printed	boretiaki
pertinacious	nanomaka	probable	nano
perturbed	kamatakiauaki	processed	katikiaki
perverted	kaubunrangaki	proclaimed	takaeakinaki
pestered	kakaiaki	productive	kimarimari
petulant	reberake	profitable	maneuna
philanthropic	kakaianga	profitless	manouna
pierced	teke	prohibited	kamabuaki
piled	kakiriuataoaki	projected	rebeaki
pillaged	taebaiaki	prolific	kimarimari
pitted	kirimaruarua	promiscuous	renganaki
pitying	nanoanga	promising	berita
placed	katukaki	pronounced	atongaki
placid	maem	proportional	kaborere
planned	iangoaki	protruding	katangibu
planted	unikaki	proud	kainikatonga
plastered	rebuaki	proven	kakoaua
playful	makei	provident	banganibai
pleasant	moringa	proximal	kan
plenteous	kimarimari	publicized	tabanga
plugged	tunganaki	puckered	kabatutu
plundered	tirioboraki	pudgy	kaubiroto
poised	kamwaneauaki	puerile	manrerei
poisonous	kabutika	puffed	kiritibutibu
polite	aboabo	pugnacious	unin
polyhedral	kiritoatoa	pulverized	bubuaki
ponderous	rawatakaei	pumped	bamaki
populated	kainaki	punctured	nekeaki
possible	konaki	purified	kaitiakaki
poured	kabwaroaki	putrid	maung
powdery	bubu	puzzled	kennanoaki
practical	maneuna	quaint	baikoraki
practiced	atakinaki	qualified	manikorakiaki
practised	kataneiaiaki	quelled	toabaraki
pragmatic	banganuaru	quenched	kamateaki
predicted	karamakinaki	racial	nanoutu
preferred	rineaki	radiated	kiakiaki
prehistoric	nabawe	ranked	aekaki
preoccupied	keinano	ransacked	unaenaeaki
prepared	abinaki	raped	kabainrangaki
prescribed	tuaki	rare	burenibwai
presented	kaonoaki	rascally	aonikai
preserved	botuakinaki	raspy	karakara
pressed	riba	rated	boaki
prevailing	toka	ratified	kateimatoaki
priceless	kakawaki	rational	nanowana

Reference: Webster's Online Dictionary (www.websters-online-dictionary.org)

scientific	kata	shouldered	aonangaki
scorched	batata	shriveled	kinikon
scored	katanetaneaki	shrivelled	ku
scorned	kaberetokoaki	shrunk	mangingi
scornful	kaonako	sightless	mataki
scoured	karaneboneboaki	signed	iranikaiaki
scraped	karakaraki	silly	nanobaba
scratched	kaukeukeaki	simulated	bwakaki
screened	nunaki	sinful	bure
scrumptious	kangkang	singular	bainanti
scrupulous	kikinto	skeptical	nanobebebebe
scummy	rannake	skilful	inaguínagu
sealed	au	skilled	rabakau
seared	kataneaki	skinned	nananga
seasick	nimarawarawa	slain	kamarua
seated	katukaki	slanted	taiaganoro
sectioned	marangaki	slashed	kirimotimoti
secured	kamaneakaki	sleepless	mweuti
seeded	kakoraki	sleepy	manango
segregated	kamarangaki	sliced	bwerebwereaki
seized	raweaki	slimy	mona
selfish	nanoriba	sloped	bateteaki
senile	taribaba	slopped	takareburebuaki
sensational	kamimi	slothful	taningaroti
sensed	kamatebwaiaki	smashed	kaibakoaki
senseless	tokoie	smeared	kabiraki
sensible	wanawana	smothered	taonaki
sensitive	binainga	smudged	kabiraki
sensuous	kaibabaru	snapped	motikaki
sent	kanakoa	snubbed	kaberetokoaki
serendipitous	neiranraoi	softened	katitaki
serviced	mwakuriaki	soiled	betingaingai
settled	kaiakinaki	sorrowful	nanokawaki
sewed	itutu	sorry	mango
shaded	nunaki	sorted	aekaki
shadowed	nu	sought	kakera
shadowy	nu	soundless	nanokirokiro
shady	nu	southbound	maiaki
shamed	kamamaeaki	spaced	uki
shameless	kakauara	spacious	mawa
shared	tibwaki	spattered	bururuaki
sharpened	taitaimaki	specified	kaonotaki
shaved	korobuaiaki	speckled	katantanaki
sheepish	kirarang	spellbound	maraia
shielded	otaotangaki	spherical	mronron
shifty	matanikimoa	spicy	reka
shocked	katonginakoaki	spiked	bouaki
shortened	karakoaki	spiky	kakang

spineless	nimaoriori	studied	kekeiakiaki
spirited	kukurei	stumpy	reka
spiteful	nanobuaka	stung	ewara
splashed	tebekaki	stupefied	kamataanoanoaki
splintered	tourikaki	stylish	kateke
spoiled	mka	submissive	inataba
spoken	taetae	substantial	kakanato
spotless	itiwewe	subtracted	anaiaki
sprawled	inraki	suckled	kamammaki
sprinkled	nurakiaki	suggested	winaki
spurned	kaberetokoaki	sunburnt	mwae
squalid	mangori	superabundant	taotira
squared	toatoanaki	supernatural	kakanaugaki
squashed	tiraki	supervisory	tararuaia
stabilized	kamwaneauaki	supplied	kamariboaki
stacked	kiruatao	supposed	katautauaki
standardized	maninaki	surmounted	kamatereaki
stark	banin	surprised	kamimiaki
startled	auba	surrendered	konaakiaki
starved	kabakiaki	susceptible	kainoki
stationary	teitei	suspected	bukunaki
steamed	kabuaneaki	suspended	katiobabaeaki
steamy	taribubu	sustained	ronaki
steely	kima	swallowed	nimaki
stemmed	kaunaki	swampy	neinei
sticky	mona	sweaty	maono
stifled	rabunaki	sweetened	karewiaki
stimulated	kakeiakaki	swelled	titibengaua
stinking	maung	swept	taeaki
stirred	takarebutataki	tactless	witakanana
stitched	itutuaki	talented	rabakau
stocked	kamariboaki	tall	ananau
stocky	kaubiroto	tamed	kamananaki
stolen	kakamwaruaki	tangled	karaiaki
stony	kauatibu	tapped	karebwerebweaki
stooped	baokoko	tarnished	kawanreaki
stopped	tokiaki	tasteless	mammam
stored	kaikoaki	tasty	katekeria
strengthened	nonoaki	tattered	maeae
strenuous	nanomwane	teased	kaenaenaki
stretchable	rena	temperamental	kibaura
stretched	rarati	tempered	kabaketeaki
strewn	inroa	tenderized	katotoaki
stringy	kiriwaka	tentative	kata
striped	matamatanaki	terrible	kakurere
stripped	raeraeaki	terrific	abakaei
stubborn	bakatoki	terrified	kakunaingaki

Reference: Webster's Online Dictionary (www.websters-online-dictionary.org)

terrifying	kakamaku	tribal	nanoutu
tested	ukeukeaki	tried	kekiaki
testy	kakaiun	trimmed	tirikaiaki
thawed	kamaraki	trodden	matiraua
thickened	atamaumauaki	troubled	katabetabeaki
thievish	kimao	troublesome	kameio
thinned	bakikangengeaki	troubling	karuanano
thorny	kakang	truncated	bakuaki
threaded	waeaki	trusted	onimakinaki
thrifty	rako	trusting	onimakina
thrilled	kakukureiaki	tumbled	bwakaki
thriving	maiuroaroa	turned	raiaki
thunderous	kaorakora	twined	binokaiaki
thwarted	kaberetokoaki	typed	koriaki
tied	ramaneaki	ugly	me
tightened	kimraki	ulterior	kiriaria
tilted	taiaganoroaki	unapproachable	kateinang
timid	ninikoria	unavailing	manouna
tinted	nunaki	unbalanced	kanenge
tiresome	kaboati	unbecoming	buaka
tiring	kakau	unblemished	itiwewe
titanic	abakaei	unburdened	taenang
toasted	kakunnaki	uncanny	kameio
toilsome	kamou	unclear	maewe
tolerant	nanomawa	uncommon	tare
toothless	wibarubaru	unconditional	matatoka
tormented	bainikirinaki	unconscious	mamataro
torpid	nibiongong	unconventional	tare
torrid	kabuebue	uncooked	oraora
tortured	kamarakaki	uncovered	tangenge
toughened	katikintakaeaki	uncultured	nonoro
towering	ananau	uncured	mwaka
traced	katotoaki	undecided	tine
tracked	niniboiaki	undercooked	waka
traded	bobaiaki	underdone	mata
traditional	manrea	underhanded	matanikimoa
trained	reireiaki	undersized	kimotoitoi
trampled	touaki	undignified	kakauara
transformed	onikaki	undivided	tabanin
transposed	uomaniaki	undressed	taebaki
trapped	taokabiaki	uneasy	mwerengau
traveled	buta	unenlightened	nonoro
treacherous	babakanikawai	unequal	bobuaka
treasured	kaotabaeaki	unequaled	moaniba
treated	ngengetaiaki	unfaithful	ruannano
treeless	wara	unfathomable	nano
tremendous	abakaei	unfavorable	ra
triangular	turaiangkor	unfolded	takinaki

unfortunate	tekebuaka	vexatious	kameio
unfruitful	aomate	vicious	buakaka
ungrateful	bangaaomata	virile	tabomane
unhappy	kawa	vivid	maiureirei
unified	maitiaki	voluminous	tabati
unimportant	mangori	voracious	babakanikora
uninhabited	rereua	waggish	kirirnang
unintelligent	anua	waisted	urabaki
unintentional	nanobebebe	warmed	kangibueaki
unjust	ribuaka	washed	tebokaki
unkept	bakarae	watered	katimtimaki
unkind	manibuaka	watertight	au
unloaded	urakinaki	watery	titi
unlucky	tekera	wavy	rabi
unmindful	nanotiotio	weakened	kangoreaki
unoccupied	noumangang	webbed	takareau
unpredictable	iteratera	wedged	tenaki
unpremeditated	taeremea	weightless	mwemwe
unqualified	babanga	whacked	oroaki
unreal	winanti	whispered	maningongoaki
unripe	mai	whitened	kamainainaki
unsightly	bureti	whitish	mai
unskillful	babanga	wicked	ioawa
unsociable	ninikuraroa	willful	nanomwaka
unsteady	bebe	withdrawn	rikakiaki
unsure	iraaua	woeful	rainanoanga
untangled	tanaraki	wooded	tokobuakoako
untidy	baitangako	wormy	ino
untwisted	rai	worthwhile	materaoi
unusual	bainataei	wreathed	biriaki
unwanted	moakakung	wriggling	takariroriro
unwilling	nanobebebebe	wrought	karaoaki
uplifted	ingaki	younger	karimwi
used	kawaiaki	youthful	ataei
useful	raroi	yummy	kangkang
vaccinated	itinaki		
varied	kaangitanneneaki		
varnished	ranebonebo		
vast	mawa		
veiled	karabaki		
venerable	mangoieta		
venerated	karineaki		
venomous	kamamate		
verbose	kabararia		
verdant	baroro		
verified	kamatebwaiaki		
versatile	takarua		

Made in the USA
Charleston, SC
25 September 2016